# Paul Kimmel's
## Accounting Course Design

Paul Kimmel, co-author on several Wiley accounting titles, teaches at University of Wisconsin — Madison using Wiley's online course in a flipped-classroom format.

**Wiley's online course was developed with the student experience in mind.**

See how Paul uses four key elements to focus his course on developing his students' success.

### Guided Learning

EXAMPLE:

Paul customizes his learning path to highlight and structure pre-assignments, post-assignments and discussions, adaptive practice, exam practice, and quizzing.

The **flexible, linear learning path** enables you to control what your students see, when they see it, and in what order. This makes it very clear for students to understand what they're supposed to complete. This is especially vital for online classes. **Having a clear path to learn reduces the risk of "losing" students, keeping them engaged and on track in your** course.

### Information Retention

EXAMPLE:

Paul assigns Interactive Tutorials ahead of pre-lecture assignments so students come to class ready to actively participate.

**Interactive Tutorials** provide students with a self-paced lecture walkthrough of the chapters. Broken into small chunks, students must respond to integrated questions correctly or exhaust attempts before moving on, enhancing the retention of information. **Trying to solve a problem before being taught the solution is frustrating but improves retention.**

### Continuous Practice

EXAMPLE:

Paul uses Adaptive Practice as a capstone activity at the end of each week to improve retention.

**Adaptive Practice** is a powerful learning tool that provides feedback, showing the areas students need to work on. **To improve learning, employ dynamic (adaptive) testing rather than static testing. Without feedback students often overestimate their competence and don't see a need to try to improve.**

### Just-in-Time Homework Help

EXAMPLE:

Paul assigns post-assignment problems supported by Solution Walkthrough Videos.

**Solution Walkthrough Videos** provide students with 24/7 just-in-time homework support and enable you to assign more difficult homework questions. **Longer, multi-learning objective problems with video support help students consolidate their understanding.**

WILEY

# Paul Kimmel's
## Accounting Course Design

## Course Design Suggestions from *Make It Stick\**

✓ Trying to solve a problem before being taught the solution improves retention.

✓ Testing (active retrieval) doesn't just measure learning, it strengthens memory.

✓ Spaced "testing" results in greater retention.

✓ Providing feedback strengthens testing more than testing alone.

*Make It Stick*; Brown, Roediger, and McDaniel, 2014.

## Considerations for a Flipped Classroom
Based on Paul Kimmel's course with two in-person lectures per week.

### EXAMPLE WEEKLY SCHEDULE

| | | |
|---|---|---|
| **SUNDAY** | Online | Complete first pre-assignment. Due Monday before class. |
| **MONDAY** | In Class | Students do at least two exercises in class on blank sheet (i.e., conditions faced in a test). |
| **TUESDAY** | Online | Complete second pre-assignment. Due Wednesday before class. |
| **WEDNESDAY** | In Class | Students do at least two exercises in class on blank sheet. |
| **THURSDAY/FRIDAY** | Online | Complete post-assignment. Due Friday night. |
| **FRIDAY/SATURDAY** | Online | Complete adaptive practice assignment. |

# Account Classification and Presentation

| Account Title | Classification | Financial Statement | Normal Balance |
|---|---|---|---|
| **A** | | | |
| Accounts Payable | Current Liability | Balance Sheet | Credit |
| Accounts Receivable | Current Asset | Balance Sheet | Debit |
| Accumulated Depreciation—Buildings | Plant Asset—Contra | Balance Sheet | Credit |
| Accumulated Depreciation—Equipment | Plant Asset—Contra | Balance Sheet | Credit |
| Administrative Expenses | Operating Expense | Income Statement | Debit |
| Advertising Expense | Operating Expense | Income Statement | Debit |
| Allowance for Doubtful Accounts | Current Asset—Contra | Balance Sheet | Credit |
| Amortization Expense | Operating Expense | Income Statement | Debit |
| **B** | | | |
| Bad Debt Expense | Operating Expense | Income Statement | Debit |
| Bonds Payable | Long-Term Liability | Balance Sheet | Credit |
| Buildings | Plant Asset | Balance Sheet | Debit |
| **C** | | | |
| Cash | Current Asset | Balance Sheet | Debit |
| Common Stock | Stockholders' Equity | Balance Sheet | Credit |
| Copyrights | Intangible Asset | Balance Sheet | Debit |
| Cost of Goods Sold | Cost of Goods Sold | Income Statement | Debit |
| **D** | | | |
| Debt Investments | Current Asset/Long-Term Investment | Balance Sheet | Debit |
| Depreciation Expense | Operating Expense | Income Statement | Debit |
| Discount on Bonds Payable | Long-Term Liability—Contra | Balance Sheet | Debit |
| Dividend Revenue | Other Income | Income Statement | Credit |
| Dividends | Temporary account closed to Retained Earnings | Retained Earnings Statement | Debit |
| Dividends Payable | Current Liability | Balance Sheet | Credit |
| **E** | | | |
| Equipment | Plant Asset | Balance Sheet | Debit |
| **F** | | | |
| Freight-Out | Operating Expense | Income Statement | Debit |
| **G** | | | |
| Gain on Disposal of Plant Assets | Other Income | Income Statement | Credit |
| Goodwill | Intangible Asset | Balance Sheet | Debit |
| **I** | | | |
| Income Summary | Temporary account closed to Retained Earnings | Not Applicable | (1) |
| Income Tax Expense | Income Tax Expense | Income Statement | Debit |
| Income Taxes Payable | Current Liability | Balance Sheet | Credit |
| Insurance Expense | Operating Expense | Income Statement | Debit |
| Interest Expense | Other Expense | Income Statement | Debit |
| Interest Payable | Current Liability | Balance Sheet | Credit |
| Interest Receivable | Current Asset | Balance Sheet | Debit |
| Interest Revenue | Other Income | Income Statement | Credit |
| Inventory | Current Asset | Balance Sheet (2) | Debit |

*(continued)*

# Account Classification and Presentation *(continued)*

| Account Title | Classification | Financial Statement | Normal Balance |
|---|---|---|---|
| **L** | | | |
| Land | Plant Asset | Balance Sheet | Debit |
| Loss on Disposal of Plant Assets | Other Expense | Income Statement | Debit |
| **M** | | | |
| Maintenance and Repairs Expense | Operating Expense | Income Statement | Debit |
| Mortgage Payable | Long-Term Liability | Balance Sheet | Credit |
| **N** | | | |
| Notes Payable | Current Liability/<br>Long-Term Liability | Balance Sheet | Credit |
| **P** | | | |
| Patents | Intangible Asset | Balance Sheet | Debit |
| Paid-in Capital in Excess of Par—Common Stock | Stockholders' Equity | Balance Sheet | Credit |
| Paid-in Capital in Excess of Par—Preferred Stock | Stockholders' Equity | Balance Sheet | Credit |
| Preferred Stock | Stockholders' Equity | Balance Sheet | Credit |
| Premium on Bonds Payable | Long-Term Liability—Adjunct | Balance Sheet | Credit |
| Prepaid Insurance | Current Asset | Balance Sheet | Debit |
| Prepaid Rent | Current Asset | Balance Sheet | Debit |
| **R** | | | |
| Rent Expense | Operating Expense | Income Statement | Debit |
| Retained Earnings | Stockholders' Equity | Balance Sheet and Retained Earnings Statement | Credit |
| **S** | | | |
| Salaries and Wages Expense | Operating Expense | Income Statement | Debit |
| Salaries and Wages Payable | Current Liability | Balance Sheet | Credit |
| Sales Discounts | Revenue—Contra | Income Statement | Debit |
| Sales Returns and Allowances | Revenue—Contra | Income Statement | Debit |
| Sales Revenue | Revenue | Income Statement | Credit |
| Selling Expenses | Operating Expense | Income Statement | Debit |
| Service Revenue | Revenue | Income Statement | Credit |
| Short-Term Investments | Current Asset | Balance Sheet | Debit |
| Stock Investments | Current Asset/Long-Term Investment | Balance Sheet | Debit |
| Supplies | Current Asset | Balance Sheet | Debit |
| Supplies Expense | Operating Expense | Income Statement | Debit |
| **T** | | | |
| Treasury Stock | Stockholders' Equity | Balance Sheet | Debit |
| **U** | | | |
| Unearned Service Revenue | Current Liability | Balance Sheet | Credit |
| Utilities Expense | Operating Expense | Income Statement | Debit |

(1) The normal balance for Income Summary will be credit when there is a net income, debit when there is a net loss. The Income Summary account does not appear on any financial statement.

(2) If a periodic system is used, Inventory also appears on the income statement in the calculation of cost of goods sold.

The following is a sample chart of accounts. It does not represent a comprehensive chart of all the accounts used in this text but rather those accounts that are commonly used. This sample chart of accounts is for a company that generates service revenue as well as sales revenue. It uses the perpetual approach to inventory. If a periodic system was used, the following temporary accounts would be needed to record inventory purchases: Purchases, Freight-In, Purchase Returns and Allowances, and Purchase Discounts.

## Chart of Accounts

| Assets | Liabilities | Stockholders' Equity | Revenues | Expenses |
|---|---|---|---|---|
| Cash | Notes Payable | Common Stock | Service Revenue | Administrative Expenses |
| Accounts Receivable | Accounts Payable | Paid-in Capital in Excess of Par—Common Stock | Sales Revenue | Amortization Expense |
| Allowance for Doubtful Accounts | Unearned Service Revenue | | Sales Discounts | |
| | Salaries and Wages Payable | Preferred Stock | Sales Returns and Allowances | Bad Debt Expense |
| Interest Receivable | Interest Payable | Paid-in Capital in Excess of Par—Preferred Stock | Interest Revenue | Cost of Goods Sold |
| Inventory | Dividends Payable | Treasury Stock | Gain on Disposal of Plant Assets | Depreciation Expense |
| Supplies | Income Taxes Payable | Retained Earnings | | Freight-Out |
| Prepaid Insurance | Bonds Payable | Dividends | | Income Tax Expense |
| Prepaid Rent | Discount on Bonds Payable | Income Summary | | Insurance Expense |
| Land | Premium on Bonds Payable | | | Interest Expense |
| Equipment | Mortgage Payable | | | Loss on Disposal of Plant Assets |
| Accumulated Depreciation—Equipment | | | | Maintenance and Repairs Expense |
| Buildings | | | | Rent Expense |
| Accumulated Depreciation—Buildings | | | | Salaries and Wages Expense |
| Copyrights | | | | Selling Expenses |
| Goodwill | | | | Supplies Expense |
| Patents | | | | Utilities Expense |

# Financial & Managerial Accounting

**Fourth Edition**

**JERRY J. WEYGANDT PhD, CPA**
University of Wisconsin—Madison
Madison, Wisconsin

**PAUL D. KIMMEL PhD, CPA**
University of Wisconsin—Madison
Madison, Wisconsin

**JILL E. MITCHELL MS, MEd, CIA**
Northern Virginia Community College
Annandale, Virginia

WILEY

## DEDICATED TO

Our spouses, Enid, Merlynn, and Sean,
for their love, support, and encouragement.

| | |
|---|---|
| VICE PRESIDENT, EDITORIAL AND PRODUCT MANAGEMENT | Michael McDonald |
| EXECUTIVE EDITOR | Zoe Craig |
| EDITOR | Veronica Schram |
| COURSE CONTENT DEVELOPER | Jenny Welter |
| INSTRUCTIONAL DESIGNER | Matt Origoni |
| MARKETING MANAGER | Christina Koop |
| EDITORIAL SUPERVISOR | Terry Ann Tatro |
| PROGRAM ASSISTANT | Natalie Munoz |
| SENIOR MANAGER COURSE DEVELOPMENT AND PRODUCTION | Ed Brislin |
| EXECUTIVE MANAGING EDITOR | Karen Staudinger |
| SENIOR PRODUCTION EDITOR | Rachel Conrad |
| SENIOR DESIGNER | Jon Boylan |
| COVER IMAGE | sharply_done/Getty Images |

This book was set in 9.5/12 STIX Two Text by Lumina Datamatics, Inc.

Founded in 1807, John Wiley & Sons, Inc. has been a valued source of knowledge and understanding for more than 200 years, helping people around the world meet their needs and fulfill their aspirations. Our company is built on a foundation of principles that include responsibility to the communities we serve and where we live and work. In 2008, we launched a Corporate Citizenship Initiative, a global effort to address the environmental, social, economic, and ethical challenges we face in our business. Among the issues we are addressing are carbon impact, paper specifications and procurement, ethical conduct within our business and among our vendors, and community and charitable support. For more information, please visit our website: www.wiley.com/go/citizenship.

ISBN-13: 978-1-119-75252-3

The inside back cover will contain printing identification and country of origin if omitted from this page. In addition, if the ISBN on the back cover differs from the ISBN on this page, the one on the back cover is correct.

Printed in America.

SKY10021848_102020

# Brief Contents

## Available in Wiley's Online Course and Wiley Custom:

Dear Student,

**Why This Course?** Remember your biology course in high school? Did you have one of those "invisible man" models (or maybe something more high-tech than that) that gave you the opportunity to look "inside" the human body? This accounting course offers something similar. To understand a business, you have to understand the financial insides of a business organization. An accounting course will help you understand the essential financial components of businesses. Whether you are looking at a large multinational company like **Apple** or **Starbucks** or a single-owner software consulting business or coffee shop, knowing the fundamentals of accounting will help you understand what is happening. As an employee, a manager, an investor, a business owner, or a director of your own personal finances—any of which roles you will have at some point in your life—you will make better decisions for having taken this course.

> "Whether you are looking at a large multinational company like **Apple** or **Starbucks** or a single-owner software consulting business or coffee shop, knowing the fundamentals of accounting will help you understand what is happening."

**Why This Text?** Your instructor has chosen this text for you because of the authors' trusted reputation. The authors have worked hard to provide instructional material that is engaging, timely, and accurate.

**How to Succeed?** We've asked many students and many instructors whether there is a secret for success in this course. The nearly unanimous answer turns out to be not much of a secret: "Do the homework." This is one course where doing is learning. The more time you spend on the homework assignments—using the various tools that this text provides—the more likely you are to learn the essential concepts, techniques, and methods of accounting.

Good luck in this course. We hope you enjoy the experience and that you put to good use throughout a lifetime of success the knowledge you obtain in this course. We are sure you will not be disappointed.

Jerry J. Weygandt
Paul D. Kimmel
Jill E. Mitchell

# Author Commitment

**JERRY J. WEYGANDT, PhD, CPA**, is Arthur Andersen Alumni Emeritus Professor of Accounting at the University of Wisconsin—Madison. He holds a Ph.D. in accounting from the University of Illinois. Articles by Professor Weygandt have appeared in *The Accounting Review, Journal of Accounting Research, Accounting Horizons, Journal of Accountancy*, and other academic and professional journals. These articles have examined such financial reporting issues as accounting for price-level adjustments, pensions, convertible securities, stock option contracts, and interim reports. Professor Weygandt is author of other accounting and financial reporting texts and is a member of the American Accounting Association, the American Institute of Certified Public Accountants, and the Wisconsin Society of Certified Public Accountants. He has served on numerous committees of the American Accounting Association and as a member of the editorial board of the Accounting Review; he also has served as President and Secretary-Treasurer of the American Accounting Association. In addition, he has been actively involved with the American Institute of Certified Public Accountants and has been a member of the Accounting Standards Executive Committee (AcSEC) of that organization. He has served on the FASB task force that examined the reporting issues related to accounting for income taxes and served as a trustee of the Financial Accounting Foundation. Professor Weygandt has received the Chancellor's Award for Excellence in Teaching and the Beta Gamma Sigma Dean's Teaching Award. He is on the board of directors of M & I Bank of Southern Wisconsin. He is the recipient of the Wisconsin Institute of CPA's Outstanding Educator's Award and the Lifetime Achievement Award. In 2001 he received the American Accounting Association's Outstanding Educator Award.

**PAUL D. KIMMEL, PhD, CPA**, received his bachelor's degree from the University of Minnesota and his doctorate in accounting from the University of Wisconsin. He was an Associate Professor at the University of Wisconsin—Milwaukee for more than 25 years and is now a Senior Lecturer at the University of Wisconsin—Madison. He has public accounting experience with Deloitte & Touche (Minneapolis). He was the recipient of the UWM School of Business Advisory Council Teaching Award and the Reggie Taite Excellence in Teaching Award, and a three-time winner of the Outstanding Teaching Assistant Award at the University of Wisconsin. He is also a recipient of the Elijah Watts Sells Award for Honorary Distinction for his results on the CPA exam. He is a member of the American Accounting Association and the Institute of Management Accountants and has published articles in *Accounting Review, Accounting Horizons, Advances in Management Accounting, Managerial Finance, Issues in Accounting Education*, and *Journal of Accounting Education*, as well as other journals. His research interests include accounting for financial instruments and innovation in accounting education.

**JILL E. MITCHELL, MS, MEd, CIA**, is a Professor of Accounting at Northern Virginia Community College (NOVA), where she has taught face-to-face, hybrid, and online courses since 2008. Since 2009, she has been an adjunct instructor at George Mason University (GMU). She is a past president of the Washington, D.C. Chapter of the Accounting and Financial Women's Alliance (AFWA), and she served on the board of directors of the Virginia Society of CPAs (VSCPA). She is a member of the American Accounting Association (AAA) and the Institute of Internal Auditors. Jill serves on the AAA Education Committee and is the co-chair for the Conference on Teaching and Learning in Accounting (CTLA). Prior to joining the faculty at NOVA, Jill was a senior auditor with Ernst & Young's Business Risk Services practice in Miami, Florida. She is a certified internal auditor and earned an MS in Accountancy from the University of Virginia and a BBA in Management Information Systems from the University of Georgia honors program. Recently, she earned an MEd in Instructional Design Technology from GMU. Jill is a recipient of the Outstanding Faculty Award, the Commonwealth's highest honor for faculty of Virginia's universities and colleges presented by the State Council of Higher Education for Virginia; the Virginia Community College System Chancellor's Award for Teaching Excellence; the AFWA's Women Who Count Award; the AAA Two-Year College Educator of the Year Award; and the AAA/J. Michael and Mary Anne Cook/Deloitte Foundation Prize, the foremost recognition of an individual who consistently demonstrates the attributes of a superior teacher in the discipline of accounting.

# New to This Edition: Data Analytics

The authors carefully considered how to thoughtfully and meaningfully integrate data analytics into the accounting course, and are pleased to provide the following data analytics resources.

## Data Analytics in the Real World

Real-world examples that illustrate engaging situations in companies are provided throughout the text.

---

### Data Analytics Insight    The Walt Disney Company

Paulbr/Getty Images

#### Using Data in Its Own World

**The Walt Disney Company** makes fun seem effortless at its theme parks, but there is a magic mountain of data collection going on behind the scenes. For example, Disney employs behavioral analytics, which uses data to both predict and influence customer behavior, in countless ways. Disney collects the data through its "MagicBands" worn by visitors to the parks. While the MagicBands provide visitors with many benefits (e.g., delivering customized itineraries, reducing wait lines, and providing customer recognition by Disney characters), these bands are also delivering continual information to the company about the locations, activities, eating habits, and purchases of Disney visitors.

Disney uses the MagicBand information to support daily adjustments of operations as well as long-term planning. For example, the company can use this information to monitor park usage and subsequently encourage visitors to change their itineraries to different activities that will require a shorter wait time. If customers are waiting in line, they aren't happy—and they also aren't spending money. Long-term planning uses of MagicBand information include designing new attractions and updating menu options in response to supply and demand.

**Source**: Randerson112358, "How Disney World Uses Big Data," *medium.com* (May 18, 2019)

**What is behavioral analytics, and how does Disney use it to minimize lines at its theme parks? (Answer is available at the end of the chapter.)**

---

## Data Analytics and Decision-Making

The text also provides numerous discussions on how managers are increasingly relying on data analytics to make decisions using accounting information.

---

Companies have never had so much available data. In many companies, virtually every aspect of operations—the employees, the customers, even the manufacturing equipment—leaves a data trail. However, while "big data" can be impressive, it can also be overwhelming.

- Having all the data in the world will not necessarily lead to better results.
- The trick is having the skills and know-how to use the data in ways that result in more productive (and happier) employees, more satisfied customers, and more profitable operations.

It is therefore not surprising that one of the most rapidly growing areas of business today is data analytics. **Data analytics** is the use of techniques, which often combine software and statistics, to analyze data to make informed decisions.

Throughout the remainder of this text, we continue to offer many examples of how successful companies are using data analytics. We also provide examples of one analytical tool, data visualizations. **Data visualizations** often help managers acquire a more intuitive understanding of (1) the relationships between variables and (2) business trends.

---

# Data Analytics in Action

Most chapters offer *Data Analytics in Action* problems, to offer students the opportunity to see how they might use data analytics to help solve realistic business problems. Excel templates for each of the *Data Analytics in Action* problems provide students a framework for solving the problem. *Data Analytics in Excel* videos provide students with step-by-step guidance in performing the Excel skills they will need to solve these problems.

**Using Data Visualization to Analyze Changes over Time**

**DA6.1**  Data visualization can be used to analyze company changes over time.

**Example:** Recall the Feature Story "Where Is That Spare Bulldozer Blade?" presented in the chapter. **Caterpillar** continues to enhance its inventory management by improving its product sustainability in two ways. First, it is rebuilding used parts to like-new condition. Second, the company is remanufacturing usable inventory parts when customers trade-in or dispose of their used equipment. These actions not only reduce inventory costs but also enable Caterpillar to participate in the circular economy, where manufacturers take responsibility for their products at the end of the product lives. As noted in its 2019 sustainability report, Caterpillar has a goal of 20% growth in both rebuilding and remanufacturing from 2013 to 2020.

Has Caterpillar reached this goal? A line chart can help you visualize the company's progress over time. What information can you obtain by examining the following chart?

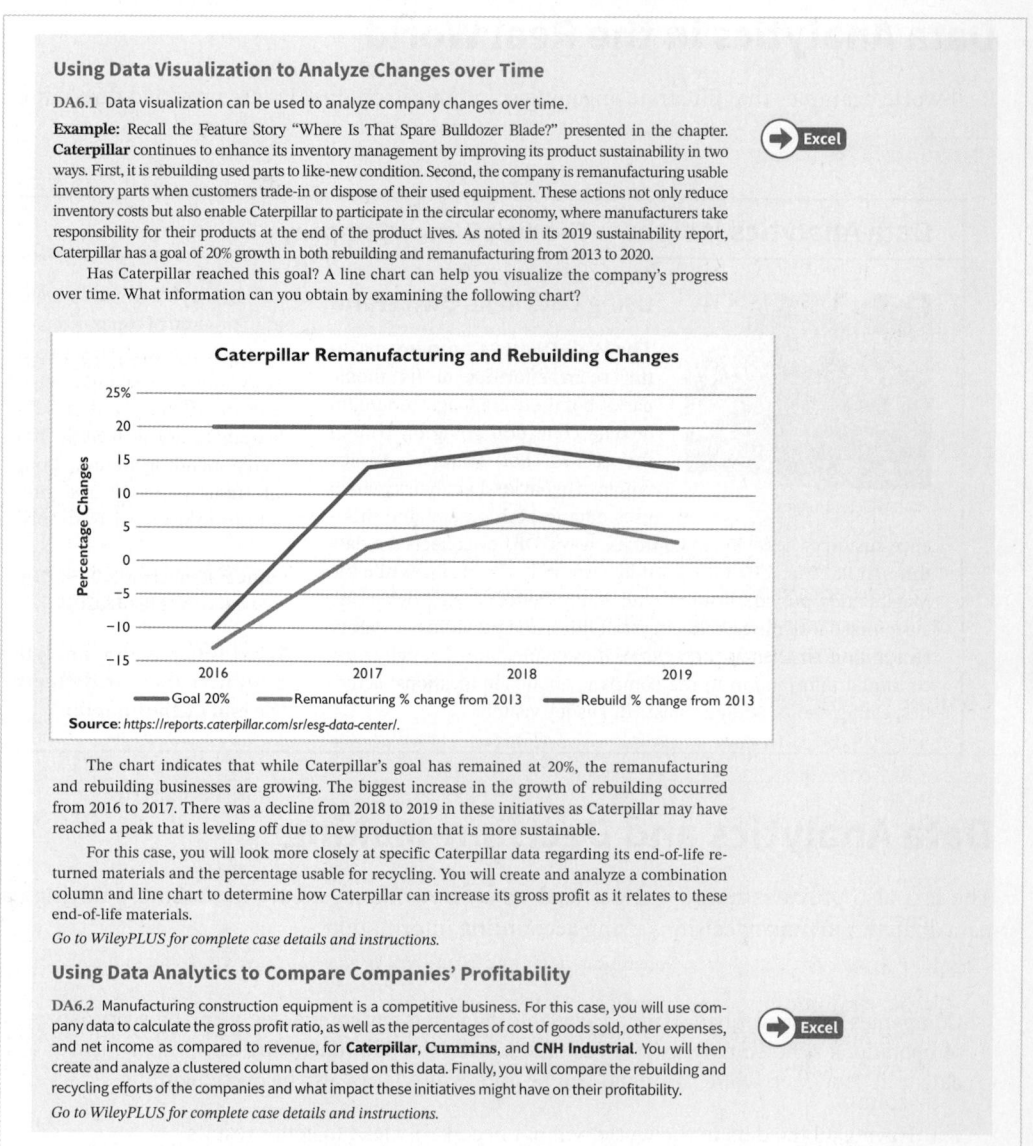

**Source**: *https://reports.caterpillar.com/sr/esg-data-center/.*

The chart indicates that while Caterpillar's goal has remained at 20%, the remanufacturing and rebuilding businesses are growing. The biggest increase in the growth of rebuilding occurred from 2016 to 2017. There was a decline from 2018 to 2019 in these initiatives as Caterpillar may have reached a peak that is leveling off due to new production that is more sustainable.

For this case, you will look more closely at specific Caterpillar data regarding its end-of-life returned materials and the percentage usable for recycling. You will create and analyze a combination column and line chart to determine how Caterpillar can increase its gross profit as it relates to these end-of-life materials.

*Go to WileyPLUS for complete case details and instructions.*

**Using Data Analytics to Compare Companies' Profitability**

**DA6.2**  Manufacturing construction equipment is a competitive business. For this case, you will use company data to calculate the gross profit ratio, as well as the percentages of cost of goods sold, other expenses, and net income as compared to revenue, for **Caterpillar**, **Cummins**, and **CNH Industrial**. You will then create and analyze a clustered column chart based on this data. Finally, you will compare the rebuilding and recycling efforts of the companies and what impact these initiatives might have on their profitability.

*Go to WileyPLUS for complete case details and instructions.*

# Data Visualization Homework Assignments

**PowerBI and Tableau visualizations** accompanied by questions are available with most chapters. PowerBI and Tableau visualizations allow students to interpret visualizations and think critically about data.

# Data Analytics Module

An **accounting-specific data analytics module** with interactive lessons, case studies, and videos is part of the Wiley online course. The module has been prepared using industry-validated content to help students develop the professional competencies needed for the changing workforce.

# New to This Edition: Chapter-by-Chapter Changes

**Chapter 1: Accounting in Action**

- NEW introductory discussion of how financial statement users can use data analytics to improve decision-making.

**Chapter 2: The Recording Process**

- NEW Helpful Hints, to reinforce student understanding of key concepts.
- NEW Accounting Across the Organization box, on **Hain Celestial Group**'s failure to provide income information to users, which resulted in a significant drop in its stock price.
- Re-ordered example transactions so payment of dividends is last, which is more reflective of real-world practices.

**Chapter 3: Adjusting the Accounts**

- NEW discussion and illustration of the five-step revenue recognition process.
- NEW business and markets news videos from **Bloomberg** that reference real-world news and decision-making related to accounting concepts. With accompanying multiple-choice and discussion questions.

**Chapter 4: Completing the Accounting Cycle**

- Updated definition of worksheet to include its most common form, an electronic spreadsheet.
- Simplified illustration of the closing process for improved understanding.
- NEW end-of-chapter problems that review portions of the accounting cycle that are not worksheet-based.

**Chapter 5: Accounting for Merchandising Operations**

- NEW section on how companies use data analytics to improve business decision-making regarding their policies on credit sales, sales returns and allowances, and sales discounts.
- NEW Comprehensive Accounting Cycle Review for the perpetual inventory method.
- NEW business and markets news videos from **Bloomberg** that reference real-world news and decision-making related to accounting concepts. With accompanying multiple-choice and discussion questions.

**Chapter 6: Inventories**

- NEW DO IT!s at end of each cost flow method discussion, so students can immediately check their understanding of the FIFO, LIFO, and average-cost methods.
- NEW illustration showing **Walmart**'s recent inventory disclosure, using retail inventory method.

- NEW Data Analytics in Action problems allow students to perform basic data analytics and data visualization.
- NEW business and markets news videos from **Bloomberg** that reference real-world news and decision-making related to accounting concepts. With accompanying multiple-choice and discussion questions.

**Chapter 7: Fraud, Internal Control, and Cash**

- NEW section on how data analytics helps improve internal controls.
- NEW discussion of recent FASB on restricted cash presentation in the statement of cash flows.
- NEW Data Analytics in Action problems allow students to perform basic data analytics and data visualization.
- NEW business and markets news videos from **Bloomberg** that reference real-world news and decision-making related to accounting concepts. With accompanying multiple-choice and discussion questions.

**Chapter 8: Accounting for Receivables**

- NEW Feature Story on how **Nike** has increased its sales through its credit policies.
- NEW section on data analytics and receivables management.
- NEW discussion of FASB expected credit loss model, which requires that companies measure expected uncollectible accounts and record bad debt expense on all receivables, even those with a low risk of loss.
- NEW business and markets news videos from **Bloomberg** that reference real-world news and decision-making related to accounting concepts. With accompanying multiple-choice and discussion questions.

**Chapter 9: Plant Assets, Natural Resources, and Intangible Assets**

- NEW Feature Story on how equipment can determine financial success in the airline industry.
- NEW discussion and International Note on use of historical cost principle and cash equivalent price in determining the cost of plant assets.
- NEW DO IT!s at end of subsections of depreciation methods, so students can immediately test their understanding of how to calculate straight-line, declining-balance, and units-of-activity depreciation methods.
- NEW discussion and illustration on depreciation disclosure in the notes to the financial statements.

- Expanded discussion of how companies must disclose in the financial statements significant changes in depreciation estimates.
- Moved "Sale of Plant Assets" section before "Retirement of Plant Assets" section for more logical organization of topics.
- Expanded discussion of description of intangible assets and how to account for them.
- NEW Data Analytics in Action problems allow students to perform basic data analytics and data visualization.
- NEW business and markets news videos from **Bloomberg** that reference real-world news and decision-making related to accounting concepts. With accompanying multiple-choice and discussion questions.

## Chapter 10: Liabilities

- NEW Feature Story on how debt has both helped and hurt **General Motors** and **Ford**.
- NEW discussion of leases and related EOC material.
- NEW discussion of bank line of credit disclosure.
- NEW business and markets news videos from **Bloomberg** that reference real-world news and decision-making related to accounting concepts. With accompanying multiple-choice and discussion questions.

## Chapter 11: Corporations: Organization, Stock Transactions, and Stockholders' Equity

- NEW discussion on hybrid forms of business organization.
- NEW discussion on how investors monitor a company's dividend practices.
- NEW discussion on how payment of stock dividend can be viewed as merely a publicity gesture.
- NEW People, Planet, and Profit Insight box on the upward trend of shareholder proposals on corporate responsibility.
- NEW Investor Insight box, on how companies that pay dividends can increase investor wealth.
- NEW Data Analytics in Action problems allow students to perform basic data analytics and data visualization.
- NEW business and markets news videos from **Bloomberg** that reference real-world news and decision-making related to accounting concepts. With accompanying multiple-choice and discussion questions.

## Chapter 12: Statement of Cash Flows

- Added more T-accounts and journal entries to increase understandability of preparing the statement of cash flows using the indirect method.
- Used **Apple** financial statements for example in how to analyze the statement of cash flows using free cash flow calculation, for increased student engagement.
- NEW Data Analytics in Action problems allow students to perform basic data analytics and data visualization.

- NEW business and markets news videos from **Bloomberg** that reference real-world news and decision-making related to accounting concepts. With accompanying multiple-choice and discussion questions.

## Chapter 13: Financial Statement Analysis

- NEW presentation of discontinued operations on the income statement (previously on the statement of comprehensive income) as well as format of the statement of comprehensive income.
- NEW illustration showing the financial ratio classifications, for improved student understanding and engagement.
- Comprehensive example, as well as explanations of ratio calculations, now included in the chapter instead of an appendix.
- NEW business and markets news videos from **Bloomberg** that reference real-world news and decision-making related to accounting concepts. With accompanying multiple-choice and discussion questions.

## Chapter 14: Managerial Accounting

- NEW section on the value of data analytics in helping managers understand the relationship between CVP variables and business trends.
- NEW Data Analytics Insight box on how **Disney** uses its MagicBands as a source of data to analyze the behavior of its customers.
- Expanded discussion within "Manufacturing Costs" section to ensure student understanding of raw materials versus direct materials as well as what is considered to be manufacturing overhead. Also updated Illustration 1.4 (assignment of costs to cost categories) to include an explanation for each cost classification, again to ensure student understanding.
- Moved up discussion of balance sheet (before income statement) in "Manufacturing Costs in Financial Statements" section for more logical presentation of topics.
- Updated each "Managerial Accounting Today" section subtopic for the latest information on service industries, lean manufacturing, balanced scorecard, ethics, and social responsibility.
- NEW Data Analytics in Action problems allow students to perform basic data analytics and data visualization.
- NEW business and markets news videos from **Bloomberg** that reference real-world news and decision-making related to accounting concepts. With accompanying multiple-choice and discussion questions.

## Chapter 15: Job Order Costing

- NEW Data Analytics Insight box on how **Autodesk** uses data analytics to improve its software and profitability.
- More discussion on assigning raw materials costs and assigning factory labor costs, to improve student understanding.

- Updated time ticket discussion for more recent process involving scanning of employee identification codes.
- NEW Data Analytics in Action problems allow students to perform basic data analytics and data visualization.

### Chapter 16: Process Costing

- Production cost report now has the "Cost Reconciliation Schedule" section to include costs to be accounted for, not just costs accounted for.
- Throughout, have carefully scrutinized discussion to ensure complete student understanding. For example, in the "Transfer to Next Department" section, have added explanation of what department transfers entail.

### Chapter 17: Activity-Based Costing

- NEW data analytics discussion added to section of identifying cost drivers.
- NEW Data Analytics Insight box on how companies such as **GE** and **UPS** use data analytics to help reduce non-value-added activities.
- NEW section ("Assigning Nonmanufacturing Overhead Costs") and income statement presentations, to help highlight differences between traditional costing and activity-based costing.

### Chapter 18: Cost-Volume-Profit

- NEW discussion on CVP and the use of data analytics, using **DHL Express** as an example.
- NEW expanded highlighted equations, to show more detailed calculations for improved understanding.
- NEW expanded explanation of what CVP analysis is.
- NEW illustration and discussion on how a GAAP income statement differs from a CVP income statement.
- NEW discussion on the variable cost ratio.
- Updated Service Company Insight box to feature more recent information on the business of music promotion (and using Drake as an example instead of the Rolling Stones) and computing the break-even point.
- Enhanced end-of-chapter assignments by offering students more opportunities to prepare CVP income statements, as well as a new problem on regression analysis.
- NEW Data Analytics in Action problems allow students to perform basic data analytics and data visualization.
- NEW business and markets news videos from **Bloomberg** that reference real-world news and decision-making related to accounting concepts. With accompanying multiple-choice and discussion questions.

### Chapter 19: Cost-Volume-Profit Analysis: Additional Issues

- NEW Data Analytics Insight box on how **Caesars Entertainment** uses data analytics to determine how to maximize profits from its customers.

- NEW Data Analytics in Action problems allow students to perform basic data analytics and data visualization.

### Chapter 20: Incremental Analysis

- Highlighted the decision rules, as well as additional factors to consider, for incremental analysis decisions.
- NEW business and markets news videos from **Bloomberg** that reference real-world news and decision-making related to accounting concepts. With accompanying multiple-choice and discussion questions.

### Chapter 21: Pricing

- NEW Data Analytics Insight box on how **Big Data Pricing** helps customers use data analytics to improve dynamic pricing practices.
- NEW Data Analytics in Action problem allows students to perform basic data analytics and data visualization.

### Chapter 22: Budgetary Planning

- NEW Data Analytics Insight box on how **Dickey's Barbecue Pit** uses data analytics to improve restaurant sales performance.
- NEW Data Analytics in Action problem allows students to perform basic data analytics and data visualization.
- NEW business and markets news videos from **Bloomberg** that reference real-world news and decision-making related to accounting concepts. With accompanying multiple-choice and discussion questions.

### Chapter 23: Budgetary Control and Responsibility Accounting

- NEW Data Analytics Insight boxes on rolling forecasts and zero-based budgeting.
- Updated section on "Judgmental Factors in ROI" with "Alternative Measures of ROI Inputs" for more precise discussion and improved student understanding.
- NEW Data Analytics in Action problems allow students to perform basic data analytics and data visualization.
- NEW business and markets news videos from **Bloomberg** that reference real-world news and decision-making related to accounting concepts. With accompanying multiple-choice and discussion questions.

### Chapter 24: Standard Costs and Balanced Scorecard

- NEW Data Analytics Insight box on how manufacturing companies are using technology such as 5G cellular to improve the amount and speed of data collection to improve operations.
- NEW highlighted applications of determining standard costs in "A Case Study" section, for improved student understanding.
- NEW Data Analytics in Action problem allows students to perform basic data analytics and data visualization.
- NEW business and markets news videos from **Bloomberg** that reference real-world news and decision-making related

to accounting concepts. With accompanying multiple-choice and discussion questions.

## Chapter 25: Planning for Capital Investments

- NEW Data Analytics Insight box on how **Electronic Arts** uses data from its current online video games to help it develop future products.

- Improved illustration showing computation of cash payback period by including detailed steps and computations.

- NEW Management Insight box on 5G and how it presents a risky investment to telecom companies.

- NEW Data Analytics in Action problems allow students to perform basic data analytics and data visualization.

- NEW business and markets news videos from **Bloomberg** that reference real-world news and decision-making related to accounting concepts. With accompanying multiple-choice and discussion questions.

## Appendix H: Investments

- NEW DO IT!s added to appendix discussion as well as end-of-chapter material.

- NEW Review and Practice section includes multiple-choice questions followed by annotated solutions, practice brief exercises with solutions, practice exercises with solutions, and a practice problem with solution.

When you think of accounting, you probably don't think of sports. So why do we have a photo of surfboards on our cover? It's because this image represents active learning that's best accomplished through full engagement, commitment, and practice. Through the integrated learning experience with the text and online course materials, *Financial & Managerial Accounting, Fourth Edition,* takes the same approach many coaches do, by helping students not only master key concepts first but understand why they're important. In this way, students appreciate the importance of accounting basics and develop a solid foundation of knowledge. This leads to better student retention and sets them up for success in future careers.

**In this new edition, all content has been carefully reviewed and revised to ensure maximum student understanding.** At the same time, the time-tested features that have proven to be of most help to students have been retained, such as the following.

## Financial Statement Transaction Illustrations

Throughout the text, carefully crafted illustrations demonstrate the analysis of business transactions. Each illustration clearly walks the student through the process of (1) basic analysis, (2) equation analysis, and (3) debit-credit analysis, as well as shows the (4) general journal entry and (5) general ledger posting.

# Infographic Learning

Over half of the text is visual, providing students alternative ways of learning about accounting.

**Revenue Recognition**

Service performed

Customer requests service → Cash received

Revenue should be recognized in the accounting period in which the service is performed.

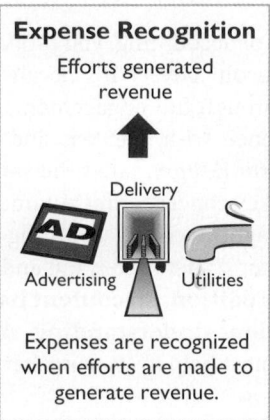

**Expense Recognition**

Efforts generated revenue

Advertising — Delivery — Utilities

Expenses are recognized when efforts are made to generate revenue.

# Real-World Decision-Making

Real-world examples, which illustrate engaging situations in companies, are provided throughout the text. Answers to the critical thinking questions are now available at the end of each chapter.

---

## People, Planet, and Profit Insight    BrightFarms

### Gardens in the Sky

Agatha Koroglu/ Shutterstock.com

The United Nations' Food and Agriculture Organization estimates that by 2050, roughly 70% of people will live in cities. This means that more food will need to be hauled farther to get it to the consumer. To address the lack of farmable land and reduce the cost of transporting produce, some companies, such as New York-based **BrightFarms**, are building urban greenhouses. BrightFarms' mission is "to grow food in the same communities where it's consumed." In doing so, the company says it uses 80% less water, 90% less land, and 95% less shipping fuel than long-distance, field-grown produce.

This sounds great, but do the numbers work? Some variable costs are reduced. For example, the use of pesticides, herbicides, fuel costs for shipping, and water are all reduced.

Soil erosion is a non-issue since plants are grown hydroponically (in a solution of water and minerals), and land requirements are reduced because of vertical structures. But, some fixed costs are higher. First, there is the cost of the building. Also, multistory buildings require artificial lighting for plants on lower floors.

Rooftop greenhouses on existing city structures already appear financially viable. For example, a 15,000 square-foot rooftop greenhouse in Brooklyn already produces roughly 30 tons of vegetables per year for local residents.

**Sources:** "Vertical Farming: Does It Really Stack Up?" *The Economist* (December 9, 2010); Jane Black, "BrightFarms Idea: Greenhouses That Cut Short the Path from Plant to Grocery Shelf," *The Washington Post* (May 7, 2013); and *BrightFarms.com* (2019).

**What are some of the variable and fixed costs that are impacted by hydroponic farming? (Answer is available at the end of the chapter.)**

# DO IT! Exercises

DO IT! Exercises in the body of the text prompt students to stop and review key concepts. They outline the Action Plan necessary to complete the exercise as well as show a detailed solution.

---

### DO IT! 3 | Adjusting Entries for Accruals

Micro Computer Services Inc. began operations on August 1, 2022. At the end of August 2022, management prepares monthly financial statements. The following information relates to August.

1. At August 31, the company owed its employees $800 in salaries and wages that will be paid on September 1.

2. On August 1, the company borrowed $30,000 from a local bank on a 1-year note payable. The annual interest rate is 10%. Interest will be paid with the note at maturity.

3. Revenue for services performed but unrecorded for August totaled $1,100.

Prepare the adjusting entries needed at August 31, 2022.

**ACTION PLAN**

- Make adjusting entries at the end of the period to recognize revenues for services performed and for expenses incurred.

- Don't forget to make adjusting entries for accruals. Adjusting entries for accruals will increase both a balance sheet and an income statement account.

**Solution**

| | | |
|---|---|---|
| 1. Salaries and Wages Expense | 800 | |
|    Salaries and Wages Payable | | 800 |
|     (To record accrued salaries) | | |
| 2. Interest Expense | 250 | |
|    Interest Payable | | 250 |
|     (To record accrued interest: | | |
|     $30,000 \times 10\% \times \frac{1}{12} = \$250$) | | |
| 3. Accounts Receivable | 1,100 | |
|    Service Revenue | | 1,100 |
|     (To record revenue for services performed) | | |

Related exercise material: **BE3.10, BE3.11, BE3.12, DO IT! 3.3**, E3.5, E3.6, E3.7, E3.8, E3.9, E3.10, E3.11, E3.12, E3.13, E3.14, E3.15, E3.17, E3.18, E3.19, **and E3.20.**

---

# Review and Practice

Each chapter concludes with a Review and Practice section which includes a review of learning objectives, key terms glossary, practice multiple-choice questions with annotated solutions, practice brief exercises with solutions, practice exercises with solutions, and a practice problem with a solution.

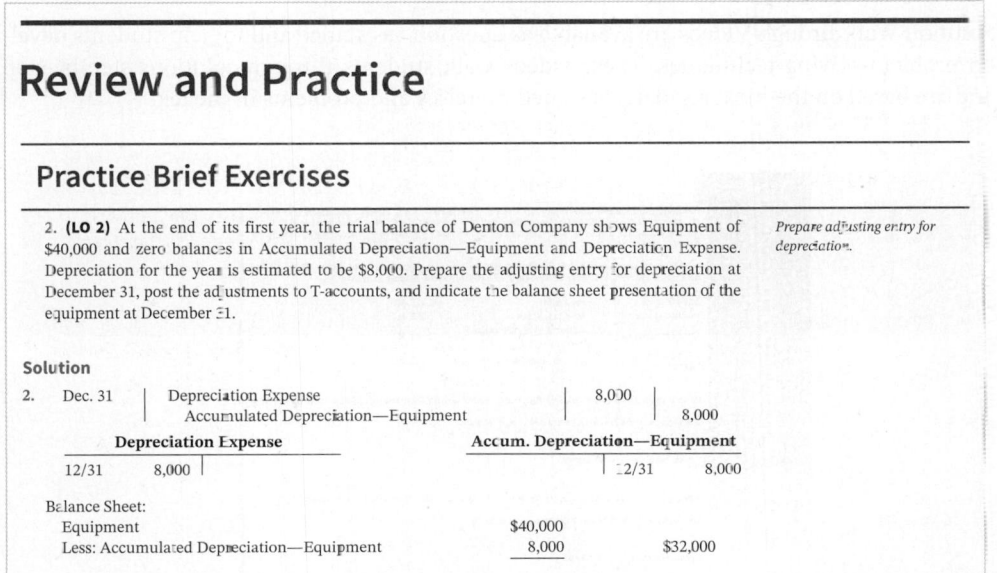

# Review and Practice

## Practice Brief Exercises

2. **(LO 2)** At the end of its first year, the trial balance of Denton Company shows Equipment of $40,000 and zero balances in Accumulated Depreciation—Equipment and Depreciation Expense. Depreciation for the year is estimated to be $8,000. Prepare the adjusting entry for depreciation at December 31, post the adjustments to T-accounts, and indicate the balance sheet presentation of the equipment at December 31.

*Prepare adjusting entry for depreciation.*

**Solution**

| | | | | |
|---|---|---|---|---|
| 2. Dec. 31 | Depreciation Expense | | 8,000 | |
| |    Accumulated Depreciation—Equipment | | | 8,000 |

| Depreciation Expense | | Accum. Depreciation—Equipment | |
|---|---|---|---|
| 12/31 | 8,000 | 12/31 | 8,000 |

Balance Sheet:
| | | |
|---|---|---|
| Equipment | $40,000 | |
| Less: Accumulated Depreciation—Equipment | 8,000 | $32,000 |

# Engaging Digital Tools

Digital study tools in Wiley's online course include the following.

## Real-World Company Videos

Real-world company videos feature both small businesses and larger companies to help students apply content and see how business owners apply concepts from the text in the real world. New to this edition are news videos from **Bloomberg** that reference real-world news and decision-making related to accounting concepts, with accompanying multiple-choice and discussion questions.

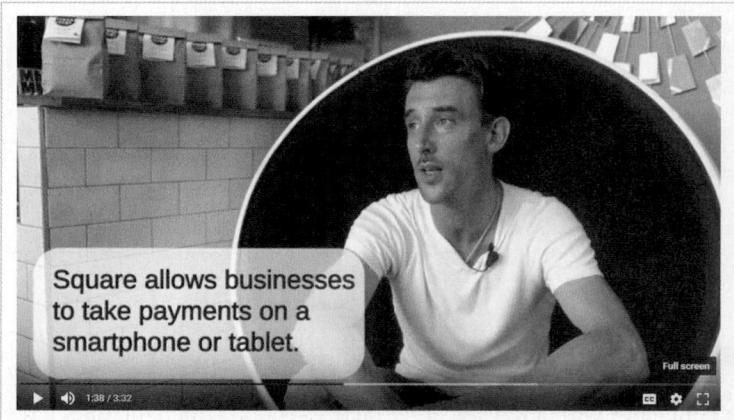

**Source:** YouTube.

## Solution Walkthrough Videos

Solution Walkthrough Videos are available as question assistance and to help students develop problem-solving techniques. These videos walk students through solutions step-by-step and are based on the most regularly assigned exercises and problems in the text.

**Source:** YouTube.

# Interactive Tutorials

Interactive tutorials are voice-guided reviews of topics in each learning objective. Checkpoints in the tutorials require students to review and solve simple self-assessment exercises.

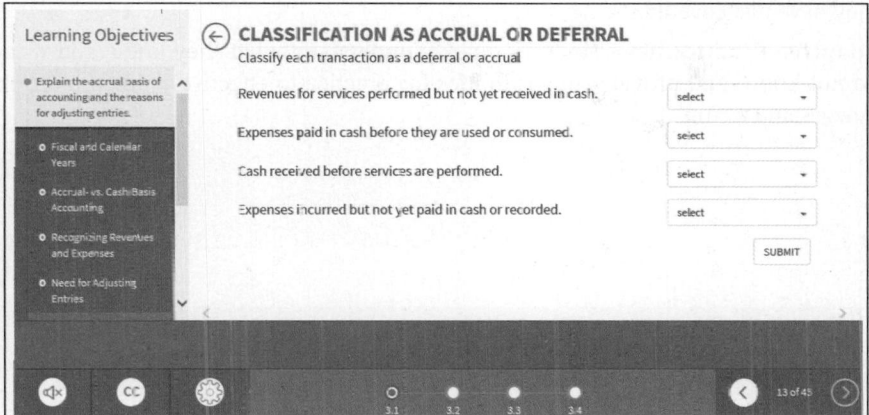

# Gradable Excel Questions

Gradable Excel questions for each chapter provide students an opportunity to practice Excel skills in the context of solving accounting problems.

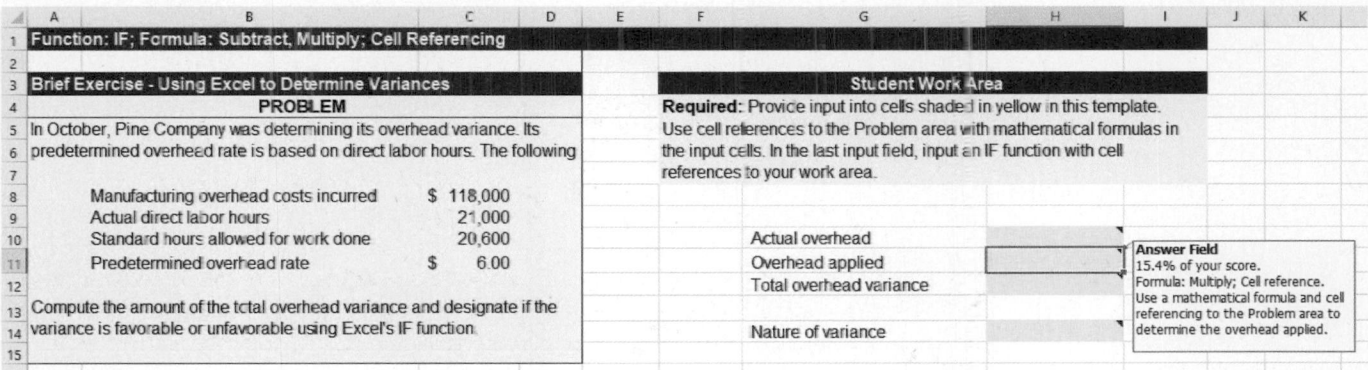

# Data Visualization Homework Assignments

**PowerBI and Tableau visualizations** accompanied by questions are available with most chapters. PowerBI and Tableau visualizations allow students to interpret visualizations and think critically about data.

In addition, other learning opportunities in Wiley's online course include the following.

- **Accounting-Specific Data Analytics Module** offers interactive lessons, case studies, and videos. The module has been prepared using industry-validated content to help students develop the professional competencies needed for the changing workforce.
- **Cookie Creations** is a continuing case that spans across the financial accounting chapters and shows how a small business grows.
- **Waterways Corporation** is a continuing case that spans across the managerial accounting chapters and offers students the opportunity to see how a small business might use managerial accounting to operate effectively.

- **Wiley Accounting Updates** (wileyaccountingupdates.com) provide faculty and students with weekly curated news articles and suggested discussion questions.

- **Flashcards and Crossword Puzzles** help students study and master basic vocabulary and concepts.

- **Student Practice** quickly and effectively assesses student understanding of the material they have just covered.

- **Adaptive Practice** helps students quickly understand what they know and what they do not know, and provides opportunities for practice to effectively prepare for class or quizzes and exams.

# Contents

# 24 Standard Costs and Balanced Scorecard 24-1

# 25 Planning for Capital Investments 25-1

## Available in Wiley's Online Course and Wiley Custom:

# Acknowledgments

*Financial & Managerial Accounting* has benefited greatly from the input of focus group participants, manuscript reviewers, users, ancillary authors, and proofers. We greatly appreciate the constructive suggestions and innovative ideas of uses and reviewers and the creativity and accuracy of the ancillary authors and checkers.

## Users and Reviewers

Shawn Abbott, *College of the Siskiyous*
Joseph Adamo, *Cazenovia College*
Dawn Addington, *Central New Mexico Community College*
Pushpa Agrawal, *University of Nebraska—Kearney*
Sol Ahiarah, *SUNY—Buffalo State*
Lynn Almond, *Virginia Polytechnic Institute*
Elizabeth Ammann, *Lindenwood University*
Joe Atallah, *Coastline Community College*
Timothy Baker, *California State University—Fresno*
Lisa Banks, *Mott Community College*
Joyce Barden, *DeVry University*
Melody Barta, *Evergreen Valley College*
Jeffrey Beatty, *Fresno City College*
Linda Bell, *Park University*
David Bojarsky, *California State University—Long Beach*
Jack Borke, *University of Wisconsin—Platteville*
Anna Boulware, *St. Charles Community College*
Bruce Bradford, *Fairfield University*
Linda Bressler, *University of Houston—Downtown*
Ann K. Brooks, *University of New Mexico*
Robert Brown, *Evergreen Valley College*
Leroy Bugger, *Edison State College*
Melodi Bunting, *Edgewood College*
Lisa Capozzoli, *College of DuPage*
Renee Castrigano, *Cleveland State University*
Wanda Causseaux, *Siena College*
Sandy Cereola, *James Madison University*
Gayle Chaky, *Dutchess Community College*
Amy Chang, *San Francisco State University*
Julie Chenier, *Louisiana State University—Baton Rouge*
James Chiafery, *University of Massachusetts—Boston*
Bea Chiang, *The College of New Jersey*
Cheryl Clark, *Point Park University*
Toni Clegg, *Delta College*
Maxine Cohen, *Bergen Community College*
Arthur College, *Evergreen Valley College*
Stephen Collins, *University of Massachusetts—Lowell*
Solveg Cooper, *Cuesta College*
William Cooper, *North Carolina A&T State University*
Cheryl Copeland, *California State University, Fresno*
Alan E. Davis, *Community College of Philadelphia*
Steven Day, *Dixie State University*
Larry DeGaetano, *Montclair State University*
Michael Deschamps, *MiraCosta College*
Bettye Desselle, *Texas Southern University*

Judy Dewitt, *Central Michigan University*
Cyril Dibie, *Tarrant County College—Arlington*
Jean Dunn, *Rady School of Management at University of California—San Diego*
Ron Dustin, *Fresno City College*
Barbara Eide, *University of Wisconsin—La Crosse*
Dennis Elam, *Texas A&M University—San Antonio*
James Emig, *Villanova University*
Janet Farler, *Pima Community College*
Charmaine Felder, *Brandman University*
Anthony Fortini, *Camden County College*
Jeanne Franco, *Paradise Valley Community College*
Chad Frawley, *Rutgers University—Northeast Normal*
Patrick Geer, *Hawkeye Community College*
Vicki Greshik, *University of Jamestown*
Andrew Griffith, *Iona College*
Jeffrey Haber, *Iona College*
John Hogan, *Fisher College*
Bambi Hora, *University of Central Oklahoma*
M.A. Houston, *Wright State University*
Jeff Hsu, *St. Louis Community College—Meramec*
Kimberly Hurt, *Central Community College*
Hussein Issa, *Rutgers Business School*
Janet Jamieson, *University of Dubuque*
Kevin Jones, *Drexel University*
Don Kovacic, *California State University—San Marcos*
Lynn Krausse, *Bakersfield College*
Craig Krenek, *Elmhurst College*
Jeffrey T. Kunz, *Carroll University*
Steven LaFave, *Augsburg College*
Eric Lee, *University of Northern Iowa*
Jason Lee, *SUNY Plattsburgh*
Harold Little, *Western Kentucky University*
Dennis Lopez, *University of Texas—San Antonio*
Lisa Ludlum, *Western Illinois University*
Michael J. MacDonald, *University of Wisconsin—Whitewater*
Suneel Maheshwari, *Marshall University*
Lois Mahoney, *Eastern Michigan University*
Diane Marker, *University of Toledo*
Tom Marsh, *Northern Virginia Community College*
Christian Mastilak, *Xavier University*
Josephine Mathias, *Mercer County Community College*
Edward McGinnis, *American River College*
Florence McGovern, *Bergen Community College*
Pam Meyer, *University of Louisiana—Lafayette*
Mary Michel, *Manhattan College*
Joan Miller, *William Paterson University*
Jill Misuraca, *University of Tampa*
Earl Mitchell, *Santa Ana College*
Syed Moiz, *University of Wisconsin—Platteville*
Brigitte Muehlmann, *Babson College*
Linda Mullins, *Georgia State University Perimeter College*
Johnna Murray, *University of Missouri—St. Louis*
Michael Newman, *University of Houston*

Lee Nicholas, *University of Northern Iowa*
Rosemary Nurre, *College of San Mateo*
Cindy Nye, *Bellevue University*
Gary Olsen, *Carroll University*
Sarah O'Rourke, *Rutgers Business School*
Glenn Pate, *Palm Beach State College*
Nori Pearson, *Washington State University*
Joe Pecore, *Rady School of Management at University of California—San Diego*
Dawn Peters, *Southwestern Illinois College*
DeAnne Peterson, *University of Wisconsin—Eau Claire*
Judy Peterson, *Monmouth College*
Timothy Peterson, *Gustavus Adolphus College*
Robert Rambo, *Roger Williams University*
Jim Resnik, *Bergen Community College*
Jorge Romero, *Towson University*
Luther Ross, *Central Piedmont Community College*
Maria Roxas, *Central Connecticut State University*
Robert Russ, *Northern Kentucky University*
Christina Ryan, *College of New Jersey*
Susan Sadowski, *Shippensburg University*
Susan Sandblom, *Scottsdale Community College*
Richard Sarkisian, *Camden County College*
Marshall Saunders, *Rutgers Business School*
Karl Schindl, *University of Wisconsin—Manitowoc*
Debbie Seifert, *Illinois State University*
Carl F. Shultz, *Rider University*
Valerie Simmons, *University of Southern Mississippi*
Gregory Sinclair, *San Francisco State University*
Mike Skaff, *College of the Sequoias*
Charles Skender, *University of North Carolina—Chapel Hill*
Karyn Smith, *Georgia Perimeter College*
Kathleen J. Smith, *University of Nebraska—Kearney*
Patrick Stegman, *College of Lake County*
Richard Steingart, *San Jose State University*
Gracelyn Stuart-Tuggle, *Palm Beach State University*
Karen Tabak, *Maryville University*
Diane Tanner, *University of North Florida*
Tom Thompson, *Savannah Technical College*
Mike Tyler, *Barry University*
Jin Ulmer, *Angelina College*
Linda Vaello, *University of Texas—San Antonio*
Manuel Valle, *City College of San Francisco*
Huey L. Van Dine, *Bergen Community College*
Joan Van Hise, *Fairfield University*
Claire Veal, *University of Texas—San Antonio*
Sheila Viel, *University of Wisconsin—Milwaukee*
Suzanne Ward, *University of Louisiana—Lafayette*
Evan Wasserman, *Rutgers Business School*
Dan Way, *Central Piedmont Community College*
Geri B. Wink, *Colorado State University—Pueblo*
Catherine Wyatt, *Lumina Datamatics*

## Online Course Developers and Reviewers

Carole Brandt-Fink
Heidi Hansel
Laura McNally
Melanie Yon

## Ancillary Authors, Contributors, Proofers, and Accuracy Checkers

Ellen Bartley, *St. Joseph's College*
LuAnn Bean, *Florida Institute of Technology*
Debby Bloom, *Queens University*
Jack Borke, *University of Wisconsin—Platteville*
Ann K. Brooks, *University of New Mexico*
Melodi Bunting, *Edgewood College*
Bea Chiang, *The College of New Jersey*
Lawrence Chui, *University of St. Thomas*
Carleton Donchess, *Bridgewater State University*
Dina El Mahdy, *Morgan State University*
James Emig, *Villanova University*
Mary Ewanechko, *Monroe Community College*
Larry Falcetto, *Emporia State University*
Vicki Greshik, *University of Jamestown*
Michael Griffin, *University of Massachusetts—Dartmouth*
Heidi Hansel, *Kirkwood Community College*
Coby Harmon, *University of California—Santa Barbara*
William Heninger, *Brigham Young University*
Lisa Hewes, *Northern Arizona University*
Derek Jackson, *St. Mary's University of Minnesota*
Craig Krenek, *Elmhurst College*
Y. Robert Lin, *California State University—East Bay*
Lisa Ludlum, *Western Illinois University*
Kirk Lynch, *Sandhills Community College*
Donald R. Majors II, *Elmhurst College and Utica College*
Susanna Matson, *Southern New Hampshire University*
Jill Misuraca, *University of Tampa*
Barbara Muller, *Arizona State University*
Linda Mullins, *Georgia State University—Perimeter College*
Yvonne Phang, *Borough of Manhattan Community College*
David Polster, *Oakton Community College*
Laura Prosser, *Black Hills State University*
Angela Sandberg, *Shorter University*
Margaret Shackell, *Forsyth Technical Community College*
Vincent Shea, *St. John's University*
Alice Sineath, *University of Maryland University College*
Teresa Speck, *St. Mary's University of Minnesota*
Lynn Stallworth, *Appalachian State University*
Diane Tanner, *University of North Florida*
Sheila Viel, *University of Wisconsin—Milwaukee*
Dick Wasson, *Southwestern College*
Lori Grady Zaher, *Bucks County Community College*

## Advisory Board

Jimmy Carmenate, *Florida International University*
Sandra Cereola, *James Madison University*
Norma Holter, *Towson University*
Frank Ilett, *Boise State University*
Christine Kloezeman, *Glendale Community College*
Johnna Murray, *University of Missouri—St. Louis*
Nori Pearson, *Washington State University*
Karen Russom, *Lone Star College—Greenspoint*
Joel Sneed, *University of Oregon*

We thank Benjamin Huegel and Teresa Speck of St. Mary's University for their extensive efforts in the preparation of the homework materials related to Current Designs. We also appreciate the considerable support provided to us by the following people at Current Designs: Mike Cichanowski, Jim Brown, Diane Buswell, and Jake Greseth. We also benefited from the assistance and suggestions provided to us by Joan Van Hise in the preparation of materials related to sustainability.

We appreciate the exemplary support and commitment given to us by executive editor Zoe Craig, editor Veronica Schram, marketing manager Christina Koop, course content developer Jenny Welter, instructional designer Matt Origoni, senior course production operations specialist Nicole Repasky, editorial supervisor Terry Ann Tatro, designer Jon Boylan, program assistant Natalie Munoz, senior production editor Rachel Conrad, and Julie Perry, Cindy Durand, Amy Kopperude, Jennifer Collins, Jennifer Collins, Gladys Soto, and Richard Bretan at Lumina. All of these professionals provided innumerable services that helped the text take shape.

We will appreciate suggestions and comments from users—instructors and students alike. You can send your thoughts and ideas about the text to us via email at: AccountingAuthors@yahoo.com.

**Paul D. Kimmel**
Madison, Wisconsin

**Jerry J. Weygandt**
Madison, Wisconsin

**Jill E. Mitchell**
Annandale, Virginia

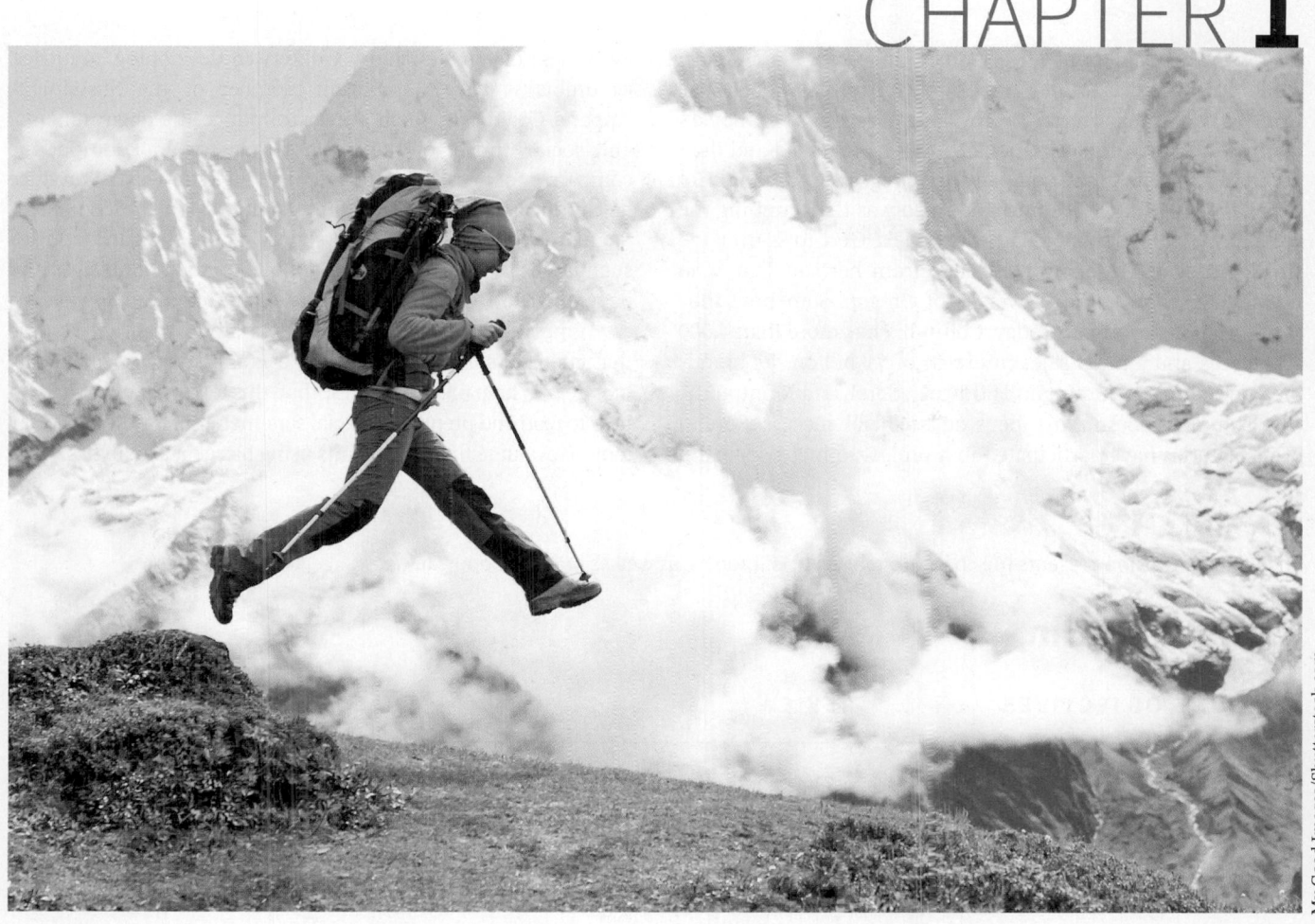

## CHAPTER 1

My Good Images/Shutterstock.com

# Accounting in Action

The **Chapter Preview** describes the purpose of the chapter and highlights major topics.

## Chapter Preview

The following Feature Story about **Columbia Sportswear Company** highlights the importance of having good financial information and knowing how to use it to make effective business decisions. Whatever your pursuits or occupation, the need for financial information is inescapable. You cannot earn a living, spend money, buy on credit, make an investment, or pay taxes without receiving, using, or dispensing financial information. Good decision-making depends on good information. The purpose of this chapter is to show you that accounting is the system used to provide useful financial information.

The **Feature Story** helps you picture how the chapter topic relates to the real world of accounting and business.

## Feature Story

### Knowing the Numbers

Many students who take this course do not plan to be accountants. If you are in that group, you might be thinking, "If I'm not going to be an accountant, why do I need to know accounting?" Well, consider this quote from Harold Geneen, the former chairman of **IT&T**: "To be good at your business, you have to know the numbers—cold." In business, accounting and financial statements are the means for communicating the numbers. If you don't know how to read financial statements, you can't really know your business.

Knowing the numbers is sometimes even a matter of corporate survival. Consider the story of **Columbia Sportswear Company**, headquartered in Portland, Oregon. Gert Boyle's family fled Nazi Germany when she was 13 years old and then purchased a small hat company in Oregon, Columbia Hat Company. In 1971, Gert's husband, who was then running the company, died suddenly of a heart attack. Gert took over the small, struggling company with help from her son Tim, who was then a senior at the University of Oregon. Somehow, they kept the company afloat. Today, Columbia has more than 4,000 employees and annual sales in excess of $1 billion. Its brands include Columbia, Mountain Hardwear, Sorel, and Montrail.

Columbia doesn't just focus on financial success. Several of its factories have participated in a project to increase health awareness of female factory workers in developing countries. Columbia is also a founding member of the Sustainable Apparel Coalition, which strives to reduce the environmental and social impact of the apparel industry. In addition, the company monitors all of the independent factories that produce its products to ensure that they comply with the company's Standards of Manufacturing Practices. These standards address such issues as forced labor, child labor, harassment, wages and benefits, health and safety, and the environment.

Employers such as Columbia Sportswear generally assume that managers in all areas of the company are "financially literate." To help prepare you for that, this text will help you learn how to read and prepare financial statements, and how to use key tools to evaluate financial results using basic data analytics.

---

The **Chapter Outline** presents the chapter's topics and subtopics, as well as practice opportunities.

# Chapter Outline

| LEARNING OBJECTIVES | REVIEW | PRACTICE |
|---|---|---|
| **LO 1** Identify the activities and users associated with accounting. | • Three activities <br> • Who uses accounting data | **DO IT! 1** Basic Concepts |
| **LO 2** Explain the building blocks of accounting: ethics, principles, and assumptions. | • Ethics <br> • GAAP <br> • Measurement principles <br> • Assumptions | **DO IT! 2** Building Blocks of Accounting |
| **LO 3** State the accounting equation, and define its components. | • Assets <br> • Liabilities <br> • Stockholders' equity | **DO IT! 3** Stockholders' Equity Effects |
| **LO 4** Analyze the effects of business transactions on the accounting equation. | • Accounting transactions <br> • Transaction analysis <br> • Summary of transactions | **DO IT! 4** Tabular Analysis |
| **LO 5** Describe the four financial statements and how they are prepared. | • Income statement <br> • Retained earnings statement <br> • Balance sheet <br> • Statement of cash flows | **DO IT! 5** Financial Statement Items |

**Go to the Review and Practice section at the end of the chapter for a review of key concepts and practice applications with solutions.**

**Visit WileyPLUS for additional tutorials and practice opportunities.**

# Accounting Activities and Users

> **LEARNING OBJECTIVE 1**
>
> Identify the activities and users associated with accounting.

What consistently ranks as one of the top career opportunities in business? What frequently rates among the most popular majors on campus? What was the undergraduate degree chosen by **Nike** founder Phil Knight, **Home Depot** co-founder Arthur Blank, former acting director of the **Federal Bureau of Investigation (FBI)** Thomas Pickard, and numerous members of Congress? Accounting.[1] Why did these people choose accounting? They wanted to understand what was happening financially to their organizations. Accounting is the financial information system that provides these insights. In short, to understand your organization, you have to know the numbers.

    **Accounting** consists of three basic activities—it **identifies, records, and communicates** the economic events of an organization to interested users. Let's take a closer look at these three activities.

**Essential terms** are printed in blue when they first appear, and are defined in the end-of-chapter **Glossary Review**.

## Three Activities

    As a starting point to the accounting process, a company **identifies the economic events relevant to its business**. Examples of economic events are the sale of snack chips by **PepsiCo**, the provision of telephone services by **AT&T**, and the payment of wages by **Facebook**.

    Once a company like PepsiCo identifies economic events, it **records** those events in order to provide a history of its financial activities. Recording consists of keeping a **systematic, chronological diary of events**, measured in dollars and cents. In recording, PepsiCo also classifies and summarizes economic events.

    Finally, PepsiCo **communicates** the collected information to interested users by means of **accounting reports**. The most common of these reports are called **financial statements**. To make the reported financial information meaningful, PepsiCo reports the recorded data in a standardized way. It accumulates information resulting from similar transactions. For example, PepsiCo accumulates all sales transactions over a certain period of time and reports the data as one amount in the company's financial statements. Such data are said to be reported **in the aggregate**. By presenting the recorded data in the aggregate, the accounting process simplifies a multitude of transactions and makes a series of activities understandable and meaningful.

    A vital element in communicating economic events is the accountant's ability to **analyze and interpret** the reported information. Analysis involves use of ratios, percentages, graphs, and charts to highlight significant financial trends and relationships. Interpretation involves **explaining the uses, meaning, and limitations of reported data**. Appendices A–E show the financial statements of **Apple Inc.**, **PepsiCo, Inc.**, **The Coca-Cola Company**, **Amazon.com, Inc.**, and **Walmart Inc.**, respectively. (In addition, in the *A Look at IFRS* section at the end of each chapter, the French company **LVMH—Louis Vuitton** is analyzed.) We refer to these statements at various places throughout the text. At this point, these financial statements probably strike you as complex and confusing. By the end of this course, you'll be surprised at your ability to understand, analyze, and interpret them.

---

[1]The appendix to this chapter describes job opportunities for accounting majors and explains why accounting is such a popular major.

**Illustration 1.1** summarizes the activities of the accounting process.

**The activities of the accounting process**

You should understand that the accounting process **includes** the bookkeeping function. **Bookkeeping** usually involves **only** the recording of economic events. It is therefore just one part of the accounting process. In total, accounting involves **the entire process of identifying**, **recording**, **and communicating economic events**.[2]

HELPFUL HINT

**Throughout this text, we will highlight examples where accounting information is used to support business decisions using data analytics.**

**Helpful Hints** further clarify concepts being discussed.

# Who Uses Accounting Data

Accounting software systems collect vast amounts of data about the economic events experienced by a company and about the parties with whom the company engages, such as suppliers and customers. Business decision-makers take advantage of this wealth of data by using data analytics to make more informed business decisions. **Data analytics** involves analyzing data, often employing both software and statistics, to draw inferences. As both data access and analytical software improve, the use of data analytics to support decisions is becoming increasingly common at virtually all types of companies (see **Helpful Hint**).

   **Users** of accounting information can be divided broadly into two groups: internal users and external users.

## Internal Users

**Internal users** of accounting information are the managers who plan, organize, and run a business. These include **marketing managers, production supervisors, finance directors, and company officers.** In running a business, internal users must answer many important questions, as shown in **Illustration 1.2**.

   To answer these and other questions, internal users need detailed information on a timely basis. **Managerial accounting** provides internal reports to help users make decisions about their companies. Examples are financial comparisons of operating alternatives, projections of income from new sales campaigns, and forecasts of cash needs for the next year.

---

[2]The origins of accounting are generally attributed to the work of Luca Pacioli, an Italian Renaissance mathematician. Pacioli was a close friend and tutor to Leonardo da Vinci and a contemporary of Christopher Columbus. In his 1494 text *Summa de Arithmetica, Geometria*, *Proportione et Proportionalite*, Pacioli described a system to ensure that financial information was recorded efficiently and accurately.

**ILLUSTRATION 1.2** Questions that internal users ask

### Questions Asked by Internal Users

Snacks   Beverages

| **Finance** | **Marketing** | **Human Resources** | **Management** |
|---|---|---|---|
| Is cash sufficient to pay dividends to Microsoft stockholders? | What price should Apple charge for an iPhone to maximize the company's net income? | Can General Motors afford to give its employees pay raises this year? | Which PepsiCo product line is the most profitable? Should any product lines be eliminated? |

**Accounting Across the Organization** boxes demonstrate applications of accounting information in various business functions.

---

## Accounting Across the Organization    Clif Bar & Company

iStock.com/Dan Moore

### Owning a Piece of the Bar

The original Clif Bar® energy bar was created in 1990 after six months of experimentation by Gary Erickson and his mother in her kitchen. Today, the company has approximately 1,000 employees and was named one of the leading Landor's Breakaway Brands®. One of **Clif Bar & Company**'s proudest moments was the creation of an employee stock ownership plan (ESOP) in 2010. This plan gives its employees 20% ownership of the company. The ESOP also resulted in Clif Bar enacting an open-book management program, including the commitment to educate all employee-owners about its finances. Armed with basic accounting knowledge, employees are more aware of the financial impact of their actions, which leads to better decisions.

**What are the benefits to the company and to the employees of making the financial statements available to all employees? (Answer is available near the end of the chapter.)**

---

## External Users

**External users** are individuals and organizations outside a company who want financial information about the company. The two most common types of external users are investors and creditors. **Investors** (owners) use accounting information to decide whether to buy, hold, or sell ownership shares of a company. **Creditors** (such as suppliers and bankers) use accounting information to evaluate the risks of granting credit or lending money. Illustration 1.3 shows some questions that investors and creditors may ask.

**ILLUSTRATION 1.3** Questions that external users ask

### Questions Asked by External Users

| **Investors** | **Investors** | **Creditors** |
|---|---|---|
| Is General Electric earning satisfactory income? | How does Disney compare in size and profitability with WarnerMedia? | Will United Airlines be able to pay its debts as they come due? |

**Financial accounting** answers these questions. It provides economic and financial information for investors, creditors, and other external users. The information needs of external users vary considerably. **Taxing authorities**, such as the Internal Revenue Service, want to know whether the company complies with tax laws. **Customers** are interested in whether a company like **Tesla, Inc.** will continue to honor product warranties and support its product lines. **Labor unions**, such as the **Major League Baseball Players Association**, want to know whether the owners have the ability to pay increased wages and benefits.

**Regulatory agencies**, such as the Securities and Exchange Commission or the Federal Trade Commission, want to know whether the company is operating within prescribed rules.

---

**ACTION PLAN**

- **Review the basic concepts discussed.**
- **Develop an understanding of the key terms used.**

The **DO IT!** exercises ask you to put newly acquired knowledge to work. They outline the **Action Plan** necessary to complete the exercise, and they show a **Solution**.

## DO IT! 1 | Basic Concepts

Indicate whether each of the five statements presented below is true or false. If false, indicate how to correct the statement.

1. The three steps in the accounting process are identification, recording, and communication.
2. Bookkeeping encompasses all steps in the accounting process.
3. Accountants prepare, but do not interpret, financial reports.
4. The two most common types of external users are investors and company officers.
5. Managerial accounting activities focus on reports for internal users.

### Solution

1. True.  2. False. Bookkeeping involves only the recording step.  3. False. Accountants analyze and interpret information in reports as part of the communication step.  4. False. The two most common types of external users are investors and creditors.  5. True.

Related exercise material: **DO IT! 1.1, E1.1, and E1.2.**

---

# The Building Blocks of Accounting

---

**LEARNING OBJECTIVE 2**

Explain the building blocks of accounting: ethics, principles, and assumptions.

---

A doctor follows certain protocols in treating a patient's illness. An architect follows certain structural guidelines in designing a building. Similarly, an accountant follows certain standards in reporting financial information. These standards are based on specific principles and assumptions. For these standards to work, however, a fundamental business concept must be present—ethical behavior.

## Ethics in Financial Reporting

People won't gamble in a casino if they think it is "rigged." Similarly, people won't play the stock market if they think share prices are rigged. At one time, the financial press was full of articles about financial scandals at **Enron**, **WorldCom**, **HealthSouth**, and **AIG**. As more scandals came to light, a mistrust of financial reporting in general seemed to be developing.

One article in the *Wall Street Journal* noted that "repeated disclosures about questionable accounting practices have bruised investors' faith in the reliability of earnings reports, which in turn has sent stock prices tumbling." Imagine trying to carry on a business or invest money if you could not depend on the financial statements to be honestly prepared. Information would have no credibility. There is no doubt that a sound, well-functioning economy depends on accurate and dependable financial reporting.

United States regulators and lawmakers were very concerned that the economy would suffer if investors lost confidence in corporate accounting because of unethical financial reporting. In response, Congress passed the **Sarbanes-Oxley Act (SOX)** to reduce unethical corporate behavior and decrease the likelihood of future corporate scandals. As a result of SOX, top management must now certify the accuracy of financial information. In addition, penalties for fraudulent financial activity are much more severe. Also, SOX increased the independence requirements of the outside auditors who review the accuracy of corporate financial statements and increased the oversight role of boards of directors (see **Ethics Note**).

The standards of conduct by which actions are judged as right or wrong, honest or dishonest, fair or not fair, are **ethics**. Effective financial reporting depends on sound ethical behavior. To sensitize you to ethical situations in business and to give you practice at solving ethical dilemmas, we address ethics in a number of ways in this text:

1. A number of the *Feature Stories* and other parts of the text discuss the central importance of ethical behavior to financial reporting.

2. *Ethics Insight* boxes and marginal *Ethics Notes* highlight ethics situations and issues in actual business settings.

3. Many of the *People, Planet, and Profit Insight* boxes focus on ethical issues that companies face in measuring and reporting social and environmental issues.

4. At the end of the chapter, an *Ethics Case* simulates a business situation and asks you to put yourself in the position of a decision-maker in that case.

When analyzing these various ethics cases and your own ethical experiences, you should apply the three steps outlined in **Illustration 1.4**.

> **Ethics Notes** help sensitize you to some of the ethical issues in accounting.

> **ETHICS NOTE**
>
> Circus-founder P.T. Barnum is alleged to have said, "Trust everyone, but cut the deck." What Sarbanes-Oxley does is to provide measures (like cutting the deck of playing cards) that help ensure that fraud will not occur.

**ILLUSTRATION 1.4**  **Steps in analyzing ethics cases and situations**

**1. Recognize an ethical situation and the ethical issues involved.**

Use your personal ethics to identify ethical situations and issues. Some businesses and professional organizations provide written codes of ethics for guidance in some business situations.

**2. Identify and analyze the principal elements in the situation.**

Identify the **stakeholders**—persons or groups who may be harmed or benefited. Ask the question: What are the responsibilities and obligations of the parties involved?

**3. Identify the alternatives, and weigh the impact of each alternative on various stakeholders.**

Select the most ethical alternative, considering all the consequences. Sometimes there will be one right answer. Other situations involve more than one right solution; these situations require an evaluation of each and a selection of the best alternative.

**Insight** boxes provide examples of business situations from various perspectives—ethics, investor, international, and corporate social responsibility. Guideline answers to the critical thinking questions as well as additional questions are available in WileyPLUS.

## Ethics Insight   Dewey & LeBoeuf LLP

### I Felt the Pressure—Would You?

Alliance Images/
Shutterstock.com

"I felt the pressure." That's what some of the employees of the now-defunct law firm of **Dewey & LeBoeuf LLP** indicated when they helped to overstate revenue and use accounting tricks to hide losses and cover up cash shortages. These employees worked for the former finance director and former chief financial officer (CFO) of the firm. Here are some of their comments:

- "I was instructed by the CFO to create invoices, knowing they would not be sent to clients. When I created these invoices, I knew that it was inappropriate."

- "I intentionally gave the auditors incorrect information in the course of the audit."

What happened here is that a small group of lower-level employees over a period of years carried out the instructions of their bosses. Their bosses, however, seemed to have no concern about unethical practices as evidenced by various e-mails with one another in which they referred to their financial manipulations as accounting tricks, cooking the books, and fake income.

**Sources:** Ashby Jones, "Guilty Pleas of Dewey Staff Detail the Alleged Fraud," *Wall Street Journal* (March 28, 2014); and Sara Randazzo, "Dewey CFO Escapes Jail Time in Fraud Case Sentencing," *Wall Street Journal* (October 10, 2017).

**Why did these employees lie, and what do you believe should be their penalty for these lies?** (Answer is available near the end of the chapter.)

# Generally Accepted Accounting Principles

The accounting profession has developed standards that are generally accepted and universally practiced. This common set of standards is called **generally accepted accounting principles (GAAP)**. These standards indicate how to report economic events.

The primary accounting standard-setting body in the United States is the **Financial Accounting Standards Board (FASB)**. The **Securities and Exchange Commission (SEC)** is the agency of the U.S. government that oversees U.S. financial markets and accounting standard-setting bodies. The SEC relies on the FASB to develop accounting standards, which public companies must follow. Many countries outside of the United States have adopted the accounting standards issued by the **International Accounting Standards Board (IASB)**. These standards are called **International Financial Reporting Standards (IFRS)** (see **International Note**).

As markets become more global, it is often desirable to compare the results of companies from different countries that report using different accounting standards. In order to increase comparability, the two standard-setting bodies have made efforts to reduce the differences between U.S. GAAP and IFRS. However, it seems likely that there will continue to be two sets of financial reporting standards in the world for the foreseeable future due to both the FASB and the IASB taking different approaches to various financial reporting issues. We highlight any major differences between GAAP and IFRS in *International Notes* as part of the text discussion as well as provide a more in-depth analysis in the *A Look at IFRS* section at the end of each chapter.

## International Insight

Toru Hanai/Pool/Getty Images

### The Korean Discount

If you think that accounting standards don't matter, consider recent events in South Korea. For many years, international investors complained that the financial reports of South Korean companies were inadequate and inaccurate. Accounting practices there often resulted in huge differences between stated revenues and actual revenues. Because investors did not have faith in the accuracy of the numbers, they were unwilling to pay as much for the shares of these companies relative to shares of comparable companies in different countries. This difference in share price was often referred to as the "Korean discount."

In response, Korean regulators decided that companies would have to comply with international accounting standards.

This change was motivated by a desire to "make the country's businesses more transparent" in order to build investor confidence and spur economic growth. Many other Asian countries, including China, India, and Japan, have also decided either to adopt international standards or to create standards that are based on the international standards.

**Source:** Evan Ramstad, "End to 'Korea Discount'?" *Wall Street Journal* (March 16, 2007).

**What is meant by the phrase "make the country's businesses more transparent"? Why would increasing transparency spur economic growth? (Answer is available near the end of the chapter.)**

# Measurement Principles

GAAP generally uses one of two measurement principles, the historical cost principle or the fair value principle. Selection of which principle to follow generally relates to trade-offs between relevance and faithful representation (see **Helpful Hint**). **Relevance** means that financial information is capable of making a difference in a decision. **Faithful representation** means that the numbers and descriptions match what really existed or happened—they are factual.

## Historical Cost Principle

The **historical cost principle** (or cost principle) dictates that companies record assets at their cost. This is true not only at the time the asset is purchased but also over the time the asset is held. For example, if **Best Buy** purchases land for $360,000, the company initially reports it in its accounting records at $360,000. But what does Best Buy do if, by the end of the next year, the fair value of the land has increased to $400,000? Under the historical cost principle, it continues to report the land at $360,000.

## Fair Value Principle

The **fair value principle** states that assets and liabilities should be reported at fair value (the price received to sell an asset or settle a liability). Fair value information may be more useful than historical cost for certain types of assets and liabilities. For example, certain investment securities are reported at fair value because market price information is usually readily available for these types of assets.

In determining which measurement principle to use, companies weigh the factual nature of cost figures versus the relevance of fair value. In general, most companies choose to use cost. Only in situations where assets are actively traded, such as investment securities, do companies apply the fair value principle extensively.

# Assumptions

Assumptions provide a foundation for the accounting process. Two main assumptions are the **monetary unit assumption** and the **economic entity assumption**.

## Monetary Unit Assumption

The **monetary unit assumption** requires that companies include in the accounting records only transaction data that can be expressed in money terms. This assumption enables accounting to quantify (measure) economic events. The monetary unit assumption is vital to applying the historical cost principle.

This assumption prevents the inclusion of some relevant information in the accounting records. For example, the health of a company's owner, the quality of service, and the morale of employees are not included. The reason: Companies cannot quantify this information in monetary terms. Though this information is important, companies record only events that can be measured in money.

## Economic Entity Assumption

**An economic entity can be any organization or unit in society.** It may be a company (such as **Crocs, Inc.**), a governmental unit (the state of Ohio), a municipality (Seattle), a school district (St. Louis District 48), or a church (Southern Baptist). The **economic entity assumption** requires that the activities of the entity be kept separate and distinct from the activities of its owner and all other economic entities (see **Ethics Note**). To illustrate, Sally Rider, owner of Sally's Boutique, must keep her personal living costs separate from the expenses of her business. Similarly, **J. Crew** and **Gap Inc.** are segregated into separate economic entities for accounting purposes.

**Proprietorship**   A business owned by one person is generally **a proprietorship**. The owner is often the manager/operator of the business. Small service-type businesses (plumbing companies, beauty salons, and auto repair shops), farms, and small retail stores (antique shops, clothing stores, and used-book stores) are often proprietorships. **Usually, only a relatively small amount of money (capital) is necessary to start in business as a proprietorship. The owner (proprietor) receives any profits, suffers any losses, and is personally liable for all debts of the business.** There is no legal distinction between the business as an economic unit and the owner, but the accounting records of the business activities are kept separate from the personal records and activities of the owner.

**Partnership** A business owned by two or more persons associated as partners is a **partnership**. In most respects, a partnership is like a proprietorship except that more than one owner is involved. Typically, a partnership agreement (written or oral) sets forth such terms as initial investment, duties of each partner, division of net income (or net loss), and settlement to be made upon death or withdrawal of a partner. Each partner generally has unlimited personal liability for the debts of the partnership. **Like a proprietorship, for accounting purposes the partnership transactions must be kept separate from the personal activities of the partners.** Partnerships are often used to organize retail and service-type businesses, including professional practices (lawyers, doctors, architects, and certified public accountants).

**Corporation** A business organized as a separate legal entity under state corporation law and having ownership divided into transferable shares of stock is a **corporation**. The holders of the shares (stockholders) **enjoy limited liability**; that is, they are not personally liable for the debts of the corporate entity. Stockholders **may transfer all or part of their ownership shares to other investors at any time** (i.e., sell their shares). The ease with which ownership can change adds to the attractiveness of investing in a corporation. Because ownership can be transferred without dissolving the corporation, the corporation **enjoys an unlimited life**.

Although the combined number of proprietorships and partnerships in the United States is more than five times the number of corporations, the revenue produced by corporations is eight times greater. Most of the largest companies in the United States—for example, **ExxonMobil**, **Ford**, **Walmart Inc.**, **Citigroup**, and **Apple**—are corporations.

## Accounting Across the Organization

blublaf/E+/Getty Images

### Spinning the Career Wheel

How will the study of accounting help you? A working knowledge of accounting is desirable for virtually every field of business. Some examples of how accounting is used in business careers include:

**General management:** Managers at **Ford Motors**, **Massachusetts General Hospital**, **California State University–Fullerton**, a **McDonald's** franchise, and a **Trek** bike shop all need to understand accounting data in order to make wise business decisions.

**Marketing:** Marketing specialists at **Procter & Gamble** must be sensitive to costs and benefits, which accounting helps them

quantify and understand. Making a sale is meaningless unless it is a profitable sale.

**Finance:** Do you want to be a banker for **Citicorp**, an investment analyst for **Goldman Sachs**, or a stockbroker for **Merrill Lynch**? These fields rely heavily on accounting knowledge to analyze financial statements. In fact, it is difficult to get a good job in a finance function without two or three courses in accounting.

**Real estate:** Are you interested in being a real estate broker for **Prudential Real Estate**? Because a third party—the bank—is almost always involved in financing a real estate transaction, brokers must understand the numbers involved: Can the buyer afford to make the payments to the bank? Does the cash flow from an industrial property justify the purchase price? What are the tax benefits of the purchase?

**How might accounting help you? (Answer is available near the end of the chapter.)**

---

### ACTION PLAN

- Review the discussion of ethics and financial reporting standards.
- Develop an understanding of the key terms used.

## DO IT! 2 | Building Blocks of Accounting

Indicate whether each of the five statements presented below is true or false. If false, indicate how to correct the statement.

1. Congress passed the Sarbanes-Oxley Act to reduce unethical behavior and decrease the likelihood of future corporate scandals.
2. The primary accounting standard-setting body in the United States is the Financial Accounting Standards Board (FASB).

3. The historical cost principle dictates that companies record assets at their cost. In later periods, however, the fair value of the asset must be used if its fair value is higher than its cost.

4. Relevance means that financial information matches what really happened; the information is factual.

5. A business owner's personal expenses must be separated from expenses of the business to comply with accounting's economic entity assumption.

**Solution**

**1.** True.   **2.** True.   **3.** False. The historical cost principle dictates that companies record assets at their cost. Under the historical cost principle, the company must also use cost in later periods. **4.** False. Faithful representation, not relevance, means that financial information matches what really happened; the information is factual.   **5.** True.

Related exercise material: **DO IT! 1.2, E1.3, and E1.4.**

# The Accounting Equation

## LEARNING OBJECTIVE 3
State the accounting equation, and define its components.

The two basic elements of a business are what it owns and what it owes. **Assets** are the resources a business owns. For example, **Google** has total assets of approximately $93.8 billion. Liabilities and stockholders' equity are the rights or claims against these resources. Thus, Google has $93.8 billion of claims against its $93.8 billion of assets. Claims of those to whom the company owes money (creditors) are called **liabilities**. Claims of owners are called **stockholders' equity**. Google has liabilities of $22.1 billion and stockholders' equity of $71.7 billion.

We can express the relationship of assets, liabilities, and stockholders' equity as an equation, as shown in **Illustration 1.5**.

| Assets | = | Liabilities | + | Stockholders' Equity |
|--------|---|-------------|---|----------------------|

**ILLUSTRATION 1.5**

**The basic accounting equation**

This relationship is the **basic accounting equation**. Assets must equal the sum of liabilities and stockholders' equity. Liabilities appear before stockholders' equity in the basic accounting equation because they are paid first if a business is liquidated.

The accounting equation applies to all **economic entities** regardless of size, nature of business, or form of business organization. It applies to a small proprietorship such as a corner grocery store as well as to a giant corporation such as **PepsiCo**. The equation provides the **underlying framework** for recording and summarizing economic events.

Let's look in more detail at the categories in the basic accounting equation.

## Assets

As noted above, **assets** are resources a business owns. The business uses its assets in carrying out such activities as production and sales. The common characteristic possessed by all assets is **the capacity to provide future services or benefits**. In a business, that service potential or future economic benefit eventually results in cash inflows (receipts). For example, consider Campus Pizza, a local restaurant. It owns a delivery truck that provides economic benefits from delivering pizzas. Other assets of Campus Pizza include tables, chairs, jukebox, cash register, oven, tableware, and, of course, cash.

# Liabilities

**Liabilities** are claims against assets—that is, existing debts and obligations. Businesses of all sizes usually borrow money and purchase merchandise on credit. These economic activities result in payables of various sorts:

- Campus Pizza, for instance, purchases cheese, sausage, flour, and beverages on credit from suppliers. These obligations are called **accounts payable**.
- Campus Pizza also has a **note payable** to First National Bank for the money borrowed to purchase the delivery truck.
- Campus Pizza may also have **salaries and wages payable** to employees and **sales and real estate taxes payable** to the local government.

All of these persons or entities to whom Campus Pizza owes money are its **creditors**.

Creditors may legally force the liquidation of a business that does not pay its debts. In that case, the law requires that creditor claims be paid **before** ownership claims.

# Stockholders' Equity

The ownership claim on a corporation's total assets is **stockholders' equity** (see **Helpful Hint**). It is equal to total assets minus total liabilities. Here is why: The assets of a business are claimed by either creditors or stockholders. To find out what belongs to stockholders, we subtract creditors' claims (the liabilities) from the assets. The remainder is the stockholders' claim on the assets—stockholders' equity. It is often referred to as **residual equity**—that is, the equity "left over" after creditors' claims are satisfied.

The stockholders' equity section of a corporation's balance sheet generally consists of (1) common stock and (2) retained earnings.

## Common Stock

A corporation may obtain funds by selling shares of stock to investors. **Common stock** is the term used to describe the total amount paid in by stockholders for the shares they purchase.

## Retained Earnings

The **retained earnings** section of the balance sheet is determined by three items: revenues, expenses, and dividends.

**Revenues** Revenues **are the increases in assets or decreases in liabilities resulting from the sale of goods or the performance of services in the normal course of business** (see **Helpful Hint**). Revenues usually result in an increase in an asset. They may arise from different sources and are called various names depending on the nature of the business. Campus Pizza, for instance, has two categories of sales revenues—pizza sales and beverage sales. Other titles for and sources of revenue common to many businesses are sales, fees, services, commissions, interest, dividends, royalties, and rent.

**Expenses** Expenses are the cost of assets consumed or services used in the process of generating revenue. **They are decreases in stockholders' equity that result from operating the business** (see **Helpful Hint**). Like revenues, expenses take many forms and are called various names depending on the type of asset consumed or service used. For example, Campus Pizza recognizes the following types of expenses: cost of ingredients (flour, cheese, tomato paste, meat, mushrooms, etc.); cost of beverages; wages expense; utilities expense (electric, gas, and water expense); telephone expense; delivery expense (gasoline, repairs, licenses, etc.); supplies expense (napkins, detergents, aprons, etc.); rent expense; interest expense; and property tax expense.

**Dividends** Net income represents an increase in net assets which are then available to distribute to stockholders. The distribution of cash or other assets to stockholders is called a **dividend**. Dividends reduce retained earnings. However, dividends are **not an expense**.

**HELPFUL HINT**

In some situations, accountants use the term *owner's equity* and in others *owners' equity*. Owner's refers to one owner (the case with a sole proprietorship), and *owners'* refers to multiple owners (the case with partnerships). The term *stockholders' equity* refers to ownership in corporations.

**HELPFUL HINT**

The effect of revenues is positive—an increase in stockholders' equity coupled with an increase in assets or a decrease in liabilities.

**HELPFUL HINT**

The effect of expenses is negative—a decrease in stockholders' equity coupled with a decrease in assets or an increase in liabilities.

A corporation first determines its revenues and expenses and then computes net income or net loss. If it has net income and decides it has no better use for that income, a corporation may decide to distribute a dividend to its owners (the stockholders).

In summary, the principal sources (increases) of stockholders' equity are investments by stockholders and revenues from business operations. In contrast, reductions (decreases) in stockholders' equity result from expenses and dividends. These relationships are shown in **Illustration 1.6.**

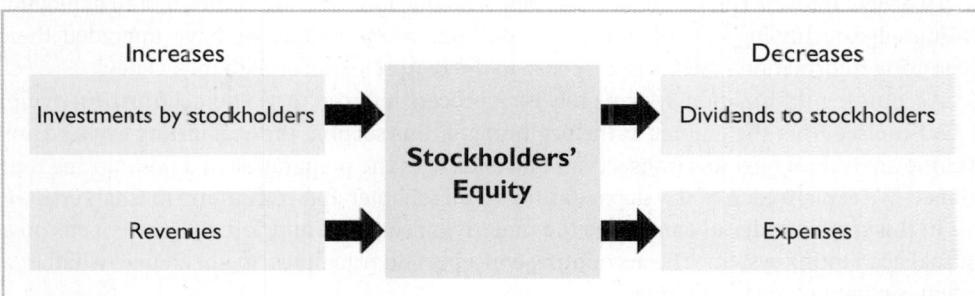

**ILLUSTRATION 1.6**

**Increases and decreases in stockholders' equity**

---

## DO IT! 3 | Stockholders' Equity Effects

Classify the following items as issuance of stock (I), dividends (D), revenues (R), or expenses (E). Then indicate whether each item increases or decreases stockholders' equity.

1. Rent Expense.              3. Dividends.
2. Service Revenue.           4. Salaries and Wages Expense.

### Solution

1. Rent Expense is an expense (E); it decreases stockholders' equity.    2. Service Revenue is revenue (R); it increases stockholders' equity.    3. Dividends is a distribution to stockholders (D); it decreases stockholders' equity.    4. Salaries and Wages Expense is an expense (E); it decreases stockholders' equity.

Related exercise material: **BE1.1, BE1.2, BE1.3, BE1.4, BE1.5, DO IT! 1.3, and E1.5.**

**ACTION PLAN**
- **Understand the sources of revenue.**
- **Understand what causes expenses.**
- **Review the rules for changes in stockholders' equity.**
- **Recognize that dividends are distributions of cash or other assets to stockholders.**

---

# Analyzing Business Transactions

**LEARNING OBJECTIVE 4**

Analyze the effects of business transactions on the accounting equation.

| Analyze business transactions | JOURNALIZE | POST | TRIAL BALANCE | ADJUSTING ENTRIES | ADJUSTED TRIAL BALANCE | FINANCIAL STATEMENTS | CLOSING ENTRIES | POST-CLOSING TRIAL BALANCE |

This **accounting cycle graphic** illustrates the steps companies follow each period to record transactions and eventually prepare financial statements.

The system of collecting and processing transaction data and communicating financial information to decision-makers is known as the **accounting information system.** Factors that shape an accounting information system include the nature of the company's business, the types of transactions, the size of the company, the volume of data, and the information demands of management and others.

Most businesses use computerized accounting systems—sometimes referred to as electronic data processing (EDP) systems. These systems handle all the steps involved in the recording process, from initial data entry to preparation of the financial statements. In order to remain competitive, companies continually improve their accounting systems to provide accurate and timely data for decision-making. For example, in a recent annual report, **Tootsie Roll** stated, "We also invested in additional processing and data storage hardware during the year. We view information technology as a key strategic tool, and are committed to deploying leading edge technology in this area." In addition, many companies have upgraded their accounting information systems in response to the requirements of Sarbanes-Oxley.

Accounting information systems rely on a process referred to as **the accounting cycle**. As you can see from the graphic at the beginning of this section, the accounting cycle begins with the analysis of business transactions and ends with the preparation of a post-closing trial balance. We explain each of the steps, starting in this chapter and continuing in Chapters 2–4.

In this text, in order to emphasize the underlying concepts and principles, we focus on a manual accounting system. The accounting concepts and principles do not change whether a system is computerized or manual.

## Accounting Transactions

**Transactions** (**business transactions**) are a business's economic events recorded by accountants. Transactions may be external or internal. **External transactions** involve economic events between the company and some outside enterprise. For example, Campus Pizza's purchase of cooking equipment from a supplier, payment of monthly rent to the landlord, and sale of pizzas to customers are external transactions. **Internal transactions** are economic events that occur entirely within one company. The use of cooking and cleaning supplies are internal transactions for Campus Pizza.

Companies carry on many activities that do not represent business transactions. Examples are hiring employees, responding to e-mails, talking with customers, and placing merchandise orders. Some of these activities may lead to business transactions: Employees will earn wages, and suppliers will deliver ordered merchandise. The company must analyze each event to find out if it affects the components of the accounting equation. If it does, the company will record the transaction. **Illustration 1.7** demonstrates the transaction identification process.

**ILLUSTRATION 1.7** **Transaction identification process**

Each transaction must have a dual effect on the accounting equation. For example, if an asset is increased, there must be a corresponding:

- Decrease in another asset, *or*
- Increase in a specific liability, *or*
- Increase in stockholders' equity.

Two or more items could be affected. For example, as one asset is increased $10,000, another asset could decrease $6,000 and a liability could increase $4,000. Any change in a liability or ownership claim is subject to similar analysis.

# Transaction Analysis

To demonstrate how to analyze transactions in terms of the accounting equation, we will review the business activities of Softbyte Inc., a smartphone app development business, during its first month of operations. As part of this analysis, we will expand the basic accounting equation. This will allow us to better illustrate the impact of transactions on stockholders' equity. Recall that stockholders' equity is comprised of two parts: common stock and retained earnings. Common stock is affected when the company issues new shares of stock in exchange for cash. Retained earnings is affected when the company earns revenue, incurs expenses, or pays dividends. **Illustration 1.8** shows the **expanded accounting equation**.

**ILLUSTRATION 1.8** **Expanded accounting equation**

If you are tempted to skip ahead after you've read a few of the following transaction analyses, don't do it (see **Helpful Hint**). Each has something unique to teach, something you'll need later. (We assure you that we've kept them to the minimum needed!)

**Transaction 1. Investment of Cash by Stockholders** Ray and Barbara Neal start a smartphone app development company that they incorporate as Softbyte Inc. On September 1, 2020, they invest $15,000 cash in the business in exchange for $15,000 of common stock. The common stock indicates the ownership interest that the Neals have in Softbyte Inc. This transaction results in an equal increase in both assets and stockholders' equity.

**HELPFUL HINT**

Study these transactions until you are sure you understand them. They are not difficult, but understanding them is important to your success in this course. The ability to analyze transactions in terms of the basic accounting equation is essential in accounting.

| Basic Analysis | The asset Cash increases $15,000, and stockholders' equity (specifically, Common Stock) increases $15,000. |
|---|---|

| Equation Analysis | | Assets | = | Liabilities | + | Stockholders Equity | |
|---|---|---|---|---|---|---|---|
| | | Cash | = | | | Common Stock | |
| | (1) | +$15,000 | = | | | +$15,000 | Issued Stock |

Observe that the equality of the basic equation has been maintained. Note also that the source of the increase in stockholders' equity (in this case, issued stock) is indicated. Why does this matter? Because investments by stockholders do not represent revenues, and they are excluded in determining net income. Therefore, it is necessary to make clear that the increase is an investment rather than revenue from operations. Additional investments (i.e., investments made by stockholders after the corporation has been initially formed) have the same effect on stockholders' equity as the initial investment.

### Transaction 2. Purchase of Equipment for Cash

Softbyte Inc. purchases computer equipment for $7,000 cash. This transaction results in an equal increase and decrease in total assets, though the composition of assets changes.

| Basic Analysis | The asset Cash decreases $7,000, and the asset Equipment increases $7,000. |
|---|---|

| | | Assets | | | = | Liabilities | + | Stockholders' Equity |
|---|---|---|---|---|---|---|---|---|
| | | Cash | + | Equipment | = | | | Common Stock |
| | | $15,000 | | | | | | $15,000 |
| Equation Analysis | (2) | −7,000 | | +$7,000 | | | | |
| | | $ 8,000 | + | $7,000 | = | | | $15,000 |
| | | | $15,000 | | | | | |

Observe that total assets are still $15,000. Common stock also remains at $15,000, the amount of the original investment.

### Transaction 3. Purchase of Supplies on Credit

Softbyte Inc. purchases headsets (and other computer accessories expected to last several months) for $1,600 from Mobile Solutions. Mobile Solutions agrees to allow Softbyte to pay this bill in October. This transaction is a purchase on account (a credit purchase). Assets increase because of the expected future benefits of using the headsets and computer accessories, and liabilities increase by the amount due Mobile Solutions.

| Basic Analysis | The asset Supplies increases $1,600, and the liability Accounts Payable increases $1,600. |
|---|---|

| | | Assets | | | | | = | Liabilities | + | Stockholders' Equity |
|---|---|---|---|---|---|---|---|---|---|---|
| | | Cash | + | Supplies | + | Equipment | = | Accounts Payable | + | Common Stock |
| Equation Analysis | | $8,000 | | | | $7,000 | | | | $15,000 |
| | (3) | | | +$1,600 | | | | +$1,600 | | |
| | | $8,000 | + | $1,600 | + | $7,000 | = | $1,600 | + | $15,000 |
| | | | | $16,600 | | | | | $16,600 | |

Total assets are now $16,600. This total is matched by a $1,600 creditor's claim and a $15,000 ownership claim.

### Transaction 4. Services Performed for Cash

Softbyte Inc. receives $1,200 cash from customers for app development services it has performed. This transaction represents Softbyte's principal revenue-producing activity. Recall that **revenue increases stockholders' equity**.

| Basic Analysis | | The asset Cash increases $1,200, and stockholders' equity increases $1,200 due to Service Revenue. |
|---|---|---|

| | | Assets | | | | | = | Liabilities + | | | Stockholders' Equity | | | | |
|---|---|---|---|---|---|---|---|---|---|---|---|---|---|---|---|
| | | | | | | | | Accounts | + | Common | + | Retained Earnings | | | |
| | | Cash | + Supplies + | Equipment | = | | | Payable | | Stock | | Rev. | − Exp. − | Div. | |
| Equation Analysis | | $8,000 | $1,600 | $7,000 | | | | $1,600 | | $15,000 | | | | | |
| | (4) | +1,200 | | | | | | | | | | +$1,200 | | | Service Revenue |
| | | $9,200 + | $1,600 + | $7,000 | = | | | $1,600 | + | $15,000 | + | $1,200 | | | |
| | | | $17,800 | | | | | | | $17,800 | | | | | |

The two sides of the equation balance at $17,800. Service Revenue is included in determining Softbyte's net income.

Note that we do not have room to give details for each individual revenue and expense account in this illustration. Thus, revenues (and expenses when we get to them) are summarized under one column heading for Revenues and one for Expenses. However, it is important to keep track of the category (account) titles affected (e.g., Service Revenue) as they will be needed when we prepare financial statements later in the chapter.

**Transaction 5. Purchase of Advertising on Credit**   Softbyte Inc. receives a bill for $250 from the *Daily News* for advertising on its online website but postpones payment until a later date. This transaction results in an increase in liabilities and a decrease in stockholders' equity.

| Basic Analysis | | The liability Accounts Payable increases $250, and stockholders' equity decreases $250 due to Advertising Expense. |
|---|---|---|

| | | Assets | | | | | = | Liabilities + | | | Stockholders' Equity | | | | |
|---|---|---|---|---|---|---|---|---|---|---|---|---|---|---|---|
| | | | | | | | | Accounts | + | Common | + | Retained Earnings | | | |
| | | Cash | + Supplies + | Equipment | = | | | Payable | | Stock | | Rev. | − Exp. − | Div. | |
| Equation Analysis | | $9,200 | $1,600 | $7,000 | | | | $1,600 | | $15,000 | | $1,200 | | | |
| | (5) | | | | | | | +250 | | | | | −$250 | | Advertising Expense |
| | | $9,200 + | $1,600 + | $7,000 | = | | | $1,850 | + | $15,000 | + | $1,200 | − $250 | | |
| | | | $17,800 | | | | | | | $17,800 | | | | | |

The two sides of the equation still balance at $17,800. Retained Earnings decreases when Softbyte incurs the expense. Expenses do not have to be paid in cash at the time they are incurred. When Softbyte pays at a later date, the liability Accounts Payable will decrease and the asset Cash will decrease (see Transaction 8). The cost of advertising is an expense (rather than an asset) because Softbyte has used the benefits. Advertising Expense is included in determining net income.

**Transaction 6. Services Performed for Cash and Credit**   Softbyte Inc. performs $3,500 of app development services for customers. The company receives cash of $1,500 from customers, and it bills the balance of $2,000 on account. This transaction results in an equal increase in assets and stockholders' equity.

**Basic Analysis**

Three specific items are affected: The asset Cash increases $1,500, the asset Accounts Receivable increases $2,000, and stockholders' equity increases $3,500 due to Service Revenue.

**Equation Analysis**

| | Assets | | | | = | Liabilities | + | | Stockholders' Equity | | |
|---|---|---|---|---|---|---|---|---|---|---|---|
| | Cash + | Accounts Receivable | + Supplies + | Equipment = | | Accounts Payable | + | Common Stock | + | Retained Earnings | |
| | | | | | | | | | | Rev. − Exp. − Div. | |
| | $9,200 | | $1,600 | $7,000 | | $1,850 | | $15,000 | | $1,200    $250 | |
| (6) | +1,500 | +$2,000 | | | | | | | | +3,500 | Service Revenue |
| | $10,700 + | $2,000 + | $1,600 + | $7,000 = | | $1,850 + | | $15,000 + | | $4,700 − $250 | |
| | | $21,300 | | | | | | $21,300 | | | |

Softbyte recognizes $3,500 in revenues when it performs the service. In exchange for this service, it received $1,500 in Cash and Accounts Receivable of $2,000. This Accounts Receivable represents customers' promises to pay $2,000 to Softbyte in the future. When it later receives collections on account, Softbyte will increase Cash and will decrease Accounts Receivable (see Transaction 9).

**Transaction 7. Payment of Expenses**  Softbyte Inc. pays the following expenses in cash for September: office rent $600, salaries and wages of employees $900, and utilities $200. These payments result in an equal decrease in assets and stockholders' equity.

**Basic Analysis**

The asset Cash decreases $1,700, and stockholders' equity decreases $1,700 due to the following expenses: Rent Expense, Salaries and Wages Expense, and Utilities Expense.

**Equation Analysis**

| | Assets | | | | = | Liabilities | − | | Stockholders' Equity | | |
|---|---|---|---|---|---|---|---|---|---|---|---|
| | Cash + | Accounts Receivable | + Supplies + | Equipment = | | Accounts Payable | + | Common Stock | + | Retained Earnings | |
| | | | | | | | | | | Rev. − Exp. − Div. | |
| | $10,700 | $2,000 | $1,600 | $7,000 | | $1,850 | | $15,000 | | $4,700    $250 | |
| (7) | −1,700 | | | | | | | | | −600 | Rent Exp. |
| | | | | | | | | | | −900 | Sal./Wages Exp. |
| | | | | | | | | | | −200 | Utilities Exp. |
| | $9,000 + | $2,000 + | $1,600 + | $7,000 = | | $1,850 + | | $15,000 + | | $4,700 − $1,950 | |
| | | $19,600 | | | | | | $19,600 | | | |

The two sides of the equation now balance at $19,600. Three lines are required in the analysis to indicate the different types of expenses that have been incurred.

**Transaction 8. Payment of Accounts Payable**  Softbyte Inc. pays its $250 *Daily News* bill in cash. The company previously (in Transaction 5) recorded the bill as an increase in Accounts Payable and a decrease in stockholders' equity.

**Basic Analysis**

This cash payment "on account" decreases the asset Cash by $250 and also decreases the liability Accounts Payable by $250.

**Equation Analysis**

| | Assets | | | | = | Liabilities | + | | Stockholders' Equity | | |
|---|---|---|---|---|---|---|---|---|---|---|---|
| | Cash + | Accounts Receivable | + Supplies + | Equipment = | | Accounts Payable | + | Common Stock | + | Retained Earnings | |
| | | | | | | | | | | Rev. −Exp. − Div. | |
| | $9,000 | $2,000 | $1,600 | $7,000 | | $1,850 | | $15,000 | | $4,700    $1,950 | |
| (8) | −250 | | | | | −250 | | | | | |
| | $8,750 + | $2,000 + | $1,600 + | $7,000 = | | $1,600 + | | $15,000 + | | $4,700 − $1,950 | |
| | | $19,350 | | | | | | $19,350 | | | |

Observe that the payment of a liability related to an expense that has previously been recorded does not affect stockholders' equity. Softbyte recorded the expense (in Transaction 5) and should not record it again.

**Transaction 9. Receipt of Cash on Account**  Softbyte Inc. receives $600 in cash from customers who had been billed for services (in Transaction 6). Transaction 9 does not change total assets, but it changes the composition of those assets.

| Basic Analysis | The asset Cash increases $600, and the asset Accounts Receivable decreases $600. |
| --- | --- |

| | | Assets | | | | = Liabilities + | | Stockholders' Equity | | | |
| --- | --- | --- | --- | --- | --- | --- | --- | --- | --- | --- | --- |
| | | Cash + | Accounts Receivable | + Supplies + | Equipment = | Accounts Payable | + | Common Stock | + | Retained Earnings | |
| | | | | | | | | | | Rev. − Exp. − Div. | |
| Equation Analysis | | $8,750 | $2,000 | $1,600 | $7,000 | $1,600 | | $15,000 | | $4,700  $1,950 | |
| | (9) | +600 | −600 | | | | | | | | |
| | | $9,350 + | $1,400 | + $1,600 + | $7,000 = | $1,600 | + | $15,000 | + | $4,700 − $1,950 | |
| | | | $19,350 | | | | | $19,350 | | | |

Note that the collection of an account receivable for services previously billed and recorded does not affect stockholders' equity. Softbyte already recorded this revenue (in Transaction 6) and should not record it again.

**Transaction 10. Dividends**  The corporation pays a dividend of $1,300 in cash to Ray and Barbara Neal, the stockholders of Softbyte Inc. This transaction results in an equal decrease in assets and stockholders' equity.

| Basic Analysis | The asset Cash decreases $1,300, and stockholders' equity decreases $1,300 due to dividends. |
| --- | --- |

| | | Assets | | | | = Liabilities + | | Stockholders' Equity | | | |
| --- | --- | --- | --- | --- | --- | --- | --- | --- | --- | --- | --- |
| | | Cash + | Accounts Receivable | + Supplies + | Equipment = | Accounts Payable | + | Common Stock | + | Retained Earnings | |
| | | | | | | | | | | Rev. − Exp. − Div. | |
| Equation Analysis | | $9,350 | $1,400 | $1,600 | $7,000 | $1,600 | | $15,000 | | $4,700  $1,950 | |
| | (10) | −1,300 | | | | | | | | − $1,300 | Dividends |
| | | $8,050 + | $1,400 | + $1,600 + | $7,000 = | $1,600 | + | $15,000 | + | $4,700 − $1,950 − $1,300 | |
| | | | $18,050 | | | | | $18,050 | | | |

Note that the dividend reduces retained earnings, which is part of stockholders' equity. **Dividends are not expenses**. Like stockholders' investments, dividends are excluded in determining net income.

# Summary of Transactions

**Illustration 1.9** summarizes the September transactions of Softbyte Inc. to show their cumulative effect on the basic accounting equation. It also indicates the transaction number and the specific effects of each transaction. Finally, Illustration 1.9 demonstrates a number of significant facts:

1. Each transaction must be analyzed in terms of its effect on:
   a. The three components of the basic accounting equation (assets, liabilities, and stockholders' equity).
   b. Specific types (kinds) of items within each component (such as the asset Cash).

2. The two sides of the equation must always be equal.

3. The Common Stock and Retained Earnings columns indicate the causes of each change in the stockholders' claim on assets.

**ILLUSTRATION 1.9** Tabular summary of Softbyte Inc. transactions

| Trans-action | Cash | + | Accounts Receivable | + Supplies + | Equipment | = Accounts Payable | + Common Stock | + Rev. | − Exp. | − Div. | |
|---|---|---|---|---|---|---|---|---|---|---|---|
| | | | | **Assets** | | **= Liabilities +** | | **Stockholders' Equity** | | | |
| | | | | | | | | **Retained Earnings** | | | |
| (1) | +$15,000 | | | | | | + $15,000 | | | | Issued Stock |
| (2) | −7,000 | | | | +$7,000 | | | | | | |
| (3) | | | | +$1,600 | | +$1,600 | | | | | |
| (4) | +1,200 | | | | | | | +$1,200 | | | Service Revenue |
| (5) | | | | | | +250 | | | −$250 | | Adver. Expense |
| (6) | +1,500 | | +$2,000 | | | | | +3,500 | | | Service Revenue |
| (7) | −1,700 | | | | | | | | −600 | | Rent Expense |
| | | | | | | | | | −900 | | Sal./Wages Exp. |
| | | | | | | | | | −200 | | Utilities Expense |
| (8) | −250 | | | | | −250 | | | | | |
| (9) | +600 | | −600 | | | | | | | | |
| (10) | −1,300 | | | | | | | | | −$1,300 | Dividends |
| | $ 8,050 + | | $1,400 + | $1,600 + | $7,000 | = $1,600 + | $15,000 + | $4,700 − | $1,950 − | $1,300 | |

$18,050                                    $18,050

There! You made it through transaction analysis. If you feel a bit shaky on any of the transactions, it might be a good idea at this point to get up, take a short break, and come back again for a brief (10- to 15-minute) review of the transactions, to make sure you understand them before you go on to the next section.

---

**ACTION PLAN**

- Analyze the effects of each transaction on the accounting equation.
- Use appropriate category names (not descriptions).
- Keep the accounting equation in balance.

## DO IT! 4 | Tabular Analysis

Transactions made by Virmari & Co., a public accounting firm, for the month of August are shown below. Prepare a tabular analysis which shows the effects of these transactions on the expanded accounting equation, similar to that shown in Illustration 1.9.

1. Virmari sold shares of common stock for $25,000 cash.
2. The company purchased $7,000 of office equipment on credit.
3. The company received $8,000 cash in exchange for services performed.
4. The company paid $850 for this month's rent.
5. The company paid a dividend of $1,000 in cash to stockholders.

### Solution

| Trans-action | Cash | + | Equipment | = | Accounts Payable | + | Common Stock | + | Rev. | − | Exp. | − | Div. | |
|---|---|---|---|---|---|---|---|---|---|---|---|---|---|---|
| | | **Assets** | | **=** | **Liabilities** | **+** | | **Stockholders' Equity** | | | | | | |
| | | | | | | | | | **Retained Earnings** | | | | | |
| (1) | +$25,000 | | | | | | +$25,000 | | | | | | | |
| (2) | | | +$7,000 | | +$7,000 | | | | | | | | | |
| (3) | +8,000 | | | | | | | | +$8,000 | | | | | Service Revenue |
| (4) | −850 | | | | | | | | | | −$850 | | | Rent Expense |
| (5) | −1,000 | | | | | | | | | | | | −$1,000 | Dividends |
| | $31,150 + | | $7,000 | = | $7,000 | + | $25,000 | + | $8,000 | − | $850 | − | $1,000 | |

$38,150                                    $38,150

Related exercise material: **BE1.6, BE1.7, BE1.8, BE1.9, DO IT! 1.4, E1.6, E1.7, and E1.8.**

# The Financial Statements

Companies prepare four financial statements from the summarized accounting data (see **Helpful Hint**):

1. An **income statement** presents the revenues and expenses and resulting net income or net loss for a specific period of time.
2. A **retained earnings statement** summarizes the changes in retained earnings for a specific period of time.
3. A **balance sheet** reports the assets, liabilities, and stockholders' equity of a company at a specific date.
4. A **statement of cash flows** summarizes information about the cash inflows (receipts) and outflows (payments) for a specific period of time.

These statements provide relevant financial data for internal and external users. **Illustration 1.10** shows the financial statements of Softbyte Inc. Note that the statements shown in Illustration 1.10 are interrelated:

1. Net income of $2,750 on the **income statement** is added to the beginning balance of retained earnings in the **retained earnings statement**.
2. Retained earnings of $1,450 at the end of the reporting period shown in the **retained earnings statement** is reported on the **balance sheet**.
3. Cash of $8,050 on the **balance sheet** is reported on the **statement of cash flows**.

Also, explanatory notes and supporting schedules are an integral part of every set of financial statements. We illustrate these notes and schedules in later chapters of this text.

Be sure to carefully examine the format and content of each statement in Illustration 1.10. We describe the essential features of each in the following sections (see **International Note**).

## Income Statement

The income statement reports the success or profitability of the company's operations over a specific period of time (see **Alternative Terminology**). For example, Softbyte Inc.'s income statement is dated "For the Month Ended September 30, 2022." It is prepared from the data appearing in the revenue and expense columns of Illustration 1.9. The heading of the statement identifies the company, the type of statement, and the time period covered by the statement.

The income statement lists revenues first, followed by expenses. Finally, the statement shows net income (or net loss). When revenues exceed expenses, **net income** results. When expenses exceed revenues, a **net loss** results.

Although practice varies, we have chosen in our illustrations and homework solutions to list expenses in order of magnitude. (We will consider alternative formats for the income statement in later chapters.)

Note that the income statement does not include investment and dividend transactions between the stockholders and the business in measuring net income. For example, as explained earlier, the cash dividend from Softbyte Inc. was not regarded as a business expense. This type of transaction is considered a reduction of retained earnings, which causes a decrease in stockholders' equity.

**ILLUSTRATION 1.10**
**Financial statements and their interrelationships**

**The heading of each statement identifies the company, the type of statement, and the specific date or time period covered by the statement.**

**Note that final sums are double-underlined, and negative amounts (in the statement of cash flows) are presented in parentheses.**

**The arrows in this illustration show the interrelationships of the four financial statements.**

**1. Net income is computed first and is needed to determine the ending balance in retained earnings.**

**2. The ending balance in retained earnings is needed in preparing the balance sheet.**

**3. The cash shown on the balance sheet is needed in preparing the statement of cash flows.**

---

### Softbyte Inc.
### Income Statement
### For the Month Ended September 30, 2022

| | | |
|---|---:|---:|
| Revenues | | |
| Service revenue | | $4,700 |
| Expenses | | |
| Salaries and wages expense | $900 | |
| Rent expense | 600 | |
| Advertising expense | 250 | |
| Utilities expense | 200 | |
| Total expenses | | 1,950 |
| Net income | | $2,750 |

### Softbyte Inc.
### Retained Earnings Statement
### For the Month Ended September 30, 2022

| | |
|---|---:|
| Retained earnings, September 1 | $ –0– |
| Add: Net income | 2,750 |
| | 2,750 |
| Less: Dividends | 1,300 |
| Retained earnings, September 30 | $1,450 |

### Softbyte Inc.
### Balance Sheet
### September 30, 2022

**Assets**

| | | |
|---|---:|---:|
| Cash | | $ 8,050 |
| Accounts receivable | | 1,400 |
| Supplies | | 1,600 |
| Equipment | | 7,000 |
| Total assets | | $18,050 |

**Liabilities and Stockholders' Equity**

| | | |
|---|---:|---:|
| Liabilities | | |
| Accounts payable | | $ 1,600 |
| Stockholders' equity | | |
| Common stock | $15,000 | |
| Retained earnings | 1,450 | 16,450 |
| Total liabilities and stockholders' equity | | $18,050 |

### Softbyte Inc.
### Statement of Cash Flows
### For the Month Ended September 30, 2022

| | | |
|---|---:|---:|
| Cash flows from operating activities | | |
| Cash receipts from revenues | | $ 3,300 |
| Cash payments for expenses | | (1,950) |
| Net cash provided by operating activities | | 1,350 |
| Cash flows from investing activities | | |
| Purchase of equipment | | (7,000) |
| Cash flows from financing activities | | |
| Sale of common stock | $15,000 | |
| Payment of cash dividends | (1,300) | 13,700 |
| Net increase in cash | | 8,050 |
| Cash at the beginning of the period | | 0 |
| Cash at the end of the period | | $ 8,050 |

# Retained Earnings Statement

Softbyte Inc.'s retained earnings statement reports the changes in retained earnings for a specific period of time. The time period is the same as that covered by the income statement ("For the Month Ended September 30, 2022"). Data for the preparation of the retained earnings statement come from the retained earnings columns of the tabular summary (Illustration 1.9) and from the income statement (Illustration 1.10).

The first line of the statement shows the beginning retained earnings amount. Then come net income and dividends. The retained earnings ending balance is the final amount on the statement. The information provided by this statement indicates the reasons why retained earnings increased or decreased during the period. If there is a net loss, it is deducted with dividends in the retained earnings statement.

# Balance Sheet

Softbyte Inc.'s balance sheet reports the assets, liabilities, and stockholders' equity at a specific date (September 30, 2022). The company prepares the balance sheet from the column headings and the month-end data shown in the last line of the tabular summary (Illustration 1.9).

Observe that the balance sheet lists assets at the top, followed by liabilities and stockholders' equity. Total assets must equal total liabilities and stockholders' equity. Softbyte Inc. reports only one liability, Accounts Payable, on its balance sheet. In most cases, there will be more than one liability. When two or more liabilities are involved, a customary way of listing is as shown in **Illustration 1.11**.

|  |  |
|---|---|
| **Liabilities** | |
| Notes payable | $10,000 |
| Accounts payable | 63,000 |
| Salaries and wages payable | 18,000 |
| **Total liabilities** | **$91,000** |

**ILLUSTRATION 1.11**

**Presentation of liabilities**

The balance sheet is like a snapshot of the company's financial condition at a specific moment in time (usually the month-end or year-end).

# Statement of Cash Flows

The primary purpose of a **statement of cash flows** is to provide financial information about the cash receipts and cash payments of a company for a specific period of time (see **Helpful Hint**). To help investors, creditors, and others in their analysis of a company's cash position, the statement of cash flows reports the cash effects of a company's **operating, investing, and financing activities**. In addition, the statement shows the net increase or decrease in cash during the period, and the amount of cash at the end of the period.

Reporting the sources, uses, and change in cash is useful because investors, creditors, and others want to know what is happening to a company's most liquid resource. The statement of cash flows provides answers to the following simple but important questions.

> **HELPFUL HINT**
>
> The statement of cash flows helps users determine if the company generates enough cash from operations to fund its investing activities.

1. Where did cash come from during the period?
2. What was cash used for during the period?
3. What was the change in the cash balance during the period?

As shown in Softbyte Inc.'s statement of cash flows in Illustration 1.10, cash increased $8,050 during the period. Net cash provided by operating activities increased cash $1,350 (cash receipts from revenue less cash payments for expenses). Cash flow from investing activities decreased cash $7,000 (purchase of equipment). Cash flow from financing activities increased cash $13,700 (sale of common stock less payment of cash dividends). At this time, you need not be concerned with how these amounts are determined. Chapter 12 will examine in detail how the statement is prepared.

## People, Planet, and Profit Insight

iStock.com/Marek
Uliasz

### Beyond Financial Statements

Should we expand our financial statements beyond the income statement, retained earnings statement, balance sheet, and statement of cash flows? Some believe we should take into account ecological and social performance, in addition to financial results, in evaluating a company. The argument is that a company's responsibility lies with anyone who is influenced by its actions. In other words, a company should be interested in benefiting many different parties, instead of only maximizing stockholders' interests.

A socially responsible business does not exploit or endanger any group of individuals. It follows fair trade practices, provides safe environments for workers, and bears responsibility for environmental damage. Granted, measurement of these factors is difficult. How to report this information is also controversial. But, many interesting and useful efforts are underway. Throughout this text, we provide additional insights into how companies are attempting to meet the challenge of measuring and reporting their contributions to society, as well as their financial results, to stockholders.

**Why might a company's stockholders be interested in its environmental and social performance? (Answer is available near the end of the chapter.)**

---

**ACTION PLAN**

- **Remember the basic accounting equation: assets must equal liabilities plus stockholders' equity.**
- **Review previous financial statements to determine how total assets, net income, and stockholders' equity are computed.**

## DO IT! 5 | Financial Statement Items

Presented below is selected information related to Flanagan Corporation at December 31, 2022. Flanagan reports financial information monthly.

| | | | |
|---|---|---|---|
| Equipment | $10,000 | Utilities Expense | $ 4,000 |
| Cash | 8,000 | Accounts Receivable | 9,000 |
| Service Revenue | 36,000 | Salaries and Wages Expense | 7,000 |
| Rent Expense | 11,000 | Notes Payable | 16,500 |
| Accounts Payable | 2,000 | Dividends | 5,000 |

**a.** Determine the total assets of Flanagan at December 31, 2022.

**b.** Determine the net income that Flanagan reported for December 2022.

**c.** Determine the stockholders' equity of Flanagan at December 31, 2022.

### Solution

**a.** The total assets are $27,000, comprised of Cash $8,000, Accounts Receivable $9,000, and Equipment $10,000.

**b.** Net income is $14,000, computed as follows.

| | | |
|---|---|---|
| Revenues | | |
| Service revenue | | $36,000 |
| Expenses | | |
| Rent expense | $11,000 | |
| Salaries and wages expense | 7,000 | |
| Utilities expense | 4,000 | |
| Total expenses | | 22,000 |
| Net income | | $14,000 |

**c.** The ending stockholders' equity of Flanagan Corporation is $8,500. By rewriting the accounting equation, we can compute stockholders' equity as assets minus liabilities, as follows.

| | | |
|---|---|---|
| Total assets [as computed in (a)] | | $27,000 |
| Less: Liabilities | | |
| Notes payable | $16,500 | |
| Accounts payable | 2,000 | 18,500 |
| Stockholders' equity | | $ 8,500 |

Note that it is not possible to determine the corporation's stockholders' equity in any other way, because the beginning total for stockholders' equity is not provided.

Related exercise material: **BE1.10, BE1.11, DO IT! 1.5, E1.9, E1.10, E1.11, E1.12, E1.13, E1.14, E1.15, E1.16, and E1.17.**

| Appendix 1A | # Career Opportunities in Accounting |
| --- | --- |

**LEARNING OBJECTIVE \*6**

Explain the career opportunities in accounting.

Why is accounting such a popular major and career choice? First, there are a lot of jobs. In many cities in recent years, the demand for accountants exceeded the supply. Not only are there a lot of jobs, but there are a wide array of opportunities. As one accounting organization observed, "accounting is one degree with 360 degrees of opportunity."

Accounting is also hot because it is obvious that accounting matters. Interest in accounting has increased, ironically, because of the attention caused by the accounting failures of companies such as **Enron** and **WorldCom**. These widely publicized scandals revealed the important role that accounting plays in society. Most people want to make a difference, and an accounting career provides many opportunities to contribute to society. Finally, the Sarbanes-Oxley Act (SOX) significantly increased the accounting and internal control requirements for corporations. This dramatically increased demand for professionals with accounting training.

Accountants are in such demand that it is not uncommon for accounting students to have accepted a job offer a year before graduation. As the following discussion reveals, the job options of people with accounting degrees are virtually unlimited.

## Public Accounting

Individuals in **public accounting** offer expert service to the general public, in much the same way that doctors serve patients and lawyers serve clients. A major portion of public accounting involves **auditing**. In auditing, a certified public accountant (CPA) examines company financial statements and provides an opinion as to how accurately the financial statements present the company's results and financial position. Analysts, investors, and creditors rely heavily on these "audit opinions," which CPAs have the exclusive authority to issue.

**Taxation** is another major area of public accounting. The work that tax specialists perform includes tax advice and planning, preparing tax returns, and representing clients before governmental agencies such as the Internal Revenue Service.

A third area in public accounting is **management consulting**. It ranges from installing basic accounting software or highly complex enterprise resource planning systems, to performing support services for major marketing projects and merger and acquisition activities.

Many CPAs are entrepreneurs. They form small- or medium-sized practices that frequently specialize in tax or consulting services.

## Private Accounting

Instead of working in public accounting, you might choose to be an employee of a for-profit company such as **Starbucks**, **Google**, or **PepsiCo**. In **private** (or **managerial**) **accounting**, you would be involved in activities such as cost accounting (finding the cost of producing specific products), budgeting, accounting information system design and support, and tax planning and preparation. You might also be a member of your company's internal audit team. In response to SOX, the internal auditors' job of reviewing the company's operations to ensure compliance with company policies and to increase efficiency has taken on increased importance.

Alternatively, many accountants work for not-for-profit organizations such as the **Red Cross** or the **Bill and Melinda Gates Foundation**, or for museums, libraries, or performing arts organizations.

# Governmental Accounting

Another option is to pursue one of the many accounting opportunities in governmental agencies. For example, the Internal Revenue Service (IRS), Federal Bureau of Investigation (FBI), and Securities and Exchange Commission (SEC) all employ accountants. The FBI has a stated goal that at least 15% of its new agents should be CPAs. There is also a very high demand for accounting educators at public colleges and universities and in state and local governments.

# Forensic Accounting

**Forensic accounting** uses accounting, auditing, and investigative skills to conduct investigations into theft and fraud. It is listed among the top 20 career paths of the future. The job of forensic accountants is to catch the perpetrators of the estimated $600 billion per year of theft and fraud occurring at U.S. companies. This includes tracing money-laundering and identity-theft activities as well as tax evasion. Insurance companies hire forensic accountants to detect frauds such as arson, and law offices employ forensic accountants to identify marital assets in divorces. Forensic accountants often have FBI, IRS, or similar government experience.

# "Show Me the Money"

How much can a new accountant make? Take a look at the average salaries for college graduates in public and private accounting shown in **Illustration 1A.1**. Keep in mind if you also have a CPA license, you'll make 10–15% more when you start out.

**ILLUSTRATION 1A.1**

Salary estimates for jobs in public and corporate accounting

| Employer | Jr. Level (0–3 yrs.) | Sr. Level (4–6 yrs.) |
|---|---|---|
| Public accounting (large firm) | $63,250–$83,250 | $78,500–$106,500 |
| Public accounting (medium firm) | $56,500–$67,750 | $70,500–$96,000 |
| Public accounting (small company) | $51,500–$60,500 | $63,750–$81,500 |
| Corporate accounting (large company) | $53,750–$69,500 | $68,750–$87,750 |

**Illustration 1A.2** lists some examples of upper-level salaries for managers in corporate accounting. Note that geographic region, experience, education, CPA certification, and company size each play a role in determining salary.

**ILLUSTRATION 1A.2**

Upper-level management salaries in corporate accounting

| Position | Large Company | Small to Medium Company |
|---|---|---|
| Chief financial officer | $207,000–$465,750 | $105,250–$208,750 |
| Corporate controller | $140,000–$224,750 | $92,000–$161,250 |
| Tax manager | $112,000–$158,250 | $88,000–$124,750 |

The **Review and Practice** section provides opportunities for students to review key concepts and terms as well as complete multiple-choice questions, exercises, and a comprehensive problem. Detailed solutions are also included.

# Review and Practice

## Learning Objectives Review

**1 Identify the activities and users associated with accounting.**

Accounting is an information system that identifies, records, and communicates the economic events of an organization to interested users. The major users and uses of accounting are as follows. (a) Management uses accounting information to plan, organize, and run the business. (b) Investors (owners) decide whether to buy, hold, or sell their financial interests on the basis of accounting data. (c) Creditors (suppliers and bankers) evaluate the risks of granting credit or lending money on the basis of accounting information. Other groups that use accounting information are taxing authorities, regulatory agencies, customers, and labor unions.

**2  Explain the building blocks of accounting: ethics, principles, and assumptions.**

Ethics are the standards of conduct by which actions are judged as right or wrong. Effective financial reporting depends on sound ethical behavior. Generally accepted accounting principles are a common set of standards used by accountants. The primary accounting standard-setting body in the United States is the Financial Accounting Standards Board. The monetary unit assumption requires that companies include in the accounting records only transaction data that can be expressed in terms of money. The economic entity assumption requires that the activities of each economic entity be kept separate from the activities of its owner(s) and other economic entities.

**3  State the accounting equation, and define its components.**

The basic accounting equation is:

$$\text{Assets} = \text{Liabilities} + \text{Stockholders' Equity}$$

Assets are resources a business owns. Liabilities are creditorship claims on total assets. Stockholders' equity is the ownership claim on total assets.

**4  Analyze the effects of business transactions on the accounting equation.**

Each business transaction must have a dual effect on the accounting equation. For example, if an individual asset increases, there must be a corresponding (1) decrease in another asset, or (2) increase in a specific liability, or (3) increase in stockholders' equity.

The expanded accounting equation is:

$$\text{Assets} = \text{Liabilities} + \text{Common Stock}$$
$$+ \text{Revenues} - \text{Expenses} - \text{Dividends}$$

Common stock is affected when the company issues new shares of stock in exchange for cash. Revenues are increases in assets resulting from income-earning activities. Expenses are the costs of assets consumed or services used in the process of earning revenue. Dividends are payments the company makes to its stockholders.

**5  Describe the four financial statements and how they are prepared.**

An income statement presents the revenues and expenses and resulting net income or net loss for a specific period of time. A retained earnings statement summarizes the changes in retained earnings for a specific period of time. A balance sheet reports the assets, liabilities, and stockholders' equity at a specific date. A statement of cash flows summarizes information about the cash inflows (receipts) and outflows (payments) for a specific period of time.

**\*6  Explain the career opportunities in accounting.**

Accounting offers many different jobs in fields such as public and private accounting, governmental accounting, and forensic accounting. Accounting is a popular major because there are many different types of jobs, with unlimited potential for career advancement.

## Glossary Review

**Accounting**  The information system that identifies, records, and communicates the economic events of an organization to interested users. (p. 1-3).

**Accounting information system**  The system of collecting and processing transaction data and communicating financial information to decision-makers. (p. 1-13).

**Assets**  Resources a business owns. (p. 1-11).

**\*Auditing**  The examination of financial statements by a certified public accountant in order to express an opinion as to how accurately the financial statements present the company's results and financial position. (p. 1-25).

**Balance sheet**  A financial statement that reports the assets, liabilities, and stockholders' equity at a specific date. (p. 1-21).

**Basic accounting equation**  Assets = Liabilities + Stockholders' equity. (p. 1-11).

**Bookkeeping**  A part of accounting that involves only the recording of economic events. (p. 1-4).

**Common stock**  Term used to describe the total amount paid in by stockholders for the shares they purchase. (p. 1-12).

**Corporation**  A business organized as a separate legal entity under state corporation law, having ownership divided into transferable shares of stock. (p. 1-10).

**Data analytics**  The use of software and statistics to draw inferences from data. (p. 1-4).

**Dividend**  A distribution by a corporation to its stockholders. (p. 1-12).

**Economic entity assumption**  An assumption that requires that the activities of the entity be kept separate and distinct from the activities of its owner and all other economic entities. (p. 1-9).

**Ethics**  The standards of conduct by which one's actions are judged as right or wrong, honest or dishonest, fair or not fair. (p. 1-7).

**Expanded accounting equation**  Assets = Liabilities + Common stock + Revenues − Expenses − Dividends. (p. 1-15).

**Expenses**  The cost of assets consumed or services used in the process of generating revenue. (p. 1-12).

**Fair value principle**  An accounting principle stating that assets and liabilities should be reported at fair value (the price received to sell an asset or settle a liability). (p. 1-9).

**Faithful representation**  Numbers and descriptions match what really existed or happened—they are factual. (p. 1-8).

**Financial accounting**  The field of accounting that provides economic and financial information for investors, creditors, and other external users. (p. 1-5).

**Financial Accounting Standards Board (FASB)** A private organization that establishes generally accepted accounting principles (GAAP) in the United States. (p. 1-8).

**\*Forensic accounting** An area of accounting that uses accounting, auditing, and investigative skills to conduct investigations into theft and fraud. (p. 1-26).

**Generally accepted accounting principles (GAAP)** Common standards that indicate how to report economic events. (p. 1-8).

**Historical cost principle** An accounting principle that states that companies should record assets at their cost. (p. 1-9).

**Income statement** A financial statement that presents the revenues and expenses and resulting net income or net loss of a company for a specific period of time. (p. 1-21).

**International Accounting Standards Board (IASB)** An accounting standard-setting body that issues standards adopted by many countries outside of the United States. (p. 1-8).

**International Financial Reporting Standards (IFRS)** International accounting standards set by the International Accounting Standards Board (IASB). (p. 1-8).

**Liabilities** Creditor claims against total assets. (p. 1-12).

**\*Management consulting** An area of public accounting ranging from development of accounting and computer systems to support services for marketing projects and merger and acquisition activities. (p. 1-25).

**Managerial accounting** The field of accounting that provides internal reports to help users make decisions about their companies. (p. 1-4).

**Monetary unit assumption** An assumption stating that companies include in the accounting records only transaction data that can be expressed in terms of money. (p. 1-9).

**Net income** The amount by which revenues exceed expenses. (p. 1-21).

**Net loss** The amount by which expenses exceed revenues. (p. 1-21).

**Partnership** A business owned by two or more persons associated as partners. (p. 1-10).

**\*Private (or managerial) accounting** An area of accounting within a company that involves such activities as cost accounting, budgeting, design and support of accounting information systems, and tax planning and preparation. (p. 1-25).

**Proprietorship** A business owned by one person. (p. 1-9).

**\*Public accounting** An area of accounting in which the accountant offers expert service to the general public. (p. 1-25).

**Relevance** Financial information that is capable of making a difference in a decision. (p. 1-8).

**Retained earnings statement** A financial statement that summarizes the changes in retained earnings for a specific period of time. (p. 1-21).

**Revenues** The increases in assets or decreases in liabilities resulting from the sale of goods or the performance of services in the normal course of business. (p. 1-12).

**Sarbanes-Oxley Act (SOX)** Law passed by Congress intended to reduce unethical corporate behavior. (p. 1-6).

**Securities and Exchange Commission (SEC)** A governmental agency that oversees U.S. financial markets and accounting standard-setting bodies. (p. 1-8).

**Statement of cash flows** A financial statement that summarizes information about the cash inflows (receipts) and cash outflows (payments) for a specific period of time. (p. 1-21).

**Stockholders' equity** The ownership claim on a corporation's total assets. (p. 1-12).

**\*Taxation** An area of public accounting involving tax advice, tax planning, preparing tax returns, and representing clients before governmental agencies. (p. 1-25).

**Transactions** The economic events of a business that are recorded by accountants. (p. 1-14).

## Practice Multiple-Choice Questions

**1. (LO 1)** Which of the following is **not** a step in the accounting process?

  **a.** Identification.      **c.** Recording.

  **b.** Economic entity.      **d.** Communication.

**2. (LO 1)** Which of the following statements about users of accounting information is **incorrect**?

  **a.** Management is an internal user.

  **b.** Taxing authorities are external users.

  **c.** Present creditors are external users.

  **d.** Regulatory authorities are internal users.

**3. (LO 2)** The historical cost principle states that:

  **a.** assets should be initially recorded at cost and adjusted when the fair value changes.

  **b.** activities of an entity are to be kept separate and distinct from its owner.

  **c.** assets should be recorded at their cost.

  **d.** only transaction data capable of being expressed in terms of money be included in the accounting records.

**4. (LO 2)** Which of the following statements about basic assumptions is **correct**?

  **a.** Basic assumptions are the same as accounting principles.

  **b.** The economic entity assumption states that there should be a particular unit of accountability.

  **c.** The monetary unit assumption enables accounting to measure employee morale.

  **d.** Partnerships are not economic entities.

**5. (LO 2)** The three types of business entities are:

  **a.** proprietorships, small businesses, and partnerships.

  **b.** proprietorships, partnerships, and corporations.

  **c.** proprietorships, partnerships, and large businesses.

  **d.** financial, manufacturing, and service companies.

**6. (LO 3)** Net income will result during a time period when:

  **a.** assets exceed liabilities.

  **b.** assets exceed revenues.

  **c.** expenses exceed revenues.

  **d.** revenues exceed expenses.

**7. (LO 3)** As of December 31, 2022, Reed Company has assets of $3,500 and stockholders' equity of $1,500. What are the liabilities for Reed Company as of December 31, 2022?

   **a.** $1,500.

   **b.** $1,000.

   **c.** $2,500.

   **d.** $2,000.

**8. (LO 4)** Performing services on account will have the following effects on the components of the basic accounting equation:

   **a.** increase assets and decrease stockholders' equity.

   **b.** increase assets and increase stockholders' equity.

   **c.** increase assets and increase liabilities.

   **d.** increase liabilities and increase stockholders' equity.

**9. (LO 4)** Which of the following events is **not** recorded in the accounting records?

   **a.** Equipment is purchased on account.

   **b.** An employee is terminated.

   **c.** A cash investment is made into the business.

   **d.** The company pays a cash dividend.

**10. (LO 4)** During 2022, Seisor Company's assets decreased $50,000 and its liabilities decreased $90,000. Its stockholders' equity therefore:

   **a.** increased $40,000.    **c.** decreased $40,000.

   **b.** decreased $140,000.    **d.** increased $140,000.

**11. (LO 4)** Payment of an account payable affects the components of the accounting equation in the following way.

   **a.** Decreases stockholders' equity and decreases liabilities.

   **b.** Increases assets and decreases liabilities.

   **c.** Decreases assets and increases stockholders' equity.

   **d.** Decreases assets and decreases liabilities.

**12. (LO 5)** Which of the following statements is **false**?

   **a.** A statement of cash flows summarizes information about the cash inflows (receipts) and outflows (payments) for a specific period of time.

   **b.** A balance sheet reports the assets, liabilities, and stockholders' equity at a specific date.

   **c.** An income statement presents the revenues, expenses, changes in stockholders' equity, and resulting net income or net loss for a specific period of time.

   **d.** A retained earnings statement summarizes the changes in retained earnings for a specific period of time.

**13. (LO 5)** On the last day of the period, Alan Cesska Company buys a $900 machine on credit. This transaction will affect the:

   **a.** income statement only.

   **b.** balance sheet only.

   **c.** income statement and retained earnings statement only.

   **d.** income statement, retained earnings statement, and balance sheet.

**14. (LO 5)** The financial statement that reports assets, liabilities, and stockholders' equity is the:

   **a.** income statement.

   **b.** retained earnings statement.

   **c.** balance sheet.

   **d.** statement of cash flows.

**\*15. (LO 6)** Services performed by a public accountant include:

   **a.** auditing, taxation, and management consulting.

   **b.** auditing, budgeting, and management consulting.

   **c.** auditing, budgeting, and cost accounting.

   **d.** auditing, budgeting, and management consulting.

## Solutions

**1. b.** Economic entity is not one of the steps in the accounting process. The other choices are true because (a) identification is the first step in the accounting process, (c) recording is the second step in the accounting process, and (d) communication is the third and final step in the accounting process.

**2. d.** Regulatory authorities are external, not internal, users of accounting information. The other choices are true statements.

**3. c.** The historical cost principle states that assets should be recorded at their cost. The other choices are incorrect because (a) the historical cost principle does not say that assets should be adjusted for changes in fair value, (b) describes the economic entity assumption, and (d) describes the monetary unit assumption.

**4. b.** The economic entity assumption states that there should be a particular unit of accountability. The other choices are incorrect because (a) basic assumptions are not the same as accounting principles, (c) the monetary unit assumption allows accounting to measure economic events, and (d) partnerships are economic entities.

**5. b.** Proprietorships, partnerships, and corporations are the three types of business entities. Choices (a) and (c) are incorrect because small and large businesses only denote the sizes of businesses. Choice (d) is incorrect because financial, manufacturing, and service companies are types of businesses, not business entities.

**6. d.** Net income results when revenues exceed expenses. The other choices are incorrect because (a) assets and liabilities are not used in the computation of net income; (b) revenues, not assets, are included in the computation of net income; and (c) when expenses exceed revenues, a net loss results.

**7. d.** Using a variation of the basic accounting equation, Assets − Stockholders' equity = Liabilities, $3,500 − $1,500 = $2,000. Therefore, choices (a) $1,500, (b) $1,000, and (c) $2,500 are incorrect.

**8. b.** When services are performed on account, assets are increased and stockholders' equity is increased. The other choices are incorrect because when services are performed on account (a) stockholders' equity is increased, not decreased; (c) liabilities are not affected; and (d) stockholders' equity is increased and liabilities are not affected.

**9. b.** If an employee is terminated, this represents an activity of a company, not a business transaction. Assets, liabilities, and stockholders' equity are not affected. Thus, there is no effect on the accounting equation. The other choices are incorrect because they are all recorded: (a) when equipment is purchased on account, both assets and liabilities increase; (c) when a cash investment is made into a business, both assets and stockholders' equity increase; and (d) when a dividend is paid, both assets and stockholders' equity decrease.

**10. a.** Using the basic accounting equation, Assets = Liabilities + Stockholders' equity, −$50,000 = −$90,000 + Stockholders' equity, so stockholders' equity increased $40,000, not (b) decreased $140,000, (c) decreased $40,000, or (d) increased $140,000.

**11. d.** Payment of an account payable results in an equal decrease of assets (cash) and liabilities (accounts payable). The other choices are incorrect because payment of an account payable (a) does not affect stockholders' equity, (b) does not increase assets, and (c) does not affect stockholders' equity.

**12. c.** An income statement represents the revenues, expenses, and resulting net income or net loss for a specific period of time but not the changes in stockholders' equity. The other choices are true statements.

**13. b.** This transaction will cause assets to increase by $900 and liabilities to increase by $900. The other choices are incorrect because this transaction (a) will have no effect on the income statement, (c) will have no effect on the income statement or the retained earnings statement, and (d) will affect the balance sheet but not the income statement or the retained earnings statement.

**14. c.** The balance sheet is the statement that reports assets, liabilities and stockholders' equity. The other choices are incorrect because (a) the income statement reports revenues and expenses, (b) the retained earnings statement reports details about stockholders' equity, and (d) the statement of cash flows reports inflows and outflows of cash.

**\*15. a.** Auditing, taxation, and management consulting are all services performed by public accountants. The other choices are incorrect because public accountants do not perform budgeting or cost accounting.

---

## Practice Brief Exercises

*Use basic accounting equation.*

**1. (LO 3)** At the beginning of the year, Ortiz Company had total assets of $900,000 and total liabilities of $440,000. Answer the following questions.

    **a.** If total assets decreased $100,000 during the year and total liabilities increased $80,000 during the year, what is the amount of stockholders' equity at the end of the year?

    **b.** During the year, total liabilities decreased $100,000, and stockholders' equity increased $200,000. What is the amount of total assets at the end of the year?

    **c.** If total assets increased $50,000 during the year and stockholders' equity increased $60,000 during the year, what is the amount of total liabilities at the end of the year?

### Solution

**1. a.** ($900,000 − $440,000) − $100,000 − $80,000 = $280,000 stockholders' equity

    **b.** $900,000 − $100,000 + $200,000 = $1,000,000 total assets

    **c.** $440,000 − $60,000 + $50,000 = $430,000 total liabilities

*Determine effect of transactions on basic accounting equation.*

**2. (LO 4)** The following are three business transactions. Create a table with rows (a), (b), and (c), and columns for assets, liabilities, and stockholders' equity. For each column, indicate whether the transactions increased (+), decreased (−), or had no effect (NE) on assets, liabilities, and stockholders' equity.

    **a.** Purchased equipment on account.

    **b.** Payment of cash dividends.

    **c.** Paid expenses in cash.

### Solution

|  | Assets | Liabilities | Stockholders' Equity |
|---|---|---|---|
| **2. a.** | + | + | NE |
| **b.** | − | NE | − |
| **c.** | − | NE | − |

*Determine effect of transactions on basic accounting equation.*

**3. (LO 4)** Follow the same format as in **Practice Brief Exercise 2**. Determine the effect on assets, liabilities, and stockholders' equity of the following three transactions.

    **a.** Performed accounting services for clients for cash.

    **b.** Borrowed cash from a bank on a note payable.

    **c.** Paid cash for rent for the month.

**Solution**

|       | Assets | Liabilities | Stockholders' Equity |
|-------|:------:|:-----------:|:--------------------:|
| 3. a. |   +    |     NE      |          +           |
| b.    |   +    |     +       |          NE          |
| c.    |   −    |     NE      |          −           |

**4. (LO 5)** Indicate whether the following items would appear on the income statement (IS), balance sheet (BS), or retained earnings statement (RES).

*Determine where items appear on financial statements.*

a. ____ Common stock.

b. ____ Cash.

c. ____ Salaries and wages expense.

d. ____ Service revenue.

e. ____ Accounts payable.

**Solution**

4. a.  __BS__  Common stock.

b.  __BS__  Cash.

c.  __IS__  Salaries and wages expense.

d.  __IS__  Service revenue.

e.  __BS__  Accounts payable.

**5. (LO 5)** Presented below in alphabetical order are balance sheet items for Feagler Company at December 31, 2022. Prepare a balance sheet following the format of Illustration 1.10.

*Prepare a balance sheet.*

| | |
|---|---:|
| Accounts receivable | $12,500 |
| Cash | 38,000 |
| Common stock | 5,000 |
| Notes payable | 40,000 |
| Retained earnings | 5,500 |

**Solution**

5.

**Feagler Company**
**Balance Sheet**
**December 31, 2022**

**Assets**

| | | |
|---|---:|---:|
| Cash | | $38,000 |
| Accounts receivable | | 12,500 |
| Total assets | | $50,500 |

**Liabilities and Stockholders' Equity**

| | | |
|---|---:|---:|
| Liabilities | | |
| Notes payable | $40,000 | |
| Total liabilities | | $40,000 |
| Stockholders' equity | | |
| Common stock | 5,000 | |
| Retained earnings | 5,500 | 10,500 |
| Total liabilities and stockholders' equity | | $50,500 |

# Practice Exercises

**1. (LO 3, 4)** Selected transactions for Beale Lawn Care Company are as follows.

*Analyze the effect of transactions.*

1. Sold common stock for cash to start business.
2. Paid monthly utilities.
3. Purchased land on account.

4. Billed customers for services performed.

5. Paid dividends.

6. Received cash from customers billed in (4).

7. Incurred utilities expense on account.

8. Purchased equipment for cash.

9. Received cash from customers when service was performed.

### Instructions

List the numbers of the above transactions and describe the effect of each transaction on assets, liabilities, and stockholders' equity. For example, the first answer is (1) Increase in assets and increase in stockholders' equity.

### Solution

1. 1.  Increase in assets and increase in stockholders' equity.

   2.  Decrease in assets and decrease in stockholders' equity.

   3.  Increase in assets and increase in liabilities.

   4.  Increase in assets and increase in stockholders' equity.

   5.  Decrease in assets and decrease in stockholders' equity.

   6.  Increase in assets and decrease in assets.

   7.  Increase in liabilities and decrease in stockholders' equity.

   8.  Increase in assets and decrease in assets.

   9.  Increase in assets and increase in stockholders' equity.

*Analyze the effect of transactions on assets, liabilities, and stockholders' equity.*

2. **(LO 3, 4)** Hayes Computer Timeshare Company entered into the following transactions during May 2022.

1.  Purchased office equipment for $10,000 from Office Outfitters on account.

2.  Paid $3,000 cash for May rent on storage space.

3.  Received $12,000 cash from customers for contracts billed in April.

4.  Performed services for Bayliss Construction Company for $4,000 cash.

5.  Paid Southern Power Co. $10,000 cash for energy usage in May.

6.  Stockholders invested an additional $30,000 in the business.

7.  Paid Office Outfitters for the equipment purchased in (1) above.

8.  Incurred advertising expense for May of $1,500 on account.

### Instructions

Indicate with the appropriate letter whether each of the transactions above results in:

a.  An increase in assets and a decrease in assets.

b.  An increase in assets and an increase in stockholders' equity.

c.  An increase in assets and an increase in liabilities.

d.  A decrease in assets and a decrease in stockholders' equity.

e.  A decrease in assets and a decrease in liabilities.

f.  An increase in liabilities and a decrease in stockholders' equity.

g.  An increase in stockholders' equity and a decrease in liabilities.

### Solution

| 2. | 1. c | 3. a | 5. d | 7. e |
|----|------|------|------|------|
|    | 2. d | 4. b | 6. b | 8. f |

## Practice Problem

**(LO 4, 5)** Legal Services Inc. was incorporated on July 1, 2022. During the first month of operations, the following transactions occurred.

*Prepare a tabular presentation and financial statements.*

1.  Legal Services issued common stock in exchange for cash of $10,000.
2.  Paid $800 for July rent on office space.
3.  Purchased office equipment on account $3,000.
4.  Performed legal services for clients for cash $1,500.
5.  Borrowed $700 cash from a bank on a note payable.
6.  Performed legal services for client on account $2,000.
7.  Paid monthly expenses: salaries $500, utilities $300, and advertising $100.

### Instructions

a.  Prepare a tabular summary of the transactions.
b.  Prepare the income statement, retained earnings statement, and balance sheet at July 31, 2022, for Legal Services Inc.

### Solution

a.

| Trans-action | Cash | + | Accounts Receivable | + | Equipment | = | Notes Payable | + | Accounts Payable | + | Common Stock | + | Rev. | − | Exp. | − | Div. | |
|---|---|---|---|---|---|---|---|---|---|---|---|---|---|---|---|---|---|---|
| | | | | | | | | | | | | | Retained Earnings | | | | | |
| (1) | −$10,000 | | | | | = | | | | | +$10,000 | | | | | | | Issued Stock |
| (2) | −800 | | | | | | | | | | | | | | −$800 | | | Rent Expense |
| (3) | | | | | +$3,000 | = | | | +$3,000 | | | | | | | | | |
| (4) | +1,500 | | | | | | | | | | | | +$1,500 | | | | | Service Revenue |
| (5) | +700 | | | | | | +$700 | | | | | | | | | | | |
| (6) | | | +$2,000 | | | | | | | | | | +2,000 | | | | | Service Revenue |
| (7) | −500 | | | | | | | | | | | | | | −500 | | | Sal./Wages Exp. |
| | −300 | | | | | | | | | | | | | | −300 | | | Utilities Expense |
| | −100 | | | | | | | | | | | | | | −100 | | | Advertising Expense |
| | $10,500 | + | $2,000 | + | $3,000 | = | $700 | + | $3,000 | + | $10,000 | + | $3,500 | − | $1,700 | | | |

$15,500

$15,500

b.

**Legal Services Inc.**
**Income Statement**
**For the Month Ended July 31, 2022**

| | | |
|---|---|---|
| Revenues | | |
| Service revenue | | $3,500 |
| Expenses | | |
| Rent expense | $800 | |
| Salaries and wages expense | 500 | |
| Utilities expense | 300 | |
| Advertising expense | 100 | |
| Total expenses | | 1,700 |
| Net income | | $1,800 |

**Legal Services Inc.**
**Retained Earnings Statement**
**For the Month Ended July 31, 2022**

| | |
|---|---|
| Retained earnings, July 1 | $ –0– |
| Add: Net income | 1,800 |
| Retained earnings, July 31 | $1,800 |

| Legal Services Inc. |||
| --- | --- | --- |
| **Balance Sheet** |||
| **July 31, 2022** |||
| **Assets** |||
| Cash | | $10,500 |
| Accounts receivable | | 2,000 |
| Equipment | | 3,000 |
| Total assets | | $15,500 |
| **Liabilities and Stockholders' Equity** |||
| Liabilities | | |
| Notes payable | $ 700 | |
| Accounts payable | 3,000 | |
| Total liabilities | | $ 3,700 |
| Stockholders' equity | | |
| Common stock | 10,000 | |
| Retained earnings | 1,800 | 11,800 |
| Total liabilities and stockholders' equity | | $15,500 |

Brief Exercises, DO IT! Exercises, Exercises, Problems, Data Analytics Activities, and many additional resources are available for practice in WileyPLUS.

## Questions

**1.** "Accounting is ingrained in our society and it is vital to our economic system." Explain why this statement is true or false.

**2.** Identify and describe the activities in the accounting process.

**3. a.** Who are internal users of accounting data?

**b.** How does accounting provide relevant data to these users?

**4.** What uses of financial accounting information are made by (a) investors and (b) creditors?

**5.** "Bookkeeping and accounting are the same." Explain why this statement is true or false.

**6.** Harper Travel Agency purchased land for $85,000 cash on December 10, 2022. At December 31, 2022, the land's value has increased to $93,000. What amount should be reported for land on Harper's balance sheet at December 31, 2022? Explain.

**7.** What is the monetary unit assumption?

**8.** What is the economic entity assumption?

**9.** What are the three basic forms of profit-oriented business organizations?

**10.** Juana Perez is the owner of a successful printing shop. Recently, her business has been increasing, and Juana has been thinking about changing the organization of her business from a proprietorship to a corporation. Discuss some of the advantages Juana would enjoy if she were to incorporate her business.

**11.** What is the basic accounting equation?

**12. a.** Define the terms assets, liabilities, and stockholders' equity.

**b.** What items affect stockholders' equity?

**13.** Which of the following items are liabilities of jewelry stores?

**a.** Cash.

**b.** Accounts payable.

**c.** Dividends.

**d.** Accounts receivable.

**e.** Supplies.

**f.** Equipment.

**g.** Salaries and wages payable.

**h.** Service revenue.

**i.** Rent expense.

**14.** Can a business enter into a transaction in which only the left side of the basic accounting equation is affected? If so, give an example.

**15.** Are the following events recorded in the accounting records? Explain your answer in each case.

**a.** The president of the company dies.

**b.** Supplies are purchased on account.

**c.** An employee is fired.

16. Indicate how the following business transactions affect the basic accounting equation.

    **a.** Paid cash for janitorial services.

    **b.** Purchased equipment for cash.

    **c.** Invested cash in the business for stock.

    **d.** Paid accounts payable in full.

17. Listed below are some items found in the financial statements of Jonas Co. Indicate in which financial statement(s) the following items would appear.

    **a.** Service revenue.

    **b.** Equipment.

    **c.** Advertising expense.

    **d.** Accounts receivable.

    **e.** Retained earnings.

    **f.** Salaries and wages payable.

18. In February 2022, Rachel Paige invested an additional $10,000 in Drumlin Company. Drumlin's accountant, Liz Cooke, recorded this receipt as an increase in cash and revenues. Is this treatment appropriate? Why or why not?

19. "A company's net income appears directly on the income statement and the retained earnings statement, and it is included indirectly in the company's balance sheet." Do you agree? Explain.

20. Monique Enterprises had a stockholders' equity balance of $158,000 at the beginning of the period. At the end of the accounting period, the stockholders' equity balance was $198,000.

    **a.** Assuming no additional investment or dividends during the period, what is the net income for the period?

    **b.** Assuming an additional investment of $16,000 but no dividends during the period, what is the net income for the period?

21. Summarized operations for Lakeview Co. for the month of July are as follows.

    Revenues recognized: for cash $30,000; on account $70,000. Expenses incurred: for cash $26,000; on account $38,000. Indicate for Lakeview Co. (a) the total revenues, (b) the total expenses, and (c) net income for the month of July.

22. The basic accounting equation is Assets = Liabilities + Stockholders' equity. Replacing the words in that equation with dollar amounts, what is **Apple**'s accounting equation at September 29, 2018?

# Brief Exercises

**BE1.1 (LO 3), AP** The following is the basic accounting equation. Determine the missing amounts.

*Use basic accounting equation.*

| Assets | = | Liabilities | + | Stockholders' Equity |
|---|---|---|---|---|
| **a.** $78,000 | | $50,000 | | ? |
| **b.** ? | | $45,000 | | $70,000 |
| **c.** $94,000 | | ? | | $60,000 |

**BE1.2 (LO 3), AP** Given the accounting equation, answer each of the following questions.

*Use basic accounting equation.*

    **a.** The liabilities of Holland Company are $120,000 and its stockholders' equity is $232,000. What is the amount of Holland Company's total assets?

    **b.** The total assets of Holland Company are $190,000 and its stockholders' equity is $86,000. What is the amount of its total liabilities?

    **c.** The total assets of Holland Company are $600,000 and its liabilities are equal to one-half of its total assets. What is the amount of Holland Company's stockholders' equity?

**BE1.3 (LO 3), AP** At the beginning of the year, Canon Company had total assets of $870,000 and total liabilities of $500,000. Answer the following questions.

*Use basic accounting equation.*

    **a.** If total assets increased $150,000 during the year and total liabilities decreased $80,000, what is the amount of stockholders' equity at the end of the year?

    **b.** During the year, total liabilities increased $100,000 and stockholders' equity decreased $66,000. What is the amount of total assets at the end of the year?

    **c.** If total assets decreased $80,000 and stockholders' equity increased $120,000 during the year, what is the amount of total liabilities at the end of the year?

**BE1.4 (LO 3), AP** Use the accounting equation to answer each of the following questions.

*Solve accounting equation.*

    **a.** The liabilities of Olga Company are $90,000. Common stock account is $150,000; dividends are $40,000; revenues, $450,000; and expenses, $320,000. What is the amount of Olga Company's total assets?

    **b.** The total assets of Lafayette Company are $57,000. Common stock account is $23,000; dividends are $7,000; revenues, $50,000; and expenses, $35,000. What is the amount of the company's total liabilities?

    **c.** The total assets of Dierdorf Co. are $600,000 and its liabilities are equal to two-thirds of its total assets. What is the amount of Dierdorf Co.'s stockholders' equity?

*Identify assets, liabilities, and stockholders' equity.*

**BE1.5 (LO 3), C** Indicate whether each of the following items is an asset (A), liability (L), or part of stockholders' equity (SE).

_____ **a.** Accounts receivable        _____ **d.** Supplies

_____ **b.** Salaries and wages payable        _____ **e.** Dividends

_____ **c.** Equipment        _____ **f.** Notes payable

*Determine effect of transactions on basic accounting equation.*

**BE1.6 (LO 4), C** The following are three business transactions. Create a table with rows (a), (b), and (c), and columns for assets, liabilities, and stockholders' equity. For each column, indicate whether the transactions increased (+), decreased (−), or had no effect (NE) on assets, liabilities, and stockholders' equity.

**a.** Purchased supplies on account.

**b.** Received cash for performing a service.

**c.** Paid expenses in cash.

*Determine effect of transactions on accounting equation.*

**BE1.7 (LO 4), C** The following are three business transactions. Create a table with rows (a), (b), and (c), and columns for assets, liabilities, and stockholders' equity. For each column, indicate whether the transactions increased (+), decreased (−), or had no effect (NE) on assets, liabilities, and stockholders' equity.

**a.** Stockholders invested cash in the business for common stock.

**b.** Paid a cash dividend.

**c.** Received cash from a customer who had previously been billed for services performed.

*Classify items affecting stockholders' equity.*

**BE1.8 (LO 4), C** Classify each of the following items as dividends (D), revenue (R), or expense (E).

_____ **a.** Advertising expense        _____ **e.** Dividends

_____ **b.** Service revenue        _____ **f.** Rent revenue

_____ **c.** Insurance expense        _____ **g.** Utilities expense

_____ **d.** Salaries and wages expense

*Determine effect of transactions on stockholders' equity.*

**BE1.9 (LO 4), C** The following are three transactions. Mark each transaction as affecting common stock (C), dividends (D), revenue (R), expense (E), or not affecting stockholders' equity (NSE).

_____ **a.** Received cash for services performed

_____ **b.** Paid cash to purchase equipment

_____ **c.** Paid employee salaries

*Prepare a balance sheet.*

**BE1.10 (LO 5), AP** In alphabetical order below are balance sheet items for Ellerby Company at December 31, 2022. Prepare a balance sheet, following the format of Illustration 1.10.

| | |
|---|---|
| Accounts payable | $85,000 |
| Accounts receivable | 72,500 |
| Cash | 44,000 |
| Common stock | 21,500 |
| Retained earnings | 10,000 |

*Determine where items appear on financial statements.*

**BE1.11 (LO 5), C** Indicate whether the following items would appear on the income statement (IS), balance sheet (BS), or retained earnings statement (RE).

_____ **a.** Notes payable        _____ **d.** Cash

_____ **b.** Advertising expense        _____ **e.** Service revenue

_____ **c.** Common stock        _____ **f.** Dividends

# DO IT! Exercises

*Review basic concepts.*

**DO IT! 1.1 (LO 1), K** Indicate whether each of the following five statements is true or false. If false, indicate how to correct the statement.

1. The three steps in the accounting process are identification, recording, and examination.

2. The accounting process includes the bookkeeping function.

3. Managerial accounting provides reports to help investors and creditors evaluate a company.

4. The two most common types of external users are investors and creditors.

5. Internal users include human resource managers.

**DO IT! 1.2 (LO 2), K** Indicate whether each of the following five statements is true or false. If false, indicate how to correct the statement.

*Review basic concepts.*

1. Congress passed the Sarbanes-Oxley Act to ensure that investors invest only in companies that will be profitable.

2. The standards of conduct by which actions are judged as loyal or disloyal are ethics.

3. The primary accounting standard-setting body in the United States is the Securities and Exchange Commission (SEC).

4. The historical cost principle dictates that companies record assets at their cost and continue to report them at their cost over the time the assets are held.

5. The monetary unit assumption requires that companies record only transactions that can be measured in money terms.

**DO IT! 1.3 (LO 3), K** Classify the following items as issuance of stock (I), dividends (D), revenues (R), or expenses (E). Then indicate whether each item increases or decreases stockholders' equity.

*Evaluate effects of transactions on stockholders' equity.*

1. Dividends.     3. Advertising expense.

2. Rent revenue.     4. Stockholders invest cash in the business.

**DO IT! 1.4 (LO 4), AP** Transactions made by Morlan and Co., a law firm, for the month of March are as follows. Prepare a tabular analysis that shows the effects of these transactions on the accounting equation, similar to that shown in Illustration 1.9.

*Prepare tabular analysis.*

1. The company performed $23,000 of services for customers, on credit.

2. The company received $23,000 in cash from customers who had been billed for services (in transaction 1).

3. The company received a bill for $1,800 of advertising, but will not pay it until a later date.

4. The company paid a dividend of $5,000 in cash to stockholders.

**DO IT! 1.5 (LO 5), AP** The following is selected information related to Garryowen Company at December 31, 2022. Garryowen reports financial information monthly.

*Determine specific amounts on the financial statements.*

| Accounts Payable | $ 3,000 | Salaries and Wages Expense | $16,500 |
|---|---|---|---|
| Cash | 9,000 | Notes Payable | 25,000 |
| Advertising Expense | 6,000 | Rent Expense | 9,800 |
| Service Revenue | 54,000 | Accounts Receivable | 13,500 |
| Equipment | 29,000 | Dividends | 7,500 |

a. Determine the total assets of Garryowen Company at December 31, 2022.

b. Determine the net income that Garryowen Company reported for December 2022.

c. Determine the stockholders' equity of Garryowen Company at December 31, 2022.

# Exercises

**E1.1 (LO 1), C** Callison Company performs the following accounting tasks during the year.

*Classify the three activities of accounting.*

_____ Analyzing and interpreting information.

_____ Classifying economic events.

_____ Explaining uses, meaning, and limitations of data.

_____ Keeping a systematic chronological diary of events.

_____ Measuring events in dollars and cents.

_____ Preparing accounting reports.

_____ Reporting information in a standard format.

_____ Selecting economic activities relevant to the company

_____ Summarizing economic events.

Accounting is "an information system that **identifies, records**, and **communicates** the economic events of an organization to interested users."

**Instructions**

Categorize the accounting tasks performed by Callison as relating to either the identification (I), recording (R), or communication (C) aspects of accounting.

*Identify users of accounting information.*

**E1.2 (LO 1), C a.** The following are users of financial statements.

_____ Customers                              _____ Securities and Exchange Commission

_____ Internal Revenue Service              _____ Store manager

_____ Labor unions                          _____ Suppliers

_____ Marketing manager                     _____ Vice president of finance

_____ Production supervisor

**Instructions**

Identify the users as being either **external users (E)** or **internal users (I)**.

**b.** The following questions could be asked by an internal user or an external user.

_____ Can we afford to give our employees a pay raise?

_____ Did the company earn a satisfactory income?

_____ Do we need to borrow in the near future?

_____ How does the company's profitability compare to other companies?

_____ What does it cost us to manufacture each unit produced?

_____ Which product should we emphasize?

_____ Will the company be able to pay its short-term debts?

**Instructions**

Identify each of the questions as being more likely asked by an **internal user (I)** or an **external user (E)**.

*Discuss ethics and the historical cost principle.*

**E1.3 (LO 2), C** Sam Cresco, president of Cresco Company, has instructed Sharon Gross, the head of the accounting department for Cresco Company, to report the company's land in the company's accounting reports at its fair value of $170,000 instead of its cost of $100,000. Cresco says, "Showing the land at $170,000 will make our company look like a better investment when we try to attract new investors next month."

**Instructions**

Explain the ethical situation involved for Sharon Gross, identifying the stakeholders and the alternatives.

*Use accounting concepts.*

**E1.4 (LO 2), C** The following situations involve accounting principles and assumptions.

**1.** Tina Company owns buildings that are worth substantially more than they originally cost. In an effort to provide more relevant information, Tina reports the buildings at fair value in its accounting reports.

**2.** Fayette Company includes in its accounting records only transaction data that can be expressed in terms of money.

**3.** Omar Shariff, president of Omar's Oasis, records his personal living costs as expenses of the Oasis.

**Instructions**

For each of the three situations, state if the accounting method used is correct or incorrect. If correct, identify which principle or assumption supports the method used. If incorrect, identify which principle or assumption has been violated.

*Classify accounts as assets, liabilities, and stockholders' equity.*

**E1.5 (LO 3), C** Bailey Cleaners has the following balance sheet items.

| | |
|---|---|
| Accounts payable | Accounts receivable |
| Cash | Notes payable |
| Equipment | Salaries and wages payable |
| Supplies | Common stock |

**Instructions**

Classify each item as an asset, liability, or stockholders' equity.

*Analyze the effect of transactions.*

**E1.6 (LO 4), C** Selected transactions for Verdent Lawn Care Company are as follows.

**1.** Sold common stock for cash to start business.

**2.** Paid monthly rent.

**3.** Purchased equipment on account.

4. Billed customers for services performed.

5. Paid dividends.

6. Received cash from customers billed in (4).

7. Incurred advertising expense on account.

8. Purchased additional equipment for cash.

9. Received cash from customers when service was performed.

**Instructions**

List the numbers of the above transactions and describe the effect of each transaction on assets, liabilities, and stockholders' equity. For example, the first answer is (1) Increase in assets and increase in stockholders' equity.

**E1.7 (LO 4), C** Keystone Computer Timeshare Company entered into the following transactions during May 2022.

1. Purchased computers for $20,000 from Data Equipment on account.

2. Paid $3,000 cash for May rent on storage space.

3. Received $15,000 cash from customers for contracts billed in April.

4. Performed computer services for Ryan Construction Company for $2,700 cash.

5. Paid Midland Power Co. $11,000 cash for energy usage in May.

6. Stockholders invested an additional $32,000 in the business.

7. Paid Data Equipment for the computers purchased in (1) above.

8. Incurred advertising expense for May of $840 on account.

*Analyze the effect of transactions on assets, liabilities, and stockholders' equity.*

**Instructions**

Indicate with the appropriate letter whether each of the transactions results in:

a. An increase in assets and a decrease in assets.

b. An increase in assets and an increase in stockholders' equity.

c. An increase in assets and an increase in liabilities.

d. A decrease in assets and a decrease in stockholders' equity.

e. A decrease in assets and a decrease in liabilities.

f. An increase in liabilities and a decrease in stockholders' equity.

g. An increase in stockholders' equity and a decrease in liabilities.

**E1.8 (LO 4, 5), AP** Writing An analysis of the transactions made by Foley & Co., a certified public accounting firm, for the month of August is as follows. Each increase and decrease in stockholders' equity is explained.

*Analyze transactions and compute net income.*

| | Assets | | | | = Liabilities + | | Stockholders' Equity | | | |
|---|---|---|---|---|---|---|---|---|---|---|
| Cash | + Accounts Receivable | + Supplies | + Equipment = | Accounts Payable | + Common Stock | + | Retained Earnings | | | |
| | | | | | | | Rev. | − Exp. | − | Div. |
| 1. +$15,000 | | | | | +$15,000 | | | | |
| 2.  −2,000 | | | +$5,000 | +$3,000 | | | | | |
| 3.  −750 | | +$750 | | | | | | | |
| 4.  +4,900 | +$4,500 | | | | | +$9,400 | | | Service Revenue |
| 5.  −1,500 | | | | −1,500 | | | | | |
| 6.  −2,000 | | | | | | | | −$2,000 | |
| 7.  −850 | | | | | | | −S 850 | | Rent Expense |
| 8.  +450 | −450 | | | | | | | | |
| 9.  −3,900 | | | | | | | −3,900 | | Sal./Wages Expense |
| 10. | | | | +500 | | | −500 | | Utilities Expense |

**Instructions**

a. Describe each transaction that occurred for the month.

b. Determine how much stockholders' equity increased for the month.

c. Compute the amount of net income for the month.

*Prepare financial statements.*

**E1.9 (LO 5), AP** An analysis of transactions for Foley & Co., a certified public accounting firm, for the month of August is as follows. Assume that August is the company's first month of business.

| | Assets | | | | = Liabilities + | Stockholders' Equity | | | | | |
|---|---|---|---|---|---|---|---|---|---|---|---|
| | Cash | + Accounts Receivable | + Supplies | + Equipment = | Accounts Payable | + Common Stock | + | Retained Earnings | | | |
| | | | | | | | | Rev. − | Exp. − | Div. | |
| 1. | +$15,000 | | | | | +$15,000 | | | | | |
| 2. | −2,000 | | | +$5,000 | +$3,000 | | | | | | |
| 3. | −750 | | +$750 | | | | | | | | |
| 4. | +4,900 | +$4,500 | | | | | | +$9,400 | | | Service Revenue |
| 5. | −1,500 | | | | −1,500 | | | | | | |
| 6. | −2,000 | | | | | | | | | −$2,000 | |
| 7. | −850 | | | | | | | | −$ 850 | | Rent Expense |
| 8. | +450 | −450 | | | | | | | | | |
| 9. | −3,900 | | | | | | | | −3,900 | | Sal./Wages Expense |
| 10. | | | | | +500 | | | | −500 | | Utilities Expense |

### Instructions

Prepare an income statement and a retained earnings statement for August and a balance sheet at August 31, 2022.

*Determine net income (or loss).*

**E1.10 (LO 5), AP** Toth Company had the following assets and liabilities on the dates indicated.

| December 31 | Total Assets | Total Liabilities |
|---|---|---|
| 2021 | $400,000 | $260,000 |
| 2022 | $480,000 | $300,000 |
| 2023 | $590,000 | $400,000 |

Toth began business on January 1, 2021, with an investment of $100,000 from stockholders.

### Instructions

From an analysis of the change in stockholders' equity during the year, compute the net income (or loss) for:

**a.** 2021, assuming Toth paid $15,000 in dividends for the year.

**b.** 2022, assuming stockholders made an additional investment of $50,000 and Toth paid no dividends in 2022.

**c.** 2023, assuming stockholders made an additional investment of $15,000 and Toth paid dividends of $30,000 in 2023.

*Analyze financial statements items.*

**E1.11 (LO 5), AN** Two items are omitted from each of the following summaries of balance sheet and income statement data for two corporations for the year 2022, Plunkett Co. and Herring Enterprises.

| | Plunkett Co. | Herring Enterprises |
|---|---|---|
| Beginning of year: | | |
| Total assets | $ 97,000 | $122,000 |
| Total liabilities | 85,000 | (c) |
| Total stockholders' equity | (a) | 75,000 |
| End of year: | | |
| Total assets | 160,000 | 180,000 |
| Total liabilities | 120,000 | 50,000 |
| Total stockholders' equity | 40,000 | 130,000 |
| Changes during year in stockholders' equity: | | |
| Additional investment | (b) | 25,000 |
| Dividends | 15,000 | (d) |
| Total revenues | 215,000 | 100,000 |
| Total expenses | 175,000 | 55,000 |

### Instructions

Determine the missing amounts.

**E1.12 (LO 5), AP** The following information relates to La Greca Co. for the year 2022.

*Prepare income statement and retained earnings statement.*

| | | | |
|---|---|---|---|
| Retained earnings, January 1, 2022 | $48,000 | Advertising expense | $ 1,800 |
| Dividends during 2022 | 5,000 | Rent expense | 10,400 |
| Service revenue | 62,500 | Utilities expense | 3,100 |
| Salaries and wages expense | 28,000 | | |

**Instructions**

After analyzing the data, prepare an income statement and a retained earnings statement for the year ending December 31, 2022.

**E1.13 (LO 5), AN** Robyn Howser is the bookkeeper for Madison Company. Robyn has been trying to determine the correct balance sheet for Madison Company, shown as follows.

*Correct an incorrectly prepared balance sheet.*

**Madison Company**
**Balance Sheet**
**December 31, 2022**

| Assets | | Liabilities | |
|---|---|---|---|
| Cash | $14,000 | Accounts payable | $15,000 |
| Supplies | 3,000 | Accounts receivable | (8,500) |
| Equipment | 48,000 | Common stock | 50,000 |
| Total assets | $65,000 | Retained earnings | 8,500 |
| | | Total liabilities and stockholders' equity | $65,000 |

**Instructions**

Prepare a correct balance sheet.

**E1.14 (LO 5), AP** Wyco Park, a public camping ground near the Four Corners National Recreation Area, has compiled the following financial information as of December 31, 2022.

*Compute net income and prepare a balance sheet.*

| | | | |
|---|---|---|---|
| Revenues during 2022—camping fees | $140,000 | Notes payable | $ 60,000 |
| Revenues during 2022—general store | 47,000 | Expenses during 2022 | 150,000 |
| Accounts payable | 11,000 | Supplies on hand | 2,500 |
| Cash on hand | 20,000 | Common stock | 20,000 |
| Original cost of equipment | 105,500 | Retained earnings | ? |
| Fair value of equipment | 140,000 | | |

**Instructions**

a. Determine Wyco Park's net income for 2022.

b. Prepare a balance sheet for Wyco Park as of December 31, 2022.

**E1.15 (LO 5), AP** The following financial information is related to the 2022 operations of Louisa Cruise Company.

*Prepare an income statement.*

| | |
|---|---|
| Maintenance and repairs expense | $ 92,000 |
| Utilities expense | 10,000 |
| Salaries and wages expense | 142,000 |
| Advertising expense | 3,500 |
| Ticket revenue | 328,000 |

**Instructions**

Prepare the 2022 income statement for Louisa Cruise Company.

**E1.16 (LO 5), AP** The following information is related to Alexis and Ryans, Attorneys at Law.

*Prepare a retained earnings statement.*

| | |
|---|---|
| Retained earnings, January 1, 2022 | $ 23,000 |
| Legal service revenue—2022 | 340,000 |
| Total expenses—2022 | 211,000 |
| Assets, January 1, 2022 | 85,000 |
| Liabilities, January 1, 2022 | 62,000 |
| Assets, December 31, 2022 | 168,000 |
| Liabilities, December 31, 2022 | 80,000 |
| Dividends—2022 | 64,000 |

**Instructions**

Prepare the 2022 retained earnings statement for Alexis and Ryans, Attorneys at Law.

*Prepare a cash flow statement.*

**E1.17 (LO 5), AP** This information is for Paulo Company for the year ended December 31, 2022.

| | |
|---|---:|
| Cash received from revenues from customers | $600,000 |
| Cash received for issuance of common stock | 280,000 |
| Cash paid for new equipment | 115,000 |
| Cash dividends paid | 18,000 |
| Cash paid for expenses | 430,000 |
| Cash balance 1/1/22 | 30,000 |

**Instructions**

Prepare the 2022 statement of cash flows for Paulo Company (see Illustration 1.10).

*Identify cash flow activities.*

**E1.18 (LO 5), C** The statement of cash flows classifies each transaction as an operating activity, an investing activity, or a financing activity. Operating activities are the types of activities the company performs to generate profits. Investing activities include the purchase of long-lived assets such as equipment or the purchase of investment securities. Financing activities are borrowing money, issuing shares of stock, and paying dividends.

Presented below are the following transactions.

1. Issued stock for $20,000 cash.

2. Issued note payable for $12,000 cash.

3. Purchased office equipment for $11,000 cash.

4. Received $15,000 cash for services performed.

5. Paid $1,000 cash for rent.

6. Paid $600 cash dividend to stockholders.

7. Paid $5,700 cash for salaries.

**Instructions**

Classify each of these transactions as operating, investing, or financing activities.

# Problems

*Analyze transactions and compute net income.*

Excel templates for selected exercises and problems provide students a framework for solving in Excel.

**Check figures** provide a key number to let you know you are on the right track.

a. Total assets $13,560

b. Net income $4,010

*Analyze transactions and prepare income statement, retained earnings statement, and balance sheet.*

**P1.1 (LO 4), AP** Fredonia Repair Inc. was started on May 1. A summary of May transactions is presented as follows.

1. Stockholders invested $10,000 cash in the business in exchange for common stock.

2. Purchased equipment for $5,000 cash.

3. Paid $400 cash for May office rent.

4. Paid $300 cash for supplies.

5. Incurred $250 of advertising costs in the *Beacon News* on account.

6. Received $4,700 in cash from customers for repair service.

7. Declared and paid a $700 cash dividend.

8. Paid part-time employee salaries $1,000.

9. Paid utility bills $140.

10. Performed repair services worth $1,100 on account.

11. Collected cash of $120 for services billed in transaction (10).

**Instructions**

a. Prepare a tabular analysis of the transactions using the following column headings: Cash, Accounts Receivable, Supplies, Equipment, Accounts Payable, Common Stock, and Retained Earnings (with separate columns for Revenues, Expenses, and Dividends). Include margin explanations for any changes in stockholders' equity. Revenue is called Service Revenue.

b. From an analysis of the Retained Earnings columns, compute the net income or net loss for May.

**P1.2 (LO 4, 5), AP** On August 31, the balance sheet of La Brava Veterinary Clinic showed Cash $9,000, Accounts Receivable $1,700, Supplies $600, Equipment $6,000, Accounts Payable $3,600, Common Stock $13,000, and Retained Earnings $700. During September, the following transactions occurred.

1. Paid $2,900 cash for accounts payable due.

2. Collected $1,300 of accounts receivable.

3. Purchased additional equipment for $2,100, paying $800 in cash and the balance on account.

4. Recognized revenue of $7,300, of which $2,500 is collected in cash and the balance is due in October.

5. Declared and paid a $400 cash dividend.

6. Paid salaries $1,700, rent for September $900, and advertising expense $200.

7. Incurred utilities expense for month on account $170.

8. Received $10,000 from Capital Bank on a 6-month note payable.

### Instructions

a. Prepare a tabular analysis of the September transactions beginning with August 31 balances. The column headings should be as follows: Cash + Accounts Receivable + Supplies + Equipment = Notes Payable + Accounts Payable + Common Stock + Retained Earnings + Revenues − Expenses − Dividends.

b. Prepare an income statement for September, a retained earnings statement for September, and a balance sheet at September 30, 2022.

*a. Ending cash $15,900*

*b. Net income $4,330*
*Total assets $29,800*

**P1.3 (LO 5), AP** On May 1, Nimbus Flying School, a company that provides flying lessons, was started by using common stock in exchange for cash of $45,000. Following are the assets and liabilities of the company on May 31, 2022, and the revenues and expenses for the month of May.

*Prepare income statement, retained earnings statement, and balance sheet.*

| | | | |
|---|---|---|---|
| Cash | $ 4,650 | Notes Payable | $28,000 |
| Accounts Receivable | 7,400 | Rent Expense | 900 |
| Equipment | 64,000 | Maintenance and | |
| Service Revenue | 6,800 | Repairs Expense | 350 |
| Advertising Expense | 500 | Gasoline Expense | 2,500 |
| Accounts Payable | 1,400 | Utilities Expense | 400 |

No additional investments were made in May, but the company paid dividends of $500 during the month.

### Instructions

a. Prepare an income statement and a retained earnings statement for the month of May and a balance sheet at May 31.

b. Prepare an income statement and a retained earnings statement for May assuming the following data are not included above: (1) $900 worth of services were performed and billed but not collected at May 31, and (2) $1,500 of gasoline expense was incurred but not paid.

*a. Net income $2,150*
*Total assets $76,050*

*b. Net income $1,550*

**P1.4 (LO 4, 5), AP** Nancy Tercek started a delivery service, Tercek Deliveries, on June 1, 2022. The following transactions occurred during the month of June.

*Analyze transactions and prepare financial statements.*

| June | 1 | Stockholders invested $10,000 cash in the business in exchange for common stock. |
|---|---|---|
| | 2 | Purchased a used van for deliveries for $14,000. Nancy paid $2,000 cash and signed a note payable for the remaining balance. |
| | 3 | Paid $500 for office rent for the month. |
| | 5 | Performed $4,800 of services on account. |
| | 9 | Declared and paid $300 in cash dividends. |
| | 12 | Purchased supplies for $150 on account. |
| | 15 | Received a cash payment of $1,250 for services performed on June 5. |
| | 17 | Purchased gasoline for $100 on account. |
| | 20 | Received $1,500 cash for services performed. |
| | 23 | Made a cash payment of $500 on the note payable. |
| | 26 | Paid $250 for utilities. |
| | 29 | Paid for the gasoline purchased on account on June 17. |
| | 30 | Paid $1,000 for employee salaries. |

### Instructions

a. Show the effects of the previous transactions on the accounting equation using the following format.

*a. Total assets $25,800*

| | | Assets | | | = | Liabilities | + | | | Stockholders' Equity | | | | |
|---|---|---|---|---|---|---|---|---|---|---|---|---|---|---|
| | | Accounts | | | | Notes | | Accounts | | Common | | Retained Earnings | | |
| Date | Cash + | Receivable | + Supplies + | Equipment = | | Payable | + | Payable | + | Stock | + | Rev. − | Exp. − | Div. |

Include margin explanations for any changes in stockholders' equity in your analysis.

b. Prepare an income statement for the month of June.

c. Prepare a balance sheet at June 30, 2022.

*b. Net income $4,450*

*c. Cash $8,100*

*Determine financial statement amounts and prepare retained earnings statement.*

**P1.5 (LO 4, 5), AP** Writing Financial statement information about four different companies is as follows.

| | Donatello Company | Leonardo Company | Michelangelo Company | Raphael Company |
|---|---|---|---|---|
| **January 1, 2022** | | | | |
| Assets | $ 75,000 | $110,000 | (g) | $150,000 |
| Liabilities | 48,000 | (d) | $ 75,000 | (j) |
| Stockholders' equity | (a) | 60,000 | 45,000 | 100,000 |
| **December 31, 2022** | | | | |
| Assets | (b) | 137,000 | 200,000 | (k) |
| Liabilities | 55,000 | 75,000 | (h) | 80,000 |
| Stockholders' equity | 40,000 | (e) | 130,000 | 140,000 |
| **Stockholders' equity changes in year** | | | | |
| Additional investment | (c) | 15,000 | 10,000 | 15,000 |
| Dividends | 6,000 | (f) | 14,000 | 10,000 |
| Total revenues | 350,000 | 420,000 | (i) | 500,000 |
| Total expenses | 335,000 | 382,000 | 342,000 | (l) |

**Instructions**

a. Determine the missing amounts. (*Hint:* For example, to solve for (a), Assets – Liabilities = Stockholders' equity = $27,000.)

*b. Retained earnings (ending) $7,000*

b. Prepare the retained earnings statement for Leonardo Company. Assume beginning retained earnings was $20,000.

c. Write a memorandum explaining the sequence for preparing financial statements and the interrelationship of the retained earnings statement with the income statement and balance sheet.

---

## Continuing Case

leungchopan/
Shutterstock.com

The **Cookie Creations** case starts in this chapter and continues through Chapter 13. You also can find this problem in WileyPLUS.

### Cookie Creations

**CC1** Natalie Koebel spent much of her childhood learning the art of cookie-making from her grandmother. They passed many happy hours mastering every type of cookie imaginable and later creating new recipes that were both healthy and delicious. Now at the start of her second year in college, Natalie is investigating various possibilities for starting her own business as part of the requirements of the entrepreneurship program in which she is enrolled.

A long-time friend insists that Natalie has to include cookies in her business plan. After a series of brainstorming sessions, Natalie settles on the idea of operating a cookie-making school. She will start on a part-time basis and offer her services in people's homes. Now that she has started thinking about it, the possibilities seem endless. During the fall, she will concentrate on holiday cookies. She will offer individual lessons and group sessions (which will probably be more entertainment than education for the participants). Natalie also decides to include children in her target market.

The first difficult decision is coming up with the perfect name for her business. Natalie settles on "Cookie Creations" and then moves on to more important issues.

**Instructions**

a. What form of business organization—proprietorship, partnership, or corporation—do you recommend that Natalie use for her business? Discuss the benefits and weaknesses of each form and give the reasons for your choice.

b. Will Natalie need accounting information? If yes, what information will she need and why? How often will she need this information?

c. Identify specific asset, liability, and stockholders' equity accounts that Cookie Creations will likely use to record its business transactions.

d. Should Natalie open a separate bank account for the business? Why or why not?

# Expand Your Critical Thinking

## Financial Reporting Problem:  Apple Inc.

**CT1.1** The financial statements of **Apple Inc.** for 2018 are presented in Appendix A. The complete annual report, including the notes to the financial statements, is available at the company's website.

**Instructions**

Refer to Apple's financial statements and answer the following questions.

    **a.** What were Apple's total assets at September 29, 2018? At September 30, 2017?

    **b.** How much cash (and cash equivalents) did Apple have on September 29, 2018?

    **c.** What amount of accounts payable did Apple report on September 29, 2018? On September 30, 2017?

    **d.** What were Apple's net sales in 2016? In 2017? In 2018?

    **e.** What is the amount of the change in Apple's net income from 2017 to 2018?

## Comparative Analysis Problem: PepsiCo, Inc. vs. The Coca-Cola Company

**CT1.2** **PepsiCo**'s financial statements are presented in Appendix B. Financial statements of **The Coca-Cola Company** are presented in Appendix C. The complete annual reports of PepsiCo and Coca-Cola, including the notes to the financial statements, are available at each company's respective website.

**Instructions**

    **a.** Based on the information contained in these financial statements, determine the following for each company.

        **1.** Total assets at December 29, 2018, for PepsiCo and for Coca-Cola at December 31, 2018.

        **2.** Accounts (notes) receivable, net at December 29, 2018, for PepsiCo and at December 31, 2018, for Coca-Cola.

        **3.** Net revenues for the year ended in 2018.

        **4.** Net income for the year ended in 2018.

    **b.** What conclusions concerning the two companies can be drawn from these data?

## Comparative Analysis Problem: Amazon.com, Inc. vs. Walmart Inc.

**CT1.3** **Amazon.com, Inc.**'s financial statements are presented in Appendix D. Financial statements of **Walmart Inc.** are presented in Appendix E. The complete annual reports of Amazon and Walmart, including the notes to the financial statements, are available at each company's respective website.

**Instructions**

    **a.** Based on the information contained in these financial statements, determine the following for each company.

        **1.** Total assets at December 31, 2018, for Amazon and for Walmart at January 31, 2019.

        **2.** Receivables (net) at December 31, 2018, for Amazon and for Walmart at January 31, 2019.

        **3.** Net sales (product only) for year ended in 2018 (2019 for Walmart).

        **4.** Net income for the year ended in 2018 (2019 for Walmart).

    **b.** What conclusions concerning these two companies can be drawn from these data?

## Decision-Making Across the Organization

**CT1.4** Kathy and James Mohr, local golf stars, opened the Chip-Shot Driving Range Company on March 1, 2022. They invested $25,000 cash and received common stock in exchange for their investment. A caddy shack was constructed for cash at a cost of $8,000, and $800 was spent on golf balls and golf clubs. The Mohrs leased five acres of land at a cost of $1,000 per month and paid the first month's rent. During the first month, advertising costs totaled $750, of which $150 was unpaid at March 31, and $400 was paid to members of the high-school golf team for retrieving golf balls. All revenues from customers were deposited in the company's bank account. On March 15, Kathy and James received a dividend of $1,000. A $100 utility bill was received on March 31 but was not paid. On March 31, the balance in the company's bank account was $18,900.

Kathy and James thought they had a pretty good first month of operations. But, their estimates of profitability ranged from a loss of $6,100 to net income of $2,450.

**Instructions**

With the class divided into groups, answer the following.

a. How could the Mohrs have concluded that the business operated at a loss of $6,100? Was this a valid basis on which to determine net income?

b. How could the Mohrs have concluded that the business operated at a net income of $2,450? (*Hint:* Prepare a balance sheet at March 31.) Was this a valid basis on which to determine net income?

c. Without preparing an income statement, determine the actual net income for March.

d. What was the revenue recognized in March?

## Communication Activity

**CT1.5** Ashley Hirano, the bookkeeper for New York Company, has been trying to develop the correct balance sheet for the company. The company's balance sheet is shown as follows.

**New York Company**
**Balance Sheet**
**For the Month Ended December 31, 2022**

| Assets | | Liabilities | |
|---|---|---|---|
| Equipment | $25,500 | Common stock | $22,000 |
| Cash | 9,000 | Accounts receivable | (6,000) |
| Supplies | 2,000 | Retained earnings | 2,000 |
| Accounts payable | (8,000) | Notes payable | 10,500 |
| | $28,500 | | $28,500 |

**Instructions**

Explain to Ashley Hirano in a memo why the original balance sheet is incorrect and what should be done to correct it.

## Ethics Case

**CT1.6** After numerous campus interviews, Greg Thorpe, a senior at Great Northern College, received two office interview invitations from the Baltimore offices of two large firms. Both firms offered to cover his out-of-pocket expenses (travel, hotel, and meals). He scheduled the interviews for both firms on the same day, one in the morning and one in the afternoon. At the conclusion of each interview, he submitted to both firms his total out-of-pocket expenses for the trip to Baltimore: mileage $112 (280 miles at $0.40), hotel $130, meals $36, and parking and tolls $18, for a total of $296. He believes this approach is appropriate. If he had made two trips, his cost would have been two times $296. He is also certain that neither firm knew he had visited the other on that same trip. Within 10 days, Greg received two checks in the mail, each in the amount of $296.

**Instructions**

a. Who are the stakeholders (affected parties) in this situation?

b. What are the ethical issues in this case?

c. What would you do in this situation?

## All About You

**CT1.7** Some people are tempted to make their finances look worse to get college financial aid. Companies sometimes also manage their financial numbers in order to accomplish certain goals. Earnings management is the planned timing of revenues, expenses, gains, and losses to smooth out bumps in net income. In managing earnings, companies' actions vary from being within the range of ethical activity to being both unethical and illegal attempts to mislead investors and creditors.

**Instructions**

Provide responses for each of the following questions.

a. Discuss whether you think each of the following actions, taken to increase the chances of receiving financial aid, is ethical.

1. Spend the student's assets and income first, before spending parents' assets and income.

2. Accelerate necessary expenses to reduce available cash. For example, if you need a new car buy it before applying for financial aid.

3. State that a truly financially dependent child is independent.

4. Have a parent take an unpaid leave of absence for long enough to get below the "threshold" level of income.

b. What are some reasons why a **company** might want to overstate its earnings?

c. What are some reasons why a **company** might want to understate its earnings?

d. Under what circumstances might an otherwise ethical person decide to illegally overstate or understate earnings?

**CT1.8** When companies need money, they go to investors or creditors. Before investors or creditors will give a company cash, they want to know the company's financial position and performance. They want to see the company's financial statements—the balance sheet and the income statement. When students need money for school, they often apply for financial aid. When you apply for financial aid, you must submit your own version of a financial statement—the Free Application for Federal Student Aid (FAFSA) form.

Suppose you have $4,000 in cash and $4,000 in credit card bills. The more cash and other assets that you have, the less likely you are to get financial aid. Also, if you have a lot of consumer debt (credit card bills), schools are less likely to loan you money. To increase your chances of receiving aid, should you use the cash to pay off your credit card bills and therefore make yourself look "worse off" to the financial aid decision-makers?

**YES:** You are playing within the rules. You are not hiding assets. You are simply restructuring your assets and liabilities to best conform with the preferences that are built into the federal aid formulas.

**NO:** You are engaging in a transaction solely to take advantage of a loophole in the federal aid rules. In doing so, you are potentially depriving someone who is actually worse off than you from receiving aid.

**Instructions**

Write a response indicating your position regarding this situation. Provide support for your view.

## FASB Codification Activity

**CT1.9** The FASB has developed the Financial Accounting Standards Board Accounting Standards Codification (or more simply "the Codification"). The FASB's primary goal in developing the Codification is to provide in one place all the authoritative literature related to a particular topic. To provide easy access to the Codification, the FASB also developed the Financial Accounting Standards Board Codification Research System (CRS). CRS is an online, real-time database that provides easy access to the Codification. The Codification and the related CRS provide a topically organized structure, subdivided into topic, subtopics, sections, and paragraphs, using a numerical index system.

You may find this system useful in your present and future studies, and so we have provided an opportunity to use this online system as part of the *Expand Your Critical Thinking* section.

**Instructions**

Academic access to the FASB Codification is available through university subscriptions, obtained from the American Accounting Association. This subscription covers an unlimited number of students within a single institution. Once this access has been obtained by your school, you should log in and familiarize yourself with the resources that are accessible at the FASB Codification site.

## Considering People, Planet, and Profit

**CT1.10** Although **Clif Bar & Company** is not a public company, it does share its financial information with its employees as part of its open-book management approach. Further, although it does not publicly share its financial information, it does provide a different form of an annual report to external users. In this report, the company provides information regarding its sustainability efforts.

**Instructions**

Go to the Who We Are page of the Clif Bar website and identify the five aspirations.

### Answers to Insight and Accounting Across the Organization Questions

**Owning a Piece of the Bar  Q:** What are the benefits to the company and to the employees of making the financial statements available to all employees?  **A:** If employees can read and use financial reports, a company will benefit in the following ways. The **marketing department** will make better decisions about products to offer and prices to charge. The **finance department** will make better decisions about debt and equity financing and how much to distribute in dividends. The **production department** will make better decisions about when to buy new equipment and how much inventory to produce. The **human resources department** will be better able to determine whether employees can be given raises. Finally, **all employees** will be better informed about the basis on which they are evaluated, which will increase employee morale.

**I Felt the Pressure—Would You?  Q:** Why did these employees lie, and what do you believe should be their penalty for these lies?  **A:**  They felt pressured by their supervisors to make the company's financial statements look better than warranted. They should be prosecuted for fraudulent activities under the Sarbanes-Oxley Act, as they knowingly misstated financial statement data.

**The Korean Discount  Q:** What is meant by the phrase "make the country's business more transparent"? Why would increasing transparency spur economic growth?  **A:** Transparency refers to the extent to which outsiders have knowledge regarding a company's financial performance and financial position. If a company lacks transparency, its financial reports do not adequately inform investors of critical information that is needed to make investment decisions. If corporate transparency is increased, investors would be more willing to supply the financial capital that businesses need in order to grow, which would spur the country's economic growth.

**Spinning the Career Wheel  Q:** How might accounting help you?  **A:** You will need to understand financial reports in any enterprise with which you are associated. Whether you become a manager, a doctor, a lawyer, a social worker, a teacher, an engineer, an architect, or an entrepreneur, a working knowledge of accounting is relevant.

**Beyond Financial Statements  Q:** Why might a company's stockholders be interested in its environmental and social performance?  **A:** Many companies now recognize that being a socially responsible organization is not only the right thing to do, but it also is good for business. Many investment professionals understand, for example, that environmental, social, and proper corporate governance of companies affects the performance of their investment portfolios. For example, **British Petroleum**'s oil spill disaster is a classic example of the problems that can occur for a company and its stockholders. BP's stock price was slashed, its dividend reduced, its executives replaced, and its reputation badly damaged. It is interesting that socially responsible investment funds are now gaining momentum in the marketplace such that companies now recognize this segment as an important investment group.

# A Look at IFRS

### LEARNING OBJECTIVE 7
Describe the impact of international accounting standards on U.S. financial reporting.

Most agree that there is a need for one set of international accounting standards. Here is why:

**Multinational corporations.** Today's companies view the entire world as their market. For example, **Coca-Cola**, **Intel**, and **McDonald's** generate more than 50% of their sales outside the United States. Many foreign companies, such as **Toyota**, **Nestlé**, and **Sony**, find their largest market to be the United States.

**Mergers and acquisitions.**  The mergers between **Fiat/Chrysler** and **Vodafone/Mannesmann** suggest that we will see even more such business combinations of companies from different countries in the future.

**Information technology.**  As communication barriers continue to topple through advances in technology, companies and individuals in different countries and markets are becoming more comfortable buying and selling goods and services from one another.

**Financial markets.**  Financial markets are of international significance today. Whether it is currency, equity securities (stocks), bonds, or derivatives, there are active markets throughout the world trading these types of instruments.

## Key Points

Following are the key similarities and differences between GAAP and IFRS as related to accounting fundamentals.

### Similarities

- The basic techniques for recording business transactions are the same for U.S. and international companies.
- Both international and U.S. accounting standards emphasize transparency in financial reporting. Both sets of standards are primarily driven by meeting the needs of investors and creditors.
- The three most common forms of business organizations, proprietorships, partnerships, and corporations, are also found in countries that use international accounting standards.

### Differences

- International standards are referred to as International Financial Reporting Standards (IFRS), developed by the International Accounting Standards Board. Accounting standards in the United States are referred to as generally accepted accounting principles (GAAP) and are developed by the Financial Accounting Standards Board.
- IFRS tends to be simpler in its accounting and disclosure requirements; some people say it is more "principles-based." GAAP is more detailed; some people say it is more "rules-based."
- The internal control standards applicable to Sarbanes-Oxley (SOX) apply only to large public companies listed on U.S. exchanges. There is continuing debate as to whether non-U.S. companies should have to comply with this extra layer of regulation.

# IFRS Practice

## IFRS Self-Test Questions

1. Which of the following is **not** a reason why a single set of high-quality international accounting standards would be beneficial?
   a. Mergers and acquisition activity.
   b. Financial markets.
   c. Multinational corporations.
   d. GAAP is widely considered to be a superior reporting system.

2. The Sarbanes-Oxley Act determines:
   a. international tax regulations.

   b. internal control standards as enforced by the IASB.
   c. internal control standards of U.S. publicly traded companies.
   d. U.S. tax regulations.

3. IFRS is considered to be more:
   a. principles-based and less rules-based than GAAP.
   b. rules-based and less principles-based than GAAP.
   c. detailed than GAAP.
   d. None of the answer choices is correct.

## IFRS Exercises

**IFRS1.1** Who are the two key international players in the development of international accounting standards? Explain their role.

**IFRS1.2** What is the benefit of a single set of high-quality accounting standards?

## International Financial Reporting Problem: Louis Vuitton

**IFRS1.3** The financial statements of **Louis Vuitton** are presented in Appendix F. The complete consolidated financial statements, including the notes to its financial statements, are available at the company's website.

### Instructions

Visit Louis Vuitton's corporate website and answer the following questions from the company's 2018 consolidated financial statements.

   a. What accounting firm performed the audit of Louis Vuitton's financial statements?
   b. What is the address of the company's corporate headquarters?
   c. What is the company's reporting currency?

## Answers to IFRS Self-Test Questions

1. d   2. c   3. a

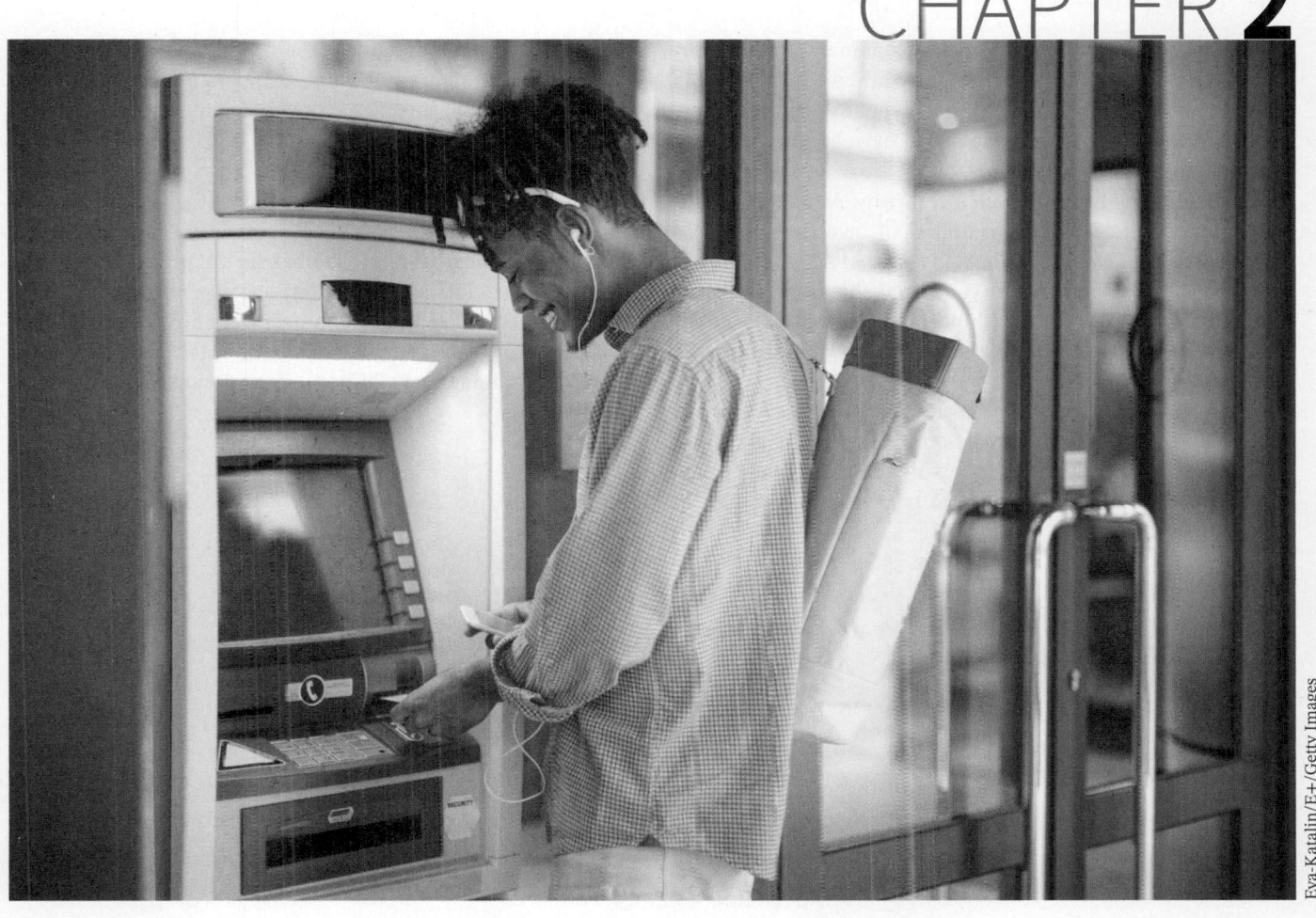

## CHAPTER 2

Eva-Katalin/E+/Getty Images

# The Recording Process

## Chapter Preview

In Chapter 1, we analyzed business transactions in terms of the accounting equation, and we presented the cumulative effects of these transactions in tabular form. Imagine a company like **MF Global** (as in the following Feature Story) using the same tabular format as Softbyte Inc. to keep track of its transactions. In a single day, MF Global engaged in thousands of business transactions. To record each transaction this way would be impractical, expensive, and unnecessary. Instead, companies use a set of procedures and records to keep track of transaction data more easily. This chapter introduces and illustrates these basic procedures and records.

## Feature Story

### Accidents Happen

How organized are you financially? Take a short quiz. Answer yes or no to each question:

- Does your wallet contain so many cash machine receipts that you've been declared a walking fire hazard?

- Do you wait until your debit card is denied before checking the status of your funds?

- Do you verify the accuracy of your checking account about as often as you clean the space behind your refrigerator?

If you think it is hard to keep track of the many transactions that make up **your** life, imagine how difficult it is for a big corporation to do so. Not only that, but now consider how important it is for a large company to have good accounting records, especially if it has control of **your** life savings. **MF Global Holdings Ltd** was such a company. As a large invest-ment broker, it held billions of dollars of investments for cli-ents. If you had *your* life savings invested at MF Global, you might be slightly displeased if you heard this from one of its representatives: "You know, I kind of remember an account for someone with a name like yours—now what did we do with that?"

Unfortunately, that is almost exactly what happened to MF Global's clients shortly before it filed for bankruptcy. During the days immediately following the bankruptcy filing, regulators and auditors struggled to piece things together. In the words of one regulator, "Their books are a disaster . . . we're trying to figure out what numbers are real numbers." One company that considered buying an interest in MF Global walked away from the deal because it "couldn't get a sense of what was on the balance sheet." That company said the information that should have been instantly available instead took days to produce.

It now appears that MF Global did not properly segregate customer accounts from company accounts. And, because of its sloppy recordkeeping, customers were not protected when the company had financial troubles. Total customer losses were approximately $1 billion. As you can see, accounting matters!

**Source:** S. Patterson and A. Lucchetti, "Inside the Hunt for MF Global Cash," *Wall Street Journal Online* (November 11, 2011).

# Chapter Outline

| LEARNING OBJECTIVES | REVIEW | PRACTICE |
|---|---|---|
| **LO 1** Describe how accounts, debits, and credits are used to record business transactions. | • Debits and credits<br>• Stockholders' equity relationships<br>• Summary of debit/credit rules | **DO IT! 1** Normal Account Balances |
| **LO 2** Indicate how a journal is used in the recording process. | • The recording process<br>• The journal | **DO IT! 2** Recording Business Activities |
| **LO 3** Explain how a ledger and posting help in the recording process. | • The ledger<br>• Posting<br>• Chart of accounts<br>• The recording process illustrated<br>• Summary illustration of journalizing and posting | **DO IT! 3** Posting |
| **LO 4** Prepare a trial balance. | • Limitations of a trial balance<br>• Locating errors<br>• Dollar signs and underlining | **DO IT! 4** Trial Balance |

**Go to the Review and Practice section at the end of the chapter for a review of key concepts and practice applications with solutions.**

**Visit WileyPLUS for additional tutorials and practice opportunities.**

# Accounts, Debits, and Credits

An **account** is an individual accounting record of increases and decreases in a specific asset, liability, or stockholders' equity item. For example, Softbyte Inc. (the company discussed in Chapter 1) would have separate accounts for Cash, Accounts Receivable, Accounts Payable, Service Revenue, Salaries and Wages Expense, and so on. (Note that whenever we are referring to a specific account, we capitalize the name.)

In its simplest form, an account consists of three parts: (1) a title, (2) a left or debit side, and (3) a right or credit side. Because the format of an account resembles the letter T, we refer to it as a **T-account**. **Illustration 2.1** shows the basic form of an account.

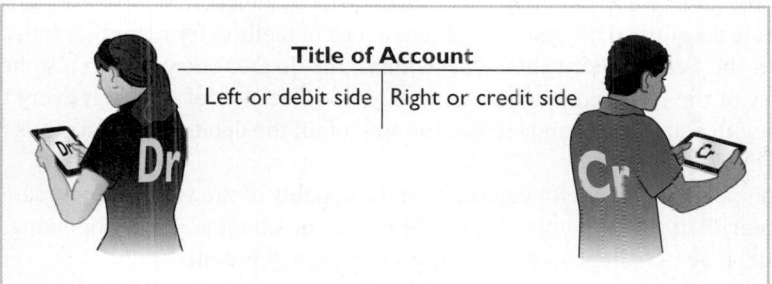

**Title of Account**

Left or debit side | Right or credit side

**ILLUSTRATION 2.1**

**Basic form of account**

We use this form often throughout this text to explain basic accounting relationships.

## Debits and Credits

The term **debit** indicates the left side of an account, and **credit** indicates the right side. They are commonly abbreviated as **Dr.** for debit and **Cr.** for credit. They **do not** mean increase or decrease, as is commonly thought. We use the terms **debit** and **credit** repeatedly in the recording process to describe **where** entries are made in accounts. For example, the act of entering an amount on the left side of an account is called **debiting** the account. Making an entry on the right side is **crediting** the account.

When comparing the totals of the two sides, an account shows a **debit balance** if the total of the debit amounts exceeds the credits. An account shows a **credit balance** if the credit amounts exceed the debits. Note the position of the debit side and credit side in Illustration 2.1.

The procedure of recording debits and credits in an account is shown in **Illustration 2.2** for the transactions affecting the Cash account of Softbyte Inc. The data are taken from the Cash column of the tabular summary in Illustration 1.9.

**ILLUSTRATION 2.2**

**Tabular summary and account form for Softbyte's Cash account**

**Tabular Summary**

| Cash |
|---|
| $15,000 |
| **−7,000** |
| 1,200 |
| 1,500 |
| −1,700 |
| −250 |
| 600 |
| −1,300 |
| $ 3,050 |

**Account Form**

| Cash | | | |
|---|---|---|---|
| (Debits) | 15,000 | (Credits) | 7,000 |
| | 1,200 | | 1,700 |
| | 1,500 | | 250 |
| | 600 | | 1,300 |
| Balance | 8,050 | | |
| **(Debit)** | | | |

Every positive item in the tabular summary represents a receipt of cash. Every negative amount represents a payment of cash. **Notice that in the account form, we record the increases in cash as debits and the decreases in cash as credits.** For example, the $15,000 receipt of cash (in blue) is debited to Cash, and the –$7,000 payment of cash (in red) is credited to Cash.

Having increases on one side and decreases on the other reduces recording errors and helps in determining the totals of each side of the account as well as the account balance. The balance is determined by netting the two sides (subtracting one amount from the other). The account balance, a debit of $8,050, indicates that Softbyte had $8,050 more increases than decreases in cash. In other words, Softbyte started with a balance of zero and now has $8,050 in its Cash account.

## Debit and Credit Procedure

In Chapter 1, you learned the effect of a transaction on the basic accounting equation. Remember that each transaction must affect two or more accounts to keep the basic accounting equation in balance. In other words, **for each transaction, debits must equal credits**. The equality of debits and credits provides the basis for the **double-entry system** of recording transactions (see **International Note**).

Under the double-entry system, the dual (two-sided) effect of each transaction is recorded in appropriate accounts. This system provides a logical method for recording transactions. As discussed in the Feature Story about **MF Global**, the double-entry system also helps ensure the accuracy of the recorded amounts as well as the detection of errors. If every transaction is recorded with equal debits and credits, the sum of all the debits to the accounts must equal the sum of all the credits.

The double-entry system for determining the equality of the accounting equation is much more efficient than the plus/minus procedure used in Chapter 1. The following discussion illustrates debit and credit procedures in the double-entry system.

## Dr./Cr. Procedures for Assets and Liabilities

In Illustration 2.2 for Softbyte Inc., increases in Cash—an asset—are entered on the left side, and decreases in Cash are entered on the right side. We know that both sides of the basic equation (Assets = Liabilities + Stockholders' Equity) must be equal. It therefore follows that increases and decreases in liabilities have to be recorded **opposite from** increases and decreases in assets. Thus, increases in liabilities are entered on the right or credit side, and decreases in liabilities are entered on the left or debit side. The effects that debits and credits have on assets and liabilities are summarized in **Illustration 2.3**.

**ILLUSTRATION 2.3**

**Debit and credit effects—assets and liabilities**

| Debits | Credits |
| --- | --- |
| Increase assets | Decrease assets |
| Decrease liabilities | Increase liabilities |

**Asset accounts normally show debit balances.** That is, debits to a specific asset account should exceed credits to that account. Likewise, **liability accounts normally show credit balances.** That is, credits to a liability account should exceed debits to that account. The **normal balance** of an account is on the side where an increase in the account is recorded. **Illustration 2.4** shows the normal balances for assets and liabilities.

**ILLUSTRATION 2.4**

**Normal balances—assets and liabilities**

Knowing the normal balance in an account may help when you are trying to identify errors (see **Helpful Hint**). For example, a credit balance in an asset account such as Land or a debit balance in a liability account such as Salaries and Wages Payable usually indicates an error. Occasionally, though, an abnormal balance may be correct. The Cash account, for example, will have a credit balance when a company has overdrawn its bank balance by spending more than it has in its account.

## Stockholders' Equity

As Chapter 1 indicated, there are five subdivisions of stockholders' equity: common stock, retained earnings, dividends, revenues, and expenses. In a double-entry system, companies keep accounts for each of these subdivisions, as explained below.

**Common Stock**   Companies issue **common stock** in exchange for the owners' investment paid in to the corporation. Credits increase the Common Stock account, and debits decrease it. For example, when an owner invests cash in the business in exchange for shares of the corporation's stock, the company debits (increases) Cash and credits (increases) Common Stock.

   **Illustration 2.5** shows the rules of debit and credit for the Common Stock account.

| Debits | Credits |
|---|---|
| Decrease Common Stock | Increase Common Stock |

**ILLUSTRATION 2.5**

Debit and credit effects— common stock

**Illustration 2.6** shows the normal balance for Common Stock.

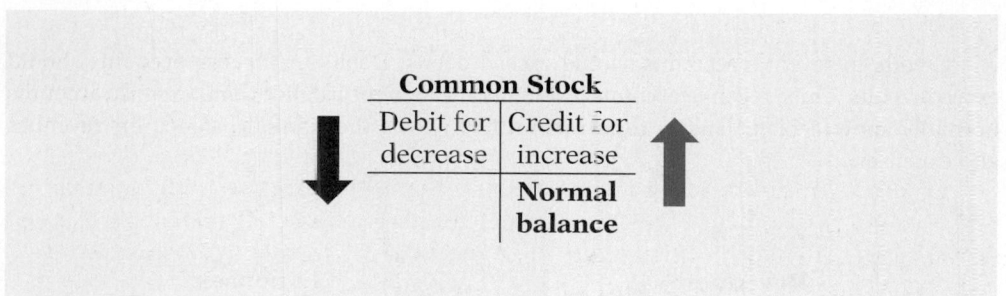

**ILLUSTRATION 2.6**

Normal balance—common stock

**Retained Earnings**   **Retained earnings** is net income that is kept (retained) in the business. It represents the portion of stockholders' equity that the company has accumulated through the profitable operation of the business. Credits (net income) increase the Retained Earnings account, and debits (dividends or net losses) decrease it, as **Illustration 2.7** shows (see **Helpful Hint**).

**ILLUSTRATION 2.7**

Debit and credit effects and normal balance—retained earnings

**Dividends**   A **dividend** is a company's distribution to its stockholders on a pro rata (equal) basis. The most common form of a distribution is a **cash dividend**. Dividends reduce the stockholders' claims on retained earnings. Debits increase the Dividends account, and credits decrease it. **Illustration 2.8** shows the normal balance for Dividends.

ILLUSTRATION 2.8

**ILLUSTRATION 2.8**

**Debit and credit effect and normal balance—dividends**

**HELPFUL HINT**

Because revenues increase stockholders' equity, a revenue account has the same debit/credit rules as the Common Stock account. Expenses have the opposite effect.

**Revenues and Expenses**   The purpose of earning revenues is to benefit the stockholders of the business. When a company recognizes revenues, stockholders' equity increases. Revenues are a subdivision of stockholders' equity and provide information as to **why** stockholders' equity increased. Credits increase revenue accounts and debits decrease them. Therefore, **the effect of debits and credits on revenue accounts is the same as their effect on stockholders' equity** (see **Helpful Hint**).

Expenses have the opposite effect. Expenses decrease stockholders' equity. Since expenses decrease net income and revenues increase it, it is logical that the increase and decrease sides of expense accounts should be the opposite of revenue accounts. Thus, expense accounts are increased by debits and decreased by credits. **Illustration 2.9** shows the rules of debits and credits for revenues and expenses.

**ILLUSTRATION 2.9**

**Debit and credit effects— revenues and expenses**

| Debits | Credits |
| --- | --- |
| Decrease revenues | Increase revenues |
| Increase expenses | Decrease expenses |

Credits to revenue accounts should exceed debits. Debits to expense accounts should exceed credits. Thus, revenue accounts normally show credit balances, and expense accounts normally show debit balances. **Illustration 2.10** shows the normal balance for revenues and expenses.

**ILLUSTRATION 2.10**

**Normal balances—revenues and expenses**

---

**Investor Insight**   Chicago Cubs

Jonathan Daniel/Getty Images Sport/Getty Images

**Keeping Score**

The **Chicago Cubs** baseball team probably has these major revenue and expense accounts:

| Revenues | Expenses |
| --- | --- |
| Admissions (ticket sales) | Players' salaries |
| Concessions | Administrative salaries |
| Television and radio | Travel |
| Advertising | Ballpark maintenance |

**Do you think that the Chicago Bears** football team would be likely to have the same major revenue and expense accounts as the Cubs? **(Answer is available near the end of the chapter.)**

# Stockholders' Equity Relationships

As Chapter 1 indicated, companies report the subdivisions of stockholders' equity in various places in the financial statements:

- Common stock and retained earnings in the stockholders' equity section of the balance sheet.
- Dividends on the retained earnings statement.
- Revenues and expenses on the income statement.

Dividends, revenues, and expenses are eventually transferred to retained earnings at the end of the period. As a result, a change in any one of these three items affects stockholders' equity. **Illustration 2.11** shows the relationships related to stockholders' equity.

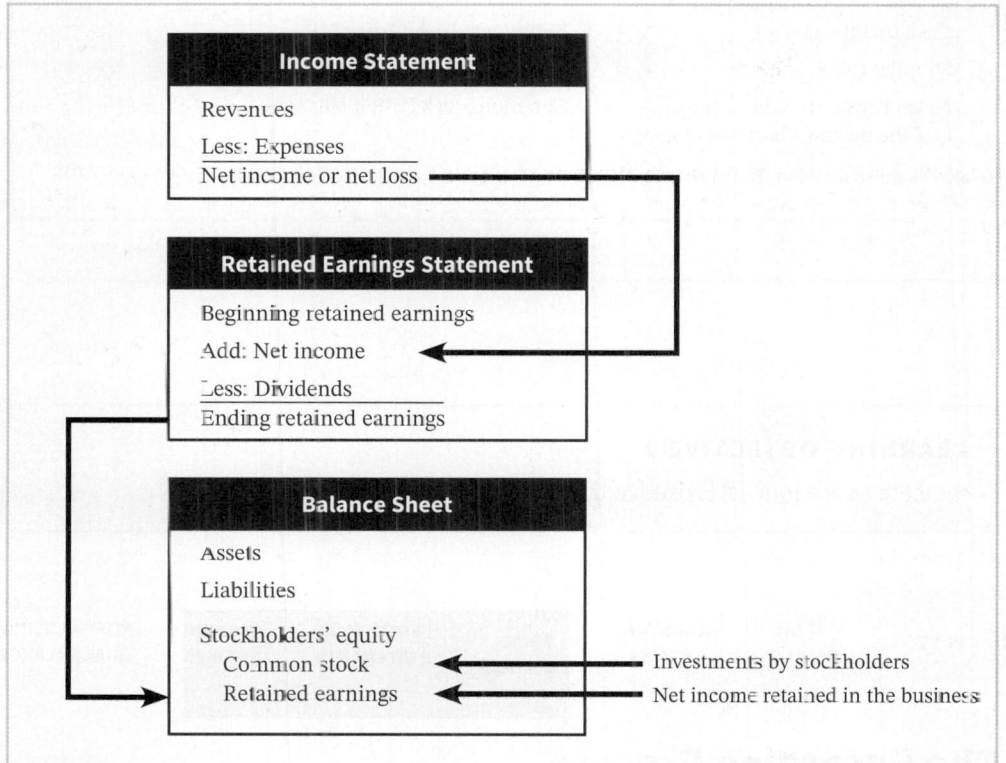

**ILLUSTRATION 2.11**

**Stockholders' equity relationships**

# Summary of Debit/Credit Rules

**Illustration 2.12** summarizes the debit/credit rules and effects on each type of account. **Study this diagram carefully.** It will help you understand the fundamentals of the double-entry system (see **Helpful Hint**). No matter what the transaction, total debits must equal total credits in order to keep the accounting equation in balance.

**HELPFUL HINT**

You may want to bookmark Illustration 2.12. You probably will refer to it often.

**ILLUSTRATION 2.12**   **Summary of debit/credit rules**

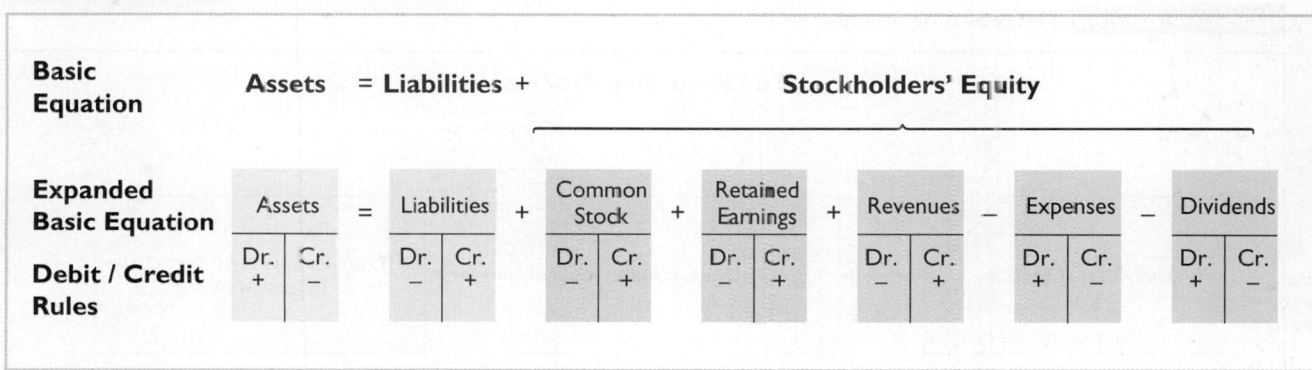

**ACTION PLAN**

• Determine the types of accounts needed. Kate will need asset accounts for each different type of asset she invests in the business, and liability accounts for any debts she incurs.

• Understand the types of stockholders' equity accounts. When Kate begins the business, she will need only Common Stock. Later, she will need other stockholders' equity accounts.

## DO IT! 1 | Normal Account Balances

Kate Browne, president of Hair It Is, Inc., has just rented space in a shopping mall in which she will open and operate a beauty salon. A friend has advised Kate to set up a double-entry set of accounting records in which to record all of her business transactions.

Identify the balance sheet accounts that Hair It Is, Inc. will likely use to record the transactions needed to establish and open the business. Also, indicate whether the normal balance of each account is a debit or a credit.

### Solution

Hair It Is, Inc. would likely use the following accounts to record the transactions needed to ready the beauty salon for opening day:

Cash (debit balance)                     Equipment (debit balance)

Supplies (debit balance)                 Accounts Payable (credit balance)

Notes Payable (credit balance),          Common Stock (credit balance)
   if the business borrows money

Related exercise material: **BE2.1, BE2.2, BE2.5, DO IT! 2.1, E2.1, E2.2, E2.4, and E2.7.**

# The Journal

**LEARNING OBJECTIVE 2**

Indicate how a journal is used in the recording process.

ANALYZE ▸ **Journalize the transactions** ▸ POST ▸ TRIAL BALANCE ▸ ADJUSTING ENTRIES ▸ ADJUSTED TRIAL BALANCE ▸ FINANCIAL STATEMENTS ▸ CLOSING ENTRIES ▸ POST-CLOSING TRIAL BALANCE

## The Recording Process

Although it is possible to enter transaction information directly into the accounts, few businesses do so. Practically every business uses the basic steps shown in **Illustration 2.13** in the recording process (an integral part of the accounting cycle):

1. Analyze each transaction in terms of its effect on the accounts.
2. Enter the transaction information in a journal.
3. Transfer the journal information to the appropriate accounts in the ledger.

**ILLUSTRATION 2.13** The recording process

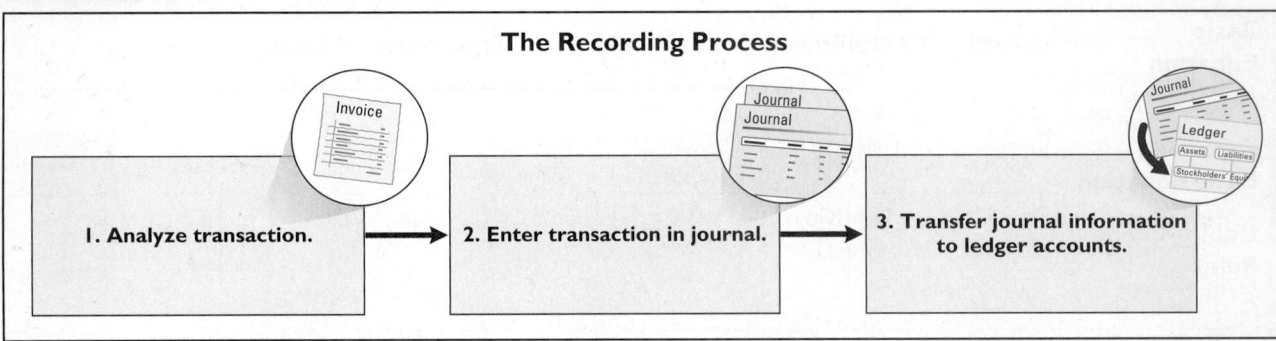

**The Recording Process**

1. Analyze transaction. → 2. Enter transaction in journal. → 3. Transfer journal information to ledger accounts.

The steps in the recording process occur repeatedly. In Chapter 1, we illustrated the first step, the analysis of transactions, and will give further examples in this and later chapters. The other two steps in the recording process are explained in the next sections.

# The Journal

Companies initially record transactions in chronological order (the order in which they occur) Thus, the **journal** is referred to as the book of original entry. For each transaction, the journal shows the debit and credit effects on specific accounts (see **Helpful Hint**).

Companies may use various kinds of journals, but every company has the most basic form of journal, a **general journal**. Typically, a general journal has spaces for dates, account titles and explanations, references, and two amount columns. See the format of the journal in Illustration 2.14. *Whenever we use the term "journal" in this text, we mean the general journal unless we specify otherwise.*

The journal makes several significant contributions to the recording process:

1. It discloses in one place the **complete effects of a transaction**.
2. It provides a **chronological record** of transactions.
3. It helps to **prevent or locate errors** because the debit and credit amounts for each entry can be easily compared.

**HELPFUL HINT**

In a computerized system, journals are kept as files, and accounts are recorded in electronic databases.

## Journalizing

Entering transaction data in the journal is known as **journalizing**. Companies make separate journal entries for each transaction. A complete entry consists of (1) the date of the transaction, (2) the accounts and amounts to be debited and credited, and (3) a brief explanation of the transaction.

**Illustration 2.14** shows the technique of journalizing, using the first two transactions of Softbyte Inc. On September 1, stockholders invested $15,000 cash in the corporation in exchange for common stock, and Softbyte purchased computer equipment for $7,000 cash. The number J1 indicates that these two entries are recorded on the first page of the journal. Illustration 2.14 shows the standard form of journal entries for these two transactions. (The boxed numbers correspond to explanations in the list below the illustration.)

| GENERAL JOURNAL | | | | J1 |
|---|---|---|---|---|
| **Date** | **Account Titles and Explanation** | **Ref.** | **Debit** | **Credit** |
| 2022 | | **5** | | |
| Sept. 1 | **2** Cash | | 15,000 | |
| **1** | **3**　Common Stock | | | 15,000 |
| | **4**　　(Issued common stock for cash) | | | |
| 1 | Equipment | | 7,000 | |
| | Cash | | | 7,000 |
| | (Purchase of equipment for cash) | | | |

**ILLUSTRATION 2.14**

**Technique of journalizing**

**1** The date of the transaction is entered in the Date column.

**2** The debit account title (that is, the account to be debited) is entered first at the extreme left margin of the column headed "Account Titles and Explanation," and the amount of the debit is recorded in the Debit column.

**3** The credit account title (that is, the account to be credited) is indented and entered on the next line in the column headed "Account Titles and Explanation," and the amount of the credit is recorded in the Credit column.

**4** A brief explanation of the transaction appears on the line below the credit account title. A space is left between journal entries. The blank space separates individual journal entries and makes the entire journal easier to read.

**5** The column titled Ref. (which stands for Reference) is left blank when the journal entry is made. This column is used later when the journal entries are transferred to the ledger accounts

**It is important to use correct and specific account titles in journalizing.** Erroneous account titles lead to incorrect financial statements. However, some flexibility exists initially in selecting account titles. The main criterion is that each title must appropriately describe the content of the account. Once a company chooses the specific title to use, it should record under that account title all later transactions involving the account. *In homework problems, you should use specific account titles when they are given.* When account titles are not given, you may select account titles that identify the nature and content of each account. The account titles used in journalizing should not contain explanations such as Cash Paid or Cash Received.

## Simple and Compound Entries

Some entries involve only two accounts, one debit and one credit. (See, for example, the entries in Illustration 2.14.) This type of entry is called a **simple entry**. Some transactions, however, require more than two accounts in journalizing. An entry that requires three or more accounts is a **compound entry**. To illustrate, assume that on July 1, Butler Company purchases a delivery truck costing $14,000. It pays $8,000 cash now and agrees to pay the remaining $6,000 on account (to be paid later). **Illustration 2.15** shows this compound entry.

**ILLUSTRATION 2.15**

Compound journal entry

| GENERAL JOURNAL | | | | J1 |
|---|---|---|---|---|
| **Date** | **Account Titles and Explanation** | **Ref.** | **Debit** | **Credit** |
| 2022<br>July 1 | Equipment | | 14,000 | |
| | Cash | | | 8,000 |
| | Accounts Payable | | | 6,000 |
| | (Purchased truck for cash with balance on account) | | | |

In a compound entry, the standard format requires that all debits be listed before the credits.

---

**ACTION PLAN**

- **Understand which activities need to be recorded and which do not. Any activities that affect assets, liabilities, or stockholders' equity should be recorded in a journal.**

- **Analyze the effects of transactions on asset, liability, and stockholders' equity accounts.**

## DO IT! 2 | Recording Business Activities

As president and sole stockholder, Kate Browne engaged in the following activities in establishing her salon, Hair It Is, Inc.:

1. Opened a bank account in the name of Hair It Is, Inc. and deposited $20,000 of her own money in this account in exchange for shares of common stock.

2. Purchased equipment on account (to be paid in 30 days) for a total cost of $4,800.

3. Interviewed three people for the position of hair stylist.

Prepare the journal entries to record the transactions.

### Solution

The three activities would be recorded as follows.

| | | | |
|---|---|---|---|
| 1. | Cash | 20,000 | |
| | Common Stock | | 20,000 |
| | (Issued common stock for cash) | | |
| 2. | Equipment | 4,800 | |
| | Accounts Payable | | 4,800 |
| | (Purchase of equipment on account) | | |

3. No entry because no transaction has occurred.

Related exercise material: **BE2.3, BE2.4, BE2.5, BE2.6, DO IT! 2.2, E2.3, E2.5, E2.6, E2.7, E2.8, E2.9, E2.12, E2.13, E2.14, and E2.17.**

# The Ledger and Posting

**LEARNING OBJECTIVE 3**

Explain how a ledger and posting help in the recording process

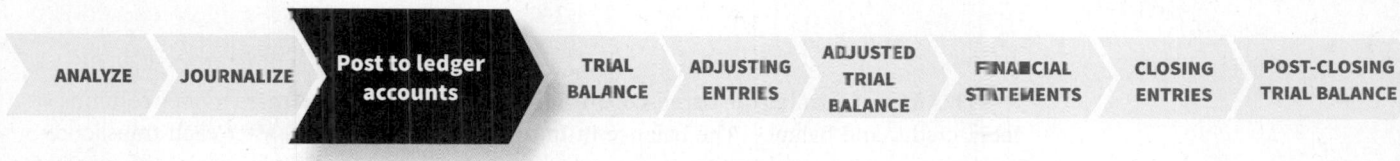

| ANALYZE | JOURNALIZE | **Post to ledger accounts** | TRIAL BALANCE | ADJUSTING ENTRIES | ADJUSTED TRIAL BALANCE | FINANCIAL STATEMENTS | CLOSING ENTRIES | POST-CLOSING TRIAL BALANCE |

## The Ledger

The entire group of accounts maintained by a company is the **ledger**. The ledger provides the balance in each of the accounts as well as keeps track of changes in these balances.

Companies may use various kinds of ledgers, but every company has a general ledger. A **general ledger** contains all the asset, liability, and stockholders' equity accounts, as shown in **Illustration 2.16**. *Whenever we use the term "ledger" in this text, we are referring to the general ledger unless we specify otherwise.*

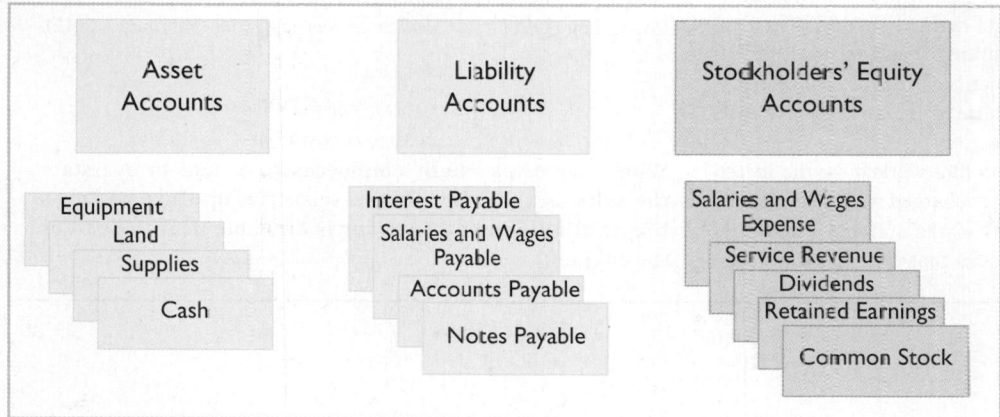

| Asset Accounts | Liability Accounts | Stockholders' Equity Accounts |

Equipment
Land
Supplies
Cash

Interest Payable
Salaries and Wages Payable
Accounts Payable
Notes Payable

Salaries and Wages Expense
Service Revenue
Dividends
Retained Earnings
Common Stock

**ILLUSTRATION 2.16**

**The general ledger, which contains all of a company's accounts**

Companies arrange the ledger in the sequence in which they present the accounts in the financial statements, beginning with the balance sheet accounts. First in order are the asset accounts, followed by liability accounts, stockholders' equity accounts, revenues, and expenses. Each account is numbered for easier identification.

The ledger provides the balance in each of the accounts. For example, the Cash account shows the amount of cash available to meet current obligations. The Accounts Receivable account shows amounts due from customers. The Accounts Payable account shows amounts owed to creditors.

## Standard Form of Account

The simple T-account form used in accounting texts is often very useful for illustration purposes. However, in practice, the account forms used in ledgers are much more structured. **Illustration 2.17** shows a typical form, using assumed data from a cash account.

**Three-column form of account**

| CASH | | | | | NO. 101 |
|---|---|---|---|---|---|
| Date | Explanation | Ref. | Debit | Credit | Balance |
| 2022 | | | | | |
| June 1 | | | 25,000 | | 25,000 |
| 2 | | | | 8,000 | 17,000 |
| 3 | | | 4,200 | | 21,200 |
| 9 | | | 7,500 | | 28,700 |
| 17 | | | | 11,700 | 17,000 |
| 20 | | | | 250 | 16,750 |
| 30 | | | | 7,300 | 9,450 |

This format is called the **three-column form of account**. It has three money columns—debit, credit, and balance. The balance in the account is determined after each transaction. Companies use the explanation space and reference columns to provide special information about the transaction.

---

**Ethics Insight   Credit Suisse Group**

iordani/Shutterstock.com

### A Convenient Overstatement

Sometimes a company's investment securities suffer a permanent decline in value below their original cost. When this occurs, the company is supposed to reduce the recorded value of the securities on its balance sheet ("write them down" in common financial lingo) and record a loss. It appears, however, that during the financial crisis of 2008, employees at some financial institutions chose to look the other way as the value of their investments skidded.

A number of Wall Street traders that worked for the investment bank **Credit Suisse Group** were charged with intentionally overstating the value of securities that had suffered declines of approximately $2.85 billion. One reason that they may have been reluctant to record the losses is out of fear that the company's shareholders and clients would panic if they saw the magnitude of the losses. However, personal self-interest might have been equally to blame—the bonuses of the traders were tied to the value of the investment securities.

**Source:** S. Pulliam, J. Eaglesham, and M. Siconolfi, "U.S. Plans Changes on Bond Fraud," *Wall Street Journal Online* (February 1, 2012).

**What incentives might employees have had to overstate the value of these investment securities on the company's financial statements? (Answer is available near the end of the chapter.)**

---

## Posting

The procedure of transferring journal entries to the ledger accounts is called **posting. This phase of the recording process accumulates the effects of journalized transactions into the individual accounts.** Posting involves the following steps.

1. In the **ledger**, in the appropriate columns of the account(s) debited, enter the date, journal page, and debit amount shown in the journal.

2. In the reference column of the **journal**, write the account number to which the debit amount was posted.

3. In the **ledger**, in the appropriate columns of the account(s) credited, enter the date, journal page, and credit amount shown in the journal.

4. In the reference column of the **journal**, write the account number to which the credit amount was posted.

**Illustration 2.18** shows these four steps using Softbyte Inc.'s first journal entry. The boxed numbers indicate the sequence of the steps.

**ILLUSTRATION 2.18**

**Posting a journal entry**

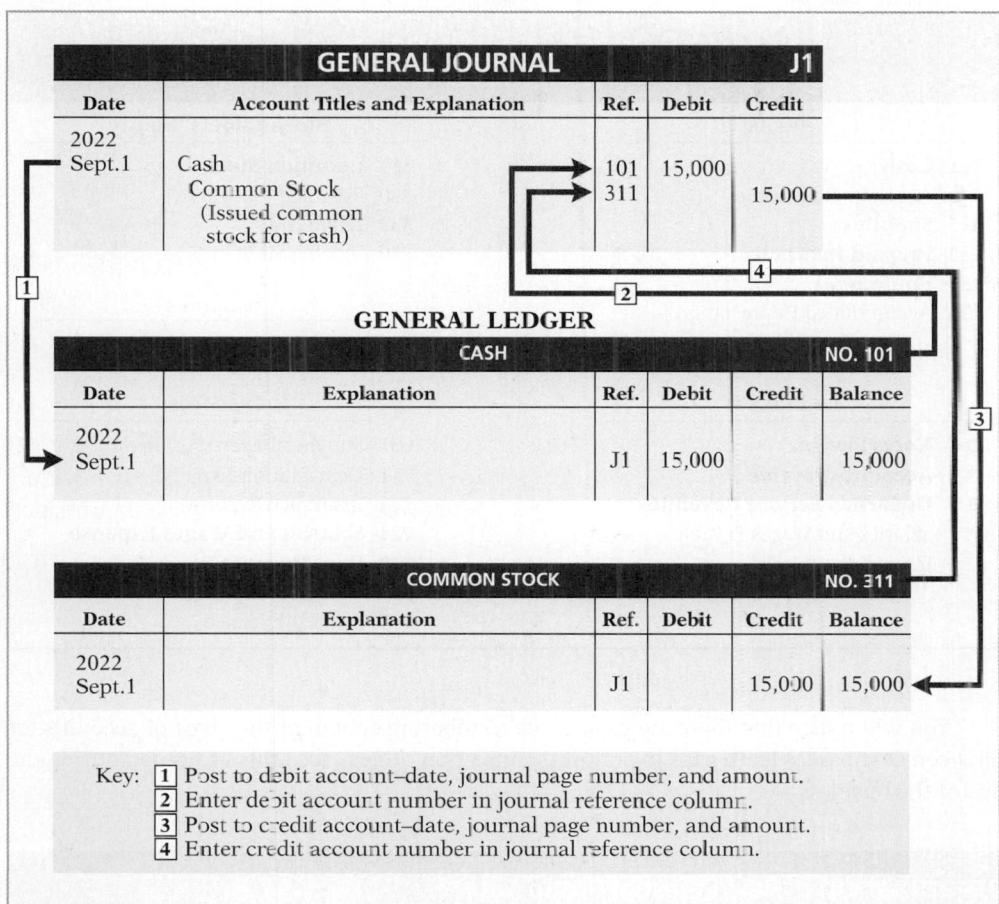

Posting should be performed in chronological order. That is, the company should post all the debits and credits of one journal entry before proceeding to the next journal entry. Postings should be made on a timely basis to ensure that the ledger is up-to-date. *In homework problems, you can journalize all transactions before posting any of the journal entries.*

The reference column of a ledger account indicates the journal page from which the transaction was posted. (After the last entry has been posted, the accountant should scan the reference column **in the journal**, to confirm that all postings have been made.) The explanation space of the ledger account is used infrequently because an explanation already appears in the journal.

## Chart of Accounts

The number and type of accounts differ for each company. The number of accounts depends on the amount of detail management desires. For example, the management of one company may want a single account for all types of utility expense. Another may keep separate expense accounts for each type of utility, such as gas, electricity, and water. Similarly, a small company like Softbyte Inc. will have fewer accounts than a corporate giant like **Dell**. Softbyte may be able to manage and report its activities in 20 to 30 accounts, while Dell may require thousands of accounts to keep track of its worldwide activities.

Most companies have a **chart of accounts**. This chart lists the accounts and the account numbers that identify their location in the ledger. The numbering system that identifies the accounts usually starts with the balance sheet accounts and follows with the income statement accounts.

In this and the next two chapters, we will be explaining the accounting for Pioneer Advertising Inc. (a service company). Accounts 101–199 indicate asset accounts; 200–299 indicate liabilities; 301–350 indicate stockholders' equity accounts; 400–499, revenues; 601–799, expenses; 800–899, other revenues; and 900–999, other expenses. **Illustration 2.19** shows Pioneer's chart of accounts. Accounts listed in red are used in this chapter; accounts shown in black are explained in later chapters.

**ILLUSTRATION 2.19**
**Chart of accounts for Pioneer Advertising Inc.**

## Pioneer Advertising Inc.
### Chart of Accounts

| Assets | | Stockholders' Equity | |
|---|---|---|---|
| 101 | **Cash** | 311 | **Common Stock** |
| 112 | Accounts Receivable | 320 | Retained Earnings |
| 126 | **Supplies** | 332 | **Dividends** |
| 130 | **Prepaid Insurance** | 350 | Income Summary |
| 157 | **Equipment** | | |
| 158 | Accumulated Depreciation— | | **Revenues** |
| | Equipment | 400 | **Service Revenue** |

| Liabilities | | Expenses | |
|---|---|---|---|
| 200 | **Notes Payable** | 631 | Supplies Expense |
| 201 | **Accounts Payable** | 711 | Depreciation Expense |
| 209 | **Unearned Service Revenue** | 722 | Insurance Expense |
| 212 | Salaries and Wages Payable | 726 | **Salaries and Wages Expense** |
| 230 | Interest Payable | 729 | **Rent Expense** |
| | | 732 | **Utilities Expense** |
| | | 905 | Interest Expense |

You will notice that there are gaps in the numbering system of the chart of accounts for Pioneer. Companies leave gaps to permit the insertion of new accounts as needed during the life of the business.

## Accounting Across the Organization    Hain Celestial Group

### It Starts with the Transaction

Keith Homan/
Shutterstock.com

Recording financial transactions in a company's records should be straightforward. If a company determines that a transaction involves revenue, it records revenue. If it has an expense, then it records an expense. However, sometimes this is difficult to do. For example, for more than a year, **Hain Celestial Group** (an organic food company) did not provide income information to investors and regulators. The reason was that the company discovered revenue irregularities and said it could not release financial results until it determined when and how to record revenue for certain transactions. When Hain missed four deadlines for reporting earnings information, the food company suffered a 34% drop in its stock price. As one analyst noted, it was hard to fathom why a seemingly simple revenue recognition issue took one year to resolve.

In other situations, outright fraud may occur. For example, regulators charged **Obsidian Energy** for fraudulently moving millions of dollars in expenses from operating expenses to capital expenditure accounts. By understating reported operating expenses, Obsidian made it appear that it was efficiently managing its costs as well as increasing its income.

These examples demonstrate that "getting the basic transaction right" is the foundation for relevant and representationally faithful financial statements. Starting with an incorrect or inappropriate transaction leads to distortions in the financial statements.

**Sources:** Shawn Tully, "The Mystery of Hain Celestial's Accounting," *Fortune.com* (August 20, 2016); and Kelly Cryderman, "U.S. Charges Obsidian, Formerly Penn West, with Accounting Fraud," *Globe and Mail* (June 28, 2017).

**Why is it important for companies to record financial transactions completely and accurately? (Answer is available near the end of the chapter.)**

# The Recording Process Illustrated

Illustrations **2.20** through **2.29** show the basic steps in the recording process, using the October transactions of Pioneer Advertising Inc. A basic analysis, an equation analysis, and a debit-credit analysis precede the journal entry and posting of each transaction. For simplicity, we use the T-account form to show the posting instead of the standard account form.

Study these transaction analyses carefully. **The purpose of transaction analysis is first to identify the type of account involved, and then to determine whether to make a debit or a credit to the account.** You should always perform this type of analysis before preparing a journal entry. Doing so will help you understand the journal entries discussed in this chapter as well as more complex journal entries in later chapters (see **Helpful Hint**).

In addition, an Accounting Cycle Tutorial is available in WileyPLUS. It provides an interactive presentation of the steps in the accounting cycle, using the Pioneer example shown in Illustrations 2.20 through 2.29.

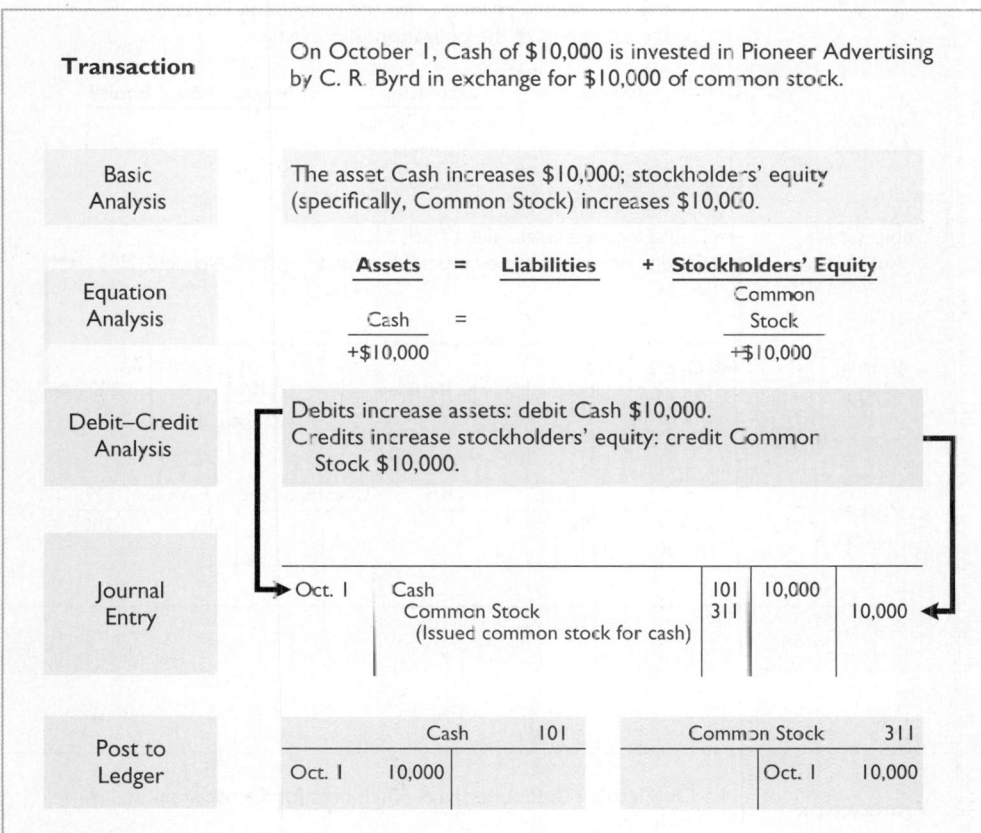

**ILLUSTRATION 2.20**

**Investment of cash by stockholders**

**Cash flow analyses** show the impact of each transaction on cash.

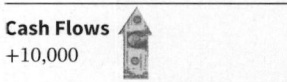

**Cash Flows**
+10,000

**HELPFUL HINT**

Follow these steps:

1. Determine what type of account is involved.
2. Determine what items increased or decreased and by how much.
3. Translate the increases and decreases into debits and credits.

**ILLUSTRATION 2.21**

**Purchase of office equipment**

**Cash Flows**
no effect

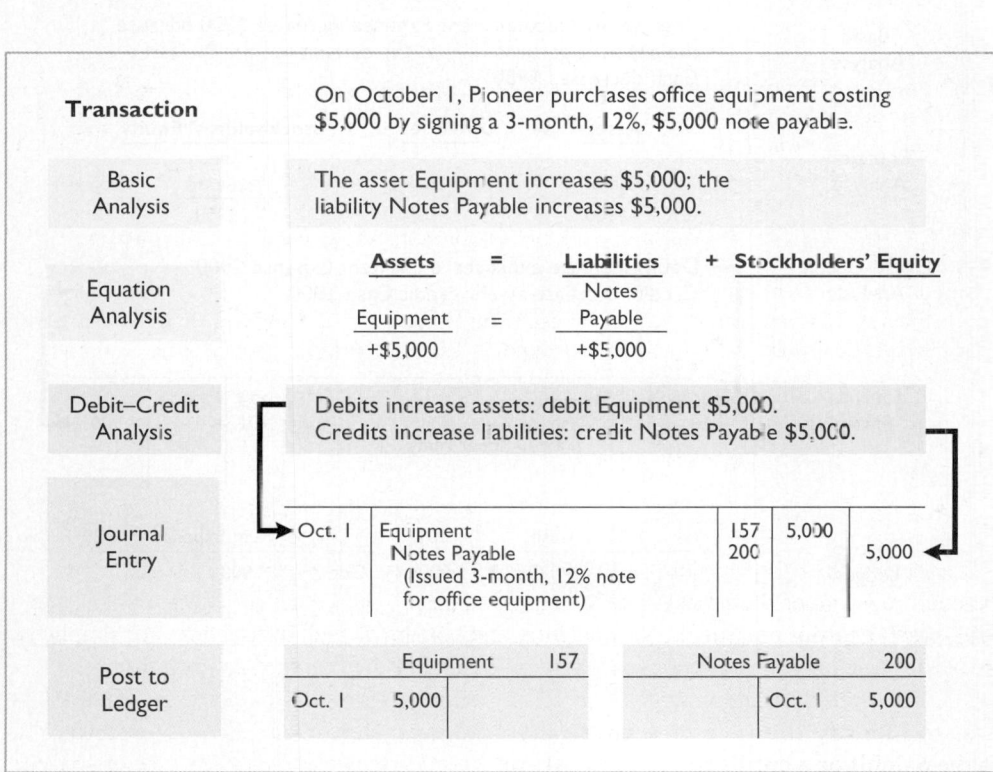

**ILLUSTRATION 2.22**

**Receipt of cash for future service**

Many liabilities have the word "payable" in their title. But, note that Unearned Service Revenue is considered a liability even though the word *payable* is not used.

**Cash Flows**
+1,200

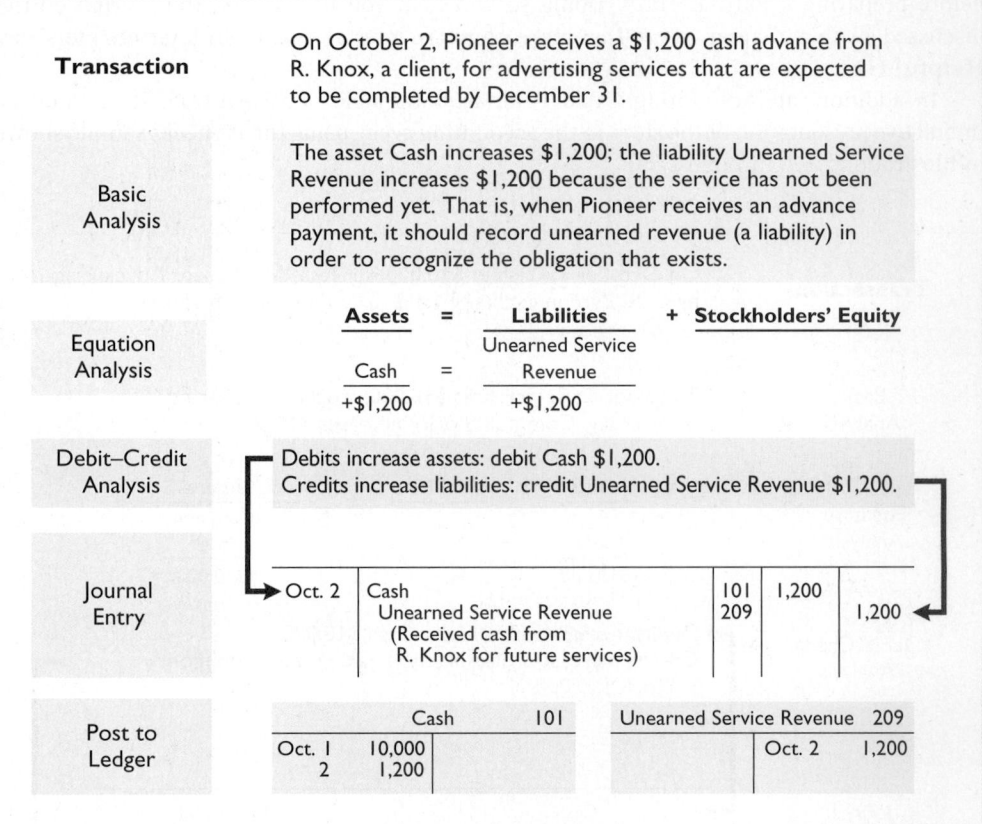

| | |
|---|---|
| **Transaction** | On October 2, Pioneer receives a $1,200 cash advance from R. Knox, a client, for advertising services that are expected to be completed by December 31. |
| **Basic Analysis** | The asset Cash increases $1,200; the liability Unearned Service Revenue increases $1,200 because the service has not been performed yet. That is, when Pioneer receives an advance payment, it should record unearned revenue (a liability) in order to recognize the obligation that exists. |

**Equation Analysis**

| Assets | = | Liabilities | + | Stockholders' Equity |
|---|---|---|---|---|
| | | Unearned Service | | |
| Cash | = | Revenue | | |
| +$1,200 | | +$1,200 | | |

**Debit–Credit Analysis**

Debits increase assets: debit Cash $1,200.
Credits increase liabilities: credit Unearned Service Revenue $1,200.

**Journal Entry**

| Oct. 2 | Cash | 101 | 1,200 | |
|---|---|---|---|---|
| | Unearned Service Revenue | 209 | | 1,200 |
| | (Received cash from | | | |
| | R. Knox for future services) | | | |

**Post to Ledger**

| Cash | | 101 | | Unearned Service Revenue | 209 |
|---|---|---|---|---|---|
| Oct. 1 | 10,000 | | | | Oct. 2 | 1,200 |
| 2 | 1,200 | | | | |

---

**ILLUSTRATION 2.23**

**Payment of monthly rent**

**Cash Flows**
−900

| | |
|---|---|
| **Transaction** | On October 3, Pioneer pays office rent for October in cash, $900. |
| **Basic Analysis** | The expense account Rent Expense increases $900 because the payment pertains only to the current month; the asset Cash decreases $900. |

**Equation Analysis**

| Assets | = | Liabilities | + | Stockholders' Equity |
|---|---|---|---|---|
| | | | | Rent |
| Cash | = | | | Expense |
| −$900 | | | | −$900 |

**Debit–Credit Analysis**

Debits increase expenses: debit Rent Expense $900.
Credits decrease assets: credit Cash $900.

**Journal Entry**

| Oct. 3 | Rent Expense | 729 | 900 | |
|---|---|---|---|---|
| | Cash | 101 | | 900 |
| | (Paid October rent) | | | |

**Post to Ledger**

| Cash | | 101 | | | Rent Expense | 729 |
|---|---|---|---|---|---|---|
| Oct. 1 | 10,000 | Oct. 3 | 900 | | Oct. 3 | 900 |
| 2 | 1,200 | | | | | |

| **Transaction** | On October 4, Pioneer pays $600 for a one-year insurance policy that will expire next year on September 30. |
|---|---|

| **Basic Analysis** | The asset Cash decreases $600. Payments of expenses that will benefit more than one accounting period are prepaid expenses or prepayments. When a company makes a payment, it debits an asset account in order to show the service or benefit that will be received in the future. Therefore, the asset Prepaid Insurance is increased $600. |
|---|---|

**Equation Analysis**

| Assets | = | Liabilities | + | Stockholders' Equity |
|---|---|---|---|---|
| Cash + Prepaid Insurance | | | | |
| −$600   +$600 | | | | |

**Cash Flows**
−600

**Debit–Credit Analysis**

Debits increase assets: debit Prepaid Insurance $600.
Credits decrease assets: credit Cash $600.

**Journal Entry**

| Oct. 4 | Prepaid Insurance | 130 | 600 | |
|---|---|---|---|---|
| | Cash | 101 | | 600 |
| | (Paid one-year policy; effective date October 1) | | | |

**Post to Ledger**

| Cash | 101 | | Prepaid Insurance | 130 |
|---|---|---|---|---|
| Oct. 1  10,000 | Oct. 3  900 | Oct. 4  600 | | |
| 2   1,200 | 4   600 | | | |

| **Transaction** | On October 5, Pioneer purchases an estimated 3-month supply of advertising materials on account from Aero Supply for $2,500. |
|---|---|

| **Basic Analysis** | The asset Supplies increases $2,500; the liability Accounts Payable increases $2,500. |
|---|---|

**Equation Analysis**

| Assets | = | Liabilities | + | Stockholders' Equity |
|---|---|---|---|---|
| Supplies | = | Accounts Payable | | |
| +$2,500 | | +$2,500 | | |

**Cash Flows**
no effect

**Debit–Credit Analysis**

Debits increase assets: debit Supplies $2,500.
Credits increase liabilities: credit Accounts Payable $2,500.

**Journal Entry**

| Oct. 5 | Supplies | 126 | 2,500 | |
|---|---|---|---|---|
| | Accounts Payable | 201 | | 2,500 |
| | (Purchased supplies on account from Aero Supply) | | | |

**Post to Ledger**

| Supplies | 126 | Accounts Payable | 201 |
|---|---|---|---|
| Oct. 5  2,500 | | Oct. 5 | 2,500 |

**ILLUSTRATION 2.26**

**Hiring of employees**

---

**Cash Flows**
no effect

---

| | |
|---|---|
| **Event** | On October 9, Pioneer hires four employees to begin work on October 15. Each employee is to receive a weekly salary of $500 for a 5-day work week, payable every 2 weeks—first payment made on October 26. |
| **Basic Analysis** | This is a business **event**; a business transaction has not occurred. There is only an agreement between the employer and the employees to enter into a business transaction beginning on October 15. Thus, a debit–credit analysis is not needed because there is no accounting entry (see October 26 transaction for first entry). |

**ILLUSTRATION 2.27**

**Receipt of cash for services performed**

---

**Cash Flows**
+10,000

---

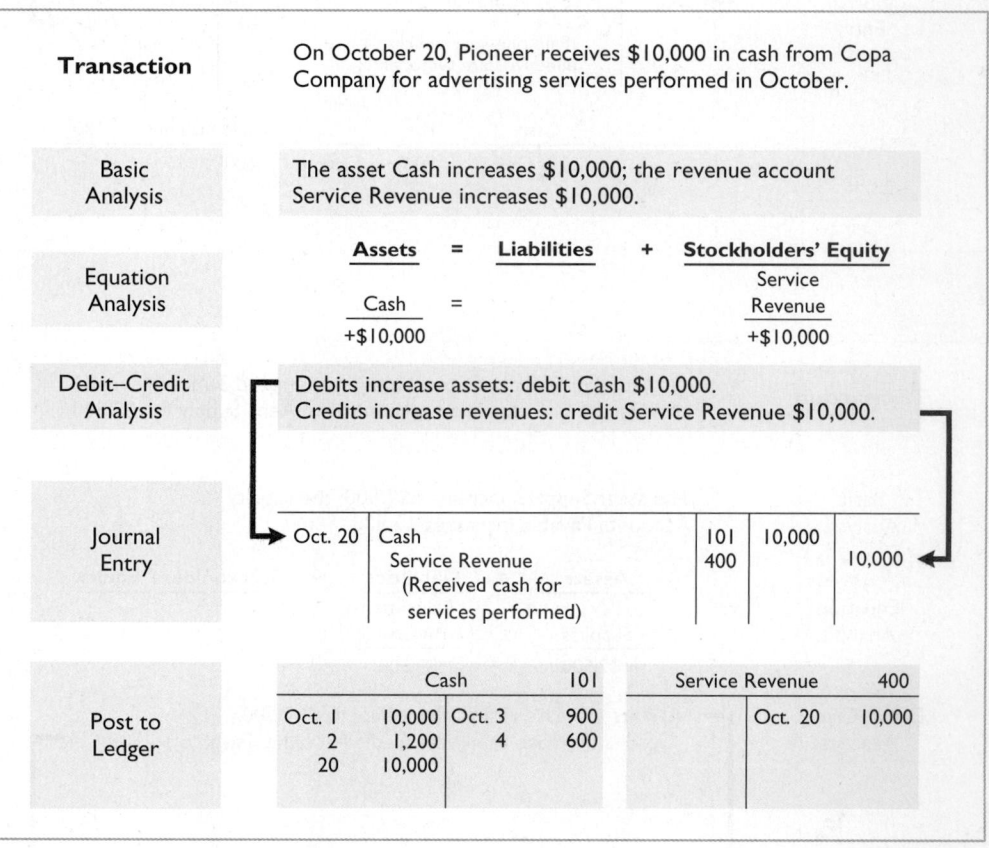

| | |
|---|---|
| **Transaction** | On October 20, Pioneer receives $10,000 in cash from Copa Company for advertising services performed in October. |
| **Basic Analysis** | The asset Cash increases $10,000; the revenue account Service Revenue increases $10,000. |

**Equation Analysis**

| **Assets** | = | **Liabilities** | + | **Stockholders' Equity** |
|---|---|---|---|---|
| | | | | Service |
| Cash | = | | | Revenue |
| +$10,000 | | | | +$10,000 |

**Debit–Credit Analysis**

Debits increase assets: debit Cash $10,000.
Credits increase revenues: credit Service Revenue $10,000.

**Journal Entry**

| Oct. 20 | Cash | 101 | 10,000 | |
|---|---|---|---|---|
| | Service Revenue | 400 | | 10,000 |
| | (Received cash for services performed) | | | |

**Post to Ledger**

| | Cash | | 101 | | Service Revenue | | 400 |
|---|---|---|---|---|---|---|---|
| Oct. 1 | 10,000 | Oct. 3 | 900 | | Oct. 20 | | 10,000 |
| 2 | 1,200 | 4 | 600 | | | | |
| 20 | 10,000 | | | | | | |

**ILLUSTRATION 2.28**
**Payment of salaries**

**Transaction**

On October 26, Pioneer owes employee salaries of $4,000 and pays them in cash (see October 9 event).

**Basic Analysis**

The expense account Salaries and Wages Expense increases $4,000; the asset Cash decreases $4,000.

**Equation Analysis**

| **Assets** | = | **Liabilities** | + | **Stockholders' Equity** |
|---|---|---|---|---|
| Cash | = | | | Salaries and Wages Expense |
| −$4,000 | | | | −$4,000 |

**Cash Flows**
−4,000

**Debit–Credit Analysis**

Debits increase expenses: debit Salaries and Wages Expense $4,000.
Credits decrease assets: credit Cash $4,000.

**Journal Entry**

| Oct. 26 | Salaries and Wages Expense | 726 | 4,000 | |
|---|---|---|---|---|
| | Cash | 101 | | 4,000 |
| | (Paid salaries to date) | | | |

**Post to Ledger**

| Cash | | | 101 | | Salaries and Wages Expense | 726 |
|---|---|---|---|---|---|---|
| Oct. 1 | 10,000 | Oct. 3 | 900 | Oct. 26 | 4,000 | |
| 2 | 1,200 | 4 | 600 | | | |
| 20 | 10,000 | 26 | 4,000 | | | |

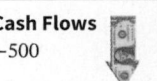

---

**ILLUSTRATION 2.29**
**Declaration and payment of dividend**

**Transaction**

On October 31, Pioneer's board of directors declares and pays a $500 cash dividend to stockholders.

**Basic Analysis**

The Dividends account increases $500; the asset Cash decreases $500.

**Equation Analysis**

| **Assets** | = | **Liabilities** | + | **Stockholders' Equity** |
|---|---|---|---|---|
| Cash | = | | | Dividends |
| −$500 | | | | −$500 |

**Cash Flows**
−500

**Debit–Credit Analysis**

Debits increase dividends: debit Dividends $500.
Credits decrease assets: credit Cash $500.

**Journal Entry**

| Oct. 31 | Dividends | 332 | 500 | |
|---|---|---|---|---|
| | Cash | 101 | | 500 |
| | (Declared and paid a cash dividend) | | | |

**Post to Ledger**

| Cash | | | 101 | | Dividends | 332 |
|---|---|---|---|---|---|---|
| Oct. 1 | 10,000 | Oct. 3 | 900 | Oct. 31 | 500 | |
| 2 | 1,200 | 4 | 600 | | | |
| 20 | 10,000 | 26 | 4,000 | | | |
| | | 31 | 500 | | | |

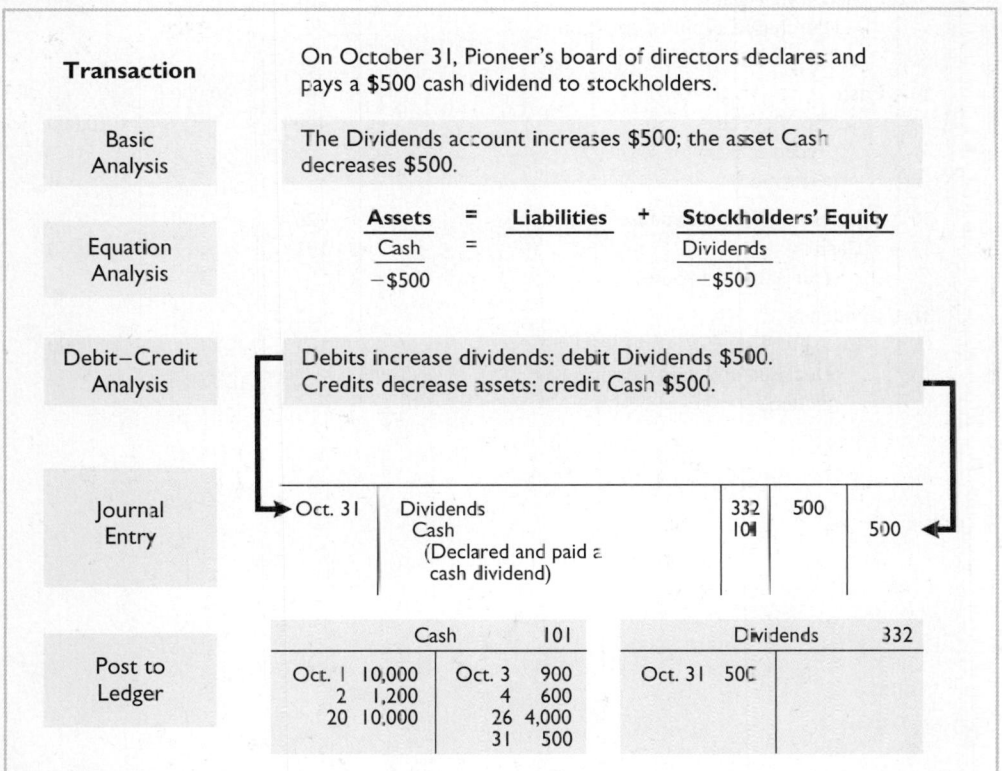

# Summary Illustration of Journalizing and Posting

**Illustration 2.30** shows the journal for Pioneer Advertising Inc. for October.

**ILLUSTRATION 2.30**

**General journal entries**

| | | GENERAL JOURNAL | | | PAGE J1 |
|---|---|---|---|---|---|
| **Date** | | **Account Titles and Explanation** | **Ref.** | **Debit** | **Credit** |
| 2022 | | | | | |
| Oct. | 1 | Cash | 101 | 10,000 | |
| | |     Common Stock | 311 | | 10,000 |
| | |       (Issued common stock for cash) | | | |
| | 1 | Equipment | 157 | 5,000 | |
| | |     Notes Payable | 200 | | 5,000 |
| | |       (Issued 3-month, 12% note for | | | |
| | |       office equipment) | | | |
| | 2 | Cash | 101 | 1,200 | |
| | |     Unearned Service Revenue | 209 | | 1,200 |
| | |       (Received advance from R. Knox | | | |
| | |       for future services) | | | |
| | 3 | Rent Expense | 729 | 900 | |
| | |     Cash | 101 | | 900 |
| | |       (Paid cash for October office rent) | | | |
| | 4 | Prepaid Insurance | 130 | 600 | |
| | |     Cash | 101 | | 600 |
| | |       (Paid one-year policy; effective | | | |
| | |       date October 1) | | | |
| | 5 | Supplies | 126 | 2,500 | |
| | |     Accounts Payable | 201 | | 2,500 |
| | |       (Purchased supplies on account | | | |
| | |       from Aero Supply) | | | |
| | 20 | Cash | 101 | 10,000 | |
| | |     Service Revenue | 400 | | 10,000 |
| | |       (Received cash for services | | | |
| | |       performed) | | | |
| | 26 | Salaries and Wages Expense | 726 | 4,000 | |
| | |     Cash | 101 | | 4,000 |
| | |       (Paid salaries to date) | | | |
| | 31 | Dividends | 332 | 500 | |
| | |     Cash | 101 | | 500 |
| | |       (Declared and paid a cash | | | |
| | |       dividend) | | | |

**Illustration 2.31** shows the ledger, with all balances in red.

**ILLUSTRATION 2.31**  General ledger

## GENERAL LEDGER

| | Cash | | | | No. 101 |
|---|---|---|---|---|---|
| Date | Explanation | Ref. | Debit | Credit | Balance |
| 2022 | | | | | |
| Oct. 1 | | J1 | 10,000 | | 10,000 |
| 2 | | J1 | 1,200 | | 11,200 |
| 3 | | J1 | | 900 | 10,300 |
| 4 | | J1 | | 600 | 9,700 |
| 20 | | J1 | 10,000 | | 19,700 |
| 26 | | J1 | | 4,000 | 15,700 |
| 31 | | J1 | | 500 | **15,200** |

| | Supplies | | | | No. 126 |
|---|---|---|---|---|---|
| Date | Explanation | Ref. | Debit | Credit | Balance |
| 2022 | | | | | |
| Oct. 5 | | J1 | 2,500 | | **2,500** |

| | Prepaid Insurance | | | | No. 130 |
|---|---|---|---|---|---|
| Date | Explanation | Ref. | Debit | Credit | Balance |
| 2022 | | | | | |
| Oct. 4 | | J1 | 600 | | **600** |

| | Equipment | | | | No. 157 |
|---|---|---|---|---|---|
| Date | Explanation | Ref. | Debit | Credit | Balance |
| 2022 | | | | | |
| Oct. 1 | | J1 | 5,000 | | **5,000** |

| | Notes Payable | | | | No. 200 |
|---|---|---|---|---|---|
| Date | Explanation | Ref. | Debit | Credit | Balance |
| 2022 | | | | | |
| Oct. 1 | | J1 | | 5,000 | **5,000** |

| | Accounts Payable | | | | No. 201 |
|---|---|---|---|---|---|
| Date | Explanation | Ref. | Debit | Credit | Balance |
| 2022 | | | | | |
| Oct. 5 | | J1 | | 2,500 | **2,500** |

| | Unearned Service Revenue | | | | No. 209 |
|---|---|---|---|---|---|
| Date | Explanation | Ref. | Debit | Credit | Balance |
| 2022 | | | | | |
| Oct. 2 | | J1 | | 1,200 | **1,200** |

| | Common Stock | | | | No. 311 |
|---|---|---|---|---|---|
| Date | Explanation | Ref. | Debit | Credit | Balance |
| 2022 | | | | | |
| Oct. 1 | | J1 | | 10,000 | **10,000** |

| | Dividends | | | | No. 332 |
|---|---|---|---|---|---|
| Date | Explanation | Ref. | Debit | Credit | Balance |
| 2022 | | | | | |
| Oct. 31 | | J1 | 500 | | **500** |

| | Service Revenue | | | | No. 400 |
|---|---|---|---|---|---|
| Date | Explanation | Ref. | Debit | Credit | Balance |
| 2022 | | | | | |
| Oct. 20 | | J1 | | 10,000 | **10,000** |

| | Salaries and Wages Expense | | | | No. 726 |
|---|---|---|---|---|---|
| Date | Explanation | Ref. | Debit | Credit | Balance |
| 2022 | | | | | |
| Oct. 26 | | J1 | 4,000 | | **4,000** |

| | Rent Expense | | | | No. 729 |
|---|---|---|---|---|---|
| Date | Explanation | Ref. | Debit | Credit | Balance |
| 2022 | | | | | |
| Oct. 3 | | J1 | 900 | | **900** |

## DO IT! 3 | Posting

Kate Browne recorded the following transactions in a general journal during the month of March.

| Mar. 4 | Cash | 2,280 | |
|---|---|---|---|
| | Service Revenue | | 2,280 |
| 15 | Salaries and Wages Expenses | 400 | |
| | Cash | | 400 |
| 19 | Utilities Expense | 92 | |
| | Cash | | 92 |

Post these entries to the Cash account of the general ledger to determine its ending balance. The beginning balance of Cash on March 1 was $600.

### Solution

**Cash**

| | | | |
|---|---|---|---|
| 3/1 Bal. | 600 | 3/15 | 400 |
| 3/4 | 2,280 | 3/19 | 92 |
| 3/31 Bal. | 2,388 | | |

Related exercise material: **BE2.7, BE2.8, DO IT! 2.3, E2.10, E2.11, E2.14, and E2.17.**

**ACTION PLAN**

- Recall that posting involves transferring the journalized debits and credits to specific accounts in the ledger.

- Determine the ending balance by netting the total debits and credits.

# The Trial Balance

## LEARNING OBJECTIVE 4
Prepare a trial balance.

ANALYZE ▶ JOURNALIZE ▶ POST ▶ **Prepare a trial balance** ▶ ADJUSTING ENTRIES ▶ ADJUSTED TRIAL BALANCE ▶ FINANCIAL STATEMENTS ▶ CLOSING ENTRIES ▶ POST-CLOSING TRIAL BALANCE

A **trial balance** is a list of accounts and their balances at a given time. Companies usually prepare a trial balance at the end of an accounting period. They list accounts in the order in which they appear in the ledger. Debit balances appear in the left column and credit balances in the right column. The totals of the two columns must be equal.

**The trial balance proves the mathematical equality of debits and credits after posting.** Under the double-entry system, this equality occurs when the sum of the debit account balances equals the sum of the credit account balances. **A trial balance may also uncover errors in journalizing and posting.** For example, a trial balance may well have detected the error at **MF Global** discussed in the Feature Story. **In addition, a trial balance is useful in the preparation of financial statements**, as we will explain in the next two chapters.

The steps for preparing a trial balance are:

1. List the account titles and their balances in the appropriate debit or credit column.

2. Total the debit and credit columns.

3. Verify the equality of the two columns.

Illustration 2.32 shows the trial balance prepared from Pioneer Advertising's ledger (see **Helpful Hint**). Note that the total debits equal the total credits.

**ILLUSTRATION 2.32**

**A trial balance**

**HELPFUL HINT**

Note that the order of presentation in the trial balance is:
- Assets
- Liabilities
- Stockholders' equity
- Revenues
- Expenses

## Pioneer Advertising Inc.
### Trial Balance
### October 31, 2022

|  | Debit | Credit |
|---|---|---|
| Cash | $15,200 |  |
| Supplies | 2,500 |  |
| Prepaid Insurance | 600 |  |
| Equipment | 5,000 |  |
| Notes Payable |  | $ 5,000 |
| Accounts Payable |  | 2,500 |
| Unearned Service Revenue |  | 1,200 |
| Common Stock |  | 10,000 |
| Dividends | 500 |  |
| Service Revenue |  | 10,000 |
| Salaries and Wages Expense | 4,000 |  |
| Rent Expense | 900 |  |
|  | **$28,700** | **$28,700** |

A trial balance is a necessary checkpoint for uncovering certain types of errors. For example, if only the debit portion of a journal entry has been posted, the trial balance would bring this error to light.

## Limitations of a Trial Balance

A trial balance does not guarantee freedom from recording errors, however. Numerous errors may exist even though the totals of the trial balance columns agree (see **Ethics Note**). For example, the trial balance may balance even when:

1. A transaction is not journalized.
2. A correct journal entry is not posted.
3. A journal entry is posted twice.
4. Incorrect accounts are used in journalizing or posting.
5. Offsetting errors are made in recording the amount of a transaction.

As long as equal debits and credits are posted, even to the wrong account or in the wrong amount, the total debits will equal the total credits. **The trial balance does not prove that the company has recorded all transactions or that the ledger is correct.**

> **ETHICS NOTE**
>
> **An error is the result of an unintentional mistake; it is neither ethical nor unethical. An irregularity is an intentional misstatement, which is viewed as unethical.**

## Locating Errors

Errors in a trial balance generally result from mathematical mistakes, incorrect postings or simply transcribing data incorrectly. What do you do if you are faced with a trial balance that does not balance? First, determine the amount of the difference between the two columns of the trial balance. After this amount is known, the following steps are often helpful:

1. If the error is $1, $10, $100, or $1,000, re-add the trial balance columns and recompute the account balances.
2. If the error is divisible by 2, scan the trial balance to see whether a balance equal to half the error has been entered in the wrong column.
3. If the error is divisible by 9, retrace the account balances on the trial balance to see whether they are incorrectly copied from the ledger. For example, if a balance was $12 and it was listed as $21, a $9 error has been made. Reversing the order of numbers is called a **transposition error**.
4. If the error is not divisible by 2 or 9, scan the ledger to see whether an account balance in the amount of the error has been omitted from the trial balance, and scan the journal to see whether a posting of that amount has been omitted.

## Dollar Signs and Underlining

Note that dollar signs do not appear in journals or ledgers. Dollar signs are typically used only in the trial balance and the financial statements. Generally, a dollar sign is shown only for the first item in the column and for the total of that column. A single line (a totaling rule) is placed under the column of figures to be added or subtracted. Total amounts are double-underlined to indicate they are final sums.

## Investor Insight   Fannie Mae

iStock.com/Enviromatic

### Why Accuracy Matters

While most companies record transactions very carefully, the reality is that mistakes still happen. For example, bank regulators fined **Bank One Corporation** (now **JPMorgan Chase**) $1.8 million because they felt that the unreliability of the bank's accounting system caused it to violate regulatory requirements.

Also, in recent years **Fannie Mae**, the government-chartered mortgage association, announced a series of large accounting errors. These announcements caused alarm among investors, regulators, and politicians because they fear that the errors may suggest larger, undetected problems. This is important because the home-mortgage market depends on Fannie Mae to buy hundreds of billions of dollars of mortgages each year from banks, thus enabling the banks to issue new mortgages.

Finally, before a major overhaul of its accounting system, the financial records of **Waste Management, Inc.** were in such disarray that of the company's 57,000 employees, 10,000 were receiving pay slips that were in error.

The Sarbanes-Oxley Act was created to minimize the occurrence of errors like these by increasing every employee's responsibility for accurate financial reporting.

**In order for these companies to prepare and issue financial statements, their accounting equations (debits and credits) must have been in balance at year-end. How could these errors or misstatements have occurred? (Answer is available near the end of the chapter.)**

---

## ACTION PLAN

- **Determine normal balances and list accounts in the order they appear in the ledger.**
- **Accounts with debit balances appear in the left column, and those with credit balances in the right column.**
- **Total the debit and credit columns to prove equality.**

## DO IT! 4 │ Trial Balance

The following accounts come from the ledger of SnowGo Corporation at December 31, 2022.

| | | | | | | |
|---|---|---|---|---|---|---|
| 157 | Equipment | $88,000 | | 311 | Common Stock | $20,000 |
| 332 | Dividends | 8,000 | | 212 | Salaries and | |
| 201 | Accounts Payable | 22,000 | | | Wages Payable | 2,000 |
| 726 | Salaries and | | | 200 | Notes Payable | |
| | Wages Expense | 42,000 | | | (due in 3 months) | 19,000 |
| 112 | Accounts Receivable | 4,000 | | 732 | Utilities Expense | 3,000 |
| 400 | Service Revenue | 95,000 | | 130 | Prepaid Insurance | 6,000 |
| | | | | 101 | Cash | 7,000 |

Prepare a trial balance in good form.

### Solution

**SnowGo Corporation**
**Trial Balance**
**December 31, 2022**

| | Debit | Credit |
|---|---|---|
| Cash | $ 7,000 | |
| Accounts Receivable | 4,000 | |
| Prepaid Insurance | 6,000 | |
| Equipment | 88,000 | |
| Notes Payable | | $ 19,000 |
| Accounts Payable | | 22,000 |
| Salaries and Wages Payable | | 2,000 |
| Common Stock | | 20,000 |
| Dividends | 8,000 | |
| Service Revenue | | 95,000 |
| Utilities Expense | 3,000 | |
| Salaries and Wages Expense | 42,000 | |
| | $158,000 | $158,000 |

Related exercise material: **BE2.9, BE2.10, DO IT! 2.4, E2.11, E2.12, E2.13, E2.14, E2.15, E2.16, and E2.17.**

# Review and Practice

## Learning Objectives Review

**1  Describe how accounts, debits, and credits are used to record business transactions.**

An account is a record of increases and decreases in specific asset, liability, and stockholders' equity items. The terms debit and credit are synonymous with left and right. Assets, dividends, and expenses are increased by debits and decreased by credits. Liabilities, common stock, retained earnings, and revenues are increased by credits and decreased by debits.

**2  Indicate how a journal is used in the recording process.**

The basic steps in the recording process are (a) analyze each transaction for its effects on the accounts, (b) enter the transaction information in a journal, and (c) transfer the journal information to the appropriate accounts in the ledger.

The initial accounting record of a transaction is entered in a journal before the data are entered in the accounts. A journal (a) discloses in one place the complete effects of a transaction, (b) provides a chronological record of transactions, and (c) prevents or locates errors because the debit and credit amounts for each entry can be easily compared.

**3  Explain how a ledger and posting help in the recording process.**

The ledger is the entire group of accounts maintained by a company. The ledger provides the balance in each of the accounts as well as keeps track of changes in these balances. Posting is the transfer of journal entries to the ledger accounts. This phase of the recording process accumulates the effects of journalized transactions in the individual accounts.

**4  Prepare a trial balance.**

A trial balance is a list of accounts and their balances at a given time. Its primary purpose is to prove the equality of debits and credits after posting. A trial balance also uncovers errors in journalizing and posting and is useful in preparing financial statements.

## Glossary Review

**Account**  A record of increases and decreases in specific asset, liability, or stockholders' equity items. (p. 2-3).

**Chart of accounts**  A list of accounts and the account numbers that identify their location in the ledger. (p. 2-13).

**Common stock**  Issued in exchange for the owners' investment paid in to corporation. (p. 2-5)

**Compound entry**  A journal entry that involves three or more accounts. (p. 2-10).

**Credit**  The right side of an account. (p. 2-3).

**Debit**  The left side of an account. (p. 2-3).

**Dividend**  A distribution by a corporation to its stockholders on a pro rata (equal) basis. (p. 2-5).

**Double-entry system**  A system that records in appropriate accounts the dual effect of each transaction. (p. 2-4).

**General journal**  The most basic form of journal. (p. 2-9).

**General ledger**  A ledger that contains all asset, liability, and stockholders' equity accounts. (p. 2-11).

**Journal**  An accounting record in which transactions are initially recorded in chronological order. (p. 2-9).

**Journalizing**  The entering of transaction data in the journal. (p. 2-9).

**Ledger**  The entire group of accounts maintained by a company. (p. 2-11).

**Normal balance**  An account balance on the side where an increase in the account is recorded. (p. 2-4).

**Posting**  The procedure of transferring journal entries to the ledger accounts. (p. 2-12).

**Retained earnings**  Net income that is kept (retained) in the business. (p. 2-5).

**Simple entry**  A journal entry that involves only two accounts. (p. 2-10).

**T-account**  The basic form of an account, consisting of (1) a title, (2) a left or debit side, and (3) a right or credit side. (p. 2-3).

**Three-column form of account**  A form with columns for debit, credit, and balance amounts in an account. (p. 2-12).

**Trial balance**  A list of accounts and their balances at a given time. (p. 2-22).

## Practice Multiple-Choice Questions

**1. (LO 1)** Which of the following statements about an account is **true**?

   **a.** The right side of an account is the debit, or increase, side.

   **b.** An account is an individual accounting record of increases and decreases in specific asset, liability, and stockholders' equity items.

   **c.** There are separate accounts for specific assets and liabilities but only one account for stockholders' equity items.

   **d.** The left side of an account is the credit, or decrease, side.

**2. (LO 1)** Debits:

   **a.** increase both assets and liabilities.

   **b.** decrease both assets and liabilities.

   **c.** increase assets and decrease liabilities.

   **d.** decrease assets and increase liabilities.

**3. (LO 1)** A revenue account:

   **a.** is increased by debits.

   **b.** is decreased by credits.

   **c.** has a normal balance of a debit.

   **d.** is increased by credits.

**4. (LO 1)** Accounts that normally have debit balances are:

   **a.** assets, expenses, and revenues.

   **b.** assets, expenses, and common stock.

   **c.** assets, liabilities, and dividends.

   **d.** assets, dividends, and expenses.

**5. (LO 1)** The expanded accounting equation is:

   **a.** Assets + Liabilities = Common Stock + Retained Earnings + Revenues + Expenses + Dividends.

   **b.** Assets = Liabilities + Common Stock + Retained Earnings + Revenues − Expenses + Dividends.

   **c.** Assets = Liabilities − Common Stock − Retained Earnings − Revenues − Expenses − Dividends.

   **d.** Assets = Liabilities + Common Stock + Retained Earnings + Revenues − Expenses − Dividends.

**6. (LO 1)** Which of the following is **not** part of the recording process?

   **a.** Analyzing transactions.

   **b.** Preparing an income statement.

   **c.** Entering transactions in a journal.

   **d.** Posting journal entries.

**7. (LO 2)** Which of the following statements about a journal is **false**?

   **a.** It is not a book of original entry.

   **b.** It provides a chronological record of transactions.

   **c.** It helps to locate errors because the debit and credit amounts for each entry can be readily compared.

   **d.** It discloses in one place the complete effect of a transaction.

**8. (LO 2)** The purchase of supplies on account should result in:

   **a.** a debit to Supplies Expense and a credit to Cash.

   **b.** a debit to Accounts Payable and a credit to Supplies Expense.

   **c.** a debit to Supplies and a credit to Accounts Payable.

   **d.** a debit to Supplies and a credit to Accounts Receivable.

**9. (LO 3)** The order of the accounts in the ledger is:

   **a.** assets, revenues, expenses, liabilities, common stock, dividends.

   **b.** assets, liabilities, common stock, dividends, revenues, expenses.

   **c.** common stock, assets, revenues, expenses, liabilities, dividends.

   **d.** revenues, assets, expenses, liabilities, common stock, dividends.

**10. (LO 3)** A ledger:

   **a.** contains only asset and liability accounts.

   **b.** should show accounts in alphabetical order.

   **c.** is a collection of the entire group of accounts maintained by a company.

   **d.** is a book of original entry.

**11. (LO 3)** Posting:

   **a.** normally occurs before journalizing.

   **b.** transfers ledger transaction data to the journal.

   **c.** is an optional step in the recording process.

   **d.** transfers journal entries to ledger accounts.

**12. (LO 3)** Before posting a payment of $5,000, the Accounts Payable of Chola Corporation had a normal balance of $18,000. The balance after posting this transaction was:

   **a.** $13,000.          **c.** $23,000.

   **b.** $5,000.           **d.** Cannot be determined.

**13. (LO 4)** A trial balance:

   **a.** is a list of accounts with their balances at a given time.

   **b.** proves the mathematical accuracy of journalized transactions.

   **c.** will not balance if a correct journal entry is posted twice.

   **d.** proves that all transactions have been recorded.

**14. (LO 4)** A trial balance will not balance if:

   **a.** a correct journal entry is posted twice.

   **b.** the purchase of supplies on account is debited to Supplies and credited to Cash.

   **c.** a $100 cash dividend is debited to Dividends for $1,000 and credited to Cash for $100.

   **d.** a $450 payment on account is debited to Accounts Payable for $45 and credited to Cash for $45.

**15. (LO 4)** The trial balance of Stevens Corporation had accounts with the following normal balances: Cash $5,000, Service Revenue $85,000, Salaries and Wages Payable $4,000, Salaries and Wages Expense $40,000, Rent Expense $10,000, Common Stock $42,000, Dividends $13,000, and Equipment $61,000. In preparing a trial balance, based on these amounts only, the total in the debit column is:

   **a.** $116,000.          **c.** $129,000.

   **b.** $118,000.          **d.** $131,000.

## Solutions

**1. b.** An account is an individual accounting record of increases and decreases in specific asset, liability, and stockholders' equity items. The other choices are incorrect because (a) the right side of the account is the credit side, not the debit side, and can be the increase or the decrease side, depending on the classification of the account; (c) there are also separate accounts for different stockholders' equity items; and (d) the left side of the account is the debit side, not the credit side, and can be either the decrease or the increase side, depending on the specific classification of the account.

**2. c.** Debits increase assets but they decrease liabilities. The other choices are incorrect because debits (a) decrease, not increase, liabilities; (b) increase, not decrease, assets; and (d) increase, not decrease, assets and decrease, not increase, liabilities.

**3. d.** A revenue account is increased by credits. The other choices are incorrect because a revenue account (a) is increased by credits, not debits; (b) is decreased by debits, not credits; and (c) has a normal balance of a credit, not a debit.

**4. d.** Assets, dividends, and expenses all have normal debit balances. The other choices are incorrect because (a) revenues have normal credit balances, (b) common stock has a normal credit balance, and (c) liabilities have normal credit balances.

**5. d.** The expanded accounting equation is Assets = Liabilities + Common Stock + Retained Earnings + Revenues − Expenses − Dividends. The other choices are therefore incorrect.

**6. b.** Preparing an income statement is not part of the recording process. Choices (a) analyzing transactions, (c) entering transactions in a journal, and (d) posting journal entries are all part of the recording process.

**7. a.** The journal is a book of original entry. The other choices are true statements.

**8. c.** The purchase of supplies on account results in a debit to Supplies and a credit to Accounts Payable. The other choices are incorrect because the purchase of supplies on account results in (a) a debit to Supplies, not Supplies Expense, and a credit to Accounts Payable, not Cash; (b) a debit to Supplies, not Accounts Payable; and (d) a credit to Accounts Payable, not Accounts Receivable.

**9. b.** The correct order of the accounts in the ledger is assets, liabilities, common stock, dividends, revenues, expenses. The other choices are incorrect because they do not reflect this order. The order of the accounts in the ledger is (1) balance sheet accounts: assets, liabilities, and stockholders' equity accounts (common stock and dividends), and then (2) income statement accounts: revenues and expenses.

**10. c.** A ledger is a collection of all the accounts maintained by a company. The other choices are incorrect because a ledger (a) contains all account types—assets, liabilities, stockholders' equity, revenue, and expense accounts—not just asset and liability accounts; (b) usually shows accounts in account number order, not alphabetical order; and (d) is not a book of original entry because entries made in the ledger come from the journals (the books of original entry).

**11. d.** Posting transfers journal entries to ledger accounts. The other choices are incorrect because posting (a) occurs after journalizing, (b) transfers journal transaction data to the ledger, and (c) is not an optional step in the recording process.

**12. a.** The balance is $13,000 ($18,000 normal balance − $5,000 payment), not (b) $5,000 or (c) $23,000. Choice (d) is incorrect because the balance can be determined.

**13. a.** A trial balance is a list of accounts with their balances at a given time. The other choices are incorrect because (b) the trial balance does not prove that journalized transactions are mathematically correct; (c) if a journal entry is posted twice, the trial balance will still balance; and (d) the trial balance does not prove that all transactions have been recorded.

**14. c.** The trial balance will not balance in this case because the debit of $1,000 to Dividends is not equal to the credit of $100 to Cash. The other choices are incorrect because (a) if a correct journal entry is posted twice, the trial balance will still balance; (b) if the purchase of supplies on account is debited to Supplies and credited to Cash, Cash and Accounts Payable will be understated but the trial balance will still balance; and (d) since the debit and credit amounts are the same, the trial balance will still balance but both Accounts Payable and Cash will be overstated.

**15. c.** The total debit column = $5,000 (Cash) + $40,000 (Salaries and Wages Expense) + $10,000 (Rent Expense) + $13,000 (Dividends) + $61,000 (Equipment) = $129,000, not (a) $116,000, (b) $118,000, or (d) $131,000.

## Practice Brief Exercises

**1. (LO 1)** Transactions for the Potter Company for the month of May are presented below. Identify the accounts to be debited and credited for each transaction.

*Identify accounts to be debited and credited.*

| May | 1 | Stockholders invested $22,000 cash in the business in exchange for common stock. |
| | 6 | Paid office rent of $900. |
| | 12 | Performed consulting services and billed client $4,400. |
| | 18 | Purchased equipment on account for $1,200. |

### Solution

**1.**

| | | **Account Debited** | **Account Credited** |
|---|---|---|---|
| May | 1 | Cash | Common Stock |
| | 6 | Rent Expense | Cash |
| | 12 | Accounts Receivable | Service Revenue |
| | 18 | Equipment | Accounts Payable |

**2. (LO 2)** Using the data from **Practice Brief Exercise 1**, journalize the transactions (omit explanations).

*Journalize transactions.*

**Solution**

| | | | | |
|---|---|---|---|---|
| 2. May | 1 | Cash | 22,000 | |
| | | Common Stock | | 22,000 |
| | 6 | Rent Expense | 900 | |
| | | Cash | | 900 |
| | 12 | Accounts Receivable | 4,400 | |
| | | Service Revenue | | 4,400 |
| | 18 | Equipment | 1,200 | |
| | | Accounts Payable | | 1,200 |

*Post journal entries to T-accounts.*

**3. (LO 3)** Selected transactions for Carlos Santana Company are presented in journal form as follows. Post the transactions to T-accounts. Make one T-account for each and determine each account's ending balance.

| | | | J1 |
|---|---|---|---|

| Date | Account Titles and Explanation | Ref. | Debit | Credit |
|---|---|---|---|---|
| June 6 | Cash | | 22,000 | |
| | Common Stock | | | 22,000 |
| | (Investment of cash in business) | | | |
| 13 | Accounts Receivable | | 8,200 | |
| | Service Revenue | | | 8,200 |
| | (Billed for services performed) | | | |
| 14 | Cash | | 3,700 | |
| | Accounts Receivable | | | 3,700 |
| | (Received cash in payment of account) | | | |

**Solution**

3.

| Cash | | | |
|---|---|---|---|
| 6/6 | 22,000 | | |
| 6/14 | 3,700 | | |
| Bal. 25,700 | | | |

| Accounts Receivable | | | |
|---|---|---|---|
| 6/13 | 8,200 | 6/14 | 3,700 |
| Bal. 4,500 | | | |

| Service Revenue | | | |
|---|---|---|---|
| | | 6/13 | 8,200 |
| | | Bal. 8,200 | |

| Common Stock | | | |
|---|---|---|---|
| | | 6/6 | 22,000 |
| | | Bal. 22,000 | |

*Post journal entries to standard form of account.*

**4. (LO 3)** Selected journal entries for Carlos Santana Company are presented in **Practice Brief Exercise 3**. Post the transactions using the standard form of account.

**Solution**

**4. Cash**

| Date | Explanation | Ref. | Debit | Credit | Balance |
|---|---|---|---|---|---|
| June 6 | | J1 | 22,000 | | 22,000 |
| 14 | | J1 | 3,700 | | 25,700 |

**Accounts Receivable**

| Date | Explanation | Ref. | Debit | Credit | Balance |
|---|---|---|---|---|---|
| June 13 | | J1 | 8,200 | | 8,200 |
| 14 | | J1 | | 3,700 | 4,500 |

**Service Revenue**

| Date | Explanation | Ref. | Debit | Credit | Balance |
|---|---|---|---|---|---|
| June 13 | | J1 | | 8,200 | 8,200 |

**Common Stock**

| Date | Explanation | Ref. | Debit | Credit | Balance |
|---|---|---|---|---|---|
| June 6 | | J1 | | 22,000 | 22,000 |

**5. (LO 4)** From the following ledger accounts, prepare a trial balance for Bundy Company at December 31, 2022. List the accounts in the order shown in the text. All account balances are normal.

*Prepare a trial balance.*

| | | | |
|---|---|---|---|
| Accounts Receivable | $10,000 | Salaries and Wages Expense | $ 2,300 |
| Supplies | 4,100 | Rent Expense | 1,200 |
| Accounts Payable | 3,500 | Common Stock | 10,200 |
| Dividends | 1,100 | Cash | 6,000 |
| Service Revenue | 11,000 | | |

**Solution**

5.

**Bundy Company**
**Trial Balance**
**December 31, 2020**

| | Debit | Credit |
|---|---|---|
| Cash | $ 6,000 | |
| Accounts Receivable | 10,000 | |
| Supplies | 4,100 | |
| Accounts Payable | | S 3,500 |
| Common Stock | | 10,200 |
| Dividends | 1,100 | |
| Service Revenue | | 11,000 |
| Salaries and Wages Expense | 2,300 | |
| Rent Expense | 1,200 | |
| | **$24,700** | **$24,700** |

# Practice Exercises

**1. (LO 1)** The following is information related to Conan Real Estate Agency.

*Analyze transactions and determine their effect on accounts.*

Oct. 1 Arnold Conan begins business as a real estate agent with a cash investment of $18,000 in exchange for common stock.
    2 Hires an administrative assistant.
    3 Purchases office equipment for $1,700, on account.
    6 Sells a house and lot for B. Clinton; bills B. Clinton S4,200 for realty services performed.
    27 Pays $900 on the balance related to the transaction of October 3.
    30 Pays the administrative assistant $2,800 in salary for October.

**Instructions**

Journalize the transactions. (You may omit explanations.)

**Solution**

1.

| | | GENERAL JOURNAL | | | J1 |
|---|---|---|---|---|---|
| Date | | Account Titles and Explanation | Ref. | Debit | Credit |
| Oct. | 1 | Cash | | 18,000 | |
| | | Common Stock | | | 18,000 |
| | 2 | No entry required | | | |
| | 3 | Equipment | | 1,700 | |
| | | Accounts Payable | | | 1,700 |
| | 6 | Accounts Receivable | | 4,200 | |
| | | Service Revenue | | | 4,200 |
| | 27 | Accounts Payable | | 900 | |
| | | Cash | | | 900 |
| | 30 | Salaries and Wages Expense | | 2,800 | |
| | | Cash | | | 2,800 |

*Journalize transactions from account data and prepare a trial balance.*

**2. (LO 2, 4)** The following T-accounts summarize the ledger of Garfunkle Landscaping Company at the end of the first month of operations.

| Cash | | | No. 101 |
|---|---|---|---|
| 4/1 | 18,000 | 4/15 | 700 |
| 4/12 | 800 | 4/25 | 1,400 |
| 4/29 | 700 | | |
| 4/30 | 1,200 | | |

| Unearned Service Revenue | | No. 209 |
|---|---|---|
| | 4/30 | 1,200 |

| Accounts Receivable | | | No. 112 |
|---|---|---|---|
| 4/7 | 3,800 | 4/29 | 700 |

| Common Stock | | No. 311 |
|---|---|---|
| | 4/1 | 18,000 |

| Supplies | | No. 126 |
|---|---|---|
| 4/4 | 1,900 | |

| Service Revenue | | No. 400 |
|---|---|---|
| | 4/7 | 3,800 |
| | 4/12 | 800 |

| Accounts Payable | | | No. 201 |
|---|---|---|---|
| 4/25 | 1,400 | 4/4 | 1,900 |

| Salaries and Wages Expense | | No. 726 |
|---|---|---|
| 4/15 | 700 | |

**Instructions**

a. Prepare the complete general journal (including explanations) from which the postings to Cash were made.

b. Prepare a trial balance at April 30, 2022.

**Solution**

**2. a.**

**GENERAL JOURNAL**

| Date | Account Titles and Explanation | Ref. | Debit | Credit |
|---|---|---|---|---|
| Apr. 1 | Cash | | 18,000 | |
| |     Common Stock | | | 18,000 |
| |     (Issued common stock for cash) | | | |
| 12 | Cash | | 800 | |
| |     Service Revenue | | | 800 |
| |     (Received cash for services performed) | | | |
| 15 | Salaries and Wages Expense | | 700 | |
| |     Cash | | | 700 |
| |     (Paid salaries to date) | | | |
| 25 | Accounts Payable | | 1,400 | |
| |     Cash | | | 1,400 |
| |     (Paid creditors on account) | | | |
| 29 | Cash | | 700 | |
| |     Accounts Receivable | | | 700 |
| |     (Received cash in payment of account) | | | |
| 30 | Cash | | 1,200 | |
| |     Unearned Service Revenue | | | 1,200 |
| |     (Received cash for future services) | | | |

**b.**

**Garfunkle Landscaping Company**
**Trial Balance**
**April 30, 2022**

| | Debit | Credit |
|---|---|---|
| Cash | $18,600 | |
| Accounts Receivable | 3,100 | |
| Supplies | 1,900 | |
| Accounts Payable | | $ 500 |
| Unearned Service Revenue | | 1,200 |
| Common Stock | | 18,000 |
| Service Revenue | | 4,600 |
| Salaries and Wages Expense | 700 | |
| | $24,300 | $24,300 |

# Practice Problem

**(LO 1, 2, 3, 4)** Bob Sample and other student investors opened Campus Laundromat Inc on September 1, 2022. During the first month of operations, the following transactions occurred.

*Journalize transactions, post, and prepare a trial balance.*

| Sept. | 1 | Stockholders invested $20,000 cash in the business in exchange for common stock. |
|---|---|---|
| | 2 | The company paid $1,000 cash for store rent for September. |
| | 3 | Purchased washers and dryers for $25,000, paying $10,000 in cash and signing a $15,000, 6-month, 12% note payable. |
| | 4 | Paid $1,200 for a one-year accident insurance policy. |
| | 10 | Received a $200 bill from the *Daily News* for advertising the opening of the laundromat. |
| | 20 | Declared and paid a $700 cash dividend to stockholders. |
| | 30 | The company determined that cash receipts for laundry services for the month were $6,200. |

The chart of accounts for the company is the same as that for Pioneer Advertising Inc. (Illustration 2.19), plus No. 610 Advertising Expense.

## Instructions

a. Journalize the September transactions. (Use J1 for the journal page number.)

b. Open ledger accounts and post the September transactions.

c. Prepare a trial balance at September 30, 2022.

## Solution

a.

**GENERAL JOURNAL**                                                          J1

| Date | | Account Titles and Explanation | Ref. | Debit | Credit |
|---|---|---|---|---|---|
| 2022 | | | | | |
| Sept. | 1 | Cash | 101 | 20,000 | |
| | | Common Stock | 311 | | 20,000 |
| | | (Issued common stock for cash) | | | |
| | 2 | Rent Expense | 729 | 1,000 | |
| | | Cash | 101 | | 1,000 |
| | | (Paid September rent) | | | |
| | 3 | Equipment | 157 | 25,000 | |
| | | Cash | 101 | | 10,000 |
| | | Notes Payable | 200 | | 15,000 |
| | | (Purchased laundry equipment for cash and 6-month, 12% note payable) | | | |
| | 4 | Prepaid Insurance | 130 | 1,200 | |
| | | Cash | 101 | | 1,200 |
| | | (Paid one-year insurance policy) | | | |
| | 10 | Advertising Expense | 610 | 200 | |
| | | Accounts Payable | 201 | | 200 |
| | | (Received bill from *Daily News* for advertising) | | | |
| | 20 | Dividends | 332 | 700 | |
| | | Cash | 101 | | 700 |
| | | (Declared and paid a cash dividend) | | | |
| | 30 | Cash | 101 | 6,200 | |
| | | Service Revenue | 400 | | 6,200 |
| | | (Received cash for services performed) | | | |

b.

**GENERAL LEDGER**

#### Cash — No. 101

| Date | Explanation | Ref. | Debit | Credit | Balance |
|------|-------------|------|-------|--------|---------|
| 2022 | | | | | |
| Sept. 1 | | J1 | 20,000 | | 20,000 |
| 2 | | J1 | | 1,000 | 19,000 |
| 3 | | J1 | | 10,000 | 9,000 |
| 4 | | J1 | | 1,200 | 7,800 |
| 20 | | J1 | | 700 | 7,100 |
| 30 | | J1 | 6,200 | | 13,300 |

#### Prepaid Insurance — No. 130

| Date | Explanation | Ref. | Debit | Credit | Balance |
|------|-------------|------|-------|--------|---------|
| 2022 | | | | | |
| Sept. 4 | | J1 | 1,200 | | 1,200 |

#### Equipment — No. 157

| Date | Explanation | Ref. | Debit | Credit | Balance |
|------|-------------|------|-------|--------|---------|
| 2022 | | | | | |
| Sept. 3 | | J1 | 25,000 | | 25,000 |

#### Notes Payable — No. 200

| Date | Explanation | Ref. | Debit | Credit | Balance |
|------|-------------|------|-------|--------|---------|
| 2022 | | | | | |
| Sept. 3 | | J1 | | 15,000 | 15,000 |

#### Accounts Payable — No. 201

| Date | Explanation | Ref. | Debit | Credit | Balance |
|------|-------------|------|-------|--------|---------|
| 2022 | | | | | |
| Sept. 10 | | J1 | | 200 | 200 |

#### Common Stock — No. 311

| Date | Explanation | Ref. | Debit | Credit | Balance |
|------|-------------|------|-------|--------|---------|
| 2022 | | | | | |
| Sept. 1 | | J1 | | 20,000 | 20,000 |

#### Dividends — No. 332

| Date | Explanation | Ref. | Debit | Credit | Balance |
|------|-------------|------|-------|--------|---------|
| 2022 | | | | | |
| Sept. 20 | | J1 | 700 | | 700 |

#### Service Revenue — No. 400

| Date | Explanation | Ref. | Debit | Credit | Balance |
|------|-------------|------|-------|--------|---------|
| 2022 | | | | | |
| Sept. 30 | | J1 | | 6,200 | 6,200 |

#### Advertising Expense — No. 610

| Date | Explanation | Ref. | Debit | Credit | Balance |
|------|-------------|------|-------|--------|---------|
| 2022 | | | | | |
| Sept. 10 | | J1 | 200 | | 200 |

#### Rent Expense — No. 729

| Date | Explanation | Ref. | Debit | Credit | Balance |
|------|-------------|------|-------|--------|---------|
| 2022 | | | | | |
| Sept. 2 | | J1 | 1,000 | | 1,000 |

c.

**Campus Laundromat Inc.**
**Trial Balance**
**September 30, 2022**

| | Debit | Credit |
|---|-------|--------|
| Cash | $13,300 | |
| Prepaid Insurance | 1,200 | |
| Equipment | 25,000 | |
| Notes Payable | | $15,000 |
| Accounts Payable | | 200 |
| Common Stock | | 20,000 |
| Dividends | 700 | |
| Service Revenue | | 6,200 |
| Advertising Expense | 200 | |
| Rent Expense | 1,000 | |
| | $41,400 | $41,400 |

Brief Exercises, DO IT! Exercises, Exercises, Problems, Data Analytics Activities, and many additional resources are available for practice in WileyPLUS.

## Questions

1. Describe the parts of a T-account.

2. "The terms debit and credit mean increase and decrease, respectively." Explain why this statement is true or false.

3. Tom Dingel, a fellow student, contends that the double-entry system means each transaction must be recorded twice. Is Tom correct? Explain.

4. Olga Conrad, a beginning accounting student, believes debit balances are favorable and credit balances are unfavorable. Is Olga correct? Discuss.

5. State the rules of debit and credit as applied to (a) asset accounts, (b) liability accounts, and (c) the stockholders' equity accounts (revenue, expenses, dividends, common stock, and retained earnings).

6. What is the normal balance for each of the following accounts? (a) Accounts Receivable. (b) Cash. (c) Dividends. (d) Accounts Payable. (e) Service Revenue. (f) Salaries and Wages Expense. (g) Common Stock.

7. Indicate whether each of the following accounts is an asset, a liability, or a stockholders' equity account and whether it has a normal debit or credit balance: (a) Accounts Receivable, (b) Accounts Payable, (c) Equipment, (d) Dividends, and (e) Supplies.

8. For the following transactions, indicate the account debited and the account credited.

   **a.** Supplies are purchased on account.

   **b.** Cash is received on signing a note payable.

   **c.** Employees are paid salaries in cash.

9. Indicate whether the following accounts generally will have (a) debit entries only, (b) credit entries only, or (c) both debit and credit entries.

   (1) Cash.

   (2) Accounts Receivable.

   (3) Dividends.

   (4) Accounts Payable.

   (5) Salaries and Wages Expense.

   (6) Service Revenue.

10. What are the basic steps in the recording process?

11. What are the advantages of using a journal in the recording process?

12. **a.** When entering a transaction in the journal, should the debit or credit be written first?

   **b.** Which should be indented, the debit or credit?

13. Describe a compound entry, and provide an example.

14. **a.** Should business transaction debits and credits be recorded directly in the ledger accounts?

   **b.** What are the advantages of first recording transactions in the journal and then posting to the ledger?

15. The account number is entered as the last step in posting the amounts from the journal to the ledger. What is the advantage of this step?

16. Journalize the following business transactions.

   **a.** Mark Stein invests $9,000 cash in the business in exchange for shares of common stock.

   **b.** Insurance of $800 is paid for the year.

   **c.** Supplies of $2,000 are purchased on account.

   **d.** Cash of $7,800 is received for services performed.

17. **a.** What is a ledger?

   **b.** What is a chart of accounts and why is it important?

18. What is a trial balance and what are its purposes?

19. Juan Kirby is confused about how accounting information flows through the accounting system. He believes the flow of information is as follows.

   **a.** Debits and credits are posted to the ledger.

   **b.** A business transaction occurs.

   **c.** Information is entered in the journal.

   **d.** Financial statements are prepared.

   **e.** The trial balance is prepared.

Is Juan correct? If not, indicate to Juan the proper flow of the information.

20. Two students are discussing the use of a trial balance. They wonder whether the following errors, each considered separately, would prevent the trial balance from balancing. What would you tell them?

   **a.** The bookkeeper debited Cash for $600 and credited Salaries and Wages Expense for $600 for payment of wages.

   **b.** Cash collected on account was debited to Cash for $900 and Service Revenue was credited for $90.

21. What are the normal balances for **Apple**'s Cash, Accounts Payable, and Interest Expense accounts?

## Brief Exercises

**BE2.1 (LO 1), C** For each of the following accounts indicate the effects of (a) a debit and (b) a credit on the accounts and (c) the normal balance of the account.

*Indicate debit and credit effects and normal balance.*

1. Accounts Payable.
2. Advertising Expense.
3. Service Revenue.
4. Accounts Receivable.
5. Common Stock.
6. Dividends.

**BE2.2 (LO 1), C** Transactions for the Sheldon Cooper Company, which provides welding services, for the month of June are presented as follows. Identify the accounts to be debited and credited for each transaction.

*Identify accounts to be debited and credited.*

June 1 Sheldon Cooper invests $4,000 cash in exchange for shares of common stock in a small welding business.
2 Purchases equipment on account for $1,200.
3 Pays $800 cash to landlord for June rent.
12 Bills P. Leonard $300 after completing welding work done on account.

*Journalize transactions.*

**BE2.3 (LO 2), AP** Transactions for the Sheldon Cooper Company, which provides welding services, for the month of June are presented as follows. Journalize the transactions. (You may omit explanations.)

June 1 Sheldon Cooper invests $4,000 cash in exchange for shares of common stock in a small welding business.
2 Purchases equipment on account for $1,200.
3 Pays $800 cash to landlord for June rent.
12 Bills P. Leonard $300 after completing welding work done on account.

*Identify and explain steps in recording process.*

**BE2.4 (LO 2), C** Writing Evan Saunders, a fellow student, is unclear about the basic steps in the recording process. Identify and briefly explain the steps in the order in which they occur.

*Indicate basic and debit-credit analysis.*

**BE2.5 (LO 2), C** Bombeck Inc. has the following transactions during August of the current year. Indicate (a) the effect on the accounting equation and (b) the debit-credit analysis (as illustrated in the chapter).

Aug. 1 Opens an office as a financial advisor, investing $5,000 in cash in exchange for common stock.
4 Pays insurance in advance for 6 months, $1,800 cash.
16 Receives $1,900 from clients for services performed.
27 Pays secretary $1,000 salary.

*Journalize transactions.*

**BE2.6 (LO 2), AP** Bombeck Inc. has the following transactions during August of the current year. Journalize the transactions. (You may omit explanations.)

Aug. 1 Opens an office as a financial advisor, investing $5,000 in cash in exchange for common stock.
4 Pays insurance in advance for 6 months, $1,800 cash.
16 Receives $1,900 from clients for services performed.
27 Pays secretary $1,000 salary.

*Post journal entries to T-accounts.*

**BE2.7 (LO 3), AP** The following selected transactions for Nikolai Company are presented in journal form. Post the transactions to T-accounts. Make one T-account for each item and determine each account's ending balance.

|  |  |  |  |  | J1 |
|---|---|---|---|---|---|
| **Date** | **Account Titles and Explanation** | **Ref.** | **Debit** | **Credit** |
| May 5 | Accounts Receivable |  | 5,000 |  |
|  | Service Revenue |  |  | 5,000 |
|  | (Billed for services performed) |  |  |  |
| 12 | Cash |  | 2,100 |  |
|  | Accounts Receivable |  |  | 2,100 |
|  | (Received cash in payment of account) |  |  |  |
| 15 | Cash |  | 3,200 |  |
|  | Service Revenue |  |  | 3,200 |
|  | (Received cash for services performed) |  |  |  |

*Post journal entries to standard form of account.*

**BE2.8 (LO 3), AP** Selected journal entries for Nikolai Company are presented as follows. Post the transactions using the standard form of account.

|  |  |  |  |  | J1 |
|---|---|---|---|---|---|
| **Date** | **Account Titles and Explanation** | **Ref.** | **Debit** | **Credit** |
| May 5 | Accounts Receivable |  | 5,000 |  |
|  | Service Revenue |  |  | 5,000 |
|  | (Billed for services performed) |  |  |  |
| 12 | Cash |  | 2,100 |  |
|  | Accounts Receivable |  |  | 2,100 |
|  | (Received cash in payment of account) |  |  |  |
| 15 | Cash |  | 3,200 |  |
|  | Service Revenue |  |  | 3,200 |
|  | (Received cash for services performed) |  |  |  |

**BE2.9 (LO 4), AP** From the following ledger balances, prepare a trial balance for the Favre Company at June 30, 2022. List the accounts in the order as indicated in the chapter. All account balances are normal. *Prepare a trial balance.*

Accounts Payable $7,000, Cash $5,200, Common Stock $20,000, Dividends $800, Equipment $17,000, Service Revenue $6,000, Accounts Receivable $3,000, Salaries and Wages Expense $6,000, and Rent Expense $1,000.

**BE2.10 (LO 4), AN** An inexperienced bookkeeper prepared the following trial balance. Prepare a correct trial balance, assuming all account balances are normal. *Prepare a correct trial balance.*

### Erika Company
### Trial Balance
### December 31, 2022

|  | Debit | Credit |
|---|---|---|
| Cash | $16,800 | |
| Prepaid Insurance | | $ 3,500 |
| Accounts Payable | | 3,000 |
| Unearned Service Revenue | 4,200 | |
| Common Stock | | 13,000 |
| Dividends | | 4,500 |
| Service Revenue | | 25,600 |
| Salaries and Wages Expense | 18,600 | |
| Rent Expense | | 2,400 |
| | $39,600 | $52,000 |

## DO IT! Exercises

**DO IT! 2.1 (LO 1), C** James Mayaguez has just rented space in a strip mall. In this space, he will open a photography studio to be called Picture This! A friend has advised James to set up a double-entry set of accounting records in which to record all of his business transactions. *Identify normal balances.*

Identify the balance sheet accounts that James will likely need to record the transactions needed to open his business (a corporation). Indicate whether the normal balance of each account is a debit or credit.

**DO IT! 2.2 (LO 2), AP** James Mayaguez engaged in the following activities in establishing his photography studio, Picture This! *Record business activities.*

1. Opened a bank account in the name of Picture This! and deposited $8,000 of his own money into this account in exchange for common stock.

2. Purchased photography supplies at a total cost of $1,600. The business paid $300 in cash and the balance is on account.

3. Obtained estimates on the cost of photography equipment from three different manufacturers.

Prepare the journal entries to record the transactions. You may omit explanations.

**DO IT! 2.3 (LO 3), AP** James Mayaguez recorded the following transactions during the month of April. *Post transaction.*

| April 3 | Cash | 3,900 | |
|---|---|---|---|
| | Service Revenue | | 3,900 |
| 16 | Rent Expense | 600 | |
| | Cash | | 600 |
| 20 | Salaries and Wages Expense | 500 | |
| | Cash | | 500 |

Post these entries to the Cash T-account of the general ledger to determine the ending balance in cash. The beginning balance in cash on April 1 was $1,600.

**DO IT! 2.4 (LO 4), AP** The following accounts are taken from the ledger of Chillin' Company at December 31, 2022. *Prepare a trial balance.*

| 200 | Notes Payable | $20,000 | 101 | Cash | $6,000 |
|---|---|---|---|---|---|
| 311 | Common Stock | 25,000 | 120 | Supplies | 5,000 |
| 157 | Equipment | 76,000 | 522 | Rent Expense | 2,000 |
| 332 | Dividends | 8,000 | 220 | Salaries and Wages Payable | 3,000 |
| 726 | Salaries and Wages Expense | 38,000 | 201 | Accounts Payable | 9,000 |
| 400 | Service Revenue | 86,000 | 112 | Accounts Receivable | 8,000 |

Prepare a trial balance in good form.

## Exercises

*Analyze statements about accounting and the recording process.*

**E2.1 (LO 1), K** Faith Dillon has prepared the following list of statements about accounts.

1. An account is an accounting record of either a specific asset or a specific liability.

2. An account shows only increases, not decreases, in the item it relates to.

3. Some items, such as cash and accounts receivable, are combined into one account.

4. An account has a left, or credit side, and a right, or debit side.

5. A simple form of an account consisting of just the account title, the left side, and the right side is called a T-account.

**Instructions**

Identify each statement as true or false. If false, indicate how to correct the statement.

*Identify debits, credits, and normal balances.*

**E2.2 (LO 1), C** Selected transactions for L. Takemoto, an interior decorating firm, in its first month of business, are as follows.

| Jan. | 2  | Stockholders invested $15,000 cash in the business in exchange for common stock. |
|------|----|-----------------------------------------------------------------------------------|
|      | 3  | Purchased used car for $8,200 cash for use in the business. |
|      | 9  | Purchased supplies on account for $500. |
|      | 11 | Billed customers $1,800 for services performed. |
|      | 16 | Paid $200 cash for advertising. |
|      | 20 | Received $780 cash from customers billed on January 11. |
|      | 23 | Paid creditor $300 cash on balance owed. |
|      | 28 | Declared and paid a $500 cash dividend. |

**Instructions**

For each transaction indicate the following.

a. The basic type of account debited and credited (asset, liability, stockholders' equity).

b. The specific account debited and credited (Cash, Rent Expense, Service Revenue, etc.).

c. Whether the specific account is increased or decreased.

d. The normal balance of the specific account.

Use the following format, in which the January 2 transaction is given as an example.

| | Account Debited | | | | Account Credited | | | |
|---|---|---|---|---|---|---|---|---|
| Date | (a) Basic Type | (b) Specific Account | (c) Effect | (d) Normal Balance | (a) Basic Type | (b) Specific Account | (c) Effect | (d) Normal Balance |
| Jan. 2 | Asset | Cash | Increase | Debit | Stockholders' Equity | Common Stock | Increase | Credit |

*Journalize transactions.*

**E2.3 (LO 2), AP** Data for L. Takemoto, interior decorating, are presented as follows.

| Jan. | 2  | Stockholders invested $15,000 cash in the business in exchange for common stock. |
|------|----|-----------------------------------------------------------------------------------|
|      | 3  | Purchased used car for $8,200 cash for use in the business. |
|      | 9  | Purchased supplies on account for $500. |
|      | 11 | Billed customers $1,800 for services performed. |
|      | 16 | Paid $200 cash for advertising. |
|      | 20 | Received $780 cash from customers billed on January 11. |
|      | 23 | Paid creditor $300 cash on balance owed. |
|      | 28 | Declared and paid a $500 cash dividend. |

**Instructions**

Journalize the transactions using journal page J1. (You may omit explanations.)

**E2.4 (LO 1), C** The following information is related to Lexington Real Estate Agency.

*Analyze transactions and determine their effect on accounts.*

Oct. 1 Diane Lexington begins business as a real estate agent with a cash investment of $20,000 in exchange for common stock.
2 Hires an administrative assistant.
3 Purchases office furniture for $2,300, on account.
6 Sells a house and lot for N. Fennig; bills N. Fennig $3,600 for realty services performed.
27 Pays $850 on the balance related to the transaction of October 3.
30 Pays the administrative assistant $2,500 in salary for October.

**Instructions**

Prepare the debit-credit analysis for each transaction as illustrated in the chapter.

**E2.5 (LO 2), AP** Transaction data for Lexington Real Estate Agency are presented as follows.

*Journalize transactions.*

Oct. 1 Diane Lexington begins business as a real estate agent with a cash investment of $20,000 in exchange for common stock.
2 Hires an administrative assistant.
3 Purchases office furniture for $2,300, on account.
6 Sells a house and lot for N. Fennig; bills N. Fennig $3,600 for realty services performed.
27 Pays $850 on the balance related to the transaction of October 3.
30 Pays the administrative assistant $2,500 in salary for October.

**Instructions**

Journalize the transactions. (You may omit explanations.)

**E2.6 (LO 1, 2), AP** Fredo Industries had the following transactions.

*Analyze transactions and journalize.*

1. Borrowed $5,000 from the bank by signing a note.
2. Paid $2,500 cash for a computer.
3. Purchased $450 of supplies on account.

**Instructions**

a. Indicate what accounts are increased and decreased by each transaction.
b. Journalize each transaction. (Omit explanations.)

**E2.7 (LO 1, 2), AP** Leppard Enterprises had the following selected transactions.

*Analyze transactions and journalize.*

1. Kim Leppard invested $5,000 cash in the business in exchange for common stock.
2. Paid office rent of $950.
3. Performed consulting services and billed a client $4,700.
4. Declared and paid a $600 cash dividend.

**Instructions**

a. Indicate the effect each transaction has on the accounting equation (Assets = Liabilities + Stockholders' Equity), using plus and minus signs.
b. Journalize each transaction. (Omit explanations.)

**E2.8 (LO 2), AP** Selected transactions for Sophie's Dog Care are as follows during the month of March.

*Journalize a series of transactions.*

March 1 Paid monthly rent of $1,200.
3 Performed services for $140 on account.
5 Performed services for $75 cash.
8 Purchased equipment for $600. The company paid $80 cash and the balance was on account.
12 Received cash from customers billed on March 3.
14 Paid salaries and wages to employees of $525.
22 Paid utilities of $72.
24 Borrowed $1,500 from Grafton State Bank by signing a note.
27 Paid $220 to repair service for plumbing repairs.
28 Paid balance amount owed from equipment purchase on March 8.
30 Paid $1,800 for 6 months of insurance.

**Instructions**

Journalize the transactions. Do not provide explanations.

*Record journal entries.*

**E2.9 (LO 2), AP** On April 1, Adventures Travel Agency, Inc. began operations. The following transactions were completed during the month.

1. Stockholders invested $24,000 in the business in exchange for common stock.
2. Obtained a bank loan for $7,000 by issuing a note payable.
3. Paid $11,000 cash to buy equipment.
4. Paid $1,200 cash for April office rent.
5. Paid $1,450 for supplies.
6. Purchased $600 of advertising in the *Daily Herald,* on account.
7. Performed services for $18,000: cash of $2,000 was received from customers, and the balance of $16,000 was billed to customers on account.
8. Paid $400 cash dividend to stockholders.
9. Paid the utility bill for the month, $2,000.
10. Paid *Daily Herald* the amount due in transaction (6).
11. Paid $40 of interest on the bank loan obtained in transaction (2).
12. Paid employees' salaries and wages, $6,400.
13. Received $12,000 cash from customers billed in transaction (7).

**Instructions**

Journalize the transactions. Do not provide explanations.

*Analyze statements about the ledger.*

**E2.10 (LO 3), C** Meghan Selzer has prepared the following list of statements about the general ledger.

1. The general ledger contains all the asset and liability accounts, but no stockholders' equity accounts.
2. The general ledger is sometimes referred to as simply the ledger.
3. The accounts in the general ledger are arranged in alphabetical order.
4. Each account in the general ledger is numbered for easier identification.
5. The general ledger is a book of original entry.

**Instructions**

Identify each statement as true or false. If false, indicate how to correct the statement.

*Post journal entries and prepare a trial balance.*

**E2.11 (LO 3, 4), AP** Selected transactions from the journal of Kati Tillman, investment broker, are presented as follows.

| Date | | Account Titles and Explanation | Ref. | Debit | Credit |
|---|---|---|---|---|---|
| Aug. | 1 | Cash | | 6,000 | |
| | | Common Stock | | | 6,000 |
| | | (Issued common stock for cash) | | | |
| | 10 | Cash | | 2,700 | |
| | | Service Revenue | | | 2,700 |
| | | (Received cash for services performed) | | | |
| | 12 | Equipment | | 5,000 | |
| | | Cash | | | 800 |
| | | Notes Payable | | | 4,200 |
| | | (Purchased office equipment for cash and notes payable) | | | |
| | 25 | Account Receivable | | 1,600 | |
| | | Service Revenue | | | 1,600 |
| | | (Billed clients for services performed) | | | |
| | 31 | Cash | | 880 | |
| | | Accounts Receivable | | | 880 |
| | | (Receipt of cash on account) | | | |

**Instructions**

a. Post the transactions to T-accounts.

b. Prepare a trial balance at August 31, 2022.

**E2.12 (LO 2, 4), AP** The following T-accounts summarize the ledger of Santana Landscaping Company at the end of its first month of operations.

*Journalize transactions from account data and prepare a trial balance.*

| Cash | | | No. 101 |
|---|---|---|---|
| 4/1 | 10,000 | 4/15 | 720 |
| 4/12 | 900 | 4/25 | 1,500 |
| 4/29 | 400 | | |
| 4/30 | 1,000 | | |

| Accounts Receivable | | | No. 112 |
|---|---|---|---|
| 4/7 | 3,200 | 4/29 | 400 |

| Supplies | | | No. 126 |
|---|---|---|---|
| 4/4 | 1,800 | | |

| Accounts Payable | | | No. 201 |
|---|---|---|---|
| 4/25 | 1,500 | 4/4 | 1,800 |

| Unearned Service Revenue | | | No. 209 |
|---|---|---|---|
| | | 4/30 | 1,000 |

| Common Stock | | | No. 311 |
|---|---|---|---|
| | | 4/1 | 10,000 |

| Service Revenue | | | No. 400 |
|---|---|---|---|
| | | 4/7 | 3,200 |
| | | 4/12 | 900 |

| Salaries and Wages Expense | | | No. 726 |
|---|---|---|---|
| 4/15 | 720 | | |

**Instructions**

a. Prepare the complete general journal (including explanations) from which the postings to Cash were made.

b. Prepare a trial balance at April 30, 2022.

**E2.13 (LO 2, 4), AP** The ledger for Higgs Co. is as follows.

*Journalize transactions from account data and prepare a trial balance.*

| Cash | | | No. 101 |
|---|---|---|---|
| 10/1 | 5,000 | 10/4 | 400 |
| 10/10 | 730 | 10/12 | 1,500 |
| 10/10 | 3,000 | 10/15 | 280 |
| 10/20 | 500 | 10/30 | 300 |
| 10/25 | 2,000 | 10/31 | 500 |

| Accounts Receivable | | | No. 112 |
|---|---|---|---|
| 10/6 | 800 | 10/20 | 500 |
| 10/20 | 910 | | |

| Supplies | | | No. 126 |
|---|---|---|---|
| 10/4 | 400 | | |

| Equipment | | | No. 157 |
|---|---|---|---|
| 10/3 | 2,000 | | |

| Notes Payable | | | No. 200 |
|---|---|---|---|
| | | 10/10 | 3,000 |

| Accounts Payable | | | No. 201 |
|---|---|---|---|
| 10/12 | 1,500 | 10/3 | 2,000 |

| Common Stock | | | No. 311 |
|---|---|---|---|
| | | 10/1 | 5,000 |
| | | 10/25 | 2,000 |

| Dividends | | | No. 332 |
|---|---|---|---|
| 10/30 | 300 | | |

| Service Revenue | | | No. 400 |
|---|---|---|---|
| | | 10/6 | 800 |
| | | 10/10 | 730 |
| | | 10/20 | 910 |

| Salaries and Wages Expense | | | No. 726 |
|---|---|---|---|
| 10/31 | 500 | | |

| Rent Expense | | | No. 729 |
|---|---|---|---|
| 10/15 | 280 | | |

**Instructions**

a. Reproduce the journal entries for the transactions that occurred on October 1, 10, and 20, and provide explanations for each.

b. Determine the October 31 balance for each of the accounts above, and prepare a trial balance at October 31, 2022.

**E2.14 (LO 2, 3), AP** Selected transactions for Alvarado Company during its first month in business are as follows.

*Prepare journal entries and post using standard account form.*

| Sept. | 1 | Stockholders invested $10,000 cash in the business in exchange for common stock. |
|---|---|---|
| | 5 | Purchased equipment for $12,000 paying $4,000 in cash and the balance on account. |
| | 25 | Paid $2,400 cash on balance owed for equipment. |
| | 30 | Declared and paid a $500 cash dividend. |

Alvarado's chart of accounts shows No. 101 Cash, No. 157 Equipment, No. 201 Accounts Payable, No. 311 Common Stock, and No. 332 Dividends.

**Instructions**

a. Journalize the transactions on page J1 of the journal. (Omit explanations.)

b. Post the transactions using the standard account form.

*Analyze errors and their effects on trial balance.*

**E2.15 (LO 4), AN** The bookkeeper for Brooks Equipment Repair made a number of errors in journalizing and posting, as the following describes.

1. A credit posting of $450 to Accounts Receivable was omitted.

2. A debit posting of $750 for Prepaid Insurance was debited to Insurance Expense.

3. A collection from a customer of $100 in payment of its account owed was journalized and posted as a debit to Cash $100 and a credit to Service Revenue $100.

4. A credit posting of $300 to Property Taxes Payable was made twice.

5. A cash purchase of supplies for $250 was journalized and posted as a debit to Supplies $25 and a credit to Cash $25.

6. A debit of $525 to Advertising Expense was posted as $552.

**Instructions**

For each error:

a. Indicate whether the trial balance will balance.

b. If the trial balance will not balance, indicate the amount of the difference.

c. Indicate the trial balance column that will have the larger total.

Consider each error separately. Use the following form, in which error (1) is given as an example.

| | (a) | (b) | (c) |
|---|---|---|---|
| **Error** | **In Balance** | **Difference** | **Larger Column** |
| (1) | No | $450 | debit |

*Prepare a trial balance.*

**E2.16 (LO 4), AP** The accounts in the ledger of Time Is Money Delivery Service contain the following balances on July 31, 2022.

| | | | |
|---|---|---|---|
| Accounts Receivable | $10,642 | Prepaid Insurance | $ 1,968 |
| Accounts Payable | 8,396 | Maintenance and Repairs Expense | 961 |
| Cash | ? | Service Revenue | 10,610 |
| Equipment | 49,360 | Dividends | 700 |
| Gasoline Expense | 758 | Common Stock | 40,000 |
| Utilities Expense | 523 | Salaries and Wages Expense | 4,428 |
| Notes Payable | 26,450 | Salaries and Wages Payable | 815 |
| | | Retained Earnings | 4,636 |

**Instructions**

Prepare a trial balance with the accounts arranged as illustrated in the chapter and fill in the missing amount for Cash.

*Journalize transactions, post transactions to T-accounts, and prepare trial balance.*

**E2.17 (LO 2, 3, 4), AP** Beyers Corporation provides security services. Selected transactions for Beyers are as follows.

Oct. 
1    Issued common stock in exchange for $66,000 cash from investors.

2    Hired part-time security consultant. Salary will be $2,000 per month. First day of work will be October 15.

4    Paid one month of rent for building for $2,000.

7    Purchased equipment for $18,000, paying $4,000 cash and the balance on account.

8    Paid $500 for advertising.

10   Received bill for equipment repair cost of $390.

12   Provided security services for event for $3,200 on account.

16   Purchased supplies for $410 on account.

21   Paid balance due from October 7 purchase of equipment.

24   Received and paid utility bill for $148.

27   Received payment from customer for October 12 services performed.

31   Paid employee salaries and wages of $5,100.

## Instructions

a. Journalize the transactions. Do not provide explanations.

b. Post the transactions to T-accounts.

c. Prepare a trial balance at October 31, 2022. (*Hint:* Compute ending balances of T-accounts first.)

# Problems

**P2.1 (LO 2), AP** Grandview Park was started on April 1 by R. S. Francis and associates. The following selected events and transactions occurred during April.

*Journalize a series of transactions.*

| | |
|---|---|
| Apr. 1 | Stockholders invested $50,000 cash in the business in exchange for common stock. |
| 4 | Purchased land costing $34,000 for cash. |
| 8 | Incurred advertising expense of $1,800 on account. |
| 11 | Paid salaries to employees $1,500. |
| 12 | Hired park manager at a salary of $3,500 per month, effective May 1. |
| 13 | Paid $2,400 cash for a one-year insurance policy. |
| 17 | Declared and paid a $1,400 cash dividend. |
| 20 | Received $5,700 in cash for admission fees. |
| 25 | Sold 100 coupon books for $30 each. Each book contains 10 coupons that entitle the holder to one admission to the park. |
| 30 | Received $3,900 in cash admission fees. |
| 30 | Paid $840 on balance owed for advertising incurred on April 8. |

Grandview uses the following accounts: Cash, Prepaid Insurance, Land, Accounts Payable, Unearned Service Revenue, Common Stock, Dividends, Service Revenue, Advertising Expense, and Salaries and Wages Expense.

## Instructions

Journalize the April transactions.

**P2.2 (LO 2, 3, 4), AP** Julia Dumars is a licensed CPA. During the first month of operations of her business, Julia Dumars, Inc. the following events and transactions occurred.

*Journalize transactions, post, and prepare a trial balance.*

| | |
|---|---|
| May 1 | Stockholders invested $20,000 cash in exchange for common stock. |
| 2 | Hired a secretary-receptionist at a salary of $2,000 per month. |
| 3 | Purchased $1,500 of supplies on account from Vincent Supply Company. |
| 7 | Paid office rent of $900 cash for the month. |
| 11 | Completed a tax assignment and billed client $2,800 for services performed. |
| 12 | Received $3,500 advance on a management consulting engagement. |
| 17 | Received cash of $1,200 for services performed for Orville Co. |
| 31 | Paid secretary-receptionist $2,000 salary for the month. |
| 31 | Paid 40% of balance due Vincent Supply Company. |

Julia uses the following chart of accounts: No. 101 Cash, No. 112 Accounts Receivable, No. 126 Supplies, No. 201 Accounts Payable, No. 209 Unearned Service Revenue, No. 311 Common Stock, No. 400 Service Revenue, No. 726 Salaries and Wages Expense, and No. 729 Rent Expense.

## Instructions

a. Journalize the transactions.

b. Post to the ledger accounts.

c. Prepare a trial balance on May 31, 2022.

*c. Trial balance totals $28,400*

*Journalize and post transactions and prepare a trial balance.*

**P2.3 (LO 2, 3, 4), AP** Tom Zopf owns and manages a computer repair service, which had the following trial balance on December 31, 2021 (the end of its fiscal year).

**Tablette Repair Service, Inc.**
**Trial Balance**
**December 31, 2021**

|                        | Debit     | Credit    |
|------------------------|-----------|-----------|
| Cash                   | $ 8,000   |           |
| Accounts Receivable    | 15,000    |           |
| Supplies               | 11,000    |           |
| Prepaid Rent           | 3,000     |           |
| Equipment              | 21,000    |           |
| Accounts Payable       |           | $17,000   |
| Common Stock           |           | 30,000    |
| Retained Earnings      |           | 11,000    |
|                        | $58,000   | $58,000   |

Summarized transactions for January 2022 were as follows.

1. Advertising costs, paid in cash, $1,000.
2. Additional supplies acquired on account $3,600.
3. Miscellaneous expenses, paid in cash, $1,700.
4. Cash collected from customers in payment of accounts receivable $13,000.
5. Cash paid to creditors for accounts payable due $14,400.
6. Repair services performed during January: for cash $5,000; on account $9,000.
7. Wages for January, paid in cash, $3,000.
8. Dividends during January were $1,600.

**Instructions**

a. Open T-accounts for each of the accounts listed in the trial balance, and enter the opening balances for 2022.

b. Prepare journal entries to record each of the January transactions. (Omit explanations.)

c. Post the journal entries to the accounts in the ledger. (Add accounts as needed.)

*d. Trial balance totals $61,200*

d. Prepare a trial balance as of January 31, 2022.

*Prepare a correct trial balance.*

**P2.4 (LO 4), AN** The following trial balance of Dominic Company does not balance.

**Dominic Company**
**Trial Balance**
**May 31, 2022**

|                              | Debit     | Credit    |
|------------------------------|-----------|-----------|
| Cash                         | $ 3,850   |           |
| Accounts Receivable          |           | $ 2,750   |
| Prepaid Insurance            | 700       |           |
| Equipment                    | 12,000    |           |
| Accounts Payable             |           | 4,500     |
| Unearned Service Revenue     | 560       |           |
| Common Stock                 |           | 11,700    |
| Service Revenue              | 8,690     |           |
| Salaries and Wages Expense   | 4,200     |           |
| Advertising Expense          |           | 1,100     |
| Utilities Expense            | 800       |           |
|                              | $30,800   | $20,050   |

Your review of the ledger reveals that each account has a normal balance. You also discover the following errors.

1. The totals of the debit sides of Prepaid Insurance, Accounts Payable, and Utilities Expense were each understated $100.

2. Transposition errors were made in Accounts Receivable and Service Revenue. Based on postings made, the correct balances were $2,570 and $8,960, respectively.

3. A debit posting to Salaries and Wages Expense of $200 was omitted.

4. A $1,000 cash dividend was debited to Common Stock for $1,000 and credited to Cash for $1,000.

5. A $520 purchase of supplies on account was debited to Equipment for $520 and credited to Cash for $520.

6. A cash payment of $450 for advertising was debited to Advertising Expense for $45 and credited to Cash for $45.

7. A collection from a customer for $420 was debited to Cash for $420 and credited to Accounts Payable for $420.

### Instructions

Prepare a correct trial balance. Note that the chart of accounts includes the following: Dividends and Supplies. (*Hint:* It helps to prepare the correct journal entry for the transaction described and compare it to the mistake made.)

*Trial balance totals $26,720*

**P2.5 (LO 2, 3, 4), AP** The Palace Theater opened on April 1. All facilities were completed on March 31. At this time, the ledger showed No. 101 Cash $6,000, No. 140 Land $12,000, No. 145 Buildings (concession stand, projection room, ticket booth, and screen) $8,000, No. 157 Equipment $6,000, No. 201 Accounts Payable $2,000, No. 275 Mortgage Payable $10,000, and No. 311 Common Stock $20,000. During April, the following events and transactions occurred.

*Journalize transactions, post, and prepare a trial balance.*

Apr. 2   Paid film rental of $800 on first movie.
3   Ordered two additional films at $950 each.
9   Received $1,800 cash from admissions.
10   Made $2,000 payment on mortgage and $1,000 for accounts payable due.
11   Palace Theater contracted with Dever Company to operate the concession stand. Dever is to pay 18% of gross concession receipts (payable monthly) for the rental of the concession stand.
12   Paid advertising expenses $320.
20   Received one of the films ordered on April 3 and was billed $950. The film will be shown in April.
25   Received $5,200 cash from admissions.
29   Paid salaries $1,600.
30   Received statement from Dever showing gross concession receipts of $1,000 and the balance due to the Palace Theater of $180 ($1,000 × 18%) for April. Dever paid one-half of the balance due and will remit the remainder on May 5.
30   Prepaid $1,000 rental on special film to be run in May.

In addition to the accounts identified above, the chart of accounts shows No. 112 Accounts Receivable, No. 136 Prepaid Rent, No. 400 Service Revenue, No. 429 Rent Revenue, No. 610 Advertising Expense, No. 726 Salaries and Wages Expense, and No. 729 Rent Expense.

### Instructions

a. Enter the beginning balances in the ledger as of April 1. Insert a check mark (✓) in the reference column of the ledger for the beginning balance.

b. Journalize the April transactions.

c. Post the April journal entries to the ledger. Assume that all entries are posted from page 1 of the journal.

d. Prepare a trial balance on April 30, 2022.

*d. Trial balance totals $37,130*

---

## Continuing Case

### Cookie Creations

(*Note:* This is a continuation of the Cookie Creations case from Chapter 1.)

**CC2** After researching the different forms of business organization, Natalie Koebel decides to operate "Cookie Creations" as a corporation. She then starts the process of getting the business running.

*Go to WileyPLUS for complete case details and instructions.*

leungchopan/
Shutterstock.com

# Expand Your Critical Thinking

## Financial Reporting Problem: Apple Inc.

**CT2.1** The financial statements of **Apple Inc.** are presented in Appendix A. The complete annual report, including the notes to the financial statements, is available at the company's website.

Apple's financial statements contain the following selected accounts, stated in millions of dollars.

Accounts Payable     Cash and Cash Equivalents
Accounts Receivable     Research and Development Expense
Property, Plant, and Equipment  Inventories

### Instructions

**a.** Answer the following questions.

 1. What is the increase and decrease side for each account?

 2. What is the normal balance for each account?

**b.** Identify the probable other account in the transaction and the effect on that account when:

 1. Accounts Receivable is decreased.

 2. Accounts Payable is decreased.

 3. Inventories are increased.

**c.** Identify the other account(s) that ordinarily would be involved when:

 1. Research and Development Expense is increased.

 2. Property, Plant, and Equipment is increased.

## Comparative Analysis Problem: PepsiCo, Inc. vs. The Coca-Cola Company

**CT2.2** **PepsiCo**'s financial statements are presented in Appendix B. Financial statements of **The Coca-Cola Company** are presented in Appendix C. The complete annual reports of PepsiCo and Coca-Cola, including the notes to the financial statements, are available at each company's respective website.

### Instructions

**a.** Based on the information contained in the financial statements, determine the normal balance of the listed accounts for each company.

| PepsiCo | Coca-Cola |
|---|---|
| 1. Inventory | 1. Accounts Receivable |
| 2. Property, Plant, and Equipment | 2. Cash and Cash Equivalents |
| 3. Accounts Payable | 3. Cost of Goods Sold (expense) |
| 4. Interest Expense | 4. Sales (revenue) |

**b.** Identify the other account ordinarily involved when:

 1. Accounts Receivable is increased.

 2. Salaries and Wages Payable is decreased.

 3. Property, Plant, and Equipment is increased.

 4. Interest Expense is increased.

## Comparative Analysis Problem: Amazon.com, Inc. vs. Walmart Inc.

**CT2.3** **Amazon.com, Inc.**'s financial statements are presented in Appendix D. Financial statements of **Walmart Inc.** are presented in Appendix E. The complete annual reports of Amazon and Walmart, including the notes to the financial statements, are available at each company's respective website.

**Instructions**

a. Based on the information contained in the financial statements, determine the normal balance of the listed accounts for each company.

| Amazon | Walmart |
|---|---|
| 1. Interest Expense | 1. Product Revenues |
| 2. Cash and Cash Equivalents | 2. Inventories |
| 3. Accounts Payable | 3. Cost of Sales |

b. Identify the other account ordinarily involved when:

1. Accounts Receivable is increased.

2. Interest Expense is increased.

3. Salaries and Wages Payable is decreased.

4. Service Revenue is increased.

## Real-World Focus

**CT2.4** Much information about specific companies is available on the Internet. Such information includes basic descriptions of the company's location, activities, industry, financial health, and financial performance.

**Instructions**

Go to the **Yahoo! Finance** website, type in a company name (or use the index to find a company name), and then answer the following questions.

a. What is the company's industry?

b. What are the company's total sales?

c. What is the company's net income?

d. What are the names of four of the company's competitors?

e. Choose one of these competitors.

f. What is this competitor's name? What are its sales? What is its net income?

g. Which of these two companies is larger by size of sales? Which one reported higher net income?

**CT2.5** The January 27, 2011, edition of the *New York Times* contains an article by Richard Sandomir entitled "N.F.L. Finances, as Seen Through Packers' Records." The author of the article discusses the fact that the **Green Bay Packers** are the only NFL team that publicly publishes its annual report.

**Instructions**

Read the article and answer the following questions.

a. Why are the Green Bay Packers the only professional football team to publish and distribute an annual report?

b. Why is the football players' labor union particularly interested in the Packers' annual report?

c. In addition to the players' labor union, what other outside party might be interested in the annual report?

d. Even though the Packers' revenue increased, the company's operating profit fell significantly. How does the article explain this decline?

## Decision-Making Across the Organization

**CT2.6** Dyanna Craig operates Craig Riding Academy. The academy's primary sources of revenue are riding fees and lesson fees, which are paid on a cash basis. Dyanna also boards horses for owners, who are billed monthly for boarding fees. In a few cases, boarders pay in advance of expected use. For its revenue transactions, the academy maintains the following accounts: Cash, Accounts Receivable, and Service Revenue.

The academy owns 10 horses, a stable, a riding corral, riding equipment, and office equipment. These assets are accounted for in these accounts: Horses, Buildings, and Equipment.

The academy also maintains the following accounts: Supplies, Prepaid Insurance, Accounts Payable, Salaries and Wages Expense, Advertising Expense, Utilities Expense, and Maintenance and Repairs Expense.

Dyanna pays periodic cash dividends to stockholders. To record stockholders' equity in the business and dividends, three accounts are maintained: Common Stock, Retained Earnings, and Dividends.

During the first month of operations, an inexperienced bookkeeper was employed. Dyanna Craig asks you to review the following 8 entries of the 50 entries made during the month. In each case, the explanation for the entry is correct.

| | | | | |
|---|---|---|---|---|
| May | 1 | Cash | 18,000 | |
| | |   Common Stock | | 18,000 |
| | |     (Issued common stock for $18,000 cash) | | |
| | 5 | Cash | 250 | |
| | |   Service Revenue | | 250 |
| | |     (Received $250 cash for lessons provided) | | |
| | 7 | Cash | 300 | |
| | |   Service Revenue | | 300 |
| | |     (Received $300 for boarding of horses beginning June 1) | | |
| | 14 | Equipment | 80 | |
| | |   Cash | | 800 |
| | |     (Purchased desk and other office equipment for $800 cash) | | |
| | 15 | Salaries and Wages Expense | 400 | |
| | |   Cash | | 400 |
| | |     (Issued dividend checks to stockholders) | | |
| | 20 | Cash | 148 | |
| | |   Service Revenue | | 184 |
| | |     (Received $184 cash for riding fees) | | |
| | 30 | Maintenance and Repairs Expense | 75 | |
| | |   Accounts Payable | | 75 |
| | |     (Received bill of $75 from carpenter for repair services performed) | | |
| | 31 | Supplies | 1,700 | |
| | |   Cash | | 1,700 |
| | |     (Purchased an estimated 2-month supply of feed and hay for $1,700 on account) | | |

### Instructions

With the class divided into groups, answer the following.

**a.** Identify each journal entry that is correct. For each journal entry that is incorrect, prepare the entry that should have been made by the bookkeeper.

**b.** Which of the incorrect entries would prevent the trial balance from balancing?

**c.** What was the correct net income for May, assuming the bookkeeper reported net income of $4,500 after posting all 50 entries? (Errors only occur on the 8 entries above.)

**d.** What was the correct cash balance at May 31, assuming the bookkeeper reported a balance of $12,475 after posting all 50 entries (and the only errors occurred in the items listed above)?

## Communication Activity

**CT2.7** Keller's Maid Company offers home-cleaning service. Two recurring transactions for the company are billing customers for services performed and paying employee salaries. For example, on March 15, bills totaling $6,000 were sent to customers and $2,000 was paid in salaries to employees.

### Instructions

Write a memo to your instructor that explains and illustrates the steps in the recording process for each of the March 15 transactions. Use the format illustrated in the chapter under the heading, "The Recording Process Illustrated."

## Ethics Cases

**CT2.8** Meredith Ward is the assistant chief accountant at Frazier Company, a manufacturer of computer chips and cellular phones. The company presently has total sales of $20 million. It is the end of the first quarter. Meredith is hurriedly trying to prepare a trial balance so that quarterly financial statements can be prepared and released to management and the regulatory agencies. The total credits on the trial balance exceed the debits by $1,000. In order to meet the 4 P.M. deadline, Meredith decides to force the debits and credits into balance by adding the amount of the difference to the Equipment account. She chooses Equipment because it is one of the larger account balances; percentage-wise, it will be the least misstated. Meredith "plugs" the difference! She believes that the difference will not affect anyone's decisions. She wishes that she had another few days to find the error but realizes that the financial statements are already late.

**Instructions**

a. Who are the stakeholders in this situation?

b. What are the ethical issues involved in this case?

c. What are Meredith's alternatives?

**CT2.9** If you haven't already done so, in the not-too-distant future you will prepare a résumé. In some ways, your résumé is like a company's annual report. Its purpose is to enable others to evaluate your past, in an effort to predict your future.

A résumé is your opportunity to create a positive first impression. It is important that it be impressive—but it should also be accurate. In order to increase their job prospects, some people are tempted to "inflate" their résumés by overstating the importance of some past accomplishments or positions. In fact, you might even think that "everybody does it" and that if you don't do it, you will be at a disadvantage.

David Edmondson, the president and CEO of well-known electronics retailer **Radio Shack**, overstated his accomplishments by claiming that he had earned a bachelor of science degree, when in fact he had not. Apparently, his employer had not done a background check to ensure the accuracy of his résumé. Should Radio Shack have fired him?

**YES:** Radio Shack is a publicly traded company. Investors, creditors, employees, and others doing business with the company will not trust it if its leader is known to have poor integrity. The "tone at the top" is vital to creating an ethical organization.

**NO:** Mr. Edmondson had been a Radio Shack employee for 11 years. He had served the company in a wide variety of positions, and had earned the position of CEO through exceptional performance. While the fact that he lied 11 years earlier on his résumé was unfortunate, his service since then made this past transgression irrelevant. In addition, the company was in the midst of a massive restructuring, which included closing 700 of its 7,000 stores. It could not afford additional upheaval at this time.

**Instructions**

Write a response indicating your position regarding this situation. Provide support for your view.

## All About You

**CT2.10** Every company needs to plan in order to move forward. Its top management must consider where it wants the company to be in 3 to 5 years. Like a company, you need to think about where you want to be 3 to 5 years from now, and you need to start taking steps now in order to get there.

**Instructions**

Provide responses to each of the following items.

a. Where would you like to be working in 3 to 5 years? Describe your plan for getting there by identifying between 5 and 10 specific steps that you need to take.

b. In order to get the job you want, you will need a résumé. Your résumé is the equivalent of a company's annual report. It needs to provide relevant and representationally faithful information about your past accomplishments so that employers can decide whether to "invest" in you. Do a search on the Internet to find a good résumé format. What are the basic elements of a résumé?

c. A company's annual report provides information about a company's accomplishments. In order for investors to use the annual report, the information must provide a faithful representation; that is, users must have faith that the information is accurate and believable. How can you provide assurance that the information on your résumé is a faithful representation of your accomplishments?

d. Prepare a résumé assuming that you have accomplished the 5 to 10 specific steps you identified in part (a). Also, provide evidence that would give assurance that the information is a faithful representation of your accomplishments.

### Considering People, Planet, and Profit

**CT2.11** Auditors provide a type of certification of corporate financial statements. Certification is used in many other aspects of business as well. For example, it plays a critical role in the sustainability movement. The February 7, 2012, issue of the *New York Times* contained an article by S. Amanda Caudill entitled "Better Lives in Better Coffee," which discusses the role of certification in the coffee business.

#### Instructions

Read the article (available online) and then answer the following questions.

a. The article mentions three different certification types that coffee growers can obtain from three different certification bodies. Using financial reporting as an example, what potential problems might the existence of multiple certification types present to coffee purchasers?

b. According to the author, which certification is most common among coffee growers? What are the possible reasons for this?

c. What social and environmental benefits are coffee certifications trying to achieve? Are there also potential financial benefits to the parties involved?

## Answers to Insight and Accounting Across the Organization Questions

**Keeping Score  Q:** Do you think that the Chicago Bears football team would be likely to have the same major revenue and expense accounts as the Cubs?  **A:** Because their businesses are similar—professional sports—many of the revenue and expense accounts for the baseball and football teams might be similar.

**A Convenient Overstatement  Q:** What incentives might employees have to overstate the value of these investment securities on the company's financial statements?  **A:** One reason that they may have been reluctant to record the losses is out of fear that the company's shareholders and clients would panic if they saw the magnitude of the losses. However, personal self-interest might have been equally to blame—the bonuses of the traders were tied to the value of the investment securities.

**It Starts with the Transaction  Q:** Why is it important to record financial transactions completely and accurately?  **A:** If companies fail to record transactions completely and accurately, financial statements will no longer be relevant and representationally faithful. And if investors cannot trust the resultant financial statements, a drop in the company's stock price will often occur.

**Why Accuracy Matters  Q:** In order for these companies to prepare and issue financial statements, their accounting equations (debits and credits) must have been in balance at year-end. How could these errors or misstatements have occurred?  **A:** A company's accounting equation (its books) can be in balance yet its financial statements have errors or misstatements because entire transactions were not recorded, transactions were recorded at wrong amounts, transactions were recorded in the wrong accounts, and/or transactions were recorded in the wrong accounting period. Audits of financial statements uncover some but obviously not all errors or misstatements.

# A Look at IFRS

### LEARNING OBJECTIVE 5
Compare the procedures for the recording process under GAAP and IFRS.

International companies use the same set of procedures and records to keep track of transaction data. Thus, the material in Chapter 2 dealing with the account, general rules of debit and credit, and steps in the recording process—the journal, ledger, and chart of accounts—is the same under both GAAP and IFRS.

### Key Points

Following are the key similarities and differences between GAAP and IFRS as related to the recording process.

### Similarities

- Transaction analysis is the same under IFRS and GAAP.
- Both the IASB and the FASB go beyond the basic definitions provided in the text for the key elements of financial statements, that is, assets, liabilities, equity, revenues and expenses. The implications of the expanded definitions are discussed in more advanced accounting courses.
- As shown in the text, dollar signs are typically used only in the trial balance and the financial statements. The same practice is followed under IFRS, using the currency of the country where the reporting company is headquartered.
- A trial balance under IFRS follows the same format as shown in the text.

### Differences

- IFRS relies less on historical cost and more on fair value than do FASB standards.
- Internal controls are a system of checks and balances designed to prevent and detect fraud and errors. While most public U.S. companies have these systems in place, many non-U.S. companies have never completely documented the controls nor had an independent auditor attest to their effectiveness.

# IFRS Practice

## IFRS Self-Test Questions

1. Which statement is **correct** regarding IFRS?
   - a. IFRS reverses the rules of debits and credits, that is, debits are on the right and credits are on the left.
   - b. IFRS uses the same process for recording transactions as GAAP.
   - c. The chart of accounts under IFRS is different because revenues follow assets.
   - d. None of the above statements are correct.

2. The expanded accounting equation under IFRS is as follows:
   - a. Assets = Liabilities + Common Stock + Retained Earnings + Revenues − Expenses + Dividends.
   - b. Assets + Liabilities = Common Stock + Retained Earnings + Revenues − Expenses − Dividends.
   - c. Assets = Liabilities + Common Stock + Retained Earnings + Revenues − Expenses − Dividends.
   - d. Assets = Liabilities + Common Stock + Retained Earnings − Revenues − Expenses − Dividends.

3. A trial balance:
   - a. is the same under IFRS and GAAP.
   - b. proves that transactions are recorded correctly.
   - c. proves that all transactions have been recorded.
   - d. will not balance if a correct journal entry is posted twice.

4. One difference between IFRS and GAAP is that:
   - a. GAAP uses accrual-accounting concepts and IFRS uses primarily the cash basis of accounting.
   - b. IFRS uses a different posting process than GAAP.
   - c. IFRS uses more fair value measurements than GAAP.
   - d. the limitations of a trial balance are different between IFRS and GAAP.

5. The general policy for using proper currency signs (dollar, yen, pound, etc.) is the same for both IFRS and this text. This policy is as follows:
   - a. Currency signs only appear in ledgers and journal entries.
   - b. Currency signs are only shown in the trial balance.
   - c. Currency signs are shown for all compound journal entries.
   - d. Currency signs are shown in trial balances and financial statements.

## International Financial Reporting Problem: Louis Vuitton

**IFRS2.1** The financial statements of **Louis Vuitton** are presented in Appendix F. The complete consolidated financial statements, including the notes to its financial statements, are available at the company's website.

### Instructions

Describe in which statement each of the following items is reported, and the position in the statement (e.g., current asset).

- a. Other operating income and expenses.
- b. Cash and cash equivalents.
- c. Trade accounts payable.
- d. Cost of net financial debt.

## Answers to IFRS Self-Test Questions

1. b   2. c   3. a   4. c   5. d

## CHAPTER 3

Rudy Archuleta/Redux Pictures

# Adjusting the Accounts

## Chapter Preview

In Chapter 1, you learned a neat little formula: Net income = Revenues − Expenses. In Chapter 2, you learned some rules for recording revenue and expense transactions. Guess what? Things are not really that nice and neat. In fact, it is often difficult for companies to determine in what time period they should report some revenues and expenses. In other words, in measuring net income, timing is everything.

## Feature Story

### Keeping Track of Groupons

Who doesn't like buying things at a discount? That's why it's not surprising that three years after it started as a company, **Groupon, Inc.** was estimated to be worth $16 billion. This translates into an average increase in value of almost $15 million per day.

Now consider that Groupon had previously been estimated to be worth even more than that. What happened?

Well, accounting regulators and investors began to question the way that Groupon had accounted for some of its transactions. Groupon sells coupons ("groupons"), so how hard can it be to account for that? It turns out that accounting for coupons is not as easy as you might think.

First, consider what happens when Groupon makes a sale. Suppose it sells a groupon for $30 for Highrise Hamburgers. When it receives the $30 from the customer, it must turn over half of that amount ($15) to Highrise Hamburgers. So should Groupon record revenue for the full $30 or just $15? Until recently,

Groupon recorded the full $30. But, in response to an SEC ruling on the issue, Groupon now records revenue of $15 instead. This caused Groupon to restate its previous financial statements. This restatement reduced annual revenue by $312.9 million.

A second issue is a matter of timing. When should Groupon record this $15 revenue? Should it record the revenue when it sells the groupon, or must it wait until the customer uses the groupon at Highrise Hamburgers? The accounting becomes even more complicated when you consider the company's loyalty programs. Groupon offers free or discounted groupons to its subscribers for doing things such as referring new customers or participating in promotions. These grou-pons are to be used for future purchases, yet the company must record the expense at the time the customer receives the groupon.

Finally, Groupon, like all other companies, relies on many estimates in its financial reporting. For example, Groupon reports that "estimates are utilized for, but not limited to, stock-based compensation, income taxes, valuation of acquired goodwill and intangible assets, customer refunds, contingent liabilities and the depreciable lives of fixed assets." It notes that "actual results could differ materially from those estimates." So, next time you use a coupon, think about what that means for the company's accountants!

## Chapter Outline

| LEARNING OBJECTIVES | REVIEW | PRACTICE |
|---|---|---|
| **LO 1** Explain the accrual basis of accounting and the reasons for adjusting entries. | • Fiscal and calendar years<br>• Accrual- vs. cash-basis accounting<br>• Recognizing revenues and expenses<br>• Need for adjusting entries<br>• Types of adjusting entries | **DO IT! 1** Timing Concepts |
| **LO 2** Prepare adjusting entries for deferrals. | • Prepaid expenses<br>• Unearned revenues | **DO IT! 2** Adjusting Entries for Deferrals |
| **LO 3** Prepare adjusting entries for accruals. | • Accrued revenues<br>• Accrued expenses<br>• Summary of basic relationships | **DO IT! 3** Adjusting Entries for Accruals |
| **LO 4** Describe the nature and purpose of an adjusted trial balance. | • Preparing the adjusted trial balance<br>• Preparing financial statements | **DO IT! 4** Trial Balance |

**Go to the Review and Practice section at the end of the chapter for a review of key concepts and practice applications with solutions.**

**Visit WileyPLUS for additional tutorials and practice opportunities.**

# Accrual-Basis Accounting and Adjusting Entries

### LEARNING OBJECTIVE 1

Explain the accrual basis of accounting and the reasons for adjusting entries.

If we could wait to prepare financial statements until a company ended its operations, no adjustments would be needed. At that point, we could easily determine its final balance sheet and the amount of lifetime income it earned.

However, most companies need feedback about how well they are performing during a period of time. For example, management usually wants monthly financial statements. The Internal Revenue Service requires all businesses to file annual tax returns. Therefore, **accountants divide the economic life of a business into artificial time periods**. This convenient assumption is referred to as the **time period assumption** (see **Alternative Terminology**).

Many business transactions affect more than one of these arbitrary time periods. For example, a new building purchased by **Citigroup** or a new airplane purchased by **Delta Air Lines** will be used for many years. It would not make sense to expense the full cost of these items at the time of purchase because they will be used for many subsequent periods. Instead, companies must allocate the costs to the periods of use (how much of the cost of a building or an airplane contributed to operations this year?).

> **ALTERNATIVE TERMINOLOGY**
>
> The time period assumption is also called the *periodicity assumption*.

**Time Period Assumption**

## Fiscal and Calendar Years

Both small and large companies prepare financial statements periodically in order to assess their financial condition and results of operations. **Accounting time periods are generally a month, a quarter, or a year.** Monthly and quarterly time periods are called **interim periods**. Most large companies must prepare both quarterly and annual financial statements.

An accounting time period that is one year in length is a **fiscal year**. A fiscal year usually begins with the first day of a month and ends 12 months later on the last day of a month. Many businesses use the **calendar year** (January 1 to December 31) as their fiscal period. Some do not. Companies whose fiscal year differs from the calendar year include **Delta Air Lines**, June 30, and **The Walt Disney Company**, September 30. Sometimes a company's year-end will vary from year to year. For example, **PepsiCo**'s fiscal year ends on the Friday closest to December 31, which was December 30 in 2017 and December 29 in 2018.

## Accrual- versus Cash-Basis Accounting

What you will learn in this chapter is **accrual-basis accounting**. Under the accrual basis, companies record transactions that change a company's financial statements **in the periods in which the events occur**. For example, using the accrual basis to determine net income means companies recognize revenues when they perform services (rather than when they receive cash). It also means recognizing expenses when incurred (rather than when paid).

An alternative to the accrual basis is the cash basis. Under **cash-basis accounting**, companies record revenue at the time they receive cash. They record an expense at the time they pay out cash. The cash basis seems appealing due to its simplicity, but it often produces misleading financial statements. For example, it fails to record revenue for a company that has performed services but has not yet received payment. As a result, the cash basis may not recognize revenue in the period that a performance obligation is satisfied.

**Accrual-basis accounting is required by generally accepted accounting principles (GAAP).** Individuals and some small companies, however, do use cash-basis accounting. The cash basis is justified for small businesses because they often have few receivables and payables. Medium and large companies use accrual-basis accounting.

## Recognizing Revenues and Expenses

It can be difficult to determine when to report revenues and expenses. The revenue recognition principle and the expense recognition principle help in this task.

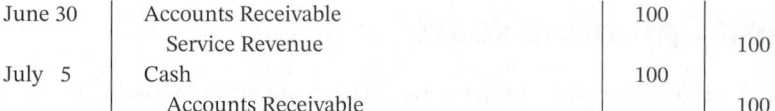

## Revenue Recognition Principle

When a company agrees to perform a service or sell a product to a customer, it has a **performance obligation**. When the company meets this performance obligation, it recognizes revenue. The **revenue recognition principle** therefore requires that companies recognize revenue in the accounting period in which the performance obligation is satisfied. A company satisfies its performance obligation by performing a service or providing a good to a customer.

To illustrate, assume Conrad Dry Cleaners performs cleaning services for $100 on June 30, but customers do not claim and pay for their clothes until July 5. Under the revenue recognition principle, Conrad records revenue on June 30 when it satisfies its performance obligation, which is when it performs the service, not in July when it receives the cash. At June 30, Conrad would report a receivable on its balance sheet and revenue in its income statement for the service performed. The journal entries would be as follows.

| | | | |
|---|---|---|---|
| June 30 | Accounts Receivable | 100 | |
| | Service Revenue | | 100 |
| July 5 | Cash | 100 | |
| | Accounts Receivable | | 100 |

### Five-Step Revenue Recognition Process—Sierra Corporation Example

Revenue recognition results from a five-step process. This process can best be illustrated with an example. Assume that Sierra Corporation signs a contract with the Lewis family to provide guide services for a one-week backpacking trip for $1,500. **Illustration 3.1** shows the five steps that Sierra follows to recognize revenue.

**ILLUSTRATION 3.1** Five steps of revenue recognition

As indicated, Step 5 is when Sierra recognizes revenue related to providing the guide services to the Lewis family. At this point, Sierra completes the trip and satisfies its performance obligation.

## Expense Recognition Principle

Accountants follow a simple rule in recognizing expenses: "Let the expenses follow the revenues." Thus, expense recognition is tied to revenue recognition. In the dry cleaning example, this means that Conrad should report the salary expense incurred in performing the June 30 cleaning service in the same period in which it recognizes the service revenue. The critical issue in expense recognition is when the expense makes its contribution to revenue. This may or may not be the same period in which the expense is paid. If Conrad does not pay the salary incurred on June 30 until July, it would report salaries payable on its June 30 balance sheet.

This practice of expense recognition is referred to as the **expense recognition principle**. It requires that companies recognize expenses in the period in which they make efforts (consume assets or incur liabilities) to generate revenue. The term matching is sometimes used in expense recognition to indicate the relationship between the effort expended and the revenue generated. **Illustration 3.2** summarizes the revenue and expense recognition principles.

**Expense Recognition**

Efforts generated revenue

Advertising   Delivery   Utilities

Expenses are recognized when efforts are made to generate revenue.

**ILLUSTRATION 3.2**  GAAP relationships in revenue and expense recognition

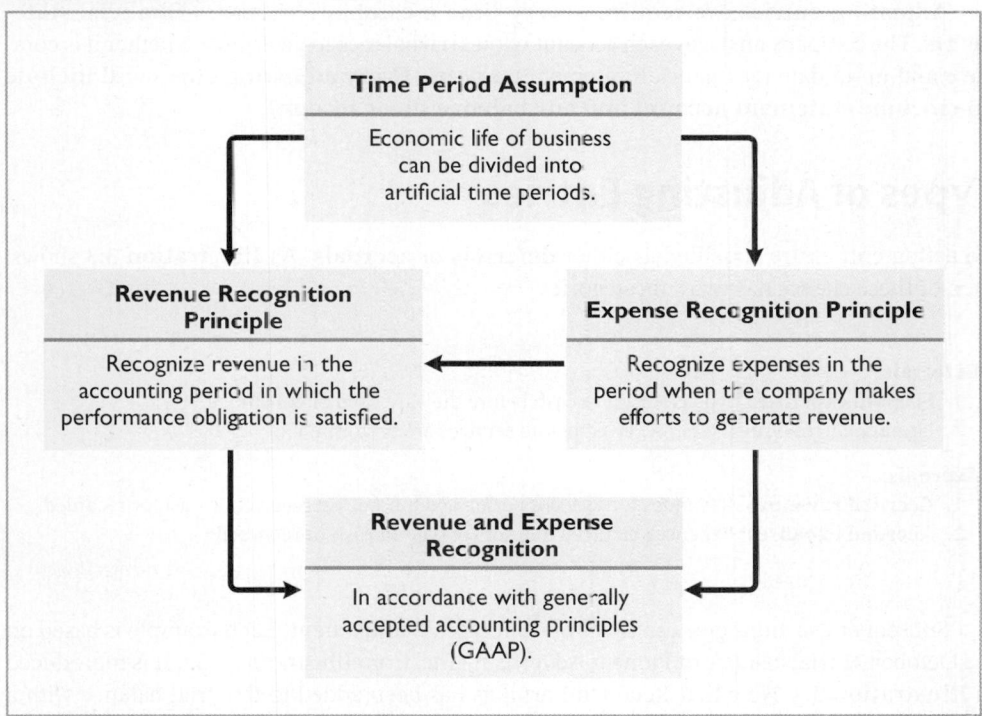

**Time Period Assumption**

Economic life of business can be divided into artificial time periods.

**Revenue Recognition Principle**

Recognize revenue in the accounting period in which the performance obligation is satisfied.

**Expense Recognition Principle**

Recognize expenses in the period when the company makes efforts to generate revenue.

**Revenue and Expense Recognition**

In accordance with generally accepted accounting principles (GAAP).

## Investor Insight     Apple Inc.

### Reporting Revenue Accurately

Until recently, electronics manufacturer **Apple** was required to spread the revenues from iPhone sales over the two-year period following the sale of the phone. Accounting standards required this because Apple was obligated to provide software updates after the phone was sold. Since Apple had service obligations after the initial date of sale, it was forced to spread the revenue over a two-year period.

PhotoAlto/James Hardy/ Getty Images

As a result, the rapid growth of iPhone sales was not fully reflected in the revenue amounts reported in Apple's income statement. A new accounting standard now enables Apple to report much more of its iPhone revenue at the point of sale. It was estimated that under the new rule revenues would have been about 17% higher and earnings per share almost 50% higher.

**In the past, why was it argued that Apple should spread the recognition of iPhone revenue over a two-year period, rather than recording it upfront? (Answer is available near the end of the chapter.)**

## The Need for Adjusting Entries

In order for revenues to be recorded in the period in which the performance obligations are satisfied and for expenses to be recognized in the period in which they are incurred, companies make adjusting entries. **Adjusting entries ensure that the revenue recognition and expense recognition principles are followed.**

Adjusting entries are necessary because the **trial balance**—the first pulling together of the transaction data—may not contain up-to-date and complete data. This is true for several reasons:

1. Some events are not recorded daily because it is not efficient to do so. Examples are the use of supplies and the earning of wages by employees.
2. Some costs are not recorded during the accounting period because these costs expire with the passage of time rather than as a result of recurring daily transactions. Examples are charges related to the use of buildings and equipment, rent, and insurance.
3. Some items may be unrecorded. An example is a utility service bill that will not be received until the next accounting period.

**Adjusting entries are required every time a company prepares financial statements.** The company analyzes each account in the trial balance to determine whether it is complete and up-to-date for financial statement purposes. **Every adjusting entry will include one income statement account and one balance sheet account.**

# Types of Adjusting Entries

Adjusting entries are classified as either **deferrals** or **accruals**. As **Illustration 3.3** shows, each of these classes has two subcategories.

**ILLUSTRATION 3.3**

Categories of adjusting entries

**Deferrals:**
1. **Prepaid expenses:** Expenses paid in cash before they are used or consumed.
2. **Unearned revenues:** Cash received before services are performed.

**Accruals:**
1. **Accrued revenues:** Revenues for services performed but not yet received in cash or recorded.
2. **Accrued expenses:** Expenses incurred but not yet paid in cash or recorded.

Subsequent sections give examples of each type of adjustment. Each example is based on the October 31 trial balance of Pioneer Advertising Inc. from Illustration 2.32. It is reproduced in **Illustration 3.4**. Note that Retained Earnings has been added to this trial balance with a zero balance. We will explain its use later.

**ILLUSTRATION 3.4**

Trial balance

## Pioneer Advertising Inc.
### Trial Balance
### October 31, 2022

|  | Debit | Credit |
| --- | --- | --- |
| Cash | $15,200 | |
| Supplies | 2,500 | |
| Prepaid Insurance | 600 | |
| Equipment | 5,000 | |
| Notes Payable | | $ 5,000 |
| Accounts Payable | | 2,500 |
| Unearned Service Revenue | | 1,200 |
| Common Stock | | 10,000 |
| Retained Earnings | | –0– |
| Dividends | 500 | |
| Service Revenue | | 10,000 |
| Salaries and Wages Expense | 4,000 | |
| Rent Expense | 900 | |
| | $28,700 | $28,700 |

We assume that Pioneer uses an accounting period of one month. Thus, monthly adjusting entries are made. The entries are dated October 31.

## DO IT! 1 | Timing Concepts

Below is a list of concepts in the left column, with a description of the concept in the right column. There are more descriptions provided than concepts. Match the description to the concept.

1. _____ Accrual-basis accounting.
2. _____ Calendar year.
3. _____ Time period assumption.
4. _____ Expense recognition principle.

a. Monthly and quarterly time periods.

b. Recognize efforts (expenses) in the period in which a company uses assets or incurs liabilities to generate results (revenues).

c. Accountants divide the economic life of a business into artificial time periods.

d. Companies record revenues when they receive cash and record expenses when they pay out cash.

e. An accounting time period that starts on January 1 and ends on December 31.

f. Companies record transactions in the period in which the events occur.

**Solution**

1. f  2. e  3. c  4. b

Related exercise material: **BE3.1, BE3.2, BE3.3, BE3.4, DO IT! 3.1, E3.1, E3.2, E3.3, E3.4, and E3.5.**

# Adjusting Entries for Deferrals

### LEARNING OBJECTIVE 2

Prepare adjusting entries for deferrals.

ANALYZE → JOURNALIZE → POST → TRIAL BALANCE → **Journalize and post adjusting entries: deferrals/accruals** → ADJUSTED TRIAL BALANCE → FINANCIAL STATEMENTS → CLOSING ENTRIES → POST-CLOSING TRIAL BALANCE

To defer means to postpone or delay. **Deferrals** are expenses or revenues that are recognized at a date later than the point when cash was originally exchanged. Companies make adjusting entries for deferred expenses to record the portion that was incurred during the period. Companies also make adjusting entries for deferred revenues to record services performed during the period. The two types of deferrals are prepaid expenses and unearned revenues.

## Prepaid Expenses

When companies pay a future expense that will benefit more than one accounting period, they record an asset called **prepaid expenses** or **prepayments**. When expenses are prepaid, an asset account is increased (debited) to show the service or benefit that the company will receive in the future. Examples of common prepayments are insurance, supplies, advertising, and rent. In addition, companies make prepayments when they purchase buildings and equipment.

**Prepaid expenses are costs that expire either with the passage of time** (e.g., rent and insurance) **or through use** (e.g., supplies). The expiration of these costs does not require daily entries, which would be impractical and unnecessary. Accordingly, companies postpone the recognition of such cost expirations until they prepare financial statements. At each statement date, they make adjusting entries to record the expenses applicable to the current accounting period and to show the remaining amounts in the asset accounts.

Prior to adjustment, assets are overstated and expenses are understated. Therefore, as shown in **Illustration 3.5**, **an adjusting entry for prepaid expenses results in an increase (a debit) to an expense account and a decrease (a credit) to an asset account**.

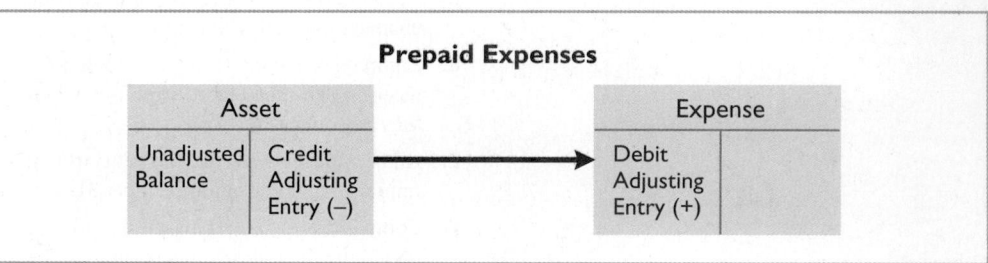

Let's look in more detail at some specific types of prepaid expenses, beginning with supplies.

## Supplies

**Supplies**

Oct. 5

Supplies purchased; record asset

Oct. 31
Supplies used; record supplies expense

The purchase of supplies, such as paper and envelopes, results in an increase (a debit) to an asset account. During the accounting period, the company uses supplies. Rather than record supplies expense as the supplies are used, companies recognize supplies expense at the **end** of the accounting period. At the end of the accounting period, the company counts the remaining supplies. The difference between the unadjusted balance in the Supplies (asset) account and the actual cost of supplies on hand represents the supplies used (an expense) for that period.

Recall from Chapter 2 that Pioneer Advertising Inc. purchased supplies costing $2,500 on October 5. Pioneer recorded the purchase by increasing (debiting) the asset Supplies. This account shows a balance of $2,500 in the October 31 trial balance. An inventory count at the close of business on October 31 reveals that $1,000 of supplies are still on hand. Thus, the cost of supplies used is $1,500 ($2,500 − $1,000). This use of supplies decreases an asset, Supplies. It also decreases stockholders' equity by increasing an expense account, Supplies Expense (see **Helpful Hint**). This is shown in **Illustration 3.6**.

**ILLUSTRATION 3.6**

**Adjustment for supplies**

**HELPFUL HINT**

Due to their nature, adjusting entries have **no effect** on cash flows. As a result, we do not show the cash flow effects in these illustrations.

After adjustment, the asset account Supplies shows a balance of $1,000, which is equal to the cost of supplies on hand at the statement date. In addition, Supplies Expense shows a balance of $1,500, which equals the cost of supplies used in October. **If Pioneer does not make the adjusting entry, October expenses are understated and net income is overstated by $1,500. Moreover, both assets and stockholders' equity will be overstated by $1,500 on the October 31 balance sheet.**

## Insurance

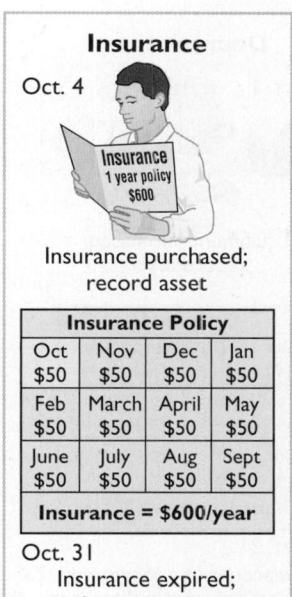

Companies purchase insurance to protect themselves from losses due to fire, theft, and unforeseen events. Insurance must be paid in advance, often for multiple months. The cost of insurance (premiums) paid in advance is recorded as an increase (debit) in the asset account Prepaid Insurance. At the financial statement date, companies increase (debit) Insurance Expense and decrease (credit) Prepaid Insurance for the cost of insurance that has expired during the period.

On October 4, Pioneer Advertising paid $600 for a one-year fire insurance policy. Coverage began on October 1. Pioneer recorded the payment by increasing (debiting) Prepaid Insurance. This account shows a balance of $600 in the October 31 trial balance. Insurance of $50 ($600 ÷ 12) expires each month. The expiration of prepaid insurance decreases an asset, Prepaid Insurance. It also decreases stockholders' equity by increasing an expense account, Insurance Expense.

As shown in **Illustration 3.7**, the asset Prepaid Insurance shows a balance of $550, which represents the unexpired cost for the remaining 11 months of coverage. At the same time, the balance in Insurance Expense equals the insurance cost that expired in October. **If Pioneer does not make this adjustment, October expenses are understated by $50 and net income is overstated by $50. Moreover, both assets and stockholders' equity will be overstated by $50 on the October 31 balance sheet.**

**ILLUSTRATION 3.7** **Adjustment for insurance**

## Depreciation

A company typically owns a variety of assets that have long lives, such as buildings, equipment, and motor vehicles. The period of service is referred to as the **useful life** of the asset. Because a building is expected to be of service for many years, it is recorded as an asset, rather than an expense, on the date it is acquired. As explained in Chapter 1, companies record such assets at **cost**, as required by the historical cost principle. To follow the expense recognition principle, companies allocate a portion of this cost to an expense during each period of the asset's useful life. **Depreciation** is the process of allocating the cost of an asset to expense over its useful life.

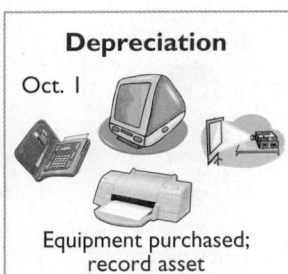

### Depreciation

Oct. 1

Equipment purchased; record asset

| Equipment | | | |
|---|---|---|---|
| Oct $40 | Nov $40 | Dec $40 | Jan $40 |
| Feb $40 | March $40 | April $40 | May $40 |
| June $40 | July $40 | Aug $40 | Sept $40 |
| Depreciation = $480/year | | | |

Oct. 31

Depreciation recognized; record depreciation expense

**Need for Adjustment** The acquisition of a long-lived asset is essentially a long-term prepayment for the use of that asset. An adjusting entry for depreciation is needed to recognize the cost that has been used (an expense) during the period and to report the unused cost (an asset) at the end of the period. One very important point to understand: **Depreciation is an allocation concept, not a valuation concept.** That is, depreciation **allocates an asset's cost to the periods in which it is used. Depreciation does not attempt to report the actual change in the value of the asset.**

For Pioneer Advertising, assume that depreciation on the equipment is $480 a year, or $40 per month. As shown in **Illustration 3.8**, rather than decrease (credit) the asset account directly, Pioneer instead credits Accumulated Depreciation—Equipment. Accumulated Depreciation is called a **contra asset account**. Such an account is offset against an asset account on the balance sheet. Thus, the Accumulated Depreciation—Equipment account offsets the asset account Equipment. **This account keeps track of the total amount of depreciation expense taken over the life of the asset.** To keep the accounting equation in balance, Pioneer decreases stockholders' equity by increasing an expense account, Depreciation Expense.

**ILLUSTRATION 3.8** Adjustment for depreciation

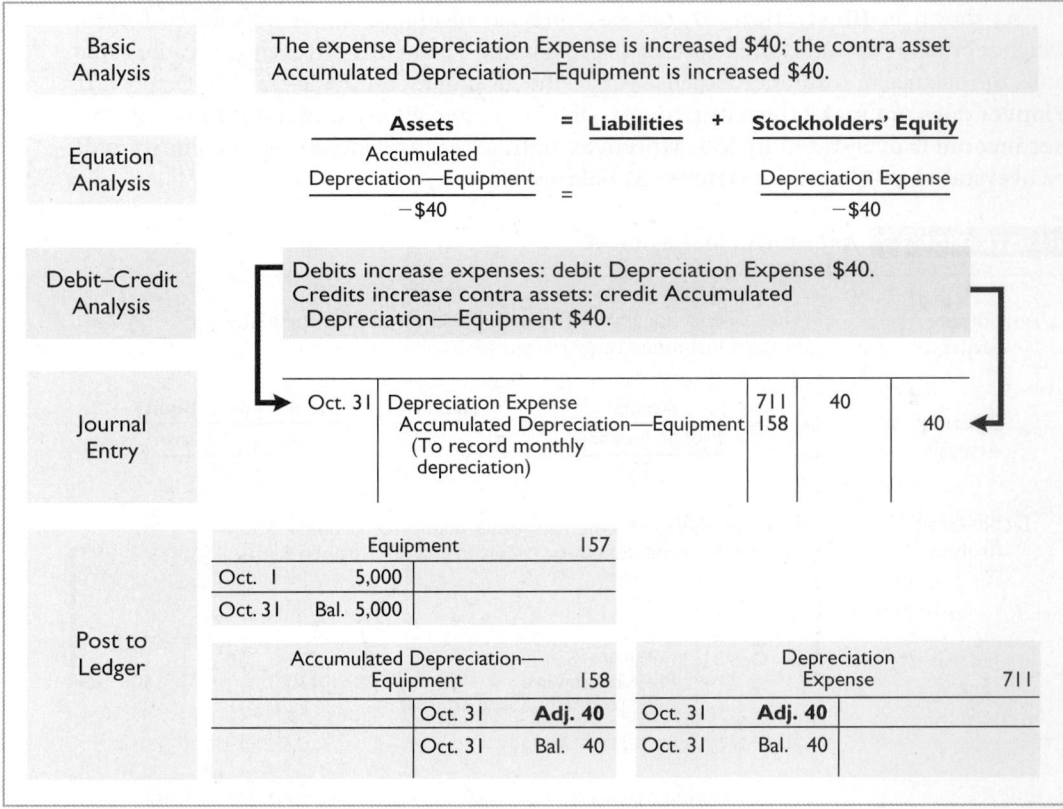

The balance in the Accumulated Depreciation—Equipment account will increase $40 each month, and the balance in Equipment remains $5,000.

**Statement Presentation** As indicated, Accumulated Depreciation—Equipment is a contra asset account (see **Helpful Hint**). It is offset against Equipment on the balance sheet. The normal balance of a contra asset account is a credit. A theoretical alternative to using a contra asset account would be to decrease (credit) the asset account by the amount of depreciation each period. But using the contra account is preferable for a simple reason: It discloses **both** the original cost of the equipment **and** the total cost that has been expensed to date. Thus, in the balance sheet, Pioneer deducts Accumulated Depreciation—Equipment from the related asset account, as shown in **Illustration 3.9**.

**HELPFUL HINT**

All contra accounts have increases, decreases, and normal balances opposite to the account to which they relate.

| | |
|---|---|
| Equipment | $5,000 |
| Less: Accumulated depreciation—equipment | 40 |
| | **$4,960** |

**ILLUSTRATION 3.9**
**Balance sheet presentation of accumulated depreciation**

**Book value** is the difference between the cost of any depreciable asset and its related accumulated depreciation (see **Alternative Terminology**). In Illustration 3.9, the book value of the equipment at the balance sheet date is $4,960. The book value and the fair value of the asset are generally two different values. As noted earlier, **the purpose of depreciation is not valuation but a means of cost allocation**.

Depreciation expense identifies the portion of an asset's cost that expired during the period (in this case, in October). The accounting equation shows that **without this adjusting entry, total assets, total stockholders' equity, and net income are overstated by $40 and depreciation expense is understated by $40**.

**Illustration 3.10** summarizes the accounting for prepaid expenses.

**ALTERNATIVE TERMINOLOGY**

Book value is also referred to as *carrying value*.

## Accounting for Prepaid Expenses

| Examples | Reason for Adjustment | Accounts Before Adjustment | Adjusting Entry |
|---|---|---|---|
| Insurance, supplies, advertising, rent, depreciation | Prepaid expenses originally recorded in asset accounts have been used. | Assets overstated. Expenses understated. | Dr. Expenses Cr. Assets or Contra Assets |

**ILLUSTRATION 3.10**
**Accounting for prepaid expenses**

# Unearned Revenues

When companies receive cash before services are performed, they record a liability by increasing (crediting) a liability account called **unearned revenues**. In other words, a **company now has a performance obligation** (liability) to perform a service for one of its customers. Items like rent, magazine subscriptions, and customer deposits for future service may result in unearned revenues. Airlines such as **United, Southwest**, and **Delta**, for instance, treat receipts from the sale of tickets as unearned revenue until the flight service is provided.

Unearned revenues are the opposite of prepaid expenses. Indeed, unearned revenue on the books of one company is likely to be a prepaid expense on the books of the company that has made the advance payment. For example, if identical accounting periods are assumed, a landlord will have unearned rent revenue when a tenant has prepaid rent.

When a company receives payment for services to be performed in a future accounting period, it increases (credits) an unearned revenue (a liability) account to recognize the liability that exists. The company subsequently recognizes revenues when it performs the service. During the accounting period, it is not practical to make daily entries as the company performs services. Instead, the company delays recognition of revenue until the adjustment process. Then, the company makes an adjusting entry to record the revenue for services performed during the period and to show the liability that remains at the end of the accounting period. Typically, prior to adjustment, liabilities are overstated and revenues are understated. Therefore, as shown in **Illustration 3.11**, the adjusting entry for unearned revenues results in a decrease (a debit) to a liability account and an increase (a credit) to a revenue account.

Pioneer Advertising received $1,200 on October 2 from R. Knox for advertising services expected to be completed by December 31. Pioneer credited the payment to Unearned Service Revenue. This liability account shows a balance of $1,200 in the October 31 trial balance. From an evaluation of the services Pioneer performed for Knox during October, the company determines that it should recognize $400 of revenue in October. The liability (Unearned Service Revenue) is therefore decreased, and stockholders' equity (Service Revenue) is increased.

As shown in **Illustration 3.12**, the liability Unearned Service Revenue now shows a balance of $800. That amount represents the remaining advertising services Pioneer is

**Unearned Revenues**

Oct. 2

Thank you in advance for your work

I will finish by Dec. 31

$1,200

Cash is received in advance; liability is recorded

Oct. 31
Some service has been performed; some revenue is recorded

ILLUSTRATION 3.11

**Adjusting entries for unearned revenues**

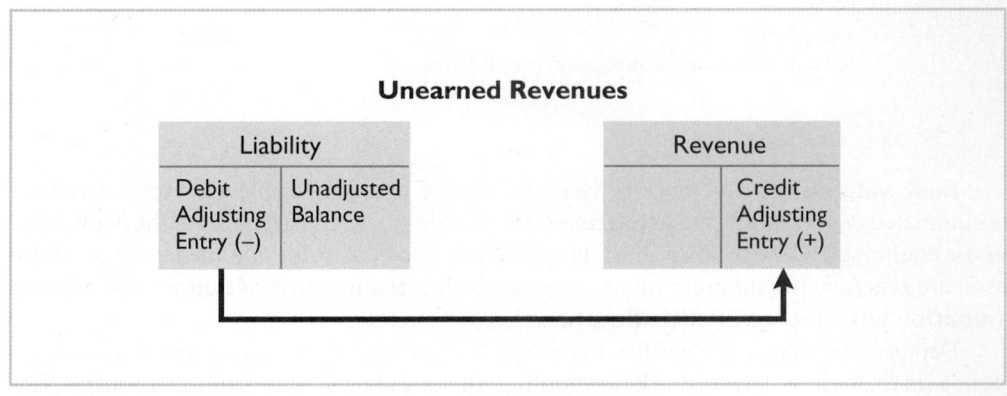

**Unearned Revenues**

| Liability | | Revenue |
|---|---|---|
| Debit Adjusting Entry (−) | Unadjusted Balance | Credit Adjusting Entry (+) |

obligated to perform in the future. At the same time, Service Revenue shows total revenue recognized in October of $10,400. **Without this adjustment, revenues and net income are understated by $400 in the income statement. Moreover, liabilities will be overstated and stockholders' equity will be understated by $400 on the October 31 balance sheet.**

ILLUSTRATION 3.12 **Service revenue accounts after adjustment**

| Basic Analysis | The liability Unearned Service Revenue is decreased $400; the revenue Service Revenue is increased $400. |
|---|---|

| Equation Analysis | Assets = Liabilities + Stockholders' Equity |
|---|---|
| | Unearned Service Revenue −$400 · · · Service Revenue +$400 |

| Debit–Credit Analysis | Debits decrease liabilities: debit Unearned Service Revenue $400. Credits increase revenues: credit Service Revenue $400. |
|---|---|

| Journal Entry | Oct. 31 | Unearned Service Revenue | 209 | 400 | |
|---|---|---|---|---|---|
| | | Service Revenue | 400 | | 400 |
| | | (To record revenue for services performed) | | | |

**Post to Ledger**

| Unearned Service Revenue 209 | | | | Service Revenue 400 | | |
|---|---|---|---|---|---|---|
| Oct. 31 | **Adj. 400** | Oct. 2 | 1,200 | | Oct. 31 | 10,000 |
| | | | | | 31 **Adj. 400** |
| | | Oct. 31 | Bal. 800 | | Oct. 31 | Bal. 10,400 |

Illustration 3.13 summarizes the accounting for unearned revenues.

ILLUSTRATION 3.13

**Accounting for unearned revenues**

## Accounting for Unearned Revenues

| Examples | Reason for Adjustment | Accounts Before Adjustment | Adjusting Entry |
|---|---|---|---|
| Rent, magazine subscriptions, customer deposits for future service | Unearned revenues recorded in liability accounts are now recognized as revenue for services performed. | Liabilities overstated. Revenues understated. | Dr. Liabilities   Cr. Revenues |

## Accounting Across the Organization    Best Buy

iStock.com/Skip Odonnell

### Turning Gift Cards into Revenue

Those of you who are marketing majors (and even most of you who are not) know that gift cards are among the hottest marketing tools in merchandising today. Customers purchase gift cards and give them to someone for later use. In a recent year, gift-card sales were expected to exceed $124 billion.

Although these programs are popular with marketing executives, they create accounting questions. Should revenue be recorded at the time the gift card is sold, or when it is exercised? How should expired gift cards be accounted

for? In a recent balance sheet, **Best Buy** reported unearned revenue related to gift cards of $427 million.

**Source:** "2014 Gift Card Sales to Top $124 Billion, But Growth Slowing," *PR Newswire* (December 10, 2014).

**Suppose that Robert Jones purchases a $100 gift card at Best Buy on December 24, 2021, and gives it to his wife, Mary Jones, on December 25, 2021. On January 3, 2022, Mary uses the card to purchase a $100 smart speaker. When do you think Best Buy should recognize revenue and why? (Answer is available near the end of the chapter.)**

## DO IT! 2 | Adjusting Entries for Deferrals

The ledger of Hammond Inc. on March 31, 2022, includes these selected accounts before adjusting entries are prepared.

|  | Debit | Credit |
|---|---|---|
| Prepaid Insurance | $ 3,600 | |
| Supplies | 2,800 | |
| Equipment | 25,000 | |
| Accumulated Depreciation—Equipment | | $5,000 |
| Unearned Service Revenue | | 9,200 |

An analysis of the accounts shows the following.

1. Insurance expires at the rate of $100 per month.

2. Supplies on hand total $800.

3. The equipment depreciates $200 a month.

4. During March, services were performed for $4,000 of the unearned service revenue reported.

Prepare the adjusting entries for the month of March.

### ACTION PLAN

- **Make adjusting entries at the end of the period for revenues recognized and expenses incurred in the period.**

- **Don't forget to make adjusting entries for deferrals. Failure to adjust for deferrals leads to overstatement of the asset or liability and understatement of the related expense or revenue.**

### Solution

| | | Debit | Credit |
|---|---|---|---|
| 1. | Insurance Expense | 100 | |
| | Prepaid Insurance | | 100 |
| | (To record insurance expired) | | |
| 2. | Supplies Expense ($2,800 − $800) | 2,000 | |
| | Supplies | | 2,000 |
| | (To record supplies used) | | |
| 3. | Depreciation Expense | 200 | |
| | Accumulated Depreciation—Equipment | | 200 |
| | (To record monthly depreciation) | | |
| 4. | Unearned Service Revenue | 4,000 | |
| | Service Revenue | | 4,000 |
| | (To record revenue for services performed) | | |

Related exercise material: **BE3.5, BE3.6, BE3.7, BE3.8, BE3.9, DO IT! 3.2, E3.5, E3.6, E3.7, E3.8, E3.9, E3.10, E3.11, E3.12, E3.13, E3.14, E3.15, and E3.16.**

# Adjusting Entries for Accruals

> **LEARNING OBJECTIVE 3**
> Prepare adjusting entries for accruals.

ANALYZE › JOURNALIZE › POST › **TRIAL BALANCE** › **Journalize and post adjusting entries: deferrals/accruals** › **ADJUSTED TRIAL BALANCE** › **FINANCIAL STATEMENTS** › **CLOSING ENTRIES** › **POST-CLOSING TRIAL BALANCE**

**Accrued Revenues**

My fee is $200

Revenue and receivable are recorded for unbilled services

Nov. 10

$200

Cash is received; receivable is reduced

The second category of adjusting entries is **accruals**. Prior to an accrual adjustment, the revenue account (and the related asset account) or the expense account (and the related liability account) are understated. Thus, the adjusting entry for accruals will **increase both a balance sheet and an income statement account.**

## Accrued Revenues

Revenues for services performed but not yet recorded at the statement date are **accrued revenues**. Accrued revenues may accumulate (accrue) with the passing of time, as in the case of interest revenue. These are unrecorded because the earning of interest does not involve daily transactions. Companies do not record interest revenue on a daily basis because it is often impractical to do so. Accrued revenues also may result from services that have been performed but not yet billed or collected, as in the case of commissions and fees. These may be unrecorded because only a portion of the total service has been performed and the clients will not be billed until the service has been completed.

An adjusting entry records the receivable that exists at the balance sheet date and the revenue for the services performed during the period. Prior to adjustment, both assets and revenues are understated. As shown in **Illustration 3.14**, **an adjusting entry for accrued revenues results in an increase (a debit) to an asset account and an increase (a credit) to a revenue account** (see **Helpful Hint**).

**ILLUSTRATION 3.14**

**Adjusting entries for accrued revenues**

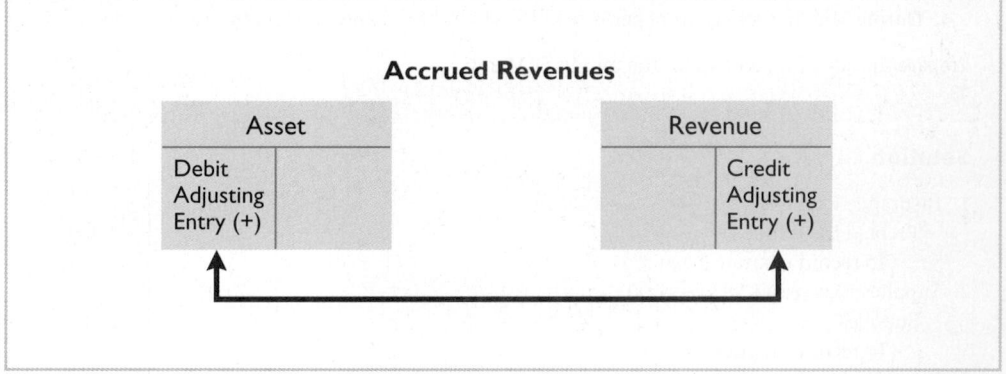

**Accrued Revenues**

| Asset | | Revenue | |
|---|---|---|---|
| Debit Adjusting Entry (+) | | | Credit Adjusting Entry (+) |

HELPFUL HINT

**For accruals, there may have been no prior entry, and the accounts requiring adjustment may both have zero balances prior to adjustment.**

In October, Pioneer Advertising Inc. performed services worth $200 that were not billed to clients on or before October 31. Because these services were not billed, they were not recorded. The accrual of unrecorded service revenue increases an asset account, Accounts Receivable. It also increases stockholders' equity by increasing a revenue account, Service Revenue, as shown in **Illustration 3.15**.

The asset Accounts Receivable shows that clients owe Pioneer $200 at the balance sheet date. The balance of $10,600 in Service Revenue represents the total revenue for services performed by Pioneer during the month ($10,000 + $400 + $200). **Without the adjusting**

**ILLUSTRATION 3.15** Adjustment for accrued revenue

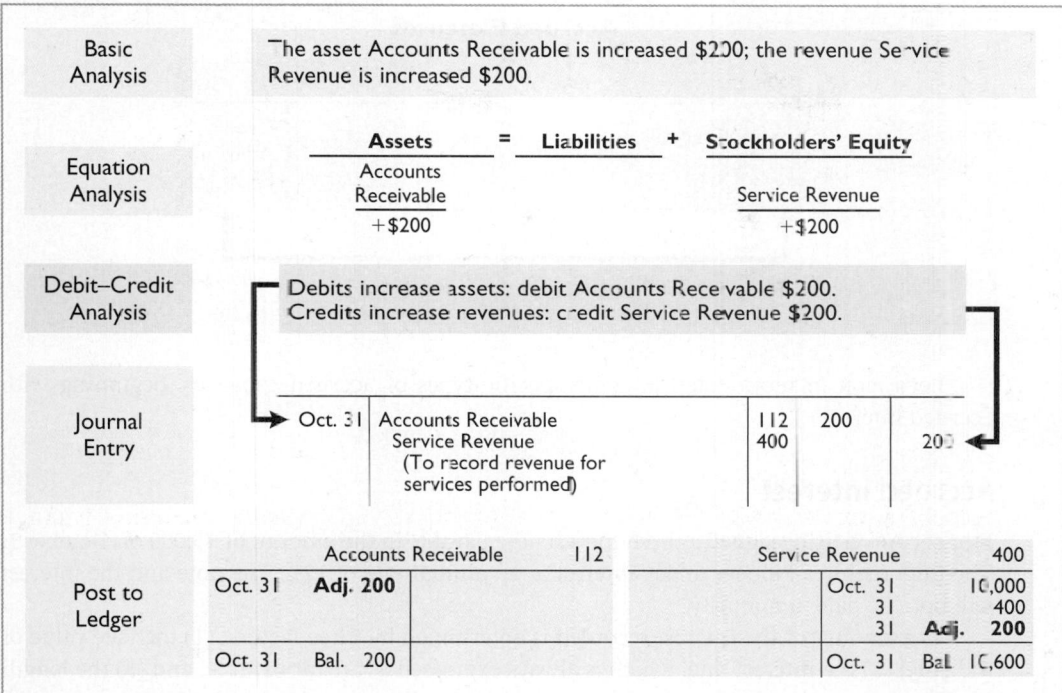

| | |
|---|---|
| Basic Analysis | The asset Accounts Receivable is increased $200; the revenue Service Revenue is increased $200. |

**Equation Analysis**

| Assets | = | Liabilities | + | Stockholders' Equity |
|---|---|---|---|---|
| Accounts Receivable | | | | Service Revenue |
| +$200 | | | | +$200 |

**Debit–Credit Analysis**

Debits increase assets: debit Accounts Receivable $200.
Credits increase revenues: credit Service Revenue $200.

**Journal Entry**

| Oct. 31 | Accounts Receivable | 112 | 200 | |
|---|---|---|---|---|
| | Service Revenue | 400 | | 200 |
| | (To record revenue for services performed) | | | |

**Post to Ledger**

| Accounts Receivable | 112 | | Service Revenue | | 400 |
|---|---|---|---|---|---|
| Oct. 31  **Adj. 200** | | | Oct. 31 | | 10,000 |
| | | | 31 | | 400 |
| | | | 31 | **Adj.** | **200** |
| Oct. 31  Bal. 200 | | | Oct. 31 | Bal. | 10,600 |

entry, assets and stockholders' equity on the balance sheet and revenues and net income on the income statement are understated.

On November 10, Pioneer receives cash of $200 for the services performed in October and makes the following entry.

| Nov. 10 | Cash | 200 | |
|---|---|---|---|
| | Accounts Receivable | | 200 |
| | (To record cash collected on account) | | |

The company records the collection of the receivables by a debit (increase) to Cash and a credit (decrease) to Accounts Receivable.

**Illustration 3.16** summarizes the accounting for accrued revenues.

## Accounting for Accrued Revenues

| Examples | Reason for Adjustment | Accounts Before Adjustment | Adjusting Entry |
|---|---|---|---|
| Interest, rent, services | Services performed but not yet received in cash or recorded. | Assets understated. Revenues understated. | Dr. Assets    Cr. Revenues |

## Accrued Expenses

Expenses incurred but not yet paid or recorded at the statement date are called **accrued expenses**. Interest, taxes, and salaries are common examples of accrued expenses.

Companies make adjustments for accrued expenses to record the obligations that exist at the balance sheet date and to recognize the expenses that apply to the current accounting period (see **Ethics Note**). Prior to adjustment, both liabilities and expenses are understated. Therefore, as **Illustration 3.17** shows, **an adjusting entry for accrued expenses results in an increase (a debit) to an expense account and an increase (a credit) to a liability account**.

**Equation analyses** summarize the effects of transactions on the three elements of the accounting equation, as well as the effect on cash flows.

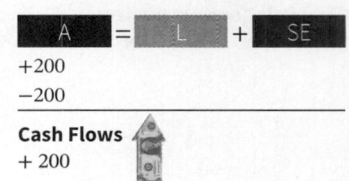

| A | = | L | + | SE |
|---|---|---|---|---|
| +200 | | | | |
| −200 | | | | |

**Cash Flows**
+ 200

**ILLUSTRATION 3.16**

**Accounting for accrued revenues**

**ETHICS NOTE**

A report released by **Fannie Mae**'s board of directors stated that improper adjusting entries at the mortgage-finance company resulted in delayed recognition of expenses caused by interest rate changes. The motivation for such accounting apparently was the desire to hit earnings estimates.

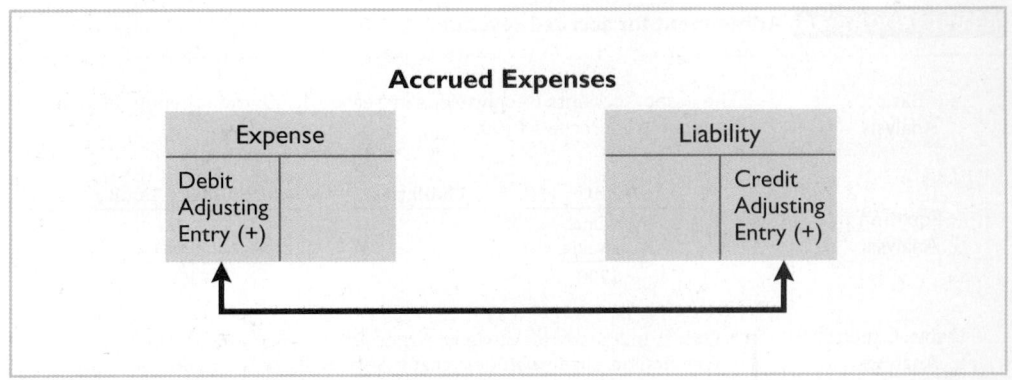

Let's look in more detail at some specific types of accrued expenses, beginning with accrued interest.

## Accrued Interest

Pioneer Advertising signed a three-month note payable in the amount of $5,000 on October 1. The note requires Pioneer to pay interest at an annual rate of 12%. The note and the interest will both be paid at maturity.

The amount of the interest recorded is determined by three factors: (1) the face value of the note; (2) the interest rate, which is always expressed as an annual rate; and (3) the length of time the note is outstanding. For Pioneer, the total interest due on the $5,000 note at its maturity date three months in the future is $150 ($5,000 $\times$ 12% $\times$ $\frac{3}{12}$), or $50 for one month (see **Helpful Hint**). **Illustration 3.18** shows the formula for computing monthly interest expense and its application to Pioneer for the month of October.

> **HELPFUL HINT**
>
> In computing interest, we express the time period as a fraction of a year.

| Face Value of Note | × | Annual Interest Rate | × | Time in Terms of One Year | = | Interest |
|---|---|---|---|---|---|---|
| $5,000 | × | 12% | × | $\frac{1}{12}$ | = | $50 |

As **Illustration 3.19** shows, the accrual of interest at October 31 increases a liability account, Interest Payable. It also decreases stockholders' equity by increasing an expense account, Interest Expense.

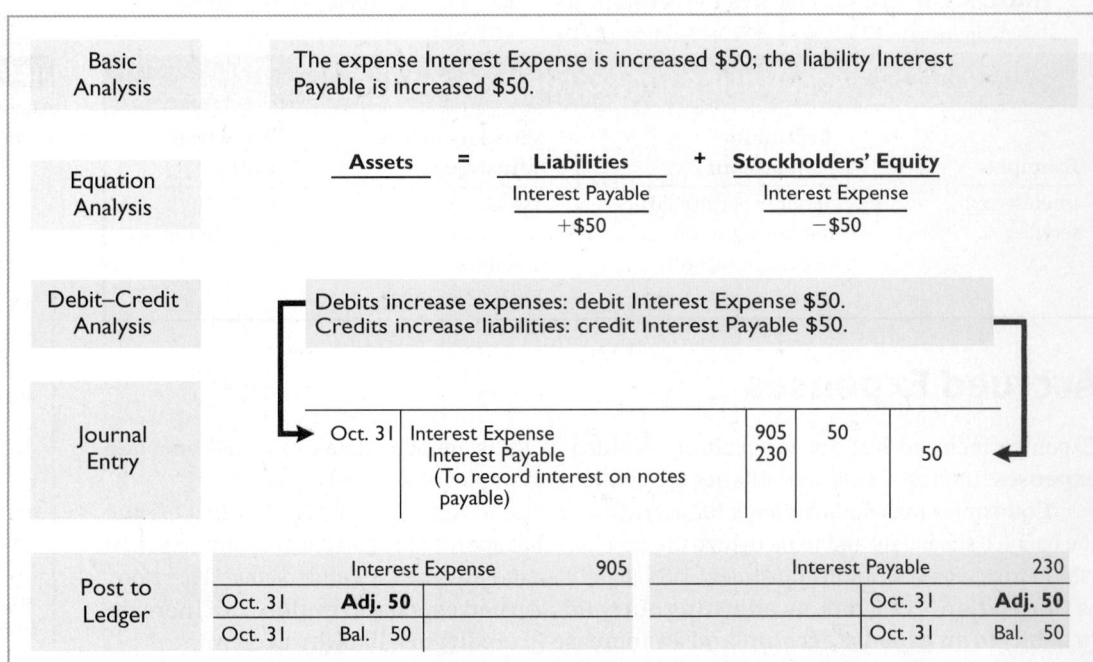

Interest Expense shows the interest charges for the month of October. Interest Payable shows the amount of interest the company owes at the statement date. Pioneer will not pay the interest until the note comes due at the end of three months. Companies use the Interest Payable account, instead of crediting Notes Payable, to disclose the two different types of obligations—interest and principal—in the accounts and statements. **Without this adjusting entry, liabilities and interest expense are understated, and net income and stockholders' equity are overstated.**

## Accrued Salaries and Wages

Companies pay for some types of expenses, such as employee salaries and wages, after the services have been performed. Pioneer Advertising paid salaries and wages on October 26 for its employees' first two weeks of work (October 15–October 26). The next payment of salaries will not occur until November 9. As **Illustration 3.20** shows, three working days of unpaid salaries and wages remain in October (October 29–31).

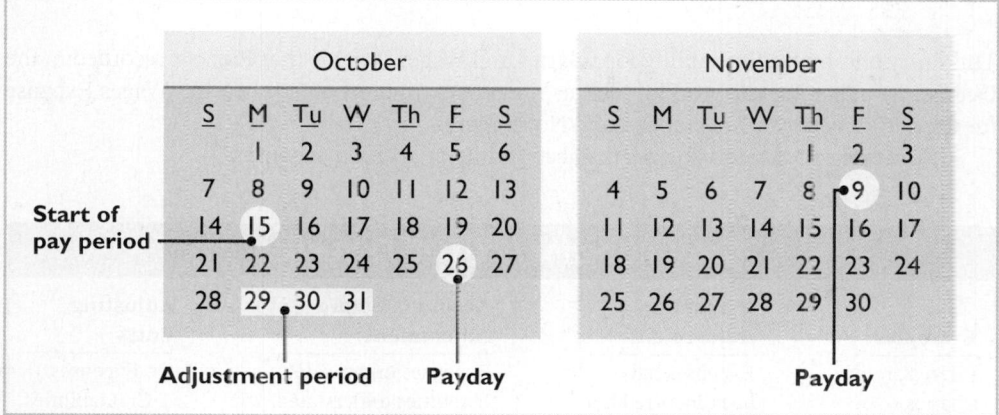

**ILLUSTRATION 3.20**

**Calendar showing Pioneer's pay periods**

At October 31, the salaries and wages for these three days represent an accrued expense and a related liability to Pioneer. The employees receive total salaries and wages of $2,000 for a five-day work week, or $400 per day. Thus, accrued salaries and wages at October 31 are $1,200 ($400 × 3). This accrual increases a liability, Salaries and Wages Payable. It also decreases stockholders' equity by increasing an expense account, Salaries and Wages Expense, as shown in **Illustration 3.21**.

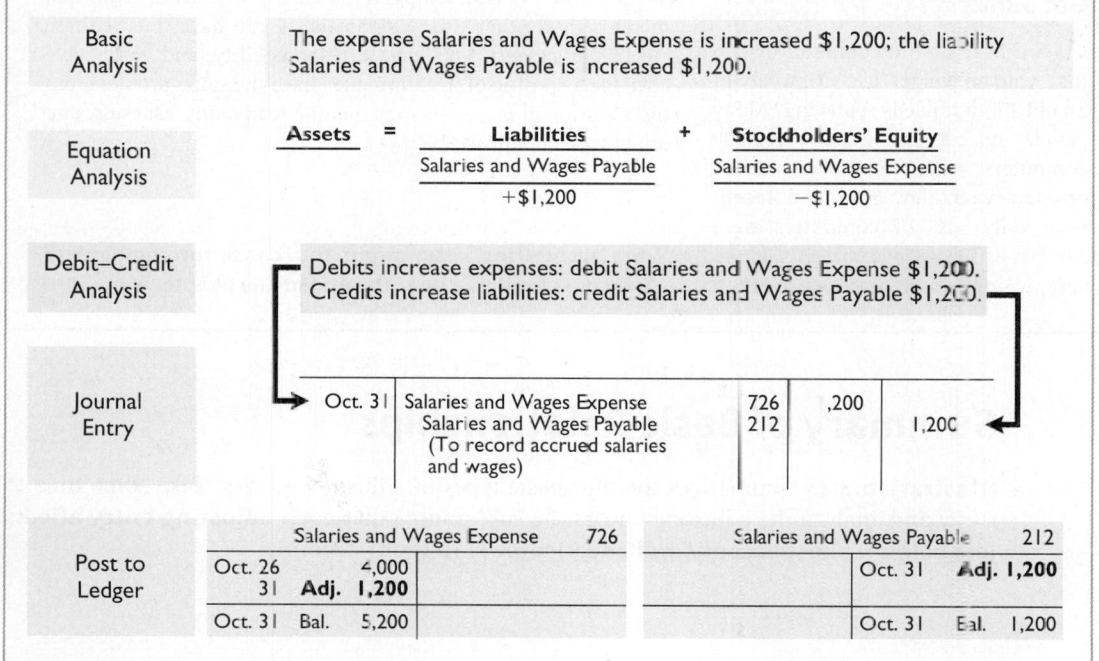

**ILLUSTRATION 3.21**

**Adjustment for accrued salaries and wages**

After this adjustment, the balance in Salaries and Wages Expense of $5,200 (13 days × $400) is the actual salary and wages expense for October. The balance in Salaries and Wages Payable of $1,200 is the amount of the liability for salaries and wages Pioneer owes as of October 31. **Without the $1,200 adjustment for salaries and wages, Pioneer's expenses are understated $1,200 and its liabilities are understated $1,200.**

Pioneer pays salaries and wages every two weeks. Consequently, the next payday is November 9, when the company will again pay total salaries and wages of $4,000. The payment consists of $1,200 of salaries and wages payable at October 31 plus $2,800 of salaries and wages expense for November (7 working days, as shown in the November calendar × $400). Therefore, Pioneer makes the following entry on November 9.

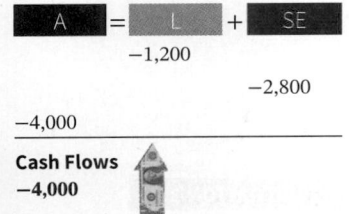

A = L + SE
−1,200
−2,800
−4,000

**Cash Flows**
**−4,000**

| Nov. 9 | Salaries and Wages Payable | 1,200 | |
| | Salaries and Wages Expense | 2,800 | |
| | Cash | | 4,000 |
| | (To record November 9 payroll) | | |

This entry eliminates the liability for Salaries and Wages Payable that Pioneer recorded in the October 31 adjusting entry, and it records the proper amount of Salaries and Wages Expense for the period between November 1 and November 9.

**Illustration 3.22** summarizes the accounting for accrued expenses.

**ILLUSTRATION 3.22**

**Accounting for accrued expenses**

## Accounting for Accrued Expenses

| Examples | Reason for Adjustment | Accounts Before Adjustment | Adjusting Entry |
|---|---|---|---|
| Interest, rent, salaries | Expenses have been incurred but not yet paid in cash or recorded. | Expenses understated. Liabilities understated. | Dr. Expenses Cr. Liabilities |

## People, Planet, and Profit Insight

### Got Junk?

Do you have an old computer or two that you no longer use? How about an old TV that needs replacing? Many people do. Approximately 163,000 computers and televisions become obsolete each day. Yet, in a recent year, only 11% of computers were recycled. It is estimated that 75% of all computers ever sold are sitting in storage somewhere, waiting to be disposed of. Each

iStock.com/Nathan Gleave

of these old TVs and computers is loaded with lead, cadmium, mercury, and other toxic chemicals. If you have one of these electronic gadgets, you have a responsibility, and a probable cost, for disposing of it. Companies have the same problem, but their discarded materials may include lead paint, asbestos, and other toxic chemicals.

**What accounting issue might this cause for companies? (Answer is available near the end of the chapter.)**

## Summary of Basic Relationships

**Illustration 3.23** summarizes the four basic types of adjusting entries. Take some time to study and analyze the adjusting entries. Be sure to note that **each adjusting entry affects one balance sheet account and one income statement account.**

| Type of Adjustment | Accounts Before Adjustment | Adjusting Entry |
|---|---|---|
| **Prepaid expenses** | Assets overstated. Expenses understated. | Dr. Expenses Cr. Assets or Contra Assets |
| **Unearned revenues** | Liabilities overstated. Revenues understated. | Dr. Liabilities Cr. Revenues |
| **Accrued revenues** | Assets understated. Revenues understated. | Dr. Assets Cr. Revenues |
| **Accrued expenses** | Expenses understated. Liabilities understated. | Dr. Expenses Cr. Liabilities |

**ILLUSTRATION 3.23**

**Summary of adjusting entries**

Illustrations **3.24** and **3.25** show the journalizing and posting of adjusting entries for Pioneer Advertising Inc. on October 31 (see **Helpful Hint**). The ledger identifies all adjustments by the reference J2 because they have been recorded on page 2 of the general journal. The company may insert a center caption "Adjusting Entries" between the last transaction entry and the first adjusting entry in the journal. When you review the general ledger in Illustration 3.25, note that the entries highlighted in red are the adjustments.

**HELPFUL HINT**

(1) Adjusting entries should not involve debits or credits to Cash.
(2) Evaluate whether the adjustment makes sense. For example, an adjustment to recognize supplies used should increase Supplies Expense.
(3) Double-check all computations.
(4) Each adjusting entry affects one balance sheet account and one income statement account.

**ILLUSTRATION 3.24**   **General journal showing adjusting entries**

| | GENERAL JOURNAL | | | | J2 |
|---|---|---|---|---|---|
| **Date** | **Account Titles and Explanation** | | **Ref.** | **Debit** | **Credit** |
| 2022 | | Adjusting Entries | | | |
| Oct. 31 | Supplies Expense | | 631 | 1,500 | |
| | Supplies | | 126 | | 1,500 |
| | (To record supplies used) | | | | |
| 31 | Insurance Expense | | 722 | 50 | |
| | Prepaid Insurance | | 130 | | 50 |
| | (To record insurance expired) | | | | |
| 31 | Depreciation Expense | | 711 | 40 | |
| | Accumulated Depreciation—Equipment | | 158 | | 40 |
| | (To record monthly depreciation) | | | | |
| 31 | Unearned Service Revenue | | 209 | 400 | |
| | Service Revenue | | 400 | | 400 |
| | (To record revenue for services performed) | | | | |
| 31 | Accounts Receivable | | 112 | 200 | |
| | Service Revenue | | 400 | | 200 |
| | (To record revenue for services performed) | | | | |
| 31 | Interest Expense | | 905 | 50 | |
| | Interest Payable | | 230 | | 50 |
| | (To record interest on notes payable) | | | | |
| 31 | Salaries and Wages Expense | | 726 | 1,200 | |
| | Salaries and Wages Payable | | 212 | | 1,200 |
| | (To record accrued salaries and wages) | | | | |

**ILLUSTRATION 3.25**  **General ledger after adjustment**

## GENERAL LEDGER

### Cash — No. 101

| Date | Explanation | Ref. | Debit | Credit | Balance |
|---|---|---|---|---|---|
| 2022 | | | | | |
| Oct. 1 | | J1 | 10,000 | | 10,000 |
| 2 | | J1 | 1,200 | | 11,200 |
| 3 | | J1 | | 900 | 10,300 |
| 4 | | J1 | | 600 | 9,700 |
| 20 | | J1 | 10,000 | | 19,700 |
| 26 | | J1 | | 4,000 | 15,700 |
| 31 | | J1 | | 500 | 15,200 |

### Accounts Receivable — No. 112

| Date | Explanation | Ref. | Debit | Credit | Balance |
|---|---|---|---|---|---|
| 2022 | | | | | |
| Oct. 31 | Adj. entry | J2 | 200 | | 200 |

### Supplies — No. 126

| Date | Explanation | Ref. | Debit | Credit | Balance |
|---|---|---|---|---|---|
| 2022 | | | | | |
| Oct. 5 | | J1 | 2,500 | | 2,500 |
| 31 | Adj. entry | J2 | | 1,500 | 1,000 |

### Prepaid Insurance — No. 130

| Date | Explanation | Ref. | Debit | Credit | Balance |
|---|---|---|---|---|---|
| 2022 | | | | | |
| Oct. 4 | | J1 | 600 | | 600 |
| 31 | Adj. entry | J2 | | 50 | 550 |

### Equipment — No. 157

| Date | Explanation | Ref. | Debit | Credit | Balance |
|---|---|---|---|---|---|
| 2022 | | | | | |
| Oct. 1 | | J1 | 5,000 | | 5,000 |

### Accumulated Depreciation—Equipment — No. 158

| Date | Explanation | Ref. | Debit | Credit | Balance |
|---|---|---|---|---|---|
| 2022 | | | | | |
| Oct. 31 | Adj. entry | J2 | | 40 | 40 |

### Notes Payable — No. 200

| Date | Explanation | Ref. | Debit | Credit | Balance |
|---|---|---|---|---|---|
| 2022 | | | | | |
| Oct. 1 | | J1 | | 5,000 | 5,000 |

### Accounts Payable — No. 201

| Date | Explanation | Ref. | Debit | Credit | Balance |
|---|---|---|---|---|---|
| 2022 | | | | | |
| Oct. 5 | | J1 | | 2,500 | 2,500 |

### Unearned Service Revenue — No. 209

| Date | Explanation | Ref. | Debit | Credit | Balance |
|---|---|---|---|---|---|
| 2022 | | | | | |
| Oct. 2 | | J1 | | 1,200 | 1,200 |
| 31 | Adj. entry | J2 | 400 | | 800 |

### Salaries and Wages Payable — No. 212

| Date | Explanation | Ref. | Debit | Credit | Balance |
|---|---|---|---|---|---|
| 2022 | | | | | |
| Oct. 31 | Adj. entry | J2 | | 1,200 | 1,200 |

### Interest Payable — No. 230

| Date | Explanation | Ref. | Debit | Credit | Balance |
|---|---|---|---|---|---|
| 2022 | | | | | |
| Oct. 31 | Adj. entry | J2 | | 50 | 50 |

### Common Stock — No. 311

| Date | Explanation | Ref. | Debit | Credit | Balance |
|---|---|---|---|---|---|
| 2022 | | | | | |
| Oct. 1 | | J1 | | 10,000 | 10,000 |

### Retained Earnings — No. 320

| Date | Explanation | Ref. | Debit | Credit | Balance |
|---|---|---|---|---|---|
| 2022 | | | | | |

### Dividends — No. 332

| Date | Explanation | Ref. | Debit | Credit | Balance |
|---|---|---|---|---|---|
| 2022 | | | | | |
| Oct. 31 | | J1 | 500 | | 500 |

### Service Revenue — No. 400

| Date | Explanation | Ref. | Debit | Credit | Balance |
|---|---|---|---|---|---|
| 2022 | | | | | |
| Oct. 20 | | J1 | | 10,000 | 10,000 |
| 31 | Adj. entry | J2 | | 400 | 10,400 |
| 31 | Adj. entry | J2 | | 200 | 10,600 |

### Supplies Expense — No. 631

| Date | Explanation | Ref. | Debit | Credit | Balance |
|---|---|---|---|---|---|
| 2022 | | | | | |
| Oct. 31 | Adj. entry | J2 | 1,500 | | 1,500 |

### Depreciation Expense — No. 711

| Date | Explanation | Ref. | Debit | Credit | Balance |
|---|---|---|---|---|---|
| 2022 | | | | | |
| Oct. 31 | Adj. entry | J2 | 40 | | 40 |

### Insurance Expense — No. 722

| Date | Explanation | Ref. | Debit | Credit | Balance |
|---|---|---|---|---|---|
| 2022 | | | | | |
| Oct. 31 | Adj. entry | J2 | 50 | | 50 |

### Salaries and Wages Expense — No. 726

| Date | Explanation | Ref. | Debit | Credit | Balance |
|---|---|---|---|---|---|
| 2022 | | | | | |
| Oct. 26 | | J1 | 4,000 | | 4,000 |
| 31 | Adj. entry | J2 | 1,200 | | 5,200 |

### Rent Expense — No. 729

| Date | Explanation | Ref. | Debit | Credit | Balance |
|---|---|---|---|---|---|
| 2022 | | | | | |
| Oct. 3 | | J1 | 900 | | 900 |

### Interest Expense — No. 905

| Date | Explanation | Ref. | Debit | Credit | Balance |
|---|---|---|---|---|---|
| 2022 | | | | | |
| Oct. 31 | Adj. entry | J2 | 50 | | 50 |

## DO IT! 3 | Adjusting Entries for Accruals

Micro Computer Services Inc. began operations on August 1, 2022. At the end of August 2022, management prepares monthly financial statements. The following information relates to August.

1. At August 31, the company owed its employees $800 in salaries and wages that will be paid on September 1.

2. On August 1, the company borrowed $30,000 from a local bank on a 1-year note payable. The annual interest rate is 10%. Interest will be paid with the note at maturity.

3. Revenue for services performed but unrecorded for August totaled $1,100.

Prepare the adjusting entries needed at August 31, 2022.

**ACTION PLAN**

- Make adjusting entries at the end of the period to recognize revenues for services performed and for expenses incurred.
- Don't forget to make adjusting entries for accruals. Adjusting entries for accruals will increase both a balance sheet and an income statement account.

### Solution

| | | |
|---|---|---|
| 1. Salaries and Wages Expense | 800 | |
|     Salaries and Wages Payable | | 800 |
|      (To record accrued salaries) | | |
| 2. Interest Expense | 250 | |
|     Interest Payable | | 250 |
|      (To record accrued interest: | | |
|      $30,000 \times 10\% \times \frac{1}{12} = \$250$) | | |
| 3. Accounts Receivable | 1,100 | |
|     Service Revenue | | 1,100 |
|      (To record revenue for services performed) | | |

Related exercise material: **BE3.10, BE3.11, BE3.12, DO IT! 3.3, E3.5, E3.6, E3.7, E3.8, E3.9, E3.10 E3.11, E3.12, E3.13, E3.14, E3.15, E3.17, E3.18, E3.19, and E3.20.**

# Adjusted Trial Balance and Financial Statements

## LEARNING OBJECTIVE 4

Describe the nature and purpose of an adjusted trial balance.

| ANALYZE | JOURNALIZE | POST | TRIAL BALANCE | ADJUSTING ENTRIES | **Adjusted trial balance** | **Prepare financial statements** | JOURNALIZE AND POST CLOSING ENTRIES | PREPARE A POST-CLOSING TRIAL BALANCE |
|---|---|---|---|---|---|---|---|---|

After a company has journalized and posted all adjusting entries, it prepares another trial balance from the ledger accounts. This trial balance is called an **adjusted trial balance**. It shows the balances of all accounts, including those adjusted, at the end of the accounting period. The purpose of an adjusted trial balance is to **prove the equality** of the total debit balances and the total credit balances in the ledger after all adjustments. Because the accounts now contain all data needed for financial statements, the adjusted trial balance is the **primary basis for the preparation of financial statements**.

# Preparing the Adjusted Trial Balance

**Illustration 3.26** presents the adjusted trial balance for Pioneer Advertising Inc. prepared from the ledger accounts in Illustration 3.25. The amounts affected by the adjusting entries are highlighted in red. Compare these amounts to those in the unadjusted trial balance in Illustration 3.4. In this comparison, you will see that there are more accounts in the adjusted trial balance as a result of the adjusting entries made at the end of the month.

**ILLUSTRATION 3.26**

**Adjusted trial balance**

**Pioneer Advertising Inc.**
**Adjusted Trial Balance**
**October 31, 2022**

|  | Debit | Credit |
|---|---|---|
| Cash | $15,200 | |
| Accounts Receivable | 200 | |
| Supplies | 1,000 | |
| Prepaid Insurance | 550 | |
| Equipment | 5,000 | |
| Accumulated Depreciation—Equipment | | $     40 |
| Notes Payable | | 5,000 |
| Accounts Payable | | 2,500 |
| Interest Payable | | 50 |
| Unearned Service Revenue | | 800 |
| Salaries and Wages Payable | | 1,200 |
| Common Stock | | 10,000 |
| Retained Earnings | | –0– |
| Dividends | 500 | |
| Service Revenue | | 10,600 |
| Salaries and Wages Expense | 5,200 | |
| Supplies Expense | 1,500 | |
| Rent Expense | 900 | |
| Insurance Expense | 50 | |
| Interest Expense | 50 | |
| Depreciation Expense | 40 | |
| | $30,190 | $30,190 |

# Preparing Financial Statements

**Companies can prepare financial statements directly from the adjusted trial balance.** **Illustrations 3.27** and **3.28** present the interrelationships of data in the adjusted trial balance and the financial statements.

As Illustration 3.27 shows, companies prepare the income statement from the revenue and expense accounts. Next, they use the Retained Earnings and Dividends accounts and the net income (or net loss) from the income statement to prepare the retained earnings statement.

**ILLUSTRATION 3.27** **Preparation of the income statement and retained earnings statement from the adjusted trial balance**

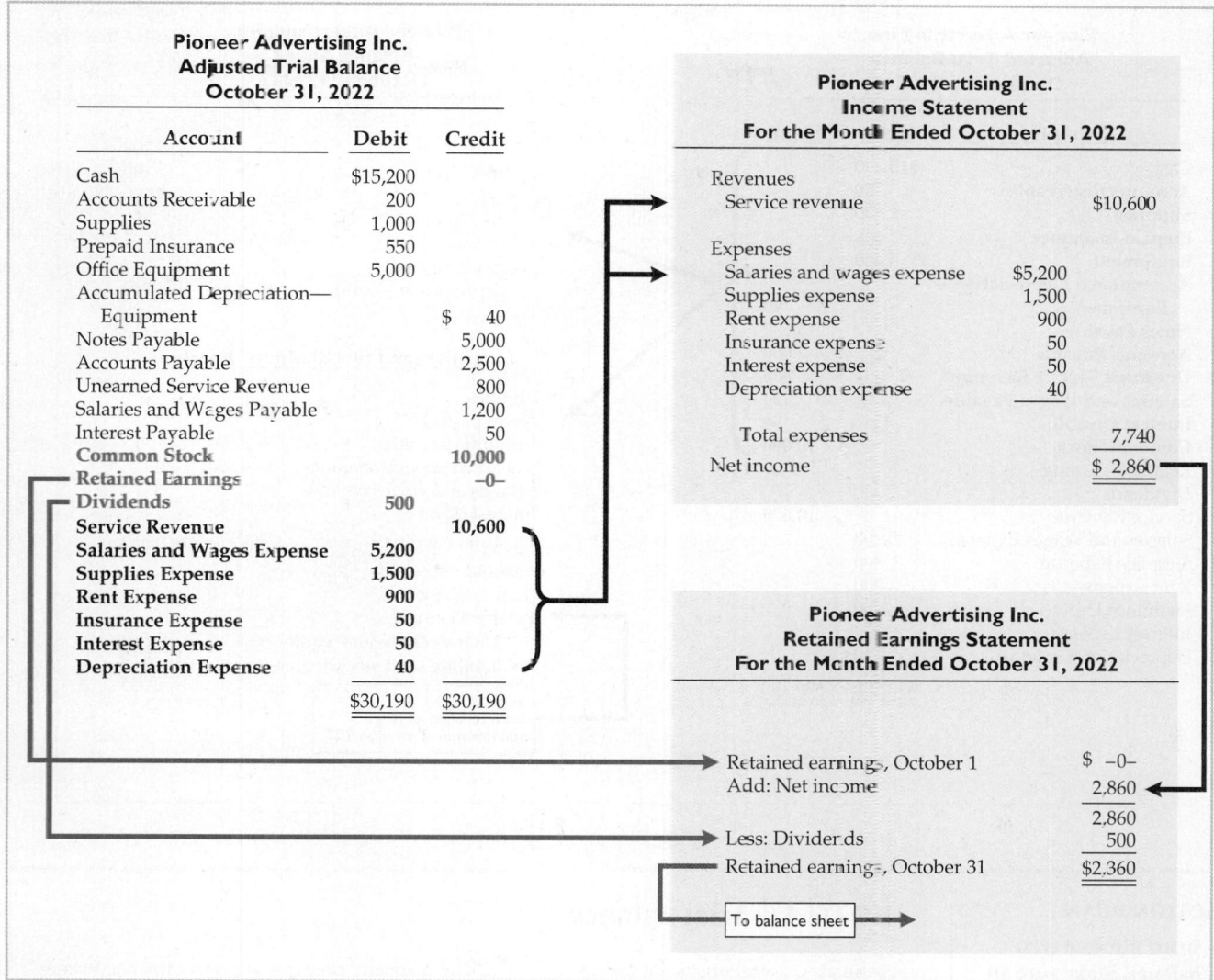

As **Illustration 3.28** shows, companies then prepare the balance sheet from the asset and liability accounts and the ending retained earnings balance as reported in the retained earnings statement.

**ILLUSTRATION 3.28** **Preparation of the balance sheet from the adjusted trial balance**

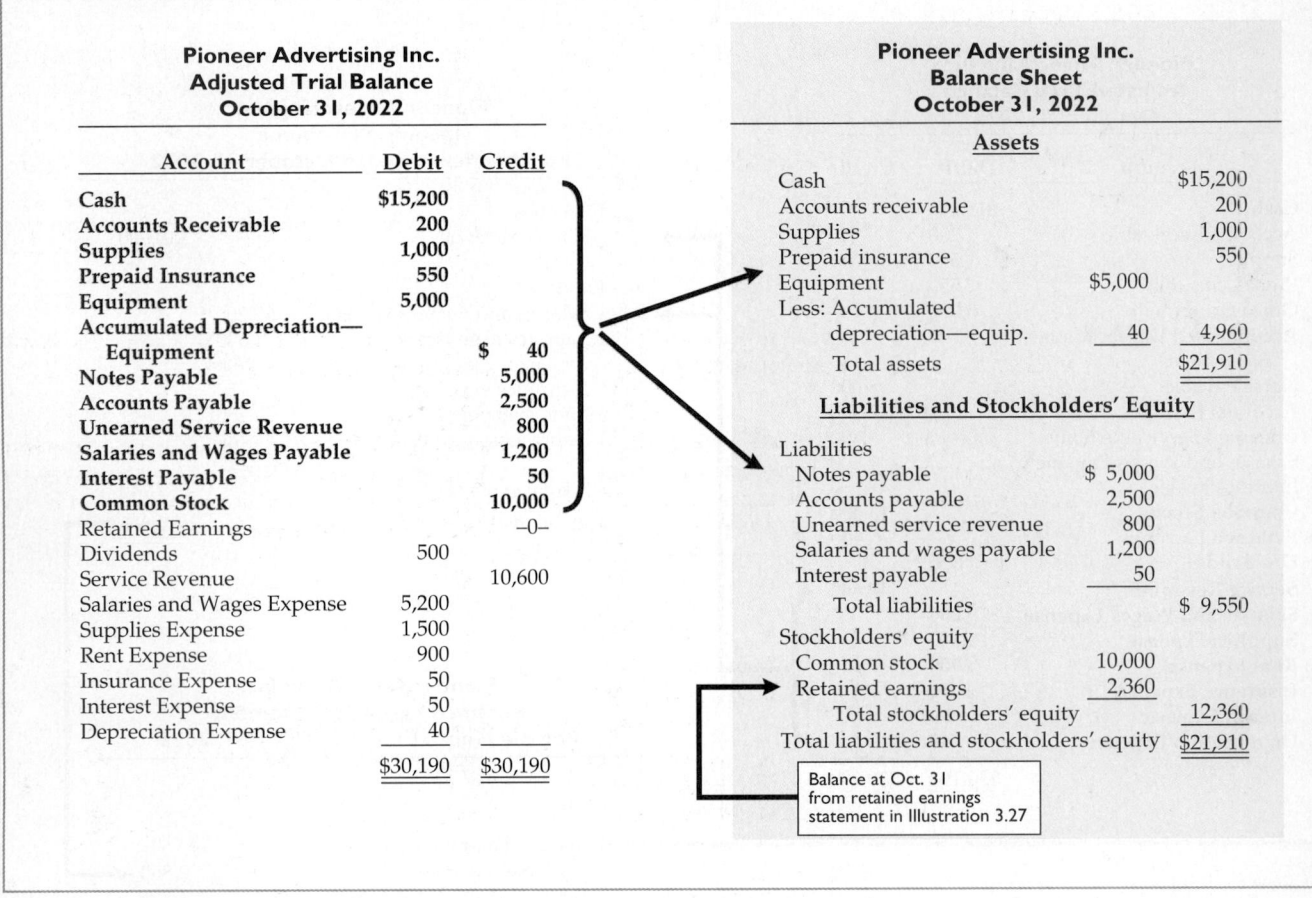

**ACTION PLAN**

- In an adjusted trial balance, make sure all asset, liability, revenue, and expense accounts are properly stated.

- To determine the ending balance in Retained Earnings, add net income and subtract dividends.

## DO IT! 4 | Trial Balance

Skolnick Co. was organized on April 1, 2022. The company prepares quarterly financial statements. The adjusted trial balance amounts at June 30 are shown below.

| | Debit | | Credit |
|---|---|---|---|
| Cash | $ 6,700 | Accumulated Depreciation— | |
| Accounts Receivable | 600 | Equipment | $ 850 |
| Prepaid Rent | 900 | Notes Payable | 5,000 |
| Supplies | 1,000 | Accounts Payable | 1,510 |
| Equipment | 15,000 | Salaries and Wages Payable | 400 |
| Dividends | 600 | Interest Payable | 50 |
| Salaries and Wages Expense | 9,400 | Unearned Rent Revenue | 500 |
| Rent Expense | 1,500 | Common Stock | 14,000 |
| Depreciation Expense | 850 | Service Revenue | 14,200 |
| Supplies Expense | 200 | Rent Revenue | 800 |
| Utilities Expense | 510 | | |
| Interest Expense | 50 | | |
| | $37,310 | | $37,310 |

**a.** Determine the net income for the quarter April 1 to June 30.

**b.** Determine the total assets and total liabilities at June 30, 2022, for Skolnick Co.

**c.** Determine the amount that appears for retained earnings at June 30, 2022.

### Solution

**a.** The net income is determined by adding revenues and subtracting expenses. The net income is computed as follows.

| | | |
|---|---:|---:|
| Revenues | | |
| Service revenue | $14,200 | |
| Rent revenue | 800 | |
| Total revenues | | $15,000 |
| Expenses | | |
| Salaries and wages expense | 9,400 | |
| Rent expense | 1,500 | |
| Depreciation expense | 850 | |
| Utilities expense | 510 | |
| Supplies expense | 200 | |
| Interest expense | 50 | |
| Total expenses | | 12,510 |
| Net income | | $ 2,490 |

**b.** Total assets and liabilities are computed as follows.

| Assets | | | | Liabilities | |
|---|---:|---:|---|---|---:|
| Cash | | $ 6,700 | | Notes payable | $5,000 |
| Accounts receivable | | 600 | | Accounts payable | 1,510 |
| Supplies | | 1,000 | | Unearned rent | |
| Prepaid rent | | 900 | | revenue | 500 |
| Equipment | $15,000 | | | Salaries and wages | |
| Less: Accumulated | | | | payable | 400 |
| depreciation— | | | | Interest payable | 50 |
| equipment | 850 | 14,150 | | | |
| Total assets | | $23,350 | | Total liabilities | $7,460 |

**c.**

| | |
|---|---:|
| Retained earnings, April 1 | $ 0 |
| Add: Net income | 2,490 |
| Less: Dividends | 600 |
| Retained earnings, June 30 | $ 1,890 |

Related exercise material: **BE3 13, BE3.14, DO IT! 3.4, E3.18, and E3.19.**

---

| Appendix 3A |
|---|

# Adjusting Entries for the Alternative Treatment of Deferrals

**LEARNING OBJECTIVE *5**

Prepare adjusting entries for the alternative treatment of deferrals.

In discussing adjusting entries for prepaid expenses and unearned revenues, we illustrated transactions for which companies made the initial entries to balance sheet accounts. In the case of prepaid expenses, the company debited the prepayment to an asset account. In the case of unearned revenue, the company credited a liability account to record the cash received.

Some companies use an alternative treatment. (1) When a company prepays an expense, it debits that amount to an expense account. (2) When it receives payment for future services, it credits the amount to a revenue account. In this appendix, we describe the circumstances that justify such entries and the different adjusting entries that may be required. This alternative treatment of prepaid expenses and unearned revenues has the same effect on the financial statements as the procedures described in the chapter.

# Prepaid Expenses

Prepaid expenses become expired costs either through the passage of time (e.g., insurance) or through consumption (e.g., advertising supplies). If at the time of purchase the company expects to consume the supplies before the next financial statement date, **it may choose to debit (increase) an expense account rather than an asset account. This alternative treatment is simply more convenient.**

Assume that Pioneer Advertising Inc. expects that it will use before the end of the month all of the supplies purchased on October 5. A debit of $2,500 to Supplies Expense (rather than to the asset account Supplies) on October 5 will eliminate the need for an adjusting entry on October 31. At October 31, the Supplies Expense account will show a balance of $2,500, which is the cost of supplies used between October 5 and October 31.

But what if the company does not use all the supplies? For example, what if an inventory of $1,000 of advertising supplies remains on October 31? Obviously, the company would need to make an adjusting entry. Prior to adjustment, the expense account Supplies Expense is overstated $1,000, and the asset account Supplies is understated $1,000. Thus, Pioneer makes the following adjusting entry.

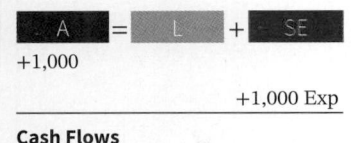

+1,000

                +1,000 Exp

**Cash Flows**
no effect

| Oct. 31 | Supplies | 1,000 | |
| |     Supplies Expense | | 1,000 |
| |       (To record supplies inventory) | | |

**Illustration 3A.1** shows the accounts after the company posts the adjusting entry.

| Supplies | | | Supplies Expense | | |
|---|---|---|---|---|---|
| 10/31 **Adj.** 1,000 | | 10/5 2,500 | 10/31 **Adj.** 1,000 | | |
| | | 10/31 **Bal.** 1,500 | | | |

After adjustment, the asset account Supplies shows a balance of $1,000, which is equal to the cost of supplies on hand at October 31. In addition, Supplies Expense shows a balance of $1,500. This is equal to the cost of supplies used between October 5 and October 31. Without the adjusting entry, expenses are overstated and net income is understated by $1,000 in the October income statement. Also, both assets and stockholders' equity are understated by $1,000 on the October 31 balance sheet.

**Illustration 3A.2** compares the entries and accounts for advertising supplies in the two adjustment approaches.

| | Prepayment Initially Debited to Asset Account (per chapter) | | | Prepayment Initially Debited to Expense Account (per appendix) | | |
|---|---|---|---|---|---|---|
| Oct. 5 | Supplies | 2,500 | | Oct. 5 | Supplies Expense | 2,500 | |
| | Accounts Payable | | 2,500 | | Accounts Payable | | 2,500 |
| Oct. 31 | Supplies Expense | 1,500 | | Oct. 31 | Supplies | 1,000 | |
| | Supplies | | 1,500 | | Supplies Expense | | 1,000 |

After Pioneer posts the entries, the accounts appear as shown in **Illustration 3A.3**.

| (per chapter) Supplies | | | (per appendix) Supplies | | |
|---|---|---|---|---|---|
| 10/5 2,500 | 10/31 **Adj.** 1,500 | | 10/31 **Adj.** 1,000 | | |
| 10/31 **Bal.** 1,000 | | | | | |

| Supplies Expense | | | Supplies Expense | | |
|---|---|---|---|---|---|
| 10/31 **Adj.** 1,500 | | | 10/5 2,500 | 10/31 **Adj.** 1,000 | |
| | | | 10/31 **Bal.** 1,500 | | |

Note that the account balances under each alternative are the same at October 31: Supplies $1,000 and Supplies Expense $1,500.

# Unearned Revenues

Unearned revenues are recognized as revenue at the time services are performed. Similar to the case for prepaid expenses, companies may credit (increase) a revenue account when they receive cash for future services.

To illustrate, assume that Pioneer Advertising Inc. received $1,200 for future services on October 2. Pioneer expects to perform the services before October 31.[1] In such a case, the company credits Service Revenue. If Pioneer in fact performs the service before October 31, no adjustment is needed.

However, if at the statement date Pioneer has not performed $800 of the services, it would make an adjusting entry (see **Helpful Hint**). Without the entry, the revenue account Service Revenue is overstated $800, and the liability account Unearned Service Revenue is understated $800. Thus, Pioneer makes the following adjusting entry.

**HELPFUL HINT**

The required adjusted balances here are Service Revenue $400 and Unearned Service Revenue $800.

| Oct. 31 | Service Revenue | 800 | |
| |    Unearned Service Revenue | | 800 |
| |     (To record unearned service revenue) | | |

A = L + SE

−800 Rev

+800

**Cash Flows**
no effect

**Illustration 3A.4** shows the accounts after Pioneer posts the adjusting entry.

| Unearned Service Revenue | | | Service Revenue | | |
|---|---|---|---|---|---|
| | 10/31 **Adj.** 800 | | 10/31 **Adj.** 800 | 10/2 | 1,200 |
| | | | | 10/31 **Bal.** | 400 |

**ILLUSTRATION 3A.4**

**Accounts after adjustment**

The liability account Unearned Service Revenue shows a balance of $800. This equals the services that will be performed in the future. In addition, the balance in Service Revenue equals the services performed in October. Without the adjusting entry, both revenues and net income are overstated by $800 in the October income statement. Also, liabilities are understated by $800 and stockholders' equity is overstated by $800 on the October 31 balance sheet.

**Illustration 3A.5** compares the entries and accounts for initially recording unearned service revenue in (1) a liability account or (2) a revenue account.

| Unearned Service Revenue Initially Credited to Liability Account (per chapter) | | | Unearned Service Revenue Initially Credited to Revenue Account (per appendix) | | |
|---|---|---|---|---|---|
| Oct. 2 | Cash | 1,200 | Oct. 2 | Cash | 1,200 |
| |   Unearned Service Revenue | 1,200 | |   Service Revenue | 1,200 |
| Oct. 31 | Unearned Service Revenue | 400 | Oct. 31 | Service Revenue | 800 |
| |   Service Revenue | 400 | |   Unearned Service Revenue | 800 |

**ILLUSTRATION 3A.5**

**Adjustment approaches—a comparison**

---

[1]This example focuses only on the alternative treatment of unearned revenues. For simplicity, we have ignored the entries to Service Revenue pertaining to the immediate recognition of revenue ($10,000) and the adjusting entry for accrued revenue ($200).

After Pioneer posts the entries, the accounts appear as shown in **Illustration 3A.6**.

**ILLUSTRATION 3A.6**
**Comparison of accounts**

| | (per chapter) | | | | | (per appendix) | | |
|---|---|---|---|---|---|---|---|---|
| | **Unearned Service Revenue** | | | | | **Unearned Service Revenue** | | |
| 10/31 **Adj.** 400 | 10/2 | 1,200 | | | | 10/31 **Adj.** | 800 |
| | 10/31 **Bal.** | 800 | | | | | |

| | **Service Revenue** | | | | **Service Revenue** | | |
|---|---|---|---|---|---|---|---|
| | 10/31 **Adj.** | 400 | | 10/31 **Adj.** 800 | 10/2 | 1,200 |
| | | | | | 10/31 **Bal.** | 400 |

Note that the balances in the accounts are the same under the two alternatives: Unearned Service Revenue $800 and Service Revenue $400.

## Summary of Additional Adjustment Relationships

**Illustration 3A.7** provides a summary of basic relationships for deferrals.

**ILLUSTRATION 3A.7** **Summary of basic relationships for deferrals**

| Type of Adjustment | Reason for Adjustment | Account Balances before Adjustment | Adjusting Entry |
|---|---|---|---|
| 1. Prepaid expenses | (a) Prepaid expenses initially recorded in asset accounts have been used. | Assets overstated. Expenses understated. | Dr. Expenses Cr. Assets |
| | (b) **Prepaid expenses initially recorded in expense accounts have not been used.** | **Assets understated. Expenses overstated.** | **Dr. Assets Cr. Expenses** |
| 2. Unearned revenues | (a) Unearned revenues initially recorded in liability accounts are now recognized as revenue. | Liabilities overstated. Revenues understated. | Dr. Liabilities Cr. Revenues |
| | (b) **Unearned revenues initially recorded in revenue accounts are still unearned.** | **Liabilities understated. Revenues overstated.** | **Dr. Revenues Cr. Liabilities** |

Alternative adjusting entries **do not apply** to accrued revenues and accrued expenses because **no entries occur before companies make these types of adjusting entries**.

---

**Appendix 3B**

# Financial Reporting Concepts

**LEARNING OBJECTIVE *6**
Discuss financial reporting concepts.

This appendix provides a summary of the concepts in action used in this text. In addition, it provides other useful concepts which accountants use as a basis for recording and reporting financial information.

## Qualities of Useful Information

The FASB completed the first phase of a project in which it developed a conceptual framework to serve as the basis for future accounting standards. The framework begins by stating that the primary objective of financial reporting is to provide financial information that is **useful** to investors and creditors for making decisions about providing capital. Useful information should possess two fundamental qualities, relevance and faithful representation, as shown in **Illustration 3B.1**.

| "Tell me what I need to know." | **Relevance** Accounting information has **relevance** if it would make a difference in a business decision. Information is considered relevant if it provides information that has **predictive value**, that is, helps provide accurate expectations about the future, and has **confirmatory value**, that is, confirms or corrects prior expectations. **Materiality** is a company-specific aspect of relevance. An item is material when its **size** makes it likely to influence the decision of an investor or creditor. |
|---|---|
|  | **Faithful Representation** **Faithful representation** means that information accurately depicts what really happened. To provide a faithful representation, information must be **complete** (nothing important has been omitted), **neutral** (is not biased toward one position or another), and **free from error**. |

## Enhancing Qualities

In addition to the two fundamental qualities, the FASB also describes a number of enhancing qualities of useful information. These include **comparability**, **verifiability**, **timeliness**, and **understandability**. In accounting, **comparability** results when different companies use the same accounting principles. Another type of comparability is consistency. **Consistency** means that a company uses the same accounting principles and methods from year to year. Information is **verifiable** if independent observers, using the same methods, obtain similar results. For accounting information to have relevance, it must be **timely**. That is, it must be available to decision-makers before it loses its capacity to influence decisions. For example, public companies like **Google** or **Best Buy** provide their annual reports to investors within 60 days of their year-end. Information has the quality of **understandability** if it is presented in a clear and concise fashion, so that reasonably informed users of that information can interpret it and comprehend its meaning.

# Assumptions in Financial Reporting

To develop accounting standards, the FASB relies on some key assumptions, as shown in **Illustration 3B.2**. These include assumptions about the monetary unit, economic entity, time period, and going concern.

# Principles in Financial Reporting

## Measurement Principles

GAAP generally uses one of two measurement principles, the historical cost principle or the fair value principle. Selection of which principle to follow generally relates to trade-offs between relevance and faithful representation.

**Historical Cost Principle** The **historical cost principle** (or cost principle, discussed in Chapter 1) dictates that companies record assets at their cost. This is true not only at the time the asset is purchased but also over the time the asset is held. For example, if land that was purchased for $30,000 increases in value to $40,000, it continues to be reported at $30,000.

**Fair Value Principle** The **fair value principle** (discussed in Chapter 1) indicates that assets and liabilities should be reported at fair value (the price received to sell an asset or settle a liability). Fair value information may be more useful than historical cost for certain types of assets and liabilities. For example, certain investment securities are reported at fair value

**Monetary Unit Assumption** The **monetary unit assumption** requires that only those things that can be expressed in money are included in the accounting records. This means that certain important information needed by investors, creditors, and managers, such as customer satisfaction, is not reported in the financial statements. This assumption relies on the monetary unit remaining relatively stable in value.

**Economic Entity Assumption** The **economic entity assumption** states that every economic entity can be separately identified and accounted for. In order to assess a company's performance and financial position accurately, it is important to not blur company transactions with personal transactions (especially those of its managers) or transactions of other companies.

**Time Period Assumption** Notice that the income statement, retained earnings statement, and statement of cash flows all cover periods of one year, and the balance sheet is prepared at the end of each year. The **time period assumption** states that the life of a business can be divided into artificial time periods and that useful reports covering those periods can be prepared for the business.

**Going Concern Assumption** The **going concern assumption** states that the business will remain in operation for the foreseeable future. Of course, many businesses do fail, but in general it is reasonable to assume that the business will continue operating.

because market price information is often readily available for these types of assets. In choosing between cost and fair value, two qualities that make accounting information useful for decision-making are used—relevance and faithful representation. In determining which measurement principle to use, the factual nature of cost figures are weighed versus the relevance of fair value. In general, most assets follow the historical cost principle because fair values may not be representationally faithful. Only in situations where assets are actively traded, such as investment securities, is the fair value principle applied.

## Revenue Recognition Principle

The **revenue recognition principle** requires that companies recognize revenue in the accounting period in which the performance obligation is satisfied. As discussed earlier in the chapter, in a service company, revenue is recognized at the time the service is performed. In a merchandising company, the performance obligation is generally satisfied when the goods transfer from the seller to the buyer (discussed in Chapter 5). At this point, the sales transaction is complete and the sales price is established.

## Expense Recognition Principle

The **expense recognition principle** (discussed earlier in the chapter) dictates that companies recognize expense in the period in which they make efforts to generate revenue. Thus, expenses follow revenues.

## Full Disclosure Principle

The **full disclosure principle** (discussed in Chapter 11) requires that companies disclose all circumstances and events that would make a difference to financial statement users. If an important item cannot reasonably be reported directly in one of the four types of financial statements, then it should be discussed in notes that accompany the statements.

## Cost Constraint

Providing information is costly. In deciding whether companies should be required to provide a certain type of information, accounting standard-setters consider the **cost constraint**. It weighs the cost that companies will incur to provide the information against the benefit that financial statement users will gain from having the information available.

# Review and Practice

## Learning Objectives Review

**1  Explain the accrual basis of accounting and the reasons for adjusting entries.**

The time period assumption indicates that the economic life of a business is divided into artificial time periods. Accrual-basis accounting means that companies record events that change a company's financial statements in the periods in which those events occur, rather than in the periods in which the company receives or pays cash.

Companies make adjusting entries at the end of an accounting period. Such entries ensure that companies recognize revenues in the period in which the performance obligation is satisfied and recognize expenses in the period in which they are incurred. The major types of adjusting entries are deferrals (prepaid expenses and unearned revenues) and accruals (accrued revenues and accrued expenses).

**2  Prepare adjusting entries for deferrals.**

Deferrals are either prepaid expenses or unearned revenues. Companies make adjusting entries for deferrals to record the portion of the prepayment that represents the expense incurred or the revenue for services performed in the current accounting period.

**3  Prepare adjusting entries for accruals.**

Accruals are either accrued revenues or accrued expenses. Companies make adjusting entries for accruals to record revenues for services performed and expenses incurred in the current accounting period that have not been recognized through daily entries.

**4  Describe the nature and purpose of an adjusted trial balance.**

An adjusted trial balance shows the balances of all accounts, including those that have been adjusted, at the end of an accounting period. Its purpose is to prove the equality of the total debit balances and total credit balances in the ledger after all adjustments.

**\*5  Prepare adjusting entries for the alternative treatment of deferrals.**

Companies may initially debit prepayments to an expense account. Likewise, they may credit unearned revenues to a revenue account. At the end of the period, these accounts may be overstated. An adjusting entry for prepaid expenses is a debit to an asset account and a credit to an expense account. An adjusting entry for unearned revenues is a debit to a revenue account and a credit to a liability account.

**\*6  Discuss financial reporting concepts.**

To be judged useful, information should have the primary characteristics of relevance and faithful representation. In addition, it should be comparable, consistent, verifiable, timely, and understandable.

The **monetary unit assumption** requires that companies include in the accounting records only transaction data that can be expressed in terms of money. The **economic entity assumption** states that economic events can be identified with a particular unit of accountability. The **time period assumption** states that the economic life of a business can be divided into artificial time periods and that meaningful accounting reports can be prepared for each period. The **going concern assumption** states that the company will continue in operation long enough to carry out its existing objectives and commitments.

The **historical cost principle** states that companies should record assets at their cost. The **fair value principle** indicates that assets and liabilities should be reported at fair value. The **revenue recognition principle** requires that companies recognize revenue in the accounting period in which the performance obligation is satisfied. The **expense recognition principle** dictates that efforts (expenses) be matched with results (revenues). The **full disclosure principle** requires that companies disclose circumstances and events that matter to financial statement users.

The **cost constraint** weighs the cost that companies incur to provide a type of information against its benefits to financial statement users.

## Glossary Review

**Accrual-basis accounting** Accounting basis in which companies record transactions that change a company's financial statements in the periods in which the events occur. (p. 3-3).

**Accruals** Adjusting entries for either accrued revenues or accrued expenses. (p. 3-6).

**Accrued expenses** Expenses incurred but not yet paid in cash or recorded. (p. 3-15).

**Accrued revenues** Revenues for services performed but not yet received in cash or recorded. (p. 3-14).

**Adjusted trial balance** A list of accounts and their balances after the company has made all adjustments. (p. 3-21).

**Adjusting entries** Entries made at the end of an accounting period to ensure that companies follow the revenue recognition and expense recognition principles. (p. 3-5).

**Book value** The difference between the cost of a depreciable asset and its related accumulated depreciation. (p. 3-11).

**Calendar year** An accounting period that extends from January 1 to December 31. (p. 3-3).

**Cash-basis accounting** Accounting basis in which companies record revenue when they receive cash and an expense when they pay out cash. (p. 3-3).

**\*Comparability** Ability to compare the accounting information of different companies because they use the same accounting principles. (p. 3-29).

**\*Consistency** Use of the same accounting principles and methods from year to year within a company. (p. 3-29).

**Contra asset account** An account offset against an asset account on the balance sheet. (p. 3-10).

**\*Cost constraint** Constraint that weighs the cost that companies will incur to provide the information against the benefit that financial statement users will gain from having the information available. (p. 3-31).

**Deferrals** Adjusting entries for either prepaid expenses or unearned revenues. (p. 3-6).

**Depreciation** The process of allocating the cost of an asset to expense over its useful life. (p. 3-9).

**\*Economic entity assumption** An assumption that every economic entity can be separately identified and accounted for. (p. 3-30).

**Expense recognition principle** The principle that companies recognize expense in the period in which they make efforts (consume assets or incur liabilities) to generate revenue. (pp. 3-5, 3-30).

**\*Fair value principle** An accounting principle that assets and liabilities should be reported at fair value (the price received to sell an asset or settle a liability). (p. 3-29).

**\*Faithful representation** Information that accurately depicts what really happened. (p. 3-29).

**Fiscal year** An accounting period that is one year in length. (p. 3-3).

**\*Full disclosure principle** An accounting principle that dictates that companies disclose circumstances and events that make a difference to financial statement users. (p. 3-30).

**\*Going concern assumption** The assumption that the company will continue in operation for the foreseeable future. (p. 3-30).

**\*Historical cost principle** An accounting principle that states that companies should record assets at their cost. (p. 3-29).

**Interim periods** Monthly or quarterly accounting time periods. (p. 3-3).

**\*Materiality** A company-specific aspect of relevance. An item is material when its size makes it likely to influence the decision of an investor or creditor. (p. 3-29).

**\*Monetary unit assumption** An assumption that requires that only those things that can be expressed in money are included in the accounting records. (p. 3-30).

**Prepaid expenses (prepayments)** Future expenses paid in cash before they are used or consumed. (p. 3-7).

**\*Relevance** The quality of information that indicates the information makes a difference in a decision. (p. 3-29).

**Revenue recognition principle** The principle that companies recognize revenue in the accounting period in which the performance obligation is satisfied. (pp. 3-4, 3-30).

**\*Timely** Describes information that is available to decision-makers before it loses its capacity to influence decisions. (p. 3-29).

**Time period assumption** An assumption that accountants can divide the economic life of a business into artificial time periods. (pp. 3-3, 3-30).

**\*Understandability** Describes information that is presented in a clear and concise fashion so that users can interpret it and comprehend its meaning. (p. 3-29).

**Unearned revenues** A liability recorded for cash received before services are performed. (p. 3-11).

**Useful life** The length of service of a long-lived asset. (p. 3-9).

**\*Verifiable** Describes information that occurs when independent observers, using the same methods, obtain similar results. (p. 3-29).

## Practice Multiple-Choice Questions

1. **(LO 1)** The revenue recognition principle states that:
   a. revenue should be recognized in the accounting period in which a performance obligation is satisfied.
   b. expenses should be matched with revenues.
   c. the economic life of a business can be divided into artificial time periods.
   d. the fiscal year should correspond with the calendar year.

2. **(LO 1)** The time period assumption states that:
   a. companies must wait until the calendar year is completed to prepare financial statements.
   b. companies use the fiscal year to report financial information.
   c. the economic life of a business can be divided into artificial time periods.
   d. companies record information in the time period in which the events occur.

3. **(LO 1)** Which of the following statements about the accrual basis of accounting is **false**?
   a. Events that change a company's financial statements are recorded in the periods in which the events occur.
   b. Revenue is recognized in the period in which services are performed.

c. This basis is in accordance with generally accepted accounting principles.

d. Revenue is recorded only when cash is received, and expense is recorded only when cash is paid.

**4. (LO 1)** The principle or assumption dictating that efforts (expenses) should be recognized in the period in which a company consumes assets or incurs liabilities to generate revenue is the:

a. expense recognition principle.

b. cost assumption.

c. time period assumption.

d. revenue recognition principle.

**5. (LO 1)** Adjusting entries are made to ensure that:

a. expenses are recognized in the period in which they are incurred.

b. revenues are recorded in the period in which services are performed.

c. balance sheet and income statement accounts have correct balances at the end of an accounting period.

d. All the responses above are correct.

**6. (LO 1)** Each of the following is a major type (or category) of adjusting entries **except**:

a. prepaid expenses.     c. accrued expenses.

b. accrued revenues.     d. recognized revenues.

**7. (LO 2)** The trial balance shows Supplies $1,350 and Supplies Expense $0. If $600 of supplies are on hand at the end of the period, the adjusting entry is:

a. Supplies                          600
      Supplies Expense                        600

b. Supplies                          750
      Supplies Expense                        750

c. Supplies Expense                  750
      Supplies                                750

d. Supplies Expense                  600
      Supplies                                600

**8. (LO 2)** Adjustments for prepaid expenses:

a. decrease assets and increase revenues.

b. decrease expenses and increase assets.

c. decrease assets and increase expenses.

d. decrease revenues and increase assets.

**9. (LO 2)** Accumulated Depreciation is:

a. a contra asset account.

b. an expense account.

c. a stockholders' equity account.

d. a liability account.

**10. (LO 2)** Rivera Company computes depreciation on delivery equipment at $1,000 for the month of June. The adjusting entry to record this depreciation is as follows.

a. Depreciation Expense               1,000
      Accumulated Depreciation—
         Rivera Company                           1,000

b. Depreciation Expense               1,000
      Equipment                                  1,000

c. Depreciation Expense               1,000
      Accumulated Depreciation—
         Equipment                                1,000

d. Equipment Expense                  1,000
      Accumulated Depreciation—
         Equipment                                1,000

**11. (LO 2)** Adjustments for unearned revenues:

a. decrease liabilities and increase revenues.

b. have an assets-and-revenues-account relationship.

c. increase assets and increase revenues.

d. decrease revenues and decrease assets.

**12. (LO 3)** Adjustments for accrued revenues:

a. have a liabilities-and-revenues-account relationship.

b. have an assets-and-revenues-account relationship.

c. decrease assets and revenues.

d. decrease liabilities and increase revenues.

**13. (LO 3)** Anika Wilson earned a salary of $400 for the last week of September. She will be paid on October 1. The adjusting entry for Anika's employer at September 30 is:

a. No entry is required.

b. Salaries and Wages Expense         400
      Salaries and Wages Payable               400

c. Salaries and Wages Expense         400
      Cash                                     400

d. Salaries and Wages Payable         400
      Cash                                     400

**14. (LO 4)** Which of the following statements is **incorrect** concerning the adjusted trial balance?

a. An adjusted trial balance proves the equality of the total debit balances and the total credit balances in the ledger after all adjustments are made.

b. The adjusted trial balance provides the primary basis for the preparation of financial statements.

c. The adjusted trial balance lists the account balances segregated by assets and liabilities.

d. The adjusted trial balance is prepared after the adjusting entries have been journalized and posted.

*15. (LO 5)** The trial balance shows Supplies $0 and Supplies Expense $1,500. If $800 of supplies are on hand at the end of the period, the adjusting entry is:

a. debit Supplies $800 and credit Supplies Expense $800.

b. debit Supplies Expense $800 and credit Supplies $800.

c. debit Supplies $700 and credit Supplies Expense $700.

d. debit Supplies Expense $700 and credit Supplies $700.

*16. (LO 6)** Neutrality is a component of:

|   | Faithful Representation | Relevance |
|---|---|---|
| a. | Yes | Yes |
| b. | No | No |
| c. | Yes | No |
| d. | No | Yes |

*17. (LO 6)** Which item is a constraint in financial accounting?

a. Comparability.          c. Cost.

b. Materiality.            d. Consistency.

## Solutions

**1. a.** Revenue should be recognized in the accounting period in which a performance obligation is satisfied. The other choices are incorrect because (b) defines the expense recognition principle, (c) describes the time period assumption, and (d) a company's fiscal year does not need to correspond with the calendar year.

**2. c.** The economic life of a business can be divided into artificial time periods. The other choices are incorrect because (a) companies report their activities on a more frequent basis and not necessarily based on a calendar year; (b) companies report financial information more frequently than annually, such as monthly or quarterly, in order to evaluate results of operations; and (d) this statement describes accrual-basis accounting.

**3. d.** Under the accrual basis of accounting, revenue is recognized when the performance obligation is satisfied, not when cash is received, and expense is recognized when incurred, not when cash is paid. The other choices are true statements.

**4. a.** The expense recognition principle dictates that companies recognize expenses in the period in which they make efforts to generate revenue. The other choices are incorrect because (b) there is no cost assumption, but the historical cost principle states that assets should be recorded at their cost; (c) the time period assumption states that the economic life of a business can be divided into artificial time periods; and (d) the revenue recognition principle indicates that revenue should be recognized in the accounting period in which a performance obligation is satisfied.

**5. d.** Adjusting entries are made for all the reasons noted in choices (a), (b), and (c). These choices are all true statements, but (d) is the best answer.

**6. d.** Unearned revenues, not recognized revenues, is one of the major categories of adjusting entries. The other choices all list one of the major categories of adjusting entries.

**7. c.** Debiting Supplies Expense for $750 and crediting Supplies for $750 ($1,350 − $600) will decrease Supplies and increase Supplies Expense. The other choices are incorrect because (a) will increase Supplies and decrease Supplies Expense and also for the wrong amounts, (b) will increase Supplies and decrease Supplies Expense, and (d) will cause Supplies to have an incorrect balance of $750 ($1,350 − $600) and Supplies Expense to have an incorrect balance of $600 ($0 + $600).

**8. c.** Adjustments for prepaid expenses decrease assets and increase expenses. The other choices are incorrect because an adjusting entry for prepaid expenses (a) increases expenses, not revenues; (b) increases, not decreases, expenses and decreases, not increases, assets; and (d) increases, not decreases, revenues and decreases, not increases, assets.

**9. a.** Accumulated Depreciation is a contra asset account; it is offset against an asset account on the balance sheet. The other choices are incorrect because Accumulated Depreciation is not (b) an expense account or reported on the income statement, (c) a stockholders' equity account, or (d) a liability account.

**10. c.** The adjusting entry is to debit Depreciation Expense and credit Accumulated Depreciation—Equipment. The other choices are incorrect because (a) the contra asset account title includes the asset being depreciated, not the company name; (b) the credit should be to the contra asset account, not directly to the asset; and (d) the debit for this entry should be Depreciation Expense, not Equipment Expense.

**11. a.** Adjustments for unearned revenues will consist of a debit (decrease) to unearned revenues (a liability) and a credit (increase) to a revenue account. Choices (b), (c), and (d) are incorrect because adjustments for unearned revenues will increase revenues but will have no effect on assets.

**12. b.** Adjustments for accrued revenues will have an assets-and-revenues-account relationship. Choices (a) and (d) are incorrect because adjustments for accrued revenues have no effect on liabilities. Choice (c) is incorrect because these adjustments will increase, not decrease, both assets and revenues.

**13. b.** The adjusting entry should be to debit Salaries and Wages Expense for $400 and credit Salaries and Wages Payable for $400. The other choices are incorrect because (a) if an adjusting entry is not made, the amount of money owed (liability) that is shown on the balance sheet will be understated and the amount of salaries and wages expense will also be understated; (c) the credit account is incorrect as adjusting entries never affect cash; and (d) the debit account should be Salaries and Wages Expense and the credit account should be Salaries and Wages Payable. Adjusting entries never affect cash.

**14. c.** The accounts on the trial balance can be segregated by the balance in the account—either debit or credit—not whether they are assets or liabilities. All accounts in the ledger are included in the adjusted trial balance, not just assets and liabilities. The other choices are true statements.

*15. **a.** This adjusting entry correctly states the Supplies account at $800 ($0 + $800) and the Supplies Expense account at $700 ($1,500 − $800). The other choices are incorrect because (b) will cause the Supplies account to have a credit balance (assets have a normal debit balance) and the Supplies Expense account to be stated at $2,300, which is too high; (c) will result in a $700 balance in the Supplies account ($100 too low) and an $800 balance in the Supplies Expense account ($100 too high); and (d) will cause the Supplies account to have a credit balance (assets have a normal debit balance) and the Supplies Expense account to be stated at $2,200, which is too high.

*16. **c.** Neutrality is one of the enhancing qualities that makes information more representationally faithful, not more relevant. Therefore, choices (a), (b), and (d) are incorrect.

*17. **c.** Cost is a constraint in financial accounting. The other choices are all enhancing qualities of useful information.

---

# Practice Brief Exercises

*Indicate why adjusting entries are needed.*

**1. (LO 1)** The ledger of Dey Company includes the following accounts. Explain why each account may need adjustment.

**a.** Supplies.

**b.** Unearned Service Revenue.

**c.** Salaries and Wages Payable.

**d.** Interest Payable.

**Solution**

1. **a.** Supplies: to recognize supplies used during the period.

   **b.** Unearned Service Revenue: to record revenue for services performed.

   **c.** Salaries and Wages Payable: to recognize salaries and wages accrual to employees at the end of a reporting period.

   **d.** Interest Payable: to recognize interest accrued but unpaid on notes payable.

2. **(LO 2)** At the end of its first year, the trial balance of Denton Company shows Equipment of $40,000 and zero balances in Accumulated Depreciation—Equipment and Depreciation Expense. Depreciation for the year is estimated to be $8,000. Prepare the adjusting entry for depreciation at December 31, post the adjustments to T-accounts, and indicate the balance sheet presentation of the equipment at December 31.

*Prepare adjusting entry for depreciation.*

**Solution**

2.   Dec. 31   | Depreciation Expense                         | 8,000 |
     |          |     Accumulated Depreciation—Equipment   |       | 8,000

| **Depreciation Expense** | | **Accum. Depreciation—Equipment** | |
|---|---|---|---|
| 12/31    8,000 | | | 12/31    8,000 |

Balance Sheet:

| | | |
|---|---|---|
| Equipment | $40,000 | |
| Less: Accumulated Depreciation—Equipment | 8,000 | $32,000 |

3. **(LO 3)** You are asked to prepare the following accrual adjusting entries at December 31.

   1. Services performed but not recorded are $4,200.

   2. Utility expenses incurred but not paid or recorded are $660.

   3. Salaries and wages earned by employees of $3,000 are unpaid.

   Use the following account titles: Accounts Payable, Accounts Receivable, Service Revenue, Salaries and Wages Expense, Salaries and Wages Payable, and Utilities Expense.

*Prepare adjusting entries for accruals.*

**Solution**

3.   Dec. 31   | Accounts Receivable              | 4,200 |
     |          |     Service Revenue           |       | 4,200
     |   31     | Utilities Expense             | 660   |
     |          |     Accounts Payable          |       | 660
     |   31     | Salaries and Wages Expense    | 3,000 |
     |          |     Salaries and Wages Payable |       | 3,000

4. **(LO 1, 2, 3)** The trial balance for Blair Company includes the following balance sheet accounts. Identify the accounts that may require adjustment. For each account that requires adjustment, indicate (a) the type of adjusting entry (prepaid expense, unearned revenue, accrued revenue, or accrued expense) and (b) the related account in the adjusting entry.

*Analyze accounts in an unadjusted trial balance.*

|   |   |
|---|---|
| Accounts Receivable | Interest Payable |
| Supplies | Unearned Service Revenue |
| Prepaid Insurance | |

**Solution**

4.

| **Account** | **Type of Adjustment** | **Related Account** |
|---|---|---|
| Accounts Receivable | Accrued Revenue | Service Revenue |
| Supplies | Prepaid Expense | Supplies Expense |
| Prepaid Insurance | Prepaid Expense | Insurance Expense |
| Interest Payable | Accrued Expense | Interest Expense |
| Unearned Service Revenue | Unearned Revenue | Service Revenue |

*Prepare an income statement from an adjusted trial balance.*

**5. (LO 4)** The adjusted trial balance of Harmony Company includes the following accounts at December 31, 2022: Cash $12,000, Retained Earnings $22,000, Dividends $3,000, Service Revenue $41,000, Rent Expense $900, Salaries and Wages Expense $6,000, Supplies Expense $700, and Depreciation Expense $1,800. Prepare an income statement for the year.

**Solution**

5.

**Harmony Company**
**Income Statement**
**For the Year Ended December 31, 2022**

| | | |
|---|---:|---:|
| Revenues | | |
| Service revenue | | $41,000 |
| Expenses | | |
| Salaries and wages expense | $6,000 | |
| Rent expense | 900 | |
| Depreciation expense | 1,800 | |
| Supplies expense | 700 | |
| Total expenses | | 9,400 |
| Net income | | $31,600 |

# Practice Exercises

*Prepare adjusting entries.*

**1. (LO 2, 3)** Wendy Penn, D.D.S., opened a dental practice on January 1, 2022. During the first month of operations, the following transactions occurred.

1. Performed services for patients totaling $785, which had not yet been recorded.

2. Utility expenses incurred but not paid or recorded prior to January 31 totaled $250.

3. Purchased dental equipment on January 1 for $90,000, paying $25,000 in cash and signing a $65,000, 3-year note payable. The equipment depreciates $500 per month. Interest is $550 per month and will be paid when the note is repaid.

4. Purchased a 1-year malpractice insurance policy on January 1 for $15,000.

5. Purchased $1,700 of dental supplies. On January 31, determined that $300 of supplies were on hand.

**Instructions**

Prepare the adjusting entries on January 31. Account titles are Accumulated Depreciation—Equipment, Depreciation Expense, Service Revenue, Accounts Receivable, Insurance Expense, Interest Expense, Interest Payable, Prepaid Insurance, Supplies, Supplies Expense, Utilities Expense, and Utilities Payable.

**Solution**

| | | | | |
|---|---|---|---:|---:|
| 1. | Jan. 31 | Accounts Receivable | 785 | |
| | | Service Revenue | | 785 |
| | 31 | Utilities Expense | 250 | |
| | | Utilities Payable | | 250 |
| | 31 | Depreciation Expense | 500 | |
| | | Accumulated Depreciation—Equipment | | 500 |
| | 31 | Interest Expense | 550 | |
| | | Interest Payable | | 550 |
| | 31 | Insurance Expense ($15,000 ÷ 12) | 1,250 | |
| | | Prepaid Insurance | | 1,250 |
| | 31 | Supplies Expense ($1,700 – $300) | 1,400 | |
| | | Supplies | | 1,400 |

**2. (LO 2, 3, 4)** The income statement of Bragg Co. for the month of July shows net income of $1,400 based on Service Revenue $5,500, Salaries and Wages Expense $2,300, Supplies Expense $1,200, and Utilities Expense $600. In reviewing the statement, you discover the following.

*Prepare correct income statement.*

1. Insurance expired during July of $450 was omitted.

2. Supplies expense includes $300 of supplies that are still on hand at July 31.

3. Depreciation on equipment of $180 was omitted.

4. Unpaid salaries and wages at July 31 of $400 were not included.

5. Services performed but unrecorded totaled $600.

**Instructions**

Prepare a correct income statement for July 2022.

**Solution**

2.

**Bragg Co.**
**Income Statement**
**For the Month Ended July 31, 2022**

| | | |
|---|---:|---:|
| Revenues | | |
| Service revenue ($5,500 + $600) | | $6,100 |
| Expenses | | |
| Salaries and wages expense ($2,300 + $400) | $2,700 | |
| Supplies expense ($1,200 – $300) | 900 | |
| Utilities expense | 600 | |
| Insurance expense | 450 | |
| Depreciation expense | 180 | |
| Total expenses | | 4,830 |
| Net income | | $1,270 |

# Practice Problem

**(LO 2, 3)** The Green Thumb Lawn Care Inc. began operations on April 1. At April 30, the trial balance shows the following balances for selected accounts.

*Prepare adjusting entries from selected data.*

| | |
|---|---:|
| Prepaid Insurance | $ 3,600 |
| Equipment | 28,000 |
| Notes Payable | 20,000 |
| Unearned Service Revenue | 4,200 |
| Service Revenue | 1,800 |

Analysis reveals the following additional data.

1. Prepaid insurance is the cost of a 2-year insurance policy, effective April 1.

2. Depreciation on the equipment is $500 per month.

3. The note payable is dated April 1. It is a 6-month, 12% note. Interest will be paid upon note repayment.

4. Seven customers paid for the company's 6-month lawn service package of $600 beginning in April. The company performed services for these customers in April

5. Lawn services performed for other customers but not recorded at April 30 totaled $1,500.

**Instructions**

Prepare the adjusting entries for the month of April. Show computations.

**Solution**

| | | GENERAL JOURNAL | | | J1 |
|---|---|---|---|---|---|

| Date | Account Titles and Explanation | Ref. | Debit | Credit |
|---|---|---|---|---|
| | *Adjusting Entries* | | | |
| Apr. 30 | Insurance Expense | | 150 | |
| |    Prepaid Insurance | | | 150 |
| |    (To record insurance expired: | | | |
| |    $3,600 \div 24 = \$150$ per month) | | | |
| 30 | Depreciation Expense | | 500 | |
| |    Accumulated Depreciation—Equipment | | | 500 |
| |    (To record monthly depreciation) | | | |
| 30 | Interest Expense | | 200 | |
| |    Interest Payable | | | 200 |
| |    (To record interest on notes payable: | | | |
| |    $\$20,000 \times 12\% \times \frac{1}{12} = \$200$) | | | |
| 30 | Unearned Service Revenue | | 700 | |
| |    Service Revenue | | | 700 |
| |    (To record revenue for services | | | |
| |    performed: $\$600 \div 6 = \$100$; | | | |
| |    $\$100$ per month $\times 7 = \$700$) | | | |
| 30 | Accounts Receivable | | 1,500 | |
| |    Service Revenue | | | 1,500 |
| |    (To record revenue for services | | | |
| |    performed) | | | |

---

**Brief Exercises, DO IT! Exercises, Exercises, Problems, Data Analytics Activities, and many additional resources are available for practice in WileyPLUS.**

*Note:* All asterisked Questions, Exercises, and Problems relate to material in the appendices to this chapter.

## Questions

**1. a.** How does the time period assumption affect an accountant's analysis of business transactions?

**b.** Explain the terms fiscal year, calendar year, and interim periods.

**2.** Identify and state two generally accepted accounting principles that relate to adjusting the accounts.

**3.** What are the five steps of the revenue recognition principle?

**4.** Susan Zupan, a lawyer, accepts a legal engagement in March, performs the work in April, and is paid in May. If Zupan's law firm prepares monthly financial statements, when should it recognize revenue from this engagement? Why?

**5.** Why do accrual-basis financial statements provide more useful information than cash-basis statements?

**6.** In completing the engagement in Question 4, Zupan incurs and pays no costs in March, incurs and pays $2,000 of costs in April, and pays $2,500 of costs in May (incurred in April). How much expense should the firm deduct from revenues in the month when it recognizes the revenue? Why?

**7.** "Adjusting entries are required by the historical cost principle of accounting." Explain why this statement is true or false.

**8.** Why may a trial balance not contain up-to-date and complete financial information?

**9.** Distinguish between the two categories of adjusting entries, and identify the types of adjustments applicable to each category.

**10.** What is the debit/credit effect of a prepaid expense adjusting entry?

**11.** "Depreciation is a valuation process that results in the reporting of the fair value of the asset." Explain why this statement is true or false.

**12.** Explain the differences between depreciation expense and accumulated depreciation.

**13.** J. Brownlee Company purchased equipment for $18,000. By the current balance sheet date, $6,000 had been depreciated. Indicate the balance sheet presentation of the data.

**14.** What is the debit/credit effect of an unearned revenue adjusting entry?

**15.** Whistler Corp. performed services for a customer but has not yet recorded payment or recorded any entry related to the work. Which of the following accounts are involved in the adjusting entry: (a) asset, (b) liability, (c) revenue, or (d) expense? For the accounts selected, indicate whether they would be debited or credited in the entry.

**16.** A company fails to recognize an expense incurred but not paid. Indicate which of the following accounts is debited and which is credited in the adjusting entry: (a) asset, (b) liability, (c) revenue, or (d) expense.

**17.** A company makes an accrued revenue adjusting entry for $900 and an accrued expense adjusting entry for $700. How much was net income understated prior to these entries? Explain.

**18.** On January 9, a company pays $5,000 for salaries and wages of which $2,000 was reported as Salaries and Wages Payable on December 31. Give the entry to record the payment.

**19.** For each of the following items before adjustment, indicate the type of adjusting entry (prepaid expense, unearned revenue, accrued revenue, or accrued expense) that is needed to correct the misstatement. If an item could result in more than one type of adjusting entry, indicate each of the types.

    **a.** Assets are understated.

    **b.** Liabilities are overstated.

    **c.** Liabilities are understated.

    **d.** Expenses are understated.

    **e.** Assets are overstated.

    **f.** Revenue is understated.

**20.** One-half of the adjusting entry is given below. Indicate the account title for the other half of the entry.

    **a.** Salaries and Wages Expense is debited.

    **b.** Depreciation Expense is debited.

    **c.** Interest Payable is credited.

    **d.** Supplies is credited.

    **e.** Accounts Receivable is debited.

    **f.** Unearned Service Revenue is debited.

**21.** "An adjusting entry may affect more than one balance sheet or income statement account." Explain why this statement is true or false.

**22.** Why is it possible to prepare financial statements directly from an adjusted trial balance?

**\*23.** Dashan Company debits Supplies Expense for all purchases of supplies and credits Rent Revenue for all advanced rentals. For each type of adjustment, give the adjusting entry.

**\*24. a.** What is the primary objective of financial reporting?

    **b.** Identify the characteristics of useful accounting information.

**\*25.** Dan Fineman, the president of King Company, is pleased. King substantially increased its net income in 2022 while keeping its unit inventory relatively the same. Howard Gross, chief accountant, cautions Dan, however. Gross says that since King changed its method of inventory valuation, there is a consistency problem and it is difficult to determine whether King is better off. Is Gross correct? Why or why not?

**\*26.** What is the distinction between comparability and consistency?

**\*27.** Describe the constraint inherent in the presentation of accounting information.

**\*28.** Laurie Belk is president of Better Books. She has no accounting background. Belk cannot understand why fair value is not used as the basis for all accounting measurement and reporting. Discuss.

**\*29.** What is the economic entity assumption? Give an example of its violation.

## Brief Exercises

**BE3.1 (LO 1), K** Number the following steps of the revenue recognition process (from 1–5) to place in the correct order.

    **a.** _____ Allocate the transaction price to the separate performance obligations.

    **b.** _____ Identify the contract with customers.

    **c.** _____ Identify the separate performance obligations in the contract.

    **d.** _____ Recognize revenue when each performance obligation is satisfied.

    **e.** _____ Determine the transaction price.

*Identify the order of the five steps in the revenue recognition process.*

**BE3.2 (LO 1), C** Transactions that affect net income do not necessarily affect cash. Identify the effect, if any, that each of the following transactions would have upon cash and net income. The first transaction has been completed as an example.

*Identify impact of transactions on cash and net income.*

| | Cash | Net Income |
|---|---|---|
| **a.** Purchased $100 of supplies for cash. | −$100 | $0 |
| **b.** Recorded an adjusting entry to record use of $20 of the above supplies. | | |
| **c.** Made sales of $1,300, all on account. | | |
| **d.** Received $800 from customers in payment of their accounts. | | |
| **e.** Purchased equipment for cash, $2,500. | | |
| **f.** Recorded depreciation of building for period used, $600. | | |

*Indicate why adjusting entries are needed.*

**BE3.3 (LO 1), C** The ledger of Melmann Company includes the following accounts. Explain why each account may require adjustment.

    **a.** Prepaid Insurance.

    **b.** Depreciation Expense.

    **c.** Unearned Service Revenue.

    **d.** Interest Payable.

*Identify the major types of adjusting entries.*

**BE3.4 (LO 1), AN** Cortina Company accumulates the following adjustment data at December 31. Indicate (1) the type of adjustment (prepaid expense, accrued revenue, and so on) and (2) the status of the accounts before adjustment (for example, "assets understated and revenues understated").

    **a.** Supplies of $400 are on hand. Supplies account shows $1,600 balance.

    **b.** Services performed but unbilled total $700.

    **c.** Interest of $300 has accumulated (and not been paid) on a note payable.

    **d.** Rent collected in advance totaling $1,100 has been earned.

*Prepare adjusting entry for supplies.*

**BE3.5 (LO 2), AP** Lahey Advertising Company's trial balance at December 31 shows Supplies $8,800 and Supplies Expense $0. On December 31, there are $1,100 of supplies on hand. Prepare the adjusting entry at December 31 and, using T-accounts, enter the balances in the accounts, post the adjusting entry, and indicate the adjusted balance in each account.

*Prepare adjusting entry for depreciation.*

**BE3.6 (LO 2), AP** At the end of its first year, the trial balance of Rayburn Company shows Equipment $22,000 and zero balances in Accumulated Depreciation—Equipment and Depreciation Expense. Depreciation for the year is estimated to be $2,750. Prepare the annual adjusting entry for depreciation at December 31, post the adjustments to T-accounts, and indicate the balance sheet presentation of the equipment at December 31.

*Prepare adjusting entry for prepaid expense.*

**BE3.7 (LO 2), AP** On July 1, 2022, Ling Co. pays $12,400 to Marsh Insurance Co. for a 2-year insurance contract. Both companies have fiscal years ending December 31. For Ling Co., journalize and post the entry on July 1 and the annual adjusting entry on December 31.

*Prepare adjusting entry for unearned revenue.*

**BE3.8 (LO 2), AP** On July 1, 2022, Ling Co. pays $12,400 to Marsh Insurance Co. for a 2-year insurance contract. Both companies have fiscal years ending December 31. Journalize and post the entry on July 1 and the annual adjusting entry on December 31 for Marsh Insurance Co. Marsh uses the accounts Unearned Service Revenue and Service Revenue.

*Prepare adjusting entries for deferrals.*

**BE3.9 (LO 2), AP** The unadjusted trial balance of Northern Exposure Inc. had these balances for the following selected accounts: Supplies $3,100, Unearned Service Revenue $8,200, and Prepaid Rent $1,200. At the end of the period, a count showed $500 of supplies on hand. Services of $2,900 had been performed related to the unearned revenue account, and one month's rent, worth $400, had been consumed by Northern Exposure. Record the required adjusting entries related to these events.

*Prepare adjusting entries for accruals.*

**BE3.10 (LO 3), AP** The bookkeeper for Tran Company asks you to prepare the following accrual adjusting entries at December 31. Use these account titles: Service Revenue, Accounts Receivable, Interest Expense, Interest Payable, Salaries and Wages Expense, and Salaries and Wages Payable.

    **a.** Interest on notes payable of $300 should be accrued.

    **b.** Services performed but unbilled totals $1,700.

    **c.** Salaries of $780 earned by employees have not been recorded or paid.

*Prepare adjusting entries for accruals.*

**BE3.11 (LO 3), AP** At December 31 of the current year, Cullen Corporation had a number of items that were not reflected in its accounting records. Maintenance and repair costs of $770 were incurred but not paid. Utilities costing $240 were used but not paid, and use of a warehouse space worth $1,900 was provided to a tenant who had not been billed as of the end of the month. Record the required adjusting entries related to these events.

*Analyze accounts in a trial balance.*

**BE3.12 (LO 2, 3), AN** The trial balance of Woods Company includes the following balance sheet accounts. Identify the accounts that might require adjustment. For each account that requires adjustment, indicate (1) the type of adjusting entry (prepaid expense, unearned revenue, accrued revenue, and accrued expense) and (2) the related account in the adjusting entry.

    **a.** Accounts Receivable.                   **e.** Dividends.

    **b.** Prepaid Insurance.                      **f.** Interest Payable.

    **c.** Cash.                                **g.** Unearned Service Revenue.

    **d.** Accumulated Depreciation—Equipment.

**BE3.13 (LO 4), AP** The adjusted trial balance of Levin Corporation at December 31, 2022, includes the following selected accounts: Retained Earnings $17,200, Dividends $6,000, Service Revenue $32,600, Salaries and Wages Expense $14,000, Insurance Expense $1,800, Rent Expense $3,900, Supplies Expense $1,500, and Depreciation Expense $1,000. Prepare an income statement for the year.

*Prepare an income statement from an adjusted trial balance.*

**BE3.14 (LO 4), AP** The adjusted trial balance of Sharp Corporation at December 31, 2022, includes the following accounts: Retained Earnings $18,000 and Dividends $7,000. The balance in Retained Earnings is the balance as of January 1. Prepare a retained earnings statement for the year assuming net income is $9,000.

*Prepare a retained earnings statement from an adjusted trial balance.*

**\*BE3.15 (LO 5), AP** Mayes Company records all prepayments in income statement accounts. At April 30, the trial balance shows Supplies Expense $2,800, Service Revenue $9,200, and zero balances in related balance sheet accounts. Prepare the adjusting entries at April 30 assuming (a) $700 of supplies on hand and (b) $3,000 of service revenue should be reported as unearned.

*Prepare adjusting entries under alternative treatment of deferrals.*

**\*BE3.16 (LO 6), C** The accompanying chart shows the qualitative characteristics of useful accounting information. Fill in the blanks.

*Identify characteristics of useful information.*

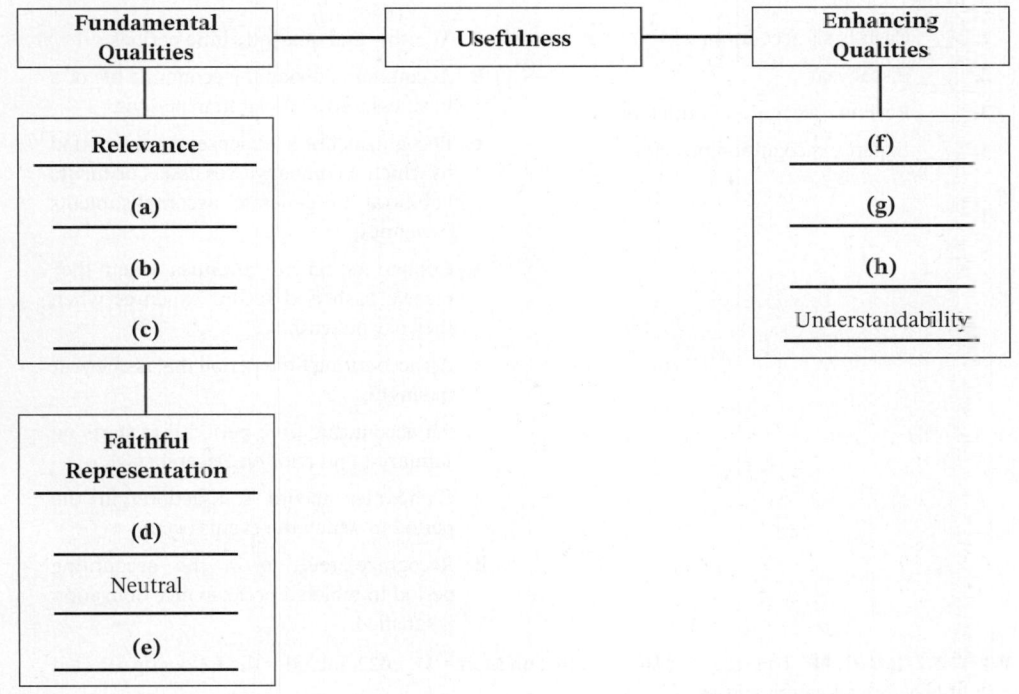

**\*BE3.17 (LO 6), C** Given the characteristics of useful accounting information, complete each of the following statements.

*Identify characteristics of useful information.*

**a.** For information to be _____, it should have predictive value, confirmatory value, and be material.

**b.** _____ means that information accurately depicts what really happened

**c.** _____ means using the same accounting principles and methods from year to year within a company.

**\*BE3.18 (LO 6), C** Here are some qualitative characteristics of useful accounting information:

*Identify characteristics of useful information.*

1. Predictive value
2. Neutral
3. Verifiable
4. Timely

Match each qualitative characteristic to one of the following statements.

_____ **a.** Accounting information should help provide accurate expectations about future events.

_____ **b.** Accounting information cannot be selected, prepared, or presented to favor one set of interested users over another.

_____ **c.** Independent observers, using the same methods, are able to obtain similar results.

_____ **d.** Accounting information must be available to decision-makers before it loses its capacity to influence their decisions.

*Define full disclosure principle.*

**\* BE3.19 (LO 6), K** Select the response that completes the following statement correctly. The full disclosure principle dictates that:

**a.** financial statements should disclose all assets at their cost.

**b.** financial statements should disclose only those events that can be measured in currency.

**c.** financial statements should disclose all events and circumstances that would matter to users of financial statements.

**d.** financial statements should not be relied on unless an auditor has expressed an unqualified opinion on them.

## DO IT! Exercises

*Identify timing concepts.*

**DO IT! 3.1 (LO 1), C** The following is a list of concepts in the left column, with a description of the concept in the right column. There are more descriptions provided than concepts. Match the description to the concept.

**1.** _____ Cash-basis accounting.

**2.** _____ Fiscal year.

**3.** _____ Revenue recognition principle.

**4.** _____ Expense recognition principle.

**a.** Monthly and quarterly time periods.

**b.** Accountants divide the economic life of a business into artificial time periods.

**c.** Recognize efforts (expenses) in the period in which a company uses assets or incurs liabilities to generate accomplishments (revenues).

**d.** Companies record revenues when they receive cash and record expenses when they pay out cash.

**e.** An accounting time period that is one year in length.

**f.** An accounting time period that starts on January 1 and ends on December 31.

**g.** Companies record transactions in the period in which the events occur.

**h.** Recognize revenue in the accounting period in which a performance obligation is satisfied.

*Prepare adjusting entries for deferrals.*

**DO IT! 3.2 (LO 2), AP** The ledger of Herrera, Inc. on March 31, 2022, includes the following selected accounts before adjusting entries.

|  | Debit | Credit |
| --- | --- | --- |
| Prepaid Insurance | $ 2,400 | |
| Supplies | 2,500 | |
| Equipment | 30,000 | |
| Unearned Service Revenue | | $9,000 |

An analysis of the accounts shows the following.

**1.** Insurance expires at the rate of $300 per month.

**2.** Supplies on hand total $1,100.

**3.** The equipment depreciates at $500 per month.

**4.** During March, services were performed for two-fifths of the unearned service revenue.

Prepare the adjusting entries for the month of March.

*Prepare adjusting entries for accruals.*

**DO IT! 3.3 (LO 3), AP** Javier Computer Services began operations in July 2022. At the end of the month, the company prepares monthly financial statements. It has the following information for the month.

**1.** At July 31, the company owed employees $1,300 in salaries that the company will pay in August.

**2.** On July 1, the company borrowed $20,000 from a local bank on a 10-year note. The annual interest rate is 12%. Interest is paid annually.

**3.** Service revenue unrecorded in July totaled $2,400.

Prepare the adjusting entries needed at July 31, 2022.

**DO IT! 3.4 (LO 4), AP** Lumina Company was organized on April 1, 2022. The company prepares quarterly financial statements. The adjusted trial balance at June 30 is shown here.

*Calculate amounts from trial balance.*

| | Debit | | Credit |
|---|---|---|---|
| Cash | $ 5,360 | Accumulated Depreciation— | |
| Accounts Receivable | 480 | Equipment | $ 700 |
| Prepaid Rent | 720 | Notes Payable | 4,000 |
| Supplies | 920 | Accounts Payable | 790 |
| Equipment | 12,000 | Salaries and Wages Payable | 300 |
| Dividends | 500 | Interest Payable | 40 |
| Salaries and Wages Expense | 7,400 | Unearned Rent Revenue | 400 |
| Rent Expense | 1,200 | Common Stock | 11,200 |
| Depreciation Expense | 700 | Service Revenue | 11,360 |
| Supplies Expense | 160 | Rent Revenue | 1,100 |
| Utilities Expense | 410 | | $29,890 |
| Interest Expense | 40 | | |
| | $29,890 | | |

a. Determine the net income for the quarter April 1 to June 30.

b. Determine the total assets and total liabilities at June 30, 2022, for Lumina Company.

c. Determine the amount that appears for Retained Earnings at June 30, 2022.

# Exercises

**E3.1 (LO 1), C** Ian Muse has prepared the following list of statements about the time period assumption.

*Explain the time period assumption.*

1. Adjusting entries would not be necessary if a company's life were not divided into artificial time periods.

2. The IRS requires companies to file annual tax returns.

3. Accountants divide the economic life of a business into artificial time periods, but all transactions affect only one of these periods.

4. Accounting time periods are generally a month, a quarter, or a year.

5. A time period lasting one year is called an interim period.

6. All fiscal years are calendar years, but not all calendar years are fiscal years.

**Instructions**

Identify each statement as true or false. If false, indicate how to correct the statement.

**E3.2 (LO 1), E Writing** On numerous occasions, proposals have surfaced to put the federal government on the accrual basis of accounting. This is no small issue. If this basis were used, it would mean that billions in unrecorded liabilities would have to be booked, and the federal deficit would increase substantially.

*Distinguish between cash and accrual basis of accounting.*

**Instructions**

a. What is the difference between accrual-basis accounting and cash-basis accounting?

b. Why would politicians prefer the cash basis over the accrual basis?

c. Write a letter to your senator explaining why the federal government should adopt the accrual basis of accounting.

**E3.3 (LO 1), AP** Primo Industries collected $105,000 from customers in 2022. Of the amount collected, $25,000 was for services performed in 2021. In addition, Primo performed services worth $40,000 in 2022, which will not be collected until 2023.

*Compute cash and accrual accounting income.*

Primo Industries also paid $72,000 for expenses in 2022. Of the amount paid, $30,000 was for expenses incurred on account in 2021. In addition, Primo incurred $42,000 of expenses in 2022, which will not be paid until 2023.

### Instructions

a. Compute 2022 cash-basis net income.

b. Compute 2022 accrual-basis net income.

*Identify point of revenue recognition.*

**E3.4 (LO 1), C** The following independent situations require professional judgment for determining when to recognize revenue from the transactions.

a. **Southwest Airlines** sells you an advance-purchase airline ticket in September for your flight home in December.

b. **Ultimate Electronics** sells you a home theater on a "no money down and full payment in three months" promotional deal.

c. The **Toronto Blue Jays** sell season tickets online to games in the Skydome. Fans can purchase the tickets at any time, although the season doesn't officially begin until April. The major league baseball season runs from April through October.

d. **RBC Financial Group** loans money on August 1. The loan and the interest are repayable in full in November.

e. In August, a customer orders a sweater from the **Target** website, paying with a Target credit card. The sweater arrives in September. Target sends a bill in October and receives payment in October.

### Instructions

Determine when revenue should be recognized in each of the above situations.

*Determine the type of adjusting entry needed.*

**E3.5 (LO 2, 3), AP** Hart Corporation encounters the following situations:

1. Hart collects $1,300 from a customer in 2022 for services to be performed in 2023.

2. Hart incurs utility expense which is not yet paid in cash or recorded.

3. Hart's employees worked 3 days in 2022 but will not be paid until 2023.

4. Hart performs services for customers but has not yet received cash or recorded the transaction.

5. Hart paid $2,400 rent on December 1 for the 4 months starting December 1.

6. Hart received cash for future services and recorded a liability until the service was performed.

7. Hart performed consulting services for a client in December 2022. On December 31, it had not billed the client for services performed of $1,200.

8. Hart paid cash for an expense and recorded an asset until the item was used up.

9. Hart purchased $900 of supplies in 2022; at year-end, $400 of supplies remain unused.

10. Hart purchased equipment on January 1, 2022; the equipment will be used for 5 years.

11. Hart borrowed $10,000 on October 1, 2022, signing an 8% 1-year note payable. Both the interest and the note will be paid in 1 year.

### Instructions

Identify what type of adjusting entry (prepaid expense, unearned revenue, accrued expense, or accrued revenue) is needed in each situation at December 31, 2022.

*Prepare adjusting entries from selected data.*

**E3.6 (LO 2, 3), AN** Verne Cova Company has the following balances in selected accounts on December 31, 2022.

| | |
|---|---|
| Accounts Receivable | $    –0– |
| Accumulated Depreciation—Equipment | –0– |
| Equipment | 7,000 |
| Interest Payable | –0– |
| Notes Payable | 10,000 |
| Prepaid Insurance | 2,100 |
| Salaries and Wages Payable | –0– |
| Supplies | 2,450 |
| Unearned Service Revenue | 30,000 |

All the accounts have normal balances. The following information has been gathered at December 31, 2022.

1. Verne Cova Company borrowed $10,000 by signing a 12%, 1-year note on September 1, 2022. Interest will be paid when the note is repaid.

2. A count of supplies on December 31, 2022, indicates that supplies of $900 are on hand.

3. Depreciation on the equipment for 2022 is $1,000.

4. Verne Cova paid $2,100 for 12 months of insurance coverage on June 1, 2022.

5. On December 1, 2022, Verne Cova collected $30,000 for consulting services to be performed evenly from December 1, 2022, through March 31, 2023.

6. Verne Cova performed consulting services for a client in December 2022. The client will be billed $4,200.

7. Verne Cova pays its employees total salaries of $9,000 every Monday for the preceding 5-day week (Monday through Friday). On Monday, December 29, employees were paid for the week ending December 26. All employees worked the last 3 days of 2022.

## Instructions

Prepare adjusting entries for the seven items described above. Verne Cova prepares adjustments annually.

**E3.7 (LO 2, 3), AN** Wang Company accumulates the following adjustment data at December 31. *Identify types of adjustments and accounts before adjustment.*

a. Services performed but unbilled total $600.

b. Store supplies of $160 are on hand. The supplies account shows a $1,900 balance.

c. Utility expenses of $275 are unpaid and unrecorded.

d. Services performed of $490 have been collected in advance.

e. Salaries of $620 are unpaid and unrecorded.

f. Prepaid insurance totaling $400 has expired.

## Instructions

For each item, indicate (1) the type of adjustment (prepaid expense, unearned revenue, accrued revenue, or accrued expense) and (2) the status of the accounts before adjustment (overstated or understated).

**E3.8 (LO 2, 3), AP** The ledger of Howard Rental Agency on March 31 of the current year includes the *Prepare adjusting entries from selected* following selected accounts before adjusting entries have been prepared. *account data.*

|  | Debit | Credit |
| --- | --- | --- |
| Supplies | $ 3,000 | |
| Prepaid Insurance | 3,600 | |
| Equipment | 25,000 | |
| Accumulated Depreciation—Equipment | | $ 8,400 |
| Notes Payable | | 20,000 |
| Unearned Rent Revenue | | 12,400 |
| Rent Revenue | | 60,000 |
| Interest Expense | 0 | |
| Salaries and Wages Expense | 14,000 | |

An analysis of the accounts shows the following.

1. The equipment depreciates $280 per month.

2. Half of the unearned rent revenue was earned during the quarter.

3. Interest of $400 should be accrued on the notes payable.

4. Supplies on hand total $850.

5. Insurance expires at the rate of $400 per month.

## Instructions

Prepare the adjusting entries at March 31, assuming that adjusting entries are made quarterly. Additional accounts are Depreciation Expense, Insurance Expense, Interest Payable, and Supplies Expense

**E3.9 (LO 2, 3), AP** Al Medina, D.D.S., opened an incorporated dental practice on January 1, 2022. During *Prepare adjusting entries.* the first month of operations, the following transactions occurred.

1. Performed services for patients who had dental plan insurance. At January 31, $760 of such services was completed but not yet billed to the insurance companies.

2. Utility expenses incurred but not paid or recorded prior to January 31 totaled $450.

3. Purchased dental equipment on January 1 for $80,000, paying $20,000 in cash and signing a $60,000, 3-year note payable (interest is paid each December 31). The equipment depreciates $400 per month. Interest is $500 per month.

4. Purchased a 1-year malpractice insurance policy on January 1 for $24,000.

5. Purchased $1,750 of dental supplies (recorded as increase to Supplies). On January 31, determined that $550 of supplies were on hand.

### Instructions

Prepare the adjusting entries on January 31. Account titles are Accumulated Depreciation—Equipment, Depreciation Expense, Service Revenue, Accounts Receivable, Insurance Expense, Interest Expense, Interest Payable, Prepaid Insurance, Supplies, Supplies Expense, Utilities Expense, and Accounts Payable.

*Prepare adjusting entries.*

**E3.10 (LO 2, 3), AN** The trial balance for Pioneer Advertising Inc. is shown in Illustration 3.4. Instead of the adjusting entries shown in the text at October 31, assume the following adjustment data.

1. Supplies on hand at October 31 total $500.
2. Expired insurance for the month is $100.
3. Depreciation for the month is $50.
4. Services related to unearned service revenue in October worth $600 were performed.
5. Services performed but not recorded at October 31 are $300.
6. Interest to be accrued at October 31 is $95.
7. Salaries to be accrued at October 31 are $1,625.

### Instructions

Prepare the adjusting entries for the items above.

*Prepare adjusting entries from selected account data.*

**E3.11 (LO 2, 3), AP** The ledger of Armour Lake Lumber Supply on July 31, 2022, includes the following selected accounts before adjusting entries have been prepared.

|  | Debit | Credit |
| --- | --- | --- |
| Supplies | $ 24,000 | |
| Prepaid Rent | 3,600 | |
| Buildings | 250,000 | |
| Accumulated Depreciation—Buildings | | $140,000 |
| Unearned Service Revenue | | 11,500 |

An analysis of the company's accounts shows the following.

1. Supplies on hand at the end of the month totaled $18,600.
2. The balance in Prepaid Rent represents 4 months of rent costs.
3. Employees were owed $3,100 related to unpaid and unrecorded salaries and wages.
4. Depreciation on buildings is $6,000 per year.
5. During the month, the company satisfied obligations worth $4,700 related to the Unearned Service Revenue account.
6. Unpaid and unrecorded maintenance and repairs costs were $2,300.

### Instructions

Prepare the adjusting entries at July 31 assuming that adjusting entries are made monthly. Use additional accounts as needed.

*Prepare a correct income statement.*

**E3.12 (LO 2, 3), AN** The income statement of Norski Co. for the month of July shows net income of $2,000 based on Service Revenue $5,500, Salaries and Wages Expense $2,100, Supplies Expense $900, and Utilities Expense $500. In reviewing the statement, you discover the following:

1. Insurance expired during July of $350 was omitted.
2. Supplies expense includes $200 of supplies that are still on hand at July 31.
3. Depreciation on equipment of $150 was omitted.
4. Unpaid wages at July 31 of $360 were not included.
5. Services performed but unrecorded totaled $700.

### Instructions

Prepare a correct income statement for July 2022.

**E3.13 (LO 2, 3), AN** Selected accounts of Villa Company are shown here.

*Journalize basic transactions and adjusting entries.*

**Supplies Expense**

| | | | |
|---|---|---|---|
| July 31 | 750 | | |

**Salaries and Wages Payable**

| | | | |
|---|---|---|---|
| | | July 31 | 1,000 |

**Salaries and Wages Expense**

| | | | |
|---|---|---|---|
| July 15 | 1,000 | | |
| 31 | 1,000 | | |

**Accounts Receivable**

| | | | |
|---|---|---|---|
| July 31 | 500 | | |

**Service Revenue**

| | | | |
|---|---|---|---|
| | | July 14 | 3,800 |
| | | 31 | 900 |
| | | 31 | 500 |

**Unearned Service Revenue**

| | | | |
|---|---|---|---|
| July 31 | 900 | July 1 | Bal. 1,500 |
| | | 20 | 600 |

**Supplies**

| | | | |
|---|---|---|---|
| July 1 | Bal. 1,100 | July 31 | 750 |
| 10 | 200 | | |

### Instructions

After analyzing the accounts, journalize (a) the July transactions and (b) the adjusting entries that were made on July 31. (*Hint:* July transactions were for cash.)

**E3.14 (LO 2, 3), AN** This is a partial adjusted trial balance of Ramon Company.

*Analyze adjusted data.*

**Ramon Company**
**Adjusted Trial Balance (partial)**
**January 31, 2022**

| | Debit | Credit |
|---|---|---|
| Supplies | $ 700 | |
| Prepaid Insurance | 1,560 | |
| Salaries and Wages Payable | | $1,060 |
| Unearned Service Revenue | | 750 |
| Supplies Expense | 950 | |
| Insurance Expense | 520 | |
| Salaries and Wages Expense | 1,800 | |
| Service Revenue | | 4,000 |

### Instructions

Answer these questions assuming the year begins January 1.

**a.** If the amount in Supplies Expense is the January 31 adjusting entry and $300 of supplies was purchased in January, what was the balance in Supplies on January 1?

**b.** If the amount in Insurance Expense is the January 31 adjusting entry and the original insurance premium was for 1 year, what was the total premium and when was the policy purchased?

**c.** If $2,500 of salaries owed were paid in January, what was the balance in Salaries and Wages Payable at December 31, 2021?

**d.** If $1,800 was received in January for services performed in January (no services are performed on credit), what was the balance in Unearned Service Revenue at December 31, 2021?

**E3.15 (LO 2, 3), AN** On December 31, 2022, Waters Company prepared an income statement and balance sheet, but failed to take into account three adjusting entries. The balance sheet showed total assets $150,000, total liabilities $70,000, and stockholders' equity $80,000. The incorrect income statement showed net income of $70,000.

*Determine effect of adjusting entries.*

The data for the three adjusting entries were:

**1.** Salaries and wages amounting to $10,000 for the last 2 days in December were not paid and not recorded. The next payroll will be in January.

**2.** Rent payments of $8,000 were received for two months in advance on December 1. The entire amount was credited to Unearned Rent Revenue when received.

**3.** Depreciation expense for 2022 is $9,000.

**Instructions**

Complete the following table to correct the financial statement amounts shown (indicate deductions with parentheses).

| Item | Net Income | Total Assets | Total Liabilities | Stockholders' Equity |
|---|---|---|---|---|
| Incorrect amounts | $70,000 | $150,000 | $70,000 | $80,000 |
| Effects of: | | | | |
| Salaries and wages | ——— | ——— | ——— | ——— |
| Rent revenue | ——— | ——— | ——— | ——— |
| Depreciation | ——— | ——— | ——— | ——— |
| Correct balances | ═══ | ═══ | ═══ | ═══ |

*Prepare and post transaction and adjusting entries for prepayments.*

**E3.16 (LO 2), AP** Action Quest Games Inc. adjusts its accounts annually. The following information is available for the year ended December 31, 2022.

1. Purchased a 1-year insurance policy on June 1 for $1,800 cash.

2. Paid $6,500 on August 31 for 5 months' rent in advance.

3. On September 4, received $3,600 cash in advance from a corporation to sponsor a game each month for a total of 9 months for the most improved students at a local school.

4. Signed a contract for cleaning services starting December 1 for $1,000 per month. Paid for the first 2 months on November 30. (*Hint:* Use the account Prepaid Cleaning to record prepayments.)

5. On December 5, received $1,500 in advance from a gaming club. Determined that on December 31, $475 of these games had not yet been played.

**Instructions**

a. For each of the above transactions, prepare the journal entry to record the initial transaction.

b. For each of the above transactions, prepare the adjusting journal entry that is required on December 31. (*Hint:* Use the account Service Revenue for item 3 and Repairs and Maintenance Expense for item 4.)

c. Post the journal entries in parts (a) and (b) to T-accounts and determine the final balance in each account. (*Note:* Posting to the Cash account is not required.)

*Prepare adjusting and subsequent entries for accruals.*

**E3.17 (LO 3), AP** Greenock Limited has the following information available for accruals for the year ended December 31, 2022. The company adjusts its accounts annually.

1. The December utility bill for $425 was unrecorded on December 31. Greenock paid the bill on January 11.

2. Greenock is open 7 days a week and employees are paid a total of $3,500 every Monday for a 7-day (Monday–Sunday) workweek. December 31 is a Thursday, so employees will have worked 4 days (Monday, December 28–Thursday, December 31) that they have not been paid for by year-end. Employees will be paid next on January 4.

3. Greenock signed a $45,000, 5% bank loan on November 1, 2021, due in 2 years. Interest is payable on the first day of each following month. (For example, interest incurred during November would be paid on December 1.)

4. Greenock receives a fee from Pizza Shop next door for all pizzas sold to customers using Greenock's facility. The amount owed for December is $300, which Pizza Shop will pay on January 4. (*Hint:* Use the Service Revenue account.)

5. Greenock rented some of its unused warehouse space to a client for $6,000 a month, payable the first day of the following month. It received the rent payment for the month of December on January 2.

**Instructions**

a. For each situation, prepare the adjusting entry required at December 31. (Round all calculations to the nearest dollar.)

b. For each situation, prepare the journal entry to record the subsequent cash transaction in 2023.

**E3.18 (LO 2, 3, 4), AP** The trial balances before and after adjustment for Ryan Company at the end of the fiscal year are as follows.

*Prepare adjusting entries.*

**Ryan Company**
**Trial Balance**
**August 31, 2022**

| | Before Adjustment | | After Adjustment | |
|---|---|---|---|---|
| | Dr. | Cr. | Dr. | Cr. |
| Cash | $10,900 | | $10,900 | |
| Accounts Receivable | 8,800 | | 9,400 | |
| Supplies | 2,500 | | 500 | |
| Prepaid Insurance | 4,000 | | 2,500 | |
| Equipment | 16,000 | | 16,000 | |
| Accumulated Depreciation—Equipment | | $ 3,600 | | $ 4,800 |
| Accounts Payable | | 5,800 | | 5,800 |
| Salaries and Wages Payable | | 0 | | 1,100 |
| Unearned Rent Revenue | | 1,800 | | 800 |
| Common Stock | | 10,000 | | 10,000 |
| Retained Earnings | | 5,500 | | 5,500 |
| Dividends | 2,800 | | 2,800 | |
| Service Revenue | | 34,000 | | 34,600 |
| Rent Revenue | | 12,100 | | 13,100 |
| Salaries and Wages Expense | 17,000 | | 18,100 | |
| Supplies Expense | 0 | | 2,000 | |
| Rent Expense | 10,800 | | 10,800 | |
| Insurance Expense | 0 | | 1,500 | |
| Depreciation Expense | 0 | | 1,200 | |
| | $72,800 | $72,800 | $75,700 | $75,700 |

**Instructions**

Prepare the adjusting entries that were made.

**E3.19 (LO 4), AP** The unadjusted and adjusted trial balance for Ryan Company are as follows.

*Prepare financial statements from adjusted trial balance.*

**Ryan Company**
**Trial Balance**
**August 31, 2022**

| | Before Adjustment | | After Adjustment | |
|---|---|---|---|---|
| | Dr. | Cr. | Dr. | Cr. |
| Cash | $10,900 | | $10,900 | |
| Accounts Receivable | 8,800 | | 9,400 | |
| Supplies | 2,500 | | 500 | |
| Prepaid Insurance | 4,000 | | 2,500 | |
| Equipment | 16,000 | | 16,000 | |
| Accumulated Depreciation—Equipment | | $ 3,600 | | $ 4,800 |
| Accounts Payable | | 5,800 | | 5,800 |
| Salaries and Wages Payable | | 0 | | 1,100 |
| Unearned Rent Revenue | | 1,800 | | 800 |
| Common Stock | | 10,000 | | 10,000 |
| Retained Earnings | | 5,500 | | 5,500 |
| Dividends | 2,800 | | 2,800 | |
| Service Revenue | | 34,000 | | 34,600 |
| Rent Revenue | | 12,100 | | 13,100 |
| Salaries and Wages Expense | 17,000 | | 18,100 | |
| Supplies Expense | 0 | | 2,000 | |
| Rent Expense | 10,800 | | 10,800 | |
| Insurance Expense | 0 | | 1,500 | |
| Depreciation Expense | 0 | | 1,200 | |
| | $72,800 | $72,800 | $75,700 | $75,700 |

## Instructions

Prepare the income and retained earnings statements for the year and the balance sheet at August 31.

*Record transactions on accrual basis; convert revenue to cash receipts.*

**E3.20 (LO 2, 3), AP** The following data are taken from the comparative balance sheets of Cascade Billiards Club, which prepares its financial statements using the accrual basis of accounting.

| Account Name | 12/31/22 Balance | 12/31/21 Balance |
|---|---|---|
| Accounts Receivable (from members) | $14,000 | $ 9,000 |
| Unearned Service Revenue | 17,000 | 25,000 |

Members are billed based upon their use of the club's facilities. Unearned service revenues arise from the sale of gift certificates, which members can apply to their future use of club facilities. The 2022 income statement for the club showed that service revenue of $161,000 was recorded during the year.

### Instructions

(*Hint:* You will probably find it helpful to use T-accounts to analyze these data.)

a. Prepare journal entries for each of the following events that took place during 2022.

1. Accounts receivable from 2021 were all collected.

2. Gift certificates outstanding at the end of 2021 were all redeemed.

3. An additional $38,000 worth of gift certificates were sold during 2022. A portion of these was used by the recipients during the year; the remainder was still outstanding at the end of 2022.

4. Services performed for members for 2022 were billed to members.

5. Accounts receivable for 2022 (i.e., those billed in item [4] above) were partially collected.

b. Determine the amount of cash received by the club, with respect to member services, during 2022.

*Journalize adjusting entries.*

*\*E3.21 (LO 5), AP** Prior to adjustments, Aaron Lynch Company has the following balances in selected accounts on December 31, 2022.

| | |
|---|---|
| Service Revenue | $40,000 |
| Insurance Expense | 2,700 |
| Supplies Expense | 2,450 |

All the accounts have normal balances. Aaron Lynch Company debits prepayments to expense accounts when paid, and credits unearned revenues to revenue accounts when received. The following information has been gathered at December 31, 2022.

1. Aaron Lynch Company paid $2,700 for 12 months of insurance coverage on June 1, 2022.

2. On December 1, 2022, Aaron Lynch Company collected $40,000 for consulting services to be performed from December 1, 2022, through March 31, 2023.

3. A count of supplies on December 31, 2022, indicates that supplies of $900 are on hand.

### Instructions

Prepare the adjusting entries needed at December 31, 2022. Adjustments are prepared annually.

*Journalize transactions and adjusting entries.*

*\*E3.22 (LO 5), AP** At Cambridge Company, prepayments are debited to expense when paid, and unearned revenues are credited to revenue when cash is received. During January of the current year, the following transactions occurred.

| Jan. | 2 | Paid $1,920 for fire insurance protection for the year. |
|---|---|---|
| | 10 | Paid $1,700 for supplies. |
| | 15 | Received $6,100 for services to be performed in the future. |

On January 31, it is determined that $2,500 of the services were performed and that there are $650 of supplies on hand.

### Instructions

a. Journalize and post the January transactions. (Use T-accounts.)

b. Journalize and post the adjusting entries at January 31.

c. Determine the ending balance in each of the accounts.

*Identify accounting assumptions and principles.*

*\*E3.23 (LO 6), K** The following are the assumptions and principles discussed in Appendix 3B.

1. Full disclosure principle.
2. Going concern assumption.
3. Monetary unit assumption.

4. Time period assumption.
5. Historical cost principle.
6. Economic entity assumption.

## Instructions

Identify by number the accounting assumption or principle that is described below. Do not use a number more than once.

_____ **a.** Indicates that a business is expected to operate indefinitely into the future.

_____ **b.** Indicates that personal and business record keeping should be separately maintained.

_____ **c.** Assumes that the monetary unit is the "measuring stick" used to report on financial performance.

_____ **d.** Separates financial information into time periods for reporting purposes.

_____ **e.** Measurement basis used when a reliable estimate of fair value is not available.

_____ **f.** Dictates that companies should disclose all circumstances and events that make a difference to financial statement users.

\* **E3.24 (LO 6), C** Rosman Co. had three major business transactions during 2022.

**a.** Reported, at its fair value of $260,000, land with a cost of $208,000.

**b.** The president of Rosman Co., Jay Rosman, purchased a truck for personal use and charged it to the company's Salaries and Wages Expense account.

**c.** Rosman Co. wanted to make its 2022 income look better, so it added 2 more weeks to the year (a 54-week year). Previous years were 52 weeks.

*Identify the assumption or principle that has been violated.*

## Instructions

In each situation, identify the assumption or principle that has been violated, if any, and discuss what the company should have done.

\* **E3.25 (LO 6), K** The following characteristics, assumptions, principles, and constraint guide the FASB when it creates accounting standards.

*Identify financial accounting concepts and principles.*

| | |
|---|---|
| Relevance | Expense recognition principle |
| Faithful representation | Time period assumption |
| Comparability | Going concern assumption |
| Consistency | Historical cost principle |
| Monetary unit assumption | Full disclosure principle |
| Economic entity assumption | Materiality |

Match each item above with a description below.

**1.** _____ Ability to easily evaluate one company's results relative to another's.

**2.** _____ Requirement that a company will continue to operate for the foreseeable future.

**3.** _____ The judgment concerning whether an item's size is large enough to matter to decision-makers.

**4.** _____ The reporting of all information that would make a difference to financial statement users.

**5.** _____ The practice of preparing financial statements at regular intervals.

**6.** _____ The quality of information that indicates the information makes a difference in a decision.

**7.** _____ A belief that items should be reported on the balance sheet at the price that was paid to acquire them.

**8.** _____ A company's use of the same accounting principles and methods from year to year.

**9.** _____ Tracing accounting events to particular companies.

**10.** _____ The desire to minimize bias in financial statements.

**11.** _____ Reporting only those things that can be measured in monetary units.

**12.** _____ Dictates that efforts (expenses) be recognized in the period in which a company uses assets or incurs liabilities to generate results (revenues).

\* **E3.26 (LO 6), E** Writing Net Nanny Software International Inc., headquartered in Vancouver, Canada, specializes in Internet safety and computer security products for both the home and commercial markets. In a recent balance sheet, it reported a retained earnings deficit of $5,678,288 (in U.S. dollars). It has reported only net losses since its inception. In spite of these losses, Net Nanny's shares of stock have traded anywhere from a high of $3.70 to a low of $0.32 on the Canadian Venture Exchange.

Net Nanny's financial statements have historically been prepared in Canadian dollars. Recently, the company adopted the U.S. dollar as its reporting currency.

*Comment on the objective and qualitative characteristics of accounting information.*

**Instructions**

**a.** What is the objective of financial reporting? How does this objective meet or not meet Net Nanny's investors' needs?

**b.** Why would investors want to buy Net Nanny's shares if the company has consistently reported losses over the last few years? Include in your answer an assessment of the relevance of the information reported on Net Nanny's financial statements.

**c.** Comment on how the change in reporting information from Canadian dollars to U.S. dollars likely affected the readers of Net Nanny's financial statements. Include in your answer an assessment of the comparability of the information.

*Comment on the objective and qualitative characteristics of financial reporting.*

**\* E3.27 (LO 6), E Writing** A friend of yours, Ana Gehrig, recently completed an undergraduate degree in science and has just started working with an international biotechnology company. Ana tells you that the owners of the business are trying to secure new sources of financing which are needed in order for the company to proceed with development of a new healthcare product. Ana said that her boss told her that the company must put together a report to present to potential investors.

Ana thought that the company should include in this package the detailed scientific findings related to the Phase I clinical trials for this product. She said, "I know that the biotech industry sometimes has only a 10% success rate with new products, but if we report all the scientific findings, everyone will see what a sure success this is going to be! The president was talking about the importance of following some set of accounting principles. Why do we need to look at some accounting rules? What they need to realize is that we have scientific results that are quite encouraging, some of the most talented employees around, and the start of some really great customer relationships. We haven't made any sales yet, but we will. We just need the funds to get through all the clinical testing and get government approval for our product. Then these investors will be quite happy that they bought in to our company early!"

**Instructions**

**a.** What is accounting information?

**b.** Comment on how Ana's suggestions for what should be reported to prospective investors conforms to the qualitative characteristics of accounting information. Do you think that the things that Ana wants to include in the information for investors will conform to financial reporting guidelines?

## Problems

*Prepare adjusting entries, post to ledger accounts, and prepare an adjusted trial balance.*

**P3.1 (LO 2, 3, 4), AP** Deanna Nardelli started her own consulting firm, Nardelli Consulting, on May 1, 2022. The unadjusted trial balance at May 31 is as follows.

**Nardelli Consulting**
**Trial Balance**
**May 31, 2022**

| Account Number | | Debit | Credit |
|---|---|---|---|
| 101 | Cash | $ 4,500 | |
| 112 | Accounts Receivable | 6,000 | |
| 126 | Supplies | 1,900 | |
| 130 | Prepaid Insurance | 3,600 | |
| 149 | Equipment | 11,400 | |
| 201 | Accounts Payable | | $ 2,200 |
| 209 | Unearned Service Revenue | | 2,000 |
| 311 | Common Stock | | 20,000 |
| 400 | Service Revenue | | 7,500 |
| 726 | Salaries and Wages Expense | 3,400 | |
| 729 | Rent Expense | 900 | |
| | | $31,700 | $31,700 |

In addition to those accounts listed on the trial balance, the chart of accounts for Nardelli Consulting also contains the following accounts and account numbers: No. 150 Accumulated Depreciation—Equipment, No. 212 Salaries and Wages Payable, No. 631 Supplies Expense, No. 717 Depreciation Expense, No. 722 Insurance Expense, and No. 732 Utilities Expense.

Other data:

1. $900 of supplies have been used during the month.

2. Utilities expense incurred but not paid or recorded on May 31, 2022, $250.

3. An insurance policy for 2 years was purchased on May 1.

4. $400 of the balance in the unearned service revenue account remains unearned at the end of the month.

5. May 31 is a Wednesday, and employees are paid on Fridays. Nardelli Consulting has two employees, who are paid $900 each for a 5-day work week.

6. The equipment has a 5-year life with no salvage value. It is being depreciated at $190 per month for 60 months.

7. Invoices representing $1,700 of services performed during the month have not been recorded as of May 31.

### Instructions

a. Prepare the adjusting entries for the month of May. Use J4 as the page number for your journal.

b. Enter the totals from the trial balance as beginning account balances and place a check mark in the posting reference column. Post the adjusting entries to the ledger accounts.

c. Prepare an adjusted trial balance at May 31, 2022.

*c. Adj. trial balance $34,920*

**P3.2 (LO 2, 3, 4), AP** The Skyline Motel opened for business on May 1, 2022. Its trial balance before adjustment on May 31 is as follows.

*Prepare adjusting entries, post, and prepare adjusted trial balance and financial statements.*

**Skyline Motel**
**Trial Balance**
**May 31, 2022**

| Account Number | | Debit | Credit |
|---|---|---|---|
| 101 | Cash | $ 3,500 | |
| 126 | Supplies | 2,080 | |
| 130 | Prepaid Insurance | 2,400 | |
| 140 | Land | 12,000 | |
| 141 | Buildings | 60,000 | |
| 149 | Equipment | 15,000 | |
| 200 | Notes Payable | | $40,000 |
| 201 | Accounts Payable | | 11,180 |
| 208 | Unearned Rent Revenue | | 3,300 |
| 311 | Common Stock | | 35,000 |
| 429 | Rent Revenue | | 10,300 |
| 610 | Advertising Expense | 600 | |
| 726 | Salaries and Wages Expense | 3,300 | |
| 732 | Utilities Expense | 900 | |
| | | $99,780 | $99,780 |

In addition to those accounts listed on the trial balance, the chart of accounts for Skyline Motel also contains the following accounts and account numbers: No. 142 Accumulated Depreciation—Buildings, No. 150 Accumulated Depreciation—Equipment, No. 212 Salaries and Wages Payable, No. 230 Interest Payable, No. 619 Depreciation Expense, No. 631 Supplies Expense, No. 718 Interest Expense, and No. 722 Insurance Expense.

Other data:

1. Prepaid insurance is a 1-year policy starting May 1, 2022.

2. A count of supplies shows $750 of unused supplies on May 31.

3. Annual depreciation is $3,000 on the buildings and $1,500 on equipment.

4. The note payable interest rate is 12%. (The note was taken out on May 1 and will be repaid along with interest in 2 years.)

5. Two-thirds of the unearned rent revenue has been earned.

6. Salaries and wages of $750 are unpaid and unrecorded at May 31.

## Instructions

a. Journalize the adjusting entries on May 31.

b. Prepare a ledger using the three-column form of account. Enter the trial balance amounts and post the adjusting entries. (Use J1 as the posting reference.)

c. Prepare an adjusted trial balance on May 31.

d. Prepare an income statement and a retained earnings statement for the month of May and a balance sheet at May 31.

*c. Adj. trial balance $101,305*
*d. Net income $4,645*
  *Ending retained*
    *earnings $4,645*
  *Total assets $93,075*

*Prepare adjusting entries and financial statements.*

**P3.3 (LO 2, 3, 4), AP** Everett Co. was organized on July 1, 2022. Quarterly financial statements are prepared. The unadjusted and adjusted trial balances as of September 30 are shown as follows.

**Everett Co.**
**Trial Balance**
**September 30, 2022**

|  | Unadjusted | | Adjusted | |
| --- | --- | --- | --- | --- |
|  | Dr. | Cr. | Dr. | Cr. |
| Cash | $ 8,700 |  | $ 8,700 |  |
| Accounts Receivable | 10,400 |  | 11,500 |  |
| Supplies | 1,500 |  | 650 |  |
| Prepaid Rent | 2,200 |  | 1,200 |  |
| Equipment | 18,000 |  | 18,000 |  |
| Accumulated Depreciation—Equipment |  | $ –0– |  | $ 700 |
| Notes Payable |  | 10,000 |  | 10,000 |
| Accounts Payable |  | 2,500 |  | 2,500 |
| Salaries and Wages Payable |  | –0– |  | 725 |
| Interest Payable |  | –0– |  | 100 |
| Unearned Rent Revenue |  | 1,900 |  | 1,050 |
| Common Stock |  | 22,000 |  | 22,000 |
| Dividends | 1,600 |  | 1,600 |  |
| Service Revenue |  | 16,000 |  | 17,100 |
| Rent Revenue |  | 1,410 |  | 2,260 |
| Salaries and Wages Expense | 8,000 |  | 8,725 |  |
| Rent Expense | 1,900 |  | 2,900 |  |
| Depreciation Expense |  |  | 700 |  |
| Supplies Expense |  |  | 850 |  |
| Utilities Expense | 1,510 |  | 1,510 |  |
| Interest Expense |  |  | 100 |  |
|  | $53,810 | $53,810 | $56,435 | $56,435 |

## Instructions

a. Journalize the adjusting entries that were made.

b. Prepare an income statement and a retained earnings statement for the 3 months ending September 30 and a balance sheet at September 30.

c. If the note bears interest at 12%, how many months has it been outstanding? (The note and interest will be paid in 2 years.)

*b. Net income $4,575*
  *Ending retained*
    *earnings $2,975*
  *Total assets $39,350*

*Prepare adjusting entries.*

**P3.4 (LO 2, 3), AP** A review of the ledger of Lewis Company at December 31, 2022, produces the following data pertaining to the preparation of annual adjusting entries.

1. Prepaid Insurance $15,200. The company has separate insurance policies on its buildings and its motor vehicles. Policy B4564 on the building was purchased on July 1, 2021, for $9,600. The policy has a term of 3 years. Policy A2958 on the vehicles was purchased on January 1, 2022, for $7,200. This policy has a term of 2 years.

*1. Insurance expense $6,800*

2. Unearned Rent Revenue $429,000. The company began subleasing office space in its new building on November 1, 2022. At December 31, the company had the following rental contracts that are paid in full for the entire term of the lease.

*2. Rent revenue $84,000*

| Date | Term (in months) | Monthly Rent Payment | Number of Leases |
| --- | --- | --- | --- |
| Nov. 1 | 9 | $5,000 | 5 |
| Dec. 1 | 6 | $8,500 | 4 |

3. Notes Payable $40,000. This balance consists of a note for 6 months at an annual interest rate of 7%, dated November 1. Interest will be paid at note maturity. (Round to nearest dollar.)

4. Salaries and Wages Payable $0. There are eight salaried employees. Salaries are paid every Monday for the prior week. Five employees receive a salary of $600 each per week, and three employees earn $700 each per week. Assume December 31 is a Tuesday. Employees do not work weekends. All employees worked the last 2 days of December.

3. Interest expense $467

4. Salaries and wages expense $2,040

**Instructions**

Prepare the adjusting entries at December 31, 2022.

**P3.5 (LO 2, 3, 4), AP** On November 1, 2022, the account balances of Schilling Equipment Repair were as follows.

*Journalize transactions and follow through accounting cycle to preparation of financial statements.*

| No. |  | Debit | No. |  | Credit |
|-----|----|-------|-----|----|--------|
| 101 | Cash | $ 2,400 | 154 | Accumulated Depreciation—Equipment | $ 2,000 |
| 112 | Accounts Receivable | 4,250 | 201 | Accounts Payable | 2,500 |
| 126 | Supplies | 1,800 | 209 | Unearned Service Revenue | 1,200 |
| 153 | Equipment | 12,000 | 212 | Salaries and Wages Payable | 700 |
|  |  |  | 311 | Common Stock | 10,000 |
|  |  |  | 320 | Retained Earnings | 3,050 |
|  |  | $20,450 |  |  | $20,450 |

During November, the following summary transactions were completed.

| Nov. | 8 | Paid $1,700 for salaries due employees, of which $700 is for October salaries. |
|------|----|-----|
|  | 10 | Received $3,420 cash from customers on account. |
|  | 12 | Received $3,100 cash for services performed in November. |
|  | 15 | Purchased equipment on account $2,000. |
|  | 17 | Purchased supplies on account $700. |
|  | 20 | Paid creditors on account $2,700. |
|  | 22 | Paid November rent $400. |
|  | 25 | Paid salaries $1,700. |
|  | 27 | Performed services on account and billed customers $1,900 for these services. |
|  | 29 | Received $600 from customers for future service. |

Adjustment data consist of:

1. Supplies on hand $1,400.
2. Accrued salaries payable $350.
3. Depreciation for the month is $200.
4. Services related to unearned service revenue of $1,250 were performed.

**Instructions**

a. Enter the November 1 balances in the ledger accounts.

b. Journalize the November transactions.

c. Post to the ledger accounts. Use J1 for the posting reference. Use the following additional accounts: No. 407 Service Revenue, No. 615 Depreciation Expense, No. 631 Supplies Expense, No. 726 Salaries and Wages Expense, and No. 729 Rent Expense.

d. Prepare a trial balance at November 30.

e. Journalize and post adjusting entries.

f. Prepare an adjusted trial balance.

g. Prepare an income statement and a retained earnings statement for November and a balance sheet at November 30.

d. Trial balance $25,350

f. Adj. trial balance $25,900

g. Net income $1,500
Ending retained
 earnings $5,450
Total assets $18,950

*Prepare adjusting entries, adjusted trial balance, and financial statements using Appendix 3A.*

**＊P3.6 (LO 2, 3, 4, 5), AP** Sommer Graphics Company was organized on January 1, 2022, by Krystal Sommer. At the end of the first 6 months of operations, the unadjusted trial balance contained the accounts shown below.

| | Debit | | Credit |
|---|---|---|---|
| Cash | $ 8,600 | Notes Payable | $ 20,000 |
| Accounts Receivable | 14,000 | Accounts Payable | 9,000 |
| Equipment | 45,000 | Common Stock | 22,000 |
| Insurance Expense | 2,700 | Rent Revenue | 52,100 |
| Salaries and Wages Expense | 30,000 | Service Revenue | 6,000 |
| Supplies Expense | 3,700 | | |
| Advertising Expense | 1,900 | | |
| Rent Expense | 1,500 | | |
| Utilities Expense | 1,700 | | |
| | $109,100 | | $109,100 |

Analysis reveals the following additional data.

1. The $3,700 balance in Supplies Expense represents supplies purchased in January. At June 30, $1,500 of supplies are on hand.

2. The note payable was issued on February 1. It is a 9%, 6-month note. Interest is paid when the note matures.

3. The balance in Insurance Expense is the premium on a 1-year policy, dated March 1, 2022.

4. Service Revenue is credited when cash is received from customers. At June 30, service revenue of $1,300 remains unearned.

5. Revenue for services performed but unrecorded at June 30 totals $2,000.

6. Depreciation is $2,250 per year.

b. Adj. trial balance $112,975

c. Net income $18,725
   Ending retained
      earnings $18,725
   Total assets $71,775

**Instructions**

a. Journalize the adjusting entries at June 30. (Assume adjustments are recorded every 6 months.)

b. Prepare an adjusted trial balance.

c. Prepare an income statement and a retained earnings statement for the 6 months ended June 30 and a balance sheet at June 30.

---

## Continuing Case

leungchopan/
Shutterstock.com

### Cookie Creations

(*Note:* This is a continuation of the Cookie Creations case from Chapters 1 and 2.)

**CC3** It is the end of November and Natalie has been in touch with her grandmother. Her grandmother asked Natalie how well things went in her first month of business. Natalie, too, would like to know if her business has been profitable or not during November. Natalie realizes that in order to determine Cookie Creations' income, she must first make adjustments.

*Go to WileyPLUS for complete case details and instructions.*

---

## Expand Your Critical Thinking

---

### Financial Reporting Problem: Apple Inc.

**CT3.1** The financial statements of **Apple Inc.** are presented in Appendix A. The complete annual report, including the notes to the financial statements, is available at the company's website.

**Instructions**

a. Using the consolidated financial statements and related information, identify items that may result in adjusting entries for prepayments.

**b.** Using the consolidated financial statements and related information, identify items that may result in adjusting entries for accruals.

**c.** What has been the trend since 2016 for net income?

## Comparative Analysis Problem:

## PepsiCo, Inc. vs. The Coca-Cola Company

**CT3.2 PepsiCo**'s financial statements are presented in Appendix B. Financial statements of **The Coca-Cola Company** are presented in Appendix C. The complete annual reports of PepsiCo and Coca-Cola, including the notes to the financial statements, are available at each company's respective website.

### Instructions

Based on information contained in these financial statements, determine the following for each company.

**a.** Net increase (decrease) in property, plant, and equipment (net) from 2017 to 2018.

**b.** Increase (decrease) in selling, general, and administrative expenses from 2017 to 2018.

**c.** Increase (decrease) in long-term debt (obligations) from 2017 to 2018.

**d.** Increase (decrease) in net income from 2017 to 2018.

**e.** Increase (decrease) in cash and cash equivalents from 2017 to 2018.

## Comparative Analysis Problem:

## Amazon.com, Inc. vs. Walmart Inc.

**CT3.3 Amazon.com, Inc.**'s financial statements are presented in Appendix D. Financial statements of **Walmart Inc.** are presented in Appendix E. The complete annual reports of Amazon and Walmart, including the notes to the financial statements, are available at each company's respective website.

### Instructions

Based on information contained in these financial statements, determine the following for each company.

**1. a.** Increase (decrease) in interest expense from 2017 to 2018.

**b.** Increase (decrease) in net income from 2017 to 2018.

**c.** Increase (decrease) in cash flow from operating activities from 2017 to 2018.

**2.** Cash flow from operating activities and net income for each company is different. What are some possible reasons for these differences?

## Real-World Focus

**CT3.4** No financial decision-maker should ever rely solely on the financial information reported in the annual report to make decisions. It is important to keep abreast of financial news. This activity demonstrates how to search for financial news on the Internet.

### Instructions

Go to the **Yahoo! Finance** website and then type in either Walmart, Target Corp., or Kmart. Choose **News**, select an article that sounds interesting to you and that would be relevant to an investor in these companies, and then answer the following questions.

**a.** What was the source of the article (e.g., Reuters, Businesswire, Prnewswire)?

**b.** Assume that you are a personal financial planner and that one of your clients owns stock in the company. Write a brief memo to your client summarizing the article and explaining the implications of the article for your client's investment.

**CT3.5** The July 6, 2011, edition of the *Wall Street Journal Online* includes an article by Michael Rapaport entitled "U.S. Firms Clash Over Accounting Rules." The article discusses why some U.S. companies favored adoption of International Financial Reporting Standards (IFRS) while other companies opposed it.

### Instructions

Read the article and answer the following questions.

**a.** The article says that the switch to IFRS tends to be favored by "larger companies, big accounting firms, and rule makers." What reasons are given for favoring the switch?

**b.** What two reasons are given by many smaller companies that oppose the switch?

c. What criticism of IFRS is raised with regard to regulated companies?

d. Explain what is meant by "condorsement."

## Decision-Making Across the Organization

**CT3.6** Abby Park was organized on April 1, 2021, by Trudy Crawford. Trudy is a good manager but a poor accountant. From the trial balance prepared by a junior accountant, Trudy prepared the following income statement for the quarter that ended March 31, 2022.

**Abby Park**
**Income Statement**
**For the Quarter Ended March 31, 2022**

| | | |
|---|---:|---:|
| Revenues | | |
|     Rent revenue | | $83,000 |
| Operating expenses | | |
|     Advertising expense | $ 4,200 | |
|     Salaries and wages expense | 27,600 | |
|     Utilities expense | 1,500 | |
|     Depreciation expense | 800 | |
|     Maintenance and repairs expense | 2,800 | |
|       Total operating expenses | | 36,900 |
| Net income | | $46,100 |

Trudy knows that something is wrong with the statement because net income has never exceeded $20,000 in any one quarter. Knowing that you are an experienced accountant, she asks you to review the income statement and other data.

You first look at the trial balance. In addition to the account balances reported above in the income statement, the ledger contains the following additional selected balances at March 31, 2022.

| | |
|---|---:|
| Supplies | $ 4,500 |
| Prepaid Insurance | 7,200 |
| Notes Payable | 20,000 |

You then make inquiries and discover the following.

1. Rent revenue includes advanced rentals for summer occupancy of $21,000.

2. There were $600 of supplies on hand at March 31.

3. Prepaid Insurance represents a 1-year policy dated January 1, 2022.

4. The mail on April 1, 2022, included the following bills: advertising for week of March 24, $110; repairs made March 10, $1,040; and March utilities, $240.

5. Salaries and wages expense total $290 per day. At March 31, 2 days' salaries and wages have been incurred but not paid or recorded.

6. The note payable is a 3-month, 17% note dated January 1, 2022. (Interest is paid at note maturity.)

### Instructions

With the class divided into groups, answer the following.

a. Prepare a correct income statement for the quarter ended March 31, 2022.

b. Explain to Trudy the generally accepted accounting principles that she did not recognize in preparing her income statement and their effect on her results.

## Communication Activity

**CT3.7** In reviewing the accounts of Gloria Jean Co. at the end of the year, you discover that adjusting entries have not been made.

### Instructions

Write a memo to Gloria Jean Hall, the owner of Gloria Jean Co., that explains the following: the nature and purpose of adjusting entries, why adjusting entries are needed, and the types of adjusting entries that may be made.

## Ethics Case

**CT3.8** Kellner Company is a pesticide manufacturer. Its sales declined greatly this year due to the passage of legislation outlawing the sale of several of Kellner's chemical pesticides. In the coming year, Kellner will have environmentally safe and competitive chemicals to replace these discontinued products. Sales in the next year are expected to greatly exceed those from any prior years. The decline in sales and profits appears to be a one-year aberration. But even so, the company president fears a large dip in the current year's profits. He believes that such a dip could cause a significant drop in the market price of Kellner's stock and make the company a takeover target.

To avoid this possibility, the company president calls in Melissa Ray, controller, to discuss this period's year-end adjusting entries. He urges her to accrue every possible revenue and to defer as many expenses as possible. He says to Melissa, "We need the revenues this year, and next year can easily absorb expenses deferred from this year. We can't let our stock price be hammered down!" Melissa didn't get around to recording the adjusting entries until January 17, but she dated the entries December 31 as if they were recorded then. Melissa also made every effort to comply with the president's request.

### Instructions

a. Who are the stakeholders in this situation?

b. What are the ethical considerations of (1) the president's request and (2) Melissa dating the adjusting entries December 31?

c. Can Melissa accrue revenues and defer expenses and still be ethical?

## All About You

**CT3.9** Companies must report or disclose in their financial statements information about all liabilities, including potential liabilities related to environmental cleanup. There are many situations in which you will be asked to provide personal financial information about your assets, liabilities, revenue, and expenses. Sometimes you will face difficult decisions regarding what to disclose and how to disclose it.

### Instructions

Suppose that you are putting together a loan application to purchase a home. Based on your income and assets, you qualify for the mortgage loan, but just barely. How would you address each of the following situations in reporting your financial position for the loan application? Provide responses for each of the following situations.

a. You signed a guarantee for a bank loan that a friend took out for $20,000. If your friend doesn't pay, you will have to pay. Your friend has made all of the payments so far, and it appears he will be able to pay in the future.

b. You were involved in an auto accident in which you were at fault. There is the possibility that you may have to pay as much as $50,000 as part of a settlement. The issue will not be resolved before the bank processes your mortgage request.

c. The company for which you work isn't doing very well, and it has recently laid off employees. You are still employed, but it is quite possible that you will lose your job in the next few months.

## Considering People, Planet, and Profit

**CT3.10** Many companies have potential pollution or environmental-disposal problems—not only for electronic gadgets, but also for the lead paint or asbestos they sold. How do we fit these issues into the accounting equation? Are these costs and related liabilities that companies should report?

**YES:** As more states impose laws holding companies responsible, and as more courts levy pollution-related fines, it becomes increasingly likely that companies will have to pay large amounts in the future.

**NO:** The amounts still are too difficult to estimate. Putting inaccurate estimates on the financial statements reduces their usefulness. Instead, why not charge the costs later, when the actual environmental cleanup or disposal occurs, at which time the company knows the actual cost?

### Instructions

Write a response indicating your position regarding this situation. Provide support for your view.

### FASB Codification Activity

**CT3.11** If your school has a subscription to the FASB Codification, log in and prepare responses to the following.

**Instructions**

Access the glossary ("Master Glossary") to answer the following.

**a.** What is the definition of revenue?

**b.** What is the definition of compensation?

### Answers to Insight and Accounting Across the Organization Questions

**Reporting Revenue Accurately Q:** In the past, why was it argued that Apple should spread the recognition of iPhone revenue over a two-year period, rather than recording it upfront? **A:** Apple promises to provide software updates over the life of the phone's use. Because this represents an unfulfilled performance obligation, it was argued that Apple should spread its revenue recognition over a two-year estimated life of the phone.

**Turning Gift Cards into Revenue Q:** Suppose that Robert Jones purchases a $100 gift card at Best Buy on December 24, 2021, and gives it to his wife, Mary Jones, on December 25, 2021. On January 3, 2022, Mary uses the card to purchase a $100 smart speaker. When do you think Best Buy should recognize revenue and why? **A:** According to the revenue recognition principle, companies should recognize revenue when the performance obligation is satisfied. In this case, revenue results when Best Buy provides the goods. Thus, when Best Buy receives cash in exchange for the gift card on December 24, 2021, it should recognize a liability, Unearned Sales Revenue, for $100. On January 3, 2022, when Mary Jones exchanges the card for merchandise, Best Buy should recognize revenue and eliminate $100 from the balance in the Unearned Sales Revenue account.

**Got Junk? Q:** What accounting issue might this cause for companies? **A:** The balance sheet should provide a fair representation of what a company owns and what it owes. If significant obligations of the company are not reported on the balance sheet, the company's net worth (its equity) will be overstated. While it is true that it is not possible to estimate the **exact** amount of future environmental cleanup costs, it is becoming clear that companies will be held accountable. Therefore, it seems reasonable to accrue for environmental costs. Recognition of these liabilities provides a more accurate picture of the company's financial position. It also has the potential to improve the environment. As companies are forced to report these amounts on their financial statements, they will start to look for more effective and efficient means to reduce toxic waste and therefore reduce their costs.

# A Look at IFRS

---

**LEARNING OBJECTIVE 7**

Compare the procedures for adjusting entries under GAAP and IFRS.

---

The procedure used to adjust the accounting records is essentially the same among countries.

## Key Points

Following are the key similarities and differences between GAAP and International Financial Reporting Standards (IFRS) as related to accrual accounting.

### Similarities

- In this chapter, you learned accrual-basis accounting applied under GAAP. Companies applying IFRS also use accrual-basis accounting to ensure that they record transactions that affect a company's financial statements in the period in which events occur.

- Similar to GAAP, cash-basis accounting is not allowed under IFRS.

- IFRS also divides the economic life of companies into artificial time periods. Under both GAAP and IFRS, this is referred to as the **time period assumption**.

- The **general** revenue recognition principle required by GAAP that is used in this text is similar to that used under IFRS.

- Revenue recognition fraud is a major issue in U.S. financial reporting. The same situation occurs in other countries, as evidenced by revenue recognition breakdowns at Dutch software company **Baan NV**, Japanese electronics giant **NEC**, and Dutch grocer **Ahold NV**.

**Differences**

- Under IFRS, revaluation (using fair value) of items such as land and buildings is permitted. IFRS allows depreciation based on revaluation of assets, which is not permitted under GAAP.

- The terminology used for revenues and gains, and expenses and losses, differs somewhat between IFRS and GAAP. For example, income under IFRS includes both revenues, which arise during the normal course of operating activities, and gains, which arise from activities outside of the normal sales of goods and services. The term "income" is not used this way under GAAP. Instead, under GAAP income refers to the net difference between revenues and expenses.

- Under IFRS, expenses include both those costs incurred in the normal course of operations as well as losses that are not part of normal operations. This is in contrast to GAAP, which defines each separately.

# IFRS Practice

## IFRS Self-Test Questions

1. IFRS:
   a. uses accrual accounting.
   b. uses cash-basis accounting.
   c. allows revenue to be recognized when a customer makes an order.
   d. requires that revenue not be recognized until cash is received.

2. Which of the following statements is **false**?
   a. IFRS employs the time period assumption.
   b. IFRS employs accrual accounting.
   c. IFRS requires that revenues and costs must be capable of being measured reliably.
   d. IFRS uses the cash basis of accounting.

3. GAAP and IFRS require that revenue be recognized:
   a. when the performance obligation is satisfied.
   b. upon receipt of cash from customers.

   c. under cash-basis accounting.
   d. when it is earned and realized.

4. Which of the following is **false**?
   a. Under IFRS, the term income describes both revenues and gains.
   b. Under IFRS, the term expenses includes losses.
   c. Under IFRS, companies do not engage in the adjusting process.
   d. Under IFRS, revenue recognition fraud is a major issue.

5. Accrual-basis accounting:
   a. is optional under IFRS.
   b. results in companies recording transactions that affect a company's financial statements in the period in which events occur.
   c. has been eliminated as a result of the IASB/FASB joint projects.
   d. is no different than cash-basis accounting.

## International Financial Reporting Problem: Louis Vuitton

**IFRS3.1** The financial statements of **Louis Vuitton** are presented in Appendix F. The complete consolidated financial statements, including the notes to its financial statements, are available at the company's website.

**Instructions**

Use Louis Vuitton's 2018 consolidated financial statements to answer the following questions.

    **a.** From the notes to the financial statements, how does the company determine the amount of revenue to record at the time of a sale?

    **b.** From the notes to the financial statements, how does the company determine the provision for product returns?

    **c.** Using the consolidated income statement and consolidated statement of financial position, identify items that may result in adjusting entries for deferrals.

    **d.** Using the consolidated income statement, identify two items that may result in adjusting entries for accruals.

**Answers to IFRS Self-Test Questions**

**1.** a   **2.** d   **3.** a   **4.** c   **5.** b

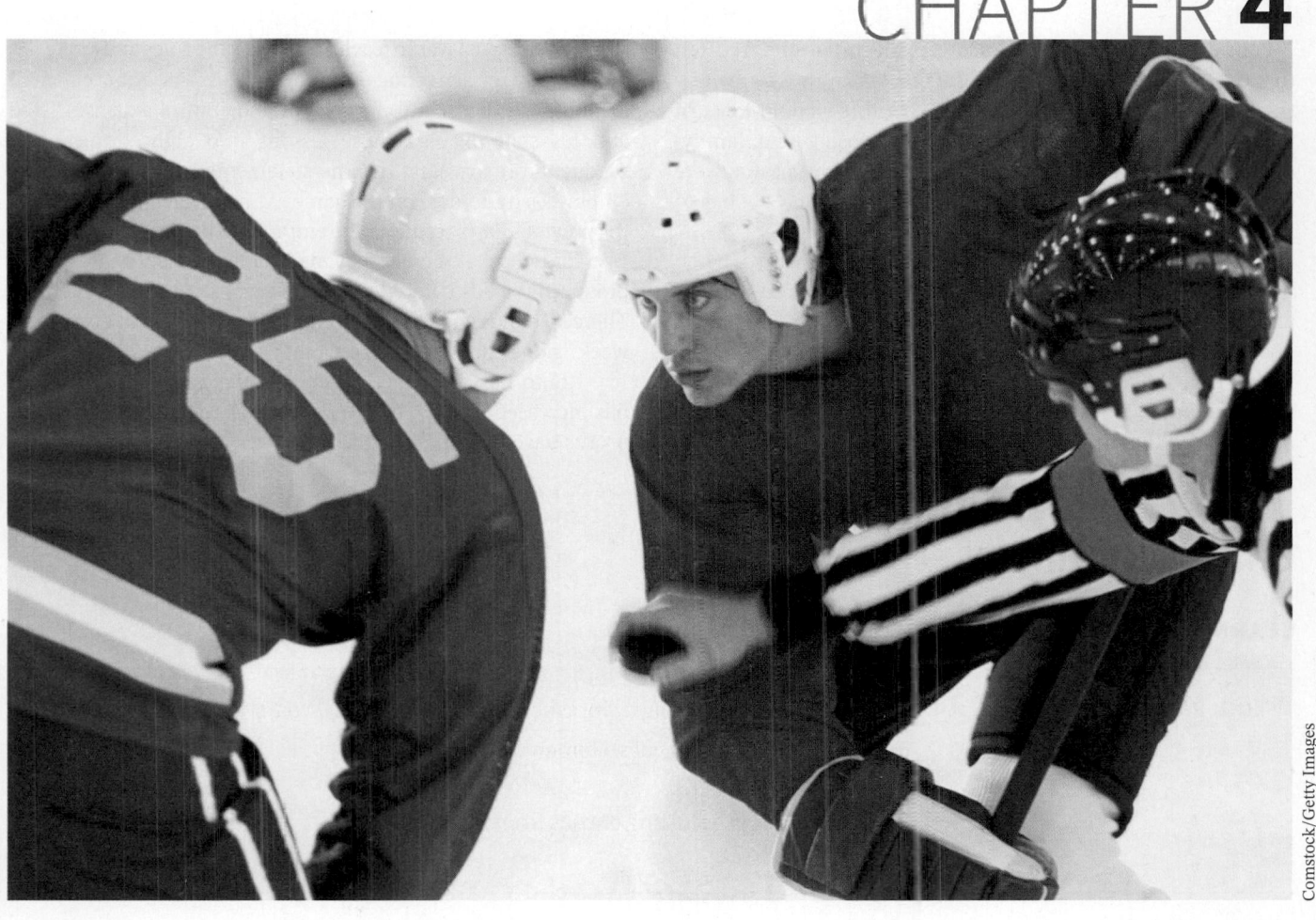

## CHAPTER 4

Comstock/Getty Images

# Completing the Accounting Cycle

## Chapter Preview

As the following Feature Story highlights, at **Rhino Foods, Inc.**, financial statements help employees understand what is happening in the business. In Chapter 3, we prepared financial statements directly from the adjusted trial balance. However, with so many details involved in the end-of-period accounting procedures, it is easy to make errors. One way to minimize errors in the records and to simplify the end-of-period procedures is to use a worksheet.

In this chapter, we will explain the role of the worksheet in accounting. We also will study the remaining steps in the accounting cycle, especially the closing process, again using Pioneer Advertising Inc. as an example. Then we will consider correcting entries and classified balance sheets.

## Feature Story

### Everyone Likes to Win

When Ted Castle was a hockey coach at the University of Vermont, his players were self-motivated by their desire to win.

But at **Rhino Foods, Inc.**, a bakery-foods company he founded in Burlington, Vermont, he discovered that manufacturing-line workers were not so self-motivated. Ted thought, what if he turned the food-making business into more like a hockey game, with rules, strategies, and trophies?

In a game, knowing the score is all-important. Ted felt that only if the employees know the score—know exactly how the business is doing daily, weekly, monthly—could he turn food-making into a game. But Rhino is a closely held, family-owned business, and its financial statements and profits were confidential. Ted wondered, should he open Rhino's books to the employees?

A consultant put Ted's concerns in perspective when he said, "Imagine you're playing touch football. You play for an hour or two, and the whole time I'm sitting there with a book, keeping score. All of a sudden I blow the whistle, and I say, 'OK, that's it. Everybody go home.' I close my book and walk away. How would you feel?" Ted opened his books and revealed the financial statements to his employees.

The next step was to teach employees the rules and strategies of how to "win" at making food. The first lesson: "Your opponent at Rhino is expenses. You must cut and control expenses." Ted and his staff distilled those lessons into daily scorecards—production reports and income statements—that keep Rhino's employees up-to-date on the game. At noon each day, Ted posts the previous day's results at the entrance to the production room. Everyone checks whether they made or lost money on what they produced the day before. And it's not just an academic exercise: There's a bonus check for each employee at the end of every four-week "game" that meets profitability guidelines.

Rhino has flourished since the first game. Employment has increased from 20 to 130 people, while both revenues and profits have grown dramatically.

# Chapter Outline

| LEARNING OBJECTIVES | REVIEW | PRACTICE |
|---|---|---|
| **LO 1** Prepare a worksheet. | • Steps in preparing a worksheet<br>• Preparing financial statements from a worksheet<br>• Preparing adjusting entries from a worksheet | **DO IT! 1** Worksheet |
| **LO 2** Prepare closing entries and a post-closing trial balance. | • Preparing closing entries<br>• Posting closing entries<br>• Preparing a post-closing trial balance | **DO IT! 2** Closing Entries |
| **LO 3** Explain the steps in the accounting cycle and how to prepare correcting entries. | • Summary of the accounting cycle<br>• Reversing entries<br>• Correcting entries | **DO IT! 3** Correcting Entries |
| **LO 4** Identify the sections of a classified balance sheet. | • Current assets<br>• Long-term investments<br>• Property, plant, and equipment<br>• Intangible assets<br>• Current liabilities<br>• Long-term liabilities<br>• Stockholders' (owners') equity | **DO IT! 4** Balance Sheet Classifications |

**Go to the Review and Practice section at the end of the chapter for a review of key concepts and practice applications with solutions.**

**Visit WileyPLUS for additional tutorials and practice opportunities.**

# The Worksheet

**LEARNING OBJECTIVE 1**

Prepare a worksheet.

We have used T-accounts and trial balances to arrive at the amounts used to prepare financial statements. Accountants, however, frequently use a spreadsheet, called a worksheet, to determine these amounts. A **worksheet** is a multiple-column spreadsheet that may be used in the adjustment process and in preparing financial statements (see **Helpful Hint**).

As its name suggests, the worksheet is a working tool for the accountant. **A worksheet is not a permanent accounting record**; it is neither a journal nor a part of the general ledger. The worksheet is merely a supplemental spreadsheet that is used to make it easier to prepare adjusting entries and the financial statements.

**Illustration 4.1** shows the basic form of a worksheet and the five steps for preparing it. The steps are performed in sequence. **The use of a worksheet is optional.** When a company chooses to use one, it prepares financial statements directly from the worksheet. It enters the adjustments in the worksheet columns and then journalizes and posts the adjustments after it has prepared the financial statements. Thus, worksheets make it possible to provide the financial statements to management and other interested parties at an earlier date.

**HELPFUL HINT**

Companies generally computerize worksheets using a spreadsheet program such as Microsoft Excel.

**ILLUSTRATION 4.1**    **Form and procedure for a worksheet**

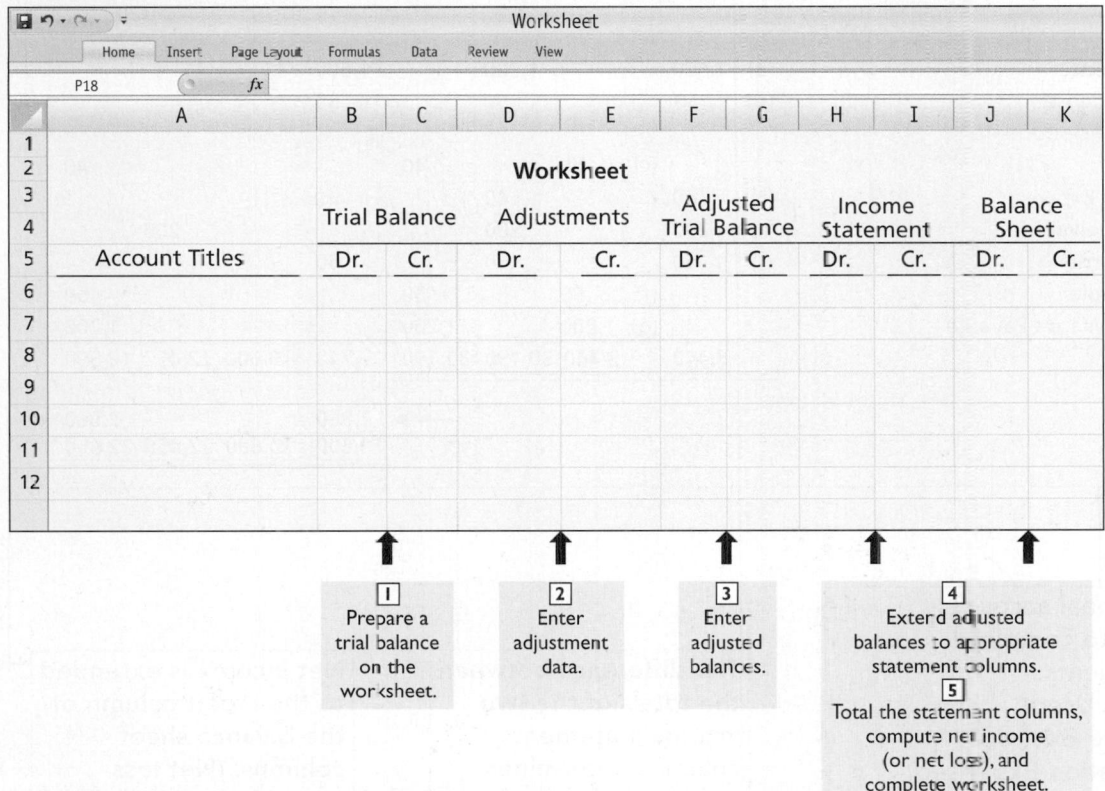

## Steps in Preparing a Worksheet

We will use the October 31 trial balance and adjustment data of Pioneer Advertising Inc. from Chapter 3 to illustrate how to prepare a worksheet. We describe each step of the process and demonstrate these steps in **Illustration 4.2**.

**ILLUSTRATION 4.2** **Preparing a worksheet**

Pioneer Advertising

| | Home | Insert | Page Layout | Formulas | Data | Review | View |

P18

### Pioneer Advertising Inc.
### Worksheet
### For the Month Ended October 31, 2022

| Account Titles | Trial Balance Dr. | Trial Balance Cr. | Adjustments Dr. | Adjustments Cr. | Adjusted Trial Balance Dr. | Adjusted Trial Balance Cr. | Income Statement Dr. | Income Statement Cr. | Balance Sheet Dr. | Balance Sheet Cr. |
|---|---|---|---|---|---|---|---|---|---|---|
| Cash | 15,200 | | | | 15,200 | | | | 15,200 | |
| Supplies | 2,500 | | | (a) 1,500 | 1,000 | | | | 1,000 | |
| Prepaid Insurance | 600 | | | (b) 50 | 550 | | | | 550 | |
| Equipment | 5,000 | | | | 5,000 | | | | 5,000 | |
| Notes Payable | | 5,000 | | | | 5,000 | | | | 5,000 |
| Accounts Payable | | 2,500 | | | | 2,500 | | | | 2,500 |
| Unearned Service Revenue | | 1,200 | (d) 400 | | | 800 | | | | 800 |
| Common Stock | | 10,000 | | | | 10,000 | | | | 10,000 |
| Dividends | 500 | | | | 500 | | | | 500 | |
| Service Revenue | | 10,000 | | (d) 400 | | 10,600 | | 10,600 | | |
| | | | | (e) 200 | | | | | | |
| Salaries and Wages Expense | 4,000 | | (g) 1,200 | | 5,200 | | 5,200 | | | |
| Rent Expense | 900 | | | | 900 | | 900 | | | |
| Totals | 28,700 | 28,700 | | | | | | | | |
| | | | | | | | | | | |
| Supplies Expense | | | (a) 1,500 | | 1,500 | | 1,500 | | | |
| Insurance Expense | | | (b) 50 | | 50 | | 50 | | | |
| Accum. Depreciation— | | | | | | | | | | |
| Equipment | | | | (c) 40 | | 40 | | | | 40 |
| Depreciation Expense | | | (c) 40 | | 40 | | 40 | | | |
| Accounts Receivable | | | (e) 200 | | 200 | | | | 200 | |
| Interest Expense | | | (f) 50 | | 50 | | 50 | | | |
| Interest Payable | | | | (f) 50 | | 50 | | | | 50 |
| Salaries and Wages Payable | | | | (g) 1,200 | | 1,200 | | | | 1,200 |
| Totals | | | 3,440 | 3,440 | 30,190 | 30,190 | 7,740 | 10,600 | 22,450 | 19,590 |
| | | | | | | | | | | |
| Net Income | | | | | | | 2,860 | | | 2,860 |
| Totals | | | | | | | 10,600 | 10,600 | 22,450 | 22,450 |

Add additional accounts as needed to complete the adjustments:
(a) Supplies Used.
(b) Insurance Expired.
(c) Depreciation Expensed.
(d) Service Revenue Recognized.
(e) Service Revenue Accrued.
(f) Interest Accrued.
(g) Salaries Accrued.

The difference between the totals of the two income statement columns determines net income or net loss.

Net income is extended to the credit column of the balance sheet columns. (Net loss would be extended to the debit column.)

**Step 1**  # Prepare a Trial Balance on the Worksheet

Enter all ledger accounts with balances in the account titles column. Enter debit and credit amounts from the ledger in the trial balance columns. Illustration 4.2 shows the worksheet trial balance for Pioneer Advertising Inc. This trial balance is the same one that appears in Illustration 2.32 and Illustration 3.4.

**Step 2**  # Enter the Adjustments in the Adjustments Columns

When using a worksheet, enter all adjustments in the adjustments columns. In entering the adjustments, use applicable trial balance accounts. If additional accounts are needed, insert them on the lines immediately below the trial balance totals. A different letter identifies the debit and credit for each adjusting entry. The term used to describe this process is **keying. Companies do not journalize the adjustments until after they complete the worksheet and prepare the financial statements.**

The adjustments for Pioneer are the same as the adjustments in Illustration 3.24. They are keyed in the adjustments columns of the worksheet as follows.

a. Pioneer debits an additional account, Supplies Expense, $1,500 for the cost of supplies used, and credits Supplies $1,500.

b. Pioneer debits an additional account, Insurance Expense, $50 for the insurance that has expired, and credits Prepaid Insurance $50.

c. The company needs two additional depreciation accounts. It debits Depreciation Expense $40 for the month's depreciation, and credits Accumulated Depreciation—Equipment $40.

d. Pioneer debits Unearned Service Revenue $400 for services performed, and credits Service Revenue $400.

e. Pioneer debits an additional account, Accounts Receivable, $200 for services performed but not billed, and credits Service Revenue $200.

f. The company needs two additional accounts relating to interest. It debits Interest Expense $50 for accrued interest, and credits Interest Payable $50.

g. Pioneer debits Salaries and Wages Expense $1,200 for accrued salaries, and credits an additional account, Salaries and Wages Payable, $1,200.

After Pioneer has entered all the adjustments, the adjustments columns are totaled to prove their equality.

**Step 3**  # Enter Adjusted Balances in the Adjusted Trial Balance Columns

Pioneer determines the adjusted balance of an account by combining the amounts entered in the first four columns of the worksheet for each account. For example, the Prepaid Insurance account in the trial balance columns has a $600 debit balance and a $50 credit in the adjustments columns. The result is a $550 debit balance recorded in the adjusted trial balance columns. **For each account, the amount in the adjusted trial balance columns is the**

**balance that will appear in the ledger after journalizing and posting the adjusting entries.** The balances in these columns are the same as those in the adjusted trial balance in Illustration 3.26.

After Pioneer has entered all account balances in the adjusted trial balance columns, the columns are totaled to prove their equality. If the column totals do not agree, the financial statement columns will not balance and the financial statements will be incorrect.

## Step 4   Extend Adjusted Trial Balance Amounts to Appropriate Financial Statement Columns

**HELPFUL HINT**

**Every adjusted trial balance amount must be extended to one of the four statement columns.**

The fourth step is to extend adjusted trial balance amounts to the income statement and balance sheet columns of the worksheet (see **Helpful Hint**). Pioneer enters balance sheet accounts in the appropriate balance sheet debit and credit columns. For instance, it enters Cash in the balance sheet debit column, and Notes Payable in the balance sheet credit column. Pioneer extends Accumulated Depreciation—Equipment to the balance sheet credit column. The reason is that accumulated depreciation is a contra asset account with a credit balance.

Pioneer extends the balances in Common Stock and Retained Earnings, if any, to the balance sheet credit column. In addition, it extends the balance in Dividends to the balance sheet debit column because it is a stockholders' equity account with a debit balance.

The company enters the expense and revenue accounts such as Salaries and Wages Expense and Service Revenue in the appropriate income statement columns.

## Step 5   Total the Statement Columns, Compute the Net Income (or Net Loss), and Complete the Worksheet

The company now must total each of the financial statement columns. The net income or net loss for the period is the difference between the totals of the two income statement columns. If total credits exceed total debits, the result is net income. In such a case, as shown in Illustration 4.2, the company inserts the words "Net Income" in the account titles space. It then enters the amount in the income statement debit column and the balance sheet credit column. **The debit amount balances the income statement columns; the credit amount balances the balance sheet columns.** In addition, the credit in the balance sheet column indicates the increase in stockholders' equity resulting from net income.

What if total debits exceed total credits in the income statement columns? In that case, the company has a net loss. It enters the amount of the net loss in the income statement credit column and the balance sheet debit column.

After entering the net income or net loss, the company determines new column totals. The totals shown in the debit and credit income statement columns will match. So will the totals shown in the debit and credit balance sheet columns. If either the income statement columns or the balance sheet columns are not equal after the net income or net loss has been entered, there is an error in the worksheet.

# Preparing Financial Statements from a Worksheet

After a company has completed a worksheet, it has at hand all the data required for preparation of financial statements. The income statement is prepared from the income statement columns. The retained earnings statement and balance sheet are prepared from the balance sheet columns. **Illustration 4.3** shows the financial statements prepared from Pioneer Advertising's

**ILLUSTRATION 4.3**

**Financial statements from a worksheet**

## Pioneer Advertising Inc.
### Income Statement
### For the Month Ended October 31, 2022

| | | |
|---|---:|---:|
| Revenues | | |
| Service revenue | | $10,600 |
| Expenses | | |
| Salaries and wages expense | $5,200 | |
| Supplies expense | 1,500 | |
| Rent expense | 900 | |
| Insurance expense | 50 | |
| Interest expense | 50 | |
| Depreciation expense | 40 | |
| Total expenses | | 7,740 |
| Net income | | $ 2,860 |

## Pioneer Advertising Inc.
### Retained Earnings Statement
### For the Month Ended October 31, 2022

| | |
|---|---:|
| Retained earnings, October 1 | $ –0– |
| Add: Net income | 2,860 |
| | 2,860 |
| Less: Dividends | 500 |
| Retained earnings, October 31 | $2,360 |

## Pioneer Advertising Inc.
### Balance Sheet
### October 31, 2022

| Assets | | |
|---|---:|---:|
| Cash | | $15,200 |
| Accounts receivable | | 200 |
| Supplies | | 1,000 |
| Prepaid insurance | | 550 |
| Equipment | $ 5,000 | |
| Less: Accumulated depreciation—equipment | 40 | 4,960 |
| Total assets | | $21,910 |
| **Liabilities and Stockholders' Equity** | | |
| Liabilities | | |
| Notes payable | $ 5,000 | |
| Accounts payable | 2,500 | |
| Interest payable | 50 | |
| Unearned service revenue | 800 | |
| Salaries and wages payable | 1,200 | |
| Total liabilities | | $ 9,550 |
| Stockholders' equity | | |
| Common stock | 10,000 | |
| Retained earnings | 2,360 | |
| Total stockholders' equity | | 12,360 |
| Total liabilities and stockholders' equity | | $21,910 |

worksheet. At this point, the company has not journalized or posted adjusting entries. Therefore, ledger balances for some accounts are not the same as the financial statement amounts.

The amount shown for common stock on the worksheet does not change from the beginning to the end of the period unless the company issues additional stock during the period. Because there was no balance in Pioneer's retained earnings, the account is not listed on the worksheet. Only after dividends and net income (or loss) are posted to retained earnings does this account have a balance at the end of the first year of the business.

Using a worksheet, companies can prepare financial statements before they journalize and post adjusting entries. **However, the completed worksheet is not a substitute for formal financial statements.** The format of the data in the financial statement columns of the worksheet is not the same as the format of the financial statements. **A worksheet is essentially a working tool of the accountant**; companies do not distribute it to management and other parties.

## Preparing Adjusting Entries from a Worksheet

**HELPFUL HINT**

Note that writing the explanation of the adjustment at the bottom of the worksheet is not required.

**A worksheet is not a journal, and it cannot be used as a basis for posting to ledger accounts.** To adjust the accounts, the company must journalize the adjustments and post them to the ledger. **The adjusting entries are prepared from the adjustments columns of the worksheet.** The reference letters in the adjustments columns and the explanations of the adjustments at the bottom of the worksheet help identify the adjusting entries (see **Helpful Hint**). The journalizing and posting of adjusting entries **follow** the preparation of financial statements when a worksheet is used. The adjusting entries on October 31 for Pioneer Advertising Inc. are the same as those shown in Illustration 3.24.

---

**ACTION PLAN**

- **Balance sheet: Extend assets to debit column. Extend liabilities to credit column. Extend contra assets to credit column. Extend Dividends account to debit column.**

- **Income statement: Extend expenses to debit column. Extend revenues to credit column.**

### DO IT! 1 | Worksheet

Susan Elbe is preparing a worksheet. Explain to Susan how she should extend the following adjusted trial balance accounts to the financial statement columns of the worksheet.

| | |
|---|---|
| Cash | Dividends |
| Accumulated Depreciation—Equipment | Service Revenue |
| Accounts Payable | Salaries and Wages Expense |

#### Solution

Income statement debit column—Salaries and Wages Expense
Income statement credit column—Service Revenue
Balance sheet debit column—Cash; Dividends
Balance sheet credit column—Accumulated Depreciation—Equipment; Accounts Payable

Related exercise material: **BE4.1, BE4.2, BE4.3, DO IT! 4.1, E4.1, E4.2, E4.3, E4.5, and E4.6.**

---

# Closing the Books

**LEARNING OBJECTIVE 2**
Prepare closing entries and a post-closing trial balance.

ANALYZE ▶ JOURNALIZE ▶ POST ▶ TRIAL BALANCE ▶ ADJUSTING ENTRIES ▶ ADJUSTED TRIAL BALANCE ▶ PREPARE FINANCIAL STATEMENTS ▶ **Journalize and post closing entries** ▶ **Prepare a post-closing trial balance**

At the end of the accounting period, the company makes the accounts ready for the next period. This is called **closing the books**. In closing the books, the company distinguishes between temporary and permanent accounts.

**Temporary accounts** relate only to a given accounting period. They include all income statement accounts and the Dividends account. **The company closes all temporary accounts at the end of the period.**

In contrast, **permanent accounts** relate to one or more future accounting periods. They consist of all balance sheet accounts, including stockholders' equity accounts. **Permanent accounts are not closed from period to period.** Instead, the company carries forward the balances of permanent accounts into the next accounting period. **Illustration 4.4** identifies the accounts in each category (see **Alternative Terminology**).

**ALTERNATIVE TERMINOLOGY**

Temporary accounts are sometimes called *nominal accounts*, and permanent accounts are sometimes called *real accounts*.

**ILLUSTRATION 4.4**
**Temporary versus permanent accounts**

**TEMPORARY**
These accounts are closed.

All revenue accounts

All expense accounts

Dividends

**PERMANENT**
These accounts are not closed.

All asset accounts

All liability accounts

Stockholders' equity

# Preparing Closing Entries

At the end of the accounting period, the company transfers temporary account balances to the permanent stockholders' equity account, Retained Earnings, by means of closing entries.

**Closing entries** formally recognize in the ledger the transfer of net income (or net loss) and Dividends to Retained Earnings. The retained earnings statement shows the results of these entries. **Closing entries also produce a zero balance in each temporary account.** The temporary accounts are then ready to accumulate data in the next accounting period separate from the data of prior periods. Permanent accounts are not closed.

**Journalizing and posting closing entries is a required step in the accounting cycle** (see Illustration 4.11). The company performs this step after it has prepared financial statements. In contrast to the steps in the cycle that you have already studied, companies generally journalize and post closing entries **only at the end of the annual accounting period**. Thus, all temporary accounts will contain data for the entire accounting period.

In preparing closing entries, companies could close each income statement account directly to Retained Earnings. However, to do so would result in excessive detail in the permanent Retained Earnings account. Instead, companies close the revenue and expense accounts to another temporary account, **Income Summary**, and then transfer the resulting net income or net loss from this account to Retained Earnings (see **Helpful Hint**).

Companies **record closing entries in the general journal**. A center caption, Closing Entries, inserted in the journal between the last adjusting entry and the first closing entry, identifies these entries. Then the company posts the closing entries to the ledger accounts.

Companies generally prepare closing entries directly from the adjusted balances in the ledger. They could prepare separate closing entries for each nominal account, but the following four entries accomplish the desired result more efficiently:

**HELPFUL HINT**

The Income Summary account is used only in the closing process. This temporary account has a zero balance at the end of the process.

1. Debit each revenue account for its balance, and credit Income Summary for total revenues.
2. Debit Income Summary for total expenses, and credit each expense account for its balance.
3. Debit Income Summary and credit Retained Earnings for the amount of net income.
4. Debit Retained Earnings for the balance in the Dividends account, and credit Dividends for the same amount (see **Helpful Hint**).

**HELPFUL HINT**

The Dividends account is closed directly to Retained Earnings and *not* to Income Summary because dividends are not an expense.

If there were a net loss (because expenses exceeded revenues), entry 3 would be reversed: there would be a credit to Income Summary and a debit to Retained Earnings. **Illustration 4.5** presents a diagram of the closing process. In it, the boxed numbers refer to the four entries required in the closing process.

**ILLUSTRATION 4.5**

**Diagram of closing process—corporation**

Key:
1 Close Revenues to Income Summary.
2 Close Expenses to Income Summary.
3 Close Income Summary to Retained Earnings.
4 Close Dividends to Retained Earnings.

## Closing Entries Illustrated

In practice, companies generally prepare closing entries only at the end of the annual accounting period. However, to illustrate the journalizing and posting of closing entries, we will assume that Pioneer Advertising Inc. closes its books monthly. **Illustration 4.6** shows the closing entries at October 31. (The numbers in parentheses before each entry correspond to the four entries diagrammed in Illustration 4.5.)

**ILLUSTRATION 4.6**

**Closing entries journalized**

| GENERAL JOURNAL | | | | | J3 |
|---|---|---|---|---|---|
| Date | | Account Titles and Explanation | Ref. | Debit | Credit |
| | | **Closing Entries** | | | |
| 2022 | | (1) | | | |
| Oct. | 31 | Service Revenue | 400 | 10,600 | |
| | | Income Summary | 350 | | 10,600 |
| | | **(To close revenue account)** | | | |
| | | (2) | | | |
| | 31 | Income Summary | 350 | 7,740 | |
| | | Supplies Expense | 631 | | 1,500 |
| | | Depreciation Expense | 711 | | 40 |
| | | Insurance Expense | 722 | | 50 |
| | | Salaries and Wages Expense | 726 | | 5,200 |
| | | Rent Expense | 729 | | 900 |
| | | Interest Expense | 905 | | 50 |
| | | **(To close expense accounts)** | | | |
| | | (3) | | | |
| | 31 | Income Summary | 350 | 2,860 | |
| | | Retained Earnings | 320 | | 2,860 |
| | | **(To close net income to retained earnings)** | | | |
| | | (4) | | | |
| | 31 | Retained Earnings | 320 | 500 | |
| | | Dividends | 332 | | 500 |
| | | **(To close dividends to retained earnings)** | | | |

Note that the amounts for Income Summary in entries (1) and (2) are the totals of the income statement credit and debit columns, respectively, in the worksheet.

A couple of cautions in preparing closing entries: (1) Avoid unintentionally doubling the revenue and expense balances rather than zeroing them by ensuring that each revenue account is debited and each expense account is credited. (2) Do not close Dividends through the Income Summary account. **Dividends are not an expense, and they are not a factor in determining net income.**

## Posting Closing Entries

**Illustration 4.7** shows the posting of the closing entries and the underlining (ruling) of the accounts. Note that all temporary accounts have zero balances after posting the closing entries. In addition, you should realize that the balance in Retained Earnings represents the accumulated undistributed net income of the corporation at the end of the accounting period. This balance is shown on the balance sheet and is the ending amount reported on the retained earnings statement, as shown in Illustration 4.3. Pioneer Advertising uses the Income Summary account only in closing (see **Helpful Hint**). It does not journalize and post entries to this account during the year.

As part of the closing process, Pioneer totals, balances, and double-underlines its temporary accounts—revenues, expenses, and dividends, as shown in T-account form in Illustration 4.7. It does not close its permanent accounts—assets, liabilities, and stockholders'

**ILLUSTRATION 4.7**    **Posting of closing entries**

| Supplies Expense | | | 631 |
|---|---|---|---|
| | 1,500 | | |
| Bal. | 1,500 | (2) | 1,500 |

| Depreciation Expense | | | 711 |
|---|---|---|---|
| | 40 | | |
| Bal. | 40 | (2) | 40 |

| Insurance Expense | | | 722 |
|---|---|---|---|
| | 50 | | |
| Bal. | 50 | (2) | 50 |

| Salaries and Wages Expense | | | 726 |
|---|---|---|---|
| | 4,000 | | |
| | 1,200 | | |
| Bal. | 5,200 | (2) | 5,200 |

| Rent Expense | | | 729 |
|---|---|---|---|
| | 900 | | |
| Bal. | 900 | (2) | 900 |

| Interest Expense | | | 905 |
|---|---|---|---|
| | 50 | | |
| Bal. | 50 | (2) | 50 |

| Income Summary | | | 350 |
|---|---|---|---|
| (2) | 7,740 | (1) | 10,600 |
| (3) | 2,860 | Bal. | 2,860 |

| Retained Earnings | | | 320 |
|---|---|---|---|
| (4) | 500 | | |
| | | (3) | 2,860 |
| | | Bal. | 2,360 |

| Dividends | | | 332 |
|---|---|---|---|
| | 500 | | |
| Bal. | 500 | (4) | 500 |

| Service Revenue | | | 400 |
|---|---|---|---|
| | | | 10,000 |
| | | | 400 |
| | | | 200 |
| (1) | 10,600 | Bal. | 10,600 |

Key:
1 Close Revenues to Income Summary.
2 Close Expenses to Income Summary.
3 Close Income Summary to Retained Earnings.
4 Close Dividends to Retained Earnings.

equity (Common Stock and Retained Earnings). Instead, Pioneer draws a single underline beneath the current-period entries for the permanent accounts. The account balance is then entered below the single underline and is carried forward to the next period (for example, see Retained Earnings).

---

### Accounting Across the Organization   Cisco Systems

iStock.com/Steve Cole

#### Performing the Virtual Close

Technology has dramatically shortened the closing process. Recent surveys have reported that the average company now takes only 6 to 7 days to close, rather than the previous 20 days. But a few companies do much better. **Cisco Systems** can perform a "virtual close"—closing within 24 hours on any day in the quarter. The same is true at **Lockheed Martin**, which improved its closing time by 85% in just the last few years. Managers at these companies emphasize that this increased speed has not reduced the accuracy and completeness of the data.

This is not just showing off. Knowing exactly where you are financially at any time allows a company to respond faster than its competitors. It also means that the hundreds of people who used to spend 10 to 20 days each quarter tracking transactions can now be more usefully employed on other projects, such as mining data for business intelligence to find new business opportunities.

**Who else benefits from a shorter closing process? (Answer is available near the end of the chapter.)**

---

## Preparing a Post-Closing Trial Balance

After Pioneer Advertising Inc. has journalized and posted all closing entries, it prepares another trial balance, called a **post-closing trial balance**, from the ledger. The post-closing trial balance lists permanent accounts and their balances after the journalizing and posting of closing entries. The purpose of the post-closing trial balance is **to prove the equality of the permanent account balances carried forward into the next accounting period**. Since all temporary accounts will have zero balances, **the post-closing trial balance will contain only permanent—balance sheet—accounts**.

**Illustration 4.8** shows the post-closing trial balance for Pioneer Advertising Inc.

**ILLUSTRATION 4.8**

**Post-closing trial balance**

### Pioneer Advertising Inc.
#### Post-Closing Trial Balance
#### October 31, 2022

|  | Debit | Credit |
|---|---|---|
| Cash | $15,200 |  |
| Accounts Receivable | 200 |  |
| Supplies | 1,000 |  |
| Prepaid Insurance | 550 |  |
| Equipment | 5,000 |  |
| Accumulated Depreciation—Equipment |  | $    40 |
| Notes Payable |  | 5,000 |
| Accounts Payable |  | 2,500 |
| Unearned Service Revenue |  | 800 |
| Salaries and Wages Payable |  | 1,200 |
| Interest Payable |  | 50 |
| Common Stock |  | 10,000 |
| Retained Earnings |  | 2,360 |
|  | $21,950 | $21,950 |

Pioneer prepares the post-closing trial balance from the permanent accounts in the ledger.

**Illustration 4.9** shows the permanent accounts in Pioneer's general ledger.

**ILLUSTRATION 4.9**  General ledger, permanent accounts

## (Permanent Accounts Only)

### GENERAL LEDGER

**Cash** — No. 101

| Date | | Explanation | Ref. | Debit | Credit | Balance |
|---|---|---|---|---|---|---|
| 2022 | | | | | | |
| Oct. | 1 | | J1 | 10,000 | | 10,000 |
| | 2 | | J1 | 1,200 | | 11,200 |
| | 3 | | J1 | | 900 | 10,300 |
| | 4 | | J1 | | 600 | 9,700 |
| | 20 | | J1 | | 500 | 9,200 |
| | 26 | | J1 | | 4,000 | 5,200 |
| | 31 | | J1 | 10,000 | | **15,200** |

**Accounts Receivable** — No. 112

| Date | | Explanation | Ref. | Debit | Credit | Balance |
|---|---|---|---|---|---|---|
| 2022 | | | | | | |
| Oct. | 31 | Adj. entry | J2 | **200** | | **200** |

**Supplies** — No. 126

| Date | | Explanation | Ref. | Debit | Credit | Balance |
|---|---|---|---|---|---|---|
| 2022 | | | | | | |
| Oct. | 5 | | J1 | 2,500 | | 2,500 |
| | 31 | Adj. entry | J2 | | **1,500** | **1,000** |

**Prepaid Insurance** — No. 130

| Date | | Explanation | Ref. | Debit | Credit | Balance |
|---|---|---|---|---|---|---|
| 2022 | | | | | | |
| Oct. | 4 | | J1 | 600 | | 600 |
| | 31 | Adj. entry | J2 | | 50 | 550 |

**Equipment** — No. 157

| Date | | Explanation | Ref. | Debit | Credit | Balance |
|---|---|---|---|---|---|---|
| 2022 | | | | | | |
| Oct. | 1 | | J1 | 5,000 | | **5,000** |

**Accumulated Depreciation—Equipment** — No. 158

| Date | | Explanation | Ref. | Debit | Credit | Balance |
|---|---|---|---|---|---|---|
| 2022 | | | | | | |
| Oct. | 31 | Adj. entry | J2 | | **40** | **40** |

**Notes Payable** — No. 200

| Date | | Explanation | Ref. | Debit | Credit | Balance |
|---|---|---|---|---|---|---|
| 2022 | | | | | | |
| Oct. | 1 | | J1 | | 5,000 | **5,000** |

**Accounts Payable** — No. 201

| Date | | Explanation | Ref. | Debit | Credit | Balance |
|---|---|---|---|---|---|---|
| 2022 | | | | | | |
| Oct. | 5 | | J1 | | 2,500 | **2,500** |

**Unearned Service Revenue** — No. 209

| Date | | Explanation | Ref. | Debit | Credit | Balance |
|---|---|---|---|---|---|---|
| 2022 | | | | | | |
| Oct. | 2 | | J1 | | 1,200 | 1,200 |
| | 31 | Adj. entry | J2 | **400** | | **800** |

**Salaries and Wages Payable** — No. 212

| Date | | Explanation | Ref. | Debit | Credit | Balance |
|---|---|---|---|---|---|---|
| 2022 | | | | | | |
| Oct. | 31 | Adj. entry | J2 | | **1,200** | **1,200** |

**Interest Payable** — No. 230

| Date | | Explanation | Ref. | Debit | Credit | Balance |
|---|---|---|---|---|---|---|
| 2022 | | | | | | |
| Oct. | 31 | Adj. entry | J2 | | **50** | **50** |

**Common Stock** — No. 311

| Date | | Explanation | Ref. | Debit | Credit | Balance |
|---|---|---|---|---|---|---|
| 2022 | | | | | | |
| Oct. | 1 | | J1 | | 10,000 | **10,000** |

**Retained Earnings** — No. 320

| Date | | Explanation | Ref. | Debit | Credit | Balance |
|---|---|---|---|---|---|---|
| 2022 | | | | | | |
| Oct. | 1 | | | | | –0– |
| | 31 | Closing entry | J3 | | 2,860 | 2,860 |
| | 31 | Closing entry | J3 | 500 | | 2,360 |

*Note:* The permanent accounts for Pioneer Advertising Inc. are shown here; the temporary accounts are shown in Illustration 4.10. Both permanent and temporary accounts are part of the general ledger; we separate them here to aid in learning.

A post-closing trial balance provides evidence that the company has properly journalized and posted the closing entries. It also shows that the accounting equation is in balance at the end of the accounting period. However, like the trial balance, it does not prove that Pioneer has recorded all transactions or that the ledger is correct. For example, the post-closing trial balance will still balance even if a transaction is not journalized and posted or if a transaction is journalized and posted twice.

The remaining accounts in the general ledger are temporary accounts, shown in **Illustration 4.10**. After Pioneer correctly posts the closing entries, each temporary account has a zero balance. These accounts are double-underlined to finalize the closing process.

**ILLUSTRATION 4.10** General ledger, temporary accounts

## (Temporary Accounts Only)

### GENERAL LEDGER

| Dividends | | | | | No. 332 |
|---|---|---|---|---|---|
| Date | Explanation | Ref. | Debit | Credit | Balance |
| 2022 | | | | | |
| Oct. 20 | | J1 | 500 | | 500 |
| 31 | **Closing entry** | J3 | | 500 | –0– |

| Income Summary | | | | | No. 350 |
|---|---|---|---|---|---|
| Date | Explanation | Ref. | Debit | Credit | Balance |
| 2022 | | | | | |
| Oct. 31 | **Closing entry** | J3 | | 10,600 | 10,600 |
| 31 | **Closing entry** | J3 | 7,740 | | 2,860 |
| 31 | **Closing entry** | J3 | 2,860 | | –0– |

| Service Revenue | | | | | No. 400 |
|---|---|---|---|---|---|
| Date | Explanation | Ref. | Debit | Credit | Balance |
| 2022 | | | | | |
| Oct. 31 | | J1 | | 10,000 | 10,000 |
| 31 | Adj. entry | J2 | | 400 | 10,400 |
| 31 | Adj. entry | J2 | | 200 | 10,600 |
| 31 | **Closing entry** | J3 | 10,600 | | –0– |

| Supplies Expense | | | | | No. 631 |
|---|---|---|---|---|---|
| Date | Explanation | Ref. | Debit | Credit | Balance |
| 2022 | | | | | |
| Oct. 31 | Adj. entry | J2 | 1,500 | | 1,500 |
| 31 | **Closing entry** | J3 | | 1,500 | –0– |

| Depreciation Expense | | | | | No. 711 |
|---|---|---|---|---|---|
| Date | Explanation | Ref. | Debit | Credit | Balance |
| 2022 | | | | | |
| Oct. 31 | Adj. entry | J2 | 40 | | 40 |
| 31 | **Closing entry** | J3 | | 40 | –0– |

| Insurance Expense | | | | | No. 722 |
|---|---|---|---|---|---|
| Date | Explanation | Ref. | Debit | Credit | Balance |
| 2022 | | | | | |
| Oct. 31 | Adj. entry | J2 | 50 | | 50 |
| 31 | **Closing entry** | J3 | | 50 | –0– |

| Salaries and Wages Expense | | | | | No. 726 |
|---|---|---|---|---|---|
| Date | Explanation | Ref. | Debit | Credit | Balance |
| 2022 | | | | | |
| Oct. 26 | | J1 | 4,000 | | 4,000 |
| 31 | Adj. entry | J2 | 1,200 | | 5,200 |
| 31 | **Closing entry** | J3 | | 5,200 | –0– |

| Rent Expense | | | | | No. 729 |
|---|---|---|---|---|---|
| Date | Explanation | Ref. | Debit | Credit | Balance |
| 2022 | | | | | |
| Oct. 3 | | J1 | 900 | | 900 |
| 31 | **Closing entry** | J3 | | 900 | –0– |

| Interest Expense | | | | | No. 905 |
|---|---|---|---|---|---|
| Date | Explanation | Ref. | Debit | Credit | Balance |
| 2022 | | | | | |
| Oct. 31 | Adj. entry | J2 | 50 | | 50 |
| 31 | **Closing entry** | J3 | | 50 | –0– |

*Note:* The temporary accounts for Pioneer Advertising Inc. are shown here. Illustration 4.9 shows the permanent accounts. Both permanent and temporary accounts are part of the general ledger; we separate them here to aid in learning.

---

**ACTION PLAN**

- **Close revenue and expense accounts to Income Summary.**
- **Close Income Summary to Retained Earnings.**
- **Close Dividends to Retained Earnings.**

## DO IT! 2 | Closing Entries

Hancock Company has the following balances in selected accounts of its adjusted trial balance.

| | | | |
|---|---|---|---|
| Accounts Payable | $27,000 | Dividends | $15,000 |
| Service Revenue | 98,000 | Retained Earnings | 42,000 |
| Rent Expense | 22,000 | Accounts Receivable | 38,000 |
| Salaries and Wages Expense | 51,000 | Supplies Expense | 7,000 |

Prepare the closing entries at December 31.

### Solution

| Dec. 31 | Service Revenue | 98,000 | |
|---|---|---|---|
| | Income Summary | | 98,000 |
| | (To close revenue account to Income Summary) | | |

| 31 | Income Summary | 80,000 | |
|---|---|---|---|
| | Salaries and Wages Expense | | 51,000 |
| | Rent Expense | | 22,000 |
| | Supplies Expense | | 7,000 |
| | (To close expense accounts to Income Summary) | | |

| 31 | Income Summary ($98,000 − $80,000) | 18,000 | |
| | Retained Earnings | | 18,000 |
| | (To close net income to retained earnings) | | |
| 31 | Retained Earnings | 15,000 | |
| | Dividends | | 15,000 |
| | (To close dividends to retained earnings) | | |

Related exercise material: **BE4.4, BE4.5, BE4.6, BE4.7, DO IT! 4.2, E4.4, E4.7 E4.8, and E4.11.**

# The Accounting Cycle and Correcting Entries

**LEARNING OBJECTIVE 3**

Explain the steps in the accounting cycle and how to prepare correcting entries.

## Summary of the Accounting Cycle

**Illustration 4.11** summarizes the steps in the accounting cycle. You can see that the cycle begins with the analysis of business transactions and ends with the preparation of a post-closing trial balance. Companies perform the steps in the cycle in sequence and repeat them in each accounting period.

Steps 1–3 may occur daily during the accounting period. Companies perform Steps 4–7 on a periodic basis, such as monthly, quarterly, or annually. Steps 8 and 9—closing entries and a post-closing trial balance—usually take place only at the end of a company's **annual** accounting period.

There are also two **optional steps** in the accounting cycle. As you have seen, companies may use a worksheet in preparing adjusting entries and financial statements. In addition, they may use reversing entries, as explained below.

## Reversing Entries—An Optional Step

Some accountants prefer to reverse certain adjusting entries by making a **reversing entry** at the beginning of the next accounting period. A reversing entry is the exact opposite of the adjusting entry made in the previous period. **Use of reversing entries is an optional bookkeeping procedure; it is not a required step in the accounting cycle.** Accordingly, we have chosen to cover this topic in Appendix 4A at the end of this chapter.

## Correcting Entries—An Avoidable Step

Unfortunately, errors may occur in the recording process. Companies should correct errors, **as soon as they discover them**, by journalizing and posting **correcting entries** (see **Ethics Note**). If the accounting records are free of errors, no correcting entries are needed.

You should recognize several differences between correcting entries and adjusting entries. First, adjusting entries are an integral part of the accounting cycle. Correcting entries, on the other hand, are unnecessary if the records are error-free. Second, companies journalize and post adjustments **only at the end of an accounting period**. In contrast, companies make correcting entries **whenever they discover an error**. Finally, adjusting entries always affect at least one balance sheet account and one income statement account. In contrast, correcting entries may involve any combination of accounts in need of correction. **Correcting entries must be posted before closing entries.**

**ETHICS NOTE**

When companies find errors in previously released income statements, they restate those numbers. Perhaps because of the increased scrutiny caused by Sarbanes-Oxley, in a recent year companies filed a record 1,195 restatements.

**ILLUSTRATION 4.11**

**Required steps in the accounting cycle**

# The Accounting Cycle

To determine the correcting entry, it is useful to compare the incorrect entry with the correct entry. Doing so helps identify the accounts and amounts that should—and should not—be corrected. After comparison, the accountant makes an entry to correct the accounts. The following two cases for Mercato Co. illustrate this approach.

## Case 1

On May 10, Mercato Co. journalized and posted a $50 cash collection on account from a customer as a debit to Cash $50 and a credit to Service Revenue $50 (see **Illustration 4.12**). The company discovered the error on May 20, when the customer paid the remaining balance in full.

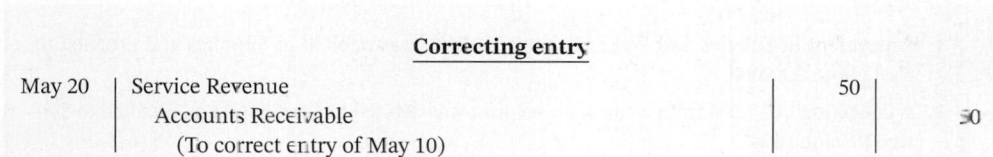

| Incorrect Entry (May 10) | | | Correct Entry (May 10) | | |
|---|---|---|---|---|---|
| Cash | 50 | | Cash | 50 | |
| Service Revenue | | 50 | Accounts Receivable | | 50 |

**ILLUSTRATION 4.12**
**Comparison of entries**

Comparison of the incorrect entry with the correct entry reveals that the debit to Cash $50 is correct. However, the $50 credit to Service Revenue should have been credited to Accounts Receivable. As a result, both Service Revenue and Accounts Receivable are overstated in the ledger. Mercato makes the correcting entry shown in **Illustration 4.13**.

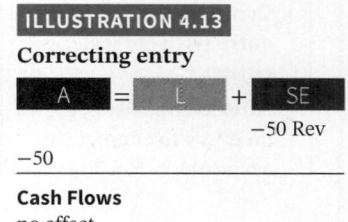

**Correcting entry**

| May 20 | Service Revenue | 50 | |
|---|---|---|---|
| | Accounts Receivable | | 50 |
| | (To correct entry of May 10) | | |

**ILLUSTRATION 4.13**
**Correcting entry**

A = L + SE

−50 Rev

−50

**Cash Flows**
no effect

## Case 2

On May 18, Mercato purchased on account equipment costing $450. The transaction was journalized and posted as a debit to Equipment $45 and a credit to Accounts Payable $45 (see **Illustration 4.14**). The error was discovered on June 3, when Mercato received the monthly statement for May from the creditor.

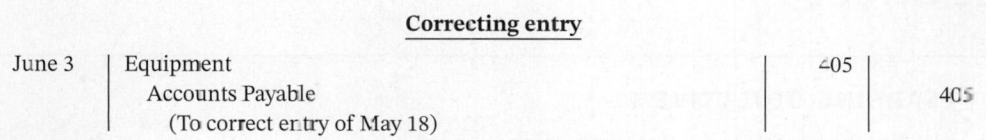

| Incorrect Entry (May 18) | | | Correct Entry (May 18) | | |
|---|---|---|---|---|---|
| Equipment | 45 | | Equipment | 450 | |
| Accounts Payable | | 45 | Accounts Payable | | 450 |

**ILLUSTRATION 4.14**
**Comparison of entries**

Comparison of the two entries shows that two accounts are incorrect. Equipment is understated $405, and Accounts Payable is understated $405. Mercato makes the correcting entry shown in **Illustration 4.15**.

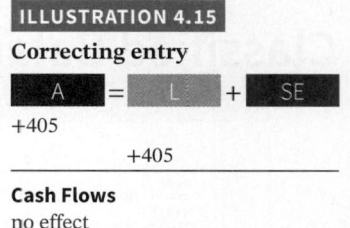

**Correcting entry**

| June 3 | Equipment | 405 | |
|---|---|---|---|
| | Accounts Payable | | 405 |
| | (To correct entry of May 18) | | |

**ILLUSTRATION 4.15**
**Correcting entry**

A = L + SE

+405

+405

**Cash Flows**
no effect

Instead of preparing one correcting entry, **it is possible to reverse the incorrect entry and then prepare the correct entry**. This approach will result in more entries and postings than a correcting entry, but it will accomplish the desired result.

## Accounting Across the Organization Yale Express

### Lost in Transportation

iStock.com/christian Lagereek

**Yale Express**, a short-haul trucking firm, turned over much of its cargo to local truckers to complete deliveries. Yale collected the entire delivery charge. When billed by the local trucker, Yale sent payment for the final phase to the local trucker. Yale used a cutoff period of 20 days into the next accounting period in making its adjusting entries for accrued liabilities. That is, it waited 20 days to receive the local truckers' bills to determine the amount of the unpaid but incurred delivery charges as of the balance sheet date.

On the other hand, **Republic Carloading**, a nationwide, long-distance freight forwarder, frequently did not receive transportation bills from truckers to whom it passed on cargo until months after the year-end. In making its year-end adjusting entries, Republic waited for months in order to include all of these outstanding transportation bills.

When Yale Express merged with Republic Carloading, Yale's vice president employed the 20-day cutoff procedure for both firms. As a result, millions of dollars of Republic's accrued transportation bills went unrecorded. When the company detected the error and made correcting entries, these and other errors changed a reported profit of $1.14 million into a loss of $1.88 million!

**What might Yale Express's vice president have done to produce more accurate financial statements without waiting months for Republic's outstanding transportation bills? (Answer is available near the end of the chapter.)**

---

### ACTION PLAN

- **Compare the incorrect entry with correct entry.**
- **After comparison, make an entry to correct the accounts.**

## DO IT! 3 | Correcting Entries

Sanchez Company discovered the following errors made in January 2022.

1. A payment of Salaries and Wages Expense of $600 was debited to Supplies and credited to Cash, both for $600.

2. A collection of $3,000 from a client on account was debited to Cash $200 and credited to Service Revenue $200.

3. The purchase of supplies on account for $860 was debited to Supplies $680 and credited to Accounts Payable $680.

Correct the errors without reversing the incorrect entry.

### Solution

| | | Debit | Credit |
|---|---|---|---|
| 1. | Salaries and Wages Expense | 600 | |
| | Supplies | | 600 |
| 2. | Service Revenue | 200 | |
| | Cash | 2,800 | |
| | Accounts Receivable | | 3,000 |
| 3. | Supplies ($860 − $680) | 180 | |
| | Accounts Payable | | 180 |

Related exercise material: **BE4.8, BE4.9, DO IT! 4.3, E4.10, E4.12, and E4.13.**

---

# Classified Balance Sheet

> **LEARNING OBJECTIVE 4**
>
> Identify the sections of a classified balance sheet.

The balance sheet presents a snapshot of a company's financial position at a point in time. To improve users' understanding of a company's financial position, companies often use a classified balance sheet. A **classified balance sheet** groups together similar assets and similar liabilities, using a number of standard classifications and sections. This is useful because items within a group have similar economic characteristics. A classified balance sheet generally contains the standard classifications listed in **Illustration 4.16**.

| Assets | Liabilities and Stockholders' Equity |
|---|---|
| Current assets | Current liabilities |
| Long-term investments | Long-term liabilities |
| Property, plant, and equipment | Stockholders' equity |
| Intangible assets | |

**ILLUSTRATION 4.16**

**Standard balance sheet classifications**

These groupings help financial statement readers determine such things as (1) whether the company has enough assets to pay its debts as they come due, and (2) the claims of short- and long-term creditors on the company's total assets. Many of these groupings can be seen in the balance sheet of Franklin Corporation shown in **Illustration 4.17**. In the sections that follow, we explain each of these groupings.

**ILLUSTRATION 4.17**

**Classified balance sheet**

## Franklin Corporation
### Balance Sheet
### October 31, 2022

#### Assets

| | | | |
|---|---|---:|---:|
| **Current assets** | | | |
| Cash | | $ 6,600 | |
| Debt investments | | 2,000 | |
| Accounts receivable | | 7,000 | |
| Notes receivable | | 1,000 | |
| Inventory | | 3,000 | |
| Supplies | | 2,100 | |
| Prepaid insurance | | 400 | |
| Total current assets | | | $22,100 |
| **Long-term investments** | | | |
| Stock investments | | 5,200 | |
| Investment in real estate | | 2,000 | 7,200 |
| **Property, plant, and equipment** | | | |
| Land | | 10,000 | |
| Equipment | $24,000 | | |
| Less: Accumulated depreciation— equipment | 5,000 | 19,000 | 29,000 |
| **Intangible assets** | | | |
| Patents | | | 3,100 |
| Total assets | | | $61,400 |

#### Liabilities and Stockholders' Equity

| | | | |
|---|---|---:|---:|
| **Current liabilities** | | | |
| Notes payable | | $11,000 | |
| Accounts payable | | 2,100 | |
| Unearned service revenue | | 900 | |
| Salaries and wages payable | | 1,600 | |
| Interest payable | | 450 | |
| Total current liabilities | | | $16,050 |
| **Long-term liabilities** | | | |
| Mortgage payable | | 10,000 | |
| Notes payable | | 1,300 | |
| Total long-term liabilities | | | 11,300 |
| Total liabilities | | | 27,350 |
| **Stockholders' equity** | | | |
| Common stock | | 20,000 | |
| Retained earnings | | 14,050 | |
| Total stockholders' equity | | | 34,050 |
| Total liabilities and stockholders' equity | | | $61,400 |

# Current Assets

**Current assets** are assets that a company expects to convert to cash or use up within one year or its operating cycle, whichever is longer. In Illustration 4.17, Franklin Corporation had current assets of $22,100. For most businesses, the cutoff for classification as current assets is one year from the balance sheet date. For example, accounts receivable are current assets because the company will collect them and convert them to cash within one year. Supplies is a current asset because the company expects to use them up in operations within one year.

Some companies use a period longer than one year to classify assets and liabilities as current because they have an operating cycle longer than one year. The **operating cycle** of a company is the average time that it takes to purchase inventory, sell it on account, and then collect cash from customers. For most businesses, this cycle takes less than a year so they use a one-year cutoff. But for some businesses, such as vineyards or airplane manufacturers, this period may be longer than a year. **Except where noted, we will assume that companies use one year to determine whether an asset or liability is current or long-term.**

Common types of current assets are (1) cash, (2) investments (such as short-term U.S. government securities), (3) receivables (notes receivable, accounts receivable, and interest receivable), (4) inventories, and (5) prepaid expenses (supplies and insurance). **On the balance sheet, companies usually list these items in the order in which they expect to convert them into cash** (*follow this rule when doing your homework*). **Illustration 4.18** presents the current assets of **Southwest Airlines Co.**

**ILLUSTRATION 4.18**

Current assets section

Real World

| Southwest Airlines Co.<br>Balance Sheet (partial)<br>(in millions) | |
|---|---:|
| **Current assets** | |
| Cash and cash equivalents | $1,355 |
| Short-term investments | 1,797 |
| Accounts receivable | 419 |
| Inventories | 467 |
| Prepaid expenses and other current assets | 418 |
| Total current assets | $4,456 |

# Long-Term Investments

**Long-term investments** are generally (1) investments in stocks and bonds of other companies that are held for more than one year, (2) long-term assets such as land or buildings that a company is not currently using in its operating activities, and (3) long-term notes receivable (see **Alternative Terminology**). In Illustration 4.17, Franklin Corporation reported total long-term investments of $7,200 on its balance sheet.

**Alphabet Inc.** reported long-term investments in its balance sheet, as shown in **Illustration 4.19**.

**ILLUSTRATION 4.19**

Long-term investments section

Real World

| Alphabet Inc.<br>Balance Sheet (partial)<br>(in millions) | |
|---|---:|
| **Long-term investments** | |
| Non-marketable investments | $5,183 |

# Property, Plant, and Equipment

**Property, plant, and equipment** are assets with relatively long useful lives that a company is currently using in operating the business (see **Alternative Terminology**). This category includes land, buildings, machinery and equipment, delivery equipment, and furniture. In Illustration 4.17, Franklin Corporation reported property, plant, and equipment of $29,000.

**Depreciation** is the practice of allocating the cost of assets to a number of years. Companies do this by systematically assigning a portion of an asset's cost as an expense each year (rather than expensing the full purchase price in the year of purchase). The assets that the company depreciates are reported on the balance sheet at cost less accumulated depreciation. The **accumulated depreciation** account shows the total amount of depreciation that the company has expensed thus far in the asset's life. In Illustration 4.17, Franklin Corporation reported accumulated depreciation of $5,000 related to its equipment.

**Illustration 4.20** presents the property, plant, and equipment of **Tesla Motors, Inc.** *In your homework, present each accumulated depreciation account immediately below the related plant asset, as shown in Illustration 4.17.*

### Tesla Motors, Inc.
**Balance Sheet (partial)**
**(in thousands)**

| Property, plant, and equipment | |
|---|---|
| Machinery, equipment and office furniture | $322,394 |
| Tooling | 230,385 |
| Leasehold improvements | 94,763 |
| Building and building improvements | 67,707 |
| Land | 45,020 |
| Computer equipment and software | 42,073 |
| Construction in progress | 76,294 |
| | 878,636 |
| Less: Accumulated depreciation | 140,142 |
| Total | $738,494 |

**ILLUSTRATION 4.20**
**Property, plant, and equipment section**
Real World

## Intangible Assets

Many companies have long-lived assets that do not have physical substance yet often are very valuable. We call these assets **intangible assets** (see **Helpful Hint**). One significant intangible asset is goodwill. Others include patents, copyrights, and trademarks or trade names that give the company **exclusive right** of use for a specified period of time. In Illustration 4.17, Franklin Corporation reported intangible assets of $3,100.

**Illustration 4.21** shows the intangible assets of media and theme park giant **The Walt Disney Company** in a recent year.

**HELPFUL HINT**
Sometimes intangible assets are reported under a broader heading called "Other assets."

### The Walt Disney Company
**Balance Sheet (partial)**
**(in millions)**

| Intangible assets and goodwill | |
|---|---|
| Character/franchise intangibles and copyrights | $ 5,830 |
| Other amortizable intangible assets | 903 |
| Less: Accumulated amortization | 1,204 |
| Net amortizable intangible assets | 5,529 |
| FCC licenses | 667 |
| Trademarks | 1,218 |
| Other indefinite lived intangible assets | 20 |
| | 7,434 |
| Goodwill | 27,881 |
| | $35,315 |

**ILLUSTRATION 4.21**
**Intangible assets section**
Real World

## People, Planet, and Profit Insight

iStock.com/Gehringj

### Regaining Goodwill

After falling to unforeseen lows amidst scandals, recalls, and economic crises, the reputation of corporate America is recovering in the eyes of the American public. Overall corporate reputation is experiencing rehabilitation as the American public gives high marks overall to corporate America, specific industries, and the largest number of individual companies in a dozen years. This is according to the findings of the *2011 Harris Interactive RQ Study*, which measures the reputations of the 60 most visible companies in the United States.

The survey focuses on six reputational dimensions that influence reputation and consumer behavior. Four of these dimensions, along with the five corporations that ranked highest within each, are as follows.

- **Social Responsibility:** (1) Whole Foods Market, (2) Johnson & Johnson, (3) Google, (4) The Walt Disney Company, (5) Procter & Gamble Co.
- **Emotional Appeal:** (1) Johnson & Johnson, (2) Amazon.com, (3) UPS, (4) General Mills, (5) Kraft Foods
- **Financial Performance:** (1) Google, (2) Berkshire Hathaway, (3) Apple, (4) Intel, (5) The Walt Disney Company
- **Products and Services:** (1) Intel Corporation, (2) 3M Company, (3) Johnson & Johnson, (4) Google, (5) Procter & Gamble Co.

**Source:** www.harrisinteractive.com.

**Name two industries today that are probably rated low on the reputational characteristics of "being trusted" and "having high ethical standards." (Answer is available near the end of the chapter.)**

# Current Liabilities

**ETHICS NOTE**

A company that has more current assets than current liabilities can increase the ratio of current assets to current liabilities by using cash to pay off some current liabilities. This gives the appearance of being more liquid. Do you think this move is ethical?

In the liabilities and stockholders' equity section of the balance sheet, the first grouping is current liabilities. **Current liabilities** are obligations that the company is to pay within the coming year or its operating cycle, whichever is longer (see **Ethics Note**). Common examples are accounts payable, salaries and wages payable, notes payable, interest payable, and income taxes payable. Also included as current liabilities are current maturities of long-term obligations—payments to be made within the next year on long-term obligations. In Illustration 4.17, Franklin Corporation reported five different types of current liabilities, for a total of $16,050.

Illustration 4.22 shows the current liabilities section adapted from the balance sheet of **The Marcus Corporation.**

**ILLUSTRATION 4.22**

**Current liabilities section**

`Real World`

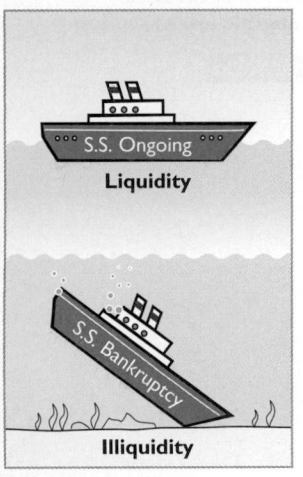

| The Marcus Corporation | |
|---|---|
| Balance Sheet (partial) | |
| (in thousands) | |
| **Current liabilities** | |
| Notes payable | $ 239 |
| Accounts payable | 24,242 |
| Current maturities of long-term debt | 57,250 |
| Other current liabilities | 27,477 |
| Income taxes payable | 11,215 |
| Salaries and wages payable | 6,720 |
| Total current liabilities | $127,143 |

Users of financial statements look closely at the relationship between current assets and current liabilities. This relationship is important in evaluating a company's **liquidity**—its ability to pay obligations expected to be due within the next year. When current assets exceed current liabilities, the likelihood of paying the liabilities is favorable. When the reverse is true, short-term creditors may not be paid, and the company may ultimately be forced into bankruptcy.

iStock.com/Jorge Salcedo

### Can a Company Be Too Liquid?

There actually is a point where a company can be too liquid—that is, it can have too much working capital (current assets less current liabilities). While it is important to be liquid enough to be able to pay short-term bills as they come due, a company does not want to tie up its cash in extra inventory or receivables that are not earning the company money.

By one estimate from the **REL Consultancy Group**, the thousand largest U.S. companies have on their books cumula- tive excess working capital of $764 billion. Based on this figure, companies could have reduced debt by 36% or increased net income by 9%. Given that managers throughout a company are interested in improving profitability, it is clear that they should have an eye toward managing working capital. They need to aim for a "Goldilocks solution"—not too much, not too little, but just right.

**Source:** K. Richardson, "Companies Fall Behind in Cash Management," *Wall Street Journal* (June 19, 2007).

**What can various company managers do to ensure that working capital is managed efficiently to maximize net income? (Answer is available near the end of the chapter.)**

## Long-Term Liabilities

**Long-term liabilities (long-term debt)** are obligations that a company expects to pay **after** one year. Liabilities in this category include bonds payable, mortgages payable, long-term notes payable, lease liabilities, and pension liabilities. Many companies report long-term debt maturing after one year as a single amount in the balance sheet and show the details of the debt in notes that accompany the financial statements. Others list the various types of long-term liabilities. In Illustration 4.17, Franklin Corporation reported long-term liabilities of $11,300.

Illustration 4.23 shows the long-term liabilities that **Nike, Inc**. reported in its balance sheet in a recent year.

**ILLUSTRATION 4.23**

**Long-term liabilities section**

**Real World**

### Nike, Inc.
#### Balance Sheet (partial)
#### (in millions)

| Long-term liabilities | |
|---|---|
| Bonds payable | $1,106 |
| Notes payable | 51 |
| Deferred income taxes and other | 1,544 |
| Total long-term liabilities | $2,701 |

## Stockholders' (Owners') Equity

The content of the owners' equity section varies with the form of business organization. In a proprietorship, there is one capital account. In a partnership, there is a capital account for each partner. Corporations divide owners' equity into two accounts—Common Stock (sometimes referred to as Capital Stock) and Retained Earnings. Corporations record stockholders' investments in the company by debiting an asset account (typically Cash) and crediting the Common Stock account. They record in the Retained Earnings account income retained for use in the business. Corporations combine the Common Stock and Retained Earnings accounts and report them on the balance sheet as **stockholders' equity**. (We discuss these corporation accounts in later chapters.) **Nordstrom, Inc.** recently reported its stockholders' equity section as shown in **Illustration 4.24**.

**Nordstrom, Inc.**
Balance Sheet (partial)
($ in thousands)

| Stockholders' equity | |
|---|---|
| Common stock, 271,331 shares | $ 685,934 |
| Retained earnings | 1,406,747 |
| Total stockholders' equity | $2,092,681 |

---

**ACTION PLAN**

- Analyze whether each financial statement item is an asset, liability, or stockholders' equity.
- Determine whether asset and liability items are short-term or long-term.

## DO IT! 4 | Balance Sheet Classifications

The following accounts were taken from the financial statements of Callahan Company.

_____ Salaries and wages payable
_____ Service revenue
_____ Interest payable
_____ Goodwill
_____ Debt investments (short-term)
_____ Mortgage payable (due in 3 years)

_____ Stock investments (long-term)
_____ Equipment
_____ Accumulated depreciation—equipment
_____ Depreciation expense
_____ Common stock
_____ Unearned service revenue

Match each of the accounts to its proper balance sheet classification, shown below. If the item would not appear on a balance sheet, use "NA."

Current assets (CA)
Long-term investments (LTI)
Property, plant, and equipment (PPE)
Intangible assets (IA)

Current liabilities (CL)
Long-term liabilities (LTL)
Stockholders' equity (SE)

### Solution

| | | | | |
|---|---|---|---|---|
| __CL__ | Salaries and wages payable | __LTI__ | Stock investments (long-term) |
| __NA__ | Service revenue | __PPE__ | Equipment |
| __CL__ | Interest payable | __PPE__ | Accumulated depreciation—equipment |
| __IA__ | Goodwill | | |
| __CA__ | Debt investments (short-term) | __NA__ | Depreciation expense |
| __LTL__ | Mortgage payable (due in 3 years) | __SE__ | Common stock |
| | | __CL__ | Unearned service revenue |

Related exercise material: **BE4.10, BE4.11, DO IT! 4.4, E4.9, E4.14, E4.15, E4.16, and E4.17.**

---

**Appendix 4A**  # Reversing Entries

**LEARNING OBJECTIVE *5**
Prepare reversing entries.

After preparing the financial statements and closing the books, it is often helpful to reverse some of the adjusting entries before recording the regular transactions of the next period. Such entries are **reversing entries**. Companies make **a reversing entry at the beginning of the next accounting period**. Each reversing entry **is the exact opposite of the adjusting entry made in the previous period**. The recording of reversing entries is an **optional step** in the accounting cycle.

The purpose of reversing entries is to simplify the recording of a subsequent transaction related to an adjusting entry. For example, in Chapter 3, the payment of salaries after an adjusting entry resulted in two debits: one to Salaries and Wages Payable and the other to Salaries and Wages Expense. With reversing entries, the company can debit the entire subsequent payment to Salaries and Wages Expense. **The use of reversing entries does not change the amounts reported in the financial statements.** What it does is simplify the recording of subsequent transactions.

# Reversing Entries Example

Companies most often use reversing entries to reverse two types of adjusting entries: accrued revenues and accrued expenses. To illustrate the optional use of reversing entries for accrued expenses, we will use the salaries expense transactions for Pioneer Advertising Inc. as illustrated in Chapters 2, 3, and 4. The transaction and adjustment data are as follows.

1. October 26 (initial salary entry): Pioneer pays $4,000 of salaries and wages earned between October 15 and October 26.
2. October 31 (adjusting entry): Salaries and wages earned between October 29 and October 31 are $1,200. The company will pay these in the November 9 payroll.
3. November 9 (subsequent salary entry): Salaries and wages paid are $4,000. Of this amount, $1,200 applied to accrued salaries and wages payable, and $2,800 was earned between November 1 and November 9.

**Illustration 4A.1** shows the entries with and without reversing entries.

**ILLUSTRATION 4A.1**  Comparative entries—without and with reversing

| Without Reversing Entries (per chapter) | | | With Reversing Entries (per appendix) | | |
|---|---|---|---|---|---|
| Initial Salary Entry | | | Initial Salary Entry | | |
| Oct. 26 | Salaries and Wages Expense | 4,000 | Oct. 26 | (Same entry) | |
|  | Cash | 4,000 |  | | |
| Adjusting Entry | | | Adjusting Entry | | |
| Oct. 31 | Salaries and Wages Expense | 1,200 | Oct. 31 | (Same entry) | |
|  | Salaries and Wages Payable | 1,200 |  | | |
| Closing Entry | | | Closing Entry | | |
| Oct. 31 | Income Summary | 5,200 | Oct. 31 | (Same entry) | |
|  | Salaries and Wages Expense | 5,200 |  | | |
| Reversing Entry | | | Reversing Entry | | |
| Nov. 1 | No reversing entry is made. | | Nov. 1 | Salaries and Wages Payable | 1,200 |
|  | | |  | Salaries and Wages Expense | 1,200 |
| Subsequent Salary Entry | | | Subsequent Salary Entry | | |
| Nov. 9 | Salaries and Wages Payable | 1,200 | Nov. 9 | Salaries and Wages Expense | 4,000 |
|  | Salaries and Wages Expense | 2,800 |  | Cash | 4,000 |
|  | Cash | 4,000 |  | | |

The first three entries are the same whether or not Pioneer uses reversing entries. The last two entries are different. The November 1 **reversing entry** eliminates the $1,200 balance in Salaries and Wages Payable created by the October 31 adjusting entry. The reversing entry also creates a $1,200 credit balance in the Salaries and Wages Expense account. As you know, it is unusual for an expense account to have a credit balance. The balance is correct in this instance, though, because it anticipates that the entire amount of the first salaries and wages payment in the new accounting period will be debited to Salaries and Wages Expense. This debit will eliminate the credit balance. The resulting debit balance in the expense account will equal the salaries and wages expense incurred in the new accounting period ($2,800 in this example).

If Pioneer makes reversing entries, it can debit all cash payments of expenses to the expense account. This means that on November 9 (and every payday) Pioneer can debit Salaries and Wages Expense for the amount paid, without regard to any accrued salaries and wages payable. Being able to make the **same entry each time** simplifies the recording process. The company can record subsequent transactions as if the related adjusting entry had never been made.

**Illustration 4A.2** shows the posting of the entries with reversing entries.

`ILLUSTRATION 4A.2` **Postings with reversing entries**

| Salaries and Wages Expense | | | | | |
|---|---|---|---|---|---|
| 10/26 Paid | 4,000 | | | | |
| 31 Adjusting | 1,200 | | | | |
| Bal. | 5,200 | 10/31 | Closing | 5,200 | |
| 11/9 Paid | 4,000 | **11/1** | **Reversing** | **1,200** | |

| Salaries and Wages Payable | | | | |
|---|---|---|---|---|
| **11/1** | **Reversing** | **1,200** | 10/31 Adjusting | 1,200 |

A company can also use reversing entries for accrued revenue adjusting entries. For Pioneer, the adjusting entry was Accounts Receivable (Dr.) $200 and Service Revenue (Cr.) $200. Thus, the reversing entry on November 1 is:

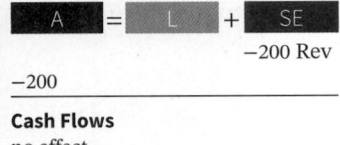

**Cash Flows**
no effect

| | | | | |
|---|---|---|---|---|
| Nov. 1 | Service Revenue | | 200 | |
| | Accounts Receivable | | | 200 |
| | (To reverse October 31 adjusting entry) | | | |

When Pioneer collects the accrued service revenue, it debits Cash and credits Service Revenue.

# Review and Practice

## Learning Objectives Review

### 1 Prepare a worksheet.

The steps in preparing a worksheet are as follows. (a) Prepare a trial balance on the worksheet. (b) Enter the adjustments in the adjustments columns. (c) Enter adjusted balances in the adjusted trial balance columns. (d) Extend adjusted trial balance amounts to appropriate financial statement columns. (e) Total the statement columns, compute net income (or net loss), and complete the worksheet.

### 2 Prepare closing entries and a post-closing trial balance.

Closing the books occurs at the end of an accounting period. The process is to journalize and post closing entries and then underline and balance all accounts. In closing the books, companies make separate entries to close revenues and expenses to Income Summary, Income Summary to Retained Earnings, and Dividends to Retained Earnings. Only temporary accounts are closed. A post-closing trial balance contains the balances in permanent accounts that are carried forward to the next accounting period. The purpose of this trial balance is to prove the equality of these balances.

### 3 Explain the steps in the accounting cycle and how to prepare correcting entries.

The required steps in the accounting cycle are (1) analyze business transactions, (2) journalize the transactions, (3) post to ledger accounts, (4) prepare a trial balance, (5) journalize and post adjusting entries, (6) prepare an adjusted trial balance, (7) prepare financial statements, (8) journalize and post closing entries, and (9) prepare a post-closing trial balance.

One way to determine the correcting entry is to compare the incorrect entry with the correct entry. After comparison, the company makes a correcting entry to correct the accounts. An alternative to one correcting entry is to reverse the incorrect entry and then prepare the correct entry.

---

**4   Identify the sections of a classified balance sheet.**

---

A classified balance sheet categorizes assets as current assets; long-term investments; property, plant, and equipment; and intangible assets. Liabilities are classified as either current or long-term. There is also a stockholders (owners') equity section, which varies with the form of business organization.

---

**\*5   Prepare reversing entries.**

---

Reversing entries are the opposite of the adjusting entries made in the preceding period. Some companies choose to make reversing entries at the beginning of a new accounting period to simplify the recording of later transactions related to the adjusting entries. In most cases, only accrued adjusting entries are reversed.

## Glossary Review

**Classified balance sheet** A balance sheet that contains standard classifications or sections. (p. 4-18).

**Closing entries** Entries made at the end of an accounting period to transfer the balances of temporary accounts to a permanent stockholders' equity account, Retained Earnings. (p. 4-9).

**Correcting entries** Entries to correct errors made in recording transactions. (p. 4-15).

**Current assets** Assets that a company expects to convert to cash or use up within one year or its operating cycle, whichever is longer. (p. 4-20).

**Current liabilities** Obligations that a company expects to pay within the coming year or its operating cycle, whichever is longer. (p. 4-22).

**Income Summary** A temporary account used in closing revenue and expense accounts. (p. 4-9).

**Intangible assets** Long-lived assets that do not have physical substance. (p. 4-21).

**Liquidity** The ability of a company to pay obligations expected to be due within the next year. (p. 4-22).

**Long-term investments** Generally, (1) investments in stocks and bonds of other companies that are normally held for many years; (2) long-term assets, such as land and buildings, not currently being used in operating activities; and (3) long-term notes receivable. (p. 4-20).

**Long-term liabilities** Obligations that a company expects to pay after one year. (p. 4-23).

**Operating cycle** The average time that it takes to purchase inventory, sell it on account, and then collect cash from customers. (p. 4-20).

**Permanent (real) accounts** Accounts that relate to one or more future accounting periods. Consist of all balance sheet accounts. Balances are carried forward to the next accounting period. (p. 4-9).

**Post-closing trial balance** A list of permanent accounts and their balances after a company has journalized and posted closing entries. (p. 4-12).

**Property, plant, and equipment** Assets with relatively long useful lives that are currently being used in operations. (p. 4-20).

**Reversing entry** An entry, made at the beginning of the next accounting period that is the exact opposite of the adjusting entry made in the previous period. (p. 4-15).

**Stockholders' equity** The ownership claim of shareholders on total assets. It is to a corporation what owner's equity is to a proprietorship. (p. 4-23).

**Temporary (nominal) accounts** Accounts that relate only to a given accounting period. Consist of all income statement accounts, the Dividends account, and the Income Summary account. All temporary accounts are closed at the end of the accounting period. (p. 4-9).

**Worksheet** A multiple-column form that may be used in making adjustments and in preparing financial statements. (p. 4-3).

## Practice Multiple-Choice Questions

1. **(LO 1)** Which of the following statements is **incorrect** concerning the worksheet?

    a. The worksheet is essentially a working tool of the accountant.

    b. The worksheet is distributed to management and other interested parties.

    c. The worksheet cannot be used as a basis for posting to ledger accounts.

    d. Financial statements can be prepared directly from the worksheet before journalizing and posting the adjusting entries.

2. **(LO 1)** In a worksheet, net income is entered in the following columns:

    a. income statement (Dr.) and balance sheet (Dr.).

    b. income statement (Cr.) and balance sheet (Dr.).

    c. income statement (Dr.) and balance sheet (Cr.).

    d. income statement (Cr.) and balance sheet (Cr.).

3. **(LO 1)** In the unadjusted trial balance of its worksheet for the year ended December 31, 2022, Knox Company reported Equipment of $120,000. The year-end adjusting entries require an adjustment of $15,000 for depreciation expense for the equipment. After the adjusted

trial balance is completed, what amount should be shown in the financial statement columns?

    **a.** A debit of $105,000 for Equipment in the balance sheet column.

    **b.** A credit of $15,000 for Depreciation Expense in the income statement column.

    **c.** A debit of $120,000 for Equipment in the balance sheet column.

    **d.** A debit of $15,000 for Accumulated Depreciation—Equipment in the balance sheet column.

**4. (LO 2)** An account that will have a zero balance after closing entries have been journalized and posted is:

    **a.** Service Revenue.

    **b.** Supplies.

    **c.** Prepaid Insurance.

    **d.** Accumulated Depreciation—Equipment.

**5. (LO 2)** When a net loss has occurred, Income Summary is:

    **a.** debited and Retained Earnings is credited.

    **b.** credited and Retained Earnings is debited.

    **c.** debited and Dividends is credited.

    **d.** credited and Dividends is debited.

**6. (LO 2)** The closing process involves separate entries to close (1) expenses, (2) dividends, (3) revenues, and (4) income summary. The correct sequencing of the entries is:

    **a.** (4), (3), (2), (1).

    **b.** (1), (2), (3), (4).

    **c.** (3), (1), (4), (2).

    **d.** (3), (2), (1), (4).

**7. (LO 2)** Which types of accounts will appear in the post-closing trial balance?

    **a.** Permanent (real) accounts.

    **b.** Temporary (nominal) accounts.

    **c.** Accounts shown in the income statement columns of a worksheet.

    **d.** None of these answer choices is correct.

**8. (LO 3)** All of the following are required steps in the accounting cycle **except**:

    **a.** journalizing and posting closing entries.

    **b.** preparing financial statements.

    **c.** journalizing the transactions.

    **d.** preparing a worksheet.

**9. (LO 3)** The proper order of the following steps in the accounting cycle is:

    **a.** prepare unadjusted trial balance, journalize transactions, post to ledger accounts, journalize and post adjusting entries.

    **b.** journalize transactions, prepare unadjusted trial balance, post to ledger accounts, journalize and post adjusting entries.

    **c.** journalize transactions, post to ledger accounts, prepare unadjusted trial balance, journalize and post adjusting entries.

    **d.** prepare unadjusted trial balance, journalize and post adjusting entries, journalize transactions, post to ledger accounts.

**10. (LO 3)** When Ramirez Company purchased supplies worth $5,000, it incorrectly recorded a credit to Supplies for $5,000 and a debit to Cash for $5,000. Before correcting this error:

    **a.** Cash is overstated and Supplies is overstated.

    **b.** Cash is understated and Supplies is understated.

    **c.** Cash is understated and Supplies is overstated.

    **d.** Cash is overstated and Supplies is understated.

**11. (LO 3)** Cash of $100 received at the time the service was performed was journalized and posted as a debit to Cash $100 and a credit to Accounts Receivable $100. Assuming the incorrect entry is not reversed, the correcting entry is:

    **a.** debit Service Revenue $100 and credit Accounts Receivable $100.

    **b.** debit Accounts Receivable $100 and credit Service Revenue $100.

    **c.** debit Cash $100 and credit Service Revenue $100.

    **d.** debit Accounts Receivable $100 and credit Cash $100.

**12. (LO 4)** The correct order of presentation in a classified balance sheet for the following current assets is:

    **a.** accounts receivable, cash, prepaid insurance, inventory.

    **b.** cash, inventory, accounts receivable, prepaid insurance.

    **c.** cash, accounts receivable, inventory, prepaid insurance.

    **d.** inventory, cash, accounts receivable, prepaid insurance.

**13. (LO 4)** A company has purchased a tract of land. It expects to build a production plant on the land in approximately 5 years. During the 5 years before construction, the land will be idle. The land should be reported as:

    **a.** property, plant, and equipment.

    **b.** land expense.

    **c.** a long-term investment.

    **d.** an intangible asset.

**14. (LO 4)** In a classified balance sheet, assets are usually classified using the following categories:

    **a.** current assets; long-term assets; property, plant, and equipment; and intangible assets.

    **b.** current assets; long-term investments; property, plant, and equipment; and tangible assets.

    **c.** current assets; long-term investments; tangible assets; and intangible assets.

    **d.** current assets; long-term investments; property, plant, and equipment; and intangible assets.

**15. (LO 4)** Current assets are listed:

    **a.** by expected conversion to cash.    **c.** by longevity.

    **b.** by importance.    **d.** alphabetically.

**\*16. (LO 5)** On December 31, Kevin Hartman Company correctly made an adjusting entry to recognize $2,000 of accrued salaries payable. On January 3 of the next year, total salaries of $3,400 were paid. Assuming the correct reversing entry was made on January 1, the entry on January 8 will result in a credit to Cash $3,400 and the following debit(s):

**a.** Salaries and Wages Payable $1,400 and Salaries and Wages Expense $2,000.

**b.** Salaries and Wages Payable $2,000 and Salaries and Wages Expense $1,400.

**c.** Salaries and Wages Expense $3,400.

**d.** Salaries and Wages Payable $3,400.

### Solutions

**1. b.** The worksheet is a working tool of the accountant; it is not distributed to management and other interested parties. The other choices are all true statements.

**2. c.** Net income is entered in the Dr. column of the income statement and the Cr. column of the balance sheet. The other choices are incorrect because net income is entered in the (a) Cr. (not Dr.) column of the balance sheet, (b) Dr. (not Cr.) column of the income statement and in the Cr. (not Dr.) column of the balance sheet, and (d) Dr. (not Cr.) column of the income statement.

**3. c.** A debit of $120,000 for Equipment would appear in the balance sheet column. The other choices are incorrect because (a) Equipment, less accumulated depreciation of $15,000, would total $105,000 under assets on the balance sheet, not on the worksheet; (b) a debit, not credit, for Depreciation Expense would appear in the income statement column; and (d) a credit, not debit, of $15,000 for Accumulated Depreciation—Equipment would appear in the balance sheet column.

**4. a.** The Service Revenue account will have a zero balance after closing entries have been journalized and posted because it is a temporary account. The other choices are incorrect because (b) Supplies, (c) Prepaid Insurance, and (d) Accumulated Depreciation—Equipment are all permanent accounts and therefore not closed in the closing process.

**5. b.** The effect of a net loss is a credit to Income Summary and a debit to Retained Earnings. The other choices are incorrect because (a) Income Summary is credited, not debited, and Retained Earnings is debited, not credited; (c) Income Summary is credited, not debited, and Dividends is not affected; and (d) Retained Earnings, not Dividends, is debited.

**6. c.** The correct order is (3) revenues, (1) expenses, (4) income summary, and (2) dividends. Therefore, choices (a), (b), and (d) are incorrect.

**7. a.** Permanent accounts appear in the post-closing trial balance. The other choices are incorrect because (b) temporary accounts and (c) income statement accounts are closed to a zero balance and are therefore not included in the post-closing trial balance. Choice (d) is wrong as there is a correct answer for this question.

**8. d.** Preparing a worksheet is not a required step in the accounting cycle. The other choices are all required steps in the accounting cycle.

**9. c.** The proper order of the steps in the accounting cycle is (1) journalize transactions, (2) post to ledger accounts, (3) prepare unadjusted trial balance, and (4) journalize and post adjusting entries. Therefore, choices (a), (b), and (d) are incorrect.

**10. d.** This entry causes Cash to be overstated and Supplies to be understated. Supplies should have been debited (increasing supplies) and Cash should have been credited (decreasing cash). The other choices are incorrect because (a) Supplies is understated, not overstated; (b) Cash is overstated, not understated; and (c) Cash is overstated, not understated, and Supplies is understated, not overstated.

**11. b.** The correcting entry is to debit Accounts Receivable $100 and credit Service Revenue $100. The other choices are incorrect because (a) Service Revenue should be credited, not debited, and Accounts Receivable should be debited, not credited; (c) Service Revenue should be credited for $100, and Cash should not be included in the correcting entry as it was recorded properly; and (d) Accounts Receivable should be debited for $100 and Cash should not be included in the correcting entry as it was recorded properly.

**12. c.** Companies list current assets on the balance sheet in the order of liquidity: cash, accounts receivable, inventory, and prepaid insurance. Therefore, choices (a), (b), and (d) are incorrect.

**13. c.** Long-term investments include long-term assets such as land that a company is not currently using in its operating activities. The other choices are incorrect because (a) land is reported as property, plant, and equipment only if it is being currently used in the business; (b) land is an asset, not an expense; and (d) land has physical substance and thus is a tangible asset.

**14. d.** These are the categories usually used in a classified balance sheet. The other choices are incorrect because the categories (a) "long-term assets" and (b) and (c) "tangible assets" are generally not used.

**15. a.** Current assets are listed in order of their liquidity, not (b) by importance, (c) by longevity, or (d) alphabetically.

**\*16. c.** The use of reversing entries simplifies the recording of the first payroll following the end of the year by eliminating the need to make an entry to the Salaries and Wages Payable account. The other choices are incorrect because (a) Salaries and Wages Payable is not part of the payroll entry on January 8, and the debit to Salaries and Wages Expense should be for $3,400, not $2,000; and (b) and (d) the Salaries and Wages Expense account, not the Salaries and Wages Payable account, should be debited.

## Practice Brief Exercises

**1. (LO 2)** The ledger of Quintana Company contains the following balances: Retained Earnings $40,000, Dividends $3,000, Service Revenue $65,000, Salaries and Wages Expense $39,000, and Maintenance and Repairs Expense $9,000. Prepare the closing entries at December 31.

*Prepare closing entries from ledger balances.*

**Solutions**

| | | | | |
|---|---|---|---|---|
| **1.** | Dec. 31 | Service Revenue | 65,000 | |
| | | Income Summary | | 65,000 |
| | 31 | Income Summary | 48,000 | |
| | | Salaries and Wages Expense | | 39,000 |
| | | Maintenance and Repairs Expense | | 9,000 |
| | 31 | Income Summary | 17,000 | |
| | | Retained Earnings | | 17,000 |
| | 31 | Retained Earnings | 3,000 | |
| | | Dividends | | 3,000 |

*Prepare correcting entries.*

**2. (LO 3)** At Shields Company, the following errors were discovered after the transactions had been journalized and posted. Prepare the correcting entries.

 a. A service rendered to a customer for $780 cash was recorded as a debit to Cash $780 and a credit to Accounts Receivable $780.

 b. The purchase of equipment on account for $1,730 was recorded as a debit to Equipment $1,370 and a credit to Accounts Payable $1,370.

**Solutions**

| | | | |
|---|---|---|---|
| **2. a.** | Accounts Receivable | 780 | |
| | Service Revenue | | 780 |
| **b.** | Equipment ($1,730 − $1,370) | 360 | |
| | Accounts Payable | | 360 |

*Prepare the current assets section of a balance sheet.*

**3. (LO 4)** The balance sheet debit column of the worksheet for Miguel Company includes the following accounts: Accounts Receivable $25,000, Prepaid Insurance $7,000, Cash $8,000, Supplies $11,000, and Stock Investments (short-term) $14,000. Prepare the current assets section of the balance sheet, listing the accounts in proper sequence.

**Solutions**

3.

**Miguel Company**
**Balance Sheet(partial)**

| | |
|---|---|
| Current assets | |
| Cash | $ 8,000 |
| Stock investments | 14,000 |
| Accounts receivable | 25,000 |
| Supplies | 11,000 |
| Prepaid insurance | 7,000 |
| Total current assets | $65,000 |

# Practice Exercises

*Journalize and post closing entries and prepare a post-closing trial balance.*

**1. (LO 2)** Arapaho Company ended its fiscal year on July 31, 2022. The company's adjusted trial balance as of the end of its fiscal year is as follows.

**Arapaho Company**
**Adjusted Trial Balance**
**July 31, 2022**

| No. | Account Titles | Debit | Credit |
|---|---|---|---|
| 101 | Cash | $ 15,940 | |
| 112 | Accounts Receivable | 8,580 | |
| 157 | Equipment | 16,900 | |
| 158 | Accumulated Depreciation—Equipment | | $ 7,500 |
| 201 | Accounts Payable | | 4,420 |
| 208 | Unearned Rent Revenue | | 1,600 |
| 311 | Common Stock | | 20,500 |
| 320 | Retained Earnings | | 25,000 |
| 332 | Dividends | 14,000 | |
| 400 | Service Revenue | | 64,000 |
| 429 | Rent Revenue | | 5,500 |
| 711 | Depreciation Expense | 4,500 | |
| 726 | Salaries and Wages Expense | 54,700 | |
| 732 | Utilities Expense | 13,900 | |
| | | $128,520 | $128,520 |

## Instructions

a. Prepare the closing entries using page J15 in a general journal.

b. Post to Retained Earnings and No. 350 Income Summary accounts. (Use the three-column form.)

c. Prepare a post-closing trial balance at July 31, 2022.

## Solution

1. a.

**GENERAL JOURNAL** J15

| Date | Account Titles | Ref. | Debit | Credit |
|---|---|---|---|---|
| July 31 | Service Revenue | 400 | 64,000 | |
| | Rent Revenue | 429 | 5,500 | |
| | Income Summary | 350 | | 69,500 |
| | (To close revenue accounts) | | | |
| 31 | Income Summary | 350 | 73,100 | |
| | Depreciation Expense | 711 | | 4,500 |
| | Salaries and Wages Expense | 726 | | 54,700 |
| | Utilities Expense | 732 | | 13,900 |
| | (To close expense accounts) | | | |
| 31 | Retained Earnings ($73,100 − $69,500) | 320 | 3,600 | |
| | Income Summary | 350 | | 3,600 |
| | (To close net loss to retained earnings) | | | |
| 31 | Retained Earnings | 320 | 14,000 | |
| | Dividends | 332 | | 14,000 |
| | (To close dividends to retained earnings) | | | |

b.

**Retained Earnings** No. 320

| Date | Explanation | Ref. | Debit | Credit | Balance |
|---|---|---|---|---|---|
| July 31 | Balance | | | | 25,000 |
| 31 | Close net loss | J15 | 3,600 | | 21,400 |
| 31 | Close dividends | J15 | 14,000 | | 7,400 |

**Income Summary** No. 350

| Date | Explanation | Ref. | Debit | Credit | Balance |
|---|---|---|---|---|---|
| July 31 | Close revenue | J15 | | 69,500 | 69,500 |
| 31 | Close expenses | J15 | 73,100 | | (3,600) |
| 31 | Close net loss | J15 | | 3,600 | 0 |

**c.**

### Arapaho Company
#### Post-Closing Trial Balance
#### July 31, 2022

|  | Debit | Credit |
|---|---|---|
| Cash | $15,940 |  |
| Accounts Receivable | 8,580 |  |
| Equipment | 16,900 |  |
| Accumulated Depreciation—Equipment |  | $ 7,500 |
| Accounts Payable |  | 4,420 |
| Unearned Rent Revenue |  | 1,600 |
| Common Stock |  | 20,500 |
| Retained Earnings |  | 7,400 |
|  | $41,420 | $41,420 |

*Prepare financial statements.*

**2. (LO 4)** The adjusted trial balance for Arapaho Company is presented in **Practice Exercise 1**.

**Instructions**

**a.** Prepare an income statement and a retained earnings statement for the year ended July 31, 2022.

**b.** Prepare a classified balance sheet at July 31, 2022.

**Solution**

**2. a.**

### Arapaho Company
#### Income Statement
#### For the Year Ended July 31, 2022

| Revenues |  |  |
|---|---|---|
| Service revenue | $64,000 |  |
| Rent revenue | 5,500 |  |
| Total revenues |  | $69,500 |
| Expenses |  |  |
| Salaries and wages expense | 54,700 |  |
| Utilities expense | 13,900 |  |
| Depreciation expense | 4,500 |  |
| Total expenses |  | 73,100 |
| Net loss |  | ($ 3,600) |

### Arapaho Company
#### Retained Earnings Statement
#### For the Year Ended July 31, 2022

| Retained earnings, August 1, 2021 |  | $25,000 |
|---|---|---|
| Less: Net loss | $ 3,600 |  |
| Dividends | 14,000 | 17,600 |
| Retained earnings, July 31, 2022 |  | $ 7,400 |

b.

## Arapaho Company
### Balance Sheet
### July 31, 2022

### Assets

| | | |
|---|---:|---:|
| Current assets | | |
| Cash | $15,940 | |
| Accounts receivable | 8,580 | |
| Total current assets | | $24,520 |
| Property, plant, and equipment | | |
| Equipment | 16,900 | |
| Less: Accumulated depreciation—equipment | 7,500 | 9,400 |
| Total assets | | $33,920 |

### Liabilities and Stockholders' Equity

| | | |
|---|---:|---:|
| Current liabilities | | |
| Accounts payable | $ 4,420 | |
| Unearned rent revenue | 1,600 | |
| Total current liabilities | | $ 6,020 |
| Stockholders' equity | | |
| Common stock | 20,500 | |
| Retained earnings | 7,400 | |
| Total stockholders' equity | | 27,900 |
| Total liabilities and stockholders' equity | | $33,920 |

## Practice Problem

**(LO 1, 2, 4)**  At the end of its first month of operations, Pampered Pet Service Inc. has the following unadjusted trial balance.

*Prepare worksheet and classified balance sheet, and journalize closing entries.*

## Pampered Pet Service Inc.
### August 31, 2022
### Trial Balance

| | Debit | Credit |
|---|---:|---:|
| Cash | $ 5,400 | |
| Accounts Receivable | 2,800 | |
| Supplies | 1,300 | |
| Prepaid Insurance | 2,400 | |
| Equipment | 60,000 | |
| Notes Payable | | $40,000 |
| Accounts Payable | | 2,400 |
| Common Stock | | 30,000 |
| Dividends | 1,000 | |
| Service Revenue | | 4,900 |
| Salaries and Wages Expense | 3,200 | |
| Utilities Expense | 800 | |
| Advertising Expense | 400 | |
| | $77,300 | $77,300 |

Other data:

1. Insurance expires at the rate of $200 per month.
2. $1,000 of supplies are on hand at August 31.
3. Monthly depreciation on the equipment is $900.
4. Interest of $500 on the notes payable has accrued during August.

**Instructions**

a. Prepare a worksheet.

b. Prepare a classified balance sheet assuming $35,000 of the notes payable are long-term.

c. Journalize the closing entries.

**Solution**

a.

**Pampered Pet Service Inc.**
**Worksheet**
**For the Month Ended August 31, 2022**

| Account Titles | Trial Balance Dr. | Trial Balance Cr. | Adjustments Dr. | Adjustments Cr. | Adjusted Trial Balance Dr. | Adjusted Trial Balance Cr. | Income Statement Dr. | Income Statement Cr. | Balance Sheet Dr. | Balance Sheet Cr. |
|---|---|---|---|---|---|---|---|---|---|---|
| Cash | 5,400 | | | | 5,400 | | | | 5,400 | |
| Accounts Receivable | 2,800 | | | | 2,800 | | | | 2,800 | |
| Supplies | 1,300 | | | (b) 300 | 1,000 | | | | 1,000 | |
| Prepaid Insurance | 2,400 | | | (a) 200 | 2,200 | | | | 2,200 | |
| Equipment | 60,000 | | | | 60,000 | | | | 60,000 | |
| Notes Payable | | 40,000 | | | | 40,000 | | | | 40,000 |
| Accounts Payable | | 2,400 | | | | 2,400 | | | | 2,400 |
| Common Stock | | 30,000 | | | | 30,000 | | | | 30,000 |
| Dividends | 1,000 | | | | 1,000 | | | | 1,000 | |
| Service Revenue | | 4,900 | | | | 4,900 | | 4,900 | | |
| Salaries and Wages Expense | 3,200 | | | | 3,200 | | 3,200 | | | |
| Utilities Expense | 800 | | | | 800 | | 800 | | | |
| Advertising Expense | 400 | | | | 400 | | 400 | | | |
| Totals | 77,300 | 77,300 | | | | | | | | |
| Insurance Expense | | | (a) 200 | | 200 | | 200 | | | |
| Supplies Expense | | | (b) 300 | | 300 | | 300 | | | |
| Depreciation Expense | | | (c) 900 | | 900 | | 900 | | | |
| Accumulated Depreciation—Equipment | | | | (c) 900 | | 900 | | | | 900 |
| Interest Expense | | | (d) 500 | | 500 | | 500 | | | |
| Interest Payable | | | | (d) 500 | | 500 | | | | 500 |
| Totals | | | 1,900 | 1,900 | 78,700 | 78,700 | 6,300 | 4,900 | 72,400 | 73,800 |
| Net Loss | | | | | | | | 1,400 | 1,400 | |
| Totals | | | | | | | 6,300 | 6,300 | 73,800 | 73,800 |

Explanation: (a) insurance expired, (b) supplies used, (c) depreciation expensed, and (d) interest accrued.

b.

**Pampered Pet Service Inc.**
**Balance Sheet**
**August 31, 2022**

**Assets**

| | | |
|---|---|---|
| Current assets | | |
| Cash | $ 5,400 | |
| Accounts receivable | 2,800 | |
| Supplies | 1,000 | |
| Prepaid insurance | 2,200 | |
| Total current assets | | $11,400 |
| Property, plant, and equipment | | |
| Equipment | 60,000 | |
| Less: Accumulated depreciation—equipment | 900 | 59,100 |
| Total assets | | $70,500 |

### Liabilities and Stockholders' Equity

Current liabilities
    Notes payable                                $ 5,000
    Accounts payable                        2,400
    Interest payable                          500

| | | |
|---|---|---|
| Total current liabilities | | $ 7,900 |
| Long-term liabilities | | |
| Notes payable | | 35,000 |
| Total liabilities | | 42,900 |
| Stockholders' equity | | |
| Common stock | 30,000 | |
| Retained earnings | (2,400)* | |
| Total stockholders' equity | | 27,600 |
| Total liabilities and stockholders' equity | | $70,500 |

*Net loss of $1,400 plus dividends of $1,000 equals negative retained earnings (deficit).

**c.**

| Aug. 31 | Service Revenue | 4,900 | |
|---|---|---|---|
| |    Income Summary | | 4,900 |
| |    (To close revenue account) | | |
| 31 | Income Summary | 6,300 | |
| |    Salaries and Wages Expense | | 3,200 |
| |    Depreciation Expense | | 900 |
| |    Utilities Expense | | 800 |
| |    Interest Expense | | 500 |
| |    Advertising Expense | | 400 |
| |    Supplies Expense | | 300 |
| |    Insurance Expense | | 200 |
| |    (To close expense accounts) | | |
| 31 | Retained Earnings | 1,400 | |
| |    Income Summary | | 1,400 |
| |    (To close net loss to retained earnings) | | |
| 31 | Retained Earnings | 1,000 | |
| |    Dividends | | 1,000 |
| |    (To close dividends to retained earnings) | | |

Brief Exercises, DO IT! Exercises, Exercises, Problems, Data Analytics Activities, and many additional resources are available for practice in WileyPLUS.

*Note:* All asterisked Questions, Exercises, and Problems relate to material in the appendix to the chapter.

## Questions

1. "A worksheet is a permanent accounting record and its use is required in the accounting cycle." Do you agree? Explain.

2. Explain the purpose of the worksheet.

3. What is the relationship, if any, between the amount shown in the adjusted trial balance column for an account and that account's ledger balance?

4. If a company's revenues are $125,000 and its expenses are $113,000, in which financial statement columns of the worksheet will the net income of $12,000 appear? When expenses exceed revenues, in which columns will the difference appear?

5. Why is it necessary to prepare formal financial statements if all of the data are in the statement columns of the worksheet?

6. Identify the account(s) debited and credited in each of the four closing entries, assuming the company has net income for the year.

7. Describe the nature of the Income Summary account and identify the types of summary data that may be posted to this account.

**8.** What are the content and purpose of a post-closing trial balance?

**9.** Which of the following accounts would not appear in the post-closing trial balance? Interest Payable, Equipment, Depreciation Expense, Dividends, Unearned Service Revenue, Accumulated Depreciation—Equipment, and Service Revenue.

**10.** Distinguish between a reversing entry and an adjusting entry. Are reversing entries required?

**11.** Indicate, in the sequence in which they are made, the three required steps in the accounting cycle that involve journalizing.

**12.** Identify, in the sequence in which they are prepared, the three trial balances that are used in the accounting cycle.

**13.** How do correcting entries differ from adjusting entries?

**14.** What standard classifications are used in preparing a classified balance sheet?

**15.** What is meant by the term "operating cycle"?

**16.** Define current assets. What basis is used for arranging individual items within the current assets section?

**17.** Distinguish between long-term investments and property, plant, and equipment.

**18.** (a) What is the term used to describe the owners' equity section of a corporation? (b) Identify the two owners' equity accounts in a corporation and indicate the purpose of each.

**19.** Using **Apple**'s annual report, determine its current liabilities at September 30, 2017, and September 29, 2018. Were current liabilities higher or lower than current assets in these two years?

**\*20.** Cigale Company prepares reversing entries. If the adjusting entry for interest payable is reversed, what type of an account balance, if any, will there be in Interest Payable and Interest Expense after the reversing entry is posted?

**\*21.** At December 31, accrued salaries payable totaled $3,500. On January 10, total salaries of $8,000 are paid. (a) Assume that reversing entries are made at January 1. Give the January 10 entry, and indicate the Salaries and Wages Expense account balance after the entry is posted. (b) Repeat part (a) assuming reversing entries are not made.

## Brief Exercises

*List the steps in preparing a worksheet.*

**BE4.1 (LO 1), K** The steps in using a worksheet are presented in random order below. List the steps in the proper order by placing numbers 1–5 in the blank spaces.

**a.** _____ Prepare a trial balance on the worksheet.

**b.** _____ Enter adjusted balances.

**c.** _____ Extend adjusted balances to appropriate statement columns.

**d.** _____ Total the statement columns, compute net income (loss), and complete the worksheet.

**e.** _____ Enter adjustment data.

*Prepare partial worksheet.*

**BE4.2 (LO 1), AP** The ledger of Clayton Company includes the following unadjusted balances: Prepaid Insurance $3,000, Service Revenue $58,000, and Salaries and Wages Expense $25,000. Adjusting entries are required for (a) expired insurance $1,800; (b) services performed $1,100, but unbilled and uncollected; and (c) accrued salaries payable $800. Enter the unadjusted balances and adjustments into a worksheet and complete the worksheet for all accounts. (Note: You will need to add the following accounts: Accounts Receivable, Salaries and Wages Payable, and Insurance Expense.)

*Identify worksheet columns for selected accounts.*

**BE4.3 (LO 1), C** The following selected accounts appear in the adjusted trial balance columns of the worksheet for Goulet Company: Accumulated Depreciation—Equipment, Depreciation Expense, Common Stock, Dividends, Service Revenue, Supplies, and Accounts Payable. Indicate the financial statement column (income statement Dr., balance sheet Cr., etc.) to which each balance should be extended.

*Prepare closing entries from ledger balances.*

**BE4.4 (LO 2), AP** The ledger of Rios Company contains the following balances: Retained Earnings $30,000, Dividends $2,000, Service Revenue $50,000, Salaries and Wages Expense $27,000, and Supplies Expense $7,000. Prepare the closing entries at December 31.

*Post closing entries; underline and balance T-accounts.*

**BE4.5 (LO 2), AP** The ledger of Rios Company contains the following balances: Retained Earnings $30,000, Dividends $2,000, Service Revenue $50,000, Salaries and Wages Expense $27,000, and Supplies Expense $7,000. Enter the balances in T-accounts, post the closing entries, and underline and balance the accounts.

*Journalize and post closing entries using the three-column form of account.*

**BE4.6 (LO 2), AP** The income statement for Weeping Willow Golf Club for the month ending July 31 shows Service Revenue $16,400, Salaries and Wages Expense $8,200, Maintenance and Repairs Expense $2,500, and Net Income $5,700. Prepare the entries to close the revenue and expense accounts. Post the entries to the revenue and expense accounts, and complete the closing process for these accounts using the three-column form of account.

*Identify post-closing trial balance accounts.*

**BE4.7 (LO 2), C** The following selected accounts appear in the adjusted trial balance columns of the worksheet for Goulet Company: Accumulated Depreciation—Equipment, Depreciation Expense, Common Stock, Dividends, Service Revenue, Supplies, and Accounts Payable. Identify the accounts that would be included in a post-closing trial balance.

**BE4.8 (LO 3), K** The steps in the accounting cycle are listed in random order below. List the steps in proper sequence, assuming no worksheet is prepared, by placing numbers 1–9 in the blank spaces.

*List the required steps in the accounting cycle in sequence.*

a. _____ Prepare a trial balance.

b. _____ Journalize the transactions.

c. _____ Journalize and post closing entries.

d. _____ Prepare financial statements.

e. _____ Journalize and post adjusting entries.

f. _____ Post to ledger accounts.

g. _____ Prepare a post-closing trial balance.

h. _____ Prepare an adjusted trial balance.

i. _____ Analyze business transactions.

**BE4.9 (LO 3), AP** At Creighton Company, the following errors were discovered after the transactions had been journalized and posted. Prepare the correcting entries.

*Prepare correcting entries.*

1. A collection on account from a customer for $870 was recorded as a debit to Cash $870 and a credit to Service Revenue $870.

2. The purchase of store supplies on account for $1,570 was recorded as a debit to Supplies $1,750 and a credit to Accounts Payable $1,750.

**BE4.10 (LO 4), AP** The balance sheet debit column of the worksheet for Hamidi Company includes the following accounts: Accounts Receivable $12,500, Prepaid Insurance $3,600, Cash $4,100, Supplies $5,200, and Debt Investments (short-term) $6,700. Prepare the current assets section of the balance sheet, listing the accounts in proper sequence.

*Prepare the current assets section of a balance sheet.*

**BE4.11 (LO 4), C** The following are the major balance sheet classifications:

*Classify accounts on balance sheet.*

Current assets (CA)    Current liabilities (CL)
Long-term investments (LTI)    Long-term liabilities (LTL)
Property, plant, and equipment (PPE)    Stockholders' equity (SE)
Intangible assets (IA)

Match each of the following accounts to its proper balance sheet classification.

_____ Accounts payable         _____ Income taxes payable
_____ Accounts receivable      _____ Debt investments (long-term)
_____ Accumulated depreciation—buildings    _____ Land
_____ Buildings                _____ Inventory
_____ Cash                     _____ Patents
_____ Copyrights               _____ Supplies

*BE4.12 (LO 5), AP** At October 31, Burgess Company made an accrued expense adjusting entry of $2,100 for salaries. Prepare the reversing entry on November 1, and indicate the balances in Salaries and Wages Payable and Salaries and Wages Expense after posting the reversing entry.

*Prepare reversing entries.*

## DO IT! Exercises

**DO IT! 4.1 (LO 1), C** Bradley Decker is preparing a worksheet. Explain to Bradley how he should extend the following adjusted trial balance accounts to the financial statement columns of the worksheet.

*Prepare a worksheet.*

Service Revenue          Accounts Receivable
Notes Payable            Accumulated Depreciation—Buildings
Common Stock             Utilities Expense

**DO IT! 4.2 (LO 2), AP** Paloma Company shows the following balances in selected accounts of its adjusted trial balance.

*Prepare closing entries.*

| | | | |
|---|---|---|---|
| Supplies | $32,000 | Service Revenue | $108,000 |
| Supplies Expense | 6,000 | Salaries and Wages Expense | 40,000 |
| Accounts Receivable | 12,000 | Utilities Expense | 8,000 |
| Dividends | 22,000 | Rent Expense | 18,000 |
| Retained Earnings | 70,000 | | |

Prepare the closing entries at December 31.

*Prepare correcting entries.*

**DO IT! 4.3 (LO 3), AN** Hanson Company has an inexperienced accountant. During the first months on the job, the accountant made the following errors in journalizing transactions. All entries were posted as made.

1. The purchase of supplies for $650 cash was debited to Equipment $210 and credited to Cash $210.

2. A $500 dividend was debited to Salaries and Wages Expense $900 and credited to Cash $900.

3. A payment on account of $820 to a creditor was debited to Accounts Payable $280 and credited to Cash $280.

Prepare the correcting entries.

*Match accounts to balance sheet classifications.*

**DO IT! 4.4 (LO 4), C** The following accounts were taken from the financial statements of Lee Company.

| | |
|---|---|
| _____ Interest revenue | _____ Common stock |
| _____ Utilities payable | _____ Accumulated depreciation—equipment |
| _____ Accounts payable | _____ Equipment |
| _____ Supplies | _____ Salaries and wages expense |
| _____ Bonds payable | _____ Debt investments (long-term) |
| _____ Goodwill | _____ Unearned rent revenue |

Match each of the accounts to its proper balance sheet classification, as shown below. If the item would not appear on a balance sheet, use "NA."

| | |
|---|---|
| Current assets (CA) | Current liabilities (CL) |
| Long-term investments (LTI) | Long-term liabilities (LTL) |
| Property, plant, and equipment (PPE) | Stockholders' equity (SE) |
| Intangible assets (IA) | |

# Exercises

*Complete the worksheet.*

**E4.1 (LO 1), AP** The trial balance columns of the worksheet for Nanduri Company at June 30, 2022, are as follows.

**Nanduri Company**
**Worksheet**
**For the Month Ended June 30, 2022**

| Account Titles | Trial Balance Dr. | Cr. |
|---|---|---|
| Cash | 2,320 | |
| Accounts Receivable | 2,440 | |
| Supplies | 1,880 | |
| Accounts Payable | | 1,120 |
| Unearned Service Revenue | | 240 |
| Common Stock | | 3,600 |
| Service Revenue | | 2,400 |
| Salaries and Wages Expense | 560 | |
| Miscellaneous Expense | 160 | |
| | 7,360 | 7,360 |

Other data:

1. A physical count reveals $500 of supplies on hand.

2. $100 of the unearned revenue is still unearned at month-end.

3. Accrued salaries are $210.

**Instructions**

Enter the trial balance on a worksheet and complete the worksheet.

**E4.2 (LO 1), AP** The adjusted trial balance columns of the worksheet for DeSousa Company are as follows.

*Complete the worksheet.*

**DeSousa Company**
**Worksheet (partial)**
**For the Month Ended April 30, 2022**

| Account Titles | Adjusted Trial Balance | | Income Statement | | Balance Sheet | |
|---|---|---|---|---|---|---|
| | Dr. | Cr. | Dr. | Cr. | Dr. | Cr. |
| Cash | 10,000 | | | | | |
| Accounts Receivable | 7,840 | | | | | |
| Prepaid Rent | 2,280 | | | | | |
| Equipment | 23,050 | | | | | |
| Accumulated Depreciation—Equip. | | 4,921 | | | | |
| Notes Payable (due in October 2022) | | 5,700 | | | | |
| Accounts Payable | | 4,920 | | | | |
| Common Stock | | 20,000 | | | | |
| Retained Earnings | | 7,960 | | | | |
| Dividends | 3,650 | | | | | |
| Service Revenue | | 15,590 | | | | |
| Salaries and Wages Expense | 10,840 | | | | | |
| Rent Expense | 760 | | | | | |
| Depreciation Expense | 671 | | | | | |
| Interest Expense | 57 | | | | | |
| Interest Payable | | 57 | | | | |
| Totals | 59,148 | 59,148 | | | | |

**Instructions**

Complete the worksheet.

**E4.3 (LO 1, 4), AP** Worksheet data for DeSousa Company are presented in E4.2.

*Prepare financial statements from worksheet.*

**Instructions**

Prepare an income statement, a retained earnings statement and a classified balance sheet.

**E4.4 (LO 2), AP** Worksheet data for DeSousa Company are presented in E4.2.

*Journalize and post closing entries and prepare a post-closing trial balance.*

**Instructions**

a. Journalize the closing entries at April 30.

b. Post the closing entries to Income Summary and Retained Earnings. (Use T-accounts.)

c. Prepare a post-closing trial balance at April 30.

**E4.5 (LO 1), AP** The adjustments columns of the worksheet for Misra Company are shown here.

*Prepare adjusting entries from financial statement columns, and extend balances to worksheet columns.*

| Account Titles | Adjustments | |
|---|---|---|
| | Debit | Credit |
| Accounts Receivable | 1,100 | |
| Prepaid Insurance | | 300 |
| Accumulated Depreciation—Equipment | | 900 |
| Salaries and Wages Payable | | 500 |
| Service Revenue | | 1,100 |
| Salaries and Wages Expense | 500 | |
| Insurance Expense | 300 | |
| Depreciation Expense | 900 | |
| | 2,800 | 2,800 |

**Instructions**

a. Prepare the adjusting entries.

b. Assuming the adjusted trial balance amount for each account is normal, indicate the financial statement column to which each balance should be extended.

*Derive adjusting entries from spreadsheet data.*

**E4.6 (LO 1), AN** Selected spreadsheet data for Elsayed Company are presented here.

| Account Titles | Trial Balance | | Adjusted Trial Balance | |
| --- | --- | --- | --- | --- |
| | Dr. | Cr. | Dr. | Cr. |
| Accounts Receivable | ? | | 34,000 | |
| Prepaid Insurance | 26,000 | | 20,000 | |
| Supplies | 7,000 | | ? | |
| Accumulated Depreciation—Equipment | | 12,000 | | ? |
| Salaries and Wages Payable | | ? | | 5,600 |
| Service Revenue | | 88,000 | | 97,000 |
| Insurance Expense | | | ? | |
| Depreciation Expense | | | 10,000 | |
| Supplies Expense | | | 4,500 | |
| Salaries and Wages Expense | ? | | 49,000 | |

**Instructions**

a. Fill in the missing amounts.

b. Prepare the adjusting entries that were made.

*Prepare closing entries and a post-closing trial balance.*

**E4.7 (LO 2), AP** Kay Magill Company had the following adjusted trial balance.

**Kay Magill Company**
**Adjusted Trial Balance**
**For the Year Ended June 30, 2022**

| Account Titles | Adjusted Trial Balance | |
| --- | --- | --- |
| | Debit | Credit |
| Cash | $ 3,712 | |
| Accounts Receivable | 3,904 | |
| Supplies | 480 | |
| Accounts Payable | | $ 1,556 |
| Unearned Service Revenue | | 160 |
| Common Stock | | 4,000 |
| Retained Earnings | | 1,760 |
| Dividends | 628 | |
| Service Revenue | | 4,300 |
| Salaries and Wages Expense | 1,344 | |
| Miscellaneous Expense | 256 | |
| Supplies Expense | 1,900 | |
| Salaries and Wages Payable | | 448 |
| | $12,224 | $12,224 |

**Instructions**

a. Prepare closing entries at June 30, 2022.

b. Prepare a post-closing trial balance.

*Journalize and post closing entries and prepare a post-closing trial balance.*

**E4.8 (LO 2), AP** Plevin Company ended its fiscal year on July 31, 2022. The company's adjusted trial balance as of the end of its fiscal year is shown as follows.

**Plevin Company**
**Adjusted Trial Balance**
**July 31, 2022**

| No. | Account Titles | Debit | Credit |
|---|---|---|---|
| 101 | Cash | $ 9,840 | |
| 112 | Accounts Receivable | 8,780 | |
| 157 | Equipment | 15,900 | |
| 158 | Accumulated Depreciation—Equip. | | $ 7,400 |
| 201 | Accounts Payable | | 4,220 |
| 208 | Unearned Rent Revenue | | 1,800 |
| 311 | Common Stock | | 20,000 |
| 320 | Retained Earnings | | 25,200 |
| 332 | Dividends | 16,000 | |
| 400 | Service Revenue | | 64,000 |
| 429 | Rent Revenue | | 6,500 |
| 711 | Depreciation Expense | 8,000 | |
| 726 | Salaries and Wages Expense | 55,700 | |
| 732 | Utilities Expense | 14,900 | |
| | | $129,120 | $129,120 |

## Instructions

**a.** Prepare the closing entries using page J15.

**b.** Post to the Retained Earnings and No. 350 Income Summary accounts. (Use the three-column form.)

**c.** Prepare a post-closing trial balance at July 31.

**E4.9 (LO 4), AP** The adjusted trial balance for Plevin Company is presented in E4.8.

*Prepare financial statements.*

## Instructions

**a.** Prepare an income statement and a retained earnings statement for the year

**b.** Prepare a classified balance sheet at July 31.

**E4.10 (LO 3), C** Janis Engle has prepared the following list of statements about the accounting cycle.

*Answer questions related to the accounting cycle.*

1. "Journalize the transactions" is the first step in the accounting cycle.

2. Reversing entries are a required step in the accounting cycle.

3. Correcting entries do not have to be part of the accounting cycle.

4. If a worksheet is prepared, some steps of the accounting cycle are incorporated into the worksheet.

5. The accounting cycle begins with the analysis of business transactions and ends with the preparation of a post-closing trial balance.

6. All steps of the accounting cycle occur daily during the accounting period.

7. The step of "post to the ledger accounts" occurs before the step of "journalize the transactions."

8. Closing entries must be prepared before financial statements can be prepared.

## Instructions

Identify each statement as true or false. If false, indicate how to correct the statement.

**E4.11 (LO 2), AP** Selected accounts for Heather's Salon are presented here. All June 30 postings are from closing entries.

*Prepare closing entries.*

| Salaries and Wages Expense | | | |
|---|---|---|---|
| 6/10 | 3,200 | | |
| 6/28 | 5,600 | | |
| Bal. | 8,800 | 6/30 | 8,800 |

| Service Revenue | | | |
|---|---|---|---|
| | | 6/15 | 9,700 |
| | | 6/24 | 8,400 |
| 6/30 | 18,100 | Bal. | 18,100 |

| Retained Earnings | | | |
|---|---|---|---|
| 6/30 | 2,500 | 6/1 | 13,000 |
| | | 6/30 | 5,000 |
| | | Bal. | 15,500 |

| Supplies Expense | | | |
|---|---|---|---|
| 6/12 | 600 | | |
| 6/24 | 700 | | |
| Bal. | 1,300 | 6/30 | 1,300 |

| Rent Expense | | | |
|---|---|---|---|
| 6/1 | 3,000 | | |
| Bal. | 3,000 | 6/30 | 3,000 |

| Dividends | | | |
|---|---|---|---|
| 6/13 | 1,000 | | |
| 6/25 | 1,500 | | |
| Bal. | 2,500 | 6/30 | 2,500 |

**Instructions**

a. Prepare the closing entries that were made.

b. Post the closing entries to Income Summary.

*Prepare correcting entries.*

**E4.12 (LO 3), AN** Andrew Clark Company discovered the following errors made in January 2022.

1. A payment of Salaries and Wages Expense of $700 was debited to Equipment and credited to Cash, both for $700.

2. A collection of $1,000 from a client on account was debited to Cash $100 and credited to Service Revenue $100.

3. The purchase of equipment on account for $760 was debited to Equipment $670 and credited to Accounts Payable $670.

**Instructions**

a. Correct the errors by reversing the incorrect entry and preparing the correct entry.

b. Correct the errors without reversing the incorrect entry.

*Prepare correcting entries.*

**E4.13 (LO 3), AN** Keenan Company has an inexperienced accountant. During the first 2 weeks on the job, the accountant made the following errors in journalizing transactions. All entries were posted as made.

1. A payment on account of $840 to a creditor was debited to Accounts Payable $480 and credited to Cash $480.

2. The purchase of supplies on account for $560 was debited to Equipment $56 and credited to Accounts Payable $56.

3. A $500 cash dividend was debited to Salaries and Wages Expense $500 and credited to Cash $500.

**Instructions**

Prepare the correcting entries.

*Prepare a classified balance sheet.*

**E4.14 (LO 4), AP** Writing The adjusted trial balance for Martell Bowling Alley at December 31, 2022, contains the following accounts.

|  | Debit |  |  | Credit |
|---|---|---|---|---|
| Buildings | $128,800 | Common Stock |  | $ 90,000 |
| Accounts Receivable | 14,520 | Retained Earnings |  | 25,000 |
| Prepaid Insurance | 4,680 | Accumulated Depreciation—Buildings |  | 42,600 |
| Cash | 18,040 | Accounts Payable |  | 12,300 |
| Equipment | 62,400 | Notes Payable |  | 97,780 |
| Land | 67,000 | Accumulated Depreciation—Equipment |  | 18,720 |
| Insurance Expense | 780 | Interest Payable |  | 2,600 |
| Depreciation Expense | 7,360 | Service Revenue |  | 17,180 |
| Interest Expense | 2,600 |  |  | $306,180 |
|  | $306,180 |  |  |  |

**Instructions**

a. Prepare a classified balance sheet; assume that $22,000 of the note payable will be paid in 2023.

b. Comment on the liquidity of the company.

*Classify accounts on balance sheet.*

**E4.15 (LO 4), C** The following are the major balance sheet classifications.

Current assets (CA)

Long-term investments (LTI)

Property, plant, and equipment (PPE)

Intangible assets (IA)

Current liabilities (CL)

Long-term liabilities (LTL)

Stockholders' equity (SE)

## Instructions

Classify each of the following accounts taken from Raman Company's balance sheet.

| | |
|---|---|
| _____ Accounts payable | _____ Accumulated depreciation—equipment |
| _____ Accounts receivable | _____ Buildings |
| _____ Cash | _____ Land (in use) |
| _____ Common stock | _____ Notes payable (due in 2 years) |
| _____ Patents | _____ Supplies |
| _____ Salaries and wages payable | _____ Equipment |
| _____ Inventory | _____ Prepaid expenses |
| _____ Stock investments | |
| (to be sold in 7 months) | |

**E4.16 (LO 4), AP** The following items were taken from the financial statements of D. Gygi Company. (All amounts are in thousands.)

*Prepare a classified balance sheet.*

| | | | |
|---|---|---|---|
| Long-term debt | S 1,000 | Accumulated depreciation—equipment | $ 5,655 |
| Prepaid insurance | 880 | Accounts payable | 1,444 |
| Equipment | 11,500 | Notes payable (due after 2023) | 400 |
| Stock investments (long-term) | 264 | Common stock | 10,000 |
| Debt investments (short-term) | 3,690 | Retained earnings | 2,955 |
| Notes payable (due in 2023) | 500 | Accounts receivable | 1,696 |
| Cash | 2,668 | Inventory | 1,256 |

## Instructions

Prepare a classified balance sheet in good form as of December 31, 2022.

**E4.17 (LO 4), AP** These financial statement items are for Norsted Company at year-end, July 31, 2022.

*Prepare financial statements.*

| | | | |
|---|---|---|---|
| Salaries and wages payable | $ 2,080 | Notes payable (long-term) | $ 1,800 |
| Salaries and wages expense | 51,700 | Cash | 14,200 |
| Utilities expense | 22,600 | Accounts receivable | 9,780 |
| Equipment | 30,400 | Accumulated depreciation—equipment | 6,000 |
| Accounts payable | 4,100 | Dividends | 3,000 |
| Service revenue | 62,000 | Depreciation expense | 4,000 |
| Rent revenue | 8,500 | Retained earnings (beginning of the year) | 21,200 |
| Common stock | 30,000 | | |

## Instructions

a. Prepare an income statement and a retained earnings statement for the year.

b. Prepare a classified balance sheet at July 31.

**\* E4.18 (LO 5), AP** Reblin Company pays salaries of $12,000 every Monday for the preceding 5-day week (Monday through Friday). Assume December 31 falls on a Tuesday, so Reblin's employees have worked 2 days without being paid at the end of the fiscal year.

*Use reversing entries.*

## Instructions

a. Assume the company does not use reversing entries. Prepare the December 31 adjusting entry and the entry on Monday, January 6, when Reblin pays the payroll.

b. Assume the company does use reversing entries. Prepare the December 31 adjusting entry, the January 1 reversing entry, and the entry on Monday, January 6, when Reblin pays the payroll.

**\* E4.19 (LO 2, 5), AP** On December 31, the adjusted trial balance of Cisneros Employment Agency shows the following selected data.

*Prepare closing and reversing entries.*

| | | | |
|---|---|---|---|
| Accounts Receivable | $24,500 | Service Revenue | $92,500 |
| Interest Expense | 8,300 | Interest Payable | 2,000 |

Analysis shows that adjusting entries were made to (1) accrue $5,000 of service revenue and (2) accrue $2,000 interest expense.

## Instructions

a. Prepare the closing entries for the temporary accounts shown above at December 31.

b. Prepare the reversing entries on January 1.

    **c.** Post the entries in (a) and (b), excluding the Income Summary account. Underline and balance the accounts. (Use T-accounts.)

    **d.** Prepare the entries to record (1) the collection of the accrued revenue on January 10 and (2) the payment of all interest due ($2,000) on January 15.

    **e.** Post the entries in (d) to the temporary accounts.

---

## Problems

---

*Prepare a worksheet, financial statements, and adjusting and closing entries.*

**P4.1 (LO 1, 2, 4), AP**  The trial balance columns of the worksheet for Lampert Roofing at March 31, 2022, are as follows.

**Lampert Roofing**
**Worksheet**
**For the Month Ended March 31, 2022**

| Account Titles | Trial Balance | |
| --- | --- | --- |
| | Dr. | Cr. |
| Cash | 4,500 | |
| Accounts Receivable | 3,200 | |
| Supplies | 2,000 | |
| Equipment | 11,000 | |
| Accumulated Depreciation—Equipment | | 1,250 |
| Accounts Payable | | 2,500 |
| Unearned Service Revenue | | 550 |
| Common Stock | | 10,000 |
| Retained Earnings | | 2,900 |
| Dividends | 1,100 | |
| Service Revenue | | 6,300 |
| Salaries and Wages Expense | 1,300 | |
| Miscellaneous Expense | 400 | |
| | 23,500 | 23,500 |

Other data:

    **1.** A physical count reveals only $550 of roofing supplies on hand.

    **2.** Depreciation for March is $250.

    **3.** Unearned service revenue amounted to $210 at March 31.

    **4.** Accrued salaries are $700.

**Instructions**

a. Adjusted trial balance $24,450

    **a.** Enter the trial balance on a worksheet and complete the worksheet.

b. Net income $2,540
Total assets $17,750

    **b.** Prepare an income statement and a retained earnings statement for the month of March and a classified balance sheet at March 31.

    **c.** Journalize the adjusting entries from the adjustments columns of the worksheet.

    **d.** Journalize the closing entries from the financial statement columns of the worksheet.

*Complete worksheet; prepare financial statements, closing entries, and post-closing trial balance.*

**P4.2 (LO 1, 2, 4), AP**  The adjusted trial balance columns of the worksheet for Alshwer Company are as follows.

**Alshwer Company**
**Worksheet**
**For the Year Ended December 31, 2022**

| Account No. | Account Titles | Adjusted Trial Balance | |
|---|---|---|---|
| | | Dr. | Cr. |
| 101 | Cash | 5,300 | |
| 112 | Accounts Receivable | 10,800 | |
| 126 | Supplies | 1,500 | |
| 130 | Prepaid Insurance | 2,000 | |
| 157 | Equipment | 27,000 | |
| 158 | Accumulated Depreciation—Equipment | | 5,600 |
| 200 | Notes Payable | | 15,000 |
| 201 | Accounts Payable | | 6,100 |
| 212 | Salaries and Wages Payable | | 2,400 |
| 230 | Interest Payable | | 600 |
| 311 | Common Stock | | 10,000 |
| 320 | Retained Earnings | | 3,000 |
| 332 | Dividends | 7,000 | |
| 400 | Service Revenue | | 61,000 |
| 610 | Advertising Expense | 8,400 | |
| 631 | Supplies Expense | 4,000 | |
| 711 | Depreciation Expense | 5,600 | |
| 722 | Insurance Expense | 3,500 | |
| 726 | Salaries and Wages Expense | 28,000 | |
| 905 | Interest Expense | 600 | |
| | Totals | 103,700 | 103,700 |

## Instructions

a. Complete the worksheet by extending the balances to the financial statement columns.

b. Prepare an income statement, a retained earnings statement, and a classified balance sheet. (*Note:* $5,000 of the notes payable become due in 2023.)

c. Prepare the closing entries. Use J14 for the journal page.

d. Post the closing entries. (Use the three-column form of account.) Income Summary is account No. 350.

e. Prepare a post-closing trial balance.

a. Net income $10,900

b. Current assets $19,600
   Current liabilities $14,100

e. Post-closing trial balance
   $46,600

**P4.3 (LO 1, 2, 3, 4), AP** Heidi Jara opened Jara's Cleaning Service on July 1, 2022. During July, the following transactions were completed.

*Complete all steps in accounting cycle.*

July 1 Stockholders invested $20,000 cash in the business in exchange for common stock.
1 Purchased used truck for $9,000, paying $4,000 cash and the balance on account.
3 Purchased cleaning supplies for $2,100 on account.
5 Paid $1,800 cash on a 1-year insurance policy effective July 1.
12 Billed customers $4,500 for cleaning services.
18 Paid $1,500 cash on amount owed on truck and $1,400 on amount owed on cleaning supplies.
20 Paid $2,500 cash for employee salaries.
21 Collected $3,400 cash from customers billed on July 12.
25 Billed customers $6,000 for cleaning services.
31 Paid $350 for the monthly gasoline bill for the truck.
31 Paid a $5,600 cash dividend.

The chart of accounts for Jara's Cleaning Service contains the following accounts: No. 101 Cash, No. 112 Accounts Receivable, No. 126 Supplies, No. 130 Prepaid Insurance, No. 157 Equipment, No. 158 Accumulated Depreciation—Equipment, No. 201 Accounts Payable, No. 212 Salaries and Wages Payable, No. 311 Common Stock, No. 320 Retained Earnings, No. 332 Dividends, No. 350 Income Summary, No. 400 Service Revenue, No. 631 Supplies Expense, No. 633 Gasoline Expense, No. 711 Depreciation Expense, No. 722 Insurance Expense, and No. 726 Salaries and Wages Expense.

## Instructions

a. Journalize and post the July transactions. Use page J1 for the journal and the three-column form of account.

b. Prepare a trial balance at July 31 on a worksheet.

b. Trial balance $34,700

c. Adjusted trial balance
$38,900

c. Enter the following adjustments on the worksheet and complete the worksheet.

1. Unbilled and uncollected revenue for services performed at July 31 were $2,700.

2. Depreciation on equipment for the month was $500.

3. One-twelfth of the insurance expired.

4. An inventory count shows $600 of cleaning supplies on hand at July 31.

5. Unpaid employee salaries of $1,000 should be accrued.

d. Net income $7,200
Total assets $26,800

d. Prepare an income statement and a retained earnings statement for July and a classified balance sheet at July 31.

e. Journalize and post adjusting entries. Use page J2 for the journal.

g. Post-closing trial balance
$27,300

f. Journalize and post closing entries and complete the closing process. Use page J3 for the journal.

g. Prepare a post-closing trial balance at July 31.

*Complete worksheet; prepare classified balance sheet, entries, and post-closing trial balance.*

**P4.4 (LO 1, 2, 4), AP** Jarmuz Management Services began business on January 1, 2021, with a capital investment of $90,000. The company manages condominiums for owners (service revenue) and rents space in its own office building (rent revenue). The trial balance and adjusted trial balance columns of the worksheet at the end of 2022 are as follows.

**Jarmuz Management Services**
**Worksheet**
**For the Year Ended December 31, 2022**

| Account Titles | Trial Balance Dr. | Trial Balance Cr. | Adjusted Trial Balance Dr. | Adjusted Trial Balance Cr. |
|---|---|---|---|---|
| Cash | 13,800 | | 13,800 | |
| Accounts Receivable | 28,300 | | 28,300 | |
| Prepaid Insurance | 3,600 | | 2,400 | |
| Land | 67,000 | | 67,000 | |
| Buildings | 127,000 | | 127,000 | |
| Equipment | 59,000 | | 59,000 | |
| Accounts Payable | | 12,500 | | 12,500 |
| Unearned Rent Revenue | | 6,000 | | 1,500 |
| Notes Payable | | 120,000 | | 120,000 |
| Common Stock | | 90,000 | | 90,000 |
| Retained Earnings | | 54,000 | | 54,000 |
| Dividends | 22,000 | | 22,000 | |
| Service Revenue | | 90,700 | | 90,700 |
| Rent Revenue | | 29,000 | | 33,500 |
| Salaries and Wages Expense | 42,000 | | 42,000 | |
| Advertising Expense | 20,500 | | 20,500 | |
| Utilities Expense | 19,000 | | 19,000 | |
| Totals | 402,200 | 402,200 | | |
| Insurance Expense | | | 1,200 | |
| Depreciation Expense | | | 6,600 | |
| Accumulated Depreciation—Buildings | | | | 3,000 |
| Accumulated Depreciation—Equipment | | | | 3,600 |
| Interest Expense | | | 10,000 | |
| Interest Payable | | | | 10,000 |
| Totals | | | 418,800 | 418,800 |

**Instructions**

a. Total current assets $44,500

a. Prepare a classified balance sheet. (*Note:* $30,000 of the notes payable is due for payment next year.)

b. Journalize the adjusting entries.

c. Journalize the closing entries.

d. Post-closing trial balance
$297,500

d. Prepare a post-closing trial balance.

**P4.5 (LO 2, 4), AP** The completed financial statement columns of the spreadsheet for Fleming Company are as follows.

*Prepare financial statements, closing entries, and post-closing trial balance.*

**Fleming Company**
**For the Year Ended December 31, 2022**

| Account No. | Account Titles | Income Statement Dr | Cr | Balance Sheet Dr | Cr |
|---|---|---|---|---|---|
| 101 | Cash | | | 8,900 | |
| 112 | Accounts Receivable | | | 10,800 | |
| 130 | Prepaid Insurance | | | 2,800 | |
| 157 | Equipment | | | 24,000 | |
| 158 | Accumulated Depreciation—Equip. | | | | 4,500 |
| 201 | Accounts Payable | | | | 9,000 |
| 212 | Salaries and Wages Payable | | | | 2,400 |
| 311 | Common Stock | | | | 12,000 |
| 320 | Retained Earnings | | | | 7,500 |
| 332 | Dividends | | | 11,000 | |
| 400 | Service Revenue | | 60,000 | | |
| 622 | Maintenance and Repairs Expense | 1,600 | | | |
| 711 | Depreciation Expense | 3,100 | | | |
| 722 | Insurance Expense | 1,800 | | | |
| 726 | Salaries and Wages Expense | 30,000 | | | |
| 732 | Utilities Expense | 1,400 | | | |
| | Totals | 37,900 | 60,000 | 57,500 | 35,400 |
| | Net Income | 22,100 | | | 22,100 |
| | | 60,000 | 60,000 | 57,500 | 57,500 |

## Instructions

a. Prepare an income statement, a retained earnings statement, and a classified balance sheet.

b. Prepare the closing entries.

c. Post the closing entries and underline and balance the accounts. (Use T-accounts.) Income Summary is account No. 350.

d. Prepare a post-closing trial balance.

a. Ending retained earnings $18,600
Total current assets $22,500

d. Post-closing trial balance $46,500

**P4.6 (LO 3), AP** Len Kumar started his own consulting firm, Kumar Consulting, on June 1, 2022. The trial balance at June 30 is as follows.

*Prepare adjusting entries, post to ledger accounts, and prepare adjusted trial balance.*

**Kumar Consulting**
**Trial Balance**
**June 30, 2022**

| | Debit | Credit |
|---|---|---|
| Cash | $ 6,850 | |
| Accounts Receivable | 7,000 | |
| Supplies | 2,000 | |
| Prepaid Insurance | 2,880 | |
| Equipment | 15,000 | |
| Accounts Payable | | $ 4,230 |
| Unearned Service Revenue | | 5,200 |
| Common Stock | | 22,000 |
| Service Revenue | | 8,300 |
| Salaries and Wages Expense | 4,000 | |
| Rent Expense | 2,000 | |
| | $39,730 | $39,730 |

In addition to those accounts listed on the trial balance, the chart of accounts for Kumar also contains the following accounts: Accumulated Depreciation—Equipment, Salaries and Wages Payable, Depreciation Expense, Insurance Expense, Utilities Expense, and Supplies Expense.

Other data:

1. Supplies on hand at June 30 total $720.

2. A utility bill for $180 has not been recorded and will not be paid until next month.

3. The insurance policy is for a year.

4. Services were performed for $4,100 of unearned service revenue by the end of the month.

5. Salaries of $1,250 are accrued at June 30.

6. The equipment has a 5-year life with no salvage value and is being depreciated at $250 per month for 60 months.

7. Invoices representing $3,900 of services performed by Kumar during the month have not been recorded as of June 30.

### Instructions

a. Prepare the adjusting entries for the month of June.

b. Service rev. $16,300

b. Post the adjusting entries to the ledger accounts. Enter the totals from the trial balance as beginning account balances. (Use T-accounts.)

c. Tot. trial balance $45,310

c. Prepare an adjusted trial balance at June 30, 2022.

*Prepare adjusting entries, adjusted trial balance, and financial statements.*

**P4.7 (LO 2, 4), AP** The Moto Hotel opened for business on May 1, 2022. Here is its trial balance before adjustment on May 31.

**Moto Hotel**
**Trial Balance**
**May 31, 2022**

| | Debit | Credit |
|---|---|---|
| Cash | $ 2,500 | |
| Supplies | 2,600 | |
| Prepaid Insurance | 1,800 | |
| Land | 15,000 | |
| Buildings | 70,000 | |
| Equipment | 16,800 | |
| Accounts Payable | | $ 4,700 |
| Unearned Rent Revenue | | 3,300 |
| Notes Payable | | 36,000 |
| Common Stock | | 60,000 |
| Rent Revenue | | 9,000 |
| Salaries and Wages Expense | 3,000 | |
| Utilities Expense | 800 | |
| Advertising Expense | 500 | |
| | $113,000 | $113,000 |

Other data:

1. Insurance expires at the rate of $450 per month.

2. A count of supplies shows $1,050 of unused supplies on May 31.

3. Annual depreciation is $3,600 on the building and $3,000 on equipment.

4. The interest rate of the notes payable is 6%. (The note was taken out on May 1 and will be repaid in 2025.)

5. Unearned rent of $2,500 has been earned.

6. Salaries of $900 are accrued and unpaid at May 31.

### Instructions

a. Journalize the adjusting entries on May 31.

c. Rent revenue $11,500
Tot. adj. trial balance $114,630

b. Prepare a ledger using T-accounts. Enter the trial balance amounts and post the adjusting entries.

c. Prepare an adjusted trial balance on May 31.

d. Net income $3,570

d. Prepare (1) an income statement and (2) a retained earnings statement for the month of May and (3) a classified balance sheet at May 31.

e. If Moto closed its accounts monthly, which accounts should be closed in May?

**P4.8 (LO 2, 4), AP** Salt Creek Golf Inc. was organized on July 1, 2022. Quarterly financial statements are prepared. The trial balance and adjusted trial balance on September 30 are shown as follows.

*Prepare adjusting entries and financial statements; identify accounts to be closed.*

**Salt Creek Golf Inc.**
**Trial Balance**
**September 30, 2022**

| | Unadjusted | | Adjusted | |
|---|---|---|---|---|
| | Dr. | Cr. | Dr. | Cr. |
| Cash | $ 6,700 | | $ 6,700 | |
| Accounts Receivable | 400 | | 1,000 | |
| Supplies | 1,200 | | 180 | |
| Prepaid Rent | 1,800 | | 900 | |
| Equipment | 15,000 | | 15,000 | |
| Accumulated Depreciation—Equipment | | | | $ 350 |
| Notes Payable | | $ 5,000 | | 5,000 |
| Accounts Payable | | 1,070 | | 1,070 |
| Salaries and Wages Payable | | | | 600 |
| Interest Payable | | | | 50 |
| Unearned Rent Revenue | | 1,000 | | 800 |
| Common Stock | | 14,000 | | 14,000 |
| Retained Earnings | | 0 | | 0 |
| Dividends | 600 | | 600 | |
| Service Revenue | | 14,100 | | 14,700 |
| Rent Revenue | | 700 | | 900 |
| Salaries and Wages Expense | 8,800 | | 9,400 | |
| Rent Expense | 900 | | 1,800 | |
| Depreciation Expense | | | 350 | |
| Supplies Expense | | | 1,020 | |
| Utilities Expense | 470 | | 470 | |
| Interest Expense | | | 50 | |
| | $35,870 | $35,870 | $37,470 | $37,470 |

## Instructions

a. Journalize the adjusting entries that were made.

b. Prepare an income statement and a retained earnings statement for the 3 months ending September 30 and a classified balance sheet at September 30.

c. Identify which accounts should be closed on September 30, assuming Salt Creek Golf closes its books quarterly.

d. If the note bears interest at 12%, how many months has it been outstanding?

b. Net income        $2,510
   Tot. assets        $23,430

**P4.9 (LO 2, 4), AP** On November 1, 2022, the following were the account balances of Soho Equipment Repair.

*Journalize transactions and follow through accounting cycle to preparation of financial statements.*

| | Debit | | Credit |
|---|---|---|---|
| Cash | $ 2,790 | Accumulated Depreciation—Equipment | $ 500 |
| Accounts Receivable | 2,910 | Accounts Payable | 2,300 |
| Supplies | 1,120 | Unearned Service Revenue | 400 |
| Equipment | 10,000 | Salaries and Wages Payable | 620 |
| | | Common Stock | 10,000 |
| | | Retained Earnings | 3,000 |
| | $16,820 | | $16,820 |

During November, the following summary transactions were completed.

Nov. 8    Paid $1,220 for salaries due employees, of which $600 is for November and $620 is for October salaries payable.

10    Received $1,800 cash from customers in payment of account.

12    Received $3,700 cash for services performed in November.

15    Purchased store equipment on account $3,600.

17    Purchased supplies on account $1,300.

20    Paid creditors $2,500 of accounts payable due.

22    Paid November rent $480.

25    Paid salaries $1,000.

27    Performed services on account worth $900 and billed customers.

29    Received $750 from customers for services to be performed in the future.

Adjustment data:

1. Supplies on hand are valued at $1,100.

2. Accrued salaries payable are $480.

3. Depreciation for the month is $250.

4. Services were performed to satisfy $500 of unearned service revenue.

**Instructions**

a. Enter the November 1 balances in the ledger accounts. (Use T-accounts.)

b. Journalize the November transactions.

c. Post to the ledger accounts. Use the following additional accounts: Service Revenue, Depreciation Expense, Supplies Expense, Salaries and Wages Expense, and Rent Expense.

d. Prepare a trial balance at November 30.

e. Journalize and post adjusting entries.

f. Prepare an adjusted trial balance.

g. Prepare an income statement and a retained earnings statement for November and a classified balance sheet at November 30.

f. Cash             $3,840
   Tot. adj. trial
      balance      $24,680
g. Net income     $970

*Analyze errors and prepare correcting entries and trial balance.*

**P4.10 (LO 3), AN** Dao Vang, CPA, was retained by Universal Cable to prepare financial statements for April 2022. Vang accumulated all the ledger balances per Universal's records and found the following.

**Universal Cable**
**Trial Balance**
**April 30, 2022**

| | Debit | Credit |
|---|---|---|
| Cash | $ 4,100 | |
| Accounts Receivable | 3,200 | |
| Supplies | 800 | |
| Equipment | 10,600 | |
| Accumulated Depreciation—Equip. | | $ 1,350 |
| Accounts Payable | | 2,100 |
| Salaries and Wages Payable | | 700 |
| Unearned Service Revenue | | 890 |
| Common Stock | | 10,000 |
| Retained Earnings | | 2,900 |
| Service Revenue | | 5,450 |
| Salaries and Wages Expense | 3,300 | |
| Advertising Expense | 600 | |
| Miscellaneous Expense | 290 | |
| Depreciation Expense | 500 | |
| | $23,390 | $23,390 |

Dao Vang reviewed the records and found the following errors.

1. Cash received from a customer on account was recorded as $950 instead of $590.

2. A payment of $75 for advertising expense was entered as a debit to Miscellaneous Expense $75 and a credit to Cash $75.

3. The first salary payment in April was for $1,900, which included $700 of salaries payable on March 31. The payment was recorded as a debit to Salaries and Wages Expense $1,900 and a credit to Cash $1,900. (No reversing entries were made on April 1.)

4. The purchase on account of a printer costing $310 was recorded as a debit to Supplies and a credit to Accounts Payable for $310.

5. A cash payment of repair expense on equipment for $95 was recorded as a debit to Equipment $69 and a credit to Cash $69.

### Instructions

a. Prepare an analysis of each error showing (1) the incorrect entry, (2) the correct entry, and (3) the correcting entry. Items 4 and 5 occurred on April 30, 2022.

b. Prepare a correct trial balance.

*b.  Trial balance $22,690*

## Continuing Case

### Cookie Creations

(*Note:* This is a continuation of the Cookie Creations case from Chapters 1 through 3.)

**CC4** Natalie had a very busy December. At the end of the month, after journalizing and posting the December transactions and adjusting entries, Natalie then prepared an adjusted trial balance.

*Go to WileyPLUS for complete case details and instructions.*

leungchopan/
Shutterstock.com

## Comprehensive Accounting Cycle Review

**ACR4.1**  Mike Greenberg opened Kleene Window Washing Inc. on July 1, 2022. During July, the following transactions occurred.

*Complete all steps in accounting cycle.*

July   1   Issued 12,000 shares of common stock for $12,000 cash.
     1   Purchased used truck for $8,000, paying $2,000 cash and the balance on account.
     3   Purchased cleaning supplies for $900 on account.
     5   Paid $1,800 cash on a 1-year insurance policy effective July 1.
    12   Billed customers $3,700 for cleaning services performed.
    18   Paid $1,000 cash on amount owed on truck and $500 on amount owed on cleaning supplies.
    20   Paid $2,000 cash for employee salaries.
    21   Collected $1,500 cash from customers billed on July 12.
    25   Billed customers $2,500 for cleaning services performed.
    31   Paid $290 for maintenance of the truck during month.
    31   Declared and paid $600 cash dividend.

The chart of accounts for Kleene Window Washing contains the following accounts: Cash, Accounts Receivable, Supplies, Prepaid Insurance, Equipment, Accumulated Depreciation—Equipment, Accounts Payable, Salaries and Wages Payable, Common Stock, Retained Earnings, Dividends, Income Summary, Service Revenue, Maintenance and Repairs Expense, Supplies Expense, Depreciation Expense, Insurance Expense, and Salaries and Wages Expense.

### Instructions

a. Journalize the July transactions.

b. Post to the ledger accounts. (Use T-accounts.)

c. Prepare a trial balance at July 31.

d. Journalize the following adjustments.

   1. Services performed but unbilled and uncollected at July 31 were $1,700.

   2. Depreciation on equipment for the month was $180.

   3. One-twelfth of the insurance expired.

    **4.** A count shows $320 of cleaning supplies on hand at July 31.

    **5.** Accrued but unpaid employee salaries were $400.

**e.** Post adjusting entries to the T-accounts.

f. Cash $5,410

**f.** Prepare an adjusted trial balance.

g. Tot. assets $21,500

**g.** Prepare the income statement and a retained earnings statement for July and a classified balance sheet at July 31.

**h.** Journalize and post closing entries and complete the closing process.

**i.** Prepare a post-closing trial balance at July 31.

*Complete all steps in accounting cycle.*

**ACR4.2** Lars Linken opened Lars Cleaners on March 1, 2022. During March, the following transactions occurred.

Mar. 1    Issued 10,000 shares of common stock for $15,000 cash.

    1    Borrowed $6,000 cash by signing a 6-month, 6%, $6,000 note payable. Interest will be paid the first day of each subsequent month.

    1    Purchased a used truck for $8,000 cash.

    2    Paid $1,500 cash to cover rent from March 1 through May 31.

    3    Paid $2,400 cash on a 6-month insurance policy effective March 1.

    6    Purchased cleaning supplies for $2,000 on account.

   14    Billed customers $3,700 for cleaning services performed.

   18    Paid $500 on amount owed on cleaning supplies.

   20    Paid $1,750 cash for employee salaries.

   21    Collected $1,600 cash from customers billed on March 14.

   28    Billed customers $4,200 for cleaning services performed.

   31    Paid $350 for gas and oil used in the truck during the month (use Maintenance and Repairs Expense).

   31    Declared and paid a $900 cash dividend.

The chart of accounts for Lars Cleaners contains the following accounts: Cash, Accounts Receivable, Supplies, Prepaid Insurance, Prepaid Rent, Equipment, Accumulated Depreciation—Equipment, Accounts Payable, Salaries and Wages Payable, Notes Payable, Interest Payable, Common Stock, Retained Earnings, Dividends, Income Summary, Service Revenue, Maintenance and Repairs Expense, Supplies Expense, Depreciation Expense, Insurance Expense, Salaries and Wages Expense, Rent Expense, and Interest Expense.

**Instructions**

**a.** Journalize the March transactions.

**b.** Post to the ledger accounts. (Use T-accounts.)

**c.** Prepare a trial balance at March 31.

**d.** Journalize the following adjustments.

    **1.** Services performed but unbilled and uncollected at March 31 were $200.

    **2.** Depreciation on equipment for the month was $250.

    **3.** One-sixth of the insurance expired.

    **4.** An inventory count shows $280 of cleaning supplies on hand at March 31.

    **5.** Accrued but unpaid employee salaries were $1,080.

    **6.** One month of the prepaid rent has expired.

    **7.** One month of interest expense related to the note payable has accrued and will be paid April 1. (*Hint:* Use the formula from Illustration 3.18 to compute interest.)

**e.** Post adjusting entries to the T-accounts.

f. Tot. adj. trial balance $31,960

**f.** Prepare an adjusted trial balance.

g. Tot. assets $24,730

**g.** Prepare the income statement and a retained earnings statement for March and a classified balance sheet at March 31.

**h.** Journalize and post closing entries and complete the closing process.

**i.** Prepare a post-closing trial balance at March 31.

**ACR4.3** On August 1, 2022, the following were the account balances of B&E Repair Services.

*Journalize transactions and follow through accounting cycle to preparation of financial statements.*

| | **Debit** | | **Credit** |
|---|---|---|---|
| Cash | $ 6,040 | Accumulated Depreciation—Equipment | $ 500 |
| Accounts Receivable | 2,910 | Accounts Payable | 2 300 |
| Notes Receivable | 4,000 | Unearned Service Revenue | 1 260 |
| Supplies | 1,030 | Salaries and Wages Payable | 1 420 |
| Equipment | 10,000 | Common Stock | 12 000 |
| | | Retained Earnings | 6 400 |
| | $23,980 | | $23 980 |

During August, the following transactions occurred.

Aug. 1   Paid $400 cash for advertising in local newspapers. Advertising flyers will be included with newspapers delivered during August and September.
  3   Paid August rent $380.
  5   Received $1,200 cash from customers in payment on account.
  10   Paid $3,120 for salaries due employees, of which $1,700 is for August and $1,420 is for July salaries payable.
  12   Received $2,800 cash for services performed in August.
  15   Purchased store equipment on account $2,000.
  20   Paid creditors $2,000 of accounts payable due.
  22   Purchased supplies on account $800.
  25   Paid $2,900 cash for employees' salaries.
  27   Billed customers $3,760 for services performed.
  29   Received $780 from customers for services to be performed in the future.

Adjustment data:

1. A count shows supplies on hand of $960.
2. Accrued but unpaid employees' salaries are $1,540.
3. Depreciation on equipment for the month is $320.
4. Services were performed to satisfy $800 of unearned service revenue.
5. One month's worth of advertising services has been received.
6. One month of interest revenue related to the $4,000 note receivable should be accrued. The 4-month note has a 6% annual interest rate. (*Hint:* Use the formula from Illustration 3.18 to compute interest.)

**Instructions**

a. Enter the August 1 balances in the ledger accounts. (Use T-accounts.)
b. Journalize the August transactions.
c. Post to the ledger accounts. B&B's chart of accounts includes Prepaid Advertising, Interest Receivable, Service Revenue, Interest Revenue, Advertising Expense, Depreciation Expense, Supplies Expense, Salaries and Wages Expense, and Rent Expense.
d. Prepare a trial balance at August 31.
e. Journalize and post adjusting entries.
f. Prepare an adjusted trial balance.
g. Prepare an income statement and a retained earnings statement for August and a classified balance sheet at August 31.
h. Journalize and post closing entries and complete the closing process.
i. Prepare a post-closing trial balance at August 31.

f. Cash $2,020
   Tot. adj. trial
     balance $32,580

g. Net loss $530

**ACR4.4** At June 30, 2022, the end of its most recent fiscal year, Green River Computer Consultants' post-closing trial balance was as follows:

*Record and post transaction, adjusting, and closing journal entries; prepare adjusted trial balance and financial statements.*

| | **Debit** | **Credit** |
|---|---|---|
| Cash | $5,230 | |
| Accounts receivable | 1,200 | |
| Supplies | 690 | |
| Accounts payable | | $ 400 |
| Unearned service revenue | | 1,120 |
| Common stock | | 3,600 |
| Retained earnings | | 2,000 |
| | $7,120 | $7,120 |

The company underwent a major expansion in July. New staff was hired and more financing was obtained. Green River conducted the following transactions during July 2022, and adjusts its accounts monthly.

July  1   Purchased equipment, paying $4,000 cash and signing a 2-year note payable for $20,000. The equipment has a 4-year useful life. The note has a 6% interest rate, with interest payable on the first day of each following month.

2   Issued 20,000 shares of common stock for $50,000 cash.

3   Paid $3,600 cash for a 12-month insurance policy effective July 1.

3   Paid the first 2 months' rent (July and August 2022) for an annual lease of office space for $4,000 per month.

6   Paid $3,800 for supplies.

9   Visited client offices and agreed on the terms of a consulting project. Green River will bill the client, Connor Productions, on the 20th of each month for services performed.

10   Collected $1,200 cash on account from Milani Brothers. This client was billed in June when Green River performed the service.

13   Performed services for Fitzgerald Enterprises. This client paid $1,120 in advance last month. All services relating to this payment are now completed.

14   Paid $400 cash for a utility bill. This related to June utilities that were accrued at the end of June.

16   Met with a new client, Thunder Bay Technologies. Received $12,000 cash in advance for future services to be performed.

18   Paid semi-monthly salaries for $11,000.

20   Performed services worth $28,000 on account and billed customers.

20   Received a bill for $2,200 for advertising services received during July. The amount is not due until August 15.

23   Performed the first phase of the project for Thunder Bay Technologies. Recognized $10,000 of revenue from the cash advance received July 16.

27   Received $15,000 cash from customers billed on July 20.

Adjustment data:

1.  Adjustment of prepaid insurance.

2.  Adjustment of prepaid rent.

3.  Supplies used, $1,250.

4.  Equipment depreciation, $500 per month.

5.  Accrual of interest on note payable. (*Hint:* Use the formula from Illustration 3.18 to compute interest.)

6.  Salaries for the second half of July, $11,000, to be paid on August 1.

7.  Estimated utilities expense for July, $800 (invoice will be received in August).

8.  Income tax for July, $1,200, will be paid in August. (*Hint:* Use the accounts Income Tax Expense and Income Taxes Payable.)

The chart of accounts for Green River Computer Consultants contains the following accounts: Cash, Accounts Receivable, Supplies, Prepaid Insurance, Prepaid Rent, Equipment, Accumulated Depreciation—Equipment, Accounts Payable, Notes Payable, Interest Payable, Income Taxes Payable, Salaries and Wages Payable, Unearned Service Revenue, Common Stock, Retained Earnings, Income Summary, Service Revenue, Supplies Expense, Depreciation Expense, Insurance Expense, Salaries and Wages Expense, Advertising Expense, Income Tax Expense, Interest Expense, Rent Expense, and Utilities Expense.

### Instructions

a.  Enter the July 1 balances in the ledger accounts. (Use T-accounts.)

b.  Journalize the July transactions.

c.  Post to the ledger accounts.

d.  Prepare a trial balance at July 31.

e.  Journalize and post adjusting entries for the month ending July 31.

f.  Prepare an adjusted trial balance.

g.  Prepare an income statement and a retained earnings statement for July and a classified balance sheet at July 31.

h.  Journalize and post closing entries and complete the closing process.

i.  Prepare a post-closing trial balance at July 31.

g. Net income $6,770
   Tot. assets $99,670

# Expand Your Critical Thinking

### Financial Reporting Problem: Apple Inc.

**CT4.1**  The financial statements of **Apple Inc.** are presented in Appendix A. The complete annual report, including the notes to the financial statements, is available at the company's website.

**Instructions**

Answer the questions below using Apple's Consolidated Balance Sheets.

   **a.** What were Apple's total current assets at September 29, 2018, and September 30, 2017?

   **b.** Are assets that Apple included under current assets listed in proper order? Explain.

   **c.** How are Apple's assets classified?

   **d.** What was Apple's "Cash and cash equivalents" at September 29, 2018?

   **e.** What were Apple's total current liabilities at September 29, 2018, and September 30, 2017?

### Comparative Analysis Problem: PepsiCo, Inc. vs. The Coca-Cola Company

**CT4.2**  **PepsiCo**'s financial statements are presented in Appendix B. Financial statements of **The Coca-Cola Company** are presented in Appendix C. The complete annual reports of PepsiCo and Coca-Cola, including the notes to the financial statements, are available at each company's respective website.

**Instructions**

   **a.** Based on the information contained in these financial statements, determine each of the following for PepsiCo at December 29, 2018, and for Coca-Cola at December 31, 2018.

   **1.** Total current assets.

   **2.** Net amount of property, plant, and equipment (land, buildings, and equipment).

   **3.** Total current liabilities.

   **4.** Total equity.

   **b.** What conclusions concerning the companies' respective financial positions can be drawn?

### Comparative Analysis Problem: Amazon.com, Inc. vs. Walmart Inc.

**CT4.3**  **Amazon.com, Inc.**'s financial statements are presented in Appendix D. Financial statements of **Walmart Inc.** are presented in Appendix E. The complete annual reports of Amazon and Walmart, including the notes to the financial statements, are available at each company's respective website.

**Instructions**

   **a.** Based on the information contained in these financial statements, determine the following for Amazon at December 31, 2018, and Walmart at January 31, 2019.

   **1.** Total current assets.

   **2.** Net amount of property and equipment (fixed assets).

   **3.** Total current liabilities.

   **4.** Total equity.

   **b.** What conclusions concerning these two companies can be drawn from these data?

### Real-World Focus

**CT4.4**  Numerous companies have established home pages on the Internet, e.g., the soda companies **Capt'n Eli Soda** and **Cheerwine**.

**Instructions**

Examine the home pages of any two companies and answer the following questions.

   **a.** What type of information is available?

   **b.** Is any accounting-related information presented?

   **c.** Would you describe the home page as informative, promotional, or both? Why?

## Decision-Making Across the Organization

**CT4.5** Whitegloves Janitorial Service was started 2 years ago by Lynn Sanders. Because business has been exceptionally good, Lynn decided on July 1, 2022, to expand operations by acquiring an additional truck and hiring two more assistants. To finance the expansion, Lynn obtained on July 1, 2022, a $25,000, 10% bank loan, payable $10,000 on July 1, 2023, and the balance on July 1, 2024. The terms of the loan require the borrower to have $10,000 more current assets than current liabilities at December 31, 2022. If these terms are not met, the bank loan will be refinanced at 15% interest. At December 31, 2022, the accountant for Whitegloves Janitorial Service Inc. prepared the following balance sheet.

**Whitegloves Janitorial Service**
**Balance Sheet**
**December 31, 2022**

| Assets | | | Liabilities and Stockholders' Equity | | |
|---|---|---|---|---|---|
| Current assets | | | Current liabilities | | |
| Cash | $ 6,500 | | Notes payable | $10,000 | |
| Accounts receivable | 9,000 | | Accounts payable | 2,500 | |
| Supplies | 5,200 | | Total current liabilities | | $12,500 |
| Prepaid insurance | 4,800 | | Long-term liability | | |
| Total current assets | | $25,500 | Notes payable | | 15,000 |
| Property, plant, and equipment | | | Total liabilities | | 27,500 |
| Equipment (net) | 22,000 | | Stockholders' equity | | |
| Delivery trucks (net) | 34,000 | | Common stock | 30,000 | |
| Total property, plant, and equipment | | 56,000 | Retained earnings | 24,000 | |
| | | | Total stockholders' equity | | 54,000 |
| Total assets | | $81,500 | Total liabilities and stockholders' equity | | $81,500 |

Lynn presented the balance sheet to the bank's loan officer on January 2, 2023, confident that the company had met the terms of the loan. The loan officer was not impressed. She said, "We need financial statements audited by a CPA." A CPA was hired and immediately realized that the balance sheet had been prepared from a trial balance and not from an adjusted trial balance. The adjustment data at the balance sheet date consisted of the following.

1. Unbilled janitorial services performed were $3,700.
2. Janitorial supplies on hand were $2,500.
3. Prepaid insurance was a 3-year policy dated January 1, 2022.
4. December expenses incurred but unpaid and unrecorded at December 31, $500.
5. Interest on the bank loan was not recorded.
6. The amounts for property, plant, and equipment presented in the balance sheet were reported net of accumulated depreciation (cost less accumulated depreciation). These amounts included accumulated depreciation of $4,000 for cleaning equipment and $5,000 for delivery trucks as of January 1, 2022. Depreciation expense for 2022 was $2,000 for cleaning equipment and $5,000 for delivery trucks.

### Instructions

With the class divided into groups, answer the following.

a. Prepare a correct balance sheet.
b. Were the terms of the bank loan met? Explain.

## Communication Activity

**CT4.6** The accounting cycle is important in understanding the accounting process.

### Instructions

Write a memorandum to your instructor that lists the steps of the accounting cycle in the order they should be completed. End with a paragraph that explains the optional steps in the cycle.

## Ethics Case

**CT4.7** As the controller of Take No Prisoners Perfume Company, you discover a misstatement that overstated net income in the prior year's financial statements. The misleading financial statements appear in the company's annual report, which was issued to banks and other creditors less than a month ago. After much thought about the consequences of telling the president, Jeb Wilde, about this misstatement, you gather your courage to inform him. Jeb says, "Hey! What they don't know won't hurt them. But, just so we set the record straight, we'll adjust this year's financial statements for last year's misstatement. We can absorb that misstatement better in this year than in last year anyway! Just don't make such a mistake again."

**Instructions**

a. Who are the stakeholders in this situation?

b. What are the ethical issues in this situation?

c. What would you do as a controller in this situation?

## All About You

**CT4.8** Companies prepare balance sheets in order to know their financial position at a specific point in time. This enables them to make a comparison to their position at previous points in time, and gives them a basis for planning for the future. In order to evaluate your financial position, you need to prepare a personal balance sheet. Assume that you have compiled the following information regarding your finances. (*Note:* Some of the items might not be used in your personal balance sheet.)

| | |
|---|---:|
| Amount owed on student loan (long-term) | $ 5,000 |
| Balance in checking account | 1,200 |
| Certificate of deposit (6-month) | 3,000 |
| Annual earnings from part-time job | 11,300 |
| Automobile | 7,000 |
| Balance on automobile loan (current portion) | 1,500 |
| Balance on automobile loan (long-term portion) | 4,000 |
| Home computer | 800 |
| Amount owed to you by younger brother | 300 |
| Balance in money market account | 1,800 |
| Annual tuition | 6,400 |
| Video and stereo equipment | 1,250 |
| Balance owed on credit card (current portion) | 150 |
| Balance owed on credit card (long-term portion) | 1,650 |

**Instructions**

Prepare a personal balance sheet using the format you have learned for a classified balance sheet for a company. For the equity account, use Owner's Equity and determine its balance using the accounting equation.

## FASB Codification Activity

**CT4.9** If your school has a subscription to the FASB Codification, log in and prepare responses to the following.

**Instructions**

a. Access the glossary ("Master Glossary") at the FASB Codification website to answer the following.

    1. What is the definition of current assets?

    2. What is the definition of current liabilities?

b. A company wants to offset its accounts payable against its cash account and show a cash amount net of accounts payable on its balance sheet. Identify the criteria (found in the FASB Codification) under which a company has the right of set off. Does the company have the right to offset accounts payable against the cash account?

## Answers to Insight and Accounting Across the Organization Questions

**Performing the Virtual Close** Q: Who else benefits from a shorter closing process? Q: Investors benefit from a shorter closing process. The shorter the closing, the sooner the company can report its financial results. This means that the financial information is timelier and therefore more relevant to investors.

**Lost in Translation  Q:** What might Yale Express's vice president have done to produce more accurate financial statements without waiting months for Republic's outstanding transportation bills? **A:** Yale's vice president could have engaged his accountants and auditors to prepare an adjusting entry based on an estimate of the outstanding transportation bills. (The estimate could have been made using past experience and the current volume of business.)

**Regaining Goodwill  Q:** Name two industries today that are probably rated low on the reputational characteristics of "being trusted" and "having high ethical standards." **A:** Two possible industries are financial companies (**Goldman Sachs** or **AIG**) and oil companies (**BP**).

**Can a Company Be Too Liquid?  Q:** What can various company managers do to ensure that working capital is managed efficiently to maximize net income? **A:** Marketing and sales managers must understand that by extending generous repayment terms, they are expanding the company's receivables balance and slowing the company's cash flow. Production managers must strive to minimize the amount of excess inventory on hand. Managers must coordinate efforts to speed up the collection of receivables, while also ensuring that the company pays its payables on time but never too early.

# A Look at IFRS

---

### LEARNING OBJECTIVE 6
Compare the procedures for the closing process under GAAP and IFRS.

---

The classified balance sheet, although generally required internationally, contains certain variations in format when reporting under IFRS.

## Key Points

Following are the key similarities and differences between GAAP and IFRS related to the closing process and the financial statements.

### Similarities

- The procedures of the closing process are applicable to all companies, whether they are using IFRS or GAAP.
- IFRS generally requires a classified statement of financial position similar to the classified balance sheet under GAAP.
- IFRS follows the same guidelines as this text for distinguishing between current and non-current assets and liabilities.

### Differences

- IFRS recommends but does not require the use of the title "statement of financial position" rather than "balance sheet."
- The format of statement of financial position information is often presented differently under IFRS. Although no specific format is required, many companies that follow IFRS present statement of financial position information in this order:
  - Non-current assets
  - Current assets
  - Equity
  - Non-current liabilities
  - Current liabilities
- Under IFRS, current assets are usually listed in the reverse order of liquidity. For example, under GAAP cash is listed first, but under IFRS it is listed last.
- IFRS has many differences in terminology from what is shown in your text. For example, in the following sample statement of financial position, notice in the investment category that stock is called shares.

## Franklin AG
### Statement of Financial Position
### October 31, 2022

### Assets

**Intangible assets**

| | | | |
|---|---|---|---|
| Patents | | | € 3,100 |

**Property, plant, and equipment**

| | | | |
|---|---|---|---|
| Land | | €10,000 | |
| Equipment | €24,000 | | |
| Less: Accumulated depreciation | 5,000 | 19,000 | 29,000 |

**Long-term investments**

| | | | |
|---|---|---|---|
| Share investments | | 5,200 | |
| Investment in real estate | | 2,000 | 7,200 |

**Current assets**

| | | | |
|---|---|---|---|
| Prepaid insurance | | 400 | |
| Supplies | | 2,100 | |
| Inventory | | 3,000 | |
| Notes receivable | | 1,000 | |
| Accounts receivable | | 7,000 | |
| Debt investments | | 2,000 | |
| Cash | | 6,600 | 22,100 |
| Total assets | | | €61,400 |

### Equity and Liabilities

**Equity**

| | | | |
|---|---|---|---|
| Share capital | | €20,000 | |
| Retained earnings | | 14,050 | €34,050 |

**Non-current liabilities**

| | | | |
|---|---|---|---|
| Mortgage payable | | 10,000 | |
| Notes payable | | 1,300 | 11,300 |

**Current liabilities**

| | | | |
|---|---|---|---|
| Notes payable | | 11,000 | |
| Accounts payable | | 2,100 | |
| Salaries and wages payable | | 1,600 | |
| Unearned service revenue | | 900 | |
| Interest payable | | 450 | 16,050 |
| Total equity and liabilities | | | €61,400 |

- Both GAAP and IFRS are increasing the use of fair value to report assets. However, at this point IFRS has adopted it more broadly. As examples, under IFRS companies can apply fair value to property, plant, and equipment, and in some cases to intangible assets.

# IFRS Practice

## IFRS Self-Test Questions

1. A company has purchased a tract of land and expects to build a production plant on the land in approximately 5 years. During the 5 years before construction, the land will be idle. Under IFRS, the land should be reported as:
   a. land expense.
   b. property, plant, and equipment.
   c. an intangible asset.
   d. a long-term investment.

2. Current assets under IFRS are listed generally:
   a. by importance.
   b. in the reverse order of their expected conversion to cash.
   c. by longevity.
   d. alphabetically.

3. Companies that follow IFRS:
   a. use the term stock instead of shares for investments.
   b. may offset assets against liabilities and show net assets and net liabilities on their statements of financial position, rather than the underlying detailed line items.

c. may report non-current assets before current assets on the statement of financial position.

d. do not have any guidelines as to what should be reported on the statement of financial position.

4. Companies that follow IFRS to prepare a statement of financial position generally use the following order of classification:

a. current assets, current liabilities, non-current assets, non-current liabilities, equity.

b. non-current assets, non-current liabilities, current assets, current liabilities, equity.

c. non-current assets, current assets, equity, non-current liabilities, current liabilities.

d. equity, non-current assets, current assets, non-current liabilities, current liabilities.

## IFRS Exercises

**IFRS4.1** In what ways does the format of a statement of financial of position under IFRS often differ from a balance sheet presented under GAAP?

**IFRS4.2** What term is commonly used under IFRS in reference to the balance sheet?

**IFRS4.3** The statement of financial position for Sundell Company at December 31, 2022, includes the following accounts (in British pounds): Accounts Receivable £12,500, Prepaid Insurance £3,600, Cash £15,400, Supplies £5,200, and Debt Investments (short-term) £6,700. Prepare the current assets section of the statement of financial position, listing the accounts in proper sequence.

**IFRS4.4** The following information is available for Lessila Bowling Alley at December 31, 2022.

| | | | |
|---|---|---|---|
| Buildings | $128,800 | Share Capital | $100,000 |
| Accounts Receivable | 14,520 | Retained Earnings (beginning) | 15,000 |
| Prepaid Insurance | 4,680 | Accumulated Depreciation—Buildings | 42,600 |
| Cash | 18,040 | Accounts Payable | 12,300 |
| Equipment | 62,400 | Notes Payable | 97,780 |
| Land | 64,000 | Accumulated Depreciation—Equipment | 18,720 |
| Insurance Expense | 780 | Interest Payable | 2,600 |
| Depreciation Expense | 7,360 | Bowling Revenues | 14,180 |
| Interest Expense | 2,600 | | |

Prepare a classified statement of financial position. Assume that $13,900 of the notes payable will be paid in 2023.

## International Comparative Analysis Problem: Apple vs. Louis Vuitton

**IFRS4.5** The financial statements of **Louis Vuitton** are presented in Appendix F. The complete consolidated financial statements, including the notes to its financial statements, are available at the company's website.

### Instructions

Identify five differences in the format of the statement of financial position used by Louis Vuitton compared with that of a company, such as **Apple**, that follows GAAP. (Apple's financial statements are available in Appendix A.)

### Answers to IFRS Self-Test Questions

1. d  2. b  3. c  4. c

iStock.com/omgimages

# Accounting for Merchandising Operations

## Chapter Preview

Merchandising is one of the largest and most influential industries in the United States. It is likely that a number of you will work for a merchandiser. Therefore, understanding the financial statements of merchandising companies is important. In this chapter, you will learn the basics about reporting merchandising transactions. In addition, you will learn how to prepare and analyze a commonly used form of the income statement—the multiple-step income statement.

## Feature Story

### Buy Now, Vote Later

Have you ever shopped for outdoor gear at an **REI (Recreational Equipment, Inc.)** store? If so, you might have been surprised if a salesclerk asked if you were a member. A

member? What do you mean a member? REI is a consumer cooperative, or "co-op" for short. To figure out what that means, consider this:

As a cooperative, the Company is owned by its members. Each member is entitled to one vote in the election of the Company's Board of Directors. Recent data show that we have more than 18 million members.

Voting rights? Now that's something you don't get from shopping at **Walmart**. REI members get other benefits as well, including sharing in the company's profits through a dividend at the end of the year. The more you spend, the bigger your dividend.

Since REI is a co-op, you might also wonder whether management's incentives might be a little different than at other stores. Management is still concerned about making a profit, as it ensures the long-term viability of the company. REI's members also want the company to be run efficiently, so that prices remain low. In order for its members to evaluate just how well management is doing, REI publishes an audited annual report, just like publicly traded companies do.

How well is this business model working for REI? Well, it has consistently been rated as one of the best places to work in the United States by *Fortune* magazine. It is one of only five companies named each year since the list was created in 1998. Also, REI had sustainable business practices long before social responsibility became popular at other companies. As the CEO's stewardship report states, "we reduced the absolute amount of energy we use despite opening four new stores and growing our business; we grew the amount of FSC-certified paper we use to 58.4 percent of our total paper footprint—including our cash register receipt paper; we facilitated 2.2 million volunteer hours and we provided $3.7 million to more than 330 conservation and recreation nonprofits."

So, while REI, like other retailers, closely monitors its financial results, it also strives to succeed in other areas. And, with over 10 million votes at stake, REI's management knows that it has to deliver.

# Chapter Outline

| LEARNING OBJECTIVES | REVIEW | PRACTICE |
|---|---|---|
| **LO 1** Describe merchandising operations and inventory systems. | • Operating cycles <br> • Flow of costs | **DO IT! 1** Merchandising Operations and Inventory Systems |
| **LO 2** Record purchases under a perpetual inventory system. | • Freight costs <br> • Purchase returns and allowances <br> • Purchase discounts <br> • Summary of purchasing transactions | **DO IT! 2** Purchase Transactions |
| **LO 3** Record sales under a perpetual inventory system. | • Sales returns and allowances <br> • Sales discounts <br> • Data analytics and credit sales | **DO IT! 3** Sales Transactions |
| **LO 4** Apply the steps in the accounting cycle to a merchandising company. | • Adjusting entries <br> • Closing entries <br> • Summary of merchandising entries | **DO IT! 4** Closing Entries |
| **LO 5** Prepare a multiple-step income statement. | • Multiple-step income statement <br> • Single-step income statement <br> • Classified balance sheet | **DO IT! 5** Multiple-Step Income Statement |

**Go to the Review and Practice section at the end of the chapter for a review of key concepts and practice applications with solutions.**

**Visit WileyPLUS for additional tutorials and practice opportunities.**

# Merchandising Operations and Inventory Systems

## LEARNING OBJECTIVE 1
Describe merchandising operations and inventory systems.

**REI**, **Walmart Inc.**, and **Amazon.com** are called merchandising companies because they buy and sell merchandise rather than perform services as their primary source of revenue. Merchandising companies that purchase and sell directly to consumers are called **retailers**. Merchandising companies that sell to retailers are known as **wholesalers**. For example, retailer **Walgreens** might buy goods from wholesaler **McKesson**. Retailer **Office Depot** might buy office supplies from wholesaler **United Stationers**. The primary source of revenue for merchandising companies is the sale of merchandise, often referred to simply as **sales revenue** or **sales**. A merchandising company has two categories of expenses: cost of goods sold and operating expenses.

**Cost of goods sold** is the total cost of merchandise sold during the period. This expense is directly related to the revenue recognized from the sale of goods. **Illustration 5.1** shows the income measurement process for a merchandising company. The items in the two blue boxes are unique to a merchandising company; they are not used by a service company.

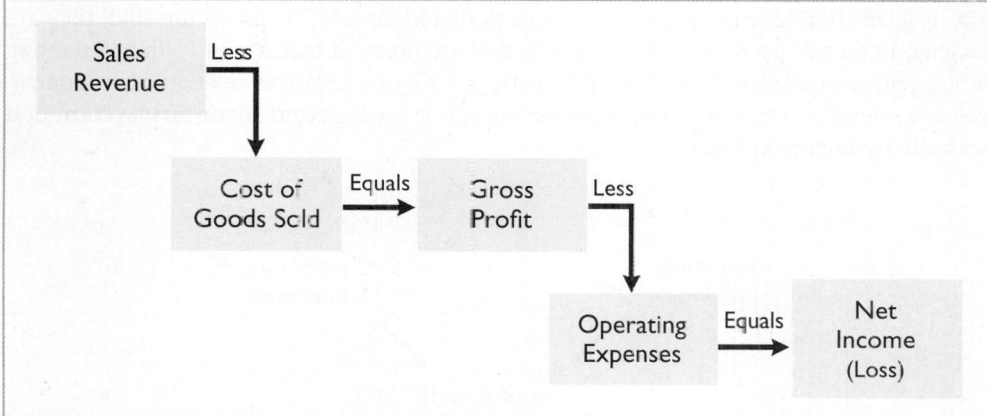

**ILLUSTRATION 5.1**

**Income measurement process for a merchandising company**

## Operating Cycles

The operating cycle of a merchandising company is ordinarily longer than that of a service company. The purchase of merchandise inventory and its eventual sale lengthen the cycle. **Illustration 5.2** shows the operating cycle of a service company.

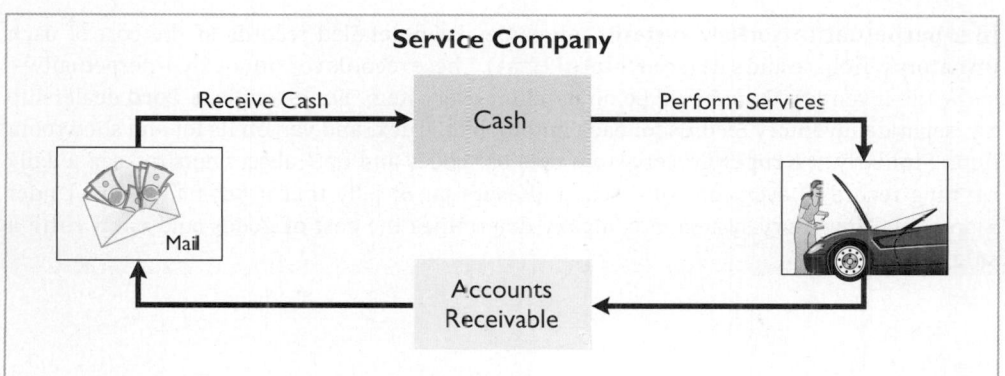

**ILLUSTRATION 5.2**

**Operating cycle for a service company**

Illustration 5.3 shows the operating cycle of a merchandising company.

**ILLUSTRATION 5.3**

Operating cycle for a merchandising company

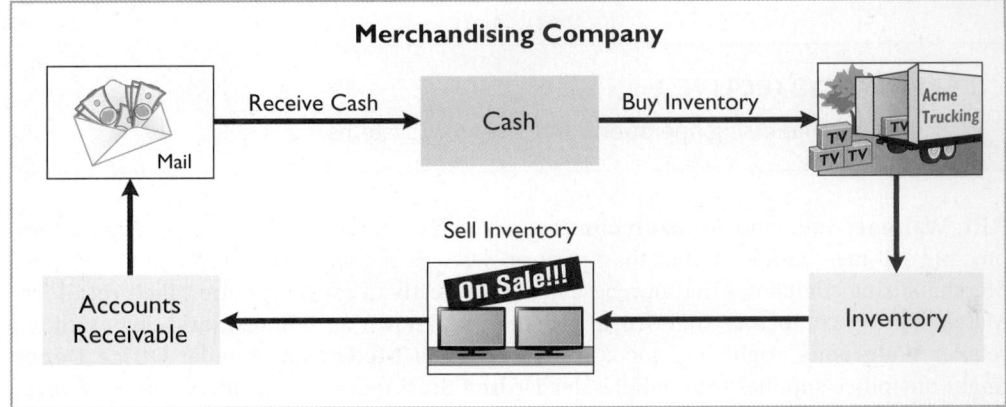

Note that the added asset account for a merchandising company is the Inventory account. Companies report inventory as a current asset on the balance sheet.

## Flow of Costs

The flow of costs for a merchandising company is as follows. Beginning inventory plus the cost of goods purchased is the cost of goods available for sale. As goods are sold, they are assigned to cost of goods sold. Those goods that are not sold by the end of the accounting period represent ending inventory. **Illustration 5.4** describes these relationships. Companies use one of two systems to account for inventory: a **perpetual inventory system** or a **periodic inventory system**.

**ILLUSTRATION 5.4**

Flow of costs

## Perpetual System

HELPFUL HINT

Even under perpetual inventory systems, companies take a physical inventory count. This is done as a control procedure to verify inventory levels, in order to detect theft or "shrinkage."

In a **perpetual inventory system**, companies keep detailed records of the cost of each inventory purchase and sale (see **Helpful Hint**). These records continuously—perpetually—show the inventory that should be on hand for every item. For example, a **Ford** dealership has separate inventory records for each automobile, truck, and van on its lot and showroom floor. Similarly, a **Kroger** grocery store uses bar codes and optical scanners to keep a daily running record of every box of cereal and every jar of jelly that it buys and sells. Under a perpetual inventory system, a company determines the cost of goods sold **each time a sale occurs**.

## Periodic System

In a **periodic inventory system**, companies do not keep detailed inventory records of the goods on hand throughout the period. Instead, they determine the cost of goods sold **only at the end of the accounting period**—that is, periodically. At that point, the company takes a physical inventory count to determine the cost of goods on hand.

To determine the cost of goods sold under a periodic inventory system, the following steps are necessary:

1. Determine the cost of goods on hand at the beginning of the accounting period.
2. Add to it the cost of goods purchased.
3. Subtract the cost of goods on hand as determined by the physical inventory count at the end of the accounting period.

**Illustration 5.5** compares the sequence of activities and the timing of the cost of goods sold computation under the two inventory systems.

**ILLUSTRATION 5.5**

**Comparing perpetual and periodic inventory systems**

## Advantages of the Perpetual System

Companies that sell merchandise with high unit values, such as automobiles, furniture, and major home appliances, have traditionally used perpetual systems. The growing use of computers and electronic scanners has enabled many more companies to install perpetual inventory systems. The perpetual inventory system is so named because the accounting records continuously—perpetually—show the quantity and cost of the inventory that should be on hand at any time.

A perpetual inventory system provides better control over inventories than a periodic system. Since the inventory records show the quantities that should be on hand, the company can count the goods at any time to see whether the amount of goods actually on hand agrees with the inventory records. If shortages are uncovered, the company can investigate immediately. Although a perpetual inventory system requires both additional clerical work and expense to maintain the subsidiary records, a computerized system can minimize this cost. Much of **Amazon.com**'s success is attributed to its sophisticated inventory system.

Some businesses find it either unnecessary or uneconomical to invest in a sophisticated, computerized perpetual inventory system such as Amazon's. Many small merchandising businesses now use basic accounting software, which provides some of the essential benefits of a perpetual inventory system. Also, managers of some small businesses still find that they can control their merchandise and manage day-to-day operations using a periodic inventory system.

**Because of the widespread use of the perpetual inventory system, we illustrate it in this chapter.** We discuss and illustrate the periodic system in Appendix 5B.

---

**Investor Insight**    Morrow Snowboards, Inc.

iStock.com/Ben Blankenburg

### Improving Stock Appeal

Investors are often eager to invest in a company that has a hot new product. However, when snowboard-maker **Morrow Snowboards, Inc.** (now part of **K2 Sports**) issued shares of stock to the public for the first time, some investors expressed reluctance to invest in Morrow because of a number of accounting control problems. To reduce investor concerns, Morrow implemented a perpetual inventory system to improve its control over inventory. In addition, the company stated that it would perform a physical inventory count every quarter until it felt that its perpetual inventory system was reliable.

**If a perpetual system keeps track of inventory on a daily basis, why do companies ever need to do a physical count? (Answer is available near the end of the chapter.)**

---

**ACTION PLAN**
- **Review merchandising concepts.**
- **Understand the flow of costs in a merchandising company.**

### DO IT! 1 | Merchandising Operations and Inventory Systems

Indicate whether the following statements are true or false. If false, indicate how to correct the statement.

1. The primary source of revenue for a merchandising company results from performing services for customers.
2. The operating cycle of a service company is usually shorter than that of a merchandising company.
3. Sales revenue less cost of goods sold equals gross profit.
4. Ending inventory plus the cost of goods purchased equals cost of goods available for sale.

#### Solution

1. False. The primary source of revenue for a service company (not a merchandising company) results from performing services for customers. Merchandising companies sell products.   2. True.
3. True.   4. False. Beginning inventory plus the cost of goods purchased equals cost of goods available for sale.

Related exercise material: **BE5.1, BE5.2, DO IT! 5.1, and E5.1.**

---

# Recording Purchases Under a Perpetual System

### LEARNING OBJECTIVE 2
Record purchases under a perpetual inventory system.

Companies purchase inventory using cash or credit (on account). They normally record purchases when they receive the goods from the seller. Every purchase should be supported by business documents that provide written evidence of the transaction. Each cash purchase should be supported by a canceled check or a cash register receipt indicating the items purchased and amounts paid. Companies record cash purchases by an increase in Inventory and a decrease in Cash.

A **purchase invoice** should support each credit purchase. This invoice indicates the total purchase price and other relevant information. However, the purchaser does not prepare a separate purchase invoice. Instead, the purchaser uses as a purchase invoice a copy of the sales invoice sent by the seller. In **Illustration 5.6**, for example, Sauk Stereo (the buyer) uses as a purchase invoice the sales invoice prepared by PW Audio Supply, Inc. (the seller).

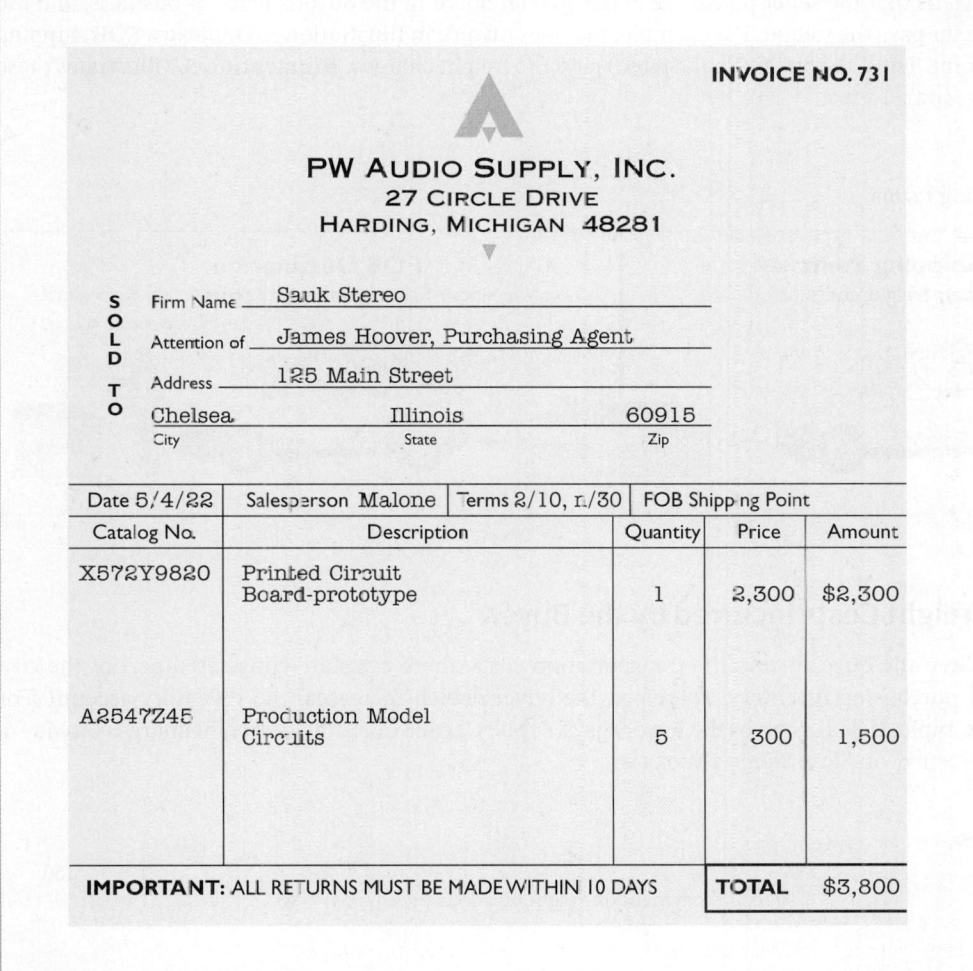

**ILLUSTRATION 5.6**
**Sales invoice used as purchase invoice by Sauk Stereo**

To better understand the contents of this invoice, identify these items:
1. Seller
2. Invoice date
3. Purchaser
4. Salesperson
5. Credit terms
6. Freight terms
7. Goods sold: catalog number, description, quantity, price per unit
8. Total invoice amount

Sauk Stereo makes the following journal entry to record its purchase from PW Audio Supply on account. The entry increases (debits) Inventory and increases (credits) Accounts Payable.

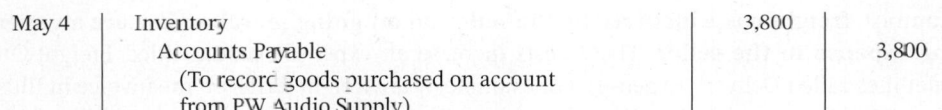

| May 4 | Inventory | 3,800 | |
| | Accounts Payable | | 3,800 |
| | (To record goods purchased on account from PW Audio Supply) | | |

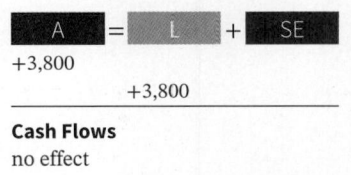

Under the perpetual inventory system, companies record purchases of merchandise for resale in the Inventory account. Not all purchases are debited to Inventory, however. Recall that companies record purchases of assets acquired for use and not for resale, such as supplies and equipment, as increases to specific asset accounts rather than to Inventory. For example, to record the purchase of materials used to make shelf signs or for cash register receipt paper, Sauk Stereo would increase (debit) Supplies.

# Freight Costs

The sales agreement should indicate who—the seller or the buyer—is to pay for transporting the goods to the buyer's place of business. When a common carrier such as a railroad, trucking company, or airline transports the goods, the carrier prepares a freight bill in accord with the sales agreement.

Freight terms are expressed as either FOB shipping point or FOB destination. The letters FOB mean **free on board**. Thus, **FOB shipping point** means that the seller places the goods free on board the carrier, and the buyer pays the freight costs. Conversely, **FOB destination** means that the seller places the goods free on board to the buyer's place of business, and the seller pays the freight. For example, the sales invoice in Illustration 5.6 indicates FOB shipping point. Thus, the buyer (Sauk Stereo) pays the freight charges. **Illustration 5.7** illustrates these shipping terms.

**ILLUSTRATION 5.7** Shipping terms

## Freight Costs Incurred by the Buyer

When the buyer incurs the transportation costs, these costs are considered part of the cost of purchasing inventory. Therefore, the buyer debits (increases) the Inventory account. For example, if Sauk Stereo (the buyer) pays Public Carrier Co. $150 for freight charges on May 6, the entry on Sauk Stereo's books is:

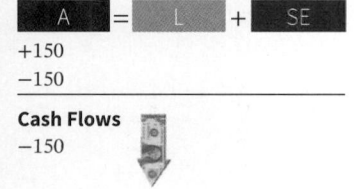

| May 6 | Inventory | 150 | |
| | Cash | | 150 |
| | (To record payment of freight on goods purchased) | | |

Thus, any freight costs incurred by the buyer are part of the cost of merchandise purchased. The reason: Inventory cost should include all costs to acquire the inventory, including freight necessary to deliver the goods to the buyer. Companies recognize these costs as cost of goods sold when inventory is sold.

## Freight Costs Incurred by the Seller

In contrast, **freight costs incurred by the seller on outgoing merchandise are an operating expense to the seller**. These costs increase an expense account titled Freight-Out (sometimes called Delivery Expense). For example, if the freight terms on the invoice in Illustration 5.6 had required PW Audio Supply (the seller) to pay the freight charges, the entry by PW Audio Supply would be:

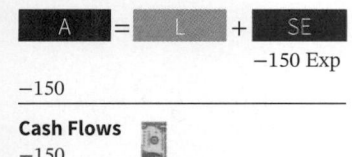

| May 4 | Freight-Out (or Delivery Expense) | 150 | |
| | Cash | | 150 |
| | (To record payment of freight on goods sold) | | |

When the seller pays the freight charges, the seller will usually establish a higher invoice price for the goods to cover the shipping expense.

## Purchase Returns and Allowances

A purchaser may be dissatisfied with the merchandise received because the goods are damaged or defective, of inferior quality, or do not meet the purchaser's specifications. In such cases, the purchaser may return the goods to the seller for credit if the sale was made on credit, or for a cash refund if the purchase was for cash. This transaction is known as a **purchase return**. Alternatively, the purchaser may choose to keep the merchandise if the seller is willing to grant an allowance (deduction) from the purchase price. This transaction is known as a **purchase allowance**.

Assume that Sauk Stereo returned goods costing $300 to PW Audio Supply on May 8. The following entry by Sauk Stereo for the returned merchandise decreases (debits) Accounts Payable and decreases (credits) Inventory.

| May 8 | Accounts Payable | 300 | |
| | Inventory | | 300 |
| | (To record return of goods purchased from PW Audio Supply) | | |

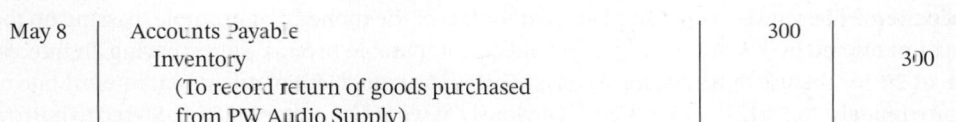

A = L + SE
−300
−300

**Cash Flows**
no effect

Because Sauk Stereo increased Inventory when the goods were received, Inventory is now decreased when Sauk Stereo returns the goods.

Suppose instead that Sauk Stereo chose to keep the goods after being granted a $50 allowance (reduction in price). It would reduce (debit) Accounts Payable and reduce (credit) Inventory for $50.

## Purchase Discounts

The credit terms of a purchase on account may permit the buyer to claim a cash discount for prompt payment. The buyer calls this cash discount a **purchase discount**. This incentive offers advantages to both parties. The purchaser saves money, and the seller is able to shorten its operating cycle by converting the accounts receivable into cash more quickly.

**Credit terms** specify the amount of the cash discount and time period in which it is offered. They also indicate the time period in which the purchaser is expected to pay the full invoice price if the discount is not taken. In the sales invoice in Illustration 5.6, credit terms are 2/10, n/30, which is read "two-ten, net thirty" (see **Helpful Hint**). This means that the buyer may take a 2% cash discount on the invoice price, less ("net of") any returns or allowances, if payment is made within 10 days of the invoice date (the **discount period**). Otherwise, the invoice price, less any returns or allowances, is due 30 days from the invoice date.

Alternatively, the discount period may extend to a specified number of days following the month in which the sale occurs. For example, 1/10 EOM (end of month) means that a 1% discount is available if the invoice is paid within the first 10 days of the next month.

When the seller elects not to offer a cash discount for prompt payment, credit terms will specify only the maximum time period for paying the balance due. For example, the invoice may state the time period as n/30, n/60, or n/10 EOM. This means, respectively, that the buyer must pay the net amount in 30 days, 60 days, or within the first 10 days of the next month.

When the buyer pays an invoice within the discount period, the amount of the discount decreases Inventory. Why? Because companies record inventory at cost, and by paying within the discount period, the buyer has reduced its cost. To illustrate, assume Sauk Stereo pays the balance due of $3,500 (gross invoice price of $3,800 less purchase returns and allowances of $300) on May 14, the last day of the discount period. Since the terms are 2/10, n/30, the cash discount is $70 ($3,500 × 2%) and Sauk Stereo pays $3,430 ($3,500 − $70). The entry Sauk Stereo makes to record its May 14 payment decreases (debits) Accounts Payable by the

> **HELPFUL HINT**
>
> The term *net* in "net 30" means the remaining amount due after subtracting any sales returns and allowances and partial payments.

net amount owed, reduces (credits) Inventory by the $70 discount, and reduces (credits) Cash by the net amount paid.

| | | A | = | L | + | SE |
|---|---|---|---|---|---|---|
| | | | | −3,500 | | |
| −3,430 | | | | | | |
| −70 | | | | | | |

**Cash Flows**
−3,430

| May 14 | Accounts Payable | 3,500 | |
|---|---|---|---|
| | Cash | | 3,430 |
| | Inventory | | 70 |
| | (To record payment within discount period) | | |

If Sauk Stereo failed to take the discount and instead made full payment of $3,500 on June 3 (after the expiration of the discount period), it would debit Accounts Payable and credit Cash for $3,500 each.

| | | A | = | L | + | SE |
|---|---|---|---|---|---|---|
| | | | | −3,500 | | |
| −3,500 | | | | | | |

**Cash Flows**
−3,500

| June 3 | Accounts Payable | 3,500 | |
|---|---|---|---|
| | Cash | | 3,500 |
| | (To record payment with no discount taken) | | |

A merchandising company should usually take all available discounts. Passing up the discount may be viewed as **paying interest** for use of the money. For example, passing up the discount offered by PW Audio Supply would be comparable to Sauk Stereo paying an interest rate of 2% for the use of $3,500 for 20 days. This is the equivalent of an annual interest rate of approximately 36.5% [2% × (365 ÷ 20)]. Obviously, it would be better for Sauk Stereo to borrow at prevailing bank interest rates of 6% to 10% than to lose the discount.

## Summary of Purchasing Transactions

The following T-account (with transaction descriptions in red) provides a summary of the effect of the previous transactions on Inventory. Sauk Stereo originally purchased $3,800 of inventory on account. It then returned $300 of goods. It paid $150 in freight charges, and finally, it received a $70 discount off the balance owed because it paid within the discount period. This results in a balance in Inventory of $3,580.

| | | Inventory | | | |
|---|---|---|---|---|---|
| Purchase | May 4 | 3,800 | May 8 | 300 | Purchase return |
| Freight-in | 6 | 150 | 14 | 70 | Purchase discount |
| Balance | | 3,580 | | | |

---

**ACTION PLAN**

- **Purchaser records goods at cost.**
- **When goods are returned, purchaser reduces Inventory.**

### DO IT! 2 | Purchase Transactions

On September 5, De La Hoya Company buys merchandise on account from Junot Diaz Company. The purchase price of the goods paid by De La Hoya is $1,500, and the cost to Diaz Company was $800. On September 8, De La Hoya returns defective goods with a selling price of $200. Record the transactions on the books of De La Hoya Company.

**Solution**

| Sept. 5 | Inventory | 1,500 | |
|---|---|---|---|
| | Accounts Payable | | 1,500 |
| | (To record goods purchased on account) | | |
| 8 | Accounts Payable | 200 | |
| | Inventory | | 200 |
| | (To record return of defective goods) | | |

Related exercise material: **BE5.3, BE5.5, DO IT! 5.2, E5.2, E5.3, E5.4, and E5.11.**

# Recording Sales Under a Perpetual System

**LEARNING OBJECTIVE 3**
Record sales under a perpetual inventory system.

In accordance with the revenue recognition principle, companies record sales revenue when the performance obligation is satisfied. Typically, the performance obligation is satisfied when the goods transfer from the seller to the buyer. At this point, the sales transaction is complete and the sales price established.

Sales may be made on credit or for cash. A **business document** should support every sales transaction, to provide written evidence of the sale. **Cash register documents** provide evidence of cash sales. A **sales invoice**, like the one shown in Illustration 5.6, provides support for a credit sale. The original copy of the invoice goes to the customer, and the seller keeps a copy for use in recording the sale. The invoice shows the date of sale, customer name, total sales price, and other relevant information.

The seller makes two entries for each sale. **The first entry records the sale**: The seller increases (debits) Cash (or Accounts Receivable if a credit sale) and also increases (credits) Sales Revenue. **The second entry records the cost of the merchandise sold**: The seller increases (debits) Cost of Goods Sold and also decreases (credits) Inventory for the cost of those goods. As a result, the Inventory account will show at all times the amount of inventory that should be on hand.

To illustrate a credit sales transaction, PW Audio Supply, Inc. records its May 4 sale of $3,800 to Sauk Stereo (see Illustration 5.6) as follows (assume the merchandise cost PW Audio Supply $2,400).

| May 4 | Accounts Receivable | 3,800 | |
| | Sales Revenue | | 3,800 |
| | (To record credit sale to Sauk Stereo per invoice #731) | | |
| 4 | Cost of Goods Sold | 2,400 | |
| | Inventory | | 2,400 |
| | (To record cost of merchandise sold on invoice #731 to Sauk Stereo) | | |

A = L + SE
+3,800
+3,800 Rev
**Cash Flows** no effect

A = L + SE
−2,400 Exp
−2,400
**Cash Flows** no effect

For internal decision-making purposes, merchandising companies may use more than one sales revenue account. For example, PW Audio Supply may decide to keep separate sales revenue accounts for its sales of TVs, Blu-ray players, and headsets. **REI** might use separate accounts for camping gear, children's clothing, and ski equipment—or it might have even more narrowly defined accounts. By using separate sales revenue accounts for major product lines, rather than a single combined sales revenue account, company management can more closely monitor sales trends and respond to changes in sales patterns more strategically. For example, if TV sales are increasing while Blu-ray player sales are decreasing, PW Audio Supply might reevaluate both its advertising and pricing policies on these items to ensure they are optimal.

On its income statement presented to outside investors, a merchandising company normally would report only a single sales figure—the sum of all of its individual sales revenue accounts. This is done for two reasons. First, providing detail on all of its individual sales revenue accounts would add considerable length to its income statement. Second, companies do not want their competitors to know the details of their operating results. However, **Microsoft** recently expanded its disclosure of revenue from three to five types. The reason: The additional categories enabled financial statement users to better evaluate the growth of the company's consumer and Internet businesses (see **Ethics Note**).

**ETHICS NOTE**
Many companies are trying to improve the quality of their financial reporting. For example, **General Electric** now provides more detail on its revenues and operating profits.

At the end of "Anatomy of a Fraud" stories, which describe some recent real-world frauds, we discuss the missing control activities that would likely have prevented or uncovered the fraud.

---

### Anatomy of a Fraud[1]

Holly Harmon was a cashier at a national superstore for only a short time when she began stealing merchandise using three methods. Under the first method, her husband or friends took UPC labels from cheaper items and put them on more expensive items. Holly then scanned the goods at the register. Using the second method, Holly scanned an item at the register but then voided the sale and left the merchandise in the shopping cart. A third approach was to put goods into large plastic containers. She scanned the plastic containers but not the goods within them. After Holly quit, a review of past surveillance tapes enabled the store to observe the thefts and to identify the participants.

**Total take: $12,000**

**The Missing Controls**

**Human resource controls.** A background check would have revealed Holly's previous criminal record. She would not have been hired as a cashier.

**Physical controls.** Software can flag high numbers of voided transactions or a high number of sales of low-priced goods. Random comparisons of video records with cash register records can ensure that the goods reported as sold on the register are the same goods that are shown being purchased on the video recording. Finally, employees should be aware that they are being monitored.

**Source:** Adapted from Wells, *Fraud Casebook* (2007), pp. 251–259.

---

## Sales Returns and Allowances

We now look at the "flip side" of purchase returns and allowances, which the seller records as **sales returns and allowances**. These are transactions where the seller either accepts goods back from the buyer (a return) or grants a reduction in the purchase price (an allowance) so the buyer will keep the goods. PW Audio Supply's entries to record returned goods involve two journal entries: (1) an increase (debit) in Sales Returns and Allowances (a contra account to Sales Revenue) and a decrease (credit) in Accounts Receivable at the $300 selling price, and (2) an increase (debit) in Inventory (assume a $140 cost) and a decrease (credit) in Cost of Goods Sold, as shown below (assuming that the goods were not defective).

A = L + SE
−300          −300 Rev
**Cash Flows**
no effect

A = L + SE
+140          +140 Exp
**Cash Flows**
no effect

| May 8 | Sales Returns and Allowances | 300 | |
| | Accounts Receivable | | 300 |
| | (To record credit granted to Sauk Stereo for returned goods) | | |

| 8 | Inventory | 140 | |
| | Cost of Goods Sold | | 140 |
| | (To record cost of goods returned) | | |

If Sauk Stereo returns goods because they are damaged or defective, then PW Audio Supply's entry to Inventory and Cost of Goods Sold should be for the fair value of the returned goods, rather than their cost. For example, if the returned goods were defective and had a fair value of $50, PW Audio Supply would debit Inventory for $50 and credit Cost of Goods Sold for $50.

What happens if the goods are not returned but the seller grants the buyer an allowance by reducing the purchase price? In this case, the seller debits Sales Returns and Allowances and credits Accounts Receivable for the amount of the allowance. An allowance has no impact on Inventory or Cost of Goods Sold since no items are returned.

---

[1] The "Anatomy of a Fraud" stories in this text are adapted from *Fraud Casebook: Lessons from the Bad Side of Business,* edited by Joseph T. Wells (Hoboken, NJ: John Wiley & Sons, Inc., 2007). Used by permission. The names of some of the people and organizations in the stories are fictitious, but the facts in the stories are true.

Sales Returns and Allowances is a **contra revenue account** to Sales Revenue. This means that it is offset against a revenue account on the income statement. The normal balance of Sales Returns and Allowances is a debit. Companies use a contra account, instead of debiting Sales Revenue, to track separately in the accounts and to report separately in the income statement the amount of sales returns and allowances. Disclosure of this information is important to management. Excessive returns and allowances may suggest problems—inferior merchandise, inaccuracies in filling orders, errors in billing customers, or delivery or shipment mistakes. Moreover, a decrease (debit) recorded directly to Sales Revenue would obscure the relative importance of sales returns and allowances as a percentage of sales. It also could distort comparisons between total sales in different accounting periods.

At the end of the accounting period, if the company anticipates that future sales returns and allowances will be material, the company should make an adjusting entry to estimate the amount of these returns. In some industries, such as those relating to the sale of books and periodicals, returns are often material. The accounting for situations where returns must be estimated is addressed in advanced accounting courses.

# Sales Discounts

As mentioned in our discussion of purchase transactions, the seller may offer the customer a cash discount—called by the seller a **sales discount**—for the prompt payment of the balance due. Like a purchase discount, a sales discount is based on the invoice price less returns and allowances, if any. The seller increases (debits) the Sales Discounts account for discounts that are taken. For example, PW Audio Supply makes the following entry to record the cash receipt on May 14 from Sauk Stereo within the discount period.

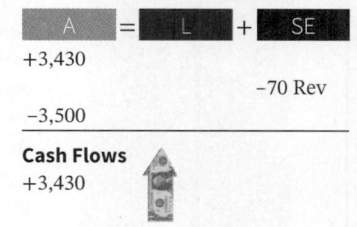

| May 14 | Cash | 3,430 | | +3,430 |
| | Sales Discounts | 70 | | −70 Rev |
| | Accounts Receivable | | 3,500 | −3,500 |
| | (To record collection within the discount period from Sauk Stereo) | | | |

Cash Flows +3,430

Like Sales Returns and Allowances, Sales Discounts is a **contra revenue account** to Sales Revenue. Its normal balance is a debit. PW Audio Supply uses this account, instead of debiting Sales Revenue, to track the amount of cash discounts taken by customers. If Sauk Stereo does not take the discount, PW Audio Supply increases (debits) Cash for $3,500 and decreases (credits) Accounts Receivable for the same amount at the date of collection.

At the end of the accounting period, if the amount of potential discounts is material, the company should make an adjusting entry to estimate the discounts. This would not usually be the case for sales discounts but might be necessary for other types of discounts, such as volume discounts, which are addressed in more advanced accounting courses.

The following T-accounts summarize the three sales-related transactions and show their combined effect on net sales for PW Audio Supply.

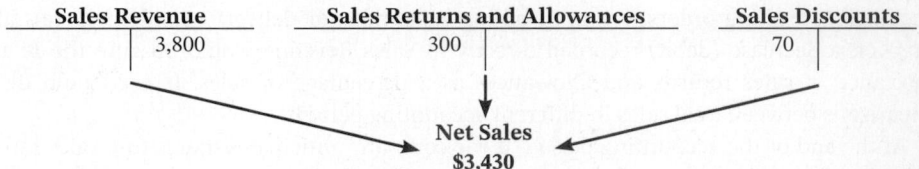

| Sales Revenue | Sales Returns and Allowances | Sales Discounts |
|---|---|---|
| 3,800 | 300 | 70 |

Net Sales
$3,430

# Data Analytics and Credit Sales

Increased access to ever larger amounts of data about customers, suppliers, products, and virtually every other aspect of a business has resulted in a greater reliance by companies on data analytics to support business decisions. Credit sales, sales returns and allowances, and sales discounts all provide rich opportunities for the use of data analytics.

First, the decision of whom to grant credit is very important. Offering credit to customers can substantially increase sales opportunities. However, some credit customers will ultimately not be able to pay the amounts owed. So offering credit to customers has costs. Effectively analyzing data regarding current as well as potential customers can help a company expand its sales base while minimizing the risk of unpaid receivables.

Similarly, companies must develop policies regarding sales return practices. Merchandisers know that generous return policies can enhance customer loyalty. But if returns become common, the company's profitability will suffer. In recent years, companies such as **Best Buy**, **REI**, and **Costco** have all refined their customer return policies, sometimes with unique rules for specific product types, as a result of data analytics applied to their data on product returns.

Finally, sales discounts are offered to customers to encourage early payment of receivables. Offering these discounts is costly. To achieve the optimal cost-benefit balance on sales discounts, companies statistically analyze past discount practices to determine how large the discount should be, how long the payment period should be, and other factors.

---

**People, Planet, and Profit Insight**   PepsiCo

Helen Sessions/Alamy Stock Photo

### Selling Green

Here is a question an executive of PepsiCo was asked: Should **PepsiCo** market green? The executive indicated that the company should, as he believes it's the No. 1 thing consumers all over the world care about. Here are some of his thoughts on this issue:

"Sun Chips are part of the food business I run. It's a 'healthy snack.' We decided that Sun Chips, if it's a healthy snack, should be made in facilities that have a net-zero footprint. In other words, I want off the electric grid everywhere we make Sun Chips. We did that. Sun Chips should be made in a facility that puts back more water than it uses. It does that. And we partnered with our suppliers and came out with the world's first compostable chip package.

Now, there was an issue with this package: It was louder than the New York subway, louder than jet engines taking off. What would a company that's committed to green do: walk away or stay committed? If your people are passionate, they're going to fix it for you as long as you stay committed. Six months later, the compostable bag has half the noise of our current package.

So the view today is: we should market green, we should be proud to do it . . . it has to be a 360-degree process, both internal and external. And if you do that, you can monetize environmental sustainability for the shareholders."

**Source:** "Four Problems—and Solutions," *Wall Street Journal* (March 7, 2011), p. R2.

**What is meant by "monetize environmental sustainability" for shareholders? (Answer is available near the end of the chapter.)**

## DO IT! 3 | Sales Transactions

On September 5, De La Hoya Company buys merchandise on account from Junot Diaz Company. The selling price of the goods is $1,500, and the cost to Diaz Company was $800. On September 8, De La Hoya returns defective goods with an initial selling price of $200 and a fair value of $30. Record the transactions on the books of Junot Diaz Company.

**Solution**

| | | | |
|---|---|---|---|
| Sept. 5 | Accounts Receivable | 1,500 | |
| | Sales Revenue | | 1,500 |
| | (To record credit sale) | | |
| 5 | Cost of Goods Sold | 800 | |
| | Inventory | | 800 |
| | (To record cost of goods sold) | | |
| 8 | Sales Returns and Allowances | 200 | |
| | Accounts Receivable | | 200 |
| | (To record credit granted for receipt of returned goods) | | |
| 8 | Inventory | 30 | |
| | Cost of Goods Sold | | 30 |
| | (To record fair value of goods returned) | | |

**ACTION PLAN**

- Seller records both the sale and the cost of goods sold at the time of the sale.
- When goods are returned, the seller records the return in a contra account, Sales Returns and Allowances, and reduces Accounts Receivable.
- Any goods returned increase Inventory and reduce Cost of Goods Sold. Defective or damaged inventory is recorded at fair value (scrap value).

Related exercise material: **BE5.3, BE5.4, DO IT! 5.3, E5.3, E5.4, E5.5, and E5.11.**

# The Accounting Cycle for a Merchandising Company

Up to this point, we have illustrated the basic entries for transactions relating to purchases and sales in a perpetual inventory system. Now we consider the remaining steps in the accounting cycle for a merchandising company. Each of the required steps described in Chapter 4 for service companies applies to merchandising companies. Appendix 5A to this chapter shows the use of a worksheet by a merchandiser (an optional step).

## Adjusting Entries

A merchandising company generally has the same types of adjusting entries as a service company. However, a merchandiser using a perpetual system will require one additional adjustment to make the records agree with the actual inventory on hand. Here's why: At the end of each period, for control purposes, a merchandising company that uses a perpetual system will take a physical count of its goods on hand. The company's unadjusted balance in Inventory usually does not agree with the actual amount of inventory on hand. The perpetual inventory records may be incorrect due to recording errors, theft, or waste. Thus, the company needs to adjust the perpetual records to make the recorded inventory amount agree with the inventory on hand. **This involves adjusting Inventory and Cost of Goods Sold.**

For example, suppose that PW Audio Supply, Inc. has an unadjusted balance of $40,500 in Inventory. Through a physical count, PW Audio Supply determines that its actual merchandise inventory at December 31 is $40,000. The company would make an adjusting entry as follows.

| | | | |
|---|---|---|---|
| Dec. 31 | Cost of Goods Sold | 500 | |
| | Inventory ($40,500 – $40,000) | | 500 |
| | (To adjust inventory to physical count) | | |

| A | = | L | + | SE |
|---|---|---|---|---|
| −500 | | | | |
| | | | | −500 Exp |

**Cash Flows**
no effect

# Closing Entries

A merchandising company, like a service company, closes to Income Summary all accounts that affect net income. In journalizing, the company credits all temporary accounts with debit balances, and debits all temporary accounts with credit balances. It also closes both Income Summary and Dividends to Retained Earnings. The following are the closing entries for PW Audio Supply using assumed amounts from its year-end adjusted trial balance. Recall that Cost of Goods Sold is an expense account with a normal debit balance, and Sales Returns and Allowances and Sales Discounts are contra revenue accounts with normal debit balances (see **Helpful Hint**).

| | | | | |
|---|---|---|---:|---:|
| Dec. 31 | Sales Revenue | | 480,000 | |
| | Income Summary | | | 480,000 |
| | (To close income statement accounts with credit balances) | | | |
| 31 | Income Summary | | 450,000 | |
| | Sales Returns and Allowances | | | 12,000 |
| | Sales Discounts | | | 8,000 |
| | Cost of Goods Sold | | | 316,000 |
| | Salaries and Wages Expense | | | 64,000 |
| | Freight-Out | | | 7,000 |
| | Advertising Expense | | | 16,000 |
| | Utilities Expense | | | 17,000 |
| | Depreciation Expense | | | 8,000 |
| | Insurance Expense | | | 2,000 |
| | (To close income statement accounts with debit balances) | | | |
| 31 | Income Summary | | 30,000 | |
| | Retained Earnings | | | 30,000 |
| | (To close net income to retained earnings) | | | |
| 31 | Retained Earnings | | 15,000 | |
| | Dividends | | | 15,000 |
| | (To close dividends to retained earnings) | | | |

After PW Audio Supply has posted the closing entries, all temporary accounts have zero balances. Also, Retained Earnings has a balance that is carried over to the next period.

# Summary of Merchandising Entries

**Illustration 5.8** summarizes the entries for the merchandising accounts using a perpetual inventory system.

**ILLUSTRATION 5.8**  Daily recurring and adjusting and closing entries

| | Transactions | Daily Recurring Entries | Dr. | Cr. |
|---|---|---|---|---|
| **Sales Transactions** | Selling merchandise to customers. | Cash or Accounts Receivable | XX | |
| | | Sales Revenue | | XX |
| | | Cost of Goods Sold | XX | |
| | | Inventory | | XX |
| | Granting sales returns or allowances to customers. | Sales Returns and Allowances | XX | |
| | | Cash or Accounts Receivable | | XX |
| | | Inventory | XX | |
| | | Cost of Goods Sold | | XX |
| | Paying freight costs on sales; FOB destination. | Freight-Out | XX | |
| | | Cash | | XX |
| | Receiving payment from customers within discount period. | Cash | XX | |
| | | Sales Discounts | XX | |
| | | Accounts Receivable | | XX |

*(continues)*

**ILLUSTRATION 5.8** *(continued)*

| | Transactions | Daily Recurring Entries | Dr. | Cr. |
|---|---|---|---|---|
| | Purchasing merchandise for resale. | Inventory<br>    Cash or Accounts Payable | XX | XX |
| **Purchase Transactions** | Paying freight costs on merchandise purchased; FOB shipping point. | Inventory<br>    Cash | XX | XX |
| | Receiving purchase returns or allowances from suppliers. | Cash or Accounts Payable<br>    Inventory | XX | XX |
| | Paying suppliers within discount period. | Accounts Payable<br>    Inventory<br>    Cash | XX | XX<br>XX |

| Events | Adjusting and Closing Entries | Dr. | Cr. |
|---|---|---|---|
| Adjust because book amount is higher than the inventory amount determined to be on hand. | Cost of Goods Sold<br>    Inventory | XX | XX |
| Closing temporary accounts with credit balances. | Sales Revenue<br>    Income Summary | XX | XX |
| Closing temporary accounts with debit balances. | Income Summary<br>    Sales Returns and Allowances<br>    Sales Discounts<br>    Cost of Goods Sold<br>    Freight-Out<br>    Expenses | XX | XX<br>XX<br>XX<br>XX<br>XX |

# DO IT! 4 | Closing Entries

The adjusted trial balance of Celine's Sports Wear Shop at December 31 shows Inventory $25,000, Sales Revenue $162,400, Sales Returns and Allowances $4,800, Sales Discounts $3,600, Cost of Goods Sold $110,000, Rent Revenue $6,000, Freight-Out $1,800, Rent Expense $8,800, and Salaries and Wages Expense $22,000. Prepare the closing entries for the income statement accounts.

### ACTION PLAN

- Close all temporary accounts with credit balances to Income Summary by debiting these accounts.
- Close all temporary accounts with debit balances, except dividends, to Income Summary by crediting these accounts.

## Solution

The two closing entries are:

| | | | |
|---|---|---|---|
| Dec. 31 | Sales Revenue | 162,400 | |
| | Rent Revenue | 6,000 | |
| |     Income Summary | | 168,400 |
| |       (To close accounts with credit balances) | | |
| | | | |
| 31 | Income Summary | 151,000 | |
| |     Cost of Goods Sold | | 110,000 |
| |     Sales Returns and Allowances | | 4,800 |
| |     Sales Discounts | | 3,600 |
| |     Freight-Out | | 1,800 |
| |     Rent Expense | | 8,800 |
| |     Salaries and Wages Expense | | 22,000 |
| |       (To close accounts with debit balances) | | |

Related exercise material: **BE5.6, BE5.7, DO IT! 5.4, E5.6, E5.7, and E5.8.**

# Multiple-Step Income Statement

---

**LEARNING OBJECTIVE 5**

Prepare a multiple-step income statement.

---

Merchandising companies widely use the classified balance sheet introduced in Chapter 4 and one of two forms for the income statement. This section explains the preparation of these financial statements by merchandisers.

## Multiple-Step Income Statement

The **multiple-step income statement** is so named because it shows several steps in determining net income. Two of these steps relate to the company's principal operating activities. A multiple-step statement also distinguishes between **operating** and **nonoperating activities**. Finally, the statement highlights intermediate components of net income and shows subgroupings of expenses.

### Income Statement Presentation of Sales

The multiple-step income statement begins by presenting **sales revenue**. It then deducts contra revenue accounts—sales returns and allowances and sales discounts—from sales revenue to arrive at **net sales**. **Illustration 5.9** presents the sales section for PW Audio Supply, Inc., using assumed data from its adjusted trial balance at year-end.

**ILLUSTRATION 5.9**

**Computation of net sales**

| Sales | | |
|---|---:|---:|
| Sales revenue | | $480,000 |
| Less: Sales returns and allowances | $12,000 | |
| Sales discounts | 8,000 | 20,000 |
| **Net sales** | | **$460,000** |

## Gross Profit

ALTERNATIVE TERMINOLOGY

**Gross profit is sometimes referred to as *gross margin*.**

From Illustration 5.1, you learned that companies deduct cost of goods sold from sales revenue to determine **gross profit** (see **Alternative Terminology**). For this computation, companies use **net sales** (which takes into consideration Sales Returns and Allowances and Sales Discounts) as the amount of sales revenue. On the basis of the sales data in Illustration 5.9 (net sales of $460,000) and cost of goods sold under the perpetual inventory system (assume $316,000), PW Audio Supply's gross profit is $144,000, computed as shown in **Illustration 5.10**.

**ILLUSTRATION 5.10**

**Computation of gross profit**

| | |
|---|---:|
| Net sales | $460,000 |
| Cost of goods sold | 316,000 |
| **Gross profit** | **$144,000** |

We also can express a company's gross profit as a percentage, called the **gross profit rate**. To do so, we divide the amount of gross profit by net sales. For PW Audio Supply, the **gross profit rate** is 31.3%, computed as shown in **Illustration 5.11**.

**ILLUSTRATION 5.11**

**Gross profit rate formula and computation**

| Gross Profit | ÷ | Net Sales | = | Gross Profit Rate |
|:---:|:---:|:---:|:---:|:---:|
| $144,000 | ÷ | $460,000 | = | 31.3% |

Analysts generally consider the gross profit **rate** to be more useful than the gross profit **amount**. The rate expresses a more meaningful (qualitative) relationship between net sales and gross profit. For example, a gross profit of $1,000,000 may sound impressive. But if it is the result of a gross profit rate of only 7%, it is not so impressive. The gross profit rate tells how many cents of each net sales dollar contribute to gross profit.

Gross profit represents the **merchandising profit** of a company. It is not a measure of the overall profitability because operating expenses are not yet deducted. But managers and other interested parties closely watch the amount and trend of gross profit. They compare current gross profit with amounts reported in past periods. They also compare the company's gross profit rate with rates of competitors and with industry averages. Such comparisons provide information about the effectiveness of a company's purchasing function and the soundness of its pricing policies.

## Operating Expenses and Income from Operations

**Operating expenses** are the next component in measuring net income for a merchandising company. They are the expenses incurred in the process of earning sales revenue. These expenses are similar in merchandising and service companies. Companies sometimes segregate operating expenses into selling expenses and administrative expenses to provide additional information. Selling expenses include such items as expenses for sales salaries and advertising. Administrative expenses include such items as insurance expense, utility expense, and freight-out.

At PW Audio Supply, operating expenses were $114,000. The company determines its income from operations by subtracting operating expenses from gross profit. Thus, as **Illustration 5.12** shows, income from operations is $30,000.

| | | |
|---|---:|---:|
| Gross profit | | $144,000 |
| **Operating expenses** | | |
| Salaries and wages expense | 64,000 | |
| Utilities expense | 17,000 | |
| Advertising expense | 16,000 | |
| Depreciation expense | 8,000 | |
| Freight-out | 7,000 | |
| Insurance expense | 2,000 | |
| **Total operating expenses** | | 114,000 |
| Income from operations | | $ 30,000 |

**ILLUSTRATION 5.12**

**Operating expenses in computing income from operations**

## Nonoperating Activities

**Nonoperating activities** consist of various revenues and expenses and gains and losses that are unrelated to the company's main line of operations. When nonoperating items are included, the label "**Income from operations**" (or "Operating income") precedes them. This label clearly identifies the results of the company's normal operations, an amount determined by subtracting cost of goods sold and operating expenses from net sales. The results of nonoperating activities are shown in the categories "**Other revenues and gains**" and "**Other expenses and losses**." **Illustration 5.13** lists examples of each.

**ILLUSTRATION 5.13**

**Other items of nonoperating activities**

### Other Revenues and Gains

**Interest revenue** from notes receivable and marketable securities.

**Dividend revenue** from investments in common stock.

**Rent revenue** from subleasing a portion of the store.

**Gain** from the sale of property, plant, and equipment.

### Other Expenses and Losses

**Interest expense** on notes and loans payable.

**Casualty losses** from recurring causes, such as vandalism and accidents.

**Loss** from the sale or abandonment of property, plant, and equipment.

**Loss** from strikes by employees and suppliers.

Merchandising companies report the nonoperating activities in the income statement immediately after the company's operating activities. **Illustration 5.14** shows these sections for PW Audio Supply, Inc., using assumed data. The net amount resulting from Other revenues and gains and Other expenses and losses is added to or subtracted from Income from operations to arrive at net income. The net income amount is the so-called "bottom line" of a company's income statement.

**ILLUSTRATION 5.14**

**Multiple-step income statement**

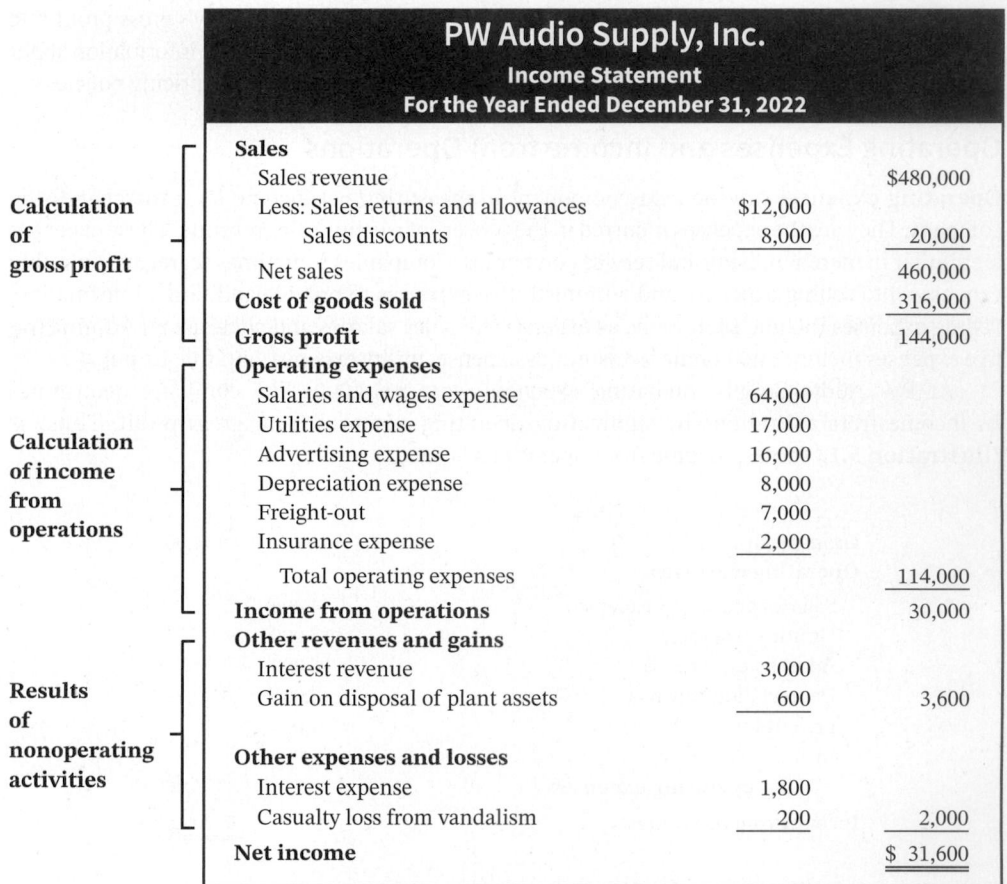

| **PW Audio Supply, Inc.** | | | |
| --- | --- | --- | --- |
| **Income Statement** | | | |
| **For the Year Ended December 31, 2022** | | | |
| **Sales** | | | |
| Sales revenue | | | $480,000 |
| Less: Sales returns and allowances | | $12,000 | |
| Sales discounts | | 8,000 | 20,000 |
| Net sales | | | 460,000 |
| **Cost of goods sold** | | | 316,000 |
| **Gross profit** | | | 144,000 |
| **Operating expenses** | | | |
| Salaries and wages expense | | 64,000 | |
| Utilities expense | | 17,000 | |
| Advertising expense | | 16,000 | |
| Depreciation expense | | 8,000 | |
| Freight-out | | 7,000 | |
| Insurance expense | | 2,000 | |
| Total operating expenses | | | 114,000 |
| **Income from operations** | | | 30,000 |
| **Other revenues and gains** | | | |
| Interest revenue | | 3,000 | |
| Gain on disposal of plant assets | | 600 | 3,600 |
| **Other expenses and losses** | | | |
| Interest expense | | 1,800 | |
| Casualty loss from vandalism | | 200 | 2,000 |
| **Net income** | | | $ 31,600 |

- Calculation of gross profit
- Calculation of income from operations
- Results of nonoperating activities

---

## Ethics Insight     IBM

ImageRite RF/Getty Images

### Disclosing More Details

After **Enron**, increased investor criticism and regulator scrutiny forced many companies to improve the clarity of their financial disclosures. For example, **IBM** began providing more detail regarding its "Other gains and losses." It had previously included these items in its selling, general, and administrative expenses, with little disclosure. For example, previously if IBM sold off one of its buildings at a gain, it included this gain in the selling, general, and administrative expense line item, thus reducing that expense. This made it appear that the company had done a better job of controlling operating expenses than it actually had.

As another example, when **eBay** sold the remainder of its investment in **Skype** to **Microsoft**, it reported a gain in "Other revenues and gains" of $1.7 billion. Since eBay's total income from operations was $2.4 billion, it was very important that the gain from the Skype sale not be buried in operating income.

**Why have investors and analysts demanded more accuracy in isolating "Other gains and losses" from operating items? (Answer is available near the end of the chapter.)**

The distinction between operating and nonoperating activities is crucial to many external users of financial data. These users view operating income as sustainable and many nonoperating activities as non-recurring (see **Ethics Note**). Therefore, when forecasting next year's income, analysts put the most weight on this year's income from operations and less weight on this year's nonoperating activities.

# Single-Step Income Statement

Another income statement format is the **single-step income statement**. The statement is so named because only one step—subtracting total expenses from total revenues—is required in determining net income.

In a single-step statement, all data are classified into two categories: (1) **revenues**, which include both operating revenues and other revenues and gains; and (2) **expenses**, which include cost of goods sold, operating expenses, and other expenses and losses. **Illustration 5.15** shows a single-step statement for PW Audio Supply, Inc.

**ILLUSTRATION 5.15**

Single-step income statement

### PW Audio Supply, Inc.
#### Income Statement
#### For the Year Ended December 31, 2022

| | | |
|---|---:|---:|
| **Revenues** | | |
| Net sales | | $460,000 |
| Interest revenue | | 3,000 |
| Gain on disposal of plant assets | | 600 |
| Total revenues | | 463,600 |
| **Expenses** | | |
| Cost of goods sold | $316,000 | |
| Operating expenses | 114,000 | |
| Interest expense | 1,800 | |
| Casualty loss from vandalism | 200 | |
| Total expenses | | 432,000 |
| **Net income** | | $ 31,600 |

There are two primary reasons for using the single-step format. (1) A company does not realize any type of profit or income until total revenues exceed total expenses, so it makes sense to divide the statement into these two categories. (2) The format is simpler and easier to read. *For homework problems, however, you should use the single-step format only when specifically instructed to do so.*

# Classified Balance Sheet

In the balance sheet, merchandising companies report inventory as a current asset immediately below accounts receivable. Recall from Chapter 4 that companies generally list current asset items in the order of their closeness to cash (liquidity). Inventory is less close to cash than accounts receivable because the goods must first be sold and then collection made from the customer. **Illustration 5.16** presents the assets section of a classified balance sheet for PW Audio Supply, Inc.

**ILLUSTRATION 5.16** Assets section of a classified balance sheet

### PW Audio Supply, Inc
#### Balance Sheet (Partial)
#### December 31, 2022

**Assets**

| | | |
|---|---:|---:|
| Current assets | | |
| Cash | | $ 9,500 |
| Accounts receivable | | 16,100 |
| **Inventory** | | 40,000 |
| Prepaid insurance | | 1,800 |
| Total current assets | | 67,400 |
| Property, plant, and equipment | | |
| Equipment | $80,000 | |
| Less: Accumulated depreciation—equipment | 24,000 | 56,000 |
| Total assets | | $123,400 |

> The $40,000 is the cost of the inventory on hand, not its expected selling price.

---

**ACTION PLAN**

- Subtract cost of goods sold from net sales to determine gross profit.
- Subtract operating expenses from gross profit to determine income from operations.
- Add/subtract nonoperating items to determine net income.

## DO IT! 5 | Multiple-Step Income Statement

The following information is available for Art Center Corp. for the year ended December 31, 2022.

| | | | | |
|---|---:|---|---|---:|
| Other revenues and gains | $ 8,000 | | Sales revenue | $462,000 |
| Other expenses and losses | 3,000 | | Operating expenses | 187,000 |
| Cost of goods sold | 147,000 | | Sales discounts | 20,000 |

Prepare a multiple-step income statement for Art Center Corp.

**Solution**

### Art Center Corp.
#### Income Statement
#### For the Year Ended December 31, 2022

| | | |
|---|---:|---:|
| Sales | | |
| Sales revenue | | $462,000 |
| Sales discounts | | 20,000 |
| Net sales | | 442,000 |
| Cost of goods sold | | 147,000 |
| Gross profit | | 295,000 |
| Operating expenses | | 187,000 |
| Income from operations | | 108,000 |
| Other revenues and gains | $8,000 | |
| Other expenses and losses | 3,000 | 5,000 |
| Net income | | $113,000 |

Related exercise material: **BE5.8, BE5.9, BE5.10, DO IT! 5.5, E5.9, E5.10, E5.12, E5.13, and E5.14.**

| Appendix 5A | # Merchandising Company Worksheet |
|---|---|

---

**LEARNING OBJECTIVE *6**

Prepare a worksheet for a merchandising company.

---

## Using a Worksheet

As indicated in Chapter 4, a worksheet enables companies to prepare financial statements before they journalize and post adjusting entries. The steps in preparing a worksheet for a merchandising company are the same as for a service company. **Illustration 5A.1** shows the

**ILLUSTRATION 5A.1** **Worksheet for merchandising company—perpetual inventory system**

PW Audio Supply

Home    Insert    Page Layout    Formulas    Data    Review    View

P18          fx

| | A | B | C | D | E | F | G | H | I | J | K |
|---|---|---|---|---|---|---|---|---|---|---|---|
| 1 | | | | | | | | | | | |
| 2 | | | | | **PW Audio Supply, Inc.** | | | | | | |
| 3 | | | | | **Worksheet** | | | | | | |
| 4 | | | | | **For the Year Ended December 31, 2022** | | | | | | |
| 5 | | Trial Balance | | Adjustments | | Adjusted Trial Balance | | Income Statement | | Balance Sheet | |
| 6 | | | | | | | | | | | |
| 7 | Accounts | Dr. | Cr. | Dr. | Cr. | Dr. | Cr. | Dr. | Cr. | Dr. | Cr. |
| 8 | Cash | 9,500 | | | | 9,500 | | | | 9,500 | |
| 9 | Accounts Receivable | 16,100 | | | | 16,100 | | | | 16,100 | |
| 10 | Inventory | 40,500 | | | (a)    500 | 40,000 | | | | 40,000 | |
| 11 | Prepaid Insurance | 3,800 | | | (b) 2,000 | 1,800 | | | | 1,800 | |
| 12 | Equipment | 80,000 | | | | 80,000 | | | | 80,000 | |
| 13 | Accumulated Depreciation—Equipment | | 16,000 | | (c) 8,000 | | 24,000 | | | | 24,000 |
| 14 | Accounts Payable | | 20,400 | | | | 20,400 | | | | 20,400 |
| 15 | Common Stock | | 50,000 | | | | 50,000 | | | | 50,000 |
| 16 | Retained Earnings | | 33,000 | | | | 33,000 | | | | 33,000 |
| 17 | Dividends | 15,000 | | | | 15,000 | | | | 15,000 | |
| 18 | Sales Revenue | | 480,000 | | | | 480,000 | | 480,000 | | |
| 19 | Sales Returns and Allowances | 12,000 | | | | 12,000 | | 12,000 | | | |
| 20 | Sales Discounts | 8,000 | | | | 8,000 | | 8,000 | | | |
| 21 | Cost of Goods Sold | 315,500 | | (a)    500 | | 316,000 | | 316,000 | | | |
| 22 | Freight-Out | 7,000 | | | | 7,000 | | 7,000 | | | |
| 23 | Advertising Expense | 16,000 | | | | 16,000 | | 16,000 | | | |
| 24 | Salaries and Wages Expense | 59,000 | | (d) 5,000 | | 64,000 | | 64,000 | | | |
| 25 | Utilities Expense | 17,000 | | | | 17,000 | | 17,000 | | | |
| 26 | Totals | 599,400 | 599,400 | | | | | | | | |
| 27 | Insurance Expense | | | (b) 2,000 | | 2,000 | | 2,000 | | | |
| 28 | Depreciation Expense | | | (c) 8,000 | | 8,000 | | 8,000 | | | |
| 29 | Salaries and Wages Payable | | | | (d) 5,000 | | 5,000 | | | | 5,000 |
| 30 | Totals | | | 15,500 | 15,500 | 612,400 | 612,400 | 450,000 | 480,000 | 162,400 | 132,400 |
| 31 | Net Income | | | | | | | 30,000 | | | 30,000 |
| 32 | Totals | | | | | | | 480,000 | 480,000 | 162,400 | 162,400 |
| 33 | | | | | | | | | | | |
| 34 | | | | | | | | | | | |

Key: (a) Adjustment to inventory on hand. (b) Insurance expired. (c) Depreciation expense. (d) Salaries and wages accrued.

worksheet for PW Audio Supply, Inc. (excluding nonoperating items). The unique accounts for a merchandiser using a **perpetual inventory system** are in red.

### Trial Balance Columns

Data for the trial balance come from the ledger balances of PW Audio Supply at December 31. The amount shown for Inventory, $40,500, is the year-end inventory amount from the perpetual inventory system.

### Adjustments Columns

A merchandising company generally has the same types of adjustments as a service company. As you see in the worksheet, adjustments (b), (c), and (d) are for insurance, depreciation, and salaries and wages. Pioneer Advertising Inc., as illustrated in Chapters 3 and 4, also had these adjustments. Adjustment (a) was required to adjust the perpetual inventory carrying amount to the actual count.

After PW Audio Supply enters all adjustments data on the worksheet, it establishes the equality of the adjustments column totals. It then extends the balances in all accounts to the adjusted trial balance columns.

### Adjusted Trial Balance

The adjusted trial balance shows the balance of all accounts after adjustment at the end of the accounting period.

### Income Statement Columns

Next, the merchandising company transfers the accounts and balances that affect the income statement from the adjusted trial balance columns to the income statement columns. PW Audio Supply shows Sales Revenue of $480,000 in the credit column. It shows the contra revenue accounts Sales Returns and Allowances $12,000 and Sales Discounts $8,000 in the debit column. The difference of $460,000 is the net sales shown on the income statement (Illustration 5.14).

Finally, the company totals all the credits in the income statement column and compares those totals to the total of the debits in the income statement column. If the credits exceed the debits, the company has net income. PW Audio Supply has net income of $30,000. If the debits exceed the credits, the company would report a net loss.

### Balance Sheet Columns

The major difference between the balance sheets of a service company and a merchandiser is inventory. PW Audio Supply shows the ending inventory amount of $40,000 in the balance sheet debit column. The information to prepare the retained earnings statement is also found in these columns. That is, the retained earnings beginning balance is $33,000. Dividends are $15,000. Net income results when the total of the debit column exceeds the total of the credit column in the balance sheet columns. A net loss results when the total of the credits exceeds the total of the debit balances.

---

| Appendix 5B | # Periodic Inventory System |
|---|---|

---

**LEARNING OBJECTIVE \*7**

Record purchases and sales under a periodic inventory system.

---

As described in this chapter, companies may use one of two basic systems of accounting for inventories: (1) the perpetual inventory system or (2) the periodic inventory system. In the chapter, we focused on the characteristics of the perpetual inventory system. In this appendix, we discuss and illustrate the **periodic inventory system**. One key difference between the two systems is the point at which the company computes cost of goods sold. For a visual reminder of this difference, refer back to Illustration 5.5.

# Determining Cost of Goods Sold Under a Periodic System

Determining cost of goods sold is different when a periodic inventory system is used rather than a perpetual system. As you have seen, a company using a **perpetual system** makes an entry to record cost of goods sold and to reduce inventory each time a sale is made. A company using a **periodic system** does not record cost of goods sold with each sale. Instead, at the end of the period, the company performs a count to determine the ending balance of inventory. It then **calculates cost of goods sold by subtracting ending inventory from the cost of goods available for sale**. Cost of goods available for sale is the sum of beginning inventory plus purchases, as shown in **Illustration 5B.1**.

Beginning inventory
+ Cost of goods purchased
Cost of goods available for sale
− Ending inventory
**Cost of goods sold**

Another difference between the two approaches is that the perpetual system directly adjusts the Inventory account for any transaction that affects inventory (such as purchases, freight costs, returns, and discounts). The periodic system does not do this. Instead, it uses separate accounts for purchases, freight costs, returns, and discounts. These various accounts are shown in Illustration 5B.2, which presents the calculation of cost of goods sold for PW Audio Supply, Inc., using the periodic approach and assumed data.

Note that the basic elements from Illustration 5B.1 are highlighted in **Illustration 5B.2**. You will learn more in Chapter 6 about how to determine cost of goods sold using the periodic system.

### PW Audio Supply, Inc.
#### Cost of Goods Sold
#### For the Year Ended December 31, 2022

| | | | |
|---|---|---|---|
| Cost of goods sold | | | |
| Inventory, January 1 | | | $ 36,000 |
| Purchases | | $325,000 | |
| Less: Purchase returns and allowances | $10,400 | | |
| Purchase discounts | 6,800 | 17,200 | |
| Net purchases | | 307,800 | |
| Add: Freight-in | | 12,200 | |
| Cost of goods purchased | | | 320,000 |
| Cost of goods available for sale | | | 356,000 |
| Less: Inventory, December 31 | | | 40,000 |
| **Cost of goods sold** | | | **$316,000** |

The use of the periodic inventory system does not affect the form of presentation in the balance sheet. As under the perpetual system, a company reports inventory in the current assets section. PW Audio Supply would report inventory of $40,000 at December 31, 2022.

# Recording Merchandise Transactions

In a **periodic inventory system**, companies record revenues from the sale of merchandise when sales are made, just as in a perpetual system. Unlike the perpetual system, however, companies **do not record the cost of the merchandise sold**. Instead, they take a physical inventory count at the **end of the period** to determine (1) the cost of the merchandise then on hand and (2) the cost of the goods sold during the period. And, **under a periodic system, companies record purchases of merchandise in the Purchases account rather than in the Inventory account**. Purchase returns and allowances, purchase discounts, and freight costs on purchases are recorded in separate accounts as well.

To illustrate the recording of merchandise transactions under a periodic inventory system, we will use purchase/sales transactions between PW Audio Supply, Inc. and Sauk Stereo, as illustrated for the perpetual inventory system in this chapter.

# Recording Purchases of Merchandise

**HELPFUL HINT**

Be careful not to debit purchases of equipment or supplies to a Purchases account.

On the basis of the sales invoice (Illustration 5.6) and receipt of the merchandise ordered from PW Audio Supply, Sauk Stereo records the $3,800 purchase as follows (see **Helpful Hint**).

| May 4 | Purchases | 3,800 | |
|---|---|---|---|
| |     Accounts Payable | | 3,800 |
| |       (To record goods purchased on account | | |
| |       from PW Audio Supply) | | |

Purchases is a temporary account whose normal balance is a debit. Recall that all temporary accounts are closed during the closing process.

## Freight Costs

When the purchaser directly incurs the freight costs, it debits the account Freight-In (or Transportation-In). For example, if Sauk Stereo pays Public Carrier Co. $150 for freight charges on its purchase from PW Audio Supply on May 6, the entry on Sauk Stereo's books is as follows.

| May 6 | Freight-In (Transportation-In) | 150 | |
|---|---|---|---|
| |     Cash | | 150 |
| |       (To record payment of freight on goods | | |
| |       purchased) | | |

Like Purchases, Freight-In is a temporary account whose normal balance is a debit. **Freight-In is part of cost of goods purchased.** The reason is that cost of goods purchased should include any freight charges necessary to bring the goods to the purchaser. Freight costs are not subject to a purchase discount. Purchase discounts apply only to the invoice cost of the merchandise.

## Purchase Returns and Allowances

Sauk Stereo returns goods costing $300 to PW Audio Supply and prepares the following entry to recognize the return.

| May 8 | Accounts Payable | 300 | |
|---|---|---|---|
| |     Purchase Returns and Allowances | | 300 |
| |       (To record return of goods purchased | | |
| |       from PW Audio Supply) | | |

Purchase Returns and Allowances is a temporary account whose normal balance is a credit.

## Purchase Discounts

On May 14, Sauk Stereo pays the balance due on account to PW Audio Supply, taking the 2% cash discount allowed by PW Audio Supply for payment within 10 days. Sauk Stereo records the payment and discount as follows.

| May 14 | Accounts Payable ($3,800 − $300) | 3,500 | |
| | Purchase Discounts ($3,500 × .02) | | 70 |
| | Cash | | 3,430 |
| | (To record payment within the discount period) | | |

Purchase Discounts is a temporary account whose normal balance is a credit.

# Recording Sales of Merchandise

The seller, PW Audio Supply, records the sale of $3,800 of merchandise to Sauk Stereo on May 4 (sales invoice No. 731, Illustration 5.6) as follows.

| May 4 | Accounts Receivable | 3,800 | |
| | Sales Revenue | | 3,800 |
| | (To record credit sales per invoice #731 to Sauk Stereo) | | |

## Sales Returns and Allowances

To record the returned goods received from Sauk Stereo on May 8, PW Audio Supply records the $300 sales return as follows. Note that there is no second entry for Cost of Goods Sold and Inventory.

| May 8 | Sales Returns and Allowances | 300 | |
| | Accounts Receivable | | 300 |
| | (To record credit granted to Sauk Stereo for returned goods) | | |

## Sales Discounts

On May 14, PW Audio Supply receives payment of $3,430 on account from Sauk Stereo. PW Audio Supply honors the 2% cash discount and records the payment of Sauk Stereo's account receivable in full as follows.

| May 14 | Cash | 3,430 | |
| | Sales Discounts ($3,500 × .02) | 70 | |
| | Accounts Receivable ($3,800 − $300) | | 3,500 |
| | (To record collection within 2/10, n/30 discount period from Sauk Stereo) | | |

## Comparison of Entries—Perpetual vs. Periodic

**Illustration 5B.3** summarizes the periodic inventory entries shown in this appendix and compares them to the perpetual system entries from the chapter. Entries that differ in the two systems are shown in color.

**ILLUSTRATION 5B.3** **Comparison of entries for perpetual and periodic inventory systems**

### Entries on Sauk Stereo's Books

| | Transaction | Perpetual Inventory System | | | Periodic Inventory System | | |
|---|---|---|---|---|---|---|---|
| May 4 | Purchase of merchandise on credit. | Inventory<br>  Accounts Payable | 3,800 | 3,800 | Purchases<br>  Accounts Payable | 3,800 | 3,800 |
| 6 | Freight costs on purchases. | Inventory<br>  Cash | 150 | 150 | Freight-In<br>  Cash | 150 | 150 |
| 8 | Purchase returns and allowances. | Accounts Payable<br>  Inventory | 300 | 300 | Accounts Payable<br>  Purchase Returns and<br>    Allowances | 300 | 300 |
| 14 | Payment on account with a discount. | Accounts Payable<br>  Cash<br>  Inventory | 3,500 | 3,430<br>70 | Accounts Payable<br>  Cash<br>  Purchase Discounts | 3,500 | 3,430<br>70 |

### Entries on PW Audio Supply's Books

| | Transaction | Perpetual Inventory System | | | Periodic Inventory System | | |
|---|---|---|---|---|---|---|---|
| May 4 | Sale of merchandise on credit. | Accounts Receivable<br>  Sales Revenue | 3,800 | 3,800 | Accounts Receivable<br>  Sales Revenue | 3,800 | 3,800 |
| | | Cost of Goods Sold<br>  Inventory | 2,400 | 2,400 | No entry for Cost of Goods Sold and Inventory | | |
| 8 | Return of merchandise sold. | Sales Returns and<br>  Allowances<br>  Accounts Receivable | 300 | 300 | Sales Returns and<br>  Allowances<br>  Accounts Receivable | 300 | 300 |
| | | Inventory<br>  Cost of Goods Sold | 140 | 140 | No entry for Cost of Goods Sold and Inventory | | |
| 14 | Cash received on account with a discount. | Cash<br>Sales Discounts<br>  Accounts Receivable | 3,430<br>70 | 3,500 | Cash<br>Sales Discounts<br>  Accounts Receivable | 3,430<br>70 | 3,500 |

# Journalizing and Posting Closing Entries

For a merchandising company, like a service company, all accounts that affect the determination of net income are closed to Income Summary. Data for the preparation of closing entries may be obtained from the income statement columns of the worksheet. In journalizing, all debit column amounts are credited, and all credit columns amounts are debited. To close the merchandise inventory in a periodic inventory system:

1. The beginning inventory balance is debited to Income Summary and credited to Inventory.
2. The ending inventory balance, as determined by the physical count, is debited to Inventory and credited to Income Summary.

The two entries for PW Audio Supply are as follows.

(1)

| | | | |
|---|---|---|---|
| Dec. 31 | Income Summary | 36,000 | |
| | Inventory | | 36,000 |
| | (To close beginning inventory) | | |

(2)

| | | | |
|---|---|---|---|
| 31 | Inventory | 40,000 | |
| | Income Summary | | 40,000 |
| | (To record ending inventory) | | |

Illustration 5B.4 shows the Inventory and Income Summary accounts after posting.

| Inventory | | | | | Income Summary | | | | |
|-----------|-----|--------|-------|-------|--------|-------|-------|-------|-------|
| 1/1 | Bal. | 36,000 | 12/31 | Close | 36,000 | 12/31 | Close | 36,000 | 12/31 | Close | 40,000 |

| Inventory | | | | |
|-----------|------|--------|-------|-------|
| 1/1 | Bal. | 36,000 | 12/31 | Close 36,000 |
| 12/31 | Close | **40,000** | | |
| 12/31 | Bal. | 40,000 | | |

| Income Summary | | | | |
|----------------|-------|--------|-------|-------|
| 12/31 | Close | **36,000** | 12/31 | Close **40,000** |

Often, the closing of Inventory is included with other closing entries, as shown below for PW Audio Supply (see **Helpful Hint**). (*Close Inventory with other accounts in homework problems unless stated otherwise.*)

**HELPFUL HINT**

Except for merchandise inventory, the easiest way to prepare the first two closing entries is to identify the temporary accounts by their balances and then prepare one entry for the credits and one for the debits.

| Dec. 31 | Inventory (Dec. 31) | 40,000 | |
|---------|---------------------|--------|---|
| | Sales Revenue | 480,000 | |
| | Purchase Returns and Allowances | 10,400 | |
| | Purchase Discounts | 6,800 | |
| |     Income Summary | | 537,200 |
| |       (To record ending inventory and close accounts with credit balances) | | |
| 31 | Income Summary | 507,200 | |
| |     Inventory (Jan. 1) | | **36,000** |
| |     Sales Returns and Allowances | | 12,000 |
| |     Sales Discounts | | 8,000 |
| |     Purchases | | 325,000 |
| |     Freight-In | | 12,200 |
| |     Salaries and Wages Expense | | 64,000 |
| |     Freight-Out | | 7,000 |
| |     Advertising Expense | | 16,000 |
| |     Utilities Expense | | 17,000 |
| |     Depreciation Expense | | 8,000 |
| |     Insurance Expense | | 2,000 |
| |       (To close beginning inventory and other income statement accounts with debit balances) | | |
| 31 | Income Summary | 30,000 | |
| |     Retained Earnings | | 30,000 |
| |       (To transfer net income to retained earnings) | | |
| 31 | Retained Earnings | 15,000 | |
| |     Dividends | | 15,000 |
| |       (To close dividends to retained earnings) | | |

After the closing entries are posted, all temporary accounts have zero balances. In addition, Retained Earnings has a credit balance of $48,000: beginning balance + net income − dividends ($33,000 + $30,000 − $15,000). The Inventory account has a $40,000 balance, which corresponds to the physical count.

# Using a Worksheet

As indicated in Chapter 4, a worksheet enables companies to prepare financial statements before journalizing and posting adjusting entries. The steps in preparing a worksheet for a merchandising company are the same as they are for a service company.

## Trial Balance Columns

Data for the trial balance come from the ledger balances of PW Audio Supply at December 31. The amount shown for Inventory, $36,000, is the beginning inventory amount from the periodic inventory system.

## Adjustments Columns

A merchandising company generally has the same types of adjustments as a service company. As you see in the worksheet in **Illustration 5B.5**, adjustments (a), (b), and (c) are for insurance, depreciation, and salaries and wages. These adjustments were also required for Pioneer Advertising Inc., as illustrated in Chapters 3 and 4. The unique accounts for a merchandiser using a **periodic inventory system** are shown in capital red letters. Note, however, that this example excludes nonoperating items.

After all adjustment data are entered on the worksheet, the equality of the adjustment column totals is established. The balances in all accounts are then extended to the adjusted trial balance columns.

**ILLUSTRATION 5B.5** Worksheet for merchandising company—periodic inventory system

PW Audio Supply, Inc.
Worksheet
For the Year Ended December 31, 2022

| Accounts | Trial Balance Dr. | Trial Balance Cr. | Adjustments Dr. | Adjustments Cr. | Adjusted Trial Balance Dr. | Adjusted Trial Balance Cr. | Income Statement Dr. | Income Statement Cr. | Balance Sheet Dr. | Balance Sheet Cr. |
|---|---|---|---|---|---|---|---|---|---|---|
| Cash | 9,500 | | | | 9,500 | | | | 9,500 | |
| Accounts Receivable | 16,100 | | | | 16,100 | | | | 16,100 | |
| INVENTORY | 36,000 | | | | 36,000 | | 36,000 | 40,000 | 40,000 | |
| Prepaid Insurance | 3,800 | | | (a) 2,000 | 1,800 | | | | 1,800 | |
| Equipment | 80,000 | | | | 80,000 | | | | 80,000 | |
| Accumulated Depreciation—Equipment | | 16,000 | | (b) 8,000 | | 24,000 | | | | 24,000 |
| Accounts Payable | | 20,400 | | | | 20,400 | | | | 20,400 |
| Common Stock | | 50,000 | | | | 50,000 | | | | 50,000 |
| Retained Earnings | | 33,000 | | | | 33,000 | | | | 33,000 |
| Dividends | 15,000 | | | | 15,000 | | | | 15,000 | |
| SALES REVENUE | | 480,000 | | | | 480,000 | | 480,000 | | |
| SALES RETURNS AND ALLOWANCES | 12,000 | | | | 12,000 | | 12,000 | | | |
| SALES DISCOUNTS | 8,000 | | | | 8,000 | | 8,000 | | | |
| PURCHASES | 325,000 | | | | 325,000 | | 325,000 | | | |
| PURCHASE RETURNS AND ALLOWANCES | | 10,400 | | | | 10,400 | | 10,400 | | |
| PURCHASE DISCOUNTS | | 6,800 | | | | 6,800 | | 6,800 | | |
| FREIGHT-IN | 12,200 | | | | 12,200 | | 12,200 | | | |
| Freight-Out | 7,000 | | | | 7,000 | | 7,000 | | | |
| Advertising Expense | 16,000 | | | | 16,000 | | 16,000 | | | |
| Salaries and Wages Expense | 59,000 | | (c) 5,000 | | 64,000 | | 64,000 | | | |
| Utilities Expense | 17,000 | | | | 17,000 | | 17,000 | | | |
| Totals | 616,600 | 616,600 | | | | | | | | |
| Insurance Expense | | | (a) 2,000 | | 2,000 | | 2,000 | | | |
| Depreciation Expense | | | (b) 8,000 | | 8,000 | | 8,000 | | | |
| Salaries and Wages Payable | | | | (c) 5,000 | | 5,000 | | | | 5,000 |
| Totals | | | 15,000 | 15,000 | 629,600 | 629,600 | 507,200 | 537,200 | 162,400 | 132,400 |
| Net Income | | | | | | | 30,000 | | | 30,000 |
| Totals | | | | | | | 537,200 | 537,200 | 162,400 | 162,400 |

Key: (a) Insurance expired. (b) Depreciation expense. (c) Salaries and wages accrued.

## Income Statement Columns

Next, PW Audio Supply transfers the accounts and balances that affect the income statement from the adjusted trial balance columns to the income statement columns. The company shows Sales Revenue of $480,000 in the credit column. It shows the contra revenue accounts, Sales Returns and Allowances of $12,000 and Sales Discounts of $8,000, in the debit column. The difference of $460,000 is the net sales shown on the income statement (Illustration 5.9). Similarly, Purchases of $325,000 and Freight-In of $12,200 are extended to the debit column. The contra purchase accounts, Purchase Returns and Allowances of $10,400 and Purchase Discounts of $6,800, are extended to the credit columns.

The worksheet procedures for the Inventory account merit specific comment as follows.

1. The beginning balance, $36,000, is extended from the adjusted trial balance column to the **income statement debit column**. From there, it can be added in reporting cost of goods available for sale in the income statement.

2. The ending inventory, $40,000, is added to the worksheet by an **income statement credit and a balance sheet debit**. The credit makes it possible to deduct ending inventory from the cost of goods available for sale in the income statement to determine cost of goods sold. The debit means the ending inventory can be reported as an asset on the balance sheet.

These two procedures are specifically shown in **Illustration 5B.6**.

|  |  | Income Statement | | Balance Sheet | |
|---|---|---|---|---|---|
|  |  | Dr. | Cr. | Dr. | Cr. |
| Inventory | (1) | 36,000 | 40,000 ⟵ (2) ⟶ | 40,000 |  |

**ILLUSTRATION 5B.6**

Worksheet procedures for inventories

The computation for cost of goods sold, taken from the items in the income statement column in Illustration 5B.5, is shown in **Illustration 5B.7** (see **Helpful Hint**).

| Debit Column | | Credit Column | |
|---|---|---|---|
| Beginning inventory | $ 36,000 | Ending inventory | $40,000 |
| Purchases | 325,000 | Purchase returns and allowances | 10,400 |
| Freight-in | 12,200 | Purchase discounts | 6,800 |
| Total debits | 373,200 | Total credits | $57,200 |
| Less: Total credits | 57,200 |  |  |
| **Cost of goods sold** | **$316,000** |  |  |

**ILLUSTRATION 5B.7**

Computation of cost of goods sold from worksheet columns

**HELPFUL HINT**

In a periodic system, cost of goods sold is a computation—it is not a separate account with a balance.

Finally, PW Audio Supply totals all the credits in the income statement column and compares these totals to the total of the debits in the income statement column. If the credits exceed the debits, the company has net income. PW Audio Supply has net income of $30,000. If the debits exceed the credits, the company would report a net loss.

## Balance Sheet Columns

The major difference between the balance sheets of a service company and a merchandising company is inventory. PW Audio Supply shows ending inventory of $40,000 in the balance sheet debit column. The information to prepare the retained earnings statement is also found in these columns. That is, the retained earnings beginning balance is $33,000. Dividends are $15,000. Net income results when the total of the debit column exceeds the total of the credit column in the balance sheet columns. A net loss results when the total of the credits exceeds the total of the debit balances.

# Review and Practice

## Learning Objectives Review

**1 Describe merchandising operations and inventory systems.**

Because of inventory, a merchandising company has sales revenue, cost of goods sold, and gross profit. To account for inventory, a merchandising company must choose between a perpetual and a periodic inventory system.

**2 Record purchases under a perpetual inventory system.**

The company debits the Inventory account for all purchases of merchandise and freight-in, and credits it for purchase discounts and purchase returns and allowances.

**3 Record sales under a perpetual inventory system.**

When a merchandising company sells inventory, it debits Accounts Receivable (or Cash) and credits Sales Revenue for the **selling price** of the merchandise. At the same time, it debits Cost of Goods Sold and credits Inventory for the **cost** of the inventory items sold. Sales Returns and Allowances and Sales Discounts are debited and are contra revenue accounts.

**4 Apply the steps in the accounting cycle to a merchandising company.**

Each of the required steps in the accounting cycle for a service company applies to a merchandising company. A worksheet is again an optional step. Under a perpetual inventory system, the company must adjust the Inventory account to agree with the physical count.

**5 Prepare a multiple-step income statement.**

A multiple-step income statement shows numerous steps in determining net income, including nonoperating activities sections. A single-step income statement classifies all data under two categories, revenues or expenses, and determines net income in one step.

**\*6 Prepare a worksheet for a merchandising company.**

The steps in preparing a worksheet for a merchandising company are the same as for a service company. The unique accounts for a merchandiser are Inventory, Sales Revenue, Sales Returns and Allowances, Sales Discounts, and Cost of Goods Sold.

**\*7 Record purchases and sales under a periodic inventory system.**

In recording purchases under a periodic system, companies must make entries for (a) cash and credit purchases, (b) purchase returns and allowances, (c) purchase discounts, and (d) freight costs using separate accounts and *not* the Inventory account. In recording sales, companies must make entries for (a) cash and credit sales, (b) sales returns and allowances, and (c) sales discounts only. The Inventory and Cost of Goods Sold accounts are not used.

## Glossary Review

**Contra revenue account**   An account that is offset against a revenue account on the income statement. (p. 5-13).

**Cost of goods sold**   The total cost of merchandise sold during the period. (p. 5-3).

**FOB destination**   Freight terms indicating that the seller places the goods free on board to the buyer's place of business, and the seller pays the freight. (p. 5-8).

**FOB shipping point**   Freight terms indicating that the seller places goods free on board the carrier, and the buyer pays the freight costs. (p. 5-8).

**Gross profit**   The excess of net sales over the cost of goods sold. (p. 5-18).

**Gross profit rate**   Gross profit expressed as a percentage, calculated by dividing the amount of gross profit by net sales. (p. 5-18).

**Income from operations**   Income from a company's principal operating activity, determined by subtracting cost of goods sold and operating expenses from gross profit. (p. 5-19).

**Multiple-step income statement**   An income statement that shows several steps in determining net income. (p. 5-18).

**Net sales**   Sales revenue less sales returns and allowances and sales discounts. (p. 5-18).

**Nonoperating activities**   Various revenues, expenses, gains, and losses that are unrelated to a company's main line of operations. (p. 5-19).

**Operating expenses**   Expenses incurred in the process of earning sales revenue. (p. 5-19).

**Other expenses and losses**   A nonoperating-activities section of the income statement that shows expenses and losses unrelated to the company's main line of operations. (p. 5-19).

**Other revenues and gains**   A nonoperating-activities section of the income statement that shows revenues and gains unrelated to the company's main line of operations. (p. 5-19).

**Periodic inventory system**   An inventory system under which the company does not keep detailed inventory records in the Inventory account throughout the accounting period but determines the cost of goods sold only at the end of an accounting period. (p. 5-5).

**Perpetual inventory system**   An inventory system under which the company keeps detailed records of the cost of each inventory purchase and sale in the Inventory account, and the records continuously show the inventory that should be on hand. (p. 5-4).

**Purchase allowance**   A deduction made to the selling price of merchandise, granted by the seller so that the buyer will keep the merchandise. (p. 5-9).

**Purchase discount**   A cash discount claimed by a buyer for prompt payment of a balance due. (p. 5-9).

**Purchase invoice**   A document that supports each credit purchase. (p. 5-7).

**Purchase return**   A return of goods from the buyer to the seller for a cash or credit refund. (p. 5-9)

**Sales discount**   A reduction given by a seller for prompt payment of a credit sale. (p. 5-13).

**Sales invoice**   A document that supports each credit sale. (p. 5-11).

**Sales returns and allowances**   Purchase returns and allowances from the seller's perspective. See *Purchase return* and *Purchase allowance*. (p. 5-12).

**Sales revenue (Sales)**   The primary source of revenue in a merchandising company. (p. 5-3).

**Single-step income statement**   An income statement that shows only one step in determining net income. (p. 5-21).

## Practice Multiple-Choice Questions

1. **(LO 1)** Gross profit will result if:
   a. operating expenses are less than net income.
   b. net sales are greater than operating expenses.
   c. net sales are greater than cost of goods sold.
   d. operating expenses are greater than cost of goods sold.

2. **(LO 2)** Under a perpetual inventory system, when goods are purchased for resale by a company:
   a. purchases on account are debited to Inventory.
   b. purchases on account are debited to Purchases.
   c. purchase returns are debited to Purchase Returns and Allowances.
   d. freight costs are debited to Freight-Out.

3. **(LO 3)** The sales revenue accounts that normally have a debit balance are:
   a. Sales Discounts.
   b. Sales Returns and Allowances.
   c. both Sales Discounts and Sales Returns and Allowances.
   d. neither Sales Discounts nor Sales Returns and Allowances.

4. **(LO 3)** A credit sale of $750 is made on June 13, terms 2/10, net/30. A return of $50 is granted on June 16. The amount received as payment in full on June 23 is:
   a. $700.            c. $685.
   b. $686.            d. $650.

5. **(LO 2)** Which of the following accounts will normally appear in the ledger of a merchandising company that uses a perpetual inventory system?
   a. Purchases.       c. Cost of Goods Sold.
   b. Freight-In.      d. Purchase Discounts.

6. **(LO 3)** To record the sale of goods for cash in a perpetual inventory system:
   a. only one journal entry is necessary to record cost of goods sold and reduction of inventory.
   b. only one journal entry is necessary to record the receipt of cash and the sales revenue.
   c. two journal entries are necessary: one to record the receipt of cash and sales revenue, and one to record the cost of goods sold and reduction of inventory.
   d. two journal entries are necessary: one to record the receipt of cash and reduction of inventory, and one to record the cost of goods sold and sales revenue.

7. **(LO 4)** The steps in the accounting cycle for a merchandising company are the same as those in a service company **except**:
   a. an additional adjusting journal entry for inventory may be needed in a merchandising company.
   b. closing journal entries are not required for a merchandising company.
   c. a post-closing trial balance is not required for a merchandising company.
   d. a multiple-step income statement is required for a merchandising company.

8. **(LO 5)** The multiple-step income statement for a merchandising company shows each of the following items **except**:
   a. gross profit.
   b. cost of goods sold.
   c. a sales section.
   d. an investing activities section.

**9. (LO 5)** If net sales are $400,000, cost of goods sold is $310,000, and operating expenses are $60,000, the gross profit is:

    **a.** $30,000.           **c.** $340,000.

    **b.** $90,000.           **d.** $400,000.

**10. (LO 5)** A single-step income statement:

    **a.** reports gross profit.

    **b.** does not report cost of goods sold.

    **c.** reports sales revenue and all other revenues and gains in the revenues section of the income statement.

    **d.** reports income from operations separately.

**11. (LO 5)** Which of the following appears on both a single-step and a multiple-step income statement?

    **a.** Inventory.           **c.** Income from operations.

    **b.** Gross profit.           **d.** Cost of goods sold.

**\*12. (LO 6)** In a worksheet using a perpetual inventory system, Inventory is shown in the following columns:

    **a.** adjusted trial balance debit and balance sheet debit.

    **b.** income statement debit and balance sheet debit.

    **c.** income statement credit and balance sheet debit.

    **d.** income statement credit and adjusted trial balance debit.

**\*13. (LO 7)** In determining cost of goods sold in a periodic system:

    **a.** purchase discounts are deducted from net purchases.

    **b.** freight-out is added to net purchases.

    **c.** purchase returns and allowances are deducted from net purchases.

    **d.** freight-in is added to net purchases.

**\*14. (LO 7)** If beginning inventory is $60,000, cost of goods purchased is $380,000, and ending inventory is $50,000, cost of goods sold is:

    **a.** $390,000.           **c.** $330,000.

    **b.** $370,000.           **d.** $420,000.

**\*15. (LO 7)** When goods are purchased for resale by a company using a periodic inventory system:

    **a.** purchases on account are debited to Inventory.

    **b.** purchases on account are debited to Purchases.

    **c.** purchase returns are debited to Purchase Returns and Allowances.

    **d.** freight costs are debited to Purchases.

## Solutions

**1. c.** Gross profit will result if net sales are greater than cost of goods sold. The other choices are incorrect because (a) operating expenses and net income are not used in the computation of gross profit; (b) gross profit results when net sales are greater than cost of goods sold, not operating expenses; and (d) gross profit results when net sales, not operating expenses, are greater than cost of goods sold.

**2. a.** Under a perpetual inventory system, when a company purchases goods for resale, purchases on account are debited to the Inventory account, not (b) Purchases or (c) Purchase Returns and Allowances. Choice (d) is incorrect because freight costs related to purchases are also debited to the Inventory account, not the Freight-Out account.

**3. c.** Both Sales Discounts and Sales Returns and Allowances normally have a debit balance. Choices (a) and (b) are both correct, but (c) is the better answer. Choice (d) is incorrect as both Sales Discounts and Sales Returns and Allowances, not neither, are correct.

**4. b.** The amount of $686 is paid within 10 days of the purchase ($750 − $50) − [($750 − $50) × 2%]. The other choices are incorrect because (a) does not consider the discount of $14; (c) the amount of the discount is based upon the amount after the return is granted ($700 × 2%), not the amount before the return of merchandise ($750 × 2%); and (d) does not constitute payment in full on June 23.

**5. c.** The Cost of Goods Sold account normally appears in the ledger of a merchandising company using a perpetual inventory system. The other choices are incorrect because (a) the Purchases account, (b) the Freight-In account, and (d) the Purchase Discounts account all appear in the ledger of a merchandising company that uses a periodic inventory system.

**6. c.** Two journal entries are necessary: one to record the receipt of cash and sales revenue, and one to record the cost of goods sold and reduction of inventory. The other choices are incorrect because (a) only considers the recognition of the expense and ignores the revenue,

(b) only considers the recognition of revenue and leaves out the expense or cost of merchandise sold, and (d) the receipt of cash and sales revenue, not reduction of inventory, are paired together, and the cost of goods sold and reduction of inventory, not sales revenue, are paired together.

**7. a.** An additional adjusting journal entry for inventory may be needed in a merchandising company to adjust for a physical inventory count, but it is not needed for a service company. The other choices are incorrect because (b) closing journal entries and (c) a post-closing trial balance are required for both types of companies. Choice (d) is incorrect because while a multiple-step income statement is not required for a merchandising company, it is useful to distinguish income generated from operating the business versus income or loss from non-recurring, nonoperating items.

**8. d.** An investing activities section appears on the statement of cash flows, not on a multiple-step income statement. Choices (a) gross profit, (b) cost of goods sold, and (c) a sales section are all items reported on a multiple-step income statement.

**9. b.** Gross profit = Net sales of $400,000 − Cost of goods sold $310,000 = $90,000, not (a) $30,000, (c) $340,000, or (d) $400,000.

**10. c.** Both sales revenue and "Other revenues and gains" are reported in the revenues section of a single-step income statement. The other choices are incorrect because (a) gross profit is not reported on a single-step income statement, (b) cost of goods sold is included in the expenses section of a single-step income statement, and (d) income from operations is not shown separately on a single-step income statement.

**11. d.** Cost of goods sold appears on both a single-step and a multiple-step income statement. The other choices are incorrect because (a) inventory does not appear on either a single-step or a multiple-step income statement and (b) gross profit and (c) income from operations appear on a multiple-step income statement but not on a single-step income statement.

**12. a.** In a worksheet using a perpetual inventory system, inventory is shown in the adjusted trial balance debit column and in the balance sheet debit column. The other choices are incorrect because the Inventory account is not shown in the income statement columns.

**\*13. d.** In determining cost of goods sold in a periodic system, freight-in is added to net purchases. The other choices are incorrect because (a) purchase discounts are deducted from purchases, not net purchases; (b) freight-out is a cost of sales, not a cost of purchases; and (c) purchase returns and allowances are deducted from purchases, not net purchases.

**\*14. a.** Beginning inventory of $60,000 + Cost of goods purchased $380,000 − Ending inventory $50,000 = Cost of goods sold $390,000, not (b) $370,000, (c) $330,000, or (d) $420,000.

**\*15. b.** Purchases for resale are debited to the Purchases account. The other choices are incorrect because (a) purchases on account are debited to Purchases, not Inventory; (c) Purchase Returns and Allowances are always credited; and (d) freight costs are debited to Freight-In, not Purchases.

## Practice Brief Exercises

**1. (LO 1, 4)** The following are the components in determining cost of goods sold for (a) Frazier Company, (b) Todd Company, and (c) Abreu Enterprises. Determine the missing amounts.

*Compute the missing amounts in determining cost of goods sold.*

|   | Beginning Inventory | Purchases | Cost of Goods Available for Sale | Ending Inventory | Cost of Goods Sold |
|---|---|---|---|---|---|
| a. | $120,000 | $150,000 | ? | ? | $160,000 |
| b. | $ 50,000 | ? | $125,000 | $45,000 | ? |
| c. | ? | $220,000 | $330,000 | $61,000 | ? |

### Solution

**1. a.** Cost of goods available for sale = $120,000 + $150,000 = $270,000
  Ending inventory = $270,000 − $160,000 = $110,000

**b.** Purchases = $125,000 − $50,000 = $75,000
  Cost of goods sold = $125,000 − $45,000 = $80,000

**c.** Beginning inventory = $330,000 − $220,000 = $110,000
  Cost of goods sold = $330,000 − $61,000 = $269,000

**2. (LO 2)** Prepare the journal entries to record the following transactions on Robertson Company's books using a perpetual inventory system.

*Journalize purchase transactions.*

  **a.** On March 2, Melky Company sold $800,000 of merchandise to Robertson Company, terms 2/10, n/30.

  **b.** On March 6, Robertson Company returned $100,000 of the merchandise purchased on March 2.

  **c.** On March 12, Robertson Company paid the balance due to Melky Company.

### Solution

| **2. a.** | Inventory | 800,000 | |
|---|---|---|---|
| | Accounts Payable | | 800,000 |
| **b.** | Accounts Payable | 100,000 | |
| | Inventory | | 100,000 |
| **c.** | Accounts Payable ($800,000 − $100,000) | 700,000 | |
| | Inventory ($700,000 × 2%) | | 14,000 |
| | Cash ($700,000 − $14,000) | | 686,000 |

**3. (LO 3)** Prepare the journal entries to record the following transactions on Wendel Company's books using a perpetual inventory system.

*Journalize sales transactions.*

  **a.** On March 2, Wendel Company sold $700,000 of merchandise to Krista Company, terms 2/10, n/30. The cost of the merchandise sold was $460,000.

  **b.** On March 6, Krista Company returned $80,000 of the merchandise purchased on March 2. The cost of the merchandise returned was $54,000.

  **c.** On March 12, Wendel Company received the balance due from Krista Company.

**Solution**

**3. a.** March  2 | Accounts Receivable | 700,000 |
| | Sales Revenue | | 700,000 |

| | 2 | Cost of Goods Sold | 460,000 |
| | | Inventory | | 460,000 |

**b.** | 6 | Sales Returns and Allowances | 80,000 |
| | | Accounts Receivable | | 80,000 |

| | 6 | Inventory | 54,000 |
| | | Cost of Goods Sold | | 54,000 |

**c.** | 12 | Cash ($620,000 − $12,400) | 607,600 |
| | | Sales Discounts ($620,000 × 2%) | 12,400 |
| | | Accounts Receivable ($700,000 − $80,000) | | 620,000 |

*Prepare closing entries.*

**4. (LO 4)** Cabrera Company uses the perpetual inventory system and has the following account balances: Sales Revenue $300,000, Sales Returns and Allowances $10,000, Cost of Goods Sold $174,000, and Inventory $50,000. Prepare the entries to record the closing of these items to Income Summary.

**Solution**

**4.** | Sales Revenue | 300,000 |
| | Income Summary | | 300,000 |

| Income Summary | 184,000 |
| | Cost of Goods Sold | | 174,000 |
| | Sales Returns and Allowances | | 10,000 |

*Compute net sales, gross profit, income from operations, and gross profit rate.*

**5. (LO 5)** Assume Yoan Company has the following reported amounts: Sales revenue $400,000, Sales discounts $10,000, Cost of goods sold $234,000, and Operating expenses $60,000. Compute the following: (a) net sales, (b) gross profit, (c) income from operations, and (d) gross profit rate. (Round to one decimal place.)

**Solution**

**5. a.** Net sales = $400,000 − $10,000 = $390,000

   **b.** Gross profit = $390,000 − $234,000 = $156,000

   **c.** Income from operations = $156,000 − $60,000 = $96,000

   **d.** Gross profit rate = $156,000 ÷ $390,000 = 40%

# Practice Exercises

*Prepare purchase and sales entries.*

**1. (LO 2, 3)** On June 10, Vareen Company purchased $8,000 of merchandise on account from Harrah Company, FOB shipping point, terms 3/10, n/30. Vareen pays the freight costs of $400 on June 11. Damaged goods totaling $300 are returned to Harrah for credit on June 12. The fair value of these goods is $70. On June 19, Vareen pays Harrah Company in full, less the purchase discount. Both companies use a perpetual inventory system.

## Instructions

**a.** Prepare separate entries for each transaction on the books of Vareen Company.

**b.** Prepare separate entries for each transaction for Harrah Company. The merchandise purchased by Vareen on June 10 had cost Harrah $4,800.

## Solution

**1. a.**

| June 10 | Inventory | 8,000 | |
| | Accounts Payable | | 8,000 |
| 11 | Inventory | 400 | |
| | Cash | | 400 |

| | | | | |
|---|---|---|---:|---:|
| 12 | Accounts Payable | | 300 | |
| | Inventory | | | 300 |
| 19 | Accounts Payable ($8,000 − $300) | | 7,700 | |
| | Inventory ($7,700 × 3%) | | | 231 |
| | Cash ($7,700 − $231) | | | 7,469 |

**b.**

| | | | | |
|---|---|---|---:|---:|
| June 10 | Accounts Receivable | | 8,000 | |
| | Sales Revenue | | | 8,000 |
| | Cost of Goods Sold | | 4,800 | |
| | Inventory | | | 4,800 |
| 12 | Sales Returns and Allowances | | 300 | |
| | Accounts Receivable | | | 300 |
| | Inventory | | 70 | |
| | Cost of Goods Sold | | | 70 |
| 19 | Cash ($7,700 − $231) | | 7,469 | |
| | Sales Discounts ($7,700 × 3%) | | 231 | |
| | Accounts Receivable ($8,000 − $300) | | | 7,700 |

**2. (LO 5)** In its income statement for the year ended December 31, 2022, Marten Company reported the following condensed data.

*Prepare multiple-step and single-step income statements.*

| | | | | |
|---|---:|---|---:|
| Interest expense | $ 70,000 | Net sales | $2,200,000 |
| Operating expenses | 725,000 | Interest revenue | 25,000 |
| Cost of goods sold | 1,300,000 | Loss on disposal of plant assets | 17,000 |

### Instructions

a. Prepare a multiple-step income statement.

b. Prepare a single-step income statement.

### Solution

**2. a.**

**Marten Company**
**Income Statement**
**For the Year Ended December 31, 2022**

| | | |
|---|---:|---:|
| Net sales | | $2,200,000 |
| Cost of goods sold | | 1,300,000 |
| Gross profit | | 900,000 |
| Operating expenses | | 725,000 |
| Income from operations | | 175,000 |
| Other revenues and gains | | |
| Interest revenue | | 25,000 |
| Other expenses and losses | | |
| Interest expense | $70,000 | |
| Loss on disposal of plant assets | 17,000 | 87,000 |
| Net income | | $ 113,000 |

**b.**

**Marten Company**
**Income Statement**
**For the Year Ended December 31, 2022**

| | | |
|---|---:|---:|
| Revenues | | |
| Net sales | | $2,200,000 |
| Interest revenue | | 25,000 |
| Total revenues | | 2,225,000 |
| Expenses | | |
| Cost of goods sold | $1,300,000 | |
| Operating expenses | 725,000 | |
| Interest expense | 70,000 | |
| Loss on disposal of plant assets | 17,000 | |
| Total expenses | | 2,112,000 |
| Net income | | $ 113,000 |

## Practice Problem

*Prepare a multiple-step income statement.*

**(LO 5)** The adjusted trial balance columns of Falcetto Company for the year ended December 31, 2022, are as follows.

| | Debit | | Credit |
|---|---|---|---|
| Cash | 14,500 | Accumulated Depreciation— | |
| Accounts Receivable | 11,100 | Equipment | 18,000 |
| Inventory | 29,000 | Notes Payable | 25,000 |
| Prepaid Insurance | 2,500 | Accounts Payable | 10,600 |
| Equipment | 95,000 | Common Stock | 50,000 |
| Dividends | 12,000 | Retained Earnings | 31,000 |
| Sales Returns and Allowances | 6,700 | Sales Revenue | 536,800 |
| Sales Discounts | 5,000 | Interest Revenue | 2,500 |
| Cost of Goods Sold | 363,400 | | 673,900 |
| Freight-Out | 7,600 | | |
| Advertising Expense | 12,000 | | |
| Salaries and Wages Expense | 56,000 | | |
| Utilities Expense | 18,000 | | |
| Rent Expense | 24,000 | | |
| Depreciation Expense | 9,000 | | |
| Insurance Expense | 4,500 | | |
| Interest Expense | 3,600 | | |
| | 673,900 | | |

### Instructions

Prepare a multiple-step income statement for Falcetto Company.

### Solution

**Falcetto Company**
**Income Statement**
**For the Year Ended December 31, 2022**

| | | |
|---|---|---|
| Sales | | |
| Sales revenue | | $536,800 |
| Less: Sales returns and allowances | $ 6,700 | |
| Sales discounts | 5,000 | 11,700 |
| Net sales | | 525,100 |
| Cost of goods sold | | 363,400 |
| Gross profit | | 161,700 |
| Operating expenses | | |
| Salaries and wages expense | 56,000 | |
| Rent expense | 24,000 | |
| Utilities expense | 18,000 | |
| Advertising expense | 12,000 | |
| Depreciation expense | 9,000 | |
| Freight-out | 7,600 | |
| Insurance expense | 4,500 | |
| Total operating expenses | | 131,100 |
| Income from operations | | 30,600 |
| Other revenues and gains | | |
| Interest revenue | | 2,500 |
| Other expenses and losses | | |
| Interest expense | | 3,600 |
| Net income | | $ 29,500 |

Brief Exercises, DO IT! Exercises, Exercises, Problems, Data Analytics Activities, and many additional resources are available for practice in WileyPLUS.

*Note:* All asterisked Questions, Exercises, and Problems relate to material in the appendices to the chapter

## Questions

1. (a) "The steps in the accounting cycle for a merchandising company are different from the accounting cycle for a service company." (b) "The measurement of net income for a merchandising company is conceptually the same as for a service company." Explain why each statement is true or false.

2. Why is the normal operating cycle for a merchandising company likely to be longer than for a service company?

3. What components of revenues and expenses are different between merchandising and service companies?

4. How does income measurement differ between a merchandising and a service company?

5. When is cost of goods sold determined in a perpetual inventory system?

6. Distinguish between FOB shipping point and FOB destination. Identify the freight terms that will result in a debit to Inventory by the buyer and a debit to Freight-Out by the seller.

7. Explain the meaning of the credit terms 2/10, n/30.

8. Goods costing $2,000 are purchased on account on July 15 with credit terms of 2/10, n/30. On July 18, a $200 credit memo is received from the supplier for damaged goods. Give the journal entry on July 24 to record payment of the balance due within the discount period using a perpetual inventory system.

9. Masie Ascot believes revenues from credit sales may be recorded before they are collected in cash. Explain why Masie is correct or incorrect.

10. (a) What is the primary source document for recording (1) cash sales and (2) credit sales? (b) Using XXs for amounts, give the journal entry for each of the transactions in part (a).

11. A credit sale is made on July 10 for $900, terms 1/15, n/30. On July 12 the purchaser returns $100 of goods for credit. Give the journal entry on July 19 to record the receipt of the balance due within the discount period.

12. Explain why the Inventory account will usually require adjustment at year-end for a merchandiser that uses the perpetual inventory system.

13. Prepare the closing entries for the Sales Revenue account, assuming a balance of $200,000 and the Cost of Goods Sold account with a $145,000 balance.

14. What merchandising account(s) will appear in the post-closing trial balance?

15. Minnick Co. has net sales of $105,000, cost of goods sold of $70,000, and operating expenses of $20,000. What is its gross profit and its gross profit rate?

16. Scribe Company reports net sales of $800,000, gross profit of $560,000, and net income of $230,000. What are its operating expenses, assuming that there are no nonoperating activities?

17. Identify the distinguishing features of a multiple-step income statement for a merchandising company.

18. Identify the sections of a multiple-step income statement that relate to (a) operating activities, and (b) nonoperating activities.

19. How does the single-step form of income statement differ from the multiple-step form?

20. What title does **Apple** use for gross profit? By how much did its 2018 gross profit change, and in what direction, when compared to 2017?

*21. Indicate the columns of the worksheet in a perpetual system in which (a) inventory and (b) cost of goods sold will be shown.

*22. Identify the accounts that are added to or deducted from Purchases in a periodic system to determine the cost of goods purchased. For each account, indicate whether it is added or deducted.

*23. On July 15, a company purchases on account goods costing $1,900, with credit terms of 2/10, n/30. On July 18, the company receives a $400 credit memo from the supplier for damaged goods. Give the journal entry on July 24 to record payment of the balance due within the discount period assuming a periodic inventory system.

## Brief Exercises

**BE5.1 (LO 1), AP** The following are the components in determining cost of goods sold. Determine the missing amounts.

*Compute missing amounts in determining cost of goods sold.*

|  | Beginning Inventory | Purchases | Cost of Goods Available for Sale | Ending Inventory | Cost of Goods Sold |
|---|---|---|---|---|---|
| a. | $80,000 | $100,000 | ? | ? | $120,000 |
| b. | $50,000 | ? | $115,000 | $35,000 | ? |
| c. | ? | $110,000 | $160,000 | $29,000 | ? |

*Compute missing amounts in determining net income.*

**BE5.2 (LO 1), AP** The following are the components in Gates Company's income statement. Determine the missing amounts, assuming that there are no nonoperating activities.

| | Sales Revenue | Cost of Goods Sold | Gross Profit | Operating Expenses | Net Income |
|---|---|---|---|---|---|
| a. | $ 75,000 | ? | $ 30,000 | ? | $12,100 |
| b. | $108,000 | $70,000 | ? | ? | $29,500 |
| c. | ? | $71,900 | $109,600 | $46,200 | ? |

*Journalize perpetual inventory entries.*

**BE5.3 (LO 2, 3), AP** Rita Company buys merchandise on account from Linus Company. The selling price of the goods is $900, and the cost of the goods is $590. Both companies use perpetual inventory systems. Journalize the transaction on the books of both companies.

*Journalize sales transactions.*

**BE5.4 (LO 3), AP** Prepare the journal entries to record the following transactions on Borst Company's books using a perpetual inventory system.

a. On March 2, Borst Company sold $800,000 of merchandise on account to McLeena Company, terms 2/10, n/30. The cost of the merchandise sold was $540,000.

b. On March 6, McLeena Company returned $140,000 of the merchandise purchased on March 2. The cost of the returned merchandise was $94,000.

c. On March 12, Borst Company received the balance due from McLeena Company.

*Journalize purchase transactions.*

**BE5.5 (LO 2), AP** Prepare the journal entries to record the following transactions on McLeena Company's books under a perpetual inventory system.

a. On March 2, Borst Company sold $800,000 of merchandise on account to McLeena Company, terms 2/10, n/30. The cost of the merchandise sold was $540,000.

b. On March 6, McLeena Company returned $140,000 of the merchandise purchased on March 2. The cost of the returned merchandise was $94,000.

c. On March 12, Borst Company received the balance due from McLeena Company.

*Prepare adjusting entry for inventory.*

**BE5.6 (LO 4), AP** At year-end, the perpetual inventory records of Litwin Company showed merchandise inventory of $98,000. The company determined, however, that its actual inventory on hand was $95,700. Record the necessary adjusting entry.

*Prepare closing entries for accounts.*

**BE5.7 (LO 4), AP** Hudson Company has the following account balances: Sales Revenue $195,000, Sales Discounts $2,000, Cost of Goods Sold $117,000, and Inventory $40,000. Prepare the entries to record the closing of these accounts to Income Summary under a perpetual inventory system.

*Prepare sales section of income statement.*

**BE5.8 (LO 5), AP** Barto Company provides the following information for the month ended October 31, 2022; sales on credit $300,000, cash sales $150,000, sales discounts $5,000, and sales returns and allowances $19,000. Prepare the sales section of a multiple-step income statement based on this information.

*Explain the presentation of a multiple-step income statement.*

**BE5.9 (LO 5), C** Writing Explain where each of the following items would appear on a multiple-step income statement: gain on disposal of plant assets, cost of goods sold, depreciation expense, and sales returns and allowances.

*Compute net sales, gross profit, income from operations, and gross profit rate.*

**BE5.10 (LO 5), AP** Assume Kader Company has the following reported amounts: Sales revenue $510,000, Sales returns and allowances $15,000, Cost of goods sold $330,000, and Operating expenses $110,000. Compute the following: (a) net sales, (b) gross profit, (c) income from operations, and (d) gross profit rate. (Round to one decimal place.)

*Identify worksheet columns for selected accounts.*

**\*BE5.11 (LO 6), C** Presented below is the format of a partial worksheet using the perpetual inventory system presented in Appendix 5A.

| Trial Balance | | Adjusted Trial Balance | | Income Statement | | Balance Sheet | |
|---|---|---|---|---|---|---|---|
| Dr. | Cr. | Dr. | Cr. | Dr. | Cr. | Dr. | Cr. |

Indicate where the following items will appear on the worksheet: (a) Cash, (b) Inventory, (c) Sales revenue, and (d) Cost of goods sold.

*Example:*
Cash: Trial balance debit column; Adjusted trial balance debit column; and Balance sheet debit column.

*Compute net purchases and cost of goods purchased.*

**\*BE5.12 (LO 7), AP** Assume that Space Company uses a periodic inventory system and has these account balances: Purchases $404,000, Purchase Returns and Allowances $13,000, Purchase Discounts $9,000, and Freight-In $16,000. Determine net purchases and cost of goods purchased.

**\*BE5.13 (LO 7), AP** Assume that Space Company uses a periodic inventory system and has these account balances: Purchases $404,000, Purchase Returns and Allowances $13,000, Purchase Discounts $9,000, and Freight-In $16,000. Assume also that Space Company has beginning inventory of $60,000, ending inventory of $90,000, and net sales of $612,000. Determine the amounts to be reported for cost of goods sold and gross profit.

*Compute cost of goods sold and gross profit.*

**\*BE5.14 (LO 7), AP** Prepare the journal entries to record these transactions on Kimble Company's books using a periodic inventory system.

*Journalize purchase transactions.*

   **a.** On March 2, Kimble Company purchased $800,000 of merchandise on account from Poe Company, terms 2/10, n/30.

   **b.** On March 6, Kimble Company returned $130,000 of the merchandise purchased on March 2.

   **c.** On March 12, Kimble Company paid the balance due to Poe Company.

**\*BE5.15 (LO 7), AP** A. Hall Company has the following merchandise account balances: Sales Revenue $180,000, Sales Discounts $2,000, Purchases $120,000, and Purchases Returns and Allowances $30,000. In addition, it has a beginning inventory of $40,000 and an ending inventory of $30,000. Prepare the entries to record the closing of these items to Income Summary using the periodic inventory system.

*Prepare closing entries for merchandise accounts.*

**\*BE5.16 (LO 7), C** The following is the format of a partial worksheet using the periodic inventory system presented in Appendix 5B.

*Identify worksheet columns for selected accounts.*

| Trial Balance | | Adjusted Trial Balance | | Income Statement | | Balance Sheet | |
|---|---|---|---|---|---|---|---|
| Dr. | Cr. | Dr. | Cr. | Dr. | Cr. | Dr. | Cr. |

Indicate where the following items will appear on the worksheet: (a) Cash, (b) Beginning inventory, (c) Accounts payable, and (d) Ending inventory.

*Example*
Cash: Trial balance debit column; Adjustment trial balance debit column; and Balance sheet debit column.

# DO IT! Exercises

**DO IT! 5.1 (LO 1), C** Indicate whether the following statements are true or false. If false, indicate how to correct the statement.

*Answer general questions about merchandisers.*

   **1.** A merchandising company reports gross profit but a service company does not.

   **2.** Under a periodic inventory system, a company determines the cost of goods sold each time a sale occurs.

   **3.** A service company is likely to use accounts receivable but a merchandising company is not likely to do so.

   **4.** Under a periodic inventory system, the cost of goods on hand at the beginning of the accounting period plus the cost of goods purchased less the cost of goods on hand at the end of the accounting period equals cost of goods sold.

**DO IT! 5.2 (LO 2), AF** On October 5, Iverson Company buys merchandise on account from Lasse Company. The selling price of the goods is $5,000, and the cost to Lasse Company is $3,000. On October 8, Iverson returns defective goods with a selling price of $640 and a fair value of $240. Record the transactions on the books of Iverson Company.

*Record transactions of purchasing company.*

**DO IT! 5.3 (LO 3), AP** On October 5, Iverson Company buys merchandise on account from Lasse Company. The selling price of the goods is $5,000, and the cost to Lasse Company is $3,000. On October 8, Iverson returns defective goods with a selling price of $640 and a fair value of $240. Record the transactions on the books of Lasse Company.

*Record transactions of selling company.*

**DO IT! 5.4 (LO 4), AF** The adjusted trial balance of Optique Boutique at December 31 shows Inventory $21,000, Sales Revenue $156,000, Sales Returns and Allowances $4,000, Sales Discounts $3,000, Cost of Goods Sold $92,400, Interest Revenue $5,000, Freight-Out $1,500, Utilities Expense $7,400, and Salaries and Wages Expense $19,500. Prepare the closing entries for Optique for these accounts.

*Prepare closing entries for a merchandising company.*

*Prepare a multiple-step income statement.*

**DO IT! 5.5 (LO 5), AP** The following information is available for Berlin Corp. for the year ended December 31, 2022:

| | | | |
|---|---|---|---|
| Other revenues and gains | $ 12,700 | Sales revenue | $592,000 |
| Other expenses and losses | 13,300 | Operating expenses | 186,000 |
| Cost of goods sold | 156,000 | Sales returns and allowances | 40,000 |

Prepare a multiple-step income statement for Berlin Corp.

# Exercises

*Answer general questions about merchandisers.*

**E5.1 (LO 1), C** Mr. Etemadi has prepared the following list of statements about service companies and merchandisers.

1. Measuring net income for a merchandiser is conceptually the same as for a service company.
2. For a merchandiser, sales less operating expenses is called gross profit.
3. For a merchandiser, the primary source of revenue is the sale of inventory.
4. Sales salaries and wages is an example of an operating expense.
5. The operating cycle of a merchandiser is the same as that of a service company.
6. In a perpetual inventory system, no detailed inventory records of goods on hand are maintained in the Inventory account.
7. In a periodic inventory system, the cost of goods sold is determined only at the end of the reporting period.
8. A periodic inventory system provides better control over inventories than a perpetual system.

**Instructions**

Identify each statement as true or false. If false, indicate how to correct the statement.

*Journalize purchase transactions.*

**E5.2 (LO 2), AP** Information related to Rice Co. is presented below.

1. On April 5, purchased merchandise on account from Jax Company for $28,000, terms 2/10, net/30, FOB shipping point.
2. On April 6, paid freight costs of $700 on merchandise purchased from Jax.
3. On April 7, purchased equipment on account for $30,000.
4. On April 8, returned $3,600 of merchandise to Jax Company.
5. On April 15, paid the amount due to Jax Company in full.

**Instructions**

a. Prepare the journal entries to record these transactions on the books of Rice Co. under a perpetual inventory system.
b. Assume that Rice Co. paid the balance due to Jax Company on May 4 instead of April 15. Prepare the journal entry to record this payment.

*Journalize perpetual inventory entries.*

**E5.3 (LO 2, 3), AP** Assume that on September 1, **Office Depot** had an inventory that included a variety of calculators. The company uses a perpetual inventory system. During September, these transactions occurred.

Sept.  6   Purchased calculators from Dragoo Co. at a total cost of $1,600, on account, terms n/30, FOB shipping point.
  9   Paid freight of $50 on calculators purchased from Dragoo Co.
  10   Returned calculators to Dragoo Co. for $66 credit because they did not meet specifications.
  12   Sold calculators costing $520 for $690 to Fryer Book Store, on account, terms n/30.
  14   Granted credit of $45 to Fryer Book Store for the return of one calculator that was not ordered. The calculator cost $34.
  20   Sold calculators costing $570 for $760 to Heasley Card Shop, on account, terms n/30.

**Instructions**

Journalize the September transactions for Office Depot.

**E5.4 (LO 2, 3), AP** On June 10, Pais Company purchased $9,000 of merchandise on account from McGiver Company, FOB shipping point, terms 3/10, n/30. Pais pays the freight costs of $400 on June 11. Goods totaling $600 are returned to McGiver for credit on June 12. On June 19, Pais pays McGiver Company in full, less the discount. Both companies use a perpetual inventory system.

*Journalize perpetual inventory entries.*

**Instructions**

a.  Prepare separate entries for each transaction on the books of Pais Company.

b.  Prepare separate entries for each transaction for McGiver Company. The merchandise purchased by Pais on June 10 cost McGiver $5,000, and the goods returned cost McGiver $310.

**E5.5 (LO 3), AP** The following transactions are for Alonzo Company.

*Journalize sales transactions.*

1.  On December 3, Alonzo Company sold $500,000 of merchandise to Arte Co., on account, terms 1/10, n/30. The cost of the merchandise sold was $330,000.

2.  On December 8, Arte Co. was granted an allowance of $25,000 for merchandise purchased on December 3.

3.  On December 13, Alonzo Company received the balance due from Arte Co.

**Instructions**

a.  Prepare the journal entries to record these transactions on the books of Alonzo Company using a perpetual inventory system.

b.  Assume that Alonzo Company received the balance due from Arte Co. on January 2 of the following year instead of December 13. Prepare the journal entry to record the receipt of payment on January 2.

**E5.6 (LO 4, 5), AP** The adjusted trial balance of Doge Company shows the following data pertaining to sales at the end of its fiscal year October 31, 2022: Sales Revenue $900,000, Freight-Out $14,000, Sales Returns and Allowances $22,000, and Sales Discounts $13,500.

*Prepare sales section and closing entries.*

**Instructions**

a.  Prepare the sales section of the multiple-step income statement.

b.  Prepare separate closing entries for (1) sales revenue, and (2) the contra accounts to sales revenue.

**E5.7 (LO 4), AP** Juan Morales Company had the following account balances at year-end: Cost of Goods Sold $60,000, Inventory $15,000, Utilities Expense $29,000, Sales Revenue $115,000, Sales Discounts $1,200, and Sales Returns and Allowances $1,700. A physical count of inventory determines that merchandise inventory on hand is $13,900.

*Prepare adjusting and closing entries.*

**Instructions**

a.  Prepare the adjusting entry necessary as a result of the physical count.

b.  Prepare closing entries.

**E5.8 (LO 4), AP** Presented below is selected information related to Garland Co. for the year ended January 31, 2022.

*Prepare adjusting and closing entries.*

| | | | |
|---|---|---|---|
| Ending inventory per perpetual records | $ 21,600 | Insurance expense | $ 12,000 |
| | | Rent expense | 20,000 |
| Ending inventory actually on hand | 21,000 | Salaries and wages expense | 55,000 |
| | | Sales discounts | 10,000 |
| Cost of goods sold | 218,000 | Sales returns and allowances | 13,000 |
| Freight-out | 7,000 | Sales revenue | 380,000 |

**Instructions**

a.  Prepare the necessary adjusting entry for inventory.

b.  Prepare the necessary closing entries.

**E5.9 (LO 5), AP** Presented below is selected information for Lien Co. for the month of January 2022.

*Prepare an income statement and calculate the gross profit rate.*

| | | | |
|---|---|---|---|
| Cost of goods sold | $212,000 | Rent expense | $ 32,000 |
| Freight-out | 7,000 | Sales discounts | 8,000 |
| Insurance expense | 12,000 | Sales returns and allowances | 20,000 |
| Salaries and wages expense | 60,000 | Sales revenue | 370,000 |

**Instructions**

a.  Prepare an income statement using the format presented in Illustration 5.14.

b.  Compute the gross profit rate.

*Prepare income statements.*

**E5.10 (LO 5), AP** In its income statement for the year ended December 31, 2022, Laine Inc. reported the following condensed data.

| | | | |
|---|---|---|---|
| Operating expenses | $ 725,000 | Interest revenue | $ 33,000 |
| Cost of goods sold | 1,256,000 | Loss on disposal of plant assets | 17,000 |
| Interest expense | 70,000 | Net sales | 2,200,000 |

**Instructions**

a. Prepare a multiple-step income statement.

b. Prepare a single-step income statement.

*Prepare correcting entries for sales and purchases.*

**E5.11 (LO 2, 3), AN** An inexperienced accountant for Huang Company made the following errors in recording merchandising transactions.

1. A $195 refund to a customer for faulty merchandise was debited to Sales Revenue $195 and credited to Cash $195.

2. A $180 credit purchase of supplies was debited to Inventory $180 and credited to Cash $180.

3. A $215 sales discount was debited to Sales Revenue.

4. A cash payment of $20 for freight on merchandise purchases was debited to Freight-Out $200 and credited to Cash $200. Huang uses the perpetual inventory system.

**Instructions**

Prepare separate correcting entries for each error, assuming that the incorrect entry is not reversed. (Omit explanations.)

*Compute various income measures.*

**E5.12 (LO 5), AP** In 2022, Matt Cruz Company had net sales of $900,000 and cost of goods sold of $522,000. Operating expenses were $225,000, and interest expense was $11,000. Cruz prepares a multiple-step income statement.

**Instructions**

a. Compute Cruz's gross profit.

b. Compute the gross profit rate. Why is this rate computed by financial statement users?

c. What is Cruz's income from operations and net income?

d. If Cruz prepared a single-step income statement, what amount would it report for net income?

e. In what section of its classified balance sheet should Cruz report inventory?

*Compute missing amounts and compute gross profit rate.*

**E5.13 (LO 5), AN** Financial information is presented here for two different companies.

| | Yoste Company | Noone Company |
|---|---|---|
| Sales revenue | $90,000 | $    (d) |
| Sales returns and allowances | (a) | 5,000 |
| Net sales | 84,000 | 100,000 |
| Cost of goods sold | 58,000 | (e) |
| Gross profit | (b) | 40,000 |
| Operating expenses | 14,380 | (f) |
| Net income | (c) | 17,000 |

**Instructions**

a. Fill in the missing amounts. Assume that there are no nonoperating activities.

b. Calculate the gross profit rate for each company. (Round to one decimal place.)

*Compute missing amounts.*

**E5.14 (LO 5), AN** The following financial information is presented for three different companies.

| | Allen Cosmetics | Bast Grocery | Corr Wholesalers |
|---|---|---|---|
| Sales revenue | $90,000 | $    (e) | $122,000 |
| Sales returns and allowances | (a) | 5,000 | 12,000 |
| Net sales | 86,000 | 95,000 | (i) |
| Cost of goods sold | 56,000 | (f) | (j) |
| Gross profit | (b) | 38,000 | 24,000 |
| Operating expenses | 15,000 | (g) | 18,000 |
| Income from operations | (c) | (h) | (k) |
| Other expenses and losses | 4,000 | 7,000 | (l) |
| Net income | (d) | 11,000 | 5,000 |

## Instructions

Determine the missing amounts.

***E5.15 (LO 6), AP*** Presented below are selected accounts for Salazar Company as reported in the worksheet using a perpetual inventory system at the end of May 2022.

*Complete worksheet using a perpetual inventory system.*

| Accounts | Adjusted Trial Balance | | Income Statement | | Balance Sheet | |
|---|---|---|---|---|---|---|
| | Dr. | Cr. | Dr. | Cr. | Dr. | Cr. |
| Cash | 11,000 | | | | | |
| Inventory | 76,000 | | | | | |
| Sales Revenue | | 480,000 | | | | |
| Sales Returns and Allowances | 10,000 | | | | | |
| Sales Discounts | 9,000 | | | | | |
| Cost of Goods Sold | 300,000 | | | | | |

## Instructions

Complete the worksheet by extending amounts reported in the adjusted trial balance to the appropriate columns in the worksheet. Do not total individual columns.

***E5.16 (LO 6), AP*** The trial balance columns of the worksheet using a perpetual inventory system for Marquez Company at June 30, 2022, are as follows.

*Prepare a worksheet using a perpetual inventory system.*

**Marquez Company**
**Worksheet**
**For the Month Ended June 30, 2022**

| Account Titles | Trial Balance | |
|---|---|---|
| | Debit | Credit |
| Cash | 1,920 | |
| Accounts Receivable | 2,440 | |
| Inventory | 11,640 | |
| Accounts Payable | | 1,120 |
| Common Stock | | 3,500 |
| Sales Revenue | | 42,500 |
| Cost of Goods Sold | 20,560 | |
| Utilities Expense | 10,560 | |
| | 47,120 | 47,120 |

Adjustment data:

Utility costs incurred on account, but not yet recorded, total $1,500.

## Instructions

Enter the trial balance on a worksheet and complete the worksheet.

***E5.17 (LO 7), AP*** The adjusted trial balance of Mendez Company at the end of its fiscal year, August 31, 2022, includes these accounts: Inventory $18,700, Purchases $154,000, Sales Revenue $190,000, Freight-In $8,000, Sales Returns and Allowances $3,000, Freight-Out $1,000, and Purchase Returns and Allowances $5,000. The ending inventory is $21,000.

*Prepare cost of goods sold section.*

## Instructions

Prepare a cost of goods sold section on the income statement for the year ending August 31, 2022 (periodic inventory system).

***E5.18 (LO 7), AP*** On January 1, 2022, Christel Madan Corporation had inventory of $50,000. At December 31, 2022, Christel Madan had the following account balances.

*Compute various income statement items.*

| | |
|---|---|
| Freight-in | $ 4,000 |
| Purchases | 509,000 |
| Purchase discounts | 6,000 |
| Purchase returns and allowances | 2,000 |
| Sales revenue | 840,000 |
| Sales discounts | 5,000 |
| Sales returns and allowances | 10,000 |

At December 31, 2022, Christel Madan determines that its ending inventory is $60,000. Christel Madan uses the periodic inventory system.

**Instructions**

a. Compute Christel Madan's 2022 gross profit.

b. Compute Christel Madan's 2022 operating expenses if net income is $130,000 and there are no non-operating activities.

*Prepare cost of goods sold section.*

**\*E5.19 (LO 7), AN** Below is a series of cost of goods sold sections for companies B, M, O, and S.

|  | **B** | **M** | **O** | **S** |
|---|---|---|---|---|
| Beginning inventory | $ 250 | $ 120 | $ 700 | $    (j) |
| Purchases | 1,500 | 1,080 | (g) | 43,590 |
| Purchase returns and allowances | 80 | (d) | 290 | (k) |
| Net purchases | (a) | 1,040 | 7,410 | 42,290 |
| Freight-in | 130 | (e) | (h) | 2,240 |
| Cost of goods purchased | (b) | 1,230 | 8,050 | (l) |
| Cost of goods available for sale | 1,800 | 1,350 | (i) | 49,530 |
| Ending inventory | 310 | (f) | 1,150 | 6,230 |
| Cost of goods sold | (c) | 1,230 | 7,600 | 43,300 |

**Instruction**

Fill in the lettered blanks to complete the cost of goods sold sections.

*Journalize purchase transactions.*

**\*E5.20 (LO 7), AP** This information relates to Alfie Co.

1. On April 5, purchased merchandise from Bach Company for $27,000, on account, terms 2/10, net/30, FOB shipping point.

2. On April 6, paid freight costs of $1,200 on merchandise purchased from Bach Company.

3. On April 7, purchased equipment on account for $30,000.

4. On April 8, returned $3,600 of the April 5 merchandise to Bach Company.

5. On April 15, paid the amount due to Bach Company in full.

**Instructions**

a. Prepare the journal entries to record these transactions on the books of Alfie Co. using a periodic inventory system.

b. Assume that Alfie Co. paid the balance due to Bach Company on May 4 instead of April 15. Prepare the journal entry to record this payment.

*Journalize purchase transactions.*

**\*E5.21 (LO 7), AP** The following information is related to Lor Co.

1. On April 5, purchased merchandise on account from Garcia Company for $19,000, terms 2/10, net/30, FOB shipping point.

2. On April 6, paid freight costs of $800 on merchandise purchased from Garcia.

3. On April 7, purchased equipment on account from Holifield Mfg. Co. for $23,000.

4. On April 8, returned merchandise that cost $4,000 to Garcia Company.

5. On April 15, paid the amount due to Garcia Company in full.

**Instructions**

a. Prepare the journal entries to record the preceding transactions on the books of Lor Co. using a periodic inventory system.

b. Assume that Lor Co. paid the balance due to Garcia Company on May 4 instead of April 15. Prepare the journal entry to record this payment.

*Complete worksheet.*

**\*E5.22 (LO 6, 7), AP** The following are selected accounts for B. Midler Company as reported in the worksheet at the end of May 2022. Ending inventory is $75,000.

| Accounts | Adjusted Trial Balance | | Income Statement | | Balance Sheet | |
|---|---|---|---|---|---|---|
|  | Dr. | Cr. | Dr. | Cr. | Dr. | Cr. |
| Cash | 9,000 |  |  |  |  |  |
| Inventory | 80,000 |  |  |  |  |  |
| Purchases | 240,000 |  |  |  |  |  |
| Purchase Returns and Allowances |  | 30,000 |  |  |  |  |
| Sales Revenue |  | 450,000 |  |  |  |  |
| Sales Returns and Allowances | 10,000 |  |  |  |  |  |
| Sales Discounts | 5,000 |  |  |  |  |  |
| Rent Expense | 42,000 |  |  |  |  |  |

## Instructions

Complete the worksheet by extending amounts reported in the adjusted trial balance columns to the appropriate columns in the worksheet. The company uses the periodic inventory system.

## Problems

**P5.1 (LO 2, 3), AP**  Powell's Warehouse distributes hardback books to retail stores and extends credit terms of 2/10, n/30 to all of its customers. During the month of June, the following merchandising transactions occurred.

*Journalize purchase and sales transactions under a perpetual inventory system.*

| June | 1 | Purchased books on account for $1,040 from Catlin Publishers, terms 2/10, n/30. |
|---|---|---|
| | 3 | Sold books on account to Garfunkle Bookstore for $1,200. The cost of the books sold was $720. |
| | 6 | Received $40 credit for books returned to Catlin Publishers. |
| | 9 | Paid Catlin Publishers in full. |
| | 15 | Received payment in full from Garfunkle Bookstore. |
| | 17 | Sold books on account to Bell Tower for $1,200. The cost of the merchandise sold was $730. |
| | 20 | Purchased books on account for $800 from Priceless Book Publishers, terms 1/15, n/30. |
| | 24 | Received payment in full from Bell Tower. |
| | 26 | Paid Priceless Book Publishers in full. |
| | 28 | Sold books on account to General Bookstore for $1,300. The cost of the merchandise sold was $780. |
| | 30 | Granted General Bookstore $130 credit for books returned costing $80. |

## Instructions

Journalize the transactions for the month of June for Powell's Warehouse using a perpetual inventory system.

**P5.2 (LO 2, 3, 5), AP**  Winters Hardware Store completed the following merchandising transactions in the month of May. At the beginning of May, the ledger of Winters showed Cash of $8,000 and Common Stock of $8,000.

*Journalize, post, and prepare a partial income statement.*

| May | 1 | Purchased merchandise on account from Black Wholesale Supply for $8,000, terms 1/10, n/30. |
|---|---|---|
| | 2 | Sold merchandise on account $4,400, terms 2/10, n/30. The cost of the merchandise sold was $3,300. |
| | 5 | Received credit from Black Wholesale Supply for merchandise returned $200. |
| | 9 | Received collections in full, less discounts, from customers billed on May 2. |
| | 10 | Paid Black Wholesale Supply in full, less discount. |
| | 11 | Purchased supplies for cash $900. |
| | 12 | Purchased merchandise for cash $3,100. |
| | 15 | Received $230 refund for return of poor-quality merchandise from supplier on cash purchase. |
| | 17 | Purchased merchandise on account from Wilhelm Distributors for $2,500, terms 2/10, n/30, FOB shipping point. |
| | 19 | Paid freight on May 17 purchase $250. |
| | 24 | Sold merchandise for cash $5,500. The merchandise sold had a cost of $4,100. |
| | 25 | Purchased merchandise on account from Clasps, Inc. for $800, terms 3/10, n/30. |
| | 27 | Paid Wilhelm Distributors in full, less discount. |
| | 29 | Made refunds to cash customers for returned merchandise $124. The returned merchandise cost $90. |
| | 31 | Sold merchandise on account for $1,280 terms n/30. The cost of the merchandise sold was $830. |

Winters Hardware's chart of accounts includes the following: No. 101 Cash, No. 112 Accounts Receivable, No. 120 Inventory, No. 126 Supplies, No. 201 Accounts Payable, No. 311 Common Stock, No. 401 Sales Revenue, No. 412 Sales Returns and Allowances, No. 414 Sales Discounts, and No. 505 Cost of Goods Sold.

## Instructions

a. Journalize the transactions using a perpetual inventory system.

b. Enter the beginning cash and common stock balances and post the transactions. (Use J1 for the journal reference.)

c. Prepare an income statement through gross profit for the month of May 2022.

c. Gross profit $2,828

*Prepare financial statements and adjusting and closing entries.*

**P5.3 (LO 4, 5), AP** The Deluxe Store is located in midtown Madison. At the end of the company's fiscal year on November 30, 2022, the following accounts with normal balances appeared in two of its trial balances.

| | Unadjusted | Adjusted |
|---|---|---|
| Accounts Payable | $ 25,200 | $ 25,200 |
| Accounts Receivable | 30,500 | 30,500 |
| Accumulated Depr.—Equip. | 34,000 | 45,000 |
| Cash | 26,000 | 26,000 |
| Common Stock | 40,000 | 40,000 |
| Cost of Goods Sold | 507,000 | 507,000 |
| Dividends | 10,000 | 10,000 |
| Freight-Out | 6,500 | 6,500 |
| Equipment | 146,000 | 146,000 |
| Depreciation Expense | | 11,000 |
| Insurance Expense | | 7,000 |
| Interest Expense | 6,400 | 6,400 |
| Interest Revenue | 8,000 | 8,000 |
| Inventory | 29,000 | 29,000 |
| Notes Payable | 37,000 | 37,000 |
| Prepaid Insurance | 10,500 | 3,500 |
| Property Tax Expense | | 2,500 |
| Property Taxes Payable | | 2,500 |
| Rent Expense | 15,000 | 15,000 |
| Retained Earnings | 61,700 | 61,700 |
| Salaries and Wages Expense | 96,000 | 96,000 |
| Sales Commissions Expense | 6,500 | 11,000 |
| Sales Commissions Payable | | 4,500 |
| Sales Returns and Allowances | 8,000 | 8,000 |
| Sales Revenue | 700,000 | 700,000 |
| Utilities Expense | 8,500 | 8,500 |

**Instructions**

*a. Net income $29,100*
*Retained earnings $80,800*
*Total assets $190,000*

**a.** Prepare a multiple-step income statement, a retained earnings statement, and a classified balance sheet. Notes payable are due in 2025. The Deluxe Store uses the perpetual inventory system.

**b.** Journalize the adjusting entries that were made.

**c.** Journalize the closing entries that are necessary.

*Journalize, post, and prepare a trial balance.*

**P5.4 (LO 2, 3, 4), AP** At the beginning of the current season on April 1, the ledger of Granite Hills Pro Shop showed Cash $2,500, Inventory $3,500, and Common Stock $6,000. The following transactions were completed during April 2022.

| Apr. | 5 | Purchased golf discs, bags, and other inventory on account from Arnie Co. $1,500, FOB shipping point, terms 3/10, n/60. |
|---|---|---|
| | 7 | Paid freight on the Arnie purchase $80. |
| | 9 | Received credit from Arnie Co. for merchandise returned $200. |
| | 10 | Sold merchandise on account for $1,340, terms n/30. The merchandise sold had a cost of $820. |
| | 12 | Purchased disc golf shirts and other accessories on account from Woods Sportswear $830, terms 1/10, n/30. |
| | 14 | Paid Arnie Co. in full, less discount. |
| | 17 | Received credit from Woods Sportswear for merchandise returned $30. |
| | 20 | Made sales on account to members for $810, terms n/30. The cost of the merchandise sold was $550. |
| | 21 | Paid Woods Sportswear in full, less discount. |
| | 27 | Granted an allowance to members for clothing that did not fit $80. |
| | 30 | Received payments on account from members $1,220. |

The chart of accounts for the store includes the following: No. 101 Cash, No. 112 Accounts Receivable, No. 120 Inventory, No. 201 Accounts Payable, No. 311 Common Stock, No. 401 Sales Revenue, No. 412 Sales Returns and Allowances, and No. 505 Cost of Goods Sold.

## Instructions

a. Journalize the April transactions using a perpetual inventory system.

b. Enter the beginning balances in the ledger accounts and post the April transactions. (Use J1 for the journal reference.)

c. Prepare a trial balance on April 30, 2022.

*P5.5 **(LO 4, 5, 6), AP** The trial balance of Valdez Fashion Center contained the following accounts at November 30, the end of the company's fiscal year. Valdez adjusts its accounts annually and uses the perpetual inventory system.

*Complete accounting cycle beginning with a worksheet.*

c. Total debits $8,150

### Valdez Fashion Center
### Trial Balance
### November 30, 2022

|  | Debit | Credit |
|---|---|---|
| Cash | $ 8,700 | |
| Accounts Receivable | 30,700 | |
| Inventory | 44,700 | |
| Supplies | 6,200 | |
| Equipment | 133,000 | |
| Accumulated Depreciation—Equipment | | $ 28,000 |
| Notes Payable | | 51,000 |
| Accounts Payable | | 48,500 |
| Common Stock | | 50,000 |
| Retained Earnings | | 40,000 |
| Dividends | 12,000 | |
| Sales Revenue | | 755,200 |
| Sales Returns and Allowances | 8,800 | |
| Cost of Goods Sold | 497,400 | |
| Salaries and Wages Expense | 140,000 | |
| Advertising Expense | 24,400 | |
| Utilities Expense | 14,000 | |
| Maintenance and Repairs Expense | 12,100 | |
| Freight-Out | 16,700 | |
| Rent Expense | 24,000 | |
| Totals | $972,700 | $972,700 |

Adjustment data:

1. Supplies on hand totaled $2,000.

2. Annual depreciation is $11,500 on the equipment.

3. Interest of $4,000 is accrued on notes payable at November 30.

4. Inventory actually on hand is $44,400.

## Instructions

a. Enter the trial balance on a worksheet, and complete the worksheet.

b. Prepare a multiple-step income statement and a retained earnings statement for the year, and a classified balance sheet as of November 30, 2022. Notes payable of $20,000 are due in January 2023.

c. Journalize the adjusting entries.

d. Journalize the closing entries.

e. Prepare a post-closing trial balance.

a. Adj. trial balance $988,200
   Net loss $2,200

b. Gross profit $248,700
   Total assets $179,300

*P5.6 **(LO 5, 7), AP** At the end of Oates Department Store's fiscal year on November 30, 2022, these accounts appeared in its adjusted trial balance.

*Determine cost of goods sold and gross profit under periodic approach.*

| | |
|---|---|
| Freight-In | $ 5,060 |
| Inventory | 41,300 |
| Purchases | 613,000 |
| Purchase Discounts | 7,000 |
| Purchase Returns and Allowances | 6,760 |
| Sales Revenue | 902,000 |
| Sales Returns and Allowances | 20,000 |

Additional facts:

1. Per a physical count, merchandise inventory on November 30, 2022, is $36,200.

2. Note that Oates Department Store uses a periodic system.

### Instructions

Prepare an income statement through gross profit for the year ended November 30, 2022.

*Gross profit $272,600*

*Calculate missing amounts and assess profitability.*

**\*P5.7 (LO 5, 7), AN** Zhou Inc. operates a retail operation that purchases and sells snowmobiles, among other outdoor products. The company purchases all inventory on credit and uses a periodic inventory system. The Accounts Payable account is used for recording inventory purchases only; all other current liabilities are accrued in separate accounts. You are provided with the following selected information for the fiscal years 2020 through 2023, inclusive.

| | 2020 | 2021 | 2022 | 2023 |
|---|---|---|---|---|
| **Income Statement Data** | | | | |
| Net sales revenue | | $96,890 | $     (e) | $82,220 |
| Cost of goods sold | | (a) | 28,060 | 26,490 |
| Gross profit | | 67,800 | 59,620 | (i) |
| Operating expenses | | 63,640 | (f) | 52,870 |
| Net income | | $    (b) | $ 3,510 | $     (j) |
| **Balance Sheet Data** | | | | |
| Inventory | $13,000 | $     (c) | $14,700 | $     (k) |
| Accounts payable | 5,800 | 6,500 | 4,600 | (l) |
| **Additional Information** | | | | |
| Purchases of merchandise inventory on account | | $25,890 | $     (g) | $24,050 |
| Cash payments to suppliers | | (d) | (h) | 24,650 |

*c. $9,800*
*g. $32,960*
*i. $55,730*

### Instructions

a. Calculate the missing amounts. Assume that there are no nonoperating activities.

b. Sales declined over the 3-year fiscal period, 2021–2023. Does that mean that profitability necessarily also declined? Explain, computing the gross profit rate and the profit margin (Net income ÷ Net sales revenue) for each fiscal year to help support your answer. (Round to one decimal place.)

*Journalize, post, and prepare trial balance and partial income statement using periodic approach.*

**\*P5.8 (LO 7), AP** At the beginning of the current season on April 1, the ledger of Granite Hills Pro Shop showed Cash $2,500, Inventory $3,500, and Common Stock $6,000. These transactions occurred during April 2022.

| Apr. | 5 | Purchased golf bags, clubs, and balls on account from Arnie Co. $1,500, terms 3/10, n/60, FOB shipping point. |
|---|---|---|
| | 7 | Paid freight on Arnie Co. purchases $80. |
| | 9 | Received credit from Arnie Co. for merchandise returned $200. |
| | 10 | Sold merchandise on account to members $1,340, terms n/30. |
| | 12 | Purchased golf shoes, sweaters, and other accessories on account from Woods Sportswear $830, terms 1/10, n/30. |
| | 14 | Paid Arnie Co. in full. |
| | 17 | Received credit from Woods Sportswear for merchandise returned $30. |
| | 20 | Made sales on account to members $810, terms n/30. |
| | 21 | Paid Woods Sportswear in full. |
| | 27 | Granted credit to customers for clothing that did not fit properly $80. |
| | 30 | Received payments on account from members $1,220. |

The chart of accounts for the pro shop includes Cash, Accounts Receivable, Inventory, Accounts Payable, Common Stock, Sales Revenue, Sales Returns and Allowances, Purchases, Purchase Returns and Allowances, Purchase Discounts, and Freight-In.

### Instructions

a. Journalize the April transactions using a periodic inventory system.

b. Using T-accounts, enter the beginning balances in the ledger accounts and post the April transactions.

*c. Tot. trial balance $8,427*

c. Prepare a trial balance on April 30, 2022.

*d. Gross profit $700*

d. Prepare an income statement through gross profit, assuming merchandise inventory on hand at April 30 is $4,263.

## Continuing Case

### Cookie Creations

leungchopan/
Shutterstock.com

(*Note:* This is a continuation of the Cookie Creations case from Chapters 1 through 4.)

**CC5** Because Natalie has had such a successful first few months, she is considering other opportunities to develop her business. One opportunity is to become the exclusive distributor of a line of fine European mixers. The current cost of a mixer is approximately $525 (U.S.), and Natalie would sell each one for $1,050. Natalie comes to you for advice on how to account for these mixers.

*Go to WileyPLUS for complete case details and instructions.*

## Comprehensive Accounting Cycle Review

**ACR5.1** On December 1, 2022, Divine Distributing Company had the following account balances.

| | Debit | | Credit |
|---|---|---|---|
| Cash | $ 7,200 | Accumulated Depreciation— | |
| Accounts Receivable | 4,600 | Equipment | $ 2,200 |
| Inventory | 12,000 | Accounts Payable | 4,500 |
| Supplies | 1,200 | Salaries and Wages Payable | 1,000 |
| Equipment | 22,000 | Common Stock | 15,000 |
| | $47,000 | Retained Earnings | 24,300 |
| | | | $47,000 |

During December, the company completed the following transactions.

| Dec. | 6 | Paid $1,600 for salaries and wages due employees, of which $600 is for December and $1,000 is for November salaries and wages payable. |
|---|---|---|
| | 8 | Received $1,900 cash from customers in payment of account (no discount allowed). |
| | 10 | Sold merchandise for cash $6,300. The cost of the merchandise sold was $4,100. |
| | 13 | Purchased merchandise on account from Hecht Co. $9,000, terms 2/10, n/30. |
| | 15 | Purchased supplies for cash $2,000. |
| | 18 | Sold merchandise on account $12,000, terms 3/10, n/30. The cost of the merchandise sold was $8,000. |
| | 20 | Paid salaries and wages $1,800. |
| | 23 | Paid Hecht Co. in full, less discount. |
| | 27 | Received collections in full, less discounts, from customers billed on December 18. |

Adjustment data:

1. Accrued salaries and wages payable were $800.
2. Depreciation was $200 per month.
3. Supplies on hand were $1,500.

### Instructions

a. Journalize the December transactions using a perpetual inventory system.

b. Enter the December 1 balances in the ledger T-accounts and post the December transactions. Use these additional accounts: Cost of Goods Sold, Depreciation Expense, Salaries and Wages Expense, Sales Revenue, Sales Discounts, and Supplies Expense.

c. Journalize and post adjusting entries.

d. Prepare an adjusted trial balance.

e. Prepare an income statement and a retained earnings statement for December and a classified balance sheet at December 31.

d. Totals $65,300

e. Net income $740

**ACR5.2** On November 1, 2022, IKonk, Inc. had the following account balances. The company uses the perpetual inventory method.

| | Debit | | Credit |
|---|---|---|---|
| Cash | $ 9,000 | Accumulated Depreciation— | |
| Accounts Receivable | 2,240 | Equipment | $ 1,000 |
| Supplies | 860 | Accounts Payable | 3,400 |
| Equipment | 25,000 | Unearned Service Revenue | 4,000 |
| | $37,100 | Salaries and Wages Payable | 1,700 |
| | | Common Stock | 20,000 |
| | | Retained Earnings | 7,000 |
| | | | $37,100 |

During November, the following transactions were completed.

Nov. 8 Paid $3,550 for salaries and wages, of which $1,850 is for November and $1,700 is for October.
10 Received $1,900 cash from customers in payment of account. No discount was allowed.
11 Purchased merchandise on account from Dimas Discount Supply for $8,000, terms 2/10, n/30.
12 Sold merchandise on account for $5,500, terms 2/10, n/30. The cost of the merchandise sold was $4,000.
15 Received credit from Dimas Discount Supply for merchandise returned $300.
19 Received collections in full, less discounts, from customers billed on sales of $5,500 on November 12.
20 Paid Dimas Discount Supply in full, less discount.
22 Received $2,300 cash for services performed in November.
25 Purchased equipment on account $5,000.
27 Purchased supplies on account $1,700.
28 Paid creditors $3,000 of accounts payable due. No discount was taken.
29 Paid November rent $375.
29 Paid salaries and wages $1,300.
29 Performed services on account and billed customers $700 for those services.
29 Received $675 from customers for services to be performed in the future.

Adjustment data:

1. Supplies on hand total $1,600.
2. Accrued salaries and wages payable are $500.
3. Depreciation for the month is $250.
4. $650 of services related to unearned service revenue was performed by month-end.

**Instructions**

a. Enter the November 1 balances in ledger T-accounts.

b. Journalize the November transactions.

c. Post to the ledger accounts. You will need to add some accounts.

d. Journalize and post adjusting entries.

e. Tot. adj. trial bal. $49,025    e. Prepare an adjusted trial balance at November 30.

f. Tot. assets $38,430    f. Prepare a multiple-step income statement and a retained earnings statement for November and a classified balance sheet at November 30.

g. Journalize and post closing entries.

# Expand Your Critical Thinking

## Financial Reporting Problem: Apple Inc.

**CT5.1** The financial statements of **Apple Inc.** are presented in Appendix A. The complete annual report, including the notes to the financial statements, is available at the company's website.

**Instructions**

Answer the following questions using Apple's Consolidated Statements of Operations.

a. What was the percentage change in (1) net sales and in (2) net income from 2016 to 2017 and from 2017 to 2018?

**b.** What was the company's gross profit rate in 2016, 2017, and 2018?

**c.** What was the company's percentage of net income to net sales in 2016, 2017, and 2018? Comment on any trend in this percentage.

## Comparative Analysis Problem: PepsiCo, Inc. vs. The Coca-Cola Company

**CT5.2** **PepsiCo**'s financial statements are presented in Appendix B. Financial statements of **The Coca-Cola Company** are presented in Appendix C. The complete annual reports of PepsiCo and Coca-Cola, including the notes to the financial statements, are available at each company's respective website.

### Instructions

**a.** Based on the information contained in these financial statements, determine each of the following for each company.

    **1.** Gross profit for 2018.

    **2.** Gross profit rate for 2018.

    **3.** Income from operations (or operating profit) for 2018.

    **4.** Percentage change in operating profit from 2017 to 2018.

**b.** What conclusions concerning the relative profitability of the two companies can you draw from these data?

## Comparative Analysis Problem: Amazon.com, Inc. vs. Walmart Inc.

**CT5.3** **Amazon.com, Inc.**'s financial statements are presented in Appendix D. Financial statements of **Walmart Inc.** are presented in Appendix E. (Use Walmart's January 31, 2019, financial statements for comparative purposes.) The complete annual reports of Amazon and Walmart, including the notes to the financial statements, are available at each company's respective website.

### Instructions

**a.** Based on the information contained in these financial statements, determine each of the following for each company. Use Amazon's net product sales and Walmart's net sales to compute gross profit information.

    **1.** Gross profit for 2018.

    **2.** Gross profit rate for 2018.

    **3.** Operating income for 2018.

    **4.** Percentage change in operating income from 2017 to 2018.

**b.** What conclusions concerning the relative profitability of the two companies can you draw from these data?

## Real-World Focus

**CT5.4** No financial decision-maker should ever rely solely on the financial information reported in a company's annual report to make decisions. It is important to keep abreast of financial news. This activity demonstrates how to search for financial news on the Internet.

### Instructions

Search the Internet for an article on either **PepsiCo** or **Coca-Cola** that sounds interesting to you and that would be relevant to an investor in these companies. Then, answer the following questions.

**a.** What was the source of the article (e.g., Reuters, Businesswire, PR Newswire)?

**b.** Assume that you are a personal financial planner and that one of your clients owns stock in the company. Write a brief memo to your client, summarizing the article and explaining the implications of the article for his or her investment.

## Decision-Making Across the Organization

**CT5.5** Three years ago, Karen Suez and her brother-in-law Reece Jones opened Gigasales Department Store. For the first two years, business was good, but the following condensed income results for 2022 were disappointing.

**Gigasales Department Store**
**Income Statement**
**For the Year Ended December 31, 2022**

| | | |
|---|---:|---:|
| Net sales | | $700,000 |
| Cost of goods sold | | 560,000 |
| Gross profit | | 140,000 |
| Operating expenses | | |
| Selling expenses | $100,000 | |
| Administrative expenses | 20,000 | 120,000 |
| Net income | | $ 20,000 |

Karen believes the problem lies in the relatively low gross profit rate (gross profit divided by net sales) of 20%. Reece believes the problem is that operating expenses are too high.

Karen thinks the gross profit rate can be improved by making two changes for 2023. She does not anticipate that these changes will have any effect on operating expenses.

1. Increase average selling prices by 15%. This increase is expected to lower sales volume so that net sales will increase only 4%.

2. Buy merchandise in larger quantities and take all purchase discounts. These changes to selling prices and purchasing practices are expected to increase the gross profit rate from 20% to a new rate of 25%.

Reece thinks expenses can be cut by making the following two changes for 2023. He feels that these changes will not have any effect on net sales or cost of goods sold.

1. Cut the 2022 sales salaries of $60,000 in half and give sales personnel a commission of 2% of net sales.

2. Reduce store deliveries to one day per week rather than twice a week. This change will reduce 2022 delivery expenses of $40,000 by 40%. (Recall that delivery costs to customers are selling expenses.)

Karen and Reece come to you for help in deciding the best way to improve net income.

**Instructions**

With the class divided into groups, answer the following.

a. Prepare a condensed income statement for 2023, assuming (1) Karen's changes are implemented and (2) Reece's ideas are adopted.

b. What is your recommendation to Karen and Reece?

c. Prepare a condensed income statement for 2023, assuming both sets of proposed changes are made.

d. Discuss the impact that other factors might have. For example, would increasing the quantity of inventory increase costs? Would a salary cut affect employee morale? Would decreased morale affect sales? Would decreased store deliveries decrease customer satisfaction? What other suggestions might be considered?

## Communication Activity

CT5.6 The following events are in chronological order.

1. Aikan decides to buy a surfboard.

2. He calls Surfing Hawaii Co. to inquire about its surfboards.

3. Two days later, he requests Surfing Hawaii Co. to make a surfboard.

4. Three days later, Surfing Hawaii Co. sends him a purchase order to fill out.

5. He sends back the purchase order.

6. Surfing Hawaii Co. receives the completed purchase order.

7. Surfing Hawaii Co. completes the surfboard.

8. Aikan picks up the surfboard.

9. Surfing Hawaii Co. bills Aikan.

10. Surfing Hawaii Co. receives payment from Aikan.

### Instructions

In a memorandum to the president of Surfing Hawaii Co., answer the following.

a. When should Surfing Hawaii Co. record the sale?

b. Suppose that with his purchase order, Aikan is required to make a down payment. Would that change your answer?

## Ethics Case

**CT5.7** Tabitha Andes was just hired as the assistant treasurer of Southside Stores, a specialty chain store that has nine retail stores concentrated in one metropolitan area. Among other things, the payment of all invoices is centralized in one of the departments Tabitha will manage. Her primary responsibility is to maintain the company's high credit rating by paying all bills when due and to take advantage of all cash discounts.

Pete Wilson, the former assistant treasurer who has been promoted to treasurer, is training Tabitha in her new duties. He instructs Tabitha that she is to continue the practice of preparing all checks "net of discount" and dating the checks the last day of the discount period. "But," Pete continues, "we always hold the checks at least 4 days beyond the discount period before mailing them. That way, we get another 4 days of interest on our money. Most of our creditors need our business and don't complain. And, if they scream about our missing the discount period, we blame it on the mailroom or the post office. We've only lost one discount out of every hundred we take that way. I think everybody does it. By the way, welcome to our team!"

### Instructions

a. What are the ethical considerations in this case?

b. What stakeholders are harmed or benefitted?

c. Should Tabitha continue the practice started by Pete? Does she have any choice?

## All About You

**CT5.8** There are many situations in business where it is difficult to determine the proper period in which to record revenue. Suppose that after graduation with a degree in finance, you take a job as a manager at a consumer electronics store called FarWest Electronics. The company has expanded rapidly in order to compete with **Best Buy**.

FarWest has also begun selling gift cards. The cards are available in any dollar amount and allow the holder of the card to purchase an item for up to 2 years from the time the card is purchased. If the card is not used during that 2 years, it expires.

### Instructions

At what point should the revenue from the gift cards be recognized? Include the reasoning to support your answers.

## FASB Codification Activity

**CT5.9** If your school has a subscription to the FASB Codification, log in and prepare responses to the following.

### Instructions

a. Access the glossary ("Master Glossary") to answer the following:

1. What is the definition provided for inventory?

2. What is a customer?

b. What guidance does the Codification provide concerning reporting inventories above cost?

### Answers to Insight and Accounting Across the Organization Questions

**Improving Stock Appeal  Q:** If a perpetual system keeps track of inventory on a daily basis, why do companies ever need to do a physical count?  **A:** A perpetual system keeps track of all sales and purchases on a continuous basis. This provides a constant record of the number of units in the inventory. However, if employees make errors in recording sales or purchases, or if there is theft, the inventory value will not be correct. As a consequence, all companies do a physical count of inventory at least once a year.

**The Point of No Return?  Q:** If a company expects significant returns, what are the implications for revenue recognition?  **A:** If a company expects significant returns, it should make an adjusting entry at the end of the year to increase Sales Returns and Allowances by the estimated amount of sales returns. This is necessary to not overstate the amount of revenue recognized in the period.

**Selling Green  Q:** What is meant by "monetize environmental sustainability" for shareholders?  **A:** By marketing green, not only does PepsiCo help the environment in the long run, but it also leads to long-term profitability as well. In other words, sound sustainability practices are good business and lead to sound financial results.

**Disclosing More Details  Q:** Why have investors and analysts demanded more accuracy in isolating "Other gains and losses" from operating items?  **A:** Greater accuracy in the classification of operating versus nonoperating ("Other gains and losses") items permits investors and analysts to judge the real operating margin, the results of continuing operations, and management's ability to control operating expenses.

# A Look at IFRS

---

**LEARNING OBJECTIVE 8**

Compare the accounting for merchandising under GAAP and IFRS.

---

The basic accounting entries for merchandising are the same under both GAAP and IFRS. The income statement is a required statement under both sets of standards. The basic format is similar although some differences do exist.

## Key Points

Following are the key similarities and differences between GAAP and IFRS related to inventories.

**Similarities**

- Under both GAAP and IFRS, a company can choose to use either a perpetual or a periodic inventory system.
- The definition of inventories is basically the same under GAAP and IFRS.
- As indicated above, the basic accounting entries for merchandising are the same under both GAAP and IFRS.
- Both GAAP and IFRS require that income statement information be presented for multiple years. For example, IFRS requires that 2 years of income statement information be presented, whereas GAAP requires 3 years.

**Differences**

- Under GAAP, companies generally classify income statement items by function. Classification by function leads to descriptions like administration, distribution, and manufacturing. Under IFRS, companies must classify expenses either by nature or by function. Classification by nature leads to descriptions such as the following: salaries, depreciation expense, and utilities expense. If a company uses the functional-expense method on the income statement, disclosure by nature is required in the notes to the financial statements.
- Presentation of the income statement under GAAP follows either a single-step or multiple-step format. IFRS does not mention a single-step or multiple-step approach.
- Under IFRS, revaluation of land, buildings, and intangible assets is permitted.

# IFRS Practice

## IFRS Self-Test Questions

1. Which of the following would **not** be included in the definition of inventory under IFRS?

    **a.** Photocopy paper held for sale by an office-supply store.

    **b.** Stereo equipment held for sale by an electronics store.

    **c.** Used office equipment held for sale by the human resources department of a plastics company.

    **d.** All of the answer choices would meet the definition.

2. Which of the following would **not** be a line item of a company reporting costs by nature?

    **a.** Depreciation expense.       **c.** Interest expense.

    **b.** Salaries expense.            **d.** Manufacturing expense.

3. Which of the following would **not** be a line item of a company reporting costs by function?

    **a.** Administration.             **c.** Utilities expense.

    **b.** Manufacturing.              **d.** Distribution.

4. Which of the following statements is **false**?

    **a.** IFRS specifically requires use of a multiple-step income statement.

    **b.** Under IFRS, companies can use either a perpetual or periodic system.

    **c.** IFRS does not require the use of a single-step income statement.

    **d.** IFRS does not prohibit the revaluation of land.

## IFRS Exercises

**IFRS5.1** Explain the difference between the "nature-of-expense" and "function-of-expense" classifications.

**IFRS5.2** For each of the following income statement line items, state whether the item is a "by nature" expense item or a "by function" expense item.

| | |
|---|---|
| _____ Cost of goods sold. | _____ Utilities expense. |
| _____ Depreciation expense. | _____ Delivery expense. |
| _____ Salaries and wages expense. | _____ General and administrative expenses. |
| _____ Selling expenses. | |

## International Financial Reporting Problem: Louis Vuitton

**IFRS5.3** The financial statements of **Louis Vuitton** are presented in Appendix F. The complete consolidated financial statements, including the notes to its financial statements, are available at the company's website.

### Instructions

Use Louis Vuitton's 2018 consolidated financial statements to answer the following questions.

**a.** Does Louis Vuitton use a multiple-step or a single-step income statement format? Explain how you made your determination.

**b.** Instead of "interest expense," what label does Louis Vuitton use for interest costs that it incurs?

**c.** Using the notes to the company's financial statements, determine the following:

1. Composition of the inventory.

2. Amount of inventory (net).

### Answers to IFRS Self-Test Questions

1. c   2. d   3. c   4. a

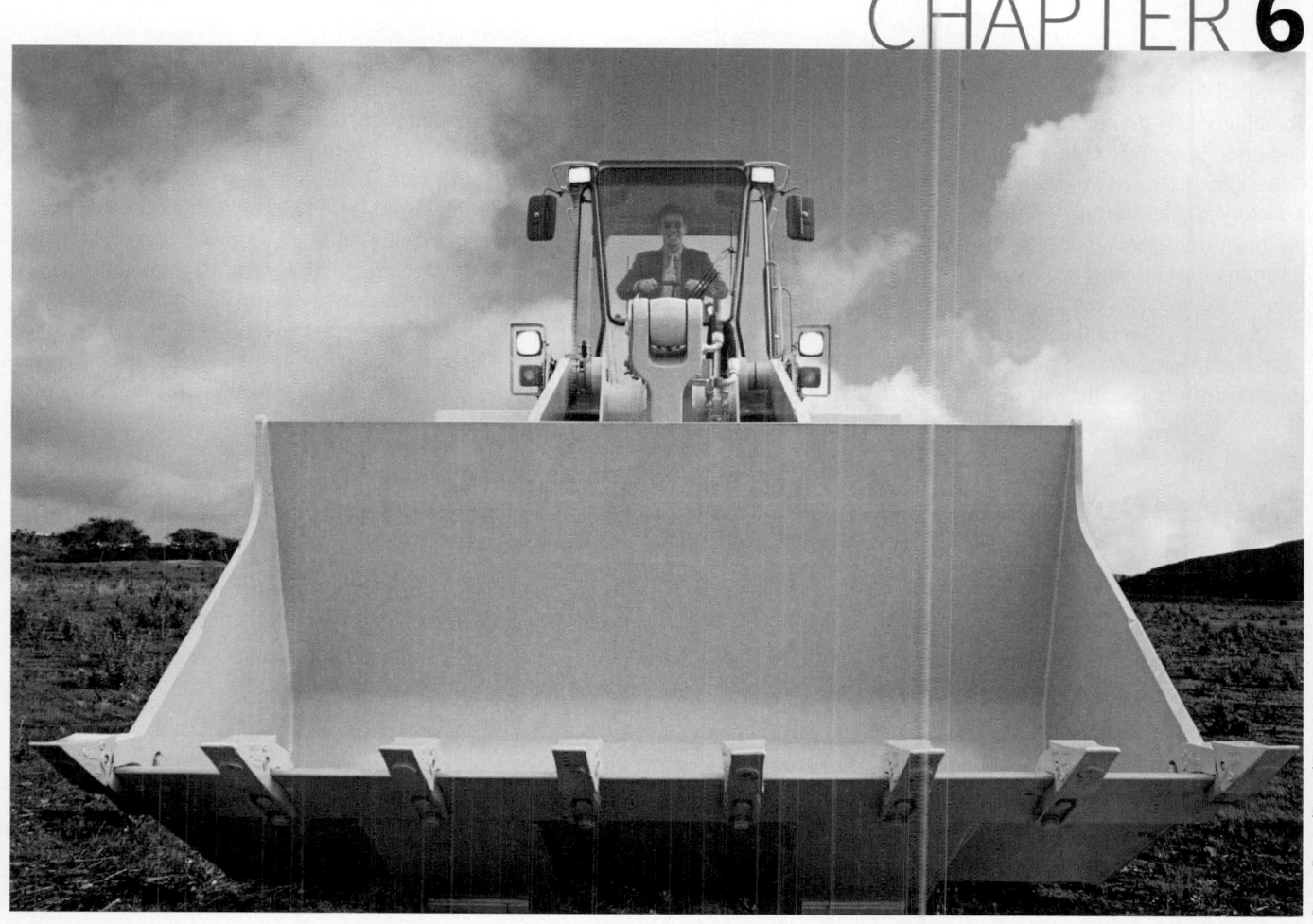

## CHAPTER 6

James Porter/Stone/Getty Images

# Inventories

## Chapter Preview

In the previous chapter, we discussed the accounting for merchandise inventory using a perpetual inventory system. In this chapter, we explain the methods used to calculate the cost of inventory on hand at the balance sheet date and the cost of goods sold.

## Feature Story

### "Where Is That Spare Bulldozer Blade?"

Let's talk inventory—big, bulldozer-size inventory. **Caterpillar Inc.** is the world's largest manufacturer of construction and mining equipment, diesel and natural gas engines, and industrial gas turbines. It sells its products in over 200 countries, making it one of the most successful U.S. exporters. More

than 70% of its productive assets are located domestically, and nearly 50% of its sales are foreign.

In the past, Caterpillar's profitability suffered, but today it is very successful. A big part of this turnaround can be attributed to effective management of its inventory. Imagine what it costs Caterpillar to have too many bulldozers sitting around in inventory—a situation the company definitely wants to avoid. Yet Caterpillar must also make sure it has enough inventory to meet demand.

At one time during a 7-year period, Caterpillar's sales increased by 100% while its inventory increased by only 50%. To achieve this dramatic reduction in the amount of resources tied up in inventory while continuing to meet customers' needs, Caterpillar used a two-pronged approach. First, it completed a factory modernization program, which greatly increased its production efficiency. The program reduced by 60% the amount of inventory the company processes at any one time. It also reduced by an incredible 75% the time it takes to manufacture a part.

Second, Caterpillar dramatically improved its parts distribution system. It ships more than 100,000 items daily from its 23 distribution centers strategically located around the world (10 million square feet of warehouse space—remember, we're talking bulldozers). The company can virtually guarantee that it can get any part to anywhere in the world within 24 hours.

These changes led to record exports, profits, and revenues for Caterpillar. It would seem that things couldn't be better. But industry analysts, as well as the company's managers, thought otherwise. In order to maintain Caterpillar's position as the industry leader, management began another major overhaul of inventory production and inventory management processes. The goal: to cut the number of repairs in half, increase productivity by 20%, and increase inventory turnover by 40%.

In short, Caterpillar's ability to manage its inventory has been a key reason for its past success and will very likely play a huge part in its future profitability as well.

## Chapter Outline

| LEARNING OBJECTIVES | REVIEW | PRACTICE |
|---|---|---|
| **LO 1** Discuss how to classify and determine inventory. | • Classifying inventory<br>• Determining inventory quantities | **DO IT! 1** Rules of Ownership |
| **LO 2** Apply inventory cost flow methods and discuss their financial effects. | • Specific identification<br>• Cost flow assumptions<br>• Financial statement and tax effects<br>• Using inventory cost flow methods consistently | **DO IT! 2** Cost Flow Methods |
| **LO 3** Indicate the effects of inventory errors on the financial statements. | • Income statement effects<br>• Balance sheet effects | **DO IT! 3** Inventory Errors |
| **LO 4** Explain the statement presentation and analysis of inventory. | • Presentation<br>• Lower-of-cost-or-net realizable value<br>• Analysis | **DO IT! 4a** LCNRV<br>**DO IT! 4b** Inventory Turnover |

**Go to the Review and Practice section at the end of the chapter for a review of key concepts and practice applications with solutions.**

**Visit WileyPLUS for additional tutorials and practice opportunities.**

# Classifying and Determining Inventory

### LEARNING OBJECTIVE 1
Discuss how to classify and determine inventory.

Two important steps in the reporting of inventory at the end of the accounting period are the classification of inventory based on its degree of completeness and the determination of inventory amounts.

# Classifying Inventory

How a company classifies its inventory depends on whether the firm is a merchandiser or a manufacturer. In a **merchandising** company, such as those described in Chapter 5, inventory consists of many different items. For example, in a grocery store, canned goods, dairy products, meats, and produce are just a few of the inventory items on hand. These items have two common characteristics: (1) they are owned by the company, and (2) they are in a form ready for sale to customers in the ordinary course of business. Thus, merchandisers need only one inventory classification, **merchandise inventory**, to describe the many different items that make up the total inventory.

In a **manufacturing** company, some inventory may not yet be ready for sale. As a result, manufacturers usually classify inventory into three categories: finished goods, work in process, and raw materials. **Finished goods inventory** is manufactured items that are completed and ready for sale. **Work in process** is that portion of manufactured inventory that has been placed into the production process but is not yet complete. **Raw materials** are the basic goods that will be used in production but have not yet been placed into production.

For example, **Caterpillar** classifies earth-moving tractors completed and ready for sale as **finished goods**. It classifies the tractors on the assembly line in various stages of production as **work in process**. The steel, glass, tires, and other components that are on hand waiting to be used in the production of tractors are identified as **raw materials** (see **Helpful Hint**). **Illustration 6.1** shows an adapted excerpt from Note 7 of Caterpillar's annual report.

**HELPFUL HINT**

Regardless of the classification, companies report all inventories under Current Assets on the balance sheet.

**ILLUSTRATION 6.1**
Composition of Caterpillar's inventory

| (millions of dollars) | December 31 | | |
| --- | --- | --- | --- |
| | 2018 | 2017 | 2016 |
| Raw materials | $ 3,382 | $ 2,802 | $2,102 |
| Work in process | 2,674 | 2,254 | 1,719 |
| Finished goods | 5,241 | 4,761 | 4,575 |
| Other | 232 | 201 | 217 |
| **Total inventories** | **$11,529** | **$10,018** | **$8,614** |

**By observing the levels and changes in the levels of these three inventory types, financial statement users can gain insight into management's production plans**. For example, low levels of raw materials and high levels of finished goods suggest that management believes it has enough inventory on hand and production will be slowing down—perhaps in anticipation of a recession. Conversely, high levels of raw materials and low levels of finished goods probably signal that management is planning to step up production.

Many companies have significantly lowered inventory levels and costs using **just-in-time (JIT) inventory** methods. Under a just-in-time method, companies manufacture or purchase goods only when needed. **Dell** is famous for having developed a system for making computers in response to individual customer requests. Even though it makes each computer to meet each customer's particular specifications, Dell is able to assemble the computer and put it on a truck in less than 48 hours. The success of the JIT system depends on reliable suppliers. By integrating its information systems with those of its suppliers, Dell reduced its inventories to nearly zero. This is a huge advantage in an industry where products become obsolete nearly overnight.

The accounting concepts discussed in this chapter apply to the inventory classifications of both merchandising and manufacturing companies. Our focus here is on merchandise inventory. Additional issues specific to manufacturing companies are discussed in managerial accounting courses.

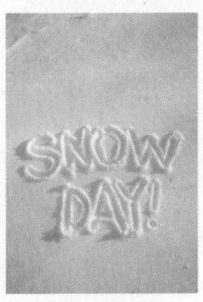

### A Big Hiccup

JIT can save a company a lot of money, but it isn't without risk. An unexpected disruption in the supply chain can cost a company a lot of money. Japanese automakers experienced just such a disruption when a 6.8-magnitude earthquake caused major damage to the company that produces 50% of their piston rings. The rings themselves cost only $1.50, but you can't make a car without them. As a result, the automakers were forced to shut down production for a few days—a loss of tens of thousands of cars.

iStock.com/PeskyMonkey

Similarly, a major snowstorm halted production at the Canadian plants of **Ford**. A Ford spokesperson said, "Because the plants run with just-in-time inventory, we don't have large stockpiles of parts sitting around. When you have a somewhat significant disruption, you can pretty quickly run out of parts."

**Sources:** Amy Chozick, "A Key Strategy of Japan's Car Makers Backfires," *Wall Street Journal* (July 20, 2007); and Kate Linebaugh, "Canada Military Evacuates Motorists Stranded by Snow," *Wall Street Journal* (December 15, 2010).

**What steps might the companies take to avoid such a serious disruption in the future? (Answer is available near the end of the chapter.)**

# Determining Inventory Quantities

**ETHICS NOTE**

**In a famous fraud, a salad oil company filled its storage tanks mostly with water. The oil rose to the top, so auditors thought the tanks were full of oil. The company also said it had more tanks than it really did: It repainted numbers on the tanks to confuse auditors.**

Companies take a physical inventory at the end of the accounting period. Taking a physical inventory involves actually counting, weighing, or measuring each kind of inventory on hand (see **Ethics Note**). If using a perpetual system, companies might take a physical inventory at other times during the accounting period for the following reasons:

1. To check the accuracy of their perpetual inventory records.
2. To determine the amount of inventory lost due to wasted raw materials, shoplifting, or employee theft.

Companies using a periodic inventory system take a physical inventory for **two different purposes**: to determine the inventory on hand at the balance sheet date, and to determine the cost of goods sold for the period.

Determining inventory quantities involves two steps: (1) taking a physical inventory of goods on hand and (2) determining the ownership of goods.

## Taking a Physical Inventory

In many companies, taking an inventory is a formidable task. Retailers such as **Target**, **True Value Hardware**, or **Home Depot** have thousands of different inventory items. An inventory count is generally more accurate when goods are not being sold or received during the counting. Consequently, companies often "take inventory" when the business is closed or when business is slow. Many retailers close early on a chosen day in January—after the holiday sales and returns, when inventories are at their lowest level—to count inventory. **Walmart Inc.**, for example, has a year-end of January 31.

## Determining Ownership of Goods

One challenge in computing inventory quantities is determining what inventory a company owns. To determine ownership of goods, two questions must be answered: Do all of the goods included in the count belong to the company? Does the company own any goods that were not included in the count?

**Goods in Transit**  A complication in determining ownership is **goods in transit** (on board a truck, train, ship, or plane) at the end of the period. The company may have purchased goods that have not yet been received, or it may have sold goods that have not yet been delivered

## Ethics Insight    Leslie Fay

### Falsifying Inventory to Boost Income

Managers at women's apparel maker **Leslie Fay** were convicted of falsifying inventory records to boost net income in an attempt to increase management bonuses. In another case, executives at **Craig Electronics** were accused of defrauding lenders by manipulating inventory records. The indictment said the company classified "defective goods as new or refurbished" and claimed that

iStock.com/Greg Brookes

it owned certain shipments "from overseas suppliers" when, in fact, Craig either did not own the shipments or the shipments did not exist.

**What effect does an overstatement of inventory have on a company's financial statements? (Answer is available near the end of the chapter.)**

---

to its customer. To arrive at an accurate count, the company must determine ownership of these goods.

Goods in transit should be included in the inventory of the company that has legal title to the goods. Legal title is determined by the terms of the sale, as shown in **Illustration 6.2** and described below.

**ILLUSTRATION 6.2** Terms of sale

1. When the terms are **FOB (free on board) shipping point**, ownership of the goods passes to the buyer when the public carrier accepts the goods from the seller.

2. When the terms are **FOB destination**, ownership of the goods remains with the seller until the goods reach the buyer.

If goods in transit at the statement date are ignored, inventory quantities may be seriously miscounted. Assume, for example, that Hargrove Company has 20,000 units of inventory on hand on December 31. It also has the following goods in transit:

1. Sales of 1,500 units shipped December 31 FOB destination.

2. Purchases of 2,500 units shipped FOB shipping point by the seller on December 31.

Hargrove has legal title to both the 1,500 units sold and the 2,500 units purchased. If the company ignores the units in transit, it would understate inventory quantities by 4,000 units (1,500 + 2,500).

As we will see later in the chapter, inaccurate inventory counts affect not only the inventory amount shown on the balance sheet but also the cost of goods sold calculation on the income statement.

**Consigned Goods** In some lines of business, it is common to hold the goods of other parties and try to sell the goods for them for a fee, but without taking ownership of the goods. These are called **consigned goods**.

For example, you might have a used car that you would like to sell. If you take the item to a dealer, the dealer might be willing to put the car on its lot and charge you a commission if it is sold. Under this agreement, the dealer **would not take ownership** of the car, which would still belong to you. Therefore, if an inventory count were taken, the car would not be included in the dealer's inventory because the dealer does not own it.

Many car, boat, and antique dealers sell goods on consignment to keep their inventory costs down and to avoid the risk of purchasing an item that they will not be able to sell. Today, even some manufacturers are making consignment agreements with their suppliers in order to keep their inventory levels low. For example, prior to filing bankruptcy, **Sports Authority Inc.** became embroiled in lawsuits with suppliers over goods that it was holding on consignment. A judge ruled that Sports Authority had to comply with the suppliers' wishes since the consigned goods belonged to the suppliers.

## Anatomy of a Fraud

Ted Nickerson, CEO of clock manufacturer Dally Industries, had expensive tastes. To support this habit, Ted took out large loans, which he collateralized with his shares of Dally Industries stock. If the price of Dally's stock fell, he was required to provide the bank with more shares of stock. To achieve target net income figures and thus maintain the stock price, Ted coerced employees in the company to alter inventory figures. Inventory quantities were manipulated by changing the amounts on inventory control tags after the year-end physical inventory count. For example, if a tag said there were 20 units of a particular item, the tag was changed to 220. Similarly, the unit costs that were used to determine the value of ending inventory were increased from, for example, $125 per unit to $1,250. Both of these fraudulent changes had the effect of increasing the amount of reported ending inventory. This reduced cost of goods sold and increased net income.

**Total take: $245,000**

**The Missing Control**

**Independent internal verification.** The company should have spot-checked its inventory records periodically, verifying that the number of units in the records agreed with the amount on hand and that the unit costs agreed with vendor price sheets.

**Source:** Adapted from Wells, *Fraud Casebook* (2007), pp. 502–509.

---

ACTION PLAN

• Apply the rules of ownership to goods held on consignment.

• Apply the rules of ownership to goods in transit.

## DO IT! 1 | Rules of Ownership

Hasbeen Company completed its inventory count. It arrived at a total inventory value of $200,000. As a new member of Hasbeen's accounting department, you have been given the information listed below. Discuss how this information affects the reported cost of inventory.

1. Hasbeen included in the inventory goods held on consignment for Falls Co., costing $15,000.
2. The company did not include in the count purchased goods of $10,000 which were in transit (terms: FOB shipping point).
3. The company did not include in the count sold inventory with a cost of $12,000 which was in transit (terms: FOB shipping point).

### Solution

The goods of $15,000 held on consignment should be deducted from the inventory count. The goods of $10,000 purchased FOB shipping point should be added to the inventory count. Sold goods of $12,000 which were in transit FOB shipping point should not be included in the ending inventory. Thus, inventory should be reported at $195,000 ($200,000 − $15,000 + $10,000).

Related exercise material: **BE6.1, BE6.2, DO IT! 6.1, E6.1, E6.2, and E6.3.**

# Inventory Methods and Financial Effects

## LEARNING OBJECTIVE 2
Apply inventory cost flow methods and discuss their financial effects.

Inventory is accounted for at cost. Cost includes all expenditures necessary to acquire goods and place them in a condition ready for sale. For example, freight costs incurred to acquire inventory are added to the cost of inventory, but the cost of shipping goods to a customer is a selling expense.

After a company has determined the quantity of units of inventory, it applies unit costs to the quantities to compute the total cost of the inventory and the cost of goods sold. This process can be complicated if a company has purchased inventory items at different times with different costs.

For example, assume that Crivitz TV Company purchased three identical 50-inch TVs on different dates at costs of $700, $750, and $800. During the year, Crivitz sold two TVs at $1,200 each. These facts are summarized in **Illustration 6.3**.

**ILLUSTRATION 6.3**

**Data for inventory costing example**

| Purchases | | | |
|---|---|---|---|
| February 3 | 1 TV | at | $700 |
| March 5 | 1 TV | at | $750 |
| May 22 | 1 TV | at | $800 |
| **Sales** | | | |
| June 1 | 2 TVs | for | $2,400 ($1,200 × 2) |

Cost of goods sold will differ depending on which two TVs the company sold. For example, it might be $1,450 ($700 + $750), or $1,500 ($700 + $800), or $1,550 ($750 + $800). In this section, we discuss alternative costing methods available to Crivitz.

## Specific Identification

If Crivitz can positively identify which particular units it sold and which are still in ending inventory, it can use the **specific identification method** of inventory costing. For example, if Crivitz sold the TVs it purchased on February 3 and May 22, then its cost of goods sold is $1,500 ($700 + $800), and its ending inventory is $750 (see **Illustration 6.4**). Using this method, companies can accurately determine ending inventory and cost of goods sold.

**ILLUSTRATION 6.4**

**Specific identification method**

Ending inventory
$750

$700 Sold

$800 Sold

Cost of goods sold = $700 + $800 = $1,500
Ending inventory = $750

Specific identification requires that companies keep records of the original cost of each individual inventory item. Historically, specific identification was possible only when a

**ETHICS NOTE**

A major disadvantage of the specific identification method is that management may be able to manipulate net income. For example, it can boost net income by selling units purchased at a low cost, or reduce net income by selling units purchased at a high cost.

company sold a limited variety of high-unit-cost items that could be identified clearly from the time of purchase through the time of sale. Examples of such products are cars, pianos, or expensive antiques (see **Ethics Note**).

Today, bar coding, electronic product codes, and radio frequency identification make it theoretically possible to apply specific identification with nearly any type of product. The reality is, however, that this practice is still relatively rare. Instead, rather than keep track of the cost of each particular item sold, most companies make assumptions, called **cost flow assumptions**, about which units were sold.

## Cost Flow Assumptions

Because specific identification is often impractical, other cost flow methods are permitted. These differ from specific identification in that they **assume** flows of costs that may be unrelated to the physical flow of goods. There are three assumed cost flow methods:

1. First-in, first-out (FIFO).
2. Last-in, first-out (LIFO).
3. Average-cost.

**There is no accounting requirement that the cost flow assumption be consistent with the physical movement of the goods.** Company management selects the appropriate cost flow method to be used for accounting purposes.

To demonstrate the three cost flow methods, we will use a **periodic** inventory system. We assume a periodic system because **very few companies use perpetual LIFO, FIFO, or average-cost** to cost their inventory and related cost of goods sold. Instead, companies that use perpetual systems often use an assumed cost (called a standard cost) to record cost of goods sold at the time of sale. Then, at the end of the period when they count their inventory, they **recalculate cost of goods sold using periodic FIFO, LIFO, or average-cost** as shown in this chapter and adjust cost of goods sold to this recalculated number.[1]

To illustrate the three inventory cost flow methods, we will use the data for Houston Electronics' Astro condensers, shown in **Illustration 6.5**.

**ILLUSTRATION 6.5**

**Data for Houston Electronics**

### Houston Electronics
#### Astro Condensers

| Date | Explanation | Units | Unit Cost | Total Cost |
|---|---|---|---|---|
| Jan. 1 | Beginning inventory | 100 | $10 | $ 1,000 |
| Apr. 15 | Purchase | 200 | 11 | 2,200 |
| Aug. 24 | Purchase | 300 | 12 | 3,600 |
| Nov. 27 | Purchase | 400 | 13 | 5,200 |
| | Total units available for sale | 1,000 | | $12,000 |
| | Units in ending inventory | (450) | | |
| | Units sold | 550 | | |

The cost of goods sold formula in a periodic system is:

| Beginning Inventory | + | Cost of Goods Purchased | – | Ending Inventory | = | Cost of Goods Sold |
|---|---|---|---|---|---|---|

[1]Also, some companies use a perpetual system to keep track of units, but they do not make an entry for perpetual cost of goods sold. In addition, firms that employ LIFO tend to use **dollar-value LIFO**, a method discussed in upper-level courses. FIFO periodic and FIFO perpetual give the same result. Therefore, companies should not incur the additional cost to use FIFO perpetual. Few companies use perpetual average-cost because of the added cost of recordkeeping. Finally, for instructional purposes, we believe it is easier to demonstrate the cost flow assumptions under the periodic system, which makes it more pedagogically appropriate.

Houston Electronics had a total of 1,000 units available to sell during the period (beginning inventory plus purchases). The total cost of these 1,000 units is $12,000, referred to as **cost of goods available for sale**. A physical inventory taken at December 31 determined that there were 450 units in ending inventory. Therefore, Houston sold 550 units (1,000 − 450) during the period. To determine the cost of the 550 units that were sold (the cost of goods sold), we assign a cost to the ending inventory and subtract that value from the cost of goods available for sale. The value assigned to the ending inventory **depends on which cost flow method we use**. No matter which cost flow assumption we use, though, the sum of cost of goods sold plus the cost of the ending inventory must equal the cost of goods available for sale—in this case, $12,000.

## First-In, First-Out (FIFO)

The **first-in, first-out (FIFO) method** assumes that the **earliest goods** purchased are the first to be sold. FIFO often parallels the actual physical flow of merchandise. That is, it generally is good business practice to sell the oldest units first. Under the FIFO method, therefore, the **costs** of the earliest goods purchased are the first to be recognized in determining cost of goods sold. (This does not necessarily mean that the oldest units **are sold** first, but that the costs of the oldest units are **recognized** first. In a bin of picture hangers at the hardware store, for example, no one really knows, nor would it matter, which hangers are sold first.) **Illustration 6.6** shows the allocation of the cost of goods available for sale at Houston Electronics under FIFO (see **Helpful Hint**).

**ILLUSTRATION 6.6**

**Allocation of costs—FIFO method**

### Cost of Goods Available for Sale

| Date | Explanation | Units | Unit Cost | Total Cost |
|---|---|---|---|---|
| Jan. 1 | Beginning inventory | 100 | $10 | $ 1,000 |
| Apr. 15 | Purchase | 200 | 11 | 2,200 |
| Aug. 24 | Purchase | 300 | 12 | 3,600 |
| Nov. 27 | Purchase | 400 | 13 | 5,200 |
| | Total | 1,000 | | $12,000 |

**Step 1: Ending Inventory**

| Date | Units | Unit Cost | Total Cost |
|---|---|---|---|
| Nov. 27 | 400 | $13 | $5,200 |
| Aug. 24 | 50 | 12 | 600 |
| Total | 450 | | $5,800 |

**Step 2: Cost of Goods Sold**

| | |
|---|---|
| Cost of goods available for sale | $12,000 |
| Less: Ending inventory | 5,800 |
| Cost of goods sold | $ 6,200 |

$1,000 / $2,200 / $3,000 / $600 / $5,200 — Ending inventory $5,800 — Cost of goods sold $6,200

**HELPFUL HINT**
Note the sequencing of the allocation: (1) compute ending inventory, and (2) determine cost of goods sold.

Under FIFO, since it is assumed that the first goods purchased were the first goods sold, ending inventory is based on the costs of the most recent units purchased (see **Helpful Hint**). That is, **under FIFO, companies determine the cost of the ending inventory by taking the unit cost of the most recent purchase and working backward until all units of inventory have been costed**. In this example, Houston Electronics accounts for the 450 units of ending inventory using the **most recent** costs. The last purchase was 400 units at

**HELPFUL HINT**
Another way of thinking about the calculation of FIFO ending inventory is the LISH assumption—last in still here.

$13 on November 27. The remaining 50 units use the unit cost of the second most recent purchase, $12, on August 24. Next, Houston Electronics calculates cost of goods sold by subtracting the cost of the units **not sold** (ending inventory) from the cost of all goods available for sale.

Illustration 6.7 demonstrates that Houston can also calculate the cost of the 550 units sold by using the costs of the first 550 units acquired. Note that of the 300 units purchased on August 24, only 250 units are assumed sold. This agrees with our calculation of the cost of ending inventory, where 50 of these units were assumed unsold and thus included in ending inventory.

**ILLUSTRATION 6.7**

**Proof of cost of goods sold— FIFO method**

| Date | Units | Unit Cost | Total Cost |
|---|---|---|---|
| Jan. 1 | 100 | $10 | $1,000 |
| Apr. 15 | 200 | 11 | 2,200 |
| Aug. 24 | 250 | 12 | 3,000 |
| Total | 550 | | $6,200 |

---

**ACTION PLAN**

- **Understand the periodic inventory system.**
- **Allocate costs between goods sold and goods on hand (ending inventory) for the FIFO method.**
- **Compute cost of goods sold for the FIFO method.**

## DO IT! 2 | Cost Flow Methods—FIFO Method

**Part 1:** The accounting records of Shumway Ag Implements show the following data.

| | |
|---|---|
| Beginning inventory | 4,000 units at $3 |
| Purchases | 6,000 units at $4 |
| Sales | 7,000 units at $12 |

Determine the cost of goods sold during the period under a periodic inventory system using the FIFO method.

### Solution

Cost of goods available for sale = (4,000 × $3) + (6,000 × $4) = $36,000

Ending inventory = 10,000 – 7,000 = 3,000 units

Cost of goods sold FIFO: $36,000 – (3,000 × $4) = $24,000

Related exercise material: **BE6.3, BE6.4, BE6.5, BE6.6, DO IT! 6.2, E6.4, E6.5, E.6.6, E6.7, and E6.8.**

---

## Last-In, First-Out (LIFO)

The **last-in, first-out (LIFO) method** assumes that the **latest goods** purchased are the first to be sold. LIFO seldom coincides with the actual physical flow of inventory. (Exceptions include goods stored in piles, such as coal or hay, where goods are removed from the top of the pile as they are sold.) Under the LIFO method, the **costs** of the latest goods purchased are the first to be recognized in determining cost of goods sold. **Illustration 6.8** shows the allocation of the cost of goods available for sale at Houston Electronics under LIFO.

**ILLUSTRATION 6.8**

**Allocation of costs— LIFO method**

| | Cost of Goods Available for Sale | | | |
|---|---|---|---|---|
| Date | Explanation | Units | Unit Cost | Total Cost |
| Jan. 1 | Beginning inventory | 100 | $10 | $ 1,000 |
| Apr. 15 | Purchase | 200 | 11 | 2,200 |
| Aug. 24 | Purchase | 300 | 12 | 3,600 |
| Nov. 27 | Purchase | 400 | 13 | 5,200 |
| | Total | 1,000 | | $12,000 |

*(continues)*

ILLUSTRATION 6.8

*(continued)*

| Step 1: Ending Inventory | | | | Step 2: Cost of Goods Sold | |
| --- | --- | --- | --- | --- | --- |
| **Date** | **Units** | **Unit Cost** | **Total Cost** | | |
| Jan. 1 | 100 | $10 | $1,000 | Cost of goods available for sale | $12,000 |
| Apr. 15 | 200 | 11 | 2,200 | Less: Ending inventory | 5,000 |
| Aug. 24 | 150 | 12 | 1,800 | Cost of goods sold | **$ 7,000** |
| Total | 450 | | **$5,000** | | |

Under LIFO, since it is assumed that the first goods sold were those that were most recently purchased, ending inventory is based on the costs of the oldest units purchased (see **Helpful Hint**). That is, **under LIFO, companies determine the cost of the ending inventory by taking the unit cost of the earliest goods available for sale and working forward until all units of inventory have been costed**. In this example, Houston Electronics accounts for the 450 units of ending inventory using the **earliest** costs. The first purchase was 100 units at $10 in the January 1 beginning inventory. Then, 200 units were purchased at $11. The remaining 150 units needed have a $12 per unit cost (August 24 purchase). Next, Houston Electronics calculates cost of goods sold by subtracting the cost of the units **not sold** (ending inventory) from the cost of all goods available for sale.

**Illustration 6.9** demonstrates that Houston can also calculate the cost of the 550 units sold by using the costs of the last 550 units acquired. Note that of the 300 units purchased on August 24, only 150 units are assumed sold. This agrees with our calculation of the cost of ending inventory, where 150 of these units were assumed unsold and thus included in ending inventory.

**HELPFUL HINT**

Another way of thinking about the calculation of LIFO ending inventory is the FISH assumption— first in still here.

| Date | Units | Unit Cost | Total Cost |
| --- | --- | --- | --- |
| Nov. 27 | 400 | $13 | $5,200 |
| Aug. 24 | 150 | 12 | 1,800 |
| Total | 550 | | **$7,000** |

ILLUSTRATION 6.9

**Proof of cost of goods sold— LIFO method**

Under a periodic inventory system, which we are using here, **all goods purchased during the period are assumed to be available for the first sale, regardless of the date of purchase.**

**ACTION PLAN**

- Understand the periodic inventory system.
- Allocate costs between goods sold and goods on hand (ending inventory) for the LIFO method.
- Compute cost of goods sold for the LIFO method.

## DO IT! 2 | Cost Flow Methods—LIFO Method

**Part 2:** The accounting records of Shumway Ag Implements show the following data.

| | |
|---|---|
| Beginning inventory | 4,000 units at $3 |
| Purchases | 6,000 units at $4 |
| Sales | 7,000 units at $12 |

Determine the cost of goods sold during the period under a periodic inventory system using the LIFO method.

### Solution

Cost of goods available for sale = $(4,000 \times \$3) + (6,000 \times \$4) = \$36,000$

Ending inventory = $10,000 - 7,000 = 3,000$ units

Cost of goods sold LIFO: $\$36,000 - (3,000 \times \$3) = \$27,000$

Related exercise material: **BE6.3, BE6.4, BE6.5, BE6.6, DO IT! 6.2, E6.5, E6.6, E6.7, and E6.8.**

## Average-Cost

The **average-cost method** allocates the cost of goods available for sale on the basis of the **weighted-average unit cost** incurred. The average-cost method assumes that goods are similar in nature. **Illustration 6.10** presents the formula and a sample computation of the weighted-average unit cost.

**ILLUSTRATION 6.10**

Formula for weighted-average unit cost

| Cost of Goods Available for Sale | ÷ | Total Units Available for Sale | = | Weighted- Average Unit Cost |
|---|---|---|---|---|
| $12,000 | ÷ | 1,000 | = | $12 |

The company then applies the weighted-average unit cost to the units on hand to determine the cost of the ending inventory. **Illustration 6.11** shows the allocation of the cost of goods available for sale at Houston Electronics using average-cost.

**ILLUSTRATION 6.11**

Allocation of costs—average-cost method

| Cost of Goods Available for Sale | | | | |
|---|---|---|---|---|
| Date | Explanation | Units | Unit Cost | Total Cost |
| Jan. 1 | Beginning inventory | 100 | $10 | $ 1,000 |
| Apr. 15 | Purchase | 200 | 11 | 2,200 |
| Aug. 24 | Purchase | 300 | 12 | 3,600 |
| Nov. 27 | Purchase | 400 | 13 | 5,200 |
| | Total | 1,000 | | $12,000 |

| Step 1: Ending Inventory | | | Step 2: Cost of Goods Sold | |
|---|---|---|---|---|
| $12,000 ÷ 1,000 = $12 | | | Cost of goods available for sale | $12,000 |
| | | | Less: Ending inventory | 5,400 |
| Units | Unit Cost | Total Cost | Cost of goods sold | $ 6,600 |
| 450 | $12 | $5,400 | | |

**ILLUSTRATION 6.11**
(continued)

We can verify the cost of goods sold under this method by multiplying the units sold by the weighted-average unit cost ($550 \times \$12 = \$6,600$). Note that this method does **not** use the average of the unit costs. That average is $11.50 ($10 + $11 + $12 + $13 = $46; $46 \div 4$). The average-cost method instead uses the average **weighted by** the quantities purchased at each unit cost.

---

## DO IT! 2 | Cost Flow Methods—Average-Cost Method

**Part 3:** The accounting records of Shumway Ag Implements show the following data.

| | |
|---|---|
| Beginning inventory | 4,000 units at $3 |
| Purchases | 6,000 units at $4 |
| Sales | 7,000 units at $12 |

Determine the cost of goods sold during the period under a periodic inventory system using the average-cost method.

### Solution

Cost of goods available for sale = $(4,000 \times \$3) + (6,000 \times \$4) = \$36,000$
Ending inventory = $10,000 - 7,000 = 3,000$ units

Weighted-average unit cost: $[(4,000 @ \$3) + (6,000 @ \$4)] \div 10,000 = \$3.60$
Cost of goods sold average-cost: $\$36,000 - (3,000 \times \$3.60) = \$25,200$

Related exercise material: **BE6.3, BE6.4, BE6.5, BE6.6, DO IT 6.2, E6.5, E6.6, E6.7, and E6.8.**

**ACTION PLAN**
- **Understand the periodic inventory system.**
- **Allocate costs between goods sold and goods on hand (ending inventory) for the average-cost method.**
- **Compute cost of goods sold for the average-cost method.**

---

# Financial Statement and Tax Effects of Cost Flow Methods

Each of the three assumed cost flow methods is acceptable under GAAP. For example, **Reebok International Ltd.** and **Wendy's International** currently use the FIFO method of inventory costing. **Campbell Soup Company**, **Kroger**, and **Walgreens** use LIFO for part or all of their inventory. **Bristol-Myers Squibb**, **Starbucks**, and **Motorola** use the average-cost method. In fact, a company may also use more than one cost flow method at the same time for different types of inventory. **Stanley Black & Decker Manufacturing Company**, for example, uses LIFO for domestic inventories and FIFO for foreign inventories. Illustration 6.12 shows the use of the three cost flow methods in 500 large U.S. companies.

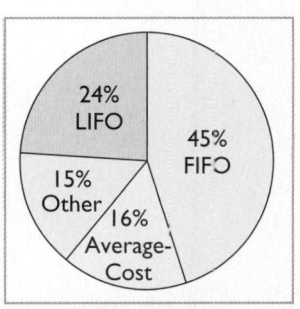

**ILLUSTRATION 6.12**

Use of cost flow methods in major U.S. companies

The reasons companies adopt different inventory cost flow methods are varied, but they usually involve one of three factors: (1) income statement effects, (2) balance sheet effects, or (3) tax effects. Analyzing financial statement and tax effects helps users determine which inventory costing method best meets the company's objectives.

## Income Statement Effects

To understand why companies might choose a particular cost flow method, let's examine the effects of the different cost flow assumptions on the financial statements of Houston Electronics. The condensed income statements in **Illustration 6.13** assume that Houston sold its 550 units for $18,500, had operating expenses of $9,000, and is subject to an income tax rate of 20%.

**ILLUSTRATION 6.13**

**Comparative effects of cost flow methods**

### Houston Electronics
#### Condensed Income Statements

|  | FIFO | LIFO | Average-Cost |
|---|---|---|---|
| Sales revenue | $18,500 | $18,500 | $18,500 |
| Beginning inventory | 1,000 | 1,000 | 1,000 |
| Purchases | 11,000 | 11,000 | 11,000 |
| Cost of goods available for sale | 12,000 | 12,000 | 12,000 |
| Ending inventory | **5,800** | **5,000** | **5,400** |
| Cost of goods sold | 6,200 | 7,000 | 6,600 |
| Gross profit | 12,300 | 11,500 | 11,900 |
| Operating expenses | 9,000 | 9,000 | 9,000 |
| Income before income taxes* | 3,300 | 2,500 | 2,900 |
| Income tax expense (20%) | 660 | 500 | 580 |
| Net income | **$ 2,640** | **$ 2,000** | **$ 2,320** |

*We are assuming that Houston Electronics is a corporation, and corporations are required to pay income taxes.

In this example, which assumes equal beginning inventories, the cost of goods available for sale ($12,000) is the same under each of the three inventory cost flow methods. However, the ending inventories and the costs of goods sold are different. This difference is due to the unit costs that the company allocated to cost of goods sold and to ending inventory. Each dollar of difference in ending inventory results in a corresponding dollar difference in income before income taxes. For Houston, an $800 difference exists between FIFO and LIFO cost of goods sold.

In periods when costs change, the cost flow assumption can have significant impacts both on income and on evaluations of income, such as the following.

1. In a period of inflation, FIFO produces a higher net income because lower unit costs of the first units purchased are matched against revenue.

2. In a period of inflation, LIFO produces a lower net income because higher unit costs of the last goods purchased are matched against revenue.

3. If costs are falling, the results from the use of FIFO and LIFO are reversed. FIFO will report the lowest net income and LIFO the highest.

4. Regardless of whether costs are rising or falling, average-cost produces net income between FIFO and LIFO.

As shown in the Houston example (Illustration 6.13), in a period of rising costs, FIFO reports the highest net income ($2,640) and LIFO the lowest ($2,000); average-cost falls between these two amounts ($2,320).

To management, higher net income is an advantage. It causes external users to view the company more favorably. In addition, management bonuses, if based on net income, will be higher. Therefore, when costs are rising (which is usually the case), companies tend to prefer FIFO because it results in higher net income.

Others believe that LIFO presents a more realistic net income number. That is, LIFO matches the more recent costs against current revenues to provide a better measure of net income. During periods of inflation, many challenge the quality of non-LIFO earnings, noting that failing to match current costs against current revenues leads to an understatement of cost of goods sold and an overstatement of net income. As some indicate, additional net income computed using FIFO creates **"paper or phantom profits"**—that is, earnings that do not really exist.

## Balance Sheet Effects

A major advantage of the FIFO method is that in a period of inflation, the costs allocated to ending inventory will approximate their current cost. For example, for Houston Electronics, 400 of the 450 units in the ending inventory are costed under FIFO at the higher November 27 unit cost of $13.

Conversely, a major shortcoming of the LIFO method is that in a period of inflation, the costs allocated to ending inventory may be significantly understated in terms of current cost. The understatement becomes greater over prolonged periods of inflation if the inventory includes goods purchased in one or more prior accounting periods. For example, **Caterpillar** has used LIFO for more than 50 years. Its balance sheet shows ending inventory of $9,700 million. But the inventory's actual current cost if FIFO had been used is $12,189 million.

## Tax Effects

We have seen that both inventory on the balance sheet and net income on the income statement are higher when companies use FIFO in a period of inflation. Yet, many companies have selected LIFO. Why? The reason is that LIFO results in the lowest income taxes (because of lower net income) during times of rising costs (see **Helpful Hint**). For example, at Houston Electronics, income taxes are $500 under LIFO, compared to $660 under FIFO. The tax savings of $160 makes more cash available for use in the business.

# Using Inventory Cost Flow Methods Consistently

Whatever cost flow method a company chooses, it should use that method consistently from one accounting period to another. This approach is often referred to as the **consistency concept**, which means that a company uses the same accounting principles and methods from year to year. Consistent application enhances the comparability of financial statements over successive time periods. In contrast, using the FIFO method one year and the LIFO method the next year would make it difficult to compare the net incomes of the two years.

Although consistent application is preferred, it does not mean that a company may never change its inventory costing method. When a company adopts a different method, it should disclose in the financial statements the change and its effects on net income. **Illustration 6.14** shows a typical disclosure, using information from recent financial statements of **Quaker Oats** (a unit of **PepsiCo**).

> **HELPFUL HINT**
> A tax rule, often referred to as the LIFO conformity rule, requires that if companies use LIFO for tax purposes they must also use it for financial reporting purposes. This means that if a company chooses the LIFO method to reduce its tax bills, it will also have to report lower net income in its financial statements.

---

### Quaker Oats
#### Notes to the Financial Statements

**Note 1:**   Effective July 1, the Company adopted the LIFO cost flow assumption for valuing the majority of U.S. Grocery Products inventories. The Company believes that the use of the LIFO method better matches current costs with current revenues. The effect of this change on the current year was to decrease net income by $16.0 million.

**ILLUSTRATION 6.14**

**Disclosure of change in cost flow method**

**Real World**

## International Insight ExxonMobil Corporation

Mike Fuentes/Bloomberg/ Getty Images

### Is LIFO Fair?

**ExxonMobil Corporation**, like many U.S. companies, uses LIFO to value its inventory for financial reporting and tax purposes. In one recent year, this resulted in a cost of goods sold figure that was $5.6 billion higher than under FIFO. By increasing cost of goods sold, ExxonMobil reduces net income, which reduces taxes. Critics say that LIFO provides an unfair "tax dodge." As Congress looks for more sources of tax revenue, some lawmakers favor the elimination

of LIFO. Supporters of LIFO argue that the method is conceptually sound because it matches current costs with current revenues. In addition, they point out that this matching provides protection against inflation.

International accounting standards do not allow the use of LIFO. Because of this, the net income of foreign oil companies such as **BP** and **Royal Dutch Shell** are not directly comparable to U.S. companies, which can make analysis difficult.

**Source:** David Reilly, "Big Oil's Accounting Methods Fuel Criticism," *Wall Street Journal* (August 8, 2006), p. C1.

**What are the arguments for and against the use of LIFO? (Answer is available near the end of the chapter.)**

### ACTION PLAN

- **Understand the periodic inventory system.**
- **Allocate costs between goods sold and goods on hand (ending inventory) for each cost flow method.**
- **Compute cost of goods sold for each method.**

## DO IT! 2 | Cost Flow Methods

**Part 4:** London Company sold 600 units of inventory in April. In addition, the following information is available.

| | | | |
|---|---|---|---|
| April 1 inventory | 250 | $10 | $ 2,500 |
| April 15 purchases | 400 | 12 | 4,800 |
| April 23 purchases | 350 | 13 | 4,550 |
| | 1,000 | | $11,850 |

Determine the cost of goods sold during the period under a periodic inventory system using (a) the FIFO method, (b) the LIFO method, and (c) the average-cost method.

### Solution

Cost of goods available for sale = $11,850
Ending inventory = 1,000 − 600 = 400 units

a. FIFO: $11,850 − $4,550 (350 × $13) − $600 (50 × $12) = $6,700
b. LIFO: $11,850 − $2,500 (250 × $10) − $1,800 (150 × $12) = $7,550
c. Weighted-average unit cost: $11,850 ($2,500 + $4,800 + $4,550) ÷ 1,000 = $11.85
   Average-cost: $11,850 − (400 × $11.85) = $7,110

Related exercise material: **BE6.3, BE6.4, BE6.5, BE6.6, DO IT! 6.2, E6.4, E6.5, E6.6, E6.7, E6.8, and E6.9.**

# Effects of Inventory Errors

### LEARNING OBJECTIVE 3
Indicate the effects of inventory errors on the financial statements.

Unfortunately, errors occasionally occur in accounting for inventory. In some cases, errors are caused by failure to count or cost the inventory correctly. In other cases, errors occur because companies do not properly recognize the transfer of legal title to goods that are in transit. When errors occur, they affect both the income statement and the balance sheet.

# Income Statement Effects

The ending inventory of one period automatically becomes the beginning inventory of the next period. Thus, inventory errors affect the computation of cost of goods sold and net income in two periods.

The effects on cost of goods sold can be computed by first entering incorrect data in the formula in **Illustration 6.15** and then substituting the correct data.

**ILLUSTRATION 6.15** **Formula for cost of goods sold**

| Beginning Inventory | + | Cost of Goods Purchased | − | Ending Inventory | = | Cost of Goods Sold |
|---|---|---|---|---|---|---|

If **beginning** inventory is understated, cost of goods sold will be understated. If **ending** inventory is understated, cost of goods sold will be overstated. **Illustration 6.16** shows the effects of inventory errors on the current year's income statement (see **Ethics Note**).

**ETHICS NOTE**

Inventory fraud increases during recessions. Such fraud includes costing inventory at amounts in excess of its actual value, or claiming to have inventory when no inventory exists. Inventory fraud usually overstates ending inventory, thereby understating cost of goods sold and creating higher net income.

| When Inventory Error: | Cost of Goods Sold Is: | Net Income Is: |
|---|---|---|
| Understates beginning inventory | Understated | Overstated |
| Overstates beginning inventory | Overstated | Understated |
| Understates ending inventory | Overstated | Understated |
| Overstates ending inventory | Understated | Overstated |

**ILLUSTRATION 6.16**

**Effects of inventory errors on current year's income statement**

An error in the ending inventory of the current period will have a **reverse effect on net income of the next accounting period**. **Illustration 6.17** shows this effect. Note that the understatement of ending inventory in 2021 results in an understatement of beginning inventory in 2022 and an overstatement of net income in 2022.

**ILLUSTRATION 6.17** **Effects of inventory errors on two years' income statements**

### Veronique Unique, Inc.
#### Condensed Income Statements

| | 2021 Incorrect | 2021 Correct | 2022 Incorrect | 2022 Correct |
|---|---|---|---|---|
| Sales revenue | $80,000 | $80,000 | $90,000 | $90,000 |
| Beginning inventory | $20,000 | $20,000 | **$12,000** | **$15,000** |
| Cost of goods purchased | 40,000 | 40,000 | 68,000 | 68,000 |
| Cost of goods available for sale | 60,000 | 60,000 | 80,000 | 83,000 |
| Ending inventory | **12,000** | **15,000** | 23,000 | 23,000 |
| Cost of goods sold | 48,000 | 45,000 | 57,000 | 60,000 |
| Gross profit | 32,000 | 35,000 | 33,000 | 30,000 |
| Operating expenses | 10,000 | 10,000 | 20,000 | 20,000 |
| Net income | $22,000 | $25,000 | $13,000 | $10,000 |

$(3,000)
Net income understated

$3,000
Net income overstated

The errors cancel. Thus, the combined total income for the 2-year period is correct.

Over the two years, though, total net income is correct because the errors **offset each other**. Notice that total net income using incorrect data is $35,000 ($22,000 + $13,000), which is the same as the total net income of $35,000 ($25,000 + $10,000) using correct data. Also note in this example that an error in the beginning inventory does not result in a corresponding error in the ending inventory for that period. The correctness of the ending inventory depends entirely on the accuracy of counting and costing the inventory at the balance sheet date under the periodic inventory system.

## Balance Sheet Effects

Companies can determine the effect of ending inventory errors on the balance sheet by using the basic accounting equation: Assets = Liabilities + Stockholders' Equity. Errors in the ending inventory have the effects shown in **Illustration 6.18**.

**ILLUSTRATION 6.18**

**Effects of ending inventory errors on balance sheet**

| Ending Inventory Error | Assets | Liabilities | Stockholders' Equity |
|---|---|---|---|
| Overstated | Overstated | No effect | Overstated |
| Understated | Understated | No effect | Understated |

The effect of an error in ending inventory on the subsequent period was shown in Illustration 6.17. Note that if the error is not corrected, the combined total net income for the two periods would be correct. Thus, total stockholders' equity reported on the balance sheet at the end of 2022 will also be correct.

---

**ACTION PLAN**

- **An ending inventory error in one period will have an equal and opposite effect on cost of goods sold and net income in the next period.**
- **After two years, the errors have offset each other.**

### DO IT! 3 | Inventory Errors

Visual Company overstated its 2021 ending inventory by $22,000. Determine the impact this error has on ending inventory, cost of goods sold, and stockholders' equity in 2021 and 2022.

**Solution**

| | 2021 | 2022 |
|---|---|---|
| Ending inventory | $22,000 overstated | No effect |
| Cost of goods sold | $22,000 understated | $22,000 overstated |
| Stockholders' equity | $22,000 overstated | No effect |

Related exercise material: **BE6.7, DO IT! 6.3, E6.9, and E6.10.**

---

# Inventory Presentation and Analysis

**LEARNING OBJECTIVE 4**

Explain the statement presentation and analysis of inventory.

## Presentation

Recall that inventory is classified in the balance sheet as a current asset immediately below accounts receivable. In a multiple-step income statement, cost of goods sold is subtracted from net sales. There also should be disclosure of (1) the major inventory classifications, (2) the basis of accounting (cost, or lower-of-cost-or-net realizable value), and (3) the cost method (FIFO, LIFO, or average-cost).

**Walmart Inc.**, for example, in its January 31, 2017, balance sheet reported inventories of $43,046 million under current assets. The accompanying notes to the financial statements, as shown in **Illustration 6.19**, disclosed the following information.

## Walmart Inc.
### Notes to the Financial Statements

**Note 1. Summary of Significant Accounting Policies**

**Inventories**

The Company values inventories at the lower of cost or market as determined primarily by the retail method of accounting, using the last-in, first-out ("LIFO") method for substantially all of the Walmart U.S. segment's inventories. The inventory at the Walmart International segment is valued primarily by the retail inventory method of accounting, using the first-in, first-out ("FIFO") method. The retail method of accounting results in inventory being valued at the lower of cost or market since permanent markdowns are immediately recorded as a reduction of the retail value of inventory. The inventory at the Sam's Club segment is valued using the LIFO method. At January 31, 2017 and 2016, the Company's inventories valued at LIFO approximate those inventories as if they were valued at FIFO.

**ILLUSTRATION 6.19**
**Inventory disclosures by Walmart**
Real World

# Lower-of-Cost-or-Net Realizable Value

The value of inventory for companies selling high-technology or fashion goods can drop very quickly due to continual changes in technology or fashion. These circumstances sometimes call for inventory valuation methods other than those presented so far. For example, at one time, purchasing managers at **Ford** decided to make a large purchase of palladium, a precious metal used in vehicle emission devices. They made this purchase because they feared a future shortage. The shortage did not materialize, and by the end of the year the cost of palladium had plummeted. Ford's inventory was then worth $1 billion less than its original cost. Do you think Ford's inventory should have been stated at cost, in accordance with the historical cost principle, or at its lower net realizable value?

As you probably reasoned, this situation requires a departure from the cost basis of accounting. When the value of inventory is lower than its cost, companies must "write down" the inventory to its net realizable value. This is done by valuing the inventory at the **lower-of-cost-or-net realizable value (LCNRV)** in the period in which the cost decline occurs. LCNRV is an example of accounting **conservatism**. Conservatism means that accountants select a method of reporting that is least likely to overstate assets and net income. Critics of accounting conservatism argue that it introduces bias into accounting numbers. This can reduce the representational faithfulness as well as the relevance of financial reports.

Under the LCNRV basis, **net realizable value** refers to the net amount that a company expects to realize (receive) from the sale of inventory. Specifically, net realizable value is the estimated selling price in the normal course of business, less estimated costs to complete and sell.

Companies apply LCNRV to the items in inventory after they have used one of the inventory costing methods (specific identification, FIFO, or average-cost) to determine cost. To illustrate the application of LCNRV, assume that Ken Tuckie TV has the following lines of merchandise with costs and net realizable values as indicated. LCNRV produces the results shown in **Illustration 6.20**. Note that the amounts shown in the final column are the lower-of-cost-or-net realizable value amounts for each item.

| | Units | Cost per Unit | Net Realizable Value per Unit | Lower-of-Cost-or-Net Realizable Value | |
|---|---|---|---|---|---|
| Flat-screen TVs | 100 | $600 | $550 | $ 55,000 | ($550 × 100) |
| Satellite radios | 500 | 90 | 104 | 45,000 | ($90 × 500) |
| DVD recorders | 850 | 50 | 48 | 40,800 | ($48 × 850) |
| DVDs | 3,000 | 5 | 6 | 15,000 | ($5 × 3,000) |
| Total inventory | | | | $155,800 | |

**ILLUSTRATION 6.20**
**Computation of lower-of-cost-or-net realizable value**

Companies that use the LIFO method or the retail inventory method (discussed in Appendix 6B and shown in Illustration 6.19) are not required to use lower-of-cost-or-net realizable value for inventory valuation. Instead, they use a lower-of-cost-or-market approach which is a more complex calculation. The computation for the lower-of-cost-or-market method is discussed in more advanced accounting courses.

---

**ACTION PLAN**

- Determine whether cost or net realizable value is lower for each inventory type.
- Sum the lowest value of each inventory type to determine the total value of inventory.

### DO IT! 4a │ LCNRV

Tracy Company sells three different types of home heating stoves (gas, wood, and pellet). The cost and net realizable value of its inventory of stoves are as follows.

| | Cost | Net Realizable Value |
|---|---|---|
| Gas | $ 84,000 | $ 79,000 |
| Wood | 250,000 | 280,000 |
| Pellet | 112,000 | 101,000 |

Determine the value of the company's inventory under the lower-of-cost-or-net realizable value approach.

#### Solution

The lowest value for each inventory type is gas $79,000, wood $250,000, and pellet $101,000. The total inventory value is the sum of these amounts, $430,000.

Related exercise material: **BE6.8, DO IT! 6.4a, E6.11, and E6.12.**

---

# Analysis

The amount of inventory carried by a company has significant economic consequences. And inventory management is a double-edged sword that requires constant attention. On the one hand, management wants to have a great variety and quantity available so that customers have a wide selection and items are always in stock. But, such a policy may incur high carrying costs (e.g., investment, storage, insurance, obsolescence, and damage). On the other hand, low inventory levels lead to stock-outs and lost sales. Common ratios used to manage and evaluate inventory levels are the inventory turnover ratio and a related measure, days in inventory.

**Inventory turnover** measures the number of times on average the inventory is sold during the period. Its purpose is to measure the liquidity of the inventory. The inventory turnover is computed by dividing cost of goods sold by the average inventory during the period. Unless seasonal factors are significant, average inventory can be computed from the beginning and ending inventory balances. For example, **Walmart** reported in its January 31, 2016, annual report a beginning inventory of $45,141 million, an ending inventory of $44,469 million, and cost of goods sold for the year ended January 31, 2016, of $360,984 million. The inventory turnover formula and computation for Walmart are shown in **Illustration 6.21**.

**ILLUSTRATION 6.21**

Inventory turnover formula and computation for Walmart

| Cost of Goods Sale | ÷ | Average Inventory | = | Inventory Turnover |
|---|---|---|---|---|
| $360,984 | ÷ | $\dfrac{\$45,141 + \$44,469}{2}$ | = | 8.1 times |

A variant of the inventory turnover is **days in inventory**. This measures the average number of days inventory is held. It is calculated as 365 divided by the inventory turnover.

For example, Walmart's inventory turnover of 8.1 times divided into 365 is 45.1 days. This is the approximate time that it takes a company to sell the inventory once it arrives at the store.

There are typical levels of inventory in every industry. Companies that are able to keep their inventory at lower levels and higher turnovers and still satisfy customer needs are the most successful.

## Accounting Across the Organization    Sony

iStock.com/Dmitry Kutlayev

### Too Many TVs or Too Few?

Financial analysts closely monitor the inventory management practices of companies. For example, some analysts following **Sony** expressed concern because the company built up its inventory of televisions in an attempt to sell 25 million liquid crystal display (LCD) TVs—a 60% increase over the prior year. In that prior year, Sony had cut its inventory levels so that its quarterly days in inventory was down to 38 days, compared to 61 days for the same quarter a year before that. Now, as a result of its inventory build-up, days

in inventory rose to 59 days. Management said that it didn't think that Sony's inventory levels were too high. However, analysts were concerned that the company would have to engage in very heavy discounting in order to sell off its inventory. Analysts noted that the losses from discounting can be "punishing."

**Source:** Daisuke Wakabayashi, "Sony Pledges to Corral Inventory," *Wall Street Journal Online* (November 2, 2010).

**For Sony, what are the advantages and disadvantages of having a low days in inventory measure? (Answer is available near the end of the chapter.)**

## DO IT! 4b | Inventory Turnover

Early in 2022, Westmoreland Company switched to a just-in-time inventory system. Its sales revenue, cost of goods sold, and inventory amounts for 2021 and 2022 are shown below.

|  | 2021 | 2022 |
|---|---|---|
| Sales revenue | $2,000,000 | $1,800,000 |
| Cost of goods sold | 1,000,000 | 910,000 |
| Beginning inventory | 290,000 | 210,000 |
| Ending inventory | 210,000 | 50,000 |

Determine the inventory turnover and days in inventory for 2021 and 2022. Discuss the changes in the amount of inventory, the inventory turnover and days in inventory, and the amount of sales across the two years.

### Solution

|  | 2021 | 2022 |
|---|---|---|
| Inventory turnover | $\dfrac{\$1,000,000}{(\$290,000 + \$210,000) \div 2} = 4$ | $\dfrac{\$910,000}{(\$210,000 + \$50,000) \div 2} = 7$ |
| Days in inventory | $365 \div 4 = 91.3$ days | $365 \div 7 = 52.1$ days |

The company experienced a very significant decline in its ending inventory as a result of the just-in-time inventory. This decline improved its inventory turnover and its days in inventory. However, its sales declined by 10%. It is possible that this decline was caused by the dramatic reduction in the amount of inventory that was on hand, which increased the likelihood of stock-outs (failure to have inventory on hand). To determine the optimal inventory level, management must weigh the benefits of reduced inventory against the potential lost sales caused by stock-outs.

Related exercise material: **BE6.9, DO IT! 6.4b, E6.12, E6.13, and E6.14.**

**ACTION PLAN**

- To find the inventory turnover, divide cost of goods sold by average inventory.
- To determine days in inventory, divide 365 days by the inventory turnover.
- Just-in-time inventory reduces the amount of inventory on hand, which reduces carrying costs. Reducing inventory levels by too much has potential negative implications for sales.

# Inventory Cost Flow Methods in Perpetual Inventory Systems

> **LEARNING OBJECTIVE *5**
> Apply the inventory cost flow methods to perpetual inventory records.

What inventory cost flow methods can companies employ if they use a perpetual inventory system? Simple—they can use any of the inventory cost flow methods described in the chapter. To illustrate the application of the three assumed cost flow methods (FIFO, LIFO, and average-cost), we will use the data shown in **Illustration 6A.1** and in this chapter for Houston Electronics' Astro condensers.

**ILLUSTRATION 6A.1**
**Inventoriable units and costs**

| | Houston Electronics | | | | |
|---|---|---|---|---|---|
| | Astro Condensers | | | | |
| Date | Explanation | Units | Unit Cost | Total Cost | Balance in Units |
| 1/1 | Beginning inventory | 100 | $10 | $ 1,000 | 100 |
| 4/15 | Purchases | 200 | 11 | 2,200 | 300 |
| 8/24 | Purchases | 300 | 12 | 3,600 | 600 |
| 9/10 | Sale | 550 | | | 50 |
| 11/27 | Purchases | 400 | 13 | 5,200 | 450 |
| | | | | $12,000 | |

# First-In, First-Out (FIFO)

Under perpetual FIFO, the company charges to cost of goods sold the cost of the earliest goods on hand **prior to each sale**. Therefore, the cost of goods sold on September 10 consists of the units on hand January 1 and the units purchased April 15 and August 24. **Illustration 6A.2** shows the inventory under a FIFO method perpetual system.

**ILLUSTRATION 6A.2**
**Perpetual system—FIFO**

| Date | Purchases | | Cost of Goods Sold | Inventory Balance (in units and cost) | |
|---|---|---|---|---|---|
| January 1 | | | | (100 @ $10) | $1,000 |
| April 15 | (200 @ $11) | $2,200 | | (100 @ $10) (200 @ $11) | $3,200 |
| August 24 | (300 @ $12) | $3,600 | | (100 @ $10) (200 @ $11) (300 @ $12) | $6,800 |
| September 10 | | | (100 @ $10) (200 @ $11) (250 @ $12) | ( 50 @ $12) | $ 600 |
| | | | **$6,200** | | |
| November 27 | (400 @ $13) | $5,200 | | ( 50 @ $12) (400 @ $13) | $5,800 |

Cost of goods sold — **$6,200**

Ending inventory — **$5,800**

The ending inventory in this situation is $5,800, and the cost of goods sold is $6,200 [(100 @ $10) + (200 @ $11) + (250 @ $12)].

Compare Illustrations 6.6 and 6A.2. You can see that the results under FIFO in a perpetual system are the **same as in a periodic system**. In both cases, the ending inventory is $5,800 and cost of goods sold is $6,200. The observation is always true: the FIFO method yields the same results for both the periodic and perpetual systems. Regardless of the system, the first costs in are the costs assigned to cost of goods sold.

## Last-In, First-Out (LIFO)

Under the LIFO method using a perpetual system, the company charges to cost of goods sold the cost of the most recent purchase **prior** to the sale. Therefore, the cost of the goods sold on September 10 consists of all the units from the August 24 and April 15 purchases plus 50 of the units in beginning inventory. **Illustration 6A.3** shows the computation of the ending inventory under the LIFO method.

**Perpetual system—LIFO**

| Date | Purchases | | Cost of Goods Sold | Inventory Balance (in units and cost) | |
|---|---|---|---|---|---|
| January 1 | | | | (100 @ $10) | $1,000 |
| April 15 | (200 @ $11) | $2,200 | | (100 @ $10) (200 @ $11) | $3,200 |
| August 24 | (300 @ $12) | $3,600 | | (100 @ $10) (200 @ $11) (300 @ $12) | $6,800 |
| September 10 | | | (300 @ $12) (200 @ $11) ( 50 @ $10) | ( 50 @ $10) | $ 500 |
| | | | $6,300 | | |
| November 27 | (400 @ $13) | $5,200 | | ( 50 @ $10) (400 @ $13) | $5,700 |

Cost of goods sold

Ending inventory

The use of LIFO in a perpetual system will usually produce cost allocations that differ from those using LIFO in a periodic system. In a perpetual system, the latest units purchased **prior to each sale** are allocated to cost of goods sold. In contrast, in a periodic system the latest units purchased **during the period** are allocated to cost of goods sold. Thus, when a purchase is made after the last sale, the LIFO method under the periodic system will apply this purchase to the period's sales. See Illustration 6.9, which shows the proof that the 400 units at $13 purchased on November 27 applied to the sale of 550 units on September 10.

Under the LIFO perpetual system in Illustration 6A.3, the 400 units at $13 purchased on November 27 are all allocated to the ending inventory. The ending inventory in this LIFO perpetual illustration is $5,700, and cost of goods sold is $6,300, as compared to the LIFO periodic Illustration 6.8, where the ending inventory is $5,000 and cost of goods sold is $7,000.

## Average-Cost

The average-cost method in a perpetual inventory system is called the **moving-average method**. Under this method, the company computes a new weighted-average unit cost **after each purchase**, by dividing the cost of goods available for sale by the units on hand. The weighted-average unit cost is then applied to (1) the units sold, to determine the cost of goods sold, and (2) the remaining units on hand, to determine the ending inventory cost. **Illustration 6A.4** shows the application of the moving-average cost method by Houston Electronics (computations of the moving-average unit cost are shown after Illustration 6A.4).

**Perpetual system— moving-average method**

| Date | Purchases | | Cost of Goods Sold | Inventory Balance (in units and cost) | |
|---|---|---|---|---|---|
| January 1 | | | | (100 @ $10) | $1,000 |
| April 15 | (200 @ $11) | $2,200 | | (300 @ $10.667) | $3,200 |
| August 24 | (300 @ $12) | $3,600 | | (600 @ $11.333) | $6,800 |
| September 10 | | | (550 @ $11.333) | (50 @ $11.333) | $ 567 |
| | | | **$6,233** | | |
| November 27 | (400 @ $13) | $5,200 | | (450 @ $12.816) | **$5,767** |

Cost of goods sold

Ending inventory

As indicated, Houston Electronics computes **a new weighted-average unit cost each time it makes a purchase**.

1. On April 15, after Houston buys 200 units for $2,200, a total of 300 units costing $3,200 ($1,000 + $2,200) are on hand. The weighted-average unit cost is $10.667 ($3,200 ÷ 300).

2. On August 24, after Houston buys 300 units for $3,600, a total of 600 units costing $6,800 ($1,000 + $2,200 + $3,600) are on hand. The weighted-average unit cost is $11.333 ($6,800 ÷ 600).

3. On September 10, to compute cost of goods sold, Houston uses this unit cost of $11.333 in costing the units sold until it makes another purchase, at which time the company computes a new unit cost. Accordingly, the unit cost of the 550 units sold on September 10 is $11.333, and the total cost of goods sold is $6,233.

4. On November 27, following the purchase of 400 units for $5,200, there are 450 units on hand costing $5,767 ($567 + $5,200) with a new weighted-average unit cost of $12.816 ($5,767 ÷ 450).

Compare this moving-average cost under the perpetual inventory system to Illustration 6.11, which shows the average-cost method under a periodic inventory system.

---

## Appendix 6B | Estimating Inventories

> **LEARNING OBJECTIVE *6**
> Describe the two methods of estimating inventories.

In the chapter, we assumed that a company would be able to physically count its inventory. What if it cannot? What if the inventory were destroyed by fire or flood, for example? In that case, the company would use an estimate to determine the cost of the lost inventory.

Two circumstances explain why companies sometimes estimate inventories. First, a casualty such as fire, flood, or earthquake may make it impossible to take a physical inventory. Second, managers may want monthly or quarterly financial statements, but a physical inventory is taken only annually. The need for estimating inventories occurs primarily with a periodic inventory system because of the absence of perpetual inventory records.

There are two widely used methods of estimating inventories: (1) the gross profit method, and (2) the retail inventory method.

### Gross Profit Method

The **gross profit method** estimates the cost of ending inventory by applying a gross profit rate to net sales. This method is relatively simple but effective. Accountants, auditors, and managers frequently use the gross profit method to test the reasonableness of the ending inventory amount. It will detect large errors.

To use this method, a company needs to know its net sales, cost of goods available for sale, and gross profit rate. The company then can estimate its gross profit for the period. **Illustration 6B.1** shows the formulas for using the gross profit method.

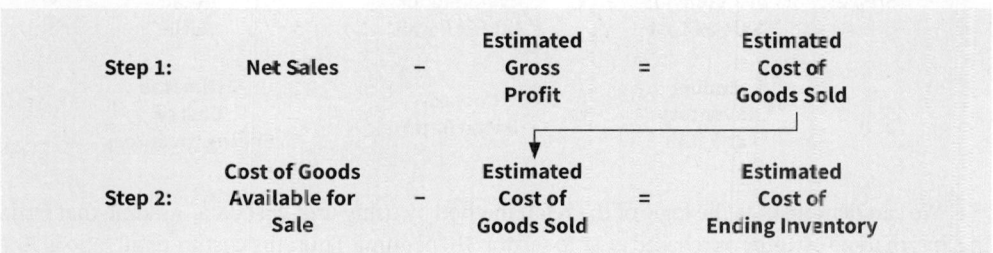

**ILLUSTRATION 6B.1**

Gross profit method formulas

To illustrate, assume that Kishwaukee Company wishes to prepare an income statement for the month of January. Its records show net sales of $200,000, beginning inventory $40,000, and cost of goods purchased $120,000. In the preceding year, the company realized a 30% gross profit rate. It expects to earn the same rate this year. Given these facts and assumptions, Kishwaukee can compute the estimated cost of the ending inventory at January 31 under the gross profit method as shown in **Illustration 6B.2**.

**ILLUSTRATION 6B.2**

Example of gross profit method

**Step 1:**

| | |
|---|---:|
| Net sales | $200,000 |
| Less: Estimated gross profit (30% × $200,000) | 60,000 |
| **Estimated cost of goods sold** | **$140,000** |

**Step 2:**

| | |
|---|---:|
| Beginning inventory | $ 40,000 |
| Cost of goods purchased | 120,000 |
| Cost of goods available for sale | 160,000 |
| Less: Estimated cost of goods sold | 140,000 |
| **Estimated cost of ending inventory** | **$ 20,000** |

The gross profit method is based on the assumption that the gross profit rate will remain constant. But, it may not remain constant, due to a change in merchandising policies or in market conditions. In such cases, the company should adjust the rate to reflect current operating conditions. In some cases, companies can obtain a more accurate estimate by applying this method on a department or product-line basis.

Note that companies should not use the gross profit method to prepare financial statements at the end of the year. These statements should be based on a physical inventory count.

# Retail Inventory Method

A retail store such as **Home Depot**, **Ace Hardware**, or **Walmart** has thousands of different types of merchandise at low unit costs. In such cases, it is difficult and time-consuming to apply unit costs to inventory quantities. An alternative is to use the **retail inventory method** to estimate the cost of inventory. Most retail companies can establish a relationship between cost and sales price. The company then applies the cost-to-retail percentage to the ending inventory at retail prices to determine inventory at cost.

Under the retail inventory method, a company's records must show both the cost and retail value of the goods available for sale. **Illustration 6B.3** presents the formulas for using the retail inventory method.

**ILLUSTRATION 6B.3**

**Retail inventory method formulas**

| | | | | | | |
|---|---|---|---|---|---|---|
| Step 1: | Goods Available for Sale at Retail | – | Net Sales | = | Ending Inventory at Retail | |
| Step 2: | Goods Available for Sale at Cost | ÷ | Goods Available for Sale at Retail | = | Cost-to-Retail Ratio | |
| Step 3: | Ending Inventory at Retail | × | Cost-to-Retail Ratio | = | Estimated Cost of Ending Inventory | |

We can demonstrate the logic of the retail method by using unit-cost data. Assume that Ortiz Inc. has marked 10 units purchased at $7 to sell for $10 per unit. Thus, the cost-to-retail ratio is 70% ($70 ÷ $100). If four units remain unsold, their retail value is $40 (4 × $10), and their cost is $28 ($40 × 70%). This amount agrees with the total cost of goods on hand on a per unit basis (4 × $7).

**Illustration 6B.4** shows application of the retail method for Valley West. Note that it is not necessary to take a physical inventory to determine the estimated cost of goods on hand at any given time.

**ILLUSTRATION 6B.4**

**Application of retail inventory method**

| | At Cost | At Retail |
|---|---|---|
| Beginning inventory | $14,000 | $ 21,500 |
| Goods purchased | 61,000 | 78,500 |
| Goods available for sale | $75,000 | 100,000 |
| Less: Net sales | | 70,000 |
| **Step (1) Ending inventory at retail =** | | **$ 30,000** |

**Step (2) Cost-to-retail ratio = $75,000 ÷ $100,000 = 75%**
**Step (3) Estimated cost of ending inventory = $30,000 × 75% = $22,500**

**HELPFUL HINT**

**In determining inventory at retail, companies use selling prices of the units.**

The retail inventory method also facilitates taking the inventory at the end of an accounting period. Valley West can value the goods on hand at the prices marked on the merchandise, and then apply the cost-to-retail ratio to the goods on hand at retail to determine the ending inventory at cost (see **Helpful Hint**).

The major disadvantage of the retail method is that it is an averaging technique. Thus, it may produce an incorrect inventory valuation if the mix of the ending inventory is not representative of the mix in the goods available for sale. Assume, for example, that the cost-to-retail ratio of 75% for Valley West consists of equal proportions of inventory items that have cost-to-retail ratios of 70%, 75%, and 80%. If the ending inventory contains only items with a 70% ratio, an incorrect inventory cost will result. Companies can minimize this problem by applying the retail method on a department or product-line basis.

# Review and Practice

## Learning Objectives Review

### 1 Discuss how to classify and determine inventory.

Merchandisers need only one inventory classification, merchandise inventory, to describe the different items that make up total inventory. Manufacturers, on the other hand, usually classify inventory into three categories: finished goods, work in process, and raw materials. To determine inventory quantities, companies (1) take a physical inventory of goods on hand and (2) determine the ownership of goods in transit or on consignment.

### 2 Apply inventory cost flow methods and discuss their financial effects.

The primary basis of accounting for inventories is cost. Cost of goods available for sale includes (a) cost of beginning inventory and (b) cost of goods purchased. The inventory cost flow methods are specific identification and three assumed cost flow methods—FIFO, LIFO, and average-cost.

When costs are rising, the first-in, first-out (FIFO) method results in lower cost of goods sold and higher net income than the other methods. The last-in, first-out (LIFO) method results in the lowest income taxes. The reverse is true when costs are falling. In the balance sheet, FIFO results in an ending inventory that is closest to current value. Inventory under LIFO is the farthest from current value.

Companies use the lower-of-cost-or-net realizable value (LCNRV) basis when the net realizable value is less than cost. Under LCNRV, companies recognize the loss in the period in which the cost decline occurs.

The inventory turnover is cost of goods sold divided by average inventory. To convert it to average days in inventory, divide 365 days by the inventory turnover.

### 3 Indicate the effects of inventory errors on the financial statements.

In the income statement of the current year: (a) If beginning inventory is understated, net income is overstated. The reverse occurs if beginning inventory is overstated. (b) If ending inventory is overstated, net income is overstated. If ending inventory is understated, net income is understated. In the following period, its effect on net income for that period is reversed, and total net income for the two years will be correct.

In the balance sheet: Ending inventory errors will have the same effect on total assets and total stockholders' equity and no effect on liabilities.

### 4 Explain the statement presentation and analysis of inventory.

Inventory is classified in the balance sheet as a current asset immediately below accounts receivable. There also should be disclosure in the notes for (1) the major inventory classifications, (2) the basis of accounting, and (3) the cost method.

### *5 Apply the inventory cost flow methods to perpetual inventory records.

Under FIFO and a perpetual inventory system, companies charge to cost of goods sold the cost of the earliest goods on hand prior to each sale. Under LIFO and a perpetual system, companies charge to cost of goods sold the cost of the most recent purchase prior to sale. Under the moving-average (average-cost) method and a perpetual system, companies compute a new weighted-average unit cost after each purchase.

### *6 Describe the two methods of estimating inventories.

The two methods of estimating inventories are the gross profit method and the retail inventory method. Under the gross profit method, companies apply a gross profit rate to net sales to determine estimated cost of goods sold. They then subtract estimated cost of goods sold from cost of goods available for sale to determine the estimated cost of the ending inventory.

Under the retail inventory method, companies compute a cost-to-retail ratio by dividing the cost of goods available for sale by the retail value of the goods available for sale. They then apply this ratio to the ending inventory at retail to determine the estimated cost of the ending inventory.

## Glossary Review

**Average-cost method** Inventory costing method that uses the weighted-average unit cost to allocate to ending inventory and cost of goods sold the cost of goods available for sale. (p. 6-12).

**Consigned goods** Goods held for sale by one party although ownership of the goods is retained by another party. (p. 6-6).

**Consistency concept** Dictates that a company use the same accounting principles and methods from year to year. (p. 6-15).

**Days in inventory** Measure of the average number of days inventory is held; calculated as 365 divided by inventory turnover. (p. 6-20).

**Finished goods inventory** Manufactured items that are completed and ready for sale. (p. 6-3).

**First-in, first-out (FIFO) method** Inventory costing method that assumes that the costs of the earliest goods purchased are the first to be recognized as cost of goods sold. (p. 6-9).

**FOB (free on board) destination** Freight terms indicating that ownership of the goods remains with the seller until the goods reach the buyer. (p. 6-5).

**FOB (free on board) shipping point** Freight terms indicating that ownership of the goods passes to the buyer when the public carrier accepts the goods from the seller. (p. 6-5).

**\*Gross profit method** A method for estimating the cost of the ending inventory by applying a gross profit rate to net sales and subtracting estimated cost of goods sold from cost of goods available for sale. (p. 6-24).

**Inventory turnover** A ratio that measures the number of times on average the inventory sold during the period; computed by dividing cost of goods sold by the average inventory during the period. (p. 6-20).

**Just-in-time (JIT) inventory** Inventory system in which companies manufacture or purchase goods only when needed for use. (p. 6-3).

**Last-in, first-out (LIFO) method** Inventory costing method that assumes the costs of the latest units purchased are the first to be allocated to cost of goods sold. (p. 6-10).

**Lower-of-cost-or-net realizable value (LCNRV)** A basis whereby inventory is stated at the lower of either its cost or its net realizable value. (p. 6-19).

**\*Moving-average method** Inventory costing method in which a new weighted-average unit cost is computed after each purchase, by dividing the cost of goods available for sale by the units on hand. (p. 6-23).

**Net realizable value** Net amount that a company expects to realize (receive) from the sale of inventory. Specifically, it is the estimated selling price in the normal course of business, less estimated costs to complete and sell. (p. 6-19)

**Raw materials** Basic goods that will be used in production but have not yet been placed into production. (p. 6-3).

**\*Retail inventory method** A method for estimating the cost of the ending inventory by applying a cost-to-retail ratio to the ending inventory at retail. (p. 6-25).

**Specific identification method** An actual physical flow costing method in which items still in inventory are specifically tracked and costed to arrive at the total cost of the ending inventory. (p. 6-7).

**Weighted-average unit cost** Average cost that is weighted by the number of units purchased at each unit cost. (p. 6-12).

**Work in process** That portion of manufactured inventory that has been placed into the production process but is not yet complete. (p. 6-3).

## Practice Multiple-Choice Questions

1. **(LO 1)** When is a physical inventory usually taken?

   a. When the company has its greatest amount of inventory.

   b. When a limited number of goods are being sold or received.

   c. At the end of the company's fiscal year.

   d. Both when a limited number of goods are being sold or received, and at the end of the company's fiscal year.

2. **(LO 1)** Which of the following should **not** be included in the physical inventory of a company?

   a. Goods held on consignment from another company.

   b. Goods shipped on consignment to another company.

   c. Goods in transit from another company shipped FOB shipping point.

   d. None of the answer choices is correct.

3. **(LO 1)** As a result of a thorough physical inventory, Railway Company determined that it had inventory of $180,000 at December 31, 2022. This count did not take into consideration the following facts: Rogers Consignment Store currently has goods worth $35,000 on its sales floor that belong to Railway but are being sold on consignment by Rogers. The selling price of these goods is $50,000. Railway purchased $13,000 of goods that were shipped on December 27, FOB destination, that will be received by Railway on January 3. Determine the correct amount of inventory that Railway should report.

   a. $230,000.              c. $228,000.

   b. $215,000.              d. $193,000.

4. **(LO 2)** Cost of goods available for sale consists of two elements: beginning inventory and:

   a. ending inventory.

   b. cost of goods purchased.

   c. cost of goods sold.

   d. All of the answer choices are correct.

5. **(LO 2)** Kam Company has the following:

   | | Units | Unit Cost |
   |---|---|---|
   | Inventory, Jan. 1 | 8,000 | $11 |
   | Purchase, June 19 | 13,000 | 12 |
   | Purchase, Nov. 8 | 5,000 | 13 |

   If 9,000 units are on hand at December 31, the cost of the ending inventory under FIFO is:

   a. $99,000.              c. $113,000.

   b. $108,000.            d. $117,000.

6. **(LO 2)** Kam Company has the following:

   | | Units | Unit Cost |
   |---|---|---|
   | Inventory, Jan. 1 | 8,000 | $11 |
   | Purchase, June 19 | 13,000 | 12 |
   | Purchase, Nov. 8 | 5,000 | 13 |

   If 9,000 units are on hand, the cost of the ending inventory under LIFO is:

   a. $113,000.            c. $99,000.

   b. $108,000.            d. $100,000.

7. **(LO 2)** Davidson Electronics has the following:

   | | Units | Unit Cost |
   |---|---|---|
   | Inventory, Jan. 1 | 5,000 | $ 8 |
   | Purchase, April 2 | 15,000 | $10 |
   | Purchase, Aug. 28 | 20,000 | $12 |

   If Davidson has 7,000 units on hand at December 31, the cost of ending inventory under the average-cost method is:

   a. $84,000.              c. $56,000.

   b. $70,000.              d. $75,250.

8. **(LO 2)** In periods of rising costs, LIFO will produce:

   a. higher net income than FIFO.

   b. the same net income as FIFO.

   c. lower net income than FIFO.

   d. higher net income than average-cost.

9. **(LO 2)** Considerations that affect the selection of an inventory costing method do **not** include:

   a. tax effects.

   b. balance sheet effects.

   c. income statement effects.

   d. perpetual vs. periodic inventory system.

10. **(LO 3)** Fran Company's ending inventory is understated $4,000. The effects of this error on the current year's cost of goods sold and net income, respectively, are:

    a. understated, overstated.        c. overstated, overstated.

    b. overstated, understated.        d. understated, understated.

11. **(LO 3)** Harold Company overstated its ending inventory by $15,000 at December 31, 2021. It did not correct the error in 2021 or 2022. As a result, Harold's stockholders' equity was:

    a. overstated at December 31, 2021, and understated at December 31, 2022.

    b. overstated at December 31, 2021, and properly stated at December 31, 2022.

    c. understated at December 31, 2021, and understated at December 31, 2022.

    d. overstated at December 31, 2021, and overstated at December 31, 2022.

12. **(LO 4)** The lower-of-cost-or-net realizable value rule for inventory is an example of the application of:

    a. the conservatism convention.

    b. the historical cost principle.

    c. the materiality concept.

    d. the economics entity assumption.

13. **(LO 4)** Norton Company purchased 1,000 widgets and has 200 widgets in its ending inventory at a cost of $91 each and a net realizable value of $80 each. The ending inventory under lower-of-cost-or-net realizable value is:

    a. $91,000.              c. $18,200.

    b. $80,000.              d. $16,000.

**14. (LO 4)** Carlos Company had beginning inventory of $80,000, ending inventory of $110,000, cost of goods sold of $285,000, and sales of $475,000. Carlos's days in inventory is:

    **a.** 73 days.

    **b.** 121.7 days.

    **c.** 102.5 days.

    **d.** 84.5 days.

**15. (LO 4)** Which of these would cause the inventory turnover to increase the most?

    **a.** Increasing the amount of inventory on hand.

    **b.** Keeping the amount of inventory on hand constant but increasing sales.

    **c.** Keeping the amount of inventory on hand constant but decreasing sales.

    **d.** Decreasing the amount of inventory on hand and increasing sales.

**\*16. (LO 5)** In a perpetual inventory system:

    **a.** LIFO cost of goods sold will be the same as in a periodic inventory system.

    **b.** average costs are a simple average of unit costs incurred.

    **c.** a new average is computed under the average-cost method after each sale.

    **d.** FIFO cost of goods sold will be the same as in a periodic inventory system.

**\*17. (LO 6)** King Company has sales of $150,000 and cost of goods available for sale of $135,000. If the gross profit rate is 30%, the estimated cost of the ending inventory under the gross profit method is:

    **a.** $15,000.

    **b.** $30,000.

    **c.** $45,000.

    **d.** $75,000.

## Solutions

**1. d.** A physical inventory is usually taken when a limited number of goods are being sold or received, and at the end of the company's fiscal year. Choice (a) is incorrect because a physical inventory count is usually taken when the company has the least, not greatest, amount of inventory. Choices (b) and (c) are correct, but (d) is the better answer.

**2. a.** Goods held on consignment should not be included because another company has title (ownership) to the goods. The other choices are incorrect because (b) goods shipped on consignment to another company and (c) goods in transit from another company shipped FOB shipping point should be included in a company's ending inventory. Choice (d) is incorrect because (a) is not included in the physical inventory.

**3. b.** The inventory held on consignment by Rogers should be included in Railway's inventory balance at cost ($35,000). The purchased goods of $13,000 should not be included in inventory until January 3 because the goods are shipped FOB destination. Therefore, the correct amount of inventory is $215,000 ($180,000 + $35,000), not (a) $230,000, (c) $228,000, or (d) $193,000.

**4. b.** Cost of goods available for sale consists of beginning inventory and cost of goods purchased, not (a) ending inventory or (c) cost of goods sold. Therefore, choice (d) is also incorrect.

**5. c.** Under FIFO, ending inventory will consist of 5,000 units from the Nov. 8 purchase and 4,000 units from the June 19 purchase. Therefore, ending inventory is (5,000 × $13) + (4,000 × $12) = $113,000, not (a) $99,000, (b) $108,000, or (d) $117,000.

**6. d.** Under LIFO, ending inventory will consist of 8,000 units from the inventory at Jan. 1 and 1,000 units from the June 19 purchase. Therefore, ending inventory is (8,000 × $11) + (1,000 × $12) = $100,000, not (a) $113,000, (b) $108,000, or (c) $99,000.

**7. d.** Under the average-cost method, total cost of goods available for sale needs to be calculated in order to determine the weighted-average unit cost. The total cost of goods available is $430,000 = (5,000 × $8) + (15,000 × $10) + (20,000 × $12). The weighted-average unit cost = ($430,000 ÷ 40,000 total units available for sale) = $10.75. Therefore, ending inventory is ($10.75 × 7,000) = $75,250, not (a) $84,000, (b) $70,000, or (c) $56,000.

**8. c.** In periods of rising costs, LIFO will produce lower net income than FIFO, not (a) higher than FIFO or (b) the same as FIFO. Choice

(d) is incorrect because in periods of rising costs, LIFO will produce lower net income than average-cost. LIFO therefore charges the highest inventory cost against revenues in a period of rising costs.

**9. d.** Perpetual vs. periodic inventory system is not one of the factors that affect the selection of an inventory costing method. The other choices are incorrect because (a) tax effects, (b) balance sheet effects, and (c) income statement effects all affect the selection of an inventory costing method.

**10. b.** Because ending inventory is too low, cost of goods sold will be too high (overstated) and since cost of goods sold (an expense) is too high, net income will be too low (understated). Therefore, the other choices are incorrect.

**11. b.** Stockholders' equity is overstated by $15,000 at December 31, 2021, and is properly stated at December 31, 2022. An ending inventory error in one period will have an equal and opposite effect on cost of goods sold and net income in the next period; after two years, the errors have offset each other. The other choices are incorrect because stockholders' equity (a) is properly stated, not understated, at December 31, 2022; (c) is overstated, not understated, by $15,000 at December 31, 2021, and is properly stated, not understated, at December 31, 2022; and (d) is properly stated at December 31, 2022, not overstated.

**12. a.** Conservatism means to use the lowest value for assets and revenues when in doubt. The other choices are incorrect because (b) historical cost means that companies value assets at the original cost, (c) materiality means that an amount is large enough to affect a decision-maker, and (d) economic entity means to keep the company's transactions separate from the transactions of other entities.

**13. d.** Under the LCNRV basis, inventory is reported at lower-of-cost-or-net realizable value. Therefore, ending inventory would be valued at 200 widgets × $80 each = $16,000 not (a) $91,000, (b) $80,000, or (c) $18,200.

**14. b.** Carlos's days in inventory = 365 ÷ Inventory turnover = 365 ÷ {$285,000 − [($80,000 + $110,000) ÷ 2]} = 121.7 days, not (a) 73 days, (c) 102.5 days, or (d) 84.5 days.

**15. d.** Decreasing the amount of inventory on hand will cause the denominator to decrease, causing inventory turnover to increase. Increasing sales will cause the numerator of the ratio to increase (higher sales means higher COGS), thus causing inventory turnover to increase even more. The other choices are incorrect because (a) increasing the amount of inventory on hand causes the denominator of the ratio to increase while the numerator stays the same, causing inventory turnover to decrease; (b) keeping the amount of inventory on hand constant but increasing sales will cause inventory turnover to increase because the numerator of the ratio will increase (higher sales means higher COGS) while the denominator stays the same, which will result in a lesser inventory increase than decreasing amount of inventory on hand and increasing sales; and (c) keeping the amount of inventory on hand constant but decreasing sales will cause inventory turnover to decrease because the numerator of the ratio will decrease (lower sales means lower COGS) while the denominator stays the same.

*16. **d.** FIFO cost of goods sold is the same under both a periodic and a perpetual inventory system. The other choices are incorrect because (a) LIFO cost of goods sold is not the same under a periodic and a perpetual inventory system; (b) average costs are based on a moving average of unit costs, not an average of unit costs; and (c) a new average is computed under the average-cost method after each purchase, not sale.

*17. **b.** COGS = Sales ($150,000) – Gross profit ($150,000 × 30%) = $105,000. Ending inventory = Cost of goods available for sale ($135,000) – COGS ($105,000) = $30,000, not (a) $15,000, (c) $45,000, or (d) $75,000.

---

## Practice Brief Exercises

*Determine ending inventory amount.*

**1. (LO 1)** Fylus Company took a physical inventory on December 31 and determined that goods costing $180,000 were on hand. Not included in the physical count were $18,000 of goods purchased from Rake Corporation, FOB destination, and $27,000 of goods sold to Shovel Company for $40,000, FOB destination. Both the Rake purchase and the Shovel sale were in transit at year-end. What amount should Fylus report as its December 31 inventory?

**Solution**

| 1. Physical inventory | $180,000 |
|---|---|
| Add: Goods sold to Shovel | 27,000 |
| Fylus ending inventory | $207,000 |

The $18,000 of goods purchased from Rake are excluded from ending inventory because the terms are FOB destination, which means Fylus takes title at the time the goods are received. Goods sold to Shovel FOB destination means that the goods are still Fylus's until delivered.

*Compute ending inventory using FIFO and LIFO.*

**2. (LO 2)** In its first month of operations, Moncada Company made three purchases of merchandise in the following sequence: (1) 200 units at $7, (2) 300 units at $8, and (3) 150 units at $9. Assuming there are 220 units on hand, compute the cost of the ending inventory under the (a) FIFO method and (b) LIFO method. Moncada use a periodic inventory system.

**Solution**

2. **a.** The ending inventory under FIFO consists of (150 units at $9) + (70 units at $8) for a total allocation of $1,910 ($1,350 + $560).

   **b.** The ending inventory under LIFO consists of (200 units at $7) + (20 units at $8) for a total allocation of $1,560 ($1,400 + $160).

*Compute inventory turnover and days in inventory.*

**3. (LO 4)** At December 31, 2022, the following information was available for Garcia Company: ending inventory $30,000, beginning inventory $42,000, cost of goods sold $240,000, and sales revenue $400,000. Calculate inventory turnover and days in inventory for Garcia Company.

**Solution**

3. Inventory turnover: $\dfrac{\$240,000}{(\$30,000 + \$42,000) \div 2} = \dfrac{\$240,000}{\$36,000} = 6.67$

Days in inventory: $\dfrac{365}{6.67} = 54.7$ days

# Practice Exercises

**1. (LO 1)** Mika Sorbiro, an auditor with Martinez CPAs, is performing a review of Sergei Company's inventory account. Sergei's did not have a good year and top management is under pressure to boost reported income. According to its records, the inventory balance at year-end was $650,000. However, the following information was not considered when determining that amount.

*Determine the correct inventory amount.*

1. Included in the company's count were goods with a cost of $200,000 that the company is holding on consignment. The goods belong to Bosnia Corporation.

2. The physical count did not include goods purchased by Sergei with a cost of $40,000 that were shipped FOB shipping point on December 28 and did not arrive at Sergei's warehouse until January 3.

3. Included in the inventory account was $15,000 of office supplies that were stored in the warehouse and were to be used by the company's supervisors and managers during the coming year.

4. The company received an order on December 28 that was boxed and was sitting on the loading dock awaiting pick-up on December 31. The shipper picked up the goods on January 1 and delivered them on January 6. The shipping terms were FOB shipping point. The goods had a selling price of $40,000 and a cost of $30,000. The goods were not included in the count because they were sitting on the dock.

5. On December 29, Sergei shipped goods with a selling price of $80,000 and a cost of $60,000 to Oman Sales Corporation FOB shipping point. The goods arrived on January 3. Oman Sales had only ordered goods with a selling price of $10,000 and a cost of $8,000. However, a Sergei's sales manager had authorized the shipment and said that if Oman wanted to ship the goods back next week, it could.

6. Included in the count was $30,000 of goods that were parts for a machine that the company no longer made. Given the high-tech nature of Sergei's products, it was unlikely that these obsolete parts had any other use. However, management would prefer to keep them on the books at cost, "since that is what we paid for them, after all."

## Instructions

Prepare a schedule to determine the correct inventory amount. Provide explanations for each item above, saying why you did or did not make an adjustment for each item.

## Solution

| | |
|---|---:|
| 1.  Ending inventory—as reported | $650,000 |
|     1. Subtract from inventory: The goods belong to Bosnia Corporation. Sergei is merely holding them for Bosnia. | (200,000) |
|     2. Add to inventory: The goods belonged to Sergei when they were shipped. | 40,000 |
|     3. Subtract from inventory: Office supplies should be carried in a separate account. They are not considered inventory held for resale. | (15,000) |
|     4. Add to inventory: The goods belong to Sergei until they are shipped (Jan. 1). | 30,000 |
|     5. Add to inventory: Oman Sales ordered goods with a cost of $8,000. Sergei should record the corresponding sales revenue of $10,000. Sergei's decision to ship extra "unordered" goods does not constitute a sale. The manager's statement that Oman could ship the goods back indicates that Sergei knows this overshipment is not a legitimate sale. The manager acted unethically in an attempt to improve Sergei's reported income by overshipping. | 52,000 |
|     6. Subtract from inventory: GAAP requires that inventory be valued at the lower-of-cost-or-net realizable value. Obsolete parts should be adjusted from cost to zero if they have no other use. | (30,000) |
| Correct inventory | $527,000 |

*Determine effects of inventory errors.*

2. **(LO 3)** Abel's Hardware reported cost of goods sold as follows.

|  | 2021 | 2022 |
|---|---|---|
| Beginning inventory | $ 20,000 | $ 30,000 |
| Cost of goods purchased | 150,000 | 175,000 |
| Cost of goods available for sale | 170,000 | 205,000 |
| Less: Ending inventory | 30,000 | 35,000 |
| Cost of goods sold | $140,000 | $170,000 |

Abel's made two errors: (1) 2021 ending inventory was overstated $2,500, and (2) 2022 ending inventory was understated $5,500.

### Instructions

Compute the correct cost of goods sold for each year.

### Solution

2.

|  | 2021 | 2022 |
|---|---|---|
| Beginning inventory | $ 20,000 | $ 27,500 |
| Cost of goods purchased | 150,000 | 175,000 |
| Cost of goods available for sale | 170,000 | 202,500 |
| Less: Corrected ending inventory | 27,500[a] | 40,500[b] |
| Cost of goods sold | $142,500 | $162,000 |

[a]$30,000 − $2,500 = $27,500; [b]$35,000 + $5,500 = $40,500

*Determine LCNRV valuation.*

3. **(LO 4)** Creve Couer Camera Inc. uses the lower-of-cost-or-net realizable value basis for its inventory. The following data are available at December 31.

|  | Units | Cost per Unit | Net Realizable Value per Unit |
|---|---|---|---|
| Cameras: |  |  |  |
| Minolta | 5 | $160 | $156 |
| Canon | 7 | 145 | 153 |
| Light Meters: |  |  |  |
| Vivitar | 12 | 120 | 114 |
| Kodak | 10 | 130 | 142 |

### Instructions

What amount should be reported for inventory on Creve Couer Camera's financial statements, assuming the lower-of-cost-or-net realizable value rule is applied?

### Solution

3.

|  | Cost per Unit | Net Realizable Value per Unit | Lower-of-Cost or-Net Realizable Value | Units | Inventory at Lower-of-Cost-or-Net Realizable Value |
|---|---|---|---|---|---|
| Cameras: |  |  |  |  |  |
| Minolta | $160 | $156 | $156 | 5 | $ 780 |
| Canon | 145 | 153 | 145 | 7 | 1,015 |
| Light Meters: |  |  |  |  |  |
| Vivitar | 120 | 114 | 114 | 12 | 1,368 |
| Kodak | 130 | 142 | 130 | 10 | 1,300 |
| Total |  |  |  |  | $4,463 |

# Practice Problems

**1. (LO 2)** Englehart Company has the following inventory purchases, and sales data for the month of March.

| | | | |
|---|---|---|---|
| Inventory: | March 1 | 200 units @ $4.00 | $ 800 |
| Purchases: | March 10 | 500 units @ $4.50 | 2,250 |
| | March 20 | 400 units @ $4.75 | 1,900 |
| | March 30 | 300 units @ $5.00 | 1,500 |
| Sales: | March 15 | 500 units | |
| | March 25 | 400 units | |

*Compute inventory and cost of goods sold using three cost flow methods in a periodic inventory system.*

The physical inventory count on March 31 shows 500 units on hand.

## Instructions

Under a **periodic inventory system**, determine the cost of inventory on hand at March 31 and the cost of goods sold for March under (a) FIFO, (b) LIFO, and (c) average-cost. (For average-cost, carry weighted-average unit cost to three decimal places.)

## Solution

1. The cost of goods available for sale is $6,450, as follows.

| | | | |
|---|---|---|---|
| Inventory: | | 200 units @ $4.00 | $ 800 |
| Purchases: | March 10 | 500 units @ $4.50 | 2,250 |
| | March 20 | 400 units @ $4.75 | 1,900 |
| | March 30 | 300 units @ $5.00 | 1,500 |
| | Total goods available for sale | | $6,450 |

**a.**

### FIFO Method

Ending inventory:

| Date | Units | Unit Cost | Total Cost | |
|---|---|---|---|---|
| March 30 | 300 | $5.00 | $1,500 | |
| March 20 | 200 | 4.75 | 950 | $2,450 |

Cost of goods sold: $6,450 − $2,450 =   $4,000

**b.**

### LIFO Method

Ending inventory:

| Date | Units | Unit Cost | Total Cost | |
|---|---|---|---|---|
| March 1 | 200 | $4.00 | $ 800 | |
| March 10 | 300 | 4.50 | 1,350 | $2,150 |

Cost of goods sold: $6,450 − $2,150 =   $4,300

**c.**

### Average-Cost Method

Weighted-average unit cost: $6,450 ÷ 1,400 = $4.607
Ending inventory: 500 × $4.607 =   $2,303.50

Cost of goods sold: $6,450 − $2,303.50 =   $4,146.50

**\*2. (LO 5) Practice Problem 1** showed cost of goods sold computations under a periodic inventory system. Now let's assume that Englehart Company uses a perpetual inventory system. The company has the same inventory, purchases, and sales data for the month of March as shown earlier:

*Compute inventory and cost of goods sold using three cost flow methods in a perpetual inventory system.*

| | | | |
|---|---|---|---|
| Inventory: | March 1 | 200 units @ $4.00 | $ 800 |
| Purchases: | March 10 | 500 units @ $4.50 | 2,250 |
| | March 20 | 400 units @ $4.75 | 1,900 |
| | March 30 | 300 units @ $5.00 | 1,500 |
| Sales: | March 15 | 500 units | |
| | March 25 | 400 units | |

The physical inventory count on March 31 shows 500 units on hand.

## Instructions

Under a **perpetual inventory system**, determine the cost of inventory on hand at March 31 and the cost of goods sold for March under (a) FIFO, (b) LIFO, and (c) moving-average cost.

## Solution

2. The cost of goods available for sale at March 31 is $6,450, as follows.

| | | | |
|---|---|---|---|
| Inventory: | | 200 units @ $4.00 | $ 800 |
| Purchases: | March 10 | 500 units @ $4.50 | 2,250 |
| | March 20 | 400 units @ $4.75 | 1,900 |
| | March 30 | 300 units @ $5.00 | 1,500 |
| Total: | | 1,400 | $6,450 |

Under a **perpetual inventory system**, the cost of goods sold under each cost flow method is as follows.

**a.**

### FIFO Method

| Date | Purchases | Cost of Goods Sold | Inventory Balance |
|---|---|---|---|
| March 1 | | | (200 @ $4.00) $ 800 |
| March 10 | (500 @ $4.50) $2,250 | | (200 @ $4.00) <br> (500 @ $4.50) } $3,050 |
| March 15 | | (200 @ $4.00) <br> (300 @ $4.50) <br> $2,150 | (200 @ $4.50) $ 900 |
| March 20 | (400 @ $4.75) $1,900 | | (200 @ $4.50) <br> (400 @ $4.75) } $2,800 |
| March 25 | | (200 @ $4.50) <br> (200 @ $4.75) <br> $1,850 | (200 @ $4.75) $ 950 |
| March 30 | (300 @ $5.00) $1,500 | | (200 @ $4.75) <br> (300 @ $5.00) } $2,450 |
| | Ending inventory $2,450 | Cost of goods sold: $2,150 + $1,850 = $4,000 | |

**b.**

### LIFO Method

| Date | Purchases | Cost of Goods Sold | Inventory Balance |
|---|---|---|---|
| March 1 | | | (200 @ $4.00) $ 800 |
| March 10 | (500 @ $4.50) $2,250 | | (200 @ $4.00) <br> (500 @ $4.50) } $3,050 |
| March 15 | | (500 @ $4.50) $2,250 | (200 @ $4.00) $ 800 |
| March 20 | (400 @ $4.75) $1,900 | | (200 @ $4.00) <br> (400 @ $4.75) } $2,700 |
| March 25 | | (400 @ $4.75) $1,900 | (200 @ $4.00) $ 800 |
| March 30 | (300 @ $5.00) $1,500 | | (200 @ $4.00) <br> (300 @ $5.00) } $2,300 |
| | Ending inventory $2,300 | Cost of goods sold: $2,250 + $1,900 = $4,150 | |

**c.**

### Moving-Average Cost Method

| Date | Purchases | Cost of Goods Sold | Inventory Balance |
|---|---|---|---|
| March 1 | | | (200 @ $ 4.00) $ 800 |
| March 10 | (500 @ $4.50) $2,250 | | (700 @ $4.357) $3,050 |
| March 15 | | (500 @ $4.357) $2,179 | (200 @ $4.357) $ 871 |
| March 20 | (400 @ $4.75) $1,900 | | (600 @ $4.618) $2,771 |
| March 25 | | (400 @ $4.618) $1,847 | (200 @ $4.618) $ 924 |
| March 30 | (300 @ $5.00) $1,500 | | (500 @ $4.848) $2,424 |
| | Ending inventory $2,424 | Cost of goods sold: $2,179 + $1,847 = $4,026 | |

Brief Exercises, DO IT! Exercises, Exercises, Problems, Data Analytics Activities, and many additional resources are available for practice in WileyPLUS.

*Note:* All asterisked Questions, Exercises, and Problems relate to material in the appendices to the chapter.

## Questions

1. "The key to successful business operations is effective inventory management." Do you agree? Explain.

2. An item must possess two characteristics to be classified as inventory by a merchandiser. What are these two characteristics?

3. Your friend Wil Juritz has been hired to help take the physical inventory in Byrd's Hardware Store. Explain to Wil what this job will entail.

4. **a.** Bonita Company ships merchandise to Myan Company on December 30. The merchandise reaches the buyer on January 6. Indicate the terms of sale that will result in the goods being included in (1) Bonita's December 31 inventory, and (2) Myan's December 31 inventory.

   **b.** Under what circumstances should Bonita Company include consigned goods in its inventory?

5. Nona Hat Shop received a shipment of hats for which it paid the wholesaler $2,970. The price of the hats was $3,000, but Nona was given a $30 cash discount and required to pay freight charges of $50. What amount should Nona record for inventory? Why?

6. Explain the difference between the terms FOB shipping point and FOB destination.

7. Ken McCall believes that the allocation of cost of goods available for sale should be based on the actual physical flow of the goods. Explain to Ken why this may be both impractical and inappropriate.

8. What is the major advantage and major disadvantage of the specific identification method of inventory costing?

9. "The selection of an inventory cost flow method is a decision made by accountants." Explain why this statement is true or false. Once a method has been selected, what accounting requirement applies?

10. Which assumed inventory cost flow method:

    **a.** usually coincides with the actual physical flow of merchandise?

    **b.** divides cost of goods available for sale by total units available for sale to determine a unit cost?

    **c.** assumes that the latest units purchased are the first to be sold?

11. In a period of rising costs, the inventory reported in Short Company's balance sheet is close to the current cost of the inventory, whereas King Company's inventory is considerably below its current cost. Identify the inventory cost flow method being used by each company. Which company probably has been reporting the higher gross profit?

12. Mamosa Corporation has been using the FIFO cost flow method during a prolonged period of inflation. During the same time period, Mamosa has been paying out all of its net income as dividends. What adverse effects may result from this policy?

13. Hank Artisan is studying for the next accounting mid-term examination. What should Hark know about (a) departing from the cost basis of accounting for inventories and (b) the meaning of "net realizable value" in the lower-of-cost-or-net realizable value method?

14. Jackson Music Center has 5 TVs on hand at the balance sheet date that cost $400 each. The net realizable value is $350 per unit. Under the lower-of-cost-or-net realizable value basis of accounting for inventories, what value should Jackson report for the TVs on the balance sheet? Why?

15. Bonnie Stores has 20 toasters on hand at the balance sheet date. Each costs $27. The net realizable value is $30 per unit. Under the lower-of-cost-or-net realizable value basis of accounting for inventories, what value should Bonnie report for the toasters on the balance sheet? Why?

16. Kuzu Company discovers in 2022 that its ending inventory at December 31, 2021, was $7,000 understated. What effect will this error have on (a) 2021 net income, (b) 2022 net income, and (c) the combined net income for the 2 years?

17. Tilton Company's balance sheet shows Inventory $162,800. What additional disclosures should be made?

18. Under what circumstances might inventory turnover be too high? That is, what possible negative consequences might occur?

19. What inventory cost flow method does **Apple** use for its inventories? (*Hint:* You will need to examine the notes for Apple's financial statements.)

*20. "When perpetual inventory records are kept, the results under the FIFO and LIFO methods are the same as they would be in a periodic inventory system." Explain why this statement is true or false.

*21. How does the average-cost method of inventory costing differ between a perpetual inventory system and a periodic inventory system?

*22. When is it necessary to estimate inventories?

*23. Both the gross profit method and the retail inventory method are based on averages. For each method, indicate the average used, how it is determined, and how it is applied.

*24. Wiggins Company has net sales of $400,000 and cost of goods available for sale of $300,000. If the gross profit rate is 35%, what is the estimated cost of the ending inventory? Show computations.

*25. Emporia Shoe Shop had goods available for sale in 2020 with a retail price of $120,000. The cost of these goods was $84,000. If sales during the period were $80,000, what is the estimated cost of ending inventory using the retail inventory method?

## Brief Exercises

*Identify items to be included in taking a physical inventory.*

**BE6.1 (LO 1), C** Peete Company identifies the following items for possible inclusion in the taking of a physical inventory. Indicate whether each item should be included or excluded from the inventory taking.

**a.** Goods shipped on consignment by Peete to another company.

**b.** Goods in transit from a supplier shipped FOB destination.

**c.** Goods sold but being held for customer pickup.

**d.** Goods held on consignment from another company.

*Determine ending inventory amount.*

**BE6.2 (LO 1), AP** Stallman Company took a physical inventory on December 31 and determined that goods costing $200,000 were on hand. Not included in the physical count were $25,000 of goods purchased from Pelzer Corporation, FOB shipping point, and $22,000 of goods sold to Alvarez Company for $30,000, FOB destination. Both the Pelzer purchase and the Alvarez sale were in transit at year-end. What amount should Stallman report as its December 31 inventory?

*Compute ending inventory using FIFO and LIFO.*

**BE6.3 (LO 2), AP** In its first month of operations, McLanie Company made three purchases of merchandise in the following sequence: (1) 300 units at $6, (2) 400 units at $8, and (3) 500 units at $9. Assuming there are 200 units on hand, compute the cost of the ending inventory under the (a) FIFO method and (b) LIFO method. McLanie uses a periodic inventory system.

*Compute the ending inventory using average-cost.*

**BE6.4 (LO 2), AP** In its first month of operations, McLanie Company made three purchases of merchandise in the following sequence: (1) 300 units at $6, (2) 400 units at $8, and (3) 500 units at $9. Assuming there are 200 units on hand, compute the cost of the ending inventory under the average-cost method. (Round weighted-average unit cost to three decimal places.)

*Explain the financial statement effect of inventory cost flow assumptions.*

**BE6.5 (LO 2), C** The management of Milque Corp. is considering the effects of inventory-costing methods on its financial statements and its income tax expense. Assuming that the cost the company pays for inventory is increasing, which method will:

**a.** Provide the highest net income?

**b.** Provide the highest ending inventory?

**c.** Result in the lowest income tax expense?

*Explain the financial statement effect of inventory cost flow assumptions.*

**BE6.6 (LO 2), AP** In its first month of operation, Hoffman Company purchased 100 units of inventory for $6, then 200 units for $7, and finally 140 units for $8. At the end of the month, 180 units remained. Compute the amount of phantom profit that would result if the company used FIFO rather than LIFO. Explain why this amount is referred to as phantom profit. The company uses the periodic system.

*Determine correct income statement amounts.*

**BE6.7 (LO 3), AN** Fennick Company reports net income of $92,000 in 2022. However, ending inventory was understated $7,000. What is the correct net income for 2022? What effect, if any, will this error have on total assets as reported in the balance sheet at December 31, 2022?

*Determine the LCNRV valuation using inventory categories.*

**BE6.8 (LO 4), AP** Wahlowitz Video Center accumulates the following cost and net realizable value data at December 31.

| Inventory Categories | Cost Data | Net Realizable Value Data |
|---|---|---|
| Cameras | $12,500 | $13,400 |
| Camcorders | 9,000 | 9,500 |
| Blu-ray players | 13,000 | 12,200 |

Compute the lower-of-cost-or-net realizable value for the company's total inventory.

*Compute inventory turnover and days in inventory.*

**BE6.9 (LO 4), AP** Suppose at December 31 of a recent year, the following information (in thousands) was available for sunglasses manufacturer **Oakley, Inc.**: ending inventory $155,377, beginning inventory $119,035, cost of goods sold $349,114, and sales revenue $761,865. Calculate the inventory turnover and days in inventory for Oakley, Inc. (Round inventory turnover to two decimal places.)

*Apply cost flow methods to a perpetual inventory system.*

***BE6.10 (LO 5), AP** Loggins Department Store uses a perpetual inventory system and had no beginning inventory. Data for product E2-D2 include the following purchases.

| Date | Number of Units | Unit Cost |
|---|---|---|
| May 7 | 50 | $10 |
| July 28 | 30 | 15 |

On June 1, Loggins sold 25 units, and on August 27, 30 more units. Compute the cost of goods sold using (a) FIFO, (b) LIFO, and (c) average-cost. (Round the cost per unit to three decimal places.)

*BE6.11 **(LO 6), AP**  At May 31, Suarez Company has net sales of $330,000 and cost of goods available for sale of $230,000. Compute the estimated cost of the ending inventory, assuming the gross profit rate is 35%.

*Apply the gross profit method.*

*BE6.12 **(LO 6), AP**  On June 30, Calico Fabrics has the following data pertaining to the retail inventory method. Goods available for sale: at cost $38,000; at retail $50,000; net sales $40,000; and ending inventory at retail $10,000. Compute the estimated cost of the ending inventory using the retail inventory method.

*Apply the retail inventory method.*

# DO IT! Exercises

**DO IT! 6.1 (LO 1), AN**  Sheldon Company just took its physical inventory on December 31. The count of inventory items on hand at the company's business locations resulted in a total inventory cost of $300,000. In reviewing the details of the count and related inventory transactions, you have discovered the following items had not been considered.

*Apply rules of ownership to determine inventory cost.*

1. Sheldon has sent inventory costing $28,000 on consignment to Richfield Company. All of this inventory was at Richfield's showrooms on December 31.

2. The company did not include in the count inventory (cost, $20,000) that was sold on December 28, terms FOB shipping point. The goods were in transit on December 31.

3. The company did not include in the count inventory (cost, $13,000) that was purchased with terms of FOB shipping point. The goods were in transit on December 31.

Compute the correct December 31 inventory.

**DO IT! 6.2 (LO 2), AP**  The accounting records of Ohm Electronics show the following data.

| | |
|---|---|
| Beginning inventory | 3,000 units at $5 |
| Purchases | 8,000 units at $7 |
| Sales | 9,400 units at $10 |

*Compute cost of goods sold under different cost flow methods.*

Determine cost of goods sold during the period under a periodic inventory system using (a) the FIFO method, (b) the LIFO method, and (c) the average-cost method. (Round unit cost to three decimal places.)

**DO IT! 6.3 (LO 3), AN**  Janus Company understated its 2021 ending inventory by $31,000. Determine the impact this error has on ending inventory, cost of goods sold, and stockholders' equity in 2021 and 2022.

*Determine effect of inventory error.*

**DO IT! 6.4a (LO 4), AP**  Jeri Company sells three different categories of tools (small, medium, and large). The cost and net realizable value of its inventory of tools are as follows.

*Compute inventory value under LCNRV.*

| | Cost | Net Realizable Value |
|---|---|---|
| Small | $ 64,000 | $ 61,000 |
| Medium | 290,000 | 260,000 |
| Large | 152,000 | 167,000 |

Determine the value of the company's inventory under the lower-of-cost-or-net realizable value approach.

**DO IT! 6.4b (LO 4), AP**  Early in 2022, Fedor Company switched to a just-in-time inventory system. Its sales revenue, cost of goods sold, and inventory amounts for 2021 and 2022 are shown below.

*Compute inventory turnover and days in inventory, and assess inventory level.*

| | 2021 | 2022 |
|---|---|---|
| Sales revenue | $3,120,000 | $3,713,000 |
| Cost of goods sold | 1,200,000 | 1,425,000 |
| Beginning inventory | 170,000 | 210,000 |
| Ending inventory | 210,000 | 90,000 |

Determine the inventory turnover and days in inventory for 2021 and 2022. Discuss the changes in the amount of inventory, the inventory turnover and days in inventory, and the amount of sales revenue across the two years.

## Exercises

*Determine the correct inventory amount.*

**E6.1 (LO 1), AN** Umatilla Bank and Trust is considering giving Pohl Company a loan. Before doing so, it decides that further discussions with Pohl's accountant may be desirable. One area of particular concern is the Inventory account, which has a year-end balance of $275,000. Discussions with the accountant reveal the following.

1. Pohl shipped goods costing $55,000 to Hemlock Company FOB shipping point on December 28. The goods are not expected to reach Hemlock until January 12. The goods were not included in the physical inventory because they were not in the warehouse.

2. The physical count of the inventory did not include goods costing $95,000 that were shipped to Pohl FOB destination on December 27 and were still in transit at year-end.

3. Pohl received goods costing $25,000 on January 2. The goods were shipped FOB shipping point on December 26 by Yanice Co. The goods were not included in the physical count.

4. Pohl shipped goods costing $51,000 to Ehler of Canada FOB destination on December 30. The goods were received in Canada on January 8. They were not included in Pohl's physical inventory.

5. Pohl received goods costing $42,000 on January 2 that were shipped FOB destination on December 29. The shipment was a rush order that was supposed to arrive December 31. This purchase was included in the ending inventory of $275,000.

### Instructions

Determine the correct inventory amount on December 31.

*Determine the correct inventory amount.*

**E6.2 (LO 1), AN** Farley Bains, an auditor with Nolls CPAs, is performing a review of Ryder Company's Inventory account. Ryder did not have a good year, and top management is under pressure to boost reported income. According to its records, the inventory balance at year-end was $740,000. However, the following information was not considered when determining that amount.

1. Included in the company's count were goods with a cost of $228,000 that the company is holding on consignment. The goods belong to Nader Corporation.

2. The physical count did not include goods purchased by Ryder with a cost of $40,000 that were shipped FOB shipping point on December 28 and did not arrive at Ryder's warehouse until January 3.

3. Included in the Inventory account was $17,000 of office supplies that were stored in the warehouse and were to be used by the company's supervisors and managers during the coming year.

4. The company received an order on December 29 that was boxed and was sitting on the loading dock awaiting pick-up on December 31. The shipper picked up the goods on January 1 and delivered them on January 6. The shipping terms were FOB shipping point. The goods had a selling price of $40,000 and a cost of $29,000. The goods were not included in the count because they were sitting on the dock.

5. Included in the count was $50,000 of goods that were parts for a machine that the company no longer made. Given the high-tech nature of Ryder's products, it was unlikely that these obsolete parts had any other use. However, management would prefer to keep them on the books at cost, "since that is what we paid for them, after all."

### Instructions

Prepare a schedule to determine the correct inventory amount. Provide explanations for each item above, stating why you did or did not make an adjustment for each item.

*Identify items in inventory.*

**E6.3 (LO 1), AN** Gato Inc. had the following inventory situations to consider at January 31, its year-end.

a. Goods held on consignment for Steele Corp. since December 12.

b. Goods shipped on consignment to Logan Holdings Inc. on January 5.

c. Goods shipped to a customer, FOB destination, on January 29 that are still in transit.

d. Goods shipped to a customer, FOB shipping point, on January 29 that are still in transit.

e. Goods purchased FOB destination from a supplier on January 25 that are still in transit.

f. Goods purchased FOB shipping point from a supplier on January 25 that are still in transit.

g. Office supplies on hand at January 31.

### Instructions

Identify which of the preceding items should be included in inventory. If the item should not be included in inventory, state in what account, if any, it should have been recorded.

**E6.4 (LO 2), AN** On December 1, Premium Electronics has three DVD players left in stock. All are identical, all are priced to sell at $35. One of the three DVD players left in stock, with serial #1012, was purchased on June 1 at a cost of $52. Another, with serial #1045, was purchased on November 1 for $48. The last player, serial #1056, was purchased on November 30 for $40.

*Calculate cost of goods sold using specific identification and FIFO periodic.*

**Instructions**

a. Calculate the cost of goods sold using the FIFO periodic inventory method assuming that two of the three players were sold by the end of December, Premium Electronics' year-end.

b. If Premium Electronics used the specific identification method instead of the FIFO method, how might it alter its earnings by "selectively choosing" which particular players to sell to the two customers? What would Premium's cost of goods sold be if the company wished to minimize earnings? Maximize earnings?

c. Which inventory method, FIFO or specific identification, do you recommend that Premium use? Explain why.

**E6.5 (LO 2), AP** Mather sells a snowboard, EZslide, that is popular with snowboard enthusiasts. The following is information relating to Mather's beginning inventory and purchases of EZslide snowboards during September. During the same month, 102 EZslide snowboards were sold. Mather uses a periodic inventory system.

*Compute inventory and cost of goods sold using periodic FIFO, LIFO, and average-cost.*

| Date | Explanation | Units | Unit Cost | Total Cost |
|---|---|---|---|---|
| Sept. 1 | Inventory | 12 | $100 | $ 1,200 |
| Sept. 12 | Purchases | 45 | 103 | 4,635 |
| Sept. 19 | Purchases | 50 | 104 | 5,200 |
| Sept. 26 | Purchases | 20 | 105 | 2,100 |
| | Totals | 127 | | $13,135 |

**Instructions**

Compute the ending inventory at September 30 and the cost of goods sold using the FIFO, LIFO, and average-cost methods. (For average-cost, round the weighted-average unit cost to three decimal places.) Prove the amount allocated to cost of goods sold under each method.

**E6.6 (LO 2), AP** Rusthe Inc. uses a periodic inventory system. Its records show the following for the month of May, in which 74 units were sold.

*Calculate inventory and cost of goods sold using FIFO, average-cost, and LIFO in a periodic inventory system.*

| Date | Explanation | Units | Unit Cost | Total Cost |
|---|---|---|---|---|
| May 1 | Inventory | 30 | $ 9 | $270 |
| 15 | Purchase | 25 | 10 | 250 |
| 24 | Purchase | 38 | 11 | 418 |
| | Total | 93 | | $938 |

**Instructions**

Calculate the ending inventory at May 31 using the (a) FIFO, (b) LIFO, and (c) average-cost methods (For average-cost, round the weighted-average unit cost to three decimal places.) Prove the amount allocated to cost of goods sold under each method.

**E6.7 (LO 2), AP** Jeters Company uses a periodic inventory system and reports the following for the month of June.

*Compute inventory and cost of goods sold using periodic FIFO, LIFO, and average-cost.*

| Date | Explanation | Units | Unit Cost | Total Cost |
|---|---|---|---|---|
| June 1 | Inventory | 120 | $5 | $ 600 |
| 12 | Purchase | 370 | 6 | 2,220 |
| 23 | Purchase | 200 | 7 | 1,400 |
| 30 | Inventory | 230 | | |

**Instructions**

a. Compute the cost of the ending inventory and the cost of goods sold under (1) FIFO, (2) LIFO, and (3) average-cost. (Round weighted-average unit cost to three decimal places.)

b. Which costing method gives the highest ending inventory? The highest cost of goods sold? Why?

c. How do the average-cost values for ending inventory and cost of goods sold relate to ending inventory and cost of goods sold for FIFO and LIFO?

d. Explain why the unit cost is not $6 per the average-cost method.

**E6.8 (LO 2), AP** Lisa Company had 100 units in beginning inventory at a total cost of $10,000. The company purchased 200 units at a total cost of $26,000. At the end of the year, Lisa had 80 units in ending inventory.

*Compute inventory under FIFO, LIFO, and average-cost.*

**Instructions**

a. Compute the cost of the ending inventory and the cost of goods sold under (1) FIFO, (2) LIFO, and (3) average-cost.

b. Which cost flow method would result in the highest net income?

c. Which cost flow method would result in inventories approximating current cost in the balance sheet?

d. Which cost flow method would result in Lisa paying the least taxes?

*Determine effects of inventory errors.*

**E6.9 (LO 3), AN** Dowell Hardware reported cost of goods sold as follows.

|  | 2022 | 2021 |
|---|---|---|
| Beginning inventory | $ 30,000 | $ 20,000 |
| Cost of goods purchased | 175,000 | 164,000 |
| Cost of goods available for sale | 205,000 | 184,000 |
| Less: Ending inventory | 37,000 | 30,000 |
| Cost of goods sold | $168,000 | $154,000 |

Dowell made two errors:

1. 2021 ending inventory was overstated by $2,000.

2. 2022 ending inventory was understated by $5,000.

**Instructions**

Compute the correct cost of goods sold for each year.

*Prepare correct income statements.*

**E6.10 (LO 3), AN** Writing Sheen Company reported these income statement data for a 2-year period.

|  | 2022 | 2021 |
|---|---|---|
| Sales revenue | $250,000 | $210,000 |
| Beginning inventory | 40,000 | 32,000 |
| Cost of goods purchased | 202,000 | 173,000 |
| Cost of goods available for sale | 242,000 | 205,000 |
| Less: Ending inventory | 55,000 | 40,000 |
| Cost of goods sold | 187,000 | 165,000 |
| Gross profit | $ 63,000 | $ 45,000 |

Sheen Company uses a periodic inventory system. The inventories at January 1, 2021, and December 31, 2022, are correct. However, the ending inventory at December 31, 2021, is overstated by $8,000.

**Instructions**

a. Prepare correct income statement data for the 2 years.

b. What is the cumulative effect of the inventory error on total gross profit for the 2 years?

c. Explain in a letter to the president of Sheen Company what has happened—that is, the nature of the error and its effect on the financial statements.

*Determine LCNRV valuation.*

**E6.11 (LO 4), AP** Digital Camera Shop Inc. uses the lower-of-cost-or-net realizable value basis for its inventory. The following data are available at December 31.

|  | Units | Cost per Unit | Net Realizable Value per Unit |
|---|---|---|---|
| Cameras |  |  |  |
| Minolta | 5 | $170 | $158 |
| Canon | 7 | 145 | 152 |
| Light Meters |  |  |  |
| Vivitar | 12 | 125 | 114 |
| Kodak | 10 | 120 | 135 |

**Instructions**

What amount should be reported for inventory on Digital Camera Shop's balance sheet, assuming the lower-of-cost-or-net realizable value rule is applied?

*Compute lower-of-cost-or-net realizable value.*

**E6.12 (LO 4), AP** Serebin Company applied FIFO to its inventory and got the following results for its ending inventory.

Cameras 100 units at a cost per unit of $65
Blu-ray players 150 units at a cost per unit of $75
iPods 125 units at a cost per unit of $80

The net realizable value of each of these products at year-end was cameras $71, Blu-ray players $67, and iPods $78.

## Instructions

Determine the amount of ending inventory at lower-of-cost-or-net realizable value.

**E6.13 (LO 4), AP** Suppose this information is available for **PepsiCo, Inc.** for 2020, 2021, and 2022.

*Compute inventory turnover, days in inventory, and gross profit rate.*

| (in millions) | 2020 | 2021 | 2022 |
|---|---|---|---|
| Beginning inventory | $ 1,926 | $ 2,290 | $ 2,522 |
| Ending inventory | 2,290 | 2,522 | 2,618 |
| Cost of goods sold | 18,038 | 20,351 | 20,099 |
| Net sales revenue | 39,474 | 43,251 | 43,232 |

## Instructions

a. Calculate the inventory turnover for 2020, 2021, and 2022. (Round to one decimal place.)

b. Calculate the days in inventory for 2020, 2021, and 2022. (Round to one decimal place.)

c. Calculate the gross profit rate for 2020, 2021, and 2022. (Round to one decimal place.)

d. Comment on any trends observed in your answers to parts (a), (b), and (c).

**E6.14 (LO 4), AP** The cost of goods sold computations for Alpha Company and Omega Company are as follows.

*Compute inventory turnover and days in inventory.*

| | Alpha Company | Omega Company |
|---|---|---|
| Beginning inventory | $ 45,000 | $ 71,000 |
| Cost of goods purchased | 200,000 | 290,000 |
| Cost of goods available for sale | 245,000 | 361,000 |
| Ending inventory | 55,000 | 69,000 |
| Cost of goods sold | $190,000 | $292,000 |

## Instructions

a. Compute inventory turnover (round to two decimal places) and days in inventory (round to nearest day) for each company.

b. Which company moves its inventory more quickly?

**\*E6.15 (LO 5), AP** Bufford Appliance uses a perpetual inventory system. For its flat-screen television sets, the January 1 inventory was 3 sets at $600 each. On January 10, Bufford purchased 6 units at $660 each. The company sold 2 units on January 8 and 4 units on January 15.

*Apply cost flow methods to a perpetual inventory system.*

## Instructions

Compute the ending inventory under (a) FIFO, (b) LIFO, and (c) moving-average cost. (For moving-average, round the weighted-average unit cost to three decimal places.)

**\*E6.16 (LO 5), AP** Inventory data for Jeters Company are presented as follows.

*Calculate inventory and cost of goods sold using three cost flow methods in a perpetual inventory system.*

| Date | Explanation | Units | Unit Cost | Total Cost |
|---|---|---|---|---|
| June 1 | Inventory | 120 | $5 | $ 600 |
| 12 | Purchase | 370 | 6 | 2,220 |
| 23 | Purchase | 200 | 7 | 1,400 |
| 30 | Inventory | 230 | | |

## Instructions

a. Calculate the cost of the ending inventory and the cost of goods sold for each cost flow assumption, using a perpetual inventory system. Assume a sale of 410 units occurred on June 15 for a selling price of $8 and a sale of 50 units on June 27 for $9. (For the moving-average method, round the weighted-average unit cost to three decimal places.)

b. How do the results differ from E6.7?

c. Why is the average unit cost not $6 [($5 + $6 + $7) ÷ 3 = $6]?

**\*E6.17 (LO 5), AP** Mather sells a snowboard, EZslide, that is popular with snowboard enthusiasts. The following is information relating to Mather's purchases of EZslide snowboards during September. During the same month, 102 EZslide snowboards were sold.

*Apply cost flow methods to a perpetual inventory system.*

| Date | Explanation | Units | Unit Cost | Total Cost |
|---|---|---|---|---|
| Sept. 1 | Inventory | 12 | $100 | $ 1,200 |
| Sept. 12 | Purchases | 45 | 103 | 4,635 |
| Sept. 19 | Purchases | 50 | 104 | 5,200 |
| Sept. 26 | Purchases | 20 | 105 | 2,100 |
| | Totals | 127 | | $13,135 |

Additional data regarding the company's sales of EZslide snowboards are provided below. Assume that Mather uses a perpetual inventory system.

| Date | | Units |
|---|---|---|
| Sept. 5 | Sale | 8 |
| Sept. 16 | Sale | 48 |
| Sept. 29 | Sale | 46 |
| | Totals | 102 |

**Instructions**

Compute ending inventory at September 30 using FIFO, LIFO, and moving-average. (For moving-average, round the weighted-average unit cost to three decimal places.)

*Use the gross profit method to estimate inventory.*

**\*E6.18 (LO 6), AP** Brenda Company reported the following information for November and December 2022.

| | November | December |
|---|---|---|
| Cost of goods purchased | $536,000 | $ 610,000 |
| Inventory, beginning-of-month | 130,000 | 120,000 |
| Inventory, end-of-month | 120,000 | ? |
| Net sales revenue | 840,000 | 1,000,000 |

Brenda's ending inventory at December 31 was destroyed in a fire.

**Instructions**

**a.** Compute the gross profit rate for November.

**b.** Using the gross profit rate for November, determine the estimated cost of inventory lost in the fire.

*Determine merchandise lost using the gross profit method of estimating inventory.*

**\*E6.19 (LO 6), AP** The inventory of Hauser Company was destroyed by fire on March 1. From an examination of the accounting records, the following data for the first 2 months of the year are obtained: Sales Revenue $51,000, Sales Returns and Allowances $1,000, Purchases $31,200, Freight-In $1,200, and Purchase Returns and Allowances $1,400.

**Instructions**

Determine the merchandise lost by fire, assuming:

**a.** A beginning inventory of $20,000 and a gross profit rate of 40% on net sales.

**b.** A beginning inventory of $30,000 and a gross profit rate of 30% on net sales.

*Determine ending inventory at cost using retail method.*

**\*E6.20 (LO 6), AP** Gepetto Shoe Store uses the retail inventory method for its two departments, Women's Shoes and Men's Shoes. The following information for each department is obtained.

| | Women's Shoes | Men's Shoes |
|---|---|---|
| Beginning inventory at cost | $ 25,000 | $ 45,000 |
| Cost of goods purchased at cost | 110,000 | 136,300 |
| Net sales | 178,000 | 185,000 |
| Beginning inventory at retail | 46,000 | 60,000 |
| Cost of goods purchased at retail | 179,000 | 185,000 |

**Instructions**

Compute the estimated cost of the ending inventory for each department under the retail inventory method.

# Problems

*Determine items and amounts to be recorded in inventory.*

**P6.1 (LO 1), AN** Pitt Limited is trying to determine its ending inventory as of February 28, 2022, the company's year-end. The accountant counted everything that was in the warehouse as of February 28, which resulted in an ending inventory of $48,000. However, she needed help in determining how to handle the following items.

**a.** On February 26, Pitt shipped to a customer goods costing $800. The goods were shipped FOB shipping point, and the customer received the goods on March 2.

**b.** On February 26, Martine Inc. shipped goods to Pitt FOB destination. The invoice price was $350 plus $25 for freight. The receiving report indicates that the goods were received by Pitt on March 2.

**c.** Pitt had $500 of inventory at a customer's warehouse "on approval." The customer was going to let Pitt know whether it wanted the merchandise by the end of the week, March 4.

**d.** Pitt also had $400 of inventory at a Belle craft shop, on consignment from Pitt.

**e.** On February 26, Pitt ordered goods costing $750. The goods were shipped FOB shipping point on February 27. Pitt received the goods on March 1.

**f.** On February 28, Pitt packaged goods and had them ready for shipping to a customer FOB destination. The invoice price was $350 plus $25 for freight; the cost of the items was $280. The goods were received by the customer on March 2.

**g.** Pitt had damaged goods set aside in the warehouse because they are no longer saleable. These goods originally cost $400 and, originally, Pitt expected to sell these items for $600.

### Instructions

For each of the above transactions, specify whether the item in question should be included in ending inventory, and if so, at what amount. For each item that is not included in ending inventory, indicate who owns it and what account, if any, it should have been recorded in.

**P6.2 (LO 2), AP** Mullins Distribution markets CDs of numerous performing artists. At the beginning of March, Mullins had in beginning inventory 2,500 CDs with a unit cost of $7. During March, Mullins made the following purchases of CDs.

| March 5 | 2,000 @ $8 | March 21 | 5,000 @ $10 |
|---|---|---|---|
| March 13 | 3,500 @ $9 | March 26 | 2,000 @ $11 |

During March 12,000 units were sold. Mullins uses a periodic inventory system.

### Instructions

**a.** Determine the cost of goods available for sale.

**b.** Determine (1) the ending inventory and (2) the cost of goods sold under each of the assumed cost flow methods (FIFO, LIFO, and average-cost). Prove the accuracy of the cost of goods sold under the FIFO and LIFO methods. (For average-cost, round the weighted-average unit cost to three decimal places.)

**c.** Which cost flow method results in (1) the highest inventory amount for the balance sheet and (2) the highest cost of goods sold for the income statement?

**P6.3 (LO 2), AP** Vista Company Inc. had a beginning inventory of 100 units of Product RST at a cost of $8 per unit. During the year, purchases were:

| Feb. 20 | 600 units at $9 | Aug. 12 | 400 units at $11 |
|---|---|---|---|
| May 5 | 500 units at $10 | Dec. 8 | 100 units at $12 |

Vista Company uses a periodic inventory system. Sales totaled 1,500 units.

### Instructions

**a.** Determine the cost of goods available for sale.

**b.** Determine the ending inventory and the cost of goods sold under each of the assumed cost flow methods (FIFO, LIFO, and average-cost). Prove the accuracy of the cost of goods sold under the FIFO and LIFO methods. (Round the weighted-average unit cost to three decimal places.)

**c.** Which cost flow method results in the lowest inventory amount for the balance sheet? The lowest cost of goods sold for the income statement?

**P6.4 (LO 2), AP** Writing The management of Felipe Inc. is reevaluating the appropriateness of using its present inventory cost flow method, which is average-cost. The company requests your help in determining the results of operations for 2022 if either the FIFO or the LIFO method had been used. For 2022, the accounting records show these data:

| Inventories | | Purchases and Sales | |
|---|---|---|---|
| Beginning (7,000 units) | $14,000 | Total net sales (180,000 units) | $747,000 |
| Ending (17,000 units) | | Total cost of goods purchased | |
| | | (190,000 units) | 466,000 |

Purchases were made quarterly as follows.

| Quarter | Units | Unit Cost | Total Cost |
|---|---|---|---|
| 1 | 50,000 | $2.20 | $110,000 |
| 2 | 40,000 | 2.35 | 94,000 |
| 3 | 40,000 | 2.50 | 100,000 |
| 4 | 60,000 | 2.70 | 162,000 |
| | 190,000 | | $466,000 |

Operating expenses were $130,000, and the company's income tax rate is 20%.

*Determine cost of goods sold and ending inventory using FIFO, LIFO, and average-cost with analysis.*

**b.** Cost of goods sold:

| FIFO | $105,000 |
|---|---|
| LIFO | $115,500 |
| Average | $109,601 |

*Determine cost of goods sold and ending inventory using FIFO, LIFO, and average-cost in a periodic inventory system and assess financial statement effects.*

**b.** Cost of goods sold:

| FIFO | $14,500 |
|---|---|
| LIFO | $15,100 |
| Average | $14,824 |

*Compute ending inventory, prepare income statements, and answer questions using FIFO and LIFO.*

## Instructions

**a.** Prepare comparative condensed income statements for 2022 under FIFO and LIFO. (Show computations of ending inventory.)

**b.** Answer the following questions for management.

1. Which cost flow method (FIFO or LIFO) produces the more meaningful inventory amount for the balance sheet? Why?

2. Which cost flow method (FIFO or LIFO) produces the more meaningful net income? Why?

3. Which cost flow method (FIFO or LIFO) is more likely to approximate the actual physical flow of goods? Why?

4. How much more cash will be available for management under LIFO than under FIFO? Why?

5. Will gross profit under the average-cost method be higher or lower than FIFO? Than LIFO? (*Note:* It is not necessary to quantify your answer.)

*a. Net income:*

*FIFO*     *$146,320*
*LIFO*     *$138,400*

*Calculate ending inventory, cost of goods sold, gross profit, and gross profit rate under a periodic inventory system; compare results.*

**P6.5 (LO 2), AP** You have the following information for Van Gogh Inc. for the month ended October 31, 2022. Van Gogh uses a periodic inventory system for inventory.

| Date | Description | Units | Unit Cost or Selling Price |
|------|-------------|-------|----------------------------|
| Oct.  1 | Beginning inventory | 60 | $24 |
| Oct.  9 | Purchase | 120 | 26 |
| Oct. 11 | Sale | 100 | 35 |
| Oct. 17 | Purchase | 100 | 27 |
| Oct. 22 | Sale | 60 | 40 |
| Oct. 25 | Purchase | 70 | 29 |
| Oct. 29 | Sale | 110 | 40 |

## Instructions

**a.** Calculate (i) ending inventory, (ii) cost of goods sold, (iii) gross profit, and (iv) gross profit rate under each of the following methods.

1. LIFO.

2. FIFO.

3. Average-cost. (Round weighted-average unit cost to three decimal places.)

**b.** Compare results for the three cost flow assumptions.

*a. Gross profit:*

*LIFO*     *$2,970*
*FIFO*     *$3,310*
*Average*   *$3,133*

*Compare specific identification, FIFO, and LIFO under a periodic inventory system; use cost flow assumption to influence gross profit.*

**P6.6 (LO 2), AP** You have the following information for Jewels Gems. Jewels uses the periodic method of accounting for its inventory transactions. Jewels only carries one brand and size of diamonds—all are identical. Each batch of diamonds purchased is carefully coded and marked with its purchase cost.

March  1    Beginning inventory 150 diamonds at a cost of $310 per diamond.
March  3    Purchased 200 diamonds at a cost of $350 each.
March  5    Sold 180 diamonds for $600 each.
March 10   Purchased 330 diamonds at a cost of $375 each.
March 25   Sold 390 diamonds for $650 each.

## Instructions

**a.** Assume that Jewels Gems uses the specific identification cost flow method.

1. Demonstrate how Jewels could maximize its gross profit for the month by specifically selecting which diamonds to sell on March 5 and March 25.

2. Demonstrate how Jewels could minimize its gross profit for the month by selecting which diamonds to sell on March 5 and March 25.

**b.** Assume that Jewels uses the FIFO cost flow assumption. Calculate cost of goods sold. How much gross profit would Jewels report under this cost flow assumption?

**c.** Assume that Jewels uses the LIFO cost flow assumption. Calculate cost of goods sold. How much gross profit would the company report under this cost flow assumption?

**d.** Which cost flow method should Jewels Gems select? Explain.

*a. Gross profit:*

*Maximum*   *$162,500*
*Minimum*   *$155,350*

*Compute ending inventory, prepare income statements, and answer questions using FIFO and LIFO.*

**P6.7 (LO 2), AN** **Writing** The management of National Inc. asks your help in determining the comparative effects of the FIFO and LIFO inventory cost flow methods. For 2022, the accounting records show these data.

| | |
|---|---|
| Inventory, January 1 (10,000 units) | $ 35,000 |
| Cost of 120,000 units purchased | 468,500 |
| Sales revenue on 98,000 units | 750,000 |
| Operating expenses | 124,000 |

Units purchased consisted of 35,000 units at $3.70 on May 10, 60,000 units at $3.90 on August 15, and 25,000 units at $4.20 on November 20. Income taxes are 20%.

**Instructions**

a. Prepare comparative condensed income statements for 2022 under FIFO and LIFO. (Show computations of ending inventory.)

b. Answer the following questions for management in the form of a business letter.

1. Which inventory cost flow method produces the inventory amount that most closely approximates the amount that would have to be paid to replace the inventory? Why?

2. Which inventory cost flow method produces the net income amount that is a more likely indicator of next period's net income? Why?

3. Which inventory cost flow method is most likely to approximate the actual physical flow of the goods? Why?

4. How much more cash will be available under LIFO than under FIFO? Why?

5. How much of the gross profit under FIFO is illusory in comparison with the gross profit under LIFO?

a. Net income:
FIFO $203,840
LIFO $191,120

***P6.8 (LO 5), AP** Bieber Inc. is a retailer operating in Calgary, Alberta. Bieber uses the perpetual inventory system. Assume that there are no credit transactions; all amounts are settled in cash. You are provided with the following information for Bieber for the month of January 2022.

*Calculate cost of goods sold, ending inventory, and gross profit for LIFO, FIFO, and moving-average under the perpetual system; compare results.*

| Date | Description | Quantity | Unit Cost or Selling Price |
|---|---|---|---|
| Dec. 31 | Ending inventory | 160 | $20 |
| Jan. 2 | Purchase | 100 | 22 |
| Jan. 6 | Sale | 180 | 40 |
| Jan. 9 | Purchase | 75 | 24 |
| Jan. 10 | Sale | 50 | 45 |
| Jan. 23 | Purchase | 100 | 25 |
| Jan. 30 | Sale | 130 | 48 |

**Instructions**

a. For each of the following cost flow assumptions, calculate (i) cost of goods sold (ii) ending inventory, and (iii) gross profit.

1. LIFO.

2. FIFO.

3. Moving-average. (Round weighted-average unit cost to three decimal places.)

b. Compare results for the three cost flow assumptions.

a. Gross profit:
LIFO $7,490
FIFO $7,865
Average $7,763

***P6.9 (LO 5), AP** Lyon Center began operations on July 1. It uses a perpetual inventory system. During July, the company had the following purchases and sales.

*Determine ending inventory under a perpetual inventory system.*

| | Purchases | | |
|---|---|---|---|
| Date | Units | Unit Cost | Sales Units |
| July 1 | 7 | $62 | |
| July 6 | | | 5 |
| July 11 | 3 | $66 | |
| July 14 | | | 3 |
| July 21 | 4 | $71 | |
| July 27 | | | 3 |

**Instructions**

a. Determine the ending inventory under a perpetual inventory system using (1) FIFO, (2) moving-average (round weighted-average unit cost to three decimal places), and (3) LIFO.

b. Which costing method produces the highest ending inventory?

a. FIFO $213
Average $207
LIFO $195

*Compute gross profit rate and inventory loss using gross profit method.*

**\*P6.10 (LO 6), AP** Suzuki Company lost all of its inventory in a fire on December 26, 2022. The accounting records showed the following inventory-related data for November and December.

| | November | December (to 12/26) |
|---|---|---|
| Net sales | $600,000 | $700,000 |
| Beginning inventory | 32,000 | 36,000 |
| Purchases | 389,000 | 420,000 |
| Purchase returns and allowances | 13,300 | 14,900 |
| Purchase discounts | 8,500 | 9,500 |
| Freight-in | 8,800 | 9,900 |
| Ending inventory | 36,000 | ? |

Suzuki is fully insured for fire losses but must prepare a report for the insurance company.

**Instructions**

a. Gross profit rate 38%

   **a.** Compute the gross profit rate for November.

   **b.** Using the gross profit rate for November, determine the estimated cost of the inventory lost in the fire.

*Compute ending inventory using retail method.*

**\*P6.11 (LO 6), AP** Dixon Books uses the retail inventory method to estimate its monthly ending inventories. The following information is available for two of its departments at **October 31, 2022**.

| | Hardcovers | | Paperbacks | |
|---|---|---|---|---|
| | Cost | Retail | Cost | Retail |
| Beginning inventory | $ 420,000 | $ 700,000 | $ 280,000 | $ 360,000 |
| Purchases | 2,135,000 | 3,200,000 | 1,155,000 | 1,540,000 |
| Freight-in | 24,000 | | 12,000 | |
| Purchase discounts | 44,000 | | 22,000 | |
| Net sales | | 3,100,000 | | 1,570,000 |

At **December 31**, Dixon Books takes a physical inventory at retail. The actual retail values of the inventories in each department are Hardcovers $790,000 and Paperbacks $335,000.

**Instructions**

a. Hardcovers: end. inv. $520,000

   **a.** Determine the estimated cost of the ending inventory for each department at **October 31**, 2022, using the retail inventory method.

   **b.** Compute the ending inventory at cost for each department at **December 31**, assuming the cost-to-retail ratios for the year are 65% for Hardcovers and 75% for Paperbacks.

# Continuing Case

leungchopan/
Shutterstock.com

## Cookie Creations

(*Note:* This is a continuation of the Cookie Creations case from Chapters 1 through 5.)

**CC6** Natalie is busy establishing both divisions of her business (cookie classes and mixer sales) and completing her business degree. Her goals for the next 11 months are to sell one mixer per month and to give two to three classes per week.

   The cost of the fine European mixers is expected to increase. Natalie has just negotiated new terms with Kzinski that include shipping costs in the negotiated purchase price (mixers will be shipped FOB destination). Natalie must choose a cost flow assumption for her mixer inventory.

*Go to WileyPLUS for complete case details and instructions.*

## Comprehensive Accounting Cycle Review

**ACR6** On December 1, 2022, Matthias Company had the following account balances.

| | Debit | | Credit |
|---|---|---|---|
| Cash | $ 4,800 | Accumulated Depreciation—Equipment | $ 1,500 |
| Accounts Receivable | 3,900 | Accounts Payable | 3,000 |
| Inventory | 1,800* | Common Stock | 20,000 |
| Equipment | 21,000 | Retained Earnings | 7,000 |
| | $31,500 | | $31,500 |

*3,000 × $0.60

The following transactions occurred during December.

Dec. 3   Purchased 4,000 units of inventory on account at a cost of $0.72 per unit.

     5   Sold 4,400 units of inventory on account for $0.90 per unit. (Matthias sold 3,000 of the $0.60 units and 1,400 of the $0.72.)

     7   Granted the December 5 customer $180 credit for 200 units of inventory returned costing $144. These units were returned to inventory.

   17   Purchased 2,200 units of inventory for cash at $0.80 each.

   22   Sold 2,000 units of inventory on account for $0.95 per unit. (Matthias sold 2,000 of the $0.72 units.)

**Adjustment data:**

1. Recognized accrued salaries payable of $400.
2. Recognized depreciation of $200 per month.

**Instructions**

a. Journalize the December transactions and adjusting entries, assuming Matthias uses the perpetual inventory system.

b. Enter the December 1 balances in the ledger T-accounts and post the December transactions. In addition to the accounts mentioned above, use the following additional accounts: Cost of Goods Sold, Depreciation Expense, Salaries and Wages Expense, Salaries and Wages Payable, Sales Revenue, and Sales Returns and Allowances.

c. Prepare an adjusted trial balance as of December 31, 2022.

d. Prepare a multiple-step income statement for December 2022 and a classified balance sheet at December 31, 2022.

e. Compute ending inventory and cost of goods sold under FIFO, assuming Matthias Company uses the periodic inventory system.

f. Compute ending inventory and cost of goods sold under LIFO, assuming Matthias Company uses the periodic inventory system.

## Data Analytics in Action

### Using Data Visualization to Analyze Changes over Time

**DA6.1** Data visualization can be used to analyze company changes over time.

**Example:** Recall the Feature Story "Where Is That Spare Bulldozer Blade?" presented in the chapter. **Caterpillar** continues to enhance its inventory management by improving its product sustainability in two ways. First, it is rebuilding used parts to like-new condition. Second, the company is remanufacturing usable inventory parts when customers trade-in or dispose of their used equipment. These actions not only reduce inventory costs but also enable Caterpillar to participate in the circular economy, where manufacturers take responsibility for their products at the end of the product lives. As noted in its 2019 sustainability report, Caterpillar has a goal of 20% growth in both rebuilding and remanufacturing from 2013 to 2020.

     Has Caterpillar reached this goal? A line chart can help you visualize the company's progress over time. What information can you obtain by examining the following chart?

Excel

Many of the next chapters include data analytics activities, which provide students opportunities to employ basic tools to analyze data.

**Caterpillar Remanufacturing and Rebuilding Changes**

**Source**: *https://reports.caterpillar.com/sr/esg-data-center/*.

The chart indicates that while Caterpillar's goal has remained at 20%, the remanufacturing and rebuilding businesses are growing. The biggest increase in the growth of rebuilding occurred from 2016 to 2017. There was a decline from 2018 to 2019 in these initiatives as Caterpillar may have reached a peak that is leveling off due to new production that is more sustainable.

For this case, you will look more closely at specific Caterpillar data regarding its end-of-life returned materials and the percentage usable for recycling. You will create and analyze a combination column and line chart to determine how Caterpillar can increase its gross profit as it relates to these end-of-life materials.

*Go to WileyPLUS for complete case details and instructions.*

### Using Data Analytics to Compare Companies' Profitability

**DA6.2** Manufacturing construction equipment is a competitive business. For this case, you will use company data to calculate the gross profit ratio, as well as the percentages of cost of goods sold, other expenses, and net income as compared to revenue, for **Caterpillar**, **Cummins**, and **CNH Industrial**. You will then create and analyze a clustered column chart based on this data. Finally, you will compare the rebuilding and recycling efforts of the companies and what impact these initiatives might have on their profitability.

*Go to WileyPLUS for complete case details and instructions.*

### Using Data Analytics to Compare Companies' Inventory Turnover

**DA6.3** Inventory turnover shows the number of times during the period a firm sells the entire dollar amount of its inventory. It is advantageous to turn over inventory more quickly to reduce the risk of obsolescence and spoilage. As such, companies often have a goal of increasing inventory turnover. For this case, you will use inventory turnover data for **Costco**, **Walmart**, **Target**, and **Amazon** to create and analyze scatter plots, as well as to calculate days' sales in inventory, to determine which company is managing its inventory levels most effectively.

*Go to WileyPLUS for complete case details and instructions.*

## Expand Your Critical Thinking

### Financial Reporting Problem: Apple Inc.

**CT6.1** The notes that accompany a company's financial statements provide informative details that would clutter the amounts and descriptions presented in the statements. Refer to the financial statements of **Apple Inc.** in Appendix A as well as its annual report. The complete annual report, including the notes to the financial statements, is available at the company's website.

**Instructions**

Answer the following questions. Complete the requirements in millions of dollars, as shown in Apple's annual report.

a. What did Apple report for the amount of inventories in its consolidated balance sheet at September 30, 2017? At September 29, 2018?

b. Compute the dollar amount of change and the percentage change in inventories between 2017 and 2018. Compute inventory as a percentage of current assets at September 29, 2018.

c. Which inventory cost flow method does Apple use? (See Notes to the Financial Statements.)

d. What is the cost of sales (cost of goods sold) reported by Apple for 2018, 2017, and 2016? Compute the percentage of cost of sales to net sales in 2018.

## Comparative Analysis Problem: PepsiCo, Inc. vs. The Coca-Cola Company

**CT6.2 PepsiCo**'s financial statements are presented in Appendix B. Financial statements of **The Coca-Cola Company** are presented in Appendix C. The complete annual reports of PepsiCo and Coca-Cola, including the notes to the financial statements, are available at each company's respective website.

**Instructions**

a. Based on the information contained in these financial statements, compute the following 2018 ratios for each company.

   1. Inventory turnover.

   2. Days in inventory.

b. What conclusions concerning the management of the inventory can you draw from these data?

## Comparative Analysis Problem: Amazon.com, Inc. vs. Walmart Inc.

**CT6.3 Amazon.com, Inc.**'s financial statements are presented in Appendix D. Financial statements of **Walmart Inc.** are presented in Appendix E. The complete annual reports of Amazon and Walmart, including the notes to the financial statements, are available at each company's respective website.

**Instructions**

a. Based on the information contained in these financial statements, compute the following ratios for each company.

   1. Inventory turnover.

   2. Days in inventory.

b. What conclusions concerning the management of the inventory can you draw from these data?

## Real-World Focus

**CT6.4** A company's annual report usually will identify the inventory method used. Knowing that you can analyze the effects of the inventory method on the income statement and balance sheet.

**Instructions**

Answer the following questions based on the current year's annual report available at **Cisco**'s website.

a. At Cisco's fiscal year-end, what was the inventory on the balance sheet?

b. How has this changed from the previous fiscal year-end?

c. How much of the inventory was finished goods?

## Decision-Making Across the Organization

**CT6.5** On April 10, 2022, fire damaged the office and warehouse of Corvet Company. Most of the accounting records were destroyed, but the following balances were determined as of March 31, 2022: inventory (January 1, 2022), $80,000; net sales revenue (January 1–March 31, 2022), $180,000; purchases (January 1–March 31, 2022), $94,000.

The company's fiscal year ends on December 31. It uses a periodic inventory system.

From an analysis of the April bank statement, you discover cancelled checks of $4,200 for cash purchases during the period April 1–10. Deposits during the same period totaled $18,500. Of that amount, 60% were collections on accounts receivable, and the balance was cash sales.

Correspondence with the company's principal suppliers revealed $12,400 of purchases on account from April 1 to April 10. Of that amount, $1,600 was for merchandise in transit on April 10 that was shipped FOB destination.

Correspondence with the company's principal customers produced acknowledgments of credit sales totaling $37,000 from April 1 to April 10. It was estimated that $5,600 of credit sales would never be acknowledged or recovered from customers.

Corvet Company reached an agreement with the insurance company that its fire-loss claim should be based on the average of the gross profit rates for the preceding 2 years. The financial statements for 2020 and 2021 showed the following data.

|  | 2021 | 2020 |
| --- | --- | --- |
| Net sales | $600,000 | $480,000 |
| Cost of goods purchased | 404,000 | 356,000 |
| Beginning inventory | 60,000 | 40,000 |
| Ending inventory | 80,000 | 60,000 |

Inventory with a cost of $17,000 was salvaged from the fire.

**Instructions**

With the class divided into groups, answer the following.

a. Determine the balances of (1) net sales revenue and (2) purchases at April 10, 2022.

*b. Determine the average gross profit rate for the years 2020 and 2021. (*Hint:* Find the gross profit rate for each year and divide the sum by 2.)

*c. Determine the inventory loss as a result of the fire, using the gross profit method.

## Communication Activity

**CT6.6** You are the controller of Small Toys Inc. Marta Johns, the president, recently mentioned to you that she found an error in the 2021 financial statements which she believes has corrected itself. She determined, in discussions with the Purchasing Department, that 2021 ending inventory was overstated by $1 million. Marta says that the 2022 ending inventory is correct. Thus, she assumes that 2022 income is correct. Marta says to you, "What happened has happened—there's no point in worrying about it anymore."

**Instructions**

You conclude that Marta is incorrect. Write a brief, tactful memo to Marta, clarifying the situation. The company uses the periodic inventory system.

## Ethics Case

**CT6.7** Nixon Wholesale Corp. uses the LIFO periodic inventory system for inventory costing purposes. In the current year, profit at Nixon is running unusually high. The corporate tax rate is also high this year, but it is scheduled to decline significantly next year. In an effort to lower the current year's net income and to take advantage of the changing income tax rate, the president of Nixon Wholesale instructs the plant accountant to recommend to the purchasing department a large purchase of inventory for delivery 3 days before the end of the year. The cost of the inventory to be purchased has doubled during the year, and the purchase will represent a major portion of the cost of goods available for sale during the period.

**Instructions**

a. What is the effect of this transaction on this year's and next year's income statement and income tax expense? Why?

b. If Nixon Wholesale had been using the FIFO method of inventory costing, would the president give the same directive?

c. Should the plant accountant order the inventory purchase to lower income? What are the ethical implications of this order?

## All About You

**CT6.8** Some of the largest business frauds ever perpetrated have involved the misstatement of inventory. Two classics were at **Leslie Fay** and **McKesson Corporation**.

**Instructions**

There is considerable information regarding inventory frauds available on the Internet. Search for information about one of the two cases mentioned above, or inventory fraud at any other company, and prepare a short explanation of the nature of the inventory fraud.

## FASB Codification Activity

**CT6.9** If your school has a subscription to the FASB Codification, log in and prepare responses to the following.

**Instructions**

  a. The primary basis for accounting for inventories is cost. How is cost defined in the Codification?
  b. What does the Codification state regarding the use of consistency in the selection or employment of a basis for inventory?

## Answers to Insight and Accounting Across the Organization Questions

**A Big Hiccup Q:** What steps might the companies take to avoid such a serious disruption in the future? **A:** The manufacturer of the piston rings should spread its manufacturing facilities across a few locations that are far enough apart that they would not all be at risk at once. In addition, the automakers might consider becoming less dependent on a single supplier as well as having weather contingency plans.

**Falsifying Inventory to Boost Income Q:** What effect does an overstatement of inventory have on a company's financial statements? **A:** The balance sheet looks stronger because inventory and retained earnings are overstated. The income statement looks better because cost of goods sold is understated and income is overstated.

**Is LIFO Fair? Q:** What are the arguments for and against the use of LIFO? **A:** Proponents of LIFO argue that it is conceptually superior because it matches the most recent cost with the most recent selling price. Critics contend that it artificially understates the company's net income and consequently reduces tax payments. Also, because most foreign companies are not allowed to use LIFO, its use by U.S. companies reduces the ability of investors to compare U.S. companies with foreign companies.

**Too Many TVs or Too Few? Q:** For Sony, what are the advantages and disadvantages of having a low days in inventory measure? **A:** If Sony has a low day in inventory, it reduces the amount of cash it has tied up in inventory. It also minimizes the risk that it will be stuck with excess inventory that could force it to provide big discounts, resulting in punishing losses. Sony also faces the risk that the TVs will become obsolete before they are sold. However, Sony increases the risk that it will encounter "stockouts," that is, it will not have adequate inventory to meet customer demand.

# A Look at IFRS

## LEARNING OBJECTIVE 7
Compare the accounting for inventories under GAAP and IFRS.

The major IFRS requirements related to accounting and reporting for inventories are the same as GAAP. The major difference is that IFRS prohibits the use of the LIFO cost flow assumption.

## Key Points

Following are the key similarities and differences between GAAP and IFRS related to inventories

**Similarities**

  • IFRS and GAAP account for inventory acquisitions at historical cost and report inventory at the lower-of-cost-or-net realizable value subsequent to acquisition.
  • Who owns the goods—goods in transit or consigned goods—as well as the costs to include in inventory are essentially accounted for the same under IFRS and GAAP.

**Differences**

- The requirements for accounting for and reporting inventories are more principles-based under IFRS. That is, GAAP provides more detailed guidelines in inventory accounting.
- A major difference between IFRS and GAAP relates to the LIFO cost flow assumption. GAAP permits the use of LIFO for inventory costing. IFRS prohibits its use. FIFO and average-cost are the only two acceptable cost flow assumptions permitted under IFRS. Both sets of standards permit specific identification where appropriate.

# IFRS Practice

## IFRS Self-Test Questions

1. Which of the following should **not** be included in the inventory of a company using IFRS?

   **a.** Goods held on consignment from another company.

   **b.** Goods shipped on consignment to another company.

   **c.** Goods in transit from another company shipped FOB shipping point.

   **d.** None of the above.

2. Which method of inventory costing is prohibited under IFRS?

   **a.** Specific identification.

   **b.** LIFO.

   **c.** FIFO.

   **d.** Average-cost.

## IFRS Exercises

**IFRS6.1** Briefly describe some of the similarities and differences between GAAP and IFRS with respect to the accounting for inventories.

**IFRS6.2** LaTour Inc. is based in France and prepares its financial statements (in euros) in accordance with IFRS. In 2022, it reported cost of goods sold of €578 million and average inventory of €154 million. Briefly discuss how analysis of LaTour's inventory turnover (and comparisons to a company using GAAP) might be affected by differences in inventory accounting between IFRS and GAAP.

## International Financial Reporting Problem: Louis Vuitton

**IFRS6.3** The financial statements of **Louis Vuitton** are presented in Appendix F. The complete consolidated financial statements, including the notes to its financial statements, are available at the company's website.

### Instructions

Using the notes to the company's 2018 consolidated financial statements, answer the following questions.

**a.** What cost flow assumption does the company use to value inventory other than wine?

**b.** What net amount of goods purchased for resale and finished products did the company report at December 31, 2018?

### Answers to IFRS Self-Test Questions

1. a   2. b

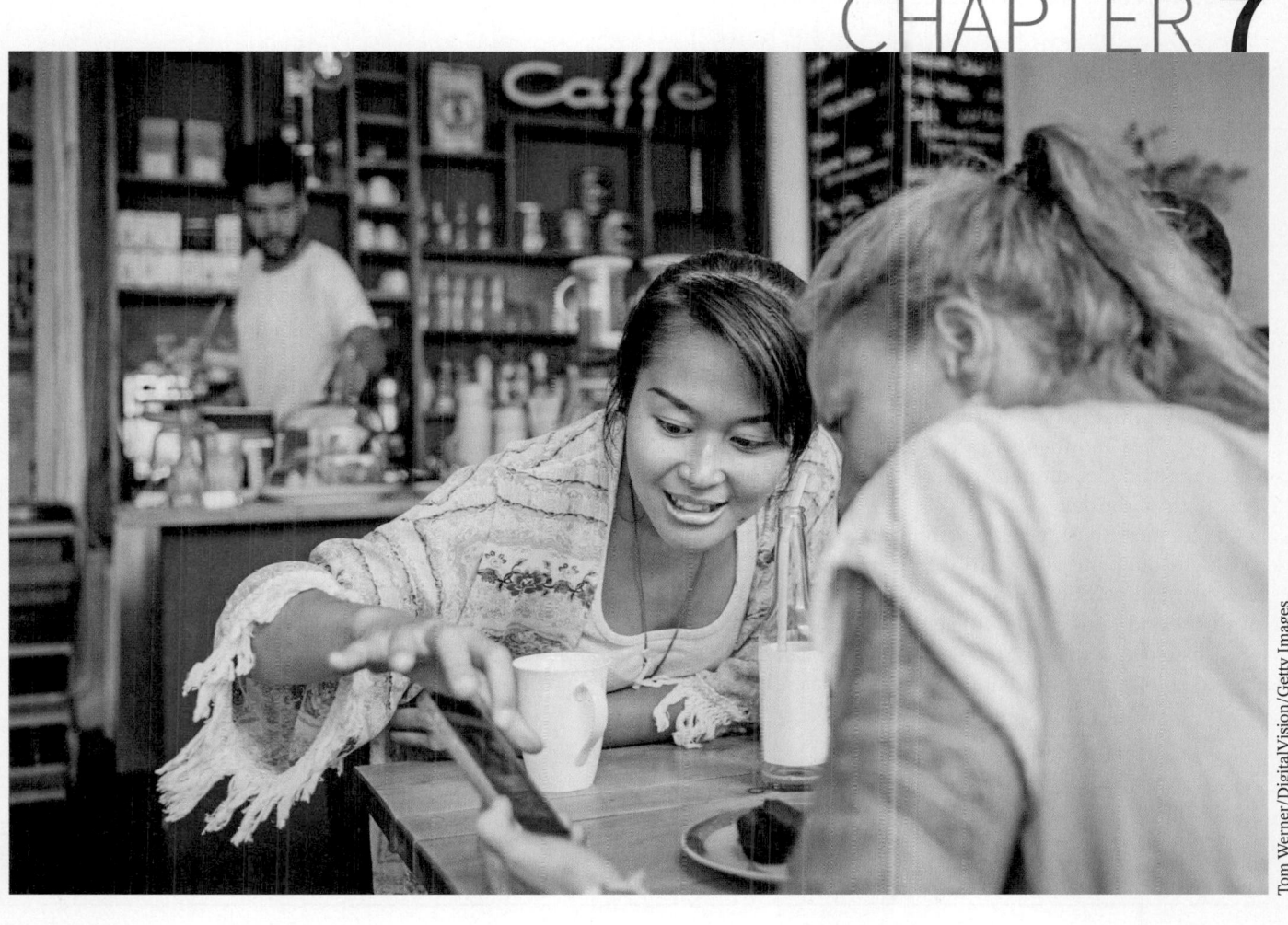

## CHAPTER 7

Tom Werner/DigitalVision/Getty Images

# Fraud, Internal Control, and Cash

## Chapter Preview

As the following Feature Story about recording cash sales at **Barriques** indicates, control of cash is important to ensure that fraud does not occur. Companies also need controls to safeguard other types of assets. For example, Barriques undoubtedly has controls to prevent the theft of food and supplies, and controls to prevent the theft of tableware and dishes from its kitchen.

In this chapter, we explain the essential features of an internal control system and how it prevents fraud. We also describe how those controls apply to a specific asset—cash. These applications include some controls with which you may be already familiar, such as the use of a bank.

# Feature Story

## Minding the Money in Madison

For many years, **Barriques** in Madison, Wisconsin, has been named the city's favorite coffeehouse. Barriques not only does a booming business in coffee but also has wonderful baked goods, delicious sandwiches, and a fine selection of wines.

"Our customer base ranges from college students to neighborhood residents as well as visitors to our capital city," says bookkeeper Kerry Stoppleworth, who joined the company shortly after it was founded in 1998. "We are unique because we have customers who come in early on their way to work for a cup of coffee and then will stop back after work to pick up a bottle of wine for dinner. We stay very busy throughout all three parts of the day."

Like most businesses where purchases are low-cost and high-volume, cash control has to be simple. "We use a computerized point-of-sale (POS) system to keep track of our inventory and allow us to efficiently ring through an order for a customer," explains Stoppleworth. "You can either scan a barcode for an item or enter in a code for items that don't

have a barcode such as cups of coffee or bakery items." The POS system also automatically tracks sales by department and maintains an electronic journal of all the sales transactions that occur during the day.

"There are two POS stations at each store, and throughout the day any of the staff may operate them," says Stoppleworth. At the end of the day, each POS station is reconciled separately. The staff counts the cash in the drawer and enters this amount into the closing totals in the POS system. The POS system then compares the cash and credit amounts, less the cash being carried forward to the next day (the float), to the shift total in the electronic journal. If there are discrepancies, a recount is done and the journal is reviewed transaction by transaction to identify the problem. The staff then creates a deposit ticket for the cash less the float and puts this in a drop safe with the electronic journal summary report for the manager to review and take to the bank the next day. Ultimately, the bookkeeper reviews all of these documents as well as the deposit receipt that the bank produces to make sure they are all in agreement.

As Stoppleworth concludes, "We keep the closing process and accounting simple so that our staff can concentrate on taking care of our customers and making great coffee and food."

# Chapter Outline

| LEARNING OBJECTIVES | REVIEW | PRACTICE |
|---|---|---|
| **LO 1** Define fraud and the principles of internal control. | • Fraud<br>• The Sarbanes-Oxley Act<br>• Internal control<br>• Principles of internal control activities<br>• Data analytics and internal controls<br>• Limitations of internal control | **DO IT! 1** Principles of Control Activities |
| **LO 2** Apply internal control principles to cash. | • Cash receipts controls<br>• Cash disbursements controls<br>• Petty cash fund | **DO IT! 2a** Control over Cash Receipts<br>**DO IT! 2b** Petty Cash Fund |
| **LO 3** Identify the control features of a bank account. | • Making bank deposits<br>• Writing checks<br>• EFT system<br>• Bank statements<br>• Reconciling the bank account | **DO IT! 3** Bank Reconciliation |
| **LO 4** Explain the reporting of cash. | • Cash equivalents<br>• Restricted cash | **DO IT! 4** Reporting Cash |

**Go to the Review and Practice section at the end of the chapter for a review of key concepts and practice applications with solutions.**

**Visit WileyPLUS for additional tutorials and practice opportunities.**

# Fraud and Internal Control

> ### LEARNING OBJECTIVE 1
> Define fraud and the principles of internal control.

The Feature Story describes many of the internal control procedures used by **Barriques**. These procedures are necessary to discourage employees from fraudulent activities.

## Fraud

A **fraud** is a dishonest act by an employee that results in personal benefit to the employee at a cost to the employer. Examples of fraud reported in the financial press include the following.

- A bookkeeper in a small company diverted $750,000 of bill payments to a personal bank account over a three-year period.
- A shipping clerk with 28 years of service shipped $125,000 of merchandise to himself.
- A computer operator embezzled $21 million from **Wells Fargo Bank** over a two-year period.
- A church treasurer "borrowed" $150,000 of church funds to finance a friend's business dealings.

Why does fraud occur? The three main factors that contribute to fraudulent activity are depicted by the **fraud triangle** in **Illustration 7.1**.

The most important element of the fraud triangle is **opportunity**. For an employee to commit fraud, the workplace environment must provide opportunities that an employee can take advantage of. Opportunities occur when the workplace lacks sufficient controls to deter and detect fraud. For example, inadequate monitoring of employee actions can create opportunities for theft and can embolden employees because they believe they will not be caught.

A second factor that contributes to fraud is **financial pressure**. Employees sometimes commit fraud because of personal financial problems caused by too much debt. Or, they might commit fraud because they want to lead a lifestyle that they cannot afford on their current salary.

The third factor that contributes to fraud is **rationalization**. In order to justify their fraud, employees rationalize their dishonest actions. For example, employees sometimes justify fraud because they believe they are underpaid while the employer is making lots of money. Employees feel justified in stealing because they believe they deserve to be paid more.

**ILLUSTRATION 7.1**
**Fraud triangle**

## The Sarbanes-Oxley Act

What can be done to prevent or to detect fraud? After numerous corporate scandals came to light in the early 2000s, Congress addressed this issue by passing the **Sarbanes-Oxley Act (SOX)**. Under SOX, all publicly traded U.S. corporations are required to maintain an adequate system of internal control. Corporate executives and boards of directors must ensure that these controls are reliable and effective. In addition, independent outside auditors must attest to the adequacy of the internal control system. Companies that fail to comply are subject to fines, and company officers can be imprisoned. SOX also created the Public Company Accounting Oversight Board (PCAOB) to establish auditing standards and regulate auditor activity.

One poll found that 60% of investors believe that SOX helps safeguard their stock investments. Many say they would be unlikely to invest in a company that fails to follow SOX requirements. Although some corporate executives have criticized the time and expense involved in following SOX requirements, SOX appears to be working well. For example, the chief accounting officer of **Eli Lilly** noted that SOX triggered a comprehensive review of how the company documents its controls. This review uncovered redundancies and pointed out controls that needed to be added. In short, it added up to time and money well spent.

# Internal Control

**Internal control** is a process designed to provide reasonable assurance regarding the achievement of company objectives related to operations, reporting, and compliance. In more detail, the purposes of internal control are to safeguard assets, enhance the reliability of accounting records, increase efficiency of operations, and ensure compliance with laws and regulations. Internal control systems have five primary components, as listed below.[1]

- **A control environment.** It is the responsibility of top management to make it clear that the organization values integrity and that unethical activity will not be tolerated. This component is often referred to as the "tone at the top."
- **Risk assessment.** Companies must identify and analyze the various factors that create risk for the business and must determine how to manage these risks.
- **Control activities.** To reduce the occurrence of fraud, management must design policies and procedures to address the specific risks faced by the company.
- **Information and communication.** The internal control system must capture and communicate all pertinent information both down and up the organization, as well as communicate information to appropriate external parties.
- **Monitoring.** Internal control systems must be monitored periodically for their adequacy. Significant deficiencies need to be reported to top management and/or the board of directors.

---

## People, Planet, and Profit Insight

iStock.com/Karl Dolenc

### And the Controls Are . . .

Internal controls are important for an effective financial reporting system. The same is true for sustainability reporting. An effective system of internal controls for sustainability reporting will help in the following ways: (1) prevent the unauthorized use of data; (2) provide reasonable assurance that the information is accurate, valid, and complete; and (3) report information that is consistent with overall sustainability accounting policies. With these types of controls, users will have the confidence that they can use the sustainability information effectively.

Some regulators are calling for even more assurance through audits of this information. Companies that potentially can cause environmental damage through greenhouse gases, as well as companies in the mining and extractive industries, are subject to reporting requirements. And, as demand for more information in the sustainability area expands, the need for audits of this information will grow.

**Why is sustainability information important to investors? (Answer is available near the end of the chapter.)**

---

# Principles of Internal Control Activities

Each of the five components of an internal control system is important. Here, we will focus on one component, the control activities. The reason? These activities are the backbone of the company's efforts to address the risks it faces, such as fraud. The specific control activities

---

[1]The Committee of Sponsoring Organizations of the Treadway Commission, "Internal Control—Integrated Framework," *www.coso.org/documents/990025P_Executive_Summary_final_may20_e.pdf*; and Stephen J. McNally, "The 2013 COSO Framework and SOX Compliance," *Strategic Finance* (June 2013).

used by a company will vary, depending on management's assessment of the risks faced. This assessment is heavily influenced by the size and nature of the company.

The six principles of control activities are as follows.

- Establishment of responsibility
- Segregation of duties
- Documentation procedures
- Physical controls
- Independent internal verification
- Human resource controls

We explain these principles in the following sections. You should recognize that they apply to most companies and are relevant to both manual and computerized accounting systems.

## Establishment of Responsibility

An essential principle of internal control is to assign responsibility to specific employees. **Control is most effective when only one person is responsible for a given task.**

To illustrate, assume that the cash on hand at the end of the day in a **Safeway** supermarket is $10 short of the cash entered in the cash register. If only one person has operated the register, the shift manager can quickly determine responsibility for the shortage. If two or more individuals have worked the register, it may be impossible to determine who is responsible for the error.

Many retailers solve this problem by having registers with multiple drawers. This makes it possible for more than one person to operate a register but still allows identification of a particular employee with a specific drawer. Only the signed-in cashier has access to his or her drawer.

Establishing responsibility often requires limiting access only to authorized personnel, and then identifying those personnel. For example, the automated systems used by many companies have mechanisms such as identifying passcodes that keep track of who made a journal entry, who entered a sale, or who went into an inventory storeroom at a particular time. Use of identifying passcodes enables the company to establish responsibility by identifying the particular employee who carried out the activity.

It's your shift now. I'm turning in my cash drawer and heading home.

**Transfer of cash drawers**

---

### Anatomy of a Fraud

Maureen Frugali was a training supervisor for claims processing at Colossal Healthcare. As a standard part of the claims-processing training program, Maureen created fictitious claims for use by trainees. These fictitious claims were then sent to the accounts payable department. After the training claims had been processed, she was to notify Accounts Payable of all fictitious claims, so that they would not be paid. However, she did not inform Accounts Payable about every fictitious claim. She created some fictitious claims for entities that she controlled (that is, she would receive the payment), and she let Accounts Payable pay her.

**Total take: $11 million**

**The Missing Control**

**Establishment of responsibility.** The healthcare company did not adequately restrict the responsibility for authorizing and approving claims transactions. The training supervisor should not have been authorized to create claims in the company's "live" system.

**Source:** Adapted from Wells, *Fraud Casebook* (2007), pp. 61–70.

---

## Segregation of Duties

Segregation of duties is indispensable in an internal control system. There are two common applications of this principle:

1. Different individuals should be responsible for related activities.
2. The responsibility for recordkeeping for an asset should be separate from the physical custody of that asset.

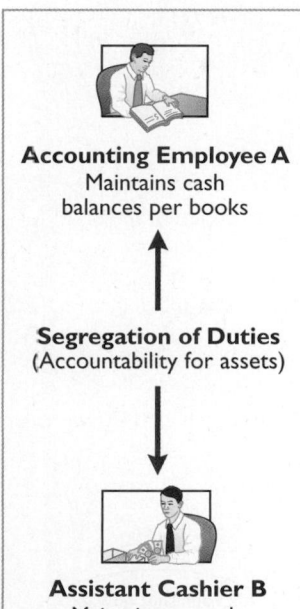

**Accounting Employee A**
Maintains cash
balances per books

**Segregation of Duties**
(Accountability for assets)

**Assistant Cashier B**
Maintains custody
of cash on hand

The rationale for segregation of duties is this: **The work of one employee should, without a duplication of effort, provide a reliable basis for evaluating the work of another employee.** For example, the personnel who design and program computerized systems should not be assigned duties related to day-to-day use of the systems. Otherwise, they could design the systems to benefit them personally and conceal the fraud through day-to-day use.

**Segregation of Related Activities**   **Making one individual responsible for related activities increases the potential for errors and irregularities.**

**Purchasing Activities**   Companies should, for example, assign related **purchasing activities** to different individuals. Related purchasing activities include ordering merchandise, approving orders, receiving goods, authorizing payment, and paying for goods or services. Various frauds are possible when one person handles related purchasing activities:

- If a purchasing agent is allowed to order goods without obtaining supervisory approval, the likelihood of the purchasing agent receiving kickbacks from suppliers increases.
- If an employee who orders goods also handles the invoice and receipt of the goods, as well as payment authorization, he or she might authorize payment for a fictitious invoice.

These abuses are less likely to occur when companies divide the purchasing tasks.

**Sales Activities**   Similarly, companies should assign related **sales activities** to different individuals. Related selling activities include making a sale, shipping (or delivering) the goods to the customer, billing the customer, and receiving payment. Various frauds are possible when one person handles related sales activities:

- If a salesperson can make a sale without obtaining supervisory approval, he or she might make sales at unauthorized prices to increase sales commissions.
- A shipping clerk who also has access to accounting records could ship goods to himself.
- A billing clerk who handles billing and receipt could understate the amount billed for sales made to friends and relatives.

These abuses are less likely to occur when companies divide the sales tasks. The salespeople make the sale, the shipping department ships the goods on the basis of the sales order, and the billing department prepares the sales invoice after comparing the sales order with the report of goods shipped.

## Anatomy of a Fraud

Lawrence Fairbanks, the assistant vice-chancellor of communications at Aesop University, was allowed to make purchases of under $2,500 for his department without external approval. Unfortunately, he also sometimes bought items for himself, such as expensive antiques and other collectibles. How did he do it? He replaced the vendor invoices he received with fake vendor invoices that he created. The fake invoices had descriptions that were more consistent with the communications department's purchases. He submitted these fake invoices to the accounting department as the basis for their journal entries and to the accounts payable department as the basis for payment.

**Total take: $475,000**

**The Missing Control**

**Segregation of duties.** The university had not properly segregated related purchasing activities. Lawrence was ordering items, receiving the items, and receiving the invoice. By receiving the invoice, he had control over the documents that were used to account for the purchase and thus was able to substitute a fake invoice.

**Source:** Adapted from Wells, *Fraud Casebook* (2007), pp. 3–15.

**Segregation of Recordkeeping from Physical Custody**   The accountant should have neither physical custody of the asset nor access to it. Likewise, the custodian of the asset should not maintain or have access to the accounting records. **The custodian of the asset is not likely to convert the asset to personal use when one employee maintains the record of the asset, and a different employee has physical custody of the asset.** The separation of accounting responsibility from the custody of assets is especially important for cash and inventories because these assets are very vulnerable to fraud.

## Anatomy of a Fraud

Angela Bauer was an accounts payable clerk for Aggasiz Construction Company. Angela prepared and issued checks to vendors and reconciled bank statements. She perpetrated a fraud in this way: She wrote checks for costs that the company had not actually incurred (e.g., fake taxes). A supervisor then approved and signed the checks. Before issuing the check, though, Angela would "white-out" the payee line on the check and change it to personal accounts that she controlled. She was able to conceal the theft because she also reconciled the bank account. That is, nobody else ever saw that the checks had been altered.

**Total take: $570,000**

**The Missing Control**

**Segregation of duties.** Aggasiz Construction Company did not properly segregate recordkeeping from physical custody. Angela had physical custody of the checks, which essentially was control of the cash. She also had recordkeeping responsibility because she prepared the bank reconciliation.

**Source:** Adapted from Wells, *Fraud Casebook* (2007), pp. 100–107.

## Documentation Procedures

Documents provide evidence that transactions and events have occurred. For example, point-of-sale terminals are networked with a company's computing and accounting records, which results in direct documentation.

Similarly, a shipping document indicates that the goods have been shipped, and a sales invoice indicates that the company has billed the customer for the goods. By requiring signatures (or initials) on the documents, the company can identify the individual(s) responsible for the transaction or event. Companies should document transactions when they occur.

Companies should establish procedures for documents. First, whenever possible, companies should use **prenumbered documents**, **and all documents should be accounted for**. Prenumbering helps to prevent a transaction from being recorded more than once, or conversely, from not being recorded at all. Second, the control system should require that employees **promptly forward source documents for accounting entries to the accounting department**. **This control measure helps to ensure timely recording of the transaction** and contributes directly to the accuracy and reliability of the accounting records.

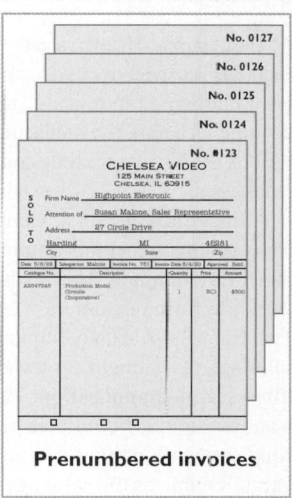

**Prenumbered invoices**

## Anatomy of a Fraud

To support their reimbursement requests for travel costs incurred, employees at Mod Fashions Corporation's design center were required to submit receipts. The receipts could include the detailed bill provided for a meal, the credit card receipt provided when the credit card payment was made, or a copy of the employee's monthly credit card bill that listed the item. A number of the designers who frequently traveled together came up with a fraud scheme: They submitted claims for the same expenses. For example, if they had a meal together that cost $200, one person submitted the detailed meal bill, another submitted the credit card receipt, and a third submitted a monthly credit card bill showing the meal as a line item. Thus, all three received a $200 reimbursement.

**Total take: $75,000**

**The Missing Control**

**Documentation procedures.** Mod Fashions should require the original, detailed receipt. It should not accept photocopies, and it should not accept credit card statements. In addition, documentation procedures could be further improved by requiring the use of a corporate credit card (rather than a personal credit card) for all business expenses.

**Source:** Adapted from Wells, *Fraud Casebook* (2007), pp. 79–90.

## Physical Controls

Use of physical controls is essential. **Physical controls** relate to the safeguarding of assets and enhance the accuracy and reliability of the accounting records. **Illustration 7.2** shows examples of these controls.

**ILLUSTRATION 7.2** **Physical controls**

### Physical Controls

Safes, vaults, and safety deposit boxes for cash and business papers

Locked warehouses and storage cabinets for inventories and records

Computer facilities with passkey access or fingerprint or eyeball scans

Alarms to prevent break-ins

Television monitors and garment sensors to deter theft

Time clocks for recording time worked

---

## Anatomy of a Fraud

At Centerstone Health, a large insurance company, the mailroom each day received insurance applications from prospective customers. Mailroom employees scanned the applications into electronic documents before the applications were processed. Once the applications were scanned, they could be accessed online by authorized employees.

Insurance agents at Centerstone Health earn commissions based upon successful applications. The sales agent's name is listed on the application. However, roughly 15% of the applications are from customers who did not work with a sales agent. Two friends—Alex, an employee in recordkeeping, and Parviz, a sales agent—thought up a way to perpetrate a fraud. Alex identified scanned applications that did not list a sales agent. After business hours, he entered the mailroom and found the hardcopy applications that did not show a sales agent. He wrote in Parviz's name as the sales agent and then rescanned the application for processing. Parviz received the commission, which the friends then split.

**Total take: $240,000**

**The Missing Control**

**Physical controls.** Centerstone Health lacked two basic physical controls that could have prevented this fraud. First, the mailroom should have been locked during nonbusiness hours, and access during business hours should have been tightly controlled. Second, the scanned applications supposedly could be accessed only by authorized employees using their passwords. However, the password for each employee was the same as the employee's user ID. Since employee user-ID numbers were available to all other employees, all employees knew each other's passwords. Thus, Alex could enter the system using another employee's password and access the scanned applications.

**Source:** Adapted from Wells, *Fraud Casebook* (2007), pp. 316–326.

---

### Independent Internal Verification

Most internal control systems provide for **independent internal verification**. This principle involves the review of data prepared by employees. To obtain maximum benefit from independent internal verification:

1. Companies should verify records periodically or on a surprise basis.
2. An employee who is independent of the personnel responsible for the information should make the verification.
3. Discrepancies and exceptions should be reported to a management level that can take appropriate corrective action.

Independent internal verification is especially useful in comparing recorded accountability with existing assets. The reconciliation of the electronic journal with the cash in the point-of-sale terminal at **Barriques** is an example of this internal control principle. Other common examples are the reconciliation of a company's cash balance per books with the cash balance per bank, and the verification of the perpetual inventory records through a count of physical inventory. **Illustration 7.3** shows the relationship between this principle and the segregation of duties principle.

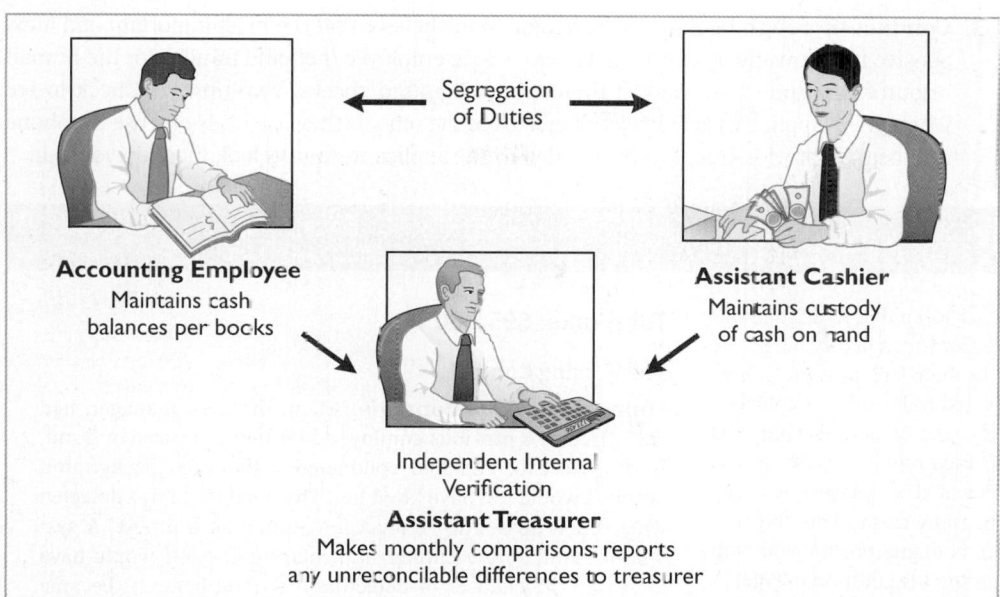

**ILLUSTRATION 7.3**

**Comparison of segregation of duties principle with independent internal verification principle**

## Anatomy of a Fraud

Bobbi Jean Donnelly, the office manager for Mod Fashions Corporation's design center, was responsible for preparing the design center budget and reviewing expense reports submitted by design center employees. Her desire to upgrade her wardrobe got the better of her, and she perpetrated a fraud that involved filing expense-reimbursement requests for her own personal clothing purchases. Bobbi Jean was able to conceal the fraud because she was responsible for reviewing all expense reports, including her own. In addition, she sometimes was given ultimate responsibility for signing off on the expense reports when her boss was "too busy." Also, because she controlled the budget, when she submitted her expenses, she coded them to budget items that she knew were running under budget, so that they would not catch anyone's attention.

**Total take: $275,000**

### The Missing Control

**Independent internal verification.** Bobbi Jean's boss should have verified her expense reports. When asked what he thought her expenses for a year were, the boss said about $10,000. At $115,000 per year, her actual expenses were more than 10 times what would have been expected. However, because he was "too busy" to verify her expense reports or to review the budget, he never noticed.

**Source:** Adapted from Wells, *Fraud Casebook* (2007), pp. 79–90.

Large companies often assign independent internal verification to internal auditors. **Internal auditors** are company employees who continuously evaluate the effectiveness of the company's internal control systems. They review the activities of departments and individuals to determine whether prescribed internal controls are being followed. They also recommend improvements when needed. For example, **WorldCom** was at one time the second largest U.S. telecommunications company. The fraud that caused its bankruptcy (the largest ever when it occurred) involved billions of dollars. It was uncovered by an internal auditor.

## Human Resource Controls

Human resource control activities include the following.

If I take a vacation, they will know that I've been stealing.

1. **Bond employees who handle cash. Bonding** involves obtaining insurance protection against theft by employees. It contributes to the safeguarding of cash in two ways. First, the insurance company carefully screens all individuals before adding them to the policy and may reject risky applicants. Second, bonded employees know that the insurance company will vigorously prosecute all offenders.

2. **Rotate employees' duties and require employees to take vacations.** These measures deter employees from attempting thefts since they will not be able to permanently conceal their improper actions. Many banks, for example, have discovered employee thefts when the employee was on vacation or assigned to a new position.

3. **Conduct thorough background checks.** Many believe that the most important and inexpensive measure any business can take to reduce employee theft and fraud is for the human resource department to conduct thorough background checks. Two tips: (1) Check to see whether job applicants actually graduated from the schools they list. (2) Never use telephone numbers for previous employers provided by the applicant. Always look them up yourself.

## Anatomy of a Fraud

Ellen Lowry was the desk manager and Josephine Rodriguez was the head of housekeeping at the Excelsior Inn, a luxury hotel. The two best friends were so dedicated to their jobs that they never took vacations, and they frequently filled in for other employees. In fact, Ms. Rodriguez, whose job as head of housekeeping did not include cleaning rooms, often cleaned rooms herself, "just to help the staff keep up." These two "dedicated" employees, working as a team, found a way to earn a little more cash. Ellen, the desk manager, provided significant discounts to guests who paid with cash. She kept the cash and did not register the guests in the hotel's computerized system. Instead, she took the room out of circulation "due to routine maintenance." Because the room did not show up as being used, it did not receive a normal housekeeping assignment. Instead, Josephine, the head of housekeeping, cleaned the rooms during the guests' stay.

**Total take: $95,000**

### The Missing Control

**Human resource controls.** Ellen, the desk manager, had been fired by a previous employer after being accused of fraud. If the Excelsior Inn had conducted a thorough background check, it would not have hired her. The hotel fraud was detected when Ellen missed work for a few days due to illness. A system of mandatory vacations and rotating days off would have increased the chances of detecting the fraud before it became so large.

**Source:** Adapted from Wells, *Fraud Casebook* (2007), pp. 145–155.

## Accounting Across the Organization

Stockbyte/Getty Images

### SOX Boosts the Role of Human Resources

Under SOX, a company needs to keep track of employees' degrees and certifications to ensure that employees continue to meet the specified requirements of a job. Also, to ensure proper employee supervision and proper separation of duties, companies must develop and monitor an organizational chart. When one corporation went through this exercise, it found that out of 17,000 employees, there were 400 people who did not report to anyone. The corporation also had 35 people who reported to each other. In addition, if an employee complains of an unfair firing and mentions financial issues at the company, the human resource department must refer the case to the company audit committee and possibly to its legal counsel.

**Why would unsupervised employees or employees who report to each other represent potential internal control threats? (Answer is available near the end of the chapter.)**

# Data Analytics and Internal Controls

Data analytics has dramatically changed many aspects of internal control practices. In the past, internal and external auditors tended to rely heavily on investigations of period-end samples of transactions to identify potential violations. Now, rather than wait for a period-end sample, many companies employ continuous monitoring of virtually every transaction. As a result, spikes in certain types of activity or developing trends are more quickly identified and investigated.

Many different aspects of journal entries can be monitored continuously. For example, systems can automatically identify who recorded a particular journal entry. This is important to ensure that the segregation of duties control principle is not violated, that is, that the entry is only made by a current (as opposed to recently terminated) employee and that the employee is authorized to make that type of entry.

Large dollar amounts in risky areas can also be flagged and investigated quickly. Recipients of payments can be easily screened to ensure, for example, that bonus amounts are correctly determined based on results and bonus formulas, and that bonuses are only paid to employees who are designated for bonus payments. Similarly, vendor payments can be easily screened to ensure that payments only go to authorized vendors and that amounts are within an anticipated range. Sophisticated models can be used to continually estimate critical measures, and those estimates are then compared to actual results to identify outliers.

# Limitations of Internal Control

Companies generally design their systems of internal control to provide **reasonable assurance** of proper safeguarding of assets and reliability of the accounting records. The concept of reasonable assurance rests on the premise that the costs of establishing control procedures should not exceed their expected benefit (see **Helpful Hint**).

To illustrate, consider shoplifting losses in retail stores. Stores could eliminate such losses by having a security guard stop and search customers as they leave the store. But store managers have concluded that the negative effects of such a procedure cannot be justified. Instead, they have attempted to control shoplifting losses by less costly procedures They post signs saying, "We reserve the right to inspect all packages" and "All shoplifters will be prosecuted." They use hidden cameras and store detectives to monitor customer activity, and they install sensor equipment at exits.

The **human element** is an important factor in every system of internal control. A good system can become ineffective as a result of employee fatigue, carelessness, or indifference. For example, a receiving clerk may not bother to count goods received and may just "fudge" the counts. Occasionally, two or more individuals may work together to get around prescribed controls. Such **collusion** can significantly reduce the effectiveness of a system, eliminating the protection offered by segregation of duties. No system of internal control is perfect.

The **size of the business** also may impose limitations on internal control. Small companies often find it difficult to segregate duties or to provide for independent internal verification. A study by the Association of Certified Fraud Examiners indicates that businesses with fewer than 100 employees are most at risk for employee theft. In fact, 29% of frauds occurred at companies with fewer than 100 employees. The median loss at small companies was $154,000, which was nearly as high as the median fraud at companies with more than 10,000 employees ($160,000). A $154,000 loss can threaten the very existence of a small company.

## DO IT! 1 | Principles of Control Activities

Identify which principles of control activities are violated in each of the following situations, and explain how each situation creates an opportunity for a fraud.

1. The person with primary responsibility for reconciling the bank account and making all bank deposits is also the company's accountant.

2. Wellstone Company's treasurer received an award for distinguished service because he had not taken a vacation in 30 years.

3. In order to save money spent on order slips and to reduce time spent keeping track of order slips, a local bar/restaurant does not buy prenumbered order slips.

**ACTION PLAN**

- **Familiarize yourself with each of the principles of control activities discussed.**
- **Understand the nature of the frauds that each principles of control activity is intended to address.**

### Solution

1. Violates the segregation of duties control principle. Recordkeeping should be separate from physical custody. As a consequence, the employee could embezzle cash and make journal entries to hide the theft.

2. Violates the human resource control principle. Key employees must take vacations. Otherwise, the treasurer, who manages the company's cash, might embezzle cash and use his position to conceal the theft.

3. Violates the documentation procedures control principle. If prenumbered documents are not used, then it is virtually impossible to account for the documents. As a consequence, an employee could write up a dinner sale, receive the cash from the customer, and then throw away the order slip and keep the cash.

Related exercise material: **BE7.1, BE7.2, BE7.3, BE7.4, DO IT! 7.1, E7.1, E7.2, E7.3, E7.5, and E7.6.**

# Cash Controls

## LEARNING OBJECTIVE 2
Apply internal control principles to cash.

Cash is the one asset that is readily convertible into any other type of asset. It also is easily concealed and transported, and is highly desired. Because of these characteristics, **cash is the asset most susceptible to fraudulent activities**. In addition, because of the large volume of cash transactions, numerous errors may occur in executing and recording them. To safeguard cash and to ensure the accuracy of the accounting records for cash, effective internal control over cash is critical.

## Cash Receipts Controls

**Illustration 7.4** shows how the internal control principles explained earlier apply to cash receipts transactions. As you might expect, companies vary considerably in how they apply these principles. To illustrate internal control over cash receipts, we will examine control activities for a retail store with both over-the-counter and mail receipts.

**ILLUSTRATION 7.4** **Application of internal control principles to cash receipts**

**Cash Receipts Controls**

**Establishment of Responsibility**
Only designated personnel are authorized to handle cash receipts (cashiers)

**Segregation of Duties**
Different individuals receive cash, record cash receipts, and hold the cash

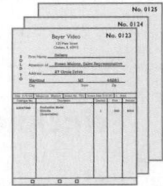

**Documentation Procedures**
Use remittance advice (mail receipts), cash register tapes or computer records, and deposit slips

**Physical Controls**
Store cash in safes and bank vaults; limit access to storage areas; use cash registers or point-of-sale terminals

**Independent Internal Verification**
Supervisors count cash receipts daily; assistant treasurer compares total receipts to bank deposits daily

**Human Resource Controls**
Bond personnel who handle cash; require employees to take vacations; conduct background checks

## Over-the-Counter Receipts

In retail businesses, control of over-the-counter receipts centers on cash registers that are visible to customers. A cash sale is entered in a cash register (or point-of-sale terminal), with the amount clearly visible to the customer. This activity prevents the sales clerk from entering a lower amount and pocketing the difference. The customer receives an itemized cash register receipt and is expected to count the change received. (One weakness at **Barriques** in the Feature Story is that customers are only given a receipt if requested.) The cash register's tape is locked in the register until a supervisor removes it. This tape accumulates the daily transactions and totals.

At the end of the clerk's shift, the clerk counts the cash and sends the cash and the count to the cashier. The cashier counts the cash, prepares a deposit slip, and deposits the cash at the bank. The cashier also sends a duplicate of the deposit slip to the accounting department to indicate cash received. The supervisor removes the cash register tape and sends it to the accounting department as the basis for a journal entry to record the cash received. (For point-of-sale systems, the accounting department receives information on daily transactions and totals through the computer network.) **Illustration 7.5** summarizes this process (see **Helpful Hint**).

**Clerk**
Enters sales, counts cash

Sends cash and count to cashier

**Supervisor**
Removes locked cash register tape

Sends cash register tape to accounting dept.

**Cashier**
Counts cash, prepares deposit slip

Deposit slip

Sends deposit slip copy to accounting dept.

**Accounting Department**
Agrees register tape to deposit slip and records journal entry

Delivers cash and deposit slip to bank

Deposit slip

Bank

This system for handling cash receipts uses an important internal control principle—segregation of recordkeeping from physical custody. The supervisor has access to the cash register tape but **not** to the cash. The clerk and the cashier have access to the cash but **not** to the register tape. In addition, the cash register tape provides documentation and enables independent internal verification. Use of these three principles of internal control (segregation of recordkeeping from physical custody, documentation, and independent internal verification) provides an effective system of internal control. Any attempt at fraudulent activity should be detected unless there is collusion among the employees.

In some instances, the amount deposited at the bank will not agree with the cash recorded in the accounting records based on the cash register tape. These differences often result because the clerk hands incorrect change back to the retail customer. In this case, the difference between the actual cash and the amount reported on the cash register tape is reported in a Cash Over and Short account. For example, suppose that the cash register tape indicated sales of $6,956.20 but the amount of cash was only $6,946.10. A cash shortfall of $10.10 exists. To account for this cash shortfall and related cash sales, the company makes the following entry.

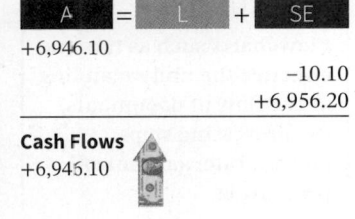

A = L + SE
+6,946.10
−10.10
+6,956.20

**Cash Flows**
+6,945.10

| | | |
|---|---|---|
| Cash | 6,946.10 | |
| Cash Over and Short | 10.10 | |
| Sales Revenue | | 6,956.20 |
| (To record cash shortfall and cash sales) | | |

Cash Over and Short is an income statement item. It is reported as miscellaneous expense when there is a cash shortfall, and as miscellaneous revenue when there is an overage. Clearly, the amount should be small. Any material amounts in this account should be investigated.

## Mail Receipts

All mail receipts should be opened in the presence of at least two mail clerks. These receipts are generally in the form of checks. A mail clerk should endorse each check "For Deposit Only." This restrictive endorsement reduces the likelihood that someone could divert the check to personal use. Banks will not give an individual cash when presented with a check that has this type of endorsement.

The mail clerks prepare, in triplicate, a list of the checks received each day. This list shows the name of the check issuer, the purpose of the payment, and the amount of the check. Each mail clerk signs the list to establish responsibility for the data. The original copy of the list, along with the checks, is then sent to the cashier's department. A copy of the list is sent to the accounting department for recording in the accounting records. The mail clerks also keep a copy.

This process provides excellent internal control for the company. By employing at least two clerks, the chance of fraud is reduced. Each clerk knows he or she is being observed by the other clerk(s). To engage in fraud, they would have to collude. The customers who submit payments also provide control because they will contact the company with a complaint if they are not properly credited for payment. Because the cashier has access to the cash but not the records, and the accounting department has access to the records but not the cash, neither can engage in undetected fraud.

---

**ACTION PLAN**

- **Differentiate among the internal control principles of (1) establishing responsibility, (2) using physical controls, and (3) independent internal verification.**

- **Design an effective system of internal control over cash receipts.**

## DO IT! 2a | Control over Cash Receipts

L. R. Cortez is concerned about the control over cash receipts in his fast-food restaurant, Big Cheese. The restaurant has two cash registers. At no time do more than two employees take customer orders and enter sales. Work shifts for employees range from 4 to 8 hours. Cortez asks your help in installing a good system of internal control over cash receipts.

### Solution

Cortez should assign a separate cash register drawer to each employee at the start of each work shift, with register totals set at zero. Each employee should have access to only the assigned register drawer to enter all sales. Each customer should be given a receipt. At the end of the shift, the employee should do a cash count. A separate employee should compare the cash count with the register tape (or point-of-sale records) to be sure they agree. In addition, Cortez should install an automated point-of-sale system that would enable the company to compare orders entered in the register to orders processed by the kitchen.

Related exercise material: **BE7.5, BE7.6, BE7.7, BE7.8, DO IT! 7.2a, E7.2, E7.3, E7.4, E7.5, and E7.6.**

# Cash Disbursements Controls

Companies disburse cash for a variety of reasons, such as to pay expenses and liabilities or to purchase assets. **Generally, internal control over cash disbursements is more effective when companies pay by check or electronic funds transfer (EFT) rather than by cash.** One exception is **payments for incidental amounts that are paid out of petty cash.**[2]

Companies generally issue checks only after following specified control procedures. **Illustration 7.6** shows how principles of internal control apply to cash disbursements.

**ILLUSTRATION 7.6**   **Application of internal control principles to cash disbursements**

**Cash Disbursements Controls**

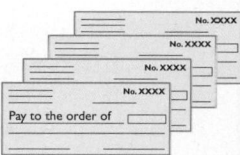

**Establishment of Responsibility**
Only designated personnel are authorized to sign checks (treasurer) and approve vendors

**Segregation of Duties**
Different individuals approve and make payments; check-signers do not record disbursements

**Documentation Procedures**
Use prenumbered checks and account for them in sequence; each check must have an approved invoice; require employees to use corporate credit cards for reimbursable expenses; stamp invoices "paid"

**Physical Controls**
Store blank checks in safes with limited access; print check amounts by machine in indelible ink

**Independent Internal Verification**
Compare checks to invoices; reconcile bank statement monthly

**Human Resource Controls**
Bond personnel who handle cash; require employees to take vacations; conduct background checks

## Voucher System Controls

Most medium and large companies use vouchers as part of their internal control over cash disbursements. A **voucher system** is a network of approvals by authorized individuals, acting independently, to ensure that all disbursements by check are proper

The system begins with the authorization to incur a cost or expense. It ends with the issuance of a check for the liability incurred. A **voucher** is an authorization form prepared for each expenditure. Companies require vouchers for all types of cash disbursements except those from petty cash.

The starting point in preparing a voucher is to fill in the appropriate information about the liability on the face of the voucher. The vendor's invoice provides most of the needed

---

[2] We explain the operation of a petty cash fund later in the chapter.

information. Then, an employee in the accounts payable department records the liability related to the voucher (in a journal called a **voucher register**) and files it according to the date on which it is to be paid. The company issues and sends a check on that date, and stamps the voucher "paid." The paid voucher is sent to the accounting department for recording (in a journal called the **check register**). A voucher system involves two journal entries, one to record the liability in the voucher register when the voucher is issued, and a second in the check register to pay the liability that relates to the voucher.

The use of a voucher system, whether done manually or electronically, improves internal control over cash disbursements. First, the authorization process inherent in a voucher system establishes responsibility. Each individual has responsibility to review the underlying documentation to ensure that it is correct. In addition, the voucher system keeps track of the documents that back up each transaction. By keeping these documents in one place, a supervisor can independently verify the authenticity of each transaction. Consider, for example, the case of Aesop University presented earlier in the Anatomy of a Fraud box. Aesop did not use a voucher system for transactions under $2,500. As a consequence, there was no independent verification of the documents, which enabled the employee to submit fake invoices to hide his unauthorized purchases.

# Petty Cash Fund

As you just learned, better internal control over cash disbursements is possible when companies make payments by check. However, using checks to pay small amounts is both impractical and a nuisance. For instance, a company would not want to write checks to pay for postage due, working lunches, or taxi fares. A common way of handling such payments, while maintaining satisfactory control, is to use a **petty cash fund** to pay relatively small amounts (see **Ethics Note**). The operation of a petty cash fund, often called an **imprest system**, involves (1) establishing the fund, (2) making payments from the fund, and (3) replenishing the fund.[3]

## Establishing the Petty Cash Fund

Two essential steps in establishing a petty cash fund are (1) appointing a petty cash custodian who will be responsible for the fund, and (2) determining the size of the fund. Ordinarily, a company expects the amount in the fund to cover anticipated disbursements for a three- to four-week period.

To establish the fund, a company issues a check payable to the petty cash custodian for the stipulated amount. For example, if Laird Company decides to establish a $100 fund on March 1, the general journal entry is as follows.

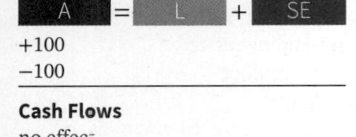

+100
−100

**Cash Flows**
no effect

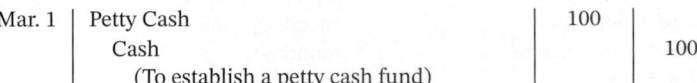

| Mar. 1 | Petty Cash | 100 | |
| |     Cash | | 100 |
| |     (To establish a petty cash fund) | | |

The fund custodian cashes the check and places the proceeds in a locked petty cash box or drawer. Most petty cash funds are established on a fixed-amount basis. The company will make no additional entries to the Petty Cash account unless management changes the stipulated amount of the fund. For example, if Laird decides on July 1 to increase the size of the fund to $250, it would debit Petty Cash $150 and credit Cash $150.

## Making Payments from the Petty Cash Fund

The petty cash custodian has the authority to make payments from the fund that conform to prescribed management policies. Usually, management limits the size of expenditures that come from petty cash. Likewise, it may not permit use of the fund for certain types of transactions (such as making short-term loans to employees).

---

[3] The term "imprest" means an advance of money for a designated purpose.

Each payment from the fund must be documented on a prenumbered petty cash receipt (or petty cash voucher), as shown in **Illustration 7.7**. The signatures of both the fund custodian and the person receiving payment are required on the receipt. If other supporting documents such as a freight bill or invoice are available, they should be attached to the petty cash receipt (see **Helpful Hint**).

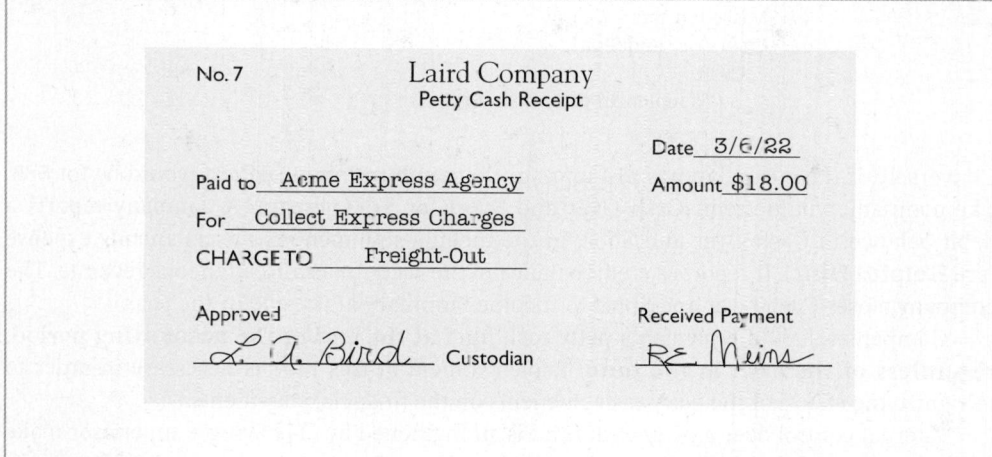

No. 7        Laird Company
Petty Cash Receipt

Paid to   Acme Express Agency      Date _3/6/22_
For    Collect Express Charges     Amount _$18.00_
CHARGE TO      Freight-Out

Approved                      Received Payment

_L. A. Bird_ Custodian           _R. E. Meins_

**ILLUSTRATION 7.7**
**Petty cash receipt**

**HELPFUL HINT**
The petty cash receipt satisfies two internal control principles: (1) establishment of responsibility (signature of custodian), and (2) documentation procedures.

The petty cash custodian keeps the receipts in the petty cash box until the fund is replenished. The sum of the petty cash receipts and the money in the fund should equal the established total at all times. Management can (and should) make surprise counts at any time by an independent person, such as an internal auditor, to determine the correctness of the fund.

The company does not make an accounting entry to record a payment when it is made from petty cash. It is considered both inexpedient and unnecessary to do so. Instead, the company recognizes the accounting effects of each payment when it replenishes the fund.

## Replenishing the Petty Cash Fund

When the money in the petty cash fund reaches a minimum level, the company replenishes the fund (see **Helpful Hint**). The petty cash custodian initiates a request for reimbursement. The custodian prepares a schedule (or summary) of the payments that have been made and sends the schedule, supported by petty cash receipts and other documentation, to the treasurer's office. The treasurer's office examines the receipts and supporting documents to verify that proper payments from the fund were made. The treasurer then approves the request and issues a check to restore the fund to its established amount. At the same time, all supporting documentation is stamped "paid" so that it cannot be submitted again for payment.

To illustrate, assume that on March 15 Laird's petty cash custodian requests a check for $87 because the fund contains $13 cash. Petty cash receipts also total $87: postage $44, freight-out $38, and miscellaneous expenses $5. This replenishment will reestablish the desired total of $100 in the fund. The journal entry to record the replenishment is as follows.

**HELPFUL HINT**
Replenishing the petty cash fund involves three internal control principles: (1) segregation of duties, (2) documentation procedures, and (3) independent internal verification.

| | | | |
|---|---|---|---|
| Mar. 15 | Postage Expense | 44 | |
| | Freight-Out | 38 | |
| | Miscellaneous Expense | 5 | |
| |     Cash | | 87 |
| |       (To replenish petty cash fund) | | |

A = L + SE
−44 Exp
−38 Exp
−5 Exp
−87

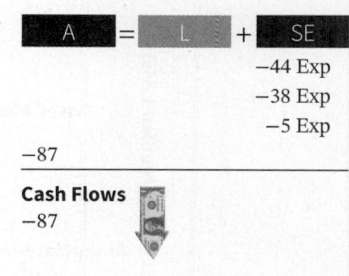

**Cash Flows**
−87

Note that the replenishment entry does not affect the Petty Cash account. Replenishment changes the composition of the fund by replacing the petty cash receipts with cash. It does not change the balance in the fund.

Occasionally, in replenishing a petty cash fund, the company may need to recognize a cash shortage or overage. This results when the total of the cash plus receipts in the petty cash box does not equal the established amount of the petty cash fund. To illustrate, assume that Laird's petty cash custodian has only $12 in cash in the fund plus the receipts as listed. The request for reimbursement would therefore be for $88 to reestablish the $100 cash total. Laird would make the following entry.

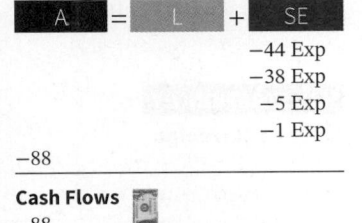

A  =  L  +  SE
−44 Exp
−38 Exp
−5 Exp
−1 Exp
−88

**Cash Flows**
−88

| Mar. 15 | Postage Expense | 44 | |
| | Freight-Out | 38 | |
| | Miscellaneous Expense | 5 | |
| | Cash Over and Short | 1 | |
| | Cash | | 88 |
| | (To replenish petty cash fund) | | |

Conversely, if the custodian has $14 in cash, the reimbursement request would be for $86. The company would credit Cash Over and Short for $1 (overage). A company reports a debit balance in Cash Over and Short in the income statement as miscellaneous expense (see **Helpful Hint**). It reports a credit balance in the account as miscellaneous revenue. The company closes Cash Over and Short to Income Summary at the end of the year.

Companies should replenish a petty cash fund **at the end of the accounting period, regardless of the cash in the fund**. Replenishment at this time is necessary in order to recognize the effects of the petty cash payments on the financial statements.

Internal control over a petty cash fund is strengthened by (1) having a supervisor make surprise counts of the fund to ascertain whether the paid petty cash receipts and fund cash equal the designated amount, and (2) cancelling or defacing the paid petty cash receipts so they cannot be resubmitted for reimbursement.

**HELPFUL HINT**

Cash over and short situations result from mathematical errors or from failure to keep accurate records.

# Ethics Insight

iStock.com/Chris Fertnig

## How Employees Steal

Occupational fraud is using your own occupation for personal gain through the misuse or misapplication of the company's resources or assets. This type of fraud is one of three types:

1. **Asset misappropriation**, such as theft of cash on hand, fraudulent disbursements, false refunds, ghost employees, personal purchases, and fictitious employees. This fraud is the most common but the least costly.

2. **Corruption**, such as bribery, illegal gratuities, and economic extortion. This fraud generally falls in the middle between asset misappropriation and financial statement fraud as regards frequency and cost.

3. **Financial statement fraud**, such as fictitious revenues, concealed liabilities and expenses, improper disclosures, and improper asset values. This fraud occurs less frequently than other types of fraud, but it is the most costly.

The following graph shows the frequency and the median loss for each type of occupational fraud. (Note that the sum of percentages exceeds 100% because some cases of fraud involved more than one type.)

**Source:** *2016 Report to the Nations on Occupational Fraud and Abuse*, Association of Certified Fraud Examiners, p. 12.

**How can companies reduce the likelihood of occupational fraud? (Answer is available near the end of the chapter.)**

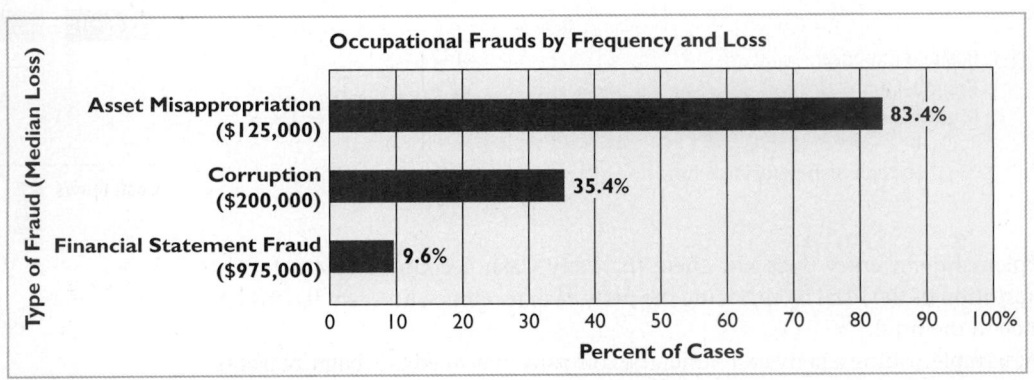

**Occupational Frauds by Frequency and Loss**

Type of Fraud (Median Loss)

Asset Misappropriation ($125,000) — 83.4%
Corruption ($200,000) — 35.4%
Financial Statement Fraud ($975,000) — 9.6%

Percent of Cases

## DO IT! 2b | Petty Cash Fund

Bateer Company established a $50 petty cash fund on July 1. On July 30, the fund had $12 cash remaining and petty cash receipts for postage $14, office supplies $10, and delivery expense to customers $15. Prepare journal entries to establish the fund on July 1 and to replenish the fund on July 30.

### Solution

| July | 1 | Petty Cash | 50 | |
|------|---|------------|----|----|
| | |     Cash | | 50 |
| | |         (To establish petty cash fund) | | |
| | | | | |
| | 30 | Postage Expense | 14 | |
| | | Supplies | 10 | |
| | | Freight-Out | 15 | |
| | |     Cash Over and Short | | 1 |
| | |     Cash ($50 – $12) | | 38 |
| | |         (To replenish petty cash) | | |

Related exercise material: **BE7.9**, **DO IT! 7.2b**, **E7.7**, and **E7.8**.

**ACTION PLAN**

- To establish the fund, set up a separate general ledger account.
- Determine how much cash is needed to replenish the fund: subtract the cash remaining from the established petty cash fund balance.
- Total the petty cash receipts. Determine any cash over or short—the difference between the cash needed to replenish the fund and the total of the petty cash receipts.
- Record the expenditures incurred according to the petty cash receipts when replenishing the fund.

# Control Features of a Bank Account

### LEARNING OBJECTIVE 3

Identify the control features of a bank account.

**The use of a bank contributes significantly to good internal control over cash.** A company safeguards its cash by using a bank as a depository and clearinghouse for checks received and checks written. The use of a bank checking account minimizes the amount of cash that must be kept on hand. It also facilitates control of cash because a double record is maintained of all bank transactions—one by the business and the other by the bank. The asset account Cash maintained by the company is the "flipside" of the bank's liability account for that company. A **bank reconciliation** is the process of comparing the bank's balance with the company's balance, and explaining the differences to make them agree.

Many companies have more than one bank account. For efficiency of operations and better control, national retailers like **Walmart** and **Target** often have regional bank accounts. Similarly, a company such as **ExxonMobil** with more than 100,000 employees may have a payroll bank account as well as one or more general bank accounts. In addition, a company may maintain several bank accounts in order to have more than one source for short-term loans.

## Making Bank Deposits

An authorized employee, such as the head cashier, should make a company's bank deposits. Each deposit must be documented by a deposit slip (ticket), as shown in **Illustration 7.8**.

**ILLUSTRATION 7.8**
**Deposit slip**

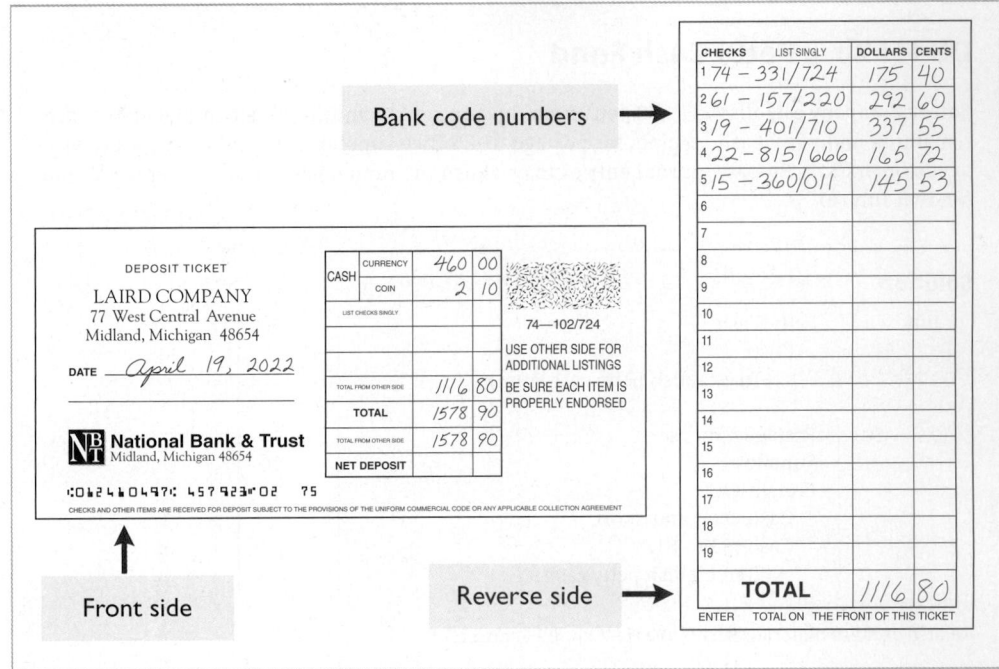

Deposit slips are prepared in duplicate. The bank retains the original; the depositor keeps the duplicate, machine-stamped by the bank to establish its authenticity.

## Writing Checks

A **check** is a written order signed by the depositor directing the bank to pay a specified sum of money to a designated recipient. There are three parties to a check: (1) the **maker** (or drawer) who issues the check, (2) the **bank** (or payer) on which the check is drawn, and (3) the **payee** to whom the check is payable. A check is a **negotiable instrument** that one party can transfer to another party by endorsement. Each check should be accompanied by an explanation of its purpose. In many companies, a remittance advice attached to the check, as shown in **Illustration 7.9**, explains the check's purpose.

**ILLUSTRATION 7.9**

**Check with remittance advice**

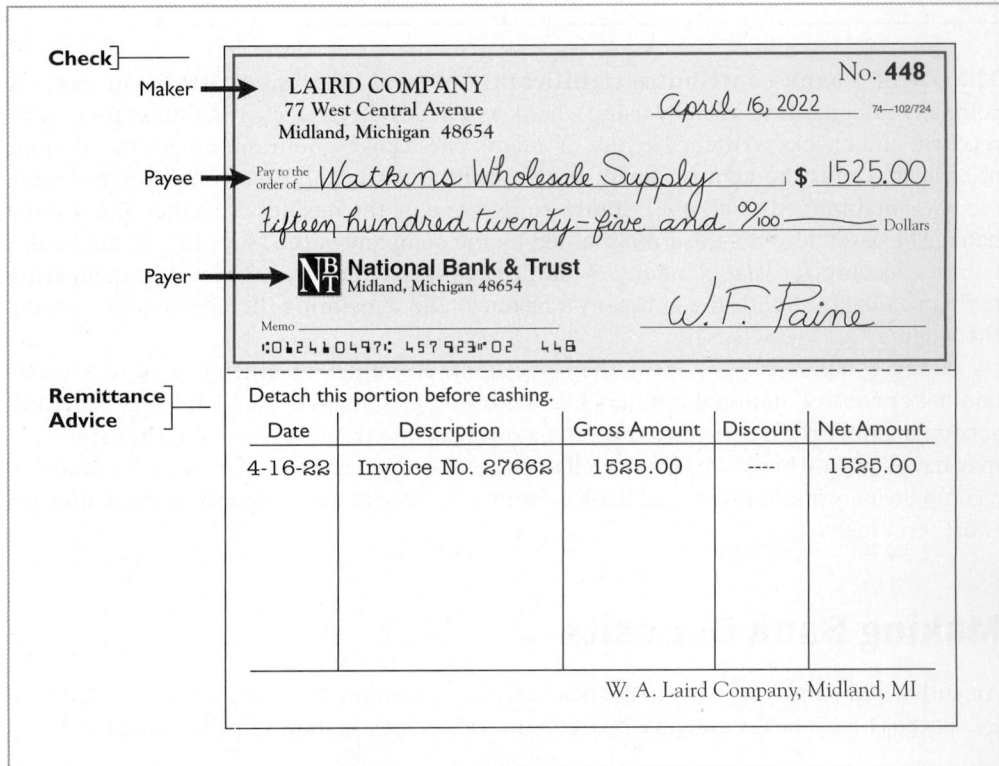

# Electronic Funds Transfer (EFT) System

It is not surprising that companies and banks have developed approaches to transfer funds among parties without the use of paper (deposit tickets, checks, etc.). Such procedures, called **electronic funds transfers (EFTs)**, are disbursement systems that use wire, telephone, or computers to transfer cash from one location to another. Use of EFT is quite common. For example, many employees receive no formal payroll checks from their employers. Instead, employers send electronic payroll data to the appropriate employee banks. Also, companies now frequently make regular payments such as those for utilities, rent, and insurance by EFT.

EFT transactions normally result in better internal control since no cash or checks are handled by company employees. This does not mean that opportunities for fraud are eliminated. In fact, the same basic principles related to internal control apply to EFT transactions. For example, without proper segregation of duties and authorizations, an employee might be able to redirect electronic payments into a personal bank account and conceal the theft with fraudulent accounting entries.

# Bank Statements

Each month, the company receives from the bank a **bank statement** showing its bank transactions and balances.[4] For example, the statement for Laird Company in **Illustration 7.10**

**ILLUSTRATION 7.10**

**Bank statement**

### National Bank & Trust
Midland, Michigan 48654     Member FDIC

**ACCOUNT STATEMENT**

LAIRD COMPANY
77 WEST CENTRAL AVENUE
MIDLAND, MICHIGAN 48654

Statement Date/Credit Line Closing Date

April 30, 2022

457923

ACCOUNT NUMBER

| Balance Last Statement | Deposits and Credits | | Checks and Debits | | Balance This Statement |
|---|---|---|---|---|---|
| | No. | Total Amount | No. | Total Amount | |
| 13,256.90 | 20 | 34,805.10 | 26 | 32,154.55 | 15,907.45 |

| Amounts Deducted from Account (debits) | | | Amounts Added to Account (credits) | | Daily Balance | |
|---|---|---|---|---|---|---|
| Date | No. | Amount | Date | Amount | Date | Amount |
| 4-2 | 435 | 644.95 | 4-2 | 4,276.85 | 4-2 | 13,888.80 |
| 4-3 | EFT | 1,000.00 | 4-3 | 2,137.50 | 4-3 | 13,249.65 |
| 4-5 | 436 | 2,260.00 | 4-5 | 1,350.47 | 4-4 | 17,063.86 |
| 4-4 | 437 | 1,185.79 | 4-7 | 988.46 | 4-5 | 15,154.33 |
| 4-3 | 438 | 776.65 | 4-8 | 1,320.28 | 4-7 | 14,648.89 |
| 4-8 | 439 | 1,781.70 | 4-9 EFT | 1,035.00 | 4-8 | 11,767.47 |
| 4-7 | 440 | 1,487.90 | 4-11 | 2,720.00 | 4-9 | 12,802.47 |
| 4-7 | EFT | 320.00 | 4-12 | 757.41 | 4-11 | 13,936.87 |
| 4-8 | 441 | 2,100.00 | 4-13 | 1,218.56 | 4-12 | 13,468.28 |
| 4-11 | 442 | 1,585.60 | | | | |
| 4-12 | 443 | 1,226.00 | | | | |
| 4-29 | NSF | 425 60 | 4-27 | 1,545.57 | 4-27 | 13,005.45 |
| 4-29 | 459 | 1,080 30 | 4-29 | 2,929.45 | 4-29 | 14,429.00 |
| 4-30 | DM | 120 00 | 4-30 | 2,128.60 | 4-30 | 15,907.45 |
| 4-30 | DM | 30 00 | | | | |
| 4-30 | 461 | 500 15 | | | | |

Symbols: **CM** Credit Memo  **EC** Error Correction  **NSF** Not Sufficient Funds  **EFT** Electronic Funds Transfer
**DM** Debit Memo  **INT** Interest Earned  **SC** Service Charge

[4]Our presentation assumes that a company makes all adjustments at the end of the month. In practice, a company may also make journal entries during the month as it reviews online information from the bank regarding its account.

shows the following: (1) checks paid and other debits (such as debit card transactions or electronic funds transfers for bill payments) that reduce the balance in the depositor's account, (2) deposits (by direct deposit, automated teller machine, or electronic funds transfer) and other credits that increase the balance in the depositor's account, and (3) the account balance after each day's transactions.

Remember that **bank statements are prepared from the** *bank's* **perspective**. For example, **every deposit the bank receives is an increase in the bank's liabilities (an account payable to the depositor)**. Therefore, in Illustration 7.10, National Bank and Trust **credits** to Laird Company every deposit it received from Laird. The reverse occurs when the bank "pays" a check issued by Laird Company on its checking account balance: Payment reduces the bank's liability and is therefore **debited** to Laird's account with the bank.

The bank statement lists in numerical sequence all paid checks along with the date the check was paid and its amount. Upon paying a check, the bank stamps the check "paid"; a paid check is sometimes referred to as a **canceled** check. In addition, the bank includes with the bank statement memoranda explaining other debits and credits it made to the depositor's account (see **Helpful Hint**).

A check that is not paid by a bank because of insufficient funds in a bank account is called an **NSF check** (not sufficient funds). The bank uses a debit memorandum when a previously deposited customer's check "bounces" because of insufficient funds. In such a case, the customer's bank marks the check NSF (not sufficient funds) and returns it to the depositor's bank. The bank then debits (decreases) the depositor's account, as shown by the symbol NSF in Illustration 7.10, and sends the NSF check and debit memorandum to the depositor as notification of the charge. The NSF check reestablishes an account receivable for the depositor and reduces its cash in the bank account.

**HELPFUL HINT**

Essentially, the bank statement is a copy of the bank's records sent to the customer or made available online for review.

## Reconciling the Bank Account

Because the bank and the company maintain independent records of the company's cash account, you might assume that the respective balances will always agree. In fact, the two balances are seldom the same at any given time, and both balances differ from the "correct or true" balance. Therefore, it is necessary to make the balance per books and the balance per bank agree with the correct or true amount—a process called **reconciling the bank account**. The need for reconciliation has two causes:

1. **Time lags** that prevent one of the parties from recording the transaction in the same period.
2. **Errors** by either party in recording transactions.

Time lags occur frequently. For example, several days may elapse between the time a company pays by check and the date the bank pays the check. Similarly, when a company uses the bank's night depository to make its deposits, there will be a difference of one day between the time the company records the receipts and the time the bank does so. A time lag also occurs whenever the bank mails a debit or credit memorandum to the company.

You might think that if a company never writes checks (for example, if a small company uses only a debit card or electronic funds transfers), it does not need to reconcile its account. However, **the possibility of errors or fraud still necessitates periodic reconciliation**. The incidence of errors or fraud depends on the effectiveness of the internal controls maintained by the company and the bank. Bank errors are infrequent. However, either party could accidentally record a $450 check as $45 or $540. In addition, the bank might mistakenly charge a check drawn by C. D. Berg to the account of C. D. Burg.

### Reconciliation Procedure

In reconciling the bank account, it is customary to reconcile the balance per books and balance per bank to their adjusted (correct or true) cash balances. **To obtain maximum benefit from a bank reconciliation, an employee who has no other responsibilities related to cash should prepare the reconciliation**. When companies do not follow the internal control principle of independent internal verification in preparing the reconciliation, cash embezzlements may escape unnoticed. For example, in the Anatomy of a Fraud box about Aggasiz Construction Company presented earlier, a bank reconciliation by someone other than Angela Bauer might have exposed her embezzlement.

Illustration 7.11 shows the reconciliation process (see **Helpful Hint**). The starting point in preparing the reconciliation is to enter the balance per bank statement and balance per books on a schedule. The following steps should reveal all the reconciling items that cause the difference between the two balances.

**HELPFUL HINT**

Deposits in transit and outstanding checks are reconciling items because of time lags.

**ILLUSTRATION 7.11**
**Bank reconciliation process**

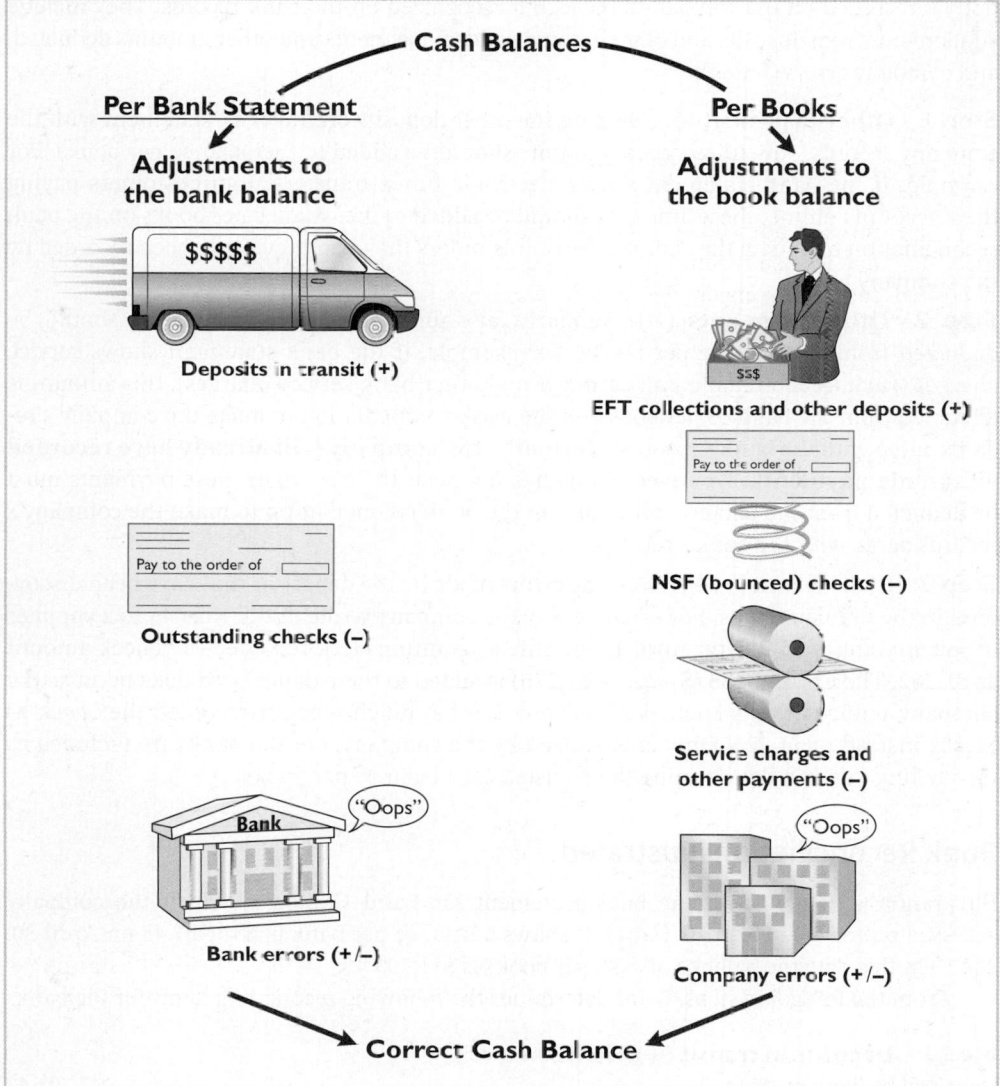

**Reconciling Items per Bank**    On the bank side of the reconciliation, the items to reconcile are deposits in transit (amounts added), outstanding checks (amounts deducted), and bank errors (if any). By adjusting the bank balance for these items, a company brings that balance up to date.

**Step 1    Deposits in transit (+).** Compare the individual deposits on the bank statement with the deposits in transit from the preceding bank reconciliation and with the deposits per company records or copies of duplicate deposit slips for the current period. Deposits recorded by the depositor that have not been recorded by the bank represent **deposits in transit**. Add these deposits to the balance per bank.

**Step 2    Outstanding checks (−).** Compare the paid checks shown on the bank statement or the paid checks returned with the bank statement with (a) checks outstanding from the preceding bank reconciliation, and (b) checks issued by the company recorded as cash payments in the current period. Issued checks recorded by the company that have not been paid by the bank represent **outstanding checks**. Deduct outstanding checks from the balance per bank.

**Step 3 Bank errors (+/−).** Note any errors made by the bank that were discovered in the previous steps. For example, if the bank processed a deposit of $1,693 as $1,639 in error, the difference of $54 ($1,693 − $1,639) is added to the balance per bank on the bank reconciliation. All errors made by the bank are reconciling items in determining the adjusted cash balance per the bank.

**Reconciling Items per Books** Reconciling items on the book side relate to amounts not yet recorded on the company's books but recognized on the bank records. They include adjustments from deposits and other amounts added, payments and other amounts deducted, and company errors (if any).

**Step 1 Other deposits (+).** Compare the other deposits on the bank statement with the company records. Any unrecorded amounts should be added to the balance per books. For example, if the bank statement shows electronic funds transfers from customers paying their accounts online, these amounts should be added to the balance per books on the bank reconciliation to update the company's records unless they had previously been recorded by the company.

**Step 2 Other payments (−).** Similarly, any unrecorded other payments should be deducted from the balance per books. For example, if the bank statement shows service charges (such as debit and credit card fees and other bank service charges), this amount is deducted from the balance per books on the bank reconciliation to make the company's records agree with the bank's records. **Normally, the company will already have recorded electronic payments.** However, if this has not been the case then these payments must be deducted from the balance per books on the bank reconciliation to make the company's records agree with the bank's records.

**Step 3 Book errors (+/−).** Note any errors made by the depositor that have been discovered in the previous steps. For example, say the company wrote check No. 443 to a supplier in the amount of $1,226 on April 12, but the accounting clerk recorded the check amount as $1,262. The error of $36 ($1,262 − $1,226) is added to the balance per books because the company reduced the balance per books by $36 too much when it recorded the check as $1,262 instead of $1,226. Only errors made by the company, not the bank, are included as reconciling items in determining the adjusted cash balance per books.

## Bank Reconciliation Illustrated

Illustration 7.10 presented the bank statement for Laird Company, which the company accessed online (see **Helpful Hint**). It shows a balance per bank of $15,907.45 on April 30, 2022. On this date the balance of cash per books is $11,709.45.

From the foregoing steps, Laird determines the following reconciling items for the bank.

**Step 1 Deposits in transit (+):** April 30 deposit
(received by bank on May 1).      $2,201.40

**Step 2 Outstanding checks (−):** No. 453, $3,000.00;
No. 457, $1,401.30; No. 460, $1,502.70.      5,904.00

**Step 3 Bank errors (+/−):** None.

Reconciling items per books are as follows:

**Step 1 Other deposits (+):** Unrecorded electronic receipt from
customer on account on April 9 determined from the bank statement.      $1,035.00

**Step 2 Other payments (−):** The electronic payments on April 3
and 7 were previously recorded by the company when they were
initiated. Unrecorded charges determined from the bank statement
are as follows:

| | |
|---|---:|
| Returned NSF check on April 29 | 425.60 |
| Debit and credit card fees on April 30 | 120.00 |
| Bank service charges on April 30 | 30.00 |

**HELPFUL HINT**

Note in the bank statement in Illustration 7.10 that the bank has paid checks No. 459 and 461, but check No. 460 is not listed. Thus, this check is outstanding. If a complete bank statement were provided, checks No. 453 and 457 also would not be listed. Laird obtains the amounts for these three checks from its cash payments records.

**Step 3   Company errors (+):** Check No. 443 was correctly written by Laird for $1,226 and was correctly paid by the bank on April 12. However, it was recorded as $1,262 on Laird's books.

36.00

**Illustration 7.12** shows Laird's bank reconciliation (see **Alternative Terminology**).

---

**Laird Company**
**Bank Reconciliation**
**April 30, 2022**

| | | |
|---|---:|---:|
| Cash balance per bank statement | | $15,907.45 |
| Add: Deposits in transit | | 2,201.40 |
| | | 18,108.85 |
| Less: Outstanding checks | | |
| No. 453 | $3,000.00 | |
| No. 457 | 1,401.30 | |
| No. 460 | 1,502.70 | 5,904.00 |
| **Adjusted cash balance per bank** | | **$12,204.85** |
| Cash balance per books | | $ 11,709.45 |
| Add: Electronic funds transfer received | $1,035.00 | |
| Error in recording check No. 443 | 36.00 | 1,071.00 |
| | | 12,780.45 |
| Less: NSF check | 425.60 | |
| Debit and credit card fees | 120.00 | |
| Bank service charge | 30.00 | 575.60 |
| **Adjusted cash balance per books** | | **$12,204.85** |

---

**ILLUSTRATION 7.12**
**Bank reconciliation**

**ALTERNATIVE TERMINOLOGY**

The terms *adjusted* cash balance, *true cash balance*, and *correct cash balance* are used interchangeably.

## Entries from Bank Reconciliation

The depositor (that is, the company) next must record each reconciling item used to determine the **adjusted cash balance per books**. If the company does not journalize and post these items, the Cash account will not show the correct balance. The adjusting entries for the Laird Company bank reconciliation on April 30 are as follows. Note that every entry involves cash.

**Collection of Electronic Funds Transfer**   A payment of an account by a customer is recorded in the same way, whether the cash is received through the mail or electronically. The entry is as follows.

| | | | |
|---|---|---:|---:|
| Apr. 30 | Cash | 1,035 | |
| | Accounts Receivable | | 1,035 |
| | (To record receipt of electronic funds transfer) | | |

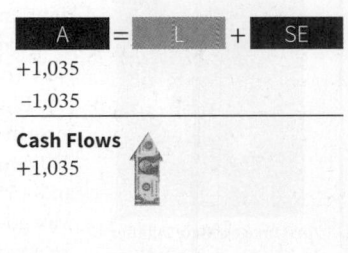

A = L + SE
+1,035
−1,035

**Cash Flows**
+1,035

**Book Error**   An examination of the cash disbursements journal shows that check No. 443 was a payment on account to Andrea Company, a supplier. The correcting entry is as follows.

| | | | |
|---|---|---:|---:|
| Apr. 30 | Cash | 36 | |
| | Accounts Payable | | 36 |
| | (To correct error in recording check No. 443) | | |

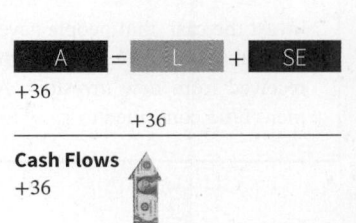

A = L + SE
+36
+36

**Cash Flows**
+36

**NSF Check** As indicated earlier, an NSF check becomes an accounts receivable to the depositor. The entry is as follows.

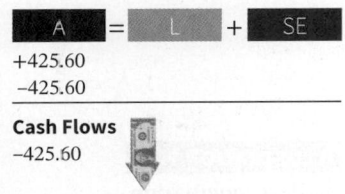

+425.60
−425.60

**Cash Flows**
−425.60

| Apr. 30 | Accounts Receivable | 425.60 | |
| | Cash | | 425.60 |
| | (To record NSF check) | | |

**Bank Charge Expense** Fees for processing debit and credit card transactions are normally debited to the Bank Charge Expense account, as are bank service charges. We have chosen to combine and record these in one journal entry, as shown below, although they also could be journalized separately.

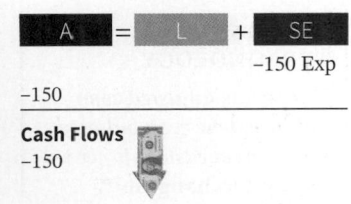

−150 Exp

−150

**Cash Flows**
−150

| Apr. 30 | Bank Charge Expense | 150 | |
| | Cash | | 150 |
| | (To record charges for debit and credit card fees of $120 and bank service charges of $30) | | |

After Laird posts the entries, the Cash account will appear as in **Illustration 7.13**. The adjusted cash balance in the ledger should agree with the adjusted cash balance per books in the bank reconciliation in Illustration 7.12.

**ILLUSTRATION 7.13**

**Adjusted balance in Cash account**

| | Cash | | | |
|---|---|---|---|---|
| Apr. 30 Bal. | 11,709.45 | Apr. 30 | 425.60 | |
| 30 | 1,035.00 | 30 | 150.00 | |
| 30 | 36.00 | | | |
| Apr. 30 Bal. | **12,204.85** | | | |

What entries does the bank make? If the company discovers any bank errors in preparing the reconciliation, it should notify the bank so the bank can make the necessary corrections on its records. The bank does not make any entries for deposits in transit or outstanding checks. Only when these items reach the bank will the bank record these items.

---

## Investor Insight

AP Images/Mary Altaffer

### Madoff's Ponzi Scheme

No recent fraud has generated more notoriety and rage than the one perpetrated by Bernard Madoff. Madoff was an elite New York investment fund manager who was highly regarded by securities regulators. Investors flocked to him because he delivered steady returns of between 10% and 15%, no matter whether the market was going up or going down. However, for many years, Madoff did not actually invest the cash that people gave to him. Instead, he was running a Ponzi scheme: He paid returns to existing investors using cash received from new investors. As long as the size of his investment fund continued to grow from new investments at a rate that exceeded the amounts that he needed to pay out in returns, Madoff was able to operate his fraud smoothly.

To conceal his misdeeds, Madoff fabricated false investment statements that were provided to investors. In addition, Madoff hired an auditor that never verified the accuracy of the investment records but automatically issued unqualified opinions each year. A competing fund manager warned the SEC a number of times over a nearly 10-year period that he thought Madoff was engaged in fraud. The SEC never aggressively investigated the allegations. Investors, many of which were charitable organizations, lost more than $18 billion. Madoff was sentenced to a jail term of 150 years.

**How was Madoff able to conceal such a giant fraud? (Answer is available near the end of the chapter.)**

## DO IT! 3 | Bank Reconciliation

Sally Kist owns Linen Kist Fabrics. Sally asks you to explain how she should treat the following reconciling items when reconciling the company's bank account: (1) a debit memorandum for an NSF check, (2) a credit memorandum for an electronic funds transfer from one of the company's customers received by the bank, (3) outstanding checks, and (4) a deposit in transit.

### Solution

Sally should treat the reconciling items as follows.

1. NSF check: Deduct from balance per books.
2. Electronic funds transfer received by bank: Add to balance per books.
3. Outstanding checks: Deduct from balance per bank.
4. Deposit in transit: Add to balance per bank.

Related exercise material: **BE7.10, BE7.11, BE7.12, BE7.13, BE7.14, BE7.15, DO IT! 7.3, E7.9, E7.10, E7.11 E7.12, and E7.13.**

# Reporting Cash

**LEARNING OBJECTIVE 4**

Explain the reporting of cash.

**Cash** consists of coins, currency (paper money), checks, money orders, and money on hand or on deposit in a bank or similar depository. Companies report cash in two different statements: the balance sheet and the statement of cash flows. The balance sheet reports the amount of cash available at a given point in time. The statement of cash flows shows the sources and uses of cash during a period of time. The statement of cash flows was introduced in Chapter 1 and will be discussed in much detail in Chapter 12. In this section, we discuss some important points regarding the presentation of cash in the balance sheet.

When presented in a balance sheet, cash on hand, cash in banks, and petty cash are often combined and reported simply as **Cash**. Because it is the most liquid asset owned by the company, cash is listed first in the current assets section of the balance sheet.

## Cash Equivalents

Many companies use the designation "Cash and cash equivalents" in reporting cash (See **Illustration 7.14** for an example.) **Cash equivalents** are short-term, highly liquid investments that are both:

1. Readily convertible to known amounts of cash, and
2. So near their maturity that their market value is relatively insensitive to changes in interest rates. (Generally, only investments with maturities of three months or less qualify under this definition.)

Examples of cash equivalents are Treasury bills, commercial paper (short-term corporate notes), and money market funds. All typically are purchased with cash that is in excess of immediate needs (see **Ethics Note**).

**ETHICS NOTE**

Recently, some companies were forced to restate their financial statements because they had too broadly interpreted which types of investments could be treated as cash equivalents. By reporting these items as cash equivalents, the companies made themselves look more liquid.

**ILLUSTRATION 7.14**

**Balance sheet presentation of cash**

**Real World**

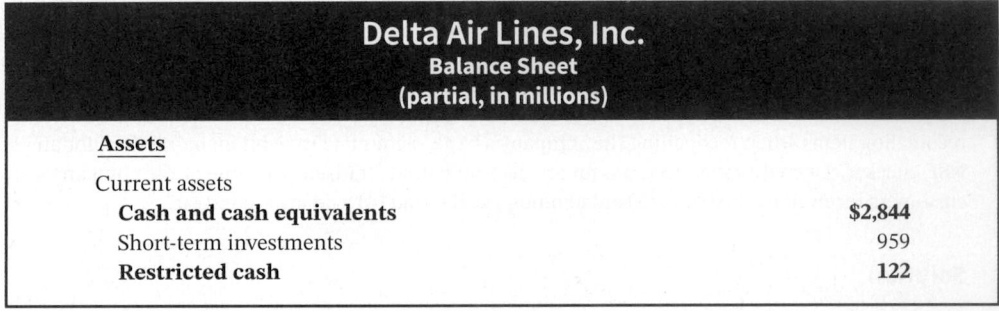

Delta Air Lines, Inc.
Balance Sheet
(partial, in millions)

| Assets | |
|---|---|
| Current assets | |
| **Cash and cash equivalents** | **$2,844** |
| Short-term investments | 959 |
| **Restricted cash** | **122** |

Occasionally, a company will have a net negative balance in its bank account. In this case, the company should report the negative balance among current liabilities. For example, farm equipment manufacturer **Ag-Chem** at one time reported "Checks outstanding in excess of cash balances" of $2,145,000 among its current liabilities.

# Restricted Cash

A company may have **restricted cash**, cash that is not available for general use but rather is restricted for a special purpose. For example, landfill companies are often required to maintain a fund of restricted cash to ensure they will have adequate resources to cover closing and clean-up costs at the end of a landfill site's useful life. **McKesson Corp.** recently reported restricted cash of $962 million to be paid out as the result of investor lawsuits.

Cash restricted in use should be reported separately on the balance sheet as restricted cash. If the company expects to use the restricted cash within the next year, it reports the amount as a current asset. When this is not the case, it reports the restricted funds as a noncurrent asset. The FASB now requires that restricted cash be included with cash and cash equivalents when reconciling the beginning and ending amounts on a statement of cash flows.

Illustration 7.14 shows restricted cash reported in the financial statements of **Delta Air Lines**. The company is required to maintain restricted cash as collateral to support insurance obligations related to workers' compensation claims. Delta does not have access to these funds for general use, and so it must report them separately, rather than as part of cash and cash equivalents.

---

**ACTION PLAN**

- **Understand how companies present cash and restricted cash on the balance sheet.**
- **Review the designations of cash equivalents and restricted cash, and how companies typically handle them.**

## DO IT! 4 | Reporting Cash

Indicate whether each of the following statements is true or false. If false, indicate how to correct the statement.

1. Cash and cash equivalents are comprised of coins, currency (paper money), money orders, and NSF checks.

2. Restricted cash is classified as either a current asset or noncurrent asset, depending on the circumstances.

3. A company may have a negative balance in its bank account. In this case, it should offset this negative balance against cash and cash equivalents on the balance sheet.

4. Because cash equivalents often include short-term investments, accounts receivable should be reported as the first item on the balance sheet.

### Solution

1. False. NSF checks should be reported as receivables, not cash and cash equivalents.   2. True.
3. False. Companies that have a negative balance in their bank accounts should report the negative balance as a current liability.   4. False. Cash equivalents are readily convertible to known amounts of cash, and so near maturity (less than 3 months) that they are considered more liquid than accounts receivable and therefore are reported before accounts receivable on the balance sheet.

Related exercise material: **BE7.16, DO IT! 7.4, E7.14, and E7.15.**

# Review and Practice

## Learning Objectives Review

### 1   Define fraud and the principles of internal control.

A fraud is a dishonest act by an employee that results in personal benefit to the employee at a cost to the employer. The fraud triangle refers to the three factors that contribute to fraudulent activity by employees: opportunity, financial pressure, and rationalization. Internal control consists of all the related methods and measures adopted within an organization to safeguard its assets, enhance the reliability of its accounting records, increase efficiency of operations, and ensure compliance with laws and regulations.

The principles of internal control are establishment of responsibility, segregation of duties, documentation procedures, physical controls, independent internal verification, and human resource controls such as bonding and requiring employees to take vacations.

### 2   Apply internal control principles to cash.

Internal controls over cash receipts include (a) designating specific personnel to handle cash; (b) assigning different individuals to receive cash, record cash, and maintain custody of cash; (c) using remittance advices for mail receipts, cash register tapes for over-the-counter receipts, and deposit slips for bank deposits; (d) using company safes and bank vaults to store cash with access limited to authorized personnel, and using cash registers or point-of-sale terminals in executing over-the-counter receipts; (e) making independent daily counts of register receipts and daily comparison of total receipts with total deposits; and (f) bonding personnel that handle cash and requiring them to take vacations.

Internal controls over cash disbursements include (a) having specific individuals such as the treasurer authorized to sign checks and approve vendors; (b) assigning different individuals to approve items for payment, make the payment, and record the payment; (c) using

prenumbered checks and accounting for all checks, with each check supported by an approved invoice; (d) storing blank checks in a safe or vault with access restricted to authorized personnel, and using a check-writing machine to imprint amounts on checks; (e) comparing each check with the approved invoice before issuing the check, and making monthly reconciliations of bank and book balances; and (f) bonding personnel who handle cash, requiring employees to take vacations, and conducting background checks.

Companies operate a petty cash fund to pay relatively small amounts of cash. They must establish the fund, make payments from the fund, and replenish the fund when the cash in the fund reaches a minimum level.

### 3   Identify the control features of a bank account.

A bank account contributes to good internal control by providing physical controls for the storage of cash. It minimizes the amount of currency that a company must keep on hand, and it creates a double record of a depositor's bank transactions. It is customary to reconcile the balance per books and balance per bank to their adjusted balances. The steps in the reconciling process are to determine deposits in transit, electronic funds transfers received by bank, outstanding checks, errors by the depositor or the bank, and unrecorded bank memoranda.

### 4   Explain the reporting of cash.

Companies list cash first in the current assets section of the balance sheet. In some cases, they report cash together with cash equivalents. Cash restricted for a special purpose is reported separately as a current asset or as a noncurrent asset, depending on when the cash is expected to be used.

## Glossary Review

**Bank reconciliation**  The process of comparing the bank's balance with the company's balance and explaining any differences to make them agree. (p. 7-19).

**Bank statement**  A monthly statement from the bank that shows the depositor's bank transactions and balances. (p. 7-21).

**Bonding**  Obtaining insurance protection against theft by employees. (p. 7-9).

**Cash**  Resources that consist of coins, currency, checks, money orders, and money on hand or on deposit in a bank or similar depository. (p. 7-27).

**Cash equivalents**  Short-term, highly liquid investments that can be converted to a specific amount of cash. (p. 7-27).

**Check**  A written order signed by a bank depositor, directing the bank to pay a specified sum of money to a designated recipient. (p. 7-20).

**Deposits in transit**  Deposits recorded by the depositor but not yet recorded by the bank. (p. 7-23).

**Electronic funds transfer (EFT)**  A disbursement system that uses wire, telephone, or computers to transfer funds from one location to another. (p. 7-21).

**Fraud**  A dishonest act by an employee that results in personal benefit to the employee at a cost to the employer. (p. 7-3).

**Fraud triangle**  The three factors that contribute to fraudulent activity by employees: opportunity, financial pressure, and rationalization. (p. 7-3).

**Internal auditors** Company employees who continuously evaluate the effectiveness of the company's internal control system. (p. 7-9).

**Internal control** A process designed to provide reasonable assurance regarding the achievement of company objectives related to operations, reporting, and compliance. (p. 7-4).

**NSF check** A check that is not paid by a bank because of insufficient funds in a customer's bank account. (p. 7-22).

**Outstanding checks** Checks issued and recorded by a company but not yet paid by the bank. (p. 7-24).

**Petty cash fund** A cash fund used to pay relatively small amounts. (p. 7-16).

**Restricted cash** Cash that must be used for a special purpose. (p. 7-28).

**Sarbanes-Oxley Act (SOX)** Regulations passed by Congress to try to reduce unethical corporate behavior. (p. 7-3).

**Voucher** An authorization form prepared for each payment in a voucher system. (p. 7-15).

**Voucher system** A network of approvals by authorized individuals acting independently to ensure that all disbursements by check are proper. (p. 7-15).

## Practice Multiple-Choice Questions

1. **(LO 1)** Which of the following is **not** an element of the fraud triangle?
   a. Rationalization.
   b. Financial pressure.
   c. Segregation of duties.
   d. Opportunity.

2. **(LO 1)** An organization uses internal control to enhance the accuracy and reliability of accounting records and to:
   a. safeguard assets.
   b. prevent fraud.
   c. produce correct financial statements.
   d. deter employee dishonesty.

3. **(LO 1)** Which of the following was **not** a result of the Sarbanes-Oxley Act?
   a. Companies must file financial statements with the Internal Revenue Service.
   b. All publicly traded companies must maintain adequate internal controls.
   c. The Public Company Accounting Oversight Board was created to establish auditing standards and regulate auditor activity.
   d. Corporate executives and board of directors must ensure that controls are reliable and effective, and they can be fined or imprisoned for failure to do so.

4. **(LO 1)** The principles of internal control do **not** include:
   a. establishment of responsibility.
   b. documentation procedures.
   c. management responsibility.
   d. independent internal verification.

5. **(LO 1)** Physical controls do **not** include:
   a. safes and vaults to store cash.
   b. independent bank reconciliations.
   c. locked warehouses for inventories.
   d. bank safety deposit boxes for important papers.

6. **(LO 1)** Which of the following control activities is **not** relevant when a company uses a computerized (rather than manual) accounting system?
   a. Establishment of responsibility.
   b. Segregation of duties.

   c. Independent internal verification.
   d. All of these control activities are relevant to a computerized system.

7. **(LO 2)** Permitting only designated personnel to handle cash receipts is an application of the principle of:
   a. segregation of duties.
   b. establishment of responsibility.
   c. independent internal verification.
   d. human resource controls.

8. **(LO 2)** The use of prenumbered checks in disbursing cash is an application of the principle of:
   a. establishment of responsibility.
   b. segregation of duties.
   c. physical controls.
   d. documentation procedures.

9. **(LO 2)** A company writes a check to replenish a $100 petty cash fund when the fund contains receipts of $94 and $4 in cash. In recording the replenishment, the company should:
   a. debit Cash Over and Short for $2.
   b. debit Petty Cash for $94.
   c. credit Cash for $94.
   d. credit Petty Cash for $2.

10. **(LO 3)** The control features of a bank account do **not** include:
   a. having bank auditors verify the correctness of the bank balance per books.
   b. minimizing the amount of cash that must be kept on hand.
   c. providing a double record of all bank transactions.
   d. safeguarding cash by using a bank as a depository.

11. **(LO 3)** In a bank reconciliation, deposits in transit are:
   a. deducted from the book balance.
   b. added to the book balance.
   c. added to the bank balance.
   d. deducted from the bank balance.

12. **(LO 3)** The reconciling item in a bank reconciliation that will result in an adjusting entry by the depositor is:
   a. outstanding checks.   c. a bank error.
   b. deposit in transit.   d. bank service charges.

**13. (LO 4)** Which of the following items in a cash drawer at November 30 is **not** cash?

    **a.** Money orders.

    **b.** Coins and currency.

    **c.** An NSF check.

    **d.** A customer check dated November 28.

**14. (LO 4)** Which of the following statements correctly describes the reporting of cash?

    **a.** Cash cannot be combined with cash equivalents.

    **b.** Restricted cash funds may be combined with cash.

    **c.** Cash is listed first in the current assets section.

    **d.** Restricted cash funds cannot be reported as a current asset.

## Solutions

**1. c.** Segregation of duties is not an element of the fraud triangle. The other choices are fraud triangle elements.

**2. a.** Safeguarding assets is one of the purposes of using internal control. The other choices are incorrect because while internal control can help to (b) prevent fraud, (c) produce correct financial statements, and (d) deter employee dishonesty, these are not the main purposes of using it.

**3. a.** Filing financial statements with the IRS is not a result of the Sarbanes-Oxley Act (SOX); SOX focuses on the prevention or detection of fraud. The other choices are results of SOX.

**4. c.** Management responsibility is not one of the principles of internal control. The other choices are true statements.

**5. b.** Independent bank reconciliations are not a physical control. The other choices are true statements.

**6. d.** Establishment of responsibility, segregation of duties, and independent internal verification are all relevant to a computerized system.

**7. b.** Permitting only designated personnel to handle cash receipts is an application of the principle of establishment of responsibility, not (a) segregation of duties, (c) independent internal verification, or (d) human resource controls.

**8. d.** The use of prenumbered checks in disbursing cash is an application of the principle of documentation procedures, not (a) establishment of responsibility, (b) segregation of duties, or (c) physical controls.

**9. a** When the replenishment check is recorded, the company should debit Cash Over and Short for the shortage of $2 (total of the receipts plus cash in the drawer ($98) versus $100), not (b) debit Petty Cash for $94, (c) credit Cash for $94, or (d) credit Petty Cash for $2.

**10. a.** Having bank auditors verify the correctness of the bank balance per books is not one of the control features of a bank account. The other choices are true statements.

**11. c.** Deposits in transit are added to the bank balance on a bank reconciliation, not (a) deducted from the book balance, (b) added to the book balance, or (d) deducted from the bank balance.

**12. d.** Because the depositor does not know the amount of the bank service charges until the bank statement is received, an adjusting entry must be made when the statement is received. The other choices are incorrect because (a) outstanding checks do not require an adjusting entry by the depositor because the checks have already been recorded in the depositor's books, (b) deposits in transit do not require an adjusting entry by the depositor because the deposits have already been recorded in the depositor's books, and (c) bank errors do not require an adjusting entry by the depositor, but the depositor does need to inform the bank of the error so it can be corrected.

**13 c.** An NSF check should not be considered cash. The other choices are true statements.

**14. c.** Cash is listed first in the current assets section. The other choices are incorrect because (a) cash and cash equivalents can be appropriately combined when reporting cash on the balance sheet, (b) restricted cash is not to be combined with cash when reporting cash on the balance sheet, and (d) restricted funds can be reported as current assets if they will be used within one year.

## Practice Brief Exercises

**1. (LO 2)** On May 31, Tyler's petty cash fund of $200 is replenished when the fund contains $7 in cash and receipts for postage $105, freight-out $49, and miscellaneous expense $40. Prepare the journal entry to record the replenishment of the petty cash fund.

*Prepare entry to replenish a petty cash fund.*

### Solution

| 1. | May 31 | Postage Expense | 105 | |
|----|--------|-----------------|-----|---|
| | | Freight-Out | 49 | |
| | | Miscellaneous Expense | 40 | |
| | |     Cash | | 193 |
| | |     Cash Over and Short | | 1 |

**2. (LO 3)** At August 31, Saladino Company has the following bank information: cash balance per bank $5,200, outstanding checks $1,462, deposits in transit $1,211, and a bank debit memo $110. Determine the adjusted cash balance per bank at July 31.

*Prepare partial bank reconciliation.*

### Solution

| 2. | Cash balance per bank | | $5,200 |
|---|---|---|---|
| | Add: Deposits in transit | | 1,211 |
| | | | 6,411 |
| | Less: Outstanding checks | | 1,462 |
| | Adjusted cash balance per bank | | $4,949 |

*Explain the statement presentation of cash balances.*

**3. (LO 4)** Zian Company has the following cash balances: Cash in Bank $18,762, Payroll Bank Account $8,000, Petty Cash $150, and Plant Expansion Fund Cash $30,000 to be used 2 years from now. Explain how each balance should be reported on the balance sheet.

### Solution

**3.** Zian Company should report Cash in Bank, Payroll Bank Account, and Petty Cash as current assets (usually combined as one Cash amount). Plant Expansion Fund Cash should be reported as a noncurrent asset, assuming the fund is not expected to be used until 2 years from now.

---

## Practice Exercises

*Indicate whether procedure is good or weak internal control.*

**1. (LO 1, 2)** Listed below are five procedures followed by Shepherd Company.

1. Total cash receipts are compared to bank deposits daily by someone who has no other cash responsibilities.

2. Time clocks are used for recording time worked by employees.

3. Employees are required to take vacations.

4. Any member of the sales department can approve credit sales.

5. Sam Hill ships goods to customers, bills customers, and receives payment from customers.

### Instructions

Indicate whether each procedure is an example of good internal control or of weak internal control. If it is an example of good internal control, indicate which internal control principle is being followed. If it is an example of weak internal control, indicate which internal control principle is violated. Use the table below.

| Procedure | IC Good or Weak? | Related Internal Control Principle |
|---|---|---|
| 1. | | |
| 2. | | |
| 3. | | |
| 4. | | |
| 5. | | |

### Solution

| 1. | Procedure | IC Good or Weak? | Related Internal Control Principle |
|---|---|---|---|
| | 1. | Good | Independent internal verification |
| | 2. | Good | Physical controls |
| | 3. | Good | Human resource controls |
| | 4. | Weak | Establishment of responsibility |
| | 5. | Weak | Segregation of duties |

*Prepare bank reconciliation and adjusting entries.*

**2. (LO 3)** The information below relates to the Cash account in the ledger of Ansel Company for June 2022.

Balance June 1—$17,450; Cash deposited—$64,000.
Balance June 30—$17,704; Checks written—$63,746.

The June bank statement shows a balance of $16,422 on June 30 and the following memoranda.

| Credits | | Debits | |
|---|---|---|---|
| Collection of electronic funds transfer | $1,530 | NSF check: Anne Adams | $425 |
| Interest earned on checking account | 35 | Safety deposit box rent | 55 |

At June 30, deposits in transit were $4,750, and outstanding checks totaled $2,383.

**Instructions**

a. Prepare the bank reconciliation at June 30.

b. Prepare the adjusting entries at June 30, assuming (1) the NSF check was from a customer on account, and (2) no interest had been accrued on the note.

**Solution**

2. **a.**

**Ansel Company**
**Bank Reconciliation**
**June 30, 2022**

| | | |
|---|---:|---:|
| Cash balance per bank statement | | $16,422 |
| Add: Deposits in transit | | 4,750 |
| | | 21,172 |
| Less: Outstanding checks | | 2,383 |
| Adjusted cash balance per bank | | $18,789 |
| | | |
| Cash balance per books | | $17,704 |
| Add: Electronic funds transfer received | $1,530 | |
| Interest earned | 35 | 1,565 |
| | | 19,369 |
| Less: NSF check | 425 | |
| Safety deposit box rent | 55 | 480 |
| Adjusted cash balance per books | | $18,789 |

**b.**

| Date | Account | Debit | Credit |
|---|---|---:|---:|
| June 30 | Cash | 1,530 | |
| |     Accounts Receivable | | 1,530 |
| 30 | Cash | 35 | |
| |     Interest Revenue | | 35 |
| 30 | Accounts Receivable (Anne Adams) | 425 | |
| |     Cash | | 425 |
| 30 | Bank Charge Expense | 55 | |
| |     Cash | | 55 |

# Practice Problem

**(LO 3)** Trillo Company's bank statement for May 2022 shows the following selected data.

| | | | |
|---|---:|---|---:|
| Balance 5/1 | $12,650 | Balance 5/31 | $14,280 |
| Debit memorandum: | | Credit memorandum: | |
|   NSF check | 175 |   Collection of electronic funds | |
| | |     transfer | 505 |

*Prepare bank reconciliation and journalize entries.*

The cash balance per books at May 31 is $13,319. Your review of the data reveals the following.

1. The NSF check was from Hup Co., a customer.

2. Outstanding checks at May 31 total $2,410.

3. Deposits in transit at May 31 total $1,752.

4. A Trillo Company check written for $352, dated May 10, cleared the bank on May 25. The company recorded this check, which was a payment on account, for $325.

**Instructions**

a. Prepare a bank reconciliation at May 31.

b. Journalize the entries required by the reconciliation.

Solution

a.

**Trillo Company**
**Bank Reconciliation**
**May 31, 2022**

| | | |
|---|---|---:|
| Cash balance per bank statement | | $14,280 |
| Add: Deposits in transit | | 1,752 |
| | | 16,032 |
| Less: Outstanding checks | | 2,410 |
| Adjusted cash balance per bank | | $13,622 |
| | | |
| Cash balance per books | | $13,319 |
| Add: Electronic funds transfer received | | 505 |
| | | 13,824 |
| Less: NSF check | $175 | |
| Error in recording check ($352 − $325) | 27 | 202 |
| Adjusted cash balance per books | | $13,622 |

b.

| | | | | |
|---|---|---|---:|---:|
| May 31 | Cash | | 505 | |
| | Accounts Receivable | | | 505 |
| | (To record receipt of electronic funds transfer) | | | |
| 31 | Accounts Receivable | | 175 | |
| | Cash | | | 175 |
| | (To record NSF check) | | | |
| 31 | Accounts Payable | | 27 | |
| | Cash | | | 27 |
| | (To correct error in recording check) | | | |

Brief Exercises, DO IT! Exercises, Exercises, Problems, Data Analytics Activities, and many additional resources are available for practice in WileyPLUS.

## Questions

**1.** A local bank reported that it lost $150,000 as the result of an employee fraud. Ray Fairburn is not clear on what is meant by an "employee fraud." Explain the meaning of fraud to Ray and give an example of a fraud that might occur at a bank.

**2.** Fraud experts often say that there are three primary factors that contribute to employee fraud. Identify the three factors and explain what is meant by each.

**3.** Identify the five components of a good internal control system.

**4.** "Internal control is concerned only with enhancing the accuracy of the accounting records." Explain why this statement is true or false.

**5.** Discuss how the Sarbanes-Oxley Act has increased the importance of internal control to top managers of a company.

**6.** What principles of internal control apply to most businesses?

**7.** In the corner grocery store, all sales clerks make change out of one cash register drawer. Is this a violation of internal control? Why?

**8.** Branden Doyle is reviewing the principle of segregation of duties. What are the two common applications of this principle?

**9.** How do documentation procedures contribute to good internal control?

**10.** What internal control objectives are met by physical controls?

**11.** (a) Explain the control principle of independent internal verification. (b) What practices are important in applying this principle?

**12.** The management of Ortiz Company asks you, the company accountant, to explain (a) the concept of reasonable assurance in internal control and (b) the importance of the human factor in internal control.

**13.** What principle(s) of internal control is (are) involved in making daily cash counts of over-the-counter receipts?

**14.** Assume that **Kohl's** installed new electronic cash registers in its department stores. How do cash registers improve internal control over cash receipts?

15. At Lazlo Wholesale Company, two mail clerks open all mail receipts. How does this strengthen internal control?

16. "To have maximum effective internal control over cash disbursements, all payments should be made by check." Explain why this statement is true or false.

17. Pauli Company's internal controls over cash disbursements provide for the treasurer to sign checks imprinted by a checkwriter after comparing the check with the approved invoice. Identify the internal control principles that are present in these controls.

18. Explain how these principles apply to cash disbursements: (a) physical controls, and (b) human resource controls.

19. (a) What is a voucher system? (b) What principles of internal control apply to a voucher system?

20. What is the essential feature of an electronic funds transfer (EFT) procedure?

21. (a) Identify the three activities that pertain to a petty cash fund, and indicate an internal control principle that is applicable to each activity. (b) When are journal entries required in the operation of a petty cash fund?

22. "The use of a bank contributes significantly to good internal control over cash." Explain why this statement is true or false.

23. Hank Cook is confused about the lack of agreement between the cash balance per books and the balance per bank. Explain the causes for the lack of agreement to Hank, and give an example of each cause.

24. Trisha Massey asks for your help concerning an NSF check. Explain to Trisha (a) what an NSF check is, (b) how it is treated in a bank reconciliation, and (c) whether it will require an adjusting entry.

25. a. Describe cash equivalents and explain how they are reported.

   b. How should restricted cash funds be reported on the balance sheet?

26. Robbins Inc. owns the following assets at the balance sheet date.

| | |
|---|---|
| Cash in bank—savings account | $ 8,000 |
| Cash on hand | 1,100 |
| Cash refund due from the IRS | 1,000 |
| Checking account balance | 12,000 |

What amount should be reported as Cash in the balance sheet?

27. What was **Apple**'s balance in cash and cash equivalents at September 29, 2018? Did it report any restricted cash? How did Apple define cash equivalents?

## Brief Exercises

**BE7.1 (LO 1), C** Match each situation with the fraud triangle factor—opportunity, financial pressure, or rationalization—that best describes it.

*Identify fraud triangle concepts.*

a. An employee's monthly credit card payments are nearly 75% of his or her monthly earnings.

b. An employee earns minimum wage at a firm that has reported record earnings for each of the last five years.

c. An employee has an expensive gambling habit.

d. An employee has check-writing and check-signing responsibilities for a small company, as well as reconciling the bank account.

**BE7.2 (LO 1), C** Shelly Eckert has prepared the following list of statements about internal control.

*Identify internal control objectives.*

a. One of the objectives of internal control is to safeguard assets from employee theft, robbery, and unauthorized use.

b. One of the objectives of internal control is to enhance the accuracy and reliability of the accounting records.

c. No laws require U.S. corporations to maintain an adequate system of internal control.

Identify each statement as true or false. If false, indicate how to correct the statement.

**BE7.3 (LO 1), C** Pat Buhn is the new owner of Young Co. She has heard about internal control but is not clear about its importance for her business. Explain to Pat the four purposes of internal control and give her one application of each purpose for Young Co.

*Explain the importance of internal control.*

**BE7.4 (LO 1), C** The internal control procedures in Dayton Company result in the following situations. Identify the principles of internal control that are being followed in each case.

*Identify internal control principles.*

a. Employees who have physical custody of assets do not have access to the accounting records.

b. Each month, the assets on hand are compared to the accounting records by an internal auditor.

c. A prenumbered shipping document is prepared for each shipment of goods to customers.

**BE7.5 (LO 2), C** Jolson Company has the following internal control procedures over cash receipts. Identify the internal control principle that is applicable to each procedure.

*Identify the internal control principles applicable to cash receipts.*

a. All over-the-counter receipts are entered in cash registers.

b. All cashiers are bonded.

    **c.** Daily cash counts are made by cashier department supervisors.

    **d.** The duties of receiving cash, recording cash, and custody of cash are assigned to different individuals.

    **e.** Only cashiers may operate cash registers.

*Make journal entries for cash overage and shortfall.*

**BE7.6 (LO 2), AP** The cash register tape for Bluestem Industries reported sales of $6,871.50. Record the journal entry that would be necessary for each of the following situations. (a) Sales per cash register tape exceeds cash on hand by $50.75. (b) Cash on hand exceeds cash reported by cash register tape by $28.32.

*Make journal entry using cash count sheet.*

**BE7.7 (LO 2), AP** While examining cash receipts information, the accounting department determined the following information: cash on hand $1,125.74 and cash sales per register tape $988.62. Prepare the required journal entry.

*Identify the internal control principles applicable to cash disbursements.*

**BE7.8 (LO 2), C** Tott Company has the following internal control procedures over cash disbursements. Identify the internal control principle that is applicable to each procedure.

    **a.** Company checks are prenumbered.

    **b.** The bank statement is reconciled monthly by an internal auditor.

    **c.** Blank checks are stored in a safe in the treasurer's office.

    **d.** Only the treasurer or assistant treasurer may sign checks.

    **e.** Check-signers are not allowed to record cash disbursement transactions.

*Prepare entry to replenish a petty cash fund.*

**BE7.9 (LO 2), AP** On March 20, Harbor's petty cash fund of $100 is replenished when the fund contains $19 in cash and receipts for postage $40, supplies $26, and travel expense $15. Prepare the journal entry to record the replenishment of the petty cash fund.

*Identify the control features of a bank account.*

**BE7.10 (LO 3), C** Luke Roye is uncertain about the control features of a bank account. Explain the control benefits of (a) a check and (b) a bank statement.

*Indicate location of reconciling items in a bank reconciliation.*

**BE7.11 (LO 3), C** The following reconciling items are applicable to the bank reconciliation for Forde Co. Indicate how each item should be shown on a bank reconciliation.

    **a.** Outstanding checks.

    **b.** Bank debit memorandum for service charge.

    **c.** Bank credit memorandum for collecting an electronic funds transfer.

    **d.** Deposits in transit.

*Identify reconciling items that require adjusting entries.*

**BE7.12 (LO 3), C** The following reconciling items are applicable to the bank reconciliation for Forde Co. Indicate (1) the items that will result in an adjustment to the depositor's records and (2) why the other items do not require adjustment.

    **a.** Outstanding checks.

    **b.** Bank debit memorandum for service charge.

    **c.** Bank credit memorandum for collecting an electronic funds transfer.

    **d.** Deposits in transit.

*Prepare partial bank reconciliation.*

**BE7.13 (LO 3), AP** At July 31, Planter Company has this bank information: cash balance per bank $7,291, outstanding checks $762, deposits in transit $1,350, and a bank service charge $40. Determine the adjusted cash balance per bank at July 31.

*Prepare partial bank reconciliation.*

**BE7.14 (LO 3), AP** At August 31, Pratt Company has a cash balance per books of $9,500 and the following additional data from the bank statement: charge for printing Pratt Company checks $35 and interest earned on checking account balance $40. In addition, Pratt Company has outstanding checks of $800. Determine the adjusted cash balance per books at August 31.

*Compute outstanding checks.*

**BE7.15 (LO 3), AN** In the month of November, Fiesta Company Inc. wrote checks in the amount of $9,750. In December, checks in the amount of $11,762 were written. In November, $8,800 of these checks were presented to the bank for payment, and $10,889 in December. There were no outstanding checks at the beginning of November. What is the amount of outstanding checks at the end of November? At the end of December?

*Explain the statement presentation of cash balances.*

**BE7.16 (LO 4), C** Spahn Company has the following cash balances: Cash in Bank $12,742, Payroll Bank Account $6,000, and Plant Expansion Fund Cash $25,000 to be used two years from now. Explain how each balance should be reported on the balance sheet.

## DO IT! Exercises

**DO IT! 7.1 (LO 1), C** Identify which control activity is violated in each of the following situations, and explain how the situation creates an opportunity for fraud or inappropriate accounting practices.

1. Once a month, the sales department sends sales invoices to the accounting department to be recorded.

2. Steve Nicoles orders merchandise for Birn Company; he also receives merchandise and authorizes payment for merchandise.

3. Several clerks at Draper's Groceries use the same cash register drawer.

*Identify violations of control activities.*

**DO IT! 7.2a (LO 2), C** Wes Unsel is concerned with control over mail receipts at Wooden Sporting Goods. All mail receipts are opened by Mel Blount. Mel sends the checks to the accounting department, where they are stamped "For Deposit Only." The accounting department records and deposits the mail receipts weekly. Wes asks for your help in establishing a good system of internal control over mail receipts.

*Design system of internal control over cash receipts.*

**DO IT! 7.2b (LO 2), AP** Wilkinson Company established a $100 petty cash fund on August 1. On August 31, the fund had $7 cash remaining and petty cash receipts for postage $31, office supplies $42, and miscellaneous expense $16. Prepare journal entries to establish the fund on August 1 and replenish the fund on August 31.

*Make journal entries for petty cash fund.*

**DO IT! 7.3 (LO 3), C** Ned Douglas owns Ned's Blankets. He asks you to explain how he should treat the following reconciling items when reconciling the company's bank account.

1. Outstanding checks.

2. A deposit in transit.

3. The bank charged to the company account a check written by another company.

4. A debit memorandum for a bank service charge.

*Explain treatment of items in bank reconciliation.*

**DO IT! 7.4 (LO 4), C** Indicate whether each of the following statements is true or false. If false, indicate how to correct the statement.

1. A company has the following assets at the end of the year: cash on hand $40,000, cash refund due from supplier $30,000, and checking account balance $22,000. Cash and cash equivalents is therefore $62,000.

2. A company that has received NSF checks should report these checks as a current liability on the balance sheet.

3. Restricted cash that is a current asset is reported as part of cash and cash equivalents.

4. A company has cash in the bank of $50,000, petty cash of $400, and stock investments of $100,000. Total cash and cash equivalents is therefore $50,400.

*Analyze statements about the reporting of cash.*

## Exercises

**E7.1 (LO 1), C** Ricci's Pizza operates strictly on a carryout basis. Customers pick up their orders at a counter where a clerk exchanges the pizza for cash. While at the counter, the customer can see other employees making the pizzas and the large ovens in which the pizzas are baked.

*Identify the principles of internal control.*

**Instructions**

Identify the six principles of internal control and give an example of each principle that you might observe when picking up your pizza. (*Note:* It may not be possible to observe all the principles.)

**E7.2 (LO 1, 2), E** The following control procedures are used at Torres Company for over-the-counter cash receipts.

*Identify internal control weaknesses over cash receipts and suggest improvements.*

1. To minimize the risk of robbery, cash in excess of $100 is stored in an unlocked briefcase in the stockroom until it is deposited in the bank.

2. All over-the-counter receipts are processed by three clerks who use a cash register with a single cash drawer.

3. The company accountant makes the bank deposit and then records the day's receipts.

4. At the end of each day, the total receipts are counted by the cashier on duty and reconciled to the cash register total.

5. Cashiers are experienced; they are not bonded.

**Instructions**

a. For each procedure, explain the weakness in internal control, and identify the control principle that is violated.

b. For each weakness, suggest a change in procedure that will result in good internal control.

*Identify internal control weaknesses over cash disbursements and suggest improvements.*

**E7.3 (LO 1, 2), E** The following control procedures are used in Bunny's Boutique Shoppe for cash disbursements.

1. Company checks are stored in an unmarked envelope on a shelf behind the cash register.

2. The store manager personally approves all payments before she signs and issues checks.

3. The store purchases used goods for resale from people that bring items to the store. Since that can occur anytime that the store is open, all employees are authorized to purchase goods for resale by disbursing cash from the register. The purchase is documented by having the store employee write on a piece of paper a description of the item that was purchased and the amount that was paid. The employee then signs the paper and puts it in the register.

4. After payment, bills are "filed" in a paid invoice folder.

5. The company accountant prepares the bank reconciliation and reports any discrepancies to the owner.

**Instructions**

a. For each procedure, explain the weakness in internal control and identify the internal control principle that is violated.

b. For each weakness, suggest a change in the procedure that will result in good internal control.

*Identify internal control weaknesses for cash disbursements and suggest improvements.*

**E7.4 (LO 2), E** At Martinez Company, checks are not prenumbered because both the purchasing agent and the treasurer are authorized to issue checks. Each signer has access to unissued checks kept in an unlocked file cabinet. The purchasing agent pays all bills pertaining to goods purchased for resale. Prior to payment, the purchasing agent determines that the goods have been received and verifies the mathematical accuracy of the vendor's invoice. After payment, the invoice is filed by vendor name and the purchasing agent records the payment in the cash disbursements journal. The treasurer pays all other bills following approval by authorized employees. After payment, the treasurer stamps all bills "paid," files them by payment date, and records the checks in the cash disbursements journal. Martinez Company maintains one checking account that is reconciled by the treasurer.

**Instructions**

a. List the weaknesses in internal control over cash disbursements.

b. Identify improvements for correcting these weaknesses.

*Indicate whether procedure is good or weak internal control.*

**E7.5 (LO 1, 2), C** Consider the following five procedures followed by Eikenberry Company.

1. Several individuals operate the cash register using the same register drawer.

2. A monthly bank reconciliation is prepared by someone who has no other cash responsibilities.

3. Joe Cockrell writes checks and also records cash payment entries.

4. One individual orders inventory, while a different individual authorizes payments.

5. Unnumbered sales invoices from credit sales are forwarded to the accounting department every four weeks for recording.

**Instructions**

Indicate whether each procedure is an example of good internal control or of weak internal control. If it is an example of good internal control, indicate which internal control principle is being followed. If it is an example of weak internal control, indicate which internal control principle is violated. Use the table below.

| Procedure | IC Good or Weak? | Related Internal Control Principle |
|---|---|---|
| 1. | | |
| 2. | | |
| 3. | | |
| 4. | | |
| 5. | | |

**E7.6 (LO 1, 2), C** The following are five procedures followed by Gilmore Company.

1. Employees are required to take vacations.

2. Any member of the sales department can approve credit sales.

3. Paul Jaggard ships goods to customers, bills customers, and receives payment from customers.

4. Total cash receipts are compared to bank deposits daily by someone who has no other cash responsibilities.

5. Time clocks are used for recording time worked by employees.

*Indicate whether procedure is good or weak internal control.*

**Instructions**

Indicate whether each procedure is an example of good internal control or of weak internal control. If it is an example of good internal control, indicate which internal control principle is being followed. If it is an example of weak internal control, indicate which internal control principle is violated. Use the table below.

| Procedure | IC Good or Weak? | Related Internal Control Principle |
|---|---|---|
| 1. | | |
| 2. | | |
| 3. | | |
| 4. | | |
| 5. | | |

**E7.7 (LO 2), AP** Setterstrom Company established a petty cash fund on May 1 for $100. The company reimbursed the fund on June 1 and July 1 with the following results.

*Prepare journal entries for a petty cash fund.*

June 1: Cash in fund $1.75. Receipts: delivery expense $31.25, postage expense $39.00, and miscellaneous expense $25.00.

July 1: Cash in fund $3.25. Receipts: delivery expense $21.00, entertainment expense $51.00, and miscellaneous expense $24.75.

On July 10, Setterstrom increased the fund from $100 to $130.

**Instructions**

Prepare journal entries for Setterstrom Company for May 1, June 1, July 1, and July 10.

**E7.8 (LO 2), AP** Horvath Company uses an imprest petty cash system. The fund was established on March 1 with a balance of $100. During March, the following petty cash receipts were found in the petty cash box.

*Prepare journal entries for a petty cash fund.*

| Date | Receipt No. | For | Amount |
|---|---|---|---|
| 3/5 | 1 | Stamps | $39 |
| 7 | 2 | Freight-Out | 21 |
| 9 | 3 | Miscellaneous Expense | 6 |
| 11 | 4 | Travel Expense | 24 |
| 14 | 5 | Miscellaneous Expense | 5 |

The fund was replenished on March 15 when the fund contained $2 in cash. On March 20, the fund was increased to $175.

**Instructions**

Journalize the entries in March that pertain to the operation of the petty cash fund.

**E7.9 (LO 3), AN** Rachel Sells is unable to reconcile the bank balance at January 31. Rachel's reconciliation is shown here.

*Prepare bank reconciliation and adjusting entries.*

| | |
|---|---|
| Cash balance per bank | $3,677.20 |
| Add: NSF check | 450.00 |
| Less: Bank service charge | 28.00 |
| Adjusted balance per bank | $4,099.20 |
| | |
| Cash balance per books | $3,975.20 |
| Less: Deposits in transit | 590.00 |
| Add: Outstanding checks | 770.00 |
| Adjusted balance per books | $4,155.20 |

**Instructions**

a. What is the proper adjusted cash balance per bank?

b. What is the proper adjusted cash balance per books?

c. Prepare the adjusting journal entries necessary to determine the adjusted cash balance per books.

*Determine outstanding checks.*

**E7.10 (LO 3), AP** At April 30, the bank reconciliation of Back 40 Company shows three outstanding checks: No. 254 $650, No. 255 $700, and No. 257 $410. The May bank statement and the May cash disbursements journal are given here.

| Bank Statement Checks Paid | | | | Cash Disbursements Journal Checks Issued | | |
|---|---|---|---|---|---|---|
| Date | Check No. | Amount | | Date | Check No. | Amount |
| 5-4 | 254 | $650 | | 5-2 | 258 | $159 |
| 5-2 | 257 | 410 | | 5-5 | 259 | 275 |
| 5-17 | 258 | 159 | | 5-10 | 260 | 925 |
| 5-12 | 259 | 275 | | 5-15 | 261 | 500 |
| 5-20 | 260 | 925 | | 5-22 | 262 | 750 |
| 5-29 | 263 | 480 | | 5-24 | 263 | 480 |
| 5-30 | 262 | 750 | | 5-29 | 264 | 360 |

### Instructions

Determine the outstanding checks at May 31.

*Prepare bank reconciliation and adjusting entries.*

**E7.11 (LO 3), AP** The following information pertains to Lance Company.

1. Cash balance per bank, July 31, $8,732.
2. July bank service charge not recorded by the depositor $45.
3. Cash balance per books, July 31, $8,768.
4. Deposits in transit, July 31, $3,500.
5. $2,023 collected from a customer for Lance Company in July by the bank through electronic funds transfer. The collection has not been recorded by Lance Company.
6. Outstanding checks, July 31, $1,486.

### Instructions

a. Prepare a bank reconciliation at July 31, 2022.
b. Journalize the adjusting entries at July 31 on the books of Lance Company.

*Prepare bank reconciliation and adjusting entries.*

**E7.12 (LO 3), AP** This information relates to the Cash account in the ledger of Howard Company.

Balance September 1—$16,400; Cash deposited—$64,000
Balance September 30—$17,600; Checks written—$62,800

The September bank statement shows a balance of $16,500 at September 30 and the following memoranda.

| Credits | | Debits | |
|---|---|---|---|
| Collection from customer of electronic funds transfer | $1,830 | NSF check: H. Kane | $560 |
| Interest earned on checking account | 45 | Safety deposit box rent | 60 |

At September 30, deposits in transit were $4,738 and outstanding checks totaled $2,383.

### Instructions

a. Prepare the bank reconciliation at September 30, 2022.
b. Prepare the adjusting entries at September 30, assuming the NSF check was from a customer on account.

*Compute deposits in transit and outstanding checks for two bank reconciliations.*

**E7.13 (LO 3), AN** The cash records of Upton Company show the following.

For July:

1. The June 30 bank reconciliation indicated that deposits in transit total $580. During July, the general ledger account Cash shows deposits of $16,900, but the bank statement indicates that only $15,600 in deposits were received during the month.
2. The June 30 bank reconciliation also reported outstanding checks of $940. During the month of July, Upton Company's books show that $17,500 of checks were issued, yet the bank statement shows that $16,400 of checks cleared the bank in July.

For September:

3. In September, deposits per the bank statement totaled $25,900, deposits per the books were $26,400, and deposits in transit at September 30 were $2,200.

4. In September, cash disbursements per the books were $23,500, checks clearing the bank were $24,000, and outstanding checks at September 30 were $2,100.

There were no bank debit or credit memoranda, and no errors were made by either the bank or Upton Company.

**Instructions**

Answer the following questions.

a. In situation 1, what were the deposits in transit at July 31?

b. In situation 2, what were the outstanding checks at July 31?

c. In situation 3, what were the deposits in transit at August 31?

d. In situation 4, what were the outstanding checks at August 31?

**E7.14 (LO 4), AP** Wynn Company has recorded the following items in its financial records.

| | |
|---|---|
| Cash in bank | $ 42,000 |
| Cash in plant expansion fund | 100,000 |
| Cash on hand | 12,000 |
| Highly liquid investments | 34,000 |
| Petty cash | 500 |
| Receivables from customers | 89,000 |
| Stock investments | 61,000 |

*Show presentation of cash in financial statements.*

The highly liquid investments had maturities of 3 months or less when they were purchased. The stock investments will be sold in the next 6 to 12 months. The plant expansion project will begin in 3 years.

**Instructions**

a. What amount should Wynn report as "Cash and cash equivalents" on its balance sheet?

b. Where should the items not included in part (a) be reported on the balance sheet?

**E7.15 (LO 4), AP** A new accountant at Wyne Inc. is trying to identify which of the amounts shown below should be reported as the current asset "Cash and cash equivalents" in the year-end balance sheet, as of April 30, 2022.

*Identify reporting of cash.*

1. $60 of currency and coin in a locked box used for incidental cash transactions.

2. A $10,000 U.S. Treasury bill, due May 31, 2022.

3. $260 of checks that Wyne has received from customers but not yet deposited.

4. $2,500 in the company's checking account.

5. $4,800 in its savings account.

6. $75 of prepaid postage in its postage meter.

7. A $25 IOU from the company receptionist.

**Instructions**

a. What amount should Wyne report for "Cash and cash equivalents" at April 30, 2022?

b. In what account(s) and in what financial statement(s) should the items not included in "Cash and cash equivalents" be reported?

# Problems

**P7.1 (LO 1, 2), C** Bolz Office Supply Company recently changed its system of internal control over cash disbursements. The system includes the following features.

*Identify internal control principles applicable to cash disbursements.*

Instead of being unnumbered and manually prepared, all checks must now be prenumbered and prepared by using the new accounts payable software purchased by the company. Before a check can be issued, each invoice must have the approval of Kathy Moon, the purchasing agent, and Robin Self, the receiving department supervisor. Checks must be signed by either Jennifer Edwards, the treasurer, or Rich Woodruff, the assistant treasurer. Before signing a check, the signer is expected to compare the amount of the check with the amount on the invoice.

After signing a check, the signer stamps the invoice PAID and inserts (within the stamp) the date, check number, and amount of the check. The "paid" invoice is then sent to the accounting department for recording.

Blank checks are stored in a safe in the treasurer's office. The combination to the safe is known only by the treasurer and assistant treasurer. Each month, the bank statement is reconciled with the general ledger cash balance by the assistant chief accountant. All employees who handle or account for cash are bonded.

## Instructions

Identify the internal control principles and their application to cash disbursements of Bolz Office Supply Company.

*Identify internal control weaknesses in cash receipts and cash disbursements.*

**P7.2 (LO 1, 2), E** Blue Bayou Middle School wants to raise money for a new sound system for its auditorium. The primary fundraising event is a dance at which the famous disc jockey Kray Zee will play classic and not-so-classic dance tunes. Grant Hill, the music and theater instructor, has been given the responsibility for coordinating the fundraising efforts. This is Grant's first experience with fundraising. He decides to put the eighth-grade choir in charge of the event; he will be a relatively passive observer.

Grant had 500 unnumbered tickets printed for the dance. He left the tickets in a box on his desk and told the choir students to take as many tickets as they thought they could sell for $5 each. In order to ensure that no extra tickets would be floating around, he told them to dispose of any unsold tickets. When the students received payment for the tickets, they were to bring the cash back to Grant and he would put it in a locked box in his desk drawer.

Some of the students were responsible for decorating the gymnasium for the dance. Grant gave each of them a key to the money box and told them that if they took money out to purchase materials, they should put a note in the box saying how much they took and what it was used for. After 2 weeks, the money box appeared to be getting full, so Grant asked Lynn Dandi to count the money, prepare a deposit slip, and deposit the money in a bank account Grant had opened.

The day of the dance, Grant wrote a check from the account to pay Kray Zee. The D.J. said, however, that he accepted only cash and did not give receipts. So Grant took $200 out of the cash box and gave it to the D.J. At the dance, Grant had Dana Uhler working at the entrance to the gymnasium, collecting tickets from students, and selling tickets to those who had not prepurchased them. Grant estimated that 400 students attended the dance.

The following day, Grant closed out the bank account, which had $250 in it, and gave that amount plus the $180 in the cash box to Principal Sanchez. Principal Sanchez seemed surprised that, after generating roughly $2,000 in sales, the dance netted only $430 in cash. Grant did not know how to respond.

## Instructions

Identify as many internal control weaknesses as you can in this scenario, and suggest how each could be addressed.

*Journalize and post petty cash fund transactions.*

**P7.3 (LO 2), AP** Kael Company maintains a petty cash fund for small expenditures. These transactions occurred during the month of August.

Aug.  1  Established the petty cash fund by writing a check payable to the petty cash custodian for $200.

15  Replenished the petty cash fund by writing a check for $175. On this date, the fund consisted of $25 in cash and these petty cash receipts: freight-out $74.40, entertainment expense $36, postage expense $33.70, and miscellaneous expense $27.50.

16  Increased the amount of the petty cash fund to $400 by writing a check for $200.

31  Replenished the petty cash fund by writing a check for $283. On this date, the fund consisted of $117 in cash and these petty cash receipts: postage expense $145, entertainment expense $90.60, and freight-out $46.40.

## Instructions

a. Journalize the petty cash transactions.

b. Post to the Petty Cash account.

c. What internal control features exist in a petty cash fund?

**P7.4 (LO 3), AP** On July 31, 2022, Keeds Company had a cash balance per books of $6,140. The statement from Dakota State Bank on that date showed a balance of $7,690.80. A comparison of the bank statement with the Cash account revealed the following facts.

*Prepare a bank reconciliation and adjusting entries.*

1. The bank service charge for July was $25.

2. The bank collected $1,520 for Keeds Company through electronic funds transfer.

3. The July 31 cash receipts of $1,193.30 were not included in the bank statement for July. These receipts were deposited by the company in a night deposit vault on July 31.

4. Company check No. 2480 issued to L. Taylor, a creditor, for $384 that cleared the bank in July was incorrectly recorded as a cash payment on July 10 for $348.

5. Checks outstanding on July 31 totaled $1,860.10.

6. On July 31, the bank statement showed an NSF charge of $575 for a check received by the company from W. Krueger, a customer, on account.

### Instructions

a. Prepare the bank reconciliation as of July 31.

b. Prepare the necessary adjusting entries at July 31.

a. Adjusted cash bal. $7,024.00

**P7.5 (LO 3), AP** The bank portion of the bank reconciliation for Bogalusa Company at October 31, 2022, is as follows.

*Prepare a bank reconciliation and adjusting entries from detailed data.*

**Bogalusa Company**
**Bank Reconciliation**
**October 31, 2022**

| | | |
|---|---|---|
| Cash balance per bank | | $12,367.90 |
| Add: Deposits in transit | | 1,530.20 |
| | | 13,898.10 |
| Less: Outstanding checks | | |

| Check Number | Check Amount | |
|---|---|---|
| 2451 | $1,260.40 | |
| 2470 | 684.20 | |
| 2471 | 844.50 | |
| 2472 | 426.80 | |
| 2474 | 1,050.00 | 4,265.90 |
| Adjusted cash balance per bank | | $ 9,632.20 |

The adjusted cash balance per bank agreed with the adjusted cash balance per books at October 31. All necessary journal entries were made at the end of October. The November bank statement showed the following checks and deposits.

| Bank Statement | | | | | |
|---|---|---|---|---|---|
| Checks and Debits | | | Deposits and Credits | | |
| Date | Number | Amount | Date | Amount | |
| 11-1 | 2470 | $   684.20 | 11-1 | $ 1,530.20 | |
| 11-2 | 2471 | 844.50 | 11-4 | 1,211.60 | |
| 11-5 | 2474 | 1,050.00 | 11-8 | 990.10 | |
| 11-4 | 2475 | 1,640.70 | 11-13 | 2,575.00 | |
| 11-8 | 2476 | 2,830.00 | 11-18 | 1,472.70 | |
| 11-10 | 2477 | 600.00 | 11-19 EFT | 2,242.00 | |
| 11-15 | 2479 | 1,750.00 | 11-21 | 2,945.00 | |
| 11-18 | 2480 | 1,330.00 | 11-25 | 2,567.30 | |
| 11-27 | 2481 | 695.40 | 11-28 | 1,650.00 | |
| 11-28 | SC | 85.00 | 11-30 | 1,186.00 | |
| 11-30 | 2483 | 575.50 | Total | $18,369.90 | |
| 11-29 | 2486 | 940.00 | | | |
| | Total | $13,025.30 | | | |

The cash records per books for November showed the following.

| Cash Payments | | | | | | | Cash Receipts | |
|---|---|---|---|---|---|---|---|---|
| Date | Number | Amount | Date | Number | Amount | | Date | Amount |
| 11-1 | 2475 | $1,640.70 | 11-20 | 2483 | $    575.50 | | 11-3 | $ 1,211.60 |
| 11-2 | 2476 | 2,830.00 | 11-22 | 2484 | 829.50 | | 11-7 | 990.10 |
| 11-2 | 2477 | 600.00 | 11-23 | 2485 | 974.80 | | 11-12 | 2,575.00 |
| 11-4 | 2478 | 538.20 | 11-24 | 2486 | 940.00 | | 11-17 | 1,472.70 |
| 11-8 | 2479 | 1,705.00 | 11-29 | 2487 | 398.00 | | 11-20 | 2,954.00 |
| 11-10 | 2480 | 1,330.00 | 11-30 | 2488 | 800.00 | | 11-24 | 2,567.30 |
| 11-15 | 2481 | 695.40 | Total | | $14,469.10 | | 11-27 | 1,650.00 |
| 11-18 | 2482 | 612.00 | | | | | 11-29 | 1,186.00 |
| | | | | | | | 11-30 | 1,304.00 |
| | | | | | | | Total | $15,910.70 |

The November bank statement contained two bank memoranda:

1. A credit of $2,242 for the collection for Bogalusa Company of an electronic funds transfer.
2. A debit for the printing of additional company checks $85.

At November 30, the cash balance per books was $11,073.80 and the cash balance per the bank statement was $17,712.50. The bank did not make any errors, but **Bogalusa Company made two errors.**

### Instructions

a. Adjusted cash bal. $13,176.80

a. Prepare a bank reconciliation at November 30, 2022.

b. Prepare the adjusting entries based on the reconciliation. (*Note:* The correction of any errors pertaining to recording checks should be made to Accounts Payable. The correction of any errors relating to recording cash receipts should be made to Accounts Receivable.)

*Prepare a bank reconciliation and adjusting entries.*

**P7.6 (LO 3), AP** Timmins Company of Emporia, Kansas, spreads herbicides and applies liquid fertilizer for local farmers. On May 31, 2022, the company's Cash account per its general ledger showed a balance of $6,738.90.

The bank statement from Emporia State Bank on that date showed the following balance.

| | Emporia State Bank | |
|---|---|---|
| **Checks and Debits** | **Deposits and Credits** | **Daily Balance** |
| XXX | XXX | 5-31    6,968.00 |

A comparison of the details on the bank statement with the details in the Cash account revealed the following facts.

1. The statement included a debit memo of $40 for the printing of additional company checks.
2. Cash sales of $883.15 on May 12 were deposited in the bank. The cash receipts entry and the deposit slip were incorrectly made for $933.15. The bank credited Timmins Company for the correct amount.
3. Outstanding checks at May 31 totaled $276.25, and deposits in transit were $1,880.15.
4. On May 18, the company issued check No. 1181 for $685 to H. Moses, on account. The check, which cleared the bank in May, was incorrectly journalized and posted by Timmins Company for $658.
5. $2,690 was collected from a customer's note receivable by the bank for Timmins Company on May 31 through electronic funds transfer.
6. Included with the canceled checks was a check issued by Tomins Company to C. Pernod for $360 that was incorrectly charged to Timmins Company by the bank.
7. On May 31, the bank statement showed an NSF charge of $380 for a check issued by Sara Ballard, a customer, to Timmins Company on account.

### Instructions

a. Adjusted cash bal. $8,931.90

a. Prepare the bank reconciliation at May 31, 2022.

b. Prepare the necessary adjusting entries for Timmins Company at May 31, 2022.

*Prepare a comprehensive bank reconciliation with theft and internal control deficiencies.*

**P7.7 (LO 1, 2, 3), AN** Daisey Company is a very profitable small business. It has not, however, given much consideration to internal control. For example, in an attempt to keep clerical and office expenses to a minimum, the company has combined the jobs of cashier and bookkeeper. As a result, Bret Turrin handles all cash receipts, keeps the accounting records, and prepares the monthly bank reconciliations.

The balance per the bank statement on October 31, 2022, was $18,380. Outstanding checks were No. 62 for $140.75, No. 183 for $180, No. 284 for $253.25, No. 862 for $190.71, No. 363 for $226.80, and No. 864 for $165.28. Included with the statement was a credit memorandum of $185 indicating the collection of a note receivable for Daisey Company by the bank on October 25. This memorandum has not been recorded by Daisey.

The company's ledger showed one Cash account with a balance of $21,877.72. The balance included undeposited cash on hand. Because of the lack of internal controls, Bret took for personal use all of the undeposited receipts in excess of $3,795.51. He then prepared the following bank reconciliation in an effort to conceal his theft of cash.

| | | |
|---|---:|---:|
| Cash balance per books, October 31 | | $21,877.72 |
| Add: Outstanding checks | | |
| No. 862 | $190.71 | |
| No. 863 | 226.80 | |
| No. 864 | 165.28 | 482.79 |
| | | 22,360.51 |
| Less: Undeposited receipts | | 3,795.51 |
| Unadjusted balance per bank, October 31 | | 18,565.00 |
| Less: Bank credit memorandum | | 185.00 |
| Cash balance per bank statement, October 31 | | $18,380.00 |

**Instructions**

a. Prepare a correct bank reconciliation. (*Hint:* Deduct the amount of the theft from the adjusted balance per books.)

*a. Adjusted cash bal. $21,018.72*

b. Indicate the three ways that Bret attempted to conceal the theft and the dollar amount involved in each method.

c. What principles of internal control were violated in this case?

## Continuing Case

### Cookie Creations

(*Note:* This is a continuation of the Cookie Creations case from Chapters 1 through 6.)

**CC7 Part 1** Natalie is struggling to keep up with the recording of her accounting transactions. She is spending a lot of time marketing and selling mixers and giving her cookie classes. Her friend John is an accounting student who runs his own accounting service. He has asked Natalie if she would like to have him do her accounting. John and Natalie meet and discuss her business.

**Part 2** Natalie decides that she cannot afford to hire John to do her accounting. One way that she can ensure that her cash account does not have any errors and is accurate and up-to-date is to prepare a bank reconciliation at the end of each month. Natalie would like you to help her.

*Go to WileyPLUS for complete case details and instructions.*

leungchopan/
Shutterstock.com

## Comprehensive Accounting Cycle Review

**ACR7** On December 1, 2022, Fullerton Company had the following account balances.

| | Debit | | Credit |
|---|---:|---|---:|
| Cash | $18,200 | Accumulated Depreciation— | |
| Notes Receivable | 2,200 | Equipment | $ 3,000 |
| Accounts Receivable | 7,500 | Accounts Payable | 6,100 |
| Inventory | 16,000 | Common Stock | 50,000 |
| Prepaid Insurance | 1,600 | Retained Earnings | 14,400 |
| Equipment | 28,000 | | |
| | $73,500 | | $73,500 |

During December, the company completed the following transactions.

Dec. 7 Received $3,600 cash from customers in payment of account (no discount allowed).
12 Purchased merchandise on account from Vance Co. $12,000, terms 1/10, n/30.
17 Sold merchandise on account $16,000, terms 2/10, n/30. The cost of the merchandise sold was $10,000.
19 Paid salaries $2,200.
22 Paid Vance Co. in full, less discount.
26 Received collections in full, less discounts, from customers billed on December 17.
31 Received $2,700 cash from customers in payment of account (no discount allowed).

**Adjustment data:**

1. Depreciation was $200 per month.
2. Insurance of $400 expired in December.

**Instructions**

a. Journalize the December transactions. (Assume a perpetual inventory system.)

b. Enter the December 1 balances in the ledger T-accounts and post the December transactions. Use these additional accounts: Cost of Goods Sold, Depreciation Expense, Insurance Expense, Salaries and Wages Expense, Sales Revenue, and Sales Discounts.

c. The statement from Jackson County Bank on December 31 showed a balance of $26,130. A comparison of the bank statement with the Cash account revealed the following facts.

1. The bank collected a note receivable of $2,200 for Fullerton Company on December 15 through electronic funds transfer.

2. The December 31 receipts were deposited in a night deposit vault on December 31. These deposits were recorded by the bank in January.

3. Checks outstanding on December 31 totaled $1,210.

4. On December 31, the bank statement showed an NSF charge of $680 for a check received by the company from L. Bryan, a customer, on account.

Prepare a bank reconciliation as of December 31 based on the available information. (*Hint:* The cash balance per books is $26,100. This can be proven by finding the balance in the Cash account from parts (a) and (b).)

d. Journalize the adjusting entries resulting from the bank reconciliation and adjustment data.

e. Post the adjusting entries to the ledger T-accounts.

f. Prepare an adjusted trial balance.

g. Prepare a multiple-step income statement for December and a classified balance sheet at December 31.

# Data Analytics in Action

## Using Data Visualization to Understand Fraud

**DA7.1** Data visualization can be used to identify the occurrence of behavioral red flags.

**Example:** Recall the "Anatomy of a Fraud" examples presented in the chapter. Most people who commit fraud leave clues, called red flags, that call attention to their actions. Sometimes, more than one red flag exists. Rarely, there are none.

Many of the red flags have common characteristics and can be divided into groups. For example, consider the following chart. Do you notice that several red flags are related to finances, while other red flags appear to have social and emotional ties? Both groups are tied to the pressure component of the fraud triangle, which will lead people to consider committing fraud.

## Behavioral Red Flags that Existed in Frauds

| Behavioral Red Flag | % of Time Flag Existed |
|---|---|
| Living beyond means | 41% |
| Financial difficulties | 29% |
| Unusually close ties with vendor/customer | 20% |
| Control issues, unwillingness to share duties | 15% |
| No behavioral red flags | 15% |
| Divorce/family problems | 14% |
| "Wheeler-dealer" attitude | 13% |
| Irritability, suspiciousness, or defensiveness | 12% |
| Addiction problems | 10% |
| Complained about inadequate pay | 9% |
| Social isolation | 7% |
| Excessive pressure from within organization | 7% |
| Past employment-related problems | 6% |
| Refusal to take vacations | 6% |
| Past legal problems | 6% |
| Complained about lack of authority | 5% |
| Other | 4% |
| Excessive family/peer pressure for success | 4% |
| Instability in life circumstances | 3% |

(Y-axis label: Behavioral Red Flags; X-axis label: % of Time Flag Existed; axis scale: 0, 5, 10, 15, 20, 25, 30, 35, 40, 45%)

**Source:** *https://www.acfe.com/report-to-the-nations/2018/default.aspx.*

Unfortunately, even with 85% of incidents showing red flags (as noted in the chart, 15% of frauds indicated no red flags), much of the fraudulent activity is not identified until a loss has occurred. Nonetheless, it is important for managers to look out for red flags to help identify fraud situations as soon as possible.

For this case, you will use data that show internal controls in place and the impact on reducing the cost to the organization of the fraud. You will create a combo clustered column and line chart and then analyze it to determine which internal controls reduced the loss by the greatest percentage.

*Go to WileyPLUS for complete case details and instructions.*

### Using Data Analytics to Determine the Impact of Internal Control Activities

**DA7.2** Fraud not only costs an organization money but also time. For this case, you will use data that provides the percentage reduction of time and percent reduction of loss for various internal control activities. You will create and analyze a column chart to identify the controls that are most effective in reducing time and fraud.

 Excel

*Go to WileyPLUS for complete case details and instructions.*

## Expand Your Critical Thinking

### Financial Reporting Problem: Apple Inc.

**CT7.1** The financial statements of **Apple Inc.** are presented in Appendix A. The complete annual report, including the notes to the financial statements, is available at the company's website.

**Instructions**

a. What comments, if any, are made about cash in the "Report of the Independent Registered Public Accounting Firm"?

b. What data about cash and cash equivalents are shown in the 2017 and 2018 consolidated balance sheets?

c. In its Notes to Consolidated Financial Statements, how does Apple define cash equivalents?

d. In "Management's Annual Report on Internal Control over Financial Reporting," what does Apple's management say about internal control for 2018?

## Comparative Analysis Problem:

## PepsiCo, Inc. vs. The Coca-Cola Company

**CT7.2** **PepsiCo**'s financial statements are presented in Appendix B. Financial statements of **The Coca-Cola Company** are presented in Appendix C. The complete annual reports of PepsiCo and Coca-Cola, including the notes to the financial statements, are available at each company's respective website.

### Instructions

a. Based on the information contained in these financial statements, determine each of the following for each company:

1. Cash and cash equivalents balance for 2018.

2. Increase (decrease) in cash and cash equivalents from 2017 to 2018 per the balance sheet.

3. Net cash provided by operating activities during the year ended December 2018 (from statement of cash flows).

b. What conclusions concerning the management of cash can be drawn from these data?

## Comparative Analysis Problem:

## Amazon.com, Inc. vs. Walmart Inc.

**CT7.3** **Amazon.com, Inc.**'s financial statements are presented in Appendix D. Financial statements of **Walmart Inc.** are presented in Appendix E. The complete annual reports of Amazon and Walmart, including the notes to the financial statements, are available at each company's respective website.

### Instructions

a. Based on the information contained in these financial statements, determine each of the following for each company:

1. Cash and cash equivalents balance at December 31, 2018, for Amazon and at January 31, 2019, for Walmart.

2. Increase (decrease) in cash and cash equivalents from 2017 to 2018 per the balance sheet.

3. Net cash provided by operating activities during the year ended December 31, 2018, for Amazon and January 31, 2019, for Walmart from the statement of cash flows.

b. What conclusions concerning the management of cash can be drawn from these data?

## Real-World Focus

**CT7.4** The **Public Company Accounting Oversight Board (PCAOB)** was created as a result of the Sarbanes-Oxley Act. It has oversight and enforcement responsibilities over accounting firms in the United States.

### Instructions

Go to the PCAOB website and then answer the following questions.

a. What is the mission of the PCAOB?

b. Briefly summarize the PCAOB's responsibilities related to inspections.

c. Briefly summarize the PCAOB's responsibilities related to enforcement.

## Decision-Making Across the Organization

**CT7.5** The board of trustees of a local church is concerned about the internal accounting controls for the offering collections made at weekly services. The trustees ask you to serve on a three-person audit team with the internal auditor of a local college and a CPA who has just joined the church.

At a meeting of the audit team and the board of trustees, you learn the following.

1. The church's board of trustees has delegated responsibility for the financial management and audit of the financial records to the finance committee. This group prepares the annual budget and approves major disbursements. It is not involved in collections or recordkeeping. No audit has been made in recent years because the same trusted employee has kept church records and served as financial secretary for 15 years. The church does not carry any fidelity insurance.

2. The collection at the weekly service is taken by a team of ushers who volunteer to serve one month. The ushers take the collection plates to a basement office at the rear of the church. They hand their plates to the head usher and return to the church service. After all plates have been turned in, the head usher counts the cash received. The head usher then places the cash in the church safe along with a notation of the amount counted. The head usher volunteers to serve for 3 months.

3. The next morning, the financial secretary opens the safe and recounts the collection. The secretary withholds $150–$200 in cash, depending on the cash expenditures expected for the week, and deposits the remainder of the collections in the bank. To facilitate the deposit, church members who contribute by check are asked to make their checks payable to "Cash."

4. Each month, the financial secretary reconciles the bank statement and submits a copy of the reconciliation to the board of trustees. The reconciliations have rarely contained any bank errors and have never shown any errors per books.

### Instructions

With the class divided into groups, answer the following.

a. Indicate the weaknesses in internal accounting control over the handling of collections.

b. List the improvements in internal control procedures that you plan to make at the next meeting of the audit team for (1) the ushers, (2) the head usher, (3) the financial secretary, and (4) the finance committee.

c. What church policies should be changed to improve internal control?

## Communication Activity

**CT7.6** As a new auditor for the CPA firm of Blacke and Whyte, you have been assigned to review the internal controls over mail cash receipts of Simon Company. Your review reveals the following. Checks are promptly endorsed "For Deposit Only," but no list of the checks is prepared by the person opening the mail. The mail is opened either by the cashier or by the employee who maintains the accounts receivable records. Mail receipts are deposited in the bank weekly by the cashier.

### Instructions

Write a letter to Frank Simon, owner of Simon Company, explaining the weaknesses in internal control and your recommendations for improving the system.

## Ethics Case

**CT7.7** You are the assistant controller in charge of general ledger accounting at Linbarger Bottling Company. Your company has a large loan from an insurance company. The loan agreement requires that the company's cash account balance be maintained at $200,000 or more, as reported monthly.

At June 30, the cash balance is $80,000, which you report to Lisa Infante, the financial vice president. Lisa excitedly instructs you to keep the cash receipts book open for one additional day for purposes of the June 30 report to the insurance company. Lisa says, "If we don't get that cash balance over $200,000, we'll default on our loan agreement. They could close us down, put us all out of our jobs!" Lisa continues, "I talked to Oconto Distributors (one of Linbarger's largest customers) this morning. They said they sent us a check for $150,000 yesterday. We should receive it tomorrow. If we include just that one check in our cash balance, we'll be in the clear. It's in the mail!"

### Instructions

a. Who will suffer negative effects if you do not comply with Lisa Infante's instructions? Who will suffer if you do comply?

b. What are the ethical considerations in this case?

c. What alternatives do you have?

## All About You

**CT7.8** The print and electronic media are full of stories about potential security risks that may arise from your computer or smartphone. It is important to keep in mind, however, that there are also many other ways that your identity can be stolen. The federal government provides many resources to help protect you from identity thieves.

**Instructions**

Search the Internet for "The Case of the Cyber Criminal" found on the U.S. Federal Trade Commission's website and then complete the case.

### FASB Codification Activity

**CT7.9**  If your school has a subscription to the FASB Codification, log in and prepare responses to the following.

    **a.** How is cash defined in the Codification?

    **b.** How are cash equivalents defined in the Codification?

    **c.** What are the disclosure requirements related to cash and cash equivalents?

### Answers to Insight and Accounting Across the Organization Questions

**And the Controls Are . . .   Q:** Why is sustainability information important to investors?  **A:** Investors, customers, suppliers, and employees want more information about companies' long-term impact on society. There is a growing awareness that sustainability issues can affect a company's financial performance. Proper reporting on sustainability issues develops a solid reputation for transparency and provides confidence to shareholders.

**SOX Boosts the Role of Human Resources   Q:** Why would unsupervised employees or employees who report to each other represent potential internal control threats?  **A:** An unsupervised employee may have a fraudulent job (or may even be a fictitious person), for example, a person drawing a paycheck without working. Or, if two employees supervise each other, there is no real separation of duties, and they can conspire to defraud the company.

**How Employees Steal   Q:** How can companies reduce the likelihood of occupational fraud?  **A:** To reduce the occurrence of occupational fraud, a company should follow the procedures discussed in this chapter. For example, to reduce fraudulent disbursements, companies should require that only designated personnel sign checks, have different personnel approve payments and make payments, ensure that check-signers do not record disbursements, use prenumbered checks and match each check to an approved invoice, store blank checks securely, reconcile the bank statement, and stamp invoices PAID.

**Madoff's Ponzi Scheme   Q:** How was Madoff able to conceal such a giant fraud?  **A:** Madoff fabricated false investment statements that were provided to investors. In addition, his auditor never verified these investment statements even though the auditor issued an unqualified opinion each year.

# A Look at IFRS

> ### LEARNING OBJECTIVE 5
> Compare the accounting for fraud, internal control, and cash under GAAP and IFRS.

Fraud can occur anywhere. Because the three main factors that contribute to fraud are universal in nature, the principles of internal control activities are used globally by companies. While Sarbanes-Oxley (SOX) does not apply to non-U.S. companies, most large international companies have internal controls similar to those presented in this chapter. IFRS and GAAP are also very similar in accounting for cash. *IAS No. 1 (revised),* "Presentation of Financial Statements," is the only standard that discusses issues specifically related to cash.

## Key Points

The following are the key similarities and differences between GAAP and IFRS related to fraud, internal control, and cash.

**Similarities**

- The fraud triangle discussed in this chapter is applicable to all international companies. Some of the major frauds on an international basis are **Parmalat** (Italy), **Royal Ahold** (the Netherlands), and **Satyam Computer Services** (India).

- Rising economic crime poses a growing threat to companies, with 34% of all organizations worldwide being victims of fraud in a recent 12-month period.

- Accounting scandals both in the United States and internationally have reignited the debate over the relative merits of GAAP, which takes a "rules-based" approach to accounting, versus IFRS, which takes a "principles-based" approach. The FASB announced that it intends to introduce more principles-based standards.

- On a lighter note, at one time the Ig Nobel Prize in Economics went to the CEOs of those companies involved in the corporate accounting scandals of that year for "adapting the mathematical concept of imaginary numbers for use in the business world." A parody of the Nobel Prizes, the Ig Nobel Prizes (read Ignoble, as in not noble) are given each year in early October for 10 achievements that "first make people laugh, and then make them think." Organized by the scientific humor magazine *Annals of Improbable Research* (*AIR*), they are presented by a group that includes genuine Nobel laureates at a ceremony at Harvard University's Sanders Theater.

- Internal controls are a system of checks and balances designed to prevent and detect fraud and errors. While most companies have these systems in place, many have never completely documented them, nor had an independent auditor attest to their effectiveness. Both of these actions are required under SOX.

- Companies find that internal control review is a costly process but badly needed. One study estimates the cost of SOX compliance for U.S. companies at over $35 billion, with audit fees doubling in the first year of compliance. At the same time, examination of internal controls indicates lingering problems in the way companies operate. One study of first compliance with the internal-control testing provisions documented material weaknesses for about 13% of companies reporting in a two-year period (*PricewaterhouseCoopers' Global Economic Crime Survey*, 2005).

- The accounting and internal control procedures related to cash are essentially the same under both IFRS and this text. In addition, the definition used for cash equivalents is the same.

- Most companies report cash and cash equivalents together under IFRS, as shown in this text. In addition, IFRS follows the same accounting policies related to the reporting of restricted cash.

**Differences**

- The SOX internal control standards apply only to companies listed on U.S. exchanges. There is continuing debate over whether foreign issuers should have to comply with this extra layer of regulation.

# IFRS Practice

## IFRS Self-Test Questions

1. Non-U.S companies that follow IFRS:
   a. do not normally use the principles of internal control activities described in this text.
   b. often offset cash with accounts payable on the balance sheet.
   c. are not required to follow SOX.
   d. None of the answer choices is correct.

2. The Sarbanes-Oxley Act applies to:
   a. all U.S. companies listed on U.S. exchanges.
   b. all companies that list stock on any stock exchange in any country.
   c. all European companies listed on European exchanges.
   d. all U.S. companies listed on U.S. exchanges and all European companies listed on European exchanges.

## IFRS Exercise

**IFRS7.1** Some people argue that the internal control requirements of the Sarbanes-Oxley Act (SOX) put U.S. companies at a competitive disadvantage to companies outside the United States. Discuss the competitive implications (both pros and cons) of SOX.

## International Financial Reporting Problem: Louis Vuitton

**IFRS7.2** The financial statements of **Louis Vuitton** are presented in Appendix F. The complete consolidated financial statements, including the notes to its financial statements, are available at the company's website.

### Instructions

Using the notes to the company's 2018 consolidated financial statements, what are Louis Vuitton's accounting policies related to cash and cash equivalents?

### Answers to IFRS Self-Test Questions

**1.** c    **2.** a

arsenik/E+/Getty Images

# Accounting for Receivables

## Chapter Preview

As indicated in the following Feature Story, receivables are a significant asset for **Nike** as well as many other retail companies. Because a large portion of sales in the United States are credit sales, receivables are important to companies in other industries as well. As a consequence, companies must pay close attention to their receivables and manage them carefully. In this chapter, you will learn what journal entries companies make when they sell products, when they collect cash from those sales, and when they write off accounts they cannot collect.

## Feature Story

### What's Cooking?

What major U.S corporation got its start 38 years ago with a waffle iron? *Hint:* It doesn't sell food. *Another hint:* Swoosh. *Another hint:* "Just do it." That's right, **Nike**. In 1971, Nike co-founder Bill Bowerman put a piece of rubber into a kitchen waffle iron,

and the trademark waffle sole was born. It seems fair to say that at Nike, "They don't make 'em like they used to."

Nike was co-founded by Bowerman and Phil Knight, a member of Bowerman's University of Oregon track team. Each began in the shoe business independently during the early 1960s. Bowerman got his start by making hand-crafted running shoes for his University of Oregon track team. Knight, after completing graduate school, started a small business importing low-cost, high-quality shoes from Japan. In 1964, the two joined forces, each contributing $500, and formed Blue Ribbon Sports, a partnership that marketed Japanese shoes.

It wasn't until 1971 that the company began manufacturing its own line of shoes. With the new shoes came a new corporate name—Nike—the Greek goddess of victory. It is hard to imagine that the company that now boasts a stable full of world-class athletes as promoters at one time had part-time employees selling shoes out of car trunks at track meets on a cash-and-carry basis.

As the business grew, Nike sold its shoes to sporting good shops and department stores on a credit basis. This necessitated receivables management. Today, with sales of $20.8 billion and accounts receivable of $3.1 billion, managing accounts receivable is vitally important to Nike's success. If it makes a major mistake with its receivables, it will definitely affect the bottom line.

In recent years, Nike has expanded its product line to a diverse range of products, including performance equipment such as soccer balls and golf clubs. While this has increased sales revenue, it has also complicated Nike's receivables management efforts. Now, instead of selling shoes at a limited number of retail outlets, it sells its vast number of products to a diverse array of stores, large and small. For example, Nike golf clubs are sold at local country clubs and golf shops across the country, while soccer equipment can be sold directly to customers through Internet sales. This diversification of its customer list complicates matters because Nike has to approve each new store or customer for credit sales, monitor cash collections, and pursue slow-paying accounts. That's a lot of work. Maybe cash-and-carry wasn't so bad after all.

# Chapter Outline

| LEARNING OBJECTIVES | REVIEW | PRACTICE |
|---|---|---|
| **LO 1** Explain how companies recognize accounts receivable. | • Types of receivables<br>• Recognizing accounts receivable | **DO IT! 1** Recognizing Accounts Receivable |
| **LO 2** Describe how companies value accounts receivable and record their disposition. | • Valuing accounts receivable<br>• Disposing of accounts receivable | **DO IT! 2a** Bad Debt Expense<br>**2b** Factoring |
| **LO 3** Explain how companies recognize, value, and dispose of notes receivable. | • Determining the maturity date<br>• Computing interest<br>• Recognizing notes receivable<br>• Valuing notes receivable<br>• Disposing of notes receivable | **DO IT! 3** Recognizing Notes Receivable |
| **LO 4** Describe the statement presentation and analysis of receivables. | • Presentation<br>• Analysis<br>• Data analytics and receivables management | **DO IT! 4** Analysis of Receivables |

**Go to the Review and Practice section at the end of the chapter for a review of key concepts and practice applications with solutions.**

**Visit WileyPLUS for additional tutorials and practice opportunities.**

# Recognition of Accounts Receivable

### LEARNING OBJECTIVE 1
Explain how companies recognize accounts receivable.

The term **receivables** refers to amounts due from individuals and companies. Receivables are claims that are expected to be collected in cash. The management of receivables is a very important activity for any company that sells goods or services on credit.

Receivables are important because they represent one of a company's most liquid assets. For many companies, receivables are also one of the largest assets. For example, receivables represent 13.7% of the current assets of pharmaceutical giant **Rite Aid**. **Illustration 8.1** lists receivables as a percentage of total assets for five other well-known companies in a recent year.

| Company | Receivables as a Percentage of Total Assets |
|---|---|
| Ford Motor Company | 43.2% |
| General Electric | 41.5 |
| Minnesota Mining and Manufacturing Company (3M) | 12.7 |
| DuPont Co. | 11.7 |
| Intel Corporation | 3.9 |

**ILLUSTRATION 8.1**
Receivables as a percentage of assets

## Types of Receivables

The relative significance of a company's receivables as a percentage of its assets depends on various factors: its industry, the time of year, whether it extends long-term financing, and its credit policies. To reflect important differences among receivables, they are frequently classified as (1) accounts receivable, (2) notes receivable, and (3) other receivables.

**Accounts receivable** are amounts customers owe on account. They result from the sale of goods and services. Companies generally expect to collect accounts receivable within 30 to 60 days. They are usually the most significant type of claim held by a company.

**Notes receivable** are a written promise (as evidenced by a formal instrument) for amounts to be received. The note normally requires the collection of interest and extends for time periods of 60–90 days or longer. Notes and accounts receivable that result from sales transactions are often called **trade receivables**.

**Other receivables** include nontrade receivables such as interest receivable, loans to company officers, advances to employees, and income taxes refundable. These do not generally result from the operations of the business. Therefore, they are generally classified and reported as separate items in the balance sheet (see **Ethics Note**).

**ETHICS NOTE**

Companies report receivables from employees separately in the financial statements. The reason: Sometimes these receivables are not the result of an "arm's-length" transaction.

## Recognizing Accounts Receivable

Recognizing accounts receivable is relatively straightforward. A service organization records a receivable when it performs a service on account. A merchandiser records accounts receivable at the point of sale of merchandise on account. When a merchandiser sells goods, it increases (debits) Accounts Receivable and increases (credits) Sales Revenue.

Recall that sellers sometimes offer sales discounts to encourage early payment by the buyer. If the buyer pays during the discount period, the receivable balance will be satisfied with a smaller cash payment. Also, the buyer might find some of the goods unacceptable and choose to return the unwanted goods. When a buyer returns goods that it previously purchased on credit, the receivable balance is reduced.

To review, assume that Jordache Co. on July 1, 2022, sells merchandise on account to Polo Company for $1,000, terms 2/10, n/30. On July 5, Polo returns merchandise with a sales price of $100 to Jordache Co. On July 11, Jordache receives payment from Polo Company for the balance due. The journal entries to record these transactions on the books of Jordache Co. are as follows (see **Helpful Hint**). **(Cost of goods sold entries are omitted.)**

**HELPFUL HINT**

These entries are the same as those described in Chapter 5. For simplicity, we have omitted inventory and cost of goods sold from this set of journal entries and from end-of-chapter material.

| July 1 | Accounts Receivable | 1,000 | |
| | Sales Revenue | | 1,000 |
| | (To record sales on account) | | |
| July 5 | Sales Returns and Allowances | 100 | |
| | Accounts Receivable | | 100 |
| | (To record merchandise returned) | | |
| July 11 | Cash ($900 − $18) | 882 | |
| | Sales Discounts ($900 × .02) | 18 | |
| | Accounts Receivable | | 900 |
| | (To record collection of accounts receivable) | | |

Some retailers issue their own credit cards. When you use a retailer's credit card (**JCPenney**, for example), the retailer charges interest on the balance due if not paid within a specified period (usually 25–30 days).

To illustrate, assume that you use your JCPenney credit card to purchase clothing with a sales price of $300 on June 1, 2022. JCPenney will increase (debit) Accounts Receivable for $300 and increase (credit) Sales Revenue for $300 (cost of goods sold entry omitted) as follows.

Cash Flows
no effect

| June 1 | Accounts Receivable | 300 | |
| | Sales Revenue | | 300 |
| | (To record sale of merchandise) | | |

Assuming that you owe $300 at the end of the month and JCPenney charges 1.5% per month on the balance due, the adjusting entry that JCPenney makes to record interest revenue of $4.50 ($300 × 1.5%) on June 30 is as follows.

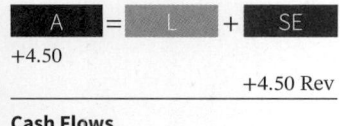

Cash Flows
no effect

| June 30 | Accounts Receivable | 4.50 | |
| | Interest Revenue | | 4.50 |
| | (To record interest on amount due) | | |

Interest revenue is often substantial for many retailers.

## Anatomy of a Fraud

Tasanee was the accounts receivable clerk for a large nonprofit foundation that provided performance and exhibition space for the performing and visual arts. Her responsibilities included activities normally assigned to an accounts receivable clerk, such as recording revenues from various sources (donations, facility rental fees, ticket revenue, and bar receipts). However, she was also responsible for handling all cash and checks from the time they were received until the time she deposited them, as well as preparing the bank reconciliation. Tasanee took advantage of her situation by falsifying bank deposits and bank reconciliations so that she could steal cash from the bar receipts. Since nobody else logged the donations or matched the donation receipts to pledges prior to Tasanee receiving them, she was able to offset the cash that was stolen against donations that she received but didn't record. Her crime was made easier by the fact that her boss, the company's controller, only did a very superficial review of the bank reconciliation

and thus didn't notice that some numbers had been cut out from other documents and taped onto the bank reconciliation.

**Total take: $1.5 million**

**The Missing Controls**

**Segregation of duties.** The foundation should not have allowed an accounts receivable clerk, whose job was to record receivables, to also handle cash, record cash, make deposits, and especially prepare the bank reconciliation.

**Independent internal verification.** The controller was supposed to perform a thorough review of the bank reconciliation. Because he did not, he was terminated from his position.

**Source:** Adapted from Wells, *Fraud Casebook* (2007), pp. 183–194.

## DO IT! 1 | Recognizing Accounts Receivable

**ACTION PLAN**
- Prepare entry to record the receivable and related return.
- Compute the sales discount and related entry.

On May 1, Wilton sold merchandise on account to Bates for $50,000 terms 3/15, n/45. On May 4, Bates returns merchandise with a sales price of $2,000. On May 14, Wilton receives payment from Bates for the balance due. Prepare journal entries to record the May transactions on Wilton's books. (You may ignore cost of goods sold entries and explanations.)

### Solution

| | | | |
|---|---|---|---|
| May 1 | Accounts Receivable | 50,000 | |
| |     Sales Revenue | | 50,000 |
| 4 | Sales Returns and Allowances | 2,000 | |
| |     Accounts Receivable | | 2,000 |
| 14 | Cash ($48,000 − $1,440) | 46,560 | |
| | Sales Discounts ($48,000 × .03) | 1,440 | |
| |     Accounts Receivable | | 48,000 |

Related exercise material: BE8.1, BE8.2, DO IT! 8.1, E8.1, E8.2, and E8.3.

# Valuation and Disposition of Accounts Receivable

### LEARNING OBJECTIVE 2

Describe how companies value accounts receivable and record their disposition.

## Valuing Accounts Receivable

Once companies record receivables in the accounts, the next question is: How should they report receivables in the financial statements? Companies report accounts receivable on the balance sheet as an asset. But determining the **amount** to report is sometimes difficult because some receivables will become uncollectible.

Each customer must satisfy the credit requirements of the seller before the credit sale is approved. Inevitably, though, some accounts receivable become uncollectible. For example, a customer may not be able to pay because of a decline in its sales revenue due to a downturn in the economy. Similarly, individuals may be laid off from their jobs or faced with unexpected hospital bills. Companies record credit losses as **Bad Debt Expense** (or Uncollectible Accounts Expense). Such losses are a normal and necessary risk of doing business on a credit basis.

When U.S. home prices fell, home foreclosures rose, and the economy in general slowed as a result of the financial crisis of 2008, lenders experienced huge increases in their bad debt expense. For example, during one quarter **Wachovia** (a large U.S. bank now owned by **Wells Fargo**) increased bad debt expense from $108 million to $408 million. Similarly, **American Express** increased its bad debt expense by 70%.

Two methods are used in accounting for uncollectible accounts: (1) the direct write-off method (not GAAP) and (2) the allowance method (GAAP). The following sections explain these methods.

### Direct Write-Off Method for Uncollectible Accounts

Under the **direct write-off method**, when a company determines a particular account to be uncollectible, it charges the loss to Bad Debt Expense. Assume, for example, that Warden Co. writes off as uncollectible M. E. Doran's $200 balance on December 12. Warden's entry is as follows.

A = L + SE

−200 Exp

−200

**Cash Flows**
no effect

| | | | | |
|---|---|---|---|---|
| Dec. 12 | Bad Debt Expense | | 200 | |
| | Accounts Receivable | | | 200 |
| | (To record write-off of M. E. Doran account) | | | |

Under this method, Bad Debt Expense will show only **actual losses** from specific customer uncollectibles. The company will report accounts receivable at its gross amount, shown in the Accounts Receivable account.

Use of the direct write-off method can reduce the relevance of both the income statement and the balance sheet. Consider the following example. In 2022, Quick Buck Computer Company decided it could increase its revenues by offering computers to college students without requiring any money down and with a no credit-approval process. On campuses across the country, it sold one million computers with a selling price of $800 each. This increased Quick Buck's revenues and receivables by $800 million. The promotion was a huge success! The 2022 balance sheet and income statement looked great. Unfortunately, during 2023, nearly 40% of the customers defaulted on their loans. This made the 2023 income statement and balance sheet look terrible. **Illustration 8.2** shows the effect of these events on the financial statements if the direct write-off method is used.

**ILLUSTRATION 8.2**

**Effects of direct write-off method**

Under the direct write-off method, companies often record bad debt expense in a period different from the period in which they record the related revenue. The method does not attempt to match bad debt expense to sales revenue in the income statement. Nor does the direct write-off method show accounts receivable in the balance sheet at the amount the company actually expects to receive in cash. **Consequently, unless uncollectibles are insignificant, the direct write-off method is not acceptable for financial reporting purposes.**

## Allowance Method for Uncollectible Accounts

The **allowance method** of accounting for uncollectibles involves estimating uncollectible accounts at the end of each period. This provides better matching of expenses with revenues on the income statement. It also ensures that companies state receivables on the balance sheet at their cash (net) realizable value. **Cash (net) realizable value** is the net amount the company expects to receive in cash. It excludes amounts that the company estimates it will not collect. Thus, this method reduces receivables in the balance sheet by the amount of estimated uncollectible receivables.

**Companies must use the allowance method for financial reporting purposes when uncollectibles are material in amount** (see **Helpful Hint**). This method has three essential features:

**HELPFUL HINT**

In this context, *material* means significant or important to financial statement users.

1. Companies **estimate** uncollectible accounts receivable. They match estimated expense **against revenues** in the same accounting period in which they record the revenues.

2. Companies debit Bad Debt Expense and credit Allowance for Doubtful Accounts through an adjusting entry at the end of each period. Allowance for Doubtful Accounts is a contra account to Accounts Receivable.

3. When companies write off a specific customer account, they debit actual uncollectibles to Allowance for Doubtful Accounts and credit that amount to Accounts Receivable.

### Recording Estimated Uncollectibles

To illustrate the allowance method, assume that Hampson Furniture has credit sales of $1,200,000 in 2022, its first year of operations. Of this amount, $200,000 of receivables remains uncollected at December 31. The credit manager estimates that $12,000 of these receivables will be uncollectible. The adjusting entry to record the estimated uncollectibles increases (debits) Bad Debt Expense and increases (credits) Allowance for Doubtful Accounts, as follows.

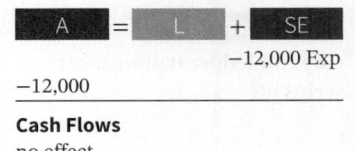

| Dec. 31 | Bad Debt Expense | 12,000 | |
| |     Allowance for Doubtful Accounts | | 12,000 |
| |        (To record estimate of uncollectible accounts) | | |

−12,000            −12,000 Exp

**Cash Flows**
no effect

Hampson reports Bad Debt Expense in the income statement as an operating expense. Thus, the estimated uncollectibles are matched with the sales revenue in 2022. Hampson records the expense in the same year it made the sales.

Allowance for Doubtful Accounts shows the estimated amount of claims on customers that the company expects will become uncollectible in the future. Companies use a contra account instead of a direct credit to Accounts Receivable because they do not know which specific customers will not pay. The credit balance in the allowance account will absorb the specific write-offs when they occur. As **Illustration 8.3** shows, the company deducts the allowance account from accounts receivable in the current assets section of the balance sheet.

| **Hampson Furniture** | | |
| **Balance Sheet (partial)** | | |
| Current assets | | |
| Cash | | $ 14,800 |
| **Accounts receivable** | $200,000 | |
| **Less: Allowance for doubtful accounts** | 12,000 | 188,000 |
| Inventory | | 310,000 |
| Supplies | | 25,000 |
| Total current assets | | $537,800 |

**ILLUSTRATION 8.3**
Presentation of allowance for doubtful accounts

The amount of $188,000 in Illustration 8.3 represents the expected **cash realizable value** of the accounts receivable at the statement date (see **Helpful Hint**). **Companies do not close Allowance for Doubtful Accounts at the end of the fiscal year as it is a permanent account.**

**HELPFUL HINT**
Cash realizable value is sometimes referred to as *accounts receivable (net).*

### Recording the Write-Off of an Uncollectible Account

Companies use various methods of collecting past-due accounts, such as letters, calls, and legal action. When they have exhausted all means of collecting a past-due account and collection appears impossible, the company writes off the account. In the credit card industry, for example, it is standard practice to write off accounts that are 210 days past due. To prevent premature or unauthorized write-offs, authorized management personnel should formally approve each write-off. **To maintain segregation of duties, the employee authorized to write off accounts should not have daily responsibilities related to cash or receivables.**

To illustrate a receivables write-off, assume that the financial vice president of Hampson Furniture authorizes a write-off of the $500 balance owed by R. A. Ware on March 1, 2023. The entry to record the write-off is as follows.

| Mar. 1 | Allowance for Doubtful Accounts | 500 | |
| |     Accounts Receivable | | 500 |
| |        (Write-off of R. A. Ware account) | | |

+500
−500

**Cash Flows**
no effect

The company does not increase Bad Debt Expense when the write-off occurs. **Under the allowance method, companies debit every specific customer write-off to Allowance for Doubtful Accounts rather than to Bad Debt Expense.** A debit to Bad Debt

Expense would be incorrect because the company has already recognized the expense when it made the adjusting entry for estimated uncollectibles. Instead, the entry to record the write-off of an uncollectible account reduces both Accounts Receivable and Allowance for Doubtful Accounts. After posting, the general ledger accounts for 2023 appear as shown in **Illustration 8.4**.

**ILLUSTRATION 8.4**

General ledger balances after write-off

| Accounts Receivable | | | | | Allowance for Doubtful Accounts | | | | |
|---|---|---|---|---|---|---|---|---|---|
| Jan. 1 Bal. | 200,000 | Mar. 1 | | **500** | Mar. 1 | | **500** | Jan. 1 Bal. | 12,000 |
| Mar. 1 Bal. | 199,500 | | | | | | | Mar. 1 Bal. | 11,500 |

A write-off affects **only balance sheet accounts**—not income statement accounts. The write-off of the account reduces both Accounts Receivable and Allowance for Doubtful Accounts. Cash realizable value in the balance sheet, therefore, remains the same, as **Illustration 8.5** shows.

**ILLUSTRATION 8.5**

Cash realizable value comparison

| | Before Write-Off | After Write-Off |
|---|---|---|
| Accounts receivable | $200,000 | $199,500 |
| Allowance for doubtful accounts | 12,000 | 11,500 |
| **Cash realizable value** | **$188,000** | **$188,000** |

### Recovery of an Uncollectible Account

Occasionally, a company collects from a customer after it has written off the account as uncollectible. The company makes two entries to record the recovery of a previously written off customer account. (1) It reverses the entry made in writing off the account. This reinstates the customer's account. (2) It journalizes the cash collection in the usual manner.

To illustrate, assume that on July 1, 2023, R. A. Ware pays the $500 amount that Hampson had written off on March 1. Hampson makes the following entries.

A = L + SE
+500
−500

**Cash Flows**
no effect

| | | | (1) | | |
|---|---|---|---|---|---|
| July 1 | Accounts Receivable | | | 500 | |
| | Allowance for Doubtful Accounts | | | | 500 |
| | (To reverse write-off of R. A. Ware account) | | | | |

A = L + SE
+500
−500

**Cash Flows**
+500

| | | | (2) | | |
|---|---|---|---|---|---|
| July 1 | Cash | | | 500 | |
| | Accounts Receivable | | | | 500 |
| | (To record collection from R. A. Ware) | | | | |

Note that the recovery of a customer account, like the write-off of a customer account, affects **only balance sheet accounts**. The net effect of the two entries above is a debit to Cash and a credit to Allowance for Doubtful Accounts for $500.

### Estimating the Allowance

For Hampson Furniture in Illustration 8.3, the amount of the expected uncollectibles was given. However, in "real life," companies must estimate the amount of expected uncollectible accounts if they use the allowance method. **Illustration 8.6** shows an excerpt from the notes to **Nike**'s financial statements discussing its use of the allowance method.

**ILLUSTRATION 8.6**
Nike's allowance method disclosure
**Real World**

### Nike, Inc.
**Notes to the Financial Statements**

*Allowance for Uncollectible Accounts Receivable*

We make ongoing estimates relating to the ability to collect our accounts receivable and maintain an allowance for estimated losses resulting from the inability of our customers to make required payments. In determining the amount of the allowance, we consider our historical level of credit losses and make judgments about the creditworthiness of significant customers based on ongoing credit evaluations. Since we cannot predict future changes in the financial stability of our customers, actual future losses from uncollectible accounts may differ from our estimates.

Frequently, companies estimate the allowance as a percentage of the outstanding receivables. Under the **percentage-of-receivables basis**, management establishes a percentage relationship between the amount of receivables and expected losses from uncollectible accounts (see **Helpful Hint**). For example, suppose Steffen Company has an ending balance in Accounts Receivable of $200,000 and an unadjusted credit balance in Allowance for Doubtful Accounts of $1,500  It estimates that 5% of its accounts receivable will eventually be uncollectible. It should report a **balance** in Allowance for Doubtful Accounts of $10,000 (.05 × $200,000)  To increase the balance in Allowance for Doubtful Accounts from its unadjusted amount of $1,500 to $10,000, the company debits (increases) Bad Debt Expense and credits (increases) Allowance for Doubtful Accounts by $8,500 ($10,000 − $1,500).

To more accurately estimate the ending balance in the allowance account, a company often prepares a schedule called **aging the accounts receivable**. This schedule classifies customer balances by the length of time they have been unpaid.

After the company arranges the accounts by age, it determines the expected uncollectible accounts by applying percentages, based on past experience, to the totals of each category. The longer a receivable is past due, the less likely it is to be collected. As a result, the estimated percentage of uncollectible accounts increases as the number of days past due increases (see **Helpful Hint**). **Illustration 8.7** shows an aging schedule for Dart Company at December 31, 2022. Note the increasing uncollectible percentages from 2% to 40%.

**HELPFUL HINT**
Where appropriate, the percentage-of-receivables basis may use only a single percentage rate.

**Allowance for Doubtful Accounts**

| | |
|---|---|
| Dec. 31 Unadj. Bal. | 1,500 |
| Dec. 31 Adj. | **8,500** |
| Dec. 31 Bal. | 10,000 |

**HELPFUL HINT**
The older categories have higher percentages because the longer an account is past due, the less likely it is to be collected.

**ILLUSTRATION 8.7**
Aging schedule

### Dart Company
### Aging Schedule
### December 31, 2022

| Customer | Total | Not Yet Due | 1–30 | 31–60 | 61–90 | Over 90 |
|---|---|---|---|---|---|---|
| T. E. Adert | $ 600 | | $ 300 | | $ 200 | $ 100 |
| R. C. Bortz | 300 | $ 300 | | | | |
| B. A. Carl | 450 | | 200 | $ 250 | | |
| O. L. Diker | 700 | 500 | | | 200 | |
| T. O. Ebbet | 600 | | | 300 | | 300 |
| Others | 36,950 | 26,200 | 5,200 | 2,450 | 1,600 | 1,500 |
| | $39,600 | $27,000 | $5,700 | $3,000 | $2,000 | $1,900 |
| Estimated percentage uncollectible | | 2% | 4% | 10% | 20% | 40% |
| Total estimated uncollectible accounts | $ 2,228 | $ 540 | $ 228 | $ 300 | $ 400 | $ 760 |

Total estimated uncollectible accounts for Dart Company ($2,228) represent the existing customer claims expected to become uncollectible in the future. Thus, this amount represents the **required balance** in Allowance for Doubtful Accounts at the balance sheet date. Accordingly, **the amount of bad debt expense that should be recorded in the adjusting entry is the difference between the required balance and the existing balance in the allowance account**. The existing, unadjusted balance in Allowance for Doubtful Accounts is the net result of the beginning balance (a normal credit balance) less the write-offs of specific accounts during the year (debits to the allowance account).

For example, if the unadjusted trial balance shows Allowance for Doubtful Accounts with a credit balance of $528, then an adjusting entry for $1,700 ($2,228 − $528) is necessary:

−1,700 Exp

−1,700

**Cash Flows**
no effect

| Dec. 31 | Bad Debt Expense | 1,700 | |
| | Allowance for Doubtful Accounts | | 1,700 |
| | (To adjust allowance account to total estimated uncollectibles) | | |

After Dart posts the adjusting entry, its accounts appear as shown in **Illustration 8.8**.

**Bad debt expense accounts after posting**

| **Bad Debt Expense** | | **Allowance for Doubtful Accounts** | |
|---|---|---|---|
| Dec. 31  Adj. **1,700** | | | Dec. 31  Unadj. |
| | | | Bal.   528 |
| | | | Dec. 31  Adj.   **1,700** |
| | | | Dec. 31  Bal.   2,228 |

An important aspect of accounts receivable management is simply maintaining a close watch on the accounts. Studies have shown that customer accounts more than 60 days past due lose approximately 50% of their value if no payment activity occurs within the next 30 days. For each additional 30 days that pass, the collectible value halves once again.

Occasionally, the allowance account will have a **debit balance** prior to adjustment. This occurs because the debits to the allowance account from write-offs during the year **exceeded** the beginning balance in the account, which was based on previous estimates for uncollectibles. In such a case, the company **adds the debit balance to the required balance** when it makes the adjusting entry. Thus, if there was a $500 **debit** balance in the allowance account before adjustment, the adjusting entry would be for $2,728 ($2,228 + $500) to arrive at an adjusted credit balance of $2,228 as shown below.

−2,728 Exp

−2,728

**Cash Flows**
no effect

| Dec. 31 | Bad Debt Expense | 2,728 | |
| | Allowance for Doubtful Accounts | | 2,728 |
| | (To adjust allowance account to total estimated uncollectibles) | | |

After Dart posts the adjusting entry, its accounts appear as shown in **Illustration 8.9**.

**Bad debt expense accounts after posting**

| **Bad Debt Expense** | | **Allowance for Doubtful Accounts** | |
|---|---|---|---|
| Dec. 31  Adj. **2,728** | | Dec. 31 Unadj. | |
| | | Bal. 500 | Dec. 31  Adj.   **2,728** |
| | | | Dec. 31  Bal.   2,228 |

The percentage-of-receivables basis provides an estimate of the cash realizable value of the receivables. The FASB now employs an expected credit loss model which requires that companies must measure expected uncollectible accounts and record bad debt expense on all receivables, even those with a low risk of loss. Companies use sophisticated models employing data analytics to arrive at accurate estimates on a timely basis.

The note in **Illustration 8.10** regarding accounts receivable comes from the annual report of the shoe company **Skechers USA**.

### Skechers USA
#### Notes to the Financial Statements

The likelihood of a material loss on an uncollectible account would be mainly dependent on deterioration in the overall economic conditions in a particular country or region. Reserves are fully provided for all probable losses of this nature. For receivables that are not specifically identified as high risk, we provide a reserve based upon our historical loss rate as a percentage of sales. Gross trade accounts receivable were $293.1 million and $241.9 million, and the allowance for bad debts, returns, sales allowances and customer chargebacks were $21.0 million and $15.9 million, at December 31, 2014 and 2013, respectively. Our credit losses charged to expense for the years ended December 31, 2014, 2013 and 2012 were $11.8 million, $2.6 million and $1.5 million, respectively. In addition, we recorded sales return and allowance expense (recoveries) for the years ended December 31, 2014, 2013 and 2012 of $2.3 million, $0.2 million and $(0.4) million, respectively.

## Ethics Insight

Christy Thompson/
Shutterstock.com

### Cookie Jar Allowances

There are many pressures on companies to achieve earnings targets. For managers, poor earnings can lead to dismissal or lack of promotion. It is thus not surprising that management may be tempted to look for ways to boost their earnings number.

One way a company can achieve greater earnings is to lower its estimate of what is needed in its Allowance for Doubtful Accounts (sometimes referred to as "tapping the cookie jar"). For example, suppose a company has an Allowance for Doubtful Accounts of $10 million and decides to reduce this balance to $9 million. As a result of this change,

Bad Debt Expense decreases by $1 million and earnings increase by $1 million.

Large banks such as **JPMorgan Chase**, **Wells Fargo**, and **Bank of America** recently decreased their Allowance for Doubtful Accounts by over $4 billion. These reductions came at a time when these big banks were still suffering from lower mortgage lending and trading activity, both of which led to lower earnings. They justified these reductions in the allowance balances by noting that credit quality and economic conditions had improved. This may be so, but it sure is great to have a cookie jar that might be tapped when a boost in earnings is needed.

**How might investors determine that a company is managing its earnings? (Answer is available near the end of the chapter.)**

## DO IT! 2a │ Bad Debt Expense

Brule Corporation has been in business for 5 years. The unadjusted trial balance at the end of the current year shows Accounts Receivable $30,000, Sales Revenue $180,000, and Allowance for Doubtful Accounts with a debit balance of $2,000. Brule estimates uncollectibles to be 10% of accounts receivable. Prepare the entry necessary to adjust Allowance for Doubtful Accounts.

### Solution

Brule should make the following entry to bring the debit balance in Allowance for Doubtful Accounts up to a normal, credit balance of $3,000 (10% × $30,000):

| | | |
|---|---|---|
| Bad Debt Expense [(10% × $30,000) + $2,000] | 5,000 | |
| Allowance for Doubtful Accounts | | 5,000 |
| (To adjust allowance account to total estimated uncollectibles) | | |

Related exercise material: **BE8.3, BE8.4, BE8.5, BE8.6, DO IT! 8.2a, E8.4, E8.5, E8.6, E8.7, and E8.8**

**ACTION PLAN**

- **Estimate the amount the company does not expect to collect.**
- **Consider the existing balance in the allowance account when using the percentage-of-receivables basis.**
- **Report receivables at their cash (net) realizable value—that is, the amount the company expects to collect in cash.**

# Disposing of Accounts Receivable

In the normal course of events, companies collect accounts receivable in cash and remove the receivables from the books. However, as credit sales and receivables have grown in significance, the "normal course of events" has changed. Companies now frequently sell their receivables to another company for cash, thereby shortening the cash-to-cash operating cycle.

Companies sell receivables for two major reasons. First, **they may be the only reasonable source of cash**. When money is tight, companies may not be able to borrow money in the usual credit markets. Or, if money is available, the cost of borrowing may be prohibitive.

A second reason for selling receivables is that **billing and collection are often time-consuming and costly**. It is often easier for a retailer to sell the receivables to another party with expertise in billing and collection matters. Credit card companies such as **MasterCard**, **Visa**, and **Discover** specialize in billing and collecting accounts receivable.

## Sale of Receivables to a Factor

A common sale of receivables is a sale to a factor. A **factor** is a finance company or bank that buys receivables from businesses and then collects the payments directly from the customers. Factoring is a multibillion dollar business.

Factoring arrangements vary widely. Typically, the factor charges a fee to the company that is selling the receivables. This fee often ranges from 1–3% of the amount of receivables purchased. To illustrate, assume that Hendredon Furniture factors $600,000 of receivables to Federal Factors. Federal Factors assesses a service charge of 2% of the amount of receivables sold. The journal entry to record the sale by Hendredon Furniture on April 2, 2022, is as follows.

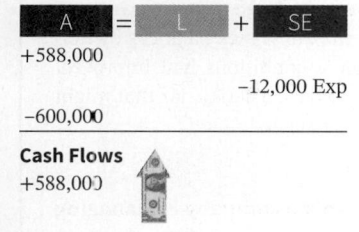

A = L + SE

+588,000

             –12,000 Exp

–600,000

**Cash Flows**
+588,000

| Apr. 2 | Cash | 588,000 | |
| | Service Charge Expense (2% × $600,000) | 12,000 | |
| |     Accounts Receivable | | 600,000 |
| |     (To record the sale of accounts receivable) | | |

If Hendredon often sells its receivables, it reports the service charge expense as an operating expense. If the company infrequently sells receivables, it may report this amount in the "Other expenses and losses" section of the income statement.

## National Credit Card Sales

Over one billion credit cards are in use in the United States—more than three credit cards for every man, woman, and child in this country. **Visa**, **MasterCard**, and **American Express** are the national credit cards that most individuals use. Three parties are involved when national credit cards are used in retail sales: (1) the credit card issuer, who is independent of the retailer; (2) the retailer; and (3) the customer. **A retailer's acceptance of a national credit card is another form of selling (factoring) the receivable**.

Illustration 8.11 shows the major advantages of national credit cards to the retailer. In exchange for these advantages, the retailer pays the credit card issuer a fee of 2–4% of the invoice price for its services (see Ethics Note).

### Accounting for Credit Card Sales

The retailer generally considers sales from the use of national credit cards as **cash sales**. The retailer must pay to the bank that issues the card a fee for processing the transactions. The retailer records the credit card slips in a similar manner as checks deposited from a cash sale.

**ILLUSTRATION 8.11**
**Advantages of credit cards to the retailer**

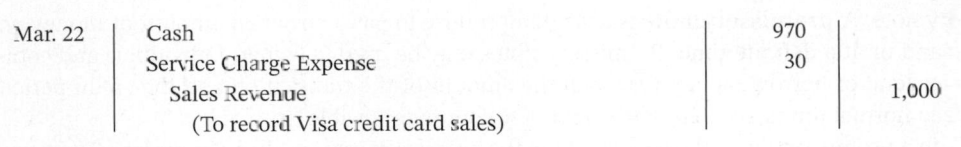

**Issuer investigates credit of customer**

Credit card issuer    Customer    Retailer

**Issuer maintains customer accounts**

**Issuer undertakes collection process and absorbs any losses**

**Retailer receives cash more quickly from credit card issuer**

To illustrate, Anita Ferreri purchases $1,000 of compact discs for her restaurant from Karen Kerr Music Co., using her Visa First Bank Card. First Bank charges a service fee of 3%. The entry to record this transaction by Karen Kerr Music on March 22, 2022, is as follows.

| Mar. 22 | Cash | 970 | |
| | Service Charge Expense | 30 | |
| | Sales Revenue | | 1,000 |
| | (To record Visa credit card sales) | | |

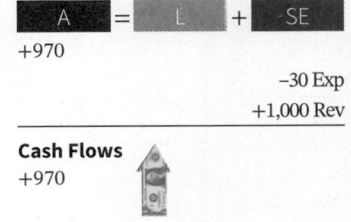

A = L + SE
+970
−30 Exp
+1,000 Rev

**Cash Flows**
+970

## Accounting Across the Organization    Nordstrom

Zibedik/iStock/ Getty Images

### How Does a Credit Card Work?

Most of you know how to use a credit card, but do you know what happens in the transaction and how the transaction is processed? Suppose that you use a **Visa** card to purchase some new ties at **Nordstrom**. The customer swipes or taps the credit card (or inserts it if it is a chip card), which allows the information to be read. The salesperson enters the amount of the purchase. The machine contacts the Visa computer, which routes the call back to the bank that issued your Visa card. The issuing bank verifies that the account exists, that the card is not stolen, and that you have not exceeded your credit limit. At this point, you then complete the sale by signing the receipt.

Visa acts as the clearing agent for the transaction. It transfers funds from the issuing bank to Nordstrom's bank account. Generally this transfer of funds from sale to the receipt of funds in the merchant's account, takes two to three days.

In the meantime, Visa puts a pending charge on your account for the amount of the tie purchase; that amount counts immediately against your available credit limit. At the end of the billing period, Visa sends you an invoice (your credit card bill), which shows the various charges you made, and the amounts that Visa expended on your behalf for the month. You then must "pay the piper" for your stylish new ties.

**Assume that Nordstrom prepares a bank reconciliation at the end of each month. If some credit card sales have not been processed by the bank, how should Nordstrom treat these transactions on its bank reconciliation? (Answer is available near the end of the chapter.)**

**ACTION PLAN**

- Consider sale of receivables to a factor.
- Weigh cost of factoring against benefit of having cash in hand.

## DO IT! 2b | Factoring

Peter M. Kell Wholesalers Co. needs to raise $120,000 in cash to safely cover next Friday's employee payroll. Kell has reached its debt ceiling with its lenders. Kell's present balance of outstanding receivables totals $750,000. Kell decides to factor $125,000 of its receivables on September 7, 2022, to alleviate this cash crunch. Record the entry that Kell would make when it raises the needed cash. (Assume a 1% service charge.)

### Solution

Assuming that Kell Co. factors $125,000 of its accounts receivable at a 1% service charge, it would make this entry:

| | | | |
|---|---|---|---|
| Sept. 7 | Cash | 123,750 | |
| | Service Charge Expense (1% × $125,000) | 1,250 | |
| |     Accounts Receivable | | 125,000 |
| |       (To record sale of receivables to factor ) | | |

Related exercise material: **BE8.7, DO IT! 8.2b, E8.9, E8.10, and E8.11.**

# Notes Receivable

---

**LEARNING OBJECTIVE 3**

Explain how companies recognize, value, and dispose of notes receivable.

---

Companies may also grant credit in exchange for a formal credit instrument known as a promissory note. A **promissory note** is a written promise to pay a specified amount of money on demand or at a definite time. Promissory notes may be used (1) when individuals and companies lend or borrow money, (2) when the amount of the transaction and the credit period exceed normal limits, or (3) in settlement of accounts receivable.

In a promissory note, the party making the promise to pay is called the **maker**. The party to whom payment is to be made is called the **payee**. The note may specifically identify the payee by name or may designate the payee simply as the bearer of the note.

In the note shown in **Illustration 8.12**, Calhoun Company is the maker and Wilma Company is the payee. To Wilma Company, the promissory note is a note receivable. To Calhoun Company, it is a note payable (see **Helpful Hint**).

**ILLUSTRATION 8.12**

**Promissory note**

**HELPFUL HINT**

For this note, the maker, Calhoun Company, debits Cash and credits Notes Payable. The payee, Wilma Company, debits Notes Receivable and credits Cash.

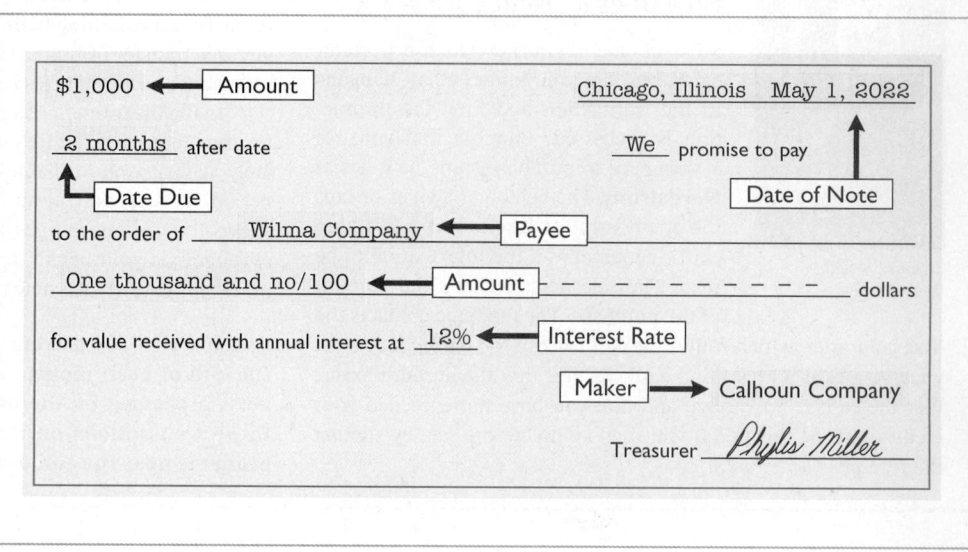

Notes receivable give the holder a stronger legal claim to assets than do accounts receivable. Like accounts receivable, notes receivable can be readily sold to another party. Promissory notes are negotiable instruments (as are checks), which means that they can be transferred to another party by endorsement.

Companies frequently accept notes receivable from customers who need to extend the payment of an outstanding account receivable. They often require such notes from high-risk customers. In some industries (such as the pleasure and sport boat industry), all credit sales are supported by notes. The majority of notes, however, originate from lending transactions.

The basic issues in accounting for notes receivable are the same as those for accounts receivable. On the following pages, we look at these issues. Before we do, however, we need to consider two issues that do not apply to accounts receivable: determining the maturity date and computing interest.

## Determining the Maturity Date

Illustration 8.13 shows three ways of stating the maturity date of a promissory note.

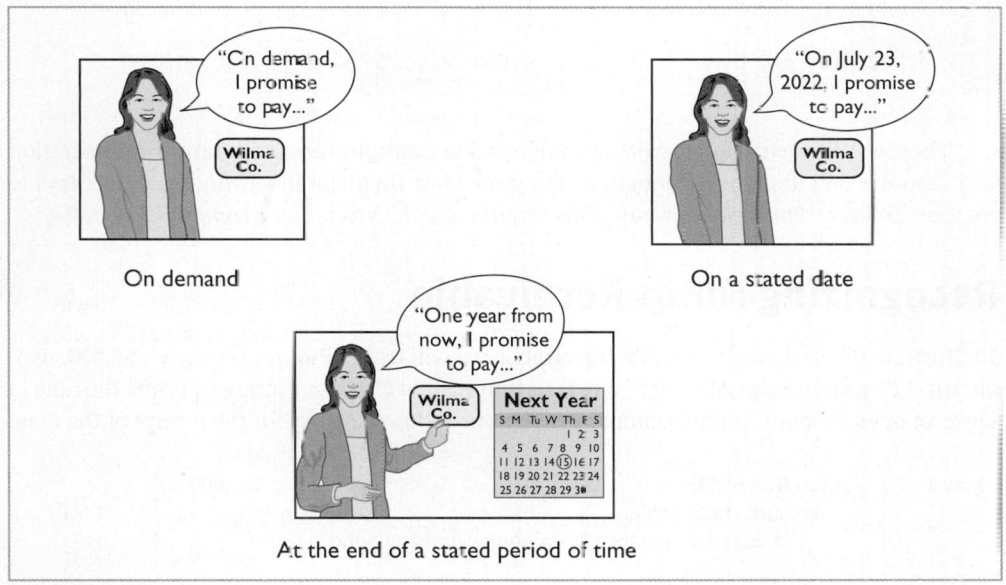

**ILLUSTRATION 8.13**

**Maturity date of different notes**

When the life of a note is expressed in terms of months, you find the date when it matures by counting the months from the date of issue. For example, the maturity date of a three-month note dated May 1 is August 1. A note drawn on the last day of a month matures on the last day of its repayment month. That is, a July 31 note due in two months matures on September 30.

When the due date is stated in terms of days, you need to count the exact number of days to determine the maturity date. In counting, **omit the date the note is issued but include the due date**. For example, the maturity date of a 60-day note dated July 17 is September 15, computed as shown in Illustration 8.14.

**ILLUSTRATION 8.14**

**Computation of maturity date**

| Term of note | | 60 days |
|---|---|---|
| July (31–17) | 14 | |
| August | 31 | 45 |
| **Maturity date: September** | | **15** |

# Computing Interest

**Illustration 8.15** gives the basic formula for computing interest on an interest-bearing note.

| Face Value of Note | × | Annual Interest Rate | × | Time in Terms of One Year | = | Interest |
|---|---|---|---|---|---|---|

The interest rate specified in a note is an **annual** rate of interest (see **Helpful Hint**). The time factor in the formula in Illustration 8.15 expresses the fraction of a year that the note is outstanding. When the maturity date is stated in days, the time factor is often the number of days divided by 360. Remember that when counting days, omit the date that the note is issued but include the due date. When the due date is stated in months, the time factor is the number of months divided by 12. **Illustration 8.16** shows computation of interest for various time periods.

| Terms of Note | Face | × | Rate | × | Time | = | Interest |
|---|---|---|---|---|---|---|---|
| $730, 12%, 120 days | $730 | × | 12% | × | $\frac{120}{360}$ | = | $ 29.20 |
| $1,000, 9%, 6 months | $1,000 | × | 9% | × | $\frac{6}{12}$ | = | $ 45.00 |
| $2,000, 6%, 1 year | $2,000 | × | 6% | × | $\frac{1}{1}$ | = | $120.00 |

There are different ways to calculate interest. For example, the computation in Illustration 8.15 assumes 360 days for the length of the year. Most financial institutions use 365 days to compute interest. *For homework problems, assume 360 days to simplify computations.*

# Recognizing Notes Receivable

To illustrate the basic entry for notes receivable, we will use Calhoun Company's $1,000, two-month, 12% promissory note dated May 1. Assuming that Calhoun Company wrote the note to settle an open account, Wilma Company makes the following entry for the receipt of the note.

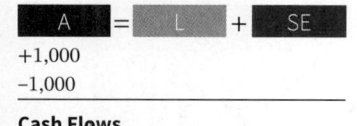

+1,000
−1,000

**Cash Flows**
no effect

| May 1 | Notes Receivable | 1,000 | |
|---|---|---|---|
| |     Accounts Receivable | | 1,000 |
| |       (To record acceptance of Calhoun Company note) | | |

The company records the note receivable at its **face value**, the value shown on the face of the note. No interest revenue is reported when the note is accepted because the revenue recognition principle requires that revenue be recognized only when the performance obligation is satisfied. Interest is therefore recognized (accrued) as time passes.

If a company lends cash in exchange for a note, the entry is a debit to Notes Receivable and a credit to Cash in the amount of the loan.

# Valuing Notes Receivable

Valuing short-term notes receivable is the same as valuing accounts receivable. Like accounts receivable, companies report short-term notes receivable at their **cash (net) realizable value**. The notes receivable allowance account is Allowance for Doubtful Accounts. The estimations involved in determining cash realizable value and in recording bad debt expense and the related allowance are done similarly to accounts receivable.

# Disposing of Notes Receivable

Notes may be held to their maturity date, at which time the face value plus accrued interest is due. In some situations, the maker of the note defaults, and the payee must make an appropriate adjustment. In other situations, similar to accounts receivable, the holder of the note speeds up the conversion to cash by selling the receivables (as described earlier in this chapter).

## Honor of Notes Receivable

A note is **honored** when its maker pays in full at its maturity date. For each interest-bearing note, the **amount due at maturity** is the face value of the note plus interest for the length of time specified on the note.

To illustrate, assume that Wolder Co. lends Higley Co. $10,000 on June 1, accepting a five-month, 9% interest note. In this situation, interest is $375 ($10,000 × 9% × $\frac{5}{12}$). The amount due, **the maturity value**, is $10,375 ($10,000 + $375). To obtain payment, Wolder (the payee) must present the note either to Higley Co. (the maker) or to the maker's agent, such as a bank. If Wolder presents the note to Higley Co. on November 1, the maturity date, Wolder's entry to record the collection is as follows.

| | | | |
|---|---|---|---|
| Nov. 1 | Cash | 10,375 | |
| | Notes Receivable | | 10,000 |
| | Interest Revenue ($10,000 × 9% × $\frac{5}{12}$) | | 375 |
| | (To record collection of Higley note and interest) | | |

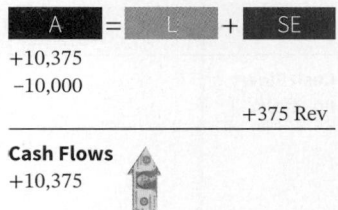

A = L + SE
+10,375
−10,000
+375 Rev

**Cash Flows**
+10,375

## Accrual of Interest Receivable

Suppose instead that Wolder Co. prepares financial statements as of September 30, necessitating an interest-adjusting entry. The timeline in **Illustration 8.17** presents the revenue analysis for this situation.

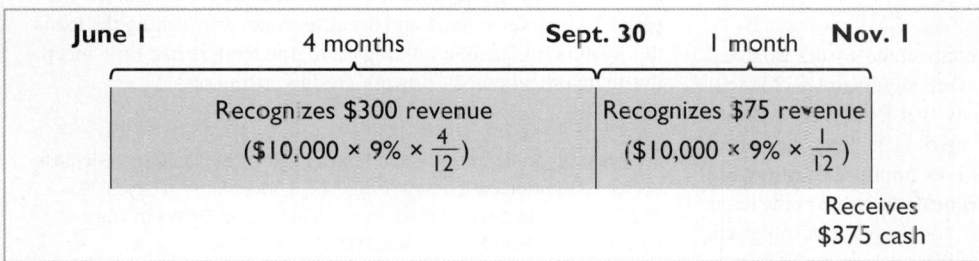

| June 1 | 4 months | Sept. 30 | 1 month | Nov. 1 |

Recognizes $300 revenue ($10,000 × 9% × $\frac{4}{12}$)    Recognizes $75 revenue ($10,000 × 9% × $\frac{1}{12}$)

Receives $375 cash

**ILLUSTRATION 8.17**

**Timeline of interest earned**

To reflect interest earned but not yet received, Wolder must accrue interest on September 30. In this case, the adjusting entry by Wolder is for four months of interest, or $300, as shown below.

| | | | |
|---|---|---|---|
| Sept. 30 | Interest Receivable ($10,000 × 9% × $\frac{4}{12}$) | 300 | |
| | Interest Revenue | | 300 |
| | (To accrue 4 months' interest on Higley note) | | |

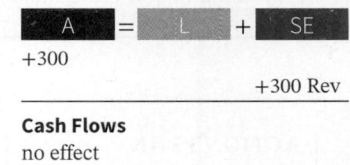

A = L + SE
+300
+300 Rev

**Cash Flows**
no effect

At the note's maturity on November 1, Wolder receives $10,375. This amount represents repayment of the $10,000 note as well as all five months of interest, or $375, as shown below. The $375 is comprised of the $300 Interest Receivable accrued on September 30 plus $75 earned during October. Wolder's entry to record the honoring of the Higley note on November 1 is as follows.

| | | | |
|---|---|---|---|
| Nov. 1 | Cash [$10,000 + ($10,000 × 9% × $\frac{5}{12}$)] | 10,375 | |
| | Notes Receivable | | 10,000 |
| | Interest Receivable | | 300 |
| | Interest Revenue ($10,000 × 9% × $\frac{1}{12}$) | | 75 |
| | (To record collection of Higley note and interest) | | |

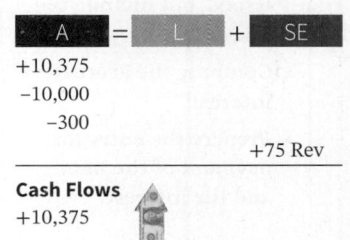

A = L + SE
+10,375
−10,000
−300
+75 Rev

**Cash Flows**
+10,375

In this case, Wolder credits Interest Receivable for the $300 that was established in the adjusting entry on September 30.

## Dishonor of Notes Receivable

A **dishonored (defaulted) note** is a note that is not paid in full at maturity. A dishonored note receivable is no longer negotiable. However, the payee still has a claim against the maker of the note for both the note and the interest. Therefore, the note holder usually transfers the customer's debt from the Notes Receivable account to an Accounts Receivable account.

To illustrate, assume that Higley Co. on November 1 indicates that it cannot pay at the present time. The entry to record the dishonor of the note depends on whether Wolder Co. expects eventual collection. If it does expect eventual collection, Wolder Co. recognizes interest revenue and debits the amount due (face value and interest) on the note to Accounts Receivable. It would make the following entry at the time the note is dishonored (assuming no previous accrual of interest).

| A | = | L | + | SE |
|---|---|---|---|---|
| +10,375 | | | | |
| −10,000 | | | | |
| | | | | +375 Rev |

**Cash Flows**
no effect

| | | | | |
|---|---|---|---|---|
| Nov. 1 | Accounts Receivable | | 10,375 | |
| | Notes Receivable | | | 10,000 |
| | Interest Revenue | | | 375 |
| | (To record the dishonor of Higley note) | | | |

If instead on November 1 there is no hope of collection, the note holder would write off the face value of the note by debiting Allowance for Doubtful Accounts. No interest revenue would be recorded because collection is not expected to occur.

---

## Accounting Across the Organization    Countrywide Financial Corporation

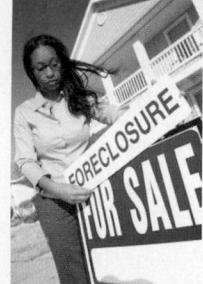

### Bad Information Can Lead to Bad Loans

Many factors contributed to the financial crisis of 2008. One significant factor that resulted in many bad loans was a failure by lenders to investigate loan customers sufficiently. For example, **Countrywide Financial Corporation** wrote many loans under its "Fast and Easy" loan program. That program allowed borrowers to provide little or no documentation for their income or their assets. Other lenders had similar programs, which earned the nickname "liars' loans." One study found that in these situations, 60% of applicants overstated

Steve Debenport/E+/ Getty Images

their incomes by more than 50% in order to qualify for a loan. Critics of the banking industry say that because loan officers were compensated for loan volume and because banks were selling the loans to investors rather than holding them, the lenders had little incentive to investigate the borrowers' creditworthiness.

**Sources:** Glenn R. Simpson and James R. Hagerty, "Countrywide Loss Focuses Attention on Underwriting," *Wall Street Journal* (April 30, 2008), p. B1; and Michael Corkery, "Fraud Seen as Driver in Wave of Foreclosures," *Wall Street Journal* (December 21, 2007), p. A1.

**What steps should the banks have taken to ensure the accuracy of financial information provided on loan applications? (Answer is available near the end of the chapter.)**

---

**ACTION PLAN**
- Count the exact number of days to determine the maturity date. Omit the date the note is issued, but include the due date.
- Compute the accrued interest.
- Prepare the entry for payment of the note and the interest.

## DO IT! 3 | Recognizing Notes Receivable

Gambit Stores accepts from Leonard Co. a $3,400, 90-day, 6% note dated May 10 in settlement of Leonard's overdue receivable. (a) What is the maturity date of the note? (b) What is the interest to be received at the maturity date? (c) What entry does Gambit make at the maturity date, assuming Leonard pays the note and interest in full at that time?

### Solution

**a.** The maturity date is August 8, computed as follows.

| Term of note: | | 90 days |
|---|---|---|
| May (31–10) | 21 | |
| June | 30 | |
| July | 31 | 82 |
| Maturity date: August | | 8 |

**b.** The interest to be received at the maturity date is $51, computed as follows.

$$\text{Face} \times \text{Rate} \times \text{Time} = \text{Interest}$$
$$\$3,400 \times 6\% \times \frac{90}{360} = \$51$$

**c.** Gambit Stores records this entry at the maturity date:

| | | |
|---|---|---|
| Cash | 3,451 | |
|     Notes Receivable | | 3,400 |
|     Interest Revenue | | 51 |
|        (To record collection of Leonard note and interest) | | |

Related exercise material: **BE8.8, BE8.9, BE8.10. DO IT! 8.3, E8.12, E8.13, E8.14, and E8.15.**

# Presentation and Analysis of Receivables

## LEARNING OBJECTIVE 4
Describe the statement presentation and analysis of receivables.

If a company has significant receivables, analysts carefully review the company's financial statement disclosures to evaluate how well the company is managing its receivables.

## Presentation

Companies should identify in the balance sheet or in the notes to the financial statements each of the major types of receivables. Short-term receivables appear in the current assets section of the balance sheet. Short-term investments appear before short-term receivables because these investments are more liquid (nearer to cash). Companies report both the gross amount of receivables and the allowance for doubtful accounts.

In the income statement, companies report bad debt expense and service charge expense as operating expenses. Interest revenue appears under "Other revenues and gains" in the nonoperating activities section of the income statement.

Presented below are examples of different types of information provided to help users understand the issues related to receivables. **Illustration 8.18**, for example, shows the composition of **Deere & Company**'s net receivables. Given that receivables represent 60% of the total assets of this heavy equipment manufacturer, investors are interested in the types of receivables and their significance.

**ILLUSTRATION 8.18**

**Balance sheet presentation of receivables**

**Real World**

| Deere & Company<br>Balance Sheet (partial)<br>(in millions) | |
|---|---|
| Receivables | |
|     Receivables from unconsolidated subsidiaries | $    30 |
|     Trade accounts and notes receivable | 3,278 |
|     Financing receivables | 27,583 |
|     Restricted financing receivables | 4,516 |
|     Other receivables | 1,500 |
| Total receivables | 37,007 |
| Less: Allowance for doubtful trade receivables | 175 |
| Net receivables | $36,832 |

**Illustration 8.19** contains an excerpt from the notes to the financial statements of **Skechers**, discussing how it monitors receivables.

**ILLUSTRATION 8.19**

Note on monitoring Skechers'
receivables

**Real World**

## Skechers USA
### Notes to the Financial Statements

To minimize the likelihood of uncollectibility, customers' credit-worthiness is reviewed periodically based on external credit reporting services, financial statements issued by the customer and our experience with the account, and it is adjusted accordingly. When a customer's account becomes significantly past due, we generally place a hold on the account and discontinue further shipments to that customer, minimizing further risk of loss.

If a company has significant concentrations of credit risk, it must discuss this risk in the notes to its financial statements. A **concentration of credit risk** is a threat of nonpayment from a single large customer or class of customers that could adversely affect the financial health of the company. **Illustration 8.20** shows an excerpt from the credit risk note from Skechers' 2015 annual report. The company reports that its five largest customers account for 14.6% of its net sales.

**ILLUSTRATION 8.20**

Excerpt from Skechers' note
on concentration of credit risk

**Real World**

## Skechers USA
### Notes to the Financial Statements

During 2015, 2014 and 2013, no customer accounted for 10.0% or more of net sales. As of December 31, 2015, one customer accounted for 10.6% of gross trade receivables. No other customer accounted for more than 10% of net trade receivables at December 31, 2015 or 2014. During 2015, 2014 and 2013, net sales to the five largest customers were approximately 14.6%, 15.7% and 18.1%, respectively.

This note to Skechers' financial statements indicates it has a relatively high concentration of credit risk. A default by any of these large customers could have a significant negative impact on its financial performance.

## Analysis

Investors and corporate managers compute financial ratios to evaluate the liquidity of a company's accounts receivable. They use the **accounts receivable turnover** to assess the liquidity of the receivables. This ratio measures the number of times, on average, the company collects accounts receivable during the period. It is computed by dividing net credit sales (net sales less cash sales) by the average net accounts receivable during the year. Unless seasonal factors are significant, average net accounts receivable outstanding can be computed from the beginning and ending balances of net accounts receivable.

For example, **Cisco Systems** recently had net sales of $37,750 million for the year. It had a beginning accounts receivable (net) balance of $5,157 million and an ending accounts receivable (net) balance of $5,344 million. Assuming that Cisco's sales were all on credit, its accounts receivable turnover is computed as shown in **Illustration 8.21**.

**ILLUSTRATION 8.21**

Accounts receivable turnover
formula and computation

| Net Credit Sales | ÷ | Average Net Accounts Receivable | = | Accounts Receivable Turnover |
|---|---|---|---|---|
| $37,750 | ÷ | $\dfrac{\$5,157 + \$5,344}{2}$ | = | 7.2 times |

The result indicates an accounts receivable turnover of 7.2 times per year. The higher the turnover, the more liquid the company's receivables.

A variant of the accounts receivable turnover that makes the liquidity even more evident is its conversion into an **average collection period** in terms of days. This is done by dividing the accounts receivable turnover into 365 days. For example, Cisco's turnover of 7.2 times is divided into 365 days, as shown in **Illustration 8.22**, to obtain approximately 51 days. This means that it takes Cisco 51 days to collect its accounts receivable.

| Days in Year | ÷ | Accounts Receivable Turnover | = | Average Collection Period in Days |
|---|---|---|---|---|
| 365 days | ÷ | 7.2 times | = | 51 days |

**ILLUSTRATION 8.22**
Average collection period for receivables formula and computation

Companies frequently use the average collection period to assess the effectiveness of a company's credit and collection policies. The general rule is that the collection period should not greatly exceed the credit term period (that is, the time allowed for payment).

# Data Analytics and Receivables Management

Opportunities abound to improve receivables management through data analytics. Software packages promise increases in working capital, improved revenues, and enhanced customer relations. So-called visualization software, which presents data in sophisticated graph format, enables managers to more quickly identify issues and obtain a deeper understanding of the factors that influence successful receivables management. Use of such software helps identify which currencies, sales representatives, customers, product lines, or geographic regions need closer attention. This sometimes enables management to do a more granular investigation of the cash-to-cash cycle time to evaluate which product lines are meeting company goals.

Data analytics of receivables is particularly valuable for predictive analysis, which allows improved evaluation of customers' risk profiles. In many instances, the company can identify risky customers and take corrective action before problems arise. Software provided by companies such as **Workday** use artificial intelligence to forecast which customers are likely to pay late.

## DO IT! 4 | Analysis of Receivables

In 2022, Lebron James Company has net credit sales of $923,795 for the year. It had a beginning accounts receivable (net) balance of $38,275 and an ending accounts receivable (net) balance of $35,988. Compute Lebron James Company's (a) accounts receivable turnover and (b) average collection period in days.

**Solution**

a.

| Net credit sales | ÷ | Average net accounts receivable | = | Accounts receivable turnover |
|---|---|---|---|---|
| $923,795 | ÷ | $\frac{\$38,275 + \$35,988}{2}$ | = | 24.9 times |

b.

| Days in year | ÷ | Accounts receivable turnover | = | Average collection period in days |
|---|---|---|---|---|
| 365 | ÷ | 24.9 times | = | 14.7 days |

Related exercise material: **BE8.11, BE8.12, DO IT! 8.4, E8.16, and E8.17.**

**ACTION PLAN**
- Review the formula to compute the accounts receivable turnover.
- Make sure that both the beginning and ending accounts receivable balances are considered in the computation.
- Review the formula to compute the average collection period in days.

# Review and Practice

## Learning Objectives Review

### 1 Explain how companies recognize accounts receivable.

Receivables are frequently classified as (1) accounts, (2) notes, and (3) other. Accounts receivable are amounts customers owe on account. Notes receivable are claims for which lenders issue formal instruments of credit as proof of the debt. Other receivables include nontrade receivables such as interest receivable, loans to company officers, advances to employees, and income taxes refundable.

Companies record accounts receivable when they perform a service on account or at the point of sale of merchandise on account. Accounts receivable are reduced by sales returns and allowances. Cash discounts reduce the amount received on accounts receivable. When interest is charged on a past due receivable, the company adds this interest to the accounts receivable balance and recognizes it as interest revenue.

### 2 Describe how companies value accounts receivable and record their disposition.

There are two methods of accounting for uncollectible accounts: the allowance method (GAAP) and the direct write-off method (not GAAP). Companies use the percentage-of-receivables basis to apply the allowance method. The percentage-of-receivables basis emphasizes the cash realizable value of the accounts receivable. An aging schedule is often used with this basis.

When a company collects an account receivable, it credits Accounts Receivable. When a company sells (factors) an account receivable, a service charge expense reduces the amount received.

### 3 Explain how companies recognize, value, and dispose of notes receivable.

For a note stated in months, the maturity date is found by counting the months from the date of issue. For a note stated in days, the number of days is counted, omitting the issue date and counting the due date. The formula for computing interest is Face value × Interest rate × Time. Interest rates are always stated in annual terms.

Companies record notes receivable at face value. In some cases, it is necessary to accrue interest prior to maturity. In this case, companies debit Interest Receivable and credit Interest Revenue.

Notes can be held to maturity. At that time the face value plus accrued interest is due, and the note is removed from the accounts. In many cases, the holder of the note speeds up the conversion by selling the receivable to another party (a factor). In some situations, the maker of the note dishonors the note (defaults), in which case the company transfers the note and accrued interest to an account receivable or writes off the note, depending on anticipated collectibility.

### 4 Describe the statement presentation and analysis of receivables.

As with accounts receivable, companies report notes receivable at their cash (net) realizable value. The notes receivable allowance account is Allowance for Doubtful Accounts. The computation and estimations involved in valuing notes receivable at cash realizable value, and in recording the proper amount of bad debt expense and the related allowance, are similar to those for accounts receivable.

Companies should identify in the balance sheet or in the notes to the financial statements each major type of receivable. Short-term receivables are considered current assets. Companies report the gross amount of receivables and the allowance for doubtful accounts. They report bad debt expense and service charge expenses in the multiple-step income statement as operating (selling) expenses. Interest revenue appears under other revenues and gains in the nonoperating activities section of the statement. Managers and investors evaluate accounts receivable for liquidity by computing a turnover ratio and an average collection period.

## Glossary Review

**Accounts receivable**   Amounts owed by customers on account. (p. 8-3).

**Accounts receivable turnover**   A measure of the liquidity of accounts receivable; computed by dividing net credit sales by average net accounts receivable. (p. 8-20).

**Aging the accounts receivable**   The analysis of receivable balances by the length of time they have been unpaid. (p. 8-9).

**Allowance method**   A GAAP method of accounting for uncollectibles that involves estimating uncollectible accounts at the end of each period. (p. 8-6).

**Average collection period**   The average amount of time that a receivable is outstanding; calculated by dividing 365 days by the accounts receivable turnover. (p. 8-21).

**Bad Debt Expense**   An expense account to record uncollectible receivables. (p. 8-5).

**Cash (net) realizable value**   The net amount a company expects to receive in cash. (p. 8-6).

**Direct write-off method**   A non-GAAP method of accounting for uncollectibles that involves expensing accounts at the time they are determined to be uncollectible. (p. 8-5).

**Dishonored (defaulted) note**   A note that is not paid in full at maturity. (p. 8-18).

**Factor**   A finance company or bank that buys receivables from businesses and then collects the payments directly from the customers. (p. 8-12).

**Maker**  The party in a promissory note who is making the promise to pay. (p. 8-14).

**Notes receivable**  Written promise (as evidenced by a formal instrument) for amounts to be received (p. 8-3).

**Other receivables**  Various forms of nontrade receivables, such as interest receivable and income taxes refundable. (p. 8-3).

**Payee**  The party to whom payment of a promissory note is to be made. (p. 8-14).

**Percentage-of-receivables basis**  A method by which management estimates what percentage of receivables will result in losses from uncollectible accounts. (p. 8-9).

**Promissory note**  A written promise to pay a specified amount of money on demand or at a definite time. (p. 8-14).

**Receivables**  Amounts due from individuals and other companies. (p. 8-3).

**Trade receivables**  Notes and accounts receivable that result from sales transactions. (p. 8-3).

## Practice Multiple-Choice Questions

**1. (LO 1)** A receivable that is evidenced by a formal instrument and that normally requires the payment of interest is a(n):

  **a.** account receivable.

  **b.** trade receivable.

  **c.** note receivable.

  **d.** classified receivable.

**2. (LO 1)** Receivables are frequently classified as:

  **a.** accounts receivable, company receivables, and other receivables.

  **b.** accounts receivable, notes receivable, and employee receivables.

  **c.** accounts receivable and general receivables.

  **d.** accounts receivable, notes receivable, and other receivables.

**3. (LO 1)** Kersee Company on June 15 sells merchandise on account to Eng Co. for $1,000, terms 2/10, n/30. On June 20, Eng Co. returns merchandise with a sales price of $300 to Kersee Company. On June 24, payment is received from Eng Co. for the balance due. What is the amount of cash received?

  **a.** $700.    **c.** $686.

  **b.** $680.    **d.** None of the above.

**4. (LO 2)** Accounts and notes receivable are reported in the current assets section of the balance sheet at:

  **a.** cash (net) realizable value.

  **b.** net book value.

  **c.** lower-of-cost-or-market value.

  **d.** invoice cost.

**5. (LO 2)** Hughes Company has a credit balance of $5,000 in its Allowance for Doubtful Accounts before any adjustments are made at the end of the year. Based on review and aging of its accounts receivable at the end of the year, Hughes estimates that $60,000 of its receivables are uncollectible. The amount of bad debt expense which should be reported for the year is:

  **a.** $5,000.    **c.** $60,000.

  **b.** $55,000.    **d.** $65,000.

**6. (LO 2)** Hughes Company has a debit balance of $5,000 in its Allowance for Doubtful Accounts before any adjustments are made at the end of the year. Based on review and aging of its accounts receivable at the end of the year, Hughes estimates that $60,000 of its receivables are uncollectible. In this situation, the amount of bad debt expense that should be reported for the year is:

  **a.** $5,000.    **c.** $60,000.

  **b.** $55,000.    **d.** $65,000.

**7. (LO 2)** Net credit sales for the month are $800,000. The accounts receivable balance is $160,000. The allowance is calculated as 7.5% of the receivables balance using the percentage-of-receivables basis.

If Allowance for Doubtful Accounts has a credit balance of $5,000 before adjustment, what is the balance after adjustment?

  **a.** $12,000.    **c.** $17,000.

  **b.** $7,000.    **d.** $31,000.

**8. (LO 2)** In 2022, Patterson Wholesale Company had net credit sales of $750,000. On January 1, 2022, Allowance for Doubtful Accounts had a credit balance of $18,000. During 2022, $30,000 of uncollectible accounts receivable were written off. Past experience indicates that the allowance should be 10% of the balance in receivables (percentage-of-receivables basis). If the accounts receivable balance was $200,000, what is the required adjustment to Allowance for Doubtful Accounts at December 31, 2022?

  **a.** $20,000.    **c.** $32,000.

  **b.** $75,000.    **d.** $30,000.

**9. (LO 2)** An analysis and aging of the accounts receivable of Prince Company at December 31 reveals the following data.

| | |
|---|---:|
| Accounts receivable | $800,000 |
| Allowance for doubtful accounts per books before adjustment | 50,000 |
| Amounts expected to become uncollectible | 65,000 |

The cash realizable value of the accounts receivable at December 31, after adjustment, is:

  **a.** $635,000.    **c.** $800,000.

  **b.** $750,000.    **d.** $735,000.

**10. (LO 2)** Which of the following statements about Visa credit card sales is **incorrect**?

  **a.** The credit card issuer makes the credit investigation of the customer.

  **b.** The retailer is not involved in the collection process.

  **c.** Two parties are involved.

  **d.** The retailer receives cash more quickly than it would from individual customers on account.

**11. (LO 2)** Good Stuff Retailers accepted $50,000 of **Citibank Visa** credit card charges for merchandise sold on July 1. Citibank charges 4% for its credit card use. The entry to record this transaction by Good Stuff Retailers will include a credit to Sales Revenue of $50,000 and a debit(s) to:

| | |
|---|---:|
| **a.** Cash | $48,000 |
| and Service Charge Expense | $2,000 |
| **b.** Accounts Receivable | $48,000 |
| and Service Charge Expense | $2,000 |
| **c.** Cash | $50,000 |
| **d.** Accounts Receivable | $50,000 |

**12. (LO 3)** One of the following statements about promissory notes is incorrect. The **incorrect** statement is:

    **a.** The party making the promise to pay is called the maker.

    **b.** The party to whom payment is to be made is called the payee.

    **c.** A promissory note is not a negotiable instrument.

    **d.** A promissory note is often required from high-risk customers.

**13. (LO 3)** Michael Co. accepts a $1,000, 3-month, 6% promissory note in settlement of an account with Tani Co. The entry to record this transaction is as follows.

| | | |
|---|---:|---:|
| **a.** Notes Receivable | 1,015 | |
|     Accounts Receivable | | 1,015 |
| **b.** Notes Receivable | 1,000 | |
|     Accounts Receivable | | 1,000 |
| **c.** Notes Receivable | 1,000 | |
|     Sales Revenue | | 1,000 |
| **d.** Notes Receivable | 1,030 | |
|     Accounts Receivable | | 1,030 |

**14. [LO 3)** Schleis Co. holds Murphy Inc.'s $10,000, 120-day, 9% note. The entry made by Schleis Co. when the note is collected, assuming no interest has been previously accrued, is:

| | | |
|---|---:|---:|
| **a.** Cash | 10,300 | |
|     Notes Receivable | | 10,300 |
| **b.** Cash | 10,000 | |
|     Notes Receivable | | 10,000 |
| **c.** Accounts Receivable | 10,300 | |
|     Notes Receivable | | 10,000 |
|     Interest Revenue | | 300 |
| **d.** Cash | 10,300 | |
|     Notes Receivable | | 10,000 |
|     Interest Revenue | | 300 |

**15. (LO 4)** Prall Corporation sells its goods on terms of 2/10, n/30. It has an accounts receivable turnover of 7. What is its average collection period (days)?

    **a.** 2,555.         **c.** 52.

    **b.** 30.           **d.** 210.

**16. (LO 4)** Eddy Corporation had net credit sales during the year of $800,000 and cost of goods sold of $500,000. The net balance of accounts receivable at the beginning of the year was $100,000, and at the end of the year it was $150,000. What were the accounts receivable turnover and the average collection period in days?

    **a.** 4.0 and 91.3 days.    **c.** 6.4 and 57 days.

    **b.** 5.3 and 68.9 days.    **d.** 8.0 and 45.6 days.

## Solutions

**1. c.** A note receivable represents claims for which formal instruments of credit are issued as evidence of the debt. The note normally requires the payment of the principal and interest on a specific date. Choices (a) account receivable, (b) trade receivable, and (d) classified receivable rarely require the payment of interest if paid within a 30-day period.

**2. d.** Receivables are frequently classified as accounts receivable, notes receivable, and other receivables. The other choices are incorrect because receivables are not frequently classified as (a) company receivables, (ɔ) employee receivables, or (c) general receivables.

**3. c.** Because payment is made within the discount period of 10 days, the amount received is $700 ($1,000 – $300 return) minus the discount of $14 ($700 × 2%), for a cash amount of $686, not (a) $700 or (b) $680. Choice (d) is wrong as there is a correct answer.

**4. a.** Accounts and notes receivable are reported in the current assets section of the balance sheet at cash (net) realizable value, not (b) net book value, (c) lower-of-cost-or-market value, or (d) invoice cost.

**5. b.** By crediting Allowance for Doubtful Accounts for $55,000, the new balance will be the required balance of $60,000. This adjusting entry debits Bad Debt Expense for $55,000 and credits Allowance for Doubtful Accounts for $55,000, not (a) $5,000, (c) $60,000, or (d) $65,000.

**6. d.** By crediting Allowance for Doubtful Accounts for $65,000, the new balance will be the required balance of $60,000. This adjusting entry debits Bad Debt Expense for $65,000 and credits Allowance for Doubtful Accounts for $65,000, not (a) $5,000, (b) $55,000, or (c) $60,000.

**7. a.** The ending balance required in the allowance account is 7.5% × $160,000, or $12,000. Since there is already a balance of $5,000 in Allowance for Doubtful Accounts, the difference of $7,000 should be added, resulting in a balance of $12,000, not (b) $7,000, (c) $17,000, or (d) $31,000.

**8. c.** After the write-offs are recorded, Allowance for Doubtful Accounts will have a debit balance of $12,000 ($18,000 credit beginning balance combined with a $30,000 debit for the write-offs). The desired balance, using the percentage-of-receivables basis, is a credit balance of $20,000 ($200,000 × 10%). In order to have an ending balance of $20,000, the required adjustment to Allowance for Doubtful Accounts is $32,000, not (a) $20,000, (b) $75,000, or (d) $30,000.

**9. d.** Accounts Receivable less the expected uncollectible amount equals the cash realizable value of $735,000 ($800,000 – $65,000), not (a) $685,000, (b) $750,000, or (c) $800,000.

**10. c.** There are three parties, not two, involved in Visa credit card sales: the credit card company, the retailer, and the customer. The other choices are true statements.

**11. a.** Credit card sales are considered cash sales. Cash is debited $48,000 for the net amount received ($50,000 – $2,000 for credit card use fee), and Service Charge Expense is debited $2,000 for the 4% credit card use fee ($50,000 × 4%). The other choices are therefore incorrect.

**12. c.** A promissory note is a negotiable instrument. The other choices are true statements.

**13. b.** Notes Receivable is recorded at face value ($1,000). No interest on the note is recorded until it is earned. Accounts Receivable is credited because no new sales have been made. The other choices are therefore incorrect.

**14. d.** Cash is debited for its maturity value [$10,000 + interest earned ($10,000 × $\frac{120}{360}$ × 9%)], Notes Receivable is credited for its face value, and Interest Revenue is credited for the amount of interest earned. The other choices are therefore incorrect.

**15. c.** Average collection period = Number of days in the year (365) ÷ Accounts receivable turnover (7) = 52 days, not (a) 2,555, (b) 30, or (d) 210.

**16. c.** The accounts receivable turnover is 6.4 {$800,000 ÷ [($100,000 + $150,000) ÷ 2]}. The average collection period in days is 57 days (365 ÷ 6.4). The other choices are therefore incorrect.

## Practice Brief Exercises

**1. (LO 1)** Record the following transactions on the books of Gonzalez Co. (Ignore cost of goods sold entries.)

*Record basic accounts receivable transactions.*

    **a.** On August 1, Gonzalez Co. sold merchandise on account to Miguel Inc. for $15,500, terms 1/10, n/30.

    **b.** On August 8, Miguel Inc. returned merchandise with a sales price of $3,100 to Gonzalez Co.

    **c.** On August 11, Miguel Inc. paid the balance due.

### Solution

| | | | |
|---|---|---|---|
| 1. a. | Accounts Receivable | 15,500 | |
| | Sales Revenue | | 15,500 |
| b. | Sales Returns and Allowances | 3,100 | |
| | Accounts Receivable | | 3,100 |
| c. | Cash ($12,400 − $124) | 12,276 | |
| | Sales Discounts ($12,400 × 1%) | 124 | |
| | Accounts Receivable ($15,500 − $3,100) | | 12,400 |

**2. (LO 2)** Sanchez Co. uses the percentage-of-receivables basis in 2022 to record bad debt expense. It estimates that 3% of accounts receivable will become uncollectible. Sales revenues are $900,000 for 2022, and sales returns and allowances are $50,000 for 2022. Accounts receivable has a balance of $139,000, and the allowance for doubtful accounts has a credit balance of $3,000. Prepare the adjusting entry to record bad debt expense in 2022.

*Prepare entry using percentage-of-receivables method.*

### Solution

| | | | |
|---|---|---|---|
| 2. | Bad Debt Expense | 1,170 | |
| | Allowance for Doubtful Accounts | | 1,170 |
| | [($139,000 × 3%) − $3,000] | | |

**3. (LO 3)** On January 20, 2022, Carlos Co. sold merchandise on account to Carson Co. for $20,000, n/30. On February 19, Carson Co. gave Carlos Co. an 8% promissory note in settlement of this account. Prepare the journal entries to record the sale and the settlement of the account receivable. (Ignore cost of goods sold entries).

*Prepare entries for notes receivable exchanged for accounts receivable.*

### Solution

| | | | | |
|---|---|---|---|---|
| 3. | Jan. 20 | Accounts Receivable | 20,000 | |
| | | Sales Revenue | | 20,000 |
| | Feb. 19 | Notes Receivable | 20,000 | |
| | | Accounts Receivable | | 20,000 |

## Practice Exercises

**1. (LO 2)** The ledger of J.C. Cobb Company at the end of the current year shows Accounts Receivable $150,000, Sales Revenue $850,000, and Sales Returns and Allowances $30,000.

*Journalize entries to record allowance for doubtful accounts using two different bases.*

### Instructions

    **a.** If J.C. Cobb uses the direct write-off method to account for uncollectible accounts, journalize the entry at December 31 if J.C. Cobb determines that M. Jack's $1,500 balance is uncollectible.

    **b.** If Allowance for Doubtful Accounts has a credit balance of $2,400 in the trial balance, journalize the adjusting entry at December 31, assuming uncollectibles are expected to be 10% of accounts receivable.

    **c.** If Allowance for Doubtful Accounts has a debit balance of $200 in the trial balance, journalize the adjusting entry at December 31, assuming uncollectibles are expected to be 6% of accounts receivable.

### Solution

**1. a.** Dec. 31

| | | |
|---|---|---|
| Bad Debt Expense | 1,500 | |
|     Accounts Receivable | | 1,500 |

    **b.** Dec. 31

| | | |
|---|---|---|
| Bad Debt Expense | 12,600 | |
|     Allowance for Doubtful Accounts | | |
|       [($150,000 × 10%) − $2,400] | | 12,600 |

    **c.** Dec. 31

| | | |
|---|---|---|
| Bad Debt Expense | 9,200 | |
|     Allowance for Doubtful Accounts | | |
|       [($150,000 × 6%) + $200] | | 9,200 |

*Journalize entries for notes receivable transactions.*

**2. (LO 3)** Troope Supply Co. has the following transactions related to notes receivable during the last 3 months of 2022.

Oct.   1    Loaned $16,000 cash to Juan Vasquez on a 1-year, 10% note.
Dec. 11    Sold goods to A. Palmer, Inc., receiving a $6,750, 90-day, 8% note.
    31    Accrued interest revenue on all notes receivable.

### Instructions

    **a.** Journalize the transactions for Troope Supply Co. (Ignore cost of goods sold entries.)

    **b.** Record the collection of the Vasquez note at its maturity in 2023.

### Solution

**2. a.**

2022

Oct.  1

| | | |
|---|---|---|
| Notes Receivable | 16,000 | |
|     Cash | | 16,000 |

Dec. 11

| | | |
|---|---|---|
| Notes Receivable | 6,750 | |
|     Sales Revenue | | 6,750 |

    31

| | | |
|---|---|---|
| Interest Receivable | 430 | |
|     Interest Revenue* | | 430 |

*Calculation of interest revenue:

Vasquez's note: $16,000 × 10% × \frac{3}{12}$ = $400

Palmer's note:    $6,750 × 8% × \frac{20}{360}$ =   30

Total accrued interest    $430

**b.**

2023

Oct.  1

| | | |
|---|---|---|
| Cash | 17,600 | |
|     Interest Receivable | | 400 |
|     Interest Revenue** | | 1,200 |
|     Notes Receivable | | 16,000 |

**$16,000 × 10% × \frac{9}{12}$

# Practice Problem

**(LO 1, 2, 3)** The following selected transactions relate to B. Dylan Corporation.

*Prepare entries for various receivables transactions.*

Mar.  1   Sold $20,000 of merchandise to Potter Company, terms 2/10, n/30.

     11   Received payment in full from Potter Company for the balance related to the March 1 sale.

     12   Accepted Juno Company's $20,000, 6-month, 12% note for balance due on outstanding accounts receivable.

     13   Made B. Dylan Corporation credit card sales for $13,200.

     15   Made Visa credit card sales totaling $6,700. A 5% service fee is charged by Visa.

Apr. 11   Sold accounts receivable of $8,000 to Harcot Factor. Harcot Factor assesses a service charge of 2% of the amount of receivables sold.

     13   Received collections of $8,200 on B. Dylan Corporation credit card sales and added finance charges of 1.5% to the remaining balances.

May  10   Wrote off as uncollectible $16,000 of accounts receivable. (B. Dylan Corporation uses the percentage-of-receivables basis to estimate uncollectibles.)

June 30   An aging schedule indicates total uncollectibles of $23,500. At June 30, the balance in the allowance account is $3,500 before adjustment.

July 16   One of the accounts receivable written off in May was from J. Simon, who pays the amount due, $4,000, in full.

## Instructions

Prepare the journal entries for the transactions. (Ignore entries for cost of goods sold.)

## Solution

| | | | |
|---|---|---:|---:|
| Mar. 1 | Accounts Receivable | 20,000 | |
| | Sales Revenue | | 20,000 |
| | (To record sales on account) | | |
| 11 | Cash | 19,600 | |
| | Sales Discounts (2% × $20,000) | 400 | |
| | Accounts Receivable | | 20,000 |
| | (To record collection of accounts receivable) | | |
| 12 | Notes Receivable | 20,000 | |
| | Accounts Receivable | | 20,000 |
| | (To record acceptance of Juno Company note) | | |
| 13 | Accounts Receivable | 13,200 | |
| | Sales Revenue | | 13,200 |
| | (To record company credit card sales) | | |
| 15 | Cash | 6,365 | |
| | Service Charge Expense (5% × $6,700) | 335 | |
| | Sales Revenue | | 6,700 |
| | (To record credit card sales) | | |
| Apr. 11 | Cash | 7,840 | |
| | Service Charge Expense (2% × $8,000) | 160 | |
| | Accounts Receivable | | 8,000 |
| | (To record sale of receivables to factor) | | |
| 13 | Cash | 8,200 | |
| | Accounts Receivable | | 8,200 |
| | (To record collection of accounts receivable) | | |
| | Accounts Receivable [($13,200 – $8,200) × 1.5%] | 75 | |
| | Interest Revenue | | 75 |
| | (To record interest on amount due) | | |
| May 10 | Allowance for Doubtful Accounts | 16,000 | |
| | Accounts Receivable | | 16,000 |
| | (To record write-off of accounts receivable) | | |

| | | | |
|---|---|---|---|
| June 30 | Bad Debt Expense ($23,500 – $3,500) | 20,000 | |
| | Allowance for Doubtful Accounts | | 20,000 |
| | (To record estimate of uncollectible accounts) | | |
| July 16 | Accounts Receivable | 4,000 | |
| | Allowance for Doubtful Accounts | | 4,000 |
| | (To reverse write-off of accounts receivable) | | |
| | Cash | 4,000 | |
| | Accounts Receivable | | 4,000 |
| | (To record collection of accounts receivable) | | |

Brief Exercises, DO IT! Exercises, Exercises, Problems, Data Analytics Activities, and many additional resources are available for practice in WileyPLUS.

## Questions

1. What is the difference between an account receivable and a note receivable?

2. What are some common types of receivables other than accounts receivable and notes receivable?

3. **Texaco** issues its own credit cards. Assume that Texaco charges you $40 interest on an unpaid balance. Prepare the journal entry that Texaco makes to record this revenue.

4. What are the essential features of the allowance method of accounting for uncollectibles?

5. Lance Morrow cannot understand why cash realizable value does not decrease when an uncollectible account is written off under the allowance method. Clarify this point for Lance.

6. What types of receivables does **Apple** report on its balance sheet? Does it use the allowance method or the direct write-off method to account for uncollectibles?

7. Sarasota Company has a credit balance of $2,200 in Allowance for Doubtful Accounts before adjustment. The total estimated uncollectibles under the percentage-of-receivables basis is $5,100. Prepare the adjusting entry to record bad debt expense.

8. How are uncollectibles accounted for under the direct write-off method? What are the disadvantages of this method?

9. Tawyna Dobbs, the vice president of sales for Tropical Pools and Spas, wants the company's credit department to be less restrictive in granting credit. "How can we sell anything when you guys won't approve anybody?" she asks. Discuss the pros and cons of easy credit. What are the accounting implications?

10. **JCPenney** accepts both its own credit cards and national credit cards. What are the advantages of accepting both types of cards?

11. An article that was published in the *Wall Street Journal* indicated that companies are selling their receivables at a record rate. Why are companies selling their receivables?

12. **Calico Corners** decides to sell $400,000 of its accounts receivable to Fast Cash Factors Inc. Fast Cash Factors assesses a service charge of 3% of the amount of receivables sold. Prepare the journal entry that Calico Corners makes to record this sale.

13. Your roommate is uncertain about the advantages of a promissory note. Compare the advantages of a note receivable with those of an account receivable.

14. How may the maturity date of a promissory note be stated?

15. Indicate the maturity date of each of the following promissory notes:

| Date of Note | Terms |
|---|---|
| a. March 13 | one year after date of note |
| b. May 4 | 3 months after date |
| c. June 20 | 30 days after date |
| d. July 1 | 60 days after date |

16. Compute the missing amounts for each of the following notes.

| Principal | Annual Interest Rate | Time | Total Interest |
|---|---|---|---|
| (a) | 6% | 60 days | $ 270 |
| $60,000 | (b) | 5 months | $2,500 |
| $50,000 | 11% | (c) | $2,750 |
| $30,000 | 8% | 3 years | (d) |

17. Mendosa Company dishonors a note at maturity. What are the options available to the lender?

18. **General Motors** has accounts receivable and notes receivable. How should the receivables be reported on the balance sheet?

19. The accounts receivable turnover is 8.14, and average net accounts receivable during the period is $400,000. What is the amount of net credit sales for the period?

# Brief Exercises

**BE8.1 (LO 1), C** The following are three receivables transactions. Indicate whether these receivables are reported as accounts receivable, notes receivable, or other receivables on a balance sheet.

*Identify different types of receivables.*

   **a.** Sold merchandise on account for $64,000 to a customer.

   **b.** Received a promissory note of $57,000 for services performed.

   **c.** Advanced $10,000 to an employee.

**BE8.2 (LO 1), AP** Record the following transactions on the books of Jarvis Co. (Omit cost of goods sold entries.)

*Record basic accounts receivable transactions.*

   **a.** On July 1, Jarvis Co. sold merchandise on account to Stacey Inc. for $23,000, terms 2/10, n/30.

   **b.** On July 8, Stacey Inc. returned merchandise with a sales price of $2,400 to Jarvis Co.

   **c.** On July 11, Stacey Inc. paid the balance due.

**BE8.3 (LO 2), AP** Bayfiew Corp uses the percentage-of-receivables basis to record bad debt expense.

*Prepare entry using the percentage-of-receivables method.*

| | |
|---|---|
| Accounts receivable (ending balance) | $550,000 (debit) |
| Allowance for doubtful accounts (unadjusted) | 4,200 (debit) |

The company estimates that 3% of accounts receivable will become uncollectible.

   **a.** Prepare the adjusting journal entry to record bad debt expense for the year.

   **b.** What is the ending (adjusted) balance in Allowance for Doubtful Accounts?

   **c.** What is the cash (net) realizable value?

**BE8.4 (LO 2), AP** At the end of 2021, Safer Co. has accounts receivable of $700,000 and an allowance for doubtful accounts of $25,000. On January 24, 2022, it is learned that the company's receivable from Madonna Inc. is not collectible and therefore management authorizes a write-off of $4,300.

*Prepare entry for write-off, and determine cash realizable value.*

   **a.** Prepare the journal entry to record the write-off.

   **b.** What is the cash realizable value of the accounts receivable (1) before the write-off and (2) after the write-off?

**BE8.5 (LO 2), AP** At the end of 2021, Safer Co. has accounts receivable of $700,000 and an allowance for doubtful accounts of $25,000. On January 24, 2022, it is learned that the company's receivable from Madonna Inc. is not collectible and therefore management authorizes a write-off of $4,300. On March 4, 2022, Safer Co. receives payment of $4,300 in full from Madonna Inc. Prepare the journal entries to record this transaction.

*Prepare entries for collection of customer account write-off.*

**BE8.6 (LO 2), AP** Byrd Co. uses the percentage-of-receivables basis to record bad debt expense and concludes that 2% of accounts receivable will become uncollectible. Accounts receivable are $400,000 at the end of the year, and the allowance for doubtful accounts has a credit balance of $2,800.

*Prepare entry using percentage-of-receivables method.*

   **a.** Prepare the adjusting journal entry to record bad debt expense for the year.

   **b.** If the allowance for doubtful accounts had a debit balance of $900 instead of a credit balance of $2,800, prepare the adjusting journal entry for bad debt expense.

**BE8.7 (LO 2), AP** Consider these transactions:

*Prepare entries for credit card sale and sale of accounts receivable.*

   **a.** Tastee Restaurant accepted a Visa card in payment of a $200 lunch bill. The bank charges a 3% fee. What entry should Tastee make?

   **b.** Martin Company sold its accounts receivable of $65,000. What entry should Martin make, given a service charge of 3% on the amount of receivables sold?

**BE8.8 (LO 3), AP** Compute interest and find the maturity date for the following notes.

*Compute interest and determine maturity dates on notes.*

| Date of Note | Face Value | Interest Rate (%) | Terms |
|---|---|---|---|
| **a.** June 10 | $80,000 | 6% | 60 days |
| **b.** July 14 | $50,000 | 7% | 90 days |
| **c.** April 27 | $12,000 | 8% | 75 days |

*Determine maturity dates and compute interest and rates on notes.*

**BE8.9 (LO 3), AN** The following are data on three promissory notes. Determine the missing amounts.

| | Date of Note | Terms | Maturity Date | Face Value | Annual Interest Rate | Total Interest |
|---|---|---|---|---|---|---|
| a. | April 1 | 60 days | ? | $600,000 | 9% | ? |
| b. | July 2 | 30 days | ? | 90,000 | ? | $600 |
| c. | March 7 | 6 months | ? | 120,000 | 10% | ? |

*Prepare entry for note receivable exchanged for accounts receivable.*

**BE8.10 (LO 3), AP** On January 10, 2022, Masterson Co. sold merchandise on account to Tompkins for $8,000, terms n/30. On February 9, Tompkins gave Masterson Co. a 7% promissory note in settlement of this account. Prepare the journal entry to record the sale and the settlement of the accounts receivable. (Omit cost of goods sold entries.)

*Prepare entry for estimated uncollectibles and classifications, and compute ratios.*

**BE8.11 (LO 2, 4), AP** During its first year of operations, Fertig Company had net credit sales of $3,000,000, of which $400,000 remained uncollected at year-end. The credit manager estimates that $18,000 of these receivables will become uncollectible.

a. Prepare the journal entry to record the estimated uncollectibles. (Assume an unadjusted balance of zero in Allowance for Doubtful Accounts.)

b. Prepare the current assets section of the balance sheet for Fertig Company, assuming that in addition to the receivables it has cash of $90,000, merchandise inventory of $180,000, and supplies of $13,000.

c. Calculate the accounts receivable turnover and average collection period. Assume that average net accounts receivable were $300,000. Explain what these measures tell us.

*Analyze accounts receivable.*

**BE8.12 (LO 4), AP** Suppose the 2022 financial statements of **3M Company** report net credit sales of $23.1 billion. Accounts receivable (net) are $3.2 billion at the beginning of the year and $3.25 billion at the end of the year. Compute 3M's accounts receivable turnover. Compute 3M's average collection period for accounts receivable in days.

# DO IT! Exercises

*Prepare entries to recognize accounts receivable.*

**DO IT! 8.1 (LO 1), AP** On March 1, Lincoln sold merchandise on account to Amelia Company for $28,000, terms 1/10, n/45. On March 6, Amelia returns merchandise with a sales price of $1,000. On March 11, Lincoln receives payment from Amelia for the balance due. Prepare journal entries to record the March transactions on Lincoln's books. (You may ignore cost of goods sold entries and explanations.)

*Prepare entry for uncollectible accounts.*

**DO IT! 8.2a (LO 2), AP** Mantle Company has been in business several years. At the end of the current year, the unadjusted trial balance shows:

| | |
|---|---|
| Accounts Receivable | $  310,000 Dr. |
| Sales Revenue | 2,200,000 Cr. |
| Allowance for Doubtful Accounts | 5,700 Cr. |

Uncollectibles are estimated to be 7% of receivables. Prepare the entry to adjust Allowance for Doubtful Accounts.

*Prepare entry for factored accounts.*

**DO IT! 8.2b (LO 2), AP** Neumann Distributors is a growing company whose ability to raise capital has not been growing as quickly as its expanding assets and sales. Neumann's local banker has indicated that the company cannot increase its borrowing for the foreseeable future. Neumann's suppliers are demanding payment for goods acquired within 30 days of the invoice date, but Neumann's customers are slow in paying for their purchases (60–90 days). As a result, Neumann has a cash flow problem.

Neumann needs $160,000 to cover next Friday's payroll. Its balance of outstanding accounts receivable totals $800,000. To alleviate this cash crunch, the company sells $170,000 of its receivables. Record the entry that Neumann would make. (Assume a 2% service charge.)

*Prepare entries for notes receivable.*

**DO IT! 8.3 (LO 3), AP** Buffet Wholesalers accepts from Gates Stores a $6,200, 4-month, 9% note dated May 31 in settlement of Gates' overdue account. The maturity date of the note is September 30. What entry does Buffet make at the maturity date, assuming Gates pays the note and interest in full at that time?

*Compute ratios for receivables.*

**DO IT! 8.4 (LO 4), AP** In 2022, Bismark Company has net credit sales of $1,600,000 for the year. It had a beginning accounts receivable (net) balance of $108,000 and an ending accounts receivable (net) balance of $120,000. Compute Bismark Company's (a) accounts receivable turnover and (b) average collection period in days.

## Exercises

**E8.1 (LO 1), AP** On January 6, Jacob Co. sells merchandise on account to Harley Inc. for $9,200, terms 1/10, n/30. On January 16, Harley pays the amount due.

*Prepare entries for recognizing accounts receivable.*

**Instructions**

Prepare the entries on Jacob Co.'s books to record the sale and related collection. (Omit cost of goods sold entries.)

**E8.2 (LO 1), AP** The following are selected transactions of Molina Company. Molina sells in large quantities to other companies and also sells its product in a small retail outlet.

*Journalize entries related to accounts receivable.*

| March | 1 | Sold merchandise on account to Dodson Company for $5,000, terms 2/10, n/30. |
|---|---|---|
| | 3 | Dodson Company returned merchandise with a sales price of $500 to Molina. |
| | 9 | Molina collected the amount due from Dodson Company from the March 1 sale. |
| | 15 | Molina sold merchandise for $400 in its retail outlet. The customer used his Molina credit card. |
| | 31 | Molina added 1.5% monthly interest to the customer's credit card balance. |

**Instructions**

Prepare journal entries for the transactions above. (Ignore cost of goods sold entries and explanations.)

**E8.3 (LO 1), AP** The following are two independent situations.

*Journalize entries for recognizing accounts receivable.*

**Instructions**

a. On January 6, Brumbaugh Co. sells merchandise on account to Pryor Inc. for $7,000, terms 2/10, n/30. On January 16, Pryor Inc. pays the amount due. Prepare the entries on Brumbaugh's books to record the sale and related collection. (Omit cost of goods sold entries.)

b. On January 10, Andrew Farley uses his Paltrow Co. credit card to purchase merchandise from Paltrow Co. for $9,000. On February 10, Farley is billed for the amount due of $9,000. On February 12, Farley pays $5,000 on the balance due. On March 10, Farley is billed for the amount due, including interest at 1% per month on the unpaid balance as of February 12. Prepare the entries on Paltrow Co.'s books related to the transactions that occurred on January 10, February 12, and March 10. (Omit cost of goods sold entries.)

**E8.4 (LO 1, 2), AP** At the beginning of the current period, Rose Corp. had balances in Accounts Receivable of $200,000 and in Allowance for Doubtful Accounts of $9,000 (credit). During the period, it had credit sales of $800,000 and collections of $763,000. It wrote off as uncollectible accounts receivable of $7,300. However, a $3,100 account previously written off as uncollectible was recovered before the end of the current period. Uncollectible accounts are estimated to total $25,000 at the end of the period. (Omit cost of goods sold entries.)

*Journalize receivables transactions.*

**Instructions**

a. Prepare the entries to record sales and collections during the period.

b. Prepare the entry to record the write-off of uncollectible accounts during the period.

c. Prepare the entries to record the recovery of the uncollectible account during the period.

d. Prepare the entry to record bad debt expense for the period.

e. Determine the ending balances in Accounts Receivable and Allowance for Doubtful Accounts.

f. What is the net realizable value of the receivables at the end of the period?

**E8.5 (LO 2), AP** The ledger of Macarty Company at the end of the current year shows Accounts Receivable $78,000, Credit Sales $310,000, and Sales Returns and Allowances $40,000.

*Journalize entries to record allowance for doubtful accounts using two different bases.*

**Instructions**

a. If Macarty uses the direct write-off method to account for uncollectible accounts, journalize the entry at December 15 if Macarty determines that Matisse's $900 balance is uncollectible.

b. If Allowance for Doubtful Accounts has a credit balance of $1,100 in the trial balance, journalize the adjusting entry at December 31, assuming uncollectibles are expected to be 10% of accounts receivable.

c. If Allowance for Doubtful Accounts has a debit balance of $500 in the trial balance, journalize the adjusting entry at December 31, assuming uncollectibles are expected to be 8% of accounts receivable.

*Determine bad debt expense, and prepare the adjusting entry.*

**E8.6 (LO 2), AP** Godfreid Company has accounts receivable of $95,400 at March 31, 2022. Credit terms are 2/10, n/30. At March 31, 2022, there is a $2,100 credit balance in Allowance for Doubtful Accounts prior to adjustment. The company uses the percentage-of-receivables basis for estimating uncollectible accounts. The company's estimates of uncollectibles are as shown below.

| | Balance, March 31 | | Estimated Percentage |
| Age of Accounts | 2022 | 2021 | Uncollectible |
| --- | --- | --- | --- |
| Current | $65,000 | $75,000 | 2% |
| 1–30 days past due | 12,900 | 8,000 | 5 |
| 31–90 days past due | 10,100 | 2,400 | 30 |
| Over 90 days past due | 7,400 | 1,100 | 50 |
| | $95,400 | $86,500 | |

**Instructions**

a. Determine the total estimated uncollectibles at March 31, 2022.

b. Prepare the adjusting entry at March 31, 2022, to record bad debt expense.

c. Discuss the implications of the changes in the aging schedule from 2021 to 2022.

*Journalize write-off and recovery.*

**E8.7 (LO 2), AP** At December 31, 2021, Blanda Company had a credit balance of $15,000 in Allowance for Doubtful Accounts. During 2022, Blanda wrote off accounts totaling $11,000. One of those accounts of $1,800 was later collected. At December 31, 2022, an aging schedule indicated that the balance in Allowance for Doubtful Accounts should be $19,000.

**Instructions**

Prepare journal entries to record the 2022 transactions of Blanda Company.

*Prepare entries for estimated uncollectibles, write-off, and recovery.*

**E8.8 (LO 2), AP** On December 31, 2021, when its Allowance for Doubtful Accounts had a debit balance of $1,400, Dallas Co. estimates that 9% of its accounts receivable balance of $90,000 will become uncollectible and records the necessary adjustment to Allowance for Doubtful Accounts. On May 11, 2022, Dallas Co. determined that B. Jared's account was uncollectible and wrote off $1,200. On June 12, 2022, Jared paid the amount previously written off.

**Instructions**

Prepare the journal entries on December 31, 2021, May 11, 2022, and June 12, 2022.

*Journalize entries for the sale of accounts receivable.*

**E8.9 (LO 2), AP** The following are two independent situations. (Ignore cost of goods sold entries.)

**Instructions**

a. On March 3, Kitselman Appliances sells $650,000 of its receivables to Ervay Factors Inc. Ervay Factors assesses a finance charge of 3% of the amount of receivables sold. Prepare the entry on Kitselman Appliances' books to record the sale of the receivables.

b. On May 10, Fillmore Company sold merchandise for $3,000 and accepted the customer's America Bank MasterCard. America Bank charges a 4% service charge for credit card sales. Prepare the entry on Fillmore Company's books to record the sale of merchandise.

*Journalize entries for credit card sales.*

**E8.10 (LO 2), AP** The following are two independent situations.

**Instructions**

a. On April 2, Jennifer Elston uses her **JCPenney** credit card to purchase merchandise from a JCPenney store for $1,500. On May 1, Elston is billed for the $1,500 amount due. Elston pays $500 on the balance due on May 3. Elston receives a bill dated June 1 for the amount due, including interest at 1.0% per month on the unpaid balance as of May 3. Prepare the entries on JCPenney Co.'s books related to the transactions that occurred on April 2, May 3, and June 1.

b. On July 4, Spangler's Restaurant accepts a Visa card for a $200 dinner bill. Visa charges a 2% service fee. Prepare the entry on Spangler's books related to this transaction.

*Journalize credit card sales.*

**E8.11 (LO 2), AP** Colaw Stores accepts both its own and national credit cards. During the year, the following selected summary transactions occurred.

| | | |
| --- | --- | --- |
| Jan. | 15 | Made Colaw credit card sales totaling $18,000. (There were no balances prior to January 15.) |
| | 20 | Made Visa credit card sales (service charge fee 2%) totaling $4,500. |
| Feb. | 10 | Collected $10,000 on Colaw credit card sales. |
| | 15 | Added finance charges of 1.5% to Colaw credit card account balances. |

**Instructions**

Journalize the transactions for Colaw Stores.

**E8.12 (LO 3), AP** Moses Supply Co. has the following transactions related to notes receivable during the last 2 months of the year. The company does not make entries to accrue interest except at December 31.

*Prepare entries for notes receivable transactions.*

Nov. 1   Loaned $60,000 cash to C. Bohr on a 12-month, 7% note.
Dec. 11   Sold goods to K. R. Fine, Inc., receiving a $3,600, 90-day, 8% note.
     16   Received a $12,000, 180-day, 9% note to settle an open account from A. Murdock.
     31   Accrued interest revenue on all notes receivable.

**Instructions**

Journalize the transactions for Moses Supply Co. (Omit cost of goods sold entries.)

**E8.13 (LO 3), AP** These transactions took place for Bramson Co.

*Journalize notes receivable transactions.*

**2021**

May 1   Received a $5,000, 12-month, 6% note in exchange for an outstanding account receivable from R. Stoney.
Dec. 31   Accrued interest revenue on the R. Stoney note.

**2022**

May 1   Received principal plus interest on the R. Stoney note. (No interest has been accrued since December 31, 2021.)

**Instructions**

Record the transactions in the general journal. The company does not make entries to accrue interest except at December 31.

**E8.14 (LO 3), AP** Vandiver Company had the following selected transactions.

*Prepare entries for notes receivable transactions.*

Apr. 1, 2022   Accepted Goodwin Company's 12-month, 6% note in settlement of a $30,000 account receivable.
July 1, 2022   Loaned $25,000 cash to Thomas Slocombe on a 9-month, 10% note.
Dec. 31, 2022   Accrued interest on all notes receivable.
Apr. 1, 2023   Received principal plus interest on the Goodwin note.
Apr. 1, 2023   Thomas Slocombe dishonored its note; Vandiver expects it will eventually collect.

**Instructions**

Prepare journal entries to record the transactions. Vandiver prepares adjusting entries once a year on December 31.

**E8.15 (LO 3), AP** On May 2, McLain Company lends $9,000 to Chang, Inc., issuing a 6-month, 7% note. At the November 2 maturity date, Chang indicates that it cannot pay.

*Journalize entries for dishonor of notes receivable.*

**Instructions**

a. Prepare the entry to record the issuance of the note.

b. Prepare the entry to record the dishonor of the note, assuming that McLain Company expects collection will occur.

c. Prepare the entry to record the dishonor of the note, assuming that McLain Company does not expect collection in the future.

**E8.16 (LO 4), AP** Eileen Corp. had the following balances in receivable accounts at October 31, 2022 (in thousands): Allowance for Doubtful Accounts $52, Accounts Receivable $2,910, Other Receivables $189, and Notes Receivable $1,353.

*Prepare a balance sheet presentation of receivables.*

**Instructions**

Prepare the balance sheet presentation of Eileen Corp.'s receivables in good form.

**E8.17 (LO 4), AN** Kerwick Company had net accounts receivable of $100,000 on January 1, 2022. The only transactions that affected accounts receivable during 2022 were net credit sales of $1,000,000. At December 31, 2022, the company had net receivables of $150,000.

*Compute accounts receivable turnover and average collection period.*

**Instructions**

a. Compute the accounts receivable turnover for 2022.

b. Compute the average collection period in days.

## Problems

*Prepare journal entries related to bad debt expense, and compute ratios.*

**P8.1 (LO 1, 2, 4), AP** At December 31, 2021, Suisse Imports reported this information on its balance sheet.

| | |
|---|---|
| Accounts receivable | $600,000 |
| Less: Allowance for doubtful accounts | 37,000 |

During 2022, the company had the following transactions related to receivables.

| | |
|---|---|
| 1. Sales on account | $2,500,000 |
| 2. Sales returns and allowances | 50,000 |
| 3. Collections of accounts receivable | 2,200,000 |
| 4. Write-offs of accounts receivable deemed uncollectible | 41,000 |
| 5. Recovery of accounts previously written off as uncollectible | 15,000 |

### Instructions

a. Prepare the journal entries to record each of these five transactions. Assume that no cash discounts were taken on the collections of accounts receivable. (Omit cost of goods sold entries.)

*b. A/R bal. $809,000*

b. Enter the January 1, 2022, balances in Accounts Receivable and Allowance for Doubtful Accounts, post the entries to the two accounts (use T-accounts), and determine the balances.

c. Prepare the journal entry to record bad debt expense for 2022, assuming that aging the accounts receivable indicates that estimated uncollectibles are $46,000.

d. Compute the accounts receivable turnover and average collection period.

*Compute bad debt expense amounts.*

**P8.2 (LO 2), AP** Writing Here is information related to Morgane Company for 2022.

| | |
|---|---|
| Total credit sales | $1,500,000 |
| Accounts receivable at December 31 | 840,000 |
| Uncollectibles written off | 37,000 |

### Instructions

a. What amount of bad debt expense will Morgane Company report if it uses the direct write-off method of accounting for uncollectibles?

*b. Bad Debt Exp. $30,600*

b. Assume that Morgane Company uses the percentage-of-receivables basis to record bad debt expense and concludes that 4% of accounts receivable will become uncollectible. What amount of bad debt expense will the company record if Allowance for Doubtful Accounts has a credit balance of $3,000?

c. Assume the same facts as in part (b), except that there is a $1,000 debit balance in Allowance for Doubtful Accounts. What amount of bad debt expense will Morgane record?

d. What is a weakness of the direct write-off method of recording bad debt expense?

*Journalize transactions related to uncollectibles.*

**P8.3 (LO 2), AP** Presented below is an aging schedule for Bryan Company at December 31, 2021.

| Customer | Total | Not Yet Due | Number of Days Past Due 1–30 | Number of Days Past Due 31–60 | Number of Days Past Due 61–90 | Number of Days Past Due Over 90 |
|---|---|---|---|---|---|---|
| Aneesh | $ 24,000 | | $ 9,000 | $15,000 | | |
| Bird | 30,000 | $ 30,000 | | | | |
| Cope | 50,000 | 5,000 | 5,000 | | $40,000 | |
| DeSpears | 38,000 | | | | | $38,000 |
| Others | 120,000 | 72,000 | 35,000 | 13,000 | | |
| | $262,000 | $107,000 | $49,000 | $28,000 | $40,000 | $38,000 |
| Estimated percentage uncollectible | | 3% | 7% | 12% | 24% | 60% |
| Total estimated uncollectibles | $ 42,400 | $ 3,210 | $ 3,430 | $ 3,360 | $ 9,600 | $22,800 |

At December 31, 2021, the unadjusted balance in Allowance for Doubtful Accounts is a credit of $8,000.

**Instructions**

a. Journalize and post the adjusting entry for uncollectibles at December 31, 2021. (Use T-accounts.)

b. Journalize and post to the allowance account these 2022 selected events and transactions:

  1. March 1, a $600 customer balance originating in 2021 is judged uncollectible.

  2. May 1, a check for $600 is received from the customer whose account was written off as uncollectible on March 1.

c. Journalize the adjusting entry for uncollectibles at December 31, 2022, assuming that the unadjusted balance in Allowance for Doubtful Accounts is a debit of $1,400 and the aging schedule indicates that total estimated uncollectibles will be $36,700.

*a. Bad Debt Exp. $34,400*

**P8.4 (LO 2), AP** Rianna.com uses the allowance method of accounting for uncollectibles. The company produced the following aging of the accounts receivable at year-end.

*Journalize transactions related to uncollectibles.*

| | | | Number of Days Outstanding | | | |
|---|---|---|---|---|---|---|
| | **Total** | **0–30** | **31–60** | **61–90** | **91–120** | **Over 120** |
| Accounts receivable | $377,000 | $222,000 | $90,000 | $38,000 | $15,000 | $12,000 |
| % uncollectible | | 1% | 4% | 5% | 8% | 10% |

**Instructions**

a. Calculate the total estimated uncollectibles based on the above information.

b. Prepare the year-end adjusting journal entry to record Bad Debt Expense using the aged uncollectible accounts receivable determined in (a). Assume the unadjusted balance in Allowance for Doubtful Accounts is a $4,000 debit.

c. Of the above accounts, $5,000 is determined to be specifically uncollectible. Prepare the journal entry to write off the uncollectible account.

d. The company collects $5,000 subsequently on a specific account that had previously been determined to be uncollectible in (c). Prepare the journal entry or entries necessary to restore the account and record the cash collection.

e. Comment on how your answers to (a)–(d) would change if Rianna.com used 3% of total accounts receivable, rather than aging the accounts receivable. What are the advantages to the company of aging the accounts receivable rather than applying a percentage to total accounts receivable?

*a. Tot. est. uncollectibles $10,120*

**P8.5 (LO 2), AP** Writing At December 31, 2022, the trial balance of Malone Company contained the following amounts before adjustment.

*Journalize entries to record transactions related to uncollectibles.*

| | **Debit** | **Credit** |
|---|---|---|
| Accounts Receivable | $180,000 | |
| Allowance for Doubtful Accounts | | $ 1,500 |
| Sales Revenue | | 875,000 |

**Instructions**

a. Prepare the adjusting entry at December 31, 2022, to record bad debt expense, assuming that the aging schedule indicates that $10,200 of accounts receivable will be uncollectible.

b. Repeat part (a), assuming that instead of a credit balance there is a $1,500 debit balance in Allowance for Doubtful Accounts.

*b. Bad Debt Exp. $11,700*

c. During the next month, January 2023, a $2,100 account receivable is written off as uncollectible. Prepare the journal entry to record the write-off.

d. Repeat part (c), assuming that Malone Company uses the direct write-off method instead of the allowance method in accounting for uncollectible accounts receivable.

e. What are the advantages of using the allowance method in accounting for uncollectible accounts as compared to the direct write-off method?

**P8.6 (LO 1, 2, 3, 4), AP** Milton Company closes its books on its July 31 year-end. The company does not make entries to accrue for interest except at its year-end. On June 30, the Notes Receivable account balance is $23,800. Notes Receivable includes the following

*Prepare entries for various credit card and notes receivable transactions.*

| Date | Maker | Face Value | Term | Maturity Date | Interest Rate |
|------|-------|-----------|------|---------------|---------------|
| April 21 | Coote Inc. | $ 6,000 | 90 days | July 20 | 8% |
| May 25 | Brady Co. | 7,800 | 60 days | July 24 | 10% |
| June 30 | BMG Corp. | 10,000 | 6 months | December 31 | 6% |

During July, the following transactions were completed.

| July | 5 | Made sales of $4,500 on Milton credit cards. |
|------|----|-----|
| | 14 | Made sales of $600 on Visa credit cards. The credit card service charge is 3%. |
| | 20 | Received payment in full from Coote Inc. on the amount due. |
| | 24 | Received payment in full from Brady Co. on the amount due. |

### Instructions

a. Journalize the July transactions and the July 31 adjusting entry to accrue interest receivable. (Interest is computed using 360 days for terms expressed in days; omit cost of goods sold entries.)

b. Enter the balances at July 1 in the receivable accounts and post the entries to all of the receivable accounts. (Use T-accounts.)

c. Show the balance sheet presentation of the receivable accounts at July 31, 2022.

b. A/R bal. $4,500

c. Tot. receivables $14,550

*Journalize various receivables transactions.*

**P8.7 (LO 1, 2, 3), AP** On January 1, 2022, Harvee Company had Accounts Receivable of $54,200 and Allowance for Doubtful Accounts of $3,700. Harvee Company prepares financial statements annually. During the year, the following selected transactions occurred.

| Jan. | 5 | Sold $4,000 of merchandise to Rian Company, terms n/30. |
|------|----|-----|
| Feb. | 2 | Accepted a $4,000, 4-month, 9% promissory note from Rian Company for balance due. |
| | 12 | Sold $12,000 of merchandise to Cato Company and accepted Cato's $12,000, 2-month, 10% note. |
| | 26 | Sold $5,200 of merchandise to Malcolm Co., terms n/10. |
| Apr. | 5 | Accepted a $5,200, 3-month, 8% note from Malcolm Co. |
| | 12 | Collected Cato Company note in full. |
| June | 2 | Collected Rian Company note in full. |
| | 15 | Sold $2,000 of merchandise to Gerri Inc. and accepted a $2,000, 6-month, 12% note. |

### Instructions

Journalize the transactions. (Omit cost of goods sold entries.)

*Calculate and interpret various ratios.*

**P8.8 (LO 4), AN** Suppose the amounts presented here are basic financial information (in millions) from the 2022 annual reports of **Nike** and **adidas**.

| | Nike | adidas |
|------|------|--------|
| Sales revenue (net) | $19,176.1 | $10,381 |
| Allowance for doubtful accounts, beginning | 78.4 | 119 |
| Allowance for doubtful accounts, ending | 110.8 | 124 |
| Accounts receivable balance (gross), beginning | 2,873.7 | 1,743 |
| Accounts receivable balance (gross), ending | 2,994.7 | 1,553 |

### Instructions

Calculate the accounts receivable turnover and average collection period for both companies. Comment on the difference in their collection experiences.

*Prepare financial statements.*

**P8.9 (LO 4), AP** The adjusted trial balance of Gibson Company for the year ended December 31, 2022, is as follows:

| | Debit | Credit |
|------|-------|--------|
| Cash | $ 6,400 | |
| Accounts Receivable | 2,700 | |
| Notes Receivable | 6,300 | |
| Inventory | 10,000 | |
| Equipment | 7,500 | |
| Allowance for Doubtful Accounts | | $ 300 |
| Accumulated Depreciation—Equipment | | 1,000 |
| Notes Payable | | 1,100 |
| Accounts Payable | | 600 |
| Common Stock | | 17,000 |

|                          | Debit    | Credit   |
|--------------------------|----------|----------|
| Retained Earnings        |          | 11,000   |
| Dividends                | 1,000    |          |
| Sales Revenue            |          | 13,000   |
| Interest Revenue         |          | 100      |
| Cost of Goods Sold       | 8,000    |          |
| Salaries and Wages Expense | 1,400  |          |
| Rent Expense             | 700      |          |
| Bad Debt Expense         | 60       |          |
| Service Charge Expense   | 40       |          |
|                          | $44,100  | $44,100  |

### Instructions

Prepare a multiple-step income statement, retained earnings statement, and classified balance sheet. The notes payable is due on January 10, 2023. The notes receivable is due on June 30, 2023. Allowance for Doubtful Accounts applies to Accounts Receivable only.

Retained earnings $12,900

## Continuing Case

### Cookie Creations

(*Note:* This is a continuation of the Cookie Creations case from Chapters 1 through 7.)

**CC8** One of Natalie's friends, Curtis Lesperance, runs a coffee shop where he sells specialty coffees and prepares and sells muffins and cookies. He is eager to buy one of Natalie's fine European mixers, which would enable him to make larger batches of muffins and cookies. However, Curtis cannot afford to pay for the mixer for at least 30 days. He asks Natalie if she would be willing to sell him the mixer on credit. Natalie comes to you for advice.

*Go to WileyPLUS for complete case details and instructions.*

Leungchopan/
Shutterstock.com

## Comprehensive Accounting Cycle Review

**ACR8** Winter Company's balance sheet at December 31, 2021, is presented as follows.

**Winter Company**
**Balance Sheet**
**December 31, 2021**

| Cash | $13,100 | Accounts payable | $ 8,750 |
|------|---------|------------------|---------|
| Accounts receivable | 19,780 | Common stock | 20,000 |
| Allowance for doubtful accounts | (800) | Retained earnings | 12,730 |
| Inventory | 9,400 |  | $41,480 |
|  | $41,480 |  |  |

During January 2022, the following transactions occurred. Winter uses the perpetual inventory system.

Jan. 1   Winter accepted a 4-month, 8% note from Merando Company in payment of Merando's $1,200 account.

3   Winter wrote off as uncollectible the accounts of Inwood Corporation ($450) and Goza Company ($280).

8   Winter purchased $17,200 of inventory on account.

11   Winter sold for $28,000 on account inventory that cost $19,600.

15   Winter sold inventory that cost $700 to Mark Lauber for $1,000. Lauber charged this amount on his Visa First Bank card. The service fee charged Winter by First Bank is 3%.

17   Winter collected $22,900 from customers on account. No sales discounts were allowed.

21   Winter paid $14,300 on accounts payable. No purchase discounts were taken.

24   Winter received payment in full ($280) from Goza Company on the account written off on January 3.

27   Winter purchased supplies for $1,400 cash.

31   Winter paid other operating expenses, $3,718.

Adjustment data:

1. Interest is recorded for the month on the note from January 1.

2. Uncollectibles are expected to be 6% of the January 31, 2022, accounts receivable.

3. A count of supplies on January 31, 2022, reveals that $560 remains unused.

**Instructions**

(You may want to set up T-accounts to determine ending balances.)

a. Prepare journal entries for the transactions listed above and adjusting entries. (Include entries for cost of goods sold using the perpetual system.)

b. Totals $74,765      **b.** Prepare an adjusted trial balance at January 31, 2022.

c. Total assets $47,473      **c.** Prepare a multiple-step income statement and a retained earnings statement for the month ended January 31, 2022, and a balance sheet as of January 31, 2022.

---

# Expand Your Critical Thinking

### Financial Reporting Problem: Apple Inc.

CT8.1 Refer to the financial statements of **Apple Inc.** in Appendix A. The complete annual report, including the notes to the financial statements, is available at the company's website.

**Instructions**

a. Calculate the accounts receivable turnover and average collection period for the year ended September 29, 2018. (Assume all sales were credit sales.)

b. Did Apple have any potentially significant credit risks during the same period as specified in (a)? (*Hint*: Refer to the notes to the financial statements.)

c. What conclusions can you draw from the information in parts (a) and (b)?

### Comparative Analysis Problem: PepsiCo, Inc. vs. The Coca-Cola Company

CT8.2 **PepsiCo, Inc.**'s financial statements are presented in Appendix B. Financial statements of **The Coca-Cola Company** are presented in Appendix C. The complete annual reports of PepsiCo and Coca-Cola, including the notes to the financial statements, are available at each company's respective website.

**Instructions**

a. Based on the information in these financial statements, compute the following 2018 ratios for each company. (Assume that all sales are credit sales and that PepsiCo's receivables on its balance sheet are all trade receivables.)

    1. Accounts receivable turnover.     2. Average collection period for receivables.

b. What conclusions about managing accounts receivable can you draw from these data?

### Comparative Analysis Problem: Amazon.com, Inc. vs. Walmart Inc.

CT8.3 **Amazon.com, Inc.**'s financial statements are presented in Appendix D. Financial statements of **Walmart Inc.** are presented in Appendix E. The complete annual reports of Amazon and Walmart, including the notes to the financial statements, are available at each company's respective website.

**Instructions**

a. Based on the information in these financial statements, compute the following ratios for each company (for the most recent year shown). (Assume all sales are credit sales.)

    1. Accounts receivable turnover.     2. Average collection period for receivables.

b. What conclusions about managing accounts receivable can you draw from these data?

### Interpreting Financial Statements

CT8.4 RLF Company sells office equipment and supplies to many organizations in the city and surrounding area on contract terms of 2/10, n/30. In the past, over 75% of the credit customers have taken advantage of the discount by paying within 10 days of the invoice date.

The number of customers taking the full 30 days to pay has increased within the last year. Current indications are that less than 60% of the customers are now taking the discount. Uncollectibles as a percentage of gross credit sales have risen from the 2.5% average in past years to about 4.5% in the current year.

The company's Finance Committee has requested more information on the collections of accounts receivable. The controller responded to this request with the following report.

**RLF Company**
**Accounts Receivable Collections**
**May 31, 2020**

The fact that some credit accounts will prove uncollectible is normal. Annual customer account write-offs have been 2.5% of gross credit sales over the past 5 years. During the last fiscal year, this percentage increased to slightly less than 4.5%. The current Accounts Receivable balance is $1,400,000. The distribution of this balance in terms of age and probability of collection is as follows.

| Proportion of Total | Age Categories | Estimated Percentage of Collection |
|---|---|---|
| 60% | not yet due | 98% |
| 22% | less than 30 days past due | 96% |
| 9% | 30 to 60 days past due | 94% |
| 5% | 61 to 120 days past due | 91% |
| 2½% | 121 to 180 days past due | 75% |
| 1½% | over 180 days past due | 30% |

Allowance for Doubtful Accounts had a credit balance of $29,500 on June 1, 2019. RLF has provided for a monthly bad debt expense accrual during the current fiscal year based on the assumption that 4.5% of gross credit sales will be uncollectible. Total gross credit sales for the 2019–2020 fiscal year amounted to $2,900,000. Write-offs of uncollectible accounts during the year totaled $102,000.

**Instructions**

a. Prepare an accounts receivable aging schedule for RLF Company using the age categories identified in the controller's report to the Finance Committee showing the following.

   1. The amount of accounts receivable outstanding for each age category and in total.

   2. The estimated amount that is uncollectible for each category and in total.

b. Compute the amount of the year-end adjustment necessary to bring Allowance for Doubtful Accounts to the balance indicated by the age analysis. Then prepare the necessary journal entry to adjust the accounting records.

c. In a recessionary environment with tight credit and high interest rates:

   1. Identify steps RLF Company might consider to improve the accounts receivable situation.

   2. Then evaluate each step identified in terms of the risks and costs involved.

## Real-World Focus

**CT8.5  Purpose:** To learn more about factoring.

**Instructions**

Go to the **Commercial Capital LLC** website, click on **Invoice Factoring**, and then answer the following questions.

   a. What are some of the benefits of factoring?

   b. What is the range of the percentages of the typical discount rate?

   c. If a company factors its receivables, what percentage of the value of the receivables can it expect to receive from the factor in the form of cash, and how quickly will it receive the cash?

## Decision-Making Across the Organization

**CT8.6**  Emilio and René Santos own Club Fandango. From its inception, Club Fandango has sold merchandise on either a cash or credit basis, but no credit cards have been accepted. During the past several months, the Santos have begun to question their credit-sales policies. First, they have lost some sales because of their refusal to accept credit cards. Second, representatives of two metropolitan banks have convinced them to accept their national credit cards. One bank, Business National Bank, has stated that (1) its credit card fee is 4% and (2) it pays the retailer 96 cents on each $1 of sales within 3 days of receiving the credit card billings.

The Santos decide to determine how much it costs to extend credit to customers. From the accounting records of the past 3 years, they accumulate these data:

|  | 2022 | 2021 | 2020 |
|---|---|---|---|
| Net credit sales | $500,000 | $600,000 | $400,000 |
| Collection agency fees for slow-paying customers | 2,900 | 2,600 | 1,600 |
| Salary of part-time accounts receivable clerk | 4,400 | 4,400 | 4,400 |

Credit and collection expenses as a percentage of net credit sales are as follows: uncollectible accounts 1.6%, billing and mailing costs .5%, and credit investigation fee on new customers .2%.

Emilio and René also determine that the average accounts receivable balance outstanding during the year is 5% of net credit sales. The Santos estimate that they could earn an average of 10% annually on cash invested in other business opportunities.

**Instructions**

With the class divided into groups, answer the following.

a. Prepare a tabulation for each year showing total credit and collection expenses in dollars and as a percentage of net credit sales.

b. Determine the net credit and collection expenses in dollars and as a percentage of net credit sales after considering the revenue not earned from other investment opportunities. (*Note:* The income lost on the cash held by the bank for 3 days is considered to be immaterial.)

c. Discuss both the financial and nonfinancial factors that are relevant to the decision.

## Communication Activity

**CT8.7** Jill Epp, a friend of yours, overheard a discussion at work about changes her employer wants to make in accounting for uncollectible accounts. Jill knows little about accounting, and she asks you to help make sense of what she heard. Specifically, she asks you to explain the differences between the percentage-of-receivables and the direct write-off methods for uncollectible accounts.

**Instructions**

In a letter of one page (or less), explain to Jill the two methods of accounting for uncollectibles. Be sure to discuss differences between these methods.

## Ethics Case

**CT8.8** The controller of Diaz Co. believes that the yearly allowance for doubtful accounts for Diaz Co. should be 2% of accounts receivable. The president of Diaz Co., nervous that the stockholders might expect the company to sustain its 10% growth rate, suggests that the controller increase the allowance for doubtful accounts to 4%. The president thinks that the lower net income, which reflects a 6% growth rate, will be a more sustainable rate for Diaz Co.

**Instructions**

a. Who are the stakeholders in this case?

b. Does the president's request pose an ethical dilemma for the controller?

c. Should the controller be concerned with Diaz Co.'s growth rate? Explain your answer.

## All About You

**CT8.9** Credit card usage in the United States is substantial. Many startup companies use credit cards as a way to help meet short-term financial needs. The most common forms of debt for startups are use of credit cards and loans from relatives.

Suppose that you start up Brothers Sandwich Shop. You invest your savings of $20,000 and borrow $70,000 from your relatives. Although sales in the first few months are good, you see that you may not have sufficient cash to pay expenses and maintain your inventory at acceptable levels, at least in the short term. You decide you may need to use one or more credit cards to fund the possible cash shortfall.

**Instructions**

a. Go to the Internet and find two sources that provide insight into how to compare credit card terms.

b. Develop a list, in descending order of importance, as to what features are most important to you in selecting a credit card for your business.

c. Examine the features of your present credit card. (If you do not have a credit card, select a likely one online for this exercise.) Given your analysis above, what are the three major disadvantages of your present credit card?

### FASB Codification Activity

**CT8.10** If your school has a subscription to the FASB Codification, log in and prepare responses to the following.

   **a.** How are receivables defined in the Codification?

   **b.** What are the conditions under which losses from uncollectible receivables (Bad Debt Expense) should be reported?

### Answers to Insight and Accounting Across the Organization Questions

**Cookie Jar Allowances Q:** How might investors determine that a company is managing its earnings? **A:** If the balance sheet reflects an increase in Accounts Receivable and a decrease in the Allowance for Doubtful Accounts, this could indicate an attempt to manage earnings by reducing the estimated uncollectible percentage.

**How Does a Credit Card Work? Q:** Assume that Nordstrom prepares a bank reconciliation at the end of each month. If some credit card sales have not been processed by the bank, how should Nordstrom treat these transactions on its bank reconciliation? **A:** Nordstrom would treat the credit card receipts as deposits in transit. It has already recorded the receipts as cash. Its bank will increase Nordstrom's cash account when it receives the receipts.

**Bad Information Can Lead to Bad Loans Q:** What steps should the banks have taken to ensure the accuracy of financial information provided on loan applications? **A:** At a minimum, the bank should have requested copies of recent income tax forms and contacted the supposed employer to verify income. To verify ownership and value of assets, it should have examined bank statements, investment statements, and title documents, and should have employed appraisers.

# A Look at IFRS

---

### LEARNING OBJECTIVE 5
Compare the accounting for receivables under GAAP and IFRS.

---

The basic accounting and reporting issues related to the recognition, measurement, and disposition of receivables are essentially the same between IFRS and GAAP.

### Key Points

Following are the key similarities and differences between GAAP and IFRS related to the accounting for receivables.

**Similarities**

- The recording of receivables, the recognition of sales returns and allowances and sales discounts, and the allowance method to record uncollectibles are the same between GAAP and IFRS.

- Both IFRS and GAAP often use the term impairment to indicate that a receivable or a percentage of receivables may not be collectible.

- The FASB and IASB have worked to implement fair value measurement for financial instruments (the amount they currently could be sold for), such as receivables. Both Boards have faced bitter opposition from various factions.

**Differences**

- Although IFRS implies that receivables with different characteristics should be reported separately, there is no standard that mandates this segregation.

- IFRS and GAAP differ in the criteria used to determine how to record a factoring transaction. IFRS uses a combination approach focused on risks and rewards and loss of control. GAAP uses loss of control as the primary criterion. In addition, IFRS permits partial derecognition of receivables; GAAP does not.

# IFRS Practice

## IFRS Self-Test Questions

1. Which of the following statements is **false** under IFRS?

   a. Receivables include equity securities purchased by the company.

   b. Receivables include credit card receivables.

   c. Receivables include amounts owed by employees as a result of company loans to employees.

   d. Receivables include amounts resulting from transactions with customers.

2. In recording a factoring transaction:

   a. IFRS focuses on loss of control.

   b. GAAP focuses on loss of control and risks and rewards.

   c. IFRS and GAAP allow partial derecognition.

   d. IFRS allows partial derecognition.

3. Under IFRS:

   a. the entry to record estimated uncollectible accounts is the same as GAAP.

   b. it is always acceptable to use the direct write-off method.

   c. all financial instruments are recorded at fair value.

   d. None of the answer choices is correct.

## International Financial Reporting Problem: Louis Vuitton

**IFRS8.1** The financial statements of **Louis Vuitton** are presented in Appendix F. The complete consolidated financial statements, including the notes to its financial statements, are available at the company's website.

### Instructions

Use the company's 2018 consolidated financial statements to answer the following questions.

   a. What is the accounting policy related to accounting for trade accounts receivable?

   b. According to the notes to the financial statements, what accounted for the difference between gross trade accounts receivable and net accounts receivable?

   c. According to the notes to the financial statements, what was the major reason why the balance in receivables increased relative to the previous year?

   d. Using information in the notes to the financial statements, determine what percentage the provision for impairment of receivables was as a percentage of gross trade receivables for 2018 and 2017. How did the ratio change from 2017 to 2018, and what does this suggest about the company's receivables?

### Answers to IFRS Self-Test Questions

1. a   2. d   3. a

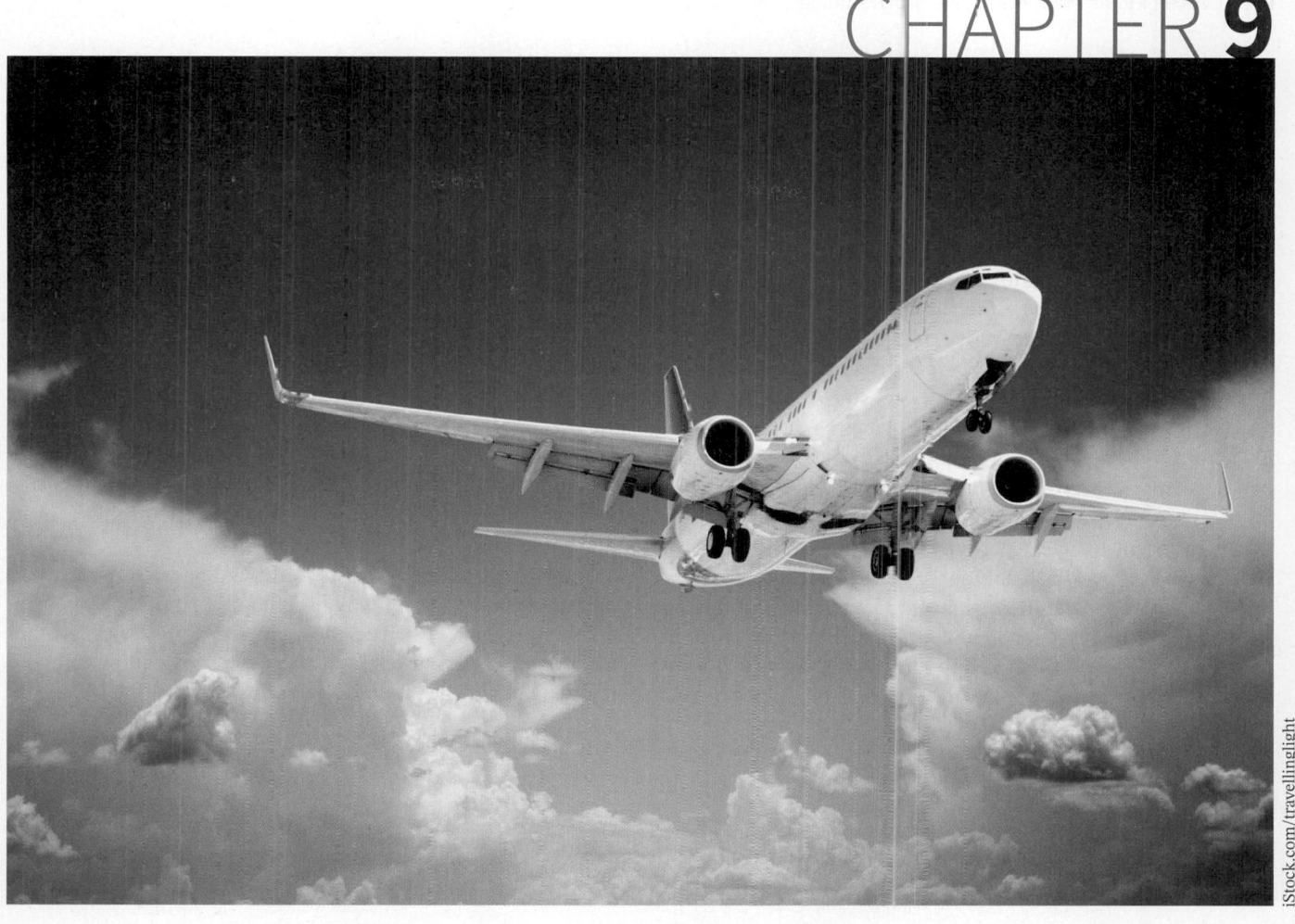

# Plant Assets, Natural Resources, and Intangible Assets

## Chapter Preview

The accounting for long-term assets has important implications for a company's reported results. In this chapter, we explain the application of the historical cost principle of accounting to property, plant, and equipment, such as **Southwest Airlines** airplanes, as well as to natural resources and intangible assets, such as the "Southwest Airlines heart" trademark. We also describe the methods that companies may use to allocate an asset's cost over its useful life. In addition, we discuss the accounting for expenditures incurred during the useful lives of assets, such as the cost of replacing tires on airplanes.

# Feature Story

## A Tale of Two Airlines

So, you're interested in starting a new business. Have you thought about the airline industry? Today, the most profitable airlines in the industry are not well-known major players like **American Airlines** and **United**. In fact, most giant, older airlines seem to be either bankrupt or on the verge of bankruptcy. In a recent year, five major airlines representing 24% of total U.S. capacity were operating under bankruptcy protection.

Not all airlines are hurting. The growth and profitability in the airline industry today is found at relative newcomers like **Southwest Airlines** and **JetBlue Airways**. These and other newer airlines compete primarily on ticket prices. During a recent five-year period, the low-fare airline market share increased by 47%, reaching 22% of U.S. airline capacity.

Southwest was the first upstart to make it big. It did so by taking a different approach. It bought small, new, fuel-efficient planes. Also, instead of the "hub-and-spoke" approach used by the major airlines, it opted for direct, short hop, no frills flights. It was all about controlling costs—getting the most out of its efficient new planes.

JetBlue, founded by former employees of Southwest, was recently ranked as the number 1 airline in the United States by the airline rating company **SkyTrax**. Management initially attempted to differentiate JetBlue by offering amenities not found on other airlines, such as seatback entertainment systems, while adopting Southwest's low-fare model. This approach was successful during JetBlue's early years, as it enjoyed both profitability and rapid growth. However, more recently the company has had to take aggressive steps to rein in costs in order to return to profitability.

In the past, upstarts such as **ValuJet** chose a different approach. The company bought planes that were 20 to 30 years old (known in the industry as *zombies*), which allowed it to quickly add planes to its fleet. ValuJet started with a $3.4 million investment and grew to be worth $630 million in its first three years.

But with high fuel costs, airlines are no longer in the market for old planes, which generally cannot be operated efficiently. Today, success in the airline business comes from owning the newest and most efficient equipment, and knowing how to get the most out of it.

# Chapter Outline

| LEARNING OBJECTIVES | REVIEW | PRACTICE |
|---|---|---|
| **LO 1** Explain the accounting for plant asset expenditures. | • Determining the cost of plant assets<br>• Expenditures during useful life | **DO IT! 1** Cost of Plant Assets |
| **LO 2** Apply depreciation methods to plant assets. | • Factors in computing depreciation<br>• Depreciation methods<br>• Depreciation and income taxes<br>• Revising periodic depreciation<br>• Impairments | **DO IT! 2a** Depreciation Methods<br>**2b** Revised Depreciation |
| **LO 3** Explain how to account for the disposal of plant assets. | • Sale of plant assets<br>• Retirement of plant assets | **DO IT! 3** Plant Asset Disposal |
| **LO 4** Describe how to account for natural resources and intangible assets. | • Natural resources<br>• Depletion<br>• Intangible assets<br>• Accounting for intangible assets<br>• Types of intangible assets<br>• Research and development costs | **DO IT! 4** Classification Concepts |
| **LO 5** Discuss how plant assets, natural resources, and intangible assets are reported and analyzed. | • Presentation<br>• Analysis | **DO IT! 5** Asset Turnover |

**Go to the Review and Practice section at the end of the chapter for a review of key concepts and practice applications with solutions.**

**Visit WileyPLUS for additional tutorials and practice opportunities.**

# Plant Asset Expenditures

**LEARNING OBJECTIVE 1**
Explain the accounting for plant asset expenditures.

**Plant assets** are resources that have three characteristics. They have physical substance (a definite size and shape), are used in the operations of a business, and are not intended for sale to customers. They are also called **property, plant, and equipment; plant and equipment**; and **fixed assets**. These assets are expected to be of use to the company for a number of years. Except for land, plant assets decline in service potential over their useful lives.

Because plant assets play a key role in ongoing operations, companies keep plant assets in good operating condition. They also replace worn-out or outdated plant assets, and expand productive resources as needed. Many companies have substantial investments in plant assets. **Illustration 9.1** shows the percentages of plant assets in relation to total assets of companies in a number of industries.

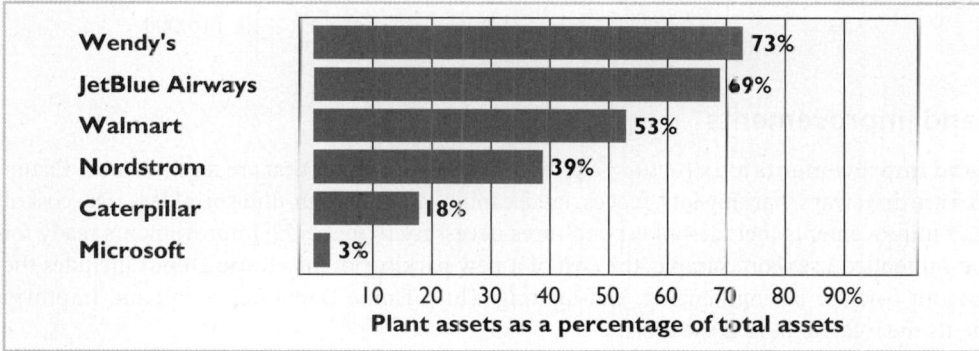

**ILLUSTRATION 9.1**

**Percentages of plant assets in relation to total assets**

# Determining the Cost of Plant Assets

The **historical cost principle** requires that companies record plant assets at cost. Thus, JetBlue Airways and Southwest Airlines record their planes at cost. **Cost consists of all expenditures necessary to acquire an asset and make it ready for its intended use.** For example, when **Boeing** buys equipment, the purchase price, freight costs paid by Boeing, and installation costs are all part of the cost of the equipment.

Cost is measured by the cash paid in a cash transaction or by the **cash equivalent price** paid when companies use noncash assets in payment. **The cash equivalent price is equal to the fair value of the asset given up or the fair value of the asset received, whichever is more clearly determinable.** Once cost is established, it becomes the basis of accounting for the plant asset over its useful life. Current fair value is not used to increase the recorded cost after acquisition. We explain the application of the historical cost principle to each of the major classes of plant assets in the following sections (see **International Note**).

**International Note**

IFRS is more flexible regarding asset valuation. Companies revalue to fair value when they believe this information is more relevant.

## Land

Companies often use **land** as a building site for a manufacturing plant or office building. The cost of land includes (1) the cash purchase price, (2) closing costs such as title and attorney fees, (3) real estate broker commissions, and (4) accrued property taxes and other liens assumed by the purchaser. For example, if the cash price is $50,000 and the purchaser agrees to pay accrued taxes of $5,000, the cost of the land is $55,000.

Companies record as debits (increases) to the Land account all necessary costs incurred to make land **ready for its intended use** (see **Helpful Hint**). When a company acquires vacant land, these costs include expenditures for clearing, draining, filling, and grading.

**HELPFUL HINT**

Management's intended use is important in applying the historical cost principle.

Sometimes the land has a building on it that must be removed before construction of a new building. In this case, the company debits to the Land account all demolition and removal costs, less any proceeds from salvaged materials.

To illustrate, assume that Hayes Company acquires real estate at a cash cost of $100,000. The property contains an old warehouse that is razed at a net cost of $6,000 ($7,500 in demolition costs less $1,500 proceeds from salvaged materials). Additional expenditures are the attorney's fee, $1,000, and the real estate broker's commission, $8,000. The cost of the land is $115,000, computed as shown in **Illustration 9.2**.

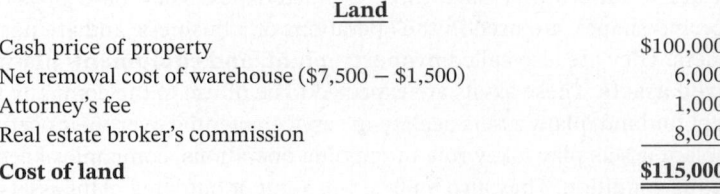

**ILLUSTRATION 9.2**
**Computation of cost of land**

| Land | |
|---|---|
| Cash price of property | $100,000 |
| Net removal cost of warehouse ($7,500 − $1,500) | 6,000 |
| Attorney's fee | 1,000 |
| Real estate broker's commission | 8,000 |
| **Cost of land** | **$115,000** |

Hayes makes the following entry to record the acquisition of the land.

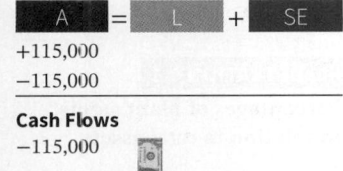

| A | = | L | + | SE |
|---|---|---|---|---|
| +115,000 | | | | |
| −115,000 | | | | |

**Cash Flows**
−115,000

| | | |
|---|---|---|
| Land | 115,000 | |
|    Cash | | 115,000 |
|      (To record purchase of land) | | |

## Land Improvements

**Land improvements** are structural additions with limited lives that are made to land. Examples are driveways, parking lots, fences, landscaping, and underground sprinklers. The cost of land improvements includes all expenditures necessary to make the improvements ready for their intended use. For example, the cost of a new parking lot for **Home Depot** includes the amount paid for paving, fencing, and lighting. Thus, Home Depot debits to Land Improvements the total of all of these costs.

Land improvements have limited useful lives. Even when well-maintained, they will eventually need to be replaced. As a result, companies expense (depreciate) the cost of land improvements over their useful lives.

## Buildings

**Buildings** are facilities used in operations, such as stores, offices, factories, warehouses, and airplane hangars. Companies debit to the Buildings account all necessary expenditures related to the purchase or construction of a building. When a building is **purchased**, such costs include the purchase price, closing costs (attorney's fee, title insurance, etc.), and the real estate broker's commission. Costs to make the building ready for its intended use include expenditures for remodeling and replacing or repairing the roof, floors, electrical wiring, and plumbing. When a new building is **constructed**, its cost consists of the contract price plus payments for architects' fees, building permits, and excavation costs.

In addition, companies charge certain interest costs to the Buildings account. Interest costs incurred to finance the project are included in the cost of the building when a significant period of time is required to get the building ready for use. In these circumstances, interest costs are considered as necessary as materials and labor. However, the inclusion of interest costs in the cost of a constructed building is **limited to interest costs incurred during the construction period**. When construction has been completed, the company records subsequent interest payments on funds borrowed to finance the construction as debits (increases) to Interest Expense.

## Equipment

**Equipment** includes assets used in operations, such as store check-out counters, office furniture, factory machinery, and delivery trucks. **JetBlue Airways**' equipment includes aircraft, in-flight entertainment systems, and trucks for ground operations. The cost of equipment consists of the cash purchase price, sales taxes, freight charges, and insurance during transit paid by the purchaser. It also includes expenditures required in assembling, installing, and testing the equipment. However, companies treat as expenses the costs of motor vehicle licenses and accident insurance on company trucks and cars. Such items are **annual recurring expenditures and do not benefit future periods**. Two criteria apply in determining the cost of equipment: (1) the frequency of the cost—one time or recurring, and (2) the benefit period— the life of the asset or one year.

To illustrate, assume that Lenard Company purchases a delivery truck on January 1 at a cash price of $22,000. Related expenditures are sales taxes $1,320, painting and lettering $500, motor vehicle license $80, and a three-year accident insurance policy $1,600. The cost of the delivery truck is $23,820, computed as shown in **Illustration 9.3**.

**ILLUSTRATION 9.3**
**Computation of cost of delivery truck**

| Delivery Truck | |
|---|---|
| Cash price | $22,000 |
| Sales taxes | 1,320 |
| Painting and lettering | 500 |
| **Cost of delivery truck** | **$23,820** |

Lenard treats the cost of a motor vehicle license as an expense and the cost of an insurance policy as a prepaid asset. Thus, the company records the purchase of the truck and related expenditures as follows.

| Equipment | 23,820 | |
|---|---|---|
| License Expense | 80 | |
| Prepaid Insurance | 1,600 | |
| Cash | | 25,500 |
| (To record purchase of delivery truck and related expenditures) | | |

A = L + SE
+23,820
−80 Exp
+1,600
−25,500

**Cash Flows**
−25,500

For another example, assume Merten Company purchases factory machinery at a cash price of $50,000. Related expenditures are sales taxes $3,000, insurance during shipping $500, and installation and testing $1,000. The cost of the factory machinery is $54,500, computed as shown in **Illustration 9.4**

**ILLUSTRATION 9.4**
**Computation of cost of factory machinery**

| Factory Machinery | |
|---|---|
| Cash price | $50,000 |
| Sales taxes | 3,000 |
| Insurance during shipping | 500 |
| Installation and testing | 1,000 |
| **Cost of factory machinery** | **$54,500** |

Thus, Merten records the purchase and related expenditures as follows.

| Equipment | 54,500 | |
|---|---|---|
| Cash | | 54,500 |
| (To record purchase of factory machinery and related expenditures) | | |

A = L + SE
+54,500
−54,500

**Cash Flows**
−54,500

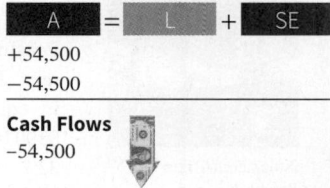

# Expenditures During Useful Life

During the useful life of a plant asset, a company may incur costs for ordinary repairs, additions, or improvements. **Ordinary repairs** are expenditures to **maintain** the operating efficiency and productive life of the asset. They usually are small amounts that occur frequently. Examples are motor tune-ups and oil changes, the painting of buildings, and the replacing of worn-out gears on machinery. Companies record such repairs as debits to Maintenance and Repairs Expense as they are incurred. Because they are immediately charged as an expense against revenues, these costs are often referred to as **revenue expenditures**.

In contrast, **additions and improvements** are costs incurred to **increase** the operating efficiency, productive capacity, or useful life of a plant asset. They are usually material in amount and occur infrequently. Additions and improvements increase the company's investment in productive facilities. Companies generally debit these amounts to the plant asset affected. They are often referred to as **capital expenditures**.

Companies must use good judgment in deciding between a revenue expenditure and capital expenditure. For example, assume that Rodriguez Co. purchases a number of wastepaper baskets. The proper accounting would appear to be to capitalize and then depreciate these wastepaper baskets over their useful lives. However, Rodriguez will generally expense these wastepaper baskets immediately. This practice is justified on the basis of **materiality**. Materiality refers to the impact of an item's size on a company's financial operations. The **materiality concept** states that if an item would not make a difference in decision-making, the company does not have to follow GAAP in reporting that item.

## Anatomy of a Fraud

Bernie Ebbers was the founder and CEO of the phone company **WorldCom**. The company engaged in a series of increasingly large, debt-financed acquisitions of other companies. These acquisitions made the company grow quickly, which made the stock price increase dramatically. However, because the acquired companies all had different accounting systems, WorldCom's financial records were a mess. When WorldCom's performance started to flatten out, Bernie coerced WorldCom's accountants to engage in a number of fraudulent activities to make net income look better than it really was and thus prop up the stock price. One of these frauds involved treating $7 billion of line costs as capital expenditures. The line costs, which were rental fees paid to other phone companies to use their phone lines, had always been properly expensed in previous years. Capitalization delayed expense recognition to future periods and thus boosted current-period profits.

**Total take: $7 billion**

### The Missing Controls

**Documentation procedures.** The company's accounting system was a disorganized collection of non-integrated systems, which resulted from a series of corporate acquisitions. Top management took advantage of this disorganization to conceal its fraudulent activities.

**Independent internal verification.** A fraud of this size should have been detected by a routine comparison of the actual physical assets with the list of physical assets shown in the accounting records.

## Accounting Across the Organization

iStock.com/Brian Raisbeck

### Many U.S. Firms Use Leases

Leases, which are formal rental agreements, allow companies to use plant assets without actually purchasing them. Leasing is big business for U.S. companies. For example, business investment in equipment in a recent year totaled $800 billion. Leasing accounted for about 33% of all business investment ($264 billion).

Who does the most leasing? Interestingly, major banks such as **Continental National Bank**, **JPMorgan Chase**, and **US Bancorp** are the major lessors. Also, many companies have established separate leasing companies, such as **Boeing Capital Corporation**, **Dell Financial Services**, and **John Deere Capital Corp**. And, as an excellent example of the magnitude of leasing, leased planes account for nearly 40% of the U.S. fleet of commercial airlines. **International Lease Finance Corporation** in Los Angeles owns more planes than any airline in the world. Leasing is also becoming increasingly common in the hotel industry. **Marriott**, **Hilton**, and **Inter-Continental** are choosing to lease hotels that are owned by someone else.

**Why might airline managers choose to lease rather than purchase their planes? (Answer is available near the end of the chapter.)**

## DO IT! 1 | Cost of Plant Assets

Assume that Drummond Heating and Cooling Co. purchases a delivery truck for $15,000 cash plus sales taxes of $900 and delivery costs of $500. The buyer also pays $200 for painting and lettering, $600 for an annual insurance policy, and $80 for a motor vehicle license. Explain how each of these costs would be accounted for.

### Solution

The first four payments ($15,000 purchase price, $900 sales taxes, $500 delivery costs, and $200 painting and lettering) are expenditures necessary to make the truck ready for its intended use. Thus, the cost of the truck is $16,600. The payment for insurance is reported as a separate asset, prepaid insurance, and allocated to expense as appropriate. The payment for the license should be treated as an expense.

Related exercise material: **BE9.1, BE9.2, BE9.3, DO IT! 9.1, E9.1, E9.2, and E9.3.**

**ACTION PLAN**

- Identify expenditures made in order to get delivery equipment ready for its intended use.
- Treat operating costs as expenses.

# Depreciation Methods

### LEARNING OBJECTIVE 2

Apply depreciation methods to plant assets.

As explained in Chapter 3, **depreciation is the process of allocating to expense the cost of a plant asset over its useful (service) life in a rational and systematic manner.** Such cost allocation enables companies to properly record expenses (efforts) with associated revenues (results) in accordance with the expense recognition principle, as shown in **Illustration 9.5.**

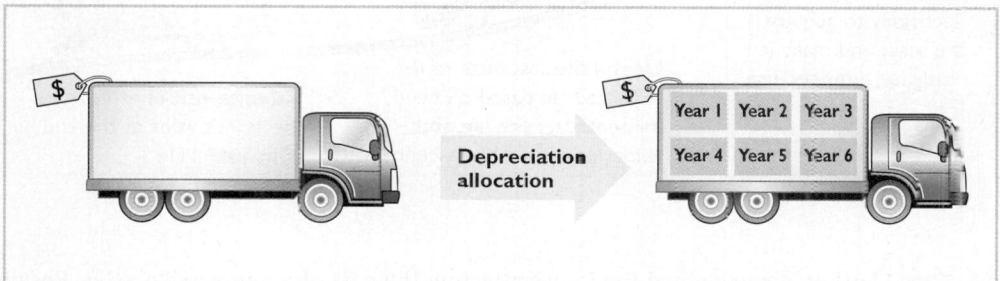

**ILLUSTRATION 9.5**

**Depreciation as a cost allocation concept**

Depreciation affects the balance sheet through accumulated depreciation, which companies report as a deduction from plant assets. It affects the income statement through depreciation expense.

It is important to understand that **depreciation is a process of cost allocation. It is not a process of asset valuation.** No attempt is made to measure the change in an asset's fair value during ownership. So, the **book value** (cost less accumulated depreciation) of a plant asset may be quite different from its **fair value.** In fact, if an asset is fully depreciated, it can have a zero book value but still have a fair value.

Depreciation applies to three classes of plant assets: land improvements, buildings, and equipment. Each asset in these classes is considered to be a **depreciable asset**. Why? Because the usefulness to the company and revenue-producing ability of each asset will decline over the asset's useful life. Depreciation **does not apply to land** because its usefulness and revenue-producing ability generally remain intact over time. In fact, in many cases, the usefulness of land increases over time because of the scarcity of good land sites. Thus, **land is not a depreciable asset**.

During a depreciable asset's useful life, its revenue-producing ability declines because of **wear and tear**. A delivery truck that has been driven 100,000 miles will be less useful to a company than one driven only 800 miles.

Revenue-producing ability may also decline because of obsolescence. **Obsolescence** occurs when an asset becomes out of date before it physically wears out. The rerouting of airlines from Chicago's Midway Airport to Chicago-O'Hare International Airport because Midway's runways were too short for giant jets is an example. Similarly, many companies replace their computers long before they originally planned to do so because technological improvements make the old hardware obsolete.

**Recognizing depreciation on an asset does not result in an accumulation of cash for replacement of the asset.** The balance in Accumulated Depreciation represents the total amount of the asset's cost that the company has charged to expense. **It is not a cash fund.**

Note that the concept of depreciation is consistent with the going concern assumption. The **going concern assumption** states that the company will continue in operation for the foreseeable future. If a company does not use a going concern assumption, then plant assets should be reported at their fair value. In that case, depreciation of these assets is not needed.

# Factors in Computing Depreciation

Three factors affect the computation of depreciation, as shown in **Illustration 9.6** (see **Helpful Hint**).

**Cost:** all expenditures necessary to acquire the asset and make it ready for intended use

**Useful life:** estimate of the expected life based on need for repair, service life, and vulnerability to obsolescence

**Salvage value:** estimate of the asset's value at the end of its useful life

1. **Cost.** Earlier, we explained the issues affecting the cost of a depreciable asset. Recall that companies record plant assets at cost, in accordance with the historical cost principle.

2. **Useful life.** **Useful life** is an estimate of the expected productive life, also called service life, of the asset for its owner. Useful life may be expressed in terms of time, units of activity (such as machine hours), or units of output. Useful life is an estimate. In making the estimate, management considers such factors as the intended use of the asset, repair and maintenance policies, and vulnerability of the asset to obsolescence. The company's past experience with similar assets is often helpful in deciding on expected useful life.

3. **Salvage value.** **Salvage value** is an estimate of the asset's value at the end of its useful life (see **Alternative Terminology**). Companies may base the value on the asset's worth as scrap or on its expected trade-in value. Like useful life, salvage value is an estimate. In making the estimate, management considers how it plans to dispose of the asset and its experience with similar assets.

# Depreciation Methods

Depreciation is generally computed using one of the following methods:

1. Straight-line.
2. Units-of-activity.
3. Declining-balance.

Each method is acceptable under generally accepted accounting principles. Management selects the method that it believes best measures an asset's contribution to revenue over its useful life. Once a company chooses a method, it should apply that method consistently over the useful life of the asset. Consistency enhances the ability to analyze financial statements over multiple years.

We will compare the three depreciation methods using the data presented in **Illustration 9.7** for a small delivery truck purchased by Barb's Florists on January 1, 2022.

| | |
|---|---|
| Cost | $13,000 |
| Expected salvage value | $1,000 |
| Estimated useful life in years | 5 |
| Estimated useful life in miles | 100,000 |

**ILLUSTRATION 9.7**

**Delivery truck data**

**Illustration 9.8** shows the use of the primary depreciation methods in a sample of the largest companies in the United States. No matter what method is used, the total amount depreciated over the useful life of the asset is its depreciable cost. **Depreciable cost** is equal to the cost of the asset less its salvage value.

## Straight-Line Method

Under the **straight-line method**, companies expense the same amount of depreciation for each year of the asset's useful life. It is measured solely by the passage of time.

To compute depreciation expense under the straight-line method, companies need to determine depreciable cost. As indicated above, **depreciable cost** is the cost of the asset less its salvage value. It represents the total amount subject to depreciation. Under the straight-line method, to determine depreciation expense, we divide depreciable cost by the asset's useful life as measured in years. **Illustration 9.9** shows the computation of the first year's depreciation expense for Barb's Florists.

**ILLUSTRATION 9.8**

**Use of depreciation methods in large U.S. companies**

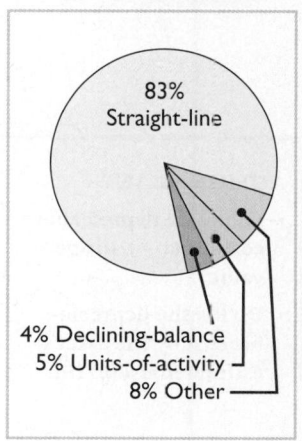

83% Straight-line

4% Declining-balance
5% Units-of-activity
8% Other

**ILLUSTRATION 9.9**  **Formula for straight-line method**

| Cost | − | Salvage Value | = | Depreciable Cost |
|---|---|---|---|---|
| $13,000 | − | $1,000 | = | $12,000 |

| Depreciable Cost | ÷ | Useful Life (in years) | = | Depreciation Expense |
|---|---|---|---|---|
| $12,000 | ÷ | 5 | = | $2,400 |

Alternatively, we also can compute an annual **rate** of depreciation. In this case, the rate is 20% (100% ÷ 5 years). When a company uses an annual straight-line rate, it applies the percentage rate to the depreciable cost of the asset. **Illustration 9.10** shows a **depreciation schedule** using an annual rate.

**Straight-line depreciation schedule**

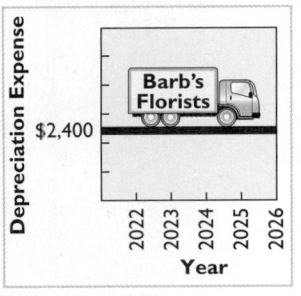

| | Computation | | | Annual | End of Year | |
|---|---|---|---|---|---|---|
| Year | Depreciable Cost | × Depreciation Rate | = | Depreciation Expense | Accumulated Depreciation | Book Value |
| 2022 | $12,000 | 20% | | **$2,400** | $ 2,400 | $10,600* |
| 2023 | 12,000 | 20 | | **2,400** | 4,800 | 8,200 |
| 2024 | 12,000 | 20 | | **2,400** | 7,200 | 5,800 |
| 2025 | 12,000 | 20 | | **2,400** | 9,600 | 3,400 |
| 2026 | 12,000 | 20 | | **2,400** | 12,000 | **1,000** |

*Book value = Cost − Accumulated depreciation = ($13,000 − $2,400).

Note that the depreciation expense of $2,400 is the same each year. The book value (computed as cost minus accumulated depreciation) at the end of the useful life is equal to the expected $1,000 salvage value.

What happens to these computations for an asset purchased **during** the year, rather than on January 1? In that case, it is necessary to **prorate the annual depreciation** on a time basis. If Barb's Florists had purchased the delivery truck on April 1, 2022, the company would own the truck for nine months of the first year (April–December). Thus, depreciation for 2022 would be $1,800 ($12,000 × 20% × $\frac{9}{12}$ of a year).

The straight-line method predominates in practice. Large companies like **Campbell Soup**, **Marriott**, and **General Mills** use the straight-line method. It is simple to apply, and it records expenses with associated revenues appropriately when the use of the asset is reasonably uniform throughout the service life. Generally, the types of assets that provide equal benefits over their useful lives are those for which daily use does not affect productivity. Examples are office furniture and fixtures, buildings, warehouses, and garages for motor vehicles.

---

**ACTION PLAN**

- Calculate depreciable cost (Cost − Salvage value).
- Divide the depreciable cost by the asset's estimated useful life.

## DO IT! 2a | Depreciation Methods—Straight-Line Depreciation

**Part 1:** On January 1, 2022, Iron Mountain Ski Corporation purchased a new snow-grooming machine for $50,000. The machine is estimated to have a 10-year life with a $2,000 salvage value. What adjusting entry would Iron Mountain Ski Corporation make at December 31, 2022, if it uses the straight-line method of depreciation and adjusts its accounts annually?

### Solution

$$\text{Depreciation expense} = \frac{\text{Cost} - \text{Salvage value}}{\text{Useful life}} = \frac{\$50,000 - \$2,000}{10} = \$4,800$$

The entry to record the first year's depreciation would be:

| Dec. 31 | Depreciation Expense | 4,800 | |
|---|---|---|---|
| | Accumulated Depreciation—Equipment | | 4,800 |
| | (To record depreciation on snow-grooming machine) | | |

Related exercise material: **BE9.4, BE9.5, and DO IT! 9.2a.**

---

## Units-of-Activity Method

Under the **units-of-activity method**, useful life is expressed in terms of the total units of production or use expected from the asset, rather than as a time period (see **Alternative Terminology**). The units-of-activity method is ideally suited to factory machinery. Manufacturing companies can measure production in units of output or in machine hours used in operating machinery. This method can also be used for such assets as delivery equipment (miles driven) and airplanes (hours in use). The units-of-activity method is generally not suitable for buildings or furniture because depreciation for these assets is more a function of time than of use (see **Helpful Hint**).

To use this method, companies estimate the total units of activity for the entire useful life, and then divide these units into depreciable cost. The resulting number represents the depreciable cost per unit. The depreciable cost per unit is then applied to the actual units of activity during the year to determine the annual depreciation expense.

To illustrate, assume that Barb's Florists drives its delivery truck 15,000 miles in the first year. **Illustration 9.11** shows the units-of-activity formula and the computation of the first year's depreciation expense

**HELPFUL HINT**

Under any method, depreciation stops when the asset's book value equals expected salvage value.

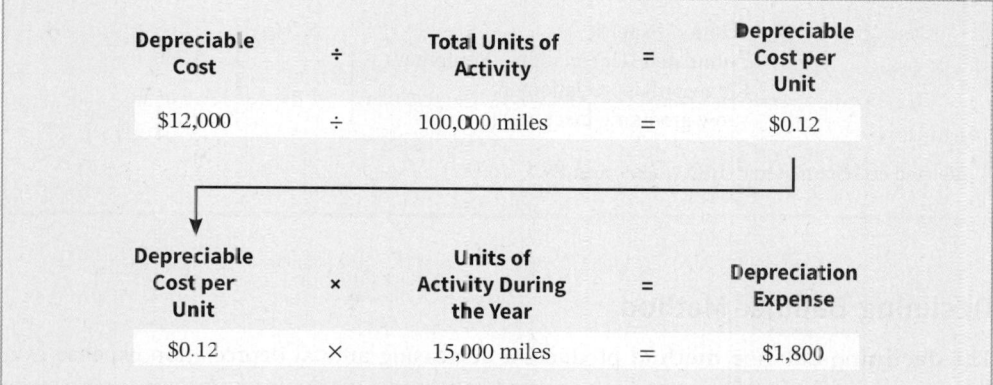

**LLUSTRATION 9.11**

Formula for units-of-activity method

Illustration 9.12 shows the units-of-activity depreciation schedule, using assumed mileage. The depreciable cost per unit remains constant for all years.

| Barb's Florists | | | | | |
|---|---|---|---|---|---|
| | Computation | | Annual | End of Year | |
| Year | Units of Activity | × Depreciable Cost/Unit = | Depreciation Expense | Accumulated Depreciation | Book Value |
| 2022 | 15,000 | $0.12 | **$1,800** | $ 1,800 | $11,200* |
| 2023 | 30,000 | 0.12 | **3,600** | 5,400 | 7,600 |
| 2024 | 20,000 | 0.12 | **2,400** | 7,800 | 5,200 |
| 2025 | 25,000 | 0.12 | **3,000** | 10,800 | 2,200 |
| 2026 | 10,000 | 0.12 | **1,200** | 12,000 | 1,000 |

*$13,000 − $1,800.

**LLUSTRATION 9.12**

Units-of-activity depreciation schedule

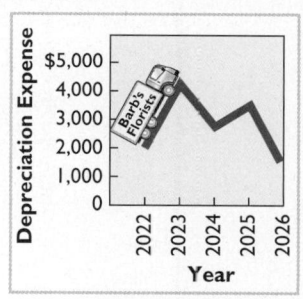

This method is easy to apply for assets purchased mid-year. In such a case, the company computes the depreciation using the productivity of the asset for the partial year.

The units-of-activity method is not nearly as popular as the straight-line method (see Illustration 9.8) primarily because it is often difficult for companies to reasonably estimate total activity. However, some very large companies, such as **Chevron** and **Boise Cascade** (a forestry company), do use this method. When the productivity of an asset varies significantly from one period to another, the units-of-activity method results in the best matching of expenses with revenues.

**ACTION PLAN**

- Calculate depreciable cost (Cost − Salvage value).
- Divide the depreciable cost by the asset's estimated useful hours.
- Multiply depreciable cost per hour by actual hours used.

## DO IT! 2a | Depreciation Methods—Units-of-Activity

**Part 2:** On January 1, 2022, Iron Mountain Ski Corporation purchased a new snow-grooming machine for $50,000. The machine is estimated to have a 100,000-hour life with a $2,000 salvage value. The machine is used for 12,000 hours during 2022. What journal entry would Iron Mountain Ski Corporation make at December 31, 2022, if it uses the units-of-activity method of depreciation and adjusts its accounts annually?

### Solution

$$\text{Depreciable cost per hour} = \frac{\text{Cost} - \text{Salvage value}}{\text{Useful life}} = \frac{\$50,000 - \$2,000}{100,000 \text{ hours}} = \$0.48/\text{hour}$$

Depreciation expense = Depreciable cost per unit × Hours of activity during the year
= $0.48 × 12,000 hours = $5,760

Iron Mountain would record the first year's depreciation as follows.

| | | | |
|---|---|---|---|
| Dec. 31 | Depreciation Expense | 5,760 | |
| | Accumulated Depreciation—Equipment | | 5,760 |
| | (To record depreciation on | | |
| | snow-grooming machine) | | |

Related exercise material: **BE9.7, E9.5, and E9.7.**

## Declining-Balance Method

The **declining-balance method** produces a decreasing annual depreciation expense over the asset's useful life. The method is so named because the periodic depreciation is based on a **declining book value** (cost less accumulated depreciation) of the asset. With this method, companies compute annual depreciation expense by multiplying the book value at the beginning of the year by the declining-balance depreciation rate. **The depreciation rate remains constant from year to year, but the book value to which the rate is applied declines each year.**

At the beginning of the first year, book value is the cost of the asset. This is because the balance in accumulated depreciation at the beginning of the asset's useful life is zero. In subsequent years, book value is the difference between cost and accumulated depreciation to date. Unlike the other depreciation methods, the declining-balance method **ignores salvage value in determining the amount to which the declining-balance rate is applied**. Salvage value, however, does limit the total depreciation that can be taken. Depreciation stops when the asset's book value equals expected salvage value.

A common declining-balance rate is double the straight-line rate. The method is often called the **double-declining-balance method**. If Barb's Florists uses the double-declining-balance method, it uses a depreciation rate of 40% (2 × the straight-line rate of 20%). **Illustration 9.13** shows the declining-balance formula and the computation of the first year's depreciation on the delivery truck.

**ILLUSTRATION 9.13**

Formula for declining-balance method

| Book Value at Beginning of Year | × | Declining-Balance Rate | = | Depreciation Expense |
|---|---|---|---|---|
| $13,000 | × | 40% | = | $5,200 |

**Illustration 9.14** shows the depreciation schedule under this method and indicates that the delivery equipment is 69% depreciated ($8,320 ÷ $12,000) at the end of the second year. Under the straight-line method, the truck would be depreciated 40% ($4,800 ÷ $12,000) at that time. Because the declining-balance method produces higher depreciation expense in the early years than in the later years, it is considered an **accelerated-depreciation method**.

## Barb's Florists

| | Computation | | | | Annual | End of Year | |
| Year | Book Value Beginning of Year | × | Depreciation Rate | = | Depreciation Expense | Accumulated Depreciation | Book Value |
|---|---|---|---|---|---|---|---|
| 2022 | $13,000 | | 40% | | **$5,200** | $ 5,200 | $7,800 |
| 2023 | 7,800 | | 40 | | **3,120** | 8,320 | 4,680 |
| 2024 | 4,680 | | 40 | | **1,872** | 10,192 | 2,808 |
| 2025 | 2,808 | | 40 | | **1,123** | 11,315 | 1,685 |
| 2026 | 1,685 | | 40 | | **685*** | 12,000 | **1,000** |

*Computation of $674 ($1 685 × 40%) is adjusted to $685 in order for book value to equal salvage value.

**ILLUSTRATION 9.14**

**Double-declining-balance depreciation schedule**

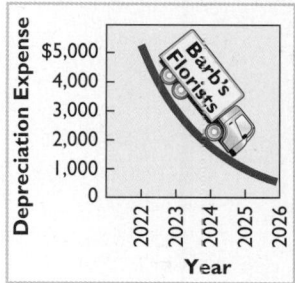

The declining-balance method is compatible with the expense recognition principle. It matches the higher depreciation expense in early years with the higher benefits received in these years. It also recognizes lower depreciation expense in later years, when the asset's contribution to revenue is less. Some assets lose usefulness rapidly because of obsolescence. In these cases, the declining-balance method provides the most appropriate depreciation amount (see **Helpful Hint**).

When a company purchases an asset during the year, it must prorate the first year's declining-balance depreciation on a time basis. For example, if Barb's Florists had purchased the truck on April 1, 2022, depreciation for 2022 would become $3,900 ($13,000 × 40% × $\frac{9}{12}$). The book value at the beginning of 2023 is then $9,100 ($13,000 − $3,900), and the 2023 depreciation is $3,640 ($9,100 × 40%). Subsequent computations would follow from those amounts.

> **HELPFUL HINT**
>
> **The method recommended for an asset that is expected to be significantly more productive in the first half of its useful life is the declining-balance method.**

---

## DO IT! 2a | Depreciation Methods—Declining-Balance

**Part 3:** On January 1, 2022, Iron Mountain Ski Corporation purchased a new snow-grooming machine for $50,000. The machine is estimated to have a 10-year life with a $2,000 salvage value. What journal entry would Iron Mountain Ski Corporation make at December 31, 2022, if it uses the double-declining-balance method of depreciation and adjusts its accounts annually?

### Solution

Depreciation rate = 2 × straight-line rate = 2 × 10% = 20%
Book value at beginning of 2022 = Cost − Accumulated depreciation = $50,000 − $0 = $50,000
Depreciation expense = Depreciation rate × Book value = 20% × $50,000 = $10,000

Iron Mountain would record the first year's depreciation as follows.

| | | | |
|---|---|---|---|
| Dec. 31 | Depreciation Expense | 10,000 | |
| | Accumulated Depreciation—Equipment | | 10,000 |
| | (To record depreciation on | | |
| | snow-grooming machine) | | |

Related exercise material **BE9.6 and E9.7.**

> **ACTION PLAN**
>
> - Calculate the declining-balance depreciation rate.
> - Determine the book value at the beginning of each year.
> - Multiply the depreciation rate by the book value.

## Comparison of Methods

**Illustration 9.15** compares annual and total depreciation expense under each of the three methods for Barb's Florists.

Annual depreciation varies considerably among the methods, but **total depreciation expense is the same ($12,000) for the five-year period** under all three methods. Each method is acceptable in accounting because each recognizes in a rational and systematic

**Comparison of depreciation methods**

| Year | Straight-Line | Units-of-Activity | Declining-Balance |
|------|---------------|-------------------|-------------------|
| 2022 | $ 2,400 | $ 1,800 | $ 5,200 |
| 2023 | 2,400 | 3,600 | 3,120 |
| 2024 | 2,400 | 2,400 | 1,872 |
| 2025 | 2,400 | 3,000 | 1,123 |
| 2026 | 2,400 | 1,200 | 685 |
| | **$12,000** | **$12,000** | **$12,000** |

manner the decline in service potential of the asset. **Illustration 9.16** graphs the depreciation expense pattern under each method.

**Patterns of depreciation expense**

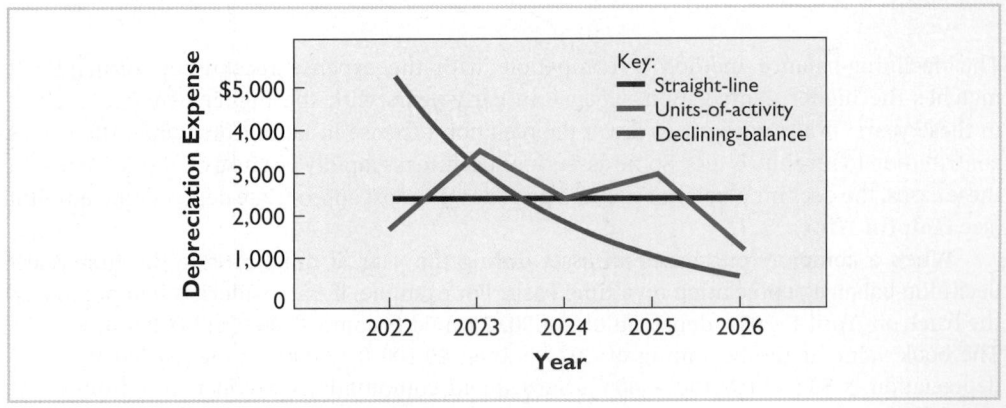

### ACTION PLAN

- For straight-line, calculate depreciable cost and then divide that by the asset's useful life.

- For units-of-activity, calculate depreciable cost, divide that by the asset's estimated useful hours, and then multiply depreciable cost per hour by actual hours used.

- For declining-balance, calculate the declining-balance depreciation rate, determine the book value at the beginning of each year, and then multiply the depreciation rate by the book value.

## DO IT! 2a  |  Depreciation Methods

**Part 4:** Mendez Corporation purchased a truck at the beginning of 2022 for $100,000. The truck is estimated to have a salvage value of $12,000 and a useful life of 160,000 miles or 8 years. It was driven 23,000 miles in 2022 and 31,000 miles in 2023. Compute depreciation expense for 2023 using the:

a.  Straight-line method.

b.  Units-of-activity method.

c.  Double-declining-balance (DDB) method.

### Solution

a. $\dfrac{\text{Cost} - \text{Salvage value}}{\text{Useful life}} = \dfrac{\$100,000 - \$12,000}{8 \text{ years}} = \$11,000$

b. $\dfrac{\text{Cost} - \text{Salvage value}}{\text{Useful life}} = \dfrac{\$100,000 - \$12,000}{160,000 \text{ miles}} = \$0.55/\text{mile}$

Depreciable cost per mile × Actual miles = $0.55 × 31,000 miles = $17,050

c. Depreciation rate = 2 × Straight-line rate = 2 × 12.5% (100% ÷ 8 years) = 25%

DDB depreciation rate × Book value at beginning of 2023
25% × $75,000* = $18,750

*Depreciation in 2022: 25% × $100,000 = $25,000; Book value at end of 2022: $100,000 − $25,000 = $75,000

Related exercise material: **BE9.4, BE9.6, BE9.7, DO IT! 9.2a, E9.5, and E9.7.**

## Depreciation and Income Taxes

### HELPFUL HINT

**Depreciation per financial statements is usually different from depreciation per tax returns.**

The Internal Revenue Service (IRS) allows corporate taxpayers to deduct depreciation expense when they compute taxable income. However, the IRS does not require taxpayers to use the same depreciation method on the tax return that is used in preparing financial statements (see **Helpful Hint**).

Many corporations use the straight-line method in their financial statements to maximize net income reported to investors. At the same time, they use a special accelerated-depreciation method on their tax returns to minimize their income taxes paid to the IRS. Taxpayers must use on their tax returns either the straight-line method or a special accelerated-depreciation method called the **Modified Accelerated Cost Recovery System** (MACRS)

## Depreciation Disclosure in the Notes

Companies must disclose the choice of depreciation method in their financial statements or in related notes that accompany the statements. **Illustration 9.17** shows excerpts from the "Property and equipment" notes from the financial statements of **Southwest Airlines**.

> ### Southwest Airlines
> #### Notes to the Financial Statements
>
> **Property and equipment** Depreciation is provided by the straight-line method to estimated residual values over periods generally ranging from 23 to 25 years for flight equipment.

**ILLUSTRATION 9.17**
**Disclosure of depreciation policies**

**Real World**

From this note, we learn that Southwest Airlines uses the straight-line method to depreciate its planes over periods of 23 to 25 years.

# Revising Periodic Depreciation

Depreciation is one example of the use of estimation in the accounting process. Management should periodically review annual depreciation expense, as well as the underlying useful life and salvage value estimates used in its computation. If wear and tear or obsolescence indicates that annual depreciation estimates are inadequate or excessive, the company should change the amount of depreciation expense.

When a change in an estimate is required, the company makes the change in **current and future years**. **It does not change depreciation in prior periods.** The rationale is that continual restatement of prior periods would adversely affect confidence in financial statements.

To determine the new annual depreciation expense, the company first computes the asset's depreciable cost at the time of the revision. It then allocates the revised depreciable cost to the remaining useful life (see **Helpful Hint**).

To illustrate, assume that Barb's Florists decides at the end of 2025 (prior to the year-end adjusting entries) to extend the useful life of the truck by one year (a total life of six years) and increase its salvage value to $2,200. The company has used the straight-line method to depreciate the asset to date. Depreciation per year was $2,400 [($13,000 − $1,000) ÷ 5]. Accumulated depreciation after three years (2022–2024) is $7,200 ($2,400 × 3), and book value is $5,800 ($13,000 − $7,200). The new annual depreciation is $1,200, computed as shown in **Illustration 9.18**.

**HELPFUL HINT**
Use a step-by-step approach: (1) determine new depreciable cost; (2) divide by remaining useful life.

| | | |
|---|---:|---|
| Book value, 1/1/25 | $ 5,800 | |
| Less: New salvage value | 2,200 | |
| Depreciable cost | $ 3,600 | |
| New remaining useful life | 3 years | (2025–2027) |
| **Revised annual depreciation ($3,600 ÷ 3)** | **$ 1,200** | |

**ILLUSTRATION 9.18**
**Revised depreciation computation**

Barb's Florists makes no journal entry for the change in useful life and salvage value estimates. On December 31, 2025, during the preparation of adjusting entries, it records depreciation expense of $1,200.

Companies must disclose in the financial statements significant changes in estimates. Although a company may have a legitimate reason for changing an estimated life, financial statement users should be aware that some companies might change an estimate simply to achieve financial statement goals. For example, extending an asset's estimated life reduces depreciation expense and increases current period income.

At one time, **AirTran Airways** (now owned by **Southwest Airlines**) increased the estimated useful lives of some of its planes from 25 to 30 years and increased the estimated lives of related aircraft parts from 5 years to 30 years. It disclosed that the change in estimate decreased its net loss for the year by approximately $0.6 million, or about $0.01 per share. Whether these changes were appropriate depends on how reasonable it is to assume that planes will continue to be used for a long time. Our Feature Story suggests that although in the past many planes lasted a long time, it is also clear that because of high fuel costs, airlines are now scrapping many of their old, inefficient planes.

## Impairments

As noted earlier, the book value of plant assets is rarely the same as the fair value. In instances where the value of a plant asset declines substantially, its fair value might fall materially below book value. This may happen because a machine has become obsolete, or the market for the product made by the machine has dried up or has become very competitive. A **permanent decline** in the fair value of an asset is referred to as an **impairment**. So as not to overstate the asset on the books, the company records a write-down, whereby the asset's book value is reduced to its new fair value during the year in which the decline in value occurs. **Disney** recorded a $200 million write-down on its action movie *John Carter*. Disney spent more than $300 million producing the film.

---

**ACTION PLAN**
- Calculate new depreciable cost.
- Divide new depreciable cost by new remaining life.

### DO IT! 2b | Revised Depreciation

Chambers Corporation purchased a piece of equipment for $36,000. It estimated a 6-year life and $6,000 salvage value. Thus, straight-line depreciation was $5,000 per year [($36,000 − $6,000) ÷ 6]. At the end of year three (before the depreciation adjustment), it estimated the new total life to be 10 years and the new salvage value to be $2,000. Compute the revised depreciation.

#### Solution

Original depreciation expense = [($36,000 − $6,000) ÷ 6] = $5,000
Accumulated depreciation after 2 years = 2 × $5,000 = $10,000
Book value = $36,000 − $10,000 = $26,000

| | |
|---|---:|
| Book value after 2 years of depreciation | $26,000 |
| Less: New salvage value | 2,000 |
| Depreciable cost | $24,000 |
| New remaining useful life (10 − 2) | 8 years |
| Revised annual depreciation ($24,000 ÷ 8) | $ 3,000 |

Related exercise material: **BE9.8, DO IT! 9.2b, and E9.8.**

---

# Plant Asset Disposals

**LEARNING OBJECTIVE 3**

Explain how to account for the disposal of plant assets.

Companies dispose of plant assets that are no longer useful to them. **Illustration 9.19** shows the three types of asset disposals.

**ILLUSTRATION 9.19** Methods of plant asset disposal

**Retirement**
Equipment is scrapped
or discarded.

**Sale**
Equipment is sold
to another party.

**Exchange**
Existing equipment is traded
for new equipment.

Whatever the disposal method, the company must determine the book value of the plant asset at the disposal date to determine the gain or loss on disposal. Recall that the book value is the difference between the cost of the plant asset and the accumulated depreciation to date. If the disposal does not occur on the first day of the year, the company must record depreciation for the fraction of the year to the date of disposal. The company then eliminates the book value by reducing (debiting) Accumulated Depreciation for the total depreciation associated with that asset to the date of disposal and reducing (crediting) the asset account for the cost of the asset.

In this chapter, we examine the accounting for the retirement and sale of plant assets. In the appendix to the chapter, we discuss and illustrate the accounting for exchanges of plant assets.

## Sale of Plant Assets

In a disposal by sale, the company compares the book value of the asset with the proceeds received from the sale. If the proceeds of the sale **exceed** the book value of the plant asset, **a gain on disposal occurs**. If the proceeds of the sale **are less than** the book value of the plant asset sold, **a loss on disposal occurs** (see Helpful Hint).

Only by coincidence will the book value and the fair value of the asset be the same when the asset is sold. Gains and losses on sales of plant assets are therefore quite common. For example, **Delta Airlines** reported a $94 million gain on the sale of five **Boeing** B727-200 aircraft and five **Lockheed Martin** L-1011-1 aircraft.

**HELPFUL HINT**

When disposing of a plant asset, the company removes in the accounting records all amounts related to the asset. This includes the original cost and the total depreciation to date in the Accumulated Depreciation account.

### Gain on Sale

To illustrate a gain on sale of plant assets, assume that on July 1, 2022, Wright Company sells office furniture for $16,000 cash. The office furniture originally cost $60,000. As of January 1, 2022, it had accumulated depreciation of $41,000. Depreciation for the first six months of 2022 is $8,000. Wright records depreciation expense and updates accumulated depreciation to July 1 with the following entry.

| | | | |
|---|---|---|---|
| July 1 | Depreciation Expense | 8,000 | |
| | Accumulated Depreciation—Equipment | | 8,000 |
| | (To record depreciation expense for the first 6 months of 2022) | | |

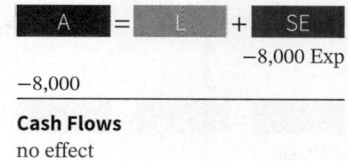

A = L + SE
−8,000 Exp
−8,000

**Cash Flows**
no effect

After the accumulated depreciation balance is updated, the company computes the gain or loss. The gain or loss is the difference between the proceeds from the sale and the book value at the date of disposal. Illustration 9.20 shows this computation for Wright Company, which has a gain on disposal of $5,000.

| | |
|---|---|
| Cost of office furniture | $60,000 |
| Less: Accumulated depreciation ($41,000 + $8,000) | 49,000 |
| Book value at date of disposal | 11,000 |
| Proceeds from sale | 16,000 |
| **Gain on disposal of plant asset** | **$ 5,000** |

**ILLUSTRATION 9.20**

**Computation of gain on disposal**

Wright records the sale and the gain on disposal of the plant asset as follows.

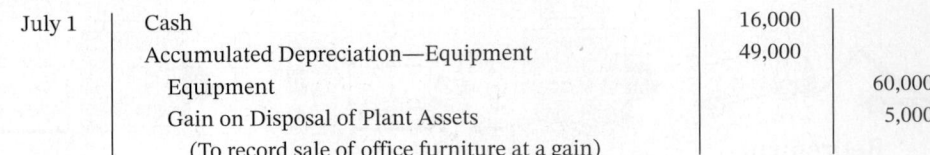

| | | | |
|---|---|---|---|
| July 1 | Cash | 16,000 | |
| | Accumulated Depreciation—Equipment | 49,000 | |
| | Equipment | | 60,000 |
| | Gain on Disposal of Plant Assets | | 5,000 |
| | (To record sale of office furniture at a gain) | | |

Companies report a gain on disposal of plant assets in the "Other revenues and gains" section of the income statement.

## Loss on Sale

Assume that instead of selling the office furniture for $16,000, Wright sells it for $9,000. In this case, Wright computes a loss of $2,000 as shown in **Illustration 9.21**.

**ILLUSTRATION 9.21**

**Computation of loss on disposal**

| | |
|---|---|
| Cost of office furniture | $60,000 |
| Less: Accumulated depreciation | 49,000 |
| Book value at date of disposal | 11,000 |
| Proceeds from sale | 9,000 |
| **Loss on disposal of plant asset** | **$ 2,000** |

Wright records the sale and the loss on disposal of the plant asset as follows.

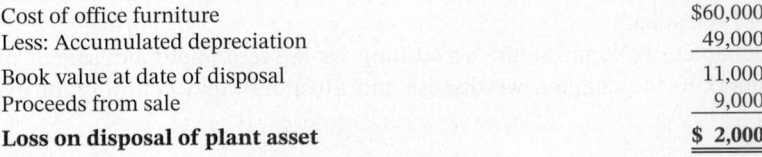

| | | | |
|---|---|---|---|
| July 1 | Cash | 9,000 | |
| | Accumulated Depreciation—Equipment | 49,000 | |
| | Loss on Disposal of Plant Assets | 2,000 | |
| | Equipment | | 60,000 |
| | (To record sale of office furniture at a loss) | | |

Companies report a loss on disposal of plant assets in the "Other expenses and losses" section of the income statement.

# Retirement of Plant Assets

To illustrate the retirement of plant assets, assume that Hobart Company retires its computer printers, which cost $32,000. The accumulated depreciation on these printers is $32,000. The equipment, therefore, is fully depreciated (zero book value). The entry to record this retirement is as follows.

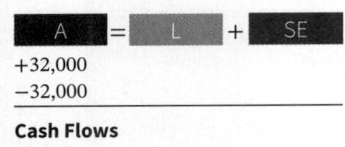

| | | |
|---|---|---|
| Accumulated Depreciation—Equipment | 32,000 | |
| Equipment | | 32,000 |
| (To record retirement of fully depreciated equipment) | | |

What happens if a fully depreciated plant asset is still useful to the company? In this case, the asset and its accumulated depreciation continue to be reported on the balance sheet, without further depreciation adjustment, until the company retires the asset. Reporting the asset and related accumulated depreciation on the balance sheet informs the financial statement reader that the asset is still in use. Once fully depreciated, no additional depreciation should be taken, even if an asset is still being used. In no situation can the accumulated depreciation on a plant asset exceed its cost.

If a company retires a plant asset before it is fully depreciated and no cash is received for scrap or salvage value, a loss on disposal occurs. For example, assume that Sunset Company discards delivery equipment that cost $18,000 and has accumulated depreciation of $14,000. The entry is as follows.

| | | |
|---|---|---|
| Accumulated Depreciation—Equipment | 14,000 | |
| Loss on Disposal of Plant Assets | 4,000 | |
|     Equipment | | 18,000 |
|       (To record retirement of delivery equipment at a loss) | | |

A = L + SE

+14,000

−4,000 Exp

−18,000

**Cash Flows**
no effect

Companies report a loss on disposal of plant assets in the "Other expenses and losses" section of the income statement.

---

## DO IT! 3 | Plant Asset Disposals

Overland Trucking has an old truck that cost $30,000 and has accumulated depreciation of $16,000 at the disposal date. Assume two different situations:

1. The company sells the old truck for $17,000 cash.
2. The truck is worthless, so the company simply retires it.

What entry should Overland use to record each scenario?

### Solution

1. Sale of truck for cash:

| | | |
|---|---|---|
| Cash | 17,000 | |
| Accumulated Depreciation—Equipment | 16,000 | |
|     Equipment | | 30,000 |
|     Gain on Disposal of Plant Assets | | 3,000 |
|       [$17,000 − ($30,000 − $16,000)] | | |
|       (To record sale of truck at a gain) | | |

2. Retirement of truck:

| | | |
|---|---|---|
| Accumulated Depreciation—Equipment | 16,000 | |
| Loss on Disposal of Plant Assets | 14,000 | |
|     Equipment | | 30,000 |
|       (To record retirement of truck at a loss) | | |

Related exercise material: **BE9.9, BE9.10, DO IT! 9.3, E9.9, and E9.10.**

**ACTION PLAN**

- Compare the asset's book value and its fair value to determine whether a gain or loss has occurred.
- Make sure that both the Equipment account and Accumulated Depreciation—Equipment are reduced upon disposal.

---

# Natural Resources and Intangible Assets

**LEARNING OBJECTIVE 4**

Describe how to account for natural resources and intangible assets.

## Natural Resources

**Natural resources** consist of standing timber and underground deposits of oil, gas, and minerals (see **Helpful Hint**). These long-lived productive assets have two distinguishing characteristics: (1) they are physically extracted in operations (such as mining, cutting, or pumping), and (2) they are replaceable only by an act of nature.

**HELPFUL HINT**

On a balance sheet, natural resources may be described more specifically as *timberlands, mineral deposits, oil reserves,* and so on.

The acquisition cost of a natural resource is the price needed to acquire the resource **and** prepare it for its intended use. For an already-discovered resource, such as an existing coal mine, cost is the price paid for the property.

# Depletion

The allocation of the cost of natural resources in a rational and systematic manner over the resource's useful life is called **depletion**. (That is, depletion is to natural resources as depreciation is to plant assets.) **Companies generally use the units-of-activity method** (learned earlier in the chapter) **to compute depletion.** The reason is that **depletion generally is a function of the units extracted during the year**.

Under the units-of-activity method, companies divide the total cost of the natural resource minus salvage value by the number of units estimated to be in the resource. The result is a **depletion cost per unit**. To compute depletion, the cost per unit is then multiplied by the number of units extracted.

To illustrate, assume that Lane Coal Company invests $5 million in a mine estimated to have 1 million tons of coal and no salvage value. **Illustration 9.22** shows the computation of the depletion cost per unit.

**ILLUSTRATION 9.22**

**Computation of depletion cost per unit**

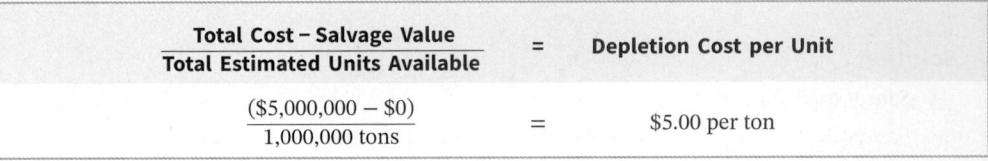

| $$\frac{\text{Total Cost} - \text{Salvage Value}}{\text{Total Estimated Units Available}}$$ | = | **Depletion Cost per Unit** |
|---|---|---|
| $$\frac{(\$5,000,000 - \$0)}{1,000,000 \text{ tons}}$$ | = | $5.00 per ton |

If Lane extracts 250,000 tons in the first year, then the depletion for the year is $1,250,000 (250,000 tons × $5). It records the depletion as follows.

A = L + SE
+1,250,000
−1,250,000

**Cash Flows**
no effect

| Inventory (coal) | 1,250,000 | |
| Accumulated Depletion | | 1,250,000 |
| (To record depletion of coal mine) | | |

Lane debits Inventory for the total depletion for the year and credits Accumulated Depletion to reduce the carrying value of the natural resource. Accumulated Depletion is a contra asset similar to Accumulated Depreciation. Lane credits Inventory when it sells the inventory and debits Cost of Goods Sold. The amount not sold remains in inventory and is reported in the current assets section of the balance sheet.

Some companies do not use an Accumulated Depletion account. In such cases, the company credits the amount of depletion directly to the natural resources account.

# Intangible Assets

**Intangible assets** are rights, privileges, and competitive advantages that result from ownership of long-lived assets that do not possess physical substance. Many companies' most valuable assets are intangible. Some widely known intangible assets are **Microsoft**'s patents, **McDonald's** franchises, the trade name iPod, and **Nike**'s trademark "swoosh."

Financial statements report numerous intangible assets. Yet, many other financially significant intangibles are not reported. To give an example, according to its financial statements in a recent year, **Google** had total stockholders' equity of $22.7 billion. But its market value—the total market value of all its shares on that same date—was roughly $178.5 billion. Thus, its actual market value was about $155.8 billion greater than the amount reported for stockholders' equity on the balance sheet. It is not uncommon for a company's reported book value to differ from its market value because balance sheets are reported at historical cost. But such an extreme difference seriously diminishes the usefulness of the balance sheet to decision-makers. In the case of Google, the difference is due to unrecorded intangibles. For many high-tech or so-called intellectual-property companies, most of their value is from intangibles, many of which are not reported under current accounting rules.

Intangibles may be evidenced by contracts, licenses, and other documents. They may arise from the following sources:

1. Government grants, such as patents, copyrights, licenses, trademarks, and trade names.
2. Acquisition of another business in which the purchase price includes a payment for goodwill.
3. Private monopolistic arrangements arising from contractual agreements, such as franchises and leases.

## Accounting for Intangible Assets

Companies record intangible assets at cost. This cost consists of all expenditures necessary for the company to acquire the right, privilege, or competitive advantage. Intangibles are categorized as having either a limited life or an indefinite life. If an intangible has a **limited life**, the company allocates its cost over the asset's useful life using a process similar to depreciation. The process of allocating the cost of intangibles is referred to as **amortization** (see **Helpful Hint**). The cost of intangible assets with **indefinite lives should not be amortized**.

To record amortization of an intangible asset, a company increases (debits) Amortization Expense and decreases (credits) the specific intangible asset. (Alternatively, some companies choose to credit a contra account, such as Accumulated Amortization. *For homework purposes, you should directly credit the specific intangible asset.*)

Intangible assets are typically amortized on a straight-line basis. For example, the legal life of a patent is 20 years. Companies **amortize the cost of a patent over its 20-year life or its useful life, whichever is shorter**. To illustrate the computation of patent amortization, assume that National Labs purchases a patent at a cost of $60,000 on June 30. If National estimates the useful life of the patent to be eight years, the annual amortization expense is $7,500 ($60,000 ÷ 8) per year. National records $3,750 ($7,500 × $\frac{6}{12}$) of amortization for the six-month period ended December 31 as follows.

| | | | |
|---|---|---|---|
| Dec. 31 | Amortization Expense | 3,750 | |
| | Patents | | 3,750 |
| | (To record patent amortization) | | |

Companies classify Amortization Expense as an operating expense in the income statement.

There is a difference between intangible assets and plant assets in determining cost. For plant assets, cost includes both the purchase price of the asset and the costs incurred in designing and constructing the asset. In contrast, the initial cost for an intangible asset includes **only the purchase price**. Companies expense any costs incurred in developing an intangible asset.

When a company has significant intangibles, analysts evaluate the reasonableness of the useful life estimates that the company discloses in the notes to its financial statements. In determining useful life, the company should consider obsolescence, inadequacy, and other factors. These may cause a patent or other intangible to become economically ineffective before the end of its legal life.

For example, suppose **Intel** purchased a patent on a new computer chip. The legal life of the patent is 20 years. From experience, however, we know that the useful life of a computer chip patent is rarely more than five years. Because new superior chips are developed so rapidly, existing chips become obsolete. Consequently, we would question the amortization expense of Intel if it amortized its patent on a computer chip for a life significantly longer than a five-year period. Amortizing an intangible over a period that is too long will understate amortization expense, overstate Intel's net income, and overstate its assets.

**HELPFUL HINT**
*Amortization* is to intangibles what *depreciation* is to plant assets and *depletion* is to natural resources.

−3,750 | | | −3,750 Exp

**Cash Flows**
no effect

# Types of Intangible Assets

## Patents

A **patent** is an exclusive right issued by the U.S. Patent Office that enables the recipient to manufacture, sell, or otherwise control an invention for a period of 20 years from the date of the grant. A patent is nonrenewable. **The initial cost of a patent is the cash or cash equivalent price paid to acquire the patent.**

The saying, "A patent is only as good as the money you're prepared to spend defending it," is very true. Many patents are subject to litigation by competitors. Any legal costs an owner incurs in successfully defending a patent in an infringement suit are considered necessary to establish the patent's validity. **The owner adds those costs to the Patents account and amortizes them over the remaining life of the patent.**

**The patent holder amortizes the cost of a patent over its 20-year legal life or its useful life, whichever is shorter.** Companies consider obsolescence and inadequacy in determining useful life. These factors may cause a patent to become economically ineffective before the end of its legal life.

## Copyrights

The federal government grants **copyrights**, which give the owner the exclusive right to reproduce and sell an artistic or published work. Copyrights last for the life of the creator plus 70 years. The cost of a copyright is the **cost of acquiring and successfully defending it**. The cost may be only the small fee paid to the U.S. Copyright Office, or it may amount to a great deal more if a copyright is acquired from another party. The useful life of a copyright generally is significantly shorter than its legal life. Therefore, copyrights usually are amortized over a relatively short period of time.

## Trademarks and Trade Names

A **trademark** or **trade name** is a word, phrase, jingle, or symbol that identifies a particular enterprise or product. Trade names like Wheaties, Monopoly, Big Mac, Kleenex, Coca-Cola, and Jeep create immediate product identification and generally enhance the sale of the product. The creator or original user may obtain exclusive legal right to the trademark or trade name by registering it with the U.S. Patent Office. Such registration provides 20 years of protection. The registration may be renewed indefinitely as long as the trademark or trade name is in use.

If a company purchases the trademark or trade name, its cost is the purchase price. If a company develops and maintains the trademark or trade name, any costs related to these activities are expensed as incurred. Because trademarks and trade names have indefinite lives, they are not amortized.

---

### Accounting Across the Organization   Google

Hattanas/
Shutterstock.com

#### We Want to Own Glass

**Google**, which trademarked the term "Google Glass," then wanted to trademark the term "Glass." Why? Because the simple word Glass has marketing advantages over the term Google Glass. It is easy to remember and is more universal. Regulators, however, balked at Google's request. They said that the possible trademark is too similar to other existing or pending software trademarks that contain the word "glass." Also, regulators suggested that the term Glass is merely descriptive and therefore lacks trademark protection. For example, regulators noted that a company that makes salsa could not trademark the term "Spicy Salsa."

**BorderStylo LLC**, which developed a Web-browser extension called Write on Glass, filed a notice of opposition to Google's request. In the end, the case will probably not be resolved because Google Glass as a company product appears to have failed.

**Source:** Jacob Gershman, "Google Wants to Own 'Glass'," *Wall Street Journal* (April 4, 2014), p. B5.

**If Google had been successful in registering the term Glass, where would this trademark be reported on its financial statements? (Answer is available near the end of the chapter.)**

## Franchises

When you fill up your tank at the corner **Shell** station, eat lunch at **Subway**, or make a reservation at a **Marriott**, you are dealing with franchises. A **franchise** is a contractual arrangement between a franchisor and a franchisee. The franchisor grants the franchisee the right to sell certain products, to perform specific services, or to use certain trademarks or trade names, usually within a designated geographic area.

Another type of franchise is a **license**. A license granted by a governmental body permits a company to use public property in performing its services. Examples are the use of city streets for a bus line or taxi service; the use of public land for telephone, electric, and cable television lines; and the use of airwaves for radio or TV broadcasting. In a recent license agreement, **FOX**, **CBS**, and **NBC** agreed to pay $27.9 billion for the right to broadcast **NFL** football games over an eight-year period. Franchises and licenses may be granted for a definite period of time, an indefinite period, or perpetually.

**When a company incurs costs in connection with the acquisition of the franchise or license, it should recognize an intangible asset.** Companies record as **operating expenses** annual payments made under a franchise agreement in the period in which they are incurred. In the case of a limited life, a company amortizes the cost of a franchise (or license) as an operating expense over the useful life. If the life is indefinite or perpetual, the cost is not amortized.

## Goodwill

Usually, the largest intangible asset that appears on a company's balance sheet is goodwill. **Goodwill** represents the value of all favorable attributes that relate to a company that are not attributable to any other specific asset. These include exceptional management, desirable location, good customer relations, skilled employees, high-quality products, and harmonious relations with labor unions. Goodwill is unique. Unlike assets such as investments and plant assets, which can be sold **individually** in the marketplace, goodwill can be identified only with the business **as a whole**.

If goodwill can be identified only with the business as a whole, how can its amount be determined? One could try to put a dollar value on the factors listed above (exceptional management, desirable location, and so on). But, the results would be very subjective, and such subjective valuations would not contribute to the reliability of financial statements. **Therefore, companies record goodwill only when an entire business is purchased. When the entire business is purchased, goodwill is the excess of cost over the fair value of the net assets (assets less liabilities) acquired.**

In recording the purchase of a business, the company debits (increases) the identifiable acquired assets at their fair values, credits liabilities at their fair values, credits cash for the purchase price, and records the difference as the cost of goodwill. **Goodwill is not amortized** because it is considered to have an indefinite life. However, goodwill must be written down if a company determines that its value has been permanently impaired.

# Research and Development Costs

**Research and development costs** are expenditures that may lead to patents, copyrights, new processes, and new products (see **Helpful Hint**). Many companies spend considerable sums of money on research and development (R&D). For example, in a recent year, **Google** spent over $9.8 billion on R&D.

Research and development costs present accounting challenges. For one thing, it is sometimes difficult to assign the costs to specific projects. Also, there are uncertainties in identifying the extent and timing of future benefits. As a result, companies usually record R&D costs **as an expense when incurred** (instead of as an asset), whether the research and development is successful or not.

To illustrate, assume that Laser Scanner Company spent $3 million on R&D that resulted in two highly successful patents. It spent $20,000 on legal fees for the patents. The company would add the lawyers' fees to the Patents account. The R&D costs however, cannot be

**HELPFUL HINT**
Research and development (R&D) costs are not intangible assets. But because they may lead to patents and copyrights, we discuss them in this section.

**International Note**

IFRS allows capitalization of some development costs. This may contribute to differences in R&D expenditures across nations.

included in the cost of the patents. Instead, the company would record the R&D costs as an expense when incurred.

Many disagree with this accounting approach (see **International Note**). They argue that expensing R&D costs leads to understated assets and net income. Others believe that capitalizing these costs will lead to highly speculative assets on the balance sheet. Who is right is difficult to determine.

---

**ACTION PLAN**

- **Know that the accounting for an intangible asset often depends on whether the item has a finite or indefinite life.**

- **Recognize the many similarities and differences between the accounting for natural resources, plant assets, and intangible assets.**

## DO IT! 4 | Classification Concepts

Match the statement with the term most directly associated with it. Use each term only once.

|   |   |
|---|---|
| Copyrights | Depletion |
| Intangible assets | Franchises |
| Research and development costs | |

1. _____ The allocation of the cost of a natural resource in a rational and systematic manner.

2. _____ Rights, privileges, and competitive advantages that result from the ownership of long-lived assets that do not possess physical substance.

3. _____ An exclusive right granted by the federal government to reproduce and sell an artistic or published work.

4. _____ A right to sell certain products or services or to use certain trademarks or trade names within a designated geographic area.

5. _____ Costs incurred by a company that often lead to patents or new products. These costs must be expensed as incurred.

### Solution

1. Depletion
2. Intangible assets
3. Copyrights

4. Franchises
5. Research and development costs

Related exercise material: **BE9.11, BE9.12, DO IT! 9.4, E9.11, E9.12, and E9.13.**

---

# Statement Presentation and Analysis

**LEARNING OBJECTIVE 5**

Discuss how plant assets, natural resources, and intangible assets are reported and analyzed.

## Presentation

Usually, companies combine plant assets and natural resources under "Property, plant, and equipment" in the balance sheet. They show intangible assets separately. **Illustration 9.23** shows the assets section from the balance sheet of Artex Company, with emphasis on the reporting of plant assets.

When a plant asset is fully depreciated, the plant asset and related accumulated depreciation should continue to be reported on the balance sheet without further depreciation or adjustment until the asset is retired. Intangibles do not usually use a contra asset account, such as the contra asset account Accumulated Depreciation used for plant

**ILLUSTRATION 9.23**

**Presentation of property, plant, and equipment, and intangible assets**

### Artex Company
**Balance Sheet (partial)**
**(in thousands)**

| | | |
|---|---:|---:|
| **Current assets** | | |
| Cash | | $ 430 |
| Accounts receivable | | 100 |
| Inventory | | 910 |
| Total current assets | | $ 1,440 |
| **Property, plant, and equipment** | | |
| Gold mine | $ 530 | |
| Less: Accumulated depletion | 210 | 320 |
| Land | | 600 |
| Buildings | 7,600 | |
| Less: Accumulated depreciation—buildings | 500 | 7,100 |
| Equipment | 3,870 | |
| Less: Accumulated depreciation—equipment | 620 | 3,250 |
| Total property, plant, and equipment | | 11,270 |
| **Intangible assets** | | |
| Patents | | 440 |
| Trademarks | | 180 |
| Goodwill | | 900 | 1,520 |
| Total assets | | $14,230 |

assets. Instead, companies record amortization of intangibles as a direct decrease (credit) to the asset account.

Companies may disclose in the balance sheet or the notes to the financial statements the major classes of assets such as land, land improvements, buildings and equipment, and accumulated depreciation (by major classes or in total). In addition, they should describe the depreciation and amortization methods that were used, as well as disclose the amount of depreciation and amortization expense for the period. *For homework purposes, use the format in Illustration 9.23 for preparing balance sheet information.*

## Analysis

Using ratios, we can analyze how efficiently a company uses its assets to generate sales. The **asset turnover** analyzes the productivity of a company's assets. It tells us how many dollars of net sales a company generates for each dollar invested in assets. This ratio is computed by dividing net sales by average total assets for the period. **Illustration 9.24** shows the computation of the asset turnover for **Procter & Gamble**. P&G's net sales for a recent year were $76,279 million. Its total ending assets were $129,495 million, and beginning assets were $144,266 million.

**ILLUSTRATION 9.24**

**Asset turnover formula and computation**

| Net Sales | ÷ | Average Total Assets | = | Asset Turnover |
|:---:|:---:|:---:|:---:|:---:|
| $76,279 | ÷ | $\dfrac{\$144,266 + \$129,495}{2}$ | = | .56 times |

Thus, each dollar invested in assets produced $0.56 in net sales for P&G. If a company is using its assets efficiently, each dollar of assets will create a high amount of net sales. This ratio varies greatly among different industries—from those that are asset-intensive (utilities) to those that are not (services).

---

## People, Planet, and Profit Insight    BHP

iStock.com/Christian Uhrig

### Sustainability Report Please

Sustainability reports identify how the company is meeting its corporate social responsibilities. Many companies, both large and small, are now issuing these reports. For example, companies such as **Disney**, **Best Buy**, **Microsoft**, **Ford**, and **ConocoPhillips** issue these reports. Presented below is an adapted section of a recent **BHP** (a global mining, oil, and gas company) sustainability report on its environmental policies. These policies are to (1) take action to address the challenges of climate change, (2) set and achieve targets that reduce pollution, and (3) enhance biodiversity by assessing and considering ecological values and land-use aspects. Here is how BHP measures the success or failure of some of these policies:

| Social Responsibility | Target | Target Date |
|---|---|---|
| Safety | • Zero work-related fatalities.<br>• Year-on-year improvement of our total recordable injury frequency (TRIF). | Annual<br>Annual |
| Health | For our most material exposures of respirable silica, diesel particulate and coal mine dust, we will achieve a 50 percent reduction in the number of workers potentially exposed as compared with the FY2017 baseline. | 30 June 2022 |
| Community | Zero significant community events. | Annual |
|  | Our social investment will contribute to improved quality of life in host communities and support achievement of the UN Sustainable Development Goals. We will invest not less than one percent of pre-tax profit (three-year rolling average) in meeting these objectives. | 30 June 2022 |
|  | Regional Indigenous Peoples Plans will be developed, which support implementation of BHP's Indigenous Peoples Strategy. Plans will include all geographically relevant assets. | 30 June 2022 |
| Climate change | Maintain FY2022 greenhouse gas (GHG) emissions at or below FY2017 levels while we continue to grow our business. | 30 June 2022 |
|  | **Longer-term goal:** In line with international commitments, BHP aims to achieve net-zero operational GHG emissions in the second half of this century. | The second half of this century. |

In addition to the environment, BHP has sections in its sustainability report that discuss people, safety, health, and community.

**Why do you believe companies issue sustainability reports? (Answer is available near the end of the chapter.)**

---

### ACTION PLAN

- **Recognize that the asset turnover analyzes the productivity of a company's assets.**
- **Know the formula Net sales ÷ Average total assets = Asset turnover.**

## DO IT! 5 | Asset Turnover

Paramour Company reported net income of $180,000, net sales of $420,000, and total assets of $460,000 on January 1, 2022, and total assets of $540,000 on December 31, 2022. Determine Paramour's asset turnover for 2022.

### Solution

The asset turnover for Paramour Company is computed as follows.

| Net Sales | ÷ | Average Total Assets | = | Asset Turnover |
|---|---|---|---|---|
| $420,000 | ÷ | $\dfrac{\$460,000 + \$540,000}{2}$ | = | .84 times |

Related exercise material: **BE9.14, DO IT! 9.5, and E9.14.**

| Appendix 9A | # Exchange of Plant Assets |

---

### LEARNING OBJECTIVE *6
Explain how to account for the exchange of plant assets.

---

Ordinarily, companies record a gain or loss on the exchange of plant assets. The rationale for recognizing a gain or loss is that most exchanges have **commercial substance**. An exchange has commercial substance if the future cash flows change as a result of the exchange.

To illustrate, Ramos Co. exchanges some of its equipment for land held by Brodhead Inc. It is likely that the timing and amount of the cash flows arising from the land will differ significantly from the cash flows arising from the equipment. As a result, both Ramos and Brodhead are in different economic positions after the exchange. Therefore, **the exchange has commercial substance**, and the companies recognize a gain or loss in the exchange. Because most exchanges have commercial substance (even when similar assets are exchanged) we illustrate only this type of situation for both a loss and a gain.

## Loss Treatment

To illustrate an exchange that results in a loss, assume that Roland Company exchanged a set of used trucks plus cash for a new semi-truck. The used trucks have a combined book value of $42,000 (cost $64,000 less $22,000 accumulated depreciation). Roland's purchasing agent, experienced in the secondhand market, indicates that the used trucks have a fair value of $26,000. In addition to the trucks, Roland must pay $17,000 for the new semi-truck. Roland computes the cost of the new semi-truck as shown in **Illustration 9A.1**.

| | |
|---|---:|
| Fair value of used trucks | $26,000 |
| Cash paid | 17,000 |
| Cost of new semi-truck | $43,000 |

**ILLUSTRATION 9A.1**
**Cost of new semi-truck**

Roland incurs a loss on disposal of plant assets of $16,000 on this exchange. The reason is that the book value of the used trucks is greater than the fair value of these trucks. **Illustration 9A.2** shows the computation.

| | |
|---|---:|
| Book value of used trucks ($64,000 − $22,000) | $42,000 |
| Fair value of used trucks | 26,000 |
| **Loss on disposal of plant assets** | **$16,000** |

**ILLUSTRATION 9A.2**
**Computation of loss on disposal**

In recording an exchange with a loss, four steps are required: (1) eliminate the book value of the asset given up, (2) record the cost of the asset acquired, (3) recognize the loss on disposal of plant assets, and (4) record cash paid or received. Roland Company thus records the exchange as follows.

| | | | |
|---|---:|---:|---|
| Equipment (new) | 43,000 | | +43,000 |
| Accumulated Depreciation—Equipment | 22,000 | | +22,000 |
| Loss on Disposal of Plant Assets | 16,000 | | −16,000 Exp |
|    Equipment (old) | | 64,000 | −64,000 |
|    Cash | | 17,000 | −17,000 |
|     (To record exchange of used trucks for semi-truck) | | | |

A = L + SE

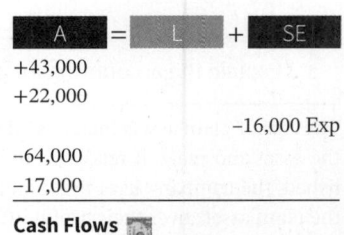

**Cash Flows**
−17,000

## Gain Treatment

To illustrate a gain situation, assume that Mark Express Delivery decides to exchange its old delivery equipment plus cash of $3,000 for new delivery equipment. The book value of the old delivery equipment is $12,000 (cost $40,000 less accumulated depreciation $28,000). The fair value of the old delivery equipment is $19,000.

The cost of the new asset is the fair value of the old asset exchanged plus any cash paid (or other consideration given up). The cost of the new delivery equipment is $22,000, computed as shown in **Illustration 9A.3**.

**ILLUSTRATION 9A.3**

**Cost of new delivery equipment**

| | |
|---|---|
| Fair value of old delivery equipment | $19,000 |
| Cash paid | 3,000 |
| **Cost of new delivery equipment** | **$22,000** |

A gain results when the fair value of the old delivery equipment is greater than its book value. For Mark Express, there is a gain of $7,000 on disposal of plant assets, computed as shown in **Illustration 9A.4**.

**ILLUSTRATION 9A.4**

**Computation of gain on disposal**

| | |
|---|---|
| Fair value of old delivery equipment | $19,000 |
| Book value of old delivery equipment ($40,000 − $28,000) | 12,000 |
| **Gain on disposal of plant assets** | **$ 7,000** |

Mark Express records the exchange as follows.

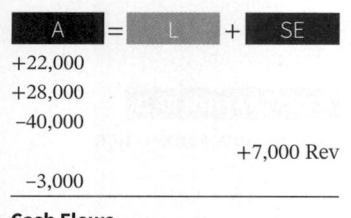

A = L + SE
+22,000
+28,000
−40,000
　　　　+7,000 Rev
−3,000

**Cash Flows**
−3,000

| | | |
|---|---|---|
| Equipment (new) | 22,000 | |
| Accumulated Depreciation—Equipment (old) | 28,000 | |
| 　Equipment (old) | | 40,000 |
| 　Gain on Disposal of Plant Assets | | 7,000 |
| 　Cash | | 3,000 |
| 　（To record exchange of old delivery equipment for new delivery equipment) | | |

In recording an exchange with a gain, the following four steps are involved: (1) eliminate the book value of the asset given up, (2) record the cost of the asset acquired, (3) recognize the gain on disposal of plant assets, and (4) record cash paid or received.

# Review and Practice

## Learning Objectives Review

### 1 Explain the accounting for plant asset expenditures.

The cost of plant assets includes all expenditures necessary to acquire the asset and make it ready for its intended use. Once cost is established, the company uses that amount as the basis of accounting for the plant assets over their useful life.

Companies incur revenue expenditures to maintain the operating efficiency and productive life of an asset. They debit these expenditures to Maintenance and Repairs Expense as incurred. Capital expenditures increase the operating efficiency, productive capacity, or expected useful life of the asset. Companies generally debit these expenditures to the plant asset affected.

## 2  Apply depreciation methods to plant assets.

Depreciation is the allocation of the cost of a plant asset to expense over its useful (service) life in a rational and systematic manner. Depreciation is not a process of valuation, nor is it a process that results in an accumulation of cash.

Three depreciation methods are:

| Method | Effect on Annual Depreciation | Formula |
|---|---|---|
| Straight-line | Constant amount | Depreciable cost ÷ Useful life (in years) |
| Units-of-activity | Varying amount | Depreciable cost per unit × Units of activity during the year |
| Declining-balance | Decreasing amount | Book value at beginning of year × Declining-balance rate |

Companies make revisions of periodic depreciation in present and future periods, not retroactively. They determine the new annual depreciation by dividing the depreciable cost at the time of the revision by the remaining useful life.

## 3  Explain how to account for the disposal of plant assets.

The accounting for disposal of a plant asset through retirement or sale is as follows. (a) Eliminate the book value of the plant asset at the date of disposal. (b) Record cash proceeds, if any. (c) Account for the difference between the book value and the cash proceeds as a gain or loss on disposal.

## 4  Describe how to account for natural resources and intangible assets.

Companies compute depletion cost per unit by dividing the total cost of the natural resource minus salvage value by the number of units estimated to be in the resource. They then multiply the depletion cost per unit by the number of units extracted and sold.

The process of allocating the cost of an intangible asset is referred to as amortization. The cost of intangible assets with indefinite lives is not amortized. Companies normally use the straight-line method for amortizing intangible assets.

## 5  Discuss how plant assets, natural resources, and intangible assets are reported and analyzed.

Companies usually combine plant assets and natural resources under property, plant, and equipment. They show intangible assets separately. Either within the balance sheet or in the notes, companies should disclose the balances of the major classes of assets, such as land, buildings, and equipment, and accumulated depreciation by major classes or in total. They also should describe the depreciation and amortization methods used, and should disclose the amount of depreciation and amortization expense for the period. The asset turnover measures the productivity of a company's assets in generating sales.

## *6  Explain how to account for the exchange of plant assets.

Ordinarily, companies record a gain or loss on the exchange of plant assets. The rationale for recognizing a gain or loss is that most exchanges have commercial substance. An exchange has commercial substance if the future cash flows change as a result of the exchange.

## Glossary Review

**Accelerated-depreciation method**  Depreciation method that produces higher depreciation expense in the early years than in the later years. (p. 9-12).

**Additions and improvements**  Costs incurred to increase the operating efficiency, productive capacity, or useful life of a plant asset. (p. 9-6).

**Amortization**  The allocation of the cost of an intangible asset to expense over its useful life in a systematic and rational manner. (p. 9-21).

**Asset turnover**  A measure of how efficiently a company uses its assets to generate sales; calculated as net sales divided by average total assets. (p. 9-25).

**Capital expenditures**  Expenditures that increase the company's investment in productive facilities. (p. 9-6).

**Cash equivalent price**  The fair value of the asset given up or the fair value of the asset received, whichever is more clearly determinable. (p. 9-3).

**Copyrights**  Exclusive grant from the federal government that allows the owner to reproduce and sell an artistic or published work. (p. 9-22).

**Declining-balance method**  Depreciation method that applies a constant rate to the declining book value of the asset and produces a decreasing annual depreciation expense over the useful life of the asset. (p. 9-12).

**Depletion**  The allocation of the cost of a natural resource in a rational and systematic manner over the resource's useful life. (p. 9-20).

**Depreciable cost**  The cost of a plant asset less its salvage value. (p. 9-9).

**Depreciation**  The process of allocating to expense the cost of a plant asset over its useful (service) life in a rational and systematic manner. (p. 9-7).

**Franchise (license)**  A contractual arrangement under which the franchisor grants the franchisee the right to sell certain products, perform specific services, or use certain trademarks or trade names, usually within a designated geographic area. (p. 9-23).

**Going concern assumption**  The company will continue in operation for the foreseeable future. (p. 9-8).

**Goodwill**  The value of all favorable attributes that relate to a company that is not attributable to any other specific asset. (p. 9-23).

**Impairment**  A permanent decline in the fair value of an asset. (p. 9-16).

**Intangible assets**  Rights, privileges, and competitive advantages that result from the ownership of long-lived assets that do not possess physical substance. (p. 9-20).

**Materiality concept**  If an item would not make a difference in decision-making, a company does not have to follow GAAP in reporting it. (p. 9-6).

**Natural resources**  Assets that consist of standing timber and underground deposits of oil, gas, and minerals. (p. 9-19).

**Ordinary repairs**  Expenditures to maintain the operating efficiency and productive life of the long-lived asset. (p. 9-5).

**Patent**  An exclusive right issued by the U.S. Patent Office that enables the recipient to manufacture, sell, or otherwise control an invention for a period of 20 years from the date of the grant. (p. 9-22).

**Plant assets** Tangible resources that are used in the operations of the business and are not intended for sale to customers. (p. 9-3).

**Research and development (R&D) costs** Expenditures that may lead to patents, copyrights, new processes, or new products. These costs are expensed as incurred. (p. 9-23).

**Revenue expenditures** Expenditures that are immediately charged against revenues as an expense. (p. 9-6).

**Salvage value** An estimate of an asset's value at the end of its useful life. (p. 9-8).

**Straight-line method** Depreciation method in which periodic depreciation is the same for each year of the asset's useful life. (p. 9-9).

**Trademark (trade name)** A word, phrase, jingle, or symbol that identifies a particular enterprise or product. (p. 9-22).

**Units-of-activity method** Depreciation method in which useful life is expressed in terms of the total units of production or use expected from an asset. (p. 9-10).

**Useful life** An estimate of the expected productive life, also called service life, of an asset. (p. 9-8).

## Practice Multiple-Choice Questions

**1. (LO 1)** Corrieten Company purchased equipment and incurred the following costs.

| | |
|---|---:|
| Cash price | $24,000 |
| Sales taxes | 1,200 |
| Insurance during transit | 200 |
| Installation and testing | 400 |
| Total costs | $25,800 |

What amount should be recorded as the cost of the equipment?

   **a.** $24,000.       **c.** $25,400.

   **b.** $25,200.       **d.** $25,800.

**2. (LO 1)** Additions to plant assets are:

   **a.** revenue expenditures.

   **b.** debited to the Maintenance and Repairs Expense account.

   **c.** debited to the Purchases account.

   **d.** capital expenditures.

**3. (LO 2)** Depreciation is a process of:

   **a.** valuation.       **c.** cash accumulation.

   **b.** cost allocation.       **d.** appraisal.

**4. (LO 2)** Cuso Company purchased equipment on January 1, 2021, at a total cost of $400,000. The equipment has an estimated salvage value of $10,000 and an estimated useful life of 5 years. The amount of accumulated depreciation at December 31, 2022, if the straight-line method of depreciation is used, is:

   **a.** $80,000.       **c.** $78,000.

   **b.** $160,000.       **d.** $156,000.

**5. (LO 2)** Kant Enterprises purchased a truck for $11,000 on January 1, 2021. The truck has an estimated salvage value of $1,000 at the end of 5 years. Using the units-of-activity method, the balance in accumulated depreciation at December 31, 2022, can be computed by the following formula:

   **a.** ($11,000 ÷ Total estimated activity) × Units of activity for 2022.

   **b.** ($10,000 ÷ Total estimated activity) × Units of activity for 2022.

   **c.** ($11,000 ÷ Total estimated activity) × Units of activity for 2021 and 2022.

   **d.** ($10,000 ÷ Total estimated activity) × Units of activity for 2021 and 2022.

**6. (LO 2)** Jefferson Company purchased a piece of equipment on January 1, 2022. The equipment cost $60,000 and has an estimated life of 8 years and a salvage value of $8,000. What was the depreciation expense for the asset for 2023 under the double-declining-balance method?

   **a.** $6,500.       **c.** $15,000.

   **b.** $11,250.       **d.** $6,562.

**7. (LO 2)** When there is a change in estimated depreciation:

   **a.** previous depreciation should be corrected.

   **b.** current and future years' depreciation should be revised.

   **c.** only future years' depreciation should be revised.

   **d.** None of the answer choices is correct.

**8. (LO 2)** Able Towing Company purchased a tow truck for $60,000 on January 1, 2022. It was originally depreciated on a straight-line basis over 10 years with an assumed salvage value of $12,000. On December 31, 2024, before adjusting entries had been made, the company decided to change the remaining estimated life to 4 years (including 2024) and the salvage value to $2,000. What was the depreciation expense for 2024?

   **a.** $6,000.       **c.** $15,000.

   **b.** $4,800.       **d.** $12,100.

**9. (LO 3)** Bennie Razor Company has decided to sell one of its old manufacturing machines on June 30, 2022. The machine was purchased for $80,000 on January 1, 2018, and was depreciated on a straight-line basis for 10 years assuming no salvage value. If the machine was sold for $26,000, what was the amount of the gain or loss recorded at the time of the sale?

   **a.** $18,000.       **c.** $22,000.

   **b.** $54,000.       **d.** $46,000.

**10. (LO 4)** Maggie Sharrer Company expects to extract 20 million tons of coal from a mine that cost $12 million. If no salvage value is expected and 2 million tons are mined in the first year, the entry to record depletion will include a:

   **a.** debit to Accumulated Depletion of $2,000,000.

   **b.** credit to Depletion Expense of $1,200,000.

   **c.** debit to Inventory of $1,200,000.

   **d.** credit to Accumulated Depletion of $2,000,000.

**11. (LO 4)** Which of the following statements is **false**?

   **a.** If an intangible asset has a finite life, it should be amortized.

   **b.** The amortization period of an intangible asset can exceed 20 years.

   **c.** Goodwill is recorded only when a business is purchased.

   **d.** Research and development costs are expensed when incurred, except when the research and development expenditures result in a successful patent.

12. **(LO 4)** Martha Beyerlein Company incurred $150,000 of research and development costs in its laboratory to develop a patent granted on January 2, 2022. On July 31, 2022, Beyerlein paid $35,000 for legal fees in a successful defense of the patent. The total amount debited to Patents through July 31, 2022, should be:

    a. $150,000.
               c. $185,000.

    b. $35,000.
               d. $170,000.

13. **(LO 5)** Indicate which of the following statements is **true**.

    a. Since intangible assets lack physical substance, they need be disclosed only in the notes to the financial statements.

    b. Goodwill should be reported as a contra account in the stockholders' equity section.

    c. Totals of major classes of assets can be shown in the balance sheet, with asset details disclosed in the notes to the financial statements.

    d. Intangible assets are typically combined with plant assets and natural resources, and shown in the property, plant, and equipment section.

14. **(LO 5)** Lake Coffee Company reported net sales of $180,000, net income of $54,000, beginning total assets of $200,000, and ending total assets of $300,000. What was the company's asset turnover?

    a. 0.90.
               c. 0.72.

    b. 0.20.
               d. 1.39.

*15. **(LO 6)** Schopenhauer Company exchanged an old machine, with a book value of $39,000 and a fair value of $35,000, and paid $10,000 cash for a similar new machine. The transaction has commercial substance. At what amount should the machine acquired in the exchange be recorded on Schopenhauer's books?

    a. $45,000.
               c. $49,000.

    b. $46,000.
               d. $50,000.

*16. **(LO 6)** In exchanges of assets in which the exchange has commercial substance:

    a. neither gains nor losses are recognized immediately.

    b. gains, but not losses, are recognized immediately.

    c. losses, but not gains, are recognized immediately.

    d. both gains and losses are recognized immediately.

## Solutions

**1. d.** All of the costs ($1,200 + $200 − $400) in addition to the cash price ($24,000) should be included in the cost of the equipment because they were necessary expenditures to acquire the asset and make it ready for its intended use. The other choices are therefore incorrect.

**2. d.** When an addition is made to plant assets, it is intended to increase productive capacity, increase the assets' useful life, or increase the efficiency of the assets. This is called a capital expenditure. The other choices are incorrect because (a) additions to plant assets are not revenue expenditures because the additions will have a long-term useful life whereas revenue expenditures are minor repairs and maintenance that do not prolong the life of the assets; (b) additions to plant assets are debited to Plant Assets, not Maintenance and Repairs Expense, because the Maintenance and Repairs Expense account is used to record expenditures not intended to increase the life of the assets; and (c) additions to plant assets are debited to Plant Assets, not Purchases, because the Purchases account is used to record assets intended for resale (inventory).

**3. b.** Depreciation is a process of allocating the cost of an asset over its useful life, not a process of (a) valuation, (c) cash accumulation, or (d) appraisal.

**4. d.** Accumulated depreciation will be the sum of 2 years of depreciation expense. Annual depreciation for this asset is ($400,000 − $10,000) ÷ 5 = $78,000. The sum of 2 years' depreciation is therefore $156,000 ($78,000 + $78,000), not (a) $80,000, (b) $160,000, or (c) $78,000.

**5. d.** The units-of-activity method takes salvage value into consideration; therefore, the depreciable cost is $10,000. This amount is divided by total estimated activity. The resulting number is multiplied by the units of activity used in 2021 and 2022 to compute the accumulated depreciation at the end of 2022, the second year of the asset's use. The other choices are therefore incorrect.

**6. b.** For the double-declining-balance method, the depreciation rate would be 25% or $\left(\frac{1}{8} \times 2\right)$. For 2022, annual depreciation expense is $15,000 ($60,000 book value × 25%); for 2023, annual depreciation expense is $11,250 [($60,000 − $15,000) × 25%], not (a) $6,500, (c) $15,000, or (d) $6,562.

**7. b.** When there is a change in estimated depreciation, the current and future years' depreciation computation should reflect the new estimates. The other choices are incorrect because (a) previous years' depreciation should not be adjusted when new estimates are made for

depreciation, and (c) when there is a change in estimated depreciation, the current and future years' depreciation computation should reflect the new estimates. Choice (d) is wrong because there is a correct answer.

**8. d.** First, calculate accumulated depreciation from January 1, 2022, through December 31, 2023, which is $9,600 {[($60,000 − $12,000) ÷ 10 years] × 2 years}. Next, calculate the revised depreciable cost, which is $48,400 ($60,000 − $9,600 − $2,000). Thus, the depreciation expense for 2024 is $12,100 ($48,400 ÷ 4), not (a) $6,000, (b) $4,800, or (c) $15,000.

**9. a.** First, the book value needs to be determined. The accumulated depreciation as of June 30, 2022, is $36,000 [($80,000 ÷ 10) × 4.5 years]. Thus, the cost of the machine less accumulated depreciation equals $44,000 ($80,000 − $36,000). The loss recorded at the time of sale is $18,000 ($26,000 − $44,000), not (b) $54,000, (c) $22,000, or (d) $46,000.

**10. c.** The amount of depletion is determined by computing the depletion per unit ($12 million ÷ 20 million tons = $0.60 per ton) and then multiplying that amount by the number of units extracted during the year (2 million tons × $0.60 = $1,200,000). This amount is debited to Inventory and credited to Accumulated Depletion. The other choices are therefore incorrect.

**11. d.** Research and development (R&D) costs are expensed when incurred, regardless of whether the research and development expenditures result in a successful patent or not. The other choices are true statements.

**12. b.** Because the $150,000 was spent developing the patent rather than buying it from another firm, it is debited to Research and Development Expense. Only the $35,000 spent on the successful defense can be debited to Patents, not (a) $150,000, (c) $185,000, or (d) $170,000.

**13. c.** Reporting only totals of major classes of assets in the balance sheet is appropriate. Additional details can be shown in the notes to the financial statements. The other choices are false statements.

**14. c.** Asset turnover = Net sales ($180,000) ÷ Average total assets [($200,000 + $300,000) ÷ 2] = 0.72 times, not (a) 0.90, (b) 0.20, or (d) 1.39 times.

*15. **a.** When an exchange has commercial substance, the debit to the new asset is equal to the fair value of the old asset plus the cash paid ($35,000 + $10,000 = $45,000), not (b) $46,000, (c) $49,000, or (d) $50,000.

*16. **d.** Both gains and losses are recognized immediately when an exchange of assets has commercial substance. The other choices are therefore incorrect.

## Practice Brief Exercises

*Compute straight-line and double-declining-balance depreciation.*

**1. (LO 2)** Fulmer Company acquires a delivery truck at a cost of $50,000 on January 1, 2022. The truck is expected to have a salvage value of $5,000 at the end of its 5-year useful life.

    **a.** Compute annual depreciation expense for the first and second years using the straight-line method.

    **b.** Compute annual depreciation expense for the first and second years using double-declining-balance.

### Solution

**1. a.** Depreciable cost of $45,000 ($50,000 − $5,000). With a 5-year useful life, annual depreciation is $9,000 ($45,000 ÷ 5). Under the straight-line method, depreciation is the same each year. Thus, depreciation is $9,000 for both the first and second years.

    **b.** The double-declining-balance rate is 40% (20% × 2), which is applied to book value at the beginning of the year. The computations are:

| | Book Value | × | Rate | = | Depreciation Expense |
|---|---|---|---|---|---|
| Year 1 | $50,000 | | 40% | | $20,000 |
| Year 2 | ($50,000 − $20,000) | | 40% | | $12,000 |

*Prepare entries for disposal by sale.*

**2. (LO 3)** Giolito Company sells equipment on August 31, 2022, for $20,000 cash. The equipment originally cost $60,000 and as of January 1, 2022, had accumulated depreciation of $38,000. Depreciation for the first 8 months of 2022 is $6,000. Prepare the journal entries to (a) update depreciation to August 31, 2022, and (b) record the sale of the equipment.

### Solution

**2. a.** Depreciation Expense      6,000
        Accumulated Depreciation—Equipment      6,000

    **b.** Cash      20,000
        Accumulated Depreciation—Equipment      44,000
            Equipment      60,000
            Gain on Disposal of Plant Assets      4,000

| | |
|---|---|
| Cost of equipment | $60,000 |
| Less: Accumulated depreciation | 44,000* |
| Book value at date of disposal | 16,000 |
| Proceeds from sale | 20,000 |
| Gain on disposal | $ 4,000 |

*$38,000 + $6,000

*Prepare amortization expense entry and balance sheet presentation for intangible assets.*

**3. (LO 4)** Lucas Company acquires a limited-life franchise for $200,000 on January 2, 2022. Its estimated useful life is 10 years. (a) Prepare the journal entry to record amortization expense for the first year. (b) Show how this franchise is reported on the balance sheet at the end of the first year.

### Solution

**3. a.** Amortization Expense ($200,000 ÷ 10)      20,000
        Franchises      20,000

    **b.** Intangible assets
        Franchises      $180,000

# Practice Exercises

**1. (LO 2)** Winston Company purchased a new machine on October 1, 2022, at a cost of $120,000. The company estimated that the machine will have a salvage value of $12,000. The machine is expected to be used for 12,000 working hours during its 4-year life.

*Determine depreciation for partial periods.*

### Instructions

Compute the depreciation expense under the following methods for the year indicated, assuming that Winston prepares adjusting entries annually.

a. Straight-line for 2022.

b. Units-of-activity for 2022, assuming machine usage was 1,700 hours.

c. Declining-balance using double the straight-line rate for 2022 and 2023.

### Solution

1.  a. Straight-line method:

$$\left(\frac{\$120,000 - \$12,000}{4}\right) = \$27,000 \text{ per year}$$

2022 depreciation $= \$27,000 \times \frac{3}{12} = \underline{\$6,750}$

b. Units-of-activity method:

$$\left(\frac{\$120,000 - \$12,000}{12,000}\right) = \$9 \text{ per hour}$$

2022 depreciation $= 1,700 \text{ hours} \times \$9 = \underline{\$15,300}$

c. Declining-balance method:

2022 depreciation $= \$120,000 \times 50\% \times \frac{3}{12} = \underline{\$15,000}$

Book value January 1, 2023 $= \$120,000 - \$15,000 = \underline{\$105,000}$

2023 depreciation $= \$105,000 \times 50\% = \underline{\$52,500}$

**2. (LO 4)** Lake Company, organized in 2022, has the following transactions related to intangible assets.

*Prepare entries to set up appropriate accounts for different intangibles; amortize intangible assets.*

| | | |
|---|---|---:|
| 1/2/22 | Purchased patent (8-year life) | $560,000 |
| 4/1/22 | Goodwill purchased (indefinite life) | 360,000 |
| 7/1/22 | Acquired 10-year franchise; expiration date 7/1/2032 | 440,000 |
| 9/1/22 | Incurred research and development costs | 85,000 |

### Instructions

Prepare the necessary entries to record these transactions. All costs incurred were for cash. Make the annual adjusting entries as of December 31, 2022, recording any necessary amortization and reflecting all balances accurately as of that date.

### Solution

| | | | | |
|---|---|---|---:|---:|
| 2. | 1/2/22 | Patents | 560,000 | |
| | | Cash | | 560,000 |
| | 4/1/22 | Goodwill | 360,000 | |
| | | Cash | | 360,000 |
| | | (Part of the entry to record purchase of another company) | | |
| | 7/1/22 | Franchises | 440,000 | |
| | | Cash | | 440,000 |
| | 9/1/22 | Research and Development Expense | 85,000 | |
| | | Cash | | 85,000 |
| | 12/31/22 | Amortization Expense | | |
| | | $\quad(\$560,000 \div 8) + [(\$440,000 \div 10) \times \frac{1}{2}]$ | 92,000 | |
| | | Patents | | 70,000 |
| | | Franchises | | 22,000 |

Ending balances. 12/31/22:
  Patents = $490,000 ($560,000 – $70,000)
  Goodwill = $360,000
  Franchises = $418,000 ($440,000 – $22,000)
  R&D expense = $85,000

# Practice Problems

*Compute depreciation under different methods.*

**1. (LO 2)** DuPage Company purchases a factory machine at a cost of $18,000 on January 1, 2022. DuPage expects the machine to have a salvage value of $2,000 at the end of its 4-year useful life.

During its useful life, the machine is expected to be used 160,000 hours. Actual annual hourly usage was 2022, 40,000; 2023, 60,000; 2024, 35,000; and 2025, 25,000.

## Instructions

Prepare depreciation schedules for the following methods: (a) straight-line, (b) units-of-activity, and (c) declining-balance using double the straight-line rate.

## Solution

**1. a.**

### Straight-Line Method

| | Computation | | | Annual | End of Year | |
| Year | Depreciable Cost* | × | Depreciation Rate | = | Depreciation Expense | Accumulated Depreciation | Book Value |
|---|---|---|---|---|---|---|---|
| 2022 | $16,000 | | 25% | | $4,000 | $ 4,000 | $14,000** |
| 2023 | 16,000 | | 25 | | 4,000 | 8,000 | 10,000 |
| 2024 | 16,000 | | 25 | | 4,000 | 12,000 | 6,000 |
| 2025 | 16,000 | | 25 | | 4,000 | 16,000 | 2,000 |

  *$18,000 – $2,000
**$18,000 – $4,000

**b.**

### Units-of-Activity Method

| | Computation | | | Annual | End of Year | |
| Year | Units of Activity | × | Depreciable Cost/Unit | = | Depreciation Expense | Accumulated Depreciation | Book Value |
|---|---|---|---|---|---|---|---|
| 2022 | 40,000 | | $0.10* | | $4,000 | $ 4,000 | $14,000 |
| 2023 | 60,000 | | 0.10 | | 6,000 | 10,000 | 8,000 |
| 2024 | 35,000 | | 0.10 | | 3,500 | 13,500 | 4,500 |
| 2025 | 25,000 | | 0.10 | | 2,500 | 16,000 | 2,000 |

  *($18,000 – $2,000) ÷ 160,000

**c.**

### Declining-Balance Method

| | Computation | | | Annual | End of Year | |
| Year | Book Value Beginning of Year | × | Depreciation Rate* | = | Depreciation Expense | Accumulated Depreciation | Book Value |
|---|---|---|---|---|---|---|---|
| 2022 | $18,000 | | 50% | | $9,000 | $ 9,000 | $9,000 |
| 2023 | 9,000 | | 50 | | 4,500 | 13,500 | 4,500 |
| 2024 | 4,500 | | 50 | | 2,250 | 15,750 | 2,250 |
| 2025 | 2,250 | | 50 | | 250** | 16,000 | 2,000 |

  *$\frac{1}{4} \times 2$
**Adjusted to $250 because ending book value should not be less than expected salvage value.

**2. (LO 3)** On January 1, 2019, Skyline Limousine Co. purchased a limo at an acquisition cost of $28,000. The vehicle has been depreciated by the straight-line method using a 4-year service life and a $4,000 salvage value. The company's fiscal year ends on December 31.

*Record disposal of plant asset.*

### Instructions

Prepare the journal entry or entries to record the disposal of the limousine assuming that it was:

a. Retired and scrapped with no salvage value on January 1, 2023.

b. Sold for $5,000 on July 1, 2022.

### Solution

| | | | |
|---|---|---:|---:|
| 2. a. 1/1/23 | Accumulated Depreciation—Equipment | 24,000 | |
| | Loss on Disposal of Plant Assets | 4,000 | |
| |     Equipment | | 28,000 |
| |     (To record retirement of limousine) | | |
| b. 7/1/22 | Depreciation Expense* | 3,000 | |
| |     Accumulated Depreciation—Equipment | | 3,000 |
| |     (To record depreciation to date | | |
| |     of disposal) | | |
| | Cash | 5,000 | |
| | Accumulated Depreciation—Equipment** | 21,000 | |
| | Loss on Disposal of Plant Assets | 2,000 | |
| |     Equipment | | 28,000 |
| |     (To record sale of limousine) | | |

$*[(\$28,000 - \$4,000) \div 4] \times \frac{1}{2}$

$**[(\$28,000 - \$4,000) \div 4] \times 3 = \$18,000; \$18,000 + \$3,000$

---

Brief Exercises, DO IT! Exercises, Exercises, Problems, Data Analytics Activities, and many additional resources are available for practice in WileyPLUS.

---

*Note:* All asterisked Questions, Exercises, and Problems relate to material in the appendix to the chapter.

## Questions

1. Ms. Harcross is uncertain about the applicability of the historical cost principle to plant assets. Explain the principle to Ms. Harcross.

2. What are some examples of land improvements?

3. Barrister Company acquires the land and building owned by Noble Company. What types of costs may be incurred to make the asset ready for its intended use if Barrister Company wants to use only the land? If it wants to use both the land and the building?

4. In a recent newspaper release, the president of Magnusson Company asserted that something has to be done about depreciation. The president said, "Depreciation does not come close to accumulating the cash needed to replace the asset at the end of its useful life." What is your response to the president?

5. Melanie is studying for the next accounting examination. She asks your help on two questions (a) What is salvage value? (b) How is salvage value used in determining depreciable cost under the straight-line method? Answer Melanie's questions.

6. Contrast the straight-line method and the units-of-activity method as to (a) useful life, and (b) the pattern of periodic depreciation over useful life.

7. Contrast the effects of the three depreciation methods on annual depreciation expense.

8. In the fourth year of an asset's 5-year useful life, the company decides that the asset will have a 6-year service life. How should the revision of this estimate be recorded? Why?

9. Distinguish between ordinary repairs and capital expenditures during an asset's useful life.

10. How is a gain or loss on the sale of a plant asset computed?

11. Marsh Corporation owns a machine that is fully depreciated but is still being used. How should Marsh account for this asset and report it in the financial statements?

12. What are natural resources, and what are their distinguishing characteristics?

13. Explain the concept of depletion and how it is computed.

14. What are the similarities and differences between the terms depreciation, depletion, and amortization?

15. Warwick Company hires an accounting intern who says that intangible assets should always be amortized over their legal lives. Is the intern correct? Explain.

16. Goodwill has been defined as the value of all favorable attributes that relate to a business that cannot be attributed to specific identifiable assets. What types of attributes could result in goodwill?

17. Kathy Malone, a business major, is working on a case problem for one of her classes. In the case problem, the company needs to raise cash to market a new product it developed. Doug Price, an engineering major, takes one look at the company's balance sheet and says, "This company has an awful lot of goodwill. Why don't you recommend that it sell some of it to raise cash?" How should Kathy respond to Doug?

18. Under what conditions is goodwill recorded? What is the proper accounting treatment for amortizing goodwill?

19. Often, research and development costs provide companies with lasting benefits. (For example, these costs can lead to the development of a patent that will increase the company's income for many years.) However, generally accepted accounting principles require that such costs be recorded as an expense when incurred. Why?

20. **McDonald's Corporation** reports total average assets of $28.9 billion and net sales of $20.5 billion. What is the company's asset turnover?

21. Peyton Corporation and Rogers Corporation operate in the same industry. Peyton uses the straight-line method to account for deprecia-tion; Rogers uses an accelerated method. Explain what complications might arise in trying to compare the results of these two companies.

22. Mesa Corporation uses straight-line depreciation for financial reporting purposes but an accelerated method for tax purposes. Is it acceptable to use different methods for the two purposes? What is Mesa Corporation's motivation for doing this?

23. You are comparing two companies in the same industry. You have determined that Gore Corp. depreciates its plant assets over a 40-year life, whereas Ross Corp. depreciates its plant assets over a 20-year life. Discuss the implications this has for comparing the results of the two companies.

24. Sosa Company is doing significant work to revitalize its ware-houses. It is not sure whether it should capitalize these costs or expense them. What are the implications for current-year net income and future net income of expensing versus capitalizing these costs?

25. What does **Apple** use as the estimated useful life on its buildings? On its machinery and equipment? (*Hint:* You will need to use the notes to Apple's financial statements, available at the company's website.)

\*26. When assets are exchanged in a transaction involving commercial substance, how is the gain or loss on disposal of plant assets computed?

\*27. Unruh Refrigeration Company trades in an old machine for a new model when the fair value of the old machine is greater than its book value. The transaction has commercial substance. Should Unruh recognize a gain on disposal of plant assets? If the fair value of the old machine is less than its book value, should Unruh recognize a loss on disposal of plant assets?

## Brief Exercises

*Determine the cost of land.*

**BE9.1 (LO 1), AP** These expenditures were incurred by Dobbin Company in purchasing land: cash price $60,000, assumed accrued taxes $5,000, attorney's fees $2,100, real estate broker's commission $3,300, and clearing and grading $3,500. What is the cost of the land?

*Determine the cost of a truck.*

**BE9.2 (LO 1), AP** Thoms Company incurs these expenditures in purchasing a truck: cash price $24,000, accident insurance (during use) $2,000, sales taxes $1,080, motor vehicle license $300, and painting and lettering $1,700. What is the cost of the truck?

*Prepare entries for delivery truck costs.*

**BE9.3 (LO 1), AP** Krieg Company had the following two transactions related to its delivery truck.

1. Paid $38 for an oil change.

2. Paid $400 to install special shelving units, which increase the operating efficiency of the truck.

Prepare Krieg's journal entries to record these two transactions.

*Compute straight-line depreciation.*

**BE9.4 (LO 2), AP** Gordon Chemicals Company acquires a delivery truck at a cost of $31,000 on January 1, 2022. The truck is expected to have a salvage value of $4,000 at the end of its 4-year useful life. Compute annual depreciation for the first and second years using the straight-line method.

*Compute depreciation and evaluate treatment.*

**BE9.5 (LO 2), AN** Ivy Company purchased land and a building on January 1, 2022. Management's best estimate of the value of the land was $100,000 and of the building $250,000. However, management told the accounting department to record the land at $230,000 and the building at $120,000. The building is being depreciated on a straight-line basis over 20 years with no salvage value. Why do you suppose man-agement requested this accounting treatment? Is it ethical?

*Compute declining-balance depreciation.*

**BE9.6 (LO 2), AP** Gordon Chemicals Company acquires a delivery truck at a cost of $31,000 on January 1, 2022. The truck is expected to have a salvage value of $4,000 at the end of its 4-year useful life. Assum-ing the declining-balance depreciation rate is double the straight-line rate, compute annual depreciation for the first and second years under the declining-balance method.

*Compute depreciation using units-of-activity method.*

**BE9.7 (LO 2), AP** Kwik Taxi Service uses the units-of-activity method in computing depreciation on its taxicabs. Each cab is expected to be driven 150,000 miles. Taxi 10 cost $27,500 and is expected to have a salvage value of $500. Taxi 10 was driven 32,000 miles in 2021 and 33,000 miles in 2022. Compute the depreciation for each year.

**BE9.8 (LO 2), AP** On January 1, 2022, the Hermann Company general ledger shows Equipment $36,000 and Accumulated Depreciation $13,600. The depreciation resulted from using the straight-line method with a useful life of 10 years and a salvage value of $2,000. On this date, the company concludes that the equipment has a remaining useful life of only 2 years with the same salvage value. Compute the revised annual depreciation.

*Compute revised depreciation.*

**BE9.9 (LO 3), AP** Prepare journal entries to record these transactions. (a) Echo Company retires its delivery equipment, which cost $41,000. Accumulated depreciation is also $41,000 on this delivery equipment. No salvage value is received. (b) Assume the same information as in part (a), except that accumulated depreciation for the equipment is $37,200 instead of $41,000

*Journalize entries for disposal of plant assets.*

**BE9.10 (LO 3), AP** Antone Company sells office equipment on July 31, 2022, for $21,000 cash. The office equipment originally cost $72,000 and as of January 1, 2022, had accumulated depreciation of $42,000. Depreciation for the first 7 months of 2022 is $4,600. Prepare the journal entries to (a) update depreciation to July 31, 2022, and (b) record the sale of the equipment.

*Journalize entries for sale of plant assets.*

**BE9.11 (LO 4), AP** Franceour Mining Co. purchased for $7 million a mine that is estimated to have 35 million tons of ore and no salvage value. In the first year, 5 million tons of ore are extracted.

a. Prepare the journal entry to record depletion for the first year.

b. Show how this mine is reported on the balance sheet at the end of the first year.

*Prepare depletion entry and balance sheet presentation for natural resources.*

**BE9.12 (LO 4), AP** Campanez Company purchases a patent for $140,000 on January 2, 2022. Its estimated useful life is 10 years.

a. Prepare the journal entry to record amortization expense for the first year.

b. Show how this patent is reported on the balance sheet at the end of the first year.

*Prepare amortization expense entry and balance sheet presentation for intangible assets.*

**BE9.13 (LO 5), AP** Information related to plant assets, natural resources, and intangible assets at the end of 2022 for Dent Company is as follows: buildings $1,100,000, accumulated depreciation—buildings $600,000, goodwill $410,000, coal mine $500,000, and accumulated depletion—coal mine $108,000. Prepare a partial balance sheet of Dent Company for these items.

*Classify long-lived assets on balance sheet.*

**BE9.14 (LO 5), AP** In a recent annual report, **Target** reported beginning total assets of $44.1 billion, ending total assets of $44.5 billion, and net sales of $63.4 billion. Compute Target's asset turnover.

*Calculate asset turnover.*

*\* **BE9.15 (LO 6), AP** Olathe Company exchanges old delivery equipment for new delivery equipment. The book value of the old delivery equipment is $31,000 (cost $61,000 less accumulated depreciation $30,000). Its fair value is $24,000, and cash of $5,000 is paid. Prepare the entry to record the exchange, assuming the transaction has commercial substance.

*Prepare entry for disposal by exchange.*

*\* **BE9.16 (LO 6), AP** Olathe Company exchanges old delivery equipment for new delivery equipment. The book value of the old delivery equipment is $31,000 (cost $61,000 less accumulated depreciation $30,000). Its fair value is $33,000, and cash of $5,000 is paid. Prepare the entry to record the exchange.

*Prepare entry for disposal by exchange.*

# DO IT! Exercises

**DO IT! 9.1 (LO 1), C** Hummer Company purchased a delivery truck. The total cash payment was $30,020, including the following items.

*Explain accounting for cost of plant assets.*

| | |
|---|---:|
| Negotiated purchase price | $24,000 |
| Installation of special shelving | 1,100 |
| Painting and lettering | 900 |
| Motor vehicle license | 180 |
| Two-year insurance policy | 2,400 |
| Sales tax | 1,440 |
| Total paid | $30,020 |

Explain how each of these costs should be accounted for.

**DO IT! 9.2a (LO 2), AP** On January 1, 2022, Salt Creek Country Club purchased a new riding mower for $15,000. The mower is expected to have a 10-year life with a $1,000 salvage value. What journal entry would Salt Creek make on December 31, 2022, if it uses straight-line depreciation?

*Calculate depreciation expense and make journal entry.*

**DO IT! 9.2b (LO 2), AP** Fordon Corporation purchased a piece of equipment for $50,000. It estimated an 8-year life and $2,000 salvage value. At the end of year 4 (before the depreciation adjustment), it estimated the new total life to be 10 years and the new salvage value to be $4,000. Compute the revised depreciation, assuming Fordon uses the straight-line method.

*Calculate revised depreciation*

*Make journal entries to record plant asset disposal.*

**DO IT! 9.3 (LO 3), AP** Bylie Company has an old factory machine that cost $50,000. The machine has accumulated depreciation of $28,000. Bylie has decided to sell the machine.

a. What entry would Bylie make to record the sale of the machine for $25,000 cash?

b. What entry would Bylie make to record the sale of the machine for $15,000 cash?

*Match classifications to concepts.*

**DO IT! 9.4 (LO 4), K** Match the statement with the term most directly associated with it. Use each term only once.

| | |
|---|---|
| Goodwill | Amortization |
| Intangible assets | Franchises |
| Research and development costs | |

1. _____ Rights, privileges, and competitive advantages that result from the ownership of long-lived assets that do not possess physical substance.

2. _____ The allocation of the cost of an intangible asset to expense in a rational and systematic manner.

3. _____ A right to sell certain products or services, or use certain trademarks or trade names, within a designated geographic area.

4. _____ Costs incurred by a company that often lead to patents or new products. These costs must be expensed as incurred.

5. _____ The excess of the cost of a company over the fair value of the net assets acquired.

*Calculate asset turnover.*

**DO IT! 9.5 (LO 5), AP** For 2022, Sale Company reported beginning total assets of $300,000 and ending total assets of $340,000. Its net income for this period was $50,000, and its net sales were $400,000. Compute the company's asset turnover for 2022.

# Exercises

*Determine cost of plant acquisitions.*

**E9.1 (LO 1), C** **Writing** The following expenditures relating to plant assets were made by Glenn Company during the first 2 months of 2022.

1. Paid $7,000 of accrued taxes at the time the plant site was acquired.
2. Paid $200 insurance to cover a possible accident loss on new factory machinery while the machinery was in transit.
3. Paid $850 sales taxes on a new delivery truck.
4. Paid $21,000 for parking lots and driveways on the new plant site.
5. Paid $250 to have the company name and slogan painted on the new delivery truck.
6. Paid $8,000 for installation of new factory machinery.
7. Paid $900 for a 2-year accident insurance policy on the new delivery truck.
8. Paid $75 motor vehicle license fee on the new truck.

**Instructions**

a. Explain the application of the historical cost principle in determining the acquisition cost of plant assets.

b. List the numbers of the transactions, and opposite each indicate the account title to which each expenditure should be debited.

*Determine property, plant, and equipment costs.*

**E9.2 (LO 1), C** Adama Company incurred the following costs.

| | |
|---|---:|
| 1. Sales tax on factory machinery purchased | $ 5,000 |
| 2. Painting of and lettering on truck immediately upon purchase | 700 |
| 3. Installation and testing of factory machinery | 2,000 |
| 4. Real estate broker's commission on land purchased | 3,500 |
| 5. Insurance premium paid for first year's insurance on new truck | 880 |
| 6. Cost of landscaping on property purchased | 7,200 |
| 7. Cost of paving parking lot for new building constructed | 17,900 |
| 8. Cost of clearing, draining, and filling land | 13,300 |
| 9. Architect's fees on self-constructed building | 10,000 |

**Instructions**

Indicate to which account Adama would debit each of the costs.

**E9.3 (LO 1), AP** On March 1, 2022, Boyd Company acquired real estate, on which it planned to construct a small office building, by paying $80,000 in cash. An old warehouse on the property was demolished at a cost of $8,200; the salvaged materials were sold for $1,700. Additional expenditures before construction began included $1,900 attorney's fee for work concerning the land purchase, $5,200 real estate broker's fee, $9,100 architect's fee, and $14,000 to put in driveways and a parking lot.

*Determine acquisition costs of land.*

**Instructions**

a. Determine the amount to be recorded as the cost of the land.

b. For each cost not used in part (a), indicate the account to be debited.

**E9.4 (LO 2), C** Alysha Monet has prepared the following list of statements about depreciation.

*Understand depreciation concepts.*

1. Depreciation is a process of asset valuation, not cost allocation.

2. Depreciation provides for the proper recording of expenses (efforts) with revenues (results).

3. The book value of a plant asset should approximate its fair value.

4. Depreciation applies to three classes of plant assets: land, buildings, and equipment.

5. Depreciation does not apply to a building because its usefulness and revenue-producing ability generally remain intact over time.

6. The revenue-producing ability of a depreciable asset will decline due to wear and tear and to obsolescence.

7. Recognizing depreciation on an asset results in an accumulation of cash for replacement of the asset.

8. The balance in accumulated depreciation represents the total cost that has been charged to expense since placing the asset in service.

9. Depreciation expense and accumulated depreciation are reported on the income statement.

10. Three factors affect the computation of depreciation: cost, useful life, and salvage value.

**Instructions**

Identify each statement as true or false. If false, indicate how to correct the statement.

**E9.5 (LO 2), AP** Yello Bus Lines uses the units-of-activity method in depreciating its buses. One bus was purchased on January 1, 2022, at a cost of $148,000. Over its 4-year useful life, the bus is expected to be driven 100,000 miles. Salvage value is expected to be $8,000.

*Compute depreciation under units-of-activity method.*

**Instructions**

a. Compute the depreciable cost per unit.

b Prepare a depreciation schedule assuming actual mileage was: 2022, 26,000; 2023, 32,000; 2024, 25,000; and 2025, 17,000.

**E9.6 (LO 2), AP** Rottino Company purchased a new machine on October 1, 2022, at a cost of $150,000. The company estimated that the machine will have a salvage value of $12,000. The machine is expected to be used for 10,000 working hours during its 5-year life.

*Determine depreciation for partial periods.*

 Excel

**Instructions**

Compute the depreciation expense under the following methods for the year indicated.

a. Straight-line for 2022.

b. Units-of-activity for 2022, assuming machine usage was 1,700 hours.

c. Declining-balance using double the straight-line rate for 2022 and 2023.

**E9.7 (LO 2), AP** Linton Company purchased a delivery truck for $34,000 on January 1, 2022. The truck has an expected salvage value of $2,000, and is expected to be driven 100,000 miles over its estimated useful life of 8 years. Actual miles driven were 15,000 in 2022 and 12,000 in 2023.

*Compute depreciation using different methods.*

**Instructions**

a. Compute depreciation expense for 2022 and 2023 using (1) the straight-line method, (2) the units-of-activity method, and (3) the double-declining-balance method.

b. Assume that Linton uses the straight-line method.

1. Prepare the journal entry to record 2022 depreciation expense.

2. Show how the truck would be reported in the December 31, 2022, balance sheet.

*Compute revised annual depreciation.*

**E9.8 (LO 2), AP** Victor Mineli, the new controller of Santorini Company, has reviewed the expected useful lives and salvage values of selected depreciable assets at the beginning of 2022. Here are his findings:

| Type of Asset | Date Acquired | Cost | Accumulated Depreciation, Jan. 1, 2022 | Useful Life (in years) | | Salvage Value | |
|---|---|---|---|---|---|---|---|
| | | | | Old | Proposed | Old | Proposed |
| Building | Jan. 1, 2014 | $700,000 | $130,000 | 40 | 58 | $50,000 | $35,000 |
| Warehouse | Jan. 1, 2017 | 120,000 | 23,000 | 25 | 20 | 5,000 | 3,600 |

All assets are depreciated by the straight-line method. Santorini Company uses a calendar year in preparing annual adjusting entries and financial statements. After discussion, management has agreed to accept Victor's proposed changes. (The "Proposed" useful life is total life, not remaining life.)

**Instructions**

a. Compute the revised annual depreciation on each asset in 2022. (Round to nearest dollar.)

b. Prepare the entry (or entries) to record depreciation on the building in 2022.

*Record disposal of equipment.*

**E9.9 (LO 3), AP** Here are selected 2022 transactions of Akron Corporation.

Jan. 1   Retired a piece of machinery that was purchased on January 1, 2012. The machine cost $62,000 and had a useful life of 10 years with no salvage value.

June 30   Sold a computer that was purchased on January 1, 2020. The computer cost $36,000 and had a useful life of 3 years with no salvage value. The computer was sold for $5,000 cash.

Dec. 31   Sold a delivery truck for $9,000 cash. The truck cost $25,000 when it was purchased on January 1, 2019, and was depreciated based on a 5-year useful life with a $4,000 salvage value.

**Instructions**

Journalize all entries required on the above dates, including entries to update depreciation on assets disposed of, where applicable. Akron Corporation uses straight-line depreciation. (Assume depreciation is up to date as of December 31, 2021).

*Journalize entries for disposal of equipment.*

**E9.10 (LO 3), AP** Pryce Company owns equipment that cost $65,000 when purchased on January 1, 2019. It has been depreciated using the straight-line method based on an estimated salvage value of $5,000 and an estimated useful life of 5 years.

**Instructions**

Prepare Pryce Company's journal entries to record the sale of the equipment in these four independent situations.

a. Sold for $31,000 on January 1, 2022.

b. Sold for $31,000 on May 1, 2022.

c. Sold for $11,000 on January 1, 2022.

d. Sold for $11,000 on October 1, 2022.

*Journalize entries for natural resources depletion.*

**E9.11 (LO 4), AP** On July 1, 2022, Friedman Inc. invested $720,000 in a mine estimated to have 900,000 tons of ore of uniform grade. During the last 6 months of 2022, 100,000 tons of ore were mined.

**Instructions**

a. Prepare the journal entry to record depletion.

b. Assume that the 100,000 tons of ore were mined, but only 80,000 units were sold. How are the costs applicable to the 20,000 unsold units reported?

*Prepare adjusting entries for amortization.*

**E9.12 (LO 4), AP** These are selected 2022 transactions for Wyle Corporation:

Jan. 1   Purchased a copyright for $120,000. The copyright has a useful life of 6 years and a remaining legal life of 30 years.

Mar. 1   Purchased a patent with an estimated useful life of 4 years and a legal life of 20 years for $54,000.

Sept. 1   Purchased a small company and recorded goodwill of $150,000. Its useful life is indefinite.

**Instructions**

Prepare all adjusting entries at December 31 to record amortization required by the events.

**E9.13 (LO 4), AP** Gill Company, organized in 2022, has the following transactions related to intangible assets.

| | | |
|---|---|---|
| 1/2/22 | Purchased patent (7-year life) | $595,000 |
| 4/1/22 | Goodwill purchased (indefinite life) | 360,000 |
| 7/1/22 | Acquired 10-year franchise; expiration date 7/1/2032 | 480,000 |
| 9/1/22 | Incurred research and development costs | 185,000 |

*Prepare entries to set up appropriate accounts for different intangibles; amortize intangible assets.*

**Instructions**

Prepare the necessary entries to record these transactions. All costs incurred were for cash. Make the adjusting entries as of December 31, 2022, recording any necessary amortization and reflecting all balances accurately as of that date.

**E9.14 (LO 5), AP** During 2022, Paola Corporation reported net sales of $3,500,000 and net income of $1,500,000. Its balance sheet reported average total assets of $1,400,000.

*Calculate asset turnover.*

**Instructions**

Calculate the asset turnover.

**\* E9.15 (LO 6), AP** Presented below are two independent transactions. Both transactions have commercial substance.

*Journalize entries for exchanges.*

1. Mercy Co. exchanged old trucks (cost $64,000 less $22,000 accumulated depreciation) plus cash of $17,000 for new trucks The old trucks had a fair value of $38,000.

2. Pence Inc. trades its used machine (cost $12,000 less $4,000 accumulated depreciation) for a new machine. In addition to exchanging the old machine (which had a fair value of $11,000), Pence also paid cash of $3,000.

**Instructions**

a. Prepare the entry to record the exchange of assets by Mercy Co.

b. Prepare the entry to record the exchange of assets by Pence Inc.

**\* E9.16 (LO 6), AP** Rizzo's Delivery Company and Overland's Express Delivery exchanged delivery trucks on January 1, 2022. Rizzo's truck cost $22,000. It has accumulated depreciation of $15,000 and a fair value of $3,000. Overland's truck cost $10,000. It has accumulated depreciation of $8,000 and a fair value of $3,000. The transaction has commercial substance.

*Journalize entries for the exchange of plant assets.*

**Instructions**

a. Journalize the exchange for Rizzo's Delivery Company.

b. Journalize the exchange for Overland's Express Delivery.

# Problems

**P9.1 (LO 1), AP** Peete Company was organized on January 1. During the first year of operations, the following plant asset expenditures and receipts were recorded in random order.

*Determine acquisition costs of land and building.*

**Debit**

| | |
|---|---|
| 1. Excavation costs for new building | $ 23,000 |
| 2. Architect's fees on building plans | 33,000 |
| 3. Full payment to building contractor | 640,000 |
| 4. Cost of real estate purchased as a plant site | 280,000 |
| 5. Cost of parking lots and driveways | 29,000 |
| 6. Accrued real estate taxes paid at time of purchase of land | 3,170 |
| 7. Installation cost of fences around property | 6,800 |
| 8. Cost of demolishing building to make land suitable for construction of new building | 31,000 |
| 9. Real estate taxes paid for the current year on land | 6,400 |
| | $1,052,370 |

**Credit**

| | |
|---|---|
| 10. Proceeds from salvage of demolished building | $ 12,000 |

### Instructions

Analyze the transactions using the following table column headings. Enter the number of each transaction in the Item column, and enter the amounts in the appropriate columns. For amounts in the Other Accounts column, also indicate the account title.

*Land $302,170*

| Item | Land | Buildings | Other Accounts |
|---|---|---|---|

*Compute depreciation under different methods.*

**P9.2 (LO 2), AP** In recent years, Jayme Company has purchased three machines. Because of frequent employee turnover in the accounting department, a different accountant was in charge of selecting the depreciation method for each machine, and various methods have been used. Information concerning the machines is summarized in the table below.

| Machine | Acquired | Cost | Salvage Value | Useful Life (in years) | Depreciation Method |
|---|---|---|---|---|---|
| 1 | Jan. 1, 2020 | $96,000 | $12,000 | 8 | Straight-line |
| 2 | July 1, 2021 | 85,000 | 10,000 | 5 | Declining-balance |
| 3 | Nov. 1, 2021 | 66,000 | 6,000 | 6 | Units-of-activity |

For the declining-balance method, Jayme Company uses the double-declining rate. For the units-of-activity method, total machine hours are expected to be 30,000. Actual hours of use in the first 3 years were 2021, 800; 2022, 4,500; and 2023, 6,000.

### Instructions

*a. Machine 2 $60,520*

**a.** Compute the amount of accumulated depreciation on each machine at December 31, 2023.

**b.** If machine 2 was purchased on April 1 instead of July 1, what would be the depreciation expense for this machine in 2021? In 2022?

*Compute depreciation under different methods.*

**P9.3 (LO 1, 2), AP** On January 1, 2022, Evers Company purchased the following two machines for use in its production process.

Machine A: The cash price of this machine was $48,000. Related expenditures also paid in cash included: sales tax $1,700, shipping costs $150, insurance during shipping $80, installation and testing costs $70, and $100 of oil and lubricants to be used with the machinery during its first year of operations. Evers estimates that the useful life of the machine is 5 years with a $5,000 salvage value remaining at the end of that time period. Assume that the straight-line method of depreciation is used.

Machine B: The recorded cost of this machine was $180,000. Evers estimates that the useful life of the machine is 4 years with a $10,000 salvage value remaining at the end of that time period.

### Instructions

**a.** Prepare the following for Machine A.

**1.** The journal entry to record its purchase on January 1, 2022.

**2.** The journal entry to record annual depreciation at December 31, 2022.

**b.** Calculate the amount of depreciation expense that Evers should record for Machine B each year of its useful life under the following assumptions.

**1.** Evers uses the straight-line method of depreciation.

*b. 2. 2022 DDB depreciation $90,000*

**2.** Evers uses the declining-balance method. The rate used is twice the straight-line rate.

**3.** Evers uses the units-of-activity method and estimates that the useful life of the machine is 125,000 units. Actual usage is as follows: 2022, 45,000 units; 2023, 35,000 units; 2024, 25,000 units; and 2025, 20,000 units.

**c.** Which method used to calculate depreciation on Machine B reports the highest amount of depreciation expense in year 1 (2022)? The highest amount in year 4 (2025)? The highest total amount over the 4-year period?

*Calculate revisions to depreciation expense.*

**P9.4 (LO 2), AP** At the beginning of 2020, Mazzaro Company acquired equipment costing $120,000. It was estimated that this equipment would have a useful life of 6 years and a salvage value of $12,000 at that time. The straight-line method of depreciation was considered the most appropriate to use with this type of equipment. Depreciation is to be recorded at the end of each year.

During 2022 (the third year of the equipment's life), the company's engineers reconsidered their expectations and estimated that the equipment's useful life would probably be 7 years (in total) instead of 6 years. The estimated salvage value was not changed at that time. However, during 2025, the estimated salvage value was reduced to $5,000.

## Instructions

Indicate how much depreciation expense should be recorded each year for this equipment, by completing the following table.

| Year | Depreciation Expense | Accumulated Depreciation |
|------|---------------------|--------------------------|
| 2020 | | |
| 2021 | | |
| 2022 | | |
| 2023 | | |
| 2024 | | |
| 2025 | | |
| 2026 | | |

**P9.5 (LO 2, 3, 5), AP** At December 31, 2022, Arnold Corporation reported the following plant assets.

| | | |
|---|---:|---:|
| Land | | $ 3,000,000 |
| Buildings | $26,500,000 | |
| Less: Accumulated depreciation—buildings | 11,925,000 | 14,575,000 |
| Equipment | 40,000,000 | |
| Less: Accumulated depreciation—equipment | 5,000,000 | 35,000,000 |
| Total plant assets | | $52,575,000 |

*2026 depreciation expense $17,900*

*Journalize equipment transactions related to purchase, sale, retirement, and depreciation.*

During 2023, the following selected cash transactions occurred.

Apr.  1   Purchased land for $2,200,000.
May   1   Sold equipment that cost $600,000 when purchased on January 1, 2016.
          The equipment was sold for $170,000.
June  1   Sold land for $1,600,000. The land cost $1,000,000.
July  1   Purchased equipment for $1,100,000.
Dec. 31   Retired equipment that cost $700,000 when purchased on December 31, 2013. No
          salvage value was received.

## Instructions

a. Journalize the transactions. (*Hint:* You may wish to set up T-accounts, post beginning balances, and then post 2023 transactions.) Arnold uses straight-line depreciation for buildings and equipment. The buildings are estimated to have a 40-year useful life and no salvage value; the equipment is estimated to have a 10-year useful life and no salvage value. Update depreciation on assets disposed of at the time of sale or retirement.

b. Record adjusting entries for depreciation for 2023.

c. Prepare the plant assets section of Arnold's balance sheet at December 31, 2023.

*c. Tot. plant assets $50,037,500*

**P9.6 (LO 3), AP** Ceda Co. has equipment that cost $80,000 and that has been depreciated $50,000.

*Record disposals.*

## Instructions

Record the disposal under the following assumptions.

a. It was discarded with no cash received.

b. It was sold for $21,000.

c. It was sold for $31,000.

*b. $9,000 loss*

**P9.7 (LO 4, 5), AP** The intangible assets section of Amato Corporation's balance sheet at December 31, 2022, is presented here.

| | |
|---|---:|
| Patents ($60,000 cost less $6,000 amortization) | $54,000 |
| Copyrights ($36,000 cost less $25,200 amortization) | 10,800 |
| Total | $64,800 |

*Prepare entries to record transactions related to acquisition and amortization of intangibles; prepare the intangible assets section and note.*

The patent was acquired in January 2022 and has a useful life of 10 years. The copyright was acquired in January 2016 and also has a useful life of 10 years. The following cash transactions may have affected intangible assets during 2023.

Jan.  2   Paid $46,800 legal costs to successfully defend the patent against infringement by another company.
Jan.–July Developed a new product, incurring $230,000 in research and development costs during February. A patent was granted for the product on July 1, and its useful life is equal to its legal life. Legal and other costs for the patent were $20,000.

Sept. 1    Paid $40,000 to a quarterback to appear in commercials advertising the company's products. The commercials aired in September.

Oct. 1    Acquired a copyright for $200,000. The copyright has a useful life and legal life of 50 years.

**Instructions**

a. Prepare journal entries to record the transactions.

b. Prepare journal entries to record the 2023 amortization expense for intangible assets.

*c. Tot. intangibles $315,300*

c. Prepare the intangible assets section of the balance sheet at December 31, 2023.

d. Prepare the note to the financial statements on Amato Corporation's intangible assets as of December 31, 2023.

*Prepare entries to correct errors in recording and amortizing intangible assets.*

**P9.8 (LO 4), AP** Due to rapid employee turnover in the accounting department, the following transactions involving intangible assets were improperly recorded by Inland Corporation.

1. Inland developed a new manufacturing process, incurring research and development costs of $160,000. The company also purchased a patent for $40,000. In early January, Inland capitalized $200,000 as the cost of the patents. Patent amortization expense of $10,000 was recorded based on a 20-year useful life.

2. On July 1, 2022, Inland purchased a small company and as a result recorded goodwill of $80,000. Inland recorded a half-year's amortization in 2022, based on a 20-year life ($2,000 amortization).

**Instructions**

Prepare all journal entries necessary to correct any errors made during 2022. Assume the books have not yet been closed for 2022.

*Calculate and comment on asset turnover.*

**P9.9 (LO 5), AP** **Writing** LaPorta Company and Lott Corporation, two corporations of roughly the same size, are both involved in the manufacture of in-line skates. Each company depreciates its plant assets using the straight-line approach. An investigation of their financial statements reveals the following information.

| | LaPorta Co. | Lott Corp. |
|---|---|---|
| Net income | $ 800,000 | $1,000,000 |
| Net sales | 1,300,000 | 1,180,000 |
| Average total assets | 2,500,000 | 2,000,000 |
| Average plant assets | 1,800,000 | 1,000,000 |

**Instructions**

*a. LaPorta .52 times*

a. For each company, calculate the asset turnover.

b. Based on your calculations in part (a), comment on the relative effectiveness of the two companies in using their assets to generate net sales.

*Prepare financial statements.*

**P9.10 (LO 5), AP** The adjusted trial balance of Feagler Company for the year ended December 31, 2022, is as follows.

| | Debit | Credit |
|---|---|---|
| Cash | $ 5,500 | |
| Accounts Receivable | 3,100 | |
| Note Receivable (due February 20, 2023) | 2,000 | |
| Inventory | 6,000 | |
| Timberland | 21,000 | |
| Land | 14,000 | |
| Equipment | 35,400 | |
| Patents | 11,000 | |
| Accumulated Depletion | | $ 3,900 |
| Allowance for Doubtful Accounts | | 1,000 |
| Accumulated Depreciation—Equipment | | 8,300 |
| Notes Payable (due January 15, 2023) | | 4,600 |
| Accounts Payable | | 2,300 |
| Common Stock | | 60,000 |
| Retained Earnings | | 8,500 |
| Sales Revenue | | 52,000 |
| Interest Revenue | | 400 |

|  | Debit | Credit |
|---|---|---|
| Cost of Goods Sold | $ 23,000 | |
| Salaries and Wages Expense | 11,400 | |
| Depreciation Expense | 2,100 | |
| Amortization Expense | 1,600 | |
| Research and Development Expense | 1,300 | |
| Bad Debt Expense | 500 | |
| License Expense | 300 | |
| Interest Expense | 800 | |
| Loss on Disposal of Plant Assets | 2,000 | |
| Total | $141,000 | $141,000 |

## Instructions

Prepare a multiple-step income statement and retained earnings statement for 2022, and a classified balance sheet as of December 31, 2022.

Net income $9,400

---

# Continuing Case

---

## Cookie Creations

(*Note:* This is a continuation of the Cookie Creations case from Chapters 1 through 8.)

**CC9** Natalie is also thinking of buying a van that will be used only for business. Natalie is concerned about the impact of the van's cost on her income statement and balance sheet. She has come to you for advice on calculating the van's depreciation.

*Go to WileyPLUS for complete case details and instructions.*

© leungchopan/
Shutterstock

---

# Comprehensive Accounting Cycle Review

---

**ACR9** Milo Corporation's unadjusted trial balance at December 1, 2022, is presented below.

|  | Debit | Credit |
|---|---|---|
| Cash | $  22,000 | |
| Accounts Receivable | 36,800 | |
| Notes Receivable | 10,000 | |
| Interest Receivable | –0– | |
| Inventory | 36,200 | |
| Prepaid Insurance | 3,600 | |
| Land | 20,000 | |
| Buildings | 150,000 | |
| Equipment | 60,000 | |
| Patent | 9,000 | |
| Allowance for Doubtful Accounts | | $      500 |
| Accumulated Depreciation—Buildings | | 50,000 |
| Accumulated Depreciation—Equipment | | 24,000 |
| Accounts Payable | | 27,300 |
| Salaries and Wages Payable | | –0– |
| Notes Payable (due April 30, 2023) | | 11,000 |
| Interest Payable | | –0– |
| Notes Payable (due in 2028) | | 35,000 |
| Common Stock | | 50,000 |
| Retained Earnings | | 63,600 |
| Dividends | 12,000 | |
| Sales Revenue | | 900,000 |
| Interest Revenue | | –0– |
| Gain on Disposal of Plant Assets | | –0– |

|                           | Debit       | Credit      |
|---------------------------|-------------|-------------|
| Bad Debt Expense          | –0–         |             |
| Cost of Goods Sold        | 630,000     |             |
| Depreciation Expense      | –0–         |             |
| Insurance Expense         | –0–         |             |
| Interest Expense          | –0–         |             |
| Other Operating Expenses  | 61,800      |             |
| Amortization Expense      | –0–         |             |
| Salaries and Wages Expense| 110,000     |             |
|                           | $1,161,400  | $1,161,400  |

The following transactions occurred during December.

Dec. 2 Purchased equipment for $16,000, plus sales taxes of $800 (paid in cash).

2 Milo sold for $3,500 equipment which originally cost $5,000. Accumulated depreciation on this equipment at January 1, 2022, was $1,800; 2022 depreciation prior to the sale of equipment was $825.

15 Milo sold for $5,000 on account inventory that cost $3,500.

23 Salaries and wages of $6,600 were paid for December.

Adjustment data:

1. Milo estimates that uncollectible accounts receivable at year-end are $4,000.

2. The note receivable is a 1-year, 8% note dated April 1, 2022. No interest has been recorded.

3. The balance in prepaid insurance represents payment of a $3,600, 6-month premium on September 1, 2022.

4. The building is being depreciated using the straight-line method over 30 years. The salvage value is $30,000.

5. The equipment owned prior to this year is being depreciated using the straight-line method over 5 years. The salvage value is 10% of cost.

6. The equipment purchased on December 2, 2022, is being depreciated using the straight-line method over 5 years, with a salvage value of $1,800.

7. The patent was acquired on January 1, 2022, and has a useful life of 9 years from that date.

8. Unpaid salaries at December 31, 2022, total $2,200.

9. Both the short-term and long-term notes payable are dated January 1, 2022, and carry a 10% interest rate. All interest is payable in the next 12 months.

10. Income tax expense was $15,000. It was unpaid at December 31.

### Instructions

a. Prepare journal entries for the transactions listed above and adjusting entries.

b. Totals $1,190,775     b. Prepare an adjusted trial balance at December 31, 2022.

c. Net income $66,150     c. Prepare a 2022 income statement and a 2022 retained earnings statement.

d. Total assets $247,850     d. Prepare a December 31, 2022, balance sheet.

---

## Data Analytics in Action

### Using Data Visualization to Analyze Types of Assets

**DA9** Data visualization can be used to identify changes in the composition of assets.

Excel

**Example:** Patents are often reported on companies' balance sheets as intangible assets. For example, consider the following chart, which shows the countries that recently had at least 100,000 patents in force.

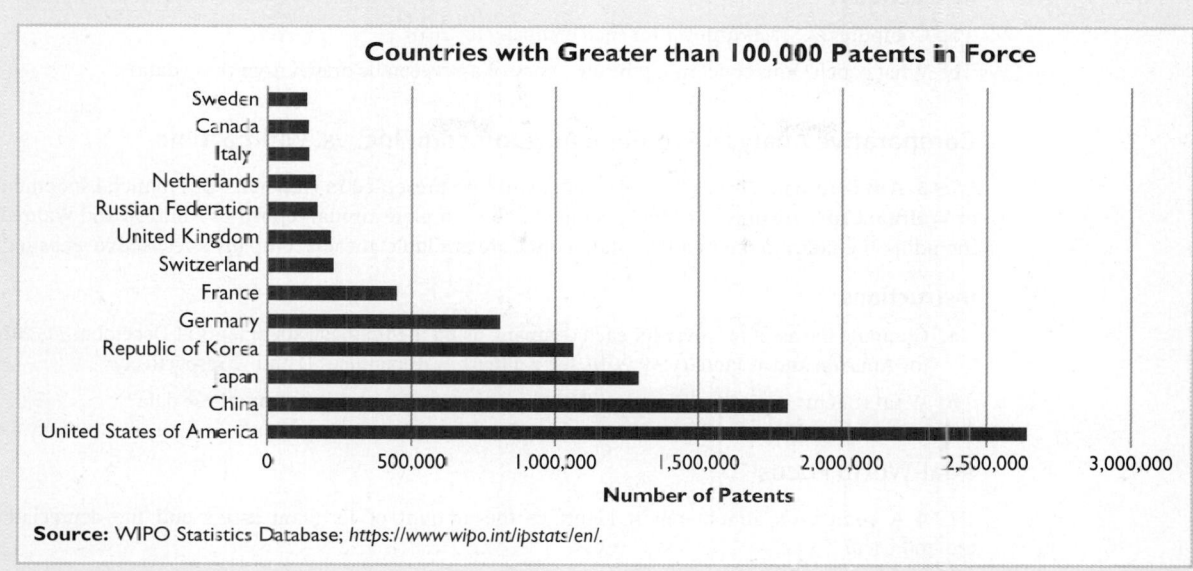

**Countries with Greater than 100,000 Patents in Force**

**Source:** WIPO Statistics Database; *https://www.wipo.int/ipstats/en/.*

For companies that have many patents, GAAP requires the amounts to be valued at historical cost on the companies' balance sheets. The market value of many of the patents owned by companies such as **Dropbox, Google**, and **Facebook** is therefore much greater than the amount reported on a company's balance sheet.

For this case, you will use data that shows the dollar value of intangible assets compared to tangible assets held by S&P 500 companies over the last 45 years. (The S&P 500 companies are a group of the largest 500 companies that trade stock on multiple U.S. stock exchanges, including the New York Stock Exchange and NASDAQ.) You will create and analyze a stacked column chart to identify trends in the types of assets held by these large companies over time.

*Go to WileyPLUS for complete case details and instructions.*

## Expand Your Critical Thinking

### Financial Reporting Problem: Apple Inc.

**CT9.1** The financial statements of **Apple Inc.** are presented in Appendix A. The complete annual report, including the notes to the financial statements, is available at the company's website.

**Instructions**

Answer the following questions.

**a.** What were the total cost and book value of property, plant, and equipment at September 29, 2018?

**b.** Using the notes to the financial statements, what method of depreciation is used by Apple for financial reporting purposes?

**c.** What was the amount of depreciation and amortization expense for each of the 3 years 2016–2018? (*Hint:* Use the statement of cash flows.)

**d.** Using the statement of cash flows, what are the amounts of property, plant, and equipment purchased in 2018 and 2017?

### Comparative Analysis Problem: PepsiCo, Inc. vs. The Coca-Cola Company

**CT9.2** **PepsiCo, Inc.**'s financial statements are presented in Appendix B. Financial statements of **The Coca-Cola Company** are presented in Appendix C. The complete annual reports of PepsiCo and Coca-Cola, including the notes to the financial statements, are available at each company's respective website.

**Instructions**

a. Compute the asset turnover for each company for 2018.

b. What conclusions concerning the efficiency of assets can be drawn from these data?

## Comparative Analysis Problem: Amazon.com, Inc. vs. Walmart Inc.

**CT9.3 Amazon.com, Inc.**'s financial statements are presented in Appendix D. Financial statements of **Walmart Inc.** are presented in Appendix E. The complete annual reports of Amazon and Walmart, including the notes to the financial statements, are available at each company's respective website.

**Instructions**

a. Compute the asset turnover for each company using the financial statements at December 31, 2018, for Amazon and at January 31, 2019, for Walmart in Appendices D and E, respectively.

b. What conclusions concerning the efficiency of assets can be drawn from these data?

## Real-World Focus

**CT9.4** A company's annual report identifies the amount of its plant assets and the depreciation method used.

**Instructions**

Select a well-known company, search the Internet for the company's website address, and then answer the following questions.

a. What is the name of the company?

b. What is the Internet address of the annual report?

c. At fiscal year-end, what is the net amount of its plant assets?

d. What is the accumulated depreciation?

e. Which method of depreciation does the company use?

## Decision-Making Across the Organization

**CT9.5** Pinson Company and Estes Company are two companies that are similar in many respects. One difference is that Pinson Company uses the straight-line method and Estes Company uses the declining-balance method at double the straight-line rate. On January 2, 2020, both companies acquired the depreciable assets shown below.

| Asset | Cost | Salvage Value | Useful Life |
|---|---|---|---|
| Buildings | $360,000 | $20,000 | 40 years |
| Equipment | 130,000 | 10,000 | 10 years |

Including the appropriate depreciation charges, annual net income for the companies in the years 2020, 2021, and 2022 and total income for the 3 years were as follows.

| | 2020 | 2021 | 2022 | Total |
|---|---|---|---|---|
| Pinson Company | $84,000 | $88,400 | $90,000 | $262,400 |
| Estes Company | 68,000 | 76,000 | 85,000 | 229,000 |

At December 31, 2022, the balance sheets of the two companies are similar except that Estes Company has more cash than Pinson Company, and the companies' net property, plant, and equipment are different.

Lynda Peace is interested in buying one of the companies. She comes to you for advice.

**Instructions**

With the class divided into groups, answer the following.

a. Determine the annual and total depreciation recorded by each company during the 3 years.

b. Assuming that Estes Company also uses the straight-line method of depreciation instead of the declining-balance method as in (a), prepare comparative income data for the 3 years.

c. Which company should Lynda Peace buy? Why?

## Communication Activity

**CT9.6** The chapter presented some concerns regarding the current accounting standards for research and development expenditures.

**Instructions**

Assume that you are either (a) the president of a company that is very dependent on ongoing research and development, writing a memo to the FASB complaining about the current accounting standards regarding research and development, or (b) the FASB member defending the current standards regarding research and development. Your memo should address the following questions.

1. By requiring expensing of R&D, do you think companies will spend less on R&D? Why or why not? What are the possible implications for the competitiveness of U.S. companies?

2. If a company makes a commitment to spend money for R&D, it must believe it has future benefits. Shouldn't these costs therefore be capitalized just like the purchase of any long-lived asset that is believed to have future benefits?

## Ethics Case

**CT9.7** Clean Aire Anti-Pollution Company is suffering declining sales of its principal product, non-biodegradable plastic cartons. The president, Wade Trumar, instructs his controller, Kate Rollins to lengthen asset lives to reduce depreciation expense. A processing line of automated plastic extruding equipment, purchased for $3.5 million in January 2022, was originally estimated to have a useful life of 8 years and a salvage value of $400,000. Depreciation has been recorded for 2 years on that basis. Wade wants the estimated life changed to 12 years total and the straight-line method continued with no change in the salvage value. Kate is hesitant to make the change, believing it is unethical to increase net income in this manner. Wade says, ' Hey, the life is only an estimate, and I've heard that our competition uses a 12-year life on their production equipment."

**Instructions**

a. Who are the stakeholders in this situation?

b. Is the proposed change in asset life unethical, or is it simply a good business practice by an astute president?

c. What is the effect of Wade's proposed change on net income in the year of change?

## All About You

**CT9.8** Companies invest substantial sums to ensure that their product is well-known to the consumer. Test your knowledge of who owns some famous brands and their impact on the financial statements.

**Instructions**

a. Provide an answer to the four multiple-choice questions below.

1. Which company owns both Taco Bell and Pizza Hut?
   a. McDonald's.            c. Yum Brands.
   b. CKE.                   d. Wendy's.

2. Dairy Queen belongs to
   a. Breyers.              c. GE.
   b. Berkshire Hathaway.   d. The Coca-Cola Company.

3. Philip Morris, the cigarette maker, is owned by:
   a. Altria.               c. Boeing.
   b. GE.                   d. ExxonMobil.

4. AOL, a major Internet provider, belongs to:
   a. Microsoft.            c. NBC.
   b. Cisco.                d. Verizon Communications.

b. How do you think the value of these brands is reported on the appropriate company's balance sheet?

### FASB Codification Activity

**CT9.9** If your school has a subscription to the FASB Codification, log in and prepare responses to the following.

  **a.** What does it mean to capitalize an item?

  **b.** What is the definition provided for an intangible asset?

  **c.** Your great-uncle, who is a CPA, is impressed that you are taking an accounting class. Based on his experience, he believes that depreciation is something that companies do based on past practice, not on the basis of authoritative guidance. Provide the authoritative literature to support the practice of fixed-asset depreciation.

### Answers to Insight and Accounting Across the Organization Questions

**Many U.S. Firms Use Leases  Q:** Why might airline managers choose to lease rather than purchase their planes?  **A:** The reasons for leasing include favorable tax treatment, better financing options, increased flexibility, reduced risk of obsolescence, and often less debt shown on the balance sheet.

**We Want to Own Glass  Q:** If Google had been successful in registering the term Glass, where would this trademark be reported on its financial statements?  **A:** The trademark would have been reported on the balance sheet under the classification, Intangible Assets.

**Sustainability Report Please  Q:** Why do you believe companies issue sustainability reports?  **A:** It is important that companies clearly describe the things they value in addition to overall profitability. Most companies recognize that the health, safety, and environmental protections of their workforce and community are important components in developing strategies for continued growth and longevity. Without a strong commitment to the principles of corporate social responsibility, it is unlikely that a company will be able to maintain long-term stability and profitability. The development of a sustainability report helps companies to consider these issues and develop measures to assess whether they are meeting their goals in this area.

# A Look at IFRS

### LEARNING OBJECTIVE 7
Compare the accounting for long-lived assets under GAAP and IFRS.

IFRS follows most of the same principles as GAAP in the accounting for property, plant, and equipment. There are, however, some significant differences in the implementation. IFRS allows the use of revaluation of property, plant, and equipment, and it also requires the use of component depreciation. In addition, there are some significant differences in the accounting for both intangible assets and impairments.

### Key Points

The following are the key similarities and differences between GAAP and IFRS as related to the accounting for long-lived assets.

**Similarities**

- The definition for plant assets for both IFRS and GAAP is essentially the same.
- Both IFRS and GAAP follow the historical cost principle when accounting for property, plant, and equipment at date of acquisition. Cost consists of all expenditures necessary to acquire the asset and make it ready for its intended use.
- Under both IFRS and GAAP, interest costs incurred during construction are capitalized. Recently, IFRS converged to GAAP requirements in this area.
- IFRS also views depreciation as an allocation of cost over an asset's useful life. IFRS permits the same depreciation methods (e.g., straight-line, accelerated, and units-of-activity) as GAAP.
- Under both GAAP and IFRS, changes in the depreciation method used and changes in useful life and salvage value are handled in current and future periods. Prior periods are not affected.

- The accounting for subsequent expenditures (such as ordinary repairs and additions) are essentially the same under IFRS and GAAP.

- The accounting for plant asset disposals is essentially the same under IFRS and GAAP.

- Initial costs to acquire natural resources are recorded in essentially the same manner under IFRS and GAAP.

- The definition of intangible assets is essentially the same under IFRS and GAAP.

- The accounting for exchanges of nonmonetary assets has recently converged between IFRS and GAAP. GAAP now requires that gains on exchanges of nonmonetary assets be recognized if the exchange has commercial substance. This is the same framework used in IFRS.

**Differences**

- IFRS uses the term **residual value** rather than salvage value to refer to an owner's estimate of an asset's value at the end of its useful life for that owner.

- IFRS allows companies to revalue plant assets to fair value at the reporting date. Companies that choose to use the revaluation framework must follow revaluation procedures. If revaluation is used, it must be applied to all assets in a class of assets. Assets that are experiencing rapid price changes must be revalued on an annual basis; otherwise, less frequent revaluation is acceptable.

- IFRS requires component depreciation. **Component depreciation** specifies that any significant parts of a depreciable asset that have different estimated useful lives should be separately depreciated. Component depreciation is allowed under GAAP but is seldom used.

- As in GAAP, under IFRS the costs associated with research and development are segregated into the two components. Costs in the research phase are always expensed under both IFRS and GAAP. Under IFRS, however, costs in the development phase are capitalized as Development Costs once technological feasibility is achieved.

- IFRS permits revaluation of intangible assets (except for goodwill). GAAP prohibits revaluation of intangible assets.

# IFRS Practice

## IFRS Self-Test Questions

1. Which of the following statements is **correct**?

   a. Both IFRS and GAAP permit revaluation of property, plant, and equipment and intangible assets (except for goodwill).

   b. IFRS permits revaluation of property, plant, and equipment and intangible assets (except for goodwill).

   c. Both IFRS and GAAP permit revaluation of property, plant, and equipment but not intangible assets.

   d. GAAP permits revaluation of property, plant, and equipment but not intangible assets.

2. Research and development costs are:

   a. expensed under GAAP.

   b. expensed under IFRS.

   c. expensed under both GAAP and IFRS.

   d. None of the answer choices is correct.

## IFRS Exercises

**IFRS9.1** What is component depreciation, and when must it be used?

**IFRS9.2** What is revaluation of plant assets? When should revaluation be applied?

**IFRS9.3** Some product development expenditures are recorded as development expenses and others as development costs. Explain the difference between these accounts and how a company decides which classification is appropriate.

## International Financial Statement Analysis: Louis Vuitton

**IFRS9.4** The financial statements of **Louis Vuitton** are presented in Appendix F. The complete consolidated financial statements, including the notes to its financial statements, are available at the company's website.

**Instructions**

Use the company's 2018 consolidated financial statements to answer the following questions.

    **a.** According to the notes to the financial statements, what method or methods does the company use to depreciate "property, plant, and equipment?" What useful lives does it use to depreciate property, plant, and equipment?

    **b.** Using the notes to the financial statements, explain how the company accounted for its intangible assets with indefinite lives.

    **c.** Using the notes to the financial statements, determine (1) the balance in Accumulated Amortization and Impairment for intangible assets (other than goodwill), and (2) the balance in Depreciation (and impairment) for property, plant, and equipment.

**Answers to IFRS Self-Test Questions**

**1.** b   **2.** a

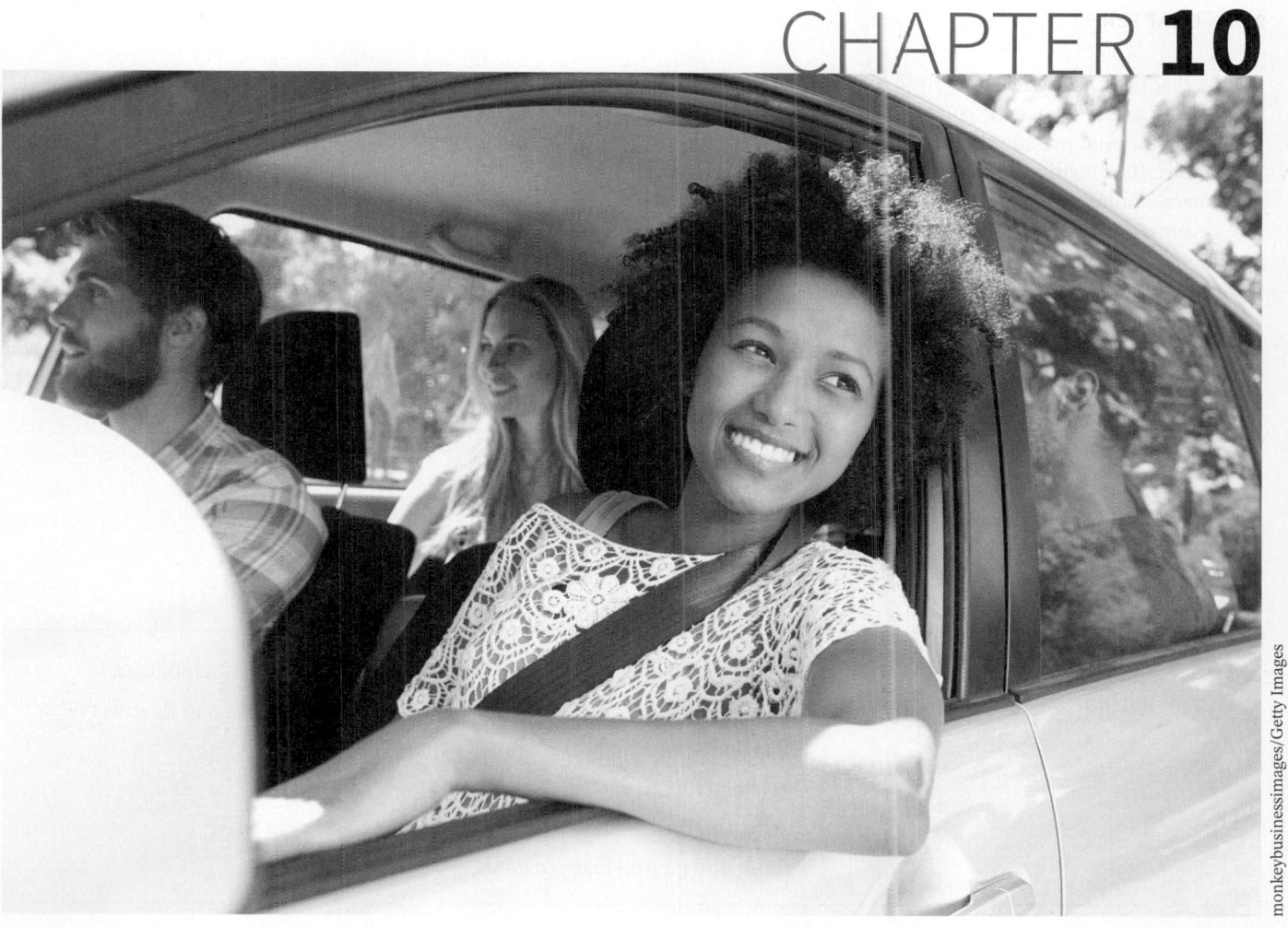

monkeybusinessimages/Getty Images

# Liabilities

## Chapter Preview

The following Feature Story suggests that **General Motors (GM)** and **Ford** accumulated tremendous amounts of debt in their pursuit of auto industry dominance. It is unlikely that they could have grown so large without this debt, but at times the debt threatened their very existence. Given this risk, why do companies borrow money? Why do they sometimes borrow short-term and other times long-term? Besides bank borrowings, what other kinds of debts do companies incur? In this chapter, we address these issues.

## Feature Story

### And Then There Were Two

Debt can help a company acquire the things it needs to grow. But, it is often the very thing that can also kill a company. A brief history of **Maxwell Car Company** illustrates the role of debt in the U.S. auto industry. In 1920, Maxwell Car Company was on the brink of financial ruin. Because it was unable to pay its bills, its creditors stepped in and took over. They hired a former **General Motors (GM)** executive named Walter Chrysler to reorganize the company. By 1925, he had taken over the company and renamed it Chrysler. By 1933, **Chrysler** was booming, with sales surpassing even those of **Ford**.

But the next few decades saw Chrysler make a series of blunders. By 1980, with its creditors pounding at the gates, Chrysler was again on the brink of financial ruin.

At that point, Chrysler brought in a former Ford executive named Lee Iacocca to save the company. Iacocca argued that the United States could not afford to let Chrysler fail because of the loss of jobs. He convinced the federal government to grant loan guarantees—promises that if Chrysler failed to pay its creditors, the government would pay them. Iacocca then streamlined operations and brought out some profitable products. Chrysler repaid all of its government-guaranteed loans by 1983, seven years ahead of the scheduled final payment.

To compete in today's global vehicle market, you must be big—really big. So in 1998, Chrysler merged with German automaker **Daimler-Benz** to form **DaimlerChrysler**. For a time, this left just two U.S.-based auto manufacturers—GM and Ford. But in 2007, DaimlerChrysler sold 81% of Chrysler to **Cerberus**, an investment group, to provide much-needed cash infusions to the automaker. In 2009, Daimler turned over its remaining stake to Cerberus. Three days later, Chrysler filed for bankruptcy. But by 2010, it was beginning to show signs of a turnaround.

The car companies are giants. GM and Ford typically rank among the top five U.S. firms in total assets. But GM and Ford accumulated truckloads of debt on their way to getting big. Although debt made it possible to get so big, the Chrysler story, and GM's bankruptcy in 2009, make it clear that debt can also threaten a company's survival.

# Chapter Outline

| LEARNING OBJECTIVES | REVIEW | PRACTICE |
|---|---|---|
| **LO 1** Explain how to account for current liabilities. | • What is a current liability?<br>• Notes payable<br>• Sales taxes payable<br>• Unearned revenues<br>• Current maturities of long-term debt<br>• Payroll and payroll taxes payable | **DO IT! 1a** Current Liabilities<br>**1b** Wages and Payroll Taxes |
| **LO 2** Describe the major characteristics of bonds. | • Types of bonds<br>• Issuing procedures<br>• Bond trading<br>• Determining the market price of a bond | **DO IT! 2** Bond Terminology |
| **LO 3** Explain how to account for bond transactions. | • Issuing bonds at face value<br>• Discount or premium on bonds<br>• Issuing bonds at a discount<br>• Issuing bonds at a premium<br>• Redeeming bonds at maturity<br>• Redeeming bonds before maturity | **DO IT! 3a** Bond Issuance<br>**3b** Bond Redemption |
| **LO 4** Explain how to account for long-term notes payable. | • Mortgage notes payable<br>• Lease liabilities | **DO IT! 4** Long-Term Notes |
| **LO 5** Discuss how liabilities are reported and analyzed. | • Presentation<br>• Analysis<br>• Debt and equity financing | **DO IT! 5** Analyzing Liabilities |

**Go to the Review and Practice section at the end of the chapter for a review of key concepts and practice applications with solutions.**

**Visit WileyPLUS for additional tutorials and practice opportunities.**

# Accounting for Current Liabilities

**LEARNING OBJECTIVE 1**
Explain how to account for current liabilities.

## What Is a Current Liability?

You have learned that liabilities are defined as "creditors' claims on total assets" and as "existing debts and obligations." Companies must settle or pay these claims, debts and obligations at some time in the future by transferring assets or services. The future date on which they are due or payable (the maturity date) is a significant feature of liabilities.

Recall that a **current liability** is a debt that a company expects to pay within one year or the operating cycle, whichever is longer. Debts that do not meet these criteria are **long-term liabilities**.

Financial statement users want to know whether a company's obligations are current or long-term. A company that has more current liabilities than current assets often lacks liquidity, or short-term debt-paying ability. In addition, users want to know the types of liabilities a company has. If a company declares bankruptcy, a specific, predetermined order of payment to creditors exists. Thus, the amount and type of liabilities are of critical importance.

The different types of current liabilities include notes payable, accounts payable, unearned revenues, and accrued liabilities such as taxes, salaries and wages, and interest payable. In the sections that follow, we discuss common types of current liabilities (see Helpful Hint).

**HELPFUL HINT**

In previous chapters, we explained the entries for accounts payable and the adjusting entries for some current liabilities.

## Notes Payable

Companies record obligations in the form of written notes as **notes payable**. Notes payable are often used instead of accounts payable because they give the lender formal proof of the obligation in case legal remedies are needed to collect the debt. Companies frequently issue notes payable to meet short-term financing needs. Notes payable usually require the borrower to pay interest.

Notes are issued for varying periods of time. **Those due for payment within one year of the balance sheet date are usually classified as current liabilities.**

To illustrate the accounting for notes payable, assume that First National Bank agrees to lend $100,000 on September 1, 2022, if Cole Williams Co. signs a $100,000, 12%, four-month note maturing on January 1. When a company issues an interest-bearing note, the amount of assets it receives upon issuance of the note generally equals the note's face value. Cole Williams therefore will receive $100,000 cash and will make the following journal entry.

| Sept. 1 | Cash | 100,000 | |
| | Notes Payable | | 100,000 |
| | (To record issuance of 12%, 4-month note to First National Bank) | | |

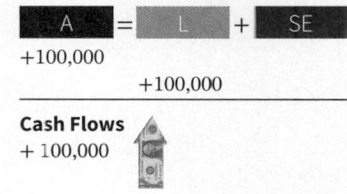

A = L + SE
+100,000
+100,000
**Cash Flows**
+ 100,000

Interest expense accrues over the life of the note, and the company must periodically record that accrual. If Cole Williams prepares financial statements annually, it makes an adjusting entry at December 31 to recognize interest expense and interest payable of $4,000 ($100,000 × 12% × $\frac{4}{12}$). **Illustration 10.1** shows the formula for computing interest and its application to Cole Williams' note.

**ILLUSTRATION 10.1**
Formula for computing interest expense

| Face Value of Note | × | Annual Interest Rate | × | Time in Terms of One Year | = | Interest |
|---|---|---|---|---|---|---|
| $100,000 | × | 12% | × | $\frac{4}{12}$ | = | $4,000 |

Cole Williams makes an adjusting entry as follows.

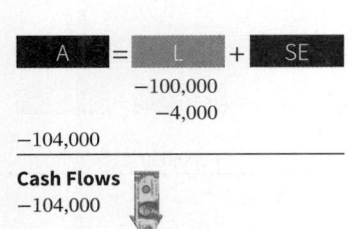

Cash Flows
no effect

| | | | |
|---|---|---|---|
| Dec. 31 | Interest Expense | 4,000 | |
| | Interest Payable | | 4,000 |
| | (To accrue interest for 4 months on First | | |
| | National Bank note) | | |

In the December 31 financial statements, the current liabilities section of the balance sheet will show notes payable $100,000 and interest payable $4,000. In addition, the company will report interest expense of $4,000 under "Other expenses and losses" in the income statement. If Cole Williams prepared financial statements monthly, the adjusting entry at the end of each month would be $1,000 ($100,000 \times 12\% \times \frac{1}{12}$).

At maturity (January 1, 2023), Cole Williams must pay the face value of the note ($100,000) plus $4,000 interest ($100,000 \times 12\% \times \frac{4}{12}$). It records payment of the note and accrued interest as follows.

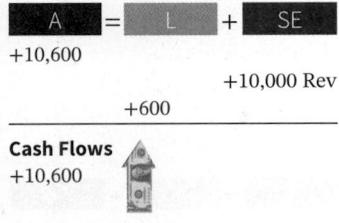

Cash Flows
−104,000

| | | | |
|---|---|---|---|
| Jan. 1 | Notes Payable | 100,000 | |
| | Interest Payable | 4,000 | |
| | Cash | | 104,000 |
| | (To record payment of First National Bank | | |
| | interest-bearing note and accrued interest at | | |
| | maturity) | | |

## Sales Taxes Payable

Many of the products we purchase at retail stores are subject to sales taxes. Many states also are now collecting sales taxes on purchases made on the Internet as well. Sales taxes are expressed as a percentage of the sales price. The selling company collects the tax from the customer when the sale occurs. Periodically (usually monthly), the retailer remits the collections to the state's department of revenue. Collecting sales taxes is important. For example, the State of New York recently sued **Sprint Corporation** for $300 million for its alleged failure to collect sales taxes on phone calls.

Under most state sales tax laws, the selling company must enter separately in the cash register the amount of the sale and the amount of the sales tax collected (see **Helpful Hint**). (Gasoline sales are a major exception.) The company then uses the cash register readings to credit Sales Revenue and Sales Taxes Payable. For example, if the March 25 cash register reading for Cooley Grocery shows sales of $10,000 and sales taxes of $600 (sales tax rate of 6%), the journal entry is as follows.

| | | | |
|---|---|---|---|
| Mar. 25 | Cash | 10,600 | |
| | Sales Revenue | | 10,000 |
| | Sales Taxes Payable | | 600 |
| | (To record daily sales and sales taxes) | | |

When the company remits the taxes to the taxing agency, it debits Sales Taxes Payable and credits Cash. The company does not report sales taxes as an expense. It simply forwards to the government the amount paid by the customers. Thus, Cooley Grocery serves only as a **collection agent** for the taxing authority.

Sometimes companies do not enter sales taxes separately in the cash register. To determine the amount of sales in such cases, divide total receipts by 100% plus the sales tax percentage. For example, assume that Cooley Grocery enters total receipts of $10,600. The receipts from the sales are equal to the sales price (100%) plus the tax percentage (6% of sales), or 1.06 times the sales total. We can compute the sales amount as follows.

$$\$10,600 \div 1.06 = \$10,000$$

Thus, we can find the sales tax amount of $600 by either (1) subtracting sales from total receipts ($10,600 − $10,000) or (2) multiplying sales by the sales tax rate ($10,000 \times .06$).

## Unearned Revenues

A magazine publisher, such as **Sports Illustrated**, receives customers' checks when they order magazines. An airline company, such as **Southwest Airlines**, often receives cash when it sells tickets for future flights. Season tickets for concerts, sporting events, and theater programs are also paid for in advance. How do companies account for customer cash payments that are received before goods are delivered or services are performed?

1. When a company receives the advance payment, it debits Cash and credits a current liability account identifying the source of the unearned revenue.

2. When the company recognizes revenue by satisfying its performance obligation, it debits an unearned revenue account and credits a revenue account.

To illustrate, assume that Superior University sells 10,000 season football tickets at $50 each for its five-game home schedule. The university makes the following entry for the sale of season tickets.

| Aug. 6 | Cash (10,000 × $50) | 500,000 | |
| |     Unearned Ticket Revenue | | 500,000 |
| |     (To record sale of 10,000 season tickets) | | |

As each game is completed, Superior records the recognition of revenue with the following entry.

| Sept. 7 | Unearned Ticket Revenue ($500,000 ÷ 5) | 100,000 | |
| |     Ticket Revenue | | 100,000 |
| |     (To record football ticket revenue) | | |

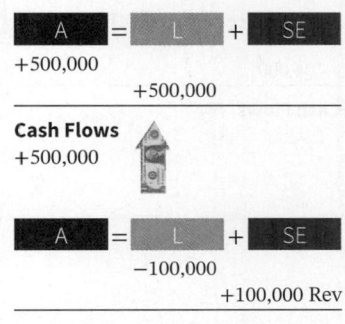

A = L + SE
+500,000
    +500,000

**Cash Flows**
+500,000

A = L + SE
−100,000
    +100,000 Rev

**Cash Flows**
no effect

The account Unearned Ticket Revenue represents unearned revenue, and Superior reports it as a current liability. As the school recognizes revenue, it reclassifies the amount from unearned revenue to Ticket Revenue. Unearned revenue is substantial for some companies. In the airline industry, for example, tickets sold for future flights represent almost 50% of total current liabilities. At **United Air Lines**, unearned ticket revenue is its largest current liability, recently amounting to over $1 billion.

**Illustration 10.2** shows specific unearned revenue and revenue accounts used in selected types of businesses.

| Type of Business | Account Title | |
| --- | --- | --- |
| | Unearned Revenue | Revenue |
| Airline | Unearned Ticket Revenue | Ticket Revenue |
| Magazine publisher | Unearned Subscription Revenue | Subscription Revenue |
| Hotel | Unearned Rent Revenue | Rent Revenue |

**ILLUSTRATION 10.2**

Unearned revenue and revenue accounts

## Current Maturities of Long-Term Debt

Companies often have a portion of long-term debt that comes due in the current year. That amount is considered a current liability. As an example, assume that Wendy Construction issues a five-year, interest-bearing $25,000 note on January 1, 2022. This note specifies that each January 1, starting January 1, 2023, Wendy should pay $5,000 of the note. When the company prepares financial statements on December 31, 2022, it should report $5,000 as a current liability and $20,000 as a long-term liability. (The $5,000 amount is the portion of the note that is due to be paid within the next 12 months.) Companies often identify current maturities of long-term debt on the balance sheet as **long-term debt due within one year**. In a recent year, **General Motors** had $724 million of such debt.

It is not necessary to prepare an adjusting entry to recognize the current maturity of long-term debt. At the balance sheet date, all obligations due within one year are classified as current, and all other obligations as long-term.

**ACTION PLAN**

- Use the interest formula: Face value of note × Annual interest rate × Time in terms of one year.

- Divide total receipts by 100% plus the tax rate to determine sales revenue; then subtract sales revenue from the total receipts.

- Determine what fraction of the total unearned rent should be recognized this year.

## DO IT! 1a | Current Liabilities

You and several classmates are studying for the next accounting examination. They ask you to answer the following questions.

1. If cash is borrowed on a $50,000, 6-month, 12% note on September 1, how much interest expense would be incurred by December 31?

2. How is the sales tax amount determined when the cash register total includes sales taxes?

3. If $15,000 is collected in advance on November 1 for 3 months' rent, what amount of rent revenue should be recognized by December 31?

**Solution**

1. $50,000 \times 12\% \times \frac{4}{12} = \$2,000$

2. First, divide the total cash register receipts by 100% plus the sales tax percentage to find the sales revenue amount. Second, subtract the sales revenue amount from the total cash register receipts to determine the sales taxes.

3. $\$15,000 \times \frac{2}{3} = \$10,000$

Related exercise material: **BE10.1, BE10.2, BE10.3, BE10.4, DO IT! 10.1a, E10.1, E10.2, E10.3, E10.4, and E10.5.**

# Payroll and Payroll Taxes Payable

Assume that Susan Alena works 40 hours this week for Pepitone Inc., earning a wage of $10 per hour. Will Susan receive a $400 check at the end of the week? Not likely. The reason: Pepitone is required to withhold amounts from her wages to pay various governmental authorities. For example, Pepitone will withhold amounts for FICA taxes (Social Security and Medicare)[1] and for federal and state income taxes. If these withholdings total $100, Susan will receive a check for only $300. **Illustration 10.3** summarizes the types of payroll deductions that normally occur for most companies.

**ILLUSTRATION 10.3**
Payroll deductions

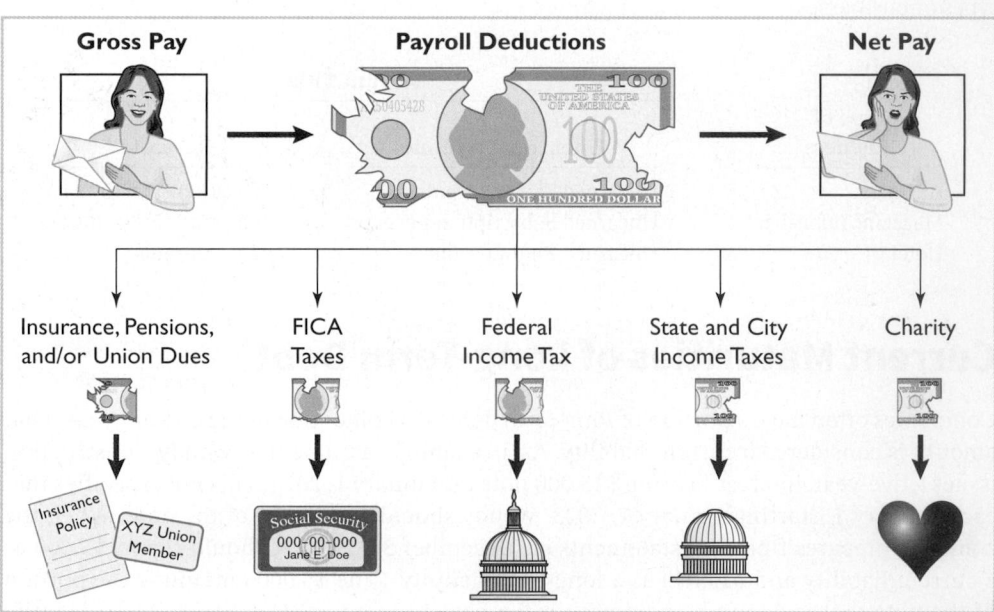

[1] Social Security and Medicare taxes are commonly called FICA taxes. In 1937, Congress enacted the Federal Insurance Contribution Act (FICA) whereby both the employee and employer must make equal contributions to Social Security and Medicare. The recent combined Social Security and Medicare rate was 7.65%. *Our examples and homework use 7.65% for both.*

As a result of these deductions, companies withhold from employee paychecks amounts that must be paid to other parties. Pepitone therefore has incurred a liability to pay these third parties and must report this liability in its balance sheet.

As a second illustration, assume that Cargo Corporation records its payroll for the week of March 7 with the journal entry shown below.

| Mar. 7 | Salaries and Wages Expense | 100,000 | |
| | FICA Taxes Payable | | 7,650 |
| | Federal Income Taxes Payable | | 21,864 |
| | State Income Taxes Payable | | 2,922 |
| | Salaries and Wages Payable | | 67,564 |
| | (To record payroll and withholding taxes for the week ending March 7) | | |

A = L + SE

−100,000 Exp

+7,650
+21,864
+2,922
+67,564

**Cash Flows**
no effect

Cargo then records payment of this payroll on March 7 as follows.

| Mar. 7 | Salaries and Wages Payable | 67,564 | |
| | Cash | | 67,564 |
| | (To record payment of the March 7 payroll) | | |

A = L + SE

−67,564

−67,564

**Cash Flows**
−67,564

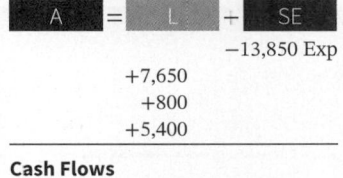

In this case, Cargo records $100,000 in salaries and wages expense. In addition, it records liabilities for the salaries and wages payable as well as liabilities to governmental agencies. Rather than pay the employees $100,000, Cargo instead must withhold the taxes and make the tax payments directly. In summary, Cargo is essentially serving as a tax collector.

In addition to the liabilities incurred as a result of withholdings, employers also incur a second type of payroll-related liability. With every payroll, the **employer** incurs liabilities to pay various **payroll taxes** levied upon the employer. These payroll taxes include the **employer's share** of FICA (Social Security and Medicare) taxes and state and federal unemployment taxes. Based on Cargo Corp.'s $100,000 payroll, the company would record the employer's expense and liability for its payroll taxes as follows.

| Mar. 7 | Payroll Tax Expense | 13,850 | |
| | FICA Taxes Payable | | 7,650 |
| | Federal Unemployment Taxes Payable | | 800 |
| | State Unemployment Taxes Payable | | 5,400 |
| | (To record employer's payroll taxes on March 7 payroll) | | |

A = L + SE

−13,850 Exp

+7,650
+800
+5,400

**Cash Flows**
no effect

Companies classify the payroll and payroll tax liability accounts as current liabilities because they must be paid to employees or remitted to taxing authorities periodically and in the near term. Taxing authorities impose substantial fines and penalties on employers if the withholding and payroll taxes are not computed correctly and paid on time.

---

## Anatomy of a Fraud

Art was a custodial supervisor for a large school district. The district was supposed to employ between 35 and 40 regular custodians, as well as 3 or 4 substitute custodians to fill in when regular custodians were absent. Instead, in addition to the regular custodians, Art "hired" 77 substitutes. In fact, almost none of these people worked for the district. Instead, Art submitted time cards for these people, collected their checks at the district office, and personally distributed the checks to the "employees." If a substitute's check was for $1,200, that person would cash the check, keep $200, and pay Art $1,000.

**Total take: $150,000**

### The Missing Controls

**Human resource controls.** Thorough background checks should be performed. No employees should begin work until they have been approved by the Board of Education and entered into the payroll system. No employees should be entered into the payroll system until they have been approved by a supervisor. All paychecks should be distributed directly to employees at the official school locations by designated employees or direct-deposited into approved employee bank accounts.

**Independent internal verification.** Budgets should be reviewed monthly to identify situations where actual costs significantly exceed budgeted amounts.

Source: Adapted from Wells, *Fraud Casebook* (2007), pp. 164–171.

**ACTION PLAN**

- Remember that wages earned by employees are an expense to the company, but withholdings reduce the amount paid to the employees.
- Payroll taxes are taxes the company incurs related to its employees.

## DO IT! 1b | Wages and Payroll Taxes

During the month of September, Lake Corporation's employees earned wages of $60,000. Withholdings related to these wages were $4,590 for FICA, $6,500 for federal income tax, and $2,000 for state income tax. Costs incurred for unemployment taxes were $90 for federal and $150 for state.

Prepare the September 30 journal entries for (a) salaries and wages expense and salaries and wages payable, assuming that all September wages will be paid in October, and (b) the company's payroll tax expense.

### Solution

**a.** To determine wages payable, reduce wages expense by the withholdings for FICA, federal income tax, and state income tax.

| | | | |
|---|---|---|---|
| Sept. 30 | Salaries and Wages Expense | 60,000 | |
| | FICA Taxes Payable | | 4,590 |
| | Federal Income Taxes Payable | | 6,500 |
| | State Income Taxes Payable | | 2,000 |
| | Salaries and Wages Payable | | 46,910 |

**b.** Payroll taxes would be for the company's share of FICA, as well as for federal and state unemployment tax.

| | | | |
|---|---|---|---|
| Sept. 30 | Payroll Tax Expense | 4,830 | |
| | FICA Taxes Payable | | 4,590 |
| | Federal Unemployment Taxes Payable | | 90 |
| | State Unemployment Taxes Payable | | 150 |

Related exercise material: **BE10.5, BE10.6, BE10.7, DO IT! 10.1b, E10.6, and E10.7.**

# Major Characteristics of Bonds

**LEARNING OBJECTIVE 2**
Describe the major characteristics of bonds.

**Long-term liabilities** are obligations that a company expects to pay more than one year in the future. In this section, we explain the accounting for the principal types of obligations reported in the long-term liabilities section of the balance sheet. These obligations often are in the form of bonds or long-term notes.

**Bonds** are a form of interest-bearing note payable issued by corporations, universities, and governmental agencies. Typically, interest payments are made to the bondholders throughout the term of the bond, and the face value is repaid upon maturity. Bonds, like common stock, are sold in small denominations (usually $1,000 or multiples of $1,000). As a result, bonds attract many investors. When a corporation issues bonds, it is borrowing money. The person who buys the bonds (the bondholder) is lending money.

## Types of Bonds

Bonds may have many different features. In the following sections, we describe the types of bonds commonly issued.

### Secured and Unsecured Bonds

**Secured bonds** have specific assets of the issuer pledged as collateral for the bonds. A bond secured by real estate, for example, is called a **mortgage bond**. A bond secured by specific assets set aside to redeem (retire) the bonds is called a **sinking fund bond**.

**Unsecured bonds**, also called **debenture bonds**, are issued against the general credit of the borrower. Companies with good credit ratings use these bonds extensively. For example, at one time, **DuPont** reported over $2 billion of debenture bonds outstanding.

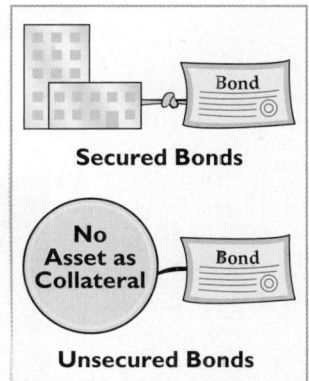

**Secured Bonds**

**Unsecured Bonds**

### Convertible and Callable Bonds

Bonds that can be converted into common stock at the bondholder's option are **convertible bonds**. Convertible bonds have features that are attractive both to bondholders and to the issuer. The conversion feature often gives bondholders an opportunity to benefit if the market price of the common stock increases substantially. Furthermore, until conversion, the bond-holder receives interest on the bond. For the issuer, the bonds sell at a higher price and pay a lower rate of interest than comparable debt securities that do not have a conversion option. Many corporations, such as **USAir**, **United States Steel**, and **General Motors**, have issued convertible bonds.

Bonds that the issuing company can redeem (buy back) at a stated dollar amount prior to maturity are **callable bonds**. Typically, bonds are repaid at the maturity date. The call feature allows companies to repay their debt early.

**Convertible Bonds**

**Callable Bonds**

## Issuing Procedures

State laws grant corporations the power to issue bonds. Both the board of directors and stockholders usually must approve bond issues. **In authorizing the bond issue, the board of directors must stipulate the number of bonds authorized, total face value, and contractual interest rate**. The total bond authorization often exceeds the number of bonds the company originally issues. This gives the corporation the flexibility to issue more bonds, if needed, to meet future cash requirements.

The **face value** is the amount of principal due at the maturity date. The **maturity date** is the date that the final payment is due to the investor from the issuing company. The **contractual interest rate**, often referred to as the **stated rate**, is the rate used to determine the amount of cash interest the issuing company pays and the investor receives. Usually, the contractual rate is stated as an annual rate.

The terms of the bond issue are set forth in a legal document called a **bond indenture**. The indenture shows the terms and summarizes the rights of the bondholders and their trustees, and the obligations of the issuing company. The **trustee** (usually a financial institution) keeps records of each bondholder, maintains custody of unissued bonds, and holds conditional title to pledged property.

In addition, the issuing company arranges for the printing of **bond certificates**. The indenture and the certificate are separate documents. As shown in **Illustration 10.4**, a bond certificate provides the following information: name of the issuer, face value (par value), contractual interest rate, and maturity date. An investment company that specializes in selling securities generally sells the bonds for the issuing company.

## Bond Trading

Bondholders have the opportunity to convert their holdings into cash at any time by selling the bonds at the current market price on national securities exchanges. **Bond prices are quoted as a percentage of the face value of the bond, which is usually $1,000**. A $1,000 face value bond with a quoted price of 97 means that the selling price of the bond is 97% of face value, or $970. Newspapers and the financial press publish bond prices and trading activity daily, as shown in **Illustration 10.5**.

**ILLUSTRATION 10.4** Bond certificate

Source: International Minerals and Chemical Corporation

**ILLUSTRATION 10.5**

**Market information for bonds**

| Issuer | Bonds | Maturity | Close | Yield |
|---|---|---|---|---|
| Time Warner Cable | 6.75 | June 15, 2039 | 116.4 | 5.49 |

> **HELPFUL HINT**
>
> The price of a $1,000 bond trading at $95\frac{1}{4}$ is $952.50.

This bond listing indicates that **Time Warner Cable** has outstanding 6.75% (contractual interest rate), $1,000 (face value) bonds that mature in 2039 (see **Helpful Hint**). They currently yield a 5.49% return. At the close of trading, the price was 116.4% of face value, or $1,164.

A corporation makes journal entries **only when it issues or buys back bonds**, when interest is accrued or paid, and when bondholders convert bonds into common stock. For example, **DuPont does not journalize** transactions between its bondholders and other investors. If Tom Smith sells his DuPont bonds to Faith Jones, DuPont does not journalize the transaction.

## Determining the Market Price of a Bond

**Same dollars at different times are not equal.**

If your company needed financing and wanted to attract investors to purchase your bonds, how would the market set the price for these bonds? To be more specific, assume that Coronet, Inc. issues a **zero-interest bond** (pays no interest) with a face value of $1,000,000 due in 20 years. For this bond, the only cash Coronet pays to bond investors is one million dollars at the end of 20 years. Would investors pay one million dollars for this bond? We hope not because one million dollars received 20 years from now is not the same as one million dollars received today.

The term **time value of money** is used to indicate the relationship between time and money—that a dollar received today is worth more than a dollar to be received at some time in the future. If you had $1 million today, you would invest it. From that investment, you would earn interest such that at the end of 20 years, you would have much more than $1 million. Thus, if someone is going to pay you $1 million 20 years from now, you would want to find its equivalent today, or its present value. In other words, you would want to determine the value today of the amount to be received in the future after taking into account current interest rates.

The current market price (present value) of a bond is the value at which it should sell in the marketplace. Market price therefore is a function of the three factors that determine present value: (1) the dollar amounts to be received, (2) the length of time until the amounts are received, and (3) the market rate of interest. The **market interest rate** is the rate investors demand for loaning funds. In most cases, the market interest rate will differ from its contractual interest rate.

To illustrate, assume that Acropolis Company on January 1, 2022, issues $100,000 of 9% bonds, due in five years, with interest payable annually at year-end. The purchaser of the bonds would receive the following two types of cash payments: (1) **principal** of $100,000 to be paid at maturity, and (2) five $9,000 **interest payments** ($100,000 × 9%) over the term of the bonds. **Illustration 10.6** shows a time diagram depicting both cash flows.

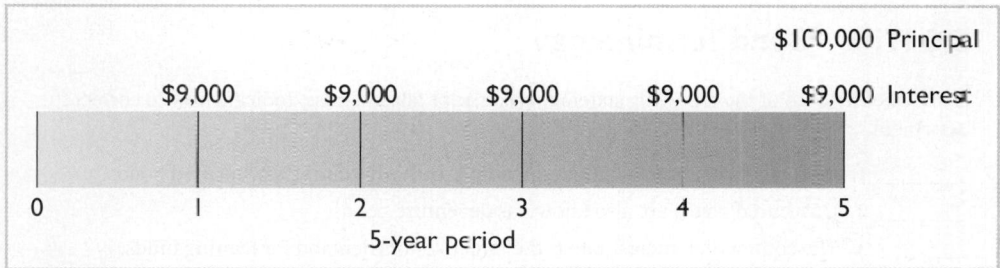

**ILLUSTRATION 10.6**

Time diagram depicting cash flows

The current market price of a bond is equal to the present value of all the future cash payments promised by the bond. **Illustration 10.7** lists and totals the present values of these amounts, assuming the market rate of interest is 9%.

| | |
|---|---|
| Present value of $100,000 received in 5 years | $ 64,993 |
| Present value of $9,000 received annually for 5 years | 35,007 |
| **Market price of bonds** | **$100,000** |

**ILLUSTRATION 10.7**

Computing the market price of bonds

Present value calculations involve the use of present value factors. Tables are available to provide the present value numbers to be used, or these values can be determined mathematically or with financial calculators.[2] Appendix G provides further discussion of the concepts and the mechanics of the time value of money computations.

## Investor Insight

### Running Hot!

alphaspirit/Shutterstock.com

Recently, the market for bonds was running hot. For example, consider these two large deals: **Apple Inc.** sold $17 billion of debt, which at the time was the largest corporate bond ever issued. But shortly thereafter, it was beaten by **Verizon Communications Inc.**, which sold $49 billion of debt. The chart highlights the increased issuance of bonds.

As one expert noted about these increases, "Companies are taking advantage of this lower-rate environment in the limited period of time it is going to be around." An interesting aspect of these bond issuances is that some companies, like

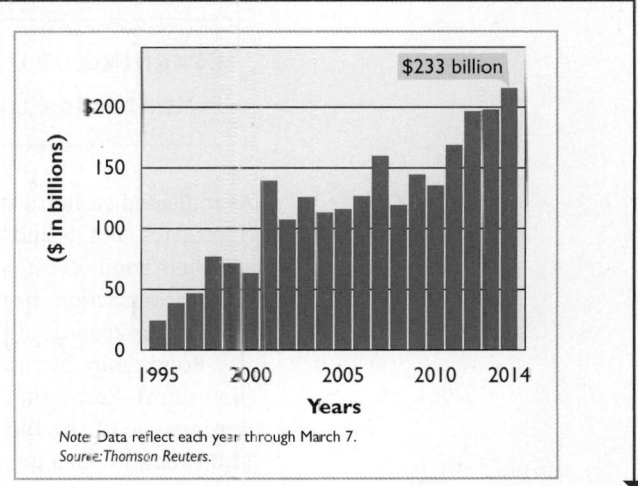

*Note:* Data reflect each year through March 7.
*Source:* Thomson Reuters.

---

[2]For those knowledgeable in the use of present value tables, the computations in the example shown in Illustration 10.7 are $100,000 × .64993 = $64,993, and $9,000 × 3.88965 = $35,007 (rounded).

**Philip Morris International**, **Medtronic**, and **Simon Property Group**, are even selling 30-year bonds. These bond issuers are benefitting from "a massive sentiment shift," says one bond expert. The belief that the economy will continue to improve is making investors more comfortable holding longer-term bonds, as they search for investments that offer better returns than U.S. Treasury bonds.

**Sources:** Vipal Monga, "The Big Number," *Wall Street Journal* (March 20, 2012), p. B5; and Mike Cherney, "Renewed Embrace of Bonds Sparks Boom," *Wall Street Journal* (March 8–9, 2014), p. B5.

**What are the advantages for companies of issuing 30-year bonds instead of 5-year bonds? (Answer is available near the end of the chapter.)**

---

**ACTION PLAN**

- Review the types of bonds and the basic terms associated with bonds.

## DO IT! 2 | Bond Terminology

State whether each of the following statements is true or false. If false, indicate how to correct the statement.

_____ **1.** Mortgage bonds and sinking fund bonds are both examples of secured bonds.

_____ **2.** Unsecured bonds are also known as debenture bonds.

_____ **3.** The contractual interest rate is the rate investors demand for loaning funds.

_____ **4.** The face value is the amount of principal the issuing company must pay at the maturity date.

_____ **5.** The market price of a bond is equal to its face value.

**Solution**

**1.** True. **2.** True. **3.** False. The contractual interest rate is used to determine the amount of cash interest the borrower pays. **4.** True. **5.** False. The market price of a bond is the value at which it should sell in the marketplace. As a result, the market price of the bond and its face value are often different.

Related exercise material: **DO IT! 10.2 and E10.8.**

---

# Accounting for Bond Transactions

### LEARNING OBJECTIVE 3

Explain how to account for bond transactions.

As indicated earlier, a corporation records bond transactions when it issues (sells) or redeems (buys back) bonds and when bondholders convert bonds into common stock. If bondholders sell their bond investments to other investors, the issuing company receives no further cash on this transaction, **nor does the issuing company journalize the transaction** (although it does keep records of the names of bondholders in some cases).

Bonds may be issued at face value, below face value (discount), or above face value (premium). Recall that bond prices for both new issues and existing bonds are quoted as **a percentage of the face value of the bond, and that face value is usually $1,000.** Thus, a $1,000 bond with a quoted price of 97 means that the selling price of the bond is 97% of face value, or $970.

## Issuing Bonds at Face Value

To illustrate the accounting for bonds issued at face value, assume that on January 1, 2022, Candlestick Inc. issues $100,000, five-year, 10% bonds at 100 (100% of face value). The entry to record the sale is as follows.

| Jan. 1 | Cash | 100,000 | |
| |     Bonds Payable | | 100,000 |
| |     (To record sale of bonds at face value) | | |

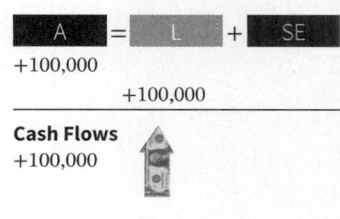

A = L + SE
+100,000
    +100,000

**Cash Flows**
+100,000

Candlestick reports bonds payable in the long-term liabilities section of the balance sheet because the maturity date is January 1, 2027 (more than one year away).

Over the term (life) of the bonds, companies make entries to record bond interest. Interest on bonds payable is computed in the same manner as interest on notes payable. Assume that interest is payable annually on January 1 on the Candlestick bonds. In that case, Candlestick accrues interest of $10,000 ($100,000 × 10%) on December 31. At December 31, Candlestick recognizes the $10,000 of interest expense incurred with the following entry.

| Dec. 31 | Interest Expense | 10,000 | |
| |     Interest Payable | | 10,000 |
| |     (To accrue bond interest) | | |

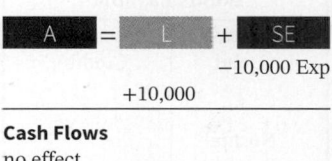

A = L + SE
           −10,000 Exp
    +10,000

**Cash Flows**
no effect

**The company classifies interest payable as a current liability** because it is scheduled for payment within the next year on January 1. When Candlestick pays the interest on January 1, 2023, it debits (decreases) Interest Payable and credits (decreases) Cash for $10,000.

Candlestick records the payment on January 1 as follows.

| Jan. 1 | Interest Payable | 10,000 | |
| |     Cash | | 10,000 |
| |     (To record payment of bond interest) | | |

A = L + SE
    −10,000
−10,000

**Cash Flows**
−10,000

## Discount or Premium on Bonds

The previous example assumed that the contractual (stated) interest rate and the market (effective) interest rate paid on the bonds were the same. Recall that the **contractual interest rate** is the rate applied to the face (par) value to arrive at the interest paid in a year. The **market interest rate** is the rate investors demand for loaning funds to the corporation. When the contractual interest rate and the market interest rate are the same, bonds sell **at face value (par value)**.

However, market interest rates change daily. The type of bond issued, the state of the economy, current industry conditions, and the company's performance all affect market interest rates. As a result, contractual and market interest rates often differ. To make bonds salable when the two rates differ, bonds sell below or above face value.

To illustrate, suppose that a company issues 10% bonds at a time when other bonds of similar risk are paying 12%. Investors will not be interested in buying the 10% bonds, so their value will fall below their face value. When a bond is sold for less than its face value, the difference between its face value and selling price is called a **discount**. As a result of the decline in the bonds' selling price, the actual interest rate incurred by the company increases to the level of the current market interest rate.

Conversely, if the market rate of interest is **lower than** the contractual interest rate, investors will have to pay more than face value for the bonds. That is, if the market rate of interest is 8% but the contractual interest rate on the bonds is 10%, the price of the bonds will be bid up. When a bond is sold for more than its face value, the difference between its face value and selling price is called a **premium. Illustration 10.8** shows these relationships.

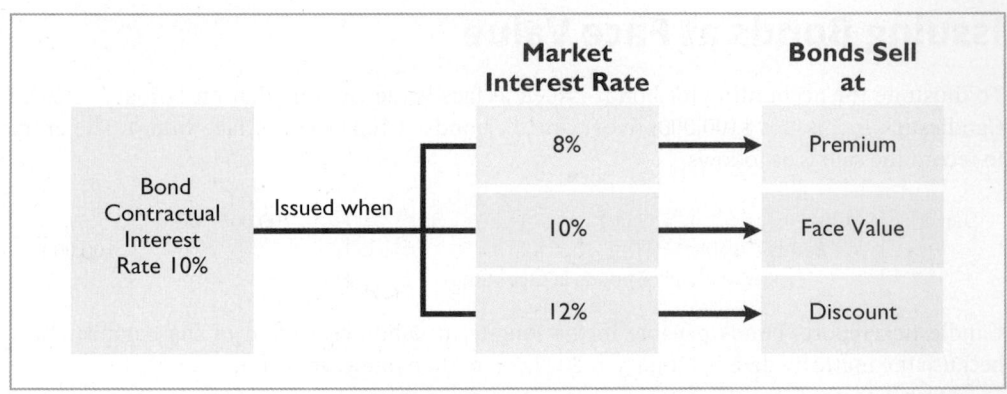

Issuance of bonds at an amount different from face value is quite common. By the time a company prints the bond certificates and markets the bonds, it will be a coincidence if the market rate and the contractual rate are the same. Thus, the issuance of bonds at a discount does not mean that the issuer's financial strength is suspect. Conversely, the sale of bonds at a premium does not indicate that the financial strength of the issuer is exceptional.

## Issuing Bonds at a Discount

**HELPFUL HINT**

**Discount on Bonds Payable**

| Increase | Decrease |
|---|---|
| Debit | Credit |
| ↓ | |
| Normal Balance | |

To illustrate issuance of bonds at a discount, assume that on January 1, 2022, Candlestick Inc. sells $100,000, five-year, 10% bonds for $98,000 (98% of face value). Interest is payable annually on January 1. The entry to record the issuance is as follows (see **Helpful Hint**).

| Jan. 1 | Cash | 98,000 | |
| | Discount on Bonds Payable | 2,000 | |
| | Bonds Payable | | 100,000 |
| | (To record sale of bonds at a discount) | | |

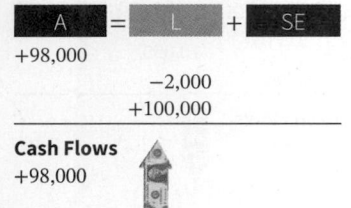

+98,000

−2,000
+100,000

**Cash Flows**
+98,000

Although Discount on Bonds Payable has a debit balance, **it is not an asset**. Rather, it is a **contra account**. This account is **deducted from bonds payable** on the balance sheet, as shown in **Illustration 10.9**.

### Candlestick Inc.
**Balance Sheet (partial)**

| Long-term liabilities | | |
|---|---|---|
| Bonds payable | $100,000 | |
| **Less: Discount on bonds payable** | **2,000** | $98,000 |

**HELPFUL HINT**

Carrying value (book value) of bonds issued at a discount is determined by subtracting the balance of the discount account from the balance of the Bonds Payable account.

The $98,000 represents the **carrying (or book) value** of the bonds (see **Helpful Hint**). On the date of issue, this amount equals the market price of the bonds.

The issuance of bonds below face value—at a discount—causes the total cost of borrowing to differ from the bond interest paid. That is, the issuing corporation must pay not only the contractual interest rate over the term of the bonds but also the face value (rather than the issuance price) at maturity. Therefore, the difference between the issuance price and face value of the bonds—the discount—is an **additional cost of borrowing**. The company records this additional cost as **interest expense** over the life of the bonds. The total cost of borrowing $98,000 for Candlestick is therefore $52,000, computed as shown in **Illustration 10.10**.

**Bonds Issued at a Discount**

| Annual interest payments | |
|---|---|
| ($100,000 × 10% = $10,000; $10,000 × 5) | $50,000 |
| Add: Bond discount ($100,000 − $98,000) | 2,000 |
| **Total cost of borrowing** | **$52,000** |

Alternatively, we can compute the total cost of borrowing as shown in **Illustration 10.11**.

| **Bonds Issued at a Discount** | |
|---|---|
| Principal at maturity | $100,000 |
| Annual interest payments ($10,000 × 5) | 50,000 |
| Cash to be paid to bondholders | 150,000 |
| Less: Cash received from bondholders | 98,000 |
| **Total cost of borrowing** | **$ 52,000** |

To follow the expense recognition principle, companies allocate bond discount to expense in each period in which the bonds are outstanding. This is referred to as **amortizing the discount**. Amortization of the discount **increases** the amount of interest expense reported each period. That is, after the company amortizes the discount, the amount of interest expense it reports in a period will exceed the contractual amount. As shown in Illustration 10.10, for the bonds issued by Candlestick, total interest expense will exceed the contractual interest by $2,000 over the life of the bonds.

As the discount is amortized, its balance declines. As a consequence, the carrying value of the bonds will increase, until at maturity the carrying value of the bonds equals their face amount. This is shown in **Illustration 10.12**. Appendices 10A and 10B at the end of this chapter discuss procedures for amortizing bond discount.

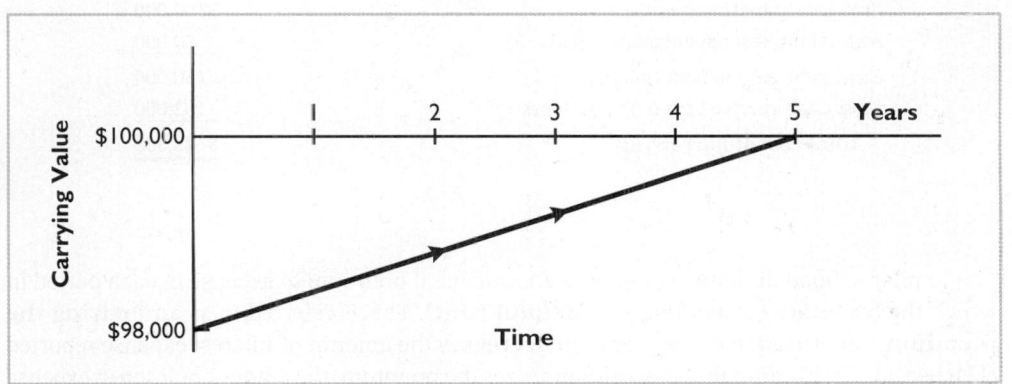

**ILLUSTRATION 10.12**

**Amortization of bond discount**

# Issuing Bonds at a Premium

To illustrate the issuance of bonds at a premium, we now assume the Candlestick Inc. bonds described above sell for $102,000 (102% of face value) rather than for $98,000. The entry to record the sale is as follows.

| Jan. 1 | Cash | 102,000 | |
|---|---|---|---|
| | Bonds Payable | | 100,000 |
| | Premium on Bonds Payable | | 2,000 |
| | (To record sale of bonds at a premium) | | |

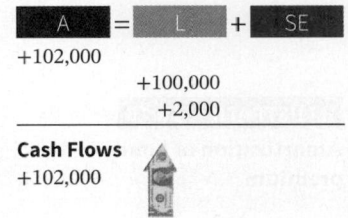

A = L + SE
+102,000      +100,000
              +2,000

**Cash Flows**
+102,000

Candlestick adds the premium on bonds payable **to the bonds payable amount** on the balance sheet, as shown in **Illustration 10.13**.

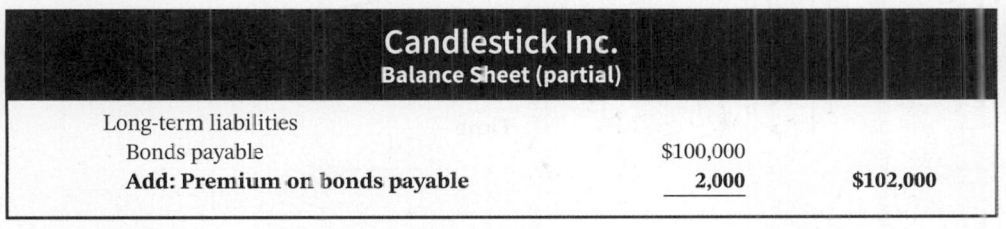

| **Candlestick Inc.** | | |
|---|---|---|
| **Balance Sheet (partial)** | | |
| Long-term liabilities | | |
| Bonds payable | $100,000 | |
| **Add: Premium on bonds payable** | 2,000 | **$102,000** |

**ILLUSTRATION 10.13**

**Statement presentation of bond premium**

The sale of bonds above face value causes the total cost of borrowing to be **less than the bond interest paid**. The reason: The borrower is not required to pay the bond premium at the maturity date of the bonds. Thus, the bond premium is considered to be **a reduction in the cost of borrowing** that reduces bond interest over the life of the bonds. The total cost of borrowing $102,000 for Candlestick is shown in **Illustration 10.14** (see **Helpful Hint**).

**ILLUSTRATION 10.14**

Total cost of borrowing—bonds issued at a premium

| Bonds Issued at a Premium | |
|---|---|
| Annual interest payments | |
| ($100,000 × 10% = $10,000; $10,000 × 5) | $50,000 |
| Less: Bond premium ($102,000 − $100,000) | 2,000 |
| **Total cost of borrowing** | **$48,000** |

Alternatively, we can compute the cost of borrowing as shown in **Illustration 10.15**.

**ILLUSTRATION 10.15**

Alternative computation of total cost of borrowing—bonds issued at a premium

| Bonds Issued at a Premium | |
|---|---|
| Principal at maturity | $100,000 |
| Annual interest payments ($10,000 × 5) | 50,000 |
| Cash to be paid to bondholders | 150,000 |
| Less: Cash received from bondholders | 102,000 |
| **Total cost of borrowing** | **$ 48,000** |

Similar to bond discount, companies allocate bond premium to expense in each period in which the bonds are outstanding (see **Helpful Hint**). This is referred to as **amortizing the premium**. Amortization of the premium **decreases** the amount of interest expense reported each period. That is, after the company amortizes the premium, the amount of interest expense it reports in a period will be less than the contractual amount. As shown in Illustration 10.14, for the bonds issued by Candlestick, contractual interest will exceed the interest expense by $2,000 over the life of the bonds.

As the premium is amortized, its balance declines. As a consequence, the carrying value of the bonds will decrease, until at maturity the carrying value of the bonds equals their face amount. This is shown in **Illustration 10.16**. Appendices 10A and 10B at the end of this chapter discuss procedures for amortizing bond premium.

**ILLUSTRATION 10.16**

Amortization of bond premium

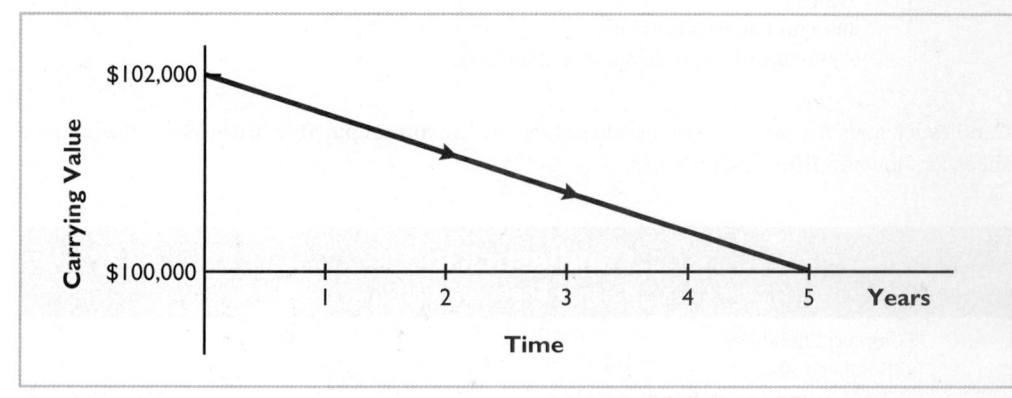

## DO IT! 3a | Bond Issuance

Giant Corporation issues $200,000 of bonds for $189,000. (a) Prepare the journal entry to record the issuance of the bonds, and (b) show how the bonds would be reported on the balance sheet at the date of issuance.

**Solution**

**a.**

| | | |
|---|---|---|
| Cash | 189,000 | |
| Discount on Bonds Payable | 11,000 | |
| Bonds Payable | | 200,000 |
| (To record sale of bonds at a discount) | | |

**b.**

Long-term liabilities

| | | |
|---|---|---|
| Bonds payable | $200,000 | |
| Less: Discount on bonds payable | 11,000 | $189,000 |

Related exercise material: **BE10.8, BE10.9, BE10.10, BE10.11, BE10.12, DO IT! 10.3a, E10.9, E10.10,** and **E10.11.**

**ACTION PLAN**

- Record cash received, bonds payable at face value, and the difference as a discount or premium.
- Report discount as a deduction from bonds payable and premium as an addition to bonds payable.

# Redeeming Bonds at Maturity

Regardless of the issue price of bonds, the book value of the bonds at maturity will equal their face value. Assuming that the company pays and records separately the interest for the last interest period, Candlestick Inc. records the redemption of its bonds at maturity as follows.

| Jan. 1 | Bonds Payable | 100,000 | |
|---|---|---|---|
| | Cash | | 100,000 |
| | (To record redemption of bonds at maturity) | | |

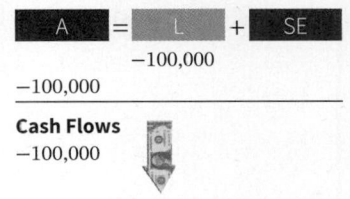

# Redeeming Bonds Before Maturity

Bonds may be redeemed before maturity. A company may decide to redeem bonds before maturity to reduce interest cost and to remove debt from its balance sheet. A company should redeem debt early only if it has sufficient cash resources.

When a company redeems bonds before maturity, it is necessary to (1) eliminate the carrying value of the bonds at the redemption date, (2) record the cash paid, and (3) recognize the gain or loss on redemption. The **carrying value** of the bonds is the face value of the bonds less any remaining bond discount or plus any remaining bond premium at the redemption date (see **Helpful Hint**).

To illustrate, assume that Candlestick Inc. has sold its bonds at a premium. At the end of the fourth period, Candlestick redeems these bonds at 103 after paying the annual interest. Assume that the carrying value of the bonds at the redemption date is $100,400 (principal $100,000 and premium $400). Candlestick records the redemption at the end of the fourth interest period (January 1, 2026) as follows.

**HELPFUL HINT**

If a bond is redeemed prior to its maturity date and its carrying value exceeds its redemption price, this results in a gain.

| Jan. 1 | Bonds Payable | 100,000 | |
|---|---|---|---|
| | Premium on Bonds Payable | 400 | |
| | Loss on Bond Redemption | 2,600 | |
| | Cash | | 103,000 |
| | (To record redemption of bonds at 103) | | |

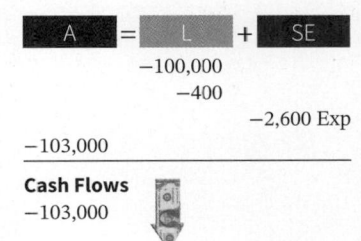

Note that the loss of $2,600 is the difference between the cash paid of $103,000 and the carrying value of the bonds of $100,400. Gains and losses from bond redemptions are reported in the income statement as "Other revenues and gains" or "Other expenses and losses."

## People, Planet, and Profit Insight

### How About Some Green Bonds?

CarpathianPrince/
Shutterstock.com

Green bonds are debt used to fund activities such as renewable-energy projects. For example, a company may use the proceeds from the sale of green bonds to clean up its manufacturing operations and cut waste (such as that related to energy consumption).

The use of green bonds has taken off as companies now have guidelines as to how to disclose and report on these green-bond proceeds. These standardized disclosures provide transparency as to how these bonds are used and their effect on overall profitability.

Investors are taking a strong interest in these bonds. Investing companies are installing socially responsible investing teams and have started to integrate sustainability into their investment processes. The disclosures of how companies are using the bond proceeds help investors to make better financial decisions.

**Source:** Ben Edwards, "Green Bonds Catch On," *Wall Street Journal* (April 3, 2014), p. C5.

**Why might standardized disclosure help investors to better understand how proceeds from the sale or issuance of bonds are used? (Answer is available near the end of the chapter.)**

---

### ACTION PLAN

- **Determine and eliminate the carrying value of the bonds.**
- **Record the cash paid.**
- **Compute and record the gain or loss (the difference between the first two items).**

### DO IT! 3b | Bond Redemption

R & B Inc. issued $500,000, 10-year bonds at a discount. Prior to maturity, when the carrying value of the bonds is $496,000, the company redeems the bonds at 98. Prepare the entry to record the redemption of the bonds.

#### Solution

There is a gain on redemption. The cash paid, $490,000 ($500,000 × 98%), is less than the carrying value of $496,000. The entry is:

| | | |
|---|---|---|
| Bonds Payable | 500,000 | |
|    Discount on Bonds Payable | | 4,000 |
|    Gain on Bond Redemption | | 6,000 |
|    Cash | | 490,000 |
|      (To record redemption of bonds at 98) | | |

Related exercise material: **BE10.13, DO IT! 10.3b, E10.12, and E10.13.**

---

# Accounting for Long-Term Notes Payable

### LEARNING OBJECTIVE 4

Explain how to account for long-term notes payable.

The use of notes payable in long-term debt financing is quite common. **Long-term notes payable** are similar to short-term interest-bearing notes payable except that the term of the notes exceeds one year. In periods of unstable interest rates, lenders may tie the interest rate on long-term notes to changes in the market rate for comparable loans.

## Mortgage Notes Payable

A long-term note may be secured by a **mortgage** that pledges title to specific assets as security for a loan. Individuals widely use **mortgage notes payable** to purchase homes, and many small and some large companies use them to acquire plant assets. At one time, approximately 18% of **McDonald's** long-term debt related to mortgage notes on land, buildings, and improvements.

Like other long-term notes payable, the mortgage loan terms may stipulate either a **fixed** or an **adjustable** interest rate. The interest rate on a fixed-rate mortgage remains the same over the life of the mortgage. The interest rate on an adjustable-rate mortgage is adjusted periodically to reflect changes in the market rate of interest. Typically, the terms require the borrower to make equal installment payments over the term of the loan. Each payment consists of (1) interest on the unpaid balance of the loan and (2) a reduction of loan principal. While the total amount of the payment remains constant, the interest decreases each period, and the portion applied to the loan principal increases.

Companies initially record mortgage notes payable at face value. They subsequently make entries for each installment payment. To illustrate, assume that Porter Technology Inc. issues a $500,000, 8%, 20-year mortgage note on December 31, 2022, to obtain needed financing for a new research laboratory. The terms provide for annual installment payments of $50,926 (not including real estate taxes and insurance). **Illustration 10.17** shows the installment payment schedule for the first four years.

| Interest Period | (A) Cash Payment | (B) Interest Expense (D) × 8% | (C) Reduction of Principal (A) − (B) | (D) Principal Balance (D) − (C) |
|---|---|---|---|---|
| Issue date | | | | $500,000 |
| 1 | $50,926 | $40,000 | $10,926 | 489,074 |
| 2 | 50,926 | 39,126 | 11,800 | 477,274 |
| 3 | 50,926 | 38,182 | 12,744 | 464,530 |
| 4 | 50,926 | 37,162 | 13,764 | 450,766 |

**ILLUSTRATION 10.17**

Mortgage installment payment schedule

Porter records the mortgage loan on December 31, 2022, as follows.

| Dec. 31 | Cash | 500,000 | |
| | Mortgage Payable | | 500,000 |
| | (To record mortgage loan) | | |

A = L + SE
+500,000
+500,000

Cash Flows
+500,000

On December 31, 2023, Porter records the first installment payment as follows.

| Dec. 31 | Interest Expense | 40,000 | |
| | Mortgage Payable | 10,926 | |
| | Cash | | 50,926 |
| | (To record annual payment on mortgage) | | |

A = L + SE
−10,926    −40,000 Exp
−50,926

Cash Flows
−50,926

**In the balance sheet, the company reports the reduction in principal for the next year as a current liability, and it classifies the remaining unpaid principal balance as a long-term liability.** At December 31, 2023, the total liability is $489,074. Of that amount, $11,800 is current and $477,274 ($489,074 − $11,800) is long-term.

# Lease Liabilities

A **lease** is a contractual agreement between a lessor (owner of a property) and a lessee (renter of the property). This arrangement gives the lessee the right to use specific property, which is owned by the **lessor**, for a specified period of time. In return for the use of the property, the **lessee** makes rental payments over the lease term to the lessor.

Leasing has grown tremendously in popularity. Today, it is the fastest growing form of capital investment. Instead of borrowing money to buy an airplane, computer, nuclear core, or satellite, a company makes periodic payments to lease these assets. Even gambling casinos lease their slot machines. The global equipment-leasing market is over a $900 billion business, with the United States accounting for about one-third of the global market.

## Accounting for Lease Arrangements

For all leases greater than one year, the lessee records a right-of-use asset and a lease liability. The lease liability is computed as the present value of the lease payments. The right-of-use asset is equal to the lease liability. To illustrate, assume that Gonzalez Company decides to lease new equipment. The lease term is four years; the economic life of the equipment is estimated to be five years. The present value of the lease payments is $190,000.

Gonzalez records the lease arrangement as follows.

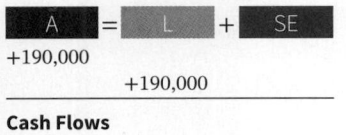

+190,000

 +190,000

**Cash Flows**
no effect

| | | |
|---|---|---|
| Right-of-Use Asset | 190,000 | |
| Lease Liability | | 190,000 |
| (To record leased asset and lease liability) | | |

## Balance Sheet Presentation

Gonzalez reports its leased asset on the balance sheet in the long-term assets section. It reports the lease liability on the balance sheet as a liability. The portion of the lease liability expected to be paid in the next year is a current liability. The remainder is classified as a long-term liability.

## Income Statement Presentation

The income statement presentation of leases by lessees depends on whether the lease is considered a finance or operating lease. The lease is a finance lease if it meets one of five criteria (discussed in more advanced accounting courses). Leases that do not meet any of these five criteria are considered operating leases.

Under finance lease treatment, the right-of-use asset is amortized (depreciated) in a fashion similar to other fixed assets, and the interest expense is determined in a fashion similar to other long-term liabilities. Under operating lease treatment, a single expense amount is determined. The calculation of this expense amount is complex and is addressed in advanced accounting courses.

---

**ACTION PLAN**

- **Record the issuance of the note as a cash receipt and a liability.**
- **Each installment payment consists of interest and payment of principal.**

### DO IT! 4 | Long-Term Notes

Cole Research issues a $250,000, 6%, 20-year mortgage note to obtain needed financing for a new lab. The terms call for annual payments of $21,796 each. Prepare the entries to record the mortgage loan and the first payment.

**Solution**

| | | |
|---|---|---|
| Cash | 250,000 | |
| Mortgage Payable | | 250,000 |
| (To record mortgage loan) | | |
| | | |
| Interest Expense | 15,000* | |
| Mortgage Payable | 6,796 | |
| Cash | | 21,796 |
| (To record annual payment on mortgage) | | |

*Interest expense = $250,000 × 6% = $15,000

Related exercise material: **BE10.14, DO IT! 10.4, and E10.14.**

# Reporting and Analyzing Liabilities

**LEARNING OBJECTIVE 5**

Discuss how liabilities are reported and analyzed.

## Presentation

Current liabilities is the first category under liabilities on the balance sheet. Companies list each of the principal types of current liabilities separately within the category. In addition, companies disclose the terms of notes payable and other key information about the individual items in the notes to the financial statements.

Companies seldom list current liabilities in the order of liquidity. The reason is that varying maturity dates may exist for specific obligations such as notes payable. Or, as a matter of custom, many companies show notes payable first and then accounts payable, regardless of amount. **Illustration 10.18** shows an example.

**ILLUSTRATION 10.18**

Balance sheet presentation of liabilities

### Marais Company
**Balance Sheet (partial)**

| Liabilities | | |
|---|---|---|
| **Current liabilities** | | |
| Notes payable | $250,000 | |
| Accounts payable | 125,000 | |
| Current maturities of long-term debt | 300,000 | |
| Salaries and wages payable | 75,000 | |
| Total current liabilities | | $ 750,000 |
| **Long-term liabilities** | | |
| Bonds payable | $1,000,000 | |
| Less: Discount on bonds payable | 80,000 | 920,000 |
| Notes payable, secured by plant assets | | 500,000 |
| Lease liability | | 440,000 |
| Total long-term liabilities | | 1,860,000 |
| Total liabilities | | $2,610,000 |

Disclosure of debt is very important. Failures at **Enron**, **WorldCom**, and **Global Crossing** have made investors very concerned about companies' debt obligations (see **Ethics Note**). Summary data regarding debts are reported in the balance sheet with detailed data (such as interest rates, maturity dates, conversion privileges, and assets pledged as collateral) reported in supporting schedules in the notes. Recall that companies should report current maturities of long-term debt as a current liability.

**ETHICS NOTE**

Some companies try to minimize the amount of debt reported on their balance sheets by not reporting certain types of commitments as liabilities. This subject is of intense interest in the financial community.

## Analysis

Careful examination of debt obligations helps you assess a company's ability to pay its current and long-term obligations. It also helps you determine whether a company can obtain debt financing in order to grow. We will use the information from the financial statements of **General Motors** (see **Illustration 10.19**) to illustrate the analysis of a company's liquidity and solvency.

**ILLUSTRATION 10.19**

Simplified balance sheets for General Motors

**Real World**

| General Motors Company Balance Sheets December 31, 2017 and 2016 (in millions) | | |
| --- | --- | --- |
| **Assets** | **2017** | **2016** |
| Total current assets | $ 68,744 | $ 76,203 |
| Noncurrent assets | 143,738 | 145,487 |
| Total assets | $212,482 | $221,690 |
| **Liabilities and Stockholders' Equity** | | |
| Total current liabilities | $ 76,890 | $ 85,181 |
| Noncurrent liabilities | 99,392 | 92,434 |
| Total liabilities | 176,282 | 177,615 |
| Total stockholders' equity | 36,200 | 44,075 |
| Total liabilities and stockholders' equity | $212,482 | $221,690 |

## Liquidity

Use of current and noncurrent classifications makes it possible to analyze a company's liquidity. **Liquidity** refers to the ability to pay maturing obligations and meet unexpected needs for cash. The relationship of current assets to current liabilities is critical in analyzing liquidity. We can express this relationship as a dollar amount (working capital) and as a ratio (the current ratio).

The excess of current assets over current liabilities is **working capital**. Illustration 10.20 shows the formula for the computation of **General Motors'** working capital (dollar amounts in millions).

**ILLUSTRATION 10.20**

Working capital formula and computation

| Current Assets | − | Current Liabilities | = | Working Capital |
| --- | --- | --- | --- | --- |
| $68,744 | − | $76,890 | = | $(8,146) |

As an absolute dollar amount, working capital offers limited informational value. For example, $1 million of working capital may be more than needed for a small company but inadequate for a large corporation. Also, $1 million of working capital may be adequate for a company at one time but inadequate at another time.

The **current ratio** permits us to compare the liquidity of different-sized companies and of a single company at different times. The current ratio is calculated as current assets divided by current liabilities. **Illustration 10.21** shows the formula for this ratio, along with its computation using General Motors' current asset and current liability data (dollar amounts in millions).

**ILLUSTRATION 10.21**

Current ratio formula and computation

| Current Assets | ÷ | Current Liabilities | = | Current Ratio |
| --- | --- | --- | --- | --- |
| $68,744 | ÷ | $76,890 | = | .89:1 |

Historically, companies and analysts considered a current ratio of 2:1 to be the standard for a good credit rating. In recent years, however, many healthy companies have maintained ratios well below 2:1 by improving management of their current assets and liabilities. General Motors' ratio of .89:1 is quite low.

Companies that keep fewer liquid assets on hand must rely on other sources of liquidity. One such source is a **bank line of credit**. A line of credit is a prearranged agreement between a company and a lender that permits the company, should it be necessary, to borrow up to an agreed-upon amount. For example, a recent disclosure regarding debt in General Motors' annual report stated that it had $12 billion of unused lines of credit.

## Solvency

Next, we look at two ratios that provide information about a company's long-run solvency. **Solvency** refers to the ability of a company to survive over a long period of time. Long-term creditors and stockholders are interested in a company's long-run solvency. Of particular interest is the company's ability to pay interest as it comes due and to repay the face value of its debt at maturity.

The **debt to assets ratio** measures the percentage of the total assets provided by creditors. It is computed by dividing total liabilities (both current and long-term liabilities) by total assets. To illustrate, we use data from Illustration 10.19. General Motors reported total liabilities of $176,282 million and total assets of $212,482 million. As shown in **Illustration 10.22**, General Motors' debt to assets ratio is 83%. The higher the percentage of debt to assets, the greater the risk that the company may be unable to meet its maturing obligation.

| Total Liabilities | ÷ | Total Assets | = | Debt to Assets Ratio |
|---|---|---|---|---|
| $176,282 | ÷ | $212,482 | = | 83% |

**ILLUSTRATION 10.22**
Debt to assets ratio

**Times interest earned** indicates the company's ability to meet interest payments as they come due. It is computed by dividing the sum of net income, interest expense, and income tax expense by interest expense. General Motors in 2017 reported a net loss of $3,882 million, interest expense of $575 million, and income tax expense of $11,533 million. As shown in **Illustration 10.23**, General Motors' times interest earned is 14.3 times. This interest coverage is considered safe.

| Net Income + Interest Expense + Income Tax Expense | ÷ | Interest Expense | = | Times Interest Earned |
|---|---|---|---|---|
| $(3,882) + $575 + $11,533 | ÷ | $575 | = | 14.3 times |

**ILLUSTRATION 10.23**
Times interest earned

### Investor Insight

iStock.com/yenwen lu

#### Debt Masking

In the wake of the financial crisis of 2008, many financial institutions are wary of reporting too much debt on their financial statements, for fear that investors will consider them too risky. The Securities and Exchange Commission (SEC) is concerned that some companies engage in "debt masking" to make it appear that they have less debt than they actually do. These companies enter into transactions at the end of the accounting period that essentially remove debt from their books. Shortly after the end of the period, they reverse the transaction and the debt goes back on their books. The *Wall Street Journal* reported that 18 large banks "had consistently lowered one type of debt at the end of each of the past five quarters, reducing it on average by 42% from quarterly peaks."

**Source:** Tom McGinty, Kate Kelly, and Kara Scannell, "Debt 'Masking' Under Fire," *Wall Street Journal Online* (April 21, 2010).

**What implications does debt masking have for an investor that is using the debt to assets ratio to evaluate a company's solvency? (Answer is available near the end of the chapter.)**

# Debt and Equity Financing

To obtain large amounts of long-term capital, corporate management has to decide whether to issue additional common stock (equity financing), bonds or notes (debt financing), or a combination of the two. This decision is important to the company, investors, and creditors. The capital structure of a company provides clues as to the potential profit that can be achieved and the risks taken by the company. Debt financing offers these advantages over common stock, as shown in **Illustration 10.24**.

**ILLUSTRATION 10.24**

Advantages of bond financing over common stock

| Bond Financing | Advantages |
|---|---|
| Ballot | 1. **Stockholder control is not affected.**<br>Bondholders do not have voting rights, so current owners (stockholders) retain full control of the company. |
| Tax Bill | 2. **Tax savings result.**<br>Bond interest is deductible for tax purposes; dividends on stock are not. |
| Income Statement / EPS | 3. **Earnings per share (EPS) may be higher.**<br>Although bond interest expense reduces net income, earnings per share often is higher under bond financing because no additional shares of common stock are issued. |

**HELPFUL HINT**

Besides corporations, governmental agencies and universities also issue bonds to raise capital.

As Illustration 10.24 shows, one reason to issue bonds is that they do not affect stockholder control. Because bondholders do not have voting rights, owners can raise capital with bonds and still maintain corporate control (see **Helpful Hint**). In addition, bonds are attractive to corporations because the cost of bond interest is tax-deductible. As a result of this tax treatment, which stock dividends do not offer, bonds may result in a lower cost of financing than equity financing.

To illustrate another advantage of bond financing, assume that Microsystems, Inc. is considering two plans for financing the construction of a new $5 million plant. Plan A involves issuance of 200,000 shares of common stock at the current market price of $25 per share. Plan B involves issuance of $5 million, 8% bonds at face value. Income before interest and taxes on the new plant will be $1.5 million. Income taxes are expected to be 30%. Microsystems currently has 100,000 shares of common stock outstanding. **Illustration 10.25** shows the alternative effects on earnings per share.

**ILLUSTRATION 10.25**

Effects on earnings per share—stocks vs. bonds

|  | Plan A<br>Issue Stock | Plan B<br>Issue Bonds |
|---|---|---|
| Income before interest and taxes | $1,500,000 | $1,500,000 |
| Interest (8% × $5,000,000) | — | 400,000 |
| Income before income taxes | 1,500,000 | 1,100,000 |
| Income tax expense (30%) | 450,000 | 330,000 |
| Net income | $1,050,000 | $ 770,000 |
| Outstanding shares | 300,000 | 100,000 |
| **Earnings per share** | **$3.50** | **$7.70** |

Note that net income is $280,000 less ($1,050,000 − $770,000) with long-term debt financing (bonds). However, earnings per share is higher because there are 200,000 fewer shares of common stock outstanding.

One disadvantage in using bonds is that the company must **pay interest** on a periodic basis. In addition, the company must also **repay the principal** at the due date. A company with fluctuating earnings and a relatively weak cash position may have great difficulty making interest payments when earnings are low. Furthermore, when the economy, stock market, or a company's revenues stagnate, debt payments can gobble up cash quickly and limit a company's ability to meet its financial obligations.

---

**ACTION PLAN**

- Use the formula for the current ratio: Current assets ÷ Current liabilities.
- Use the formula for working capital: Current assets – Current liabilities.
- Use the formula for the debt to assets ratio: Total liabilities ÷ Total assets.

## DO IT! 5 | Analyzing Liabilities

Trout Company provides you with the following balance sheet information as of December 31, 2022.

| Current assets | $10,500 | Current liabilities | $ 8,000 |
|---|---|---|---|
| Long-term assets | 24,200 | Long-term liabilities | 16,000 |
| Total assets | $34,700 | Stockholders' equity | 10,700 |
|  |  | Total liabilities and<br>stockholders' equity | $34,700 |

In addition, Trout reported net income for 2022 of $14,000, income tax expense of $2,800, and interest expense of $900.

**Instructions**

a. Compute the current ratio and working capital for Trout for 2022.

b. Assume that at the end of 2022, Trout used $2,000 cash to pay off $2,000 of accounts payable How would the current ratio and working capital have changed?

c. Compute the debt to assets ratio and the times interest earned for Trout for 2022.

**Solution**

a. Current ratio is 1.31:1 ($10,500 ÷ $8,000). Working capital is $2,500 ($10,500 − $8,000).

b. Current ratio is 1.42:1 [($10,500 − $2,000) ÷ ($8,000 − $2,000)]. Working capital is $2,500 ($8,500 − $6,000).

c. Debt to assets ratio is 69.2% ($24,000 ÷ $34,700). Times interest earned is 19.67 times [($14,000 + $2,800 + $900) ÷ $900].

Related exercise material: **BE10.18, DO IT! 10.5, E10.18, and E10.19.**

---

| Appendix 10A | # Straight-Line Amortization |

---

**LEARNING OBJECTIVE \*6**

Apply the straight-line method of amortizing bond discount and bond premium.

## Amortizing Bond Discount

To follow the expense recognition principle, companies allocate bond discount to expense in each period in which the bonds are outstanding. The **straight-line method of amortization** allocates the same amount to interest expense in each interest period. The calculation is presented in **Illustration 10A.1**.

| Bond Discount | ÷ | Number of Interest Periods | = | Bond Discount Amortization |
|---|---|---|---|---|

**ILLUSTRATION 10A.1**

**Formula for straight-line method of bond discount amortization**

In the Candlestick Inc. example, the company sold $100,000, five-year, 10% bonds on January 1, 2022, for $98,000. This resulted in a $2,000 bond discount ($100,000 − $98,000). The bond discount amortization is $400 ($2,000 ÷ 5) for each of the five amortization periods. Candlestick records the first accrual of bond interest and the amortization of bond discount on December 31 as follows.

| Dec. 31 | Interest Expense | 10,400 | |
| | Discount on Bonds Payable | | 400 |
| | Interest Payable ($100,000 × 10%) | | 10,000 |
| | (To record accrued bond interest and amortization of bond discount) | | |

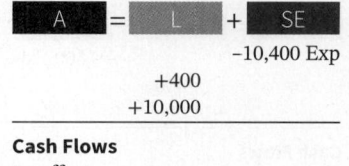

−10,400 Exp
+400
+10,000

**Cash Flows**
no effect

Over the term of the bonds, the balance in Discount on Bonds Payable will decrease annually by the same amount until it has a zero balance at the maturity date of the bonds (see **Alternative Terminology**). Thus, the carrying value of the bonds at maturity will be equal to the face value of the bonds.

Preparing a bond discount amortization schedule, as shown in **Illustration 10A.2**, is useful to determine interest expense, discount amortization, and the carrying value of the bond. As indicated, the interest expense recorded each period is $10,400. Also note that the carrying value of the bond increases $400 each period until it reaches its face value of $100,000 at the end of period 5.

**ALTERNATIVE TERMINOLOGY**

The balance in the Discount on Bonds Payable account is often referred to as *Unamortized Discount on Bonds Payable.*

**ILLUSTRATION 10A.2**

**Bond discount amortization schedule**

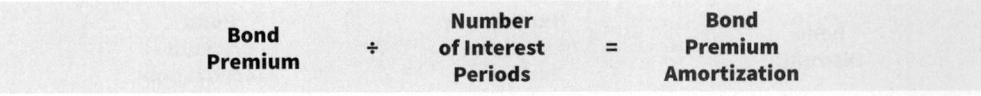

Candlestick Inc.

| Home | Insert | Page Layout | Formulas | Data | Review | View |
|---|---|---|---|---|---|---|

| P18 | | *fx* | | | | |

| | A | B | C | D | E | F |
|---|---|---|---|---|---|---|
| 1 | | | **Candlestick Inc.** | | | |
| 2 | | | **Bond Discount Amortization Schedule** | | | |
| 3 | | | **Straight-Line Method—Annual Interest Payments** | | | |
| 4 | | | **$100,000 of 10%, 5-Year Bonds** | | | |
| 5 | | | | | | |
| 6 | | (A) | (B) | (C) | (D) | (E) |
| 7 | Interest | Interest to Be Paid | Interest Expense to Be Recorded | Discount Amortization | Unamortized Discount | Bond Carrying Value |
| 8 | Periods | (10% × $100,000) | (A) + (C) | ($2,000 ÷ 5) | (D) − (C) | ($100,000 − D) |
| 9 | Issue date | | | | $2,000 | $ 98,000 |
| 10 | 1 | $10,000 | $10,400 | $ 400 | 1,600 | 98,400 |
| 11 | 2 | 10,000 | 10,400 | 400 | 1,200 | 98,800 |
| 12 | 3 | 10,000 | 10,400 | 400 | 800 | 99,200 |
| 13 | 4 | 10,000 | 10,400 | 400 | 400 | 99,600 |
| 14 | 5 | 10,000 | 10,400 | 400 | 0 | 100,000 |
| 15 | | $50,000 | $52,000 | $2,000 | | |
| 16 | | | | | | |
| 17 | Column **(A)** remains constant because the face value of the bonds ($100,000) is multiplied by the annual contractual interest rate (10%) each period. | | | | | |
| 18 | Column **(B)** is computed as the interest paid (Column A) plus the discount amortization (Column C). | | | | | |
| 19 | Column **(C)** indicates the discount amortization each period. | | | | | |
| 20 | Column **(D)** decreases each period by the same amount until it reaches zero at maturity. | | | | | |
| 21 | Column **(E)** increases each period by the amount of discount amortization until it equals the face value at maturity. | | | | | |

# Amortizing Bond Premium

The amortization of bond premium parallels that of bond discount. **Illustration 10A.3** presents the formula for determining bond premium amortization under the straight-line method.

**ILLUSTRATION 10A.3**

**Formula for straight-line method of bond premium amortization**

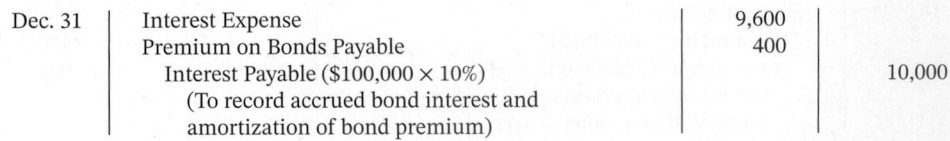

| Bond Premium | ÷ | Number of Interest Periods | = | Bond Premium Amortization |
|---|---|---|---|---|

Continuing our example, assume Candlestick Inc., sells the bonds described above for $102,000, rather than $98,000. This results in a bond premium of $2,000 ($102,000 − $100,000). The premium amortization for each interest period is $400 ($2,000 ÷ 5). Candlestick records the first accrual of interest on December 31 as follows.

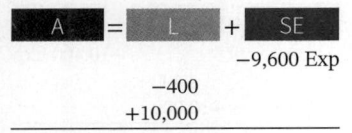

| A | = | L | + | SE |
|---|---|---|---|---|
| | | | | −9,600 Exp |
| | | −400 | | |
| | | +10,000 | | |

**Cash Flows**
no effect

| Dec. 31 | Interest Expense | 9,600 | |
|---|---|---|---|
| | Premium on Bonds Payable | 400 | |
| | Interest Payable ($100,000 × 10%) | | 10,000 |
| | (To record accrued bond interest and amortization of bond premium) | | |

Over the term of the bonds, the balance in Premium on Bonds Payable will decrease annually by the same amount until it has a zero balance at maturity.

A bond premium amortization schedule, as shown in **Illustration 10A.4**, is useful to determine interest expense, premium amortization, and the carrying value of the bond. As indicated, the interest expense Candlestick records each period is $9,600. Note that the carrying value of the bond decreases $400 each period until it reaches its face value of $100,000 at the end of period 5.

**ILLUSTRATION 10A.4**

**Bond premium amortization schedule**

| | | | Candlestick Inc. | | | |
|---|---|---|---|---|---|---|
| | Home | Insert | Page Layout   Formulas   Data   Review   View | | | |
| | P18 | | fx | | | |
| | A | B | C | D | E | F |

| | A | B | C | D | E | F |
|---|---|---|---|---|---|---|
| 1 | | | **Candlestick Inc.** | | | |
| 2 | | | **Bond Premium Amortization Schedule** | | | |
| 3 | | | **Straight-Line Method—Annual Interest Payments** | | | |
| 4 | | | **$100,000 of 10%, 5-Year Bonds** | | | |
| 5 | | | | | | |
| 6 | | (A) | (B) | (C) | (D) | (E) |
| 7 | Interest | Interest to Be Paid | Interest Expense to Be Recorded | Premium Amortization | Unamortized Premium | Bond Carrying Value |
| 8 | Periods | (10% × $100,000) | (A) – (C) | ($2,000 ÷ 5) | (D) – (C) | ($100,000 + D) |
| 9 | Issue date | | | | $2,000 | $102,000 |
| 10 | 1 | $10,000 | $ 9,600 | $ 400 | 1,600 | 101,600 |
| 11 | 2 | 10,000 | 9,600 | 400 | 1,200 | 101,200 |
| 12 | 3 | 10,000 | 9,600 | 400 | 800 | 100,800 |
| 13 | 4 | 10,000 | 9,600 | 400 | 400 | 100,400 |
| 14 | 5 | 10,000 | 9,600 | 400 | 0 | 100,000 |
| 15 | | $50,000 | $48,000 | $2,000 | | |
| 16 | | | | | | |
| 17 | Column **(A)** remains constant because the face value of the bonds ($100,000) is multiplied by the annual contractual interest rate (10%) each period. | | | | | |
| 18 | Column **(B)** is computed as the interest paid (Column A) less the premium amortization (Column C). | | | | | |
| 19 | Column **(C)** indicates the premium amortization each period. | | | | | |
| 20 | Column **(D)** decreases each period by the same amount until it reaches zero at maturity. | | | | | |
| 21 | Column **(E)** decreases each period by the amount of premium amortization until it equals the face value at maturity. | | | | | |

---

## Appendix 10B    **Effective-Interest Amortization**

---

### LEARNING OBJECTIVE *7

Apply the effective-interest method of amortizing bond discount and bond premium.

---

To follow the expense recognition principle, companies allocate bond discount and bond premium to expense in each period in which the bonds are outstanding. However, to completely comply with the expense recognition principle, interest expense **as a percentage of carrying value** should not change over the life of the bonds.

This percentage, referred to as the **effective-interest rate**, is established when the bonds are issued and remains constant in each interest period. Unlike the straight-line method, the effective-interest method of amortization accomplishes this result.

Under the **effective-interest method of amortization**, the amortization of bond discount or bond premium results in periodic interest expense equal to a constant percentage of the carrying value of the bonds. The effective-interest method results in **varying amounts** of amortization and interest expense per period but a **constant percentage rate**. In contrast, the straight-line method results in constant amounts of amortization and interest expense per period but a varying percentage rate.

Companies follow three steps under the effective-interest method:

1. Compute the **bond interest expense** by multiplying the carrying value of the bonds at the beginning of the interest period by the effective-interest rate.

2. Compute the **bond interest paid** (or accrued) by multiplying the face value of the bonds by the contractual interest rate.

3. Compute the **amortization amount** by determining the difference between the amounts computed in Steps 1 and 2.

Illustration 10B.1 depicts these steps.

Computation of amortization using effective-interest method

| (1) Bond Interest Expense | (2) Bond Interest Paid | (3) |
|---|---|---|
| $\begin{bmatrix} \text{Carrying Value} \\ \text{of Bonds at} \\ \text{Beginning of} \\ \text{Period} \end{bmatrix} \times \begin{matrix} \text{Effective-} \\ \text{Interest} \\ \text{Rate} \end{matrix}$ | $- \begin{bmatrix} \text{Face} \\ \text{Value of} \\ \text{Bond} \end{bmatrix} \times \begin{matrix} \text{Contractual} \\ \text{Interest} \\ \text{Rate} \end{matrix}$ | $= \begin{matrix} \textbf{Amortization} \\ \textbf{Amount} \end{matrix}$ |

**Both the straight-line and effective-interest methods of amortization result in the same total amount of interest expense over the term of the bonds**. Furthermore, interest expense each interest period is generally comparable in amount. However, **when the amounts are materially different**, **generally accepted accounting principles (GAAP) require use of the effective-interest method.**

**HELPFUL HINT**

Note that the amount of periodic interest expense increases over the life of the bonds when the effective-interest method is used for bonds issued at a discount. The reason is that a constant percentage is applied to an increasing bond carrying value to compute interest expense. The carrying value is increasing because of the amortization of the discount.

## Amortizing Bond Discount

In the Candlestick Inc. example, the company sold $100,000, five-year, 10% bonds on January 1, 2022, for $98,000. This resulted in a $2,000 bond discount ($100,000 − $98,000). This discount results in an effective-interest rate of approximately 10.5348%. (The effective-interest rate can be computed using the techniques shown in Appendix G.)

Preparing a bond discount amortization schedule as shown in **Illustration 10B.2** facilitates the recording of interest expense and the discount amortization. Note that interest expense as a percentage of carrying value remains constant at 10.5348% (see **Helpful Hint**).

**ILLUSTRATION 10B.2** Bond discount amortization schedule

Candlestick Inc.

| | Home | Insert | Page Layout | Formulas | Data | Review | View | | |

| | P18 | | | fx | | | | | |

| | A | B | C | D | E | F |
|---|---|---|---|---|---|---|
| 1 | | | Candlestick Inc. | | | |
| 2 | | | Bond Discount Amortization Schedule | | | |
| 3 | | | Effective-Interest Method—Annual Interest Payments | | | |
| 4 | | | 10% Bonds Issued at 10.5348% | | | |
| 5 | | | | | | |
| 6 | | (A) Interest to | (B) Interest Expense to Be Recorded | (C) Discount | (D) Unamortized | (E) Bond |
| 7 | Interest | Be Paid | (10.5348% × Preceding | Amortization | Discount | Carrying Value |
| 8 | Periods | (10% × $100,000) | Bond Carrying Value) | (B) – (A) | (D) – (C) | ($100,000 – D) |
| 9 | Issue date | | | | $2,000 | $ 98,000 |
| 10 | 1 | $10,000 | $10,324 (10.5348% × $98,000) | $ 324 | 1,676 | 98,324 |
| 11 | 2 | 10,000 | 10,358 (10.5348% × $98,324) | 358 | 1,318 | 98,682 |
| 12 | 3 | 10,000 | 10,396 (10.5348% × $98,682) | 396 | 922 | 99,078 |
| 13 | 4 | 10,000 | 10,438 (10.5348% × $99,078) | 438 | 484 | 99,516 |
| 14 | 5 | 10,000 | 10,484 (10.5348% × $99,516) | 484 | –0– | 100,000 |
| 15 | | $50,000 | $52,000 | $2,000 | | |
| 16 | | | | | | |
| 17 | Column **(A)** remains constant because the face value of the bonds ($100,000) is multiplied by the annual contractual interest rate (10%) each period. | | | | | |
| 18 | Column **(B)** is computed as the preceding bond carrying value times the annual effective-interest rate (10.5348%). | | | | | |
| 19 | Column **(C)** indicates the discount amortization each period. | | | | | |
| 20 | Column **(D)** decreases each period until it reaches zero at maturity. | | | | | |
| 21 | Column **(E)** increases each period until it equals face value at maturity. | | | | | |
| 22 | | | | | | |
| 23 | | | | | | |

For the first interest period, **Illustration 10B.3** shows the computations of bond interest expense and the bond discount amortization.

| | |
|---|---|
| Bond interest expense ($98,000 × 10.5348%) | $10,324 |
| Less: Bond interest paid ($100,000 × 10%) | 10,000 |
| **Bond discount amortization** | **$    324** |

**ILLUSTRATION 10B.3**

**Computation of bond discount amortization**

As a result, Candlestick records the accrual of interest and amortization of bond discount on December 31 as follows.

| Dec. 31 | Interest Expense | 10,324 | |
|---|---|---|---|
| | Discount on Bonds Payable | | 324 |
| | Interest Payable | | 10,000 |
| | (To record accrued interest and amortization of bond discount) | | |

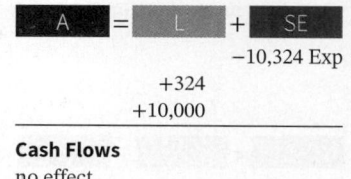

−10,324 Exp

+324
+10,000

**Cash Flows**
no effect

For the second interest period, bond interest expense will be $10,358 ($98,324 × 10.5348%), and the discount amortization will be $358. At December 31, Candlestick makes the following adjusting entry.

| Dec. 31 | Interest Expense | 10,358 | |
|---|---|---|---|
| | Discount on Bonds Payable | | 358 |
| | Interest Payable | | 10,000 |
| | (To record accrued interest and amortization of bond discount) | | |

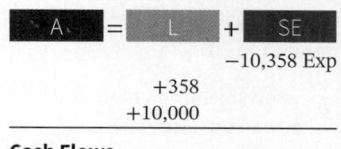

−10,358 Exp

+358
+10,000

**Cash Flows**
no effect

# Amortizing Bond Premium

Continuing our example, assume Candlestick Inc. sells the bonds described above for $102,000 rather than $98,000. This would result in a bond premium of $2,000 ($102,000 − $100,000). This premium results in an effective-interest rate of approximately 9.4794%. (The effective-interest rate can be solved for using the techniques shown in Appendix G.) **Illustration 10B.4** shows the bond premium amortization schedule.

**ILLUSTRATION 10B.4**    **Bond premium amortization schedule**

| | Interest Periods | (A) Interest to Be Paid (10% × $100,000) | (B) Interest Expense to Be Recorded (9.4794% × Preceding Bond Carrying Value) | (C) Premium Amortization (A) − (B) | (D) Unamortized Premium (D) − (C) | (E) Bond Carrying Value ($100,000 + D) |
|---|---|---|---|---|---|---|
| | | | **Candlestick Inc.** | | | |
| | | | **Bond Premium Amortization Schedule** | | | |
| | | | **Effective-Interest Method—Annual Interest Payments** | | | |
| | | | **10% Bonds Issued at 9.4794%** | | | |
| 9 | Issue date | | | | $2,000 | $102,000 |
| 10 | 1 | $10,000 | $ 9,669  (9.4794% × $102,000) | $  331 | 1,669 | 101,669 |
| 11 | 2 | 10,000 | 9,638  (9.4794% × $101,669) | 362 | 1,307 | 101,307 |
| 12 | 3 | 10,000 | 9,603  (9.4794% × $101,307) | 397 | 910 | 100,910 |
| 13 | 4 | 10,000 | 9,566  (9.4794% × $100,910) | 434 | 476 | 100,476 |
| 14 | 5 | 10,000 | 9,524 *  (9.4794% × $100,476) | 476* | –C– | 100,000 |
| 15 | | $50,000 | $48,000 | $2,000 | | |

| | |
|---|---|
| 17 | Column **(A)** remains constant because the face value of the bonds ($100,000) is multiplied by the contractual interest rate (10%) each period. |
| 18 | Column **(B)** is computed as the carrying value of the bonds times the annual effective-interest rate (9.4794%). |
| 19 | Column **(C)** indicates the premium amortization each period. |
| 20 | Column **(D)** decreases each period until it reaches zero at maturity. |
| 21 | Column **(E)** decreases each period until it equals face value at maturity. |
| 23 | *Rounded to eliminate remaining discount resulting from rounding the effective rate. |

For the first interest period, **Illustration 10B.5** shows the computations of bond interest expense and the bond premium amortization.

**ILLUSTRATION 10B.5**

**Computation of bond
premium amortization**

| | |
|---|---:|
| Bond interest paid ($100,000 × 10%) | $10,000 |
| Less: Bond interest expense ($102,000 × 9.4794%) | 9,669 |
| **Bond premium amortization** | **$ 331** |

The entry Candlestick makes on December 31 is:

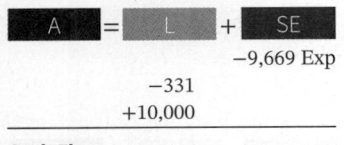

−9,669 Exp

−331
+10,000

**Cash Flows**
no effect

| Dec. 31 | Interest Expense | 9,669 | |
|---|---|---|---|
| | Premium on Bonds Payable | 331 | |
| | Interest Payable | | 10,000 |
| | (To record accrued interest and amortization of bond premium) | | |

For the second interest period, interest expense will be $9,638, and the premium amortization will be $362. Note that the amount of periodic interest expense decreases over the life of the bond when companies apply the effective-interest method to bonds issued at a premium. The reason is that a constant percentage is applied to a decreasing bond carrying value to compute interest expense. The carrying value is decreasing because of the amortization of the premium.

# Review and Practice

## Learning Objectives Review

### 1 Explain how to account for current liabilities.

A current liability is a debt that a company expects to pay within one year or the operating cycle, whichever is longer. The major types of current liabilities are notes payable, accounts payable, sales taxes payable, unearned revenues, and accrued liabilities such as taxes, salaries and wages, and interest payable.

When a promissory note is interest-bearing, the amount of assets received upon the issuance of the note is generally equal to the face value of the note. Interest expense accrues over the life of the note. At maturity, the amount paid equals the face value of the note plus accrued interest.

Companies record sales taxes payable at the time the related sales occur. The company serves as a collection agent for the taxing authority. Sales taxes are not an expense to the company. Companies initially record unearned revenues in an unearned revenue account. As a company recognizes revenue by satisfying its performance obligation, a transfer from unearned revenue to revenue occurs. Companies report the current maturities of long-term debt as a current liability in the balance sheet.

### 2 Describe the major characteristics of bonds.

Bonds can have many different features and may be secured, unsecured, convertible, or callable. The terms of the bond issue are set forth in a bond indenture, and a bond certificate provides the specific information about the bond itself.

### 3 Explain how to account for bond transactions.

When companies issue bonds, they debit Cash for the cash proceeds and credit Bonds Payable for the face value of the bonds. The account Premium on Bonds Payable shows a bond premium. Discount on Bonds Payable shows a bond discount.

When bondholders redeem bonds at maturity, the issuing company credits Cash and debits Bonds Payable for the face value of the bonds. When bonds are redeemed before maturity, the issuing company (a) eliminates the carrying value of the bonds at the redemption date, (b) records the cash paid, and (c) recognizes the gain or loss on redemption.

### 4 Explain how to account for long-term notes payable.

Long-term notes payable are similar to short-term notes payable except the term of the note payable exceeds one year. Each payment consists of (1) interest expense on the unpaid balance of the loan and (2) a reduction of loan principal. The interest expense decreases each period, while the portion applied to the loan principal increases.

### 5 Describe how liabilities are reported and analyzed.

Companies should report the nature and amount of each long-term debt in the balance sheet or in the notes accompanying the financial statements.

Companies may sell bonds to investors to raise long-term capital. Bonds offer the following advantages over common stock: (a) stockholder control is not affected, (b) tax savings result, and (c) earnings per share of common stock may be higher.

Stockholders and long-term creditors are interested in a company's long-run solvency. Debt to assets and times interest earned are two ratios that provide information about debt-paying ability and long-run solvency.

**\*6   Apply the straight-line method of amortizing bond discount and bond premium.**

The straight-line method of amortization results in a constant amount of amortization and interest expense per period.

**\*7   Apply the effective-interest method of amortizing bond discount and bond premium.**

The effective-interest method results in varying amounts of amortization and interest expense per period but a constant percentage rate of interest. When the difference between the straight-line and effective-interest method is material, GAAP requires use of the effective-interest method.

## Glossary Review

**Bond certificate**   A legal document that indicates the name of the issuer, the face value of the bonds, the contractual interest rate, and the maturity date of the bonds. (p. 10-9).

**Bond indenture**   A legal document that sets forth the terms of the bond issue. (p. 10-9).

**Bonds**   A form of interest-bearing notes payable issued by corporations, universities, and governmental entities. (p. 10-8).

**Callable bonds**   Bonds that are subject to redemption (buy back) at a stated dollar amount prior to maturity at the option of the issuer. (p. 10-9).

**Contractual interest rate**   Rate used to determine the amount of cash interest the borrower pays and the investor receives. (p. 10-9).

**Convertible bonds**   Bonds that permit bondholders to convert them into common stock at the bondholders' option. (p. 10-9).

**Current ratio**   A measure of a company's liquidity; computed as current assets divided by current liabilities (p. 10-22).

**Debenture bonds**   Bonds issued against the general credit of the borrower. Also called unsecured bonds. (p. 10-9).

**Debt to assets ratio**   A solvency measure that indicates the percentage of total assets provided by creditors; computed as total liabilities divided by total assets. (p. 10-23).

**Discount (on a bond)**   The difference between the face value of a bond and its selling price, when the bond is sold for less than its face value. (p. 10-13).

**\*Effective-interest method of amortization**   A method of amortizing bond discount or bond premium that results in periodic interest expense equal to a constant percentage of the carrying value of the bonds. (p. 10-27).

**\*Effective-interest rate**   Rate established when bonds are issued that maintains a constant value for interest expense as a percentage of bond carrying value in each interest period. (p. 10-27).

**Face value**   Amount of principal due at the maturity date of the bond. (p. 10-9).

**Long-term liabilities**   Obligations expected to be paid more than one year in the future. (p. 10-3).

**Market interest rate**   The rate investors demand for loaning funds to the corporation. (p. 10-11).

**Maturity date**   The date on which the final payment on the bond is due from the bond issuer to the investor. (p. 10-9).

**Mortgage bond**   A bond secured by real estate. (p. 10-9).

**Mortgage notes payable**   A long-term note secured by a mortgage that pledges title to specific assets as security for a loan. (p. 10-18).

**Notes payable**   Obligations in the form of written notes. (p. 10-3).

**Premium (on a bond)**   The difference between the selling price and the face value of a bond, when the bond is sold for more than its face value. (p. 10-13).

**Secured bonds**   Bonds that have specific assets of the issuer pledged as collateral. (p. 10-9).

**Sinking fund bonds**   Bonds secured by specific assets set aside to redeem them. (p. 10-9).

**\*Straight-line method of amortization**   A method of amortizing bond discount or bond premium that allocates the same amount to interest expense in each interest period. (p. 10-25).

**Times interest earned**   A solvency measure that indicates a company's ability to meet interest payments; computed by dividing the sum of net income, interest expense, and income tax expense by interest expense. (p. 10-23).

**Time value of money**   The relationship between time and money. A dollar received today is worth more than a dollar promised at some time in the future. (p. 10-10).

**Unsecured bonds**   Bonds issued against the general credit of the borrower. Also called debenture bonds. (p. 10-9).

**Working capital**   A measure of a company's liquidity; computed as current assets minus current liabilities. (p. 10-22).

## Practice Multiple-Choice Questions

**1. (LO 1)** The time period for classifying a liability as current is one year or the operating cycle, whichever is:

    **a.** longer.    **c.** probable.

    **b.** shorter.    **d.** possible.

**2. (LO 1)** To be classified as a current liability, a debt must be expected to be paid within:

    **a.** one year.

    **b.** the operating cycle.

    **c.** 2 years.

    **d.** one year or the operating cycle, whichever is longer.

**3. (LO 1)** Ottman Company borrows $88,500 on September 1, 2022, from Sandwich State Bank by signing an $88,500, 12%, one-year note, interest to be paid at maturity. What is the interest at December 31, 2022?

    **a.** $2,655.    **c.** $4,425.

    **b.** $3,540.    **d.** $10,620.

**4. (LO 1)** JD Company borrowed $70,000 on December 1 on a 6-month, 12% note, interest to be paid at maturity. At December 31:

    **a.** neither the note payable nor the interest payable is a current liability.

    **b.** the note payable is a current liability but the interest payable is not.

    **c.** the interest payable is a current liability but the note payable is not.

    **d.** both the note payable and the interest payable are current liabilities.

**5. (LO 1)** Alexis Company has total proceeds from sales of $4,515. If the proceeds include sales taxes of 5%, the amount to be credited to Sales Revenue is:

    **a.** $4,000.    **c.** $4,289.25.

    **b.** $4,300.    **d.** No correct answer given.

**6. (LO 1)** No Fault Insurance Company collected a premium of $18,000 for a 1-year insurance policy on April 1, 2022. What amount should No Fault report as a current liability for Unearned Service Revenue at December 31, 2022?

    **a.** $0.    **c.** $13,500.

    **b.** $4,500.    **d.** $18,000.

**7. (LO 1)** Employer payroll taxes do **not** include:

    **a.** federal unemployment taxes.

    **b.** state unemployment taxes.

    **c.** federal income taxes.

    **d.** FICA taxes.

**8. (LO 1)** When recording payroll:

    **a.** gross earnings are recorded as salaries and wages payable.

    **b.** net pay is recorded as salaries and wages expense.

    **c.** payroll deductions are recorded as liabilities.

    **d.** More than one of the answers is correct.

**9. (LO 2)** The term used for bonds that are unsecured is:

    **a.** callable bonds.    **c.** debenture bonds.

    **b.** U.S. Treasury bonds.    **d.** convertible bonds.

**10. (LO 3)** Karson Inc. issues 10-year bonds with a face value of $200,000. If the bonds are issued at a premium, this indicates that:

    **a.** the contractual interest rate exceeds the market interest rate.

    **b.** the market interest rate exceeds the contractual interest rate.

    **c.** the contractual interest rate and the market interest rate are the same.

    **d.** no relationship exists between the two rates.

**11. (LO 3)** On January 1, 2022, Kelly Corp. issues $200,000, 5-year, 7% bonds at face value. The entry to record the issuance of the bonds would include a:

    **a.** debit to Cash for $14,000.

    **b.** debit to Bonds Payable for $200,000.

    **c.** credit to Bonds Payable for $200,000.

    **d.** credit to Interest Expense of $14,000.

**12. (LO 3)** Prescher Corporation issued bonds that pay interest every July 1 and January 1. The entry to accrue bond interest at December 31 includes a:

    **a.** debit to Interest Payable.

    **b.** credit to Cash.

    **c.** credit to Interest Expense.

    **d.** credit to Interest Payable.

**13. (LO 3)** Goethe Corporation redeems its $100,000 face value bonds at 105 on January 1, following the payment of annual interest. The carrying value of the bonds at the redemption date is $103,745. The entry to record the redemption will include a:

    **a.** credit of $3,745 to Loss on Bond Redemption.

    **b.** debit of $3,745 to Premium on Bonds Payable.

    **c.** credit of $1,255 to Gain on Bond Redemption.

    **d.** debit of $5,000 to Premium on Bonds Payable.

**14. (LO 4)** Andrews Inc. issues a $497,000, 10%, 3-year mortgage note on January 1. The note will be paid in three annual installments of $200,000, each payable at the end of the year. What is the amount of interest expense that should be recognized by Andrews Inc. in the second year?

    **a.** $16,567.    **c.** $34,670.

    **b.** $49,700.    **d.** $346,700.

**15. (LO 4)** Howard Corporation issued a 20-year mortgage note payable on January 1, 2022. At December 31, 2022, the unpaid principal balance will be reported as:

    **a.** a current liability.

    **b.** a long-term liability.

    **c.** part current and part long-term liability.

    **d.** interest payable.

**16. (LO 5)** For 2022, Corn Flake Corporation reported net income of $300,000. Interest expense was $40,000 and income taxes were $100,000. The times interest earned was:

   **a.** 3 times.   **c.** 7.5 times.

   **b.** 4.4 times.   **d.** 11 times.

**\*17. (LO 6)** On December 31, 2022, Hurley Corporation issues $500,000, 5-year, 12% bonds at 96 with interest payable each December 31. The entry on December 31, 2023, to record payment of bond interest and the amortization of bond discount using the straight-line method will include a:

   **a.** debit to Interest Expense $30,000.

   **b.** debit to Interest Expense $60,000.

   **c.** credit to Discount on Bonds Payable $4,000.

   **d.** credit to Discount on Bonds Payable $2,000.

**\*18. (LO 6)** On December 31, 2022, Hurley Corporation issues $500,000, 5-year, 12% bonds at 96 with interest payable each December 31. What is the carrying value of the bonds at the end of the third interest period using straight-line amortization?

   **a.** $492,000.   **c.** $486,000.

   **b.** $488,000.   **d.** $464,000.

**\*19. (LO 7)** On January 1, Holly Ester Inc. issued $1,000,000, 9% bonds for $938,554. The market rate of interest for these bonds is 10%. Interest is payable annually on December 31. Holly Ester uses the effective-interest method of amortizing bond discount. At the end of the first year, Holly Ester should report unamortized bond discount of:

   **a.** $54,900.

   **b.** $57,591.

   **c.** $51,610.

   **d.** $51,000.

**\*20. (LO 7)** Dias Corporation issued $1,000,000, 14%, 5-year bonds with interest payable annually on December 31. The bonds sold for $1,072,096. The market rate of interest for these bonds was 12%. On the first interest date, using the effective-interest method, the debit entry to Interest Expense is for:

   **a.** $120,000.

   **b.** $125,581.

   **c.** $128,652.

   **d.** $140,000.

## Solutions

**1. a.** The time period for classifying a liability as current is one year or the operating cycle, whichever is longer, not (b) shorter, (c) probable, or (d) possible.

**2. d.** To be classified as a current liability, a debt must be expected to be paid within one year or the operating cycle. Choices (a) and (b) are both correct, but (d) is the better answer. Choice (c) is incorrect.

**3. b.** Accrued interest at 12/31/22 is computed as the face value ($88,500) times the interest rate (12%) times the portion of the year the debt was outstanding (4 months out of 12), or $3,540 ($88,500 × 12% × $\frac{4}{12}$), not (a) $2,655, (c) $4,425, or (d) $10,620.

**4. d.** A current liability is a debt the company reasonably expects to pay (1) from existing current assets or through the creation of other current liabilities, and (2) within the next year or the operating cycle, whichever is longer. Since both the interest payable and the note payable are expected to be paid within one year, they both will be considered current liabilities. The other choices are therefore incorrect.

**5. b.** Dividing the total proceeds ($4,515) by one plus the sales tax rate (1.05) will result in the amount of sales to be credited to the Sales Revenue account of $4,300 ($4,515 ÷ 1.05). The other choices are therefore incorrect.

**6. b.** The monthly premium is $1,500 ($18,000 ÷ 12). Because No Fault has recognized 9 months of insurance revenue (April 1–December 31), 3 months' insurance premium is still unearned. The amount that No Fault should report as Unearned Service Revenue is therefore $4,500 (3 months × $1,500), not (a) $0, (c) $13,500, or (d) $18,000.

**7. c.** Federal income taxes are an employee payroll deduction, not an employer payroll tax. The employer is merely a collection agent. The other choices are all included in employer payroll taxes.

**8. c.** Payroll deductions are recorded as liabilities. The other choices are incorrect because (a) gross earnings are recorded as salaries and wages expense, and (b) net pay is recorded as salaries and wages payable. Choice (d) is wrong as there is only one correct answer.

**9. c.** Debenture bonds are not secured by any collateral. The other choices are incorrect because (a) callable bonds can be paid off or retired by the issuer before they reach their maturity date, (b) U.S. Treasury bonds are secured by the federal government, and (d) convertible bonds permit bondholders to convert them into common stock at the bondholders' option.

**10. a.** When bonds are issued at a premium, this indicates that the contractual interest rate is higher than the market interest rate. The other choices are incorrect because (b) when the market interest rate exceeds the contractual interest rate, bonds are sold at a discount; (c) when the contractual interest rate and the market interest rate are the same, bonds will be issued at par; and (d) the relationship between the market rate of interest and the contractual rate of interest determines whether bonds are issued at par, a discount, or a premium.

**11. c.** The issuance entry for the bonds includes a debit to Cash for $200,000 and a credit to Bonds Payable for $200,000. The other choices are therefore incorrect.

**12. d.** Since the interest has not been paid, it must be accrued as an increase in expenses and liabilities. The entry would be a debit to Interest Expense and a credit to Interest Payable. The other choices are incorrect because (a) an interest accrual will increase, not decrease, Interest Payable; (b) interest accruals do not affect Cash; and (c) an interest accrual will increase, not decrease, Interest Expense.

**13. b.** The entry to record the retirement of bonds will include a debit to Bonds Payable of $100,000, a debit to Premium on Bonds Payable of $3,745 ($103,745 − $100,000), a credit to Cash of $105,000 ($100,000 × 1.05), and a debit to Loss on Bond Redemption of $1,255 ($105,000 − $103,745). The other choices are therefore incorrect.

**14. c.** In the first year, Andrews will recognize $49,700 of interest expense ($497,000 × 10%). After the first payment is made, the amount remaining on the note will be $346,700 [$497,000 principal − ($200,000 payment − $49,700 interest)]. The remaining balance ($346,700) is multiplied by the interest rate (10%) to compute the interest expense to be recognized for the second year, $34,670 ($346,700 × 10%), not (a) $16,567, (b) $49,700, or (d) $346,700.

**15. c.** Howard Corporation reports the reduction in principal for the next year as a current liability, and it classifies the remaining unpaid principal balance as a long-term liability. The other choices are therefore incorrect.

**16. d.** Times interest earned = Net income + Interest expense + Income tax expense ($300,000 + $40,000 + $100,000 = $440,000) ÷ Interest expense ($40,000), which equals 11 times, not (a) 3, (b) 4.4, or (c) 7.5 times.

**\*17. c.** [$500,000 − (96% × $500,000)] = $20,000; $20,000 ÷ 5 = $4,000 of discount to amortize annually. As a result, the entry would involve a credit to Discount on Bonds Payable $4,000. The other choices are therefore incorrect.

**\*18. a.** The carrying value of bonds increases by the amount of the periodic discount amortization. Discount amortization using the straight-line method is $4,000 each period. Total discount amortization for three periods is $12,000 ($4,000 × 3 periods) which is added to the initial carrying value ($480,000) to arrive at $492,000, the carrying value at the end of the third interest period, not (b) $488,000, (c) $486,000, or (d) $464,000.

**\*19. b.** The beginning balance of unamortized bond discount is $61,446 ($1,000,000 − $938,554). The discount amortization is $3,855, the difference between the cash interest payment of $90,000 ($1,000,000 × 9%) and the interest expense recorded of $93,855 ($938,554 × 10%). This discount amortization ($3,855) is then subtracted from the beginning balance of unamortized discount ($61,446) to arrive at a balance of $57,591 at the end of the first year, not (a) $54,900, (c) $51,610, or (d) $51,000.

**\*20. c.** The debit to Interest Expense = $1,072,096 (initial carrying value of bond) × 12% (market rate) = $128,652, not (a) $120,000, (b) $125,581, or (d) $140,000.

## Practice Brief Exercises

*Compute and record sales taxes payable.*

**1. (LO 1)** Amy Pond Discounts does not segregate sales and sales taxes at the time of sale. The cash receipts for March 17 total $19,928. All sales are subject to a 6% sales tax. Compute sales taxes payable and make the entry to record sales taxes payable and sales revenue.

### Solution

1. Sales taxes payable:
   Sales = $18,800 ($19,928 ÷ 1.06)
   Sales taxes payable = $1,128 ($18,800 × 6%)

| | | | |
|---|---|---|---|
| Mar. 17 | Cash | 19,928 | |
| | Sales Revenue | | 18,800 |
| | Sales Taxes Payable | | 1,128 |

*Compute gross earnings and net pay.*

**2. (LO 2)** Ben Borke's regular hourly wage rate is $20, and he receives an hourly rate of $30 for work in excess of 40 hours. During a January pay period, Ben works 46 hours. Ben's federal income tax withholding is $123, he has no voluntary deductions, and the FICA tax rate is 7.65%. There are no state income taxes. Compute Ben's gross earnings and net pay for the pay period.

### Solution

2. Gross earnings:

| | | |
|---|---|---|
| Regular pay (40 hours × $20) | | $800.00 |
| Overtime pay (6 hours × $30) | | 180.00 |
| Gross earnings | | $980.00 |
| Less: FICA taxes withheld ($980 × 7.65%) | $ 74.97 | |
| Federal income taxes withheld | 123.00 | 197.97 |
| Net pay | | $782.03 |

**3. (LO 3)** Kahnle Corporation issued 3,000, 7%, 5-year, $1,000 bonds dated January 1, 2022, at 100. Interest is paid each January 1. (a) Prepare the journal entry to record the sale of these bonds on January 1, 2022. (b) Prepare the adjusting journal entry on December 31, 2022, to record interest expense. (c) Prepare the journal entry on January 1, 2023, to record interest paid.

*Prepare entries for bonds issued at face value.*

**Solution**

**3. a.**  2022
Jan. 1

| | | |
|---|---|---|
| Cash | 3,000,000 | |
|     Bonds Payable (3,000 × $1,000) | | 3,000,000 |

**b.**  2022
Dec. 31

| | | |
|---|---|---|
| Interest Expense | 210,000 | |
|     Interest Payable ($3,000,000 × 7%) | | 210,000 |

**c.**  2023
Jan. 1

| | | |
|---|---|---|
| Interest Payable | 210,000 | |
|     Cash ($3,000,000 × 7%) | | 210,000 |

**4. (LO 4)** Tyler-Danish Inc. issues a $600,000, 10%, 10-year mortgage note on December 31, 2022, to obtain financing for a new building. The terms provide for annual installment payments of $97,647. Prepare the entry to record the mortgage loan on December 31, 2022, and the first installment payment on December 31, 2023.

*Prepare entries for long-term notes payable.*

**Solution**

**4.**

| Annual Interest Period | (A) Cash Payment | (B) Interest Expense (D) × 10% | (C) Reduction of Principal (A) − (B) | (D) Principal Balance (D) − (C) |
|---|---|---|---|---|
| Issue Date | | | | $600,000 |
| 1 | $97,647 | $60,000 | $37,647 | 562,353 |

2022
Dec. 31

| | | |
|---|---|---|
| Cash | 600,000 | |
|     Mortgage Payable | | 600,000 |

2023
Dec. 31

| | | |
|---|---|---|
| Interest Expense | 60,000 | |
| Mortgage Payable | 37,647 | |
|     Cash | | 97,647 |

**5. (LO 5)** The following are liabilities for Rymer Company at December 31, 2022. Prepare the long-term liabilities section of the balance sheet for Rymer Company.

*Prepare statement presentation of long-term liabilities.*

| | |
|---|---|
| Bonds payable, due 2024 | $700,000 |
| Accounts payable | 100,000 |
| Lease liability, due after 2023 | 120,000 |
| Notes payable, due 2027 | 110,000 |
| Premium on bonds payable | 40,000 |

**Solution**

**5.** Long-term liabilities*

| | | |
|---|---|---|
| Bonds payable, due 2024 | $700,000 | |
| Plus: Premium on bonds payable | 40,000 | $740,000 |
| Notes payable, due 2027 | | 110,000 |
| Lease liability | | 120,000 |
|     Total long-term liabilities | | $970,000 |

*Accounts Payable is a current liability.

# Practice Exercises

*Prepare entries for interest-bearing notes.*

**1. (LO 1)** On June 1, JetSet Company borrows $150,000 from First Bank on a 6-month, $150,000, 8% note. Interest is paid at maturity.

**Instructions**

a. Prepare the entry on June 1.

b. Prepare the adjusting entry on June 30.

c. Prepare the entry at maturity (December 1), assuming monthly adjusting entries have been made through November 30.

d. What was the total financing cost (interest expense)?

**Solution**

| | | | | |
|---|---|---|---|---|
| **1. a.** | June 1 | Cash | 150,000 | |
| | | Notes Payable | | 150,000 |
| **b.** | June 30 | Interest Expense | 1,000 | |
| | | Interest Payable | | |
| | | ($150,000 \times 8\% \times \frac{1}{12}$) | | 1,000 |
| **c.** | Dec. 1 | Notes Payable | 150,000 | |
| | | Interest Payable | | |
| | | ($150,000 \times 8\% \times \frac{6}{12}$) | 6,000 | |
| | | Cash | | 156,000 |

d. $6,000

*Prepare entries for bonds issued at face value.*

**2. (LO 3)** Global Airlines Company issued $900,000 of 8%, 10-year bonds on January 1, 2022, at face value. Interest is payable annually each January 1.

**Instructions**

Prepare the journal entries to record the following events.

a. The issuance of the bonds.

b. The accrual of interest on December 31.

c. The payment of interest on January 1, 2023.

d. The redemption of bonds at maturity, assuming interest for the last interest period has been paid and recorded.

**Solution**

| | | | | |
|---|---|---|---|---|
| **2. a.** | 2022 | | | |
| | Jan. 1 | Cash | 900,000 | |
| | | Bonds Payable | | 900,000 |
| **b.** | 2022 | | | |
| | Dec. 31 | Interest Expense | 72,000 | |
| | | Interest Payable ($900,000 \times 8\%$) | | 72,000 |
| **c.** | 2023 | | | |
| | Jan. 1 | Interest Payable | 72,000 | |
| | | Cash | | 72,000 |
| **d.** | 2032 | | | |
| | Jan. 1 | Bonds Payable | 900,000 | |
| | | Cash | | 900,000 |

*Prepare entries to record mortgage note and installment payments.*

**3. (LO 4)** Trawler Company borrowed $500,000 on December 31, 2022, by issuing a $500,000, 7% mortgage note payable. The terms call for annual installment payments of $80,000 each December 31.

**Instructions**

a. Prepare the journal entries to record the mortgage loan and the first two installment payments.

b. Indicate the amount of mortgage note payable to be reported as a current liability and as a long-term liability at December 31, 2023.

### Solution

**3. a.** 2022

| | | | |
|---|---|---|---|
| Dec. 31 | Cash | 500,000 | |
| | Mortgage Payable | | 500,000 |

2023

| | | | |
|---|---|---|---|
| Dec. 31 | Interest Expense ($500,000 × 7%) | 35,000 | |
| | Mortgage Payable | 45,000 | |
| | Cash | | 80,000 |

2024

| | | | |
|---|---|---|---|
| Dec. 31 | Interest Expense [($500,000 − $45,000) × 7%] | 31,850 | |
| | Mortgage Payable | 48,150 | |
| | Cash | | 80,000 |

**b.** Current: $48,150

Long-term: $406,850 ($500,000 − S45,000 − $48,150)

## Practice Problem

**(LO 3, 4)** Snyder Software Inc. has successfully developed a new spreadsheet software application. To produce and market the application, the company needed $1.9 million of additional financing. On January 1, 2022, Snyder borrowed money as follows.

*Prepare entries to record issuance of bonds and long-term notes, interest accrued, and bond redemption.*

1. Snyder issued $1 million, 10%, 10-year bonds at face value. Interest is payable each January 1.
2. Snyder also issued a $400,000, 6%, 15-year mortgage payable. The terms provide for annual installment payments of $41,185 on December 31.

### Instructions

1. For the 10-year, 10% bonds:

    a. Journalize the issuance of the bonds on January 1, 2022.

    b. Prepare the journal entry for interest expense in 2022.

    c. Prepare the entry for the redemption of the bonds at 101 on January 1, 2025, after paying the interest due on this date.

2. For the mortgage payable:

    a. Prepare the entry for the issuance of the note on January 1, 2022.

    b. Prepare a payment schedule for the first four installment payments.

    c. Indicate the current and noncurrent amounts for the mortgage payable at December 31, 2022.

### Solution

**1. a.** 2022

| | | | |
|---|---|---|---|
| Jan. 1 | Cash | 1,000,000 | |
| | Bonds Payable | | 1,000,000 |
| | (To record issuance of bonds) | | |

**b.** 2022

| | | | |
|---|---|---|---|
| Dec. 31 | Interest Expense | 100,000 | |
| | Interest Payable ($1,000,000 × 10%) | | 100,000 |
| | (To record accrual of annual interest) | | |

**c.** 2025

| | | | |
|---|---|---|---|
| Jan. 1 | Bonds Payable | 1,000,000 | |
| | Loss on Bond Redemption | 10,000* | |
| | Cash | | 1,010,000 |
| | (To record redemption of bonds at 101) | | |

*$1,010,000 − $1,000,000

**2. a.** 2022

| | | | | |
|---|---|---|---|---|
| Jan. 1 | Cash | | 400,000 | |
| | Mortgage Payable | | | 400,000 |
| | (To record issuance of mortgage payable) | | | |

**b.**

| Interest Period | Cash Payment | Interest Expense | Reduction of Principal | Principal Balance |
|---|---|---|---|---|
| Issue date | | | | $400,000 |
| 1 | $41,185 | $24,000 | $17,185 | 382,815 |
| 2 | 41,185 | 22,969 | 18,216 | 364,599 |
| 3 | 41,185 | 21,876 | 19,309 | 345,290 |
| 4 | 41,185 | 20,717 | 20,468 | 324,822 |

**c.** Current liability: $18,216
Long-term liability: $364,599

---

Brief Exercises, DO IT! Exercises, Exercises, Problems, Data Analytics Activities, and many additional resources are available for practice in WileyPLUS.

---

*Note:* All asterisked Questions, Exercises, and Problems relate to material in the appendices to the chapter.

---

## Questions

**1.** Jenny Perez believes a current liability is a debt that can be expected to be paid in one year. Is Jenny correct? Explain.

**2.** Rayborn Company obtains $20,000 in cash by signing a 9%, 6-month, $20,000 note payable to First Bank on July 1. Rayborn's fiscal year ends on September 30. What information should be reported for the note payable in the annual financial statements?

**3. a.** Your roommate says, "Sales taxes are reported as an expense in the income statement." Do you agree? Explain.

**b.** Leiana's Cafe has cash proceeds from sales of $8,550. This amount includes $550 of sales taxes. Give the entry to record the proceeds.

**4.** Carolina University sold 9,000 season football tickets at $100 each for its five-game home schedule. What entries should be made (a) when the tickets are sold and (b) after each game?

**5.** Identify three taxes commonly withheld by the employer from an employee's gross pay.

**6.** (a) What are long-term liabilities? Give three examples. (b) What is a bond?

**7.** Contrast the following types of bonds: (a) secured and unsecured, and (b) convertible and callable.

**8.** The following terms are important in issuing bonds: (a) face value, (b) contractual interest rate, (c) bond indenture, and (d) bond certificate. Explain each of these terms.

**9.** Describe the two major obligations related to bonds.

**10.** Assume that Acorn Inc. sold bonds with a face value of $100,000 for $104,000. Was the market interest rate equal to, less than, or greater than the bonds' contractual interest rate? Explain.

**11.** If a 6%, 10-year, $800,000 bond is issued at face value and interest is paid annually, what is the amount of the interest payment at the end of the first period?

**12.** If the Bonds Payable account has a balance of $700,000 and the Discount on Bonds Payable account has a balance of $36,000, what is the carrying value of the bonds?

**13.** Which accounts are debited and which are credited if a bond issue originally sold at a premium is redeemed before maturity at 97 immediately following the payment of interest?

**14.** Rattigan Corporation is considering issuing a convertible bond. What is a convertible bond? Discuss the advantages of a convertible bond from the standpoint of (a) the bondholders and (b) the issuing corporation.

**15.** Tim Rian, a friend of yours, has recently purchased a home for $125,000, paying $25,000 down and the remainder financed by a 6.5%, 20-year mortgage, payable at $745.57 per month. At the end of the first month, Tim receives a statement from the bank indicating that only $203.90 of principal was paid during the month. At this rate, he calculates that it will take over 40 years to pay off the mortgage. Is he right? Discuss.

**16.** (a) What is a lease agreement? (b) What are the two common types of leases?

17. Benedict Company entered into an agreement to lease 12 computers from Haley Electronics, Inc. The present value of the lease payments is $186,300. Assuming that this is a finance lease, what entry would Benedict Company make on the date of the lease agreement?

18. **a.** In general, what are the requirements for the financial statement presentation of long-term liabilities?

   **b.** What ratios may be computed to evaluate a company's liquidity and solvency?

19. Identify the liabilities classified by **Apple** as current in 2018.

20. (a) As a source of long-term financing, what are the major advantages of bonds over common stock? (b) What are the major disadvantages in using bonds for long-term financing?

21. What is liquidity? What are two measures of liquidity?

*22. Explain the straight-line method of amortizing discount and premium on bonds payable.

*23. Robbins Corporation issues $200,000 of 6%, 5-year bonds on January 1, 2022, at 103. Assuming that the straight-line method is used to amortize the premium, what is the total amount of interest expense for 2022?

*24. Honore Draper is discussing the advantages of the effective-interest method of bond amortization with her accounting staff. What points do you think Honore is making to argue her case?

*25. Dotsin Corporation issues $400,000 of 9%, 5-year bonds on January 1, 2022, at 104. If Dotsin uses the effective-interest method in amortizing the premium, will the annual interest expense increase or decrease over the life of the bonds? Explain.

# Brief Exercises

**BE10.1 (LO 1), C** Busch Company has these obligations at December 31: (a) a note payable for $100,000 due in 2 years with an annual interest rate of 6%, (b) interest payable of $6,000 on a long-term note payable due next year, and (c) accounts payable of $60,000. For each obligation, indicate whether it should be classified as a current liability, long-term liability, or both.

*Identify whether obligations are current liabilities.*

**BE10.2 (LO 1), AP** Hive Company borrows $90,000 on July 1 from the bank by signing a $90,000, 7%, 1-year note payable. Interest will be repaid at maturity. Prepare the journal entries to record (a) the proceeds of the note and (b) accrued interest at December 31, assuming adjusting entries are made only at the end of the year.

*Prepare entries for an interest-bearing note payable.*

**BE10.3 (LO 1), AP** Greenspan Supply does not segregate sales and sales taxes at the time of sale. The register total for March 16 is $10,388. All sales are subject to a 6% sales tax. Compute sales taxes payable and make the entry to record sales taxes payable and sales.

*Compute and record sales taxes payable.*

**BE10.4 (LO 1), AP** Bramble University sells 3,500 season basketball tickets at $80 each for its 10-game home schedule. Give the entry to record (a) the sale of the season tickets and (b) the revenue recognized after playing the first home game.

*Prepare entries for unearned revenues.*

**BE10.5 (LO 1), AP** Betsy Strand's regular hourly wage rate is $16, and she receives an hourly rate of $24 for work in excess of 40 hours. During a January pay period, Betsy works 47 hours. Betsy's federal income tax withholding is $95, and she has no voluntary deductions. Compute Betsy Strand's gross earnings and net pay for the pay period. Assume that the FICA tax rate is 7.65%.

*Compute gross earnings and net pay.*

**BE10.6 (LO 1), AP** Betsy Strand's regular hourly wage rate is $16, and she receives an hourly rate of $24 for work in excess of 40 hours. During a January pay period, Betsy works 47 hours. Betsy's federal income tax withholding is $95, and she has no voluntary deductions. Prepare the employer's journal entries to record (a) Betsy's pay for the period and (b) the payment of Betsy's wages. Use January 15 for the end of the pay period and the payment date. Assume that the FICA tax rate is 7.65%.

*Record a payroll and the payment of wages.*

**BE10.7 (LO 1), AP** Betsy Strand's regular hourly wage rate is $16, and she receives an hourly rate of $24 for work in excess of 40 hours. During a January pay period, Betsy works 47 hours. Betsy's federal income tax withholding is $95, and she has no voluntary deductions. Prepare the employer's journal entry to record payroll taxes for the period. Assume the FICA tax rate is 7.65%. Ignore unemployment taxes.

*Prepare entries for payroll taxes.*

**BE10.8 (LO 3), AP** Bridle Inc. issues $300,000, 10-year, 8% bonds at 98. Prepare the journal entry to record the sale of these bonds on March 1, 2022.

*Prepare entry for bonds issued.*

**BE10.9 (LO 3), AP** Ravine Company issues $400,000, 20-year, 7% bonds at 101. Prepare the journal entry to record the sale of these bonds on June 1, 2022.

*Prepare entry for bonds issued.*

**BE10.10 (LO 3), AP** Clooney Corporation issued 3,000 7%, 5-year, $1,000 bonds dated January 1, 2022, at face value. Interest is paid each January 1.

   **a.** Prepare the journal entry to record the sale of these bonds on January 1, 2022.

   **b.** Prepare the adjusting journal entry on December 31, 2022, to record interest expense.

   **c.** Prepare the journal entry on January 1, 2023, to record interest paid.

*Prepare journal entries for bonds issued at face value.*

*Prepare entries for bonds sold at a discount and a premium.*

**BE10.11 (LO 3), AP** Nasreen Company issues $2 million, 10-year, 8% bonds at 97, with interest payable each January 1.

    **a.** Prepare the journal entry to record the sale of these bonds on January 1, 2022.

    **b.** Assuming instead that the above bonds sold for 104, prepare the journal entry to record the sale of these bonds on January 1, 2022.

*Prepare entries for bonds issued.*

**BE10.12 (LO 3), AP** Frankum Company has issued three different bonds during 2022. Interest is payable annually on each of these bonds.

    **1.** On January 1, 2022, 1,000, 8%, 5-year, $1,000 bonds dated January 1, 2022, were issued at face value.

    **2.** On July 1, $900,000, 9%, 5-year bonds dated July 1, 2022, were issued at 102.

    **3.** On September 1, $400,000, 7%, 5-year bonds dated September 1, 2022, were issued at 98.

Prepare the journal entry to record each bond transaction at the date of issuance.

*Prepare entry for redemption of bonds.*

**BE10.13 (LO 3), AP** The balance sheet for Miley Consulting reports the following information on July 1, 2022.

| | | |
|---|---:|---:|
| Long-term liabilities | | |
| Bonds payable | $1,000,000 | |
| Less: Discount on bonds payable | 60,000 | $940,000 |

Miley decides to redeem these bonds at 101 after paying annual interest. Prepare the journal entry to record the redemption on July 1, 2022.

*Prepare entries for long-term notes payable.*

**BE10.14 (LO 4), AP** Jenseng Inc. issues an $800,000, 10%, 10-year mortgage note on December 31, 2022, to obtain financing for a new building. The terms provide for annual installment payments of $130,196. Prepare the entry to record the mortgage loan on December 31, 2022, and the first installment payment on December 31, 2023.

*Account for finance lease.*

**BE10.15 (LO 4), AP** Imhoff Company leases a new building from Noble Construction, Inc. The present value of the lease payments is $700,000. The lease is a finance lease. Prepare the journal entry that the lessee should make to record this transaction.

*Prepare statement presentation of long-term liabilities.*

**BE10.16 (LO 5), AP** Presented here are long-term liability items for Stevens Inc. at December 31, 2022. Prepare the long-term liabilities section of the balance sheet for Stevens Inc.

| | |
|---|---:|
| Bonds payable (due 2026) | $700,000 |
| Lease liability (due after 2023) | 70,000 |
| Notes payable (due 2024) | 80,000 |
| Discount on bonds payable | 28,000 |

*Compare bond versus stock financing.*

**BE10.17 (LO 5), AN** Moby Inc. is considering two alternatives to finance its construction of a new $2 million plant.

    **a.** Issuance of 200,000 shares of common stock at the market price of $10 per share.

    **b.** Issuance of $2 million, 8% bonds at face value.

Complete the following table, and indicate which alternative is preferable.

| | Issue Stock | Issue Bond |
|---|---:|---:|
| Income before interest and taxes | $700,000 | $700,000 |
| Interest expense from bonds | _____ | _____ |
| Income before income taxes | | |
| Income tax expense (30%) | _____ | _____ |
| Net income | $_____ | $_____ |
| Outstanding shares | _____ | 500,000 |
| Earnings per share | _____ | _____ |

*Prepare liabilities section of balance sheet.*

**BE10.18 (LO 5), AP** Presented here are liability items for O'Brian Inc. at December 31, 2022. Prepare the liabilities section of O'Brian's balance sheet.

| | | | |
|---|---:|---|---:|
| Accounts payable | $157,000 | FICA taxes payable | $ 7,800 |
| Notes payable | 20,000 | Interest payable | 40,000 |
| (due May 1, 2023) | | Notes payable (due 2024) | 80,000 |
| Bonds payable (due 2026) | 900,000 | Income taxes payable | 3,500 |
| Unearned rent revenue | 240,000 | Sales taxes payable | 1,700 |
| Discount on bonds payable | 41,000 | | |

**BE10.19 (LO 5), AN** Suppose the 2022 **adidas** financial statements contain the following selected data (in millions).

| | | | |
|---|---|---|---|
| Current assets | $4,485 | Interest expense | $169 |
| Total assets | 8,875 | Income tax expense | 113 |
| Current liabilities | 2,836 | Net income | 245 |
| Total liabilities | 5,099 | | |
| Cash | 775 | | |

Compute the following values and provide a brief interpretation of each.

   **a.** Working capital.                 **c.** Debt to assets ratio.

   **b.** Current ratio.                  **d.** Times interest earned.

**\*BE10.20 (LO 6), AP** Alpine Company issues $2 million, 10-year, 7% bonds at 99, with interest payable each December 31. The straight-line method is used to amortize bond discount.

   **a.** Prepare the journal entry to record the sale of these bonds on January 1, 2022

   **b.** Prepare the journal entry to record interest expense and bond discount amortization on December 31, 2022, assuming no previous accrual of interest.

**\*BE10.21 (LO 6), AP** Harvard Inc. issues $4 million, 5-year, 8% bonds at 102, with interest payable each January 1. The straight-line method is used to amortize bond premium.

   **a.** Prepare the journal entry to record the sale of these bonds on January 1, 2022.

   **b.** Prepare the journal entry to record interest expense and bond premium amortization on December 31, 2022, assuming no previous accrual of interest

**\*BE10.22 (LO 7), AP** **Writing** The following is the partial bond discount amortization schedule for Rohr Corp. Rohr uses the effective-interest method of amortization.

| Interest Periods | Interest to Be Paid | Interest Expense to Be Recorded | Discount Amortization | Unamortized Discount | Bond Carrying Value |
|---|---|---|---|---|---|
| Issue date | | | | $38,609 | $961,391 |
| 1 | $45,000 | $48,070 | $3,070 | 35,539 | 964,461 |
| 2 | 45,000 | 48,223 | 3,223 | 32,316 | 967,684 |

   **a.** Prepare the journal entry to record the payment of interest and the discount amortization at the end of period 1.

   **b.** Explain why interest expense is greater than interest paid.

   **c.** Explain why interest expense will increase each period.

# DO IT! Exercises

**DO IT! 10.1a (LO 1), AP** You and several classmates are studying for the next accounting exam. They ask you to answer the following questions.

1. If cash is borrowed on a $60,000, 9-month, 10% note on August 1, how much interest expense would be incurred by December 31?

2. The cash register total including sales taxes is $42,000, and the sales tax rate is 5%. What is the sales taxes payable?

3. If $42,000 is collected in advance on November 1 for 6-month magazine subscriptions, what amount of subscription revenue should be recognized on December 31?

**DO IT! 10.1b (LO 1), AP** During the month of February, Hennesey Corporation's employees earned wages of $74,000. Withholdings related to these wages were $5,661 for FICA, $7,100 for federal income tax, and $1,900 for state income tax. Costs incurred for unemployment taxes were $110 for federal and $160 for state.

   Prepare the February 28 journal entries for (a) salaries and wages expense and salaries and wages payable assuming that all February wages will be paid in March and (b) the company's payroll tax expense.

*Evaluate statements about bonds.*

**DO IT! 10.2 (LO 2), C** State whether each of the following statements is true or false. If false, indicate how to correct the statement.

_____ **1.** Mortgage bonds and sinking fund bonds are both examples of debenture bonds.

_____ **2.** Convertible bonds are also known as callable bonds.

_____ **3.** The market rate is the rate investors demand for loaning funds.

_____ **4.** Annual interest on bonds is equal to the face value times the stated rate.

_____ **5.** The present value of a bond is the value at which it should sell in the market.

*Prepare journal entry for bond issuance and show balance sheet presentation.*

**DO IT! 10.3a (LO 3), AP** Smiley Corporation issues $300,000 of bonds for $315,000. (a) Prepare the journal entry to record the issuance of the bonds, and (b) show how the bonds would be reported on the balance sheet at the date of issuance.

*Prepare entry for bond redemption.*

**DO IT! 10.3b (LO 3), AP** Farmland Corporation issued $400,000 of 10-year bonds at a discount. Prior to maturity, when the carrying value of the bonds was $388,000, the company redeemed the bonds at 99. Prepare the entry to record the redemption of the bonds.

*Prepare entries for mortgage note and installment payment on note.*

**DO IT! 10.4 (LO 4), AP** Detwiler Orchard issues a $700,000, 6%, 15-year mortgage note to obtain needed financing for a new lab. The terms call for annual payments of $72,074 each. Prepare the entries to record the mortgage loan and the first installment payment.

*Analyze liabilities.*

**DO IT! 10.5 (LO 5), AN** Grouper Company provides you with the following balance sheet information as of December 31, 2022.

| | | | | |
|---|---|---|---|---|
| Current assets | $11,500 | Current liabilities | | $12,000 |
| Long-term assets | 26,500 | Long-term liabilities | | 14,000 |
| Total assets | $38,000 | Stockholders' equity | | 12,000 |
| | | Total liabilities and stockholders' equity | | $38,000 |

In addition, Grouper reported net income for 2022 of $16,000, income tax expense of $3,200, and interest expense of $1,300.

**a.** Compute the current ratio and working capital for Grouper for 2022.

**b.** Assume that at the end of 2022, Grouper used $3,000 cash to pay off $3,000 of accounts payable. How would the current ratio and working capital have changed?

**c.** Compute the debt to assets ratio and the times interest earned ratio for Grouper for 2022. (Do not use the information from (b) to determine the solution.)

# Exercises

*Prepare entries for interest-bearing notes.*

**E10.1 (LO 1), AP** C.S. Lewis Company had the following transactions involving notes payable.

| | |
|---|---|
| July 1, 2022 | Borrows $50,000 from First National Bank by signing a 9-month, 8% note. |
| Nov. 1, 2022 | Borrows $60,000 from Lyon County State Bank by signing a 3-month, 6% note. |
| Dec. 31, 2022 | Prepares annual adjusting entries. |
| Feb. 1, 2023 | Pays principal and interest to Lyon County State Bank. |
| Apr. 1, 2023 | Pays principal and interest to First National Bank. |

### Instructions

Prepare journal entries for each of the transactions.

*Prepare entries for interest-bearing notes.*

**E10.2 (LO 1), AP** On June 1, Marchon Company Ltd. borrows $60,000 from Acme Bank on a 6-month, $60,000, 8% note. The note matures on December 1.

### Instructions

**a.** Prepare the entry on June 1.

**b.** Prepare the adjusting entry on June 30.

**c.** Prepare the entry at maturity (December 1), assuming monthly adjusting entries have been made through November 30.

**d.** What was the total financing cost (interest expense)?

**E10.3 (LO 1), AP** In performing accounting services for small businesses, you encounter the following situations pertaining to cash sales.

*Journalize sales and related taxes.*

1. Cerviq Company enters sales and sales taxes separately on its cash register. On April 10, the register totals are sales $22,000 and sales taxes $1,100.

2. Quartz Company does not segregate sales and sales taxes. Its register total for April 15 is $13,780, which includes a 6% sales tax.

**Instructions**

Prepare the entries to record the sales transactions and related taxes for (a) Cerviq Company and (b) Quartz Company.

**E10.4 (LO 1), AP** Season tickets for the Dingos are priced at $320 and include 16 home games. An equal amount of revenue is recognized after each game is played. When the season began, the amount credited to Unearned Ticket Revenue was $1,728,000. By the end of October, $1,188,000 of the Unearned Ticket Revenue had been recognized as revenue.

*Journalize unearned revenue transactions.*

**Instructions**

a. How many season tickets did the Dingos sell?

b. How many home games had the Dingos played by the end of October?

c. Prepare the entry for the initial recording of the Unearned Ticket Revenue.

d. Prepare the entry to recognize the revenue after the first home game had been played.

**E10.5 (LO 1), AP** Cassini Company Ltd. publishes a monthly sports magazine, *Fishing Preview*. Subscriptions to the magazine cost $28 per year. During November 2022, Cassini sells 6,300 subscriptions for cash, beginning with the December issue. Cassini prepares financial statements quarterly and recognizes subscription revenue at the end of the quarter. The company uses the accounts Unearned Subscription Revenue and Subscription Revenue. The company has a December 31 year-end.

*Journalize unearned subscription revenue.*

**Instructions**

a. Prepare the entry in November for the receipt of the subscriptions.

b. Prepare the adjusting entry at December 31, 2022, to record subscription revenue in December 2022.

c. Prepare the adjusting entry at March 31, 2023, to record subscription revenue in the first quarter of 2023.

**E10.6 (LO 1), AP** Dan Noll's gross earnings for the week were $1,780, his federal income tax withholding was $303, and his FICA total was $136. There were no state income taxes.

*Calculate and record net pay.*

**Instructions**

a. What was Noll's net pay for the week?

b. Journalize the entry for the recording of his pay in the general journal. (*Note:* Use Salaries and Wages Payable, not Cash.)

c. Record the issuing of the check for Noll's pay in the general journal.

**E10.7 (LO 1), AP** According to the accountant of Ulster Inc., its payroll taxes for the week were as follows: $137.68 for FICA taxes, $13.77 for federal unemployment taxes, and $92.93 for state unemployment taxes.

*Record accrual of payroll taxes.*

**Instructions**

Journalize the entry to record payroll taxes.

**E10.8 (LO 2), C** Nick Bosch has prepared the following list of statements about bonds.

*Evaluate statements about bonds.*

1. Bonds are a form of interest-bearing notes payable.

2. Secured bonds have specific assets of the issuer pledged as collateral for the bonds.

3. Secured bonds are also known as debenture bonds.

4. A conversion feature may be added to bonds to make them more attractive to bond buyers.

5. The rate used to determine the amount of cash interest the borrower pays is called the stated rate.

6. Bond prices are usually quoted as a percentage of the face value of the bond.

7. The present value of a bond is the value at which it should sell in the marketplace.

**Instructions**

Identify each statement as true or false. If false, indicate how to correct the statement.

*Prepare journal entries for issuance of bonds and payment and accrual of interest.*

**E10.9 (LO 3), AP** On August 1, 2022, Gonzaga Corporation issued $600,000, 7%, 10-year bonds at face value. Interest is payable annually on August 1. Gonzaga's year-end is December 31.

**Instructions**

Prepare journal entries to record the following events.

  **a.** The issuance of the bonds.

  **b.** The annual accrual of interest on December 31, 2022.

  **c.** The payment of interest on August 1, 2023.

*Prepare journal entries for issuance of bonds and payment and accrual of interest.*

**E10.10 (LO 3), AP** On January 1, Kirkland Company issued $300,000, 8%, 10-year bonds at face value. Kirkland's year-end is December 31. Interest is payable annually on January 1.

**Instructions**

Prepare journal entries to record the following events.

  **a.** The issuance of the bonds.

  **b.** The annual accrual of interest on December 31.

  **c.** The payment of interest on January 1.

*Prepare entries to record issuance of bonds at discount and premium.*

**E10.11 (LO 3), AP** Whitmore Company issued $500,000 of 5-year, 8% bonds at 97 on January 1, 2022. The bonds pay interest annually.

**Instructions**

  **a.** **1.** Prepare the journal entry to record the issuance of the bonds.

    **2.** Compute the total cost of borrowing for these bonds.

  **b.** Repeat the requirements from part (a), assuming the bonds were issued at 105.

*Prepare entries for bond interest and redemption.*

**E10.12 (LO 3), AP** The following information is taken from Ohlman Corp.'s balance sheet at December 31, 2021.

| | |
|---|---|
| Current liabilities | |
|   Interest payable | $ 112,000 |
| Long-term liabilities | |
|   Bonds payable, 7%, due January 1, 2024 | 1,600,000 |

Bond interest is payable annually on January 1. The bonds are callable on any interest date.

**Instructions**

  **a.** Journalize the payment of the bond interest on January 1, 2022.

  **b.** Assume that on January 1, 2022, after paying interest, Ohlman calls bonds having a face value of $600,000. The call price is 103. Record the redemption of the bonds.

  **c.** Prepare the entry to record the annual accrual of interest on December 31, 2022.

*Prepare journal entries for redemption of bonds.*

**E10.13 (LO 3), AP** The following situations are independent of each other.

**Instructions**

For each situation, prepare the appropriate journal entry for the redemption of the bonds.

  **a.** Mikhail Corporation redeemed $140,000 face value, 9% bonds on April 30, 2022, at 101. The carrying value of the bonds at the redemption date was $126,500. The bonds pay annual interest, and the interest payment due on April 30, 2022, has been made and recorded.

  **b.** Oldman, Inc., redeemed $170,000 face value, 12.5% bonds on June 30, 2022, at 98. The carrying value of the bonds at the redemption date was $184,000. The bonds pay annual interest, and the interest payment due on June 30, 2022, has been made and recorded.

*Prepare entries to record mortgage note and payments.*

**E10.14 (LO 4), AP** Yancey Co. receives $300,000 when it issues a $300,000, 10% mortgage note payable to finance the construction of a building at December 31, 2022. The terms provide for annual installment payments of $50,000 on December 31.

**Instructions**

Prepare the journal entries to record the mortgage loan and the first two payments.

*Prepare long-term liabilities section.*

**E10.15 (LO 5), AP** The adjusted trial balance for Karr Farm Corporation at the end of 2022 contained the following accounts.

| | |
|---|---:|
| Interest Payable | $   9,000 |
| Lease Liability, due after 2023 | 89,500 |
| Bonds Payable, due 2026 | 180,000 |
| Premium on Bonds Payable | 32,000 |

## Instructions

Prepare the long-term liabilities section of the balance sheet.

**E10.16 (LO 5), AP** Sanchez, Inc. reports the following liabilities (in thousands) on its December 31, 2022, balance sheet.

*Prepare liabilities section of balance sheet.*

| | | | |
|---|---:|---|---:|
| Accounts payable | $4,263.9 | Mortgage payable (due after 2023) | $6,746.7 |
| Unearned rent revenue | 1,058.1 | Notes payable (due in 2025) | 335.6 |
| Bonds payable | 1,961.2 | Salaries and wages payable | 858.1 |
| Current portion of | | Notes payable (due in 2023) | 2,563.6 |
| mortgage payable | 1,992.2 | Warranty liability—current | 1,417.3 |
| Income taxes payable | 265.2 | | |

## Instructions

a. Identify which of the above liabilities are likely current and which are likely long-term. List any items that do not fit in either category. Explain the reasoning for your selection.

b. Prepare the liabilities section of Sanchez's balance sheet as at December 31, 2022.

**E10.17 (LO 5), AN** Gilliland Airlines is considering two alternatives for the financing of a purchase of a fleet of airplanes. These two alternatives are:

*Compare two alternatives of financing—issuance of common stock vs. issuance of bonds.*

1. Issue 90,000 shares of common stock at $30 per share. (Cash dividends have not been paid nor is the payment of any contemplated.)

2. Issue 10%, 10-year bonds at face value for $2,700,000.

It is estimated that the company will generate $890,000 of income before interest and taxes as a result of this purchase. The company has an estimated tax rate of 30% and has 120,000 shares of common stock outstanding prior to the new financing.

## Instructions

Determine the effect on net income and earnings per share for these two methods of financing.

**E10.18 (LO 5), AN** Suppose the following financial data were reported by **3M Company** for 2021 and 2022 (dollars in millions).

*Calculate current ratio and working capital before and after paying accounts payable.*

**3M Company**
**Balance Sheets (partial)**

| | 2022 | 2021 |
|---|---:|---:|
| Current assets | | |
| Cash and cash equivalents | $  3,040 | $1,849 |
| Accounts receivable, net | 3,250 | 3,195 |
| Inventories | 2,639 | 3,013 |
| Other current assets | 1,866 | 1,541 |
| Total current assets | $10,795 | $9,598 |
| Current liabilities | $  4,897 | $5,839 |

## Instructions

a. Calculate the current ratio and working capital for 3M for 2021 and 2022.

b. Suppose that at the end of 2022, 3M management used $300 million cash to pay off $300 million of accounts payable. How would its current ratio and working capital have changed?

**E10.19 (LO 5), AN** Suppose **McDonald's** 2022 financial statements contain the following selected data (in millions).

*Calculate liquidity and solvency ratios; discuss impact of unrecorded obligations on liquidity and solvency.*

| | | | |
|---|---:|---|---:|
| Current assets | $ 3,416.3 | Interest expense | $  473.2 |
| Total assets | 30,224.9 | Income tax expense | 1,936.0 |
| Current liabilities | 2,938.7 | Net income | 4,551.0 |
| Total liabilities | 16,191.0 | | |

### Instructions

Compute the following values and provide a brief interpretation of each.

**a.** Working capital.   **c.** Debt to assets ratio.

**b.** Current ratio.   **d.** Times interest earned.

*Prepare journal entries to record issuance of bonds, payment of interest, amortization of premium using straight-line, and redemption at maturity.*

**\*E10.20 (LO 6), AP** Sehr Company issued $500,000, 6%, 30-year bonds on January 1, 2022, at 103. Interest is payable annually on January 1. Sehr uses straight-line amortization for bond premium or discount.

### Instructions

Prepare the journal entries to record the following events.

**a.** The issuance of the bonds.

**b.** The accrual of interest and the premium amortization on December 31, 2022.

**c.** The payment of interest on January 1, 2023.

**d.** The redemption of the bonds at maturity, assuming interest for the last interest period has been paid and recorded.

*Prepare journal entries to record issuance of bonds, payment of interest, amortization of discount using straight-line, and redemption at maturity.*

**\*E10.21 (LO 6), AP** Motley Company issued $300,000, 8%, 15-year bonds on December 31, 2021, for $288,000. Interest is payable annually on December 31. Motley uses the straight-line method to amortize bond premium or discount.

### Instructions

Prepare the journal entries to record the following events.

**a.** The issuance of the bonds.

**b.** The payment of interest and the discount amortization on December 31, 2022.

**c.** The redemption of the bonds at maturity, assuming interest for the last interest period has been paid and recorded.

*Prepare entries for issuance of bonds, payment of interest, and amortization of discount using effective-interest method.*

**\*E10.22 (LO 7), AP** Woode Corporation issued $400,000, 7%, 20-year bonds on January 1, 2022, for $360,727. This price resulted in an effective-interest rate of 8% on the bonds. Interest is payable annually on January 1. Woode uses the effective-interest method to amortize bond premium or discount.

### Instructions

Prepare the journal entries to record the following. (Round to the nearest dollar.)

**a.** The issuance of the bonds.

**b.** The accrual of interest and the discount amortization on December 31, 2022.

**c.** The payment of interest on January 1, 2023.

*Prepare entries for issuance of bonds, payment of interest, and amortization of premium using effective-interest method.*

**\*E10.23 (LO 7), AP** Hernandez Company issued $380,000, 7%, 10-year bonds on January 1, 2022, for $407,968. This price resulted in an effective-interest rate of 6% on the bonds. Interest is payable annually on January 1. Hernandez uses the effective-interest method to amortize bond premium or discount.

### Instructions

Prepare the journal entries to record the following. (Round to the nearest dollar.)

**a.** The issuance of the bonds.

**b.** The accrual of interest and the premium amortization on December 31, 2022.

**c.** The payment of interest on January 1, 2023.

## Problems

*Prepare current liability entries, adjusting entries, and current liabilities section.*

**P10.1 (LO 1, 5), AP** On January 1, 2022, the ledger of Romada Company contained these liability accounts.

| | |
|---|---|
| Accounts Payable | $42,500 |
| Sales Taxes Payable | 6,600 |
| Unearned Service Revenue | 19,000 |

During January, the following selected transactions occurred.

| | | |
|---|---|---|
| Jan. | 1 | Borrowed $18,000 in cash from Apex Bank on a 4-month, 5%, $18,000 note. Interest will be paid at maturity. |
| | 5 | Sold merchandise for cash totaling $6,254, which includes 6% sales taxes. |
| | 12 | Performed services for customers who had made advance payments of $10,000. (Credit Service Revenue.) |
| | 14 | Paid state treasurer's department for sales taxes collected in December 2021, $6,600. |
| | 20 | Sold 500 units of a new product on credit at $48 per unit, plus 6% sales tax. |

During January, the company's employees earned wages of $70,000. Withholdings related to these wages were $5,355 for FICA, $5,000 for federal income tax, and $1,500 for state income tax. The company owed no money related to these earnings for federal or state unemployment tax. Assume that wages earned during January will be paid during February. No entry had been recorded for wages or payroll tax expense as of January 31.

**Instructions**

a. Journalize the January transactions.

b. Journalize the adjusting entries at January 31 for the outstanding note payable and for salaries and wages expense and payroll tax expense.

c. Prepare the current liabilities section of the balance sheet at January 31, 2022. Assume no change in Accounts Payable.

*c. Tot. current liabilities $146,724*

**P10.2 (LO 1, 5), AP** The following are selected transactions of Blanco Company. Blanco prepares financial statements **quarterly**. Interest on all notes is paid at maturity.

*Journalize and post note transactions; show balance sheet presentation.*

| | | |
|---|---|---|
| Jan. | 2 | Purchased merchandise on account from Nunez Company, $30,000, terms 2/10, n/30. (Blanco uses the perpetual inventory system.) |
| Feb. | 1 | Issued a 9%, 2-month, $30,000 note to Nunez in payment of account. |
| Mar. | 31 | Accrued interest for 2 months on Nunez note. |
| Apr. | 1 | Paid face value and interest on Nunez note. |
| July | 1 | Purchased equipment from Marson Equipment, paying $11,000 in cash and signing a 10%, 3-month, $60,000 note. |
| Sept. | 30 | Accrued interest for 3 months on Marson note. |
| Oct. | 1 | Paid face value and interest on Marson note. |
| Dec. | 1 | Borrowed $24,000 from the Paola Bank by issuing a 3-month, 8% note with a face value of $24,000. |
| Dec. | 31 | Recognized interest expense for 1 month on Paola Bank note. |

**Instructions**

a. Prepare journal entries for the listed transactions and events.

b. Post to the accounts Notes Payable, Interest Payable, and Interest Expense.

c. Show the balance sheet presentation of notes and interest payable at December 31, 2022.

d. What is total interest expense for the year?

*d. $2,110*

**P10.3 (LO 3, 5), AP** On October 1, 2021, Kristal Corp. issued $700,000, 5%, 10-year bonds at face value. The bonds were dated October 1, 2021, and pay interest annually on October 1. Financial statements are prepared annually on December 31.

*Prepare journal entries to record issuance of bonds, interest, balance sheet presentation, and bond redemption.*

**Instructions**

a. Prepare the journal entry to record the issuance of the bonds.

b. Prepare the adjusting entry to record the accrual of interest on December 31, 2021.

c. Show the balance sheet presentation of bonds payable and bond interest payable on December 31, 2021.

d. Prepare the journal entry to record the payment of interest on October 1, 2022.

e. Prepare the adjusting entry to record the accrual of interest on December 31, 2022.

f. Assume that on January 1, 2023, Kristal pays the accrued bond interest and calls the bonds. The call price is 104. Record the payment of interest and redemption of the bonds.

*f. Loss                     $28,000*

**P10.4 (LO 3, 5), AP** Malcolm Company sold $6,000,000, 7%, 15-year bonds on January 1, 2022. The bonds were dated January 1, 2022, and pay interest each December 31. The bonds were sold at 98.

*Prepare journal entries to record issuance of bonds, show balance sheet presentation, and record bond redemption.*

## Instructions

**a.** Prepare the journal entry to record the issuance of the bonds on January 1, 2022.

**b.** At December 31, 2022, $8,000 of the bond discount had been amortized. Show the long-term liability balance sheet presentation of the bond liability at December 31, 2022.

c. Loss $224,000

**c.** At January 1, 2024, when the carrying value of the bonds was $5,896,000, the company redeemed the bonds at 102. Record the redemption of the bonds assuming that interest for the year had already been paid.

*Journalize and post note transactions; show balance sheet presentation.*

**P10.5 (LO 1, 5), AP** Ehler Corporation sells rock-climbing products and also operates an indoor climbing facility for climbing enthusiasts. During the last part of 2022, Ehler had the following transactions related to notes payable. Interest on all notes is paid at maturity.

| | |
|---|---|
| Sept.  1 | Issued a $12,000 note to Pippen to purchase inventory. The 3-month note payable bears interest of 6% and is due December 1. (Ehler uses a perpetual inventory system.) |
| Sept. 30 | Accrued interest for the Pippen note. |
| Oct.  1 | Issued a $16,500, 8%, 4-month note to Prime Bank to finance the purchase of a new climbing wall for advanced climbers. The note is due February 1. |
| Oct. 31 | Accrued interest for the Pippen note and the Prime Bank note. |
| Nov.  1 | Issued a $26,000 note and paid $8,000 cash to purchase a vehicle to transport clients to nearby climbing sites as part of a new series of climbing classes. This note bears interest of 6% and matures in 12 months. |
| Nov. 30 | Accrued interest for the Pippen note, the Prime Bank note, and the vehicle note. |
| Dec.  1 | Paid principal and interest on the Pippen note. |
| Dec. 31 | Accrued interest for the Prime Bank note and the vehicle note. |

## Instructions

**a.** Prepare journal entries for the above transactions.

b. Interest Payable $590

**b.** Post the above entries to the Notes Payable, Interest Payable, and Interest Expense accounts. (Use T-accounts.)

**c.** Show the balance sheet presentation of notes payable and interest payable at December 31.

**d.** How much interest expense relating to notes payable did Ehler incur during the year?

*Prepare journal entries to record interest payments and redemption of bonds.*

**P10.6 (LO 3), AP** The following information is taken from Hardesty's balance sheet at December 31, 2021.

| | |
|---|---|
| Current liabilities | |
| Interest payable | $ 40,000 |
| Long-term liabilities | |
| Bonds payable (8%, due January 1, 2025) | 500,000 |

Interest is payable annually on January 1. The bonds are callable on any annual interest payment date.

## Instructions

**a.** Journalize the payment of the bond interest on January 1, 2022.

b. Loss $6,000

**b.** Assume that on January 1, 2022, after paying interest, Hardesty calls bonds having a face value of $200,000. The call price is 103. Record the redemption of the bonds.

**c.** Prepare the adjusting entry on December 31, 2022, to accrue the interest on the remaining bonds.

*Prepare installment payments schedule, journal entries, and balance sheet presentation for a mortgage payable.*

**P10.7 (LO 4, 5), AP** Laverne Inc. purchased a new piece of equipment to be used in its new facility. The $370,000 piece of equipment was purchased with a $50,000 down payment and with cash received through the issuance of a $320,000, 8%, 5-year mortgage payable issued on January 1, 2022. The terms provide for annual installment payments of $80,146 each December 31.

## Instructions

(Round all computations to the nearest dollar.)

**a.** Prepare an installment payments schedule for the first three payments of the mortgage payable.

**b.** Prepare the journal entry related to the notes payable for December 31, 2022.

c. Current portion $58,910

**c.** Show the balance sheet presentation for this obligation for December 31, 2022. (*Hint:* Be sure to distinguish between the current and long-term portions of the mortgage.)

*Prepare financial statements from an adjusted trial balance.*

**P10.8 (LO 5), AP** The adjusted trial balance of Ubben Company for the year ended December 31, 2022, is as follows.

|  | Debit | Credit |
|---|---|---|
| Cash | $ 32,000 | |
| Accounts Receivable | 30,000 | |
| Inventory | 9,000 | |
| Equipment | 50,000 | |
| Allowance for Doubtful Accounts | | $  1,000 |
| Accumulated Depreciation—Equipment | | 4,000 |
| Notes Payable | | 3,000 |
| Accounts Payable | | 11,000 |
| Unearned Service Revenue | | 6,600 |
| Sales Taxes Payable | | 2,100 |
| Salaries and Wages Payable | | 1,800 |
| FICA Taxes Payable | | 500 |
| Interest Payable | | 400 |
| Bonds Payable | | 12,000 |
| Mortgage Notes Payable | | 8,000 |
| Common Stock | | 15,000 |
| Retained Earnings | | 12,900 |
| Sales Revenue | | 220,000 |
| Cost of Goods Sold | 120,000 | |
| Salaries and Wages Expense | 40,000 | |
| Depreciation Expense | 10,000 | |
| Rent Expense | 5,000 | |
| Bad Debt Expense | 1,200 | |
| Interest Expense | 300 | |
| Dividends | 200 | |
| Discount on Bonds Payable | 600 | |
| | $298,300 | $298,300 |

## Instructions

Prepare a multiple-step income statement and retained earnings statement for 2022, and a classified balance sheet as of December 31, 2022. The notes payable is due on January 10, 2023. The mortgage notes payable matures in 2028, with a principal payment of $1,000 due in March 2023.

**\*P10.9 (LO 5, 6), AP** Paris Electric sold $3,000,000, 10%, 10-year bonds on January 1, 2022. The bonds were dated January 1 and pay interest annually on January 1. Paris Electric uses the straight-line method to amortize bond premium or discount. The bonds were sold at 104.

*Prepare entries to record issuance of bonds, interest accrual, and straight-line amortization for 2 years.*

### Instructions

a. Prepare the journal entry to record the issuance of the bonds on January 1, 2022.

b. Prepare a bond premium amortization schedule for the first four interest periods.

b. Amortization $12,000

c. Prepare the journal entries for interest expense and the amortization of the premium in 2022 and 2023. Also, prepare the journal entry for interest payment in 2023.

d. Show the balance sheet presentation of the bond liability at December 31, 2023.

d. Premium on bonds payable $96,000

**\*P10.10 (LO 5, 6), AP** Fong Corporation sold $2,000,000, 7%, 5-year bonds on January 1, 2022. The bonds were dated January 1, 2022, and pay interest each January 1. Fong Corporation uses the straight-line method to amortize bond premium or discount.

*Prepare journal entries to record issuance of bonds, interest, and straight-line amortization, and show balance sheet presentation.*

### Instructions

a. Prepare all the necessary journal entries to record the issuance of the bonds and bond interest expense for 2022, assuming that the bonds sold at 102.

b. Prepare journal entries as in part (a) assuming that the bonds sold at 97.

c. Show the balance sheet presentation for the bond issue at December 31, 2022, using (1) the 102 selling price, and then (2) the 97 selling price.

Excel

*Prepare journal entries to record interest payments, straight-line discount amortization, and redemption of bonds.*

**\*P10.11 (LO 6), AP** The following information is taken from Lassen Corp.'s balance sheet at December 31, 2021.

| | | |
|---|---|---|
| Current liabilities | | |
| Interest payable | | $ 96,000 |
| Long-term liabilities | | |
| Bonds payable (4%, due January 1, 2032) | $2,400,000 | |
| Less: Discount on bonds payable | 24,000 | 2,376,000 |

Interest is payable annually on January 1. The bonds are callable on any annual interest payment date. Lassen uses straight-line amortization for any bond premium or discount. From December 31, 2021, the bonds will be outstanding for an additional 10 years (120 months).

**Instructions**

(Round all computations to the nearest dollar.)

a. Journalize the payment of bond interest on January 1, 2022.

b. Prepare the entry to amortize bond discount and to accrue the interest on December 31, 2022.

c. Loss $11,600

c. Assume that on January 1, 2023, after paying interest, Lassen Corp. calls bonds having a face value of $400,000. The call price is 102. Record the redemption of the bonds.

d. Prepare the adjusting entry at December 31, 2023, to amortize bond discount and to accrue interest on the remaining bonds.

*Prepare journal entries to record issuance of bonds, payment of interest, and amortization of bond discount using effective-interest method.*

**\*P10.12 (LO 7), AP** On January 1, 2022, Lachte Corporation issued $1,800,000 face value, 5%, 10-year bonds at $1,667,518. This price resulted in an effective-interest rate of 6% on the bonds. Lachte uses the effective-interest method to amortize bond premium or discount. The bonds pay interest each January 1.

**Instructions**

(Round all computations to the nearest dollar.)

a. Prepare the journal entry to record the issuance of the bonds on January 1, 2022.

b. Prepare an amortization table through December 31, 2024 (three interest periods) for this bond issue.

c. Interest Expense $100,051

c. Prepare the journal entry to record the accrual of interest and the amortization of the discount on December 31, 2022.

d. Prepare the journal entry to record the payment of interest on January 1, 2023.

e. Prepare the journal entry to record the accrual of interest and the amortization of the discount on December 31, 2023.

*Prepare journal entries to record issuance of bonds, payment of interest, and effective-interest amortization, and show balance sheet presentation.*

**\*P10.13 (LO 5, 7), AP** Writing On January 1, 2022, Opal Company issued $2,000,000 face value, 7%, 10-year bonds at $2,147,202. This price resulted in a 6% effective-interest rate on the bonds. Opal uses the effective-interest method to amortize bond premium or discount. The bonds pay annual interest on each January 1.

**Instructions**

a. Prepare the journal entries to record the following transactions.

1. The issuance of the bonds on January 1, 2022.

2. Accrual of interest and amortization of the premium on December 31, 2022.

3. The payment of interest on January 1, 2023.

a. 4. Interest Expense $128,162

4. Accrual of interest and amortization of the premium on December 31, 2023.

b. Show the proper long-term liabilities balance sheet presentation for the liability for bonds payable at December 31, 2023.

c. Provide the answers to the following questions in narrative form.

1. What amount of interest expense is reported for 2023?

2. Would the bond interest expense reported in 2023 be the same as, greater than, or less than the amount that would be reported if the straight-line method of amortization were used?

## Continuing Case

### Cookie Creations

(*Note:* This is a continuation of the Cookie Creations case from Chapters 1 through 9.)

**CC10** Recall that Cookie Creations sells fine European mixers that it purchases from Kzinski Supply Co. Kzinski warrants the mixers to be free of defects in material and workmanship for a period of one year from the date of original purchase. If the mixer has such a defect, Kzinski will repair or replace the mixer free of charge for parts and labor.

*Go to WileyPLUS for complete case details and instructions.*

leungchopan/
Shutterstock.com

## Comprehensive Accounting Cycle Review

**ACR10.1** Aimes Corporation's balance sheet at December 31, 2021, is presented below.

**Aimes Corporation**
**Balance Sheet**
**December 31, 2021**

| Cash | $ 30,000 | Accounts payable | $ 13,750 |
|---|---|---|---|
| Inventory | 30,750 | Interest payable | 2,500 |
| Prepaid insurance | 5,600 | Bonds payable | 50,000 |
| Equipment | 38,000 | Common stock | 25,000 |
| | $104,350 | Retained earnings | 13,100 |
| | | | $104,350 |

During 2022, the following transactions occurred. Aimes uses a perpetual inventory system.

1. Aimes paid $2,500 interest on the bonds on January 1, 2022.
2. Aimes purchased $241,100 of inventory on account.
3. Aimes sold for $480,000 cash inventory which cost $265,000. Aimes also collected $28,800 sales taxes.
4. Aimes paid $230,000 on accounts payable.
5. The prepaid insurance ($5,600) expired on July 31.
6. On August 1, Aimes paid $10,200 for insurance coverage from August 1, 2022, through July 31, 2023.
7. Aimes paid $17,000 sales taxes to the state.
8. Paid other operating expenses, $91,000.
9. Redeemed the bonds on December 31, 2022, by paying $48,000 plus $2,500 interest.
10. Issued $90,000 of 8% bonds on December 31, 2022, at 103. The bonds pay interest every June 30 and December 31.

Adjustment data:

1. Recorded the insurance expired from item 7.
2. The equipment was acquired on December 31, 2021, and will be depreciated on a straight-line basis over 5 years with a $3,000 salvage value.

### Instructions

(You may want to set up T-accounts to determine ending balances.)

a. Prepare journal entries for the transactions listed above and adjusting entries.

b. Prepare an adjusted trial balance at December 31, 2022.

c. Prepare an income statement and a retained earnings statement for the year ending December 31, 2022, and a classified balance sheet as of December 31, 2022.

| | |
|---|---|
| b. Totals | $656,450 |
| c. N.I. | $106,650 |

**ACR10.2** Writing Eastland Company and Westside Company are competing businesses. Both began operations 6 years ago and are quite similar in most respects. The current balance sheet data for the two companies are shown as follows.

|  | Eastland Company | Westside Company |
| --- | --- | --- |
| Cash | $ 63,300 | $ 48,400 |
| Accounts receivable | 304,700 | 302,500 |
| Allowance for doubtful accounts | (13,600) | –0– |
| Inventory | 463,900 | 515,200 |
| Plant and equipment | 255,300 | 257,300 |
| Accumulated depreciation—plant and equipment | (112,650) | (189,850) |
| Total assets | $960,950 | $933,550 |
| Current liabilities | $440,200 | $431,500 |
| Long-term liabilities | 78,000 | 82,000 |
| Total liabilities | 518,200 | 513,500 |
| Stockholders' equity | 442,750 | 420,050 |
| Total liabilities and stockholders' equity | $960,950 | $933,550 |

You have been engaged as a consultant to conduct a review of the two companies. Your goal is to determine which of them is in the stronger financial position. Both companies use the FIFO inventory method.

Your review of their financial statements quickly reveals that the two companies have not followed the same accounting practices. The differences and your conclusions regarding them are summarized below.

1. Eastland Company has used the allowance method of accounting for uncollectibles. A review shows that the amount of its write-offs each year has been quite close to the allowances that have been provided. It therefore seems reasonable to have confidence in its current estimate of uncollectibles.

    Westside Company has used the direct write-off method for uncollectibles, and it has been somewhat slow to write off its uncollectible accounts. Based upon an aging analysis and review of its accounts receivable, it is estimated that $18,000 of its existing accounts will probably prove to be uncollectible.

2. Eastland Company estimated a useful life of 12 years and a salvage value of $30,000 for its plant and equipment. It has been depreciating them on a straight-line basis.

    Westside Company has the same type of plant and equipment, with the same age. However, it estimated a useful life of 10 years and a salvage value of $10,000. It has been depreciating its plant and equipment using the double-declining-balance method. Westside's percentage of accumulated depreciation to plant and equipment is a better representation of cost allocation.

    Based upon engineering studies of these types of plant and equipment, you conclude that Westside's estimates and method for calculating depreciation are the more appropriate. If Eastland Company used the double-declining-balance method of depreciation, its accumulated depreciation balance would be $188,374.

3. Among its current liabilities, Eastland has included the portions of long-term liabilities that become due within the next year. Westside has not done so.

    You find that $16,000 of Westside's $82,000 of long-term liabilities are due to be repaid in the current year.

**Instructions**

a. Total assets:
   Eastland $885,226
   Westside $915,550

**a.** Revise the balance sheets presented above so that the data are comparable and reflect the current financial position for each of the two companies.

**b.** Prepare a brief report to your client stating your conclusions.

# Expand Your Critical Thinking

## Financial Reporting Problem: Apple Inc.

**CT10.1** The financial statements of **Apple Inc.** are presented in Appendix A. The complete annual report, including the notes to the financial statements, is available at the company's website.

### Instructions

Refer to Apple's financial statements and answer the following questions about current liabilities.

a. What were Apple's total current liabilities at September 29, 2018? What was the increase/decrease in Apple's total current liabilities from the prior year?

b. How much were the accounts payable at September 29, 2018?

c. What were the components of total current liabilities on September 29, 2018 (other than accounts payable already discussed in (b))?

## Comparative Analysis Problem: PepsiCo, Inc. vs. The Coca-Cola Company

**CT10.2** **PepsiCo, Inc.**'s financial statements are presented in Appendix B. Financial statements of **The Coca-Cola Company** are presented in Appendix C.

### Instructions

a. At December 29, 2018, what was PepsiCo's largest current liability? What were its total current liabilities? At December 31, 2018, what was Coca-Cola's largest current liability? What were its total current liabilities?

b. Based on information contained in those financial statements, compute the following 2018 values for each company:

1. Working capital.

2. Current ratio.

c. What conclusions concerning the relative liquidity of these companies can be drawn from these data?

d. Based on the information contained in these financial statements, compute the following 2018 ratios for each company.

1. Debt to assets.

2. Times interest earned.

e. What conclusions concerning the companies' long-run solvency can be drawn from these ratios?

## Comparative Analysis Problem: Amazon.com, Inc. vs. Walmart Inc.

**CT10.3** The financial statements of **Amazon.com, Inc.** are presented in Appendix D. Financial statements of **Walmart Inc.** are presented in Appendix E.

### Instructions

a. Based on the information contained in these financial statements, compute the current ratio for the most recent fiscal year provided for each company. What conclusions concerning the companies' liquidity can be drawn from these ratios?

b. Based on the information contained in these financial statements, compute the following ratios for each company's most recent fiscal year.

1. Debt to assets ratio.

2. Times interest earned.

What conclusions about the companies' long-run solvency can be drawn from the ratios?

### Real-World Focus

**CT10.4** Bond or debt securities pay a stated rate of interest. This rate of interest is dependent on the risk associated with the investment. Also, bond prices change when the risks associated with those bonds change. **Standard & Poor's** provides ratings for companies that issue debt securities.

**Instructions**

Go to the Standard & Poor's website and then answer the following questions.

a. Explain the meaning of an "A" rating. Explain the meaning of a "C" rating.

b. What types of things can cause a change in a company's credit rating?

c. Explain the relationship between a company's credit rating and the merit of an investment in that company's bonds.

### Decision-Making Across the Organization

*CT10.5 On January 1, 2020, Picard Corporation issued $3,000,000, 5-year, 8% bonds at 97. The bonds pay interest annually on January 1. By January 1, 2022, the market rate of interest for bonds of risk similar to those of Picard Corporation had risen. As a result, the market price of these bonds was $2,500,000 on January 1, 2022—below their carrying value of $2,946,000.

Geoff Marquis, president of the company, suggests repurchasing all of these bonds in the open market at the $2,500,000 price. But to do so the company will have to issue $2,500,000 (face value) of new 10-year, 12% bonds at par. The president asks you, as controller, "What is the feasibility of my proposed repurchase plan?"

**Instructions**

With the class divided into groups, answer the following.

a. Prepare the journal entry to redeem the 5-year bonds on January 1, 2022. Prepare the journal entry to issue the new 10-year bonds.

b. Prepare a short memo to the president in response to his request for advice. List the economic factors that you believe should be considered for his repurchase proposal.

### Communication Activity

**CT10.6** Jerry Hogan, president of Norwest, Inc., is considering the issuance of bonds to finance an expansion of his business. He has asked you to (1) discuss the advantages of bonds over common stock financing, (2) indicate the types of bonds he might issue, and (3) explain the issuing procedures used in bond transactions.

**Instructions**

Write a memo to the president, answering his request.

### Ethics Case

**CT10.7** Ken Iwig is the president, founder, and majority owner of Olathe Medical Corporation, an emerging medical technology products company. Olathe is in dire need of additional capital to keep operating and to bring several promising products to final development, testing, and production. Ken, as owner of 51% of the outstanding stock, manages the company's operations. He places heavy emphasis on research and development and on long-term growth. The other principal stockholder is Barb Lowery who, as a nonemployee investor, owns 40% of the stock. Barb would like to deemphasize the R&D functions and emphasize the marketing function, to maximize short-run sales and profits from existing products. She believes this strategy would raise the market price of Olathe's stock.

All of Ken's personal capital and borrowing power is tied up in his 51% stock ownership. He knows that any offering of additional shares of stock will dilute his controlling interest because he won't be able to participate in such an issuance. But, Barb has money and would likely buy enough shares to gain control of Olathe. She then would dictate the company's future direction, even if it meant replacing Ken as president and CEO.

The company already has considerable debt. Raising additional capital with debt will be costly, will adversely affect Olathe's credit rating, and will increase the company's reported losses due to the growth in interest expense. Barb and the other minority stockholders express opposition to the assumption of additional debt, fearing the company will be pushed to the brink of bankruptcy. Wanting to maintain his control and to preserve the direction of "his" company, Ken is doing everything to avoid a stock issuance. He is contemplating a large issuance of bonds, even if it means the bonds are issued with a high effective-interest rate.

## Instructions

**a.** Who are the stakeholders in this situation?

**b.** What are the ethical issues in this case?

**c.** What would you do if you were Ken?

## All About You

**CT10.8** Medical costs are substantial and rising. But will they be the most substantial expense over your lifetime? Not likely. Will it be housing or food? Again, not likely. The answer is taxes. On average, Americans work 107 days per year to afford their taxes. Companies, too, have large tax burdens. They look very hard at tax issues in deciding where to build their plants and where to locate their administrative headquarters.

### Instructions

**a.** Determine what your state income taxes are if your taxable income is $60,000 and you file as a single taxpayer in the state in which you live.

**b.** Assume that you own a home worth $200,000 in your community and the tax rate is 2.1%. Compute the property taxes you would pay.

**c.** Assume that the total gasoline bill for your automobile is $1,200 a year (300 gallons at $4 per gallon). What are the amounts of state and federal taxes that you pay on the $1,200?

**d.** Assume that your purchases for the year total $9,000. Of this amount, $5,000 was for food and prescription drugs. What is the amount of sales tax you would pay on these purchases? (Many states do not levy a sales tax on food or prescription drugs. Does yours?)

**e.** Determine what your FICA taxes are if your income is $60,000.

**f.** Determine what your federal income taxes are if your taxable income is $60,000 and you file as a single taxpayer.

**g.** Determine your total taxes paid based on the above calculations, and determine the percentage of income that you would pay in taxes based on the following formula: Total taxes paid ÷ Total income.

**CT10.9** Numerous articles have been written that identify early warning signs that you might be getting into trouble with your personal debt load. You can find many good articles on this topic on the Internet.

### Instructions

Find an article that identifies early warning signs of personal debt trouble. Write a summary of the article and bring your summary and the article to class to share.

## FASB Codification Activity

**CT10.10** If your school has a subscription to the FASB Codification, log in and prepare responses to the following.

**a.** What is the definition of current liabilities?

**b.** What is the definition of long-term obligation?

**c.** What guidance does the Codification provide for the disclosure of long-term liabilities?

## Answers to Insight and Accounting Across the Organization Questions

**Running Hot!** **Q:** What are the advantages for companies of issuing 30-years bonds instead of 5-year bonds? **A:** The major advantages for companies are to extend their debt and to pay low interest rates. This locks in these low rates for a considerable period of time.

**How About Some Green Bonds?** **Q:** Why might standardized disclosure help investors to better understand how proceeds from the sale or issuance of bonds are used? **A:** By requiring transparency as to how a bond's proceeds are to be used and how it will affect a company's sustainable profitability, investors will make better financial decisions.

**Debt Masking** **Q:** What implications does debt masking have for an investor that is using the debt to assets ratio to evaluate a company's solvency? **A:** Since the debt to assets ratio is calculated using financial statement numbers from the end of the accounting period, debt masking could result in investors making incorrect assumptions about a company's solvency. By engaging in debt masking, a company is misleading investors because what it is disclosing at the end of the period does not reflect what its normal financial position was during most of the accounting period.

# A Look at IFRS

---

**LEARNING OBJECTIVE 8**
Compare the accounting for liabilities under GAAP and IFRS.

---

IFRS and GAAP have similar definitions of liabilities but have a different approach for recording certain liabilities.

## Key Points

Following are the key similarities and differences between GAAP and IFRS as related to accounting for liabilities.

**Similarities**

- The basic definition of a liability under GAAP and IFRS is very similar. In a more technical way, liabilities are defined by the IASB as a present obligation of the entity arising from past events, the settlement of which is expected to result in an outflow from the entity of resources embodying economic benefits.

- The accounting for current liabilities such as notes payable, unearned revenue, and payroll taxes payable is similar between GAAP and IFRS.

- IFRS requires that companies classify liabilities as current or noncurrent on the face of the statement of financial position (balance sheet), except in industries where a **presentation** based on liquidity would be considered to provide more useful information (such as financial institutions). When current liabilities (also called short-term liabilities) are presented, they are generally presented in order of liquidity.

- Under IFRS, liabilities are classified as current if they are expected to be paid within 12 months.

- Similar to GAAP, items are normally reported in order of liquidity. Companies sometimes show liabilities before assets. Also, they will sometimes show long-term liabilities before current liabilities.

- The basic calculation for bond valuation is the same under GAAP and IFRS. In addition, the accounting for bond liability transactions is essentially the same between GAAP and IFRS.

- IFRS requires use of the effective-interest method for amortization of bond discounts and premiums. GAAP also requires the effective-interest method, except that it allows use of the straight-line method where the difference is not material. Under IFRS, companies do not use a premium or discount account but instead show the bond at its net amount. For example, if a $100,000 bond was issued at 97, under IFRS a company would record:

| | | |
|---|---|---|
| Cash | 97,000 | |
|     Bonds Payable | | 97,000 |

**Differences**

- The accounting for convertible bonds differs between IFRS and GAAP. Unlike GAAP, IFRS splits the proceeds from the convertible bond between an equity component and a debt component. The equity conversion rights are reported in equity.

  To illustrate, assume that Harris Corp. issues convertible 7% bonds with a face value of $1,000,000 and receives $1,000,000. Comparable bonds without a conversion feature would have required a 9% rate of interest. To determine how much of the proceeds would be allocated to debt and how much to equity, the promised payments of the bond obligation would be discounted at the market rate of 9%. Suppose that this results in a present value of $850,000. The entry to record the issuance would be:

| | | |
|---|---|---|
| Cash | 1,000,000 | |
|     Bonds Payable | | 850,000 |
|     Share Premium—Conversion Equity | | 150,000 |

- Under IFRS, companies sometimes will net current liabilities against current assets to show working capital on the face of the statement of financial position.

- Leases classified as operating leases under GAAP are accounted for differently under IFRS. Also, IFRS allows alternative measurement bases for right-of-use assets (e.g., the revaluation model).

- Both Boards share the same objective of recording leases by lessees and lessors according to their economic substance—that is, according to the definitions of assets and liabilities. However, GAAP for leases is much more "rules-based" with specific criteria to determine if a lease arrangement is a finance or operating lease. IFRS is more conceptual in its provisions.

# IFRS Practice

## IFRS Self-Test Questions

1. Which of the following is **false**?
    a. Under IFRS, current liabilities must always be presented before noncurrent liabilities.
    b. Under IFRS, an item is a current liability if it will be paid within the next 12 months.
    c. Under IFRS, current liabilities are sometimes netted against current assets on the statement of financial position.
    d. Under IFRS, a liability is only recognized if it is a present obligation.

2. The accounting for bonds payable is:
    a. essentially the same under IFRS and GAAP.
    b. different under IFRS as GAAP requires use of the straight-line method for amortization of bond premium and discount.
    c. the same under IFRS and GAAP, except that market prices may be different because the present value calculations are different between IFRS and GAAP.
    d. not covered by IFRS.

3. Which of the following is **true** regarding accounting for amortization of bond discount and premium?
    a. Both IFRS and GAAP must use the effective-interest method.
    b. GAAP must use the effective-interest method, but IFRS may use either the effective-interest method or the straight-line method.
    c. IFRS is required to use the effective-interest method.
    d. GAAP is required to use the straight-line method.

4. The leasing standards employed by IFRS:
    a. rely more heavily on interpretation of the conceptual meaning of assets and liabilities than GAAP.
    b. are more "rules based" than those of GAAP.
    c. employ the same "bright-line test" as GAAP.
    d. are identical to those of GAAP.

## IFRS Exercises

**IFRS10.1** Briefly describe some of the similarities and differences between GAAP and IFRS with respect to the accounting for liabilities.

**IFRS10.2** Ratzlaff Company issues (in euros) €2 million, 10-year, 8% bonds at 97, with interest payable annually on January 1.

### Instructions
a. Prepare the journal entry to record the sale of these bonds on January 1, 2022.
b. Assuming instead that the above bonds sold for 104, prepare the journal entry to record the sale of these bonds on January 1, 2022.

## International Financial Reporting Problem: Louis Vuitton

**IFRS10.3** The financial statements of **Louis Vuitton** are presented in Appendix F. The complete consolidated financial statements, including the notes to its financial statements, are available at the company's website.

### Instructions
Use the company's 2018 consolidated financial statements to answer the following questions.
a. What were the total current liabilities for the company as of December 31, 2018? What portion of these current liabilities related to provisions?
b. According to the notes to the financial statements, what is the composition of long-term gross borrowings?
c. According to the accounting policy note to the financial statements, how are borrowings measured?
d. Determine the amount of fixed-rate and adjustable-rate (floating) borrowings (gross) that the company reports.

## Answers to IFRS Self-Test Questions

1. a   2. a   3. c   4. a

## CHAPTER 11

S3studio/Getty Images

# Corporations: Organization, Stock Transactions, and Stockholders' Equity

## Chapter Preview

Corporations like **Facebook** and **Google** have substantial resources at their disposal. In fact, the corporation is the dominant form of business organization in the United States in terms of sales, earnings, and number of employees. All of the 500 largest U.S. companies are corporations. In this chapter, we look at the essential features of a corporation and explain the accounting for a corporation's capital stock transactions.

# Feature Story

## Oh Well, I Guess I'll Get Rich

Suppose you started one of the fastest-growing companies in the history of business. Now suppose that by "going public"—issuing stock of your company to outside investors who are foaming at the mouth for the chance to buy its shares—you would instantly become one of the richest people in the world. Would you hesitate?

That is exactly what Mark Zuckerberg, the founder of **Facebook**, did. Many people who start high-tech companies go public as soon as possible to cash in on their riches. But Zuckerberg was reluctant to do so. To understand why, you need to understand the advantages and disadvantages of being a public company.

The main motivation for issuing shares to the public is to raise money so you can grow your business. However, unlike a manufacturer or even an online retailer, Facebook doesn't need major physical resources, it doesn't have inventory, and it doesn't really need much money for marketing. But why not go public anyway, so the company would have some extra cash on hand—and so you personally get rich? As head of a closely held, nonpublic company, Zuckerberg was subject to far fewer regulations than a public company. Prior to going public, Zuckerberg could basically run the company however he wanted to.

For example, early in 2012, Facebook shocked the investment community by purchasing the photo-sharing service Instagram. The purchase was startling both for its speed (over a weekend) and price ($1 billion). Zuckerberg basically didn't seek anyone's approval. He thought it was a good idea, so he just did it. The structured decision-making process of a public company would make it very difficult for a public company to move that fast.

Speed is useful, but it is likely that Facebook will make even bigger acquisitions in the future. The reason: To survive among the likes of **Microsoft**, **Google**, and **Apple**, Facebook needs lots of cash. To raise that amount of money, the company really needed to go public. So in 2012, Mark Zuckerberg reluctantly made Facebook a public company, thus becoming one of the richest people in the world.

# Chapter Outline

| LEARNING OBJECTIVES | REVIEW | PRACTICE |
|---|---|---|
| **LO 1** Discuss the major characteristics of a corporation. | • Characteristics of a corporation<br>• Forming a corporation<br>• Stockholder rights<br>• Stock issue considerations<br>• Corporate capital | **DO IT! 1a** Corporate Organization<br>**1b** Corporate Capital |
| **LO 2** Explain how to account for the issuance of common, preferred, and treasury stock. | • Accounting for common stock<br>• Accounting for preferred stock<br>• Accounting for treasury stock | **DO IT! 2a** Issuance of Stock<br>**2b** Treasury Stock |
| **LO 3** Explain how to account for cash dividends, stock dividends, and stock splits. | • Cash dividends<br>• Dividend preferences<br>• Stock dividends<br>• Stock splits | **DO IT! 3a** Dividends on Preferred and Common Stock<br>**3b** Stock Dividends and Stock Splits |
| **LO 4** Discuss how stockholders' equity is reported and analyzed. | • Retained earnings<br>• Retained earnings restrictions<br>• Balance sheet presentation of stockholders' equity<br>• Analysis of stockholders' equity | **DO IT! 4a** Stockholders' Equity Section<br>**4b** Analyzing Stockholders' Equity |

**Go to the Review and Practice section at the end of the chapter for a review of key concepts and practice applications with solutions.**

**Visit WileyPLUS for additional tutorials and practice opportunities.**

# Corporate Form of Organization

**LEARNING OBJECTIVE 1**

Discuss the major characteristics of a corporation.

In 1819, Chief Justice John Marshall defined a corporation as "an artificial being, invisible, intangible, and existing only in contemplation of law." This definition is the foundation for the prevailing legal interpretation that a **corporation** is an **entity separate and distinct from its owners**.

A corporation is created by law, and its continued existence depends upon the statutes of the state in which it is incorporated. As a legal entity, a corporation has most of the rights and privileges of a person. The major exceptions relate to privileges that only a living person can exercise, such as the right to vote or to hold public office. A corporation is subject to the same duties and responsibilities as a person. For example, it must abide by the laws, and it must pay taxes.

Two common ways to classify corporations are by **purpose** and by **ownership**. A corporation may be organized for the purpose of making a profit, or it may be not-for-profit. For-profit corporations include such well-known companies as **McDonald's**, **Nike**, **PepsiCo**, and **Google**. Not-for-profit corporations are organized for charitable, medical, or educational purposes. Examples are the **Salvation Army** and the **American Cancer Society**.

Classification by ownership differentiates publicly held and privately held corporations. A **publicly held corporation** may have thousands of stockholders. Its stock is regularly traded on a national securities exchange such as the New York Stock Exchange or NASDAQ. Examples are **IBM**, **Caterpillar**, and **Apple**.

In contrast, a **privately held corporation** usually has only a few stockholders, and does not offer its stock for sale to the general public (see **Alternative Terminology**). Privately held companies are generally much smaller than publicly held companies, although some notable exceptions exist. **Cargill Inc.**, a private corporation that trades in grain and other commodities, is one of the largest companies in the United States.

**ALTERNATIVE TERMINOLOGY**

**Privately held corporations are also referred to as *closely held corporations*.**

## Characteristics of a Corporation

In 1964, when **Nike**'s founders Phil Knight and Bill Bowerman were just getting started in the running shoe business, they formed their original organization as a partnership. In 1968, they reorganized the company as a corporation. A number of characteristics distinguish corporations from proprietorships and partnerships. We explain the most important of these characteristics below.

### Separate Legal Existence

As an entity separate and distinct from its owners, the corporation acts under its own name rather than in the name of its stockholders. **Facebook** may buy, own, and sell property. It may borrow money, and it may enter into legally binding contracts in its own name. It may also sue or be sued, and it pays its own taxes.

In a partnership, the acts of the owners (partners) bind the partnership. In contrast, the acts of its owners (stockholders) do not bind the corporation unless such owners are **agents** of the corporation. For example, if you owned shares of Nike stock, you would not have the right to purchase inventory for the company unless you were designated as an agent of the corporation.

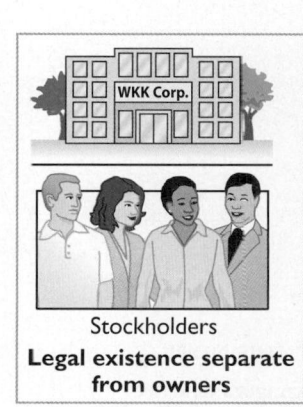

Stockholders
**Legal existence separate from owners**

### Limited Liability of Stockholders

Since a corporation is a separate legal entity, creditors have recourse only to corporate assets to satisfy their claims. The liability of stockholders is normally limited to their investment in the

Stockholders
**Limited liability of stockholders**

corporation. Creditors have no legal claim on the personal assets of the owners unless fraud has occurred. Even in the event of bankruptcy, stockholders' losses are generally limited to their capital investment in the corporation.

### Transferable Ownership Rights

**Transferable ownership rights**

Shares of capital stock represent ownership in a corporation. These shares are transferable units. Stockholders may dispose of part or all of their interest in a corporation simply by selling their stock. The transfer of an ownership interest in a partnership requires the consent of each owner. In contrast, the transfer of stock is entirely at the discretion of the stockholder. It does not require the approval of either the corporation or other stockholders.

The transfer of ownership rights between stockholders normally has no effect on the daily operating activities of the corporation. Nor does it affect the corporation's assets, liabilities, and total ownership equity. The transfer of these ownership rights is a transaction between individual owners. The company does not participate in the transfer of these ownership rights after the original sale of the capital stock.

### Ability to Acquire Capital

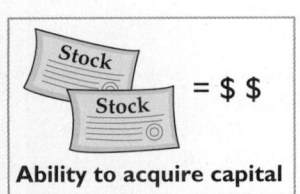

**Ability to acquire capital**

It is relatively easy for a corporation to obtain capital through the issuance of stock. Buying stock in a corporation is often attractive to an investor because a stockholder has limited liability and shares of stock are readily transferable. Also, numerous individuals can become stockholders by investing relatively small amounts of money.

### Continuous Life

**Continuous life**

The life of a corporation is stated in its charter. The life may be perpetual, or it may be limited to a specific number of years. If it is limited, the company can extend the life through renewal of the charter. Since a corporation is a separate legal entity, its continuance as a going concern is not affected by the withdrawal, death, or incapacity of a stockholder, employee, or officer. As a result, a successful company can have a continuous and perpetual life.

### Corporation Management

Stockholders legally own the corporation. However, they manage the corporation indirectly through a board of directors they elect. Mark Zuckerberg is the chairman of **Facebook**'s board of directors. The board, in turn, formulates the operating policies for the company. The board also selects officers, such as a president and one or more vice presidents, to execute policy and to perform daily management functions. As a result of the Sarbanes-Oxley Act, the board is now required to monitor management's actions more closely. Many feel that the failures of **Enron**, **WorldCom**, and **MF Global** could have been avoided by more diligent boards.

**Illustration 11.1** presents a typical organization chart showing the delegation of responsibility. The chief executive officer (CEO) has overall responsibility for managing the business. As the organization chart shows, the CEO delegates responsibility to other officers. The chief accounting officer is the **controller**. The controller's responsibilities include (1) maintaining the accounting records, (2) ensuring an adequate system of internal control, and (3) preparing financial statements, tax returns, and internal reports. The **treasurer** has custody of the corporation's funds and is responsible for maintaining the company's cash position.

The organizational structure of a corporation enables a company to hire professional managers to run the business (see **Ethics Note**). On the other hand, the separation of ownership and management often reduces an owner's ability to actively manage the company.

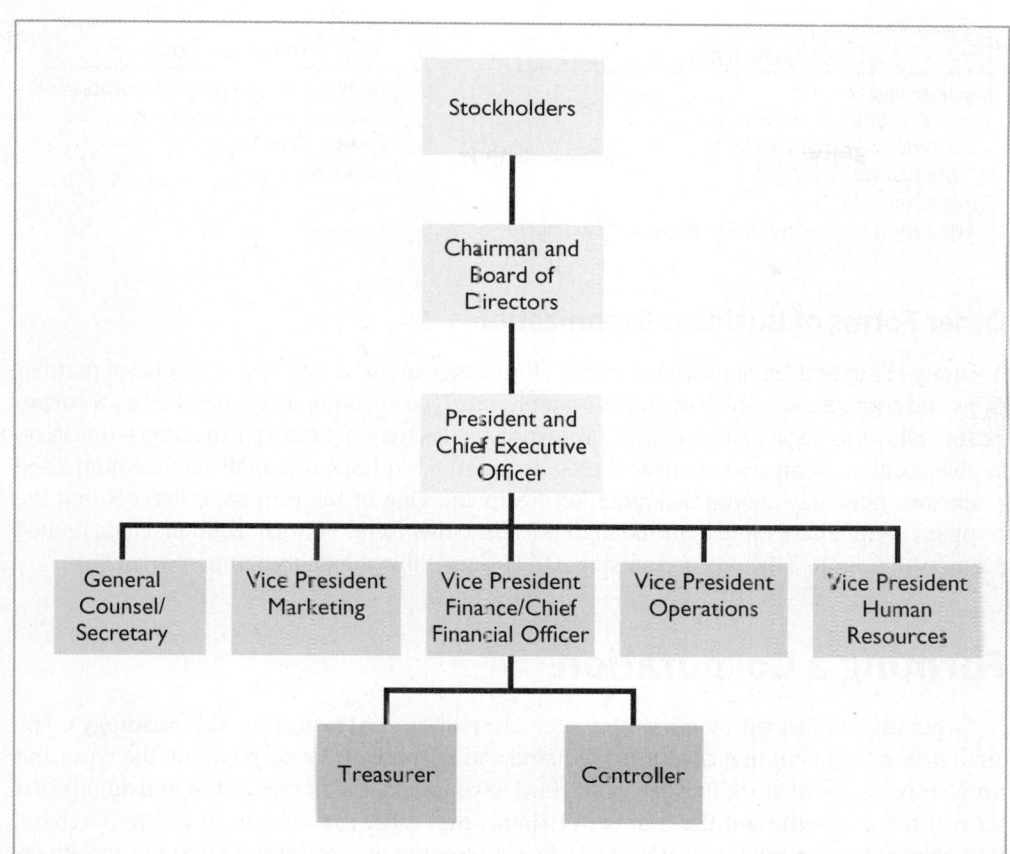

**ILLUSTRATION 11.1**

**Corporation organization chart**

## Government Regulations

A corporation is subject to numerous state and federal regulations. For example, state laws usually prescribe the requirements for issuing stock, the distributions of earnings permitted to stockholders, and the acceptable methods for buying back and retiring stock. Federal securities laws govern the sale of capital stock to the general public. Also, most publicly held corporations are required to make extensive disclosure of their financial affairs to the Securities and Exchange Commission (SEC) through quarterly and annual reports (Forms 10Q and 10K). In addition, when a corporation lists its stock on organized securities exchanges, it must comply with the reporting requirements of these exchanges. Government regulations are designed to protect the owners of the corporation.

**Government regulations**

## Additional Taxes

Owners of proprietorships and partnerships report their share of earnings on their personal income tax returns. The individual owner then pays taxes on this amount. Corporations, on the other hand, must pay federal and state income taxes **as a separate legal entity**. These taxes can be substantial. They can amount to as much as 40% of taxable income.

In addition, stockholders must pay taxes on cash dividends (pro rata distributions of net income). Thus, many argue that the government taxes corporate income **twice (double taxation)**—once at the corporate level and again at the individual level.

In summary, **Illustration 11.2** shows the advantages and disadvantages of a corporation compared to a proprietorship and a partnership.

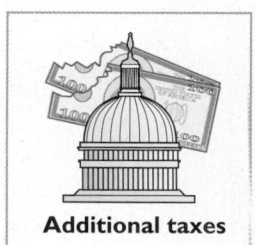

**Additional taxes**

**ILLUSTRATION 11.2**

**Advantages and disadvantages of a corporation**

| Advantages | Disadvantages |
|---|---|
| Separate legal existence | Corporation management—separation of ownership and management |
| Limited liability of stockholders | Government regulations |
| Transferable ownership rights | Additional taxes |
| Ability to acquire capital | |
| Continuous life | |
| Corporation management—professional managers | |

## Other Forms of Business Organization

A variety of "hybrid" organizational forms—forms that combine different attributes of partnerships and corporations—now exist. For example, one type of corporate form, called an **S corporation**, allows for legal treatment as a corporation but tax treatment as a partnership—that is, no double taxation. Because of changes to the S corporation's rules, more small- and medium-sized businesses now may choose S corporation treatment. One of the primary criteria is that the company cannot have more than 100 shareholders. Other forms of organization include limited partnerships, limited liability partnerships (LLPs), and limited liability companies (LLCs).

# Forming a Corporation

**ALTERNATIVE TERMINOLOGY**

The charter is often referred to as the *articles of incorporation*.

A corporation is formed by grant of a state **charter** (see **Alternative Terminology**). The charter is a document that describes the name and purpose of the corporation, the types and number of shares of stock that are authorized to be issued, the names of the individuals that formed the company, and the number of shares that these individuals agreed to purchase. Regardless of the number of states in which a corporation has operating divisions, it is incorporated in only one state.

It is to the company's advantage to incorporate in a state whose laws are favorable to the corporate form of business organization. For example, although **Facebook** has its headquarters in California, it is incorporated in Delaware. In fact, more and more corporations have been incorporating in states with rules that favor existing management. For example, **Gulf Oil** changed its state of incorporation to Delaware to thwart possible unfriendly takeovers. There, certain defensive tactics against takeovers can be approved by the board of directors alone, without a vote by shareholders.

Upon receipt of its charter from the state of incorporation, the corporation establishes **by-laws**. The by-laws establish the internal rules and procedures for conducting the affairs of the corporation. Corporations engaged in interstate commerce must also obtain a **license** from each state in which they do business. The license subjects the corporation's operating activities to the general corporation laws of the state.

Costs incurred in the formation of a corporation are called **organization costs**. These costs include legal and state fees, and promotional expenditures involved in the organization of the business. **Corporations expense organization costs as incurred.** Determining the amount and timing of future benefits is so difficult that it is standard procedure to take a conservative approach of expensing these costs immediately.

# Stockholder Rights

When chartered, the corporation may begin selling shares of stock. When a corporation has only one class of stock, it is **common stock**. Each share of common stock gives the stockholder the ownership rights pictured in **Illustration 11.3**. The articles of incorporation or the by-laws state the ownership rights of a share of stock.

Proof of stock ownership is evidenced by a form known as a **stock certificate**. As **Illustration 11.4** shows, the face of the certificate shows the name of the corporation, the stockholder's name, the class and special features of the stock, the number of shares owned, and the signatures of authorized corporate officials. Prenumbered certificates facilitate accountability. They may be issued for any quantity of shares.

**ILLUSTRATION 11.3** Ownership rights of stockholders

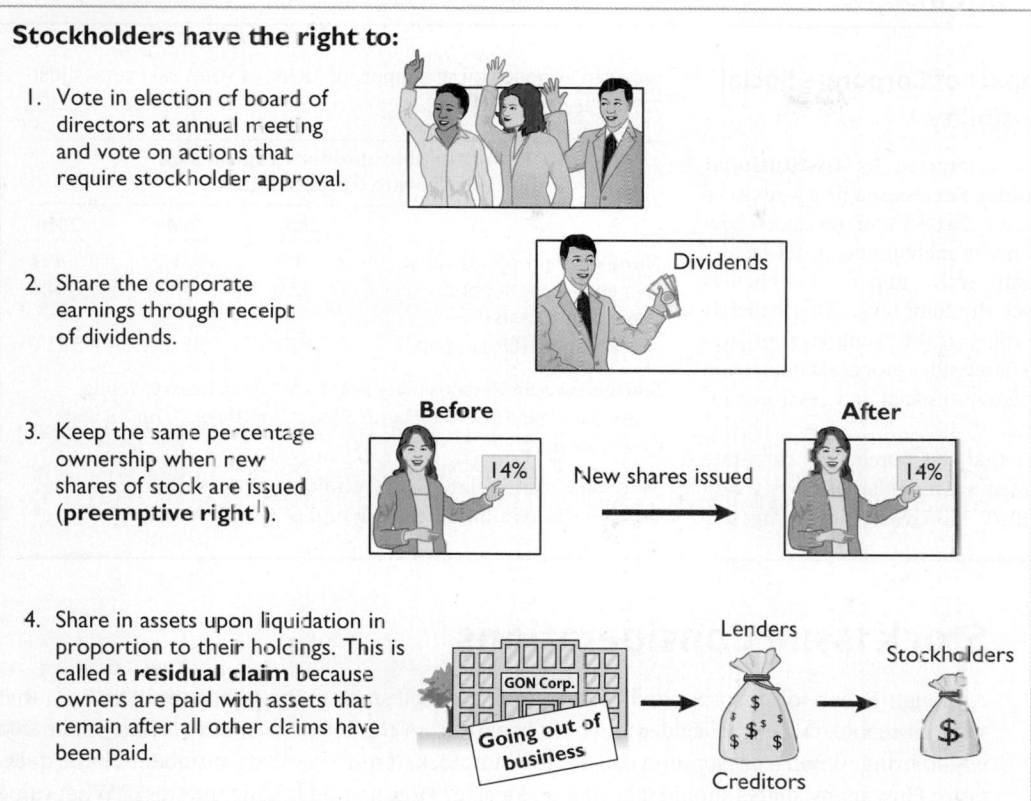

## Stockholders have the right to:

1. Vote in election of board of directors at annual meeting and vote on actions that require stockholder approval.

2. Share the corporate earnings through receipt of dividends.

3. Keep the same percentage ownership when new shares of stock are issued (**preemptive right**[1]).

4. Share in assets upon liquidation in proportion to their holdings. This is called a **residual claim** because owners are paid with assets that remain after all other claims have been paid.

**ILLUSTRATION 11.4**

**A stock certificate**

Source: The Franklin Life Insurance Company

---

[1]A number of companies have eliminated the preemptive right because they believe it makes an unnecessary and cumbersome demand on management. For example, by stockholder approval, **IBM** has dropped its preemptive right for stockholders.

---

### People, Planet, and Profit Insight

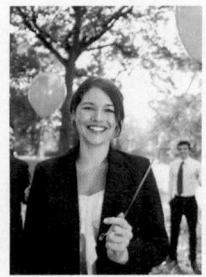

#### The Impact of Corporate Social Responsibility

A survey conducted by **Institutional Shareholder Services**, a proxy advisory firm, shows that 83% of investors now believe environmental and social factors can significantly impact shareholder value over the long term. This belief is clearly visible in the rising level of support for shareholder proposals requesting action related to social and environmental issues.

iStock.com/Robert Churchill

The following table shows that the number of corporate social responsibility (CSR) related shareholder proposals rose from 150 in 2000 to 191 in 2010. Moreover, those proposals received average voting support of 18.4% of votes cast versus just 7.5% a decade earlier.

| Trends in Shareholder Proposals on Corporate Responsibility | | | |
|---|---|---|---|
| | **2000** | **2005** | **2010** |
| Number of proposals voted | 150 | 155 | 191 |
| Average voting support | 7.5% | 9.9% | 18.4% |
| Percent proposals receiving >10% support | 16.7% | 31.2% | 52.1% |

**Source:** Investor Responsibility Research Center, Ernst & Young, *Seven Questions CEOs and Boards Should Ask About: "Triple Bottom Line" Reporting.*

**Why are CSR-related shareholder proposals increasing? (Answer is available near the end of the chapter.)**

---

## Stock Issue Considerations

Although **Facebook** incorporated in 2004, it did not sell stock to the public until 2012. At that time, Facebook evidently decided it would benefit from the infusion of cash that a public sale would bring. When a corporation decides to issue stock, it must resolve a number of basic questions: How many shares should it authorize for sale? How should it issue the stock? What value should the corporation assign to the stock? We address these questions in the following sections.

### Authorized Stock

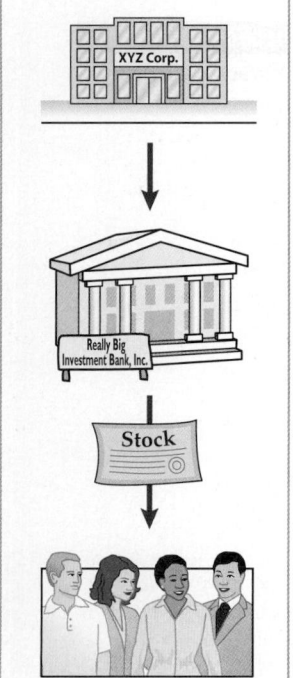

**Indirect issuance**

The charter indicates the maximum number of shares that a corporation is **authorized** to sell. The total amount of **authorized stock** at the time of incorporation normally anticipates both initial and subsequent capital needs. As a result, the number of shares authorized generally exceeds the number initially sold. If it sells all authorized stock, a corporation must obtain consent of the state to amend its charter before it can issue additional shares.

**The authorization of capital stock does not result in a formal accounting entry. The reason is that the event has no immediate effect on either corporate assets or stockholders' equity.** However, the number of authorized shares is often reported in the stockholders' equity section of the balance sheet. It is then simple to determine the number of unissued shares that the corporation can issue without amending the charter: subtract the total shares issued from the total authorized. For example, if **Advanced Micro** was authorized to sell 100,000 shares of common stock and issued 80,000 shares, 20,000 shares would remain unissued.

### Issuance of Stock

A corporation can issue common stock **directly** to investors. Alternatively, it can issue the stock **indirectly** through an investment banking firm that specializes in bringing securities to the attention of prospective investors. Direct issue is typical in closely held companies. Indirect issue is customary for a publicly held corporation.

In an indirect issue, the investment banking firm may agree to **underwrite** the entire stock issue. In this arrangement, the investment banker buys the stock from the corporation at a stipulated price and resells the shares to investors. The corporation thus avoids any risk of being unable to sell the shares. Also, it obtains immediate use of the cash received from the underwriter. The investment banking firm, in turn, assumes the risk of reselling the shares, in return for an underwriting fee.[2] For example, **Google** (the world's number-one Internet

---

[2]Alternatively, the investment banking firm may agree only to enter into a **best-efforts contract** with the corporation. In such cases, the banker agrees to sell as many shares as possible at a specified price. The corporation bears the risk of unsold stock. Under a best-efforts arrangement, the banking firm is paid a fee or commission for its services.

search engine) used underwriters when it issued a highly successful initial public offering, raising $1.67 billion. The underwriters charged a 3% underwriting fee (approximately $50 million) on Google's stock offering.

How does a corporation set the price for a new issue of stock? Among the factors to be considered are (1) the company's anticipated future earnings, (2) its expected dividend rate per share, (3) its current financial position, (4) the current state of the economy, and (5) the current state of the securities market. The calculation can be complex and is properly the subject of a finance course.

## Anatomy of a Fraud

The president, chief operating officer, and chief financial officer of **SafeNet**, a software encryption company, were each awarded employee stock options by the company's board of directors as part of their compensation package. Stock options enable an employee to buy a company's stock sometime in the future at the price that existed when the stock option was awarded. For example, suppose that you received stock options today when the stock price of your company was $30. Three years later, if the stock price rose to $100, you could "exercise" your options and buy the stock for $30 per share, thereby making $70 per share. After being awarded their stock options, the three employees changed the award dates in the company's records to dates in the past, when the company's stock was trading at historical lows. For instance, using the previous example, they would choose a past date when the stock was selling for $10 per share, rather than the $30 price on the actual award date. This would increase the profit from exercising the options to $90 per share.

### Total take: $1.7 million

#### The Missing Control

**Independent internal verification.** The company's board of directors should have ensured that the awards were properly administered. For example, the date on the minutes from the board meeting could be compared to the dates that were recorded for the awards. In addition, the dates should again be confirmed upon exercise.

## Par and No-Par Value Stocks

**Par value stock** is capital stock to which the charter has assigned a value per share. Years ago, par value determined the **legal capital** per share that a company must retain in the business for the protection of corporate creditors. That amount was not available for withdrawal by stockholders. Thus, in the past, most states required the corporation to sell its shares at par or above.

However, par value was often immaterial relative to the actual value of the company's stock—even at the time of issuance. Thus, its usefulness as a protective device to creditors was questionable. For example, **Facebook**'s par value is $0.000006 per share, yet its market price recently was $84. Thus, par has no relationship with market price. In the vast majority of cases, it is an immaterial amount. As a consequence, today many states do not require a par value. Instead, they use other means to protect creditors.

**No-par value stock** is capital stock to which the charter has not assigned a value. No-par value stock is fairly common today. For example, **Nike** and **Procter & Gamble** both have no-par stock. In many states, the board of directors assigns a **stated value** to no-par shares.

## DO IT! 1a | Corporate Organization

Indicate whether each of the following statements is true or false. If false, indicate how to correct the statement.

_____ 1. Similar to partners in a partnership, stockholders of a corporation have unlimited liability.

_____ 2. It is relatively easy for a corporation to obtain capital through the issuance of stock.

_____ 3. The separation of ownership and management is an advantage of the corporate form of business.

_____ 4. The journal entry to record the authorization of capital stock includes a credit to the appropriate capital stock account.

_____ 5. All states require a par value per share for capital stock.

**ACTION PLAN**

- Review the characteristics of a corporation to understand which are advantages and which are disadvantages.

- Understand that corporations raise capital through the issuance of stock, which can be par or no-par.

**Solution**

**1.** False. The liability of stockholders is normally limited to their investment in the corporation. **2.** True. **3.** False. The separation of ownership and management is a disadvantage of the corporate form of business. **4.** False. The authorization of capital stock does not result in a formal accounting entry. **5.** False. Many states do not require a par value.

Related exercise material: **BE11.1, DO IT! 11.1a, E11.1, and E11.2.**

# Corporate Capital

Owners' equity for a corporation is identified by various names: **stockholders' equity**, **shareholders' equity**, or **corporate capital**. The stockholders' equity section of a corporation's balance sheet consists of two parts: (1) paid-in (contributed) capital and (2) retained earnings (earned capital).

The distinction between **paid-in capital** and **retained earnings** is important from both a legal and a financial point of view. Legally, corporations can make distributions of earnings (declare dividends) out of retained earnings in all states. However, in many states they cannot declare dividends out of paid-in capital. Management, stockholders, and others often look to retained earnings for the continued existence and growth of the corporation.

## Paid-In Capital

**Paid-in capital** is the total amount of cash and other assets paid in to the corporation by stockholders in exchange for capital stock. As noted earlier, when a corporation has only one class of stock, it is **common stock**.

## Retained Earnings

**Retained earnings** is net income that a corporation retains for future use. Net income is recorded in Retained Earnings by a closing entry that debits Income Summary and credits Retained Earnings. For example, assuming that net income for Delta Robotics in its first year of operations is $130,000, the closing entry is:

−130,000 Inc
+130,000 RE

**Cash Flows**
no effect

| | | |
|---|---|---|
| Income Summary | 130,000 | |
|    Retained Earnings | | 130,000 |
|      (To close Income Summary and transfer net income | | |
|      to Retained Earnings) | | |

If Delta Robotics has a balance of $800,000 in common stock at the end of its first year, its stockholders' equity section is as shown in **Illustration 11.5**.

**ILLUSTRATION 11.5**

**Stockholders' equity section**

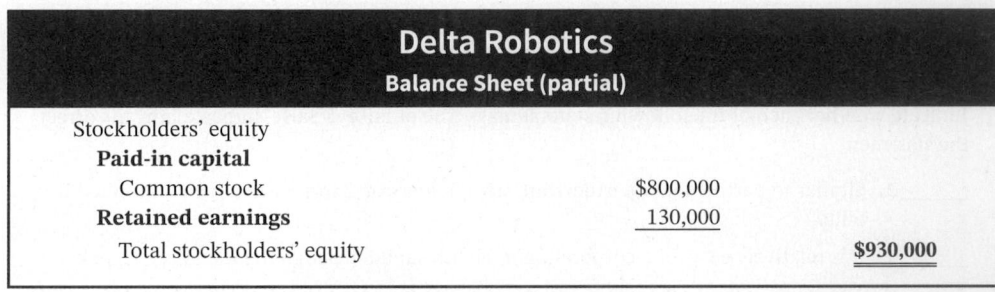

| **Delta Robotics** | | |
|---|---|---|
| **Balance Sheet (partial)** | | |
| Stockholders' equity | | |
|   **Paid-in capital** | | |
|     Common stock | $800,000 | |
|   **Retained earnings** | 130,000 | |
|     Total stockholders' equity | | **$930,000** |

**Illustration 11.6** compares the owners' equity (stockholders' equity) accounts reported on a balance sheet for a proprietorship and a corporation.

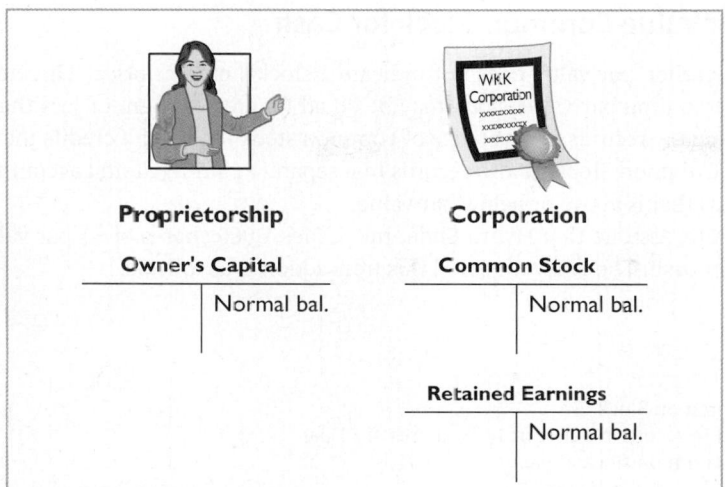

ILLUSTRATION 11.6
**Comparison of owners' equity accounts**

## DO IT! 1b | Corporate Capital

ACTION PLAN

- Record net income in Retained Earnings by a closing entry in which Income Summary is debited and Retained Earnings is credited.

- In the stockholders' equity section, show (1) paid-in capital and (2) retained earnings.

At the end of its first year of operation, Doral Corporation has $750,000 of common stock and net income of $122,000. Prepare (a) the closing entry for net income and (b) the stockholders' equity section at year-end.

### Solution

| | | |
|---|---|---|
| **a.** Income Summary | 122,000 | |
| Retained Earnings | | 122,000 |
| (To close Income Summary and transfer net income to Retained Earnings) | | |

**b.** Stockholders' equity
Paid-in capital

| | | |
|---|---|---|
| Common stock | $750,000 | |
| Retained earnings | 122,000 | |
| Total stockholders' equity | | $872,000 |

Related exercise material: **DO IT! 11.1b.**

# Accounting for Stock Issuances

### LEARNING OBJECTIVE 2

Explain how to account for the issuance of common, preferred, and treasury stock.

## Accounting for Common Stock

Let's now look at how to account for issues of common stock. The primary objectives in accounting for the issuance of common stock are (1) to identify the specific sources of paid-in capital, and (2) to maintain the distinction between paid-in capital and retained earnings. **The issuance of common stock affects only paid-in capital accounts.**

## Issuing Par Value Common Stock for Cash

As discussed earlier, par value does not indicate a stock's market price. Therefore, the cash proceeds from issuing par value stock may be equal to, greater than, or less than par value. When the company records the issuance of common stock for cash, it credits the par value of the shares to Common Stock. It also records in a separate paid-in capital account the portion of the proceeds that is above or below par value.

To illustrate, assume that Hydro-Slide, Inc. issues 1,000 shares of $1 par value common stock at par for cash. The entry to record this transaction is as follows.

Cash Flows
+1,000

| | | |
|---|---|---|
| Cash | 1,000 | |
|    Common Stock | | 1,000 |
|      (To record issuance of 1,000 shares of $1 par common stock at par) | | |

Now assume that Hydro-Slide issues an additional 1,000 shares of the $1 par value common stock for cash at $5 per share. The amount received above the par value, in this case $4 ($5 − $1), is credited to Paid-in Capital in Excess of Par—Common Stock. The entry is as follows.

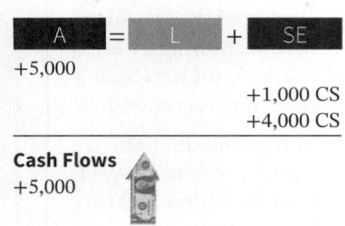

Cash Flows
+5,000

| | | |
|---|---|---|
| Cash | 5,000 | |
|    Common Stock | | 1,000 |
|    Paid-in Capital in Excess of Par—Common Stock | | 4,000 |
|      (To record issuance of 1,000 shares of $1 par common stock) | | |

**ALTERNATIVE TERMINOLOGY**

Paid-in Capital in Excess of Par is also called *Premium on Stock*.

**ILLUSTRATION 11.7**

Stockholders' equity—paid-in capital in excess of par

The total paid-in capital from these two transactions is $6,000, and the legal capital is $2,000 (see **Alternative Terminology**). Assuming Hydro-Slide, Inc. has retained earnings of $27,000, **Illustration 11.7** shows the company's stockholders' equity section.

| Hydro-Slide, Inc. Balance Sheet (partial) | |
|---|---|
| Stockholders' equity | |
|   Paid-in capital | |
|     Common stock | $ 2,000 |
|     **Paid-in capital in excess of par— common stock** | **4,000** |
|       Total paid-in capital | 6,000 |
|   Retained earnings | 27,000 |
|       Total stockholders' equity | $33,000 |

When a corporation issues stock for less than par value, it debits the account Paid-in Capital in Excess of Par—Common Stock if a credit balance exists in this account. If a credit balance does not exist, then the corporation debits to Retained Earnings the amount less than par. This situation occurs only rarely. Most states do not permit the sale of common stock below par value because stockholders may be held personally liable for the difference between the price paid upon original sale and par value.

## Issuing No-Par Common Stock for Cash

When no-par common stock has a stated value, the entries are similar to those illustrated for par value stock. The corporation credits the stated value to Common Stock. Also, when the selling price of no-par stock exceeds stated value, the corporation credits the excess to Paid-in Capital in Excess of Stated Value—Common Stock.

For example, assume that instead of $1 par value stock, Hydro-Slide, Inc. has $5 stated value no-par stock and the company issues 5,000 shares at $8 per share for cash. The entry is as follows.

| | | |
|---|---:|---:|
| Cash | 40,000 | |
|     Common Stock | | 25,000 |
|     Paid-in Capital in Excess of Stated Value—Common Stock | | 15,000 |
|       (To record issuance of 5,000 shares of $5 stated | | |
|       value no-par stock) | | |

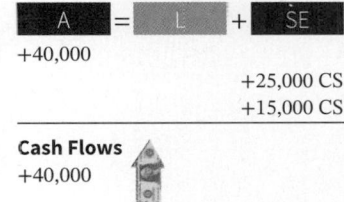

Hydro-Slide, Inc. reports Paid-in Capital in Excess of Stated Value—Common Stock as part of paid-in capital in the stockholders' equity section.

What happens when no-par stock does not have a stated value? In that case, the corporation credits the entire proceeds to Common Stock. Thus, if Hydro-Slide does not assign a stated value to its no-par stock, it records the issuance of the 5,000 shares at $8 per share for cash as follows.

| | | |
|---|---:|---:|
| Cash | 40,000 | |
|     Common Stock | | 40,000 |
|       (To record issuance of 5,000 shares of no-par stock) | | |

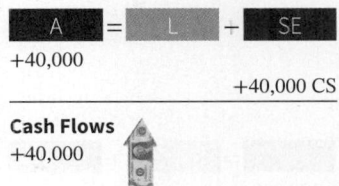

## Issuing Common Stock for Services or Noncash Assets

Corporations also may issue stock for services (compensation to attorneys or consultants) or for noncash assets (land, buildings, and equipment). In such cases, what cost should be recognized in the exchange transaction? To comply with the **historical cost principle**, in a noncash transaction **cost is the cash equivalent price**. Thus, **cost is either the fair value of the consideration given up or the fair value of the consideration received**, whichever is more clearly determinable.

To illustrate, assume that attorneys have helped Jordan Company incorporate. They have billed the company $5,000 for their services. They agree to accept 4,000 shares of $1 par value common stock in payment of their bill. At the time of the exchange, there is no established market price for the stock. In this case, the fair value of the consideration received ($5,000 attorney services) is more clearly evident. Accordingly, Jordan Company makes the following entry.

| | | |
|---|---:|---:|
| Organization Expense | 5,000 | |
|     Common Stock | | 4,000 |
|     Paid-in Capital in Excess of Par—Common Stock | | 1,000 |
|       (To record issuance of 4,000 shares of $1 par value | | |
|       stock to attorneys) | | |

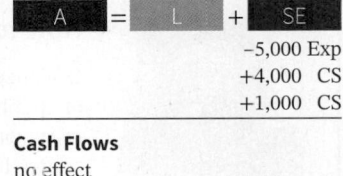

As explained earlier, organization costs are expensed as incurred.

In contrast, assume that Athletic Research Inc. is an existing publicly held corporation. Its $5 par value common stock is actively traded at $8 per share. The company issues 10,000 shares of stock to acquire land recently advertised for sale at $90,000. The most clearly evident value in this noncash transaction is the market price of the consideration given ($80,000 common stock; the advertised price of the land is not necessarily indicative of its value). The company records the transaction as follows.

| | | |
|---|---|---|
| Land | 80,000 | |
| Common Stock | | 50,000 |
| Paid-in Capital in Excess of Par—Common Stock | | 30,000 |
| (To record issuance of 10,000 shares of $5 par value stock for land) | | |

+80,000
+50,000 CS
+30,000 CS

**Cash Flows**
no effect

As illustrated in these examples, **the par value of the stock is never a factor in determining the cost of the assets or services received in noncash transactions**. This is also true of the stated value of no-par stock.

## Accounting for Preferred Stock

To appeal to a larger segment of potential investors, a corporation may issue an additional class of stock, called preferred stock. **Preferred stock** has contractual provisions that give it some preference or priority over common stock. Typically, preferred stockholders have a priority as to (1) distributions of earnings (dividends) and (2) assets in the event of liquidation. However, they generally do not have voting rights.

Like common stock, corporations may issue preferred stock for cash or for noncash assets. The entries for these transactions are similar to the entries for common stock. When a corporation has more than one class of stock, each paid-in capital account title should identify the stock to which it relates. A company might have the following accounts: Preferred Stock, Common Stock, Paid-in Capital in Excess of Par—Preferred Stock, and Paid-in Capital in Excess of Par—Common Stock.

For example, if Stine Corporation issues 10,000 shares of $10 par value preferred stock for $12 cash per share, the entry to record the issuance is as follows.

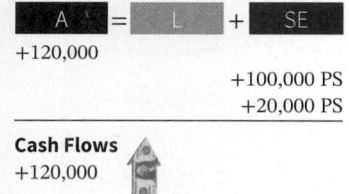

| | | |
|---|---|---|
| Cash | 120,000 | |
| Preferred Stock | | 100,000 |
| Paid-in Capital in Excess of Par—Preferred Stock | | 20,000 |
| (To record issuance of 10,000 shares of $10 par value preferred stock) | | |

+120,000
+100,000 PS
+20,000 PS

**Cash Flows**
+120,000

Preferred stock may have either a par value or no-par value. In the stockholders' equity section of the balance sheet, companies list preferred stock first because of its dividend and liquidation preferences over common stock.

---

**Investor Insight** Facebook

### How to Read Stock Quotes

Emmanuel Dunand/
AFP/Getty Images

Organized exchanges trade the stock of publicly held companies at dollar prices per share established by the interaction between buyers and sellers. For each listed security, the financial press reports the high and low prices of the stock during the year, the total volume of stock traded on a given day, the high and low prices for the day, and the closing market price, with the net change for the day. **Facebook** is listed on the NASDAQ exchange. Here is a listing for Facebook:

| | 52 Weeks | | | | | | |
|---|---|---|---|---|---|---|---|
| Stock | High | Low | Volume | High | Low | Close | Net Change |
| Facebook | 86.07 | 54.66 | 54,156,600 | 85.59 | 83.11 | 84.63 | .629 |

These numbers indicate the following. The high and low market prices for the last 52 weeks have been $86.07 and $54.66. The trading volume for the day was 54,156,600 shares. The high, low, and closing prices for that date were $85.59, $83.11, and $84.63, respectively. The net change for the day was a decrease of $0.629 per share.

**For stocks traded on organized exchanges, how are the dollar prices per share established? What factors might influence the price of shares in the marketplace? (Answer is available near the end of the chapter.)**

## DO IT! 2a | Issuance of Stock

Cayman Corporation begins operations on March 1 by issuing 100,000 shares of $1 par value common stock for cash at $12 per share. On March 15, it issues 5,000 shares of common stock to attorneys in settlement of their bill of $50,000 for organization costs. On March 28, Cayman Corporation issues 1,500 shares of $10 par value preferred stock for cash at $30 per share. Journalize the issuance of the common and preferred shares, assuming the shares are not publicly traded.

### Solution

| | | | |
|---|---|---|---|
| Mar. 1 | Cash | 1,200,000 | |
| | Common Stock (100,000 × $1) | | 100,000 |
| | Paid-in Capital in Excess of Par—Common Stock | | 1,100,000 |
| | (To record issuance of 100,000 shares at $12 per share) | | |
| Mar. 15 | Organization Expense | 50,000 | |
| | Common Stock (5,000 × $1) | | 5,000 |
| | Paid-in Capital in Excess of Par—Common Stock | | 45,000 |
| | (To record issuance of 5,000 shares for attorneys' fees) | | |
| Mar. 28 | Cash | 45,000 | |
| | Preferred Stock (1,500 × $10) | | 15,000 |
| | Paid-in Capital in Excess of Par—Preferred Stock | | 30,000 |
| | (To record issuance of 1,500 shares at $30 per share) | | |

Related exercise material: **BE11.2, BE11.3, BE11 4, BE11.5, DO IT! 11.2a, E11.3, E11.4 E11.6, and E11 8.**

**ACTION PLAN**

- In issuing shares for cash, credit Common Stock or Preferred Stock for par value per share.
- Credit any additional proceeds in excess of par to a separate paid-in capital account.
- When stock is issued for services, use the cash equivalent price.
- For the cash equivalent price, use either the fair value of what is given up or the fair value of what is received, whichever is more clearly determinable.

# Accounting for Treasury Stock

**Treasury stock** is a corporation's own stock that it has issued and subsequently reacquired from shareholders but not retired (see **Helpful Hint**). A corporation may acquire treasury stock for various reasons:

1. To reissue the shares to officers and employees under bonus and stock compensation plans.
2. To increase trading of the company's stock in the securities market. Companies expect that buying their own stock will signal that management believes the stock is underpriced, which they hope will enhance its market price.
3. To have additional shares available for use in the acquisition of other companies.
4. To reduce the number of shares outstanding and thereby increase earnings per share.

A less frequent reason for purchasing treasury shares is to eliminate hostile shareholders by buying them out.

Many corporations have treasury stock. For example, approximately 65% of U.S. companies have treasury stock. In a recent year, **Nike** purchased more than 6 million treasury shares.

## Purchase of Treasury Stock

Companies generally account for treasury stock by **the cost method**. This method uses the cost of the shares purchased to value the treasury stock. Under the cost method, the company debits **Treasury Stock** for the **price paid to reacquire the shares**. When the company disposes of the shares, it credits to Treasury Stock **the same amount** it paid to reacquire the shares.

To illustrate, assume that on January 1, 2022, the stockholders' equity section of Mead Inc. has 400,000 shares authorized and 100,000 shares of $5 par value common stock outstanding (all issued at par value) and Retained Earnings of $200,000. **Illustration 11.8** shows the stockholders' equity section before purchase of treasury stock.

**HELPFUL HINT**

Treasury shares do not have dividend rights or voting rights.

**ILLUSTRATION 11.8**

**Stockholders' equity with no treasury stock**

**Mead, Inc.**
Balance Sheet (partial)

| Stockholders' equity | |
|---|---|
| Paid-in capital | |
| Common stock, $5 par value, 400,000 shares | |
| authorized, 100,000 shares issued and outstanding | $500,000 |
| Retained earnings | 200,000 |
| Total stockholders' equity | $700,000 |

On February 1, 2022, Mead acquires 4,000 shares of its common stock at $8 per share. The entry is as follows.

−32,000 TS

−32,000

**Cash Flows**

−32,000

| Feb. 1 | Treasury Stock | 32,000 | |
|---|---|---|---|
| | Cash | | 32,000 |
| | (To record purchase of 4,000 shares of treasury stock at $8 per share) | | |

Mead debits Treasury Stock for the cost of the shares purchased ($32,000). Is the original paid-in capital account, Common Stock, affected? No, because **the number of issued shares does not change**.

In the stockholders' equity section of the balance sheet, Mead deducts treasury stock from total paid-in capital and retained earnings. Treasury Stock is a **contra stockholders' equity account**. Thus, the acquisition of treasury stock reduces stockholders' equity. The stockholders' equity section of Mead, Inc. after purchase of treasury stock is as shown in **Illustration 11.9**.

**ILLUSTRATION 11.9**

**Stockholders' equity with treasury stock**

**Mead, Inc.**
Balance Sheet (partial)

| Stockholders' equity | |
|---|---|
| Paid-in capital | |
| Common stock, $5 par value, 400,000 shares authorized, | |
| 100,000 shares issued, and 96,000 shares outstanding | $500,000 |
| Retained earnings | 200,000 |
| Total paid-in capital and retained earnings | 700,000 |
| **Less: Treasury stock (4,000 shares)** | **32,000** |
| Total stockholders' equity | $668,000 |

**ETHICS NOTE**

The purchase of treasury stock reduces the cushion for creditors. To protect creditors, many states require that a portion of retained earnings equal to the cost of the treasury stock purchased be restricted from being paid as dividends.

Mead discloses in the balance sheet both the number of shares issued (100,000) and the number of shares in the treasury (4,000). The difference is the number of shares of stock outstanding (96,000). The term **outstanding stock** means the number of shares of issued stock that are being held by stockholders.

Some maintain that companies should report treasury stock as an asset because it can be sold for cash. But under this reasoning, companies would also show unissued stock as an asset, which is clearly incorrect. Rather than being an asset, treasury stock reduces stockholder claims on corporate assets. This effect is correctly shown by reporting treasury stock as a deduction from total paid-in capital and retained earnings (see **Ethics Note**).

**HELPFUL HINT**

Treasury stock transactions are classified as capital stock transactions. As in the case when stock is issued, the income statement is not involved.

### Disposal of Treasury Stock

Treasury stock is usually sold. The accounting for its sale differs when treasury stock is sold above cost than when it is sold below cost (see **Helpful Hint**).

**Sale of Treasury Stock Above Cost**    If the selling price of the treasury stock is equal to its cost, the company records the sale of the shares by a debit to Cash and a credit to Treasury

Stock. When the selling price of the stock is greater than its cost, the company credits the difference to Paid-in Capital from Treasury Stock.

To illustrate, assume that on July 1, Mead, Inc. sells for $10 per share 1,000 of the 4,000 shares of its treasury stock previously acquired at $8 per share. The entry is as follows.

| July 1 | Cash (1,000 × $10) | 10,000 | |
| | Treasury Stock (1,000 × $8) | | 8,000 |
| | Paid-in Capital from Treasury Stock | | 2,000 |
| | (To record sale of 1,000 shares of treasury stock above cost) | | |

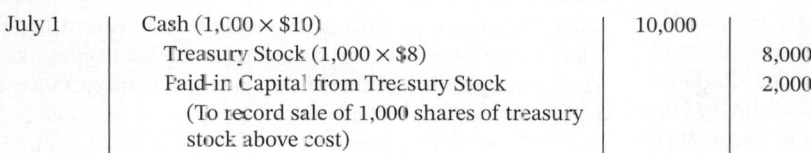

A = L + SE
+10,000
+8,000 TS
+2,000 TS

Cash Flows
+10,000

Mead does not record a $2,000 gain on sale of treasury stock because (1) gains on sales occur when **assets** are sold, and treasury stock is not an asset, and (2) a corporation does not realize a gain or suffer a loss from stock transactions with its own stockholders. Thus, companies should **not** include in net income any paid-in capital arising from the sale of treasury stock. Instead, they report Paid-in Capital from Treasury Stock separately on the balance sheet, as a part of paid-in capital.

**Sale of Treasury Stock Below Cost**   When a company sells treasury stock below its cost, it usually debits to Paid-in Capital from Treasury Stock the excess of cost over selling price. Thus, if Mead, Inc. sells an additional 800 shares of treasury stock on October 1 at $7 per share, it makes the following entry.

| Oct. 1 | Cash (800 × $7) | 5,600 | |
| | Paid-in Capital from Treasury Stock | 800 | |
| | Treasury Stock (800 × $8) | | 6,400 |
| | (To record sale of 800 shares of treasury stock below cost) | | |

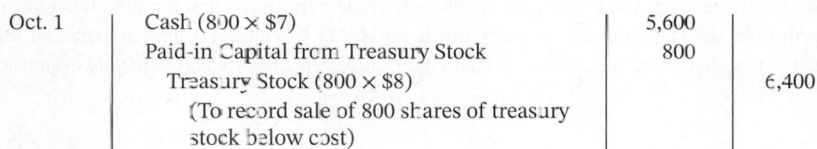

A = L + SE
+5,600
−800 TS
+6,400 TS

Cash Flows
−5,600

Observe the following from the two sales entries. (1) Mead credits Treasury Stock at cost in each entry. (2) Mead uses Paid-in Capital from Treasury Stock for the difference between cost and the resale price of the shares. (3) The original paid-in capital account, Common Stock, is not affected. **The sale of treasury stock increases both total assets and total stockholders' equity.**

**Illustration 11.10** shows the treasury stock account balances on October 1 after posting the foregoing entries.

| Treasury Stock | | | | Paid-in Capital from Treasury Stock | | | |
|---|---|---|---|---|---|---|---|
| Feb. 1 | 32,000 | July 1 | 8,000 | Oct. 1 | 800 | July 1 | 2,000 |
| | | Oct. 1 | 6,400 | | | Oct. 1 Bal. | 1,200 |
| Oct. 1 Bal. | 17,600 | | | | | | |

**ILLUSTRATION 11.10**
**Treasury stock accounts**

When a company fully depletes the credit balance in Paid-in Capital from Treasury Stock, it debits to Retained Earnings any additional excess of cost over selling price. To illustrate, assume that Mead, Inc. sells its remaining 2,200 shares at $7 per share on December 1. The excess of cost over selling price is $2,200 [2,200 × ($8 − $7)]. In this case, Mead debits $1,200 of the excess to Paid-in Capital from Treasury Stock. It debits the remainder to Retained Earnings. The entry is as follows.

| Dec. 1 | Cash (2,200 × $7) | 15,400 | |
| | Paid-in Capital from Treasury Stock | 1,200 | |
| | Retained Earnings | 1,000 | |
| | Treasury Stock (2,200 × $8) | | 17,600 |
| | (To record sale of 2,200 shares of treasury stock at $7 per share) | | |

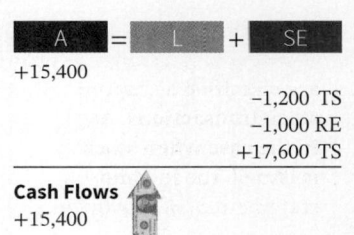

A = L + SE
+15,400
−1,200 TS
−1,000 RE
+17,600 TS

Cash Flows
+15,400

## Accounting Across the Organization   Reebok

### A Bold Repurchase Strategy

In a bold (and some would say risky) move, **Reebok** at one time bought back nearly a third of its shares. This repurchase of shares dramatically reduced Reebok's available cash. In fact, the company borrowed significant funds to accomplish the repurchase. In a press release, management stated that it was repurchasing the shares because it believed its stock was severely underpriced. The repurchase of so many shares was meant to signal management's belief in good future earnings.

Han Myung-Gu/
WireImage/Getty Images

Skeptics, however, suggested that Reebok's management was repurchasing shares to make it less likely that another company would acquire Reebok (in which case Reebok's top managers would likely lose their jobs). By depleting its cash, Reebok became a less attractive acquisition target. Acquiring companies like to purchase companies with large cash balances so they can pay off debt used in the acquisition.

**What signal might a large stock repurchase send to investors regarding management's belief about the company's growth opportunities? (Answer is available near the end of the chapter.)**

---

**ACTION PLAN**

- **Record the purchase of treasury stock at cost.**
- **When treasury stock is sold above its cost, credit the excess of the selling price over cost to Paid-in Capital from Treasury Stock. If Paid-in Capital from Treasury Stock is depleted, then debit Retained Earnings.**
- **When treasury stock is sold below its cost, debit the excess of cost over selling price to Paid-in Capital from Treasury Stock.**

## DO IT! 2b ⏐ Treasury Stock

Santa Anita Inc. purchases 3,000 shares of its $50 par value common stock for $180,000 cash on July 1. It will hold the shares in the treasury until resold. On November 1, the corporation sells 1,000 shares of treasury stock for cash at $70 per share. Journalize the treasury stock transactions.

### Solution

| | | | |
|---|---|---:|---:|
| July 1 | Treasury Stock | 180,000 | |
| |    Cash | | 180,000 |
| |     (To record the purchase of 3,000 shares at $60 per share) | | |
| Nov. 1 | Cash | 70,000 | |
| |    Treasury Stock | | 60,000 |
| |    Paid-in Capital from Treasury Stock | | 10,000 |
| |     (To record the sale of 1,000 shares of treasury stock at $70 per share) | | |

Related exercise material: **BE11.6, DO IT! 11.2b, E11.7, E11.8 and E11.9.**

---

# Cash Dividends, Stock Dividends, and Stock Splits

### LEARNING OBJECTIVE 3

Explain how to account for cash dividends, stock dividends, and stock splits.

A **dividend** is a corporation's distribution of cash or stock to its stockholders on a pro rata (proportional to ownership) basis. Pro rata means that if you own 10% of the common shares, you will receive 10% of the dividend. Dividends can take four forms: cash, property, scrip (a promissory note to pay cash), or stock. Cash dividends predominate in practice although companies also declare stock dividends with some frequency. These two forms of dividends are therefore the focus of our discussion.

Investors are very interested in a company's dividend practices. In the financial press, **dividends are generally reported quarterly as a dollar amount per share**. (Sometimes they are reported on an annual basis.) For example, the recent **quarterly** dividend rate was 24 cents per share for **Nike**, 22 cents per share for **GE**, and 25 cents per share for **Conagra Brands**.

# Cash Dividends

A **cash dividend** is a pro rata distribution of cash to stockholders. Cash dividends are not paid on treasury shares. For a corporation to pay a cash dividend, it must have the following.

1. **Retained earnings.** The legality of a cash dividend depends on the laws of the state in which the company is incorporated. Payment of cash dividends from retained earnings is legal in all states. In general, cash dividend distributions from only the balance in common stock (legal capital) are illegal.

   A dividend declared out of paid-in capital is termed a **liquidating dividend**. Such a dividend reduces or "liquidates" the amount originally paid in by stockholders. Statutes vary considerably with respect to cash dividends based on paid-in capital in excess of par or stated value. Many states permit such dividends.

2. **Adequate cash.** Recently, Facebook had a balance in retained earnings of $6,099 million but a cash balance of only $4,315 million. If it had wanted to pay a dividend equal to its retained earnings, Facebook would have had to raise $1,784 million more in cash. It would have been unlikely to do this because it would not be able to pay this much in dividends in future years. In addition, such a dividend would completely deplete Facebook's balance in retained earnings, so it would not be able to pay a dividend in the next year unless it had positive net income.

3. **Declared dividends.** A company does not pay dividends unless its board of directors decides to do so, at which point the board "declares" the dividend. The board of directors has full authority to determine the amount of income to distribute in the form of a dividend and the amount to retain in the business. Dividends do not accrue like interest on a note payable, and they are not a liability until declared.

The amount and timing of a dividend are important issues for management to consider. The payment of a large cash dividend could lead to liquidity problems for the company. On the other hand, a small dividend or a missed dividend may cause unhappiness among stockholders. Many stockholders expect to receive a reasonable cash payment from the company on a periodic basis. Many companies declare and pay cash dividends quarterly. On the other hand, a number of high-growth companies pay no dividends, preferring to conserve cash to finance future capital expenditures.

Investors monitor a company's dividend practices. For example, regular dividend boosts in the face of irregular earnings can be a warning signal. Companies with high dividends and rising debt may be borrowing money to pay shareholders. On the other hand, low dividends may not be a negative sign because it may mean the company is reinvesting in itself, which may result in high returns through increases in the stock price. Presumably, investors seeking regular dividends buy stock in companies that pay periodic dividends, and those seeking growth in the stock price (capital gains) buy stock in companies that retain their earnings rather than pay dividends

## Entries for Cash Dividends

Three dates are important in connection with dividends: (1) the declaration date, (2) the record date, and (3) the payment date. Normally, there are two to four weeks between each date. Companies make accounting entries on the declaration date and the payment date. Companies do not make any entries on the record date.

On the **declaration date**, the board of directors formally declares (authorizes) the cash dividend and announces it to stockholders. The declaration of a cash dividend **commits**

**the corporation to a legal obligation**. The company must make an entry to recognize the increase in Cash Dividends and the increase in the liability Dividends Payable.

To illustrate, assume that on December 1, 2022, the directors of Media General declare a 50 cents per share cash dividend on 100,000 outstanding shares of $10 par value common stock. The dividend is $50,000 (100,000 × $0.50). The entry to record the declaration is as follows.

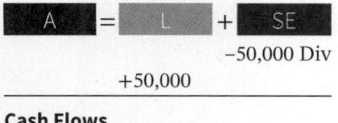

Cash Flows
no effect

**Declaration Date**

| | | | |
|---|---|---|---|
| Dec. 1 | Cash Dividends | 50,000 | |
| | Dividends Payable | | 50,000 |
| | (To record declaration of cash dividend) | | |

Media General debits the account Cash Dividends. Cash dividends decrease retained earnings. We use the specific title Cash Dividends to differentiate it from other types of dividends, such as stock dividends. Dividends Payable is a current liability. It will normally be paid within the next several months. *For homework problems, you should use the Cash Dividends account for recording dividend declarations.*

At the **record date**, the company determines ownership of the outstanding shares for dividend purposes (see **Helpful Hint**). The stockholders' records maintained by the corporation supply this information. In the interval between the declaration date and the record date, the corporation updates its stock ownership records. For Media General, the record date is December 22. No entry is required on this date because the corporation's liability recognized on the declaration date is unchanged.

**Record Date**

| | | | |
|---|---|---|---|
| Dec. 22 | No entry | | |

On the **payment date**, the company makes cash dividend payments to the stockholders of record (as of December 22) and records the payment of the dividend. If January 20 is the payment date for Media General, the entry on that date is as follows.

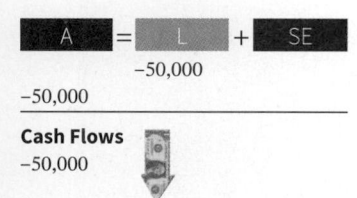

Cash Flows
−50,000

**Payment Date**

| | | | |
|---|---|---|---|
| Jan. 20 | Dividends Payable | 50,000 | |
| | Cash | | 50,000 |
| | (To record payment of cash dividend) | | |

Note that payment of the dividend reduces both current assets and current liabilities. It has no effect on stockholders' equity. The cumulative effect of the declaration and payment of a cash dividend is to **decrease both stockholders' equity and total assets**. **Illustration 11.11** summarizes the three important dates associated with dividends for Media General.

**ILLUSTRATION 11.11**
**Key dividend dates**

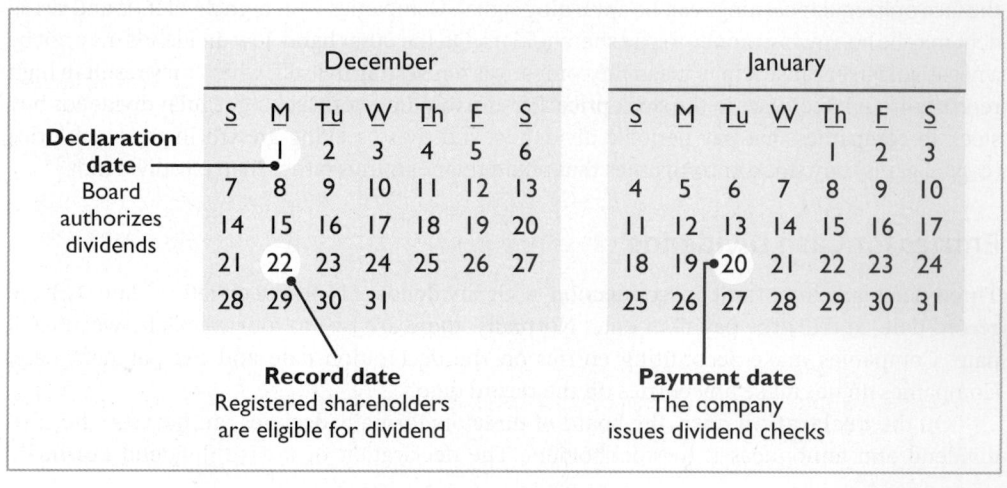

When using a Cash Dividends account, Media General should transfer the balance of that account to Retained Earnings at the end of the year by a closing entry. The entry for Media General at closing on December 31, 2022, is as follows.

| Dec. 31 | Retained Earnings | 50,000 | |
| | Cash Dividends | | 50,000 |
| | (To close Cash Dividends to Retained Earnings) | | |

---

## Investor Insight

iStock.com/Palto

### What About Dividends?

If you have some excess dollars that you want to invest, you might consider stocks that pay dividends. According to data from the **Standard & Poor's (S&P)** Dow Jones Indices, dividend income made up 33% of the monthly return of the S&P 500 between 1926 and 2015. What that means is that dividends comprise one-third of the return to shareholders.

In addition, data from 1927 to 2014 indicate that dividend payers outperformed non-dividend payers, averaging 10.4% annual growth versus 8.5%. If you do not think that difference is much, the table indicates how an annual investment of $10,000 would grow at each of these rates.

| Growth Over | 8.5% Annual Growth Rate | 10.4% Annual Growth Rate |
| --- | --- | --- |
| 10 years | $ 161,000 | $ 179,400 |
| 20 years | 524,900 | 661,800 |
| 30 years | 1,300,000 | 2,000,000 |

Some companies have strong dividend yields, such as **Ford Motor Company** and **AT&T**. Others have been increasing dividend payouts at a strong clip, such as **UPS**, **Microsoft**, and **Boeing**. Good luck in your future investing!

**Source:** Selena Maranjian, "Dividend Stocks in 2017: 7 Stats Everyone Should Know," *The Motley Fool* (December 14, 2016).

**What factors must management consider in deciding how large a dividend to pay? (Answer is available near the end of the chapter.)**

---

# Dividend Preferences

**Preferred stockholders have the right to receive dividends before common stockholders.** For example, if the dividend rate on preferred stock is $5 per share, common shareholders cannot receive any dividends in the current year until preferred stockholders have received $5 per share. The first claim to dividends does not, however, **guarantee** the payment of dividends. Dividends depend on many factors, such as adequate retained earnings and availability of cash. If a company does not pay dividends to preferred stockholders, it cannot pay dividends to common stockholders.

For preferred stock, companies state the per share dividend amount as a percentage of the par value or as a specified dollar amount. For example, **EarthLink** (before it merged with **Windstream Holdings**) specified a 3% dividend on its $100 par value preferred stock. **PepsiCo** pays $4.56 per share on its no-par preferred stock.

Most preferred stocks also have a preference on corporate assets if the corporation fails. This feature provides security for the preferred stockholder. The preference to assets may be for the par value of the shares or for a specified liquidating value. For example, **Commonwealth Edison**'s preferred stock entitles its holders to receive $31.80 per share, plus accrued and unpaid dividends, in the event of liquidation. The liquidation preference establishes the respective claims of creditors and preferred stockholders in litigation involving bankruptcy lawsuits.

I hope there's some money left when it's my turn.

Preferred        Common
stockholders   stockholders

**Dividend preferences**

## Cumulative Dividend

Preferred stock often contains a **cumulative dividend** feature. This feature stipulates that preferred stockholders must be paid both current-year dividends and any unpaid prior-year dividends before common stockholders are paid any dividends. When preferred stock is cumulative, preferred dividends not declared in a given period are called **dividends in arrears**.

To illustrate, assume that Scientific Leasing has 5,000 shares of 7%, $100 par value, cumulative preferred stock outstanding. Each $100 share pays a $7 dividend (.07 × $100 par value). The annual dividend is $35,000 (5,000 × $7 per share). If dividends are two years in arrears, preferred stockholders are entitled to receive the dividends shown in **Illustration 11.12**.

**ILLUSTRATION 11.12**

**Computation of total dividends to preferred stock**

| | |
|---|---:|
| Dividends in arrears ($35,000 × 2) | $ 70,000 |
| Current-year dividends | 35,000 |
| **Total preferred dividends** | **$105,000** |

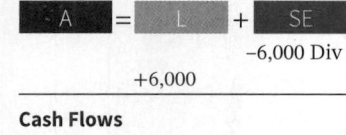

**Payment of a cumulative dividend**

Dividend in arrears

Current dividend

**Preferred stockholders**

The company cannot pay dividends to common stockholders until it pays the entire preferred dividend. In other words, companies cannot pay dividends to common stockholders while any preferred dividends are in arrears.

**Dividends in arrears are not considered a liability. No payment obligation exists until the board of directors formally declares that the corporation will pay a dividend.** However, companies should disclose in the notes to the financial statements the amount of dividends in arrears. Doing so enables investors to assess the potential impact of this commitment on the corporation's financial position.

The investment community does not look favorably on companies that are unable to meet their dividend obligations. As a financial officer noted in discussing one company's failure to pay its cumulative preferred dividend for a period of time, "Not meeting your obligations on something like that is a major black mark on your record."

## Allocating Cash Dividends Between Preferred and Common Stock

As indicated, preferred stock has priority over common stock in regard to dividends. Holders of cumulative preferred stock must be paid any unpaid prior-year dividends and their current-year dividend before common stockholders receive dividends.

To illustrate, assume that at December 31, 2022, IBR Inc. has 1,000 shares of 8%, $100 par value cumulative preferred stock outstanding. It also has 50,000 shares of $10 par value common stock outstanding. The dividend per share for preferred stock is $8 ($100 par value × 8%). The required annual dividend for preferred stock is therefore $8,000 (1,000 shares × $8). At December 31, 2022, the directors declare a $6,000 cash dividend. In this case, the entire dividend amount goes to preferred stockholders because of their dividend preference. The entry to record the declaration of the dividend is as follows.

A = L + SE

−6,000 Div

+6,000

**Cash Flows**
no effect

| Dec. 31 | Cash Dividends | 6,000 | |
|---|---|---|---|
| | Dividends Payable | | 6,000 |
| | (To record $6 per share cash dividend to preferred stockholders) | | |

Because of the cumulative feature, dividends of $2 ($8 − $6) per share are in arrears on preferred stock for 2022. IBR must pay this $2,000 of dividends to preferred stockholders before it can pay any future dividends to common stockholders. IBR should disclose dividends in arrears in the financial statements.

At December 31, 2023, IBR declares a $50,000 cash dividend. The allocation of the dividend to the two classes of stock is as shown in **Illustration 11.13**.

**ILLUSTRATION 11.13**

**Allocating dividends to preferred and common stock**

| | | |
|---|---:|---:|
| Total dividend | | $50,000 |
| Allocated to preferred stock | | |
| **Dividends in arrears, 2022 (1,000 × $2)** | $2,000 | |
| **2023 dividend (1,000 × $8)** | 8,000 | 10,000 |
| Remainder allocated to common stock | | $40,000 |

The entry to record the declaration of the dividend is as follows.

| Dec. 31 | Cash Dividends | 50,000 | |
|---|---|---|---|
| | Dividends Payable | | 50,000 |
| | (To record declaration of cash dividends of $10,000 to preferred stock and $40,000 to common stock) | | |

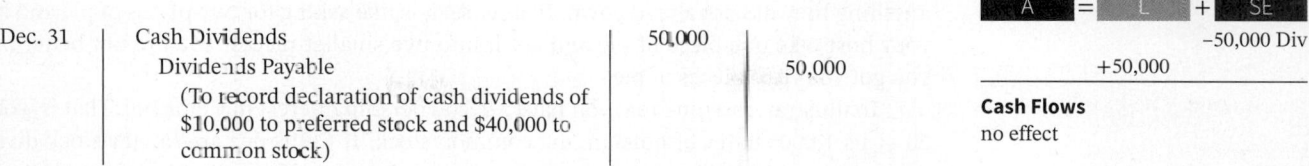

A = L + SE

−50,000 Div

+50,000

**Cash Flows**
no effect

If IBR's preferred stock is not cumulative, preferred stockholders receive only $8,000 in dividends in 2023. Common stockholders receive $42,000.

---

## DO IT! 3a | Dividends on Preferred and Common Stock

MasterMind Corporation has 2,000 shares of 6%, $100 par value preferred stock outstanding at December 31, 2022. At December 31, 2022, the company declared a $60,000 cash dividend. Determine the dividend paid to preferred stockholders and common stockholders under each of the following scenarios.

1. The preferred stock is noncumulative, and the company has not missed any dividends in previous years.
2. The preferred stock is noncumulative, and the company did not pay a dividend in each of the two previous years.
3. The preferred stock is cumulative, and the company did not pay a dividend in each of the two previous years.

### Solution

1. The company has not missed past dividends and the preferred stock is noncumulative. Thus, the preferred stockholders are paid only this year's dividend. The dividend paid to preferred stockholders would be $12,000 (2,000 × .06 × $100). The dividend paid to common stockholders would be $48,000 ($60,000 − $12,000).

2. The preferred stock is noncumulative. Thus, past unpaid dividends do not have to be paid. The dividend paid to preferred stockholders would be $12,000 (2,000 × .06 × $100). The dividend paid to common stockholders would be $48,000 ($60,000 − $12,000).

3. The preferred stock is cumulative. Thus, dividends that have been missed (dividends in arrears) must be paid. The dividend paid to preferred stockholders would be $36,000 (3 × 2,000 × .06 × $100). Of the $36,000, $24,000 relates to dividends in arrears and $12,000 relates to the current year's dividend on preferred stock. The dividend paid to common stockholders would be $24,000 ($60,000 − $36,000).

Related exercise material: **BE11.7, DO IT! 11.3a, and E11.13.**

**ACTION PLAN**

- Determine dividends on preferred shares by multiplying the dividend rate times the par value of the stock times the number of outstanding preferred shares.
- Understand the cumulative feature. If preferred stock is cumulative, then any missed dividends (dividends in arrears) and the current year's dividend must be paid to preferred stockholders before dividends are paid to common stockholders.

---

# Stock Dividends

A **stock dividend** is a pro rata (proportional to ownership) distribution of the corporation's own stock to stockholders. Whereas a company pays cash in a cash dividend, a company issues shares of stock in a stock dividend. **A stock dividend results in a decrease in retained earnings and an increase in paid-in capital.** Unlike a cash dividend, a stock dividend does not decrease total stockholders' equity or total assets.

Because a stock dividend does not result in a distribution of assets, some view it as nothing more than a publicity gesture. Stock dividends are often issued by companies that do not have adequate cash to issue a cash dividend. Such companies may not want to announce that they are not going to issue a cash dividend at their expected time. By issuing a stock dividend, they "save face" by giving the appearance of distributing a dividend. Note that since a stock dividend neither increases nor decreases the assets in the company, investors are not receiving anything they did not already own. In a sense, it is like asking for two pieces of pie and having your host take one piece of pie and cut it into two smaller pieces. You are not better off, but you got your two pieces of pie.

To illustrate, assume that you have a 2% ownership interest in Cetus Inc. That is, you own 20 of its 1,000 shares of outstanding common stock. If Cetus declares a 10% stock dividend, it would issue 100 shares (1,000 × 10%) of stock. You would receive two shares (2% × 100). Would your ownership interest change? No, it would remain at 2% (22 ÷ 1,100). **You now own more shares of stock, but your ownership interest has not changed.**

Cetus has disbursed no cash and has assumed no liabilities. What, then, are the purposes and benefits of a stock dividend? Corporations issue stock dividends generally for one or more of the following reasons.

1. To satisfy stockholders' dividend expectations without spending cash.
2. To increase the marketability of the corporation's stock. When the number of shares outstanding increases, the market price per share decreases. Decreasing the market price of the stock makes it easier for smaller investors to purchase the shares.
3. To emphasize that a company has permanently reinvested in the business a portion of stockholders' equity, which therefore is unavailable for cash dividends.

When the dividend is declared, the board of directors determines the size of the stock dividend and the value assigned to each dividend. In order to meet legal requirements, the per share amount must be at least equal to the par or stated value.

Generally, if the company issues a **small stock dividend** (less than 20–25% of the corporation's outstanding stock), the value assigned to the dividend is the fair value (market price) per share. This treatment is based on the assumption that a small stock dividend will have little effect on the market price of the shares previously outstanding. Thus, many stockholders consider small stock dividends to be distributions of earnings equal to the market price of the shares distributed. If a company issues a **large stock dividend** (greater than 20–25%), the price assigned to the dividend is the par or stated value. Small stock dividends predominate in practice. Thus, we will illustrate only entries for small stock dividends.

## Entries for Stock Dividends

To illustrate the accounting for small stock dividends, assume that Medland Corporation has a balance of $300,000 in retained earnings. It declares a 10% stock dividend on its 50,000 shares of $10 par value common stock. The current market price of its stock is $15 per share. The number of shares to be issued is 5,000 (10% × 50,000). Therefore, the total amount to be debited to Stock Dividends is $75,000 (5,000 × $15). The entry to record the declaration of the stock dividend is as follows.

| A | = | L | + | SE |
|---|---|---|---|---|
| | | | | −75,000 Div |
| | | | | +50,000 CS |
| | | | | +25,000 CS |

**Cash Flows**
no effect

| | | |
|---|---|---|
| Stock Dividends | 75,000 | |
|    Common Stock Dividends Distributable | | 50,000 |
|    Paid-in Capital in Excess of Par—Common Stock | | 25,000 |
|     (To record declaration of 10% stock dividend) | | |

Medland debits Stock Dividends for the market price of the stock issued ($15 × 5,000). (Similar to cash dividends, stock dividends decrease retained earnings.) Medland also credits Common Stock Dividends Distributable for the par value of the dividend shares ($10 × 5,000) and credits Paid-in Capital in Excess of Par—Common Stock for the excess of the market price over par ($5 × 5,000).

Common Stock Dividends Distributable is a **stockholders' equity account**. It is not a liability because assets will not be used to pay the dividend. If the company prepares a balance sheet before it issues the dividend shares, it reports the distributable account under paid-in capital as shown in **Illustration 11.14**.

| Paid-in capital | |
|---|---|
| Common stock | $500,000 |
| **Common stock dividends distributable** | **50,000** |
| Paid-in capital in excess of par—common stock | 25,000 |
| Total paid-in capital | $575,000 |

When Medland issues the dividend shares, it debits Common Stock Dividends Distributable and credits Common Stock, as follows.

| | | |
|---|---|---|
| Common Stock Dividends Distributable | 50,000 | |
| Common Stock | | 50,000 |
| (To record issuance of 5,000 shares in a stock dividend) | | |

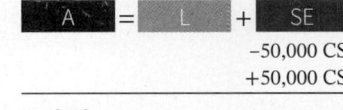

−50,000 CS
+50,000 CS

**Cash Flows**
no effect

## Effects of Stock Dividends

How do stock dividends affect stockholders' equity? They **change the composition of stockholders' equity** because they transfer a portion of retained earnings to paid-in capital. However, **total stockholders' equity remains the same**. Stock dividends also have no effect on the par or stated value per share, but the number of shares outstanding increases. **Illustration 11.15** shows these effects for Medland.

| | Before Dividend | Change | After Dividend |
|---|---|---|---|
| Stockholders' equity | | | |
| Paid-in capital | | | |
| Common stock, $10 par | $500,000 | $ 50,000 | $550,000 |
| Paid-in capital in excess of par | — | 25,000 | 25,000 |
| Total paid-in capital | 500,000 | +75,000 | 575,000 |
| Retained earnings | 300,000 | −75,000 | 225,000 |
| **Total stockholders' equity** | **$800,000** | **$     0** | **$800,000** |
| **Outstanding shares** | **50,000** | **+5,000** | **55,000** |
| **Par value per share** | **$10.00** | **$0** | **$10.00** |

In this example, total paid-in capital increases by $75,000 (50,000 shares × 10% × $15) and retained earnings decreases by the same amount. Note also that total stockholders' equity remains unchanged at $800,000. The number of shares increases by 5,000 (50,000 × 10%).

# Stock Splits

A **stock split**, like a stock dividend, involves issuance of additional shares to stockholders according to their percentage ownership. **However, a stock split results in a reduction in the par or stated value per share** (see Helpful Hint). The purpose of a stock split is to increase the marketability of the stock by lowering its market price per share. This, in turn, makes it easier for the corporation to issue additional stock.

The effect of a split on market price is generally **inversely proportional** to the size of the split. For example, after a 2-for-1 stock split, the market price of **Nike**'s stock fell from $111 to approximately $55. The lower market price stimulated market activity. Within one year, the stock was trading above $100 again. **Illustration 11.16** shows the effect of a 4-for-1 stock split for stockholders.

In a stock split, the company increases the number of shares in the same proportion that par or stated value per share decreases. For example, in a 2-for-1 split, the company exchanges one share of $10 par value stock for two shares of $5 par value stock. **A stock split does not have any effect on total paid-in capital, retained earnings, or total stockholders' equity.** However, the number of shares outstanding increases, and par value per share decreases. **Illustration 11.17** shows these effects for Medland Corporation, assuming that it splits its 50,000 shares of common stock on a 2-for-1 basis.

|  | Before Stock Split | Change | After Stock Split |
|---|---|---|---|
| Stockholders' equity |  |  |  |
| Paid-in capital |  |  |  |
| Common stock, | $500,000 |  | $500,000 |
| Paid-in capital in excess of par—common stock | –0– |  | –0– |
| Total paid-in capital | 500,000 | $ –0– | 500,000 |
| Retained earnings | 300,000 | –0– | 300,000 |
| **Total stockholders' equity** | **$800,000** | **$ –0–** | **$800,000** |
| **Outstanding shares** | **50,000** | **+50,000** | **100,000** |
| **Par value per share** | **$10.00** | **–$5.00** | **$5.00** |

A stock split does not affect the balances in any stockholders' equity accounts. Therefore, **a company does not need to journalize a stock split**.

**Illustration 11.18** summarizes the differences between stock dividends and stock splits.

| Item | Stock Dividend | Stock Split |
|---|---|---|
| Total paid-in capital | Increase | No change |
| Total retained earnings | Decrease | No change |
| Total par value (common stock) | Increase | No change |
| Par value per share | No change | Decrease |
| Outstanding shares | Increase | Increase |
| Total stockholders' equity | No change | No change |

## Investor Insight    Berkshire Hathaway

iStock.com/Hiob

### A No-Split Philosophy

Warren Buffett's company, **Berkshire Hathaway**, has two classes of shares. Until recently, the company had never split either class of stock. As a result, the class A stock had a market price of $97,000 and the class B sold for about $3,200 per share. Because the price per share is so high, the stock does not trade as frequently as the stock of other companies. Buffett has always opposed stock splits because he feels that a lower stock price attracts short-term investors. He appears to be correct. For example, while more than 6 million shares of **IBM** are exchanged on the average day, only about 1,000 class A shares of Berkshire are traded. Despite Buffett's aversion to splits, in order to accomplish a recent acquisition, Berkshire decided to split its class B shares 50 to 1.

**Source:** Scott Patterson, "Berkshire Nears Smaller Baby B's," *Wall Street Journal Online* (January 19, 2010).

**Why does Warren Buffett usually oppose stock splits? (Answer is available near the end of the chapter.)**

---

## DO IT! 3b | Stock Dividends and Stock Splits

Sing CD Company has had five years of record earnings. Due to this success, the market price of its 500,000 outstanding shares of $2 par value common stock has tripled from $15 per share to $45. During this period, paid-in capital remained the same at $2,000,000. Retained earnings increased from $1,500,000 to $10,000,000. President Joan Elbert is considering either a 10% stock dividend or a 2-for-1 stock split. She asks you to show the before-and-after effects of each option on retained earnings, total stockholders' equity, shares outstanding, and par value per share.

### Solution

The stock dividend amount is $2,250,000 [(500,000 × 10%) × $45]. The new balance in retained earnings is $7,750,000 ($10,000,000 – $2,250,000). The retained earnings balance after the stock split is the same as it was before the split: $10,000,000. Total stockholders' equity does not change. The effects on the stockholders' equity accounts are as follows.

|  | Original Balances | After Dividend | After Split |
|---|---|---|---|
| Paid-in capital | $ 2,000,000 | $ 4,250,000 | $ 2,000,000 |
| Retained earnings | 10,000,000 | 7,750,000 | 10,000,000 |
| Total stockholders' equity | $12,000,000 | $12,000,000 | $12,000,000 |
| Shares outstanding | 500,000 | 550,000 | 1,000,000 |
| Par value per share | $2.00 | $2.00 | $1.00 |

Related exercise material: **BE11.8, BE11.9, DO IT! 11.3b, E11.14, E11.15,** and **E11.16.**

### ACTION PLAN

- Calculate the stock dividend's effect on retained earnings by multiplying the number of new shares times the market price of the stock (or par value for a large stock dividend).
- Recall that a stock dividend increases the number of shares without affecting total stockholders' equity.
- Recall that a stock split only increases the number of shares outstanding and decreases the par value per share.

---

# Reporting and Analyzing Stockholders' Equity

## LEARNING OBJECTIVE 4

Discuss how stockholders' equity is reported and analyzed.

## Retained Earnings

Recall that **retained earnings** is net income that a company retains in the business. The balance in retained earnings is part of the stockholders' claim on the total assets of the corporation. It does not, however, represent a claim on any specific asset. Nor can the amount of retained earnings be associated with the balance of any asset account. For example, a $100,000 balance in retained earnings does not mean that there should be $100,000 in cash.

The reason is that the company may have used the cash resulting from the excess of revenues over expenses to purchase buildings, equipment, and other assets.

To demonstrate that retained earnings and cash may be quite different, **Illustration 11.19** shows recent amounts of retained earnings and cash in selected companies.

**ILLUSTRATION 11.19**

Retained earnings and cash balances

|  | (in millions) | |
| Company | Retained Earnings | Cash |
| --- | --- | --- |
| Facebook | $ 3,159 | $3,323 |
| Google | 61,262 | 8,989 |
| Nike | 5,695 | 3,337 |
| Starbucks | 4,130 | 2,576 |
| Amazon | 2,190 | 8,658 |

**HELPFUL HINT**

Remember that Retained Earnings is a stockholders' equity account; its normal balance is a credit.

Remember that when a company has net income, it closes net income to retained earnings. The closing entry is a debit to Income Summary and a credit to Retained Earnings.

When a company has a **net loss** (expenses exceed revenues), it also closes this amount to retained earnings. The closing entry is a debit to Retained Earnings and a credit to Income Summary (see **Helpful Hint**). To illustrate, assume that Rendle Corporation has a net loss of $400,000 in 2022. The closing entry to record this loss is as follows.

| | | |
| --- | --- | --- |
| Retained Earnings | 400,000 | |
|     Income Summary | | 400,000 |
|       (To close net loss to Retained Earnings) | | |

This closing entry is done even if it results in a debit balance in Retained Earnings. **Companies do not debit net losses to paid-in capital accounts.** To do so would destroy the distinction between paid-in and earned capital. If cumulative losses exceed cumulative income over a company's life, a debit balance in Retained Earnings results. A debit balance in Retained Earnings is identified as a **deficit**. A company reports a deficit as a deduction in the stockholders' equity section, as shown in **Illustration 11.20** for Ursula, Inc.

**ILLUSTRATION 11.20**

Stockholders' equity with deficit

### Ursula, Inc.
#### Balance Sheet (partial)

| | |
| --- | --- |
| Stockholders' equity | |
|   Paid-in capital | |
|     Common stock | $800,000 |
|     **Retained earnings (deficit)** | **(50,000)** |
| Total stockholders' equity | $750,000 |

## Retained Earnings Restrictions

The balance in retained earnings is generally available for dividend declarations. Some companies state this fact. In some circumstances, however, there may be **retained earnings restrictions**. These make a portion of the balance currently unavailable for dividends. Restrictions result from one or more of these causes: legal, contractual, or voluntary.

Companies generally disclose retained earnings restrictions in the notes to the financial statements. For example, as shown in **Illustration 11.21**, **Tektronix, Inc.**, a manufacturer of electronic measurement devices, recently had total retained earnings of $774 million, but the unrestricted portion was only $223.8 million.

## Tektronix, Inc.
### Notes to the Financial Statements

Certain of the Company's debt agreements require compliance with debt covenants. The Company had unrestricted retained earnings of $223.8 million after meeting those requirements.

**ILLUSTRATION 11.21**
**Disclosure of unrestricted retained earnings**

**Real World**

# Balance Sheet Presentation of Stockholders' Equity

In the stockholders' equity section of the balance sheet, companies report paid-in capital, retained earnings, and treasury stock. Within paid-in capital, two classifications are recognized:

1. **Capital stock**, which consists of preferred and common stock. Companies show preferred stock before common stock because of its preferential rights. They report information about the par value, shares authorized, shares issued, and shares outstanding for each class of stock.

2. **Additional paid-in capital**, which includes the excess of amounts paid in over par or stated value.

Illustration 11.22 presents the stockholders' equity section of the balance sheet of Graber Inc. (see **International Note**). The company discloses a retained earnings restriction in the notes. The stockholders' equity section for Graber Inc. includes most of the accounts discussed in this chapter. The disclosures pertaining to Graber's common stock indicate that 400,000 shares are issued, 100,000 shares are unissued (500,000 authorized less 400,000 issued), and 390,000 shares are outstanding (400,000 issued less 10,000 shares in treasury).

**International Note**
Like GAAP, companies using IFRS typically disclose separate categories of capital on the balance sheet. However, because of varying accounting treatments of certain transactions (such as treasury stock or asset revaluations), some categories used under IFRS vary from those under GAAP.

## Graber Inc.
### Balance Sheet (partial)

| | | |
|---|---:|---:|
| Stockholders' equity | | |
| Paid-in capital | | |
| Capital stock | | |
| 9% preferred stock, $100 par value, cumulative, | | |
| 10,000 shares authorized, 6,000 shares issued | | |
| and outstanding | | $ 600,000 |
| Common stock, no par, $5 stated value, | | |
| 500,000 shares authorized, 400,000 shares | | |
| issued, and 390,000 outstanding | | 2,000,000 |
| Total capital stock | | 2,600,000 |
| Additional paid-in capital | | |
| Paid-in capital in excess of par—preferred stock | $ 30,000 | |
| Paid-in capital in excess of stated value—common stock | 1,050,000 | |
| Total additional paid-in capital | | 1,080,000 |
| Total paid-in capital | | 3,680,000 |
| Retained earnings (see Note R) | | 1,050,000 |
| Total paid-in capital and retained earnings | | 4,730,000 |
| Less: Treasury stock (10,000 common shares) | | 80,000 |
| Total stockholders' equity | | $4,650,000 |
| **Note R: Retained earnings is restricted for the cost of treasury stock, $80,000.** | | |

**ILLUSTRATION 11.22**
**Stockholders' equity section of balance sheet**

## DO IT! 4a | Stockholders' Equity Section

Jennifer Corporation has issued 300,000 shares of $3 par value common stock. It is authorized to issue 600,000 shares. The paid-in capital in excess of par value on the common stock is $380,000. The corporation has reacquired 15,000 shares of common stock at a cost of $50,000 and is currently holding those shares.

The corporation also has 4,000 shares issued and outstanding of 8%, $100 par value preferred stock. It is authorized to issue 10,000 shares. The paid-in capital in excess of par value on the preferred stock is $97,000. Retained earnings is $610,000.

Prepare the stockholders' equity section of the balance sheet.

**Solution**

| Jennifer Corporation | | | |
|---|---|---|---|
| **Balance Sheet (partial)** | | | |
| Stockholders' equity | | | |
| Paid-in capital | | | |
| Capital stock | | | |
| 8% preferred stock, $100 par value, 10,000 shares authorized, 4,000 shares issued and outstanding | $400,000 | | |
| Common stock, $3 par value, 600,000 shares authorized, 300,000 shares issued, and 285,000 shares outstanding | 900,000 | | |
| Total capital stock | | $1,300,000 | |
| Additional paid-in capital | | | |
| Paid-in capital in excess of par—preferred stock | 97,000 | | |
| Paid-in capital in excess of par value—common stock | 380,000 | | |
| Total additional paid-in capital | | 477,000 | |
| Total paid-in capital | | 1,777,000 | |
| Retained earnings | | 610,000 | |
| Total paid-in capital and retained earnings | | 2,387,000 | |
| Less: Treasury stock (15,000 common shares) (at cost) | | 50,000 | |
| Total stockholders' equity | | $2,337,000 | |

Related exercise material: **BE11.11, DO IT! 11.4a, E11.19, E11.20, and E11.21.**

# Analysis of Stockholders' Equity

Investors are interested in both a company's dividend record and its earnings performance. Although those two measures are often parallel, that is not always the case. Thus, investors should investigate each one separately.

## Payout Ratio

One way that companies reward stockholders for their investment is to pay them dividends. The **payout ratio** measures the percentage of earnings a company distributes in the form of cash dividends to common stockholders. It is computed by **dividing total cash dividends declared to common shareholders by net income**.

To illustrate, **Nike**'s dividends were recently $1,133 million and net income was $4,240 million. **Illustration 11.23** shows Nike's payout ratio.

**ILLUSTRATION 11.23**

Nike's payout ratio

| Cash Dividends Declared on Common Stock | ÷ | Net Income | = | Payout Ratio |
|---|---|---|---|---|
| $1,133 | ÷ | $4,240 | = | 26.7% |

Companies attempt to set their dividend rate at a level that will be sustainable. Companies that have high growth rates are characterized by low payout ratios because they reinvest most of their net income in the business. Thus, a low payout ratio is not necessarily bad news. Companies that believe they have many good opportunities for growth, such as **Facebook** will reinvest those funds in the company rather than pay dividends. However, low dividend payments, or a cut in dividend payments, might signal that a company has liquidity or solvency problems and is trying to conserve cash by not paying dividends. Thus, investors and analysts should investigate the reason for low dividend payments.

**Illustration 11.24** lists recent payout ratios of four well-known companies.

**ILLUSTRATION 11.24**
Payout ratios of companies

| Company | Payout Ratio |
|---|---|
| Microsoft | 24.5% |
| Kellogg | 43.3% |
| Facebook | 0.0% |
| Walmart | 49.0% |

## Return on Common Stockholders' Equity

Investors and analysts can measure profitability from the viewpoint of the common stock-holder by the **return on common stockholders' equity**. This ratio, as shown in Illustration 11.25, indicates how many dollars of net income the company earned for each dollar invested by the common stockholders. It is computed by dividing **net income available to common stockholders** (which is net income minus preferred dividends) by average common stock-holders' equity.

To illustrate, **Walt Disney Company**'s beginning-of-the-year and end-of-the-year common stockholders' equity were $31,820 and $30,753 million, respectively. Its net income was $4,687 million, and no preferred stock was outstanding. The return on common stockholders' equity is computed as shown in **Illustration 11.25**.

**ILLUSTRATION 11.25**
Disney's return on common stockholders' equity

| Net Income minus Preferred Dividends | ÷ | Average Common Stockholders' Equity | = | Return on Common Stockholders' Equity |
|---|---|---|---|---|
| ($4,687 − $0) | ÷ | $\frac{(\$31,820 + \$30,753)}{2}$ | = | 15.0% |

As shown above, if a company has preferred stock, we would deduct the amount of **preferred dividends** from the company's net income to compute income available to common stockholders. Also, the par value of preferred stock is deducted from total stockholders' equity when computing the average common stockholders' equity.

## DO IT! 4b | Analyzing Stockholders' Equity

On January 1, 2022, Siena Corporation purchased 2,000 shares of treasury stock. Other information regarding Siena Corporation is provided below.

| | 2021 | 2022 |
|---|---|---|
| Net income | $110,000 | $110,000 |
| Dividends on preferred stock | 10,000 | 10,000 |
| Dividends on common stock | 2,000 | 1,600 |
| Common stockholders' equity, beginning of year | 500,000 | 400,000* |
| Common stockholders' equity, end of year | 500,000 | 400,000 |

*Adjusted for purchase of treasury stock.

(a) Compute return on common stockholders' equity for each year, and (b) discuss its change from 2021 to 2022.

**ACTION PLAN**
- Determine return on common stockholders' equity by dividing net income available to common stockholders by average common stockholders' equity.

**Solution**

**a.**

|  | 2021 | 2022 |
|---|---|---|
| Return on common stock-holders' equity | $\dfrac{(\$110{,}000 - \$10{,}000)}{(\$500{,}000 + \$500{,}000) \div 2} = 20\%$ | $\dfrac{(\$110{,}000 - \$10{,}000)}{(\$400{,}000 + \$400{,}000) \div 2} = 25\%$ |

**b.** Between 2021 and 2022, return on common stockholders' equity improved from 20% to 25%. While this would appear to be good news for the company's common stockholders, this increase should be carefully evaluated. It is important to note that net income did not change during this period. The increase in the ratio was due to the purchase of treasury shares, which reduced the denominator of the ratio. As the company repurchases its own shares, it becomes more reliant on debt and thus increases its risk.

Related exercise material: **DO IT! 11.4b, E11.22, E11.23, and E11.24.**

---

**Appendix 11A**

# Stockholders' Equity Statement

**LEARNING OBJECTIVE *5**

Describe the use and content of the stockholders' equity statement.

When balance sheets and income statements are presented by a corporation, changes in the separate accounts comprising stockholders' equity should also be disclosed. Disclosure of such changes is necessary to make the financial statements sufficiently informative for users. The disclosures may be made in an additional statement or in the notes to the financial statements.

Many corporations make the disclosures in a **stockholders' equity statement**. The statement shows the changes in **each** stockholders' equity account and in **total** stockholders' equity during the year. As shown in **Illustration 11A.1**, the stockholders' equity statement is prepared in columnar form. It contains columns for each account and for total stockholders' equity. The transactions are then identified and their effects are shown in the appropriate columns.

**ILLUSTRATION 11A.1** Stockholders' equity statement

### Hampton Corporation
#### Stockholders' Equity Statement
#### For the Year Ended December 31, 2022

|  | Common Stock ($5 Par) | Paid-in Capital in Excess of Par—Common Stock | Retained Earnings | Treasury Stock | Total |
|---|---|---|---|---|---|
| Balance January 1 | $300,000 | $200,000 | $650,000 | $(34,000) | $1,116,000 |
| Issued 5,000 shares of common stock at $15 | 25,000 | 50,000 |  |  | 75,000 |
| Declared a $40,000 cash dividend |  |  | (40,000) |  | (40,000) |
| Purchased 2,000 shares for treasury at $16 |  |  |  | (32,000) | (32,000) |
| Net income for year |  |  | 240,000 |  | 240,000 |
| Balance December 31 | $325,000 | $250,000 | $850,000 | $(66,000) | $1,359,000 |

In practice, additional columns are usually provided to show the number of shares of issued stock and treasury stock. The stockholders' equity statement for **PepsiCo** for a three-year period is shown in Appendix B. **When a stockholders' equity statement is presented, a retained earnings statement is not necessary** because the retained earnings column explains the changes in this account.

| Appendix 11B | **Book Value per Share** |
|---|---|

**LEARNING OBJECTIVE \*6**
Compute book value per share.

You have learned about a number of per share amounts in this chapter. Another per share amount of some importance is **book value per share**. It represents **the equity a common stockholder has in the net assets of the corporation** from owning one share of stock. Remember that the net assets (total assets minus total liabilities) of a corporation must be equal to total stockholders' equity. **Illustration 11B.1** shows the formula for computing book value per share when a company has only one class of stock outstanding.

| Total Stockholders' Equity | ÷ | Number of Common Shares Outstanding | = | Book Value per Share |
|---|---|---|---|---|

**ILLUSTRATION 11B.1**
Book value per share formula

Thus, if Marlo Corporation has total stockholders' equity of $1,500,000 (common stock $1,000,000 and retained earnings $500,000) and 50,000 shares of common stock outstanding, book value per share is $30 ($1,500,000 ÷ 50,000).

When a company has both preferred and common stock, the computation of book value is more complex. Since preferred stockholders have a prior claim on net assets over common stockholders, their equity must be deducted from total stockholders' equity. Then, we can determine the stockholders' equity that applies to the common stock. The computation of book value per share involves the following steps.

1. **Compute the preferred stock equity.** This equity is equal to the sum of the call price of all outstanding shares of preferred stock plus any cumulative dividends in arrears. If the preferred stock does not have a call price, the par value of the stock is used.
2. **Determine the common stock equity.** Subtract the preferred stock equity from total stockholders' equity.
3. **Determine book value per share.** Divide common stock equity by shares of common stock outstanding.

## Book Value per Share Example

We will use the stockholders' equity section of Graber Inc. shown in Illustration 11.23. Assume that Graber's preferred stock is callable at $120 per share and is cumulative, and that dividends on Graber's preferred stock were in arrears for one year, $54,000 (6,000 × $9). **Illustration 11B.2** shows the computation of preferred stock equity (Step 1 in the preceding list).

| | |
|---|---|
| Call price (6,000 shares × $120) | $720,000 |
| Dividends in arrears (6,000 shares × $9) | 54,000 |
| **Preferred stock equity** | **$774,000** |

**ILLUSTRATION 11B.2**
Computation of preferred stock equity—Step 1

The computation of book value per share (Steps 2 and 3) is shown in **Illustration 11B.3**.

| | |
|---|---|
| Total stockholders' equity | $4,760,000 |
| Less: **Preferred stock equity** | 774,000 |
| **Common stock equity** | **$3,986,000** |
| **Shares of common stock outstanding** | 390,000 |
| **Book value per share** ($3,986,000 ÷ 390,000) | **$10.22** |

**ILLUSTRATION 11B.3**
Computation of book value per share with preferred stock—Steps 2 and 3

Note that we used a call price of $120 instead of the par value of $100. Note also that the paid-in capital in excess of par value of preferred stock, $30,000, **is not assigned to the preferred stock equity**. Preferred stockholders ordinarily do not have a right to amounts paid-in in excess of par value. Therefore, such amounts are assigned to the common stock equity in computing book value per share.

# Book Value versus Market Price

Be sure you understand that **book value per share generally does not equal market price per share**. Book value generally is based on recorded costs. Market price reflects the subjective judgments of thousands of stockholders and prospective investors about a company's potential for future earnings and dividends. Market price per share may exceed book value per share, but that fact does not necessarily mean that the stock is overpriced. The correlation between book value and the annual range of a company's market price per share is often remote, as indicated by the data shown in **Illustration 11B.4**.

**ILLUSTRATION 11B.4**

Book value per share and market prices compared

| Company | Book Value (year-end) | Market Range (for the year) |
|---|---|---|
| The Limited | $13.38 | $31.03–$22.89 |
| H. J. Heinz | $ 7.48 | $40.61–$34.53 |
| Cisco Systems | $ 3.66 | $21.24–$17.01 |
| Walmart | $12.79 | $50.87–$42.31 |

Book value per share **is useful** in determining the trend of a stockholder's per share equity in a corporation. It is also significant in many contracts and in court cases where the rights of individual parties are based on cost information.

# Review and Practice

## Learning Objectives Review

**1 Discuss the major characteristics of a corporation.**

The major characteristics of a corporation are separate legal existence, limited liability of stockholders, transferable ownership rights, ability to acquire capital, continuous life, corporation management, government regulations, and additional taxes.

**2 Explain how to account for the issuance of common, preferred, and treasury stock.**

**Common Stock.** When companies record the issuance of common stock for cash, they credit the par value of the shares to Common Stock. They record in a separate paid-in capital account the portion of the proceeds that is above or below par value. When no-par common stock has a stated value, the entries are similar to those for par value stock. When no-par stock does not have a stated value, companies credit the entire proceeds to Common Stock.

**Preferred Stock.** Like common stock, companies may issue preferred stock for cash or noncash assets. The entries for these transactions are similar to the entries for common stock. Preferred stock has contractual provisions that give it priority over common stock in certain areas. Typically, preferred stockholders have preferences (1) to dividends and (2) to assets in liquidation. They usually do not have voting rights.

**Treasury Stock.** The cost method is generally used in accounting for treasury stock. Under this approach, companies debit Treasury Stock at the price paid to reacquire the shares. They credit the same amount to Treasury Stock when they sell the shares. The difference between the sales price and cost is recorded in stockholders' equity accounts, not in income statement accounts.

**3 Explain how to account for cash dividends, stock dividends, and stock splits.**

**Cash Dividends.** Companies make entries for cash dividends at the declaration date and at the payment date. At the **declaration date**, the entry is debit Cash Dividends and credit Dividends Payable. At the **payment date**, the entry is debit Dividends Payable and credit Cash.

**Stock Dividends.** At the declaration date, the entry for a small stock dividend is debit Stock Dividends, credit Paid-in Capital in

Excess of Par (or Stated Value)—Common Stock, and credit Common Stock Dividends Distributable. At the distribution date, the entry for a small stock dividend is debit Common Stock Dividends Distributable and credit Common Stock.

**Stock Splits.** A stock split reduces the par or stated value per share and increases the number of shares but does not affect balances in stockholders' equity accounts. As a result, no entry is needed.

---

**4   Discuss how stockholders' equity is reported and analyzed.**

---

Additions to retained earnings consist of net income. Deductions consist of net loss and cash and stock dividends. In some instances, portions of retained earnings are restricted, making that portion unavailable for the payment of dividends.

In the stockholders' equity section of the balance sheet, companies report paid-in capital and retained earnings and identify specific sources of paid-in capital. Within paid-in capital, companies show two classifications: capital stock and additional paid-in capital. If a corporation has treasury stock, it deducts the cost of treasury stock from total paid-in capital and retained earnings to determine total stockholders' equity.

A company's dividend record can be evaluated by looking at what percentage of net income it chooses to pay out in dividends, as measured by the payout ratio (dividends divided by net income). Earnings performance is measured with the return on common stockholders' equity (income available to common stockholders divided by average common stockholders' equity).

---

**\*5   Describe the use and content of the stockholders' equity statement.**

---

Corporations must disclose changes in stockholders' equity accounts and may choose to do so by issuing a separate stockholders' equity statement. This statement, prepared in columnar form, shows changes in each stockholders' equity account and in total stockholders' equity during the accounting period. When this statement is presented, a retained earnings statement is not necessary.

---

**\*6   Compute book value per share.**

---

Book value per share represents the equity a common stockholder has in the net assets of a corporation from owning one share of stock. When there is only common stock outstanding, the formula for computing book value per share is Total stockholders' equity ÷ Number of common shares outstanding = Book value per share.

---

## Glossary Review

---

**Authorized stock**   The amount of stock that a corporation is authorized to sell as indicated in its charter. (p. 11-8).

**\*Book value per share**   The equity a common stockholder has in the net assets of the corporation from owning one share of stock. (p. 11-33).

**Cash dividend**   A pro rata distribution of cash to stockholders. (p. 11-19).

**Charter**   A document that is issued by the state to set forth important terms and features regarding the creation of a corporation. (p. 11-6).

**Corporation**   A business organized as a legal entity separate and distinct from its owners under state corporation law. (p. 11-3).

**Cumulative dividend**   A feature of preferred stock entitling the stockholder to receive current and unpaid prior-year dividends before common stockholders receive dividends. (p. 11-21).

**Declaration date**   The date the board of directors formally declares (authorizes) a dividend and announces it to stockholders. (p. 11-19).

**Deficit**   A debit balance in Retained Earnings. (p. 11-28).

**Dividend**   A corporation's distribution of cash or stock to its stockholders on a pro rata (proportional) basis. (p. 11-18).

**Liquidating dividend**   A dividend declared out of paid-in capital. (p. 11-19).

**No-par value stock**   Capital stock that has not been assigned a value in the corporate charter. (p. 11-9).

**Organization costs**   Costs incurred in the formation of a corporation. (p. 11-6).

**Outstanding stock**   Capital stock that has been issued and is being held by stockholders. (p. 11-16).

**Paid-in capital**   Total amount of cash and other assets paid in to the corporation by stockholders in exchange for capital stock. (p. 11-10).

**Par value stock**   Capital stock that has been assigned a value per share in the corporate charter. (p. 11-9)

**Payment date**   The date dividends are transferred to stockholders. (p. 11-20).

**Payout ratio**   A measure of the percentage of earnings a company distributes in the form of cash dividends to common stockholders. (p. 11-30).

**Preferred stock**   Capital stock that has some preferences over common stock. (p. 11-14).

**Privately held corporation**   A corporation that has only a few stockholders and whose stock is not available for sale to the general public. (p. 11-3).

**Publicly held corporation**   A corporation that may have thousands of stockholders and whose stock is regularly traded on a national securities exchange. (p. 11-3).

**Record date**   The date when ownership of outstanding shares is determined for dividend purposes. (p. 11-20).

**Retained earnings**   Net income that the corporation retains for future use. (p. 11-10).

**Retained earnings restrictions**   Circumstances that make a portion of retained earnings currently unavailable for dividends. (p. 11-28).

**Return on common stockholders' equity**   A measure of profitability that shows how many dollars of net income were earned for each dollar invested by the owners; computed as net income minus preferred dividends divided by average common stockholders' equity. (p. 11-31).

**Stated value**   The amount per share assigned by the board of directors to no-par value stock. (p. 11-9).

**Stock dividend**   A pro rata distribution to stockholders of the corporation's own stock. (p. 11-23).

**\*Stockholders' equity statement**   A statement that shows the changes in each stockholders' equity account and in total stockholders' equity during the year. (p. 11-32).

**Stock split**   The issuance of additional shares of stock to stockholders according to their percentage ownership. It is accompanied by a reduction in the par or stated value per share. (p. 11-25).

**Treasury stock**   A corporation's own stock that has been issued and subsequently reacquired from shareholders by the corporation but not retired. (p. 11-15).

## Practice Multiple-Choice Questions

**1. (LO 1)** Which of the following is **not** a major advantage of a corporate form of organization?

  **a.** Separate legal existence.

  **b.** Continuous life.

  **c.** Government regulations.

  **d.** Transferable ownership rights.

**2. (LO 1)** A major **disadvantage** of a corporation is:

  **a.** limited liability of stockholders.

  **b.** additional taxes.

  **c.** transferable ownership rights.

  **d.** separate legal existence.

**3. (LO 1)** Which of the following statements is **false**?

  **a.** Ownership of common stock gives the owner a voting right.

  **b.** The stockholders' equity section begins with a paid-in capital section.

  **c.** The authorization of capital stock does not result in a formal accounting entry.

  **d.** Par value and market price of a company's stock are always the same.

**4. (LO 2)** ABC Corporation issues 1,000 shares of $10 par value common stock at $12 per share. In recording the transaction, credits are made to:

  **a.** Common Stock $10,000 and Paid-in Capital in Excess of Stated Value $2,000.

  **b.** Common Stock $12,000.

  **c.** Common Stock $10,000 and Paid-in Capital in Excess of Par $2,000.

  **d.** Common Stock $10,000 and Retained Earnings $2,000.

**5. (LO 2)** Preferred stock may have priority over common stock **except** in:

  **a.** dividends.

  **b.** assets in the event of liquidation.

  **c.** cumulative dividend features.

  **d.** voting.

**6. (LO 2)** XYZ, Inc. sells 100 shares of $5 par value treasury stock at $13 per share. If the cost of acquiring the shares was $10 per share, the entry for the sale should include credits to:

  **a.** Treasury Stock $1,000 and Paid-in Capital from Treasury Stock $300.

  **b.** Treasury Stock $500 and Paid-in Capital from Treasury Stock $800.

  **c.** Treasury Stock $1,000 and Retained Earnings $300.

  **d.** Treasury Stock $500 and Paid-in Capital in Excess of Par $800.

**7. (LO 2)** In the stockholders' equity section of the balance sheet, the cost of treasury stock is deducted from:

  **a.** total paid-in capital and retained earnings.

  **b.** retained earnings.

  **c.** total stockholders' equity.

  **d.** common stock in paid-in capital.

**8. (LO 3)** U-Bet Corporation has 10,000 shares of 8%, $100 par value, cumulative preferred stock outstanding at December 31, 2022. No dividends were declared in 2020 or 2021. If U-Bet wants to pay $375,000 of dividends in 2022, common stockholders will receive:

  **a.** $0.          **c.** $215,000.

  **b.** $295,000.    **d.** $135,000.

**9. (LO 3)** Entries for cash dividends are required on the:

  **a.** declaration date and the payment date.

  **b.** record date and the payment date.

  **c.** declaration date, record date, and payment date.

  **d.** declaration date and the record date.

**10. (LO 3)** Which of the following statements about small stock dividends is **true**?

  **a.** A debit to Retained Earnings for the par value of the shares issued should be made.

  **b.** A small stock dividend decreases total stockholders' equity.

  **c.** Market price per share should be assigned to the dividend shares.

  **d.** A small stock dividend ordinarily will have an effect on par value per share of stock.

**11. (LO 3)** Orlando Company has a beginning balance in retained earnings of $100,000. During the year, it had a net loss of $20,000, declared cash dividends of $3,000, and declared a small stock dividend that had a market value of $7,000 and a par value of $1,000. The ending balance in retained earnings is:

  **a.** $120,000.    **c.** $79,000.

  **b.** $80,000.      **d.** $70,000.

**12. (LO 4)** In the stockholders' equity section of the balance sheet, common stock is:

  **a.** listed before preferred stock.

  **b.** added to total capital stock.

  **c.** part of paid-in capital.

  **d.** part of additional paid-in capital.

**13. (LO 4)** Which of the following is **not** reported under additional paid-in capital?

  **a.** Paid-in capital in excess of par.

  **b.** Common stock.

  **c.** Paid-in capital in excess of stated value.

  **d.** Paid-in capital from treasury stock.

**14. (LO 4)** Jackson Inc. reported net income of $186,000 during 2022 and paid dividends of $26,000 on common stock. It also has 10,000 shares of 6%, $100 par value, noncumulative preferred stock outstanding and paid dividends of $60,000 on preferred stock. Common stockholders' equity was $1,200,000 on January 1, 2022, and $1,600,000 on December 31, 2022. The company's return on common stockholders' equity for 2022 is:

  **a.** 10.0%.      **c.** 7.1%.

  **b.** 9.0%.       **d.** 13.3%.

*15. **(LO 5)** When a stockholders' equity statement is presented, it is not necessary to prepare a (an):

 a. retained earnings statement.

 b. balance sheet.

 c. income statement.

 d. None of the answer choices is correct

*16. **(LO 6)** The ledger of JFK, Inc. shows common stock, common treasury stock, and no preferred stock. For this company, the formula for computing book value per share is:

 a. total paid-in capital and retained earnings divided by the number of shares of common stock issued.

 b. common stock divided by the number of shares of common stock issued.

 c. total stockholders' equity divided by the number of shares of common stock outstanding.

 d. total stockholders' equity divided by the number of shares of common stock issued.

## Solutions

1. **c.** Government regulations are a disadvantage of a corporation. The other choices are advantages of a corporation.

2. **b.** Additional taxes are a disadvantage of a corporation. The other choices are advantages of a corporation.

3. **d.** Par value has no relationship with market price, and many states today do not require a par value. The other choices are true statements.

4. **c.** Common Stock should be credited for $10,000 and Paid-in Capital in Excess of Par should be credited for $2,000. The stock is par value stock, not stated value stock, and this excess is contributed, not earned, capital. The other choices are therefore incorrect.

5. **d.** Preferred stock usually does not have voting rights and therefore does not have priority over common stock on this issue. The other choices are true statements.

6. **a.** Treasury Stock should be credited for $1,000 (100 shares × $10, the acquisition cost). Paid-in Capital from Treasury Stock should be credited for the difference between the $1,000 and the cash received of $1,300 (100 shares × $13), or $300. The other choices are therefore incorrect.

7. **a.** The cost of treasury stock is deducted from total paid-in capital and retained earnings. The other choices are therefore incorrect.

8. **d.** The preferred stockholders will receive a total of $240,000 of dividends [dividends in arrears ($80,000 × 2 years) + current-year dividends ($80,000)]. If U-Bet wants to pay a total of $375,000 in 2022, then common stockholders will receive $135,000 ($375,000 – $240,000), not (a) $0, (b) $295,000, or (c) $215,000.

9. **a.** Entries are required for dividends on the declaration date and the payment date, but not the record date. The other choices are therefore incorrect.

10. **c.** Because the stock dividend is considered small, the fair value (market price), not the par value, is assigned to the shares. The other choices are incorrect because (a) a debit to Retained Earnings for the fair value of the shares issued should be made; (b) a small stock dividend changes the composition of total stockholders' equity, but does not change the total; and (c) a small stock dividend will have no effect on par value per share.

11. **d.** The ending balance in retained earnings is $70,000. It is computed by subtracting from the beginning balance of $100,000 the following items: net loss of $20,000, cash dividends of $3,000, and stock dividends of $7,000. Note that market value of the cash dividend should be used instead of its par value. The other choices are therefore incorrect.

12. **c.** Common stock is part of paid-in capital. The other choices are incorrect because common stock (a) is listed after preferred stock, (b) is not added to total capital stock but is part of capital stock, and (d) is part of capital stock, not additional paid-in capital.

13. **b.** Common stock is reported in the capital stock section of paid-in capital, not in the additional paid-in capital section. The other choices are true statements.

14. **b.** Return on common stockholders' equity = Net income available to common stockholders ÷ Average common stockholders' equity. Net income available to common stockholders = Net income – Preferred dividends = $126,000 [$186,000 – (10,000 × .06 × $100)]. The company's return on common stockholders' equity for the year is therefore 9.0% [$126,000 ÷ ($1,200,000 + $1,600,000) ÷ 2)], not (a) 10.0%, (c) 7.1%, or (d) 13.3%.

*15. **a.** When a stockholders equity statement is presented, a retained earnings statement is unnecessary as the information would be redundant. Choices (b) balance sheet and (c) income statement are required statements. Choice (d) is wrong because there is a correct answer given.

*16. **c.** When a company has only one class of stock outstanding, Book value per share = Total stockholders' equity ÷ Number of shares of common stock outstanding. The other choices are therefore incorrect.

# Practice Brief Exercises

1. **(LO 2)** On April 10, Leury Corporation issues 3,000 shares of $5 par value common stock for cash at $14 per share. Journalize the issuance of the stock.

*Prepare entries for issuance of par value common stock.*

## Solution

| 1. April 10 | Cash (3,000 × $14) | 42,000 | |
| | Common Stock (3,000 × $5) | | 15,000 |
| | Paid-in Capital in Excess of Par— | | |
| | Common Stock (3,000 × $9) | | 27,000 |

*Prepare entries for treasury stock transactions.*

**2. (LO 2)** On June 1, Omar Corporation purchases 600 shares of its $5 par value common stock for the treasury at a cash price of $10 per share. Journalize the treasury stock transaction.

### Solution

| | | | | |
|---|---|---|---|---|
| 2. June 1 | Treasury Stock (600 × $10) | | 6,000 | |
| | Cash | | | 6,000 |

*Prepare entries for a cash dividend.*

**3. (LO 3)** Giovanni Corporation has 70,000 shares of common stock outstanding. It declares a $2 per share cash dividend on November 15 to stockholders of record on December 15. The dividend is paid on December 31. Prepare the entries on the appropriate dates to record the declaration and payment of the cash dividend.

### Solution

| | | | | |
|---|---|---|---|---|
| 3. Nov. 15 | Cash Dividends (70,000 × $2) | | 140,000 | |
| | Dividends Payable | | | 140,000 |
| Dec. 31 | Dividends Payable | | 140,000 | |
| | Cash | | | 140,000 |

*Show before-and-after effects of a stock dividend.*

**4. (LO 3)** The stockholders' equity section of Ynoa Corporation consists of common stock ($5 par) $3,000,000 and retained earnings $1,000,000. A 15% stock dividend (90,000 shares) is declared when the market price per share is $11. Show the before-and-after effects of the dividend on (a) the components of stockholders' equity, (b) shares outstanding, and (c) par value per share.

### Solution

| | Before Dividend | After Dividend |
|---|---|---|
| 4. a. Stockholders' equity | | |
| Paid-in capital | | |
| Common stock, $5 par | $3,000,000 | $3,450,000 |
| In excess of par | — | 540,000 |
| Total paid-in capital | 3,000,000 | 3,990,000 |
| Retained earnings | 1,000,000 | 10,000 |
| Total stockholders' equity | $4,000,000 | $4,000,000 |
| b. Outstanding shares | 600,000 | 690,000 |
| c. Par value per share | $5.00 | $5.00 |

*Prepare stockholders' equity section.*

**5. (LO 4)** Navarez Corporation has the following accounts at December 31: Common Stock, $2 par, 50,000 shares issued, $100,000; Paid-in Capital in Excess of Par—Common Stock $40,000; Retained Earnings $65,000; and Treasury Stock, 2,000 shares, $17,000. Prepare the stockholders' equity section of the balance sheet.

### Solution

| | |
|---|---|
| 5. Stockholders' equity | |
| Paid-in capital | |
| Common stock, $2 par value, 50,000 shares | |
| issued, and 48,000 shares outstanding | $100,000 |
| In excess of par—common stock | 40,000 |
| Total paid-in capital | 140,000 |
| Retained earnings | 65,000 |
| Total paid-in capital and retained earnings | 205,000 |
| Less: Treasury stock (2,000 common shares) | 17,000 |
| Total stockholders' equity | $188,000 |

# Practice Exercises

**1. (LO 2)** Maci Co. had the following transactions during the current period.

*Journalize issuance of common and preferred stock and purchase of treasury stock.*

Mar.   2    Issued 5,000 shares of $5 par value common stock to attorneys in payment of a bill for $35,000 for services performed in helping the company to incorporate.

June 12    Issued 60,000 shares of $5 par value common stock for cash of $370,000.

July  11    Issued 1,000 shares of $100 par value preferred stock for cash at $112 per share.

Nov. 28    Purchased 2,000 shares of treasury stock for $70,000.

### Instructions

Journalize the transactions.

### Solution

**1.**

| | | | |
|---|---|---|---|
| Mar.   2 | Organization Expense | 35,000 | |
| | Common Stock (5,000 × $5) | | 25,000 |
| | Paid-in Capital in Excess of Par— | | |
| | Common Stock | | 10,000 |
| June  12 | Cash | 370,000 | |
| | Common Stock (60,000 × $5) | | 300,000 |
| | Paid-in Capital in Excess of Par— | | |
| | Common Stock | | 70,000 |
| July   11 | Cash (1,000 × $112) | 112,000 | |
| | Preferred Stock (1,000 × $100) | | 100,000 |
| | Paid-in Capital in Excess of Par— | | |
| | Preferred Stock (1,000 × $12) | | 12,000 |
| Nov.  28 | Treasury Stock | 70,000 | |
| | Cash | | 70,000 |

**2. (LO 3, 4)** On January 1, Chong Corporation had 95,000 shares of no-par common stock issued and outstanding. The stock has a stated value of $5 per share. During the year, the following occurred.

*Journalize cash dividends; indicate statement presentation.*

Apr.   1    Issued 25,000 additional shares of common stock for $17 per share.

June 15    Declared a cash dividend of $1 per share to stockholders of record on June 30.

July  10    Paid the $1 cash dividend.

Dec.   1    Issued 2,000 additional shares of common stock for $19 per share.

     15    Declared a cash dividend on outstanding shares of $1.20 per share to stockholders of record on December 31.

### Instructions

**a.** Prepare the entries, if any, on each of the three dividend dates.

**b.** How are dividends and dividends payable reported in the financial statements prepared at December 31?

### Solution

| | | | |
|---|---|---|---|
| **2. a.** June 15 | Cash Dividends [(95,000 + 25,000) × $1] | 120,000 | |
| | Dividends Payable | | 120,000 |
| July  10 | Dividends Payable | 120,000 | |
| | Cash | | 120,000 |
| Dec.  15 | Cash Dividends [(120,000 + 2,000) × $1.20] | 146,400 | |
| | Dividends Payable | | 146,400 |

**b.** In the retained earnings statement, dividends of $266,400 ($120,000 + $146,400) will be deducted. In the balance sheet, Dividends Payable of $146,400 will be reported as a current liability.

## Practice Problem

*Journalize transactions and prepare stockholders' equity section.*

**(LO 2, 4)** Rolman Corporation is authorized to issue 1,000,000 shares of $5 par value common stock. In its first year, the company has the following stock transactions.

| | |
|---|---|
| Jan. 10 | Issued 400,000 shares of stock at $8 per share. |
| July 1 | Issued 100,000 shares of stock for land. The land had an asking price of $900,000. The stock is currently selling on a national exchange at $8.25 per share. |
| Sept. 1 | Purchased 10,000 shares of common stock for the treasury at $9 per share. |
| Dec. 1 | Sold 4,000 shares of the treasury stock at $10 per share. |

### Instructions

**a.** Journalize the transactions.

**b.** Prepare the stockholders' equity section, assuming the company had ending retained earnings of $200,000 at December 31.

### Solution

**a.**

| | | | | |
|---|---|---|---:|---:|
| Jan. 10 | Cash | | 3,200,000 | |
| | | Common Stock | | 2,000,000 |
| | | Paid-in Capital in Excess of Par—Common Stock | | 1,200,000 |
| | | (To record issuance of 400,000 shares of $5 par value stock) | | |
| July 1 | Land | | 825,000 | |
| | | Common Stock | | 500,000 |
| | | Paid-in Capital in Excess of Par—Common Stock | | 325,000 |
| | | (To record issuance of 100,000 shares of $5 par value stock for land) | | |
| Sept. 1 | Treasury Stock | | 90,000 | |
| | | Cash | | 90,000 |
| | | (To record purchase of 10,000 shares of treasury stock at cost) | | |
| Dec. 1 | Cash | | 40,000 | |
| | | Treasury Stock | | 36,000 |
| | | Paid-in Capital from Treasury Stock | | 4,000 |
| | | (To record sale of 4,000 shares of treasury stock above cost) | | |

**b.**

## Rolman Corporation
### Balance Sheet (partial)

| | | |
|---|---:|---:|
| Stockholders' equity | | |
| Paid-in capital | | |
| Capital stock | | |
| Common stock, $5 par value, 1,000,000 shares authorized, 500,000 shares issued, 494,000 shares outstanding | | $2,500,000 |
| Additional paid-in capital | | |
| In excess of par—common stock | $1,525,000 | |
| From treasury stock | 4,000 | |
| Total additional paid-in capital | | 1,529,000 |
| Total paid-in capital | | 4,029,000 |
| Retained earnings | | 200,000 |
| Total paid-in capital and retained earnings | | 4,229,000 |
| Less: Treasury stock (6,000 shares) | | 54,000 |
| Total stockholders' equity | | $4,175,000 |

Brief Exercises, DO IT! Exercises, Exercises, Problems, Data Analytics Activities, and many additional resources are available for practice in WileyPLUS.

*Note:* All asterisked Questions, Exercises, and Problems relate to material in the appendices to the chapter.

## Questions

1. Joe, a student, asks your help in understanding the following characteristics of a corporation: (a) separate legal existence, (b) limited liability of stockholders, and (c) transferable ownership rights. Explain these characteristics to Joe.

2. **a.** Your friend G. C. Jones cannot understand how the characteristic of corporation management is both an advantage and a disadvantage. Clarify this problem for G. C.

  **b.** Identify and explain two other disadvantages of a corporation.

3. **a.** The following terms pertain to the forming of a corporation: (1) charter, (2) by-laws, and (3) organization costs. Explain the terms.

  **b.** Nona James believes a corporation must be incorporated in the state in which its headquarters' office is located. Is Nona correct? Explain.

4. What are the basic ownership rights of common stockholders in the absence of restrictive provisions?

5. **a.** What are the two principal components of stockholders' equity?

  **b.** What is paid-in capital? Give three examples.

6. How does the balance sheet for a corporation differ from the balance sheet for a proprietorship?

7. The corporate charter of Gage Corporation allows the issuance of a maximum of 100,000 shares of common stock. During its first two years of operations, Gage sold 70,000 shares to shareholders and reacquired 4,000 of these shares. After these transactions, how many shares are authorized, issued, and outstanding?

8. Which is the better investment—common stock with a par value of $5 per share, or common stock with a par value of $20 per share? Why?

9. What factors help determine the market price of stock?

10. Why is common stock usually not issued at a price that is less than par value?

11. Land appraised at $80,000 is purchased by issuing 1,000 shares of $20 par value common stock. The market price of the shares at the time of the exchange, based on active trading in the securities market, is $95 per share. Should the land be recorded at $20,000, $80,000, or $95,000? Explain.

12. For what reasons might a company like **IBM** repurchase some of its stock (treasury stock)?

13. Monet, Inc. purchases 1,000 shares of its own previously issued $5 par common stock for $11,000. Assuming the shares are held in the treasury, what effect does this transaction have on (a) net income, (b) total assets, (c) total paid-in capital, and (d) total stockholders' equity?

14. Monet, Inc. purchases 1,000 shares of its own previously issued $5 par common stock for $11,000. Monet then resells this treasury stock for $16,000. What effect does this resale transaction have on (a) net income, (b) total assets, (c) total paid-in capital, and (d) total stockholders' equity?

15. **a.** What are the principal differences between common stock and preferred stock?

  **b.** Preferred stock may be cumulative. Discuss this feature.

  **c.** How are dividends in arrears presented in the financial statements?

16. Identify the events that result in credits and debits to retained earnings.

17. Indicate how each of the following accounts should be classified in the stockholders' equity section.

  **a.** Common stock.

  **b.** Paid-in capital in excess of par—common stock.

  **c.** Retained earnings.

  **d.** Treasury stock.

  **e.** Paid-in capital from treasury stock.

  **f.** Paid-in capital in excess of stated value—common stock.

  **g.** Preferred stock.

18. Jan Kimler maintains that adequate cash is the only requirement for the declaration of a cash dividend. Is Jan correct? Explain.

19. **a.** Three dates are important in connection with cash dividends. Identify these dates, and explain their significance to the corporation and its stockholders.

  **b.** Identify the accounting entries that are made for a cash dividend and the date of each entry.

20. Contrast the effects of a cash dividend and a stock dividend on a corporation's balance sheet.

21. Doris Angel asks, "Since stock dividends don't change anything, why declare them?" What is your answer to Doris?

22. Jayne Corporation has 170,000 shares of $15 par value common stock outstanding when it announces a 3-for-1 stock split. Before the split, the stock had a market price of $120 per share. After the split, how many shares of stock will be outstanding? What will be the approximate market price per share?

23. The board of directors is considering either a stock split or a stock dividend. They understand that total stockholders' equity will remain the same under either action. However, they are not sure of the different effects of the two types of actions on other aspects of stockholders' equity. Explain the differences to the board of directors.

24. What is the purpose of a retained earnings restriction? Identify the possible causes of retained earnings restrictions.

25. What is the formula for the payout ratio? What does it indicate?

*26. What is the formula for computing book value per share when a corporation has only common stock?

*27. Emko Inc.'s common stock has a par value of $1, a book value of $24, and a current market price of $18. Explain why these amounts are all different.

## Brief Exercises

*List the advantages and disadvantages of a corporation.*

**BE11.1 (LO 1), K** Angie Baden is studying for her accounting midterm examination. Identify for Angie the advantages and disadvantages of the corporate form of business organization.

*Journalize issuance of par value common stock.*

**BE11.2 (LO 2), AP** On May 10, Pilar Corporation issues 2,500 shares of $5 par value common stock for cash at $13 per share. Journalize the issuance of the stock.

*Prepare entries for issuance of no-par value common stock.*

**BE11.3 (LO 2), AP** On June 1, Noonan Inc. issues 4,000 shares of no-par common stock at a cash price of $6 per share. Journalize the issuance of the shares assuming the stock has a stated value of $1 per share.

*Prepare entries for issuance of stock in a noncash transaction.*

**BE11.4 (LO 2), AP** Lei Inc.'s $10 par value common stock is actively traded at a market price of $15 per share. Lei issues 5,000 shares to purchase land advertised for sale at $85,000. Journalize the issuance of the stock in acquiring the land.

*Journalize issuance of preferred stock.*

**BE11.5 (LO 2), AP** Layes Inc. issues 8,000 shares of $100 par value preferred stock for cash at $106 per share. Journalize the issuance of the preferred stock.

*Prepare entries for treasury stock transactions.*

**BE11.6 (LO 2), AP** On July 1, Raney Corporation purchases 500 shares of its $5 par value common stock for the treasury at a cash price of $9 per share. On September 1, it sells 300 shares of the treasury stock for cash at $11 per share. Journalize the two treasury stock transactions.

*Prepare entries for a cash dividend.*

**BE11.7 (LO 3), AP** Basse Corporation has 7,000 shares of common stock outstanding. It declares a $1 per share cash dividend on November 1 to stockholders of record on December 1. The dividend is paid on December 31. Prepare the entries on the appropriate dates to record the declaration and payment of the cash dividend.

*Prepare entries for a stock dividend.*

**BE11.8 (LO 3), AP** Langley Corporation has 50,000 shares of $10 par value common stock outstanding. It declares a 15% stock dividend on December 1 when the market price per share is $16. The dividend shares are issued on December 31. Prepare the entries for the declaration and issuance of the stock dividend.

*Show before-and-after effects of a stock dividend.*

**BE11.9 (LO 3), AP** The stockholders' equity section of Mabry Corporation's balance sheet consists of common stock ($8 par) $1,000,000 and retained earnings $300,000. A 10% stock dividend (12,500 shares) is declared when the market price per share is $19. Show the before-and-after effects of the dividend on (a) the components of stockholders' equity and (b) the shares outstanding.

*Determine retained earnings balance.*

**BE11.10 (LO 4), AP** For the year ending December 31, 2022, Soto Inc. reports net income $170,000 and cash dividends $85,000. Determine the balance in retained earnings at December 31 assuming the balance in retained earnings on January 1, 2022, was $220,000.

*Prepare a stockholders' equity section.*

**BE11.11 (LO 4), AP** Sudz Corporation has these accounts at December 31: Common Stock, $10 par, 5,000 shares issued, $50,000; Paid-in Capital in Excess of Par Value $22,000; Retained Earnings $42,000; and Treasury Stock, 500 shares, $11,000. Prepare the stockholders' equity section of the balance sheet.

*Compute book value per share.*

**\*BE11.12 (LO 6), AP** The balance sheet for Lauren Inc. shows the following: total paid-in capital and retained earnings $877,000, total stockholders' equity $817,000, common stock issued 44,000 shares, and common stock outstanding 38,000 shares. Compute the book value per share. (No preferred stock is outstanding.)

# DO IT! Exercises

**DO IT! 11.1a (LO 1), C** Indicate whether each of the following statements is true or false. If false, indicate how to correct the statement.

_____ 1. The corporation is an entity separate and distinct from its owners.

_____ 2. The liability of stockholders is normally limited to their investment in the corporation.

_____ 3. The relative lack of government regulation is an advantage of the corporate form of business.

_____ 4. There is no journal entry to record the authorization of capital stock.

_____ 5. No-par value stock is quite rare today.

*Analyze statements about corporate organization.*

**DO IT! 11.1b (LO 1), AP** At the end of its first year of operation, Goss Corporation has $1,000,000 of common stock and net income of $236,000. Prepare (a) the closing entry for net income and (b) the stockholders' equity section at year-end.

*Close net income and prepare stockholders' equity section.*

**DO IT! 11.2a (LO 2), AP** Beauty Island Corporation began operations on April 1 by issuing 60,000 shares of $5 par value common stock for cash at $13 per share. On April 19, it issued 2,000 shares of common stock to attorneys in settlement of their bill of $27,500 for organization costs. In addition, Beauty Island issued 1,000 shares of $1 par value preferred stock for $6 cash per share. Journalize the issuance of the common and preferred shares, assuming the shares are not publicly traded.

*Journalize issuance of stock.*

**DO IT! 11.2b (LO 2), AP** Fouts Corporation purchased 2,000 shares of its $10 par value common stock for $130,000 on August 1. It will hold these shares in the treasury until resold. On December 1, the corporation sold 1,200 shares of treasury stock for cash at $72 per share. Journalize the treasury stock transactions.

*Journalize treasury stock transactions.*

**DO IT! 11.3a (LO 3), AP** Herr Corporation has 3,000 shares of 8%, $100 par value preferred stock outstanding at December 31, 2022. At December 31, 2022, the company declared a $105,000 cash dividend. Determine the dividend paid to preferred stockholders and common stockholders under each of the following scenarios.

*Determine dividends paid to preferred and common stockholders.*

1. The preferred stock is noncumulative, and the company has not missed any dividends in previous years.

2. The preferred stock is noncumulative, and the company did not pay a dividend in each of the two previous years.

3. The preferred stock is cumulative, and the company did not pay a dividend in each of the two previous years.

**DO IT! 11.3b (LO 3), AP** Spears Company has had 4 years of record earnings. Due to this success, the market price of its 400,000 outstanding shares of $2 par value common stock has increased from $6 per share to $50. During this period, paid-in capital remained the same at $2,400,000. Retained earnings increased from $1,800,000 to $12,000,000. CEO Don Ames is considering either (1) a 15% stock dividend or (2) a 2-for-1 stock split. He asks you to show the before-and-after effects of each option on (a) retained earnings, (b) total stockholders' equity, and (c) par value per share.

*Determine effects of stock dividend and stock split.*

**DO IT! 11.4a (LO 4), AP** Hoyle Corporation has issued 100,000 shares of $5 par value common stock. It was authorized to sell 500,000 shares. The paid-in capital in excess of par on common stock is $263,000. The corporation has reacquired 7,000 common shares at a cost of $46,000 and is currently holding those shares.

The corporation also has 2,000 shares issued and outstanding of 9%, $100 par value preferred stock. It was authorized 10,000 shares. The paid-in capital in excess of par value on the preferred stock is $23,000. Retained earnings is $372,000. Prepare the stockholders' equity section of the balance sheet.

*Prepare stockholders' equity section.*

**DO IT! 11.4b (LO 4), AP** On January 1, 2022, Vahsholtz Corporation purchased 5,000 shares of treasury stock. Other information regarding Vahsholtz Corporation is provided as follows.

*Compute return on stockholders' equity and discuss changes.*

|  | 2022 | 2021 |
|---|---|---|
| Net income | $110,000 | $100,000 |
| Dividends on preferred stock | $ 30,000 | $ 30,000 |
| Dividends on common stock | $ 25,000 | $ 20,000 |
| Weighted-average number of common shares outstanding | 45,000 | 50,000 |
| Common stockholders' equity beginning of year | $750,000 | $600,000 |
| Common stockholders' equity end of year | $830,000 | $750,000 |

(a) Compute return on common stockholders' equity for each year, and (b) discuss the changes from 2021 to 2022.

## Exercises

*Identify characteristics of a corporation.*

**E11.1 (LO 1), C** Andrea has prepared the following list of statements about corporations.

1. A corporation is an entity separate and distinct from its owners.

2. As a legal entity, a corporation has most of the rights and privileges of a person.

3. Most of the largest U.S. corporations are privately held corporations.

4. Corporations may buy, own, and sell property; borrow money; enter into legally binding contracts; and sue and be sued.

5. The net income of a corporation is not taxed as a separate entity.

6. Creditors have a legal claim on the personal assets of the owners of a corporation if the corporation does not pay its debts.

7. The transfer of stock from one owner to another requires the approval of either the corporation or other stockholders.

8. The board of directors of a corporation legally owns the corporation.

9. The chief accounting officer of a corporation is the controller.

10. Corporations are subject to fewer state and federal regulations than partnerships or proprietorships.

### Instructions

Identify each statement as true or false. If false, indicate how to correct the statement.

*Identify characteristics of a corporation.*

**E11.2 (LO 1), C** Khalid has come to you with statements about corporations.

1. Corporation management is both an advantage and a disadvantage of a corporation compared to a proprietorship or a partnership.

2. Limited liability of stockholders, government regulations, and additional taxes are the major disadvantages of a corporation.

3. When a corporation is formed, organization costs are recorded as an asset.

4. Each share of common stock gives the stockholder the ownership rights to vote at stockholder meetings, share in corporate earnings, keep the same percentage ownership when new shares of stock are issued, and share in assets upon liquidation.

5. The number of issued shares is always greater than or equal to the number of authorized shares.

6. A journal entry is required for the authorization of capital stock.

7. Publicly held corporations usually issue stock directly to investors.

8. The trading of capital stock on a securities exchange involves the transfer of already issued shares from an existing stockholder to another investor.

9. The market price of common stock is usually the same as its par value.

10. Retained earnings is the total amount of cash and other assets paid in to the corporation by stockholders in exchange for capital stock.

### Instructions

Identify each statement as true or false. If false, indicate how to correct the statement.

*Journalize issuance of common stock.*

**E11.3 (LO 2), AP** During its first year of operations, Mona Corporation had these transactions pertaining to its common stock.

| | |
|---|---|
| Jan. 10 | Issued 30,000 shares for cash at $5 per share. |
| July 1 | Issued 60,000 shares for cash at $7 per share. |

### Instructions

a. Journalize the transactions, assuming that the common stock has a par value of $5 per share.

b. Journalize the transactions, assuming that the common stock is no-par with a stated value of $1 per share.

*Journalize issuance of common stock.*

**E11.4 (LO 2), AP** Osage Corporation issued 2,000 shares of stock.

### Instructions

Prepare the entry for the issuance under the following independent assumptions.

a. The stock had a par value of $5 per share and was issued for a total of $52,000.

b. The stock had a stated value of $5 per share and was issued for a total of $52,000.

c. The stock had no par or stated value and was issued for a total of $52,000.

d. The stock had a par value of $5 per share and was issued to attorneys for services provided during incorporation valued at $52,000.

e. The stock had a par value of $5 per share and was issued for land worth $52,000.

**E11.5 (LO 2, 3), AP** Hodge Corporation issued 100,000 shares of $20 par value, cumulative, 6% preferred stock on January 1, 2021, for $2,300,000. In December 2023, Hodge declared its first dividend of $500,000.

*Differentiate between preferred and common stock dividends.*

**Instructions**

a. Prepare Hodge's journal entry to record the issuance of the preferred stock.

b. If the preferred stock is **not** cumulative, how much of the $500,000 would be paid to **common** stockholders?

c. If the preferred stock is cumulative, how much of the $500,000 would be paid to **common** stockholders?

**E11.6 (LO 2), AP** As an auditor for the CPA firm of Hinkson and Calvert, you encounter the following situations in auditing different clients.

*Journalize noncash common stock transactions.*

1. LR Corporation is a closely held corporation whose stock is not publicly traded. On December 5, the corporation acquired land by issuing 5,000 shares of its $20 par value common stock. The owners' asking price for the land was $120,000, and the fair value of the land was $110,000.

2. Vera Corporation is a publicly held corporation whose common stock is traded on the securities markets. On June 1, it acquired land by issuing 20,000 shares of its $10 par value stock. At the time of the exchange, the land was advertised for sale at $250,000. The stock was selling at $11 per share.

**Instructions**

Prepare the journal entries for each of the situations above.

**E11.7 (LO 2), AP** Rinehart Corporation purchased from its stockholders 5,000 shares of its own previously issued stock for $255,000. It later resold 2,000 shares for $54 per share, then 2,000 more shares for $49 per share, and finally 1,000 shares for $43 per share.

*Journalize treasury stock transactions.*

**Instructions**

Prepare journal entries for the purchase of the treasury stock and the three sales of treasury stock

**E11.8 (LO 2), AP** Quay Co. had the following transactions during the current period.

*Journalize issuance of common and preferred stock and purchase of treasury stock.*

| Mar. | 2 | Issued 5,000 shares of $5 par value common stock to attorneys in payment of a bill for $30,000 for services performed in helping the company to incorporate. |
| June | 12 | Issued 60,000 shares of $5 par value common stock for cash of $375,000. |
| July | 11 | Issued 1,000 shares of $100 par value preferred stock for cash at $110 per share. |
| Nov. | 28 | Purchased 2,000 shares of treasury stock for $80,000. |

**Instructions**

Journalize the transactions.

**E11.9 (LO 2), AP** On January 1, 2022, the stockholders' equity section of Newlin Corporation shows common stock ($5 par value) $1,500,000; paid-in capital in excess of par $1,000,000; and retained earnings $1,200,000. During the year, the following treasury stock transactions occurred.

*Journalize treasury stock transactions.*

| Mar. | 1 | Purchased 50,000 shares for cash at $15 per share. |
| July | 1 | Sold 10,000 treasury shares for cash at $17 per share. |
| Sept. | 1 | Sold 8,000 treasury shares for cash at $14 per share. |

**Instructions**

a. Journalize the treasury stock transactions.

b. Restate the entry for September 1, assuming the treasury shares were sold at $12 per share.

**E11.10 (LO 2, 4), AP** Penland Corporation is authorized to issue both preferred and common stock. The par value of the preferred stock is $50. During the first year of operations, the company had the following events and transactions pertaining to its preferred stock.

*Journalize preferred stock transactions and indicate statement presentation.*

| Feb. | 1 | Issued 40,000 shares for cash at $51 per share. |
| July | 1 | Issued 60,000 shares for cash at $56 per share. |

## Instructions

a. Journalize the transactions.

b. Post to the stockholders' equity accounts. (Use T-accounts.)

c. Discuss the statement presentation of the accounts.

*Answer questions about stockholders' equity section.*

**E11.11 (LO 2, 4), C** The stockholders' equity section of Lachlin Corporation's balance sheet at December 31 is presented here.

|  |  |
|---|---:|
| **Lachlin Corporation** | |
| **Balance Sheet (partial)** | |
| Stockholders' equity | |
| Paid-in capital | |
| Preferred stock, cumulative, 10,000 shares authorized, | |
| 6,000 shares issued and outstanding | $ 600,000 |
| Common stock, no par, 750,000 shares authorized, | |
| 580,000 shares issued | 2,900,000 |
| Total paid-in capital | 3,500,000 |
| Retained earnings | 1,158,000 |
| Total paid-in capital and retained earnings | 4,658,000 |
| Less: Treasury stock (6,000 common shares) | 32,000 |
| Total stockholders' equity | $4,626,000 |

## Instructions

From a review of the stockholders' equity section, answer the following questions.

a. How many shares of common stock are outstanding?

b. Assuming there is a stated value, what is the stated value of the common stock?

c. What is the par value of the preferred stock?

d. If the annual dividend on preferred stock is $36,000, what is the dividend rate on preferred stock?

e. If dividends of $72,000 were in arrears on preferred stock, what would be the balance reported for retained earnings?

*Prepare correct entries for capital stock transactions.*

**E11.12 (LO 2), AP** Gilliam Corporation recently hired a new accountant with extensive experience in accounting for partnerships. Because of the pressure of the new job, the accountant was unable to review his understanding of corporation accounting. During the first month, the accountant made the following entries for the corporation's capital stock.

| | | | | |
|---|---|---|---:|---:|
| May 2 | Cash | | 130,000 | |
| | Capital Stock | | | 130,000 |
| | (Issued 10,000 shares of $10 par value | | | |
| | common stock at $13 per share) | | | |
| 10 | Cash | | 600,000 | |
| | Capital Stock | | | 600,000 |
| | (Issued 10,000 shares of $50 par value | | | |
| | preferred stock at $60 per share) | | | |
| 15 | Capital Stock | | 15,000 | |
| | Cash | | | 15,000 |
| | (Purchased 1,000 shares of common | | | |
| | stock for the treasury at $15 per share) | | | |
| 31 | Cash | | 8,000 | |
| | Capital Stock | | | 5,000 |
| | Gain on Sale of Stock | | | 3,000 |
| | (Sold 500 shares of treasury stock at $16 | | | |
| | per share) | | | |

## Instructions

On the basis of the explanation for each entry, prepare the entry that should have been made for the capital stock transactions.

**E11.13 (LO 3), AP**  On January 1, Graves Corporation had 60,000 shares of no-par common stock issued and outstanding. The stock has a stated value of $4 per share. During the year, the following transactions occurred.

*Journalize cash dividends; indicate statement presentation.*

Apr.  1   Issued 9,000 additional shares of common stock for $11 per share.

June 15   Declared a cash dividend of $1.50 per share to stockholders of record on June 30.

July 10   Paid the $1.50 cash dividend.

Dec.  1   Issued 4,000 additional shares of common stock for $12 per share.

15   Declared a cash dividend on outstanding shares of $1.60 per share to stockholders of record on December 31.

**Instructions**

a. Prepare the entries, if any, on each of the three dates that involved dividends.

b. How are dividends and dividends payable reported in the financial statements prepared at December 31?

**E11.14 (LO 3), AP**  On January 1, 2022, Lenne Corporation had $1,200,000 of common stock outstanding that was issued at par and retained earnings of $750,000. The company issued 30,000 shares of common stock at par on July 1 and earned net income of $400,000 for the year.

*Journalize stock dividends.*

**Instructions**

Journalize the declaration of a 15% stock dividend on December 10, 2022, for the following two independent assumptions.

a. Par value is $10 and market price is $15.

b. Par value is $5 and market price is $8.

**E11.15 (LO 3), AP**  On October 31, the stockholders' equity section of Manolo Company's balance sheet consists of common stock $648,000 and retained earnings $400,000. Manolo is considering the following two courses of action: (1) declaring a 5% stock dividend on the 81,000 $8 par value shares outstanding or (2) effecting a 2-for-1 stock split that will reduce par value to $4 per share. The current market price is $17 per share.

*Compare effects of a stock dividend and a stock split.*

**Instructions**

Prepare a tabular summary of the effects of the alternative actions on the company's stockholders' equity and outstanding shares. Use these column headings: **Before Action, After Stock Dividend**, and **After Stock Split.**

**E11.16 (LO 3), AP**  Before preparing financial statements for the current year, the chief accountant for Toso Company discovered the following errors in the accounts.

*Prepare correcting entries for dividends and a stock split.*

1. The declaration and payment of a $50,000 cash dividend was recorded as a debit to Interest Expense $50,000 and a credit to Cash $50,000.

2. A 10% stock dividend (1,000 shares) was declared on the $10 par value stock when the market price per share was $18. The only entry made was Stock Dividends (Dr.) $10,000 and Dividend Payable (Cr.) $10,000. The shares have not been issued.

3. A 4-for-1 stock split involving the issue of 400,000 shares of $5 par value common stock for 100,000 shares of $20 par value common stock was recorded as a debit to Retained Earnings $2,000,000 and a credit to Common Stock $2,000,000.

**Instructions**

Prepare the correcting entries at December 31.

**E11.17 (LO 4), AP**  On January 1, 2022, Eddy Corporation had retained earnings of $610,000. During the year, Eddy had the following selected events.

*Determine retained earnings balance.*

1. Declared cash dividends $120,000.

2. Earned net income $350,000.

3. Declared stock dividends $90,000.

**Instructions**

Determine the retained earnings balance at the end of the year.

*Determine retained earnings balance.*

**E11.18 (LO 4), AP** Newland Company reported retained earnings at December 31, 2021, of $330,000. Newland had 200,000 shares of common stock outstanding at the beginning of 2022.

The following transactions occurred during 2022.

1. A cash dividend of $0.50 per share was declared and paid.

2. A 5% stock dividend was declared and distributed when the market price per share was $15 per share.

3. Net income was $285,000.

**Instructions**

Compute the ending balance in retained earnings at the end of 2022.

*Classify stockholders' equity accounts.*

**E11.19 (LO 4), AP** The ledger of Rolling Hills Corporation contains the following accounts: Common Stock, Preferred Stock, Treasury Stock, Paid-in Capital in Excess of Par—Preferred Stock, Paid-in Capital in Excess of Stated Value—Common Stock, Paid-in Capital from Treasury Stock, and Retained Earnings.

**Instructions**

Classify each account using the following table headings.

| | Paid-in Capital | | | |
| Account | Capital Stock | Additional | Retained Earnings | Other |
| --- | --- | --- | --- | --- |

*Prepare a stockholders' equity section.*

**E11.20 (LO 4), AP** The following accounts appear in the ledger of Horner Inc. after the books are closed at December 31, 2022.

| | |
| --- | --- |
| Common Stock, no par, $1 stated value, 400,000 shares authorized; | |
| 300,000 shares issued | $ 300,000 |
| Common Stock Dividends Distributable | 30,000 |
| Paid-in Capital in Excess of Stated Value—Common Stock | 1,200,000 |
| Preferred Stock, $5 par value, 8%, 40,000 shares authorized; | |
| 30,000 shares issued | 150,000 |
| Retained Earnings | 800,000 |
| Treasury Stock (10,000 common shares) | 74,000 |
| Paid-in Capital in Excess of Par—Preferred Stock | 344,000 |

**Instructions**

Prepare the stockholders' equity section at December 31, 2022, assuming retained earnings is restricted for plant expansion in the amount of $100,000 (use Note R).

*Prepare a stockholders' equity section.*

**E11.21 (LO 4), AP** Dirk Company reported the following balances at December 31, 2021: common stock $500,000, paid-in capital in excess of par—common stock $100,000, and retained earnings $250,000. During 2022, the following transactions affected stockholders' equity.

1. Issued preferred stock with a par value of $125,000 for $200,000.

2. Purchased treasury stock (common) for $40,000.

3. Earned net income of $180,000.

4. Declared and paid cash dividends of $56,000.

**Instructions**

Prepare the stockholders' equity section of Dirk Company's December 31, 2022, balance sheet.

*Prepare an income statement and compute return on equity.*

**E11.22 (LO 4), AP** In 2022, Pennington Corporation had net sales of $600,000 and cost of goods sold of $360,000. Operating expenses were $153,000, and interest expense was $7,500. The corporation's tax rate is 30%. The corporation declared preferred dividends of $15,000 in 2022, and its average common stockholders' equity during the year was $200,000.

**Instructions**

a. Prepare a multiple-step income statement for Pennington Corporation.

b. Compute Pennington Corporation's return on common stockholders' equity for 2022.

**E11.23 (LO 4), AN**  The following financial information is available for Flintlock Corporation.

| (in millions) | 2022 | 2021 |
|---|---|---|
| Average common stockholders' equity | $2,532 | $2,591 |
| Dividends declared for common stockholders | 298 | 611 |
| Dividends declared for preferred stockholders | 40 | 40 |
| Net income | 504 | 555 |

**Instructions**

Calculate the payout ratio and return on common stockholders' equity for 2022 and 2021. Comment on your findings.

**E11.24 (LO 4), AN**  Suppose the following financial information is available for **Walgreens**.

| (in millions) | 2022 | 2021 |
|---|---|---|
| Average common stockholders' equity | $13,622.5 | $11,986.5 |
| Dividends declared for common stockholders | 471 | 394 |
| Dividends declared for preferred stockholders | 0 | 0 |
| Net income | 2,006 | 2,157 |

**Instructions**

Calculate the payout ratio and return on common stockholders' equity for 2022 and 2021. Comment on your findings.

\* **E11.25 (LO 4, 6), AP**  A recent stockholders' equity section of **Aluminum Company of America (Alcoa)** showed the following (in alphabetical order): additional paid-in capital $6,101, common stock $925, preferred stock $56, retained earnings $7,428, and treasury stock $2,828. (All dollar data are in millions.)

The preferred stock has 557,740 shares authorized, with a par value of $100 and an annual $3.75 per share cumulative dividend preference. At December 31 of the current year, 557,649 shares of preferred are issued and 546,024 shares are outstanding. There are 1.8 billion shares of $1 par value common stock authorized, of which 924.6 million are issued and 844.8 million are outstanding at December 31.

**Instructions**

a. Prepare the stockholders' equity section of the current year, including disclosure of all relevant data.

b. Compute the book value per share of common stock, assuming there are no preferred dividends in arrears. (Round to two decimals.)

\* **E11.26 (LO 6), AP**  At December 31, Gorden Corporation has total stockholders' equity of $3,200,000. Included in this total are preferred stock $500,000 and paid-in capital in excess of par—preferred stock $50,000. There are 10,000 shares of $50 par value, 8% cumulative preferred stock outstanding. At year-end, 200,000 shares of common stock are outstanding.

**Instructions**

Compute the book value per share of common stock under each of the following assumptions.

a. There are no preferred dividends in arrears, and the preferred stock does not have a call price.

b. Preferred dividends are one year in arrears, and the preferred stock has a call price of $50 per share.

# Problems

**P11.1 (LO 2, 4), AP**  DeLong Corporation was organized on January 1, 2022. It is authorized to issue 10,000 shares of 8%, $100 par value preferred stock, and 500,000 shares of no-par common stock with a stated value of $2 per share. The following stock transactions were completed during the first year.

| | |
|---|---|
| Jan. 10 | Issued 80,000 shares of common stock for cash at $4 per share. |
| Mar. 1 | Issued 5,000 shares of preferred stock for cash at $105 per share. |
| Apr. 1 | Issued 24,000 shares of common stock for land. The asking price of the land was $90,000. The fair value of the land was $85,000. |
| May 1 | Issued 80,000 shares of common stock for cash at $4.50 per share. |
| Aug. 1 | Issued 10,000 shares of common stock to attorneys in payment of their bill of $30,000 for services performed in helping the company organize. |
| Sept. 1 | Issued 10,000 shares of common stock for cash at $5 per share. |
| Nov. 1 | Issued 1,000 shares of preferred stock for cash at $109 per share. |

### Instructions

a. Journalize the transactions.

*c. Total paid-in capital $1,479,000*

b. Post to the stockholders' equity accounts. (Use T-accounts.)

c. Prepare the paid-in capital section of stockholders' equity at December 31, 2022.

*Journalize and post treasury stock transactions, and prepare stockholders' equity section.*

**P11.2 (LO 2, 4), AP** Fechter Corporation had the following stockholders' equity accounts on January 1, 2022: Common Stock ($5 par) $500,000, Paid-in Capital in Excess of Par—Common Stock $200,000, and Retained Earnings $100,000. In 2022, the company had the following treasury stock transactions.

| | |
|---|---|
| Mar. 1 | Purchased 5,000 shares at $8 per share. |
| June 1 | Sold 1,000 shares at $12 per share. |
| Sept. 1 | Sold 2,000 shares at $10 per share. |
| Dec. 1 | Sold 1,000 shares at $7 per share. |

Fechter Corporation uses the cost method of accounting for treasury stock. In 2022, the company reported net income of $30,000.

### Instructions

a. Journalize the treasury stock transactions, and prepare the closing entry at December 31, 2022, for net income.

*b. Treasury Stock $8,000*

*c. Total stockholders' equity $829,000*

b. Open accounts for (1) Paid-in Capital from Treasury Stock, (2) Treasury Stock, and (3) Retained Earnings. (Post to T-accounts.)

c. Prepare the stockholders' equity section of Fechter Corporation's balance sheet at December 31, 2022.

*Journalize and post transactions, and prepare stockholders' equity section.*

**P11.3 (LO 2, 4), AP** The stockholders' equity accounts of Castle Corporation on January 1, 2022, were as follows.

| | |
|---|---|
| Preferred Stock (8%, $50 par, cumulative, 10,000 shares authorized) | $ 400,000 |
| Common Stock ($1 stated value, 2,000,000 shares authorized) | 1,000,000 |
| Paid-in Capital in Excess of Par—Preferred Stock | 100,000 |
| Paid-in Capital in Excess of Stated Value—Common Stock | 1,450,000 |
| Retained Earnings | 1,816,000 |
| Treasury Stock (10,000 common shares) | 50,000 |

During 2022, the corporation had the following transactions and events pertaining to its stockholders' equity.

| | |
|---|---|
| Feb. 1 | Issued 25,000 shares of common stock for $120,000. |
| Apr. 14 | Sold 6,000 shares of treasury stock—common for $33,000. |
| Sept. 3 | Issued 5,000 shares of common stock for a patent valued at $35,000. |
| Nov. 10 | Purchased 1,000 shares of common stock for the treasury at a cost of $6,000. |
| Dec. 31 | Determined that net income for the year was $452,000. |

No dividends were declared during the year.

### Instructions

a. Journalize the transactions and the closing entry for net income.

b. Enter the beginning balances in the accounts, and post the journal entries to the stockholders' equity accounts. (Use T-accounts.)

*c. Total stockholders' equity $5,350,000*

c. Prepare a stockholders' equity section at December 31, 2022, including the disclosure of the preferred dividends in arrears.

**P11.4 (LO 3, 4), AP** On January 1, 2022, Geffrey Corporation had the following stockholders' equity accounts.

*Prepare dividend entries and stockholders' equity section.*

| | |
|---|---:|
| Common Stock ($20 par value, 60,000 shares issued and outstanding) | $1,200,000 |
| Paid-in Capital in Excess of Par—Common Stock | 200,000 |
| Retained Earnings | 600,000 |

During the year, the following transactions occurred.

| | | |
|---|---|---|
| Feb. | 1 | Declared a $1 cash dividend per share to stockholders of record on February 15, payable March 1. |
| Mar. | 1 | Paid the dividend declared in February. |
| Apr. | 1 | Announced a 2-for-1 stock split. Prior to the split, the market price per share was $36. |
| July | 1 | Declared a 10% stock dividend to stockholders of record on July 15, distributable July 31. On July 1, the market price of the stock was $13 per share. |
| | 31 | Issued the shares for the stock dividend. |
| Dec. | 1 | Declared a $0.50 per share dividend to stockholders of record on December 15, payable January 5, 2023. |
| | 31 | Determined that net income for the year was $350,000. |

**Instructions**

a. Journalize the transactions and the closing entries for net income and dividends.

b. Enter the beginning balances, and post the entries to the stockholders' equity accounts. (Use T-accounts.) (*Note:* Open additional stockholders' equity accounts as needed.)

c. Prepare the stockholders' equity section at December 31.

*c. Total stockholders' equity $2,224,000*

**P11.5 (LO 2, 3, 4), AP** The post-closing trial balance of Storey Corporation at December 31, 2022, contains the following stockholders' equity accounts.

*Prepare stockholders' equity section and compute allocation of dividends.*

| | |
|---|---:|
| Preferred Stock (15,000 shares issued) | $ 750,000 |
| Common Stock (250,000 shares issued) | 2,500,000 |
| Paid-in Capital in Excess of Par—Preferred Stock | 250,000 |
| Paid-in Capital in Excess of Par—Common Stock | 400,000 |
| Common Stock Dividends Distributable | 250,000 |
| Retained Earnings | 1,105,000 |

A review of the accounting records reveals the following.

1. No errors have been made in recording 2022 transactions or in preparing the closing entries.

2. Preferred stock is $50 par, 6%, and cumulative; 15,000 shares have been outstanding since January 1, 2021.

3. Authorized stock is 20,000 shares of preferred, 500,000 shares of common with a $10 par value.

4. The January 1 balance in Retained Earnings was $1,170,000.

5. On July 1, 20,000 shares of common stock were issued for cash at $16 per share.

6. A cash dividend of $250,000 was declared and properly allocated to preferred and common stock on October 1. No dividends were paid to preferred stockholders in 2021.

7. On December 31, a 10% common stock dividend was declared out of retained earnings on common stock when the market price per share was $16.

8. Net income for the year was $585,000.

9. On December 31, 2022, the directors authorized disclosure of a $200,000 restriction of retained earnings for plant expansion. (Use Note X.)

**Instructions**

a. Reproduce the Retained Earnings account (T-account) for 2022.

b. Prepare the stockholders' equity section at December 31, 2022.

c. Compute the allocation of the cash dividend to preferred and common stock.

*b. Total stockholders' equity $5,255,000*

*Prepare entries for stock transactions and prepare stockholders' equity section.*

**P11.6 (LO 2, 3, 4), AP** Irwin Corporation has been authorized to issue 20,000 shares of $100 par value, 10%, noncumulative preferred stock and 1,000,000 shares of no-par common stock. The corporation assigned a $2.50 stated value to the common stock. At December 31, 2022, the ledger contained the following post-closing balances pertaining to stockholders' equity.

| | |
|---|---:|
| Preferred Stock | $ 120,000 |
| Paid-in Capital in Excess of Par—Preferred Stock | 20,000 |
| Common Stock | 1,000,000 |
| Paid-in Capital in Excess of Stated Value—Common Stock | 1,800,000 |
| Treasury Stock (1,000 common shares) | 11,000 |
| Paid-in Capital from Treasury Stock | 1,500 |
| Retained Earnings | 82,000 |

All the preferred stock was issued for land having a fair value of $140,000. All common stock issued was for cash. In November, 1,500 shares of common stock were purchased for the treasury at a per share cost of $11. In December, 500 shares of treasury stock were sold for $14 per share. No dividends were declared in 2022.

**Instructions**

a. Prepare the journal entries for the:

 1. Issuance of preferred stock for land.

 2. Issuance of common stock for cash.

 3. Purchase of common treasury stock for cash.

 4. Sale of treasury stock for cash.

*b. Total stockholders' equity $3,012,500*

b. Prepare the stockholders' equity section at December 31, 2022.

*Prepare dividend entries and stockholders' equity section.*

**P11.7 (LO 2, 3, 4), AP** On January 1, 2022, Primo Corporation had the following stockholders' equity accounts.

| | |
|---|---:|
| Common Stock ($10 par value, 75,000 shares issued and outstanding) | $750,000 |
| Paid-in Capital in Excess of Par—Common Stock | 200,000 |
| Retained Earnings | 540,000 |

During the year, the following transactions occurred.

| | | |
|---|---|---|
| Jan. | 15 | Declared a $1 cash dividend per share to stockholders of record on January 31, payable February 15. |
| Feb. | 15 | Paid the dividend declared in January. |
| Apr. | 15 | Declared a 10% stock dividend to stockholders of record on April 30, distributable May 15. On April 15, the market price of the stock was $14 per share. |
| May | 15 | Issued the shares for the stock dividend. |
| July | 1 | Announced a 2-for-1 stock split. The market price per share at the time of the announcement was $15. (The new par value is $5.) |
| Dec. | 1 | Declared a $0.60 per share cash dividend to stockholders of record on December 15, payable January 10, 2023. |
| | 31 | Determined that net income for the year was $250,000. |

**Instructions**

a. Journalize the transactions and the closing entries for net income and dividends.

*c. Total stockholders' equity $1,566,000*

b. Enter the beginning balances, and post the entries to the stockholders' equity accounts. (*Note:* Open additional stockholders' equity accounts as needed.)

c. Prepare a stockholders' equity section at December 31, 2022.

*Prepare stockholders' equity statement.*

**\*P11.8 (LO 5), AP** On January 1, 2022, Goodhue Inc. had the following stockholders' equity balances.

| | |
|---|---:|
| Common Stock (400,000 shares issued) | $800,000 |
| Paid-in Capital in Excess of Par—Common Stock | 500,000 |
| Common Stock Dividends Distributable | 120,000 |
| Retained Earnings | 600,000 |

During 2022, the following transactions and events occurred.

1. Issued 60,000 shares of $2 par value common stock as a result of 15% stock dividend declared on December 15, 2021.

2. Issued 30,000 shares of common stock for cash at $4 per share.

3. Purchased 25,000 shares of common stock for the treasury at $5 per share.

4. Declared and paid a cash dividend of $111,000.

5. Sold 8,000 shares of treasury stock for cash at $5 per share.

6. Earned net income of $360,000.

### Instructions

Prepare a stockholders' equity statement for the year.

Total stockholders' equity
$2,304,000

\*P11.9 (LO 5, 6), AP  The following stockholders' equity accounts (post-closing) arranged alphabetically are in the ledger of Westin Corporation at December 31, 2022.

*Prepare stockholders' equity section; compute book value per share.*

| | |
|---|---:|
| Common Stock ($10 stated value) | $1,500,000 |
| Paid-in Capital from Treasury Stock | 6,000 |
| Paid-in Capital in Excess of Par—Preferred Stock | 42,400 |
| Paid-in Capital in Excess of Stated Value—Common Stock | 690,000 |
| Preferred Stock (8%, $100 par, noncumulative) | 360,000 |
| Retained Earnings | 776,000 |
| Treasury Stock—Common (7,000 shares) | 92,000 |

### Instructions

a. Prepare the stockholders' equity section of the balance sheet at December 31, 2022.

b. Compute the book value per share of the common stock, assuming the preferred stock has a call price of $110 per share.

a. Total stockholders' equity
$3,282,400

## Continuing Case

### Cookie Creations

(*Note:* This is a continuation of the Cookie Creations case from Chapters 1 through 10.)

**CC11**  After establishing their company's fiscal year-end to be October 31, Natalie and Curtis began operating Cookie & Coffee Creations Inc. on November 1, 2020. On that date, they issued both preferred and common stock. After the first year of operations, Natalie and Curtis want to prepare financial information for the year.

*Go to WileyPLUS for complete case details and instructions*

leungchopan/
Shutterstock.com

## Comprehensive Accounting Cycle Review

**ACR11.1**  Hawkeye Corporation's balance sheet at December 31, 2021, is presented as follows.

*Journalize transactions and prepare financial statements.*

**Hawkeye Corporation**
**Balance Sheet**
**December 31, 2021**

| | | | |
|---|---:|---|---:|
| Cash | $ 24,600 | Accounts payable | $ 25,600 |
| Accounts receivable | 45,500 | Common stock ($10 par) | 80,000 |
| Allowance for doubtful | | Retained earnings | 127,400 |
| accounts | (1,500) | | $233,000 |
| Supplies | 4,400 | | |
| Land | 40,000 | | |
| Buildings | 142,000 | | |
| Accumulated depreciation—buildings | (22,000) | | |
| | $233,000 | | |

During 2022, the following transactions occurred.

1. On January 1, 2022, Hawkeye issued 1,200 shares of $40 par, 7% preferred stock for $49,200.

2. On January 1, 2022, Hawkeye also issued 900 shares of the $10 par value common stock for $21,000.

3. Hawkeye performed services for $320,000 on account.

4. On April 1, 2022, Hawkeye collected cash of $36,000 in advance for services to be performed evenly from April 1, 2022, to March 31, 2023.

5. Hawkeye collected $276,000 from customers on account.

6. Hawkeye bought $35,100 of supplies on account.

7. Hawkeye paid $32,200 on accounts payable.

8. Hawkeye reacquired 400 shares of its common stock on June 1, 2022, for $28 per share.

9. Paid other operating expenses of $188,200.

10. On December 31, 2022, Hawkeye declared the annual preferred stock dividend and a $1.20 per share dividend on the outstanding common stock, all payable on January 15, 2023.

11. An account receivable of $1,700 which originated in 2021 is written off as uncollectible.

Adjustment data:

1. A count of supplies indicates that $5,900 of supplies remain unused at year-end.

2. Recorded revenue from item 4 above.

3. The allowance for doubtful accounts should have a balance of $3,500 at year end.

4. Depreciation is recorded on the building on a straight-line basis based on a 30-year life and a salvage value of $10,000.

5. The income tax rate is 30%, and the taxes remain unpaid at year-end. (*Hint:* Prepare the income statement up to income before income taxes and multiply by 30% to compute the amount.)

### Instructions

(You may want to set up T-accounts to determine ending balances.)

a. Prepare journal entries for the transactions listed above and adjusting entries.

b. Totals $740,690

c. Net income $81,970
   Tot. assets $421,000

b. Prepare an adjusted trial balance at December 31, 2022.

c. Prepare an income statement and a retained earnings statement for the year ending December 31, 2022, and a classified balance sheet as of December 31, 2022.

*Journalize transactions and prepare financial statements.*

**ACR11.2** Karen Noonan opened Clean Sweep Inc. on February 1, 2022. During February, the following transactions and events occurred.

| Feb. | 1 | Issued 5,000 shares of Clean Sweep common stock for $13,000. Each share has a $1.50 par. |
| | 1 | Borrowed $8,000 on a 2-year, 6% note payable. |
| | 1 | Paid $9,020 to purchase used floor and window cleaning equipment from a company going out of business ($4,820 was for the floor equipment and $4,200 was for the window equipment). |
| | 1 | Paid $220 for February Internet and phone services. |
| | 3 | Purchased cleaning supplies for $980 on account. |
| | 4 | Hired 4 employees. Each will be paid $480 per 5-day work week (Monday–Friday). Employees will begin working Monday, February 9. |
| | 5 | Obtained insurance coverage for $9,840 per year. Coverage runs from February 1, 2022, through January 31, 2023. Karen paid $2,460 cash for the first quarter of coverage. |
| | 5 | Discussions with the insurance agent indicated that providing outside window cleaning services would cost too much to insure. Karen sold the window cleaning equipment for $3,950 cash. |
| | 16 | Billed customers $3,900 for cleaning services performed through February 13, 2022. |
| | 17 | Received $540 from a customer for 4 weeks of cleaning services to begin February 21, 2022. (By paying in advance, this customer received 10% off the normal weekly fee of $150.) |
| | 18 | Paid $300 on amount owed on cleaning supplies. |
| | 20 | Paid $3 per share to buy 300 shares of Clean Sweep common stock from a shareholder who disagreed with management goals. The shares will be held as treasury shares. |
| | 23 | Billed customers $4,300 for cleaning services performed through February 20. |
| | 24 | Paid cash for employees' wages for 2 weeks (February 9–13 and 16–20). |
| | 25 | Collected $2,500 cash from customers billed on February 16. |
| | 27 | Paid $220 for Internet and phone services for March. (*Hint:* Use Prepaid Expenses.) |
| | 28 | Declared and paid a cash dividend of $0.20 per share. |

### Instructions

a. Journalize the February transactions. (You do not need to include an explanation for each journal entry.)

b. Post to the ledger accounts. (Use T-accounts.)

c. Totals $30,420

c. Prepare a trial balance at February 28, 2022.

d. Journalize the following adjustments. (Round all amounts to whole dollars.)

1. Services performed for customers through February 28, 2022, but unbilled and uncollected were $3,800.

2. Received notice that a customer who was billed $200 for services performed February 10 has filed for bankruptcy. Clean Sweep does not expect to collect any portion of this outstanding receivable.

3. Clean Sweep uses the allowance method to estimate bad debts. Clean Sweep estimates that 3% of its month-end receivables will not be collected.

4. Record 1 month of depreciation for the floor equipment. Use the straight-line method, an estimated life of 4 years, and $500 salvage value.

5. Record 1 month of insurance expense.

6. An inventory count shows $400 of supplies on hand at February 28.

7. One week of services were performed for the customer who paid in advance on February 17.

8. Accrue for wages owed through February 28, 2022.

9. Accrue for interest expense for 1 month.

10. Karen estimates a 20% income tax rate. [*Hint:* Prepare an income statement up to income before income taxes to help with the income tax calculation.)

e. Post adjusting entries to the T-accounts.

f. Prepare an adjusted trial balance.

g. Prepare a **multiple-step income statement, a retained earnings statement**, and a **properly classified balance sheet** as of February 28, 2022.

h. Journalize closing entries.

g. Net income $3,117
   Tot. assets $26,101

# Data Analytics in Action

## Using Data Visualization to Analyze Dividends

**DA11.1** Data visualization can be used to compare dividends and stock prices.

**Example:** Recall the *Investor Insight* box "What About Dividends?" presented in the chapter. The dividend yield ratio is the annual dividend per share divided by the market price per share. Two factors can contribute to a high dividend yield: (1) the payment of a large dividend, which causes the numerator to be large, or (2) having a low share market price, which causes the denominator to be small.

  **Ford Motor Company** is considered to have a high dividend yield. But how does Ford's dividend yield compare to its competitors? Consider the following chart, which presents the dividends per share and dividend yields for Ford, **General Motors**, **Toyota**, and **Tesla**.

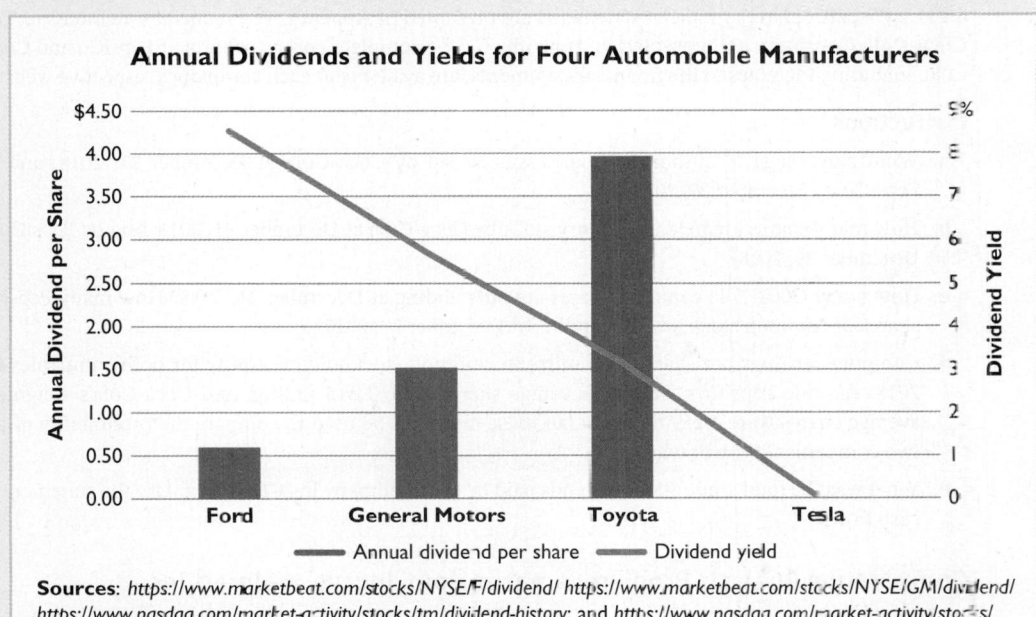

**Sources:** https://www.marketbeat.com/stocks/NYSE/F/dividend/ https://www.marketbeat.com/stocks/NYSE/GM/dividend/ https://www.nasdaq.com/market-activity/stocks/tm/dividend-history; and https://www.nasdaq.com/market-activity/stocks/tsla/dividend-history.

If you examine the pattern of dividend yields, observe that both General Motors and Toyota have higher dividends than Ford, while Tesla currently pays no dividends. The dividend yields are much higher for Ford than those of General Motors and Toyota, while Tesla has a zero yield due to not paying dividends.

For this case, you will review data for these four companies to determine how the effect of stock market prices can help explain the dividend yield. You will create and analyze a combo column and line chart to determine how an investor might balance stock prices and dividend yields when deciding which stocks to buy.

*Go to WileyPLUS for complete case details and instructions.*

### Using Data Analytics to Compare the Effect of Stock Splits

**DA11.2** Warren Buffet, the CEO of **Berkshire Hathaway**, does not believe in stock splits, as noted in the *Investor Insight* box "A No-Split Philosophy" presented in the chapter. On the other hand, **The Walt Disney Company** stock has been split a few times. For this case, you will use stock prices from both companies to create and analyze a line chart and a combo clustered column and line chart.

*Go to WileyPLUS for complete case details and instructions.*

## Expand Your Critical Thinking

### Financial Reporting Problem: Apple Inc.

**CT11.1** The stockholders' equity section of **Apple Inc.**'s balance sheet is shown in the Consolidated Statement of Financial Position in Appendix A. The complete annual report, including the notes to its financial statements, is available at the company's website.

#### Instructions

Answer the following questions.

   **a.** What is the par or stated value per share of Apple's common stock?

   **b.** What percentage of Apple's authorized common stock was issued at September 29, 2018? (Round to the nearest full percent.)

   **c.** How many shares of common stock were outstanding at September 30, 2017, and at September 29, 2018?

   **d.** Calculate the payout ratio, earnings per share, and return on common stockholders' equity for 2018.

### Comparative Analysis Problem: PepsiCo, Inc. vs. The Coca-Cola Company

**CT11.2** **PepsiCo, Inc.**'s financial statements are presented in Appendix B. Financial statements of **The Coca-Cola Company** are presented in Appendix C. The complete annual reports of PepsiCo and Coca-Cola, including the notes to the financial statements, are available at each company's respective website.

#### Instructions

   **a.** What percentage of authorized shares was issued by Coca-Cola at December 31, 2018, and by PepsiCo at December 29, 2018?

   **b.** How many shares are held as treasury stock by Coca-Cola at December 31, 2018, and by PepsiCo at December 29, 2018?

   **c.** How many Coca-Cola common shares are outstanding at December 31, 2018? How many PepsiCo shares of common stock are outstanding at December 29, 2018?

   **d.** Compute earnings per share and return on common stockholders' equity for both companies for 2018. Assume PepsiCo's weighted-average shares were 1,415 million and Coca-Cola's weighted-average shares were 4,259 million. Can these measures be used to compare the profitability of the two companies? Why or why not?

   **e.** What was the total amount of dividends paid by each company in 2018? (*Hint:* Use the statement of cash flows.)

### Comparative Analysis Problem: Amazon.com, Inc. vs. Walmart Inc.

**CT11.3** **Amazon.com, Inc.**'s financial statements are presented in Appendix D. Financial statements of **Walmart Inc.** are presented in Appendix E. The complete annual reports of Amazon and Walmart, including the notes to the financial statements, are available at each company's respective website. Assume that Walmart has 11,000 million shares authorized and has 2,878 million shares issued and outstanding.

**Instructions**

a. What percentage of authorized shares was issued by Amazon at December 31, 2018, and by Walmart at January 31, 2019?

b. How many shares are held as treasury stock by Amazon at December 31, 2018, and by Walmart at January 31, 2019?

c. How many Amazon common shares are outstanding at December 31, 2018? How many Walmart shares of common stock are outstanding at January 31, 2019?

d. What are the basic earnings per share for both Amazon and Walmart as of December 31, 2018 and January 31, 2019, respectively?

e. What was the total amount of dividends, if any, paid by Amazon for the year ending December 31, 2018? What was the total dividends paid by Walmart for the year ending January 31, 2019? (*Hint:* Use the statement of cash flows.)

## Real-World Focus

**CT11.4** Use the stockholders' equity section of an annual report and identify the major components.

**Instructions**

Select a well-known company, search the Internet for its most recent annual report, and then answer the following questions.

a. What is the company's name?

b. What classes of capital stock has the company issued?

c. For each class of stock:

   1. How many shares are authorized, issued, and/or outstanding?

   2. What is the par value?

d. What are the company's retained earnings?

e. Has the company acquired treasury stock? How many shares?

## Decision-Making Across the Organization

**CT11.5** The stockholders' meeting for Percival Corporation has been in progress for some time. The chief financial officer for Percival is presently reviewing the company's financial statements and is explaining the items that comprise the stockholders' equity section of the balance sheet for the current year. The stockholders' equity section of Percival Corporation at December 31, 2022, is as follows.

**Percival Corporation**
**Balance Sheet (partial)**
**December 31, 2022**

| | | |
|---|---:|---:|
| Paid-in capital | | |
|   Capital stock | | |
|     Preferred stock, authorized 1,000,000 shares | | |
|       cumulative, $100 par value, $8 per share, 6,000 | | |
|       shares issued and outstanding | | $ 600,000 |
|     Common stock, authorized 5,000,000 shares, $1 par | | |
|       value, 3,000,000 shares issued, and 2,700,000 outstanding | | 3,000,000 |
|     Total capital stock | | 3,600,000 |
|   Additional paid-in capital | | |
|     In excess of par—preferred stock | $ 50,000 | |
|     In excess of par—common stock | 25,000,000 | |
|     Total additional paid-in capital | | 25,050,000 |
|     Total paid-in capital | | 28,650,000 |
| Retained earnings | | 900,000 |
|     Total paid-in capital and retained earnings | | 29,550,000 |
| Less: Treasury stock (300,000 common shares) | | 9,300,000 |
|     Total stockholders' equity | | $20,250,000 |

At the meeting, stockholders have raised a number of questions regarding the stockholders' equity section.

**Instructions**

With the class divided into groups, answer the following questions as if you were the chief financial officer for Percival Corporation.

**a.** "What does the cumulative provision related to the preferred stock mean?"

**b.** "I thought the common stock was presently selling at $29.75, but the company has the stock stated at $1 per share. How can that be?"

**c.** "Why is the company buying back its common stock? Furthermore, the treasury stock has a debit balance because it is subtracted from stockholders' equity. Why is treasury stock not reported as an asset if it has a debit balance?"

## Communication Activity

**CT11.6** Earl Kent, your uncle, is an inventor who has decided to incorporate. Uncle Earl knows that you are an accounting major at U.N.O. In a recent letter to you, he ends with the question, "I'm filling out a state incorporation application. Can you tell me the difference in the following terms: (1) authorized stock, (2) issued stock, (3) outstanding stock, and (4) preferred stock?"

**Instructions**

In a brief note, differentiate for Uncle Earl among the four different stock terms. Write the letter to be friendly, yet professional.

## Ethics Case

**CT11.7** The R&D division of Pele Corp. has just developed a chemical for sterilizing the vicious Brazilian "killer bees" which are invading Mexico and the southern United States. The president of the company is anxious to get the chemical on the market to boost the company's profits. He believes his job is in jeopardy because of decreasing sales and profits. The company has an opportunity to sell this chemical in Central American countries, where the laws are much more relaxed than in the United States.

The director of Pele's R&D division strongly recommends further testing in the laboratory for side-effects of this chemical on other insects, birds, animals, plants, and even humans. He cautions the president, "We could be sued from all sides if the chemical has tragic side-effects that we didn't even test for in the labs." The president answers, "We can't wait an additional year for your lab tests. We can avoid losses from such lawsuits by establishing a separate wholly owned corporation to shield Pele from such lawsuits. We can't lose any more than our investment in the new corporation, and we'll invest in just the patent covering this chemical. We'll reap the benefits if the chemical works and is safe, and avoid the losses from lawsuits if it's a disaster." The following week, Pele creates a new wholly owned corporation called Cabo Inc., sells the chemical patent to it for $10, and watches the spraying begin.

**Instructions**

**a.** Who are the stakeholders in this situation?

**b.** Are the president's motives and actions ethical?

**c.** Can Pele shield itself against losses of Cabo Inc.?

## All About You

**CT11.8** A high percentage of Americans own stock in corporations. As a shareholder in a corporation, you will receive an annual report. One of the goals of this course is for you to learn how to navigate your way around an annual report.

**Instructions**

Use **Apple**'s 2018 annual report (see Appendix A) to answer the following questions.

**a.** What CPA firm performed the audit of Apple's financial statements?

**b.** What was the amount of Apple's earnings per share in 2018?

**c.** What were net sales in 2018?

**d.** How much cash did Apple spend on capital expenditures in 2018?

**e.** Over what life does the company depreciate its buildings?

**f.** What were the proceeds from issuance of common stock in 2018?

## FASB Codification Activity

**CT11.9** If your school has a subscription to the FASB Codification, log in and prepare responses to the following.

**a.** What is the stock dividend?

**b.** What is a stock split?

**c.** At what percentage point does the issuance of additional shares qualify as a stock dividend, as opposed to a stock split?

## Answers to Insight and Accounting Across the Organization Questions

**The Impact of Corporate Social Responsibility Q:** Why are CSR-related shareholder proposals increasing? **A:** CSR-related shareholder proposals are increasing because a recent survey indicated that 83% of investors believe that CSR factors impact shareholder value over the long term. Further, these proposals have received increasing voting support over the last 10 years.

**How to Read Stock Quotes Q:** For stocks traded on organized exchanges, how are the dollar prices per share established? What factors might influence the price of shares in the marketplace? **A:** The dollar prices per share are established by the interaction between buyers and sellers of the shares. Other factors that might influence the price of shares include the company's anticipated future earnings, its expected dividend rate per share, its current financial position, the current state of the economy, and the current state of the securities market.

**A Bold Repurchase Strategy Q:** What signal might a large stock repurchase send to investors regarding management's belief about the company's growth opportunities? **A:** When a company has many growth opportunities, it will normally conserve its cash in order to be better able to fund expansion. A large use of cash to buy back stock (and essentially shrink the company) would suggest that management was not optimistic about its growth opportunities.

**What About Dividends? Q:** What factors must management consider in deciding how large a dividend to pay? **A:** Management must consider the company's retained earnings balance and amount of cash, and balance that with stockholder expectations. The payment of a large cash dividend could lead to liquidity problems for the company. On the other hand, a small dividend may cause unhappiness among stockholders.

**A No-Split Philosophy Q:** Why does Warren Buffet usually oppose stock splits? **A:** Buffett prefers to attract shareholders who will make a long-term commitment to his company, as opposed to traders who will only hold their investment for a short period of time. He believes that a high stock price discourages short-term investment.

# A Look at IFRS

### LEARNING OBJECTIVE 7

Compare the accounting for stockholders' equity under GAAP and IFRS.

The accounting for transactions related to stockholders' equity, such as issuance of shares and purchase of treasury stock, is similar under both IFRS and GAAP. Major differences relate to terminology used, introduction of items such as revaluation surplus, and presentation of stockholders' equity information.

## Key Points

Following are the key similarities and differences between GAAP and IFRS as related to stockholders' equity, dividends, retained earnings, and income reporting.

### Similarities

- Aside from the terminology used, the accounting for the issuance of shares, the purchase of treasury stock, and dividends is similar.
- Like GAAP, IFRS does not allow a company to record gains or losses on purchases of its own shares.
- The computations related to earnings per share are essentially the same under IFRS and GAAP.

**Differences**

- Under IFRS, the term **reserves** is used to describe all equity accounts other than those arising from contributed (paid-in) capital. This would include, for example, reserves related to retained earnings, asset revaluations, and fair value differences.

- Many countries have a different mix of investor groups than in the United States. For example, in Germany, financial institutions like banks are not only major creditors of corporations but often are the largest corporate stockholders as well. In the United States, Asia, and the United Kingdom, many companies rely on substantial investment from private investors.

- There are often terminology differences for equity accounts. The following summarizes some of the common differences in terminology.

| GAAP | IFRS |
|---|---|
| Common stock | Share capital—ordinary |
| Stockholders | Shareholders |
| Par value | Nominal or face value |
| Authorized stock | Authorized share capital |
| Preferred stock | Share capital—preference |
| Paid-in capital | Issued/allocated share capital |
| Paid-in capital in excess of par—common stock | Share premium—ordinary |
| Paid-in capital in excess of par—preferred stock | Share premium—preference |
| Retained earnings | Retained earnings or Retained profits |
| Retained earnings deficit | Accumulated losses |

As an example of how similar transactions use different terminology under IFRS, consider the accounting for the issuance of 1,000 shares of $1 par value common stock for $5 per share. Under IFRS, the entry is as follows.

| | | |
|---|---|---|
| Cash | 5,000 | |
|     Share Capital—Ordinary | | 1,000 |
|     Share Premium—Ordinary | | 4,000 |

- A major difference between IFRS and GAAP relates to the account Revaluation Surplus. Revaluation surplus arises under IFRS because companies are permitted to revalue their property, plant, and equipment to fair value under certain circumstances. This account is part of general reserves under IFRS and is not considered contributed capital.

- IFRS often uses terms such as **retained profits** or **accumulated profit or loss** to describe retained earnings. The term retained earnings is also often used.

- Equity is given various descriptions under IFRS, such as shareholders' equity, owners' equity, capital and reserves, and shareholders' funds.

# IFRS Practice

## IFRS Self-Test Questions

**1.** Which of the following is **true**?

  **a.** In the United States, the primary corporate stockholders are financial institutions.

  **b.** Share capital means total assets under IFRS.

  **c.** Share Capital—Ordinary is an account used under IFRS.

  **d.** The accounting for treasury stock differs extensively between GAAP and IFRS.

**2.** Under IFRS, the amount of capital received in excess of par value would be credited to:

  **a.** Retained Earnings.

  **b.** Contributed Capital—Ordinary.

  **c.** Share Premium—Ordinary.

  **d.** Retained Profits.

**3.** Which of the following is **false**?

  **a.** Under GAAP, companies cannot record gains on transactions involving their own shares.

  **b.** Under IFRS, companies cannot record gains on transactions involving their own shares.

  **c.** Under IFRS, the statement of stockholders' equity is a required statement.

  **d.** Under IFRS, treasury shares are not permitted.

**4.** Which of the following does **not** represent a pair of GAAP/IFRS-comparable terms?

  **a.** Additional paid-in capital/Share premium.

  **b.** Treasury stock/Repurchase reserve.

  **c.** Common stock/Share capital.

  **d.** Preferred stock/Preference shares.

5. The basic accounting for cash dividends and stock dividends:

   a. is different under IFRS versus GAAP.

   b. is the same under IFRS and GAAP.

   c. differs only for the accounting for cash dividends between GAAP and IFRS.

   d. differs only for the accounting for stock dividends between GAAP and IFRS.

6. Which item is **not** considered part of reserves?

   a. Unrealized loss on available-for-sale investments

   b. Revaluation surplus.

   c. Retained earnings.

   d. Issued shares.

7. Which set of terms can be used to describe total stockholders' equity under IFRS?

   a. Shareholders' equity, capital and reserves, other comprehensive income.

   b. Capital and reserves, shareholders' equity, shareholders' funds.

   c. Capital and reserves, retained earnings, shareholders' equity.

   d. All of the answer choices are correct.

8. Earnings per share computations related to IFRS and GAAP:

   a. are essentially similar.

   b. result in an amount referred to as earnings per share.

   c. must deduct preferred (preference) dividends when computing earnings per share.

   d. All of the answer choices are correct.

## IFRS Exercises

**IFRS11.1** On May 10, Jaurez Corporation issues 1,000 shares of $10 par value ordinary shares for cash at $18 per share. Journalize the issuance of the shares.

**IFRS11.2** Meenen Corporation has the following accounts at December 31, 2022 (in euros). Share Capital—Ordinary, €10 par, 5,000 shares issued, €50,000; Share Premium—Ordinary €10,000; Retained Earnings €45,000; and Treasury Shares—Ordinary, 500 shares, €11,000. Prepare the equity section of the statement of financial position (balance sheet).

**IFRS11.3** Overton Co. had the following transactions during the current period.

| | | |
|---|---|---|
| Mar. | 2 | Issued 5,000 shares of $1 par value ordinary shares to attorneys in payment of a bill for $30,000 for services performed in helping the company to incorporate. |
| June | 12 | Issued 60,000 shares of $1 par value ordinary shares for cash of $375,000. |
| July | 11 | Issued 1,000 shares of $100 par value preference shares for cash at $110 per share. |
| Nov. | 28 | Purchased 2,000 treasury shares (ordinary) for $80,000. |

### Instructions

Journalize the above transactions.

## International Financial Reporting Problem: Louis Vuitton

**IFRS11.4** The financial statements of **Louis Vuitton** are presented in Appendix F. The complete consolidated financial statements, including the notes to its financial statements, are available at the company's website.

### Instructions

Use the company's 2018 consolidated financial statements to answer the following questions.

   a. Determine the following amounts at December 31, 2018: (1) total equity, (2) total revaluation reserve, and (3) number of treasury shares.

   b. Examine the equity section of the company's balance sheet. For each of the following, provide the comparable label that would be used under GAAP: (1) share capital and (2) share premium.

   c. Did the company declare and pay any dividends for the year ended December 31, 2018?

   d. Compute the company's return on ordinary shareholders' equity for the year ended December 31, 2018.

   e. What was Louis Vuitton's earnings per share for the year ended December 31, 2018?

### Answers to IFRS Self-Test Questions

**1.** c  **2.** c  **3.** d  **4.** b  **5.** b  **6.** d  **7.** b  **8.** d

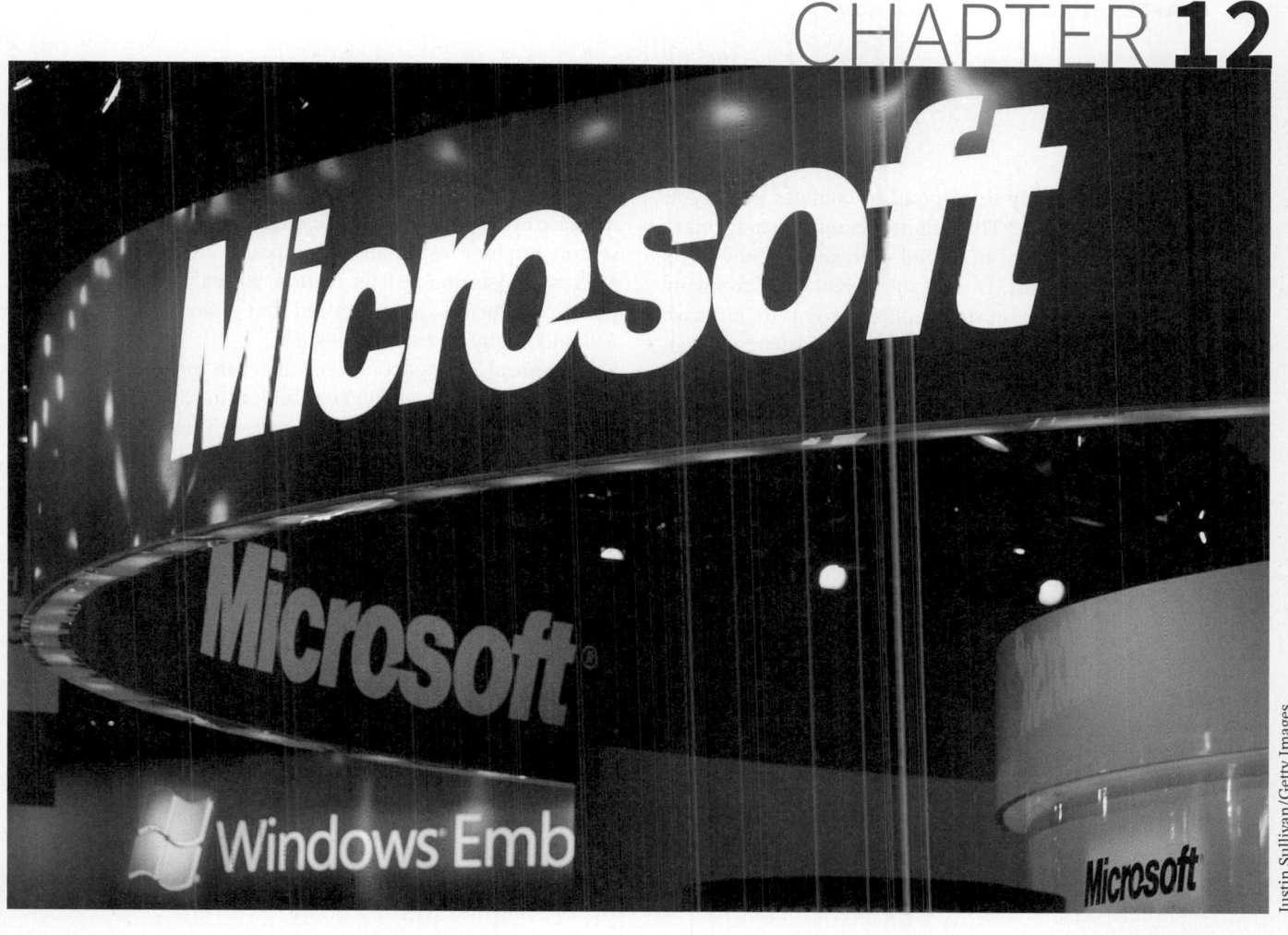

## CHAPTER 12

Justin Sullivan/Getty Images

# Statement of Cash Flows

## Chapter Preview

The balance sheet, income statement, and retained earnings statement do not always show the whole picture of the financial condition of a company or institution. In fact, looking at the financial statements of some well-known companies, a thoughtful investor might ask questions like these: How did **Eastman Kodak** finance cash dividends of $649 million in a year in which it earned only $17 million? How could **United Air Lines** purchase new planes that cost $1.9 billion in a year in which it reported a net loss of over $2 billion? How did the companies that spent a combined fantastic $4.1 trillion on mergers and acquisitions in a recent year finance those deals? Answers to these and similar questions can be found in this chapter, which presents the statement of cash flows.

# Feature Story

## Got Cash?

Companies must be ready to respond to changes quickly in order to survive and thrive. This requires careful management of cash. One company that managed cash successfully in its early years was **Microsoft**. During those years, the company paid much of its payroll with stock options (rights to purchase company stock in the future at a given price) instead of cash. This conserved cash and turned more than a thousand of its employees into millionaires.

Eventually, Microsoft had a different kind of cash problem. It reached a more "mature" stage in life, generating so much cash—roughly $1 billion per month—that it could not always figure out what to do with it. At one time, Microsoft had accumulated $60 billion.

The company said it was accumulating cash to invest in new opportunities, buy other companies, and pay off pending lawsuits. Microsoft's stockholders complained that holding all this cash was putting a drag on the company's profitability. Why? Because Microsoft had the cash invested in very low-yielding government securities. Stockholders felt that the company either should find new investment projects that would bring higher returns, or return some of the cash to stockholders.

Finally, Microsoft announced a plan to return cash to stockholders by paying a special one-time $32 billion dividend. This special dividend was so large that, according to the U.S. Commerce Department, it caused total personal income in the United States to rise by 3.7% in one month—the largest increase ever recorded by the agency. (It also made the holiday season brighter, especially for retailers in the Seattle area.) Microsoft also doubled its regular annual dividend to $3.50 per share. Further, it announced that it would spend another $30 billion buying treasury stock.

**Apple** also has encountered this cash "problem." Recently, Apple had approximately $100 billion in liquid assets (cash, cash equivalents, and investment securities). The company was generating $69 billion of cash per year from its operating activities but spending only about $10 billion on plant assets. In response to shareholder pressure, Apple announced that it would begin to pay a quarterly dividend of $2.65 per share and buy back up to $10 billion of its stock. Analysts noted that the dividend consumes only $10 billion of cash per year. This leaves Apple wallowing in cash. The rest of us should have such problems.

**Source:** "Business: An End to Growth? Microsoft's Cash Bonanza," *The Economist* (July 23, 2005), p. 61.

# Chapter Outline

| LEARNING OBJECTIVES | REVIEW | PRACTICE |
|---|---|---|
| **LO 1** Discuss the usefulness and format of the statement of cash flows. | • Usefulness of the statement of cash flows<br>• Classification of cash flows<br>• Significant noncash activities<br>• Format of the statement of cash flows | **DO IT! 1** Classification of Cash Flows |
| **LO 2** Prepare a statement of cash flows using the indirect method. | • Indirect and direct methods<br>• Indirect method—Computer Services Company<br>• Step 1: Operating activities<br>• Summary of conversion to net cash provided by operating activities<br>• Step 2: Investing and financing activities<br>• Step 3: Net change in cash | **DO IT! 2a** Cash Flows from Operating Activities<br>**DO IT! 2b** Indirect Method |
| **LO 3** Analyze the statement of cash flows. | • Free cash flow | **DO IT! 3** Free Cash Flow |

**Go to the Review and Practice section at the end of the chapter for a review of key concepts and practice applications with solutions.**

**Visit WileyPLUS for additional tutorials and practice opportunities.**

# Usefulness and Format of the Statement of Cash Flows

### LEARNING OBJECTIVE 1
Discuss the usefulness and format of the statement of cash flows.

The balance sheet, income statement, and retained earnings statement provide only limited information about a company's cash flows (cash receipts and cash payments). For example, comparative balance sheets show the net increase in property, plant, and equipment during the year. But, they do not show how the additions were financed or paid for. The income statement shows net income based on the accrual basis of accounting. But, it does not indicate the amount of cash generated by operating activities. The retained earnings statement shows cash dividends declared but not the cash dividends paid during the year. None of these statements presents a detailed summary of where cash came from and how it was used.

## Usefulness of the Statement of Cash Flows

The **statement of cash flows** reports the cash receipts, cash payments, and net change in cash resulting from operating, investing, and financing activities during a period. The information in a statement of cash flows helps investors, creditors, and others assess the following.

1. **The entity's ability to generate future cash flows.** By examining relationships between items in the statement of cash flows, investors can better predict the amounts, timing, and uncertainty of future cash flows than they can from accrual-basis data.

2. **The entity's ability to pay dividends and meet obligations.** If a company does not have adequate cash, it cannot pay employees, settle debts, or pay dividends. Employees, creditors, and stockholders should be particularly interested in this statement because it alone shows the flows of cash in a business.

3. **The reasons for the difference between net income and net cash provided (used) by operating activities.** Net income provides information on the success or failure of a business. However, some financial statement users are critical of accrual-basis net income because it requires many estimates (see **Ethics Note**). As a result, users often challenge the reliability of the number. Such is not the case with cash. Many readers of the statement of cash flows want to know the reasons for the difference between net income and net cash provided by operating activities. Then, they can assess for themselves the reliability of the net income number.

4. **The cash investing and financing transactions during the period.** By examining a company's investing and financing transactions, a financial statement reader can better understand why assets and liabilities changed during the period.

**ETHICS NOTE**

Though we discourage reliance on cash flows to the exclusion of accrual accounting, comparing net cash provided by operating activities to net income can reveal important information about the "quality" of reported net income. Such a comparison can reveal the extent to which net income provides a good measure of actual performance.

## Classification of Cash Flows

The statement of cash flows classifies cash receipts and cash payments as operating, investing, and financing activities. Transactions and other events characteristic of each kind of activity are as follows.

1. **Operating activities** include the cash effects of transactions that generate revenues and expenses. They thus enter into the determination of net income.

2. **Investing activities** include (a) acquiring and disposing of investments and property, plant, and equipment, and (b) lending money and collecting the loans.

3. **Financing activities** include (a) obtaining cash from issuing debt and repaying the amounts borrowed, and (b) obtaining cash from stockholders, repurchasing shares, and paying dividends.

The operating activities category is the most important. It shows the cash provided by company operations. This source of cash is generally considered to be the best measure of a company's ability to generate sufficient cash to continue as a going concern.

**Illustration 12.1** lists typical cash receipts and cash payments within each of the three classifications. *Study the list carefully; it will prove very useful in solving homework exercises and problems.*

**ILLUSTRATION 12.1**

**Typical receipt and payment classifications**

**Operating activities**

**Investing activities**

**Financing activities**

### Types of Cash Inflows and Outflows

**Operating activities—Income statement items**

Cash inflows:

From sale of goods or services.

From interest received and dividends received.

Cash outflows:

To suppliers for inventory.

To employees for wages.

To government for taxes.

To lenders for interest.

To others for expenses.

**Investing activities—Changes in investments and long-term assets**

Cash inflows:

From sale of property, plant, and equipment.

From sale of investments in debt or equity securities of other entities.

From collection of principal on loans to other entities.

Cash outflows:

To purchase property, plant, and equipment.

To purchase investments in debt or equity securities of other entities.

To make loans to other entities.

**Financing activities—Changes in long-term liabilities and stockholders' equity**

Cash inflows:

From sale of common and preferred stock.

From issuance of debt (bonds and notes).

Cash outflows:

To stockholders as dividends.

To redeem long-term debt or reacquire capital stock (treasury stock).

Note the following general guidelines:

1. Operating activities involve income statement items.

2. Investing activities involve cash flows resulting from changes in investments and long-term asset items.

3. Financing activities involve cash flows resulting from changes in long-term liability and stockholders' equity items.

Companies classify as operating activities some cash flows related to investing or financing activities. For example, receipts of investment revenue (interest and dividends) are classified as operating activities. So are payments of interest to lenders. Why are these considered operating activities? **Because companies report these items in the income statement, where results of operations are shown**.

# Significant Noncash Activities

Not all of a company's significant activities involve cash. Examples of significant noncash activities are as follows.

1. Direct issuance of common stock to purchase assets.

2. Conversion of bonds into common stock.

3. Direct issuance of debt to purchase assets.
4. Exchanges of plant assets.

**Companies do not report in the body of the statement of cash flows significant financing and investing activities that do not affect cash.** Instead, they report these activities in either a **separate schedule** at the bottom of the statement of cash flows or in a **separate note or supplementary schedule** to the financial statements (see **Helpful Hint**). The reporting of these noncash activities in a separate schedule satisfies the **full disclosure principle**.

*In solving homework assignments, you should present significant noncash investing and financing activities in a separate schedule at the bottom of the statement of cash flows (see the last item in Illustration 12.2 below).*

**HELPFUL HINT**

Do not include noncash investing and financing activities in the body of the statement of cash flows. Report this information in a separate schedule.

---

## Accounting Across the Organization   Target Corporation

Darren McCollester/ Getty Images

### Net *What?*

Net income is not the same as net cash provided by operating activities. The table shows some results from recent annual reports (dollars in millions), including **Target Corporation**. Note how the numbers differ greatly across the list even though all these companies engage in retail merchandising.

| Company | Net Income | Net Cash Provided by Operating Activities |
|---|---|---|
| Kohl's Corporation | $ 889 | $ 1,884 |
| Walmart Inc. | 16,669 | 25,591 |
| J. C. Penney Company, Inc. | (1,388) | (1,814) |
| Costco Wholesale Corp. | 20,391 | 3,437 |
| Target Corporation | 1,971 | 6,520 |

In general, why do differences exist between net income and net cash provided by operating activities? (Answer is available near the end of the chapter.)

---

# Format of the Statement of Cash Flows

The general format of the statement of cash flows presents the results of the three activities discussed previously—operating, investing, and financing—plus the significant noncash investing and financing activities. **Illustration 12.2** shows a widely used form of the statement of cash flows.

**ILLUSTRATION 12.2**

Format of statement of cash flows

| Company Name<br>Statement of Cash Flows<br>For the Period Covered | | |
|---|---|---|
| **Cash flows from operating activities** | | |
| (List of individual items) | XX | |
| Net cash provided (used) by operating activities | | XXX |
| **Cash flows from investing activities** | | |
| (List of individual inflows and outflows) | XX | |
| Net cash provided (used) by investing activities | | XXX |
| **Cash flows from financing activities** | | |
| (List of individual inflows and outflows) | XX | |
| Net cash provided (used) by financing activities | | XXX |
| **Net increase (decrease) in cash** | | XXX |
| **Cash at beginning of period** | | XXX |
| **Cash at end of period** | | XXX |
| **Noncash investing and financing activities** | | |
| (List of individual noncash transactions) | | XXX |

The cash flows from operating activities section always appears first, followed by the investing activities section and then the financing activities section. The sum of the operating, investing, and financing sections equals the net increase or decrease in cash for the period.

This amount is added to the beginning cash balance to arrive at the ending cash balance—the same amount reported on the balance sheet. The FASB now requires that restricted cash be included with cash and cash equivalents when reconciling the beginning and ending amounts on the statement of cash flows.

---

**ACTION PLAN**

- Identify the three types of activities used to report all cash inflows and outflows.
- Report as operating activities the cash effects of transactions that generate revenues and expenses and enter into the determination of net income.
- Report as investing activities transactions that (a) acquire and dispose of investments and long-term assets and (b) lend money and collect loans.
- Report as financing activities transactions that (a) obtain cash from issuing debt and repay the amounts borrowed and (b) obtain cash from stockholders and pay them dividends.

### DO IT! 1 | Classification of Cash Flows

During its first week, Duffy & Stevenson Company had these transactions.

1. Issued 100,000 shares of common stock at par for $800,000 cash.
2. Borrowed $200,000 from Castle Bank, signing a 5-year note bearing 8% interest.
3. Purchased two semi-trailer trucks for $170,000 cash.
4. Paid employees $12,000 for salaries and wages.
5. Collected $20,000 cash for services performed.

Classify each of these transactions by type of cash flow activity. (*Hint:* Refer to Illustration 12.1.)

**Solution**

1. Financing activity.      4. Operating activity.
2. Financing activity.      5. Operating activity.
3. Investing activity.

Related exercise material: **BE12.1, BE12.2, BE12.3, DO IT! 12.1, E12.1, E12.2, and E12.3.**

---

# Preparing the Statement of Cash Flows—Indirect Method

**LEARNING OBJECTIVE 2**

Prepare a statement of cash flows using the indirect method.

Companies prepare the statement of cash flows differently from the three other basic financial statements. First, it is not prepared from an adjusted trial balance. It requires detailed information concerning the changes in account balances that occurred between two points in time. An adjusted trial balance will not provide the necessary data. Second, the statement of cash flows deals with cash receipts and payments. As a result, the company **adjusts** the effects of the use of accrual accounting **to determine cash flows**.

The information to prepare this statement usually comes from three sources:

- **Comparative balance sheets.** Information in the comparative balance sheets indicates the amount of the changes in assets, liabilities, and stockholders' equity from the beginning to the end of the period.

- **Current income statement**. Information in this statement helps determine the amount of net cash provided or used by operating activities during the period.
- **Additional information.** Such information includes transaction data that are needed to determine how cash was provided or used during the period.

Preparing the statement of cash flows from these data sources involves three major steps, explained in **Illustration 12.3**.

**ILLUSTRATION 12.3**

**Three major steps in preparing the statement of cash flows**

**Step 1**: Determine net cash provided/used by operating activities by converting net income from an accrual basis to a cash basis.

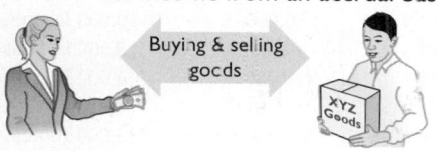
Buying & selling goods

This step involves analyzing not only the current year's income statement but also comparative balance sheets and selected additional data.

**Step 2**: Analyze changes in noncurrent asset and liability accounts and stockholders' equity accounts and report as investing and financing activities, or disclose as noncash transactions.

For Sale
Bank
Investing
Financing

This step involves analyzing comparative balance sheet data and selected additional information for their effects on cash.

**Step 3**: Compare the net change in cash on the statement of cash flows with the change in the Cash account reported on the balance sheet to make sure the amounts agree.

Year 1    Year 2    Difference

The difference between the beginning and ending cash balances can be easily computed from comparative balance sheets.

# Indirect and Direct Methods

In order to perform Step 1, a company **must convert net income from an accrual basis to a cash basis**. This conversion may be done by either of two methods: (1) the indirect method or (2) the direct method. **Both methods arrive at the same amount** for "Net cash provided by operating activities." They differ in **how** they arrive at the amount.

The **indirect method** adjusts net income for items that do not affect cash. A great majority of companies (98%) use this method. Companies favor the indirect method for two reasons: (1) it is easier and less costly to prepare, and (2) it focuses on the differences between net income and net cash flow from operating activities.

The **direct method** shows operating cash receipts and payments. It is prepared by adjusting each item in the income statement from the accrual basis to the cash basis. The FASB has expressed a preference for the direct method but allows the use of either method.

The next section illustrates the more popular indirect method. Appendix 12A illustrates the direct method.

# Indirect Method—Computer Services Company

To explain how to prepare a statement of cash flows using the indirect method, we use financial information from Computer Services Company. **Illustration 12.4** presents Computer Services' current- and previous-year balance sheets, its current-year income statement, and related financial information for the current year.

**ILLUSTRATION 12.4**

**Comparative balance sheets, income statement, and additional information for Computer Services Company**

## Computer Services Company
### Comparative Balance Sheets
### December 31

| Assets | 2022 | 2021 | Change in Account Balance Increase/Decrease |
|---|---|---|---|
| **Current assets** | | | |
| Cash | $ 55,000 | $ 33,000 | $ 22,000 Increase |
| Accounts receivable | 20,000 | 30,000 | 10,000 Decrease |
| Inventory | 15,000 | 10,000 | 5,000 Increase |
| Prepaid expenses | 5,000 | 1,000 | 4,000 Increase |
| **Property, plant, and equipment** | | | |
| Land | 130,000 | 20,000 | 110,000 Increase |
| Buildings | 160,000 | 40,000 | 120,000 Increase |
| Accumulated depreciation—buildings | (11,000) | (5,000) | 6,000 Increase |
| Equipment | 27,000 | 10,000 | 17,000 Increase |
| Accumulated depreciation—equipment | (3,000) | (1,000) | 2,000 Increase |
| Total assets | $398,000 | $138,000 | |
| **Liabilities and Stockholders' Equity** | | | |
| **Current liabilities** | | | |
| Accounts payable | $ 28,000 | $ 12,000 | $ 16,000 Increase |
| Income taxes payable | 6,000 | 8,000 | 2,000 Decrease |
| **Long-term liabilities** | | | |
| Bonds payable | 130,000 | 20,000 | 110,000 Increase |
| **Stockholders' equity** | | | |
| Common stock | 70,000 | 50,000 | 20,000 Increase |
| Retained earnings | 164,000 | 48,000 | 116,000 Increase |
| Total liabilities and stockholders' equity | $398,000 | $138,000 | |

## Computer Services Company
### Income Statement
### For the Year Ended December 31, 2022

| | | |
|---|---|---|
| Sales revenue | | $507,000 |
| Cost of goods sold | $150,000 | |
| Operating expenses (excluding depreciation) | 111,000 | |
| Depreciation expense | 9,000 | |
| Loss on disposal of plant assets | 3,000 | |
| Interest expense | 42,000 | 315,000 |
| Income before income tax | | 192,000 |
| Income tax expense | | 47,000 |
| Net income | | $145,000 |

**Additional information for 2022:**

1. Depreciation expense was comprised of $6,000 for building and $3,000 for equipment.
2. The company sold equipment with a book value of $7,000 (cost $8,000, less accumulated depreciation $1,000) for $4,000 cash.
3. Issued $110,000 of long-term bonds in direct exchange for land.
4. A building costing $120,000 was purchased for cash. Equipment costing $25,000 was also purchased for cash.
5. Issued common stock at par for $20,000 cash.
6. The company declared and paid a $29,000 cash dividend.

We now apply the three steps for preparing a statement of cash flows to the information provided for Computer Services Company.

# Step 1: Operating Activities

## Determine Net Cash Provided/Used by Operating Activities by Converting Net Income from an Accrual Basis to a Cash Basis

To determine net cash provided by operating activities under the indirect method, companies **adjust net income in numerous ways**. A useful starting point is to understand **why** net income must be converted to net cash provided by operating activities.

Under generally accepted accounting principles (GAAP), most companies use the accrual basis of accounting. This basis requires that companies record revenue when a performance obligation is satisfied and record expenses when incurred. Revenues include credit sales for which the company has not yet collected cash. Expenses incurred include some items that have not yet been paid in cash. Thus, under the accrual basis, net income is not the same as net cash provided by operating activities.

Therefore, under the **indirect method**, companies must adjust net income to convert certain items to the cash basis. The indirect method (or reconciliation method) starts with net income and converts it to net cash provided by operating activities. **Illustration 12.5** lists the three types of adjustments.

| Net Income | +/− | Adjustments | = | Net Cash Provided/ Used by Operating Activities |
|---|---|---|---|---|
| | | • **Add back noncash expenses**, such as depreciation expense and amortization expense. | | |
| | | • **Deduct gains and add losses** that resulted from investing and financing activities. | | |
| | | • **Analyze changes** to noncash current asset and current liability accounts. | | |

**ILLUSTRATION 12.5**
Three types of adjustments to convert net income to net cash provided by operating activities

We explain the three types of adjustments in the next three sections.

## Depreciation Expense

Computer Services' income statement reports depreciation expense of $9,000. Although depreciation expense reduces net income, it does not reduce cash. In other words, depreciation expense is a noncash charge. The company must add it back to net income to negate the effect of the expense to arrive at net cash provided by operating activities (see **Helpful Hint**). Computer Services reports depreciation expense in the statement of cash flows as in **Illustration 12.6**.

**HELPFUL HINT**
Depreciation is similar to any other expense in that it reduces net income. It differs in that it does not involve a current cash outflow. That is why it must be *added back* to net income to arrive at net cash provided by operating activities.

| | |
|---|---|
| Cash flows from operating activities | |
| Net income | $145,000 |
| Adjustments to reconcile net income to net cash provided by operating activities: | |
| **Depreciation expense** | 9,000 |
| Net cash provided by operating activities | $154,000 |

**ILLUSTRATION 12.6**
Adjustment for depreciation

As the first adjustment to net income in the statement of cash flows, companies frequently list depreciation and similar noncash charges such as amortization of intangible assets and bad debt expense.

## Loss on Disposal of Plant Assets

Illustration 12.1 states that cash received from the sale (disposal) of plant assets is reported in the investing activities section. Because of this, **companies eliminate from net income all gains and losses related to the disposal of plant assets, to arrive at net cash provided by operating activities.**

In our example, Computer Services' income statement reports a $3,000 loss on the disposal of plant assets (book value $7,000, less $4,000 cash received from disposal of plant assets). The journal entry to record this transaction would have been as follows.

| | | |
|---|---|---|
| Cash | 4,000 | |
| Accumulated Depreciation—Equipment | 1,000 | |
| Loss on Disposal of Plant Assets | 3,000 | |
|     Equipment | | 8,000 |

The company's loss of $3,000 should be added to net income in order to determine net cash provided by operating activities. The loss reduced net income but did not reduce cash. **Illustration 12.7** shows that the $3,000 loss is eliminated by adding $3,000 back to net income to arrive at net cash provided by operating activities. (The cash received of $4,000 will be reported in the investing activities section, as discussed later.)

**ILLUSTRATION 12.7**

**Adjustment for loss on disposal of plant assets**

| Cash flows from operating activities | | |
|---|---|---|
|   Net income | | $145,000 |
|   Adjustments to reconcile net income to net cash | | |
|     provided by operating activities: | | |
|       Depreciation expense | $9,000 | |
|       **Loss on disposal of plant assets** | **3,000** | 12,000 |
|     Net cash provided by operating activities | | $157,000 |

If a gain on disposal occurs, the company deducts the gain from net income in order to determine net cash provided by operating activities. **In the case of either a gain or a loss, companies report the actual amount of cash received from the sale in the investing activities section of the statement of cash flows.**

## Changes to Noncash Current Asset and Current Liability Accounts

A final adjustment in reconciling net income to net cash provided by operating activities involves examining all changes in current asset and current liability accounts. The accrual-accounting process records revenues in the period in which the performance obligation is satisfied and expenses as incurred. For example, Accounts Receivable reflects amounts owed to the company for sales that have been made but for which cash collections have not yet been received. Prepaid Insurance reflects insurance that has been paid for but has not yet expired (therefore has not been expensed). Similarly, Salaries and Wages Payable reflects salaries and wages expense that has been incurred but has not been paid.

As a result, companies need to adjust net income for these accruals and prepayments to determine net cash provided by operating activities. Thus, they must analyze the change in each current asset and current liability account to determine its impact on net income and cash.

**Changes in Noncash Current Assets** The adjustments required for changes in noncash current asset accounts are as follows. **Deduct from net income increases in current asset accounts, and add to net income decreases in current asset accounts, to arrive at net cash provided by operating activities.** We observe these relationships by analyzing the accounts of Computer Services.

**Decrease in Accounts Receivable** Computer Services' accounts receivable decreased by $10,000 (from $30,000 to $20,000) during the period. For Computer Services, this means that cash receipts were $10,000 higher than sales revenue. The Accounts Receivable account in **Illustration 12.8** shows that Computer Services had $507,000 in sales revenue (as reported on the income statement), but it collected $517,000 in cash.

**ILLUSTRATION 12.8**

**Analysis of accounts receivable**

| Accounts Receivable | | | | | |
|---|---|---|---|---|---|
| 1/1/22 | Balance | 30,000 | **Receipts from customers** | | **517,000** |
| | **Sales revenue** | **507,000** | | | |
| 12/31/22 | Balance | 20,000 | | | |

As shown in Illustration 12.9, to adjust net income to net cash provided by operating activities, the company **adds** to net income the decrease of $10,000 in accounts receivable. When the Accounts Receivable balance increases, cash receipts are lower than sales revenue earned under the accrual basis. Therefore, the company **deducts** from net income the amount of the increase in accounts receivable, to arrive at net cash provided by operating activities.

**Increase in Inventory** Computer Services' inventory increased $5,000 (from $10,000 to $15,000) during the period. The change in the Inventory account reflects the difference between the amount of inventory purchased and the cost of inventory sold. For Computer Services, this means that the cost of merchandise purchased exceeded the cost of goods sold by $5,000. As a result, cost of goods sold does not reflect $5,000 of cash payments made for merchandise. The company **deducts** from net income this inventory increase of $5,000 during the period, to arrive at net cash provided by operating activities (see Illustration 12.9). If inventory decreases, the company **adds** to net income the amount of the change, to arrive at net cash provided by operating activities.

**Increase in Prepaid Expenses** Computer Services' prepaid expenses increased during the period by $4,000. This means that cash paid for prepaid expenses is greater than the actual expenses reported on an accrual basis. In other words, the company has made cash payments in the current period that will not be charged to expenses until future periods. To adjust net income to net cash provided by operating activities, the company **deducts** from net income the $4,000 increase in prepaid expenses (see **Illustration 12.9**).

| | | | ILLUSTRATION 12.9 |
|---|---|---|---|
| Cash flows from operating activities | | | **Adjustments for changes in current asset accounts** |
| Net income | | $145,000 | |
| Adjustments to reconcile net income to net cash | | | |
| provided by operating activities: | | | |
| Depreciation expense | $ 9,000 | | |
| Loss on disposal of plant assets | 3,000 | | |
| **Decrease in accounts receivable** | **10,000** | | |
| **Increase in inventory** | **(5,000)** | | |
| **Increase in prepaid expenses** | **(4,000)** | 13,000 | |
| Net cash provided by operating activities | | $158,000 | |

If prepaid expenses decrease, reported expenses are greater than the expenses paid. Therefore, the company **adds** to net income the decrease in prepaid expenses, to arrive at net cash provided by operating activities.

**Changes in Current Liabilities** The adjustments required for changes in current liability accounts are as follows. **Add to net income increases in current liability accounts and deduct from net income decreases in current liability accounts, to arrive at net cash provided by operating activities.**

**Increase in Accounts Payable** For Computer Services, Accounts Payable increased by $16,000 (from $12,000 to $28,000) during the period. That means the company received $16,000 more in goods than it actually paid for. As shown in **Illustration 12.10**, to adjust net income to determine net cash provided by operating activities, the company adds to net income the $16,000 increase in Accounts Payable.

**Decrease in Income Taxes Payable** When a company incurs income tax expense but has not yet paid its taxes, it records income taxes payable. A change in the Income Taxes Payable account reflects the difference between income tax expense incurred and income tax actually paid. Computer Services' Income Taxes Payable account decreased by $2,000. That means the $47,000 of income tax expense reported on the income statement was $2,000 less than the amount of taxes paid during the period of $49,000. As shown in Illustration 12.10, to adjust net income to a cash basis, the company must reduce net income by $2,000.

Illustration 12.10 shows that after starting with net income of $145,000, the sum of all of the adjustments to net income was $27,000. This resulted in net cash provided by operating activities of $172,000.

**ILLUSTRATION 12.10**

**Adjustments for changes in current liability accounts**

| Cash flows from operating activities | | |
|---|---|---|
| Net income | | $145,000 |
| Adjustments to reconcile net income to net cash provided by operating activities: | | |
| Depreciation expense | $ 9,000 | |
| Loss on disposal of plant assets | 3,000 | |
| Decrease in accounts receivable | 10,000 | |
| Increase in inventory | (5,000) | |
| Increase in prepaid expenses | (4,000) | |
| **Increase in accounts payable** | **16,000** | |
| **Decrease in income taxes payable** | **(2,000)** | 27,000 |
| Net cash provided by operating activities | | $172,000 |

# Summary of Conversion to Net Cash Provided by Operating Activities—Indirect Method

As shown in the previous illustrations, the statement of cash flows prepared by the indirect method starts with net income. It then adds or deducts items to arrive at net cash provided by operating activities. The required adjustments are of three types:

1. Noncash charges such as depreciation and amortization.
2. Gains and losses on the disposal of plant assets.
3. Changes in noncash current asset and current liability accounts.

Illustration 12.11 provides a summary of these changes and required adjustments.

**ILLUSTRATION 12.11**

**Adjustments required to convert net income to net cash provided by operating activities**

| | | Adjustments Required to Convert Net Income to Net Cash Provided by Operating Activities |
|---|---|---|
| **Noncash Charges** | Depreciation expense | Add |
| | Amortization expense | Add |
| **Gains and Losses** | Loss on disposal of plant assets | Add |
| | Gain on disposal of plant assets | Deduct |
| **Changes in Current Assets and Current Liabilities** | Increase in current asset account | Deduct |
| | Decrease in current asset account | Add |
| | Increase in current liability account | Add |
| | Decrease in current liability account | Deduct |

## Anatomy of a Fraud

For more than a decade, the top executives at the Italian dairy products company **Parmalat** engaged in multiple frauds that overstated cash and other assets by more than $1 billion while understating liabilities by between $8 and $12 billion. Much of the fraud involved creating fictitious sources and uses of cash. Some of these activities incorporated sophisticated financial transactions with subsidiaries created with the help of large international financial institutions. However, much of the fraud employed very basic, even sloppy, forgery of documents. For example, when outside auditors requested confirmation of bank accounts (such as a fake $4.8 billion account in the Cayman Islands), documents were created on scanners, with signatures that were cut and pasted from other documents. These were then passed through a fax machine numerous times to make them look real (if difficult to read). Similarly, fictitious bills were created in order to divert funds to other businesses owned by the Tanzi family (who controlled Parmalat).

### Total take: Billions of dollars

#### The Missing Control

**Independent internal verification.** Internal auditors at the company should have independently verified bank accounts and major transfers of cash to outside companies that were controlled by the Tanzi family.

## DO IT! 2a  Cash Flows from Operating Activities

Josh's PhotoPlus reported net income of $73,000 for 2022. Included in the income statement were depreciation expense of $7,000 and a gain on disposal of plant assets of $2,500. Josh's comparative balance sheets show the following balances.

|  | 12/31/21 | 12/31/22 |
|---|---|---|
| Accounts receivable | $17,000 | $21,000 |
| Accounts payable | 6,000 | 2,200 |

Calculate net cash provided by operating activities for Josh's PhotoPlus.

### Solution

| Cash flows from operating activities | | |
|---|---|---|
| Net income | | $73,000 |
| Adjustments to reconcile net income to net cash provided by operating activities: | | |
| Depreciation expense | $ 7,000 | |
| Gain on disposal of plant assets | (2,500) | |
| Increase in accounts receivable | (4,000) | |
| Decrease in accounts payable | (3,800) | (3,300) |
| Net cash provided by operating activities | | $69,700 |

Related exercise material: **BE12.4, BE12.5, BE12.6, DO IT! 12.2a, E12.4, E12.5, E12.6, and E12.7.**

**ACTION PLAN**
- Add noncash charges such as depreciation back to net income to compute net cash provided by operating activities.
- Deduct from net income gains on the disposal of plant assets, or add losses back to net income, to compute net cash provided by operating activities.
- Use changes in noncash current asset and current liability accounts to compute net cash provided by operating activities.

# Step 2: Investing and Financing Activities

## Analyze Changes in Noncurrent Asset and Liability Accounts and Stockholders' Equity Accounts and Report as Investing and Financing Activities, or as Noncash Investing and Financing Activities

**Increase in Land**  As indicated from the change in the Land account and the additional information, Computer Services purchased land for $110,000. This activity is generally classified as an investing activity. However, by directly exchanging bonds for land, the issuance of bonds payable for land has no effect on cash. But, it is a significant noncash investing and financing activity that merits disclosure in a separate schedule (see Illustration 12.14).

**Increase in Buildings**  As the additional data indicate, Computer Services acquired an office building for $120,000 cash. This is a cash outflow reported in the investing activities section (see Illustration 12.14).

**Increase in Equipment**  The Equipment account increased $17,000. The additional information explains that this net increase resulted from two transactions: (1) a purchase of equipment for $25,000, and (2) the sale for $4,000 of equipment costing $8,000. These transactions are investing activities (see **Helpful Hint**). The company should report each transaction separately. Thus, it reports the purchase of equipment as an outflow of cash for $25,000. It reports the sale as an inflow of cash for $4,000. The T-account in **Illustration 12.12** shows the reasons for the change in this account during the year.

**HELPFUL HINT**

The investing and financing activities are measured and reported the same way under both the direct and indirect methods.

**ILLUSTRATION 12.12**

**Analysis of equipment**

| Equipment | | | | |
|---|---|---|---|---|
| 1/1/22 | Balance | 10,000 | Cost of equipment sold | 8,000 |
|  | **Purchase of equipment** | **25,000** | | |
| 12/31/22 | Balance | 27,000 | | |

| A | = | L | + | SE |
|---|---|---|---|---|

+4,000
+1,000
                    −3,000 Exp
−8,000

**Cash Flows**
+4,000

**HELPFUL HINT**

When companies issue stocks or bonds for cash, the actual proceeds will appear in the statement of cash flows as a financing inflow (rather than the par value of the stocks or face value of bonds).

**ILLUSTRATION 12.13**

**Analysis of retained earnings**

**ILLUSTRATION 12.14**

**Statement of cash flows, 2022—indirect method**

**HELPFUL HINT**

Note that in the investing and financing activities sections, positive numbers indicate cash inflows (receipts), and negative numbers indicate cash outflows (payments).

The following entry shows the details of the equipment sale transaction.

| | | |
|---|---|---|
| Cash | 4,000 | |
| Accumulated Depreciation—Equipment | 1,000 | |
| Loss on Disposal of Plant Assets | 3,000 | |
|     Equipment | | 8,000 |

**Increase in Bonds Payable** The Bonds Payable account increased $110,000. As indicated in the additional information, the company acquired land from the issuance of these bonds. It reports this noncash transaction in a separate schedule at the bottom of the statement.

**Increase in Common Stock** The balance sheet reports an increase in Common Stock of $20,000. The additional information section notes that this increase resulted from the issuance of new shares of stock for cash at par. This is a cash inflow reported in the financing activities section (see **Helpful Hint**).

**Increase in Retained Earnings** Retained earnings increased $116,000 during the year. This increase can be explained by two factors: (1) net income of $145,000 increased retained earnings, and (2) dividends declared of $29,000 decreased retained earnings. The company adjusts net income to net cash provided by operating activities in the operating activities section. The T-account shown in **Illustration 12.13** shows the reasons for the change in this account during the year.

| Retained Earnings | | | | |
|---|---|---|---|---|
| Dividends declared | 29,000 | 1/1/22 | Balance | 48,000 |
| | | | Net income | 145,000 |
| | | 12/31/22 | Balance | 164,000 |

Payment of the dividends (not the declaration) is a **cash outflow that the company reports as a financing activity**. Since the balance sheet does not report a Cash Dividends Payable account, the declared cash dividends of $29,000 must have been paid.

## Statement of Cash Flows—2022

Using the previous information, we can now prepare a statement of cash flows for 2022 for Computer Services Company as shown in **Illustration 12.14** (see **Helpful Hint**).

### Computer Services Company
#### Statement of Cash Flows—Indirect Method
#### For the Year Ended December 31, 2022

| | | |
|---|---|---|
| Cash flows from operating activities | | |
|   Net income | | $145,000 |
|   Adjustments to reconcile net income to net cash | | |
|     provided by operating activities: | | |
|     Depreciation expense | $ 9,000 | |
|     Loss on disposal of plant assets | 3,000 | |
|     Decrease in accounts receivable | 10,000 | |
|     Increase in inventory | (5,000) | |
|     Increase in prepaid expenses | (4,000) | |
|     Increase in accounts payable | 16,000 | |
|     Decrease in income taxes payable | (2,000) | 27,000 |
|       Net cash provided by operating activities | | 172,000 |
| Cash flows from investing activities | | |
|   Purchase of building | (120,000) | |
|   Purchase of equipment | (25,000) | |
|   Sale of equipment | 4,000 | |
|     Net cash used by investing activities | | (141,000) |
| Cash flows from financing activities | | |
|   Issuance of common stock | 20,000 | |
|   Payment of cash dividends | (29,000) | |
|     Net cash used by financing activities | | (9,000) |
| Net increase in cash | | 22,000 |
| Cash at beginning of period | | 33,000 |
| Cash at end of period | | $ 55,000 |
| **Noncash investing and financing activities** | | |
|   Issuance of bonds payable to purchase land | | $110,000 |

# Step 3: Net Change in Cash

## Compare the Net Change in Cash on the Statement of Cash Flows with the Change in the Cash Account Reported on the Balance Sheet to Make Sure the Amounts Agree

Illustration 12.14 indicates that the net change in cash during the period was an increase of $22,000. This agrees with the change in Cash account reported on the comparative balance sheets in Illustration 12.4.

## Accounting Across the Organization

iStock.com/Soubrette

### Burning Through Our Cash

**Box** (cloud storage), **FireEye** (cyber-security), and **MobileIron** (mobile security of data) are a few of the tech companies that recently have issued or are about to issue stock to the public. Investors now have to determine whether these tech companies have viable products and high chances for success.

An important consideration in evaluating a tech company is determining its financial flexibility—its ability to withstand adversity if an economic setback occurs. One way to measure financial flexibility is to assess a company's cash burn rate, which determines how long its cash will hold out if the company is expending more cash than it is receiving.

FireEye, for example, used cash in excess of $50 million in 2013. But the company also had over $150 million as a cash cushion, so it would have taken over 30 months for it to run out of cash. And even though Box has a much lower cash burn rate than FireEye, it still has over a year's cushion. Compare that to the tech companies in 2000, when over one-quarter of them were on track to run out of cash within a year. And many did. Fortunately, the tech companies of today seem to be better equipped to withstand an economic setback.

**Source:** Shira Ovide, "Tech Firms' Cash Hoards Cool Fears of a Meltdown," *Wall Street Journal* (May 14, 2014).

**What implications does a company's cash burn rate have for its survival? (Answer is available near the end of the chapter.)**

## DO IT! 2b | Indirect Method

Use the following information to prepare a statement of cash flows using the indirect method.

**Reynolds Company**
**Comparative Balance Sheets**
**December 31**

|  | 2022 | 2021 | Change Increase/Decrease |
|---|---|---|---|
| **Assets** | | | |
| Cash | $ 54,000 | $ 37,000 | $ 17,000 Increase |
| Accounts receivable | 68,000 | 26,000 | 42,000 Increase |
| Inventory | 54,000 | -0- | 54,000 Increase |
| Prepaid expenses | 4,000 | 6,000 | 2,000 Decrease |
| Land | 45,000 | 70,000 | 25,000 Decrease |
| Buildings | 200,000 | 200,000 | -0- |
| Accumulated depreciation—buildings | (21,000) | (11,000) | 10,000 Increase |
| Equipment | 193,000 | 68,000 | 125,000 Increase |
| Accumulated depreciation—equipment | (28,000) | (10,000) | 18,000 Increase |
| Totals | $569,000 | $386,000 | |

**ACTION PLAN**

- Determine net cash provided/used by operating activities by adjusting net income for items that did not affect cash.
- Determine net cash provided/used by investing activities and financing activities.
- Determine the net increase/decrease in cash.

| | 2022 | 2021 | Change Increase/ Decrease |
|---|---|---|---|
| **Liabilities and Stockholders' Equity** | | | |
| Accounts payable | $ 23,000 | $ 40,000 | $ 17,000 Decrease |
| Accrued expenses payable | 10,000 | –0– | 10,000 Increase |
| Bonds payable | 110,000 | 150,000 | 40,000 Decrease |
| Common stock ($1 par) | 220,000 | 60,000 | 160,000 Increase |
| Retained earnings | 206,000 | 136,000 | 70,000 Increase |
| Totals | $569,000 | $386,000 | |

### Reynolds Company
#### Income Statement
#### For the Year Ended December 31, 2022

| | | |
|---|---|---|
| Sales revenue | | $890,000 |
| Cost of goods sold | $465,000 | |
| Operating expenses | 221,000 | |
| Interest expense | 12,000 | |
| Loss on disposal of plant assets | 2,000 | 700,000 |
| Income before income taxes | | 190,000 |
| Income tax expense | | 65,000 |
| Net income | | $125,000 |

**Additional information:**

1. Operating expenses include depreciation expense of $33,000, $10,000 for the building and $23,000 for the equipment.
2. Land was sold at its book value for cash.
3. Cash dividends of $55,000 were declared and paid in 2022.
4. Equipment with a cost of $166,000 was purchased for cash. Equipment with a cost of $41,000 and a book value of $36,000 was sold for $34,000 cash.
5. Bonds of $40,000 were redeemed at their face value for cash.
6. Common stock ($1 par) was issued at par for $160,000 cash.

### Solution

### Reynolds Company
#### Statement of Cash Flows—Indirect Method
#### For the Year Ended December 31, 2022

| | | |
|---|---|---|
| Cash flows from operating activities | | |
| Net income | | $ 125,000 |
| Adjustments to reconcile net income to net cash provided by operating activities: | | |
| Depreciation expense | $ 33,000 | |
| Loss on disposal of plant assets | 2,000 | |
| Increase in accounts receivable | (42,000) | |
| Increase in inventory | (54,000) | |
| Decrease in prepaid expenses | 2,000 | |
| Decrease in accounts payable | (17,000) | |
| Increase in accrued expenses payable | 10,000 | (66,000) |
| Net cash provided by operating activities | | 59,000 |
| Cash flows from investing activities | | |
| Sale of land | 25,000 | |
| Sale of equipment | 34,000 | |
| Purchase of equipment | (166,000) | |
| Net cash used by investing activities | | (107,000) |

| Cash flows from financing activities | | |
|---|---|---|
| Redemption of bonds | (40,000) | |
| Issuance of common stock | 160,000 | |
| Payment of cash dividends | (55,000) | |
| Net cash provided by financing activities | | 65,000 |
| Net increase in cash | | 17,000 |
| Cash at beginning of period | | 37,000 |
| Cash at end of period | | $  54,000 |

Related exercise material: **BE12.4, BE12.5, BE12.6, BE12.7, DO IT! 12.2b, E12.4, E12.5, E12.6, E12.7, E12.8, and E12.9.**

# Analyzing the Statement of Cash Flows

## LEARNING OBJECTIVE 3

Analyze the statement of cash flows.

Traditionally, investors and creditors used ratios based on accrual accounting. These days, cash-based ratios are gaining increased acceptance among analysts.

## Free Cash Flow

In the statement of cash flows, net cash provided by operating activities is intended to indicate the cash-generating capability of a company. Analysts have noted, however, that **net cash provided by operating activities fails to take into account that a company must invest in new fixed assets** just to maintain its current level of operations. Companies also must at least **maintain dividends at current levels** to satisfy investors. The measurement of free cash flow provides additional insight regarding a company's cash-generating ability. **Free cash flow** describes the net cash provided by operating activities after adjustment for capital expenditures and dividends.

Consider the following example. Suppose that MPC produced and sold 10,000 personal computers this year. It reported $100,000 net cash provided by operating activities. In order to maintain production at 10,000 computers, MPC invested $15,000 in equipment. It chose to pay $5,000 in dividends. Its free cash flow was $80,000 ($100,000 − $15,000 − $5,000). The company could use this $80,000 either to purchase new assets to expand the business or to pay an $80,000 dividend and continue to produce 10,000 computers. In practice, free cash flow is often calculated with the formula in **Illustration 12.15**. (Alternative definitions also exist.)

| Free Cash Flow | = | Net Cash Provided by Operating Activities | − | Capital Expenditures | − | Cash Dividends |
|---|---|---|---|---|---|---|

**ILLUSTRATION 12.15**

Free cash flow

**Illustration 12.16** provides basic information excerpted from the 2018 statement of cash flows of **Tootsie Roll Industries**.

**ILLUSTRATION 12.16**

**Tootsie Roll's cash flow information**
**($ in thousands)**

Real World

### Tootsie Roll Industries
#### Statement of Cash Flows (partial)
#### December 31, 2018

| | | |
|---|---|---|
| Net cash provided by operating activities | | $100,929 |
| Cash flows from investing activities | | |
| Capital expenditures | $(27,612) | |
| Purchases of trading securities | (4,378) | |
| Sale of trading securities | 1,255 | |
| Sale and maturity of available for sale securities | 64,602 | |
| Net cash used in investing activities | | $ 44,510 |
| Dividends paid in cash | | $ 22,978 |

Tootsie Roll's free cash flow is computed as shown in **Illustration 12.17**. Tootsie Roll generated approximately $50.3 million of free cash flow. This is a significant amount of cash generated in a single year. It is available for the acquisition of new assets, the buyback and retirement of stock or debt, or the payment of dividends.

**ILLUSTRATION 12.17**

**Calculation of Tootsie Roll's free cash flow**
**($ in thousands)**

| | |
|---|---|
| Net cash provided by operating activities | $100,929 |
| Less: Capital expenditures | 27,612 |
| Dividends paid | 22,978 |
| Free cash flow | $ 50,339 |

Tootsie Roll's cash from operations of $100,929,000 exceeds its 2018 net income of $56,805,000 by $44,124,000. This lends credibility to Tootsie Rolls' income number as an indicator of potential future performance.

---

**ACTION PLAN**

- Compute free cash flow as Net cash provided by operating activities – Capital expenditures – Cash dividends.

## DO IT! 3 | Free Cash Flow

Chicago Corporation issued the following statement of cash flows for 2022.

### Chicago Corporation
#### Statement of Cash Flows—Indirect Method
#### For the Year Ended December 31, 2022

| | | |
|---|---|---|
| Cash flows from operating activities | | |
| Net income | | $ 19,000 |
| Adjustments to reconcile net income to net cash provided by operating activities: | | |
| Depreciation expense | $ 8,100 | |
| Loss on disposal of plant assets | 1,300 | |
| Decrease in accounts receivable | 6,900 | |
| Increase in inventory | (4,000) | |
| Decrease in accounts payable | (2,000) | 10,300 |
| Net cash provided by operating activities | | 29,300 |
| Cash flows from investing activities | | |
| Sale of investments | 1,100 | |
| Purchase of equipment | (19,000) | |
| Net cash used by investing activities | | (17,900) |

| Cash flows from financing activities | | | |
|---|---|---|---|
| Issuance of common stock | 10,000 | | |
| Payment on long-term note payable | (5,000) | | |
| Payment of cash dividends | (9,000) | | |
| Net cash used by financing activities | | (4,000) | |
| Net increase in cash | | 7,400 | |
| Cash at beginning of year | | 10,000 | |
| Cash at end of year | | $ 17,400 | |

(a) Compute free cash flow for Chicago Corporation. (b) Explain why free cash flow often provides better information than "Net cash provided by operating activities."

**Solution**

a. Free cash flow = $29,300 – $19,000 – $9,000 = $1,300

b. Net cash provided by operating activities fails to take into account that a company must invest in new plant assets just to maintain the current level of operations. Companies must also maintain dividends at current levels to satisfy investors. The measurement of free cash flow provides additional insight regarding a company's cash-generating ability.

Related exercise material: **BE12.8, BE12.9, BE12.10, BE12.11, DO IT! 12.3, E12.8**, and **E12.10**.

---

| **Appendix 12A** | # Statement of Cash Flows—Direct Method |
|---|---|

**LEARNING OBJECTIVE \*4**

Prepare a statement of cash flows using the direct method.

To explain and illustrate the direct method for preparing a statement of cash flows, we use the transactions of Computer Services Company for 2022. **Illustration 12A.1** presents information related to 2022 for the company.

To prepare a statement of cash flows under the direct method, we apply the three steps outlined in Illustration 12.3 for the indirect method.

# Step 1: Operating Activities

## Determine Net Cash Provided/Used by Operating Activities by Converting Net Income Components from an Accrual Basis to a Cash Basis

Under the **direct method**, companies compute net cash provided by operating activities by **adjusting each item in the income statement** from the accrual basis to the cash basis. To simplify and condense the operating activities section, companies **report only major classes of operating cash receipts and cash payments**. For these major classes, the difference between cash receipts and cash payments is the net cash provided by operating activities. These relationships are as shown in **Illustration 12A.2**.

An efficient way to apply the direct method is to analyze the items reported in the income statement in the order in which they are listed. We then determine cash

**ILLUSTRATION 12A.1**

Comparative balance sheets, income statement, and additional information for Computer Services Company

## Computer Services Company
### Comparative Balance Sheets
### December 31

| | 2022 | 2021 | Change in Account Balance Increase/Decrease |
|---|---|---|---|
| **Assets** | | | |
| Current assets | | | |
| Cash | $ 55,000 | $ 33,000 | $ 22,000 Increase |
| Accounts receivable | 20,000 | 30,000 | 10,000 Decrease |
| Inventory | 15,000 | 10,000 | 5,000 Increase |
| Prepaid expenses | 5,000 | 1,000 | 4,000 Increase |
| Property, plant, and equipment | | | |
| Land | 130,000 | 20,000 | 110,000 Increase |
| Buildings | 160,000 | 40,000 | 120,000 Increase |
| Accumulated depreciation—buildings | (11,000) | (5,000) | 6,000 Increase |
| Equipment | 27,000 | 10,000 | 17,000 Increase |
| Accumulated depreciation—equipment | (3,000) | (1,000) | 2,000 Increase |
| Total assets | $398,000 | $138,000 | |
| | | | |
| **Liabilities and Stockholders' Equity** | | | |
| Current liabilities | | | |
| Accounts payable | $ 28,000 | $ 12,000 | $ 16,000 Increase |
| Income taxes payable | 6,000 | 8,000 | 2,000 Decrease |
| Long-term liabilities | | | |
| Bonds payable | 130,000 | 20,000 | 110,000 Increase |
| Stockholders' equity | | | |
| Common stock | 70,000 | 50,000 | 20,000 Increase |
| Retained earnings | 164,000 | 48,000 | 116,000 Increase |
| Total liabilities and stockholders' equity | $398,000 | $138,000 | |

## Computer Services Company
### Income Statement
### For the Year Ended December 31, 2022

| | | |
|---|---|---|
| Sales revenue | | $507,000 |
| Cost of goods sold | $150,000 | |
| Operating expenses (excluding depreciation) | 111,000 | |
| Depreciation expense | 9,000 | |
| Loss on disposal of plant assets | 3,000 | |
| Interest expense | 42,000 | 315,000 |
| Income before income tax | | 192,000 |
| Income tax expense | | 47,000 |
| Net income | | $145,000 |

**Additional information for 2022:**

1. Depreciation expense was comprised of $6,000 for building and $3,000 for equipment.

2. The company sold equipment with a book value of $7,000 (cost $8,000, less accumulated depreciation $1,000) for $4,000 cash.

3. Issued $110,000 of long-term bonds in direct exchange for land.

4. A building costing $120,000 was purchased for cash. Equipment costing $25,000 was also purchased for cash.

5. Issued common stock at par for $20,000 cash.

6. The company declared and paid a $29,000 cash dividend.

**ILLUSTRATION 12A.2** | **Major classes of cash receipts and payments**

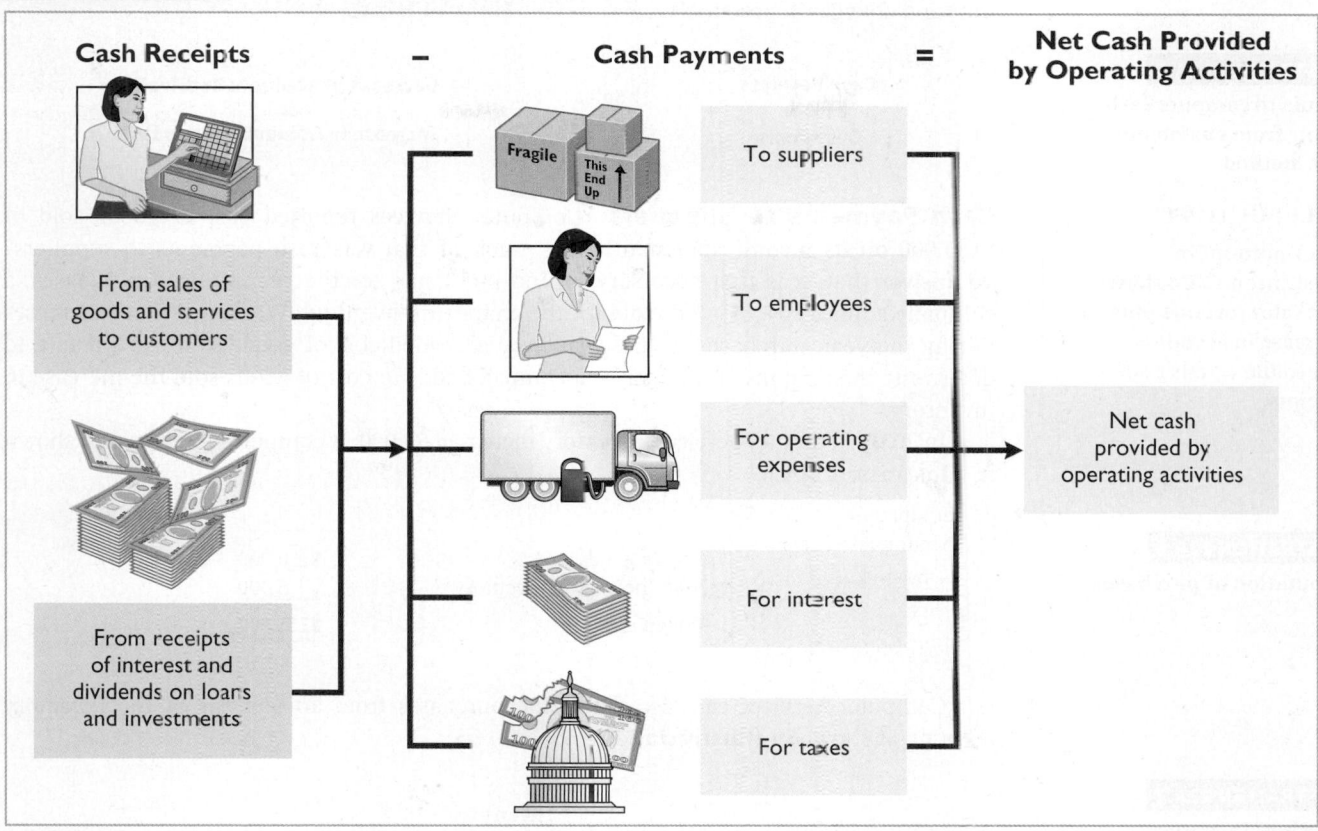

receipts and cash payments related to these revenues and expenses. The following presents the adjustments required to prepare a statement of cash flows for Computer Services Company using the direct method.

**Cash Receipts from Customers**   The income statement for Computer Services reported sales revenue from customers of $507,000. How much of that was cash receipts? To answer that, a company considers the change in accounts receivable during the year. When accounts receivable increase during the year, revenues on an accrual basis are higher than cash receipts from customers. Operations led to revenues, but not all of those revenues resulted in cash receipts.

To determine the amount of cash receipts, a company deducts from sales revenue the increase in accounts receivable. On the other hand, there may be a decrease in accounts receivable. That would occur if cash receipts from customers exceeded sales revenue. In that case, a company adds to sales revenue the decrease in accounts receivable. For Computer Services, accounts receivable decreased $10,000. Thus, cash receipts from customers were $517,000, computed as shown in **Illustration 12A.3**.

| | |
|---|---|
| Sales revenue | $507,000 |
| Add: Decrease in accounts receivable | 10,000 |
| **Cash receipts from customers** | **$517,000** |

**ILLUSTRATION 12A.3**

**Computation of cash receipts from customers**

Computer Services can also determine cash receipts from customers from an analysis of the Accounts Receivable account, as shown in **Illustration 12A.4**.

| | Accounts Receivable | | | |
|---|---|---|---|---|
| 1/1/22 | Balance | 30,000 | Receipts from customers | 517,000 |
| | Sales revenue | 507,000 | | |
| 12/31/22 | Balance | 20,000 | | |

**ILLUSTRATION 12A.4**

**Analysis of accounts receivable**

**Illustration 12A.5** shows the relationships among cash receipts from customers, sales revenue, and changes in accounts receivable (see **Helpful Hint**).

ILLUSTRATION 12A.5

**Formula to compute cash receipts from customers— direct method**

| Cash Receipts from Customers | = | Sales Revenue | + Decrease in Accounts Receivable or − Increase in Accounts Receivable |
|---|---|---|---|

**HELPFUL HINT**

The T-account in Illustration 12A.4 shows that sales revenue plus decrease in accounts receivable equals cash receipts.

**Cash Payments to Suppliers**   Computer Services reported cost of goods sold of $150,000 on its income statement. How much of that was cash payments to suppliers? To answer that, it is first necessary to find purchases for the year. To find purchases, a company adjusts cost of goods sold for the change in inventory. When inventory increases during the year, purchases for the year have exceeded cost of goods sold. As a result, to determine the amount of purchases, a company adds to cost of goods sold the increase in inventory.

In 2022, Computer Services' inventory increased $5,000. It computes purchases as shown in **Illustration 12A.6**.

ILLUSTRATION 12A.6

**Computation of purchases**

| | |
|---|---|
| Cost of goods sold | $150,000 |
| Add: Increase in inventory | 5,000 |
| **Purchases** | **$155,000** |

Computer Services can also determine purchases from an analysis of the Inventory account, as shown in **Illustration 12A.7**.

ILLUSTRATION 12A.7

**Analysis of inventory**

| | Inventory | | | | |
|---|---|---|---|---|---|
| 1/1/22 | Balance | 10,000 | Cost of goods sold | | 150,000 |
| | **Purchases** | **155,000** | | | |
| 12/31/22 | Balance | 15,000 | | | |

After computing purchases, a company can determine cash payments to suppliers. This is done by adjusting purchases for the change in accounts payable. When accounts payable increase during the year, purchases on an accrual basis are higher than they are on a cash basis. As a result, to determine cash payments to suppliers, a company deducts from purchases the increase in accounts payable. On the other hand, if cash payments to suppliers exceed purchases, there will be a decrease in accounts payable. In that case, a company adds to purchases the decrease in accounts payable. For Computer Services, cash payments to suppliers were $139,000, computed as shown in **Illustration 12A.8**.

ILLUSTRATION 12A.8

**Computation of cash payments to suppliers**

| | |
|---|---|
| Purchases | $155,000 |
| Deduct: Increase in accounts payable | 16,000 |
| **Cash payments to suppliers** | **$139,000** |

Computer Services also can determine cash payments to suppliers from an analysis of the Accounts Payable account, as shown in **Illustration 12A.9**.

ILLUSTRATION 12A.9

**Analysis of accounts payable**

| | Accounts Payable | | | | |
|---|---|---|---|---|---|
| **Payments to suppliers** | **139,000** | 1/1/22 | Balance | | 12,000 |
| | | | Purchases | | 155,000 |
| | | 12/31/22 | Balance | | 28,000 |

**HELPFUL HINT**

The T-account shows that purchases less increase in accounts payable equals payments to suppliers.

**Illustration 12A.10** shows the relationships among cash payments to suppliers, cost of goods sold, changes in inventory, and changes in accounts payable (see **Helpful Hint**).

| Cash Payments to Suppliers | = | Cost of Goods Sold | + Increase in Inventory or − Decrease in Inventory | + Decrease in Accounts Payable or − Increase in Accounts Payable |
|---|---|---|---|---|

ILLUSTRATION 12A.10

Formula to compute cash payments to suppliers—direct method

### Cash Payments for Operating Expenses

Computer Services reported on its income statement operating expenses of $111,000. How much of that amount was cash paid for operating expenses? To answer that, we need to adjust this amount for any changes in prepaid expenses and accrued expenses payable. For example, if prepaid expenses increased during the year, cash paid for operating expenses is higher than operating expenses reported on the income statement. To convert operating expenses to cash payments for operating expenses, a company adds the increase in prepaid expenses to operating expenses. On the other hand, if prepaid expenses decrease during the year, it deducts the decrease from operating expenses.

Companies must also adjust operating expenses for changes in accrued expenses payable. When accrued expenses payable increase during the year, operating expenses on an accrual basis are higher than they are on a cash basis. As a result, to determine cash payments for operating expenses, a company deducts from operating expenses an increase in accrued expenses payable. On the other hand, a company adds to operating expenses a decrease in accrued expenses payable because cash payments exceed operating expenses.

Computer Services' cash payments for operating expenses were $115,000, computed as shown in **Illustration 12A.11**.

| | |
|---|---|
| Operating expenses | $111,000 |
| Add: Increase in prepaid expenses | 4,000 |
| **Cash payments for operating expenses** | **$115,000** |

ILLUSTRATION 12A.11

Computation of cash payments for operating expenses

**Illustration 12A.12** shows the relationships among cash payments for operating expenses, changes in prepaid expenses, and changes in accrued expenses payable.

| Cash Payments for Operating Expenses | = | Operating Expenses | + Increase in Prepaid Expenses or − Decrease in Prepaid Expenses | + Decrease in Accrued Expenses Payable or − Increase in Accrued Expenses Payable |
|---|---|---|---|---|

ILLUSTRATION 12A.12

Formula to compute cash payments for operating expenses—direct method

### Depreciation Expense and Loss on Disposal of Plant Assets

Computer Services' depreciation expense in 2022 was $9,000. Depreciation expense is not shown on a statement of cash flows under the direct method because it is a noncash charge. If the amount for operating expenses includes depreciation expense, operating expenses must be reduced by the amount of depreciation to determine cash payments for operating expenses.

The loss on disposal of plant assets of $3,000 is also a noncash charge. The loss on disposal of plant assets reduces net income, but it does not reduce cash. Thus, the loss on disposal of plant assets is not shown on the statement of cash flows under the direct method.

Other charges to expense that do not require the use of cash, such as the amortization of intangible assets and bad debt expense, are treated in the same manner as depreciation.

### Cash Payments for Interest

Computer Services reported on the income statement interest expense of $42,000. Since the balance sheet did not report interest payable for 2021 or 2022, the amount reported as interest expense is the same as the amount of interest paid.

### Cash Payments for Income Taxes

Computer Services reported income tax expense of $47,000 on the income statement. Income taxes payable, however, decreased $2,000. This decrease means that income taxes paid were more than income tax expense reported in the income statement. Cash payments for income taxes were therefore $49,000 as shown in **Illustration 12A.13**.

**ILLUSTRATION 12A.13**

Computation of cash payments for income taxes

| | |
|---|---|
| Income tax expense | $47,000 |
| Add: Decrease in income taxes payable | 2,000 |
| **Cash payments for income taxes** | **$49,000** |

Computer Services can also determine cash payments for income taxes from an analysis of the Income Taxes Payable account, as shown in **Illustration 12A.14**.

**ILLUSTRATION 12A.14**

Analysis of income taxes payable

**Income Taxes Payable**

| | | | | |
|---|---|---|---|---|
| **Cash payments for income taxes** | **49,000** | 1/1/22 | Balance | 8,000 |
| | | | Income tax expense | 47,000 |
| | | 12/31/22 | Balance | 6,000 |

**Illustration 12A.15** shows the relationships among cash payments for income taxes, income tax expense, and changes in income taxes payable.

**ILLUSTRATION 12A.15**

Formula to compute cash payments for income taxes— direct method

| Cash Payments for Income Taxes | = | Income Tax Expense | { | + Decrease in Income Taxes Payable<br>or<br>− Increase in Income Taxes Payable |
|---|---|---|---|---|

The operating activities section of the statement of cash flows of Computer Services is shown in **Illustration 12A.16**.

**ILLUSTRATION 12A.16**

Operating activities section of the statement of cash flows

| | | |
|---|---|---|
| Cash flows from operating activities | | |
| Cash receipts from customers | | $517,000 |
| Less: Cash payments: | | |
| To suppliers | $139,000 | |
| For operating expenses | 115,000 | |
| For interest expense | 42,000 | |
| For income taxes | 49,000 | 345,000 |
| Net cash provided by operating activities | | $172,000 |

When a company uses the direct method, it must also provide in a **separate schedule** (not shown here) the net cash flows from operating activities as computed under the indirect method. Note that whether a company uses the indirect or direct method, the net cash provided by operating activities is the same for both methods.

# Step 2: Investing and Financing Activities

## Analyze Changes in Noncurrent Asset and Liability Accounts and Stockholders' Equity Accounts and Record as Investing and Financing Activities, or Disclose as Noncash Transactions

**Increase in Land**   As indicated from the change in the Land account and the additional information, Computer Services purchased land for $110,000 by directly exchanging bonds for the land. The exchange of bonds payable for land has no effect on cash. But, it is a significant noncash investing and financing activity that merits disclosure in a separate schedule (see Illustration 12A.18).

**Increase in Buildings**  As the additional data indicate, Computer Services acquired an office building for $120,000 cash. This is a cash outflow reported in the investing activities section (see Illustration 12A.18).

**Increase in Equipment**  The Equipment account increased $17,000. The additional information explains that this was a net increase that resulted from two transactions: (1) a purchase of equipment of $25,000, and (2) the sale for $4,000 of equipment costing $8,000. These transactions are investing activities (see **Helpful Hint**). The company should report each transaction separately. The statement in Illustration 12A.18 reports the purchase of equipment as an outflow of cash for $25,000. It reports the sale as an inflow of cash for $4,000. The T-account in **Illustration 12A.17** shows the reasons for the change in this account during the year.

**HELPFUL HINT**

The investing and financing activities are measured and reported the same under both the direct and indirect methods.

**ILLUSTRATION 12A.17**
**Analysis of equipment**

| Equipment | | | |
|---|---|---|---|
| 1/1/22 | Balance | 10,000 | Cost of equipment sold  8,000 |
| | **Purchase of equipment** | **25,000** | |
| 12/31/22 | Balance | 27,000 | |

The following entry shows the details of the equipment sale transaction.

| | | |
|---|---|---|
| Cash | 4,000 | |
| Accumulated Depreciation—Equipment | 1,000 | |
| Loss on Disposal of Plant Assets | 3,000 | |
|    Equipment | | 8,000 |

A = L + SE

+4,000
+1,000
                  −3,000 Exp
−8,000

**Cash Flows**
+4,000

**Increase in Bonds Payable**  The Bonds Payable account increased $110,000. As indicated in the additional information, the company acquired land by directly exchanging bonds for land. Illustration 12A.18 reports this noncash transaction in a separate schedule at the bottom of the statement.

**Increase in Common Stock**  The balance sheet reports an increase in Common Stock of $20,000. The additional information section notes that this increase resulted from the issuance of new shares of stock. This is a cash inflow reported in the financing activities section in Illustration 12A.18 (see **Helpful Hint**).

**Increase in Retained Earnings**  Retained earnings increased $116,000 during the year. This increase can be explained by two factors  (1) net income of $145,000 increased retained earnings, and (2) dividends of $29,000 decreased retained earnings. **Payment** of the dividends (not the declaration) is a **cash outflow that the company reports as a financing activity in Illustration 12A.18**.

**HELPFUL HINT**

When companies issue stocks or bonds for cash, the actual proceeds will appear in the statement of cash flows as a financing inflow (rather than the par value of the stocks or face value of bonds).

## Statement of Cash Flows—2022

**Illustration 12A.18** shows the statement of cash flows for Computer Services Company.

Statement of cash flows,
2022—direct method

### Computer Services Company
#### Statement of Cash Flows—Direct Method
#### For the Year Ended December 31, 2022

| | | |
|---|---:|---:|
| Cash flows from operating activities | | |
|   Cash receipts from customers | | $ 517,000 |
|   Less: Cash payments: | | |
|     To suppliers | $ 139,000 | |
|     For operating expenses | 115,000 | |
|     For income taxes | 49,000 | |
|     For interest expense | 42,000 | 345,000 |
|       Net cash provided by operating activities | | 172,000 |
| Cash flows from investing activities | | |
|   Sale of equipment | 4,000 | |
|   Purchase of building | (120,000) | |
|   Purchase of equipment | (25,000) | |
|       Net cash used by investing activities | | (141,000) |
| Cash flows from financing activities | | |
|   Issuance of common stock | 20,000 | |
|   Payment of cash dividends | (29,000) | |
|       Net cash used by financing activities | | (9,000) |
| Net increase in cash | | 22,000 |
| Cash at beginning of period | | 33,000 |
| Cash at end of period | | $ 55,000 |
| **Noncash investing and financing activities** | | |
|   Issuance of bonds payable to purchase land | | $ 110,000 |

## Step 3: Net Change in Cash

### Compare the Net Change in Cash on the Statement of Cash Flows with the Change in the Cash Account Reported on the Balance Sheet to Make Sure the Amounts Agree

Illustration 12A.18 indicates that the net change in cash during the period was an increase of $22,000. This agrees with the change in balances in the Cash account reported on the balance sheets in Illustration 12A.1.

---

| Appendix 12B |
|---|

# Worksheet for the Indirect Method

**LEARNING OBJECTIVE *5**

Use a worksheet to prepare the statement of cash flows using the indirect method.

When preparing a statement of cash flows, companies may need to make numerous adjustments to net income. In such cases, they often use **a worksheet to assemble and classify the data that will appear on the statement**. The worksheet is merely an aid in preparing the statement. Its use is optional. **Illustration 12B.1** shows the skeleton format of the worksheet for preparation of the statement of cash flows.

The following guidelines are important in preparing a worksheet.

1. In the balance sheet accounts section, **list accounts with debit balances separately from those with credit balances**. This means, for example, that Accumulated Depreciation appears under credit balances and not as a contra account under debit

ILLUSTRATION 12B.1

**Format of worksheet**

| | XYZ Company | | | |
|---|---|---|---|---|
| Home   Insert   Page Layout   Formulas   Data   Review   View | | | | |
| P18 | fx | | | |
| | A | B | C | D | E |

| | A | B | C | D | E |
|---|---|---|---|---|---|
| 1 | | **XYZ Company** | | | |
| 2 | | **Worksheet** | | | |
| 3 | | **Statement of Cash Flows for the Year Ended . . .** | | | |
| 4 | | | | | |
| 5 | | | | | |
| 6 | | End of | | | End of |
| 7 | | Last Year | Reconciling Items | | Current Year |
| 8 | Balance Sheet Accounts | Balances | Debit | Credit | Balances |
| 9 | Debit balance accounts | XX | XX | XX | XX |
| 10 | | XX | XX | XX | XX |
| 11 | Totals | XXX | | | XXX |
| 12 | Credit balance accounts | XX | XX | XX | XX |
| 13 | | XX | XX | XX | XX |
| 14 | Totals | XXX | | | XXX |
| 15 | | | | | |
| 16 | Statement of Cash | | | | |
| 17 | Flows Effects | | | | |
| 18 | Operating activities | | | | |
| 19 | Net income | | XX | | |
| 20 | Adjustments to net income | | XX | XX | |
| 21 | Investing activities | | | | |
| 22 | Receipts and payments | | XX | XX | |
| 23 | Financing activities | | | | |
| 24 | Receipts and payments | | XX | XX | |
| 25 | Totals | | XXX | XXX | |
| 26 | Increase (decrease) in cash | | (XX) | XX | |
| 27 | Totals | | XXX | XXX | |
| 28 | | | | | |

balances. Enter the beginning and ending balances of each account in the appropriate columns. Enter as reconciling items in the two middle columns the transactions that caused the change in the account balance during the year.

After all reconciling items have been entered, each line pertaining to a balance sheet account should "foot across." That is, the beginning balance plus or minus the reconciling item(s) must equal the ending balance. When this agreement exists for all balance sheet accounts, all changes in account balances have been reconciled.

2. The bottom portion of the worksheet consists of the operating, investing, and financing activities sections. It provides the information necessary to prepare the formal statement of cash flows. **Enter inflows of cash as debits in the reconciling columns. Enter outflows of cash as credits in the reconciling columns.** Thus, in this section, the sale of equipment for cash at book value appears as a debit under investing activities. Similarly, the purchase of land for cash appears as a credit under investing activities.

3. **The reconciling items shown in the worksheet are not entered in any journal or posted to any account.** They do not represent either adjustments or corrections of the balance sheet accounts. They are used only to facilitate the preparation of the statement of cash flows.

# Preparing the Worksheet

Preparing a worksheet involves a series of prescribed steps. The steps in this case are:

1. Enter in the balance sheet accounts section the balance sheet accounts and their beginning and ending balances.

2. Enter in the reconciling columns of the worksheet the data that explain the changes in the balance sheet accounts other than cash and their effects on the statement of cash flows.

3. Enter on the cash line and at the bottom of the worksheet the increase or decrease in cash. This entry should enable the totals of the reconciling columns to be in agreement.

To illustrate the preparation of a worksheet, we will use the 2022 data for Computer Services Company. Your familiarity with these data (from the chapter) should help you understand the use of a worksheet. For ease of reference, the comparative balance sheets, income statement, and selected data for 2022 are presented in **Illustration 12B.2**.

**ILLUSTRATION 12B.2**

Comparative balance sheets, income statement, and additional information for Computer Services Company

| Computer Services Company | | | |
|---|---|---|---|
| Home   Insert   Page Layout   Formulas   Data   Review   View | | | |
| P18   _fx_ | | | |
| A | B | C | D |

**Computer Services Company**
**Comparative Balance Sheets**
**December 31**

| | 2022 | 2021 | Change in Account Balance Increase/Decrease |
|---|---|---|---|
| **Assets** | | | |
| Current assets | | | |
| Cash | $ 55,000 | $ 33,000 | $ 22,000 Increase |
| Accounts receivable | 20,000 | 30,000 | 10,000 Decrease |
| Inventory | 15,000 | 10,000 | 5,000 Increase |
| Prepaid expenses | 5,000 | 1,000 | 4,000 Increase |
| Property, plant, and equipment | | | |
| Land | 130,000 | 20,000 | 110,000 Increase |
| Buildings | 160,000 | 40,000 | 120,000 Increase |
| Accumulated depreciation—buildings | (11,000) | (5,000) | 6,000 Increase |
| Equipment | 27,000 | 10,000 | 17,000 Increase |
| Accumulated depreciation—equipment | (3,000) | (1,000) | 2,000 Increase |
| Total assets | $398,000 | $138,000 | |
| | | | |
| **Liabilities and Stockholders' Equity** | | | |
| Current liabilities | | | |
| Accounts payable | $ 28,000 | $ 12,000 | $ 16,000 Increase |
| Income taxes payable | 6,000 | 8,000 | 2,000 Decrease |
| Long-term liabilities | | | |
| Bonds payable | 130,000 | 20,000 | 110,000 Increase |
| Stockholders' equity | | | |
| Common stock | 70,000 | 50,000 | 20,000 Increase |
| Retained earnings | 164,000 | 48,000 | 116,000 Increase |
| Total liabilities and stockholders' equity | $398,000 | $138,000 | |

| Computer Services Company | | | |
|---|---|---|---|
| Home   Insert   Page Layout   Formulas   Data   Review   View | | | |
| P18   _fx_ | | | |
| A | B | C | D |

**Computer Services Company**
**Income Statement**
**For the Year Ended December 31, 2022**

| | | | |
|---|---|---|---|
| Sales revenue | | | $507,000 |
| Cost of goods sold | | $150,000 | |
| Operating expenses (excluding depreciation) | | 111,000 | |
| Depreciation expense | | 9,000 | |
| Loss on disposal of plant assets | | 3,000 | |
| Interest expense | | 42,000 | 315,000 |
| Income before income taxes | | | 192,000 |
| Income tax expense | | | 47,000 |
| Net income | | | $145,000 |

**Additional information for 2022:**

1. Depreciation expense was comprised of $6,000 for building and $3,000 for equipment.

2. The company sold equipment with a book value of $7,000 (cost $8,000, less accumulated depreciation $1,000) for $4,000 cash.

3. Issued $110,000 of long-term bonds in direct exchange for land.

4. A building costing $120,000 was purchased for cash. Equipment costing $25,000 was also purchased for cash.

5. Issued common stock at par for $20,000 cash.

6. The company declared and paid a $29,000 cash dividend.

## Determining the Reconciling Items

Companies can use one of several approaches to determine the reconciling items. For example, they can first complete the changes affecting net cash provided by operating activities, and then can determine the effects of financing and investing transactions. Or they can analyze the balance sheet accounts in the order in which they are listed on the worksheet. We will follow this latter approach for Computer Services, except for cash. As indicated in Step 3, **cash is handled last**.

**Accounts Receivable** The decrease of $10,000 in accounts receivable means that cash collections from sales revenue are higher than the sales revenue reported in the income statement. To convert net income to net cash provided by operating activities, we add the decrease of $10,000 to net income. The entry in the reconciling columns of the worksheet is:

| | | | |
|---|---|---|---|
| **a.** | Operating—Decrease in Accounts Receivable | 10,000 | |
| | Accounts Receivable | | 10,000 |

**Inventory** Computer Services' inventory balance increases $5,000 during the period. The Inventory account reflects the difference between the amount of inventory that the company purchased and the amount that it sold. For Computer Services, this means that the cost of merchandise purchased exceeds the cost of goods sold by $5,000. As a result, cost of goods sold does not reflect $5,000 of cash payments made for merchandise. We deduct this inventory increase of $5,000 during the period from net income to arrive at net cash provided by operating activities. The worksheet entry is:

| | | | |
|---|---|---|---|
| **b.** | Inventory | 5,000 | |
| | Operating—Increase in Inventory | | 5,000 |

**Prepaid Expenses** An increase of $4,000 in prepaid expenses means that expenses deducted in determining net income are less than expenses that were paid in cash. We deduct the increase of $4,000 from net income in determining net cash provided by operating activities. The worksheet entry is:

| | | | |
|---|---|---|---|
| **c.** | Prepaid Expenses | 4,000 | |
| | Operating—Increase in Prepaid Expenses | | 4,000 |

**Land** The increase in land of $110,000 resulted from a purchase through the issuance of long-term bonds. The company should report this transaction as a significant noncash investing and financing activity (see **Helpful Hint**). The worksheet entry is:

| | | | |
|---|---|---|---|
| **d.** | Land | 110,000 | |
| | Bonds Payable | | 110,000 |

**HELPFUL HINT**

These amounts are asterisked in the worksheet to indicate that they result from a significant noncash transaction.

**Buildings** The cash purchase of a building for $120,000 is an investing activity cash outflow. The entry in the reconciling columns of the worksheet is:

| | | | |
|---|---|---|---|
| **e.** | Buildings | 120,000 | |
| | Investing—Purchase of Building | | 120,000 |

**Equipment** The increase in equipment of $17,000 resulted from a cash purchase of $25,000 and the disposal of plant assets (equipment) costing $8,000. The book value of the equipment was $7,000, the cash proceeds were $4,000, and a loss of $3,000 was recorded. The worksheet entries are:

| | | | |
|---|---|---|---|
| **f.** | Equipment | 25,000 | |
| | Investing—Purchase of Equipment | | 25,000 |

| | | | |
|---|---|---|---|
| **g.** | Investing—Sale of Equipment | 4,000 | |
| | Operating—Loss on Disposal of Plant Assets | 3,000 | |
| | Accumulated Depreciation—Equipment | 1,000 | |
| | Equipment | | 8,000 |

**Accounts Payable**   We must add the increase of $16,000 in accounts payable to net income to determine net cash provided by operating activities. The worksheet entry is:

| | | | |
|---|---|---|---|
| **h.** | Operating—Increase in Accounts Payable | 16,000 | |
| | Accounts Payable | | 16,000 |

**Income Taxes Payable**   When a company incurs income tax expense but has not yet paid its taxes, it records income taxes payable. A change in the Income Taxes Payable account reflects the difference between income tax expense incurred and income taxes actually paid. Computer Services' Income Taxes Payable account decreases by $2,000. That means the $47,000 of income tax expense reported on the income statement was $2,000 less than the amount of taxes paid during the period of $49,000. To adjust net income to a cash basis, we must reduce net income by $2,000. The worksheet entry is:

| | | | |
|---|---|---|---|
| **i.** | Income Taxes Payable | 2,000 | |
| | Operating—Decrease in Income Taxes | | |
| | Payable | | 2,000 |

**Bonds Payable**   The increase of $110,000 in this account resulted from the issuance of bonds for land. This is a significant noncash investing and financing activity. Worksheet entry (d) above is the only entry necessary.

**Common Stock**   The balance sheet reports an increase in Common Stock of $20,000. The additional information section notes that this increase resulted from the issuance of new shares of common stock at par for cash. This is a cash inflow reported in the financing section. The worksheet entry is:

| | | | |
|---|---|---|---|
| **j.** | Financing—Issuance of Common Stock | 20,000 | |
| | Common Stock | | 20,000 |

**Accumulated Depreciation—Buildings, and Accumulated Depreciation— Equipment**   Increases in these accounts of $6,000 and $3,000, respectively, resulted from depreciation expense. Depreciation expense is a **noncash charge that we must add to net income** to determine net cash provided by operating activities. The worksheet entries are:

| | | | |
|---|---|---|---|
| **k.** | Operating—Depreciation Expense | 6,000 | |
| | Accumulated Depreciation—Buildings | | 6,000 |
| **l.** | Operating—Depreciation Expense | 3,000 | |
| | Accumulated Depreciation—Equipment | | 3,000 |

**Retained Earnings**   The $116,000 increase in retained earnings resulted from net income of $145,000 and the declaration and payment of a $29,000 cash dividend. Net income is included in net cash provided by operating activities, and the dividends are a financing activity cash outflow. The entries in the reconciling columns of the worksheet are:

| | | | |
|---|---|---|---|
| **m.** | Operating—Net Income | 145,000 | |
| | Retained Earnings | | 145,000 |
| **n.** | Retained Earnings | 29,000 | |
| | Financing—Payment of Dividends | | 29,000 |

**Disposition of Change in Cash**   The firm's cash increased $22,000 in 2022. The final entry on the worksheet, therefore, is:

| | | | |
|---|---|---|---|
| **o.** | Cash | 22,000 | |
| | Increase in Cash | | 22,000 |

As shown in the worksheet, we enter the increase in cash in the reconciling credit column as a **balancing** amount. This entry should complete the reconciliation of the changes in the balance sheet accounts. Also, it should permit the totals of the reconciling columns to be in agreement. When all changes have been explained and the reconciling columns are in agreement, the reconciling columns are ruled to complete the worksheet. The completed worksheet for Computer Services Company is shown in **Illustration 12B.3**.

**ILLUSTRATION 12B.3**

Completed worksheet—
indirect method

| | | Computer Services Company | | |
|---|---|---|---|---|
| Home | Insert | Page Layout | Formulas | Data | Review | View |

P18    *fx*

| | A | B | C | D | E |
|---|---|---|---|---|---|
| 1 | | **Computer Services Company** | | | |
| 2 | | **Worksheet** | | | |
| 3 | | **Statement of Cash Flows for the Year Ended December 31, 2022** | | | |
| 4 | | | | | |
| 5 | | Balance | Reconciling Items | | Balance |
| 6 | Balance Sheet Accounts | 12/31/21 | Debit | Credit | 12/31/22 |
| 7 | Debits | | | | |
| 8 | Cash | 33,000 | (o) 22,000 | | 55,000 |
| 9 | Accounts Receivable | 30,000 | | (a) 10,000 | 20,000 |
| 10 | Inventory | 10,000 | (b) 5,000 | | 15,000 |
| 11 | Prepaid Expenses | 1,000 | (c) 4,000 | | 5,000 |
| 12 | Land | 20,000 | (d)110,000* | | 130,000 |
| 13 | Buildings | 40,000 | (e)120,000 | | 160,000 |
| 14 | Equipment | 10,000 | (f) 25,000 | (g) 3,000 | 27,000 |
| 15 | Total | 144,000 | | | 412,000 |
| 16 | Credits | | | | |
| 17 | Accounts Payable | 12,000 | | (h) 16,000 | 28,000 |
| 18 | Income Taxes Payable | 8,000 | (i) 2,000 | | 6,000 |
| 19 | Bonds Payable | 20,000 | | (d)110,000* | 130,000 |
| 20 | Accumulated Depreciation—Buildings | 5,000 | | (k) 6,000 | 11,000 |
| 21 | Accumulated Depreciation—Equipment | 1,000 | (g) 1,000 | (l) 3,000 | 3,000 |
| 22 | Common Stock | 50,000 | | (j) 20,000 | 70,000 |
| 23 | Retained Earnings | 48,000 | (n) 29,000 | (m)145,000 | 164,000 |
| 24 | Total | 144,000 | | | 412,000 |
| 25 | | | | | |
| 26 | Statement of Cash Flows Effects | | | | |
| 27 | Operating activities | | | | |
| 28 | Net income | | (m)145,000 | | |
| 29 | Decrease in accounts receivable | | (a) 10,000 | | |
| 30 | Increase in inventory | | | (b) 5,000 | |
| 31 | Increase in prepaid expenses | | | (c) 4,000 | |
| 32 | Increase in accounts payable | | (h) 16,000 | | |
| 33 | Decrease in income taxes payable | | | (i) 2,000 | |
| 34 | Depreciation expense | | {(k) 6,000 | | |
| 35 | | | {(l) 3,000 | | |
| 36 | Loss on disposal of plant assets | | (g) 3,000 | | |
| 37 | Investing activities | | | | |
| 38 | Purchase of building | | | (e)120,000 | |
| 39 | Purchase of equipment | | | (f) 25,000 | |
| 40 | Sale of equipment | | (g) 4,000 | | |
| 41 | Financing activities | | | | |
| 42 | Issuance of common stock | | (j) 20,000 | | |
| 43 | Payment of dividends | | | (n) 29,000 | |
| 44 | Totals | | 525,000 | 503,000 | |
| 45 | Increase in cash | | | (o) 22,000 | |
| 46 | Totals | | 525,000 | 525,000 | |
| 47 | | | | | |
| | * Significant noncash investing and financing activity. | | | | |

---

**Appendix 12C** # Statement of Cash Flows—T-Account Approach

**LEARNING OBJECTIVE *6**

Use the T-account approach to prepare a statement of cash flows.

Many people like to use T-accounts to provide structure to the preparation of a statement of cash flows. The use of T-accounts is based on the accounting equation:

**Assets = Liabilities + Stockholders' Equity**

Now, let's rewrite the left-hand side as:

**Cash + Noncash Assets = Liabilities + Stockholders' Equity**

Next, rewrite the equation by subtracting Noncash Assets from each side to isolate Cash on the left-hand side:

**Cash = Liabilities + Stockholders' Equity − Noncash Assets**

Finally, if we insert the Δ symbol (which means "change in"), we have:

**Δ Cash = Δ Liabilities + Δ Stockholders' Equity − Δ Noncash Assets**

What this means is that the change in cash is equal to the change in all of the other balance sheet accounts. Another way to think about this is that if we analyze the changes in all of the noncash balance sheet accounts, we will explain the change in the Cash account. This, of course, is exactly what we are trying to do with the statement of cash flows.

To implement this approach, first prepare a large Cash T-account with sections for operating, investing, and financing activities. Then, prepare smaller T-accounts for all of the other noncash balance sheet accounts. Insert the beginning and ending balances for each of these accounts. Once you have done this, then walk through the steps outlined in Illustration 12.3. As you walk through the steps, enter debit and credit amounts into the affected accounts. When all of the changes in the T-accounts have been explained, you are done. To demonstrate, we apply this approach to the example of Computer Services Company that is presented in the chapter. Each of the adjustments in **Illustration 12C.1** is numbered so you can follow them through the T-accounts.

1. Post net income as a debit to the operating section of the Cash T-account and a credit to Retained Earnings. Make sure to label all adjustments to the Cash T-account. It also helps to number each adjustment so you can trace all of them if you make an error.

2. Post depreciation expense as a debit to the operating section of Cash and a credit to each of the appropriate accumulated depreciation accounts.

3. Post any gains or losses on the sale of property, plant, and equipment. To do this, it is best to first prepare the journal entry that was recorded at the time of the sale and then post each element of the journal entry. For example, for Computer Services the entry was as follows.

| | | |
|---|---:|---:|
| Cash | 4,000 | |
| Accumulated Depreciation—Equipment | 1,000 | |
| Loss on Disposal of Plant Assets | 3,000 | |
|     Equipment | | 8,000 |

The $4,000 cash entry is a source of cash in the investing section of the Cash account. Accumulated Depreciation—Equipment is debited for $1,000. The Loss on Disposal of Plant Assets (equipment) is a debit to the operating section of the Cash T-account. Finally, Equipment is credited for $8,000.

4–8. Next, post each of the changes to the noncash current asset and current liability accounts. For example, to explain the $10,000 decline in Computer Services' accounts receivable, credit Accounts Receivable for $10,000 and debit the operating section of the Cash T-account for $10,000.

**ILLUSTRATION 12C.1** **T-account approach**

**Cash**

| Operating | | | | |
|---|---|---|---|---|
| (1) Net income | 145,000 | 5,000 | Inventory (5) | |
| (2) Depreciation expense | 9,000 | 4,000 | Prepaid expenses (6) | |
| (3) Loss on equipment | 3,000 | 2,000 | Income taxes payable (8) | |
| (4) Accounts receivable | 10,000 | | | |
| (7) Accounts payable | 16,000 | | | |
| Net cash provided by operating activities | 172,000 | | | |
| **Investing** | | | | |
| (3) Sold equipment | 4,000 | 120,000 | Purchased building (10) | |
| | | 25,000 | Purchased equipment (11) | |
| | | 141,000 | Net cash used by investing activities | |
| **Financing** | | | | |
| (12) Issued common stock | 20,000 | 29,000 | Dividend paid (13) | |
| | | 9,000 | Net cash used by financing activities | |
| Net increase in cash | 22,000 | | | |

| Accounts Receivable | | Inventory | | Prepaid Expenses | | Land | |
|---|---|---|---|---|---|---|---|
| 30,000 | | 10,000 | | 1,000 | | 20,000 | |
| | 10,000 (4) | (5) 5,000 | | (6) 4,000 | | (9) 110,000 | |
| 20,000 | | 15,000 | | 5,000 | | 130,000 | |

| Buildings | | Accumulated Depreciation—Buildings | | Equipment | | Accumulated Depreciation—Equipment | |
|---|---|---|---|---|---|---|---|
| 40,000 | | | 5,000 | 10,000 | | | 1,000 |
| (10) 120,000 | | | 6,000 (2) | (11) 25,000 | 8,000 (3) | (3) 1,000 | 3,000 (2) |
| 160,000 | | | 11,000 | 27,000 | | | 3,000 |

| Accounts Payable | | Income Taxes Payable | | Bonds Payable | | Common Stock | | Retained Earnings | |
|---|---|---|---|---|---|---|---|---|---|
| | 12,000 | | 8,000 | | 20,000 | | 50,000 | | 48,000 |
| | 16,000 (7) | (8) 2,000 | | | 110,000 (9) | | 20,000 (12) | | 145,000 (1) |
| | 28,000 | | 6,000 | | 130,000 | | 70,000 | (13) 29,000 | |
| | | | | | | | | | 164,000 |

9. Analyze the changes in the noncurrent accounts. Land was purchased by issuing bonds payable. This requires a debit to Land for $110,000 and a credit to Bonds Payable for $110,000. Note that this is a significant noncash event that requires disclosure at the bottom of the statement of cash flows.

10. Buildings is debited for $120,000, and the investing section of the Cash T-account is credited for $120,000 as a use of cash from investing.

11. Equipment is debited for $25,000 and the investing section of the Cash T-account is credited for $25,000 as a use of cash from investing.

12. Common Stock is credited for $20,000 for the issuance of shares of stock, and the financing section of the Cash T-account is debited for $20,000.

13. Retained Earnings is debited to reflect the payment of the $29,000 dividend, and the financing section of the Cash T-account is credited to reflect the use of Cash.

At this point, all of the changes in the noncash accounts have been explained. All that remains is to subtotal each section of the Cash T-account and compare the total change in cash with the change shown on the balance sheet. Once this is done, the information in the Cash T-account can be used to prepare a statement of cash flows.

# Review and Practice

## Learning Objectives Review

### 1 Discuss the usefulness and format of the statement of cash flows.

The statement of cash flows provides information about the cash receipts, cash payments, and net change in cash resulting from the operating, investing, and financing activities of a company during the period. Operating activities include the cash effects of transactions that enter into the determination of net income. Investing activities involve cash flows resulting from changes in investments and long-term asset items. Financing activities involve cash flows resulting from changes in long-term liability and stockholders' equity items.

### 2 Prepare a statement of cash flows using the indirect method.

The preparation of a statement of cash flows involves three major steps. (1) Determine net cash provided/used by operating activities by converting net income from an accrual basis to a cash basis. (2) Analyze changes in noncurrent asset and liability accounts and stockholders' equity accounts and report as investing and financing activities, or disclose as noncash transactions. (3) Compare the net change in cash on the statement of cash flows with the change in the Cash account reported on the balance sheet to make sure the amounts agree.

### 3 Analyze the statement of cash flows.

Free cash flow indicates the amount of cash a company generated during the current year that is available for the payment of additional dividends or for expansion.

### *4 Prepare a statement of cash flows using the direct method.

The preparation of the statement of cash flows involves three major steps. (1) Determine net cash provided/used by adjusting each item in the income statement from the accrual basis to the cash basis. (2) Analyze changes in noncurrent asset and liability accounts and stockholders' equity accounts and record as investing and financing activities, or disclose as noncash transactions. (3) Compare the net change in cash on the statement of cash flows with the change in the Cash account reported on the balance sheet to make sure the amounts agree. The direct method reports cash receipts less cash payments to arrive at net cash provided by operating activities.

### *5 Use a worksheet to prepare the statement of cash flows using the indirect method.

When there are numerous adjustments, a worksheet can be a helpful tool in preparing the statement of cash flows. Key guidelines for using a worksheet are as follows. (1) List accounts with debit balances separately from those with credit balances. (2) In the reconciling columns in the bottom portion of the worksheet, show cash inflows as debits and cash outflows as credits. (3) Do not enter reconciling items in any journal or account, but use them only to help prepare the statement of cash flows.

The steps in preparing the worksheet are as follows. (1) Enter beginning and ending balances of balance sheet accounts. (2) Enter debits and credits in reconciling columns. (3) Enter the increase or decrease in cash in two places as a balancing amount.

### *6 Use the T-account approach to prepare a statement of cash flows.

To use T-accounts to prepare the statement of cash flows: (1) prepare a large Cash T-account with sections for operating, investing, and financing activities; (2) prepare smaller T-accounts for all other noncash accounts; (3) insert beginning and ending balances for all balance sheet accounts; and (4) follows the steps in Illustration 12C.1, entering debit and credit amounts as needed.

## Glossary Review

*Direct method* A method of preparing a statement of cash flows that shows operating cash receipts and payments. It is prepared by adjusting each item in the income statement from the accrual basis to the cash basis. (pp. 12-7, 12-19).

Financing activities Cash flow activities that include (a) obtaining cash from issuing debt and repaying the amounts borrowed and (b) obtaining cash from stockholders, repurchasing shares, and paying dividends. (p. 12-3).

**Free cash flow**  Net cash provided by operating activities adjusted for capital expenditures and cash dividends paid. (p. 12-17).

**Indirect method**  A method of preparing a statement of cash flows in which net income is adjusted for items that do not affect cash, to determine net cash provided by operating activities. (pp. 12-7, 12-9).

**Investing activities**  Cash flow activities that include (a) purchasing and disposing of investments and property, plant, and equipment using cash and (b) lending money and collecting the loans. (p. 12-3).

**Operating activities**  Cash flow activities that include the cash effects of transactions that generate revenues and expenses and thus enter into the determination of net income. (p. 12-3).

**Statement of cash flows**  A basic financial statement that provides information about the cash receipts, cash payments, and net change in cash during a period, resulting from operating, investing, and financing activities. (p. 12-3).

# Practice Multiple-Choice Questions

**1. (LO 1)** Which of the following is **incorrect** about the statement of cash flows?

a. It is a fourth basic financial statement.

b. It provides information about cash receipts and cash payments of an entity during a period.

c. It reconciles the ending Cash account balance to the balance per the bank statement.

d. It provides information about the operating, investing, and financing activities of the business.

**2. (LO 1)** Which of the following is **not** reported in the statement of cash flows?

a. The net change in stockholders' equity during the year.

b. Cash payments for plant assets during the year.

c. Cash receipts from sales of plant assets during the year.

d. How acquisitions of plant assets during the year were financed.

**3. (LO 1)** The statement of cash flows classifies cash receipts and cash payments into these activities:

a. operating and nonoperating.

b. investing, financing, and operating.

c. financing, operating, and nonoperating.

d. investing, financing, and nonoperating.

**4. (LO 1)** Which is an example of a cash flow from an operating activity?

a. Payment of cash to lenders for interest.

b. Receipt of cash from the sale of common stock.

c. Payment of cash dividends to the company's stockholders.

d. None of the answer choices is correct.

**5. (LO 1)** Which is an example of a cash flow from an investing activity?

a. Receipt of cash from the issuance of bonds payable.

b. Payment of cash to repurchase outstanding common stock.

c. Receipt of cash from the sale of equipment.

d. Payment of cash to suppliers for inventory.

**6. (LO 1)** Cash dividends paid to stockholders are classified on the statement of cash flows as:

a. an operating activity.

b. an investing activity

c. a combination of an operating activity and an investing activity.

d. a financing activity.

**7. (LO 1)** Which is an example of a cash flow from a financing activity?

a. Receipt of cash from sale of land.

b. Issuance of debt for cash.

c. Purchase of equipment for cash.

d. None of the answer choices is correct.

**8. (LO 1)** Which of the following is **incorrect** about the statement of cash flows?

a. The direct method may be used to report net cash provided by operating activities.

b. The statement shows the net cash provided (used) for three categories of activity.

c. The operating section is the last section of the statement.

d. The indirect method may be used to report net cash provided by operating activities.

**Use the indirect method to solve Questions 9 through 11.**

**9. (LO 2)** Net income is $132,000, accounts payable increased $10,000 during the year, inventory decreased $6,000 during the year, and accounts receivable increased $12,000 during the year. Under the indirect method, what is net cash provided by operating activities?

a. $102,000.  c. $124,000.

b. $112,000.  d. $136,000.

**10. (LO 2)** Items that are added back to net income in determining net cash provided by operating activities under the indirect method do **not** include:

a. depreciation expense.

b. an increase in inventory.

c. amortization expense.

d. loss on disposal of plant assets.

**11. (LO 2)** The following data are available for Bill Mack Corporation.

| | |
|---|---|
| Net income | $200,000 |
| Depreciation expense | 40,000 |
| Dividends paid | 60,000 |
| Gain on sale of land | 10,000 |
| Decrease in accounts receivable | 20,000 |
| Decrease in accounts payable | 30,000 |

Net cash provided by operating activities is:

a. $160,000.  c. $240,000.

b. $220,000.  d. $280,000.

**12. (LO 2)** The following data are available for Orange Peels Corporation.

| | |
|---|---|
| Proceeds from sale of land | $100,000 |
| Proceeds from sale of equipment | 50,000 |
| Issuance of common stock | 70,000 |
| Purchase of equipment | 30,000 |
| Payment of cash dividends | 60,000 |

Net cash provided by investing activities is:

a. $120,000.      c. $150,000.

b. $130,000.      d. $190,000.

**13. (LO 2)** The following data are available for Retique!

| | |
|---|---|
| Increase in accounts payable | $ 40,000 |
| Increase in bonds payable | 100,000 |
| Sale of investment | 50,000 |
| Issuance of common stock | 60,000 |
| Payment of cash dividends | 30,000 |

Net cash provided by financing activities is:

a. $90,000.      c. $160,000.

b. $130,000.      d. $170,000.

**14. (LO 3)** The statement of cash flows should **not** be used to evaluate an entity's ability to:

a. generate net income.      c. pay dividends.

b. generate future cash flows.      d. meet obligations.

**15. (LO 3)** Free cash flow provides an indication of a company's ability to:

a. manage inventory.

b. generate cash to pay additional dividends.

c. generate cash to invest in new capital expenditures.

d. both generate cash to pay additional dividends and invest in new capital expenditures.

**Use the direct method to solve Questions 16 and 17.**

***16. (LO 4)** The beginning balance in accounts receivable is $44,000, the ending balance is $42,000, and sales during the period are $129,000. What are cash receipts from customers?

a. $127,000.

b. $129,000.

c. $131,000.

d. $141,000.

***17. (LO 4)** Which of the following items is reported on a statement of cash flows prepared by the direct method?

a. Loss on sale of building.

b. Increase in accounts receivable.

c. Depreciation expense.

d. Cash payments to suppliers.

***18. (LO 5)** In a worksheet for the statement of cash flows, a decrease in accounts receivable is entered in the reconciling columns as a credit to Accounts Receivable and a debit in the:

a. investing activities section.

b. operating activities section.

c. financing activities section.

d. None of the answer choices is correct.

***19. (LO 5)** In a worksheet for the statement of cash flows, a worksheet entry that includes a credit to accumulated depreciation will also include a:

a. credit in the operating activities section and a debit in another section.

b. debit in the operating activities section.

c. debit in the investing activities section.

d. debit in the financing activities section.

## Solutions

**1. c.** The statement of cash flows does not reconcile the ending cash balance to the balance per the bank statement. The other choices are true statements.

**2. a.** The net change in stockholders' equity during the year is not reported in the statement of cash flows. The other choices are true statements.

**3. b.** Operating, investing, and financing activities are the three classifications of cash receipts and cash payments used in the statement of cash flows. The other choices are therefore incorrect.

**4. a.** Payment of cash to lenders for interest is an operating activity. The other choices are incorrect because (b) receipt of cash from the sale of common stock is a financing activity, (c) payment of cash dividends to the company's stockholders is a financing activity, and (d) there is a correct answer.

**5. c.** Receipt of cash from the sale of equipment is an investing activity. The other choices are incorrect because (a) the receipt of cash from the issuance of bonds payable is a financing activity, (b) payment of cash to repurchase outstanding common stock is a financing activity, and (d) payment of cash to suppliers for inventory is an operating activity.

**6. d.** Cash dividends paid to stockholders are classified as a financing activity, not (a) an operating activity, (b) an investing activity, or (c) a combination of an operating and an investing activity.

**7. b.** Issuance of debt for cash is a financing activity. The other choices are incorrect because (a) the receipt of cash from the sale of land is an investing activity, (c) the purchase of equipment for cash is an investing activity, and (d) there is a correct answer.

**8. c.** The operating section of the statement of cash flows is the first, not the last, section of the statement. The other choices are true statements.

**9. d.** Net cash provided by operating activities is computed by adjusting net income for the changes in the three current asset/current liability accounts listed. An increase in accounts payable ($10,000) and a decrease in inventory ($6,000) are added to net income ($132,000), while an increase in accounts receivable ($12,000) is subtracted from net income, or $132,000 + $10,000 + $6,000 − $12,000 = $136,000, not (a) $102,000, (b) $112,000, or (c) $124,000.

**10. b.** An increase in inventory is subtracted, not added, to net income in determining net cash provided by operating activities. The other choices are incorrect because (a) depreciation expense,

(c) amortization expense, and (d) loss on disposal of plant assets are all added back to net income in determining net cash provided by operating activities.

**11. b.** Net cash provided by operating activities is $220,000 (Net income $200,000 + Depreciation expense $40,000 – Gain on sale of land $10,000 + Decrease in accounts receivable $20,000 – Decrease in accounts payable $30,000), not (a) $160,000, (c) $240,000, or (d) $280,000.

**12. a.** Net cash provided by investing activities is $120,000 (Sale of land $100,000 + Sale of equipment $50,000 – Purchase of equipment $30,000), not (b) $130,000, (c) $150,000, or (d) $190,000. Issuance of common stock and payment of cash dividends are financing activities.

**13. b.** Net cash provided by financing activities is $130,000 (Increase in bonds payable $100,000 + Issuance of common stock $60,000 – Payment of cash dividends $30,000), not (a) $90,000, (c) $160,000, or (d) $170,000. Increase in accounts payable is an operating activity and sale of investment is an investing activity.

**14. a.** The statement of cash flows is not used to evaluate an entity's ability to generate net income. The other choices are true statements.

**15. d.** Free cash flow provides an indication of a company's ability to generate cash to pay additional dividends and invest in new capital

expenditures. Choice (a) is incorrect because other measures besides free cash flow provide the best measure of a company's ability to manage inventory. Choices (b) and (c) are true statements, but (d) is the better answer.

**\*16. c.** Cash from customers amount to $131,000 ($129,000 + a decrease in accounts receivable of $2,000). The other choices are therefore incorrect.

**\*17. d.** Cash payments to suppliers are reported on a statement of cash flows prepared by the direct method. The other choices are incorrect because (a) loss on sale of building, (b) increase in accounts receivable, and (c) depreciation expense are reported in the operating activities section of the statement of cash flows when the indirect, not direct, method is used.

**\*18. b.** Because accounts receivable is a current asset, the debit belongs in the operating activities section of the worksheet, not in the (a) investing activities or (c) financing activities section. Choice (d) is incorrect as there is a right answer.

**\*19. b.** A worksheet entry that includes a credit to accumulated depreciation will also include a debit to depreciation expense. This debit in the operating activities section of the statement of cash flows will be added to the net income to determine net cash provided by operating activities. The other choices are therefore incorrect.

## Practice Brief Exercises

**1. (LO 1)** The following is a summary of the Cash account of Covey Company:

*Identify investing activity transactions.*

**Cash (Summary Form)**

| | | | |
|---|---|---|---|
| Balance, Jan. 1 | 8,000 | | |
| Receipts from customers | 364,000 | Payments for goods | 200,000 |
| Dividends on stock investments | 6,000 | Payments for operating expenses | 140,000 |
| Proceeds from sale of land | 96,000 | Purchase of equipment | 70,000 |
| Proceeds from issuance of bonds | | Taxes paid | 8,000 |
| payable | 300,000 | Dividends paid | 50,000 |
| Balance, Dec. 31 | 306,000 | | |

What amount of net cash provided (used) by investing activities should be reported in the statement of cash flows?

**Solution**

1. Cash flows from investing activities

| | |
|---|---|
| Proceeds from sale of land | $96,000 |
| Purchase of equipment | (70,000) |
| Net cash provided by investing activities | $26,000 |

Note that dividends on stock investments is classified as an operating cash flow.

**2. (LO 2)** Engel, Inc. reported net income of $1.6 million in 2022. Depreciation for the year was $140,000, accounts receivable increased $250,000, and accounts payable increased $210,000. The company also had a gain on disposal of plant assets of $19,000. Compute net cash provided by operating activities using the indirect method.

*Compute net cash provided by operating activities—indirect method.*

**Solution**

|  |  |  |
|---|---|---|
| 2. Net income |  | $1,600,000 |
| Adjustments to reconcile net income to net cash provided by operating activities |  |  |
| Depreciation expense | $ 140,000 |  |
| Gain on disposal of plant assets | (19,000) |  |
| Accounts receivable increase | (250,000) |  |
| Accounts payable increase | 210,000 | 81,000 |
| Net cash provided by operating activities |  | $1,681,000 |

*Calculate free cash flow.*

**3. (LO 3)** Goldberg Corporation reported net cash provided by operating activities of $410,000, net cash used by investing activities of $200,000 (including cash spent for equipment of $160,000), and net cash provided by financing activities of $60,000. Dividends of $110,000 were paid. Calculate free cash flow.

**Solution**

3. Free cash flow = $410,000 − $160,000 − $110,000 = $140,000

# Practice Exercises

*Prepare journal entries to determine effect on statement of cash flows.*

**1. (LO 2)** Furst Corporation had the following transactions.

1. Paid salaries of $14,000.
2. Issued 1,000 shares of $1 par value common stock for equipment worth $16,000.
3. Sold equipment (cost $10,000, accumulated depreciation $6,000) for $3,000.
4. Sold land (cost $12,000) for $16,000.
5. Issued another 1,000 shares of $1 par value common stock for $18,000.
6. Recorded depreciation of $20,000.

**Instructions**

For each transaction above, **(a)** prepare the journal entry, and **(b)** indicate how it would affect the statement of cash flows. Assume the indirect method.

**Solution**

1. 1. a.

| | | |
|---|---|---|
| Salaries and Wages Expense | 14,000 | |
| Cash | | 14,000 |

b. Salaries and wages expense is not reported separately on the statement of cash flows. It is part of the computation of net income in the income statement and is included in the net income amount on the statement of cash flows.

2. a.

| | | |
|---|---|---|
| Equipment | 16,000 | |
| Common Stock | | 1,000 |
| Paid-in Capital in Excess of Par—Common Stock | | 15,000 |

b. The issuance of common stock for equipment ($16,000) is reported as a noncash financing and investing activity at the bottom of the statement of cash flows.

**3. a.** Cash

| | | |
|---|---|---|
| Cash | 3,000 | |
| Loss on Disposal of Plant Assets | 1,000 | |
| Accumulated Depreciation—Equipment | 6,000 | |
| Equipment | | 10,000 |

**b.** The cash receipt ($3,000) is reported in the investing section. The loss ($1,000) is added to net income in the operating section.

**4. a.** Cash

| | | |
|---|---|---|
| Cash | 16,000 | |
| Land | | 12,000 |
| Gain on Disposal of Plant Assets | | 4,000 |

**b.** The cash receipt ($16,000) is reported in the investing section. The gain ($4,000) is deducted from net income in the operating section.

**5. a.** Cash

| | | |
|---|---|---|
| Cash | 18,000 | |
| Common Stock | | 1,000 |
| Paid-in Capital in Excess of Par—Common Stock | | 17,000 |

**b.** The cash receipt ($18,000) is reported in the financing section.

**6. a.** Depreciation Expense

| | | |
|---|---|---|
| Depreciation Expense | 20,000 | |
| Accumulated Depreciation—Equipment | | 20,000 |

**b.** Depreciation expense ($20,000) is added to net income in the operating section.

**2. (LO 2, 3)** Strong Corporation's comparative balance sheets are as follows.

*Prepare statement of cash flows and compute free cash flow.*

### Strong Corporation
#### Comparative Balance Sheets
#### December 31

| | 2022 | 2021 |
|---|---|---|
| Cash | $ 28,200 | $ 17,700 |
| Accounts receivable | 24,200 | 22,300 |
| Investments | 23,000 | 16,000 |
| Equipment | 60,000 | 70,000 |
| Accumulated depreciation—equipment | (14,000) | (10,000) |
| Total | $121,400 | $116,000 |
| Accounts payable | $ 19,600 | $ 11,100 |
| Bonds payable | 10,000 | 30,000 |
| Common stock | 60,000 | 45,000 |
| Retained earnings | 31,800 | 29,900 |
| Total | $121,400 | $116,000 |

Additional information:

1. Net income was $28,300. Dividends declared and paid were $26,400. Depreciation expense was $5,200.
2. Equipment which cost $10,000 and had accumulated depreciation of $1,200 was sold for $4,300.
3. All other changes in noncurrent accounts had a direct effect on cash flows, except the change in accumulated depreciation.

### Instructions

**a.** Prepare a statement of cash flows for 2022 using the indirect method.

**b.** Compute free cash flow.

**Solution**

2. **a.**

| Strong Corporation<br>Statement of Cash Flows<br>For the Year Ended December 31, 2022 | | |
|---|---|---|
| Cash flows from operating activities | | |
| Net income | | $ 28,300 |
| Adjustments to reconcile net income | | |
| to net cash provided by operating activities: | | |
| Depreciation expense | $ 5,200 | |
| Loss on disposal of plant assets | 4,500* | |
| Increase in accounts payable | 8,500 | |
| Increase in accounts receivable | (1,900) | 16,300 |
| Net cash provided by operating activities | | 44,600 |
| Cash flows from investing activities | | |
| Sale of equipment | 4,300 | |
| Purchase of investments | (7,000) | |
| Net cash used by investing activities | | (2,700) |
| Cash flows from financing activities | | |
| Issuance of common stock | 15,000 | |
| Retirement of bonds | (20,000) | |
| Payment of dividends | (26,400) | |
| Net cash used by financing activities | | (31,400) |
| Net increase in cash | | 10,500 |
| Cash at beginning of period | | 17,700 |
| Cash at end of period | | $ 28,200 |

*[$4,300 − ($10,000 − $1,200)]

**b.** Free cash flow = $44,600 − $0 − $26,400 = $18,200

---

## Practice Problem

*Prepare statement of cash flows using indirect and direct methods.*

**(LO 2, 4)** The income statement for the year ended December 31, 2022, for Kosinski Manufacturing Company contains the following condensed information.

| Kosinski Manufacturing Company<br>Income Statement<br>For the Year Ended December 31, 2022 | | |
|---|---|---|
| Sales revenue | | $6,583,000 |
| Cost of goods sold | $2,810,000 | |
| Operating expenses (excluding depreciation) | 2,086,000 | |
| Depreciation expense | 880,000 | |
| Loss on disposal of plant assets | 24,000 | 5,800,000 |
| Income before income taxes | | 783,000 |
| Income tax expense | | 353,000 |
| Net income | | $ 430,000 |

The $24,000 loss resulted from selling equipment for $270,000 cash. New equipment was purchased for $750,000 cash.

The following balances are reported on Kosinski's comparative balance sheets at December 31.

## Kosinski Manufacturing Company
### Comparative Balance Sheets (partial)

|  | 2022 | 2021 |
|---|---|---|
| Cash | $672,000 | $130,000 |
| Accounts receivable | 775,000 | 610,000 |
| Inventory | 834,000 | 867,000 |
| Accounts payable | 521,000 | 501,000 |

Income tax expense of $353 000 represents the amount paid in 2022. Dividends declared and paid in 2022 totaled $200,000.

### Instructions

a. Prepare the statement of cash flows using the indirect method.

*b. Prepare the statement of cash flows using the direct method.

### Solution

a.

## Kosinski Manufacturing Company
### Statement of Cash Flows—Indirect Method
### For the Year Ended December 31, 2022

| | | |
|---|---|---|
| Cash flows from operating activities | | |
| Net income | | $ 430,000 |
| Adjustments to reconcile net income to net cash provided by operating activities: | | |
| Depreciation expense | $ 880,000 | |
| Loss on disposal of plant assets | 24,000 | |
| Increase in accounts receivable | (165,000) | |
| Decrease in inventory | 33,000 | |
| Increase in accounts payable | 20,000 | 792,000 |
| Net cash provided by operating activities | | 1,222,000 |
| Cash flows from investing activities | | |
| Sale of equipment | 270,000 | |
| Purchase of equipment | (750,000) | |
| Net cash used by investing activities | | (480,000) |
| Cash flows from financing activities | | |
| Payment of cash dividends | (200,000) | |
| Net cash used by financing activities | | (200,000) |
| Net increase in cash | | 542,000 |
| Cash at beginning of period | | 130,000 |
| Cash at end of period | | $ 672,000 |

*b.

## Kosinski Manufacturing Company
### Statement of Cash Flows—Direct Method
### For the Year Ended December 31, 2022

| | | |
|---|---|---|
| Cash flows from operating activities | | |
| Cash collections from customers | | $6,418,000* |
| Less: Cash payments: | | |
| To suppliers | $2,757,000** | |
| For operating expenses | 2,086,000 | |
| For income taxes | 353,000 | 5,196,000 |
| Net cash provided by operating activities | | 1,222,000 |

| | | |
|---|---:|---:|
| Cash flows from investing activities | | |
| Sale of equipment | 270,000 | |
| Purchase of equipment | (750,000) | |
| Net cash used by investing activities | | (480,000) |
| Cash flows from financing activities | | |
| Payment of cash dividends | (200,000) | |
| Net cash used by financing activities | | (200,000) |
| Net increase in cash | | 542,000 |
| Cash at beginning of period | | 130,000 |
| Cash at end of period | | $ 672,000 |

*Direct-Method Computations:*

| | |
|---|---:|
| *Computation of cash collections from customers: | |
| Sales revenue | $6,583,000 |
| Deduct: Increase in accounts receivable | (165,000) |
| Cash collections from customers | $6,418,000 |
| | |
| **Computation of cash payments to suppliers | |
| Cost of goods sold per income statement | $2,810,000 |
| Deduct: Decrease in inventories | (33,000) |
| Deduct: Increase in accounts payable | (20,000) |
| Cash payments to suppliers | $2,757,000 |

**Brief Exercises, DO IT! Exercises, Exercises, Problems, Data Analytics Activities, and many additional resources are available for practice in WileyPLUS.**

*Note:* All asterisked Questions, Exercises, and Problems relate to material in the appendices to the chapter.

## Questions

**1. a.** What is a statement of cash flows?

**b.** Pat Marx maintains that the statement of cash flows is an optional financial statement. Do you agree? Explain.

**2.** What questions about cash are answered by the statement of cash flows?

**3.** Distinguish among the three types of activities reported in the statement of cash flows.

**4. a.** What are the major sources (inflows) of cash?

**b.** What are the major uses (outflows) of cash?

**5.** Why is it important to disclose certain noncash transactions? How should they be disclosed?

**6.** Helen Powell and Paul Tang were discussing the format of the statement of cash flows of Baumgarten Co. At the bottom of Baumgarten's statement of cash flows was a separate section entitled "Noncash investing and financing activities." Give three examples of significant noncash transactions that would be reported in this section.

**7.** Why is it necessary to use comparative balance sheets, a current income statement, and certain transaction data in preparing a statement of cash flows?

**8.** Contrast the advantages and disadvantages of the direct and indirect methods of preparing the statement of cash flows. Are both methods acceptable? Which method is preferred by the FASB? Which method is more popular?

**9.** When the total cash inflows exceed the total cash outflows in the statement of cash flows, how and where is this excess identified?

**10.** Describe the indirect method for determining net cash provided (used) by operating activities.

**11.** Why is it necessary to convert accrual-basis net income to cash-basis income when preparing a statement of cash flows?

**12.** The president of Murquery Company is puzzled. During the last year, the company experienced a net loss of $800,000, yet its cash increased $300,000 during the same period of time. Explain to the president how this could occur.

**13.** Identify five items that are adjustments to convert net income to net cash provided by operating activities under the indirect method.

**14.** Why and how is depreciation expense reported in a statement of cash flows prepared using the indirect method?

**15.** Why is the statement of cash flows useful?

**16.** During 2022, Slivowitz Doubleday Company converted $1,700,000 of its total $2,000,000 of bonds payable into common stock. Indicate how the transaction would be reported on a statement of cash flows, if at all.

**17.** In its 2018 statement of cash flows, what amount did **Apple** report for net cash (a) provided by operating activities, (b) used for investing activities, and (c) used for financing activities?

*__18.__ Describe the direct method for determining net cash provided by operating activities.

*__19.__ Give the formulas under the direct method for computing (a) cash receipts from customers and (b) cash payments to suppliers.

*__20.__ Harbinger Inc. reported sales of $2 million for 2022. Accounts receivable decreased $150,000 and accounts payable increased $300,000. Compute cash receipts from customers, assuming that the receivable and payable transactions are related to operations.

*__21.__ In the direct method, why is depreciation expense not reported in the cash flows from operating activities section?

*__22.__ Why is it advantageous to use a worksheet when preparing a statement of cash flows? Is a worksheet required to prepare a statement of cash flows?

## Brief Exercises

**BE12.1 (LO 1), C** Each of these items must be considered in preparing a statement of cash flows for Irvin Co. for the year ended December 31, 2022. For each item, state how it should be shown in the statement of cash flows for 2022.

*Indicate statement presentation of selected transactions.*

  **a.** Issued bonds for $200,000 cash.

  **b.** Purchased equipment for $180,000 cash.

  **c.** Sold land costing $20,000 for $20,000 cash.

  **d.** Declared and paid a $50,000 cash dividend.

**BE12.2 (LO 1), C** Classify each item as an operating, investing, or financing activity. Assume all items involve cash unless there is information to the contrary.

*Classify items by activities.*

  **a.** Purchase of equipment.

  **b.** Proceeds from sale of building.

  **c.** Redemption of bonds payable.

  **d.** Cash received from sale of goods.

  **e.** Payment of dividends.

  **f.** Issuance of common stock.

**BE12.3 (LO 1), AP** The following T-account is a summary of the Cash account of Alixon Company.

*Identify financing activity transactions.*

| Cash (Summary Form) | | | |
|---|---|---|---|
| Balance, Jan. 1 | 8,000 | | |
| Receipts from customers | 364,000 | Payments for goods | 200,000 |
| Dividends on stock investments | 6,000 | Payments for operating expenses | 140,000 |
| Proceeds from sale of equipment | 36,000 | Interest paid | 10,000 |
| Proceeds from issuance of | | Taxes paid | 8,000 |
|   bonds payable | 300,000 | Dividends paid | 40,000 |
| Balance, Dec. 31 | 316,000 | | |

What amount of net cash provided (used) by financing activities should be reported in the statement of cash flows?

**BE12.4 (LO 2), AP** Miguel, Inc. reported net income of $2.5 million in 2022. Depreciation for the year was $160,000, accounts receivable decreased $350,000, and accounts payable decreased $280,000. Compute net cash provided by operating activities using the indirect method.

*Compute net cash provided by operating activities—indirect method.*

**BE12.5 (LO 2), AP** The net income for Mongan Co. for 2022 was $280,000. For 2022, depreciation on plant assets was $70,000, and the company incurred a loss on disposal of plant assets of $28,000. Compute net cash provided by operating activities under the indirect method, assuming there were no other changes in the company's accounts.

*Compute net cash provided by operating activities—indirect method.*

**BE12.6 (LO 2), AP** The comparative balance sheets for Gale Company show these changes in noncash current asset accounts: accounts receivable decreased $80,000, prepaid expenses increased $28,000, and inventories increased $40,000. Compute net cash provided by operating activities using the indirect method, assuming that net income is $186,000.

*Compute net cash provided by operating activities—indirect method.*

*Determine cash received from sale of equipment.*

**BE12.7 (LO 2), AN** The T-accounts for Equipment and the related Accumulated Depreciation—Equipment for Goldstone Company at the end of 2022 are shown here.

| | Equipment | | | | Accum. Depr.—Equipment | | |
|---|---|---|---|---|---|---|---|
| Beg. bal. | 80,000 | Disposals | 22,000 | Disposals | 5,100 | Beg. bal. | 44,500 |
| Acquisitions | 41,600 | | | | | Depr. exp. | 12,000 |
| End. bal. | 99,600 | | | | | End. bal. | 51,400 |

In addition, Goldstone's income statement reported a loss on the disposal of plant assets of $3,500. What amount was reported on the statement of cash flows as "cash flow from sale of equipment"?

*Calculate free cash flow.*

**BE12.8 (LO 3), AP** Suppose that during 2022 **Cypress Semiconductor Corporation** reported net cash provided by operating activities of $89,303,000, cash used in investing of $43,126,000, and cash used in financing of $7,368,000. In addition, cash spent for fixed assets during the period was $25,823,000. No dividends were paid. Calculate free cash flow.

*Calculate free cash flow.*

**BE12.9 (LO 3), AP** Sprouts Corporation reported net cash provided by operating activities of $412,000, net cash used by investing activities of $250,000, and net cash provided by financing activities of $70,000. In addition, cash spent for capital assets during the period was $200,000. No dividends were paid. Calculate free cash flow.

*Calculate free cash flow.*

**BE12.10 (LO 3), AP** Suppose **Shaw Communications** reported net cash used by operating activities of $104,539,000 and sales revenue of $2,867,459,000 during 2022. Cash spent on plant asset additions during the year was $79,330,000. Calculate free cash flow.

*Calculate and analyze free cash flow.*

**BE12.11 (LO 3), AN** The management of Uhuru Inc. is trying to decide whether it can increase its dividend. During the current year, it reported net income of $875,000. It had net cash provided by operating activities of $734,000, paid cash dividends of $92,000, and had capital expenditures of $310,000. Compute the company's free cash flow, and discuss whether an increase in the dividend appears warranted. What other factors should be considered?

*Compute receipts from customers—direct method.*

\* **BE12.12 (LO 4), AP** Suppose **Columbia Sportswear Company** had accounts receivable of $299,585,000 at January 1, 2022, and $226,548,000 at December 31, 2022. Assume sales revenue was $1,244,023,000 for the year 2022. What is the amount of cash receipts from customers in 2022?

*Compute cash payments for income taxes—direct method.*

\* **BE12.13 (LO 4), AP** Hoffman Corporation reported income taxes of $370,000,000 on its 2022 income statement and income taxes payable of $277,000,000 at December 31, 2021, and $528,000,000 at December 31, 2022. What amount of cash payments were made for income taxes during 2022?

*Compute cash payments for operating expenses—direct method.*

\* **BE12.14 (LO 4), AP** Pietr Corporation reports operating expenses of $90,000, excluding depreciation expense of $15,000, for 2022. During the year, prepaid expenses decreased $7,200 and accrued expenses payable increased $4,400. Compute the cash payments for operating expenses in 2022.

# DO IT! Exercises

*Classify transactions by type of cash flow activity.*

**DO IT! 12.1 (LO 1), C** Moss Corporation had the following transactions.

1. Issued $160,000 of bonds payable.
2. Paid utilities expense.
3. Issued 500 shares of preferred stock for $45,000.
4. Sold land and a building for $250,000.
5. Loaned $30,000 to Dead End Corporation, receiving Dead End's 1-year, 12% note.

Classify each of these transactions by type of cash flow activity (operating, investing, or financing). (*Hint:* Refer to Illustration 12.1.)

*Calculate net cash from operating activities.*

**DO IT! 12.2a (LO 2), AP** PK Photography reported net income of $100,000 for 2022. Included in the income statement were depreciation expense of $6,300, patent amortization expense of $4,000, and a gain on disposal of plant assets of $3,600. PK's comparative balance sheets show the following balances.

| | 12/31/22 | 12/31/21 |
|---|---|---|
| Accounts receivable | $21,000 | $27,000 |
| Accounts payable | 9,200 | 6,000 |

Calculate net cash provided by operating activities for PK Photography.

**DO IT! 12.2b (LO 2), AN** Alex Company reported the following information for 2022.

*Prepare statement of cash flows—indirect method.*

### Alex Company
#### Comparative Balance Sheets
#### December 31

| Assets | 2022 | 2021 | Change Increase/Decrease | |
|---|---|---|---|---|
| Cash | $ 59,000 | $ 36,000 | $ 23,000 | Increase |
| Accounts receivable | 62,000 | 22,000 | 40,000 | Increase |
| Inventory | 44,000 | –0– | 44,000 | Increase |
| Prepaid expenses | 6,000 | 4,000 | 2,000 | Increase |
| Land | 55,000 | 70,000 | 15,000 | Decrease |
| Buildings | 200,000 | 200,000 | –0– | No change |
| Accumulated depreciation—buildings | (21,000) | (14,000) | 7,000 | Increase |
| Equipment | 183,000 | 68,000 | 115,000 | Increase |
| Accumulated depreciation—equipment | (28,000) | (10,000) | 18,000 | Increase |
| Totals | $560,000 | $376,000 | | |
| | | | | |
| **Liabilities and Stockholders' Equity** | | | | |
| Accounts payable | $ 43,000 | $ 40,000 | $ 3,000 | Increase |
| Accrued expenses payable | –0– | 10,000 | 10,000 | Decrease |
| Bonds payable | 100,000 | 150,000 | 50,000 | Decrease |
| Common stock ($1 par) | 230,000 | 60,000 | 170,000 | Increase |
| Retained earnings | 187,000 | 116,000 | 71,000 | Increase |
| Totals | $560,000 | $376,000 | | |

### Alex Company
#### Income Statement
#### For the Year Ended December 31, 2022

| | | |
|---|---|---|
| Sales revenue | | $941,000 |
| Cost of goods sold | $475,000 | |
| Operating expenses | 231,000 | |
| Interest expense | 12,000 | |
| Loss on disposal of plant assets | 2,000 | 720,000 |
| Income before income taxes | | 221,000 |
| Income tax expense | | 65,000 |
| Net income | | $156,000 |

Additional information:

1. Operating expenses include depreciation expense of $40,000.

2. Land was sold at its book value for cash.

3. Cash dividends of $85,000 were declared and paid in 2022.

4. Equipment with a cost of $166,000 was purchased for cash. Equipment with a cost of $51,000 and a book value of $36,000 was sold for $34,000 cash.

5. Bonds of $50,000 were redeemed at their face value for cash.

6. Common stock ($1 par) was issued at par for $170,000 cash.

Use this information to prepare a statement of cash flows using the indirect method.

*Compute and discuss free cash flow.*

**DO IT! 12.3 (LO 3), AP** Moskow Corporation issued the following statement of cash flows for 2022.

| Moskow Corporation | | |
|---|---|---|
| **Statement of Cash Flows—Indirect Method** | | |
| **For the Year Ended December 31, 2022** | | |
| Cash flows from operating activities | | |
| Net income | | $ 59,000 |
| Adjustments to reconcile net income to net cash | | |
| provided by operating activities: | | |
| Depreciation expense | $ 9,100 | |
| Decrease in accounts receivable | 9,500 | |
| Increase in inventory | (5,000) | |
| Decrease in accounts payable | (2,200) | |
| Loss on disposal of plant assets | 3,300 | 14,700 |
| Net cash provided by operating activities | | 73,700 |
| Cash flows from investing activities | | |
| Sale of investments | 3,100 | |
| Purchase of equipment | (24,200) | |
| Net cash used by investing activities | | (21,100) |
| Cash flows from financing activities | | |
| Issuance of common stock | 20,000 | |
| Payment on long-term note payable | (10,000) | |
| Payment of cash dividends | (13,000) | |
| Net cash used by financing activities | | (3,000) |
| Net increase in cash | | 49,600 |
| Cash at beginning of year | | 13,000 |
| Cash at end of year | | $ 62,600 |

**a.** Compute free cash flow for Moskow Corporation.

**b.** Explain why free cash flow often provides better information than "Net cash provided by operating activities."

# Exercises

*Classify transactions by type of activity.*

**E12.1 (LO 1), C** Kiley Corporation had these transactions during 2022.

**a.** Purchased a machine for $30,000, giving a long-term note in exchange.

**b.** Issued $50,000 par value common stock for cash.

**c.** Issued $200,000 par value common stock upon conversion of bonds having a face value of $200,000.

**d.** Declared and paid a cash dividend of $13,000.

**e.** Sold a long-term investment with a cost of $15,000 for $15,000 cash.

**f.** Collected $16,000 from sale of goods.

**g.** Paid $18,000 to suppliers.

**Instructions**

Analyze the transactions and indicate whether each transaction is an operating activity, investing activity, financing activity, or noncash investing and financing activity.

*Classify transactions by type of activity.*

**E12.2 (LO 1), C** An analysis of comparative balance sheets, the current year's income statement, and the general ledger accounts of Hailey Corp. uncovered the following items. Assume all items involve cash unless there is information to the contrary.

**a.** Exchange of land for patent.

**b.** Sale of building at book value.

**c.** Payment of dividends.

**d.** Depreciation of plant assets.

**e.** Conversion of bonds into common stock.

**f.** Issuance of capital stock.

**g.** Amortization of patent.

**h.** Issuance of bonds for land.

**i.** Purchase of land.

**j.** Loss on disposal of plant assets.

**k.** Retirement of bonds.

**Instructions**

Indicate where each item should be presented in the statement of cash flows (indirect method) using these four major classifications: operating activity (that is, the item would be listed among the adjustments to net income to determine net cash provided by operating activities under the indirect method), investing activity, financing activity, or significant noncash investing and financing activity.

**E12.3 (LO 1), AP** Cushenberry Corporation had the following transactions.

*Prepare journal entry and determine effect on cash flows.*

1. Sold land (cost $12,000) for $15,000.

2. Issued common stock at par for $20,000.

3. Recorded depreciation on buildings for $17,000.

4. Paid salaries of $9,000.

5. Issued 1,000 shares of $1 par value common stock for equipment worth $8,000.

6. Sold equipment (cost $10,000, accumulated depreciation $7,000) for $1,200.

**Instructions**

For each transaction above, (a) prepare the journal entry, and (b) indicate how it would affect the statement of cash flows using the indirect method.

**E12.4 (LO 2), AP** Sosa Company reported net income of $190,000 for 2022. Sosa also reported depreciation expense of $35,000 and a loss of $5,000 on the disposal of plant assets. The comparative balance sheets show an increase in accounts receivable of $15,000 for the year, a $17,000 increase in accounts payable, and a $4,000 increase in prepaid expenses.

*Prepare the operating activities section—indirect method.*

**Instructions**

Prepare the operating activities section of the statement of cash flows for 2022. Use the indirect method.

**E12.5 (LO 2), AP** The current sections of Sunn Inc.'s balance sheets at December 31, 2021 and 2022, are presented here. Sunn's net income for 2022 was $153,000. Depreciation expense was $27,000.

*Prepare the operating activities section—indirect method.*

|  | 2022 | 2021 |
|---|---|---|
| Current assets |  |  |
| Cash | $105,000 | $ 99,000 |
| Accounts receivable | 80,000 | 89,000 |
| Inventory | 163,000 | 172,000 |
| Prepaid expenses | 27,000 | 22,000 |
| Total current assets | $380,000 | $382,000 |
| Current liabilities |  |  |
| Accrued expenses payable | $ 15,000 | $ 5,000 |
| Accounts payable | 85,000 | 92,000 |
| Total current liabilities | $100,000 | $ 97,000 |

**Instructions**

Prepare the operating activities section of the company's statement of cash flows for the year ended December 31, 2022, using the indirect method.

**E12.6 (LO 2), AP** The following information is available for Stamos Corporation for the year ended December 31, 2022.

*Prepare statement of cash flows—indirect method.*

| | |
|---|---|
| Beginning cash balance | $ 45,000 |
| Accounts payable decrease | 3,700 |
| Depreciation expense | 162,000 |
| Accounts receivable increase | 8,200 |
| Inventory increase | 11,000 |
| Net income | 284,100 |
| Cash received for sale of land at book value | 35,000 |
| Cash dividends paid | 12,000 |
| Income taxes payable increase | 4,700 |
| Cash used to purchase building | 289,000 |
| Cash used to purchase treasury stock | 26,000 |
| Cash received from issuing bonds | 200,000 |

### Instructions

Prepare a statement of cash flows using the indirect method.

*Prepare partial statement of cash flows—indirect method.*

**E12.7 (LO 2), AN** The following three accounts appear in the general ledger of Beiber Corp. during 2022.

#### Equipment

| Date | | Debit | Credit | Balance |
|---|---|---|---|---|
| Jan. 1 | Balance | | | 160,000 |
| July 31 | Purchase of equipment | 70,000 | | 230,000 |
| Sept. 2 | Purchase of equipment | 53,000 | | 283,000 |
| Nov. 10 | Cost of equipment sold | | 49,000 | 234,000 |

#### Accumulated Depreciation—Equipment

| Date | | Debit | Credit | Balance |
|---|---|---|---|---|
| Jan. 1 | Balance | | | 71,000 |
| Nov. 10 | Accumulated depreciation on equipment sold | 16,000 | | 55,000 |
| Dec. 31 | Depreciation for year | | 28,000 | 83,000 |

#### Retained Earnings

| Date | | Debit | Credit | Balance |
|---|---|---|---|---|
| Jan. 1 | Balance | | | 105,000 |
| Aug. 23 | Dividends (cash) | 14,000 | | 91,000 |
| Dec. 31 | Net income | | 72,000 | 163,000 |

### Instructions

From the postings in the accounts, indicate how the information is reported on a statement of cash flows using the indirect method. The loss on disposal of plant assets was $8,000.

*Prepare statement of cash flows and compute free cash flow.*

**E12.8 (LO 2, 3), AP** Rojas Corporation's comparative balance sheets are presented below.

#### Rojas Corporation
#### Comparative Balance Sheets
#### December 31

| | 2022 | 2021 |
|---|---|---|
| Cash | $ 14,300 | $ 10,700 |
| Accounts receivable | 21,200 | 23,400 |
| Land | 20,000 | 26,000 |
| Buildings | 70,000 | 70,000 |
| Accumulated depreciation—buildings | (15,000) | (10,000) |
| Total | $110,500 | $120,100 |
| | | |
| Accounts payable | $ 12,370 | $ 31,100 |
| Common stock | 75,000 | 69,000 |
| Retained earnings | 23,130 | 20,000 |
| Total | $110,500 | $120,100 |

Additional information:

1. Net income was $22,630. Dividends declared and paid were $19,500.

2. No noncash investing and financing activities occurred during 2022.

3. The land was sold for cash of $4,900.

### Instructions

a. Prepare a statement of cash flows for 2022 using the indirect method.

b. Compute free cash flow.

**E12.9 (LO 2), AP** The following are comparative balance sheets for Mitch Company

*Prepare statement of cash flows—indirect method.*

### Mitch Company
### Comparative Balance Sheets
### December 31

| | 2022 | 2021 |
|---|---|---|
| **Assets** | | |
| Cash | $ 68,000 | $ 22,000 |
| Accounts receivable | 88,000 | 76,000 |
| Inventory | 167,000 | 189,000 |
| Land | 80,000 | 100,000 |
| Equipment | 260,000 | 200,000 |
| Accumulated depreciation—equipment | (66,000) | (32,000) |
| Total | $597,000 | $555,000 |
| **Liabilities and Stockholders' Equity** | | |
| Accounts payable | $ 39,000 | $ 43,000 |
| Bonds payable | 150,000 | 200,000 |
| Common stock ($1 par) | 216,000 | 179,000 |
| Retained earnings | 192,000 | 133,000 |
| Total | $597,000 | $555,000 |

Additional information:

1. Net income for 2022 was $93,000.

2. Depreciation expense was $34,000.

3. Cash dividends of $39,000 were declared and paid.

4. Bonds payable with a carrying value of $50,000 were redeemed for $50,000 cash.

5. Common stock was issued at par for $42,000 cash.

6. No equipment was sold during 2022.

7. Land was sold for its book value.

### Instructions

Prepare a statement of cash flows for 2022 using the indirect method.

**E12.10 (LO 2, 3), AP** Rodriquez Corporation's comparative balance sheets are as follows.

*Prepare statement of cash flows—indirect method and compute free cash flow.*

### Rodriquez Corporation
### Comparative Balance Sheets
### December 31

| | 2022 | 2021 |
|---|---|---|
| Cash | $ 15,200 | $ 17,700 |
| Accounts receivable | 25,200 | 22,300 |
| Investments | 20,000 | 16,000 |
| Equipment | 60,000 | 70,000 |
| Accumulated depreciation—equipment | (14,000) | (10,000) |
| Total | $106,400 | $116,000 |
| Accounts payable | $ 14,600 | $ 11,100 |
| Bonds payable | 10,000 | 30,000 |
| Common stock | 50,000 | 45,000 |
| Retained earnings | 31,800 | 29,900 |
| Total | $106,400 | $116,000 |

Additional information:

1. Net income was $18,300. Dividends declared and paid were $16,400.

2. Equipment which cost $10,000 and had accumulated depreciation of $1,200 was sold for $3,300.

3. No noncash investing and financing activities occurred during 2022.

4. Bonds were retired at their carrying value.

**Instructions**

a. Prepare a statement of cash flows for 2022 using the indirect method.

b. Compute free cash flow.

*Compute net cash provided by operating activities—direct method.*

**\*E12.11 (LO 4), AP** Zimmer Company completed its first year of operations on December 31, 2022. Its initial income statement showed that Zimmer had sales revenue of $198,000 and operating expenses of $83,000. Accounts receivable and accounts payable at year-end were $60,000 and $23,000, respectively. Assume that accounts payable related to operating expenses. Ignore income taxes.

**Instructions**

Compute net cash provided by operating activity using the direct method.

*Compute cash payments—direct method.*

**\*E12.12 (LO 4), AP** Suppose the 2022 income statement for **McDonald's Corporation** shows cost of goods sold $5,178.0 million and operating expenses (including depreciation expense of $1,216.2 million) $10,725.7 million. The comparative balance sheets for the year show that inventory decreased $5.3 million, prepaid expenses increased $42.2 million, accounts payable (inventory suppliers) increased $15.6 million, and accrued expenses payable increased $199.8 million.

**Instructions**

Using the direct method, compute (a) cash payments to suppliers and (b) cash payments for operating expenses.

*Compute cash flow from operating activities—direct method.*

**\*E12.13 (LO 4), AP** The 2022 accounting records of Megan Transport provide the following information.

| | | | |
|---|---:|---|---:|
| Payment of interest | $ 10,000 | Payment of salaries and wages | $ 53,000 |
| Cash sales | 48,000 | Depreciation expense | 16,000 |
| Receipt of dividend revenue | 18,000 | Proceeds from sale of vehicles | 812,000 |
| Payment of income taxes | 12,000 | Purchase of equipment for cash | 22,000 |
| Net income | 38,000 | Loss on sale of vehicles | 3,000 |
| Payment for merchandise | 97,000 | Payment of dividends | 14,000 |
| Payment for land | 74,000 | Payment of operating expenses | 28,000 |
| Collection of accounts receivable | 195,000 | | |

**Instructions**

Prepare the cash flows from operating activities section using the direct method.

*Calculate cash flows—direct method.*

**\*E12.14 (LO 4), AN** The following information is taken from the 2022 general ledger of Preminger Company.

| | | |
|---|---|---:|
| Rent | Rent expense | $ 30,000 |
| | Prepaid rent, January 1 | 5,900 |
| | Prepaid rent, December 31 | 7,400 |
| Salaries | Salaries and wages expense | $ 54,000 |
| | Salaries and wages payable, January 1 | 2,000 |
| | Salaries and wages payable, December 31 | 8,000 |
| Sales | Sales revenue | $160,000 |
| | Accounts receivable, January 1 | 16,000 |
| | Accounts receivable, December 31 | 7,000 |

**Instructions**

In each case, compute the amount that should be reported in the operating activities section of the statement of cash flows under the direct method.

*Prepare a worksheet.*

**\*E12.15 (LO 5), AP** Comparative balance sheets for International Company are as follows.

**International Company**
**Comparative Balance Sheets**
**December 31**

| | 2022 | 2021 |
|---|---:|---:|
| **Assets** | | |
| Cash | $ 73,000 | $ 22,000 |
| Accounts receivable | 85,000 | 76,000 |
| Inventory | 180,000 | 189,000 |
| Land | 75,000 | 100,000 |
| Equipment | 250,000 | 200,000 |
| Accumulated depreciation—equipment | (66,000) | (42,000) |
| Total | $597,000 | $545,000 |

|  | 2022 | 2021 |
|---|---|---|
| **Liabilities and Stockholders' Equity** | | |
| Accounts payable | $ 34,000 | $ 47,000 |
| Bonds payable | 150,000 | 200,000 |
| Common stock ($1 par) | 214,000 | 164,000 |
| Retained earnings | 199,000 | 134,000 |
| Total | $597,000 | $545,000 |

Additional information:

1. Net income for 2022 was $135,000.

2. Cash dividends of $70,000 were declared and paid.

3. Bonds payable with a carrying value of $50,000 were redeemed for $50,000 cash.

4. Common stock was issued at par for $50,000 cash.

5. Depreciation expense was $24,000.

6. Sales revenue for the year was $978,000.

7. Land was sold at cost, and equipment was purchased for cash.

**Instructions**

Prepare a worksheet for a statement of cash flows for 2022 using the indirect method. Enter the reconciling items directly on the worksheet, using letters to cross-reference each entry.

# Problems

**P12.1 (LO 1, 2), C** You are provided with the following information regarding events that occurred at Moore Corporation during 2022 or changes in account balances as of December 31, 2022.

*Distinguish among operating, investing, and financing activities.*

|  | (1) Statement of Cash Flow Section Affected | (2) If Operating, Did It Increase or Decrease Reported Cash from Operating Activities? |
|---|---|---|
| a. Depreciation expense was $80,000. | | |
| b. Interest Payable account increased $5,000. | | |
| c. Received $26,000 from sale of plant assets. | | |
| d. Acquired land by issuing common stock to seller. | | |
| e. Paid $17,000 cash dividend to preferred stockholders. | | |
| f. Paid $4,000 cash dividend to common stockholders. | | |
| g. Accounts Receivable account decreased $10,000. | | |
| h. Inventory increased $2,000. | | |
| i. Received $100,000 from issuing bonds payable. | | |
| j. Acquired equipment for $16,000 cash. | | |

**Instructions**

Moore prepares its statement of cash flows using the indirect method. Complete the first column of the table, indicating whether each item affects the operating activities section (O) (that is, the item would be listed among the adjustments to net income to determine net cash provided by operating activities under the indirect method), investing activities section (I), financing activities section (F), or is a noncash (NC) transaction reported in a separate schedule. For those items classified as operating activities (O), indicate whether the item is added (A) or subtracted (S) from net income to determine net cash provided by operating activities.

**P12.2 (LO 2), AN** The following account balances relate to the stockholders' equity accounts of Molder Corp. at year-end.

*Determine cash flow effects of changes in equity accounts.*

|  | 2022 | 2021 |
|---|---|---|
| Common stock, 10,500 and 10,000 shares, issued and outstanding, respectively, for 2022 and 2021 | $160,800 | $140,000 |
| Preferred stock, 5,000 shares, issued and outstanding | 125,000 | 125,000 |
| Retained earnings | 300,000 | 270,000 |

A small stock dividend was declared and issued in 2022. The market price of the shares was $8,800. Cash dividends of $20,000 were declared and paid in both 2022 and 2021. The common stock and preferred stock have no par or stated value.

**Instructions**

a. Net income $58,800

a. What was the amount of net income reported by Molder Corp. in 2022?

b. Determine the amounts of any cash inflows or outflows related to the common stock and dividend accounts in 2022.

c. Indicate where each of the cash inflows or outflows identified in (b) would be classified on the statement of cash flows.

*Prepare the operating activities section—indirect method.*

 Excel

**P12.3 (LO 2), AP** The income statement of Munsun Company is presented here.

| Munsun Company | | |
|---|---|---|
| Income Statement | | |
| For the Year Ended November 30, 2022 | | |
| Sales revenue | | $7,600,000 |
| Cost of goods sold | | |
| Beginning inventory | $1,900,000 | |
| Purchases | 4,400,000 | |
| Goods available for sale | 6,300,000 | |
| Ending inventory | 1,600,000 | |
| Total cost of goods sold | | 4,700,000 |
| Gross profit | | 2,900,000 |
| Operating expenses | | |
| Selling expenses | 450,000 | |
| Administrative expenses | 700,000 | 1,150,000 |
| Net income | | $1,750,000 |

Additional information:

1. Accounts receivable decreased $380,000 during the year, and inventory decreased $300,000.
2. Prepaid expenses increased $150,000 during the year.
3. Accounts payable to suppliers of inventory decreased $350,000 during the year.
4. Accrued expenses payable decreased $100,000 during the year.
5. Administrative expenses include depreciation expense of $110,000.

**Instructions**

Net cash provided— oper. act. $1,940,000

Prepare the operating activities section of the statement of cash flows for the year ended November 30, 2022, for Munsun Company, using the indirect method.

*Prepare the operating activities section—direct method.*

Net cash provided— oper. act. $1,940,000

*****P12.4 (LO 4), AP** Data for Munsun Company are presented in P12.3.

**Instructions**

Prepare the operating activities section of the statement of cash flows using the direct method.

*Prepare the operating activities section—indirect method.*

 Excel

**P12.5 (LO 2), AP** Rewe Company's income statement contained the following condensed information.

| Rewe Company | | |
|---|---|---|
| Income Statement | | |
| For the Year Ended December 31, 2022 | | |
| Service revenue | | $970,000 |
| Operating expenses, excluding depreciation | $614,000 | |
| Depreciation expense | 55,000 | |
| Loss on disposal of plant assets | 16,000 | 685,000 |
| Income before income taxes | | 285,000 |
| Income tax expense | | 56,000 |
| Net income | | $229,000 |

Rewe's balance sheets contained the following comparative data at December 31.

|  | 2022 | 2021 |
|---|---|---|
| Accounts receivable | $70,000 | $60,000 |
| Accounts payable | 41,000 | 32,000 |
| Income taxes payable | 13,000 | 7,000 |

Accounts payable pertain to operating expenses

## Instructions

Prepare the operating activ_ties section of the statement of cash flows using the indirect method.

*P12.6 **(LO 4), AP** Data for Rewe Company are presented in P12.5.

## Instructions

Prepare the operating activities section of the statement of cash flows using the direct method.

P12.7 **(LO 2, 3), AP** Presented here are the financial statements of Warner Company.

**Net cash provided**     $305,000

*Prepare the operating activities section—direct method.*

 **Excel**

**Net cash provided**     $305,000

*Prepare a statement of cash flows— indirect method, and compute free cash flow.*

**Excel**

### Warner Company
### Comparative Balance Sheets
### December 31

|  | 2022 | 2021 |
|---|---|---|
| **Assets** | | |
| Cash | $ 35,000 | $ 20,000 |
| Accounts receivable | 20,000 | 14,000 |
| Inventory | 28,000 | 20,000 |
| Property, plant, and equipment | 60,000 | 78,000 |
| Accumulated depreciation | (32,000) | (24,000) |
| Total | $111,000 | $108,000 |
| **Liabilities and Stockholders' Equity** | | |
| Accounts payable | $ 19,000 | $ 15,000 |
| Income taxes payable | 7,000 | 8,000 |
| Bonds payable | 17,000 | 33,000 |
| Common stock | 18,000 | 14,000 |
| Retained earnings | 50,000 | 38,000 |
| Total | $111,000 | $108,000 |

### Warner Company
### Income Statement
### For the Year Ended December 31, 2022

|  |  |  |
|---|---|---|
| Sales revenue | | $242,000 |
| Cost of goods sold | | 175,000 |
| Gross profit | | 67,000 |
| Selling expenses | $18,000 | |
| Administrative expenses | 6,000 | 24,000 |
| Income from operations | | 43,000 |
| Interest experse | | 3,000 |
| Income before income taxes | | 40,000 |
| Income tax expense | | 8,000 |
| Net income | | $ 32,000 |

Additional data:

1. Depreciation expense was $17,500.
2. Dividends declared and paid were $20,000.
3. During the year, equipment was sold for $8,500 cash. This equipment originally cost $18,000 and had accumulated depreciation of $9,500 at the time of sale.
4. Bonds were redeemed at their carrying value.
5. Common stock was issued at par for cash.

## Instructions

a. Prepare a statement of cash flows using the indirect method.
b. Compute free cash flow.

a. Net cash provided—
oper. act.     $38,500

*Prepare a statement of cash flows—direct method, and compute free cash flow.*

 Excel

*Prepare a statement of cash flows—indirect method.*

a. Net cash provided—
   oper. act.          $38,500

**\*P12.8 (LO 3, 4), AP** Data for Warner Company are presented in P12.7. Further analysis reveals the following.

1. Accounts payable pertain to merchandise suppliers.
2. All operating expenses except for depreciation were paid in cash.
3. All depreciation expense is in the selling expense category.
4. All sales and inventory purchases are on account.

**Instructions**

a. Prepare a statement of cash flows for Warner Company using the direct method.
b. Compute free cash flow.

**P12.9 (LO 2), AP** Condensed financial data of Granger Inc. follow.

**Granger Inc.**
**Comparative Balance Sheets**
**December 31**

| | 2022 | 2021 |
|---|---|---|
| **Assets** | | |
| Cash | $ 80,800 | $ 48,400 |
| Accounts receivable | 87,800 | 38,000 |
| Inventory | 112,500 | 102,850 |
| Prepaid expenses | 28,400 | 26,000 |
| Long-term investments | 138,000 | 109,000 |
| Plant assets | 285,000 | 242,500 |
| Accumulated depreciation | (50,000) | (52,000) |
| Total | $682,500 | $514,750 |
| **Liabilities and Stockholders' Equity** | | |
| Accounts payable | $102,000 | $ 67,300 |
| Accrued expenses payable | 16,500 | 21,000 |
| Bonds payable | 110,000 | 146,000 |
| Common stock | 220,000 | 175,000 |
| Retained earnings | 234,000 | 105,450 |
| Total | $682,500 | $514,750 |

**Granger Inc.**
**Income Statement Data**
**For the Year Ended December 31, 2022**

| | | |
|---|---|---|
| Sales revenue | | $388,460 |
| Less: | | |
| Cost of goods sold | $135,460 | |
| Operating expenses, excluding depreciation | 12,410 | |
| Depreciation expense | 46,500 | |
| Income tax expense | 27,280 | |
| Interest expense | 4,730 | |
| Loss on disposal of plant assets | 7,500 | 233,880 |
| Net income | | $154,580 |

Additional information:

1. New plant assets costing $100,000 were purchased for cash during the year.
2. Old plant assets having an original cost of $57,500 and accumulated depreciation of $48,500 were sold for $1,500 cash.
3. Bonds payable matured and were paid off at face value for cash.
4. A cash dividend of $26,030 was declared and paid during the year.
5. Common stock was issued at par for cash.
6. There were no significant noncash transactions.

Net cash provided—
   oper. act.         $176,930

*Prepare a statement of cash flows—direct method.*

**Instructions**

Prepare a statement of cash flows using the indirect method.

**\*P12.10 (LO 4), AP** Data for Granger Inc. are presented in P12.9. Further analysis reveals that accounts payable pertain to merchandise creditors.

**Instructions**

Prepare a statement of cash flows for Granger Inc. using the direct method.

**P12.11 (LO 2), AP** The comparative balance sheets for Spicer Company as of December 31 are as follows.

Net cash provided—
   oper. act.          $176,930

*Prepare a statement of cash flows—indirect method.*

**Spicer Company**
**Comparative Balance Sheets**
**December 31**

|  | 2022 | 2021 |
|---|---|---|
| **Assets** | | |
| Cash | $ 68,000 | $ 45,000 |
| Accounts receivable | 50,000 | 58,000 |
| Inventory | 151,450 | 142,000 |
| Prepaid expenses | 15,280 | 21,000 |
| Land | 145,000 | 130,000 |
| Buildings | 200,000 | 200,000 |
| Accumulated depreciation—buildings | (60,000) | (40,000) |
| Equipment | 225,000 | 155,000 |
| Accumulated depreciation—equipment | (45,000) | (35,000) |
| Total | $749,730 | $676,000 |
| **Liabilities and Stockholders' Equity** | | |
| Accounts payable | $ 44,730 | $ 36,000 |
| Bonds payable | 300,000 | 300,000 |
| Common stock, $1 par | 200,000 | 160,000 |
| Retained earnings | 205,000 | 180,000 |
| Total | $749,730 | $676,000 |

Additional information:

1. Operating expenses include depreciation expense of $42,000 ($20,000 of depreciation expense for buildings and $22,000 for equipment).
2. Land was sold for cash at book value.
3. Cash dividends of $12,000 were declared and paid.
4. Net income for 2022 was $37,000.
5. Equipment was purchased for $92,000 cash. In addition, equipment costing $22,000 with a book value of $10,000 was sold for $8,000 cash.
6. 40,000 shares of $1 par value common stock were issued in exchange for land with a fair value of $40,000.

**Instructions**

Prepare a statement of cash flows for the year ended December 31, 2022, using the indirect method.

Net cash provided—
   oper. act.          $94,000

*Prepare a worksheet—indirect method.*

 Excel

**\*P12.12 (LO 5), AP** Condensed financial data of Oakley Company are as follows.

**Oakley Company**
**Comparative Balance Sheets**
**December 31**

|  | 2022 | 2021 |
|---|---|---|
| **Assets** | | |
| Cash | $ 82,700 | $ 47,250 |
| Accounts receivable | 90,800 | 57,000 |
| Inventory | 126,900 | 102,650 |
| Investments | 84,500 | 87,000 |
| Equipment | 255,000 | 205,000 |
| Accumulated depreciation—equipment | (49,500) | (40,000) |
|  | $590,400 | $458,900 |
| **Liabilities and Stockholders' Equity** | | |
| Accounts payable | $ 57,700 | $ 48,280 |
| Accrued expenses payable | 12,100 | 18,830 |
| Bonds payable | 100,000 | 70,000 |
| Common stock | 250,000 | 200,000 |
| Retained earnings | 170,600 | 121,790 |
|  | $590,400 | $458,900 |

**Oakley Company**
**Income Statement**
**For the Year Ended December 31, 2022**

| | | |
|---|---:|---:|
| Sales revenue | | $297,500 |
| Gain on disposal of plant assets | | 8,750 |
| | | 306,250 |
| Less: | | |
| Cost of goods sold | $99,460 | |
| Operating expenses (excluding depreciation expense) | 14,670 | |
| Depreciation expense | 49,700 | |
| Income tax expense | 7,270 | |
| Interest expense | 2,940 | 174,040 |
| Net income | | $132,210 |

Additional information:

1. Equipment costing $97,000 was purchased for cash during the year.

2. Investments were sold at their carrying value.

3. Equipment costing $47,000 was sold for $15,550, resulting in a gain of $8,750.

4. A cash dividend of $83,400 was declared and paid during the year.

Reconciling items total
$610,210

**Instructions**

Prepare a worksheet for the statement of cash flows using the indirect method. Enter the reconciling items directly in the worksheet columns, using letters to cross-reference each entry.

## Continuing Case

### Cookie Creations

(*Note:* This is a continuation of the Cookie Creations case from Chapters 1 through 11.)

**CC12** Natalie has prepared the balance sheet and income statement of Cookie & Coffee Creations Inc. and would like you to prepare the statement of cash flows.

*Go to WileyPLUS for complete case details and instructions.*

leungchopan/
Shutterstock.com

## Data Analytics in Action

### Using Data Visualization to Analyze Cash Flows

**DA12.1** Data visualization can be used to illustrate cash flows.

**Example:** Consider the *Accounting Across the Organization* box "Burning Through Our Cash" presented in the chapter. The three tech companies listed, **Box**, **FireEye**, and **MobileIron**, have all issued stock to the public. As mentioned, prior to making investments in these companies, the investors most likely closely examined each respective company's cash flows. The investors want to be sure that these companies are able to generate enough cash to satisfy liabilities, pay dividends, and grow the company.

We can use data visualization to understand the pattern of cash flows for companies such as these. For example, consider the following chart.

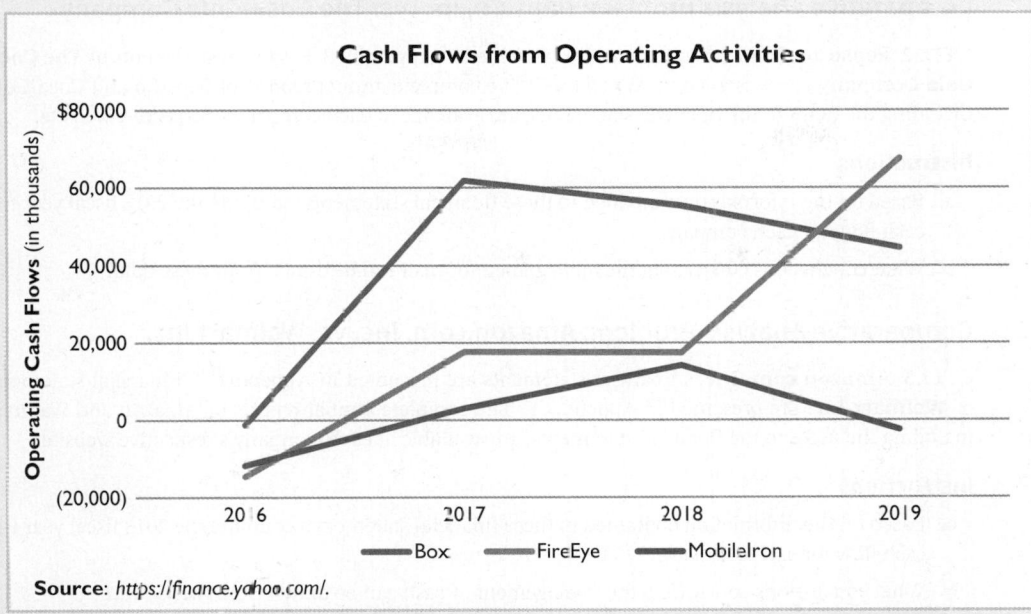

**Cash Flows from Operating Activities**

**Source:** *https://finance.yahoo.com/.*

FireEye has an upward sloping trajectory, making its operating cash flows appear more promising than the others. Box's operating cash flows have the steepest downward trend beginning in 2017, making it the company with the biggest concerns. MobileIron had a steady increase for the first two years but has taken a recent downturn, making it a second company that investors should monitor closely.

For this case, you will look more closely at the statement of cash flow data for these three companies. You will then create and analyze clustered column charts to determine what helpful information these visualizations might provide to investors.

*Go to WileyPLUS for complete case details and instructions.*

### Using Data Analytics to Evaluate Industry Cash Flows

**DA12.2**  By evaluating the cash flows of top competitors within an industry, financial statement users can make certain generalizations about that industry overall. This will help them to better analyze the cash flows of another company within that industry. For this case, you will use cash flow information from four leading pharmaceutical companies to create and analyze waterfall charts, to then make generalizations about this industry's cash flows

*Go to WileyPLUS for complete case details and instructions.*

## Expand Your Critical Thinking

### Financial Reporting Problem: Apple Inc.

**CT12.1**  The financial statements of **Apple Inc.** are presented in Appendix A.

### Instructions

Answer the following questions.

a. What was the amount of net cash provided by operating activities for the year ended September 29, 2018? For the year ended September 30, 2017?

b. What was the amount of increase or decrease in cash and cash equivalents for the year ended September 29, 2018?

c. Which method of computing net cash provided by operating activities does Apple use?

d. From your analysis of the September 29, 2018, statement of cash flows, was the change in accounts receivable a decrease or an increase? Was the change in inventories a decrease or an increase? Was the change in accounts payable a decrease or an increase?

e. What was the net cash provided (generated) by investing activities for the year ended September 29, 2018?

f. What was the amount of interest paid in the year ended September 29, 2018? What was the amount of income taxes paid for the same period?

## Comparative Analysis Problem: PepsiCo, Inc. vs. The Coca-Cola Company

**CT12.2 PepsiCo**'s financial statements are presented in Appendix B. Financial statements of **The Coca-Cola Company** are presented in Appendix C. The complete annual reports of PepsiCo and Coca-Cola, including the notes to the financial statements, are available at each company's respective website.

### Instructions

**a.** Based on the information contained in these financial statements, compute the 2018 fiscal year free cash flow for each company.

**b.** What conclusions concerning the management of cash can be drawn from these data?

## Comparative Analysis Problem: Amazon.com, Inc. vs. Walmart Inc.

**CT12.3 Amazon.com, Inc.**'s financial statements are presented in Appendix D. Financial statements of **Walmart Inc.** are presented in Appendix E. The complete annual reports of Amazon and Walmart, including the notes to the financial statements, are available at each company's respective website.

### Instructions

**a.** Based on the information contained in these financial statements, compute the 2018 fiscal year free cash flow for each company.

**b.** What conclusions concerning the management of cash can be drawn from these data?

## Decision-Making Across the Organization

**CT12.4** Pete Kent and Maria Robles are examining the following statement of cash flows for Sullivan Company for the year ended January 31, 2022.

**Sullivan Company**
**Statement of Cash Flows**
**For the Year Ended January 31, 2022**

| | |
|---|---:|
| Sources of cash | |
| From sales of merchandise | $385,000 |
| From sale of capital stock | 405,000 |
| From sale of investment (purchased below) | 80,000 |
| From depreciation | 55,000 |
| From issuance of note for truck | 20,000 |
| From interest on investments | 6,000 |
| Total sources of cash | 951,000 |
| | |
| Uses of cash | |
| For purchase of fixtures and equipment | $320,000 |
| For merchandise purchased for resale | 258,000 |
| For operating expenses (including depreciation) | 170,000 |
| For purchase of investment | 75,000 |
| For purchase of truck by issuance of note | 20,000 |
| For purchase of treasury stock | 10,000 |
| For interest on note payable | 3,000 |
| Total uses of cash | 856,000 |
| Net increase in cash | $ 95,000 |

Pete claims that Sullivan's statement of cash flows is an excellent portrayal of a superb first year, with cash increasing $95,000. Maria replies that it was not a superb first year. Rather, she says, the year was an operating failure, the statement is presented incorrectly, and $95,000 is not the actual increase in cash. The cash balance at the beginning of the year was $140,000.

### Instructions

With the class divided into groups, answer the following.

**a.** Using the data provided, prepare a statement of cash flows in proper form using the indirect method. The only noncash items in the income statement are depreciation and the gain from the sale of the investment.

**b.** With whom do you agree, Pete or Maria? Explain your position.

## Real-World Focus

**CT12.5** Purpose: Learn about the **Securities and Exchange Commission (SEC)**.

**Instructions**

Go to the SEC website, choose **About**, and then answer the following questions.

a. How many enforcement actions does the SEC take each year against securities law violators? What are typical infractions?

b. After the Depression, Congress passed the Securities Acts of 1933 and 1934 to improve investor confidence in the markets. What two "common sense" notions are these laws based on?

c. Who was the president of the United States at the time of the creation of the SEC? Who was the first SEC chairperson?

**CT12.6** You can use the Internet to view **SEC** filings.

**Instructions**

Choose a company, go to the **Yahoo! Finance** website, and then answer the following questions.

a. What company did you select?

b. What is its stock symbol? What is its selling price?

c. What recent SEC filings are available for your viewing? (*Hint:* Use the Profile link.)

d. Which filing is the most recent? What is its date?

## Communication Activity

**CT12.7** Walt Jax, the owner-president of Computer Services Company, is unfamiliar with the statement of cash flows that you, as his accountant, prepared. He asks for further explanation.

**Instructions**

Write him a brief memo explaining the form and content of the statement of cash flows as shown in Illustration 12.14.

## Ethics Case

**CT12.8** Pendleton Automotive Corp. is a medium-sized wholesaler of automotive parts. It has 10 stockholders who have been paid a total of $1 million in cash dividends for 8 consecutive years. The board's policy requires that, for this dividend to be declared, net cash provided by operating activities as reported in Pendleton Automotive's current year's statement of cash flows must exceed $1 million. President and CEO Hans Pfizer's job is secure so long as he produces annual operating cash flows to support the usual dividend.

At the end of the current year, controller Kurt Nolte presents president Hans Pfizer with some disappointing news: The net cash provided by operating activities is calculated by the indirect method to be only $970,000. The president says to Kurt, "We must get that amount above $1 million. Isn't there some way to increase operating cash flow by another $30,000?" Kurt answers, "These figures were prepared by my assistant. I'll go back to my office and see what I can do." The president replies, "I know you won't let me down, Kurt."

Upon close scrutiny of the statement of cash flows, Kurt concludes that he can get the operating cash flows above $1 million by reclassifying the proceeds from the $60,000, 2-year note payable listed in the financing activities section as "Proceeds from bank loan—$60,000." He will report the note instead as "Increase in payables—$60,000" and treat it as an adjustment to net income in the operating activities section. He returns to the president, saying, "You can tell the board to declare their usual dividend. Our net cash flow provided by operating activities is $1,030,000." "Good man, Kurt! I knew I could count on you," exults the president.

**Instructions**

a. Who are the stakeholders in this situation?

b. Was there anything unethical about the president's actions? Was there anything unethical about the controller's actions?

c. Are the board members or anyone else likely to discover the misclassification?

## All About You

**CT12.9** In this chapter, you learned that companies prepare a statement of cash flows in order to keep track of their sources and uses of cash and to help them plan for their future cash needs. Planning for short- and long-term cash needs is every bit as important for you as it is for a company.

**Instructions**

Read the online article "Financial Uh-Oh? No Problem" and then complete the following. To access this article, it may be necessary to register at no cost.

    **a.** Describe the three factors that determine how much money you should set aside for short-term needs.

    **b.** How many months of living expenses does the article suggest to set aside?

    **c.** Estimate how much you should set aside based upon your current situation. Are you closer to Cliff's scenario or to Prudence's?

## FASB Codification Activity

**CT12.10** If your school has a subscription to the FASB Codification, log in and prepare responses to the following. Use the Master Glossary to determine the proper definitions.

    **a.** What are cash equivalents?

    **b.** What are financing activities?

    **c.** What are investing activities?

    **d.** What are operating activities?

    **e.** What is the primary objective for the statement of cash flow? Is working capital the basis for meeting this objective?

    **f.** Do companies need to disclose information about investing and financing activities that do not affect cash receipts or cash payments? If so, how should such information be disclosed?

## Answers to Insight and Accounting Across the Organization Questions

**New *What*? Q:** In general, why do differences exist between net income and net cash provided by operating activities? **A:** The differences are explained by differences in the timing of the reporting of revenues and expenses under accrual accounting versus cash. Under accrual accounting, companies report revenues when the performance obligation is satisfied, even if cash has not been received, and they report expenses when incurred, even if cash has not been paid.

**Burning Through Our Cash Q:** What implications does a company's cash burn rate have for its survival? **A:** The cash burn rate is measured by the amount that cash disbursements exceed cash receipts during a year. If a company does not have a sufficient cash cushion to weather such bad times, it will be unable to pay its liabilities as they come due and will cease to exist.

# A Look at IFRS

> **LEARNING OBJECTIVE 7**
> Compare the procedures for the statement of cash flows under GAAP and IFRS.

As in GAAP, the statement of cash flows is a required statement for IFRS. In addition, the content and presentation of an IFRS statement of cash flows is similar to the one used for GAAP. However, the disclosure requirements related to the statement of cash flows are more extensive under GAAP. *IAS 7* ("Cash Flow Statements") provides the overall IFRS requirements for cash flow information.

## Key Points

Following are the key similarities and differences between GAAP and IFRS as related to the statement of cash flows.

**Similarities**

- Companies preparing financial statements under IFRS must also prepare a statement of cash flows as an integral part of the financial statements.

- Both IFRS and GAAP require that the statement of cash flows have three major sections—operating, investing, and financing activities—along with changes in cash and cash equivalents.

- Similar to GAAP, the statement of cash flows can be prepared using either the indirect or direct method under IFRS. In both U.S. and international settings, companies choose for the most part to use the indirect method for reporting net cash flows from operating activities.

- The definition of cash equivalents used in IFRS is similar to that used in GAAP. A major difference is that in certain situations, bank overdrafts are considered part of cash and cash equivalents under IFRS (which is not the case in GAAP). Under GAAP, bank overdrafts are classified as financing activities in the statement of cash flows and are reported as liabilities on the balance sheet.

### Differences

- IFRS requires that noncash investing and financing activities be excluded from the statement of cash flows. Instead, these noncash activities should be reported elsewhere. This requirement is interpreted to mean that noncash investing and financing activities should be disclosed in the notes to the financial statements instead of in the financial statements. Under GAAP, companies may present this information on the face of the statement of cash flows.

- One area where there can be substantial differences between IFRS and GAAP relates to the classification of interest dividends, and taxes. The following table indicates the differences between the two approaches.

| Item | IFRS | GAAP |
|---|---|---|
| Interest paid | Operating or financing | Operating |
| Interest received | Operating or investing | Operating |
| Dividends paid | Operating or financing | Financing |
| Dividends received | Operating or investing | Operating |
| Taxes paid | Operating—unless specific identification with financing or investing activity | Operating |

- Under IFRS, some companies present the operating section in a single line item, with a full reconciliation provided in the notes to the financial statements. This presentation is not seen under GAAP.

# IFRS Practice

## IFRS Self-Test Questions

1. Under IFRS, interest paid can be reported as:
   a. only a financing activity.
   b. a financing activity or an investing activity
   c. a financing activity or an operating activity.
   d. only an operating activity.

2. IFRS requires that noncash items:
   a. be reported in the section to which they relate, that is, a noncash investing activity would be reported in the investing section.
   b. be disclosed in the notes to the financial statements.
   c. do not need to be reported.
   d. be treated in a fashion similar to cash equivalents.

3. Under IFRS:
   a. taxes are always treated as an operating activity.
   b. the income statement uses the headings operating, investing, and financing.
   c. dividends received can be either an operating or investing activity.
   d. dividends paid can be either an operating or investing activity.

4. Which of the following is **correct?**
   a. Under IFRS, the statement of cash flows is optional.
   b. IFRS requires use of the direct method in preparing the statement of cash flows.
   c. The majority of companies following GAAP and the majority following IFRS employ the indirect method to the statement of cash flows.
   d. Under IFRS, companies offset financing activities against investing activities.

## IFRS Exercises

**IFRS12.1** Discuss the differences that exist in the treatment of bank overdrafts under GAAP and IFRS.

**IFRS12.2** Describe the treatment of each of the following items under IFRS versus GAAP.

    **a.** Interest paid               **c.** Dividends paid.

    **b.** Interest received        **d.** Dividends received.

## International Financial Reporting Problem: Louis Vuitton

**IFRS12.3** The financial statements of **Louis Vuitton** are presented in Appendix F. The complete consolidated financial statements, including the notes to its financial statements, are available at the company's website.

### Instructions

Use the company's 2018 consolidated cash flow statement to answer the following questions.

    **a.** In which section (operating, investing, or financing) does Louis Vuitton report interest paid (finance costs)?

    **b.** In which section (operating, investing, or financing) does Louis Vuitton report dividends received?

    **c.** If Louis Vuitton reported under GAAP rather than IFRS, how would its treatment of bank overdrafts differ?

### Answers to IFRS Self-Test Questions

**1.** c    **2.** b    **3.** c    **4.** c

# Financial Analysis: The Big Picture

## Chapter Preview

We can all learn an important lesson from Warren Buffett: Study companies carefully if you wish to invest. Do not get caught up in fads but instead find companies that are financially healthy. Using some of the basic decision tools presented in this text, you can perform a rudimentary analysis on any company and draw basic conclusions about its financial health. Although it would not be wise for you to bet your life savings on a company's stock relying solely on your current level of knowledge, we strongly encourage you to practice your new skills wherever possible. Only with practice will you improve your ability to interpret financial numbers.

Before we unleash you on the world of high finance, we present a few more important concepts and techniques as well as one more comprehensive review of corporate financial statements. We use all of the decision tools presented in this text to analyze a single company, with comparisons to a competitor and industry averages.

# Feature Story

## It Pays to Be Patient

A recent issue of *Forbes* magazine listed Warren Buffett as the second richest person in the world. His estimated wealth was $69 billion, give or take a few million. How much is $69 billion? If you invested $69 billion in an investment earning just 4%, you could spend $7.6 million per day—every day—forever.

So, how does Buffett spend his money? Basically, he doesn't! He still lives in the same house that he purchased in Omaha, Nebraska, in 1958 for $31,500. He still drives his own car (a Cadillac DTS). And, in case you were thinking that his kids are riding the road to Easy Street, think again. Buffett has committed to donate virtually all of his money to charity before he dies.

How did Buffett amass this wealth? Through careful investing. Buffett epitomizes a "value investor." He applies the basic techniques he learned in the 1950s from the great value investor Benjamin Graham. He looks for companies that have good long-term potential but are currently underpriced. He invests in companies that have low exposure to debt and that reinvest their earnings for future growth. He does not get caught up in fads or the latest trends.

For example, Buffett sat out on the dot-com mania in the 1990s. When other investors put lots of money into fledgling high-tech firms, Buffett didn't bite because he did not find dot-com companies that met his criteria. He didn't get to enjoy the stock price boom on the way up, but on the other hand, he didn't have to ride the price back down to Earth. When the dot-com bubble burst, everyone else was suffering from investment shock. Buffett swooped in and scooped up deals on companies that he had been following for years.

In 2012, the stock market had again reached near record highs. Buffett's returns had been significantly lagging the market. Only 26% of his investments at that time were in stock, and he was sitting on $38 billion in cash. One commentator noted that "if the past is any guide, just when Buffett seems to look most like a loser, the party is about to end."

If you think you want to follow Buffett's example and transform your humble nest egg into a mountain of cash, be warned. His techniques have been widely circulated and emulated, but never practiced with the same degree of success. You should probably start by honing your financial analysis skills. A good way for you to begin your career as a successful investor is to master the fundamentals of financial analysis discussed in this chapter.

**Source:** Jason Zweig, "Buffett Is Out of Step," *Wall Street Journal* (May 7, 2012).

# Chapter Outline

| LEARNING OBJECTIVES | REVIEW | PRACTICE |
|---|---|---|
| **LO 1**  Apply the concepts of sustainable income and quality of earnings. | • Sustainable income<br>• Quality of earnings | **DO IT!  1**  Unusual Items |
| **LO 2**  Apply horizontal analysis and vertical analysis. | • Horizontal analysis<br>• Vertical analysis | **DO IT!  2**  Horizontal Analysis |
| **LO 3**  Analyze a company's performance using ratio analysis. | • Liquidity ratios<br>• Solvency ratios<br>• Profitability ratios<br>• Financial analysis and data analytics<br>• Comprehensive example | **DO IT!  3**  Ratio Analysis |

**Go to the Review and Practice section at the end of the chapter for a targeted summary and practice applications with solutions.**

**Visit WileyPLUS for additional tutorials and practice opportunities.**

# Sustainable Income and Quality of Earnings

**LEARNING OBJECTIVE 1**

Apply the concepts of sustainable income and quality of earnings.

## Sustainable Income

The value of a company like **Google** is a function of the amount, timing, and uncertainty of its future cash flows. Google's current and past income statements are particularly useful in helping analysts predict these future cash flows. In using this approach, analysts must make sure that Google's past income numbers reflect its **sustainable income**, that is, they do not include unusual (out-of-the-ordinary) revenues, expenses, gains, and losses.

**Sustainable income** is, therefore, the most likely level of income to be obtained by a company in the future. Sustainable income differs from actual net income by the amount of unusual revenues, expenses, gains, and losses included in the current year's income. Determining sustainable income requires an understanding of discontinued operations, comprehensive income, and changes in accounting principle. Analysts are interested in sustainable income because it helps them derive an estimate of future earnings without the "noise" of unusual items.

### Discontinued Operations

**Discontinued operations** refers to the disposal of a **significant component** of a business, such as the elimination of a major class of customers or an entire activity. For example, to downsize its operations, **General Dynamics Corp.** sold its missile business to **Hughes Aircraft Co.** for $450 million. In its income statement, General Dynamics reported the sale in a separate section entitled "Discontinued operations."

When a company has discontinued operations, the company should report on its income statement both income from continuing operations and income (or loss) from discontinued operations. **The income (loss) from discontinued operations consists of two parts: the income (loss) from operations of the component and the gain (loss) on disposal of the component.** The income from continuing operations as well as the discontinued component are reported net of tax.

To illustrate, assume that during 2022 Acro Energy Inc. has income before income taxes of $800,000. During 2022, Acro discontinued and sold its unprofitable chemical division. The loss in 2022 from the chemical division's operations (net of $60,000 taxes) was $140,000. The loss on disposal of the chemical division (net of $30,000 taxes) was $70,000. Assuming a 20% tax rate on income, **Illustration 13.1** shows Acro's income statement (see **Helpful Hint**).

Note that the statement uses the caption "Income from continuing operations" and adds a new section "Discontinued operations." **The new section reports both the operating loss and the loss on disposal net of applicable income taxes.** This presentation clearly indicates the separate effects of continuing operations and discontinued operations on net income.

**ILLUSTRATION 13.1**

**Income statement**

**HELPFUL HINT**

Observe the dual disclosures: (1) the results of operation of the discontinued division must be separated from the results of continuing operations, and (2) the company must also report the gain or loss on disposal of the division.

| Acro Energy Inc. | | |
|---|---|---|
| Income Statement (partial) | | |
| For the Year Ended December 31, 2022 | | |
| Income before income taxes | | $800,000 |
| Income tax expense | | 160,000 |
| Income from continuing operations | | 640,000 |
| **Discontinued operations** | | |
| Loss from operation of chemical division, net of $40,000 income tax savings | $160,000 | |
| Loss from disposal of chemical division, net of $20,000 income tax savings | 80,000 | (240,000) |
| Net income | | $400,000 |

## Investor Insight

### What Does "Non-Recurring" Really Mean?

iStock.com/Andrey Armiagov

Many companies incur restructuring charges as they attempt to reduce costs. They often label these items in the income statement as "non-recurring" charges, to suggest that they are isolated events, unlikely to occur in future periods. The question for analysts is, are these costs really one-time, "non-recurring events" or do they reflect problems that the company will be facing for many periods in the future? If they are one-time events, then they can be largely ignored when trying to predict future earnings.

But, some companies report "one-time" restructuring charges over and over again. For example, **Procter & Gamble** reported a restructuring charge in 12 consecutive quarters, and **Motorola** had "special" charges in 14 consecutive quarters. On the other hand, other companies have a restructuring charge only once in a 5- or 10-year period. There appears to be no substitute for careful analysis of the numbers that comprise net income.

**If a company takes a large restructuring charge, what is the effect on the company's current income statement versus future ones? (Answer is available near the end of the chapter.)**

## Comprehensive Income

Most revenues, expenses, gains, and losses are included in net income. However, as discussed in earlier chapters, certain gains and losses that bypass net income are reported as part of a more inclusive earnings measure called comprehensive income. **Comprehensive income** is the sum of net income and other comprehensive income items.[1]

**Illustration of Comprehensive Income** Accounting standards require that companies adjust most investments in stocks and bonds up or down to their market price at the end of each accounting period. For example, assume that during 2022, its first year of operations, Stassi Corporation purchased **IBM** bonds for $10,500 as an investment, which it intends to sell sometime in the future. At the end of 2022, Stassi was still holding the investment, but the bonds' market price was now $8,000. In this case, Stassi is required to reduce the recorded value of its IBM investment by $2,500. The $2,500 difference is an "unrealized" loss. A gain or loss is referred to as unrealized when an asset has experienced a change in value but the owner has not sold the asset. The sale of the asset results in "realization" of the gain or loss.

---

[1]The FASB's Conceptual Framework describes comprehensive income as including all changes in stockholders' equity during a period except those changes resulting from investments by stockholders and distributions to stockholders.

Should Stassi include this $2,500 unrealized loss in net income? It depends on whether Stassi classifies the IBM bonds as a trading security or an available-for-sale security. A **trading security** is bought and held primarily for sale in the near term to generate income on short-term price differences. Companies report unrealized losses on trading securities in the "Other expenses and losses" section of the income statement. The rationale: It is likely that the company will realize the unrealized loss (or an unrealized gain), so the company should report the loss (gain) as part of net income.

If Stassi did not purchase the investment for trading purposes, it is classified as available-for-sale. **Available-for-sale securities** are held with the intent of selling them sometime in the future. Companies do not include unrealized gains or losses on available-for-sale securities in net income. Instead, they report them as part of "Other comprehensive income," which is not included in net income.

**Format** Companies report other comprehensive income in a separate statement of comprehensive income. For example, assuming that Stassi Corporation has a net income of $300,000 and a 20% tax rate, the unrealized loss would be reported below net income, net of tax, as shown in **Illustration 13.2**.

**ILLUSTRATION 13.2**
**Statement of comprehensive income**

### Stassi Corporation
#### Statement of Comprehensive Income
#### For the Year Ended December 31, 2022

| | |
|---|---|
| Net income | $300,000 |
| Other comprehensive income | |
| Unrealized loss on available-for-sale securities, net of $500 income tax savings | 2,000 |
| Comprehensive income | $298,000 |

Companies report the cumulative amount of other comprehensive income from all years as a separate component of stockholders' equity. To illustrate, assume Stassi has common stock of $3,000,000, retained earnings of $300,000, and accumulated other comprehensive loss of $2,000. (To simplify, we are assuming that this is Stassi's first year of operations. Since it has only operated for one year, the cumulative amount of other comprehensive income is this year's loss of $2,000.) **Illustration 13.3** shows the balance sheet presentation of the accumulated other comprehensive loss.

**ILLUSTRATION 13.3**
**Accumulated other comprehensive loss in stockholders' equity section**

### Stassi Corporation
#### Balance Sheet (partial)

| | |
|---|---|
| Stockholders' equity | |
| Common stock | $3,000,000 |
| Retained earnings | 300,000 |
| Total paid-in capital and retained earnings | 3,300,000 |
| **Accumulated other comprehensive loss** | **2,000** |
| Total stockholders' equity | $3,298,000 |

Note that the presentation of the accumulated other comprehensive loss is similar to the presentation of the cost of treasury stock in the stockholders' equity section. (Accumulated unrealized gains would be added in this section of the balance sheet.)

**Income Statement and Statement of Comprehensive Income** As discussed, many companies report net income and other comprehensive income in separate statements, such as those shown for Pace Corporation in **Illustration 13.4**.

**ILLUSTRATION 13.4**

Income statement and statement of comprehensive income

### Pace Corporation
#### Income Statement
#### For the Year Ended December 31, 2022

| | | |
|---|---:|---:|
| Net sales | | $440,000 |
| Cost of goods sold | | 260,000 |
| Gross profit | | 180,000 |
| Operating expenses | | 118,250 |
| Income from operations | | 61,750 |
| Other revenues and gains | | 5,600 |
| Other expenses and losses | | 9,600 |
| Income before income taxes | | 57,750 |
| Income tax expense ($57,750 × 20%) | | 11,550 |
| Income from continuing operations | | 46,200 |
| **Discontinued operations** | | |
| **Loss from operation of plastics division, net of income tax savings $18,000 ($60,000 × 20%)** | **$42,000** | |
| **Gain on disposal of plastics division, net of $15,000 income taxes ($50,000 × 20%)** | 35,000 | 7,000 |
| Net income | | $39,200 |

### Pace Corporation
#### Statement of Comprehensive Income
#### For the Year Ended December 31, 2022

| | |
|---|---:|
| Net income | $39,200 |
| **Other comprehensive income** | |
| **Unrealized gain on available-for-sale securities, net of income taxes ($15,000 × 20%)** | 10,500 |
| **Comprehensive income** | **$49,700** |

Note how the income statement shown in Illustration 13.4 presents the types of items usually found on this statement, such as net sales, cost of goods sold, operating expenses, and income taxes. Together, the income statement and statement of comprehensive income show how companies report discontinued operations and other comprehensive income (highlighted in red).

## Changes in Accounting Principle

For ease of comparison, users of financial statements expect companies to prepare their statements on a basis **consistent** with the preceding period. A **change in accounting principle** occurs when the principle used in the current year is different from the one used in the preceding year. An example is a change in inventory costing methods (such as FIFO to average-cost). Accounting rules permit a change when management can show that the new principle is preferable to the old principle.

Companies report most changes in accounting principle retroactively.[2] That is, they report the results from both the current period and previous periods using the new principle. Thus, the same principle is used in all periods. This treatment improves the ability to compare financial performance across years.

---

---

# Quality of Earnings

The quality of a company's earnings is of extreme importance to analysts. A company that has a high **quality of earnings** provides full and transparent information that will not confuse or mislead users of the financial statements.

Recent accounting scandals suggest that some companies are spending too much time managing their income and not enough time managing their business. Here are some of the factors affecting the quality of earnings.

## Alternative Accounting Methods

Variations among companies in the application of generally accepted accounting principles (GAAP) may hamper comparability and reduce quality of earnings. For example, suppose one company uses the FIFO method of inventory costing, while another company in the same industry uses LIFO. If inventory is a significant asset to both companies, it is unlikely that their current ratios are comparable. For example, if **General Motors Corporation** used FIFO instead of LIFO for inventory valuation, its inventories in a recent year would have been 26% higher, which significantly affects the current ratio (and other ratios as well).

In addition to differences in inventory costing methods, differences also exist in reporting such items as depreciation and amortization. Although these differences in accounting methods might be detectable from reading the notes to the financial statements, adjusting the financial data to compensate for the different methods is often difficult, if not impossible.

## Pro Forma Income

Companies whose stock is publicly traded are required to present their income statement following GAAP. In recent years, many companies have been also reporting a second measure of

---

[2]An exception to the general rule is a change in depreciation methods. The effects of this change are reported prospectively in current and future periods. Discussion of this approach is left for more advanced courses.

income, called pro forma income. **Pro forma income** usually excludes items that the company considers unusual or non-recurring.

For example, in a recent year, **Cisco Systems** (a high-tech company) reported a quarterly net loss under GAAP of $2.7 billion. Cisco reported pro forma income for the same quarter as a profit of $230 million. This large difference in profits between GAAP income numbers and pro forma income is not unusual. For example, during one nine-month period, the 100 largest companies on the Nasdaq stock exchange reported a total pro forma income of $19.1 billion but a total loss as measured by GAAP of $82.3 billion—a difference of about $100 billion!

To compute pro forma income, companies generally exclude any items they deem inappropriate for measuring their performance. Many analysts and investors are critical of the practice of using pro forma income because these numbers often make companies look better than they really are. As the financial press noted, pro forma numbers might be called "earnings before bad stuff." Companies, on the other hand, argue that pro forma numbers more clearly indicate sustainable income because they exclude unusual and non-recurring expenses. "Cisco's technique gives readers of financial statements a clear picture of Cisco's normal business activities," the company said in a statement issued in response to questions about its pro forma income accounting.

Recently, the SEC provided some guidance on how companies should present pro forma information. Stay tuned: Everyone seems to agree that pro forma numbers can be useful if they provide insights into determining a company's sustainable income. However, many companies have abused the flexibility that pro forma numbers allow and have used the measure as a way to put their companies in a more favorable light.

## Improper Recognition

Because some managers feel pressure from Wall Street to continually increase earnings, they manipulate earnings numbers to meet these expectations. The most common abuse is the improper recognition of revenue. One practice that some companies use is called **channel stuffing**. Offering deep discounts, companies encourage customers to buy early (stuff the channel) rather than later. This boosts the seller's earnings in the current period, but it often leads to a disaster in subsequent periods because customers have no need for additional goods. To illustrate, **Bristol-Myers Squibb** at one time indicated that it used sales incentives to encourage wholesalers to buy more drugs than they needed. As a result, the company had to issue revised financial statements showing corrected revenues and income.

Another practice is the improper capitalization of operating expenses as assets. **WorldCom** capitalized over $7 billion of operating expenses in order to report positive net income. In other situations, companies fail to report all their liabilities. **Enron** promised to make payments on certain contracts if financial difficulty developed, but these guarantees were not reported as liabilities. In addition, disclosure was so lacking in transparency that it was impossible to understand what was happening at the company.

---

**ACTION PLAN**

• Show discontinued operations and other comprehensive income net of tax.

### DO IT! 1 | Unusual Items

In its proposed 2022 income statement, AIR Corporation reports income before income taxes $400,000, unrealized gain on available-for-sale securities $100,000, income taxes $120,000 (not including unusual items), loss from operation of discontinued flower division $50,000, and loss on disposal of discontinued flower division $90,000. The income tax rate is 20%. Prepare a correct partial income statement, beginning with "Income before income taxes," and a statement of comprehensive income.

**Solution**

### AIR Corporation
#### Income Statement (partial)
#### For the Year Ended December 31, 2022

| | | |
|---|---:|---:|
| Income before income taxes | | $400,000 |
| Income tax expense | | 120,000 |
| Income from continuing operations | | 280,000 |
| Discontinued operations | | |
|   Loss from operation of flower division, | | |
|     net of $20,000 income tax savings | $20,000 | |
|   Loss on disposal of flower division, | | |
|     net of $18,000 income tax savings | 72,000 | (92,000) |
| Net income | | $188,000 |

### AIR Corporation
#### Statement of Comprehensive Income
#### For the Year Ended December 31, 2022

| | |
|---|---:|
| Net income | $188,000 |
| Other comprehensive income | |
|   Unrealized gain on available-for-sale | |
|     securities, net of $20,000 income taxes | 80,000 |
| Comprehensive income | $268,000 |

Related exercise material: **BE13.1, BE13.2, DO IT! 13.1, E13.1, and E13.2.**

# Horizontal Analysis and Vertical Analysis

### LEARNING OBJECTIVE 2
Apply horizontal analysis and vertical analysis.

In assessing the financial performance of a company, investors are interested in its core or sustainable earnings. In addition, investors are interested in making comparisons from period to period. Throughout this text, we have relied on three types of comparisons to improve the decision-usefulness of financial information:

1. **Intracompany basis.** Comparisons within a company are often useful to detect changes in financial relationships and significant trends. For example, a comparison of **Kellogg's** current year's cash amount with the prior year's cash amount shows either an increase or a decrease. Likewise, a comparison of Kellogg's year-end cash amount with the amount of its total assets at year-end shows the proportion of total assets in the form of cash.

2. **Intercompany basis.** Comparisons with other companies provide insight into a company's competitive position. For example, investors can compare Kellogg's total sales for the year with the total sales of its competitors in the breakfast cereal area, such as **General Mills**.

3. **Industry averages.** Comparisons with industry averages provide information about a company's relative position within the industry. For example, financial statement readers can compare Kellogg's financial data with the averages for its industry compiled by financial rating organizations such as **Dun & Bradstreet**, **Moody's**, and **Standard & Poor's**, or with information provided on the Internet by organizations such as **Yahoo!** on its financial site.

We use three basic tools in financial statement analysis to highlight the significance of financial statement data:

1. Horizontal analysis.
2. Vertical analysis.
3. Ratio analysis.

In previous chapters, we relied primarily on ratio analysis, supplemented with some basic horizontal and vertical analysis. In the remainder of this section, we introduce more formal forms of horizontal and vertical analysis. In the next section, we review ratio analysis in some detail.

## Horizontal Analysis

**Horizontal analysis**, also known as trend analysis, is a technique for evaluating a series of financial statement data over a period of time. Its purpose is to determine the increase or decrease that has taken place, expressed as either an amount or a percentage. For example, here are recent net sales figures (in thousands) of Chicago Cereal Company:

| 2022 | 2021 | 2020 | 2019 | 2018 |
|------|------|------|------|------|
| $11,776 | $10,907 | $10,177 | $9,614 | $8,812 |

If we assume that 2018 is the base year, we can measure all percentage increases or decreases relative to this base-period amount with the formula shown in **Illustration 13.5**.

$$\text{Change Since Base Period} = \frac{\text{Current-Year Amount} - \text{Base-Year Amount}}{\text{Base-Year Amount}}$$

Using horizontal analysis, we can determine that net sales for Chicago Cereal increased approximately 9.1% [($9,614 − $8,812) ÷ $8,812] from 2018 to 2019. Similarly, we can also determine that net sales increased by 33.6% [($11,776 − $8,812) ÷ $8,812] from 2018 to 2022.

Alternatively, we can express current-year net sales as a percentage of the base period. To do so, we divide the current-year amount by the base-year amount, as shown in **Illustration 13.6**.

$$\text{Current Results in Relation to Base Period} = \frac{\text{Current-Year Amount}}{\text{Base-Year Amount}}$$

Current-period net sales expressed as a percentage of the base period for each of the five years, using 2018 as the base period, are shown in **Illustration 13.7**.

ILLUSTRATION 13.7
**Horizontal analysis of net sales**

## Chicago Cereal Company
### Net Sales (in thousands)
### Base Period 2018

| 2022 | 2021 | 2020 | 2019 | 2018 |
|------|------|------|------|------|
| $11,776 | $10,907 | $10,177 | $9,614 | $8,812 |
| 133.6% | 123.8% | 115.5% | 109.1% | 100% |

The large increase in net sales during 2019 would raise questions regarding possible reasons for such a significant change. Chicago Cereal's 2019 notes to the financial statements explain that the company completed an acquisition of Elf Foods Company during 2019. This major acquisition would help explain the increase in net sales highlighted by horizontal analysis.

To further illustrate horizontal analysis, we use the financial statements of Chicago Cereal Company. Its two-year condensed balance sheets for 2022 and 2021, showing dollar and percentage changes, are presented in **Illustration 13.8** (see **Helpful Hint**).

ILLUSTRATION 13.8
**Horizontal analysis of balance sheets**

**HELPFUL HINT**

When using horizontal analysis, be sure to examine both dollar amount changes and percentage changes.

## Chicago Cereal Company
### Condensed Balance Sheets
### December 31 (in thousands)

| | 2022 | 2021 | Increase (Decrease) during 2022 Amount | Percent |
|---|---|---|---|---|
| **Assets** | | | | |
| Current assets | $ 2,717 | $ 2,427 | $290 | 11.9 |
| Property, plant, and equipment (net) | 2,990 | 2,816 | 174 | 6.2 |
| Other assets | 5,690 | 5,471 | 219 | 4.0 |
| Total assets | $11,397 | $10,714 | $683 | 6.4 |
| **Liabilities and Stockholders' Equity** | | | | |
| Current liabilities | $ 4,044 | $ 4,020 | $ 24 | 0.6 |
| Long-term liabilities | 4,827 | 4,625 | 202 | 4.4 |
| Total liabilities | 8,871 | 8,645 | 226 | 2.6 |
| Stockholders' equity | | | | |
| Common stock | 493 | 397 | 96 | 24.2 |
| Retained earnings | 3,390 | 2,584 | 806 | 31.2 |
| Treasury stock (cost) | (1,357) | (912) | 445 | 48.8 |
| Total stockholders' equity | 2,526 | 2,069 | 457 | 22.1 |
| Total liabilities and stockholders' equity | $11,397 | $10,714 | $683 | 6.4 |

The comparative balance sheets show that a number of changes occurred in Chicago Cereal's financial position from 2021 to 2022. In the assets section, current assets increased $290,000, or 11.9% ($290 ÷ $2,427, in thousands), and property, plant, and equipment (net) increased $174,000, or 6.2%. Other assets increased $219,000, or 4.0%. In the liabilities section, current liabilities increased $24,000, or 0.6%, while long-term liabilities increased $202,000, or 4.4%. In the stockholders' equity section, we find that retained earnings increased $806,000, or 31.2%.

**Illustration 13.9** presents two-year comparative income statements of Chicago Cereal Company for 2022 and 2021, showing dollar and percentage changes (see **Helpful Hint**).

Horizontal analysis of income statements

The increase in the Amount column of $99 results from adding and subtracting the amounts shown. In the Percent column, the 9.9% cannot be determined by adding and subtracting the percentages shown.

### Chicago Cereal Company
#### Condensed Income Statements
#### For the Years Ended December 31 (in thousands)

| | 2022 | 2021 | Increase (Decrease) during 2022 Amount | Percent |
|---|---|---|---|---|
| Net sales | $11,776 | $10,907 | $869 | 8.0 |
| Cost of goods sold | 6,597 | 6,082 | 515 | 8.5 |
| Gross profit | 5,179 | 4,825 | 354 | 7.3 |
| Selling and administrative expenses | 3,311 | 3,059 | 252 | 8.2 |
| Income from operations | 1,868 | 1,766 | 102 | 5.8 |
| Interest expense | 321 | 294 | 27 | 9.2 |
| Income before income taxes | 1,547 | 1,472 | 75 | 5.1 |
| Income tax expense | 444 | 468 | (24) | (5.1) |
| Net income | $ 1,103 | $ 1,004 | $ 99 | 9.9 |

Horizontal analysis of the income statements shows the following changes. Net sales increased $869,000, or 8.0% ($869 ÷ $10,907, in thousands). Cost of goods sold increased $515,000, or 8.5% ($515 ÷ $6,082). Selling and administrative expenses increased $252,000, or 8.2% ($252 ÷ $3,059). Overall, gross profit increased 7.3% and net income increased 9.9%. The increase in net income can be attributed to the increase in net sales and a decrease in income tax expense.

The measurement of changes from period to period in percentages is relatively straightforward and quite useful. However, complications can result in making the computations. If an item has no value in a base year or preceding year and a value in the next year, no percentage change can be computed.

## Vertical Analysis

**Vertical analysis**, also called common-size analysis, is a technique for evaluating financial statement data that expresses each item in a financial statement as a **percentage of a base amount**. For example, on a balance sheet we might express current assets as 22% of total assets (total assets being the base amount). Or, on an income statement we might express selling expenses as 16% of net sales (net sales being the base amount).

Presented in **Illustration 13.10** are the comparative balance sheets of Chicago Cereal for 2022 and 2021, analyzed vertically. The base for the asset items is **total assets**, and the base for the liability and stockholders' equity items is **total liabilities and stockholders' equity**.

Vertical analysis of balance sheets

### Chicago Cereal Company
#### Condensed Balance Sheets
#### December 31 (in thousands)

| | 2022 Amount | Percent* | 2021 Amount | Percent* |
|---|---|---|---|---|
| **Assets** | | | | |
| Current assets | $ 2,717 | 23.8 | $ 2,427 | 22.6 |
| Property, plant, and equipment (net) | 2,990 | 26.2 | 2,816 | 26.3 |
| Other assets | 5,690 | 50.0 | 5,471 | 51.1 |
| Total assets | $11,397 | 100.0 | $10,714 | 100.0 |

| | 2022 | | 2021 | |
|---|---|---|---|---|
| | Amount | Percent* | Amount | Percent* |
| **Liabilities and Stockholders' Equity** | | | | |
| Current liabilities | $ 4,044 | 35.5 | $ 4,020 | 37.5 |
| Long-term liabilities | 4,827 | 42.4 | 4,625 | 43.2 |
| Total liabilities | 8,871 | 77.9 | 8,645 | 80.7 |
| Stockholders' equity | | | | |
| Common stock | 493 | 4.3 | 397 | 3.7 |
| Retained earnings | 3,390 | 29.7 | 2,584 | 24.1 |
| Treasury stock (cost) | (1,357) | (11.9) | (912) | (8.5) |
| Total stockholders' equity | 2,526 | 22.1 | 2,069 | 19.3 |
| Total liabilities and stockholders' equity | $11,397 | 100.0 | $10,714 | 100.0 |

*Numbers have been rounded to total 100%.

**ILLUSTRATION 13.10**

*(continued)*

In addition to showing the relative size of each item on the balance sheets, vertical analysis can show the percentage change in the individual asset, liability, and stockholders' equity items. Current assets increased $290,000 from 2021 to 2022, and they increased from 22.6% to 23.8% of total assets. Property, plant, and equipment (net) decreased from 26.3% to 26.2% of total assets. Other assets decreased from 51.1% to 50.0% of total assets. Total stockholders' equity increased by $457,000 from 19.3% to 22.1% of total liabilities and stockholders' equity.

This switch to a higher percentage of equity financing has two causes.

1. While total liabilities increased by $226,000, the percentage of liabilities declined from 80.7% to 77.9% of total liabilities and stockholders' equity.

2. Retained earnings increased by $806,000, from 24.1% to 29.7% of total liabilities and stockholders' equity.

Thus, the company shifted toward equity financing by relying less on debt and by increasing the amount of retained earnings.

Vertical analysis of the comparative income statements of Chicago Cereal, shown in **Illustration 13.11**, reveals that cost of goods sold **as a percentage of net sales** increased

**Chicago Cereal Company**
**Condensed Income Statements**
**For the Years Ended December 31 (in thousands)**

| | 2022 | | 2021 | |
|---|---|---|---|---|
| | Amount | Percent* | Amount | Percent* |
| Net sales | $11,776 | 100.0 | $10,907 | 100.0 |
| Cost of goods sold | 6,597 | 56.0 | 6,082 | 55.8 |
| Gross profit | 5,179 | 44.0 | 4,825 | 44.2 |
| Selling and administrative expenses | 3,311 | 28.1 | 3,059 | 28.0 |
| Income from operations | 1,868 | 15.9 | 1,766 | 16.2 |
| Interest expense | 321 | 2.7 | 294 | 2.7 |
| Income before income taxes | 1,547 | 13.2 | 1,472 | 13.5 |
| Income tax expense | 444 | 3.8 | 468 | 4.3 |
| Net income | $ 1,103 | 9.4 | $ 1,004 | 9.2 |

*Numbers have been rounded to total 100%.

**ILLUSTRATION 13.11**

**Vertical analysis of income statements**

from 55.8% to 56.0%, and selling and administrative expenses increased from 28.0% to 28.1%. Net income as a percentage of net sales increased from 9.2% to 9.4%. Chicago Cereal's increase in net income as a percentage of sales is due primarily to the decrease in income tax expense as a percentage of sales.

Vertical analysis also enables you to compare companies of different sizes. For example, one of Chicago Cereal's competitors is Giant Mills. Giant Mills' sales are 1,000 times larger than those of Chicago Cereal. Vertical analysis enables us to meaningfully compare the condensed income statements of Chicago Cereal and Giant Mills, as shown in **Illustration 13.12**.

**ILLUSTRATION 13.12**

**Intercompany comparison by vertical analysis**

### Condensed Income Statements
#### For the Year Ended December 31, 2022

| | Chicago Cereal (in thousands) | | Giant Mills, Inc. (in millions) | |
|---|---|---|---|---|
| | **Amount** | **Percent*** | **Amount** | **Percent*** |
| Net sales | $11,776 | 100.0 | $17,910 | 100.0 |
| Cost of goods sold | 6,597 | 56.0 | 11,540 | 64.4 |
| Gross profit | 5,179 | 44.0 | 6,370 | 35.6 |
| Selling and administrative expenses | 3,311 | 28.1 | 3,474 | 19.4 |
| Income from operations | 1,868 | 15.9 | 2,896 | 16.2 |
| Interest expense | 321 | 2.7 | 196 | 1.1 |
| Income before income taxes | 1,547 | 13.2 | 2,700 | 15.1 |
| Income tax expense | 144 | 3.8 | 876 | 4.9 |
| Net income | $ 1,103 | 9.4 | $ 1,824 | 10.2 |

*Numbers have been rounded to total 100%.

Chicago Cereal's results are presented in thousands while those of Giant Mills are presented in millions. Vertical analysis eliminates the impact of this size difference for our analysis. Chicago Cereal has a higher gross profit percentage of 44.0%, compared to 35.6% for Giant Mills. But, Chicago Cereal's selling and administrative expenses are 28.1% of net sales, while those of Giant Mills are 19.4% of net sales. Looking at net income, we see that Chicago Cereal's net income as a percentage of net sales is 9.4%, compared to 10.2% for Giant Mills.

## Anatomy of a Fraud

Sometimes relationships between numbers can be used to detect fraud. Financial ratios that appear abnormal or statistical abnormalities in the numbers themselves can reveal fraud. For example, the fact that **WorldCom**'s line costs, as a percentage of either total expenses or revenues, differed significantly from those of its competitors should have alerted people to the possibility of fraud. Or, consider the case of a bank manager, who cooperated with a group of his friends to defraud the bank's credit card department. The manager's friends would apply for credit cards and then run up balances of slightly less than $5,000. The bank had a policy of allowing bank personnel to write off balances of less than $5,000 without seeking supervisor approval.

The fraud was detected by applying statistical analysis based on Benford's Law. Benford's Law states that in a random collection of numbers, the frequency of lower digits (e.g., 1, 2, or 3) should be much higher than that of higher digits (e.g., 7, 8, or 9). In this case, bank auditors analyzed the first two digits of amounts written off. There was a spike at 48 and 49, which was not consistent with what would be expected if the numbers were random.

**Total take: Thousands of dollars**

**The Missing Control**

**Independent internal verification.** While it might be efficient to allow employees to write off accounts below a certain level, it is important that these write-offs be reviewed and verified periodi-cally. Such a review would likely call attention to an employee with large amounts of write-offs, or in this case, write-offs that were frequently very close to the approval threshold.

**Source:** Mark J. Nigrini, "I've Got Your Number," *Journal of Accountancy Online* (May 1999).

---

## DO IT! 2 | Horizontal Analysis

Summary financial information for Rosepatch Company is as follows.

|  | December 31, 2022 | December 31, 2021 |
|---|---|---|
| Current assets | $234,000 | $180,000 |
| Plant assets (net) | 756,000 | 420,000 |
| Total assets | $990,000 | $600,000 |

Compute the amount and percentage changes in 2022 using horizontal analysis, assuming 2021 is the base year.

**Solution**

| | Increase in 2022 | |
|---|---|---|
| | **Amount** | **Percent** |
| Current assets | $ 54,000 | 30% [($234,000 − $180,000) ÷ $180,000] |
| Plant assets (net) | 336,000 | 80% [($756,000 − $420,000) ÷ $420,000] |
| Total assets | $390,000 | 65% [($990,000 − $600,000) ÷ $600,000] |

Related exercise material: **BE13.4, BE13.6, BE13.7, BE13.9, DO IT! 13.2, E13.3, E13.5, and E13.6.**

**ACTION PLAN**

• **Find the percentage change by dividing the amount of the increase by the 2021 amount (base year).**

---

# Ratio Analysis

---

**LEARNING OBJECTIVE 3**

Analyze a company's performance using ratio analysis.

---

**Ratio analysis** expresses the relationship among selected items of financial statement data. A **ratio** expresses the mathematical relationship between one quantity and another. The relationship is expressed in terms of either a percentage, a rate, or a simple proportion.

To illustrate, in a recent year, **Nike, Inc.** had current assets of $13,626 million and current liabilities of $3,926 million. We can find the relationship between these two measures by dividing current assets by current liabilities. The alternative means of expression are as follows.

**Percentage:** Current assets are 347% of current liabilities.
**Rate:** Current assets are 3.47 times current liabilities.
**Proportion:** The relationship of current assets to liabilities is 3.47:1.

To analyze the primary financial statements, we can use ratios to evaluate liquidity, solvency, and profitability. **Illustration 13.13** describes these classifications.

**Liquidity Ratios**

Measure short-term ability of the company to pay its maturing obligations and to meet unexpected needs for cash

**Solvency Ratios**

Measure the ability of the company to survive over a long period of time

**Profitability Ratios**

Measure the income or operating success of a company for a given period of time

Revenues — Expenses = Net income

Ratios can provide clues to underlying conditions that may not be apparent from individual financial statement components. However, a single ratio by itself is not very meaningful. Thus, in the discussion of ratios we will use the following types of comparisons.

1. **Intracompany comparisons** for two years for Chicago Cereal.
2. **Industry average comparisons** based on median ratios for the industry.
3. **Intercompany comparisons** based on Giant Mills as Chicago Cereal's principal competitor.

## Liquidity Ratios

**Liquidity ratios (Illustration 13.14)** measure the short-term ability of the company to pay its maturing obligations and to meet unexpected needs for cash. Short-term creditors such as bankers and suppliers are particularly interested in assessing liquidity.

**Liquidity Ratios**

1. Current ratio $\dfrac{\text{Current assets}}{\text{Current liabilities}}$

2. Inventory turnover $\dfrac{\text{Cost of goods sold}}{\text{Average inventory}}$

3. Days in inventory $\dfrac{\text{365 days}}{\text{Inventory turnover}}$

4. Accounts receivable turnover $\dfrac{\text{Net credit sales}}{\text{Average net accounts receivable}}$

5. Average collection period $\dfrac{\text{365 days}}{\text{Accounts receivable turnover}}$

## Solvency Ratios

**Solvency ratios (Illustration 13.15)** measure the ability of the company to survive over a long period of time. Long-term creditors and stockholders are interested in a company's long-run solvency, particularly its ability to pay interest as it comes due and to repay the balance of debt at its maturity.

**ILLUSTRATION 13.15**

**Summary of solvency ratios**

### Solvency Ratios

**6.** Debt to assets ratio

$$\frac{\text{Total liabilities}}{\text{Total assets}}$$

**7.** Times interest earned

$$\frac{\text{Net income} + \text{Interest expense} + \text{Income tax expense}}{\text{Interest expense}}$$

**8.** Free cash flow

$$\frac{\text{Net cash provided}}{\text{by operating activities}} - \frac{\text{Capital}}{\text{expenditures}} - \frac{\text{Cash}}{\text{dividends}}$$

## Profitability Ratios

**Profitability ratios (Illustration 13.16)** measure the income or operating success of a company for a given period of time. A company's income, or lack of it, affects its ability to obtain debt and equity financing, its liquidity position, and its ability to grow. As a consequence, creditors and investors alike are interested in evaluating profitability. Profitability is frequently used as the ultimate test of management's operating effectiveness.

**ILLUSTRATION 13.16**

**Summary of profitability ratios**

### Profitability Ratios

**9.** Return on common stockholders' equity

$$\frac{\text{Net income} - \text{Preferred dividends}}{\text{Average common stockholders' equity}}$$

**10.** Return on assets

$$\frac{\text{Net income}}{\text{Average total assets}}$$

**11.** Profit margin

$$\frac{\text{Net income}}{\text{Net sales}}$$

**12.** Asset turnover

$$\frac{\text{Net sales}}{\text{Average total assets}}$$

**13.** Gross profit rate

$$\frac{\text{Gross profit}}{\text{Net sales}}$$

**14.** Earnings per share

$$\frac{\text{Net income} - \text{Preferred dividends}}{\text{Weighted-average common shares outstanding}}$$

**15.** Price-earnings ratio

$$\frac{\text{Market price per share}}{\text{Earnings per share}}$$

**16.** Payout ratio

$$\frac{\text{Cash dividends paid on common stock}}{\text{Net income}}$$

## Financial Analysis and Data Analytics

In the age of "Big Data," opportunities for investors to apply data analytics to financial data are boundless. Immense quantities and types of data are available to investors. Free financial data about corporations, for example, can be obtained from the SEC's Edgar database and other sources. Alternatively, database services such as Compustat and WorldScope sell financial and other information regarding a wide range of company and industry characteristics. In addition, each day massive amounts of trading data are collected from financial exchanges.

Professional analysts employ sophisticated computerized valuation models that use financial, nonfinancial, and trading data to identify investment opportunities. Since these valuation models frequently rely heavily on accounting data, it is important to have a sound understanding of the financial accounting standards on which the numbers used in the models are based. If you desire to someday use data analytics to evaluate companies, the accounting skills and financial analysis tools acquired in this course are a good start.

## Comprehensive Example of Ratio Analysis

In this section, we provide a comprehensive review of ratios used for evaluating the financial health and performance of a company. We use the financial information in **Illustrations 13.17** through **13.20** to calculate Chicago Cereal Company's 2022 ratios. You can use these data to review the computations.

**ILLUSTRATION 13.17**

**Chicago Cereal Company's balance sheets**

### Chicago Cereal Company
#### Balance Sheets
#### December 31 (in thousands)

| | 2022 | 2021 |
|---|---|---|
| **Assets** | | |
| Current assets | | |
| Cash | $ 524 | $ 411 |
| Accounts receivable (net) | 1,026 | 945 |
| Inventory | 924 | 824 |
| Prepaid expenses and other current assets | 243 | 247 |
| Total current assets | 2,717 | 2,427 |
| Property, plant, and equipment (net) | 2,990 | 2,816 |
| Other assets | 5,690 | 5,471 |
| Total assets | $11,397 | $10,714 |

ILLUSTRATION 13.17

(continued)

| | 2022 | 2021 |
|---|---|---|
| **Liabilities and Stockholders' Equity** | | |
| Current liabilities | $ 4,044 | $ 4,020 |
| Long-term liabilities | 4,827 | 4,625 |
| Stockholders' equity—common | 2,526 | 2,069 |
| Total liabilities and stockholders' equity | $11,397 | $10,714 |

### Chicago Cereal Company
#### Condensed Income Statements
#### For the Years Ended December 31 (in thousands)

ILLUSTRATION 13.18

**Chicago Cereal Company's income statements**

| | 2022 | 2021 |
|---|---|---|
| Net sales | $11,776 | $10,907 |
| Cost of goods sold | 6,597 | 6,082 |
| Gross profit | 5,179 | 4,825 |
| Selling and administrative expenses | 3,311 | 3,059 |
| Income from operations | 1,868 | 1,766 |
| Interest expense | 321 | 294 |
| Income before income taxes | 1,547 | 1,472 |
| Income tax expense | 444 | 468 |
| Net income | $ 1,103 | $ 1,004 |

### Chicago Cereal Company
#### Condensed Statements of Cash Flows
#### For the Years Ended December 31 (in thousands)

ILLUSTRATION 13.19

**Chicago Cereal Company's statements of cash flows**

| | 2022 | 2021 |
|---|---|---|
| **Cash flows from operating activities** | | |
| Cash receipts from operating activities | $11,695 | $10,841 |
| Cash payments for operating activities | (10,192) | (9,431) |
| Net cash provided by operating activities | 1,503 | 1,410 |
| **Cash flows from investing activities** | | |
| Purchases of property, plant, and equipment | (472) | (453) |
| Other investing activities | (129) | 8 |
| Net cash used in investing activities | (601) | (445) |
| **Cash flows from financing activities** | | |
| Issuance of common stock | 163 | 218 |
| Issuance of debt | 2,179 | 721 |
| Reductions of debt | (2,011) | (650) |
| Payment of cash dividends | (475) | (450) |
| Repurchase of common stock and other items | (645) | (612) |
| Net cash provided (used) by financing activities | (789) | (773) |
| Increase (decrease) in cash and cash equivalents | 113 | 192 |
| Cash and cash equivalents at beginning of year | 411 | 219 |
| Cash and cash equivalents at end of year | $ 524 | $ 411 |

**Additional information:**

ILLUSTRATION 13.20

**Additional information for Chicago Cereal Company**

| | 2022 | 2021 |
|---|---|---|
| Weighted-average common shares outstanding (thousands) | 418.7 | 418.5 |
| Stock price at year-end | $52.92 | $50.06 |

As indicated in the chapter, we can classify ratios into three types for analysis of the primary financial statements:

1. **Liquidity ratios.** Measures of the short-term ability of the company to pay its maturing obligations and to meet unexpected needs for cash.

2. **Solvency ratios.** Measures of the ability of the company to survive over a long period of time.

3. **Profitability ratios.** Measures of the income or operating success of a company for a given period of time.

As a tool of analysis, ratios can provide clues to underlying conditions that may not be apparent from an inspection of the individual components of a particular ratio. But, a single ratio by itself is not very meaningful. Accordingly, in this discussion we use the following three comparisons.

1. **Intracompany comparisons** covering two years for Chicago Cereal (using comparative financial information from Illustrations 13.17 through 13.20). The ratios for 2021 are given and not calculated because the beginning balances are not provided for this year.

2. **Intercompany comparisons** using Giant Mills as one of Chicago Cereal's competitors.

3. **Industry average comparisons** based on **MSN.com** median ratios for manufacturers of flour and other grain mill products and comparisons with other sources. For some of the ratios that we use, industry comparisons are not available (denoted "na").

## Liquidity Ratios

Liquidity ratios measure the short-term ability of the company to pay its maturing obligations and to meet unexpected needs for cash.

- Short-term creditors such as bankers and suppliers are particularly interested in assessing liquidity.

- The measures used to determine the company's short-term debt-paying ability are the current ratio, the accounts receivable turnover, the average collection period, the inventory turnover, and days in inventory. In addition, another measure used to assess liquidity is working capital. Working capital is current assets less current liabilities.

1. **Current ratio.** The **current ratio** expresses the relationship of current assets to current liabilities, computed by dividing current assets by current liabilities. It is widely used for evaluating a company's liquidity and short-term debt-paying ability. The 2022 and 2021 current ratios for Chicago Cereal and comparative data are shown in **Illustration 13.21**.

**ILLUSTRATION 13.21** Current ratio

| Ratio | Formula | Chicago Cereal | | Giant Mills | Industry Average |
|---|---|---|---|---|---|
| | | 2022 | 2021 | 2022 | |
| Current ratio | $\dfrac{\text{Current assets}}{\text{Current liabilities}}$ | $\dfrac{\$2{,}717}{\$4{,}044} = .67$ | .60 | .67 | 1.06 |

What do the measures tell us?

- Chicago Cereal's 2022 current ratio of .67 means that for every dollar of current liabilities, it has $0.67 of current assets. (We sometimes state such ratios as .67:1 to reinforce this interpretation.)

- Its current ratio—and therefore its liquidity—increased significantly in 2022.

- Its ratio is well below the industry average but the same as that of Giant Mills.

2. **Accounts receivable turnover.** Analysts can measure liquidity by how quickly a company converts certain assets to cash. A low value for the current ratio can sometimes be compensated for if some of the company's current assets are highly liquid.

How liquid, for example, are the receivables? The ratio used to assess the liquidity of the receivables is the **accounts receivable turnover**, which measures the number of times, on average, a company collects receivables during the period. The accounts receivable turnover is computed by dividing net credit sales (net sales less cash sales) by average net accounts receivable during the year. The accounts receivable turnover for Chicago Cereal is shown in **Illustration 13.22**.

**ILLUSTRATION 13.22**  Accounts receivable turnover

| Ratio | Formula | Chicago Cereal 2022 | | 2021 | Giant Mills 2022 | Industry Average |
|---|---|---|---|---|---|---|
| Accounts receivable turnover | $\dfrac{\text{Net credit sales}}{\text{Average net accounts receivable}}$ | $\dfrac{\$11,776}{(\$1,026 + \$945) \div 2}$ = 11.9 | | 12.0 | 12.2 | 11.2 |

In computing the rate, we assumed that all Chicago Cereal's sales are credit sales.

- Its accounts receivable turnover declined slightly in 2022.
- The turnover of 11.9 times is higher than the industry average of 11.2 times, and slightly lower than Giant Mills' turnover of 12.2 times.
- A higher value suggests better liquidity because the receivables are being collected more quickly.

3. **Average collection period.**  A popular variant of the accounts receivable turnover converts it into an **average collection period** in days. This is done by dividing the accounts receivable turnover into 365 days. The average collection period for Chicago Cereal is shown in **Illustration 13.23**.

**ILLUSTRATION 13.23**  Average collection period

| Ratio | Formula | Chicago Cereal 2022 | 2021 | Giant Mills 2022 | Industry Average |
|---|---|---|---|---|---|
| Average collection period | $\dfrac{365 \text{ days}}{\text{Accounts receivable turnover}}$ | $\dfrac{365}{11.9}$ = 30.7 | 30.4 | 29.9 | 32.6 |

Chicago Cereal's 2022 accounts receivable turnover of 11.9 times is divided into 365 days to obtain approximately 31 days.

- This means that the average collection period for receivables is about 31 days.
- Its average collection period is slightly longer than that of Giant Mills and shorter than that of the industry.
- A shorter collection period means receivables are being collected more quickly and thus are more liquid.

Analysts frequently use the average collection period to assess the effectiveness of a company's credit and collection policies. The general rule is that the collection period should not greatly exceed the credit term period (i.e., the time allowed for payment, which is 30 days for many companies).

4. **Inventory turnover.**  The **inventory turnover** measures the number of times average inventory was sold during the period. Its purpose is to measure the liquidity of the inventory. A high measure indicates that inventory is being sold and replenished frequently. The inventory turnover is computed by dividing the cost of goods sold by the average inventory during the period. Unless seasonal factors are significant, average inventory can be computed using the beginning and ending inventory balances. Chicago Cereal's inventory turnover is shown in **Illustration 13.24**.

**ILLUSTRATION 13.24** Inventory turnover

| Ratio | Formula | Chicago Cereal | | Giant Mills | Industry Average |
| | | 2022 | 2021 | 2022 | |
|---|---|---|---|---|---|
| Inventory turnover | Cost of goods sold / Average inventory | $\dfrac{\$6,597}{(\$924 + \$824) \div 2} = 7.5$ | 7.9 | 7.4 | 6.7 |

Chicago Cereal's inventory turnover decreased slightly in 2022.

- The turnover of 7.5 times is higher than the industry average of 6.7 times and similar to that of Giant Mills.
- Generally, the faster the inventory turnover, the less cash is tied up in inventory and the less the chance of inventory becoming obsolete.
- A downside of high inventory turnover is that it sometimes results in lost sales because if a company keeps less inventory on hand, it is more likely to run out of inventory when it is needed.

5. **Days in inventory.** A variant of the inventory turnover is the **days in inventory**, which measures the average number of days inventory is held. The days in inventory for Chicago Cereal is shown in **Illustration 13.25**.

**ILLUSTRATION 13.25** Days in inventory

| Ratio | Formula | Chicago Cereal | | Giant Mills | Industry Average |
| | | 2022 | 2021 | 2022 | |
|---|---|---|---|---|---|
| Days in inventory | 365 days / Inventory turnover | $\dfrac{365}{7.5} = 48.7$ | 46.2 | 49.3 | 54.5 |

Chicago Cereal's 2022 inventory turnover of 7.5 divided into 365 is approximately 49 days.

- An average selling time of 49 days is faster than the industry average and similar to that of Giant Mills.
- However, inventory turnovers vary considerably among industries. For example, grocery store chains have a turnover of 10 times and an average selling period of 37 days. In contrast, jewelry stores have an average turnover of 1.3 times and an average selling period of 281 days.
- Within a company, there may even be significant differences in inventory turnover among different types of products. Thus, in a grocery store the turnover of perishable items such as produce, meats, and dairy products is faster than the turnover of soaps and detergents.

To conclude, nearly all of these liquidity measures suggest that Chicago Cereal's liquidity changed little during 2022. Its liquidity appears acceptable when compared to the industry as a whole and when compared to Giant Mills.

## Solvency Ratios

**Solvency ratios** measure the ability of the company to survive over a long period of time.

- Long-term creditors and stockholders are interested in a company's long-run solvency, particularly its ability to pay interest as it comes due and to repay the face value of debt at maturity.
- The debt to assets ratio and times interest earned provide information about debt-paying ability.
- In addition, free cash flow provides information about the company's solvency and its ability to pay additional dividends or invest in new projects.

6. **Debt to assets ratio.**   The **debt to assets ratio** measures the percentage of total financing provided by creditors. It is computed by dividing total liabilities (both current and long-term debt) by total assets. This ratio indicates the degree of financial leveraging. It also provides some indication of the company's ability to withstand losses without impairing the interests of its creditors. The higher the percentage of debt to assets, the greater the risk that the company may be unable to meet its maturing obligations. Thus, from the creditors' point of view, a low ratio of debt to assets is desirable. Chicago Cereal's debt to assets ratio is shown in **Illustration 13.26**.

**ILLUSTRATION 13.26**  Debt to assets ratio

| Ratio | Formula | Chicago Cereal 2022 | 2021 | Giant Mills 2022 | Industry Average |
|---|---|---|---|---|---|
| Debt to assets ratio | Total liabilities / Total assets | $\frac{\$8,871}{\$11,397} = 78\%$ | 81% | 55% | 55% |

Chicago Cereal's 2022 ratio means that creditors have provided financing sufficient for 78% of the company's total assets.

- Alternatively, the ratio indicates that the company would have to liquidate 78% of its assets at their book value in order to pay off all of its debts.
- Chicago Cereal's ratio is above the industry average of 55%, as well as that of Giant Mills.
- This suggests that it is less solvent than the industry average and Giant Mills. Chicago Cereal's solvency improved slightly from that in 2021.

The adequacy of this ratio is often judged in light of the company's earnings. Generally, companies with relatively stable earnings, such as public utilities, have higher debt to assets ratios than cyclical companies with widely fluctuating earnings, such as many high-tech companies.

Another ratio with a similar meaning is the **debt to equity ratio**.

- It shows the relative use of borrowed funds (total liabilities) compared with resources invested by the owners.
- If debt and assets are defined as above (all liabilities and all assets), then when the debt to assets ratio equals 50%, the debt to equity ratio is 1:1.

7. **Times interest earned.**   The **times interest earned** (also called interest coverage) indicates the company's ability to meet interest payments as they come due. It is computed by dividing the sum of net income, interest expense, and income tax expense by interest expense. Note that this ratio uses income before interest expense and income taxes because this amount represents what is available to cover interest. Chicago Cereal's times interest earned is shown in **Illustration 13.27**.

**ILLUSTRATION 13.27**  Times interest earned

| Ratio | Formula | Chicago Cereal 2022 | 2021 | Giant Mills 2022 | Industry Average |
|---|---|---|---|---|---|
| Times interest earned | (Net Income + Interest expense + Income tax expense) / Interest expense | $\frac{\$1,103 + \$321 + \$444}{\$321} = 5.8$ | 6.0 | 9.9 | 5.5 |

For Chicago Cereal, the 2022 interest coverage was 5.8 times, which indicates that income before interest and taxes was 5.8 times the amount needed for interest expense.

- This is less than the rate for Giant Mills, but it slightly exceeds the rate for the industry.
- The debt to assets ratio decreased for Chicago Cereal during 2022, and its times interest earned held relatively constant.
- A low debt to assets ratio and high times interest earned suggest better solvency.

8. **Free cash flow.** One indication of a company's solvency, as well as of its ability to pay dividends or expand operations, is the amount of excess cash it generated after investing in capital expenditures and paying dividends. This amount is referred to as **free cash flow**. For example, if you generate $100,000 of net cash provided by operating activities but you spend $30,000 on capital expenditures and pay $10,000 in dividends, you have $60,000 ($100,000 − $30,000 − $10,000) to use either to expand operations, pay additional dividends, or pay down debt. Chicago Cereal's free cash flow is shown in **Illustration 13.28**.

**ILLUSTRATION 13.28** Free cash flow

| Ratio | Formula | Chicago Cereal | | Giant Mills | Industry |
| | | 2021 | 2022 | 2022 | Average |
|---|---|---|---|---|---|
| Free cash flow | Net cash provided by operating activities − Capital expenditures − Cash dividends | $1,503 − $472 − $475 = $556 (in thousands) | $507 | $895 (in millions) | na |

Chicago Cereal's free cash flow increased slightly from 2021 to 2022.

- During both years, the net cash provided by operating activities was more than enough to allow it to acquire additional productive assets and maintain dividend payments.
- It could have used the remaining cash to reduce debt if necessary.
- Given that Chicago Cereal is much smaller than Giant Mills, we would expect Chicago Cereal's free cash flow to be substantially smaller, which it is.

## Profitability Ratios

**Profitability ratios** measure the income or operating success of a company for a given period of time.

- A company's income, or the lack of it, affects its ability to obtain debt and equity financing, its liquidity position, and its ability to grow.
- As a consequence, creditors and investors alike are interested in evaluating profitability.
- Analysts frequently use profitability as the ultimate test of management's operating effectiveness.

The relationships among measures of profitability are very important. Understanding them can help management determine where to focus its efforts to improve profitability. **Illustration 13.29** diagrams these relationships. Our discussion of Chicago Cereal's profitability is structured around this diagram.

9. **Return on common stockholders' equity (ROE).** A widely used measure of profitability from the common stockholders' viewpoint is the **return on common stockholders' equity (ROE)**. This ratio shows how many dollars of net income the company earned for each dollar invested by the owners. It is computed by dividing net income minus any

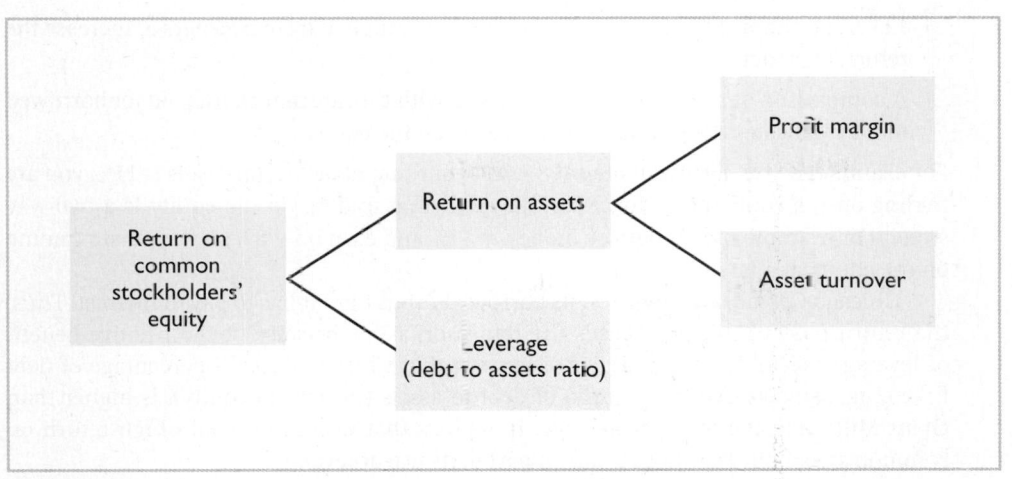

preferred dividends—that is, income available to common stockholders—by average common stockholders' equity. The return on common stockholders' equity for Chicago Cereal is shown in **Illustration 13.30**.

**ILLUSTRATION 13.30** **Return on common stockholders' equity**

| Ratio | Formula | Chicago Cereal 2022 | 2021 | Giant Mills 2022 | Industry Average |
|---|---|---|---|---|---|
| Return on common stockholders' equity | $\dfrac{\text{Net Income} - \text{Preferred dividends}}{\text{Average common stockholders' equity}}$ | $\dfrac{\$1,103 - \$0}{(\$2,526 + \$2,069) \div 2} = 48\%$ | 46% | 25% | 19% |

Chicago Cereal's 2022 return on common stockholders' equity is unusually high at 48%. The industry average is 19% and Giant Mills' return is 25%. In the subsequent sections, we investigate the causes of this high return.

10. **Return on assets.** The return on common stockholders' equity is affected by two factors: the **return on assets** and the degree of leverage. The return on assets measures the overall profitability of assets in terms of the income earned on each dollar invested in assets. It is computed by dividing net income by average total assets. Chicago Cereal's return on assets is shown in **Illustration 13.31**.

**ILLUSTRATION 13.31** **Return on assets**

| Ratio | Formula | Chicago Cereal 2022 | 2021 | Giant Mills 2022 | Industry Average |
|---|---|---|---|---|---|
| Return on assets | $\dfrac{\text{Net income}}{\text{Average total assets}}$ | $\dfrac{\$1,103}{(\$11,397 + \$10,714) \div 2} = 10.0\%$ | 9.4% | 6.2% | 5.3% |

Chicago Cereal had a 10.0% return on assets in 2022. This rate is significantly higher than that of Giant Mills and the industry average.

Note that its rate of return on common stockholders' equity (48%) is substantially higher than its rate of return on assets (10%). The reason is that it has made effective use of **leverage**.

- **Leveraging** or **trading on the equity** at a gain means that the company has borrowed money at a lower rate of interest than the rate of return it earns on the assets it purchased with the borrowed funds.

- Leverage enables management to use money supplied by nonowners to increase the return to owners.

- A comparison of the rate of return on assets with the rate of interest paid for borrowed money indicates the profitability of trading on the equity.

For example, if you borrow money at 8% and your rate of return on assets is 11%, you are trading on the equity at a gain. Note, however, that trading on the equity is a two-way street. For example, if you borrow money at 11% and earn only 8% on it, you are trading on the equity at a loss.

Chicago Cereal earns more on its borrowed funds than it has to pay in interest. Thus, the return to stockholders exceeds the return on assets because of the positive benefit of leverage. Recall from our earlier discussion that Chicago Cereal's percentage of debt financing, as measured by the ratio of debt to assets (or debt to equity), is higher than Giant Mills' and the industry average. It appears that Chicago Cereal's high return on common stockholders' equity is due in part to its use of leverage.

11. **Profit margin.** The return on assets is affected by two factors, the first of which is the profit margin. The **profit margin**, or rate of return on sales, is a measure of the percentage of each dollar of sales that results in net income. It is computed by dividing net income by net sales for the period. Chicago Cereal's profit margin is shown in **Illustration 13.32**.

ILLUSTRATION 13.32

**Profit margin**

| Ratio | Formula | Chicago Cereal | | Giant Mills | Industry |
|-------|---------|----------------|------|-------------|----------|
| | | 2022 | 2021 | 2022 | Average |
| Profit margin | $\dfrac{\text{Net income}}{\text{Net sales}}$ | $\dfrac{\$1,103}{\$11,776} = 9.4\%$ | 9.2% | 8.2% | 6.1% |

Chicago Cereal experienced a slight increase in its profit margin from 2021 to 2022 of 9.2% to 9.4%.

- Its profit margin was higher, indicating the company earned more profit out of each dollar of net sales, than the industry average and that of Giant Mills.

- High-volume (high inventory turnover) businesses such as grocery stores and pharmacy chains generally have low profit margins.

- Low-volume businesses such as jewelry stores and airplane manufacturers typically have high profit margins.

12. **Asset turnover.** The other factor that affects the return on assets is the asset turnover. The **asset turnover** measures how efficiently a company uses its assets to generate sales. It is determined by dividing net sales by average total assets for the period. The resulting number shows the dollars of net sales produced by each dollar invested in assets. **Illustration 13.33** shows the asset turnover for Chicago Cereal.

ILLUSTRATION 13.33

**Asset turnover**

| Ratio | Formula | Chicago Cereal | | Giant Mills | Industry |
|-------|---------|----------------|------|-------------|----------|
| | | 2022 | 2021 | 2022 | Average |
| Asset turnover | $\dfrac{\text{Net sales}}{\text{Average total assets}}$ | $\dfrac{\$11,776}{(\$11,397 + \$10,714) \div 2} = 1.07$ | 1.02 | .76 | .87 |

The asset turnover shows that in 2022, Chicago Cereal generated sales of $1.07 for each dollar it had invested in assets.

- The ratio rose from 2021 to 2022.

- Its asset turnover is above the industry average and that of Giant Mills.

- Asset turnovers vary considerably among industries. The average asset turnover for utility companies is .45, for example, while the grocery store industry has an average asset turnover of 3.49.

In summary, Chicago Cereal's return on assets increased from 9.4% in 2021 to 10.0% in 2022. Underlying this increase was an increased profitability on each dollar of net sales (as measured by the profit margin) and a rise in the sales-generating efficiency of its assets (as measured by the asset turnover). The combined effect of the profit margin and asset turnover yields the return on assets for Chicago Cereal shown in **Illustration 13.34.**

**ILLUSTRATION 13.34** **Composition of return on assets**

| Ratios: | Profit Margin | × | Asset Turnover | = | Return on Assets |
|---|---|---|---|---|---|
| | $\dfrac{\text{Net Income}}{\text{Net Sales}}$ | × | $\dfrac{\text{Net Sales}}{\text{Average Total Assets}}$ | = | $\dfrac{\text{Net Income}}{\text{Average Total Assets}}$ |
| **Chicago Cereal** | | | | | |
| 2022 | 9.4% | × | 1.07 times | = | 10.1%* |
| 2021 | 9.2% | × | 1.02 times | = | 9.4% |

*Difference from value in Illustration 13.31 due to rounding.

13. **Gross profit rate.**  One factor that strongly influences the profit margin is the gross profit rate. The **gross profit rate** is determined by dividing gross profit (net sales less cost of goods sold) by net sales. This rate indicates a company's ability to maintain an adequate unit selling price above its unit cost of goods sold.

As an industry becomes more competitive, this ratio typically declines.

- For example, in the early years of the personal computer industry, gross profit rates were quite high.
- Today, because of increased competition and a belief that most brands of personal computers are similar in quality, gross profit rates have become thin.
- Analysts should closely monitor gross profit rates over time.

**Illustration 13.35** shows Chicago Cereal's gross profit rate.

**ILLUSTRATION 13.35**

Gross profit rate

| Ratio | Formula | Chicago Cereal 2022 | Chicago Cereal 2021 | Giant Mills 2022 | Industry Average |
|---|---|---|---|---|---|
| Gross profit rate | $\dfrac{\text{Gross profit}}{\text{Net sales}}$ | $\dfrac{\$5,179}{\$11,776} = 44\%$ | 44% | 34% | 30% |

Chicago Cereal's gross profit rate remained constant from 2021 to 2022, and exceeded that of Giant Mills and of the industry average.

14. **Earnings per share (EPS).**  Stockholders usually think in terms of the number of shares they own or plan to buy or sell. Expressing net income earned on a per share basis provides a useful perspective for evaluating profitability. **Earnings per share** is a measure of the net income earned on each share of common stock. It is computed by dividing net income by the average number of common shares outstanding during the year.

The terms "net income per share" and "earnings per share" refer to the amount of net income applicable to each share of **common stock**. Therefore, when we compute earnings per share, if there are preferred dividends declared for the period, we must deduct them from net income to arrive at income available to the common stockholders. Chicago Cereal's earnings per share is shown in **Illustration 13.36**. There were no shares of preferred stock outstanding and no preferred stock dividends.

ILLUSTRATION 13.36
**Earnings per share**

| Ratio | Formula | Chicago Cereal 2022 | 2021 | Giant Mills 2022 | Industry Average |
|---|---|---|---|---|---|
| Earnings per share (EPS) | $\dfrac{\text{Net income} - \text{Preferred dividends}}{\text{Weighted-average common shares outstanding}}$ | $\dfrac{\$1,103 - \$0}{418.7} = \$2.63$ | $2.40 | $2.90 | na |

Note that no industry average is presented in Illustration 13.36.

- Industry data for earnings per share are not reported, and in fact the Chicago Cereal and Giant Mills ratios should not be compared.
- Such comparisons are not meaningful because of the wide variations in the number of shares of outstanding stock among companies.
- Chicago Cereal's earnings per share increased 23 cents per share in 2022. This represents a 9.6% increase from the 2021 EPS of $2.40.

15. **Price-earnings ratio.** The **price-earnings (P-E) ratio** is an oft-quoted statistic that measures the ratio of the market price of each share of common stock to the earnings per share of common stock. The price-earnings ratio reflects investors' assessments of a company's future earnings. It is computed by dividing the market price per share by earnings per share. Chicago Cereal's price-earnings ratio is shown in **Illustration 13.37**.

ILLUSTRATION 13.37
**Price-earnings ratio**

| Ratio | Formula | Chicago Cereal 2022 | 2021 | Giant Mills 2022 | Industry Average |
|---|---|---|---|---|---|
| Price-earnings ratio | $\dfrac{\text{Market price per share}}{\text{Earnings per share}}$ | $\dfrac{\$52.92}{\$2.63} = 20.1$ | 20.9 | 24.3 | 35.8 |

At the end of 2022 and 2021, the market price of Chicago Cereal's stock was $52.92 and $50.06, respectively.

- In 2022, each share of Chicago Cereal's stock sold for 20.1 times the amount that was earned on each share.
- Chicago Cereal's price-earnings ratio is lower than Giant Mills' ratio of 24.3 and lower than the industry average of 35.8 times.
- Its lower P-E ratio suggests that the market is less optimistic about Chicago Cereal than about Giant Mills, but it might also signal that Chicago Cereal's stock is underpriced.

16. **Payout ratio.** The **payout ratio** measures the percentage of earnings distributed in the form of cash dividends. It is computed by dividing cash dividends paid on common stock by net income. Companies that have high growth rates are characterized by low payout ratios because they reinvest most of their net income in the business. The payout ratio for Chicago Cereal is shown in **Illustration 13.38**.

ILLUSTRATION 13.38
**Payout ratio**

| Ratio | Formula | Chicago Cereal 2022 | 2021 | Giant Mills 2022 | Industry Average |
|---|---|---|---|---|---|
| Payout ratio | $\dfrac{\text{Cash dividends paid on common stock}}{\text{Net income}}$ | $\dfrac{\$475}{\$1,103} = 43\%$ | 45% | 54% | 37% |

The 2022 and 2021 payout ratios for Chicago Cereal are lower than that of Giant Mills (54%) but higher than the industry average (37%).

- A lower payout ratio means a company has chosen to pay out a lower percentage of its net income as dividends.

- Management has some control over the amount of dividends paid each year, and companies are generally reluctant to reduce a dividend below the amount paid in a previous year.

- The payout ratio will actually increase if a company's net income declines but the company keeps its total dividend payment the same. (Of course, unless the company returns to its previous level of profitability, maintaining this higher dividend payout ratio is probably not possible over the long run.)

Before drawing any conclusions regarding Chicago Cereal's dividend payout ratio, we should calculate this ratio over a longer period of time to evaluate any trends and also try to find out whether management's philosophy regarding dividends has changed recently. The "Selected Financial Data" section of Chicago Cereal's Management Discussion and Analysis shows that over a 5-year period, earnings per share rose 45%, while dividends per share grew only 19%.

In terms of the types of financial information available and the ratios used by various industries, what can be practically covered in this text gives you the "Titanic approach." That is, you are only seeing the tip of the iceberg compared to the vast databases and types of ratio analysis that are available electronically. The availability of information is not a problem. The real trick is to be discriminating enough to perform relevant analysis and select pertinent comparative data.

---

## DO IT! 3 | Ratio Analysis

The condensed financial statements of John Cully Company, for the years ended June 30, 2022 and 2021, are presented as follows.

### John Cully Company
#### Balance Sheets
#### June 30

| | (in thousands) | |
|---|---|---|
| | 2022 | 2021 |
| **Assets** | | |
| Current assets | | |
| Cash and cash equivalents | $ 553.3 | $ 611.6 |
| Accounts receivable (net) | 776.6 | 664.9 |
| Inventory | 768.3 | 653.5 |
| Prepaid expenses and other current assets | 204.4 | 269.2 |
| Total current assets | 2,302.6 | 2,199.2 |
| Investments | 12.3 | 12.6 |
| Property, plant, and equipment (net) | 694.2 | 647.0 |
| Other assets | 876.7 | 849.3 |
| Total assets | $3,885.8 | $3,708.1 |
| **Liabilities and Stockholders' Equity** | | |
| Current liabilities | $1,497.7 | $1,322.0 |
| Long-term liabilities | 679.5 | 637.1 |
| Stockholders' equity—common | 1,708.6 | 1,749.0 |
| Total liabilities and stockholders' equity | $3,885.8 | $3,708.1 |

**ACTION PLAN**

- Remember that the current ratio includes all current assets.

- Use average balances for turnover ratios like inventory, accounts receivable, and return on assets.

| John Cully Company | | |
| --- | --- | --- |
| Income Statements | | |
| For the Years Ended June 30 | | |

| | (in thousands) | |
| --- | --- | --- |
| | **2022** | **2021** |
| Net sales | $6,336.3 | $5,790.4 |
| Expenses | | |
| Cost of goods sold | 1,617.4 | 1,476.3 |
| Selling and administrative expenses | 4,007.6 | 3,679.0 |
| Interest expense | 13.9 | 27.1 |
| Total expenses | 5,638.9 | 5,182.4 |
| Income before income taxes | 697.4 | 608.0 |
| Income tax expense | 291.3 | 232.6 |
| Net income | $ 406.1 | $ 375.4 |

Compute the following ratios for 2022 and 2021.

    **a.** Current ratio.

    **b.** Inventory turnover. (Inventory on 6/30/20 was $599.0.)

    **c.** Profit margin.

    **d.** Return on assets. (Assets on 6/30/20 were $3,349.9.)

    **e.** Return on common stockholders' equity. (Stockholders' equity on 6/30/20 was $1,795.9.)

    **f.** Debt to assets ratio.

    **g.** Times interest earned.

### Solution

| | 2022 | 2021 |
| --- | --- | --- |
| **a.** Current ratio: | | |
| $2,302.6 ÷ $1,497.7 = | 1.5:1 | |
| $2,199.2 ÷ $1,322.0 = | | 1.7:1 |
| **b.** Inventory turnover: | | |
| $1,617.4 ÷ [($768.3 + $653.5) ÷ 2] = | 2.3 times | |
| $1,476.3 ÷ [($653.5 + $599.0) ÷ 2] = | | 2.4 times |
| **c.** Profit margin: | | |
| $406.1 ÷ $6,336.3 = | 6.4% | |
| $375.4 ÷ $5,790.4 = | | 6.5% |
| **d.** Return on assets: | | |
| $406.1 ÷ [($3,885.8 + $3,708.1) ÷ 2] = | 10.7% | |
| $375.4 ÷ [($3,708.1 + $3,349.9) ÷ 2] = | | 10.6% |
| **e.** Return on common stockholders' equity: | | |
| ($406.1 – $0) ÷ [($1,708.6 + $1,749.0) ÷ 2] = | 23.5% | |
| ($375.4 – $0) ÷ [($1,749.0 + $1,795.9) ÷ 2] = | | 21.2% |
| **f.** Debt to assets ratio: | | |
| ($1,497.7 + $679.5) ÷ $3,885.8 = | 56.0% | |
| ($1,322.0 + $637.1) ÷ $3,708.1 = | | 52.8% |
| **g.** Times interest earned: | | |
| ($406.1 + $13.9 + $291.3) ÷ $13.9 = | 51.2 times | |
| ($375.4 + $27.1 + $232.6) ÷ $27.1 = | | 23.4 times |

Related exercise material: **BE13.10, BE13.11, BE13.12, BE13.13, BE13.14, BE13.15, DO IT! 13.3, E13.7, E13.8, E13.9, E13.10, E13.11, E13.12, and E13.13.**

# Review and Practice

## Learning Objectives Review

### 1 Apply the concepts of sustainable income and quality of earnings.

Sustainable income analysis is useful in evaluating a company's performance. Sustainable income is the most likely level of income to be obtained by the company in the future and omits unusual items. Discontinued operations and other comprehensive income items are presented separately to highlight their unusual nature. Items below income from continuing operations must be presented net of tax.

A high quality of earnings provides full and transparent information that will not confuse or mislead users of the financial statements. Issues related to quality of earnings are (1) alternative accounting methods, (2) pro forma income, and (3) improper recognition.

### 2 Apply horizontal analysis and vertical analysis.

Horizontal analysis is a technique for evaluating a series of data over a period of time to determine the increase or decrease that has taken place, expressed as either a dollar amount or a percentage.

Vertical analysis is a technique that expresses each item in a financial statement as a percentage of a relevant total or a base amount.

### 3 Analyze a company's performance using ratio analysis.

Financial ratios are provided in Illustration 13.14 (liquidity), Illustration 13.15 (solvency), and Illustration 13.16 (profitability). Analysis is enhanced by intracompany, intercompany, and industry comparisons of these three classes of ratios.

## Glossary Review

**Accounts receivable turnover** A measure of the liquidity of receivables; computed as net credit sales divided by average net accounts receivable. (p. 13-21).

**Asset turnover** A measure of how efficiently a company uses its assets to generate net sales; computed as net sales divided by average total assets. (p. 13-26).

**Available-for-sale securities** Securities that are held with the intent of selling them sometime in the future. (p. 13-5).

**Average collection period** The average number of days that receivables are outstanding; calculated as accounts receivable turnover divided into 365 days. (p. 13-21).

**Change in accounting principle** Use of an accounting principle in the current year that is different from the one used in the preceding year. (p. 13-6).

**Comprehensive income** The sum of net income and other comprehensive income items. (p. 13-4)

**Current ratio** A measure used to evaluate a company's liquidity and short-term debt-paying ability; calculated as current assets divided by current liabilities. (p. 13-20).

**Days in inventory** A measure of the average number of days that inventory is held; computed as inventory turnover divided into 365 days. (p. 13-22).

**Debt to assets ratio** A measure of the percentage of total financing provided by creditors; computed as total liabilities divided by total assets. (p. 13-23).

**Discontinued operations** The disposal of a significant component of a business. (p. 13-3).

**Earnings per share** The net income earned by each share of outstanding common stock; computed as net income less preferred dividends divided by the weighted-average common shares outstanding. (p. 13-27).

**Free cash flow** A measure of solvency. Cash remaining from operating activities after adjusting for capital expenditures and dividends paid. (p. 13-24).

**Gross profit rate** Gross profit expressed as a percentage of net sales; computed as gross profit divided by net sales. (p. 13-27).

**Horizontal analysis** A technique for evaluating a series of financial statement data over a period of time to determine the increase (decrease) that has taken place, expressed as either a dollar amount or a percentage. (p. 13-10).

**Inventory turnover** A measure of the liquidity of inventory. Measures the number of times average inventory was sold during the period; computed as cost of goods sold divided by average inventory. (p. 13-21).

**Leveraging** Borrowing money at a lower rate of interest than can be earned by using the borrowed money; also referred to as *trading on the equity*. (p. 13-25).

**Liquidity ratios** Measures of the short-term ability of the company to pay its maturing current obligations and to meet unexpected needs for cash. (p. 13-16).

**Payout ratio** A measure of the percentage of earnings distributed in the form of cash dividends; calculated as cash dividends paid on common stock divided by net income. (p. 13-28).

**Price-earnings (P-E) ratio** A comparison of the market price of each share of common stock to the earnings per share; computed as the market price of the stock divided by earnings per share. (p. 13-28).

**Profitability ratios** Measures of the income or operating success of a company for a given period of time. (p. 13-17).

**Profit margin** A measure of the net income generated by each dollar of net sales; computed as net income divided by net sales. (p. 13-26).

**Pro forma income** A measure of income that usually excludes items that a company considers unusual or non-recurring. (p. 13-8).

**Quality of earnings** Indicates the level of full and transparent information that is provided to users of the financial statements. (p. 13-7).

**Ratio** The mathematical relationship between one quantity and another. The relationship may be expressed either as a percentage, a rate, or a simple proportion. (p. 13-15).

**Ratio analysis** A technique for evaluating financial statements that expresses the relationship between selected financial statement data. (p. 13-15).

**Return on assets** A profitability measure that indicates the amount of net income generated by each dollar of assets; calculated as net income divided by average total assets. (p. 13-25).

**Return on common stockholders' equity (ROE)** A measure of the dollars of net income earned for each dollar invested by the owners; computed as income available to common stockholders divided by average common stockholders' equity. (p. 13-24).

**Solvency ratios** Measures of the ability of a company to survive over a long period of time, particularly to pay interest as it comes due and to repay the balance of debt at its maturity. (p. 13-17).

**Sustainable income** The most likely level of income to be obtained by a company in the future. (p. 13-3).

**Times interest earned** A measure of a company's solvency and ability to meet interest payments as they come due; calculated as the sum of net income, interest expense, and income tax expense divided by interest expense. (p. 13-23).

**Trading on the equity** *See leveraging.* (p. 13-25).

**Trading securities** Securities bought and held primarily for sale in the near term to generate income on short-term price differences. (p. 13-5).

**Vertical analysis** A technique for evaluating financial statement data that expresses each item in a financial statement as a percentage of a base amount. (p. 13-12).

## Practice Multiple-Choice Questions

**1. (LO 1)** In reporting discontinued operations, the income statement should show in a special section:

  a. gains on the disposal of the discontinued component.

  b. losses on the disposal of the discontinued component.

  c. neither gains nor losses on the disposal of the discontinued component.

  d. both gains and losses on the disposal of the discontinued component.

**2. (LO 1)** Cool Stools Corporation has income before taxes of $400,000 and a loss on discontinued operations of $100,000. If the income tax rate is 25% on all items, the income statement should report income from continuing operations and discontinued operations, respectively, of

  a. $325,000 and $100,000.

  b. $325,000 and $75,000.

  c. $300,000 and $100,000.

  d. $300,000 and $75,000.

**3. (LO 1)** Which of the following would be considered an "Other comprehensive income" item?

  a. Gain on disposal of discontinued operations.

  b. Unrealized loss on available-for-sale securities.

  c. Loss related to flood.

  d. Net income.

**4. (LO 1)** Which situation below might indicate a company has a low quality of earnings?

  a. The same accounting principles are used each year.

  b. Revenue is recognized when the performance obligation is satisfied.

  c. Maintenance costs are capitalized and then depreciated.

  d. The company's P-E ratio is high relative to competitors.

**5. (LO 2)** In horizontal analysis, each item is expressed as a percentage of the:

  a. net income amount.

  b. stockholders' equity amount.

  c. total assets amount.

  d. base-year amount.

**6. (LO 2)** Adams Corporation reported net sales of $300,000, $330,000, and $360,000 in the years 2020, 2021, and 2022, respectively.

If 2020 is the base year, what percentage do 2022 net sales represent of the base?

  a. 77%.                    c. 120%.

  b. 108%.                   d. 130%.

**7. (LO 2)** The following schedule is a display of what type of analysis?

| | Amount | Percent |
|---|---|---|
| Current assets | $200,000 | 25% |
| Property, plant, and equipment | 600,000 | 75% |
| Total assets | $800,000 | |

  a. Horizontal analysis.        c. Vertical analysis.

  b. Differential analysis.       d. Ratio analysis.

**8. (LO 2)** In vertical analysis, the base amount for depreciation expense is generally:

  a. net sales.

  b. depreciation expense in a previous year.

  c. gross profit.

  d. fixed assets.

**9. (LO 3)** Which measure is an evaluation of a company's ability to pay current liabilities?

  a. Accounts receivable turnover.

  b. Current ratio.

  c. Both accounts receivable turnover and current ratio.

  d. None of the answer choices is correct.

**10. (LO 3)** Which measure is useful in evaluating the efficiency in managing inventories?

  a. Inventory turnover.

  b. Days in inventory.

  c. Both inventory turnover and days in inventory.

  d. None of the answer choices is correct.

**11. (LO 3)** Which of these is **not** a liquidity ratio?

  a. Current ratio.

  b. Asset turnover.

  c. Inventory turnover.

  d. Accounts receivable turnover.

**12. (LO 3)** Plano Corporation reported net income $24,000, net sales $400,000, and average assets $600,000 for 2022. What is the 2022 profit margin?

a. 6%.      c. 40%.

b. 12%.     d. 200%.

Use the following financial statement information as of the end of each year to answer Questions 13–17.

|  | 2022 | 2021 |
|---|---|---|
| Inventory | $ 54,000 | $ 48,000 |
| Current assets | 81,000 | 106,000 |
| Total assets | 382,000 | 326,000 |
| Current liabilities | 27,000 | 36,000 |
| Total liabilities | 102,000 | 88,000 |
| Common stockholders' equity | 240,000 | 198,000 |
| Net sales | 784,000 | 697,000 |
| Cost of goods sold | 306,000 | 277,000 |
| Net income | 134,000 | 90,000 |
| Income tax expense | 22,000 | 18,000 |
| Interest expense | 12,000 | 12,000 |
| Dividends paid to preferred stockholders | 4,000 | 4,000 |
| Dividends paid to common stockholders | 15,000 | 10,000 |

**13. (LO 3)** Compute the days in inventory for 2022.

a. 64.4 days.      c. 6 days.

b. 60.8 days.      d. 24 days.

**14. (LO 3)** Compute the current ratio for 2022.

a. 1.26:1.      c. 0.80:1.

b. 3.0:1.       d. 3.75:1.

**15. (LO 3)** Compute the profit margin for 2022.

a. 17.1%.      c. 37.9%.

b. 18.1%.      d. 5.9%.

**16. (LO 3)** Compute the return on common stockholders' equity for 2022.

a. 54.2%.      c. 61.2%.

b. 52.5%.      d. 59.4%.

**17. (LO 3)** Compute the times interest earned for 2022.

a. 11.2 times.      c. 14.0 times.

b. 65.3 times.      d. 13.0 times.

## Solutions

**1. d.** Gains and losses from the operations of a discontinued component and gains and losses on the disposal of the discontinued component are shown in a separate section immediately after continuing operations in the income statement. Choices (a) and (b) are correct, but (d) is the better answer. Choice (c) is wrong as there is a correct answer.

**2. d.** Income tax expense = 25% × $400,000 = $100,000; therefore, income from continuing operations = $400,000 − $100,000 = $300,000. The loss on discontinued operations is reported net of tax, $100,000 × 75% = $75,000. The other choices are therefore incorrect.

**3. b.** Unrealized gains and losses on available-for-sale securities are part of other comprehensive income. The other choices are incorrect because they are reported on the income statement as follows: (a) a gain on the disposal of discontinued operations is reported as an unusual item, (c) loss related to a flood is reported among other expenses and losses, and (d) net income is a separate line item.

**4. c.** Capitalizing and then depreciating maintenance costs suggests that a company is trying to avoid expensing certain costs by deferring them to future accounting periods to increase current-period income. The other choices are incorrect because (a) using the same accounting principles each year and (b) recognizing revenue when the performance obligation is satisfied is in accordance with GAAP. Choice (d) is incorrect because a high P-E ratio does not suggest that a firm has low quality of earnings.

**5. d.** Horizontal analysis converts each succeeding year's balance to a percentage of the base year amount, not (a) net income amount, (b) stockholders' equity amount, or (c) total assets amount.

**6. c.** The trend percentage for 2022 is 120% ($360,000 ÷ $300,000), not (a) 77%, (b) 108%, or (d) 130%.

**7. c.** The data in the schedule are a display of vertical analysis because the individual asset items are expressed as a percentage of total assets. The other choices are therefore incorrect. Horizontal analysis is a technique for evaluating a series of data over a period of time.

**8. a.** In vertical analysis, net sales is used as the base amount for income statement items, not (b) depreciation expense in a previous year, (c) gross profit, or (d) fixed assets.

**9. c.** Both the accounts receivable turnover and the current ratio measure a firm's ability to pay current liabilities. Choices (a) and (b) are correct but (c) is the better answer. Choice (d) is incorrect because there is a correct answer.

**10. c.** Both inventory turnover and days in inventory measure a firm's efficiency in managing inventories. Choices (a) and (b) are correct but (c) is the better answer. Choice (d) is incorrect because there is a correct answer.

**11. b.** Asset turnover is a measure of profitability. The other choices are incorrect because the (a) current ratio, (c) inventory turnover, and (d) accounts receivable turnover are all measures of a firm's liquidity.

**12. a.** Profit margin = Net income ($24,000) ÷ Net sales ($400,000) = 6%, not (b) 12%, (c) 40%, or (d) 200%.

**13. b.** Inventory turnover = Cost of goods sold ÷ Average inventory {$306,000 ÷ [($54,000 + $48,000) ÷ 2]} = 6 times. Thus, days in inventory = 60.8 (365 ÷ 6), not (a) 64.4, (c) 6, or (d) 24 days.

**14. b.** Current ratio = Current assets ÷ Current liabilities ($81,000 ÷ $27,000) = 3.0:1, not (a) 1.26 1, (c) 0.80:1, or (d) 3.75:1.

**15. a.** Profit margin = Net income ÷ Net sales ($134,000 ÷ $784,000) = 17.1%, not (b) 18.1%, (c) 37.9% or (d) 5.9%.

**16. d.** Return on common stockholders' equity = Net income ($134,000) − Dividends to preferred stockholders ($4,000) ÷ Average common stockholders' equity [($240,000 + $198,000) ÷ 2] = 59.4%, not (a) 54.2%, (b) 52.5%, or (c) 61.2%.

**17. c.** Times interest earned = (Net income + Interest expense + Income tax expense) ÷ Interest expense [($134,000 + $12,000 + $22,000) ÷ $12,000] = 14.0 times, not (a) 11.2, (b) 65.3, or (d) 13.0 times.

# Practice Brief Exercises

*Prepare a discontinued operations section.*

**1. (LO 1)** On September 30, Reynaldo Corporation discontinued its operations in Africa. During the year, the operating income was $100,000 before taxes. On September 1, Reynaldo disposed of its African facilities at a pretax loss of $350,000. The applicable tax rate is 20%. Show the discontinued operations section of the income statement.

**Solution**

1.

**Reynaldo Corporation**
**Income Statement (partial)**

|  |  |  |
|---|---|---|
| Income from operations of discontinued division, net of $30,000 income taxes ($100,000 × 20%) | $ 80,000 |  |
| Loss from disposal of discontinued division, net of $105,000 income tax savings ($350,000 × 20%) | 280,000 | $(200,000) |

*Prepare horizontal analysis.*

**2. (LO 2)** Using the following data from the comparative balance sheet of Alfredo Company, perform a horizontal analysis.

|  | December 31, 2022 | December 31, 2021 |
|---|---|---|
| Accounts payable | $ 300,000 | $ 200,000 |
| Common stock | 700,000 | 600,000 |
| Total liabilities and equity | 2,000,000 | 1,800,000 |

**Solution**

2.

|  | December 31, 2022 | December 31, 2021 | Increase or (Decrease) Amount | Percent* |
|---|---|---|---|---|
| Accounts payable | $ 300,000 | $ 200,000 | $100,000 | 50% |
| Common stock | 700,000 | 600,000 | 100,000 | 17 |
| Total liabilities and stockholders' equity | 2,000,000 | 1,800,000 | 200,000 | 11 |

*100 ÷ 200 = 50%; 100 ÷ 600 = 16.7%; 200 ÷ 1,800 = 11.1%

*Calculate ratios.*

**3. (LO 3)** Gonzalez Company has beginning inventory of $400,000, cost of goods sold of $2,200,000, and days in inventory of 73. What is Gonzalez' inventory turnover and ending inventory?

**Solution**

3. Days in inventory = 365 ÷ Inventory turnover
$$73 = 365 \div \text{Inventory turnover.}$$
Inventory turnover = 5 (365 ÷ 73)

Inventory turnover = Cost of goods sold ÷ Average inventory
$$5 = \$2,200,000 \div \text{Average inventory}$$
Average inventory = $2,200,000 ÷ 5 = $440,000.

Since beginning inventory is $400,000, ending inventory must be $480,000:
($400,000 + $480,000) ÷ 2 = $440,000.

## Practice Exercises

1. **(LO 2)** The comparative condensed balance sheets of Roadway Corporation are as follows.

*Prepare horizontal and vertical analyses.*

### Roadway Corporation
### Condensed Balance Sheets
### December 31

|  | 2022 | 2021 |
|---|---|---|
| **Assets** | | |
| Current assets | $ 76,000 | $ 80,000 |
| Property, plant, and equipment (net) | 99,000 | 90,000 |
| Intangible assets | 25,000 | 40,000 |
| Total assets | $200,000 | $210,000 |
| **Liabilities and Stockholders' Equity** | | |
| Current liabilities | $ 40,800 | $ 48,000 |
| Long-term liabilities | 143,000 | 150,000 |
| Stockholders' equity | 16,200 | 12,000 |
| Total liabilities and stockholders' equity | $200,000 | $210,000 |

### Instructions

a. Prepare a horizontal analysis of the balance sheet data for Roadway Corporation using 2021 as a base.

b. Prepare a vertical analysis of the balance sheet data for Roadway Corporation in columnar form for 2022.

### Solution

**1. a.**

### Roadway Corporation
### Condensed Balance Sheets
### December 31

|  | 2022 | 2021 | Increase (Decrease) | Percent Change from 2021 |
|---|---|---|---|---|
| **Assets** | | | | |
| Current assets | $ 76,000 | $ 80,000 | $ (4,000) | (5.0%) |
| Property, plant, and equipment (net) | 99,000 | 90,000 | 9,000 | 10.0% |
| Intangible assets | 25,000 | 40,000 | (15,000) | (37.5%) |
| Total assets | $200,000 | $210,000 | $(10,000) | (4.8%) |
| **Liabilities and Stockholders' Equity** | | | | |
| Current liabilities | $ 40,800 | $ 48,000 | $ (7,200) | (15.0%) |
| Long-term liabilities | 143,000 | 150,000 | (7,000) | (4.7%) |
| Stockholders' equity | 16,200 | 12,000 | 4,200 | 35.0% |
| Total liabilities and stockholders' equity | $200,000 | $210,000 | $(10,000) | (4.8%) |

**b.**

| Roadway Corporation<br>Condensed Balance Sheet<br>December 31, 2022 | | |
| :--- | ---: | ---: |
| | **Amount** | **Percent** |
| **Assets** | | |
| Current assets | $ 76,000 | 38.0% |
| Property, plant, and equipment (net) | 99,000 | 49.5% |
| Intangible assets | 25,000 | 12.5% |
| Total assets | $200,000 | 100.0% |
| | | |
| **Liabilities and Stockholders' Equity** | | |
| Current liabilities | $ 40,800 | 20.4% |
| Long-term liabilities | 143,000 | 71.5% |
| Stockholders' equity | 16,200 | 8.1% |
| Total liabilities and stockholders' equity | $200,000 | 100.0% |

*Compute ratios.*

**2. (LO 3)** Rondo Corporation's comparative balance sheets are presented here.

| Rondo Corporation<br>Balance Sheets<br>December 31 | | |
| :--- | ---: | ---: |
| | **2022** | **2021** |
| Cash | $ 5,300 | $ 3,700 |
| Accounts receivable (net) | 21,200 | 23,400 |
| Inventory | 9,000 | 7,000 |
| Land | 20,000 | 26,000 |
| Buildings | 70,000 | 70,000 |
| Accumulated depreciation—buildings | (15,000) | (10,000) |
| Total | $110,500 | $120,100 |
| | | |
| Accounts payable | $ 10,370 | $ 31,100 |
| Common stock | 75,000 | 69,000 |
| Retained earnings | 25,130 | 20,000 |
| Total | $110,500 | $120,100 |

Rondo's 2022 income statement included net sales of $120,000, cost of goods sold of $70,000, and net income of $14,000.

**Instructions**

Compute the following ratios for 2022.

a. Current ratio.

b. Accounts receivable turnover.

c. Inventory turnover.

d. Profit margin.

e. Asset turnover.

f. Return on assets.

g. Return on common stockholders' equity.

h. Debt to assets ratio.

**Solution**

2. **a.** ($5,300 + $21,200 + $9,000) ÷ $10,370 = 3.42:1

**b.** $120,000 ÷ [($21,200 + $23,400) ÷ 2] = 5.38 times

**c.** $70,000 ÷ [($9,000 + $7,000) ÷ 2] = 8.8 times

**d.** $14,000 ÷ $120,000 = 11.7%

**e.** $120,000 ÷ [($110,500 + $120,100) ÷ 2] = 1.04 times

**f.** $14,000 ÷ [($110,500 + $120,100) ÷ 2] = 12.1%

**g.** $14,000 ÷ [($100,130 + $89,000) ÷ 2] = 14.8%

**h.** $10,370 ÷ $110,500 = 9.4%

## Practice Problem

**(LO 1)** The events and transactions of Dever Corporation for the year ended December 31, 2022, resulted in the following data.

*Prepare an income statement and a statement of comprehensive income.*

| | |
|---|---:|
| Cost of goods sold | $2,600,000 |
| Net sales | 4,400,000 |
| Other expenses and losses | 9,600 |
| Other revenues and gains | 5,600 |
| Selling and administrative expenses | 1,100,000 |
| Income from operations of plastics division | 70,000 |
| Gain from disposal of plastics division | 500,000 |
| Unrealized loss on available-for-sale securities | 60,000 |

Analysis reveals the following:

1. All items are recorded before the applicable income tax rate of 20%.
2. The plastics division was sold on July 1.
3. All operating data for the plastics division have been segregated.

### Instructions

Prepare an income statement and a statement of comprehensive income for the year.

### Solution

**Dever Corporation**
**Income Statement**
**For the Year Ended December 31, 2022**

| | | |
|---|---:|---:|
| Net sales | | $4,400,000 |
| Cost of goods sold | | 2,600,000 |
| Gross profit | | 1,800,000 |
| Selling and administrative expenses | | 1,100,000 |
| Income from operations | | 700,000 |
| Other revenues and gains | | 5,600 |
| Other expenses and losses | | 9,600 |
| Income before income taxes | | 696,000 |
| Income tax expense ($696,000 × 20%) | | 139,200 |
| Income from continuing operations | | 556,800 |
| Discontinued operations | | |
|   Income from operation of plastics division, net of $14,000 | | |
|     income taxes ($70,000 × 20%) | $ 56,000 | |
|   Gain from disposal of plastics division, net of $100,000 | | |
|     income taxes ($500,000 × 20%) | 400,000 | 456,000 |
| Net income | | $1,012,800 |

**Dever Corporation**
**Statement of Comprehensive Income**
**For the Year Ended December 31, 2022**

| | | |
|---|---:|---:|
| Net income | | $1,012,800 |
| Unrealized loss on available-for-sale securities, net of $18,000 | | |
|   income tax savings ($60,000 × 20%) | | 48,000 |
| Comprehensive income | | $964,900 |

Brief Exercises, DO IT! Exercises, Exercises, Problems, Data Analytics Activities, and many additional resources are available for practice in WileyPLUS.

## Questions

1. Explain sustainable income. What relationship does this concept have to the treatment of discontinued operations on the income statement?

2. Hogan Inc. reported 2021 earnings per share of $3.26 and had no discontinued operations. In 2022, earnings per share on income from continuing operations was $2.99, and earnings per share on net income was $3.49. Do you consider this trend to be favorable? Why or why not?

3. Moosier Inc. has been in operation for 3 years and uses the FIFO method of inventory costing. During the fourth year, Moosier changes to the average-cost method for all its inventory. How will Moosier report this change?

4. What amount did **Apple** report as "Other comprehensive earnings" in its consolidated statement of comprehensive income ending September 29, 2018? By what percentage did Apple's "Comprehensive income" differ from its "Net income"?

5. Identify and explain factors that affect quality of earnings.

6. Explain how the choice of one of the following accounting methods over the other raises or lowers a company's net income during a period of continuing inflation.
   a. Use of FIFO instead of LIFO for inventory costing.
   b. Use of a 6-year life for machinery instead of a 9-year life.
   c. Use of straight-line depreciation instead of declining-balance depreciation.

7. Two popular methods of financial statement analysis are horizontal analysis and vertical analysis. Explain the difference between these two methods.

8. a. If Erin Company had net income of $300,000 in 2021 and it experienced a 24.5% increase in net income for 2022, what is its net income for 2022?
   b. If 6 cents of every dollar of Erin's revenue results in net income in 2021, what is the dollar amount of 2021 revenue?

9. a. Gina Jaimes believes that the analysis of financial statements is directed at two characteristics of a company: liquidity and profitability. Is Gina correct? Explain.
   b. Are short-term creditors, long-term creditors, and stockholders interested in primarily the same characteristics of a company? Explain.

10. a. Distinguish among the following bases of comparison: intracompany, intercompany, and industry averages.
    b. Give the principal value of using each of the three bases of comparison.

11. Name the major ratios useful in assessing (a) liquidity and (b) solvency.

12. Vern Thoms is puzzled. His company had a profit margin of 10% in 2022. He feels that this is an indication that the company is doing well. Tina Amos, his accountant, says that more information is needed to determine the company's financial well-being. Who is correct? Why?

13. What does each type of ratio measure?
    a. Liquidity ratios.
    b. Solvency ratios.
    c. Profitability ratios.

14. What is the difference between the current ratio and working capital?

15. Handi Mart, a retail store, has an accounts receivable turnover of 4.5 times. The industry average is 12.5 times. Does Handi Mart have a collection problem with its receivables?

16. Which ratios should be used to help answer each of these questions?
    a. How efficient is a company in using its assets to produce net sales?
    b. How near to sale is the inventory on hand?
    c. How many dollars of net income were earned for each dollar invested by the owners?
    d. How able is a company to meet interest charges as they become due?

17. At year-end, the price-earnings ratio of **General Motors** was 11.3, and the price-earnings ratio of **Microsoft** was 28.14. Which company did the stock market favor? Explain.

18. What is the formula for computing the payout ratio? Do you expect this ratio to be high or low for a growth company?

19. Holding all other factors constant, indicate whether each of the following changes generally signals good or bad news about a company.
    a. Increase in profit margin.
    b. Decrease in inventory turnover.
    c. Increase in current ratio.
    d. Decrease in earnings per share.
    e. Increase in price-earnings ratio.
    f. Increase in debt to assets ratio.
    g. Decrease in times interest earned.

20. The return on assets for Ayala Corporation is 7.6%. During the same year, Ayala's return on common stockholders' equity is 12.8%. What is the explanation for the difference in the two rates?

21. Which two ratios do you think should be of greatest interest in each of the following cases?
    a. A pension fund considering the purchase of 20-year bonds.
    b. A bank contemplating a short-term loan.
    c. A common stockholder.

22. Keanu Inc. has net income of $200,000, average shares of common stock outstanding of 40,000, and preferred dividends of $20,000 that were declared and paid during the period. What is Keanu's earnings per share of common stock? Fred Tyme, the president of Keanu, believes that the computed EPS of the company is high. Comment.

# Brief Exercises

**BE13.1 (LO 1), AP** On June 30, Flores Corporation discontinued its operations in Mexico. During the year, the operating income was $200,000 before taxes. On September 1, Flores disposed of the Mexico facility at a pretax loss of $640,000. The applicable tax rate is 25%. Show the discontinued operations section of Flores's income statement.

*Prepare a discontinued operations section of an income statement.*

**BE13.2 (LO 1), AP** An inexperienced accountant for Silva Corporation showed the following in the income statement: net income $337,500 and unrealized gain on available-for-sale securities (before taxes) $70,000. The unrealized gain on available-for-sale securities is subject to a 25% tax rate. Prepare a correct statement of comprehensive income.

*Prepare a statement of comprehensive income including unusual items.*

**BE13.3 (LO 1), C** On January 1, 2022, Bryce Inc. changed from the LIFO method of inventory costing to the FIFO method. Explain how this change in accounting principle should be treated in the company's financial statements.

*Indicate how a change in accounting principle is reported.*

**BE13.4 (LO 2), AP** Using these data from the comparative balance sheets of Rollaird Company, perform a horizontal analysis.

*Prepare horizontal analysis.*

|  | December 31, 2022 | December 31, 2021 |
|---|---|---|
| Accounts receivable (net) | $ 460,000 | $ 400,000 |
| Inventory | 780,000 | 650,000 |
| Total assets | 3,164,000 | 2,300,000 |

**BE13.5 (LO 2), AP** Using these data from the comparative balance sheets of Rollaird Company, perform a vertical analysis.

*Prepare vertical analysis.*

|  | December 31, 2022 | December 31, 2021 |
|---|---|---|
| Accounts receivable (net) | $ 460,000 | $ 400,000 |
| Inventory | 780,000 | 650,000 |
| Total assets | 3,164,000 | 2,800,000 |

**BE13.6 (LO 2), AP** Net income was $500,000 in 2020, $485,000 in 2021, and $518,400 in 2022. What is the percentage of change (a) from 2020 to 2021, and (b) from 2021 to 2022? Is the change an increase or a decrease?

*Calculate percentage of change.*

**BE13.7 (LO 2), AP** If Coho Company had net income of $382,800 in 2022 and it experienced a 16% increase in net income over 2021, what was its 2021 net income?

*Calculate net income.*

**BE13.8 (LO 2), AP** Vertical analysis (common-size) percentages for Palau Company's net sales, cost of goods sold, and expenses are listed here.

*Analyze change in net income.*

| Vertical Analysis | 2022 | 2021 | 2020 |
|---|---|---|---|
| Net sales | 100.0% | 100.0% | 100.0% |
| Cost of goods sold | 60.5 | 52.9 | 64.8 |
| Expenses | 25.0 | 26.6 | 27.5 |

Did Palau's net income as a percent of net sales increase, decrease, or remain unchanged over the 3-year period? Provide numerical support for your answer.

**BE13.9 (LO 2), AP** **Writing** Horizontal analysis (trend analysis) percentages for Phoenix Company's net sales, cost of goods sold, and expenses are listed here.

*Analyze change in net income.*

| Horizontal Analysis | 2022 | 2021 | 2020 |
|---|---|---|---|
| Net sales | 96.2% | 104.8% | 100.0% |
| Cost of goods sold | 101.0 | 98.0 | 100.0 |
| Expenses | 105.6 | 95.4 | 100.0 |

Explain whether Phoenix's net income increased, decreased, or remained unchanged over the 3-year period.

**BE13.10 (LO 3), AP** Suppose these selected condensed data are taken from recent balance sheets of Bob Evans Farms (in thousands).

*Calculate current ratio.*

|  | 2022 | 2021 |
|---|---|---|
| Cash | $ 13,606 | $ 7,669 |
| Accounts receivable (net) | 23,045 | 19,951 |
| Inventory | 31,087 | 31,345 |
| Other current assets | 12,522 | 11,909 |
| Total current assets | $ 80,260 | $ 70,874 |
| Total current liabilities | $245,805 | $326,203 |

Compute the current ratio for each year and comment on your results.

*Evaluate collection of accounts receivable.*

**BE13.11 (LO 3), AN** Writing The following data are taken from the financial statements of Colby Company.

|  | 2022 | 2021 |
|---|---|---|
| Accounts receivable (net), end of year | $ 550,000 | $ 540,000 |
| Net sales on account | 4,300,000 | 4,000,000 |
| Terms for all sales are 1/10, n/45 |  |  |

Compute for each year (a) the accounts receivable turnover and (b) the average collection period. What conclusions about the management of accounts receivable can be drawn from these data? At the end of 2020, accounts receivable (net) was $520,000.

*Evaluate management of inventory.*

**BE13.12 (LO 3), AN** Writing The following data were taken from the financial records of Mydorf Company.

|  | 2022 | 2021 |
|---|---|---|
| Net sales | $6,420,000 | $6,240,000 |
| Beginning inventory | 960,000 | 840,000 |
| Purchases | 4,840,000 | 4,661,000 |
| Ending inventory | 1,020,000 | 960,000 |

Compute for each year (a) the inventory turnover and (b) days in inventory. What conclusions concerning the management of the inventory can be drawn from these data?

*Calculate profitability ratios.*

**BE13.13 (LO 3), AN Staples, Inc.** is one of the largest suppliers of office products in the United States. Suppose it had net income of $738.7 million and net sales of $24,275.5 million in 2022. Its total assets were $13,073.1 million at the beginning of the year and $13,717.3 million at the end of the year. What is Staples, Inc.'s (a) asset turnover and (b) profit margin? (Round to two decimals.) Provide a brief interpretation of your results.

*Calculate profitability ratios.*

**BE13.14 (LO 3), AN** Hollie Company has stockholders' equity of $400,000 and net income of $72,000. It has a payout ratio of 18% and a return on assets of 20%. How much did Hollie pay in cash dividends, and what were its average total assets?

*Calculate and analyze free cash flow.*

**BE13.15 (LO 3), AN** Selected data taken from a recent year's financial statements of trading card company **Topps Company, Inc.** are as follows (in millions).

| | |
|---|---|
| Net sales | $326.7 |
| Current liabilities, beginning of year | 41.1 |
| Current liabilities, end of year | 62.4 |
| Net cash provided by operating activities | 10.4 |
| Total liabilities, beginning of year | 65.2 |
| Total liabilities, end of year | 73.2 |
| Capital expenditures | 3.7 |
| Cash dividends | 6.2 |

Compute the free cash flow. Provide a brief interpretation of your results.

# DO IT! Exercises

*Prepare a partial income statement and a statement of comprehensive income.*

**DO IT! 13.1 (LO 1), AP** In its proposed 2022 income statement, Hrabik Corporation reports income before income taxes $500,000, income taxes $100,000 (not including unusual items), loss on operation of discontinued music division $60,000, gain on disposal of discontinued music division $40,000, and unrealized loss on available-for-sale securities $150,000. The income tax rate is 20%. Prepare a correct partial income statement, beginning with income before income taxes, and a statement of comprehensive income for the year ended December 31, 2022.

*Prepare horizontal analysis.*

**DO IT! 13.2 (LO 2), AP** Summary financial information for Gandaulf Company is as follows.

|  | Dec. 31, 2022 | Dec. 31, 2021 |
|---|---|---|
| Current assets | $ 200,000 | $ 220,000 |
| Plant assets | 1,040,000 | 780,000 |
| Total assets | $1,240,000 | $1,000,000 |

Compute the amount and percentage changes in 2022 using horizontal analysis, assuming 2021 is the base year.

**DO IT! 13.3  (LO 3), AP**  The condensed financial statements of Murawski Company for the years 2021 and 2022 are presented as follows. (Amounts in thousands.)

*Compute ratios.*

| Murawski Company | | |
| --- | --- | --- |
| Balance Sheets | | |
| December 31 | | |
| | **2022** | **2021** |
| Current assets | | |
| Cash and cash equivalents | $ 330 | $ 360 |
| Accounts receivable (net) | 470 | 400 |
| Inventory | 460 | 390 |
| Prepaid expenses | 120 | 160 |
| Total current assets | 1,380 | 1,310 |
| Investments | 10 | 10 |
| Property, plant, and equipment (net) | 420 | 380 |
| Intangibles and other assets | 530 | 510 |
| Total assets | $2,340 | $2,210 |
| Current liabilities | $ 900 | $ 790 |
| Long-term liabilities | 410 | 380 |
| Stockholders' equity—common | 1,030 | 1,040 |
| Total liabilities and stockholders' equity | $2,340 | $2,210 |

| Murawski Company | | |
| --- | --- | --- |
| Income Statements | | |
| For the Years Ended December 31 | | |
| | **2022** | **2021** |
| Net sales | $3,800 | $3,460 |
| Expenses | | |
| Cost of goods sold | 955 | 890 |
| Selling & administrative expenses | 2,400 | 2,330 |
| Interest expense | 25 | 20 |
| Total expenses | 3,380 | 3,240 |
| Income before income taxes | 420 | 220 |
| Income tax expense | 126 | 66 |
| Net income | $ 294 | $ 154 |

Compute the following ratios for 2022 and 2021.

a. Current ratio.

b. Inventory turnover. (Inventory on 12/31/20 was $340.)

c. Profit margin.

d. Return on assets. (Assets on 12/31/20 were $1,900.)

e. Return on common stockholders' equity. (Stockholders' equity—common on 12/31/20 was $900.)

f. Debt to assets ratio.

g. Times interest earned.

## Exercises

*Prepare a correct partial income statement.*

**E13.1 (LO 1), AN** Writing For its fiscal year ending October 31, 2022, Haas Corporation reports the following partial data.

| | |
|---|---:|
| Income before income taxes | $540,000 |
| Income tax expense (20% × $420,000) | 84,000 |
| Income from continuing operations | 456,000 |
| Loss on discontinued operations | 120,000 |
| Net income | $336,000 |

The loss on discontinued operations was comprised of a $50,000 loss from operations and a $70,000 loss from disposal. The income tax rate is 20% on all items.

**Instructions**

a. Prepare a correct partial income statement, beginning with income before income taxes.

b. Explain in memo form why the original income statement data are misleading.

*Prepare a partial income statement and a statement of comprehensive income.*

**E13.2 (LO 1), AP** Trayer Corporation has income from continuing operations of $290,000 for the year ended December 31, 2022. It also has the following items (before considering income taxes).

1. An unrealized loss of $80,000 on available-for-sale securities.

2. A gain of $30,000 on the discontinuance of a division (comprised of a $10,000 loss from operations and a $40,000 gain on disposal).

Assume all items are subject to income taxes at a 20% tax rate.

**Instructions**

Prepare a partial income statement, beginning with income from continuing operations, and a statement of comprehensive income.

*Prepare horizontal analysis.*

**E13.3 (LO 2), AP** Here is financial information for Glitter Inc.

| | December 31, 2022 | December 31, 2021 |
|---|---:|---:|
| Current assets | $106,000 | $ 90,000 |
| Plant assets (net) | 400,000 | 350,000 |
| Current liabilities | 99,000 | 65,000 |
| Long-term liabilities | 122,000 | 90,000 |
| Common stock, $1 par | 130,000 | 115,000 |
| Retained earnings | 155,000 | 170,000 |

**Instructions**

Prepare a schedule showing a horizontal analysis for 2022, using 2021 as the base year.

*Prepare vertical analysis.*

**E13.4 (LO 2), AP** Operating data for Joshua Corporation are presented as follows.

| | 2022 | 2021 |
|---|---:|---:|
| Net sales | $800,000 | $600,000 |
| Cost of goods sold | 520,000 | 408,000 |
| Selling expenses | 120,000 | 72,000 |
| Administrative expenses | 60,000 | 48,000 |
| Income tax expense | 30,000 | 24,000 |
| Net income | 70,000 | 48,000 |

**Instructions**

Prepare a schedule showing a vertical analysis for 2022 and 2021.

**E13.5 (LO 2), AP** Hypothetical comparative condensed balance sheets of **Nike, Inc** are presented here.

*Prepare horizontal and vertical analyses.*

### Nike, Inc.
### Condensed Balance Sheets
### May 31
### ($ in millions)

|  | 2022 | 2021 |
|---|---|---|
| **Assets** | | |
| Current assets | $ 9,734 | $ 8,839 |
| Property, plant, and equipment (net) | 1,958 | 1,891 |
| Other assets | 1,558 | 1,713 |
| Total assets | $13,250 | $12,443 |
| **Liabilities and Stockholders' Equity** | | |
| Current liabilities | $ 3,277 | $ 3,322 |
| Long-term liabilities | 1,280 | 1,296 |
| Stockholders' equity | 8,693 | 7,325 |
| Total liabilities and stockholders' equity | $13,250 | $12,443 |

**Instructions**

a. Prepare a horizontal analysis of the balance sheet data for Nike, using 2021 as a base. (Show the amount of increase or decrease as well.)

b. Prepare a vertical analysis of the balance sheet data for Nike for 2022.

**E13.6 (LO 2), AP** Here are the comparative condensed income statements of Delaney Corporation.

*Prepare horizontal and vertical analyses.*

### Delaney Corporation
### Condensed Income Statements
### For the Years Ended December 31

|  | 2022 | 2021 |
|---|---|---|
| Net sales | $598,000 | $500,000 |
| Cost of goods sold | 477,000 | 420,000 |
| Gross profit | 121,000 | 80,000 |
| Operating expenses | 80,000 | 44,000 |
| Net income | $ 41,000 | $ 36,000 |

**Instructions**

a. Prepare a horizontal analysis of the income statement data for Delaney Corporation, using 2021 as a base. (Show the amounts of increase or decrease.)

b. Prepare a vertical analysis of the income statement data for Delaney Corporation for both years.

**E13.7 (LO 3), AP Nordstrom, Inc.** operates department stores in numerous states. Selected hypothetical financial statement data (in millions) for 2022 are presented below.

*Compute liquidity ratios.*

|  | End of Year | Beginning of Year |
|---|---|---|
| Cash and cash equivalents | $ 795 | $ 72 |
| Accounts receivable (net) | 2,035 | 1,942 |
| Inventory | 898 | 900 |
| Other current assets | 326 | 303 |
| Total current assets | $4,054 | $3,217 |
| Total current liabilities | $2,014 | $1,601 |

For the year, net credit sales were $8,258 million, cost of goods sold was $5,328 million, and net cash provided by operating activities was $1,251 million.

**Instructions**

Compute the current ratio, accounts receivable turnover, average collection period, inventory turnover, and days in inventory for the current year.

*Perform current ratio analysis.*

**E13.8 (LO 3), AP** Gwynn Incorporated had the following transactions involving current assets and current liabilities during February 2022.

Feb. 3   Collected accounts receivable of $15,000.
     7   Purchased equipment for $23,000 cash.
    11   Paid $3,000 for a 1-year insurance policy.
    14   Paid accounts payable of $12,000.
    18   Declared cash dividends of $4,000.

Additional information:
As of February 1, 2022, current assets were $120,000 and current liabilities were $40,000.

**Instructions**

Compute the current ratio as of the beginning of the month and after each transaction.

*Compute selected ratios.*

**E13.9 (LO 3), AP** Lendell Company has these comparative balance sheet data:

**Lendell Company**
**Balance Sheets**
**December 31**

|  | 2022 | 2021 |
|---|---|---|
| Cash | $ 15,000 | $ 30,000 |
| Accounts receivable (net) | 70,000 | 60,000 |
| Inventory | 60,000 | 50,000 |
| Plant assets (net) | 200,000 | 180,000 |
|  | $345,000 | $320,000 |
|  |  |  |
| Accounts payable | $ 50,000 | $ 60,000 |
| Bonds payable (15%) | 100,000 | 100,000 |
| Common stock, $10 par | 140,000 | 120,000 |
| Retained earnings | 55,000 | 40,000 |
|  | $345,000 | $320,000 |

Additional information for 2022:

1. Net income was $25,000.

2. Sales on account were $375,000. Sales returns and allowances amounted to $25,000.

3. Cost of goods sold was $198,000.

4. Net cash provided by operating activities was $48,000.

5. Capital expenditures were $25,000, and cash dividends paid were $10,000.

6. The bonds payable are due in 2035.

**Instructions**

Compute the following ratios at December 31, 2022.

a. Current ratio.

b. Accounts receivable turnover.

c. Average collection period.

d. Inventory turnover.

e. Days in inventory.

f. Free cash flow.

*Compute selected ratios.*

**E13.10 (LO 3), AP** Selected hypothetical comparative statement data for the giant bookseller **Barnes & Noble** are presented here. All balance sheet data are as of the end of the fiscal year (in millions).

|  | 2022 | 2021 |
|---|---|---|
| Net sales | $5,121.8 | $5,286.7 |
| Cost of goods sold | 3,540.6 | 3,679.8 |
| Net income | 75.9 | 135.8 |
| Accounts receivable (net) | 81.0 | 107.1 |
| Inventory | 1,203.5 | 1,358.2 |
| Total assets | 2,993.9 | 3,249.8 |
| Total common stockholders' equity | 921.6 | 1,074.7 |

**Instructions**

Compute the following ratios for 2022.

a. Profit margin.

b. Asset turnover.

c. Return on assets.

d. Return on common stockholders' equity.

e. Gross profit rate.

**E13.11 (LO 3), AP** Here is the income statement for Myers, Inc.

*Compute selected ratios.*

**Myers, Inc.**
**Income Statement**
**For the Year Ended December 31, 2022**

| | |
|---|---:|
| Net sales | $400,000 |
| Cost of goods sold | 230,000 |
| Gross profit | 170,000 |
| Expenses (including $16,000 interest and $24,000 income taxes) | 98,000 |
| Net income | $ 72,000 |

Additional information:

1. Common stock outstanding January 1, 2022, was 32,000 shares, and 40,000 shares were outstanding at December 31, 2022. (Use a simple average for weighted-average.)

2. The market price of Myers stock was $14 on December 31, 2022.

3. Cash dividends of $21,000 were declared and paid.

**Instructions**

Compute the following measures for 2022.

a. Earnings per share.

b. Price-earnings ratio.

c. Payout ratio.

d. Times interest earned.

**E13.12 (LO 3), AP** Panza Corporation experienced a fire on December 31, 2022, in which its financial records were partially destroyed. It has been able to salvage some of the records and has ascertained the following balances.

*Compute amounts from ratios.*

| | December 31, 2022 | December 31, 2021 |
|---|---:|---:|
| Cash | $ 30,000 | $ 10,000 |
| Accounts receivable (net) | 72,500 | 126,000 |
| Inventory | 200,000 | 180,000 |
| Accounts payable | 50,000 | 90,000 |
| Notes payable | 30,000 | 60,000 |
| Common stock, $100 par | 400,000 | 400,000 |
| Retained earnings | 113,500 | 101,000 |

Additional information:

1. The inventory turnover is 3.8 times.

2. The return on common stockholders' equity is 22%. The company had no additional capital accounts.

3. The accounts receivable turnover is 11.2 times.

4. The return on assets is 18%.

5. Total assets at December 31, 2021, were $605,000.

**Instructions**

Compute the following for Panza Corporation.

a. Cost of goods sold for 2022.

b. Net credit sales for 2022.

c. Net income for 2022.

d. Total assets at December 31, 2022.

*Compute ratios.*

**E13.13 (LO 3), AP** The condensed financial statements of Ness Company for the years 2021 and 2022 are as follows.

**Ness Company**
**Balance Sheets**
**December 31 (in thousands)**

|  | 2022 | 2021 |
|---|---|---|
| Current assets |  |  |
| Cash and cash equivalents | $ 330 | $ 360 |
| Accounts receivable (net) | 470 | 400 |
| Inventory | 460 | 390 |
| Prepaid expenses | 130 | 160 |
| Total current assets | 1,390 | 1,310 |
| Investments | 10 | 10 |
| Property, plant, and equipment (net) | 410 | 380 |
| Other assets | 530 | 510 |
| Total assets | $2,340 | $2,210 |
| Current liabilities | $ 820 | $ 790 |
| Long-term liabilities | 480 | 380 |
| Stockholders' equity—common | 1,040 | 1,040 |
| Total liabilities and stockholders' equity | $2,340 | $2,210 |

**Ness Company**
**Income Statements**
**For the Year Ended December 31 (in thousands)**

|  | 2022 | 2021 |
|---|---|---|
| Net sales | $3,800 | $3,460 |
| Expenses |  |  |
| Cost of goods sold | 970 | 890 |
| Selling and administrative expenses | 2,400 | 2,330 |
| Interest expense | 10 | 20 |
| Total expenses | 3,380 | 3,240 |
| Income before income taxes | 420 | 220 |
| Income tax expense | 168 | 88 |
| Net income | $ 252 | $ 132 |

Compute the following ratios for 2022 and 2021.

a. Current ratio.

b. Inventory turnover. (Inventory on December 31, 2020, was $340.)

c. Profit margin.

d. Return on assets. (Assets on December 31, 2020, were $1,900.)

e. Return on common stockholders' equity. (Stockholders' equity—common on December 31, 2020, was $900.)

f. Debt to assets ratio.

g. Times interest earned.

# Problems

**P13.1 (LO 2, 3), AN** [Writing] Here are comparative financial statement data for Duke Company and Lord Company, two competitors. All data are as of December 31, 2022, and December 31, 2021.

*Prepare vertical analysis and comment on profitability.*

|  | Duke Company | | Lord Company | |
|---|---|---|---|---|
|  | **2022** | **2021** | **2022** | **2021** |
| Net sales | $1,849,000 | | $546,000 | |
| Cost of goods sold | 1,063,200 | | 289,000 | |
| Operating expenses | 240,000 | | 82,000 | |
| Interest expense | 6,800 | | 3,600 | |
| Income tax expense | 62,000 | | 28,000 | |
| Current assets | 325,975 | $312,410 | 83,336 | $ 79,467 |
| Plant assets (net) | 526,800 | 500,000 | 139,728 | 125,812 |
| Current liabilities | 66,325 | 75,815 | 35,348 | 30,281 |
| Long-term liabilities | 113,990 | 90,000 | 29,620 | 25,000 |
| Common stock, $10 par | 500,000 | 500,000 | 120,000 | 120,000 |
| Retained earnings | 172,460 | 146,595 | 38,096 | 29,998 |

## Instructions

**a.** Prepare a vertical analysis of the 2022 income statement data for Duke Company and Lord Company.

**b.** Comment on the relative profitability of the companies by computing the 2022 return on assets and the return on common stockholders' equity for both companies.

**P13.2 (LO 3), AP** The comparative statements of Wahlberg Company are presented here.

*Compute ratios from balance sheets and income statements.*

**Wahlberg Company**
**Income Statements**
**For the Years Ended December 31**

|  | **2022** | **2021** |
|---|---|---|
| Net sales | $1,890,540 | $1,750,500 |
| Cost of goods sold | 1,058,540 | 1,006,000 |
| Gross profit | 832,000 | 744,500 |
| Selling and administrative expenses | 500,000 | 479,000 |
| Income from operations | 332,000 | 265,500 |
| Other expenses and losses | | |
|    Interest expense | 22,000 | 20,000 |
| Income before income taxes | 310,000 | 245,500 |
| Income tax expense | 92,000 | 73,000 |
| Net income | $ 218,000 | $ 172,500 |

**Wahlberg Company**
**Balance Sheets**
**December 31**

|  | **2022** | **2021** |
|---|---|---|
| **Assets** | | |
| Current assets | | |
|    Cash | $   60,100 | $  64,200 |
|    Debt investments (short-term) | 74,000 | 50,000 |
|    Accounts receivable (net) | 117,800 | 102,800 |
|    Inventory | 126,000 | 115,500 |
|    Total current assets | 377,900 | 332,500 |
| Plant assets (net) | 549,000 | 520,300 |
| Total assets | $1,026,900 | $852,800 |

|  | 2022 | 2021 |
|---|---|---|
| **Liabilities and Stockholders' Equity** | | |
| Current liabilities | | |
| Accounts payable | $ 160,000 | $145,400 |
| Income taxes payable | 43,500 | 42,000 |
| Total current liabilities | 203,500 | 187,400 |
| Bonds payable | 220,000 | 200,000 |
| Total liabilities | 423,500 | 387,400 |
| Stockholders' equity | | |
| Common stock ($5 par) | 290,000 | 300,000 |
| Retained earnings | 313,400 | 165,400 |
| Total stockholders' equity | 603,400 | 465,400 |
| Total liabilities and stockholders' equity | $1,026,900 | $852,800 |

All sales were on credit. Net cash provided by operating activities for 2022 was $220,000. Capital expenditures were $136,000, and cash dividends paid were $70,000.

**Instructions**

Compute the following ratios for 2022.

a. Earnings per share.

b. Return on common stockholders' equity.

c. Return on assets.

d. Current ratio.

e. Accounts receivable turnover.

f. Average collection period.

g. Inventory turnover.

h. Days in inventory.

i. Times interest earned.

j. Asset turnover.

k. Debt to assets ratio.

l. Free cash flow.

*Perform ratio analysis, and discuss changes in financial position and operating results.*

**P13.3 (LO 3), AN** Writing Condensed balance sheet and income statement data for Jergan Corporation are presented here.

**Jergan Corporation**
**Balance Sheets**
**December 31**

|  | 2022 | 2021 | 2020 |
|---|---|---|---|
| Cash | $ 30,000 | $ 20,000 | $ 18,000 |
| Accounts receivable (net) | 50,000 | 45,000 | 48,000 |
| Other current assets | 90,000 | 95,000 | 64,000 |
| Investments | 55,000 | 70,000 | 45,000 |
| Property, plant, and equipment (net) | 500,000 | 370,000 | 358,000 |
|  | $725,000 | $600,000 | $533,000 |
| Current liabilities | $ 85,000 | $ 80,000 | $ 70,000 |
| Long-term debt | 145,000 | 85,000 | 50,000 |
| Common stock, $10 par | 320,000 | 310,000 | 300,000 |
| Retained earnings | 175,000 | 125,000 | 113,000 |
|  | $725,000 | $600,000 | $533,000 |

**Jergan Corporation**
**Income Statements**
**For the Years Ended December 31**

|  | 2022 | 2021 |
|---|---|---|
| Sales | $740,000 | $600,000 |
| Less: Sales returns and allowances | 40,000 | 30,000 |
| Net sales | 700,000 | 570,000 |
| Cost of goods sold | 425,000 | 350,000 |
| Gross profit | 275,000 | 220,000 |
| Operating expenses (including income taxes) | 180,000 | 150,000 |
| Net income | $ 95,000 | $ 70,000 |

Additional information:

1. The market price of Jergan's common stock was $7.00, $7.50, and $8.50 for 2020, 2021, and 2022, respectively.

2. You must compute dividends declared. All declared dividends were paid in cash in the year of declaration.

## Instructions

a. Compute the following ratios for 2021 and 2022.

    1. Profit margin.

    2. Gross profit rate.

    3. Asset turnover.

    4. Earnings per share.

    5. Price-earnings ratio.

    6. Payout ratio.

    7. Debt to assets ratio

b. Based on the ratios calculated, discuss briefly the improvement or lack thereof in the financial position and operating results from 2021 to 2022 of Jergan Corporation.

**P13.4 (LO 3), AN** The following financial information is for Priscoll Company.

*Compute ratios; comment on overall liquidity and profitability.*

**Priscoll Company**
**Balance Sheets**
**December 31**

| | 2022 | 2021 |
|---|---|---|
| **Assets** | | |
| Cash | $ 70,000 | $ 65,000 |
| Debt investments (short-term) | 55,000 | 40,000 |
| Accounts receivable (net) | 104,000 | 90,000 |
| Inventory | 230,000 | 165,000 |
| Prepaid expenses | 25,000 | 23,000 |
| Land | 130,000 | 130,000 |
| Building and equipment (net) | 260,000 | 185,000 |
| Total assets | $874,000 | $698,000 |
| **Liabilities and Stockholders' Equity** | | |
| Notes payable (current) | $170,000 | $120,000 |
| Accounts payable | 65,000 | 52,000 |
| Accrued liabilities | 40,000 | 40,000 |
| Bonds payable, due 2025 | 250,000 | 170,000 |
| Common stock, $10 par | 200,000 | 200,000 |
| Retained earnings | 149,000 | 116,000 |
| Total liabilities and stockholders' equity | $874,000 | $698,000 |

**Priscoll Company**
**Income Statements**
**For the Years Ended December 31**

| | 2022 | 2021 |
|---|---|---|
| Net sales | $882,000 | $790,000 |
| Cost of goods sold | 640,000 | 575,000 |
| Gross profit | 242,000 | 215,000 |
| Operating expenses | 190,000 | 167,000 |
| Net income | $ 52,000 | $ 48,000 |

Additional information:

1. Inventory at the beginning of 2021 was $115,000.

2. Accounts receivable (net) at the beginning of 2021 were $86,000.

3. Total assets at the beginning of 2021 were $660,000.

4. No common stock transactions occurred during 2021 or 2022.

5. All sales were on credit.

## Instructions

**a.** Indicate, by using ratios, the change in liquidity and profitability of Priscoll Company from 2021 to 2022. (*Note:* Not all profitability ratios can be computed, nor can cash-basis ratios be computed.)

**b.** The following are three **independent** situations and a ratio that may be affected. For each situation, compute the affected ratio (1) as of December 31, 2022, and (2) as of December 31, 2023, after giving effect to the situation.

| Situation | Ratio |
|---|---|
| **1.** 18,000 shares of common stock were sold at par on July 1, 2023. Net income for 2023 was $54,000, and there were no dividends. | Return on common stockholders' equity |
| **2.** All of the notes payable were paid in 2023. All other liabilities remained at their December 31, 2022, levels. Total assets on December 31, 2023, were $900,000. | Debt to assets ratio |
| **3.** The market price of common stock was $9 and $12 on December 31, 2022 and 2023, respectively. Net income for 2023 was $54,000. (Use a simple average calculation for EPS). | Price-earnings ratio |

*Compute selected ratios, and compare liquidity, profitability, and solvency for two companies.*

**P13.5 (LO 3), AN** Selected hypothetical financial data of **Target** and **Walmart** for 2022 are presented here (in millions).

| | Target Corporation | Walmart Inc. |
|---|---|---|
| **Income Statement Data for Year** | | |
| Net sales | $65,357 | $408,214 |
| Cost of goods sold | 45,583 | 304,657 |
| Selling and administrative expenses | 15,101 | 79,607 |
| Interest expense | 707 | 2,065 |
| Other income (expense) | (94) | (411) |
| Income tax expense | 1,384 | 7,139 |
| Net income | $ 2,488 | $ 14,335 |
| **Balance Sheet Data (End of Year)** | | |
| Current assets | $18,424 | $ 48,331 |
| Noncurrent assets | 26,109 | 122,375 |
| Total assets | $44,533 | $170,706 |
| Current liabilities | $11,327 | $ 55,561 |
| Long-term debt | 17,859 | 44,089 |
| Total stockholders' equity | 15,347 | 71,056 |
| Total liabilities and stockholders' equity | $44,533 | $170,706 |
| **Beginning-of-Year Balances** | | |
| Total assets | $44,106 | $163,429 |
| Total stockholders' equity | 13,712 | 65,682 |
| Current liabilities | 10,512 | 55,390 |
| Total liabilities | 30,394 | 97,747 |
| **Other Data** | | |
| Average net accounts receivable | $ 7,525 | $ 4,025 |
| Average inventory | 6,942 | 33,836 |
| Net cash provided by operating activities | 5,881 | 26,249 |
| Capital expenditures | 1,729 | 12,184 |
| Cash dividends paid | 496 | 4,217 |

**Instructions**

a. For each company compute the following ratios. Assume all sales were on credit.

1. Current ratio.
2. Accounts receivable turnover.
3. Average collection period.
4. Inventory turnover.
5. Days in inventory.
6. Profit margin.

7. Asset turnover.
8. Return on assets.
9. Return on common stockholders' equity.
10. Debt to assets ratio.
11. Times interest earned.
12. Free cash flow

b. Compare the liquidity, solvency, and profitability of the two companies.

## Continuing Case

### Cookie Creations

(*Note:* This is a continuation of the Cookie Creations case from Chapters 1 through 12.)

**CC13** Natalie and Curtis have comparative balance sheets and income statements for Cookie & Coffee Creations Inc. They have been told that they can use these financial statements to prepare horizontal and vertical analyses, to calculate financial ratios, to analyze how their business is doing, and to make some decisions they have been considering.

*Go to WileyPLUS for complete case details and instructions.*

leungchopan/
Shutterstock.com

## Expand Your Critical Thinking

### Financial Reporting Problem: Apple Inc.

**CT13.1** Your parents are considering investing in **Apple Inc.** common stock. They ask you, as an accounting expert, to make an analysis of the company for them. Financial statements of Apple are presented in Appendix A. The complete annual report, including the notes to its financial statements, is available at the company's website.

**Instructions**

a. Make a 5-year trend analysis, using 2014 as the base year, of (1) net sales and (2) net income. Comment on the significance of the trend results.

b. Compute for 2018 and 2017 the (1) debt to assets ratio and (2) times interest earned. (See Note 3 for interest expense.) How would you evaluate Apple's long-term solvency?

c. Compute for 2018 and 2017 the (1) profit margin, (2) asset turnover, (3) return on assets, and (4) return on common stockholders' equity. How would you evaluate Apple's profitability? Total assets at September 24, 2016, were $321,686 million and total stockholders' equity at September 24, 2016, was $128,249 million.

d. What information outside the annual report may also be useful to your parents in making a decision about Apple?

### Comparative Analysis Problem: PepsiCo, Inc. vs. The Coca-Cola Company

**CT13.2** **PepsiCo's** financial statements are presented in Appendix B. Financial statements of **The Coca-Cola Company** are presented in Appendix C. The complete annual reports of PepsiCo and Coca-Cola, including the notes to the financial statements, are available at each company's respective website.

**Instructions**

a. Based on the information contained in these financial statements, determine each of the following for each company.

1. The percentage increase (decrease) in (i) net sales and (ii) net income from 2017 to 2018.

2. The percentage increase in (i) total assets and (ii) total common stockholders' (shareholders') equity from 2017 to 2018.

3. The basic earnings per share and price-earnings ratio for 2018. (For both PepsiCo and Coca-Cola, use the basic earnings per share.) Coca-Cola's common stock had a market price of $47.35 at the end of fiscal-year 2018, and PepsiCo's common stock had a market price of $110.48.

b. What conclusions concerning the two companies can be drawn from these data?

## Comparative Analysis Problem: Amazon.com, Inc. vs. Walmart Inc.

**CT13.3** The financial statements of **Amazon.com, Inc.** are presented in Appendix D. Financial statements of **Walmart Inc.** are presented in Appendix E.

**Instructions**

a. Based on the information in the financial statements, determine each of the following for each company:

1. The percentage increase (i) in total net sales for Amazon and net sales for Walmart, and (ii) in net income between the two most recent years provided.

2. The percentage increase (i) in total assets and (ii) in total stockholders' equity between the two most recent years provided.

3. The basic earnings per share for the most recent year provided.

b. What conclusions concerning the two companies can be drawn from these data?

## Decision-Making Across the Organization

**CT13.4** You are a loan officer for White Sands Bank of Taos. Paul Jason, president of P. Jason Corporation, has just left your office. He is interested in an 8-year loan to expand the company's operations. The borrowed funds would be used to purchase new equipment. As evidence of the company's debt-worthiness, Jason provided you with the following facts.

|  | 2022 | 2021 |
|---|---|---|
| Current ratio | 3.1 | 2.1 |
| Asset turnover | 2.8 | 2.2 |
| Net income | Up 32% | Down 8% |
| Earnings per share | $3.30 | $2.50 |

Jason is a very insistent (some would say pushy) man. When you told him that you would need additional information before making your decision, he acted offended and said, "What more could you possibly want to know?" You responded that, at a minimum, you would need complete, audited financial statements.

**Instructions**

With the class divided into groups, answer the following.

a. Explain why you would want the financial statements to be audited.

b. Discuss the implications of the ratios provided for the lending decision you are to make. That is, does the information paint a favorable picture? Are these ratios relevant to the decision?

c. List three other ratios that you would want to calculate for this company, and explain why you would use each.

## Real-World Focus

**CT13.5** You can use the Internet to employ comparative data and industry data to evaluate a company's performance and financial position.

**Instructions**

Identify two competing companies and then go to the **MarketWatch** website. Type one of the company names in the search box (e.g., **Best Buy**) and then use the information from the Profile tab to answer the following questions.

a. Evaluate the company's liquidity relative to the industry averages and to the competitor that you chose.

b. Evaluate the company's solvency relative to the industry averages and to the competitor that you chose.

c. Evaluate the company's profitability relative to the industry averages and to the competitor that you chose.

**CT13.6** The April 25, 2012, edition of the *Wall Street Journal* contains an article by Spencer Jakab entitled "Amazon's Valuation Is Hard to Justify."

### Instructions

Read the article and answer the following questions.

a. Explain what is meant by the statement that "On a split-adjusted basis, today's share price is the equivalent of $1,166."

b. The article says that **Amazon.com** nearly doubled its capital spending on items such as fulfillment centers (sophisticated warehouses where it finds, packages, and ships goods to customers). Discuss the implications that this spending would have on the company's return on assets in the short-term and in the long-term.

c. How does Amazon's P-E ratio compare to that of **Apple**, **Netflix**, and **Walmart**? What does this suggest about investors' expectations about Amazon's future earnings?

d. What factor does the article cite as a possible hurdle that might reduce Amazon's ability to raise its operating margin back to previous levels?

## Communication Activity

**CT13.7** Larry Dundee is the chief executive officer of Palmer Electronics. Dundee is an expert engineer but a novice in accounting. Dundee asks you, as an accounting student, to explain (a) the bases for comparison in analyzing Palmer's financial statements and (b) the factors affecting quality of earnings.

### Instructions

Write a memo to Larry Dundee that explains the basis for comparison and the factors affecting quality of earnings.

## Ethics Case

**CT13.8** René Kelly, president of RL Industries, wishes to issue a press release to bolster her company's image and maybe even its stock price, which has been gradually falling. As controller, you have been asked to provide a list of 20 financial ratios and other operating statistics for RL Industries' first-quarter financials and operations.

Two days after you provide the data requested, Erin Lourdes, the public relations director of RL, asks you to prove the accuracy of the financial and operating data contained in the press release written by the president and edited by Erin. In the news release, the president highlights the sales increase of 25% over last year's first quarter and the positive change in the current ratio from 1.5:1 last year to 3:1 this year. She also emphasizes that production was up 50% over the prior year's first quarter.

You note that the release contains only positive or improved ratios and none of the negative or deteriorated ratios. For instance, no mention is made that the debt to assets ratio has increased from 35% to 55%, that inventories are up 89%, and that although the current ratio improved, the accounts receivable turnover fell from 12 to 9. Nor is there any mention that the reported profit for the quarter would have been a loss had not the estimated lives of RL plant and machinery been increased by 30%. Erin emphasized, "The Pres wants this release by early this afternoon."

### Instructions

a. Who are the stakeholders in this situation?

b. Is there anything unethical in the president's actions?

c. Should you as controller remain silent? Does Erin have any responsibility?

## All About You

**CT13.9** In this chapter, you learned how to use many tools for performing a financial analysis of a company. When making personal investments, however, it is most likely that you won't be buying stocks and bonds in individual companies. Instead, when most people want to invest in stock, they buy mutual funds. By investing in a mutual fund, you reduce your risk because the fund diversifies by buying the stock of a variety of different companies, bonds, and other investments, depending on the stated goals of the fund.

Before you invest in a fund, you will need to decide what type of fund you want. For example, do you want a fund that has the potential of high growth (but also high risk), or are you looking for lower risk and a steady stream of income? Do you want a fund that invests only in U.S. companies, or do you want one that invests globally? Many resources are available to help you with these types of decisions.

**Instructions**

Do an Internet search on "Motley Fool Here's How to Determine Your Ideal Asset Allocation Strategy" and then complete the investment allocation questionnaire. Add up your total points to determine the type of investment fund that would be appropriate for you.

## FASB Codification Activity

**CT13.10** If your school has a subscription to the FASB Codification, log in and prepare responses to the following. Use the Master Glossary for determining the proper definitions.

   **a.** Discontinued operations.

   **b.** Comprehensive income.

## Answers to Insight and Accounting Across the Organization Questions

**What Does "Non-Recurring" Really Mean? Q:** If a company takes a large restructuring charge, what is the effect on the company's current income statement versus future ones? **A:** The current period's net income can be greatly diminished by a large restructuring charge. The net incomes in future periods can be enhanced because they are relieved of costs (i.e., depreciation and labor expenses) that would have been charged to them.

**More Frequent Ups and Downs Q:** When predicting future earnings, how should analysts treat the one-time charge that results from a switch to the different approach for accounting for pension plans? **A:** Because the change in principle will only happen once, it should be ignored when predicting future earnings. That is, because it will not happen again in future periods, it would not be included in estimates of future results.

**How to Manage the Current Ratio Q:** How might management influence a company's current ratio? **A:** Management can affect the current ratio by speeding up or withholding payments on accounts payable just before the balance sheet date. Management can alter the cash balance by increasing or decreasing long-term assets or long-term debt, or by issuing or purchasing common stock.

**High Ratings Can Bring Low Returns Q:** Why are credit rating agencies important to the financial markets? **A:** Credit rating agencies perform financial analysis on publicly traded companies and then publish research reports and credit ratings. Investors and creditors rely on the information provided by credit rating agencies in making investment and lending decisions.

# A Look at IFRS

> ## LEARNING OBJECTIVE 4
> Compare financial statement analysis and income statement presentation under GAAP and IFRS.

The tools of financial statement analysis are the same throughout the world. Techniques such as vertical and horizontal analysis, for example, are tools used by analysts regardless of whether GAAP- or IFRS-related financial statements are being evaluated. In addition, the ratios provided in the text are the same ones that are used internationally.

As in GAAP, the income statement is a required statement under IFRS. In addition, the content and presentation of an IFRS income statement is similar to the one used for GAAP. *IAS 1* (revised),

"Presentation of Financial Statements," provides general guidelines for the reporting of income statement information. In general, the differences in the presentation of financial statement information are relatively minor.

## Key Points

Following are the key similarities between GAAP and IFRS as related to financial statement analysis and income statement presentation. There are no significant differences between the two standards.

- The tools of financial statement analysis covered in this chapter are universal and therefore no significant differences exist in the analysis methods used.
- The basic objectives of the income statement are the same under both GAAP and IFRS. As indicated in the text, a very important objective is to ensure that users of the income statement can evaluate the sustainable income of the company. Thus, both the IASB and the FASB are interested in distinguishing normal levels of income from unusual items in order to better predict a company's future profitability.
- The basic accounting for discontinued operations is the same under IFRS and GAAP.
- The accounting for changes in accounting principles and changes in accounting estimates are the same for both GAAP and IFRS.
- Both GAAP and IFRS follow the same approach in reporting comprehensive income.

# IFRS Practice

## IFRS Self-Test Questions

1. The basic tools of financial analysis are the same under both GAAP and IFRS **except** that:

   a. horizontal analysis cannot be done because the format of the statements is sometimes different.

   b. vertical analysis cannot be done under IFRS.

   c. the current ratio cannot be computed because current liabilities are often reported before current assets in IFRS statements of position.

   d. None of the answer choices is correct.

2. Presentation of comprehensive income must be reported under IFRS in:

   a. the statement of stockholders' equity.

   b. the income statement ending with net income.

   c. the notes to the financial statements.

   d. a statement of comprehensive income.

3. In preparing its income statement for 2022, Parmalane assembles the following information.

   | | |
   |---|---|
   | Net sales | $500,000 |
   | Cost of goods sold | 300,000 |
   | Operating expenses | 40,000 |
   | Loss on discontinued operations | 20,000 |

   Ignoring income taxes, what is Parmalane's income from continuing operations for 2022 under IFRS?

   a. $260,000.

   b. $250,000.

   c. $240,000.

   d. $160,000.

## International Financial Reporting Problem: Louis Vuitton

**IFRS13.1** The financial statements of **Louis Vuitton** are presented in Appendix F. The complete consolidated financial statements, including the notes to its financial statements, are available at the company's website.

### Instructions

Use the company's 2018 consolidated financial statements to answer the following questions.

a. What was the company's profit margin for 2018? Has it increased or decreased from 2017?

b. What was the company's operating profit for 2018?

c. The company reported comprehensive income of €6,337 million in 2018. What are the other comprehensive gains and losses reported in 2018?

### Answers to IFRS Self-Test Questions

1. d   2. d   3. d

iNoppadol/Shutterstock.com

# Managerial Accounting

## Chapter Preview

This chapter focuses on issues illustrated in the following Feature Story about **Current Designs** and its parent company **Wenonah Canoe**. To succeed, the company needs to determine and control the costs of material, labor, and overhead, and understand the relationship between costs and profits. Managers often make decisions that determine their company's fate—and their own. Managers are evaluated on the results of their decisions. Managerial accounting provides tools to assist management in making decisions and evaluating the effectiveness of those decisions.

## Feature Story

### Just Add Water ... and Paddle

Mike Cichanowski grew up on the Mississippi River in Winona, Minnesota. At a young age, he learned to paddle a canoe so he could explore the river. Before long, Mike began crafting his own canoes from bent wood and fiberglass in his dad's garage. Then, when his canoe-making shop outgrew the garage, he moved it into an old warehouse. When that was going to be torn down, Mike came to a critical juncture in his life. He took out a bank loan and built his own small shop, giving birth to the company **Wenonah Canoe**.

Wenonah Canoe soon became known as a pioneer in developing techniques to get the most out of new materials such as plastics, composites, and carbon fibers—maximizing strength while minimizing weight.

In the 1990s, as kayaking became popular, Mike made another critical decision when he acquired **Current Designs**, a premier Canadian kayak manufacturer. This venture allowed Wenonah to branch out with new product lines while providing Current Designs with much-needed capacity expansion and manufacturing expertise. Mike moved Current Designs' headquarters to Minnesota and made a big (and potentially risky) investment in a new production facility. Today, the company's 90 employees produce about 12,000 canoes and kayaks per year. These are sold across the country and around the world.

Mike will tell you that business success is "a three-legged stool." The first leg is the knowledge and commitment to make a great product. Wenonah's canoes and Current Designs' kayaks are widely regarded as among the very best. The second leg is the ability to sell your product. Mike's company started off making great canoes, but it took a little longer to figure out how to sell them. The third leg is not something that most of you would immediately associate with entrepreneurial success. It is what goes on behind the scenes—accounting. Good accounting information is absolutely critical to the countless decisions, big and small, that ensure the survival and growth of the company.

Bottom line: No matter how good your product is, and no matter how many units you sell, if you don't have a firm grip on your numbers, you are up a creek without a paddle.

**Source:** *www.wenonah.com.*

 Watch the *What Is Managerial Accounting?* video in WileyPLUS for an introduction to managerial accounting and the topics presented in the remaining chapters of this text.

# Chapter Outline

| LEARNING OBJECTIVES | REVIEW | PRACTICE |
|---|---|---|
| **LO 1**  Identify the features of managerial accounting and the functions of management. | • Comparing managerial and financial accounting<br>• Management functions<br>• Organizational structure | **DO IT! 1**  Managerial Accounting Overview |
| **LO 2**  Describe the classes of manufacturing costs and the differences between product and period costs. | • Manufacturing costs<br>• Product versus period costs<br>• Illustration of cost concepts | **DO IT! 2**  Managerial Cost Concepts |
| **LO 3**  Demonstrate how to compute cost of goods manufactured and prepare financial statements for a manufacturer. | • Balance sheet<br>• Income statement<br>• Cost of goods manufactured<br>• Cost of goods manufactured schedule | **DO IT! 3**  Cost of Goods Manufactured |
| **LO 4**  Discuss trends in managerial accounting. | • Service industries<br>• Focus on the value chain<br>• Balanced scorecard<br>• Business ethics<br>• Corporate social responsibility<br>• The value of data analytics | **DO IT! 4**  Trends in Managerial Accounting |

**Go to the Review and Practice section at the end of the chapter for a targeted summary and practice applications with solutions.**

**Visit WileyPLUS for additional tutorials and practice opportunities.**

# Managerial Accounting Basics

**LEARNING OBJECTIVE 1**

Identify the features of managerial accounting and the functions of management.

**Managerial accounting** provides economic and financial information for managers and other internal users. The skills that you learn in these next chapters will be vital to your future success in business. You don't believe us? Let's look at examples of some of the crucial activities of employees at **Current Designs** and where those activities are addressed in this text.

- In order to know whether it is making a profit, Current Designs needs accurate information about the cost of each kayak (Chapters 15, 16, and 17). To be profitable, Current Designs adjusts the number of kayaks it produces in response to changes in economic conditions and consumer tastes. It needs to understand how changes in the number of kayaks it produces impact its production costs and profitability (Chapters 18 and 19).
- Further, Current Designs' managers often consider alternative courses of action. For example, should the company accept a special order from a customer, produce a particular kayak component internally or outsource it, or continue or discontinue a particular product line (Chapter 20)? Related to this decision is determining what price to charge for the kayaks (Chapter 21).
- In order to plan for the future, Current Designs prepares budgets (Chapter 22), and then compares its budgeted numbers with its actual results to evaluate performance and identify areas that need to change (Chapters 23 and 24).
- Finally, Current Designs sometimes needs to make substantial investment decisions, such as the building of a new factory or the purchase of new equipment (Chapter 25).

Someday, you are going to face decisions just like these. You may end up in sales, marketing, management, production, or finance. You may work for a company that provides medical care, produces software, or serves up mouth-watering meals. No matter what your job position or product, the skills you acquire in this class will increase your chances of business success. Put another way, in business you can either guess or you can make an informed decision. As former **Microsoft** CEO Steve Ballmer said, "If you're supposed to be making money in business and supposed to be satisfying customers and building market share, there are numbers that characterize those things. And if somebody can't speak to me quantitatively about it, then I'm nervous." These next chapters give you the skills you need to quantify information so you can make informed business decisions.

## Comparing Managerial and Financial Accounting

There are both similarities and differences between managerial and financial accounting.

- Each field of accounting deals with the economic events of a business. For example, *determining* the unit cost of manufacturing a product is part of managerial accounting. *Reporting* the total cost of goods manufactured and sold is part of financial accounting.
- Both managerial and financial accounting require that a company's economic events be quantified and communicated to interested parties.

**Illustration 14.1** summarizes the principal differences between financial accounting and managerial accounting.

ILLUSTRATION 14.1   **Differences between financial and managerial accounting**

| Feature | Financial Accounting | Managerial Accounting |
|---|---|---|
| Primary Users of Reports | External users: stockholders, creditors, and regulators. | Internal users: officers and managers. |
| Types and Frequency of Reports | External financial statements. Quarterly and annually. | Internal reports. As frequently as needed. |
| Purpose of Reports | General-purpose. | Special-purpose for specific decisions. |
| Content of Reports | Pertains to business as a whole. Highly aggregated (condensed). Limited to accrual accounting and cost data. Governed by generally accepted accounting principles (GAAP). | Pertains to subunits of the business. Very detailed. Extends beyond accrual accounting to any relevant data. Evaluated based on relevance to decisions. |
| Verification Process | Audited by CPA. | No independent audits. |

# Management Functions

Managers' activities and responsibilities can be classified into three broad functions:

1. Planning.
2. Directing.
3. Controlling.

In performing these functions, managers make decisions that have a significant impact on the organization.

**Planning** requires managers to look ahead and to establish objectives.

- These objectives are often diverse: maximizing short-term profits and market share, maintaining a commitment to environmental protection, and contributing to social programs.
- A key objective of management is to **add value** to the business under its control. Value is usually measured by the price of the company's stock and by the potential selling price of the company.

For example, **Hewlett-Packard**, in an attempt to gain a stronger foothold in the computer industry, greatly reduced its prices to compete with **Dell**.

**Directing** involves coordinating a company's diverse activities and human resources to produce a smooth-running operation.

- This function relates to implementing planned objectives and providing necessary incentives to motivate employees.
- Directing also involves selecting executives, appointing managers and supervisors, and hiring and training employees.

For example, manufacturers such as **Campbell Soup Company**, **General Motors**, and **Dell** need to coordinate purchasing, manufacturing, warehousing, and selling. Service corporations such as **American Airlines**, **Federal Express**, and **AT&T** coordinate scheduling, sales, service, and acquisitions of equipment and supplies.

The third management function, **controlling**, is the process of keeping the company's activities on track.

- In controlling operations, managers determine whether planned goals are met.
- When there are deviations from targeted objectives, managers decide what changes are needed to get back on track.

Scandals at companies like **Theranos** and **Danske Bank** attest to the fact that companies need adequate controls to ensure that the company develops and distributes accurate information.

How do managers achieve control? A smart manager in a very small operation can make personal observations, ask good questions, and know how to evaluate the answers. But using this approach in a larger organization would result in chaos. Imagine the president of **Apple** attempting to determine whether the company is meeting its planned objectives without some record of what has happened and what is expected to occur. Thus, large businesses typically use a formal system of evaluation. These systems include such features as budgets, responsibility centers, and performance evaluation reports—all of which are features of managerial accounting.

Decision-making is not a separate management function. Rather, it is the outcome of the exercise of good judgment in planning, directing, and controlling.

# Organizational Structure

Most companies prepare **organization charts** to show the interrelationships of activities and the delegation of authority and responsibility within the company. **Illustration 14.2** shows a typical organization chart.

**ILLUSTRATION 14.2**   **A typical corporate organization chart**

Stockholders own the corporation. They provide oversight indirectly through a **board of directors** they elect.

- The board formulates the operating policies for the company or organization.
- The board selects officers, such as a president and one or more vice presidents, to execute policy and to perform daily management functions.

The **chief executive officer (CEO)** has overall responsibility for managing the business. As the organization chart shows, the CEO delegates responsibilities to other officers.

Responsibilities within the company are frequently classified as either line or staff positions.

- Employees with **line positions** are directly involved in the company's primary revenue-generating operating activities. Examples of line positions include the vice president of operations, vice president of marketing, factory managers, supervisors, and production personnel.

- Employees with **staff positions** are involved in activities that support the efforts of the line employees. In a company like **General Electric** or **Facebook**, employees in finance, legal, and human resources have staff positions.

- While activities of staff employees are vital to the company, these employees are nonetheless there to support the line employees who engage in the company's primary operations.

The **chief financial officer (CFO)** is responsible for all of the accounting and finance issues the company faces. The CFO is supported by the **controller** and the **treasurer**. The controller's responsibilities include:

1. Maintaining the accounting records.
2. Ensuring an adequate system of internal control.
3. Preparing financial statements, tax returns, and internal reports.

The treasurer has custody of the corporation's funds and is responsible for maintaining the company's cash position.

Also serving the CFO is the internal audit staff. The staff's responsibilities include:

- Reviewing the reliability and integrity of financial information provided by the controller and treasurer.

- Ensuring that internal control systems are functioning properly to safeguard corporate assets.

- Investigating compliance with policies and regulations.

In many companies, these staff members also determine whether resources are used in the most economical and efficient fashion.

The vice president of operations oversees employees with line positions. For example, the company might have multiple factory managers, each of whom reports to the vice president of operations. Each factory also has department managers, such as fabricating, painting, and shipping, each of whom reports to the factory manager.

---

## Management Insight    DPR Construction

### Does a Company Need a CEO?

Can a company function without a person at the top? Nearly all companies have a CEO although some, such as **Oracle**, **Chipotle**, and **Whole Foods**, have operated with two people in the CEO position. **Samsung** even had three CEOs at the same time. On the other hand, **Abercrombie & Fitch** operated for more than two years without a CEO because its CEO unexpectedly quit and a suitable replacement was hard to find. In fact, some companies replace the CEO position with a management committee. These companies feel this structure improves decision-making and increases

Sam Edwards/Caiaimage/
Getty Images

collaboration. For example, the 4,000 employees of **DPR Construction** are overseen by an eight-person committee. Committee members are rotated off gradually but then continue to advise current members. The company notes that this approach provides more continuity over time than the sometimes sudden and harsh changes that occur when CEOs are replaced.

**Source:** Rachel Feintzeig, "Companies Manage with No CEO," *Wall Street Journal* (December 13, 2016).

**What are some of the advantages cited by companies that choose a structure that lacks a CEO? (Answer is available at the end of the chapter.)**

## DO IT! 1 | Managerial Accounting Overview

Indicate whether the following statements are true or false. If false, explain why.

1. Managerial accountants have a single role within an organization: collecting and reporting costs to management.
2. Financial accounting reports are general-purpose and intended for external users.
3. Managerial accounting reports are special-purpose and issued as frequently as needed.
4. Managers' activities and responsibilities can be classified into three broad functions: cost accounting, budgeting, and internal control.
5. Managerial accounting reports must now comply with generally accepted accounting principles (GAAP).

### Solution

1. False. Managerial accountants do determine product costs, but they are also responsible for evaluating how well the company employs its resources. As a result, when the company makes critical strategic decisions, managerial accountants serve as team members alongside personnel from production, marketing, and engineering.
2. True.
3. True.
4. False. Managers' activities are classified into three broad functions: planning, directing, and controlling. Planning requires managers to look ahead to establish objectives. Directing involves coordinating a company's diverse activities and human resources to produce a smooth-running operation. Controlling keeps the company's activities on track.
5. False. Managerial accounting reports are for internal use and thus do not have to comply with GAAP.

Related exercise material: **BE14.1, BE14.2, DO IT! 14.1, and E14.1.**

**ACTION PLAN**

- **Understand that managerial accounting is a field of accounting that provides economic and financial information for managers and other internal users.**
- **Understand that financial accounting provides information for external users.**
- **Analyze which users require which different types of information.**

# Managerial Cost Concepts

### LEARNING OBJECTIVE 2

Describe the classes of manufacturing costs and the differences between product and period costs.

In order for managers at **Current Designs** to plan, direct, and control operations effectively, they need good information. One very important type of information relates to costs. Managers should ask questions such as the following.

1. What costs are involved in making a product or performing a service?
2. If we decrease production volume, will costs change?
3. What impact will automation have on total costs?
4. How can we best control costs?

To answer these questions, managers obtain and analyze reliable and relevant cost information. The first step is to understand the various cost categories that companies use.

# Manufacturing Costs

**Manufacturing** consists of activities and processes that convert raw materials into finished goods. Contrast this type of operation with merchandising, which sells products in the form in which they are purchased.

- Manufacturing costs incurred to produce a product are classified as direct materials, direct labor, and manufacturing overhead.
- Typically, manufacturing costs are incurred at the production facility (the factory). The terms *manufacturing cost* and *product cost* are used interchangeably.

## Direct Materials

Direct Materials

To obtain the materials that will be converted into the finished product, the manufacturer purchases raw materials. **Raw materials** are the basic materials and parts used in the manufacturing process.

Raw materials that can be physically and directly associated with the finished product during the manufacturing process are **direct materials**. Examples include flour in the baking of bread, syrup in the bottling of soft drinks, and steel in the making of automobiles. A primary direct material of many Current Designs' kayaks is polyethylene powder. Some of its high-performance kayaks use Kevlar®.

Some raw materials cannot be easily associated with the finished product. These are called indirect materials. **Indirect materials** have one of two characteristics:

1. They do not physically become part of the finished product (such as polishing compounds used by Current Designs for the finishing touches on kayaks).
2. They are impractical to trace to the finished product because their physical association with the finished product is too small in terms of cost (such as cotter pins and lock washers used in kayak rudder assembly).

Companies account for indirect materials as part of **manufacturing overhead**. So, all direct materials are raw materials, but not all raw materials are direct materials.

## Direct Labor

Direct Labor

The work of factory employees that can be physically and directly associated with converting raw materials into finished goods is **direct labor**. Bottlers at **Coca-Cola**, bakers at **Hostess Brands**, and equipment operators at **Current Designs** are employees whose activities are usually classified as direct labor. **Indirect labor** refers to the work of manufacturing-related employees that has no physical association with the making of the finished product or for which it is impractical to trace costs to the goods produced. Examples include salaries and wages of factory maintenance people, factory security, product quality inspectors, and factory supervisors. While these employees work in the production facility, they are not directly involved in converting raw materials into the finished product. Like indirect materials, companies classify indirect labor as **manufacturing overhead**.

## Manufacturing Overhead

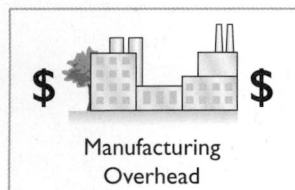

Manufacturing Overhead

**Manufacturing overhead** consists of manufacturing costs that are indirectly associated with the manufacture of the finished product.

- Manufacturing overhead includes indirect materials, indirect labor, depreciation on factory buildings and machines, and insurance, taxes, and maintenance on factory facilities.
- If the cost is manufacturing-related but cannot be classified as direct materials or direct labor, it should be considered manufacturing overhead.

One study of manufactured goods found the following magnitudes of the three different product costs as a percentage of the total product cost: direct materials 54%, direct labor 13%, and manufacturing overhead 33% (see **Alternative Terminology**). Note that the direct labor component is the smallest. This component of product cost is dropping substantially because of automation. Companies are working hard to increase productivity by decreasing labor. In some companies, direct labor has become as little as 5% of the total cost.

Tracing direct materials and direct labor costs to specific products is fairly straightforward. Good recordkeeping can tell a company how much plastic it used in making each type of gear, or how many hours of factory labor it took to assemble a part. But tracing overhead costs to specific products presents problems. How much of the purchasing agent's salary is attributable to the hundreds of different products made in the same factory? What about the grease that keeps the machines running smoothly, or the electricity costs of the factory? Boiled down to its simplest form, the question becomes: Which products cause the incurrence of which costs? In subsequent chapters, we show various methods of aggregating and allocating overhead to products as these costs cannot be directly traced.

**ALTERNATIVE TERMINOLOGY**

Some companies use terms such as *factory overhead, indirect manufacturing costs,* and *burden* instead of manufacturing overhead.

# Product versus Period Costs

Each of the manufacturing cost components—direct materials, direct labor, and manufacturing overhead—are product costs. As the term suggests, **product costs** are costs that are a necessary and integral part of producing the finished product (see **Alternative Terminology**).

- All manufacturing costs are classified as product costs.
- Companies record product costs, when incurred, as an asset called inventory.
- These costs do not become expenses until the company sells the finished goods inventory.
- At that point, the company records the expense as cost of goods sold.

**ALTERNATIVE TERMINOLOGY**

All manufacturing costs are product costs, which are also called *inventoriable* costs.

**Period costs** are costs that are matched with the revenue of a specific time period rather than included in inventory as part of the cost to produce a salable product.

- These are nonmanufacturing costs.
- Period costs include selling and administrative expenses.
- In order to determine net income, companies deduct these period costs from revenues in the period in which they are incurred.

**Illustration 14.3** summarizes these relationships and cost terms. Our main concern in this chapter is with product costs.

**ILLUSTRATION 14.3**

**Product versus period costs**

**All Costs**

**Product Costs**
Manufacturing Costs
(Inventoriable)

- Direct Materials
- Direct Labor
- Manufacturing Overhead
  - Indirect materials
  - Indirect labor
  - Other indirect costs

**Period Costs**
Nonmanufacturing Costs
(Non-Inventoriable)

- Selling Expenses
- Administrative Expenses

# Illustration of Cost Concepts

To improve your understanding of cost concepts, we illustrate them here through an extended example. Suppose you started your own snowboard factory, Terrain Park Boards. Think that's impossible? **Burton Snowboards** was started by Jake Burton Carpenter, when he was only 23 years old. Jake initially experimented with 100 different prototype designs before settling on a final design. Then Jake, along with two relatives and a friend, started making 50 boards per day in Londonderry, Vermont. Unfortunately, while they made a lot of boards in their first year, they were only able to sell 300 of them. To get by during those early years, Jake taught tennis and tended bar to pay the bills.

Illustration 14.4 shows some of the costs that your snowboard factory, Terrain Park Boards, would incur. We have classified each cost as a product cost or a period cost, as well as provided an explanation for the classification. We have also specified whether product costs are direct materials, direct labor, or manufacturing overhead.

**ILLUSTRATION 14.4**

**Assignment of costs to cost categories**

| Cost | Product Cost (direct materials, direct labor, or manufacturing overhead) | Period Cost (non-manufacturing) | Explanation |
|---|---|---|---|
| 1. Wood cores, fiberglass, and resin ($30 per board) | Direct materials | | Essential elements of finished product |
| 2. Labor to trim and shape boards ($40 per board) | Direct labor | | Physically and directly associated with converting raw materials into finished goods |
| 3. Factory equipment depreciation ($25,000) | Manufacturing overhead | | Factory cost that is not direct materials or direct labor |
| 4. Property taxes on factory building ($6,000 per year) | Manufacturing overhead | | Factory cost that is not direct materials or direct labor |
| 5. Advertising costs ($60,000 per year) | | X | Not a cost associated with producing product |
| 6. Sales commissions ($20 per board) | | X | Not a cost associated with producing product |
| 7. Factory maintenance salaries ($25,000 per year) | Manufacturing overhead | | A factory cost, but employees are not physically and directly involved with converting raw materials into finished goods |
| 8. Salary of factory manager ($70,000 per year) | Manufacturing overhead | | A factory cost, but employees are not physically and directly involved with converting raw materials into finished goods |
| 9. Cost of shipping boards to customers ($8 per board) | | X | Not a cost associated with producing product |
| 10. Salary of product quality inspector ($20,000 per year) | Manufacturing overhead | | A factory cost, but employees are not physically and directly involved with converting raw materials into finished goods |

**Total manufacturing costs** are the sum of the **product costs**—direct materials, direct labor, and manufacturing overhead—incurred in the current period. If Terrain Park Boards produces 10,000 snowboards the first year, the total manufacturing costs would be $846,000, as shown in **Illustration 14.5**.

Once it knows the total manufacturing costs, Terrain Park Boards can compute the average manufacturing cost per unit. Assuming 10,000 units, the cost to produce one snowboard is $84.60 ($846,000 ÷ 10,000 units).

| Cost Item | Manufacturing Cost |
|---|---|
| 1. Material cost ($30 × 10,000) | $300,000 |
| 2. Labor cost ($40 × 10,000) | 400,000 |
| 3. Depreciation on factory equipment | 25,000 |
| 4. Property taxes on factory building | 6,000 |
| 7. Factory maintenance salaries | 25,000 |
| 8. Salary of factory manager | 70,000 |
| 10. Salary of product quality inspector | 20,000 |
| **Total manufacturing product costs** | **$846,000** |

**ILLUSTRATION 14.5**

**Computation of total manufacturing product costs**

The cost concepts discussed in this chapter are used extensively in subsequent chapters. So study Illustration 14.4 carefully. If you do not understand any of these classifications, go back and reread the appropriate section.

---

**Service Company Insight**     Allegiant Airlines

Stephen Strathdee\
iStock.com

### Low Fares but Decent Profits

When other airlines were cutting flight service due to recession, **Allegiant Airlines** increased capacity by 21%. Sounds crazy, doesn't it? But it must have known something because while the other airlines were losing money, it was generating profits. In fact, it often has the industry's highest profit margins. Consider also that its average one-way fare is only $83. So how does it make money? As a low-budget airline, it focuses on controlling costs.

Allegiant purchases used planes for $3 million each rather than new planes for $40 million. It flies out of small towns, so wages are low and competition is nonexistent. It minimizes hotel costs by having its flight crews finish their day in their home cities. The company also only flies a route if its 150-passenger planes are nearly full (it averages about 90% of capacity). The bottom line is that Allegiant knows its costs to the penny. Knowing what your costs are might not be glamorous, but it sure beats losing money.

**Sources:** Susan Carey, "For Allegiant, Getaways Mean Profits," *Wall Street Journal Online* (February 18, 2009); and Scott Mayerowitz, "Tiny Allegiant Air Thrives on Low Costs, High Fees," *http://bigstory.ap.org* (June 28, 2013).

**What are some of the line items that would appear in the cost of services performed schedule of an airline? (Answer is available at the end of the chapter.)**

---

## DO IT! 2 | Managerial Cost Concepts

A bicycle company has these costs: tires, wages of employees who put tires on the wheels, factory building depreciation, advertising expenditures, factory machine lubricants, spokes, salary of factory manager, salary of accountant, handlebars, salaries of factory maintenance employees, and salary of product quality inspector. Classify each of these costs as a product cost or a period cost. Specify direct materials, direct labor, or manufacturing overhead for product costs.

### Solution

| Cost | Product Cost | Period Cost |
|---|---|---|
| Tires | Direct materials | |
| Wages of employees who put tires on the wheels | Direct labor | |
| Factory building depreciation | Manufacturing overhead | |
| Advertising expenditures | | X |
| Factory machine lubricants | Manufacturing overhead | |
| Spokes | Direct materials | |
| Salary of factory manager | Manufacturing overhead | |
| Salary of accountant | | X |
| Handlebars | Direct materials | |
| Salaries of factory maintenance employees | Manufacturing overhead | |
| Salary of product quality inspector | Manufacturing overhead | |

**ACTION PLAN**

- **Direct materials:** any raw materials physically and directly associated with the finished product.

- **Direct labor:** the work of factory employees directly associated with the finished product.

- **Manufacturing overhead:** any costs indirectly associated with the finished product.

- **Costs that are not product costs are period costs.**

Related exercise material: **BE14.3, BE14.4, BE14.5, BE14.6, DO IT! 14.2, E14.2, E14.3, E14.4, E14.5, E14.6, and E14.7.**

# Manufacturing Costs in Financial Statements

**LEARNING OBJECTIVE 3**
Demonstrate how to compute cost of goods manufactured and prepare financial statements for a manufacturer.

The financial statements of a manufacturer are very similar to those of a merchandiser. For example, you will find many of the same sections and same accounts in the financial statements of **Procter & Gamble** that you find in the financial statements of **Dick's Sporting Goods**. The principal differences between their financial statements occur in two places:

1. The current assets section in the balance sheet.
2. The cost of goods sold section in the income statement.

Each step in the accounting cycle for a merchandiser also applies to a manufacturer.

- For example, prior to preparing financial statements, manufacturers make adjustments.
- The adjustments are essentially the same as those of a merchandiser.

## Balance Sheet

The balance sheet for a merchandising company shows just one category of inventory. In contrast, the balance sheet for a manufacturer may have three inventory accounts, raw materials, work in process, and finished goods, as shown in **Illustration 14.6** for Current Designs' kayak inventory.

**ILLUSTRATION 14.6**  **Inventory accounts for a manufacturer**

| **Raw Materials Inventory** | **Work in Process Inventory** | **Finished Goods Inventory** |
|---|---|---|
|  |  |  |
| Shows the cost of raw materials on hand. | Shows the cost applicable to units that have been started into production but are only partially completed. | Shows the cost of completed goods on hand. |

Finished Goods Inventory is to a manufacturer what Inventory is to a merchandiser. In both cases, these represent the goods that the company has available for sale. The current assets sections presented in **Illustration 14.7** contrast the presentations of inventories for merchandising and manufacturing companies. The remainder of the balance sheet is similar for the two types of companies.

**ILLUSTRATION 14.7**    **Current assets sections of merchandising and manufacturing balance sheets**

| Merchandising Company | | |
|---|---|---|
| **Balance Sheet** | | |
| **December 31, 2022** | | |
| Current assets | | |
| Cash | | $100,000 |
| Accounts receivable (net) | | 210,000 |
| **Inventory** | | **400,000** |
| Prepaid expenses | | 22,000 |
| Total current assets | | $732,000 |

| Manufacturing Company | | |
|---|---|---|
| **Balance Sheet** | | |
| **December 31, 2022** | | |
| Current assets | | |
| Cash | | $180,000 |
| Accounts receivable (net) | | 210,000 |
| **Inventory** | | |
| **Finished goods** | $80,000 | |
| **Work in process** | 25,200 | |
| **Raw materials** | 22,800 | **128,000** |
| Prepaid expenses | | 18,000 |
| Total current assets | | $536,000 |

# Income Statement

Under a periodic inventory system, the income statements of a merchandiser and a manufacturer differ in the cost of goods sold section.

- Merchandisers compute cost of goods sold by adding the beginning inventory to the **cost of goods purchased** and subtracting the ending inventory.

- Manufacturers compute cost of goods sold by adding the beginning finished goods inventory to the **cost of goods manufactured** and subtracting the ending finished goods inventory.

**Illustration 14.8**, which assumes a periodic inventory system, shows these different methods.

**ILLUSTRATION 14.8**

**Merchandiser versus manufacturer cost of goods sold calculations**

A number of accounts are involved in determining the cost of goods manufactured. To eliminate excessive detail, income statements typically show only the total cost of goods manufactured. A separate statement, called a Cost of Goods Manufactured Schedule, presents the details (see Illustration 14.11).

**Illustration 14.9** shows the different presentations of the cost of goods sold sections for merchandising and manufacturing companies. The other sections of an income statement are similar for merchandisers and manufacturers.

**Cost of goods sold sections of merchandising and manufacturing income statements**

| Merchandising Company | |
|---|---:|
| **Income Statement (partial)** | |
| **For the Year Ended December 31, 2022** | |
| Cost of goods sold | |
| Inventory, Jan. 1 | $ 70,000 |
| Cost of goods purchased | 650,000 |
| Cost of goods available for sale | 720,000 |
| Less: Inventory, | |
| Dec. 31 | 400,000 |
| Cost of goods sold | $320,000 |

| Manufacturing Company | |
|---|---:|
| **Income Statement (partial)** | |
| **For the Year Ended December 31, 2022** | |
| Cost of goods sold | |
| Finished goods inventory, Jan. 1 | $ 90,000 |
| Cost of goods manufactured | |
| (see Illustration 14.11) | 370,000 |
| Cost of goods available for sale | 460,000 |
| Less: Finished goods inventory, | |
| Dec. 31 | 80,000 |
| Cost of goods sold | $380,000 |

# Cost of Goods Manufactured

An example may help show how companies determine the cost of goods manufactured. Assume that on January 1, **Current Designs** has a number of kayaks in various stages of production. In total, these partially completed manufactured units are called beginning **work in process inventory**. These are kayaks that were worked on during the prior year but were not completed. As a result, these kayaks will be completed during the current year. The cost of beginning work in process inventory is based on the **manufacturing costs incurred in the prior period**.

Current Designs first incurs manufacturing costs in the current year to complete the kayaks that were in process on January 1. It then incurs manufacturing costs for production of new orders. The sum of the direct materials costs, direct labor costs, and manufacturing overhead incurred in the current year is the **total manufacturing costs** for the current period.

We now have two cost amounts:

1. The cost of the beginning work in process.
2. The total manufacturing costs for the current period.

The sum of these costs is the **total cost of work in process** for the year.

At the end of the year, Current Designs may have some kayaks that are only partially completed. The costs of these unfinished units represent the cost of the **ending work in process inventory**. To find the **cost of goods manufactured**, we subtract the ending work in process inventory from the total cost of work in process. **Illustration 14.10** shows the calculation for determining the cost of goods manufactured.

**Cost of goods manufactured calculation**

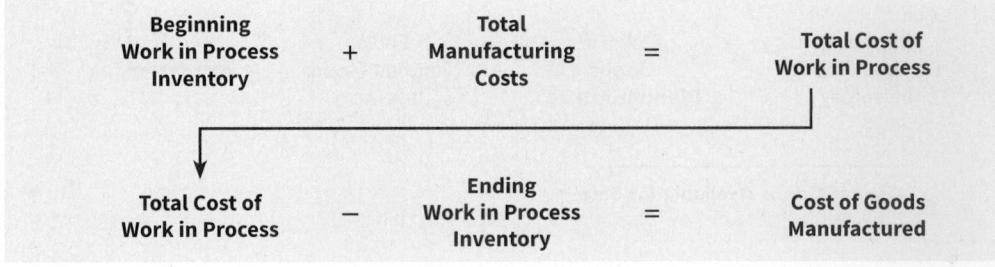

# Cost of Goods Manufactured Schedule

The **cost of goods manufactured schedule** reports cost elements used in calculating cost of goods manufactured. **Illustration 14.11** shows the schedule for Current Designs (using assumed data). The schedule presents detailed data for direct materials and for manufacturing overhead.

You should be able to distinguish between "Total manufacturing costs" and "Cost of goods manufactured."

- As Illustration 14.11 shows, total manufacturing costs is the sum of all manufacturing costs (direct materials, direct labor, and manufacturing overhead) **incurred during the period**.

- Cost of goods manufactured is the cost of those goods that were **completed during the period** and are no longer work in process; these costs relate to finished goods.

- If we add beginning work in process inventory to the total manufacturing costs incurred during the period and then subtract the ending work in process inventory (the calculation given in Illustration 14.10), we arrive at the cost of goods manufactured during the period.

- Cost of goods manufactured represents the costs related to items that were completed during the period and are therefore included in finished goods.

**ILLUSTRATION 14.11**

**Cost of goods manufactured schedule**

| Current Designs<br>Cost of Goods Manufactured Schedule<br>for the Year Ended December 31, 2022 | | |
| --- | --- | --- |
| **Work in process, January 1** | | $ 18,400 |
| **Direct materials** | | |
| Raw materials inventory, January 1 | $ 16,700 | |
| Raw materials purchases | 152,500 | |
| Total raw materials available for use | 169,200 | |
| Less: Raw materials inventory, December 31 | 22,800 | |
| Direct materials used | | $146,400* |
| **Direct labor** | | 175,600 |
| **Manufacturing overhead** | | |
| Indirect labor | 14,300 | |
| Factory repairs | 12,600 | |
| Factory utilities | 10,100 | |
| Factory depreciation | 9,440 | |
| Factory insurance | 8,360 | |
| Total manufacturing overhead | | 54,800 |
| **Total manufacturing costs** | | 376,800 |
| Total cost of work in process | | 395,200 |
| **Less: Work in process, December 31** | | 25,200 |
| **Cost of goods manufactured** | | $370,000 |

*To simplify the presentation, assumes that all raw materials used were direct materials.

## ACTION PLAN

- **Start with beginning work in process as the first item in the cost of goods manufactured schedule.**
- **Sum direct materials used, direct labor, and manufacturing overhead to determine total manufacturing costs.**
- **Sum beginning work in process and total manufacturing costs to determine total cost of work in process.**
- **Cost of goods manufactured is the total cost of work in process less ending work in process.**

## DO IT! 3 | Cost of Goods Manufactured

The following information is available for Keystone Company.

| | March 1 | March 31 |
|---|---|---|
| Raw materials inventory | $12,000 | $10,000 |
| Work in process inventory | 2,500 | 4,000 |
| Raw materials purchased in March | $ 90,000 | |
| Direct labor in March | 75,000 | |
| Manufacturing overhead in March | 220,000 | |

Prepare the cost of goods manufactured schedule for the month of March 2022. (Assume that all raw materials used were direct materials.)

### Solution

**Keystone Company**
**Cost of Goods Manufactured Schedule**
**For the Month Ended March 31, 2022**

| | | | |
|---|---|---|---|
| Work in process, March 1 | | | $ 2,500 |
| Direct materials | | | |
|   Raw materials, March 1 | $ 12,000 | | |
|   Raw materials purchases | 90,000 | | |
|   Total raw materials available for use | 102,000 | | |
|   Less: Raw materials, March 31 | 10,000 | | |
|   Direct materials used | | $ 92,000 | |
| Direct labor | | 75,000 | |
| Manufacturing overhead | | 220,000 | |
| Total manufacturing costs | | | 387,000 |
| Total cost of work in process | | | 389,500 |
| Less: Work in process, March 31 | | | 4,000 |
| Cost of goods manufactured | | | $385,500 |

Related exercise material: **BE14.7, BE14.8, BE14.9, BE14.10, DO IT! 14.3, E14.8, E14.9, E14.10, E14.11, E14.12, E14.13, E14.14, E14.15, E14.16, and E14.17.**

# Managerial Accounting Today

> **LEARNING OBJECTIVE 4**
> Discuss trends in managerial accounting.

In this rapidly changing world, managerial accounting needs to continue to innovate in order to provide managers with the information they need.

## Service Industries

Much of the U.S. economy has shifted toward an emphasis on services.

- Today, approximately 80% of U.S. workers are employed by service companies.
- Airlines, marketing agencies, cable companies, and governmental agencies are just a few examples of service companies.
- Service companies differ from manufacturing companies in that services are consumed immediately by customers.

For example, an airline uses special equipment to provide its product, but the output of that equipment is consumed immediately by the customer in the form of a flight. A marketing agency performs services for its clients that are immediately consumed by the customer in the form of a marketing plan. In contrast, a manufacturing company like **Boeing** records the airplanes that it manufactures as inventory until they are sold.

This chapter's examples feature manufacturing companies because accounting for the manufacturing environment requires the use of the broadest range of accounts. That is, the accounts used by service companies represent a subset of those used by manufacturers because service companies are not producing inventory. Neither an airline nor a marketing agency produces an inventoriable product. However, just like a manufacturer, each needs to keep track of the costs of its services in order to know whether it is generating a profit (see **Ethics Note**). An airline needs to know the cost of flight service to each destination, and a marketing agency needs to know the cost to develop a marketing plan. The techniques shown in this chapter to accumulate manufacturing costs to determine manufacturing inventory are equally useful for determining the costs of performing services.

Many of the examples we present in subsequent chapters, as well as some end-of-chapter materials, will be based on service companies.

## Focus on the Value Chain

The **value chain** refers to all business processes associated with providing a product or performing a service. **Illustration 14.12** depicts the value chain for a manufacturer.

- Note that the value chain includes both manufacturing and nonmanufacturing costs.
- Many of the most significant business innovations in recent years have resulted either directly, or indirectly, from a focus on the value chain.

For example, **lean manufacturing** was originally pioneered by Japanese automobile manufacturer **Toyota** but is now widely employed. Lean manufacturing requires a review of all business processes in an effort to increase productivity and eliminate waste, all while continually trying to improve quality.

**ILLUSTRATION 14.12**   **A manufacturer's value chain**

Research & development and product design → Acquisition of raw materials → Production → Sales and marketing → Delivery → Customer relations and subsequent services

**Manufacturing Costs**

**Just-in-time (JIT) inventory** methods, which have significantly lowered inventory levels and costs for many companies, are one innovation that resulted from the focus on the value chain.

- Under the JIT inventory method, goods are manufactured or purchased just in time for sale.
- However, JIT also necessitates increased emphasis on product quality. Because JIT companies do not have excess inventory on hand, they cannot afford to stop production because of defects or machine breakdowns. If they stop production, deliveries will be delayed and customers will be unhappy.

Partially as a consequence of JIT, many companies now focus on **total quality management (TQM)** to reduce defects in finished products, with the goal of zero defects.

**Toyota** was one of the pioneers of TQM processes as early as the 1940s. Some of the largest companies in the world, including **Ford** and **ExxonMobil**, have benefitted from these practices.

Another innovation is the **theory of constraints**.

- This involves identification of "bottlenecks"—constraints within the value chain that limit a company's profitability.
- Once a major constraint has been identified and eliminated, the company moves on to fix the next most significant constraint.

**General Motors** found that by applying the theory of constraints to its distribution system, it could more effectively meet the demands of its dealers and minimize the amount of excess inventory in its distribution system. This also reduced its need for overtime labor.

Technology has played a big role in the focus on the value chain and the implementation of lean manufacturing. For example, **enterprise resource planning (ERP) systems**, such as those provided by **SAP**, provide a comprehensive, centralized, integrated source of information to manage all major business processes—from purchasing, to manufacturing, to sales, to human resources.

- ERP systems have, in some large companies, replaced as many as 200 individual software packages.
- In addition, the focus on improving efficiency in the value chain has resulted in adoption of automated manufacturing processes.

As overhead costs have increased because of factory automation, the accuracy of overhead cost allocation to specific products has become more important. In response, managerial accountants devised an allocation approach called **activity-based costing (ABC)**.

- ABC allocates overhead based on each product's use of particular activities in making the product.
- In addition to providing more accurate product costing, ABC can contribute to increased efficiency in the value chain.

For example, suppose one of a company's overhead pools is allocated based on the number of setups that each product requires. If a particular product's cost is high because it is allocated a lot of overhead due to a high number of setups, management will be motivated to try to reduce the number of setups and thus reduce its overhead allocation. ABC is discussed further in Chapter 17.

---

## Management Insight    Inditex SA

Pixel-shot / Alamy Stock Photo

### Supplying Today's (Not Yesterday's) Fashions

In terms of total sales dollars, **Inditex SA** is the planet's largest fashion retailer. What does it do differently than its competitors? How did it double its sales over a recent seven-year period while competitors such as **Gap Inc.** stumbled badly? Inditex distinguishes itself in its value chain's ability to react quickly to constantly changing customer tastes. First, designers and commercial staff sit side by side in a massive, open workspace facility, taking direct input from sales staff around the world regarding new product ideas. Manufacturing facilities are located relatively near company headquarters, allowing more direct input and oversight into production. Also, all goods (other than online sales) are shipped straight from the production facility to stores, rather than warehouses. As a result of its unique approach to how it designs, manufactures, and distributes its goods, Inditex can actually sometimes get a new product from initial idea to the store shelf in two weeks rather than the industry norm of two to eight months. And because Inditex provides customers with designs that competitors don't have yet, it can charge higher prices while also continuing to look for ways to increase efficiency and thus cut costs.

**Source:** Patricia Kowsmann, "Fast Fashion: How a Zara Coat Went from Design to Fifth Avenue in 25 Days," *Wall Street Journal* (December 6, 2016).

**What steps has Inditex taken that make its value chain unique? (Answer is available at the end of the chapter.)**

# Balanced Scorecard

The **balanced scorecard** corrects for management's sometimes biased or limited perspective.

- This approach uses both financial and nonfinancial measures to evaluate all aspects of a company's operations in an integrated fashion.
- The performance measures are linked in a cause-and-effect fashion to ensure that they all tie to the company's overall objectives.

For example, to increase return on assets, the company could try to increase sales. To increase sales, the company could try to increase customer satisfaction. To increase customer satisfaction, the company could try to reduce product defects. Finally, to reduce product defects, the company could increase employee training. The balanced scorecard, which is discussed further in Chapter 24, is now used by many companies, including **Hilton Hotels**, **Walmart**, and **HP**.

# Business Ethics

All employees within an organization are expected to act ethically in their business activities. Given the importance of ethical behavior to corporations and their owners (stockholders), an increasing number of organizations provide codes of business ethics for their employees.

## Creating Proper Incentives

Companies like **Amazon.com**, **IBM**, and **Nike** use complex systems to monitor, control, and evaluate the actions of managers. Unfortunately, these systems and controls sometimes unwittingly create incentives for managers to take unethical actions.

- Because budgets are also used as an evaluation tool, some managers try to "game" the budgeting process by underestimating their division's predicted performance so that it will be easier to meet their performance targets.
- But, if budgets are set at unattainable levels, managers sometimes take unethical actions to meet the targets in order to receive higher compensation or, in some cases, to keep their jobs.

In a recent example, the largest bank in the United States, **Wells Fargo**, admitted that it had fired 5,300 employees for opening more than 2 million accounts without customer approval or knowledge. According to the director of the Consumer Financial Protection Bureau, "Wells Fargo employees secretly opened unauthorized accounts to hit sales targets and receive bonuses."

## Code of Ethical Standards

In response to corporate scandals, the U.S. Congress enacted the **Sarbanes-Oxley Act (SOX)** to help prevent lapses in internal control.

- CEOs and CFOs are now required to certify that financial statements give a fair presentation of the company's operating results and its financial condition.
- Top managers must certify that the company maintains an adequate system of internal controls to ensure accurate financial reports.
- Companies now pay more attention to the composition of the board of directors. In particular, the audit committee of the board of directors must be comprised entirely of independent members (that is, non-employees) and must contain at least one financial expert.
- The law substantially increases the penalties for misconduct.

To provide guidance for managerial accountants, the Institute of Management Accountants (IMA) has developed a code of ethical standards, entitled *IMA Statement of Ethical Professional Practice*. Management accountants should not commit acts in violation of these standards. Nor should they condone such acts by others within their organizations. Throughout the text, we address various ethical issues managers face.

## Corporate Social Responsibility

The balanced scorecard attempts to take a broader, more inclusive view of corporate profitability measures. Many companies, however, have begun to evaluate not just corporate profitability but also **corporate social responsibility**.

- Corporate social responsibility considers a company's efforts to employ sustainable business practices with regard to its employees, society, and the environment.
- This is sometimes referred to as the **triple bottom line** because it evaluates a company's performance with regard to **people, planet, and profit**.
- Recent reports indicate that nearly 80% of the 500 largest U.S. companies provide sustainability reports.

Make no mistake, these companies are still striving to maximize profits—in a competitive world, they won't survive long if they don't. In fact, you might recognize a few of the names on a recent list (published by Corporate Knights) of the 100 most sustainable companies in the world. Are you surprised that **General Electric**, **adidas**, **BMW**, **Coca-Cola**, or **Apple** made the list? These companies have learned that with a long-term, sustainable approach, they can maximize profits while also acting in the best interest of their employees, their communities, and the environment. In fact, a monetary bonus was provided by 87% of the companies on the list to managers that met sustainability goals. At various points within this text, we discuss situations where real companies use the very skills that you are learning to evaluate decisions from a sustainable perspective, such as in the following Insight box.

---

### People, Planet, and Profit Insight   Phantom Tac

aabeele/Shutterstock.com

#### People Matter

Many clothing factories in developing countries are known for unsafe buildings, poor working conditions, and wage and labor violations. One of the owners of **Phantom Tac**, a clothing manufacturer in Bangladesh, did make efforts to develop sustainable business practices. This owner, David Mayor, provided funding for a training program for female workers. He also developed a website to educate customers about the workers' conditions. But Phantom Tac also had to make a profit. Things got tight when one of its customers canceled orders because Phantom Tac failed a social compliance audit. The company had to quit funding the training program and the website.

Recently, Bangladesh's textile industry has seen some significant improvements in working conditions and safety standards. As Brad Adams, Asia director of **Human Rights Watch**, notes, "The (Dhaka) government has belatedly begun to register unions, which is an important first step, but it now needs to ensure that factory owners stop persecuting their leaders and actually allow them to function."

**Sources:** Jim Yardley, "Clothing Brands Sidestep Blame for Safety Lapses," *The New York Times Online* (December 30, 2013); and Palash Ghosh, "Despite Low Pay, Poor Work Conditions, Garment Factories Empowering Millions of Bangladeshi Women," *International Business Times* (March 25, 2014).

**What are some of the common problems for many clothing factories in developing countries? (Answer is available at the end of the chapter.)**

---

## The Value of Data Analytics

Companies have never had so much available data. In many companies, virtually every aspect of operations—the employees, the customers, even the manufacturing equipment—leaves a data trail. However, while "big data" can be impressive, it can also be overwhelming.

- Having all the data in the world will not necessarily lead to better results.
- The trick is having the skills and know-how to use the data in ways that result in more productive (and happier) employees, more satisfied customers, and more profitable operations.

It is therefore not surprising that one of the most rapidly growing areas of business today is data analytics. **Data analytics** is the use of techniques, which often combine software and statistics, to analyze data to make informed decisions.

Throughout the remainder of this text we continue to offer many examples of how successful companies are using data analytics. We also provide examples of one analytical tool, data visualizations. **Data visualizations** often help managers acquire a more intuitive understanding of (1) the relationships between variables and (2) business trends.

---

### Data Analytics Insight    The Walt Disney Company

Paulbr/Getty Images

#### Using Data in Its Own World

**The Walt Disney Company** makes fun seem effortless at its theme parks, but there is a magic mountain of data collection going on behind the scenes. For example, Disney employs behavioral analytics, which uses data to both predict and influence customer behavior, in countless ways. Disney collects the data through its "MagicBands" worn by visitors to the parks. While the MagicBands provide visitors with many benefits (e.g., delivering customized itineraries, reducing wait lines, and providing customer recognition by Disney characters), these bands are also delivering continual information to the company about the locations, activities, eating habits, and purchases of Disney visitors.

Disney uses the MagicBand information to support daily adjustments of operations as well as long-term planning. For example, the company can use this information to monitor park usage and subsequently encourage visitors to change their itineraries to different activities that will require a shorter wait time. If customers are waiting in line, they aren't happy—and they also aren't spending money. Long-term planning uses of MagicBand information include designing new attractions and updating menu options in response to supply and demand.

Source: Randerson112358, "How Disney World Uses Big Data," *medium.com* (May 18, 2019).

**What is behavioral analytics, and how does Disney use it to minimize lines at its theme parks? (Answer is available at the end of the chapter.)**

---

## DO IT! 4 | Trends in Managerial Accounting

Match the descriptions that follow with the corresponding terms.

**Descriptions:**

1. _____ All activities associated with providing a product or performing a service.

2. _____ A method of allocating overhead based on each product's use of activities in making the product.

3. _____ Systems implemented to reduce defects in finished products with the goal of achieving zero defects.

4. _____ A performance-measurement approach that uses both financial and nonfinancial measures, tied to company objectives, to evaluate a company's operations in an integrated fashion.

5. _____ Inventory system in which goods are manufactured or purchased just as they are needed for use or sale.

6. _____ A company's efforts to employ sustainable business practices with regard to its employees, society, and the environment.

7. _____ A code of ethical standards developed by the Institute of Management Accountants.

**Terms:**

a. Activity-based costing.

b. Balanced scorecard.

c. Corporate social responsibility.

d. Just-in-time (JIT) inventory.

e. Total quality management (TQM).

f. Statement of Ethical Professional Practice.

g. Value chain.

**ACTION PLAN**

- Develop a forward-looking view, in order to advise and provide information to various members of the organization.

- Understand current business trends and issues.

### Solution

**1.** g  **2.** a  **3.** e  **4.** b  **5.** d  **6.** c  **7.** f

Related exercise material: **BE14.11, DO IT! 14.4, and E14.18.**

# Review and Practice

## Learning Objectives Review

### 1 Identify the features of managerial accounting and the functions of management.

The *primary users* of managerial accounting reports, issued as frequently as needed, are internal users, who are officers, department heads, managers, and supervisors in the company. The purpose of these reports is to provide special-purpose information for a particular user for a specific decision. The content of managerial accounting reports pertains to subunits of the business. It may be very detailed, and may extend beyond the accrual accounting system. The reporting standard is relevance to the decision being made. No independent audits are required in managerial accounting.

The functions of management are planning, directing, and controlling. Planning requires management to look ahead and to establish objectives. Directing involves coordinating the diverse activities and human resources of a company to produce a smooth-running operation. Controlling is the process of keeping the activities on track.

### 2 Describe the classes of manufacturing costs and the differences between product and period costs.

Manufacturing costs are typically classified as either (1) direct materials, (2) direct labor, or (3) manufacturing overhead. Raw materials that can be physically and directly associated with the finished product during the manufacturing process are called direct materials. The work of factory employees that can be physically and directly associated with converting raw materials into finished goods is considered direct labor. Manufacturing overhead consists of costs that are indirectly associated with the manufacture of the finished product. Manufacturing costs are typically incurred at the manufacturing facility.

Product costs are costs that are a necessary and integral part of producing the finished product (manufacturing costs). Product costs are also called inventoriable costs. These costs do not become expenses until the company sells the finished goods inventory.

Period costs are costs that are identified with a specific time period rather than with a salable product. These costs relate to non-manufacturing costs and therefore are not inventoriable costs. They are expensed as incurred.

### 3 Demonstrate how to compute cost of goods manufactured and prepare financial statements for a manufacturer.

Companies add the cost of the beginning work in process to the total manufacturing costs for the current year to arrive at the total cost of work in process for the year. They then subtract the ending work in process from the total cost of work in process to arrive at the cost of goods manufactured.

The difference between a merchandising and a manufacturing balance sheet is in the current assets section. The current assets section of a manufacturing company's balance sheet presents three inventory accounts: finished goods inventory, work in process inventory, and raw materials inventory.

The difference between a merchandising and a manufacturing income statement is in the cost of goods sold section. A manufacturing cost of goods sold section shows beginning and ending finished goods inventories and the cost of goods manufactured.

### 4 Discuss trends in managerial accounting.

Managerial accounting has experienced many changes in recent years, including a shift toward service companies as well as an emphasis on ethical behavior. Improved practices include a focus on managing the value chain through techniques such as just-in-time inventory, total quality management, activity-based costing, and theory of constraints. The balanced scorecard is now used by many companies in order to attain a more comprehensive view of the company's operations, and companies are now evaluating their performance with regard to their corporate social responsibility. Finally, data analytics and data visualizations are important tools that help businesses identify problems and opportunities, and then make informed decisions.

## Glossary Review

**Activity-based costing (ABC)** A method of allocating overhead based on each product's use of activities in making the product. (p. 14-18).

**Balanced scorecard** A performance-measurement approach that uses both financial and nonfinancial measures, tied to company objectives, to evaluate a company's operations in an integrated fashion. (p. 14-19).

**Board of directors** The group of officials elected by the stockholders of a corporation to formulate operating policies and select officers who will manage the company. (p. 14-5).

**Chief executive officer (CEO)** Corporate officer who has overall responsibility for managing the business and delegates responsibilities to other corporate officers. (p. 14-6).

**Chief financial officer (CFO)** Corporate officer who is responsible for all of the accounting and finance issues of the company. (p. 14-6).

**Controller** Financial officer responsible for a company's accounting records, system of internal control, and preparation of financial statements, tax returns, and internal reports. (p. 14-6).

**Corporate social responsibility**   The efforts of a company to employ sustainable business practices with regard to its employees, society, and the environment. (p. 14-20).

**Cost of goods manufactured**   Total cost of work in process less the cost of the ending work in process inventory. Cost of all the items completed during the period. (p. 14-14).

**Data analytics**   The use of techniques, which often combine software and statistics, to analyze data to make informed decisions. (p. 14-20).

**Direct labor**   The work of factory employees that can be physically and directly associated with converting raw materials into finished goods. (p. 14-8).

**Direct materials**   Raw materials that can be physically and directly associated with manufacturing the finished product. (p. 14-8).

**Enterprise resource planning (ERP) system**   Software that provides a comprehensive, centralized, integrated source of information used to manage all major business processes. (p. 14-18).

**Indirect labor**   Work of factory employees that has no physical association with the finished product or for which it is impractical to trace the costs to the goods produced. (p. 14-8).

**Indirect materials**   Raw materials that do not physically become part of the finished product or that are impractical to trace to the finished product because their physical association with the finished product is too small. (p. 14-8).

**Just-in-time (JIT) inventory**   Inventory system in which goods are manufactured or purchased just in time for sale. (p. 14-17).

**Line positions**   Jobs that are directly involved in a company's primary revenue-generating operating activities. (p. 14-6).

**Managerial accounting**   A field of accounting that provides economic and financial information for managers and other internal users. (p. 14-3).

**Manufacturing overhead**   Manufacturing costs that are indirectly associated with the manufacture of the finished product. (p. 14-8).

**Period costs**   Costs that are matched with the revenue of a specific time period and charged to expense as incurred. (p. 14-9).

**Product costs**   Costs that are a necessary and integral part of producing the finished product. All manufacturing costs are classified as product costs and are included in inventory. (p. 14-9).

**Sarbanes-Oxley Act (SOX)**   Law passed by Congress intended to reduce unethical corporate behavior. (p. 14-19).

**Staff positions**   Jobs that support the efforts of line employees. (p. 14-6).

**Theory of constraints**   A specific approach used to identify and manage constraints in order to achieve the company's goals. (p. 14-18).

**Total cost of work in process**   Cost of the beginning work in process plus total manufacturing costs for the current period. (p. 14-14).

**Total manufacturing costs**   The sum of direct materials, direct labor, and manufacturing overhead incurred in the current period. (p. 14-10).

**Total quality management (TQM)**   Systems implemented to reduce defects in finished products with the goal of achieving zero defects. (p. 14-17).

**Treasurer**   Financial officer responsible for custody of a company's funds and for maintaining its cash position. (p. 14-6).

**Triple bottom line**   The evaluation of a company's social responsibility performance with regard to people, planet, and profit. (p. 14-20).

**Value chain**   All business processes associated with providing a product or performing a service. (p. 14-17).

**Work in process inventory**   Partially completed manufactured units. (p. 14-14).

## Practice Multiple-Choice Questions

1. **(LO 1)** Managerial accounting:
   a. is governed by generally accepted accounting principles.
   b. places emphasis on special-purpose information.
   c. pertains to the entity as a whole and is highly aggregated.
   d. is limited to cost data.

2. **(LO 1)** The management of an organization performs several broad functions. They are:
   a. planning, directing, and selling.
   b. planning, directing, and controlling.
   c. planning, manufacturing, and controlling.
   d. directing, manufacturing, and controlling.

3. **(LO 2)** Direct materials are a:

|     | Product Cost | Manufacturing Overhead Cost | Period Cost |
|-----|--------------|------------------------------|-------------|
| a.  | Yes          | Yes                          | No          |
| b.  | Yes          | No                           | No          |
| c.  | Yes          | Yes                          | Yes         |
| d.  | No           | No                           | No          |

4. **(LO 2)** Which of the following costs would a computer manufacturer include in manufacturing overhead?
   a. The cost of the disk drives.
   b. The wages earned by computer assemblers.
   c. The cost of the memory chips.
   d. Depreciation on testing equipment.

5. **(LO 2)** Which of the following is **not** an element of manufacturing overhead?
   a. Sales manager's salary.
   b. Factory manager's salary.
   c. Factory repairman's wages.
   d. Product inspector's salary.

6. **(LO 2)** Indirect labor is a:
   a. nonmanufacturing cost.    c. product cost.
   b. raw material cost.        d. period cost.

7. **(LO 2)** Which of the following costs are classified as a period cost?
   a. Wages paid to a factory custodian.
   b. Wages paid to a production department supervisor.
   c. Wages paid to the CEO.
   d. Wages paid to an assembly worker.

8. **(LO 3)** For the year, Redder Company has cost of goods manufactured of $600,000, beginning finished goods inventory of $200,000, and ending finished goods inventory of $250,000. The cost of goods sold is:
   a. $450,000.                 c. $550,000.
   b. $500,000.                 d. $600,000.

9. **(LO 3)** Cost of goods available for sale is a step in the calculation of cost of goods sold of:

    **a.** a merchandising company but not a manufacturing company.

    **b.** a manufacturing company but not a merchandising company.

    **c.** a merchandising company and a manufacturing company.

    **d.** neither a manufacturing company nor a merchandising company.

10. **(LO 3)** A cost of goods manufactured schedule shows beginning and ending inventories for:

    **a.** raw materials and work in process only.

    **b.** work in process only.

    **c.** raw materials only.

    **d.** raw materials, work in process, and finished goods.

11. **(LO 3)** The calculation to determine the cost of goods manufactured is:

    **a.** Beginning raw materials inventory + Total manufacturing costs − Ending work in process inventory.

    **b.** Beginning work in process inventory + Total manufacturing costs − Ending finished goods inventory.

    **c.** Beginning finished goods inventory + Total manufacturing costs − Ending finished goods inventory.

    **d.** Beginning work in process inventory + Total manufacturing costs − Ending work in process inventory.

12. **(LO 4)** After passage of the Sarbanes-Oxley Act:

    **a.** reports prepared by managerial accountants must be audited by CPAs.

    **b.** CEOs and CFOs must certify that financial statements provide a fair presentation of the company's operating results.

    **c.** the audit committee, rather than top management, is responsible for the company's financial statements.

    **d.** reports prepared by managerial accountants must comply with generally accepted accounting principles (GAAP).

13. **(LO 4)** Which of the following managerial accounting techniques attempts to allocate manufacturing overhead in a more meaningful fashion?

    **a.** Just-in-time inventory.    **c.** Balanced scorecard.

    **b.** Total quality management.    **d.** Activity-based costing.

14. **(LO 4)** Corporate social responsibility refers to:

    **a.** the practice by management of reviewing all business processes in an effort to increase productivity and eliminate waste.

    **b.** an approach used to allocate overhead based on each product's use of activities.

    **c.** the attempt by management to identify and eliminate constraints within the value chain.

    **d.** efforts by companies to employ sustainable business practices with regard to employees and the environment.

## Solutions

**1. b.** Managerial accounting emphasizes special-purpose information. The other choices are incorrect because (a) financial accounting is governed by generally accepted accounting principles, (c) financial accounting pertains to the entity as a whole and is highly aggregated, and (d) cost accounting and cost data are a subset of management accounting.

**2. b.** Planning, directing, and controlling are the broad functions performed by the management of an organization. The other choices are incorrect because (a) selling is performed by the sales group in the organization, not by management; (c) manufacturing is performed by the manufacturing group in the organization, not by management; and (d) manufacturing is performed by the manufacturing group in the organization, not by management.

**3. b.** Direct materials are a product cost only. Therefore, choices (a), (c), and (d) are incorrect as direct materials are not manufacturing overhead or a period cost.

**4. d.** Depreciation on testing equipment would be included in manufacturing overhead because it is indirectly associated with the finished product. The other choices are incorrect because (a) disk drives would be direct materials, (b) computer assembler wages would be direct labor, and (c) memory chips would be direct materials.

**5. a.** The sales manager's salary is not directly or indirectly associated with the manufacture of the finished product. The other choices are incorrect because (b) the factory manager's salary, (c) the factory repairman's wages, and (d) the product inspector's salary are all elements of manufacturing overhead.

**6. c.** Indirect labor is a product cost because it is part of the effort required to produce a product. The other choices are incorrect because (a) indirect labor is a manufacturing cost because it is part of the effort required to produce a product, (b) indirect labor is not a raw material cost because raw material costs only include direct materials and indirect materials, and (d) indirect labor is not a period cost because it is part of the effort required to produce a product.

**7. c.** Wages paid to the CEO would be included in administrative expenses and classified as a period cost. The other choices are incorrect because (a) factory custodian wages are indirect labor, which is manufacturing overhead and a product cost; (b) production department supervisor wages are indirect labor, which is manufacturing overhead and a product cost; and (d) assembly worker wages is direct labor and is a product cost.

**8. c.** Cost of goods sold is computed as Beginning finished goods inventory ($200,000) + Cost of goods manufactured ($600,000) − Ending finished goods inventory ($250,000), or $200,000 + $600,000 − $250,000 = $550,000. Therefore, choices (a) $450,000, (b) $500,000, and (d) $600,000 are incorrect.

**9. c.** Both a merchandising company (periodic inventory system) and a manufacturing company use cost of goods available for sale to calculate cost of goods sold. Therefore, choices (a) only a merchandising company, (b) only a manufacturing company, and (d) neither a manufacturing company or a merchandising company are incorrect.

**10. a.** A cost of goods manufactured schedule shows beginning and ending inventories for raw materials and work in process only. Therefore, choices (b) work in process only and (c) raw materials only are incorrect. Choice (d) is incorrect because the schedule does not include finished goods.

**11. d.** The calculation to determine the cost of goods manufactured is Beginning work in process inventory + Total manufacturing costs −

Ending work in process inventory. The other choices are incorrect because (a) raw materials inventory, (b) ending finished goods inventory, and (c) beginning finished goods inventory and ending finished goods inventory are not part of the computation.

12. **b.** CEOs and CFOs must certify that financial statements provide a fair presentation of the company's operating results. The other choices are incorrect because (a) reports prepared by financial (not managerial) accountants must be audited by CPAs; (c) SOX clarifies that top management, not the audit committee, is responsible for the company's financial statements; and (d) reports by financial (not managerial) accountants must comply with GAAP.

13. **d.** Activity-based costing attempts to allocate manufacturing overhead in a more meaningful fashion. Therefore, choices (a) just-in-time inventory, (b) total quality management, and (c) balanced scorecard are incorrect.

14. **d.** Corporate social responsibility refers to efforts by companies to employ sustainable business practices with regard to employees and the environment. The other choices are incorrect because (a) defines lean manufacturing, (b) refers to activity-based costing, and (c) describes the theory of constraints.

## Practice Brief Exercises

1. **(LO 1)** The following are selected data for Lopez Furniture.

*Classify manufacturing costs.*

| | |
|---|---|
| Utilities for manufacturing equipment | $120,000 |
| Wood | 850,000 |
| Depreciation on factory building | 220,000 |
| Wages for production workers | 391,000 |
| Fabric | 313,000 |
| Delivery expense | 144,000 |
| Property taxes on factory | 70,000 |

Using this selected data, determine total (a) direct materials, (b) direct labor, (c) manufacturing overhead, (d) product costs, and (e) period costs.

### Solution

1. **a.** Wood ($850,000) + Fabric ($313,000) = $1,163,000

   **b.** Wages for production workers, $391,000

   **c.** Utilities ($120,000) + Depreciation ($220,000) + Property taxes ($70,000) = $410,000

   **d.** Direct materials ($1,163,000) + Direct labor ($391,000) + Manufacturing overhead ($410,000) = $1,964,000

   **e.** Delivery expense, $144,000

2. **(LO 3)** Cody Cellular has the following data: direct labor $100,000, direct materials used $90,000, total manufacturing overhead $110,000, beginning work in process $15,000, and ending work in process $24,000. Compute (a) total manufacturing costs, (b) total cost of work in process, and (c) cost of goods manufactured.

*Compute total manufacturing costs and total cost of work in process.*

### Solution

2. **a.**

| | |
|---|---|
| Direct materials use | $ 90,000 |
| Direct labor | 100,000 |
| Total manufacturing overhead | 110,000 |
| Total manufacturing costs | $300,000 |

   **b.**

| | |
|---|---|
| Beginning work in process | $ 15,000 |
| Total manufacturing costs | 300,000 |
| Total cost of work in process | $315,000 |

   **c.**

| | |
|---|---|
| Total cost of work in process | $315,000 |
| Less ending work in process | (24,000) |
| Cost of goods manufactured | $291,000 |

*Prepare current assets section.*

**3. (LO 3)** The following are current asset items in alphabetical order for Asche Company's balance sheet at December 31, 2022. Prepare the current assets section (including a complete heading).

| | |
|---|---:|
| Accounts receivable | $100,000 |
| Cash | 29,000 |
| Finished goods | 47,000 |
| Prepaid expenses | 20,000 |
| Raw materials | 39,000 |
| Short-term investments | 51,000 |
| Work in process | 44,000 |

### Solution

3.

**Asche Company**
**Balance Sheet**
**December 31, 2022**

| | | |
|---|---:|---:|
| Current assets | | |
| Cash | | $ 29,000 |
| Short-term investments | | 51,000 |
| Accounts receivable | | 100,000 |
| Inventories | | |
|   Finished goods | $47,000 | |
|   Work in process | 44,000 | |
|   Raw materials | 39,000 | 130,000 |
| Prepaid expenses | | 20,000 |
|     Total current assets | | $330,000 |

# Practice Exercises

*Determine the total amount of various types of costs.*

**1. (LO 2)** Fredricks Company reports the following costs and expenses in May.

| | | | |
|---|---:|---|---:|
| Factory utilities | $ 15,600 | Direct labor | $89,100 |
| Depreciation on factory | | Sales salaries | 46,400 |
|   equipment | 12,650 | Property taxes on factory | |
| Depreciation on delivery trucks | 8,800 |   building | 2,500 |
| Indirect factory labor | 48,900 | Repairs to office equipment | 2,300 |
| Indirect materials | 80,800 | Factory repairs | 2,000 |
| Direct materials used | 137,600 | Advertising | 18,000 |
| Factory manager's salary | 13,000 | Office supplies used | 5,640 |

### Instructions

From the information, determine the total amount of:

a. Manufacturing overhead.

b. Product costs.

c. Period costs.

### Solution

**1. a.**

| | |
|---|---:|
| Factory utilities | $ 15,600 |
| Depreciation on factory equipment | 12,650 |
| Indirect factory labor | 48,900 |
| Indirect materials | 80,800 |
| Factory manager's salary | 13,000 |
| Property taxes on factory building | 2,500 |
| Factory repairs | 2,000 |
| Manufacturing overhead | $175,450 |

**b.** Direct materials used .......................... $137,600
　　Direct labor ................................... 89,100
　　Manufacturing overhead ......................... 175,450
　　Product costs ................................. $402,150

**c.** Depreciation on delivery trucks ............... $ 8,800
　　Sales salaries ................................ 46,400
　　Repairs to office equipment ................... 2,300
　　Advertising ................................... 18,000
　　Office supplies used .......................... 5,640
　　Period costs ................................. $ 81,140

**2. (LO 3)** Tommi Corporation incurred the following costs during the year.

*Compute cost of goods manufactured and sold.*

| | | | |
|---|---|---|---|
| Direct materials used in production | $120,000 | Advertising expense | $45,000 |
| Depreciation on factory | 60,000 | Property taxes on factory | 19,000 |
| Property taxes on store | 7,500 | Delivery expense | 21,000 |
| Labor costs of assembly-line workers | 110,000 | Sales commissions | 35,000 |
| Factory supplies used | 25,000 | Salaries paid to sales clerks | 50,000 |

Work in process inventory was $10,000 at January 1 and $14,000 at December 31. Finished goods inventory was $60,500 at January 1 and $50,600 at December 31. (Assume that all raw materials used were direct materials.)

**Instructions**

　　**a.** Compute cost of goods manufactured.
　　**b.** Compute cost of goods sold.

**Solution**

**2. a.** Work in process, January 1 .................................................. $ 10,000
　　　Direct materials used ........................................... $120,000
　　　Direct labor .................................................... 110,000
　　　Manufacturing overhead
　　　　Depreciation on factory ............... $60,000
　　　　Factory supplies used .................. 25,000
　　　　Property taxes on factory .............. 19,000
　　　　Total manufacturing overhead ..................................... 104,000
　　　Total manufacturing costs ........................................................ 334,000
　　　Total cost of work in process .................................................... 344,000
　　　Less: Ending work in process ................................................... 14,000
　　　Cost of goods manufactured ..................................................... $330,000

**b.** Finished goods inventory, January 1 ............................................. $ 60,500
　　Cost of goods manufactured ...................................................... 330,000
　　Cost of goods available for sale ................................................. 390,500
　　Less: Finished goods inventory, December 31 ..................................... 50,600
　　Cost of goods sold .............................................................. $339,900

# Practice Problem

**(LO 3)** Superior Company has the following cost and expense data for the year ended December 31, 2022.

*Prepare a cost of goods manufactured schedule, an income statement, and a partial balance sheet.*

| | | | |
|---|---|---|---|
| Raw materials, 1/1/22 | $ 30,000 | Property taxes, factory building | $ 6,000 |
| Raw materials, 12/31/22 | 20,000 | Sales revenue | 1,500,000 |
| Raw materials purchases | 205,000 | Delivery expenses (to customers) | 100,000 |
| Work in process, 1/1/22 | 80,000 | Sales commissions | 150,000 |
| Work in process, 12/31/22 | 50,000 | Indirect labor | 105,000 |

| | | | |
|---|---|---|---|
| Finished goods, 1/1/22 | 110,000 | Factory machinery rent | 40,000 |
| Finished goods, 12/31/22 | 120,000 | Factory utilities | 65,000 |
| Direct labor | 350,000 | Depreciation, factory building | 24,000 |
| Factory manager's salary | 35,000 | Administrative expenses | 300,000 |
| Insurance, factory | 14,000 | | |

## Instructions

a. Prepare a cost of goods manufactured schedule for Superior Company for 2022. (Assume that all raw materials used were direct materials.)

b. Prepare an income statement for Superior Company for 2022.

c. Assume that Superior Company's accounting records show the balances of the following current asset accounts: Cash $17,000, Accounts Receivable (net) $120,000, Prepaid Expenses $13,000, and Short-Term Investments $26,000. Prepare the current assets section of the balance sheet for Superior Company as of December 31, 2022.

## Solution

**a.**

**Superior Company**
**Cost of Goods Manufactured Schedule**
**For the Year Ended December 31, 2022**

| | | | |
|---|---|---|---|
| Work in process, January 1 | | | $ 80,000 |
| Direct materials | | | |
| Raw materials inventory, January 1 | $ 30,000 | | |
| Raw materials purchases | 205,000 | | |
| Total raw materials available for use | 235,000 | | |
| Less: Raw materials inventory, December 31 | 20,000 | | |
| Direct materials used | | $215,000 | |
| Direct labor | | 350,000 | |
| Manufacturing overhead | | | |
| Indirect labor | $105,000 | | |
| Factory utilities | 65,000 | | |
| Factory machinery rent | 40,000 | | |
| Factory manager's salary | 35,000 | | |
| Depreciation, factory building | 24,000 | | |
| Insurance, factory | 14,000 | | |
| Property taxes, factory building | 6,000 | | |
| Total manufacturing overhead | | 289,000 | |
| Total manufacturing costs | | | 854,000 |
| Total cost of work in process | | | 934,000 |
| Less: Work in process, December 31 | | | 50,000 |
| Cost of goods manufactured | | | $884,000 |

**b.**

**Superior Company**
**Income Statement**
**For the Year Ended December 31, 2022**

| | | |
|---|---|---|
| Sales revenue | | $1,500,000 |
| Cost of goods sold | | |
| Finished goods inventory, January 1 | $110,000 | |
| Cost of goods manufactured | 884,000 | |
| Cost of goods available for sale | 994,000 | |
| Less: Finished goods inventory, December 31 | 120,000 | |
| Cost of goods sold | | 874,000 |
| Gross profit | | 626,000 |

Operating expenses

| | | |
|---|---|---|
| Administrative expenses | 300,000 | |
| Sales commissions | 150,000 | |
| Delivery expenses | 100,000 | |
| Total operating expenses | | 550,000 |
| Net income | | $    76,000 |

c.

### Superior Company
### Balance Sheet (partial)
### December 31, 2022

| | | |
|---|---|---|
| Current assets | | |
| Cash | | $ 17,000 |
| Short-term investments | | 26,000 |
| Accounts receivable (net) | | 120,000 |
| Inventory | | |
| Finished goods | $ 120,000 | |
| Work in process | 50,000 | |
| Raw materials | 20,000 | 190,000 |
| Prepaid expenses | | 13,000 |
| Total current assets | | $366,000 |

Brief Exercises, DO IT! Exercises, Exercises, Problems, Data Analytics Activities, and many additional resources are available for practice in WileyPLUS.

## Questions

**1. a.** "Managerial accounting is a field of accounting that provides economic information for all interested parties." Is this true? Explain why or why not.

**b.** Joe Delong believes that managerial accounting serves only manufacturing firms. Is Joe correct? Explain.

**2.** Distinguish between managerial and financial accounting as to (a) primary users of reports, (b) types and frequency of reports, and (c) purpose of reports.

**3.** How do the content of reports and the verification of reports differ between managerial and financial accounting?

**4.** Linda Olsen is studying for the next accounting mid-term examination. Summarize for Linda what she should know about management functions.

**5.** "Decision-making is management's most important function." Is this true? Explain why or why not.

**6.** Explain the primary difference between line positions and staff positions, and give examples of each.

**7.** Jerry Lang is unclear as to the difference between the balance sheets of a merchandising company and a manufacturing company. Explain the difference to Jerry.

**8.** How are manufacturing costs classified?

**9.** Mel Finney claims that the distinction between direct and indirect materials is based entirely on physical association with the product. Is Mel correct? Why?

**10.** Tina Burke is confused about the differences between a product cost and a period cost. Explain the differences to Tina.

**11.** Identify the differences in the cost of goods sold section of an income statement between a merchandising company and a manufacturing company.

**12.** The determination of the cost of goods manufactured involves the following factors: (A) beginning work in process inventory, (B) total manufacturing costs, and (C) ending work in process inventory. Identify the meaning of X in the following equations:

**a.** $A + B = X$          **b.** $A + B - C = X$

**13.** Sealy Company has beginning raw materials inventory $12,000, ending raw materials inventory $15,000, and raw materials purchases $170,000. What is the cost of direct materials used?

**14.** Tate Inc. has beginning work in process $26,000, direct materials used $240,000, direct labor $220,000, total manufacturing overhead $180,000, and ending work in process $32,000. What are the total manufacturing costs?

**15.** Tate Inc. has beginning work in process $26,000, direct materials used $240,000, direct labor $220,000, total manufacturing overhead $180,000, and ending work in process $32,000. What are (a) the total cost of work in process and (b) the cost of goods manufactured?

**16.** In what order should manufacturing inventories be reported in a balance sheet?

**17.** How does the output of manufacturing operations differ from that of service operations?

**18.** Discuss whether the product costing techniques discussed in this chapter apply equally well to manufacturers and service companies.

19. What is the value chain? Describe, in sequence, the main components of a manufacturer's value chain.

20. What is an enterprise resource planning (ERP) system? What are its primary benefits?

21. Why is product quality important for companies that implement a just-in-time inventory system?

22. Explain what is meant by "balanced" in the balanced scorecard approach.

23. In what ways can the budgeting process create incentives for unethical behavior?

24. What rules were enacted under the Sarbanes-Oxley Act to address unethical accounting practices?

25. What is activity-based costing, and what are its potential benefits?

## Brief Exercises

*Distinguish between managerial and financial accounting.*

**BE14.1 (LO 1), C** Complete the following comparison table between managerial and financial accounting.

| | **Financial Accounting** | **Managerial Accounting** |
|---|---|---|
| Primary users of reports | | |
| Types of reports | | |
| Frequency of reports | | |
| Purpose of reports | | |
| Content of reports | | |
| Verification process | | |

*Identify the three management functions.*

**BE14.2 (LO 1), C** Listed below are the three functions of the management of an organization.

1. Planning.  2. Directing.  3. Controlling.

Identify which of the following statements best describes each of the above functions.

a. _____ requires management to look ahead and to establish objectives. A key objective of management is to add value to the business.

b. _____ involves coordinating the diverse activities and human resources of a company to produce a smooth-running operation. This function relates to the implementation of planned objectives.

c. _____ is the process of keeping the activities on track. Management determines whether goals are being met and what changes are necessary when there are deviations.

*Classify manufacturing costs.*

**BE14.3 (LO 2), C** Determine whether each of the following costs should be classified as direct materials (DM), direct labor (DL), or manufacturing overhead (MO).

a. _____ Frames and tires used in manufacturing bicycles.

b. _____ Wages paid to production workers.

c. _____ Insurance on factory equipment and machinery.

d. _____ Depreciation on factory equipment.

*Classify manufacturing costs.*

**BE14.4 (LO 2), C** Indicate whether each of the following costs of an automobile manufacturer would be classified as direct materials, direct labor, or manufacturing overhead.

a. _____ Windshield.

b. _____ Engine.

c. _____ Wages of assembly-line worker.

d. _____ Depreciation of factory machinery.

e. _____ Factory machinery lubricants.

f. _____ Tires.

g. _____ Steering wheel.

h. _____ Salary of painting supervisor.

*Identify product and period costs.*

**BE14.5 (LO 2), C** Identify whether each of the following costs should be classified as product costs or period costs.

a. _____ Manufacturing overhead.

b. _____ Selling expenses.

c. _____ Administrative expenses.

d. _____ Advertising expenses.

e. _____ Direct labor.

f. _____ Direct materials.

*Classify manufacturing costs.*

**BE14.6 (LO 2), C** Presented here are Rook Company's monthly manufacturing cost data related to its tablet computer product.

a. Utilities for manufacturing equipment       $116,000

b. Raw materials (CPU, chips, etc.)                  85,000

**c.** Depreciation on manufacturing building          880,000

**d.** Wages for production workers                      191,000

Enter each cost item in the following table, placing an "X" under the appropriate classification.

| | Product Costs | | |
| --- | --- | --- | --- |
| | Direct Materials | Direct Labor | Manufacturing Overhead |
| **a.** | | | |
| **b.** | | | |
| **c.** | | | |
| **d.** | | | |

**BE14.7 (LO 3), AP** Francum Company has the following data: direct labor $209,000, direct materials used $180,000, total manufacturing overhead $208,000, and beginning work in process $25,000. Compute (a) total manufacturing costs and (b) total cost of work in process.

*Compute total manufacturing costs and total cost of work in process.*

**BE14.8 (LO 3), AP** In alphabetical order, here are current asset items for Roland Company's balance sheet at December 31, 2022. Prepare the current assets section (including a complete heading).

*Prepare current assets section of balance sheet.*

| | |
| --- | --- |
| Accounts receivable | $200,000 |
| Cash | 62,000 |
| Finished goods | 91,000 |
| Prepaid expenses | 38,000 |
| Raw materials | 83,000 |
| Work in process | 87,000 |

**BE14.9 (LO 3), AP** The following are incomplete manufacturing cost data. Determine the missing amounts for these three independent situations.

*Determine missing amounts in computing total manufacturing costs.*

| | Direct Materials Used | Direct Labor | Manufacturing Overhead | Total Manufacturing Costs |
| --- | --- | --- | --- | --- |
| **1.** | $40,000 | $61,000 | $ 50,000 | ? |
| **2.** | ? | $75,000 | $140,000 | $296,000 |
| **3.** | $55,000 | ? | $111,000 | $310,000 |

**BE14.10 (LO 3), AP** Use the data from BE14.9 and the data that follow. Determine the missing amounts.

*Determine missing amounts in computing cost of goods manufactured.*

| | Total Manufacturing Costs | Work in Process (Jan. 1) | Work in Process (Dec. 31) | Cost of Goods Manufactured |
| --- | --- | --- | --- | --- |
| **1.** | ? | $120,000 | $32,000 | ? |
| **2.** | $296,000 | ? | $98,000 | $331,000 |
| **3.** | $310,000 | $463,000 | ? | $715,000 |

**BE14.11 (LO 4), C** The Sarbanes-Oxley Act (SOX) has important implications for the financial community. Explain two implications of SOX.

*Identify important regulatory changes.*

## DO IT! Exercises

**DO IT! 14.1 (LO 1), C** Indicate whether the following statements are true or false. If false, indicate how to correct the statement.

*Identify managerial accounting concepts.*

1. The board of directors has primary responsibility for daily management functions.

2. Financial accounting reports pertain to subunits of the business and are very detailed.

3. Managerial accounting reports must follow GAAP and are audited by CFAs.

4. Managers' activities and responsibilities can be classified into three broad functions: planning, directing, and controlling.

*Identify managerial cost classifications.*

**DO IT! 14.2 (LO 2), C** A music company has these costs:

| | |
|---|---|
| Advertising | Paper inserts for CD cases |
| Blank CDs | CD plastic cases |
| Depreciation of CD image burner | Salaries of sales representatives |
| Salary of factory manager | Salaries of factory maintenance employees |
| Factory supplies used | Salaries of employees who burn music onto CDs |

Classify each cost as a period or a product cost. Within the product cost category, indicate whether the cost is part of direct materials (DM), direct labor (DL), or manufacturing overhead (MO).

*Prepare cost of goods manufactured schedule.*

**DO IT! 14.3 (LO 3), AP** The following information is available for Tomlin Company.

| | | April 1 | April 30 |
|---|---|---|---|
| Raw materials inventory | | $10,000 | $14,000 |
| Work in process inventory | | 5,000 | 3,500 |
| Materials purchased in April | $ 98,000 | | |
| Direct labor in April | 80,000 | | |
| Manufacturing overhead in April | 160,000 | | |

Prepare the cost of goods manufactured schedule for the month of April 2022. (Assume that all raw materials used were direct materials.)

*Identify trends in managerial accounting.*

**DO IT! 14.4 (LO 4), C** Match the descriptions that follow with the corresponding terms.

**Descriptions:**

1. _____ Inventory system in which goods are manufactured or purchased just as they are needed for sale.

2. _____ A method of allocating overhead based on each product's use of activities in making the product.

3. _____ Systems that are especially important to firms adopting just-in-time inventory methods.

4. _____ Part of the value chain for a manufacturing company.

5. _____ The U.S. economy is trending toward this.

6. _____ A performance-measurement approach that uses both financial and nonfinancial measures, tied to company objectives, to evaluate a company's operations in an integrated fashion.

7. _____ Requires that top managers certify that the company maintains an adequate system of internal controls over financial reporting.

**Terms:**

a. Activity-based costing.
b. Balanced scorecard.
c. Total quality management (TQM).
d. Research and development, and product design.
e. Service industries.
f. Just-in-time (JIT) inventory.
g. Sarbanes-Oxley Act (SOX).

# Exercises

*Identify distinguishing features of managerial accounting.*

**E14.1 (LO 1), C** Justin Bleeber has prepared the following list of statements about managerial accounting, financial accounting, and the functions of management.

1. Financial accounting focuses on providing information to internal users.

2. Staff positions are directly involved in the company's primary revenue-generating activities.

3. Preparation of budgets is part of financial accounting.

4. Managerial accounting applies only to merchandising and manufacturing companies.

5. Both managerial accounting and financial accounting deal with many of the same economic events.

6. Managerial accounting reports are prepared only quarterly and annually.

7. Financial accounting reports are general-purpose reports.

8. Managerial accounting reports pertain to subunits of the business.

9. Managerial accounting reports must comply with generally accepted accounting principles.

10. The company treasurer reports directly to the vice president of operations.

**Instructions**

Identify each statement as true or false. If false, indicate how to correct the statement.

**E14.2 (LO 2), C** The following is a list of costs and expenses usually incurred by Barnum Corporation, a manufacturer of furniture, in its factory.

*Classify costs into three classes of manufacturing costs.*

1. Salaries for product inspectors.

2. Insurance on factory machines.

3. Property taxes on the factory building.

4. Factory repairs.

5. Upholstery used in manufacturing furniture.

6. Wages paid to assembly-line workers.

7. Factory machinery depreciation.

8. Glue, nails, paint, and other small parts used in production.

9. Factory supervisors' salaries.

10. Wood used in manufacturing furniture.

**Instructions**

Classify these items into the following categories: (a) direct materials, (b) direct labor, and (c) manufacturing overhead.

**E14.3 (LO 2), C** Trak Corporation, which manufactures bicycles, incurred the following costs.

*Identify types of costs and explain their accounting.*

| | | | |
|---|---|---|---|
| Bicycle components | $100,000 | Advertising expense | $45,000 |
| Depreciation on factory | 60,000 | Property taxes on factory | 14,000 |
| Property taxes on retail store | 7,500 | Customer delivery expense | 21,000 |
| Labor costs of assembly-line workers | 110,000 | Sales commissions | 35,000 |
| Factory supplies used | 13,000 | Salaries paid to sales clerks | 50,000 |

**Instructions**

a. Identify each of the above costs as direct materials, direct labor, manufacturing overhead, or period costs.

b. Explain the basic difference in accounting for product costs and period costs.

**E14.4 (LO 2), AP** Knight Company reports the following costs and expenses in May.

*Determine the total amount of various types of costs.*

| | | | |
|---|---|---|---|
| Factory utilities | $ 15,500 | Direct labor | $69,100 |
| Depreciation on factory | | Sales salaries | 46,400 |
| equipment | 12,650 | Property taxes on factory | |
| Depreciation on delivery trucks | 3,300 | building | 2,500 |
| Indirect factory labor | 48,900 | Repairs to office equipment | 1,300 |
| Indirect materials | 80,800 | Factory repairs | 2,000 |
| Direct materials used | 137,600 | Advertising | 15,000 |
| Factory manager's salary | 8,000 | Office supplies used | 2,640 |

**Instructions**

From the information, determine the total amount of:

a. Manufacturing overhead.

b. Product costs.

c. Period costs.

**E14.5 (LO 2), C** Gala Company is a manufacturer of laptop computers. Various costs and expenses associated with its operations are as follows.

*Classify various costs into different cost categories.*

1. Property taxes on the factory building.

2. Production superintendents' salaries.

3. Memory boards and chips used in assembling computers.

4. Depreciation on the factory equipment.

  5. Salaries for quality control inspectors.

  6. Sales commissions paid to sell laptop computers.

  7. Electrical components used in assembling computers.

  8. Wages of workers assembling laptop computers.

  9. Soldering materials used on factory assembly lines.

  10. Salaries for the night security guards for the factory building.

The company intends to classify these costs and expenses into the following categories: (a) direct materials, (b) direct labor, (c) manufacturing overhead, and (d) period costs.

**Instructions**

List the items (1) through (10). For each item, indicate the cost category to which it belongs.

*Classify various costs into different cost categories.*

**E14.6 (LO 2), C** Service The administrators of Crawford County's Memorial Hospital are interested in identifying the various costs and expenses that are incurred in producing a patient's X-ray. A list of such costs and expenses is presented here.

  1. Salaries for the X-ray machine technicians.

  2. Wages for the hospital janitorial personnel.

  3. Film costs for the X-ray machines.

  4. Property taxes on the hospital building.

  5. Salary of the X-ray technicians' supervisor.

  6. Electricity costs for the X-ray department.

  7. Maintenance and repairs on the X-ray machines.

  8. X-ray department supplies.

  9. Depreciation on the X-ray department equipment.

  10. Depreciation on the hospital building.

The administrators want these costs and expenses classified as (a) direct materials, (b) direct labor, or (c) service overhead.

**Instructions**

List the items (1) through (10). For each item, indicate the cost category to which the item belongs.

*Classify various costs into different cost categories.*

**E14.7 (LO 2), AP** Service National Express reports the following costs and expenses in June 2022 for its delivery service.

| | | | |
|---|---:|---|---:|
| Indirect materials used | $ 6,400 | Drivers' salaries | $16,000 |
| Depreciation on delivery equipment | 11,200 | Advertising | 4,600 |
| Dispatcher's salary | 5,000 | Delivery equipment repairs | 300 |
| Property taxes on office building | 870 | Office supplies | 650 |
| CEO's salary | 12,000 | Office utilities | 990 |
| Gas and oil for delivery trucks | 2,200 | Repairs on office equipment | 180 |

**Instructions**

Determine the total amount of (a) delivery service (product) costs and (b) period costs.

*Classify various costs into different cost categories.*

**E14.8 (LO 2), AP** Evilene Company makes industrial-grade brooms. It incurs the following costs.

  1. Salaries for broom inspectors.

  2. Copy machine maintenance at corporate headquarters.

  3. Hourly wages for assembly workers.

  4. Research and development for new broom types.

  5. Salary for factory manager.

  6. Depreciation on broom-assembly equipment.

  7. Salary for the CEO administrative assistant.

  8. Wood for handles.

  9. Factory cleaning supplies.

  10. Lubricants for broom-assembly factory equipment.

  11. Salaries for customer service representatives.

  12. Salaries for factory maintenance crew.

  13. Sales team golf outings with customers.

  14. Salaries for the raw materials receiving department employees.

  15. Advertising expenses.

  16. Depreciation on the CFO company car.

  17. Straw for brooms.

  18. Salaries for sales personnel.

  19. Shipping costs to customers.

**Instructions**

  **a.** Indicate whether each cost is direct materials, direct labor, manufacturing overhead, or nonmanufacturing.

  **b.** Indicate whether each cost is a product cost or a period cost.

**E14.9 (LO 3), AP** Lopez Corporation incurred the following costs during 2022.

*Compute cost of goods manufactured and sold, and discuss classification of various costs.*

| | | | |
|---|---|---|---|
| Direct materials used in product | $120,000 | Advertising expense | $45,000 |
| Depreciation on factory | 60,000 | Property taxes on factory | 14,000 |
| Property taxes on store | 7,500 | Delivery expense | 21,000 |
| Labor costs of assembly-line workers | 110,000 | Sales commissions | 35,000 |
| Factory supplies used | 23,000 | Salaries paid to sales clerks | 50,000 |

Work in process inventory was $12,000 at January 1 and $15,500 at December 31. Finished goods inventory was $60,000 at January 1 and $45,600 at December 31.

**Instructions**

  **a.** Compute cost of goods manufactured.

  **b.** Compute cost of goods sold.

  **c.** For those costs not included in the calculations in part (a) or part (b), explain how they would be classified and reported in the financial statements.

**E14.10 (LO 3), AP** An incomplete cost of goods manufactured schedule is presented here.

*Determine missing amounts in cost of goods manufactured schedule.*

**Hobbit Company**
**Cost of Goods Manufactured Schedule**
**For the Year Ended December 31, 2022**

| | | | |
|---|---|---|---|
| Work in process, January 1 | | | $210,000 |
| Direct materials | | | |
|   Raw materials inventory, January 1 | $   ? | | |
|   Raw materials purchases | 158,000 | | |
|   Total raw materials available for use | ? | | |
|   Less: Raw materials inventory, December 31 | 22,500 | | |
|   Direct materials used | | $180,000 | |
| Direct labor | | ? | |
| Manufacturing overhead | | | |
|   Indirect labor | 18,000 | | |
|   Factory depreciation | 36,000 | | |
|   Factory utilities | 68,000 | | |
|   Total manufacturing overhead | | 122,000 | |
| Total manufacturing costs | | | ? |
| Total cost of work in process | | | ? |
| Less: Work in process, December 31 | | | 31,000 |
| Cost of goods manufactured | | | $540,000 |

**Instructions**

Complete the cost of goods manufactured schedule for Hobbit Company. (Assume that all raw materials used were direct materials.)

**E14.11 (LO 3), AN** Manufacturing cost data for Copa Company are presented as follows.

*Determine the missing amount of different cost items.*

| | Case A | Case B | Case C |
|---|---|---|---|
| Direct materials used | $  (a) | $68,400 | $130,000 |
| Direct labor | 57,000 | 86,000 | (g) |
| Manufacturing overhead | 46,500 | 81,600 | 102,000 |
| Total manufacturing costs | 195,650 | (d) | 253,700 |
| Work in process 1/1/22 | (b) | 16,500 | (h) |
| Total cost of work in process | 221,500 | (e) | 337,000 |
| Work in process 12/31/22 | (c) | 11,000 | 70,000 |
| Cost of goods manufactured | 185,275 | (f) | (i) |

**Instructions**

Determine the missing amount for each letter (a) through (i).

*Determine the missing amount of different cost items, and prepare a condensed cost of goods manufactured schedule.*

**E14.12 (LO 3), AN** Incomplete manufacturing cost data for Horizon Company for 2022 are presented as follows for these four independent situations.

| | Direct Materials Used | Direct Labor | Manufac- turing Overhead | Total Manufac- turing Costs | Work in Process Jan. 1 | Work in Process Dec. 31 | Cost of Goods Manufac- tured |
|---|---|---|---|---|---|---|---|
| 1. | $117,000 | $140,000 | $ 87,000 | $ (a) | $33,000 | $ (b) | $360,000 |
| 2. | (c) | 200,000 | 132,000 | 450,000 | (d) | 40,000 | 470,000 |
| 3. | 80,000 | 100,000 | (e) | 265,000 | 60,000 | 80,000 | (f) |
| 4. | 70,000 | (g) | 75,000 | 288,000 | 45,000 | (h) | 270,000 |

**Instructions**

a. Determine the missing amount for each letter.

b. Prepare a condensed cost of goods manufactured schedule for situation (1) for the year ended December 31, 2022.

*Prepare a cost of goods manufactured schedule and a partial income statement.*

**E14.13 (LO 3), AP** Cepeda Corporation has the following cost records for June 2022.

| | | | |
|---|---|---|---|
| Indirect factory labor | $ 4,500 | Factory utilities | $ 400 |
| Direct materials used | 20,000 | Depreciation, factory equipment | 1,400 |
| Work in process, 6/1/22 | 3,000 | Direct labor | 40,000 |
| Work in process, 6/30/22 | 3,800 | Maintenance, factory equipment | 1,800 |
| Finished goods, 6/1/22 | 5,000 | Indirect materials used | 2,200 |
| Finished goods, 6/30/22 | 7,500 | Factory manager's salary | 3,000 |

**Instructions**

a. Prepare a cost of goods manufactured schedule for June 2022.

b. Prepare an income statement through gross profit for June 2022 assuming sales revenue is $92,100.

*Classify various costs into different categories and prepare cost of services performed schedule.*

**E14.14 (LO 2, 3), AP** Service Keisha Tombert, the bookkeeper for Washington Consulting, a political consulting firm, has recently completed a managerial accounting course at her local college. One of the topics covered in the course was the cost of goods manufactured schedule. Keisha wondered if such a schedule could be prepared for her firm. She realized that, as a service-oriented company, it would have no work in process inventory to consider.

Listed here are the costs her firm incurred for the month ended August 31, 2022.

| | |
|---|---|
| Supplies used on consulting contracts | $ 1,700 |
| Supplies used in the administrative offices | 1,500 |
| Depreciation on equipment used for contract work | 900 |
| Depreciation on administrative office equipment | 1,050 |
| Salaries of professionals working on contracts | 15,600 |
| Salaries of administrative office personnel | 7,700 |
| Janitorial services for professional offices | 700 |
| Janitorial services for administrative offices | 500 |
| Insurance on contract operations | 800 |
| Insurance on administrative operations | 900 |
| Utilities for contract operations | 1,400 |
| Utilities for administrative offices | 1,300 |

**Instructions**

a. Prepare a schedule of cost of contract services performed (similar to a cost of goods manufactured schedule) for the month.

b. List the costs not included in (a), and then explain how they would be classified and reported in the financial statements.

*Determine cost of goods manufactured and prepare a partial income statement.*

**E14.15 (LO 3), AP** The following information is available for Aikman Company.

| | January 1, 2022 | 2022 | December 31, 2022 |
|---|---|---|---|
| Raw materials inventory | $21,000 | | $30,000 |
| Work in process inventory | 13,500 | | 17,200 |
| Finished goods inventory | 27,000 | | 21,000 |
| Materials purchased | | $150,000 | |
| Direct labor | | 220,000 | |
| Manufacturing overhead | | 180,000 | |
| Sales revenue | | 910,000 | |

## Instructions

a. Compute cost of goods manufactured. (Assume that all raw materials used were direct materials.)

b. Prepare an income statement through gross profit.

c. Show the presentation of the ending inventories on the December 31, 2022, balance sheet.

d. How would the income statement and balance sheet of a merchandising company be different from Aikman's financial statements?

**E14.16 (LO 3), C** University Company produces collegiate apparel. From its accounting records, it prepares the following schedule and financial statements on a yearly basis.

*Indicate in which schedule or financial statement(s) different cost items would appear.*

a. Cost of goods manufactured schedule.

b. Income statement.

c. Balance sheet.

The following items are found in the company's accounting records and accompanying data.

1. Direct labor.

2. Raw materials inventory, January 1.

3. Work in process inventory, December 31.

4. Finished goods inventory, January 1.

5. Indirect labor.

6. Depreciation expense of factory machinery.

7. Work in process, January 1.

8. Finished goods inventory, December 31.

9. Factory maintenance salaries.

10. Cost of goods manufactured.

11. Depreciation expense of delivery equipment.

12. Cost of goods available for sale.

13. Direct materials used.

14. Heat and electricity for factory.

15. Repairs to roof of factory building.

16. Cost of raw materials purchases.

## Instructions

List the items (1)–(16). For each item, indicate by using the appropriate letter or letters, the schedule and/or financial statement(s) in which the item would appear.

**E14.17 (LO 3), AP** An analysis of the accounts of Roberts Company reveals the following manufacturing cost data for the month ended June 30, 2022.

*Prepare a cost of goods manufactured schedule, and present the ending inventories on the balance sheet.*

| Inventory | Beginning | Ending |
|---|---|---|
| Raw materials | $9,000 | $13,100 |
| Work in process | 5,000 | 7,000 |
| Finished goods | 9,000 | 8,000 |

Costs incurred: raw materials purchases $54,000, direct labor $47,000, manufacturing overhead $19,900. The specific overhead costs were: indirect labor $5,500, factory insurance $4,000, machinery depreciation $4,000, machinery repairs $1,800, factory utilities $3,100, and miscellaneous factory costs $1,500. (Assume that all raw materials used were direct materials.)

## Instructions

a. Prepare the cost of goods manufactured schedule for the month ended June 30, 2022.

b. Show the presentation of the ending inventories on the June 30, 2022, balance sheet.

**E14.18 (LO 3), AP** Writing McQueen Motor Company manufactures automobiles. During September 2022, the company purchased 5,000 head lamps at a cost of $15 per lamp. Fifty of these lamps were used to replace the head lamps in autos used by traveling sales staff, and 4,600 lamps were put in autos manufactured during the month.

*Determine the amount of cost to appear in various accounts, and indicate in which financial statements these accounts would appear.*

Of the autos put into production during September 2022, 90% were completed and transferred to the company's storage lot. Of the cars completed during the month, 70% were sold by September 30.

**Instructions**

a. Determine the cost of head lamps that would appear in each of the following accounts at September 30, 2022: Raw Materials, Work in Process, Finished Goods, Cost of Goods Sold, and Selling Expenses.

b. Write a short memo to the chief accountant, indicating whether and where each of the accounts in (a) would appear on the income statement or on the balance sheet at September 30, 2022.

*Identify various managerial accounting practices.*

**E14.19 (LO 4), C** The following is a list of terms related to managerial accounting practices.

1. Activity-based costing.

2. Just-in-time inventory.

3. Balanced scorecard.

4. Value chain.

**Instructions**

Match each of the terms with the statement below that best describes the term.

a. _____ A performance-measurement technique that attempts to consider and evaluate all aspects of performance using financial and nonfinancial measures in an integrated fashion.

b. _____ The group of activities associated with providing a product or performing a service.

c. _____ An approach used to reduce the cost associated with handling and holding inventory by reducing the amount of inventory on hand.

d. _____ A method used to allocate overhead to products based on each product's use of the activities that cause the incurrence of the overhead cost.

# Problems

*Classify manufacturing costs into different categories and compute the unit cost.*

**P14.1 (LO 2), AP** Ohno Company specializes in manufacturing a unique model of bicycle helmet. The model is well accepted by consumers, and the company has enough orders to keep the factory production at 10,000 helmets per month (80% of its full capacity). Ohno's monthly manufacturing costs and other expense data are as follows.

| | |
|---|---|
| Rent on factory equipment | $11,000 |
| Insurance on factory building | 1,500 |
| Raw materials used (plastics, polystyrene, etc.) | 75,000 |
| Utility costs for factory | 900 |
| Supplies used for general office | 300 |
| Wages for assembly-line workers | 58,000 |
| Depreciation on office equipment | 800 |
| Miscellaneous materials used (glue, thread, etc.) | 1,100 |
| Factory manager's salary | 5,700 |
| Property taxes on factory building | 400 |
| Advertising for helmets | 14,000 |
| Sales commissions | 10,000 |
| Depreciation on factory building | 1,500 |

**Instructions**

a. Prepare an answer sheet with the following column headings.

| | Product Costs | | | |
|---|---|---|---|---|
| Cost Item | Direct Materials | Direct Labor | Manufacturing Overhead | Period Costs |

Enter each cost item on your answer sheet, placing the dollar amount under the appropriate heading. Total the dollar amounts in each of the columns.

b. Compute the cost to produce one helmet.

*a. DM $75,000*
*DL $58,000*
*MO $22,100*
*PC $25,100*

*Classify manufacturing costs into different categories and compute the unit cost.*

**P14.2 (LO 2), AP** Bell Company has been a retailer of audio systems for the past 3 years. However, after a thorough survey of audio system markets, Bell decided to turn its retail store into an audio equipment factory. Production began October 1, 2022.

Direct materials costs for an audio system total $74 per unit. Workers on the production lines are paid $12 per hour. An audio system takes 5 labor hours to complete. In addition, the rent on the equipment used to assemble audio systems amounts to $4,900 per month. Indirect materials cost $5 per system. A supervisor was hired to oversee production; her monthly salary is $3,000.

Factory janitorial costs are $1,300 monthly. Advertising costs for the audio system will be $9,500 per month. The factory building depreciation is $7,800 per year. Property taxes on the factory building will be $9,000 per year.

**Instructions**

a. Prepare an answer sheet with the following column headings for October 2022.

| Cost Item | Product Costs | | | Period Costs |
|---|---|---|---|---|
| | Direct Materials | Direct Labor | Manufacturing Overhead | |

Assuming that Bell manufactures, on average, 1,500 audio systems per month, enter each cost item on your answer sheet, placing the dollar amount per month under the appropriate heading. Total the dollar amounts in each of the columns.

b. Compute the cost to produce one audio system.

| a. | DM | $111,000 |
|---|---|---|
| | DL | $ 90,000 |
| | MO | $ 18,100 |
| | PC | $ 9,500 |

**P14.3 (LO 3), AN** Incomplete manufacturing costs, expenses, and selling data for two different cases for the year ended December 31, 2022, are as follows.

*Determine the missing amount of different cost items, and prepare a condensed cost of goods manufactured schedule, an income statement, and a partial balance sheet.*

| | Case | |
|---|---|---|
| | 1 | 2 |
| Direct materials used | $ 9,600 | S (g) |
| Direct labor | 5,000 | 8,000 |
| Manufacturing overhead | 8,000 | 4,000 |
| Total manufacturing costs | (a) | 16,000 |
| Beginning work in process inventory | 1,000 | (h) |
| Ending work in process inventory | (b) | 3,000 |
| Sales revenue | 24,500 | (i) |
| Sales discounts | 2,500 | 1,400 |
| Cost of goods manufactured | 17,000 | 24,000 |
| Beginning finished goods inventory | (c) | 3,300 |
| Cost of goods available for sale | 22,000 | (j) |
| Cost of goods sold | (d) | (k) |
| Ending finished goods inventory | 3,400 | 2,500 |
| Gross profit | (e) | 7,000 |
| Operating expenses | 2,500 | (l) |
| Net income | (f) | 5,000 |

**Instructions**

a. Determine the missing amount for each letter.

b. Prepare a condensed cost of goods manufactured schedule for Case 1.

c. Prepare an income statement and the current assets section of the balance sheet for Case 1. Assume that in Case 1 the other items in the current assets section are as follows: Cash $3,000, Accounts Receivable (net) $15,000, Raw Materials $600. and Prepaid Expenses $400.

| b. | Ending WIP | $ 6,600 |
|---|---|---|
| c. | Current assets | $29,000 |

**P14.4 (LO 3), AP** The following data were taken from the records of Clarkson Company for the fiscal year ended June 30, 2022.

*Prepare a cost of goods manufactured schedule, a partial income statement, and a partial balance sheet.*

 Excel

| | | | |
|---|---|---|---|
| Raw Materials | | Accounts Receivable | $ 27,000 |
| Inventory 7/1/21 | $ 48,000 | Factory Insurance | 4,600 |
| Raw Materials | | Factory Machinery | |
| Inventory 6/30/22 | 39,600 | Depreciation | 16,000 |
| Finished Goods | | Factory Utilities | 27,600 |
| Inventory 7/1/21 | 96,000 | Office Utilities Expense | 8,650 |
| Finished Goods | | Sales Revenue | 534,000 |
| Inventory 6/30/22 | 75,900 | Sales Discounts | 4,200 |
| Work in Process | | Factory Manager's Salary | 58,000 |

| | | | | | |
|---|---|---|---|---|---|
| Inventory 7/1/21 | 19,800 | | Factory Property Taxes | 9,600 |
| Work in Process | | | Factory Repairs | 1,400 |
| Inventory 6/30/22 | 18,600 | | Raw Materials Purchases | 96,400 |
| Direct Labor | 139,250 | | Cash | 32,000 |
| Indirect Labor | 24,460 | | | |

### Instructions

a. CGM $386,910
b. Gross profit $122,790
c. Current assets $193,100

**a.** Prepare a cost of goods manufactured schedule. (Assume that all raw materials used were direct materials.)

**b.** Prepare an income statement through gross profit.

**c.** Prepare the current assets section of the balance sheet at June 30, 2022.

*Prepare a cost of goods manufactured schedule and a correct income statement.*

**⟶ Excel**

**P14.5 (LO 3), AN** Empire Company is a manufacturer of smartphones. Its controller resigned in October 2022. An inexperienced assistant accountant has prepared the following income statement for the month of October 2022.

---

**Empire Company**
**Income Statement**
**For the Month Ended October 31, 2022**

| | | |
|---|---:|---:|
| Sales revenue | | $780,000 |
| Less: Operating expenses | | |
| Raw materials purchases | $264,000 | |
| Direct labor cost | 190,000 | |
| Advertising expense | 90,000 | |
| Selling and administrative salaries | 75,000 | |
| Rent on factory facilities | 60,000 | |
| Depreciation on sales equipment | 45,000 | |
| Depreciation on factory equipment | 31,000 | |
| Indirect labor cost | 28,000 | |
| Utilities expense | 12,000 | |
| Insurance expense | 8,000 | 803,000 |
| Net loss | | $ (23,000) |

---

Prior to October 2022, the company had been profitable every month. The company's president is concerned about the accuracy of the income statement. As her friend, you have been asked to review the income statement and make necessary corrections. After examining other manufacturing cost data, you have acquired additional information as follows.

**1.** Inventory balances at the beginning and end of October were:

| | October 1 | October 31 |
|---|---:|---:|
| Raw materials | $18,000 | $29,000 |
| Work in process | 20,000 | 14,000 |
| Finished goods | 30,000 | 50,000 |

**2.** Only 75% of the utilities expense and 60% of the insurance expense apply to factory operations. The remaining amounts should be charged to selling and administrative activities.

### Instructions

a. CGM $581,800
b. NI $2,000

**a.** Prepare a schedule of cost of goods manufactured for October 2022. (Assume that all raw materials used were direct materials.)

**b.** Prepare a correct income statement for October 2022.

## Continuing Cases

### Current Designs

**CD14** Mike Cichanowski founded **Wenonah Canoe** and later purchased **Current Designs**, a company that designs and manufactures kayaks. The kayak-manufacturing facility is located just a few minutes from the canoe company's headquarters in Winona, Minnesota.

Current Designs makes kayaks using two different processes. The rotational molding process uses high temperature to melt polyethylene powder in a closed rotating metal mold to produce a complete kayak hull and deck in a single piece. These kayaks are less labor-intensive and less expensive for the company to produce and sell.

Its other kayaks use the vacuum-bagged composite lamination process (which we will refer to as the composite process). Layers of fiberglass or Kevlar® are carefully placed by hand in a mold and are bonded with resin. Then, a high-pressure vacuum is used to eliminate any excess resin that would otherwise add weight and reduce the strength of the finished kayak. These kayaks require a great deal of skilled labor as each boat is individually finished. The exquisite finish of the vacuum-bagged composite kayaks gave rise to Current Designs' tag line, "A work of art, made for life."

Current Designs has the following managers:

Mike Cichanowski, CEO
Diane Buswell, Controller
Deb Welch, Purchasing Manager
Bill Johnson, Sales Manager
Dave Thill, Kayak Factory Manager
Rick Thrune, Production Manager for Composite Kayaks

The company's accounting data for the most recent period is as follows.

Each of the remaining chapters includes a hypothetical case featuring **Current Designs**, the company described at the beginning of this chapter. Students can also work through this case following an **Excel tutorial** available in **WileyPLUS**. Each chapter's tutorial focuses on a different Excel function or feature.

 Excel

| | | | Product Costs | | Period Costs | Amount |
|---|---|---|---|---|---|---|
| Payee | Purpose | Direct Materials | Direct Labor | Manufacturing Overhead | | |
| Winona Agency | Property insurance for factory | | | | | 3,200 |
| Bill Johnson (sales manager) | Payroll check—payment to sales manager | | | | | 1,700 |
| Xcel Energy | Electricity for factory | | | | | 450 |
| Winona Printing | Price lists for salespeople | | | | | 85 |
| Jim Kaiser (sales representative) | Sales commissions | | | | | 1,250 |
| Dave Thill (factory manager) | Payroll check—payment to factory manager | | | | | 1,450 |
| Dana Schultz (kayak assembler) | Payroll check—payment to kayak assembler | | | | | 760 |
| Composite One | Bagging film used when kayaks are assembled; it is discarded after use | | | | | 260 |
| Fastenal | Shop supplies—brooms, paper towels, etc. | | | | | 890 |
| Ravago | Polyethylene powder which is the main ingredient for the rotational molded kayaks | | | | | 3,170 |
| Winona County | Property taxes on factory | | | | | 5,480 |
| North American Composites | Kevlar® fabric for composite kayaks | | | | | 4,930 |
| Waste Management | Trash disposal for the company office building | | | | | 660 |
| None | Record depreciation of manufacturing equipment | | | | | 4,540 |

**Instructions**

a. What are the primary information needs of each manager?

b. Name one special-purpose management accounting report that could be designed for each manager. Include the name of the report, the information it would contain, and how frequently it should be issued.

c. When Diane Buswell, controller for Current Designs, reviewed the accounting records for a recent period, she noted the cost items and amounts shown above (amounts are assumed). Enter the amount for each item in the appropriate cost category. Then sum the amounts in each cost category column.

The **Waterways case** starts in this chapter and continues in every remaining chapter. You will find the complete case for each chapter in **WileyPLUS**.

## Waterways Corporation

**WC14** Waterways Corporation is a private corporation formed for the purpose of providing the products and the services needed to irrigate farms, parks, commercial projects, and private lawns. It has a centrally located factory in a U.S. city that manufactures the products it markets to retail outlets across the nation. It also maintains a division that performs installation and warranty servicing in six metropolitan areas.

The mission of Waterways is to manufacture quality parts that can be used for effective irrigation projects that also conserve water. Through that effort, the company hopes to satisfy its customers, perform rapid and responsible service, and serve the community and the employees who represent the company in each community.

The company has been growing rapidly, so management is considering new ideas to help the company continue its growth and maintain the high quality of its products.

Waterways was founded by Will Winkman, who is the company president and chief executive officer (CEO). Working with him from the company's inception is Will's brother, Ben, whose sprinkler designs and ideas about the installation of proper systems have been a major basis of the company's success. Ben is the vice president who oversees all aspects of design and production in the company.

The factory itself is managed by Todd Senter, who hires line managers to supervise the factory employees. The factory makes all of the parts for the irrigation systems. The purchasing department is managed by Helen Hines.

The installation and training division is overseen by vice president Henry Writer, who supervises the managers of the six local installation operations. Each of these local managers hires his or her own local service people. These service employees are trained by the home office under Henry Writer's direction because of the uniqueness of the company's products.

There is a small human resources department under the direction of Sally Fenton, a vice president who handles the employee paperwork, though hiring is actually performed by the separate departments. Teresa Totter is the vice president who heads the sales and marketing area; she oversees 10 well-trained salespeople.

The accounting and finance division of the company is run by Ann Headman, who is the chief financial officer (CFO) and a company vice president. She is a member of the Institute of Management Accountants and holds a certificate in management accounting. She has a small staff of accountants, including a controller and a treasurer, and a staff of accounting input operators who maintain the financial records.

A partial list of Waterways' accounts and their balances for the month of November follows.

| | |
|---|---|
| Accounts Receivable | $ 275,000 |
| Advertising Expenses | 54,000 |
| Cash | 260,000 |
| Depreciation—Factory Equipment | 16,800 |
| Depreciation—Office Equipment | 2,400 |
| Direct Labor | 42,000 |
| Factory Utilities | 27,000 |
| Finished Goods Inventory, November 30 | 68,800 |
| Finished Goods Inventory, October 31 | 72,550 |
| Indirect Labor | 48,000 |
| Office Salaries | 325,000 |
| Office Supplies Expense | 1,600 |
| Other Administrative Expenses | 72,000 |
| Prepaid Expenses | 41,250 |
| Raw Materials Inventory, November 30 | 52,700 |
| Raw Materials Inventory, October 31 | 38,000 |
| Raw Materials Purchases | 184,500 |

| | |
|---|---|
| Rent—Factory Equipment | 47,000 |
| Repairs—Factory Equipment | 4,500 |
| Sales Revenue | 1,350,000 |
| Sales Commissions | 40,500 |
| Work in Process Inventory, October 31 | 52,700 |
| Work in Process Inventory, November 30 | 42,000 |

## Instructions

a. Based on the information given, construct an organizational chart of Waterways Corporation.

b. A list of accounts and their values are given above. From this information, prepare a cost of goods manufactured schedule, an income statement, and a partial balance sheet for Waterways Corporation for the month of November. (Assume that all raw materials used were direct materials.)

## Data Analytics in Action

### Using Data Visualization to Determine Performance

**DA14.1** Data visualization can be used to review company results.

**Example:** Recall the *Management Insight* "Supplying Today's (Not Yesterday's) Fashion" presented in the chapter. Data analytics can help **Inditex** determine how it is performing over time. For retailers, the gross margin percentage is a good measure of how the company is doing, as it indicates what percentage of sales is available to cover selling and administration costs and generate profit. From publicly available data, we can calculate Inditex's gross margin percentage [(Sales – Cost of goods sold ÷ Sales] and track it over time. What do you observe when you look at the following chart?

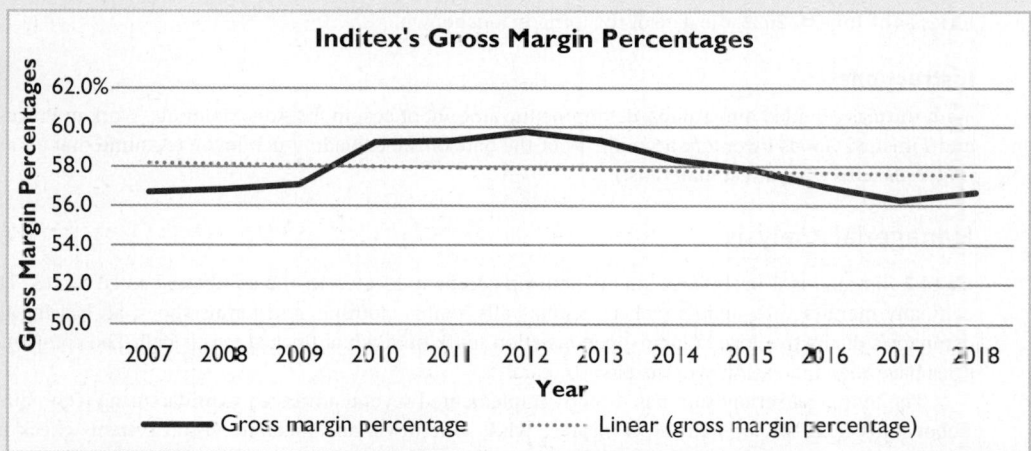

Hopefully, you immediately noticed that Inditex is able to maintain a high and stable gross margin over the time period shown. Management should be quite pleased with this. But another measure of success, revenue per employee, can provide management with even more insight concerning its sales. This case will require you calculate and graph this data for Inditex, and then analyze the results.

*Go to WileyPLUS for complete case details and instructions.*

### Data Analytics at Inditex Corporation

**DA14.2** You are excited about your upcoming job interview at **Inditex**. You realize that you need to have a better understanding of the company so that you can have several thoughtful questions prepared to ask during the interview. For this case, you will use Inditex's performance information to create several visualizations that will help increase your knowledge of the company's operations.

*Go to WileyPLUS for complete case details and instructions.*

# Expand Your Critical Thinking

## Decision-Making Across the Organization

**CT14.1** Wendall Company specializes in producing fashion outfits. On July 31, 2022, a tornado touched down at its factory and general office. The inventories in the warehouse and the factory were completely destroyed, as was the general office nearby. However, after a careful search of the disaster site the next morning, Bill Francis, the company's controller, and Elizabeth Walton, the cost accountant, were able to recover a small part of the manufacturing cost data for the current month.

"What a horrible experience," sighed Bill. "And the worst part is that we may not have enough records to use in filing an insurance claim."

"It was terrible," replied Elizabeth. "However, I managed to recover some of the manufacturing cost data that I was working on yesterday afternoon. The data indicate that our direct labor cost in July totaled $250,000 and that we had purchased $365,000 of raw materials. Also, I recall that the amount of raw materials used for July was $350,000. But I'm not sure this information will help. The rest of our records are blown away."

"Well, not exactly," said Bill. "I was working on the year-to-date income statement when the tornado warning was announced. My recollection is that our sales in July were $1,240,000 and our gross profit ratio has been 40% of sales. Also, I can remember that our cost of goods available for sale was $770,000 for July."

"Maybe we can work something out from this information!" exclaimed Elizabeth. "My experience tells me that our manufacturing overhead is usually 60% of direct labor."

"Hey, look what I just found," cried Elizabeth. "It's a copy of this June's balance sheet, and it shows that our inventories as of June 30 are Finished goods $38,000, Work in process $25,000, and Raw materials $19,000."

"Super," yelled Bill. "Let's go work something out."

In order to file an insurance claim, Wendall Company needs to determine the amount of its inventories as of July 31, 2022, the date of the tornado touchdown.

### Instructions

With the class divided into groups, determine the amount of cost in the Raw Materials, Work in Process, and Finished Goods inventory accounts as of the date of the tornado touchdown. (Assume that all raw materials used were direct materials.)

## Managerial Analysis

**CT14.2** Tenrack is a fairly large manufacturing company located in the southern United States. The company manufactures tennis rackets, tennis balls, tennis clothing, and tennis shoes, all bearing the company's distinctive logo, a large green question mark on a white flocked tennis ball. The company's sales have been increasing over the past 10 years.

The tennis racket division has recently implemented several advanced manufacturing techniques. Robot arms hold the tennis rackets in place while glue dries, and machine vision systems check for defects. The engineering and design team uses computerized drafting and testing of new products. The following managers work in the tennis racket division:

Jason Dennis, Sales Manager (supervises all sales representatives)
Peggy Groneman, Technical Specialist (supervises computer programmers)
Dave Marley, Cost Accounting Manager (supervises cost accountants)
Kevin Carson, Production Supervisor (supervises all manufacturing employees)
Sally Renner, Engineer (supervises all new-product design teams)

### Instructions

a. What are the primary information needs of each manager?

b. Which, if any, financial accounting report(s) is each likely to use?

c. Name one special-purpose management accounting report that could be designed for each manager. Include the name of the report, the information it would contain, and how frequently it should be issued.

## Real-World Focus

**CT14.3** The **Institute of Management Accountants** (IMA) is an organization dedicated to excellence in the practice of management accounting and financial management.

**Instructions**

Go to the IMA's website to locate the answers to the following questions.

a. How many members does the IMA have, and what are their job titles?

b. What are some of the benefits of joining the IMA as a student?

c. Use the chapter locator function to locate the IMA chapter nearest you, and find the name of the chapter president.

## Communication Activity

**CT14.4** Refer to P14.5 and add the following requirement.

Prepare a letter to the president of the company, Shelly Phillips, describing the changes you made. Explain clearly why net income is different after the changes. Keep the following points in mind as you compose your letter.

1. This is a letter to the president of a company, who is your friend. The style should be generally formal, but you may relax some requirements. For example, you may call the president by her first name.

2. Executives are very busy. Your letter should tell the president your main results first (for example, the amount of net income).

3. You should include brief explanations so that the president can understand the changes you made in the calculations.

## Ethics Case

**CT14.5** Steve Morgan, controller for Newton Industries, was reviewing production cost reports for the year. One amount in these reports continued to bother him—advertising. During the year, the company had instituted an expensive advertising campaign to sell some of its slower-moving products. It was still too early to tell whether the advertising campaign was successful.

There had been much internal debate as how to report advertising cost. The vice president of finance argued that advertising cost should be reported as a cost of production, just like direct materials and direct labor. He therefore recommended that this cost be identified as manufacturing overhead and reported as part of inventory costs until sold. Others disagreed. Morgan believed that this cost should be reported as an expense of the current period, so as not to overstate net income. Others argued that it should be reported as prepaid advertising and reported as a current asset.

The president finally had to decide the issue. He argued that advertising cost should be reported as inventory. His arguments were practical ones. He noted that the company was experiencing financial difficulty and that expensing this amount in the current period might jeopardize a planned bond offering. Also, by reporting the advertising cost as inventory rather than as prepaid advertising, less attention would be directed to it by the financial community.

**Instructions**

a. Who are the stakeholders in this situation?

b. What are the ethical issues involved in this situation?

c. What would you do if you were Steve Morgan?

## All About You

**CT14.6** The primary purpose of managerial accounting is to provide information useful for management decisions. Many of the managerial accounting techniques that you will learn will be useful for decisions you make in your everyday life.

**Instructions**

For each of the following managerial accounting techniques, read the definition provided and then provide an example of a personal situation that would benefit from use of this technique.

a. Break-even point (Chapter 18).

b. Budget (Chapter 22).

c. Balanced scorecard (Chapter 24).

d. Capital budgeting (Chapter 25).

## Considering Your Costs and Benefits

**CT14.7** Because of global competition, companies have become increasingly focused on reducing costs. To reduce costs and remain competitive, many companies are turning to outsourcing. Outsourcing means hiring an outside supplier to provide elements of a product or service rather than producing them internally.

Suppose you are the managing partner in a CPA firm with 30 full-time staff members. Larger firms in your community have begun to outsource basic tax-return preparation work to India. Should you outsource your basic tax-return work to India as well? You estimate that you would have to lay off six staff members if you outsource the work. The basic arguments for and against are as follows.

> **YES:** The wages paid to Indian accountants are very low relative to U.S. wages. You will not be able to compete unless you outsource.
>
> **NO:** Tax-return data are highly sensitive. Many customers will be upset to learn that their data are being emailed around the world.

### Instructions

Write a response indicating your position regarding this situation. Provide support for your view.

## Answers to Insight and Accounting Across the Organization Questions

**Does a Company Need a CEO? Q:** What are some of the advantages cited by companies that choose a structure that lacks a CEO? **A:** Companies that replace the CEO with a management committee do so because they believe that it enhances decision-making, improves collaboration, and increases management continuity by avoiding the disruptions associated with replacing a CEO.

**Low Fares but Decent Profits Q:** What are some of the line items that would appear in the cost of services performed schedule of an airline? **A:** Some of the line items that would appear in the cost of services performed schedule of an airline would be fuel, flight crew salaries, maintenance wages, depreciation on equipment, airport gate fees, and food-service costs.

**Supplying Today's (Not Yesterday's) Fashions Q:** What steps has Inditex taken that make its value chain unique? **A:** Inditex has taken numerous steps to make its supply chain more efficient and responsive. It employs an open workspace facility, where designers and commercial staff sit together and take calls regarding product ideas directly from sales employees. Production facilities are primarily located within a reasonably close distance, so management can direct and monitor production. Goods are shipped directly to stores, rather than warehouses, thus saving time and ensuring that goods are shipped to their intended targets.

**People Matter Q:** What are some of the common problems for many clothing factories in developing countries? **A:** Some of the common problems for many clothing factories in developing countries would be pressure to produce goods faster, lack of training for workers, unsafe buildings, substandard work conditions, and wage and labor violations. These problems can be exacerbated by the fact that many young women in developing countries are willing to accept low wages and working conditions that Americans consider unsafe because factory jobs offer them an opportunity to have a life that is better than that available in their villages.

**Using Data in Its Own World Q:** What is behavioral analytics, and how does Disney use it to minimize lines at its theme parks? **A:** Behavioral analytics is the use of data to predict and influence customer behavior. To minimize wait lines, and thus improve its customers' experiences, Disney uses data collected from its visitors' "MagicBands" to determine what incentives to provide to encourage customers to shift their itineraries to underutilized activities.

# Job Order Costing

## Chapter Preview

The following Feature Story about **Disney** describes how important accurate costing is to movie studios. In order to submit accurate bids on new film projects and to know whether it profited from past films, the company needs a good costing system. This chapter illustrates how costs are assigned to specific jobs, such as the production of the most recent *Avengers* movie. We begin the discussion in this chapter with an overview of the flow of costs in a job order cost accounting system. We then use a case study to explain and illustrate the documents, entries, and accounts in this type of cost accounting system.

## Feature Story

### Profiting from the Silver Screen

Have you ever had the chance to tour a movie studio? There's a lot going on! Lots of equipment and lots of people with a variety of talents. Running a film studio, whether as an independent company or part of a major corporation, is a complex and risky business. Consider **Disney**, which has produced such classics as Snow *White and the Seven Dwarfs* and such colossal successes as *Frozen*. The movie studio has, however, also seen its share of losses. Disney's *Lone Ranger* movie brought in revenues of $260 million, but its production and marketing costs were a combined $375 million—a loss of $115 million.

Every time Disney or another movie studio makes a new movie, it is creating a unique product. Ideally, each new movie should be able to stand on its own, that is, the film should generate revenues that exceed its costs. In order to know whether a particular movie is profitable, the studio must keep track of all of the costs incurred to make and market the film. These costs include such items as salaries of the writers, actors, director, producer, and production team (e.g., film crew); licensing costs; depreciation on equipment; music; studio rental; and marketing and distribution costs. If you've ever watched the credits at the end of a movie, you know the list goes on and on.

The movie studio isn't the only one with an interest in knowing a particular project's profitability. Many of the people involved in making the movie, such as the screenwriters, actors, and producers, have at least part of their compensation tied to its profitability. As such, complaints about inaccurate accounting are common in the movie industry.

In particular, a few well-known and widely attended movies reported low profits, or even losses, once the accountants got done with them. How can this be? The issue is that a large portion of a movie's costs are overhead costs that can't be directly traced to a film, such as depreciation of film equipment and sets, facility maintenance costs, and executives' salaries. Actors and others often complain that these overhead costs are overallocated to their movie and therefore negatively affect their compensation.

To reduce the risk of financial flops, many of the big studios now focus on making sequels of previous hits. This might explain why, shortly after losing money on the *Lone Ranger*, Disney decided to make more *Avengers* movies—much safer bets.

 **Watch the *Making a Hollywood Movie* video in WileyPLUS to learn more about job order costing in the real world.**

# Chapter Outline

| LEARNING OBJECTIVES | REVIEW | PRACTICE |
|---|---|---|
| **LO 1** Describe cost systems and the flow of costs in a job order system. | • Process cost system<br>• Job order cost system<br>• Job order cost flow<br>• Accumulating manufacturing costs | **DO IT! 1** Accumulating Manufacturing Costs |
| **LO 2** Use a job cost sheet to assign costs to work in process. | • Raw materials costs<br>• Factory labor costs | **DO IT! 2** Work in Process |
| **LO 3** Demonstrate how to determine and use the predetermined overhead rate. | • Predetermined overhead rate<br>• Applying manufacturing overhead | **DO IT! 3** Predetermined Overhead Rate |
| **LO 4** Prepare entries for manufacturing and service jobs completed and sold. | • Finished goods<br>• Cost of goods sold<br>• Summary of job order cost flows<br>• Job order for service companies<br>• Advantages and disadvantages of job order costing | **DO IT! 4** Completion and Sale of Jobs |
| **LO 5** Distinguish between under- and overapplied manufacturing overhead. | • Under- or overapplied manufacturing overhead | **DO IT! 5** Applied Manufacturing Overhead |

**Go to the Review and Practice section at the end of the chapter for a targeted summary and exercises with solutions.**

**Visit WileyPLUS for additional tutorials and practice opportunities.**

# Cost Accounting Systems

**LEARNING OBJECTIVE 1**

Describe cost systems and the flow of costs in a job order system.

**Cost accounting** focuses on measuring, recording, and reporting product costs for manufacturers and service costs for service organizations. Companies determine both the total cost and the unit cost of each product.

- The accuracy of the product cost information is critical to the success of the company.
- Companies use this information to determine which products to produce, what prices to charge, and how many units to produce.
- Accurate product cost information is also vital for effective evaluation of employee performance.

A **cost accounting system** consists of accounts for the various manufacturing and service costs. These accounts are fully integrated into the general ledger of a company. An important feature of a cost accounting system is the use of **a perpetual inventory system**. Such a system **provides immediate, up-to-date information on the cost of a product**.

There are two basic types of cost accounting systems:

1. A process cost system.
2. A job order cost system.

Although cost accounting systems differ widely from company to company, most involve one of these two traditional product costing systems.

## Process Cost System

A company uses a **process cost system** when it manufactures a large volume of similar products. Production is continuous. Examples of a process cost system are the manufacture of cereal by **Kellogg**, the refining of petroleum by **ExxonMobil**, and the production of ice cream by **Ben & Jerry's**.

- Process costing accumulates product-related costs **for a period of time** (such as a week or a month) instead of assigning costs to specific products or job orders.
- In process costing, companies assign the costs to departments or processes for the specified period of time.

**Illustration 15.1** shows examples of the use of a process cost system. We will discuss the process cost system further in Chapter 16.

**ILLUSTRATION 15.1** Process cost system

**Process Cost System**
Potato Chips Production

1. Harvest    2. Clean    3. Slice    4. Fry    5. Bag

Similar products are produced over a specified time period.

# Job Order Cost System

Under a **job order cost system**, the company assigns product costs to each **job** or to each **batch** of goods. An example of a job is the manufacture of a jet by **Boeing**, the production of a movie by **Disney**, or the making of a fire truck by **Pierce Manufacturing**. An example of a batch is the printing of 225 wedding invitations by a local print shop, or the printing of a weekly issue of *Fortune* magazine by a high-tech printer such as **Quad Graphics**.

- An important feature of job order costing is that each job or batch has its own distinguishing characteristics. For example, each house is custom built, each consulting engagement by a CPA firm is unique, and each printing job is different.
- **The objective is to compute the cost per job.** At each point in manufacturing a product or performing a service, the company can identify the job and its associated costs.
- A job order cost system measures product costs for each job, rather than for set time periods.

**Illustration 15.2** shows the recording of product costs in a job order cost system for Disney as it produced two different films at the same time: an animated film and an action thriller.

**ILLUSTRATION 15.2**
**Job order cost system for Disney**

Job Order Cost System
Two Jobs: Animated Film and Action Thriller

- Computer programmers
- Musical composers
- Voice-over talent
- Animation talent

Job #9501

- Actors
- Stuntpeople
- Set design
- Food caterers
- Stuntperson insurance
- Location fees

Job #9502

Each job has distinguishing characteristics and related product costs.

Can a company use both job order and process cost systems? Yes. For example, **General Motors** uses process cost accounting for its standard model cars, such as Malibu and Corvettes, and job order cost accounting for a custom-made limousine for the president of the United States.

The objective of both cost accounting systems is to provide unit cost information for product pricing, cost control, inventory valuation, and financial statement presentation.

---

## Data Analytics Insight    Autodesk

### Providing Service Through the Cloud

Kran Kanthawong/123RF

**Autodesk** is a leader in the development of computer-aided design (CAD) software in areas such as architecture, construction, production, and graphic effects. Originally, when Autodesk sold a product, it just shipped the software along with some instructions. The company then attempted to learn about customer usage of the product through surveys, customer feedback forms, error reports, and focus groups. That has now changed since Autodesk has shifted to a "software-as-a-service" (SaaS) model in which the company provides software subscriptions via the cloud.

The SaaS model allows Autodesk to maintain a continuous customer relationship as well as provides immediate access to tremendous amounts of data. The company knows which aspects of its software are being used, what needs fixing, and what features can be scaled back or eliminated. The SaaS model also allows for continuous customer revenues; in fact, one use of the data is to compute an "expected lifetime value of a customer." With that long-range strategy in mind, the data helps the company to focus on developing features that are most likely to attract big spenders, all while minimizing costs. As management notes, "We're able to now understand which parts of the system are being used most, and which are cost inefficient."

**Source:** Bernard Marr, *Big Data in Practice* (Hoboken, N.J.: John Wiley & Sons, 2016), pages 205–210.

**How does the software-as-a-service (SaaS) model change how the company collects and uses cost data in decision-making? (Answer is available at the end of the chapter.)**

# Job Order Cost Flow

We first address the flow of costs for a manufacturer (service company costs are addressed in a later section). The flow of product costs (direct materials, direct labor, and manufacturing overhead) in job order cost accounting parallels the physical flow of the materials as they are converted into finished goods and then sold (see **Illustration 15.3**).

1. Companies first **accumulate** manufacturing costs in the form of raw materials, factory labor, or manufacturing overhead.
2. They then **assign** manufacturing costs to the Work in Process Inventory account.
3. When a job is completed, the company transfers the cost of the job to Finished Goods Inventory.
4. Later, when the goods are sold, the company transfers their cost to Cost of Goods Sold, reported on the income statement.

**ILLUSTRATION 15.3**   **Flow of costs in job order costing**

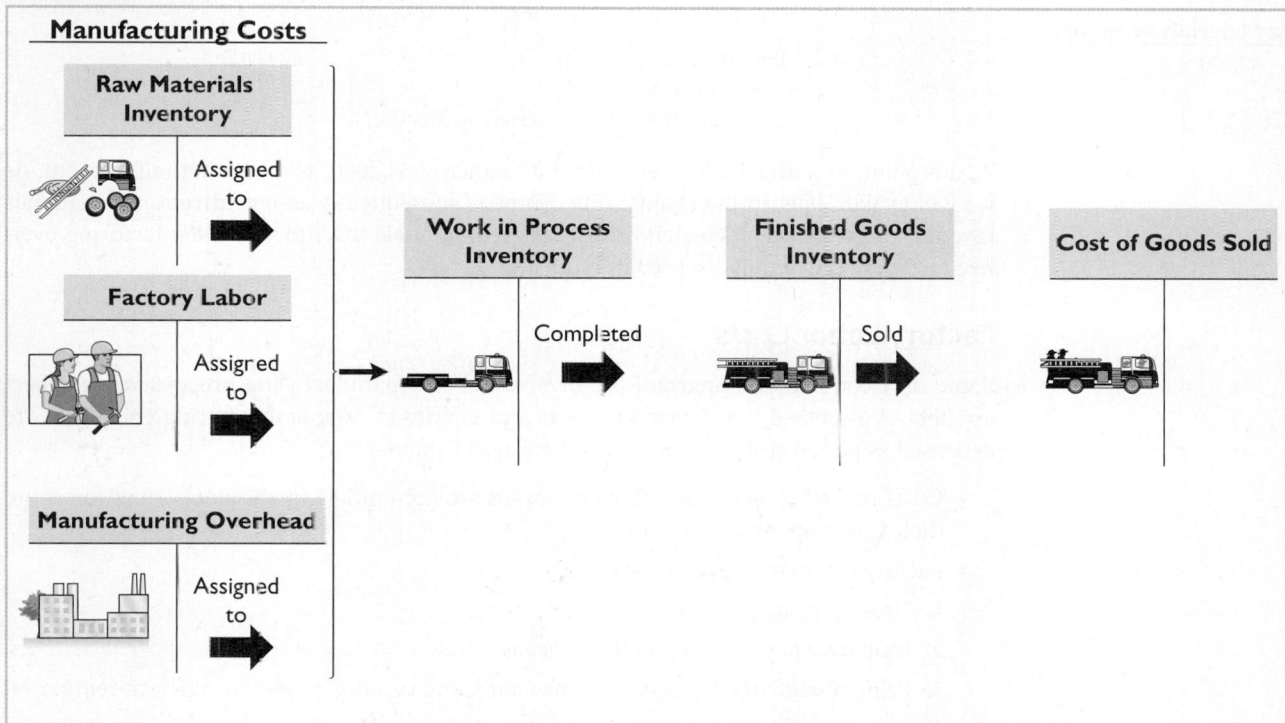

Illustration 15.3 provides a basic overview of the flow of costs in a manufacturing setting for production of a fire truck. (A more detailed presentation of the flow of costs is provided near the end of this chapter in Illustration 15.15.) There are two major steps in the flow of costs:

1. *Accumulating* the manufacturing costs incurred.
2. *Assigning* the accumulated costs to the work done.

The following discussion shows that the company accumulates manufacturing costs incurred by debits to Raw Materials Inventory, Factory Labor, and Manufacturing Overhead. The company does not attempt to associate these costs with specific jobs when it initially incurs the costs. Instead, the company makes subsequent entries to assign manufacturing costs incurred to specific jobs as they are consumed. In the remainder of this chapter, we will use a case study to explain how a job order cost system operates.

# Accumulating Manufacturing Costs

To illustrate a job order cost system, we will use the January transactions of Wallace Company, which makes custom electronic sensors for corporate safety applications (such as fire and carbon monoxide) and security applications (such as theft and corporate espionage).

## Raw Materials Costs

When Wallace receives raw materials (both direct and indirect) it has purchased from a supplier, **it debits the cost of the materials to Raw Materials Inventory**.

- The company debits Raw Materials Inventory for the invoice cost of the raw materials and freight costs chargeable to the purchaser.
- It credits Raw Materials Inventory for purchase discounts taken and purchase returns and allowances if applicable.
- Wallace makes **no effort at this point to associate the cost of these materials with specific jobs or orders**.

To illustrate, assume that Wallace purchases, on account, 2,000 lithium batteries (Stock No. AA2746) at $5 per unit ($10,000) and 800 electronic modules (Stock No. AA2850) at $40 per unit ($32,000) for a total cost of $42,000 ($10,000 + $32,000). The entry to record the receipt of this purchase on January 4 is:

**Raw Materials Inventory**

| | |
|---|---|
| 42,000 | |

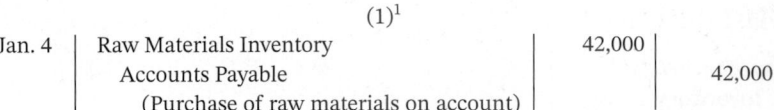

$(1)^1$

| | | | |
|---|---|---|---|
| Jan. 4 | Raw Materials Inventory | 42,000 | |
| |     Accounts Payable | | 42,000 |
| |     (Purchase of raw materials on account) | | |

At this point, Raw Materials Inventory has a balance of $42,000, as shown in the T-account. As we will explain later in the chapter, the company subsequently assigns **direct** raw materials inventory to work in process and **indirect** raw materials inventory to manufacturing overhead when the materials are used in production.

## Factory Labor Costs

Some of a company's employees are involved in the manufacturing process, while others are not. As discussed in Chapter 14, wages and salaries of nonmanufacturing employees are expensed as period costs (e.g., Salaries and Wages Expense).

- Costs related to manufacturing employees are accumulated in Factory Labor to ensure their treatment as product costs.
- Factory labor consists of three costs:
  1. Gross earning of factory workers.
  2. Employer payroll taxes on these wages.
  3. Fringe benefits (such as sick pay, pensions, and vacation pay) incurred by the employer.
- **Companies debit labor costs to Factory Labor as they incur those costs.**

To illustrate, assume that Wallace incurs $32,000 of factory labor costs. The entry to record factory labor (both direct and indirect) for the month is:

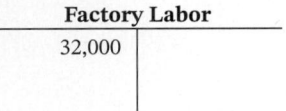

**Factory Labor**

| | |
|---|---|
| 32,000 | |

(2)

| | | | |
|---|---|---|---|
| Jan. 31 | Factory Labor | 32,000 | |
| |     Payroll Liabilities | | 32,000 |
| |     (To record factory labor costs) | | |

At this point, Factory Labor has a balance of $32,000, as shown in the T-account. The Factory Labor account accumulates all manufacturing labor costs, that is, both direct labor and indirect labor. The company subsequently assigns direct factory labor to work in process and indirect factory labor to manufacturing overhead.

## Manufacturing Overhead Costs

A company has many types of overhead costs.

- If these overhead costs, such as property taxes, depreciation, insurance, and repairs, relate to overhead costs of a nonmanufacturing facility, such as an office building, then these

---

[1] The numbers placed above the journal entries for Wallace Company are used for reference purposes in the summary provided in Illustration 15.15.

costs are expensed as period costs (e g., Property Tax Expense, Depreciation Expense, Insurance Expense, and Maintenance and Repairs Expense).

- If the costs relate to the manufacturing process, they are accumulated in Manufacturing Overhead to ensure their treatment as product costs.

Using assumed data, the summary entry for manufacturing overhead (other than indirect materials and indirect labor) for Wallace Company is:

|  | (3) |  |  |
|---|---|---|---|
| Jan. 31 | Manufacturing Overhead | 13,800 |  |
|  | Utilities Payable |  | 4,800 |
|  | Prepaid Insurance |  | 2,000 |
|  | Accounts Payable (for repairs) |  | 2,600 |
|  | Accumulated Depreciation |  | 3,000 |
|  | Property Taxes Payable |  | 1,400 |
|  | (To record manufacturing overhead costs) |  |  |

**Manufacturing Overhead**

| 13,800 | |
|---|---|

At this point, Manufacturing Overhead has a balance of $13,800, as shown in the T-account. The company subsequently assigns manufacturing overhead to work in process

---

## DO IT! 1 | Accumulating Manufacturing Costs

During the current month, Ringling Company incurs the following manufacturing costs:

a. Raw material purchases of $4,200 on account.

b. Factory labor of $18,000.

c. Factory utilities of $2,200 are payable, prepaid factory insurance of $1,800 has expired, and depreciation on the factory building is $3,500.

Prepare journal entries for each type of manufacturing cost.

### Solution

| a. Raw Materials Inventory | 4,200 |  |
|---|---|---|
| Accounts Payable |  | 4,200 |
| (Purchases of raw materials on account) |  |  |
| b. Factory Labor | 13,000 |  |
| Payroll Liabilities |  | 18,000 |
| (To record factory labor costs) |  |  |
| c. Manufacturing Overhead | 7,500 |  |
| Utilities Payable |  | 2,200 |
| Prepaid Insurance |  | 1,800 |
| Accumulated Depreciation |  | 3,500 |
| (To record manufacturing overhead costs) |  |  |

Related exercise material: BE15.1, BE15.2, DO IT! 15.1, E15.1, E15.7, E15.8, and E15.11.

**ACTION PLAN**

- In accumulating manufacturing costs, debit at least one of three accounts: Raw Materials Inventory, Factory Labor, and Manufacturing Overhead.

- Manufacturing overhead costs may be recognized daily. Or, manufacturing overhead may be recorded periodically through a summary entry.

---

# Assigning Manufacturing Costs

### LEARNING OBJECTIVE 2

Use a job cost sheet to assign costs to work in process.

Assigning manufacturing costs to work in process results in the following entries.

1. **Debits** made to Work in Process Inventory
2. **Credits** made to Raw Materials Inventory, Factory Labor, and Manufacturing Overhead.

An essential accounting record in assigning costs to jobs is a **job cost sheet**, as shown in **Illustration 15.4**. A **job cost sheet** is a form used to track the costs chargeable to a specific job and to determine the total and unit costs of the completed job.

**ILLUSTRATION 15.4** Job cost sheet

**Job Cost Sheet**

Job No. _____    Quantity _____

Item _____    Date Requested _____

For _____    Date Completed _____

| Date | Direct Materials | Direct Labor | Manufacturing Overhead |
| --- | --- | --- | --- |
| | | | |
| | | | |

Cost of completed job
  Direct materials                                              $ _____
  Direct labor                                                     _____
  Manufacturing overhead                                  _____
Total cost                                                          $ _____
Unit cost (total cost ÷ quantity)                        $ _____

Companies keep a separate job cost sheet for each job, typically as a computer file.

- The job cost sheets constitute the subsidiary ledger for the Work in Process Inventory control account in the general ledger. A **subsidiary ledger** consists of individual records for each individual item—in this case, each job.
- The Work in Process Inventory account is referred to as a **control account** because it summarizes the detailed data regarding specific jobs contained in the job cost sheets.
- **Each debit entry to Work in Process Inventory must be accompanied by a corresponding posting to one or more job cost sheets**—the assignment of direct materials, direct labor, or manufacturing overhead.

## Raw Materials Costs

Assignment of raw materials costs involves two steps:

1. Posting detailed information to individual job cost sheets.
2. Journalizing summary data in the general journal.

**Companies assign raw materials costs to jobs when their materials storeroom issues the materials in response to requests.** Requests for issuing raw materials are made by production department personnel on a prenumbered **materials requisition slip**. The materials issued may be used directly on a job, or they may be considered indirect materials.

- As **Illustration 15.5** shows, the requisition should indicate the quantity and type of materials withdrawn and the job to be charged (see **Ethics Note**).
- Note in Illustration 15.5 the specific job to be charged (Job No. 101). The materials requisition slip is also an example of the internal control of documentation (in this case, prenumbering as R247).
- The company will charge direct materials to Work in Process Inventory, and indirect materials to Manufacturing Overhead.

**ILLUSTRATION 15.5**

**Materials requisition slip**

Wallace Company
**Materials Requisition Slip**

Deliver to: _____ Assembly Department _____     Req. No.     R247
**Job to charge:** _____ **Job No. 101** _____        Date: _____ 1/6/22

| Quantity | Description | Stock No. | Cost per Unit | Total |
|---|---|---|---|---|
| 200 | Lithium batteries | AA2746 | $5.00 | $1,000 |

Requested by _Bruce Howart_          Received by _Herb Crowley_

Approved by _Kap Shin_                Costed by _Heather Remmers_

The company may use any of the inventory costing methods (FIFO, LIFO, or average-cost) in costing the requisitions **to the individual job cost sheets**. In an automated system, the requisition is entered electronically. Once approved and delivered to production, the direct materials are charged automatically to an electronic job cost record.

Periodically, the company journalizes the aggregated requisitions. For example, if Wallace uses $24,000 of direct materials and $6,000 of indirect materials in January, the entry on January 31 is:

(4)

| Jan. 31 | Work in Process Inventory | 24,000 | |
|---|---|---|---|
| | Manufacturing Overhead | 6,000 | |
| |    Raw Materials Inventory | | 30,000 |
| |      (To assign materials to jobs and overhead) | | |

This entry reduces Raw Materials Inventory by $30,000, increases Work in Process Inventory by $24,000 as the direct costs are assigned to jobs, and increases Manufacturing Overhead by $6,000, as the following shows.

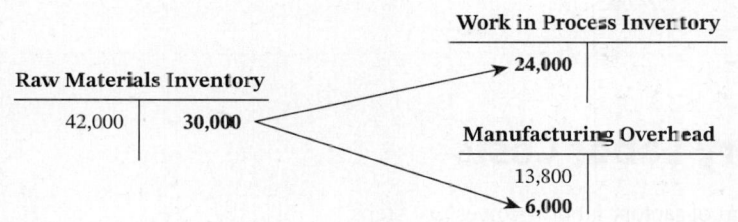

**Illustration 15.6** shows the posting of requisition slip R247 to Job No. 101 for $1,000 and other assumed postings to the job cost sheets for materials requested on other materials requisition slips. The requisition slips provide the basis for total direct materials costs of $12,000 for Job No. 101, $7,000 for Job No. 102, and $5,000 for Job No. 103. After the company has completed all postings, the sum of the direct materials columns of the job cost sheets (the **subsidiary** account amounts of $12,000, $7,000, and $5,000) should equal the direct materials debited to Work in Process Inventory (the **control** account amount of $24,000).

**ILLUSTRATION 15.6**  Job cost sheets–posting of direct materials

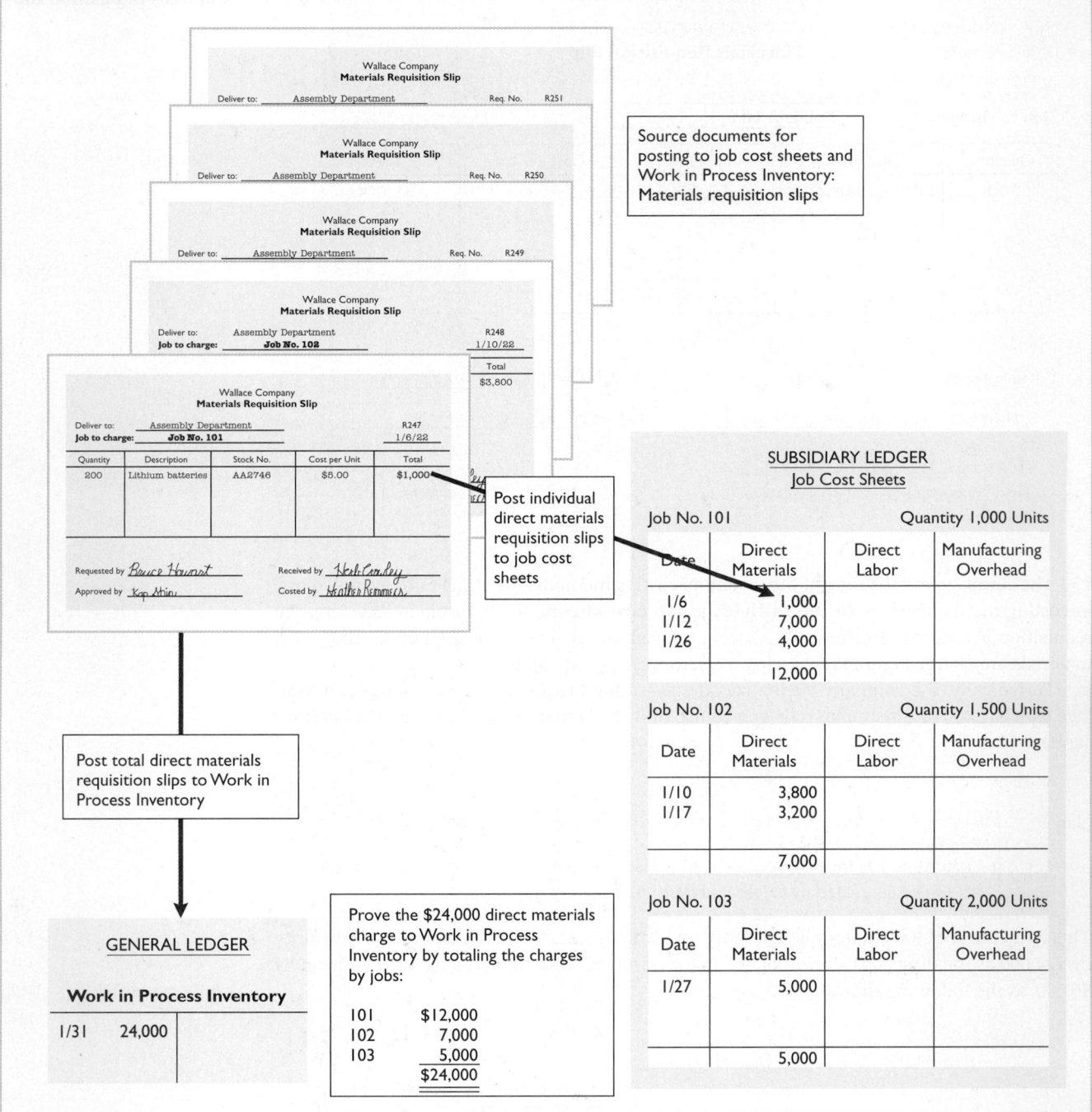

## Factory Labor Costs

Assignment of factory labor involves two steps:

1. Posting detailed information to individual job cost sheets (subsidiary ledger).
2. Journalizing summarized data in the general journal.

**Companies assign factory labor costs to specific jobs (direct labor) or to manufacturing overhead (indirect labor) on the basis of time tickets prepared when the work is performed.**

- The **time ticket** indicates the employee name, the hours worked, the account and job to be charged, and the total labor cost.

- When direct labor is involved, the time ticket must indicate the job number, as shown in **Illustration 15.7**. The employee's supervisor should approve all time tickets.
- Many companies accumulate this information through the use of bar coding and scanning devices instead of physical time tickets. When they start and end work, employees scan bar codes on their identification badges and bar codes associated with each job they work on.

**ILLUSTRATION 15.7**
**Time ticket**

**Wallace Company**
**Time Ticket**

| Employee | John Nash | | Date: | 1/6/22 |
| Charge to: | **Work in Process** | | Employee No. | 124 |
| | | | **Job No.** | **101** |

| Time | | | Hourly Rate | Total Cost |
| Start | Stop | Total Hours | | |
| --- | --- | --- | --- | --- |
| 0800 | 1200 | 4 | 10.00 | 40.00 |

Approved by  *Bob Kadler*          Costed by  *M. Cher*

The time tickets are subsequently sent to the payroll department.

- The payroll department combines the employee's hourly gross wages from the time tickets with any applicable payroll taxes and associated fringe benefits. This total direct labor cost is posted to the job cost sheets.
- In an automated system, after factory employees scan their identification codes, labor costs are automatically calculated and posted to electronic job cost sheets.
- After posting to individual job cost sheets, the company completes the assignment process with a journal entry for total labor cost. It debits Work in Process Inventory for direct labor and debits Manufacturing Overhead for indirect labor.

For example, if the $32,000 total factory labor cost consists of $28,000 of direct labor and $4,000 of indirect labor, the entry is:

(5)

| Jan. 31 | Work in Process Inventory | 28,000 | |
| | Manufacturing Overhead | 4,000 | |
| | Factory Labor | | 32,000 |
| | (To assign labor to jobs and overhead) | | |

As a result of this entry, Factory Labor is reduced by $32,000 so it has a zero balance, and labor costs are assigned to the appropriate manufacturing accounts. The entry increases Work in Process Inventory by $28,000 and increases Manufacturing Overhead by $4,000, as the following shows.

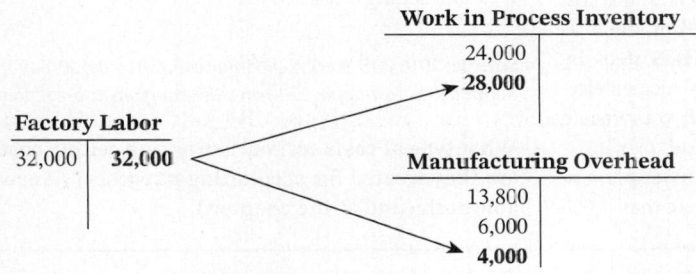

Let's assume that the labor costs chargeable to Wallace's three jobs are $15,000, $9,000, and $4,000. **Illustration 15.8** shows the Work in Process Inventory and job cost sheets after posting. As in the case of direct materials, the sum of the postings to the direct labor columns of the job cost sheets (subsidiary accounts Job 101 $15,000, Job 102 $9,000, and Job 103 $4,000) should equal the posting of direct labor to the Work in Process Inventory control account ($28,000).

**ILLUSTRATION 15.8** **Job cost sheets–direct labor**

**Management Insight    IHS**

© New Africa/Shutterstock.com

### The Cost of an iPhone? Just Tear One Apart

All companies need to know what it costs to make their own products—but a lot of companies would like to know the cost of their competitors' products as well. That's where **IHS** steps in. IHS tears apart sophisticated electronic devices to tell you what it would cost to replicate.

In the case of smartphones, which often have more than 1,000 tiny components, that is no small feat. For example, consider that the components of a recent iPhone model cost about $221. Assembly adds only about another $5. However, the difference between what you pay (almost triple the total component cost) and the "cost" is not all profit. You also have to consider the additional nonmanufacturing costs of research, design, marketing, patent fees, and selling costs.

**Source:** 2016 IHS Markit; *9to5mac.com/2016/09/20/649-iphone-7-estimated-to-cost-apple-220-heres-the-component-breakdown.*

**What type of costs are marketing and selling costs, and how are they treated for accounting purposes? (Answer is available at the end of the chapter.)**

## DO IT! 2 | Work in Process

Danielle Company is working on two job orders. The job cost sheets show the following:

Direct materials—Job 120 $6,000; Job 121 $3,600

Direct labor—Job 120 $4,000; Job 121 $2,000

Prepare the two summary entries to record the assignment of costs to Work in Process from the data on the job cost sheets.

### Solution

The two summary entries are:

| | | |
|---|---|---|
| Work in Process Inventory ($6,000 + $3,600) | 9,600 | |
|     Raw Materials Inventory | | 9,600 |
|     (To assign materials to jobs) | | |
| Work in Process Inventory ($4,000 + $2,000) | 6,000 | |
|     Factory Labor | | 6,000 |
|     (To assign labor to jobs) | | |

Related exercise material: **BE15.3, BE15.4, BE15.5, DO IT! 15.2, E15.2, E15.7, and E15.8.**

**ACTION PLAN**

- **Recognize that Work in Process Inventory is the control account for all unfinished job cost sheets.**
- **Debit Work in Process Inventory for the materials and labor charged to the job cost sheets.**
- **Credit the accounts that were debited when the manufacturing costs were accumulated.**

# Predetermined Overhead Rates

**LEARNING OBJECTIVE 3**

Demonstrate how to determine and use the predetermined overhead rate.

Companies charge the **actual** costs of direct materials and direct labor to specific jobs because these costs can be directly traced to specific jobs. In contrast, manufacturing **overhead** relates to production operations **as a whole**.

- As a result, overhead costs cannot be assigned to specific jobs on the basis of actual costs incurred because these costs cannot be traced to (identified with) specific jobs.
- Instead, companies assign (or "apply") manufacturing overhead to work in process and to specific jobs **on an estimated basis through the use of a predetermined overhead rate** (see **Alternative Terminology**).
- The **predetermined overhead rate** is based on the relationship between estimated annual overhead costs and estimated annual operating activity, expressed in terms of a common **activity base**.
- The company may state the activity in terms of direct labor costs, direct labor hours, machine hours, or any other measure that will provide an equitable basis for applying overhead costs to jobs.

**ALTERNATIVE TERMINOLOGY**

Assigning manufacturing overhead is also referred to as applying manufacturing overhead.

Companies establish the predetermined overhead rate at the beginning of the year. Small companies often use a single, company-wide predetermined overhead rate. Large companies often use rates that vary from department to department. The equation for calculating a predetermined overhead rate is shown in **Illustration 15.9**.

| Estimated Annual Overhead Costs | ÷ | Estimated Annual Operating Activity | = | Predetermined Overhead Rate |
|---|---|---|---|---|

**ILLUSTRATION 15.9**

Equation for predetermined overhead rate

Overhead consists only of indirect costs and relates to production operations as a whole. To know what "the whole" is, it might seem logical to wait until the end of the year's operations. At that time, the company knows all of its actual costs for the period. As a practical matter, though, managers cannot wait until the end of the year.

- To cost products effectively as they are completed, managers need information about product costs of specific jobs completed during the year.
- Using an estimated predetermined overhead rate enables costs to be determined for the job immediately and identifies when these costs may be different from those planned.

**Illustration 15.10** indicates how manufacturing overhead is assigned to work in process.

**ILLUSTRATION 15.10**

**Using predetermined overhead rates**

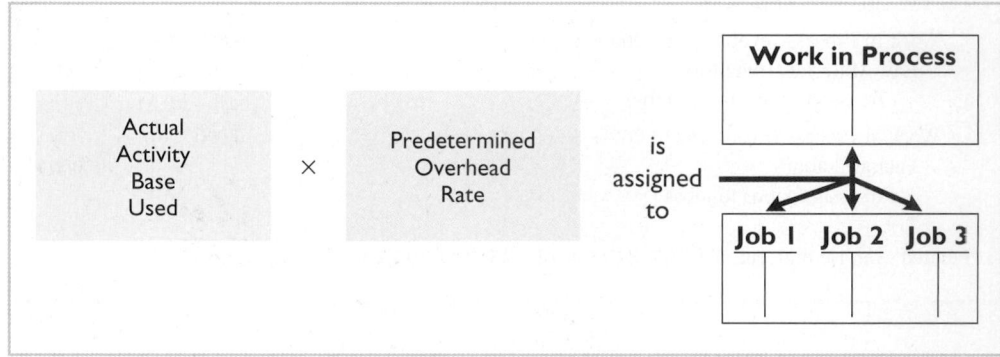

Wallace Company uses direct labor cost as the activity base. Assuming that the company estimates annual overhead costs to be $280,000 and direct labor costs for the year to be $350,000, the overhead rate is 80%, computed as shown in **Illustration 15.11**.

**ILLUSTRATION 15.11**

**Calculation of predetermined overhead rate**

| Estimated Annual Overhead Costs | ÷ | Estimated Direct Labor Cost | = | Predetermined Overhead Rate |
|---|---|---|---|---|
| $280,000 | ÷ | $350,000 | = | 80% |

This means that for every dollar of direct labor, Wallace will assign 80 cents of manufacturing overhead to a job. The use of a predetermined overhead rate enables the company to determine the approximate total cost of each job **when it completes the job**.

Historically, companies have used direct labor costs or direct labor hours as the activity base. The reason was the relatively high correlation between direct labor and manufacturing overhead.

- Today, more companies are using **machine hours as the activity base, due to increased reliance on automation in manufacturing operations**.
- Or, as mentioned in Chapter 14 (and discussed more fully in Chapter 17), many companies now use activity-based costing to more accurately assign overhead costs based on the activities that give rise to the costs.
- A company may use more than one activity base.

For example, if a job is manufactured in more than one factory department, each department may have its own overhead rate. A company might also use two bases in assigning overhead to jobs: direct materials dollars for indirect materials, and direct labor hours for such costs as insurance and supervisor salaries.

Wallace Company uses a single predetermined overhead rate and applies manufacturing overhead to work in process after it assigns direct labor costs. It also applies manufacturing overhead to specific jobs at that time. For January, Wallace applied overhead of $22,400 in response to its assignment of $28,000 of direct labor costs (direct labor cost of $28,000 × 80%). The following entry records this application.

(6)

| | | | |
|---|---|---|---|
| Jan. 31 | Work in Process Inventory | 22,400 | |
| | Manufacturing Overhead | | 22,400 |
| | (To assign overhead to jobs) | | |

This entry reduces the balance in Manufacturing Overhead and increases Work in Process Inventory by $22,400, as shown below.

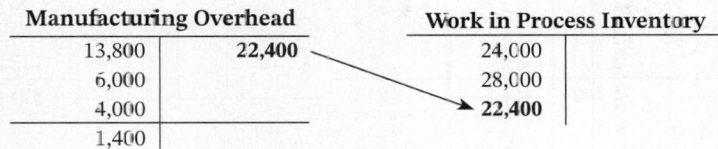

| Manufacturing Overhead | | Work in Process Inventory |
|---|---|---|
| 13,800 | **22,400** | 24,000 |
| 6,000 | | 28,000 |
| 4,000 | | **22,400** |
| 1,400 | | |

The overhead that Wallace applies to each job will be 80% of the direct labor cost of the job for the month. **Illustration 15.12** shows the Work in Process Inventory account and the job cost sheets after posting. Note that the debit of $22,400 to Work in Process Inventory equals the sum of the overhead applied to jobs: Job No. 101 $12,000 + Job No. 102 $7,200 + Job No. 103 $3,200.

**ILLUSTRATION 15.12** **Job cost sheets–manufacturing overhead applied**

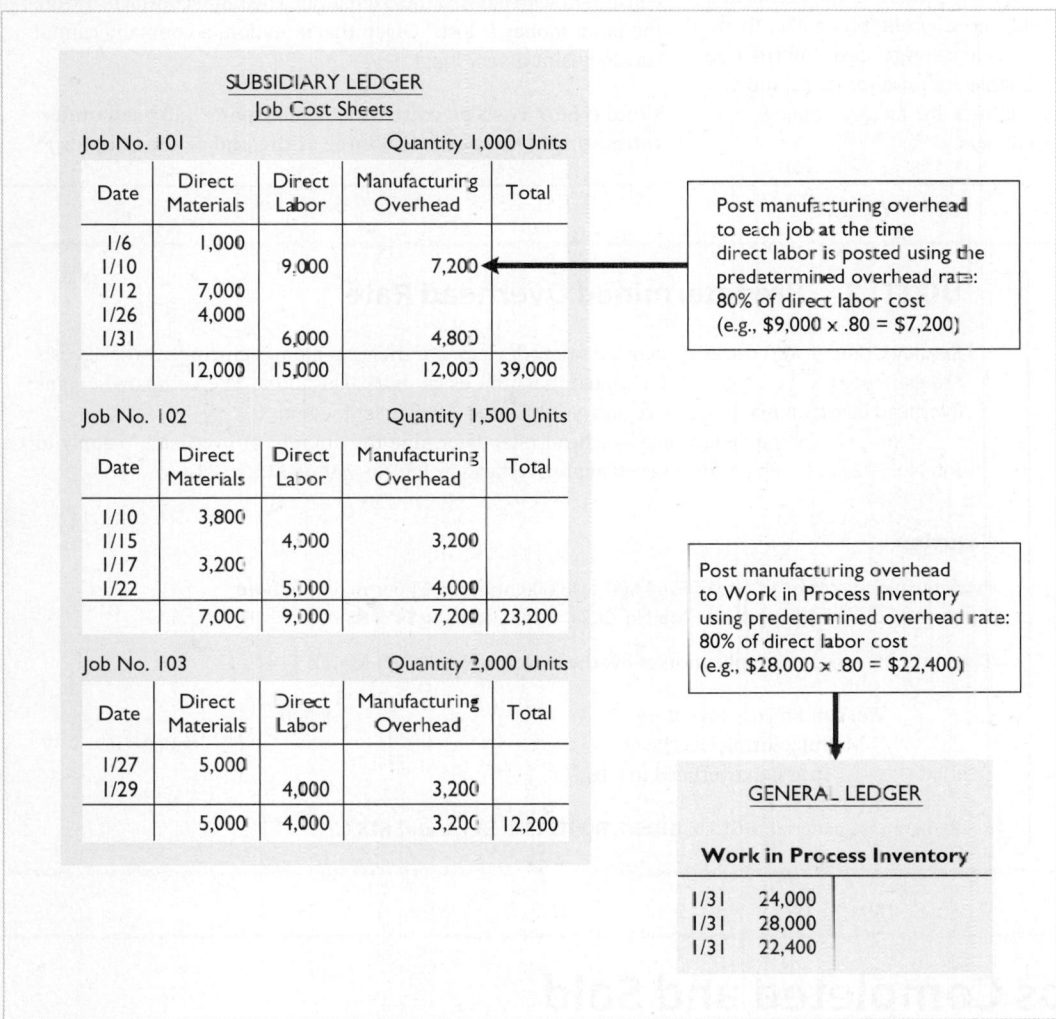

After posting the credit of $22,400 to manufacturing overhead, a debit balance remains.

- This means that the overhead applied to jobs using the predetermined rate was less than the actual amount of overhead incurred during the period.
- This situation is referred to as underapplied overhead.

We address the treatment of under- and overapplied overhead in a later section.

At the end of each month, the **balance in Work in Process Inventory should equal the sum of the costs shown on the job cost sheets of unfinished jobs**. Illustration 15.13 presents proof of the agreement of the control and subsidiary accounts for Wallace. (It assumes that all jobs are still in process.)

**ILLUSTRATION 15.13**

**Proof of job cost sheets to Work in Process Inventory**

| Work in Process Inventory | | Job Cost Sheets | |
|---|---|---|---|
| Jan. 31 | 24,000 | No. 101 | $ 39,000 |
| 31 | 28,000 | 102 | 23,200 |
| 31 | 22,400 | 103 | 12,200 |
| | **74,400** | ◄—————— | **$74,400** |

---

## Management Insight

© Tony Tremblay/
iStockphoto

### Jobs Won, Money Lost

Many companies suffer from poor cost accounting. As a result, they sometimes make products they should not be selling at all, or they buy product components that they could more profitably make themselves. Also, inaccurate cost information leads companies to misallocate capital and frustrates efforts by factory managers to improve efficiency.

For example, consider the case of a diversified company in the business of rebuilding diesel locomotives. The managers thought they were making money, but a consulting firm found that the company had seriously underestimated costs. The company bailed out of the business and not a moment too soon. Says the consultant who advised the company, "The more contracts it won, the more money it lost." Given that situation, a company cannot stay in business very long!

**What type of costs do you think the company had been underestimating? (Answer is available at the end of the chapter.)**

---

**ACTION PLAN**

- **The predetermined overhead rate is estimated annual overhead cost divided by estimated annual operating activity.**

- **Assignment of overhead to jobs is determined by multiplying the actual activity base used by the predetermined overhead rate.**

- **The entry to record the assignment of overhead transfers an amount out of Manufacturing Overhead into Work in Process Inventory.**

### DO IT! 3 | Predetermined Overhead Rate

Stanley Company produces specialized safety devices. For the year, manufacturing overhead costs are estimated to be $160,000. Estimated machine usage is 40,000 hours. The company assigns overhead based on machine hours. Job No. 302 used 2,000 machine hours.

Compute the predetermined overhead rate, determine the amount of overhead to apply to Job No. 302, and prepare the entry to apply overhead to Job No. 302 on March 31.

#### Solution

Predetermined overhead rate = $160,000 ÷ 40,000 hours = $4 per machine hour
Amount of overhead applied to Job No. 302 = 2,000 hours × $4 = $8,000

The entry to record the application of overhead to Job No. 302 on March 31 is:

| | | |
|---|---|---|
| Work in Process Inventory | 8,000 | |
| Manufacturing Overhead | | 8,000 |
| (To assign overhead to jobs) | | |

Related exercise material: **BE15.6, BE15.7, DO IT! 15.3, E15.5, and E15.6.**

---

# Entries for Jobs Completed and Sold

**LEARNING OBJECTIVE 4**

Prepare entries for manufacturing and service jobs completed and sold.

## Assigning Costs to Finished Goods

**When a job is completed**, Wallace Company summarizes the costs and completes the lower portion of the applicable job cost sheet. For example, if we assume that Wallace completes Job No. 101, a batch of electronic sensors, on January 31, the job cost sheet appears as shown in **Illustration 15.14**.

**ILLUSTRATION 15.14**
**Completed job cost sheet**

### Job Cost Sheet

Job No. 101    Quantity 1,000
Item Electronic Sensors    Date Requested January 5
For Tanner Company    Date Completed January 31

| Date | Direct Materials | Direct Labor | Manufacturing Overhead |
|---|---|---|---|
| 1/6 | $ 1,000 | | |
| 1/10 | | $ 9,000 | $ 7,200 |
| 1/12 | 7,000 | | |
| 1/26 | 4,000 | | |
| 1/31 | | 6,000 | 4,800 |
| | $12,000 | $15,000 | $12,000 |

Cost of completed job
Direct materials    $ 12,000
Direct labor    15,000
Manufacturing overhead    12,000
Total cost    $ 39,000
Unit cost ($39,000 ÷ 1,000)    $ 39.00

When a job is finished, Wallace makes an entry to transfer its total cost to Finished Goods Inventory. The entry is as follows.

(7)

| Jan. 31 | Finished Goods Inventory | 39,000 | |
| | Work in Process Inventory | | 39,000 |
| | (To record completion of Job No. 101) | | |

This entry increases Finished Goods Inventory and reduces Work in Process Inventory by $39,000, as shown in the following T-accounts.

| Work in Process Inventory | | Finished Goods Inventory |
|---|---|---|
| 24,000 | 39,000 → | 39,000 |
| 28,000 | | |
| 22,400 | | |

**Finished Goods Inventory is a control account. It controls individual finished goods records** in a finished goods subsidiary ledger, which includes all the job cost sheets for completed jobs that have not yet been sold.

## Assigning Costs to Cost of Goods Sold

Companies using a perpetual inventory system recognize cost of goods sold when each sale occurs. To illustrate the entries a company makes when it sells a completed job, assume that on January 31 Wallace Company sells on account Job No. 101. The job cost $39,000, and it sold for $50,000. The entries to record the sale and recognize cost of goods sold are:

|  |  | (8) |  |  |
|---|---|---|---|---|
| Jan. 31 | Accounts Receivable | | 50,000 | |
| | Sales Revenue | | | 50,000 |
| | (To record sale of Job No. 101) | | | |
| | | | | |
| 31 | Cost of Goods Sold | | 39,000 | |
| | Finished Goods Inventory | | | 39,000 |
| | (To record cost of Job No. 101) | | | |

This entry increases Cost of Goods Sold and reduces Finished Goods Inventory by $39,000, as shown in the T-accounts below.

| Finished Goods Inventory | | Cost of Goods Sold |
|---|---|---|
| 39,000 | 39,000 ⟶ | 39,000 |

# Summary of Job Order Cost Flows

**Illustration 15.15** shows a completed flowchart for a job order cost accounting system. All postings are keyed to entries 1–8 in the example presented in the previous pages for Wallace Company.

**ILLUSTRATION 15.15** **Flow of costs in a job order cost system**

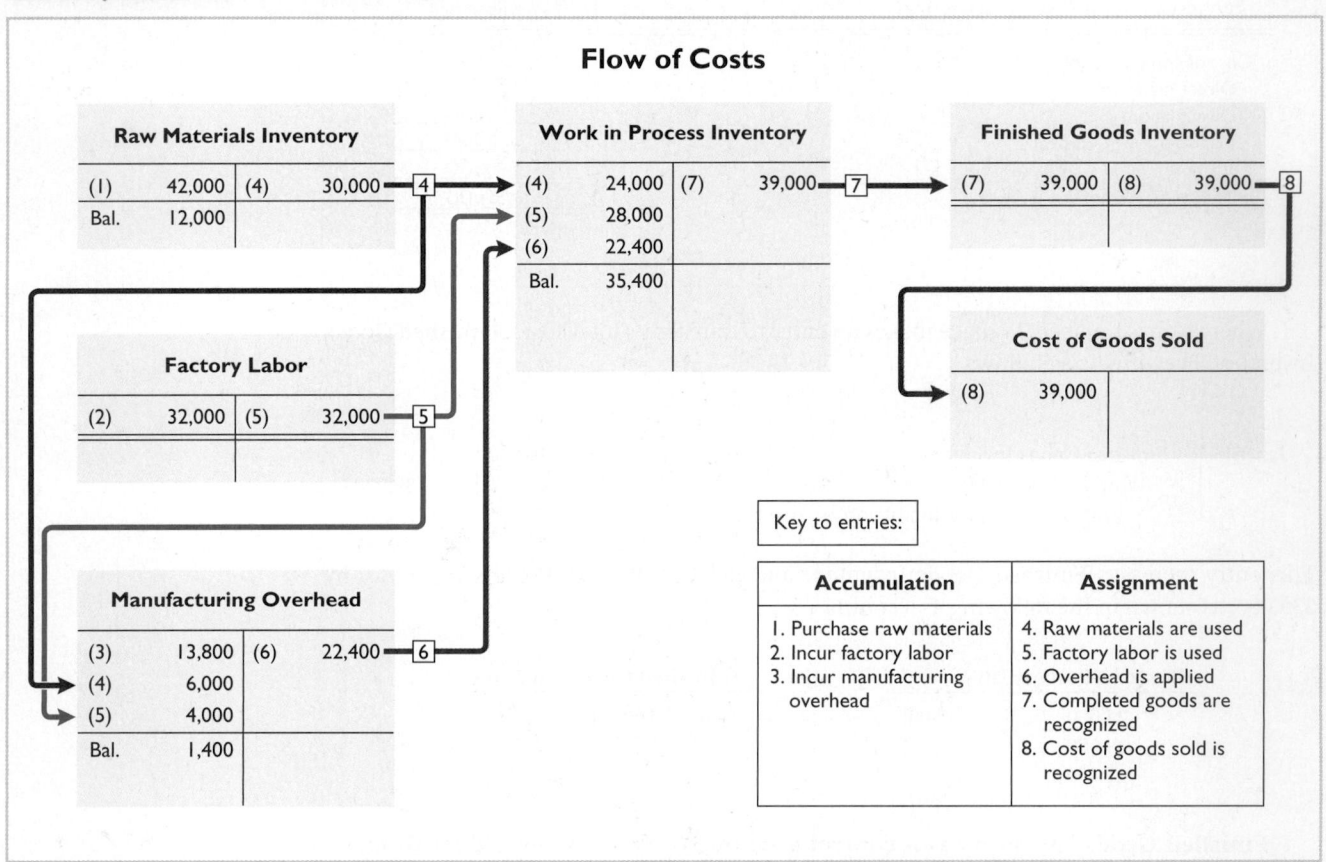

The cost flows in the diagram can be categorized as one of four types:

- **Accumulation.** The company first accumulates costs by (1) purchasing raw materials, (2) incurring labor costs, and (3) incurring manufacturing overhead costs.
- **Assignment to jobs.** Once the company has incurred manufacturing costs, it must assign them to specific jobs. For example, as it uses raw materials on specific jobs (4), the company assigns them to work in process or treats them as manufacturing overhead if the raw materials cannot be associated with a specific job. Similarly, the company either assigns factory labor (5) to work in process or treats it as manufacturing overhead if the factory labor cannot be associated with a specific job. Finally, the company assigns

manufacturing overhead (6) to work in process using a *predetermined overhead rate*. This deserves emphasis: **Do not assign overhead using actual overhead costs but instead apply overhead using a predetermined overhead rate.**

- **Completed jobs.** As jobs are completed (7), the company transfers the cost of the completed job out of Work in Process Inventory into Finished Goods Inventory.
- **When goods are sold.** As specific items are sold (8), the company transfers their cost out of Finished Goods Inventory into Cost of Goods Sold.

**Illustration 15.16** summarizes the flow of documents in a job order cost system.

**ILLUSTRATION 15.16**   **Flow of documents in a job order cost system**

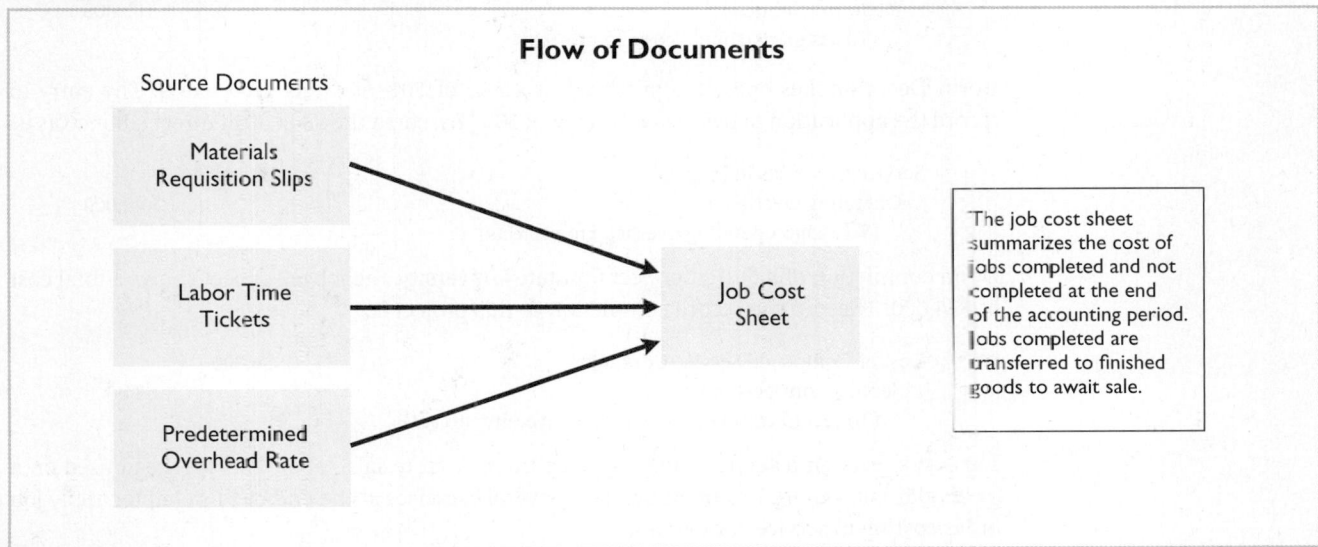

## Job Order Costing for Service Companies

Our extended job order costing example focuses on a manufacturer so that you see the flow of costs through the inventory accounts.

- Job order costing is also commonly used by service companies.
- While service companies do not have inventory, the techniques of job order costing are still quite useful in many service-industry environments.

Consider, for example, the **Mayo Clinic** (healthcare), **PricewaterhouseCoopers** (accounting), and **Goldman Sachs** (investment banking). These companies need to keep track of the cost of jobs performed for specific customers to evaluate the profitability of medical treatments, audits, or investment banking engagements.

Many service organizations bill their customers using cost-plus contracts (discussed more fully in Chapter 21).

- Cost-plus contracts mean that the customer's bill is the sum of the costs incurred on the job, plus a profit amount that is calculated as a percentage of the costs incurred.
- In order to minimize conflict with customers and reduce potential contract disputes, service companies that use cost-plus contracts must maintain accurate and up-to-date costing records.

Up-to-date cost records enable a service company to immediately notify a customer of cost overruns due to customer requests for changes to the original plan or unexpected complications. Timely recordkeeping allows the contractor and customer to consider alternatives before it is too late.

A service company that uses a job order cost system does not have inventory accounts. It does, however, use an account similar to Work in Process Inventory, referred to here as Service Contracts in Process, to record job costs prior to completion. It also uses an account called Operating Overhead, which is similar to Manufacturing Overhead. To illustrate the journal entries for a service company under a job order cost system, consider the following transactions for Dorm Decor, an interior design company. The entry to record the assignment of $9,000 of supplies to projects ($7,000 direct and $2,000 indirect) is:

| | | |
|---|---|---|
| Service Contracts in Process | 7,000 | |
| Operating Overhead | 2,000 | |
|     Supplies | | 9,000 |
|       (To assign supplies to projects) | | |

The entry to record the assignment of employee payroll costs of $100,000 ($84,000 direct and $16,000 indirect) is:

| | | |
|---|---|---|
| Service Contracts in Process | 84,000 | |
| Operating Overhead | 16,000 | |
|     Payroll Liabilities | | 100,000 |
|       (To assign personnel costs to projects) | | |

Dorm Decor applies operating overhead at a rate of 50% of direct labor costs. The entry to record the application of overhead ($84,000 × 50%) based on the $84,000 of direct labor costs is:

| | | |
|---|---|---|
| Service Contracts in Process | 42,000 | |
|     Operating Overhead | | 42,000 |
|       (To assign operating overhead to projects) | | |

Upon completion of a design project for State University, the job cost sheet shows a total cost of $34,000. The entry to record completion of this project is:

| | | |
|---|---|---|
| Cost of Completed Service Contracts | 34,000 | |
|     Service Contracts in Process | | 34,000 |
|       (To record completion of State University project) | | |

Job cost sheets for a service company keep track of materials, labor, and overhead used on a particular job, similar to a manufacturer. Several exercises at the end of this chapter apply job order costing to service companies.

---

## Service Company Insight     General Electric

© Christian Lagereek/iStockphoto

### Sales Are Nice, but Service Revenue Pays the Bills

Jet engines are one of the many products made by the industrial operations division of **General Electric (GE)**. At prices as high as $30 million per engine, you can bet that GE does its best to keep track of costs. It might surprise you that GE doesn't make much profit on the sale of each engine. So why does it bother making them? For the service revenue. During one recent year, about 75% of the division's revenues came from servicing its own products. One estimate is that the $13 billion in aircraft engines sold during a recent three-year period will generate about $90 billion in service revenue over the 30-year life of the engines. GE hopes to have 44,000 engines in service in the near future.

Because of the high product costs, both the engines themselves and the subsequent service are most likely accounted for using job order costing. Accurate service cost records are important because GE needs to generate high profit margins (estimated to be 30%) on its service jobs to make up for the low margins on the original sale. It also needs good cost records for its service jobs in order to control its costs. Otherwise, a competitor, such as **Pratt & Whitney**, might submit lower bids for service contracts and take lucrative service jobs away from GE.

**Sources:** Paul Glader, "GE's Focus on Services Faces Test," *Wall Street Journal Online* (March 3, 2009); and Steve Heller, "General Electric's Untapped Opportunity in Aviation," *The Motley Fool* (August 27, 2016).

**Why would GE use job order costing to keep track of the cost of repairing a malfunctioning engine for a major airline? (Answer is available at the end of the chapter.)**

---

# Advantages and Disadvantages of Job Order Costing

Job order costing is more precise in the assignment of costs to projects than process costing (discussed in Chapter 16). For example, assume that a construction company, Juan Company, builds 10 custom homes a year at a total cost of $2,000,000. One way to determine the cost of each home is to divide the total construction cost incurred during the year by the number of homes produced during the year. For Juan Company, an average cost of $200,000 ($2,000,000 ÷ 10) is computed. If the homes are nearly identical, then this approach is adequate for purposes of determining profit per home.

- But if the homes vary in terms of size, style, and material types, using the average cost of $200,000 to determine profit per home is inappropriate.
- Instead, Juan Company should use a job order cost system to determine the specific cost incurred to build each home and the amount of profit made on each.
- Thus, job order costing provides more useful information for determining the profitability of particular projects and for estimating costs when preparing bids on future jobs.

However, job order costing requires a significant amount of data entry. For Juan Company, it would be much easier to simply keep track of total costs incurred during the year than it is to keep track of the costs incurred on each job (each home built). Recording this information is time-consuming, and if the data is not entered accurately, the product costs are incorrect.

- In recent years, technological advances, such as bar-coding devices for both labor costs and materials, have increased the accuracy and reduced the effort needed to record costs on specific jobs.
- These innovations expand the opportunities to apply job order costing in a wider variety of business settings, thus improving management's ability to control costs and make better-informed decisions.

A common problem of all costing systems is how to assign overhead to the finished product. Overhead often represents more than 50% of a product's cost, and this cost is often difficult to assign meaningfully to the product. How, for example, is the salary of a project manager at Juan Company assigned to the various homes, which may differ in size, style, and cost of materials used?

- The accuracy of the job order cost system is largely dependent on the accuracy of the overhead allocation process.
- Even if the company does a good job of keeping track of the specific amounts of materials and labor used on each job, if the overhead costs are not assigned to individual jobs in a meaningful way, the product costing information is not useful. We address this issue in more detail in Chapter 17.

## DO IT! 4 | Completion and Sale of Jobs

During the current month, Onyx Corporation completed Job 109 and Job 112. Job 109 cost $19,000 and Job 112 cost $27,000. Job 112 was sold on account for $42,000. Journalize the entries for the completion of the two jobs and the sale of Job 112.

**ACTION PLAN**
- Debit Finished Goods Inventory for the cost of completed jobs.
- Debit Cost of Goods Sold for the cost of jobs sold.

### Solution

| | | |
|---|---|---|
| Finished Goods Inventory | 46,000 | |
| Work in Process Inventory | | 46,000 |
| (To record completion of Job 109, costing $19,000 and Job 112, costing $27,000) | | |
| Accounts Receivable | 42,000 | |
| Sales Revenue | | 42,000 |
| (To record sale of Job 112) | | |
| Cost of Goods Sold | 27,000 | |
| Finished Goods Inventory | | 27,000 |
| (To record cost of goods sold for Job 112) | | |

Related exercise material: **BE15.8, BE15.9, DO IT! 15.4, E15.2, E15.3, E15.6, E15.7,** and **E15.10.**

# Applied Manufacturing Overhead

At the end of a period, companies prepare financial statements that present aggregated data for all jobs manufactured and sold.

**HELPFUL HINT**

Companies usually prepare monthly financial statements for management use only.

- The cost of goods manufactured schedule in job order costing is the same as presented in Chapter 14 with one exception: **The schedule shows manufacturing overhead applied, rather than actual overhead costs.**
- **The company adds this amount to direct materials used and direct labor assigned to determine total manufacturing costs.**
- Companies prepare the cost of goods manufactured schedule directly from the Work in Process Inventory account (see **Helpful Hint**).

**Illustration 15.17** shows a **condensed** schedule for Wallace Company for January.

**ILLUSTRATION 15.17**

Cost of goods manufactured schedule

### Wallace Company
**Cost of Goods Manufactured Schedule**
**For the Month Ended January 31, 2022**

| | | |
|---|---:|---:|
| Work in process, January 1 | | $ –0– |
| Direct materials used | $24,000 | |
| Direct labor | 28,000 | |
| **Manufacturing overhead applied** | **22,400** | |
| Total manufacturing costs | | 74,400 |
| Total cost of work in process | | 74,400 |
| Less: Work in process, January 31 | | 35,400 |
| Cost of goods manufactured | | $39,000 |

Note that the cost of goods manufactured ($39,000) agrees with the amount transferred from Work in Process Inventory to Finished Goods Inventory in journal entry No. 7 in Illustration 15.15.

## Under- or Overapplied Manufacturing Overhead

Recall that overhead is applied based on an estimate of total annual overhead costs. This estimate will rarely be exactly equal to actual overhead incurred. Therefore, at the end of the year, after overhead has been applied to specific jobs, the Manufacturing Overhead account will likely have a remaining balance.

- When Manufacturing Overhead has a **debit balance**, overhead is said to be underapplied. **Underapplied overhead** means that the overhead applied to work in process is less than the overhead incurred.
- Conversely, when manufacturing overhead has a **credit balance**, overhead is overapplied. **Overapplied overhead** means that the overhead applied to work in process is greater than the overhead incurred.

**Illustration 15.18** shows these concepts.

**ILLUSTRATION 15.18**  Under- and overapplied overhead

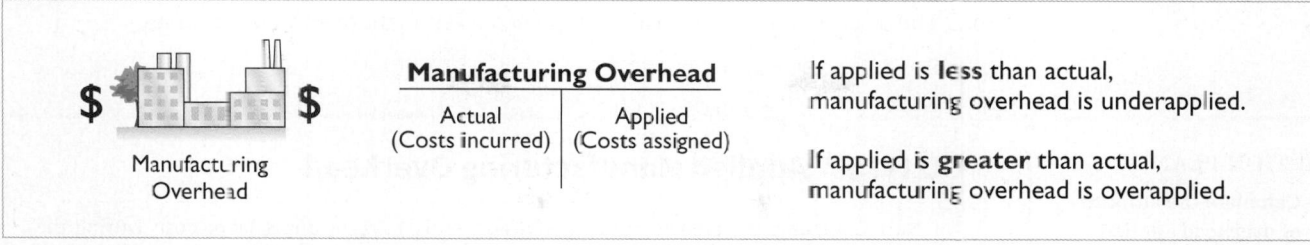

| Manufacturing Overhead | |
|---|---|
| **Actual** (Costs incurred) | **Applied** (Costs assigned) |

If applied is **less** than actual, manufacturing overhead is underapplied.

If applied is **greater** than actual, manufacturing overhead is overapplied.

## Year-End Balance

At the end of the year, all manufacturing overhead transactions are complete. There is no further opportunity for offsetting events to occur. At this point, Wallace Company eliminates any balance in Manufacturing Overhead by an adjusting entry. It considers under- or overapplied overhead to be an **adjustment to cost of goods sold.**

- Wallace **debits underapplied overhead to Cost of Goods Sold.**
- **It credits overapplied overhead to Cost of Goods Sold**. (Service organizations use Cost of Completed Service Contracts.)

To illustrate, as noted earlier in the chapter and shown below, after overhead of $22,400 has been assigned, Wallace has a $1,400 debit balance in Manufacturing Overhead at January 31. This occurred because the amount of overhead applied was less than the amount actually incurred during the period.

| Manufacturing Overhead | |
|---|---|
| 13,800 | 22,400 ]– Applied |
| Incurred — 6,000 | |
| 4,000 | |
| **1,400** | |

The adjusting entry for the underapplied overhead is:

| Jan. 31 | Cost of Goods Sold | 1,400 | |
|---|---|---|---|
| | Manufacturing Overhead | | 1,400 |
| | (To transfer underapplied overhead to cost of goods sold) | | |

After Wallace posts this entry, Manufacturing Overhead has a zero balance. In preparing an income statement for the year, Wallace reports cost of goods sold **after adjusting it** for either under- or overapplied overhead.

Illustration 15.19 presents an income statement for Wallace after adjusting for the $1,400 of underapplied overhead.

**ILLUSTRATION 15.19**

**Partial income statement**

| **Wallace Company** Income Statement (partial) For the Month Ended January 31, 2022 | | |
|---|---|---|
| Sales revenue | | $50,000 |
| Cost of goods sold | | |
| Finished goods inventory, January 1 | $   –0– | |
| **Cost of goods manufactured (see Illustration 15.17)** | 39,000 | |
| Cost of goods available for sale | 39,000 | |
| Less: Finished goods inventory, January 31 | –0– | |
| Cost of goods sold—unadjusted | 39,000 | |
| Add: Adjustment for underapplied overhead | 1,400 | |
| Cost of goods sold—adjusted | | 40,400 |
| Gross profit | | $ 9,600 |

For more accurate costing, significant under- or overapplied overhead at the end of the year should be allocated among ending work in process, finished goods, and cost of goods sold. The discussion of this allocation approach is left to more advanced courses.

---

**ACTION PLAN**

• Calculate the amount of overhead applied by multiplying the predetermined overhead rate by actual activity.

• If applied overhead is less than actual, overhead is underapplied.

• If applied overhead is greater than actual, overhead is overapplied.

## DO IT! 5 | Applied Manufacturing Overhead

For Karr Company, the predetermined overhead rate is 140% of direct labor cost. During the month, Karr incurred $90,000 of factory labor costs, of which $80,000 is direct labor and $10,000 is indirect labor. Actual overhead incurred (including indirect labor) was $119,000.

Compute the amount of manufacturing overhead applied during the month. Determine the amount of under- or overapplied manufacturing overhead.

### Solution

Manufacturing overhead applied = (140% × $80,000) = $112,000
Underapplied manufacturing overhead = ($119,000 − $112,000) = $7,000

Related exercise material: **BE15.10, DO IT! 15.5, E15.4, E15.5, E15.9, and E15.13.**

---

# Review and Practice

## Learning Objectives Review

**1   Describe cost systems and the flow of costs in a job order system.**

Cost accounting focuses on the procedures for measuring, recording, and reporting product and service costs. From the data accumulated, companies determine the total production cost and the unit cost of each product. The two basic types of cost accounting systems are process cost and job order cost.

In job order costing, companies first accumulate manufacturing costs in three accounts: Raw Materials Inventory, Factory Labor, and Manufacturing Overhead. They then assign the accumulated costs to Work in Process Inventory and eventually to Finished Goods Inventory and Cost of Goods Sold.

**2   Use a job cost sheet to assign costs to work in process.**

A job cost sheet is a form used to record the costs chargeable to a specific job and to determine the total and unit costs of the completed job. Job cost sheets constitute the subsidiary ledger for the Work in Process Inventory control account.

**3   Demonstrate how to determine and use the predetermined overhead rate.**

The predetermined overhead rate is based on the relationship between estimated annual overhead costs and estimated annual operating activity. This is expressed in terms of a common activity base, such as direct labor cost, direct labor hours, or machine hours. Companies use this rate to assign overhead costs to work in process and to specific jobs.

**4   Prepare entries for manufacturing and service jobs completed and sold.**

When jobs are completed, companies debit the cost to Finished Goods Inventory and credit it to Work in Process Inventory. When a job is sold, the entries are (a) debit Cash or Accounts Receivable and credit Sales Revenue for the selling price, and (b) debit Cost of Goods Sold and credit Finished Goods Inventory for the cost of the goods.

**5   Distinguish between under- and overapplied manufacturing overhead.**

Underapplied manufacturing overhead indicates that the overhead assigned to work in process is less than the actual overhead costs incurred. Overapplied overhead indicates that the overhead assigned to work in process is greater than the actual overhead costs incurred.

## Glossary Review

**Cost accounting** An area of accounting that focuses on measuring, recording, and reporting product and service costs. (p. 15-3).

**Cost accounting system** Manufacturing and service cost accounts that are fully integrated into the general ledger of a company. (p. 15-3).

**Job cost sheet** A form used to record the costs chargeable to a specific job and to determine the total and unit costs of the completed job. (p. 15-8).

**Job order cost system** A cost accounting system in which costs are assigned to each job or batch. (p. 15-4).

**Materials requisition slip** A document authorizing the issuance of raw materials from the storeroom to production. (p. 15-8).

**Overapplied overhead** A situation in which overhead applied to work in process is greater than the actual overhead costs incurred. (p. 15-22).

**Predetermined overhead rate** A rate based on the relationship between estimated annual overhead costs and estimated annual operating activity, expressed in terms of a common activity base. (p. 15-13).

**Process cost system** A cost accounting system used when a company manufactures a large volume of similar products. (p. 15-3).

**Time ticket** A document that indicates the employee name, the hours worked, the account and job to be charged, and the total labor cost. (p. 15-10).

**Underapplied overhead** A situation in which overhead applied to work in process is less than the actual overhead costs incurred. (p. 15-22).

## Practice Multiple-Choice Questions

**1. (LO 1)** Cost accounting focuses on the measuring, recording, and reporting of:

    **a.** product costs.

    **b.** future costs.

    **c.** manufacturing processes.

    **d.** managerial accounting decisions.

**2. (LO 1)** A company is more likely to use a job order cost system if:

    **a.** it manufactures a large volume of similar products.

    **b.** its production is continuous.

    **c.** it manufactures products with unique characteristics.

    **d.** it uses a periodic inventory system.

**3. (LO 1)** In accumulating raw materials costs, companies debit the cost of raw materials purchased in a perpetual inventory system to:

    **a.** Raw Materials Purchases.

    **b.** Raw Materials Inventory.

    **c.** Purchases.

    **d.** Work in Process.

**4. (LO 1)** When incurred, factory labor costs are debited to:

    **a.** Work in Process Inventory.

    **b.** Factory Wages Expense.

    **c.** Factory Labor.

    **d.** Payroll Liabilities.

**5. (LO 1)** The flow of costs in job order costing:

    **a.** begins with work in process inventory and ends with finished goods inventory.

    **b.** begins as soon as a sale occurs.

    **c.** parallels the physical flow of materials as they are converted into finished goods and then sold.

    **d.** is necessary to prepare the cost of goods manufactured schedule.

**6. (LO 2)** Raw materials are assigned to a job when:

    **a.** the job is sold.

    **b.** the materials are purchased.

    **c.** the materials are received from the vendor.

    **d.** the materials are issued by the materials storeroom.

**7. (LO 2)** The sources of information for assigning costs to job cost sheets are:

    **a.** invoices, time tickets, and the predetermined overhead rate.

    **b.** materials requisition slips, time tickets, and the actual overhead costs.

    **c.** materials requisition slips, payroll register, and the predetermined overhead rate.

    **d.** materials requisition slips, time tickets, and the predetermined overhead rate.

**8. (LO 2)** In recording the issuance of raw materials in a job order cost system it would be **incorrect** to:

    **a.** debit Work in Process Inventory.

    **b.** debit Finished Goods Inventory.

    **c.** debit Manufacturing Overhead.

    **d.** credit Raw Materials Inventory.

**9. (LO 2)** The entry when direct factory labor is assigned to jobs is a debit to:

    **a.** Work in Process Inventory and a credit to Factory Labor.

    **b.** Manufacturing Overhead and a credit to Factory Labor.

    **c.** Factory Labor and a credit to Manufacturing Overhead.

    **d.** Factory Labor and a credit to Work in Process Inventory.

**10. (LO 3)** The equation for computing the predetermined manufacturing overhead rate is estimated annual overhead costs divided by estimated annual operating activity, expressed as:

    **a.** direct labor cost.    **c.** machine hours.

    **b.** direct labor hours.    **d.** Any of the answer choices is correct.

**11. (LO 3)** In Crawford Company, the predetermined overhead rate is 80% of direct labor cost. During the month, Crawford incurs $210,000 of factory labor costs, of which $180,000 is direct labor and $30,000 is indirect labor. Actual overhead incurred was $200,000. The amount of overhead debited to Work in Process Inventory should be:

    **a.** $200,000.    **c.** $168,000.

    **b.** $144,000.    **d.** $160,000.

**12. (LO 4)** Mynex Company completes Job No. 26 at a cost of $4,500 and later sells it for $7,000 cash. A **correct** entry is:

    **a.** debit Finished Goods Inventory $7,000 and credit Work in Process Inventory $7,000.

    **b.** debit Cost of Goods Sold $7,000 and credit Finished Goods Inventory $7,000.

    **c.** debit Finished Goods Inventory $4,500 and credit Work in Process Inventory $4,500.

    **d.** debit Accounts Receivable $7,000 and credit Sales Revenue $7,000.

**13. (LO 5)** At the end of an accounting period, a company using a job order cost system calculates the cost of goods manufactured:

    **a.** from the job cost sheet.

    **b.** from the Work in Process Inventory account.

    **c.** by adding direct materials used, direct labor incurred, and manufacturing overhead incurred.

    **d.** from the Cost of Goods Sold account.

**14. (LO 4)** Which of the following statements is **true**?

    **a.** Job order costing requires less data entry than process costing.

    **b.** Allocation of overhead is easier under job order costing than process costing.

    **c.** Job order costing provides more precise costing for custom jobs than process costing.

    **d.** The use of job order costing has declined because more companies have adopted automated accounting systems.

**15. (LO 5)** At end of the year, a company has a $1,200 debit balance in Manufacturing Overhead. The company:

    **a.** makes an adjusting entry by debiting Manufacturing Overhead Applied for $1,200 and crediting Manufacturing Overhead for $1,200.

    **b.** makes an adjusting entry by debiting Manufacturing Overhead Expense for $1,200 and crediting Manufacturing Overhead for $1,200.

    **c.** makes an adjusting entry by debiting Cost of Goods Sold for $1,200 and crediting Manufacturing Overhead for $1,200.

    **d.** makes no adjusting entry because differences between actual overhead and the amount applied are a normal part of job order costing and will average out over the next year.

**16. (LO 5)** Manufacturing overhead is underapplied if:

    **a.** actual overhead is less than applied.

    **b.** actual overhead is greater than applied.

    **c.** the predetermined rate equals the actual rate.

    **d.** actual overhead equals applied overhead.

## Solutions

**1. a.** Cost accounting focuses on the measuring, recording, and reporting of product costs, not (b) future costs, (c) manufacturing processes, or (d) managerial accounting decisions.

**2. c.** A job costing system is more likely for products with unique characteristics. The other choices are incorrect because a process cost system is more likely for (a) large volumes of similar products or (b) if production is continuous. Choice (d) is incorrect because the choice of a costing system is not dependent on whether a periodic or perpetual inventory system is used.

**3. b.** In a perpetual inventory system, purchases of raw materials are debited to Raw Materials Inventory, not (a) Raw Materials Purchases, (c) Purchases, or (d) Work in Process.

**4. c.** When factory labor costs are incurred, they are debited to Factory Labor, not (a) Work in Process Inventory, (b) Factory Wages Expense, or (d) Payroll Liabilities (they are debited to Factory Labor and credited to Payroll Liabilities).

**5. c.** Job order costing parallels the physical flow of materials as they are converted into finished goods. The other choices are incorrect because job order costing begins (a) with raw materials, not work in process, and ends with cost of goods sold; and (b) as soon as raw materials are purchased, not when the sale occurs. Choice (d) is incorrect because the cost of goods manufactured schedule is prepared from the Work in Process Inventory account and is only a portion of the costs in a job order cost system.

**6. d.** Raw materials are assigned to a job when the materials are issued by the materials storeroom, not when (a) the job is sold, (b) the materials are purchased, or (c) the materials are received from the vendor.

**7. d.** Materials requisition slips are used to assign direct materials, time tickets are used to assign direct labor, and the predetermined overhead rate is used to assign manufacturing overhead to job cost sheets. The other choices are incorrect because (a) materials requisition slips, not invoices, are used to assign direct materials; (b) the predetermined overhead rate, not the actual overhead costs, is used to assign manufacturing overhead; and (c) time tickets, not the payroll register, are used to assign direct labor.

**8. b.** Finished Goods Inventory is debited when goods are transferred from work in process to finished goods, not when raw materials are issued for a job. Choices (a), (c), and (d) are true statements.

**9. a.** When direct factory labor is assigned to jobs, the entry is a debit to Work in Process Inventory and a credit to Factory Labor. The other choices are incorrect because (b) Work in Process Inventory, not Manufacturing Overhead, is debited; (c) Work in Process Inventory, not Factory Labor, is debited and Factory Labor, not Manufacturing Overhead, is credited; and (d) Work in Process Inventory, not Factory Labor, is debited and Factory Labor, not Work in Process Inventory, is credited.

**10. d.** Any of the activity bases mentioned can be used in computing the predetermined manufacturing overhead rate. Choices (a) direct labor cost, (b) direct labor hours, and (c) machine hours can all be used in computing the predetermined manufacturing overhead rate, but (d) is a better answer.

**11. b.** Work in Process Inventory should be debited for $144,000 ($180,000 × 80%), the amount of manufacturing overhead applied, not (a) $200,000, (c) $168,000, or (d) $160,000.

**12. c.** When a job costing $4,500 is completed, Finished Goods Inventory is debited and Work in Process Inventory is credited for $4,500. Choices (a) and (b) are incorrect because the amounts should be for the cost of the job ($4,500), not the sale amount ($7,000). Choice (d) is incorrect because the debit should be to Cash, not Accounts Receivable.

**13. b.** At the end of an accounting period, a company using a job order cost system prepares the cost of goods manufactured schedule from the Work in Process Inventory account, not (a) from the job cost sheet; (c) by adding direct materials used, direct labor incurred, and manufacturing overhead incurred; or (d) from the Cost of Goods Sold Account.

**14. c.** Job order costing provides more precise costing for custom jobs than process costing. The other choices are incorrect because (a) job order costing often requires significant data entry, (b) overhead assignment is a problem for all costing systems, and (d) the use of job order costing has increased due to automated accounting systems.

**15. c.** The company would make an adjusting entry for the underapplied overhead by debiting Cost of Goods Sold for $1,200 and crediting Manufacturing Overhead for $1,200, not by debiting

(a) Manufacturing Overhead Applied for $1,200 or (b) Manufacturing Overhead Expense for $1,200. Choice (d) is incorrect because at the end of the year, a company makes an entry to eliminate any balance in Manufacturing Overhead.

**16. b.** Manufacturing overhead is underapplied if actual overhead is greater than applied overhead. The other choices are incorrect because (a) if actual overhead is less than applied, then manufacturing overhead is overapplied; (c) if the predetermined rate equals the actual rate, the actual overhead costs incurred equal the overhead costs applied, neither over- nor underapplied; and (d) if the actual overhead equals the applied overhead, neither over- nor underapplied occurs.

## Practice Brief Exercises

**1. (LO 2)** During January, its first month of operations, Swarzak Company had factory labor of $9,000. Time tickets show that the factory labor of $9,000 was used as follows: Job 1 $3,200, Job 2 $2,600, Job 3 $2,200, and general factory use $1,000. Prepare summary journal entries to record factory labor.

*Prepare entries to record factory labor.*

### Solution

| 1. Jan. 31 | Factory Labor | 9,000 | |
| | Payroll Liabilities | | 9,000 |
| Jan. 31 | Work in Process Inventory | 8,000* | |
| | Manufacturing Overhead | 1,000 | |
| | Factory Labor | | 9,000 |

*$3,200 + $2,600 + $2,200

**2. (LO 3)** Brock Company estimates that annual manufacturing overhead costs will be $950,000. Annual direct labor cost is the base used to apply overhead, and it is estimated to be $500,000. During January, Brock incurred direct labor costs of $40,000. Prepare the entry to assign overhead to production.

*Assign manufacturing overhead to production.*

### Solution

2. Overhead rate based on direct labor cost = ($950,000 ÷ $500,000) = 190%.

| Jan. 31 | Work in Process Inventory | 76,000 | |
| | Manufacturing Overhead ($40,000 × 190%) | | 76,000 |

**3. (LO 4)** In May, Huntzinger Company completes Jobs 14, 15, and 16. Job 14 cost $40,000, Job 15 $70,000, and Job 16 $35,000. On May 31, Job 14 is sold to a customer on account for $72,000. Journalize the entries for the completion of the three jobs and the sale of Job 14.

*Prepare entries for completion and sale of jobs.*

### Solution

| 3. May 31 | Finished Goods Inventory | 145,000* | |
| | Work in Process Inventory | | 145,000 |
| 31 | Accounts Receivable | 72,000 | |
| | Sales Revenue | | 72,000 |
| 31 | Cost of Goods Sold | 40,000 | |
| | Finished Goods Inventory | | 40,000 |

*$40,000 + $70,000 + $35,000

*Prepare adjusting entries for under- and overapplied overhead.*

**4. (LO 5)** At December 31, the balances in Manufacturing Overhead are Alex Company—debit $2,200, Katz Company—credit $1,900. Prepare the adjusting entry for each company at December 31, assuming the adjustment is made to cost of goods sold.

**Solution**

4.                                    **Alex Company**

| Dec. 31 | Cost of Goods Sold | 2,200 | |
| |     Manufacturing Overhead | | 2,200 |

**Katz Company**

| Dec. 31 | Manufacturing Overhead | 1,900 | |
| |     Cost of Goods Sold | | 1,900 |

## Practice Exercises

*Analyze a job cost sheet and prepare entries for manufacturing costs.*

**1. (LO 1, 2, 3, 4)** A job cost sheet for Michaels Company is shown below.

| Job No. 92 | | | | For 2,000 Units |
|---|---|---|---|---|
| Date | | Direct Materials | Direct Labor | Manufacturing Overhead |
| Beg. bal. Jan. | 1 | 3,925 | 6,000 | 4,200 |
| | 8 | 6,000 | | |
| | 12 | | 8,500 | 6,375 |
| | 25 | 2,000 | | |
| | 27 | | 4,000 | 3,000 |
| | | 11,925 | 18,500 | 13,575 |

| Cost of completed job: | |
|---|---|
|   Direct materials | $11,925 |
|   Direct labor | 18,500 |
|   Manufacturing overhead | 13,575 |
| Total cost | $44,000 |
| Unit cost ($44,000 ÷ 2,000) | $ 22.00 |

**Instructions**

**a.** Answer the following questions.

    **1.** What was the balance in Work in Process Inventory on January 1 if this was the only unfinished job?

    **2.** If manufacturing overhead is applied on the basis of direct labor cost, what overhead rate was used in each year?

**b.** Prepare summary entries at January 31 to record the current year's transactions pertaining to Job No. 92.

**Solution**

**1. a. 1.** $14,125, or ($3,925 + $6,000 + $4,200).

    **2.** Last year 70%, or ($4,200 ÷ $6,000); this year 75% (either $6,375 ÷ $8,500 or $3,000 ÷ $4,000).

| | | | | |
|---|---|---|---|---|
| **b.** Jan. 31 | Work in Process Inventory | | 8,000 | |
| | Raw Materials Inventory | | | 8,000 |
| | ($6,000 + $2,000) | | | |
| 31 | Work in Process Inventory | | 12,500 | |
| | Factory Labor | | | 12,500 |
| | ($8,500 + $4,000) | | | |
| 31 | Work in Process Inventory | | 9,375 | |
| | Manufacturing Overhead | | | 9,375 |
| | ($6,375 + $3,000) | | | |
| 31 | Finished Goods Inventory | | 44,000 | |
| | Work in Process Inventory | | | 44,000 |

**2. (LO 3, 5)** Kwik Kopy Company applies operating overhead to photocopying jobs on the basis of machine hours used. Overhead costs are estimated to total $290,000 for the year, and machine usage is estimated at 125,000 hours.

*Compute the overhead rate and under- or overapplied overhead.*

For the year, $295,000 of overhead costs are incurred and 130,000 hours are used.

### Instructions

a. Compute the service overhead rate for the year.

b. What is the amount of under- or overapplied overhead at December 31?

c. Assuming the under- or overapplied overhead for the year is not allocated to inventory accounts, prepare the adjusting entry to assign the amount to cost of services provided.

### Solution

2. **a.** $2.32 per machine hour ($290,000 ÷ 125,000).

**b.** ($295,000) − ($2.32 × 130,000 machine hours)

$295,000 − $301,600 = $6,600 overapplied

**c.**
| | | |
|---|---|---|
| Operating Overhead | 6,600 | |
| Cost of Services Provided | | 6,600 |

## Practice Problem

**(LO 3, 5)** Cardella Company applies overhead on the basis of direct labor costs. The company estimates annual overhead costs to be $760,000 and annual direct labor costs to be $950,000. During February, Cardella works on two jobs: A16 and B17. Summary data concerning these jobs are as follows.

*Compute predetermined overhead rate, apply overhead, and calculate under- or overapplied overhead.*

### Manufacturing Costs Incurred

Purchased $54,000 of raw materials on account.

Factory labor $80,000.

Manufacturing overhead incurred exclusive of indirect materials and indirect labor $59,800. This was comprised of utilities $25,000, insurance $9,000, depreciation $10,000, and property taxes $15,800.

### Assignment of Costs

Direct materials: Job A16 $27,000, Job B17 $21,000
Indirect materials: $3,000
Direct labor: Job A16 $52,000, Job B17 $26,000
Indirect labor: $2,000

The company completed Job A16 and sold it on account for $150,000. Job B17 was only partially completed.

### Instructions

**a.** Compute the predetermined overhead rate.

**b.** Journalize the February transactions in the sequence presented in the chapter (use February 28 for all dates).

**c.** What was the amount of under- or overapplied manufacturing overhead?

### Solution

**a.**

| Estimated annual overhead costs | ÷ | Estimated annual operating activity | = | Predetermined overhead rate |
|---|---|---|---|---|
| $760,000 | ÷ | $950,000 | = | 80% |

**b.**

(1)

| Feb. 28 | Raw Materials Inventory | 54,000 | |
|---|---|---|---|
| | Accounts Payable | | 54,000 |
| | (Purchase of raw materials on account) | | |

(2)

| 28 | Factory Labor | 80,000 | |
|---|---|---|---|
| | Payroll Liabilities | | 80,000 |
| | (To record factory labor costs) | | |

(3)

| 28 | Manufacturing Overhead | 59,800 | |
|---|---|---|---|
| | Utilities Payable | | 25,000 |
| | Prepaid Insurance | | 9,000 |
| | Accumulated Depreciation | | 10,000 |
| | Property Taxes Payable | | 15,800 |
| | (To record overhead costs) | | |

(4)

| Feb. 28 | Work in Process Inventory | 48,000* | |
|---|---|---|---|
| | Manufacturing Overhead | 3,000 | |
| | Raw Materials Inventory | | 51,000 |
| | (To assign raw materials to production) | | |

*$27,000 + $21,000

(5)

| 28 | Work in Process Inventory | 78,000** | |
|---|---|---|---|
| | Manufacturing Overhead | 2,000 | |
| | Factory Labor | | 80,000 |
| | (To assign factory labor to production) | | |

**$52,000 + $26,000

(6)

| 28 | Work in Process Inventory | 62,400 | |
|---|---|---|---|
| | Manufacturing Overhead | | 62,400 |
| | (To assign overhead to jobs— | | |
| | 80% × $78,000) | | |

(7)

| 28 | Finished Goods Inventory | 120,600 | |
|---|---|---|---|
| | Work in Process Inventory | | 120,600 |
| | (To record completion of Job A16: direct materials $27,000, direct labor $52,000, and manufacturing overhead $41,600) | | |

(8)

| | | | | |
|---|---|---|---|---|
| 28 | Accounts Receivable | | 150 000 | |
| | Sales Revenue | | | 150,000 |
| | (To record sale of Job A16) | | | |
| 28 | Cost of Goods Sold | | 120,600 | |
| | Finished Goods Inventory | | | 120,600 |
| | (To record cost of sale for Job A16) | | | |

**c.** Manufacturing Overhead has a debit balance of $2,400 as shown below.

**Manufacturing Overhead**

| | | | |
|---|---|---|---|
| (3) | 59,800 | (6) | 62,400 |
| (4) | 3,000 | | |
| (5) | 2,000 | | |
| Bal. | 2,400 | | |

Thus, manufacturing overhead is underapplied for the month.

---

Brief Exercises, DO IT! Exercises, Exercises, Problems, Data Analytics Activities, and many additional resources are available for practice in WileyPlus.

---

## Questions

**1. a.** Mary Barett is not sure about the difference between cost accounting and a cost accounting system. Explain the difference to Mary.

**b.** What is an important feature of a cost accounting system?

**2. a.** Distinguish between the two types of cost accounting systems.

**b.** Can a company use both types of cost accounting systems?

**3.** What type of industry is likely to use a job order cost system? Give some examples.

**4.** What type of industry is likely to use a process cost system? Give some examples.

**5.** Your roommate asks your help in understanding the major steps in the flow of costs in a job order cost system. Identify the steps for your roommate.

**6.** "Accumulation entries to Manufacturing Overhead normally are only made daily." Is this true? Explain why or why not.

**7.** Stan Kaiser is confused about the source documents used in assigning materials and labor costs. Identify the documents and give the entry for each document.

**8.** What is the purpose of a job cost sheet?

**9.** Indicate the source documents that are used in charging costs to specific jobs.

**10.** Explain the purpose and use of a "materials requisition slip" as used in a job order cost system.

**11.** Sam Bowden believes actual manufacturing overhead costs should be charged to jobs. Is this true? Explain why or why not.

**12.** What inputs are involved in computing a predetermined overhead rate?

**13.** How can the agreement of Work in Process Inventory and job cost sheets be verified?

**14.** Jane Neff believes that the cost of goods manufactured schedule in job order cost accounting is the same as shown in Chapter 14. Is Jane correct? Explain.

**15.** Matt Litke is confused about under- and overapplied manufacturing overhead. Define the terms for Matt, and indicate the unadjusted balance in the manufacturing overhead account applicable to each term.

**16.** "At the end of the year, under- or overapplied overhead is closed to Income Summary." Is this correct? If not, indicate the customary treatment of this amount.

---

## Brief Exercises

**BE15.1 (LO 1), C** Dieker Company begins operations on January 1. Because all work is done to customer specifications, the company decides to use a job order cost system. Prepare a flowchart of a typical job order system with arrows showing the flow of costs. Identify the eight transactions.

*Prepare a flowchart of a job order cost accounting system and identify transactions.*

**BE15.2 (LO 1), AP** During January, its first month of operations, Dieker Company accumulated the following manufacturing costs: raw materials purchased $4,000 on account, factory labor incurred $6,000,

*Prepare entries for accumulating manufacturing costs.*

and factory utilities payable $2,000. Prepare separate journal entries for each type of manufacturing cost (use January 31 for all dates).

*Prepare entry for the assignment of raw materials costs.*

**BE15.3 (LO 2), AP** In January, Dieker Company requisitions raw materials for production as follows: Job 1 $900, Job 2 $1,200, Job 3 $700, and general factory use $600. Prepare a summary journal entry to record raw materials used (use January 31 as the date).

*Prepare entry for the assignment of factory labor costs.*

**BE15.4 (LO 2), AP** Factory labor information for Dieker Company is given in BE15.2. During January, time tickets show that the factory labor of $6,000 was used as follows: Job 1 $2,200, Job 2 $1,600, Job 3 $1,400, and general factory use $800. Prepare a summary journal entry to record factory labor used (use January 31 as the date).

*Prepare job cost sheets.*

**BE15.5 (LO 2), AP** Data pertaining to job cost sheets for Dieker Company are given in BE15.3 and BE15.4. Prepare the job cost sheets for each of the three jobs using the format shown in Illustration 15.8 (use January 31 as the date). (*Note:* You may omit the column for Manufacturing Overhead.)

*Compute predetermined overhead rates.*

**BE15.6 (LO 3), AP** Marquis Company estimates that annual manufacturing overhead costs will be $900,000. Estimated annual operating activity bases are direct labor cost $500,000, direct labor hours 50,000, and machine hours 100,000. Compute the predetermined overhead rate for each activity base.

*Assign manufacturing overhead to production.*

**BE15.7 (LO 3), AP** During the first quarter, Francum Company incurs the following direct labor costs: January $40,000, February $30,000, and March $50,000. For each month, prepare the entry to assign overhead to production using a predetermined rate of 70% of direct labor cost (date journal entries as of the end of the month).

*Prepare entries for completion and sale of completed jobs.*

**BE15.8 (LO 4), AP** In March, Stinson Company completes Jobs 10 and 11. Job 10 cost $20,000 and Job 11 $30,000. On March 31, Job 10 is sold to the customer for $35,000 in cash. Journalize the entries for the completion of the two jobs and the sale of Job 10 (date journal entries as of the end of the month).

*Prepare entries for payroll liabilities and operating overhead.*

**BE15.9 (LO 4), AP** Ruiz Engineering Contractors incurred employee payroll costs of $36,000 ($28,000 direct and $8,000 indirect) on an engineering project. The company applies overhead at a rate of 25% of direct labor cost. Record the entries to assign payroll liabilities and to apply overhead. Assume journal entries are made at the end of the month.

*Prepare adjusting entries for under- and overapplied overhead.*

**BE15.10 (LO 5), AP** At December 31, balances in Manufacturing Overhead are Shimeca Company—debit $1,200, Garcia Company—credit $900. Prepare the adjusting entry for each company at December 31, assuming the adjustment is made to cost of goods sold.

## DO IT! Exercises

*Prepare entries for manufacturing costs.*

**DO IT! 15.1 (LO 1), AP** During the current month, Wacholz Company incurs the following manufacturing costs.

a. Purchased raw materials of $18,000 on account.

b. Incurred factory labor of $40,000.

c. Factory utilities of $3,100 are payable, prepaid factory insurance of $2,700 has expired, and depreciation on the factory building is $9,500.

Prepare journal entries for each type of manufacturing cost. (Use a summary entry to record manufacturing overhead.)

*Assign costs to work in process.*

**DO IT! 15.2 (LO 2), AP** Milner Company is working on two job orders. The job cost sheets show the following.

|  | Job 201 | Job 202 |
|---|---|---|
| Direct materials | $7,200 | $9,000 |
| Direct labor | 4,000 | 8,000 |

Prepare the two summary entries to record the assignment of costs to Work in Process from the data on the job cost sheets.

**DO IT! 15.3 (LO 3), AP** Washburn Company produces earbuds. During the year, manufacturing overhead costs are estimated to be $200,000. Estimated machine usage is 2,500 hours. The company assigns overhead based on machine hours. Job No. 551 used 90 machine hours. Compute the predetermined overhead rate, determine the amount of overhead to apply to Job No. 551, and prepare the entry to apply overhead to Job No. 551 on January 15.

*Compute and apply the predetermined overhead rate.*

**DO IT! 15.4 (LO 4), AP** During the current month, Standard Corporation completed Job 310 and Job 312. Job 310 cost $70,000 and Job 312 cost $50,000. Job 312 was sold on account for $90,000. Journalize the entries for the completion of the two jobs and the sale of Job 312 (use January 31 for the dates).

*Prepare entries for completion and sale of jobs.*

**DO IT! 15.5 (LO 5), AP** For Eckstein Company, the predetermined overhead rate is 130% of direct labor cost. During the month, Eckstein incurred $100,000 of factory labor costs, of which $85,000 is direct labor and $15,000 is indirect labor. Actual overhead incurred was $115,000. Compute the amount of manufacturing overhead applied during the month. Determine the amount of under- or overapplied manufacturing overhead.

*Apply manufacturing overhead and determine under- or overapplication.*

# Exercises

**E15.1 (LO 1, 2), AP** Total factory labor costs related to factory workers for Larkin Company during the month of January are $90,000. Of the total accumulated cost of factory labor, 85% is related to direct labor and 15% is attributable to indirect labor.

*Prepare entries for factory labor.*

 Excel

**Instructions**

a. Prepare the January 31 entry to record the factory labor costs for the month of January.

b. Prepare the January 31 entry to assign factory labor to production.

**E15.2 (LO 1, 2, 3, 4), AP** Stine Company uses a job order cost system. On May 1, the company has a balance in Work in Process Inventory of $3,500 and two jobs in process: Job No. 429 $2,000, and Job No. 430 $1,500. During May, a summary of source documents reveals the following.

*Prepare entries for manufacturing costs.*

| Job Number | Materials Requisition Slips | | Labor Time Tickets | |
|---|---|---|---|---|
| 429 | $2,500 | | $1,900 | |
| 430 | 3,500 | | 3,000 | |
| 431 | 4,400 | $10,400 | 7,600 | $12,500 |
| General use | | 800 | | 1,200 |
| | | $11,200 | | $13,700 |

Stine Company applies manufacturing overhead to jobs at an overhead rate of 60% of direct labor cost. Job No. 429 is completed during the month.

**Instructions**

a. Prepare May 31 summary journal entries to record (1) the requisition slips, (2) the time tickets, (3) the assignment of manufacturing overhead to jobs, and (4) the completion of Job No. 429.

b. Post the entries to Work in Process Inventory, and prove the agreement of the control account with the job cost sheets. (Use a T-account.)

**E15.3 (LO 1, 2, 3, 4), AP** A job cost sheet for Ryan Company is shown as follows.

*Analyze a job cost sheet and prepare entries for manufacturing costs.*

| Job No. 92 | | | | For 2,000 Units |
|---|---|---|---|---|
| Date | | Direct Materials | Direct Labor | Manufacturing Overhead |
| Beg. bal. Jan. | 1 | 5,000 | 6,000 | 4,200 |
| | 8 | 6,000 | | |
| | 12 | | 8,000 | 6,400 |
| | 25 | 2,000 | | |
| | 27 | | 4,000 | 3,200 |
| | | 13,000 | 18,000 | 13,800 |

| Cost of completed job: | |
|---|---|
| Direct materials | $13,000 |
| Direct labor | 18,000 |
| Manufacturing overhead | 13,800 |
| Total cost | $44,800 |
| Unit cost ($44,800 ÷ 2,000) | $ 22.40 |

## Instructions

a. On the basis of this data, answer the following questions.

1. What was the balance in Work in Process Inventory on January 1 if this was the only unfinished job?

2. If manufacturing overhead is applied on the basis of direct labor cost, what overhead rate was used in each year?

b. Prepare summary entries at January 31 to record the current year's transactions pertaining to Job No. 92.

*Analyze costs of manufacturing and determine missing amounts.*

**E15.4 (LO 1, 5), AN** Manufacturing cost data for Orlando Company, which uses a job order cost system, are presented below.

| | Case A | Case B |
|---|---|---|
| Work in process 1/1/22 | $ (a) | $ 15,500 |
| Direct materials used | (b) | 83,000 |
| Direct labor | 50,000 | 140,000 |
| Manufacturing overhead applied | 42,500 | (d) |
| Total manufacturing costs | 145,650 | (e) |
| Total cost of work in process | 201,500 | (f) |
| Work in process 12/31/22 | (c) | 11,800 |
| Cost of goods manufactured | 192,300 | (g) |

## Instructions

Determine the missing amount for each letter. Assume that in both cases manufacturing overhead is applied on the basis of direct labor cost and the rate is the same.

*Compute the manufacturing overhead rate and under- or overapplied overhead.*

**E15.5 (LO 3, 5), AN** Ikerd Company applies manufacturing overhead to jobs on the basis of machine hours used. Overhead costs are estimated to total $300,000 for the year, and machine usage is estimated at 125,000 hours.

For the year, $322,000 of overhead costs are incurred, and 130,000 machine hours are used.

## Instructions

a. Compute the manufacturing overhead rate for the year.

b. What is the amount of under- or overapplied overhead at December 31?

c. Prepare the adjusting entry to assign the under- or overapplied overhead for the year to cost of goods sold.

*Analyze job cost sheet and prepare entry for completed job.*

**E15.6 (LO 1, 2, 3, 4), AP** A job cost sheet of Sandoval Company is given as follows.

**Job Cost Sheet**

JOB NO.   469                                    Quantity   <u>2,500</u>

ITEM   <u>White Lion Cages</u>              Date Requested   <u>7/2</u>

FOR   <u>Todd Company</u>                     Date Completed   <u>7/31</u>

| Date | Direct Materials | Direct Labor | Manufacturing Overhead |
|------|------------------|--------------|------------------------|
| 7/10 | 690 | | |
| 12 | 900 | | |
| 15 | | 440 | 550 |
| 22 | | 380 | 475 |
| 24 | 1,600 | | |
| 27 | 1,500 | | |
| 31 | | 540 | 675 |

Cost of completed job:

   Direct materials                  —————

   Direct Labor                     —————

   Manufacturing overhead     —————

Total cost                    —————

Unit cost                     =====

## Instructions

a. Answer the following questions.

   1. What are the source documents for direct materials, direct labor, and manufacturing overhead costs assigned to this job?

   2. Overhead is applied on the basis of direct labor cost. What is the predetermined manufacturing overhead rate?

   3. What are the total cost and the unit cost of the completed job?

b. Prepare the entry to record the completion of the job on July 31.

**E15.7 (LO 1, 2, 3, 4), AP** Crawford Corporation incurred the following transactions.

*Prepare entries for manufacturing and nonmanufacturing costs.*

1. Purchased raw materials on account $46,300.

2. Raw materials of $36,000 were requisitioned to the factory. An analysis of the materials requisition slips indicated that $6,800 was classified as indirect materials.

3. Factory labor costs incurred were $59,900.

4. Time tickets indicated that $54,000 was direct labor and $5,900 was indirect labor.

5. Manufacturing overhead costs incurred on account were $80,500.

6. Depreciation on the company's office building was $8,100.

7. Manufacturing overhead was applied at the rate of 150% of direct labor cost.

8. Goods costing $88,000 were completed and transferred to finished goods.

9. Finished goods costing $75,000 to manufacture were sold on account for $103,000.

## Instructions

Journalize the transactions. (Omit explanations.)

**E15.8 (LO 1, 2, 3, 4), AP** Enos Printing Corp. uses a job order cost system. The following data summarize the operations related to the first quarter's production.

*Prepare entries for manufacturing and nonmanufacturing costs.*

1. Materials purchased on account $192,000, and factory wages incurred $87,300.

2. Materials requisitioned and factory labor used by job:

| Job Number | Materials | Factory Labor |
|---|---|---|
| A20 | $ 35,240 | $18,000 |
| A21 | 42,920 | 22,000 |
| A22 | 36,100 | 15,000 |
| A23 | 39,270 | 25,000 |
| Indirect | 4,470 | 7,300 |
| | $158,000 | $87,300 |

3. Manufacturing overhead costs incurred on account $49,500. (*Hint*: Use Accounts Payable.)

4. Depreciation on factory equipment $14,550.

5. Depreciation on the company's office building $14,300.

6. Manufacturing overhead rate is 90% of direct labor cost.

7. Jobs completed during the quarter: A20, A21, and A23.

### Instructions

Prepare entries to record the operations summarized above. Prepare a schedule showing the individual cost elements and total cost for each job in item 7.

*Prepare a cost of goods manufactured schedule and partial financial statements.*

**E15.9 (LO 1, 5), AP** At May 31, 2022, the accounts of Lopez Company show the following.

1. May 1 inventories—finished goods $12,600, work in process $14,700, and raw materials $8,200.

2. May 31 inventories—finished goods $9,500, work in process $15,900, and raw materials $7,100.

3. Debit postings to work in process were direct materials $62,400, direct labor $50,000, and manufacturing overhead applied $40,000. (Assume that overhead applied was equal to overhead incurred.)

4. Sales revenue totaled $215,000.

### Instructions

a. Prepare a condensed cost of goods manufactured schedule for May 2022.

b. Prepare an income statement for May 2022 through gross profit.

c. Prepare the balance sheet section of the manufacturing inventories at May 31, 2022.

*Compute work in process and finished goods from job cost sheets.*

**E15.10 (LO 2, 4), AP** Tierney Company begins operations on April 1. Information from job cost sheets shows the following.

| Job Number | Manufacturing Costs Assigned | | | Month Completed |
|---|---|---|---|---|
| | April | May | June | |
| 10 | $5,200 | $4,400 | | May |
| 11 | 4,100 | 3,900 | $2,000 | June |
| 12 | 1,200 | | | April |
| 13 | | 4,700 | 4,500 | June |
| 14 | | 5,900 | 3,600 | Not complete |

Job 12 was completed in April. Job 10 was completed in May. Jobs 11 and 13 were completed in June. Each job was sold for 25% above its cost in the month following completion.

### Instructions

a. What is the balance in Work in Process Inventory at the end of each month?

b. What is the balance in Finished Goods Inventory at the end of each month?

c. What is the gross profit for May, June, and July?

*Prepare entries for service organizations.*

**E15.11 (LO 1, 3, 4), AP** **Service** The following are the job cost related accounts for the law firm of Colaw Associates and their manufacturing equivalents:

| Law Firm Accounts | Manufacturing Company Accounts |
|---|---|
| Supplies | Raw Materials Inventory |
| Payroll Liabilities | Payroll Liabilities |
| Operating Overhead | Manufacturing Overhead |
| Service Contracts in Process | Work in Process Inventory |
| Cost of Completed Service Contracts | Finished Goods Inventory |

Cost data for the month of March follow.

1. Purchased supplies on account $1,800.

2. Issued supplies $1,200 (60% direct and 40% indirect).

3. Assigned labor costs based on time tickets for the month which indicated labor costs of $70,000 (80% direct and 20% indirect).

4. Operating overhead costs incurred for cash totaled $40,000.

5. Operating overhead is applied at a rate of 90% of direct labor cost.

6. Work completed totaled $75,000.

**Instructions**

a. Journalize the transactions for March. (Omit explanations.)

b. Determine the balance of the Service Contracts in Process account. (Use a T-account.)

**E15.12 (LO 2, 3, 4), AP** `Service` Don Lieberman and Associates, a CPA firm, uses job order costing to capture the costs of its audit jobs. There were no audit jobs in process at the beginning of November. Listed below are data concerning the three audit jobs worked on during November.

*Determine cost of jobs and ending balances of a service company's accounts.*

|                      | Waters Inc. | Renolds Inc. | Bayfield Inc. |
|----------------------|-------------|--------------|---------------|
| Direct materials     | $600        | $400         | $200          |
| Auditor labor costs  | $5,400      | $6,600       | $3,375        |
| Auditor hours        | 72          | 88           | 45            |

Overhead costs are applied to jobs on the basis of auditor hours, and the predetermined overhead rate is $50 per auditor hour. The Waters Inc. job is the only incomplete job at the end of November. Actual overhead for the month was $11,000.

**Instructions**

a. Determine the cost assigned to each job.

b. Determine the balance of the Service Contracts in Process account at the end of November.

c. Calculate the ending balance of the Operating Overhead account for November.

**E15.13 (LO 3, 5), AP** `Service` Tombert Decorating uses a job order cost system to collect the costs of its interior decorating business. Each client's consultation is treated as a separate job. Overhead is applied to each job based on the number of decorator hours incurred. Listed below are data for the current year.

*Determine predetermined overhead rate, apply overhead, and determine whether balance is under- or overapplied.*

| | |
|---|---|
| Estimated overhead costs | $960,000 |
| Actual overhead costs | $982,800 |
| Estimated decorator hours | 40,000 |
| Actual decorator hours | 40,500 |

The company uses the account Operating Overhead in place of Manufacturing Overhead, and the account Service Contracts in Process in place of Work in Process Inventory.

**Instructions**

a. Compute the predetermined overhead rate.

b. Prepare the entry to apply the overhead for the year.

c. Determine whether the overhead was under- or overapplied and by how much.

## Problems

**P15.1 (LO 1, 2, 3, 4, 5), AP** Lott Company uses a job order cost system and applies overhead to production on the basis of direct labor costs. On January 1, 2022, Job 50 was the only job in process. The costs incurred prior to January 1 on this job were as follows: direct materials $20,000, direct labor $12,000, and manufacturing overhead $16,000. As of January 1, Job 49 had been completed at a cost of $90,000 and was part of finished goods inventory. There was a $15,000 balance in the Raw Materials Inventory account on January 1.

*Prepare entries and postings to job cost sheets for a job order cost system.*

During the month of January, Lott Company began production on Jobs 51 and 52, and completed Jobs 50 and 51. Jobs 49 and 50 were sold on account during the month for $122,000 and $158,000, respectively. The following additional events occurred during the month.

1. Purchased additional raw materials of $90,000 on account.

2. Incurred factory labor costs of $70,000.

3. Incurred manufacturing overhead costs as follows: depreciation on equipment $12,000 and various other manufacturing overhead costs on account $16,000.

4. Assigned direct materials and direct labor to jobs as follows.

| Job No. | Direct Materials | Direct Labor |
|---|---|---|
| 50 | $10,000 | $ 5,000 |
| 51 | 39,000 | 25,000 |
| 52 | 30,000 | 20,000 |

5. Assigned indirect materials of $17,000 and indirect labor of $20,000.

**Instructions**

a. Calculate the predetermined overhead rate for 2022, assuming Lott Company estimates total manufacturing overhead costs of $840,000, direct labor costs of $700,000, and direct labor hours of 20,000 for the year.

b. Open job cost sheets for Jobs 50, 51, and 52. Enter the January 1 balances on the job cost sheet for Job 50.

c. Prepare the journal entries to record the purchase of raw materials, the factory labor costs incurred, and the manufacturing overhead costs incurred during the month of January.

d. Prepare the journal entries to record the assignment of raw materials, factory labor, and manufacturing overhead costs to production. In assigning manufacturing overhead costs, use the overhead rate calculated in (a). Post all costs to the job cost sheets as necessary.

e. Total the job cost sheets for any job(s) completed during the month. Prepare the journal entry (or entries) to record the completion of any job(s) during the month.

f. Prepare the journal entry (or entries) to record the sale of any job(s) during the month.

g. What is the balance in the Finished Goods Inventory account at the end of the month? (*Hint*: Use a T-account for Finished Goods Inventory.) What does this balance consist of?

h. What is the amount of over- or underapplied overhead?

*e. Job 50, $69,000*
*Job 51, $94,000*

*Prepare entries in a job order cost system and partial income statement.*

**P15.2 (LO 1, 2, 3, 4, 5), AP** For the year ended December 31, 2022, the job cost sheets of Cinta Company contained the following data.

| Job Number | Explanation | Direct Materials | Direct Labor | Manufacturing Overhead | Total Costs |
|---|---|---|---|---|---|
| 7640 | Balance 1/1 | $25,000 | $24,000 | $28,800 | $ 77,800 |
| | Current year's costs | 30,000 | 36,000 | 43,200 | 109,200 |
| 7641 | Balance 1/1 | 11,000 | 18,000 | 21,600 | 50,600 |
| | Current year's costs | 43,000 | 48,000 | 57,600 | 148,600 |
| 7642 | Current year's costs | 58,000 | 55,000 | 66,000 | 179,000 |

Other data:

1. Raw materials inventory totaled $15,000 on January 1. During the year, $140,000 of raw materials were purchased on account.

2. Finished goods on January 1 consisted of Job No. 7638 for $87,000 and Job No. 7639 for $92,000.

3. Job No. 7640 and Job No. 7641 were completed during the year.

4. Job Nos. 7638, 7639, and 7641 were sold on account for $530,000.

5. Manufacturing overhead incurred on account totaled $120,000.

6. Incurred depreciation on factory machinery $8,000.

7. Assigned indirect materials of $14,000 and indirect labor of $18,000.

**Instructions**

*a. $179,000; Job 7642:*
*$179,000*

a. Prove the agreement of Work in Process Inventory with job cost sheets pertaining to unfinished work. (*Hint*: Use a single T-account for Work in Process Inventory.) Calculate each of the following, then post each to the T-account: (1) beginning balance, (2) direct materials, (3) direct labor, (4) manufacturing overhead, and (5) completed jobs.

**b.** Prepare the adjusting entry for manufacturing overhead, assuming the balance is allocated entirely to Cost of Goods Sold.

**c.** Prepare an income statement through gross profit for 2022.

**P15.3 (LO 1, 2, 3, 4, 5), AP** Case Inc. is a construction company specializing in custom patios. The patios are constructed of concrete, brick, fiberglass, and lumber, depending on customer preference. On June 1, 2022, the general ledger for Case Inc. contains the following data.

| | | | |
|---|---|---|---|
| Raw Materials Inventory | $4,200 | Manufacturing Overhead Applied | $32,640 |
| Work in Process Inventory | $5,540 | Manufacturing Overhead Incurred | $31,650 |

Subsidiary data for Work in Process Inventory on June 1 are as follows.

### Job Cost Sheets

| | Customer Job | | |
|---|---|---|---|
| **Cost Element** | **Rodgers** | **Stevens** | **Linton** |
| Direct materials | $ 600 | $ 800 | $ 900 |
| Direct labor | 320 | 540 | 580 |
| Manufacturing overhead | 400 | 675 | 725 |
| | $1,320 | $2,015 | $2,205 |

During June, raw materials purchased on account were $4,900, and $4,300 of factory wages were paid. Additional overhead costs consisted of depreciation on equipment $900 and miscellaneous costs of $400 incurred on account.

A summary of materials requisition slips and time tickets for June shows the following.

| Customer Job | Materials Requisition Slips | Time Tickets |
|---|---|---|
| Rodgers | $ 800 | $ 850 |
| Koss | 2,000 | 800 |
| Stevens | 500 | 360 |
| Linton | 1,300 | 1,200 |
| Rodgers | 300 | 390 |
| | 4,900 | 3,600 |
| General use | 1,500 | 1,200 |
| | $6,400 | $4,800 |

Overhead was assigned to jobs at the same rate of $1.25 per dollar of direct labor cost throughout the year. The patios for customers Rodgers, Stevens, and Linton were completed during June and sold for a total of $18,900. Each customer paid in full at the time of sale.

### Instructions

**a.** Journalize the June transactions: (1) purchase of raw materials, factory labor costs incurred, and manufacturing overhead costs incurred; (2) assignment of direct materials, labor, and overhead to production; and (3) completion of jobs and sale of goods.

**b.** Post the entries to Work in Process Inventory.

**c.** Reconcile the balance in Work in Process Inventory with the costs of unfinished jobs.

**d.** Prepare a cost of goods manufactured schedule for June.

**P15.4 (LO 3, 5), AP** Agassi Company uses a job order cost system in each of its three manufacturing departments. Manufacturing overhead is applied to jobs on the basis of direct labor cost in Department D, direct labor hours in Department E, and machine hours in Department K.

In establishing the predetermined overhead rates for 2022, the following estimates were made for the year.

| | Department | | |
|---|---|---|---|
| | **D** | **E** | **K** |
| Manufacturing overhead | $1,200,000 | $1,500,000 | $900,000 |
| Direct labor costs | $1,500,000 | $1,250,000 | $450,000 |
| Direct labor hours | 100,000 | 125,000 | 40,000 |
| Machine hours | 400,000 | 500,000 | 120,000 |

The following information pertains to January 2022 for each manufacturing department.

---

Side notes (right margin):

b. Amount = $6,800

c. $158,600

*Prepare entries in a job order cost system and cost of goods manufactured schedule.*

d. Cost of goods manufactured $14,740

*Compute predetermined overhead rates, apply overhead, and calculate under- or overapplied overhead.*

| | Department | | |
|---|---|---|---|
| | **D** | **E** | **K** |
| Direct materials used | $140,000 | $126,000 | $78,000 |
| Direct labor costs | $120,000 | $110,000 | $37,500 |
| Manufacturing overhead incurred | $ 99,000 | $124,000 | $79,000 |
| Direct labor hours | 8,000 | 11,000 | 3,500 |
| Machine hours | 34,000 | 45,000 | 10,400 |

a. 80%, $12, $7.50

b. $356,000, $368,000, $193,500

c. $3,000, $(8,000), $1,000

*Analyze manufacturing accounts and determine missing amounts.*

 Excel

### Instructions

**a.** Compute the predetermined overhead rate for each department.

**b.** Compute the total manufacturing costs assigned to jobs in January in each department.

**c.** Compute the under- or overapplied overhead for each department at January 31.

**P15.5 (LO 1, 2, 3, 4, 5), AN** Phillips Corporation's fiscal year ends on November 30. The following accounts are found in its job order cost accounting system for the first month of the new fiscal year.

### Raw Materials Inventory

| Dec. | 1 | Beginning balance | (a) | Dec. 31 | Requisitions | 16,850 |
|---|---|---|---|---|---|---|
| | 31 | Purchases | 17,225 | | | |
| Dec. | 31 | Ending balance | 7,975 | | | |

### Work in Process Inventory

| Dec. | 1 | Beginning balance | (b) | Dec. 31 | Jobs completed | (f) |
|---|---|---|---|---|---|---|
| | 31 | Direct materials | (c) | | | |
| | 31 | Direct labor | 8,400 | | | |
| | 31 | Overhead | (d) | | | |
| Dec. | 31 | Ending balance | (e) | | | |

### Finished Goods Inventory

| Dec. | 1 | Beginning balance | (g) | Dec. 31 | Cost of goods sold | (i) |
|---|---|---|---|---|---|---|
| | 31 | Jobs completed | (h) | | | |
| Dec. | 31 | Ending balance | (j) | | | |

### Factory Labor

| Dec. | 31 | Factory wages | 12,025 | Dec. 31 | Wages assigned | (k) |
|---|---|---|---|---|---|---|

### Manufacturing Overhead

| Dec. | 31 | Indirect materials | 2,900 | Dec. 31 | Overhead applied | (m) |
|---|---|---|---|---|---|---|
| | 31 | Indirect labor | (l) | | | |
| | 31 | Other overhead | 1,245 | | | |

Other data:

1. On December 1, two jobs were in process: Job No. 154 and Job No. 155. These jobs had combined direct materials costs of $9,750 and combined direct labor costs of $15,000. Overhead was applied at a rate that was 75% of direct labor cost.

2. During December, Job Nos. 156, 157, and 158 were started. On December 31, Job No. 158 was unfinished. This job had charges for direct materials $3,800 and direct labor $4,800, plus manufacturing overhead. All jobs, except for Job No. 158, were completed in December.

3. On December 1, Job No. 153 was in the finished goods warehouse. It had a total cost of $5,000. On December 31, Job No. 157 was the only finished job that was not sold. It had a cost of $4,000.

4. Manufacturing overhead was $1,470 underapplied in December.

c. $13,950

f. $52,450

i. $53,450

### Instructions

List the letters (a) through (m) and indicate the amount pertaining to each letter.

## Continuing Cases

### Current Designs

**CD15**   Huegel Hollow Resort has ordered 20 rotomolded kayaks from **Current Designs**. Each kayak will be formed in the rotomolded oven, cooled, and then have the excess plastic trimmed away. Then, the hatches, seat, ropes, and bungees will be attached to the kayak.

Dave Thill, the kayak factory manager, knows that manufacturing each kayak requires 54 pounds of polyethylene powder and a finishing kit (rope, seat, hardware, etc.). The polyethylene powder used in these kayaks costs $1.50 per pound, and the finishing kits cost $170 each. Each kayak will use two kinds of labor: 2 hours of more-skilled type I labor from people who run the oven and trim the plastic, and 3 hours of less-skilled type II labor from people who attach the hatches and seat and other hardware. The type I employees are paid $15 per hour, and the type II employees are paid $12 per hour. For purposes of this problem, assume that overhead is applied to all jobs at a rate of 150% of direct labor costs.

**Instructions**

Determine the total cost of the Huegel Hollow order and the cost of each individual kayak in the order. Identify costs as direct materials, direct labor, or manufacturing overhead.

### Waterways Corporation

(*Note:* This is a continuation of the Waterways case from Chapter 14.)

**WC15**   Waterways has two major public-park projects to provide with comprehensive irrigation in one of its service locations this month. Job J57 and Job K52 involve 15 acres of landscaped terrain which will require special-order sprinkler heads to meet the specifications of the project. This case asks you to help Waterways use a job order cost system to account for production of these parts.

*Go to WileyPLUS for complete case details and instructions.*

## Comprehensive Case

**CC15**   Greetings Inc., a nationally recognized retailer of greeting cards and small gift items, decides to employ Internet technology to expand its sales opportunities. For this case, you will employ traditional job order costing techniques and then evaluate the resulting product costs.

*Go to WileyPLUS for complete case details and instructions.*

**Comprehensive Cases** present realistic business situations that require students to apply topics learned in this and previous chapters.

## Data Analytics in Action

### Using Data Visualization to Analyze Profitability

**DA15.1**   Data visualization can be used to review profitability.

**Example:**   Recall the *Feature Story* "Profiting from the Silver Screen" presented at the beginning of the chapter. Data analytics can help movie executives understand industry performance. Industry experts track box office receipts, production costs, and estimated gross profit. From publicly available data, we can get an estimate of these amounts. Here are graphed data for comedy films derived from books. What do you observe?

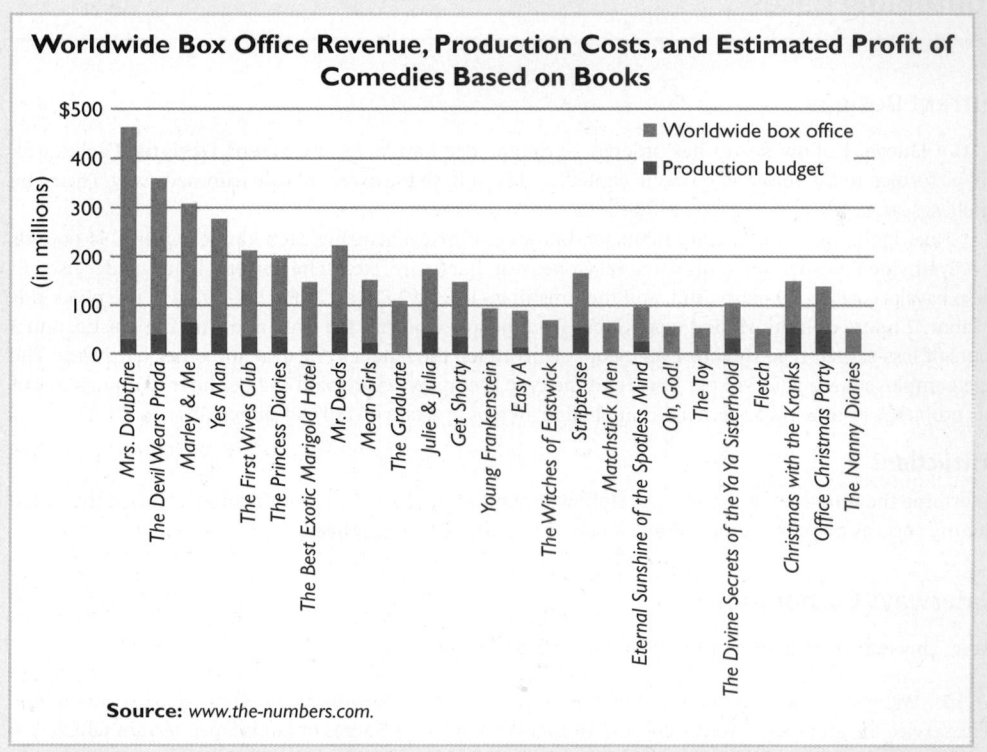

**Source:** *www.the-numbers.com.*

You can see that *Mrs. Doubtfire* has the highest box-office sales and relatively low production costs. But, does that mean it also has the highest gross profit? For this case, you will look closer at the costs and revenues for these movies by calculating gross profit and then graphing and analyzing the results.

*Go to WileyPLUS for complete case details and instructions.*

### Data Analytics at the Movies

**DA15.2** You are interested in the effect of production budget costs on the profitability of movies. For this case, you will use Excel pivot tables to summarize the production budget costs for worldwide box office receipts and the estimated gross profit, and then analyze the results.

*Go to WileyPLUS for complete case details and instructions.*

### Data Analytics at HydroHappy

**DA15.3** HydroHappy rents out giant water slides for parties and other events. HydroHappy has a team that loads and transports the requested slides on the company's trucks, assembles the slides at the customers' chosen locations, and dismantles, loads, and transports the slides back to HydroHappy's warehouse when the event is complete. In the past, HydroHappy has not kept job cost records due to having only two or three jobs per week. Now that demand is increasing, HydroHappy has purchased five new slides and runs several jobs concurrently. The company now needs to track the costs by job so it can assess the profitability of each job. For this case, you will create and analyze a pivot table and a clustered column pivot chart to identify which jobs are profitable as well as consider the factors that may have contributed to those jobs that are not.

*Go to WileyPLUS for complete case details and instructions.*

## Expand Your Critical Thinking

### Decision-Making Across the Organization

**CT15.1**   Khan Products Company uses a job order cost system. For a number of months, there has been an ongoing rift between the sales department and the production department concerning a special-order product, TC-1. TC-1 is a seasonal product that is manufactured in batches of 1,000 units. TC-1 is sold at cost plus a markup of 40% of cost.

The sales department is unhappy because fluctuating unit production costs significantly affect selling prices. Sales personnel complain that this has caused excessive customer complaints and the loss of considerable orders for TC-1.

The production department maintains that each job order must be fully costed on the basis of the costs incurred during the period in which the goods are produced. Production personnel maintain that the only real solution is for the sales department to increase sales quantities in the slack periods.

Andrea Parley, president of the company, asks you as the company accountant to collect quarterly data for the past year on TC-1 From the cost accounting system, you accumulate the following production quantity and cost data.

| Costs | Quarter | | | |
|---|---|---|---|---|
| | 1 | 2 | 3 | 4 |
| Direct materials | $100,000 | $220,000 | $ 80,000 | $200,000 |
| Direct labor | 60,000 | 132,000 | 48,000 | 120,000 |
| Manufacturing overhead | 105,000 | 153,000 | 97,000 | 125,000 |
| Total | $265,000 | $505,000 | $225,000 | $445,000 |
| Production in batches | 5 | 11 | 4 | 10 |
| Unit cost (per batch) | $ 53,000 | $ 45,909* | $ 56,250 | $ 44,500 |

*Rounded.

### Instructions

With the class divided into groups, complete the following.

**a.** What manufacturing cost element is responsible for the fluctuating unit costs? Why?

**b.** What is your recommended solution to the problem of fluctuating unit costs?

**c.** Restate the quarterly data on the basis of your recommended solution.

### Managerial Analysis

**CT15.2**   In the course of routine checking of all journal entries prior to preparing year-end reports, Betty Eller discovered several strange entries. She recalled that the president's son Joe had come in to help out during an especially busy time and that he had recorded some journal entries. She was relieved that there were only a few of his entries, and even more relieved that he had included rather lengthy explanations. The entries Joe made were:

(1)

| | | |
|---|---|---|
| Work in Process Inventory | 25,000 | |
| Cash | | 25,000 |

(This is for direct materials put into process. I don't find the record that we paid for these, so I'm crediting Cash because I know we'll have to pay for them sooner or later.)

(2)

| | | |
|---|---|---|
| Manufacturing Overhead | 12,000 | |
| Cash | | 12,000 |

(This is for bonuses paid to salespeople. I know they're part of overhead, and I can't find an account called "Non-Factory Overhead" or "Other Overhead" so I'm putting it in Manufacturing Overhead. I have the check stubs, so I know we paid these.)

(3)

| | | |
|---|---|---|
| Work in Process Inventory | 3,000 | |
| Raw Materials Inventory | | 3,000 |

(This is for the glue used in the factory. I know we used this to make the products, even though we didn't use very much on any one of the products. I got it out of inventory, so I credited an inventory account.)

### Instructions

**a.** How should Joe have recorded each of the three events?

**b.** If the entry was not corrected, which financial statements (income statement or balance sheet) would be affected? What balances would be overstated or understated? (For events (2) and (3), assume the affected units were completed and sold.)

## Real-World Focus

**CT15.3** The **Institute of Management Accountants (IMA)** sponsors a certification for management accountants, allowing them to obtain the title of Certified Management Accountant.

### Instructions

Go to the IMA website, choose **About IMA**, choose **CMA Certification**, and then **Getting Started**. Answer part (a) below. Next, choose **CMA Certification**, then **Current CMAs**, then **Maintain Your Certification**, and then click on **Download the CPE Requirements and Rules**. Answer part (b) below.

**a.** What is the experience qualification requirement?

**b.** How many hours of continuing education are required, and what types of courses qualify?

## Communication Activity

**CT15.4** You are the management accountant for Williams Company. Your company does custom carpentry work and uses a job order cost system. Williams sends detailed job cost sheets to its customers, along with an invoice. The job cost sheets show the date materials were used, the dollar cost of materials, and the hours and cost of labor. A predetermined overhead application rate is used, and the total overhead applied is also listed.

Nancy Kopay is a customer who recently had custom cabinets installed. Along with her check in payment for the work done, she included a letter. She thanked the company for including the detailed cost information but questioned why overhead was estimated. She stated that she would be interested in knowing exactly what costs were included in overhead, and she thought that other customers would, too.

### Instructions

Prepare a letter to Ms. Kopay (address: 123 Cedar Lane, Altoona, KS 66651) and tell her why you did not send her information on exact costs of overhead included in her job. Respond to her suggestion that you provide this information.

## Ethics Case

**CT15.5** Service LRF Printing provides printing services to many different corporate clients. Although LRF bids most jobs, some jobs, particularly new ones, are negotiated on a "cost-plus" basis. Cost-plus means that the buyer is willing to pay the actual cost plus a return (profit) on these costs to LRF.

Alice Reiley, controller for LRF, has recently returned from a meeting where LRF's president stated that he wanted her to find a way to charge more costs to any project that was on a cost-plus basis. The president noted that the company needed more profits to meet its stated goals this period. By charging more costs to the cost-plus projects and therefore fewer costs to the jobs that were bid, the company should be able to increase its profit for the current year.

Alice knew why the president wanted to take this action. Rumors were that he was looking for a new position and if the company reported strong profits, the president's opportunities would be enhanced. Alice also recognized that she could probably increase the cost of certain jobs by changing the basis used to assign manufacturing overhead.

### Instructions

**a.** Who are the stakeholders in this situation?

**b.** What are the ethical issues in this situation?

**c.** What would you do if you were Alice Reiley?

## All About You

**CT15.6**  Many of you will work for a small business. Some of you will even own your own business. In order to operate a small business, you will need a good understanding of managerial accounting, as well as many other skills. Much information is available to assist people who are interested in starting a new business. A great place to start is the website provided by the **Small Business Administration**, which is an agency of the federal government whose purpose is to support small businesses.

### Instructions

Go to *https://www.sba.gov/business-guide/10-steps-start-your-business/* and then list the 10 steps for starting a business.

## Considering Your Costs and Benefits

**CT15.7**  After graduating, you might decide to start a small business. As discussed in this chapter, owners of any business need to know how to calculate the cost of their products. In fact, many small businesses fail because they don't accurately calculate their product costs, so they don't know whether they are making a profit or losing money—until it's too late.

Suppose that you decide to start a landscape business. You use an old pickup truck that you've fully paid for. You store the truck and other equipment in your parents' barn, and you store trees and shrubs on their land. Your parents will not charge you for the use of these facilities for the first two years, but beginning in the third year they will charge a reasonable rent. Your mother helps you by answering phone calls and providing customers with information. She doesn't charge you for this service, but she plans on doing it for only your first two years in business. In pricing your services, should you include charges for the truck, the barn, the land, and your mother's services when calculating your product cost? The basic arguments for and against are as follows.

**YES:** If you don't include charges for these costs, your costs are understated and your profitability is overstated.

**NO:** At this point, you are not actually incurring costs related to these activities; therefore, you shouldn't record charges.

### Instructions

Write a response indicating your position regarding this situation. Provide support for your view.

## Answers to Insight and Accounting Across the Organization Questions

**Providing Service Through the Cloud  Q:** How does the software-as-a-service (SaaS) model change how the company collects and uses cost data in decision-making? **A:** Before using the SaaS model, the company relied on a sampling of customer feedback to determine product changes and enhancements. Now, the company knows the most cost-efficient ways to upgrade its software based on the significant user data it receives. The company can also use the information to evaluate its profitability with regard to specific customers or customer types.

**The Cost of an iPhone? Just Tear One Apart  Q:** What type of costs are marketing and selling costs, and how are they treated for accounting purposes? **A:** Product costs include materials, labor, and overhead. Costs not related to production, such as marketing and selling costs, are period costs. Period costs are expensed in the period that they are incurred.

**Jobs Won, Money Lost  Q:** What type of costs do you think the company had been underestimating? **A:** It is most likely that the company failed to estimate and track overhead. In a highly diversified company, overhead associated with the diesel locomotive jobs may have been "lost" in the total overhead pool for the entire company.

**Sales Are Nice, but Service Revenue Pays the Bills  Q:** Why would GE use job order costing to keep track of the cost of repairing a malfunctioning engine for a major airline? **A:** GE operates in a competitive environment. Other companies offer competing bids to win service contracts on GE's airplane engines. GE needs to know what it costs to repair engines, so that it can present competitive bids while still generating a reasonable profit.

## CHAPTER 16

Elaine Thompson/AP Photo

# Process Costing

## Chapter Preview

As the following Feature Story describes, the cost accounting system used by companies such as **Jones Soda** is **process cost accounting**. In contrast to job order cost accounting, which focuses on the individual job, process cost accounting focuses on the *processes* involved in mass-producing products that are identical or very similar in nature. The primary objective of this chapter is to explain and illustrate process costing.

## Feature Story

### The Little Guy Who Could

It isn't easy for a small company to get a foothold in the bottled beverage business. The giants, **The Coca-Cola Company** and **PepsiCo Inc.**, vigilantly defend their turf, constantly watching for new trends and opportunities. It is nearly impossible to get shelf space in stores, and

consumer tastes can change faster than a bottle of soda can lose its fizz. But **Jones Soda Co.**, headquartered in Seattle, has overcome these and other obstacles to make a name for itself. Its corporate motto is, "Run with the little guy . . . create some change."

The company started as a Canadian distributor of other companies' beverages. Soon, it decided to make its own products under the corporate name Urban Juice and Soda Company. Eventually, its name changed to Jones

Soda—the name of its most popular product. From the very start, Jones Soda was different. It sold soda from machines placed in tattoo parlors and piercing shops, and it sponsored a punk rock band as well as surfers and snowboarders. At one time, the company's product was the official drink at the **Seattle Seahawks'** stadium and was served on **Alaska Airlines**.

Today, Jones Soda makes a wide variety of products: soda-flavored candy, energy drinks, and product-promoting gear that includes t-shirts, sweatshirts, caps, shorts, and calendars. Its most profitable product is still its multi-flavored, pure cane soda with its creative labeling. If you've seen Jones Soda on a store shelf, then you know that it appears to have an infinite variety of labels. The bottle labels are actually created by customers and submitted on the company's website. (To see some of the best labels from the past, see the Gallery at the Jones Soda website.) If you would like some soda with a custom label of your own, you can design and submit a label and order a 12-pack.

Because Jones Soda has a dizzying array of product variations, keeping track of costs is of vital importance. No matter how good your products are, if you don't keep your costs under control, you are likely to fail. Jones Soda's managers need accurate cost information regarding each primary product and each variation to ensure profitability. So while its marketing approach differs dramatically from the giants, Jones Soda needs the same kind of cost information as the big guys.

 Watch the *Jones Soda* video in WileyPLUS to learn more about process costing in the real world.

## Chapter Outline

| LEARNING OBJECTIVES | REVIEW | PRACTICE |
|---|---|---|
| **LO 1** Discuss the uses of a process cost system and how it compares to a job order cost system. | • Uses of process cost systems<br>• Process costing for service companies<br>• Comparing job order and process cost systems | **DO IT! 1** Compare Job Order and Process Cost Systems |
| **LO 2** Explain the flow of costs in a process cost system and the journal entries to assign manufacturing costs. | • Process cost flow<br>• Assigning manufacturing costs | **DO IT! 2** Manufacturing Costs in Process Costing |
| **LO 3** Compute equivalent units of production. | • Weighted-average method<br>• Refinements on the method | **DO IT! 3** Equivalent Units of Production |
| **LO 4** Complete the four steps to prepare a production cost report. | • Physical unit flow<br>• Equivalent units of production<br>• Unit production costs<br>• Cost reconciliation schedule<br>• Production cost report | **DO IT! 4** Cost Reconciliation Schedule |

**Go to the Review and Practice section at the end of the chapter for a targeted summary and practice applications with solutions.**

**Visit WileyPLUS for additional tutorials and practice opportunities.**

# Overview of Process Cost Systems

**LEARNING OBJECTIVE 1**

Discuss the uses of a process cost system and how it compares to a job order cost system.

## Uses of Process Cost Systems

Companies use **process cost systems** to assign costs to similar products that are mass-produced in a continuous fashion. **Jones Soda Co.** uses a process cost system as follows.

- Production of the soda, once it begins, continues until the completed bottles of soda emerge.
- The processing is the same for the entire production run—with precisely the same amount of materials, labor, and overhead.
- Each finished bottle of soda is indistinguishable from another.

A company such as **United States Steel** uses process costing in the manufacturing of steel. **Kellogg** and **General Mills** use process costing for cereal production; **ExxonMobil** uses process costing for its oil refining. **Sherwin Williams** uses process costing for its paint products.

- At a bottling company like Jones Soda, the manufacturing process begins with the blending of ingredients.
- Next, automated machinery moves the bottles into position and fills them.
- The production process then caps, labels, packages, and forwards the bottles to the finished goods warehouse.

**Illustration 16.1** shows this process.

**ILLUSTRATION 16.1** **Manufacturing processes**

For Jones Soda, as well as the other companies just mentioned, once production begins, it continues until the finished product emerges. Each unit of finished product is like every other unit. In comparison, a job order cost system assigns costs to a *specific job*. Examples are the construction of a customized home, the making of a movie, or the manufacturing of a specialized machine. **Illustration 16.2** provides examples of companies that primarily use either a process cost system or a job order cost system.

ILLUSTRATION 16.2 Process cost and job order cost companies and products

| Process Cost System | | | Job Order Cost System | | |
|---|---|---|---|---|---|
| **Company** | **Product** | | **Company** | **Product** | |
| Jones Soda, PepsiCo | Soft drinks | | Young & Rubicam, J. Walter Thompson | Advertising | |
| ExxonMobil, Royal Dutch Shell | Oil | | Disney, Warner Bros. | Movies | |
| Intel, Advanced Micro Devices | Computer chips | | Center Ice Consultants, Ice Pro | Ice rinks | |
| Dow Chemical, DuPont | Chemicals | | Kaiser Permanente, Mayo Clinic | Patient health care | |

## Process Costing for Service Companies

When considering service companies, you might initially think of specific, nonroutine tasks, such as rebuilding an automobile engine, consulting on a business acquisition, or defending a major lawsuit. However, many service companies perform repetitive, routine work. For example, **Jiffy Lube** regularly performs oil changes. **H&R Block** focuses on the routine aspects of basic tax practice.

- Service companies that perform individualized, nonroutine services will probably benefit from using a job order cost system.
- Those that perform routine, repetitive services would probably prefer a process cost system.

## Similarities and Differences Between Job Order Cost and Process Cost Systems

In a job order cost system, companies assign costs to each job. In a process cost system, companies track costs through a series of connected manufacturing processes or departments, rather than by individual jobs. Thus, companies use process cost systems when they produce a large volume of uniform or relatively homogeneous products. **Illustration 16.3** shows the basic flow of costs in these two systems.

ILLUSTRATION 16.3 Job order cost and process cost flow

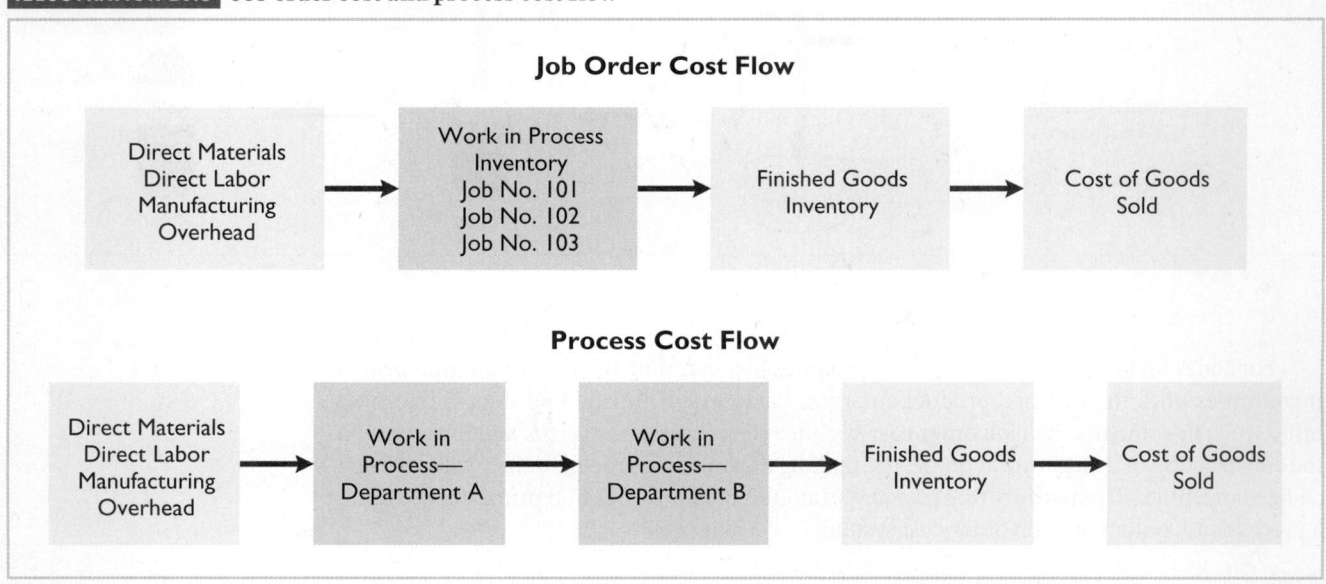

The following analysis highlights the basic similarities and differences between these two systems.

## Similarities

Job order cost and process cost systems are similar in three ways:

1. **The manufacturing cost components.** Both costing systems track three manufacturing cost components—direct materials, direct labor, and manufacturing overhead.
2. **The accumulation of the costs of materials, labor, and overhead.** Both costing systems record the acquisition of raw materials as a debit to Raw Materials Inventory, incurred factory labor as a debit to Factory Labor, and actual manufacturing overhead costs incurred as debits to Manufacturing Overhead.
3. **The flow of costs.** As noted above, both systems accumulate all manufacturing costs by debits to Raw Materials Inventory, Factory Labor, and Manufacturing Overhead. Both systems then assign these costs to the same accounts—Work in Process Inventory, Finished Goods Inventory, and Cost of Goods Sold. **The methods of assigning costs, however, differ significantly**. These differences are explained and illustrated later in the chapter.

## Differences

The differences between a job order cost and a process cost system are as follows.

1. **The number of work in process inventory accounts used.** A job order cost system uses only one work in process inventory account. A process cost system uses multiple work in process inventory accounts.
2. **Documents used to track costs.** A job order cost system charges costs to individual jobs and summarizes them in a job cost sheet. A process cost system summarizes costs in a production cost report for each department; there are no job cost sheets.
3. **The point at which costs are totaled.** A job order cost system totals costs when the job is completed. A process cost system totals costs at the end of a period of time.
4. **Unit cost computations.** In a job order cost system, the unit cost is the total cost per job divided by the units produced for that job. In a process cost system, the unit cost is total manufacturing costs for the period divided by the equivalent units produced during the period.

**Illustration 16.4** summarizes the major differences between a job order cost and a process cost system.

| Feature | Job Order Cost System | Process Cost System |
|---|---|---|
| **Work in process inventory accounts** | One work in process inventory account | Multiple work in process inventory accounts |
| **Documents used** | Job cost sheets | Production cost reports |
| **Determination of total manufacturing costs** | Each job | Each period |
| **Unit-cost computations** | Cost of each job ÷ Units produced for the job | The sum of materials costs and conversion costs, each divided by their respective equivalent units |

**ILLUSTRATION 16.4**

Job order versus process cost systems

## DO IT! 1 | Compare Job Order and Process Cost Systems

Indicate whether each of the following statements is true or false.

1. A law firm is likely to use process costing for major lawsuits.
2. A manufacturer of paintballs is likely to use process costing.
3. Both job order and process costing determine product costs at the end of a period of time, rather than when a product is completed.
4. Process costing does not keep track of manufacturing overhead.

### Solution

1. False.  2. True.  3. False.  4. False.

Related exercise material: **DO IT! 16.1 and E16.1.**

# Process Cost Flow and Assigning Costs

**LEARNING OBJECTIVE 2**

Explain the flow of costs in a process cost system and the journal entries to assign manufacturing costs.

## Process Cost Flow

**Illustration 16.5** shows the flow of costs in the process cost system for Tyler Company. Tyler manufactures roller blade and skateboard wheels that it sells to manufacturers and retail outlets. Manufacturing consists of two processes: machining and assembly. The Machining Department shapes, hones, and drills the raw materials. The Assembly Department assembles and packages the wheels.

**ILLUSTRATION 16.5** Flow of costs in process cost system

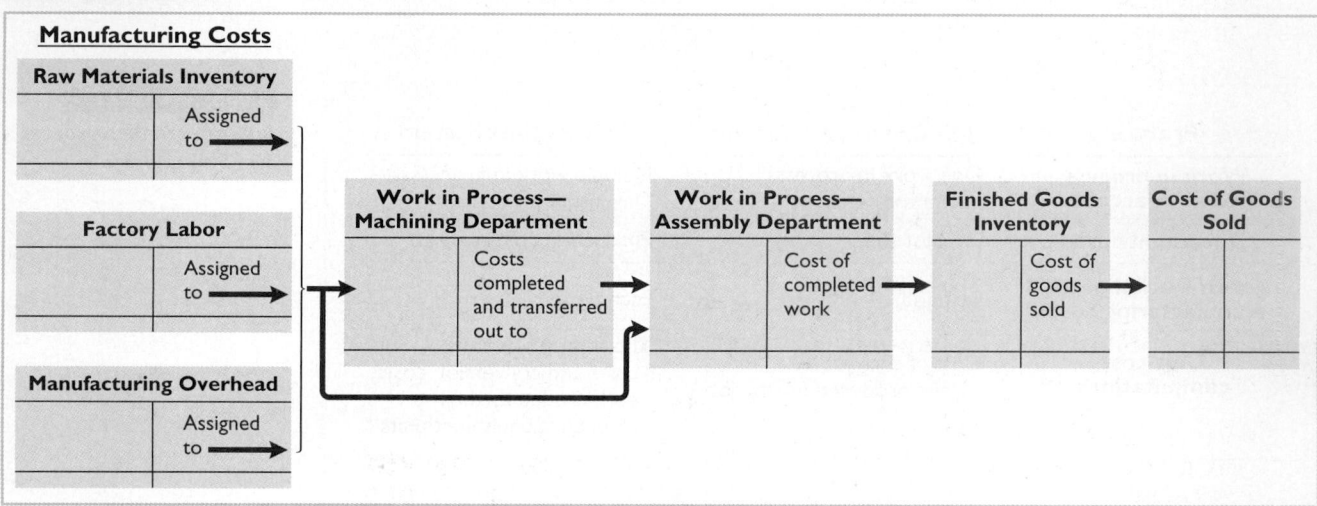

As the flow of costs indicates, the company can assign direct materials, direct labor, and manufacturing overhead in both the Machining and Assembly Departments. When it finishes its work, the Machining Department transfers the partially completed units to the Assembly Department. The Assembly Department completes the goods and then transfers them to the finished goods inventory. Upon sale, Tyler removes the goods from the finished goods inventory. Within each department, a similar set of activities is performed on each unit processed.

# Assigning Manufacturing Costs—Journal Entries

As indicated, the accumulation of the costs of direct materials, direct labor, and manufacturing overhead is the same in a process cost system as in a job order cost system. That is, both systems follow these procedures:

- Debit all raw materials acquired to Raw Materials Inventory at the time of purchase.
- Debit all factory labor to Factory Labor as labor costs are incurred.
- Debit overhead costs to Manufacturing Overhead as these costs are incurred.

However, the assignment of the three manufacturing cost components to work in process inventory accounts in a process cost system is different from a job order cost system. Here, we look at how companies assign these manufacturing cost components in a process cost system.

## Materials Costs

All direct materials issued for production are a materials cost to the producing department. A process cost system may use materials requisition slips, but **it generally requires fewer requisitions than in a job order cost system. The materials are used for processes rather than for specific jobs** and therefore typically are for larger quantities.

Materials

- At the beginning of the first process, a company usually adds most of the materials needed for production.
- However, other materials may be added at various points.

For example, in the manufacture of **Hershey** candy bars, the chocolate and other ingredients are added at the beginning of the first process, and the wrappers and cartons are added at the end of the packaging process.

Tyler Company adds materials at the beginning of each process. Suppose at the beginning of the current period that Tyler adds $50,000 of direct materials to the machining process and $20,000 of direct materials to the assembly process. Tyler makes the following entry to record the direct materials used.

| | | |
|---|---|---|
| Work in Process—Machining | 50,000 | |
| Work in Process—Assembly | 20,000 | |
|    Raw Materials Inventory | | 70,000 |
|      (To record direct materials used) | | |

## Factory Labor Costs

In a process cost system, as in a job order cost system, companies may use time tickets to determine the cost of labor assignable to production departments. Since they assign labor costs to a process rather than a job, they can obtain, from the payroll register or departmental payroll summaries, the labor cost chargeable to a process.

Factory Labor

Suppose that Tyler Company incurs factory labor charges of $20,000 in the machining process and $13,000 in the assembly process. The entry to assign direct labor costs to machining and assembly for Tyler is as follows.

| | | |
|---|---|---|
| Work in Process—Machining | 20,000 | |
| Work in Process—Assembly | 13,000 | |
|    Factory Labor | | 33,000 |
|      (To assign direct labor to production) | | |

Manufacturing
Overhead

## Manufacturing Overhead Costs

The objective in assigning overhead in a process cost system is to allocate the overhead costs to the production departments on an objective and equitable basis. That basis is the activity that "drives" or causes the costs.

- A primary driver of overhead costs in continuous manufacturing operations is **machine time used**, not direct labor.
- Thus, companies **widely use machine hours** in assigning manufacturing overhead costs using predetermined overhead rates.

Assume that based on machine hours that Tyler Company assigns overhead of $45,000 to the machining process and $17,000 to the assembly process. Tyler's entry to assign overhead to the two processes is as follows.

| | | |
|---|---|---|
| Work in Process—Machining | 45,000 | |
| Work in Process—Assembly | 17,000 | |
|     Manufacturing Overhead | | 62,000 |
|       (To assign overhead to production) | | |

### Management Insight    Caterpillar

© SweetyMommy/
iStockphoto

#### Choosing a Cost Driver

In one of its automated cost centers, **Caterpillar** inputs work into the cost center, where robotic machines process it and transfer the completed job to the next cost center without human intervention. One person tends all of the machines and spends more time maintaining machines than operating them. In such cases, overhead rates based on direct labor hours may be misleading. Surprisingly, some companies continue to assign manufacturing overhead on the basis of direct labor despite the fact that there is no cause-and-effect relationship between labor and overhead.

**What is the result if a company uses the wrong "cost driver" to assign manufacturing overhead? (Answer is available at the end of the chapter.)**

## Transfer to Next Department

When work in process items have received all the necessary inputs from one department, they progress to the next department. In our example, Tyler Company needs an entry to record the cost of the goods transferred out of the Machining Department. In this case, the transfer is to the Assembly Department. Suppose Tyler transfers goods with a recorded cost of $87,000 from machining to assembly. Tyler makes the following entry.

| | | |
|---|---|---|
| Work in Process—Assembly | 87,000 | |
|     Work in Process—Machining | | 87,000 |
|       (To record transfer of units to the Assembly Department) | | |

## Transfer to Finished Goods

Suppose the Assembly Department completes units with a recorded cost of $114,000 and then transfers them to the finished goods warehouse. The entry for this transfer is as follows.

| | | |
|---|---|---|
| Finished Goods Inventory | 114,000 | |
|     Work in Process—Assembly | | 114,000 |
|       (To record transfer of completed units to finished goods) | | |

## Transfer to Cost of Goods Sold

Suppose Tyler Company sells finished goods with a recorded cost of $27,000. It records the cost of goods sold as follows.

| | | |
|---|---|---|
| Cost of Goods Sold | 27,000 | |
|   Finished Goods Inventory | | 27,000 |
|     (To record cost of units sold) | | |

---

### DO IT! 2 | Manufacturing Costs in Process Costing

Ruth Company manufactures ZEBO through two processes: blending and bottling. In June, direct materials used were Blending $18,000 and Bottling $4,000. Direct labor costs were Blending $12,000 and Bottling $5,000. Manufacturing overhead costs assigned were Blending $6,000 and Bottling $2,500. The Blending Department transfers units completed at a cost of $19,000 to the Bottling Department. The Bottling Department transfers units completed at a cost of $11,000 to Finished Goods. Journalize the assignment of these costs to the two processes and the transfer of units as appropriate

**ACTION PLAN**
- In process cost accounting, keep separate work in process inventory accounts for each process.
- When the costs are assigned to production, debit the separate work in process inventory accounts.
- Transfer cost of completed units to the next process or to Finished Goods.

#### Solution

The entries are:

| | | |
|---|---|---|
| Work in Process—Blending | 18,000 | |
| Work in Process—Bottling | 4,000 | |
|   Raw Materials Inventory | | 22,000 |
|     (To record direct materials used) | | |
| | | |
| Work in Process—Blending | 12,000 | |
| Work in Process—Bottling | 5,000 | |
|   Factory Labor | | 17,000 |
|     (To assign direct labor to production) | | |
| | | |
| Work in Process—Blending | 6,000 | |
| Work in Process—Bottling | 2,500 | |
|   Manufacturing Overhead | | 8,500 |
|     (To assign overhead to production) | | |
| | | |
| Work in Process—Bottling | 19,000 | |
|   Work in Process—Blending | | 19,000 |
|     (To record transfer of units to the Bottling Department) | | |
| | | |
| Finished Goods Inventory | 11,000 | |
|   Work in Process—Bottling | | 11,000 |
|     (To record transfer of units to finished goods) | | |

Related exercise material: **BE16.1, BE16.2, BE16.3, DO IT! 16.2, E16.2, and E16.4.**

---

# Equivalent Units

### LEARNING OBJECTIVE 3
Compute equivalent units of production.

Suppose you have a work-study job in the office of your college's president, and she asks you to compute the cost of instruction per full-time equivalent student at your college. The college's vice president for finance provides the information shown in **Illustration 16.6.**

**ILLUSTRATION 16.6**

**Information for full-time student example**

| Costs: | |
| Total annual cost of instruction | $9,000,000 |
| Student population: | |
| Full-time students | 900 |
| Part-time students | 1,000 |

Part-time students take 60% of the classes of full-time students during the year. **Illustration 16.7** shows how to compute the number of full-time equivalent students per year.

**ILLUSTRATION 16.7**

**Full-time equivalent unit computation**

| Full-Time Students | + | Equivalent Units of Part-Time Students | = | Full-Time Equivalent Students |
|---|---|---|---|---|
| 900 | + | (1,000 × 60%) | = | 1,500 |

The cost of instruction per full-time equivalent student is therefore the total cost of instruction ($9,000,000) divided by the number of full-time equivalent students (1,500), which is $6,000 ($9,000,000 ÷ 1,500).

A process cost system uses the same idea, called equivalent units of production.

- **Equivalent units of production** measure the work done during the period, expressed in fully completed units.
- Companies use this measure to determine the cost per unit of a completed product.

# Weighted-Average Method

The equation to compute equivalent units of production is shown in **Illustration 16.8**.

**ILLUSTRATION 16.8**

**Equivalent units of production equation**

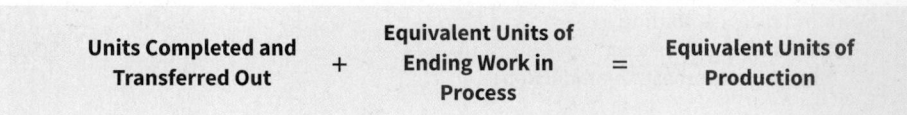

| Units Completed and Transferred Out | + | Equivalent Units of Ending Work in Process | = | Equivalent Units of Production |
|---|---|---|---|---|

To better understand this concept of equivalent units, consider the following two separate examples.

**Example 1.** In a specific period, the entire production efforts of Sullivan Company's Blending Department resulted in ending work in process of 4,000 units that are 60% complete as to materials, labor, and overhead. The equivalent units of production for the Blending Department are therefore 2,400 units (4,000 × 60%).

**Example 2.** The production efforts of Kori Company's Packaging Department during the period resulted in 10,000 units completed and transferred out, and 5,000 units in ending work in process that are 70% completed. The equivalent units of production are therefore 13,500 [10,000 + (5,000 × 70%)].

This method of computing equivalent units is referred to as the **weighted-average method**. It considers the degree of completion (weighting) of the units completed and transferred out and the ending work in process.

# Refinements on the Weighted-Average Method

**Kellogg Company** has produced Eggo® Waffles since 1970. Three departments produce these waffles: Mixing, Baking, and Freezing/Packaging. The Mixing Department combines dry ingredients, including flour, salt, and baking powder, with liquid ingredients, including eggs and vegetable oil, to make waffle batter. **Illustration 16.9** provides information related to the Mixing Department at the end of June. Note that separate unit cost computations are needed for materials and conversion costs whenever the two types of costs do not occur in the process at the same time.

| Mixing Department | | | |
|---|---|---|---|
| | | **Percentage Complete** | |
| | **Physical Units** | **Direct Materials** | **Conversion Costs** |
| Work in process, June 1 | 100,000 | 100% | 70% |
| Started into production | 800,000 | | |
| Total units to be accounted for | 900,000 | | |
| Units completed and transferred out | 700,000 | | |
| Work in process, June 30 | 200,000 | 100% | 60% |
| Total units accounted for | 900,000 | | |

**ILLUSTRATION 16.9**

**Information for Mixing Department**

Illustration 16.9 indicates that the beginning work in process is 100% complete as to materials cost and 70% complete as to conversion costs (see **Ethics Note**). **Conversion costs are the sum of direct labor costs and manufacturing overhead costs.** In other words, Kellogg adds both the dry and liquid ingredients (materials) at the beginning of the waffle-making process, and the conversion costs (labor and overhead) related to the mixing of these ingredients are incurred uniformly and are 70% complete. The ending work in process is 100% complete as to materials cost and 60% complete as to conversion costs.

We then use the Mixing Department information to determine equivalent units.

- **In computing equivalent units, the beginning work in process is not part of the equivalent units of production calculation.**
- The units transferred out to the Baking Department are fully complete as to both materials and conversion costs. The ending work in process is fully complete as to materials but only 60% complete as to conversion costs.
- We therefore need to make **two equivalent units computations**: one for direct materials and the other for conversion costs.

**Illustration 16.10** shows these computations.

**ETHICS NOTE**

An unethical manager might use incorrect completion percentages when determining equivalent units. This results in either raising or lowering costs. Since completion percentages are somewhat subjective, this form of income manipulation can be difficult to detect.

| Mixing Department | | |
|---|---|---|
| | **Equivalent Units** | |
| | **Materials** | **Conversion Costs** |
| Units completed and transferred out | 700,000 | 700,000 |
| Work in process, June 30 | | |
| 200,000 × 100% | 200,000 | |
| 200,000 × 60% | | 120,000 |
| Total equivalent units | 900,000 | 820,000 |

**ILLUSTRATION 16.10**

**Computation of equivalent units—Mixing Department**

We can refine the earlier equation used to compute equivalent units of production (Illustration 16.8) to show the computations for materials and for conversion costs, as shown in **Illustration 16.11.**

**ILLUSTRATION 16.11**
**Refined equivalent units of production calculation**

| Units Completed and Transferred Out— Materials | + | Equivalent Units of Ending Work in Process—Materials | = | Equivalent Units of Production— Materials |
|---|---|---|---|---|
| Units Completed and Transferred Out— Conversion Costs | + | Equivalent Units of Ending Work in Process—Conversion Costs | = | Equivalent Units of Production— Conversion Costs |

---

## People, Planet, and Profit Insight     General Electric

© Nicole Hofmann/ iStockphoto

### Haven't I Seen That Before?

For a variety of reasons, many companies, including **General Electric**, are making a big push to remanufacture goods that have been thrown away. Items getting a second chance include cell phones, computers, home appliances, car parts, vacuum cleaners, and medical equipment. Businesses have figured out that profit margins on remanufactured goods are significantly higher than on new goods.

As prices of commodities such as copper and steel increase, reusing parts makes more sense. Also, as more local governments initiate laws requiring that electronics and appliances be recycled rather than thrown away, the cost of remanufacturing declines because the gathering of used goods becomes far more efficient.

Besides benefitting the manufacturer, remanufacturing provides goods at a much lower price to consumers, reduces waste going to landfills, saves energy, reuses scarce resources, and reduces emissions. For example, it was estimated that a remanufactured car starter results in about 50% less carbon dioxide emissions than making a new one.

**Source:** James R. Hagerty and Paul Glader, "From Trash Heap to Store Shelf," *Wall Street Journal Online* (January 24, 2011).

**In what ways might the relative composition (direct materials, direct labor, and manufacturing overhead) of a remanufactured product's cost differ from that of a newly made product? (Answer is available at the end of the chapter.)**

---

**ACTION PLAN**

• **To measure the work done during the period, expressed in fully completed units, compute equivalent units of production.**

• **Use the appropriate equation: Units completed and transferred out + Equivalent units of ending work in process = Equivalent units of production.**

## DO IT! 3 | Equivalent Units of Production

The Fabricating Department for Outdoor Essentials has the following production and cost data for the current month.

| Beginning Work in Process | Units Completed and Transferred Out | Ending Work in Process |
|---|---|---|
| –0– | 15,000 | 10,000 |

All direct materials are entered at the beginning of the process. The ending work in process units are 30% complete as to conversion costs. Compute the equivalent units of production for (a) materials and (b) conversion costs.

### Solution

a. Since direct materials are entered at the beginning of the process, ending work in process equals 10,000 equivalent units. Thus, 15,000 completed units + 10,000 equivalent units = 25,000 equivalent units of production for materials.

b. Since ending work in process is only 30% complete as to conversion costs, ending work in process equals 3,000 equivalent units (10,000 units × 30%). Thus, 15,000 completed units + 3,000 equivalent units = 18,000 equivalent units of production for conversion costs.

Related exercise material: **BE16.4, BE16.5, DO IT! 16.3, E16.5, E16.6, E16.8, E16.9, E16.10, E16.11, E16.13, E16.14, and E16.15.**

# The Production Cost Report

**LEARNING OBJECTIVE 4**

Complete the four steps to prepare a production cost report.

As mentioned earlier, companies using a process cost system prepare a production cost report for each department.

- A **production cost report** is the key document that management uses to understand the activities in a department.
- It shows the production quantity and cost data related to that department using process costing.

For example, in producing Eggo® Waffles, **Kellogg Company** uses three production cost reports: Mixing, Baking, and Freezing/Packaging. **Illustration 16.12** shows the flow of costs to make an Eggo® Waffle and the related production cost reports for each department.

**ILLUSTRATION 16.12**  **Flow of costs in making Eggo® Waffles**

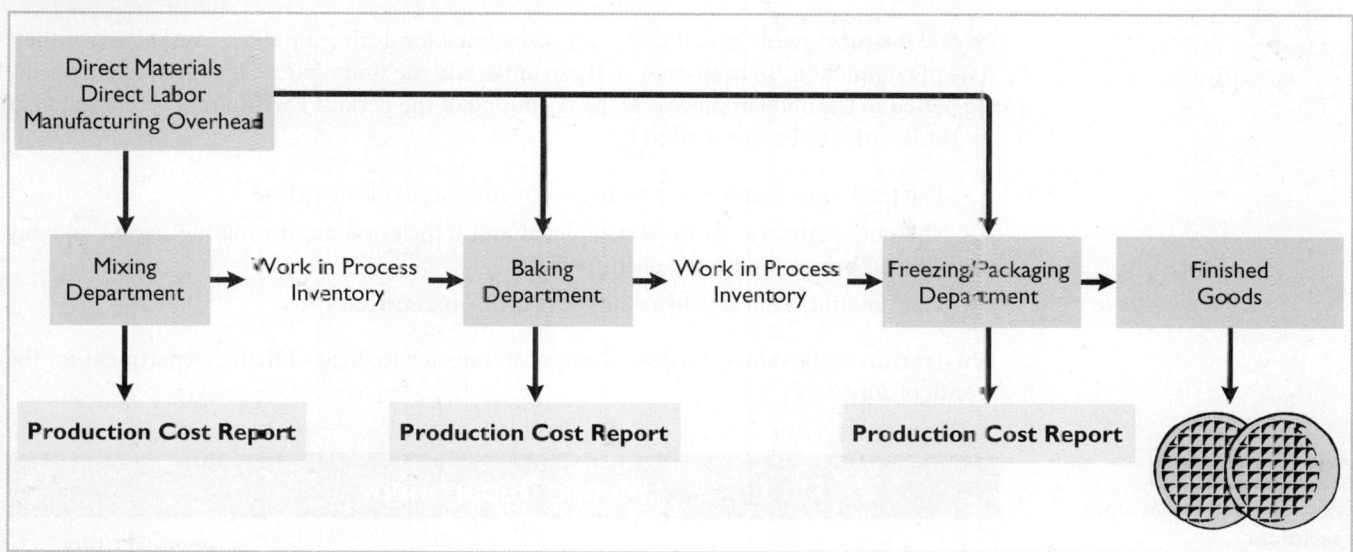

In order to complete a production cost report, the company must perform four steps, which as a whole make up the process cost system.

1. Compute the physical unit flow.
2. Compute the equivalent units of production.
3. Compute unit production costs.
4. Prepare a cost reconciliation schedule.

**Illustration 16.13** shows assumed data for the Mixing Department at **Kellogg Company** for the month of June. We will use this information to complete a production cost report for the Mixing Department.

ILLUSTRATION 16.13

Unit and cost data—Mixing Department

| Mixing Department | |
|---|---|
| **Physical Units** | |
| Work in process, June 1 | 100,000 |
| Direct materials: 100% complete | |
| Conversion costs: 70% complete | |
| Units started into production during June | 800,000 |
| Units completed and transferred out to Baking Department | 700,000 |
| Work in process, June 30 | 200,000 |
| Direct materials: 100% complete | |
| Conversion costs: 60% complete | |
| **Costs** | |
| Work in process, June 1 | |
| Direct materials: 100% complete | $ 50,000 |
| Conversion costs: 70% complete | 35,000 |
| Cost of work in process, June 1 | $ 85,000 |
| Costs incurred during production in June | |
| Direct materials | $400,000 |
| Conversion costs | 170,000 |
| Costs incurred in June | $570,000 |

# Compute the Physical Unit Flow (Step 1)

**Physical units** are the actual units to be accounted for during a period, irrespective of their state of completion. To keep track of these units, add the units started into production during the period to the units in process at the beginning of the period. This amount is referred to as the **total units to be accounted for**.

- The total units then are accounted for by the output of the period.
- The output consists of units completed and transferred out during the period and any units in process at the end of the period.
- This amount is referred to as the **total units accounted for**.

Illustration 16.14 shows the flow of physical units for Kellogg's Mixing Department for the month of June.

ILLUSTRATION 16.14

Physical unit flow—Mixing Department

| Mixing Department | |
|---|---|
| | **Physical Units** |
| Units to be accounted for | |
| Work in process, June 1 | 100,000 |
| Started into production | 800,000 |
| Total units to be accounted for | **900,000** |
| Units accounted for | |
| Completed and transferred out | 700,000 |
| Work in process, June 30 | 200,000 |
| Total units accounted for | **900,000** |

The records indicate that the Mixing Department must account for 900,000 physical units. Of this sum, 700,000 units were completed and transferred to the Baking Department, and 200,000 units were still in process.

# Compute the Equivalent Units of Production (Step 2)

Once the physical flow of the units is established, Kellogg must measure the Mixing Department's output in terms of equivalent units of production. The Mixing Department adds all direct materials at the beginning of the process, and it incurs conversion costs uniformly throughout the process (see **Helpful Hint**). Thus, we need two computations of equivalent units of production: one for materials and one for conversion costs. These computations are shown in **Illustration 16.15**. Recall that these computations ignore beginning work in process.

**HELPFUL HINT**

Materials are not always added at the beginning of the process. For example, materials are sometimes added uniformly during the process.

|  | Equivalent Units | |
|---|---|---|
|  | **Materials** | **Conversion Costs** |
| Units completed and transferred out | 700,000 | 700,000 |
| Work in process, June 30 | | |
| 200,000 × 100% | 200,000 | |
| 200,000 × 60% | | 120,000 |
| Total equivalent units | **900,000** | **820,000** |

**ILLUSTRATION 16.15**

Computation of equivalent units—Mixing Department

# Compute Unit Production Costs (Step 3)

Armed with the knowledge of the equivalent units of production, we can now compute the unit production costs.

- **Unit production costs** are costs expressed in terms of equivalent units of production.
- When equivalent units of production are different for direct materials and conversion costs, we compute three unit costs: (1) materials, (2) conversion, and (3) total manufacturing.

The computation of total materials cost related to Eggo® Waffles is shown in **Illustration 16.16**.

| | |
|---|---|
| Work in process, June 1 | |
| Direct materials cost | $ 50,000 |
| Costs added to production during June | |
| Direct materials cost | 400,000 |
| Total materials cost | **$450,000** |

**ILLUSTRATION 16.16**

Total materials cost computation

Illustration 16.17 shows the computation of unit materials cost.

| Total Materials Cost | ÷ | Equivalent Units of Materials | = | Unit Materials Cost |
|---|---|---|---|---|
| $450,000 | ÷ | 900,000 | = | $0.50 |

**ILLUSTRATION 16.17**

Unit materials cost computation

Illustration 16.18 shows the computation of total conversion costs for June.

| | |
|---|---|
| Work in process, June 1 | |
| Conversion costs | $ 35,000 |
| Costs added to production during June | |
| Conversion costs | 170,000 |
| Total conversion costs | **$205,000** |

**ILLUSTRATION 16.18**

Total conversion costs computation

The computation of unit conversion cost is shown in **Illustration 16.19**.

**ILLUSTRATION 16.19**

**Unit conversion cost computation**

| Total Conversion Costs | ÷ | Equivalent Units of Conversion Costs | = | Unit Conversion Cost |
|---|---|---|---|---|
| $205,000 | ÷ | 820,000 | = | $0.25 |

Total manufacturing cost per unit is therefore computed as shown in **Illustration 16.20**.

**ILLUSTRATION 16.20**

**Total manufacturing cost per unit**

| Unit Materials Cost | + | Unit Conversion Cost | = | Total Manufacturing Cost per Unit |
|---|---|---|---|---|
| $0.50 | + | $0.25 | = | $0.75 |

# Prepare a Cost Reconciliation Schedule (Step 4)

We are now ready to determine the cost of goods completed and transferred out of the Mixing Department to the Baking Department and the costs that remain in ending work in process inventory for the Mixing Department. Kellogg charged total costs of $655,000 to the Mixing Department in June, calculated as shown in **Illustration 16.21**.

**ILLUSTRATION 16.21**

**Costs charged to Mixing Department**

| | |
|---|---|
| Costs to be accounted for | |
| Work in process, June 1 | $ 85,000 |
| Started into production | 570,000 |
| Total costs to be accounted for | **$655,000** |

The company then prepares a cost reconciliation schedule (see **Illustration 16.22**) to assign these costs to (a) units completed and transferred out to the Baking Department and (b) ending work in process.

**ILLUSTRATION 16.22**

**Cost reconciliation schedule—Mixing Department**

| Mixing Department Cost Reconciliation Schedule | | |
|---|---|---|
| Costs accounted for | | |
| Completed and transferred out (700,000 × $0.75) | | $525,000 |
| Work in process, June 30 | | |
| Materials (200,000 × $0.50) | $100,000 | |
| Conversion costs (120,000 × $0.25) | 30,000 | 130,000 |
| Total costs accounted for | | **$655,000** |

Kellogg uses the total manufacturing cost per unit, $0.75, in costing the **units completed** and transferred to the Baking Department. In contrast, the unit materials cost and the unit conversion cost are needed in costing **units in process**. The **cost reconciliation schedule** shows that the **total costs accounted for** (Illustration 16.22) equal the **total costs to be accounted for** (Illustration 16.21).

# Preparing the Production Cost Report

At this point, Kellogg is ready to prepare the production cost report for the Mixing Department. As indicated earlier, this report is an internal document for management that shows production quantity and cost data for a production department. **Illustration 16.23** shows the completed production cost report for the Mixing Department and identifies the four steps used in preparing it (see **Helpful Hint**).

- Production cost reports provide a basis for evaluating the productivity of a department.
- In addition, managers can use the cost data to assess whether unit costs and total costs are reasonable.
- By comparing the quantity and cost data with predetermined goals, top management can also judge whether current performance is meeting planned objectives.

**HELPFUL HINT**

The four steps in preparing a production cost report:
1. Compute the physical unit flow.
2. Compute the equivalent units of production.
3. Compute unit production costs.
4. Prepare a cost reconciliation schedule.

**ILLUSTRATION 16.23** Production cost report

### Mixing Department
### Production Cost Report
### For the Month Ended June 30, 2022

|  | | | Equivalent Units | | |
|---|---|---|---|---|---|
|  |  | Physical Units | Materials | Conversion Costs | |
| 6 | **Quantities** | | | | |
| 7 | Units to be accounted for | Step 1 | Step 2 | | |
| 8 | Work in process, June 1 | 100,000 | | | |
| 9 | Started into production | 800,000 | | | |
| 10 | Total units to be accounted for | 900,000 | | | |
| 11 | Units accounted for | | | | |
| 12 | Completed and transferred out | 700,000 | 700,000 | 700,000 | |
| 13 | Work in process, June 30 | 200,000 | 200,000 | 120,000 | (200,000 × 60%) |
| 14 | Total units accounted for | 900,000 | 900,000 | 820,000 | |

| | **Costs** | | Materials | Conversion Costs | Total |
|---|---|---|---|---|---|
| 16 | **Unit costs** Step 3 | | | | |
| 17 | Total cost | (a) | $450,000 | $205,000 | $655,000 |
| 18 | Equivalent units | (b) | 900,000 | 820,000 | |
| 19 | Unit costs [(a) ÷ (b)] | | $0.50 | $0.25 | $0.75 |

| | **Cost Reconciliation Schedule** Step 4 | | | | |
|---|---|---|---|---|---|
| 21 | Costs to be accounted for | | | | |
| 22 | Work in process, June 1 | | | | $ 85,000 |
| 23 | Started into production | | | | 570,000 |
| 24 | Total costs to be accounted for | | | | $655,000 |
| 25 | Costs accounted for | | | | |
| 26 | Completed and transferred out (700,000 × $0.75) | | | | $525,000 |
| 27 | Work in process, June 30 | | | | |
| 28 | Materials (200,000 × $0.50) | | | $100,000 | |
| 29 | Conversion costs (120,000 × $0.25) | | | 30,000 | 130,000 |
| 30 | Total costs accounted for | | | | $655,000 |

# Costing Systems—Final Comments

Companies often use a combination of a process cost and a job order cost system.

- Called **operations costing**, this hybrid system is similar to process costing in its assumption that standardized methods are used to manufacture the product.
- At the same time, the product may have some customized, individual features that require the use of a job order cost system.

Consider, for example, **Ford Motor Company**. Each vehicle at a given factory goes through the same assembly line, but Ford uses different materials (such as seat coverings, paint, and tinted glass) for different vehicles. Similarly, **Kellogg**'s Pop-Tarts® toaster pastries go through numerous standardized processes—mixing, filling, baking, frosting, and packaging. The pastry dough, though, comes in different flavors—plain, chocolate, and graham—and fillings include Smucker's® real fruit, chocolate fudge, vanilla creme, brown sugar cinnamon, and s'mores.

A cost-benefit trade-off occurs as a company decides which costing system to use. A job order cost system, for example, provides detailed information related to the cost of the product.

- Because each job has its own distinguishing characteristics, the system can provide an accurate cost per job.
- This information is useful in controlling costs and pricing products.
- However, the cost of implementing a job order cost system is often expensive because of the accounting costs involved.

On the other hand, for a company like **Intel**, is there a benefit in knowing whether the cost of the one-hundredth computer chip produced is different from the one-thousandth chip produced? Probably not. An average cost of the product will suffice for control and pricing purposes.

In summary, when deciding to use one of these systems or a combination system, a company must weigh the costs of implementing the system against the benefits from the additional information provided.

---

**ACTION PLAN**

- Assign the total manufacturing cost of $15 per unit to the 12,000 units completed and transferred out.
- Assign the materials cost and conversion costs based on equivalent units of production to units in ending work in process.

## DO IT! 4 | Cost Reconciliation Schedule

In March, Rodayo Manufacturing had the following unit production costs in its Assembly Department: materials $6 and conversion costs $9. On March 1, it had no work in process. During March, the Assembly Department completed and transferred out 12,000 units. As of March 31, 800 units that were 25% complete as to conversion costs and 100% complete as to materials were in ending work in process in the Assembly Department. Assign the costs to the units completed and transferred out and to work in process at the end of the month.

### Solution

The assignment of costs is as follows.

| | | |
|---|---:|---:|
| Costs accounted for | | |
|   Completed and transferred out (12,000 × $15) | | $180,000 |
|   Work in process, March 31 | | |
|     Materials (800 × $6) | $4,800 | |
|     Conversion costs (200* × $9) | 1,800 | 6,600 |
| Total costs accounted for | | $186,600 |

*800 × 25%

Related exercise material: **BE16.6, BE16.7, BE16.8, BE16.9, DO IT! 16.4, E16.3, E16.5, E16.6, E16.7, E16.8, E16.9, E16.10, E16.11, E16.13, E16.14,** and **E16.15.**

# Appendix 16A | FIFO Method for Equivalent Units

**LEARNING OBJECTIVE *5**

Compute equivalent units using the FIFO method.

In this chapter, we demonstrated the weighted-average method of computing equivalent units. Some companies use a different method, referred to as the **first-in, first-out (FIFO) method**, to compute equivalent units. The purpose of this appendix is to illustrate how companies use the FIFO method to prepare a production cost report.

## Equivalent Units Under FIFO

Under the FIFO method, companies compute equivalent units on a first-in, first-out basis. Some companies favor the FIFO method because the FIFO cost assumption usually corresponds to the actual physical flow of the goods. Under the FIFO method, companies therefore assume that the beginning work in process is completed before new work is started.

Using the FIFO method, equivalent units are the sum of the work performed to:

1. Finish the units of beginning work in process inventory.
2. Complete the units started into production during the period (referred to as the **units started and completed**).
3. Start, but only partially complete, the units in ending work in process inventory.

Normally, in a process cost system, some units will always be in process at both the beginning and the end of the period.

### Illustration

**Illustration 16A.1** shows the physical flow of units for the Assembly Department of Shutters Inc. In addition, it indicates the degree of completion of the work in process inventory accounts in regard to conversion costs.

| Assembly Department | |
|---|---:|
| | **Physical Units** |
| Units to be accounted for | |
| Work in process, June 1 (40% complete) | 500 |
| Started into production | 8,000 |
| Total units to be accounted for | **8,500** |
| Units accounted for | |
| Completed and transferred out | 8,100 |
| Work in process, June 30 (75% complete) | 400 |
| Total units accounted for | **8,500** |

**ILLUSTRATION 16A.1**

**Physical unit flow—Assembly Department**

In Illustration 16A.1, the units completed and transferred out (8,100) plus the units in ending work in process (400) equal the total units to be accounted for (8,500). Using FIFO, we then compute equivalent units of production for conversion costs for the Assembly Department as follows.

1. The 500 units of beginning work in process were 40% complete. Thus 300 equivalent units (500 units × 60%) were required to complete the beginning inventory that was completed and transferred out.
2. The units started and completed during the current month are **the units transferred out minus the units in beginning work in process**. For the Assembly Department, units started and completed are 7,600 (8,100 − 500). These 7,600 physical units equate to 7,600 equivalent units.

3. The 400 units of ending work in process were 75% complete. Thus, equivalent units were 300 (400 × 75%).

Equivalent units for conversion costs for the Assembly Department are 8,200, computed as shown in **Illustration 16A.2**.

**ILLUSTRATION 16A.2**

**Computation of equivalent units—FIFO method**

| | Assembly Department | | |
|---|---|---|---|
| Production Data | Work Added Physical Units | Equivalent This Period | Units |
| Work in process, June 1 | 500 | 60% | 300 |
| Started and completed | 7,600 | 100% | 7,600 |
| Work in process, June 30 | 400 | 75% | 300 |
| Total | 8,500 | | 8,200 |

# Comprehensive Example

To provide a complete illustration of the FIFO method, we will use the data for the Mixing Department at **Kellogg Company** for the month of June, as shown in **Illustration 16A.3**.

**ILLUSTRATION 16A.3**

**Unit and cost data—Mixing Department**

| Mixing Department | |
|---|---|
| **Physical Units** | |
| Work in process, June 1 | 100,000 |
|   Direct materials: 100% complete | |
|   Conversion costs: 70% complete | |
| Units started into production during June | 800,000 |
| Units completed and transferred out to Baking Department | 700,000 |
| Work in process, June 30 | 200,000 |
|   Direct materials: 100% complete | |
|   Conversion costs: 60% complete | |
| **Costs** | |
| Work in process, June 1 | |
|   Direct materials: 100% complete | $ 50,000 |
|   Conversion costs: 70% complete | 35,000 |
| Cost of work in process, June 1 | $ 85,000 |
| Costs incurred during production in June | |
|   Direct materials | $400,000 |
|   Conversion costs | 170,000 |
| Costs incurred in June | $570,000 |

## Compute the Physical Unit Flow (Step 1)

**Illustration 16A.4** shows the physical flow of units for Kellogg's Mixing Department for the month of June.

**ILLUSTRATION 16A.4**

**Physical unit flow—Mixing Department**

| Mixing Department | |
|---|---|
| | Physical Units |
| Units to be accounted for | |
|   Work in process, June 1 | 100,000 |
|   Started into production | 800,000 |
| Total units to be accounted for | 900,000 |
| Units accounted for | |
|   Completed and transferred out | 700,000 |
|   Work in process, June 30 | 200,000 |
| Total units accounted for | 900,000 |

Under the FIFO method, companies often expand the physical units schedule, as shown in **Illustration 16A.5**, to explain the completed and transferred-out section.

- As a result, this section reports the beginning work in process and the units started and completed.
- These two items further explain the completed and transferred-out section.

| Mixing Department | |
|---|---|
| | **Physical Units** |
| Units to be accounted for | |
| Work in process, June 1 | 100,000 |
| Started into production | 800,000 |
| Total units to be accounted for | **900,000** |
| Units accounted for | |
| Completed and transferred out | |
| **Work in process, June 1** | **100,000** |
| **Started and completed** | **600,000** |
| | **700,000** |
| Work in process, June 30 | 200,000 |
| Total units accounted for | **900,000** |

The records indicate that the Mixing Department must account for 900,000 units. Of this sum, 700,000 units were completed and transferred to the Baking Department and 200,000 units were still in process.

## Compute Equivalent Units of Production (Step 2)

As with the method presented in the chapter, once they determine the physical flow of the units, companies need to determine equivalent units of production. The Mixing Department adds materials at the beginning of the process, and it incurs conversion costs uniformly throughout the process (see **Helpful Hint**). Thus, Kellogg must make two computations of equivalent units: one for materials and one for conversion costs.

**Equivalent Units for Materials**   Since Kellogg adds materials at the beginning of the process, no additional materials costs are required to complete the beginning work in process. In addition, 100% of the materials costs has been incurred on the ending work in process. **Illustration 16A.6** shows the computation of equivalent units for materials.

**HELPFUL HINT**

As noted earlier, materials are not always added at the beginning of the process. For example, companies sometimes add materials uniformly during the process.

| Mixing Department—Materials | | | |
|---|---|---|---|
| **Production Data** | **Physical Units** | **Direct Materials Added This Period** | **Equivalent Units** |
| Work in process, June 1 | 100,000 | –0– | –0– |
| Started and completed | 600,000 | 100% | **600,000** |
| Work in process, June 30 | 200,000 | 100% | **200,000** |
| Total | 900,000 | | **800,000** |

**Equivalent Units for Conversion Costs**   The 100,000 units of beginning work in process were 70% complete in terms of conversion costs. Thus, the Mixing Department required 30,000 equivalent units [(100,000 units × (100% – 70%)] of conversion costs to complete the beginning inventory. In addition, the 200,000 units of ending work in process were 60% complete in terms of conversion costs. Thus, the equivalent units for conversion costs is 750,000, computed as shown in **Illustration 16A.7**.

**Computation of equivalent units—conversion costs**

| Mixing Department—Conversion Costs | | | |
|---|---|---|---|
| Production Data | Physical Units | Work Added This Period | Equivalent Units |
| Work in process, June 1 | 100,000 | 30% | **30,000** |
| Started and completed | 600,000 | 100% | **600,000** |
| Work in process, June 30 | 200,000 | 60% | **120,000** |
| Total | 900,000 | | **750,000** |

## Compute Unit Production Costs (Step 3)

Armed with the knowledge of the equivalent units of production, Kellogg can now compute the unit production costs.

- Unit production costs are costs expressed in terms of equivalent units of production.
- When equivalent units of production are different for materials and conversion costs, companies compute three unit costs: (1) materials, (2) conversion, and (3) total manufacturing.

Under the FIFO method, the unit costs of production are based entirely on the production costs incurred during the month. Thus, the costs in the beginning work in process are not relevant because they were incurred on work done in the preceding month. As Illustration 16A.3 indicated, the costs incurred during production in June were as shown in **Illustration 16A.8**.

ILLUSTRATION 16A.8

**Costs incurred during production in June**

| | |
|---|---|
| Direct materials | $400,000 |
| Conversion costs | 170,000 |
| Total costs incurred during June | $570,000 |

**Illustration 16A.9** shows the computation of unit materials cost, unit conversion costs, and total unit cost related to Eggo® Waffles.

ILLUSTRATION 16A.9

**Unit cost computations— Mixing Department**

| (1) | Total Materials Cost | ÷ | Equivalent Units of Materials | = | Unit Materials Cost |
|---|---|---|---|---|---|
| | $400,000 | ÷ | 800,000 | = | $0.50 |
| (2) | Total Conversion Costs | ÷ | Equivalent Units of Conversion Costs | = | Unit Conversion Cost |
| | $170,000 | ÷ | 750,000 | = | $0.227 (rounded)* |
| (3) | Unit Materials Cost | + | Unit Conversion Cost | = | Total Manufacturing Cost per Unit |
| | $0.50 | + | $0.227 | = | $0.727 |

*For homework problems, round unit costs to three decimal places.*

As shown, the unit costs are $0.50 for materials, $0.227 for conversion costs, and $0.727 for total manufacturing costs.

## Prepare a Cost Reconciliation Schedule (Step 4)

Kellogg is now ready to determine the cost of goods transferred out of the Mixing Department to the Baking Department and the costs in ending work in process. The total costs charged to the Mixing Department in June are $655,000, calculated as shown in **Illustration 16A.10** (see Illustration 16A.3 for further detail).

| Costs to be accounted for | |
|---|---|
| Work in process, June 1 | $ 85,000 |
| Started into production | 570,000 |
| Total costs to be accounted for | $655,000 |

**ILLUSTRATION 16A.10**
**Costs charged to Mixing Department**

Kellogg next prepares a cost reconciliation schedule to assign these costs to (1) units completed and transferred out to the Baking Department and (2) ending work in process. Under the FIFO method, the first goods to be completed during the period are the units in beginning work in process.

- Thus, the cost of the beginning work in process is always assigned to the goods transferred to the next department (or finished goods, if processing is complete).
- Under the FIFO method, ending work in process also will be assigned only the production costs incurred in the current period.

**Illustration 16A.11** shows a cost reconciliation schedule for the Mixing Department.

### Mixing Department
#### Cost Reconciliation Schedule

| | | |
|---|---|---|
| Costs accounted for | | |
| Completed and transferred out | | |
| Work in process, June 1 | | $ 85,000 |
| Costs to complete beginning work in process | | |
| Conversion costs (30,000 × $0.227) | | 6,810 |
| Total costs | | 91,810 |
| Units started and completed (600,000 × $0.727)* | | 435,950** |
| Total costs completed and transferred out | | 527,760 |
| Work in process, June 30 | | |
| Materials (200,000 × $0.50) | $100,000 | |
| Conversion costs (120,000 × $0.227) | 27,240 | 127,240 |
| Total costs accounted for | | **$655,000** |

*Any rounding errors should be adjusted in the "Units started and completed" calculation.
**Minus $250 rounding difference.

**ILLUSTRATION 16A.11**
**Cost reconciliation report**

As you can see, the total costs accounted for ($655,000 from Illustration 16A.11) equal the total costs to be accounted for ($655,000 from Illustration 16A.10).

## Preparing the Production Cost Report

At this point, Kellogg is ready to prepare the production cost report for the Mixing Department. This report is an internal document for management that shows production quantity and cost data for a production department.

As discussed previously, there are four steps in preparing a production cost report:

1. Compute the physical unit flow.
2. Compute the equivalent units of production.
3. Compute unit production costs.
4. Prepare a cost reconciliation schedule.

**Illustration 16A.12** shows the production cost report for the Mixing Department, with the four steps identified in the report.

As indicated in the chapter, production cost reports provide a basis for evaluating the productivity of a department (see **Helpful Hint**). In addition, managers can use the cost data to assess whether unit costs and total costs are reasonable. By comparing the quantity and cost data with predetermined goals, top management can also judge whether current performance is meeting planned objectives.

**HELPFUL HINT**

The two self-checks in the report are (1) total physical units accounted for must equal the total units to be accounted for, and (2) total costs accounted for must equal the total costs to be accounted for.

**ILLUSTRATION 16A.12** Production cost report—FIFO method

| | A | B | C | D | E |
|---|---|---|---|---|---|
| | | | | Mixing Department | |
| | Home Insert Page Layout Formulas Data Review View | | | | |
| | P18 | fx | | | |
| 1 | | **Mixing Department** | | | |
| 2 | | **Production Cost Report** | | | |
| 3 | | **For the Month Ended June 30, 2022** | | | |
| 4 | | **Equivalent Units** | | | |
| 5 | | Physical Units | Materials | Conversion Costs | |
| 6 | **Quantities** | | | | |
| 7 | Units to be accounted for | Step 1 | Step 2 | | |
| 8 | Work in process (WIP), June 1 | 100,000 | | | |
| 9 | Started into production | 800,000 | | | |
| 10 | Total units to be accounted for | 900,000 | | | |
| 11 | Units accounted for | | | | |
| 12 | Completed and transferred out | | | | |
| 13 | Work in process, June 1 | 100,000 | 0 | 30,000 | |
| 14 | Started and completed | 600,000 | 600,000 | 600,000 | |
| 15 | Work in process, June 30 | 200,000 | 200,000 | 120,000 | |
| 16 | Total units accounted for | 900,000 | 800,000 | 750,000 | |
| 17 | **Costs** | | | | |
| 18 | **Unit costs** Step 3 | | Materials | Conversion Costs | Total |
| 19 | Costs in June (excluding beginning WIP) (a) | | $400,000 | $170,000 | $570,000 |
| 20 | Equivalent units (b) | | 800,000 | 750,000 | |
| 21 | Unit costs [(a) ÷ (b)] | | $0.50 | $0.227 | $0.727 |
| 22 | **Cost Reconciliation Schedule** Step 4 | | | | |
| 23 | Costs to be accounted for | | | | |
| 24 | Work in process, June 1 | | | | $ 85,000 |
| 25 | Started into production | | | | 570,000 |
| 26 | Total costs to be accounted for | | | | $655,000 |
| 27 | Costs accounted for | | | | |
| 28 | Completed and transferred out | | | | |
| 29 | Work in process, June 1 | | | $ 85,000 | |
| 30 | Costs to complete beginning work in process | | | | |
| 31 | Conversion costs (30,000 × $0.227) | | | 6,810 | $ 91,810 |
| 32 | Units started and completed (600,000 × $0.727)* | | | | 435,950 |
| 33 | Total costs completed and transferred out | | | | 527,760 |
| 34 | Work in process, June 30 | | | | |
| 35 | Materials (200,000 × $0.50) | | | 100,000 | |
| 36 | Conversion costs (120,000 × $0.227) | | | 27,240 | 127,240 |
| 37 | Total costs accounted for | | | | $655,000 |
| 38 | | | | | |
| 39 | *Any rounding errors should be adjusted in the "Units started and completed" calculation | | | | |

# FIFO and Weighted-Average

The weighted-average method of computing equivalent units has **one major advantage**: It is simple to understand and apply.

- In cases where prices do not fluctuate significantly from period to period, the weighted-average method will be very similar to the FIFO method.

- In addition, companies that have been using just-in-time procedures effectively for inventory control purposes will have minimal inventory balances. In this case, differences between the weighted-average and the FIFO methods will not be material.

Conceptually, the FIFO method is superior to the weighted-average method because it measures **current performance** using only costs incurred in the current period.

- Managers are, therefore, not held responsible for costs from prior periods over which they may not have had control.
- In addition, the FIFO method **provides current cost information**, which the company can use to establish **more accurate pricing strategies** for goods manufactured and sold in the current period.

# Review and Practice

## Learning Objectives Review

### 1 Discuss the uses of a process cost system and how it compares to a job order cost system.

Companies that mass-produce similar products in a continuous fashion use process cost systems. Once production begins, it continues until the finished product emerges. Each unit of finished product is indistinguishable from every other unit.

Job order cost systems are similar to process cost systems in three ways. (1) Both systems track the same cost components—direct materials, direct labor, and manufacturing overhead. (2) Both accumulate costs in the same accounts—Raw Materials Inventory, Factory Labor, and Manufacturing Overhead. (3) Both assign accumulated costs to the same accounts—Work in Process, Finished Goods Inventory, and Cost of Goods Sold. However, the methods used to assign costs differ significantly.

There are four main differences between the two cost systems. (1) A process cost system uses separate work in process inventory accounts for each department or manufacturing process, rather than only one work in process inventory account used in a job order cost system. (2) A process cost system summarizes costs in a production cost report for each department. A job order cost system charges costs to individual jobs and summarizes them in a job cost sheet. (3) Costs are totaled at the end of a time period in a process cost system but at the completion of a job in a job order cost system. (4) A process cost system calculates unit cost as Total manufacturing costs for the period ÷ Equivalent units of production for the period. A job order cost system calculates unit cost as Total cost per job ÷ Units produced.

### 2 Explain the flow of costs in a process cost system and the journal entries to assign manufacturing costs.

A process cost system assigns manufacturing costs for raw materials, labor, and overhead to work in process inventory accounts for various departments or manufacturing processes. It transfers the costs of partially completed units from one department to another as those units move through the manufacturing process. The system transfers the costs of completed work to Finished Goods Inventory. Finally, when inventory is sold, the system transfers the costs to Cost of Goods Sold.

Entries to assign the costs of direct materials, direct labor, and manufacturing overhead consist of credits to Raw Materials Inventory, Factory Labor, and Manufacturing Overhead, and debits to Work in Process Inventory for each department. Entries to record the cost of goods transferred to another department are a credit to Work in Process Inventory for the department whose work is finished and a debit to Work in Process Inventory for the department to which the goods are transferred. The entry to record units completed and transferred to the warehouse is a credit to Work in Process Inventory for the department whose work is finished and a debit to Finished Goods Inventory. The entry to record the sale of goods is a credit to Finished Goods Inventory and a debit to Cost of Goods Sold.

### 3 Compute equivalent units of production.

Equivalent units of production measure work done during a period, expressed in fully completed units. Companies use this measure to determine the cost per unit of completed product. Equivalent units are the sum of units completed and transferred out plus equivalent units of ending work in process.

### 4 Complete the four steps to prepare a production cost report.

The four steps to complete a production cost report are as follows. (1) Compute the physical unit flow—that is, the total physical units to be accounted for. (2) Compute the equivalent units of production separately for direct materials and conversion costs. (3) Compute the unit production costs per equivalent units of production. (4) Prepare a cost reconciliation schedule, which shows that the total costs accounted for equal the total costs to be accounted for.

The production cost report contains both quantity and cost data for a production department over a specific period. There are four sections in the report: (1) flow of physical units, (2) equivalent units determination, (3) unit costs, and (4) cost reconciliation schedule.

### *5 Compute equivalent units using the FIFO method.

Equivalent units under the FIFO method are the sum of the work performed to (1) finish the units of beginning work in process inventory, if any; (2) complete some of the units started into production during the period; and (3) start, but only partially complete, the units in ending work in process inventory.

## Glossary Review

**Conversion costs** The sum of direct labor costs and manufacturing overhead costs. (p. 16-11).

**Cost reconciliation schedule** A schedule that shows that the total costs accounted for equal the total costs to be accounted for. (p. 16-16).

**Equivalent units of production** A measure of the work done during the period, expressed in fully completed units. (p. 16-10).

**Operations costing** A combination of a process cost and a job order cost system in which products are manufactured primarily by standardized methods, with some customization. (p. 16-18).

**Physical units** Actual units to be accounted for during a period, irrespective of their state of completion. (p. 16-14).

**Process cost system** An accounting system used to assign costs to similar products that are mass-produced in a continuous fashion. (p. 16-3).

**Production cost report** An internal report for management that shows both production quantity and cost data for a production department using process costing. (p. 16-13).

**Total units accounted for** The sum of the units completed and transferred out during the period plus the units in process at the end of the period. (p. 16-14).

**Total units to be accounted for** The sum of the units started into production during the period plus the units in process at the beginning of the period. (p. 16-14).

**Unit production costs** Costs expressed in terms of equivalent units of production. (p. 16-15).

**Weighted-average method** Method of computing equivalent units of production that considers the degree of completion (weighting) of the units completed and transferred out and the ending work in process. (p. 16-10).

## Practice Multiple-Choice Questions

1. **(LO 1)** Which of the following items is **not** characteristic of a process cost system?
   a. Once production begins, it continues until the finished product emerges.
   b. The products produced are heterogeneous in nature.
   c. The focus is on continually producing homogeneous products.
   d. When the finished product emerges, all units have precisely the same amount of materials, labor, and overhead.

2. **(LO 1)** Indicate which of the following statements is **not** correct.
   a. Both a job order and a process cost system track the same three manufacturing cost components—direct materials, direct labor, and manufacturing overhead.
   b. A job order cost system uses only one work in process inventory account, whereas a process cost system uses multiple work in process inventory accounts.
   c. Manufacturing costs are accumulated the same way in a job order and in a process cost system.
   d. Manufacturing costs are assigned the same way in a job order and in a process cost system.

3. **(LO 2)** In a process cost system, the flow of costs is:
   a. work in process, cost of goods sold, finished goods.
   b. finished goods, work in process, cost of goods sold.
   c. finished goods, cost of goods sold, work in process.
   d. work in process, finished goods, cost of goods sold.

4. **(LO 2)** In making journal entries to assign direct materials costs, a company using process costing:
   a. debits Finished Goods Inventory.
   b. often debits two or more work in process inventory accounts.

   c. generally credits two or more work in process inventory accounts.
   d. credits Finished Goods Inventory.

5. **(LO 2)** In a process cost system, manufacturing overhead:
   a. is assigned to finished goods at the end of each accounting period.
   b. is assigned to a work in process inventory account for each job as the job is completed.
   c. is assigned to a work in process inventory account for each production department on the basis of a predetermined overhead rate.
   d. is assigned to a work in process inventory account for each production department as overhead costs are incurred.

6. **(LO 3)** Conversion costs are the sum of:
   a. fixed and variable overhead costs.
   b. direct labor costs and overhead costs.
   c. direct material costs and overhead costs.
   d. direct labor and indirect labor costs.

7. **(LO 3)** The Mixing Department's production efforts during the period resulted in 20,000 units completed and transferred out, and 5,000 units in ending work in process 60% complete as to materials and conversion costs. Beginning inventory is 1,000 units, 40% complete as to materials and conversion costs. The equivalent units of production for materials are:
   a. 22,600.              c. 24,000.
   b. 23,000.              d. 25,000.

**8. (LO 3)** In RYZ Company, there are zero units in beginning work in process, 7,000 units started into production, and 500 units in ending work in process 20% completed. The physical units to be accounted for are:

**a.** 7,000.

**c.** 7,500.

**b.** 7,360.

**d.** 7,340.

**9. (LO 3)** Mora Company has 2,000 units in beginning work in process, 20% complete as to conversion costs, 23,000 units completed and transferred out to finished goods, and 3,000 units in ending work in process $33\frac{1}{3}$ % complete as to conversion costs.

The beginning inventory and ending inventory are fully complete as to materials costs. Equivalent units for materials and conversion costs are, respectively:

**a.** 22,000, 24,000.

**c.** 26,000, 24,000.

**b.** 24,000, 26,000.

**d.** 26,000, 26,000.

**10. (LO 4)** Fortner Company has no beginning work in process; 9,000 units are completed and transferred out, and 3,000 units in ending work in process are one-third finished as to conversion costs and fully complete as to materials cost. If total materials cost is $60,000, the unit materials cost is:

**a.** $5.00.

**b.** $5.45 rounded.

**c.** $6.00.

**d.** No correct answer is given.

**11. (LO 4)** Largo Company has unit costs of $10 for materials and $30 for conversion costs. If there are 2,500 units in ending work in process, 40% complete as to conversion costs and fully complete as to materials cost, the total cost assignable to the ending work in process inventory is:

**a.** $45,000.

**c.** $75,000.

**b.** $55,000.

**d.** $100,000.

**12. (LO 4)** A production cost report:

**a.** is an external report.

**b.** shows both the production quantity and cost data related to a department.

**c.** shows equivalent units of production but not physical units.

**d.** contains six sections.

**13. (LO 4)** In a production cost report, units to be accounted for are calculated as:

**a.** Units started into production + Units in ending work in process.

**b.** Units started into production − Units in beginning work in process.

**c.** Units completed and transferred out + Units in beginning work in process.

**d.** Units started into production + Units in beginning work in process.

***14. (LO 5)** Hollins Company uses the FIFO method to compute equivalent units. It has 2,000 units in beginning work in process, 20% complete as to conversion costs, 25,000 units started and completed, and 3,000 units in ending work in process, 30% complete as to conversion costs. All units are 100% complete as to materials. Equivalent units for materials and conversion costs are, respectively:

**a.** 28,000 and 26,600.

**b.** 28,000 and 27,500.

**c.** 27,000 and 26,200.

**d.** 27,000 and 29,600.

***15. (LO 5)** KLM Company uses the FIFO method to compute equivalent units. It has no beginning work in process; 9,000 units are started and completed and 3,000 units in ending work in process are one-third completed as to conversion costs. All material is added at the beginning of the process. If total materials cost is $60,000, the unit materials cost is:

**a.** $5.00.

**b.** $6.00.

**c.** $6.67 (rounded).

**d.** No correct answer is given.

***16. (LO 5)** Toney Company uses the FIFO method to compute equivalent units of production. It has unit costs of $10 for materials and $30 for conversion costs. If there are 2,500 units in ending work in process, 100% complete as to materials and 40% complete as to conversion costs, the total cost assignable to the ending work in process inventory is:

**a.** $45,000.

**c.** $75,000.

**b.** $55,000.

**d.** $100,000.

## Solutions

**1. b.** The products produced are homogeneous, not heterogeneous, in nature. Choices (a), (c), and (d) are incorrect because they all represent characteristics of a process cost system.

**2. d.** Manufacturing costs are not assigned the same way in a job order and in a process cost system. Choices (a), (b), and (c) are true statements.

**3. d.** In a process cost system, the flow of costs is work in process, finished goods, cost of goods sold. Therefore, choices (a), (b), and (c) are incorrect.

**4. b.** The debit is often to two or more work in process inventory accounts, not (a) a debit to Finished Goods Inventory, (c) credits to two or more work in process inventory accounts, or (d) a credit to Finished Goods Inventory.

**5. c.** In a process cost system, manufacturing overhead is assigned to a work in process inventory account for each production department on the basis of a predetermined overhead rate, not (a) to a finished goods account, (b) as the job is completed, or (d) as overhead costs are incurred.

**6. b.** Conversion costs are the sum of labor costs and overhead costs, not the sum of (a) fixed and variable overhead costs, (c) direct material costs and overhead costs, or (d) direct labor and indirect labor costs.

**7. b.** For materials, the equivalent units of production is the sum of units completed and transferred out (20,000) and the equivalent units of ending work in process inventory (5,000 units × 60%), or 20,000 + 3,000 = 23,000 units, not (a) 22,600 units, (c) 24,000 units, or (d) 25,000 units.

**8. a.** There are 7,000 physical units to be accounted for (0 units in beginning inventory + 7,000 units started), not (b) 7,360, (c) 7,500, or (d) 7,340.

**9. c.** The equivalent units for materials are 26,000 (23,000 units completed and transferred out plus 3,000 in ending work in process inventory). The equivalent units for conversion costs are 24,000 (23,000 completed and transferred out plus $33\frac{1}{3}$% of the ending work in process inventory, or 1,000). Therefore, choices (a) 22,000, 24,000; (b) 24,000, 26,000; and (d) 26,000, 26,000 are incorrect.

**10. a.** $60,000 ÷ (9,000 + 3,000 units) = $5.00 per unit, not (b) $5.45 (rounded), (c) $6.00, or (d) no correct answer is given.

**11. b.** [(2,500 units × 100% complete) × $10] + [(2,500 units × 40% complete) × $30], or $25,000 + $30,000 = $55,000, not (a) $45,000, (c) $75,000, or (d) $100,000.

**12. b.** A production cost report shows the flow of units and costs assigned to a department and costs accounted for as well as the production quantity. The other choices are incorrect because a production cost report (a) is an internal, not external, report; (c) does show physical units; and (d) is prepared in four steps and does not contain six sections.

**13. d.** In a production cost report, units to be accounted for are calculated as Units started in production + Units in beginning work in process, not (a) Units in ending work in process, (b) minus Units in beginning work in process, or (c) Units completed and transferred out.

**\*14. b.** The equivalent units for materials are 28,000 [25,000 started and completed + (3,000 × 100%)]. The equivalent units for conversion costs are 27,500 [(2,000 × 80%) + 25,000 + (3,000 × 30%)]. Therefore, choices (a) 28,000, 26,600; (c) 27,000, 26,200; and (d) 27,000, 29,600 are incorrect.

**\*15. a.** Unit materials cost is $5.00 [$60,000 ÷ (9,000 + 3,000)]. Therefore, choices (b) $6.00, (c) $6.67 (rounded), and (d) no correct answer are incorrect.

**\*16. b.** The total cost assignable to the ending work in process is $55,000 [($10 × 2,500) + ($30 × 2,500 × 40%)]. Therefore, choices (a) $45,000, (c) $75,000, and (d) $100,000 are incorrect.

## Practice Brief Exercises

*Journalize the assignment of materials.*

**1. (LO 2)** Jeremiah Industries purchased $70,000 of raw materials on account. Supporting records show that the Assembly Department used $43,000 of the raw materials and the Finishing Department used the remainder. Prepare the journal entries relating to raw materials.

### Solution

| 1. Raw Materials Inventory | 70,000 | |
|---|---|---|
| Accounts Payable | | 70,000 |
| Work in Process—Assembly Department | 43,000 | |
| Work in Process—Finishing Department | 27,000 | |
| Raw Materials Inventory | | 70,000 |

*Compute equivalent units of production.*

**2. (LO 3)** The Cooking Department of Caleb Foods has the following production data for October: beginning work in process 3,000 units that are 100% complete as to materials and 30% complete as to conversion costs; units completed and transferred out 10,000 units; and ending work in process 6,000 units that are 100% complete as to materials and 60% complete as to conversion costs. Compute the equivalent units of production for (a) materials and (b) conversion costs for the month of October.

### Solution

| 2. | (a) Materials | (b) Conversion Costs |
|---|---|---|
| Units completed and transferred out | 10,000 | 10,000 |
| Work in process, November 30 | | |
| Materials (6,000 × 100%) | 6,000 | |
| Conversion costs (6,000 × 60%) | | 3,600 |
| Total equivalent units | 16,000 | 13,600 |

**3. (LO 4)** Smith Company has the following production data for April: units completed and transferred out 50,000, and ending work in process 8,000 units that are 100% complete for materials and 30% complete for conversion costs. If unit materials cost is $3 and unit conversion cost is $8, determine the costs to be assigned to the units completed and transferred out and the units in ending work in process.

*Compute costs to units completed and transferred out and to work in process.*

### Solution

| 3. | Assignment of Costs | Equivalent Units | Unit Cost | | |
|---|---|---|---|---|---|
| | Completed and transferred out | | | | |
| | Completed and transferred out | 50,000 | $11* | | $550,000 |
| | Work in process, 4/30 | | | | |
| | Materials | 8,000 | 3 | $24,000 | |
| | Conversion costs | 2,400** | 8 | 19,200 | 43,200 |
| | Total costs | | | | $593,200 |

\* $3 + $8; ** 8,000 × 30%

**4. (LO 4)** Production costs chargeable to the Finishing Department in July in Lethbridge-Stewart Manufacturing are materials $60,000, labor $29,500, and overhead $11,000. Equivalent units of production are materials 30,000 and conversion costs 27,000. Production records indicate that 25,000 units were completed and transferred out, and 5,000 units in ending work in process were 40% complete as to conversion costs and 100% complete as to materials.

   **a.** Compute the unit costs for materials and conversion costs.

   **b.** Prepare the "costs accounted for" section of a cost reconciliation schedule.

*Prepare unit costs and cost reconciliation schedule.*

### Solution

**4. a.**

| Total materials costs | ÷ | Equivalent units of materials | = | Unit materials cost |
|---|---|---|---|---|
| $60,000 | | 30,000 | | $2.00 |

| Total conversion costs* | ÷ | Equivalent units of conversion costs | = | Unit conversion cost |
|---|---|---|---|---|
| $40,500 | | 27,000 | | $1.50 |

*$29,500 + $11,000

**b.** Costs accounted for:

| | | |
|---|---|---|
| Completed and transferred out (25,000 × $3.50*) | | $ 87,500 |
| Work in process | | |
| Materials (5,000 × $2.00) | $10,000 | |
| Conversion costs (2,000** × $1.50) | 3,000 | 13,000 |
| Total costs accounted for | | $100,500 |

*$2.00 + $1.50; **5,000 × 40%

## Practice Exercises

**1. (LO 2)** Armando Company manufactures pizza sauce through two production departments: Cooking and Canning. In each process, materials and conversion costs are incurred evenly throughout the process. For the month of April, the work in process inventory accounts show the following debits.

*Journalize transactions.*

| | Cooking | Canning |
|---|---|---|
| Beginning work in process | $ -0- | $ 4,000 |
| Direct materials | 25,000 | 8,000 |
| Direct labor | 8,500 | 7,500 |
| Manufacturing overhead | 29,000 | 25,800 |
| Costs transferred in | | 55,000 |

### Instructions

Journalize the April transactions, using April 30 as the date.

**Solution**

1.

| | | | | |
|---|---|---|---|---|
| April 30 | Work in Process—Cooking | | 25,000 | |
| | Work in Process—Canning | | 8,000 | |
| |    Raw Materials Inventory | | | 33,000 |
| 30 | Work in Process—Cooking | | 8,500 | |
| | Work in Process—Canning | | 7,500 | |
| |    Factory Labor | | | 16,000 |
| 30 | Work in Process—Cooking | | 29,000 | |
| | Work in Process—Canning | | 25,800 | |
| |    Manufacturing Overhead | | | 54,800 |
| 30 | Work in Process—Canning | | 55,000 | |
| |    Work in Process—Cooking | | | 55,000 |

*Prepare a production cost report.*

2. **(LO 3, 4)** The Sanding Department of Jo Furniture Company has the following production and manufacturing cost data for March 2022, the first month of operation.

    Production: 15,000 units started in period; 11,000 units completed and transferred out; 4,000 units in ending work in process that are 100% complete as to materials and 25% complete as to conversion costs.

    Manufacturing costs: Materials $48,000; labor $42,000; and overhead $36,000.

**Instructions**

Prepare a production cost report for March 2022. All direct materials are added at the beginning of the process, and conversion costs are incurred uniformly throughout the process.

**Solution**

2.

**Jo Furniture Company**
**Sanding Department**
**Production Cost Report**
**For the Month Ended March 31, 2022**

| | | Equivalent Units | |
|---|---|---|---|
| **Quantities** | **Physical Units** | **Materials** | **Conversion Costs** |
| Units to be accounted for | | | |
|   Work in process, March 1 | 0 | | |
|   Started into production | 15,000 | | |
| Total units to be accounted for | 15,000 | | |
| Units accounted for | | | |
|   Completed and transferred out | 11,000 | 11,000 | 11,000 |
|   Work in process, March 31 | 4,000 | 4,000 | 1,000 (4,000 × 25%) |
| Total units accounted for | 15,000 | 15,000 | 12,000 |

| **Costs** | **Materials** | **Conversion Costs** | **Total** |
|---|---|---|---|
| Unit costs | | | |
|   Total cost | $48,000 | $78,000* | $126,000 |
|   Equivalent units | 15,000 | 12,000 | |
|   Unit costs | $3.20 | $6.50 | $9.70 |

(continues)

*(continued)*

**Cost Reconciliation Schedule**

Costs to be accounted for

| | | |
|---|---|---|
| Work in process, March 1 | | $ 0 |
| Started into production | | 126,000 |
| Total costs to be accounted for | | $126,000 |

Costs accounted for

| | | |
|---|---|---|
| Completed and transferred out (11,000 × $9.70) | | $106,700 |
| Work in process, March 31 | | |
| Materials (4,000 × $3.20) | $12,800 | |
| Conversion costs (1,000 × $6.50) | 6,500 | 19,300 |
| Total costs accounted for | | $126,000 |

*$42,000 + $36,000

---

# Practice Problem

**(LO 3, 4)**   Karlene Industries produces plastic ice cube trays in two processes: heating and stamping. All materials are added at the beginning of the Heating Department process, and conversion costs are incurred uniformly throughout the process. Karlene uses the weighted-average method to compute equivalent units of production.

On November 1, the Heating Department had in process 1,000 trays that were 70% complete. During November, it started into production 12,000 trays. On November 30, 2022, 2,000 trays that were 60% complete as to conversion costs were in process.

The following cost information for the Heating Department was also available.

*Prepare a production cost report and journalize.*

| Work in process, November 1: | | Costs incurred in November: | |
|---|---|---|---|
| Materials | $ 640 | Direct materials | $3,000 |
| Conversion costs | 360 | Direct labor | 2,300 |
| Cost of work in process, Nov. 1 | $1,000 | Manufacturing overhead | 4,050 |

## Instructions

a. Prepare a production cost report for the Heating Department for the month of November 2022, using the weighted-average method.

b. Journalize the transfer of costs from the Heating Department to the Stamping Department.

## Solution

a.

**Karlene Industries**
**Heating Department**
**Production Cost Report**
**For the Month Ended November 30, 2022**

| | | Equivalent Units | |
|---|---|---|---|
| | Physical Units | Materials | Conversion Costs |
| **Quantities** | Step 1 | Step 2 | |
| Units to be accounted for | | | |
| Work in process, November 1 | 1,000 | | |
| Started into production | 12,000 | | |
| Total units to be accounted for | 13,000 | | |
| Units accounted for | | | |
| Completed and transferred out | 11,000* | 11,000 | 11,000 |
| Work in process, November 30 | 2,000 | 2,000 | 1,200** |
| Total units accounted for | 13,000 | 13,000 | 12,200 |

*13,000 − 2,000; **2,000 × 60%

*(continues)*

*(continued)*

| Costs | | | Conversion | |
|---|---|---|---|---|
| **Unit costs** Step 3 | | **Materials** | **Costs** | **Total** |
| Total cost | (a) | $ 3,640* | $ 6,710** | $10,350 |
| Equivalent units | (b) | 13,000 | 12,200 | |
| Unit costs [(a) ÷ (b)] | | $0.28 | $0.55 | $0.83 |

**Cost Reconciliation Schedule** Step 4

| | | | |
|---|---|---|---|
| Costs to be accounted for | | | |
|   Work in process, November 1 | | | $ 1,000 |
|   Started into production | | | 9,350*** |
| Total costs to be accounted for | | | $10,350 |
| Costs accounted for | | | |
|   Completed and transferred out | | | |
|     (11,000 × $0.83) | | | $ 9,130 |
|   Work in process, November 30 | | | |
|     Materials (2,000 × $0.28) | | $560 | |
|     Conversion costs (1,200 × $0.55) | | 660 | 1,220 |
| Total costs accounted for | | | $10,350 |

  \*$640 + $3,000
 \*\*$360 + $2,300 + $4,050
\*\*\*$3,000 + $2,300 + $4,050

| | | | |
|---|---|---|---|
| **b.** Work in Process—Stamping | | 9,130 | |
|     Work in Process—Heating | | | 9,130 |
|       (To record transfer of units to the Stamping | | | |
|       Department) | | | |

Brief Exercises, DO IT! Exercises, Exercises, Problems, Data Analytics Activities, and many additional resources are available for practice in WileyPLUS.

*Note:* All asterisked Questions, Exercises, and Problems relate to material in the appendix to this chapter.

## Questions

1. Identify which costing system—job order or process cost—the following companies would primarily use: (a) **Quaker Oats**, (b) **Jif Peanut Butter**, (c) **Gulf Craft** (luxury yachts), and (d) **Warner Bros. Motion Pictures**.

2. Contrast the primary focus of job order cost accounting and of process cost accounting.

3. What are the similarities between a job order and a process cost system?

4. Your roommate is confused about the features of process cost accounting. Identify and explain the distinctive features for your roommate.

5. Sam Bowyer believes there are no significant differences in the flow of costs between job order cost accounting and process cost accounting. Is Sam correct? Explain.

6. **a.** What source documents are used in assigning (1) materials and (2) labor to production in a process cost system?

  **b.** What criterion and basis are commonly used in assigning overhead to processes?

7. At Ely Company, overhead is assigned to production departments at the rate of $5 per machine hour. In July, machine hours were 3,000 in the Machining Department and 2,400 in the Assembly Department. Prepare the entry to assign overhead to production.

8. Mark Haley is uncertain about the steps used to prepare a production cost report. State the procedures that are required in the sequence in which they are performed.

9. John Harbeck is confused about computing physical units. Explain to John how physical units to be accounted for and physical units accounted for are determined.

10. What is meant by the term "equivalent units of production"?

11. How are equivalent units of production computed?

12. Coats Company had zero units of beginning work in process. During the period, 9,000 units were completed and transferred out, and there were 600 units of ending work in process. How many units were started into production?

13. Sanchez Co. has zero units of beginning work in process. During the period, 12,000 units were completed and transferred out, and there were 500 units of ending work in process one-fifth complete as to conversion cost and 100% complete as to materials cost. What were the equivalent units of production for (a) materials and (b) conversion costs?

14. Hindi Co. started 3,000 units during the period. Its beginning inventory is 500 units one-fourth complete as to conversion costs and 100% complete as to materials costs. Its ending inventory is 300 units one-fifth complete as to conversion costs and 100% complete as to materials costs. How many units were completed and transferred out this period?

15. Clauss Company completes and transfers out 14,000 units and has 2,000 units of ending work in process that are 25% complete as to conversion costs. Materials are entered at the beginning of the process, and there is no beginning work in process. Assuming unit materials costs of $3 and unit conversion costs of $5, what are the costs to be assigned to units (a) completed and transferred out and (b) in ending work in process?

16. **a.** Ann Quinn believes the production cost report is an external report for stockholders. Is Ann correct? Explain.

**b.** Identify the sections in a production cost report.

17. What purposes are served by a production cost report?

18. At Trent Company, there are 800 units of ending work in process that are 100% complete as to materials and 40% complete as to conversion costs. If the unit cost of materials is $3 and the total costs assigned to the 800 units is $6,000, what is the per unit conversion cost?

19. What is the difference between operations costing and a process cost system?

20. How does a company decide whether to use a job order or a process cost system?

*21. Soria Co. started and completed 2,000 units for the period. Its beginning inventory is 800 units 25% complete and its ending inventory is 400 units 20% complete. Soria uses the FIFO method to compute equivalent units. How many units were completed and transferred out this period?

*22. Reyes Company completes and transfers out 12,000 units and has 2,000 units of ending work in process that are 25% complete as to conversion costs. Materials are entered at the beginning of the process, and there is no beginning work in process. Reyes uses the FIFO method to compute equivalent units. Assuming unit materials costs of $3 and unit conversion costs of $7, what are the costs to be assigned to units (a) completed and transferred out and (b) in ending work in process?

## Brief Exercises

**BE16.1 (LO 2), AP** Warner Company purchases $50,000 of raw materials on account, and it incurs $60,000 of factory labor costs. Journalize the two transactions on March 31, assuming the labor costs are not paid until April.

*Journalize entries for accumulating costs.*

**BE16.2 (LO 2), AP** Data for Warner Company are given in BE16.1. Supporting records show that (a) the Assembly Department used $24,000 of direct materials and $35,000 of direct labor, and (b) the Finishing Department used the remainder. Journalize the assignment of the costs to the processing departments on March 31.

*Journalize the assignment of materials and labor costs.*

**BE16.3 (LO 2), AP** Direct labor data for Warner Company are given in BE16.2. Manufacturing overhead is assigned to departments on the basis of 160% of direct labor costs. Journalize the assignment of overhead to the Assembly and Finishing Departments.

*Journalize the assignment of overhead costs.*

**BE16.4 (LO 3), AP** Goode Company has the following production data for selected months.

*Compute equivalent units of production.*

| Month | Beginning Work in Process | Units Completed and Transferred Out | Ending Work in Process Units | % Complete as to Conversion Cost |
|---|---|---|---|---|
| January | –0– | 35,000 | 10,000 | 40% |
| March | –0– | 40,000 | 8,000 | 75 |
| July | –0– | 45,000 | 16,000 | 25 |

Compute equivalent units of production for materials and conversion costs, assuming that materials are entered at the beginning of the process and that conversion costs are incurred uniformly throughout the process.

**BE16.5 (LO 3), AP** The Smelting Department of Kiner Company has the following production data for November.

*Compute equivalent units of production.*

Beginning work in process 2,000 units that are 100% complete as to materials and 20% complete as to conversion costs; units completed and transferred out 9,000 units; and ending work in process 7,000 units that are 100% complete as to materials and 40% complete as to conversion costs.

Compute the equivalent units of production for (a) materials and (b) conversion costs for the month of November.

**BE16.6 (LO 4), AP** In Mordica Company, total materials costs are $33,000, and total conversion costs are $54,000 for June. Equivalent units of production are materials 10,000 and conversion costs 12,000. Compute the unit costs for materials, conversion costs, and total manufacturing costs.

*Compute unit costs of production.*

**BE16.7 (LO 4), AP** Trek Company has the following production data for April: units completed and transferred out 40,000, and ending work in process 5,000 units that are 100% complete for materials and 40% complete for conversion costs. If unit materials cost is $4 and unit conversion cost is $7, determine the costs to be assigned to the units completed and transferred out and the units in ending work in process.

*Assign costs to units completed and transferred out and to work in process.*

*Compute unit costs.*

**BE16.8 (LO 4), AP** Production costs of the Finishing Department in June in Hollins Company are materials $12,000, labor $29,500, and overhead $18,000. Equivalent units of production are materials 20,000 and conversion costs 19,000. Compute the unit costs for materials and conversion costs for June.

*Prepare cost reconciliation schedule.*

**BE16.9 (LO 4), AP** Data for Hollins Company are given in BE16.8. Production records indicate that 18,000 units were completed and transferred out, and 2,000 units in ending work in process were 50% complete as to conversion costs and 100% complete as to materials. Prepare the "costs accounted for" section of a cost reconciliation schedule.

*Assign costs to units completed and transferred out and to work in process.*

**\*BE16.10 (LO 5), AP** Pix Company has the following production data for March 2022: no beginning work in process, units started and completed 30,000, and ending work in process 5,000 units that are 100% complete for materials and 40% complete for conversion costs. Pix uses the FIFO method to compute equivalent units. If unit materials cost is $6 and unit conversion cost is $10, determine the costs to be assigned to the units completed and transferred out and the units in ending work in process. The total costs to be assigned are $530,000.

*Prepare a partial production cost report using the FIFO method.*

**\*BE16.11 (LO 5), AP** Using the data in BE16.10, prepare the "costs accounted for" section of the production cost report for Pix Company using the FIFO method.

# DO IT! Exercises

*Compare job order and process cost systems.*

**DO IT! 16.1 (LO 1), C** Indicate whether each of the following statements is true or false.

1. Many hospitals use job order costing for small, routine medical procedures.
2. A manufacturer of computer flash drives would use a job order cost system.
3. A process cost system uses multiple work in process inventory accounts.
4. A process cost system keeps track of costs on job cost sheets.

*Assign and journalize manufacturing costs.*

**DO IT! 16.2 (LO 2), AP** Kopa Company manufactures CH-21 through two processes: mixing and packaging. In July, the following costs were assigned.

|  | Mixing | Packaging |
|---|---|---|
| Direct materials used | $10,000 | $28,000 |
| Direct labor costs | 8,000 | 36,000 |
| Manufacturing overhead costs | 12,000 | 54,000 |

Units completed at a cost of $21,000 in the Mixing Department are transferred to the Packaging Department. Units completed at a cost of $106,000 in the Packaging Department are transferred to Finished Goods. Journalize the assignment of these costs to the two processes and the transfer of units as appropriate.

*Compute equivalent units.*

**DO IT! 16.3 (LO 3), AP** The Assembly Department for Right Pens has the following production data for the current month.

| Beginning Work in Process | Units Completed and Transferred Out | Ending Work in Process |
|---|---|---|
| –0– | 20,000 | 10,000 |

Materials are entered at the beginning of the process. The ending work in process units are 70% complete as to conversion costs. Compute the equivalent units of production for (a) materials and (b) conversion costs.

*Prepare cost reconciliation schedule.*

**DO IT! 16.4 (LO 4), AP** In March, Kelly Company had the following unit production costs: materials $10 and conversion costs $8. On March 1, it had no work in process. During March, Kelly completed and transferred out 22,000 units. As of March 31, 4,000 units that were 40% complete as to conversion costs and 100% complete as to materials were in ending work in process.

a. Compute the total units to be accounted for.
b. Compute the equivalent units of production for materials and conversion costs.
c. Prepare a cost reconciliation schedule, including the costs of units completed and transferred out and the costs of units in work in process, for March 2022.

# Exercises

**E16.1 (LO 1), C** Robert Wilkins has prepared the following list of statements about process cost accounting.   *Understand process cost accounting.*

1. Process cost systems are used to apply costs to similar products that are mass-produced in a continuous fashion.

2. A process cost system is used when each finished unit is indistinguishable from another.

3. Companies that produce soft drinks, movies, and computer chips would all use process cost accounting.

4. In a process cost system, costs are tracked by individual jobs.

5. Job order costing and process costing track different manufacturing cost components.

6. Both job order costing and process costing account for direct materials, direct labor, and manufacturing overhead.

7. Costs flow through the accounts in the same basic way for both job order costing and process costing.

8. In a process cost system, only one work in process inventory account is used.

9. In a process cost system, costs are summarized in a job cost sheet.

10. In a process cost system, the unit cost is the sum of materials costs and conversion costs, each divided by their respective equivalent units.

## Instructions

Identify each statement as true or false. If false, indicate how to correct the statement.

**E16.2 (LO 2), AP** Harrelson Company manufactures pizza sauce through two production departments:   *Journalize transactions.*
Cooking and Canning. In each process, materials and conversion costs are incurred evenly throughout
the process. For the month of April, the work in process inventory accounts show the following debits.

|  | Cooking | Canning |
|---|---|---|
| Beginning work in process | $ –0– | $ 4,000 |
| Direct materials | 21,000 | 9,000 |
| Direct labor | 8,500 | 7,000 |
| Manufacturing overhead | 31,500 | 25,800 |
| Costs transferred in |  | 53,000 |

## Instructions

Journalize the April transactions, using April 30 as the date.

**E16.3 (LO 2, 3, 4), AP** The ledger of American Company has the following work in process inventory   *Answer questions on costs and production.*
account.

**Work in Process—Painting**

| 5/1 | Balance | 3,590 | 5/31 | Completed and transferred out | ? |
|---|---|---|---|---|---|
| 5/31 | Direct materials | 5,160 | | | |
| 5/31 | Direct labor | 2,530 | | | |
| 5/31 | Manufacturing overhead | 1,380 | | | |
| 5/31 | Balance | ? | | | |

Production records show that there were 400 units in the beginning inventory, 30% complete, 1,600 units
started into production, and 1,700 units completed and transferred out. The beginning work in process
had materials cost of $2,040 and conversion costs of $1,550. The units in ending inventory were 40%
complete as to conversion costs. Materials are entered at the beginning of the painting process, and conversion costs are incurred uniformly throughout the process.

## Instructions

a. How many units are in process at May 31?

b. What is the unit materials cost for May?

c. What is the unit conversion cost for May?

d. What is the total cost of units completed and transferred out in May?

e. What is the cost of the May 31 work in process inventory?

*Journalize transactions for two processes.*

**E16.4 (LO 2), AP** Schrager Company has two production departments: Cutting and Assembly. July 1 inventories are Raw Materials $4,200, Work in Process—Cutting $2,900, Work in Process—Assembly $10,600, and Finished Goods $31,000. During July, the following transactions occurred.

1. Purchased $62,500 of raw materials on account.

2. Incurred $60,000 of factory labor. (Credit Wages Payable.)

3. Incurred $70,000 of manufacturing overhead; $40,000 was paid and the remainder is unpaid.

4. Requisitioned materials for Cutting $15,700 and Assembly $8,900.

5. Used factory labor for Cutting $33,000 and Assembly $27,000.

6. Applied overhead at the rate of $18 per machine hour. Machine hours were Cutting 1,680 and Assembly 1,720.

7. Transferred goods costing $67,600 from the Cutting Department to the Assembly Department.

8. Completed and transferred goods costing $134,900 from Assembly to Finished Goods Inventory.

9. Sold goods costing $150,000 for $200,000 on account.

**Instructions**

Journalize the transactions. (Omit explanations and dates.)

*Compute physical units and equivalent units of production.*

**E16.5 (LO 3, 4), AP** In Shady Company, materials are entered at the beginning of each process, and conversion costs are incurred uniformly throughout the process. Work in process inventories, with the percentage of work done on conversion costs, and production data for its Sterilizing Department in selected months during 2022 are as follows.

| | Beginning Work in Process | | Units Completed and | Ending Work in Process | |
|---|---|---|---|---|---|
| Month | Units | Conversion Cost% | Transferred Out | Units | Conversion Cost% |
| January | –0– | — | 11,000 | 2,000 | 60 |
| March | –0– | — | 12,000 | 3,000 | 30 |
| May | –0– | — | 14,000 | 7,000 | 80 |
| July | –0– | — | 10,000 | 1,500 | 40 |

**Instructions**

a. For January and May, compute the physical units to be accounted for and the physical units accounted for.

b. Compute the equivalent units of production for (1) materials and (2) conversion costs for each month.

*Determine equivalent units, unit costs, and assignment of costs.*

**E16.6 (LO 3, 4), AP** The Cutting Department of Cassel Company has the following production and cost data for July.

| Production | Costs | |
|---|---|---|
| 1. Completed and transferred out 12,000 units. | Beginning work in process | $  –0– |
| 2. 3,000 units in ending working in process are 60% complete as to conversion costs and 100% complete as to materials at July 31. | Direct materials | 45,000 |
| | Direct labor | 16,200 |
| | Manufacturing overhead | 18,300 |

Materials are entered at the beginning of the process. Conversion costs are incurred uniformly throughout the process.

**Instructions**

a. Determine the equivalent units of production for (1) materials and (2) conversion costs.

b. Compute unit costs and prepare a cost reconciliation schedule.

*Prepare a production cost report.*

**E16.7 (LO 3, 4), AP** The Sanding Department of Quik Furniture Company has the following production and manufacturing cost data for March 2022, the first month of operation.

*Production:* 7,000 units completed and transferred out; 3,000 units in ending work in process are 100% complete as to materials and 20% complete as to conversion costs.

*Manufacturing costs:* Materials $33,000; labor $21,000; and overhead $36,000.

## Instructions

Prepare a production cost report.

**E16.8 (LO 3, 4), AP** The Blending Department of Luongo Company has the following cost and production data for the month of April.

*Determine equivalent units, unit costs, and assignment of costs.*

Costs:

Work in process, April 1

| | |
|---|---|
| Direct materials: 100% complete | $100,000 |
| Conversion costs: 20% complete | 70,000 |
| Cost of work in process, April 1 | $170,000 |

Costs incurred during production in April

| | |
|---|---|
| Direct materials | $ 800,000 |
| Conversion costs | 365,000 |
| Costs incurred in April | $1,165,000 |

Units completed and transferred out totaled 17,000. Ending work in process was 1,000 units that are 100% complete as to materials and 40% complete as to conversion costs.

### Instructions

a. Compute the equivalent units of production for (1) materials and (2) conversion costs for the month of April.

b. Compute the unit costs for the month.

c. Determine the costs to be assigned to the units completed and transferred out and in ending work in process.

**E16.9 (LO 3, 4), AP** Baden Company has gathered the following information.

*Determine equivalent units, unit costs, and assignment of costs.*

| | |
|---|---|
| Units in beginning work in process | –0– |
| Units started into production | 36,000 |
| Units in ending work in process | 6,000 |
| Percent complete in ending work in process: | |
| Conversion costs | 40% |
| Materials | 100% |
| Costs incurred: | |
| Direct materials | $72,000 |
| Direct labor | $61,000 |
| Overhead | $101,000 |

### Instructions

a. Compute equivalent units of production for materials and for conversion costs.

b. Determine the unit costs of production.

c. Show the assignment of costs to units completed and transferred out and to work in process at the end of the period.

**E16.10 (LO 3, 4), AP** Overton Company has gathered the following information. All materials are added at the beginning of the process, and conversion costs are incurred uniformly throughout the process.

*Determine equivalent units, unit costs, and assignment of costs.*

| | |
|---|---|
| Units in beginning work in process | 20,000 |
| Units started into production | 164,000 |
| Units in ending work in process | 24,000 |
| Percent complete in ending work in process: | |
| Conversion costs | 60% |
| Materials | 100% |
| Cost of beginning work in process, plus costs incurred during the period: | |
| Direct materials | $101,200 |
| Direct labor | $164,800 |
| Overhead | $184,000 |

### Instructions

a. Compute equivalent units of production for materials and for conversion costs.

b. Determine the unit costs of production.

c. Show the assignment of costs to units completed and transferred out and to work in process at the end of the period.

*Compute equivalent units, unit costs, and costs assigned.*

**E16.11 (LO 3, 4), AP** The Polishing Department of Major Company has the following production and manufacturing cost data for September. All materials are added at the beginning of the process, and conversion costs are incurred uniformly throughout the process.

*Production:* Beginning inventory 1,600 units that are 100% complete as to materials and 30% complete as to conversion costs; units started during the period are 42,900; ending inventory of 5,000 units 10% complete as to conversion costs.

*Manufacturing costs:* Beginning inventory costs, comprised of $20,000 of materials and $43,180 of conversion costs; materials costs added in Polishing during the month, $175,800; labor and overhead applied in Polishing during the month, $125,680 and $257,140, respectively.

**Instructions**

a. Compute the equivalent units of production for materials and conversion costs for the month of September.

b. Compute the unit costs for materials and conversion costs for the month.

c. Determine the costs to be assigned to the units completed and transferred out and to work in process at the end of September.

*Explain the production cost report.*

**E16.12 (LO 4), S** Writing David Skaros has recently been promoted to production manager. He has just started to receive various managerial reports, including the production cost report that you prepared. It showed that his department had 2,000 equivalent units in ending inventory. His department has had a history of not keeping enough inventory on hand to meet demand. He has come to you, very angry, and wants to know why you credited him with only 2,000 units when he knows he had at least twice that many on hand.

**Instructions**

Explain to him why his production cost report showed only 2,000 equivalent units in ending inventory. Write an informal memo. Be kind and explain very clearly why he is mistaken.

*Prepare a production cost report.*

**E16.13 (LO 3, 4), AP** The Welding Department of Healthy Company has the following production and manufacturing cost data for February 2022. All materials are added at the beginning of the process.

| Manufacturing Costs | | | Production Data | |
|---|---|---|---|---|
| Beginning work in process | | | Beginning work in process | 15,000 units |
|    Materials | $18,000 | | Units completed and transferred out | 55,000 |
|    Conversion costs | 14,175 | $ 32,175 | Units started in production | 51,000 |
| Costs added during month | | | Ending work in process | 11,000 units |
|    Direct materials | | 180,000 | | |
|    Direct labor | | 67,380 | | |
|    Manufacturing overhead | | 61,445 | | |
| | | $341,000 | | |

**Instructions**

Beginning work in process and ending work in process were 10% and 20% complete with respect to conversion costs, respectively. Prepare a production cost report for the Welding Department for the month of February.

*Determine equivalent units, unit costs, and assignment of costs.*

**\*E16.14 (LO 5), AP** The Cutting Department of Lasso Company has the following production and cost data for August.

| Production | Costs | |
|---|---|---|
| 1. Started and completed 10,000 units. | Beginning work in process | $ –0– |
| 2. Started 2,000 units that are 40% | Costs added during month | |
|    complete at August 31. |    Direct materials | 45,000 |
| |    Direct labor | 13,600 |
| |    Manufacturing overhead | 16,100 |

Materials are entered at the beginning of the process. Conversion costs are incurred uniformly during the process. Lasso Company uses the FIFO method to compute equivalent units.

**Instructions**

a. Determine the equivalent units of production for (1) materials and (2) conversion costs.

b. Compute unit costs and prepare the cost reconciliation schedule at the end of August.

*E16.15 **(LO 5), AP** The Smelting Department of Polzin Company has the following production and cost data for September.

*Compute equivalent units, unit costs, and costs assigned.*

> *Production:* Beginning work in process 2,000 units that are 100% complete as to materials and 20% complete as to conversion costs; units started and completed 9,000 units; and ending work in process 1,000 units that are 100% complete as to materials and 40% complete as to conversion costs.

> *Manufacturing costs:* Work in process, September 1, $15,200; materials $60,000, conversion costs $132,000.

Polzin uses the FIFO method to compute equivalent units. All direct materials are added at the beginning of the process. Conversion costs are incurred uniformly throughout the process.

**Instructions**

a. Compute the equivalent units of production for (1) materials and (2) conversion costs for the month of September.

b. Compute the unit costs for the month.

c. Determine the costs to be assigned to the units completed and transferred out and to work in process units at the end of the month.

*E16.16 **(LO 5), AP** The ledger of Hasgrove Company has the following work in process inventory account.

*Answer questions on costs and production.*

**Work in Process—Painting**

| 3/1 | Balance | 3,680 | 3/31 | Completed and transferred out | ? |
| 3/31 | Direct materials | 6,600 | | | |
| 3/31 | Direct labor | 2,400 | | | |
| 3/31 | Manufacturing overhead | 1,150 | | | |
| 3/31 | Balance | ? | | | |

Production records show that there were 800 units in the beginning inventory, 30% complete, 1,100 units started, and 1,500 units completed and transferred out. The units in ending inventory were 40% complete. Materials are added at the beginning of the painting process, and conversion costs are incurred uniformly throughout the process. Hasgrove uses the FIFO method to compute equivalent units.

**Instructions**

Answer the following questions

a. How many units are in process at March 31?

b. What is the unit materials cost for March?

c. What is the unit conversion cost for March?

d. What is the total cost of units started in February and completed in March?

e. What is the total cost of units started and completed in March?

f. What is the cost of the March 31 ending inventory?

*E16.17 **(LO 5), AP** The Welding Department of Majestic Company has the following production and manufacturing cost data for February 2022. All materials are added at the beginning of the process, and conversion costs are incurred uniformly throughout the process. Majestic uses the FIFO method to compute equivalent units of production.

*Prepare a production cost report for a second process.*

| **Manufacturing Costs** | | **Production Data** | |
|---|---|---|---|
| Beginning work in process | $ 32,175 | Beginning work in process | 15,000 units |
| Costs added during month | | Units completed and transferred out | 54,000 |
| Direct materials | 192,000 | Units started in production | 64,000 |
| Direct labor | 35,100 | Ending work in process | 25,000 units |
| Manufacturing overhead | 68,400 | | |

**Instructions**

Beginning work in process and ending work in process were 10% and 20% complete with respect to conversion costs, respectively. Prepare a production cost report for the Welding Department for February 2022.

# Problems

*Journalize transactions.*

**P16.1 (LO 2), AP** Fire Out Company manufactures its product, Vitadrink, through two manufacturing processes: Mixing and Packaging. All materials are added at the beginning of each process, and conversion costs are incurred uniformly throughout the process. On October 1, 2022, inventories consisted of Raw Materials $26,000, Work in Process—Mixing $0, Work in Process—Packaging $250,000, and Finished Goods $289,000. The beginning inventory for Packaging consisted of 10,000 units that were 50% complete as to conversion costs and fully complete as to materials. During October, 50,000 units were started into production in the Mixing Department, and the following transactions were completed.

1. Purchased $300,000 of raw materials on account.
2. Issued direct materials for production: Mixing $210,000 and Packaging $45,000.
3. Incurred labor costs of $278,900. (Use Wages Payable.)
4. Used factory labor: Mixing $182,500 and Packaging $96,400.
5. Incurred $810,000 of manufacturing overhead on account.
6. Applied manufacturing overhead on the basis of $23 per machine hour. Machine hours were 28,000 in Mixing and 6,000 in Packaging.
7. Transferred 45,000 units from Mixing to Packaging at a cost of $979,000.
8. Completed and transferred 53,000 units from Packaging to Finished Goods at a cost of $1,315,000.
9. Sold goods costing $1,604,000 for $2,500,000 on account.

## Instructions

Journalize the October transactions.

*Complete four steps necessary to prepare a production cost report.*

**P16.2 (LO 3, 4), AP** Rosenthal Company manufactures bowling balls through two processes: Molding and Packaging. In the Molding Department, the urethane, rubber, plastics, and other materials are molded into bowling balls. In the Packaging Department, the balls are placed in cartons and sent to the finished goods warehouse. All materials are added at the beginning of each process. Labor and manufacturing overhead are incurred uniformly throughout each process. Production and cost data for the Molding Department during June 2022 are presented below.

| Production Data | June |
|---|---|
| Beginning work in process units | –0– |
| Units started into production | 22,000 |
| Ending work in process units | 2,000 |
| Percent complete as to conversion—ending inventory | 40% |

| Cost Data | |
|---|---|
| Direct materials used in June | $198,000 |
| Direct labor incurred in June | 53,600 |
| Manufacturing overhead assigned in June | 112,800 |
| Total | $364,400 |

## Instructions

a. Prepare a schedule showing physical units of production.

b. Determine the equivalent units of production for materials and conversion costs.

c. Compute the unit costs of production.

d. Determine the costs to be assigned to the units completed and transferred out and to work in process for June.

e. Prepare a production cost report for the Molding Department for the month of June.

c. Materials $9.00
CC $8.00
d. Completed and
transferred out $340,000
Ending WIP $ 24,400

*Complete four steps necessary to prepare a production cost report.*

**P16.3 (LO 3, 4), AP** Thakin Industries Inc. manufactures dorm furniture in separate processes. In each process, materials are added at the beginning, and conversion costs are incurred uniformly. Production and cost data for the first process in making a product are as follows.

|  | Cutting Department |
|---|---|
| **Production Data—July** | T12-Tables |
| Work in process units, July 1 | –0– |
| Units started into production | 20,000 |
| Work in process units, July 31 | 5,000 |
| Work in process percent complete as to conversion, July 31 | 60% |

| **Cost Data—July** | |
|---|---|
| Work in process, July 1 | $ –0– |
| Direct materials used in July | 380,000 |
| Direct labor incurred in July | 234,400 |
| Manufacturing overhead assigned in July | 104,000 |
| Total | $718,400 |

## Instructions

**a. 1.** Compute the physical units of production.

**2.** Compute equivalent units of production for materials and for conversion costs.

**3.** Determine the unit costs of production for July.

**4.** Show the assignment of costs to units completed and transferred out and to work in process for July.

**b.** Prepare the production cost report for July 2022.

*a. 3. Materials $19*
*CC $18*
*4. Completed and transferred out $629,000*
*Ending WIP $ 89,400*

**P16.4 (LO 3, 4), AP** Rivera Company has several processing departments. Costs to be accounted for in the Assembly Department for November 2022 totaled $2,280,000 as follows.

*Assign costs and prepare production cost report.*

| Work in process, November 1 | | |
|---|---|---|
| Materials | $79,000 | |
| Conversion costs | 48,150 | $ 127,150 |
| Direct materials added during November | | 1,589,000 |
| Direct labor incurred during November | | 225,920 |
| Manufacturing overhead assigned during November | | 337,930 |
| | | $2,280,000 |

Production records show that 35,000 units were in beginning work in process 30% complete as to conversion costs, 660,000 units were started into production, and 25,000 units were in ending work in process 40% complete as to conversion costs. Materials are added at the beginning of each process, and conversion costs are incurred uniformly throughout the process.

## Instructions

**a.** Determine the equivalent units of production and the unit production costs for the Assembly Department.

**b.** Determine the assignment of costs to goods completed and transferred out and to work in process for November.

**c.** Prepare a production cost report for the Assembly Department for November 2022.

*b. Completed and transferred out $2,211,000*
*Ending WIP $ 69,000*

**P16.5 (LO 3, 4), AP** Polk Company manufactures basketballs. The first step is the production of internal rubber bladders. Materials are added at the beginning of the production process, and conversion costs are incurred uniformly. Production and cost data for the Bladder Department for July 2022 are as follows.

*Determine equivalent units and unit costs and assign costs.*

| **Production Data—Basketballs** | Units | Percentage Complete |
|---|---|---|
| Work in process units, July 1 | 500 | 60% |
| Units started into production | 1,000 | |
| Work in process units, July 31 | 600 | 40% |

*(continued)*

*(continued)*

**Cost Data—Basketballs**

| | | |
|---|---|---|
| Work in process, July 1 | | |
| Materials | $750 | |
| Conversion costs | 600 | $1,350 |
| Costs added during July | | |
| Direct materials | | 2,400 |
| Direct labor | | 1,580 |
| Manufacturing overhead | | 1,240 |

### Instructions

a. Calculate the following.

1. The equivalent units of production for materials and conversion costs.

2. The unit costs of production for materials and conversion costs.

3. The assignment of costs to units completed and transferred out and to work in process at the end of the accounting period.

b. Prepare a production cost report for the month of July for the basketballs.

*a. 2. Materials           $2.10*
*3. Completed and*
*transferred out   $4,590*
*Ending WIP        $1,980*

*Compute equivalent units and complete production cost report.*

**P16.6 (LO 3, 4), AP** Hamilton Processing Company uses the weighted-average method and manufactures a single product—an industrial carpet shampoo used by many universities. The manufacturing activity for the month of October has just been completed. A partially completed production cost report for the month of October for the Mixing and Cooking Department is as follows. Beginning work in process is 100% complete for direct materials and 70% complete for conversion costs. Ending work in process is 60% complete for direct materials and 40% complete for conversion costs.

**Hamilton Processing Company**
**Mixing and Cooking Department**
**Production Cost Report**
**For the Month Ended October 31, 2022**

| | | Equivalent Units | |
|---|---|---|---|
| **Quantities** | **Physical Units** | **Materials** | **Conversion Costs** |
| Units to be accounted for | | | |
| Work in process, October 1 | | | |
| (100% materials, 70% conversion costs) | 20,000 | | |
| Started into production | 150,000 | | |
| Total units to be accounted for | 170,000 | | |
| Units accounted for | | | |
| Completed and transferred out | 120,000 | ? | ? |
| Work in process, October 31 | | | |
| (60% materials, 40% conversion costs) | 50,000 | ? | ? |
| Total units accounted for | 170,000 | ? | ? |

| **Costs** | | | |
|---|---|---|---|
| Unit costs | **Materials** | **Conversion Costs** | **Total** |
| Total cost | $240,000 | $105,000 | $345,000 |
| Equivalent units | ? | ? | |
| Unit costs | $   ? + | $   ? = | $   ? |

*(continues)*

(continued)

| Cost Reconciliation Schedule | Physical Units | Equivalent Units Materials | Conversion Costs | |
|---|---|---|---|---|
| Costs to be accounted for | | | | |
| Work in process, October 1 | | | | $ 30,000 |
| Started into production | | | | 315,000 |
| Total costs to be accounted for | | | | $345,000 |
| Costs accounted for | | | | |
| Completed and transferred out | | | | $ ? |
| Work in process, October 31 | | | | |
| Materials | | $ ? | | |
| Conversion costs | | ? | ? | |
| Total costs accounted for | | $ ? | | $ ? |

## Instructions

a. Prepare a schedule that shows how the equivalent units were computed so that you can complete the "Quantities: Units accounted for" equivalent units section shown in the production cost report, and compute October unit costs.

b. Complete the production cost report for October 2022.

a.  Materials          $1.60
b.  Completed and
      transferred out   $282,000
    Ending WIP          $ 63,000

*P16.7 (LO 5), AP Owen Company manufactures bicycles and tricycles. For both products, materials are added at the beginning of the production process, and conversion costs are incurred uniformly. Owen Company uses the FIFO method to compute equivalent units. Production and cost data for the Assembly Department for March are as follows.

*Determine equivalent units and unit costs and assign costs for processes; prepare production cost report.*

| Production Data—Bicycles | Units | Percentage Complete as to Conversion Costs |
|---|---|---|
| Work in process units, March 1 | 200 | 80% |
| Units started into production | 1,000 | |
| Work in process units, March 31 | 300 | 40% |

| Cost Data—Bicycles | |
|---|---|
| Work in process, March 1 | $19,280 |
| Costs added during March | |
| Direct materials | 50,000 |
| Direct labor | 25,900 |
| Manufacturing overhead | 30,000 |

| Production Data—Tricycles | Units | Percentage Complete as to Conversion Costs |
|---|---|---|
| Work in process units, March 1 | 100 | 75% |
| Units started into production | 1,000 | |
| Work in process units, March 31 | 60 | 25% |

| Cost Data—Tricycles | |
|---|---|
| Work in process, March 1 | $ 6,125 |
| Costs added during March | |
| Direct materials | 30,000 |
| Direct labor | 14,300 |
| Manufacturing overhead | 20,000 |

## Instructions

a. Calculate the following for both the bicycles and the tricycles.

   1. The equivalent units of production for materials and conversion costs.

   2. The unit costs of production for materials and conversion costs.

   3. The assignment of costs to units completed and transferred out and to work in process at the end of the accounting period.

b. Prepare a production cost report for March 2022 for the bicycles only.

a.  Bicycles:
    1. Materials       1,000
    2. Materials       $50
    3. Completed and
       transferred out  $102,380
    Ending WIP          $ 22,800

# Continuing Cases

### Current Designs

**CD16** Building a kayak using the composite method is a very labor-intensive process. In the Fabrication Department, the kayaks go through several steps as employees carefully place layers of Kevlar® in a mold and then use resin to fuse together the layers. The excess resin is removed with a vacuum process, and the upper shell and lower shell are removed from the molds and assembled. The seat, hatch, and other components are added in the Finishing Department.

At the beginning of April, **Current Designs** had 30 kayaks in process in the Fabrication Department. Rick Thrune, the production manager, estimated that about 80% of the materials costs had been added to these boats, which were about 50% complete with respect to the conversion costs. The cost of this inventory had been calculated to be $8,400 in materials and $9,000 in conversion costs.

During April, 72 boats were started into production. At the end of the month, the 35 kayaks in the ending inventory were 20% complete as to materials and 40% complete as to conversion costs.

A review of the accounting records for April showed that materials with a cost of $17,500 had been requisitioned by the Fabrication Department and that the conversion costs for the month were $39,600.

#### Instructions

Complete a production cost report for April 2022 for the Fabrication Department using the weighted-average method. Direct materials and conversion costs are incurred uniformly throughout the process.

### Waterways Corporation

(*Note:* This is a continuation of the Waterways case from Chapters 14–15.)

**WC16** Because most of the parts for its irrigation systems are standard, Waterways handles the majority of its manufacturing as a process cost system. There are multiple process departments. Three of these departments are the Molding, Cutting, and Welding Departments. All items eventually end up in the Packaging Department, which prepares items for sale in kits or individually. This case asks you to help Waterways calculate equivalent units and prepare a production cost report.

*Go to WileyPLUS for complete case details and instructions.*

# Expand Your Critical Thinking

### Decision-Making Across the Organization

**CT16.1** Florida Beach Company manufactures sunscreen, called NoTan, in 11-ounce plastic bottles. NoTan is sold in a competitive market. As a result, management is very cost-conscious. NoTan is manufactured through two processes: mixing and filling. Materials are added at the beginning of each process, and labor and manufacturing overhead occur uniformly throughout each process. Unit costs are based on the cost per gallon of NoTan using the weighted-average method.

On June 30, 2022, Mary Ritzman, the chief accountant for the past 20 years, opted to take early retirement. Her replacement, Joe Benili, had extensive accounting experience with motels in the area but only limited contact with manufacturing accounting. During July, Joe correctly accumulated the following production quantity and cost data for the Mixing Department.

*Production quantities:* Work in process, July 1, 8,000 gallons 75% complete as to conversion costs; started into production 100,000 gallons; work in process, July 31, 5,000 gallons 20% complete. All materials are added at the beginning of the process.

*Production costs:* Beginning work in process $88,000, comprised of $21,000 of materials costs and $67,000 of conversion costs; incurred in July: materials $573,000, conversion costs $765,000.

Joe then prepared a production cost report on the basis of physical units started into production. His report showed a unit manufacturing cost of $14.26 per gallon of NoTan. The management of Florida Beach was surprised at the high unit cost. The president comes to you, as Mary's top assistant, to review Joe's report and prepare a correct report if necessary.

**Instructions**

With the class divided into groups, answer the following questions.

    **a.** Show how Joe arrived at the unit manufacturing cost of $14.26 per gallon of NoTan.

    **b.** What error(s) did Joe make in preparing his production cost report?

    **c.** Prepare a correct production cost report for July.

## Managerial Analysis

**CT16.2** Harris Furniture Company manufactures living room furniture through two departments: Framing and Upholstering. Materials are added at the beginning of each process, and conversion costs are incurred uniformly throughout the process. For May, the following cost data are obtained from the two work in process inventory accounts.

| | Framing | Upholstering |
|---|---|---|
| Work in process, May 1 | $   –0– | $   ? |
| Materials | 450,000 | ? |
| Conversion costs | 261,000 | 330,000 |
| Costs transferred in | –0– | 600,000 |
| Costs completed and transferred out | 600,000 | ? |
| Work in process, May 31 | 111,000 | ? |

**Instructions**

Answer the following questions using the weighted-average method.

    **a.** If 3,000 sofas were started into production in Framing on May 1 and 2,500 sofas were completed and transferred to Upholstering, what was the unit cost of materials for May in the Framing Department?

    **b.** Using the data in part (a), what was the per unit conversion cost of the sofas completed and transferred to Upholstering?

    **c.** Continuing the assumptions in (a) above, what is the percentage of completion as to conversion costs of the units in process at May 31 in the Framing Department?

## Real-World Focus

**CT16.3** Paintball is now played around the world. The process of making paintballs is actually quite similar to the process used to make certain medical pills. In fact, paintballs were previously often made at the same factories that made pharmaceuticals.

**Instructions**

Do an Internet search on "video of paintball production," view that video, and then complete the following.

    **a.** Describe in sequence the primary steps used to manufacture paintballs.

    **b.** Explain the costs incurred by the company that would fall into each of the following categories: materials, labor, and overhead. Of these categories, which do you think would be the greatest cost in making paintballs?

    **c.** Discuss whether a paintball manufacturer would use job order costing or process costing.

## Communication Activity

**CT16.4** Diane Barone was a good friend of yours in high school and is from your home town. While you chose to major in accounting when you both went away to college, she majored in marketing and management. You are now the accounting manager for the Snack Foods Division of Melton Enterprises. Your friend Diane was promoted to regional sales manager for the same division of Melton. Diane recently telephoned you. She explained that she was familiar with job cost sheets, which had been used by the Special Projects Division where she had formerly worked. She was, however, very uncomfortable with the production cost reports prepared by your division. She emailed you a list of her particular questions:

    **1.** Since Melton occasionally prepares snack foods for special orders in the Snack Foods Division, why don't we track costs of the orders separately?

    **2.** What is an equivalent unit of production?

    **3.** Why am I getting four production cost reports? Isn't there one work in process inventory account?

### Instructions

Prepare a memo to Diane. Answer her questions and include any additional information you think would be helpful. You may write informally but do use proper grammar and punctuation.

## Ethics Case

**CT16.5** R. B. Dillman Company manufactures a high-tech component used in Bluetooth speakers that passes through two production processing departments, Molding and Assembly. Department managers are partially compensated on the basis of units of product completed and transferred out relative to units of product put into production. This was intended as encouragement to be efficient and to minimize waste.

Jan Wooten is the department head in the Molding Department, and Tony Ferneti is her quality control inspector. During the month of June, Jan hired three new employees who were not yet technically skilled. As a result, many of the units produced in June had minor molding defects. In order to maintain the department's normal high rate of completion, Jan told Tony to pass through inspection and on to the Assembly Department all units that had defects nondetectable to the human eye. "Company and industry tolerances on this product are too high anyway," says Jan. "Less than 2% of the units we produce are subjected in the market to the stress tolerance we've designed into them. The odds of those 2% being any of this month's units are even less. Anyway, we're saving the company money."

### Instructions

a. Who are the potential stakeholders involved in this situation?

b. What alternatives does Tony have in this situation? What might the company do to prevent this situation from occurring?

## Considering People, Planet, and Profit

**CT16.6** When an oil refinery in Texas City, Texas, on the Houston Ship Channel exploded, it killed 15 people and sent a plume of smoke hundreds of feet into the air. The blast started as a fire in the section of the factory that increased the octane of the gasoline that was produced at the refinery. The Houston Ship Channel is the main waterway that allows commerce to flow from the Gulf of Mexico into Houston.

The Texas Commission on Environmental Quality expressed concern about the release of nitrogen oxides, benzene, and other known carcinogens as a result of the blast. Neighbors of the factory complained that the factory had been emitting carcinogens for years and that the regulators had ignored their complaints about emissions and unsafe working conditions.

### Instructions

Answer the following questions.

a. What costs might the company face as a result of the accident?

b. How might the company have reduced the costs associated with the accident?

## Answers to Insight and Accounting Across the Organization Questions

**Choosing a Cost Driver  Q:** What is the result if a company uses the wrong "cost driver" to assign manufacturing overhead?  **A:** Incorrect assignment of manufacturing overhead will result in some products receiving too much overhead and others receiving too little.

**Haven't I Seen That Before?  Q:** In what ways might the relative composition (direct materials, direct labor, and manufacturing overhead) of a remanufactured product's cost differ from that of a newly made product?  **A:** We would expect that the direct materials costs would be substantially reduced since the bulk of the physical product is being reused. Because remanufacturing a product requires identification and replacement of malfunctioning components, the direct labor component might increase while the level of automation might decrease. This process might not be as easily automated as the production of a new product.

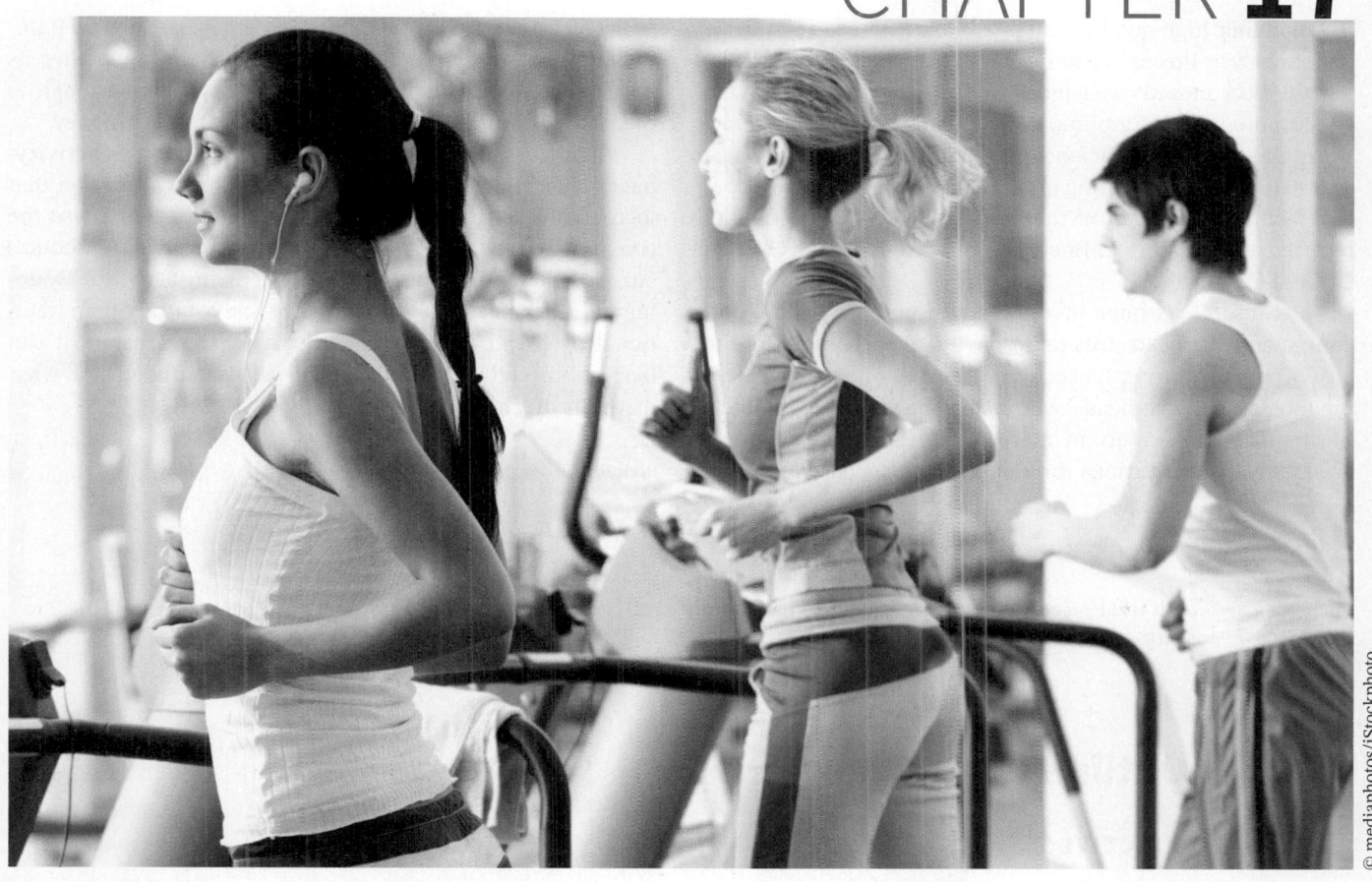

© mediaphotos/iStockphoto

# Activity-Based Costing

## Chapter Preview

As indicated in the following Feature Story about **Precor**, the traditional costing systems described in earlier chapters are not the best answer for every company. Precor suspected that its traditional costing system was masking significant differences in its real cost structure, so it sought a new method of assigning overhead costs. Similar searches by other companies for ways to improve operations and gather more accurate cost data for decision-making have resulted in the development of powerful management tools, including **activity-based costing (ABC)**. The primary objective of this chapter is to explain and illustrate activity-based costing.

## Feature Story

### Precor Is on Your Side

Do you feel like the whole world is conspiring against your efforts to get in shape? Is it humanly possible to resist the constant barrage of advertisements and fast-food servers who pleasantly encourage us to "supersize" it? Lest we think that we have no allies in our battle against the bulge, consider **Precor**.

Ever since it made the first ergonomically sound rowing machine in 1980, Precor's sole mission has been to provide high-quality exercise equipment. It makes elliptical trainers, exercise bikes, rowing machines, treadmills, multi-station strength systems, and many other forms of equipment designed to erase the cumulative effects of a fast-food nation. Its equipment has been used in **Hilton** hotels and **Gold's Gym** franchises.

Building high-quality fitness equipment requires sizable investments by Precor in buildings and machinery. For example, when Precor moved its facilities from Valencia, California, to Greensboro, North Carolina, the company installed low-flow water fixtures, high-efficiency heating and cooling systems, and state-of-the-art lighting in its $26 million, 230,000-square-foot facility. As a result of these efforts, Precor's new facility received a Leadership in Energy and Efficient Design (LEED) CI Gold Certification.

Because of its huge investments in property, plant, and equipment, overhead costs represent a large percentage of the cost of manufacturing Precor's exercise equipment. The combination of high overhead costs and a wide variety of products means that it is important that Precor assigns its overhead accurately to its various products. Without accurate cost

information, Precor will not know whether its elliptical trainers and recumbent bicycles are making money, whether its AMT 100i adaptive motion trainer is priced high enough to cover its costs, or if its 240i Stretchtrainer is losing money.

To increase the accuracy of its costs, Precor uses **activity-based costing**. This is a method of overhead allocation that focuses on identifying the types of activities that cause the company to incur costs. It then assigns overhead to products based on their relative usage of cost-incurring activities. By doing this, the allocation of overhead is less arbitrary than traditional overhead allocation methods. In short, before it can help us burn off the pounds, Precor needs to understand what drives its overhead costs.

**Source:** *www.precor.com.*

 Watch the *Precor* video in WileyPLUS to learn more about activity-based costing.

# Chapter Outline

| LEARNING OBJECTIVES | REVIEW | PRACTICE |
|---|---|---|
| **LO 1** Discuss the difference between traditional costing and activity-based costing. | • Traditional costing systems<br>• Illustration of a traditional system<br>• Need for a new approach<br>• Activity-based costing | **DO IT! 1** Costing Systems |
| **LO 2** Apply activity-based costing to a manufacturer. | • Identify and classify activities and allocate overhead to cost pools<br>• Identify cost drivers<br>• Compute activity-based overhead rates<br>• Assign overhead costs<br>• Comparing unit costs | **DO IT! 2** Apply ABC to Manufacturer |
| **LO 3** Explain the benefits and limitations of activity-based costing. | • Advantage of multiple cost pools<br>• Advantage of enhanced cost control<br>• Advantage of better management decisions<br>• Limitations of ABC | **DO IT! 3** Classify Activity Levels |
| **LO 4** Apply activity-based costing to service industries. | • Traditional costing example<br>• ABC example | **DO IT! 4** Apply ABC to Service Company |

**Go to the Review and Practice section at the end of the chapter for a targeted summary and practice applications with solutions.**

**Visit WileyPLUS for additional tutorials and practice opportunities.**

# Traditional vs. Activity-Based Costing

### LEARNING OBJECTIVE 1
Discuss the difference between traditional costing and activity-based costing.

## Traditional Costing Systems

It is probably impossible to determine the *exact* cost of a product or service. However, in order to achieve improved management decisions, companies strive to provide decision-makers with the most accurate cost estimates they can.

- The most accurate estimate of product cost occurs when the costs are traced directly to the actual product or service.
- Direct materials and direct labor costs are the easiest to trace directly to the product through the use of material requisition forms and payroll time sheets.
- Overhead costs, on the other hand, are an indirect or common cost that generally cannot be easily or directly traced to individual products or services. Instead, companies use estimates to assign overhead costs to products and services.

Often, the most difficult part of computing accurate unit costs is determining the proper amount of **overhead cost** to assign to each product, service, or job.

- In our coverage of job order costing in Chapter 15 and of process costing in Chapter 16, we used a single or plantwide overhead rate throughout the year for the entire factory operation. That rate was called the **predetermined overhead rate**.
- For job order costing, we assumed that **direct labor (cost or hours)** was the relevant activity base for assigning all overhead costs to jobs. For process costing, we frequently assumed that **machine hours** was the relevant activity base for assigning all overhead to the process or department.

**Illustration 17.1** displays a simplified (one-stage) traditional costing system relying on direct labor to assign overhead.

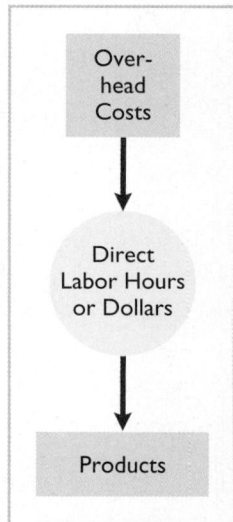

**Traditional one-stage costing system**

## Illustration of a Traditional Costing System

To illustrate a traditional costing system, assume that Atlas Company produces two abdominal fitness products—the Ab Bench and the Ab Coaster. Each year, the company produces 25,000 Ab Benches but only 5,000 Ab Coasters (to simplify our example, we assume that all units manufactured in a year are sold in that same year). Each unit produced requires one hour of direct labor, for a total of 30,000 labor hours (25,000 + 5,000). The direct labor cost is $12 per unit for each product. Total direct labor costs are $360,000 [$12 × (25,000 + 5,000)].

The direct materials cost per unit is $40 for the Ab Bench and $30 for the Ab Coaster. Therefore, the per unit direct materials and direct labor costs are $52 for the Ab Bench and $42 for the Ab Coaster, as shown in **Illustration 17.2**. Total direct materials costs are $1,150,000 [($40 × 25,000) + ($30 × 5,000)].

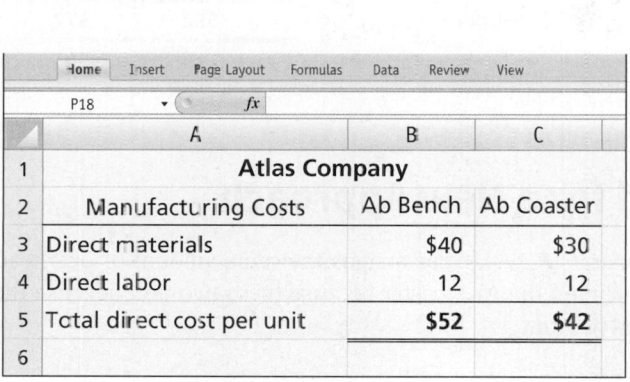

**Direct costs per unit— traditional costing**

| Manufacturing Costs | Ab Bench | Ab Coaster |
|---|---|---|
| Direct materials | $40 | $30 |
| Direct labor | 12 | 12 |
| Total direct cost per unit | $52 | $42 |

**Atlas Company**

Atlas expects to incur annual manufacturing overhead costs of $900,000. It sells the Ab Bench for $200 and the Ab Coaster for $170. Using this information, plus assumed data regarding selling and administrative expenses, a multiple-step income statement is provided in **Illustration 17.3**.

**Income statement for Atlas Company**

### Atlas Company
### Income Statement
### For the Year Ended December 31, 2022

| | | |
|---|---:|---:|
| Sales | | $5,850,000 |
| Cost of goods sold* | | |
|    Direct materials | $1,150,000 | |
|    Direct labor | 360,000 | |
|    Manufacturing overhead | 900,000 | 2,410,000 |
| Gross profit | | 3,440,000 |
| Selling and administrative expenses | | |
|    Administrative expenses | 450,000 | |
|    Selling expenses | 360,000 | 810,000 |
| Net income | | $2,630,000 |

*Because we have assumed that all goods produced during the period were sold, the cost of goods manufactured is equal to the cost of goods sold.

As discussed, the cost of direct materials and direct labor can be directly traced to each product. However, manufacturing overhead cannot be traced directly; instead, it must be assigned using a predetermined overhead rate in order to determine product cost.

Atlas assigns overhead using a single predetermined overhead rate based on the 30,000 direct labor hours it expects to use this year. Thus, the predetermined overhead rate is $30 per direct labor hour ($900,000 ÷ 30,000 direct labor hours).

Since both products require one direct labor hour per unit, both products are assigned overhead costs of $30 per unit under traditional costing. **Illustration 17.4** shows the total unit costs for the Ab Bench and the Ab Coaster.

**Total unit costs— traditional costing**

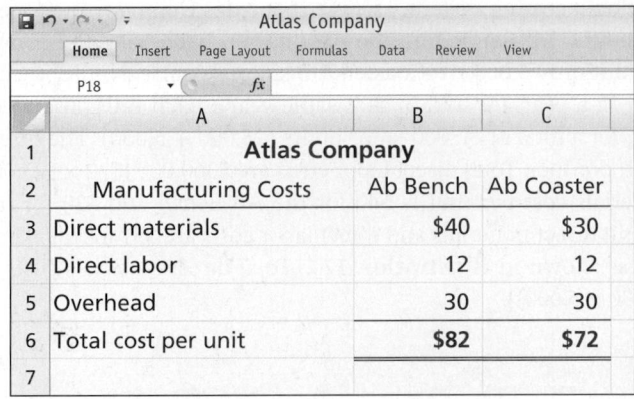

| Manufacturing Costs | Ab Bench | Ab Coaster |
|---|---:|---:|
| Direct materials | $40 | $30 |
| Direct labor | 12 | 12 |
| Overhead | 30 | 30 |
| Total cost per unit | $82 | $72 |

## The Need for a New Approach

As shown in Illustration 17.4, Atlas assigns the same amount of overhead costs per unit to both the Ab Bench and the Ab Coaster because these two products use the same amount of direct labor hours per unit.

- Historically, the use of direct labor as the activity base seemed to make sense as direct labor made up a large portion of total manufacturing cost.
- Also, there often was a correlation between direct labor and the incurrence of overhead cost.
- Direct labor thus became the most popular basis for allocating overhead.

However, using a single rate based on direct labor hours may not be the best approach for Atlas to assign its overhead.

In recent years, manufacturers and service providers have experienced tremendous changes. Advances in computerized systems, technological innovations, global competition, and automation have altered the manufacturing environment drastically.

- As a result, the amount of direct labor used in many industries has greatly decreased, and total overhead costs resulting from depreciation on expensive equipment and machinery, utilities, repairs, and maintenance have significantly increased.
- When there is less (or no) correlation between direct labor and overhead costs incurred, plantwide predetermined overhead rates based on direct labor are misleading.

Companies that use overhead rates based on direct labor when this correlation does not exist experience significant product cost distortions.

To minimize such distortions, many companies began to use machine hours instead of labor hours as the basis to assign overhead in an automated manufacturing environment. But, even machine hours may not serve as a good basis for plantwide allocation of overhead costs. For example, product design and engineering costs are not correlated with machine hours but instead with the number of different items a company produces.

- Companies that have complex processes need to use multiple allocation bases to compute accurate product costs.
- An overhead cost allocation method that uses multiple bases is **activity-based costing**.

## Activity-Based Costing

**Activity-based costing (ABC)** is an approach for allocating overhead costs. Specifically, ABC allocates overhead to multiple activity cost pools and then assigns the activity cost pools to products and services by means of cost drivers. In using ABC, you need to understand the following concepts.

---

### Key Concepts

**Activity.**   Any event, action, transaction, or work sequence that incurs costs when producing a product or performing a service.

**Activity cost pool.**   The overhead cost attributed to a distinct activity (e.g., ordering materials or setting up machines).

**Cost driver.**   Any factor or activity that has a direct cause-effect relationship with the resources consumed.

---

Activity-based costing involves the following four steps, as shown in **Illustration 17.5**.

- Step 1 allocates overhead costs to activity cost pools. Examples of overhead cost pools are ordering materials, setting up machines, assembling products, and inspecting products.
- Steps 2–4 assign the overhead in the activity cost pools to products, using cost drivers.

The cost drivers are activities undertaken to produce goods or perform services, which cause the company to consume resources. Examples are number of purchase orders, number of machine setups, labor hours, and number of inspections.

ILLUSTRATION 17.5

**The four steps of activity-based costing**

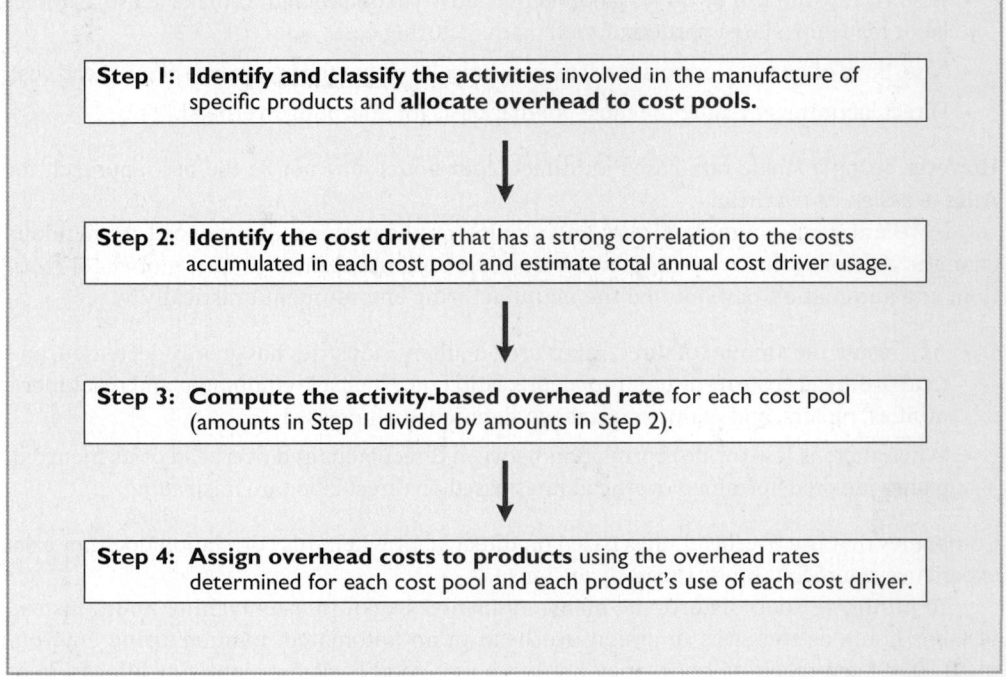

**Step 1:** **Identify and classify the activities** involved in the manufacture of specific products and **allocate overhead to cost pools.**

**Step 2:** **Identify the cost driver** that has a strong correlation to the costs accumulated in each cost pool and estimate total annual cost driver usage.

**Step 3:** **Compute the activity-based overhead rate** for each cost pool (amounts in Step 1 divided by amounts in Step 2).

**Step 4:** **Assign overhead costs to products** using the overhead rates determined for each cost pool and each product's use of each cost driver.

**Illustration 17.6** shows examples of activities, and possible cost drivers to measure them, for a company that manufactures two types of equipment—lawn mowers and snow throwers.

ILLUSTRATION 17.6

**Activities and related cost drivers**

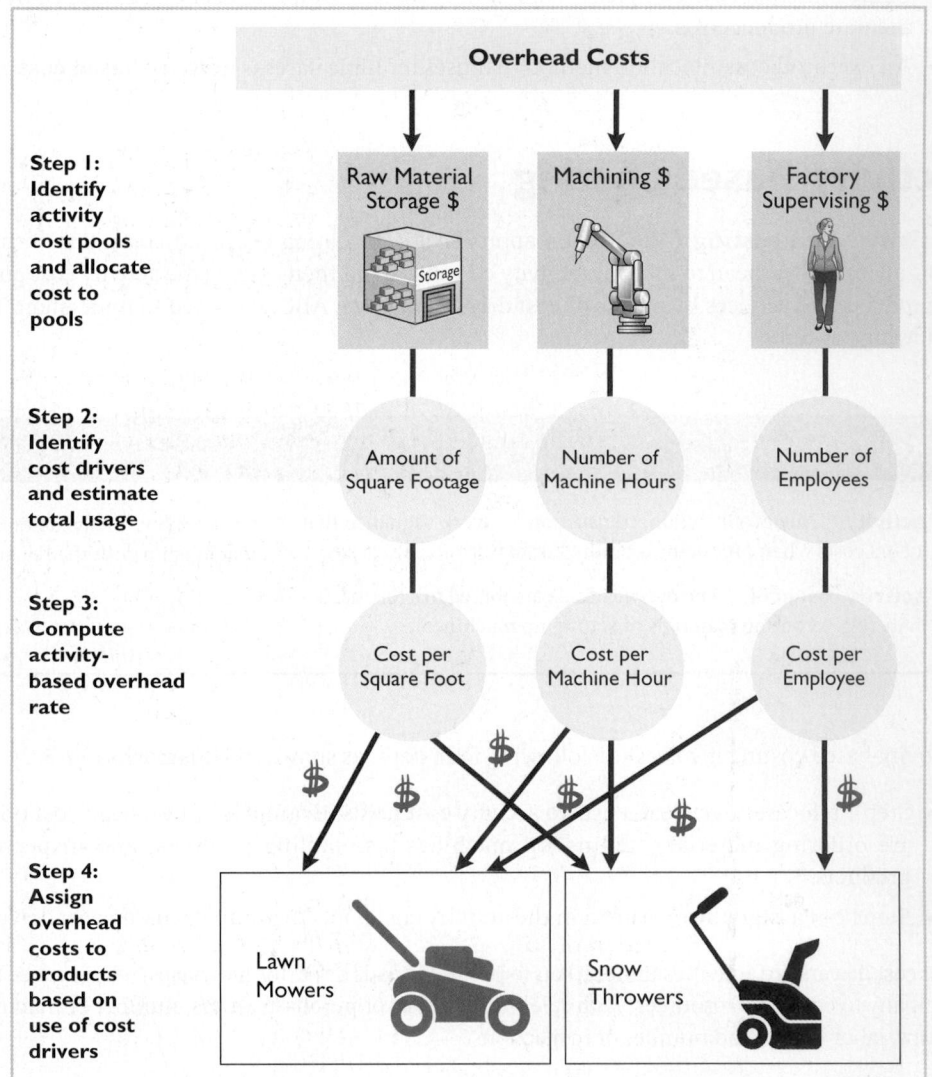

- In the first step, the company allocates overhead costs to activity cost pools. In this simplified example, the company has identified three activity cost pools: raw material storage, machining, and factory supervising.
- After the costs are allocated to the activity cost pools, the company uses cost drivers to determine the costs to assign to the individual products based on each product's use of each activity. For example, if lawn mowers require more activity by the machining department, as measured by the number of machine hours, then more of the overhead costs from the machining pool are assigned to the lawn mowers.
- The more complex a product's manufacturing operation, the more activities and cost drivers it is likely to have. If there is little or no correlation between changes in the cost driver and consumption of the overhead cost, inaccurate product costs are inevitable.

---

### DO IT! 1 | Costing Systems

Indicate whether the following statements are true or false.

1. A traditional costing system assigns overhead by means of multiple overhead rates.
2. Direct materials and direct labor costs are easier to trace to products than overhead.
3. As manufacturing processes have become more automated, more companies have chosen to assign overhead on the basis of direct labor costs.
4. In activity-based costing, an activity is any event, action, transaction, or work sequence that incurs cost when producing goods or performing services.

#### Solution

1. False.  2. True.  3. False.  4. True.

Related exercise material: **BE17.1, BE17.2, DO IT! 17.1, E17.1, and E17.2.**

**ACTION PLAN**
- **Understand that a traditional costing system assigns overhead on the basis of a single predetermined overhead rate.**
- **Understand that an ABC system allocates overhead to identified activity cost pools and then assigns costs to products using related cost drivers that measure the resources consumed.**

---

# ABC and Manufacturers

## LEARNING OBJECTIVE 2
Apply activity-based costing to a manufacturer.

In this section, we present a simple case example that compares activity-based costing with traditional costing. It illustrates how ABC eliminates the cost distortions that can occur in traditional overhead cost allocation.

- As you study this example, you should understand that ABC does not *replace* an existing job order or process cost system.
- What ABC does is to segregate overhead into various cost pools in an effort to provide more accurate cost information.

As a result, ABC supplements—rather than replaces—these cost systems.

Let's return to our Atlas Company example. Using the information from Illustration 17.4, we can calculate unit costs under ABC. As shown earlier in Illustration 17.5, activity-based costing involves the following four steps.

1. **Identify and classify the activities** involved in the manufacture of specific products and **allocate overhead to cost pools**.

2. **Identify the cost driver** that has a strong correlation to the costs accumulated in each cost pool and estimate total annual cost driver usage.

3. **Compute the activity-based overhead rate** for each cost pool.

4. **Assign overhead costs to products** using the overhead rates determined for each cost pool and each product's use of each cost driver.

# Identify and Classify Activities and Allocate Overhead to Cost Pools (Step 1)

Activity-based costing starts with an analysis of the activities needed to manufacture a product or perform a service.

- This analysis should identify all resource-consuming activities.
- It requires documenting every activity undertaken to accomplish a task.

Atlas Company identifies four activity cost pools: manufacturing, machine setups, purchase ordering, and factory maintenance.

Next, the company allocates overhead costs directly to the appropriate activity cost pool. For example, Atlas allocates all overhead costs directly associated with machine setups (such as salaries, supplies, and depreciation) to the setup cost pool. **Illustration 17.7** shows the four cost pools, along with the estimated overhead allocated to each cost pool. Note that the total estimated overhead is $900,000 under either traditional costing or ABC.

**ILLUSTRATION 17.7**

**Activity cost pools and estimated overhead**

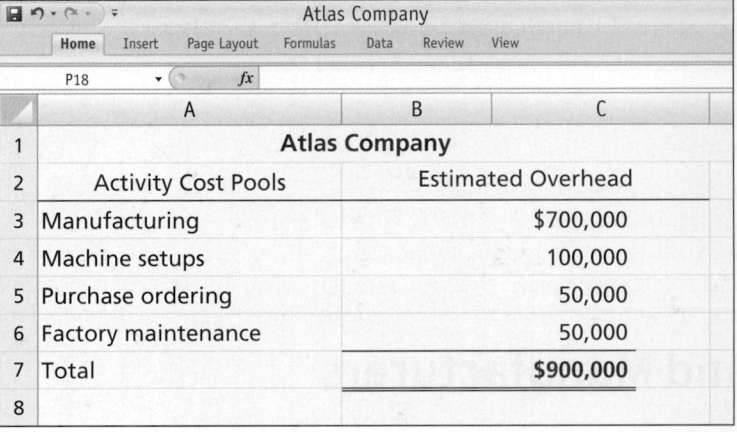

| Atlas Company | |
| --- | --- |
| Activity Cost Pools | Estimated Overhead |
| Manufacturing | $700,000 |
| Machine setups | 100,000 |
| Purchase ordering | 50,000 |
| Factory maintenance | 50,000 |
| Total | **$900,000** |

# Identify Cost Drivers (Step 2)

After costs are allocated to the activity cost pools, the company must identify the cost drivers for each cost pool. The cost driver must accurately measure the actual consumption of the activity by the various products.

- To achieve accurate costing, a **high degree of correlation** must exist between the cost driver and the actual consumption of the overhead costs in the cost pool.
- This is an area that has benefited greatly from company data collection efforts at nearly every stage of the value chain.
- By applying analytics to this data, the company can increase the likelihood that cost drivers are closely related to resource consumption.

Availability and ease of obtaining data relating to the cost driver is an important factor that must be considered in its selection.

**Illustration 17.8** shows the cost drivers that Atlas Company identifies and their total estimated use per activity cost pool. For example, the cost driver for the machine setup cost pool is the number of setups. A product that requires more setups will cause more setup costs to be incurred, and it therefore should be assigned more overhead costs from the setup cost pool. The total number of setups is estimated to be 2,000 for the year.

| Activity Cost Pools | Cost Drivers | Estimated Use of Cost Drivers per Activity |
|---|---|---|
| Manufacturing | Machine hours | 50,000 machine hours |
| Machine setups | Number of setups | 2,000 setups |
| Purchase ordering | Number of purchase orders | 2,500 purchase orders |
| Factory maintenance | Square footage | 25,000 square feet |

**ILLUSTRATION 17.8**
Cost drivers and their estimated use

# Compute Activity-Based Overhead Rates (Step 3)

Next, the company computes an **activity-based overhead rate** per cost driver by dividing the estimated overhead per activity by the number of cost drivers estimated to be used per activity.

- This step is similar to calculating a predetermined overhead rate under the traditional costing approach except that instead of one rate for the company, there is one rate per cost pool.
- **Illustration 17.9** shows the equation for this computation.

$$\frac{\text{Estimated Overhead per Activity}}{\text{Estimated Use of Cost Drivers per Activity}} = \text{Activity-Based Overhead Rate}$$

**ILLUSTRATION 17.9**
Equation for computing activity-based overhead rate

Atlas Company computes its activity-based overhead rates by using the estimated overhead per activity cost pool, shown in Illustration 17.7, and the estimated use of cost drivers per activity, shown in Illustration 17.8. These computations are presented in **Illustration 17.10**. For example, $100,000 was allocated to the machine setup pool, and the estimated number of annual setups is 2,000. The activity-based rate for machine setups is therefore $50 per setup ($100,000 ÷ 2,000 setups).

**ILLUSTRATION 17.10**  Computation of activity-based overhead rates

| Activity Cost Pools | Estimated Overhead | Estimated Use of Cost Drivers per Activity | Activity-Based Overhead Rates |
|---|---|---|---|
| Manufacturing | $700,000 | 50,000 machine hours | $14 per machine hour |
| Machine setups | 100,000 | 2,000 setups | $50 per setup |
| Purchase ordering | 50,000 | 2,500 purchase orders | $20 per order |
| Factory maintenance | 50,000 | 25,000 square feet | $2 per square foot |
| Total | $900,000 | | |

# Assign Overhead Costs to Products (Step 4)

In allocating overhead costs, the company must know the use of cost drivers **for each product**. Because of its low volume and higher number of components, the Ab Coaster requires more setups and purchase orders than the Ab Bench. **Illustration 17.11** shows the use of cost drivers per product for each of Atlas Company's products. Note that of the 2,000 estimated total setups, 500 result from producing the Ab Bench and 1,500 result from the Ab Coaster.

**ILLUSTRATION 17.11** Use of cost drivers per product

| Activity Cost Pools | Cost Drivers | Estimated Use of Cost Drivers per Activity | Use of Cost Drivers per Product: Ab Bench | Use of Cost Drivers per Product: Ab Coaster |
|---|---|---|---|---|
| Manufacturing | Machine hours | 50,000 machine hours | 30,000 | 20,000 |
| Machine setups | Number of setups | 2,000 setups | 500 | 1,500 |
| Purchase ordering | Number of purchase orders | 2,500 purchase orders | 750 | 1,750 |
| Factory maintenance | Square feet | 25,000 square feet | 10,000 | 15,000 |

To assign overhead costs to each product, Atlas multiplies the activity-based overhead rates per cost driver (Illustration 17.10) by the number of cost drivers used per product (Illustration 17.11). **Illustration 17.12** shows the overhead cost assigned to each product. For example, of the total of $100,000 allocated to the machine setup pool, $25,000 (500 setups × $50) is assigned to the Ab Bench and $75,000 (1,500 setups × $50) is assigned to the Ab Coaster.

**ILLUSTRATION 17.12** Allocation of activity cost pools to products

| Activity Cost Pools | Ab Bench: Use of Cost Drivers per Product | × Ab Bench: Activity-Based Overhead Rates | = Ab Bench: Cost Assigned | Ab Coaster: Use of Cost Drivers per Product | × Ab Coaster: Activity-Based Overhead Rates | = Ab Coaster: Cost Assigned |
|---|---|---|---|---|---|---|
| Manufacturing | 30,000 | $14 | $420,000 | 20,000 | $14 | $280,000 |
| Machine setups | 500 | $50 | 25,000 | 1,500 | $50 | 75,000 |
| Purchase ordering | 750 | $20 | 15,000 | 1,750 | $20 | 35,000 |
| Factory maintenance | 10,000 | $2.00 | 20,000 | 15,000 | $2.00 | 30,000 |
| Total costs assigned (a) | | | $480,000 | | | $420,000 |
| Units produced (b) | | | 25,000 | | | 5,000 |
| Overhead cost per unit [(a)÷(b)], rounded | | | $19.20 | | | $84.00 |

Of the total overhead costs of $900,000 shown in Illustration 17.7, $480,000 was assigned to the Ab Bench and $420,000 to the Ab Coaster. Under ABC, the overhead cost per unit is $19.20 ($480,000 ÷ 25,000) for the Ab Bench and $84.00 ($420,000 ÷ 5,000) for the Ab Coaster. We see next how this per unit amount substantially differs from that computed under a traditional costing system.

# Comparing Unit Costs

Illustration 17.13 compares the unit costs for Atlas Company's Ab Bench and Ab Coaster under traditional costing and ABC.

| Manufacturing Costs | Ab Bench | | Ab Coaster | |
|---|---|---|---|---|
| | Traditional Costing | ABC | Traditional Costing | ABC |
| Direct materials | $40.00 | $40.00 | $30.00 | $ 30.00 |
| Direct labor | 12.00 | 12.00 | 12.00 | 12.00 |
| Overhead | 30.00 | 19.20 | 30.00 | 84.00 |
| Total cost per unit | $82.00 | $71.20 | $72.00 | $126.00 |

Overstated
$10.80

Understated
$54.00

**ILLUSTRATION 17.13**

**Comparison of unit product costs**

The comparison shows that unit costs under traditional costing are different and often misleading.

- Traditional costing overstates the cost of producing the Ab Bench by $10.80 per unit and understates the cost of producing the Ab Coaster by $54 per unit.
- These differences are attributable to how Atlas assigns manufacturing overhead across the two systems.

Using a traditional costing system, each product was assigned the same amount of overhead ($30) because both products use the same amount of the cost driver (direct labor hours). In contrast, ABC assigns overhead to products based on multiple cost drivers. For example, under ABC, Atlas assigns 75% of the costs of equipment setups to Ab Coasters because Ab Coasters were responsible for 75% (1,500 ÷ 2,000) of the total number of setups.

Note that activity-based costing does not change the amount of total manufacturing overhead costs.

- Under both traditional costing and ABC, Atlas spends the same amount of overhead—$900,000.
- However, ABC assigns manufacturing overhead costs in a more accurate manner.

Thus, ABC helps Atlas avoid some negative consequences of a traditional costing system, such as overpricing its Ab Benches and thereby possibly losing market share to competitors. Atlas has also been sacrificing profitability by underpricing the Ab Coaster.

Companies that move from traditional costing to ABC often have similar experiences as ABC shifts costs from high-volume products to low-volume products. This shift occurs because traditional overhead allocation uses volume-driven bases such as labor hours or machine hours. The traditional approach ignores the fact that many overhead costs are not correlated with volume. In addition, ABC recognizes products' use of resources, which also increases the accuracy of product costs.

## Management Insight

© CGinspiration/ iStockphoto

### ABC Evaluated

Surveys of companies often show ABC usage of approximately 50%. Yet, in recent years, articles about ABC have expressed mixed opinions regarding its usefulness. To evaluate ABC practices and user satisfaction with ABC, a survey was conducted of 348 companies worldwide. Some of the interesting findings included the following: ABC methods are widely used across the entire value chain rather than being primarily used to assign production-specific costs; only 25% of non-ABC companies think they are accurately tracing the costs of activities, while 70% of ABC companies think their company does

this well; and respondents felt that ABC provides greater support for financial, operational, and strategic decisions. More than 87% of respondents said that their ideal costing system would include some form of ABC. Since this significantly exceeds the 50% of the respondents actually using it, ABC usage may well increase in the future.

**Source:** William Stratton, Denis Desroches, Raef Lawson, and Toby Hatch, "Activity-Based Costing Is It Still Relevant?" *Management Accounting Quarterly* (Spring, 2009, pp. 31–39.

**What might explain why so many companies say that ideally they would use ABC, but they haven't adopted it yet? (Answer is available at the end of the chapter.)**

## DO IT! 2 | Apply ABC to Manufacturer

Casey Company has five activity cost pools and two products. It estimates production of 200,000 units of its automobile scissors jack and 80,000 units of its truck hydraulic jack. Having identified its activity cost pools and the cost drivers for each cost pool, Casey Company accumulated the following data relative to those activity cost pools and cost drivers.

| Annual Overhead Data | | | | Use of Cost Drivers per Product | |
|---|---|---|---|---|---|
| Activity Cost Pools | Cost Drivers | Estimated Overhead | Estimated Use of Cost Drivers per Activity | Scissors Jacks | Hydraulic Jacks |
| Ordering and receiving | Purchase orders | $ 200,000 | 2,500 orders | 1,000 | 1,500 |
| Machine setup | Setups | 600,000 | 1,200 setups | 500 | 700 |
| Machining | Machine hours | 2,000,000 | 800,000 machine hours | 300,000 | 500,000 |
| Assembling | Parts | 1,800,000 | 3,000,000 parts | 1,800,000 | 1,200,000 |
| Inspecting and testing | Tests | 700,000 | 35,000 tests | 20,000 | 15,000 |
| | | $5,300,000 | | | |

**ACTION PLAN**

- Determine the activity-based overhead rate by dividing the estimated overhead per activity by the estimated use of cost drivers per activity.

Using the above data, do the following.

a. Prepare a schedule showing the computations of the activity-based overhead rates per cost driver.

b. Prepare a schedule assigning each activity's overhead cost to the two products.

c. Compute the overhead cost per unit for each product.

d. Comment on the comparative overhead cost per unit.

### Solution

a. Computations of activity-based overhead rates per cost driver:

| Activity Cost Pools | Estimated Overhead | ÷ | Estimated Use of Cost Drivers per Activity | = | Activity-Based Overhead Rates |
|---|---|---|---|---|---|
| Ordering and receiving | $ 200,000 | | 2,500 purchase orders | | $80 per order |
| Machine setup | 600,000 | | 1,200 setups | | $500 per setup |
| Machining | 2,000,000 | | 800,000 machine hours | | $2.50 per machine hour |
| Assembling | 1,800,000 | | 3,000,000 parts | | $0.60 per part |
| Inspecting and testing | 700,000 | | 35,000 tests | | $20 per test |
| | $5,300,000 | | | | |

b. Assignment of each activity's overhead cost to products using ABC:

| Activity Cost Pools | Scissors Jacks | | | Hydraulic Jacks | | |
|---|---|---|---|---|---|---|
| | Use of Cost Drivers per Product × | Activity-Based Overhead Rates | = Cost Assigned | Use of Cost Drivers per Product × | Activity-Based Overhead Rates | = Cost Assigned |
| Ordering and receiving | 1,000 | $80 | $ 80,000 | 1,500 | $80 | $ 120,000 |
| Machine setup | 500 | $500 | 250,000 | 700 | $500 | 350,000 |
| Machining | 300,000 | $2.50 | 750,000 | 500,000 | $2.50 | 1,250,000 |
| Assembling | 1,800,000 | $0.60 | 1,080,000 | 1,200,000 | $0.60 | 720,000 |
| Inspecting and testing | 20,000 | $20 | 400,000 | 15,000 | $20 | 300,000 |
| Total assigned costs | | | $2,560,000 | | | $2,740,000 |

c. Computation of overhead cost per unit:

| | Scissors Jack | Hydraulic Jack |
|---|---|---|
| Total costs assigned (a) | $2,560,000 | $2,740,000 |
| Total units produced (b) | 200,000 | 80,000 |
| Overhead cost per unit (a ÷ b) | $12.80 | $34.25 |

d. These data show that the total overhead assigned to 80,000 hydraulic jacks exceeds the overhead assigned to 200,000 scissors jacks. The overhead cost per hydraulic jack is $34.25, but it is only $12.80 per scissors jack.

Related exercise material: **BE17.3, BE17.4, BE17.5, BE17.6, BE17.7, DO IT! 17.2, E17.3, E17.4, E17.5, E17.6, E17.7, and E17.8.**

**ACTION PLAN**

- Assign the overhead of each activity cost pool to the individual products by multiplying the use of cost driver per product times the activity-based overhead rate.
- Determine overhead cost per unit by dividing the overhead assigned to each product by the number of units of that product.

# ABC Benefits and Limitations

**LEARNING OBJECTIVE 3**
Explain the benefits and limitations of activity-based costing.

ABC has three primary benefits:

1. ABC employs more cost pools and therefore results in more accurate product costing.
2. ABC leads to enhanced control over overhead costs.
3. ABC supports better management decisions.

## The Advantage of Multiple Cost Pools

The main mechanism by which ABC increases product cost accuracy is the use of multiple cost pools. Instead of one plantwide pool (or even several departmental pools) and a single cost driver, companies use numerous activity cost pools with more relevant cost drivers. Thus, costs are assigned more accurately on the basis of the cost drivers used to produce each product.

Note that in the Atlas Company example, the *manufacturing* cost pool reflected multiple manufacturing activities, including machining, assembling, and painting. These activities were included in a single pool for simplicity.

- If we had instead broken the manufacturing pool into multiple pools, we would have used cost drivers specific to each pool.
- This would lead to more accurate overhead allocation.

In many companies, the number of activities—and thus the number of pools—can be substantial. For example, **Clark-Hurth** (a division of **Clark Equipment Company**), a manufacturer of axles and transmissions, identified over 170 activities. **Compumotor** (a division of **Parker Hannifin**) identified over 80 activities in just the procurement function of its Material Control Department. **Illustration 17.14** shows a more likely "split" of the activities that were included in Atlas's manufacturing cost pool, reflecting separate pools and drivers for each of those activities.

**ILLUSTRATION 17.14** **A more detailed view of Atlas's manufacturing activities**

## Assigning Nonmanufacturing Overhead Costs

To simplify our presentation and to enable a direct comparison of overhead allocation under traditional costing versus activity-based costing, we assume that Atlas Company only assigned manufacturing overhead costs to products. Consider again the multiple-step income statement presented for Atlas Company, shown in **Illustration 17.15**.

**ILLUSTRATION 17.15** **Income statement for Atlas Company showing manufacturing and nonmanufacturing costs**

### Atlas Company
#### Income Statement
#### For the Year Ended December 31, 2022

| | | |
|---|---:|---:|
| Sales | | $5,850,000 |
| Cost of goods sold* | | |
|    Direct materials | $1,150,000 | |
|    Direct labor | 360,000 | |
|    Manufacturing overhead | 900,000 | 2,410,000 |
| Gross profit | | 3,440,000 |
| Selling and administrative expenses | | |
|    Administrative expenses | 450,000 | |
|    Selling expenses | 360,000 | 810,000 |
| Net income | | $2,630,000 |

*Because we have assumed that all goods produced during the period were sold, the cost of goods manufactured is equal to the cost of goods sold.

The nonmanufacturing overhead costs included in selling and administrative expenses represent a significant portion of the company's costs.

- Generally accepted accounting principles (GAAP) requires that these costs be expensed during the current period as period costs, rather than assigning these costs to products.

- However, to gain a better understanding of product and/or customer profitability, many companies use activity-based costing to assign some nonmanufacturing costs to products or customers.

- For example, if shipping costs are included in the selling expenses category, those costs can usually be directly traced to specific products. Note that the incurrence of other costs included in selling expenses can vary considerably across products or customers.

For example, suppose that Atlas sells its products to three different types of customers: (1) "big box" stores, (2) workout facilities, and (3) individuals via online sales. The demands on the company's sales resources (e.g., order taking, order filling, sales calls, travel, and warranty costs) might vary considerably across these three sales channels. To evaluate the relative profitability of each of these three sales channels, Atlas could use activity-based costing to allocate the sales costs to these three customer types for internal decision-making purposes.

## Classification of Activity Levels

To gain the full advantage of having multiple cost pools, the costs within the pool must be correlated with the driver. To achieve this, a company's managers often characterize activities as belonging to one of the following four activity-level groups when designing an ABC system.

1. **Unit-level activities** are performed for each unit of production. For example, the assembly of cell phones is a unit-level activity because the amount of assembly the company performs increases with each additional cell phone assembled.
2. **Batch-level activities** are performed every time a company produces another batch of a product. For example, suppose that to start processing a new batch of ice cream, an ice cream producer needs to set up its machines. The amount of time spent setting up and cleaning up machines increases with the number of batches produced, not with the number of units produced.
3. **Product-level activities** are performed every time a company produces a new type of product. For example, before a pharmaceutical company can produce and sell a new type of medicine, it must undergo very substantial product tests to ensure the product is effective and safe. The amount of time spent on testing activities increases with the number of products the company produces.
4. **Facility-level activities** are required to support or sustain an entire production process. Consider, for example, a hospital. The hospital building must be insured and heated, and the property taxes must be paid, no matter how many patients the hospital treats. These costs do not vary as a function of the number of units, batches, or products.

Companies may achieve greater accuracy in overhead cost allocation to products by recognizing these four different levels of activities and, from them, developing specific activity cost pools and their related cost drivers. **Illustration 17.16** depicts this four-level activity hierarchy, along with the types of activities and examples of cost drivers for those activities at each level.

Note that sometimes the classification of an activity will depend on the context. For example, in some circumstances, inspection is a batch-level activity that is driven by the number of batches or setups. This is because the company will have to ensure that the setup was done properly and did not cause a deviation from product specifications. However, inspection can also be a unit-level activity that is driven by the number of units produced.

# The Advantage of Enhanced Cost Control

Some companies experiencing the benefits of activity-based costing have applied it to a broader range of management activities. **Activity-based management (ABM)** extends the use of ABC from product costing to a comprehensive management tool that focuses on reducing costs and improving processes and decision-making.

**ILLUSTRATION 17.16**

**Hierarchy of activity levels**

| Four Levels | Types of Activities | Examples of Cost Drivers |
|---|---|---|
| **Unit-Level Activities** | | |
| | Machine-related<br>  Drilling, cutting, milling,<br>  trimming, pressing | Machine hours |
| | Labor-related<br>  Assembling, painting,<br>  sanding, sewing | Direct labor hours or cost |
| **Batch-Level Activities** | | |
| | Equipment setups | Number of setups or setup time |
| | Purchase ordering | Number of purchase orders |
| | Inspection | Number of setups |
| | Materials handling | Number of material moves |
| **Product-Level Activities** | | |
| | Product design | Number of product designs |
| | Engineering changes | Number of changes |
| **Facility-Level Activities** | | |
| | Factory management salaries | Number of employees managed |
| | Factory depreciation | Square footage |
| | Property taxes | Square footage |
| | Utilities | Square footage |

For example, in developing an ABC system, managers increase their awareness of the activities performed by the company in its production and supporting processes.

- Many companies now employ lean manufacturing practices, which require that the companies review all business processes in an effort to increase productivity and eliminate waste.
- As part of this process, managers classify activities as value-added or non-valued-added.

**Value-added activities** are essential activities of **a company's operations** that increase the perceived value of a product or service to customers. Examples for the manufacture of **Precor** exercise equipment include engineering design, machining, assembly, assembly supervision, and painting. Supervision of a value-added activity is itself a value-added activity, as it coordinates and manages the value-added activity with a goal of improving operations. Thus, since assembly is a value-added activity, supervision of assembly is also value-added. Examples of value-added activities in a service company include performing surgery at a hospital, performing legal research at a law firm, and delivering packages by a freight company.

**Non–value-added activities** are nonessential activities that, if eliminated, would not reduce the perceived value of a company's product or service. These activities simply **add cost to, or increase the time spent on, a product or service without increasing its perceived value**. One example is inventory storage. If a company **eliminated the need** to store inventory, it would not reduce the value of its product, but it would decrease its product costs. Similarly, inspections are a non–value-added activity. A company can eliminate the need for inspections by improving its production process. Thus, the elimination of inspection would not reduce the value of the product. Other examples include moving materials, work in process, or finished goods from one location to another in the factory during the production process; waiting for manufacturing equipment to become available; and fixing defective goods under warranty.

Companies often use **activity flowcharts** to help identify the ABC activities, such as the one shown in **Illustration 17.17**. The top part of this flowchart identifies activities as

**ILLUSTRATION 17.17**   Analyzing non–value-added activities to improve operations

## Heartland Company
### Activity Flowchart

**Activities**

| NVA | NVA | NVA | NVA | VA | | NVA | NVA | VA | NVA | NVA | NVA | VA |
|---|---|---|---|---|---|---|---|---|---|---|---|---|
| Receive and Inspect Materials | Move and Store Materials | Move Materials to Production and Wait | Set Up Machines | Machining | | Inspect | Move and Wait | Assembly | Inspect and Test | Move to Storage | Store Finished Goods | Package and Ship |
| | | | | Drill | Lathe | | | | | | | |

| | | | | | | | | | | | | | |
|---|---|---|---|---|---|---|---|---|---|---|---|---|---|
| Current Days | 1 | 12 | 2.5 | 1.5 | 2 | 1 | 0.2 | 6 | 2 | 0.3 | 0.5 | 14 | 1 |

⟵————————————— *Total Current Average Time = 44 days* —————————————⟶

| | | | | | | | | | | | | | |
|---|---|---|---|---|---|---|---|---|---|---|---|---|---|
| Proposed Days | 1 | 4 | 1.5 | 1.5 | 2 | 1 | 0.2 | 2 | 2 | 0.3 | 0.5 | 10 | 1 |

⟵————————————— *Total Proposed Average Time = 27 days* —————————————⟶

**Proposed reduction in non–value-added time = 17 days**

VA = Value-added        NVA = Non–value-added

value-added (highlighted in red) or non–value-added. Two rows in the lower part of the flowchart show the number of days spent on each activity. The first row shows the number of days spent on each activity under the current manufacturing process. The second row shows the number of days estimated to be spent on each activity under management's proposed reengineered manufacturing process.

- The proposed changes would reduce time spent on non–value-added activities by 17 days.
- This 17-day improvement is due entirely to moving inventory more quickly through the non–value-added processes—that is, by reducing inventory time in moving, storage, and waiting.

Appendix 17A discusses a just-in-time inventory system, which some companies use to eliminate non–value-added activities related to inventory.

Not all activities labeled non–value-added are totally wasteful, nor can they be totally eliminated. For example, although inspection time is a non–value-added activity from a customer's perspective, few companies would eliminate their quality control functions. Similarly, moving and waiting time is non–value-added, but it would be impossible to completely eliminate in most instances. Nevertheless, when managers recognize the non–value-added characteristic of these activities, they are motivated to minimize them as much as possible. Attention to such matters is part of the growing practice of activity-based management, which helps managers concentrate on **continuous improvement** of operations and activities.

## Management Insight    General Mills

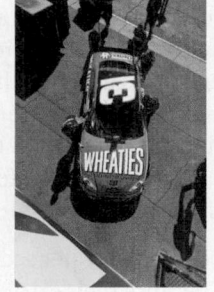
© Action Sports Photography/Shutterstock.com

### What Does NASCAR Have to Do with Breakfast Cereal?

Often the best way to improve a process is to learn from observing a different process. Production-line technicians from food producer **General Mills** were flown to North Carolina to observe firsthand how race-car pit crews operate. In a NASCAR race, the value-added activity is driving toward the finish line; any time spent in the pit is non–value-added. Every split second saved in the pit increases the chances of winning. From what the General Mills technicians learned at the car race, as well as other efforts, they were able to reduce setup time from 5 hours to just 20 minutes.

**What are the benefits of reducing setup time? (Answer is available at the end of the chapter.)**

# The Advantage of Better Management Decisions

Managers extend the use of ABC via activity-based management (ABM) for both strategic and operational decisions or perspectives. For example, returning to Atlas Company, its managers might use ABC information about its Ab Benches and Ab Coasters to improve the efficiency of its operations. For example, after realizing that both products require a high volume of setup hours—as well as the costs of these hours—they might want to reduce the hours required to set up production runs. Such information may lead managers to increase the number of units produced with each setup or to optimize production schedules for the two products.

ABC also helps managers evaluate employees, departments, and business units.

- Atlas, for example, might use ABC information about salespeople's activities related to customer visits, number of orders, and post-sales customer service. Such information informs managers about how much effort salespeople are exerting, as well as how efficient they are in dealing with customers.

- Similarly, Atlas might use ABC information about each department's use of shared resources, like inventory space. Such information lets managers know which departments are the most efficient, which in turn leads to sharing best-practices information within the company.

ABC information also helps Atlas to establish **performance standards** within the company, as well as **benchmark** its performance against other companies.

The implications of ABC are not limited to operational decisions. The differences in profitability between the Ab Benches and Ab Coasters may suggest a need to change the company's product mix. Such considerations, in turn, have implications for Atlas's marketing strategy. ABM may guide managers in considering different target customer markets for the two products. Or, managers might consider bundling the two products into a "home gym" set. As another, more extreme, example, managers might consider outsourcing production for one of the products or dropping one of the product lines altogether.

It is often the case that ABM for one perspective has implications for another perspective.

- For instance, the strategic decision to drop a product line is usually followed by operational decisions regarding what to do with employees' time or the machinery and equipment originally used to manufacture the dropped product.

- Similarly, increases in employees' efficiency following from operational decisions often lead to changes in employee hiring and compensation strategy.

The interrelated nature of the strategic and operational perspectives often means that a decision is not made until the cascading implications of that decision are also identified and considered.

# Some Limitations and Knowing When to Use ABC

ABC can be very beneficial, but it is not without its limitations.

1. **ABC can be expensive to use.** The increased cost of identifying multiple activities and applying numerous cost drivers discourages many companies from using ABC.

2. **ABC systems are more complex than traditional systems.**

3. **Some arbitrary allocations remain.** Even though more overhead costs can be assigned directly to products through ABC, some overhead costs might still be assigned by fairly arbitrary cost drivers. For example, Atlas Company allocated $50,000 of overhead pertaining to insurance and property taxes to the facility management cost pool. Atlas assigned this $50,000 using square footage used by each product (10,000 square feet for Ab Benches and 15,000 square feet for Ab Coasters). A more accurate driver of insurance costs might be replacement costs of production equipment for each product type. However, such information may not be readily available, and Atlas must make do with square footage.

So companies must ask, is the cost of implementation greater than the benefit of greater accuracy? For some companies, there may be no need to consider ABC at all because their existing system is sufficient.

In light of these limitations, how does a company know when to use ABC? The presence of one or more of the following factors would point to possible use:

1. Product lines differ greatly in volume and manufacturing complexity.

2. Product lines are numerous and diverse, requiring various degrees of support services.

3. Overhead costs constitute a significant portion of total costs.

4. The manufacturing process or the number of products has changed significantly, for example, from labor-intensive to capital-intensive due to automation.

5. Production or marketing managers are ignoring data provided by the existing system and are instead using "bootleg" costing data or other alternative data when pricing or making other product decisions.

Ultimately, it is important to realize that the redesign and installation of a product costing system is a significant decision that requires considerable cost and a major effort to accomplish.

- Financial managers need to be cautious and deliberate when initiating changes in costing systems, giving careful consideration to the relative costs and benefits.

- A key factor in implementing a successful ABC system is the support of top management, especially given that the benefits of ABC are not completely visible until *after* it has been implemented.

---

## Data Analytics Insight

Istudioworkstock/
Shutterstock.com

### Delivering People and Packages

In the past, one of the main barriers to implementing ABC was the high cost of data collection needed to determine cost pools, cost drivers, and activity usage. But today's automated systems collect data on virtually every aspect of a company's operations, thus helping a company to more easily implement ABC and employ ABM. This data can also help companies employ ABM by reducing non–value-added activities.

For example, for airlines, nonscheduled maintenance and repairs is a significant non–value-added activity that causes many flight delays. In response, **General Electric (GE)**, which makes many of the engines used in passenger jets, now equips its jet engines with sensors, which makes it possible to predict when parts are likely to fail. The airline can then preemptively schedule maintenance and preorder parts as needed.

Data analytics can also help to streamline operations and improve efficiency in package delivery. The goal of a package delivery company is to get packages to the destination in a cost-effective and timely fashion. And when these packages contain medical supplies, this goal can take on an added urgency as some medical supplies expire very quickly. **UPS** handles this issue by placing sensors on high-priority medical packages, which allows the company to continuously track the packages. UPS couples this with continuous data regarding weather patterns and other potential delivery disruptions to determine if the company should reroute any of these packages to avoid delays.

**Sources:** Sara Castellanos, "UPS to Use Sensors That Can Track Medical Packages at All Times," *Wall Street Journal Online* (November 20, 2019); and Bernard Marr, *Big Data in Practice* (Hoboken, N.J.: John Wiley & Sons, 2016), pp. 125–129.

**How do big data and data analytics help companies implement and employ ABC and ABM? (Answer is available at the end of this chapter.)**

---

## DO IT! 3 | Classify Activity Levels

Morgan Toy Company manufactures six primary product lines of toys in its Morganville factory. As a result of an activity analysis, the accounting department has identified eight activity cost pools. Each of the toy products is produced in large batches, with the whole factory devoted to one product at a time. Classify each of the following activities as either unit-level, batch-level, product-level, or facility-level: (a) engineering design, (b) machine setup, (c) toy design, (d) interviews of prospective factory managers, (e) inspections after each setup, (f) polishing parts, (g) assembling parts, and (h) health and safety.

### ACTION PLAN

- You should use unit-level activities for each unit of product, batch-level activities for each batch of product, product-level activities for an entire product line, and facility-level activities for across the entire range of products.

### Solution

    **a.** Product-level.  **b.** Batch-level.  **c.** Product-level.  **d.** Facility-level.  **e.** Batch-level.
    **f.** Unit-level.  **g.** Unit-level.  **h.** Facility-level.

Related exercise material: **BE17.10, BE17.11, BE17.12, DO IT! 17.3, E17.12, and E17.3.**

# ABC and Service Industries

> **LEARNING OBJECTIVE 4**
>
> Apply activity-based costing to service industries.

Although initially developed and implemented by manufacturers, activity-based costing has been widely adopted in service industries as well. ABC is used by airlines, railroads, hotels, hospitals, banks, insurance companies, telephone companies, and financial services firms.

- The overall objective of ABC in service firms is no different than it is in a manufacturing company.
- That objective is to identify the key activities that generate costs and to keep track of how many of those activities are completed for each service performed (by job, service, contract, or customer).

The general approach to identifying activities, activity cost pools, and cost drivers is the same for service companies and for manufacturers. Also, the labeling of activities as value-added and non–value-added, and the attempt to reduce or eliminate non–value-added activities as much as possible, is just as valid in service industries as in manufacturing operations. What sometimes makes implementation of activity-based costing difficult in service industries is that, compared to manufacturers, **a larger proportion of overhead costs are company-wide costs** that cannot be easily traced to specific services performed by the company.

To illustrate the application of activity-based costing to a service company contrasted to traditional costing, we use a public accounting firm. This illustration is applicable to any service firm that performs numerous services for a client as part of a job, such as a law, consulting, or architectural firm.

## Traditional Costing Example

Assume that the public accounting firm of Check and Doublecheck prepares the condensed annual budget shown in **Illustration 17.18**. The firm engages in a number of services, including audit, tax, and computer consulting.

The cost of the professional service performed is usually based on direct labor. Under traditional costing, direct labor is the basis for overhead application to each job. As shown

**ILLUSTRATION 17.18**

**Condensed annual budget of a service firm under traditional costing**

### Check and Doublecheck, CPAs
#### Annual Budget

| | | |
|---|---:|---:|
| Revenue | | $4,000,000 |
| Direct labor | $1,200,000 | |
| Overhead (estimated) | 600,000 | |
| Total costs | | 1,800,000 |
| Operating income | | $2,200,000 |

$$\frac{\text{Estimated overhead}}{\text{Direct labor cost}} = \text{Predetermined overhead rate}$$

$$\frac{\$600,000}{\$1,200,000} = 50\%$$

in Illustration 17.18, the predetermined overhead rate of 50% is calculated by dividing the total estimated overhead cost by the total direct labor cost. To determine the operating income earned on any job, Check and Doublecheck applies overhead at the rate of 50% of actual direct professional labor costs incurred. For example, assume that Check and Doublecheck records $140,000 of actual direct professional labor cost during its audit of Plano Molding Company, which was billed an audit fee of $260,000. Under traditional costing, using 50% as the rate for applying overhead to the job, Check and Doublecheck would compute applied overhead and operating income related to the Plano Molding Company audit as shown in **Illustration 17.19**.

**ILLUSTRATION 17.19**

**Overhead applied under traditional costing system**

| Check and Doublecheck, CPAs | | |
|---|---|---|
| Plano Molding Company Audit | | |
| Revenue | | $260,000 |
| Less: Direct professional labor | $140,000 | |
| Applied overhead (50% × $140,000) | 70,000 | 210,000 |
| Operating income | | $ 50,000 |

This example, under traditional costing, uses only one cost driver (direct labor cost) to determine the overhead application rate.

## Activity-Based Costing Example

Under *activity-based costing*, Check and Doublecheck distributes its estimated annual overhead costs of $600,000 to three activity cost pools. The firm computes activity-based overhead rates per cost driver by dividing the amount allocated to each activity overhead cost pool by the estimated number of cost drivers used per activity. **Illustration 17.20** shows an annual overhead budget using an ABC system.

**ILLUSTRATION 17.20**   **Condensed annual budget of a service firm under activity-based costing**

| | | | | Check and Doublecheck, CPAs | | | |
|---|---|---|---|---|---|---|---|
| | | | | Annual Overhead Budget | | | |
| Activity Cost Pools | Cost Drivers | Estimated Overhead | ÷ | Estimated Use of Cost Drivers per Activity | = | Activity-Based Overhead Rates | |
| Administration | Number of partner-hours | $335,000 | | 3,350 | | $100 per partner-hour | |
| Customer development | Revenue billed | 160,000 | | $4,000,000 | | $0.04 per $1 of revenue | |
| Recruiting and training | Direct professional hours | 105,000 | | 30,000 | | $3.50 per professional hour | |
| | | $600,000 | | | | | |

The assignment of the individual overhead activity rates to the actual number of activities used in the performance of the Plano Molding Company audit results in total overhead assigned of $57,200, as shown in **Illustration 17.21**.

| | Check and Doublecheck CPA | | | | |
|---|---|---|---|---|---|

**Check and Doublecheck, CPAs**
**Plano Molding Company Audit**

| | Activity Cost Pools | Cost Drivers | Use of Drivers | Activity-Based Overhead Rates | Cost Assigned |
|---|---|---|---|---|---|
| 6 | Administration | Number of partner-hours | 335 | $100.00 | $33,500 |
| 7 | Customer development | Revenue billed | $260,000 | $0.04 | 10,400 |
| 8 | Recruiting and training | Direct professional hours | 3,800 | $3.50 | 13,300 |
| 9 | | | | | $57,200 |

Under activity-based costing, Check and Doublecheck assigns overhead costs of $57,200 to the Plano Molding Company audit, as compared to $70,000 under traditional costing. **Illustration 17.22** compares total costs and operating margins under the two costing systems.

**Check and Doublecheck, CPAs**
**Plano Molding Company Audit**

| | Traditional Costing | | ABC | |
|---|---|---|---|---|
| Revenue | | $260,000 | | $260,000 |
| Expenses | | | | |
| Direct professional labor | $140,000 | | $140,000 | |
| Applied overhead | 70,000 | | 57,200 | |
| Total expenses | | 210,000 | | 197,200 |
| Operating income | | $ 50,000 | | $ 62,800 |
| Profit margin | | 19.2% | | 24.2% |

Illustration 17.22 shows that the assignment of overhead costs under traditional costing and ABC is different.

- The total cost assigned to performing the audit of Plano Molding Company is greater under traditional costing by $12,800 ($70,000 − $57,200), and the profit margin is significantly lower.

- Traditional costing understates the profitability of the audit.

## Service Company Insight    American Airlines

Image by tookapic from Pixabay

### Traveling Light

Have you flown on **American Airlines** since baggage fees have been implemented? Did the fee make you so mad that you swore that the next time you flew, you would pack fewer clothes so you could use a carry-on bag instead? That is exactly how American Airlines (and the other airlines that charge baggage fees) hoped that you would react. Baggage handling is extremely labor-intensive. All that tagging, sorting, loading on carts, loading in planes, unloading, and sorting again add up to about $9 per bag. Baggage handling also involves equipment costs: sorters, carts, conveyors, tractors, and storage facilities. That's about another $4 of equipment-related overhead per bag. Finally, there is the additional fuel cost of a 40-pound item—about $2 in fuel for a 3-hour flight. These costs add up to $15 ($9 + $4 + $2).

Since airlines have implemented their baggage fees, fewer customers are checking bags. Not only does this save the airlines money, it also increases the amount of space available for hauling cargo. An airline can charge at least $80 for hauling a small parcel for same-day delivery service.

For those bags that do still get checked-in by customers, **Alaska Airlines** has reduced its costs by employing barcode scanning of every bag that goes on and off a plane to speed up its sorting process.

**Source:** Scott McCartney, "What It Costs an Airline to Fly Your Luggage," *Wall Street Journal* (November 25, 2008); and Scott McCartney, "The Best and Worst Airlines of 2016" *Wall Street Journal* (January 11, 2017).

**Why do airlines charge even higher rates for heavier bags, bags that are odd shapes (e.g., ski bags), and bags with hazardous materials in them? (Answer is available at the end of the chapter.)**

## DO IT! 4 | Apply ABC to Service Company

We Carry It, Inc. is a trucking company. It provides local, short-haul, and long-haul services. The company has developed the following three cost pools.

| Activity Cost Pools | Cost Drivers | Estimated Overhead | Estimated Use of Cost Drivers per Activity |
|---|---|---|---|
| Loading and unloading | Number of pieces | $ 70,000 | 100,000 pieces |
| Travel | Miles driven | 250,000 | 500,000 miles |
| Logistics | Hours | 60,000 | 2,000 hours |

a. Compute the activity-based overhead rate for each pool.

b. Determine the overhead assigned to Job A1027, which has 150 pieces and requires 200 miles of driving and 0.75 hours of logistics.

### Solution

a. The activity based overhead rates are as follows.

| Activity Cost Pools | Estimated Overhead | ÷ | Estimated Use of Cost Drivers per Activity | = | Activity-Based Overhead Rate |
|---|---|---|---|---|---|
| Loading and unloading | $ 70,000 | | 100,000 pieces | | $0.70 per piece |
| Travel | 250,000 | | 500,000 miles | | $0.50 per mile |
| Logistics | 60,000 | | 2,000 hours | | $30 per hour |

b. The overhead applied to job A1027 is $(150 \times \$0.70) + (200 \times \$0.50) + (0.75 \times \$30) = \$227.50$

Related exercise material: **BE17.12, DO IT! 17.4, E17.14, E17.15, and E17.17.**

---

| Appendix 17A | # Just-in-Time Processing |
|---|---|

**LEARNING OBJECTIVE *5**

Explain just-in-time (JIT) processing.

---

Traditionally, continuous process manufacturing has been based on a **just-in-case** philosophy: Inventories of raw materials are maintained *just in case* some items are of poor quality or a key supplier is shut down by a strike. Similarly, subassembly parts are manufactured and stored *just in case* they are needed later in the manufacturing process. Finished goods are completed and stored *just in case* unexpected and rush customer orders are received. This philosophy often results in a "**push approach**," in which raw materials and subassembly parts are pushed through each process. Traditional processing often results in the buildup of extensive manufacturing inventories.

Primarily in response to foreign competition, many U.S. firms have switched to **just-in-time (JIT) processing**.

- JIT manufacturing is dedicated to having the right amounts of materials, parts, or products just as they are needed.
- JIT first hit the United States in the early 1980s when automobile companies adopted it to compete with foreign automakers. Many companies, including **Dell**, **Caterpillar**, and **Harley-Davidson**, now successfully use JIT.
- Under JIT processing, companies receive raw materials **just in time** for use in production, they complete subassembly parts **just in time** for use in finished goods, and they complete finished goods **just in time** to be sold.

**Illustration 17A.1** shows the sequence of activities in just-in-time processing.

**ILLUSTRATION 17A.1** **Just-in-time processing**

# Objective of JIT Processing

An ultimate objective of JIT is to eliminate manufacturing inventories. Inventories have an adverse effect on net income because they tie up funds and storage space that could be put to more productive uses. JIT strives to eliminate inventories by using a "**pull approach**" in manufacturing.

- This approach begins with the customer placing an order with the company, which starts the process of pulling the product through the manufacturing process.
- A computer at the final workstation sends a signal to the preceding workstation.

- This signal indicates the exact materials (parts and subassemblies) needed to complete the production of a specified product for a specified time period, such as an eight-hour shift.
- The next-preceding process, in turn, sends its signal to other processes back up the line.

The goal is a smooth, continuous flow in the manufacturing process, with no buildup of inventories at any point.

## Elements of JIT Processing

There are three important elements in JIT processing:

1. **Dependable suppliers.** Suppliers must be willing to deliver on short notice exact quantities of raw materials according to precise quality specifications (even including multiple deliveries within the same day) (see **Helpful Hint**). Suppliers must also be willing to deliver the raw materials at specified workstations rather than at a central receiving department. This type of purchasing requires constant and direct communication. Such communication is facilitated by an online computer linkage between the company and its suppliers.

2. **A multiskilled work force.** Under JIT, machines are often strategically grouped into work cells or workstations. Much of the work is automated. As a result, one worker may operate and maintain several different types of machines.

3. **A total quality control system.** The company must establish total quality control throughout the manufacturing operations (see **Helpful Hint**). Total quality control means **no defects**. Since the pull approach signals only required quantities, any defects at any workstation will shut down operations at subsequent workstations. Total quality control requires continuous monitoring by both line employees and supervisors at each workstation.

**HELPFUL HINT**
Buyer leverage is important in finding dependable suppliers. Companies like GM and GE have more success than smaller companies.

**HELPFUL HINT**
Without its emphasis on quality control, JIT would be impractical or even impossible. In JIT, quality is engineered into the production process.

## Benefits of JIT Processing

The major benefits of implementing JIT processing are as follows.

1. Significant reduction or elimination of manufacturing inventories.
2. Enhanced product quality.
3. Reduction or elimination of rework costs and inventory storage costs.
4. Production cost savings from the improved flow of goods through the processes.

The effects in many cases have been dramatic. For example, after using JIT for two years, a major division of **Hewlett-Packard** found that work in process inventories (in dollars) were down 82%, scrap/rework costs were down 30%, space utilization improved by 40%, and labor efficiency improved 50%. As indicated, JIT not only reduces inventory but also enables a company to manufacture a better product faster and with less waste.

One of the major accounting benefits of JIT is the elimination of separate raw materials and work in process inventory accounts.

- These accounts are replaced by **one account**, Raw and In-Process Inventory.
- All materials and conversion costs are charged to this account.
- The reduction (or elimination) of in-process inventories results in a simpler computation of equivalent units of production.

A significant potential downside of JIT is the higher risk of not having materials when they are needed. As noted above, JIT requires dependable suppliers. But even dependable suppliers cannot overcome unexpected situations, such as natural disasters, that disrupt the supply chain.

# Review and Practice

## Learning Objectives Review

### 1  Discuss the difference between traditional costing and activity-based costing.

A traditional costing system assigns overhead to products on the basis of predetermined plantwide or departmentwide rates such as direct labor or machine hours. An ABC system allocates overhead to identified activity cost pools and then assigns costs to products using related cost drivers that measure the activities (resources) consumed.

The development of an activity-based costing system involves the following four steps. (1) Identify and classify the major activities involved in the manufacture of specific products and allocate overhead to cost pools. (2) Identify the cost driver that has a strong correlation to the costs accumulated in each cost pool and estimate total annual cost driver usage. (3) Compute the activity-based overhead rate for each cost pool. (4) Assign overhead costs to products using the overhead rates determined for each cost pool and each product's use of each cost driver.

### 2  Apply activity-based costing to a manufacturer.

To identify activity cost pools, a company must perform an analysis of each operation or process, documenting and timing every task, action, or transaction. Cost drivers identified for assigning activity cost pools must (a) accurately measure the actual consumption of the activity by the various products and (b) have related data easily available. The overhead allocated to each activity cost pool is divided by the estimated use of cost drivers to determine the activity-based overhead rate for each pool. Overhead is assigned to products by multiplying a particular product's estimated use of a cost driver by the activity-based overhead rate. This is done for each activity cost pool and then summed.

### 3  Explain the benefits and limitations of activity-based costing.

Features of ABC that make it a more accurate product costing system include (1) the increased number of cost pools used to assign overhead (including use of the activity-level hierarchy), (2) the enhanced control over overhead costs (including identification of non–value-added activities), and (3) the better management decisions it makes possible. The limitations of ABC are (1) the higher analysis and measurement costs that accompany multiple activity centers and cost drivers, and (2) the necessity still to assign some costs arbitrarily.

### 4  Apply activity-based costing to service industries.

The overall objective of using ABC in service industries is no different than for manufacturing industries—that is, improved costing of services performed (by job, service, contract, or customer). The general approach to costing is the same: analyze operations, identify activities, accumulate overhead costs by activity cost pools, and identify and use cost drivers to assign the cost pools to the services.

### *5  Explain just-in-time (JIT) processing.

JIT is a processing system dedicated to having on hand the right materials and products just at the time they are needed, thereby reducing the amount of inventory and the time inventory is held. One of the principal accounting effects is that one account, Raw and In-Process Inventory, replaces both the raw materials and work in process inventory accounts.

## Glossary Review

**Activity**  Any event, action, transaction, or work sequence that incurs costs when producing a product or performing a service. (p. 17-5).

**Activity-based costing (ABC)**  A costing system that allocates overhead to multiple activity cost pools and assigns the activity cost pools to products or services by means of cost drivers. (p. 17-5).

**Activity-based management (ABM)**  Extends ABC from product costing to a comprehensive management tool that focuses on reducing costs and improving processes and decision-making. (p. 17-15).

**Activity cost pool**  The overhead cost attributed to a distinct type of activity or related activities. (p. 17-5).

**Batch-level activities**  Activities performed for each batch of products rather than for each unit. (p. 17-15).

**Cost driver**  Any factor or activity that has a direct cause–effect relationship with the resources consumed. In ABC, cost drivers are used to assign activity cost pools to products or services. (p. 17-5).

**Facility-level activities**  Activities required to support or sustain an entire production process. (p. 17-15).

*__Just-in-time (JIT) processing__  A processing system dedicated to having the right amount of materials, parts, or products arrive as they are needed, thereby reducing the amount of inventory. (p. 17-23).

**Non–value-added activity**  A nonessential activity that, if eliminated, would not reduce the perceived value of a company's product or service. (p. 17-16).

**Product-level activities**  Activities performed in support of an entire product line but not always performed every time a new unit or batch of products is produced. (p. 17-15).

**Unit-level activities**  Activities performed for each unit of production. (p. 17-15).

**Value-added activity**  An essential activity that increases the perceived value of a product or service to a customer. (p. 17-16).

## Practice Multiple-Choice Questions

1. **(LO 1)** Activity-based costing (ABC):

   a. can be used only in a process cost system.

   b. focuses on units of production.

   c. focuses on activities needed to produce a good or perform a service.

   d. uses only a single basis of allocation.

2. **(LO 1)** Activity-based costing:

   a. is the initial phase of converting to a just-in-time operating environment.

   b. can be used only in a job order costing system.

   c. is a two-stage overhead cost allocation system that identifies activity cost pools and cost drivers.

   d. uses direct labor as its primary cost driver.

3. **(LO 1)** Any activity that causes resources to be consumed is called a:

   a. just-in-time activity.

   b. facility-level activity.

   c. cost driver.

   d. non–value-added activity.

4. **(LO 2)** Which of the following would be the **best** cost driver for the assembling cost pool?

   a. Number of product lines.

   b. Number of parts.

   c. Number of orders.

   d. Amount of square footage.

5. **(LO 2)** The overhead rate for machine setups is $100 per setup. Products A and B have 80 and 60 setups, respectively. The overhead assigned to each product is:

   a. Product A $8,000, Product B $8,000.

   b. Product A $8,000, Product B $6,000.

   c. Product A $6,000, Product B $6,000.

   d. Product A $6,000, Product B $8,000.

6. **(LO 2)** Donna Crawford Co. has identified inspections as an activity cost pool to which it has allocated estimated overhead of $1,920,000. It has estimated use of cost drivers for that activity to be 160,000 inspections. Widgets require 40,000 inspections, gadgets 30,000 inspections, and targets 90,000 inspections. The overhead assigned to each product is:

   a. Widgets $40,000, gadgets $30,000, targets $90,000.

   b. Widgets $640,000, gadgets $640,000, targets $640,000.

   c. Widgets $360,000, gadgets $480,000, targets $1,080,000.

   d. Widgets $480,000, gadgets $360,000, targets $1,080,000.

7. **(LO 3)** A frequently cited limitation of activity-based costing is:

   a. ABC results in more cost pools being used to assign overhead costs to products.

   b. certain overhead costs remain to be assigned by means of some arbitrary volume-based cost driver such as labor or machine hours.

   c. ABC leads to poorer management decisions.

   d. ABC results in less control over overhead costs.

8. **(LO 3)** A company should consider using ABC if:

   a. overhead costs constitute a small portion of total product costs.

   b. it has only a few product lines that require similar degrees of support services.

   c. direct labor constitutes a significant part of the total product cost and a high correlation exists between direct labor and changes in overhead costs.

   d. its product lines differ greatly in volume and manufacturing complexity.

9. **(LO 3)** A nonessential activity that adds costs to the product but does not increase its perceived value is a:

   a. value-added activity.

   b. cost driver.

   c. cost/benefit activity.

   d. non–value-added activity.

10. **(LO 3)** The following activity is value-added:

    a. storage of raw materials.

    b. moving parts from machine to machine.

    c. producing a necessary product component on a machine.

    d. All of the above.

11. **(LO 3)** A relevant facility-level cost driver for factory heating costs is:

    a. machine hours.

    b. direct materials.

    c. floor space.

    d. direct labor cost.

12. **(LO 4)** The first step in the development of an activity-based costing system for a service company is:

    a. identify and classify activities and allocate overhead to cost pools.

    b. assign overhead costs to products.

    c. identify cost drivers.

    d. compute overhead rates.

*13. **(LO 5)** Under just-in-time processing:

    a. raw materials are received just in time for use in production.

    b. subassembly parts are completed just in time for use in assembling finished goods.

    c. finished goods are completed just in time to be sold.

    d. All of the answer choices are correct.

*14. **(LO 5)** The primary objective of just-in-time processing is to:

    a. accumulate overhead in activity cost pools.

    b. eliminate or reduce all manufacturing inventories.

    c. identify relevant activity cost drivers.

    d. identify value-added activities.

## Solutions

**1. c.** Focusing on activities needed to produce a good or perform a service is an accurate statement about activity-based costing. The other choices are incorrect because ABC (a) can be used in either a process cost or a job order cost system; (b) focuses on activities performed to produce a product, not on units of production; and (d) uses multiple bases of allocation, not just a single basis of allocation.

**2. c.** ABC is a two-stage overhead cost allocation system that identifies activity cost pools and cost drivers. The other choices are incorrect because ABC (a) is not necessarily part of the conversion to a just-in-time operating environment, (b) can be used in either a process cost or a job order cost system, and (d) uses other activities in addition to direct labor as cost drivers.

**3. c.** Activities that cause resources to be consumed are called cost drivers, not (a) just-in-time activities, (b) facility-level activities, or (d) non–value-added activities.

**4. b.** The number of parts would be the best cost driver for the assembling cost pool as it has a higher degree of correlation with the actual consumption of the overhead costs, that is, the assembling of parts, than (a) number of product lines, (c) number of orders, or (d) amount of square footage.

**5. b.** The overhead assigned to Product A is $8,000 ($100 × 80) and to Product B is $6,000 ($100 × 60), not (a) $8,000, $8,000; (c) $6,000, $6,000; or (d) $6,000, $8,000.

**6. d.** The overhead assigned to widgets is $480,000 [($1,920,000 ÷ 160,000) × 40,000], to gadgets is $360,000 [($1,920,000 ÷ 160,000) × 30,000], and to targets is $1,080,000 [($1,920,000 ÷ 160,000) × 90,000]. Therefore, choices (a) $40,000, $30,000, and $90,000; (b) $640,000, $640,000, and $640,000; and (c) $360,000, $480,000, and $1,080,000 are incorrect.

**7. b.** A limitation of ABC is that certain overhead costs remain to be assigned by means of some arbitrary volume-based cost driver. The other choices are incorrect because (a) more cost pools is an advantage of ABC, (c) ABC can lead to better management decisions, and (d) ABC results in more control over overhead costs.

**8. d.** A company should consider using ABC if its product lines differ greatly in volume and manufacturing complexity. For choices (a), (b), and (c), a traditional costing system should be sufficient and less expensive to implement.

**9. d.** Non–value-added activities add costs to a product but do not increase its perceived value, not (a) value-added activities, (b) cost drivers, or (c) cost/benefit activities.

**10. c.** Producing a necessary product component on a machine is a value-added activity as it is an integral part of manufacturing a product. Choices (a) and (b) are non–value-added activities, so therefore choice (d) is incorrect as well.

**11. c.** Floor space is a relevant facility-level cost driver for factory heating costs as a larger space will result in higher heating costs. The other choices are incorrect because (a) machine hours, (b) direct materials, and (d) direct labor cost are all unit-level cost drivers.

**12. a.** The first step in developing an ABC system is to identify and classify activities and allocate overhead to cost pools. The other choices are incorrect because (b) is Step 4, (c) is Step 2, and (d) is Step 3.

**\*13. d.** All of the choices are accurate statements about just-in-time processing.

**\*14. b.** Eliminating or reducing all manufacturing inventories is the primary objective of just-in-time processing. The other choices are incorrect because choices (a), (c), and (d) are part of the process of implementing an ABC system.

---

# Practice Brief Exercises

---

*Compute activity-based overhead rates.*

**1. (LO 2)** Franco Company identifies three activities in its manufacturing process: machine setups, machining, and inspections. Estimated annual overhead cost for each activity is $280,000, $140,000, and $39,000, respectively. The cost driver for each activity and the estimated annual usage are number of setups 1,400, machine hours 7,000, and number of inspections 1,300. Compute the overhead rate for each activity.

**Solution**

**1.**

| | |
|---|---|
| Machine setups | $280,000 ÷ 1,400 = $200 per setup |
| Machining | $140,000 ÷ 7,000 = $20 per machine hour |
| Inspections | $ 39,000 ÷ 1,300 = $30 per inspection |

**2. (LO 2)** Dodge Inc. uses activity-based costing as the basis for information to set prices for its six lines of seasonal coats. Compute the activity-based overhead rates using the following budgeted data for each of the activity cost pools.

*Compute activity-based overhead rates.*

| Activity Cost Pools | Estimated Overhead | Estimated Use of Cost Drivers per Activity |
|---|---|---|
| Designing | $ 300,000 | 6,000 designer hours |
| Sizing and cutting | 3,000,000 | 150,000 machine hours |
| Stitching and trimming | 1,200,000 | 40,000 labor hours |
| Wrapping and packing | 420,000 | 28,000 finished units |

**Solution**

**2.**

| Activity Cost Pool | Estimated Overhead | ÷ | Estimated Use of Cost Drivers per Activity | = | Activity-Based Overhead Rates |
|---|---|---|---|---|---|
| Designing | $ 300,000 | | 6,000 designer hours | | $50.00 per designer hour |
| Sizing and cutting | 3,000,000 | | 150,000 machine hours | | $20.00 per machine hour |
| Stitching and trimming | 1,200,000 | | 40,000 labor hours | | $30.00 per labor hour |
| Wrapping and packing | 420,000 | | 28,000 finished units | | $15 per finished unit |

**3. (LO 2)** Rankle, Inc. a manufacturer of tofu-based hot dogs, employs activity-based costing. The budgeted data for each of the activity cost pools is provided below for the year 2022.

*Compute activity-based overhead rates.*

| Activity Cost Pools | Estimated Overhead | Estimated Use of Cost Drivers per Activity |
|---|---|---|
| Ordering and receiving | $ 280,000 | 5,600 orders |
| Food processing | 1,400,000 | 40,000 machine hours |
| Packaging | 560,000 | 22,400 labor hours |

For 2022, the company had 5,400 orders and used 41,000 machine hours, and labor hours totaled 23,000. What is the total overhead applied?

**Solution**

**3.**

| Activity Cost Pool | Estimated Overhead | ÷ | Estimated Use of Cost Drivers per Activity | = | Activity-Based Overhead Rates |
|---|---|---|---|---|---|
| Ordering and receiving | $ 280,000 | | 5,600 orders | | $50.00 per order |
| Food processing | 1,400,000 | | 40,000 machine hours | | $35.00 per machine hour |
| Packaging | 560,000 | | 22,400 labor hours | | $25.00 per labor hour |

| Cost Drivers | × | Overhead Rates | = | Total Overhead Applied |
|---|---|---|---|---|
| 5,400 orders | | $50.00 | | $ 270,000 |
| 41,000 machine hours | | $35.00 | | 1,435,000 |
| 23,000 labor hours | | $25.00 | | 575,000 |
| | | | | $2,280,000 |

# Practice Exercises

*Assign overhead using traditional costing and ABC.*

1. **(LO 1, 2)** Domestic Fabrics has budgeted overhead costs of $955,000. It has assigned overhead on a plantwide basis to its two products (wool and cotton) using direct labor hours which are estimated to be 477,500 for the current year. The company has decided to experiment with activity-based costing and has created two activity cost pools and related activity cost drivers. These two cost pools are cutting (cost driver is machine hours) and machine setups (cost driver is number of machine setups). Overhead allocated to the cutting cost pool is $400,000, and $555,000 is allocated to the machine setups cost pool. Additional information regarding cost driver usage related to these pools is as follows.

|  | Wool | Cotton | Total |
|---|---|---|---|
| Machine hours | 100,000 | 100,000 | 200,000 |
| Number of machine setups | 1,000 | 500 | 1,500 |

### Instructions

a. Determine the amount of overhead assigned to the wool product line and the cotton product line using activity-based costing.

b. What is the difference between the allocation of overhead to the wool and cotton product lines using activity-based costing versus the traditional approach, assuming direct labor hours were incurred evenly between the wool and cotton?

### Solution

1. a.

| Activity Cost Pools | Cost Drivers | Estimated Overhead |
|---|---|---|
| Cutting | Machine hours | $400,000 |
| Machine setups | Number of machine setups | 555,000 |

Activity-based overhead rates:

| Cutting | Machine Setups |
|---|---|
| $\dfrac{\$400,000}{200,000} = \$2$ per machine hour | $\dfrac{\$555,000}{1,500} = \$370$ per setup |

|  | Wool | Cotton |
|---|---|---|
| Activity-based costing |  |  |
| Cutting |  |  |
| 100,000 × $2 | $200,000 |  |
| 100,000 × $2 |  | $200,000 |
| Machine setups |  |  |
| 1,000 × $370 | 370,000 |  |
| 500 × $370 |  | 185,000 |
| Total cost assigned | $570,000 | $385,000 |

b. $\dfrac{\text{Estimated overhead}}{\text{Direct labors hours}} = \dfrac{\$955,000}{477,500} = \$2$ per direct labor hour

|  | Wool | Cotton |
|---|---|---|
| Traditional costing |  |  |
| 238,750* × $2 | $477,500 |  |
| 238,750 × $2 |  | $477,500 |

*477,500 ÷ 2

The wool product line is assigned $92,500 ($570,000 − $477,500) more overhead cost when an activity-based costing system is used. As a result, the cotton product line is assigned $92,500 ($477,500 − $385,000) less.

*Assign overhead using traditional costing and ABC.*

2. **(LO 1, 2, 3)** Organic Products, Inc., uses a traditional product costing system to assign overhead costs uniformly to all products. To meet Food and Drug Administration (FDA) requirements and to assure its customers of safe, sanitary, and nutritious food, Organic engages in a high level of quality control. Organic assigns its quality-control overhead costs to all products at a rate of 20% of direct

labor costs. Its direct labor cost for the month of June for its low-calorie dessert line is $55,000. In response to repeated requests from its financial vice president, Organic management agrees to adopt activity-based costing. Data relating to the low-calorie dessert line for the month of June are as follows.

| Activity Cost Pools | Cost Drivers | Overhead Rate | Cost Drivers Used per Activity |
|---|---|---|---|
| Inspections of material received | Number of pounds | $ 0.70 per pound | 6,000 pounds |
| In-process inspections | Number of servings | $ 0.35 per serving | 10,000 servings |
| FDA certification | Customer orders | $13.00 per order | 450 orders |

## Instructions

**a.** Compute the quality-control overhead cost to be assigned to the low-calorie dessert product line for the month of June using (1) the traditional product costing system (direct labor cost is the cost driver), and (2) activity-based costing.

**b.** By what amount does the traditional product costing system undercost or overcost the low-calorie dessert line?

## Solution

2. **a. 1.** Traditional product costing system:

$55,000 × .20 = $11,000. Quality-control overhead costs assigned in June to the low-calorie dessert line are $11,000.

   **2.** Activity-based costing system:

| Activity Cost Pools | Cost Drivers Used | × | Activity-Based Overhead Rate | = | Overhead Cost Assigned |
|---|---|---|---|---|---|
| Inspections of material received | 6,000 | | $ 0.70 | | $ 4,200 |
| In-process inspections | 10,000 | | 0.35 | | 3,500 |
| FDA certification | 450 | | 13.00 | | 5,850 |
| Total assigned cost for June | | | | | $13,550 |

**b.** As compared to ABC, the traditional costing system undercosts the quality-control overhead cost assigned to the low-calorie dessert product line by $2,550 ($13,550 − $11,000) in the month of June. That is a 23.2% ($2,550 ÷ $11,000) understatement.

## Practice Problem

**(LO 2)** Spreadwell Paint Company manufactures two high-quality base paints: an *oil-based* paint and a *latex* paint. Both are housepaints and are manufactured only in a neutral white color. Spreadwell sells the white base paints to franchised retail paint and decorating stores where pigments are added to tint (color) the paint as the customer desires. The oil-based paint is made with organic solvents (petroleum products) such as mineral spirits or turpentine. The latex paint is made with water; synthetic resin particles are suspended in the water, and dry and harden when exposed to air.

Spreadwell uses the same processing equipment to produce both paints in different production runs. Between batches, the vats and other processing equipment must be washed and cleaned.

After analyzing the company's entire operations, Spreadwell's accountants and production managers have identified activity cost pools and accumulated annual budgeted overhead costs by pool as follows.

*Assign overhead and compute unit costs.*

| Activity Cost Pools | Estimated Overhead |
|---|---|
| Purchasing | $ 240,000 |
| Processing (weighing and mixing, grinding, thinning and drying, straining) | 1,400,000 |
| Packaging (quarts, gallons, and 5-gallons) | 580,000 |
| Testing | 240,000 |
| Storage and inventory control | 180,000 |
| Washing and cleaning equipment | 560,000 |
| Total annual budgeted overhead | $3,200,000 |

Following further analysis, activity cost drivers were identified, and their estimated use by activity, as well as use by product, were scheduled as follows.

| Activity Cost Pools | Cost Drivers | Estimated Cost Drivers per Activity | Use of Drivers per Product Oil-Based | Use of Drivers per Product Latex |
|---|---|---|---|---|
| Purchasing | Purchase orders | 1,500 orders | 800 | 700 |
| Processing | Gallons processed | 1,000,000 gallons | 400,000 | 600,000 |
| Packaging | Containers filled | 400,000 containers | 180,000 | 220,000 |
| Testing | Number of tests | 4,000 tests | 2,100 | 1,900 |
| Storing | Avg. gals. on hand | 18,000 gallons | 10,400 | 7,600 |
| Washing | Number of batches | 800 batches | 350 | 450 |

Spreadwell has budgeted 400,000 gallons of oil-based paint and 600,000 gallons of latex paint for processing during the year.

**Instructions**

a. Prepare a schedule showing the computations of the activity-based overhead rates.

b. Prepare a schedule assigning each activity's overhead cost pool to each product.

c. Compute the overhead cost per unit for each product.

**Solution**

a. Computations of activity-based overhead rates:

| Activity Cost Pools | Estimated Overhead | ÷ | Estimated Use of Cost Drivers | = | Activity-Based Overhead Rates |
|---|---|---|---|---|---|
| Purchasing | $ 240,000 | | 1,500 orders | | $160 per order |
| Processing | 1,400,000 | | 1,000,000 gallons | | $1.40 per gallon |
| Packaging | 580,000 | | 400,000 containers | | $1.45 per container |
| Testing | 240,000 | | 4,000 tests | | $60 per test |
| Storing | 180,000 | | 18,000 gallons | | $10 per gallon |
| Washing | 560,000 | | 800 batches | | $700 per batch |
| | $3,200,000 | | | | |

b. Assignment of activity cost pools to products:

| Activity Cost Pools | Oil-Based Paint Use of Drivers | Oil-Based Paint Overhead Rates | Oil-Based Paint Cost Assigned | Latex Paint Use of Drivers | Latex Paint Overhead Rates | Latex Paint Cost Assigned |
|---|---|---|---|---|---|---|
| Purchasing | 800 | $160 | $ 128,000 | 700 | $160 | $ 112,000 |
| Processing | 400,000 | $1.40 | 560,000 | 600,000 | $1.40 | 840,000 |
| Packaging | 180,000 | $1.45 | 261,000 | 220,000 | $1.45 | 319,000 |
| Testing | 2,100 | $60 | 126,000 | 1,900 | $60 | 114,000 |
| Storing | 10,400 | $10 | 104,000 | 7,600 | $10 | 76,000 |
| Washing | 350 | $700 | 245,000 | 450 | $700 | 315,000 |
| Total overhead assigned | | | $1,424,000 | | | $1,776,000 |

**c.** Computation of overhead cost assigned per unit:

|  | Oil-Based Paint | Latex Paint |
|---|---|---|
| Total overhead cost assigned | $1,424,000 | $1,776,000 |
| Total gallons produced | 400,000 | 600,000 |
| Overhead cost per gallon | $3.56 | $2.96 |

Brief Exercises, DO IT! Exercises, Exercises, Problems, Data Analytics Activities, and many additional resources are available for practice in WileyPLUS.

*Note:* All asterisked Questions, Exercises, and Problems relate to material in the appendix to the chapter.

## Questions

1. Under what conditions is direct labor a valid basis for allocating overhead?

2. What has happened in recent industrial history to reduce the usefulness of direct labor as the primary basis for allocating overhead to products?

3. In an automated manufacturing environment, what basis of overhead allocation is frequently more relevant than direct labor hours?

4. What is generally true about overhead allocation to products versus low-volume products under a traditional costing system?

5. What are the principal differences between activity-based costing (ABC) and traditional product costing?

6. What is the equation for computing activity-based overhead rates?

7. What steps are involved in developing an activity-based costing system?

8. Explain the preparation and use of a value-added/non–value-added activity flowchart in an ABC system.

9. What is an activity cost pool?

10. What is a cost driver?

11. What makes a cost driver accurate and appropriate?

12. What is the calculation for assigning activity cost pools to products?

13. What are the primary benefits of activity-based costing?

14. What are the limitations of activity-based costing?

15. Under what conditions is ABC generally the superior overhead costing system?

16. What refinement has been made to enhance the efficiency and effectiveness of ABC for use in managing costs?

17. Of what benefit is classifying activities as value-added or non–value-added?

18. In what ways is the application of ABC to service industries the same as its application to manufacturing companies?

19. What is the relevance of the classification of levels of activity to ABC?

*20. **a.** Describe the philosophy and approach of just-in-time processing.

   **b.** Identify the major elements of JIT processing.

## Brief Exercises

**BE17.1 (LO 1), AP** `Service` Digger Inc. sells a high-speed retrieval system for mining information. It provides the following information for the year.

*Identify differences between costing systems.*

|  | Budgeted | Actual |
|---|---|---|
| Overhead cost | $975,000 | $950,000 |
| Machine hours | 50,000 | 45,000 |
| Direct labor hours | 100,000 | 92,000 |

Overhead is applied on the basis of direct labor hours. (a) Compute the predetermined overhead rate. (b) Determine the amount of overhead applied for the year. (c) Explain how an activity-based costing system might differ in terms of computing a predetermined overhead rate.

*Identify differences between costing systems.*

**BE17.2 (LO 1), AP** Finney Inc. has conducted an analysis of overhead costs related to one of its product lines using a traditional costing system (volume-based) and an activity-based costing system. Here are its results.

|  | Traditional Costing | ABC |
|---|---|---|
| Sales revenue | $600,000 | $600,000 |
| Overhead costs: |  |  |
| Product RX3 | $ 34,000 | $ 50,000 |
| Product Y12 | 36,000 | 20,000 |
|  | $ 70,000 | $ 70,000 |

Explain how a difference in the overhead costs between the two systems may have occurred.

*Identify cost drivers.*

**BE17.3 (LO 2), AP** Splash Co. identifies the following activities that pertain to manufacturing overhead for its production of water polo balls: materials handling, machine setups, factory machine maintenance, factory supervision, and quality control. For each activity, identify an appropriate cost driver.

*Identify cost drivers.*

**BE17.4 (LO 2), AP** Mason Company manufactures four products in a single production facility. The company uses activity-based costing. The following activities have been identified through the company's activity analysis: (a) inventory control, (b) machine setups, (c) employee training, (d) quality inspections, (e) materials orderings, (f) drilling operations, and (g) factory maintenance.

For each activity, name a cost driver that might be used to assign overhead costs to products.

*Compute activity-based overhead rates.*

**BE17.5 (LO 2), AP** Morgana Company identifies three activities in its manufacturing process: machine setups, machining, and inspections. Estimated annual overhead cost for each activity is $150,000, $375,000, and $87,500, respectively. The cost driver for each activity and the estimated annual usage are number of setups 2,500, machine hours 25,000, and number of inspections 1,750. Compute the overhead rate for each activity.

*Compute activity-based overhead rates.*

**BE17.6 (LO 2), AP** Weisman, Inc. uses activity-based costing as the basis for information to set prices for its six lines of seasonal coats. Compute the activity-based overhead rates using the following budgeted data for each of the activity cost pools.

| Activity Cost Pools | Estimated Overhead | Estimated Use of Cost Drivers per Activity |
|---|---|---|
| Sizing and cutting | $ 4,000,000 | 160,000 machine hours |
| Stitching and trimming | 1,440,000 | 80,000 labor hours |
| Wrapping and packing | 336,000 | 32,000 finished units |

*Compute overhead applied.*

**BE17.7 (LO 2), AP** Spud, Inc., a manufacturer of gourmet snacks, employs activity-based costing. The budgeted data for each of the activity cost pools is provided below for the year 2022.

| Activity Cost Pools | Estimated Overhead | Estimated Use of Cost Drivers per Activity |
|---|---|---|
| Ordering and receiving | $ 84,000 | 12,000 orders |
| Food processing | 480,000 | 60,000 machine hours |
| Packaging | 1,760,000 | 40,000 labor hours |

For 2022, the company had 7,000 orders for its gourmet snacks and used 40,000 machine hours; labor hours totaled 25,000. What is the total overhead applied?

*Classify activities as value- or non–value-added.*

**BE17.8 (LO 3), AP** Rich Novelty Company identified the following activities in its production and support operations. Classify each of these activities as either value-added or non–value-added.

a. Machine setup.  d. Moving work in process.

b. Design engineering.  e. Inspecting and testing.

c. Storing inventory.  f. Painting and packing.

*Classify service company activities as value- or non–value-added.*

**BE17.9 (LO 3, 4), AN** Service Pine and Danner is an architectural firm that is contemplating the implementation of activity-based costing. The following activities are performed daily by staff architects. Classify these activities as value-added or non–value-added: (a) designing and drafting, 3 hours; (b) staff meetings, 1 hour; (c) on-site supervision, 2 hours; (d) lunch, 1 hour; (e) consultation with client on specifications, 1.5 hours; and (f) entertaining a prospective client for dinner, 2 hours.

*Classify activities according to level.*

**BE17.10 (LO 3, 4), AN** Service Kwik Pix is a large digital processing center that serves 130 outlets in grocery stores, service stations, camera and photo shops, and drug stores in 16 nearby towns. Kwik Pix operates 24 hours a day, 6 days a week. Classify each of the following activity costs of Kwik Pix as either unit-level, batch-level, product-level, or facility-level.

a. Color printing materials.

b. Photocopy paper.

c. Depreciation of machinery (assume units-of-activity depreciation).

d. Setups for enlargements.

e. Supervisor's salary.

f. Ordering materials.

g. Pickup and delivery.

h. Commission to dealers.

i. Insurance on building.

j. Loading developing machines.

**BE17.11 (LO 3), AP** FixIt, Inc. operates 20 injection molding machines in the production of tool boxes of four different sizes, named the Apprentice, the Handyman, the Journeyman, and the Professional. Classify each of the following costs as unit-level, batch-level, product-level, or facility-level. *(in right margin:)* *Classify activities according to level.*

a. First-shift supervisor's salary.

b. Powdered raw plastic.

c. Dies for casting plastic components.

d. Depreciation on injection molding machines (assume units-of-activity depreciation).

e. Changing dies on machines.

f. Moving components to assembly department.

g. Engineering design.

h. Employee health and medical insurance coverage.

**BE17.12 (LO 3, 4), AP** Spin Cycle Architecture uses three activity pools to apply overhead to its projects. Each activity has a cost driver used to assign the overhead costs to the projects. The activities and related overhead costs are as follows: initial concept formation $40,000, design $300,000, and construction oversight $100,000. The cost drivers and estimated use are as follows. *(in right margin:)* *Compute rates and activity levels.*

| Activities | Cost Drivers | Estimated Use of Cost Drivers per Activity |
|---|---|---|
| Initial concept formation | Number of project changes | 20 |
| Design | Square feet | 150,000 |
| Construction oversight | Number of months | 100 |

a. Compute the predetermined overhead rate for each activity.

b. Classify each of these activities as unit-level, batch-level, product-level, or facility-level.

## DO IT! Exercises

**DO IT! 17.1 (LO 1), K** Indicate whether the following statements are true or false. *(in right margin:)* *Identify characteristics of traditional and ABC systems.*

a. The reasoning behind ABC cost allocation is that products consume activities and activities consume resources.

b. Activity-based costing is an approach for allocating direct labor to products.

c. In today's increasingly automated environment, direct labor is never an appropriate basis for allocating costs to products.

d. A cost driver is any factor or activity that has a direct cause-effect relationship with resources consumed.

e. Activity-based costing segregates overhead into various cost pools in an effort to provide more accurate cost information.

**DO IT! 17.2 (LO 2), AP** Flynn Industries has three activity cost pools and two products. It estimates production of 3,000 units of Product BC113 and 1,500 of Product AD908. Having identified its activity cost pools and the cost drivers for each pool, Flynn accumulated the following data relative to those activity cost pools and cost drivers. *(in right margin:)* *Compute activity-based overhead rates and assign overhead using ABC.*

| Annual Overhead Data | | | | Use of Cost Drivers per Product | |
|---|---|---|---|---|---|
| Activity Cost Pools | Cost Drivers | Estimated Overhead | Estimated Use of Cost Drivers per Activity | Product BC113 | Product AD908 |
| Machine setup | Setups | $ 16,000 | 40 | 25 | 15 |
| Machining | Machine hours | 110,000 | 5,000 | 1,000 | 4,000 |
| Packing | Orders | 30,000 | 500 | 150 | 350 |

Using the above data, do the following:

a. Prepare a schedule showing the computations of the activity-based overhead rates per cost driver.

b. Prepare a schedule assigning each activity's overhead cost to the two products.

c. Compute the overhead cost per unit for each product. (Round to nearest cent.)

d. Comment on the comparative overhead cost per product.

*Classify activities according to level.*

**DO IT! 17.3 (LO 3), C** Adamson Company manufactures four lines of garden tools. As a result of an activity analysis, the accounting department has identified eight activity cost pools. Each of the product lines is produced in large batches, with the whole factory devoted to one product at a time. Classify each of the following activities or costs as either unit-level, batch level, product-level, or facility-level.

a. Machining parts.

b. Product design.

c. Factory maintenance.

d. Machine setup.

e. Assembling parts.

f. Purchasing raw materials.

g. Factory property taxes.

h. Painting garden tools.

*Apply ABC to service company.*

**DO IT! 17.4 (LO 4), AP** Service  Ready Ride is a trucking company. It provides local, short-haul, and long-haul services. It has developed the following three cost pools.

| Activity Cost Pools | Cost Drivers | Estimated Overhead | Estimated Use of Cost Driver per Activity |
|---|---|---|---|
| Loading and unloading | Number of pieces | $ 90,000 | 90,000 |
| Travel | Miles driven | 450,000 | 600,000 |
| Logistics | Hours | 75,000 | 3,000 |

a. Compute the activity-based overhead rates for each pool.

b. Determine the overhead assigned to Job XZ3275, which has 150 pieces and requires 200 miles of driving and 0.75 hours of logistics.

# Exercises

*Assign overhead using traditional costing and ABC.*

**E17.1 (LO 1, 2), AP** Saddle Inc. has two types of handbags: standard and custom. The controller has decided to use a plantwide overhead rate based on direct labor costs. The president has heard of activity-based costing and wants to see how the results would differ if this system were used. Two activity cost pools were developed: machining (machine hours) and machine setup (number of setups). The total estimated machine hours is 2,000, and the total estimated number of setups is 500. Presented below is information related to each product's use of cost drivers.

| | Standard | Custom |
|---|---|---|
| Direct labor costs | $50,000 | $100,000 |
| Machine hours | 1,000 | 1,000 |
| Number of setups | 100 | 400 |

Total estimated overhead costs are $240,000. Overhead cost allocated to the machining activity cost pool is $140,000, and $100,000 is allocated to the machine setup activity cost pool.

## Instructions

a. Compute the overhead rate using the traditional (plantwide) approach.

b. Compute the overhead rates using the activity-based costing approach.

c. Determine the difference in allocation between the two approaches.

*Explain difference between traditional and activity-based costing.*

**E17.2 (LO 1), AP** Ayala Inc. has conducted the following analysis related to its product lines, using a traditional costing system (volume-based) and an activity-based costing system. The traditional and the activity-based costing systems assign the same amount of direct materials and direct labor costs.

| Products | Sales Revenue | Total Costs Traditional | Total Costs ABC |
|---|---|---|---|
| Product 540X | $180,000 | $55,000 | $50,000 |
| Product 137Y | 160,000 | 50,000 | 35,000 |
| Product 249S | 70,000 | 15,000 | 35,000 |

## Instructions

a. For each product line, compute operating income using the traditional costing system.

b. For each product line, compute operating income using the activity-based costing system.

c. Using the following calculation, compute the percentage difference in operating income for each of the product lines of Ayala: [Operating Income (ABC) − Operating Income (traditional cost)] ÷ Operating Income (traditional cost). (Round to two decimals.)

d. Provide a rationale as to why the costs for Product 540X are approximately the same using either the traditional or activity-based costing system.

**E17.3 (LO 1, 2), AN** EcoFabrics has budgeted overhead costs of $945,000. It has assigned overhead on a plantwide basis to its two products (wool and cotton) using direct labor hours which are estimated to be 450,000 for the current year. The company has decided to experiment with activity-based costing and has created two activity cost pools and related activity cost drivers. These two cost pools are cutting (cost driver is machine hours) and design (cost driver is number of setups). Total estimated machine hours is 200,000, and total estimated number of setups is 1,500. Overhead allocated to the cutting cost pool is $360,000, and $585,000 is allocated to the design cost pool. Additional information related to product usage by these pools is as follows.

*Assign overhead using traditional costing and ABC.*

| | Wool | Cotton |
|---|---|---|
| Machine hours | 100,000 | 100,000 |
| Number of setups | 1,000 | 500 |

## Instructions

a. Determine the amount of overhead assigned to the wool product line and the cotton product line using activity-based costing.

b. What amount of overhead would be assigned to the wool and cotton product lines using the traditional approach, assuming direct labor hours were incurred evenly between the wool and cotton? How does this compare with the amount assigned using ABC in part (a)?

**E17.4 (LO 1, 2), AN** Altex Inc. manufactures two products: car wheels and truck wheels. To determine the amount of overhead to assign to each product line, the controller, Robert Hermann, has developed the following information.

*Assign overhead using traditional costing and ABC.*

 Excel

| | Car | Truck |
|---|---|---|
| Estimated wheels produced | 40,000 | 10,000 |
| Direct labor hours per wheel | 1 | 3 |

Total estimated overhead costs for the two product lines are $770,000.

## Instructions

a. Compute the overhead cost assigned to the car wheels and truck wheels, assuming that direct labor hours is used to assign overhead costs.

b. Hermann is not satisfied with the traditional method of allocating overhead because he believes that most of the overhead costs relate to the truck wheels product line because of its complexity. He therefore develops the following three activity cost pools and related cost drivers to better understand these costs.

| Activity Cost Pools | Estimated Overhead Costs | Estimated Use of Cost Drivers |
|---|---|---|
| Setting up machines | $220,000 | 1,000 setups |
| Assembling | 280,000 | 70,000 labor hours |
| Inspection | 270,000 | 1,200 inspections |

Compute the activity-based overhead rates for these three cost pools.

c. Compute the cost that is assigned to the car wheels and truck wheels product lines using an activity-based costing system, given the following information.

**Use of Cost Drivers per Product**

|  | Car | Truck |
|---|---|---|
| Number of setups | 200 | 800 |
| Direct labor hours | 40,000 | 30,000 |
| Number of inspections | 100 | 1,100 |

**d.** What do you believe Hermann should do?

*Assign overhead using traditional costing and ABC.*

**E17.5 (LO 1, 2), AN** Perdon Corporation manufactures safes—large mobile safes, and large walk-in stationary bank safes. As part of its annual budgeting process, Perdon is analyzing the profitability of its two products. Part of this analysis involves estimating the amount of overhead to be assigned to each product line. The information shown below relates to overhead.

|  | Mobile Safes | Walk-In Safes |
|---|---|---|
| Units planned for production | 200 | 50 |
| Material moves per product line | 300 | 200 |
| Purchase orders per product line | 450 | 350 |
| Direct labor hours per product line | 800 | 1,700 |

**Instructions**

**a.** The total estimated manufacturing overhead was $260,000. Under traditional costing (which assigns overhead on the basis of direct labor hours), what amount of manufacturing overhead costs are assigned to:

  **1.** One mobile safe?

  **2.** One walk-in safe?

**b.** The total estimated manufacturing overhead of $260,000 was comprised of $160,000 for materials handling costs and $100,000 for purchasing activity costs. Under activity-based costing (ABC):

  **1.** What amount of materials handling costs are assigned to:

    **a.** One mobile safe?

    **b.** One walk-in safe?

  **2.** What amount of purchasing activity costs are assigned to:

    **a.** One mobile safe?

    **b.** One walk-in safe?

**c.** Compare the amount of overhead assigned to one mobile safe and to one walk-in safe under the traditional costing approach versus under ABC.

*Identify activity cost pools and cost drivers.*

**E17.6 (LO 2), AN** Santana Corporation manufactures snowmobiles in its Blue Mountain, Wisconsin, factory. The following costs are budgeted for the first quarter's operations.

| | |
|---|---|
| Machine setup, indirect materials | $ 4,000 |
| Inspections | 16,000 |
| Tests | 4,000 |
| Insurance, factory | 110,000 |
| Engineering design | 140,000 |
| Depreciation, machinery | 520,000 |
| Machine setup, indirect labor | 20,000 |
| Property taxes on factory | 29,000 |
| Factory heating | 19,000 |
| Electricity, factory lighting | 21,000 |
| Engineering prototypes | 60,000 |
| Depreciation, factory | 210,000 |
| Electricity, machinery | 36,000 |
| Machine maintenance wages | 19,000 |

**Instructions**

Classify the above costs of Santana Corporation into activity cost pools using the following: engineering, machinery, machine setup, quality control, factory costs. Next, identify a cost driver that may be used to assign each cost pool to each line of snowmobiles.

**E17.7 (LO 2), AN** Rojas Vineyards in Oakville, California, produces three varieties of wine: merlot, viognier, and pinot noir. The winemaster, Russel Hansen, has identified the following activities as cost pools for accumulating overhead and assigning it to products.

*Identify activity cost drivers.*

1. Spraying. The vines are sprayed with organic pesticides for protection against insects and fungi.

2. Harvesting. The grapes are hand-picked, placed in carts, and transported to the crushers.

3. Stemming and crushing. Cartfuls of bunches of grapes of each variety are separately loaded into machines that remove stems and gently crush the grapes.

4. Pressing and filtering. The crushed grapes are transferred to presses that mechanically remove the juices and filter out bulk and impurities.

5. Fermentation. The grape juice, by variety, is fermented in either stainless-steel tanks or oak barrels.

6. Aging. The wines are aged in either stainless-steel tanks or oak barrels for one to three years depending on variety.

7. Bottling and corking. Bottles are machine-filled and corked.

8. Labeling and boxing. Each bottle is labeled, as is each nine-bottle case, with the name of the vintner, vintage, and variety.

9. Storing. Packaged and boxed bottles are stored awaiting shipment.

10. Shipping. The wine is shipped to distributors and private retailers.

11. Heating and air-conditioning of plant and offices.

12. Maintenance of production equipment. Repairs, replacements, and general maintenance are performed in the off-season.

**Instructions**

For each of Rojas Vineyards' activity cost pools, identify a probable cost driver that might be used to assign overhead costs to its three wine varieties.

**E17.8 (LO 2), AN** Wilmington, Inc. manufactures five models of kitchen appliances. The company is installing activity-based costing and has identified the following activities performed at its Mesa factory.

*Identify activity cost drivers.*

1. Designing new models.

2. Purchasing raw materials and parts.

3. Storing and managing inventory.

4. Receiving and inspecting raw materials and parts.

5. Interviewing and hiring new personnel.

6. Machine forming sheet steel into appliance parts.

7. Manually assembling parts into appliances.

8. Training all employees of the company.

9. Insuring all tangible fixed assets.

10. Supervising production.

11. Maintaining and repairing machinery and equipment.

12. Painting and packaging finished appliances.

Having analyzed its Mesa factory operations for purposes of installing activity-based costing, Wilmington, Inc. identified its activity cost centers. It now needs to identify relevant activity cost drivers in order to assign overhead costs to its products.

**Instructions**

Using the activities listed above, identify for each activity one or more cost drivers that might be used to assign overhead to Wilmington's five products.

**E17.9 (LO 2, 3), AP** Writing Air United, Inc. manufactures two products: missile range instruments and space pressure gauges. During April, 50 range instruments and 300 pressure gauges were produced, and overhead costs of $94,500 were estimated. An analysis of estimated overhead costs reveals the following activities.

*Compute overhead rates and assign overhead using ABC.*

 Excel

| Activities | Cost Drivers | Total Cost |
|---|---|---|
| 1. Materials handling | Number of requisitions | $40,000 |
| 2. Machine setups | Number of setups | 21,500 |
| 3. Quality inspections | Number of inspections | 33,000 |
| | | $94,500 |

The cost driver volume for each product was as follows.

| Cost Drivers | Instruments | Gauges | Total |
|---|---|---|---|
| Number of requisitions | 400 | 600 | 1,000 |
| Number of setups | 200 | 300 | 500 |
| Number of inspections | 200 | 400 | 600 |

### Instructions

a. Determine the overhead rate for each activity.

b. Assign the manufacturing overhead costs for April to the two products using activity-based costing.

c. Write a memorandum to the president of Air United explaining the benefits of activity-based costing.

*Assign overhead using traditional costing and ABC.*

**E17.10 (LO 1, 2, 3), AP** Kragan Clothing Company manufactures its own designed and labeled athletic wear and sells its products through catalog sales and retail outlets. While Kragan has for years used activity-based costing in its manufacturing activities, it has always used traditional costing in assigning its selling costs to its product lines. Selling costs have traditionally been assigned to Kragan's product lines at a rate of 70% of direct materials costs. Its direct materials costs for the month of March for Kragan's "high-intensity" line of athletic wear are $400,000. The company has decided to extend activity-based costing to its selling costs (for internal decision-making only). Data relating to the "high-intensity" line of products for the month of March are as follows.

| Activity Cost Pools | Cost Drivers | Overhead Rate | Number of Cost Drivers Used per Activity |
|---|---|---|---|
| Sales commissions | Dollar sales | $0.05 per dollar sales | $900,000 |
| Advertising—TV | Minutes | $300 per minute | 250 |
| Advertising—Internet | Column inches | $10 per column inch | 2,000 |
| Catalogs | Catalogs mailed | $2.50 per catalog | 60,000 |
| Cost of catalog sales | Catalog orders | $1 per catalog order | 9,000 |
| Credit and collection | Dollar sales | $0.03 per dollar sales | 900,000 |

### Instructions

a. Compute the selling costs to be assigned to the "high-intensity" line of athletic wear for the month of March (1) using the traditional product costing system (direct materials cost is the cost driver), and (2) using activity-based costing.

b. By what amount does the traditional product costing system undercost or overcost the "high-intensity" product line relative to costing under ABC?

*Assign overhead using traditional costing and ABC.*

**E17.11 (LO 1, 2, 3), AP** Health 'R Us, Inc., uses a traditional product costing system to assign overhead costs uniformly to all its packaged multigrain products. To meet Food and Drug Administration requirements and to assure its customers of safe, sanitary, and nutritious food, Health 'R Us engages in a high level of quality control. Health 'R Us assigns its quality-control overhead costs to all products at a rate of 17% of direct labor costs. Its direct labor cost for the month of June for its low-calorie breakfast line is $70,000. In response to repeated requests from its financial vice president, Health 'R Us's management agrees to adopt activity-based costing. Data relating to the low-calorie breakfast line for the month of June are as follows.

| Activity Cost Pools | Cost Drivers | Overhead | Number of Cost Drivers Used per Activity |
|---|---|---|---|
| Inspections of material received | Number of pounds | $0.90 per pound | 6,000 pounds |
| In-process inspections | Number of servings | $0.33 per serving | 10,000 servings |
| FDA certification | Customer orders | $12.00 per order | 420 orders |

### Instructions

a. Compute the quality-control overhead cost to be assigned to the low-calorie breakfast product line for the month of June (1) using the traditional product costing system (direct labor cost is the cost driver), and (2) using activity-based costing.

b. By what amount does the traditional product costing system undercost or overcost the low-calorie breakfast line relative to costing under ABC?

**E17.12 (LO 3), AN** Having itemized its costs for the first quarter of next year's budget, Santana Corporation desires to install an activity-based costing system. First, it identified the activity cost pools in which to accumulate factory overhead. Second, it identified the relevant cost drivers. (This was done in E17.6.)

*Classify activities by level.*

**Instructions**

Using the activity cost pools identified in E17.6, classify each of those cost pools as either unit-level, batch-level, product-level, or facility-level.

**E17.13 (LO 3), AN** William Mendel & Sons, Inc. is a small manufacturing company in La Jolla that uses activity-based costing. Mendel & Sons accumulates overhead in the following activity cost pools.

*Classify activities by level.*

1. Hiring personnel.
2. Managing parts inventory.
3. Purchasing.
4. Testing prototypes.
5. Designing products.
6. Setting up equipment.
7. Training employees.
8. Inspecting machined parts after each setup.
9. Machining.
10. Assembling.

**Instructions**

For each activity cost pool, indicate whether the activity cost pool would be unit-level, batch-level, product-level, or facility-level.

**E17.14 (LO 4), AP** Service Venus Creations sells window treatments (shades, blinds, and awnings) to both commercial and residential customers. The following information relates to its budgeted operations for the current year.

*Assign overhead using traditional costing and ABC.*

|  | **Commercial** | | **Residential** | |
| --- | --- | --- | --- | --- |
| Revenues |  | $300,000 |  | $480,000 |
| Direct materials costs | $ 30,000 |  | $ 50,000 |  |
| Direct labor costs | 100,000 |  | 300,000 |  |
| Overhead costs | 85,000 | 215,000 | 150,000 | 500,000 |
| Operating income (loss) |  | $ 85,000 |  | ($ 20,000) |

The controller, Peggy Kingman, is concerned about the residential product line. She cannot understand why this line is not more profitable given that the installations of window coverings are less complex for residential customers. In addition, the residential client base resides in close proximity to the company office, so travel costs are not as expensive on a per client visit for residential customers. As a result, she has decided to take a closer look at the overhead costs assigned to the two product lines to determine whether a more accurate product costing model can be developed. Here are the three activity cost pools and related information she developed:

| Activity Cost Pools | Estimated Overhead | Cost Drivers |
| --- | --- | --- |
| Scheduling and travel | $85,000 | Hours of travel |
| Setup time | 90,000 | Number of setups |
| Supervision | 60,000 | Direct labor cost |

| **Use of Cost Drivers per Product** | | |
| --- | --- | --- |
|  | **Commercial** | **Residential** |
| Scheduling and travel | 750 hours | 500 hours |
| Setup time | 350 setups | 250 setups |

**Instructions**

a. Compute the activity-based overhead rates for each of the three cost pools, and determine the overhead cost assigned to each product line.

b. Compute the operating income for each product line, using the activity-based overhead rates.

c. What do you believe Peggy Kingman should do?

**E17.15 (LO 4), AP** Service Snap Prints Company is a small printing and copying firm with three high-speed offset printing presses, five copiers (two color and three black-and-white), one collator, one cutting and folding machine, and one fax machine. To improve its pricing practices, owner-manager Terry Morton is installing activity-based costing. Additionally, Terry employs five employees: two printers/

*Identify activity cost pools.*

designers, one receptionist/bookkeeper, one salesperson/copy-machine operator, and one janitor/delivery clerk. Terry can operate any of the machines and, in addition to managing the entire operation, he performs the training, designing, selling, and marketing functions.

### Instructions

As Snap Prints' independent accountant who prepares tax forms and quarterly financial statements, you have been asked to identify the activities that would be used to accumulate overhead costs for assignment to jobs and customers. Using your knowledge of a small printing and copying firm (and some imagination), identify at least 12 activity cost pools as the start of an activity-based costing system for Snap Prints Company.

*Classify service company activities as value-added or non–value-added.*

**E17.16 (LO 3, 4), AN** Service Lasso and Markowitz is a law firm that is initiating an activity-based costing system. Sam Lasso, the senior partner and strong supporter of ABC, has prepared the following list of activities performed by a typical attorney in a day at the firm.

| Activities | Hours |
|---|---|
| Writing contracts and letters | 1.5 |
| Attending staff meetings | 0.5 |
| Taking depositions | 1.0 |
| Doing research | 1.0 |
| Traveling to/from court | 1.0 |
| Contemplating legal strategy | 1.0 |
| Eating lunch | 1.0 |
| Litigating a case in court | 2.5 |
| Entertaining a prospective client | 1.5 |

### Instructions

Classify each of the activities listed by Sam Lasso as value-added or non–value-added, and defend your classification. How much was value-added time and how much was non–value-added?

*Apply ABC to service company.*

**E17.17 (LO 4), AP** Service Manzeck Company operates a snow-removal service. The company owns five trucks, each of which has a snow plow in the front to plow driveways and a snow thrower in the back to clear sidewalks. Because plowing snow is very tough on trucks, the company incurs significant maintenance costs. Truck depreciation and maintenance represents a significant portion of the company's overhead. The company removes snow at residential locations, in which case the drivers spend the bulk of their time walking behind the snow-thrower machine to clear sidewalks. On commercial jobs, the drivers spend most of their time plowing. Manzeck assigns overhead based on labor hours. Total estimated overhead costs for the year are $42,000. Total estimated labor hours are 1,500 hours. The average residential property requires 0.5 hours of labor, while the average commercial property requires 2.5 hours of labor. The following additional information is available.

| Activity Cost Pools | Cost Drivers | Estimated Overhead | Estimated Use of Cost Drivers per Activity |
|---|---|---|---|
| Plowing | Square yards of surface plowed | $38,000 | 200,000 |
| Snow throwing | Linear feet of sidewalk cleared | $ 4,000 | 50,000 |

### Instructions

a. Determine the predetermined overhead rate under traditional costing.

b. Determine the amount of overhead assigned to the average residential job using traditional costing based on labor hours.

c. Determine the activity-based overhead rates for each cost pool.

d. Determine the amount of overhead assigned to the average residential job using activity-based costing. Assume that the average residential job has 20 square yards of plowing and 60 linear feet of snow throwing.

e. Discuss your findings from parts (b) and (d).

# Problems

**P17.1 (LO 1, 2, 3), AP** Combat Fire, Inc. manufactures steel cylinders and nozzles for two models of fire extinguishers: (1) a home fire extinguisher and (2) a commercial fire extinguisher. The *home model* is a high-volume (54,000 units), half-gallon cylinder that holds 2 1/2 pounds of multi-purpose dry chemical at 480 PSI. The *commercial model* is a low-volume (10,200 units), two-gallon cylinder that holds 10 pounds of multi-purpose dry chemical at 390 PSI. Both products require 1.5 hours of direct labor for completion. Therefore, total annual direct labor hours are 96,300 or [1.5 hours × (54,000 + 10,200)]. Estimated annual manufacturing overhead is $1,584,280. Thus, the predetermined overhead rate is $16.45 or ($1,584,280 ÷ 96,300) per direct labor hour. The direct materials cost per unit is $18.50 for the home model and $26.50 for the commercial model. The direct labor cost is $19 per unit for both the home and the commercial models.

The company's managers identified six activity cost pools and related cost drivers and accumulated overhead by cost pool as follows.

*Assign overhead using traditional costing and ABC; compute unit costs; classify activities as value- or non–value-added.*

| Activity Cost Pools | Cost Drivers | Estimated Overhead | Estimated Use of Cost Drivers | Use of Drivers by Product | |
|---|---|---|---|---|---|
| | | | | Home | Commercial |
| Receiving | Pounds | $ 80,400 | 335,000 | 215,000 | 120,000 |
| Forming | Machine hours | 150,500 | 35,000 | 27,000 | 8,000 |
| Assembling | Number of parts | 412,300 | 217,000 | 165,000 | 52,000 |
| Testing | Number of tests | 51,000 | 25,500 | 15,500 | 10,000 |
| Painting | Gallons | 52,580 | 5,258 | 3,680 | 1,578 |
| Packing and shipping | Pounds | 337,500 | 335,000 | 215,000 | 120,000 |
| | | $1,584,280 | | | |

## Instructions

**a.** Under traditional product costing, compute the total unit cost of each product. Prepare a simple comparative schedule of the individual costs by product (similar to Illustration 17.4).

**b.** Under ABC, prepare a schedule showing the computations of the activity-based overhead rates (per cost driver).

**c.** Prepare a schedule assigning each activity's overhead cost pool to each product based on the use of cost drivers. (Include a computation of overhead cost per unit, rounding to the nearest cent.)

**d.** Compute the total cost per unit for each product under ABC.

**e.** Classify each of the activities as a value-added activity or a non–value-added activity.

**f.** Comment on (1) the comparative overhead cost per unit for the two products under ABC, and (2) the comparative total costs per unit under traditional costing and ABC.

a. Unit cost—H.M. $62.18

c. Cost assigned—H.M. $1,086,500

d. Cost/unit—H.M. $57.62

**P17.2 (LO 2), AP** **Writing** Schultz Electronics manufactures two ultra-high-definition television models: the Royale, which sells for $1,600, and a new model, the Majestic, which sells for $1,300. The production cost computed per unit under traditional costing for each model in 2022 was as follows.

*Assign overhead to products using ABC and evaluate decision.*

| Traditional Costing | Royale | Majestic |
|---|---|---|
| Direct materials | $ 700 | $420 |
| Direct labor (S20 per hour) | 120 | 100 |
| Manufacturing overhead ($38 per DLH) | 228 | 190 |
| Total per unit cost | $1,048 | $710 |

In 2022, Schultz manufactured 25,000 units of the Royale and 10,000 units of the Majestic. The overhead rate of $38 per direct labor hour was determined by dividing total estimated manufacturing overhead of $7,600,000 by the total direct labor hours (200,000) for the two models.

Under traditional costing, the gross profit on the models was Royale $552 ($1,600 − $1,048) and Majestic $590 ($1,300 − $710). Because of this difference, management is considering phasing out the Royale model and increasing the production of the Majestic model.

Before finalizing its decision, management asks Schultz's controller to prepare an analysis using activity-based costing (ABC). The controller accumulates the following information about overhead for the year ended December 31, 2022.

| Activity Cost Pools | Cost Drivers | Estimated Overhead | Estimated Use of Cost Drivers | Activity Based Overhead Rate |
|---|---|---|---|---|
| Purchasing | Number of orders | $1,200,000 | 40,000 | $30/order |
| Machine setups | Number of setups | 900,000 | 18,000 | $50/setup |
| Machining | Machine hours | 4,800,000 | 120,000 | $40/hour |
| Quality control | Number of inspections | 700,000 | 28,000 | $25/inspection |

The cost drivers used for each product were:

| Cost Drivers | Royale | Majestic | Total |
|---|---|---|---|
| Purchase orders | 17,000 | 23,000 | 40,000 |
| Machine setups | 5,000 | 13,000 | 18,000 |
| Machine hours | 75,000 | 45,000 | 120,000 |
| Inspections | 11,000 | 17,000 | 28,000 |

### Instructions

a. Royale $4,035,000

b. Cost/unit—Royale $981.40

*Assign overhead costs using traditional costing and ABC; compare results.*

a. Assign the total 2022 manufacturing overhead costs to the two products using activity-based costing (ABC) and determine the overhead cost per unit.

b. What was the cost per unit and gross profit of each model using ABC?

c. Are management's future plans for the two models sound? Explain.

**P17.3 (LO 1, 2), AN** Writing Shaker Stairs Co. designs and builds factory-made premium wooden stairways for homes. The manufactured stairway components (spindles, risers, hangers, hand rails) permit installation of stairways of varying lengths and widths. All are of white oak wood. Budgeted manufacturing overhead costs for the year 2022 are as follows.

| Overhead Cost Pools | Amount |
|---|---|
| Purchasing | $ 75,000 |
| Handling materials | 82,000 |
| Production (cutting, milling, finishing) | 210,000 |
| Setting up machines | 105,000 |
| Inspecting | 90,000 |
| Inventory control (raw materials and finished goods) | 126,000 |
| Utilities | 180,000 |
| Total budgeted overhead costs | $868,000 |

For the last 4 years, Shaker Stairs Co. has been charging overhead to products on the basis of machine hours. For the year 2022, 100,000 machine hours are budgeted.

Jeremy Nolan, owner-manager of Shaker Stairs Co., recently directed his accountant, Bill Seagren, to implement the activity-based costing system that he has repeatedly proposed. At Jeremy Nolan's request, Bill and the production foreman identify the following cost drivers and their usage for the previously budgeted overhead cost pools.

| Activity Cost Pools | Cost Drivers | Estimated Use of Cost Drivers |
|---|---|---|
| Purchasing | Number of orders | 600 |
| Handling materials | Number of moves | 8,000 |
| Production (cutting, milling, finishing) | Direct labor hours | 100,000 |
| Setting up machines | Number of setups | 1,250 |
| Inspecting | Number of inspections | 6,000 |
| Inventory control (raw materials and finished goods) | Number of components | 168,000 |
| Utilities | Square feet occupied | 90,000 |

Steve Hannon, sales manager, has received an order for 250 stairways from Community Builders, Inc., a large housing development contractor. At Steve's request, Bill prepares cost estimates for producing components for 250 stairways so Steve can submit a contract price per stairway to Community Builders. He accumulates the following data for the production of 250 stairways.

| | |
|---|---:|
| Direct materials | $103,600 |
| Direct labor | $112,000 |
| Machine hours | 14,500 |
| Direct labor hours | 5,000 |
| Number of purchase orders | 60 |
| Number of material moves | 800 |
| Number of machine setups | 100 |
| Number of inspections | 450 |
| Number of components | 16,000 |
| Number of square feet occupied | 8,000 |

## Instructions

**a.** Compute the predetermined overhead rate using traditional costing with machine hours as the basis.

**b.** What is the manufacturing cost per stairway under traditional costing? (Round to the nearest cent.)

**c.** What is the manufacturing cost per stairway under the proposed activity-based costing? (Round to the nearest cent. Prepare all of the necessary schedules.)

**d.** Which of the two costing systems is preferable in pricing decisions and why?

*b.  Cost/stairway $1,365.84*

*c.  Cost/stairway $1,139.80*

**P17.4 (LO 1, 2), AN** Benton Corporation produces two grades of non-alcoholic wine from grapes that it buys from California growers. It produces and sells roughly 3,000,000 liters per year of a low-cost, high-volume product called CoolDay. It sells this in 600,000 5-liter jugs. Benton also produces and sells roughly 300,000 liters per year of a low-volume, high-cost product called LiteMist. LiteMist is sold in 1-liter bottles. Based on recent data, the CoolDay product has not been as profitable as LiteMist. Management is considering dropping the inexpensive CoolDay line so it can focus more attention on the LiteMist product. The LiteMist product already demands considerably more attention than the CoolDay line.

*Assign overhead costs using traditional costing and ABC; compare results.*

Jack Eller, president and founder of Benton, is skeptical about this idea. He points out that for many decades the company produced only the CoolDay line and that it was always quite profitable. It wasn't until the company started producing the more complicated LiteMist wine that the profitability of CoolDay declined. Prior to the introduction of LiteMist, the company had basic equipment, simple production procedures, and virtually no need for quality control. Because LiteMist is bottled in 1-liter bottles, it requires considerably more time and effort, both to bottle and to label and box than does CoolDay. The company must bottle and handle 5 times as many bottles of LiteMist to sell the same quantity as CoolDay. CoolDay requires 1 month of aging; LiteMist requires 1 year. CoolDay requires cleaning and inspection of equipment every 10,000 liters; LiteMist requires such maintenance every 600 liters.

Jack has asked the accounting department to prepare an analysis of the cost per liter using the traditional costing approach and using activity-based costing. The following information was collected.

| | CoolDay | LiteMist |
|---|---:|---:|
| Direct materials per liter | $0.40 | $1.20 |
| Direct labor cost per liter | $0.50 | $0.90 |
| Direct labor hours per liter | 0.05 | 0.09 |
| Total direct labor hours | 150,000 | 27,000 |

| Activity Cost Pools | Cost Drivers | Estimated Overhead | Estimated Use of Cost Drivers | Use of Cost Drivers per Product | |
|---|---|---:|---:|---:|---:|
| | | | | CoolDay | LiteMist |
| Grape processing | Cart of grapes | $ 145,860 | 6,600 | 6,000 | 600 |
| Aging | Total months | 396,000 | 6,600,000 | 3,000,000 | 3,600,000 |
| Bottling and corking | Number of bottles | 270,000 | 900,000 | 600,000 | 300,000 |
| Labeling and boxing | Number of bottles | 189,000 | 900,000 | 600,000 | 300,000 |
| Maintain and inspect equipment | Number of inspections | 240,800 | 800 | 350 | 450 |
| | | $1,241,660 | | | |

**Instructions**

Answer each of the following questions. (Round all calculations to three decimal places.)

a. Cost/liter—C.D. $1.251

**a.** Under traditional product costing using direct labor hours, compute the total manufacturing cost per **liter** of both products.

**b.** Under ABC, prepare a schedule showing the computation of the activity-based overhead rates (per cost driver).

c. Overhead cost/liter—
C.D. $.241

**c.** Prepare a schedule assigning each activity's overhead cost pool to each product, based on the use of cost drivers. Include a computation of overhead cost per liter.

**d.** Compute the total manufacturing cost per liter for both products under ABC.

**e.** Write a memo to Jack Eller discussing the implications of your analysis for the company's plans. In this memo, provide a brief description of ABC as well as an explanation of how the traditional approach can result in distortions.

*Assign overhead costs to services using traditional costing and ABC; compute overhead rates and unit costs; compare results.*

**P17.5 (LO 1, 2, 3, 4), AN** Service  Lewis and Stark is a public accounting firm that offers two primary services, auditing and tax-return preparation. A controversy has developed between the partners of the two service lines as to who is contributing the greater amount to the bottom line. The area of contention is the assignment of overhead. The tax partners argue for assigning overhead on the basis of 40% of direct labor dollars, while the audit partners argue for implementing activity-based costing. The partners agree to use next year's budgeted data for purposes of analysis and comparison. The following overhead data are collected to develop the comparison.

| Activity Cost Pools | Cost Drivers | Estimated Overhead | Estimated Use of Cost Drivers | Use of Cost Drivers per Service | |
|---|---|---|---|---|---|
| | | | | Audit | Tax |
| Employee training | Direct labor dollars | $216,000 | $1,800,000 | $1,100,000 | $700,000 |
| Typing and secretarial | Number of reports/ forms | 76,200 | 2,500 | 800 | 1,700 |
| Computing | Number of minutes | 204,000 | 60,000 | 27,000 | 33,000 |
| Facility rental | Number of employees | 142,500 | 40 | 22 | 18 |
| Travel | Per expense reports | 81,300 | Trace directly | 56,000 | 25,300 |
| | | $720,000 | | | |

**Instructions**

**a.** Using traditional product costing as proposed by the tax partners, compute the total overhead cost assigned to both services (audit and tax) of Lewis and Stark.

b. (2) Cost assigned—Tax $337,441

**b. 1.** Using activity-based costing, prepare a schedule showing the computations of the activity-based overhead rates (per cost driver). (*Hint:* As a result of breaking out travel costs as a separate cost pool, travel costs can now be traced directly to services provided. Thus, an overhead rate is not needed.)

**2.** Prepare a schedule assigning each activity's overhead cost pool to each accounting service based on the use of the cost drivers.

c. Difference—Audit $57,441

**c.** Comment on the comparative overhead cost for the two services under both traditional costing and ABC.

---

## Continuing Cases

### Current Designs

**CD17** As you learned in the previous chapters, Current Designs has two main product lines—composite kayaks, which are handmade and very labor-intensive, and rotomolded kayaks, which require less labor but employ more expensive equipment. Current Designs' controller, Diane Buswell, is now evaluating several different methods of assigning overhead to these products. It is important to ensure that costs are appropriately assigned to the company's products. At the same time, the system that is used must not be so complex that its costs are greater than its benefits.

Diane has decided to use the following activities and costs to evaluate the methods of assigning overhead.

Current Designs Activity Cost Pools

| | A | B |
|---|---|---|
| 1 | | |
| 2 | Activities | Cost |
| 3 | Designing new models | $121,100 |
| 4 | Creating and testing prototypes | 152,000 |
| 5 | Creating molds for kayaks | 188,500 |
| 6 | Operating oven for the rotomolded kayaks | 40,000 |
| 7 | Operating the vacuum line for the composite kayaks | 28,000 |
| 8 | Supervising production employees | 180,000 |
| 9 | Curing time (the time that is needed for the chemical processes to finish before the next step in the production process; many of these costs are related to the space required in the building) | 190,400 |
| 10 | Total | $900,000 |

As Diane examines the data, she decides that the cost of operating the oven for the rotomolded kayaks and the cost of operating the vacuum line for the composite kayaks can be directly assigned to each of these product lines and do not need to be assigned with the other costs.

## Instructions

For purposes of this analysis, assume that Current Designs uses $234,000 in direct labor costs to produce 1,000 composite kayaks and $286,000 in direct labor costs to produce 4,000 rotomolded kayaks each year.

a. One method of assigning overhead would assign the common costs to each product line by using an assignment basis such as the number of employees working on each type of kayak or the amount of factory space used for the production of each type of kayak. Diane knows that about 50% of the area of the factory and 50% of the employees work on the composite kayaks, and the remaining space and other employees work on the rotomolded kayaks. Using this information and remembering that the costs of operating the oven and vacuum line have been directly assigned, determine the total amount to be assigned to the composite kayak line and the rotomolded kayak line, and the amount to be assigned to each of the units in each line.

b. Another method of assigning overhead is to use direct labor dollars as an assignment basis. Remembering that the costs of the oven and the vacuum line have been assigned directly to the product lines, allocate the remaining costs using direct labor dollars as the allocation basis. Then, determine the amount of overhead that should be assigned to each unit of each product line using this method.

c. Activity-based costing requires a cost driver for each cost pool. Use the following information to assign the costs to the product lines using the activity-based costing approach.

Current Designs Cost Drivers

| | A | B | C | D |
|---|---|---|---|---|
| 1 | | | | |
| 2 | Activity Cost Pools | Cost Drivers | Driver Amount for Composite Kayaks | Driver Amount for Rotomolded Kayaks |
| 3 | Designing new models | Number of models | 3 | 1 |
| 4 | Creating and testing prototypes | Number of prototypes | 6 | 2 |
| 5 | Creating molds for kayaks | Number of molds | 12 | 1 |
| 6 | Supervising production employees | Number of employees | 12 | 12 |
| 7 | Curing time | Number of days of curing time | 15,000 | 2,000 |
| 8 | | | | |

What amount of overhead should be assigned to each composite kayak using this method? What amount of overhead should be assigned to each rotomolded kayak using this method?

**d.** Which of the three methods do you think Current Designs should use? Why?

## Waterways Corporation

(*Note:* This is a continuation of the Waterways case from Chapters 14–16.)

**WC17** Waterways looked into ABC as a method of costing because of the variety of items it produces and the many different activities in which it is involved. This case asks you to help Waterways use an activity-based costing system to account for its production activities.

*Go to WileyPLUS for complete case details and instructions.*

## Comprehensive Case

**CC17** In Chapter 15, you used job order costing techniques to help Greetings Inc., a retailer of greeting cards and small gift items, expand its operations. Your next task is to help the new unit, Wall Décor, become profitable through the use of activity-based costing. In this case, you will have the opportunity to discuss the cost/benefit trade-offs between simple ABC systems versus refined systems, and the potential benefit of using capacity rather than estimated sales when allocating fixed overhead costs.

*Go to WileyPLUS for complete case details and instructions.*

## Expand Your Critical Thinking

### Decision-Making Across the Organization

**CT17.1** `Service` East Valley Hospital is a primary medical care facility and trauma center that serves 11 small, rural midwestern communities within a 40-mile radius. The hospital offers all the medical/surgical services of a typical small hospital. It has a staff of 18 full-time doctors and 20 part-time visiting specialists. East Valley has a payroll of 150 employees consisting of technicians, nurses, therapists, managers, directors, administrators, dieticians, secretaries, data processors, and janitors.

**Instructions**

With the class divided into groups, discuss and answer the following.

**a.** Using your (limited, moderate, or in-depth) knowledge of a hospital's operations, identify as many **activities** as you can that would serve as the basis for implementing an activity-based costing system.

**b.** For each of the activities listed in (a), identify a **cost driver** that would serve as a valid measure of the resources consumed by the activity.

### Managerial Analysis

**CT17.2** Ideal Manufacturing Company has supported a research and development (R&D) department that has for many years been the sole contributor to the company's new farm machinery products. The R&D activity is an overhead cost center that performs services only to in-house manufacturing departments (four different product lines), all of which produce agricultural/farm/ranch-related machinery products.

The department has never sold its services to outside companies. But, because of its long history of success, larger manufacturers of agricultural products have approached Ideal to hire its R&D department for special projects. Because the costs of operating the R&D department have been spiraling uncontrollably, Ideal's management is considering entertaining these outside approaches to absorb the increasing costs. However, (1) management doesn't have any cost basis for charging R&D services to outsiders, and (2) it needs to gain control of its R&D costs. Management decides to implement an activity-based costing system in order to determine the charges for both outsiders and in-house users of the department's services.

R&D activities fall into four pools with the following annual costs.

| | |
|---|---|
| Market analysis | $1,050,000 |
| Product design | 2,350,000 |
| Product development | 3,600,000 |
| Prototype testing | 1,400,000 |

Activity analysis determines that the appropriate cost drivers and their usage for the four activities are:

| Activities | Cost Drivers | Total Estimated Drivers |
|---|---|---|
| Market analysis | Hours of analysis | 15,000 hours |
| Product design | Number of designs | 2,500 designs |
| Product development | Number of products | 90 products |
| Prototype testing | Number of tests | 500 tests |

**Instructions**

a. Compute the activity-based overhead rate for each activity cost pool.

b. How much cost would be charged to an in-house manufacturing department that consumed 1,800 hours of market analysis time, was provided 280 designs relating to 10 products, and requested 92 engineering tests?

c. How much cost would serve as the basis for pricing an R&D bid with an outside company on a contract that would consume 800 hours of analysis time, require 178 designs relating to 3 products, and result in 70 engineering tests?

d. What is the benefit to Ideal Manufacturing of applying activity-based costing to its R&D activity for both in-house and outside charging purposes?

## Real-World Focus

**CT17.3** **Service** An article in *Cost Management*, by Kocakulah, Bartlett, and Albin entitled "ABC for Calculating Mortgage Loan Servicing Expenses" (July/August 2009, p. 36), discusses a use of ABC in the financial services industry.

**Instructions**

Read the article (obtain online or at your library) and then answer the following questions.

a. What are some of the benefits of ABC that relate to the financial services industry?

b. What are three things that the company's original costing method did not take into account?

c. What were some of the cost drivers used by the company in the ABC approach?

## Ethics Case

**CT17.4** Curtis Rich, the cost accountant for Hi-Power Mower Company, recently installed activity-based costing at Hi-Power's St. Louis lawn tractor (riding mower) factory where three models—the 8-horsepower Bladerunner, the 12-horsepower Quickcut, and the 18-horsepower Supercut—are manufactured. Curtis's new product costs for these three models show that the company's traditional costing system had been significantly undercosting the 18-horsepower Supercut. This was due primarily to the lower sales volume of the Supercut compared to the Bladerunner and the Quickcut.

Before completing his analysis and reporting these results to management, Curtis is approached by his friend Ed Gray, who is the production manager for the 18-horsepower Supercut model. Ed has heard from one of Curtis's staff about the new product costs and is upset and worried for his job because the new costs show the Supercut to be losing, rather than making, money.

At first, Ed condemns the new cost system, whereupon Curtis explains the practice of activity-based costing and why it is more accurate than the company's present system. Even more worried now, Ed begs Curtis, "Massage the figures just enough to save the line from being discontinued. You don't want me to lose my job, do you? Anyway, nobody will know."

Curtis holds firm but agrees to recompute all his calculations for accuracy before submitting his costs to management.

**Instructions**

a. Who are the stakeholders in this situation?

b. What, if any, are the ethical considerations in this situation?

c. What are Curtis's ethical obligations to the company? To his friend?

## All About You

**CT17.5** There are many resources available on the Internet to assist people in time management. Some of these resources are designed specifically for college students.

**Instructions**

Do an Internet search of Dartmouth College's time-management video. Watch the video and then answer the following questions.

a. What are the main tools of time management for students, and what is each used for?

b. At what time of day are students most inclined to waste time? What time of day is the best for studying complex topics?

c. How can employing time-management practices be a "liberating" experience?

d. Why is goal-setting important? What are the characteristics of good goals, and what steps should you take to help you develop your goals?

## Considering Your Costs and Benefits

**CT17.6** As discussed in the chapter, the principles underlying activity-based costing have evolved into the broader approach known as *activity-based management*. One of the common practices of activity-based management is to identify all business activities, classify each activity as either a value-added or a non–value-added activity, and then try to reduce or eliminate the time spent on non–value-added activities. Consider the implications of applying this same approach to your everyday life, at work and at school. How do you spend your time each day? How much of your day is spent on activities that help you accomplish your objectives, and how much of your day is spent on activities that do not add value?

Many self-help books and websites offer suggestions on how to improve your time management. Should you minimize the "non–value-added" hours in your life by adopting the methods suggested by these sources? The basic arguments for and against are as follows.

**YES:** There are a limited number of hours in a day. You should try to maximize your chances of achieving your goals by eliminating the time that you waste.

**NO:** Life is about more than working yourself to death. Being an efficiency expert doesn't guarantee that you will be happy. Schedules and daily planners are too constraining.

**Instructions**

Write a response indicating your position regarding this situation. Provide support for your view.

## Answers to Insight and Accounting Across the Organization Questions

**ABC Evaluated  Q:** What might explain why so many companies say that ideally they would use ABC, but they haven't adopted it yet? **A:** As noted in the chapter, implementation of an ABC system can be very expensive. It may be difficult to justify an expenditure for a system that allocates overhead costs more accurately. The benefits of more accurate costing may not be as obvious as some of the other things a company might spend its money on, such as a machine that produces goods more efficiently.

**What Does NASCAR Have to Do with Breakfast Cereal?  Q:** What are the benefits of reducing setup time? **A:** Setup time is a non–value-added activity that costs race-car pit crews valuable time in their goal of winning races. Similarly, by reducing the time spent on their setups, companies like General Mills can reduce their non–value-added costs.

**Delivering People and Packages  Q:** How do big data and data analytics help companies implement and employ ABC and ABM? **A:** The data collected by automated systems can be used by companies to help identify the cost pools, cost drivers, and activity usage needed to implement ABC. In addition, data collected by these same systems can help companies identify and reduce non–value-added activities.

**Traveling Light  Q:** Why do airlines charge even higher rates for heavier bags, bags that are odd shapes (e.g., ski bags), and bags with hazardous materials in them? **A:** Each of these factors increases the costs to the airlines. Heavier baggage is more difficult to handle, thus increasing labor costs. It also uses up more fuel. Bags that are odd shapes complicate handling both for humans and machines. In addition, odd shapes take up more space in the cargo area. Finally, hazardous materials require special handling and storage procedures. All of these factors should be considered by an airline when it decides how much to charge for special baggage.

blackCAT/E+/Getty Images

# Cost-Volume-Profit

## Chapter Preview

As the following Feature Story indicates, to manage any size business you must understand how costs respond to changes in sales volume (quantity sold) and the effect of costs and revenues on profits. A prerequisite to understanding cost-volume-profit (CVP) relationships is knowledge of how costs behave. In this chapter, we first explain the considerations involved in cost behavior analysis. Then, we discuss and illustrate CVP analysis.

## Feature Story

### Don't Worry—Just Get Big

It wasn't that Jeff didn't have a good job. He was a vice president at a Wall Street firm. But, despite his good position, he quit his job, moved to Seattle, and started an online retailer, which he named **Amazon.com**. Like any good entrepreneur, Jeff Bezos kept his initial investment small. Operations were run out of his garage. And, to avoid the need for a warehouse, he took orders for books and had them shipped from other distributors' warehouses.

By its fourth month, Amazon was selling 100 books a day. In its first full year, it had $15.7 million in sales. The next year, sales increased eightfold. Two years later, sales were $1.6 billion.

Although its sales growth was impressive, Amazon's ability to lose money was equally amazing. One analyst nicknamed it *Amazon.bomb*, while another, predicting its demise, called it *Amazon.toast*. Why was it losing money?

The company used every available dollar to reinvest in itself. It built massive warehouses and bought increasingly sophisticated (and expensive) computers and equipment to improve its distribution system. This desire to grow as fast as possible was captured in a T-shirt slogan at its company picnic, which read "Eat another hot dog, get big fast." This buying binge was increasing the company's fixed costs at a rate that exceeded its sales growth. Skeptics predicted that Amazon would soon run out of cash. It didn't.

At the end of one year, even as it announced record profits, Amazon's share price fell by 9%. Why? Because although the company was predicting that its sales revenue in the next quarter would increase by at least 28%, it predicted that its operating profit would fall by at least 2% and perhaps by as much as 34%. The company made no apologies. It explained that it was in the process of expanding from 39 distribution centers to 52. As Amazon's finance chief noted, "You're not as productive on those assets for some time. I'm very pleased with the investments we're making and we've shown over our history that we've been able to make great returns on the capital we invest in." Or, in the words of Jeff Bezos, "It's a fixed cost business and so what I could see from the internal metrics at a certain volume level we would cover our fixed costs, and we would **be profitable**." In other words, eat another hot dog.

**Sources:** Christine Frey and John Cook, "How Amazon.com Survived, Thrived and Turned a Profit," *Seattle Post* (January 28, 2008); Stu Woo, "Sticker Shock Over Amazon Growth," *Wall Street Journal* (January 28, 2011); Miriam Guttfried, "Amazon's Never-Ending Story," *Wall Street Journal* (April 25, 2014); and John Stoll, "Why Investors Don't Care That Snap and Lyft Are Hemorrhaging Money," *Wall Street Journal* (April 26, 2019).

 Watch the *Southwest Airlines* video in WileyPLUS to learn more about cost-volume-profit analysis in the real world.

# Chapter Outline

| LEARNING OBJECTIVES | REVIEW | PRACTICE |
|---|---|---|
| **LO 1** Explain variable, fixed, and mixed costs and the relevant range. | • Variable costs<br>• Fixed costs<br>• Relevant range<br>• Mixed costs | **DO IT! 1** Types of Costs |
| **LO 2** Apply the high-low method to determine the components of mixed costs. | • High-low method<br>• Identifying variable and fixed costs | **DO IT! 2** High-Low Method |
| **LO 3** Prepare a CVP income statement to determine contribution margin. | • Basic components<br>• CVP income statement | **DO IT! 3** CVP Income Statement |
| **LO 4** Compute the break-even point using three approaches. | • Mathematical equation<br>• Contribution margin techniques<br>• Graphic presentation | **DO IT! 4** Break-Even Analysis |
| **LO 5** Determine the sales required to earn target net income and determine margin of safety. | • Target net income<br>• Margin of safety<br>• CVP and data analytics | **DO IT! 5** Break-Even Point, Margin of Safety, and Target Net Income |

**Go to the Review and Practice section at the end of the chapter for a targeted summary and practice applications with solutions.**

**Visit WileyPLUS for additional tutorials and practice opportunities.**

# Cost Behavior Analysis

---

**LEARNING OBJECTIVE 1**

Explain variable, fixed, and mixed costs and the relevant range.

---

**Cost behavior analysis** is the study of how specific costs respond to changes in the level of business activity.

- Some costs change when activity changes, and others remain the same. For example, for an airline company such as **Southwest** or **United**, the longer the flight, the higher the fuel costs. On the other hand, **Massachusetts General Hospital**'s costs to staff the emergency room on any given night are relatively constant regardless of the number of patients treated.

- A knowledge of cost behavior helps management plan operations and decide between alternative courses of action.

- Cost behavior analysis applies to all types of entities.

The starting point in cost behavior analysis is measuring the key business activities. Activity levels may be expressed in terms of sales dollars (in a retail company), miles driven (in a trucking company), room occupancy (in a hotel), or dance classes taught (by a dance studio). Many companies use more than one measurement base. A manufacturer, for example, may use direct labor hours or units of output for manufacturing costs, and sales revenue or units sold for selling expenses.

For an activity level to be useful in cost behavior analysis, changes in the level or volume of activity should be correlated with changes in costs.

- The activity level selected is referred to as the activity index or driver.

- The **activity index** identifies the activity that causes changes in the behavior of costs.

- With an appropriate activity index, companies can classify the behavior of costs in response to changes in activity levels into three categories: variable, fixed, or mixed.

*Unless specifically stated otherwise, our examples and end-of-chapter material use the volume (quantity) of output (e.g., goods produced or services provided) as the activity index.*

## Variable Costs

**Variable costs** are costs that vary **in total** directly and proportionately with changes in the activity level.

- If the level increases 10%, total variable costs will increase 10%. If the level of activity decreases by 25%, variable costs will decrease 25%.

- Examples of variable costs include direct materials and direct labor for a manufacturer; cost of goods sold, sales commissions, and freight-out for a merchandiser; and gasoline in airline and trucking companies.

- A variable cost may also be defined as a cost that **remains the same *per unit* at every level of activity**. This means that the unit variable cost is constant.

To illustrate the behavior of a variable cost, assume that Damon Company manufactures cell phones that contain cameras. Damon purchases the cameras, a direct material, from a supplier for $10 each. **The activity index is the number of cell phones produced**. As Damon manufactures each phone, the total cost of cameras installed in phones increases by $10. As part (a) of **Illustration 18.1** shows, total cost of the cameras will be $20,000 (2,000 × $10) if Damon produces 2,000 phones, and $100,000 when it produces

**ILLUSTRATION 18.1**

**Behavior of total and unit variable costs; unit variable costs remain constant**

10,000 phones. We can also see that the unit variable costs remain the same as the level of activity changes. As part (b) of Illustration 18.1 shows, the unit variable cost of $10 for the cameras is the same whether Damon produces 2,000 or 10,000 phones.

Companies that rely heavily on labor either to manufacture a product or perform a service, such as **Hilton** and **Marriott**, are likely to have a high percentage of variable costs related to direct labor. In contrast, companies that use a high proportion of machinery and equipment in producing revenue, such as **AT&T** and **Duke Energy**, may have a lower percentage of variable costs related to direct labor.

## Fixed Costs

**Fixed costs** are costs that **remain the same in total** regardless of changes in the activity level.

- Examples include property taxes, insurance, rent, supervisory salaries, and straight-line depreciation on buildings and equipment.
- Because total fixed costs remain constant as activity changes, it follows that **fixed costs *per unit* vary inversely with activity: As volume increases, unit cost declines, and vice versa**.

To illustrate the behavior of fixed costs, assume that Damon Company leases its productive facilities at a rental cost of $10,000 per month. Total fixed costs of the facilities remain a constant $10,000 at every level of activity, as part (a) of **Illustration 18.2** shows. But, **on**

**ILLUSTRATION 18.2**

**Behavior of total and unit fixed costs**

**a per unit basis, the cost of rent declines as activity increases**, as part (b) of Illustration 18.2 shows. At 2,000 units, the unit cost per cell phone is $5 ($10,000 ÷ 2,000). When Damon produces 10,000 cell phones, the unit cost of the rent is only $1 per phone ($10,000 ÷ 10,000).

The trend for many manufacturers is to have more fixed costs and fewer variable costs. This trend is the result of increased use of automation and less use of employee direct labor. As a result, depreciation and rent charges (fixed costs) increase, whereas direct labor costs (variable costs) decrease.

---

## People, Planet, and Profit Insight    BrightFarms

Agatha Koroglu/
Shutterstock.com

### Gardens in the Sky

The United Nations' Food and Agriculture Organization estimates that by 2050, roughly 70% of people will live in cities. This means that more food will need to be hauled farther to get it to the consumer. To address the lack of farmable land and reduce the cost of transporting produce, some companies, such as New York-based **BrightFarms**, are building urban greenhouses. BrightFarms' mission is "to grow food in the same communities where it's consumed." In doing so, the company says it uses 80% less water, 90% less land, and 95% less shipping fuel than long-distance, field-grown produce.

This sounds great, but do the numbers work? Some variable costs are reduced. For example, the use of pesticides, herbicides, fuel costs for shipping, and water are all reduced.

Soil erosion is a non-issue since plants are grown hydroponically (in a solution of water and minerals), and land requirements are reduced because of vertical structures. But, some fixed costs are higher. First, there is the cost of the building. Also, multistory buildings require artificial lighting for plants on lower floors.

Rooftop greenhouses on existing city structures already appear financially viable. For example, a 15,000 square-foot rooftop greenhouse in Brooklyn already produces roughly 30 tons of vegetables per year for local residents.

**Sources:** "Vertical Farming: Does It Really Stack Up?" *The Economist* (December 9, 2010); Jane Black, "BrightFarms Idea: Greenhouses That Cut Short the Path from Plant to Grocery Shelf," *The Washington Post* (May 7, 2013); and *BrightFarms.com* (2019).

**What are some of the variable and fixed costs that are impacted by hydroponic farming? (Answer is available at the end of the chapter.)**

---

# Relevant Range

In Illustration 18.1 part (a), a straight line is drawn throughout the entire range of the activity index for total variable costs. In essence, the assumption is that the costs are **linear**.

- If a relationship is linear (that is, straight-line), then changes in the activity index will result in a direct, proportional change in the total variable costs.
- For example, if the activity level doubles, the total variable costs double.

It is now necessary to ask: Is the straight-line relationship realistic? In most business situations, a straight-line relationship **does not exist** for variable costs throughout the entire range of possible activity.

- At abnormally low levels of activity, it may be impossible to be cost-efficient. Small-scale operations may not allow the company to obtain quantity discounts for raw materials or to use specialized labor.
- At abnormally high levels of activity, unit labor costs may increase sharply because of overtime pay. Also, at high activity levels, unit materials costs may jump significantly because of excess spoilage caused by worker fatigue.

As a result, in the real world, the relationship between the behavior of variable costs and changes in the activity level is often **curvilinear**, as shown in part (a) of **Illustration 18.3**. In the curved sections of the line, a change in the activity index will **not** result in a direct, proportional change in the total variable costs. That is, a doubling of the activity index will not result in an exact doubling of the total variable costs. The total variable costs may be more than double, or they may be less than double.

**Nonlinear behavior of variable and fixed costs**

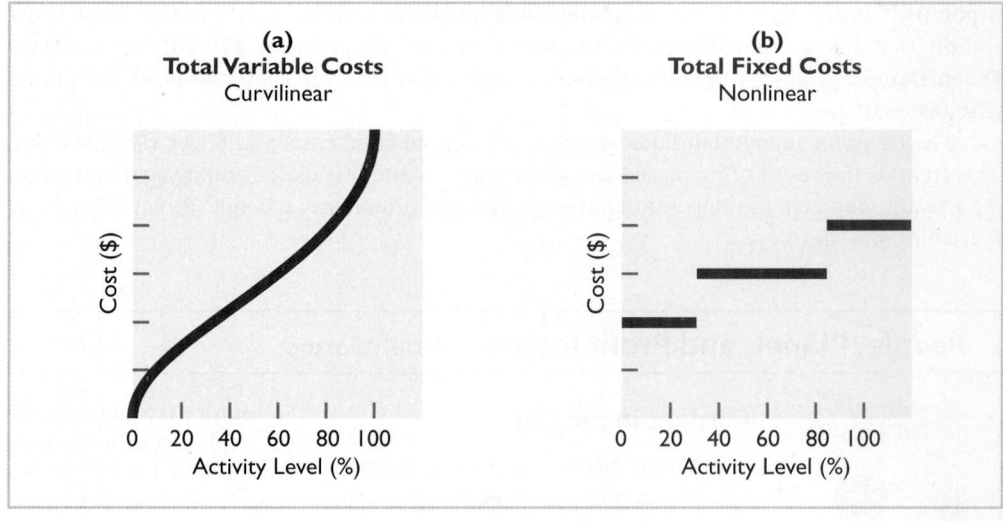

Total fixed costs also do not have a straight-line relationship over the entire range of activity. Some fixed costs will not change. But it is possible for management to change other fixed costs (see **Helpful Hint**). For example, in some instances, salaried employees (fixed) are replaced with freelance workers (variable). Some costs are step costs. For example, once a company exceeds certain levels of activity, it may have to add an additional warehouse or more machinery. Illustration 18.3 part (b) shows an example of step-cost behavior of total fixed costs through all potential levels of activity.

For most companies, operating at almost zero or at 100% capacity is the exception rather than the rule. Instead, companies often operate over a somewhat narrower range, such as 40–80% of capacity. For example, the average occupancy rate for hotels is between 50% and 80%. Airlines calculate their capacity using a measure called a load factor (which combines the number of available seats and the miles flown); this measure has risen to an average of 80% or higher for some airlines in recent years.

**HELPFUL HINT**

Fixed costs that may be changed by managers include research, such as new product development, and management training programs.

**ALTERNATIVE TERMINOLOGY**

The relevant range is also called the *normal* or *practical range*.

- The range over which a company expects to operate during a year is called the **relevant range** of the activity index (see **Alternative Terminology**).
- Within the relevant range, as both diagrams in **Illustration 18.4** show, a straight-line relationship generally exists for both variable and fixed costs between 40% and 80% of capacity.

**Linear behavior within relevant range**

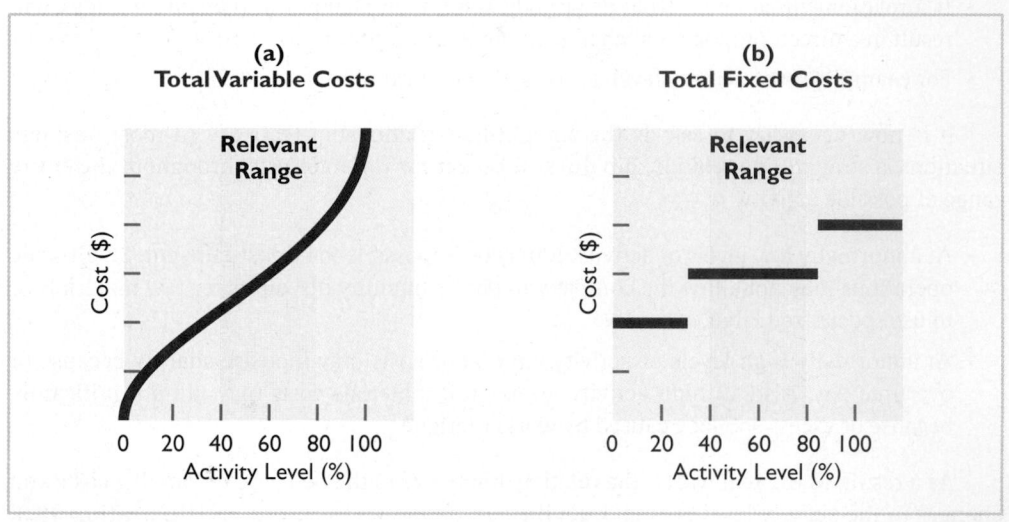

As you can see, although the linear (straight-line) relationship may not be completely realistic, **the linear assumption produces useful data for CVP analysis as long as the level of activity remains within the relevant range.**

# Mixed Costs

**Mixed costs** are costs that contain both variable-cost and fixed-cost components. **Mixed costs, therefore, change in total but not proportionately with changes in the activity level.** For example, each month the electric bill includes a flat service fee plus a usage charge.

The rental of a **U-Haul** truck is another good example of a mixed cost. Assume that local rental terms for a 17-foot truck, including insurance, are $50 per day plus 50 cents per mile. When determining the cost of a one-day rental:

- The fixed-cost component is the cost of having the truck available ($50 per day charge).
- The variable-cost component is the cost of actually using the truck (50 cents per mile driven).

The graphic presentation of the rental cost for a one-day rental is shown in **Illustration 18.5**.

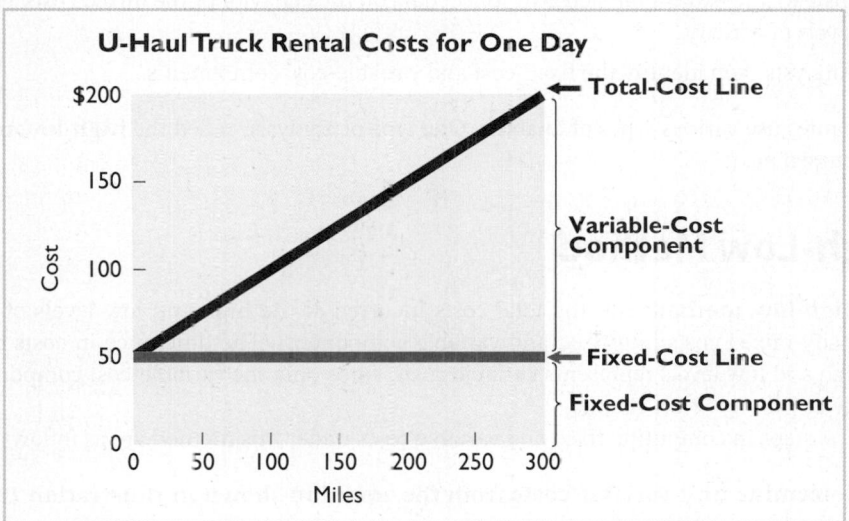

**Behavior of a mixed cost**

---

## DO IT! 1 | Types of Costs

Helena Company reports the following total costs at two levels of production.

|  | 10,000 Units | 20,000 Units |
|---|---|---|
| Direct materials | $20,000 | $40,000 |
| Maintenance | 8,000 | 10,000 |
| Direct labor | 17,000 | 34,000 |
| Indirect materials | 1,000 | 2,000 |
| Depreciation (straight-line) | 4,000 | 4,000 |
| Utilities | 3,000 | 5,000 |
| Rent | 6,000 | 6,000 |

Classify each cost as variable, fixed, or mixed.

### Solution

Direct materials, direct labor, and indirect materials are variable costs because the total cost doubles with the doubling in activity.

Depreciation and rent are fixed costs because the total cost does not vary with the change in activity.

Maintenance and utilities are mixed costs because the total cost changes, but the change is not proportional to the change in activity.

Related exercise material: **BE18.1, BE18.2, BE18.3, DO IT! 18.1, E18.1, E18.2, E18.4, and E18.6.**

**ACTION PLAN**
- **Recall that a variable cost varies in total directly and proportionately with each change in activity level.**
- **Recall that a fixed cost remains the same in total with each change in activity level.**
- **Recall that a mixed cost changes in total but not proportionately with each change in activity level.**

# Mixed Costs Analysis

**LEARNING OBJECTIVE 2**

Apply the high-low method to determine the components of mixed costs.

For purposes of cost-volume-profit analysis, **mixed costs must be classified into their fixed and variable components**. How does management make the classification?

- One possibility is to determine the variable and fixed components each time a mixed cost is incurred. But because of time and cost constraints, this approach is rarely followed.
- Instead, the usual approach is to collect data on the behavior of the mixed costs at various levels of activity.
- Analysts then identify the fixed-cost and variable-cost components.

Companies use various types of analysis. One type of analysis, called the **high-low method**, is discussed next.

## High-Low Method

The **high-low method** uses the total costs incurred at the high and low levels of activity to classify mixed costs into fixed and variable components. The difference in costs between the high and low levels represents variable costs, since only the variable-cost component can change as activity levels change.

The steps in computing fixed and variable costs under this method are as follows.

1. **Determine unit variable costs from the equation shown in** Illustration 18.6. This is the slope of the cost function.

**ILLUSTRATION 18.6**

**Equation for unit variable costs using high-low method**

| Change in Total Costs at High versus Low Activity Level | ÷ | High minus Low Activity Level | = | Unit Variable Costs |
|---|---|---|---|---|

To illustrate, assume that Metro Transit Company has the maintenance costs and mileage data for its fleet of buses over a six-month period shown in Illustration 18.7.

**ILLUSTRATION 18.7**

**Assumed maintenance costs and mileage data**

| Month | Miles Driven | Total Cost | Month | Miles Driven | Total Cost |
|---|---|---|---|---|---|
| January | 20,000 | $30,000 | April | 50,000 | $63,000 |
| February | 40,000 | 48,000 | May | 30,000 | 42,000 |
| March | 35,000 | 49,000 | June | 43,000 | 61,000 |

The high level of activity is 50,000 miles in April, and the low level of activity is 20,000 miles in January. The maintenance costs at these two levels are $63,000 and $30,000, respectively. The difference in maintenance costs is $33,000 ($63,000 − $30,000), and the difference in miles is 30,000 (50,000 − 20,000). Therefore, for Metro Transit, unit variable costs are $1.10, computed as follows.

| Change in Total Costs at High versus Low Activity Level | | High minus Low Activity Level | | Unit Variable Costs |
|---|---|---|---|---|
| $33,000 | ÷ | 30,000 miles | = | $1.10 per mile |

2. **Determine the total fixed costs by subtracting the total variable costs at either the high or the low activity level from the total cost at that activity level.**

**Illustration 18.8** shows the computations for Metro Transit.

**ILLUSTRATION 18.8**

**High-low method computation of fixed costs**

| | | High | Low |
|---|---|---|---|
| | | **Activity Level** | |
| 4 Total cost | | $63,000 | $30,000 |
| 5 Less: | Variable costs | | |
| 6 | 50,000 × $1.10 | 55,000 | |
| 7 | 20,000 × $1.10 | | 22,000 |
| 8 Total fixed costs | | **$ 8,000** | **$ 8,000** |

For example, at the 50,000-mile level of activity, variable costs are 50,000 × $1.10 = $55,000. To determine the fixed costs of $8,000, we subtract the variable costs of $55,000 from the total cost of $63,000. **Total maintenance costs are therefore $8,000 per month of fixed costs plus $1.10 per mile of variable costs.** This is represented by the following total cost equation.

| Total maintenance costs | = | **Fixed-Cost Component** $8,000 | + | **Variable-Cost Component** ($1.10 × Miles driven) |
|---|---|---|---|---|

For example, at 45,000 miles, estimated maintenance costs would be $8,000 fixed and $49,500 variable ($1.10 × 45,000), for a total of $57,500.

The graph in **Illustration 18.9** plots the six-month data for Metro Transit Company.

**ILLUSTRATION 18.9**

**Scatter plot for Metro Transit Company**

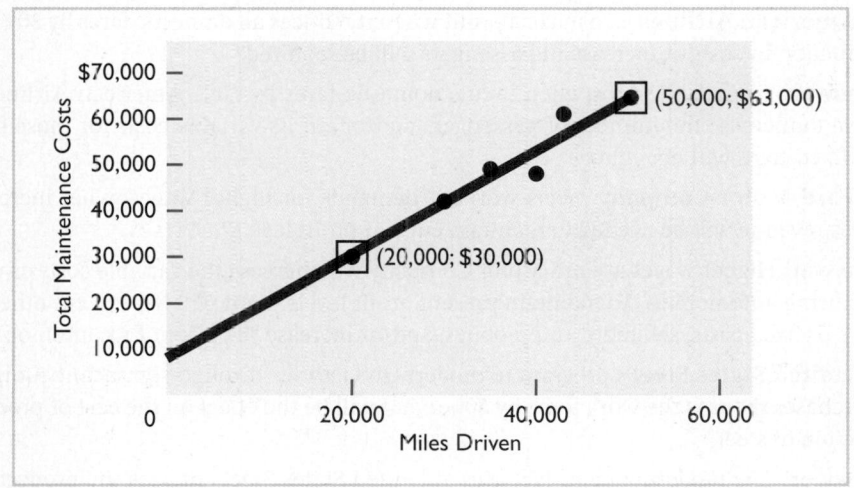

- The red line drawn in the graph connects the high and low data points (in squares) and therefore represents the equation that we just solved using the high-low method.
- The red, "high-low" line intersects the y-axis at $8,000 (the fixed-cost level), and it rises by its slope of $1.10 per unit (the unit variable costs).

- Note that not all data points fall exactly on the plotted line. A completely different line would result if we chose to draw a line through any two of the other data points. That is, by choosing two other data points, we would end up with a different estimate of fixed costs and different unit variable costs.

- Thus, from this scatter plot, we can see that while the high-low method is simple, the result is rather arbitrary.

A better approach, which uses information from all the data points to estimate fixed and variable costs, is called *regression analysis*. A discussion of regression analysis is provided in Appendix 18A as well as in the Excel video available in WileyPLUS.

---

**Management Insight    Kroger**

### Are Robotic Workers More Humane?

phonlamaiphoto/Adobe Stock Photos

Warehouse distribution centers for large retailers and grocers employ more than 800,000 people in the United States. But many companies, such as grocer **Kroger**, have a hard time finding and retaining warehouse workers. One reason? Studies have shown that some warehouse workers walk up to 20 miles and lift 50,000 pounds during a single day. As a result, as the needs for storage increase and companies are faced with the proposition of building massive new warehouses, some companies are choosing instead to invest in robotic warehousing systems.

Robots can provide many advantages over their human counterparts. Robots need aisles that are less than 30 inches wide, as opposed to traditional warehouse aisles that are 10 to 12 feet wide. Moving at speeds of up to 25 miles per hour, robots can drop off and retrieve warehouse cases about five times as fast as a human. Robotic systems cut labor costs by about 80%, and they cut warehouse size anywhere from 25% to 40%. However, a fully automated system costs between $40 to $80 million, so the switch to robotic systems is not a trivial decision.

**Source:** Robbie Whelan, "Fully Autonomous Robots: The Warehouse Workers of the Near Future," *Wall Street Journal* (September 20, 2016).

**How would a company's variable and fixed costs change if it adopts a robotic system? (Answer is available at the end of the chapter.)**

---

# Importance of Identifying Variable and Fixed Costs

Why is it important to identify costs as either variable or fixed components? The answer may become apparent if we look at the following four business decisions.

1. If **American Airlines** is to make a profit when it reduces all domestic fares by 30%, what reduction in costs or increase in passengers will be required?

   **Answer**: To make a profit when it cuts domestic fares by 30%, American Airlines will have to increase the number of passengers and/or cut its variable costs for those flights. Its fixed costs will not change.

2. If **Ford Motor Company** meets workers' demands for higher wages, what increase in sales revenue will be needed to maintain current profit levels?

   **Answer**: Higher wages at Ford Motor Company will increase the variable costs of manufacturing automobiles. To maintain present profit levels, Ford will have to cut other variable or fixed costs, sell more automobiles, and/or increase the price of its automobiles.

3. If **United States Steel**'s program to modernize factories through significant equipment purchases reduces the work force by 50%, what will be the effect on the cost of producing one ton of steel?

   **Answer**: The modernizing of factories at United States Steel changes the proportion of fixed and variable costs of producing one ton of steel. Fixed costs increase because of higher depreciation charges, whereas variable costs decrease due to the reduction in the number of steelworkers and related direct labor costs.

4. What happens if **Kellogg's** increases its advertising expenses but cannot increase prices because of competitive pressure?

   **Answer**: Sales volume must be increased to cover the increase in fixed advertising costs.

## DO IT! 2 | High-Low Method

Byrnes Company accumulates the following data concerning a mixed cost, using units produced as the activity level.

| | Units Produced | Total Cost |
|---|---|---|
| March | 9,800 | $14,740 |
| April | 8,500 | 13,250 |
| May | 7,000 | 11,100 |
| June | 7,600 | 12,000 |
| July | 8,100 | 12,460 |

a. Compute the variable-cost and fixed-cost components using the high-low method.

b. Using the information from your answer to part (a), write the cost equation.

c. Estimate the total cost if the company produces 8,000 units.

**ACTION PLAN**
- Determine the highest and lowest levels of activity.
- Compute unit variable cost as Change in total costs ÷ Change in activity level = Unit variable cost.
- Compute fixed cost as Total cost − (Unit variable cost × Units produced) = Total fixed cost.

### Solution

a. Unit variable cost: $(\$14{,}740 - \$11{,}100) \div (9{,}800 - 7{,}000) = \$1.30$

  Fixed cost: $\$14{,}740 - (\$1.30 \times 9{,}800 \text{ units}) = \$2{,}000$
  OR $\$11{,}100 - (\$1.30 \times 7{,}000 \text{ units}) = \$2{,}000$

b. Cost $= \$2{,}000 + (\$1.30 \times \text{units produced})$

c. Total cost to produce 8,000 units: $\$2{,}000 + \$10{,}400 (\$1.30 \times 8{,}000 \text{ units}) = \$12{,}400$

Related exercise material: **BE18.4, BE18.5, DO IT 18.2, E18.3, and E18.5.**

# Cost-Volume-Profit Analysis

Prepare a CVP income statement to determine contribution margin.

**Cost-volume-profit (CVP) analysis** is the study of the effects of changes in costs and volume (quantity) on a company's profits.

- CVP analysis is important in profit planning.
- It also is a critical factor in management decisions such as setting selling prices, determining product mix, and maximizing use of production facilities.

## Basic Components

CVP analysis considers the interrelationships among the components—production/sales quantity, unit selling price, unit variable costs, total fixed costs, and sales mix—shown in **Illustration 18.10**. Note that management can modify operations to impact these components. But, it needs to do so with a solid understanding of how any operational changes will impact net income. This is CVP analysis.

The following assumptions underlie each CVP analysis.

1. The behavior of both costs and revenues is linear throughout the relevant range of the activity index.
2. Costs can be classified accurately as either variable or fixed.

**ILLUSTRATION 18.10** Components of CVP analysis

3. Changes in activity are the only factors that affect costs.

4. All units produced are sold.

5. When more than one type of product is sold, the sales mix will remain constant. That is, the percentage that each product represents of total sales will stay the same. Sales mix complicates CVP analysis because different products will have different cost relationships. In this chapter, we assume a single product. In Chapter 19, however, we examine the sales mix more closely.

When these assumptions are not valid, the CVP analysis may be inaccurate.

## CVP Income Statement

Because CVP is so important for decision-making, management often wants this information reported in a **cost-volume-profit (CVP) income statement** format for internal use.

- The CVP income statement classifies costs as variable or fixed and computes a contribution margin.
- **Contribution margin (CM)** is the amount of revenue remaining after deducting variable costs. It is often stated both as a total amount and on a per unit basis.

We use Vargo Electronics Company to illustrate a CVP income statement and to contrast it with an income statement reported under generally accepted accounting principles (GAAP). Vargo Electronics produces cell phones. **Illustration 18.11** presents relevant data for the cell phones sold by this company in June 2022.

**ILLUSTRATION 18.11**

**Selling and cost data for Vargo Electronics**

| | | |
|---|---:|---:|
| Unit selling price per cell phone | | $500 |
| | | |
| Unit variable costs | | |
| Direct materials | $185 | |
| Direct labor | 100 | |
| Sales personnel commissions | 15 | |
| Total unit variable costs | | $300 |
| | | |
| Monthly fixed costs | | |
| Manufacturing overhead | $ 40,000 | |
| CEO salary | 150,000 | |
| Sales salaries | 10,000 | |
| Total monthly fixed costs | | $200,000 |
| | | |
| Units sold | | 1,600 |

Note that in Illustration 18.11, as well as in the applications and assignment material of CVP analysis that follow, **we assume that the term "costs" includes all costs and expenses related to production and sale of the product. That is, costs include manufacturing product costs plus selling and administrative period expenses.**

**Illustration 18.12** compares the traditional GAAP income statement for Vargo Electronics with its CVP income statement.

**ILLUSTRATION 18.12**   **GAAP income statement versus CVP income statement**

**(a)**

**Vargo Electronics Company**
GAAP Income Statement
For the Month Ended June 30, 2022

| | | |
|---|---|---|
| Sales (1,600 × $500) | | $800,000 |
| Cost of goods sold | | |
| Direct materials (1,600 × $185) | $296,000 | |
| Direct labor (1,600 × $100) | 160,000 | |
| Manufacturing overhead | 40,000 | 496,000 |
| **Gross profit** | | **304,000** |
| Operating expenses | | |
| Sales commissions (1,600 × $15) | 24,000 | |
| Sales personnel salaries | 10,000 | |
| CEO salary | 150,000 | 184,000 |
| **Net income** | | **$120,000** |

**(b)**

**Vargo Electronics Company**
CVP Income Statement
For the Month Ended June 30, 2022

| | | |
|---|---|---|
| Sales (1,600 × $500) | | $800,000 |
| Variable costs | | |
| Direct materials (1,600 × $185) | $296,000 | |
| Direct labor (1,600 × $100) | 160,000 | |
| Sales commissions (1,600 × $15) | 24,000 | 480,000 |
| **Contribution margin** | | **320,000** |
| Fixed costs | | |
| Manufacturing overhead | 40,000 | |
| Sales personnel salaries | 10,000 | |
| CEO salary | 150,000 | 200,000 |
| **Net income** | | **$120,000** |

While both income statements arrive at the same net income of $120,000, the components of each income statement are grouped differently to emphasize different aspects of the company's operations.

- The GAAP income statement differentiates between **product costs** (those included in cost of goods sold) and **period costs** (those listed in operating expenses). The CVP statement differentiates between **variable costs** and **fixed costs**.
- The GAAP income statement emphasizes **gross profit** (the difference between the amount received for goods sold and the cost of producing/purchasing these goods). Gross profit represents the net amount available to cover the company's operating expenses.
- The CVP income statement highlights **contribution margin** (the difference between the amount received for goods sold and the company's variable costs). Contribution margin represents the net amount available to cover fixed costs.

Subsequent illustrations show that sometimes per unit amounts and percentage of sales amounts are included in separate columns in a CVP statement to facilitate CVP analysis. *Homework assignments specify which columns to present.*

## Unit Contribution Margin

**Illustration 18.13** shows the equation for **unit contribution margin** and the computation for Vargo Electronics.

| Unit Selling Price | − | Unit Variable Costs | = | Unit Contribution Margin |
|---|---|---|---|---|
| $500 | − | $300 | = | $200 |

**ILLUSTRATION 18.13**

**Equation for unit contribution margin**

Unit contribution margin indicates that for every cell phone sold, the selling price exceeds the unit variable costs by $200.

- Vargo generates $200 of contribution margin per unit to cover fixed costs and contribute to net income.
- Because Vargo has fixed costs of $200,000, it must sell 1,000 cell phones ($200,000 ÷ $200) to cover its fixed costs

- At the point where total contribution margin exactly equals fixed costs (sale of 1,000 cell phones), Vargo will report net income of zero.
- At this point, referred to as the **break-even point**, total costs (variable plus fixed) exactly equal total revenue.

**Illustration 18.14** shows Vargo's condensed CVP income statement, which assumes that June sales were at the point where net income equals zero. For Vargo, this point occurs when sales volume is 1,000 units. It shows a contribution margin of $200,000. A separate per unit column was added, which shows a unit contribution margin of $200 ($500 − $300).

**ILLUSTRATION 18.14**

CVP income statement, with zero net income (1,000 cell phones sold)

### Vargo Electronics Company
#### CVP Income Statement
#### For the Month Ended June 30, 2022

|  | Total | Per Unit |
|---|---|---|
| Sales (1,000 × $500) | $500,000 | $500 |
| Variable costs (1,000 × $300) | 300,000 | 300 |
| **Contribution margin** | 200,000 | **$200** |
| Fixed costs | 200,000 | |
| **Net income** | $ –0– | |

It follows that for every cell phone sold above the break-even point of 1,000 units, **net income increases by the amount of the unit contribution margin, $200**. For example, assume that Vargo sold one more cell phone, for a total of 1,001 cell phones sold. In this case, Vargo reports net income of $200, as shown in **Illustration 18.15**.

**ILLUSTRATION 18.15**

CVP income statement, with net income and per unit data (1,001 cell phones sold)

### Vargo Electronics Company
#### CVP Income Statement
#### For the Month Ended June 30, 2022

|  | Total | Per Unit |
|---|---|---|
| Sales (1,001 × $500) | $500,500 | $500 |
| Variable costs (1,001 × $300) | 300,300 | 300 |
| **Contribution margin** | 200,200 | **$200** |
| Fixed costs | 200,000 | |
| **Net income** | $ 200 | |

## Contribution Margin Ratio

Many managers use the contribution margin ratio in CVP analysis. The contribution margin ratio is the contribution margin expressed as a percentage of sales. **Illustration 18.16** presents the same information as Illustration 18.14 but with a column added that presents percentage of sales information.

**ILLUSTRATION 18.16**

CVP income statement, with net income and percent of sales data (1,000 cell phones sold)

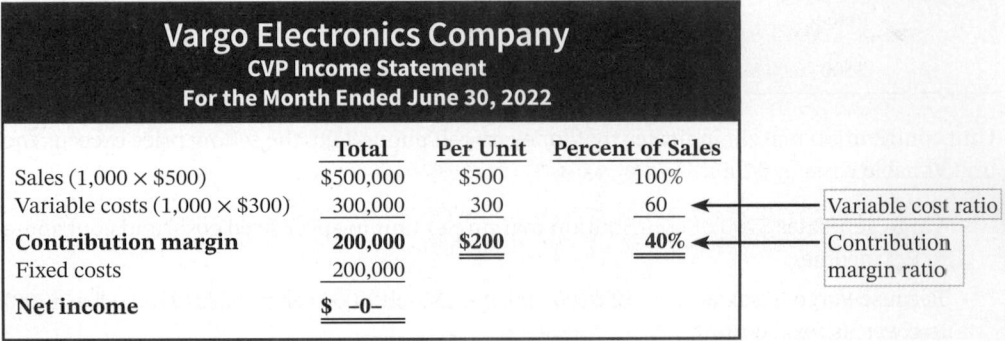

### Vargo Electronics Company
#### CVP Income Statement
#### For the Month Ended June 30, 2022

|  | Total | Per Unit | Percent of Sales |  |
|---|---|---|---|---|
| Sales (1,000 × $500) | $500,000 | $500 | 100% | |
| Variable costs (1,000 × $300) | 300,000 | 300 | 60 | ← Variable cost ratio |
| **Contribution margin** | 200,000 | **$200** | **40%** | ← Contribution margin ratio |
| Fixed costs | 200,000 | | | |
| **Net income** | $ –0– | | | |

- This column shows that Vargo has a **variable cost ratio**, that is, variable costs expressed as a percentage of sales, of 60%. This tells us that for every dollar of sales, Vargo incurs variable costs of 60 cents.

- When this percentage is subtracted from 100%, we arrive at Vargo's contribution margin ratio of 40%. This tells us that for every dollar of sales, Vargo earns a contribution margin of 40 cents.

Alternatively, the **contribution margin ratio** can be determined by dividing the unit contribution margin by the unit selling price. **Illustration 18.17** shows the ratio for Vargo Electronics.

| Unit Contribution Margin | ÷ | Unit Selling Price | = | Contribution Margin Ratio |
|:---:|:---:|:---:|:---:|:---:|
| $200 | ÷ | $500 | = | 40% |

**ILLUSTRATION 18.17**
Equation for contribution margin ratio

- The contribution margin ratio of 40% means that Vargo generates 40 cents of contribution margin with each dollar of sales. That is, $0.40 of each sales dollar (40% × $1) is available to apply to fixed costs and to contribute to net income.

- This expression of contribution margin is very helpful in determining the effect of changes in sales on net income. For example, if Vargo's sales increase $100,000, net income will increase $40,000 (40% × $100,000).

- Thus, by using the contribution margin ratio, managers can quickly determine increases in net income from any change in sales.

We can also see this effect through a CVP income statement. Assume that Vargo's current sales are $500,000 and it wants to know the effect of a $100,000 (200-unit) increase in sales. Vargo prepares the comparative CVP income statement analysis shown in **Illustration 18.18**.

**ILLUSTRATION 18.18** **Comparative CVP income statements**

**Vargo Electronics Company**
**CVP Income Statement**
**For the Month Ended June 30, 2022**

| | No Change | | | With $100,000 Increase in Sales | | |
|---|---|---|---|---|---|---|
| | Total | Per Unit | Percent of Sales | Total | Per Unit | Percent of Sales |
| Sales | $500,000 | $500 | 100% | $600,000 | $500 | 100% |
| Variable costs | 300,000 | 300 | 60 | 360,000 | 300 | 60% |
| **Contribution margin** | **200,000** | **$200** | **40%** | **240,000** | **$200** | **40%** |
| Fixed costs | 200,000 | | | 200,000 | | |
| **Net income** | **$ –0–** | | | **$ 40,000** | | |

As sales increase, variable costs also increase.

- We can employ Vargo's variable cost ratio of 60% to determine that the $100,000 increase in sales results in a $60,000 (60% × $100,000) increase in variable costs.

- Since fixed costs do not increase, the resulting increase in net income is the difference between the increase in sales and the increase in variable costs of $40,000 ($100,000 − $60,000).

- Alternatively, the $40,000 increase in net income can be calculated on either a unit contribution margin basis (200 units × $200 per unit) or using the contribution margin ratio times the increase in sales dollars (40% × $100,000).

- Note that the unit contribution margin and contribution margin as a percentage of sales (that is, the contribution margin ratio) remain unchanged by the increase in sales.

Study these CVP income statements carefully. The concepts presented in these statements are used extensively in this and later chapters.

**ACTION PLAN**

- Provide a heading with the name of the company, name of statement, and period covered.
- Subtract variable costs from sales to determine contribution margin. Subtract fixed costs from contribution margin to determine net income.
- Express sales, variable costs, and contribution margin on a per unit basis.
- Express sales, variable costs, and contribution margin as a percentage of sales.

## DO IT! 3 | CVP Income Statement

Ampco Industries produces and sells a cell phone-operated thermostat. Information regarding the costs and sales of thermostats during September 2022 are provided below.

| | |
|---|---|
| Unit selling price of thermostat | $85 |
| Unit variable costs | $32 |
| Total monthly fixed costs | $190,000 |
| Units sold | 4,000 |

Prepare a CVP income statement for Ampco Industries for the month of September. Provide total, per unit, and percent of sales values.

### Solution

**Ampco Industries**
**CVP Income Statement**
**For the Month Ended September 30, 2022**

| | Total | Per Unit | Percent of Sales |
|---|---|---|---|
| Sales | $340,000 | $85 | 100.00% |
| Variable costs | 128,000 | 32 | 37.65 |
| Contribution margin | 212,000 | $53 | 62.35% |
| Fixed costs | 190,000 | | |
| Net income | $ 22,000 | | |

Related exercise material: **BE18.6, BE18.7, DO IT! 18.3, and E18.7.**

# Break-Even Analysis

### LEARNING OBJECTIVE 4

Compute the break-even point using three approaches.

A key relationship in CVP analysis is the level of activity at which total revenues equal total costs (both fixed and variable)—the **break-even point**. At this volume of sales, the company will realize no income but will suffer no loss. The process of finding the break-even point is called **break-even analysis**. Knowledge of the break-even point is useful to management when it considers decisions such as whether to introduce new product lines, change sales prices on established products, or enter new market areas.

The break-even point can be:

1. Computed from a mathematical equation.
2. Computed by using contribution margin techniques.
3. Derived from a cost-volume-profit (CVP) graph.

The break-even point can be expressed either in **sales units** (quantity) or **sales dollars**.

## Mathematical Equation

**Illustration 18.19** shows a common profit equation used as the basis for CVP analysis. This equation expresses net income as sales minus variable and fixed costs.

**ILLUSTRATION 18.19**
**Profit equation for break-even point**

| Sales | − | Variable Costs | − | Fixed Costs | = | Net Income |
|---|---|---|---|---|---|---|
| $500Q | − | $300Q | − | $200,000 | = | $0 |

- Sales is expressed as the unit selling price ($500) times the quantity of units sold (Q).
- Variable costs are determined by multiplying the unit variable costs ($300) by the quantity of units sold (Q).
- When net income is set to zero, as it is in this illustration, this equation can be used to calculate the break-even point.

As shown in Illustration 18.14, net income equals zero when the contribution margin (sales minus variable costs) is equal to fixed costs. To reflect this, **Illustration 18.20** rewrites the equation with contribution margin (sales minus variable costs) on the left side, and fixed costs and net income of zero on the right. We can then compute the break-even point **in sales units** by **using the unit selling price** and **unit variable costs** and solving for the quantity (Q).

**ILLUSTRATION 18.20**
**Computation of break-even point in sales units**

| Sales | − | Variable Costs | − | Fixed Costs | = | Net Income |
|---|---|---|---|---|---|---|
| $500Q | − | $300Q | − | $200,000 | = | $0 ← Profit equation set to zero |
| $500Q | − | $300Q | = | $200,000 | + | $0 ← Total contribution margin = Fixed costs |
| $200Q | = | $200,000 ← | | Solve for Q to determine break-even quantity | | |

$$Q = \frac{\$200,000}{\$200} = \frac{\textbf{Fixed Costs}}{\textbf{Unit Contribution Margin}}$$ ← Equation for break-even point in sales units

$$Q = 1,000 \text{ units}$$

where

| Q | = | quantity of units sold |
|---|---|---|
| $500 | = | unit selling price |
| $300 | = | unit variable costs |
| $200,000 | = | total fixed costs |

Thus, Vargo Electronics must sell 1,000 cell phones to break even.

To find the amount of **sales dollars** required to break even, we multiply the units sold at the break-even point times the unit selling price, as shown below.

$$1,000 \times \$500 = \$500,000 \text{ (break-even point in sales dollars)}$$

# Contribution Margin Techniques

Many managers employ contribution margin analysis to compute the break-even point. This can be a shortcut to the mathematical equation method discussed above.

## Unit Contribution Margin: Break-Even Point in Sales Units

The final step in Illustration 18.20 divides fixed costs by the unit contribution margin (highlighted in red). Thus, rather than walk through all of the steps of the equation approach, we can simply employ the equation shown in **Illustration 18.21**.

| Fixed Costs | ÷ | Unit Contribution Margin | = | Break-Even Point in Sales Units |
|---|---|---|---|---|
| $200,000 | ÷ | $200 | = | 1,000 units |

Why does this equation work?

- The unit contribution margin is the net amount by which the unit selling price exceeds the unit variable costs.
- Every sale generates this much (in this case, $200 per unit) to cover fixed costs (in this case, $200,000).
- Consequently, if we divide fixed costs ($200,000) by the unit contribution margin ($200), we know how many units we need to sell to break even (1,000 units).

## Contribution Margin Ratio: Break-Even Point in Sales Dollars

When a company has numerous products, it is not practical to determine the unit contribution margin for each product. In this case, we instead use the contribution margin ratio to determine the break-even point in total sales dollars (rather than sales units).

- Recall that the contribution margin ratio is the **percentage** of each dollar of sales that is available to cover fixed costs and generate net income.
- Therefore, **to determine the sales dollars needed to cover fixed costs,** we divide fixed costs by the contribution margin ratio, as shown in **Illustration 18.22.**

**ILLUSTRATION 18.22**

**Equation for break-even point in sales dollars using contribution margin ratio**

| Fixed Costs | ÷ | Contribution Margin Ratio | = | Break-Even Point in Sales Dollars |
|---|---|---|---|---|
| $200,000 | ÷ | 40% | = | $500,000 |

To apply this equation to Vargo Electronics, consider that its 40% contribution margin ratio means that for every dollar sold, it generates 40 cents of contribution margin. The question is, how many sales dollars does Vargo need in order to generate total contribution margin of $200,000 to pay off fixed costs?

- We divide the fixed costs of $200,000 by the 40 cents of contribution margin generated by each dollar of sales to arrive at $500,000 ($200,000 ÷ 40%).
- To prove this result, if we generate 40 cents of contribution margin for each dollar of sales, then the total contribution margin generated by $500,000 in sales is $200,000 ($500,000 × 40%), just enough to cover the total fixed costs.

---

## Service Company Insight    Flightserve

EXTREME-
PHOTOGRAPHER/E+/
Getty Images

### Charter Flights Offer a Good Deal

The Internet is wringing inefficiencies out of nearly every industry. While commercial aircraft spend roughly 4,000 hours a year in the air, chartered aircraft are flown only 500 hours annually. That means that they are sitting on the ground—not making any money—about 90% of the time.

One company, **Flightserve**, saw a business opportunity in that fact. For about the same cost as a first-class ticket, Flightserve matches up executives with charter flights in small "private jets." The executive gets a more comfortable ride and avoids the hassle of big airports. Flightserve noted that the average charter jet has eight seats. When all eight seats are full, the company has an 80% profit margin. It breaks even at an average of 3.3 full seats per flight. Another company, **NetJets**, uses an alternative approach to increase utilization of jets and thus reduce fixed costs. It offers shared ownership in private jets.

**Sources:** "Jet Set Go," *The Economist* (March 18, 2000), p. 68; and Doug Gollan, "How NetJets' Private Jet Service Is Making Itself Whole Again," *Forbes* (June 3, 2015).

**How did Flightserve determine that it would break even with 3.3 seats full per flight? (Answer is available at the end of the chapter.)**

# Graphic Presentation

An effective way to understand the break-even point is to prepare a break-even graph. Because this graph also shows costs, volume, and profits, it is referred to as a **cost-volume-profit (CVP) graph**.

- Sales volume is represented along the horizontal axis.
- This axis should extend to the maximum level of expected sales.
- Both total revenues (sales) and total costs (fixed plus variable) are represented on the vertical axis (in dollars).

An example of a CVP graph is shown in **Illustration 18.23**.

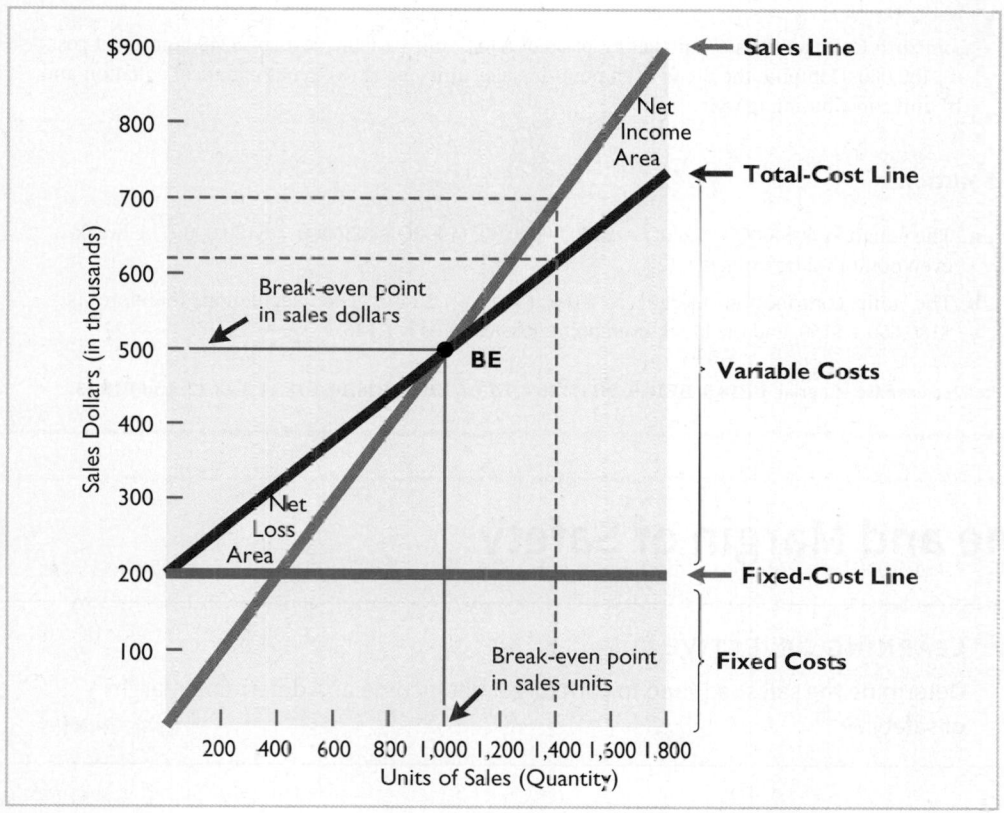

**ILLUSTRATION 18.23**

**Vargo Electronics' CVP graph**

The construction of the graph, using the data for Vargo Electronics, is as follows.

1. Plot the sales line (shown in brown), starting at the zero activity level. For every cell phone sold, total revenue increases by $500. For example, at 200 units, sales are $100,000. At the upper level of activity (1,800 units), sales are $900,000. The sales line is assumed to be linear through the full range of activity. **It has a slope equal to the unit selling price.**

2. Plot the total fixed costs using a horizontal line (shown in green). For the cell phones, this line is plotted at $200,000. The fixed costs are the same at every level of activity.

3. Plot the total-cost line (shown in red). This starts at the fixed-cost line at zero activity. It increases by the variable costs at each level of activity. For each cell phone, variable costs are $300. Thus, at 200 units, total variable costs are $60,000 ($300 × 200) and the total cost is $260,000 ($60,000 + $200,000). At 1,800 units, total variable costs are $540,000 ($300 × 1,800) and total cost is $740,000 ($540,000 + $200,000). On the graph, the amount of the variable costs can be derived from the difference between the total-cost and fixed-cost lines at each level of activity. **The total-cost line has a slope equal to the unit variable costs. It has a y-intercept, at the point of zero units sold, equal to the fixed costs of $200,000.**

4. Determine the break-even point from the intersection of the total-cost line and the sales line at point BE. The break-even point in sales dollars is found by drawing a horizontal line from the break-even point to the vertical axis. The break-even point in sales units is found by

drawing a vertical line from the break-even point to the horizontal axis. For the cell phones, the break-even point is $500,000 of sales, or 1,000 units. At this sales level, Vargo will cover costs but make no profit.

The CVP graph also shows both the net income and net loss areas. Thus, the amount of net income or net loss at each level of sales can be derived from the sales and total-cost lines.

A CVP graph is useful because the effects of a change in any component in the CVP analysis can be quickly seen. For example, a 10% increase in the unit selling price will change the location of the sales line. Likewise, the effects on total costs of wage increases can be quickly observed.

---

**ACTION PLAN**

- **Apply the profit equation: Sales − Variable costs − Fixed costs = Net income.**

- **Apply the break-even equation: Fixed costs ÷ Unit contribution margin = Break-even point in sales units.**

## DO IT! 4 | Break-Even Analysis

Lombardi Company has a unit selling price of $400, unit variable costs of $240, and fixed costs of $180,000. Compute the break-even point in sales units using (a) a mathematical equation and (b) unit contribution margin.

### Solution

a. The equation is $400Q − $240Q − $180,000 = $0; ($400Q − $240Q) = $180,000. The break-even point in sales units is 1,125.

b. The unit contribution margin is $160 ($400 − $240). The calculation therefore is $180,000 ÷ $160, and the break-even point in sales units is 1,125.

Related exercise material: **BE18.8, BE18.9, DO IT! 18.4, E18.8, E18.9, E18.10, E18.11, E18.12, and E18.13.**

---

# Target Net Income and Margin of Safety

---

### LEARNING OBJECTIVE 5
Determine the sales required to earn target net income and determine margin of safety.

---

## Target Net Income

Rather than simply striving to "breaking even," management usually sets an income objective often called **target net income**. It then determines the sales necessary to achieve this specified level of income by using one of the three approaches discussed earlier.

### Mathematical Equation

We know that at the break-even point no profit or loss results for the company. By adding an amount for target net income to the same basic equation, we obtain the equation shown in **Illustration 18.24** for determining required sales.

**ILLUSTRATION 18.24**

**Equation for sales to meet target net income**

| Sales | − | Variable Costs | − | Fixed Costs | = | Target Net Income |
|-------|---|---------------|---|-------------|---|-------------------|

Recall that once the break-even point has been reached so that fixed costs are covered, each additional unit sold increases net income by the amount of the unit contribution margin. We can rewrite the equation with contribution margin (sales minus variable costs) on the left-hand side, and fixed costs and target net income on the right. Assuming that target net income is $120,000 for Vargo Electronics, the computation of required sales in units is as shown in **Illustration 18.25.**

**ILLUSTRATION 18.25**

**Computation of required sales units to achieve target net income**

| | Sales | − | Variable Costs | − | Fixed Costs | = | Target Net Income |
|---|---|---|---|---|---|---|---|
| | $500Q | − | $300Q | − | $200,000 | = | $120,000 |
| | $500Q | − | $300Q | | | = | $200,000 + $120,000 |

$$\$200Q = \$200,000 + \$120,000$$

$$Q = \frac{\$200,000 + \$120,000}{\$200} = \frac{\textbf{Fixed Costs + Target Net Income}}{\textbf{Unit Contribution Margin}}$$

$$Q = 1,600$$

where

$Q$ = quantity of units sold
$\$500$ = unit selling price
$\$300$ = unit variable costs
$\$200,000$ = total fixed costs
$\$120,000$ = target net income

Vargo must sell 1,600 units to achieve target net income of $120,000. The sales dollars required to achieve the target net income is found by multiplying the units sold by the unit selling price [(1,600 × $500) = $800,000].

## Contribution Margin Techniques

As in the case of the break-even point, we can compute the sales units or sales dollars required to meet a target net income. The calculation to compute required sales in units for Vargo Electronics using the unit contribution margin can be seen in the final step of the approach in Illustration 18.25 (shown in red). We simply divide the sum of fixed costs and target net income by the unit contribution margin. **Illustration 18.26** shows this for Vargo.

**ILLUSTRATION 18.26**

**Equation for sales units required to achieve target net income using unit contribution margin**

| $\left(\begin{array}{c}\textbf{Fixed Costs +}\\\textbf{Target Net Income}\end{array}\right)$ | ÷ | Unit Contribution Margin | = | Sales Units |
|---|---|---|---|---|
| ($200,000 + $120,000) | ÷ | $200 | = | 1,600 units |

To achieve its desired target net income of $120,000, Vargo must sell 1,600 cell phones.

**Illustration 18.27** presents the equation to compute the required sales dollars for Vargo using the contribution margin ratio.

**ILLUSTRATION 18.27**

**Equation for sales dollars required to achieve target net income using contribution margin ratio**

| $\left(\begin{array}{c}\textbf{Fixed Costs −}\\\textbf{Target Net Income}\end{array}\right)$ | ÷ | Contribution Margin Ratio | = | Sales Dollars |
|---|---|---|---|---|
| ($200,000 + $120,000) | ÷ | 40% | = | $800,000 |

To achieve its desired target net income of $120,000, Vargo must generate sales of $800,000.

## Graphic Presentation

We also can use the CVP graph in Illustration 18.23 to find the sales required to meet target net income.

- In the net income area of the graph, the distance between the sales line and the total-cost line at any point equals net income.
- We can find required sales by analyzing the differences between the two lines until the desired net income is found.

For example, suppose Vargo Electronics sells 1,400 cell phones. Illustration 18.23 shows that a vertical line drawn at 1,400 units intersects the sales line at $700,000 and the total-cost line at $620,000. The difference between the two amounts represents the net income (profit) of $80,000.

# Margin of Safety

Suppose that your company has been operating at a profit, but you are concerned that business might slow down in the coming year. You would like to know how far your sales could fall before you begin losing money. **Margin of safety** is the difference between actual or expected sales, and sales at the break-even point.

- It measures the "cushion" that a particular level of sales provides above the break-even point.
- It tells us how far sales could fall before the company begins operating at a loss.
- The margin of safety is expressed in dollars or as a ratio.

The equation for stating the **margin of safety in dollars** is actual (or expected) sales minus break-even sales. **Illustration 18.28** shows the computation for Vargo Electronics, assuming that actual (or expected) sales are $750,000.

**ILLUSTRATION 18.28**

Equation for margin of safety in dollars

| Actual (or Expected) Sales | − | Break-Even Sales | = | Margin of Safety in Dollars |
|---|---|---|---|---|
| $750,000 | − | $500,000 | = | $250,000 |

Vargo's margin of safety is $250,000. Its sales could fall by $250,000 before it operates at a loss.

The **margin of safety ratio** is the margin of safety in dollars divided by actual (or expected) sales. **Illustration 18.29** shows the equation and computation for determining the margin of safety ratio.

**ILLUSTRATION 18.29**

Equation for margin of safety ratio

| Margin of Safety in Dollars | ÷ | Actual (or Expected) Sales | = | Margin of Safety Ratio |
|---|---|---|---|---|
| $250,000 | ÷ | $750,000 | = | 33% |

This means that the company's sales could fall by 33% before it operates at a loss.

**The higher the margin of safety in dollars or the margin of safety ratio, the lower the risk that the company will operate at a loss.** Management evaluates the adequacy of the margin of safety in terms of such factors as the vulnerability of the product to competitive pressures or a potential downturn in the economy.

## CVP and Data Analytics

Data analytics plays an important role in CVP analysis. Consider that to perform CVP analysis meaningfully, you need to collect data that you have confidence is accurate. For example, the shipping company **DHL Express**, a competitor to **UPS** and **FedEx**, at one point lacked data of sufficient quality to accurately distinguish between fixed and variable costs, information crucial to performing CVP analysis.

- The company then made a big investment in data collection and analysis, which enabled it to determine the cost and profitability of every shipment.
- Over time, the company was able to refine its abilities to use this data so that it can now link the profitability of what is being shipped to the cost of shipping it.
- This helps DHL Express determine what size airplanes it should use for particular shipments, which leads to better cost control and profitability.

### Service Company Insight  Drake

Image Press Agency/ Alamy Stock Photo

**How a Music Promoter Makes Money**

Computations of the break-even point and margin of safety are important for service companies. Consider how the promoter for the musician Drake might use the break-even point and margin of safety in planning a concert. For example, say one show should bring in ticket sales of $2.45 million, and the promoter guarantees $1.2 million to Drake. In addition, 20% of ticket sales goes to the venue in which the performance is staged. Add another $400,000 for other costs such as insurance, ticket takers, parking attendants, advertising, and so on. All of these costs must be considered in determining whether the show should go on.

**What amount of sales dollars are required for the promoter to break even? (Answer is available at the end of the chapter.)**

## DO IT! 5 | Break-Even Point, Margin of Safety, and Target Net Income

Zootsuit Inc. makes travel bags that sell for $56 each. For the coming year, management expects fixed costs to total $320,000 and variable costs to be $42 per unit. Compute the following: (a) break-even point in sales dollars using the contribution margin (CM) ratio; (b) the margin of safety and margin of safety ratio assuming actual sales are $1,382,400; and (c) the sales dollars required to earn net income of $410,000.

### Solution

a. Contribution margin ratio = [($56 − $42) ÷ $56] = 25%

Break-even point in sales dollars = $320,000 ÷ 25% = $1,280,000

b. Margin of safety = $1,382,400 − $1,280,000 = $102,400

Margin of safety ratio = $102,400 ÷ $1,382,400 = 7.4%

c. Sales dollars = ($320,000 + $410,000) ÷ 25% = $2,920,000

Related exercise material: **BE18.10, BE18.11, BE18.12, DO IT! 18.5, E18.14, E18.15, E18.16, and E18.17.**

---

| Appendix 18A | # Regression Analysis |

### LEARNING OBJECTIVE *6

Apply regression analysis to determine the components of mixed costs.

The high-low method is often used to estimate fixed and variable costs for a mixed-cost situation.

- An advantage of the high-low method is that it is easy to apply.
- But, how accurate and reliable is the estimated cost equation that it produces?

For example, consider the example shown in **Illustration 18A.1**, which indicates the cost equation line produced by the high-low method for Metro Transit Company's maintenance costs. How well does the high-low method represent the relationship between miles driven and total cost? This line is close to nearly all of the data points. Therefore, in this case, the high-low method provides a cost equation that is a very good fit for this data set. It identifies fixed and variable costs in an accurate and reliable way.

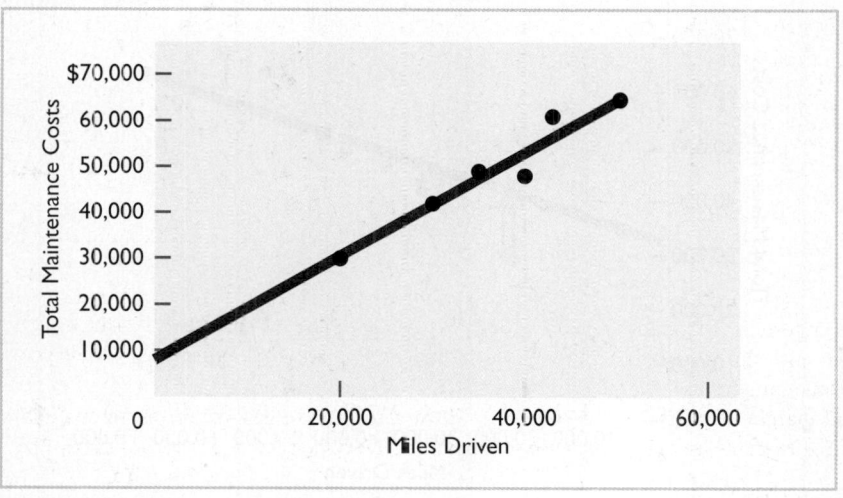

**ILLUSTRATION 18A.1**

**Scatter plot for Metro Transit Company (total maintenance costs as a function of miles driven)**

While the high-low method works well for the Metro Transit data set, a weakness of this method is that it employs only two data points and ignores the rest.

- If those two data points are representative of the entire data set, then the high-low method provides reasonable results (as seen in Illustration 18A.1).
- But, if the high and low data points are not representative of the rest of the data set, then the results are misleading.

To illustrate, assume that Hanson Trucking Company has 12 months of maintenance cost data, as shown in **Illustration 18A.2**.

**ILLUSTRATION 18A.2**

**Maintenance costs and mileage data for Hanson Trucking Company**

| Month | Miles Driven | Total Cost | Month | Miles Driven | Total Cost |
|---|---|---|---|---|---|
| January | 20,000 | $30,000 | July | 15,000 | $39,000 |
| February | 40,000 | 49,000 | August | 28,000 | 41,000 |
| March | 35,000 | 46,000 | September | 60,000 | 72,000 |
| April | 50,000 | 63,000 | October | 55,000 | 67,000 |
| May | 30,000 | 42,000 | November | 19,000 | 29,000 |
| June | 43,000 | 52,000 | December | 65,000 | 63,000 |

The high and low activities are 65,000 miles in December and 15,000 miles in July. The maintenance costs at these two levels are $63,000 and $39,000, respectively. The difference in maintenance costs is $24,000 ($63,000 − $39,000), and the difference in miles is 50,000 (65,000 − 15,000). Therefore, for Hanson Trucking, unit variable costs under the high-low method are $0.48 ($24,000 ÷ 50,000). To determine total variable costs, we multiply the number of miles by cost per mile. For example, at the low activity level of 15,000 miles, total variable costs are $7,200 (15,000 × $0.48). To determine fixed costs, we subtract total variable costs at the low activity level from the total cost at the low activity level ($39,000) as follows.

$$\text{Fixed costs} = \$39,000 - (\$0.48 \times 15,000) = \$31,800$$

Therefore, the cost equation based on the high-low method for this data produces the following calculation:

| | | **Fixed Costs** | | **Variable Costs** |
|---|---|---|---|---|
| Maintenance costs | = | **Intercept** | + | **Slope × Quantity** |
| | = | $31,800 | + | ($0.48 × Miles driven) |

**Illustration 18A.3** shows a scatter plot of the data with a line representing the high-low method cost equation.

**ILLUSTRATION 18A.3**

**Scatter plot for Hanson Trucking Company (total maintenance costs as a function of miles driven)**

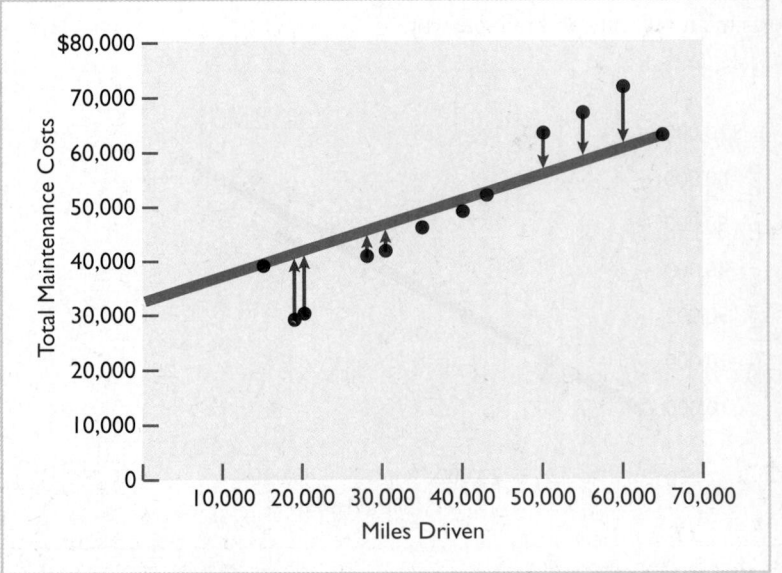

- Note that most of the data points for Hanson Trucking are a significant distance from the line.
- For example, at 19,000 miles, the observed maintenance cost is $29,000, but the equation predicts $40,920 [$31,800 + ($0.48 × 19,000)]. That is a difference of $11,920 ($40,920 − $29,000).
- In this case, the high-low method cost equation does not provide a good representation of the actual relationship between miles driven and maintenance costs.

To derive a more representative cost equation, the company should employ regression analysis.

**Regression analysis** is a statistical approach that estimates the cost equation by employing information from **all** data points, not just the highest and lowest ones. While it involves mathematical analysis taught in statistics courses (which we will not address here), we can provide you with a basic understanding of how regression analysis works.

Consider Illustration 18A.3, which highlights the distance that each data point is from the high-low cost equation line. Regression analysis determines a cost equation that results in a line that minimizes the sum of the squared distances from the line to the data points.

Many software packages perform regression analysis. In **Illustration 18A.4**, we use the **Intercept** and **Slope** functions in Excel to estimate the regression equation for the Hanson Trucking Company data.[1] The Excel video provided in WileyPLUS demonstrates the use of the Intercept and Slope functions.

| | A | B | C | D |
|---|---|---|---|---|
| | Month | Miles Driven | Total Maintenance Costs | |
| 2 | January | 20,000 | 30,000 | |
| 3 | February | 40,000 | 49,000 | |
| 4 | March | 35,000 | 46,000 | |
| 5 | April | 50,000 | 63,000 | |
| 6 | May | 30,000 | 42,000 | |
| 7 | June | 43,000 | 52,000 | |
| 8 | July | 15,000 | 39,000 | |
| 9 | August | 28,000 | 41,000 | |
| 10 | September | 60,000 | 72,000 | |
| 11 | October | 55,000 | 67,000 | |
| 12 | November | 19,000 | 29,000 | |
| 13 | December | 65,000 | 63,000 | |
| 14 | | | | |
| 15 | | Formula | | |
| 16 | Intercept | =INTERCEPT(C2:C13,B2:B13) | 18,502 | |
| 17 | Slope | =SLOPE(C2:C13,B2:B13) | 0.81 | |
| 18 | | | | |

**ILLUSTRATION 18A.4**

**Excel spreadsheet for Hanson Trucking Company (total maintenance costs)**

The cost equation based on the regression results is:

| | | Fixed Costs | | Variable Costs |
|---|---|---|---|---|
| | | Intercept | + | Slope × Quantity |
| Total maintenance costs | = | | | |
| | = | $18,502 | + | ($0.81 × Miles driven) |

Compare this to the cost equation based on the use of the high-low cost approach:

| | | Fixed Costs | | Variable Costs |
|---|---|---|---|---|
| | | Intercept | + | Slope × Quantity |
| Total maintenance costs | = | | | |
| | = | $31,800 | + | ($0.48 × Miles driven) |

---

[1] To use the Intercept and Slope functions in Excel, enter your data in two columns in an Excel spreadsheet. The first column should be your "X" independent variable (miles driven, cells B2 to B13 in our example). The second column should be your "Y" dependent variable (maintenance costs, cells C2 to C13 in our example). Next, in a separate cell, choosing from Excel's statistical functions, enter =Intercept(C2:C13,B2:B13) and in a different cell enter =Slope(C2:C13,B2:B13)

As **Illustration 18A.5** shows, the intercept and slope differ significantly between the regression equation (green) and the high-low equation (red).[2]

**ILLUSTRATION 18A.5** Comparison of cost equation lines from regression analysis versus high-low method

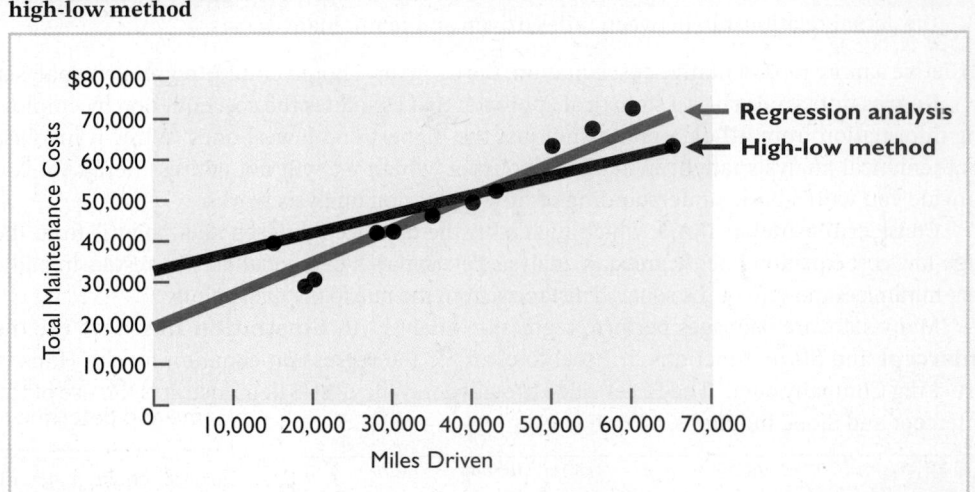

- The regression cost equation line does not include the high and low data points but instead follows a path that minimizes the cumulative distance from all of the data points.
- By doing so, it provides a cost equation that is more representative of the relationship between miles driven and total maintenance costs than the high-low method.

Why should managers care about the accuracy of the cost equation? Managers make many decisions that require that mixed costs be separated into fixed and variable components. Inaccurate classifications of these costs might cause a manager to make an inappropriate decision. For example, Hanson Trucking Company's break-even point differs significantly depending on which of these two cost equations was used. If Hanson Trucking relies on the high-low method, it would have a distorted view of the level of sales it would need in order to break even. In addition, misrepresentation for fixed and variable costs could result in inappropriate decisions, such as whether to discontinue a product line. It would also result in inaccurate product costing under activity-based costing.

While regression analysis usually provides more reliable estimates of the cost equation, it does have its limitations.

1. The regression approach that we applied above assumes a linear relationship between the variables (that is, an increase or decrease in one variable results in a proportional increase or decrease in the other). If the actual relationship differs significantly from linearity, then linear regression can provide misleading results. (Nonlinear regression is addressed in advanced statistics courses.)

2. Regression estimates can be severely influenced by "outliers"—data points that differ significantly from the rest of the observations. It is therefore good practice to plot data points in a scatter graph to identify outliers and then investigate the reasons why they differ. In some cases, outliers must be adjusted for or eliminated.

3. Regression estimation is most accurate when it is based on a large number of data points. However, collecting data can be time-consuming and costly. In some cases, there simply are not enough observable data points to arrive at a reliable estimate.

---

[2] To plot a scatter graph in Excel, highlight the data and then click on Scatter under the Insert tab. To draw the cost equation line, click on the scatter plot, then select Layout and Trendline. In order to get the cost equation line to intercept the Y axis, under Trendline Options in the Backward field, enter the lowest value of your X variable. For example, for Hanson Trucking, we entered 15,000.

# Review and Practice

## Learning Objectives Review

**1   Explain variable, fixed, and mixed costs and the relevant range.**

Variable costs are costs that vary in total directly and proportionately with changes in the activity index. Fixed costs are costs that remain the same in total regardless of changes in the activity index.

The relevant range is the range of activity in which a company expects to operate during a year. It is important in CVP analysis because the behavior of costs is assumed to be linear throughout the relevant range.

Mixed costs change in total but not proportionately with changes in the activity level. For purposes of CVP analysis, mixed costs must be classified into their fixed and variable components.

**2   Apply the high-low method to determine the components of mixed costs.**

Determine the unit variable costs by dividing the change in total costs at the highest and lowest levels of activity by the difference in activity at those levels. Then, determine fixed costs by subtracting total variable costs from the amount of total costs at either the highest or lowest level of activity.

**3   Prepare a CVP income statement to determine contribution margin.**

The five components of CVP analysis are (1) volume or level of activity (quantity), (2) unit selling price, (3) unit variable costs, (4) total fixed costs, and (5) sales mix. Contribution margin is the amount of revenue remaining after deducting variable costs. It is identified in a CVP income statement, which classifies costs as variable or fixed. It can be expressed as a total amount, as a per unit amount, or as a ratio.

**4   Compute the break-even point using three approaches.**

At the break-even point, sales revenue equals total costs, resulting in a net income of zero. The break-even point can be (a) computed from a mathematical equation, (b) computed by using a contribution margin technique, and (c) derived from a CVP graph.

**5   Determine the sales required to earn target net income and determine margin of safety.**

The general equation for required sales is Sales − Variable costs − Fixed costs = Target net income. Two other equations are (1) Sales in units = (Fixed costs + Target net income) ÷ Unit contribution margin, and (2) Sales dollars = (Fixed costs + Target net income) ÷ Contribution margin ratio.

Margin of safety is the difference between actual or expected sales and sales at the break-even point. The equations for margin of safety metrics are (1) Actual (or expected) sales − Break-even sales = Margin of safety in dollars, and (2) Margin of safety in dollars ÷ Actual (expected) sales = Margin of safety ratio.

**\*6   Apply regression analysis to determine the components of mixed costs.**

The high-low method provides a quick estimate of the cost equation for a mixed cost. However, the high-low method is based on only the highest and lowest data points. Regression analysis provides an estimate of the cost equation based on all data points. The cost equation line that results from regression analysis minimizes the sum of the (squared) distances of all of the data points from the cost equation line. Computer programs such as Excel enable easy estimation of the cost equation with regression.

## Glossary Review

**Activity index** The activity that causes changes in the behavior of costs. (p. 18-3).

**Break-even point** The level of activity at which total revenue equals total costs, yielding a net income of zero. (p. 18-14).

**Contribution margin (CM)** The amount of revenue remaining after deducting variable costs. (p. 18-12).

**Contribution margin ratio** The percentage of each dollar of sales that is available to apply to fixed costs and contribute to net income; calculated as unit contribution margin divided by unit selling price, or as total contribution margin divided by total sales. (p. 18-15).

**Cost behavior analysis** The study of how specific costs respond to changes in the level of business activity. (p. 18-3).

**Cost-volume-profit (CVP) analysis** The study of the effects of changes in costs and volume (quantity) on a company's profits. (p. 18-11).

**Cost-volume-profit (CVP) graph** A graph showing the relationship between costs, volume, and profits. (p. 18-19).

**Cost-volume-profit (CVP) income statement** A statement for internal use that classifies costs as fixed or variable and reports contribution margin in the body of the statement. (p. 18-12).

**Fixed costs** Costs that remain the same in total regardless of changes in the activity level. (p. 18-4).

**High-low method** A mathematical calculation that uses the total costs incurred at the high and low levels of activity to classify mixed costs into fixed and variable components. (p. 18-8).

**Margin of safety** The difference between actual or expected sales, and sales at the break-even point. (p. 18-22).

**Mixed costs** Costs that contain both a variable-cost and a fixed-cost component and change in total but not proportionately with changes in the activity level. (p. 18-7).

*Regression analysis A statistical approach that estimates the cost equation by employing information from all data points to find the cost equation line that minimizes the sum of the squared distances from the line to all the data points. (p. 18-25).

Relevant range The range of the activity index over which the company expects to operate during the year. (p. 18-6).

Target net income The income objective set by management. (p. 18-20).

Unit contribution margin The amount of revenue remaining per unit after deducting variable costs; calculated as unit selling price minus unit variable costs. (p. 18-13).

Variable cost ratio Variable costs expressed as a percentage of sales. (p. 18-15).

Variable costs Costs that vary in total directly and proportionately with changes in the activity level. (p. 18-3).

## Practice Multiple-Choice Questions

1. **(LO 1)** Variable costs are costs that:
   a. vary in total directly and proportionately with changes in the activity level but do not remain the same per unit at every activity level.
   b. remain the same per unit and in total at every activity level.
   c. neither vary in total directly and proportionately with changes in the activity level nor remain the same per unit at every activity level.
   d. both vary in total directly and proportionately with changes in the activity level and remain the same per unit at every activity level.

2. **(LO 2)** The relevant range is:
   a. the range of activity in which variable costs will be curvilinear.
   b. the range of activity in which fixed costs will be curvilinear.
   c. the range over which the company expects to operate during a year.
   d. usually from zero to 100% of operating capacity.

3. **(LO 1, 2)** Mixed costs consist of a:
   a. variable-cost component and a fixed-cost component.
   b. fixed-cost component and a product-cost component.
   c. period-cost component and a product-cost component.
   d. variable-cost component and a period-cost component.

4. **(LO 1, 2)** Your cell phone service provider offers a plan that is classified as a mixed cost. The cost for 1,000 minutes in a month is $50. If you use 2,000 minutes this month, your cost will be:
   a. $50.                 c. more than $100.
   b. $100.                d. between $50 and $100.

5. **(LO 2)** Kendra Corporation's total utility costs during the past year were $1,200 during its highest month and $600 during its lowest month. These costs corresponded with 10,000 units of production during the high month and 2,000 units during the low month. What are the fixed cost and unit variable cost of its utility costs using the high-low method?
   a. $0.075 variable and $450 fixed.
   b. $0.120 variable and $0 fixed.
   c. $0.300 variable and $0 fixed.
   d. $0.060 variable and $600 fixed.

6. **(LO 3)** Which of the following is **not** involved in CVP analysis?
   a. Sales mix.              c. Fixed costs per unit.
   b. Unit selling price.     d. Volume or level of activity (quantity).

7. **(LO 3)** When comparing a GAAP income statement to a CVP income statement:

   a. net income will always be greater on the GAAP statement.
   b. net income will always be less on the GAAP statement.
   c. net income will always be identical on both.
   d. net income will be greater or less depending on the sales volume.

8. **(LO 3)** Contribution margin:
   a. is revenue remaining after deducting fixed and variable costs.
   b. may not be expressed as unit contribution margin.
   c. is sales less cost of goods sold.
   d. is revenue remaining after deducting variable costs and may be expressed as unit contribution margin.

9. **(LO 3)** Cournot Company sells 100,000 wrenches for $12 a unit. Fixed costs are $300,000, and net income is $200,000. What should be reported as variable costs in the CVP income statement?
   a. $700,000.              c. $500,000.
   b. $900,000.              d. $1,000,000.

10. **(LO 4)** Gossen Company is planning to sell 200,000 pliers for $4 per unit. The contribution margin ratio is 25%. If Gossen will break even at this level of sales, what are the fixed costs?
    a. $100,000.             c. $200,000.
    b. $160,000.             d. $300,000.

11. **(LO 4)** Brownstone Company's contribution margin ratio is 30%. If Brownstone's sales revenue is $100 greater than its break-even sales dollars, its net income:
    a. will be $100.         c. will be $30.
    b. will be $70.          d. cannot be determined without knowing fixed costs.

12. **(LO 5)** The mathematical equation for computing required sales to obtain target net income is:
    a. Variable costs + Target net income.
    b. Variable costs + Fixed costs + Target net income.
    c. Fixed costs + Target net income.
    d. No correct answer is given.

13. **(LO 5)** Margin of safety is computed as:
    a. Actual sales − Break-even sales.
    b. Contribution margin − Fixed costs.
    c. Break-even point in sales dollars − Variable costs.
    d. Actual sales − Contribution margin.

14. **(LO 5)** Marshall Company had actual sales of $600,000 when the break-even point in sales dollars was $420,000. What is the margin of safety ratio?
    a. 25%.                  c. $33\frac{1}{3}$%.
    b. 30%.                  d. 45%.

## Solutions

**1. d.** Variable costs vary in total directly and proportionately with changes in the activity level and remain the same per unit at every activity level. Choices (a) and (b) are only partially correct. Choice (c) is incorrect as it is the opposite of (d).

**2. c.** The relevant range is the range over which the company expects to operate during a year. The other choices are incorrect because the relevant range is the range over which (a) variable costs are expected to be linear, not curvilinear, and (b) the company expects fixed costs to remain the same. Choice (d) is incorrect because this answer does not specifically define relevant range.

**3. a.** Mixed costs consist of a variable-cost component and a fixed-cost component, not (b) a product-cost component, (c) a period-cost component or a product-cost component, or (d) a period-cost component.

**4. d.** Your cost will include the fixed-cost component (flat service fee), which does not increase, plus the variable-cost component (usage charge) for the additional 1,000 minutes, which will increase your cost to between $50 and $100. Therefore, choices (a) $50, (b) $100, and (c) more than $100 are incorrect.

**5. a.** Unit variable cost is $0.075 [($1,200 − $600) ÷ (10,000 − 2,000)] and fixed is $450 [($1,200 − ($0.075 × 10,000)]. Therefore, choices (b) $0.120 variable and $0 fixed, (c) $0.300 variable and $0 fixed, and (d) $0.060 variable and $600 fixed are incorrect.

**6. c.** Total fixed costs, not fixed costs per unit, are involved in CVP analysis. Choices (a) sales mix, (b) unit selling price, and (d) volume or level of activity are all involved in CVP analysis.

**7. c.** Net income will always be identical on both a GAAP income statement and a CVP income statement. Therefore, choices (a), (b), and (d) are incorrect statements.

**8. d.** Contribution margin is revenue remaining after deducting variable costs and it may be expressed on a per unit basis. Choices (a) and (b) are incorrect because (a) includes fixed costs and (b) contribution margin can be expressed on a per unit basis. Choice (c) is incorrect because it defines gross profit, not contribution margin.

**9. a.** Contribution margin is equal to fixed costs plus net income ($300,000 + $200,000 = $500,000). Since variable costs are the difference between total sales ($1,200,000) and contribution margin ($500,000), $700,000 must be the amount of variable costs in the CVP income statement. Therefore, choices (b) $900,000, (c) $500,000, and (d) $1,000,000 are incorrect.

**10. c.** Fixed costs ÷ Contribution margin ratio = Break-even point in sales dollars. Solving for fixed costs, (200,000 × $4) × .25 = $200,000, not (a) $100,000, (b) $160,000, or (d) $300,000.

**11. c.** If Brownstone's sales revenue is $100 greater than its break-even sales dollars, its net income will be $30 or ($100 × 30%), not (a) $100 or (b) $70. Choice (d) is incorrect because net income can be determined without knowing fixed costs.

**12. b.** The correct equation is Sales = Variable costs + Fixed costs + Target net income. The other choices are incorrect because (a) needs fixed costs added, (c) needs variable costs added, and (c) there is a correct answer given (b).

**13. a.** Margin of safety is computed as Actual sales − Break-even point in sales dollars. Therefore, choices (b) Contribution margin − Fixed costs, (c) Break-even sales − Variable costs, and (d) Actual sales − Contribution margin are incorrect.

**14. b.** The margin of safety ratio is computed by dividing the margin of safety in dollars of $180,000 ($600,000 − $420,000) by actual sales of $600,000. The result is 30% ($180,000 ÷ $600,000), not (a) 25%, (c) $33\frac{1}{3}$%, or (d) 45%.

## Practice Brief Exercises

**1. (LO 2)** Benji Company accumulates the following data concerning a mixed cost, using miles as the activity level.

*Determine variable- and fixed-cost components using the high-low method.*

| | Miles Driven | Total Cost | | Miles Driven | Total Cost |
|---|---|---|---|---|---|
| January | 7,500 | $20,000 | March | 8,500 | $22,000 |
| February | 8,200 | 21,100 | April | 8,300 | 21,750 |

Compute the variable-cost and fixed-cost components using the high-low method.

### Solution

**1.**

| High | | Low | | Difference |
|---|---|---|---|---|
| $22,000 | − | $20,000 | = | $2,000 |
| 8,500 | − | 7,500 | = | 1,000 |

Unit variable costs per mile = $2,000 ÷ 1,000 = $2.00.

| | High | Low |
|---|---|---|
| Total cost | $22,000 | $20,000 |
| Less: Variable costs | | |
| 8,500 × $2.00 | 17,000 | |
| 7,500 × $2.00 | | 15,000 |
| Total fixed costs | $ 5,000 | $ 5,000 |

Mixed cost is $5,000 plus $2.00 per mile.

*Determine missing amounts for contribution margin.*

**2. (LO 3)** Determine the missing amounts.

| Unit Selling Price | Unit Variable Costs | Unit Contribution Margin | Contribution Margin Ratio |
|---|---|---|---|
| $800 | $520 | (a) | (b) |
| 500 | (c) | $200 | (d) |
| (e) | (f) | 450 | 45% |

**Solution**

**2. a.** ($800 − $520) = $280

**b.** ($280 ÷ $800) = 35%

**c.** ($500 − $200) = $300

**d.** ($200 ÷ $500) = 40%

**e.** ($450 ÷ 45%) = $1,000

**f.** ($1,000 − $450) = $550

*Prepare CVP income statement.*

**3. (LO 3)** Kitty Cora makes and sells biscuit batter by the batch. The unit selling price is $10 per batch. The following data pertain to the month ended June 30, 2022.

| | |
|---|---|
| Fixed costs | $ 75,000 |
| Variable costs | 300,000 |
| Net income | 125,000 |

Prepare a CVP income statement for the month ended June 30, 2022. Include columns for per batch and percent of sales information.

**Solution**

3.

**Kitty Cora**
**CVP Income Statement**
**For the Month Ended June 30, 2022**

| | Total | Per Batch | Percent of Sales |
|---|---|---|---|
| Sales | $500,000 | $10 | 100% |
| Variable costs | 300,000 | 6 | 60 |
| Contribution margin | 200,000 | $ 4 | 40% |
| Fixed costs | 75,000 | | |
| Net income | $125,000 | | |

*Compute the break-even point.*

**4. (LO 4)** Jacob Company has a unit selling price of $600, unit variable costs of $216, and fixed costs of $2,438,400. Compute the break-even point in sales units using (a) the mathematical equation and (b) unit contribution margin.

**Solution**

**4. a.** $600Q − $216Q − $2,438,400 = $0

$384Q = $2,438,400

Q = 6,350 units

**b.** Unit contribution margin = $600 − $216 = $384

= $2,438,400 ÷ $384 = 6,350 units

*Compute the margin of safety and margin of safety ratio.*

**5. (LO 5)** For Posh Company, actual sales are $1,500,000, and break-even sales are $1,300,000. Compute (a) the margin of safety in dollars and (b) the margin of safety ratio.

**Solution**

**5. a.** Margin of safety = $1,500,000 − $1,300,000 = $200,000

**b.** Margin of safety ratio = $200,000 ÷ $1,500,000 = 13.3%

## Practice Exercises

1. **(LO 1, 2)** The controller of Teton Industries has collected the following monthly cost data for use in analyzing the behavior of maintenance costs.

*Determine fixed-cost and variable-cost components using the high-low method and prepare graph.*

| Month | Total Maintenance Costs | Total Machine Hours |
|---|---|---|
| January | $2,900 | 300 |
| February | 3,000 | 400 |
| March | 3,600 | 600 |
| April | 4,300 | 790 |
| May | 3,200 | 500 |
| June | 4,500 | 800 |

### Instructions

a. Determine the fixed-cost and unit variable-cost components using the high-low method.

b. Prepare a graph showing the behavior of maintenance costs, and identify the fixed-cost and variable-cost components. Use 200 unit increments and $1,000 cost increments.

### Solution

1. a. **Total Maintenance Costs:**

$$\frac{\$4,500 - \$2,900}{800 - 300} = \frac{\$1,600}{500} = \$3.20 \text{ unit variable costs per machine hour}$$

| | 800 Machine Hours | 300 Machine Hours |
|---|---|---|
| Total costs | $4,500 | $2,900 |
| Less: Variable costs | | |
| 800 × $3.20 | 2,560 | |
| 300 × $3.20 | | 960 |
| Total fixed costs | $1,940 | $1,940 |

Thus, total maintenance costs are $1,940 per month plus $3.20 per machine hour.

The cost equation is:

Total maintenance costs = $1,940 + ($3.20 × Machine hours)

b.

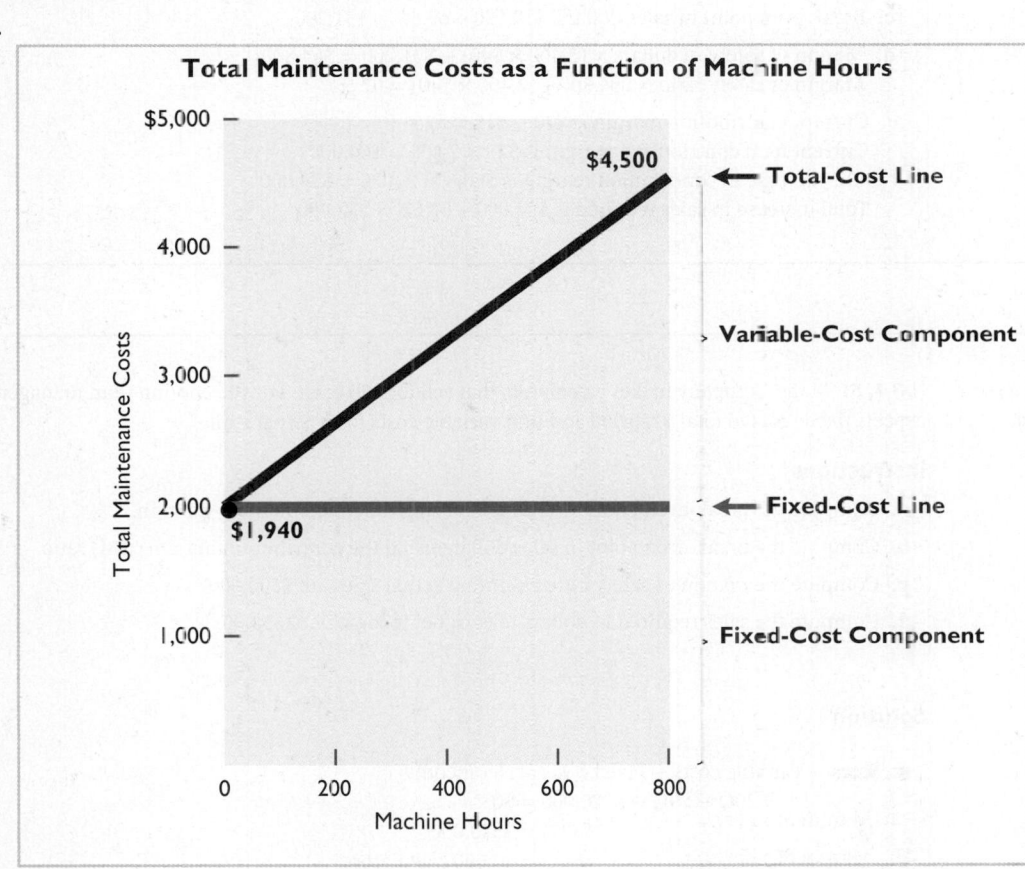

*Determine contribution margin ratio, break-even point in sales dollars, and margin of safety.*

**2. (LO 3, 4, 5)** Zion Seating Co., a manufacturer of chairs, had the following data for the year ended December 31, 2022:

| | |
|---|---|
| Sales | 2,400 chairs |
| Unit selling price | $40 per chair |
| Unit variable costs | $15 per chair |
| Fixed costs | $19,500 |

**Instructions**

a. Prepare a CVP income statement with columns for per unit and percent of sales information.

b. What is the contribution margin ratio?

c. What is the break-even point in sales dollars?

d. What is the margin of safety in dollars and the margin of safety ratio?

e. If the company wishes to increase its total dollar contribution margin by 40% in 2023, by how much will it need to increase its sales if unit contribution margin remains constant?

(CGA adapted)

**Solution**

2. a.

**Zion Seating Co.**
**CVP Income Statement**
**For the Month Ended December 31, 2022**

| | Total | Per Batch | Percent of Sales |
|---|---|---|---|
| Sales (2,400 × $40) | $96,000 | $40 | 100.0% |
| Variable costs (2,400 × $15) | 36,000 | 15 | 37.5 |
| Contribution margin | 60,000 | $25 | 62.5% |
| Fixed costs | 19,500 | | |
| Net income | $40,500 | | |

b. Contribution margin ratio = Unit contribution margin ÷ Unit selling price
($40 − $15) ÷ $40 = 62.5%

c. Break-even point in sales dollars: $19,500 ÷ 62.5% = $31,200

d. Margin of safety in dollars = (2,400 × $40) − $31,200 = $64,800
Margin of safety ratio = $64,800 ÷ (2,400 × $40) = 67.5%

e. Current contribution margin is $40 − $15 = $25
Current total contribution margin is $25 × 2,400 = $60,000
40% increase in contribution margin is $60,000 × 40% = $24,000
Total increase in sales required is $24,000 ÷ 62.5% = $38,400

# Practice Problem

*Compute break-even point, contribution margin ratio, margin of safety, and sales for target net income.*

**(LO 4, 5)** Mabo Company makes calculators that sell for $20 each. For the coming year, management expects fixed costs to total $220,000 and unit variable costs to be $9 per unit.

**Instructions**

a. Compute the break-even point in sales units using the mathematical equation.

b. Compute the break-even point in sales dollars using the contribution margin (CM) ratio.

c. Compute the margin of safety ratio assuming actual sales are $500,000.

d. Compute the sales required in dollars to earn net income of $165,000.

**Solution**

a. Sales − Variable costs − Fixed costs = Net income
$20Q − $9Q − $220,000 = $0
$11Q = $220,000
Q = 20,000 calculators

b. Unit contribution margin = Unit selling price − Unit variable costs

$$\$11 = \$20 - \$9$$

Contribution margin ratio = Unit contribution margin ÷ Unit selling price

$$55\% = \$11 \div \$20$$

Break-even point in sales dollars = Fixed costs ÷ Contribution margin ratio

$$= \$220,000 \div 55\%$$
$$= \$400,000$$

c. Margin of safety ratio = $\dfrac{\text{Actual sales} - \text{Break-even sales}}{\text{Actual sales}}$

$$= \frac{\$500,000 - \$400,000}{\$500,000}$$
$$= 20\%$$

d. Sales − Variable costs − Fixed costs = Net income

$$\$20Q - \$9Q - \$220,000 = \$165,000$$
$$\$11Q = \$385,000$$
$$Q = 35,000 \text{ calculators}$$

35,000 calculators × $20 = $700,000 required sales

OR

(Fixed costs + Target net income) ÷ Contribution margin ratio = Sales in dollars

$$(\$220,000 + \$165,000) \div 0.55 = \$700,000$$

---

**Brief Exercises, DO IT! Exercises, Exercises, Problems, Data Analytics Activities, and many additional resources are available for practice in WileyPLUS.**

---

*Note:* All asterisked Questions, Exercises, and Problems relate to material in the appendix to this chapter.

## Questions

**1. a.** What is cost behavior analysis?

**b.** Why is cost behavior analysis important to management?

**2. a.** Scott Winter asks your help in understanding the term "activity index." Explain the meaning and importance of this term for Scott.

**b.** State the two ways that variable costs may be defined.

**3.** Contrast the effects of changes in the activity level on total fixed costs and on unit fixed costs.

**4.** J.P. Alexander claims that the relevant range concept is important only for variable costs.

**a.** Explain the relevant range concept.

**b.** Is J.P.'s claim correct? Explain why or why not.

**5.** "The relevant range is indispensable in cost behavior analysis." Is this true? Why or why not?

**6.** Adam Antal is confused. He does not understand why rent on his apartment is a fixed cost and rent on a Hertz rental truck is a mixed cost. Explain the difference to Adam.

**7.** How should mixed costs be classified in CVP analysis? What approach is used to effect the appropriate classification?

**8.** At the high and low levels of activity during the month, direct labor hours are 90,000 and 40,000, respectively. The related costs are $165,000 and $100,000. What are the fixed costs and unit variable costs?

**9.** "Cost-volume-profit (CVP) analysis is based entirely on unit costs." Is this true? Explain why or why not.

**10.** Faye Dunn defines contribution margin as the amount of profit available to cover operating expenses. Is there any truth in this definition? Discuss.

**11.** Marshall Company's GWhiz calculator sells for $40. Unit variable costs are estimated to be $26. What are the unit contribution margin and the contribution margin ratio?

**12.** "Break-even analysis is of limited use to management because a company cannot survive by just breaking even." Is this true? Explain why or why not.

**13.** Total fixed costs are $26,000 for Daz Inc. It has a unit contribution margin of $15 and a contribution margin ratio of 25%. Compute the break-even point in sales dollars.

**14.** Feggy Turnbull asks your help in constructing a CVP graph. Explain to Peggy (a) how the break-even point is plotted, and (b) how the level of activity and sales dollars at the break-even point are determined.

**15.** Define the term "margin of safety." If Revere Company expects to sell 1,250 units of its product at $12 per unit, and break-even sales for the product are $13,200, what is the margin of safety ratio?

**16.** Huang Company's break-even point in sales dollars is $500,000. Assuming fixed costs are $180,000, what sales revenue is needed to achieve a target net income of $90,000?

**17.** The GAAP income statement for Pace Company for the year ended December 31, 2022, shows sales $900,000, cost of goods sold $600,000, and operating expenses $200,000. Assuming all costs and expenses are 70% variable and 30% fixed, prepare a CVP income statement through contribution margin.

**\*18.** James Brooks estimated the unit variable-cost and fixed-cost components of his company's utility costs using the high-low method. He is concerned that the cost equation that resulted from the high-low method might not provide an accurate representation of his company's utility costs. What is the inherent weakness of the high-low method? What alternative approach might Brooks use, and what are its advantages?

*19. Mary Webster owns and manages a company that provides trenching services. Her clients are companies that need to lay power lines, gas lines, and fiber optic cable. Because trenching machines require considerable maintenance due to the demanding nature of the work, Mary has created a scatter plot that displays her monthly maintenance costs. If Mary were to estimate a cost equation line using regression analysis for the data in her scatter plot, what primary characteristic would that line display?

*20. What are some of the limitations of regression analysis?

## Brief Exercises

*Classify costs as variable, fixed, or mixed.*

**BE18.1 (LO 1), C** Monthly production costs in Dilts Company for two levels of production are as follows.

| Cost | 2,000 Units | 4,000 Units |
|---|---|---|
| Indirect labor | $10,000 | $20,000 |
| Supervisory salaries | 5,000 | 5,000 |
| Maintenance | 4,000 | 6,000 |

Indicate which costs are variable, fixed, and mixed, and give the reason for each answer.

*Diagram the behavior of costs within the relevant range.*

**BE18.2 (LO 1), AN** For Lodes Company, the relevant range of production is 40–80% of capacity. At 40% of capacity, variable costs are $4,000 and fixed costs are $6,000. At 80% capacity, the same variable and fixed costs are $8,000 and $6,000, respectively. Diagram the behavior of each cost within the relevant range assuming the behavior is linear.

*Diagram the behavior of a mixed cost.*

**BE18.3 (LO 1), AN** For Wesland Company, a mixed cost is $15,000 plus $18 per direct labor hour. Diagram the behavior of the fixed cost and total cost using increments of 500 hours up to 2,500 hours on the horizontal axis and increments of $15,000 up to $60,000 on the vertical axis.

*Determine unit variable costs and fixed costs using the high-low method.*

**BE18.4 (LO 2), AP** Bruno Company accumulates the following data concerning a mixed cost, using miles as the activity level.

| | Miles Driven | Total Cost | | Miles Driven | Total Cost |
|---|---|---|---|---|---|
| January | 8,000 | $14,150 | March | 8,500 | $15,000 |
| February | 7,500 | 13,500 | April | 8,200 | 14,490 |

Compute the unit variable costs and fixed costs using the high-low method for this mixed cost.

*Determine unit variable costs and fixed costs using the high-low method.*

**BE18.5 (LO 2), AP** Markowis Corp. has collected the following data concerning its maintenance costs for the past 6 months.

| | Units Produced | Total Maintenance Costs |
|---|---|---|
| July | 18,000 | $36,000 |
| August | 32,000 | 48,000 |
| September | 36,000 | 55,000 |
| October | 22,000 | 38,000 |
| November | 40,000 | 74,500 |
| December | 38,000 | 62,000 |

Compute the unit variable costs and fixed costs using the high-low method for this mixed cost.

*Determine missing amounts for contribution margin.*

**BE18.6 (LO 3), AN** Determine the missing amounts.

| | Unit Selling Price | Unit Variable Costs | Unit Contribution Margin | Contribution Margin Ratio |
|---|---|---|---|---|
| 1. | $640 | $352 | (a) | (b) |
| 2. | $300 | (c) | $93 | (d) |
| 3. | (e) | (f) | $325 | 25% |

*Prepare CVP income statement.*

**BE18.7 (LO 3), AP** Russell Inc. had sales of $2,200,000 for the first quarter of 2022 (it sold 220,000 units). In making the sales, the company incurred the following costs and expenses.

| | Variable | Fixed |
|---|---|---|
| Cost of goods sold | $920,000 | $440,000 |
| Selling expenses | 70,000 | 45,000 |
| Administrative expenses | 88,000 | 98,000 |

Prepare a CVP income statement for the quarter ended March 31, 2022. Include columns for per unit and percent of sales information.

*Compute the break-even point in sales units.*

**BE18.8 (LO 4), AP** Rice Company has a unit selling price of $520, unit variable costs of $286, and fixed costs of $163,800. Compute the break-even point in sales units using (a) the mathematical equation and (b) unit contribution margin.

**BE18.9 (LO 4), AP** Presto Corp. had total variable costs of $180,000, total fixed costs of $110,000, and total revenues of $300,000. Compute the required sales dollars to break even.

*Compute the break-even point in sales dollars.*

**BE18.10 (LO 5), AP** For Flynn Company, variable costs are 70% of sales, and fixed costs are $195,000. Management's net income goal is $75,000. Compute the required sales dollars needed to achieve management's target net income of $75,000. (Use the contribution margin technique.)

*Compute sales for target net income.*

**BE18.11 (LO 5), AP** For Astoria Company, actual sales are $1,000,000, and break-even sales are $800,000. Compute (a) the margin of safety in dollars and (b) the margin of safety ratio.

*Compute the margin of safety in dollars and the margin of safety ratio.*

**BE18.12 (LO 5), AP** Deines Corporation has fixed costs of $480,000. It has a unit selling price of $6, unit variable costs of $4.40, and a target net income of $1,500,000. Compute the required sales in units to achieve its target net income.

*Compute the required sales in units for target net income.*

**\*BE18.13 (LO 6), AP** Stiever Corporation's maintenance costs are shown here.

*Compute unit variable costs and fixed costs using regression analysis.*

| | Units Produced | Total Cost |
|---|---|---|
| July | 18,000 | $32,000 |
| August | 32,000 | 48,000 |
| September | 36,000 | 55,000 |
| October | 22,000 | 38,000 |
| November | 40,000 | 66,100 |
| December | 38,000 | 62,000 |

Compute the unit variable costs and fixed costs using regression analysis for this mixed cost. Present your solution in the form of a cost equation. (We recommend that you use the Intercept and Slope functions in Excel.)

## DO IT! Exercises

**DO IT! 18.1 (LO 1), C** Amanda Company reports the following total costs at two levels of production.

*Classify types of costs.*

| | 5,000 Units | 10,000 Units |
|---|---|---|
| Indirect labor | $ 3,000 | $ 6,000 |
| Property taxes | 7,000 | 7,000 |
| Direct labor | 28,000 | 56,000 |
| Direct materials | 22,000 | 44,000 |
| Depreciation (straight-line) | 4,000 | 4,000 |
| Utilities | 5,000 | 8,000 |
| Maintenance | 9,000 | 11,000 |

Classify each cost as variable, fixed, or mixed.

**DO IT! 18.2 (LO 2), AP** Westerville Company accumulates the following data concerning a mixed cost, using units produced as the activity level.

*Compute costs using high-low method and estimate total cost.*

| | Units Produced | Total Cost |
|---|---|---|
| March | 10,000 | $18,000 |
| April | 9,000 | 16,650 |
| May | 10,500 | 18,580 |
| June | 8,800 | 16,200 |
| July | 9,500 | 17,100 |

a. Compute the unit variable costs and fixed costs using the high-low method.
b. Using the information from your answer to part (a), write the cost equation.
c. Estimate the total cost if the company produces 9,200 units.

**DO IT! 18.3 (LO 3), AP** Cedar Grove Industries produces and sells cell phone-operated home security systems. Information regarding the costs and sales during May 2022 is as follows.

*Prepare CVP income statement.*

| | |
|---|---|
| Unit selling price | $45.00 |
| Unit variable costs | $21.60 |
| Total monthly fixed costs | $120,000 |
| Units sold | 8,000 |

Prepare a CVP income statement for Cedar Grove Industries for the month of May. Provide total, per unit, and percent of sales values.

**DO IT! 18.4 (LO 4), AP** Snow Cap Company has a unit selling price of $250, unit variable costs of $170, and fixed costs of $160,000. Compute the break-even point in sales units using (a) the mathematical equation and (b) unit contribution margin.

*Compute break-even point in sales units.*

**DO IT! 18.5 (LO 4, 5), AP** Presto Company makes radios that sell for $30 each. For the coming year, management expects fixed costs to total $220,000 and unit variable costs to be $18.

*Compute break-even point, margin of safety ratio, and sales for target net income.*

a. Compute the break-even point in sales dollars using the contribution margin (CM) ratio.
b. Compute the margin of safety ratio assuming actual sales are $800,000.
c. Compute the sales dollars required to earn net income of $140,000.

# Exercises

*Define and classify variable, fixed, and mixed costs.*

**E18.1 (LO 1), C** Bonita Company manufactures a single product. Annual production costs incurred in the manufacturing process are shown here for two levels of production.

| | Costs Incurred | | | |
|---|---|---|---|---|
| **Production in Units** | **5,000** | | **10,000** | |
| | **Total** | **Unit** | **Total** | **Unit** |
| **Production Costs** | **Cost** | **Cost** | **Cost** | **Cost** |
| Direct materials | $8,000 | $1.60 | $16,000 | $1.60 |
| Direct labor | 9,500 | 1.90 | 19,000 | 1.90 |
| Utilities | 2,000 | 0.40 | 3,300 | 0.33 |
| Rent | 4,000 | 0.80 | 4,000 | 0.40 |
| Maintenance | 800 | 0.16 | 1,400 | 0.14 |
| Supervisory salaries | 1,000 | 0.20 | 1,000 | 0.10 |

**Instructions**

a. Define the terms variable costs, fixed costs, and mixed costs.

b. Classify each cost above as either variable, fixed, or mixed.

*Diagram cost behavior, determine relevant range, and classify costs.*

**E18.2 (LO 1), AP** Shingle Enterprises is considering manufacturing a new product. It projects the cost of direct materials and rent for a range of output as follows.

| Output in Units | Rent Cost | Direct Materials |
|---|---|---|
| 1,000 | $ 5,000 | $ 4,000 |
| 2,000 | 5,000 | 7,200 |
| 3,000 | 8,000 | 9,000 |
| 4,000 | 8,000 | 12,000 |
| 5,000 | 8,000 | 15,000 |
| 6,000 | 8,000 | 18,000 |
| 7,000 | 8,000 | 21,000 |
| 8,000 | 8,000 | 24,000 |
| 9,000 | 10,000 | 29,300 |
| 10,000 | 10,000 | 35,000 |
| 11,000 | 10,000 | 44,000 |

**Instructions**

a. Diagram the anticipated behavior of each cost for outputs ranging from 1,000 to 11,000 units.

b. Determine the relevant range of activity for this product based on the cost behavior of each input.

c. Calculate the unit variable costs within the relevant range.

d. Indicate the fixed cost within the relevant range.

*Determine fixed costs and unit variable costs using the high-low method and prepare graph.*

**E18.3 (LO 1, 2), AN** The controller of Norton Industries has collected the following monthly cost data for use in analyzing the behavior of maintenance costs.

| Month | Total Maintenance Costs | Total Machine Hours |
|---|---|---|
| January | $2,700 | 300 |
| February | 3,000 | 350 |
| March | 3,600 | 500 |
| April | 4,500 | 690 |
| May | 3,200 | 400 |
| June | 5,500 | 700 |

**Instructions**

a. Determine the fixed costs and unit variable costs using the high-low method for this mixed cost.

b. Prepare a graph showing the behavior of maintenance costs, and identify the fixed-cost and unit variable-cost components. Use 100-hour increments and $1,000-cost increments.

**E18.4 (LO 1), C** Family Furniture Corporation incurred the following costs.

*Classify variable, fixed, and mixed costs.*

1. Wood used in the production of furniture.

2. Fuel used in delivery trucks.

3. Straight-line depreciation on factory building.

4. Screws used in the production of furniture.

5. Sales staff salaries.

6. Sales commissions.

7. Property taxes.

8. Insurance on buildings.

9. Hourly wages of furniture craftsmen.

10. Salaries of factory supervisors.

11. Utilities expense.

12. Telephone bill.

**Instructions**

Identify the costs above as variable, fixed, or mixed.

**E18.5 (LO 1, 2), AP** The controller of Hall Industries has collected the following monthly cost data for use in analyzing the behavior of maintenance costs.

*Determine fixed costs and unit variable costs using the high-low method and prepare graph.*

| Month | Total Maintenance Costs | Total Machine Hours |
|---|---|---|
| January | $2,640 | 3,500 |
| February | 3,000 | 4,000 |
| March | 3,600 | 6,000 |
| April | 4,500 | 7,900 |
| May | 3,200 | 5,000 |
| June | 4,620 | 8,000 |

**Instructions**

a. Determine the fixed costs and unit variable costs using the high-low method for this mixed cost.

b. Prepare a graph showing the behavior of maintenance costs and identify the fixed-cost and variable-cost components. Use 2,000-hour increments and $1,000-cost increments.

**E18.6 (LO 1), AP** PCB Corporation manufactures a single product. Monthly production costs incurred in the manufacturing process are shown below for the production of 3,000 units.

*Determine fixed, variable, and mixed costs.*

| | |
|---|---|
| Direct materials | $ 7,500 |
| Direct labor | 18,000 |
| Utilities | 2,100 |
| Property taxes | 1,000 |
| Indirect labor | 4,500 |
| Supervisory salaries | 1,900 |
| Maintenance | 1,100 |
| Depreciation (straight-line) | 2,400 |

The utilities and maintenance costs are mixed costs. The fixed components of these costs are $300 and $200, respectively.

**Instructions**

a. Identify the above costs as variable, fixed, or mixed.

b. Calculate the expected costs when production is 5,000 units.

**E18.7 (LO 3), K** Writing  Marty Moser wants Moser Company to use CVP analysis to study the effects of changes in costs and volume on the company. Marty has heard that certain assumptions must be valid in order for CVP analysis to be useful.

*Explain assumptions underlying CVP analysis.*

**Instructions**

Prepare a memo to Marty Moser concerning the assumptions that underlie CVP analysis.

*Compute break-even point in sales units and in sales dollars.*

**E18.8 (LO 3, 4), AP** `Service` All That Blooms provides environmentally friendly lawn services for homeowners. Its operating costs are as follows.

| | |
|---|---|
| Depreciation (straight-line) | $1,400 per month |
| Advertising | $200 per month |
| Insurance | $2,000 per month |
| Weed and feed materials | $12 per lawn |
| Direct labor | $10 per lawn |
| Fuel | $2 per lawn |

All That Blooms charges $60 per treatment for the average single-family lawn. For the month ended July 31, 2022, the company had total sales of $7,200.

**Instructions**

a. Prepare a CVP income statement for the month ended July 31, 2022. Include columns for per unit and percent of sales information.

b. Determine the company's break-even point in (1) number of lawns serviced per month and (2) sales dollars.

*Compute break-even point in sales units and in sales dollars.*

→ Excel

**E18.9 (LO 3, 4), AP** `Service` The Palmer Acres Inn is trying to determine its break-even point during its off-peak season. The inn has 50 rooms that it rents at $60 a night. Operating costs are as follows.

| | |
|---|---|
| Salaries | $5,900 per month |
| Property tax | $1,100 per month |
| Depreciation (straight-line) | $1,000 per month |
| Maintenance | $100 per month |
| Maid service | $14 per room |
| Other costs | $28 per room |

**Instructions**

Determine the inn's break-even point in (a) number of rented rooms per month and (b) sales dollars.

*Compute contribution margin and break-even point.*

**E18.10 (LO 3, 4), AP** `Service` In the month of March, Style Salon serviced 560 clients at an average price of $120. During the month, fixed costs were $21,024 and variable costs were 60% of sales.

**Instructions**

a. Determine the total contribution margin in dollars, the unit contribution margin, and the contribution margin ratio.

b. Using the contribution margin technique, compute the break-even point in sales dollars and in sales units.

*Compute break-even point.*

**E18.11 (LO 3, 4), AP** `Service` Spencer Kars provides shuttle service between 4 hotels near a medical center and an international airport. Spencer Kars uses two 10-passenger vans to offer 12 round trips per day. A recent month's activity in the form of a cost-volume-profit income statement is as follows.

| | | |
|---|---:|---:|
| Sales (1,500 passengers) | | $36,000 |
| Variable costs | | |
| Fuel | $ 5,040 | |
| Tolls and parking | 3,100 | |
| Maintenance | 860 | 9,000 |
| Contribution margin | | 27,000 |
| Fixed costs | | |
| Salaries | 15,700 | |
| Depreciation (straight-line) | 1,300 | |
| Insurance | 1,000 | 18,000 |
| Net income | | $ 9,000 |

**Instructions**

a. Calculate the break-even point in (1) sales dollars and (2) number of passengers.

b. Without calculations, determine the contribution margin at the break-even point.

*Compute unit variable costs, contribution margin ratio, and increase in fixed costs.*

**E18.12 (LO 3, 4), AP** In 2021, Manhoff Company had a break-even point of $350,000 based on a unit selling price of $5 and fixed costs of $112,000. In 2022, the unit selling price and the unit variable costs did not change, but the break-even point increased to $420,000.

**Instructions**

a. Compute the unit variable costs and the contribution margin ratio for 2021.

b. Compute the increase in fixed costs for 2022.

**E18.13 (LO 3, 4), AP** Billings Company has the following information available for September 2022. *Prepare CVP income statements.*

| | |
|---|---|
| Unit selling price of video game consoles | $400 |
| Unit variable costs | $280 |
| Total fixed costs | $54,000 |
| Units sold | 600 |

**Instructions**

a. Compute the unit contribution margin.

b. Prepare a CVP income statement. Include columns for per unit and percent of sales information.

c. Compute Billings' break-even point in sales units.

d. Prepare a CVP income statement for the break-even point. Include columns for per unit and percent of sales information

**E18.14 (LO 3), AP** Risky Corporation had sales of $3,000,000 for the year ended December 31, 2022. The unit selling price was $15. In making the sales, the company incurred the following costs and expenses. *Prepare GAAP income statement and CVP income statement.*

| | Variable | Fixed |
|---|---|---|
| Cost of goods sold | $600 000 | $800,000 |
| Selling expenses | 120 000 | 60,000 |
| Administrative expenses | 240 000 | 80,000 |

**Instructions**

a. Prepare a GAAP income statement.

b. Prepare a CVP income statement. Include columns for per unit and percent of sales information

**E18.15 (LO 4, 5), AP** Naylor Company had $210,000 of net income in 2021 when the unit selling price was $140, the unit variable costs were $90, and the fixed costs were $570,000. Management expects per unit data and total fixed costs to remain the same in 2022. The president of Naylor Company is under pressure from stockholders to increase net income by $62,400 in 2022. *Compute various components to derive target net income under different assumptions.*

**Instructions**

a. Compute the number of units sold in 2021.

b. Compute the number of units that would have to be sold in 2022 to reach the stockholders' desired net income.

c. Assume that Naylor Company sells the same number of units in 2022 as it did in 2021. What would the selling price have to be in order to reach the stockholders' desired net income, assuming the unit variable costs and fixed costs remain at 2021 levels?

**E18.16 (LO 5), AP** Yams Company reports the following operating results for the month of August: sales $400,000 (5,000 units), variable costs $240,000, and fixed costs $90,000. Management is considering the following independent courses of action to increase net income. *Compute net income under different alternatives.*

1. Increase the unit selling price by 10% with no change in total variable costs, fixed costs, or units sold.

2. Reduce variable costs to 55% of sales while holding fixed costs, quantity, and unit selling price constant.

**Instructions**

Compute the net income to be earned under each alternative  Which course of action will produce the higher net income?

**E18.17 (LO 4, 5), AP** Glacial Company estimates that variable costs will be 62.5% of sales, and fixed costs will total $600,000. The unit selling price of the product is $4. *Prepare a CVP graph and compute break-even point and margin of safety.*

**Instructions**

a. Compute the break-even point in (1) sales units and (2) sales dollars.

b. Prepare a CVP graph, assuming maximum sales of $3,200,000. (*Note:* Use $400,000 increments for sales and costs and 100,000 increments for units.)

c. Assuming actual sales are $2 million, compute the margin of safety (1) in dollars and (2) as a ratio.

*Determine contribution margin ratio, break-even point in sales dollars, and margin of safety.*

**E18.18 (LO 3, 4, 5), AP** Felde Bucket Co., a manufacturer of rain barrels, had the following data for 2021:

| | |
|---|---|
| Sales quantity | 2,500 barrels |
| Unit selling price | $40 per barrel |
| Unit variable costs | $24 per barrel |
| Fixed costs | $19,500 |

**Instructions**

a. What is the contribution margin ratio?

b. What is the break-even point in sales dollars?

c. What is the margin of safety in sales dollars and as a ratio?

d. If the company wishes to increase its total dollar contribution margin by 30% in 2022, by how much will it need to increase its sales dollars if all other factors (other than sales quantity) remain constant?

(CGA adapted)

*Determine fixed costs and unit variable costs using regression analysis, prepare scatter plot, and estimate cost at particular level of activity.*

**\* E18.19 (LO 6), AP** The controller of Standard Industries has collected the following monthly cost data for analyzing the behavior of electricity costs.

| | Total Electricity Costs | Total Machine Hours |
|---|---|---|
| January | $2,500 | 300 |
| February | 3,000 | 350 |
| March | 3,600 | 500 |
| April | 4,500 | 690 |
| May | 3,200 | 400 |
| June | 4,900 | 700 |
| July | 4,100 | 650 |
| August | 3,800 | 520 |
| September | 5,100 | 680 |
| October | 4,200 | 630 |
| November | 3,300 | 350 |
| December | 6,100 | 720 |

**Instructions**

a. Determine the fixed costs and unit variable costs using regression analysis. (We recommend the use of Excel.)

b. Prepare a scatter plot using Excel. Present the cost equation line estimated in part (a).

c. What electricity cost does the cost equation estimate for a level of activity of 500 machine hours? By what amount does this differ from March's observed cost for 500 machine hours?

## Problems

*Determine fixed costs and unit variable costs using high-low method, and estimate cost at particular level of activity.*

**P18.1 (LO 1, 2), AP** The controller of Rather Production has collected the following monthly cost data for analyzing the behavior of electricity costs.

| | Total Electricity Costs | Total Machine Hours |
|---|---|---|
| January | $2,500 | 300 |
| February | 3,000 | 350 |
| March | 3,600 | 500 |
| April | 4,500 | 690 |
| May | 3,200 | 400 |
| June | 4,900 | 700 |
| July | 4,100 | 650 |
| August | 3,800 | 520 |
| September | 5,100 | 680 |
| October | 4,200 | 630 |
| November | 3,300 | 350 |
| December | 5,860 | 720 |

**Instructions**

  **a.** Determine the fixed costs and unit variable costs using the high-low method.

  **b.** What electricity cost does the cost equation estimate for a level of activity of 500 machine hours? By what amount does this differ from March's observed cost for 500 machine hours?

  **c.** What electricity cost does the cost equation estimate for a level of activity of 700 machine hours? By what amount does this differ from June's observed cost for 700 machine hours?

*a. VC $8*

**P18.2 (LO 1, 2, 3, 4), AN** Service Vin Diesel owns the Fredonia Barber Shop. He employs four barbers and pays each a base salary of $1,250 per month. One of the barbers serves as the manager and receives an extra $500 per month. In addition to the base salary, each barber also receives a commission of $4.50 per haircut.

    Other costs are as follows.

*Determine unit variable costs and fixed costs, compute break-even point, prepare a CVP graph, and determine net income.*

|  |  |
|---|---|
| Advertising | $200 per month |
| Rent | $1,100 per month |
| Barber supplies | $0.30 per haircut |
| Utilities | $175 per month plus $0.20 per haircut |
| Magazines | $25 per month |

Vin currently charges $10 per haircut.

**Instructions**

  **a.** Determine the unit variable costs per haircut and the total monthly fixed costs.

  **b.** Compute the break-even point in sales units and in sales dollars.

  **c.** Prepare a CVP graph, assuming a maximum of 1,800 haircuts in a month. Use increments of 300 haircuts on the horizontal axis and $3,000 on the vertical axis.

  **d.** Determine net income, assuming 1,600 haircuts are given in a month.

*a. VC $5*

**P18.3 (LO 3, 4, 5), AP** Jorge Company bottles and distributes B-Lite, a diet soft drink. The beverage is sold for 50 cents per 16-ounce bottle to retailers. For the year 2022, management estimates the following revenues and costs.

*Prepare a CVP income statement and compute break-even point, contribution margin ratio, margin of safety ratio, and sales for target net income.*

Excel

| | | | |
|---|---|---|---|
| Sales | $1,800,000 | Selling expenses—variable | $70,000 |
| Direct materials | 430,000 | Selling expenses—fixed | 65,000 |
| Direct labor | 360,000 | Administrative expenses— | |
| Manufacturing overhead— | | variable | 20,000 |
| variable | 380,000 | Administrative expenses— | |
| Manufacturing overhead— | | fixed | 60,000 |
| fixed | 280,000 | | |

**Instructions**

  **a.** Prepare a CVP income statement for 2022 based on management's estimates. Include columns for per unit and percent of sales information.

  **b.** Compute the break-even point in (1) sales units and (2) sales dollars.

  **c.** Compute the contribution margin ratio and the margin of safety ratio. (Round to nearest full percent.)

  **d.** Determine the sales dollars required to earn net income of $180,000.

*b. (1) 2,700,000 units*

*c. CM ratio 30%*

**P18.4 (LO 4), E** Tanek Corp.'s sales slumped badly in 2022. For the first time in its history, it operated at a loss. The company's income statement showed the following results from selling 500,000 units of product: sales $2,500,000, total costs and expenses $2,590,000, and net loss $90,000. Costs and expenses consisted of the following amounts.

*Compute break-even point under alternative courses of action.*

| | Total | Variable | Fixed |
|---|---|---|---|
| Cost of goods sold | $2,140,000 | $1,590,000 | $550,000 |
| Selling expenses | 250,000 | 92,000 | 158,000 |
| Administrative expenses | 200,000 | 68,000 | 132,000 |
| | $2,590,000 | $1,750,000 | $840,000 |

Management is considering the following independent alternatives for 2023.

  **1.** Increase the unit selling price 20% with no change in total costs, total expenses, and sales volume.

  **2.** Change the compensation of sales personnel from fixed annual salaries totaling $140,000 to total salaries of $60,000 plus a 5% commission on sales. All other total costs, total expenses, and total sales remain unchanged.

**Instructions**

a. Compute the break-even point in sales dollars for 2022.

b. Alternative 1 $2,000,000

b. Compute the break-even point in sales dollars under each of the alternative courses of action. (Round all ratios to nearest full percent.) Which course of action do you recommend?

*Compute break-even point and margin of safety ratio, and prepare a CVP income statement before and after changes in business environment.*

**P18.5 (LO 3, 4, 5), E** Mary Willis is the advertising manager for Bargain Shoe Store. She is currently working on a major promotional campaign. Her ideas include the installation of a new lighting system and increased display space that will add $29,000 in fixed costs to the $270,000 currently spent. In addition, Mary is proposing that a 5% price decrease ($40 to $38) will produce a 25% increase in sales volume (20,000 to 25,000). Variable costs will remain at $25 per pair of shoes. Management is impressed with Mary's ideas but concerned about the effects that these changes will have on the break-even point and the margin of safety.

**Instructions**

a. Prepare a CVP income statement for current operations and after Mary's changes are introduced. (Show column for total amounts only.) Would you make the changes suggested?

b. Compute the current break-even point in sales units, and compare it to the break-even point in sales units if Mary's ideas are implemented.

c. Current margin of safety ratio 10%

c. Compute the margin of safety ratio for current operations and after Mary's changes are introduced. (Round to nearest full percent.)

*Compute contribution margin, fixed costs, break-even point, sales for target net income, and margin of safety ratio.*

**P18.6 (LO 3, 4, 5), AN** Viejol Corporation has collected the following information after its first year of operations. Sales were $1,600,000 on 100,000 units, selling expenses $250,000 (40% variable and 60% fixed), direct materials $490,000, direct labor $290,000, administrative expenses $270,000 (20% variable and 80% fixed), and manufacturing overhead $380,000 (70% variable and 30% fixed). Top management has asked you to do a CVP analysis so that it can make plans for the coming year. It has projected that unit sales will increase by 10% next year.

**Instructions**

a. Compute (1) the contribution margin for the current year and the projected year, and (2) the fixed costs for the current year and the projected year. Unit selling price, unit variable costs, and fixed costs are estimated to remain unchanged.

b. 120,000 units

b. Compute the break-even point in sales units and sales dollars for the current year.

c. The company has a target net income of $145,000. What is the required sales in dollars for the company to meet its target?

d. If the company meets its target net income number, by what percentage could its sales fall before it is operating at a loss? That is, what is its margin of safety ratio?

*Determine variable and fixed costs.*

**P18.7 (LO 1, 3, 5), E** Kaiser Industries carries no inventories. Its product is manufactured only when a customer's order is received. It is then shipped immediately after it is made. For its fiscal year ended October 31, 2022, Kaiser's break-even point was $1.5 million. On sales of $1.5 million, its GAAP income statement showed a gross profit of $242,500, direct materials cost of $500,000, and direct labor costs of $625,000. The contribution margin was $180,000, and variable manufacturing overhead was $62,500.

**Instructions**

a. 2. $70,000

a. Calculate the following:

  1. Variable selling and administrative expenses.

  2. Fixed manufacturing overhead.

  3. Fixed selling and administrative expenses.

b. Ignoring your answer to part (a), assume that fixed manufacturing overhead was $100,000 and the fixed selling and administrative expenses were $80,000. The marketing vice president feels that if the company increased its advertising, sales could be increased by 20%. What is the maximum increased advertising cost the company can incur and still report the same income as before the advertising expenditure, assuming that the contribution margin ratio remains unchanged?

(CGA adapted)

*Determine fixed costs and unit variable costs using regression analysis, and estimate cost at particular level of activity.*

\*P18.8 (LO 1, 2, 6), AP The controller of Brokaw Production has collected the following monthly cost data for analyzing the behavior of utility costs.

|  | Total Utility Costs | Total Machine Hours |
|---|---|---|
| January | $3,200 | 400 |
| February | 4,700 | 550 |
| March | 4,000 | 500 |
| April | 2,100 | 790 |
| May | 3,600 | 450 |
| June | 5,300 | 700 |
| July | 5,500 | 690 |
| August | 5,100 | 620 |
| September | 7,400 | 880 |
| October | 4,600 | 610 |
| November | 3,000 | 350 |
| December | 6,700 | 820 |

### Instructions

a. Determine the fixed costs and unit variable costs using regression analysis. (We recommend the use of Excel.)

a. VC $5.7343

b. Prepare a scatter plot using Excel. Present the cost equation line estimated in part (a).

c. What utility cost does the cost equation estimate for a level of activity of 500 machine hours? By what amount does this differ from March's observed cost for 500 machine hours?

d. What utility cost does the cost equation estimate for a level of activity of 700 machine hours? By what estimate does this differ from June's observed cost for 700 machine hours?

## Continuing Cases

### Current Designs

**CD18**  Bill Johnson, sales manager, and Diane Buswell, controller, at Current Designs are beginning to analyze the cost considerations for one of the composite models of the kayak division. They have provided the following production and operational costs necessary to produce one composite kayak.

 Excel

| | Current Designs—Cost Information | |
|---|---|---|
| Home   Insert   Page Layout   Formulas   Data   Review   View | | |
| B7        fx | | |
| | A | B | C |
| 1 | Kevlar® | $250 per kayak | |
| 2 | Resin and supplies | $100 per kayak | |
| 3 | Finishing kit (seat, rudder, ropes, etc.) | $170 per kayak | |
| 4 | Direct labor | $420 per kayak | |
| 5 | Selling and administrative expenses—variable | $400 per kayak | |
| 6 | Selling and administrative expenses—fixed | $119,700 per year | |
| 7 | Manufacturing overhead—fixed | $240,000 per year | |
| 8 | | | |

Bill and Diane have asked you to provide a cost-volume-profit analysis, to help them finalize the budget projections for the upcoming year. Bill has informed you that the selling price of the composite kayak will be $2,000.

### Instructions

a. Calculate unit variable costs.

b. Determine the unit contribution margin.

c. Using the unit contribution margin, determine the break-even point in sales units for this product line.

d. Assume that Current Designs would like to earn net income of $270,600 on this product line. Using the unit contribution margin, calculate the number of units that need to be sold to achieve this goal.

e. Based on the most recent sales forecast, Current Designs expects to sell 1,000 units of this model. Using your results from part (c), calculate the margin of safety in dollars and the margin of safety ratio.

### Waterways Corporation

(*Note:* This is a continuation of the Waterways case from Chapters 14–17.)

**WC18** The Vice President for Sales and Marketing at Waterways Corporation is planning for production needs to meet sales demand in the coming year. He is also trying to determine how the company's profits might be increased in the coming year. This case asks you to use cost-volume-profit concepts to help Waterways understand contribution margins of some of its products and decide whether to mass-produce any of them.

*Go to WileyPLUS for complete case details and instructions.*

## Data Analytics in Action

### Using Data Visualization to Analyze Costs

 Excel

**DA18.1** Data visualization can be used to compare options.

**Example:** Consider the *Management Insight* box "Are Robotic Workers More Humane?" presented in the chapter. Data analytics can help **Kroger** determine if using robots in its warehouse would be a cost-effective decision. Consider the following chart, which compares income effects in both a manual and a robotic system. When using human labor in a manual system, we see that labor costs are substantial. When a robotic system is utilized, we see that depreciation is a larger cost item, and labor is much less.

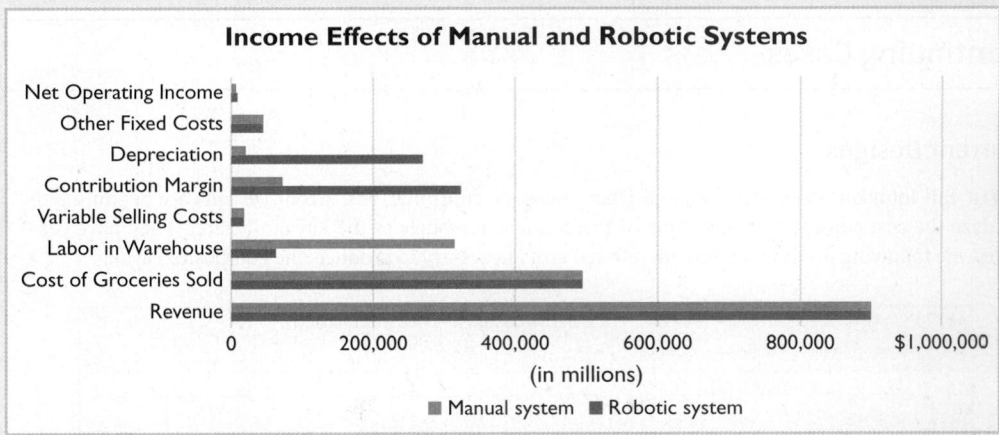

If we assume that revenues will increase 40% due to an increased sales volume, what effect will we see on net operating income? As shown in the following chart, the increase in net operating income is larger in an automated system. This is because the labor increase was a smaller dollar amount than the respective increase in a manual system, coupled with no increase in total fixed costs. This effect is often referred to as **operating leverage**, which is discussed further in Chapter 19.

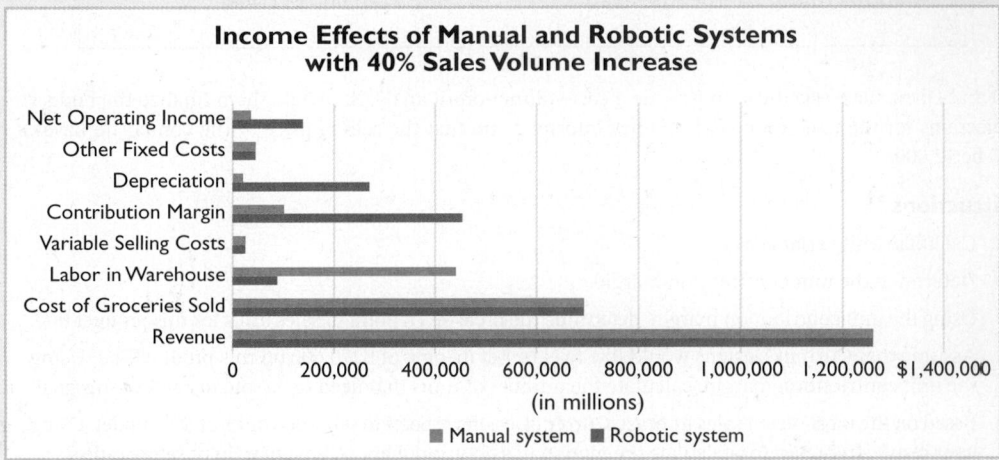

For this case, you will use an approach similar to that used in the example just presented. You will help a fast food restaurant evaluate the benefits of installing a kiosk in the lobby to automate customer orders, thus reducing the need for cashiers. This case requires you to compare income statement data for traditional and digital ordering for the restaurant, and then create and analyze a bar chart.

*Go to WileyPLUS for complete case details and instructions.*

## Data Analytics at HydroHappy

**DA18.2** HydroHappy management wants to examine its largest non–value-added cost, selling costs, to see if it can identify a better cost driver in an effort to lower its total selling costs. The company currently uses the number of sales calls as its cost driver. For this case, you will generate scatter charts, as well as use Excel's Slope and Intercept functions, to help HydroHappy determine the best cost driver for selling costs.

*Go to WileyPLUS for complete case details and instructions.*

# Expand Your Critical Thinking

## Decision-Making Across the Organization

**CT18.1** Creative Ideas Company has decided to introduce a new product. The new product can be manufactured by either a capital-intensive method or a labor-intensive method. The manufacturing method will not affect the quality of the product. The estimated manufacturing costs by the two methods are as follows.

|  | Capital-Intensive | Labor-Intensive |
|---|---|---|
| Direct materials | $5 per unit | $5.50 per unit |
| Direct labor | $6 per unit | $8.00 per unit |
| Variable overhead | $3 per unit | $4.50 per unit |
| Fixed manufacturing costs | $2,524,000 | $1,550,000 |

Creative Ideas' market research department has recommended an introductory unit sales price of $32. The selling expenses are estimated to be $502,000 annually plus S2 for each unit sold, regardless of manufacturing method.

### Instructions

With the class divided into groups, answer the following.

a. Calculate the estimated break-even point in annual unit sales of the new product if Creative Ideas Company uses the:

1. Capital-intensive manufacturing method.

2. Labor-intensive manufacturing method.

b. Determine the annual unit sales volume at which Creative Ideas Company would be indifferent between the two manufacturing methods.

c. Explain the circumstance under which Creative Ideas should employ each of the two manufacturing methods.

(CMA adapted)

## Managerial Analysis

**CT18.2** The condensed income statement for the Peri and Paul partnership for 2022 is as follows.

**Peri and Paul Company**
**Income Statement**
**For the Year Ended December 31, 2022**

| | | |
|---|---|---|
| Sales (240,000 units) | | $1,200,000 |
| Cost of goods sold | | 800,000 |
| Gross profit | | 400,000 |
| Operating expenses | | |
| Selling | $300,000 | |
| Administrative | 152,500 | 452,500 |
| Net loss | | $ (52,500) |

A cost behavior analysis indicates that 75% of the cost of goods sold are variable and 40% of the selling expenses are variable. Administrative expenses are $92,500 fixed.

**Instructions**

(Round to nearest unit, cent, and percentage, where necessary. Use the CVP income statement format in computing net income.)

a. Compute the break-even point in sales dollars and in sales units for 2022.

b. Peri has proposed a plan to get the partnership "out of the red" and improve its profitability. She feels that the quality of the product could be substantially improved by spending $0.32 more per unit on better raw materials. The unit selling price could be increased to $5.25. Peri estimates that sales volume would increase by 25%. Compute net income under Peri's proposal and the break-even point in sales dollars.

c. Paul was a marketing major in college. He believes that sales volume can be increased only by intensive advertising and promotional campaigns. He therefore proposed the following plan as an alternative to Peri's: (1) increase unit variable selling expenses to $0.575, (2) lower the unit selling price by $0.25, and (3) increase fixed selling expenses by $51,000. Paul quoted an old marketing research report that said that sales volume would increase by 60% if these changes were made. Compute net income under Paul's proposal and the break-even point in sales dollars.

d. Which plan should be accepted? Explain your answer.

## Real-World Focus

**CT18.3 The Coca-Cola Company** hardly needs an introduction. A line taken from the cover of a recent annual report says it all: If you measured time in servings of Coca-Cola, "a billion Coca-Cola's ago was yesterday morning." On average, every U.S. citizen drinks 363 8-ounce servings of Coca-Cola products each year. Coca-Cola's primary line of business is the making and selling of syrup to bottlers. These bottlers then sell the finished bottles and cans of Coca-Cola to retailers.

In the annual report of Coca-Cola, the following information was provided.

---

### The Coca-Cola Company
#### Management Discussion

Our gross margin declined to 61 percent this year from 62 percent in the prior year, primarily due to costs for materials such as sweeteners and packaging.

The increases [in selling expenses] in the last two years were primarily due to higher marketing expenditures in support of our Company's volume growth.

We measure our sales volume in two ways: (1) gallon shipments of concentrates and syrups and (2) unit cases of finished product (bottles and cans of Coke sold by bottlers).

---

**Instructions**

Answer the following questions.

a. Are sweeteners and packaging a variable cost or a fixed cost? What is the impact on the contribution margin of an increase in the per unit cost of sweeteners or packaging? What are the implications for profitability?

b. In your opinion, are Coca-Cola's marketing expenditures a fixed cost, variable cost, or mixed cost? Give justification for your answer.

c. Which of the two measures cited for measuring volume represents the activity index as defined in this chapter? Why might Coca-Cola use two different measures?

## Communication Activity

**CT18.4** Your roommate asks for your help on the following questions about CVP analysis equations.

a. How can the mathematical equation for the break-even point provide a result for units sold and sales dollars?

b. How do the equations differ for unit contribution margin and contribution margin ratio?

c. How can contribution margin techniques be used to determine the break-even point in sales units and in sales dollars?

**Instructions**

Write a memo to your roommate stating the relevant equations and answering each question.

## Ethics Case

**CT18.5** Scott Bestor is an accountant for Westfield Company. Early this year, Scott made a highly favorable projection of sales and net income over the next 3 years for Westfield's hot-selling computer PLEX. Based on the projections Scott presented to senior management, the company decided to expand production in this area. This decision led to dislocations of some factory personnel, who were reassigned to one of the company's newer factories in another state. However, no one was fired, and in fact the company expanded its workforce slightly.

Unfortunately, Scott rechecked his projection computations a few months later and found that he had made an error that would have reduced his projections substantially. Luckily, sales of PLEX have exceeded projections so far, and management is satisfied with its decision. Scott, however, is not sure what to do. Should he confess his honest mistake and jeopardize his possible promotion? He suspects that no one will catch the error because PLEX sales have exceeded his projections, and it appears that net income will materialize close to his projections.

**Instructions**

**a.** Who are the stakeholders in this situation?

**b.** Identify the ethical issues involved in this situation.

**c.** What are the possible alternative actions for Scott? What would you do in Scott's position?

## All About You

**CT18.6** Cost-volume-profit analysis can also be used in making personal financial decisions. For example, the purchase of a new car is one of your biggest personal expenditures. It is important that you carefully analyze your options.

Suppose that you are considering the purchase of a hybrid vehicle. Let's assume the following facts. The hybrid will initially cost an additional $4,500 above the cost of a traditional vehicle. On average, the hybrid will get 50 miles per gallon of gas, and the traditional car will get 30 miles per gallon. Also, assume that the cost of gas is $2.50 per gallon.

**Instructions**

Using the facts above, answer the following questions.

**a.** For gasoline, what is the unit variable cost of going one mile in the hybrid car? What is the unit variable cost of going one mile in the traditional car?

**b.** Using the information in part (a), if "miles" is your unit of measure, what is the differential between the hybrid vehicle and the traditional vehicle? That is, express the variable cost savings on a per-mile basis.

**c.** How many miles would you have to drive in order to break even on your investment in the hybrid car?

**d.** What other factors might you want to consider?

## Answers to Insight and Accounting Across the Organization Questions

**Gardens in the Sky Q:** What are some of the variable and fixed costs that are impacted by hydroponic farming? **A:** Compared to traditional methods, hydroponic farming would reduce the use of pesticides, herbicides, fuel, and water. Soil erosion would be eliminated, and land requirements would drop. But, fixed costs related to constructing greenhouses, suitable vertical planters, as well as investments in artificial lighting could be high.

**Are Robotic Workers More Humane? Q:** How would a company's variable and fixed costs change if it adopts a robotic system? **A:** If a company adopts a fully autonomous robotic system, its labor costs (a variable cost) could drop by 80%. Its fixed costs related to the size of its warehouse facility would drop, because autonomous systems require less space. However, other fixed costs would increase significantly as a result of its investment in the robotic equipment.

**Charter Deals Offer a Good Deal Q:** How did FlightServe determine that it would break even with 3.3 seats full per flight? **A:** FlightServe determined its break-even point with the following equation: Fixed costs ÷ Contribution margin per seat occupied = Break-even point in seats.

**How a Music Promoter Makes Money Q:** What amount of sales dollars are required for the promoter to break even? **A:** Fixed costs = $1,200,000 + $400,000 = $1,600,000 and contribution margin ratio = 80%. Therefore, the break-even point in sales dollars = $1,600,000 ÷ .80 = $2,000,000.

© bikeriderlondon/Shutterstock.com

# Cost-Volume-Profit Analysis: Additional Issues

## Chapter Preview

As the following Feature Story about **Whole Foods Market** suggests, the relationship between a company's fixed and variable costs can have a huge impact on its profitability. In particular, the trend toward cost structures dominated by fixed costs has significantly increased the volatility of many companies' net income. The purpose of this chapter is to demonstrate additional uses of cost-volume-profit analysis in making sound business decisions.

## Feature Story

### Not Even a Flood Could Stop It

America has had a reputation as a country populated with people who won't buy a restaurant meal unless it can be ordered from the driver's seat of a car. Customers want to receive said "meal" 30 seconds later from a drive-up window and then consume the bagged product while driving one-handed down an eight-lane freeway. This is actually a fairly accurate depiction of the restaurant preferences (and eating habits) of one of the authors of this text. However, given the success of **Whole Foods Market** (now owned by **Amazon.com**), this certainly cannot be true of all Americans.

Whole Foods Market began humbly in 1978 as a natural-foods store called SaferWay. (Get it? A play on **SafeWay** grocery stores.) It was founded in Austin, Texas, by 25-year-old John Mackey (a self-described college dropout) and 21-year-old Renee Lawson Hardy. They financed the first store by borrowing $45,000 from family and friends. The early days were "interesting." First, John and Renee got kicked out of their apartment for storing grocery products there. No problem—they just moved into the store. They bathed in the store's dishwasher with an attached hose. They did whatever it took to keep their costs down and the store going.

Two years later, John and Renee merged SaferWay with another store to form the first Whole Foods Market. The store's first year was very successful. Well, that is, until everything in the store was completely destroyed by Austin's biggest flood in more than 70 years. They lost $400,000 in goods—and they had no insurance. But within 28 days, with tons of volunteer work and supportive creditors and vendors, the store reopened.

Today, Whole Foods operates approximately 500 stores. The size of the average store has actually declined in recent years. While huge stores (up to 80,000 square feet) were successful in a few cities, in most locations the fixed costs of such a large facility made it hard to achieve profit targets. Then, when sales became sluggish during the financial crisis of 2008, the company determined that it could reduce its fixed costs, such as rent and utility costs, by reducing its average store size by about 20%. However, with fewer square feet, managers must keep a closer eye on the sales mix. They need to be aware of the relative contribution margins of each product line to maximize the profit per square foot while still providing the products its customers want.

Why is a company as successful as Whole Foods so concerned about controlling costs? The answer is that the grocery business runs on very thin margins. So while we doubt that anybody is bathing in the store's dishwashers anymore, Whole Foods is as vigilant about its costs today as it was during its first year of operations.

 Watch the *Whole Foods Market* video in WileyPLUS to learn more about the use of cost-volume-profit analysis in a changing business environment.

# Chapter Outline

| LEARNING OBJECTIVES | REVIEW | PRACTICE |
|---|---|---|
| **LO 1** Apply basic CVP concepts. | • Basic concepts<br>• Business environment | **DO IT! 1** CVP Analysis |
| **LO 2** Explain the term sales mix and its effects on break-even sales. | • Break-even in units<br>• Break-even in dollars | **DO IT! 2** Sales Mix Break-Even |
| **LO 3** Determine sales mix when a company has limited resources. | • Contribution margin per unit<br>• Theory of constraints | **DO IT! 3** Sales Mix with Limited Resources |
| **LO 4** Indicate how operating leverage affects profitability. | • Contribution margin ratio<br>• Break-even point<br>• Margin of safety ratio<br>• Operating leverage | **DO IT! 4** Operating Leverage |

**Go to the Review and Practice section at the end of the chapter for a targeted summary and practice applications with solutions.**

**Visit WileyPLUS for additional tutorials and practice opportunities.**

# Basic CVP Concepts

---

**LEARNING OBJECTIVE 1**

Apply basic CVP concepts.

---

As indicated in Chapter 18, cost-volume-profit (CVP) analysis is the study of the effects of changes in costs and volume on a company's profit.

- CVP analysis is important to profit planning.
- It is also a critical factor in determining product mix, maximizing use of production facilities, and setting selling prices.

## Basic Concepts

Before we introduce additional issues of CVP analysis, let's review some of the basic concepts that you learned in Chapter 18—specifically, break-even analysis, target net income, and margin of safety. As in Chapter 18, we use Vargo Electronics Company to illustrate these concepts.

### Break-Even Analysis

Vargo Electronics' CVP income statement (**Illustration 19.1**) shows that total contribution margin (sales minus variable expenses) is $320,000, and the company's unit contribution margin is $200. Recall that contribution margin can also be expressed in the form of the **contribution margin ratio** (contribution margin divided by sales), which in the case of Vargo is 40% ($200 ÷ $500).

| Vargo Electronics Company | | | |
|---|---|---|---|
| CVP Income Statement | | | |
| For the Month Ended June 30, 2022 | | | |
| | Total | Per Unit | Percent of Sales |
| Sales | $800,000 | $500 | 100% |
| Variable expenses | | | |
| Cost of goods sold | $400,000 | | |
| Selling expenses | 60,000 | | |
| Administrative expenses | 20,000 | | |
| Total variable expenses | 480,000 | 300 | 60 |
| **Contribution margin** | 320,000 | $200 | 40% |
| Fixed expenses | | | |
| Cost of goods sold | 120,000 | | |
| Selling expenses | 40,000 | | |
| Administrative expenses | 40,000 | | |
| Total fixed expenses | 200,000 | | |
| **Net income** | $120,000 | | |

**ILLUSTRATION 19.1**

**Detailed CVP income statement**

**Illustration 19.2** demonstrates how to compute Vargo's break-even point in sales units (using unit contribution margin).

| Fixed Costs | ÷ | Unit Contribution Margin | = | Break-Even Point in Sales Units |
|---|---|---|---|---|
| $200,000 | ÷ | $200 | = | 1,000 units |

**ILLUSTRATION 19.2**

**Break-even point in sales units**

**Illustration 19.3** shows the computation for the break-even point in sales dollars (using contribution margin ratio).

**ILLUSTRATION 19.3**
**Break-even point in sales dollars**

| Fixed Costs | ÷ | Contribution Margin Ratio | = | Break-Even Point in Sales Dollars |
|---|---|---|---|---|
| $200,000 | ÷ | .40 | = | $500,000 |

When a company is in its early stages of operation, its primary goal is to break even. Failure to break even will lead eventually to financial failure.

## Target Net Income

Once a company achieves its break-even point, it then sets a sales goal that will generate a target net income. For example, assume that Vargo's management has a target net income of $250,000. **Illustration 19.4** shows the required sales in units to achieve its target net income.

**ILLUSTRATION 19.4** Target net income in units

| (Fixed Costs + Target Net Income) | ÷ | Unit Contribution Margin | = | Sales in Units |
|---|---|---|---|---|
| ($200,000 + $250,000) | ÷ | $200 | = | 2,250 units |

**Illustration 19.5** uses the contribution margin ratio to compute the required sales in dollars.

**ILLUSTRATION 19.5** Target net income in dollars

| (Fixed Costs + Target Net Income) | ÷ | Contribution Margin Ratio | = | Sales in Dollars |
|---|---|---|---|---|
| ($200,000 + $250,000) | ÷ | .40 | = | $1,125,000 |

In order to achieve net income of $250,000, Vargo has to sell 2,250 cell phones, for a total price of $1,125,000.

## Margin of Safety

Another measure managers use to assess profitability is the margin of safety.

- The **margin of safety** tells us **how far sales can drop** before the company will be operating at a loss.
- Managers like to have a sense of how much cushion they have between their current situation and operating at a loss.
- The margin of safety can be expressed in dollars or as a ratio.

In Illustration 19.1, for example, Vargo reported sales of $800,000. At that sales level, its margin of safety in dollars and as a ratio are as shown in **Illustrations 19.6** and 19.7.

**ILLUSTRATION 19.6** Margin of safety in dollars

| Actual (Expected) Sales | − | Break-Even Sales | = | Margin of Safety in Dollars |
|---|---|---|---|---|
| $800,000 | − | $500,000 | = | $300,000 |

As **Illustration 19.7** indicates (as does Illustration 19.6), Vargo's sales could drop by $300,000, or 37.5%, before the company would operate at a loss.

**ILLUSTRATION 19.7** Margin of safety as a ratio

| Margin of Safety in Dollars | ÷ | Actual (Expected) Sales | = | Margin of Safety as a Ratio |
|---|---|---|---|---|
| $300,000 | ÷ | $800,000 | = | 37.5% |

# CVP and Changes in the Business Environment

To better understand how CVP analysis works, let's look at three independent cases that might occur at Vargo Electronics. Each case uses the original cell phone sales and cost data, shown in **Illustration 19.8**.

| | |
|---|---|
| Unit selling price | $500 |
| Unit variable costs | $300 |
| Total fixed costs | $200,000 |
| Break-even sales | $500,000 or 1,000 units |

**ILLUSTRATION 19.8**

Original cell phone sales and cost data

## Case I

A competitor is offering a 10% discount on the selling price of its cell phones. Management must decide whether to offer a similar discount.

**Question:** What effect will a 10% discount on selling price have on the break-even point for cell phones?

**Answer:** A 10% discount on selling price reduces the unit selling price to $450 [$500 − ($500 × 10%)]. Unit variable costs remain unchanged at $300. Thus, the unit contribution margin is $150 ($450 − $300). Assuming no change in fixed costs, break-even sales are 1,333 units, computed as shown in **Illustration 19.9**.

| Fixed Costs | ÷ | Unit Contribution Margin | = | Break-Even Sales |
|---|---|---|---|---|
| $200,000 | ÷ | $150 | = | 1,333 units (rounded) |

**ILLUSTRATION 19.9**

Computation of break-even sales in units

For Vargo, this change requires monthly sales to increase by 333 units, or 33⅓%, in order to break even. In reaching a conclusion about offering a 10% discount to customers, management must determine how likely it is to achieve the increased sales. Also, management should estimate the possible loss of sales if the competitor's discount price is not matched.

## Case II

To meet the threat of foreign competition, management invests in new robotic equipment that will lower the amount of direct labor required to make cell phones. The company estimates that total fixed costs will increase by 30% and that unit variable costs will decrease by 30%.

**Question:** What effect will the new equipment have on the sales volume required to break even?

**Answer:** Total fixed costs become $260,000 [$200,000 + ($200,000 × 30%)]. The unit variable costs become $210 [$300 − ($300 × 30%)]. Thus, the unit contribution margin is $290 ($500 − $210). The new break-even point is approximately 897 units, computed as shown in **Illustration 19.10**.

| Fixed Costs | ÷ | Unit Contribution Margin | = | Break-Even Sales |
|---|---|---|---|---|
| $260,000 | ÷ | ($500 − $210) | = | 897 units (rounded) |

**ILLUSTRATION 19.10**

Computation of break-even sales in units

These changes appear to be advantageous for Vargo. The break-even point is reduced by 103 units (1,000 − 897).

## Case III

Vargo's principal supplier of raw materials has just announced a price increase. The higher cost is expected to increase the unit variable costs of cell phones by $25. Management decides that it does not want to increase the selling price of the cell phones. It plans a cost-cutting program that will save $17,500 in fixed costs per month. Vargo is currently realizing monthly net income of $80,000 on sales of 1,400 cell phones.

**Question:** What increase in units sold will be needed to maintain the same level of net income?

**Answer:** The unit variable costs increase to $325 ($300 + $25). Fixed costs are reduced to $182,500 ($200,000 − $17,500). Because of the change in variable costs, the unit contribution margin becomes $175 ($500 − $325). **Illustration 19.11** shows the computation of the required number of units sold to achieve the target net income.

**ILLUSTRATION 19.11**

**Computation of required sales**

| $\left(\begin{array}{c}\text{Fixed Costs + Target}\\\text{Net Income}\end{array}\right)$ | ÷ | Unit Contribution Margin | = | Sales in Units |
|---|---|---|---|---|
| ($182,500 + $80,000) | ÷ | $175 | = | 1,500 |

To achieve the required sales, Vargo Electronics will have to sell 1,500 cell phones, an increase of 100 units. If this does not seem to be a reasonable expectation, management will either have to make further cost reductions or accept less net income if the selling price remains unchanged.

We hope that the concepts reviewed in this section are now familiar to you. We are now ready to examine additional ways that companies use CVP analysis to assess profitability and to help in making effective business decisions.

---

## Management Insight   Amazon.com

Warchi/Getty Images

### Don't Just Look—Buy Something

When analyzing an Internet business such as **Amazon.com**, analysts closely watch the so-called "conversion rate." This rate is calculated by dividing the number of people who actually take a desired action at an Internet site (e.g., buy something) by the total number of people who visit the site. Average conversion rates are from 3% to 5%. A rate below 2% is poor, while a rate above 10% is great.

Conversion rates have an obvious effect on the break-even point. Suppose you spend $10,000 on your site, which then attracts 5,000 visitors. If you get a 2% conversion rate (100 purchases), your site costs $100 per purchase ($10,000 ÷ 100). A 4% conversion rate lowers your cost to $50 per transaction, and an 8% conversion rate

gets you down to $25. One recent study estimates that the average conversion rate for e-commerce is 1.6% but that it can vary considerably. Other studies show that conversion rates increase if the site has an easy-to-use interface, fast-performing screens, a convenient ordering process, and advertising that is both clever and clear.

**Sources:** J. William Gurley, "The One Internet Metric That Really Counts," *Fortune* (March 6, 2000), p. 392; Milind Mody, "Chief Mentor: How Startups Can Win Customers Online," *Wall Street Journal* (May 11, 2011); and Neil Patel, "What Is a Good Conversion Rate? The Answer Might Surprise You," *The Daily Egg* (updated October 23, 2018).

**Besides increasing their conversion rates, what steps can online merchants use to lower their break-even points? (Answer is available at the end of the chapter.)**

## DO IT! 1 | CVP Analysis

Krisanne Company reports the following operating results for the month of June.

**Krisanne Company**
**CVP Income Statement**
**For the Month Ended June 30, 2022**

|  | Total | Per Unit | Percent of Sales |
|---|---|---|---|
| Sales (5,000 units) | $300,000 | $60 | 100% |
| Variable costs | 180,000 | 36 | 60 |
| Contribution margin | 120,000 | $24 | 40% |
| Fixed expenses | 100,000 |  |  |
| Net income | $ 20,000 |  |  |

To increase net income, management is considering reducing the selling price by 10%, with no changes to unit variable costs or fixed costs. Management is confident that this change will increase unit sales by 25%.

Using the contribution margin technique, compute the break-even point in sales units and sales dollars and the margin of safety in dollars (a) assuming no changes to sales price or costs, and (b) assuming changes to sales price and volume as described above. (c) Comment on your findings.

**Solution**

a. Assuming no changes to sales price or costs:

Break-even point in sales units = 4,167 units (rounded) ($100,000 ÷ $24)
Break-even point in sales dollars = $250,000 ($100,000 ÷ .40$^a$)
Margin of safety in dollars = $50,000 ($300,000 − $250,000)

$^a$$24 ÷ $60

b. Assuming changes to sales price and volume:

Break-even point in sales units = 5,556 units (rounded) ($100,000 ÷ $18$^b$)
Break-even point in sales dollars = $300,000 ($100,000 ÷ ($18 ÷ $54$^c$))
Margin of safety in dollars = $37,500 ($337,500$^d$ − $300,000)

$^b$$60 − (.10 × $60) − $36 = $18
$^c$$60 − (.10 × $60)
$^d$5,000 + (.25 × 5,000) = 6,250 units, 6,250 units × $54 = $337 500

c. The increase in the break-even point and the decrease in the margin of safety indicate that management should not implement the proposed change. The increase in sales volume will result in contribution margin of $112,500 (6,250 × $18), which is $7,500 ($120,000 − $112,500) less than the current amount.

Related exercise material: **BE19.3, BE19.4, BE19.5, BE19.6, DO IT! 19.1, E19.1, E19.2, E19.3, E19.4, and E19.5.**

# Sales Mix and Break-Even Sales

## LEARNING OBJECTIVE 2

Explain the term sales mix and its effects on break-even sales.

To this point, our discussion of CVP analysis has assumed that a company sells only one product. However, most companies sell multiple products.

- When a company sells multiple products, it is important that management understands the financial implications of its sales mix.
- **Sales mix** is the relative percentage in which a company sells its products.

For example, suppose 80% of **Hewlett Packard**'s unit sales are printers and the other 20% are PCs. Its sales mix is 80% printers to 20% PCs.

Sales mix is important to managers because different products often have substantially different contribution margins. For example, **Ford**'s SUVs and F150 pickup trucks have higher contribution margins compared to its economy cars. Similarly, first-class tickets sold by **United Airlines** provide substantially higher contribution margins than coach-class tickets.

## Break-Even Sales in Units

Companies can compute break-even sales for a mix of two or more products by determining the **weighted-average unit contribution margin of all the products**. Returning to our example from Chapter 18, assume that Vargo Electronics Company sells not only cell phones but high-definition TVs as well. Vargo sells its two products in the following amounts: 1,500 cell phones and 500 TVs, for a total of 2,000 units. **Illustration 19.12** shows the sales mix, expressed as a percentage of the 2,000 total units sold.

**ILLUSTRATION 19.12**
**Sales mix as a percentage of units sold**

| Cell Phones | TVs |
|---|---|
| 1,500 units ÷ 2,000 units = 75% | 500 units ÷ 2,000 units = 25% |

That is, 75% of the 2,000 units sold are cell phones, and 25% of the 2,000 units sold are TVs.

**Illustration 19.13** shows additional information related to Vargo. The unit contribution margin for cell phones is $200; for TVs, it is $500. Vargo's fixed costs total $275,000.

**ILLUSTRATION 19.13**
**Per unit data—sales mix**

| Unit Data | Cell Phones | TVs |
|---|---|---|
| Selling price | $500 | $1,000 |
| Variable costs | 300 | 500 |
| Contribution margin | $200 | $500 |
| Sales mix—units | 75% | 25% |
| Fixed costs = $275,000 | | |

To compute break-even for Vargo, we must determine the weighted-average unit contribution margin for the two products.

- We use the **weighted-average**, as opposed to a simple average, because Vargo sells three times as many cell phones as TVs.
- As a result, in determining an average unit contribution margin, three times as much weight should be placed on the contribution margin of the cell phones as on the TVs.

The weighted-average contribution margin for a sales mix of 75% cell phones and 25% TVs is $275, which is computed as shown in **Illustration 19.14**.

**ILLUSTRATION 19.14**  **Weighted-average unit contribution margin**

| Cell Phones | | | | TVs | | | | |
|---|---|---|---|---|---|---|---|---|
| ( Unit Contribution Margin | × | Sales Mix Percentage ) | + | ( Unit Contribution Margin | × | Sales Mix Percentage ) | = | Weighted-Average Unit Contribution Margin |
| ($200 | × | .75) | + | ($500 | × | .25) | = | $275 |

Similar to our calculation in the single-product setting, we can compute the break-even point in sales units by dividing the fixed costs by the weighted-average unit contribution margin of $275. **Illustration 19.15** shows the computation of break-even sales in units for Vargo, assuming $275,000 of fixed costs.

| Fixed Costs | ÷ | Weighted-Average Unit Contribution Margin | = | Break-Even Point in Sales Units |
|---|---|---|---|---|
| $275,000 | ÷ | $275 | = | 1,000 units |

**ILLUSTRATION 19.15**

**Break-even point in sales units**

Illustration 19.15 shows the break-even point for Vargo is 1,000 units—cell phones and TVs combined. Management needs to know how many of the 1,000 units sold are cell phones and how many are TVs. Applying the sales mix percentages that we computed previously of 75% for cell phones and 25% for TVs, these 1,000 units would be comprised of 750 cell phones (.75 × 1,000 units) and 250 TVs (.25 × 1,000). This is verified by the computations in **Illustration 19.16**, which shows that the total contribution margin is $275,000 when 1,000 units are sold. As required at the break-even point, this contribution margin equals the fixed costs of $275,000.

| Product | Unit Sales | × | Unit Contribution Margin | = | Total Contribution Margin |
|---|---|---|---|---|---|
| Cell phones | 750 | × | $200 | = | $150,000 |
| TVs | 250 | × | 500 | = | 125,000 |
| | **1,000** | | | | **$275,000** |

**ILLUSTRATION 19.16**

**Break-even proof—sales units**

Management should continually review and update the company's sales mix.

- At any level of units sold, **net income will be greater if higher contribution margin units are sold rather than lower contribution margin units**.
- For Vargo, TVs produce a higher contribution margin.
- Consequently, if Vargo sells 700 cell phones instead of 750, and 300 TVs instead of 250 (a sales mix of 70% cell phones and 30% TVs), net income would be higher than in the current sales mix even though total units sold (1,000 units) are the same.

An analysis of these relationships shows that a shift from low-margin sales to high-margin sales may increase net income even though there is a decline in total units sold. Likewise, a shift from high- to low-margin sales may result in a decrease in net income even though there is an increase in total units sold.

---

**Data Analytics Insight**    **Caesars Entertainment**

### Taking No Chances with Its Profits

To navigate in a constantly changing casino environment, many casinos rely heavily on data analytics to improve profitability. For example, **Caesars Entertainment** says it can trace and collect data on 85% of the dollars spent in its casinos. This helps the company optimize its sale mix while also gaining a precise understanding of its customer base.

Maz Day/Shutterstock.com

Optimizing the sales mix is vital in this business. In fact, data analytics provides evidence that refutes the popular view that casinos make significant profits from wealthy "high-rollers" losing big money at the gaming tables. Instead, it's the sales from food, beverages, lodging, and concerts that help the casinos rake in the money. Further, through data analysis, Caesars has determined that it gets 80% of its revenues and nearly 100% of its profits from "normal" as opposed to "high-roller" customers. With that in mind, the company can then also use data analytics to determine what types of incentives are the most effective in motivating targeted customer types to spend more money on specific goods and services. For Caesars, chance is limited to its gaming tables, not its profits.

**Source:** Berbard Marr, *Big Data in Practice* (Hoboken, N.J.: John Wiley and Sons, 2016), pp. 181–187.

**How does big data correct management's view on two misconceptions about where today's casinos make their money? (Answer is available at the end of the chapter.)**

---

# Break-Even Sales in Dollars

The calculation of the break-even point presented for Vargo Electronics in the previous section works well if a company has only a *small number* of products. In contrast, consider **3M**, the maker of Post-it Notes, which has more than 30,000 products. In order to calculate the break-even point for 3M using a weighted-average unit contribution margin, we would need to calculate 30,000 different unit contribution margins. That is not realistic.

- Therefore, for a company with many products, we calculate the break-even point in terms of sales dollars (rather than units sold), using sales information for divisions or product lines (rather than individual products).

- This requires that we compute both sales mix as a percentage of total dollar sales (rather than units sold) and the contribution margin ratio (rather than unit contribution margin).

To illustrate, suppose that Kale Garden Supply Company has two divisions—Indoor Plants and Outdoor Plants. Each division has hundreds of different types of plants and plant-care products. **Illustration 19.17** provides the information necessary for determining the sales mix percentages for the two divisions of Kale Garden Supply.

**ILLUSTRATION 19.17**   Cost-volume-profit data for Kale Garden Supply

| | Indoor Plant Division | Percent of Sales | Outdoor Plant Division | Percent of Sales | Company Total | Percent of Sales |
|---|---|---|---|---|---|---|
| Sales | $200,000 | 100% | $800,000 | 100% | $1,000,000 | 100% |
| Variable costs | 120,000 | 60 | 560,000 | 70 | 680,000 | 68 |
| Contribution margin | $ 80,000 | 40% | $240,000 | 30% | $ 320,000 | 32% |
| Sales mix percentage (in sales dollars) (Division sales ÷ Total sales) | $\frac{\$200,000}{\$1,000,000} = .20$ | | $\frac{\$800,000}{\$1,000,000} = .80$ | | | |

**Illustration 19.18** shows the contribution margin ratio for each division (40% and 30%) and for the combined company (32%), which is computed by dividing the total contribution margin by total sales. (These amounts are also listed in Illustration 19.17.)

**ILLUSTRATION 19.18**
Contribution margin ratio for each division

|  | Indoor Plant Division | Outdoor Plant Division | Company Total |
|---|---|---|---|
| Contribution margin ratio (Contribution margin ÷ Sales) | $\frac{\$80,000}{\$200,000} = .40$ | $\frac{\$240,000}{\$800,000} = .30$ | $\frac{\$320,000}{\$1,000,000} = .32$ |

Note that the contribution margin ratio of 32% for the total company is a weighted average of the individual contribution margin ratios of the two divisions (40% and 30%).

- To illustrate, in **Illustration 19.19** we multiply each division's contribution margin ratio by its sales mix percentage, based on sales dollars, and then total these amounts.
- The calculation in Illustration 19.19 is useful because it enables us to determine how the break-even point changes when the sales mix changes.

**ILLUSTRATION 19.19**  Calculation of weighted-average contribution margin

| Indoor Plant Division | | | | Outdoor Plant Division | | | | Weighted-Average Contribution Margin Ratio |
|---|---|---|---|---|---|---|---|---|
| (Contribution Margin Ratio | × | Sales Mix Percentage) | + | (Contribution Margin Ratio | × | Sales Mix Percentage) | = | Weighted-Average Contribution Margin Ratio |
| (.40 | × | .20) | + | (.30 | × | .80) | = | .32 |

Kale Garden Supply's break-even point in sales dollars is computed by dividing its fixed costs of $300,000 by the weighted-average contribution margin ratio of 32%, as shown in **Illustration 19.20**.

| Fixed Costs | ÷ | Weighted-Average Contribution Margin Ratio | = | Break-Even Point in Sales Dollars |
|---|---|---|---|---|
| $300,000 | ÷ | .32 | = | $937,500 |

**ILLUSTRATION 19.20**
Calculation of break-even point in sales dollars

This break-even point is based on the sales mix of 20% to 80%. We can determine the amount of sales contributed by each division by multiplying the sales mix percentage of each division by the total sales figure. Of the company's total break-even sales of $937,500, a total of $187,500 (.20 × $937,500) will come from the Indoor Plant Division, and $750,000 (.80 × $937,500) will come from the Outdoor Plant Division.

What would be the impact on the break-even point if a higher percentage of Kale Garden Supply's sales were to come from the Indoor Plant Division?

- Because the Indoor Plant Division enjoys a higher contribution margin ratio, this change in the sales mix would result in a higher weighted-average contribution margin ratio and consequently a lower break-even point in sales dollars.
- For example, if the sales mix changes to 50% for the Indoor Plant Division and 50% for the Outdoor Plant Division, the weighted-average contribution margin ratio would be 35% [(.40 × .50) + (.30 × .50)]. The new, lower, break-even point is $857,143 ($300,000 ÷ .35).
- The opposite would occur if a higher percentage of sales were expected from the Outdoor Plant Division.

As you can see, the information provided using CVP analysis can help managers better understand the impact of sales mix on profitability.

## Management Insight    Chipotle

Stockbroker/MBI/
Alamy Stock Photo

### Wouldn't You Rather Have a Chicken Burrito?

Restaurants serve a variety of products, and they certainly don't all have the same contribution margin. Obviously, restaurants would prefer that you buy products that provide them with a higher margin. For example, beef burritos cost more at **Chipotle**—so they provide a higher margin right? Wrong. Even though Chipotle charges more for beef burritos, the price difference still doesn't cover the higher raw materials cost of beef relative to chicken. So Chipotle's chicken products have a higher contribution margin than their beef entrees. At one point, Chipotle increased its price on its beef entrees relative to chicken by 40 cents, resulting in about an 80-cent price difference. The price increase still didn't cover the difference in raw materials costs, but management hoped that the higher price would cause some people to switch to chicken.

**Source:** Adam Levine-Weinberg, "Why Investors Will Love Chipotle Mexican Grill, Inc.'s Price Increase," *The Motley Fool* (May 31, 2014).

**If Chipotle's customers switch from beef to chicken, what will happen to its revenues and its net income? (Answer is available at the end of the chapter.)**

---

### ACTION PLAN

- **The sales mix is the relative percentage of each product sold in units.**
- **The weighted-average unit contribution margin is the sum of the unit contribution margins multiplied by the respective sales mix percentage.**
- **Determine the break-even point in sales units by dividing the fixed costs by the weighted-average unit contribution margin.**
- **Determine the number of units of each model to sell by multiplying the total break-even units by the respective sales mix percentage for each product.**

## DO IT! 2 | Sales Mix Break-Even

Manzeck Bicycles International produces and sells three different types of mountain bikes. Information regarding the three models is shown below.

|  | Pro | Intermediate | Standard | Total |
|---|---|---|---|---|
| Units sold | 5,000 | 10,000 | 25,000 | 40,000 |
| Selling price | $800 | $500 | $350 | |
| Variable costs | $500 | $300 | $250 | |

The company's total fixed costs to produce the bicycles are $7,500,000.

a. Determine the sales mix as a function of units sold for the three products.

b. Determine the weighted-average unit contribution margin.

c. Determine the total number of units that the company must sell to break even.

d. Determine the number of units of each model that the company must sell to break even.

### Solution

a. The sales mix percentages as a function of units sold are:

| Pro | Intermediate | Standard |
|---|---|---|
| $\dfrac{5,000}{40,000} = 12.5\%$ | $\dfrac{10,000}{40,000} = 25\%$ | $\dfrac{25,000}{40,000} = 62.5\%$ |

b. The weighted-average unit contribution margin is:

$$[.125 \times (\$800 - \$500)] + [.25 \times (\$500 - \$300)] + [.625 \times (\$350 - \$250)] = \$150$$

c. The break-even point in sales units is:

$$\frac{\$7,500,000}{\$150} = 50,000 \text{ units}$$

d. The break-even units to sell for each product are:

| Pro: | 50,000 units × 12.5% | = | 6,250 units |
|---|---|---|---|
| Intermediate: | 50,000 units × 25% | = | 12,500 units |
| Standard: | 50,000 units × 62.5% | = | 31,250 units |
| | | | 50,000 units |

Related exercise material: **BE19.7, BE19.8, BE19.9, BE19.10, DO IT! 19.2, E19.6, E19.7, E19.8, E19.9, and E19.10.**

# Sales Mix with Limited Resources

---

**LEARNING OBJECTIVE 3**

Determine sales mix when a company has limited resources.

---

In the previous discussion, we assumed a certain sales mix and then determined the break-even point given that sales mix. We now discuss how limited resources influence the sales-mix decision.

- All companies have resource limitations.
- The limited resource may be floor space in a retail department store, raw materials, direct labor hours, or machine capacity in a manufacturing company.
- When a company has limited resources, management must decide which products to make and sell in order to maximize net income.

To illustrate, recall that Vargo Electronics manufactures cell phones and TVs. The limiting resource is machine capacity, which is 3,600 hours per month. **Illustration 19.21** shows that each TV requires more than three times as many machine hours as one cell phone.

|  | Cell Phones | TVs |
|---|---|---|
| Unit contribution margin | $200 | $500 |
| Machine hours required per unit | .2 | .625 |

**ILLUSTRATION 19.21**

**Contribution margin and machine hours**

The TVs may appear to be more profitable since they have a higher unit contribution margin ($500) than the cell phones ($200). However, the cell phones take fewer machine hours to produce than the TVs.

- Therefore, it is necessary to find the **contribution margin per unit of limited resource**—in this case, contribution margin per machine hour (see **Helpful Hint**).
- This is obtained by dividing the unit contribution margin of each product by the number of units of the limited resource required for each product, as shown in **Illustration 19.22**.

**HELPFUL HINT**

CM alone is not enough to make this decision. The key factor is CM per unit of limited resource.

|  | Cell Phones | TVs |
|---|---|---|
| Unit contribution margin (a) | $ 200 | $500 |
| Machine hours required (b) | 0.2 | 0.625 |
| **Contribution margin per unit of limited resource [(a) ÷ (b)]** | **$1,000** | **$800** |

**ILLUSTRATION 19.22**

**Contribution margin per unit of limited resource**

The computation shows that the cell phones have a higher contribution margin per unit of limited resource. This would suggest that, given sufficient demand for cell phones, Vargo should shift the sales mix to produce more cell phones or increase machine capacity.

As indicated in Illustration 19.22, the constraint for the production of the TVs is the number of machine hours available to produce them.

- In addressing this problem, we have taken the limited number of machine hours as a given and have attempted to maximize the contribution margin given the constraint.
- One question that Vargo should ask, however, is whether this constraint can be reduced or eliminated.

- If Vargo is able to increase machine capacity from 3,600 hours to 4,200 hours, the additional 600 hours could be used to produce either the cell phones or TVs.

The total contribution margin that results from producing more cell phones versus more TVs is found by multiplying the additional machine hours by the contribution margin per unit of limited resource, as shown in **Illustration 19.23**.

**ILLUSTRATION 19.23**

**Incremental analysis—computation of total contribution margin**

| | Cell Phones | TVs |
|---|---|---|
| Machine hours (a) | 600 | 600 |
| Contribution margin per unit of limited resource (b) | $ 1,000 | $ 800 |
| **Contribution margin [(a) × (b)]** | **$600,000** | **$480,000** |

From this analysis, we can see that to maximize net income, all of the increased capacity should be used to make and sell the cell phones (assuming sufficient demand exists for the cell phones).

Vargo's manufacturing constraint might be due to a bottleneck in production or to poorly trained machine operators.

- In addition to finding ways to solve those problems, the company should consider other possible solutions, such as outsourcing part of the production, acquiring additional new equipment (discussed in Chapter 25), or striving to eliminate any non–value-added activities (see Chapter 17).
- As discussed in Chapter 14, this approach is referred to as the **theory of constraints**, which is a specific approach used to identify and manage constraints in order to achieve the company's goals.
- According to this theory, a company must continually identify its constraints and find ways to reduce or eliminate them, where appropriate.

---

## Management Insight    Macy's

Svetlana
Kolpakova/123RF

### Something Smells

When fragrance sales went flat, retailers such as **Macy's** turned up the heat on fragrance manufacturers. They reduced the amount of floor space devoted to fragrances, leaving fragrance manufacturers fighting each other for the smaller space. The retailer doesn't just choose the fragrance with the highest contribution margin. Instead, it chooses the fragrance with the highest contribution margin per square foot for a given period of time. In this game, a product with a lower contribution margin, but a higher turnover, could well be the winner.

**What is the limited resource for a retailer, and what implications does this have for sales mix? (Answer is available at the end of the chapter.)**

---

**ACTION PLAN**

- **Calculate the contribution margin per unit of limited resource for each product.**

## DO IT! 3 | Sales Mix with Limited Resources

Carolina Corporation manufactures and sells three different types of high-quality sealed ball bearings for mountain bike wheels. The bearings vary in terms of their quality specifications—primarily with respect to their smoothness and roundness. They are referred to as Fine, Extra-Fine, and Super-Fine bearings. Machine time is limited. More machine time is required to manufacture the Extra-Fine and Super-Fine bearings. The following information is also provided.

| | Product | | |
|---|---|---|---|
| | **Fine** | **Extra-Fine** | **Super-Fine** |
| Selling price | $6.00 | $10.00 | $16.00 |
| Variable costs and expenses | 4.00 | 6.50 | 11.00 |
| Contribution margin | $2.00 | $ 3.50 | $ 5.00 |
| Machine hours required | 0.02 | 0.04 | 0.08 |

**a.** Ignoring the machine time constraint, what strategy would appear optimal?

**b.** What is the contribution margin per unit of limited resource for each type of bearing?

**c.** If additional machine time could be obtained, how should the additional capacity be used?

### Solution

**a.** The Super-Fine bearings have the highest unit contribution margin. Thus, ignoring any manufacturing constraints, it would appear that the company should shift toward production of more Super-Fine units.

**b.** The contribution margin per unit of limited resource (machine hours) is calculated as:

| | **Fine** | **Extra-Fine** | **Super-Fine** |
|---|---|---|---|
| $\dfrac{\text{Unit contribution margin}}{\text{Limited resource consumed per unit}}$ | $\dfrac{\$2}{.02} = \$100$ | $\dfrac{\$3.5}{.04} = \$87.50$ | $\dfrac{\$5}{08} = \$62.50$ |

**c.** The Fine bearings have the highest contribution margin per unit of limited resource (machine time) even though they have the lowest unit contribution margin. Given the resource constraint, any additional capacity should be used to make Fine bearings, assuming that the market can absorb additional units.

Related exercise material: **BE19.11, BE19.12, DO IT! 19.3, E19.11, E19.12,** and **E19.13.**

# Operating Leverage and Profitability

### LEARNING OBJECTIVE 4
Indicate how operating leverage affects profitability.

**Cost structure** refers to the relative proportion of fixed versus variable costs that a company incurs. Cost structure can have a significant effect on profitability. For example, computer equipment manufacturer **Cisco Systems** substantially reduced its fixed costs by outsourcing much of its production. By minimizing its fixed costs, Cisco is now less susceptible to economic swings. However, as the following discussion shows, its reduced reliance on fixed costs reduced its ability to experience the incredible profitability that it used to have during economic booms.

The choice of cost structure should be carefully considered as there are many ways that companies can influence it.

- By acquiring sophisticated robotic equipment, many companies have reduced their use of manual labor.
- Similarly, by investing heavily in computers and online technology, some brokerage firms, such as **E*Trade**, have reduced their reliance on human brokers. In so doing, they have increased their reliance on fixed costs (through depreciation on the robotic equipment or computer equipment) and reduced their reliance on variable costs (the variable employee labor cost).
- Alternatively, by outsourcing their production, some companies have reduced their fixed costs and increased their variable costs. **Nike**, for example, does very little manufacturing

but instead outsources the manufacture of nearly all of its shoes and clothing. It has consequently converted many of its fixed costs into variable costs and therefore changed its cost structure.

Consider the following example of Vargo Electronics and one of its competitors, New Wave Company. Both make consumer electronics. Vargo uses a traditional, labor-intensive manufacturing process. New Wave has invested in a completely automated system. The factory employees are involved only in setting up, adjusting, and maintaining the machinery. **Illustration 19.24** shows CVP income statements for each company.

**ILLUSTRATION 19.24**

CVP income statements for two companies

| | Vargo Electronics | Percent of Sales | New Wave Company | Percent of Sales |
|---|---|---|---|---|
| Sales | $800,000 | 100% | $800,000 | 100% |
| Variable costs | 480,000 | 60 | 160,000 | 20 |
| Contribution margin | 320,000 | 40% | 640,000 | 80% |
| Fixed costs | 200,000 | | 520,000 | |
| Net income | $120,000 | | $120,000 | |

Both companies have the same sales and the same net income.

- But, notice that Vargo has much higher variable costs ($480,000) than New Wave ($160,000).
- Conversely, Vargo has much lower fixed costs ($200,000) than New Wave ($520,000).
- Because of these differences in cost structures, Vargo and New Wave differ greatly in how their net income is affected by sales increases or decreases.

Let's evaluate the impact of cost structure on the profitability of the two companies.

## Effect on Contribution Margin Ratio

First let's look at the contribution margin ratio. **Illustration 19.25** shows the computation of the contribution margin ratio for each company (which can also be seen in Illustration 19.24).

**ILLUSTRATION 19.25**

Contribution margin ratio for two companies

| | Contribution Margin | ÷ | Sales | = | Contribution Margin Ratio |
|---|---|---|---|---|---|
| Vargo Electronics | $320,000 | ÷ | $800,000 | = | 40% |
| New Wave | $640,000 | ÷ | $800,000 | = | 80% |

Because of its lower variable costs, New Wave has a contribution margin ratio of 80% versus only 40% for Vargo Electronics.

- That means that with every dollar of sales, New Wave generates 80 cents of contribution margin (and thus an 80-cent increase in net income), versus only 40 cents for Vargo.
- However, it also means that for every dollar that sales decline, New Wave loses 80 cents in net income, whereas Vargo will lose only 40 cents.
- New Wave's cost structure, which relies more heavily on fixed costs, makes its net income more sensitive to changes in sales revenue.

# Effect on Break-Even Point

The difference in cost structure also affects the break-even point. The break-even point for each company is calculated in **Illustration 19.26**.

| | Fixed Costs | ÷ | Contribution Margin Ratio | = | Break-Even Point in Sales Dollars |
|---|---|---|---|---|---|
| Vargo Electronics | $200,000 | ÷ | .40 | = | $500,000 |
| New Wave | $520,000 | ÷ | .80 | = | $650,000 |

**ILLUSTRATION 19.26**
**Computation of break-even point for two companies**

New Wave's break-even point is $650,000 versus only $500,000 for Vargo Electronics. That means that New Wave needs to generate $150,000 ($650,000 − $500,000) more in sales than Vargo before it breaks even. This higher break-even point makes New Wave riskier than Vargo. A company cannot survive for very long unless it at least breaks even.

# Effect on Margin of Safety Ratio

We can also evaluate the relative impact that changes in sales would have on the two companies by computing the margin of safety ratio. **Illustration 19.27** shows the computation of the **margin of safety ratio** for the two companies.

| | (Actual Sales | − | Break-Even Sales) | ÷ | Actual Sales | = | Margin of Safety Ratio |
|---|---|---|---|---|---|---|---|
| Vargo Electronics | ($800,000 | − | $500,000) | ÷ | $800,000 | = | 38% |
| New Wave | ($800,000 | − | $650,000) | ÷ | $800,000 | = | 19% |

**ILLUSTRATION 19.27**
**Computation of margin of safety ratio for two companies**

The difference in the margin of safety ratio reflects the difference in risk between the two companies. Vargo Electronics could sustain a 38% decline in sales before it would be operating at a loss. New Wave could sustain only a 19% decline in sales before it would be operating "in the red."

# Operating Leverage

**Operating leverage** refers to the extent to which a company's net income reacts to a given change in sales.

- Companies that have higher fixed costs relative to variable costs have higher operating leverage.
- When a company's sales revenue is increasing, high operating leverage is a good thing because it means that profits will increase rapidly.
- But when sales are declining, too much operating leverage can have devastating consequences.

## Degree of Operating Leverage

How can we compare operating leverage between two companies?

- The **degree of operating leverage** provides a measure of a company's potential for volatile earnings and can be used to compare companies.
- Degree of operating leverage is computed by dividing contribution margin by net income.

This equation is presented in **Illustration 19.28** and applied to our two manufacturers of cell phones.

**ILLUSTRATION 19.28**

**Computation of degree of operating leverage**

|  | Contribution Margin | ÷ | Net Income | = | Degree of Operating Leverage |
|---|---|---|---|---|---|
| Vargo Electronics | $320,000 | ÷ | $120,000 | = | 2.67 |
| New Wave | $640,000 | ÷ | $120,000 | = | 5.33 |

Vargo Electronics' degree of operating leverage is 2.67 versus 5.33 for New Wave. Its higher degree of operating leverage means that New Wave's net income reacts more to changes in sales. In fact, New Wave's earnings would go up (or down) by two times (5.33 ÷ 2.67 = 2.00) as much as Vargo Electronics' with an equal increase (or decrease) in sales. For example, suppose both companies experience a 10% decrease in sales. Vargo's net income will decrease by 26.7% (2.67 × 10%), while New Wave's will decrease by 53.3% (5.33 × 10%). Thus, New Wave's higher operating leverage exposes it to greater earnings volatility risk.

You should be careful not to conclude from this analysis that a cost structure that relies on higher fixed costs, and consequently has higher operating leverage, is necessarily bad.

- Internet music companies **Pandora** and **Spotify** have very little operating leverage. Some have suggested that they have limited potential for net income growth. When their revenues grow, their variable costs (very significant fees for the right to use music) grow proportionally.
- When used carefully, operating leverage can add considerably to a company's profitability.

For example, computer equipment manufacturer **Komag** enjoyed a 66% increase in net income when its sales increased by only 8%. As one commentator noted, "Komag's fourth quarter illustrates the company's significant operating leverage; a small increase in sales leads to a big profit rise." However, as our illustration demonstrates, increased reliance on fixed costs increases a company's risk.

---

## People, Planet, and Profit Insight

### Solar Power Generates More Than Electricity

When homeowners first began to put solar panels on their homes, electric utility companies encouraged them to do so. The power companies saw this as an opportunity to reduce their fixed investment in power-generating equipment. When a homeowner generated more electricity than the household needed, the extra electricity went into the grid, and the homeowner was compensated by the power company. It seemed to be a win-win situation.

Alessandro2802/ Getty Images

But, now that solar power has become so widespread, power companies are concerned that they might have excess power-generating capacity and that they won't be able to charge customers enough to cover their fixed costs. So the power companies have been reducing the amount that they pay homeowners for excess electricity generated by solar power. They are arguing that a larger portion of customers' bills should be fixed charges, as opposed to charges that vary with use. The power companies say that since so much of their costs are fixed costs, they need a dependable income stream to cover their fixed costs. Environmentalists worry that if a large percentage of a customer's bill is fixed (that is, doesn't vary with usage), then the customer won't have an incentive to conserve energy.

**How do the homeowner solar panels represent a form of outsourcing? At what point did this create a dilemma for power companies? (Answer is available at the end of the chapter.)**

## DO IT! 4 | Operating Leverage

Rexfield Corp., a company specializing in crime scene investigations, is contemplating an investment in automated mass-spectrometers. Its current process relies on a high number of lab technicians. The new equipment would employ a computerized expert system. The company's CEO has requested a comparison of the old technology versus the new technology. The accounting department has prepared the following CVP income statements for use in your analysis.

| | CSI Equipment | |
| --- | --- | --- |
| | Old | New |
| Sales | $2,000,000 | $2,000,000 |
| Variable costs | 1,400,000 | 600,000 |
| Contribution margin | 600,000 | 1,400,000 |
| Fixed costs | 400,000 | 1,200,000 |
| Net income | $ 200,000 | $ 200,000 |

Use the information provided above to do the following.

**a.** Compute the degree of operating leverage for the company under each scenario.

**b.** Discuss your results.

### Solution

**a.**

| | Contribution Margin | ÷ | Net Income | = | Degree of Operating Leverage |
| --- | --- | --- | --- | --- | --- |
| Old | $600,000 | ÷ | $200,000 | = | 3.00 |
| New | $1,400,000 | ÷ | $200,000 | = | 7.00 |

**b.** The degree of operating leverage measures the company's sensitivity to changes in sales. By switching to a cost structure dominated by fixed costs, the company would significantly increase its operating leverage. As a result, with a percentage change in sales, its percentage change in net income would be 2.33 (7.00 ÷ 3.00) times as much with the new technology as it would under the old.

Related exercise material: **BE19.13, BE19.14, BE19.15, DO IT! 19.4, E19.14, E19.15, and E19.16.**

---

| **Appendix 19A** | # Absorption Costing versus Variable Costing |
| --- | --- |

### LEARNING OBJECTIVE *5

Explain the differences between absorption costing and variable costing.

In earlier chapters, we classified both variable and fixed manufacturing costs as product costs. In job order costing, for example, a job is assigned the costs of direct materials, direct labor, and **both** variable and fixed manufacturing overhead.

- This costing approach is referred to as **full** or **absorption costing**.
- It is so named because all manufacturing costs are charged to, or absorbed by, the product.
- Absorption costing is the approach required for external reporting under generally accepted accounting principles.

In this appendix, we now present an alternative approach, **variable costing**, which is consistent with the cost-volume-profit material presented in Chapters 18 and 19, and therefore readily supports CVP analysis.

- Under **variable costing**, only direct materials, direct labor, and variable manufacturing overhead costs are considered product costs.
- Companies using variable costing recognize fixed manufacturing overhead costs as period costs (expenses) when incurred.
- Companies may not use variable costing for external financial reports because generally accepted accounting principles require that fixed manufacturing overhead be accounted for as a product cost.

**Illustration 19A.1** shows the difference between absorption costing and variable costing. Under both absorption and variable costing, selling and administrative expenses are period costs.

**ILLUSTRATION 19A.1**

Difference between absorption costing and variable costing

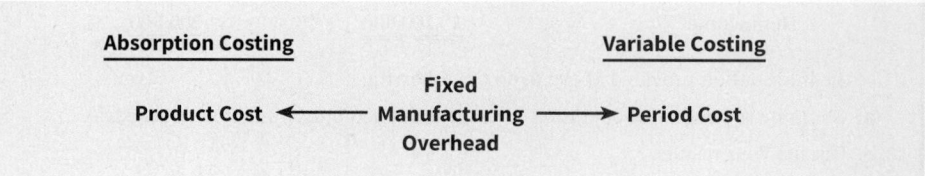

**Absorption Costing** — Product Cost ← Fixed Manufacturing Overhead → Period Cost — **Variable Costing**

# Example Comparing Absorption Costing with Variable Costing

To illustrate absorption and variable costing, assume that Premium Products Corporation manufactures a polyurethane sealant, called Fix-It, for car windshields. Relevant data for Fix-It in January 2022, the first month of production, are shown in **Illustration 19A.2**.

**ILLUSTRATION 19A.2**

Sealant sales and cost data for Premium Products Corporation

| | |
|---|---|
| Selling price | $20 per unit. |
| Units | Produced 30,000; sold 20,000; beginning inventory zero. |
| Unit variable costs | Manufacturing $9 (direct materials $5, direct labor $3, and variable overhead $1). Selling and administrative expenses $2. |
| Fixed costs | Manufacturing overhead $120,000. Selling and administrative expenses $15,000. |

The per unit manufacturing cost under each costing approach is computed in **Illustration 19A.3**.

**ILLUSTRATION 19A.3**

Computation of per unit manufacturing cost

| Type of Cost | Absorption Costing | Variable Costing |
|---|---|---|
| Direct materials | $ 5 | $5 |
| Direct labor | 3 | 3 |
| Variable manufacturing overhead | 1 | 1 |
| **Fixed manufacturing overhead** ($120,000 ÷ 30,000 units produced) | 4 | 0 |
| **Manufacturing cost per unit** | **$13** | **$9** |

The manufacturing cost per unit is $4 higher ($13 − $9) for absorption costing.

- This occurs because fixed manufacturing overhead costs are a product cost under absorption costing.
- Under variable costing, they are, instead, a period cost, and so they are expensed.

Based on these data, each unit sold and each unit remaining in inventory on the balance sheet is costed under absorption costing at $13 and under variable costing at $9.

## Absorption Costing Example

**Illustration 19A.4** shows the income statement for Premium Products using absorption costing. It shows that cost of goods manufactured is $390,000, computed by multiplying the 30,000 units produced times the manufacturing cost per unit of $13 (see Illustration 19A.3). Cost of goods sold is $260,000, after subtracting ending inventory of $130,000.

- Notice that the ending inventory of $130,000 includes fixed manufacturing overhead costs of $40,000 (10,000 × $4).
- Under absorption costing, $40,000 of the fixed manufacturing overhead is deferred to a future period as part of the cost of ending inventory.
- We will see that this is the primary difference between absorption costing and variable costing.

**ILLUSTRATION 19A.4**

**Absorption costing income statement**

### Premium Products Corporation
#### Income Statement
#### For the Month Ended January 31, 2022
#### Absorption Costing

| | | |
|---|---:|---:|
| Sales (20,000 units × $20) | | $400,000 |
| Cost of goods sold | | |
| Inventory, January 1 | $   –0– | |
| Cost of goods manufactured (30,000 units × $13) | 390,000* | |
| Cost of goods available for sale | 390,000 | |
| **Less: Inventory, January 31 (10,000 units × $13)** | **130,000** | |
| Cost of goods sold (20,000 units × $13) | | 260,000 |
| Gross profit | | 140,000 |
| Variable selling and administrative expenses | | |
| (20,000 × $2) | 40,000 | |
| Fixed selling and administrative expenses | 15,000 | 55,000 |
| **Net income** | | **$ 85,000** |

*(30,000 units × $9) variable + $120,000 fixed

## Variable Costing Example

As **Illustration 19A.5** shows, companies use the cost-volume-profit format in preparing a variable costing income statement. The variable manufacturing cost of $270,000 is computed by multiplying the 30,000 units produced times variable manufacturing cost of $9 per unit (see Illustration 19A.3). As in absorption costing, both variable and fixed selling and administrative expenses are treated as period costs.

**Variable costing income statement**

| Premium Products Corporation Income Statement For the Month Ended January 31, 2022 Variable Costing | | |
|---|---|---|
| Sales (20,000 units × $20) | | $400,000 |
| Variable cost of goods sold | | |
| Inventory, January 1 | $ –0– | |
| Variable cost of goods manufactured (30,000 units × $9) | 270,000 | |
| Variable cost of goods available for sale | 270,000 | |
| **Less: Inventory, January 31 (10,000 units × $9)** | **90,000** | |
| Variable cost of goods sold | 180,000 | |
| Variable selling and administrative expenses (20,000 units × $2) | 40,000 | 220,000 |
| Contribution margin | | 180,000 |
| Fixed manufacturing overhead | 120,000 | |
| Fixed selling and administrative expenses | 15,000 | 135,000 |
| **Net income** | | **$ 45,000** |

**There is one primary difference between variable and absorption costing: Under variable costing, companies charge the fixed manufacturing overhead as an expense in the current period.**

- Fixed manufacturing overhead costs of the current period, therefore, are not deferred to future periods through the ending inventory.
- As a result, absorption costing will show a **higher net income number** than variable costing **whenever units produced exceed units sold**.

This difference can be seen in the income statements in Illustrations 19A.4 and 19A.5. Note the difference in the computation of the January 31 ending inventory: $9 per unit times 10,000 units in Illustration 19A.5, $13 per unit times 10,000 units in Illustration 19A.4. This translates into a $40,000 difference in the ending inventories ($130,000 under absorption costing versus $90,000 under variable costing), which results in the $40,000 difference in net income. Under absorption costing, expensing $40,000 of the fixed overhead costs (10,000 units × $4) has been deferred (delayed) to a future period as part of inventory on the balance sheet. In contrast, under variable costing, all fixed manufacturing costs are expensed in the current period.

- As shown, when units produced exceed units sold, income under absorption costing is *higher*.
- When units produced are less than units sold, income under absorption costing is *lower*.
- When units produced and sold are the same, net income will be *equal* under the two costing approaches. In this case, there is no increase in ending inventory. So fixed overhead costs of the current period are not deferred to future periods through the ending inventory.

## Net Income Effects

To further illustrate the concepts underlying absorption and variable costing, we will look at an extended example using Overbay Inc., a manufacturer of special-purpose drones. We assume that production volume stays the same each year over the 3-year period, but the number of units sold varies each year.

## 2021 Results

As indicated in **Illustration 19A.6**, the variable manufacturing cost per drone is $240,000, and the fixed manufacturing overhead cost per drone is $60,000 (assuming 10 drones). Total manufacturing cost per drone under absorption costing is therefore $300,000 ($240,000 + $60,000). Overbay also has variable selling and administrative expenses of $5,000 per drone. The fixed selling and administrative expenses are $80,000.

**ILLUSTRATION 19A.6**

**Information for Overbay Inc.**

| | 2021 | 2022 | 2023 |
|---|---|---|---|
| **Volume information** | | | |
| Drones in beginning inventory | 0 | 0 | 2 |
| Drones produced | 10 | 10 | 10 |
| Drones sold | 10 | 8 | 12 |
| Drones in ending inventory | 0 | 2 | 0 |
| | | | |
| **Financial information** | | | |
| Selling price per drone | $400,000 | | |
| Variable manufacturing cost per drone | $240,000 | | |
| Fixed manufacturing overhead for the year | $600,000 | | |
| Fixed manufacturing overhead per drone | $ 60,000 ($600,000 ÷ 10) | | |
| Variable selling and administrative expenses per drone | $ 5,000 | | |
| Fixed selling and administrative expenses | $ 80,000 | | |

An absorption costing income statement for 2021 for Overbay Inc. is shown in **Illustration 19A.7**.

**ILLUSTRATION 19A.7**

**Absorption costing income statement—2021**

| Overbay Inc. Income Statement For the Year Ended December 31, 2021 Absorption Costing | | |
|---|---|---|
| Sales (10 drones × $400,000) | | $4,000,000 |
| Cost of goods sold (10 drones × $300,000) | | 3,000,000 |
| Gross profit | | 1,000,000 |
| Variable selling and administrative expenses (10 drones × $5,000) | $50,000 | |
| Fixed selling and administrative expenses | 80,000 | 130,000 |
| Net income | | $ 870,000 |

Overbay reports net income of $870,000 under absorption costing.

Under a variable costing system, the income statement follows a cost-volume-profit (CVP) format. In this case, the manufacturing cost is comprised solely of the variable manufacturing costs of $240,000 per drone. The entire amount of fixed manufacturing overhead costs of $600,000 for the year are expensed in 2021. As in absorption costing, the fixed and variable selling and administrative expenses are period costs expensed in 2021. A variable costing income statement for Overbay Inc. for 2021 is shown in **Illustration 19A.8**.

ILLUSTRATION 19A.8
**Variable costing income
statement—2021**

## Overbay Inc.
### Income Statement
### For the Year Ended December 31, 2021
### Variable Costing

| | | |
|---|---:|---:|
| Sales (10 drones × $400,000) | | $4,000,000 |
| Variable cost of goods sold | | |
| (10 drones × $240,000) | $2,400,000 | |
| Variable selling and administrative expenses | | |
| (10 drones × $5,000) | 50,000 | 2,450,000 |
| Contribution margin | | 1,550,000 |
| Fixed manufacturing overhead | 600,000 | |
| Fixed selling and administrative expenses | 80,000 | 680,000 |
| Net income | | $ 870,000 |

As shown in Illustration 19A.8, the variable costing net income of $870,000 is the same as the absorption costing net income computed in Illustration 19A.7.

- **When the numbers of units produced and sold are the same, net income is equal under the two costing approaches.**
- Because no increase in ending inventory occurs, no fixed manufacturing overhead costs incurred in 2021 are deferred to future periods as part of ending inventory using absorption costing.

## 2022 Results

In 2022, Overbay produced 10 drones but sold only eight drones. As a result, there are two drones in ending inventory. The absorption costing income statement for 2022 is shown in **Illustration 19A.9.**

ILLUSTRATION 19A.9
**Absorption costing income
statement—2022**

## Overbay Inc.
### Income Statement
### For the Year Ended December 31, 2022
### Absorption Costing

| | | |
|---|---:|---:|
| Sales (8 drones × $400,000) | | $3,200,000 |
| Cost of goods sold (8 drones × $300,000) | | 2,400,000 |
| Gross profit | | 800,000 |
| Variable selling and administrative expenses | | |
| (8 drones × $5,000) | $40,000 | |
| Fixed selling and administrative expenses | 80,000 | 120,000 |
| Net income | | $ 680,000 |

Under absorption costing, the ending inventory of two drones is $600,000 ($300,000 × 2). As shown in Illustration 19A.6, each unit of ending inventory includes $60,000 ($600,000 ÷ 10) of fixed manufacturing overhead. Therefore, fixed manufacturing overhead costs of $120,000 ($60,000 × 2 drones) are deferred until a future period.

The variable costing income statement for 2022 is shown in **Illustration 19A.10.**

**Overbay Inc.**
**Income Statement**
**For the Year Ended December 31, 2022**
**Variable Costing**

| | | |
|---|---|---|
| Sales (8 drones × $400,000) | | $3,200,000 |
| Variable cost of goods sold | | |
| (8 drones × $240,000) | $1,920,000 | |
| Variable selling and administrative expenses | | |
| (8 drones × $5,000) | 40,000 | 1,960,000 |
| Contribution margin | | 1,240,000 |
| Fixed manufacturing overhead | 600,000 | |
| Fixed selling and administrative expenses | 80,000 | 680,000 |
| Net income | | $ 560,000 |

**ILLUSTRATION 19A.10**

**Variable costing income statement—2022**

As shown in Illustrations 19A.9 and 19A.10, because the number of units produced (10) exceeds units sold (8), net income under absorption costing ($680,000) is higher than net income under variable costing ($560,000).

- The reason: The cost of the ending inventory is higher under absorption costing than under variable costing because fixed manufacturing overhead cost is retained in ending inventory.
- In 2022, under absorption costing, fixed manufacturing overhead of $120,000 is deferred and carried to future periods as part of inventory.
- Under variable costing, the $120,000 is expensed in the current period, and therefore the difference in the two net income numbers is $120,000 ($680,000 − $560,000).

## 2023 Results

In 2023, Overbay produced 10 drones and sold 12 (10 drones from the current year's production and 2 drones from the beginning inventory). As a result, there are no drones in ending inventory. The absorption costing income statement for 2023 is shown in **Illustration 19A.11**.

**Overbay Inc.**
**Income Statement**
**For the Year Ended December 31, 2023**
**Absorption Costing**

| | | |
|---|---|---|
| Sales (12 drones × $400,000) | | $4,800,000 |
| Cost of goods sold (12 drones × $300,000) | | 3,600,000 |
| Gross profit | | 1,200,000 |
| Variable selling and administrative expenses | | |
| (12 drones × $5,000) | $60,000 | |
| Fixed selling and administrative expenses | 80,000 | 140,000 |
| Net income | | $1,060,000 |

**ILLUSTRATION 19A.11**

**Absorption costing income statement—2023**

Fixed manufacturing costs of $720,000 ($60,000 × 12 drones) are expensed as part of cost of goods sold in 2023. This $720,000 includes $120,000 of fixed manufacturing costs incurred during 2022 and included in beginning inventory, plus $600,000 of fixed manufacturing costs incurred during 2023. Given this result for the absorption costing statement, what would you now expect the result to be under variable costing? Let's take a look.

The variable costing income statement for 2023 is shown in **Illustration 19A.12**.

### Overbay Inc.
#### Income Statement
#### For the Year Ended December 31, 2023
#### Variable Costing

| | | |
|---|---:|---:|
| Sales (12 drones × $400,000) | | $4,800,000 |
| Variable cost of goods sold | | |
| (12 drones × $240,000) | $2,880,000 | |
| Variable selling and administrative expenses | | |
| (12 drones × $5,000) | 60,000 | 2,940,000 |
| Contribution margin | | 1,860,000 |
| Fixed manufacturing overhead | 600,000 | |
| Fixed selling and administrative expenses | 80,000 | 680,000 |
| Net income | | $1,180,000 |

When drones produced (10) are less than drones sold (12), net income under absorption cost-ing ($1,060,000) is less than net income under variable costing ($1,180,000).

- This difference of $120,000 ($1,180,000 − $1,060,000) results because $120,000 of fixed manufacturing overhead costs in beginning inventory are charged to 2023 under absorption costing, in addition to the $600,000 of fixed manufacturing overhead incurred during the current period.
- Under variable costing, there is no fixed manufacturing overhead cost in beginning or ending inventory.

**Illustration 19A.13** summarizes the results of the three years.

| | Net Income Under Two Costing Approaches | | |
|---|---|---|---|
| | **2021**<br>**Units Produced =**<br>**Units Sold** | **2022**<br>**Units Produced >**<br>**Units Sold** | **2023**<br>**Units Produced <**<br>**Units Sold** |
| Absorption costing | $870,000 | $680,000 | $ 1,060,000 |
| Variable costing | 870,000 | 560,000 | 1,180,000 |
| Difference | $ −0− | $120,000 | $ (120,000) |

This relationship between production and sales and its effect on net income under the two costing approaches is shown in **Illustration 19A.14**.

ILLUSTRATION 19A.14

Summary of income effects
under absorption costing and
variable costing

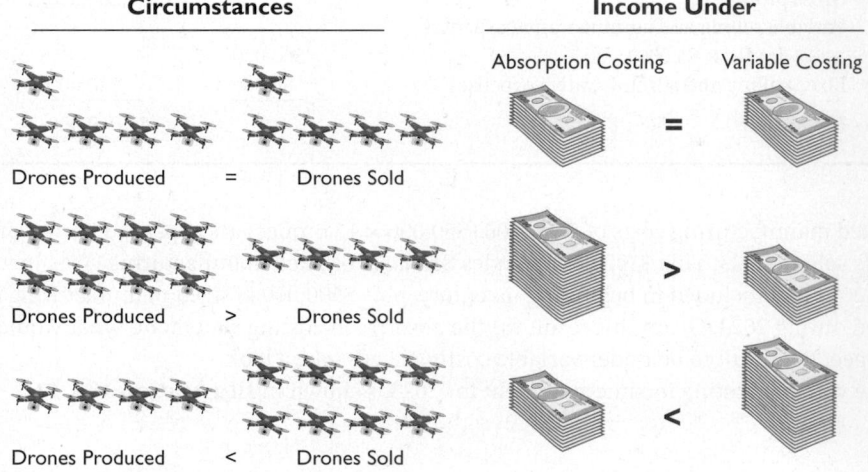

# Decision-Making Concerns

**Generally accepted accounting principles require that absorption costing be used for the costing of inventory for external reporting purposes.**

- Net income measured under GAAP (absorption costing) is often used internally to evaluate performance, justify cost reductions, or evaluate new projects.
- Some companies, however, have recognized that net income calculated using GAAP does not highlight differences between variable and fixed costs and may lead to poor business decisions. These companies use variable costing for internal reporting purposes.

The following discussion and example highlight a significant problem related to the use of absorption costing for decision-making purposes.

When production exceeds sales, absorption costing reports a higher net income than variable costing. The reason is that some fixed manufacturing costs are not expensed in the current period but are deferred to future periods as part of inventory. As a result, **management may be tempted to overproduce in a given period in order to increase net income.** Although net income will increase, this decision to overproduce may not be in the company's best interest.

- Suppose, for example, a division manager's compensation is based on the division's net income. In such a case, the manager may decide to meet the net income targets by producing more units than will be sold.
- While this overproduction may increase the manager's compensation, the buildup of inventories in the long run will lead to additional costs to the company.
- Variable costing avoids this situation because net income under variable costing is unaffected by changes in production levels, as the following illustration shows.

For example, say that Warren Lund, a division manager of Walker Enterprises, is under pressure to boost the performance of the Lighting Division in 2022. Unfortunately, recent profits have not met expectations. The expected sales for this year are 20,000 units. As he plans for the year, Warren has to decide whether to produce 20,000 or 30,000 units. **Illustration 19A.15** presents the facts available for the division.

| | |
|---|---|
| Beginning inventory | 0 |
| Expected sales in units | 20,000 |
| Selling price per unit | $15 |
| Variable manufacturing cost per unit | $6 |
| Fixed manufacturing overhead cost (total) | $60,000 |
| **Fixed manufacturing overhead costs per unit** | |
| Based on 20,000 units produced | $3 per unit ($60,000 ÷ 20,000 units) |
| Based on 30,000 units produced | $2 per unit ($60,000 ÷ 30,000 units) |
| **Total manufacturing cost per unit** | |
| Based on 20,000 units produced | $9 per unit ($6 variable + $3 fixed) |
| Based on 30,000 units produced | $8 per unit ($6 variable + $2 fixed) |
| **Selling and administrative expenses** | |
| Variable selling and administrative expenses per unit | $1 |
| Fixed selling and administrative expenses | $15,000 |

**Illustration 19A.16** shows the division's results based on the two possible levels of output under absorption costing.

## Lighting Division
### Income Statement
### For the Year Ended December 31, 2022
### Absorption Costing

|  | 20,000 Produced | 30,000 Produced |
|---|---|---|
| Sales (20,000 units × $15) | $300,000 | $300,000 |
| Cost of goods sold | 180,000* | 160,000** |
| Gross profit | 120,000 | 140,000 |
| Variable selling and administrative expenses | | |
| (20,000 units × $1) | 20,000 | 20,000 |
| Fixed selling and administrative expenses | 15,000 | 15,000 |
| Net income | $ 85,000 | $105,000 |

*20,000 units × $9; see red content in Illustration 19A.15.
**20,000 units × $8; see red content in Illustration 19A.15.

If the Lighting Division produces and sells 20,000 units, its net income under absorption costing is $85,000. If it produces 30,000 units but sells only 20,000 units, its net income is $105,000. By producing 30,000 units, the division has inventory of 10,000 units. This excess inventory causes net income to increase $20,000 because $20,000 of fixed costs (10,000 units × $2) are not charged to the current year, but are deferred to future periods.

What do you think Warren Lund might do in this situation?

- Given his concern about the profit numbers of the Lighting Division, he may be tempted to produce more units than are needed.

- Although this increased production will increase 2022 net income, it may be costly to the company in the long run because holding excess inventory is costly.

Now let's evaluate the same situation under variable costing. **Illustration 19A.17** shows a variable costing income statement for production at both 20,000 and 30,000 units, using the information from Illustration 19A.15.

## Lighting Division
### Income Statement
### For the Year Ended December 31, 2022
### Variable Costing

|  | 20,000 Produced | 30,000 Produced |
|---|---|---|
| Sales (20,000 units × $15) | $300,000 | $300,000 |
| Variable cost of goods sold (20,000 units × $6) | 120,000 | 120,000 |
| Variable selling and administrative expenses | | |
| (20,000 units × $1) | 20,000 | 20,000 |
| Contribution margin | 160,000 | 160,000 |
| Fixed manufacturing overhead | 60,000 | 60,000 |
| Fixed selling and administrative expenses | 15,000 | 15,000 |
| Net income | $ 85,000 | $ 85,000 |

From this example, we see that under variable costing, net income is not affected by the number of units produced. Net income is $85,000 whether the division produces 20,000 or 30,000 units. Why? Because fixed manufacturing overhead is treated as a period expense.

- Unlike absorption costing, no fixed manufacturing overhead is deferred through inventory buildup.

- Therefore, under variable costing, production does not increase income; sales do.
- As a result, if the company uses variable costing, managers like Warren Lund cannot affect profitability by increasing production.

# Potential Advantages of Variable Costing

Variable costing has a number of potential advantages relative to absorption costing:

1. Net income computed under variable costing is unaffected by changes in production levels. As a result, it is much easier to understand the impact of fixed and variable costs on the computation of net income when variable costing is used.

2. The use of variable costing is consistent with the cost-volume-profit material presented in Chapters 18 and 19 and therefore readily supports CVP analysis.

3. Net income computed under variable costing is closely tied to changes in sales levels (not production levels) and therefore provides a more realistic assessment of the company's success or failure during a period.

4. The presentation of fixed-cost and variable-cost components on the face of the variable costing income statement makes it easier to identify these costs and understand their effect on the business. Under absorption costing, the allocation of fixed costs to inventory makes it difficult to evaluate the impact of fixed costs on the company's results.

Companies that use just-in-time processing techniques to minimize their inventories will not have significant differences between absorption and variable costing net income.

---

## DO IT! 5 | Variable Costing

Franklin Company produces and sells tennis balls. The following costs are available for the year ended December 31, 2022. The company has no beginning inventory. In 2022, 8,000,000 units were produced, but only 7,500,000 units were sold. The unit selling price was $0.50 per ball. Costs and expenses were as follows.

| | |
|---|---|
| Unit variable costs | |
| Direct materials | $0.10 |
| Direct labor | 0.05 |
| Variable manufacturing overhead | 0.08 |
| Variable selling and administrative expenses | 0.02 |
| Annual fixed costs and expenses | |
| Manufacturing overhead | $500,000 |
| Selling and administrative expenses | 100,000 |

a. Compute the manufacturing cost of one unit of product using variable costing.

b. Prepare a 2022 income statement for Franklin Company using variable costing.

### Solution

a. The cost of one unit of product under variable costing would be:

| | |
|---|---|
| Direct materials | $0.10 |
| Direct labor | 0.05 |
| Variable manufacturing overhead | 0.08 |
| | **$0.23** |

**ACTION PLAN**

- Recall that under variable costing, only variable manufacturing costs are treated as manufacturing (product) costs.

- Subtract all fixed costs, both manufacturing overhead and selling and administrative expenses, as period costs.

**b.** The variable costing income statement would be as follows.

**Franklin Company**
**Income Statement**
**For the Year Ended December 31, 2022**
**Variable Costing**

| | | |
|---|---:|---:|
| Sales (7,500,000 × $0.50) | | $3,750,000 |
| Variable cost of goods sold (7,500,000 × $0.23) | $1,725,000 | |
| Variable selling and administrative expenses | | |
|   (7,500,000 × .02) | 150,000 | 1,875,000 |
| Contribution margin | | 1,875,000 |
| Fixed manufacturing overhead | 500,000 | |
| Fixed selling and administrative expenses | 100,000 | 600,000 |
| Net income | | $1,275,000 |

Related exercise material: **BE19.16, BE19.17, BE19.18, BE19.19, E19.17, E19.18, and E19.19.**

# Review and Practice

## Learning Objectives Review

### 1 Apply basic CVP concepts.

The CVP income statement classifies costs and expenses as variable or fixed and reports contribution margin in the body of the statement. Contribution margin is the amount of revenue remaining after deducting variable costs. It can be expressed as a per unit amount or as a ratio. The break-even point in sales units is fixed costs divided by unit contribution margin. The break-even point in sales dollars is fixed costs divided by the contribution margin ratio. These equations can also be used to determine sales units or sales dollars needed to achieve target net income, simply by adding target net income to fixed costs before dividing by the contribution margin. Margin of safety indicates how much sales can decline before the company is operating at a loss. It can be expressed in dollar terms or as a percentage.

### 2 Explain the term sales mix and its effects on break-even sales.

Sales mix is the relative proportion in which each product is sold when a company sells more than one product. For a company with a small number of different products, break-even sales in units is determined by using the weighted-average unit contribution margin of all the products. If the company sells many different products, then calculating the break-even point using unit information is not practical. Instead, in a company with many products, break-even sales in dollars is calculated using the weighted-average contribution margin ratio.

### 3 Determine sales mix when a company has limited resources.

When a company has limited resources, it is necessary to find the contribution margin per unit of limited resource. This amount is then multiplied by the units of limited resource to determine which product maximizes net income.

### 4 Indicate how operating leverage affects profitability.

Operating leverage refers to the degree to which a company's net income reacts to a change in sales. Operating leverage is determined by a company's relative use of fixed versus variable costs. Companies with high fixed costs relative to variable costs have high operating leverage. A company with high operating leverage experiences a sharp increase (decrease) in net income with a given increase (decrease) in sales. The degree of operating leverage is measured by dividing contribution margin by net income.

### *5 Explain the differences between absorption costing and variable costing.

Under absorption costing, fixed manufacturing costs are product costs. Under variable costing, fixed manufacturing costs are period costs.

If production volume exceeds sales volume, net income under absorption costing will exceed net income under variable costing by the amount of fixed manufacturing costs included in ending inventory that results from units produced but not sold during the period. If production volume is less than sales volume, net income under absorption costing will be less than under variable costing by the amount of fixed manufacturing costs included in the units sold during the period that were not produced during the period.

The use of variable costing is consistent with cost-volume-profit analysis. Net income under variable costing is unaffected by changes in production levels. Instead, it is closely tied to changes in sales. The presentation of fixed costs in the variable costing approach makes it easier to identify fixed costs and to evaluate their impact on the company's profitability.

## Glossary Review

*Absorption costing   A costing approach in which all manufacturing costs are charged to the product. (p. 19-19).

Cost structure   The relative proportion of fixed versus variable costs that a company incurs. (p. 19-15).

Degree of operating leverage   A measure of the extent to which a company's net income reacts to a change in sales. It is calculated by dividing contribution margin by net income. (p. 19-18).

Operating leverage   The extent to which a company's net income reacts to a change in sales. Operating leverage is determined by a company's relative use of fixed versus variable costs. (p. 19-17).

Sales mix   The relative percentage in which a company sells its multiple products. It can be calculated based on unit sales or sales revenue. (p. 19-8).

Theory of constraints   A specific approach used to identify and manage constraints in order to achieve the company's goals. (p. 19-14).

*Variable costing   A costing approach in which only variable manufacturing costs are product costs, and fixed manufacturing costs are period costs (expenses). (p. 19-20).

## Practice Multiple-Choice Questions

**1. (LO 1)** Which one of the following is the format of a CVP income statement?

   a. Sales − Variable costs = Fixed costs + Net income.

   b. Sales − Fixed costs − Variable costs − Operating expenses = Net income.

   c. Sales − Cost of goods sold − Operating expenses = Net income.

   d. Sales − Variable costs − Fixed costs = Net income.

**2. (LO 1)** Croc Catchers calculates its contribution margin to be less than zero. Which statement is **true**?

   a. Its fixed costs are less than the unit variable costs.

   b. Its profits are greater than its total costs.

   c. The company should sell more units.

   d. Its selling price is less than its variable costs.

**3. (LO 1)** Which one of the following describes the break-even point?

   a. It is the point where total sales equal total variable plus total fixed costs.

   b. It is the point where the contribution margin equals zero.

   c. It is the point where total variable costs equal total fixed costs.

   d. It is the point where total sales equal total fixed costs.

**4. (LO 1)** The following information is available for Chap Company.

| | |
|---|---|
| Sales | $350,000 |
| Cost of goods sold | $120,000 |
| Total fixed expenses | $60,000 |
| Total variable expenses | $100,000 |

Which amount would you find on Chap's CVP income statement?

   a. Contribution margin of $250,000.

   b. Contribution margin of $190,000.

   c. Gross profit of $230,000.

   d. Gross profit of $190,000.

**5. (LO 1)** Gabriel Corporation has fixed costs of $180,000 and unit variable costs of $8.50. It has a target income of $268,000. How many units must it sell at $12 per unit to achieve its target net income?

   a. 51,429 units.          c. 76,571 units.

   b. 128,000 units.          d. 21,176 units.

**6. (LO 1)** Mackey Corporation has fixed costs of $150,000 and unit variable costs of $9. If sales price per unit is $12, what is break-even sales in dollars?

   a. $200,000.          c. $480,000.

   b. $450,000.          d. $600,000.

**7. (LO 2)** Sales mix is:

   a. important to sales managers but not to accountants.

   b. easier to analyze on absorption costing income statements.

   c. a measure of the relative percentage of a company's variable costs to its fixed costs.

   d. a measure of the relative percentage in which a company's products are sold.

**8. (LO 2)** Net income will be:

   a. greater if more higher-contribution margin units are sold than lower-contribution margin units.

   b. greater if more lower-contribution margin units are sold than higher-contribution margin units.

   c. equal as long as total sales remain equal, regardless of which products are sold.

   d. unaffected by changes in the mix of products sold.

**9. (LO 3)** If the unit contribution margin is $15 and it takes 3.0 machine hours to produce the unit, the contribution margin per unit of limited resource is:

   a. $25.          c. $4.

   b. $5.          d. None of the answer choices are correct.

**10. (LO 3)** MEM manufactures two products. Product X has a contribution margin of $26 and requires 4 hours of machine time. Product Y has a contribution margin of $14 and requires 2 hours of machine time. Assuming that machine time is limited to 3,000 hours, how should MEM allocate the machine time to maximize its income?

   a. Use 1,500 hours to produce X and 1,500 hours to produce Y.

   b. Use 2,250 hours to produce X and 750 hours to produce Y.

   c. Use 3,000 hours to produce only X.

   d. Use 3,000 hours to produce only Y.

11. **(LO 3)** When a company has a limited resource, it should apply additional capacity of that resource to providing more units of the product or service that has:

    **a.** the highest contribution margin.

    **b.** the highest selling price.

    **c.** the highest gross profit.

    **d.** the highest unit contribution margin of that limited resource.

12. **(LO 4)** The degree of operating leverage:

    **a.** can be computed by dividing total contribution margin by net income.

    **b.** provides a measure of the company's earnings volatility.

    **c.** affects a company's break-even point.

    **d.** All of the answer choices are correct.

13. **(LO 4)** A high degree of operating leverage:

    **a.** indicates that a company has a larger percentage of variable costs relative to its fixed costs.

    **b.** is computed by dividing fixed costs by contribution margin.

    **c.** exposes a company to greater earnings volatility risk.

    **d.** exposes a company to less earnings volatility risk.

14. **(LO 4)** Stevens Company has a degree of operating leverage of 3.5 at a sales level of $1,200,000 and net income of $200,000. If Stevens' sales fall by 10%, Stevens can be expected to experience a:

    **a.** decrease in net income of $70,000.

    **b.** decrease in contribution margin of $7,000.

    **c.** decrease in operating leverage of 35%.

    **d.** decrease in net income of $175,000.

*15. **(LO 5)** Fixed manufacturing overhead costs are recognized as:

    **a.** period costs under absorption costing.

    **b.** product costs under absorption costs.

    **c.** product costs under variable costing.

    **d.** part of ending inventory costs under both absorption and variable costing.

*16. **(LO 5)** Net income computed under absorption costing will be:

    **a.** higher than net income computed under variable costing in all cases.

    **b.** equal to net income computed under variable costing in all cases.

    **c.** higher than net income computed under variable costing when units produced are greater than units sold.

    **d.** higher than net income computed under variable costing when units produced are less than units sold.

## Solutions

1. **d.** The format of a CVP income statement is Sales − Variable costs − Fixed costs = Net income. Therefore, choices (a), (b), and (c) are incorrect.

2. **d.** If contribution margin is less than zero, selling price is less than variable costs. The other choices are incorrect because if contribution margin is less than zero (a) selling price, not fixed costs, is less than variable costs; (b) neither profits or total costs can be determined from the contribution margin amount; and (c) selling more units will only increase the negativity of the contribution margin.

3. **a.** The break-even point is the point where total sales equal total variable costs plus total fixed costs. Choices (b), (c), and (d) are therefore incorrect.

4. **a.** The CVP income statement would show Sales ($350,000) − Total variable expenses ($100,000) = Contribution margin ($250,000), not (b) contribution margin of $190,000. Choices (c) and (d) are incorrect because gross profit does not appear on a CVP income statement.

5. **b.** Required sales in units to achieve net income = ($180,000 + $268,000)/($12 − $8.50) = 128,000 units, not (a) 51,429 units, (c) 76,571 units, or (d) 21,176 units.

6. **d.** Fixed costs ($150,000) ÷ Contribution margin ratio ($3 ÷ $12) = $600,000, not (a) $200,000, (b) $450,000, or (c) $480,000.

7. **d.** Sales mix is the relative percentage in which a company sells its multiple products. The other choices are incorrect because (a) sales mix is also important to accountants, and (b) absorption costing income statements are not needed. Choice (c) is an incorrect definition of sales mix.

8. **a.** Net income will be greater if more higher contribution margin units are sold than lower contribution units. Choices (b), (c), and (d) are therefore incorrect statements.

9. **b.** The contribution margin per unit of limited resource is Unit contribution margin ($15) ÷ Units of limited resource (3.0 machine hours) = $5, not (a) $25, (c) $4, or (d) none of the above.

10. **d.** Unit contribution margin of Product X ($26 ÷ 4) < unit contribution margin of Product Y ($14 ÷ 2), so the machine time should be applied toward the product with the higher unit contribution margin. Choices (a), (b), and (c) are incorrect because these options will not maximize MEM's income.

11. **d.** The company should apply additional capacity of the limited resource to providing more units of the product or service that has the highest unit contribution margin of that limited resource, not (a) the highest contribution margin, (b) the highest selling price, or (c) the highest gross profit.

12. **d.** All of the above statements about operating leverage are true. So while choices (a), (b), and (c) are true statements, choice (d) is the better answer.

13. **c.** A high degree of operating leverage exposes a company to greater earnings volatility risk. The other choices are incorrect because a high degree of operating leverage (a) means a company has higher fixed costs relative to variable costs, not vice versa; (b) is computed by dividing contribution margin by net income, not fixed costs by contribution margin; and (d) exposes a company to greater, not less, earnings volatility risk.

14. **a.** Net income ($200,000) × Operating leverage (3.5) × Decrease in sales (10%) = decrease in net income of $70,000, not (b) decrease in contribution margin of $7,000, (c) decrease in operating leverage of 35%, or (d) decrease in net income of $175,000.

*15. **b.** Under absorption costing, fixed manufacturing overhead costs and variable manufacturing overhead costs are both product costs. The other choices are incorrect because (a) fixed manufacturing overhead costs are recognized as product costs under absorption costing, not period costs; (c) under variable costing, fixed manufacturing costs are recognized as period costs; and (d) fixed manufacturing costs are part of ending inventory under absorption costing only.

*16. **c.** Net income is higher under absorption costing than under variable costing when units produced exceed units sold, not

(a) higher in all cases, (b) equal to net income under variable costing in all cases, or (d) higher when units produced are less than units sold.

## Practice Brief Exercises

1. **(LO 2)** Wifi Corporation sells three different models of a wifi extender. Model W5 sells for $60 and has variable costs of $45. Model W10 sells for $90 and has variable costs of $70. Model W15 sells for $300 and has variable costs of $260. The sales mix of the three models is W5, 50%; W10, 20%; and W15, 30%. What is the weighted-average unit contribution margin?

*Compute weighted-average unit contribution margin based on sales mix.*

**Solution**

1.

| Model | Sales Mix Percentage | Unit Contribution Margin | Weighted-Average Unit Contribution Margin |
|-------|------|-------|-------|
| W5 | 50% | $15 ($60 − $45) | $ 7.50 |
| W10 | 20% | $20 ($90 − $70) | 4.00 |
| W15 | 30% | $40 ($300 − $260) | 12.00 |
| | | | $23.50 |

2. **(LO 2)** Information for Wifi Corporation is given in **Practice Brief Exercise 1**. If the company has fixed costs of $246,750, how many units of each model must the company sell in order to break even?

*Compute break-even point in sales units for company with multiple products.*

**Solution**

2.    Total break-even = ($246,750 ÷ $23.50*) = 10,500 units

*Computed in **Practice Brief Exercise 1**

**Sales Units**

| | | |
|---|---|---|
| Units of W5 | = .50 × 10,500 = | 5,250 |
| Units of W10 | = .20 × 10,500 = | 2,100 |
| Units of W15 | = .30 × 10,500 = | 3,150 |
| | | 10,500 |

3. **(LO 3)** In Familia Company, data concerning two products are unit contribution margin— Product A $15, Product B $20; machine hours required for one unit—Product A 3, Product B 4. Compute the contribution margin per unit of limited resource for each product.

*Show allocation of limited resources.*

**Solution**

3.

| | Product A | Product B |
|---|---|---|
| Unit contribution margin (a) | $15 | $20 |
| Machine hours required (b) | 3 | 4 |
| Contribution margin per unit of limited resource [(a) ÷ (b)] | $ 5 | $ 5 |

4. **(LO 4)** Rachel Potato Chips is considering the purchase of a new automated potato-cutting machine. The new machine will reduce variable labor costs but will increase depreciation expense. Contribution margin is expected to increase from $150,000 to $225,000. Net income is expected to be the same at $50,000. Compute the degree of operating leverage before and after the purchase of the new equipment. Interpret your results.

*Compute degree of operating leverage.*

**Solution**

4. Degree of operating
   leverage (old) = $150,000 ÷ $50,000 = 3

   Degree of operating
   leverage (new) = $225,000 ÷ $50,000 = 4.5

   If Rachel's sales change, the resulting change in net income will be 1.5 times (4.5 ÷ 3) higher with the new machine than under the old system.

# Practice Exercises

*Compute break-even point in sales units for a company with more than one product.*

**1. (LO 2)** Yard-King manufactures lawnmowers, weed-trimmers, and chainsaws. Its sales mix and unit contribution margins are as follows.

| | Sales Mix | Unit Contribution Margin |
|---|---|---|
| Lawnmowers | 30% | $35 |
| Weed-trimmers | 50 | 25 |
| Chainsaws | 20 | 50 |

Yard-King has fixed costs of $4,620,000.

**Instructions**

Compute the number of units of each product that Yard-King must sell in order to break even under this product mix.

**Solution**

1.

| | Sales Mix Percentage | Unit Contribution Margin | Weighted-Average Contribution Margin |
|---|---|---|---|
| Lawnmowers | 30% | $35 | $10.50 |
| Weed-trimmers | 50 | 25 | 12.50 |
| Chainsaws | 20 | 50 | 10.00 |
| | | | $33.00 |

Total break-even sales in units = $4,620,000 ÷ $33.00 = 140,000 units

| | Sales Mix Percentage | | Total Break-Even Sales | | Sales Needed per Product |
|---|---|---|---|---|---|
| Lawnmowers | 30% | × | 140,000 units | = | 42,000 units |
| Weed-trimmers | 50 | × | 140,000 | = | 70,000 |
| Chainsaws | 20 | × | 140,000 | = | 28,000 |
| Total units | | | | | 140,000 units |

*Compute contribution margin and determine the product to be manufactured.*

**2. (LO 3)** Rene Company manufactures and sells three products. Relevant per unit data concerning each product are given below.

| | Product | | |
|---|---|---|---|
| | A | B | C |
| Selling price | $12 | $13 | $15 |
| Variable costs and expenses | $ 4 | $ 8 | $ 9 |
| Machine hours to produce | 2 | 1 | 2 |

## Instructions

**a.** Compute the contribution margin per unit of limited resource (machine hours) for each product.

**b.** Assuming 4,500 additional machine hours are available, which product should be manufactured and why?

**c.** Prepare an analysis showing the total contribution margin if the additional hours are (1) divided equally among the products, and (2) allocated entirely to the product identified in (b) above.

## Solution

**2. a.**

| | Product | | |
|---|---|---|---|
| | **A** | **B** | **C** |
| Unit contribution margin (a) | $8 | $5 | $6 |
| Machine hours required (b) | 2 | 1 | 2 |
| Contribution margin per unit of limited resource (a) ÷ (b) | $4 | $5 | $3 |

**b.** Product B should be manufactured because it results in the highest contribution margin per machine hour.

**c. 1.**

| | Product | | |
|---|---|---|---|
| | **A** | **B** | **C** |
| Machine hours (a) (4,500 ÷ 3) | 1,500 | 1,500 | 1,500 |
| Contribution margin per unit of limited resource (b) | $   4 | $   5 | $   3 |
| Total contribution margin [(a)] × [(b)] | $6,000 | $7,500 | $4,500 |

The total contribution margin is $18,000 ($6,000 + $7,500 + $4,500)

**2.**

| | Product |
|---|---|
| | **B** |
| Machine hours (a) | 4,500 |
| Contribution margin per unit of limited resource (b) | $   5 |
| Total contribution margin [(a) × (b)] | $22,500 |

**3. (LO 4)** The CVP income statements shown below are available for Vericelli Company and Boone Company.

*Compute degree of operating leverage and evaluate impact of alternative cost structures on net income.*

| | Vericelli Co. | Boone Co. |
|---|---|---|
| Sales revenue | $600,000 | $600,000 |
| Variable costs | 320,000 | 120,000 |
| Contribution margin | 280,000 | 480,000 |
| Fixed costs | 180,000 | 380,000 |
| Net income | $100,000 | $100,000 |

## Instructions

**a.** Compute the degree of operating leverage for each company and interpret your results.

**b.** Assuming that sales revenue increases by 10%, prepare a variable costing income statement for each company.

**c.** Discuss how the cost structure of these two companies affects their operating leverage and profitability.

**Solution**

3. **a.**

| | Contribution Margin | ÷ | Net Income | = | Degree of Operating Leverage |
|---|---|---|---|---|---|
| Vericelli | $280,000 | ÷ | $100,000 | = | 2.8 |
| Boone | 480,000 | ÷ | 100,000 | = | 4.8 |

Boone has a higher degree of operating leverage. Its earnings would increase (decrease) by a greater amount than Vericelli if each experienced an equal increase (decrease) in sales.

**b.**

| | Vericelli Co. | Boone Co. |
|---|---|---|
| Sales revenue | $660,000* | $660,000 |
| Variable costs | 352,000** | 132,000*** |
| Contribution margin | 308,000 | 528,000 |
| Fixed costs | 180,000 | 380,000 |
| Net income | $128,000 | $148,000 |

*$600,000 × 1.1    **$320,000 × 1.1    ***$120,000 × 1.1

**c.** Each company experienced a $60,000 increase in sales. However, because of Boone's higher operating leverage, it experienced a $48,000 ($148,000 − $100,000) increase in net income while Vericelli experienced only a $28,000 ($128,000 − $100,000) increase. This is what we would have expected since Boone's degree of operating leverage exceeds that of Vericelli.

# Practice Problem

*Determine sales mix with limited resources.*

**(LO 3)** Francis Corporation manufactures and sells three different types of water-sport wakeboards. The boards vary in terms of their quality specifications—primarily with respect to their smoothness and finish. They are referred to as Smooth, Extra-Smooth, and Super- Smooth boards. Machine time is limited. More machine time is required to manufacture the Extra-Smooth and Super-Smooth boards. Additional information on a per unit basis is provided below.

| | Product | | |
|---|---|---|---|
| | Smooth | Extra-Smooth | Super-Smooth |
| Selling price | $60 | $100 | $160 |
| Variable costs and expenses | 50 | 75 | 130 |
| Contribution margin | $10 | $ 25 | $ 30 |
| Machine hours required | 0.25 | 0.40 | 0.60 |

Total fixed costs: $234,000

## Instructions

Answer each of the following questions.

**a.** Ignoring the machine time constraint, what strategy would appear optimal?

**b.** What is the contribution margin per unit of limited resource for each type of board?

**c.** If additional machine time could be obtained, how should the additional capacity be used?

## Solution

**a.** The Super-Smooth boards have the highest unit contribution margin. Thus, ignoring any manufacturing constraints, it would appear that the company should shift toward production of more Super-Smooth units.

**b.** The contribution margin per unit of limited resource is calculated as follows.

| | Smooth | Extra-Smooth | Super-Smooth |
|---|---|---|---|
| $\dfrac{\text{Unit contribution margin}}{\text{Limited resource consumed per unit}}$ | $\dfrac{\$10}{.25} = \$40$ | $\dfrac{\$25}{.40} = \$62.50$ | $\dfrac{\$30}{.60} = \$50$ |

**c.** The Extra-Smooth boards have the highest contribution margin per unit of limited resource. Given the resource constraint, any additional capacity should be used to make Extra-Smooth boards.

---

Brief Exercises, DO IT! Exercises, Exercises, Problems, Data Analytics Activities, and many additional resources are available for practice in WileyPLUS.

---

*Note:* All asterisked Questions, Exercises, and Problems relate to material in the appendix to this chapter.

## Questions

**1.** What is meant by CVP analysis?

**2.** Provide three examples of management decisions that benefit from CVP analysis.

**3.** Distinguish between a traditional GAAP income statement and a CVP income statement.

**4.** Describe the features of a CVP income statement that make it more useful for management decision-making than the traditional GAAP income statement that is prepared for external users.

**5.** The traditional GAAP income statement for Wheat Company shows sales $900,000, cost of goods sold $500,000, and operating expenses $200,000. Assuming all costs and expenses are 75% variable and 25% fixed, prepare a CVP income statement through contribution margin.

**6.** If management chooses to reduce its selling price to match that of a competitor, how will the break-even point be affected?

**7.** What is meant by the term sales mix? How does sales mix affect the calculation of the break-even point?

**8.** Performance Company sells two types of performance tires. The lower-priced model is guaranteed for only 50,000 miles; the higher-priced model is guaranteed for 150,000 miles. The unit contribution margin on the higher-priced tire is twice as high as that of the lower-priced tire. If the sales mix shifts so that the company begins to sell more units of the lower-priced tire, explain how the company's break-even point in units will change.

**9.** What approach should be used to calculate the break-even point of a company that has many products?

**10.** How is the contribution margin per unit of limited resource computed?

**11.** What is the theory of constraints? Provide some examples of possible constraints for a manufacturer.

**12.** What is meant by "cost structure?" Explain how a company's cost structure affects its break-even point.

**13.** What is operating leverage? How does a company increase its operating leverage?

**14.** How does the replacement of manual labor with automated equipment affect a company's cost structure? What implications does this have for its operating leverage and break-even point?

**15.** What is a measure of operating leverage, and how is it calculated?

**16.** Pine Company has a degree of operating leverage of 8. Fir Company has a degree of operating leverage of 4. Interpret these measures.

**\*17.** Distinguish between absorption costing and variable costing.

**\*18. a.** What is the major rationale for the use of variable costing?

　　　**b.** Discuss why variable costing cannot be used for financial reporting purposes.

**\*19.** Doe Rowan Corporation sells one product, its waterproof hiking boot. It began operations in the current year and had an ending inventory of 8,500 units. The company sold 20,000 units throughout the year. Fixed manufacturing overhead is $5 per unit, and total manufacturing cost per unit is $20 (including fixed manufacturing overhead costs). What is the difference in net income between absorption and variable costing?

**\*20.** If production equals sales, what, if any, is the difference between net income under absorption costing versus under variable costing?

**\*21.** If production is greater than sales, how does absorption costing net income differ from variable costing net income?

**\*22.** In the long run, will net income be higher or lower under variable costing compared to absorption costing?

## Brief Exercises

*Determine missing amounts for contribution margin.*

**BE19.1 (LO 1), AN** Determine the missing amounts.

| | Unit Selling Price | Unit Variable Costs | Unit Contribution Margin | Contribution Margin Ratio |
|---|---|---|---|---|
| 1. | $250 | $180 | (a) | (b) |
| 2. | $500 | (c) | $200 | (d) |
| 3. | (e) | (f) | $330 | 30% |

*Prepare CVP income statement.*

**BE19.2 (LO 1), AP** Hamby Inc. has sales of $2,000,000 for the first quarter of 2022. In making the sales, the company incurred the following costs and expenses.

| | Variable | Fixed |
|---|---|---|
| Cost of goods sold | $760,000 | $600,000 |
| Selling expenses | 95,000 | 60,000 |
| Administrative expenses | 79,000 | 66,000 |

Prepare a CVP income statement for the quarter ended March 31, 2022.

*Compute the break-even point.*

**BE19.3 (LO 1), AP** Eastland Corp. had total variable costs of $150,000, total fixed costs of $120,000, and total revenues of $250,000. Compute the required sales in dollars to break even.

*Compute the break-even point.*

**BE19.4 (LO 1), AP** Dilts Company has a unit selling price of $400, unit variable costs of $250, and fixed costs of $210,000. Compute the break-even point in sales units using (a) the mathematical equation and (b) unit contribution margin.

*Compute sales for target net income.*

**BE19.5 (LO 1), AP** For Rivera Company, variable costs are 70% of sales, and fixed costs are $210,000. Management's net income goal is $60,000. Compute the required sales needed to achieve management's target net income of $60,000. (Use the mathematical equation approach.)

*Compute the margin of safety and the margin of safety ratio.*

**BE19.6 (LO 1), AP** For Kosko Company, actual sales are $1,200,000 and break-even sales are $960,000. Compute (a) the margin of safety in dollars and (b) the margin of safety ratio.

*Compute weighted-average unit contribution margin based on sales mix.*

**BE19.7 (LO 2), AP** NoFly Corporation sells three different models of a mosquito "zapper." Model A12 sells for $50 and has variable costs of $35. Model B22 sells for $100 and has variable costs of $70. Model C124 sells for $400 and has variable costs of $300. The sales mix of the three models is A12, 60%: B22, 15%; and C124, 25%. What is the weighted-average unit contribution margin?

*Compute break-even point in sales units for company with multiple products.*

**BE19.8 (LO 2), AP** Information for NoFly Corporation is given in BE19.7. If the company has fixed costs of $269,500, how many units of each model must the company sell in order to break even?

*Compute break-even point in sales dollars for company with multiple product lines.*

**BE19.9 (LO 2), AP** Dixie Candle Supply makes candles. The sales mix (as a percentage of total dollar sales) of its three product lines is birthday candles 30%, standard tapered candles 50%, and large scented candles 20%. The contribution margin ratio of each candle type is shown below.

| Candle Type | Contribution Margin Ratio |
|---|---|
| Birthday | 20% |
| Standard tapered | 30% |
| Large scented | 45% |

a. What is the weighted-average contribution margin ratio?

b. If the company's fixed costs are $450,000 per year, what is the sales dollar amount of each type of candle that must be sold to break even?

*Determine weighted-average contribution margin.*

**BE19.10 (LO 2), AP** Faune Furniture Co. consists of two divisions, Bedroom Division and Dining Room Division. The results of operations for the most recent quarter are:

| | Bedroom Division | Dining Room Division | Total |
|---|---|---|---|
| Sales | $500,000 | $750,000 | $1,250,000 |
| Variable costs | 225,000 | 450,000 | 675,000 |
| Contribution margin | $275,000 | $300,000 | $ 575,000 |

a. Determine the company's sales mix based on sales revenue.

b. Determine the company's weighted-average contribution margin ratio.

**BE19.11 (LO 3), AP** In Marshall Company, data concerning two products are unit contribution margin— Product A $10, Product B $12; machine hours required for one unit—Product A 2, Product B 3. Compute the contribution margin per unit of limited resource for each product.

*Show allocation of limited resources.*

**BE19.12 (LO 3), AP** Sage Corporation manufactures two products with the following characteristics.

*Show allocation of limited resources.*

|  | Unit Contribution Margin | Machine Hours Required for Production |
|---|---|---|
| Product 1 | $42 | .15 hours |
| Product 2 | $32 | .10 hours |

If Sage's machine hours are limited to 2,000 per month, determine which product it should produce.

**BE19.13 (LO 4), AP** Sam's Shingle Corporation is considering the purchase of a new automated shingle-cutting machine. The new machine will reduce variable labor costs but will increase depreciation expense. Contribution margin is expected to increase from $200,000 to $240,000. Net income is expected to be the same at $40,000. Compute the degree of operating leverage before and after the purchase of the new equipment. Interpret your results.

*Compute degree of operating leverage.*

**BE19.14 (LO 4), AP** Presented below are variable costing income statements for Diggs Company and Doggs Company. They are in the same industry, with the same net incomes, but different cost structures.

*Compute break-even point with change in operating leverage.*

|  | Diggs Co. | Doggs Co. |
|---|---|---|
| Sales | $200,000 | $200,000 |
| Variable costs | 80,000 | 50,000 |
| Contribution margin | 120,000 | 150,000 |
| Fixed costs | 75,000 | 105,000 |
| Net income | $ 45,000 | $ 45,000 |

Compute the break-even point in sales dollars for each company and comment on your findings.

**BE19.15 (LO 4), AP** The degree of operating leverage for Montana Corp. and APK Co. are 1.6 and 5.4, respectively. Both have net incomes of $50,000. Determine their respective contribution margins.

*Determine contribution margin from degree of operating leverage.*

**\*BE19.16 (LO 5), AP** The Rock Company produces basketballs. It incurred the following costs during the year.

*Compute product costs under variable costing.*

| Direct materials | $14,400 |
|---|---|
| Direct labor | $25,600 |
| Fixed manufacturing overhead | $12,000 |
| Variable manufacturing overhead | $29,400 |
| Selling costs | $21,000 |

What are the total product costs for the company under variable costing?

**\*BE19.17 (LO 5), AP** Information concerning The Rock Company is provided in BE19.16. What are the total product costs for the company under absorption costing?

*Compute product costs under absorption costing.*

**\*BE19.18 (LO 5), AP** Burns Company incurred the following costs during the year: direct materials $20 per unit; direct labor $14 per unit; variable manufacturing overhead $15 per unit; variable selling and administrative costs $8 per unit; fixed manufacturing overhead $128,000; and fixed selling and administrative costs $10,000. Burns produced 8,000 units and sold 6,000 units. Determine the manufacturing cost per unit under (a) absorption costing and (b) variable costing.

*Determine manufacturing cost per unit under absorption and variable costing.*

**\*BE19.19 (LO 5), AP** **Writing** Harris Company's fixed overhead costs are $4 per unit, and its variable overhead costs are $8 per unit. In the first month of operations, 50,000 units are produced, and 46,000 units are sold. Write a short memo to the chief financial officer explaining which costing approach will produce the higher income and what the difference will be.

## DO IT! Exercises

*Compute the break-even point and margin of safety under different alternatives.*

**DO IT! 19.1 (LO 1), AP** Victoria Company reports the following operating results for the month of April.

**Victoria Company**
**CVP Income Statement**
**For the Month Ended April 30, 2022**

|  | Total | Per Unit | Percent of Sales |
|---|---|---|---|
| Sales (9,000 units) | $450,000 | $50 | 100% |
| Variable costs | 270,000 | 30 | 60 |
| Contribution margin | 180,000 | $20 | 40% |
| Fixed expenses | 150,000 |  |  |
| Net income | $ 30,000 |  |  |

Management is considering the following course of action to increase net income: Reduce the selling price by 4%, with no changes to unit variable costs or fixed costs. Management is confident that this change will increase unit sales by 20%.

Using the contribution margin technique, compute the break-even point in sales units and sales dollars and margin of safety in dollars:

a. Assuming no changes to selling price or costs, and

b. Assuming changes to sales price and volume as described above.

Comment on your findings.

*Compute sales mix, weighted-average contribution margin, and break-even point.*

**DO IT! 19.2 (LO 2), AP** Snow Cap Springs produces and sells water filtration systems for homeowners. Information regarding its three models is shown below.

|  | Basic | Basic Plus | Premium | Total |
|---|---|---|---|---|
| Units sold | 750 | 450 | 300 | 1,500 |
| Selling price | $250 | $400 | $800 |  |
| Variable costs | $195 | $285 | $415 |  |

The company's total fixed costs to produce the filtration systems are $180,700.

a. Determine the sales mix as a function of units sold for the three products.

b. Determine the weighted-average unit contribution margin.

c. Determine the total number of units that the company must produce to break even.

d. Determine the number of units of each model that the company must produce to break even.

*Determine sales mix with limited resources.*

**DO IT! 19.3 (LO 3), AP** Zoom Corporation manufactures and sells three different types of binoculars. They are referred to as Good, Better, and Best binoculars. Grinding and polishing time is limited. More time is required to grind and polish the lenses used in the Better and Best binoculars. Additional information is provided below.

|  | Product | | |
|---|---|---|---|
|  | Good | Better | Best |
| Selling price | $90.00 | $330.00 | $900.00 |
| Variable costs and expenses | 50.00 | 180.00 | 480.00 |
| Contribution margin | $40.00 | $150.00 | $420.00 |
| Grinding and polishing time required | 0.5 hrs | 1.5 hrs | 6 hrs |

a. Ignoring the time constraint, what strategy would appear to be optimal?

b. What is the contribution margin per unit of limited resource for each type of binocular?

c. If additional grinding and polishing time could be obtained, how should the additional capacity be used?

*Determine operating leverage.*

**DO IT! 19.4 (LO 4), AP** Bergen Hospital is contemplating an investment in an automated surgical system. Its current process relies on the a number of skilled physicians. The new equipment would employ a computer robotic system operated by a technician. The company requested an analysis of the old technology versus the new technology. The accounting department has prepared the following CVP income statements for use in your analysis.

|  | Old | New |
|---|---|---|
| Sales | $3,000,000 | $3,000,000 |
| Variable costs | 1,600,000 | 700,000 |
| Contribution margin | 1,400,000 | 2,300,000 |
| Fixed costs | 1,000,000 | 1,900,000 |
| Net income | $ 400,000 | $ 400,000 |

**a.** Compute the degree of operating leverage for the company under each scenario.

**b.** Discuss your results.

## Exercises

**E19.1 (LO 1), AP** Service  The Soma Inn is trying to determine its break-even point. The inn has 75 rooms that are rented at $50 a night. Operating costs are as follows.

*Compute break-even point and margin of safety.*

| Salaries | $10,600 per month |
|---|---|
| Utilities | 2,400 per month |
| Depreciation | 1,500 per month |
| Maintenance | 800 per month |
| Maid service | 8 per room |
| Other costs | 34 per room |

### Instructions

**a.** Determine the inn's break-even point in (1) number of rented rooms per month and (2) sales dollars.

**b.** If the inn plans on renting an average of 50 rooms per day (assuming a 30-day month), what is (1) the monthly margin of safety in dollars and (2) the margin of safety ratio?

**E19.2 (LO 1), AP** Service  In the month of June, Jose Hebert's Beauty Salon gave 4,000 haircuts, shampoos, and hair colorings at an average price of $30 each. During the month, fixed costs were $16,800 and variable costs were 75% of sales.

*Compute contribution margin, break-even point, and margin of safety.*

### Instructions

**a.** Determine the contribution margin in dollars, per unit and as a ratio.

**b.** Using the contribution margin technique, compute the break-even point in sales dollars and in sales units.

**c.** Compute the margin of safety in dollars and as a ratio.

**E19.3 (LO 1), AP** Barnes Company reports the following operating results for the month of August: sales $325,000 (units 5,000); variable costs $210,000; and fixed costs $75,000. Management is considering the following independent courses of action to increase net income.

*Compute net income under different alternatives.*

**1.** Increase selling price by 10% with no change in total variable costs or sales volume.

**2.** Reduce variable costs to 58% of sales.

**3.** Reduce fixed costs by $15,000.

### Instructions

Compute the net income to be earned under each alternative. Which course of action will produce the highest net income?

**E19.4 (LO 1), AP** Service  Comfi Airways, Inc., a small two-plane passenger airline, has asked for your assistance in some basic analysis of its operations. Both planes seat 10 passengers each, and they fly commuters from Comfi's base airport to the major city in the state, Metropolis. Each month, 40 round-trip flights are made. The following is a recent month's activity in the form of a cost-volume-profit income statement.

*Compute break-even point and prepare CVP income statement.*

| | | |
|---|---:|---:|
| Fare revenues (400 passenger flights) | | $48,000 |
| Variable costs | | |
| Fuel | $14,000 | |
| Snacks and drinks | 800 | |
| Landing fees | 2,000 | |
| Supplies and forms | 1,200 | 18,000 |
| Contribution margin | | 30,000 |
| Fixed costs | | |
| Depreciation | 3,000 | |
| Salaries | 15,000 | |
| Advertising | 500 | |
| Airport hangar fees | 1,750 | 20,250 |
| Net income | | $ 9,750 |

### Instructions

a. Calculate the break-even point in (1) sales dollars and (2) number of passenger flights.

b. Without calculations, determine the contribution margin at the break-even point.

c. If ticket prices were decreased by 10%, passenger flights would increase by 25%. However, total variable costs would increase by the same percentage as passenger flights. Should the ticket price decrease be adopted?

*Prepare a CVP income statement before and after changes in business environment.*

**E19.5 (LO 1), AP**  Carey Company had sales in 2021 of $1,500,000 on 60,000 units. Variable costs totaled $900,000, and fixed costs totaled $500,000.

A new raw material is available that will decrease the unit variable costs by 20% (or $3). However, to process the new raw material, fixed operating costs will increase by $100,000. Management feels that one-half of the decline in the unit variable costs should be passed on to customers in the form of a sales price reduction. The marketing department expects that this sales price reduction will result in a 5% increase in the number of units sold.

### Instructions

Prepare a projected CVP income statement for 2022 (a) assuming the changes have not been made, and (b) assuming that changes are made as described.

*Compute break-even point in sales units for a company with more than one product.*

**E19.6 (LO 2), AP**  Yard Tools manufactures lawnmowers, weed-trimmers, and chainsaws. Its sales mix and unit contribution margin are as follows.

| | Sales Mix | Unit Contribution Margin |
|---|:---:|:---:|
| Lawnmowers | 20% | $30 |
| Weed-trimmers | 50% | $20 |
| Chainsaws | 30% | $40 |

Yard Tools has fixed costs of $4,200,000.

### Instructions

Compute the number of units of each product that Yard Tools must sell in order to break even under this product mix.

*Compute service line break-even point and target net income in dollars for a company with more than one service.*

**E19.7 (LO 2), AN** Service  PDQ Repairs has 200 auto-maintenance service outlets nationwide. It performs primarily two lines of service: oil changes and brake repair. Oil change–related services represent 70% of its sales and provide a contribution margin ratio of 20%. Brake repair represents 30% of its sales and provides a 40% contribution margin ratio. The company's fixed costs are $15,600,000 (that is, $78,000 per service outlet).

### Instructions

a. Calculate the dollar amount of each type of service that the company must provide in order to break even.

b. The company has a desired net income of $52,000 per service outlet. What is the dollar amount of each type of service that must be performed by each service outlet to meet its target net income per outlet?

*Compute break-even point in sales dollars for a company with more than one service.*

**E19.8 (LO 2), AN** Service  Express Delivery is a rapidly growing delivery service. Last year, 80% of its revenue came from the delivery of mailing "pouches" and small, standardized delivery boxes (which provides a 20% contribution margin). The other 20% of its revenue came from delivering non-standardized boxes (which provides a 70% contribution margin). With the rapid growth of Internet retail sales, Express believes that there are great opportunities for growth in the delivery of non-standardized boxes. The company has fixed costs of $12,000,000.

**Instructions**

a. What is the company's break-even point in total sales dollars? At the break-even point, how much of the company's sales are provided by each type of service?

b. The company's management would like to hold its fixed costs constant but shift its sales mix so that 60% of its revenue comes from the delivery of non-standardized boxes and the remainder from pouches and small boxes. If this were to occur, what would be the company's break-even sales, and what amount of sales would be provided by each service type?

**E19.9 (LO 2), AP** Tiger Golf Accessories sells golf shoes, gloves, and a laser-guided range-finder that measures distance. Shown below are unit cost and sales data.

*Compute break-even point in sales units for a company with multiple products.*

|  | Pairs of Shoes | Pairs of Gloves | Range-Finder |
|---|---|---|---|
| Unit sales price | $100 | $30 | $260 |
| Unit variable costs | 60 | 10 | 200 |
| Unit contribution margin | $ 40 | $20 | $ 60 |
| Sales mix | 35% | 55% | 10% |

Fixed costs are $620,000.

**Instructions**

a. Compute the break-even point in sales units for the company.

b. Determine the number of units to be sold at the break-even point for each product line.

c. Verify that the mix of sales units determined in (b) will generate a zero net income.

**E19.10 (LO 2), AP** Personal Electronix sells computer tablets and MP3 players. The business is divided into two divisions along product lines. CVP income statements for a recent quarter's activity are presented below.

*Determine break-even point in sales dollars for two divisions.*

|  | Tablet Division | MP3 Player Division | Total |
|---|---|---|---|
| Sales | $600,000 | $400,000 | $1,000,000 |
| Variable costs | 420,000 | 260,000 | 680,000 |
| Contribution margin | $180,000 | $140,000 | 320,000 |
| Fixed costs |  |  | 120,000 |
| Net income |  |  | $ 200,000 |

**Instructions**

a. Determine the sales mix percentage based on sales revenue and contribution margin ratio for each division.

b. Calculate the company's weighted-average contribution margin ratio.

c. Calculate the company's break-even point in sales dollars.

d. Determine the sales level in dollars for each division at the break-even point.

**E19.11 (LO 3), AN** Mars Company manufactures and sells three products. Relevant per unit data concerning each product are given below.

*Compute contribution margin and determine the product to be manufactured.*

|  | Product | | |
|---|---|---|---|
|  | A | B | C |
| Selling price | $9 | $12 | $15 |
| Variable costs and expenses | $3 | $10 | $12 |
| Machine hours to produce | 2 | 1 | 2 |

**Instructions**

a. Compute the contribution margin per unit of limited resource (machine hours) for each product.

b. Assuming 3,000 additional machine hours are available, which product should be manufactured?

c. Prepare an analysis showing the total contribution margin if the additional hours are (1) divided equally among the products, and (2) allocated entirely to the product identified in (b) above.

*Compute contribution margin and determine the products to be manufactured.*

**E19.12 (LO 3), AN** Dalton Inc. produces and sells three products. Unit data concerning each product are shown below.

| | Product | | |
|---|---|---|---|
| | **D** | **E** | **F** |
| Selling price | $200 | $300 | $250 |
| Direct labor costs | 30 | 80 | 35 |
| Other variable costs | 95 | 80 | 145 |

The company has 2,000 hours of labor available to build inventory in anticipation of the company's peak season. Management is trying to decide which product should be produced. The direct labor hourly rate is $10.

**Instructions**

a. Determine the number of direct labor hours per unit.

b. Determine the contribution margin per direct labor hour.

c. Determine which product should be produced and the total contribution margin for that product.

*Compute contribution margin and determine the products to be manufactured.*

**E19.13 (LO 3), AN** Helena Company manufactures and sells two products. Relevant per unit data concerning each product follow.

| | Product | |
|---|---|---|
| | **Basic** | **Deluxe** |
| Selling price | $40 | $52 |
| Variable costs | $22 | $24 |
| Machine hours | 0.5 | 0.8 |

**Instructions**

a. Compute the contribution margin per machine hour for each product.

b. If 1,000 additional machine hours are available, which product should Helena manufacture?

c. Prepare an analysis showing the total contribution margin if the additional hours are:

1. Divided equally between the products.

2. Allocated entirely to the product identified in part (b).

*Compute degree of operating leverage and evaluate impact of alternative cost structures on net income.*

**E19.14 (LO 4), AN** The single-column CVP income statements shown below are available for Armstrong Company and Contador Company.

| | **Armstrong Co.** | **Contador Co.** |
|---|---|---|
| Sales | $500,000 | $500,000 |
| Variable costs | 240,000 | 50,000 |
| Contribution margin | 260,000 | 450,000 |
| Fixed costs | 160,000 | 350,000 |
| Net income | $100,000 | $100,000 |

**Instructions**

a. Compute the degree of operating leverage for each company and interpret your results.

b. Assuming that sales revenue increases by 10%, restate the single-column CVP income statement from above for each company.

c. Discuss how the cost structure of these two companies affects their operating leverage and profitability.

*Compute degree of operating leverage and evaluate impact of alternative cost structures on net income and margin of safety.*

**E19.15 (LO 4), AN** Service Casas Modernas of Juarez, Mexico, is contemplating a major change in its cost structure. Currently, all of its drafting work is performed by skilled draftsmen. Rafael Jiminez, Casas' owner, is considering replacing the draftsmen with a computerized drafting system. However, before making the change, Rafael would like to know the consequences of the change, since the volume of business varies significantly from year to year. Shown below are CVP income statements for each alternative.

| | **Manual System** | **Computerized System** |
|---|---|---|
| Sales | $1,500,000 | $1,500,000 |
| Variable costs | 1,200,000 | 600,000 |
| Contribution margin | 300,000 | 900,000 |
| Fixed costs | 100,000 | 700,000 |
| Net income | $ 200,000 | $ 200,000 |

## Instructions

**a.** Determine the degree of operating leverage for each alternative.

**b.** Which alternative would produce the higher net income if sales increased by $150,000?

**c.** Using the margin of safety ratio, determine which alternative could sustain the greater decline in sales before operating at a loss.

**E19.16 (LO 4), AN** An investment banker is analyzing two companies that specialize in the production and sale of candied yams. Traditional Yams uses a labor-intensive approach, and Auto-Yams uses a mechanized system. CVP income statements for the two companies are shown below.

*Compute degree of operating leverage and impact on net income of alternative cost structures.*

|  | Traditional Yams | Auto-Yams |
| --- | --- | --- |
| Sales | $400,000 | $400,000 |
| Variable costs | 320,000 | 160,000 |
| Contribution margin | 80,000 | 240,000 |
| Fixed costs | 30,000 | 190,000 |
| Net income | $ 50,000 | $ 50,000 |

The investment banker is interested in acquiring one of these companies. However, she is concerned about the impact that each company's cost structure might have on its profitability.

## Instructions

**a.** Calculate each company's degree of operating leverage. Determine which company's cost structure makes it more sensitive to changes in sales volume.

**b.** Determine the effect on each company's net income if sales decrease by 15% and if sales increase by 10%. Do not prepare income statements.

**c.** Which company should the investment banker acquire? Discuss.

*E19.17 (LO 5), AP** Siren Company builds custom fishing lures for sporting goods stores. In its first year of operations, 2022, the company incurred the following costs.

*Compute product cost and prepare an income statement under variable and absorption costing.*

 **Excel**

### Unit Variable Costs

| | |
| --- | --- |
| Direct materials | $7.50 |
| Direct labor | $3.45 |
| Variable manufacturing overhead | $5.80 |
| Variable selling and administrative expenses | $3.90 |

### Annual Fixed Costs

| | |
| --- | --- |
| Fixed manufacturing overhead | $225,000 |
| Fixed selling and administrative expenses | $210,100 |

Siren Company sells the fishing lures for $25. During 2022, the company sold 80,000 lures and produced 90,000 lures.

## Instructions

**a.** Assuming the company uses variable costing, calculate Siren's manufacturing cost per unit for 2022.

**b.** Prepare a variable costing income statement for 2022.

**c.** Assuming the company uses absorption costing, calculate Siren's manufacturing cost per unit for 2022.

**d.** Prepare an absorption costing income statement for 2022.

*E19.18 (LO 5), AN** Langdon Company produced 9,000 units during the past year, but only 8,200 of the units were sold. The following additional information is also available.

*Determine ending inventory under variable costing and determine whether absorption or variable costing would result in higher net income.*

| | |
| --- | --- |
| Direct materials used | $79,000 |
| Direct labor incurred | $30,000 |
| Variable manufacturing overhead | $21,500 |
| Fixed manufacturing overhead | $45,000 |
| Fixed selling and administrative expenses | $70,000 |
| Variable selling and administrative expenses | $10,000 |

There was no work in process inventory at the beginning and end of the year, nor did Langdon have any beginning finished goods inventory.

**Instructions**

a. What would be Langdon Company's finished goods inventory cost on December 31 under variable costing?

b. Which costing method, absorption or variable costing, would show a higher net income for the year? By what amount?

*Compute manufacturing cost under absorption and variable costing and explain difference.*

\*E19.19 **(LO 5), AN** Crate Express Co. produces wooden crates used for shipping products by ocean liner. In 2022, Crate Express incurred the following costs.

| | |
|---|---:|
| Wood used in crate production | $54,000 |
| Nails (considered insignificant and a variable expense) | 350 |
| Direct labor | 43,000 |
| Utilities for the factory: | |
| $1,500 each month, | |
| plus $0.50 for each kilowatt-hour used each month | |
| Rent expense for the factory for the year | 21,400 |

Assume Crate Express used an average 500 kilowatt-hours each month over the past year.

**Instructions**

a. What is Crate Express's total manufacturing cost if it uses a variable costing approach?

b. What is Crate Express's total manufacturing cost if it uses an absorption costing approach?

c. What accounts for the difference in manufacturing costs between these two costing approaches?

# Problems

*Compute break-even point under alternative courses of action.*

P19.1 **(LO 1), AN** Midlands Inc. had a bad year in 2021. For the first time in its history, it operated at a loss. The company's income statement showed the following results from selling 80,000 units of product: net sales $2,000,000; total costs and expenses $2,235,000; and net loss $235,000. Costs and expenses consisted of the following.

| | Total | Variable | Fixed |
|---|---:|---:|---:|
| Cost of goods sold | $1,568,000 | $1,050,000 | $ 518,000 |
| Selling expenses | 517,000 | 92,000 | 425,000 |
| Administrative expenses | 150,000 | 58,000 | 92,000 |
| | $2,235,000 | $1,200,000 | $1,035,000 |

Management is considering the following independent alternatives for 2022.

1. Increase unit selling price 25% with no change in costs and expenses.

2. Change the compensation of salespersons from fixed annual salaries totaling $200,000 to total salaries of $40,000 plus a 5% commission on net sales.

3. Purchase new high-tech factory machinery that will change the proportion between variable and fixed cost of goods sold to 50:50.

**Instructions**

a. Compute the break-even point in sales dollars for 2021.

b. (2) $2,500,000

b. Compute the break-even point in sales dollars under each of the alternative courses of action for 2022. (Round to the nearest dollar.) Which course of action do you recommend?

*Compute break-even point and margin of safety ratio, and prepare a CVP income statement before and after changes in business environment.*

P19.2 **(LO 1), AN** Lorge Corporation has collected the following information after its first year of sales. Sales were $1,500,000 on 100,000 units; selling expenses $250,000 (40% variable and 60% fixed); direct materials $511,000; direct labor $290,000; administrative expenses $270,000 (20% variable and 80% fixed); and manufacturing overhead $350,000 (70% variable and 30% fixed). Top management has asked you to do a CVP analysis so that it can make plans for the coming year. It has projected that unit sales will increase by 10% next year.

**Instructions**

a. Compute (1) the contribution margin for the current year and the projected year, and (2) the fixed costs for the current year. (Assume that fixed costs will remain the same in the projected year.)

b. Compute the break-even point in sales units and sales dollars for the first year.

*b. 157,000 units*

c. The company has a target net income of $200,000. What is the required sales in dollars for the company to meet its target?

d. If the company meets its target net income number, by what percentage could its sales fall before it is operating at a loss? That is, what is its margin of safety ratio?

e. The company is considering a purchase of equipment that would reduce its direct labor costs by $104,000 and would change its manufacturing overhead costs to 30% variable and 70% fixed (assume total manufacturing overhead cost is $350,000, as above). It is also considering switching to a pure commission basis for its sales staff. This would change selling expenses to 90% variable and 10% fixed (assume total selling expense is $250,000, as above). Compute (1) the contribution margin and (2) the contribution margin ratio, and recompute (3) the break-even point in sales dollars. Comment on the effect each of management's proposed changes has on the break-even point.

*e. (3) $1,735,714*

**P19.3 (LO 2), AN** Serv ce  The Grand Inn is a restaurant in Flagstaff, Arizona. It specializes in south-western style meals in a moderate price range. Paul Weld, the manager of Grand, has determined that during the last 2 years the sales mix and contribution margin ratio of its offerings are as follows.

*Determine break-even sales under alternative sales strategies and evaluate results.*

|  | Percent of Total Sales | Contribution Margin Ratio |
|---|---|---|
| Appetizers | 15% | 50% |
| Main entrees | 50% | 25% |
| Desserts | 10% | 50% |
| Beverages | 25% | 80% |

Paul is considering a variety of options to try to improve the profitability of the restaurant. His goal is to generate a target net income of $117,000. The company has fixed costs of $1,053,000 per year.

**Instructions**

a. Calculate the total restaurant sales and the sales of each product line that would be necessary to achieve the desired target net income.

*a. Total sales $2,600,000*

b. Paul believes the restaurant could greatly improve its profitability by reducing the complexity and selling price of its entrees to increase the number of clients that it serves. It would then more heavily market its appetizers and beverages. He is proposing to reduce the contribution margin ratio on the main entrees to 10% by dropping the average selling price. He envisions an expansion of the restau-rant that would increase fixed costs by $585,000. At the same time, he is proposing to change the sales mix to the following.

*b. Total sales $3,375,000*

|  | Percent of Total Sales | Contribution Margin Ratio |
|---|---|---|
| Appetizers | 25% | 50% |
| Main entrees | 25% | 10% |
| Desserts | 10% | 50% |
| Beverages | 40% | 80% |

Compute the total restaurant sales, and the sales of each product line that would be necessary to achieve the desired target net income of $117,000.

c. Suppose that Paul reduces the selling price on entrees and increases fixed costs as proposed in part (b), but customers are not swayed by the marketing efforts and the sales mix remains what it was in part (a). Compute the total restaurant sales and the sales of each product line that would be necessary to achieve the desired target net income. Comment on the potential risks and benefits of this strategy.

**P19.4 (LO 3), AN** Tanek Industries manufactures and sells three different models of wet-dry shop vac-uum cleaners. Although the shop vacs vary in terms of quality and features, all are good sellers. Tanek is currently operating at full capacity with limited machine time.

Sales and production information relevant to each model follows.

*Determine sales mix with limited resources.*

|  | Product | | |
|---|---|---|---|
|  | **Economy** | **Standard** | **Deluxe** |
| Selling price | $30 | $50 | $100 |
| Variable costs and expenses | $16 | $20 | $ 46 |
| Machine hours required | 0.5 | 0.8 | 1.6 |

### Instructions

**b.** Economy $28

**a.** Ignoring the machine time constraint, which single product should Tanek Industries produce?

**b.** What is the contribution margin per unit of limited resource for each product?

**c.** If additional machine time could be obtained, how should the additional time be used?

*Compute degree of operating leverage and evaluate impact of operating leverage on financial results.*

**P19.5 (LO 4), AN** Writing The following single-column CVP income statements are available for Blanc Company and Noir Company.

|  | **Blanc Company** | **Noir Company** |
|---|---|---|
| Sales | $500,000 | $500,000 |
| Variable costs | 280,000 | 180,000 |
| Contribution margin | 220,000 | 320,000 |
| Fixed costs | 170,000 | 270,000 |
| Net income | $ 50,000 | $ 50,000 |

### Instructions

a. BE, Blanc $386,364
   BE, Noir $421,875

b. DOL, Blanc 4.4
   DOL, Noir 6.4

**a.** Compute the break-even point in sales dollars and the margin of safety ratio (round to 3 places) for each company.

**b.** Compute the degree of operating leverage for each company and interpret your results.

**c.** Assuming that sales revenue increases by 20%, restate the CVP income statement for each company.

**d.** Assuming that sales revenue decreases by 20%, restate the CVP income statement for each company.

**e.** Discuss how the cost structure of these two companies affects their operating leverage and profitability.

*Determine contribution margin, break-even point, target sales, and degree of operating leverage.*

**P19.6 (LO 1, 4), AN** Bonita Beauty Corporation manufactures cosmetic products that are sold through a network of sales agents. The agents are paid a commission of 18% of sales. The income statement for the year ending December 31, 2022, is as follows.

**Bonita Beauty Corporation**
**Income Statement**
**For the Year Ended December 31, 2022**

| | | |
|---|---|---|
| Sales | | $75,000,000 |
| Cost of goods sold | | |
| Variable | $31,500,000 | |
| Fixed | 8,610,000 | 40,110,000 |
| Gross margin | | 34,890,000 |
| Selling and marketing expenses | | |
| Commissions | 13,500,000 | |
| Fixed costs | 10,260,000 | 23,760,000 |
| Operating income | | $11,130,000 |

The company is considering hiring its own sales staff to replace the network of agents. It will pay its salespeople a commission of 8% and incur additional fixed costs of $7.5 million.

### Instructions

a. $47,175,000

**a.** Under the current policy of using a network of sales agents, calculate the Bonita Beauty Corporation's break-even point in sales dollars for the year 2022.

**b.** Calculate the company's break-even point in sales dollars for the year 2022 if it hires its own sales force to replace the network of agents.

c. Calculate the degree of operating leverage at sales of $75 million if (1) Bonita Beauty uses sales agents, and (2) Bonita Beauty employs its own sales staff. Describe the advantages and disadvantages of each alternative.

d. Calculate the estimated sales volume in sales dollars that would generate an identical net income for the year ending December 31, 2022, regardless of whether Bonita Beauty Corporation employs its own sales staff and pays them an 8% commission or continues to use the independent network of agents. (*Hint:* Set up an equation, with the net income formula employing independent agents as one side of the equation and the net income formula employing the company's own sales staff as the other side of the equation. Before solving, eliminate those aspects that are the same on each side of the equation as they do not vary under the two alternatives.)

(CMA-Canada adapted)

*c. (2) 3.37*

\*P19.7 **(LO 5), AN** Writing Jackson Company produces plastic that is used for injection-molding applications such as gears for small motors. In 2021, the first year of operations, Jackson produced 4,000 tons of plastic and sold 3,500 tons. In 2022, the production and sales results were exactly reversed. In each year, the selling price per ton was $2,000, variable manufacturing costs were 15% of the sales price of units produced, variable selling expenses were 10% of the selling price of units sold, fixed manufacturing costs were $2,800,000, and fixed administrative expenses were $500,000.

*Prepare income statements under absorption costing and variable costing for a company with beginning inventory, and reconcile differences.*

### Instructions

a. Prepare income statements for each year using variable costing. (Use the format from Illustration 19A.5.)

b. Prepare income statements for each year using absorption costing. (Use the format from Illustration 19A.4.)

c. Reconcile the differences each year in net income under the two costing approaches.

d. Comment on the effects of production and sales on net income under the two costing approaches.

*a. 2022 $2,700,000*

*b. 2022 $2,350,000*

\*P19.8 **(LO 5), AN** Writing Dilithium Batteries is a division of Enterprise Corporation. The division manufactures and sells a long-life battery used in a wide variety of applications. During the coming year, it expects to sell 60,000 units for $30 per unit. Nyota Uthura is the division manager. She is considering producing either 60,000 or 90,000 units during the period. Other information is presented in the schedule.

*Prepare absorption and variable costing income statements and reconcile differences between absorption and variable costing income statements when sales level and production level change. Discuss relative usefulness of absorption costing versus variable costing.*

### Division Information for 2022

| | |
|---|---:|
| Beginning inventory | 0 |
| Expected sales in units | 60,000 |
| Selling price per unit | $30 |
| Variable manufacturing costs per unit | $12 |
| Fixed manufacturing overhead costs (total) | $540,000 |
| Fixed manufacturing overhead costs per unit: | |
| Based on 60,000 units | $9 per unit ($540,000 ÷ 60,000) |
| Based on 90,000 units | $6 per unit ($540,000 ÷ 90,000) |
| | |
| Manufacturing costs per unit: | |
| Based on 60,000 units | $21 per unit ($12 variable + $9 fixed) |
| Based on 90,000 units | $18 per unit ($12 variable + $6 fixed) |
| Variable selling and administrative expenses | $2 |
| Fixed selling and administrative expenses (total) | $50,000 |

### Instructions

a. Prepare an absorption costing income statement, with one column showing the results if 60,000 units are produced and one column showing the results if 90,000 units are produced.

b. Prepare a variable costing income statement, with one column showing the results if 60,000 units are produced and one column showing the results if 90,000 units are produced.

c. Reconcile the difference in net incomes under the two approaches and explain what accounts for this difference.

d. Discuss the relative usefulness of the variable costing income statements versus the absorption costing income statements for decision making and for evaluating the manager's performance.

*a. 90,000 units: NI $550,000*

*b. 90,000 units: NI $370,000*

## Continuing Cases

### Current Designs

**CD19** **Current Designs** manufactures two different types of kayaks, rotomolded kayaks and composite kayaks. The following information is available for each product line.

|  | Rotomolded | Composite |
|---|---|---|
| Unit selling price | $950 | $2,000 |
| Unit variable costs | $570 | $1,340 |

The company's fixed costs are $820,000. An analysis of the sales mix identifies that rotomolded kayaks make up 80% of the total units sold.

#### Instructions

a. Determine the weighted-average unit contribution margin for Current Designs.

b. Determine the break-even point in sales units for Current Designs and identify how many units of each type of kayak will be sold at the break-even point. (Round to the nearest whole number.)

c. Assume that the sales mix changes, and rotomolded kayaks now make up 70% of total units sold. Calculate the total number of units that would need to be sold to earn a net income of $2,000,000 and identify how many units of each type of kayak will be sold at this level of income. (Round to the nearest whole number.)

d. Assume that Current Designs will have sales of $3,000,000 with two-thirds of the sales dollars in rotomolded kayaks and one-third of the sales dollars in composite kayaks. Assuming $660,000 of fixed costs are allocated to the rotomolded kayaks and $160,000 to the composite kayaks, prepare a CVP income statement for each product line.

e. Using the information in part (d), calculate the degree of operating leverage for each product line and interpret your findings. (Round to two decimal places.)

### Waterways Corporation

(*Note:* This is a continuation of the Waterways case from Chapters 14–18.)

**WC19** This case asks you to perform break-even analysis based on Waterways' sales mix and to make sales mix decisions related to Waterways' use of its productive facilities. An optional extension of the case (related to the chapter appendix) also asks you to prepare a variable costing income statement and an absorption costing income statement.

*Go to WileyPLUS for complete case details and instructions.*

## Data Analytics in Action

### Using Data Visualization to Analyze Revenues

**DA19.1** Data visualization can be used to identify business expansion opportunities.

**Example:** Recall the *Data Analytics Insight* box "Taking No Chances with Its Profits" presented in the chapter. Data analytics can help companies know where opportunities lie. For example, while **Caesars Entertainment** uses data analytics to maximize its in-house profitability, other gaming companies may look to expand through outside operations. For example, consider the following chart, which shows gaming revenue by state in 2018, 2009, and 2001.

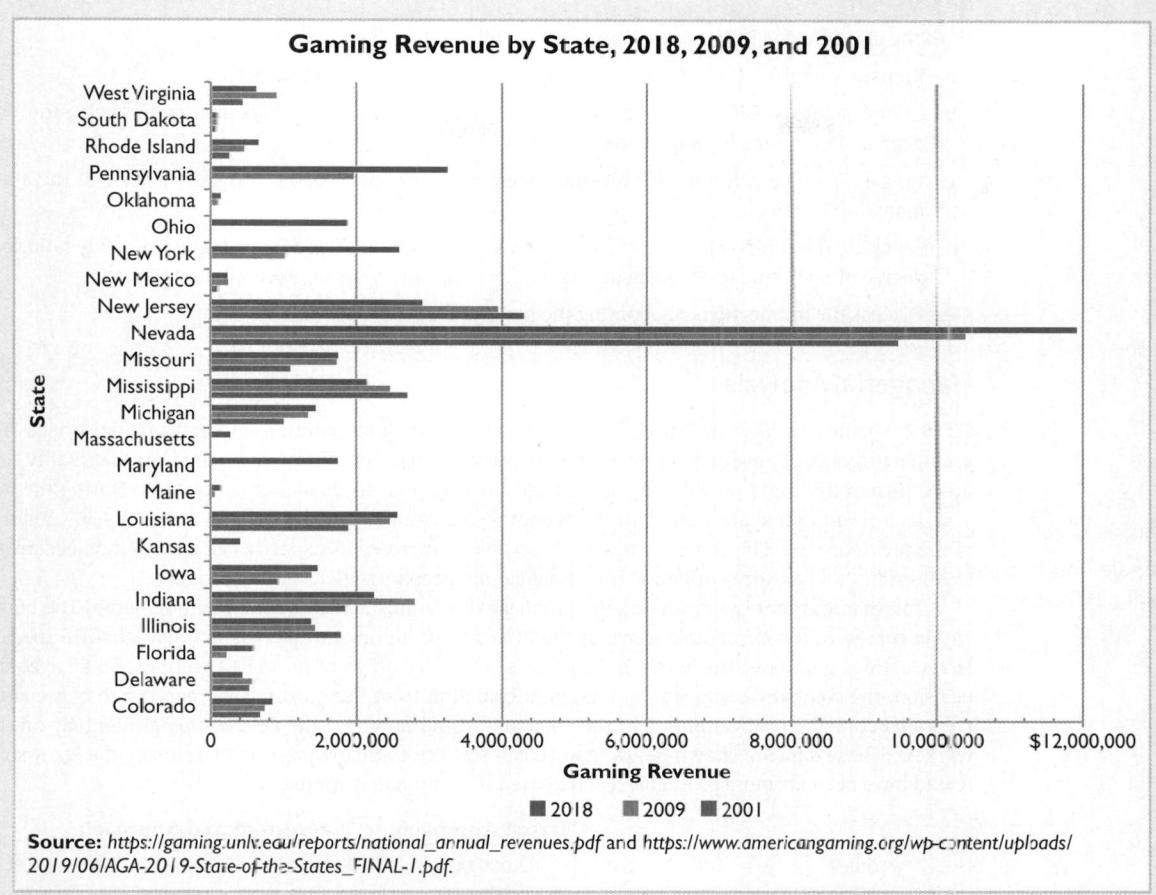

**Gaming Revenue by State, 2018, 2009, and 2001**

*y-axis: State; x-axis: Gaming Revenue (0; 2,000,000; 4,000,000; 6,000,000; 8,000,000; 10,000,000; $12,000,000)*

States listed top to bottom: West Virginia, South Dakota, Rhode Island, Pennsylvania, Oklahoma, Ohio, New York, New Mexico, New Jersey, Nevada, Missouri, Mississippi, Michigan, Massachusetts, Maryland, Maine, Louisiana, Kansas, Iowa, Indiana, Illinois, Florida, Delaware, Colorado

Legend: ■ 2018   ■ 2009   ■ 2001

**Source:** *https://gaming.unlv.edu/reports/national_annual_revenues.pdf* and *https://www.americangaming.org/wp-content/uploads/2019/06/AGA-2019-State-of-the-States_FINAL-1.pdf.*

You can see that some states have grown their gaming revenue significantly, while other states show a declining gaming revenue. Managers look for states that have growth potential when deciding where to expand.

For this case, you will take a closer look at this data, to identify which states hold potential for further expansion of gaming revenue. This case requires you to create and analyze a column chart.

*Go to WileyPLUS for complete case details and instructions.*

### Data Analytics at HydroHappy

**DA19.2**   HydroHappy management wants to examine the profitability of its small retail shop near the beach in St. Thomas, Virgin Islands. The shop rents and sells two unique products, boogie boards and skim boards, referred to by the locals as a "Boogie" and a "Skimmy." Even though the rental operations are profitable, the retail operations may not be covering the related costs. On average, the company sells two Skimmy boards for every one Boogie. For this case, you will prepare a break-even analysis for HydroHappy's two products by using data for forecasted sales. You will also create a CVP graph to forecast the company's total sales revenue, fixed costs, and total variable costs in order to determine the profitability of HydroHappy's retail sales operation.

*Go to WileyPLUS for complete case details and instructions.*

## Expand Your Critical Thinking

### Decision-Making Across the Organization

**CT19.1**   E-Z Seats manufactures swivel seats for customized vans. It currently manufactures 10,000 seats per year, which it sells for $500 per seat. It incurs unit variable costs of $200 per seat and fixed costs of $2,000,000. It is considering automating the upholstery process, which is now largely manual. It estimates that if it does so, its fixed costs will be $3,000,000, and its unit variable costs will decline to $100 per seat.

**Instructions**

With the class divided into groups, complete the following activities.

a. Prepare a single-column CVP income statement based on current activity.

b. Compute the contribution margin ratio, break-even point in sales dollars, margin of safety ratio, and degree of operating leverage based on current activity.

c. Prepare a single-column CVP income statement assuming that the company invests in the automated upholstery system.

d. Compute the contribution margin ratio, break-even point in sales dollars, margin of safety ratio, and degree of operating leverage assuming the new upholstery system is implemented.

e. Discuss the implications of adopting the new system.

## Managerial Analysis

**CT19.2** For nearly 20 years, Specialized Coatings has provided painting and galvanizing services for manufacturers in its region. Manufacturers of various metal products have relied on the quality and quick turnaround time provided by Specialized Coatings and its 20 skilled employees. During the last year, as a result of a sharp upturn in the economy, the company's sales have increased by 30% relative to the previous year. The company has not been able to increase its capacity fast enough, so Specialized Coatings has had to turn work away because it cannot keep up with customer requests.

Top management is considering the purchase of a sophisticated robotic painting booth. The booth would represent a considerable move in the direction of automation versus manual labor. If Specialized Coatings purchases the booth, it would most likely lay off 15 of its skilled painters. To analyze the decision, the company compiled production information from the most recent year and then prepared a parallel compilation assuming that the company would purchase the new equipment and lay off the workers. Those data are shown below. As you can see, the company projects that during the last year it would have been far more profitable if it had used the automated approach.

| | Current Approach | Automated Approach |
|---|---|---|
| Sales | $2,000,000 | $2,000,000 |
| Variable costs | 1,500,000 | 1,000,000 |
| Contribution margin | 500,000 | 1,000,000 |
| Fixed costs | 380,000 | 800,000 |
| Net income | $ 120,000 | $ 200,000 |

**Instructions**

a. Compute and interpret the contribution margin ratio under each approach.

b. Compute the break-even point in sales dollars under each approach. Discuss the implications of your findings.

c. Using the current level of sales, compute the margin of safety ratio under each approach and interpret your findings.

d. Determine the degree of operating leverage for each approach at current sales levels. How much would the company's net income decline under each approach with a 10% decline in sales?

e. At what level of sales would the company's net income be the same under either approach?

f. Discuss the issues that the company must consider in making this decision.

## Real-World Focus

**CT19.3** At one time, **Del Monte Foods Company** reported three separate operating segments: consumer products (which includes a variety of canned foods including tuna, fruit, and vegetables); pet products (which includes pet food and snacks and veterinary products); and soup and infant-feeding products (which includes soup, broth, and infant feeding and pureed products).

In its annual report, Del Monte uses absorption costing. As a result, information regarding the relative composition of its fixed and variable costs is not available. We have assumed that $860.3 million of its total operating expenses of $1,920.3 million are fixed and have allocated the remaining variable costs across the three divisions. Sales data, along with assumed expense data, are provided below.

|  | (in millions) | |
|---|---|---|
|  | **Sales** | **Variable Costs** |
| Consumer products | $1,031.8 | $ 610 |
| Pet products | 837.3 | 350 |
| Soup and infant-feeding products | 302.0 | 100 |
|  | $2,171.1 | $1,060 |

### Instructions

a. Compute each segment's contribution margin ratio and the sales mix.

b. Using the information computed in part (a), compute the company's break-even point in sales dollars, and then determine the amount of sales that would be generated by each division at the break-even point.

**CT19.4** **Service**  The external financial statements published by publicly traded companies are based on absorption cost accounting. As a consequence, it is very difficult to gain an understanding of the relative composition of the companies' fixed and variable costs. It is possible, however, to learn about a company's sales mix and the relative profitability of its various divisions. This exercise looks at the financial statements of **FedEx Corporation**.

### Instructions

Go to the FedEx website to access the company's 2019 annual report and then use it to answer the following questions.

a. Read page 64 of the report under the heading "Reportable Segments." What are the four reportable segments of the company?

b. Page 69 of the report shows an income statement for the FedEx Ground segment, which lists the operating expenses. Assuming that rentals, depreciation, and "other" are all fixed costs, prepare a variable costing income statement for 2019.

c. Using the information from part (b), compute the segment's contribution margin ratio and the break-even point in sales dollars.

## Communication Activity

**CT19.5** Easton Corporation makes two different boat anchors—a traditional fishing anchor and a high-end yacht anchor—using the same production machinery. The contribution margin of the yacht anchor is three times as high as that of the other product. The company is currently operating at full capacity and has been doing so for nearly two years. Bjorn Borg, the company's CEO, wants to cut back on production of the fishing anchor so that the company can make more yacht anchors. He says that this is a "no-brainer" because the contribution margin of the yacht anchor is so much higher.

### Instructions

Write a short memo to Bjorn Borg describing the analysis that the company should do before it makes this decision and any other considerations that would affect the decision.

## Ethics Case

\*CT19.6 Brett Stern was hired during January 2022 to manage the home products division of Hi-Tech Products. As part of his employment contract, he was told that he would get $5,000 of additional bonus for every 1% increase that the division's profits exceeded those of the previous year.

Soon after coming on board, Brett met with his factory managers and explained that he wanted the factory to be run at full capacity. Previously, the factory had employed just-in-time inventory practices and had consequently produced units only as they were needed. Brett stated that under previous management the company had missed out on too many sales opportunities because it didn't have enough inventory on hand. Because previous management had employed just-in-time inventory practices, when Brett came on board there was virtually no beginning inventory. The unit selling price and unit variable costs remained the same from 2021 to 2022. The following additional information is also provided.

|                                              | **2021**      | **2022**      |
|----------------------------------------------|--------------:|--------------:|
| Net income                                   | $ 300,000     | $ 525,000     |
| Units produced                               | 25,000        | 30,000        |
| Units sold                                   | 25,000        | 25,000        |
| Fixed manufacturing overhead costs           | $1,350,000    | $1,350,000    |
| Fixed manufacturing overhead costs per unit  | $     54      | $     45      |

**Instructions**

a. Calculate Brett's bonus based on the net income shown above.

b. Recompute the 2021 and 2022 results using variable costing.

c. Recompute Brett's 2022 bonus under variable costing.

d. Were Brett's actions unethical? Do you think any actions need to be taken by the company?

## All About You

**CT19.7** **Service** Many of you will some day own your own business. One rapidly growing opportunity is no-frills workout centers. Such centers attract customers who want to take advantage of state-of-the-art fitness equipment but do not need the other amenities of full-service health clubs. One way to own your own fitness business is to buy a franchise. **Snap Fitness** is a Minnesota-based business that offers franchise opportunities. For a very low monthly fee ($26, without an annual contract), customers can access a Snap Fitness center 24 hours a day.

The Snap Fitness website indicates that start-up costs range from $60,000 to $184,000. This initial investment covers the following pre-opening costs: franchise fee, grand opening marketing, leasehold improvements, utility/rent deposits, and training.

**Instructions**

a. Suppose that Snap Fitness estimates that each location incurs $4,000 per month in fixed operating expenses plus $1,460 to lease equipment. A recent newspaper article describing no-frills fitness centers indicated that a Snap Fitness site might require only 300 members to break even. Using the information provided above and your knowledge of CVP analysis, estimate the amount of variable costs. (When performing your analysis, assume that the only fixed costs are the estimated monthly operating expenses and the equipment lease.)

b. Using the information from part (a), what would monthly sales in members and dollars have to be to achieve a target net income of $3,640 for the month?

c. Provide five examples of variable costs for a fitness center.

d. Go to a fitness-business website, such as **Snap Fitness** or **Anytime Fitness**, and find information about purchasing a franchise. Summarize the franchise information needed to decide whether entering into a franchise agreement would be a good idea.

## Considering People, Planet, and Profit

**CT19.8** Many politicians, scientists, economists, and businesspeople have become concerned about the potential implications of global warming. The largest source of the emissions thought to contribute to global warming is from coal-fired power plants. The cost of alternative energy has declined, but it is still higher than coal. In 1980, wind-powered electricity cost 80 cents per kilowatt hour. Using today's highly efficient turbines with rotor diameters of up to 125 meters, the cost can be as low as 4 cents (about the same as coal), or as much as 20 cents in places with less wind.

Some people have recently suggested that conventional cost comparisons are not adequate because they do not take environmental costs into account. For example, while coal is a very cheap energy source, it is also a significant contributor of greenhouse gases. Should environmental costs be incorporated into decision calculations when planners evaluate new power plants? The basic arguments for and against are as follows.

**YES:** As long as environmental costs are ignored, renewable energy will appear to be too expensive relative to coal

**NO:** If one country decides to incorporate environmental costs into its decision-making process but other countries do not, the country that does so will be at a competitive disadvantage because its products will cost more to produce.

## Instructions

Write a response indicating your position regarding this situation. Provide support for your view.

## Answers to Insight and Accounting Across the Organization Questions

**Don't Just Look—Buy Something Q:** Besides increasing their conversion rates, what steps can online merchants use to lower their break-even points? **A:** In theory, one of the principal advantages of online retailers is that they can minimize their investment in "bricks and mortar" and thus minimize their fixed costs. Some online merchants never even handle the merchandise they sell. Instead, they simply provide a centralized location for customers to view merchandise and to place orders. The online retailer then forwards the order to the supplier, and the supplier ships it directly to the customer. However, some online merchants that originally planned on employing this model have since found it necessary to build their own warehouses and distribution centers to ensure timely and dependable product delivery. This increases their fixed costs and consequently increases their break-even point.

**Taking No Chances with Its Profits** Q: How does big data correct management's view on two misconceptions about where today's casinos make their money? **A:** Because Caesars has vast amounts of data regarding its customers and their spending patterns, it now knows that it makes most of its money from (1) everyday customers rather than wealthy high-rollers and (2) activities other than gambling (e.g., sales of food, beverages, lodging, and concerts).

**Wouldn't You Rather Have a Chicken Burrito? Q:** If Chipotle's customers switch from beef to chicken, what will happen to its revenues and its net income? **A:** Since chicken products sell for less, the company's revenues would fall. But since the contribution margin on chicken products is higher, the company's net income would rise.

**Something Smells Q:** What is the limited resource for a retailer, and what implications does this have for sales mix? **A:** For retailers, the limited resource is not just shelf space, but shelf space per day. At first, you might think that a product that is small and has a high contribution margin would be the product of choice. But, you also have to factor in the amount of time that a product sits on the shelf. For example, suppose products A and B are the same size. Product A has twice the contribution margin as product B, but product A sits on the shelf five times as long as product B. In this case, once time spent on the shelf is taken into account, product B's superior turnover more than makes up for its lower contribution margin.

**Solar Power Generates More Than Electricity Q:** How do the homeowner solar panels represent a form of outsourcing? At what point did this create a dilemma for power companies? **A:** In effect, the power companies were outsourcing part of the power-generating responsibility to homeowners. They were paying a fee to the homeowner for excess electricity, but the fee paid was less than the rate charged to the end-user. The dilemma arose because the power companies were not able to reduce their fixed costs fast enough as the supply of excess power from homeowners became significant.

# Incremental Analysis

## Chapter Preview

An important purpose of management accounting is to provide managers with relevant information for decision-making. Companies of all sorts must make product decisions. **Unilever**, the world's largest supplier of teas, considered exiting the tea industry in the developed world. **Little Caesars** decided to team up with **DoorDash** to deliver its pizzas. **Quaker Oats** decided to sell off a line of beverages, at a price more than $1 billion less than it paid for that product line only a few years before.

This chapter explains management's decision-making process and a decision-making approach called incremental analysis. The use of incremental analysis is demonstrated in a variety of situations.

## Feature Story

### Keeping It Clean

When you think of new, fast-growing, San Francisco companies, you probably think of fun products like smartphones, social networks, and game apps. You don't tend to think of

soap. In fact, given that some of the biggest, most powerful companies in the world dominate the soap market (e.g., **Proctor & Gamble**, **Clorox**, and **Unilever**), starting a new soap company seems like an outrageously bad idea. But that didn't dissuade Adam Lowry and Eric Ryan from giving it a try. The long-time friends and former roommates combined their skills (Adam's chemical engineering and Eric's design and marketing) to start **Method Products**. Their goal: selling environmentally friendly soaps that actually remove dirt.

Within a year of its formation, the company had products on the shelves at **Target** stores. Within five years, Method was cited by numerous business publications as one of the fastest-growing companies in the country. It was easy—right? Wrong. Running a company is never easy. In addition, because of Method's commitment to sustainability, all of its business decisions are just a little more complex than usual. For example, the company wanted to use solar power to charge the batteries for the forklifts used in its factories. No problem, just put solar panels on the buildings. But because Method outsources its manufacturing, it doesn't actually own factory buildings. In fact, the company that does Method's manufacturing doesn't own the buildings either. Solution— Method parked old semi-trailers next to the factories and installed solar panels on those.

Since Method insists on using natural products and sustainable production practices, its production costs are higher than those of companies that don't adhere to these standards. Adam and Eric insist, however, that this actually benefits them because they have to be far more careful about controlling costs and far more innovative in solving problems. Consider Method's laundry detergent. It is eight times stronger than normal detergent, so it can be sold in a substantially smaller package. This reduces both its packaging and shipping costs. In fact, when the cost of the raw materials used for soap production jumped by as much as 40%, Method actually viewed it as an opportunity to grab market share. It determined that it could offset the cost increases in other places in its supply chain, thus absorbing the cost much easier than its big competitors.

In these and other instances, Adam and Eric identified their alternative courses of action, determined what was relevant to each choice and what wasn't, and then carefully evaluated the incremental costs and revenues of each alternative. When you are small and your competitors have some of the biggest marketing budgets in the world, you can't afford to make very many mistakes.

 **Video**   Watch the *Method Products* video in WileyPLUS to learn more about incremental analysis in the real world.

## Chapter Outline

| LEARNING OBJECTIVES | REVIEW | PRACTICE |
|---|---|---|
| **LO 1** Describe management's decision-making process and incremental analysis. | • Incremental analysis approach<br>• How incremental analysis works<br>• Qualitative factors<br>• Relationship of incremental analysis and activity-based costing<br>• Types of incremental analysis | **DO IT! 1** Incremental Analysis |
| **LO 2** Analyze the relevant costs in accepting an order at a special price. | • Special price<br>• Available capacity | **DO IT! 2** Special Orders |
| **LO 3** Analyze the relevant costs in a make-or-buy decision. | • Make or buy<br>• Opportunity cost | **DO IT! 3** Make or Buy |
| **LO 4** Analyze the relevant costs and revenues in determining whether to sell or process materials further. | • Single-product case<br>• Multiple-product case | **DO IT! 4** Sell or Process Further |
| **LO 5** Analyze the relevant costs to be considered in repairing, retaining, or replacing equipment. | • Repair, retain, or replace equipment<br>• Sunk costs | **DO IT! 5** Repair or Replace Equipment |
| **LO 6** Analyze the relevant costs in deciding whether to eliminate an unprofitable segment or product. | • Unprofitable segments<br>• Avoidable fixed costs<br>• Effect of contribution margin | **DO IT! 6** Unprofitable Segments |

**Go to the Review and Practice section at the end of the chapter for a targeted summary and practice applications with solutions.**

**Visit WileyPLUS for additional tutorials and practice opportunities.**

# Decision-Making and Incremental Analysis

## LEARNING OBJECTIVE 1
Describe management's decision-making process and incremental analysis.

Making decisions is an important management function.

- However, management's decision-making process does not always follow a set pattern because decisions vary significantly in their scope, urgency, and importance.
- It is possible, though, to identify some steps that are frequently involved in the process. These steps are shown in **Illustration 20.1**.

**ILLUSTRATION 20.1**  **Steps in management's decision-making process**

1. Identify the problem and assign responsibility → 2. Determine and evaluate possible courses of action → 3. Make a decision → 4. Review results of the decision

Accounting's contribution to the decision-making process occurs primarily in Steps 2 and 4—evaluating possible courses of action and reviewing results.

- In Step 2, for each possible course of action, relevant revenue and cost data are provided. These show the expected overall effect on net income.
- In Step 4, internal reports are prepared that review the actual impact of the decision.

In making business decisions, management ordinarily considers both financial and nonfinancial information. **Financial** information is related to revenues and costs and their effect on the company's overall profitability. **Nonfinancial** information relates to such factors as the effect of the decision on employee turnover, the environment, or the overall image of the company in the community. (These are considerations that we touched on in our Chapter 14 discussion of corporate social responsibility.)

## Incremental Analysis Approach

**Decisions involve a choice among alternative courses of action.** Suppose you face the personal financial decision of whether to purchase or lease a car. The financial data relate to the cost of leasing versus the cost of purchasing. For example, leasing involves periodic lease payments; purchasing requires "upfront" payment of the purchase price. In other words, the financial information relevant to the decision are the data that vary in the future among the possible alternatives.

- The process used to identify the financial data that change under alternative courses of action is called **incremental analysis** (see **Alternative Terminology**).
- In some cases, you will find that when you use incremental analysis, both costs **and** revenues vary.
- In other cases, only costs **or** revenues vary.

Just as your decision to buy or lease a car affects your future financial situation, similar decisions, on a larger scale, affect a company's future. Incremental analysis identifies the

**ALTERNATIVE TERMINOLOGY**

Incremental analysis is also called *differential analysis* because the analysis focuses on differences.

probable effects of those decisions on future earnings. Such analysis inevitably involves estimates and uncertainty. Gathering data for incremental analyses may involve market analysts, engineers, and accountants. In quantifying the data, the accountant must produce the most reliable information available.

# How Incremental Analysis Works

The basic approach in incremental analysis is shown in **Illustration 20.2**.

**ILLUSTRATION 20.2** Basic approach in incremental analysis

| | Alternative A | Alternative B | Net Income Increase (Decrease) |
|---|---|---|---|
| Revenues | $125,000 | $110,000 | $ (15,000) |
| Costs | 100,000 | 80,000 | 20,000 |
| Net income | $ 25,000 | $ 30,000 | $ 5,000 |

This example compares Alternative B with Alternative A. The net income column shows the differences between the alternatives. In this case, incremental revenue will be $15,000 less under Alternative B than under Alternative A. But a $20,000 incremental cost savings will be realized.[1] Thus, Alternative B will produce $5,000 more net income than Alternative A.

In the following pages, you will encounter three important cost concepts used in incremental analysis:

1. **Relevant cost and revenues.** In incremental analysis, the only factors to be considered are those costs and revenues that differ across alternatives. Those factors are called **relevant costs and revenues**. Costs and revenues that do not differ across alternatives can be ignored when trying to choose between alternatives.

2. **Opportunity cost.** Often in choosing one course of action, the company must give up the opportunity to benefit from some other course of action. For example, if a machine is used to make one type of product, the benefit of making another type of product with that machine is lost. This lost potential benefit is referred to as **opportunity cost**.

3. **Sunk cost.** Costs that have already been incurred and will not be changed or avoided by any present or future decisions are referred to as **sunk costs**. For example, the amount you spent in the past to purchase or repair a laptop should have no bearing on your decision whether to buy a new laptop. **Sunk costs are not relevant costs.**

Incremental analysis sometimes involves changes that at first glance might seem contrary to your intuition.

- Sometimes variable costs **do not change** under the alternative courses of action. For example, direct labor, normally a variable cost, is not a relevant cost in deciding between the acquisition of two new factory machines if each asset requires the same amount of direct labor.

- Sometimes fixed costs **do change**. For example, rent expense, normally a fixed cost, is a relevant cost in a decision whether to continue occupancy of a building or to purchase or lease a new building.

---

[1]Although income taxes are sometimes important in incremental analysis, they are ignored in the chapter for simplicity's sake.

It is also important to understand that **the approaches to incremental analysis discussed in this chapter do not take into consideration the time value of money**. That is, amounts to be paid or received in future years are not discounted for the cost of interest in this chapter. The effect of the time value of money on decisions is addressed in Chapter 25 and Appendix G.

---

## Service Company Insight    American Express

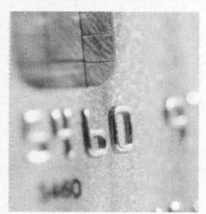

iStock.com/Jani Bryson

### That Letter from AmEx Might Not Be a Bill

No doubt every one of you has received an invitation from a credit card company to open a new account—some of you have probably received three in one day. But how many of you have received an offer of $300 to close out your credit card account? **American Express** decided to offer some of its customers $300 if they would give back their credit card. You could receive the $300 even if you hadn't paid off your balance yet, as long as you agreed to give up your credit card. Apparently, these customers cost more than they are worth.

In some instances, it's the customer that initiates a similar deal. Customers that are swimming in debt are sometimes able to negotiate a lower settlement amount with credit card companies.

**Sources:** Aparajita Saha-Bubna and Lauren Pollock, "AmEx Offers Some Holders $300 to Pay and Leave," *Wall Street Journal Online* (February 23, 2009); and Satta Sarmah Hightower, "How to Negotiate Debt with Your Credit Card Company," *creditkarma.com* (updated August 12, 2019).

**What are the relevant costs that American Express would need to know in order to determine to whom to make this offer? (Answer is available at the end of the chapter.)**

---

# Qualitative Factors

In this chapter, we focus primarily on the quantitative factors that affect a decision—those attributes that can be easily expressed in terms of numbers or dollars. However, many of the decisions involving incremental analysis have important qualitative features. Though not easily measured, they should not be ignored.

- Consider, for example, the potential effects of the make-or-buy decision or of the decision to eliminate a line of business on existing employees and the community in which the plant is located.
- The cost savings that may be obtained from outsourcing or from eliminating a plant should be weighed against these qualitative attributes.
- One example would be the cost of lost morale that might result.

For example, Al "Chainsaw" Dunlap was a so-called "turnaround" artist who went into many companies, identified inefficiencies (using incremental analysis techniques), and tried to correct these problems to improve corporate profitability. Along the way, he laid off thousands of employees at numerous companies. As head of **Sunbeam**, it was Al Dunlap who lost his job because his Draconian approach failed to improve Sunbeam's profitability. It was reported that Sunbeam's employees openly rejoiced for days after his departure. Clearly, qualitative factors can matter.

# Relationship of Incremental Analysis and Activity-Based Costing

In Chapter 17, we noted that many companies have shifted to activity-based costing to allocate overhead costs to products. The primary reason for using activity-based costing is that it results in a more accurate allocation of overhead.

- The concepts presented in this chapter are completely consistent with the use of activity-based costing.
- In fact, activity-based costing results in more accurate costing and, therefore, improved incremental analysis.

# Types of Incremental Analysis

A number of different types of decisions involve incremental analysis. The more common types of decisions are whether to:

1. Accept an order at a special price.
2. Make or buy component parts or finished products.
3. Sell products or process them further.
4. Repair, retain, or replace equipment.
5. Eliminate an unprofitable business segment or product.

We consider each of these types of decisions in the following pages.

---

**ACTION PLAN**

- Past costs that cannot be changed as a result of any present or future action are sunk costs.
- Benefits lost by choosing one option over another are opportunity costs.

## DO IT! 1 | Incremental Analysis

Owen T Corporation is comparing two different options. The company currently operates under Option 1, with revenues of $80,000 per year, maintenance expenses of $5,000 per year, and operating expenses of $38,000 per year. Option 2 provides revenues of $80,000 per year, maintenance expenses of $12,000 per year, and operating expenses of $32,000 per year. Option 1 employs a piece of equipment that was upgraded 2 years ago at a cost of $22,000. If Option 2 is chosen, it will free up resources that will increase revenues by $3,000.

Complete the following table to show the change in income from choosing Option 2 versus Option 1. Designate any sunk costs with an "S."

| | Option 1 | Option 2 | Net Income Increase (Decrease) | Sunk (S) |
|---|---|---|---|---|
| Revenues | | | | |
| Maintenance expenses | | | | |
| Operating expenses | | | | |
| Equipment upgrade | | | | |
| Opportunity cost | | | | |

**Solution**

| | Option 1 | Option 2 | Net Income Increase (Decrease) | Sunk (S) |
|---|---|---|---|---|
| Revenues | $80,000 | $80,000 | $ 0 | |
| Maintenance expenses | 5,000 | 12,000 | (7,000) | |
| Operating expenses | 38,000 | 32,000 | 6,000 | |
| Cost of past equipment upgrade | 22,000 | 0 | 0 | S |
| Opportunity cost | 3,000 | 0 | 3,000 | |
| | | | $ 2,000 | |

Related exercise material: **BE20.1, BE20.2, DO IT! 20.1, E20.1, and E20.18.**

---

# Special Orders

**LEARNING OBJECTIVE 2**

Analyze the relevant costs in accepting an order at a special price.

Sometimes a company has an opportunity to obtain additional business if it is willing to make a price concession to a specific customer or make a special accommodation for a potential new customer. **In this case, the basic decision rule is to accept the special order if the incremental price exceeds the incremental costs to complete the order.**

To illustrate, assume that Sunbelt Company produces 100,000 Smoothie blenders per month, which is 80% of plant capacity. Variable manufacturing costs are $8 per unit. Fixed manufacturing costs are $400,000, or $4 per unit. The Smoothie blenders are normally sold directly to retailers at $20 each. Kensington Co. (a foreign wholesaler) has offered to purchase an additional 2,000 blenders from Sunbelt at $11 per unit. Management has determined that acceptance of the offer would not affect normal sales of the product, and the additional units can be manufactured without increasing plant capacity. What should management do?

If management makes its decision on the basis of the total cost per unit of $12 ($8 variable + $4 fixed), the order would be rejected because costs per unit ($12) exceed revenues per unit ($11) by $1 per unit. However, since the units can be produced within existing plant capacity, the special order **will not increase fixed costs**. Let's identify the relevant data for the decision.

- The variable manufacturing costs increase $16,000 ($8 × 2,000).
- The expected revenue increases $22,000 ($11 × 2,000).

Thus, as shown in **Illustration 20.3**, Sunbelt increases its net income by $6,000 by accepting this special order (see **Helpful Hint**).

**ILLUSTRATION 20.3**  **Incremental analysis—accepting an order at a special price**

| | Reject Order | Accept Order | Net Income Increase (Decrease) |
|---|---|---|---|
| Revenues | $0 | $22,000 | $ 22,000 |
| Costs | 0 | 16,000 | (16,000) |
| Net income | $0 | $ 6,000 | $ 6,000 |

## Additional Considerations

Decisions regarding special orders often need to take into account other factors beyond costs and revenues. For example, consider the following.

- We assume that sales of the product in other markets **would not be affected by this special order**. If other sales were affected, then Sunbelt would have to consider the change in profit due to lost sales in making the decision.
- If Sunbelt is operating **at full capacity**, it is likely that the special order would be rejected. Under such circumstances, the company would have to expand plant capacity. In that case, the special order would have to absorb these additional fixed manufacturing costs as well as the variable manufacturing costs.

## DO IT! 2 | Special Orders

Cobb Company incurs costs of $28 per unit ($18 variable and $10 fixed) to make a product that normally sells for $42. A foreign wholesaler offers to buy 5,000 units at $25 each. The special order results in additional shipping costs of $1 per unit. Compute the increase or decrease in net income Cobb realizes by accepting the special order, assuming Cobb has excess operating capacity. Should Cobb Company accept the special order?

**ACTION PLAN**

- Identify all costs that would change as a result of accepting the order, and net this amount against the change in revenues.

**Solution**

| | Reject | Accept | Net Income Increase (Decrease) |
|---|---|---|---|
| Revenues | $-0- | $125,000* | $125,000 |
| Costs | -0- | 95,000** | (95,000) |
| Net income | $-0- | $ 30,000 | $ 30,000 |

*5,000 × $25
**(5,000 × $18) + (5,000 × $1)

The analysis indicates net income increases by $30,000; therefore, Cobb Company should accept the special order.

Related exercise material: **BE20.3, DO IT! 20.2, E20.2, E20.3, and E20.4.**

# Make or Buy

**LEARNING OBJECTIVE 3**

Analyze the relevant costs in a make-or-buy decision.

When a manufacturer assembles component parts to produce a finished product, management must decide whether to make or buy the components. The decision to buy parts or services is often referred to as outsourcing. For example, as discussed in the Feature Story, a company such as **Method Products** may either make or buy the soaps used in its products. Similarly, **Hewlett-Packard Corporation** may make or buy the electronic circuitry, cases, and printer heads for its printers. At one time, **Boeing** sold some of its commercial aircraft factories in an effort to cut production costs and focus on engineering and final assembly rather than manufacturing. The decision to make or buy components should be made on the basis of incremental analysis.

Baron Company makes motorcycles. **Illustration 20.4** shows the annual costs it incurs in producing 25,000 ignition switches for motorcycles.

**ILLUSTRATION 20.4**

**Annual product cost data**

| | |
|---|---|
| Direct materials | $ 50,000 |
| Direct labor | 75,000 |
| Variable manufacturing overhead | 40,000 |
| Fixed manufacturing overhead | 60,000 |
| Total manufacturing costs | $225,000 |
| **Total cost per unit ($225,000 ÷ 25,000)** | **$9.00** |

Instead of making its own switches at a cost of $9, Baron Company might purchase the ignition switches from Ignition, Inc. at a price of $8 per unit. Should management do this?

- A review of operations indicates that if the ignition switches are purchased from Ignition, Inc., *all* of Baron's variable costs but only $10,000 of its fixed manufacturing costs will be eliminated (avoided).

- Thus, $50,000 of the fixed manufacturing costs remain if the ignition switches are purchased.

The relevant costs for incremental analysis are shown in **Illustration 20.5.**

**ILLUSTRATION 20.5**   Incremental analysis—make or buy

Incremental Analysis - Make or buy

Home   Insert   Page Layout   Formulas   Data   Review   View

P18   fx

| | A | B | C | D |
|---|---|---|---|---|
| 1 | | Make | Buy | Net Income Increase (Decrease) |
| 2 | Direct materials | $ 50,000 | $ 0 | $ 50,000 |
| 3 | Direct labor | 75,000 | 0 | 75,000 |
| 4 | Variable manufacturing costs | 40,000 | 0 | 40,000 |
| 5 | Fixed manufacturing costs | 60,000 | 50,000 | 10,000 |
| 6 | Purchase price (25,000 × $8) | 0 | 200,000 | (200,000) |
| 7 | Total annual cost | $225,000 | $250,000 | $ (25,000) |
| 8 | | | | |

This analysis indicates that Baron Company incurs $25,000 of additional costs by buying the ignition switches rather than making them. Therefore, Baron should continue to make the ignition switches even though the total manufacturing cost is $1 higher per unit than the purchase price. The primary cause of this result is that, even if the company purchases the ignition switches, it will still have fixed costs of $50,000 to absorb.

# Opportunity Cost

The previous make-or-buy analysis is complete only if it is assumed that the productive capacity used to make the ignition switches cannot be converted to another purpose. If there is an opportunity to use this productive capacity in some other manner, then this opportunity cost must be considered. As indicated earlier, **opportunity cost** is the lost potential benefit that could have been obtained by following an alternative course of action.

To illustrate, assume that through buying the switches, Baron Company can use the released productive capacity to generate additional income of $38,000 from producing a different product.

- This lost income is an additional cost of continuing to make the switches in the make-or-buy decision.

- This $38,000 opportunity cost is therefore added to the "Make" column for comparison.

As shown in **Illustration 20.6**, it is now advantageous to buy the ignition switches because the company's income would increase by $13,000.

**ILLUSTRATION 20.6**   Incremental analysis—make or buy, with opportunity cost

Incremental Analysis - Make or buy with opportunity cost

Home   Insert   Page Layout   Formulas   Data   Review   View

P18   fx

| | A | B | C | D |
|---|---|---|---|---|
| 1 | | Make | Buy | Net Income Increase (Decrease) |
| 2 | Total annual cost* | $225,000 | $250,000 | $(25,000) |
| 3 | **Opportunity cost** | **38,000** | 0 | 38,000 |
| 4 | Total cost | $263,000 | $250,000 | $ 13,000 |
| 5 | *From Illustration 20.5. | | | |
| 6 | | | | |

## Additional Considerations

In the make-or-buy decision, it is important for management to also take into account qualitative factors.

- For instance, buying may be the most economically feasible solution, but such action could result in the closing of a manufacturing plant and laying off many good workers.

- In addition, management must assess the supplier's ability to satisfy the company's quality control standards at the quoted price per unit on a timely basis.

## Management Insight

Nerthuz/iStock/Getty Images Plus/Getty Images

### Batteries Are Included!

Top managers at every major car manufacturer face a massive make-or-buy decision. For example, consider the production of electric cars. By far, the most expensive component in an electric car is the battery, which costs about $7,500. The battery is critical to vehicle performance since it determines both the power and range of the vehicle. **Mercedes** and **Volkswagen** plan to make their own batteries, but **General Motors**, **BMW**, and **Renault** have decided to buy their batteries from suppliers such as Panasonic and Samsung.

It is not an easy decision. Battery production requires huge investments in plant assets and research and development. **Nissan** learned the hard way that making your own batteries can be a risky venture. It made a big investment in battery production for its electric car, the Leaf, but then suffered huge losses when sales of the Leaf were far below projections. Alternatively, **Tesla**, which only makes electric cars, has fully committed to making its own batteries. In fact, it often describes itself as a battery company.

**Source:** Stephen Wilmot, "Auto Companies: Better with Batteries Not Included," *Wall Street Journal* (December 19, 2016).

**What are the factors that companies must consider in deciding whether to make or to buy the batteries for their vehicles? (Answer is available at the end of the chapter.)**

---

### ACTION PLAN

• **Look for the costs that change.**

• **Ignore the costs that do not change.**

• **Use the format in the chapter for your answer.**

• **Recognize that opportunity cost can make a difference.**

## DO IT! 3 | Make or Buy

Juanita Company must decide whether to make or buy some of its components for the appliances it produces. The costs of producing 166,000 electrical cords for its appliances are as follows.

| | | | |
|---|---|---|---|
| Direct materials | $90,000 | Variable overhead | $32,000 |
| Direct labor | 20,000 | Fixed overhead | 24,000 |

Instead of making the electrical cords at an average cost per unit of $1.00 ($166,000 ÷ 166,000), the company has an opportunity to buy the cords at $0.90 per unit. If the company purchases the cords, all variable costs and one-fourth of the fixed costs are eliminated.

**a.** Prepare an incremental analysis showing whether the company should make or buy the electrical cords.

**b.** Will your answer be different if the released productive capacity of the production facility will generate additional income of $5,000?

### Solution

**a.**

| | Make | Buy | Net Income Increase (Decrease) |
|---|---|---|---|
| Direct materials | $ 90,000 | $ –0– | $ 90,000 |
| Direct labor | 20,000 | –0– | 20,000 |
| Variable manufacturing costs | 32,000 | –0– | 32,000 |
| Fixed manufacturing costs | 24,000 | 18,000* | 6,000 |
| Purchase price | –0– | 149,400** | (149,400) |
| Total cost | $166,000 | $167,400 | $ (1,400) |

*$24,000 × .75
**166,000 × $0.90

This analysis indicates that Juanita Company will incur $1,400 of additional costs if it buys the electrical cords rather than making them.

**b.**

| | Make | Buy | Net Income Increase (Decrease) |
|---|---|---|---|
| Total cost | $166,000 | $167,400 | $(1,400) |
| Opportunity cost | 5,000 | –0– | 5,000 |
| Total cost | $171,000 | $167,400 | $ 3,600 |

Yes, the answer is different. The analysis shows that net income increases by $3,600 if Juanita Company purchases the electrical cords rather than making them.

Related exercise material: **BE20.4, DO IT! 20.3, E20.5, E20.6, E20.7, and E20.8.**

# Sell or Process Further

---

**LEARNING OBJECTIVE 4**

Analyze the relevant costs and revenues in determining whether to sell or process materials further.

---

Many manufacturers have the option of selling products at a given point in the production cycle or continuing to process with the expectation of selling them at a later point at a higher price. For example, a bicycle manufacturer such as **Trek** could sell its bicycles to retailers either unassembled or assembled. A furniture manufacturer such as **IKEA** could sell its furniture to stores either unfinished or finished. The sell-or-process-further decision should be made on the basis of incremental analysis. The basic decision rule is: **Process further as long as the incremental revenue from such processing exceeds the incremental processing costs.**

## Single-Product Case

Assume, for example, that Woodmasters Inc. makes tables. It sells unfinished tables for $50. The cost to manufacture an unfinished table is $35, computed as shown in **Illustration 20.7**.

| | |
|---|---:|
| Direct materials | $15 |
| Direct labor | 10 |
| Variable manufacturing overhead | 6 |
| Fixed manufacturing overhead | 4 |
| **Manufacturing cost per unit** | **$35** |

**ILLUSTRATION 20.7**
**Per unit cost of unfinished table**

Woodmasters currently has unused productive capacity that is expected to continue indefinitely. Some of this capacity could be used to finish the tables and sell them at $60 per unit.

- For a finished table, direct materials will increase $2 and direct labor costs will increase $4.
- Variable manufacturing overhead costs will increase by $2.40 (60% of direct labor).
- No increase is anticipated in fixed manufacturing overhead.

Should the company sell the unfinished tables, or should it process them further (see **Helpful Hint**)? **Illustration 20.8** shows the incremental analysis on a per unit basis.

**HELPFUL HINT**

Current net income is known. Net income from processing further is an estimate. In making its decision, management could add a "risk" factor for the estimate.

**ILLUSTRATION 20.8**   **Incremental analysis—sell or process further**

Incremental Analysis - Sell or process further

| | A | B | C | D |
|---|---|---|---|---|
| | | Sell Unfinished | Process Further | Net Income Increase (Decrease) |
| 2 | Unit selling price | $50.00 | $60.00 | $10.00 |
| 3 | Cost per unit | | | |
| 4 | Direct materials | 15.00 | 17.00 | (2.00) |
| 5 | Direct labor | 10.00 | 14.00 | (4.00) |
| 6 | Variable manufacturing overhead | 6.00 | 8.40 | (2.40) |
| 7 | Fixed manufacturing overhead | 4.00 | 4.00 | 0.00 |
| 8 | Total | 35.00 | 43.40 | (8.40) |
| 9 | Net income per unit | $15.00 | $16.60 | $ 1.60 |

It would be advantageous for Woodmasters to process the tables further. The incremental revenue of $10.00 from the additional processing is $1.60 higher than the incremental processing costs of $8.40. This results in an increase to net income of $1.60 per unit.

# Multiple-Product Case

Sell-or-process-further decisions are particularly applicable to processes that produce multiple products simultaneously.

- In many industries, a number of end-products are produced from a single raw material and a common production process.
- These multiple end-products are commonly referred to as **joint products**.

For example, in the meat-packing industry, **Armour** processes a cow or pig into meat, internal organs, hides, bones, and fat products. In the petroleum industry, **ExxonMobil** refines crude oil to produce gasoline, lubricating oil, kerosene, paraffin, and ethylene.

**Illustration 20.9** presents a joint product situation for Marais Creamery involving a decision **to sell or process further** cream and skim milk. Cream and skim milk are joint products that result from the processing of raw milk. The company must decide whether to sell the cream or process it further into cottage cheese. It must also decide whether to sell the skim milk or process it further into condensed milk.

**ILLUSTRATION 20.9** **Joint production process—Creamery**

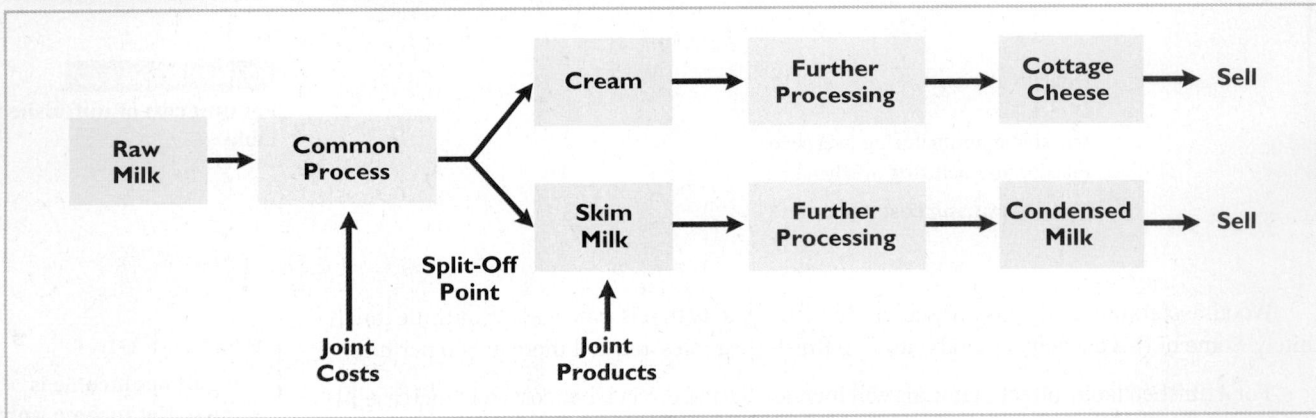

Marais incurs many costs prior to the manufacture of the cream and skim milk. All costs incurred prior to the point at which the two products are separately identifiable (the **split-off point**) are called **joint costs**.

- For purposes of determining the cost of each product, joint product costs must be allocated to the individual products.
- This is frequently done based on the relative sales value of the joint products.
- While this allocation is important for determination of product cost, **it is irrelevant for any sell-or-process-further decisions; joint product costs are sunk costs**. That is, they have already been incurred, and they cannot be changed or avoided by any subsequent decision.

Should Marais sell the cream or process it further into cottage cheese? **Illustration 20.10** provides the daily cost and revenue data for Marais Creamery related to this decision.

**ILLUSTRATION 20.10**

**Cost and revenue data per day for cream**

| Costs (per day) | |
|---|---:|
| Joint cost allocated to cream | $ 9,000 |
| Cost to process cream into cottage cheese | 10,000 |
| **Revenues from Products (per day)** | |
| Cream | $19,000 |
| Cottage cheese | 27,000 |

From this information, we can determine whether the company should simply sell the cream or process it further into cottage cheese. **Illustration 20.11** shows the necessary analysis.

**ILLUSTRATION 20.11**   **Analysis of whether to sell cream or process into cottage cheese**

| | Incremental Analysis - Sell or process further - Cream or cottage cheese | | | |
| --- | --- | --- | --- | --- |
| | Home   Insert   Page Layout   Formulas   Data   Review   View | | | |
| | P18              fx | | | |
| | A | B | C | D |
| 1 | | Sell | Process Further | Net Income Increase (Decrease) |
| 2 | Sales per day | $19,000 | $27,000 | $ 8,000 |
| 3 | Cost per day to process cream into cottage cheese | 0 | 10,000 | (10,000) |
| 4 | Net income per day | $19,000 | $17,000 | $ (2,000) |
| 5 | | | | |

- Note that the joint cost of $9,000 that is allocated to the cream is not included in this decision.
- It is not relevant to the decision because it is a sunk cost.
- It has been incurred in the past and will remain the same no matter whether the cream is subsequently processed into cottage cheese or not.

From this analysis, we can see that Marais should not process the cream further because it will sustain an incremental loss of $2,000.

Should Marais sell the skim milk or process it further into condensed milk? **Illustration 20.12** provides the daily cost and revenue data for the company related to this decision.

**ILLUSTRATION 20.12**

**Cost and revenue data per day for skim milk**

| Costs (per day) | |
| --- | --- |
| Joint cost allocated to skim milk | $ 5,000 |
| Cost to process skim milk into condensed milk | 8,000 |
| **Revenues from Products (per day)** | |
| Skim milk | $11,000 |
| Condensed milk | 26,000 |

**Illustration 20.13** shows that Marais Company should process the skim milk into condensed milk, as it will increase net income by $7,000.

**ILLUSTRATION 20.13**   **Analysis of whether to sell skim milk or process into condensed milk**

| | Incremental Analysis - Sell or process further - Skim milk or condensed milk | | | |
| --- | --- | --- | --- | --- |
| | Home   Insert   Page Layout   Formulas   Data   Review   View | | | |
| | P18              fx | | | |
| | A | B | C | D |
| 1 | | Sell | Process Further | Net Income Increase (Decrease) |
| 2 | Sales per day | $11,000 | $26,000 | $15,000 |
| 3 | Cost per day to process skim milk into condensed milk | 0 | 8,000 | (8,000) |
| 4 | Net income per day | $11,000 | $18,000 | $ 7,000 |
| 5 | | | | |

- Again, note that the $5,000 of joint cost allocated to the skim milk is irrelevant in deciding whether to sell or process further.
- The joint cost remains the same, whether or not further processing is performed.

## Additional Considerations

The decision on whether to sell or process further needs to be reevaluated as market conditions change. For example, if the price of skim milk increases relative to the price of condensed milk, it may become more profitable to sell the skim milk rather than process it into condensed milk.

- Consider French food company **Danone SA**, which was heavily invested in organic milk production. As consumers of organic milk shifted to milk substitutes (e.g., almond milk), Danone chose to process more of its organic milk into organic cheese, yogurt, and creamer.
- Similarly, oil refineries, such as the **Port Arthur Refinery** in Texas, must also constantly reassess which products to produce from the oil they receive at their plants as market conditions change.

**ACTION PLAN**

- **Identify the revenues that change as a result of painting the rocking chair.**
- **Identify all costs that change as a result of painting the rocking chair, and net the amount against the revenues.**

## DO IT! 4 | Sell or Process Further

Easy Does It manufactures unpainted furniture for the do-it-yourself (DIY) market. It currently sells a child's rocking chair for $25. Production costs per unit are $12 variable and $8 fixed. Easy Does It is considering painting the rocking chair and selling it for $35. Variable costs to paint each chair are expected to be $9, and fixed costs are expected to be $2.

Prepare an analysis showing whether Easy Does It should sell unpainted or painted chairs.

**Solution**

| | Sell | Process Further | Net Income Increase (Decrease) |
|---|---|---|---|
| Revenues | $25 | $35 | $10 |
| Variable costs | 12 | 21[a] | (9) |
| Fixed costs | 8 | 10[b] | (2) |
| Net income | $ 5 | $ 4 | $(1) |

[a]$12 + $9; [b]$8 + $2

The analysis indicates that the rocking chair should be sold unpainted because net income per chair will be $1 greater.

Related exercise material: **BE20.5, BE20.6, DO IT! 20.4, E20.9, E20.10, E20.11, and E20.12.**

# Repair, Retain, or Replace Equipment

**LEARNING OBJECTIVE 5**

Analyze the relevant costs to be considered in repairing, retaining, or replacing equipment.

Management often has to decide whether to continue using an asset, repair it, or replace it. For example, **Delta Airlines** must decide whether to replace old jets with new, more fuel-efficient ones. **The basic decision rule is that the company should choose the option that results in the lowest cost (and thus the highest income) over the relevant time period.**

To illustrate, assume that Jeffcoat Company has a factory machine that originally cost $110,000. It has a balance in Accumulated Depreciation of $70,000, so the machine's book value is $40,000. It has a remaining useful life of four years. The company is considering replacing this machine with a new machine.

- A new machine is available that costs $120,000. It is expected to have zero salvage value at the end of its four-year useful life.

- If the new machine is acquired, variable manufacturing costs are expected to decrease from $160,000 to $125,000 annually (that is, $640,000 versus $500,000 over the four-year period). The old unit could be sold for $5,000.

- The costs that are relevant to this decision are the four-year variable manufacturing costs ($640,000 versus $500,000), the cost of the new machine ($120,000), and the amount that could be received from the sale of the old machine ($5,000).

Illustration 20.14 shows the incremental analysis for the **four-year period**.

**ILLUSTRATION 20.14**  **Incremental analysis—retain or replace equipment**

Incremental Analysis - Retain or replace equipment

| A | B | C | D | E | F |
|---|---|---|---|---|---|
| 1 | Retain Equipment | | Replace Equipment | | Net Income Increase (Decrease) |
| 2 Variable manufacturing costs | $640,000 ª | | $500,000 ᵇ | | $140,000 |
| 3 New machine cost | | | 120,000 | | (120,000) |
| 4 Sale of old machine | | | (5,000) | | 5,000 |
| 5   Total | $640,000 | | $615,000 | | $ 25,000 |
| 6 | | | | | |
| 7 ª4 years × $160,000 | | | | | |
| 8 ᵇ4 years × $125,000 | | | | | |
| 9 | | | | | |

In this case, it would be to the company's advantage to replace the equipment.

- The lower variable manufacturing costs due to replacement more than offset the cost of the new equipment.

- Note that the $5,000 received from the sale of the old machine is relevant to the decision because it will only be received if the company chooses to replace its equipment.

In general, any trade-in allowance or cash disposal value of existing assets is relevant to the decision to retain or replace equipment.

One other point should be mentioned regarding Jeffcoat's decision: **The book value of the old machine does not affect the decision.**

- Book value is a **sunk cost**, which is a cost that cannot be changed by any present or future decision.

- **Sunk costs are not relevant in incremental analysis.**

## Additional Considerations

Sometimes, decisions regarding whether to replace equipment are clouded by behavioral decision-making errors. For example, suppose a manager spent $90,000 repairing a machine two months ago. Suppose that the machine now breaks down again.

- The manager might be inclined to think that because the company recently spent a large amount of money to repair the machine, the machine should be repaired again rather than replaced.

- However, the amount spent in the past to repair the machine is irrelevant to the current decision. It is a sunk cost.

Similarly, suppose a manager spent $5,000,000 to purchase a machine. Six months later, a new machine comes on the market that is significantly more efficient than the one recently purchased. The manager might be inclined to think that he or she should not buy the new machine because of the recent purchase. In fact, the manager might fear that buying a different machine so quickly might call into question the merit of the previous decision.

- Again, the fact that the company recently bought a machine is not relevant.
- Instead, the manager should use incremental analysis to determine whether the savings generated by the efficiencies of the new machine would justify its purchase.

## DO IT! 5 | Repair or Replace Equipment

Rochester Roofing is faced with a decision. The company relies very heavily on the use of its 60-foot extension lift for work on large homes and commercial properties. Last year, the company spent $60,000 refurbishing the lift. It has just determined that another $40,000 of repair work is required. Alternatively, Rochester Roofing has found a newer used lift that is for sale for $170,000. The company estimates that both the old and new lifts would have useful lives of 6 years. However, the new lift is more efficient and thus would reduce operating expenses from $70,000 to $50,000 each year. The company could also rent the new lift to other contractors for about $2,000 per year. The old lift is not suitable for rental. The old lift could currently be sold for $25,000 if the new lift is purchased. The new lift and old lift are estimated to have salvage values of zero if used for another 6 years. Prepare an incremental analysis that shows whether the company should repair or replace the equipment.

### Solution

| | Retain Equipment | Replace Equipment | Net Income Increase (Decrease) |
|---|---|---|---|
| Operating expenses | $420,000* | $300,000** | $120,000 |
| Repair costs | 40,000 | | 40,000 |
| Rental revenue | | $(12,000)*** | 12,000 |
| New machine cost | | 170,000 | (170,000) |
| Sale of old machine | | (25,000) | 25,000 |
| Total cost | $460,000 | $433,000 | $ 27,000 |

*6 years × $70,000
**6 years × $50,000
***6 years × $2,000

The analysis indicates that purchasing the new machine would increase net income for the 6-year period by $27,000.

Related exercise material: **BE20.7, DO IT! 20.5, E20.13, and E20.14.**

# Eliminate Unprofitable Segment or Product

**LEARNING OBJECTIVE 6**

Analyze the relevant costs in deciding whether to eliminate an unprofitable segment or product.

Management sometimes must decide whether to eliminate an unprofitable business segment or product. For example, airlines such as **Delta** sometimes stop servicing certain cities or cut back on the number of flights. **Goodyear** quit producing several brands in the low-end tire market, and **adidas** eliminated its **Rockport** division. Again, the key is to **focus on the relevant costs—the data that change under the alternative courses of action** (see Helpful Hint).

To illustrate, assume that Venus Company manufactures tennis racquets in three models: Pro, Master, and Champ. Pro and Master are profitable lines. Champ (highlighted in red in the table below) operates at a loss. Condensed income statement data are as shown in **Illustration 20.15.**

| | Pro | Master | Champ | Total |
|---|---|---|---|---|
| Sales | $800,000 | $300,000 | **$100,000** | $1,200,000 |
| Variable costs | 520,000 | 210,000 | **90,000** | 820,000 |
| Contribution margin | 280,000 | 90,000 | **10,000** | 380,000 |
| Fixed costs | 80,000 | 50,000 | **30,000** | 160,000 |
| Net income | $200,000 | $ 40,000 | **$ (20,000)** | $ 220,000 |

**ILLUSTRATION 20.15**

**Segment income data**

You might think that total net income will increase by $20,000 to $240,000 if the unprofitable Champ line of racquets is eliminated. However, **net income may actually decrease if the Champ line is discontinued.**

- The reason is that the company's total fixed costs will be the same whether or not the Champ line is discontinued.
- That is, the fixed costs allocated to the Champ racquets cannot be eliminated, so they will have to be absorbed by the other products.

To illustrate, assume that the $30,000 of fixed costs applicable to the unprofitable segment are instead allocated $\frac{2}{3}$ to the Pro model and $\frac{1}{3}$ to the Master model if the Champ model is eliminated. Fixed costs will increase to $100,000 ($80,000 + $20,000) in the Pro line and to $60,000 ($50,000 + $10,000) in the Master line. **Illustration 20.16** shows the revised income statement.

| | Pro | Master | Total |
|---|---|---|---|
| Sales | $800,000 | $300,000 | $1,100,000 |
| Variable costs | 520,000 | 210,000 | 730,000 |
| Contribution margin | 280,000 | 90,000 | 370,000 |
| Fixed costs | **100,000** | **60,000** | 160,000 |
| Net income | $180,000 | $ 30,000 | $ 210,000 |

**ILLUSTRATION 20.16**

**Income data after eliminating unprofitable product line**

Total net income would decrease $10,000 ($220,000 − $210,000). This result is also obtained in the incremental analysis of the Champ racquets shown in **Illustration 20.17**.

**ILLUSTRATION 20.17** Incremental analysis—eliminating unprofitable segment with no reduction in fixed costs

| | A | B | C | D |
|---|---|---|---|---|
| 1 | | Continue | Eliminate | Net Income Increase (Decrease) |
| 2 | Sales | $100,000 | $ 0 | $(100,000) |
| 3 | Variable costs | 90,000 | 0 | 90,000 |
| 4 | Contribution margin | 10,000 | 0 | (10,000) |
| 5 | Fixed costs | 30,000 | 30,000 | 0 |
| 6 | Net income | $ (20,000) | $(30,000) | $ (10,000) |
| 7 | | | | |

The loss in net income is attributable to the Champ line's $10,000 contribution margin ($220,000 − $210,000), which will not be realized if the segment is discontinued.

Assume the same facts as above, except now assume that $22,000 of the fixed costs attributed to the Champ line can be eliminated if the line is discontinued. **Illustration 20.18** presents the incremental analysis based on this revised assumption.

**ILLUSTRATION 20.18** Incremental analysis—eliminating unprofitable segment with reduction in fixed costs

| | Incremental Analysis - Eliminating an unprofitable segment | | |
|---|---|---|---|
| Home Insert Page Layout Formulas Data Review View | | | |
| P18 | fx | | |
| A | B | C | D |
| 1 | Continue | Eliminate | Net Income Increase (Decrease) |
| 2 Sales | $100,000 | $ 0 | $(100,000) |
| 3 Variable costs | 90,000 | 0 | 90,000 |
| 4 Contribution margin | 10,000 | 0 | (10,000) |
| 5 Fixed costs | 30,000 | 8,000 | 22,000 |
| 6 Net income | $ (20,000) | $(8,000) | $ 12,000 |
| 7 | | | |

In this case, because the company is able to eliminate some of its fixed costs by eliminating the division, it can increase its net income by $12,000. **This occurs because the $22,000 savings that results from the eliminated fixed costs exceeds the $10,000 in lost contribution margin by $12,000 ($22,000 − $10,000).**

## Additional Considerations

In deciding on the future status of an unprofitable segment, management should consider the effect of elimination on related product lines. For example, companies might retain high-quality product lines that are individually unprofitable because of the reputational benefits that carry over to lower-end products. In our previous tennis racquet example, the Pro and Master lines might benefit from the fact that the Champ line is used by recognized tennis professionals. Other considerations are as follows:

- It may be possible for continuing product lines to obtain some or all of the sales lost by the discontinued product line.
- In some businesses, services or products may be linked—for example, free checking accounts at a bank, or coffee at a donut shop.
- In addition, management should consider the effect of eliminating the product line on employees who may have to be discharged or retrained.

## Service Company Insight    Amazon.com

iStock.com/klenger

### Giving Away the Store?

In an earlier chapter, we discussed **Amazon.com**'s incredible growth. However, some analysts have questioned whether some of the methods that Amazon uses to increase its sales make good business sense. For example, a few years ago, Amazon initiated a "Prime" free-shipping subscription program. For an annual fee, Amazon's customers get free shipping on as many goods as they want to buy. At the time, CEO Jeff Bezos promised that the program would be costly in the short-term but benefit the company in the long-term. Six years later, it was true that Amazon's sales had grown considerably. It was also estimated that its Prime customers buy two to three times as much as non-Prime customers. But, its shipping costs rose from

2.8% of sales to 4% of sales, which is remarkably similar to the drop in its gross margin from 24% to 22.3%. Amazon's order fulfillment center uses 30,000 robots and more than 100 million square feet of space. It generates significant fees from merchants that sell on its site and rely on its fulfillment services.

**Sources:** Martin Peers, "Amazon's Prime Numbers," *Wall Street Journal Online* (February 3, 2011); and Evan Niu, "Ever Wonder How Amazon.com Pays for All of That Free Shipping?" *The Motley Fool* (October 26, 2015).

**What are the relevant revenues and costs that Amazon should consider relative to the decision whether to offer the Prime free-shipping subscription? (Answer is available at the end of the chapter.)**

## DO IT! 6 | Unprofitable Segments

Lambert, Inc. manufactures several types of accessories. For the year, the knit hats and scarves line had sales of $400,000, variable expenses of $310,000, and fixed expenses of $120,000. Therefore, the knit hats and scarves line had a net loss of $30,000. If Lambert eliminates the knit hats and scarves line, $20,000 of fixed costs will remain. Prepare an analysis showing whether the company should eliminate the knit hats and scarves line.

### Solution

| | Continue | Eliminate | Net Income Increase (Decrease) |
|---|---|---|---|
| Sales | $400,000 | $ 0 | $(400,000) |
| Variable costs | 310,000 | 0 | 310,000 |
| Contribution margin | 90,000 | 0 | (90,000) |
| Fixed costs | 120,000 | 20,000 | 100,000 |
| Net income | $(30,000) | $(20,000) | $ 10,000 |

The analysis indicates that Lambert should eliminate the knit hats and scarves line because net income will increase $10,000.

Related exercise material: **BE20.8, DO IT! 20.6, E20.15, E20.16, and E20.17.**

# Review and Practice

## Learning Objectives Review

### 1 Describe management's decision-making process and incremental analysis.

Management's decision-making process consists of (a) identifying the problem and assigning responsibility for the decision, (b) determining and evaluating possible courses of action, (c) making the decision, and (d) reviewing the results of the decision. Incremental analysis identifies financial data that change under alternative courses of action. These data are relevant to the decision because they vary across the possible alternatives.

### 2 Analyze the relevant costs in accepting an order at a special price.

The relevant costs are those that change if the order is accepted. The relevant information in accepting an order at a special price is the difference between the variable manufacturing costs to produce the special order and expected revenues. Any changes in fixed costs, opportunity cost, or other incremental costs or savings (such as additional shipping) should be considered.

### 3 Analyze the relevant costs in a make-or-buy decision.

In a make-or-buy decision, the relevant costs are (a) the variable manufacturing costs that will be saved as well as changes to fixed manufacturing costs, (b) the purchase price, and (c) opportunity cost.

### 4 Analyze the relevant costs and revenues in determining whether to sell or process materials further.

The decision rule for whether to sell or process materials further is: Process further as long as the incremental revenue from processing exceeds the incremental processing costs.

### 5 Analyze the relevant costs to be considered in repairing, retaining, or replacing equipment.

The relevant costs to be considered in determining whether equipment should be repaired, retained, or replaced are the effects on variable costs and the cost of the new equipment. Also, any disposal value of the existing asset must be considered.

### 6 Analyze the relevant costs in deciding whether to eliminate an unprofitable segment or product.

In deciding whether to eliminate an unprofitable segment or product, the relevant costs are the variable costs that drive the contribution margin, if any, produced by the segment or product. Opportunity cost and reduction of fixed expenses must also be considered.

## Glossary Review

**Incremental analysis** The process of identifying the financial data that change under alternative courses of action. (p. 20-3).

**Joint costs** For joint products, all costs incurred prior to the point at which the two products are separately identifiable (known as the split-off point). (p. 20-12).

**Joint products** Multiple end-products produced from a single raw material and a common production process. (p. 20-12).

**Opportunity cost** The potential benefit that is lost when one course of action is chosen rather than an alternative course of action. (p. 20-4).

**Relevant costs and revenues** Those costs and revenues that differ across alternatives. (p. 20-4).

**Sunk cost** A cost incurred in the past that cannot be changed or avoided by any present or future decision. (p. 20-4).

## Practice Multiple-Choice Questions

**1. (LO 1)** Three of the steps in management's decision-making process are (1) review results of decision, (2) determine and evaluate possible courses of action, and (3) make the decision. The steps are carried out in the following order:

   **a.** (1), (2), (3).         **c.** (2), (1), (3).

   **b.** (3), (2), (1).         **d.** (2), (3), (1).

**2. (LO 1)** Incremental analysis is the process of identifying the financial data that:

   **a.** do not change under alternative courses of action.

   **b.** change under alternative courses of action.

   **c.** are mixed under alternative courses of action.

   **d.** No correct answer is given.

**3. (LO 1)** In making business decisions, management ordinarily considers:

   **a.** quantitative factors but not qualitative factors.

   **b.** financial information only.

   **c.** both financial and nonfinancial information.

   **d.** relevant costs, opportunity cost, and sunk costs.

**4. (LO 1)** A company is considering the following alternatives:

| | Alternative A | Alternative B |
| --- | --- | --- |
| Revenues | $50,000 | $50,000 |
| Variable costs | 24,000 | 24,000 |
| Fixed costs | 12,000 | 15,000 |

Which of the following are relevant in choosing between these alternatives?

   **a.** Revenues, variable costs, and fixed costs.

   **b.** Variable costs and fixed costs.

   **c.** Variable costs only.

   **d.** Fixed costs only.

**5. (LO 2)** It costs a company $14 of variable costs and $6 of fixed costs to produce product Z200, which sells for $30. A foreign buyer offers to purchase 3,000 units at $18 each. If the special offer is accepted and produced with unused capacity, net income will:

   **a.** decrease $6,000.       **c.** increase $12,000.

   **b.** increase $6,000.       **d.** increase $9,000.

**6. (LO 2)** It costs a company $14 of variable costs and $6 of fixed costs to produce product Z200. Product Z200 sells for $30. A buyer offers to purchase 3,000 units at $18 each. The seller will incur special shipping costs of $5 per unit. If the special offer is accepted and produced with unused capacity, net income will:

   **a.** increase $3,000.       **c.** decrease $12,000.

   **b.** increase $12,000.      **d.** decrease $3,000.

**7. (LO 3)** Jobart Company is currently operating at full capacity. It is considering buying a part from an outside supplier rather than making it in-house. If Jobart purchases the part, it can use the released productive capacity to generate additional income of $30,000 from producing a different product. When conducting incremental analysis in this make-or-buy decision, the company should:

   **a.** ignore the $30,000.

   **b.** add $30,000 to other costs in the "Make" column.

   **c.** add $30,000 to other costs in the "Buy" column.

   **d.** subtract $30,000 from the other costs in the "Make" column.

**8. (LO 3)** In a make-or-buy decision, relevant costs are:

   **a.** manufacturing costs that will be saved.

   **b.** the purchase price of the units.

   **c.** the opportunity cost.

   **d.** All of the answer choices are correct.

**9. (LO 3)** Derek is performing incremental analysis in a make-or-buy decision for Item X. If Derek buys Item X, he can use its released productive capacity to produce Item Z. Derek will sell Item Z for $12,000 and incur production costs of $8,000. Derek's incremental analysis should include an opportunity cost of:

   **a.** $12,000.         **c.** $4,000.

   **b.** $8,000.          **d.** $0.

**10. (LO 4)** The decision rule in a sell-or-process-further decision is: Process further as long as the incremental revenue from processing exceeds:

   **a.** incremental processing costs.

   **b.** variable processing costs.

   **c.** fixed processing costs.

   **d.** No correct answer is given.

**11. (LO 4)** Walton, Inc. makes an unassembled product that it currently sells for $55. Production costs are $20. Walton is considering assembling the product and selling it for $68. The cost to assemble the product is estimated at $12. What decision should Walton make?

    **a.** Sell before assembly; net income per unit will be $12 greater.

    **b.** Sell before assembly; net income per unit will be $1 greater.

    **c.** Process further; net income per unit will be $13 greater.

    **d.** Process further; net income per unit will be $1 greater.

**12. (LO 5)** In a decision to retain or replace equipment, the book value of the old equipment is a (an):

    **a.** opportunity cost.     **c.** incremental cost.

    **b.** sunk cost.     **d.** marginal cost.

**13. (LO 6)** If an unprofitable segment is eliminated:

    **a.** net income will always increase.

    **b.** variable costs of the eliminated segment will have to be absorbed by other segments.

    **c.** fixed costs allocated to the eliminated segment will have to be absorbed by other segments.

    **d.** net income will always decrease.

**14. (LO 6)** A segment of Hazard Inc. has the following data.

| | |
|---|---|
| Sales | $200,000 |
| Variable expenses | 140,000 |
| Fixed expenses | 100,000 |

If this segment is eliminated, what will be the effect on the remaining company? Assume that 50% of the fixed expenses will be eliminated and the rest will be allocated to the segments of the remaining company.

    **a.** $120,000 increase.

    **b.** $10,000 decrease.

    **c.** $50,000 increase.

    **d.** $10,000 increase.

## Solutions

**1. d.** The order of the steps in the decision process is (2) determine and evaluate possible courses of action, (3) make the decision, and (1) review the results of decision. Choices (a), (b), and (c) list the steps in the incorrect order.

**2. b.** Incremental analysis is the process of identifying the financial data that change under alternative courses of action, not the financial data that (a) do not change or (c) are mixed. Choice (d) is wrong as there is a correct answer given.

**3. c.** Management ordinarily considers both financial and nonfinancial information in making business decisions. The other choices are incorrect because they are all limited to financial data and do not consider nonfinancial information.

**4. d.** Fixed costs are the only relevant factor, that is, the only factor that differs across Alternatives A and B. The other choices are incorrect because they list either revenues, variable costs, or both, which are the same amounts for both alternatives.

**5. c.** If the special offer is accepted and produced with unused capacity, unit variable costs = $14 and income per unit = ($18 − $14), so net income will increase by $12,000 (3,000 × $4), not (a) decrease $6,000, (b) increase $6,000, or (d) increase $9,000.

**6. d.** If the special offer is accepted and produced with unused capacity, unit variable costs = $19 ($14 variable + $5 shipping costs) and income per unit = −$1 ($18 − $19), so net income will decrease by $3,000 (3,000 × −$1), not (a) increase $3,000, (b) increase $12,000, or (c) decrease $12,000.

**7. b.** Jobart Company should add $30,000 to other costs in the "Make" column as it represents lost income of continuing to make the part in-house. The other choices are incorrect because the $30,000 (a) should not be ignored as it is an opportunity cost, (c) represents potential lost income if the company continues to make the part instead of buying it so

therefore should not be placed in the "Buy" column, and (d) should be added to, not subtracted from, the other costs in the "Make" column.

**8. d.** All the costs in choices (a), (b), and (c) are relevant in a make-or-buy decision. So although choices (a), (b), and (c) are true statements, choice (d) is a better answer.

**9. c.** Derek's opportunity cost in its make-or-buy decision is $12,000 (revenue for Item Z) − $8,000 (production costs for Item Z) = $4,000, not (a) $12,000, (b) $8,000, or (d) $0.

**10. a.** The decision rule in a sell-or-process-further decision is to process further as long as the incremental revenue from such processing exceeds incremental processing costs, not (b) variable processing costs or (c) fixed processing costs. Choice (d) is wrong as there is a correct answer given.

**11. d.** If Walton processes further, net income per unit will increase $13 ($68 − $55), which is $1 more than its additional production costs ($12). The other choices are therefore incorrect.

**12. b.** In the decision to retain or replace equipment, the book value of the old equipment is a sunk cost (it reflects the original cost less accumulated depreciation, neither of which is relevant to the decision), not (a) an opportunity cost, (c) an incremental cost, or (d) a marginal cost.

**13. c.** Even though the segment is eliminated, the fixed costs allocated to that segment will still have to be covered. This is done by having other segments absorb the fixed costs of that segment. Choices (a) and (d) are incorrect because net income can either increase or decrease if a segment is eliminated. Choice (b) is incorrect because when a segment is eliminated, the variable costs of that segment will also be eliminated and will not need to be absorbed by other segments.

**14. b.** If the segment continues, net income = −$40,000 ($200,000 − $140,000 − $100,000). If the segment is eliminated, the contribution margin will also be eliminated but $50,000 ($100,000 × .50) of the fixed costs will remain. Therefore, the effect of eliminating the segment will be a $10,000 decrease not (a) a $120,000 increase, (c) a $50,000 increase, or (d) a $10,000 increase.

# Practice Brief Exercises

*Determine whether to make or buy a part.*

**1. (LO 3)** Flavia Industries incurs unit costs of $24 ($18 variable and $6 fixed) in making an assembly part for its finished product. A supplier offers to make 20,000 units of the assembly part at $17 per unit. If the offer is accepted, Flavia will save all variable costs but no fixed costs. Prepare an analysis showing the total cost saving, if any, Flavia will realize by buying the part.

### Solution

1.

|  | Make | Buy | Net Income Increase (Decrease) |
|---|---|---|---|
| Variable manufacturing costs | $360,000 | $ –0– | $360,000 |
| Fixed manufacturing costs | 120,000 | 120,000 | –0– |
| Purchase price | –0– | 340,000 | (340,000) |
| Total annual cost | $480,000 | $460,000 | $ 20,000 |

The decision should be to buy the part.

*Determine whether to sell or process further.*

**2. (LO 4)** Fast Speed Bicycle Inc. makes parts for unfinished bicycles that it sells for $125. Production costs are $40 variable and $20 fixed. Because of unused capacity, Fast Speed is considering finishing the bicycles and selling them for $200. Additional variable finishing costs are expected to be $65 with no increase in fixed costs. Prepare an analysis on a per unit basis showing whether Fast Speed should sell unfinished or unfinished bicycles.

### Solution

2.

|  | Sell | Process Further | Net Income Increase (Decrease) |
|---|---|---|---|
| Unit selling price | $125 | $200 | $75 |
| Cost per unit |  |  |  |
| Variable | 40 | 105 | (65) |
| Fixed | 20 | 20 | 0 |
| Total | 60 | 125 | (65) |
| Net income per unit | $ 65 | $ 75 | $10 |

The bicycles should be processed further because the incremental revenues exceed incremental costs by $10 per unit.

*Determine whether to eliminate an unprofitable segment.*

**3. (LO 6)** Hava Racquets Company manufactures pickleball racquets in four different models. For the year, the SoftNet line had a net loss of $40,000 from sales of $250,000, variable costs of $180,000, and fixed costs of $110,000. If the SoftNet line is eliminated, $30,000 of fixed costs will remain. Prepare an analysis showing whether the SoftNet Line should be eliminated.

### Solution

3.

|  | Continue | Eliminate | Net Income Increase (Decrease) |
|---|---|---|---|
| Sales | $250,000 | $ –0– | $(250,000) |
| Variable costs | 180,000 | –0– | 180,000 |
| Contribution margin | 70,000 | –0– | (70,000) |
| Fixed costs | 110,000 | 30,000 | 80,000 |
| Net income | $ (40,000) | $(30,000) | $ 10,000 |

The SoftNet product line should be eliminated because $80,000 of fixed cost is eliminated whereas only $70,000 of contribution margin is realized if the line is continued. The $70,000 related to the contribution margin is lower than the $80,000 savings related to fixed costs. Therefore, a savings of $10,000 results from eliminating SoftNet.

# Practice Exercises

**1. (LO 3)** Maningly Inc. has been manufacturing its own lampshades for its table lamps. The company is currently operating at 100% of capacity. Variable manufacturing overhead is charged to production at the rate of 50% of direct labor cost. The direct materials and direct labor cost per unit to make the lampshades are $4 and $6, respectively. Normal production is 50,000 table lamps per year.

*Use incremental analysis for make-or-buy decision.*

A supplier offers to make the lampshades at a price of $13.50 per unit. If Maningly accepts the supplier's offer, all variable manufacturing costs will be eliminated. But, the $50,000 of fixed manufacturing overhead currently being charged to the lampshades will have to be absorbed by other products.

### Instructions

**a.** Prepare the incremental analysis for the decision to make or buy the lampshades.

**b.** Should Maningly buy the lampshades?

**c.** Would your answer be different in (b) if the productive capacity released by not making the lampshades could be used to produce income of $40,000?

### Solution

**1. a.**

|  | Make | Buy | Net Income Increase (Decrease) |
|---|---|---|---|
| Direct materials (50,000 × $4.00) | $200,000 | $ -0- | $ 200,000 |
| Direct labor (50,000 × $6.00) | 300,000 | -0- | 300,000 |
| Variable manufacturing costs |  |  |  |
| ($300,000 × 50%) | 150,000 | -0- | 150,000 |
| Fixed manufacturing costs | 50,000 | 50,000 | -0- |
| Purchase price (50,000 × $13.50) | -0- | 675,000 | (675,000) |
| Total annual cost | $700,000 | $725,000 | $ (25,000) |

**b.** No, Maningly should not purchase the lampshades. As indicated by the incremental analysis, it would cost the company $25,000 more to purchase the lampshades.

**c.** Yes, by purchasing the lampshades, a total cost saving of $15,000 will result as shown below.

|  | Make | Buy | Net Income Increase (Decrease) |
|---|---|---|---|
| Total annual cost (from (a)) | $700,000 | $725,000 | $(25,000) |
| Opportunity cost | 40,000 | -0- | 40,000 |
| Total cost | $740,000 | $725,000 | $ 15,000 |

**2. (LO 4)** A company manufactures three products using the same production process. The costs incurred up to the split-off point are $200,000. These costs are allocated to the products on the basis of their sales value at the split-off point. The number of units produced, the selling prices per unit of the three products at the split-off point and after further processing, and the additional processing costs are as follows.

*Use incremental analysis for whether to sell or process materials further.*

| Product | Number of Units Produced | Selling Price at Split-Off | Selling Price after Processing | Additional Processing Costs |
|---|---|---|---|---|
| D | 3,000 | $11.00 | $15.00 | $14,000 |
| E | 6,000 | 12.00 | 16.20 | 16,000 |
| F | 2,000 | 19.40 | 24.00 | 9,000 |

### Instructions

**a.** Which information is relevant to the decision on whether or not to process the products further? Explain why this information is relevant.

**b.** Which product(s) should be processed further and which should be sold at the split-off point?

**c.** Would your decision be different if the company was using the quantity of output to allocate joint costs? Explain.

(CGA adapted)

## Solution

**2. a.** The costs that are relevant in this decision are the incremental revenues and the incremental costs associated with processing the material past the split-off point. Any costs incurred up to the split-off point are sunk costs and therefore irrelevant to this decision.

**b.** Revenue after further processing:
Product D: $45,000 (3,000 units × $15.00 per unit)
Product E: $97,200 (6,000 units × $16.20 per unit)
Product F: $48,000 (2,000 units × $24.00 per unit)

Revenue at split-off:
Product D: $33,000 (3,000 units × $11.00 per unit)
Product E: $72,000 (6,000 units × $12.00 per unit)
Product F: $38,800 (2,000 units × $19.40 per unit)

|  | D | E | F |
|---|---|---|---|
| Incremental revenue | $ 12,000[a] | $ 25,200[b] | $ 9,200[c] |
| Incremental cost | (14,000) | (16,000) | (9,000) |
| Increase (decrease) in profit | $ (2,000) | $ 9,200 | $ 200 |

[a]$45,000 – $33,000; [b]$97,200 – $72,000; [c]$48,000 – $38,800

Products E and F should be processed further, but Product D should not be processed further.

**c.** The decision would remain the same. It does not matter how the joint costs are allocated because joint costs are irrelevant to this decision.

*Use incremental analysis for retaining or replacing equipment.*

**3. (LO 5)** Tek Enterprises uses a computer to process its payroll. Lately, business has been so good that it takes an extra 3 hours per night, plus every third Saturday, to process. Management is considering updating its computer with a faster model that would eliminate all of the overtime processing.

|  | Current Machine | New Machine |
|---|---|---|
| Original purchase cost | $ 9,000 | $12,000 |
| Accumulated depreciation | 2,000 | — |
| Estimated annual operating costs | 16,000 | 12,000 |
| Useful life | 6 years | 6 years |

If sold now, the current machine would have a salvage value of $3,000. If operated for the remainder of its useful life, the current machine would have zero salvage value. The new machine is expected to have zero salvage value after 6 years.

## Instructions
Should the current machine be replaced? (Ignore the time value of money.)

## Solution

3.

|  | Retain Machine | Replace Machine | Net Income Increase (Decrease) |
|---|---|---|---|
| Operating costs | $96,000* | $72,000** | $24,000 |
| New machine cost | -0- | 12,000 | (12,000) |
| Salvage value (old) | -0- | (3,000) | 3,000 |
| Total | $96,000 | $81,000 | $15,000 |

*$16,000 × 6
**$12,000 × 6

The current machine should be replaced. The incremental analysis shows that net income for the 6-year period will be $15,000 higher by replacing the current machine.

*Use incremental analysis for elimination of division.*

**4. (LO 6)** Benai Lorenzo, a recent graduate of Bonita's accounting program, evaluated the operating performance of Wasson Company's six divisions. Benai made the following presentation to the Wasson board of directors and suggested the Ortiz Division be eliminated. "If the Ortiz Division is eliminated," she said, "our total profits would increase by $23,870."

| | The Other Five Divisions | Ortiz Division | Total |
|---|---|---|---|
| Sales | $1,654,200 | $ 96,200 | $1,760,400 |
| Cost of goods sold | 978,520 | 76,470 | 1,054,990 |
| Gross profit | 635,680 | 19,730 | 705,410 |
| Operating expenses | 527,940 | 43,600 | 571,540 |
| Net income | $ 157,740 | $(23,870) | $ 133,870 |

In the Ortiz Division, cost of goods sold is $70,000 variable and $6,470 fixed, and operating expenses are $15,000 variable and $28,600 fixed. None of the Ortiz Division's fixed costs will be eliminated if the division is discontinued.

### Instructions

Is Benai right about eliminating the Ortiz Division? Prepare an incremental analysis schedule to support your answer.

### Solution

**4.**

| | Continue | Eliminate | Net Income Increase (Decrease) |
|---|---|---|---|
| Sales | $ 96,200 | $ -0- | $(96,200) |
| Variable expenses | | | |
| Cost of goods sold | 70,000 | -0- | 70,000 |
| Operating expenses | 15,000 | -0- | 15,000 |
| Total variable | 85,000 | -0- | 85,000 |
| Contribution margin | 11,200 | -0- | (11,200) |
| Fixed expenses | | | |
| Cost of goods sold | 6,470 | 6,470 | -0- |
| Operating expenses | 28,600 | 28,600 | -0- |
| Total fixed | 35,070 | 35,070 | -0- |
| Net income (loss) | $(23,870) | $(35,070) | $(11,200) |

Benai is incorrect. The incremental analysis shows that net income will be $11,200 less if the Ortiz Division is eliminated. This amount equals the contribution margin that would be lost by discontinuing the division.

## Practice Problem

**(LO 2)** Walston Company produces kitchen cabinets for homebuilders across the western United States. The cost of producing 5,000 cabinets is as follows.

*Use incremental analysis for a special order.*

| Materials | $ 500,000 |
|---|---|
| Labor | 250,000 |
| Variable overhead | 100,000 |
| Fixed overhead | 400,000 |
| Total | $1,250,000 |

Walston also incurs selling expenses of $20 per cabinet. Wellington Corp. has offered Walston $165 per cabinet for a special order of 1,000 cabinets. The cabinets would be sold to homebuilders in the eastern United States and thus would not conflict with Walston's current sales. Selling expenses per cabinet would be only $5 per cabinet. Walston has available capacity to do the work.

### Instructions

a. Prepare an incremental analysis for the special order.

b. Should Walston accept the special order? Why or why not?

**Solution**

a. Relevant costs per unit would be:

| | |
|---|---|
| Materials | $500,000 \div 5,000 = \$100$ |
| Labor | $250,000 \div 5,000 = \quad 50$ |
| Variable overhead | $100,000 \div 5,000 = \quad 20$ |
| Selling expenses | $\underline{\quad\quad 5}$ |
| Total relevant cost per unit | $\underline{\$175}$ |

| | Reject Order | Accept Order | Net Income Increase (Decrease) |
|---|---|---|---|
| Revenues | $-0- | $165,000* | $ 165,000 |
| Costs | -0- | 175,000** | (175,000) |
| Net income | $\underline{\$-0-}$ | $\underline{\$(10,000)}$ | $\underline{\$\ (10,000)}$ |

*$165 \times 1,000$; **$175 \times 1,000$

b. Walston should reject the offer. The incremental benefit of $165 per cabinet is less than the incremental cost of $175. By accepting the order, Walston's net income would actually decline by $10,000.

---

Brief Exercises, DO IT! Exercises, Exercises, Problems, Data Analytics Activities, and many additional resources are available for practice in WileyPLUS.

---

# Questions

**1.** What steps are frequently involved in management's decision-making process?

**2.** Your roommate, Anna Polis, contends that accounting contributes to most of the steps in management's decision-making process. Is your roommate correct? Explain.

**3.** "Incremental analysis involves the accumulation of information concerning a single course of action." Is this true? Explain why or why not.

**4.** Sydney Greene asks for your help concerning the relevance of variable and fixed costs in incremental analysis. Help Sydney with her problem.

**5.** What data are relevant in deciding whether to accept an order at a special price?

**6.** Emil Corporation has an opportunity to buy parts at $9 each that currently cost $12 to make. What manufacturing costs are relevant to this make-or-buy decision?

**7.** Define the term "opportunity cost." How may this cost be relevant in a make-or-buy decision?

**8.** What is the decision rule in deciding whether to sell a product or process it further?

**9.** What are joint products? What accounting issue results from the production process that creates joint products?

**10.** How are allocated joint costs treated when making a sell-or-process-further decision?

**11.** Your roommate, Gale Dunham, is confused about sunk costs. Explain to your roommate the meaning of sunk costs and their relevance to a decision to retain or replace equipment.

**12.** Huang Inc. has one product line that is unprofitable. What circumstances may cause overall company net income to be lower if the unprofitable product line is eliminated?

# Brief Exercises

*Identify the steps in management's decision-making process.*

**BE20.1 (LO 1), K** The steps in management's decision-making process are listed in random order below. Indicate the order in which the steps should be executed.

_____ Make a decision.          _____ Review results of the decision.

_____ Identify the problem and assign          _____ Determine and evaluate possible courses
            responsibility.                                              of action.

*Determine incremental changes.*

**BE20.2 (LO 1), AP** Bogart Company is considering two alternatives. Alternative A will have revenues of $160,000 and costs of $100,000. Alternative B will have revenues of $180,000 and costs of $125,000. Compare Alternative A to Alternative B showing incremental revenues, costs, and net income.

**BE20.3 (LO 2), AP** At Bargain Electronics, it costs $30 per unit ($20 variable and $10 fixed) to make an MP3 player that normally sells for $45. A foreign wholesaler offers to buy 3,000 units at $25 each. Bargain Electronics will incur special shipping costs of $3 per unit. Assuming that Bargain Electronics has excess operating capacity, indicate the net income (loss) Bargain Electronics would realize by accepting the special order.

*Determine whether to accept a special order.*

**BE20.4 (LO 3), AP** Manson Industries incurs unit costs of $8 ($5 variable and $3 fixed) in making an assembly part for its finished product. A supplier offers to make 10,000 of the assembly part at $6 per unit. If the offer is accepted, Manson will save all variable costs but no fixed costs. Prepare an analysis showing the total cost saving, if any, that Manson will realize by buying the part.

*Determine whether to make or buy a part.*

**BE20.5 (LO 4), AP** Pine Street Inc. makes unfinished bookcases that it sells for $62. Production costs are $36 variable and $10 fixed. Because it has unused capacity, Pine Street is considering finishing the bookcases and selling them for $70. Variable finishing costs are expected to be $6 per unit with no increase in fixed costs. Prepare an analysis on a per unit basis showing whether Pine Street should sell unfinished or finished bookcases.

*Determine whether to sell or process further.*

**BE20.6 (LO 4), AP** Each day, Adama Corporation processes 1 ton of a secret raw material into two resulting products, AB1 and XY1. When it processes 1 ton of the raw material, the company incurs joint processing costs of $60,000. It allocates $25,000 of these costs to AB1 and $35,000 of these costs to XY1. The resulting AB1 can be sold for $100,000. Alternatively, it can be processed further to make AB2 at an additional processing cost of $45,000, and sold for $150,000. Each day's batch of XY1 can be sold for $95,000. Or, it can be processed further to create XY2, at an additional processing cost of $50,000, and sold for $130,000. Discuss what products Adama Corporation should make.

*Determine whether to sell or process further, joint products.*

**BE20.7 (LO 5), AP** Bryant Company has a factory machine with a book value of $90,000 and a remaining useful life of 5 years. It can be sold for $30,000. A new machine is available at a cost of $400,000. This machine will have a 5-year useful life with no salvage value. The new machine will lower annual variable manufacturing costs from $600,000 to $500,000. Prepare an analysis showing whether the old machine should be retained or replaced.

*Determine whether to retain or replace equipment.*

**BE20.8 (LO 6), AP** Lisah, Inc. manufactures golf clubs in three models. For the year, the Big Bart line has a net loss of $10,000 from sales $200,000, variable costs $180,000, and fixed costs $30,000. If the Big Bart line is eliminated, $20,000 of fixed costs will remain. Prepare an analysis showing whether the Big Bart line should be eliminated.

*Determine whether to eliminate an unprofitable segment.*

## DO IT! Exercises

**DO IT! 20.1 (LO 1), AN** Nathan T Corporation is comparing two different options. Nathan T currently uses Option 1, with revenues of $65,000 per year, maintenance expenses of $5,000 per year, and operating expenses of $26,000 per year. Option 2 provides revenues of $60,000 per year, maintenance expenses of $5,000 per year, and operating expenses of $22,000 per year. Option 1 employs a piece of equipment which was upgraded 2 years ago at a cost of $17,000. If Option 2 is chosen, it will free up resources that will bring in an additional $4,000 of revenue. Complete the following table to show the change in income from choosing Option 2 versus Option 1. Designate sunk costs with an "S."

*Determine incremental costs.*

|  | Option 1 | Option 2 | Net Income Increase (Decrease) | Sunk (S) |
|---|---|---|---|---|
| Revenues |  |  |  |  |
| Maintenance expenses |  |  |  |  |
| Operating expenses |  |  |  |  |
| Equipment upgrade |  |  |  |  |
| Opportunity cost |  |  |  |  |

**DO IT! 20.2 (LO 2), AN** Maize Company incurs a cost of $35 per unit, of which $20 is variable, to make a product that normally sells for $58. A foreign wholesaler offers to buy 6,000 units at $30 each. Maize will incur additional costs of $4 per unit to imprint a logo and to pay for shipping. Compute the increase or decrease in net income Maize will realize by accepting the special order, assuming Maize has sufficient excess operating capacity. Should Maize Company accept the special order?

*Evaluate special order.*

**DO IT! 20.3 (LO 3), AN** Wilma Company must decide whether to make or buy some of its components. The costs of producing 60,000 switches for its generators are as follows.

*Evaluate make-or-buy opportunity.*

| | | | |
|---|---|---|---|
| Direct materials | $30,000 | Variable overhead | $45,000 |
| Direct labor | 42,000 | Fixed overhead | 60,000 |

Instead of making the switches at an average cost of $2.95 ($177,000 ÷ 60,000), the company has an opportunity to buy the switches at $2.70 per unit. If the company purchases the switches, all the variable costs and one-fourth of the fixed costs will be eliminated. (a) Prepare an incremental analysis showing whether the company should make or buy the switches. (b) Would your answer be different if the released productive capacity will generate additional income of $34,000?

*Sell or process further.*

**DO IT! 20.4 (LO 4), AP** Mesa Verde manufactures unpainted furniture for the do-it-yourself (DIY) market. It currently sells a table for $75. Production costs per unit are $40 variable and $10 fixed. Mesa Verde is considering staining and sealing the table to sell it for $100. Unit variable costs to finish each table are expected to be an additional $19 per table, and fixed costs are expected to be an additional $3 per table. Prepare an analysis showing whether Mesa Verde should sell stained or finished tables.

*Repair or replace equipment.*

**DO IT! 20.5 (LO 5), AP** Darcy Roofing is faced with a decision. The company relies very heavily on the use of its 60-foot extension lift for work on large homes and commercial properties. Last year, Darcy Roofing spent $60,000 refurbishing the lift. It has just determined that another $50,000 of repair work is required. Alternatively, it has found a newer used lift that is for sale for $170,000. The company estimates that both lifts would have useful lives of 5 years. The new lift is more efficient and thus would reduce operating expenses from $90,000 to $60,000 each year. Darcy Roofing could also rent out the new lift for about $10,000 per year. The old lift is not suitable for rental. The old lift could currently be sold for $15,000 if the new lift is purchased. The new lift and old lift are estimated to have salvage values of zero if used for another 6 years. Prepare an incremental analysis showing whether the company should repair or replace the equipment.

*Analyze whether to eliminate unprofitable segment.*

**DO IT! 20.6 (LO 6), AP** Gator Corporation manufactures several types of accessories. For the year, the gloves and mittens line had sales of $500,000, variable expenses of $370,000, and fixed expenses of $150,000. Therefore, the gloves and mittens line had a net loss of $20,000. If Gator eliminates the line, $38,000 of fixed costs will remain. Prepare an analysis showing whether the company should eliminate the gloves and mittens line.

# Exercises

*Analyze statements about decision-making and incremental analysis.*

**E20.1 (LO 1), C** As a study aid, your classmate Pascal Adams has prepared the following list of statements about decision-making and incremental analysis.

1. The first step in management's decision-making process is, "Determine and evaluate possible courses of action."

2. The final step in management's decision-making process is to actually make the decision.

3. Accounting's contribution to management's decision-making process occurs primarily in evaluating possible courses of action and in reviewing the results.

4. In making business decisions, management ordinarily considers only financial information because it is objectively determined.

5. Decisions involve a choice among alternative courses of action.

6. The process used to identify the financial data that change under alternative courses of action is called incremental analysis.

7. Costs that are the same under all alternative courses of action sometimes affect the decision.

8. When using incremental analysis, some costs will always change under alternative courses of action, but revenues will not.

9. Variable costs will change under alternative courses of action, but fixed costs will not.

## Instructions

Identify each statement as true or false. If false, indicate how to correct the statement.

*Use incremental analysis for special-order decision.*

**E20.2 (LO 2), AN** Gruden Company produces golf discs which it normally sells to retailers for $7 each. The cost of manufacturing 20,000 golf discs is:

| | |
|---|---|
| Materials | $ 10,000 |
| Labor | 30,000 |
| Variable overhead | 20,000 |
| Fixed overhead | 40,000 |
| Total | $100,000 |

Gruden also incurs 5% sales commission ($0.35) on each disc sold.

McGee Corporation offers Gruden $4.80 per disc for 5,000 discs. McGee would sell the discs under its own brand name in foreign markets not yet served by Gruden. If Gruden accepts the offer, it will incur a one-time fixed cost of $6,000 due to the rental of an imprinting machine. No sales commission will result from the special order.

**Instructions**

a. Prepare an incremental analysis for the special order.

b. Should Gruden accept the special order? Why or why not?

c. What assumptions underlie the decision made in part (b)?

**E20.3 (LO 2), AN** Moonbeam Company manufactures toasters. For the first 8 months of 2022, the company reported the following operating results while operating at 75% of plant capacity:

*Use incremental analysis for special order.*

| | |
|---|---:|
| Sales (350,000 units) | $4,375,000 |
| Cost of goods sold | 2,600,000 |
| Gross profit | 1,775,000 |
| Operating expenses | 840,000 |
| Net income | $ 935,000 |

Cost of goods sold was 70% variable and 30% fixed; operating expenses were 80% variable and 20% fixed.

In September, Moonbeam receives a special order for 15,000 toasters at $7.60 each from Luna Company of Ciudad Juarez. Acceptance of the order would result in an additional $3,000 of shipping costs but no increase in fixed costs.

**Instructions**

a. Prepare an incremental analysis for the special order.

b. Should Moonbeam accept the special order? Why or why not?

**E20.4 (LO 2), AN** Klean Fiber Company is the creator of Y-Go, a technology that weaves silver into its fabrics to kill bacteria and odor on clothing while managing heat. Y-Go has become very popular in undergarments for sports activities. Operating at capacity, the company can produce 1,000,000 Y-Go undergarments a year. The per unit and the total costs for an individual garment when the company operates at full capacity are as follows.

*Use incremental analysis for special order.*

| | Per Undergarment | Total |
|---|---:|---:|
| Direct materials | $2.00 | $2,000,000 |
| Direct labor | 0.75 | 750,000 |
| Variable manufacturing overhead | 1.00 | 1,000,000 |
| Fixed manufacturing overhead | 1.50 | 1,500,000 |
| Variable selling expenses | 0.25 | 250,000 |
| Totals | $5.50 | $5,500,000 |

The U.S. Army has approached Klean Fiber and expressed an interest in purchasing 250,000 Y-Go undergarments for soldiers in extremely warm climates. The Army would pay the unit cost for direct materials, direct labor, and variable manufacturing overhead costs. In addition, the Army has agreed to pay an additional $1 per undergarment to cover all other costs and provide a profit. Presently, Klean Fiber is operating at 70% capacity and does not have any other potential buyers for Y-Go. If Klean Fiber accepts the Army's offer, it will not incur any variable selling expenses related to this order.

**Instructions**

Using incremental analysis, determine whether Klean Fiber should accept the Army's offer.

**E20.5 (LO 3), AN** Pottery Ranch Inc. has been manufacturing its own finials for its curtain rods. The company is currently operating at 100% of capacity, and variable manufacturing overhead is charged to production at the rate of 70% of direct labor cost. The direct materials and direct labor cost per unit to make a pair of finials are $4 and $5, respectively. Normal production is 30,000 curtain rods per year.

*Use incremental analysis for make-or-buy decision.*

Excel

A supplier offers to make a pair of finials at a price of $12.95 per unit. If Pottery Ranch accepts the supplier's offer, all variable manufacturing costs will be eliminated, but the $45,000 of fixed manufacturing overhead currently being charged to the finials will have to be absorbed by other products.

**Instructions**

a. Prepare the incremental analysis for the decision to make or buy the finials.

b. Should Pottery Ranch buy the finials?

c. Would your answer be different in (b) if the productive capacity released by not making the finials could be used to produce income of $20,000?

*Use incremental analysis for make-or-buy decision.*

**E20.6 (LO 3), E** Jobs, Inc. has recently started the manufacture of Tri-Robo, a three-wheeled robot that can scan a home for fires and gas leaks and then transmit this information to a smartphone. The cost structure to manufacture 20,000 Tri-Robos is as follows.

|  | Cost |
|---|---|
| Direct materials ($50 per robot) | $1,000,000 |
| Direct labor ($40 per robot) | 800,000 |
| Variable overhead ($6 per robot) | 120,000 |
| Allocated fixed overhead ($30 per robot) | 600,000 |
| Total | $2,520,000 |

Jobs is approached by Tienh Inc., which offers to make Tri-Robo for $115 per unit or $2,300,000.

**Instructions**

a. Using incremental analysis, determine whether Jobs should accept this offer under each of the following independent assumptions.

1. Assume that $405,000 of the fixed overhead cost can be avoided.

2. Assume that none of the fixed overhead can be avoided. However, if the robots are purchased from Tienh Inc., Jobs can use the released productive resources to generate additional income of $375,000.

b. Describe the qualitative factors that might affect the decision to purchase the robots from an outside supplier.

*Prepare incremental analysis for make-or-buy decision.*

**E20.7 (LO 3), E** Riggs Company purchases sails and produces sailboats. It currently produces 1,200 sailboats per year, operating at normal capacity, which is about 80% of full capacity. Riggs purchases sails at $250 each, but the company is considering using the excess capacity to manufacture the sails instead. The manufacturing cost per sail would be $100 for direct materials, $80 for direct labor, and $90 for overhead. The $90 overhead is based on $78,000 of annual fixed overhead that is allocated using normal capacity.

The president of Riggs has come to you for advice. "It would cost me $270 to make the sails," she says, "but only $250 to buy them. Should I continue buying them, or have I missed something?"

**Instructions**

a. Prepare a per unit analysis of the differential costs. Briefly explain whether Riggs should make or buy the sails.

b. If Riggs suddenly finds an opportunity to rent out the unused capacity of its factory for $77,000 per year, would your answer to part (a) change? Briefly explain.

c. Identify three qualitative factors that should be considered by Riggs in this make-or-buy decision.

(CGA adapted)

*Prepare incremental analysis concerning make-or-buy decision.*

**E20.8 (LO 3), E** Innova uses 1,000 units of the component IMC2 every month to manufacture one of its products. The unit costs incurred to manufacture the component are as follows.

| Direct materials | $ 65.00 |
|---|---|
| Direct labor | 45.00 |
| Overhead | 126.50 |
| Total | $236.50 |

Overhead costs include variable material handling costs of $6.50, which are applied to products on the basis of direct material costs. The remainder of the overhead costs are applied on the basis of direct labor dollars and consist of 60% variable costs and 40% fixed costs.

A vendor has offered to supply the IMC2 component at a price of $200 per unit.

**Instructions**

a. Should Innova purchase the component from the outside vendor if Innova's unused facilities remain idle?

b. Should Innova purchase the component from the outside vendor if it can use its facilities to manufacture another product? What information will Innova need to make an accurate decision? Show your calculations.

c. What are the qualitative factors that Innova will have to consider when making this decision?

(CGA adapted)

*Use incremental analysis for further processing of materials decision.*

**E20.9 (LO 4), AN** Anna Garden recently opened her own basketweaving studio. She sells finished baskets in addition to selling the raw materials needed by customers to weave baskets of their own. Unfortunately, owing to space limitations, Anna is unable to carry all the varieties of kits originally assembled and must choose between two basic packages.

The Basic Kit includes undyed, uncut reeds (with dye included) for weaving one basket. This basic package costs Anna $16 and sells for $30. The second kit, called Stage 2, includes cut reeds that have already been dyed. With this kit the customer need only soak the reeds and weave the basket. Anna produces the Stage 2 kit by using the materials included in the Basic Kit. Because she is more efficient at cutting and dying reeds than her average customer, Anna is able to produce two Stage 2 kits in one hour from one Basic Kit. (She values her time at $18 per hour.) The Stage 2 kit sells for $36.

### Instructions

Determine whether Anna's basketweaving studio should carry the Basic Kit with undyed and uncut reeds or the Stage 2 kit with reeds already dyed and cut. Prepare an incremental analysis to support your answer.

**E20.10 (LO 4), AN** Stahl Inc. produces three separate products from a common process costing $100.000. Each of the products can be sold at the split-off point or can be processed further and then sold for a higher price. Shown here are cost and selling price data for a recent period.

*Determine whether to sell or process further, joint products.*

| | Sales Value at Split-Off Point | Cost to Process Further | Sales Value after Further Processing |
|---|---|---|---|
| Product 10 | $60,000 | $100,000 | $190,000 |
| Product 12 | 15,000 | 30,000 | 35,000 |
| Product 14 | 55,000 | 150,000 | 215,000 |

### Instructions

a. Determine total net income if all products are sold at the split-off point.

b. Determine total net income if all products are sold after further processing.

c. Using incremental analysis, determine which products should be sold at the split-off point and which should be processed further.

d. Determine total net income using the results from (c) and explain why the net income is different from that determined in (b).

**E20.11 (LO 4), AN** Kirk Minerals processes materials extracted from mines. The most common raw material that it processes results in three joint products: Spock, Uhura, and Sulu. Each of these products can be sold as is, or each can be processed further and sold for a higher price. The company incurs joint costs of $180,000 to process one batch of the raw material that produces the three joint products. The following cost and sales information is available for one batch of each product.

*Determine whether to sell or process further, joint products.*

| | Sales Value at Split-Off Point | Allocated Joint Costs | Cost to Process Further | Sales Value of Processed Product |
|---|---|---|---|---|
| Spock | $210,000 | $40,000 | $110,000 | $300,000 |
| Uhura | 300,000 | 60,000 | 85,000 | 400,000 |
| Sulu | 455,000 | 80,000 | 250,000 | 800,000 |

### Instructions

Determine whether each of the three joint products should be sold as is, or processed further.

**E20.12 (LO 4), E** A company manufactures three products using the same production process. The costs incurred up to the split-off point are $200,000. These costs are allocated to the products on the basis of their sales value at the split-off point. The number of units produced, the selling prices per unit of the three products at the split-off point and after further processing, and the additional processing costs are as follows.

*Prepare incremental analysis for whether to sell or process materials further.*

| Product | Number of Units Produced | Selling Price at Split-Off | Selling Price after Processing | Additional Processing Costs |
|---|---|---|---|---|
| D | 4,000 | $10.00 | $15.00 | $14,000 |
| E | 6,000 | 11.60 | 16.20 | 20,000 |
| F | 2,000 | 19.40 | 22.60 | 9,000 |

### Instructions

a. Which information is relevant to the decision on whether or not to process the products further? Explain why this information is relevant.

**b.** Which product(s) should be processed further and which should be sold at the split-off point?

**c.** Would your decision be different if the company was using the quantity of output to allocate joint costs? Explain.

(CGA adapted)

*Use incremental analysis for retaining or replacing equipment decision.*

**E20.13 (LO 5), E** Service On January 2, 2021, Twilight Hospital purchased a $100,000 special radiology scanner from Bella Inc. The scanner had a useful life of 4 years and was estimated to have no disposal value at the end of its useful life. The straight-line method of depreciation is used on this scanner. Annual operating costs with this scanner are $105,000.

Approximately one year later, the hospital is approached by Dyno Technology salesperson Jacob Cullen, who indicated that purchasing the scanner in 2021 from Bella Inc. was a mistake. He points out that Dyno has a scanner that will save Twilight Hospital $25,000 a year in operating expenses over its 3-year useful life. Jacob notes that the new scanner will cost $110,000 and has the same capabilities as the scanner purchased last year. The hospital agrees that both scanners are of equal quality. The new scanner will have no disposal value. Jacob agrees to buy the old scanner from Twilight Hospital for $50,000.

### Instructions

**a.** If Twilight Hospital sells its old scanner on January 2, 2022, compute the gain or loss on the sale.

**b.** Using incremental analysis, determine if Twilight Hospital should purchase the new scanner on January 2, 2022.

**c.** Explain why Twilight Hospital might be reluctant to purchase the new scanner, regardless of the results indicated by the incremental analysis in (b).

*Use incremental analysis for retaining or replacing equipment decision.*

**E20.14 (LO 5), AN** Johnson Enterprises uses a computer to handle its sales invoices. Lately, business has been so good that it takes an extra 3 hours per night, plus every third Saturday, to keep up with the volume of sales invoices. Management is considering updating its computer with a faster model that would eliminate all of the overtime processing.

| | Current Machine | New Machine |
| --- | --- | --- |
| Original purchase cost | $15,000 | $25,000 |
| Accumulated depreciation | $ 6,000 | — |
| Estimated annual operating costs | $25,000 | $20,000 |
| Remaining useful life | 5 years | 5 years |

If sold now, the current machine would have a salvage value of $6,000. If operated for the remainder of its useful life, the current machine would have zero salvage value. The new machine is expected to have zero salvage value after 5 years.

### Instructions

Prepare an incremental analysis to determine whether the current machine should be replaced.

*Use incremental analysis concerning elimination of division.*

**E20.15 (LO 6), AN** Veronica Mars, a recent graduate of Bell's accounting program, evaluated the operating performance of Dunn Company's six divisions. Veronica made the following presentation to Dunn's board of directors and suggested the Percy Division be eliminated. "If the Percy Division is eliminated," she said, "our total profits would increase by $26,000."

| | The Other Five Divisions | Percy Division | Total |
| --- | --- | --- | --- |
| Sales | $1,664,200 | $100,000 | $1,764,200 |
| Cost of goods sold | 978,520 | 76,000 | 1,054,520 |
| Gross profit | 685,680 | 24,000 | 709,680 |
| Operating expenses | 527,940 | 50,000 | 577,940 |
| Net income | $ 157,740 | $(26,000) | $ 131,740 |

In the Percy Division, cost of goods sold is $61,000 variable and $15,000 fixed, and operating expenses are $30,000 variable and $20,000 fixed. None of the Percy Division's fixed costs will be eliminated if the division is discontinued.

### Instructions

Is Veronica right about eliminating the Percy Division? Prepare a schedule to support your answer.

*Use incremental analysis for elimination of a product line.*

**E20.16 (LO 6), AN** Cawley Company makes three models of tasers. Information on the three products is given here.

| | Tingler | Shocker | Stunner |
|---|---|---|---|
| Sales | $300,000 | $500,000 | $200,000 |
| Variable expenses | 150,000 | 200,000 | 145,000 |
| Contribution margin | 150,000 | 300,000 | 55,000 |
| Fixed expenses | 120,000 | 230,000 | 95,000 |
| Net income | $ 30,000 | $ 70,000 | $ (40,000) |

Fixed expenses consist of $300,000 of common costs allocated to the three products based on relative sales, as well as direct fixed expenses unique to each model of $30,000 (Tingler), $80,000 (Shocker), and $35,000 (Stunner). The common costs will be incurred regardless of how many models are produced. The direct fixed expenses would be eliminated if that model is phased out.

James Watt, an executive with the company, feels the Stunner line should be discontinued to increase the company's net income.

### Instructions

a. Compute current net income for Cawley Company.

b. Compute net income by product line and in total for Cawley Company if the company discontinues the Stunner product line. (*Hint:* Allocate the $300,000 common costs to the two remaining product lines based on their relative sales.)

c. Should Cawley eliminate the Stunner product line? Why or why not?

**E20.17 (LO 6), AN** Tharp Company operates a small factory in which it manufactures two products: C and D. Production and sales results for last year were as follows.

*Prepare incremental analysis concerning keeping or dropping a product to maximize operating income.*

| | C | D |
|---|---|---|
| Units sold | 9,000 | 20,000 |
| Unit selling price | $95 | $75 |
| Unit variable costs | 50 | 40 |
| Unit fixed costs | 24 | 24 |

For purposes of simplicity, the firm averages total fixed costs over the total number of units of C and D produced and sold.

The research department has developed a new product (E) as a replacement for product D. Market studies show that Tharp Company could sell 10,000 units of E next year at a price of $115; unit variable costs of E are $45. The introduction of product E will lead to a 10% increase in demand for product C and discontinuation of product D. If the company does not introduce the new product, it expects next year's results to be the same as last year's.

### Instructions

Should Tharp Company introduce product E next year? Explain why or why not. Show calculations to support your decision.

(CMA–Canada adapted)

**E20.18 (LO 1, 2, 3, 4, 5, 6), C** The following costs relate to a variety of different decision situations.

*Identify relevant costs for different decisions.*

| Cost | Decision |
|---|---|
| 1. Unavoidable fixed overhead | Eliminate an unprofitable segment |
| 2. Direct labor | Make or buy |
| 3. Original cost of old equipment | Equipment replacement |
| 4. Joint production costs | Sell or process further |
| 5. Opportunity cost | Accepting a special order |
| 6. Segment manager's salary | Eliminate an unprofitable segment (manager will be terminated) |
| 7. Cost of new equipment | Equipment replacement |
| 8. Incremental production costs | Sell or process further |
| 9. Direct materials | Equipment replacement (the amount of materials required does not change) |
| 10. Rent expense | Purchase or lease a building |

### Instructions

For each cost listed above, indicate if it is relevant or not to the related decision. For those costs determined to be irrelevant, briefly explain why.

## Problems

*Use incremental analysis for special order and identify nonfinancial factors in the decision.*

**P20.1 (LO 2), E** Writing ThreePoint Sports Inc. manufactures basketballs for the Women's National Basketball Association (WNBA). For the first 6 months of 2022, the company reported the following operating results while operating at 80% of plant capacity and producing 120,000 units.

| | Amount |
|---|---|
| Sales | $4,800,000 |
| Cost of goods sold | 3,600,000 |
| Selling and administrative expenses | 405,000 |
| Net income | $ 795,000 |

Fixed costs for the period were cost of goods sold $960,000, and selling and administrative expenses $225,000.

In July, normally a slack manufacturing month, ThreePoint Sports receives a special order for 10,000 basketballs at $28 each from the Greek Basketball Association (GBA). Acceptance of the order would increase variable selling and administrative expenses $0.75 per unit because of shipping costs but would not increase fixed costs and expenses.

### Instructions

a. NI increase $37,500

   **a.** Prepare an incremental analysis for the special order.

   **b.** Should ThreePoint Sports Inc. accept the special order? Explain your answer.

   **c.** What is the minimum selling price on the special order to produce net income of $5.00 per ball?

   **d.** What nonfinancial factors should management consider in making its decision?

*Use incremental analysis related to make or buy, consider opportunity cost, and identify nonfinancial factors.*

**P20.2 (LO 3), E** Writing The management of Shatner Manufacturing Company is trying to decide whether to continue manufacturing a part or to buy it from an outside supplier. The part, called CISCO, is a component of the company's finished product.

The following information was collected from the accounting records and production data for the year ending December 31, 2022.

   **1.** 8,000 units of CISCO were produced in the Machining Department.

   **2.** Variable manufacturing costs applicable to the production of each CISCO unit were: direct materials $4.80, direct labor $4.30, indirect labor $0.43, utilities $0.40.

   **3.** Fixed manufacturing costs applicable to the production of CISCO were:

| Cost Item | Direct | Allocated | Total |
|---|---|---|---|
| Depreciation | $2,100 | $ 900 | $3,000 |
| Property taxes | 500 | 200 | 700 |
| Insurance | 900 | 600 | 1,500 |
| | $3,500 | $1,700 | $5,200 |

All variable manufacturing and direct fixed costs will be eliminated if CISCO is purchased. Allocated costs will not be eliminated if CISCO is purchased. So if CISCO is purchased, the fixed manufacturing costs allocated to CISCO will have to be absorbed by other production departments.

   **4.** The lowest quotation for 8,000 CISCO units from a supplier is $80,000.

   **5.** If CISCO units are purchased, freight and inspection costs would be $0.35 per unit, and receiving costs totaling $1,300 per year would be incurred by the Machining Department.

### Instructions

a. NI (decrease) $(1,160)

   **a.** Prepare an incremental analysis for CISCO. Your analysis should have columns for (1) Make CISCO, (2) Buy CISCO, and (3) Net Income Increase/(Decrease).

   **b.** Based on your analysis, what decision should management make?

c. NI increase $1,840

   **c.** Would the decision be different if Shatner Company has the opportunity to produce $3,000 of net income with the facilities currently being used to manufacture CISCO? Show computations.

   **d.** What nonfinancial factors should management consider in making its decision?

*Determine if product should be sold or processed further.*

→ Excel

**P20.3 (LO 4), AN** Thompson Industrial Products Inc. (TIPI) is a diversified industrial-cleaner processing company. The company's Dargan plant produces two products, a table cleaner and a floor cleaner, from a common set of chemical inputs (CDG). Each week, 900,000 ounces of chemical input are processed at a cost of $210,000 into 600,000 ounces of floor cleaner and 300,000 ounces of table cleaner. The floor cleaner has no market value until it is converted into a polish with the trade name FloorShine. The additional processing costs for this conversion amount to $240,000.

FloorShine sells at $20 per 30-ounce bottle. The table cleaner can be sold for $17 per 25-ounce bottle. However, the table cleaner can be converted into two other products by adding 300,000 ounces of another compound (TCP) to the 300,000 ounces of table cleaner. This joint process will yield 300,000 ounces each of table stain remover (TSR) and table polish (TP). The additional processing costs for this process amount to $100,000. Both table products can be sold for $14 per 25-ounce bottle.

The company decided not to process the table cleaner into TSR and TP based on the following analysis.

| | | Process Further | | |
| | Table Cleaner | Table Stain Remover (TSR) | Table Polish (TP) | Total |
|---|---|---|---|---|
| Production in ounces | 300,000 | 300,000 | 300,000 | |
| Revenues | $204,000 | $168,000 | $168,000 | $336,000 |
| Costs: | | | | |
| CDG costs | 70,000* | 52,500 | 52,500 | 105,000** |
| TCP costs | -0- | 50,000 | 50,000 | 100,000 |
| Total costs | 70,000 | 102,500 | 102,500 | 205,000 |
| Weekly gross profit | $134,000 | $ 65,500 | $ 65,500 | $131,000 |

*If table cleaner is not processed further, it is allocated $\frac{1}{3}$ of the $210,000 of CDG cost, which is equal to $\frac{1}{3}$ of the total physical output.

**If table cleaner is processed further, total physical output is 1,200,000 ounces. TSR and TP combined account for 50% of the total physical output and are each allocated 25% of the CDG cost.

### Instructions

a. Determine if management made the correct decision to not process the table cleaner further by doing the following.

1. Calculate the company's total weekly gross profit assuming the table cleaner is not processed further.

2. Calculate the company's total weekly gross profit assuming the table cleaner is processed further.

3. Compare the resulting net incomes and comment on management's decision.

b. Using incremental analysis, determine if the table cleaner should be processed further.

(CMA adapted)

*a. 2. Gross profit $186,000*

**P20.4 (LO 5), S** `Service` `Writing` At the beginning of last year (2021), Richter Condos installed a mechanized elevator for its tenants. The owner of the company, Ron Richter, recently returned from an industry equipment exhibition where he watched a computerized elevator demonstrated. He was impressed with the elevator's speed, comfort of ride, and cost efficiency. Upon returning from the exhibition, he asked his purchasing agent to collect price and operating cost data on the new elevator. In addition, he asked the company's accountant to provide him with cost data on the company's elevator. This information is presented here.

*Compute gain or loss, and determine if equipment should be replaced.*

| | Old Elevator | New Elevator |
|---|---|---|
| Purchase price | $120,000 | $160,000 |
| Estimated salvage value | -0- | -0- |
| Estimated useful life | 5 years | 4 years |
| Depreciation method | Straight-line | Straight-line |
| Annual operating costs other than depreciation: | | |
| Variable | $35,000 | $10,000 |
| Fixed | 23,000 | 8,500 |

Annual revenues are $240,000, and selling and administrative expenses are $29,000, regardless of which elevator is used. If the old elevator is replaced now, at the beginning of 2022, Richter Condos will be able to sell it for $25,000.

**Instructions**

a. Determine any gain or loss if the old elevator is replaced.

b. Prepare a 4-year summarized income statement for each of the following assumptions:

1. The old elevator is retained.

b. 2. NI $539,000

2. The old elevator is replaced.

c. NI increase $23,000

c. Using incremental analysis, determine if the old elevator should be replaced.

d. Write a memo to Ron Richter explaining why any gain or loss should be ignored in the decision to replace the old elevator.

*Prepare incremental analysis concerning elimination of divisions.*

**P20.5 (LO 6), AN** Brislin Company has four operating divisions. During the first quarter of 2022, the company reported aggregate income from operations of $213,000 and the following divisional results.

| | Division | | | |
|---|---|---|---|---|
| | **I** | **II** | **III** | **IV** |
| Sales | $250,000 | $200,000 | $500,000 | $450,000 |
| Cost of goods sold | 200,000 | 192,000 | 300,000 | 250,000 |
| Selling and administrative expenses | 75,000 | 60,000 | 60,000 | 50,000 |
| Income (loss) from operations | $(25,000) | $(52,000) | $140,000 | $150,000 |

Analysis reveals the following percentages of variable costs in each division.

| | **I** | **II** | **III** | **IV** |
|---|---|---|---|---|
| Cost of goods sold | 70% | 90% | 80% | 75% |
| Selling and administrative expenses | 40 | 60 | 50 | 60 |

Discontinuance of any division would save 50% of the fixed costs and expenses for that division.

Top management is very concerned about the unprofitable divisions (I and II). Consensus is that one or both of the divisions should be discontinued.

**Instructions**

a. Contribution margin I $80,000

a. Compute the contribution margin for Divisions I and II.

b. Prepare an incremental analysis concerning the possible discontinuance of (1) Division I and (2) Division II. What course of action do you recommend for each division?

c. Income III $132,800

c. Prepare a columnar condensed income statement for Brislin Company, assuming Division II is eliminated. (Use the CVP format.) Division II's unavoidable fixed costs are allocated equally to the continuing divisions.

d. Reconcile the total income from operations ($213,000) with the total income from operations without Division II.

# Continuing Cases

## Current Designs

**CD20 Current Designs** faces a number of important decisions that require incremental analysis. Consider each of the following situations independently.

### Situation 1

Recently, Mike Cichanowski, owner and CEO of Current Designs, received a phone call from the president of a brewing company. He was calling to inquire about the possibility of Current Designs producing "floating coolers" for a promotion his company was planning. These coolers resemble kayaks but are about one-third the size. They are used to float food and beverages while paddling down the river on a weekend leisure trip. The company would be interested in purchasing 100 coolers for the upcoming summer. It is willing to pay $250 per cooler. The brewing company would pick up the coolers upon completion of the order.

Mike met with Diane Buswell, controller, to identify how much it would cost Current Designs to produce the coolers. After careful analysis, the following costs were identified.

| | |
|---|---|
| Direct materials | $80/unit |
| Direct labor | $60/unit |
| Variable overhead | $20/unit |

Current Designs would be able to modify an existing mold to produce the coolers. The cost of these modifications would be approximately $3,000.

### Instructions

a. Assuming that the company has available capacity, prepare an incremental analysis to determine whether Current Designs should accept this special order to produce the coolers.

b. Discuss additional factors that Mike and Diane should consider if Current Designs is currently operating at full capacity.

### Situation 2

Current Designs is always working to identify ways to increase efficiency while becoming more environmentally conscious. During a recent brainstorming session, one employee suggested to Diane Buswell, controller, that the company should consider replacing the current rotomold oven as a way to realize savings from reduced energy consumption. The oven operates on natural gas, using 17,000 therms of natural gas for an entire year. A new, energy-efficient rotomold oven would operate on 15,000 therms of natural gas for an entire year. After seeking out price quotes from a few suppliers, Diane determined that it would cost approximately $250,000 to purchase a new, energy-efficient rotomold oven. She determines that the expected useful life of the new oven would be 10 years, and it would have no salvage value at the end of its useful life. Current Designs would be able to sell the current oven for $10,000.

### Instructions

a. Prepare an incremental analysis to determine if Current Designs should purchase the new rotomold oven, assuming that the average price for natural gas over the next 10 years will be $0.65 per therm.

b. Diane is concerned that natural gas prices might increase at a faster rate over the next 10 years. If the company projects that the average natural gas price of the next 10 years could be as high as $0.85 per therm, discuss how that might change your conclusion in (a).

### Situation 3

One of Current Designs' competitive advantages is found in the ingenuity of its owner and CEO, Mike Cichanowski. His involvement in the design of kayak molds and production techniques has led to Current Designs being recognized as an industry leader in the design and production of kayaks. This ingenuity was evident in an improved design of one of the most important components of a kayak, the seat. The "Revolution Seating System" is a one-of-a-kind, rotating axis seat that gives unmatched, full-contact, under-leg support. It is quickly adjustable with a lever-lock system that allows for a customizable seat position that maximizes comfort for the rider.

Having just designed the "Revolution Seating System," Current Designs must now decide whether to produce the seats internally or buy them from an outside supplier. The costs for Current Designs to produce the seats are as follows.

| | | | |
|---|---|---|---|
| Direct materials | $20/unit | Direct labor | $15/unit |
| Variable overhead | $12/unit | Fixed overhead | $20,000 |

Current Designs will need to produce 3,000 seats this year; 25% of the fixed overhead will be avoided if the seats are purchased from an outside vendor. After soliciting prices from outside suppliers, the company determined that it will cost $50 to purchase a seat from an outside vendor.

### Instructions

a. Prepare an incremental analysis showing whether Current Designs should make or buy the "Revolution Seating System."

b. Would your answer in (a) change if the productive capacity released by not making the seats could be used to produce income of $20,000?

## Waterways Corporation

(*Note:* This is a continuation of the Waterways case from Chapters 14–19.)

**WC20** Waterways Corporation is considering various business opportunities. It wants to make the best use of its production facilities to maximize income. This case asks you to help Waterways do incremental analysis on these various opportunities.

*Go to WileyPLUS for complete case details and instructions.*

# Expand Your Critical Thinking

## Decision-Making Across the Organization

**CT20.1** Aurora Company is considering the purchase of a new machine. The invoice price of the machine is $140,000, freight charges are estimated to be $4,000, and installation costs are expected to be $6,000. Salvage value of the new equipment is expected to be zero after a useful life of 5 years. Existing equipment could be retained and used for an additional 5 years if the new machine is not purchased. At that time, the salvage value of the equipment would be zero. If the new machine is purchased now, the existing machine would have to be scrapped. Aurora's accountant, Lisah Huang, has accumulated the following data regarding annual sales and expenses with and without the new machine.

1. Without the new machine, Aurora can sell 12,000 units of product annually at a per unit selling price of $100. If the new machine is purchased, the number of units produced and sold would increase by 10%, and the selling price would remain the same.

2. The new machine is faster than the old machine, and it is more efficient in its usage of materials. With the old machine the gross profit rate will be 25% of sales, whereas the rate will be 30% of sales with the new machine.

3. Annual selling expenses are $180,000 with the current equipment. Because the new equipment would produce a greater number of units to be sold, annual selling expenses are expected to increase by 10% if it is purchased.

4. Annual administrative expenses are expected to be $100,000 with the old machine, and $113,000 with the new machine.

5. The current book value of the existing machine is $36,000. Aurora uses straight-line depreciation.

### Instructions

With the class divided into groups, prepare an incremental analysis for the 5 years showing whether Aurora should keep the existing machine or buy the new machine. (Ignore income tax effects.)

## Managerial Analysis

**CT20.2** MiniTek manufactures private-label small electronic products, such as alarm clocks, calculators, kitchen timers, stopwatches, and automatic pencil sharpeners. Some of the products are sold as sets, and others are sold individually. Products are studied as to their sales potential, and then cost estimates are made. The Engineering Department develops production plans, and then production begins. The company has generally had very successful product introductions. Only two products introduced by the company have been discontinued.

One of the products currently sold is a multi-alarm clock. The clock has four alarms that can be programmed to sound at various times and for varying lengths of time. The company has experienced a great deal of difficulty in making the circuit boards for the clocks. The production process has never operated smoothly. The product is unprofitable at the present time, primarily because of warranty repairs and product recalls. Two models of the clocks were recalled, for example, because they sometimes caused an electric shock when the alarms were being shut off. The Engineering Department is attempting to revise the manufacturing process, but the revision will take another 6 months at least.

The clocks were very popular when they were introduced, and since they are private-label, the company has not suffered much from the recalls. Presently, the company has a very large order for several items from BigMart. The order includes 5,000 of the multi-alarm clocks. When the company suggested that BigMart purchase the clocks from another manufacturer, BigMart threatened to rescind the entire order unless the clocks were included.

The company has therefore investigated the possibility of having another company make the clocks for them. The clocks were bid for the BigMart order based on an estimated $6.90 cost to manufacture:

| | |
|---|---|
| Circuit board, 1 each @ $2.00 | $2.00 |
| Plastic case, 1 each @ $0.80 | 0.80 |
| Alarms, 4 @ $0.15 each | 0.60 |
| Labor, 15 minutes @ $12/hour | 3.00 |
| Overhead, $2.00 per labor hour | 0.50 |

MiniTek could purchase clocks to fill the BigMart order for $10 from Trans-Tech Asia, a Korean manufacturer with a very good quality record. Trans-Tech has offered to reduce the price to $7.50 after MiniTek has been a customer for 6 months, placing an order of at least 1,000 units per month. If MiniTek becomes a "preferred customer" by purchasing 15,000 units per year, the price would be reduced still further to $4.50.

Omega Products, a local manufacturer, has also offered to make clocks for MiniTek. They have offered to sell 5,000 clocks for $5 each. However, Omega Products has been in business for only 6 months. They have experienced significant turnover in their labor force, and the local press has reported that the owners may face tax evasion charges soon. The owner of Omega Products is an electronics engineer, however, and the quality of the clocks is likely to be good.

If MiniTek decides to purchase the clocks from either Trans-Tech or Omega, all the costs to manufacture could be avoided, except a total of $1,000 in overhead costs for machine depreciation. The machinery is fairly new, and has no alternate use.

**Instructions**

a. What is the difference in profit under each of the alternatives if the clocks are to be sold for $14.50 each to BigMart?

b. What are the most important nonfinancial factors that MiniTek should consider when making this decision?

c. What do you think MiniTek should do in regard to the BigMart order? What should it do in regard to continuing to manufacture the multi-alarm clocks? Be prepared to defend your answer.

## Real-World Focus

**CT20.3**  Founded in 1983 and foreclosed in 1996, **Beverly Hills Fan Company** was located in Woodland Hills, California. With 23 employees and sales of less than $10 million, the company was relatively small. Management felt that there was potential for growth in the upscale market for ceiling fans and lighting. They were particularly optimistic about growth in Mexican and Canadian markets.

Presented here is information from the president's letter in one of the company's last annual reports.

### Beverly Hills Fan Company
#### President's Letter

An aggressive product development program was initiated during the past year resulting in new ceiling fan models planned for introduction this year. Award winning industrial designer Ron Rezek created several new fan models for the Beverly Hills Fan and L.A. Fan lines, including a new Showroom Collection, designed specifically for the architectural and designer markets. Each of these models has received critical acclaim, and order commitments for this year have been outstanding. Additionally, our Custom Color and special order fans continued to enjoy increasing popularity and sales gains as more and more customers desire fans that match their specific interior decors. Currently, Beverly Hills Fan Company offers a product line of over 100 models of contemporary, traditional, and transitional ceiling fans.

**Instructions**

a. What points did the company management need to consider before deciding to offer the special-order fans to customers?

b. How would have incremental analysis been employed to assist in this decision?

## Communication Activity

**CT20.4**  Hank Jewell is a production manager at a metal fabricating factory. Last night, he read an article about a new piece of equipment that would dramatically reduce his division's costs. Hank was very excited about the prospect, and the first thing he did this morning was to bring the article to his supervisor, Preston Thiese, the factory manager. The following conversation occurred:

Hank:  Preston, I thought you would like to see this article on the new PDD1130; they've made some fantastic changes that could save us millions of dollars.

Preston:  I appreciate your interest, Hank, but I actually have been aware of the new machine for 2 months. The problem is that we just bought a new machine last year. We spent $2 million on that machine, and it was supposed to last us 12 years. If we replace it now, we would have to write its book value off of the books for a huge loss. If I go to top management now and say that I want a new machine, they will fire me. I think we should use our existing machine for a couple of years, and then when it becomes obvious that we have to have a new machine, I will make the proposal.

**Instructions**

Hank just completed a course in managerial accounting, and he believes that Preston is making a big mistake. Write a memo from Hank to Preston explaining Preston's decision-making error.

### Ethics Case

**CT20.5** Blake Romney became chief executive officer of Peters Inc. 2 years ago. At the time, the company was reporting lagging profits, and Blake was brought in to "stir things up." The company has three divisions: electronics, fiber optics, and plumbing supplies. Blake has no interest in plumbing supplies, and one of the first things he did was to put pressure on his accountants to reallocate some of the company's fixed costs away from the other two divisions to the plumbing division. This had the effect of causing the plumbing division to report losses during the last 2 years; in the past it had always reported low, but acceptable, net income. Blake felt that this reallocation would shine a favorable light on him in front of the board of directors because it meant that the electronics and fiber optics divisions would look like they were improving. Given that these are "businesses of the future," he believed that the stock market would react favorably to these increases, while not penalizing the poor results of the plumbing division. Without this shift in the allocation of fixed costs, the profits of the electronics and fiber optics divisions would not have improved. But now the board of directors has suggested that the plumbing division be closed because it is reporting losses. This would mean that nearly 500 employees, many of whom have worked for Peters their whole lives, would lose their jobs.

#### Instructions

    **a.** If a division is reporting losses, does that necessarily mean that it should be closed?

    **b.** Was the reallocation of fixed costs across divisions unethical?

    **c.** What should Blake do?

### All About You

**CT20.6** Managerial accounting techniques can be used in a wide variety of settings. As we have frequently pointed out, you can use them in many personal situations. They also can be useful in trying to find solutions for societal issues that appear to be hard to solve.

#### Instructions

Read the *Fortune* article, "The Toughest Customers: How Hardheaded Business Metrics Can Help the Hard-Core Homeless," by Cait Murphy (do an Internet search on the title), and then answer the following questions.

    **a.** How does the article define "chronic" homelessness?

    **b.** In what ways does homelessness cost a city money? What are the estimated costs of a chronic homeless person to various cities?

    **c.** What are the steps suggested to address the problem?

    **d.** What is the estimated cost of implementing this program in New York? What results have been seen?

    **e.** In terms of incremental analysis, frame the relevant costs in this situation.

### Considering Your Costs and Benefits

**CT20.7** School costs money. Is this an expenditure that you should have avoided? On average, a year of tuition at a public four-year college costs about $10,000, and a year of tuition at a public two-year college costs about $5,000. If you did not go to college, you might avoid mountains of school-related debt. In fact, each year, about 600,000 students decide to drop out of school. Many of them never return. Suppose that you are working two jobs and going to college, and that you are not making ends meet. Your grades are suffering due to your lack of available study time. You feel depressed. Should you drop out of school?

    **YES:** You can always go back to school. If your grades are bad and you are depressed, what good is school doing you anyway?

    **NO:** Once you drop out, it is very hard to get enough momentum to go back. Dropping out will dramatically reduce your long-term opportunities. It is better to stay in school, even if you take only one class per semester. While you cannot go back and redo your initial decision, you can look at some facts to evaluate the wisdom of your decision.

#### Instructions

Write a response indicating your position regarding this situation. Provide support for your view.

### Answers to Insight and Accounting Across the Organization Questions

**That Letter from AmEx Might Not Be a Bill** **Q:** What are the relevant costs that American Express would need to know in order to determine to whom to make this offer? **A:** Clearly, American Express would make this offer to those customers that are most likely to default on their bills. The most important relevant cost would be the "expected loss" that an at-risk customer posed. If a customer has a high probability of defaulting and if the expected loss exceeds the $300 cost, then American Express can probably save money by paying that customer to quit using its card so that the customer doesn't ring up an even bigger bill.

**Batteries Are Included!** Q: What are the factors that companies must consider in deciding whether to make or to buy the batteries for their vehicles? **A:** The quantitative factors include whether the avoidable costs, both variable and fixed, of making the batteries are less than the purchase price of the batteries. In addition, the avoidable costs must be increased if there are any opportunity costs associated with making the batteries. The choice should be the alternative with the least cost. However, there are qualitative factors that may impact the decision. What if some skilled employees would lose their jobs if the batteries are purchased? In addition, management must assess the supplier's ability to meet the company's production schedule as well as its quality control standards at the quoted unit price.

**Giving Away the Store?** Q: What are the relevant revenues and costs that Amazon should consider relative to the decision whether to offer the Prime free-shipping subscription? **A:** The relevant revenues to consider would be the estimated change in revenue that would result from offering free shipping and the cost of the annual fee for a Prime subscription. The relevant costs would be the estimated additional shipping costs that the company would incur.

## CHAPTER 21

Rawpixel.com/Adobe Stock

# Pricing

## Chapter Preview

As the following Feature Story about **Zappos.com** indicates, few management decisions are more important than setting prices. **Intel**, for example, must sell computer chips at a price that is high enough to cover its costs and ensure a reasonable profit. But if the price is too high, the chips will not sell. In this chapter, we examine two types of pricing situations. The first part of the chapter addresses pricing for goods sold or services provided to external parties. The second part of the chapter addresses pricing decisions managers face when they sell goods to other divisions within the company.

## Feature Story

### They've Got Your Size—and Color

Nick Swinmurn was shopping for a pair of shoes. He found a store with the right style, but not the right color. The next store had the right color, but not the right size. After visiting numerous stores, he went home, figuring he would buy them online.

After all, it was 1999, so you could buy everything online, right? Well, apparently not shoes. After an exhaustive search, Nick still came up shoeless.

Nick lived in San Francisco, where in 1999 everybody with even half an idea started an Internet company and became a millionaire. Or so it seemed. So Nick started **Zappos.com.** The company is dedicated to providing the best selection in shoes in terms of brands, styles, colors, size, and, most importantly, service.

To make sure that Zappos had a fighting chance of evolving from a half-baked idea to a thriving business, Nick brought in Tony Hsieh. At the age of 24, Tony had developed and recently sold a business to **Microsoft** for $265 million. Tony then brought in Alfred Lin to manage the company's finances. Tony and Alfred first met when Tony was running a pizza business and Alfred was Tony's best pizza customer. Together, Tony and Alfred have run Zappos based on 10 basic principles:

1. Deliver WOW through service.
2. Embrace and drive change.
3. Create fun and a little weirdness.
4. Be adventurous, creative, and open-minded.
5. Pursue growth and learning.
6. Build open and honest relationships with communication.
7. Build a positive team and family spirit.
8. Do more with less.
9. Be passionate and determined.
10. Be humble.

Are you looking for a pair of size 6 Giuseppe Zanotti heels for $1,295 or a pair of Keen size 17 sandals for $95? Zappos is committed to having what you want and getting it to you as fast as possible. Providing this kind of service is not cheap, however. It means having vast warehouses and sophisticated order processing systems. The company's price has to cover its costs and provide a reasonable profit yet still be competitive. If the price is too high, Zappos loses business. Too low and the company could lose its shirt (or in this case, shoes).

**Source:** *www.zappos.com.*

 **Video** Watch the *Zappos.com* video in WileyPLUS to learn more about how the company sets prices.

## Chapter Outline

| LEARNING OBJECTIVES | REVIEW | PRACTICE |
|---|---|---|
| **LO 1** Compute a target cost when the market determines a product price. | • Establishing a target cost | **DO IT! 1** Target Costing |
| **LO 2** Compute a target selling price using cost-plus pricing. | • Cost-plus pricing<br>• Limitations of cost-plus pricing<br>• Variable-cost pricing | **DO IT! 2** Target Selling Price |
| **LO 3** Use time-and-material pricing to determine the cost of services provided. | • Calculate labor rate<br>• Calculate material loading charge<br>• Calculate charges for a particular job | **DO IT! 3** Time-and-Material Pricing |
| **LO 4** Determine a transfer price using the negotiated, cost-based, and market-based approaches. | • Negotiated transfer prices<br>• Cost-based transfer prices<br>• Market-based transfer prices<br>• Effect of outsourcing on transfer pricing<br>• Transfers between divisions in different countries | **DO IT! 4** Transfer Pricing |

**Go to the Review and Practice section at the end of the chapter for a targeted summary and practice applications with solutions.**

**Visit WileyPLUS for additional tutorials and practice opportunities.**

# Target Costing

### LEARNING OBJECTIVE 1
Compute a target cost when the market determines a product price.

Establishing the price for any good or service is affected by many factors. Take the pharmaceutical industry as an example. Its approach to profitability has been to:

- Spend heavily on research and development in an effort to find and patent a few new drugs.
- Price them high.
- Market them aggressively.

Individuals in the United States sometimes question whether these prices are too high. For example, the price of EpiPens® received considerable criticism. The drug companies counter that they need to set these prices high to cover their substantial financial risks to develop these products. **Illustration 21.1** indicates the many factors that can affect pricing decisions.

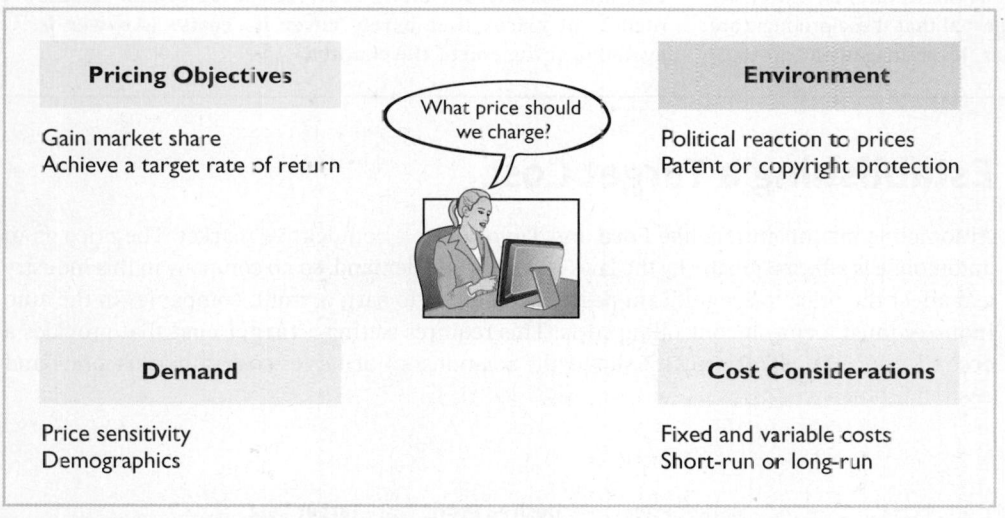

**Pricing Objectives**

Gain market share
Achieve a target rate of return

*What price should we charge?*

**Environment**

Political reaction to prices
Patent or copyright protection

**Demand**

Price sensitivity
Demographics

**Cost Considerations**

Fixed and variable costs
Short-run or long-run

**ILLUSTRATION 21.1**

**Pricing factors**

**In the long run, a company must price its product to cover its costs and earn a reasonable profit.**

- But to price its product appropriately, it must have a good understanding of market forces at work.
- In most cases, a company does not set the prices.
- Instead, the price is set by the competitive market (the laws of supply and demand).

For example, a company such as **Chevron** or **ExxonMobil** cannot set the price of gasoline by itself. These companies are called **price takers** because the price of gasoline is set by market forces (the supply of oil and the demand by customers). This is the case for any product that is not easily differentiated from competing products, such as farm products (corn or wheat) or minerals (coal or sand).

In other situations, the company sets the prices:

- When the product is specially made for a customer. An example would be a unique dress designed by **Versace** or **Armani**.
- When there are few or no other producers capable of manufacturing a similar item. An example would be a company that has a patent or copyright on a unique process, such as computer chips by **Intel**.

- When it effectively differentiates its product or service from others. For example, even in a competitive market like coffee, **Starbucks** has been able to differentiate its product and charge a premium for a cup of java.

---

## Management Insight   Amazon.com

Cyberstock/Alamy Stock Photo

### Pricing to Sell

Managers at **Amazon.com** make many different pricing decisions for products with vastly different characteristics. For example, Amazon provides "cloud services" to both corporate and retail clients, as well as video rental, book sales, and order fulfillment services for thousands of different vendors. It also has produced and sold some of its own electronic devices, with varying degrees of success. For example, Amazon produced the Fire smartphone, which it tried unsuccessfully to sell for the same premium price as the iPhone (eventually, it had to offer steep discounts before it discontinued its sales).

On the other end of the price spectrum, Amazon has offered tablets and e-reader devices (such as the Kindle) for extremely low prices. In fact, some have suggested that these products are sold below cost. Why would Amazon's management do that?

Because the company makes money on the services delivered by tablets and e-readers, such as e-books and movies. (This is similar to **Google**, which provides many of its services for free but then makes advertising revenue as people use its free services.) In fact, even on its cheapest electronic devices, Amazon is cognizant of its costs. Although it desired to set the target price of its cheapest Kindle at $50, "the e-reader screen technology from its vendors ultimately proved too expensive to drop the retail price." Ultimately, Amazon decided it could not price the Kindle below $79.

**Source:** Greg Bensinger, "Amazon to Release $50 Tablet as It Struggles to Sell Pricier Devices," *Wall Street Journal* (September 7, 2015).

**Why did Amazon choose to charge a premium price for its Fire smartphone but offers some of its tablet and Kindle models at prices that barely cover its costs? (Answer is available at the end of the chapter.)**

---

# Establishing a Target Cost

Automobile manufacturers like **Ford** and **Toyota** face a competitive market. The price of an automobile is affected greatly by the laws of supply and demand, so no company in this industry can affect the price to a significant degree. Therefore, to earn a profit, companies in the auto industry must focus on controlling costs. This requires setting a **target cost** that provides a desired profit. **Illustration 21.2** shows the relationship of target cost to market price and desired profit.

**ILLUSTRATION 21.2**

**Target cost as related to price and profit**

> **Market Price   —   Desired Profit   =   Target Cost**

Assuming it reaches sales targets, if **General Motors** can produce its automobiles for its target cost (or less), it will meet its profit goal. If it cannot achieve its target cost, it will fail to achieve the desired profit, which will disappoint its stockholders.

In a competitive market, a company generally establishes and uses a target cost as follows.

1. **Chooses the segment of the market it wants to compete in—that is, its market niche.** For example, it may choose between selling luxury goods or economy goods in order to focus its efforts on one segment or the other.
2. **Conducts market research.** This determines the features its product should have, and what the market price is for a product with those features.
3. **Determines its target cost by setting a desired profit.** The difference between the market price and the desired profit is the target cost of the product (shown in Illustration 21.2).
4. **Assembles a team of employees with expertise in a variety of areas (production and operations, marketing, and finance).** The team's task is to design and develop a product that can meet quality specifications while not exceeding the target cost.

Thus, the target cost includes all product and period costs necessary to make and market the product or service.

## Service Company Insight    Disney

Tomas Abad/Alamy
Stock Photo

### How Much Did You Pay for That Seat?

Pricing decisions are now frequently made by sophisticated computer algorithms. This is true for airlines, hotels, and even Broadway shows. Pricing for these service businesses is particularly important because no revenue is earned on an unused airplane seat, hotel room, or theater seat. These algorithms, which are based on models derived from vast amounts of data from previous customer experiences, strive to determine the best price to charge to fill the seats and maximize revenue. Prices are very dynamic, changing daily or hourly. As a result, it is not unusual to sit directly next to somebody that paid significantly more (or less) than you did on an airplane.

Experts says that the algorithm that **Disney** employs to determine ticket prices for its Broadway show *The Lion King* is among the best in the business. Disney's pricing model enabled *The Lion King* to nearly double its revenues within six years. As a consequence, the company is very reluctant to reveal specific information about its formulas.

**Source:** Patrick Healy, "Ticket Pricing Puts 'Lion King' Atop Broadway's Circle of Life," *The New York Times* (March 17, 2014).

**What factors must the managers of a Broadway show consider when setting prices? (Answer is available at the end of the chapter.)**

---

## DO IT! 1 | Target Costing

Fine Line Phones is considering introducing a fashion cover for its phones. Market research indicates that 200,000 units can be sold if the price is no more than $20. If Fine Line decides to produce the covers, it will need to invest $1,000,000 in new production equipment. Fine Line requires a minimum rate of return of 25% on all investments.

Determine the target cost per unit for the cover.

### Solution

The desired profit for this new product line is as follows.

| Invested assets | × | Minimum rate of return | = | Desired profit |
|---|---|---|---|---|
| $1,000,000 | × | 25% | = | $250,000 |

Each cover must therefore result in $1.25 of profit ($250,000 ÷ 200,000 units). The target cost per unit for the cover can then be calculated as follows.

| Market price | – | Desired profit | = | Target cost per unit |
|---|---|---|---|---|
| $20 | – | $1.25 | = | $18.75 per unit |

Related exercise material: **BE21.1, DO IT! 21.1, E21.1, and E21.2.**

**ACTION PLAN**

- **Recall that Market price – Desired profit = Target cost.**
- **The minimum rate of return is a company's desired profit.**

---

# Cost-Plus and Variable-Cost Pricing

### LEARNING OBJECTIVE 2

Compute a target selling price using cost-plus pricing.

## Cost-Plus Pricing

As discussed, in a competitive product environment, the price of a product is set by the market. In order to achieve its desired profit, the company focuses on achieving a target cost.

- In a less competitive environment, companies have a greater ability to set the product price.
- Commonly, when a company sets a product price, it does so as a function of, or relative to, the cost of the product or service. This is referred to as **cost-plus pricing**.

- Under cost-plus pricing, a company first determines a cost base and then adds a **markup** to the cost base to determine the **target selling price**.

If the cost base includes all of the costs required to produce and sell the product, then the markup represents the desired profit.

- The size of the markup (profit) depends on the return the company hopes to generate on the amount it has invested.
- In determining the optimal markup, the company must also consider competitive and market conditions, political and legal issues, and other relevant factors.
- Once the company has determined its cost base and its desired markup, it can add the two together to determine the target selling price.

**Illustration 21.3** presents the basic cost-plus pricing equation.

**ILLUSTRATION 21.3**

**Cost-plus pricing equation**

$$\text{Cost} \quad + \quad \text{Markup} \quad = \quad \text{Target Selling Price}$$

To illustrate, assume that Thinkmore Products, Inc. is in the process of setting a selling price on its new video camera pen. It is a functioning pen that records up to 2 hours of audio and video. The unit variable cost estimates for the video camera pen are as shown in **Illustration 21.4**.

**ILLUSTRATION 21.4**

**Unit variable cost**

|  | Per Unit |
|---|---|
| Direct materials | $23 |
| Direct labor | 17 |
| Variable manufacturing overhead | 12 |
| Variable selling and administrative expenses | 8 |
| Unit variable cost | **$60** |

To produce and sell its product, Thinkmore incurs fixed manufacturing overhead of $350,000 and fixed selling and administrative expenses of $300,000. To determine the unit cost, we divide total fixed costs by the number of units the company expects to produce. **Illustration 21.5** shows the computation of unit fixed cost for Thinkmore, assuming the production of 10,000 units.

**ILLUSTRATION 21.5**

**Unit fixed cost, 10,000 units**

|  | Total Costs | ÷ | Budgeted Volume | = | Unit Cost |
|---|---|---|---|---|---|
| Fixed manufacturing overhead | $350,000 | ÷ | 10,000 | = | $35 |
| Fixed selling and administrative expenses | 300,000 | ÷ | 10,000 | = | 30 |
| Unit fixed cost (at 10,000 units) |  |  |  |  | **$65** |

Management is ultimately evaluated based on its ability to generate a high return on the company's investment. This is frequently expressed as a return on investment (ROI) percentage, calculated as income divided by the average amount invested in a product or service. A higher percentage reflects a greater success in generating profits from the investment in a product or service. Chapter 23 provides a more in-depth discussion of the use of ROI to evaluate the performance of investment center managers.

- To achieve a desired ROI percentage, a product's markup should be determined by calculating the desired ROI per unit.
- This is calculated by multiplying the desired ROI percentage times the amount invested to produce the product, and then dividing this by the number of units produced.

**Illustration 21.6** shows the computation used to determine a markup amount based on a desired ROI per unit for Thinkmore, assuming that the company expects to produce 10,000 units, desires a 20% ROI, and invests $2,000,000.

ILLUSTRATION 21.6

**Calculation of markup based on desired ROI per unit**

| Desired ROI Percentage × Amount Invested | = | Markup (Desired ROI per Unit) |
|---|---|---|
| Units Produced | | |
| $\dfrac{20\% \times \$2,000,000}{10,000 \text{ units}}$ | = | $40 |

Thinkmore expects to receive income of $400,000 (20% × $2,000,000) on its $2,000,000 investment. On a per unit basis, the markup based on the desired ROI per unit is $40 ($400,000 ÷ 10,000 units). Given the unit costs shown above, **Illustration 21.7** computes the sales price to be $165.

ILLUSTRATION 21.7

**Computation of selling price, 10,000 units**

| | Per Unit |
|---|---|
| Variable cost | $ 60 |
| Fixed cost | 65 |
| Total cost | 125 |
| Markup (desired ROI per unit) | 40 |
| Unit selling price (at 10,000 units) | **$165** |

In most cases, companies like Thinkmore use a markup percentage on cost to determine the selling price. **Illustration 21.8** presents the equation to compute the markup percentage to achieve a desired ROI of $40 per unit.

ILLUSTRATION 21.8

**Computation of markup percentage**

| Markup (Desired ROI per Unit) | ÷ | Total Unit Cost | = | Markup Percentage |
|---|---|---|---|---|
| $40 | ÷ | $125 | = | 32% |

Using a 32% markup on cost, Thinkmore would compute the target selling price as shown in **Illustration 21.9**.

ILLUSTRATION 21.9

**Computation of selling price—markup approach**

| Total Unit Cost | + | ( Total Unit Cost | × | Markup Percentage ) | = | Target Selling Price |
|---|---|---|---|---|---|---|
| $125 | — | ($125 | × | 32%) | = | $165 |

Thinkmore should set the selling price for its video camera pen at $165.

## Limitations of Cost-Plus Pricing

The cost-plus pricing approach has a major advantage: It is simple to compute.

- However, the cost model does not give consideration to the demand side. That is, will customers pay the price Thinkmore Products computed for its video camera pen?
- In addition, sales volume plays a large role in determining unit costs. The lower the sales volume, for example, the higher the price Thinkmore must charge to meet its desired ROI.

To illustrate, if the budgeted sales volume was 5,000 instead of 10,000, Thinkmore's unit variable costs would remain the same. However, the unit fixed cost would change as shown in **Illustration 21.10**.

ILLUSTRATION 21.10

**Unit fixed cost, 5,000 units**

| | Total Costs | ÷ | Budgeted Volume | = | Unit Cost |
|---|---|---|---|---|---|
| Fixed manufacturing overhead | $350,000 | ÷ | 5,000 | = | $ 70 |
| Fixed selling and administrative expenses | 300,000 | ÷ | 5,000 | = | 60 |
| Unit fixed cost (at 5,000 units) | | | | | **$130** |

As indicated in Illustration 21.5, the unit fixed cost for 10,000 units was $65. However, at a lower sales volume of 5,000 units, the unit fixed cost increases to $130. Thinkmore's desired 20% ROI now results in a $80 ROI per unit [(20% × $2,000,000) ÷ 5,000]. Thinkmore computes the selling price at 5,000 units as shown in **Illustration 21.11**.

ILLUSTRATION 21.11

**Computation of selling price, 5,000 units**

| | Per Unit |
|---|---|
| Variable cost | $ 60 |
| Fixed cost | 130 |
| Total cost | 190 |
| Markup (desired ROI per unit) | 80 |
| Unit selling price (at 5,000 units) | **$270** |

As shown, the lower the budgeted volume, the higher the unit price. The reason: Fixed costs and ROI are spread over fewer units, and therefore the fixed cost and ROI per unit increase. In this case, at 5,000 units, Thinkmore would have to mark up its total unit costs 42.11% to earn a desired ROI of $80 per unit, as shown below.

$$42.11\% = \frac{\$80 \text{ (desired ROI per unit)}}{\$190 \text{ (total unit cost)}}$$

The target selling price would then be $270, as indicated earlier:

$$\$190 + (\$190 \times 42.11\%) = \$270$$

The opposite effect will occur if budgeted volume is higher (say, 12,000 units) because fixed costs and ROI can be spread over more units. As a result, the cost-plus model of pricing will achieve its desired ROI only when Thinkmore sells the quantity it budgeted. If actual volume is much less than budgeted volume, Thinkmore may sustain losses unless it can raise its prices.

## Variable-Cost Pricing

In determining the target price for Thinkmore Products' video camera pen, we calculated the cost base by including all costs incurred. This approach is referred to as **full-cost pricing**.

- Instead of using full costs to set prices, some companies simply add a markup to their variable costs (thus excluding fixed manufacturing and fixed selling and administrative costs).

- Using **variable-cost pricing** as the basis for setting prices avoids the problem of using uncertain cost information (as discussed above for Thinkmore) related to unit fixed cost computations.

- Variable-cost pricing also is helpful in pricing special orders or when excess capacity exists.

The major disadvantage of variable-cost pricing is that managers may set the price too low and consequently fail to cover their fixed costs. In the long run, failure to cover fixed costs will lead to losses. As a result, companies that use variable-cost pricing must adjust their markups to make sure that the price set will provide a fair return. The use of variable costs as the basis for setting prices is discussed in Appendix 21A.

---

## Management Insight   Parker Hannifin

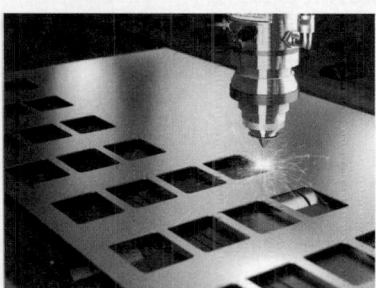

tiero/Getty Images

### At Least It Was Simple

For nearly 90 years, **Parker Hannifin** used the same simple approach to price its industrial parts. It calculated the production cost, then added on a percentage of the cost (about 35%) to arrive at the price. It didn't matter if a product was a premium product or a standard product. And if Parker reduced its production costs, it then also cut the price for the product.

The problem with this approach was that it made it difficult for the company to ever substantially increase its profit margins. So the company's CEO decided to break with tradition and implement strategic pricing schemes similar to those used by retailers. It determined that for about one-third of its products, the company had a competitive advantage that would allow it to charge a higher markup. For example, there might be limited competition for the product, its product might be of higher quality, or it might have the ability to produce a product faster. The company determined that the price increases raised net income by $200 million—not bad considering that net income was $130 million before the price increases.

**Source:** Timothy Aeppel, "Changing the Formula: Seeking Perfect Prices, CEO Tears Up the Rules." *Wall Street Journal Online* (March 27, 2007).

**What kind of help might the sales staff need in implementing this new approach? (Answer is available at the end of the chapter.)**

---

## DO IT! 2   Target Selling Price

Air Corporation produces air purifiers. The following unit cost information is available: direct materials $16, direct labor $18, variable manufacturing overhead $11, variable selling and administrative expenses $6. Fixed selling and administrative expenses are $50,000, and fixed manufacturing overhead is $150,000. Using a 45% markup percentage on total unit cost and assuming 10,000 units, compute the target selling price.

### Solution

| | |
|---|---|
| Direct materials | $16 |
| Direct labor | 18 |
| Variable manufacturing overhead | 11 |
| Variable selling and administrative expenses | 6 |
| Fixed selling and administrative expenses | 5* |
| Fixed manufacturing overhead | 15** |
| Total unit cost | $71 |

$$\text{Total unit cost} + \left(\text{Total unit cost} \times \text{Markup percentage}\right) = \text{Target selling price}$$

$$\$71 + (\$71 \times 45\%) = \underline{\$102.95}$$

*$50,000 ÷ 10,000; **$150,000 ÷ 10,000

**ACTION PLAN**

- Calculate the unit total cost.
- Multiply the unit total cost by the markup percentage, then add this amount to the unit total cost to determine the target selling price.

Related exercise material **BE21.2, BE21.3, BE21.4, BE21.5, DO IT! 21.2, E21.3, E21.4, E21.5, E21.6, and E21.7.**

# Time-and-Material Pricing

Another variation on cost-plus pricing is **time-and-material pricing**.

- Under this approach, the company sets two pricing rates—one for the **labor** used on a job and another for the **material**.
- The labor rate includes the hourly rate paid for direct labor time and other employee costs.
- The material charge is based on the cost of direct parts and materials used and a **material loading charge** for related overhead costs.

Time-and-material pricing is widely used in service industries, especially professional firms such as public accounting, law, engineering, and consulting firms, as well as construction companies, repair shops, and printers.

To illustrate a time-and-material pricing situation, assume the data shown in **Illustration 21.12** for Lake Holiday Marina, a boat and motor repair shop.

**ILLUSTRATION 21.12**

**Total annual budgeted time and material costs**

### Lake Holiday Marina
#### Budgeted Costs for the Year 2022

| | Time Charges | Material Loading Charges* |
|---|---|---|
| Mechanics' wages and benefits | $103,500 | — |
| Parts manager's salary and benefits | — | $11,500 |
| Office employee's salary and benefits | 20,700 | 2,300 |
| Other overhead (supplies, depreciation, property taxes, advertising, utilities) | 26,800 | 14,400 |
| Total budgeted costs | $151,000 | $28,200 |

*The material loading charges exclude the invoice cost of the materials.

Using time-and-material pricing involves three steps:

1. Calculate the per hour labor charge.
2. Calculate the charge for obtaining and holding materials.
3. Calculate the charges for a particular job.

**Step 1: Calculate the Labor Rate** The first step for time-and-material pricing is to determine a charge for labor time. The charge for labor time is expressed as a rate per hour of labor. This rate includes:

1. The direct labor cost of the employees, including hourly pay rate plus fringe benefits.
2. Selling, administrative, and similar overhead costs.
3. An allowance for a desired profit or ROI per hour of employee time.

In some industries, such as repair shops for autos and boats, the same hourly labor rate is charged regardless of which employee performs the work. In other industries, the rate that is charged is adjusted according to classification or level of the employee. A public accounting firm, for example, would charge different rates for the services of an assistant, senior manager, or partner. A law firm would charge different rates for the work of a paralegal, associate, or partner.

**Illustration 21.13** shows computation of the hourly charges for Lake Holiday Marina during 2022. The marina budgets 5,000 annual labor hours in 2022, and it desires a profit margin of $8 per hour of labor.

**ILLUSTRATION 21.13**   **Computation of hourly time-charge rate**

| | | Lake Holiday Marina | | | | |
|---|---|---|---|---|---|---|
| | Home   Insert   Page Layout   Formulas   Data   Review   View | | | | | |
| | P18   *fx* | | | | | |
| | A | B | C | D | E | F |
| 1 | Per Hour | Total Cost | ÷ | Total Hours | = | Per Hour Charge |
| 2 | Hourly labor rate for repairs | | | | | |
| 3 | Mechanics' wages and benefits | $103,500 | ÷ | 5,000 | = | $20.70 |
| 4 | Overhead costs | | | | | |
| 5 | Office employee's salary and benefits | 20,700 | ÷ | 5,000 | = | 4.14 |
| 6 | Other overhead | 26,800 | ÷ | 5,000 | = | 5.36 |
| 7 | Total hourly cost | $151,000 | ÷ | 5,000 | = | 30.20 |
| 8 | Profit margin | | | | | 8.00 |
| 9 | Rate charged per hour of labor | | | | | $38.20 |
| 10 | | | | | | |

To determine the labor charge for a job, the marina multiplies this rate of $38.20 by the number of hours of labor used.

## Step 2: Calculate the Material Loading Charge   The charge for materials typically includes the invoice price of any materials used on the job plus a material loading charge.

- The **material loading charge** covers the costs of purchasing, receiving, handling, and storing materials, plus any desired profit margin on the materials themselves.
- The material loading charge is expressed as a **percentage** of the total estimated costs of parts and materials for the year.
- To determine this percentage, the company:
  1. Estimates its total annual costs for purchasing, receiving, handling, and storing materials.
  2. Divides this amount by the total estimated cost of parts and materials.
  3. Adds a desired profit margin on the materials themselves.

**Illustration 21.14** shows the computation of the material loading charge used by Lake Holiday Marina during 2022. The marina estimates that the total invoice cost of parts and

**ILLUSTRATION 21.14**   **Computation of material loading charge**

| | | Lake Holiday Marina | | | | |
|---|---|---|---|---|---|---|
| | Home   Insert   Page Layout   Formulas   Data   Review   View | | | | | |
| | P18   *fx* | | | | | |
| | A | B | C | D | E | F |
| 1 | | Material Loading Charges | ÷ | Total Invoice Cost, Parts and Materials | = | Material Loading Percentage |
| 2 | Overhead costs | | | | | |
| 3 | Parts manager's salary and benefits | $11,500 | | | | |
| 4 | Office employee's salary | 2,300 | | | | |
| 5 | | 13,800 | ÷ | $120,000 | = | 11.50% |
| 6 | | | | | | |
| 7 | Other overhead | 14,400 | ÷ | 120,000 | = | 12.00% |
| 8 | | $28,200 | ÷ | 120,000 | = | 23.50% |
| 9 | Profit margin | | | | | 20.00% |
| 10 | Material loading percentage | | | | | 43.50% |
| 11 | | | | | | |

materials used in 2022 will be $120,000. The marina desires a 20% profit margin on the invoice cost of parts and materials.

The marina's material loading charge on any particular job is 43.50% multiplied by the cost of materials used on the job. For example, if the marina used $100 of parts, the additional material loading charge would be $43.50.

**Step 3: Calculate Charges for a Particular Job**   The charges for any particular job are the sum of:

1. The labor charge.
2. The charge for the materials.
3. The material loading charge.

For example, suppose that Lake Holiday Marina prepares a price quotation to estimate the cost to refurbish a used 28-foot pontoon boat. Lake Holiday Marina estimates the job will require 50 hours of labor and $3,600 in parts and materials. **Illustration 21.15** shows the marina's price quotation.

**Price quotation for time and material**

| Lake Holiday Marina | | |
|---|---|---|
| **Time-and-Material Price Quotation** | | |
| Job: Marianne Perino, repair of 28-foot pontoon boat | | |
| Labor charges: 50 hours @ $38.20 | | $1,910 |
| Material charges | | |
| Cost of parts and materials | $3,600 | |
| Material loading charge (43.5% × $3,600) | 1,566 | 5,166 |
| Total price of labor and material | | $7,076 |

Included in the $7,076 price quotation for the boat repair are charges for labor costs, overhead costs, materials costs, materials handling and storage costs, and a profit margin on both labor and parts. Lake Holiday Marina used labor hours as a basis for computing the time rate. Other companies, such as machine shops, plastic molding shops, and printers, might use machine hours.

## Service Company Insight   Button Worldwide

Don Bayley/iStockphoto

### It Ain't Like It Used to Be

For many decades, professionals in most service industries used some form of hourly based price, regardless of the outcome. But the financial crisis of 2008 brought an end to that practice. Many customers now demand that bills be tied to actual performance, rather than to the amount of hours worked.

For example, communications company **Button Worldwide**, which used to charge about $15,000 or more per month as its "retainer fee," now instead charges based on achieving particular outcomes. For example, the company might charge $10,000 if it obtains a desirable public speaking engagement for a company executive. Similarly, a digital marketing agency reduced its hourly fee from $135 to $80, but it gets a bonus if it achieves specified increases in the sales volume on a customer's website.

**Source:** Simona Covel, "Firms Try Alternative to Hourly Fees," *Wall Street Journal Online* (April 2, 2009).

**What implications does this have for a service company's need for managerial accounting? (Answer is available at the end of the chapter.)**

## DO IT! 3 | Time-and-Material Pricing

ACTION PLAN
- **Calculate the labor charge.**
- **Calculate the material loading charge.**
- **Compute the bill for specific repair.**

Presented below are data for Harmon Electrical Repair Shop for next year.

| | |
|---|---|
| Repair-technicians' wages | $130,000 |
| Fringe benefits | 30,000 |
| Overhead | 20,000 |

The desired profit margin per labor hour is $10. The material loading charge is 40% of invoice cost. Harmon estimates that 8,000 labor hours will be worked next year. If Harmon repairs a TV that takes 4 hours to repair and uses parts costing $50, compute the bill for this job.

### Solution

| | Total Cost | ÷ | Total Hours | = | Per Hour Charge |
|---|---|---|---|---|---|
| Repair-technicians' wages | $130,000 | ÷ | 8,000 | = | $16.25 |
| Fringe benefits | 30,000 | ÷ | 8,000 | = | 3.75 |
| Overhead | 20,000 | ÷ | 8,000 | = | 2.50 |
| | $180,000 | ÷ | 8,000 | = | 22.50 |
| Profit margin | | | | | 10.00 |
| Rate charged per hour of labor | | | | | $32.50 |

| | | |
|---|---|---|
| Job: Repair TV | | |
| Labor charges  4 hours @ $32.50 | | $130 |
| Material charges | | |
| Cost of parts and materials | $50 | |
| Material loading charge (40% × $50) | 20 | 70 |
| Total price of labor and material | | $200 |

Related exercise material: **BE21.6, DO IT! 21.3, E21.8, E21.9, and E21.10.**

---

# Transfer Prices

### LEARNING OBJECTIVE 4
Determine a transfer price using the negotiated, cost-based, and market-based approaches.

In today's global economy, growth is often vital to survival. Some companies grow "vertically," meaning they expand in the direction of either their suppliers or customers. For example, a manufacturer of bicycles like **Trek** may acquire a bicycle component manufacturer or a chain of bicycle shops. A movie production company like **Walt Disney** or **WarnerMedia** may acquire a movie theater chain or a cable television company.

- Divisions within vertically integrated companies often transfer goods or services to other divisions in the company.
- When goods are transferred between divisions of the same company, the price used to record the transaction is the **transfer price**.

**Illustration 21.16** shows transfers between divisions for Aerobic Bicycle Company. As shown, the Component Division sells goods to the Company's Assembly Division, as well as to outside parties. Units sold to the Assembly Division are recorded at the transfer price.

**ILLUSTRATION 21.16**

**Transfer pricing example**

The primary objective of transfer pricing is the same as that of pricing a product to an outside party.

- The objective is to maximize the return to the company.
- An additional objective of transfer pricing is to measure divisional performance accurately.

Setting a transfer price is complicated because of competing interests among divisions within the company. For example, in the case of the bicycle company shown in Illustration 21.16, setting the transfer price high will benefit the Component Division (the selling division) but will hurt the Assembly Division (the purchasing division).

There are three possible approaches for determining a transfer price:

1. Negotiated transfer prices.
2. Cost-based transfer prices.
3. Market-based transfer prices.

Conceptually, a negotiated transfer price should work best, but due to practical considerations, companies often use the other two methods.

## Negotiated Transfer Prices

A **negotiated transfer price** is determined through agreement of division managers. To illustrate negotiated transfer pricing, we examine Alberta Company. Until recently, Alberta focused exclusively on making rubber soles for work boots and hiking boots. It sold these rubber soles to boot manufacturers for $18 per sole and had a variable cost of $11 per sole.

- Last year, the company decided to take advantage of its strong reputation by expanding into the business of making hiking boots.
- As a consequence of this expansion, the company is now structured as two independent divisions, the Boot Division and the Sole Division.
- The company compensates the manager of each division based on achievement of profitability targets for that division.

The Boot Division manufactures leather uppers for hiking boots and attaches these uppers to rubber soles. Its variable costs, not including the sole, are $35 per boot. During its first year, the Boot Division purchased its rubber soles from an outside supplier for $17 per sole so as not to disrupt the operations of the Sole Division. However, top management now wants the Sole Division to provide at least some of the soles used by the Boot Division. **Illustration 21.17** shows the computation of the contribution margin per unit for each division when the Boot Division purchases soles from an outside supplier for $17 and the Sole Division sells to outside customers for $18 per sole.

| Boot Division | | Sole Division | |
| --- | --- | --- | --- |
| Selling price of boot | $90 | Selling price of sole | $18 |
| Variable cost of boot (not including sole) | 35 | Variable cost per sole | 11 |
| Cost of sole purchased from outside supplier | 17 | | |
| **Contribution margin per unit** | **$38** | **Contribution margin per unit** | **$ 7** |

**Total contribution margin per unit $45** ($38 + $7)

ILLUSTRATION 21.17

**Computation of contribution margin for two divisions, when Boot Division purchases soles from an outside supplier**

This information indicates that the contribution margin per unit for the Boot Division is $38 and for the Sole Division is $7. The total contribution margin per unit is $45 ($38 + $7).

Now let's ask the question, "What would be a fair transfer price if the Sole Division sold 10,000 soles to the Boot Division?" The answer depends on how busy the Sole Division is—that is, whether it has excess capacity.

## No Excess Capacity

Assume that the Sole Division has no excess capacity and produces and sells 80,000 soles to outside customers. As indicated in Illustration 21.17, the Sole Division charges outside customers $18 and has a variable cost of $11, so its contribution margin on units sold to outside customers is $7 ($18 − $11). Since the Sole Division has no excess capacity, if it chooses to sell 10,000 units to the Boot Division, it would have to forgo sales of 10,000 units to outside customers.

- The contribution margin on sales to outside customers that would be forgone as a result of an internal transfer is referred to as the **opportunity cost**.
- Therefore, the Sole Division must receive from the Boot Division a payment that will at least cover its variable cost of $11 per sole **plus** its contribution margin—opportunity cost— of $7 per sole.
- The sum of the variable cost and the opportunity cost is referred to as the **minimum transfer price**.
- If the Sole Division cannot recover the minimum transfer price, it should not sell its soles to the Boot Division.

The minimum transfer price that would be acceptable to the Sole Division is $18, as shown in **Illustration 21.18**.

| Variable Cost | + | Opportunity Cost | = | Minimum Transfer Price |
| --- | --- | --- | --- | --- |
| $11 | + | $7 | = | $18 |

ILLUSTRATION 21.18

**Minimum transfer price equation—no excess capacity**

From the perspective of the Boot Division (the buyer), the most it will pay is what the sole would cost from an outside supplier. In this case, therefore, the Boot Division would pay no more than $17. As shown in **Illustration 21.19**, an acceptable transfer price is not available in this situation.

**No Excess Capacity**

I will pay no more than $17 (cost from outside supplier).

Transfer price of $17

I must receive at least my variable cost of $11 plus my opportunity cost of $7—or $18.

Boot Division        **No Deal**        Sole Division

ILLUSTRATION 21.19

**Transfer price negotiations— no excess capacity**

## Excess Capacity

What happens if the Sole Division **has excess capacity**? For example, assume the Sole Division can produce 80,000 soles but can sell only 70,000 soles in the open market. As a result, it has available capacity of 10,000 units. Because it has excess capacity, the Sole Division could provide 10,000 units to the Boot Division without losing its $7 contribution margin on these units. Therefore, as **Illustration 21.20** shows, the minimum price it would now accept is $11.

**Minimum transfer price equation—excess capacity**

| Variable Cost | + | Opportunity Cost | = | Minimum Transfer Price |
|:---:|:---:|:---:|:---:|:---:|
| $11 | + | $0 | = | $11 |

In this case, the Boot Division and the Sole Division should negotiate a transfer price within the range of $11 to $17, as shown in **Illustration 21.21**.

**Transfer pricing negotiations— excess capacity**

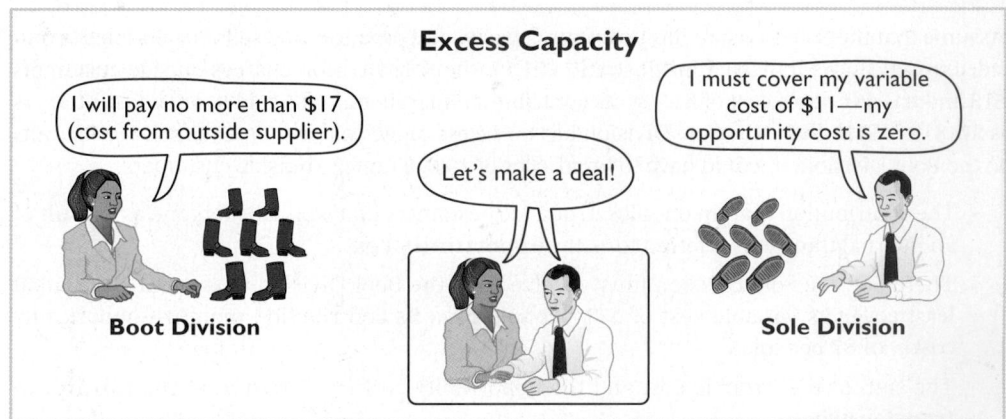

**Given excess capacity**, Alberta Company will increase its overall net income if the Boot Division purchases the 10,000 soles internally. This is true as long as the Sole Division's variable cost is less than the outside price of $17.

- The Sole Division will receive a positive contribution margin from any transfer price above its variable cost of $11.
- The Boot Division will benefit from any price below $17.
- At any transfer price above $17, the Boot Division will go to an outside supplier, a solution that would be undesirable to both divisions as well as to the company as a whole.

## Variable Costs

In the minimum transfer price equation, **variable cost is defined as the variable cost of units sold *internally***.

- In some instances, the variable cost of units sold internally will differ from the variable cost of units sold externally. For example, companies often can avoid some variable selling expenses when units are sold internally. In this case, the variable cost of units sold internally will be lower than that of units sold externally.
- Alternatively, the variable cost of units sold internally could be higher than normal if the internal division requests a special order that requires more expensive materials or additional labor. For example, assume that the Boot Division designs a new high-margin, heavy-duty boot. The sole for this boot will use denser rubber with an intricate lug design. Alberta Company is not aware of any supplier that currently makes such a sole, nor does it feel that any other supplier can meet its quality expectations. As a consequence, there is no available market price to use as the transfer price.

We can, however employ the equation for the minimum transfer price to assist in arriving at a reasonable solution. After evaluating the special sole, the Sole Division determines that its variable cost would be $19 per sole. The Sole Division is at full capacity. The Sole Division's opportunity cost at full capacity is the $7 ($18 − $11) per sole that it earns producing the standard sole and selling it to an outside customer. Therefore, the minimum transfer price that the Sole Division would be willing to accept for the special-order sole is as shown in **Illustration 21.22**

| Variable Cost | + | Opportunity Cost | = | Minimum Transfer Price |
|---|---|---|---|---|
| $19 | + | $7 | = | $26 |

**ILLUSTRATION 21.22**

**Minimum transfer price equation—special order**

The transfer price of $26 provides the Sole Division with enough revenue to cover its increased variable cost and its opportunity cost (contribution margin on its standard sole).

## Units Transferred Are Unequal to Units Forgone

In some situations, when the division has no excess capacity, the number of units transferred internally differs from the number units forgone on sales to outside parties. This occurs if characteristics of the units transferred internally differ from standard units, and thus differ in terms of the amount of manufacturing resources required for production. For example, suppose that the Boot Division requests 7,000 units of a special, high-endurance sole that requires more manufacturing resources than a standard sole. To produce 7,000 units of the special sole for the Boot Division, the Sole Division will have to forgo sales of 10,000 units of its standard sole to outside customers.

- When the number of units transferred internally differs from the number of units of external sales forgone, a company must compute the opportunity cost per unit transferred internally.
- This is accomplished by first computing the total contribution margin on all units forgone and then dividing by the number of units transferred internally.

The calculation for the opportunity cost, applied to the special order from the Boot Division, is shown in **Illustration 21.23**.

| [(Selling Price − Variable Cost) × Units Forgone] | ÷ | Units Transferred Internally | = | Opportunity Cost |
|---|---|---|---|---|
| [($18 − $11) × 10,000] | ÷ | 7,000 | = | $10 |

**ILLUSTRATION 21.23**

**Opportunity cost if units sold are unequal to units forgone**

Notice that, because the number of units forgone exceeds the number of units that will be transferred internally, the opportunity cost per unit of $10 exceeds the opportunity cost per unit of $7 that we computed previously on a standard unit.

## Summary of Negotiated Transfer Pricing

Under negotiated transfer pricing, the selling division establishes a minimum transfer price, and the purchasing division establishes a maximum transfer price. This system provides a sound basis for establishing a transfer price because both divisions are better off if the proper decision-making rules are used. However, companies often do not use negotiated transfer pricing because:

- Market price information is sometimes not easily obtainable.
- A lack of trust between the two negotiating divisions may lead to a breakdown in the negotiations.
- Negotiations often lead to different pricing strategies from division to division, which is cumbersome and sometimes costly to implement.

Many companies, therefore, often use simple systems based on cost or market information to develop transfer prices.

## Cost-Based Transfer Prices

An alternative to negotiated transfer pricing is cost-based pricing.

- A **cost-based transfer price** is based on the costs incurred by the division producing the goods or services.
- A cost-based transfer price can be based on variable costs alone, or on variable costs plus fixed costs.
- In some cases, the selling division may add a markup.

The cost-based approach sometimes results in improper transfer prices. Improper transfer prices can reduce company profits and provide unfair evaluations of division performance. To illustrate, assume that Alberta Company requires the division to use a transfer price based on the variable cost of the sole. With no excess capacity, the contribution margins per unit for the two divisions are as shown in **Illustration 21.24**.

**ILLUSTRATION 21.24**

**Cost-based transfer price—10,000 units**

| Boot Division | | Sole Division | |
|---|---|---|---|
| Selling price of boot | $90 | Selling price of sole | $11 |
| Variable cost of boot (not including sole) | 35 | Variable cost per sole | 11 |
| Cost of sole purchased from sole division | 11 | **Contribution margin** | |
| **Contribution margin per unit** | **$44** | **per unit** | **$ 0** |

Total contribution margin per unit **$44** ($44 + $0)

This cost-based transfer system is a bad deal for the Sole Division as it reports no profit on the transfer of 10,000 soles to the Boot Division.

- If the Sole Division could sell these soles to an outside customer, it would make $70,000 [10,000 × ($18 − $11)].
- The Boot Division, on the other hand, is delighted. Its contribution margin per unit increases from $38 to $44, or $6 per boot.
- Thus, this transfer price results in an unfair evaluation of these two divisions.

Further examination of this example reveals that this transfer price reduces the company's overall profits. The Sole Division lost a contribution margin per unit of $7 (Illustration 21.17), and the Boot Division experiences only a $6 increase in its contribution margin per unit. Overall, Alberta Company loses $10,000 [10,000 boots × ($7 − $6)]. **Illustration 21.25** illustrates this deficiency.

**ILLUSTRATION 21.25**

**Cost-based transfer price results—no excess capacity**

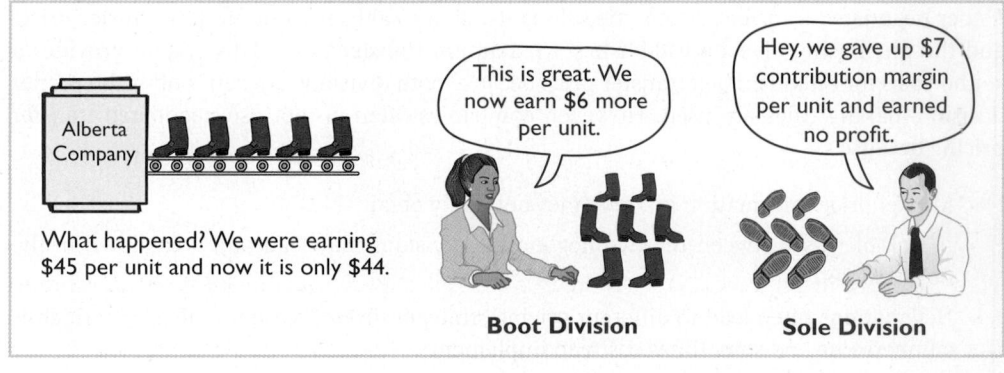

The overall results change if the Sole Division **has excess capacity**. In this case, the Sole Division continues to report a zero profit on these 10,000 units but does not lose the $7 per unit of contribution margin (because it had excess capacity). The Boot Division gains $6. So overall, the company is better off by $60,000 (10,000 × $6). However, with a cost-based system, the Sole Division continues to report a zero profit on these 10,000 units.

The cost-based approach has disadvantages:

- A cost-based system does not reflect the division's true profitability.
- **It does not provide adequate incentive for the Sole Division to control costs**. The division's costs are simply passed on to the next division.

Despite these disadvantages, the cost system is simple to understand and easy to use because the information is already available in the accounting system. In addition, market information is sometimes not available, so the only alternative is some type of cost-based system. As a result, cost-based transfer prices are the most common method used by companies to establish transfer prices.

## Market-Based Transfer Prices

The **market-based transfer price** is based on existing market prices of competing goods or services.

- A market-based system is often considered the best approach because it is objective and generally provides the proper economic incentives.
- For example, if the Sole Division can charge the market price, it is indifferent as to whether soles are sold to outside customers or internally to the Boot Division—it does not lose any contribution margin.
- Similarly, the Boot Division pays a price for the soles that is at or reasonably close to market.

When the Sole Division has no excess capacity, the market-based system works reasonably well. The Sole Division receives market price, and the Boot Division pays market price.

If the Sole Division has excess capacity, however, the market-based system can lead to actions that are not in the best interest of the company. The minimum transfer price that the Sole Division should receive is its variable cost plus its opportunity cost. If the Sole Division has excess capacity, its opportunity cost is zero. However, under the market-based system, the Sole Division transfers the goods at the market price of $18, for a contribution margin per unit of $7 ($18 − $11). The Boot Division manager has to accept the $18 sole price. This price may not accurately reflect a fair cost of the sole, given that the Sole Division had excess capacity. As a result, the Boot Division may overprice its boots in the market if it uses the market price of the sole plus a markup in setting the price of the boot. This action can lead to losses for Alberta overall.

As indicated earlier, in many cases, there simply is not a well-defined market for the good or service being transferred. When this is the case, a reasonable market value cannot be developed, so companies often resort to a cost-based system.

## Effect of Outsourcing on Transfer Pricing

An increasing number of companies rely on **outsourcing**.

- Outsourcing involves contracting with an external party to provide a good or service, rather than performing the work internally.
- Some companies have taken outsourcing to the extreme by outsourcing all of their production. Many of these so-called **virtual companies** have well-established brand names though they do not manufacture any of their own products.

Companies use incremental analysis (Chapter 20) to determine whether outsourcing is profitable. When companies outsource, fewer components are transferred internally between divisions. This reduces the need for transfer prices.

# Transfers Between Divisions in Different Countries

As more companies "globalize" their operations, an increasing number of intercompany transfers are between divisions that are located in different countries. One estimate suggests that 60% of trade between countries is simply transfers between company divisions. Differences in tax rates across countries can complicate the determination of the appropriate transfer price.

- A company pays income tax in the country in which it generates revenue.
- Some companies intentionally shift income from divisions located in countries with high tax rates to divisions located in countries with low tax rates.

Appendix 21B discusses in more detail transfer pricing issues that occur when goods are exchanged between divisions in different countries.

---

## Data Analytics Insight   Big Data Pricing

### Setting the Optimal Price

Studio Romantic/
Shutterstock.com

Product pricing has benefitted greatly from the use of big data and data analytics. One example is dynamic pricing, where companies rapidly adjust a product's prices across customers or across time based on changing market conditions. Dynamic pricing has been used by ride-sharing services such as **Uber**, hotel chains such as **Marriott**, and sports teams such as the **San Francisco Giants**.

As you might expect, the concept of dynamic pricing ties in very well with data analytics. For example, consider **Big Data Pricing**, which provides consulting services to assist companies in obtaining optimal pricing. In its promotional materials, Big Data Pricing advertises that it helps companies to "gain access to deep pricing and technical expertise to help drive ROI, pricing process improvement, business adoption and optimize performance." To accomplish this, employees at Big Data Pricing employ a variety of software platforms, including Salesforce CPQ, Vendavo, Price f(x), Vistex, Tableau, and Lumira.

Finally, consider that a recent job opening at Big Data Pricing required the following qualifications: "deep analytical skills, critical thinking, excellent communication skills, work collaboratively, willingness to learn." So, a combination of data analytical skills and an understanding of pricing models could very well be your ticket to a good job!

**Sources:** *www.bigdatapricing.com* (March 2020).

**What is dynamic pricing, and why would the use of dynamic pricing require data analytics? (Answer is available at the end of the chapter.)**

---

## DO IT! 4 │ Transfer Pricing

**ACTION PLAN**

- **Determine whether the company is at full capacity or not.**
- **Determine variable cost and opportunity cost.**
- **Apply minimum transfer price equation.**

The clock division of Control Central Corporation manufactures clocks and then sells them to customers for $10 per unit. Its unit variable cost is $4, and its unit fixed cost is $2.50. Management would like the clock division to transfer 8,000 of these clocks to another division within the company at a price of $5. The clock division could avoid $0.50 per clock of variable packaging costs by selling internally.

a. Determine the minimum transfer price, assuming the clock division is not operating at full capacity.

b. Determine the minimum transfer price, assuming the clock division is operating at full capacity.

### Solution

a. If the clock division is not operating at full capacity, the opportunity cost for the clocks is $0. Since internal sales will eliminate $0.50 of packaging costs, the variable cost per clock is $3.50 ($4 − $0.50).

$$\text{Minimum transfer price} = \text{Variable cost} + \text{Opportunity cost}$$
$$\$3.50 = \$3.50 + \$0$$

**b.** If the clock division is already operating at full capacity, the opportunity cost for the clocks is $6 ($10 − $4). Since internal sales will eliminate $0.50 of packaging costs, the variable cost per clock is $3.50 ($4 − $0.50).

$$\text{Minimum transfer price} = \text{Variable cost} + \text{Opportunity cost}$$
$$\$9.50 = \$3.50 + \$6$$

Related exercise material: **BE21.7, BE21.8, BE21.9, DO IT! 21.4, E21.11, E21.12, E21.13, E21.14, and E21.15.**

---

## Appendix 21A | Absorption-Cost and Variable-Cost Pricing

### LEARNING OBJECTIVE *5
Determine prices using absorption-cost pricing and variable-cost pricing.

In determining the target price for Thinkmore Products' video camera pen in the chapter, we calculated the cost base **by including all costs incurred**. This approach is referred to as **full-cost pricing**.

- Using total cost as the basis of the markup makes sense conceptually. In the long run, the price must cover all costs and provide a reasonable profit.
- However, total cost is difficult to determine in practice. This is because period costs (selling and administrative expenses) are difficult to trace to a specific product.
- Activity-based costing can be used to overcome this difficulty to some extent.

In practice, companies sometimes use two other cost approaches: (1) absorption-cost pricing or (2) variable-cost pricing. Absorption-cost pricing is more popular than variable-cost pricing.[1] We illustrate both approaches because both have merit.

## Absorption-Cost Pricing

**Absorption-cost pricing** is consistent with generally accepted accounting principles (GAAP). The reason: It includes both variable and fixed manufacturing costs as product costs.

- **Absorption-cost pricing excludes from this cost base both variable and fixed selling and administrative costs.**
- Thus, companies must somehow provide for selling and administrative costs plus the target ROI. They do this through the markup.

The **first step** in absorption-cost pricing is to compute the unit **manufacturing cost**. For Thinkmore Products, this amounts to $87 per unit at a volume of 10,000 units, as shown in **Illustration 21A.1**.

| | Per Unit |
|---|---|
| Direct materials | $23 |
| Direct labor | 17 |
| Variable manufacturing overhead | 12 |
| Fixed manufacturing overhead ($350,000 ÷ 10,000) | 35 |
| Total unit manufacturing cost (absorption cost) | $87 |

**ILLUSTRATION 21A.1**
Computation of unit manufacturing cost

[1]For a discussion of cost-plus pricing, see Eunsup Skim and Ephraim F. Sudit, "How Manufacturers Price Products," *Management Accounting* (February 1995), pp. 37–39; and V. Govindarajan and R.N. Anthony, "How Firms Use Cost Data in Pricing Decisions," *Management Accounting* (65, no. 1), pp. 30–36.

In addition, Thinkmore provides the information given in **Illustration 21A.2** regarding selling and administrative expenses per unit and desired ROI per unit.

**ILLUSTRATION 21A.2**

**Other selling and administrative expense information**

| | |
|---|---|
| Variable selling and administrative expenses | $ 8 |
| Fixed selling and administrative expenses ($300,000 ÷ 10,000) | 30 |
| Total selling and administrative expenses per unit | $38 |
| Desired ROI per unit (see Illustration 21.6) | $40 |

The **second step** in absorption-cost pricing is to compute the markup percentage using the equation in **Illustration 21A.3**. Note that when companies use manufacturing cost per unit as the cost base to compute the markup percentage, the **percentage must cover the desired ROI and also the selling and administrative expenses**.

**ILLUSTRATION 21A.3**

**Markup percentage— absorption-cost pricing**

| Desired ROI per Unit | + | Selling and Administrative Expenses per Unit | = | Markup Percentage | × | Manufacturing Cost per Unit |
|---|---|---|---|---|---|---|
| $40 | + | $38 | = | **MP** | × | $87 |

Solving, we find:

$$MP = (\$40 + \$38) \div \$87 = 89.66\%$$

The **third** and final **step** is to set the target selling price. Using a markup percentage of 89.66% and absorption-cost pricing, Thinkmore computes the target selling price as shown in **Illustration 21A.4**.

**ILLUSTRATION 21A.4**

**Computation of target price— absorption-cost pricing**

| Manufacturing Cost per Unit | + | ( Markup Percentage | × | Manufacturing Cost per Unit ) | = | Target Selling Price |
|---|---|---|---|---|---|---|
| $87 | + | (89.66% | × | $87) | = | $165 |

Using a target price of $165 will produce the desired 20% return on investment for Thinkmore on its video camera pen at a volume level of 10,000 units, as shown in **Illustration 21A.5**.

**ILLUSTRATION 21A.5**

**Proof of 20% ROI— absorption-cost pricing**

### Thinkmore Products, Inc.
#### Budgeted Absorption-Cost Income Statement

| | |
|---|---|
| Revenue (10,000 camera pens × $165) | $1,650,000 |
| Cost of goods sold (10,000 camera pens × $87) | 870,000 |
| Gross profit | 780,000 |
| Selling and administrative expenses [10,000 camera pens × ($8 + $30)] | 380,000 |
| Net income | **$ 400,000** |

#### Budgeted ROI

$$\frac{\text{Net income}}{\text{Invested assets}} = \frac{\$400,000}{\$2,000,000} = 20\%$$

#### Markup Percentage

$$\frac{\text{Net income} + \text{Selling and administrative expenses}}{\text{Cost of goods sold}} = \frac{\$400,000 + \$380,000}{\$870,000} = 89.66\%$$

Because of the fixed-cost component, if Thinkmore sells more than 10,000 units, the ROI will be greater than 20%. If it sells fewer than 10,000 units, the ROI will be less than 20%. The markup percentage is also verified by adding $400,000 (the net income) and $380,000 (selling and administrative expenses) and then dividing by $870,000 (the cost of goods sold or the cost base).

Most companies that use cost-plus pricing use either absorption cost or full cost as the basis. The reasons for this tendency are as follows.

1. Absorption-cost information is most readily provided by a company's cost accounting system. Because absorption-cost data already exist in general ledger accounts, it is cost-effective to use the data for pricing.

2. Basing the cost-plus calculation on only variable costs could encourage managers to set too low a price to boost sales. There is the fear that if managers use only variable costs, they will substitute variable costs for full costs, which can lead to repeated price cutting.

3. Absorption-cost or full-cost pricing provides the most defensible base for justifying prices to all interested parties—managers, customers, and government.

# Variable-Cost Pricing

Under **variable-cost pricing**, the cost base consists of all of the **variable costs** associated with a product, including variable selling and administrative costs.

- **Because fixed costs are not included in the base, the markup must provide for all fixed costs (manufacturing, and selling and administrative) and the target ROI.**
- Variable-cost pricing is more useful for making short-run decisions because it considers variable-cost and fixed-cost behavior patterns separately.

The **first step** in variable-cost pricing is to compute the unit variable cost. For Thinkmore Products, this amounts to $60 per unit, as shown in **Illustration 21A.6**.

|  | Per Unit |
| --- | --- |
| Direct materials | $23 |
| Direct labor | 17 |
| Variable manufacturing overhead | 12 |
| Variable selling and administrative expense | 8 |
| Total unit variable cost | $60 |

**ILLUSTRATION 21A.5**

**Computation of unit variable cost**

The **second step** in variable-cost pricing is to compute the markup percentage. **Illustration 21A.7** shows the calculation for the markup percentage. For Thinkmore, fixed costs include fixed manufacturing overhead of $35 per unit ($350,000 ÷ 10,000) and fixed selling and administrative expenses of $30 per unit ($300,000 ÷ 10,000).

| Desired ROI per Unit | + | Unit Fixed Cost | = | Markup Percentage | × | Unit Variable Cost |
| --- | --- | --- | --- | --- | --- | --- |
| $40 | + | ($35 + $30) | = | MP | × | $60 |

**ILLUSTRATION 21A.7**

**Computation of markup percentage—variable-cost pricing**

Solving, we find:

$$MP = \frac{\$40 + (\$35 + \$30)}{\$60} = 175\%$$

The **third step** is to set the target selling price. Using a markup percentage of 175% and the variable-cost approach, Thinkmore computes the selling price as shown in **Illustration 21A.8**.

**ILLUSTRATION 21A.8**

**Computation of target price— variable-cost pricing**

| Unit Variable Cost | + | ( Markup Percentage | × | Unit Variable Cost ) | = | Target Selling Price |
|---|---|---|---|---|---|---|
| $60 | + | (175% | × | $60) | = | $165 |

Using a target price of $165 will produce the desired 20% return on investment for Thinkmore on its video camera pen at a volume level of 10,000 units, as shown in **Illustration 21A.9**.

**ILLUSTRATION 21A.9**

**Proof of 20% ROI— variable-cost approach**

### Thinkmore Products, Inc.
#### Budgeted Variable-Cost Income Statement

| | | |
|---|---|---|
| Revenue (10,000 camera pens × $165) | | $1,650,000 |
| Variable costs (10,000 camera pens × $60) | | 600,000 |
| Contribution margin | | 1,050,000 |
| Fixed manufacturing overhead | $350,000 | |
| Fixed selling and administrative expenses | 300,000 | 650,000 |
| Net income | | **$ 400,000** |

**Budgeted ROI**

$$\frac{\text{Net income}}{\text{Invested assets}} = \frac{\$400,000}{\$2,000,000} = \textbf{20\%}$$

**Markup Percentage**

$$\frac{\text{Net income} + \text{Fixed costs}}{\text{Variable costs}} = \frac{\$400,000 + \$650,000}{\$600,000} = \textbf{175\%}$$

Under any of the three pricing approaches we have looked at (full-cost, absorption-cost, and variable-cost), the desired ROI will be attained only if the budgeted sales volume for the period is attained.

- None of these approaches guarantees a profit or a desired ROI.
- Achieving a desired ROI is the result of many factors, some of which are beyond the company's control, such as market conditions, political and legal issues, customers' tastes, and competitive actions.

Because absorption-cost pricing includes allocated fixed costs, it does not make clear how the company's costs will change as volume changes. To avoid blurring the effects of cost behavior on net income, some managers therefore prefer variable-cost pricing. The specific reasons for using variable-cost pricing, even though the basic accounting data are less accessible, are as follows.

1. Variable-cost pricing, being based on variable cost, is more consistent with cost-volume-profit analysis used by managers to measure the profit implications of changes in price and volume.
2. Variable-cost pricing provides the type of data managers need for pricing special orders. It reveals the incremental effect of accepting one more order.
3. Variable-cost pricing avoids arbitrary allocation of common fixed costs (such as executive salaries) to individual product lines.

# Appendix 21B | Transfers Between Divisions in Different Countries

### LEARNING OBJECTIVE *6

Explain issues involved in transferring goods between divisions in different countries.

Companies must pay income tax in the country where they generate the income.

- In order to maximize income and minimize income tax, some companies attempt to report more income in countries with low tax rates, and less income in countries with high tax rates.
- They accomplish this by adjusting the transfer prices they use on internal transfers between divisions located in different countries.
- They allocate more contribution margin to the division in the low-tax-rate country, and allocate less to the division in the high-tax-rate country.

To illustrate, suppose that Alberta's Boot Division is located in a country with a corporate tax rate of 10%, and the Sole Division is located in a country with a tax rate of 30%. To maximize the company's combined after-tax profit, it would want to shift income from the Sole Division to the Boot Division because the Boot Division is taxed at a lower rate. **Illustration 21B.1** compares the after-tax contribution margin to the company using a transfer price of $18 versus a transfer price of $11.

**ILLUSTRATION 21B.1**

**After-tax contribution margin per unit under alternative transfer prices**

### At $18 Transfer Price

| Boot Division | | Sole Division | |
|---|---|---|---|
| Selling price of boot | $90.00 | Selling price of sole | $18.00 |
| Variable cost of boot (not including sole) | 35.00 | Variable cost per sole | 11.00 |
| Cost of sole purchased internally | 18.00 | | |
| Before-tax contribution margin | 37.00 | Before-tax contribution margin | 7.00 |
| Tax at 10% | 3.70 | Tax at 30% | 2.10 |
| After-tax contribution margin | $33.30 | After-tax contribution margin | $ 4.90 |

Before-tax total contribution margin per unit to company = $37 + $7 = **$44**
After-tax total contribution margin per unit to company = $33.30 + $4.90 = **$38.20**

### At $11 Transfer Price

| Boot Division | | Sole Division | |
|---|---|---|---|
| Selling price of boot | $90.00 | Selling price of sole | $11.00 |
| Variable cost of boot (not including sole) | 35.00 | Variable cost per sole | 11.00 |
| Cost of sole purchased internally | 11.00 | | |
| Before-tax contribution margin | 44.00 | Before-tax contribution margin | 0.00 |
| Tax at 10% | 4.40 | Tax at 30% | 0.00 |
| After-tax contribution margin | $39.60 | After-tax contribution margin | $ 0.00 |

Before-tax total contribution margin per unit to company = $44 + $0 = **$44**
After-tax total contribution margin per unit to company = $39.60 + $0 = **$39.60**

Note that the **before-tax** total contribution margin to Alberta Company is $44 regardless of whether the transfer price is $18 or $11. However, the **after-tax** total contribution margin to Alberta Company is $38.20 using the $18 transfer price and $39.60 using the $11 transfer price. The reason: When Alberta uses the $11 transfer price, more of the contribution margin is attributed to the division that is in the country with the lower tax rate, so the company pays $1.40 less per unit in taxes [($3.70 + $2.10) − $4.40].

As this analysis shows, Alberta Company would be better off using the $11 transfer price. However, this presents some concerns.

- The Sole Division manager will not be happy with an $11 transfer price. This price may lead to unfair evaluations of the Sole Division's manager.

- The company must ask whether it is legal and ethical to use an $11 transfer price when the market price clearly is higher than that.

Additional consideration of international transfer pricing is discussed in advanced accounting courses.

# Review and Practice

## Learning Objectives Review

### 1 Compute a target cost when the market determines a product price.

To compute a target cost, the company determines its target selling price. Once the target selling price is set, it determines its target cost by setting a desired profit. The difference between the target price and desired profit is the target cost of the product.

### 2 Compute a target selling price using cost-plus pricing.

Cost-plus pricing involves establishing a cost base and adding to this cost base a markup to determine a target selling price. The cost-plus pricing equation is expressed as follows: Target selling price = Cost + (Markup percentage × Cost).

### 3 Use time-and-material pricing to determine the cost of services provided.

Under time-and-material pricing, two pricing rates are set—one for the labor used on a job and another for the material. The labor rate includes direct labor time and other employee costs. The material charge is based on the cost of direct parts and materials used and a material loading charge for related overhead costs.

### 4 Determine a transfer price using the negotiated, cost-based, and market-based approaches.

The negotiated price is determined through agreement of division managers. Under a cost-based approach, the transfer price may be based on variable cost alone or on variable costs plus fixed costs. Companies may add a markup to these numbers. The cost-based approach often leads to poor performance evaluations and purchasing decisions. The advantage of the cost-based system is its simplicity. A market-based transfer price is based on existing competing market prices and services. A market-based system is often considered the best approach because it is objective and generally provides the proper economic incentives.

### *5 Determine prices using absorption-cost pricing and variable-cost pricing.

Absorption-cost pricing uses total manufacturing cost as the cost base and provides for selling and administrative costs plus the target ROI through the markup. The target selling price is computed as: Manufacturing cost per unit + (Markup percentage × Manufacturing cost per unit).

Variable-cost pricing uses all of the variable costs, including selling and administrative costs, as the cost base and provides for fixed costs and target ROI through the markup. The target selling price is computed as: Unit variable cost + (Markup percentage × Unit variable cost).

### *6 Explain issues involved in transferring goods between divisions in different countries.

Companies must pay income tax in the country where they generate the income. In order to maximize income and minimize income tax, many companies prefer to report more income in countries with low tax rates, and less income in countries with high tax rates. This is accomplished by adjusting the transfer prices they use on internal transfers between divisions located in different countries.

## Glossary Review

**\*Absorption-cost pricing**  An approach to pricing that defines the cost base as the manufacturing cost; it excludes both variable and fixed selling and administrative costs. (p. 21-21).

**Cost-based transfer price**  A transfer price that uses as its foundation the costs incurred by the division producing the goods. (p. 21-18).

**Cost-plus pricing**  A process whereby a product's selling price is determined by adding a markup to a cost base. (p. 21-5).

**Full-cost pricing**  An approach to pricing that defines the cost base as all costs incurred. (p. 21-8).

**Market-based transfer price**  A transfer price that is based on existing market prices of competing products. (p. 21-19).

**Markup**  The amount added to a product's cost base to determine the product's selling price. (p. 21-5).

**Material loading charge**  A charge added to cover the cost of purchasing, receiving, handling, and storing materials, plus any desired profit margin on the materials themselves. (p. 21-11).

**Negotiated transfer price**  A transfer price that is determined by the agreement of the division managers. (p. 21-14).

**Opportunity cost**  The contribution margin on sales to outside customers that would be forgone as a result of an internal transfer. (p. 21-15).

**Outsourcing**  Contracting with an external party to provide a good or service, rather than performing the work internally. (p. 21-19).

**Target cost**  The cost that will provide the desired profit on a product when the seller does not have control over the product's price. (p. 21-4).

**Target selling price**  The selling price that will provide the desired profit on a product when the seller has the ability to determine the product's price. (p. 21-6).

**Time-and-material pricing**  An approach to cost-plus pricing in which the company uses two pricing rates, one for the labor used on a job and another for the material. (p. 21-10).

**Transfer price**  The price used to record the transfer of goods between two divisions of a company. (p. 21-13).

**Variable-cost pricing**  An approach to pricing that defines the cost base as all variable costs; it excludes both fixed manufacturing and fixed selling and administrative costs. (pp. 21-8, 21-23).

## Practice Multiple-Choice Questions

1. **(LO 1)** Target cost related to price and profit means that:
   a. cost and desired profit must be determined before selling price.
   b. cost and selling price must be determined before desired profit.
   c. price and desired profit must be determined before costs.
   d. costs can be achieved only if the company is at full capacity.

2. **(LO 1)** Classic Toys has examined the market for toy train locomotives. It believes there is a market niche in which it can sell locomotives at $80 each. It estimates that it could sell 10,000 of these locomotives annually. Variable costs to make a locomotive are expected to be $25. Classic anticipates a profit of $15 per locomotive. The target cost for the locomotive is:
   a. $80.
   b. $65.
   c. $40.
   d. $25.

3. **(LO 1, 2)** In a competitive, common-product environment, a seller would most likely use:
   a. time-and-material pricing.
   b. variable costing.
   c. target costing.
   d. cost-plus pricing.

4. **(LO 2)** Cost-plus pricing means that:
   a. Selling price = Variable cost + (Markup percentage + Variable cost).
   b. Selling price = Cost + (Markup percentage × Cost).
   c. Selling price = Manufacturing cost + (Markup percentage + Manufacturing cost).
   d. Selling price = Fixed cost + (Markup percentage × Fixed cost).

5. **(LO 2)** Adler Company is considering developing a new product. The company has gathered the following information on this product.

| | |
|---|---|
| Expected total unit cost | $25 |
| Estimated investment for new product | $500,000 |
| Desired ROI | 10% |
| Expected number of units to be produced and sold | 1,000 |

   Given this information, the desired markup percentage and selling price are:
   a. markup percentage 10%; selling price $55.
   b. markup percentage 200%; selling price $75.
   c. markup percentage 10%; selling price $50.
   d. markup percentage 100%; selling price $55.

6. **(LO 2)** Mystique Co. provides the following information for the new product it recently introduced.

| | |
|---|---|
| Total unit cost | $30 |
| Desired ROI per unit | $10 |
| Target selling price | $40 |

   What would be Mystique Co.'s percentage markup on cost?
   a. 125%.
   b. 75%.
   c. 33⅓%.
   d. 25%.

7. **(LO 3)** Crescent Electrical Repair has decided to price its work on a time-and-material basis. It estimates the following costs for the year related to labor.

| | |
|---|---|
| Technician wages and benefits | $100,000 |
| Office employee's salary and benefits | $ 40,000 |
| Other overhead | $ 80,000 |

Crescent desires a profit margin of $10 per labor hour and budgets 5,000 hours of repair time for the year. The office employee's salary, benefits, and other overhead costs should be divided evenly between time charges and material loading charges. Crescent labor charge per hour would be:

a. $42.   c. $32.

b. $34.   d. $30.

**8. (LO 3)** Time-and-material pricing would most likely be used by a:

a. garden-fertilizer producer.

b. lawn-mower manufacturer.

c. tree farm.

d. lawn-care provider.

**9. (LO 3)** When a company uses time-and-material pricing, the material loading charge is expressed as a percentage of:

a. the total estimated labor costs for the year.

b. the total estimated costs of parts and materials for the year.

c. the total estimated overhead costs for the year.

d. the total estimated costs of parts, materials, and labor for the year.

**10. (LO 4)** The Plastics Division of Weston Company manufactures plastic molds and then sells them to customers for $70 per unit. Its unit variable cost is $30, and its unit fixed cost is $10. Management would like the Plastics Division to transfer 10,000 of these molds to another division within the company at a price of $40. The Plastics Division is operating at full capacity. What is the minimum transfer price that the Plastics Division should accept?

a. $10.   c. $40.

b. $30.   d. $70.

**11. (LO 4)** Assume the same information as Question 10, except that the Plastics Division has available capacity of 10,000 units for plastic moldings. What is the minimum transfer price that the Plastics Division should accept?

a. $10.   c. $40.

b. $30.   d. $70.

**12. (LO 4)** The most common method used to establish transfer prices is the:

a. negotiated transfer pricing approach.

b. opportunity costing transfer pricing approach.

c. cost-based transfer pricing approach.

d. market-based transfer pricing approach.

*13. **(LO 5)** AST Electrical provides the following cost information related to its production of electronic circuit boards.

|  | Per Unit |
| --- | --- |
| Variable manufacturing cost | $40 |
| Fixed manufacturing cost | $30 |
| Variable selling and administrative expenses | $ 8 |
| Fixed selling and administrative expenses | $12 |
| Desired ROI per unit | $15 |

What is its markup percentage assuming that AST Electrical uses absorption-cost pricing?

a. 16.67%.   c. 54.28%.

b. 50%.   d. 118.75%.

*14. **(LO 5)** Assume the same information as Question 13 and determine AST Electrical's markup percentage using variable-cost pricing.

a. 16.67%.   c. 54.28%.

b. 50%.   d. 118.75%.

*15. **(LO 6)** Global Industries transfers parts between divisions in two countries, Eastland and Westland. Eastland's tax rate is 8%, and Westland's tax rate is 16%. If Global desired to minimize tax payments and maximize net income, it might consider establishing transfer prices that:

a. allocate contribution margin equally between Eastland and Westland.

b. allocate more contribution margin to Eastland.

c. allocate more contribution margin to Westland.

d. allocate half as much contribution margin to Eastland as it does to Westland.

## Solutions

**1. c.** The selling price and the desired profit must be decided before costs are determined. Therefore, the other choices are incorrect.

**2. b.** The target cost for the locomotive is selling price less desired profit or $80 − $15 = $65, not (a) $80, (c) $40, or (d) $25.

**3. c.** A seller would most likely use target costing in a competitive common-product environment as the price is set by the market. In a less competitive environment, companies have a greater ability to set the product price and therefore could use (a) time-and-material pricing, (b) variable costing, or (d) cost-plus pricing.

**4. b.** In cost-plus pricing, Selling price = Cost + (Markup percentage × Cost). The other choices are therefore incorrect.

**5. b.** The desired markup percentage = [(.10 × $500,000) ÷ 1,000] ÷ $25 = 200%. The selling price = $25 + $50 = $75. The other choices are therefore incorrect.

**6. c.** The percentage markup on cost = ($10 ÷ $30) = 33⅓%, not (a) 125%, (b) 75%, or (d) 25%.

**7. a.** The labor charge per hour = $10 + {[$100,000 + .5($40,000) + .5($80,000)] ÷ 5,000} = $42, not (b) $34, (c), $32, or (d) $30.

**8. d.** A lawn-care provider would be most likely to use time-and-material pricing as it is a service company. The other choices provide products rather than services.

**9. b.** In time-and-material pricing, the material loading charge is expressed as a percentage of the total estimated costs of parts and materials for the year. Therefore, the other choices are incorrect.

**10. d.** The minimum transfer price the Plastics Division should accept = Unit variable cost + Opportunity cost per unit. Since the Plastics Division is operating at full capacity, the opportunity cost per unit is equal to the contribution margin per unit of $40 (selling price of $70 − unit variable cost of $30). The minimum transfer price is therefore $30 + $40 = $70, not (a) $10, (b) $30, or (c) $40.

**11. b.** Since we assume the Plastics Division has excess capacity of 10,000 units, the minimum transfer price is equal to the unit variable cost of $30, not (a) $10, (c) $40, or (d) $70.

**12. c.** The most common method to establish transfer prices is the cost-based transfer pricing approach as it is simple to use, easy to understand, and has available cost data. Negotiated transfer pricing and market-based transfer pricing are considered better approaches but often are not used because of lack of market price information or other considerations.

**\*13. b.** Using the absorption-cost approach, add the desired ROI per unit ($15) and selling and administrative expenses per unit ($20) = $35 per unit, then divide that by the manufacturing cost per unit ($70), which equals the markup percentage of 50%, not (a) 16.67%, (c) 54.28%, or (d) 118.75%.

**\*14. d.** Using variable-cost pricing, add the desired ROI per unit ($15), fixed manufacturing costs per unit ($30) and fixed selling and administrative expenses per unit ($12) = $57, then divide that by the total unit variable costs ($40 + $8) = $57 ÷ $48 = 118.75%, not (a) 16.67%, (b) 50%, or (c) 54.28%.

**\*15. b.** To minimize tax payments and maximize net income, Global's transfer prices might allocate more contribution margin to Eastland as it has a lower tax rate. (Note that the legal and ethical ramifications of this action would need to be considered.) The other choices are therefore incorrect.

# Practice Brief Exercises

**1. (LO 2)** During the current year, Winston Corporation expects to produce 15,000 units and has budgeted the following: net income $500,000, variable costs $800,000, and fixed costs $700,000. It has invested assets of $2,000,000. The company's budgeted ROI was 20%. What was its budgeted markup percentage using a full-cost approach?

*Compute ROI and markup percentage.*

## Solution

1. The markup percentage is equal to desired ROI per unit divided by total unit cost. The desired ROI per unit is computed as follows.

$$\text{Desired ROI per unit} = \frac{\$2,000,000 \times 30\%}{15,000 \text{ units}} = \$40$$

The total unit cost is computed as follows.

$$\text{Total unit cost} = \frac{\$800,000 + \$700,000}{15,000 \text{ units}} = \$100$$

The budgeted markup percentage is computed as follows.

$$\frac{\text{Desired ROI per unit}}{\text{Total unit cost}} = \frac{\$40}{\$100} = 40\%$$

**2. (LO 3)** Tanner Bicycle Repair charges $28 per hour of labor. It has a material loading percentage of 30%. On a recent job replacing the rear wheel and sprocket of a racing bike, Tanner worked 8 hours and used parts with a cost of $450. Calculate Tanner's total bill.

*Use time-and-material pricing to determine bill.*

## Solution

2. Tanner's total bill would equal:

$$(8 \text{ hours} \times \$28) + \$450 + (\$450 \times 30\%) = \$809$$

**3. (LO 4)** The Memory Division of Ellie International produces a computer memory element that it sells to its customers for $30 per unit. Its unit variable cost is $18, and its unit fixed cost is $7. Top management of Ellie International would like the Memory Division to transfer 7,000 units to another division within the company at a price of $21. The Memory Division has sufficient excess capacity to provide the units. What is the minimum transfer price that the Memory Division should accept?

*Determine minimum transfer price.*

## Solution

3. If the division has excess capacity, then its opportunity cost is zero. In this case, the minimum transfer price is:

$$\text{Minimum transfer price} = \$18 + \$0 = \$18$$

*Determine minimum transfer price for special order.*

**4. (LO 4)** Use the data from **Practice Brief Exercise 3** but assume that the units being requested are special high-performance units and that the division's unit variable cost would be $21 (rather than $18). Assume the division is operating at full capacity. What is the minimum transfer price that the Memory Division should accept?

**Solution**

**4.** The minimum transfer price is equal to the division's variable cost plus its opportunity cost. In this case, the minimum transfer price is:

$$\text{Minimum transfer price} = \$21 + (\$30 - \$18) = \$33$$

# Practice Exercises

*Use cost-plus pricing to determine various amounts.*

**1. (LO 2)** Notown Recording Studio rents studio time to musicians in 2-hour blocks. Each session includes the use of the studio facilities, a digital recorded CD of the performance, and a professional music producer/mixer. Anticipated annual volume is 1,000 sessions. The company has invested $2,300,000 in the studio and expects a return on investment (ROI) of 15%. Budgeted costs for the coming year are as follows.

| | Per Session | Total |
|---|---|---|
| Direct materials (CDs, etc.) | $ 20 | |
| Direct labor | 400 | |
| Variable overhead | 50 | |
| Fixed overhead | | $950,000 |
| Variable selling and administrative expenses | 40 | |
| Fixed selling and administrative expenses | | 540,000 |

**Instructions**

**a.** Determine the total cost per session.

**b.** Determine the desired ROI per session.

**c.** Calculate the markup percentage on the total cost per session.

**d.** Calculate the target price per session.

**Solution**

**1. a.** Total cost per session:

| | Per Session |
|---|---|
| Direct materials | $ 20 |
| Direct labor | 400 |
| Variable overhead | 50 |
| Fixed overhead ($950,000 ÷ 1,000) | 950 |
| Variable selling & administrative expenses | 40 |
| Fixed selling & administrative expenses ($540,000 ÷ 1,000) | 540 |
| Total cost per session | $2,000 |

**b.** Desired ROI per session = (15% × $2,300,000) ÷ 1,000 = $345

**c.** Markup percentage on total cost per session = $345 ÷ $2,000 = 17.25%

**d.** Target price per session = $2,000 + ($2,000 × 17.25%) = $2,345

*Determine minimum transfer price.*

**2. (LO 4)** Mercury Corporation manufactures car audio systems. It is a division of Country-Wide Motors, which manufactures vehicles. Mercury sells car audio systems to other divisions of Country-Wide, as well as to other vehicle manufacturers and retail stores. The following information is available for Mercury's standard unit: unit variable cost $31, unit fixed cost $23, and unit selling price to outside customer $85. Country-Wide currently purchases a standard unit from an outside supplier for $80. Because of quality concerns and to ensure a reliable supply, the top management of Country-Wide has ordered Mercury to provide 200,000 units per year at a transfer price of $30 per unit. Mercury is already operating at full capacity. Mercury can avoid $2 per unit of variable selling costs by selling the unit internally.

### Instructions

a. What is the minimum transfer price that Mercury should accept?

b. What is the potential loss to the corporation as a whole resulting from this forced transfer?

c. How should the company resolve this situation?

### Solution

2. a. The minimum transfer price that Mercury should accept is:

Minimum transfer price = ($31 − $2) + ($85 − $31) = $83

b. The lost contribution margin per unit to the company is:

| | |
|---|---|
| Contribution margin lost by Mercury | |
| {($85 − $31) − [$30 − ($31 − $2)]} | $53 |
| Increased contribution margin to vehicle division ($80 − $30) | 50 |
| Net loss in contribution margin | $ 3 |

Total lost contribution margin is $3 × 200,000 units = $600,000

c. If management insists that it wants Mercury to provide the car audio systems and Mercury is operating at full capacity, then it must be willing to pay the minimum transfer price for those units. Otherwise, it will penalize the managers of Mercury by not giving them adequate credit for their contribution to the corporation's contribution margin.

## Practice Problem

**(LO 4)** Revco Electronics is a division of International Motors, an automobile manufacturer. Revco produces car radio/CD players. Revco sells its products to other divisions of International Motors, as well as to other car manufacturers and electronics distributors. The following information is available regarding Revco's car radio/CD player.

*Determine minimum transfer price under different situations.*

| | |
|---|---|
| Selling price of car radio/CD player to external customers | $49 |
| Unit variable cost | $28 |
| Capacity | 200,000 units |

### Instructions

Determine whether the goods should be transferred internally or purchased externally and what the appropriate transfer price should be under each of the following **independent** situations.

a. Revco Electronics is operating at full capacity. There is a saving of $4 per unit for variable cost if the car radio is made for internal sale. International Motors can purchase a comparable car radio from an outside supplier for $47.

b. Revco Electronics has sufficient existing capacity to meet the needs of International Motors. International Motors can purchase a comparable car radio from an outside supplier for $47.

c. International Motors wants to purchase a special-order car radio/CD player with additional features. It needs 15,000 units. Revco Electronics has determined that the additional unit variable cost would be $12. Revco Electronics has no spare capacity. It will have to forgo sales of 15,000 units to external parties in order to provide this special order.

### Solution

a. Revco Electronics' opportunity cost (its lost contribution margin) would be $21 ($49 − $28). Using the equation for minimum transfer price, we determine:

| Minimum transfer price | = | Variable cost | + | Opportunity cost |
|---|---|---|---|---|
| $45 | = | ($28 − $4) | + | $21 |

Since this minimum transfer price is less than the $47 it would cost if International Motors purchases from an external party, internal transfer should take place. Revco Electronics and International Motors should negotiate a transfer price between $45 and $47.

**b.** Since Revco Electronics has available capacity, its opportunity cost (its lost contribution margin) would be $0. Using the equation for minimum transfer price, we determine the following.

$$\begin{array}{ccccc} \text{Minimum transfer price} & = & \text{Variable cost} & + & \text{Opportunity cost} \\ \$28 & = & \$28 & + & \$0 \end{array}$$

Since International Motors can purchase the unit for $47 from an external party, the most it would be willing to pay would be $47. It is in the best interest of the company as a whole, as well as the two divisions, for a transfer to take place. The two divisions must reach a negotiated transfer price between $28 and $47 that recognizes the costs and benefits to each party and is acceptable to both.

**c.** Revco Electronics' opportunity cost (its lost contribution margin per unit) would be $21 ($49 − $28). Its variable cost would be $40 ($28 + $12). Using the equation for minimum transfer price, we determine the following.

$$\begin{array}{ccccc} \text{Minimum transfer price} & = & \text{Variable cost} & + & \text{Opportunity cost} \\ \$61 & = & \$40 & + & \$21 \end{array}$$

Note that in this case Revco Electronics has no available capacity. Its management may decide that it does not want to provide this special order because to do so will require that it cut off the supply of the standard unit to some of its existing customers. This may anger those customers and result in the loss of customers.

---

## Brief Exercises, DO IT! Exercises, Exercises, Problems, Data Analytics Activities, and many additional resources are available for practice in WileyPLUS.

---

*Note:* All asterisked Questions, Exercises, and Problems relate to material in the appendices to this chapter.

---

## Questions

**1.** What are the two types of pricing environments for sales to external parties?

**2.** In what situation does a company place the greatest focus on its target cost? How is the target cost determined?

**3.** What is the basic equation to determine the target selling price in cost-plus pricing?

**4.** Benz Corporation produces a filter that has a unit cost of $18. The company would like a 30% markup. Using cost-plus pricing, determine the unit selling price.

**5.** What is the basic equation for the markup percentage?

**6.** Stanley Corporation manufactures an electronic switch for dishwashers. The unit cost base, excluding selling and administrative expenses, is $60. The unit cost of selling and administrative expenses is $15. The company's desired ROI per unit is $6. Calculate its markup percentage on total unit cost.

**7.** Sheen Co. manufactures a standard cabinet for a Blu-ray player. The unit variable cost is $16. The unit fixed cost is $9. The desired ROI per unit is $6. Compute the markup percentage on total unit cost and the target selling price for the cabinet.

**8.** In what circumstances is time-and-material pricing most often used?

**9.** What is the material loading charge? How is it expressed?

**10.** What is a transfer price? Why is determining a fair transfer price important to division managers?

**11.** When setting a transfer price, what objective(s) should the company have in mind?

**12.** What are the three approaches for determining transfer prices?

**13.** Describe the cost-based approach to transfer pricing. What is the strength of this approach? What are the weaknesses of this approach?

**14.** What is the general equation for determining the minimum transfer price that the selling division should be willing to accept?

**15.** When determining the minimum transfer price, what is meant by the "opportunity cost"?

**16.** In what circumstances will a negotiated transfer price be used instead of a market-based price?

**\*17.** What costs are excluded from the cost base when absorption-cost pricing is used to determine the markup percentage?

**\*18.** Marie Corporation manufactures a fiber optic connector. The unit variable cost is $16. The unit fixed cost is $9. The company's desired ROI per unit is $3. Compute the markup percentage using variable-cost pricing.

**\*19.** Explain how companies use transfer pricing between divisions located in different countries to reduce tax payments, and discuss the propriety of this approach.

## Brief Exercises

**BE21.1 (LO 1), AP** Ortega Company manufactures computer hard drives. The market for hard drives is very competitive. The current market price for a computer hard drive is $45. Ortega would like a profit of $10 per drive. How can Ortega accomplish this objective?

*Compute target cost.*

**BE21.2 (LO 2), AP** Mussatto Corporation produces snowboards. The following unit cost information is available: direct materials $12, direct labor $8, variable manufacturing overhead $6, fixed manufacturing overhead $14, variable selling and administrative expenses $4, and fixed selling and administrative expenses $12. Using a 30% markup percentage on total unit cost, compute the target selling price.

*Use cost-plus pricing to determine selling price.*

**BE21.3 (LO 2), AP** Jaymes Corporation produces high-performance rotors. It expects to produce 50,000 rotors in the coming year. It has invested $10,000,000 to produce rotors. The company has a required return on investment of 12%. What is its ROI per unit?

*Compute ROI per unit.*

**BE21.4 (LO 2), AP** Morales Corporation produces microwave ovens. The following unit cost information is available: direct materials $36, direct labor $24, variable manufacturing overhead $18, fixed manufacturing overhead $40, variable selling and administrative expenses $14, and fixed selling and administrative expenses $28. Its desired ROI per unit is $30. Compute its markup percentage using a total-cost approach.

*Compute markup percentage.*

**BE21.5 (LO 2), AP** During the current year, Chudrick Corporation expects to produce 10,000 units and has budgeted the following: net income $300,000, variable costs $1,100,000, and fixed costs $100,000. It has invested assets of $1,500,000. The company's budgeted ROI was 20%. What was its budgeted markup percentage using a full-cost approach?

*Compute ROI and markup percentage.*

**BE21.6 (LO 3), AP** `Service` Rooney Small Engine Repair charges $42 per hour of labor. It has a material loading percentage of 40%. On a recent job replacing the engine of a riding lawnmower, Rooney worked 10.5 hours and used parts with a cost of $700. Calculate Rooney's total bill.

*Use time-and-material pricing to determine bill.*

**BE21.7 (LO 4), AP** The Heating Division of Kobe International produces a heating element that it sells to its customers for $45 per unit. Its unit variable cost is $25, and its unit fixed cost is $10. Top management of Kobe International would like the Heating Division to transfer 15,000 heating units to another division within the company at a price of $29. The Heating Division is operating at full capacity. What is the minimum transfer price that the Heating Division should accept?

*Determine minimum transfer price.*

**BE21.8 (LO 4), AP** Use the data from BE21.7 but assume that the Heating Division has sufficient excess capacity to provide the 15,000 heating units to the other division. What is the minimum transfer price that the Heating Division should accept?

*Determine minimum transfer price with excess capacity.*

**BE21.9 (LO 4), AP** Use the data from BE21.7 but assume that the units being requested are special high-performance units, and the division's unit variable cost would be $27 (rather than $25). What is the minimum transfer price that the Heating Division should accept?

*Determine minimum transfer price for special order.*

*****BE21.10 (LO 5), AP** Using the data in BE21.4, compute the markup percentage using absorption-cost pricing.

*Compute markup percentage using absorption-cost pricing.*

*****BE21.11 (LO 5), AP** Using the data in BE21.4, compute the markup percentage using variable-cost pricing.

*Compute markup percentage using variable-cost pricing.*

## DO IT! Exercises

**DO IT! 21.1 (LO 1), AP** Maize Water is considering introducing a water filtration device for its 20-ounce water bottles. Market research indicates that 1,000,000 units can be sold if the price is no more than $3. If Maize Water decides to produce the filters, it will need to invest $2,000,000 in new production equipment. Maize Water requires a minimum rate of return of 16% on all investments.
  Determine the target cost for the filter.

*Determine target cost.*

*Use cost-plus pricing to determine various amounts.*

**DO IT! 21.2 (LO 2), AP** Gundy Corporation produces area rugs. The following unit cost information is available: direct materials $18, direct labor $9, variable manufacturing overhead $5, fixed manufacturing overhead $6, variable selling and administrative expenses $3, and fixed selling and administrative expenses $7.

Using a 30% markup on total per unit cost, compute the target selling price.

*Use time-and-material pricing to determine bill.*

**DO IT! 21.3 (LO 3), AP** Service The following information relates to labor for Verde Appliance Repair Shop.

| | |
|---|---|
| Repair-technicians' wages | $110,000 |
| Fringe benefits | 40,000 |
| Overhead | 50,000 |

The desired profit margin per hour is $20. The material loading charge is 60% of invoice cost. Verde estimates that 5,000 labor hours will be worked next year. If Verde repairs a dishwasher that takes 1.5 hours to repair and uses parts that cost $70, compute the bill for the job.

*Determine transfer prices.*

**DO IT! 21.4 (LO 4), AP** The fastener division of Southern Fasteners manufactures zippers and then sells them to customers for $8 per unit. Its unit variable cost is $3, and its unit fixed cost is $1.50. Management would like the fastener division to transfer 12,000 of these zippers to another division within the company at a price of $3. The fastener division could avoid $0.20 per zipper of variable packaging costs by selling internally.

Determine the minimum transfer price (a) assuming the fastener division is not operating at full capacity, and (b) assuming the fastener division is operating at full capacity.

# Exercises

*Compute target cost.*

**E21.1 (LO 1), AP** Mesa Cheese Company has developed a new cheese slicer called Slim Slicer. The company plans to sell this slicer through its online website. Given market research, Mesa believes that it can charge $20 for the Slim Slicer. Prototypes of the Slim Slicer, however, are costing $22. By using cheaper materials and gaining efficiencies in mass production, Mesa believes it can reduce Slim Slicer's cost substantially. Mesa wishes to earn a return of 40% of the selling price.

## Instructions

a. Compute the target cost for the Slim Slicer.

b. When is target costing particularly helpful in deciding whether to produce a given product?

*Compute target cost.*

**E21.2 (LO 1), AP** Eckert Company is involved in producing and selling high-end golf equipment. The company has recently been involved in developing various types of laser guns to measure yardages on the golf course. One small laser gun, called LittleLaser, appears to have a very large potential market. Because of competition, Eckert does not believe that it can charge more than $90 for LittleLaser. At this price, Eckert believes it can sell 100,000 of these laser guns. Eckert will require an investment of $8,000,000 to manufacture, and the company wants an ROI of 20%.

## Instructions

Determine the target cost for one LittleLaser.

*Compute target cost and cost-plus pricing.*

**E21.3 (LO 1, 2), AP** Leno Company makes swimsuits and sells these suits directly to retailers. Although Leno has a variety of suits, it does not make the Performance suit used by highly skilled swimmers. The market research department believes that a strong market exists for this type of suit. The department indicates that the Performance suit would sell for approximately $100. Given its experience, Leno believes the Performance suit would have the following manufacturing costs.

| | |
|---|---|
| Direct materials | $ 25 |
| Direct labor | 30 |
| Manufacturing overhead | 45 |
| Total costs | $100 |

**Instructions**

a. Assume that Leno uses cost-plus pricing, setting the selling price 25% above its costs. (1) What would be the price charged for the Performance swimsuit? (2) Under what circumstances might Leno consider manufacturing the Performance swimsuit given this approach?

b. Assume that Leno uses target costing. What is the price that Leno would charge the retailer for the Performance swimsuit?

c. What is the highest acceptable manufacturing cost Leno would be willing to incur to produce the Performance swimsuit, if it desired a profit of $25 per unit? (Assume target costing.)

**E21.4 (LO 2), AP** Kaspar Corporation makes a commercial-grade cooking griddle. The following information is available for Kaspar Corporation's anticipated annual volume of 30,000 units.

*Use cost-plus pricing to determine selling price.*

Excel

| | Per Unit | Total |
|---|---|---|
| Direct materials | $17 | |
| Direct labor | 8 | |
| Variable manufacturing overhead | 11 | |
| Fixed manufacturing overhead | | $300,000 |
| Variable selling and administrative expenses | 4 | |
| Fixed selling and administrative expenses | | 150,000 |

The company uses a 40% markup percentage on total cost.

**Instructions**

a. Compute the total unit cost.

b. Compute the target selling price.

**E21.5 (LO 2), AP** Schopp Corporation makes a mechanical stuffed alligator that sings the Martian national anthem. The following information is available for Schopp Corporation's anticipated annual volume of 500,000 units.

*Use cost-plus pricing to determine various amounts.*

Excel

| | Per Unit | Total |
|---|---|---|
| Direct materials | $ 7 | |
| Direct labor | 11 | |
| Variable manufacturing overhead | 15 | |
| Fixed manufacturing overhead | | $3,000,000 |
| Variable selling and administrative expenses | 14 | |
| Fixed selling and administrative expenses | | 1,500,000 |

The company has a desired ROI of 25%. It has invested assets of $28,000,000.

**Instructions**

a. Compute the total unit cost.

b. Compute the desired ROI per unit.

c. Compute the markup percentage using total unit cost.

d. Compute the target selling price.

**E21.6 (LO 2), AP** Service  Alma's Recording Studio rents studio time to musicians in 2-hour blocks. Each session includes the use of the studio facilities, a digital recording of the performance, and a professional music producer/mixer. Anticipated annual volume is 1,000 sessions. The company has invested $2,352,000 in the studio and expects a return on investment (ROI) of 20%. Budgeted costs for the coming year are as follows.

*Use cost-plus pricing to determine various amounts.*

| | Per Session | Total |
|---|---|---|
| Direct materials (CDs, etc.) | $ 20 | |
| Direct labor | 400 | |
| Variable overhead | 50 | |
| Fixed overhead | | $950,000 |
| Variable selling and administrative expenses | 40 | |
| Fixed selling and administrative expenses | | 500,000 |

**Instructions**

a. Determine the total cost per session.

b. Determine the desired ROI per session.

c. Calculate the markup percentage on the total cost per session.

d. Calculate the target price per session.

*Use cost-plus pricing to determine various amounts.*

**E21.7 (LO 2), AP** Gibbs Corporation produces industrial robots for high-precision manufacturing. The following information is given for Gibbs Corporation.

|  | Per Unit | Total |
|---|---|---|
| Direct materials | $380 | |
| Direct labor | 290 | |
| Variable manufacturing overhead | 72 | |
| Fixed manufacturing overhead | | $1,500,000 |
| Variable selling and administrative expenses | 55 | |
| Fixed selling and administrative expenses | | 324,000 |

The company has a desired ROI of 20%. It has invested assets of $54,000,000. It anticipates production of 3,000 units per year.

**Instructions**

a. Compute the unit cost of the fixed manufacturing overhead and the fixed selling and administrative expenses.

b. Compute the desired ROI per unit. (Round to the nearest dollar.)

c. Compute the target selling price.

*Use time-and-material pricing to determine bill.*

**E21.8 (LO 3), AP** Service Second Chance Welding rebuilds spot welders for manufacturers. The following budgeted cost data for 2022 is available for Second Chance.

|  | Time Charges | Material Loading Charges |
|---|---|---|
| Technicians' wages and benefits | $228,000 | — |
| Parts manager's salary and benefits | — | $42,500 |
| Office employee's salary and benefits | 38,000 | 9,000 |
| Other overhead | 15,200 | 24,000 |
| Total budgeted costs | $281,200 | $75,500 |

The company desires a $30 profit margin per hour of labor and a 20% profit margin on parts. It has budgeted for 7,600 hours of repair time in the coming year, and estimates that the total invoice cost of parts and materials in 2022 will be $400,000.

**Instructions**

a. Compute the rate charged per hour of labor.

b. Compute the material loading percentage. (Round to three decimal places.)

c. Pace Corporation has requested an estimate to rebuild its spot welder. Second Chance estimates that it would require 40 hours of labor and $2,000 of parts. Compute the total estimated bill.

*Use time-and-material pricing to determine bill.*

**E21.9 (LO 3), AP** Service Rey Custom Electronics (RCE) sells and installs complete security, computer, audio, and video systems for homes. On newly constructed homes it provides bids using time-and-material pricing. The following budgeted cost data are available.

|  | Time Charges | Material Loading Charges |
|---|---|---|
| Technicians' wages and benefits | $150,000 | — |
| Parts manager's salary and benefits | — | $34,000 |
| Office employee's salary and benefits | 30,000 | 15,000 |
| Other overhead | 15,000 | 42,000 |
| Total budgeted costs | $195,000 | $91,000 |

The company has budgeted for 6,250 hours of technician time during the coming year. It desires a $38 profit margin per hour of labor and an 80% profit on parts. It estimates the total invoice cost of parts and materials in 2022 will be $700,000.

**Instructions**

a. Compute the rate charged per hour of labor.

b. Compute the material loading percentage.

c.  RCE has just received a request for a bid on a security and home entertainment system from Buil Builders on a $1,200,000 new home. The company estimates that the job would require 80 hours of labor and $40,000 of parts. Compute the total estimated bill.

**E21.10 (LO 3), AP** `Service` Wasson's Classic Cars restores classic automobiles to showroom status. Budgeted data for the current year are as follows.

*Use time-and-material pricing to determine bill.*

|  | Time Charges | Material Loading Charges |
|---|---|---|
| Restorers' wages and fringe benefits | $270,000 | — |
| Purchasing agent's salary and fringe benefits | — | $ 67,500 |
| Administrative salaries and fringe benefits | 54,000 | 21,960 |
| Other overhead costs | 24,000 | 77,490 |
| Total budgeted costs | $348,000 | $166,950 |

The company anticipated that the restorers would work a total of 12,000 hours this year. Expected parts and materials were $1,260,000.

In late January, the company experienced a fire in its facilities that destroyed most of the accounting records. The accountant remembers that the hourly labor rate was $70.00 and that the material loading charge was 83.25%.

**Instructions**

a.  Determine the profit margin per hour on labor.

b.  Determine the profit margin on materials.

c.  Determine the total price of labor and materials on a job that was completed after the fire that required 150 hours of labor and $60,000 in parts and materials.

**E21.11 (LO 4), AP** `Writing` Chen Company's Small Motor Division manufactures a number of small motors used in household and office appliances. The Household Division of Chen then assembles and packages such items as blenders and juicers. Both divisions are free to buy and sell any of their components internally or externally. The following costs relate to small motor LN233 on a per unit basis.

*Determine minimum transfer price.*

| | |
|---|---|
| Unit fixed cost | $ 5 |
| Unit variable cost | 11 |
| Unit selling price | 35 |

**Instructions**

a.  Assuming that the Small Motor Division has excess capacity, compute the minimum acceptable price for the transfer of small motor LN233 to the Household Division.

b.  Assuming that the Small Motor Division does not have excess capacity, compute the minimum acceptable price for the transfer of the small motor to the Household Division.

c.  Explain why the level of capacity in the Small Motor Division has an effect on the transfer price.

**E21.12 (LO 4), AN** The Cycle Division of Ayala Company has the following unit data related to its most recent cycle, the Roadbuster.

*Determine effect on income from transfer price.*

| | | |
|---|---|---|
| Selling price | | $2,200 |
| Variable cost of goods sold | | |
| Body frame | $300 | |
| Other variable costs | 900 | 1,200 |
| Contribution margin | | $1,000 |

Presently, the Cycle Division buys its body frames from an outside supplier. However, Ayala has another division, FrameBody, that makes body frames for other cycle companies. The Cycle Division believes that FrameBody's product is suitable for its new Roadbuster cycle. Presently, FrameBody sells its frames for $350 per frame. The variable cost for FrameBody is $270. The Cycle Division is willing to pay $280 to purchase the frames from FrameBody.

**Instructions**

a.  Assume that FrameBody has excess capacity and is able to meet all of the Cycle Division's needs. If the Cycle Division buys 1,000 frames from FrameBody, determine the following: (1) effect on the income of the Cycle Division, (2) effect on the income of FrameBody, and (3) effect on the income of Ayala.

**b.** Assume that FrameBody does not have excess capacity and therefore would lose sales if the frames were sold to the Cycle Division. If the Cycle Division buys 1,000 frames from FrameBody, determine the following: (1) effect on the income of the Cycle Division, (2) effect on the income of FrameBody, and (3) effect on the income of Ayala.

*Determine minimum transfer price.*

**E21.13 (LO 4), AP** Benson Corporation manufactures car stereos. It is a division of Berna Motors, which manufactures vehicles. Benson sells car stereos to Berna, as well as to other vehicle manufacturers and retail stores. The following information is available for Benson's standard unit: unit variable cost $37, unit fixed cost $23, and unit selling price to outside customer $86. Berna currently purchases a standard unit from an outside supplier for $80. Because of quality concerns and to ensure a reliable supply, the top management of Berna has ordered Benson to provide 200,000 units per year at a transfer price of $35 per unit. Benson is already operating at full capacity. Benson can avoid $3 per unit of variable selling costs by selling the unit internally.

**Instructions**

Answer each of the following questions.

**a.** What is the minimum transfer price that Benson should accept?

**b.** What is the potential loss to the corporation as a whole resulting from this forced transfer?

**c.** How should the company resolve this situation?

*Compute minimum transfer price.*

**E21.14 (LO 4), AP** The Bathtub Division of Kirk Plumbing Corporation has recently approached the Faucet Division with a proposal. The Bathtub Division would like to make a special "ivory" tub with gold-plated fixtures for the company's 50-year anniversary. It would make only 5,000 of these units. It would like the Faucet Division to make the fixtures and provide them to the Bathtub Division at a transfer price of $160. If sold externally, the estimated unit variable cost would be $140. However, by selling internally, the Faucet Division would save $6 per unit on variable selling expenses. The Faucet Division is currently operating at full capacity. Its standard unit sells for $50 per unit and has variable costs of $29.

**Instructions**

Compute the minimum transfer price that the Faucet Division should be willing to accept, and discuss whether it should accept this offer.

*Determine minimum transfer price.*

**E21.15 (LO 4), AP** Service The Appraisal Department of Jean Bank performs appraisals of business properties for loans being considered by the bank and appraisals for home buyers that are financing their purchase through some other financial institution. The department charges $160 per home appraisal, and its variable costs are $130 per appraisal.

Recently, Jean Bank has opened its own Home-Loan Department and wants the Appraisal Department to perform 1,200 appraisals on all Jean Bank–financed home loans. Bank management feels that the cost of these appraisals to the Home-Loan Department should be $150. The variable cost per appraisal to the Home-Loan Department would be $8 less than those performed for outside customers due to savings in administrative costs.

**Instructions**

**a.** Determine the minimum transfer price, assuming the Appraisal Department has excess capacity.

**b.** Determine the minimum transfer price, assuming the Appraisal Department has no excess capacity.

**c.** Assuming the Appraisal Department has no excess capacity, should management force the department to charge the Home-Loan Department only $150? Discuss.

*Determine minimum transfer price under different situations.*

**E21.16 (LO 4), AP** Crede Inc. has two divisions. Division A makes and sells student desks. Division B manufactures and sells reading lamps.

Each desk has a reading lamp as one of its components. Division A can purchase reading lamps at a cost of $10 from an outside vendor. Division A needs 10,000 lamps for the coming year.

Division B has the capacity to manufacture 50,000 lamps annually. Sales to outside customers are estimated at 40,000 lamps for the next year. Reading lamps are sold at $12 each. Variable costs are $7 per lamp and include $1 of variable sales costs that are not incurred if lamps are sold internally to Division A. The total amount of fixed costs for Division B is $80,000.

**Instructions**

Consider the following independent situations.

**a.** What should be the minimum transfer price accepted by Division B for the 10,000 lamps and the maximum transfer price paid by Division A? Justify your answer.

b. Suppose Division B could use the excess capacity to produce and sell externally 15,000 units of a new product at a unit selling price of $7. The unit variable cost for this new product is $5. What should be the minimum transfer price accepted by Division B for the 10,000 lamps and the maximum transfer price paid by Division A? Justify your answer.

c. If Division A needs 15,000 lamps instead of 10,000 during the next year. what should be the minimum transfer price accepted by Division B and the maximum transfer price paid by Division A? Justify your answer.

(CGA adapted)

**E21.17 (LO 4), AP** Twyla Company is a multidivisional company. Its managers have full responsibility for profits and complete autonomy to accept or reject transfers from other divisions. Division A produces a subassembly part for which there is a competitive market. Division B currently uses this subassembly for a final product that is sold outside at $2,400. Division A charges Division B market price for the part, which is $1,500 per unit. Variable costs are $1,100 and $1,200 for Divisions A and B, respectively.

*Determine minimum transfer price under different situations.*

The manager of Division B feels that Division A should transfer the part at a lower price than market because at market, Division B is unable to make a profit.

**Instructions**

a. Calculate Division B's contribution margin if transfers are made at the market price, and calculate the company's total contribution margin.

b. Assume that Division A can sell all its production in the open market. Should Division A transfer the goods to Division B? If so, at what price?

c. Assume that Division A can sell in the open market only 500 units at $1,500 per unit out of the 1,000 units that it can produce every month. Assume also that a 20% reduction in price is necessary to sell all 1,000 units each month. Should transfers be made? If so, how many units should the division transfer and at what price? To support your decision, submit a schedule that compares the total company contribution margins under the following three different alternatives. Alternative 1: maintain price, no transfers; Alternative 2: cut price, no transfers; and Alternative 3: maintain price and transfers.

(CMA-Canada adapted)

**\*E21.18 (LO 5), AP** Information for Schopp Corporation is given in E21.5.

*Compute total unit cost, ROI, and markup percentages using absorption-cost pricing and variable-cost pricing.*

**Instructions**

Using the information given in E21.5, complete the following.

a. Compute the total unit cost.

b. Compute the desired ROI per unit.

c. Using absorption-cost pricing, compute the markup percentage.

d. Using variable-cost pricing, compute the markup percentage.

**\*E21.19 (LO 5), AP** Rap Corporation produces outdoor portable fireplace units. The following unit cost information is available: direct materials $20, direct labor $25, variable manufacturing overhead $14, fixed manufacturing overhead $21, variable selling and administrative expenses $9, and fixed selling and administrative expenses $11. The company's ROI per unit is $24.

*Compute markup percentage using absorption-cost pricing and variable-cost pricing.*

**Instructions**

Compute Rap Corporation's markup percentage using (a) absorption-cost pricing and (b) variable-cost pricing.

**\*E21.20 (LO 5), AP** Information for Gibbs Corporation is given in E21.7.

*Compute various amounts using absorption-cost pricing and variable-cost pricing.*

**Instructions**

Using the information given in E21.7, answer the following.

a. Compute the cost per unit of the fixed manufacturing overhead and the fixed selling and administrative expenses.

b. Compute the desired ROI per unit. (Round to the nearest dollar.)

c. Compute the markup percentage and target selling price using absorption-cost pricing. (Round the markup percentage to three decimal places.)

d. Compute the markup percentage and target selling price using variable-cost pricing. (Round the markup percentage to three decimal places.)

# Problems

*Use cost-plus pricing to determine various amounts.*

**P21.1 (LO 2), AP** National Corporation needs to set a target price for its newly designed product M14–M16. The following data relate to this new product.

| | Per Unit | Total |
|---|---|---|
| Direct materials | $25 | |
| Direct labor | 40 | |
| Variable manufacturing overhead | 10 | |
| Fixed manufacturing overhead | | $1,440,000 |
| Variable selling and administrative expenses | 5 | |
| Fixed selling and administrative expenses | | 960,000 |

These costs are based on a budgeted volume of 80,000 units produced and sold each year. National uses cost-plus pricing methods to set its target selling price. The markup percentage on total unit cost is 40%.

## Instructions

*a. Unit variable cost $80*

a. Compute the total unit variable cost, total unit fixed cost, and total unit cost for M14–M16.

b. Compute the desired ROI per unit for M14–M16.

c. Compute the target selling price for M14–M16.

d. Compute unit variable cost, unit fixed cost, and unit total cost assuming that 60,000 M14–M16s are produced and sold during the year.

*Use cost-plus pricing to determine various amounts.*

**P21.2 (LO 2), AP** Lovell Computer Parts Inc. is in the process of setting a selling price on a new component it has just designed and developed. The following cost estimates for this new component have been provided by the accounting department for a budgeted volume of 50,000 units.

| | Per Unit | Total |
|---|---|---|
| Direct materials | $50 | |
| Direct labor | 26 | |
| Variable manufacturing overhead | 20 | |
| Fixed manufacturing overhead | | $600,000 |
| Variable selling and administrative expenses | 19 | |
| Fixed selling and administrative expenses | | 400,000 |

Lovell Computer Parts management requests that the total unit cost be used in cost-plus pricing its products. On this particular product, management also directs that the target price be set to provide a 25% return on investment (ROI) on invested assets of $1,000,000.

## Instructions

(Round all calculations to two decimal places.)

a. Compute the markup percentage and target selling price that will allow Lovell Computer Parts to earn its desired ROI of 25% on this new component.

*b. Target selling price $146.25*

b. Assuming that the volume is 40,000 units, compute the markup percentage and target selling price that will allow Lovell Computer Parts to earn its desired ROI of 25% on this new component.

*Use time-and-material pricing to determine bill.*

**P21.3 (LO 3), AP** Service  Sutton's Electronic Repair Shop has budgeted the following time and material for 2022.

| Sutton's Electronic Repair Shop Budgeted Costs for the Year 2022 | | |
|---|---|---|
| | **Time Charges** | **Material Loading Charges** |
| Shop employees' wages and benefits | $108,000 | — |
| Parts manager's salary and benefits | — | $25,400 |
| Office employee's salary and benefits | 23,500 | 13,600 |
| Overhead (supplies, depreciation, advertising, utilities) | 26,000 | 16,000 |
| Total budgeted costs | $157,500 | $55,000 |

Sutton's budgets 5,000 hours of repair time in 2022 and will bill a profit of $10 per labor hour along with a 25% profit markup on the invoice cost of parts. The estimated invoice cost for parts to be used is $100,000.

On January 5, 2022, Sutton's is asked to submit a price estimate to fix a 72-inch flat-screen TV. Sutton's estimates that this job will consume 4 hours of labor and $200 in parts.

**Instructions**

a. Compute the labor rate for Sutton's Electronic Repair Shop for the year 2022.

b. Compute the material loading charge percentage for Sutton's Electronic Repair Shop for the year 2022.

c. Prepare a time-and-material price quotation for fixing the flat-screen TV.

*c. $526*

**P21.4 (LO 4), AP** Service Writing Word Wizard is a publishing company with a number of different book lines. Each line has contracts with a number of different authors. The company also owns a printing operation called Quick Press. The book lines and the printing operation each operate as a separate profit center. The printing operation earns revenue by printing books by authors under contract with the book lines owned by Word Wizard, as well as authors under contract with other companies. The printing operation bills out at $0.01 per page, and a typical book requires 500 pages of print. A manager from Business Books, one of Word Wizard's book lines, has approached the manager of the printing operation offering to pay $0.007 per page for 1,500 copies of a 500-page book. The book line pays outside printers $0.009 per page. The printing operation's variable cost per page is $0.004.

*Determine minimum transfer price with no excess capacity and with excess capacity.*

**Instructions**

Determine whether the printing should be done internally or externally, and the appropriate transfer price, under each of the following situations.

a. Assume that the printing operation is booked solid for the next 2 years, and it would have to cancel an obligation with an outside customer in order to meet the needs of the internal division.

b. Assume that the printing operation has available capacity.

c. The top management of Word Wizard believes that the printing operation should always do the printing for the company's authors. On a number of occasions, it has forced the printing operation to cancel jobs with outside customers in order to meet the needs of its own lines. Discuss the pros and cons of this approach.

d. Calculate the change in contribution margin to each division, and to the company as a whole, if top management forces the printing operation to accept the $0.007 per page transfer price when it has no available capacity.

*d. Loss to company $(750)*

**P21.5 (LO 4), AP** Gutierrez Company makes various electronic products. The company is divided into a number of autonomous divisions that can either sell to internal units or sell externally. All divisions are located in buildings on the same piece of property. The Board Division has offered the Chip Division $21 per unit to supply it with chips for 40,000 boards. It has been purchasing these chips for $22 per unit from outside suppliers. The Chip Division receives $22.50 per unit for sales made to outside customers on this type of chip. The variable cost of chips sold externally by the Chip Division is $14.50. It estimates that it will save $4.50 per chip of selling expenses on units sold internally to the Board Division. The Chip Division has no excess capacity.

*Determine minimum transfer price with no excess capacity.*

**Instructions**

a. Calculate the minimum transfer price that the Chip Division should accept. Discuss whether it is in the Chip Division's best interest to accept the offer.

b. Suppose that the Chip Division decides to reject the offer. What are the financial implications for each division, and for the company as a whole, of this decision?

*b. Total loss to company $(160,000)*

**P21.6 (LO 4), AP** Comm Devices (CD) is a division of Worldwide Communications, Inc. CD produces restaurant pagers and other personal communication devices. These devices are sold to other Worldwide divisions, as well as to other communication companies. CD was recently approached by the manager of the Personal Communications Division regarding a request to make a special emergency-response pager designed to receive signals from anywhere in the world. The Personal Communications Division has requested that CD produce 12,000 units of this special pager. The following facts are available regarding the Comm Devices Division.

*Determine minimum transfer price under different situations.*

| | |
|---|---|
| Selling price of standard pager | $95 |
| Variable cost of standard pager | 50 |
| Additional variable cost of special pager | 30 |

### Instructions

For each of the following independent situations, calculate the minimum transfer price, and discuss whether the internal transfer should take place or whether the Personal Communications Division should purchase the pager externally.

a. The Personal Communications Division has offered to pay the CD Division $105 per pager. The CD Division has no available capacity. The CD Division would have to forgo sales of 10,000 pagers to existing customers in order to meet the request of the Personal Communications Division. (*Note:* The number of special pagers to be produced does not equal the number of existing pagers that would be forgone.)

*b. Minimum transfer price $140*

b. The Personal Communications Division has offered to pay the CD Division $150 per pager. The CD Division has no available capacity. The CD Division would have to forgo sales of 16,000 pagers to existing customers in order to meet the request of the Personal Communications Division. (*Note:* The number of special pagers to be produced does not equal the number of existing pagers that would be forgone.)

c. The Personal Communications Division has offered to pay the CD Division $100 per pager. The CD Division has available capacity.

*Compute the target price using absorption-cost pricing and variable-cost pricing.*

**\*P21.7 (LO 5), AP** Stent Corporation needs to set a target price for its newly designed product EverReady. The following data relate to this new product.

|  | Per Unit | Total |
| --- | --- | --- |
| Direct materials | $20 | |
| Direct labor | 40 | |
| Variable manufacturing overhead | 10 | |
| Fixed manufacturing overhead | | $1,600,000 |
| Variable selling and administrative expenses | 5 | |
| Fixed selling and administrative expenses | | 1,120,000 |

The costs shown above are based on a budgeted volume of 80,000 units produced and sold each year. Stent uses cost-plus pricing methods to set its target selling price. Because some managers prefer absorption-cost pricing and others prefer variable-cost pricing, the accounting department provides information under both approaches using a markup of 50% on absorption cost and a markup of 80% on variable cost.

### Instructions

*a. Markup $45*

a. Compute the target price for one unit of EverReady using absorption-cost pricing.

*b. Markup $60*

b. Compute the target price for one unit of EverReady using variable-cost pricing.

*Compute various amounts using absorption-cost pricing and variable-cost pricing.*

**\*P21.8 (LO 5), AP** **Writing** Anderson Windows Inc. is in the process of setting a target price on its newly designed tinted window. Cost data relating to the window at a budgeted volume of 4,000 units are as follows.

|  | Per Unit | Total |
| --- | --- | --- |
| Direct materials | $100 | |
| Direct labor | 70 | |
| Variable manufacturing overhead | 20 | |
| Fixed manufacturing overhead | | $120,000 |
| Variable selling and administrative expenses | 10 | |
| Fixed selling and administrative expenses | | 102,000 |

Anderson Windows uses cost-plus pricing methods that are designed to provide the company with a 25% ROI on its tinted window line. A total of $1,016,000 in assets is committed to production of the new tinted window.

### Instructions

*a. 45%*

a. Compute the markup percentage under absorption-cost pricing that will allow Anderson Windows to realize its desired ROI.

b. Compute the target price of the window under absorption-cost pricing, and show proof that the desired ROI is realized.

c. Compute the markup percentage under variable-cost pricing that will allow Anderson Windows to realize its desired ROI. (Round to three decimal places.)

d. Compute the target price of the window under variable-cost pricing, and show proof that the desired ROI is realized.

e. Since both absorption-cost pricing and variable-cost pricing produce the same target price and provide the same desired ROI, why do both methods exist? Isn't one method clearly superior to the other?

## Continuing Cases

### Current Designs

**CD21**  As a service to its customers, **Current Designs** repairs damaged kayaks. This is especially valuable to customers that have made a significant investment in the composite kayaks. To price the repair jobs, Current Designs uses time-and-material pricing with a desired profit margin of $20 per labor hour and a 50% materials loading charge.

Recently, Bill Johnson, Vice President of Sales and Marketing, received a phone call from a dealer in Brainerd, Minnesota. The dealer has a customer who recently damaged his composite kayak and would like an estimate of the cost to repair it. After the dealer emailed pictures of the damage, Bill reviewed the pictures with the repair technician and determined that the total materials charges for the repair would be $100. Bill estimates that the job will take 3 labor hours to complete. Following is the budgeted cost data for Current Designs:

| | |
|---|---|
| Repair-technician wages | $30,000 |
| Fringe benefits | 10,000 |
| Overhead | 10,000 |

Current Designs has allocated 2,000 hours of repair time for the upcoming year. The customer has agreed to transport the kayak to the Winona production facility for the repairs.

**Instructions**

Determine the price that Current Designs would charge to complete the repairs for the customer.

### Waterways Corporation

(*Note:* This is a continuation of the Waterways case from Chapters 14–20.)

**WC21**  Waterways Corporation competes in a market economy in which its products must be sold at market prices. Its emphasis is therefore on manufacturing its products at a cost that allows the company to earn its desired profit. This case asks you to consider a pricing situation for Waterways' projects.

*Go to WileyPLUS for complete case details and instructions.*

## Comprehensive Case

**CC21**  Greetings, Inc., a retailer of greeting cards and small gift items, needs to change its transfer pricing strategy for its Wall Décor division. In this case, you will have the opportunity to evaluate profitability using two different transfer pricing approaches and comment on the terms of the proposed transfer pricing agreement.

*Go to WileyPLUS for complete case details and instructions.*

## Data Analytics in Action

### Using Data Visualization to Analyze Trends

**DA21**  Data visualization can help Broadway theatre analysts to understand ticket prices.

**Example:**  Recall the *Service Company Insight* box "How Much Did You Pay for That Seat?" presented in the chapter. As discussed, ticket prices are dynamic and respond quickly to changes in demand. For example, take a look at the following chart. How might you explain some of the biggest drops in ticket prices in the first week of 2020?

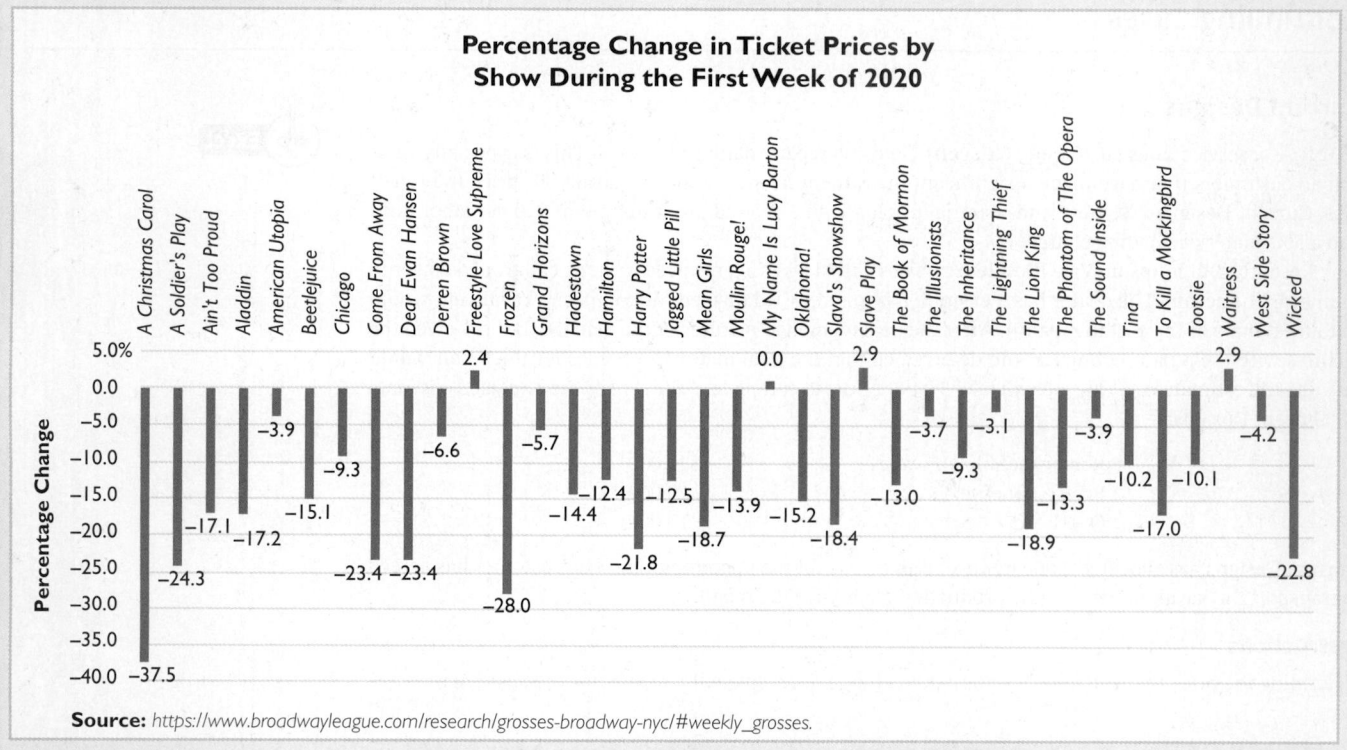

**Source:** *https://www.broadwayleague.com/research/grosses-broadway-nyc/#weekly_grosses.*

You can see that *A Christmas Carol* has the biggest average weekly price drop. However, we would expect this drop. The show would have had its highest sales and prices in November and December, during the holiday season.

Using data analytics to get big-picture results often leads to additional analysis. In this case, you will use tree map visualizations and a combo chart to delve deeper into the possible causes and effects of dynamic Broadway ticket prices.

*Go to WileyPlus for complete case details and instructions.*

# Expand Your Critical Thinking

## Decision-Making Across the Organization

**CT21.1** Lanier Manufacturing has multiple divisions that make a wide variety of products. Recently, the Bearing Division and the Wheel Division argued over a transfer price. The Wheel Division needed bearings for garden tractor wheels. It normally buys its bearings from an outside supplier for $25 per set. However, the company's top management just initiated a campaign to persuade the different divisions to buy their materials from within the company whenever possible. As a result, Hank Sherril, the purchasing manager for the Wheel Division, received a letter from the vice president of Purchasing, ordering him to contact the Bearing Division to discuss buying bearings from this division.

To comply with this request, Hank from the Wheel Division called Mary Plimpton of the Bearing Division, to request the price for 15,000 bearings. Mary responded that the bearings normally sell for $36 per set. However, Mary noted that the Bearing Division would save $3 on marketing costs by selling internally and would pass this cost savings on to the Wheel Division. She further commented that the Bearing Division was at full capacity and therefore would not be able to provide any bearings presently. In the future, if the Bearing Division had available capacity, it would be happy to provide bearings.

Hank responded indignantly, "Thanks but no thanks." He said, "We can get all the bearings we need from Falk Manufacturing for $25 per set, and its quality is acceptable for our product." Mary snorted back, "Falk makes low-quality bearings. We incur a total unit cost of $22 unit for units we sell externally. Our bearings can withstand heat of 2,000 degrees centigrade and are good to within .00001 centimeters. If you guys are happy buying low-quality bearings, then go ahead and buy from Falk."

Two weeks later, Hank's boss from the central office stopped in to find out whether he had placed an order with the Bearing Division. Hank responded that he would sooner buy his bearings from his worst enemy than from the Bearing Division.

## Instructions

With the class divided into groups, prepare answers to the following.

**a.** Why might the company's top management want the divisions to start doing more business with one another?

**b.** Under what conditions should a buying division be forced to buy from an internal supplier? Under what conditions should a selling division be forced to sell to an internal division rather than to an outside customer?

**c.** The vice president of Purchasing thinks that this problem should be resolved by forcing the Bearing Division to sell to the Wheel Division at its cost of $22. Is this a good solution for the Wheel Division? Is this a good solution for the Bearing Division? Is this a good solution for the company?

**d.** Provide at least two other possible solutions to this problem. Discuss the merits and drawbacks of each.

## Managerial Analysis

**CT21.2** **Service** Construction on the Bonita Full-Service Car Wash is nearing completion. The owner is Dave Kear, a retired accounting professor. The car wash is strategically located on a busy street that separates an affluent suburban community from a middle-class community. It has two state-of-the-art stalls. Each stall can provide anything from a basic two-stage wash and rinse to a five-stage luxurious bath. It is all "touchless," that is, there are no brushes to potentially damage the car. Outside each stall, there is also a 400-horsepower vacuum. Dave likes to joke that these vacuums are so strong that they will pull the carpet right out of your car if you aren't careful.

Dave has some important decisions to make before he can open the car wash. First, he knows that there is one drive-through car wash only a 10-minute drive away. It is attached to a gas station; it charges $5 for a basic wash, and $4 if you also buy at least 8 gallons of gas. It is a "brush"-type wash with rotating brush heads. There is also a self-serve "stand outside your car and spray until you are soaked" car wash a 15-minute drive away from Dave's location. He went over and tried this out. He went through $3 in quarters to get the equivalent of a basic wash. He knows that both of these locations always have long lines, which is one reason why he decided to build a new car wash.

Dave is planning to offer three levels of wash service—Basic, Deluxe, and Premium. The Basic is all automated; it requires no direct intervention by employees. The Deluxe is all automated except that at the end an employee will wipe down the car and will put a window treatment on the windshield that reduces glare and allows rainwater to run off more quickly. The Premium level is a "pampered" service. This will include all the services of the Deluxe, plus a special wax after the machine wax, and an employee will vacuum the car, wipe down the entire interior, and wash the inside of the windows. To provide the Premium service, Dave will have to hire a couple of "car wash specialists" to do the additional pampering.

Dave has pulled together the following estimates, based on data he received from the local Chamber of Commerce and information from a trade association.

|  | Per Unit | Total |
| --- | --- | --- |
| Direct materials per Basic wash | $0.30 | |
| Direct materials per Deluxe wash | 0.80 | |
| Direct materials per Premium wash | 1.10 | |
| Direct labor per Basic wash | na | |
| Direct labor per Deluxe wash | 0.40 | |
| Direct labor per Premium wash | 2.40 | |
| Variable overhead per Basic wash | 0.10 | |
| Variable overhead per Deluxe and Premium washes | 0.20 | |
| Fixed overhead | | $117,000 |
| Variable selling and administrative expenses all washes | 0.10 | |
| Fixed selling and administrative expenses | | 130,500 |

The total estimated number of washes of any type is 45,000. Dave has invested assets of $393,750. He would like a return on investment (ROI) of 20%.

## Instructions

Complete the following.

**a.** Identify the issues that Dave must consider in deciding on the price of each level of service of his car wash. Also discuss what issues he should consider in deciding on what levels of service to provide.

**b.** Dave estimates that of the total 45,000 washes, 20,000 will be Basic, 20,000 will be Deluxe, and 5,000 will be Premium. Calculate the selling price, using cost-plus pricing, that Dave should use for each type of wash to achieve his desired ROI of 20%.

**c.** During the first year, instead of selling 45,000 washes, Dave sold 43,000 washes. He was quite accurate in his estimate of first-year sales, but he was way off on the types of washes that he sold. He sold 3,000 Basic, 31,000 Deluxe, and 9,000 Premium. His actual total fixed expenses were as he expected, and his unit variable cost was as estimated. Calculate Dave's actual net income and his actual ROI. (Round to two decimal places.)

**d.** Dave is using a traditional approach to allocate overhead. As a consequence, he is allocating overhead equally to all three types of washes, even though the Basic wash is considerably less complicated and uses very little of the technical capabilities of the machinery. What should Dave do to determine more accurate unit costs? How will this affect his pricing and, consequently, his sales?

### Real-World Focus

**CT21.3 Merck & Co., Inc.** is a global, research-driven pharmaceutical company that discovers, develops, manufactures, and markets a broad range of human and animal health products. The following are excerpts from the financial review section of the company's annual report.

---

## Merck & Co., Inc.
### Financial Review Section (partial)

In the United States, the Company has been working with private and governmental employers to slow the increase of health care costs.

Outside of the United States, in difficult environments encumbered by government cost containment actions, the Company has worked with payers to help them allocate scarce resources to optimize health care outcomes, limiting potentially detrimental effects of government actions on sales growth.

Several products face expiration of product patents in the near term.

The Company, along with other pharmaceutical manufacturers, received a notice from the Federal Trade Commission (FTC) that it was conducting an investigation into pricing practices.

---

### Instructions

Complete the following.

**a.** Based on the above excerpts from Merck's annual report, discuss some unique pricing issues faced by companies that operate in the pharmaceutical industry.

**b.** What are some reasons why the same company often sells identical drugs for dramatically different prices in different countries? How can the same drug used for both humans and animals cost significantly different prices?

**c.** Suppose that Merck has just developed a revolutionary new drug. Discuss the steps it would go through in setting a price. Include a discussion of the information it would need to gather, and the issues it would need to consider.

### Communication Activity

**CT21.4** Service Jane Fleming recently graduated from college with a degree in landscape architecture. Her father runs a tree, shrub, and perennial-flower nursery, and her brother has a business delivering topsoil, mulch, and compost. Jane has decided that she would like to start a landscape business. She believes that she can generate a nice profit for herself, while providing an opportunity for both her brother's and father's businesses to grow.

One potential problem that Jane is concerned about is that her father and brother tend to charge the highest prices of any local suppliers for their products. She is hoping that she can demonstrate that it would be in her interest, as well as theirs, for them to sell to her at a discounted price.

### Instructions

Write a memo to Jane explaining what information she must gather, and what issues she must consider, in working out an arrangement with her father and brother. In your memo, discuss how this situation differs from a "standard" transfer pricing problem, but also how it has many of the characteristics of a transfer pricing problem.

## Ethics Case

**CT21.5** Service Jumbo Airlines operates out of three main "hub" airports in the United States. Recently, Econo Airlines began operating a flight from Reno, Nevada, into Jumbo's Metropolis hub for $190. Jumbo Airlines offers a price of $425 for the same route. The management of Jumbo is not happy about Econo invading its turf. In fact, Jumbo has driven off nearly every other competing airline from its hub, so that today 90% of flights into and out of Metropolis are Jumbo Airline flights. Econo is able to offer a lower fare because its pilots are paid less, it uses older planes, and it has lower overhead costs. Econo has been in business for only 6 months, and it services only two other cities. It expects the Metropolis route to be its most profitable.

Jumbo estimates that it would have to charge $210 just to break even on this flight. It estimates that Econo can break even at a price of $160. Within one day of Econo's entry into the market, Jumbo dropped its price to $140, whereupon Econo matched its price. They both maintained this fare for a period of 9 months, until Econo went out of business. As soon as Econo went out of business, Jumbo raised its fare back to $425.

**Instructions**

Answer each of the following questions.

- **a.** Who are the stakeholders in this case?
- **b.** What are some of the reasons why Econo's break-even point is lower than that of Jumbo?
- **c.** What are the likely reasons why Jumbo was able to offer this price for this period of time, while Econo could not?
- **d.** What are some of the possible courses of action available to Econo in this situation?
- **e.** Do you think that this kind of pricing activity is ethical? What are the implications for the stakeholders in this situation?

## Considering Your Costs and Benefits

**CT21.6** The January 2011 issue of *Strategic Finance* includes an article by J. Lockhart, A. Taylor. K. Thomas, B. Levetsovitis, and J. Wise entitled "When a Higher Price Pays Off."

**Instructions**

Read the article and then complete the following.

- **a.** Explain what is meant by a "low-cost" supplier versus a "low-priced" supplier.
- **b.** **Clarus Technologies'** products are typically priced significantly higher than its competitors' products. How is it able to overcome the initial "sticker shock"?
- **c.** List the five categories of costs that the authors used to compare the Tornado to competing products. Give examples of specific types of costs in each category.
- **d.** The article discusses full-cost accounting as developed by the **Environmental Protection Agency (EPA)**. What are the characteristics of this approach, and what implications does the approach used in this article have for corporate social responsibility?

## Answers to Insight and Accounting Across the Organization Questions

**Pricing to Sell  Q:** Why did Amazon choose to charge a premium price for its Fire smartphone but offers some of its tablet and Kindle models at prices that barely cover its costs?  **A:** Amazon can sell its tablets and Kindles for very low prices because it can generate significant additional revenue on e-book sales and movie rentals when people use those devices. But the Fire smartphone had much less potential for subsequent revenue, so its sales price needed to cover its costs and provide a reasonable profit.

**How Much Did You Pay for That Seat?  Q:** What factors must the managers of a Broadway show consider when setting prices?  **A:** Because an empty seat represents revenue that can never be recovered, Broadway shows use dynamic pricing. This is an algorithmic program that takes into account factors beyond costs of production. These include, but are not limited to, how many empty seats remain to be filled (capacity), how close the sale is to the performance beginning (time), how popular the show is (demand), and even weather conditions. All of these factors are considered when setting prices for empty seats up to the time of the performance in order to maximize revenues.

**At Least It Was Simple  Q:** What kind of help might the sales staff need in implementing this new approach?  **A:** Many customers might object to the price increases, and some might even threaten to buy a competing product. The company needs to provide the sales staff with justifications for the product. For example, salespeople need evidence to demonstrate that the superior quality of the product justified the higher price.

**It Ain't Like It Used to Be  Q:** What implications does this have for a service company's need for managerial accounting?  **A:** When service companies billed by the hour, they were better able to ensure their profitability because labor hours is their primary cost. But when billing schemes become performance-based, the company cannot be assured that the bill will cover its hourly costs. As a consequence, companies will need to be far more accurate in their estimates of the likelihood of achieving desired outcomes, or their costs may well exceed their revenues.

**Setting the Optimal Price  Q:** What is dynamic pricing, and why would the use of dynamic pricing require data analytics?  **A:** Dynamic pricing involves the practice of using different prices across customers or across time to maximize profits. To benefit from dynamic pricing, a company would need to have large amounts of customer data, as well as information regarding changes in product demand under different market conditions. For example, a sports team might factor in the impact of weather, day of the week, and a team's winning percentage, based on significant data from past events, to determine the optimal prices for a particular game.

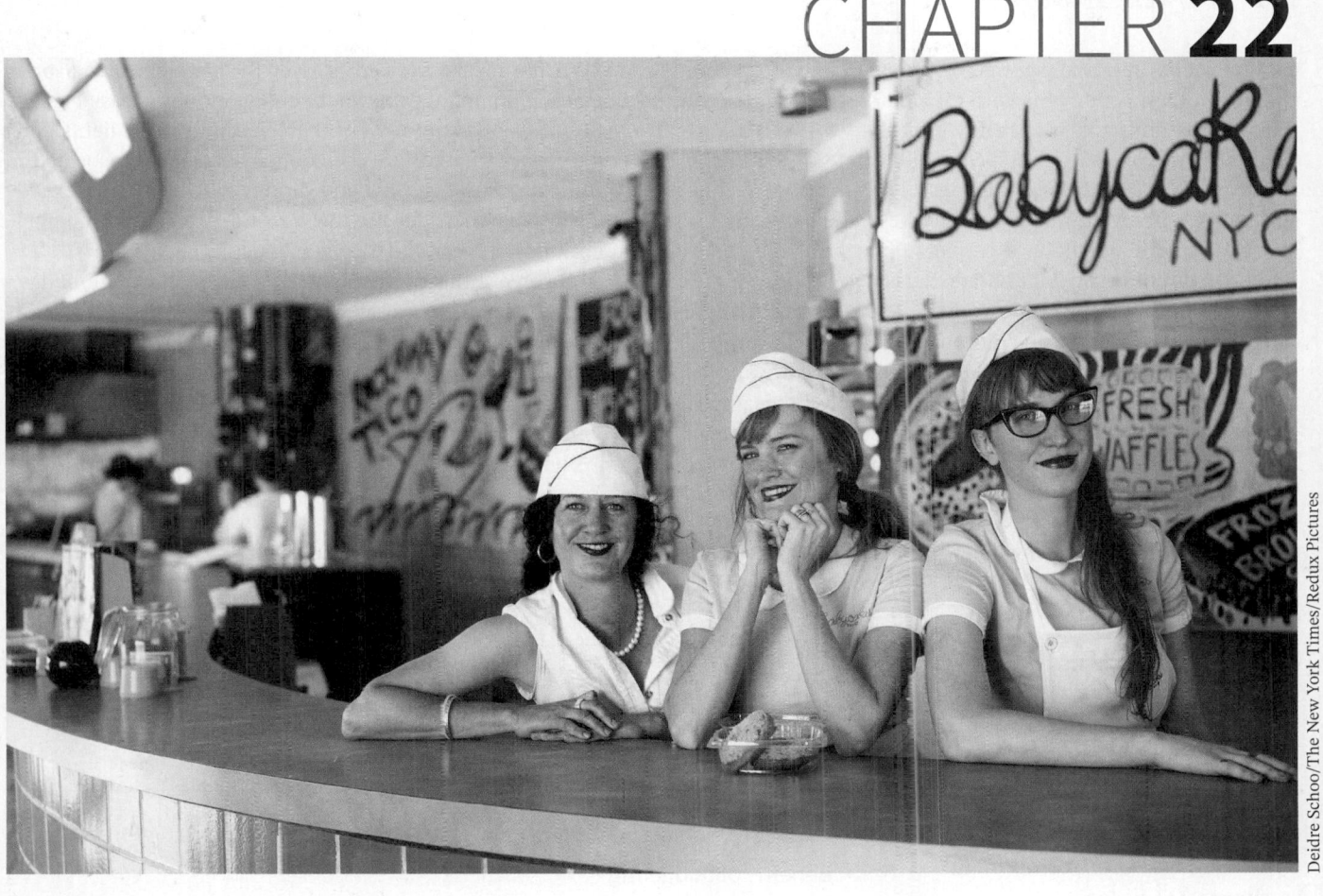

## CHAPTER 22

Deidre Schoo/The New York Times/Redux Pictures

# Budgetary Planning

## Chapter Preview

As the following Feature Story about **Erin McKenna's Bakery NYC** (formerly **BabyCakes NYC**) indicates, budgeting is critical to financial well-being. As a student, you budget your study time and your money. Families budget income and expenses. Governmental agencies budget revenues and expenditures. Businesses use budgets in planning and controlling their operations.

Our primary focus in this chapter is the use of budgeting as a planning tool by management. Through budgeting, it should be possible for management to maintain enough cash to pay creditors as well as have sufficient raw materials to meet production requirements and adequate finished goods to meet expected sales.

## Feature Story

### What's in Your Cupcake?

The best business plans often result from meeting a basic human need. Many people would argue that cupcakes aren't necessarily essential to support life. But if you found out that allergies were going to deprive you forever of cupcakes, you might view baked goods in a whole new light. Such was the dilemma faced by Erin McKenna. When she found that her wheat allergies prevented her from consuming most baked sweets, she decided to open a bakery that met her needs. Her vegan and kosher bakery, **Erin McKenna's Bakery NYC**, advertises that it is refined-sugar-free, gluten-free, wheat-free, soy-free, dairy-free, and egg-free. So if you're one of the more than 10 million Americans with a food allergy or some other dietary constraint, this is probably the bakery for you.

Those of you that have spent a little time in the kitchen might wonder what kind of ingredients Erin McKenna's Bakery uses. To avoid the gluten in wheat, the company uses **Bob's Red Mill** rice flour, a garbanzo/fava bean mix, or oat flours. How does Erin McKenna's Bakery get all those great frosting colors without artificial dyes? The company achieves pink with beets, green with chlorophyll, yellow with turmeric, and blue/purple with red cabbage. To eliminate dairy and soy, the bakers use rice and coconut milk. And finally, to accomplish over-the-top deliciousness without refined sugar, the company uses agave nectar (a sweetener derived from cactus) and evaporated cane juice (often referred to as organic or unrefined sugar).

With cupcakes priced at over $3 per item and a brisk business, you might think that making money is easy for Erin McKenna's Bakery. But all of these specialty ingredients don't come cheap. In addition, the company's shops are located in Manhattan, Los Angeles, and Orlando, so rent isn't exactly inexpensive either. Despite these costs, Erin's first store made a profit its first year and did even better in later years.

To achieve this profitability, Erin relies on careful budgeting. First, she estimates sales. Then, she determines her needs for materials, labor, and overhead. Prices for raw materials can fluctuate significantly, so Erin needs to update her budget accordingly. Finally, she has to budget for other products such as her cookbooks, baking kits, and T-shirts. Without a budget, Erin's business might not be so sweet.

 Watch the *BabyCakes NYC* video in WileyPLUS to learn more about real-world budgetary planning.

# Chapter Outline

| LEARNING OBJECTIVES | REVIEW | PRACTICE |
|---|---|---|
| **LO 1** State the essentials of effective budgeting and the components of the master budget. | • Budgeting and accounting<br>• Benefits of budgeting<br>• Effective budgeting essentials<br>• Master budget | **DO IT! 1** Budget Terminology |
| **LO 2** Prepare budgets for sales, production, and direct materials. | • Sales budget<br>• Production budget<br>• Direct materials budget | **DO IT! 2** Sales, Production, and Direct Materials Budgets |
| **LO 3** Prepare budgets for direct labor, manufacturing overhead, and selling and administrative expenses, and a budgeted income statement. | • Direct labor budget<br>• Manufacturing overhead budget<br>• Selling and administrative expense budget<br>• Budgeted income statement | **DO IT! 3** Budgeted Income Statement |
| **LO 4** Prepare a cash budget and a budgeted balance sheet. | • Cash budget<br>• Budgeted balance sheet | **DO IT! 4** Cash Budget |
| **LO 5** Apply budgeting principles to nonmanufacturing companies. | • Merchandisers<br>• Service companies<br>• Not-for-profit organizations | **DO IT! 5** Merchandise Purchases Budget |

**Go to the Review and Practice section at the end of the chapter for a targeted summary and practice applications with solutions.**

**Visit WileyPLUS for additional tutorials and practice opportunities.**

# Effective Budgeting and the Master Budget

> **LEARNING OBJECTIVE 1**
>
> State the essentials of effective budgeting and the components of the master budget.

As explained in Chapter 14, **planning** is the process of establishing company-wide objectives. A successful organization makes both long-term and short-term plans. These plans establish the objectives of the company and the proposed approach to accomplish them.

A **budget** is a formal written statement of management's plans for a specified future time period, expressed in financial terms.

- It represents the primary method of communicating agreed-upon objectives throughout the organization.
- Once adopted, a budget becomes an important basis for evaluating performance.
- It promotes efficiency and serves as a deterrent to waste and inefficiency.

We consider the role of budgeting as a **control device** in Chapter 23.

## Budgeting and Accounting

Accounting information makes major contributions to the budgeting process. From the accounting records, companies obtain historical data on revenues, costs, and expenses. These data are helpful in formulating future budget goals.

Accountants are responsible for presenting management's budgeting goals in financial terms.

- Accountants translate management's plans and communicate the budget to employees throughout the company.
- They prepare periodic budget reports that provide the basis for measuring performance and comparing actual results with planned objectives.

The budget itself and the administration of the budget, however, are entirely management responsibilities.

## The Benefits of Budgeting

The primary benefits of budgeting are as follows.

1. It requires all levels of management to **plan ahead** and to formalize goals on a recurring basis.
2. It provides **definite objectives** for evaluating performance at each level of responsibility.
3. It creates an **early warning system** for potential problems so that management can make changes before things get out of hand.
4. It facilitates the **coordination of activities** within the business. It does this by correlating the goals of each segment with overall company objectives. Thus, the company can integrate production and sales promotion with expected sales.
5. It results in greater **management awareness** of the entity's overall operations and the impact on operations of external factors, such as economic trends.
6. It **motivates personnel** throughout the organization to meet planned objectives.

A budget is an aid to management; it is not a *substitute* for management. A budget cannot operate or enforce itself. Companies can realize the benefits of budgeting only when managers carefully administer budgets.

# Essentials of Effective Budgeting

Effective budgeting depends on a **sound organizational structure**. In such a structure, authority and responsibility for all phases of operations are clearly defined. Budgets based on **research and analysis** are more likely to result in realistic goals that will contribute to the growth and profitability of a company. And, the effectiveness of a budget program is directly related to its **acceptance by all levels of management**.

Once adopted, the budget is an important tool for evaluating performance. Managers should systematically and periodically review variations between actual and expected results to determine their cause(s). However, individuals should not be held responsible for variations that are beyond their control.

## Length of the Budget Period

The budget period is not necessarily one year in length. **A budget may be prepared for any period of time.** Various factors influence the length of the budget period:

- The type of budget.
- The nature of the organization.
- The need for periodic appraisal.
- Prevailing business conditions.

The budget period should be long enough to provide an attainable goal under normal business conditions. Ideally, the time period should minimize the impact of seasonal or cyclical fluctuations. On the other hand, the budget period should not be so long that reliable estimates are impossible.

The **most common budget period is one year**. The annual budget, in turn, is often supplemented by monthly and quarterly budgets. Many companies use **continuous 12-month budgets**. These budgets drop the month just ended and add a future month. One benefit of continuous budgeting is that it keeps management planning a full year ahead.

---

## Accounting Across the Organization

Thinkstock/Stockbyte/
Getty Images

### Businesses Often Feel Too Busy to Plan for the Future

A study by Willard & Shullman Group Ltd. found that less than 14% of businesses with fewer than 500 employees do an annual budget or have a written business plan. For many small businesses, the basic assumption is that, "As long as I sell as much as I can, and keep my employees paid, I'm doing OK." A few small business owners even say that they see no need for budgeting and planning. Most small business owners, though, say that they understand that budgeting and planning are critical for survival and growth. But given the long hours that they already work addressing day-to-day challenges, they also say that they are "just too busy to plan for the future."

**Describe a situation in which a business "sells as much as it can" but cannot "keep its employees paid." (Answer is available at the end of the chapter.)**

---

## The Budgeting Process

The development of the budget for the coming year generally starts several months before the end of the current year. The budgeting process usually begins with the collection of data from each organizational unit of the company. Past performance is often the starting point from which future budget goals are formulated.

The budget is developed within the framework of a **sales forecast**.

- This forecast shows potential sales for the industry and the company's expected share of such sales.
- Sales forecasting involves a consideration of various factors:

1. General economic conditions.
2. Industry trends.
3. Market research studies.
4. Anticipated advertising and promotion.
5. Previous market share.
6. Changes in prices.
7. Technological developments.

- The input of sales personnel and top management is essential to the sales forecast.

In small companies like **Erin McKenna's Bakery NYC**, the budgeting process is often informal. In larger companies, a **budget committee** has responsibility for coordinating the preparation of the budget.

- The committee ordinarily includes the president, treasurer, chief accountant (controller), and management personnel from each of the major areas of the company, such as sales, production, and research.
- The budget committee serves as a review board where managers can defend their budget goals and requests. Differences are reviewed, modified if necessary, and reconciled.
- The budget is then put in its final form by the budget committee, approved, and distributed.

## Budgeting and Human Behavior

A budget can have a significant impact on human behavior. If done well, it can inspire managers to higher levels of performance. However, if done poorly, budgets can discourage additional effort and pull down the morale of managers. Why do these diverse effects occur? The answer is found in how the budget is developed and administered.

In developing the budget, each level of management should be invited to participate. This "bottom-to-top" approach is referred to as **participative budgeting**.

- One benefit of participative budgeting is that lower-level managers have more detailed knowledge of their specific area and thus are able to provide more accurate budgetary estimates.
- When lower-level managers participate in the budgeting process, they are more likely to perceive the resulting budget as fair.
- The overall goal is to reach agreement on a budget that the managers consider fair and achievable, but which also meets the corporate goals set by top management. When this goal is met, the budget will provide positive motivation for the managers.

In contrast, if managers view the budget as unfair and unrealistic, they may feel discouraged and uncommitted to budget goals. The risk of having unrealistic budgets is generally greater when the budget is developed from top management down to lower management than vice versa. **Illustration 22.1** shows the flow of budget data from bottom to top under participative budgeting.

At one time, in an effort to revive its plummeting stock price, **WarnerMedia**'s top management determined and publicly announced bold (and ultimately unattainable) new financial goals for the coming year. Unfortunately, these goals were not reached. The next year, the company hired a new CEO who said the company would now set reasonable goals. The new budgets were developed with participative budgeting. Each operating unit set what it felt were optimistic but attainable goals. In the words of one manager, using this approach created a sense of teamwork.

**ILLUSTRATION 22.1** Flow of budget data under participative budgeting

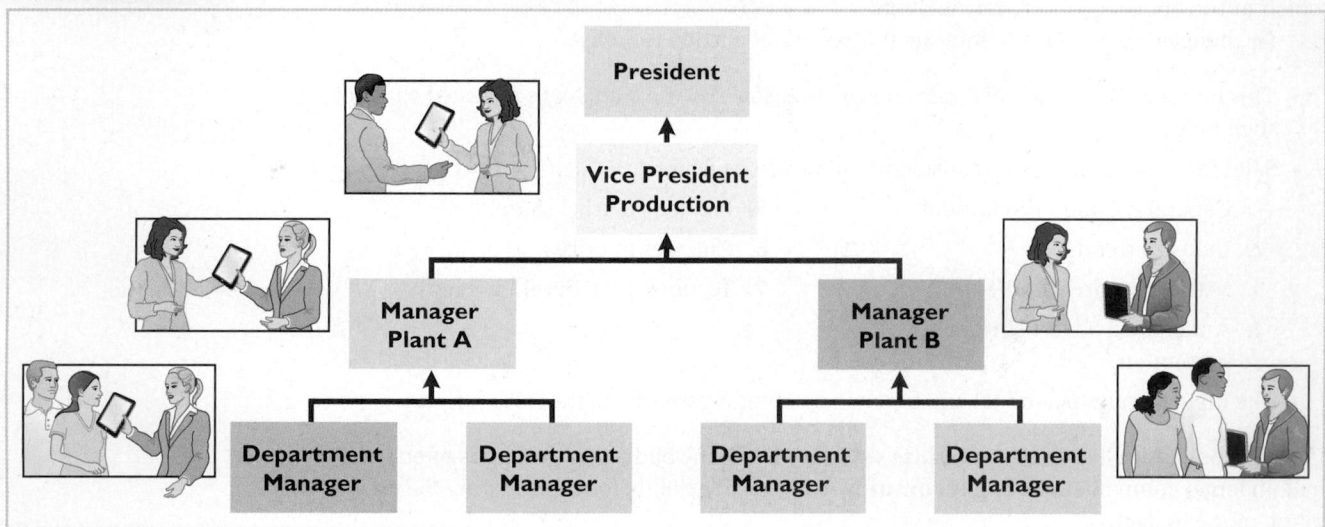

Participative budgeting does, however, have potential disadvantages.

1. The "give and take" of participative budgeting is time-consuming (and thus more costly). Under a "top-down" approach, the budget can be more quickly developed by top management and then dictated to lower-level managers.

2. Participative budgeting can foster budgetary "gaming" through **budgetary slack**, which occurs when managers intentionally underestimate budgeted revenues or overestimate budgeted expenses in order to make it easier to achieve budgetary goals for their division.

To minimize budgetary slack, higher-level managers must carefully review and thoroughly question the budget projections provided to them by employees whom they supervise.

For the budget to be effective, top management must completely support the budget. The budget is an important tool for evaluating performance. It also can be used as a positive aid in achieving projected goals. The effect of an evaluation is positive when top management tempers criticism with advice and assistance. In contrast, a manager is likely to respond negatively if top management uses the budget exclusively to assess blame. A budget should not be used as a pressure device to force improved performance (see **Ethics Note**). In sum, a budget can be a manager's friend or foe.

**ETHICS NOTE**

Unrealistic budgets can lead to unethical employee behavior such as cutting corners on the job or distorting internal financial reports.

## Budgeting and Long-Range Planning

Budgeting and long-range planning have three significant differences:

1. **The time period involved**. The maximum length of a budget is usually one year, and budgets are often prepared for shorter periods of time, such as a month or a quarter. In contrast, long-range planning usually encompasses a period of at least five years (see **Helpful Hint**).

2. **Emphasis**. Budgeting focuses on achieving specific short-term goals, such as meeting annual profit objectives. **Long-range planning**, on the other hand:
   - Identifies long-term goals.
   - Selects strategies to achieve those goals.
   - Develops policies and plans to implement the strategies.

In long-range planning, management also considers anticipated trends in the economic and political environment and how the company should cope with them.

**HELPFUL HINT**

A budget has more detail and is more concerned with short-term goals than a long-range plan.

3. **The amount of detail presented**. Budgets, as you will see in this chapter, can be very detailed. Long-range plans contain considerably less detail as the data are intended more for a review of progress toward long-term goals than as a basis of control for achieving specific results. The primary objective of long-range planning is to develop the best strategy to maximize the company's performance over an extended future period.

# The Master Budget

The term "budget" is actually a shorthand term to describe a variety of budget documents. All of these documents are combined into a master budget. The **master budget** is a set of interrelated budgets that constitutes a plan of action for a specified time period.

The master budget contains two classes of budgets:

1. **Operating budgets**, which are the individual budgets that result in the preparation of the budgeted income statement. These budgets establish goals for the company's sales and production personnel.

2. **Financial budgets**, which focus primarily on the cash resources needed to fund expected operations and planned capital expenditures. Financial budgets include the capital expenditure budget, the cash budget, and the budgeted balance sheet.

**Illustration 22.2** shows the individual budgets included in a master budget and the sequence in which they are prepared. The company first develops the operating budgets, beginning with the sales budget. Then, it prepares the financial budgets. In this chapter, we explain and illustrate each budget shown in Illustration 22.2 except the capital expenditure budget. That budget is discussed under the topic of capital budgeting in Chapter 25.

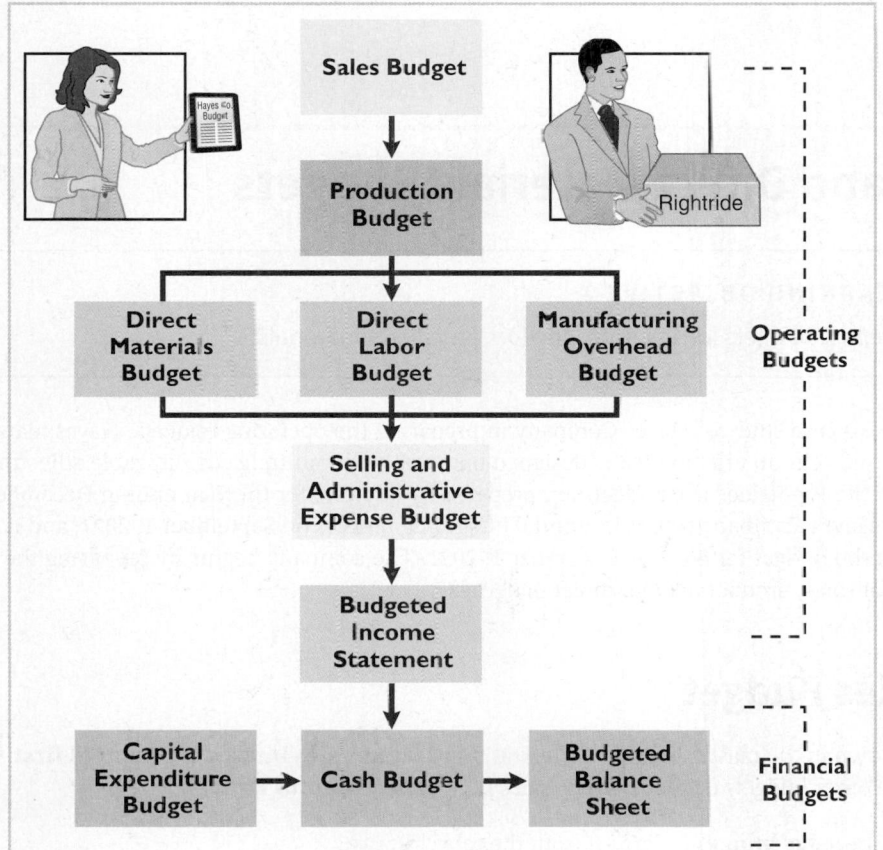

**ILLUSTRATION 22.2**

**Components of the master budget**

**ACTION PLAN**

- **Understand the budgeting process, including the importance of the sales forecast.**
- **Understand the difference between an operating budget and a financial budget.**
- **Differentiate budgeting from long-range planning.**
- **Realize that the master budget is a set of interrelated budgets.**

### DO IT! 1 | Budget Terminology

Use this list of terms to complete the sentences that follow.

| | |
|---|---|
| Long-range planning | Participative budgeting |
| Sales forecast | Operating budgets |
| Master budget | Financial budgets |

1. A _____ shows potential sales for the industry and a company's expected share of such sales.

2. _____ are used as the basis for the preparation of the budgeted income statement.

3. The _____ is a set of interrelated budgets that constitutes a plan of action for a specified time period.

4. _____ identifies long-term goals, selects strategies to achieve these goals, and develops policies and plans to implement the strategies.

5. Lower-level managers are more likely to perceive results as fair and achievable under a _____ approach.

6. _____ focus primarily on the cash resources needed to fund expected operations and planned capital expenditures.

#### Solution

1. Sales forecast.
2. Operating budgets.
3. Master budget.
4. Long-range planning.
5. Participative budgeting.
6. Financial budgets.

Related exercise material: **BE22.1, DO IT! 22.1, and E22.1.**

---

# Sales, Production, and Direct Materials Budgets

### LEARNING OBJECTIVE 2
Prepare budgets for sales, production, and direct materials.

We use a case study of Hayes Company in preparing the operating budgets. Hayes manufactures and sells an ergonomically designed bike seat with multiple customizable adjustments, called the Rightride. The budgets are prepared by quarters for the year ending December 31, 2022. Hayes Company begins its annual budgeting process on September 1, 2021, and it completes the budget for 2022 by December 1, 2021. The company begins by preparing the budgets for sales, production, and direct materials.

**HELPFUL HINT**

For a retail or manufacturing company, the sales budget is the starting point for the master budget. It sets the level of activity for other functions such as production and purchasing.

## Sales Budget

As shown in the master budget in Illustration 22.2, **the sales budget is prepared first**. Each of the other budgets depends on the sales budget (see **Helpful Hint**).

- The **sales budget** is derived from the sales forecast.
- It represents management's best estimate of sales revenue for the budget period.
- An inaccurate sales budget may adversely affect net income.

For example, an overly optimistic sales budget may result in excessive inventories that may have to be sold at reduced prices. In contrast, an unduly pessimistic sales budget may result in loss of sales revenue due to inventory shortages.

For example, at one time **Amazon.com** significantly underestimated demand for its e-book reader, the Kindle. As a consequence, it did not produce enough Kindles and was completely sold out well before the holiday shopping season. Not only did this represent a huge lost opportunity for Amazon, but it exposed the company to potential competitors, who were eager to provide customers with alternatives to the Kindle.

Forecasting sales is challenging. For example, consider the forecasting challenges faced by major sports arenas, whose revenues depend on the success of the home team. **Madison Square Garden**'s revenues from April to June were $193 million during a year when the New York Knicks made the NBA playoffs. But revenues were only $133.2 million a couple of years later when the team did not make the playoffs. Or, consider the challenges faced by Hollywood movie producers in predicting the complicated revenue stream produced by a new movie. Movie theater ticket sales represent only 20% of total revenue. The bulk of revenue comes from global sales, video-on-demand streaming, television rights, merchandising products, and videogames, all of which are difficult to forecast.

The sales budget is prepared by multiplying the expected unit sales volume for each product by its anticipated unit selling price. Hayes Company expects sales volume to be 3,000 units in the first quarter, with 500-unit increases in each succeeding quarter. **Illustration 22.3** shows the sales budget for the year, by quarter, based on a unit selling price of $60.

**ILLUSTRATION 22.3**

Sales budget

**Hayes Company Sales Budget**

Home | Insert | Page Layout | Formulas | Data | Review | View

P18

|  | A | B | C | D | E | F |
|---|---|---|---|---|---|---|
| 1 | | **Hayes Company** | | | | |
| 2 | | **Sales Budget** | | | | |
| 3 | | **For the Year Ending December 31, 2022** | | | | |
| 4 | | Quarter | | | | |
| 5 | | 1 | 2 | 3 | 4 | Year |
| 6 | Expected sales units | 3,000 | 3,500 | 4,000 | 4,500 | 15,000 |
| 7 | Unit selling price | × $60 | × $60 | × $60 | × $60 | × $60 |
| 8 | Total sales | $180,000 | $210,000 | $240,000 | $270,000 | $900,000 |

Some companies classify the anticipated sales revenue as cash or credit sales and by geographic regions, territories, or salespersons.

## Service Company Insight

MarsBars/iStock/Getty Images Plus/Getty Images

### The Implications of Budgetary Optimism

Companies aren't the only ones that need to estimate revenues. Governments at all levels (e.g., local, state, and federal) prepare annual budgets. Most are required to submit balanced budgets, that is, estimated revenues are required to cover anticipated expenditures. Estimating government revenues can be very difficult. For example, at one time, the median state government overestimated revenues by 10.2%, with four state governments missing by more than 25%.

What makes estimation so difficult for governments? Most states rely on income taxes, which fluctuate widely with economic gyrations. Some states rely on sales taxes, which are problematic because the laws regarding sales taxes haven't fully adjusted for the shift from manufacturing to service companies and from brick-and-mortar stores to online sales.

**Sources:** Conor Dougherty, "States Fumble Revenue Forecasts," *Wall Street Journal Online* (March 2, 2011); and Elizabeth McNichol, "Improving State Revenue Forecasting: Best Practices for a More Trusted and Reliable Revenue Estimate," *Center on Budget and Policy Priorities* (September 4, 2014).

**Why is it important that government budgets accurately estimate future revenues during economic downturns? (Answer is available at the end of the chapter.)**

# Production Budget

The **production budget** shows the number of units of a product to produce to meet anticipated sales demand. Production requirements are determined from the equation shown in **Illustration 22.4.**[1]

**ILLUSTRATION 22.4**

Production requirements equation

| Expected Sales Units | + | Desired Ending Finished Goods Units | − | Beginning Finished Goods Units | = | Required Production Units |
|---|---|---|---|---|---|---|

**Illustration 22.5** shows the production budget for Hayes Company, which is based on the equation shown in Illustration 22.4.

**ILLUSTRATION 22.5** Production budget

| | A | B | C | D | E | F |
|---|---|---|---|---|---|---|
| | | Hayes Company Production Budget | | | | |
| 1 | | **Hayes Company** | | | | |
| 2 | | Production Budget | | | | |
| 3 | | For the Year Ending December 31, 2022 | | | | |
| 4 | | | Quarter | | | |
| 5 | | 1 | 2 | 3 | 4 | Year |
| 6 | Expected sales units (Illustration 22.3) | 3,000 | 3,500 | 4,000 | 4,500 | |
| 7 | Add: Desired ending finished goods units[a] | 700 | 800 | 900 | 1,000[b] | |
| 8 | Total required units | 3,700 | 4,300 | 4,900 | 5,500 | |
| 9 | Less: Beginning finished goods units[c] | 600 | 700 | 800 | 900 | |
| 10 | **Required production units** | **3,100** | **3,600** | **4,100** | **4,600** | **15,400** |
| 11 | | | | | | |
| 12 | [a]20% of next quarter's sales | | | | | |
| 13 | [b]Expected 2023 first-quarter sales, 5,000 units × .20 | | | | | |
| 14 | [c]20% of estimated first-quarter 2022 sales units | | | | | |

- In the first quarter, expected sales are 3,000 units.
- Hayes Company believes it should maintain an ending inventory equal to 20% of the next quarter's budgeted sales volume to ensure a continuous supply. The ending finished goods inventory for the first quarter is 700 units (.20 × anticipated second-quarter sales of 3,500 units).
- If we then subtract the beginning finished goods units of 600 units (20% of first-quarter sales), we arrive at required production of 3,100 units.

**An accurate estimate of the amount of ending inventory required to meet demand is essential in scheduling production requirements.** Excessive inventories in one quarter may lead to cutbacks in production and employee layoffs in a subsequent quarter. On the other hand, inadequate inventories may result either in added costs for overtime work or in lost sales.

The production budget, in turn, provides the basis for the budgeted costs for each manufacturing cost component, as explained in the following discussion.

# Direct Materials Budget

The **direct materials budget** shows both the quantity and cost of direct materials to be purchased. The first step toward computing the cost of direct materials purchases is to compute the direct materials units required for production. **Illustration 22.6** shows the equation for this amount.

---

[1] This equation ignores any work in process inventories, which are assumed to be nonexistent in Hayes Company.

| Units to Be Produced | × | Direct Materials Units per Unit of Unit Produced | = | Direct Materials Units Required for Production |
|---|---|---|---|---|

**ILLUSTRATION 22.6**
Equation for direct materials units required for production

Employing this equation, Illustration 22.9 shows the following.

- For Hayes Company's first quarter of production, there are 3,100 units to be produced.
- Each unit produced requires two pounds of raw materials.
- Therefore, the units of direct materials required for production is 6,200 pounds (3,100 × 2).

Next we can compute the direct materials units to be purchased using the equation shown in **Illustration 22.7**.

| Direct Materials Units Required for Production | + | Desired Ending Direct Materials Units | − | Beginning Direct Materials Units | = | Direct Materials Units to Be Purchased |
|---|---|---|---|---|---|---|

**ILLUSTRATION 22.7**
Equation for direct materials units to be purchased

Employing this equation, Illustration 22.9 shows the following.

- For Hayes Company's first quarter of production, the direct materials units required for production is 6,200 pounds (computed above).
- To that we add the desired ending direct materials units. For Hayes, this is assumed to be 10% of the next quarter's production requirements. or 720 pounds (.10 × 7,200).
- Then, we subtract the beginning direct materials units of 620 pounds (10% of this quarter's production requirements of 6,200) to arrive at the direct materials units to be purchased of 6,300 pounds.

Finally, to arrive at the cost of direct materials purchases, we employ the equation shown in **Illustration 22.8**.

| Direct Materials Units to Be Purchased | × | Cost per Direct Materials Unit | = | Cost of Direct Materials Purchases |
|---|---|---|---|---|

**ILLUSTRATION 22.8**
Equation for cost of direct materials purchases

Hayes Company's direct materials cost is $4 per pound. Employing this equation, Illustration 22.9 shows that for Hayes' first quarter of production, the cost of direct materials pur-

**ILLUSTRATION 22.9**  Direct materials budget

### Hayes Company
### Direct Materials Budget
### For the Year Ending December 31, 2022

| | Quarter 1 | 2 | 3 | 4 | Year |
|---|---|---|---|---|---|
| Units to be produced (Illustration 22.5) | 3,100 | 3,600 | 4,100 | 4,600 | |
| Direct materials units per unit produced | × 2 | × 2 | × 2 | × 2 | |
| Direct materials units required for production | 6,200 | 7,200 | 8,200 | 9,200 | |
| Add: Desired ending direct materials (pounds)[a] | 720 | 820 | 920 | 1,020[c] | |
| Total materials required | 6,920 | 8,020 | 9,120 | 10,220 | |
| Less: Beginning direct materials (pounds) | 620[b] | 720 | 820 | 920 | |
| Direct materials units to be purchased (pounds) | 6,300 | 7,300 | 8,300 | 9,300 | |
| Cost per pound | × $4 | × $4 | × $4 | × $4 | |
| Cost of direct materials purchases | $25,200 | $29,200 | $33,200 | $37,200 | $124,800 |

[a]10% of next quarter's production requirements
[b]10% of estimated first-quarter pounds needed for production
[c]Total pounds needed for production is assumed to be 10,200 for the first quarter of 2023

chases is computed by multiplying the units to be purchased of 6,300 pounds by the cost per direct materials unit of $4 per pound, to arrive at $25,200 (6,300 × $4).

**The desired ending inventory is again a key component in the budgeting process.** For example, inadequate inventories could result in temporary shutdowns of production. Hayes Company is located in close proximity to its suppliers. It therefore believes that an ending inventory of raw materials equal to 10% of the next quarter's production requirements is adequate to meet its needs.

---

## Management Insight

iStock.com/William Wang

### Betting That Prices Won't Fall

Sometimes things happen that cause managers to reevaluate their normal purchasing patterns. Consider, for example, the predicament that businesses faced when the price of many raw materials skyrocketed. Rubber, cotton, oil, corn, wheat, steel, copper, and spices—prices for seemingly everything were going straight up. Anticipating that prices might continue to go up, many managers decided to stockpile much larger quantities of raw materials to avoid paying even higher prices in the future.

For example, after cotton prices rose 92%, one manager of a printed T-shirt manufacturer decided to stockpile a huge supply of plain T-shirts in anticipation of additional price increases. While he normally has about 30 boxes of T-shirts in inventory, he purchased 2,500 boxes. Similarly, the supply chain disruptions caused by COVID-19 created many difficult purchasing decisions for companies.

**Source:** Liam Pleven and Matt Wirz, "Companies Stock Up as Commodities Prices Rise," *Wall Street Journal Online* (February 3, 2011).

**What are the potential downsides of stockpiling a huge amount of raw materials? (Answer is available at the end of the chapter.)**

---

### ACTION PLAN

- **Know the form and content of the sales budget.**
- **Prepare the sales budget first, as the basis for the other budgets.**
- **Determine the units that must be produced to meet anticipated sales.**
- **Know how to compute the beginning and ending finished goods units.**
- **Determine the materials required to meet production needs.**
- **Know how to compute the beginning and ending direct materials units.**

## DO IT! 2 | Sales, Production, and Direct Materials Budgets

Soriano Company is preparing its master budget for 2022. Relevant data pertaining to its sales, production, and direct materials budgets are as follows.

*Sales.* Sales for the year are expected to total 1,200,000 units. Quarterly sales, as a percentage of total sales, are 20%, 25%, 30%, and 25%, respectively. The unit selling price is expected to be $50 for the first three quarters and $55 beginning in the fourth quarter. Sales in the first quarter of 2023 are expected to be 10% higher than the budgeted sales for the first quarter of 2022.

*Production.* Management desires to maintain the ending finished goods inventories at 25% of the next quarter's budgeted sales volume.

*Direct materials.* Each unit requires 3 pounds of raw materials at a cost of $5 per pound. Management desires to maintain raw materials inventories at 5% of the next quarter's production requirements. Assume the production requirements for the first quarter of 2023 are 810,000 pounds.

Prepare the sales, production, and direct materials budgets by quarters for 2022.

### Solution

**Soriano Company Sales Budget**

|  | Quarter | | | | Year |
|---|---|---|---|---|---|
|  | 1 | 2 | 3 | 4 |  |
| Expected unit sales[a] | 240,000 | 300,000 | 360,000 | 300,000 | 1,200,000 |
| Unit selling price | × $50 | × $50 | × $50 | × $55 |  |
| **Total sales** | **$12,000,000** | **$15,000,000** | **$18,000,000** | **$16,500,000** | **$61,500,000** |

**Soriano Company**
**Sales Budget**
**For the Year Ending December 31, 2022**

[a]Specified quarterly percentage times annual units, e.g., first quarter of .20 × 1,200,000

Soriano Company Production Budget

Home  Insert  Page Layout  Formulas  Data  Review  View

P18  fx

## Soriano Company
## Production Budget
## For the Year Ending December 31, 2022

| | 1 | 2 | 3 | 4 | Year |
|---|---|---|---|---|---|
| | | | Quarter | | |
| Expected unit sales | 240,000 | 300,000 | 360,000 | 300,000 | |
| Add: Desired ending finished goods units[a] | 75,000 | 90,000 | 75,000 | 66,000[b] | |
| Total required units | 315,000 | 390,000 | 435,000 | 366,000 | |
| Less: Beginning finished goods units | 60,000[c] | 75,000 | 90,000 | 75,000 | |
| **Required production units** | **255,000** | **315,000** | **345,000** | **291,000** | **1,206,000** |

[a]25% of next quarter's unit sales
[b]Estimated first-quarter 2023 sales units: 240,000 + (240,000 × .10) = 264,000; 264,000 × .25
[c]25% of estimated first-quarter 2022 sales units (240,000 × .25)

Soriano Company Direct Materials Budget

Home  Insert  Page Layout  Formulas  Data  Review  View

P18  fx

## Soriano Company
## Direct Materials Budget
## For the Year Ending December 31, 2022

| | 1 | 2 | 3 | 4 | Year |
|---|---|---|---|---|---|
| | | | Quarter | | |
| Units to be produced | 255,000 | 315,000 | 345,000 | 291,000 | |
| Direct materials per unit | × 3 | × 3 | × 3 | × 3 | |
| Total pounds needed for production | 765,000 | 945,000 | 1,035,000 | 873,000 | |
| Add: Desired ending direct materials (pounds) | 47,250 | 51,750 | 43,650 | 40,500[a] | |
| Total materials required | 812,250 | 996,750 | 1,078,650 | 913,500 | |
| Less: Beginning direct materials (pounds) | 38,250[b] | 47,250 | 51,750 | 43,650 | |
| Direct materials purchases | 774,000 | 949,500 | 1,026,900 | 869,850 | |
| Cost per pound | × $5 | × $5 | × $5 | × $5 | |
| **Total cost of direct materials purchases** | **$3,870,000** | **$4,747,500** | **$5,134,500** | **$4,349,250** | **$18,101,250** |

[a]Estimated first-quarter 2023 production requirements: 810,000 × .05 = 40,500
[b]5% of estimated first-quarter pounds needed for production

Related exercise material: **BE22.2, BE22.3, BE22.4, DO IT! 22.2**, E22.2, E22.3, E22.4, E22.5, E22.6, E22.7, and E22.8.

# Direct Labor, Manufacturing Overhead, and S&A Expense Budgets

> **LEARNING OBJECTIVE 3**
> Prepare budgets for direct labor, manufacturing overhead, and selling and administrative expenses, and a budgeted income statement.

As shown in Illustration 22.2, the operating budgets culminate with preparation of the budgeted income statement. Before we can do that, we need to prepare budgets for direct labor, manufacturing overhead, and selling and administrative expenses.

## Direct Labor Budget

Like the direct materials budget, the **direct labor budget** contains the quantity (hours) and cost of direct labor necessary to meet production requirements. The total direct labor cost is derived from the equation shown in **Illustration 22.10**.

$$\begin{array}{c} \text{Units} \\ \text{to Be} \\ \text{Produced} \end{array} \times \begin{array}{c} \text{Direct Labor} \\ \text{Hours} \\ \text{per Unit} \end{array} \times \begin{array}{c} \text{Direct} \\ \text{Labor Cost} \\ \text{per Hour} \end{array} = \begin{array}{c} \text{Total Direct} \\ \text{Labor Cost} \end{array}$$

Direct labor hours are determined based on the units to be produced as reported in the production budget. For example, in the first quarter, 3,100 units are to be produced. At Hayes Company, two hours of direct labor are required to produce each unit of finished goods. The anticipated hourly wage rate is $10. **Illustration 22.11** employs the equation in Illustration 22.10 using these data.

**ILLUSTRATION 22.11**  Direct labor budget

| | Hayes Company Direct Labor Budget | | | | | |
|---|---|---|---|---|---|---|
| | Home  Insert  Page Layout  Formulas  Data  Review  View | | | | | |
| | P18  *fx* | | | | | |
| | A | B | C | D | E | F |
| 1 | **Hayes Company** | | | | | |
| 2 | **Direct Labor Budget** | | | | | |
| 3 | **For the Year Ending December 31, 2022** | | | | | |
| 4 | | Quarter | | | | |
| 5 | | 1 | 2 | 3 | 4 | Year |
| 6 | Units to be produced (Illustration 22.5) | 3,100 | 3,600 | 4,100 | 4,600 | |
| 7 | Direct labor time (hours) per unit | × 2 | × 2 | × 2 | × 2 | |
| 8 | Total required direct labor hours | 6,200 | 7,200 | 8,200 | 9,200 | |
| 9 | Direct labor cost per hour | × $10 | × $10 | × $10 | × $10 | |
| 10 | **Total direct labor cost** | **$62,000** | **$72,000** | **$82,000** | **$92,000** | **$308,000** |
| 11 | | | | | | |

- Each of the 3,100 units produced in the first quarter requires two hours of labor per unit, for a total of 6,200 hours (3,100 × 2).
- Each hour of labor costs $10, for a total cost of $62,000 (6,200 × $10).

The direct labor budget is critical in maintaining a labor force that can meet the expected levels of production (see **Helpful Hint**). Maintaining steady employment levels benefits employers because it reduces hiring and training costs. A steady employment level also keeps employees' morale high since it reduces their income concerns.

**HELPFUL HINT**

An important assumption in Illustration 22.11 is that the company can add to and subtract from its work force as needed so that the $10 per hour labor cost applies to a wide range of possible production activity.

# Manufacturing Overhead Budget

The **manufacturing overhead budget** shows the expected manufacturing overhead costs for the budget period. As **Illustration 22.12** shows, **this budget distinguishes between variable and fixed overhead costs**.

**ILLUSTRATION 22.12**

Manufacturing overhead budget

**Hayes Company Manufacturing Overhead Budget**

| | Quarter 1 | Quarter 2 | Quarter 3 | Quarter 4 | Year |
|---|---|---|---|---|---|
| | **Hayes Company** | | | | |
| | **Manufacturing Overhead Budget** | | | | |
| | **For the Year Ending December 31, 2022** | | | | |
| Direct labor hours (Illustration 22.11) | 6,200 | 7,200 | 8,200 | 9,200 | 30,800 |
| **Variable costs** | | | | | |
| Indirect materials ($1.00/hour) | $ 6,200 | $ 7,200 | $ 8,200 | $ 9,200 | $ 30,800 |
| Indirect labor ($1.40/hour) | 8,680 | 10,080 | 11,480 | 12,880 | 43,120 |
| Utilities ($0.40/hour) | 2,480 | 2,880 | 3,280 | 3,680 | 12,320 |
| Maintenance ($0.20/hour) | 1,240 | 1,440 | 1,640 | 1,840 | 6,160 |
| Total variable costs | 18,600 | 21,600 | 24,600 | 27,600 | 92,400 |
| **Fixed costs** | | | | | |
| Supervisory salaries | 20,000 | 20,000 | 20,000 | 20,000 | 80,000 |
| Depreciation | 3,800 | 3,800 | 3,800 | 3,800 | 15,200 |
| Property taxes and insurance | 9,000 | 9,000 | 9,000 | 9,000 | 36,000 |
| Maintenance | 5,700 | 5,700 | 5,700 | 5,700 | 22,800 |
| Total fixed costs | 38,500 | 38,500 | 38,500 | 38,500 | 154,000 |
| **Total manufacturing overhead** | **$57,100** | **$60,100** | **$63,100** | **$66,100** | **$246,400** |
| Manufacturing overhead rate per direct labor hour ($246,400 ÷ 30,800) | | | | | **$8** |

- Hayes Company expects variable costs to fluctuate with production volume on the basis of the following rates per direct labor hour: indirect materials $1.00, indirect labor $1.40, utilities $0.40, and maintenance $0.20.

- Thus, for the 6,200 direct labor hours needed to produce 3,100 units, budgeted indirect materials are $6,200 (6,200 × $1), and budgeted indirect labor is $8,680 (6,200 × $1.40).

- Hayes also recognizes that some maintenance is fixed (the amounts reported for fixed costs are assumed for our example).

At Hayes Company, overhead is applied to production on the basis of direct labor hours. Thus, as Illustration 22.12 shows, the budgeted annual rate is $8 per hour ($246,400 ÷ 30,800). Note that the accuracy of budgeted overhead cost estimates can be greatly improved by employing activity-based costing.

# Selling and Administrative Expense Budget

Hayes Company combines its operating expenses into one budget, the **selling and administrative expense budget**. This budget (**Illustration 22.13**) projects anticipated selling and administrative expenses for the budget period. It also classifies expenses as either variable or fixed.

**ILLUSTRATION 22.13** Selling and administrative expense budget

| | A | B | C | D | E | F |
|---|---|---|---|---|---|---|
| | | | | Quarter | | |
| 5 | | 1 | 2 | 3 | 4 | Year |
| 6 | Budgeted sales in units (Illustration 22.3) | 3,000 | 3,500 | 4,000 | 4,500 | 15,000 |
| 7 | Variable expenses | | | | | |
| 8 | Sales commissions ($3 per unit) | $ 9,000 | $10,500 | $12,000 | $13,500 | $ 45,000 |
| 9 | Freight-out ($1 per unit) | 3,000 | 3,500 | 4,000 | 4,500 | 15,000 |
| 10 | Total variable expenses | 12,000 | 14,000 | 16,000 | 18,000 | 60,000 |
| 11 | Fixed expenses | | | | | |
| 12 | Advertising | 5,000 | 5,000 | 5,000 | 5,000 | 20,000 |
| 13 | Sales salaries | 15,000 | 15,000 | 15,000 | 15,000 | 60,000 |
| 14 | Office salaries | 7,500 | 7,500 | 7,500 | 7,500 | 30,000 |
| 15 | Depreciation | 1,000 | 1,000 | 1,000 | 1,000 | 4,000 |
| 16 | Property taxes and insurance | 1,500 | 1,500 | 1,500 | 1,500 | 6,000 |
| 17 | Total fixed expenses | 30,000 | 30,000 | 30,000 | 30,000 | 120,000 |
| 18 | Total selling and administrative expenses | $42,000 | $44,000 | $46,000 | $48,000 | $180,000 |

Heading: Hayes Company / Selling and Administrative Expense Budget / For the Year Ending December 31, 2022

- In this case, the variable expense rates per unit of sales are sales commissions $3 and freight-out $1.
- Variable expenses per quarter are based on the unit sales from the sales budget (see Illustration 22.3).

Hayes expects sales in the first quarter to be 3,000 units. Sales commissions expense is therefore $9,000 (3,000 × $3), and freight-out is $3,000 (3,000 × $1) (fixed expenses are based on assumed data).

# Budgeted Income Statement

The **budgeted income statement** is the important end-product of the operating budgets.

- This budget indicates the expected profitability of operations for the budget period.
- The budgeted income statement provides the basis for evaluating company performance.

Budgeted income statements often act as a call to action. For example, a board member at **XM Satellite Radio** felt that budgeted costs were too high relative to budgeted revenues. When management refused to cut its marketing and programming costs, the board member resigned. He felt that without the cuts, the company risked financial crisis.

As you would expect, the budgeted income statement is prepared from the various operating budgets. For example, to find the cost of goods sold, Hayes Company must first determine the total unit cost of producing one Rightride bicycle seat, as shown in **Illustration 22.14**.

**ILLUSTRATION 22.14**

Computation of total unit cost

| Cost Component | Illustration | Quantity | Unit Cost | Total |
|---|---|---|---|---|
| Direct materials | 22.9 | 2 pounds | $ 4.00 | $ 8.00 |
| Direct labor | 22.11 | 2 hours | $10.00 | 20.00 |
| Manufacturing overhead | 22.12 | 2 hours | $ 8.00 | 16.00 |
| Total unit cost | | | | $44.00 |

Hayes then determines cost of goods sold by multiplying the units sold by the unit cost. Its budgeted cost of goods sold is $660,000 (15,000 × $44). All data for the income statement come from the individual operating budgets except the following: (1) interest expense is expected to be $100, and (2) income taxes are estimated to be $12,000. **Illustration 22.15** shows the budgeted multiple-step income statement.

**ILLUSTRATION 22.15**

**Budgeted multiple-step income statement**

### Hayes Company
**Budgeted Income Statement**
**For the Year Ending December 31, 2022**

| | |
|---|---:|
| Sales (Illustration 22.3) | $900,000 |
| Cost of goods sold (15,000 × $44) | 660,000 |
| Gross profit | 240,000 |
| Selling and administrative expenses (Illustration 22.13) | 180,000 |
| Income from operations | 60,000 |
| Interest expense | 100 |
| Income before income taxes | 59,900 |
| Income tax expense | 12,000 |
| Net income | $ 47,900 |

## Data Analytics Insight    Dickey's Barbecue Pit

mphillips007/Getty Images

### That's Some Tasty Data!

What could be better than big data covered in luscious barbecue sauce? Consider **Dickey's Barbecue Pit**, which operates more than 500 restaurants in the United States. The company employs a sophisticated data collection and analysis system that helps it to choose the best menu options to meet customer tastes in specific locations, create budgets, and make rapid adjustments on a daily basis so that individual restaurants as well as the company as a whole can hit budgeted targets. If the data indicate that results at a specific restaurant are subpar, the company can quickly implement training or operational support, tailored to the particular aspects of operations that need to change, to get that location back on track.

Further, if sales at a specific restaurant have been low and inventory is accumulating, the system can text known customers in that restaurant's area with promotions that will spur sales until inventory returns to desired levels. Of particular importance is that the system's dashboard is easily understood and used by employees at all levels of the company. This creates a more participative environment where employees feel like they are contributing to the success of the company.

**Source:** Bernard Marr, *Big Data in Practice* (Hoboken, N.J.: John Wiley and Sons, 2016), pp. 175–180.

**Why are flexibility and ease of use important to this application of big data and data analytics? (Answer is available at the end of the chapter.)**

## DO IT! 3 | Budgeted Income Statement

Soriano Company is preparing its budgeted income statement for 2022. Relevant data pertaining to its sales, production, and direct materials budgets can be found in **DO IT! 2**.

In addition, Soriano budgets 0.5 hours of direct labor per unit, labor costs at $15 per hour, and manufacturing overhead at $25 per direct labor hour. Its budgeted selling and administrative expenses for 2022 are $12,000,000.

**a.** Calculate the budgeted total unit cost.

**b.** Prepare the budgeted multiple-step income statement for 2022. (Ignore income taxes.)

### Solution

**a.**

| Cost Component | Quantity | Unit Cost | Total |
|---|---|---|---:|
| Direct materials | 3.0 pounds | $ 5 | $15.00 |
| Direct labor | 0.5 hours | 15 | 7.50 |
| Manufacturing overhead | 0.5 hours | 25 | 12.50 |
| **Total unit cost** | | | **$35.00** |

**ACTION PLAN**

- **Recall that total unit cost consists of direct materials, direct labor, and manufacturing overhead.**
- **Recall that direct materials costs are included in the direct materials budget.**
- **Know the form and content of the income statement.**
- **Use the total unit sales information from the sales budget to compute annual sales and cost of goods sold.**

b.

|  |  |
|---|---|
| **Soriano Company** | |
| **Budgeted Income Statement** | |
| **For the Year Ending December 31, 2022** | |
| Sales (1,200,000 units from sales budget) | $61,500,000 |
| Cost of goods sold (1,200,000 × $35.00/unit) | 42,000,000 |
| Gross profit | 19,500,000 |
| Selling and administrative expenses | 12,000,000 |
| Net income | $ 7,500,000 |

Related exercise material: **BE22.8, DO IT! 22.3, E22.11, and E22.13.**

# Cash Budget and Budgeted Balance Sheet

**LEARNING OBJECTIVE 4**

Prepare a cash budget and a budgeted balance sheet.

As shown in Illustration 22.2, the financial budgets consist of the capital expenditure budget, the cash budget, and the budgeted balance sheet. We will discuss the capital expenditure budget in Chapter 25.

## Cash Budget

The **cash budget** shows anticipated cash flows.

- Because cash is so vital, this budget is often considered to be the most important financial budget.
- The cash budget contains three sections (cash receipts, cash disbursements, and financing) and the beginning and ending cash balances, as shown in **Illustration 22.16** (see **Helpful Hint**).

**ILLUSTRATION 22.16**

**Basic form of a cash budget**

**HELPFUL HINT**

The cash budget is prepared after the other budgets because the information generated by the other budgets dictates the expected inflows and outflows of cash.

| | A | B | C |
|---|---|---|---|
| 1 | **Any Company** | | |
| 2 | **Cash Budget** | | |
| 3 | Beginning cash balance | $X,XXX | |
| 4 | **Add: Cash receipts** (itemized) | X,XXX | |
| 5 | Total available cash | X,XXX | |
| 6 | **Less: Cash disbursements** (itemized) | X,XXX | |
| 7 | Excess (deficiency) of available cash over cash disbursements | X,XXX | |
| 8 | **Financing** | X,XXX | |
| 9 | Ending cash balance | $X,XXX | |

1. The **cash receipts section** includes expected receipts from the company's principal source(s) of revenue. These are usually cash sales and collections from customers on credit sales. This section also shows anticipated receipts of interest and dividends, and proceeds from planned sales of investments, plant assets, and the company's capital stock.

2. The **cash disbursements section** shows expected cash payments. Such payments include direct materials, direct labor, manufacturing overhead, and selling and administrative expenses. This section also includes projected payments for income taxes, dividends, investments, and plant assets.

3. The **financing section** shows expected borrowings and the repayment of the borrowed funds plus interest. Companies need this section when there is a cash deficiency or when the cash balance is below management's minimum required balance.

Data in the cash budget are prepared in sequence. The ending cash balance of one period becomes the beginning cash balance for the next period. Companies obtain data for preparing the cash budget from other budgets and from information provided by management. In practice, cash budgets are often prepared for the year on a monthly basis.

To minimize detail, we assume that Hayes Company prepares an annual cash budget by quarters. To prepare the cash budget, it is useful to prepare a schedule for collections from customers. This schedule is based on the following assumption:

Sales (Illustration 22.3): 60% are collected in the quarter sold and 40% are collected in the following quarter. Accounts receivable of $60,000 at December 31, 2021, are expected to be collected in full in the first quarter of 2022.

The schedule of cash collections from customers in **Illustration 22.17** applies this assumption.

- In the first quarter, Hayes collects the $60,000 that was outstanding at the beginning of the quarter, as well as an additional $108,000 (.60 × $180,000), which is 60% of the first-quarter sales of $180,000.

- Total receipts in the first quarter are $168,000 ($60,000 + $108,000).

- In the second quarter, the company collects the remaining 40% of first-quarter sales of $72,000 (.40 × $180,000) as well as $126,000 (.60 × $210,000), which is 60% of second-quarter sales of $210,000.

- Second-quarter receipts are $198,000 ($72,000 + $126,000).

**ILLUSTRATION 22.17**

**Collections from customers**

| | A | B | C | D | E | F |
|---|---|---|---|---|---|---|
| | | | | Hayes Company | | |
| | Home  Insert  Page Layout  Formulas  Data  Review  View | | | | | |
| | P18 | fx | | | | |
| 1 | | | **Hayes Company** | | | |
| 2 | | | Schedule of Expected Collections from Customers | | | |
| 3 | | | For the Year Ending December 31, 2022 | | | |
| 4 | | | | Collections by Quarter | | |
| 5 | | Salesª | 1 | 2 | 3 | 4 |
| 6 | Accounts receivable, 12/31/21 | | $ 60,000 | | | |
| 7 | First quarter | $180,000 | 108,000ᵇ | $ 72,000ᶜ | | |
| 8 | Second quarter | 210,000 | | 126,000 | $ 84,000 | |
| 9 | Third quarter | 240,000 | | | 144,000 | $ 96,000 |
| 10 | Fourth quarter | 270,000 | | | | 162,000 |
| 11 | **Total collections** | | $168,000 | $198,000 | $228,000 | $258,000 |
| 12 | | | | | | |
| 13 | ªPer Illustration 22.3; ᵇ$180,000 × .60; ᶜ$180,000 × .40 | | | | | |
| 14 | | | | | | |

Next, it is useful to prepare a schedule of expected cash payments for direct materials, based on this second assumption:

Direct materials (Illustration 22.9): 50% are paid in the quarter purchased and 50% are paid in the following quarter. Accounts payable of $10,600 at December 31, 2021, are expected to be paid in full in the first quarter of 2022.

The schedule of cash payments for direct materials in **Illustration 22.18** applies this second assumption.

**ILLUSTRATION 22.18**

**Payments for direct materials**

| | Hayes Company | | | | |
|---|---|---|---|---|---|
| Home   Insert   Page Layout   Formulas   Data   Review   View | | | | | |
| P18 | fx | | | | |
| | A | B | C | D | E | F |
| 1 | **Hayes Company** | | | | | |
| 2 | **Schedule of Expected Payments for Direct Materials** | | | | | |
| 3 | **For the Year Ending December 31, 2022** | | | | | |
| 4 | | | Payments by Quarter | | | |
| 5 | | Purchases[a] | 1 | 2 | 3 | 4 |
| 6 | Accounts payable, 12/31/21 | | $10,600 | | | |
| 7 | First quarter | $25,200 | 12,600[b] | $12,600[c] | | |
| 8 | Second quarter | 29,200 | | 14,600 | $14,600 | |
| 9 | Third quarter | 33,200 | | | 16,600 | $16,600 |
| 10 | Fourth quarter | 37,200 | | | | 18,600 |
| 11 | **Total payments** | | **$23,200** | **$27,200** | **$31,200** | **$35,200** |
| 12 | | | | | | |
| 13 | [a]Per Illustration 22.9; [b]$25,200 × .50; [c]$25,200 × .50 | | | | | |

- In the first quarter, Hayes pays the balance of its beginning accounts payable balance of $10,600 as well as pays $12,600, which is 50% of its first-quarter purchases of $25,200.
- The total payments in the first quarter are $23,200 ($10,600 + $12,600).
- In the second quarter, it pays $12,600 (.50 × $25,200) for the remaining 50% of its first-quarter purchases as well as $14,600 (.50 × $29,200) for 50% of the second-quarter purchases.
- Total payments in the second quarter are $27,200 ($12,600 + $14,600).

The preparation of Hayes Company's cash budget is based on the following additional assumptions.

1. The January 1, 2022, cash balance is expected to be $38,000. Hayes wishes to maintain a balance of at least $15,000.
2. Short-term investment securities are expected to be sold for $2,000 cash in the first quarter.
3. Direct labor (Illustration 22.11): 100% is paid in the quarter incurred.
4. Manufacturing overhead (Illustration 22.12) and selling and administrative expenses (Illustration 22.13): All items except depreciation are paid in the quarter incurred.
5. Management plans to purchase a truck in the second quarter for $10,000 cash.
6. Hayes makes equal quarterly payments of its estimated $12,000 annual income taxes.
7. Loans are repaid in the earliest quarter in which there is sufficient cash (that is, when the cash on hand exceeds the $15,000 minimum required balance).

**Illustration 22.19** shows the cash budget for Hayes Company. The budget indicates that Hayes will need $3,000 of financing in the second quarter to maintain a minimum cash balance of $15,000. Since there is an excess of available cash over disbursements of $22,500 at the end of the third quarter, the borrowing, plus $100 interest, is repaid in this quarter.

**A cash budget contributes to more effective cash management.** It shows managers when additional financing is necessary well before the actual need arises. And, it indicates when excess cash is available for investments or other purposes.

**ILLUSTRATION 22.19**   Cash budget

Hayes Company Cash Budget

| Home | Insert | Page Layout | Formulas | Data | Review | View |

P18

| | A | B | C | D | E |
|---|---|---|---|---|---|
| 1 | | **Hayes Company** | | | |
| 2 | | **Cash Budget** | | | |
| 3 | | **For the Year Ending December 31, 2022** | | | |
| 4 | | Quarter | | | |
| 5 | | 1 | 2 | 3 | 4 |
| 6 | Beginning cash balance | $ 38,000 | $ 25,500 | $ 15,000 | $ 19,400 |
| 7 | **Add: Receipts** | | | | |
| 8 | Collections from customers | 168,000 | 198,000 | 228,000 | 258,000 |
| 9 | Sale of investment securities | 2,000 | 0 | 0 | 0 |
| 10 | Total receipts | 170,000 | 198,000 | 228,000 | 258,000 |
| 11 | Total available cash | 208,000 | 223,500 | 243,000 | 277,400 |
| 12 | **Less: Disbursements** | | | | |
| 13 | Direct materials | 23,200 | 27,200 | 31,200 | 35,200 |
| 14 | Direct labor | 62,000 | 72,000 | 82,000 | 92,000 |
| 15 | Manufacturing overhead | 53,300[a] | 56,300 | 59,300 | 62,300 |
| 16 | Selling and administrative expenses | 41,000[b] | 43,000 | 45,000 | 47,000 |
| 17 | Purchase of truck | 0 | 10,000 | 0 | 0 |
| 18 | Income tax expense | 3,000 | 3,000 | 3,000 | 3,000 |
| 19 | Total disbursements | 182,500 | 211,500 | 220,500 | 239,500 |
| 20 | Excess (deficiency) of available cash over cash disbursements | 25,500 | 12,000 | 22,500 | 37,900 |
| 21 | **Financing** | | | | |
| 22 | Add: Borrowings | 0 | 3,000 | 0 | 0 |
| 23 | Less: Repayments including interest | 0 | 0 | 3,100 | 0 |
| 24 | Ending cash balance | $ 25,500 | $ 15,000 | $ 19,400 | $ 37,900 |
| 25 | | | | | |
| 26 | [a]$57,100 − $3,800 depreciation; [b]$42,000 − $1,000 depreciation | | | | |
| 27 | | | | | |

## Management Insight   Kraft Heinz

### Starting from Scratch

Violka08/iStock/Getty Images Plus/Getty Images

An increasing number of companies, including the giant food company **Kraft Heinz**, have adopted "zero-based budgeting." This budgeting approach requires that the budgeting process start from scratch, rather than using the previous year's budget as a starting point. Every proposed cost must be justified, not just the large expenses. For example, **Pilgrim's Pride Corp.** "scrutinized how much paper it used to print documents, how much soap employees used to wash their hands, and how much Gatorade hourly employees at one processing facility drank during breaks."

The move toward zero-based budgeting is due in part to pressure by shareholders to increase company performance, as well as management fear that if a company's operations aren't lean, it will be taken over by outside investors. Proponents point toward zero-based budgeting's ability to reduce wasteful spending practices such as first-class plane flights. But critics suggest that it often results in significant layoffs, destroys employee morale, and potentially reduces a company's ability to pursue growth opportunities. **Coca-Cola** recently implemented zero-based budgeting but calls it "zero-based work" to try to disassociate its efforts from some of the negative connotations associated with zero-based budgeting.

**Source:** David Kesmodel and Annie Gasparro, "Kraft-Heinz Deal Shows Brazilian Buyout Firm's Cost-Cutting Recipe," *Wall Street Journal* (March 2015).

**What are some of the pros and cons of zero-based budgeting? (Answer is available at the end of the chapter.)**

## Budgeted Balance Sheet

The **budgeted balance sheet** is a projection of financial position at the end of the budget period. This budget is developed from the budgeted balance sheet for the preceding year and the budgets for the current year. For Hayes Company, pertinent data from the budgeted balance sheet at December 31, 2021, are as follows.

| | | | |
|---|---|---|---|
| Buildings and equipment | $182,000 | Common stock | $225,000 |
| Accumulated depreciation | 28,800 | Retained earnings | 46,480 |

**Illustration 22.20** shows Hayes Company's budgeted classified balance sheet at December 31, 2022.

**ILLUSTRATION 22.20**

**Budgeted classified balance sheet**

## Hayes Company
### Budgeted Balance Sheet
### December 31, 2022

**Assets**

| | | |
|---|---|---|
| Current assets | | |
| Cash | | $ 37,900 |
| Accounts receivable | | 108,000 |
| Finished goods inventory | | 44,000 |
| Raw materials inventory | | 4,080 |
| Total current assets | | 193,980 |
| Property, plant, and equipment | | |
| Buildings and equipment | $192,000 | |
| Less: Accumulated depreciation | 48,000 | 144,000 |
| Total assets | | $337,980 |

**Liabilities and Stockholders' Equity**

| | | |
|---|---|---|
| Liabilities | | |
| Accounts payable | | $ 18,600 |
| Stockholders' equity | | |
| Common stock | $225,000 | |
| Retained earnings | 94,380 | |
| Total stockholders' equity | | 319,380 |
| Total liabilities and stockholders' equity | | $337,980 |

The computations and sources of the amounts are explained as follows.

- **Cash:** Ending cash balance $37,900, shown in the cash budget (Illustration 22.19).
- **Accounts receivable:** 40% of fourth-quarter sales $270,000, shown in the schedule of expected collections from customers (Illustration 22.17).
- **Finished goods inventory:** Desired ending inventory 1,000 units, shown in the production budget (Illustration 22.5) times the total unit cost $44 (shown in Illustration 22.14).
- **Raw materials inventory:** Desired ending inventory 1,020 pounds, times the cost per pound $4, shown in the direct materials budget (Illustration 22.9).
- **Buildings and equipment:** December 31, 2021, balance $182,000, plus purchase of truck for $10,000 (Illustration 22.19).
- **Accumulated depreciation:** December 31, 2021, balance $28,800, plus $15,200 depreciation shown in manufacturing overhead budget (Illustration 22.12) and $4,000 depreciation shown in selling and administrative expense budget (Illustration 22.13).
- **Accounts payable:** 50% of fourth-quarter purchases $37,200, shown in schedule of expected payments for direct materials (Illustration 22.18).
- **Common stock:** Unchanged from the beginning of the year.
- **Retained earnings:** December 31, 2021, balance $46,480, plus net income $47,900, shown in budgeted income statement (Illustration 22.15).

After budget data are entered into the computer, Hayes prepares the various budgets (sales, cash, etc.), as well as the budgeted financial statements. Using spreadsheets, management can also perform "what if" (sensitivity) analyses based on different hypothetical assumptions. For example, suppose that sales managers project that sales will be 10% higher in the coming quarter. What impact does this change have on the rest of the budgeting process and the financing needs of the business? The impact of the various assumptions on the budget is quickly determined by the spreadsheet. Armed with these analyses, managers make more informed decisions about the impact of various projects. They also anticipate future problems and business opportunities. As seen in this chapter, budgeting is an excellent use of computer spreadsheets.

## DO IT! 4 | Cash Budget

Martian Company management wants to maintain a minimum monthly cash balance of $15,000. At the beginning of March, the cash balance is $16,500, expected cash receipts for March are $210,000, and cash disbursements are expected to be $220,000. How much cash, if any, must be borrowed to maintain the desired minimum monthly balance?

### Solution

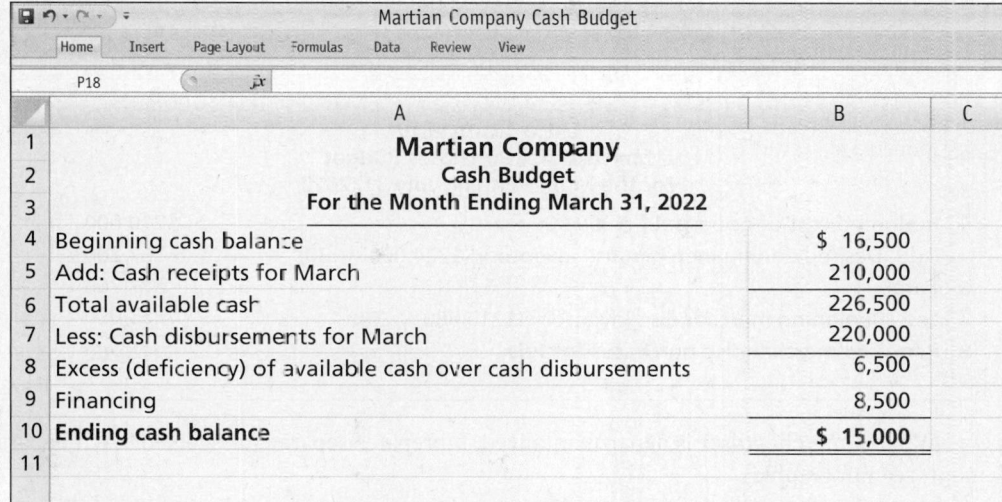

| | A | B | C |
|---|---|---|---|
| 1 | **Martian Company** | | |
| 2 | **Cash Budget** | | |
| 3 | **For the Month Ending March 31, 2022** | | |
| 4 | Beginning cash balance | $ 16,500 | |
| 5 | Add: Cash receipts for March | 210,000 | |
| 6 | Total available cash | 226,500 | |
| 7 | Less: Cash disbursements for March | 220,000 | |
| 8 | Excess (deficiency) of available cash over cash disbursements | 6,500 | |
| 9 | Financing | 8,500 | |
| 10 | **Ending cash balance** | $ 15,000 | |
| 11 | | | |

To maintain the desired minimum cash balance of $15,000, Martian Company must borrow $8,500 of cash.

Related exercise material: **BE22.9, DO IT! 22.4, E22.14, E22.15, and E22.16.**

**ACTION PLAN**

- **Write down the basic form of the cash budget, starting with the beginning cash balance, adding cash receipts for the period, deducting cash disbursements, and identifying the needed financing to achieve the desired minimum ending cash balance.**
- **Insert the data given into the outlined form of the cash budget.**

# Budgeting in Nonmanufacturing Companies

### LEARNING OBJECTIVE 5
Apply budgeting principles to nonmanufacturing companies.

Budgeting is not limited to manufacturers. Budgets are also used by merchandisers, service companies, and not-for-profit organizations.

## Merchandisers

As in manufacturing operations, the sales budget for a merchandiser is both the starting point and the key factor in the development of the master budget. The major differences between the master budgets of a merchandiser and a manufacturer are as follows.

1. A merchandiser **uses a merchandise purchases budget instead of a production budget**.
2. A merchandiser **does not use the manufacturing budgets (direct materials, direct labor, and manufacturing overhead)**.

The **merchandise purchases budget** shows the estimated cost of goods to be purchased to meet expected sales. The equation for determining budgeted merchandise purchases is as shown in **Illustration 22.21**.

**ILLUSTRATION 22.21**

Merchandise purchases equation

| Budgeted Cost of Goods Sold | + | Desired Ending Merchandise Inventory | − | Beginning Merchandise Inventory | = | Required Merchandise Purchases |
|---|---|---|---|---|---|---|

To illustrate, assume that the budget committee of Lima Company is preparing the merchandise purchases budget for July 2022. It estimates that budgeted sales will be $300,000 in July and $320,000 in August. Cost of goods sold is expected to be 70% of sales—that is, $210,000 in July (.70 × $300,000) and $224,000 in August (.70 × $320,000). The company's desired ending inventory is 30% of the following month's cost of goods sold. Required merchandise purchases for July are $214,200, computed as shown in **Illustration 22.22**.

**ILLUSTRATION 22.22**

Merchandise purchases budget

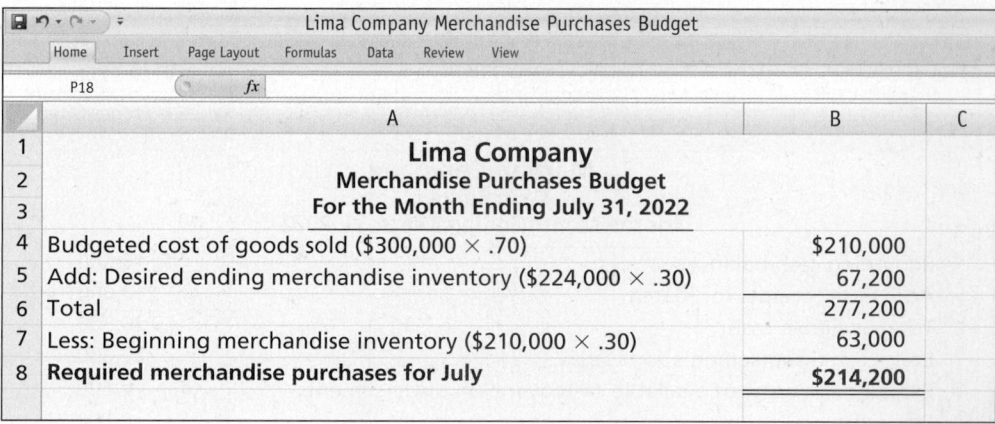

**Lima Company**
**Merchandise Purchases Budget**
**For the Month Ending July 31, 2022**

| | A | B |
|---|---|---|
| 4 | Budgeted cost of goods sold ($300,000 × .70) | $210,000 |
| 5 | Add: Desired ending merchandise inventory ($224,000 × .30) | 67,200 |
| 6 | Total | 277,200 |
| 7 | Less: Beginning merchandise inventory ($210,000 × .30) | 63,000 |
| 8 | **Required merchandise purchases for July** | **$214,200** |

When a merchandiser is departmentalized, it prepares separate budgets for each department (see infographic).

- For example, a grocery store prepares sales budgets and purchases budgets for each of its major departments, such as meats, dairy, and produce.
- The store then combines these budgets into a master budget for the store.

When a retailer has branch stores, it prepares a separate master budget for each store. Then, it incorporates these budgets into master budgets for the company as a whole.

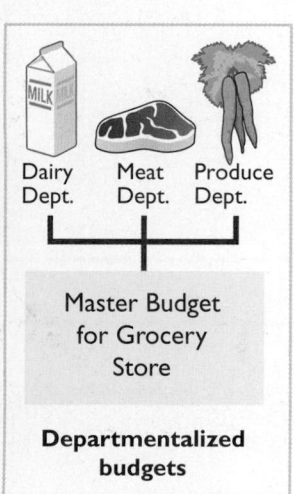

Departmentalized budgets

# Service Companies

In a service company, such as a public accounting firm, a law office, or a medical practice, the critical factor in budgeting is **coordinating professional staff needs with anticipated services**.

- If a firm is overstaffed, labor costs may be disproportionately high, profits may be lower because of the additional salaries, and staff turnover sometimes increases because of lack of challenging work.
- If a service company is understaffed, it may lose revenue because existing and prospective client needs for service cannot be met, and professional staff may seek other jobs because of excessive workloads.

Suppose that Stephan Lawn and Plowing Service estimates that it will service 300 small lawns, 200 medium lawns, and 100 large lawns during the month of July. It estimates its direct labor needs as 1 hour per small lawn, 1.75 hours for a medium lawn, and 2.75 hours for a large lawn. Its average cost for direct labor is $15 per hour. Stephan prepares a direct labor budget as shown in **Illustration 22.23**.

Service companies can obtain budget data for service revenue from **expected output** or **expected input**.

- When output is used, it is necessary to determine the expected billings of clients for services performed. In a public accounting firm, for example, output is the sum of its billings in auditing, tax, and consulting services.

| ↻ ⤵ ▾ | Stephan Lawn and Plowing Service Direct Labor Budget | | | |
|---|---|---|---|---|
| Home   Insert   Page Layout   Formulas   Data   Review   View | | | | |
| P18        fx | | | | |

| | A | B | C | D | E |
|---|---|---|---|---|---|
| 1 | **Stephan Lawn and Plowing Service** | | | | |
| 2 | **Direct Labor Budget** | | | | |
| 3 | **For the Month Ending July 31, 2022** | | | | |
| 4 | | Small | Medium | Large | Total |
| 5 | Lawns to be serviced | 300 | 200 | 100 | |
| 6 | Direct labor time (hours) per lawn | × 1 | × 1.75 | × 2.75 | |
| 7 | Total required direct labor hours | 300 | 350 | 275 | |
| 8 | Direct labor cost per hour | × $15 | × $15 | × $15 | |
| 9 | **Total direct labor cost** | **$4,500** | **$5,250** | **$4,125** | **$13,875** |

**ILLUSTRATION 22.23**
**Direct labor budget for service company**

- When input data are used, each professional staff member projects his or her billable time. The firm then applies billing rates to billable time to produce expected service revenue.

# Not-for-Profit Organizations

Budgeting is just as important for not-for-profit organizations as for profit-oriented businesses. The budget process, however, is different. In most cases, not-for-profit entities budget **on the basis of cash flows (expenditures and receipts), rather than on a revenue and expense basis**.

- The starting point in the process is usually expenditures, not receipts. Management's task generally is to find the receipts needed to support the planned expenditures.
- The activity index is also likely to be significantly different. For example, in a not-for-profit entity, such as a university, budgeted faculty positions may be based on full-time equivalent students or credit hours expected to be taught in a department.

For some governmental units, voters approve the budget. In other cases, such as state governments and the federal government, legislative approval is required. After the budget is adopted, it must be followed. Overspending is often illegal. In governmental budgets, authorizations tend to be on a line-by-line basis. That is, the budget for a municipality may have a specified authorization for police and fire protection, garbage collection, street paving, and so on. The line-item authorization of governmental budgets significantly limits the amount of discretion management can exercise. The city manager often cannot use savings from one line item, such as street paving, to cover increased spending in another line item, such as snow removal.

## Service Company Insight    Museum of Contemporary Art

ZUMA Press, Inc./
Alamy Stock Photo

### Budget Shortfalls as Far as the Eye Can See

All organizations need to stick to budgets. The **Museum of Contemporary Art** in Los Angeles learned this the hard way. Over a 10-year period, its endowment shrank from $50 million to $6 million as its newly hired director strove to build the museum's reputation through spending. The director consistently ran budget deficits, which eventually threatened the museum's survival.

The most recent recession created budgeting challenges for nearly all governmental agencies. Tax revenues dropped rapidly as earnings declined and unemployment skyrocketed. At the same time, sources of debt financing dried up. Even **Princeton** **University**, with the largest endowment per student of any U.S. university ($2 million per student), experienced a 25% drop in the value of its endowment when the financial markets plunged. Because the endowment supports 45% of the university's $1.25 billion budget, when the endowment fell the university had to make cuts. Many raises were capped at $2,000, administrative budgets were cut by 5%, and major construction projects were put on hold.

**Sources:** Edward Wyatt and Jori Finkel, "Soaring in Art, Museum Trips Over Finances," *Wall Street Journal Online* (December 4, 2008); Stu Woo, "California's Plans to Close Gap Become More Drastic," *Wall Street Journal Online* (January 8, 2009); and John Hechinger, "Princeton Cuts Budget as Endowment Slides," *Wall Street Journal Online* (January 9, 2009).

**Why would a university's budgeted scholarships probably fall when the stock market suffers a serious drop? (Answer is available at the end of the chapter.)**

**ACTION PLAN**

- Begin with budgeted cost of goods sold.
- Add desired ending merchandise inventory.
- Subtract beginning merchandise inventory.

# DO IT! 5 | Merchandise Purchases Budget

Becker Company estimates that 2022 sales will be $15,000 in quarter 1, $20,000 in quarter 2, and $25,000 in quarter 3. Cost of goods sold is 80% of sales. Management desires to have ending finished goods inventory equal to 15% of the next quarter's expected cost of goods sold. Prepare a merchandise purchases budget by quarter for the first six months of 2022.

## Solution

Becker Company Merchandise Purchases Budget

Home | Insert | Page Layout | Formulas | Data | Review | View

P18    $fx$

|  | A | B | C | D |
|---|---|---|---|---|
| 1 | **Becker Company** | | | |
| 2 | **Merchandise Purchases Budget** | | | |
| 3 | **For the Six Months Ending June 30, 2022** | | | |
| 4 | | Quarter | | |
| 5 | | 1 | 2 | Six Months |
| 6 | Budgeted cost of goods sold (sales × .80) | $12,000 | $16,000 | |
| 7 | Add: Desired ending merchandise inventory (15% of next quarter's cost of goods sold) | 2,400 | 3,000 | |
| 8 | Total | 14,400 | 19,000 | |
| 9 | Less: Beginning merchandise inventory (15% this quarter's cost of goods sold) | 1,800 | 2,400 | |
| 10 | **Required merchandise purchases** | **$12,600** | **$16,600** | **$29,200** |

Related exercise material: **BE22.10, DO IT! 22.5, E22.19, E22.20, and E22.21.**

---

# Review and Practice

## Learning Objectives Review

### 1 State the essentials of effective budgeting and the components of the master budget.

The primary benefits of budgeting are that it (a) requires management to plan ahead, (b) provides definite objectives for evaluating performance, (c) creates an early warning system for potential problems, (d) facilitates coordination of activities, (e) results in greater management awareness, and (f) motivates personnel to meet planned objectives. The essentials of effective budgeting are (a) sound organizational structure, (b) research and analysis, and (c) acceptance by all levels of management.

The master budget consists of the following budgets: (a) sales, (b) production, (c) direct materials, (d) direct labor, (e) manufacturing overhead, (f) selling and administrative expense, (g) budgeted income statement, (h) capital expenditure budget, (i) cash budget, and (j) budgeted balance sheet.

### 2 Prepare budgets for sales, production, and direct materials.

The sales budget is derived from sales forecasts. The production budget starts with budgeted sales units, adds desired ending finished goods inventory, and subtracts beginning finished goods inventory to arrive at the required number of units to be produced. The direct materials budget starts with the direct materials units (e.g., pounds) required for budgeted production, adds desired ending direct materials units, and subtracts beginning direct materials units to arrive at required direct materials units to be purchased. This amount is multiplied by the direct materials cost (e.g., cost per pound) to arrive at the total cost of direct materials purchases.

**3 Prepare budgets for direct labor, manufacturing overhead, and selling and administrative expenses, and a budgeted income statement.**

The direct labor budget starts with the units to be produced as determined in the production budget. This amount is multiplied by the direct labor hours per unit and the direct labor cost per hour to arrive at the total direct labor cost. The manufacturing overhead budget lists all of the individual types of overhead costs, distinguishing between fixed and variable costs. The selling and administrative expense budget lists all of the individual types of selling and administrative expense items, distinguishing between fixed and variable costs. The budgeted income statement is prepared from the various operating budgets. Cost of goods sold is determined by calculating the budgeted cost to produce one unit, then multiplying this amount by the number of units sold.

**4 Prepare a cash budget and a budgeted balance sheet.**

The cash budget has three sections (receipts, disbursements, and financing) and the beginning and ending cash balances. Receipts and payments sections are determined after preparing separate schedules for collections from customers and payments to suppliers. The budgeted balance sheet is developed from the budgeted balance sheet from the preceding year and the various budgets for the current year.

**5 Apply budgeting principles to nonmanufacturing companies.**

Budgeting may be used by merchandisers for development of a merchandise purchases budget. In service companies, budgeting is a critical factor in coordinating staff needs with anticipated services. In not-for-profit organizations, the starting point in budgeting is usually expenditures, not receipts

## Glossary Review

**Budget** A formal written statement of management's plans for a specified future time period, expressed in financial terms. (p. 22-3).

**Budgetary slack** The amount by which a manager intentionally underestimates budgeted revenues or overestimates budgeted expenses in order to make it easier to achieve budgetary goals. (p. 22-6).

**Budget committee** A group responsible for coordinating the preparation of the budget. (p. 22-5).

**Budgeted balance sheet** A projection of financial position at the end of the budget period. (p. 22-21).

**Budgeted income statement** An estimate of the expected profitability of operations for the budget period. (p. 22-16).

**Cash budget** A projection of anticipated cash flows. (p. 22-18).

**Direct labor budget** A projection of the quantity and cost of direct labor necessary to meet production requirements. (p. 22-14).

**Direct materials budget** An estimate of the quantity and cost of direct materials to be purchased. (p. 22-13).

**Financial budgets** Individual budgets that focus primarily on the cash resources needed to fund expected operations and planned capital expenditures. (p. 22-7).

**Long-range planning** A formalized process of identifying long-term goals, selecting strategies to achieve those goals, and developing policies and plans to implement the strategies. (p. 22-6).

**Manufacturing overhead budget** An estimate of expected manufacturing overhead costs for the budget period. (p. 22-15).

**Master budget** A set of interrelated budgets that constitutes a plan of action for a specific time period. (p. 22-7).

**Merchandise purchases budget** The estimated cost of goods to be purchased by a merchandiser to meet expected sales. (p. 22-24).

**Operating budgets** Individual budgets that result in a budgeted income statement. (p. 22-7).

**Participative budgeting** A budgetary approach that starts with input from lower-level managers and works upward so that managers at all levels participate. (p. 22-5).

**Production budget** A projection of the units that must be produced to meet anticipated sales. (p. 22-10).

**Sales budget** An estimate of expected sales revenue for the budget period. (p. 22-8).

**Sales forecast** The projection of potential sales for the industry and the company's expected share of such sales. (p. 22-5).

**Selling and administrative expense budget** A projection of anticipated selling and administrative expenses for the budget period. (p. 22-15).

## Practice Multiple-Choice Questions

1. **(LO 1)** Which of the following is **not** a benefit of budgeting?
   a. Management can plan ahead.
   b. An early warning system is provided for potential problems.
   c. It enables disciplinary action to be taken at every level of responsibility.
   d. The coordination of activities is facilitated.

2. **(LO 1)** A budget:
   a. is the responsibility of management accountants.
   b. is the primary method of communicating agreed-upon objectives throughout an organization.
   c. ignores past performance because it represents management's plans for a future time period.
   d. may promote efficiency but has no role in evaluating performance.

3. **(LO 1)** The essentials of effective budgeting do **not** include:
   a. top-down budgeting.
   b. management acceptance.

c. research and analysis.

d. sound organizational structure.

**4. (LO 1)** Compared to budgeting, long-range planning generally has the:

a. same amount of detail.  c. same emphasis.

b. longer time period.  d. same time period.

**5. (LO 2)** A sales budget is:

a. derived from the production budget.

b. management's best estimate of sales revenue for the year.

c. not the starting point for the master budget.

d. prepared only for credit sales.

**6. (LO 2)** The equation for the production budget is budgeted sales in units plus:

a. desired ending merchandise inventory less beginning merchandise inventory.

b. beginning finished goods units less desired ending finished goods units.

c. desired ending direct materials units less beginning direct materials units.

d. desired ending finished goods units less beginning finished goods units.

**7. (LO 2)** Direct materials inventories are kept in pounds in Byrd Company, and the total pounds of direct materials needed for production is 9,500. If the beginning inventory is 1,000 pounds and the desired ending inventory is 2,200 pounds, the total number of pounds to be purchased is:

a. 9,400.

b. 9,500.

c. 9,700.

d. 10,700.

**8. (LO 3)** The equation for computing the direct labor budget is to multiply the direct labor cost per hour by the:

a. total required direct labor hours.

b. physical units to be produced.

c. equivalent units to be produced.

d. No correct answer is given.

**9. (LO 3)** Each of the following budgets is used in preparing the budgeted income statement **except** the:

a. sales budget.

b. selling and administrative expense budget.

c. capital expenditure budget.

d. direct labor budget.

**10. (LO 3)** The budgeted income statement is:

a. the end-product of the operating budgets.

b. the end-product of the financial budgets.

c. the starting point of the master budget.

d. dependent on cash receipts and cash disbursements.

**11. (LO 4)** The budgeted balance sheet is:

a. developed from the budgeted balance sheet for the preceding year and the budgets for the current year.

b. the last operating budget prepared.

c. used to prepare the cash budget.

d. All of the answer choices are correct.

**12. (LO 4)** The format of a cash budget is:

a. Beginning cash balance + Cash receipts + Cash from financing − Cash disbursements = Ending cash balance.

b. Beginning cash balance + Cash receipts − Cash disbursements +/− Financing = Ending cash balance.

c. Beginning cash balance + Net income − Cash dividends = Ending cash balance.

d. Beginning cash balance + Cash revenues − Cash expenses = Ending cash balance.

**13. (LO 4)** Expected direct materials purchases in Read Company are $70,000 in the first quarter and $90,000 in the second quarter. Forty percent of the purchases are paid in cash as incurred, and the balance is paid in the following quarter. The budgeted cash payments for purchases in the second quarter are:

a. $96,000.  c. $78,000.

b. $90,000.  d. $72,000.

**14. (LO 5)** The budget for a merchandiser differs from a budget for a manufacturer because:

a. a merchandise purchases budget replaces the production budget, and the other manufacturing budgets are not used.

b. the manufacturing budgets are not applicable, except the production budget is still used.

c. a merchandise purchases budget replaces the production budget (and the other manufacturing budgets are not used), and the manufacturing budgets are not applicable (except the production budget is still used).

d. None of the answer choices is correct.

**15. (LO 5)** In most cases, not-for-profit entities:

a. prepare budgets using the same steps as those used by profit-oriented businesses.

b. know budgeted cash receipts at the beginning of a time period, so they budget only for expenditures.

c. begin the budgeting process by budgeting expenditures rather than receipts.

d. can ignore budgets because they are not expected to generate net income.

## Solutions

1. **c.** Budgeting does not necessarily enable disciplinary action to be taken at every level of responsibility. The other choices are all benefits of budgeting.

2. **b.** A budget is the primary method of communicating agreed-upon objectives throughout an organization. The other choices are

incorrect because (a) a budget is the responsibility of all levels of management, not management accountants; (c) past performance is not ignored in the budgeting process but instead is the starting point from which future budget goals are formulated; and (d) the budget not only may promote efficiency but is an important tool for evaluating performance.

**3. a.** Top-down budgeting is not one of the essentials of effective budgeting. The other choices are true statements.

**4. b.** Long-range planning generally encompasses a period of at least 5 years whereas budgeting usually covers a period of 1 year. The other choices are incorrect because budgeting and long-range planning (a) do not have the same amount of detail, (c) do not have the same emphasis, and (d) do not cover the same time period.

**5. b.** A sales budget is management's best estimate of sales revenue for the year. The other choices are incorrect because a sales budget (a) is the first budget prepared and is the one budget that is not derived from any other budget, (c) is the starting point for the master budget, and (d) is prepared for both cash and credit sales.

**6. d.** The equation for the production budget is budgeted sales in units plus desired ending finished goods units less beginning finished goods units. The other choices are therefore incorrect.

**7. d.** Pounds to be purchased = Amount needed for production (9,500) + Desired ending inventory (2,200) − Beginning inventory (1,000) = 10,700, not (a) 9,400, (b) 9,500, or (c) 9,700.

**8. a.** Direct labor cost = Direct labor cost per hour × Total required direct labor hours. The other choices are therefore incorrect.

**9. c.** The capital expenditure budget is not used in preparing the budgeted income statement. The other choices are true statements.

**10. a.** The budgeted income statement is the end-product of the operating budgets, not (b) the end-product of the financial budgets,

(c) the starting point of the master budget, or (d) dependent on cash receipts and cash disbursements.

**11. a.** The budgeted balance sheet is developed from the budgeted balance sheet for the preceding year and the budgets for the current year. The other choices are therefore incorrect.

**12. b.** The format of a cash budget is Beginning cash balance + Cash receipts − Cash disbursements +/− Financing = Ending cash balance. The other choices are therefore incorrect.

**13. c.** Budgeted cash payments for the second quarter = Purchases for the first quarter ($42,000; $70,000 × .60) + 40% of the purchases for the second quarter ($36,000; $90,000 × .40) = $78,000, not (a) $96,000, (b) $90,000, or (d) $72,000

**14. a.** The budget for a merchandiser uses a merchandise purchases budget in place of a production budget, and the other manufacturing budgets are not used. It is true the manufacturing budgets are not applicable for a merchandiser, but it is not true the production budget is still used, so choice (b) is not correct.

**15. c.** In most cases, not-for-profit entities begin the budgeting process by budgeting expenditures rather than receipts. The other choices are incorrect because in most cases not-for-profit entities (a) prepare budgets using different, not the same, steps as those used by profit-oriented enterprises; (b) budget for both expenditures and receipts; and (d) cannot ignore budgets.

## Practice Brief Exercises

**1. (LO 2)** Romana Company estimates that unit sales will be 20,000 in quarter 1, 24,000 in quarter 2, 27,000 in quarter 3, and 33,000 in quarter 4. Management desires to have an ending finished goods inventory equal to 20% of the next quarter's expected unit sales. Prepare a production budget by quarters for the first 6 months of 2022.

*Prepare a production budget for two quarters.*

### Solution

1.

**Romana Company**
**Production Budget**
**For the Six Months Ending June 30, 2022**

|  | Quarter | | Six |
| --- | --- | --- | --- |
|  | 1 | 2 | Months |
| Expected unit sales | 20,000 | 24,000 |  |
| Add: Desired ending finished goods | 4,800[a] | 5,400[c] |  |
| Total required units | 24,800 | 29,400 |  |
| Less: Beginning finished goods inventory | 4,000[b] | 4,800 |  |
| Required production units | 20,800 | 24,600 | 45,400 |

[a]24,000 × .2; [b]20,000 × .2; [c]27,000 × .2

**2. (LO 3)** For Jovanka Company, units to be produced are 7,000 in quarter 1 and 9,800 in quarter 2. It takes 2.2 hours to make a finished unit, and the expected hourly wage rate is $20 per hour. Prepare a direct labor budget by quarters for the 6 months ending June 30, 2022.

*Prepare a direct labor budget for 2 quarters.*

**Solution**

2.

**Jovanka Company**
**Direct Labor Budget**
**For the Six Months Ending June 30, 2022**

|  | Quarter | | Six |
|---|---|---|---|
|  | 1 | 2 | Months |
| Units to be produced | 7,000 | 9,800 | |
| Direct labor time (hours) per unit | × 2.2 | × 2.2 | |
| Total required direct labor hours | 15,400 | 21,560 | |
| Direct labor cost per hour | × $20 | × $20 | |
| Total direct labor cost | $308,000 | $431,200 | $739,200 |

*Prepare data for a cash budget.*

**3. (LO 4)** Vislor Industries expects credit sales for January, February, and March to be $165,000, $200,000, and $220,000, respectively. It is expected that 70% of the sales will be collected in the month of sale, and 30% will be collected in the following month. Compute cash collections from customers for each month.

**Solution**

3.

|  | Collections from Customers | | |
|---|---|---|---|
| **Credit Sales** | **January** | **February** | **March** |
| January, $165,000 | $115,500 | $ 49,500 | |
| February, $200,000 | | 140,000 | $ 60,000 |
| March, $220,000 | | | 154,000 |
| | $115,500 | $189,500 | $214,000 |

*Determine required merchandise purchases for 1 month.*

**4. (LO 5)** Turlough Wholesalers is preparing its merchandise purchases budget. Budgeted sales are $300,000 for June and $380,000 for July. Cost of goods sold is expected to be 60% of sales. The company's desired ending inventory is 25% of the following month's cost of goods sold. Compute the required purchases for June.

**Solution**

4.

| Budgeted cost of goods sold ($300,000 × 60%) | $180,000 |
|---|---|
| Add: Desired ending inventory ($380,000 × 60% × 25%) | 57,000 |
| Total inventory required | 237,000 |
| Less: Beginning inventory ($300,000 × 60% × 25%) | 45,000 |
| Required merchandise purchases for June | $192,000 |

# Practice Exercises

*Prepare production and direct materials budgets by quarter for 6 months.*

**1. (LO 2)** On January 1, 2022, the Heche Company budget committee has reached agreement on the following data for the 6 months ending June 30, 2022.

Sales units: First quarter 5,000; second quarter 6,000; third quarter 7,000
Ending raw materials inventory: 40% of the next quarter's production requirements
Ending finished goods inventory: 30% of the next quarter's expected sales units
Third-quarter 2022 production: 7,500 units

The ending raw materials and finished goods inventories at December 31, 2021, follow the same percentage relationships to production and sales that are desired for 2022. Two pounds of raw materials are required to make each unit of finished goods. Raw materials purchased are expected to cost $5 per pound.

## Instructions

   **a.** Prepare a production budget by quarters for the 6-month period ended June 30, 2022.

   **b.** Prepare a direct materials budget by quarters for the 6-month period ended June 30, 2022.

## Solution

**1. a.**

Heche Company Production Budget

| | Home | Insert | Page Layout | Formulas | Data | Review | View | | |
|---|---|---|---|---|---|---|---|---|---|

P18    *fx*

| | A | B | C | D |
|---|---|---|---|---|
| 1 | **Heche Company** | | | |
| 2 | **Production Budget** | | | |
| 3 | **For the Six Months Ending June 30, 2022** | | | |
| 4 | | Quarter | | |
| 5 | | 1 | 2 | Six Months |
| 6 | Expected unit sales | 5,000 | 6,000 | |
| 7 | Add: Desired ending finished goods units | 1,800$^{(1)}$ | 2,100$^{(2)}$ | |
| 8 | Total required units | 6,800 | 8,100 | |
| 9 | Less: Beginning finished goods units | 1,500$^{(3)}$ | 1,800 | |
| 10 | **Required production units** | 5,300 | 6,300 | 11,600 |
| 11 | | | | |
| 12 | $^{(1)}.30 \times 6,000;^{(2)}.30 \times 7,000;^{(3)}.30 \times 5,000$ | | | |

**b.**

Heche Company Direct Materials Budget

| | Home | Insert | Page Layout | Formulas | Data | Review | View | | |
|---|---|---|---|---|---|---|---|---|---|

P18    *fx*

| | A | B | C | D |
|---|---|---|---|---|
| 1 | **Heche Company** | | | |
| 2 | **Direct Materials Budget** | | | |
| 3 | **For the Six Months Ending June 30, 2022** | | | |
| 4 | | Quarter | | |
| 5 | | 1 | 2 | Six Months |
| 6 | Units to be produced | 5,300 | 6,300 | |
| 7 | Direct materials per unit | × 2 | × 2 | |
| 8 | Total pounds needed for production | 10,600 | 12,600 | |
| 9 | Add: Desired ending direct materials (pounds) | 5,040$^{(1)}$ | 6,000$^{(2)}$ | |
| 10 | Total materials required | 15,640 | 18,600 | |
| 11 | Less: Beginning direct materials (pounds) | 4,240$^{(3)}$ | 5,040 | |
| 12 | Direct materials purchase | 11,400 | 13,560 | |
| 13 | Cost per pound | × $5 | × $5 | |
| 14 | **Total cost of direct materials purchase** | **$57,000** | **$67,800** | **$124,800** |
| 15 | | | | |
| 16 | $^{(1)}.40 \times 12,600;^{(2)}.40 \times (7,500 \times 2); ^{(3)}.40 \times 10,600$ | | | |
| 17 | | | | |

**2. (LO 4)** Jake Company expects to have a cash balance of $45,000 on January 1, 2022. Relevant monthly budget data for the first 2 months of 2022 are as follows.    *Prepare a cash budget for 2 months.*

    Collections from customers: January $100,000, February $160,000.

    Payments for direct materials: January $60,000, February $80,000.

    Direct labor: January $30,000, February $45,000. Wages are paid in the month they are incurred.

    Manufacturing overhead: January $26,000, February $31,000. These costs include depreciation of $1,000 per month. All other overhead costs are paid as incurred.

    Selling and administrative expenses: January $15,000, February $20,000. These costs are exclusive of depreciation. They are paid as incurred.

    Sales of marketable securities in January are expected to realize $10,000 in cash. Jake Company has a line of credit at a local bank that enables it to borrow up to $25,000. The company wants to maintain a minimum monthly cash balance of $25,000.

**Instructions**

Prepare a cash budget for January and February.

**Solution**

2.

| | Jake Company Cash Budget | | |
|---|---|---|---|
| | Home   Insert   Page Layout   Formulas   Data   Review   View | | |
| | P18         fx | | |
| | A | B | C |
| 1 | **Jake Company** | | |
| 2 | **Cash Budget** | | |
| 3 | **For the Two Months Ending February 28, 2022** | | |
| 4 | | January | February |
| 5 | Beginning cash balance | $ 45,000 | $ 25,000 |
| 6 | Add: Receipts | | |
| 7 |    Collections from customers | 100,000 | 160,000 |
| 8 |    Sale of marketable securities | 10,000 | 0 |
| 9 |       Total receipts | 110,000 | 160,000 |
| 10 | Total available cash | 155,000 | 185,000 |
| 11 | Less: Disbursements | | |
| 12 |    Direct materials | 60,000 | 80,000 |
| 13 |    Direct labor | 30,000 | 45,000 |
| 14 |    Manufacturing overhead | 25,000* | 30,000 |
| 15 |    Selling and administrative expenses | 15,000 | 20,000 |
| 16 |       Total disbursements | 130,000 | 175,000 |
| 17 | Excess (deficiency) of available cash over cash | | |
| 18 |    Disbursements | 25,000 | 10,000 |
| 19 | Financing | | |
| 20 |    Borrowings | 0 | 15,000 |
| 21 |    Repayments | 0 | 0 |
| 22 | **Ending cash balance** | **$ 25,000** | **$ 25,000** |
| 23 | | | |
| | *$26,000 – $1,000 | | |

# Practice Problems

*Prepare sales and production budgets.*

**1. (LO 2)** Asheville Company is preparing its master budget for 2022. Relevant data pertaining to its sales and production budgets are as follows.

**Sales.**   Sales for the year are expected to total 2,100,000 units. Quarterly sales, as a percentage of total sales, are 15%, 25%, 35%, and 25%, respectively. The unit selling price is expected to be $70 for the first three quarters and $75 beginning in the fourth quarter. Sales in the first quarter of 2023 are expected to be 10% higher than the budgeted sales volume for the first quarter of 2022.

**Production.**   Management desires to maintain ending finished goods inventories at 20% of the next quarter's budgeted sales volume.

**Instructions**

Prepare the sales budget and production budget by quarters for 2022.

**Solution**

1.

| | | | | | |
|---|---|---|---|---|---|
| ▣ ᴺ · ᴺ · ⬝ | Asheville Company Sales Budget and Production Budget | | | | |
| Home   Insert   Page Layout   Formulas   Data   Review   View | | | | | |
| P18   ⬤   *fx* | | | | | |
| | A | B | C | D | E | F |

| | A | B | C | D | E | F |
|---|---|---|---|---|---|---|
| 1 | | **Asheville Company** | | | | |
| 2 | | **For the Year Ending December 31, 2022** | | | | |
| 3 | | **Sales Budget** | | | | |
| 4 | | Quarter | | | | |
| 5 | | 1 | 2 | 3 | 4 | Year |
| 6 | Expected unit sales[a] | 315,000 | 525,000 | 735,000 | 525,000 | 2,100,000 |
| 7 | Unit selling price | × $70 | × $70 | × $70 | × $75 | |
| 8 | Total sales | $22,050,000 | $36,750,000 | $51,450,000 | $39,375,000 | $149,625,000 |
| 9 | | | | | | |
| 10 | | **Production Budget** | | | | |
| 11 | Expected unit sales | 315,000 | 525,000 | 735,000 | 525,000 | |
| 11 | Add: Desired ending finished goods units | 105,000 | 147,000 | 105,000 | 69,300[b] | |
| 12 | Total required units | 420,000 | 672,000 | 840,000 | 594,300 | |
| 13 | Less: Beginning finshed goods units | 63,000[c] | 105,000 | 147,000 | 105,000 | |
| 14 | **Required production units** | **357,000** | **567,000** | **693,000** | **489,300** | **2,106,300** |
| 15 | | | | | | |
| 16 | [a]Expected first-quarter unit sales 2,100,000 × .15; second and fourth quarters 2,100,000 × .25; | | | | | |
| 17 | third quarter 2,100,000 × .35 | | | | | |
| 18 | [b]Estimated first-quarter 2023 sales volume 315,000 + (315,000 × .10) = 346,500; 346,500 × .20 | | | | | |
| 19 | [c]20% of estimated first-quarter 2022 sales units (315,000 × .20) | | | | | |

2. **(LO 3, 4)** Barrett Company has completed all operating budgets other than the income statement for 2022. Selected data from these budgets follow.

*Prepare budgeted cost of goods sold, income statement, and balance sheet.*

Sales: $300,000
Purchases of raw materials: $145,000
Ending inventory of raw materials: $15,000
Direct labor: $40,000
Manufacturing overhead: $73,000, including $3,000 of depreciation expense
Selling and administrative expenses: $36,000 including depreciation expense of $1,000
Interest expense: $1,000
Principal payment on note: $2,000
Dividends declared: $2,000
Income tax rate: 30%

Other information:

Assume that there are no work-in-process or finished goods inventories.
Year-end accounts receivable: 4% of 2022 sales.
Year-end accounts payable: 50% of ending inventory of raw materials.
Interest, direct labor, manufacturing overhead, and selling and administrative expenses other than depreciation are paid as incurred.
Dividends declared and income taxes for 2022 will not be paid until 2023.

**Barrett Company**
**Balance Sheet**
**December 31, 2021**

## Assets

| | | |
|---|---|---|
| Current assets | | |
| Cash | | $20,000 |
| Raw materials inventory | | 10,000 |
| Total current assets | | 30,000 |
| Property, plant, and equipment | | |
| Equipment | $40,000 | |
| Less: Accumulated depreciation | 4,000 | 36,000 |
| Total assets | | $66,000 |

## Liabilities and Stockholders' Equity

| | | |
|---|---|---|
| Liabilities | | |
| Accounts payable | $ 5,000 | |
| Notes payable | 22,000 | |
| Total liabilities | | $27,000 |
| Stockholders' equity | | |
| Common stock | 25,000 | |
| Retained earnings | 14,000 | |
| Total stockholders' equity | | 39,000 |
| Total liabilities and stockholders' equity | | $66,000 |

### Instructions

**a.** Calculate budgeted cost of goods sold.

**b.** Prepare a budgeted multiple-step income statement for the year ending December 31, 2022.

**c.** Prepare a budgeted classified balance sheet as of December 31, 2022.

### Solution

**2. a.** Beginning raw materials + Purchases − Ending raw materials = Cost of direct materials used
($10,000 + $145,000 − $15,000 = $140,000)
Direct materials used + Direct labor + Manufacturing overhead = Cost of goods sold ($140,000 + $40,000 + $73,000 = $253,000)

**b.**

**Barrett Company**
**Budgeted Income Statement**
**For the Year Ending December 31, 2022**

| | |
|---|---|
| Sales | $300,000 |
| Cost of goods sold | 253,000 |
| Gross profit | 47,000 |
| Selling and administrative expenses | 36,000 |
| Income from operations | 11,000 |
| Interest expense | 1,000 |
| Income before income tax expense | 10,000 |
| Income tax expense (30%) | 3,000* |
| Net income | $ 7,000 |

*$10,000 × .30

c.

**Barrett Company**
**Budgeted Balance Sheet**
**December 31, 2022**

### Assets

Current assets
  Cash[(1)] ............................................................ $17,500
  Accounts receivable (.04 × $300,000) .................. 12,000
  Raw materials inventory .................................. 15,000

  Total current assets ....................................... 44,500
Property, plant, and equipment
  Equipment ................................ $40,000
  Less: Accumulated depreciation[(2)] ..... 8,000 ...... 32,000

  Total assets .................................................. $76,500

### Liabilities and Stockholders' Equity

Liabilities
  Accounts payable (.50 × $15,000) ......... $ 7,500
  Income taxes payable (see income statement) .. 3,000
  Dividends payable ....................... 2,000
  Note payable ($22,000 − $2,000) ......... 20,000

  Total liabilities .......................................... $32,500
Stockholders' equity
  Common stock ........................... 25,000
  Retained earnings[(3)] ................... 19,000

  Total stockholders' equity ............................. 44,000

  Total liabilities and stockholders' equity .......... $76,500

[(1)]Beginning cash balance ....................................... $ 20,000
  Add: Receipts
    Collections from customers [(1 − .04) × $300,000 sales)] ... 288,000

  Total available cash ......................................... 308,000
  Less: Disbursements
    Direct materials ($5,000 + $145,000 − $7,500) ... $142,500
    Direct labor .................................... 40,000
    Manufacturing overhead ($73,000 − $3,000) ....... 70,000
    Selling and administrative expenses ($36,000 − $1,000) .. 35,000

  Total disbursements .......................................... 287,500

  Excess of available cash over cash disbursements ...... 20,500
  Financing
  Less: Repayment of principal and interest .............. 3,000

  Ending cash balance ......................................... $ 17,500

[(2)]$4,000 + $3,000 − $1,000

[(3)]Beginning retained earnings + Net income − Dividends declared = Ending retained earnings ($14,000 + $7,000 − $2,000 = $19,000)

Brief Exercises, DO IT! Exercises, Exercises, Problems, Data Analytics Activities, and many additional resources are available for practice in WileyPLUS.

## Questions

1. **a.** What is a budget?
   **b.** How does a budget contribute to good management?

2. Kate Cey and Joe Coulter are discussing the benefits of budgeting. They ask you to identify the primary benefits of budgeting. Comply with their request.

3. Jane Gilligan asks your help in understanding the essentials of effective budgeting. Identify the essentials for Jane.

4. **a.** "Accounting plays a relatively unimportant role in budgeting." Is this true? Explain why or why not.

   **b.** What responsibilities does management have in budgeting?

5. What criteria are helpful in determining the length of the budget period? What is the most common budget period?

6. Lori Wilkins maintains that the only difference between budgeting and long-range planning is time. Is this true? Explain why or why not.

7. What is participative budgeting? What are its potential benefits? What are its potential disadvantages?

8. What is budgetary slack? What incentive do managers have to create budgetary slack?

9. Distinguish between a master budget and a sales forecast.

10. What budget is the starting point in preparing the master budget? What may result if this budget is inaccurate?

11. "The production budget shows both unit production data and unit cost data." Is this true? Explain why or why not.

12. Alou Company has 20,000 beginning finished goods units. Budgeted sales units are 160,000. If management desires 15,000 ending finished goods units, what are the required units of production?

13. In preparing the direct materials budget for Quan Company, management concludes that required purchases are 64,000 units. If 52,000 direct materials units are required in production and there are 9,000 units of beginning direct materials, what are the desired units of ending direct materials?

14. The production budget of Justus Company calls for 80,000 units to be produced. If it takes 45 minutes to make one unit and the

direct labor rate is $16 per hour, what is the total budgeted direct labor cost?

15. Ortiz Company's manufacturing overhead budget shows total variable costs of $198,000 and total fixed costs of $162,000. Total production in units is expected to be 150,000. It takes 20 minutes to make one unit, and the direct labor rate is $15 per hour. Express the manufacturing overhead rate as (a) a percentage of direct labor cost, and (b) an amount per direct labor hour.

16. Everly Company's variable selling and administrative expenses are 12% of net sales. Fixed expenses are $50,000 per quarter. The sales budget shows expected sales of $200,000 and $240,000 in the first and second quarters, respectively. What are the total budgeted selling and administrative expenses for each quarter?

17. For Goody Company, the budgeted cost for one unit of product is direct materials $10, direct labor $20, and manufacturing overhead 80% of direct labor cost. If 25,000 units are expected to be sold at $65 each, what is the budgeted gross profit?

18. Indicate the supporting schedules used in preparing a budgeted income statement through gross profit for a manufacturer.

19. Identify the three sections of a cash budget. What balances are also shown in this budget?

20. Noterman Company has credit sales of $600,000 in January. Past experience suggests that 40% is collected in the month of sale, 50% in the month following the sale, and 10% in the second month following the sale. Compute the cash collections from January sales in January, February, and March.

21. What is the equation for determining required merchandise purchases for a merchandiser?

22. How might expected revenues in a service company be computed?

## Brief Exercises

*Prepare a diagram of a master budget.*

**BE22.1 (LO 1), AN** Maris Company uses the following budgets: balance sheet, capital expenditure, cash, direct labor, direct materials, income statement, manufacturing overhead, production, sales, and selling and administrative expense. Prepare a diagram of the interrelationships of the budgets in the master budget. Indicate whether each budget is an operating or a financial budget.

*Prepare a sales budget.*

**BE22.2 (LO 2), AP** Paige Company estimates that unit sales will be 10,000 in quarter 1, 14,000 in quarter 2, 15,000 in quarter 3, and 18,000 in quarter 4. Using a unit selling price of $70, prepare the sales budget by quarters for the year ending December 31, 2022.

*Prepare a production budget for 2 quarters.*

**BE22.3 (LO 2), AP** Paige Company estimates that unit sales will be 10,000 in quarter 1, 14,000 in quarter 2, 15,000 in quarter 3, and 18,000 in quarter 4. The unit selling price is $70. Management desires to have an ending finished goods inventory equal to 25% of the next quarter's expected unit sales. Prepare a production budget by quarters for the first 6 months of 2022.

*Prepare a direct materials budget for 1 month.*

**BE22.4 (LO 2), AP** Perine Company has 2,000 pounds of raw materials in its December 31, 2021, ending inventory. Required production for January and February of 2022 are 4,000 and 5,000 units, respectively. Two pounds of raw materials are needed for each unit, and the estimated cost per pound is $6. Management desires an ending inventory equal to 25% of next month's materials requirements. Prepare the direct materials budget for January.

*Prepare a direct labor budget for 2 quarters.*

**BE22.5 (LO 3), AP** For Gundy Company, units to be produced are 5,000 in quarter 1 and 7,000 in quarter 2. It takes 1.6 hours to make a finished unit, and the expected hourly wage rate is $15 per hour. Prepare a direct labor budget by quarters for the 6 months ending June 30, 2022.

*Prepare a manufacturing overhead budget.*

**BE22.6 (LO 3), AP** For Roche Inc., variable manufacturing overhead costs are expected to be $20,000 in the first quarter of 2022, with $5,000 increments in each of the remaining three quarters. Fixed overhead costs are estimated to be $40,000 in each quarter. Prepare the manufacturing overhead budget by quarters and in total for the year.

**BE22.7 (LO 3), AP** Elbert Company classifies its selling and administrative expense budget into variable and fixed components. Variable expenses are expected to be $24,000 in the first quarter, and $4,000 increments are expected in the remaining quarters of 2022. Fixed expenses are expected to be $40,000 in each quarter. Prepare the selling and administrative expense budget by quarters and in total for 2022.

*Prepare a selling and administrative expense budget.*

**BE22.8 (LO 3), AP** North Company has completed all of its operating budgets. The sales budget for the year shows 50,000 units and total sales of $2,250,000. The total cost of producing one unit is $25. Selling and administrative expenses are expected to be $300,000. Interest is estimated to be $10,000. Income taxes are estimated to be $200,000. Prepare a budgeted multiple-step income statement for the year ending December 31, 2022.

*Prepare a budgeted income statement for the year.*

**BE22.9 (LO 4), AP** Kaspar Industries expects credit sales for January, February, and March to be $220,000, $260,000, and $300,000, respectively. It is expected that 75% of the sales will be collected in the month of sale, and 25% will be collected in the following month. Compute cash collections from customers for each month.

*Prepare data for a cash budget.*

**BE22.10 (LO 5), AP** Moore Wholesalers is preparing its merchandise purchases budget. Budgeted sales are $400,000 for April and $480,000 for May. Cost of goods sold is expected to be 65% of sales. The company's desired ending inventory is 20% of the following month's cost of goods sold. Compute the required purchases for April.

*Determine required merchandise purchases for 1 month.*

## DO IT! Exercises

**DO IT! 22.1 (LO 1), K** Use this list of terms to complete the sentences that follow.

*Identify budget terminology.*

| | |
|---|---|
| Long-range plans | Participative budgeting |
| Sales forecast | Operating budgets |
| Master budget | Financial budgets |

1. _____ establish goals for the company's sales and production personnel.
2. The _____ is a set of interrelated budgets that constitutes a plan of action for a specified time period.
3. _____ reduces the risk of having unrealistic budgets.
4. _____ include the cash budget and the budgeted balance sheet.
5. The budget is formed within the framework of a _____.
6. _____ contain considerably less detail than budgets.

**DO IT! 22.2 (LO 2), AP** Pargo Company is preparing its master budget for 2022. Relevant data pertaining to its sales, production and direct materials budgets are as follows.

*Prepare sales, production, and direct materials budgets.*

**Sales.** Sales for the year are expected to total 1,000,000 units. Quarterly sales are 20%, 25%, 25%, and 30%, respectively. The unit selling price is expected to be $40 for the first three quarters and $45 beginning in the fourth quarter. Sales in the first quarter of 2023 are expected to be 20% higher than the budgeted sales for the first quarter of 2022.

**Production.** Management desires to maintain the ending finished goods inventories at 25% of the next quarter's budgeted sales volume.

**Direct materials.** Each unit requires 2 pounds of raw materials at a cost of $12 per pound. Management desires to maintain raw materials inventories at 10% of the next quarter's production requirements. Assume the production requirements for first quarter of 2023 are 450,000 pounds.

Prepare the sales, production, and direct materials budgets by quarters for 2022.

**DO IT! 22.3 (LO 3), AP** Pargo Company is preparing its budgeted income statement for 2022. Relevant data pertaining to its sales, production, and direct materials budgets can be found in **DO IT! 22.2**

*Calculate budgeted total unit cost and prepare budgeted income statement.*

In addition, Pargo budgets 0.3 hours of direct labor per unit, labor costs at $15 per hour, and manufacturing overhead at $20 per direct labor hour. Its budgeted selling and administrative expenses for 2022 are $6,000,000.

a. Calculate the budgeted total unit cost.
b. Prepare the budgeted multiple-step income statement for 2022. (Ignore income taxes.)

**DO IT! 22.4 (LO 4), AP** Batista Company management wants to maintain a minimum monthly cash balance of $25,000. At the beginning of April, the cash balance is $25,000, expected cash receipts for

*Determine amount of financing needed.*

April are $245,000, and cash disbursements are expected to be $255,000. How much cash, if any, must be borrowed to maintain the desired minimum monthly balance?

*Prepare merchandise purchases budget.*

**DO IT! 22.5 (LO 5), AP** Zeller Company estimates that 2022 sales will be $40,000 in quarter 1, $48,000 in quarter 2, and $58,000 in quarter 3. Cost of goods sold is 50% of sales. Management desires to have ending merchandise inventory equal to 10% of the next quarter's expected cost of goods sold. Prepare a merchandise purchases budget by quarter for the first 6 months of 2022.

# Exercises

*Explain the concept of budgeting.*

**E22.1 (LO 1), C** Writing Trusler Company has always done some planning for the future, but the company has never prepared a formal budget. Now that the company is growing larger, it is considering preparing a budget.

**Instructions**

Write a memo to Jim Dixon, the president of Trusler Company, in which you define budgeting, identify the budgets that comprise the master budget, identify the primary benefits of budgeting, and discuss the essentials of effective budgeting.

*Prepare a sales budget for 2 quarters.*

**E22.2 (LO 2), AP** Edington Electronics Inc. produces and sells two models of calculators, XQ-103 and XQ-104. The calculators sell for $15 and $25, respectively. Because of the intense competition Edington faces, management budgets sales semiannually. Its projections for the first 2 quarters of 2022 are as follows.

| | Unit Sales | |
| --- | --- | --- |
| **Product** | **Quarter 1** | **Quarter 2** |
| XQ-103 | 20,000 | 22,000 |
| XQ-104 | 12,000 | 15,000 |

No changes in selling prices are anticipated.

**Instructions**

Prepare a sales budget for the 2 quarters ending June 30, 2022. List the products and show units, selling price, and total sales by product and in total for each quarter and for the 6 months.

*Prepare a sales budget for 4 quarters.*

**E22.3 (LO 2), AP** Service Thome and Crede, CPAs, are preparing their service revenue (sales) budget for the coming year (2022). The practice is divided into three departments: auditing, tax, and consulting. Billable hours for each department, by quarter, are provided here.

| **Department** | **Quarter 1** | **Quarter 2** | **Quarter 3** | **Quarter 4** |
| --- | --- | --- | --- | --- |
| Auditing | 2,300 | 1,600 | 2,000 | 2,400 |
| Tax | 3,000 | 2,200 | 2,000 | 2,500 |
| Consulting | 1,500 | 1,500 | 1,500 | 1,500 |

Average hourly billing rates are auditing $80, tax $90, and consulting $110.

**Instructions**

Prepare the service revenue (sales) budget for 2022 by listing the departments and showing billable hours, billable rate, and total revenue for each quarter and the year in total.

*Prepare quarterly production budgets.*

**E22.4 (LO 2), AP** Turney Company produces and sells automobile batteries, the heavy-duty HD-240. The 2022 sales forecast is as follows.

| Quarter | HD-240 |
| --- | --- |
| 1 | 5,000 |
| 2 | 7,000 |
| 3 | 8,000 |
| 4 | 10,000 |

The January 1, 2022, inventory of HD-240 is 2,000 units. Management desires an ending inventory each quarter equal to 40% of the next quarter's sales. Sales in the first quarter of 2023 are expected to be 25% higher than sales in the same quarter in 2022.

**Instructions**

Prepare quarterly production budgets for each quarter and in total for 2022.

**E22.5 (LO 2), AP** DeWitt Industries has adopted the following production budget for the first 4 months of 2022.

*Prepare a direct materials purchases budget.*

| Month | Units | Month | Units |
| --- | --- | --- | --- |
| January | 10,000 | March | 5,000 |
| February | 8,000 | April | 4,000 |

Each unit requires 2 pounds of raw materials costing $3 per pound. On December 31, 2021, the ending raw materials inventory was 4,000 pounds. Management wants to have a raw materials inventory at the end of the month equal to 20% of next month's production requirements.

**Instructions**

Prepare a direct materials purchases budget by month for the first quarter.

**E22.6 (LO 2), AP** On January 1, 2022, the Hardin Company budget committee has reached agreement on the following data for the 6 months ending June 30, 2022.

*Prepare production and direct materials budgets by quarters for 6 months.*

Sales units: First quarter 5,000, second quarter 6,000, third quarter 7,000.

Ending raw materials inventory: 40% of the next quarter's production requirements.

Ending finished goods inventory: 25% of the next quarter's expected sales units.

Third-quarter production: 7,200 units.

The ending raw materials and finished goods inventories at December 31, 2021, follow the same percentage relationships to production and sales that occur in 2022. Three pounds of raw materials are required to make each unit of finished goods. Raw materials purchased are expected to cost $4 per pound.

**Instructions**

a. Prepare a production budget by quarters for the 6-month period ended June 30, 2022.

b. Prepare a direct materials budget by quarters for the 6-month period ended June 30, 2022.

**E22.7 (LO 2), AP** Rensing Ltd. estimates sales for the second quarter of 2022 will be as follows.

*Calculate raw materials purchases in dollars.*

| Month | Units |
| --- | --- |
| April | 2,550 |
| May | 2,675 |
| June | 2,390 |

The target ending inventory of finished products is as follows.

| | |
| --- | --- |
| March 31 | 2,000 |
| April 30 | 2,230 |
| May 31 | 2,200 |
| June 30 | 2,310 |

Two units of materials are required for each unit of finished product. Production for July is estimated at 2,700 units to start building inventory for the fall sales period. Rensing's policy is to have an inventory of raw materials at the end of each month equal to 50% of the following month's production requirements. Raw materials are expected to cost $4 per unit throughout the period.

**Instructions**

Calculate the May raw materials purchases in dollars.

(CGA adapted)

**E22.8 (LO 2), AP** Fuqua Company's sales budget projects unit sales of part 198Z of 10,000 units in January, 12,000 units in February, and 13,000 units in March. Each unit of part 198Z requires 4 pounds of materials, which cost $2 per pound. Fuqua Company desires its ending raw materials inventory to equal 40% of the next month's production requirements, and its ending finished goods inventory to equal 20% of the next month's expected unit sales. These goals were met at December 31, 2021.

*Prepare a production and a direct materials budget.*

**Instructions**

a. Prepare a production budget for January and February 2022.

b. Prepare a direct materials budget for January 2022.

*Prepare a direct labor budget.*

**E22.9 (LO 3), AP** Rodriguez, Inc., is preparing its direct labor budget for 2022 from the following production budget based on a calendar year.

| Quarter | Units | | Quarter | Units |
|---|---|---|---|---|
| 1 | 20,000 | | 3 | 35,000 |
| 2 | 25,000 | | 4 | 30,000 |

Each unit requires 1.5 hours of direct labor.

**Instructions**

Prepare a direct labor budget for 2022. Wage rates are expected to be $16 for the first 2 quarters and $18 for quarters 3 and 4.

*Prepare production and direct labor budgets.*

**E22.10 (LO 2, 3), AP** Lowell Company makes and sells artistic frames for pictures. The controller is responsible for preparing the master budget and has accumulated the following information for 2022.

| | January | February | March | April | May |
|---|---|---|---|---|---|
| Estimated unit sales | 12,000 | 14,000 | 13,000 | 11,000 | 11,000 |
| Unit selling price | $50.00 | $47.50 | $47.50 | $47.50 | $47.50 |
| Direct labor hours per unit | 2.0 | 2.0 | 1.5 | 1.5 | 1.5 |
| Direct labor cost per hour | $8.00 | $8.00 | $8.00 | $9.00 | $9.00 |

Lowell has a labor contract that calls for a wage increase to $9.00 per hour on April 1. New labor-saving machinery has been installed and will be fully operational by March 1.

Lowell expects to begin the year with 17,600 frames on hand and has a policy of carrying an end-of-month inventory of 100% of the following month's sales, plus 40% of the second following month's sales.

**Instructions**

Prepare a production budget and a direct labor budget for Lowell Company by month and for the first quarter of the year. The direct labor budget should include direct labor hours.

(CMA-Canada adapted)

*Prepare a manufacturing overhead budget for the year.*

**E22.11 (LO 3), AP** Atlanta Company is preparing its manufacturing overhead budget for 2022. Relevant data consist of the following.

Units to be produced (by quarters): 10,000, 12,000, 14,000, 16,000.

Direct labor: time is 1.5 hours per unit.

Variable overhead costs per direct labor hour: indirect materials $0.80, indirect labor $1.20, and maintenance $0.50.

Fixed overhead costs per quarter: supervisory salaries $41,250, depreciation $15,000, and maintenance $12,000.

**Instructions**

Prepare the manufacturing overhead budget for the year, showing quarterly data.

*Prepare a selling and administrative expense budget for 2 quarters.*

**E22.12 (LO 3), AP** Kirkland Company combines its operating expenses for budget purposes in a selling and administrative expense budget. For the first 6 months of 2022, the following data are available.

1. Sales: 20,000 units quarter 1; 22,000 units quarter 2.

2. Variable costs per dollar of sales: sales commissions 5%, delivery expense 2%, and advertising 3%.

3. Fixed costs per quarter: sales salaries $12,000, office salaries $8,000, depreciation $4,200, insurance $1,500, utilities $800, and repairs expense $500.

4. Unit selling price: $20.

**Instructions**

Prepare a selling and administrative expense budget by quarters for the first 6 months of 2022.

**E22.13 (LO 3), AP** Fultz Company has accumulated the following budget data for the year 2022.

*Prepare a budgeted income statement for the year.*

1. Sales: 30,000 units, unit selling price $85.

2. Cost of one unit of finished goods: direct materials 1 pound at $5 per pound, direct labor 3 hours at $15 per hour, and manufacturing overhead $5 per direct labor hour.

3. Inventories (raw materials only): beginning, 10,000 pounds; ending, 15,000 pounds.

4. Selling and administrative expenses: $170,000; interest expense: $30,000.

5. Income taxes: 20% of income before income taxes.

**Instructions**

a. Prepare a schedule showing the computation of cost of goods sold for 2022.

b. Prepare a budgeted multiple-step income statement for 2022.

**E22.14 (LO 4), AP** Danner Company expects to have a cash balance of $45,000 on January 1, 2022. Relevant monthly budget data for the first 2 months of 2022 are as follows.

*Prepare a cash budget for 2 months.*

Collections from customers: January $85,000, February $150,000.

Payments for direct materials: January $50,000, February $75,000.

Direct labor: January $30,000, February $45,000. Wages are paid in the month they are incurred.

Manufacturing overhead: January $21,000, February $25,000. These costs include depreciation of $1,500 per month. All other overhead costs are paid as incurred.

Selling and administrative expenses: January $15,000, February $20,000. These costs are exclusive of depreciation. They are paid as incurred.

Sales of marketable securities in January are expected to realize $12,000 in cash. Danner Company has a line of credit at a local bank that enables it to borrow up to $25,000. The company wants to maintain a minimum monthly cash balance of $20,000.

**Instructions**

Prepare a cash budget for January and February.

**E22.15 (LO 4), AP** Deitz Corporation is projecting a cash balance of $30,000 in its December 31, 2021, balance sheet. Deitz's schedule of expected collections from customers for the first quarter of 2022 shows total collections of $185,000. The schedule of expected payments for direct materials for the first quarter of 2022 shows total payments of $43,000. Other information gathered for the first quarter of 2022 is sale of equipment $3,000, direct labor $70,000, manufacturing overhead $35,000, selling and administrative expenses $45,000, and purchase of securities $14,000. Deitz wants to maintain a balance of at least $25,000 cash at the end of each quarter.

*Prepare a cash budget.*

**Instructions**

Prepare a cash budget for the first quarter.

**E22.16 (LO 4), AN** The controller of Trenshaw Company wants to improve the company's control system by preparing a month-by-month cash budget. The following information is for the month ending July 31, 2022.

*Prepare cash budget for a month.*

| | |
|---|---|
| June 30, 2022, cash balance | $45,000 |
| Dividends to be declared on July 15* | 12,000 |
| Cash expenditures to be paid in July for operating expenses | 40,800 |
| Amortization expense in July | 4,500 |
| Cash collections to be received in July | 90,000 |
| Merchandise purchases to be paid in cash in July | 56,200 |
| Equipment to be purchased for cash in July | 20,000 |

*Dividends are payable 30 days after declaration to shareholders of record on the declaration date.

Trenshaw Company wants to keep a minimum cash balance of $25,000.

**Instructions**

a. Prepare a cash budget for the month ended July 31, 2022, and indicate how much money, if any, Trenshaw Company will need to borrow to meet its minimum cash requirement.

b. Explain how cash budgeting can reduce the cost of short-term borrowing.

(CGA adapted)

*Prepare schedules of expected collections and payments.*

**E22.17 (LO 4), AP** Nieto Company's budgeted sales and direct materials purchases are as follows.

| | Budgeted Sales | Budgeted D.M. Purchases |
|---|---|---|
| January | $200,000 | $30,000 |
| February | 220,000 | 36,000 |
| March | 250,000 | 38,000 |

Nieto's sales are 30% cash and 70% credit. Credit sales are collected 10% in the month of sale, 50% in the month following sale, and 36% in the second month following sale; 4% are uncollectible. Nieto's purchases are 50% cash and 50% on account. Purchases on account are paid 40% in the month of purchase, and 60% in the month following purchase.

**Instructions**

a. Prepare a schedule of expected collections from customers for March.

b. Prepare a schedule of expected payments for direct materials for March.

*Prepare schedules for cash receipts and cash payments, and determine ending balances for balance sheet.*

**E22.18 (LO 4, 5), AP** Service Green Landscaping Inc. is preparing its budget for the first quarter of 2022. The next step in the budgeting process is to prepare a cash receipts schedule and a cash payments schedule. To that end, the following information has been collected.

Clients usually pay 60% of their fee in the month that service is performed, 30% the month after, and 10% the second month after receiving service.

Actual service revenue for 2021 and expected service revenues for 2022 are November 2021, $80,000; December 2021, $90,000; January 2022, $100,000; February 2022, $120,000; and March 2022, $140,000.

Purchases of landscaping supplies (direct materials) are paid 60% in the month of purchase and 40% the following month. Actual purchases for 2021 and expected purchases for 2022 are December 2021, $14,000; January 2022, $12,000; February 2022, $15,000; and March 2022, $18,000.

**Instructions**

a. Prepare the following schedules for each month in the first quarter of 2022 and for the quarter in total:

   1. Expected collections from clients.

   2. Expected payments for landscaping supplies.

b. Determine the following balances at March 31, 2022:

   1. Accounts receivable.

   2. Accounts payable.

*Prepare a cash budget for 2 quarters.*

**E22.19 (LO 4, 5), AP** Service Pletcher Dental Clinic is a medium-sized dental service specializing in family dental care. The clinic is currently preparing the master budget for the first 2 quarters of 2022. All that remains in this process is the cash budget. The following information has been collected from other portions of the master budget and elsewhere.

| | |
|---|---|
| Beginning cash balance | $ 30,000 |
| Required minimum cash balance | 25,000 |
| Payment of income taxes (2nd quarter) | 4,000 |
| Professional salaries: | |
| 1st quarter | 140,000 |
| 2nd quarter | 140,000 |
| Interest from investments (2nd quarter) | 7,000 |
| Overhead costs: | |
| 1st quarter | 77,000 |
| 2nd quarter | 100,000 |
| Selling and administrative costs, including | |
| $2,000 depreciation: | |
| 1st quarter | 50,000 |
| 2nd quarter | 70,000 |
| Purchase of equipment (2nd quarter) | 50,000 |
| Sale of equipment (1st quarter) | 12,000 |
| Collections from patients: | |
| 1st quarter | 235,000 |
| 2nd quarter | 380,000 |
| Interest payments (2nd quarter) | 200 |

**Instructions**

Prepare a cash budget for each of the first two quarters of 2022.

**E22.20 (LO 5), AP** Service In May 2022, the budget committee of Grand Stores assembles the following data in preparation of budgeted merchandise purchases for the month of June.

1. Expected sales: June $500,000, July $600,000.

2. Cost of goods sold is expected to be 75% of sales.

3. Desired ending merchandise inventory is 30% of the following (next) month's cost of goods sold.

4. The beginning inventory at June 1 will be the desired amount.

*Prepare a purchases budget and budgeted income statement for a merchandiser.*

**Instructions**

a. Compute the budgeted merchandise purchases for June.

b. Prepare the budgeted multiple-step income statement for June through gross profit.

**E22.21 (LO 5), AP** Emeric and Ellie's Painting Service estimates that it will paint 10 small homes, 5 medium homes, and 2 large homes during the month of June 2022. The company estimates its direct labor needs as 40 hours per small home, 70 hours for a medium home, and 120 hours for a large home. Its average cost for direct labor is $18 per hour.

*Prepare a direct labor budget for a service company.*

**Instructions**

Prepare a direct labor budget for Emeric and Ellie's Painting Service for June 2022.

## Problems

**P22.1 (LO 2, 3), AP** Cook Farm Supply Company manufactures and sells a pesticide called Snare. The following data are available for preparing budgets for Snare for the first 2 quarters of 2022.

*Prepare budgeted income statement and supporting budgets.*

1. Sales: quarter 1, 40,000 bags; quarter 2, 56,000 bags. Selling price is $60 per bag.

2. Direct materials: each bag of Snare requires 4 pounds of Gumm at a cost of $3.80 per pound and 6 pounds of Tarr at $1.50 per pound.

3. Desired inventory levels

| Type of Inventory | January 1 | April 1 | July 1 |
|---|---|---|---|
| Snare (bags) | 8,000 | 15,000 | 18,000 |
| Gumm (pounds) | 9,000 | 10,000 | 13,000 |
| Tarr (pounds) | 14,000 | 20,000 | 25,000 |

4. Direct labor: direct labor time is 15 minutes per bag at an hourly rate of $16 per hour.

5. Selling and administrative expenses are expected to be 15% of sales plus $175,000 per quarter.

6. Interest expense is $100,000 for the 2 quarters.

7. Income taxes are expected to be 20% of income before income taxes.

Your assistant has prepared two budgets: (1) the manufacturing overhead budget shows expected costs to be 125% of direct labor cost, and (2) the direct materials budget for Tarr shows the cost of Tarr purchases to be $297,000 in quarter 1 and $439,500 in quarter 2.

**Instructions**

Prepare the budgeted multiple-step income statement for the first 6 months and all required operating budgets by quarters. (*Note:* Use variable and fixed in the selling and administrative expense budget.) Do not prepare the manufacturing overhead budget or the direct materials budget for Tarr.

Net income $1,007,040
Cost per bag $33.20

**P22.2 (LO 2, 3), AP** Deleon Inc. is preparing its annual budgets for the year ending December 31, 2022. Accounting assistants furnish the following data.

*Prepare sales, production, direct materials, direct labor, and income statement budgets.*

| | Product JB 50 | Product JB 60 |
|---|---|---|
| Sales budget: | | |
| Anticipated volume in units | 400,000 | 200,000 |
| Unit selling price | $20 | $25 |
| Production budget: | | |
| Desired ending finished goods units | 30,000 | 15,000 |
| Beginning finished goods units | 25,000 | 10,000 |

| | Product JB 50 | Product JB 60 |
|---|---|---|
| Direct materials budget: | | |
| Direct materials per unit (pounds) | 2 | 3 |
| Desired ending direct materials pounds | 30,000 | 10,000 |
| Beginning direct materials pounds | 40,000 | 15,000 |
| Cost per pound | $3 | $4 |
| Direct labor budget: | | |
| Direct labor time per unit | 0.4 | 0.6 |
| Direct labor rate per hour | $12 | $12 |
| Budgeted income statement: | | |
| Total unit cost | $13 | $20 |

An accounting assistant has prepared the detailed manufacturing overhead budget and the selling and administrative expense budget. The latter shows selling expenses of $560,000 for product JB 50 and $360,000 for product JB 60, and administrative expenses of $540,000 for product JB 50 and $340,000 for product JB 60. Interest expense is $150,000 (not allocated to products). Income taxes are expected to be 20%.

a. Total sales $13,000,000
b. Required production units:
   JB 50, 405,000
   JB 60, 205,000
c. Total cost of direct materials purchases $4,840,000
d. Total direct labor cost $3,420,000
e. Net income $1,480,000

### Instructions

Prepare the following budgets for the year. Show data for each product. Quarterly budgets should not be prepared.

a. Sales.

b. Production.

c. Direct materials.

d. Direct labor.

e. Multiple-step income statement (*Note:* income taxes are not allocated to the products).

*Prepare sales and production budgets and compute cost per unit under two plans.*

**P22.3 (LO 2), E** Hill Industries had sales in 2021 of $6,800,000 and gross profit of $1,100,000. Management is considering two alternative budget plans to increase its gross profit in 2022.

Plan A would increase the unit selling price from $8.00 to $8.40. Sales volume would decrease by 125,000 units from its 2021 level. Plan B would decrease the unit selling price by $0.50. The marketing department expects that the sales volume would increase by 130,000 units.

At the end of 2021, Hill has 40,000 units of inventory on hand. If Plan A is accepted, the 2022 ending inventory should be 35,000 units. If Plan B is accepted, the ending inventory should be 60,000 units. Each unit produced will cost $1.50 in direct labor, $1.30 in direct materials, and $1.20 in variable overhead. The fixed overhead for 2022 should be $1,895,000.

### Instructions

c. Unit cost: Plan A $6.63
   Plan B $5.90
d. Gross profit:
   Plan A $1,283,250
   Plan B $1,568,000

a. Prepare a sales budget for 2022 under each plan.

b. Prepare a production budget for 2022 under each plan.

c. Compute the production cost per unit under each plan. Why is the cost per unit different for the two plans? (Round to two decimals.)

d. Which plan should be accepted? (*Hint:* Compute the gross profit under each plan.)

*Prepare cash budget for 2 months.*

**P22.4 (LO 4), AP** Colter Company prepares monthly cash budgets. Relevant data from operating budgets for 2022 are as follows.

| | January | February |
|---|---|---|
| Sales | $360,000 | $400,000 |
| Direct materials purchases | 120,000 | 125,000 |
| Direct labor | 90,000 | 100,000 |
| Manufacturing overhead | 70,000 | 75,000 |
| Selling and administrative expenses | 79,000 | 85,000 |

All sales are on account. Collections are expected to be 50% in the month of sale, 30% in the first month following the sale, and 20% in the second month following the sale. Sixty percent (60%) of direct materials purchases are paid in cash in the month of purchase, and the balance due is paid in the month following the purchase. All other items above are paid in the month incurred except for selling and administrative expenses, which include $1,000 of depreciation per month.

Other data:

1. Credit sales: November 2021, $250,000; December 2021, $320,000.

2. Purchases of direct materials: December 2021, $100,000.

3. Other receipts: January—collection of December 31, 2021, notes receivable $15,000; February—proceeds from sale of securities $6,000.

4. Other disbursements: February—payment of $6,000 cash dividend.

The company's cash balance on January 1, 2022, is expected to be $60,000. The company wants to maintain a minimum cash balance of $50.000.

**Instructions**

a. Prepare schedules for (1) expected collections from customers and (2) expected payments for direct materials purchases for January and February.

b. Prepare a cash budget for January and February in columnar form.

**P22.5 (LO 5), AP** The budget committee of Suppar Company collects the following data for its San Miguel Store in preparing budgeted income statements for May and June 2022.

1. Sales for May are expected to be $800,000. Sales in June and July are expected to be 5% higher than the preceding month.

2. Cost of goods sold is expected to be 75% of sales.

3. Company policy is to maintain ending merchandise inventory at 10% of the following month's cost of goods sold.

4. Operating expenses are estimated to be as follows:

| | |
|---|---|
| Sales salaries | $35,000 per month |
| Advertising | 6% of monthly sales |
| Delivery expense | 2% of monthly sales |
| Sales commissions | 5% of monthly sales |
| Rent expense | $5,000 per month |
| Depreciation | $800 per month |
| Utilities | $600 per month |
| Insurance | $500 per month |

5. Interest expense is $2,000 per month. Income taxes are estimated to be 20% of income before income taxes.

**Instructions**

a. Prepare the merchandise purchases budget for each month in columnar form.

b. Prepare budgeted multiple-step income statements for each month in columnar form. Show in the statements the details of cost of goods sold.

**P22.6 (LO 3, 4), AP** Krause Industries' balance sheet at December 31, 2021, is presented here.

**Krause Industries**
**Balance Sheet**
**December 31, 2021**

**Assets**

| | | |
|---|---|---|
| Current assets | | |
| Cash | | $ 7,500 |
| Accounts receivable | | 73,500 |
| Finished goods inventory (1,500 units) | | 24,000 |
| Total current assets | | 105,000 |
| Property, plant, and equipment | | |
| Equipment | $40,000 | |
| Less: Accumulated depreciation | 10,000 | 30,000 |
| Total assets | | $135,000 |

**Liabilities and Stockholders' Equity**

| | | |
|---|---|---|
| Liabilities | | |
| Notes payable | | $ 25,000 |
| Accounts payable | | 45,000 |
| Total liabilities | | 70,000 |
| Stockholders' equity | | |
| Common stock | $40,000 | |
| Retained earnings | 25,000 | |
| Total stockholders' equity | | 65,000 |
| Total liabilities and stockholders' equity | | $135,000 |

*Side margin notes:*

a. January: collections $326,000; payments $112,000

b. Ending cash balance: January $51,000 February $50,000

*Prepare purchases and income statement budgets for a merchandiser.*

a. Purchases: May $603,000 June $633,150

b. Net income: May $41,680 June $45,520

*Prepare budgeted cost of goods sold, income statement, retained earnings, and balance sheet.*

Budgeted data for the year 2022 include the following.

|  | 2022 | |
|---|---|---|
|  | **Quarter 4** | **Total** |
| Sales budget (8,000 units at $32) | $76,800 | $256,000 |
| Direct materials used | 17,000 | 62,500 |
| Direct labor | 12,500 | 50,900 |
| Manufacturing overhead applied | 10,000 | 48,600 |
| Selling and administrative expenses | 18,000 | 75,000 |

To meet sales requirements and to have 2,500 units of finished goods on hand at December 31, 2022, the production budget shows 9,000 required units of output. The total unit cost of production is expected to be $18. Krause uses the first-in, first-out (FIFO) inventory costing method. Interest expense is expected to be $3,500 for the year. Income taxes are expected to be 20% of income before income taxes. In 2022, the company expects to declare and pay an $8,000 cash dividend.

The company's cash budget shows an expected cash balance of $13,180 at December 31, 2022. All sales and purchases are on account. It is expected that 60% of quarterly sales are collected in cash within the quarter and the remainder is collected in the following quarter. Direct materials purchased from suppliers are paid 50% in the quarter incurred and the remainder in the following quarter. Purchases in the fourth quarter were the same as the materials used. In 2022, the company expects to purchase additional equipment costing $9,000. A total of $4,000 of depreciation expense on equipment is included in the budget data and split equally between manufacturing overhead and selling and administrative expenses. Krause expects to pay $8,000 on the outstanding notes payable balance plus all interest due and payable to December 31 (included in interest expense $3,500, above). Accounts payable at December 31, 2022, includes amounts due suppliers (see above) plus other accounts payable relating to manufacturing overhead of $7,200. Unpaid income taxes at December 31 will be $5,000.

**Instructions**

Net income $29,200
Total assets $123,900

Prepare a budgeted statement of cost of goods sold, budgeted multiple-step income statement, and retained earnings statement for 2022, and a budgeted classified balance sheet at December 31, 2022.

## Continuing Cases

### Current Designs

**CD22** Diane Buswell is preparing the 2022 budget for one of **Current Designs**' rotomolded kayaks. Extensive meetings with members of the sales department and executive team have resulted in the following unit sales projections for 2022.

| | |
|---|---|
| Quarter 1 | 1,000 kayaks |
| Quarter 2 | 1,500 kayaks |
| Quarter 3 | 750 kayaks |
| Quarter 4 | 750 kayaks |

Current Designs' policy is to have finished goods ending inventory in a quarter equal to 20% of the next quarter's anticipated sales. Preliminary sales projections for 2023 are 1,100 units for the first quarter and 1,500 units for the second quarter. Ending inventory of finished goods at December 31, 2021, will be 200 rotomolded kayaks.

Production of each kayak requires 54 pounds of polyethylene powder and a finishing kit (rope, seat, hardware, etc.). Company policy is that the ending inventory of polyethylene powder should be 25% of the amount needed for production in the next quarter. Assume that the ending inventory of polyethylene powder on December 31, 2021, is 19,400 pounds. The finishing kits can be assembled as they are needed. As a result, Current Designs does not maintain a significant inventory of the finishing kits.

The polyethylene powder used in these kayaks costs $1.50 per pound, and the finishing kits cost $170 each. Production of a single kayak requires 2 hours of time by more experienced, type I employees and 3 hours of finishing time by type II employees. The type I employees are paid $15 per hour, and the type II employees are paid $12 per hour.

Selling and administrative expenses for this line are expected to be $45 per unit sold plus $7,500 per quarter. Manufacturing overhead is assigned at 150% of labor costs.

**Instructions**

Prepare the production budget, direct materials budget, direct labor budget, manufacturing overhead budget, and selling and administrative budget for this product line by quarter and in total for 2022.

## Waterways Corporation

(*Note:* This is a continuation of the Waterways case from Chapters 14–21.)

**WC22** Waterways Corporation is preparing its budget for the coming year, 2022. The first step is to plan for the first quarter of that coming year. The company has gathered information from its managers in preparation of the budgeting process. This case asks you to prepare the various budgets that comprise the master budget for 2022.

*Go to WileyPLUS for complete case details and instructions.*

## Comprehensive Cases

**CC22.1** Service  Auburn Circular Club is planning a major fundraiser that it hopes will become a successful annual event: sponsoring a professional rodeo. For this case, you will encounter many managerial accounting issues that would be common for a start-up business, such as CVP analysis (Chapter 18), incremental analysis (Chapter 20), and budgetary planning (this chapter).

**CC22.2** Sweats Galore is a new business venture that will make custom sweatshirts using a silk-screen process. In helping the company's owner, Michael Woods, set up his business, you will have the opportunity to apply your understanding of CVP relationships (Chapter 18) and budgetary planning (this chapter).

*Go to WileyPLUS for complete details and instructions for both cases.*

## Data Analytics in Action

### Data Analytics at HydroHappy

**DA22**  HydroHappy has developed a new marketing plan that looks very promising for increased sales for the upcoming summer months. The biggest concern is that the production facility will not have the capacity to handle the additional production needed. For this case, you will generate Excel pivot tables and pivot line charts to analyze company capacity for estimated increased production levels.

 Excel

*Go to WileyPLUS for complete case details and instruction*

## Expand Your Critical Thinking

### Decision-Making Across the Organization

**CT22.1** Palmer Corporation operates on a calendar-year basis. It begins the annual budgeting process in late August when the president establishes targets for the total dollar sales and net income before taxes for the next year.

The sales target is given first to the marketing department. The marketing manager formulates a sales budget by product line in both units and dollars. From this budget, sales quotas by product line in units and dollars are established for each of the corporation's sales districts. The marketing manager also estimates the cost of the marketing activities required to support the target sales volume and prepares a tentative marketing expense budget.

The executive vice president uses the sales and profit targets, the sales budget by product line, and the tentative marketing expense budget to determine the dollar amounts that can be devoted to manufacturing and corporate office expense. The executive vice president prepares the budget for corporate expenses. She then forwards to the production department the product-line sales budget in units and the total dollar amount that can be devoted to manufacturing.

The production manager meets with the factory managers to develop a manufacturing plan that will produce the required units when needed within the cost constraints set by the executive vice president. The budgeting process usually comes to a halt at this point because the production department does not consider the financial resources allocated to be adequate.

When this standstill occurs, the vice president of finance, the executive vice president, the marketing manager, and the production manager meet together to determine the final budgets for each of the areas. This normally results in a modest increase in the total amount available for manufacturing costs and cuts in the marketing expense and corporate office expense budgets. The total sales and net income figures proposed by the president are seldom changed. Although the participants are seldom pleased with the compromise, these budgets are final. Each executive then develops a new detailed budget for the operations in his or her area.

None of the areas has achieved its budget in recent years. Sales often run below the target. When budgeted sales are not achieved, each area is expected to cut costs so that the president's profit target can be met. However, the profit target is seldom met because costs are not cut enough. In fact, costs often run above the original budget in all functional areas (marketing, production, and corporate office).

The president is disturbed that Palmer has not been able to meet the sales and profit targets. He hires a consultant with considerable experience with companies in Palmer's industry. The consultant reviews the budgets for the past 4 years. He concludes that the product line sales budgets were reasonable and that the cost and expense budgets were adequate for the budgeted sales and production levels.

### Instructions

With the class divided into groups, complete the following.

a. Discuss how the budgeting process employed by Palmer Corporation contributes to the failure to achieve the president's sales and profit targets.

b. Suggest how Palmer Corporation's budgeting process could be revised to correct the problems.

c. Should the functional areas be expected to cut their costs when sales volume falls below budget? Explain your answer.

(CMA adapted)

## Managerial Analysis

**CT22.2** Elliot & Hesse Inc. manufactures ergonomic devices for computer users. Some of its more popular products include anti-glare filters and privacy filters (for computer monitors) and keyboard stands with wrist rests. Over the past 5 years, it experienced rapid growth, with sales of all products increasing 20% to 50% each year.

Last year, some of the primary manufacturers of computers began introducing new products with some of the ergonomic designs, such as anti-glare filters and wrist rests, already built in. As a result, sales of Elliot & Hesse's accessory devices have declined somewhat. The company believes that the privacy filters will probably continue to show growth, but that the other products will probably continue to decline. When the next year's budget was prepared, increases were built into research and development so that replacement products could be developed or the company could expand into some other product line. Some product lines being considered are general-purpose ergonomic devices including back supports, foot rests, and sloped writing pads.

The most recent results have shown that sales decreased more than was expected for the anti-glare filters. As a result, the company may have a shortage of funds. Top management has therefore asked that all expenses be reduced 10% to compensate for these reduced sales. Summary budget information is as follows.

| | |
|---|---:|
| Direct materials | $240,000 |
| Direct labor | 110,000 |
| Insurance | 50,000 |
| Depreciation | 90,000 |
| Machine repairs | 30,000 |
| Sales salaries | 50,000 |
| Office salaries | 80,000 |
| Factory salaries (indirect labor) | 50,000 |
| Total | $700,000 |

## Instructions

Using the information above, answer the following questions.

a. What are the implications of reducing each of the costs? For example, if the company reduces direct materials costs, it may have to do so by purchasing lower-quality materials. This may affect sales in the long run.

b. Based on your analysis in (a), what do you think is the best way to obtain the $70,000 in cost savings requested? Be specific. Are there any costs that cannot or should not be reduced? Why?

## Real-World Focus

**CT22.3** Information regarding many approaches to budgeting can be found online. The following activity investigates the merits of "zero-based" budgeting, as discussed by Michael LaFaive, Director of Fiscal Policy of the **Mackinac Center for Public Policy**.

### Instructions

Read the article at the Mackinac website and then answer the following questions.

a. How does zero-based budgeting differ from standard budgeting procedures?

b. What are some potential advantages of zero-based budgeting?

c. What are some potential disadvantages of zero-based budgeting?

d. How often do departments in Oklahoma undergo zero-based budgeting?

## Communication Activity

**CT22.4** Service In order to better serve their rural patients, Drs. Joe and Rick Parcells (brothers) began giving safety seminars. Especially popular were their "emergency-preparedness" talks given to farmers. Many people asked whether the "kit" of materials the doctors recommended for common farm emergencies was commercially available.

After checking with several suppliers, the doctors realized that no other company offered the supplies they recommended in their seminars, packaged in the way they described. Their wives, Megan and Sue, agreed to make a test package by ordering supplies from various medical supply companies and assembling them into a "kit" that could be sold at the seminars. When these kits proved a runaway success, the sisters-in-law decided to market them. At the advice of their accountant, they organized this venture as a separate company, called Life Protection Products (LPP), with Megan Parcells as CEO and Sue Parcells as Secretary-Treasurer.

LPP soon started receiving requests for the kits from all over the country, as word spread about their availability. Even without advertising, LPP was able to sell its full inventory every month. However, the company was becoming financially strained. Megan and Sue had about $100,000 in savings, and they invested about half that amount initially. They believed that this venture would allow them to make money. However, at the present time, only about $30,000 of the cash remains, and the company is constantly short of cash.

Megan has come to you for advice. She does not understand why the company is having cash flow problems. She and Sue have not even been withdrawing salaries. However, they have rented a local building and have hired two more full-time workers to help them cope with the increasing demand. They do not think they could handle the demand without this additional help.

Megan is also worried that the cash problems mean that the company may not be able to support itself. She has prepared the cash budget shown below. All seminar customers pay for their products in full at the time of purchase. In addition, several large companies have ordered the kits for use by employees who work in remote sites. They have requested credit terms and have been allowed to pay in the month following the sale. These large purchasers amount to about 25% of the sales at the present time. LPP purchases the materials for the kits about 2 months ahead of time. Megan and Sue are considering slowing the growth of the company by simply purchasing less materials, which will mean selling fewer kits.

The workers are paid weekly. Megan and Sue need about $15,000 cash on hand at the beginning of the month to pay for purchases of raw materials. Right now they have been using cash from their savings, but as noted, only $30,000 is left.

**Life Protection Products**
**Cash Budget**
**For the Quarter Ending June 30, 2022**

|  | April | May | June |
|---|---|---|---|
| Cash balance, beginning | $15,000 | $15,000 | $15,000 |
| Cash received |  |  |  |
|    From prior month sales | 5,000 | 7,500 | 12,500 |
|    From current sales | 15,000 | 22,500 | 37,500 |
| Total cash on hand | 35,000 | 45,000 | 65,000 |
| Cash payments |  |  |  |
|    To employees | 3,000 | 3,000 | 3,000 |
|    For products | 25,000 | 35,000 | 45,000 |
|    Miscellaneous expenses | 5,000 | 6,000 | 7,000 |
|    Postage | 1,000 | 1,000 | 1,000 |
| Total cash payments | 34,000 | 45,000 | 56,000 |
| Cash balance | $ 1,000 | $ 0 | $ 9,000 |
| Borrow from savings | $14,000 | $15,000 | $ 1,000 |
| Borrow from bank? | $ 0 | $ 0 | $ 5,000 |

**Instructions**

Write a response to Megan Parcells. Explain why LPP is short of cash. Will this company be able to support itself? Explain your answer. Make any recommendations you deem appropriate.

## Ethics Case

**CT22.5** You are an accountant in the budgetary, projections, and special projects department of Fernetti Conductor, Inc., a large manufacturing company. The president, Richard Brown, asks you on very short notice to prepare some sales and income projections covering the next 2 years of the company's much-heralded new product lines. He wants these projections for a series of speeches he is making while on a 2-week trip to eight East Coast brokerage firms. The president hopes to bolster Fernetti's stock sales and price.

    You work 23 hours in 2 days to compile the projections, hand-deliver them to the president, and are swiftly but graciously thanked as he departs. A week later, you find time to go over some of your computations and discover a miscalculation that makes the projections grossly overstated. You quickly inquire about the president's itinerary and learn that he has made half of his speeches and has half yet to make. You are in a quandary as to what to do.

**Instructions**

a. What are the consequences of telling the president of your gross miscalculations?

b. What are the consequences of not telling the president of your gross miscalculations?

c. What are the ethical considerations to you and the president in this situation?

## All About You

**CT22.6** In order to get your personal finances under control, you need to prepare a personal budget. Assume that you have compiled the following information regarding your expected cash flows for a typical month.

| | | | |
|---|---|---|---|
| Rent payment | $ 500 | Miscellaneous costs | $210 |
| Interest income | 50 | Savings | 50 |
| Income tax withheld | 300 | Eating out | 150 |
| Electricity bill | 85 | Telephone and Internet costs | 125 |
| Groceries | 100 | Student loan payments | 375 |
| Wages earned | 2,500 | Entertainment costs | 250 |
| Insurance | 100 | Transportation costs | 150 |

**Instructions**

Using the information above, prepare a personal budget. In preparing this budget, use the format included in the "Steps to Creating a Household Budget" article available at **the balance**'s website (go to the site and do a search for the article). Just skip any unused line items.

## Considering Your Costs and Benefits

**CT22.7** You might hear people say that they "need to learn to live within a budget." The funny thing is that most people who say this haven't actually prepared a personal budget, nor do they intend to. Instead, what they are referring to is a vaguely defined, poorly specified collection of rough ideas of how much they should spend on various aspects of their lives. However, you can't live within or even outside of something that doesn't exist. With that in mind, let's take a look at one aspect of personal-budget templates.

Many personal-budget worksheet templates that are provided for college students treat student loans as an income source. See, for example, the template included in the "Steps to Creating a Household Budget" article available at **the balance**'s website. Based on your knowledge of accounting, is this correct?

**YES:** Student loans provide a source of cash, which can be used to pay costs. As the saying goes, "It all spends the same." Therefore, student loans are income.

**NO:** Student loans must eventually be repaid; therefore, they are not income. As the name indicates, they are loans.

### Instructions

Write a response indicating your position regarding this situation. Provide support for your view.

## Answers to Insight and Accounting Across the Organization Questions

**Businesses Often Feel Too Busy to Plan for the Future  Q:** Describe a situation in which a business "sells as much as it can" but cannot "keep its employees paid."  **A:** It may come as a surprise to some that companies that are experiencing rapid sales growth often have inadequate cash to pay their employees. This occurs because the company must buy increasingly large amounts of supplies, equipment, and inventory to meet anticipated increased demand. But, the cash the company is collecting is based on its lower sales levels in the past. As a consequence, even though the company's sales are growing, the company might fail due to inadequate cash to pay its employees. Thus, it is especially important for rapidly growing businesses to prepare budgets.

**The Implications of Budgetary Optimism  Q:** Why is it important that government budgets accurately estimate future revenues during economic downturns?  **A:** Accuracy of government revenue estimates is especially important during economic downturns because most governments must balance their budgets. If anticipated revenues in one period do not match expectations, then the shortfall must be made up in the next period. This can result in much steeper, more disruptive cuts than might have been necessary had the government anticipated the revenue decline more accurately and consequently started cutting expenditures sooner.

**Betting That Prices Won't Fall  Q:** What are the potential downsides of stockpiling a huge amount of raw materials?  **A:** If prices continue to go up, these managers will avoid paying higher prices until their inventory runs out. However, it is a risky strategy. First, prices fluctuate. If a price goes up by 90% in a year, it can also go down by 90%. If this happens, the managers will be stuck with overpriced raw materials. Second, if the economy slows down, it might take a lot longer to sell their inventory than the managers had planned. There are many costs associated with holding large quantities of inventory. The additional storage, insurance, and handling costs can be very expensive, and obsolescence can occur.

**That's Some Tasty Data!  Q:** Why are flexibility and ease of use important to this application of big data and data analytics?  **A:** Flexibility and ease of use are important for a couple of reasons. First, the company operates stores in different regions of the country. Customer tastes can vary, so what is optimal in one area might not be in another. Second, the technological skillset of employees at different levels and positions in the company can vary a lot. In order to be most useful, it is important that the system be able to collect data from and provide data to all relevant employees, no matter their technological abilities.

**Starting from Scratch  Q:** What are some of the pros and cons of zero-based budgeting?  **A:** Proponents of zero-based budgeting point toward its success at reducing wasteful spending by questioning the necessity of every expenditure. But critics point toward instances where zero-based budgeting has devastated employee morale, resulted in large employee layoffs, and stifled company growth.

**Budget Shortfalls as Far as the Eye Can See  Q:** Why would a university's budgeted scholarships probably fall when the stock market suffers a serious drop?  **A:** Scholarships typically cannot be paid out of the "principal" portion of donations made to scholarship endowment funds. Instead, scholarships are usually funded through earnings generated by endowment investments. Any excess earnings above current-year scholarship needs can be used for scholarships in subsequent years. But a serious drop in the value of endowment investments can wipe out previous earnings, in some cases completely eliminating funds available for scholarships.

## CHAPTER 23

Edvard Nalbantjan/Shutterstock.com

# Budgetary Control and Responsibility Accounting

## Chapter Preview

In Chapter 22, we discussed the use of budgets for planning. We now consider how budgets are used by management to control operations. In the following Feature Story on **The Roxy Hotel Tribeca**, we see that management uses the budget to adapt to the business environment. This chapter focuses on two aspects of management control: (1) budgetary control and (2) responsibility accounting.

## Feature Story

### Pumpkin Madeleines and a Movie

Perhaps no place in the world has a wider variety of distinctive, high-end accommodations than New York City. It's tough to set yourself apart in the Big Apple, but unique is what **The Roxy Hotel Tribeca** is all about.

When you walk through the doors of this triangular-shaped building, nestled in one of Manhattan's most affluent neighborhoods, you immediately encounter a striking eight-story atrium. Although the hotel was completely renovated, it still maintains its funky mid-century charm. Just consider the always hip hotel bar. Besides serving up cocktails until 2 a.m., the bar also provides food. These are not the run-of-the-mill, chain-hotel, borderline edibles. The chef is famous for tantalizing delectables such as duck rillettes, sea salt baked branzino, housemade pappardelle, and pumpkin madeleines.

Another thing that really sets the hotel apart is its private screening room. As a guest, you can enjoy plush leather seating, state-of-the-art projection, and digital surround sound, all while viewing a cult classic from the hotel's film series. In fact, on Sundays, free screenings are available to guests and non-guests alike on a first-come-first-served basis.

To attract and satisfy a discerning clientele, The Roxy Hotel Tribeca's management incurs higher and more unpredictable costs than those of a standard hotel. As fun as it might be to run a high-end hotel, management cannot be cavalier about spending money. To maintain profitability, management closely monitors costs and revenues to make sure that they track with budgeted amounts. Further, because of unexpected fluctuations in demand for rooms (think hurricanes or bitterly cold winter weather), management must sometimes revise forecasts and budgets and adapt quickly. To evaluate performance and identify when changes need to be made, the budget needs to be flexible.

 Watch the *Tribeca Grand* video in WileyPLUS to learn more about real-world budgeting.

# Chapter Outline

| LEARNING OBJECTIVES | REVIEW | PRACTICE |
|---|---|---|
| **LO 1** Describe budgetary control and static budget reports. | • Budgetary control<br>• Static budget reports | **DO IT! 1** Static Budget Reports |
| **LO 2** Prepare flexible budget reports. | • Why flexible budgets?<br>• Developing the flexible budget<br>• Flexible budget—a case study<br>• Flexible budget reports | **DO IT! 2** Flexible Budgets |
| **LO 3** Apply responsibility accounting to cost and profit centers. | • Controllable vs. noncontrollable revenues and costs<br>• Principles of performance evaluation<br>• Responsibility reporting system<br>• Types of responsibility centers | **DO IT! 3** Profit Center Responsibility Report |
| **LO 4** Evaluate performance in investment centers. | • Return on investment (ROI)<br>• Responsibility report<br>• Alternative measures of ROI inputs<br>• Improving ROI | **DO IT! 4** Performance Evaluation |

**Go to the Review and Practice section at the end of the chapter for a targeted summary and practice applications with solutions.**

**Visit WileyPLUS for additional tutorials and practice opportunities.**

# Budgetary Control and Static Budget Reports

**LEARNING OBJECTIVE 1**
Describe budgetary control and static budget reports.

## Budgetary Control

One of management's responsibilities is to control company operations. Control consists of the steps taken by management to see that planned objectives are met. We now ask: How do budgets contribute to control of operations?

The use of budgets in controlling operations is known as **budgetary control**.

- Such control takes place by means of **budget reports** that compare actual results with planned objectives.
- The use of budget reports is based on the belief that planned objectives lose much of their potential value without some monitoring of progress along the way.
- Just as your professors give midterm exams to evaluate your progress, top management requires periodic reports on the progress of department managers toward planned objectives.

Budget reports provide management with feedback on operations and are prepared as frequently as needed.

- The feedback for a crucial objective, such as having enough cash on hand to pay bills, may be made daily.
- For other objectives, such as meeting budgeted annual sales and operating expenses, monthly budget reports may suffice.

From these reports, management analyzes any differences between actual and planned results and determines their causes. Management then takes corrective action, or it decides to modify future plans. Budgetary control involves the activities shown in **Illustration 23.1**.

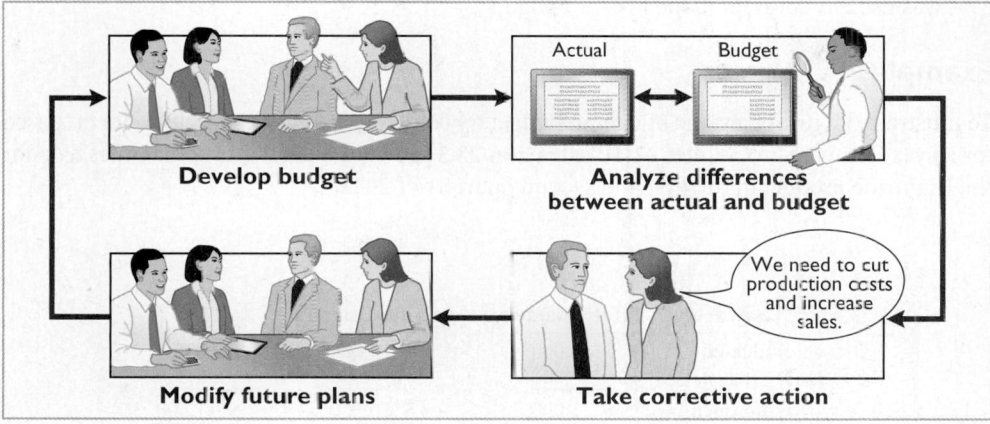

**ILLUSTRATION 23.1**
**Budgetary control activities**

Develop budget

Analyze differences between actual and budget

Modify future plans

Take corrective action

We need to cut production costs and increase sales.

Budgetary control works best when a company has a formalized reporting system. The reporting system does the following.

1. Identifies the name of the budget report, such as the sales budget or the manufacturing overhead budget.

2. States the frequency of the report, such as weekly or monthly.

3. Specifies the purpose of the report.

4. Indicates the primary recipient(s) of the report.

**Illustration 23.2** provides a partial budgetary control system for a manufacturing company. Note the frequency of the reports and their emphasis on control. For example, there is a daily report on scrap and a weekly report on labor.

**ILLUSTRATION 23.2** Budgetary control reporting system

| Name of Report | Frequency | Purpose | Primary Recipient(s) |
|---|---|---|---|
| Sales | Weekly | Determine whether sales goals are met | Top management and sales manager |
| Labor | Weekly | Control direct and indirect labor costs | Vice president of production and production department managers |
| Scrap | Daily | Determine efficient use of materials | Production manager |
| Departmental overhead costs | Monthly | Control overhead costs | Department manager |
| Selling expenses | Monthly | Control selling expenses | Sales manager |
| Income statement | Monthly and quarterly | Determine whether income goals are met | Top management |

## Static Budget Reports

You learned in Chapter 22 that the master budget formalizes management's planned objectives for the coming year. When used in budgetary control, each budget included in the master budget is considered to be static.

• A **static budget** is a projection of budget data **at a single level of activity before actual activity occurs**.

• These budgets do not consider data for different levels of activity.

• As a result, companies compare actual results with budget data at the activity level that was used in developing the master budget.

### Examples

To illustrate the role of a static budget in budgetary control, we will use selected data prepared for Hayes Company in Chapter 22. **Illustration 23.3** provides budget and actual sales data for the Rightride product in the first and second quarters of 2022.

**ILLUSTRATION 23.3**

Budget and actual sales data

| Sales | First Quarter | Second Quarter | Total |
|---|---|---|---|
| Budgeted | $180,000 | $210,000 | $390,000 |
| Actual | 179,000 | 199,500 | 378,500 |
| Difference | $ 1,000 | $ 10,500 | $ 11,500 |

**ALTERNATIVE TERMINOLOGY**

The difference between budget and actual is sometimes called a *budget variance*.

The sales budget report for Hayes' first quarter is shown in **Illustration 23.4**. The right-most column reports the difference between the budgeted and actual amounts (see **Alternative Terminology**).

**ILLUSTRATION 23.4**

**Sales budget report—first quarter**

**Hayes Company Sales Budget Report**

| Product Line | Budget | Actual | Difference<br>Favorable F<br>Unfavorable U |
|---|---|---|---|
| Rightride[a] | $180,000 | $179,000 | **$1,000 U** |

[a]In practice, each product line would be included in the report.

The report shows that sales are $1,000 under budget—an unfavorable result.

- This difference is less than 1% of budgeted sales ($1,000 ÷ $180,000 = .0056, or 0.56%).
- Top management's reaction to differences is often influenced by the materiality (significance) of the difference.
- Since the difference of $1,000 is immaterial in this case, we assume that Hayes management takes no specific corrective action.

**Illustration 23.5** shows the sales budget report for the second quarter. It contains one new feature: cumulative year-to-date information. This report indicates that sales for the second quarter are $10,500 below budget. This is 5% of budgeted sales ($10,500 ÷ $210,000). Top management may now conclude that the difference between budgeted and actual sales requires investigation.

**ILLUSTRATION 23.5**   Sales budget report—second quarter

**Hayes Company Sales Budget Report**

**Hayes Company**
**Sales Budget Report**
**For the Quarter Ended June 30, 2022**

| Product Line | Second Quarter | | | Year-to-Date | | |
|---|---|---|---|---|---|---|
| | Budget | Actual | Difference<br>Favorable F<br>Unfavorable U | Budget | Actual | Difference<br>Favorable F<br>Unfavorable U |
| Rightride | $210,000 | $199,500 | **$10,500 U** | $390,000 | $378,500 | **$11,500 U** |

Management's analysis should start by:
- Asking the sales manager the cause(s) of the shortfall.
- Considering the need for corrective action.

For example, management may attempt to increase sales by offering sales incentives to customers or by increasing the advertising of Rightrides. Or, if management concludes that a downturn in the economy is responsible for the lower sales, it may modify planned sales and profit goals for the remainder of the year.

## Uses and Limitations

From these examples, you can see that a master sales budget is useful in evaluating the performance of a sales manager. It is now necessary to ask: Is the master budget appropriate for evaluating a manager's performance in controlling costs? Recall that in a static

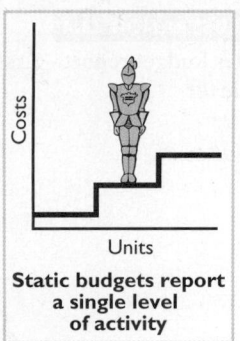

**Static budgets report a single level of activity**

budget, data are not modified or adjusted, regardless of changes in activity. It follows, then, that a static budget is appropriate in evaluating a manager's effectiveness in controlling costs when:

1. The actual level of activity closely approximates the master budget activity level, and/or
2. The behavior of the costs in response to changes in activity is fixed.

A static budget report is, therefore, appropriate for **fixed manufacturing costs** and for **fixed selling and administrative expenses**. But, as you will see shortly, static budget reports may not be a proper basis for evaluating a manager's performance in controlling variable costs.

**ACTION PLAN**

- **Classify each cost as variable or fixed**
- **Determine the difference as favorable or unfavorable.**
- **Determine the difference in total variable costs, total fixed costs, and total costs.**

## DO IT! 1 | Static Budget Reports

Lawler Company expects to produce 5,000 units of product CV93 during the current month. Budgeted variable manufacturing costs per unit are direct materials $6, direct labor $15, and overhead $24. Monthly budgeted fixed manufacturing overhead costs are $10,000 for depreciation and $5,000 for supervision.

In the current month, Lawler actually produced 5,500 units and incurred the following costs: direct materials $33,900, direct labor $74,200, variable overhead $120,500, depreciation $10,000, and supervision $5,000.

Prepare a static budget report. (*Hint:* The Budget column is based on estimated production of 5,000 units while the Actual column is the actual costs incurred during the period.) Were costs controlled? Discuss limitations of this budget.

**Solution**

Lawler Company

|  | A | B | C | D | |
|---|---|---|---|---|---|
| 1 | | | | Difference | |
| 2 | | | | Favorable - F | |
| 3 | | Budget | Actual | Unfavorable - U | |
| 4 | Production in units | 5,000 | 5,500 | | |
| 5 | | | | | |
| 6 | Variable costs | | | | |
| 7 | Direct materials ($6) | $ 30,000 | $ 33,900 | $3,900 | U |
| 8 | Direct labor ($15) | 75,000 | 74,200 | 800 | F |
| 9 | Overhead ($24) | 120,000 | 120,500 | 500 | U |
| 10 | Total variable costs | 225,000 | 228,600 | 3,600 | U |
| 11 | | | | | |
| 12 | Fixed costs | | | | |
| 13 | Depreciation | 10,000 | 10,000 | 0 | |
| 14 | Supervision | 5,000 | 5,000 | 0 | |
| 15 | Total fixed costs | 15,000 | 15,000 | 0 | |
| 16 | Total costs | $240,000 | $243,600 | $3,600 | U |
| 17 | | | | | |
| 18 | | | | | |

The static budget indicates that actual variable costs exceeded budgeted amounts by $3,600. Fixed costs were exactly as budgeted. The static budget gives the impression that the company did not control its variable costs. However, the static budget does not give consideration to the fact that the company produced 500 more units than planned. As a result, the static budget is not a good tool to evaluate variable costs. It is, however, a good tool to evaluate fixed costs as those should not vary with changes in production volume.

Related exercise material: **BE23.1, BE23.2, DO IT! 23.1, and E23.2.**

# Flexible Budget Reports

## LEARNING OBJECTIVE 2

Prepare flexible budget reports.

In contrast to a static budget, which is based on one level of activity, a **flexible budget** projects budget data for various levels of activity.

- In essence, **the flexible budget is a series of static budgets at different levels of activity**.
- The flexible budget recognizes that the budgetary process is more useful if it is adaptable to changed operating conditions.

Flexible budgets can be prepared for each of the types of budgets included in the master budget. For example, **Marriott Hotels** can budget revenues and net income on the basis of 60%, 80%, and 100% of room occupancy. Similarly, **American Van Lines** can budget its operating expenses on the basis of various levels of truck-miles driven. **Duke Energy** can budget revenue and net income on the basis of estimated billions of kwh (kilowatt hours) of residential, commercial, and industrial electricity generated. In the following pages, we will illustrate a flexible budget for manufacturing overhead.

**Flexible budgets are static budgets at different activity levels**

## Why Flexible Budgets?

Assume that you are the manager in charge of manufacturing overhead in the Assembly Department of Barton Robotics. In preparing the manufacturing overhead budget for 2022, you prepare the static budget shown in **Illustration 23.6** based on a production volume of 10,000 units of robotic controls (see **Helpful Hint**).

**HELPFUL HINT**

The master budget described in Chapter 22 is based on a static budget.

**ILLUSTRATION 23.6**

**Static overhead budget**

| Barton Robotics<br>Manufacturing Overhead Budget (Static)<br>Assembly Department<br>For the Year Ended December 31, 2022 | |
|---|---|
| Budgeted production in units (robotic controls) | 10,000 |
| | |
| Budgeted costs | |
| Indirect materials | $  250,000 |
| Indirect labor | 260,000 |
| Utilities | 190,000 |
| Depreciation | 280,000 |
| Property taxes | 70,000 |
| Supervision | 50,000 |
| | $1,100,000 |

Fortunately for the company, the demand for robotic controls has increased, and Barton produces and sells 12,000 units during the year rather than 10,000. You are elated! Increased sales means increased profitability, which should mean a bonus or a raise for you and the employees in your department. Unfortunately, a comparison of Assembly Department actual and budgeted costs has put you on the spot. **Illustration 23.7** shows the budget report.

**ILLUSTRATION 23.7**

**Overhead static budget report**

**Barton Robotics**

| | A | B | C | D | E |
|---|---|---|---|---|---|
| 1 | | **Barton Robotics** | | | |
| 2 | | **Manufacturing Overhead Static Budget Report** | | | |
| 3 | | **For the Year Ended December 31, 2022** | | | |
| 4 | | | | Difference | |
| 5 | | Budget | Actual | Favorable - F<br>Unfavorable - U | |
| 6 | Production in units | 10,000 | 12,000 | | |
| 7 | | | | | |
| 8 | Costs | | | | |
| 9 | Indirect materials | $ 250,000 | $ 295,000 | $ 45,000 | U |
| 10 | Indirect labor | 260,000 | 312,000 | 52,000 | U |
| 11 | Utilities | 190,000 | 225,000 | 35,000 | U |
| 12 | Depreciation | 280,000 | 280,000 | 0 | |
| 13 | Property taxes | 70,000 | 70,000 | 0 | |
| 14 | Supervision | 50,000 | 50,000 | 0 | |
| 15 | | $1,100,000 | $1,232,000 | $132,000 | U |
| 16 | | | | | |

This comparison uses budgeted cost data based on the original activity level (10,000 robotic controls).

- It indicates that the costs incurred by the Assembly Department are significantly **over budget** for three of the six overhead costs.
- There is a total unfavorable difference of $132,000, which is 12% over budget ($132,000 ÷ $1,100,000).

Your supervisor is very unhappy. Instead of sharing in the company's success, you may find yourself looking for another job. What went wrong?

When you calm down and carefully examine the manufacturing overhead budget, you identify the problem: The budget data are not relevant!

- At the time the budget was developed, the company anticipated that only 10,000 units would be produced. Instead, 12,000 units were actually produced.
- Comparing actual costs incurred at a production level of 12,000 units with budgeted variable costs at an expected production level of 10,000 units is meaningless (see **Helpful Hint**).

**HELPFUL HINT**

A static budget is not useful for performance evaluation if a company has substantial variable costs.

- As production increases, the budget allowances for variable costs should increase proportionately. The variable costs in this example are indirect materials, indirect labor, and utilities.

Analyzing the budget data for these costs at 10,000 units, you arrive at the unit variable cost results shown in **Illustration 23.8**.

**ILLUSTRATION 23.8**

**Unit variable costs**

| Item | Budgeted<br>Cost | ÷ | Budgeted Number<br>of Units | = | Unit<br>Variable Cost |
|---|---|---|---|---|---|
| Indirect materials | $250,000 | | 10,000 | | $25 |
| Indirect labor | 260,000 | | 10,000 | | 26 |
| Utilities | 190,000 | | 10,000 | | 19 |
| | $700,000 | | | | $70 |

Using these unit variable costs, **Illustration 23.9** calculates the budgeted variable costs at 12,000 units.

| Item | Unit Variable Cost × Actual Units = | Budgeted Variable Costs |
|---|---|---|
| Indirect materials | $25 × 12,000 | $300,000 |
| Indirect labor | $26 × 12,000 | 312,000 |
| Utilities | $19 × 12,000 | 228,000 |
| | | $840,000 |

**ILLUSTRATION 23.9**
Budgeted variable costs, 12,000 units

Because fixed costs do not change in total as activity changes, the budgeted amounts for these costs remain the same. **Illustration 23.10** shows the budget report based on the flexible budget for **12,000 units** of production. (Compare this with Illustration 23.7.)

**ILLUSTRATION 23.10**
Overhead flexible budget report

**Barton Robotics**
**Manufacturing Overhead Flexible Budget Report**
**For the Year Ended December 31, 2022**

| | Budget | Actual | Difference Favorable - F Unfavorable - U | |
|---|---|---|---|---|
| Production in units | 12,000 | 12,000 | | |
| | | | | |
| Variable costs | | | | |
| Indirect materials ($25) | $ 300,000 | $ 295,000 | $5,000 | F |
| Indirect labor ($26) | 312,000 | 312,000 | 0 | |
| Utilities ($19) | 228,000 | 225,000 | 3,000 | F |
| Total variable costs | 840,000 | 832,000 | 8,000 | F |
| | | | | |
| Fixed costs | | | | |
| Depreciation | 280,000 | 280,000 | 0 | |
| Property taxes | 70,000 | 70,000 | 0 | |
| Supervision | 50,000 | 50,000 | 0 | |
| Total fixed costs | 400,000 | 400,000 | 0 | |
| Total costs | $1,240,000 | $1,232,000 | $8,000 | F |

This flexible budget report indicates that the Assembly Department's costs are **under budget**—a favorable difference. Instead of worrying about being fired, you may be in line for a bonus or a raise after all! As this analysis shows, the only appropriate comparison is between actual costs at 12,000 units of production and budgeted costs at 12,000 units. Flexible budget reports provide this comparison.

# Developing the Flexible Budget

The flexible budget uses the master budget as its basis. To develop the flexible budget, management uses the following steps.

1. Identify the activity index and the relevant range of activity.
2. Identify the variable costs, and determine the budgeted variable cost per unit of activity for each cost.
3. Identify the fixed costs, and determine the budgeted amount for each cost.
4. Prepare the budget for selected increments of activity within the relevant range.

The activity index chosen should have a strong relationship with the costs being budgeted. That is, an increase in the activity index should coincide with an increase in costs. For manufacturing overhead costs, for example, the activity index is usually the same as the index used in developing the predetermined overhead rate—that is, direct labor hours or machine hours. For selling and administrative expenses, the activity index usually is sales or net sales.

The choice of the increment of activity is largely a matter of judgment. For example, if the relevant range is 8,000 to 12,000 direct labor hours, increments of 1,000 hours may be selected. The flexible budget is then prepared for each increment within the relevant range.

---

### Service Company Insight    NBCUniversal

KlaraBstock/
Shutterstock.com

#### Just What the Doctor Ordered?

Nobody is immune from the effects of declining revenues—not even movie stars. When the number of viewers of a popular medical drama declined by almost 20%, **Fox Broadcasting** said it wanted to cut the license fee that it paid to **NBCUniversal** by 20%.

What would NBCUniversal do in response? It might cut the size of the show's cast, which would reduce the payroll costs associated with the show. Or, it could reduce the number of episodes that take advantage of the full cast. Alternatively, it might threaten to quit providing the show to Fox altogether and instead present the show on its own NBC-affiliated channels. As consumers continue to shift to alternative entertainment sources, television executives will need to make creative adjustments in order to maintain profitability.

**Sources:** Sam Schechner, "Media Business Shorts: NBCU, Fox Taking Scalpel to 'House'," *Wall Street Journal Online* (April 17, 2011); and Rick Porter, "TV LongView: Five Years of Network Ratings Declines in Context," *The Hollywood Reporter* (September 21, 2019).

**How might the use of flexible budgets help to identify the best solution to this problem? (Answer is available at the end of the chapter.)**

---

## Flexible Budget—A Case Study

To illustrate the flexible budget, we use Fox Company. Fox's management uses a **flexible budget for monthly comparisons** of actual and budgeted manufacturing overhead costs of the Finishing Department. The master budget for the year ending December 31, 2022, shows expected **annual** operating capacity of 120,000 direct labor hours and the overhead costs shown in **Illustration 23.11**.

**ILLUSTRATION 23.11**

**Master budget data**

| Variable Costs | | Fixed Costs | |
|---|---|---|---|
| Indirect materials | $180,000 | Depreciation | $180,000 |
| Indirect labor | 240,000 | Supervision | 120,000 |
| Utilities | 60,000 | Property taxes | 60,000 |
| Total | $480,000 | Total | $360,000 |

The four steps for developing the flexible budget are applied as follows.

**Step 1   Identify the activity index and the relevant range of activity.** Management has found that there is a strong relationship between direct labor hours and variable manufacturing overhead costs. Thus, the activity index is direct labor hours. The relevant range is 8,000–12,000 direct labor hours per **month**.

**Step 2   Identify the variable costs, and determine the budgeted variable cost per unit of activity for each cost.** A cost is variable if total costs vary directly as a result of a change in the activity index, which is direct labor in this case. In this example, indirect materials, indirect labor, and utilities are variable costs. The variable cost per unit is found by dividing each total budgeted cost by the direct labor hours used in preparing the annual master budget (120,000 hours). **Illustration 23.12** shows the computations for Fox Company.

**ILLUSTRATION 23.12**

**Computation of variable cost per direct labor hour**

| Variable Costs | Total Budgeted Cost ÷ Budgeted Direct Labor Hours | = | Variable Cost per Direct Labor Hour |
|---|---|---|---|
| Indirect materials | $180,000 ÷ 120,000 | | **$1.50** |
| Indirect labor | $240,000 ÷ 120,000 | | **2.00** |
| Utilities | $60,000 ÷ 120,000 | | **0.50** |
| Total | | | **$4.00** |

**Step 3    Identify the fixed costs, and determine the budgeted amount for each cost.** A cost is fixed if the total cost does not vary as a result of changes in the activity index. In this example, depreciation, supervision, and property taxes are fixed costs. Since Fox desires **monthly budget data**, it divides each annual budgeted cost by 12 to find the monthly amounts. Therefore, the monthly budgeted fixed costs are depreciation $15,000 ($180,000 ÷ 12), supervision $10,000 ($120,000 ÷ 12), and property taxes $5,000 ($60,000 ÷ 12).

**Step 4    Prepare the budget for selected increments of activity within the relevant range.** Management prepares the budget in increments of 1,000 direct labor hours.

Illustration 23.13 shows Fox's flexible budget.

**ILLUSTRATION 23.13**

**Monthly overhead flexible budget**

| | B | C | D | E | F |
|---|---|---|---|---|---|
| **Fox Company** | | | | | |
| **Monthly Manufacturing Overhead Flexible Budget** | | | | | |
| **Finishing Department** | | | | | |
| **For Months During the Year 2022** | | | | | |
| Activity level | | | | | |
| Direct labor hours | 8,000 | 9,000 | 10,000 | 11,000 | 12,000 |
| Variable costs | | | | | |
| Indirect materials ($1.50)[a] | $12,000[b] | $13,500 | $15,000 | $16,500 | $18,000 |
| Indirect labor ($2.00)[a] | 16,000[c] | 18,000 | 20,000 | 22,000 | 24,000 |
| Utilities ($0.50)[a] | 4,000[d] | 4,500 | 5,000 | 5,500 | 6,000 |
| Total variable costs | 32,000 | 36,000 | 40,000 | 44,000 | 48,000 |
| Fixed costs | | | | | |
| Depreciation | 15,000 | 15,000 | 15,000 | 15,000 | 15,000 |
| Supervision | 10,000 | 10,000 | 10,000 | 10,000 | 10,000 |
| Property taxes | 5,000 | 5,000 | 5,000 | 5,000 | 5,000 |
| Total fixed costs | 30,000 | 30,000 | 30,000 | 30,000 | 30,000 |
| Total costs | $62,000 | $66,000 | $70,000 | $74,000 | $78,000 |

[a]Cost per direct labor hour; [b]8,000 x $1.50; [c]8,000 x $2.00; [d]8,000 x $0.50

Fox uses the cost equation shown in **Illustration 23.14** to determine total budgeted costs at any level of activity.

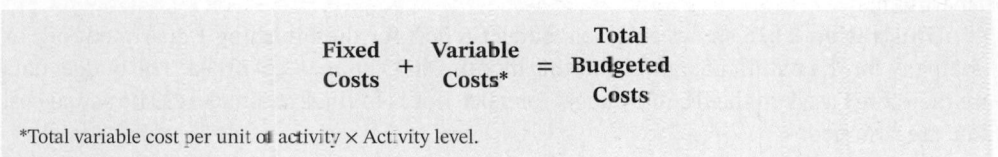

$$\text{Fixed Costs} + \text{Variable Costs*} = \text{Total Budgeted Costs}$$

*Total variable cost per unit of activity × Activity level.

**ILLUSTRATION 23.14**

**Cost equation for total budgeted costs**

For Fox, fixed costs are $30,000 per month, and total variable cost per direct labor hour is $4 ($1.50 + $2.00 + $0.50).

- At 9,000 direct labor hours, total budgeted costs are $66,000 [$30,000 + ($4 × 9,000)].
- At 8,622 direct labor hours, total budgeted costs are $64,488 [$30,000 − ($4 × 8,622)] (see **Helpful Hint**).

Total budgeted costs can also be shown graphically, as in **Illustration 23.15**.

**HELPFUL HINT**

Using the data given for Fox, the amount of total costs to be budgeted for 10,600 direct labor hours would be $30,000 fixed + $42,400 variable (10,600 × $4) = $72,400 total.

**ILLUSTRATION 23.15**

**Graphic flexible budget data highlighting 10,000 and 12,000 activity levels**

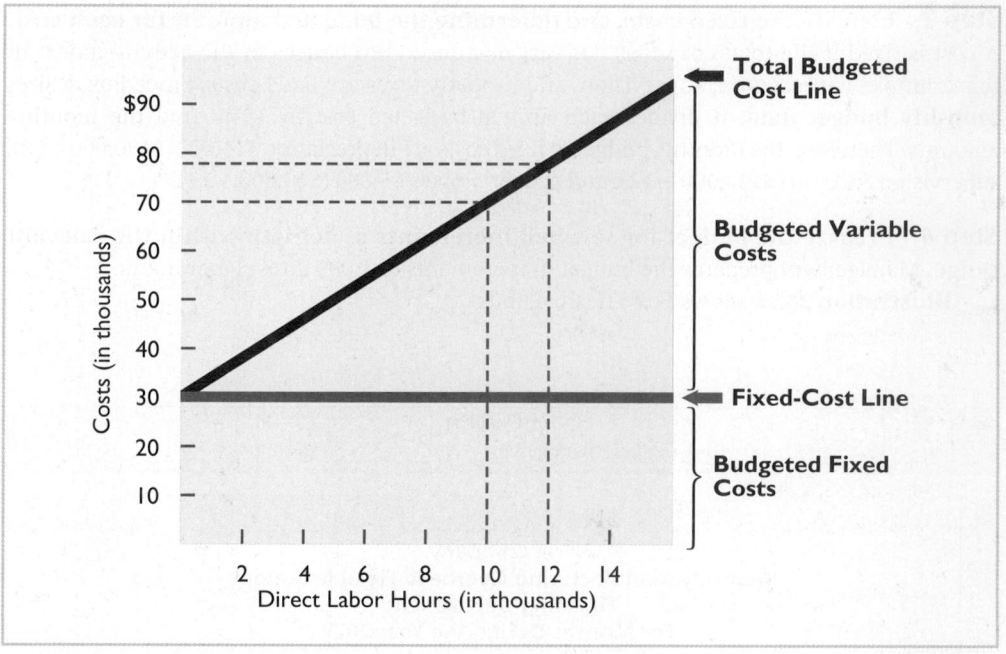

- In the graph, the horizontal axis represents the activity index, and costs are indicated on the vertical axis.
- The graph highlights two activity levels (10,000 and 12,000).
- As shown, total budgeted costs at these activity levels are $70,000 [$30,000 + ($4 × 10,000)] and $78,000 [$30,000 + ($4 × 12,000)], respectively.

# Flexible Budget Reports

Flexible budget reports are another type of internal report. The flexible budget report consists of two sections:

1. Production data for a selected activity index, such as direct labor hours.
2. Cost data for variable and fixed costs.

The report provides a basis for evaluating a manager's performance in two areas: production control and cost control. Flexible budget reports are widely used in production and service departments.

    **Illustration 23.16** shows a flexible budget report for the Finishing Department of Fox Company for the month of January. In this month, 9,000 hours are worked. The budget data are therefore based on the flexible budget for 9,000 hours in Illustration 23.13. The actual cost data are assumed.

    How appropriate is this report in evaluating the Finishing Department manager's performance in controlling overhead costs? The report clearly provides a more reliable basis than a static budget.

- Both actual and budget costs are based on the activity level worked during January.
- Since variable costs generally are incurred directly by the department, the difference between the budget allowance for those hours and the actual costs is the responsibility of the department manager.

**ILLUSTRATION 23.16**
**Overhead flexible budget report**

**Fox Company**

Home   Insert   Page Layout   Formulas   Data   Review   View

P18

| | A | B | C | D | E |
|---|---|---|---|---|---|
| 1 | | | Fox Company | | |
| 2 | | Manufacturing Overhead Flexible Budget Report | | | |
| 3 | | Finishing Department | | | |
| 4 | | For the Month Ended January 31, 2022 | | | |
| 5 | | | | Difference | |
| 6 | | Budget at | Actual costs at | Favorable - F | |
| 7 | Direct labor hours (DLH) | 9,000 DLH | 9,000 DLH | Unfavorable - U | |
| 8 | | | | | |
| 9 | Variable costs | | | | |
| 10 | Indirect materials ($1.50)[a] | $13,500 | $14,000 | $ 500 | U |
| 11 | Indirect labor ($2.00)[a] | 18,000 | 17,000 | 1,000 | F |
| 12 | Utilities ($0.50)[a] | 4,500 | 4,600 | 100 | U |
| 13 | Total variable costs | 36,000 | 35,600 | 400 | F |
| 14 | | | | | |
| 15 | Fixed costs | | | | |
| 16 | Depreciation | 15,000 | 15,000 | 0 | |
| 17 | Supervision | 10,000 | 10,000 | 0 | |
| 18 | Property taxes | 5,000 | 5,000 | 0 | |
| 19 | Total fixed costs | 30,000 | 30,000 | 0 | |
| 20 | Total costs | $66,000 | $65,600 | $ 400 | F |
| 21 | | | | | |
| 22 | [a]Cost per direct labor hour | | | | |

In subsequent months, Fox Company will prepare other flexible budget reports. For each month, the budget data are based on the actual activity level attained. In February, that level may be 11,000 direct labor hours, in July 10,000, and so on.

Note that this flexible budget is based on a single cost driver. A more accurate budget often can be developed using activity-based costing (see Chapter 17).

---

## Data Analytics Insight

### These Forecasts Move with the Times!

Many companies now supplement their annual static budgets with rolling forecasts. Although budgets are detailed documents, they are typically only prepared annually and thus can

Solarbeamk/Shutterstock.com

quickly lose usefulness as business conditions change. In contrast, rolling forecasts are less detailed, focus on those elements that management believes are the most important, and are usually updated monthly. As a result rolling forecasts can help improve management's ability to respond to changing business conditions and enable creation of scenarios where management can experiment with "what if" questions.

Forecasts are forward-looking, covering a period of time anywhere from 4 to 18 months. And while long-term forecasts might provide more insight, shorter-term forecasts are more accurate. To create and update these short-term rolling forecasts, companies rely heavily on big data. For example, companies must identify the most significant value-drivers in creating rolling forecasts; data analytics can help to verify the accuracy of the data used. For many companies, a well-developed rolling forecast system, based on data analytics, is invaluable.

**Source:** Robert Freedman, "How to Transition from a Static to a Rolling Forecast," *CFO Dive* (December 4, 2019).

**In what ways are budgets and rolling forecasts similar, and in what ways do they differ? (Answer is available at the end of the chapter.)**

## DO IT! 2 | Flexible Budgets

In Strassel Company's flexible budget graph, the fixed-cost line and the total budgeted cost line intersect the vertical axis at $36,000. The total budgeted cost line is $186,000 at an activity level of 50,000 direct labor hours. Compute total budgeted costs at 30,000 direct labor hours.

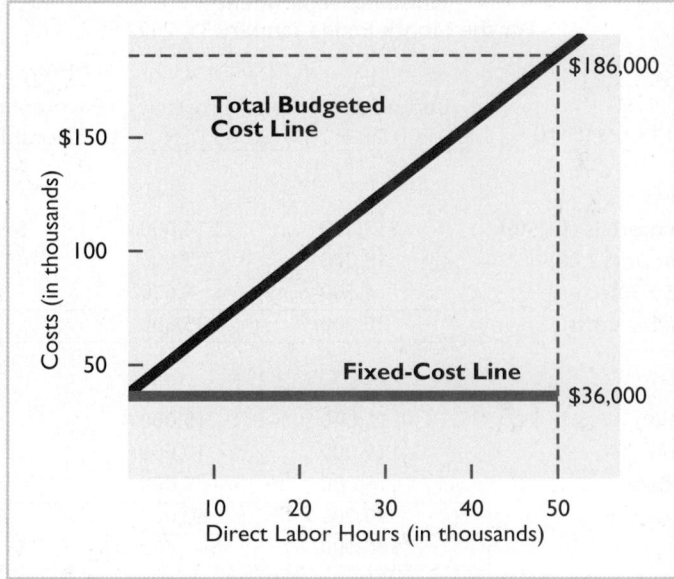

### Solution

Using the graph, fixed costs are $36,000, and variable costs are $3 per direct labor hour [($186,000 − $36,000) ÷ 50,000]. Thus, at 30,000 direct labor hours, total budgeted costs are $126,000 [$36,000 + ($3 × 30,000)].

Related exercise material: **BE23.4, DO IT! 23.2, E23.3, and E23.5.**

# Responsibility Accounting and Responsibility Centers

**LEARNING OBJECTIVE 3**

Apply responsibility accounting to cost and profit centers.

Like budgeting, responsibility accounting is an important part of management accounting.

• **Responsibility accounting** involves identifying and reporting costs (and revenues, where relevant) on the basis of the manager who has the authority to make the day-to-day decisions about the items.

• Under responsibility accounting, a manager's performance is evaluated on matters directly under that manager's control.

Responsibility accounting can be used at every level of management in which the following conditions exist.

1. Costs and revenues can be directly associated with the specific level of management responsibility.

2. The costs and revenues can be controlled by employees at the level of responsibility with which they are associated.

3. Budget data can be developed for evaluating the manager's effectiveness in controlling the costs and revenues.

**Illustration 23.17** depicts levels of responsibility for controlling costs.

**ILLUSTRATION 23.17**

**Responsibility for controllable costs at varying levels of management**

Under responsibility accounting, any individual who controls a specified set of activities can be a responsibility center. Thus, responsibility accounting may extend from the lowest level of control to the top strata of management. Once responsibility is established, the company first measures and reports the effectiveness of the individual's performance for the specified activity. It then reports that measure upward throughout the organization (see **Helpful Hint**).

Responsibility accounting is especially valuable in a decentralized company.

- **Decentralization** means that the control of operations is delegated to many managers throughout the organization.

- The term **segment** (or **division**) is sometimes used to identify an area of responsibility in decentralized operations.

Under responsibility accounting, companies prepare segment reports periodically, such as monthly, quarterly, and annually, to evaluate managers' performance.

Responsibility accounting is an essential part of any effective system of budgetary control. The reporting of costs and revenues under responsibility accounting differs from budgeting in two respects:

1. A distinction is made between controllable and noncontrollable items.

2. Performance reports either emphasize or include only items controllable by the individual manager.

Responsibility accounting applies to both for-profit and not-for-profit entities. For-profit entities seek to maximize net income. Not-for-profit entities wish to provide services as cost-efficiently as possible.

**HELPFUL HINT**

All companies use responsibility accounting. Without some form of responsibility accounting, there would be chaos in discharging management's control function.

---

**Management Insight**   Cisco Systems

fluxfoto/Getty Images

### Competition versus Collaboration

Many compensation and promotion programs encourage competition among employees for pay raises. To get ahead, you have to perform better than your fellow employees. While this may encourage hard work, it does not foster collaboration, and it can lead to distrust and disloyalty. Such negative effects have led some companies to believe that cooperation and collaboration, not competition, are essential in order to succeed in today's work environment.

As a consequence, many companies explicitly include measures of collaboration in their performance measures. For example, **Procter & Gamble** measures collaboration in employees' annual performance reviews. At **Cisco Systems**, the assessment of an employee's teamwork can affect the annual bonus by as much as 20%. A recent concern is that employees have become swamped in a confusing array of collaboration tools from Box Inc., Slack Technologies, Microsoft, Alphabet, and Facebook. In response, companies are trying to simplify the collaboration process.

**Sources:** Carol Hymowitz, "Rewarding Competitors Over Collaboration No Longer Makes Sense," *Wall Street Journal* (February 13, 2006); and Jay Greene, "Beware Collaboration—Tool Overload," *Wall Street Journal* (March 12, 2017).

**How might managers of separate divisions be able to reduce division costs through collaboration? (Answer is available at the end of the chapter.)**

---

## Controllable versus Noncontrollable Revenues and Costs

All costs and revenues are controllable at some level of responsibility within a company. This truth underscores the adage by the CEO of any organization that "the buck stops here" (see **Helpful Hint**). Under responsibility accounting, the critical issue is **whether the cost or revenue is controllable at the level of responsibility with which it is associated**. A cost over which a manager has control is called a **controllable cost**. From this definition, it follows that:

1. All costs are controllable by top management because of the broad range of its authority.
2. Fewer costs are controllable as one moves down to each lower level of managerial responsibility because of the manager's decreasing authority.

In general, **costs incurred directly by a level of responsibility are controllable at that level** (see **Helpful Hint**). In contrast, costs incurred indirectly and allocated to a responsibility level are **noncontrollable costs** at that level.

## Principles of Performance Evaluation

Performance evaluation is at the center of responsibility accounting. It is a management function that compares actual results with budget goals. It involves both behavioral and reporting principles.

### Management by Exception

**Management by exception** means:

- Top management's review of a budget report is focused either entirely or primarily on significant differences between actual results and planned objectives.
- This approach enables top management to focus on problem areas.

For example, many companies now use online reporting systems for employees to file their travel and entertainment expense reports. In addition to significantly reducing reporting time, the online system enables managers to quickly analyze variances from travel budgets. This cuts down on expense account "padding" such as spending too much on meals or falsifying documents for costs that were never actually incurred.

Under management by exception, top management does not investigate every difference. For this approach to be effective, there must be guidelines for identifying which differences to investigate. The usual criteria are materiality and controllability.

**Materiality**   Without quantitative guidelines, management would have to investigate every budget difference regardless of the amount.

- Materiality is usually expressed as a percentage difference from budget. For example, management may set the percentage difference at 5% for important items and 10% for other items.
- Managers will investigate all differences either over or under budget by the specified percentage. Costs over budget warrant investigation to determine why they were not controlled. Likewise, costs under budget merit investigation to determine whether costs critical to profitability are being curtailed.

For example, if maintenance costs are budgeted at $80,000 but only $40,000 is spent, major unexpected breakdowns in productive facilities may occur in the future. Or, as discussed in Chapter 22, cost might be under budget due to budgetary slack.

Alternatively, a company may specify a single percentage difference from budget for all items and supplement this guideline with a minimum dollar limit. For example, the exception criteria may be stated at 5% of budget or more than $10,000.

**Controllability of the Item**   Exception guidelines are more restrictive for controllable items than for items the manager cannot control.

- In fact, there may be no guidelines for noncontrollable items.
- For example, a large unfavorable difference between actual and budgeted property tax expense may not be flagged for investigation because the only possible causes are an unexpected increase in the tax rate or in the assessed value of the property.
- An investigation into the difference would be useless: The manager cannot control either cause.

## Behavioral Principles

The human factor is critical in evaluating performance. Behavioral principles include the following.

1. **Managers of responsibility centers should have direct input into the process of establishing budget goals of their area of responsibility.** Without such input, managers may view the goals as unrealistic or arbitrarily set by top management. Such views adversely affect the managers' motivation to meet the targeted objectives.

2. **The evaluation of performance should be based entirely on matters that are controllable by the manager being evaluated.** Criticism of a manager on matters outside his or her control reduces the effectiveness of the evaluation process. It leads to negative reactions by the manager and to doubts about the fairness of the company's evaluation policies.

3. **Top management should support the evaluation process.** As explained earlier, the evaluation process begins at the lowest level of responsibility and extends upward to the highest level of management. Managers quickly lose faith in the process when top management ignores, overrules, or bypasses established procedures for evaluating a manager's performance.

4. **The evaluation process must allow managers to respond to their evaluations.** Evaluation is not a one-way street. Managers should have the opportunity to defend their performance. Evaluation without feedback is both impersonal and ineffective.

5. **The evaluation should identify both good and poor performance.** Praise for good performance is a powerful motivating factor for a manager. This is especially true when a manager's compensation includes rewards for meeting budget goals.

## Reporting Principles

Performance evaluation under responsibility accounting should be based on certain reporting principles. These principles pertain primarily to the internal reports that provide the basis for evaluating performance. Performance reports should:

- Contain only data that are controllable by the manager of the responsibility center.
- Provide accurate and reliable budget data to measure performance.
- Highlight significant differences between actual results and budget goals.
- Be tailor-made for the intended evaluation by ensuring only controllable costs are included.
- Be prepared at reasonable time intervals.

In recent years, companies have come under increasing pressure from influential shareholder groups to do a better job of linking executive pay to corporate performance. For example, at one time software maker **Siebel Systems** unveiled an incentive plan after lengthy discussions with the California Public Employees' Retirement System. One unique feature of the plan is that managers' targets will be publicly disclosed at the beginning of each year for investors to evaluate.

---

### Data Analytics Insight

chombosan / Alamy Stock Photo

#### Hitting the Road with Zero-Based Budgeting

The automotive industry has enjoyed a relatively stable business model for almost 100 years. But now it is threatened by changes coming from multiple fronts. Managers at auto manufacturers must decide whether they are going to expend massive investments in electric vehicles, autonomous vehicles, and mobility as a service. Such large outlays of company resources would necessitate diverting funds away from some current activities. How will these managers determine what to invest in and what to drop?

One possible tool these managers might use is zero-based budgeting. This approach requires that "all costs and expenses be reassessed and justified in terms of their contribution to the business' overall value." This determination relies heavily on data analytic models that employ large amounts of data from a wide variety of sources to predict future business trends. Proponents of "zero-basing" argue that it enables companies to rapidly redeploy limited resources when the business environment is constantly changing. But, zero-based budgeting has been criticized by some as being unnecessarily disruptive, time-consuming, and expensive. Zero-based budgeting might be especially problematic in the automotive industry, where a company culture is well-established. Big changes can stir up big emotions.

**Source:** Global Strategy Group, KPMG International Cooperative, "Zero Basing in Automotive," *Realizing Value Series* (2018).

**What are some of the pros and cons of employing zero-based budgeting? (Answer is available at the end of the chapter.)**

---

# Responsibility Reporting System

A **responsibility reporting system** involves the preparation of a report for each level of responsibility in the company's organization chart. To illustrate such a system, we use the partial organization chart and production departments of Francis Chair Company in **Illustration 23.18**.

The responsibility reporting system begins with the lowest level of responsibility for controlling costs and moves upward to each higher level. (Illustration 23.19 details the connections between levels). A brief description of the four reports for Francis Chair is as follows.

1. **Report D** is typical of reports that go to department managers. Similar reports are prepared for the managers of the Assembly and Enameling Departments.
2. **Report C** is an example of reports that are sent to factory managers. It shows the costs of the Chicago factory that are controllable at the second level of responsibility. In addition, Report C shows summary data for each department that is controlled by the factory manager. Similar reports are prepared for the Detroit and St. Louis factory managers.
3. **Report B** illustrates the reports at the third level of responsibility. It shows the controllable costs of the vice president of production and summary data on the three assembly factories for which this officer is responsible. Similar reports are prepared for the vice presidents of sales and finance.

**ILLUSTRATION 23.18**   Partial organization chart

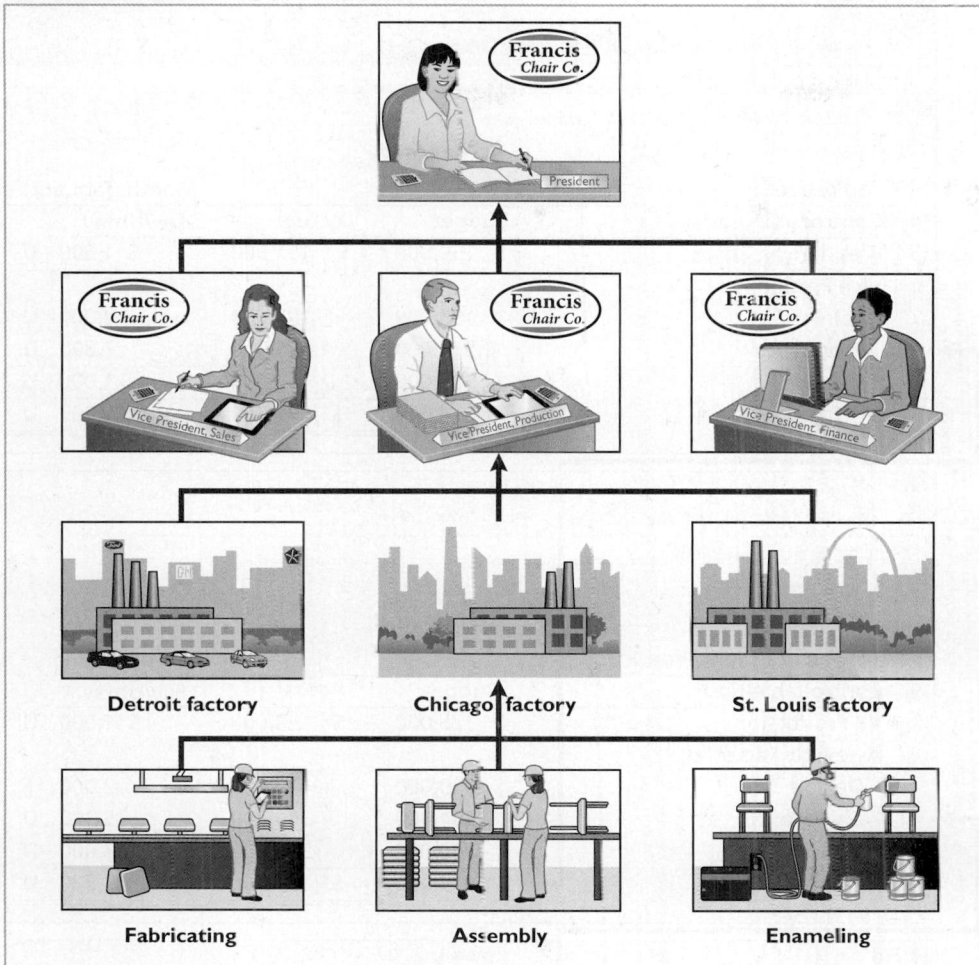

**Report A**
President sees summary data of vice presidents.

**Report B**
Vice president sees summary of controllable costs in his/her functional area.

**Report C**
Factory manager sees summary of controllable costs for each department in the factory.

**Report D**
Department manager sees controllable costs of his/her department.

4. **Report A** is typical of reports that go to the top level of responsibility—the president. It shows the controllable costs and expenses of this office and summary data on the vice presidents that are accountable to the president.

A responsibility reporting system permits management by exception at each level of responsibility. And, each higher level of responsibility can obtain the detailed report for each lower level of responsibility. For example, the vice president of production in Francis Chair may request the Chicago factory manager's report because this factory is $5,300 over budget.

This type of reporting system also permits comparative evaluations. In **Illustration 23.19**, the Chicago factory manager can easily rank the department managers' effectiveness in controlling manufacturing costs. Comparative rankings provide further incentive for a manager to control costs.

# Types of Responsibility Centers

There are three basic types of responsibility centers: cost centers, profit centers, and investment centers. These classifications indicate the nature of the responsibility the manager has for the performance of the center.

1. A **cost center** incurs costs (and expenses) but does not directly generate revenues.
   - Managers of cost centers have the authority to incur costs.
   - They are evaluated on their ability to control costs.
   - **Cost centers are usually either production departments or service departments.**

**ILLUSTRATION 23.19** Responsibility reporting system

**Report A**
President sees summary
data of vice presidents.

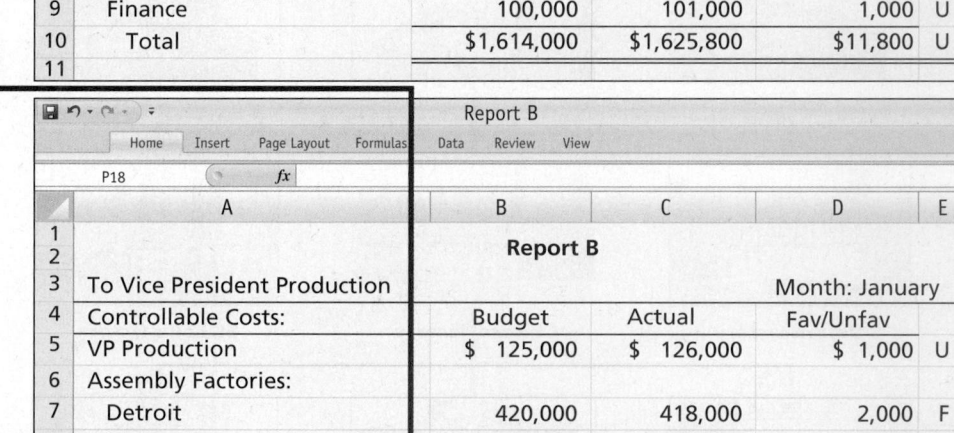

| Report A | | | | |
| --- | --- | --- | --- | --- |
| To President | | | Month: January | |
| Controllable Costs: | Budget | Actual | Fav/Unfav | |
| President | $ 150,000 | $ 151,500 | $ 1,500 | U |
| Vice Presidents: | | | | |
| Sales | 185,000 | 187,000 | 2,000 | U |
| **Production** | **1,179,000** | **1,186,300** | **7,300** | U |
| Finance | 100,000 | 101,000 | 1,000 | U |
| Total | $1,614,000 | $1,625,800 | $11,800 | U |

**Report B**
Vice president sees sum-
mary of controllable costs
in his/her functional area.

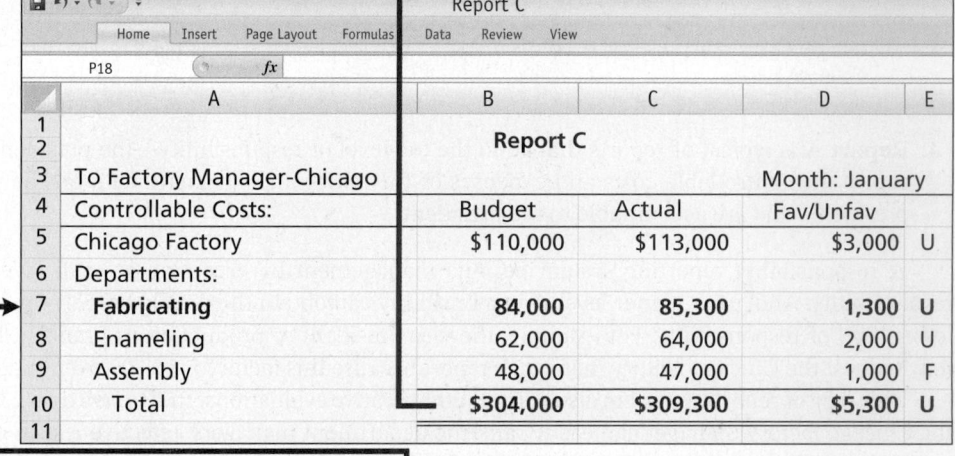

| Report B | | | | |
| --- | --- | --- | --- | --- |
| To Vice President Production | | | Month: January | |
| Controllable Costs: | Budget | Actual | Fav/Unfav | |
| VP Production | $ 125,000 | $ 126,000 | $ 1,000 | U |
| Assembly Factories: | | | | |
| Detroit | 420,000 | 418,000 | 2,000 | F |
| **Chicago** | **304,000** | **309,300** | **5,300** | U |
| St. Louis | 330,000 | 333,000 | 3,000 | U |
| Total | $1,179,000 | $1,186,300 | $ 7,300 | U |

**Report C**
Factory manager sees sum-
mary of controllable costs
for each department in the
factory.

| Report C | | | | |
| --- | --- | --- | --- | --- |
| To Factory Manager-Chicago | | | Month: January | |
| Controllable Costs: | Budget | Actual | Fav/Unfav | |
| Chicago Factory | $110,000 | $113,000 | $3,000 | U |
| Departments: | | | | |
| **Fabricating** | **84,000** | **85,300** | **1,300** | U |
| Enameling | 62,000 | 64,000 | 2,000 | U |
| Assembly | 48,000 | 47,000 | 1,000 | F |
| Total | $304,000 | $309,300 | $5,300 | U |

**Report D**
Department manager sees
controllable costs of
his/her department.

| Report D | | | | |
| --- | --- | --- | --- | --- |
| To Fabricating Dept. Manager | | | Month: January | |
| Controllable Costs: | Budget | Actual | Fav/Unfav | |
| Direct Materials | $20,000 | $20,500 | $ 500 | U |
| Direct Labor | 40,000 | 41,000 | 1,000 | U |
| Overhead | 24,000 | 23,800 | 200 | F |
| Total | $84,000 | $85,300 | $1,300 | U |

Production departments participate directly in making the product. Service departments provide only support services. In a **Ford Motor Company** manufacturing facility. the welding, painting, and assembling departments are production departments. Ford's maintenance and human resources departments are service departments. Both the production departments and service departments are cost centers.

2. A **profit center** incurs costs (and expenses) and also generates revenues.

   - Managers of profit centers are judged on the profitability of their centers.
   - Examples of profit centers include the individual departments of a retail store, such as clothing, furniture, and automotive products, and branch offices of banks (see **Helpful Hint**).

3. Like a profit center, an **investment center** incurs costs (and expenses) and generates revenues. In addition, an investment center has control over decisions regarding the assets available for use.

   - Investment center managers are evaluated on both the profitability of the center and the rate of return earned on the assets used.
   - Investment centers are often associated with subsidiary companies.

Utility company **Duke Energy** has operating divisions such as electric utility, energy trading, and natural gas. Investment center managers control or significantly influence investment decisions related to such matters as plant expansion and entry into new market areas.

**Illustration 23.20** depicts the three types of responsibility centers.

**HELPFUL HINT**

The jewelry department of **Macy's** department store is a profit center, while the makeup department of a movie studio is a cost center.

**ILLUSTRATION 23.20**  **Types of responsibility centers**

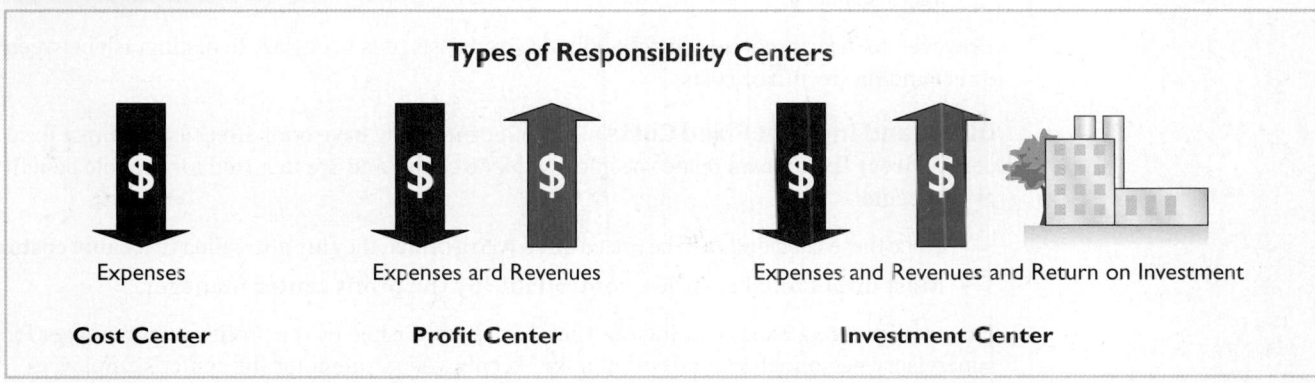

**Types of Responsibility Centers**

| Expenses | Expenses and Revenues | Expenses and Revenues and Return on Investment |
|---|---|---|
| **Cost Center** | **Profit Center** | **Investment Center** |

## Responsibility Accounting for Cost Centers

The evaluation of a manager's performance for cost centers is based on his or her ability to meet budgeted goals for controllable costs. **Responsibility reports for cost centers compare actual controllable costs with flexible budget data.**

**Illustration 23.21** shows a responsibility report. The report is adapted from the flexible budget report for Fox Company in Illustration 23.16. It assumes that the Finishing Department manager is able to control all manufacturing overhead costs except depreciation, property taxes, and his own monthly salary of $6,000. The remaining $4,000 ($10,000 − $6,000) of supervision costs are assumed to apply to other supervisory personnel within the Finishing Department, whose salaries are controllable by the manager.

- The report in Illustration 23.21 includes **only controllable costs**, and no distinction is made between variable and fixed costs.
- The responsibility report continues the concept of management by exception.
- In this case, top management may request an explanation of the $1,000 favorable difference in indirect labor and/or the $500 unfavorable difference in indirect materials if considered significant.

**ILLUSTRATION 23.21**
**Responsibility report for a cost center**

| | Fox Company<br>Finishing Department<br>Responsibility Report<br>For the Month Ended January 31, 2022 | | | |
|---|---|---|---|---|
| | | | Difference<br>Favorable - F | |
| Controllable Costs | Budget | Actual | Unfavorable - U | |
| Indirect materials | $13,500 | $14,000 | $ 500 | U |
| Indirect labor | 18,000 | 17,000 | 1,000 | F |
| Utilities | 4,500 | 4,600 | 100 | U |
| **Supervision** | **4,000** | **4,000** | 0 | |
| Total | $40,000 | $39,600 | $ 400 | F |

## Responsibility Accounting for Profit Centers

To evaluate the performance of a profit center manager, upper management needs detailed information about both controllable revenues and controllable costs.

- The operating revenues earned by a profit center, such as sales, are controllable by the manager.
- All variable costs (and expenses) incurred by the center are also controllable by the manager because they vary with sales.

However, to determine the controllability of fixed costs, it is necessary to distinguish between direct and indirect fixed costs.

### Direct and Indirect Fixed Costs
A profit center may have both direct and indirect fixed costs. **Direct fixed costs** relate specifically to one center and are incurred for the sole benefit of that center.

- Since these fixed costs can be traced directly to a center, they are also called **traceable costs**.
- **Most direct fixed costs are controllable by the profit center manager**.

Examples of direct fixed costs include the salaries established by the profit center manager for supervisory personnel and the cost of a timekeeping department for the center's employees.

In contrast, **indirect fixed costs** pertain to a company's overall operating activities and are incurred for the benefit of more than one profit center.

- When preparing budgets, a company allocates indirect fixed costs to profit centers on some type of equitable basis.
- Because these fixed costs apply to more than one center, they are also called **common costs**.
- **Most indirect fixed costs are not controllable by the profit center manager and are therefore not reported in the responsibility report**.

For example, property taxes on a building occupied by more than one center may be allocated on the basis of square feet of floor space used by each center. Or, the costs of a company's human resources department may be allocated to profit centers on the basis of the number of employees in each center.

### Responsibility Report
The responsibility report for a profit center shows budgeted and actual **controllable revenues and costs**. The report is prepared using the cost-volume-profit income statement explained in Chapter 18 (see **Helpful Hint**). In the report:

1. Controllable fixed costs are deducted from contribution margin.
2. The excess of contribution margin over controllable fixed costs is identified as **controllable margin**.
3. Noncontrollable fixed costs, such as indirect fixed costs, are not reported.

**HELPFUL HINT**

Recognize that we are emphasizing *financial* measures of performance. Companies are now making an effort to also stress *nonfinancial* performance measures such as product quality, labor productivity, market growth, materials' yield, manufacturing flexibility, and technological capability.

Illustration 23.22 shows the responsibility report for the manager of the Marine Division, a profit center of Mantle Company. For the year, the Marine Division also had $60,000 of indirect fixed costs that were not controllable by the profit center manager and therefore were omitted from the report.

**ILLUSTRATION 23.22**

**Responsibility report for profit center**

Mantle Company

| | Budget | Actual | Difference Favorable - F Unfavorable - U | |
|---|---|---|---|---|
| Sales | $1,200,000 | $1,150,000 | $50,000 | U |
| Variable costs | | | | |
| Cost of goods sold | 500,000 | 490,000 | 10,000 | F |
| Selling and administrative | 160,000 | 156,000 | 4,000 | F |
| Total | 660,000 | 646,000 | 14,000 | F |
| Contribution margin | 540,000 | 504,000 | 36,000 | J |
| **Controllable fixed costs** | | | | |
| Cost of goods sold | 100,000 | 100,000 | 0 | |
| Selling and administrative | 80,000 | 80,000 | 0 | |
| Total | 180,000 | 180,000 | 0 | |
| **Controllable margin** | $ 360,000 | $ 324,000 | $36,000 | U |

Mantle Company / Marine Division / Responsibility Report / For the Year Ended December 31, 2022

Controllable margin is considered to be the best measure of the manager's performance **in controlling revenues and costs**.

- The report in Illustration 23.22 shows that the manager's performance was below budgeted expectations by 10% ($36,000 ÷ $360,000) of the budgeted controllable margin.
- Top management would likely investigate the causes of this unfavorable result.
- Note that the responsibility report for the division manager does not show the Marine Division's noncontrollable indirect fixed costs of $60,000 because the manager cannot control these costs.

Management also may choose to see **monthly** responsibility reports for profit centers. In addition, responsibility reports may include cumulative year-to-date results.

## DO IT! 3 | Profit Center Responsibility Report

Midwest Division operates as a profit center. It reports the following for the year:

| | Budget | Actual |
|---|---|---|
| Sales | $1,500,000 | $1,700,000 |
| Variable costs | 700,000 | 800,000 |
| Controllable fixed costs | 400,000 | 400,000 |
| Noncontrollable fixed costs | 200,000 | 200,000 |

Prepare a responsibility report for the Midwest Division for December 31, 2022.

**ACTION PLAN**
- Deduct variable costs from sales to show contribution margin.
- Deduct controllable fixed costs from the contribution margin to show controllable margin.
- Do not report noncontrollable fixed costs.

**Solution**

| | | Midwest Division Responsibility Report | | |
|---|---|---|---|---|
| Home Insert Page Layout Formulas Data Review View | | | | |
| P18 | *fx* | | | |
| | A | B | C | D | E |
| 1 | | Midwest Division | | | |
| 2 | | Responsibility Report | | | |
| 3 | | For the Year Ended December 31, 2022 | | | |
| 4 | | | | Difference | |
| 5 | | Budget | Actual | Favorable F Unfavorable U | |
| 6 | Sales | $1,500,000 | $1,700,000 | $200,000 | F |
| 7 | Variable costs | 700,000 | 800,000 | 100,000 | U |
| 8 | Contribution margin | 800,000 | 900,000 | 100,000 | F |
| 9 | Controllable fixed costs | 400,000 | 400,000 | 0 | |
| 10 | **Controllable margin** | **$ 400,000** | **$ 500,000** | **$100,000** | F |
| 11 | | | | | |

Related exercise material: **BE23.7, BE23.8, DO IT! 23.3, and E23.15.**

# Investment Centers

---

**LEARNING OBJECTIVE 4**

Evaluate performance in investment centers.

---

As explained earlier, an investment center manager can control or significantly influence decisions regarding the amount and nature of assets available for use in operations.

- Thus, the primary basis for evaluating the performance of a manager of an investment center is **return on investment (ROI)**.
- The return on investment is considered to be a useful performance measurement because it shows the **effectiveness of the manager in utilizing the assets at his or her disposal**.

## Return on Investment (ROI)

The equation for computing ROI for an investment center, together with assumed illustrative data, is shown in **Illustration 23.23**.

**ILLUSTRATION 23.23**

**ROI equation**

| Controllable Margin | ÷ | Average Operating Assets | = | Return on Investment (ROI) |
|---|---|---|---|---|
| $1,000,000 | ÷ | $5,000,000 | = | 20% |

The two factors that determine ROI are controllable margin and average operating assets. Both factors in the equation are controllable by the investment center manager.

- Operating assets consist of current assets and factory assets used in operations by the center and controlled by the manager.
- Nonoperating assets such as idle factory assets and land held for future use are excluded.

- Average operating assets are usually based on the cost or book value of the assets at the beginning and end of the year.

Based on these assigned values, the ROI of 20% indicates that, on average, the segment generates 20 cents of profit for every dollar invested in assets.

# Responsibility Report

The scope of the investment center manager's responsibility significantly affects the content of the performance report.

- Since an investment center is an independent entity for operating purposes, **all fixed costs are controllable by its manager**. For example, the manager is responsible for depreciation on investment center assets.
- Therefore, more fixed costs are identified as controllable in the performance report for an investment center manager than in a performance report for a profit center manager.
- The report also shows budgeted and actual ROI below controllable margin.

To illustrate this responsibility report, we will now assume that the Marine Division of Mantle Company is an investment center. It has budgeted and actual average operating assets of $2,000,000. The manager can control $60,000 of additional fixed costs that were not controllable when the division was a profit center. **Illustration 23.24** shows the division's responsibility report.

**ILLUSTRATION 23.24**

**Responsibility report for investment center**

| | Budget | Actual | Difference<br>Favorable - F<br>Unfavorable - U | |
|---|---|---|---|---|
| Sales | $ 1,200,000 | $ 1,150,000 | $ 50,000 | U |
| Variable costs | | | | |
|   Cost of goods sold | 500,000 | 490,000 | 10,000 | F |
|   Selling and administrative | 160,000 | 156,000 | 4,000 | F |
|   Total | 660,000 | 646,000 | 14,000 | F |
| Contribution margin | 540,000 | 504,000 | 36,000 | U |
| **Controllable fixed costs** | | | | |
|   Cost of goods sold | 100,000 | 100,000 | 0 | |
|   Selling and administrative | 80,000 | 80,000 | 0 | |
|   **Other fixed costs** | 60,000 | 60,000 | 0 | |
|   Total | 240,000 | 240,000 | 0 | |
| **Controllable margin** | $ 300,000 | $ 264,000 | $ 36,000 | U |
| **Return on investment** | 15.0% | 13.2% | 1.8% | U |
| | (a) | (b) | (c) | |

$$\text{(a) } \frac{\$\ 300,000}{\$\ 2,000,000} \qquad \text{(b) } \frac{\$\ 264,000}{\$\ 2,000,000} \qquad \text{(c) } \frac{\$\ 36,000}{\$\ 2,000,000}$$

The report shows that the manager's performance based on ROI was below budget expectations by 1.8% (15.0% versus 13.2%). Top management would likely want explanations for this unfavorable result.

# Alternative Measures of ROI Inputs

The inputs to ROI can be measured in a variety of ways.

1. **Valuation of operating assets.**

   • Operating asset measures include acquisition cost, book value, appraised value, or fair value. The first two bases are readily available from the accounting records.

   • Each of the alternative values for operating assets can provide a reliable basis for evaluating a manager's performance as long as it is consistently applied between reporting periods.

2. **Margin (income) measure.**

   • Possible income measures include controllable margin, income from operations, or net income.

   • When computing ROI for a responsibility report, the best option is to use controllable margin since it is computed using only controllable costs. Income from operations and net income include noncontrollable costs in their computation.

# Improving ROI

The manager of an investment center can improve ROI by increasing controllable margin, and/or reducing average operating assets. To illustrate, we use the assumed data for the Laser Division of Berra Company shown in **Illustration 23.25**.

**Assumed data for Laser Division**

| | |
|---|---|
| Sales | $2,000,000 |
| Variable costs | 1,100,000 |
| Contribution margin (45%) | 900,000 |
| Controllable fixed costs | 300,000 |
| Controllable margin (a) | $ 600,000 |
| Average operating assets (b) | $5,000,000 |
| Return on investment (a) ÷ (b) | **12%** |

## Increasing Controllable Margin

Controllable margin can be increased by increasing sales or by reducing variable and controllable fixed costs as follows.

1. **Increase sales 10%.** Sales will increase $200,000 ($2,000,000 × .10). Assuming no change in the contribution margin percentage of 45% ($900,000 ÷ $2,000,000), contribution margin will increase $90,000 ($200,000 × .45). Controllable margin will also increase by $90,000 because controllable fixed costs will not change. Thus, controllable margin becomes $690,000 ($600,000 + $90,000). The new ROI is 13.8%, computed as shown in **Illustration 23.26**.

**ROI computation—increase in sales**

$$ROI = \frac{\text{Controllable margin}}{\text{Average operating assets}} = \frac{\$690,000}{\$5,000,000} = \textbf{13.8\%}$$

   • An increase in sales benefits both the investment center and the company if it results in new business.

   • It would not benefit the company if the increase was achieved at the expense of other investment centers.

2. **Decrease variable and fixed costs 10%.** Total costs decrease $140,000 [($1,100,000 + $300,000) × .10]. This reduction results in a corresponding increase in controllable margin. Thus, controllable margin becomes $740,000 ($600,000 + $140,000). The new ROI is 14.8%, computed as shown in **Illustration 23.27**.

$$ROI = \frac{\text{Controllable margin}}{\text{Average operating assets}} = \frac{\$740,000}{\$5,000,000} = \textbf{14.8\%}$$

**ILLUSTRATION 23.27**
**ROI computation—decrease in costs**

- This course of action is clearly beneficial when the reduction in costs is the result of eliminating waste and inefficiency.
- But, a reduction in costs that results from cutting expenditures on vital activities, such as required maintenance and inspections, is not likely to be acceptable to top management.

## Reducing Average Operating Assets

Assume that average operating assets are reduced 10% or $500,000 ($5,000,000 × .10). Average operating assets become $4,500,000 ($5,000,000 – $500,000). Since controllable margin remains unchanged at $600,000, the new ROI is 13.3%, computed as shown in **Illustration 23.28**.

$$ROI = \frac{\text{Controllable margin}}{\text{Average operating assets}} = \frac{\$600,000}{\$4,500,000} = \textbf{13.3\%}$$

**ILLUSTRATION 23.28**
**ROI computation—decrease in operating assets**

Reductions in operating assets may or may not be prudent.

- It is beneficial to eliminate overinvestment in inventories and to dispose of excessive factory assets.
- However, it is unwise to reduce inventories below expected needs or to dispose of essential factory assets.

---

## Management Insight

rh2010/Adobe Stock

### Is Your Job a Game?

As discussed in this chapter, the things you are held accountable for depend on your job responsibilities. Similarly, the form of a company's incentive and compensation structure varies depending on your level within the organization. If you are the chief executive officer (CEO), it is likely that a significant portion of your pay (about 30%) will be in the form of a stock-based bonus. This bonus is usually tied to overall company performance, typically measured by earnings per share and shareholder returns.

If you are a lower-level employee, your raises and bonuses might be structured similar to the incentives in video games. This so-called "gamification" has the ability to incentivize not just the most obvious aspect of your job but also many of the other functions that your manager deems important. For example, rather than just reward you for total sales made, your bonus under gamification might change if you "accurately enter their client's information into a sales tracker, assess the quality of sales leads or track how often they are going to sales meetings." It can also provide "points" for things like whether you lead a healthy lifestyle, collaborate with co-workers, and improve interpersonal skills.

**Sources:** Scott Thurm, "CEO Pay More Closely Matches Firms' Results," *Wall Street Journal* (September 11, 2013); and Farhad Manjoo, "The Gamification of the Office Approaches," *Wall Street Journal* (January 12, 2014).

**Why is the reward system of top managers tied to different types of measures than those of lower-level managers? (Answer is available at the end of the chapter.)**

---

## DO IT! 4 | Performance Evaluation

Metro Industries reported the following results for 2022.

| | |
|---|---|
| Sales | $400,000 |
| Variable costs | 320,000 |
| Controllable fixed costs | 40,800 |
| Average operating assets | 280,000 |

Management is considering the following two independent courses of action in 2023 in order to maximize the return on investment for this division.

**ACTION PLAN**

Recall key equations:
- **Sales – Variable costs = Contribution margin.**
- **Contribution margin – Controllable fixed costs = Controllable margin.**
- **Return on investment = Controllable margin ÷ Average operating assets.**

1. Reduce average operating assets by $80,000, with no change in controllable margin.
2. Increase sales $80,000, with no change in the contribution margin percentage.

For each proposed course of action:

a. Compute the controllable margin and the return on investment for 2022.
b. Compute the controllable margin and the expected return on investment for 2023.

### Solution

a. Return on investment for 2022:

| | |
|---|---:|
| Sales | $400,000 |
| Variable costs | 320,000 |
| Contribution margin | 80,000 |
| Controllable fixed costs | 40,800 |
| Controllable margin | $ 39,200 |

$$\text{Return on investment} \quad \frac{\$39,200}{\$280,000} \quad = \quad 14\%$$

b. Expected return on investment for alternative 1:

$$\frac{\$39,200}{\$280,000 - \$80,000} \quad = \quad 19.6\%$$

Expected return on investment for alternative 2:

| | |
|---|---:|
| Sales ($400,000 + $80,000) | $480,000 |
| Variable costs ($320,000 ÷ $400,000 × $480,000) | 384,000 |
| Contribution margin | 96,000 |
| Controllable fixed costs | 40,800 |
| Controllable margin | $ 55,200 |

$$\text{Return on investment} \quad \frac{\$55,200}{\$280,000} \quad = \quad 19.7\%$$

Related exercise material: **BE23.9, BE23.10, DO IT! 23.4, E23.16, and E23.17.**

---

| Appendix 23A |
|---|

# ROI versus Residual Income

**LEARNING OBJECTIVE *5**

Explain the difference between ROI and residual income.

Although most companies use ROI to evaluate investment performance, ROI has a significant disadvantage. To illustrate, let's look at the Electronics Division of Pujols Company. It has an ROI of 20%, computed as shown in **Illustration 23A.1**.

**ILLUSTRATION 23A.1**

**ROI computation**

| Controllable Margin | ÷ | Average Operating Assets | = | Return on Investment (ROI) |
|:---:|:---:|:---:|:---:|:---:|
| $1,000,000 | ÷ | $5,000,000 | = | 20% |

The Electronics Division is considering producing a new product, a GPS device (hereafter referred to as Tracker) for its boats. To produce Tracker, operating assets will have to increase $2,000,000. Tracker is expected to generate an additional $260,000 of controllable margin. **Illustration 23A.2** shows how Tracker will affect ROI.

| | Without Tracker | Tracker | With Tracker |
|---|---|---|---|
| Controllable margin (a) | $1,000,000 | $260,000 | $1,260,000 |
| Average operating assets (b) | $5,000,000 | $2,000,000 | $7,000,000 |
| Return on investment [(a) ÷ (b)] | 20% | 13% | 18% |

**ILLUSTRATION 23A.2**

ROI comparison

The investment in Tracker reduces ROI from 20% to 18%.

Let's suppose that you are the manager of the Electronics Division and must make the decision to produce or not produce Tracker.

- If you were evaluated using ROI, you probably would not produce Tracker because your ROI would drop from 20% to 18%.
- The problem with this ROI analysis is that it ignores an important variable: the minimum rate of return on a company's operating assets.
- The **minimum rate of return** is the rate at which the Electronics Division can cover its costs and earn a profit.

Assuming that the Electronics Division has a minimum rate of return of 10%, it should probably invest in Tracker because its ROI of 13% is greater than 10%.

# Residual Income Compared to ROI

To evaluate performance using the minimum rate of return, companies use the residual income approach. **Residual income** is the income that remains after subtracting from the controllable margin the minimum rate of return on a company's average operating assets. The residual income for Tracker would be computed as shown in **Illustration 23A.3**.

| Controllable Margin | − | ( Minimum Rate of Return × Average Operating Assets ) | = | Residual Income |
|---|---|---|---|---|
| $260,000 | − | (10% × $2,000,000) | = | $60,000 |

**ILLUSTRATION 23A.3**

Residual income computation

As shown, the residual income related to the Tracker investment is $60,000. **Illustration 23A.4** indicates how the division's residual income changes as the additional investment in Tracker is made.

| | Without Tracker | Tracker | With Tracker |
|---|---|---|---|
| Controllable margin (a) | $1,000,000 | $260,000 | $1,260,000 |
| Average operating assets × 10% (b) | 500,000 | 200,000 | 700,000 |
| Residual income [(a) − (b)] | $ 500,000 | $ 60,000 | **$ 560,000** |

**ILLUSTRATION 23A.4**

Residual income comparison

This example illustrates how performance evaluation based on ROI can be misleading and can even cause managers to reject projects that would actually increase income for the company. As a result, many companies such as **Coca-Cola**, **Briggs & Stratton**, **Eli Lilly**, and **Siemens AG** use residual income (or a variant often referred to as economic value added) to evaluate investment alternatives and measure company performance.

## Residual Income Weakness

It might appear from the above discussion that the goal of any company should be to maximize the total amount of residual income in each division. This goal, however, ignores the fact that one division might use substantially fewer assets to attain the same level of residual income as another division. For example, we know that to produce Tracker, the Electronics Division of Pujols Company used $2,000,000 of average operating assets to generate $260,000 of controllable margin. Now let's say a different division produced a product called SeaDog, which used $4,000,000 to generate $460,000 of controllable margin, as shown in **Illustration 23A.5**.

**ILLUSTRATION 23A.5**

**Comparison of two products**

| | Tracker | SeaDog |
|---|---|---|
| Controllable margin (a) | $260,000 | $460,000 |
| Average operating assets × 10% (b) | 200,000 | 400,000 |
| Residual income [(a) − (b)] | **$ 60,000** | **$ 60,000** |

If the performance of these two investments were evaluated using residual income, they would be considered equal:

- Both products have the same total residual income.
- This ignores, however, the fact that SeaDog required **twice** as many operating assets to achieve the same level of residual income.

# Review and Practice

## Learning Objectives Review

### 1 Describe budgetary control and static budget reports.

Budgetary control consists of (a) preparing periodic budget reports that compare actual results with planned objectives, (b) analyzing the differences to determine their causes, (c) taking appropriate corrective action, and (d) modifying future plans, if necessary.

Static budget reports are useful in evaluating the progress toward planned sales and profit goals. They are also appropriate in assessing a manager's effectiveness in controlling costs when (a) actual activity closely approximates the master budget activity level, and/or (b) the behavior of the costs in response to changes in activity is fixed.

### 2 Prepare flexible budget reports.

To develop the flexible budget, it is necessary to do the following. (a) Identify the activity index and the relevant range of activity. (b) Identify the variable costs, and determine the budgeted variable cost per unit of activity for each cost. (c) Identify the fixed costs, and determine the budgeted amount for each cost. (d) Prepare the budget for selected increments of activity within the relevant range. Flexible budget reports permit an evaluation of a manager's performance in controlling production and costs.

**3   Apply responsibility accounting to cost and profit centers.**

Responsibility accounting involves accumulating and reporting revenues and costs on the basis of the individual manager who has the authority to make the day-to-day decisions about the items. The evaluation of a manager's performance is based on the matters directly under the manager's control. In responsibility accounting, it is necessary to distinguish between controllable and noncontrollable fixed costs and to identify three types of responsibility centers: cost, profit, and investment.

Responsibility reports for cost centers compare actual costs with flexible budget data. The reports show only controllable costs, and no distinction is made between variable and fixed costs. Responsibility reports show contribution margin, controllable fixed costs, and controllable margin for each profit center.

**4   Evaluate performance in investment centers.**

The primary basis for evaluating performance in investment centers is return on investment (ROI). The equation for computing ROI for investment centers is Controllable margin ÷ Average operating assets.

**\*5   Explain the difference between ROI and residual income.**

ROI is controllable margin divided by average operating assets. Residual income is the income that remains after subtracting the minimum rate of return on a company's average operating assets. ROI sometimes provides misleading results because profitable investments are often rejected when the investment reduces ROI but increases overall profitability.

## Glossary Review

**Budgetary control**   The use of budgets to control operations. (p. 23-3).

**Controllable cost**   A cost over which a manager has control. (p. 23-16).

**Controllable margin**   Contribution margin less controllable fixed costs. (p. 23-22).

**Cost center**   A responsibility center that incurs costs but does not directly generate revenues. (p. 23-19).

**Decentralization**   Organizational structure in which control of operations is delegated to many managers throughout the organization. (p. 23-15).

**Direct fixed costs**   Costs that relate specifically to a responsibility center and are incurred for the sole benefit of the center. (p. 23-22).

**Flexible budget**   A projection of budget data for various levels of activity. (p. 23-7).

**Indirect fixed costs**   Costs that are incurred for the benefit of more than one profit center. (p. 23-22).

**Investment center**   A responsibility center that incurs costs, generates revenues, and has control over decisions regarding the assets available for use. (p. 23-21).

**Management by exception**   The review of budget reports by top management focused entirely or primarily on significant differences between actual results and planned objectives. (p. 23-16).

**Noncontrollable costs**   Costs incurred indirectly and allocated to a responsibility level that are not controllable at that level. (p. 23-16).

**Profit center**   A responsibility center that incurs costs and also generates revenues. (p. 23-21).

**\*Residual income**   The income that remains after subtracting from the controllable margin the minimum rate of return on a company's average operating assets. (p. 23-29).

**Responsibility accounting**   A part of management accounting that involves identifying and reporting revenues and costs on the basis of the manager who has the authority to make the day-to-day decisions about the items. (p. 23-14).

**Responsibility reporting system**   The preparation of reports for each level of responsibility in the company's organization chart. (p. 23-18).

**Return on investment (ROI)**   A measure of management's effectiveness in utilizing assets at its disposal in an investment center. (p. 23-24).

**Segment (or division)**   An area of responsibility in decentralized operations. (p. 23-15).

**Static budget**   A projection of budget data at one level of activity. (p. 23-4).

## Practice Multiple-Choice Questions

1. **(LO 1)** Budgetary control involves all but one of the following:
   a. modifying future plans.
   b. analyzing differences.
   c. using static budgets but **not** flexible budgets.
   d. determining differences between actual and planned results.

2. **(LO 1)** Depending on the nature of the report, budget reports are prepared:
   a. daily.
   b. weekly.
   c. monthly.
   d. All of the answer choices are correct.

3. **(LO 1)** A production manager in a manufacturing company would most likely receive a:

   **a.** sales report.

   **b.** income statement.

   **c.** scrap report.

   **d.** shipping department overhead report.

4. **(LO 1)** A static budget is:

   **a.** a projection of budget data at several levels of activity within the relevant range of activity.

   **b.** a projection of budget data at a single level of activity.

   **c.** compared to a flexible budget in a budget report.

   **d.** never appropriate in evaluating a manager's effectiveness in controlling costs.

5. **(LO 1)** A static budget is useful in controlling costs when cost behavior is:

   **a.** mixed.        **c.** variable.

   **b.** fixed.        **d.** linear.

6. **(LO 2)** At zero direct labor hours in a flexible budget graph, the total budgeted cost line intersects the vertical axis at $30,000. At 10,000 direct labor hours, a horizontal line drawn from the total budgeted cost line intersects the vertical axis at $90,000. Fixed and variable costs may be expressed as:

   **a.** $30,000 fixed plus $6 per direct labor hour variable.

   **b.** $30,000 fixed plus $9 per direct labor hour variable.

   **c.** $60,000 fixed plus $3 per direct labor hour variable.

   **d.** $60,000 fixed plus $6 per direct labor hour variable.

7. **(LO 2)** At 9,000 direct labor hours, the flexible budget for indirect materials (a variable cost) is $27,000. If $28,000 of indirect materials costs are incurred at 9,200 direct labor hours, the flexible budget report should show the following difference for indirect materials:

   **a.** $1,000 unfavorable.    **c.** $400 favorable.

   **b.** $1,000 favorable.      **d.** $400 unfavorable.

8. **(LO 3)** Under responsibility accounting, the evaluation of a manager's performance is based on matters that the manager:

   **a.** directly controls.

   **b.** directly and indirectly controls.

   **c.** indirectly controls.

   **d.** has shared responsibility for with another manager.

9. **(LO 3)** Responsibility centers include:

   **a.** cost centers.

   **b.** profit centers.

   **c.** investment centers.

   **d.** All of the answer choices are correct.

10. **(LO 3)** Responsibility reports for cost centers:

    **a.** distinguish between fixed and variable costs.

    **b.** use static budget data.

    **c.** include both controllable and noncontrollable costs.

    **d.** include only controllable costs.

11. **(LO 3)** The accounting department of a manufacturing company is an example of:

    **a.** a cost center.

    **b.** a profit center.

    **c.** an investment center.

    **d.** a contribution center.

12. **(LO 3)** To evaluate the performance of a profit center manager, upper management needs detailed information about:

    **a.** controllable costs.

    **b.** controllable revenues.

    **c.** controllable costs and revenues.

    **d.** controllable costs and revenues and average operating assets.

13. **(LO 3)** In a responsibility report for a profit center, controllable fixed costs are deducted from contribution margin to show:

    **a.** profit center margin.    **c.** net income.

    **b.** controllable margin.      **d.** income from operations.

14. **(LO 4)** In the equation for return on investment (ROI), the factors for controllable margin and operating assets are, respectively:

    **a.** controllable margin percentage and total operating assets.

    **b.** controllable margin dollars and average operating assets.

    **c.** controllable margin dollars and total assets.

    **d.** controllable margin percentage and average operating assets.

15. **(LO 4)** A manager of an investment center can improve ROI by:

    **a.** increasing average operating assets.

    **b.** reducing sales.

    **c.** increasing variable costs.

    **d.** reducing variable and/or controllable fixed costs.

## Solutions

1. **c.** Budgetary control involves using flexible budgets and sometimes static budgets. The other choices are all part of budgetary control.

2. **d.** Budget reports are prepared daily, weekly, or monthly. The other choices are correct, but choice (d) is the better answer.

3. **c.** A production manager in a manufacturing company would most likely receive a scrap report. The other choices are incorrect because (a) top management or a sales manager would most likely receive a sales report, (b) top management would most likely receive

an income statement, and (d) a department manager would most likely receive a shipping department overhead report.

4. **b.** A static budget is a projection of budget data at a single level of activity. The other choices are incorrect because a static budget (a) is a projection of budget data at a single level of activity, not at several levels of activity within the relevant range of activity; (c) is not compared to a flexible budget in a budget report; and (d) is appropriate in evaluating a manager's effectiveness in controlling fixed costs.

5. **b.** A static budget is useful for controlling fixed costs. The other choices are incorrect because a static budget is not useful for controlling (a) mixed costs, (c) variable costs, or (d) linear costs.

**6. a.** The intersection point of $90,000 is total budgeted costs, or budgeted fixed costs plus budgeted variable costs. Fixed costs are $30,000 (amount at zero direct labor hours), so budgeted variable costs are $60,000 [$90,000 (Total costs) − $30,000 (Fixed costs)]. Budgeted variable costs ($60,000) divided by total activity level (10,000 direct labor hours) gives the variable cost per unit of $6 per direct labor hour. The other choices are therefore incorrect.

**7. d.** Budgeted indirect materials per direct labor hour (DLH) is $3 ($27,000 ÷ 9,000). At an activity level of 9,200 direct labor hours, budgeted indirect materials are $27,600 (9,200 × $3 per DLH) but actual indirect materials costs are $28,000, resulting in a $400 unfavorable difference. The other choices are therefore incorrect.

**8. a.** The evaluation of a manager's performance is based only on matters that the manager directly controls. The other choices are therefore incorrect as they include indirect controls and shared responsibility.

**9. d.** Cost centers, profit centers, and investment centers are all responsibility centers. The other choices are correct, but choice (d) is the better answer.

**10. d.** Responsibility reports for cost centers report only controllable costs; they (a) do not distinguish between fixed and variable costs; (b) use flexible budget data, not static budget data; and (c) do not include noncontrollable costs.

**11. a.** The accounting department of a manufacturing company is an example of a cost center, not (b) a profit center, (c) an investment center, or (d) contribution center.

**12. c.** To evaluate the performance of a profit center manager, upper management needs detailed information about controllable costs and revenues, not just (a) controllable costs or (b) controllable revenues. Choice (d) is incorrect because upper management does not need information about average operating assets.

**13. b.** Contribution margin less controllable fixed costs is the controllable margin, not (a) the profit center margin, (c) net income, or (d) income from operations.

**14. b.** The factors in the equation for ROI are controllable margin dollars and average operating assets. The other choices are therefore incorrect.

**15. d.** Reducing variable or controllable fixed costs will cause the controllable margin to increase, which is one way a manager of an investment center can improve ROI. The other choices are incorrect because (a) increasing average operating assets will lower ROI; (b) reducing sales will cause contribution margin to go down, thereby decreasing controllable margin since there will be less contribution margin to cover controllable fixed costs and resulting in lower ROI; and (c) increasing variable costs will cause the contribution margin to be lower, thereby decreasing controllable margin and resulting in lower ROI.

## Practice Brief Exercises

**1. (LO 2)** Borusa Company expects to produce 600,000 units of its product Eldrad in 2022. Monthly production is expected to range from 40,000 to 50,000 units. Budgeted variable manufacturing costs per unit are direct materials $4, direct labor $5, and overhead $8. Budgeted fixed manufacturing costs per unit are $2 for depreciation and $1.50 for supervision. Prepare a flexible manufacturing budget for the relevant range value using 10,000-unit increments.

*Prepare a flexible budget for variable costs.*

### Solution

1.

**Borusa Company**
**Monthly Flexible Manufacturing Budget**
**For the Year 2022**

| | | | |
|---|---|---|---|
| Activity level | | | |
| Finished units | 40,000 | 50,000 | 60,000 |
| Variable costs | | | |
| Direct materials ($4) | $160,000 | $ 200,000 | $ 240,000 |
| Direct labor ($5) | 200,000 | 250,000 | 300,000 |
| Overhead ($8) | 320,000 | 400,000 | 480,000 |
| Total variable costs ($17) | 680,000 | 850,000 | 1,020,000 |
| Fixed costs | | | |
| Depreciation* | 100,000 | 100,000 | 100,000 |
| Supervision** | 75,000 | 75,000 | 75,000 |
| Total fixed costs | 175,000 | 175,000 | 175,000 |
| Total costs | $855,000 | $1,025,000 | $1,195,000 |

*($2 × 600,000) − 12; **($1.50 × 600,000) ÷ 12

*Prepare a responsibility report for a profit center.*

**2. (LO 3)** Goth Company accumulates the following summary data for the year ending December 31, 2022, for its Chancellor Division, which it operates as a profit center: sales—$2,000,000 budget, $1,940,000 actual; variable costs—$1,000,000 budget, $980,000 actual; and controllable fixed costs—$300,000 budget, $317,000 actual. Prepare a responsibility report for the Chancellor Division.

**Solution**

2.

**Goth Company**
**Chancellor Division**
**Responsibility Report**
**For the Year Ended December 31, 2022**

|  | Budget | Actual | Difference<br>Favorable F<br>Unfavorable U |
|---|---|---|---|
| Sales | $2,000,000 | $1,940,000 | $   60,000 U |
| Variable costs | 1,000,000 | 980,000 | 20,000 F |
| Contribution margin | 1,000,000 | 960,000 | 40,000 U |
| Controllable fixed costs | 300,000 | 317,000 | 17,000 U |
| Controllable margin | $   700,000 | $   643,000 | $   57,000 U |

*Compute return on investment using the ROI equation.*

**3. (LO 4)**  For its three investment centers, Usher Company accumulates the following data.

|  | I | II | III |
|---|---|---|---|
| Sales | $2,000,000 | $4,000,000 | $4,000,000 |
| Controllable margin | 1,200,000 | 2,100,000 | 2,400,000 |
| Average operating assets | 4,000,000 | 7,000,000 | 9,600,000 |

Compute the return on investment (ROI) for each center.

**Solution**

3.

I   ($1,200,000 ÷ $4,000,000) = 30%
II   ($2,100,000 ÷ $7,000,000) = 30%
III   ($2,400,000 ÷ $9,600,000) = 25%

# Practice Exercises

*Prepare flexible manufacturing overhead budget.*

**1. (LO 2)** Felix Company uses a flexible budget for manufacturing overhead based on direct labor hours. Variable manufacturing overhead costs per direct labor hour are as follows.

| Indirect labor | $0.70 |
|---|---|
| Indirect materials | 0.50 |
| Utilities | 0.40 |

Budgeted fixed overhead costs per month are supervision $4,000, depreciation $3,000, and property taxes $800. The company believes it will normally operate in a range of 7,000–10,000 direct labor hours per month.

**Instructions**

Prepare a monthly flexible manufacturing overhead budget for 2022 for the expected range of activity, using increments of 1,000 direct labor hours.

**Solution**

1.

Felix Company
**Monthly Flexible Manufacturing Overhead Budget**
For the Year 2022

| Activity level | | | | |
|---|---|---|---|---|
| Direct labor hours | 7,000 | 8,000 | 9,000 | 10,000 |
| Variable costs | | | | |
| Indirect labor ($.70) | $ 4,900 | $ 5,600 | $ 6,300 | $ 7,000 |
| Indirect materials ($.50) | 3,500 | 4,000 | 4,500 | 5,000 |
| Utilities ($.40) | 2,800 | 3,200 | 3,600 | 4,000 |
| Total variable costs ($1.60) | 11,200 | 12,800 | 14,400 | 16,000 |
| Fixed costs | | | | |
| Supervision | 4,000 | 4,000 | 4,000 | 4,000 |
| Depreciation | 3,000 | 3,000 | 3,000 | 3,000 |
| Property taxes | 800 | 800 | 800 | 800 |
| Total fixed costs | 7,800 | 7,800 | 7,800 | 7,800 |
| Total costs | $19,000 | $20,600 | $22,200 | $23,800 |

2. **(LO 4)** The White Division of Mesin Company reported the following data for the current year.

*Compute ROI for current year and for possible future changes.*

| | |
|---|---|
| Sales | $3,000,000 |
| Variable costs | 2,400,000 |
| Controllable fixed costs | 400,000 |
| Average operating assets | 5,000,000 |

Top management is unhappy with the investment center's return on investment (ROI). It asks the manager of the White Division to submit plans to improve ROI in the next year. The manager believes it is feasible to consider the following independent courses of action.

1. Increase sales by $300,000 with no change in the contribution margin percentage.

2. Reduce variable costs by $100,000.

3. Reduce average operating assets by 4%.

**Instructions**

a. Compute the return on investment (ROI) for the current year.

b. Using the ROI equation, compute the ROI under each of the proposed courses of action. (Round to one decimal.)

**Solution**

2. **a.** Controllable margin = ($3,000,000 − $2,400,000 − $400,000) = $200,000
   ROI = $200,000 ÷ $5,000,000 = 4%

   **b. 1.** Contribution margin percentage is 20%, or [($3,000,000 − $2,400,000) ÷ $3,000,000]
   Increase in controllable margin = $300,000 × 20% = $60,000
   ROI = ($200,000 + $60,000) ÷ $5,000,000 = 5.2%

   2. ($200,000 + $100,000) ÷ $5,000,000 = 6%

   3. $200,000 ÷ [$5,000,000 − ($5,000,000 × .04)] = 4.2%

# Practice Problem

**(LO 2)** Glenda Company uses a flexible budget for manufacturing overhead based on direct labor hours. For 2022, the master overhead budget for the Packaging Department based on 300,000 direct labor hours was as follows.

*Prepare flexible budget report.*

| Variable Costs | | Fixed Costs | |
|---|---|---|---|
| Indirect labor | $360,000 | Supervision | $ 60,000 |
| Supplies and lubricants | 150,000 | Depreciation | 24,000 |
| Maintenance | 210,000 | Property taxes | 18,000 |
| Utilities | 120,000 | Insurance | 12,000 |
| | $840,000 | | $114,000 |

During July, 24,000 direct labor hours were worked. The company incurred the following variable costs in July: indirect labor $30,200, supplies and lubricants $11,600, maintenance $17,500, and utilities $9,200. Actual fixed overhead costs were the same as monthly budgeted fixed costs.

### Instructions

Prepare a flexible budget report for the Packaging Department for July.

### Solution

**Glenda Company**
**Manufacturing Overhead Budget Report (Flexible)**
**Packaging Department**
**For the Month Ended July 31, 2022**

| | | | Difference |
|---|---|---|---|
| | Budget | Actual Costs | Favorable F |
| Direct labor hours (DLH) | 24,000 DLH | 24,000 DLH | Unfavorable U |
| Variable costs | | | |
| Indirect labor ($1.20[a]) | $28,800 | $30,200 | $1,400 U |
| Supplies and lubricants ($0.50[a]) | 12,000 | 11,600 | 400 F |
| Maintenance ($0.70[a]) | 16,800 | 17,500 | 700 U |
| Utilities ($0.40[a]) | 9,600 | 9,200 | 400 F |
| Total variable | 67,200 | 68,500 | 1,300 U |
| Fixed costs | | | |
| Supervision | 5,000[b] | 5,000 | –0– |
| Depreciation | 2,000[b] | 2,000 | –0– |
| Property taxes | 1,500[b] | 1,500 | –0– |
| Insurance | 1,000[b] | 1,000 | –0– |
| Total fixed | 9,500 | 9,500 | –0– |
| Total costs | $76,700 | $78,000 | $1,300 U |

[a]$360,000 ÷ 300,000; $150,000 ÷ 300,000; $210,000 ÷ 300,000; $120,000 ÷ 300,000
[b]Annual cost divided by 12

Brief Exercises, DO IT! Exercises, Exercises, Problems, Data Analytics Activities, and many additional resources are available for practice in WileyPLUS.

*Note:* All asterisked Questions, Exercises, and Problems relate to material in the appendix to the chapter.

## Questions

**1. a.** What is budgetary control?

**b.** Fred Barone is describing budgetary control. What steps should be included in Fred's description?

**2.** The following purposes are part of a budgetary reporting system: (a) Determine efficient use of materials. (b) Control overhead costs. (c) Determine whether income objectives are being met. For each purpose, indicate the name of the report, the frequency of the report, and the primary recipient(s) of the report.

**3.** How may a budget report for the second quarter differ from a budget report for the first quarter?

**4.** Ken Bay questions the usefulness of a master sales budget in evaluating sales performance. Is there justification for Ken's concern? Explain.

**5.** Under what circumstances may a static budget be an appropriate basis for evaluating a manager's effectiveness in controlling costs?

**6.** "A flexible budget is really a series of static budgets." Is this true? Explain why or why not.

**7.** The static manufacturing overhead budget based on 40,000 direct labor hours shows budgeted indirect labor costs of $54,000. During March, the department incurs $64,000 of indirect labor while working 45,000 direct labor hours. Is this a favorable or unfavorable performance? Why?

**8.** A static overhead budget based on 40,000 direct labor hours shows Factory Insurance $6,500 as a fixed cost. At the 50,000 direct labor hours worked in March factory insurance costs were $6,300. Is this a favorable or unfavorable performance? Why?

**9.** Megan Pedigo is confused about how a flexible budget is prepared. Identify the steps for Megan.

**10.** Cali Company has prepared a graph of flexible budget data. At zero direct labor hours, the total budgeted cost line intersects the vertical axis at $20,000. At 10,000 direct labor hours, the line drawn from the total budgeted cost line intersects the vertical axis at $85,000. How may the fixed and variable costs be expressed?

**11.** The flexible budget calculation is fixed costs $50,000 plus variable costs of $4 per direct labor hour. What is the total budgeted cost at (a) 9,000 hours and (b) 12,345 hours?

**12.** What is management by exception? What criteria may be used in identifying exceptions?

**13.** What is responsibility accounting? Explain the purpose of responsibility accounting.

**14.** Eve Rooney is studying for an accounting examination. Describe for Eve what conditions are necessary for responsibility accounting to be used effectively.

**15.** Distinguish between controllable and noncontrollable costs.

**16.** How do responsibility reports differ from budget reports?

**17.** What is the relationship, if any, between a responsibility reporting system and a company's organization chart?

**18.** Distinguish among the three types of responsibility centers.

**19.** (a) What costs are included in a performance report for a cost center? (b) In the report, are variable and fixed costs identified?

**20.** How do direct fixed costs differ from indirect fixed costs? Are both types of fixed costs controllable?

**21.** Jane Nott is confused about controllable margin reported in an income statement for a profit center. How is this margin computed, and what is its primary purpose?

**22.** What is the primary basis for evaluating the performance of the manager of an investment center? Indicate the equation for this basis.

**23.** Explain the ways in which ROI can be improved.

**24.** Indicate two behavioral principles that pertain to (a) the manager being evaluated and (b) top management.

**\*25.** What is a major disadvantage of using ROI to evaluate investment and company performance?

**\*26.** What is residual income, and what is one of its major weaknesses?

## Brief Exercises

**BE23.1 (LO 1), AP** For the quarter ended March 31, 2022, Croix Company accumulates the following sales data for its newest guitar, The Edge: $315,000 budget; $305,000 actual. Prepare a static budget report for the quarter.

*Prepare static budget report.*

**BE23.2 (LO 1), AP** For the quarter ended March 31, 2022, Croix Company accumulates the following sales data for its newest guitar, The Edge: $315,000 budget; $305,000 actual. In the second quarter, budgeted sales were $380,000, and actual sales were $384,000. Prepare a static budget report for the second quarter and for the year to date.

*Prepare static budget report for 2 quarters.*

**BE23.3 (LO 2), E** In Rooney Company, direct labor is $20 per hour. The company expects to operate at 10,000 direct labor hours each month. In January 2022, direct labor totaling $206,000 is incurred in working 10,400 hours. Prepare (a) a static budget report and (b) a flexible budget report. Evaluate the usefulness of each report.

*Show usefulness of flexible budgets in evaluating performance.*

**BE23.4 (LO 2), AP** Gundy Company expects to produce 1,200,000 units of Product XX in 2022. Monthly production is expected to range from 80,000 to 120,000 units. Budgeted variable manufacturing costs per unit are direct materials $5, direct labor $6, and overhead $8. Budgeted fixed manufacturing costs per unit for depreciation are $2 and for supervision are $1. Prepare a flexible manufacturing budget for the relevant range value using 20,000 unit increments.

*Prepare a flexible budget for variable costs.*

**BE23.5 (LO 2), AN** Gundy Company expects to produce 1,200,000 units of Product XX in 2022. Monthly production is expected to range from 80,000 to 120,000 units. Budgeted variable manufacturing costs per unit are direct materials $5, direct labor $6, and overhead $8. Budgeted fixed manufacturing costs per unit for depreciation are $2 and for supervision are $1. In March 2022, the company incurs the following costs in producing 100,000 units: direct materials $520,000, direct labor $596,000, and variable overhead $805,000. Actual fixed costs were equal to budgeted fixed costs. Prepare a flexible budget report for March. Were costs controlled?

*Prepare flexible budget report.*

*Prepare a responsibility report for a cost center.*

**BE23.6 (LO 3), AP** In the Assembly Department of Hannon Company, budgeted and actual manufacturing overhead costs for the month of April 2022 were as follows.

|  | Budget | Actual |
|---|---|---|
| Indirect materials | $16,000 | $14,300 |
| Indirect labor | 20,000 | 20,600 |
| Utilities | 10,000 | 10,850 |
| Supervision | 5,000 | 5,000 |

All costs are controllable by the department manager. Prepare a responsibility report for April for the cost center.

*Prepare a responsibility report for a profit center.*

**BE23.7 (LO 3), AP** Torres Company accumulates the following summary data for the year ending December 31, 2022, for its Water Division, which it operates as a profit center: sales—$2,000,000 budget, $2,080,000 actual; variable costs—$1,000,000 budget, $1,050,000 actual; and controllable fixed costs—$300,000 budget, $305,000 actual. Prepare a responsibility report for the Water Division for the year ending December 31, 2022.

*Prepare a responsibility report for an investment center.*

**BE23.8 (LO 4), AP** For the year ending December 31, 2022, Cobb Company accumulates the following data for the Plastics Division, which it operates as an investment center: contribution margin—$700,000 budget, $710,000 actual; controllable fixed costs—$300,000 budget, $302,000 actual. Average operating assets for the year were $2,000,000. Prepare a responsibility report for the Plastics Division beginning with contribution margin for the year ending December 31, 2022.

*Compute return on investment using the ROI equation.*

**BE23.9 (LO 4), AP** For its three investment centers, Gerrard Company accumulates the following data:

|  | I | II | III |
|---|---|---|---|
| Sales | $2,000,000 | $4,000,000 | $ 4,000,000 |
| Controllable margin | 1,400,000 | 2,000,000 | 3,600,000 |
| Average operating assets | 5,000,000 | 8,000,000 | 10,000,000 |

Compute the return on investment (ROI) for each center.

*Compute return on investment under changed conditions.*

**BE23.10 (LO 4), AP** For its three investment centers, Gerrard Company accumulates the following data:

|  | I | II | III |
|---|---|---|---|
| Sales | $2,000,000 | $4,000,000 | $ 4,000,000 |
| Controllable margin | 1,400,000 | 2,000,000 | 3,600,000 |
| Average operating assets | 5,000,000 | 8,000,000 | 10,000,000 |

The company expects the following changes for investment centers I, II, and III in the next year: investment center I to increase sales 15%, investment center II to decrease controllable fixed costs $400,000, and investment center III to decrease average operating assets $400,000. Compute the expected return on investment (ROI) for each center. Assume investment center I has a contribution margin percentage of 70%.

*Compute ROI and residual income.*

**\*BE23.11 (LO 5), AP** Sterling, Inc. reports the following financial information for its sports clothing segment.

| Average operating assets | $3,000,000 |
|---|---|
| Controllable margin | $630,000 |
| Minimum rate of return | 10% |

Compute the return on investment and the residual income for the segment.

*Compute ROI and residual income.*

**\*BE23.12 (LO 5), AP** Presented here is information related to the Southern Division of Lumber, Inc.

| Contribution margin | $1,200,000 |
|---|---|
| Controllable margin | $800,000 |
| Average operating assets | $4,000,000 |
| Minimum rate of return | 15% |

Compute the Southern Division's return on investment and residual income.

# DO IT! Exercises

*Prepare and evaluate a static budget report.*

**DO IT! 23.1 (LO 1), AP** Wade Company estimates that it will produce 6,000 units of product IOA during the current month. Budgeted variable manufacturing costs per unit are direct materials $7, direct labor $13, and overhead $18. Monthly budgeted fixed manufacturing overhead costs are $8,000 for depreciation and $3,800 for supervision.

In the current month, Wade actually produced 6,500 units and incurred the following costs: direct materials $38,850, direct labor $76,440, variable overhead $116,640, depreciation $8,000 and supervision $4,000.

Prepare a static budget report. *Hint:* The Budget column is based on estimated production while the Actual column is the actual cost incurred during the period. (*Note:* You do not need to prepare the heading.) Were costs controlled? Discuss limitations of the budget.

**DO IT! 23.2 (LO 2), AP** In Pargo Company's flexible budget graph, the fixed-cost line and the total budgeted cost line intersect the vertical axis at $90,000. The total budgeted cost line is $350,000 at an activity level of 50,000 direct labor hours. Compute total budgeted costs at 55,000 direct labor hours.

*Compute total budgeted costs in flexible budget.*

**DO IT! 23.3 (LO 3), AP** The Rockies Division operates as a profit center. It reports the following for the year ending December 31, 2022.

*Prepare a responsibility report.*

| | Budget | Actual |
|---|---|---|
| Sales | $2,000,000 | $1,890,000 |
| Variable costs | 800,000 | 760,000 |
| Controllable fixed costs | 550,000 | 550,000 |
| Noncontrollable fixed costs | 250,000 | 250,000 |

Prepare a responsibility report for the Rockies Division at December 31, 2022.

**DO IT! 23.4 (LO 4), AP** The service division of Raney Industries reported the following results for 2022.

*Compute ROI and expected return on investments.*

| | |
|---|---|
| Sales | $500,000 |
| Variable costs | 300,000 |
| Controllable fixed costs | 75,000 |
| Average operating assets | 625,000 |

Management is considering the following independent courses of action in 2023 in order to maximize the return on investment for this division.

1. Reduce average operating assets by $125,000, with no change in controllable margin.
2. Increase sales $100,000, with no change in the contribution margin percentage.
a. Compute the controllable margin and the return on investment for 2022.
b. Compute the controllable margin and the expected return on investment for 2023 for each proposed alternative.

# Exercises

**E23.1 (LO 1, 2), K** Connie Rice has prepared the following list of statements about budgetary control.

*Understand the concept of budgetary control.*

1. Budget reports compare actual results with planned objectives.
2. All budget reports are prepared on a weekly basis.
3. Management uses budget reports to analyze differences between actual and planned results and to determine their causes.
4. As a result of analyzing budget reports, management may either take corrective action or modify future plans.
5. Budgetary control works best when a company has an informal reporting system.
6. The primary recipients of the sales report are the sales manager and the production supervisor.
7. The primary recipient of the scrap report is the production manager.
8. A static budget is a projection of budget data at a single level of activity.
9. Top management's reaction to unfavorable differences is not influenced by the materiality of the difference.
10. A static budget is not appropriate in evaluating a manager's effectiveness in controlling costs unless the actual activity level approximates the static budget activity level or the behavior of the costs is fixed

## Instructions

Identify each statement as true or false. If false, indicate how to correct the statement.

*Prepare and evaluate static budget report.*

**E23.2 (LO 1), AN** Crede Company budgeted selling expenses of $30,000 in January, $35,000 in February, and $40,000 in March. Actual selling expenses were $31,200 in January, $34,525 in February, and $46,000 in March. The company considers any difference that is less than 5% of the budgeted amount to be immaterial.

**Instructions**

a. Prepare a selling expense report that compares budgeted and actual amounts by month and for the year to date.

b. What is the purpose of the report prepared in (a), and who would be the primary recipient?

c. What would be the likely result of management's analysis of the report?

*Prepare flexible manufacturing overhead budget.*

**E23.3 (LO 2), AP** Myers Company uses a flexible budget for manufacturing overhead based on direct labor hours. Variable manufacturing overhead costs per direct labor hour are as follows.

| | |
|---|---|
| Indirect labor | $1.00 |
| Indirect materials | 0.70 |
| Utilities | 0.40 |

Fixed overhead costs per month are supervision $4,000, depreciation $1,200, and property taxes $800. The company believes it will normally operate in a range of 7,000–10,000 direct labor hours per month.

**Instructions**

Prepare a monthly manufacturing overhead flexible budget for 2022 for the expected range of activity, using increments of 1,000 direct labor hours.

*Prepare flexible budget reports for manufacturing overhead costs, and comment on findings.*

**E23.4 (LO 2), AN** Writing Using the information in E23.3, assume that in July 2022, Myers Company incurs the following manufacturing overhead costs.

| **Variable Costs** | | **Fixed Costs** | |
|---|---|---|---|
| Indirect labor | $8,800 | Supervision | $4,000 |
| Indirect materials | 5,800 | Depreciation | 1,200 |
| Utilities | 3,200 | Property taxes | 800 |

**Instructions**

a. Prepare a flexible budget performance report, assuming that the company worked 9,000 direct labor hours during the month.

b. Prepare a flexible budget performance report, assuming that the company worked 8,500 direct labor hours during the month.

c. Comment on your findings.

*Prepare flexible selling expense budget.*

**E23.5 (LO 2), AP** Fallon Company uses flexible budgets to control its selling expenses. Monthly sales are expected to range from $170,000 to $200,000. Variable costs and their percentage relationship to sales are sales commissions 6%, advertising 4%, travel 3%, and delivery 2%. Fixed selling expenses will consist of sales salaries $35,000, depreciation on delivery equipment $7,000, and insurance on delivery equipment $1,000.

**Instructions**

Prepare a monthly selling expense flexible budget for each $10,000 increment of sales within the relevant range for the year ending December 31, 2022.

*Prepare flexible budget reports for selling expenses.*

**E23.6 (LO 2), AN** Writing The actual selling expenses incurred in March 2022 by Fallon Company are as follows.

| **Variable Expenses** | | **Fixed Expenses** | |
|---|---|---|---|
| Sales commissions | $11,000 | Sales salaries | $35,000 |
| Advertising | 6,900 | Depreciation | 7,000 |
| Travel | 5,100 | Insurance | 1,000 |
| Delivery | 3,450 | | |

**Instructions**

a. Prepare a flexible budget performance report for March using the budget data in E23.5, assuming that March sales were $170,000.

b. Prepare a flexible budget performance report, assuming that March sales were $180,000.

c. Comment on the importance of using flexible budgets in evaluating the performance of the sales manager.

**E23.7 (LO 2), AP** Appliance Possible Inc. (AF) is a manufacturer of toaster ovens. To improve control over operations, the president of AP wants to begin using a flexible budgeting system, rather than using only the current master budget. The following data are available for AP's expected costs at production levels of 90,000, 100,000, and 110,000 units.

Prepare flexible budget.

| | | |
|---|---|---|
| Variable costs | | |
| Manufacturing | $6 per unit | |
| Administrative | $4 per unit | |
| Selling | $3 per unit | |
| Fixed costs | | |
| Manufacturing | $160,000 | |
| Administrative | $80,000 | |

**Instructions**

a. Prepare a flexible budget for each of the possible production levels: 90,000, 100,000, and 110,000 units.

b. If AP sells the toaster ovens for $16 each, how many units will it have to sell to make a profit of $60,000 before taxes?

(CGA adapted)

**E23.8 (LO 1, 2), E** **Service** **Writing** Rensing Groomers is in the dog-grooming business. Its operating costs are described by the following equations:

Prepare flexible budget report; compare<br>flexible and static budgets.

| | |
|---|---|
| Grooming supplies (variable) | $y = \$0 + \$5x$ |
| Direct labor (variable) | $y = \$0 + \$14x$ |
| Overhead (mixed) | $y = \$10,000 + \$1x$ |

Milo, the owner, has determined that direct labor is the cost driver for all three categories of costs.

**Instructions**

a. Prepare a flexible budget for activity levels of 550, 600, and 700 direct labor hours.

b. Explain why the flexible budget is more informative than the static budget.

c. Calculate the total cost per direct labor hour at each of the activity levels specified in part (a).

d. The groomers at Rensing normally work a total of 650 direct labor hours during each month. Each grooming job normally takes a groomer 1.3 hours. Milo wants to earn a profit equal to 40% of the costs incurred. Determine what he should charge each pet owner for grooming.

(CGA adapted)

**E23.9 (LO 1, 2), E** As sales manager, Joe Batista was given the following static budget report for selling expenses in the Clothing Department of Soria Company for the month of October.

Prepare flexible budget report, and<br>answer question.

**Soria Company**
**Clothing Department**
**Budget Report**
**For the Month Ended October 31, 2022**

| | Budget | Actual | Difference<br>Favorable F<br>Unfavorable U |
|---|---|---|---|
| Sales in units | 8,000 | 10,000 | 2,000 F |
| Variable expenses | | | |
| Sales commissions | $ 2,400 | $ 2,600 | $ 200 U |
| Advertising expense | 720 | 850 | 130 U |
| Travel expense | 3,600 | 4,100 | 500 U |
| Free samples given out | 1,600 | 1,400 | 200 F |
| Total variable | 8,320 | 8,950 | 630 U |
| Fixed expenses | | | |
| Rent | 1,500 | 1,500 | –0– |
| Sales salaries | 1,200 | 1,200 | –0– |
| Office salaries | 800 | 800 | –0– |
| Depreciation—autos (sales staff) | 500 | 500 | –0– |
| Total fixed | 4,000 | 4,000 | –0– |
| Total expenses | $12,320 | $12,950 | $ 630 U |

As a result of this budget report, Joe was called into the president's office and congratulated on his fine sales performance. He was reprimanded, however, for allowing his costs to get out of control. Joe knew something was wrong with the performance report that he had been given. However, he was not sure what to do, and comes to you for advice.

**Instructions**

a. Prepare a budget report based on flexible budget data to help Joe.

b. Should Joe have been reprimanded? Explain.

*Prepare flexible budget and responsibility report for manufacturing overhead.*

**E23.10 (LO 2, 3), AP** Chubbs Inc.'s manufacturing overhead budget for the first quarter of 2022 contained the following data.

| Variable Costs | | Fixed Costs | |
|---|---|---|---|
| Indirect materials | $12,000 | Supervisory salaries | $36,000 |
| Indirect labor | 10,000 | Depreciation | 7,000 |
| Utilities | 8,000 | Property taxes and insurance | 8,000 |
| Maintenance | 6,000 | Maintenance | 5,000 |

Actual variable costs were indirect materials $13,500, indirect labor $9,500, utilities $8,700, and maintenance $5,000. Actual fixed costs equaled budgeted costs except for property taxes and insurance, which were $8,300. The actual activity level equaled the budgeted level.

All costs are considered controllable by the production department manager except for depreciation, and property taxes and insurance.

**Instructions**

a. Prepare a manufacturing overhead flexible budget report for the first quarter.

b. Prepare a responsibility report for the first quarter.

*Prepare and discuss a responsibility report.*

**E23.11 (LO 2, 3), AP** Service Writing UrLink Company is a newly formed company specializing in high-speed Internet service for home and business. The owner, Lenny Kirkland, divided the company into two segments: Home Internet Service and Business Internet Service. Each segment is run by its own supervisor, while basic selling and administrative services are shared by both segments.

Lenny has asked you to help him create a performance reporting system that will allow him to measure each segment's performance in terms of its profitability. To that end, the following information has been collected on the Home Internet Service segment for the first quarter of 2022.

| | Budget | Actual |
|---|---|---|
| Service revenue | $25,000 | $26,200 |
| Allocated portion of: | | |
|   Building depreciation | 11,000 | 11,000 |
|   Advertising | 5,000 | 4,200 |
|   Billing | 3,500 | 3,000 |
|   Property taxes | 1,200 | 1,000 |
| Material and supplies | 1,600 | 1,200 |
| Supervisory salaries | 9,000 | 9,500 |
| Insurance | 4,000 | 3,900 |
| Wages | 3,000 | 3,250 |
| Gas and oil | 2,800 | 3,400 |
| Equipment depreciation | 1,500 | 1,300 |

**Instructions**

a. Prepare a responsibility report for the first quarter of 2022 for the Home Internet Service segment.

b. Write a memo to Lenny Kirkland discussing the principles that should be used when preparing performance reports.

*State total budgeted cost equations, and prepare flexible budget graph.*

**E23.12 (LO 2), AP** Venetian Company has two production departments, Fabricating and Assembling. At a department managers' meeting, the controller uses flexible budget graphs to explain total budgeted costs. A separate graph based on direct labor hours is used for each department. The graphs show the following.

1. At zero direct labor hours, the total budgeted cost line and the fixed-cost line intersect the vertical axis at $50,000 in the Fabricating Department and $40,000 in the Assembling Department.

2. At normal capacity of 50,000 direct labor hours, the line drawn from the total budgeted cost line intersects the vertical axis at $150,000 in the Fabricating Department and $120,000 in the Assembling Department.

### Instructions

a. State the total budgeted cost equation for each department.

b. Compute the total budgeted cost for each department, assuming actual direct labor hours worked were 53,000 and 47,000, in the Fabricating and Assembling Departments, respectively.

c. Prepare the flexible budget graph for the Fabricating Department, assuming the maximum direct labor hours in the relevant range is 100,000. Use increments of 10,000 direct labor hours on the horizontal axis and increments of $50,000 on the vertical axis.

**E23.13 (LO 3), AP** Fey Company's organization chart includes the president; the vice president of production; three assembly factories—Dallas, Atlanta, and Tucson; and two departments within each factory—Machining and Finishing. Budget and actual manufacturing cost data for July 2022 are as follows.

*Prepare reports in a responsibility reporting system.*

*Finishing Department—Dallas:* direct materials $42,500 actual, $44,000 budget; direct labor $83,400 actual, $82,000 budget; manufacturing overhead $51,000 actual, $49,200 budget.

*Machining Department—Dallas:* total manufacturing costs $220,000 actual, $219,000 budget.

*Atlanta Factory:* total manufacturing costs $424,000 actual, $420,000 budget.

*Tucson Factory:* total manufacturing costs $494,200 actual, $496,500 budget.

The Dallas factory manager's office costs were $95,000 actual and $92,000 budget. The vice president of production's office costs were $132,000 actual and $130,000 budget. Office costs are not allocated to departments and factories.

### Instructions

Using the format shown in Illustration 23.19, prepare the reports in a responsibility system for:

a. The Finishing Department—Dallas.

b. The factory manager—Dallas.

c. The vice president of production.

**E23.14 (LO 3), AN** The Mixing Department manager of Malone Company is able to control all overhead costs except rent, property taxes, and salaries. Budgeted monthly overhead costs for the Mixing Department, in alphabetical order, are:

*Prepare a responsibility report for a cost center.*

| Indirect labor | $12,000 | Property taxes | $ 1,000 |
| Indirect materials | 7,700 | Rent | 1,800 |
| Lubricants | 1,675 | Salaries | 10,000 |
| Maintenance | 3,500 | Utilities | 5,000 |

Actual costs incurred for January 2022 are indirect labor $12,250, indirect materials $10,200, lubricants $1,650, maintenance $3,500, property taxes $1,100, rent $1,800, salaries $10,000, and utilities $6,400.

### Instructions

a. Prepare a responsibility report for January 2022.

b. What would be the likely result of management's analysis of the report?

**E23.15 (LO 3), AN** Horatio Inc. has three divisions which are operated as profit centers. Actual operating data for the divisions listed alphabetically are as follows.

*Compute missing amounts in responsibility reports for three profit centers, and prepare a report.*

| Operating Data | Women's Shoes | Men's Shoes | Children's Shoes |
|---|---|---|---|
| Contribution margin | $270,000 | (3) | $180,000 |
| Controllable fixed costs | 100,000 | (4) | (5) |
| Controllable margin | (1) | $ 90,000 | 95,000 |
| Sales | 600,000 | 450,000 | (6) |
| Variable costs | (2) | 320,000 | 250,000 |

### Instructions

a. Compute the missing amounts. Show computations.

b. Prepare a responsibility report for the Women's Shoes Division assuming (1) the data are for the month ended June 30, 2022, and (2) all data equal budget except variable costs which are $5,000 over budget.

*Prepare a responsibility report for a profit center, and compute ROI.*

**E23.16 (LO 3, 4), AP** The Sports Equipment Division of Harrington Company is operated as a profit center. Sales for the division were budgeted for 2022 at $900,000. The only variable costs budgeted for the division were cost of goods sold ($440,000) and selling and administrative ($60,000). Fixed costs were budgeted at $100,000 for cost of goods sold, $90,000 for selling and administrative, and $70,000 for non-controllable fixed costs. Actual results for these items were:

| | |
|---|---:|
| Sales | $880,000 |
| Cost of goods sold | |
|    Variable | 408,000 |
|    Fixed | 105,000 |
| Selling and administrative | |
|    Variable | 61,000 |
|    Fixed | 66,000 |
| Noncontrollable fixed | 90,000 |

### Instructions

a. Prepare a responsibility report for the Sports Equipment Division for 2022.

b. Assume the division is an investment center, and average operating assets were $1,000,000. The noncontrollable fixed costs are controllable at the investment center level. Compute ROI using the actual amounts.

*Compute ROI for current year and for possible future changes.*

**E23.17 (LO 4), AP** The South Division of Wiig Company reported the following data for the current year.

| | |
|---|---:|
| Sales | $3,000,000 |
| Variable costs | 1,950,000 |
| Controllable fixed costs | 600,000 |
| Average operating assets | 5,000,000 |

Top management is unhappy with the investment center's return on investment (ROI). It asks the manager of the South Division to submit plans to improve ROI in the next year. The manager believes it is feasible to consider the following independent courses of action.

1. Increase sales by $300,000 with no change in the contribution margin percentage.

2. Reduce variable costs by $150,000.

3. Reduce average operating assets by 6.25%.

### Instructions

a. Compute the return on investment (ROI) for the current year.

b. Using the ROI equation, compute the ROI under each of the proposed courses of action. (Round to one decimal.)

*Prepare a responsibility report for an investment center.*

**E23.18 (LO 4), AP** Service Writing The Dinkle and Frizell Dental Clinic provides both preventive and orthodontic dental services. The two owners, Reese Dinkle and Anita Frizell, operate the clinic as two separate investment centers: Preventive Services and Orthodontic Services. Each of them is in charge of one of the centers: Reese for Preventive Services and Anita for Orthodontic Services. Each month, they prepare an income statement for the two centers to evaluate performance and make decisions about how to improve the operational efficiency and profitability of the clinic.

Recently, they have been concerned about the profitability of the Preventive Services operations. For several months, it has been reporting a loss. The responsibility report for the month of May 2022 is shown here.

| | Actual | Difference from Budget | |
|---|---:|---:|---|
| Service revenue | $40,000 | $1,000 | F |
| Variable costs | | | |
|    Filling materials | 5,000 | 100 | U |
|    Novocain | 3,900 | 100 | U |
|    Supplies | 1,900 | 350 | F |
|    Dental assistant wages | 2,500 | 0 | |
|    Utilities | 500 | 110 | U |
| Total variable costs | 13,800 | 40 | F |

|  | Actual | Difference from Budget |
|---|---|---|
| Fixed costs | | |
| Allocated portion of receptionist's salary | $ 3,000 | $ 200 U |
| Dentist salary | 9,800 | 400 U |
| Equipment depreciation | 6,000 | 0 |
| Allocated portion of building depreciation | 15,000 | 1,000 U |
| Total fixed costs | 33,800 | 1,500 U |
| Operating income (loss) | $(7,600) | $ 560 U |

In addition, the owners know that the investment in operating assets at the beginning of the month was $82,400, and it was $77,600 at the end of the month. They have asked for your assistance in evaluating their current performance reporting system.

**Instructions**

a. Prepare an investment center responsibility report for the Preventative Services segment for May 2022.

b. Write a memo to the owners discussing the deficiencies of their current reporting system.

**E23.19 (LO 4), AN** Service The Ferrell Transportation Company uses a responsibility reporting system to measure the performance of its three investment centers: Planes, Taxis, and Limos. Segment performance is measured using a system of responsibility reports and return on investment calculations. The allocation of resources within the company and the segment managers' bonuses are based in part on the results shown in these reports.

Recently, the company was the victim of a computer virus that deleted portions of the company's accounting records. This was discovered when the current period's responsibility reports were being prepared. The printout of the actual operating results, with question marks for missing amounts, appeared as follows.

*Prepare missing amounts in responsibility reports for three investment centers.*

|  | Planes | Taxis | Limos |
|---|---|---|---|
| Service revenue | $ ? | $500,000 | $ ? |
| Variable costs | 5,500,000 | ? | 300,000 |
| Contribution margin | ? | 250,000 | 480,000 |
| Controllable fixed costs | 1,500,000 | ? | ? |
| Controllable margin | ? | 80,000 | 210,000 |
| Average operating assets | 25,000,000 | ? | 1,500,000 |
| Return on investment | 12% | 10% | ? |

**Instructions**

Determine the missing pieces of information above.

**\*E23.20 (LO 5), AN** Presented here is selected information for three regional divisions of Medina Company.

*Compare ROI and residual income.*

|  | Divisions | | |
|---|---|---|---|
|  | North | West | South |
| Contribution margin | $300,000 | $500,000 | $400,000 |
| Controllable margin | $140,000 | $360,000 | $210,000 |
| Average operating assets | $1,000,000 | $2,000,000 | $1,500,000 |
| Minimum rate of return | 13% | 16% | 10% |

**Instructions**

a. Compute the return on investment for each division.

b. Compute the residual income for each division.

c. Assume that each division has an investment opportunity that would provide a rate of return of 16%.

1. If ROI is used to measure performance, which division or divisions will probably make the additional investment?

2. If residual income is used to measure performance, which division or divisions will probably make the additional investment?

*Fill in information related to ROI and residual income.*

**\*E23.21 (LO 5), AN** The following is selected financial information for two divisions of Samberg Brewing.

| | Lager | Lite Lager |
|---|---|---|
| Contribution margin | $500,000 | $300,000 |
| Controllable margin | 200,000 | (c) |
| Average operating assets | (a) | $1,200,000 |
| Minimum rate of return | (b) | 11% |
| Return on investment | 16% | (d) |
| Residual income | $100,000 | $156,000 |

**Instructions**

Supply the missing information for the lettered items.

## Problems

*Prepare flexible budget and budget report for manufacturing overhead.*

 Excel

**P23.1 (LO 2), AN** Writing Bumblebee Company estimates that 300,000 direct labor hours will be worked during the coming year, 2022, in the Packaging Department. On this basis, the following budgeted manufacturing overhead cost data are computed for the year.

| Fixed Overhead Costs | | Variable Overhead Costs | |
|---|---|---|---|
| Supervision | $ 96,000 | Indirect labor | $126,000 |
| Depreciation | 72,000 | Indirect materials | 90,000 |
| Insurance | 30,000 | Repairs | 69,000 |
| Rent | 24,000 | Utilities | 72,000 |
| Property taxes | 18,000 | Lubricants | 18,000 |
| | $240,000 | | $375,000 |

It is estimated that direct labor hours worked each month will range from 27,000 to 36,000 hours.

During October, 27,000 direct labor hours were worked, and the following overhead costs were incurred.

Fixed overhead costs: supervision $8,000, depreciation $6,000, insurance $2,460, rent $2,000, and property taxes $1,500.

Variable overhead costs: indirect labor $12,432, indirect materials $7,680, repairs $6,100, utilities $6,840, and lubricants $1,920.

**Instructions**

a. Total costs: DLH 27,000, $53,750; DLH 36,000, $65,000
b. Total cost $1,182 U

**a.** Prepare a monthly manufacturing overhead flexible budget for each increment of 3,000 direct labor hours over the relevant range for the year ending December 31, 2022.

**b.** Prepare a flexible budget report for October.

**c.** Comment on management's efficiency in controlling manufacturing overhead costs in October.

*Prepare flexible budget, budget report, and graph for manufacturing overhead.*

**P23.2 (LO 2), E** Zelmer Company manufactures tablecloths. Sales have grown rapidly over the past 2 years. As a result, the president has installed a budgetary control system for 2022. The following data were used in developing the master manufacturing overhead budget for the Ironing Department, which is based on an activity index of direct labor hours.

| Variable Costs | Rate per Direct Labor Hour | Annual Fixed Costs | |
|---|---|---|---|
| Indirect labor | $0.40 | Supervision | $48,000 |
| Indirect materials | 0.50 | Depreciation | 18,000 |
| Factory utilities | 0.30 | Insurance | 12,000 |
| Factory repairs | 0.20 | Rent | 30,000 |

The master overhead budget was prepared in the expectation that 480,000 direct labor hours will be worked during the year. In June, 41,000 direct labor hours were worked. At that level of activity, actual costs were as shown below.

Variable—per direct labor hour: indirect labor $0.44, indirect materials $0.48, factory utilities $0.32, and factory repairs $0.25.

Fixed: same as budgeted.

## Instructions

a. Prepare a monthly manufacturing overhead flexible budget for the year ending December 31, 2022, assuming production levels range from 35,000 to 50,000 direct labor hours. Use increments of 5,000 direct labor hours.

b. Prepare a budget report for June comparing actual results with budget data based on the flexible budget.

c. Were costs effectively controlled? Explain

d. State the equation for computing the total budgeted costs for the Ironing Department.

e. Prepare the flexible budget graph, showing total budgeted costs at 35,000 and 45,000 direct labor hours. Use increments of 5,000 direct labor hours on the horizontal axis and increments of $10,000 on the vertical axis.

**P23.3 (LO 1, 2), AN** Ratchet Company uses budgets in controlling costs. The August 2022 budget report for the company's Assembling Department is as follows.

**Ratchet Company**
**Budget Report**
**Assembling Department**
**For the Month Ended August 31, 2022**

| Manufacturing Costs | Budget | Actual | Difference Favorable F Unfavorable U |
|---|---|---|---|
| Variable costs | | | |
| Direct materials | $ 48,000 | $ 47,000 | $1,000 F |
| Direct labor | 54,000 | 51,200 | 2,800 F |
| Indirect materials | 24,000 | 24,200 | 200 U |
| Indirect labor | 13,000 | 17,500 | 500 F |
| Utilities | 15,000 | 14,900 | 100 F |
| Maintenance | 12,000 | 12,400 | 400 U |
| Total variable | 171,000 | 167,200 | 3,800 F |
| Fixed costs | | | |
| Rent | 12,000 | 12,000 | –0– |
| Supervision | 17,000 | 17,000 | –0– |
| Depreciation | 6,000 | 6,000 | –0– |
| Total fixed | 35,000 | 35,000 | –0– |
| Total costs | $206,000 | $202,200 | $3,800 F |

The monthly budget amounts in the report were based on an expected production of 60,000 units per month or 720,000 units per year. The Assembling Department manager is pleased with the report and expects a raise, or at least praise for a job well done. The company president, however, is unhappy with the results for August because only 58,000 units were produced.

## Instructions

a. State the total monthly budgeted cost equation.

b. Prepare a budget report for August using flexible budget data. Why does this report provide a better basis for evaluating performance than the report based on static budget data?

c. In September, 64,000 units were produced. Prepare the budget report using flexible budget data, assuming (1) each variable cost was 10% higher than its actual cost in August, and (2) fixed costs were the same in September as in August.

**P23.4 (LO 3), AN** Writing Clarke Inc. operates the Patio Furniture Division as a profit center. Operating data for this division for the year ended December 31, 2022, are shown here.

| | Budget | Difference from Budget |
|---|---|---|
| Sales | $2,500,000 | $50,000 F |
| Cost of goods sold | | |
| Variable | 1,300,000 | 41,000 F |
| Controllable fixed | 200,000 | 3,000 U |
| Selling and administrative | | |
| Variable | 220,000 | 6,000 U |
| Controllable fixed | 50,000 | 2,000 U |
| Noncontrollable fixed costs | 70,000 | 4,000 U |

### Margin notes

a. Total costs: 35,000 DLH, $58,000; 50,000 DLH, $79,000

b. Total cost:
   Budget $66,400
   Actual $70,090

*State total budgeted cost equation, and prepare flexible budget reports for 2 time periods.*

 Excel

b. Total budgeted cost $200,300

c. Total cost:
   Budget $217,400
   Actual $218,920

*Prepare responsibility report for a profit center.*

In addition, Clarke incurs $180,000 of indirect fixed costs that were budgeted at $175,000. Twenty percent (20%) of these costs are allocated to the Patio Furniture Division.

**Instructions**

a. Contribution margin $85,000 F
   Controllable margin $80,000 F

**a.** Prepare a responsibility report for the Patio Furniture Division for the year.

**b.** Comment on the manager's performance in controlling revenues and costs.

**c.** Identify any costs excluded from the responsibility report and explain why they were excluded.

*Prepare responsibility report for an investment center, and compute ROI.*

**P23.5 (LO 4), E** Optimus Company manufactures a variety of tools and industrial equipment. The company operates through three divisions. Each division is an investment center. Operating data for the Home Division for the year ended December 31, 2022, and relevant budget data are as follows.

| | Actual | Comparison with Budget |
|---|---|---|
| Sales | $1,400,000 | $100,000 favorable |
| Variable cost of goods sold | 665,000 | 45,000 unfavorable |
| Variable selling and administrative expenses | 125,000 | 25,000 unfavorable |
| Controllable fixed cost of goods sold | 170,000 | On target |
| Controllable fixed selling and administrative expenses | 80,000 | On target |

Average operating assets for the year for the Home Division were $2,000,000, which was also the budgeted amount.

**Instructions**

a. Controllable margin:
   Budget $330
   Actual $360

**a.** Prepare a responsibility report (in thousands of dollars) for the Home Division.

**b.** Evaluate the manager's performance. Which items will likely be investigated by top management?

**c.** Compute the expected ROI in 2022 for the Home Division, assuming the following independent changes to actual data.

  **1.** Variable selling and administrative expenses are decreased by 4%.

  **2.** Average operating assets are decreased by 10%.

  **3.** Sales are increased by $200,000, and this increase is expected to increase contribution margin by $80,000.

*Prepare reports for cost centers under responsibility accounting, and comment on performance of managers.*

**P23.6 (LO 3), AN** Durham Company uses a responsibility reporting system. It has divisions in Denver, Seattle, and San Diego. Each division has three production departments: Cutting, Shaping, and Finishing. The responsibility for each department rests with a manager who reports to the division production manager. Each division manager reports to the vice president of production. There are also vice presidents for marketing and finance. All vice presidents report to the president.

In January 2022, controllable actual and budget manufacturing overhead cost data for the departments and divisions were as shown here.

| Manufacturing Overhead | Actual | Budget |
|---|---|---|
| Individual costs—Cutting Department—Seattle | | |
| Indirect labor | $ 73,000 | $ 70,000 |
| Indirect materials | 47,900 | 46,000 |
| Maintenance | 20,500 | 18,000 |
| Utilities | 20,100 | 17,000 |
| Supervision | 22,000 | 20,000 |
| | $183,500 | $171,000 |
| Total costs | | |
| Shaping Department—Seattle | $158,000 | $148,000 |
| Finishing Department—Seattle | 210,000 | 205,000 |
| Denver division | 678,000 | 673,000 |
| San Diego division | 722,000 | 715,000 |

Additional overhead costs were incurred as follows: Seattle division production manager—actual costs $52,500, budget $51,000; vice president of production—actual costs $65,000, budget $64,000; president—actual costs $76,400, budget $74,200. These expenses are not allocated.

The vice presidents who report to the president, other than the vice president of production, had the following expenses.

| Vice President | Actual | Budget |
|---|---|---|
| Marketing | $133,600 | $130,000 |
| Finance | 109,000 | 104,000 |

## Instructions

Using the format in Illustration 23.19, prepare the following responsibility reports.

a. Manufacturing overhead—Cutting Department manager—Seattle division.

b. Manufacturing overhead—Seattle division manager.

c. Manufacturing overhead—vice president of production.

d. Manufacturing overhead and expenses—president.

a. $12,500 U

b. $29,000 U

c. $42,000 U

d. $52,800 U

*P23.7  **(LO 5), AN**  Writing  Sentinel Industries has manufactured prefabricated houses for over 20 years. The houses are constructed in sections to be assembled on customers' lots. Sentinel expanded into the precut housing market when it acquired Jensen Company. one of its suppliers. In this market, various types of lumber are precut into the appropriate lengths, banded into packages, and shipped to customers' lots for assembly. Sentinel designated the Jensen Division as an investment center.

*Compare ROI and residual income.*

Sentinel uses return on investment (ROI) as a performance measure with investment defined as average operating assets. Management bonuses are based in part on ROI. All investments are expected to earn a minimum rate of return of 18%. Jensen's ROI has ranged from 20.1% to 23.5% since it was acquired. Jensen had an investment opportunity in 2022 that had an estimated ROI of 19%. Jensen management decided against the investment because it believed the investment would decrease the division's overall ROI.

Selected financial information for Jensen is presented here. The division's average operating assets were $12,300,000 for the year 2022.

**Sentinel Industries**
**Jensen Division**
**Selected Financial Information**
**For the Year Ended December 31, 2022**

| | |
|---|---|
| Sales | $24,000,000 |
| Contribution margin | 9,100,000 |
| Controllable margin | 2,460,000 |

## Instructions

a. Calculate the following performance measures for 2022 for the Jensen Division.

   1. Return on investment (ROI).

   2. Residual income.

b. Would the management of Jensen Division have been more likely to accept the investment opportunity it had in 2022 if residual income were used as a performance measure instead of ROI? Explain your answer.

a. ROI 20%

(CMA adapted)

---

# Continuing Cases

---

## Current Designs

**CD23** The **Current Designs** staff has prepared the annual manufacturing budget for the rotomolded line based on an estimated annual production of 4,000 kayaks during 2022. Each kayak will require 54 pounds of polyethylene powder and a finishing kit (rope, seat, hardware, etc.). The polyethylene powder used in these kayaks costs $1.50 per pound, and the finishing kits cost $170 each. Each kayak will use two kinds of labor—2 hours of type I labor from people who run the oven and trim the plastic, and 3 hours of work from type II workers who attach the hatches and seat and other hardware. The type I employees are paid $15 per hour, and the type II are paid $12 per hour.

Manufacturing overhead is budgeted at $396,000 for 2022, broken down as follows.

| | |
|---|---|
| Variable costs | |
| Indirect materials | $ 40,000 |
| Manufacturing supplies | 53,800 |
| Maintenance and utilities | 88,000 |
| | 181,800 |
| | |
| Fixed costs | |
| Supervision | 90,000 |
| Insurance | 14,400 |
| Depreciation | 109,800 |
| | 214,200 |
| Total | $396,000 |

During the first quarter, ended March 31, 2022, 1,050 units were actually produced with the following costs.

| | |
|---|---|
| Polyethylene powder | $ 87,000 |
| Finishing kits | 178,840 |
| Type I labor | 31,500 |
| Type II labor | 39,060 |
| Indirect materials | 10,500 |
| Manufacturing supplies | 14,150 |
| Maintenance and utilities | 26,000 |
| Supervision | 20,000 |
| Insurance | 3,600 |
| Depreciation | 27,450 |
| Total | $438,100 |

### Instructions

**a.** Prepare the annual manufacturing budget for 2022, assuming that 4,000 kayaks will be produced.

**b.** Prepare the flexible budget for manufacturing for the quarter ended March 31, 2022. Assume activity levels of 900, 1,000, and 1,050 units.

**c.** Assuming the rotomolded line is treated as a cost center, prepare a flexible budget report for manufacturing for the quarter ended March 31, 2022, when 1,050 units were produced. (Round all budgeted amounts to the nearest dollar.)

## Waterways Corporation

(*Note:* This is a continuation of the Waterways case from Chapters 14–22.)

**WC23** Waterways Corporation is continuing its budget preparations. This case gives you static budget information as well as actual overhead costs, and asks you to calculate amounts related to budgetary control and responsibility accounting.

*Go to WileyPLUS for complete case details and instructions.*

## Data Analytics in Action

### Using Data Visualization for Budgeting

**DA23.1** Data visualization can be used to help improve forecasts.

**Example:** Recall the section "Flexible Budget—A Case Study" presented in the chapter. Flexible budgeting is useful because it enables managers to evaluate performance in light of changing conditions. But the ability to react quickly to changing conditions is even more important. For example, consider the following charts, which present quarterly data for Honda sales in four regional markets.

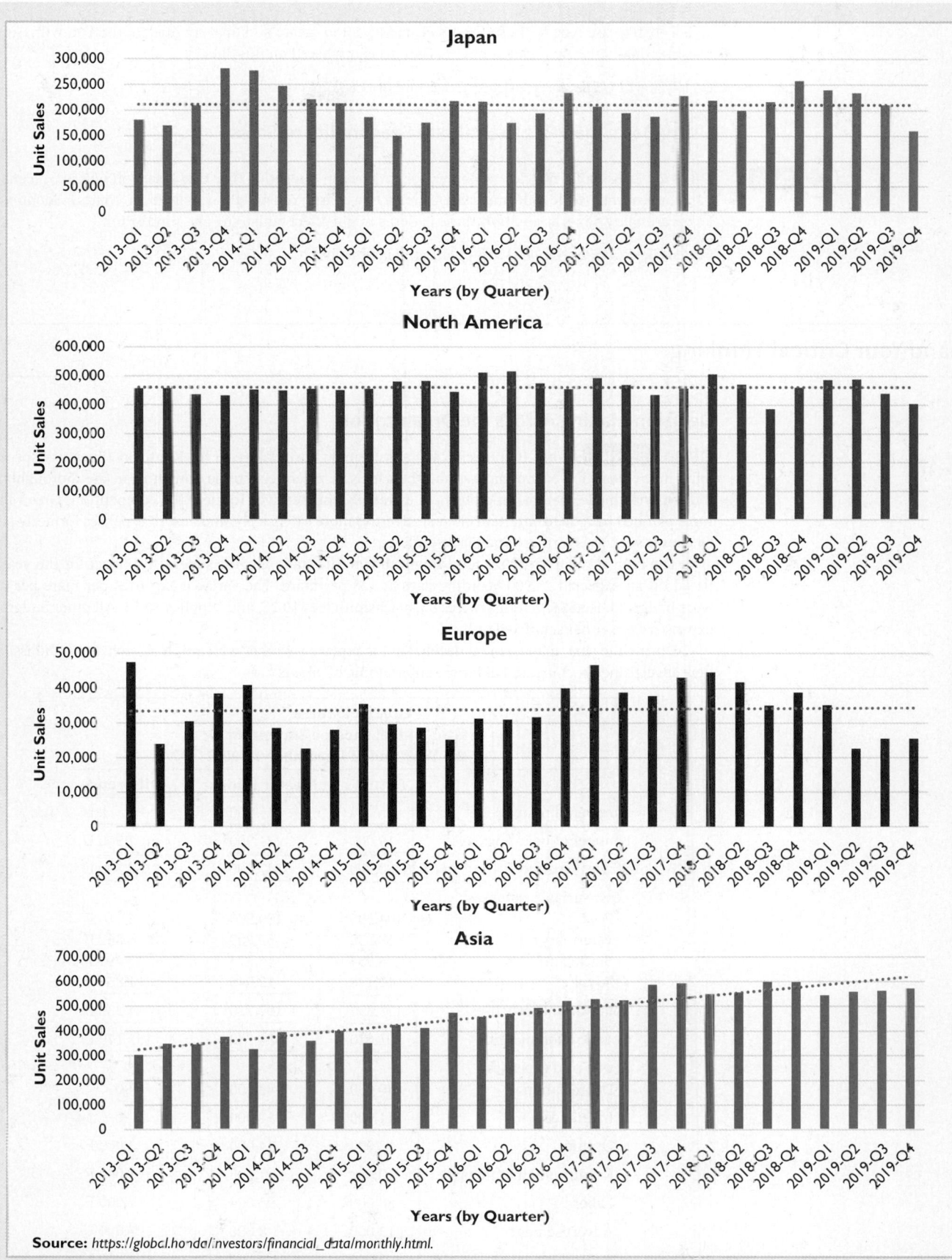

**Source:** *https://global.honda/investors/financial_data/monthly.html.*

    While the number of vehicles sold differs by region, the trends shown are used in forecasting sales and accompanying budgets. In examining the above charts, it appears that some regions will likely be more difficult to budget than others. For example, sales in Europe are the most volatile, as shown by the changing heights of the columns, and Japan is somewhat erratic. On the other hand, North America's and Asia's upward trends are much more consistent, making it easier to forecast sales in those regions.

For this case, you will use Excel's Forecast tool to create and analyze line charts. You will also consider qualitative factors that might affect decisions based on this data.

*Go to WileyPLUS for complete case details and instructions.*

### Using Data Analytics to Evaluate Seasonality of Sales

**DA23.2** Seasonality of sales can have a big impact on budgeting. For this case, you will use recent data for **Honda**'s worldwide unit sales to create line charts. You will then analyze the charts to identify any seasonality patterns and how these patterns might affect budgeting and production.

*Go to WileyPLUS for complete case details and instructions.*

---

# Expand Your Critical Thinking

### Decision-Making Across the Organization

**CT23.1** [Service] Green Pastures is a 400-acre farm on the outskirts of the Kentucky Bluegrass, specializing in the boarding of broodmares and their foals. A recent economic downturn in the thoroughbred industry has made the boarding business extremely competitive. To meet the competition, Green Pastures planned in 2022 to entertain clients, advertise more extensively, and absorb expenses formerly paid by clients such as veterinary and blacksmith fees.

The budget report for 2022 follows. As shown, the static income statement budget for the year is based on an expected 21,900 boarding days at $25 per mare. The variable expenses per mare per day were budgeted: feed $5, veterinary fees $3, blacksmith fees $0.25, and supplies $0.55. All other budgeted expenses were either semifixed or fixed.

During the year, management decided not to replace a worker who quit in March, but it did issue a new advertising brochure and did more entertaining of clients.[1]

|  | Actual | Master Budget | Difference |
|---|---|---|---|
| **Green Pastures** | | | |
| **Static Budget Income Statement** | | | |
| **For the Year Ended December 31, 2022** | | | |
| Number of mares | 52 | 60 | 8 U |
| Number of boarding days | 19,000 | 21,900 | 2,900 U |
| Service revenue | $380,000 | $547,500 | $167,500 U |
| Less: Variable expenses | | | |
| Feed | 104,390 | 109,500 | 5,110 F |
| Veterinary fees | 58,838 | 65,700 | 6,862 F |
| Blacksmith fees | 4,984 | 5,475 | 491 F |
| Supplies | 10,178 | 12,045 | 1,867 F |
| Total variable expenses | 178,390 | 192,720 | 14,330 F |
| Contribution margin | 201,610 | 354,780 | 153,170 U |
| Less: Fixed expenses | | | |
| Depreciation | 40,000 | 40,000 | –0– |
| Insurance | 11,000 | 11,000 | –0– |
| Utilities | 12,000 | 14,000 | 2,000 F |
| Repairs and maintenance | 10,000 | 11,000 | 1,000 F |
| Labor | 88,000 | 95,000 | 7,000 F |
| Advertisement | 12,000 | 8,000 | 4,000 U |
| Entertainment | 7,000 | 5,000 | 2,000 U |
| Total fixed expenses | 180,000 | 184,000 | 4,000 F |
| Net income | $ 21,610 | $170,780 | $149,170 U |

[1]Data for this case are adapted from Hans Sprohge, John Talbott, Paul Rosenfield, and Frederick Gill, "New Applications for Variance Analysis," *Journal of Accountancy* (AICPA: New York, April 1989), pp. 137–141.

**Instructions**

With the class divided into groups, answer the following.

a. Based on the static budget report:

   1. What was the primary cause(s) of the decline in net income?

   2. Did management do a good, average, or poor job of controlling expenses?

   3. Were management's decisions to stay competitive sound?

b. Prepare a flexible budget report for the year.

c. Based on the flexible budget report, answer the three questions in part (a) above.

d. What course of action do you recommend for the management of Green Pastures?

## Managerial Analysis

**CT23.2** Lanier Company manufactures expensive watch cases sold as souvenirs. Three of its sales departments are Retail Sales, Wholesale Sales, and Outlet Sales. The Retail Sales Department is a profit center. The Wholesale Sales Department is a cost center. Its managers merely take orders from customers who purchase through the company's wholesale catalog. The Outlet Sales Department is an investment center because each manager is given full responsibility for an outlet store location. The manager can hire and discharge employees, purchase, maintain, and sell equipment, and in general is fairly independent of company control.

Mary Gammel is a manager in the Retail Sales Department. Stephen Flott manages the Wholesale Sales Department. Jose Gomez manages the Golden Gate Club outlet store in San Francisco. The following are the budget responsibility reports for each of the three departments.

**Budget**

|  | Retail Sales | Wholesale Sales | Outlet Sales |
|---|---|---|---|
| Sales | $ 750,000 | $ 400,000 | $200,000 |
| Variable costs |  |  |  |
| Cost of goods sold | 150,000 | 100,000 | 25,000 |
| Advertising | 100,000 | 30,000 | 5,000 |
| Sales salaries | 75,000 | 15,000 | 3,000 |
| Printing | 10,000 | 20,000 | 5,000 |
| Travel | 20,000 | 30,000 | 2,000 |
| Fixed costs |  |  |  |
| Rent | 50,000 | 30,000 | 10,000 |
| Insurance | 5,000 | 2,000 | 1,000 |
| Depreciation | 75,000 | 100,000 | 40,000 |
| Investment in assets | 1,000,000 | 1,200,000 | 800,000 |

**Actual Results**

|  | Retail Sales | Wholesale Sales | Outlet Sales |
|---|---|---|---|
| Sales | $ 750,000 | $ 400,000 | $200,000 |
| Variable costs |  |  |  |
| Cost of goods sold | 192,000 | 122,000 | 26,500 |
| Advertising | 100,000 | 30,000 | 5,000 |
| Sales salaries | 75,000 | 15,000 | 3,000 |
| Printing | 10,000 | 20,000 | 5,000 |
| Travel | 14,000 | 21,000 | 1,500 |
| Fixed costs |  |  |  |
| Rent | 40,000 | 50,000 | 12,300 |
| Insurance | 5,000 | 2,000 | 1,000 |
| Depreciation | 80,000 | 90,000 | 56,000 |
| Investment in assets | 1,000,000 | 1,200,000 | 800,000 |

**Instructions**

a. Determine which of the items should be included in the responsibility report for each of the three managers.

b. Compare the budgeted measures with the actual results. Decide which results should be called to the attention of each manager.

## Real-World Focus

**CT23.3 CA Technologies**, the world's leading business software company, delivers the end-to-end infrastructure to enable e-business through innovative technology, services, and education. Recently, CA Technologies had 19,000 employees worldwide and revenue of over $6 billion.

The following information is from the company's annual report.

---

### CA Technologies
#### Management Discussion

The Company has experienced a pattern of business whereby revenue for its third and fourth fiscal quarters reflects an increase over first- and second-quarter revenue. The Company attributes this increase to clients' increased spending at the end of their calendar year budgetary periods and the culmination of its annual sales plan. Since the Company's costs do not increase proportionately with the third- and fourth-quarters' increase in revenue, the higher revenue in these quarters results in greater profit margins and income. Fourth-quarter profitability is traditionally affected by significant new hirings, training, and education expenditures for the succeeding year.

---

### Instructions

a. Why don't the company's costs increase proportionately as the revenues increase in the third and fourth quarters?

b. What type of budgeting seems appropriate for the CA Technologies situation?

## Communication Activity

**CT23.4** The manufacturing overhead budget for Fleming Company contains the following items.

| Variable costs | | Fixed costs | |
|---|---|---|---|
| Indirect materials | $22,000 | Supervision | $17,000 |
| Indirect labor | 12,000 | Inspection costs | 1,000 |
| Maintenance expense | 10,000 | Insurance expense | 2,000 |
| Manufacturing supplies | 6,000 | Depreciation | 15,000 |
| Total variable | $50,000 | Total fixed | $35,000 |

The budget was based on an estimated 2,000 units being produced. During the past month, 1,500 units were produced, and the following costs incurred.

| Variable costs | | Fixed costs | |
|---|---|---|---|
| Indirect materials | $22,500 | Supervision | $18,400 |
| Indirect labor | 13,500 | Inspection costs | 1,200 |
| Maintenance expense | 8,200 | Insurance expense | 2,200 |
| Manufacturing supplies | 5,000 | Depreciation | 14,700 |
| Total variable | $49,200 | Total fixed | $36,500 |

### Instructions

a. Determine which items would be controllable by Fred Bedner, the production manager.

b. How much should have been spent during the month for the manufacture of the 1,500 units?

c. Prepare a flexible manufacturing overhead budget report for Mr. Bedner.

d. Prepare a responsibility report. Include only the costs that would have been controllable by Mr. Bedner. Assume that the supervision cost above includes Mr. Bedner's monthly salary of $10,000, both at budget and actual. In an attached memo, describe clearly for Mr. Bedner the areas in which his performance needs to be improved.

## Ethics Case

**CT23.5** American Products Corporation participates in a highly competitive industry. In order to meet this competition and achieve profit goals, the company has chosen the decentralized form of organization. Each manager of a decentralized investment center is measured on the basis of profit contribution, market penetration, and return on investment. Failure to meet the objectives established by corporate management for these measures has not been acceptable and usually has resulted in demotion or dismissal of an investment center manager.

An anonymous survey of managers in the company revealed that the managers feel the pressure to compromise their personal ethical standards to achieve the corporate objectives. For example, at certain factory locations there was pressure to reduce quality control to a level which could not assure that all unsafe products would be rejected. Also, sales personnel were encouraged to use questionable sales tactics to obtain orders, including gifts and other incentives to purchasing agents.

The chief executive officer is disturbed by the survey findings. In his opinion, such behavior cannot be condoned by the company. He concludes that the company should do something about this problem.

### Instructions

a. Who are the stakeholders (the affected parties) in this situation?

b. Identify the ethical implications, conflicts, or dilemmas in the above described situation.

c. What might the company do to reduce the pressures on managers and to decrease the ethical conflicts?

(CMA adapted)

## All About You

**CT23.6** It is one thing to prepare a personal budget; it is another thing to stick to it. Financial planners have suggested various mechanisms to provide support for enforcing personal budgets. One approach is called "envelope budgeting."

### Instructions

Do an Internet search on "envelope system money management" and then complete the following.

a. Summarize the process of envelope budgeting.

b. Evaluate whether you think you would benefit from envelope budgeting. What do you think are its strengths and weaknesses relative to your situation?

## Considering Your Costs and Benefits

**CT23.7** Preparing a personal budget is a great first step toward control over your personal finances. It is especially useful to prepare a budget when you face a big decision. For most people, the biggest decision they will ever make is whether to purchase a house. The percentage of people in the United States who own a home is high compared to many other countries. This is partially the result of U.S. government programs and incentives that encourage home ownership. For example, the interest on a home mortgage is tax-deductible, subject to some limitations.

Before purchasing a house, you should first consider whether buying it is the best choice for you. Suppose you just graduated from college and are moving to a new community. Should you immediately buy a new home?

**YES:** If I purchase a home, I am making my housing cost more like a "fixed cost," thus minimizing increases in my future housing costs. Also, I benefit from the appreciation in my home's value. Although recent turbulence in the economy has caused home prices in many communities to decline, I know that over the long term, home prices have increased across the country.

**NO:** I just moved to a new town, so I don't know the housing market. I am new to my job, so I don't know whether I will like it or my new community. Also, if my job does go well, it is likely that my income will increase in the next few years, so I will able to afford a better house if I wait. Therefore, the flexibility provided by renting is very valuable to me at this point in my life.

### Instructions

Write a response indicating your position regarding this situation. Provide support for your view.

## Answers to Insight and Accounting Across the Organization Questions

**Just What the Doctor Ordered?** **Q:** How might the use of flexible budgets help to identify the best solution to this problem? **A:** A fixed budget assumes a particular level of activity. In the case of television shows, the number of viewers can impact revenues and costs. NBCUniversal could prepare alternative budgets at varying levels of activities and assume various cost structures depending on the number of cast members and other factors. Experimenting with different scenarios could help the network identify an approach that maintains an acceptable level of income as revenues decline.

**These Forecasts Move with the Times!** **Q:** In what ways are budgets and rolling forecasts similar, and in what ways do they differ? **A:** Budgets and forecasts both are forward-looking documents that describe future performance. Budgets are more detailed, static documents that are typically only updated once per year. Rolling forecasts are less detailed, focus only on the more important elements of a business, and are usually updated monthly.

**Competition versus Collaboration** **Q:** How might managers of separate divisions be able to reduce division costs through collaboration? **A:** Division managers might reduce costs by sharing design and marketing resources, or by jointly negotiating with suppliers. In addition, they can reduce the need to hire and lay off employees by sharing staff across divisions as human resource needs change.

**Hitting the Road with Zero-Based Budgeting** **Q:** What are some of the pros and cons of employing zero-based budgeting? **A:** One advantage of zero-based budgeting is that it forces a company to focus its resources on those operational aspects that are most likely to be successful in creating value. It also allows a company to react more quickly to change. Potential disadvantages are that zero-based budgeting can be very disruptive, time-consuming, and costly.

**Is Your Job a Game?** **Q:** Why is the reward system of top managers tied to different types of measures than those of lower-level managers? **A:** Managers should only be held responsible for those things over which they have control. Since the CEO is the top person in the company, he or she is responsible for the overall performance of the company. As a consequence, the CEO's bonus can be tied to measures of the company's general performance, such as earnings per share and shareholder return. Bonuses for lower-level managers need to be tied to those factors that they can control.

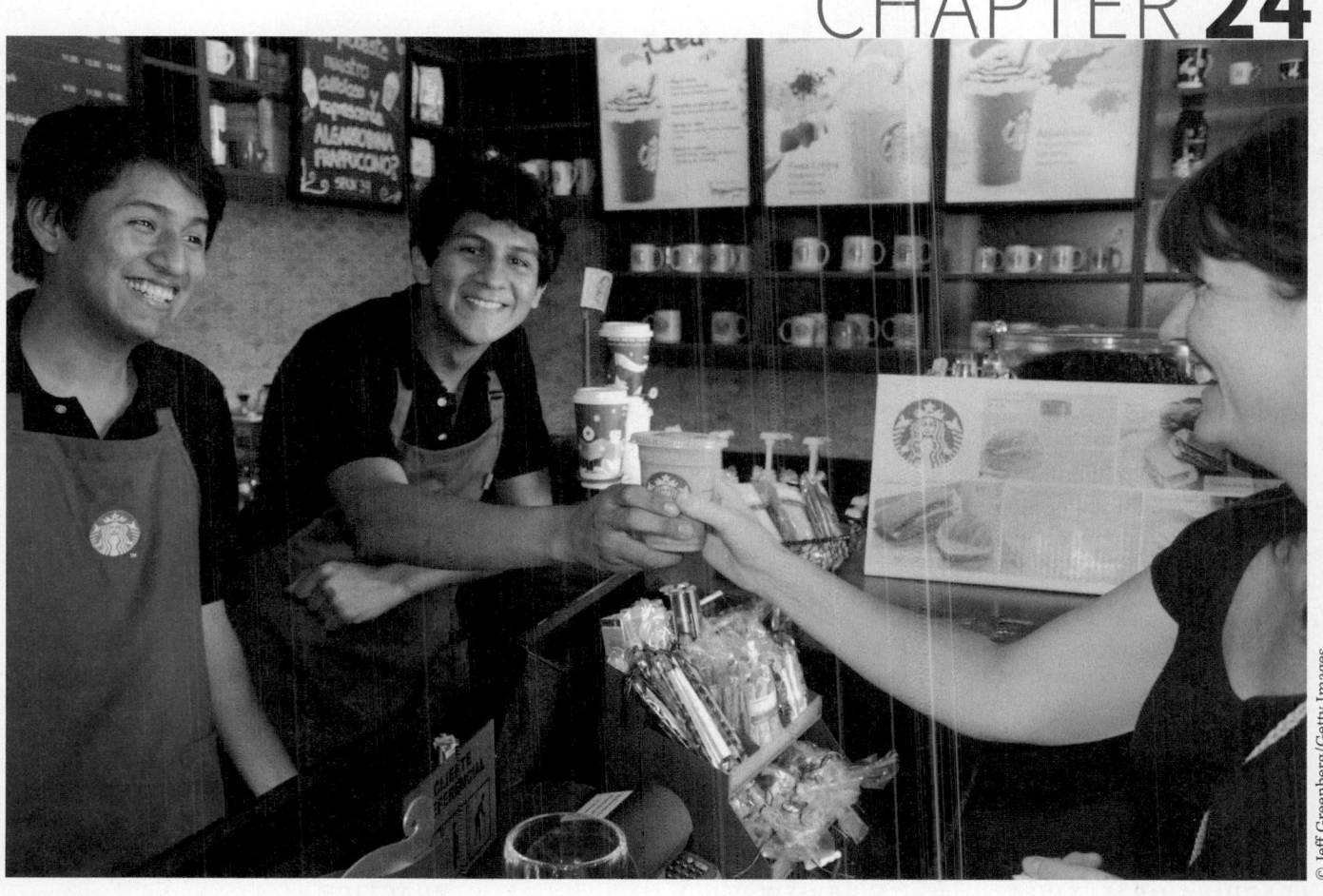

## CHAPTER 24

© Jeff Greenberg/Getty Images

# Standard Costs and Balanced Scorecard

## Chapter Preview

Standards are a fact of life. You met the admission standards for the school you are attending. The vehicle that you drive had to meet certain governmental emissions standards. The hamburgers and salads that you eat in a restaurant have to meet certain health and nutritional standards before they can be sold. As described in the following Feature Story, **Starbucks** has standards for the costs of its materials, labor, and overhead. The reason for standards in these cases is very simple: They help to ensure that overall product quality is high while keeping costs under control.

In this chapter, we continue the study of controlling costs. You will learn how to evaluate performance using standard costs and a balanced scorecard.

# Feature Story

## 80,000 Different Caffeinated Combinations

When Howard Schultz purchased a small Seattle coffee-roasting business in 1987, he set out to create a new kind of company. He also saw the store as a place where you could order a beverage, custom-made to your unique tastes, in an environment that would give you the sense that you had escaped, if only momentarily, from the chaos we call life. Schultz believed that the company would prosper if employees shared in its success.

In a little more than 20 years, Howard Schultz's company, **Starbucks**, grew from that one store to over 17,000 locations in 54 countries. That is an incredible rate of growth, and it didn't happen by accident. While Starbucks does everything it can to maximize the customer's experience, behind the scenes it needs to control costs. Consider the almost infinite options of beverage combinations and variations at Starbucks. The company must determine the most efficient way to make each beverage, it must communicate these methods in the form of standards to its employees, and it must then evaluate whether those standards are being met.

Schultz's book, *Onward: How Starbucks Fought for Its Life Without Losing Its Soul*, describes a painful period in which Starbucks had to close 600 stores and lay off thousands of employees. When a prominent shareholder suggested that the company eliminate its employee healthcare plan, as so many other companies had done, Schultz refused. Schultz feels that providing health care to the company's employees is an essential part of the standard cost of a cup of Starbucks' coffee.

 In WileyPLUS, watch the *Starbucks* video to learn more about how the company sets standards; watch the *Southwest Airlines* video to learn more about the real-world use of the balanced scorecard.

# Chapter Outline

| LEARNING OBJECTIVES | REVIEW | PRACTICE |
|---|---|---|
| **LO 1** Describe standard costs. | • Distinguishing between standards and budgets<br>• Setting standard costs | **DO IT! 1** Standard Costs |
| **LO 2** Determine direct materials variances. | • Analyzing and reporting variances<br>• Calculating direct materials variances | **DO IT! 2** Direct Materials Variances |
| **LO 3** Determine direct labor and total manufacturing overhead variances. | • Direct labor variances<br>• Manufacturing overhead variances | **DO IT! 3** Labor and Manufacturing Overhead Variances |
| **LO 4** Prepare variance reports and balanced scorecards. | • Reporting variances<br>• Income statement presentation of variances<br>• Balanced scorecard | **DO IT! 4** Reporting Variances |

**Go to the Review and Practice section at the end of the chapter for a targeted summary and practice applications with solutions.**

**Visit WileyPLUS for additional tutorials and practice opportunities.**

# Overview of Standard Costs

Standards are common in business.

- Standards established internally by a company may extend to personnel matters, such as employee absenteeism and ethical codes of conduct, quality control standards for products, and standard costs for goods and services.

- In managerial accounting, **standard costs** are predetermined unit costs, which companies use as measures of performance.

We focus on manufacturing operations in this chapter. But you should recognize that standard costs also apply to many types of service businesses as well. For example, a fast-food restaurant such as **McDonald's** knows the price it should pay for pickles, beef, buns, and other ingredients. It also knows how much time it should take an employee to prepare and serve hamburgers. If the company pays too much for pickles or if employees take too much time to prepare Big Macs, McDonald's notices the deviations from standards and takes corrective action. Not-for-profit entities, such as universities, charitable organizations, and governmental agencies, also may use standard costs as measures of performance.

Standard costs offer a number of advantages to an organization, as shown in **Illustration 24.1**.

- The organization will realize these advantages only when standard costs are carefully established and prudently used.

**ILLUSTRATION 24.1**  Advantages of standard costs

**Advantages of Standard Costs**

Facilitate management planning

Promote greater economy by making employees more "cost-conscious"

Useful in setting selling prices

Contribute to management control by providing basis for evaluation of cost control

Useful in highlighting variances in management by exception

Simplify costing of inventories and reduce clerical costs

- Using standards as a way to place blame can have a negative effect on managers and employees.
- To minimize this effect, many companies offer wage incentives to those who meet the standards.

# Distinguishing Between Standards and Budgets

Both **standards** and **budgets** are predetermined costs, and both contribute to management planning and control. There is a difference, however, in the way the terms are expressed.

- A standard is a **unit** amount.
- A budget is a **total** amount.

Thus, it is customary to state that the **standard cost** of direct labor for a unit of product is, say, $10. If the company produces 5,000 units of the product, the $50,000 of direct labor is the **budgeted** labor cost. A standard is the budgeted **cost per unit** of product. A standard is therefore concerned with each individual cost component that makes up the entire budget.

There are important accounting differences between budgets and standards.

- Except in the application of manufacturing overhead to jobs and processes, budget data are not journalized in cost accounting systems.
- In contrast, as we illustrate in the appendix to this chapter, standard costs may be incorporated into cost accounting systems.
- A company may report its inventories at standard cost in its financial statements, but it would not report inventories at budgeted costs.

# Setting Standard Costs

The setting of standard costs to produce a unit of product is a difficult task. It requires input from all persons who have responsibility for costs and quantities.

- To determine the standard cost of direct materials, management consults purchasing agents, product managers, quality control engineers, and production supervisors.
- In setting the standard cost for direct labor, managers obtain pay rate data from the payroll department.
- Industrial engineers generally determine the labor time requirements.
- The managerial accountant provides important input for the standard-setting process by accumulating historical cost data and by knowing how costs respond to changes in activity levels.

To be effective in controlling costs, standard costs need to be current at all times. Thus, standards are under continuous review. They should change whenever managers determine that the existing standard is not a good measure of performance. Circumstances that warrant revision of a standard include changed wage rates resulting from a new union contract, a change in product specifications, and the implementation of a new manufacturing method.

### Ideal versus Normal Standards

Companies set standards at one of two levels: ideal or normal.

- **Ideal standards** represent optimum levels of performance under perfect operating conditions.
- **Normal standards** represent efficient levels of performance that are attainable under expected operating conditions.

Some managers believe ideal standards will stimulate workers to ever-increasing improvement. However, most managers believe that ideal standards lower the morale of the workforce because they are difficult, if not impossible, to meet (see **Ethics Note**). Very few companies use ideal standards.

Most companies that use standards set them at a normal level. Properly set, normal standards should be **rigorous but attainable**. Normal standards allow for rest periods, machine breakdowns, and other "normal" contingencies in the production process. In the remainder of this chapter, we will assume that standard costs are set at a normal level.

## A Case Study

To establish the standard cost of producing a product:

- Determine standards for each manufacturing cost component—direct materials, direct labor, and manufacturing overhead.
- Derive the standard for each component from the standard price to be paid and the standard quantity to be used.

To illustrate, we use an extended example. Xonic Beverage Company uses standard costs to measure performance at the production facility of its caffeinated energy drink, Xonic Tonic. Xonic produces one-gallon containers of concentrated syrup that it sells to coffee and smoothie shops, and other retail outlets. The syrup is mixed with ice water or ice "slush" before serving. The potency of the beverage varies depending on the amount of concentrated syrup used.

**Direct Materials**   The **direct materials price standard** is the cost per finished unit of product of direct materials that should be incurred.

- This standard is based on the purchasing department's best estimate of the **cost of raw materials**.
- This cost is frequently based on current purchase prices.
- The price standard also includes an amount for related costs such as receiving, storing, and handling.

**Illustration 24.2** shows the materials price standard per pound of material for Xonic Tonic.

| Item | Price |
| --- | --- |
| Purchase price, net of discounts | $2.70 |
| Freight | 0.20 |
| Receiving and handling | 0.10 |
| **Standard direct materials price per pound** | **$3.00** |

**ILLUSTRATION 24.2**

**Setting direct materials price standard**

The **direct materials quantity standard** is the quantity of direct materials that management determines should be used per unit of finished goods.

- This standard is expressed as a physical measure, such as pounds, barrels, or board feet.
- In setting the standard, management considers both the quality and quantity of materials required to manufacture the product.
- The standard includes allowances for unavoidable waste and normal spoilage.

The standard quantity per unit for Xonic Tonic is shown in **Illustration 24.3**.

**ILLUSTRATION 24.3**

**Setting direct materials quantity standard**

| Item | Quantity (Pounds) |
|---|---|
| Required materials | 3.5 |
| Allowance for waste | 0.4 |
| Allowance for spoilage | 0.1 |
| **Standard direct materials quantity per unit** | **4.0** |

**The standard direct materials cost per unit is the standard direct materials price times the standard direct materials quantity.** For Xonic, the standard direct materials cost per gallon of Xonic Tonic is $12 ($3 × 4 pounds), as follows.

**Standard Direct Materials Cost per Gallon**

| Standard Direct Materials Price (SP) | × | Standard Direct Materials Quantity (SQ) | = | Standard Direct Materials Cost |
|---|---|---|---|---|
| $3 per lb | × | 4 lbs per gallon | = | $12 per gallon |

**Direct Labor**  The **direct labor price standard** is the rate per hour that should be incurred for direct labor (see **Alternative Terminology**).

**ALTERNATIVE TERMINOLOGY**

The direct labor price standard is also called the *direct labor rate standard*.

- This standard is based on current wage rates, adjusted for anticipated changes such as cost of living adjustments (COLAs).
- The price standard also generally includes employer payroll taxes and fringe benefits, such as paid holidays and vacations.

For Xonic, the direct labor price standard is as shown in **Illustration 24.4**.

**ILLUSTRATION 24.4**

**Setting direct labor price standard**

| Item | Price |
|---|---|
| Hourly wage rate | $12.50 |
| COLA | 0.25 |
| Payroll taxes | 0.75 |
| Fringe benefits | 1.50 |
| **Standard direct labor rate per hour** | **$15.00** |

The **direct labor quantity standard** is the time that management determines should be required to make one unit of the product (see **Alternative Terminology**).

**ALTERNATIVE TERMINOLOGY**

The direct labor quantity standard is also called the *direct labor efficiency standard*.

- This standard is especially critical in labor-intensive companies.
- Allowances should be made in this standard for rest periods, cleanup, machine setup, and machine downtime.

Illustration 24.5 shows the direct labor quantity standard for Xonic.

**ILLUSTRATION 24.5**

**Setting direct labor quantity standard**

| Item | Quantity (Hours) |
|---|---|
| Actual production time | 1.5 |
| Rest periods and cleanup | 0.2 |
| Setup and downtime | 0.3 |
| **Standard direct labor hours per unit** | **2.0** |

**The standard direct labor cost per unit of finished product is the standard direct labor rate times the standard direct labor hours.** For Xonic, the standard direct labor cost per gallon is $30 ($15 × 2 hours), as follows.

### Standard Direct Labor Cost per Gallon

| Standard Direct Labor Rate (SP) | × | Standard Direct Labor Hours (SQ) | = | Standard Direct Labor Cost |
|---|---|---|---|---|
| $15 per hour | × | 2 hours per gallon | = | $30 per gallon |

**Manufacturing Overhead**   For manufacturing overhead, companies use a **standard predetermined overhead rate** in setting the standard.

- This overhead rate is determined by dividing budgeted overhead costs by an expected standard activity index.
- For example, the index may be standard direct labor hours or standard machine hours.

As discussed in Chapter 17, many companies employ activity-based costing (ABC) to allocate overhead costs. Because ABC uses multiple activity indices to allocate overhead costs, it results in a better correlation between activities and costs incurred than do other methods. As a result, the use of ABC can significantly improve the usefulness of standard costing for management decision-making.

Xonic uses standard direct labor hours as the activity index. The company expects to produce 13,200 gallons of Xonic Tonic during the year at normal capacity. **Normal capacity is** the average activity output that a company should experience over the long run. Since it takes two direct labor hours for each gallon, total standard direct labor hours are 26,400 (13,200 gallons × 2 hours).

At normal capacity of 26,400 direct labor hours, overhead costs are budgeted to be $132,000. Of that amount, $79,200 are variable and $52,800 are fixed. **Illustration 24.6** shows computation of the standard predetermined overhead rates for Xonic.

**Calculating the overhead rate**

Overhead ÷ Standard activity index

| Budgeted Overhead Costs | Amount | ÷ | Standard Direct Labor Hours | = | Overhead Rate per Direct Labor Hour |
|---|---|---|---|---|---|
| Variable | $ 79,200 | | 26,400 | | $3.00 |
| Fixed | 52,800 | | 26,400 | | 2.00 |
| Total | $132,000 | | 26,400 | | **$5.00** |

**ILLUSTRATION 24.6**

Computing predetermined overhead rates

**The standard manufacturing overhead cost per unit is the predetermined overhead rate times the activity index quantity standard.** For Xonic, which uses direct labor hours as its activity index, the standard manufacturing overhead cost per gallon of Xonic Tonic is $10 ($5 × 2 hours), as follows.

### Standard Manufacturing Overhead Cost per Gallon

| Predetermined Overhead Rate (SP) | × | Standard Direct Labor Hours (SQ) | = | Overhead Rate per Direct Labor Hour |
|---|---|---|---|---|
| $5 | × | 2 hours | = | $10 |

**Total Standard Cost per Unit**   After a company has established the standard quantity and price per unit of finished product for each cost component, it can determine the total standard cost. The total standard cost per unit is the sum of the standard costs of direct materials, direct labor, and manufacturing overhead. The total standard cost per gallon of Xonic Tonic is $52, as the standard cost card in **Illustration 24.7** shows.

**ILLUSTRATION 24.7**

**Standard cost per gallon of Xonic Tonic**

| Product: Xonic Tonic | | Unit Measure: Gallon | | |
|---|---|---|---|---|
| **Manufacturing Cost Components** | **Standard** | | | |
| | **Quantity** | **× Price** | **=** | **Cost** |
| Direct materials | 4 pounds | $3.00 | | $12.00 |
| Direct labor | 2 hours | $15.00 | | 30.00 |
| Manufacturing overhead | 2 hours* | $5.00 | | 10.00 |
| | | | | $52.00 |

*Overhead assigned based on direct labor hours

The company prepares a standard cost card for each product. This card provides the basis for determining variances from standards.

---

## DO IT! 1 | Standard Costs

Ridette Inc. accumulated the following standard cost data concerning product Cty31.

Direct materials per unit: 1.5 pounds at $4 per pound
Direct labor per unit: 0.25 hours at $13 per hour.
Manufacturing overhead: allocated based on direct labor hours at a predetermined rate of $15.60 per direct labor hour.

Compute the standard cost of one unit of product Cty31.

### Solution

| Manufacturing Cost Components | **Standard** | | | |
|---|---|---|---|---|
| | **Quantity** | **× Price** | **=** | **Cost** |
| Direct materials | 1.5 pounds | $ 4.00 | | $ 6.00 |
| Direct labor | 0.25 hours | $13.00 | | 3.25 |
| Manufacturing overhead | 0.25 hours | $15.60 | | 3.90 |
| Total | | | | $13.15 |

Related exercise material: **BE24.2, BE24.3, DO IT! 24.1, E24.1, E24.2, and E24.3.**

---

# Direct Materials Variances

**LEARNING OBJECTIVE 2**

Determine direct materials variances.

## Analyzing and Reporting Variances

One of the major management uses of standard costs is to identify variances from standards. **Variances** are the differences between total actual costs and total standard costs (see **Alternative Terminology**).

To illustrate, assume that in producing 1,000 gallons of Xonic Tonic in the month of June, Xonic incurred the costs listed in **Illustration 24.8**.

| Direct materials | $13,020 |
|---|---|
| Direct labor | 31,080 |
| Variable overhead | 6,500 |
| Fixed overhead | 4,400 |
| Total actual costs | $55,000 |

**ILLUSTRATION 24.8**
**Actual production costs**

Companies determine total standard costs by multiplying the units produced by the standard cost per unit. The total standard cost of Xonic Tonic is $52,000 (1,000 gallons × $52). Thus, the total variance is $3,000, as shown in **Illustration 24.9**.

| Actual costs | $55,000 |
|---|---|
| Less: Standard costs | 52,000 |
| **Total variance** | **$ 3,000** |

**ILLUSTRATION 24.9**
**Computation of total variance**

Note that the variance is expressed in total dollars, not on a per unit basis.

When actual costs exceed standard costs, the variance is **unfavorable**.

- The $3,000 variance in June for Xonic Tonic is unfavorable.
- An unfavorable variance has a negative connotation as it reduces profit. It suggests that the company paid too much for one or more of the manufacturing cost components or that it used the components inefficiently.

If actual costs are less than standard costs, the variance is **favorable**.

- A favorable variance has a positive connotation as it increases profit.
- It suggests efficiencies in incurring manufacturing costs and in using direct materials, direct labor, and manufacturing overhead.

However, be careful. A favorable variance could be obtained by using inferior materials. In printing wedding invitations, for example, a favorable variance could result from using an inferior grade of paper. Or, a favorable variance might be achieved in installing tires on an automobile assembly line by tightening only half of the lug bolts. A variance is not favorable if the company has sacrificed quality control standards.

- To interpret a variance, you must analyze its components.
- A variance can result from differences related to the cost of materials, labor, or overhead.

**Illustration 24.10** shows that the total variance is the sum of the materials, labor, and overhead variances.

| Materials Variance | + | Labor Variance | + | Overhead Variance | = | Total Variance |
|---|---|---|---|---|---|---|

**ILLUSTRATION 24.10**
**Components of total variance**

In the following discussion, you will see that the materials variance and the labor variance are the sum of variances resulting from price differences and quantity differences. **Illustration 24.11** shows a format for computing the price and quantity variances.

Note that the left side of the matrix is actual cost (actual quantity times actual price). The right hand is standard cost (standard quantity times standard price). The difference between these two amounts (shown in the blue box in Illustration 24.11) is the total materials or labor variance. The only additional component you need in order to compute the price and quantity variances is the middle component, the actual quantity at the standard price.

- To compute the price variance, we hold the quantity constant (at the actual quantity) but vary the price (actual versus standard).
- Similarly, to compute the quantity variance, we hold the price constant (at the standard price) but vary the quantity (actual versus standard).

## Calculating Direct Materials Variances

Part of Xonic's total variance of $3,000 is due to a materials variance.

- In completing the order for 1,000 gallons of Xonic Tonic, the company used 4,200 pounds of direct materials. From Illustration 24.3, we know that Xonic's standards require it to use 4 pounds of materials per gallon produced, so it should have only used 4,000 (4 × 1,000) pounds of direct materials to produce 1,000 gallons.
- The direct materials were purchased at a price of $3.10 per unit. Illustration 24.2 shows that the standard cost of each pound of direct materials is $3 instead of the $3.10 actually paid.

**Illustration 24.12** shows that the **total materials variance** is computed as the difference between the amount paid (actual quantity times actual price) and the amount that should have been paid based on standards (standard quantity times standard price of materials).

**ILLUSTRATION 24.12**

**Equation for total materials variance**

| $\left(\begin{array}{c}\text{Actual Quantity}\\ \times \text{ Actual Price}\end{array}\right)$ | − | $\left(\begin{array}{c}\text{Standard Quantity}\\ \times \text{ Standard Price}\end{array}\right)$ | = | Total Materials Variance |
|---|---|---|---|---|
| (AQ) × (AP) | | (SQ) × (SP) | | (TMV) |
| (4,200 × $3.10) | − | (4,000* × $3.00) | | |
| $13,020 | − | $12,000 | = | $1,020 U |

*1,000 units × 4 pounds

Thus, for Xonic, the total materials variance is $1,020 ($13,020 − $12,000) unfavorable (abbreviated as "U"). It is unfavorable because the actual cost exceeded the standard cost.

The total materials variance could be caused by differences in the price paid (price variance) for the materials or by differences in the amount of materials used (quantity variance). **Illustration 24.13** shows that the total materials variance is the sum of the materials price variance and the materials quantity variance.

| Materials Price Variance + Materials Quantity Variance = Total Materials Variance |

**ILLUSTRATION 24.13**

Components of total materials variance

The materials price variance results from a difference between the actual price and the standard price. **Illustration 24.14** shows that the **materials price variance** is computed as the difference between the actual amount paid (actual quantity of materials times actual price) and the standard amount that should have been paid for the materials used (actual quantity of materials times standard price).[1]

$$\left(\begin{array}{c}\text{Actual Quantity}\\ \times \text{ Actual Price}\end{array}\right) - \left(\begin{array}{c}\text{Actual Quantity}\\ \times \text{ Standard Price}\end{array}\right) = \begin{array}{c}\text{Materials Price}\\ \text{Variance}\end{array}$$

| (AQ) × (AP) | | (AQ) × (SP) | | (MPV) |
| (4,200 × $3.10) | − | (4,200 × $3.00) | | |
| $13,020 | − | $12,600 | = | $420 U |

**ILLUSTRATION 24.14**

Equation for materials price variance

For Xonic, the materials price variance is $420 ($13,020 − $12,600) unfavorable.

Another way of thinking about the price variance is that we are holding the quantity constant at the actual quantity and varying the price. Thus, the price variance can also be computed by multiplying the actual quantity purchased by the difference between the actual and standard price per unit (see **Helpful Hint**). The computation in this case is 4,200 × ($3.10 − $3.00) = $420 U.

- As seen in Illustration 24.13, the other component of the materials variance is the quantity variance.
- The quantity variance results from differences between the amount of material actually used and the amount that should have been used.

**HELPFUL HINT**

The alternative equation is:
$$\boxed{AQ} \times \boxed{AP - SP} = \boxed{MPV}$$

As shown in **Illustration 24.15**, the **materials quantity variance** is computed as the difference between the standard cost of the actual quantity (actual quantity times standard price) and the standard cost of the amount that should have been used (standard quantity times standard price for materials).

$$\left(\begin{array}{c}\text{Actual Quantity}\\ \times \text{ Standard Price}\end{array}\right) - \left(\begin{array}{c}\text{Standard Quantity}\\ \times \text{ Standard Price}\end{array}\right) = \begin{array}{c}\text{Materials}\\ \text{Quantity Variance}\end{array}$$

| (AQ) × (SP) | | (SQ) × (SP) | | (MQV) |
| (4,200 × $3.00) | − | (4,000 × $3.00) | | |
| $12,600 | − | $12,000 | = | $600 U |

**ILLUSTRATION 24.15**

Equation for materials quantity variance

Thus, for Xonic, the materials quantity variance is $600 ($12,600 − $12,000) unfavorable.

The quantity variance can also be computed by applying the standard price to the difference between actual and standard quantities used (see **Helpful Hint**). The computation in this example is $3.00 × (4,200 − 4,000) = $600 U.

**Illustration 24.16** summarizes the total materials variance of $1,020 U.

**HELPFUL HINT**

The alternative equation is:
$$\boxed{SP} \times \boxed{AQ - SQ} = \boxed{MQV}$$

| Materials price variance | $ 420 U |
| Materials quantity variance | 600 U |
| **Total materials variance** | **$1,020 U** |

**ILLUSTRATION 24.16**

Summary of materials variances

---

[1]Assume that all materials purchased during the period are used in production and that no units remain in inventory at the end of the period.

Companies sometimes use a matrix to analyze a variance.

- **When the matrix is used, a company computes the amounts using the equations for each cost component first and then computes the variances.**
- The matrix provides a convenient structure for determining each variance.

**Illustration 24.17** shows the completed matrix for the direct materials variance for Xonic.

**ILLUSTRATION 24.17** **Matrix for direct materials variances**

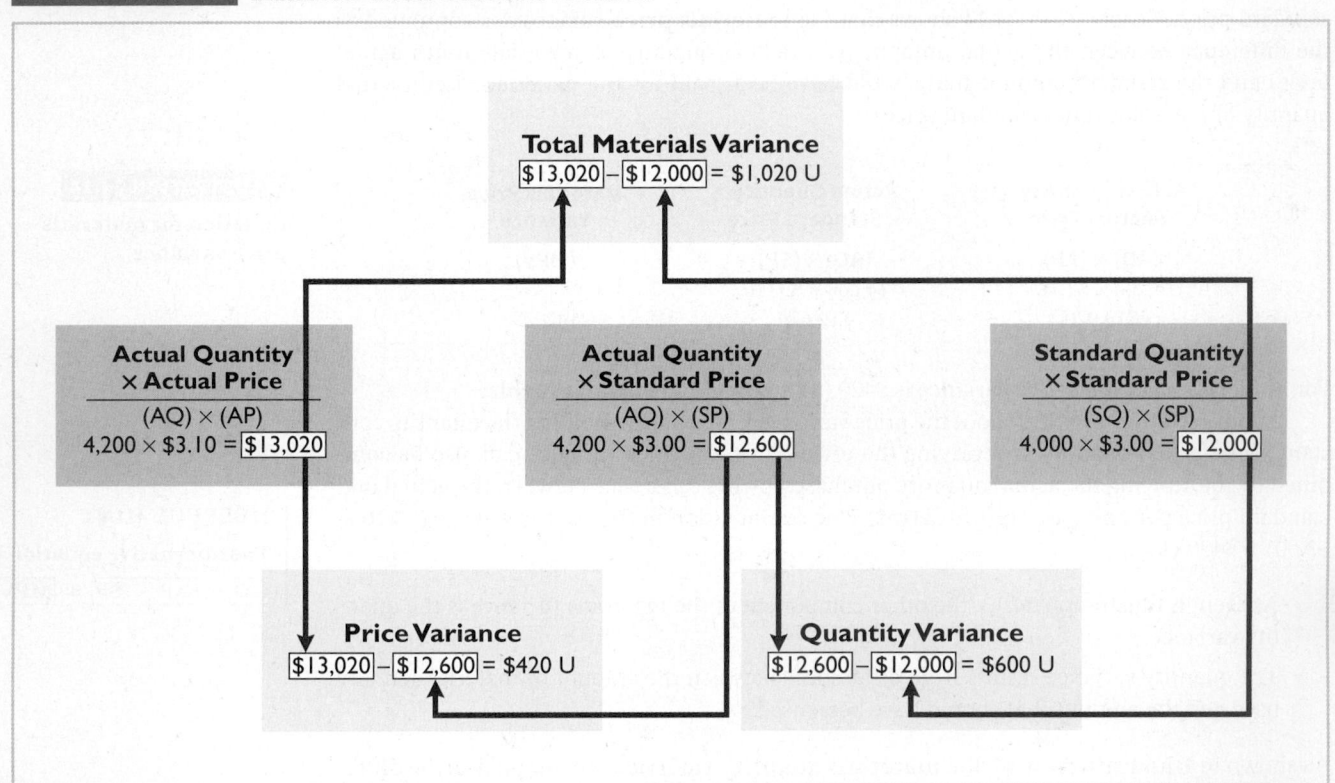

**Total Materials Variance**
$13,020 − $12,000 = $1,020 U

**Actual Quantity × Actual Price**
(AQ) × (AP)
4,200 × $3.10 = $13,020

**Actual Quantity × Standard Price**
(AQ) × (SP)
4,200 × $3.00 = $12,600

**Standard Quantity × Standard Price**
(SQ) × (SP)
4,000 × $3.00 = $12,000

**Price Variance**
$13,020 − $12,600 = $420 U

**Quantity Variance**
$12,600 − $12,000 = $600 U

## Causes of Materials Variances

What are the causes of a variance? The causes may relate to both internal and external factors.

**Materials Price Variances** The investigation of a **materials price variance usually begins in the purchasing department**.

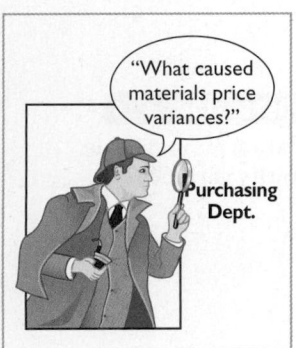

"What caused materials price variances?" Purchasing Dept.

- Many factors affect the price paid for raw materials, such as the availability of quantity and cash discounts, the quality of the materials requested, and the delivery method used.
- To the extent that these factors are considered in setting the price standard, the purchasing department is responsible for any variances.
- However, a variance may be beyond the control of the purchasing department. Sometimes, for example, prices may rise faster than expected, or actions by groups over which the company has no control, such as the OPEC nations' oil price increases, may cause an unfavorable variance.

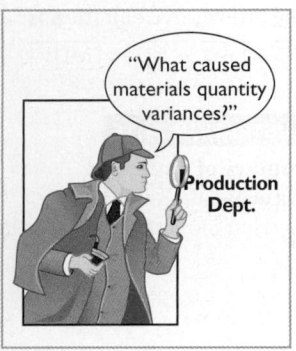

"What caused materials quantity variances?" Production Dept.

For example, during a recent year, **Kraft Foods** and **Kellogg Company** both experienced unfavorable materials price variances when the cost of dairy and wheat products jumped unexpectedly. There are also times when a production department may be responsible for the price variance. This may occur when a rush order forces the company to pay a higher price for the materials.

**Materials Quantity Variances** The starting point for determining the cause(s) of a significant **materials quantity variance is in the production department**.

- If the variances are due to inexperienced workers, faulty machinery, or carelessness, the production department is responsible.
- However, if the materials obtained by the purchasing department were of inferior quality, then the purchasing department is responsible.

---

### DO IT! 2 | Direct Materials Variances

The standard cost of Wonder Walkers includes two units of direct materials at $8.00 per unit. During July, the company buys 22,000 units of direct materials at $7.50 and uses those materials to produce 10,000 Wonder Walkers. Compute the total, price, and quantity variances for materials.

#### Solution

Standard quantity = 10,000 × 2 = 20,000
Substituting amounts into the equations, the variances are:

Total materials variance = (22,000 × $7.50) − (20,000 × $8.00) = $5,000 unfavorable
Materials price variance = (22,000 × $7.50) − (22,000 × $8.00) = $11,000 favorable
Materials quantity variance = (22,000 × $8.00) − (20,000 × $8.00) = $16,000 unfavorable

Related exercise material: **BE24.4, DO IT! 24.2, and E24.5.**

**ACTION PLAN**

Use the equations for computing each of the materials variances:

- Total materials variance = (AQ × AP) − (SQ × SP)
- Materials price variance = (AQ × AP) − (AQ × SP)
- Materials quantity variance = (AQ × SP) − (SQ × SP)

---

# Direct Labor and Manufacturing Overhead Variances

**LEARNING OBJECTIVE 3**
Determine direct labor and total manufacturing overhead variances.

## Direct Labor Variances

The process of determining direct labor variances is the same as for determining the direct materials variances. In completing the Xonic Tonic order, the company incurred 2,100 direct labor hours. The standard hours allowed for the units produced were 2,000 hours (1,000 gallons × 2 hours). The standard labor rate was $15 per hour, and the actual labor rate was $14.80.

- The total labor variance is the difference between the amount actually paid for labor versus the amount that should have been paid.
- **Illustration 24.18** shows that the **total labor variance** is computed as the difference between the amount actually paid for labor (actual hours times actual rate) and the amount that should have been paid (standard hours times standard rate for labor).

The total labor variance is $1,080 ($31,080 − $30,000) unfavorable.

| $\begin{pmatrix} \text{Actual Hours} \\ \times \text{Actual Rate} \end{pmatrix}$ | − | $\begin{pmatrix} \text{Standard Hours} \\ \times \text{Standard Rate} \end{pmatrix}$ | = | Total Labor Variance |
|:---:|:---:|:---:|:---:|:---:|
| (AH) × (AR) | | (SH) × (SR) | | (TLV) |
| (2,100 × $14.80) | − | (2,000 × $15.00) | | |
| $31,080 | − | $30,000 | = | $1,080 U |

**ILLUSTRATION 24.18**

Equation for total labor variance

The total labor variance is caused by differences in the labor rate (labor price variance) or differences in labor hours (labor quantity variance). **Illustration 24.19** shows that the total labor variance is the sum of the labor price variance and the labor quantity variance.

**ILLUSTRATION 24.19**
**Components of total labor variance**

| Labor Price Variance | + | Labor Quantity Variance | = | Total Labor Variance |
|---|---|---|---|---|

- The labor price variance results from the difference between the rate paid to workers and the rate that was supposed to be paid.
- **Illustration 24.20** shows that the **labor price variance** is computed as the difference between the actual amount paid (actual hours times actual rate) and the amount that should have been paid for the number of hours worked (actual hours times standard rate for labor).

**ILLUSTRATION 24.20**
**Equation for labor price variance**

| $\left(\begin{array}{c}\text{Actual Hours}\\ \times\text{ Actual Rate}\end{array}\right)$ | − | $\left(\begin{array}{c}\text{Actual Hours}\\ \times\text{ Standard Rate}\end{array}\right)$ | = | Labor Price Variance |
|---|---|---|---|---|
| (AH) × (AR) | | (AH) × (SR) | | (LPV) |
| (2,100 × $14.80) | − | (2,100 × $15.00) | | |
| $31,080 | − | $31,500 | = | $420 F |

**HELPFUL HINT**

The alternative equation is:
$$\boxed{\text{AH}} \times \boxed{\text{AR} - \text{SR}} = \boxed{\text{LPV}}$$

For Xonic, the labor price variance is $420 ($31,080 − $31,500) favorable.

The labor price variance can also be computed by multiplying actual hours worked by the difference between the actual pay rate and the standard pay rate (see **Helpful Hint**). The computation in this example is 2,100 × ($15.00 − $14.80) = $420 F.

The other component of the total labor variance is the labor quantity variance.

- The labor quantity variance results from the difference between the actual number of labor hours and the number of hours that should have been worked for the quantity produced.
- **Illustration 24.21** shows that the **labor quantity variance** is computed as the difference between the amount that should have been paid for the hours worked (actual hours times standard rate) and the amount that should have been paid for the amount of hours that should have been worked (standard hours times standard rate for labor).

**ILLUSTRATION 24.21**
**Equation for labor quantity variance**

| $\left(\begin{array}{c}\text{Actual Hours}\\ \times\text{ Standard Rate}\end{array}\right)$ | − | $\left(\begin{array}{c}\text{Standard Hours}\\ \times\text{ Standard Rate}\end{array}\right)$ | = | Labor Quantity Variance |
|---|---|---|---|---|
| (AH) × (SR) | | (SH) × (SR) | | (LQV) |
| (2,100 × $15.00) | − | (2,000 × $15.00) | | |
| $31,500 | − | $30,000 | = | $1,500 U |

**HELPFUL HINT**

The alternative equation is:
$$\boxed{\text{SR}} \times \boxed{\text{AH} - \text{SH}} = \boxed{\text{LQV}}$$

Thus, for Xonic, the labor quantity variance is $1,500 ($31,500 − $30,000) unfavorable.

The same result can be obtained by multiplying the standard rate by the difference between actual hours worked and standard hours allowed (see **Helpful Hint**). In this case, the computation is $15.00 × (2,100 − 2,000) = $1,500 U.

**Illustration 24.22** summarizes the total direct labor variance of $1,080 U.

**ILLUSTRATION 24.22**
**Summary of labor variances**

| | |
|---|---|
| Labor price variance | $   420 F |
| Labor quantity variance | 1,500 U |
| **Total direct labor variance** | **$1,080 U** |

These results can also be obtained from the matrix in **Illustration 24.23**.

**ILLUSTRATION 24.23**    Matrix for direct labor variances

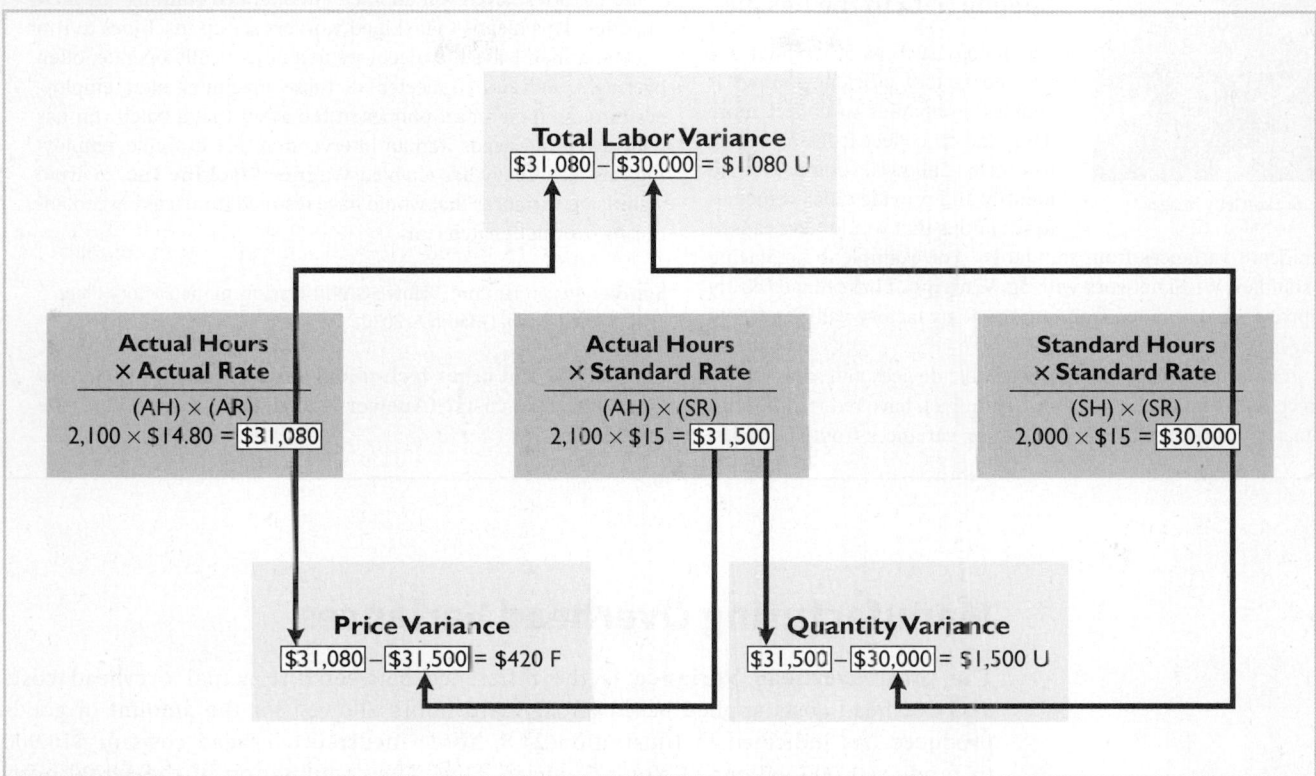

## Causes of Labor Variances

Labor variances can result from a variety of factors.

**Labor Price Variances**    **Labor price variances** usually result from two factors:

1. Paying workers **different wages than expected**.
2. **Misallocation of workers**.

In companies where pay rates are determined by union contracts, labor price variances should be infrequent. When workers are not unionized, there is a much higher likelihood of such variances. The responsibility for these variances rests with the manager who authorized the wage change.

Misallocation of the workforce refers to using skilled workers in place of unskilled workers and vice versa.

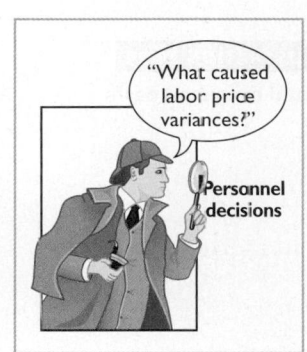

- The use of an inexperienced worker instead of an experienced one will result in a favorable price variance because of the lower pay rate of the unskilled worker.
- An unfavorable price variance would result if a skilled worker were substituted for an inexperienced one.

The production department generally is responsible for labor price variances resulting from misallocation of the workforce.

**Labor Quantity Variances**    **Labor quantity variances** relate to the **efficiency of workers**. The cause of a quantity variance generally can be traced to the production department.

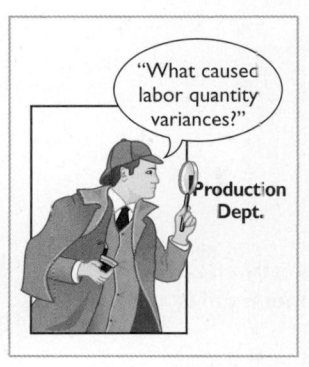

- The causes of an unfavorable variance may be poor training, worker fatigue, faulty machinery, or carelessness, and are the responsibility of the **production department**.
- However, if the excess time is due to inferior materials, the responsibility falls outside the production department and resides instead with the purchasing department.

---

**Data Analytics Insight**    Whirlpool

### Speedy Data to the Rescue!

Technology such as 5G cellular has boosted factory efficiency. How? It enables companies to collect more data, and to collect it faster, which has often allowed companies to identify and provide quick remedies to situations that would have caused

Iaremenko/Getty Images

significant variances from standards. For example, by replacing its standard Wi-Fi network with 5g, **Whirlpool** has reduced costly stoppages that resulted from autonomous factory vehicles losing their network connection.

Other technology, such as wearable devices and sensors that detect heat, sound, and even worker fatigue, have reduced injuries to factory workers while also reducing variances from standards.

Some factories have even adopted "unattended running" in their factories. This means that skilled workers set up machines to run a job and then leave the machines to automatically operate, often overnight. Sensors connected to these machines alert employees through their smart phones in the event that a batch run has gone awry and needs human intervention. For example, employing this technology has enabled **Wagner Machine Inc.** to avoid significant variances that would have resulted from leaking coolant during overnight batch runs.

**Source:** Austen Hufford, "How 5G Will Transform the Factory Floor," *Wall Street Journal* (March 5, 2020).

**How do 5G and other technology reduce specific variances from standard costs? (Answer is available at the end of the chapter.)**

---

# Manufacturing Overhead Variances

The **total overhead variance** is the difference between the actual overhead costs and overhead costs applied based on standard hours allowed for the amount of goods produced. As indicated in Illustration 24.8, Xonic incurred overhead costs of $10,900 to produce 1,000 gallons of Xonic Tonic in June. The computation of the actual overhead is comprised of a variable and a fixed component. **Illustration 24.24** shows this computation.

**ILLUSTRATION 24.24**

**Actual overhead costs**

| | |
|---|---:|
| Variable overhead | $ 6,500 |
| Fixed overhead | 4,400 |
| **Total actual overhead** | **$10,900** |

To find the total overhead variance in a standard costing system, we determine the overhead costs applied based on standard hours allowed.

- **Standard hours allowed** are the hours that *should* have been worked for the units produced.
- Overhead costs for Xonic Tonic are applied based on direct labor hours. Because it takes two hours of direct labor to produce one gallon of Xonic Tonic, for the 1,000-gallon Xonic Tonic order, the standard hours allowed are 2,000 hours (1,000 gallons × 2 hours).
- We then apply the predetermined overhead rate to the 2,000 standard hours allowed.

Recall from Illustration 24.6 that the amount of budgeted overhead costs at normal capacity of $132,000 was divided by normal capacity of 26,400 direct labor hours, to arrive at a predetermined overhead rate of $5 ($132,000 ÷ 26,400). The predetermined rate of $5 is then multiplied by the 2,000 standard hours allowed, to determine the overhead costs applied.

**Illustration 24.25** shows the equation for the total overhead variance and the calculation for Xonic for the month of June.

| | Actual Overhead | − | Overhead Applied* | = | Total Overhead Variance |
|---|---|---|---|---|---|
| | $10,900 | − | $10,000 | = | $900 U |
| | ($6,500 + $4,400) | | ($5 × 2,000 hours) | | |

*Based on standard hours allowed.

**ILLUSTRATION 24.25**

**Equation for total overhead variance**

Thus, for Xonic, the total overhead variance is $900 unfavorable.

The overhead variance is generally analyzed through a price and a quantity variance.

- The name usually given to the price variance is the **overhead controllable variance**.
- The quantity variance is referred to as the **overhead volume variance**.

Appendix 24B discusses how the total overhead variance can be broken down into these two variances.

## Causes of Manufacturing Overhead Variances

One reason for an overhead variance relates to over- or underspending on overhead items. For example, overhead may include indirect labor for which a company paid wages higher than the standard labor price allowed. Or, the price of electricity to run the company's machines increased, and the company did not anticipate this additional cost.

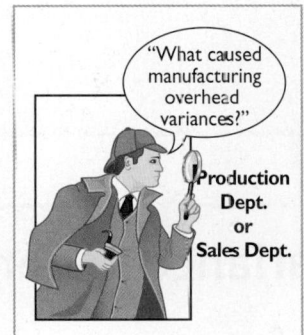

- Companies should investigate any spending variances to determine whether they will continue in the future.
- Generally, the responsibility for these variances rests with the production department.

The overhead variance can also result from the inefficient use of overhead.

- For example, the flow of materials through the production process may be impeded because of a lack of skilled labor to perform the necessary production tasks, due to a lack of planning. In this case, the production department is responsible for the cause of the variance.
- On the other hand, overhead can also be underutilized because of a lack of sales orders. When the cause is a lack of sales orders, the responsibility rests outside the production department and resides instead with the sales department.

For example, at one point **Chrysler** experienced a very significant unfavorable overhead variance because factory capacity was maintained at excessively high levels, due to overly optimistic sales forecasts.

---

### People, Planet, and Profit Insight   Starbucks

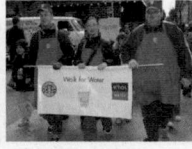

Archer Colin/SIPA/ NewsCom

#### What's Brewing at Starbucks?

It's easy for a company to say it's committed to corporate social responsibility. But **Starbucks** actually spells out measurable goals. In its annual *Global Social Impact Report*, the company describes its goals, its achievements, and even its shortcomings related to corporate social responsibility. For example, Starbucks discussed its goal of getting 100% of its electricity from renewable sources. It also has numerous goals related to purchasing coffee from sources that are certified as responsibly grown and ethically traded, providing funds for loans to coffee farmers, and fostering partnerships to provide training to 200,000 farmers on ecologically friendly growing.

In those instances where it didn't achieve its goals, Starbucks set new goals and described steps it would take to achieve them. You can view the company's *Global Social Impact Report* at the Starbucks website.

**Source:** "2018 Global Social Impact Report," *Starbucks.com.*

**What implications does Starbucks' commitment to corporate social responsibility have for the standard cost of a cup of coffee? (Answer is available at the end of the chapter.)**

**ACTION PLAN**

Use the equations for computing each of the variances.

- Total labor variance = (AH × AR) − (SH × SR)
- Labor price variance = (AH × AR) − (AH × SR)
- Labor quantity variance = (AH × SR) − (SH × SR)
- Total overhead variance = Actual overhead − Overhead applied*

*Based on standard hours allowed.

## DO IT! 3 | Labor and Manufacturing Overhead Variances

The standard cost of Product YY includes 3 hours of direct labor at $12.00 per hour. The predetermined overhead rate is $20.00 per direct labor hour. During July, the company incurred 3,500 hours of direct labor at an average rate of $12.40 per hour and $71,300 of manufacturing overhead costs. It produced 1,200 units.

**a.** Compute the total, price, and quantity variances for labor.

**b.** Compute the total overhead variance.

### Solution

Substituting amounts into the equations, the variances are:

Total labor variance = (3,500 × $12.40) − (3,600 × $12.00) = $200 unfavorable

Labor price variance = (3,500 × $12.40) − (3,500 × $12.00) = $1,400 unfavorable

Labor quantity variance = (3,500 × $12.00) − (3,600 × $12.00) = $1,200 favorable

Total overhead variance = $71,300 − $72,000* = $700 favorable

*(1,200 × 3 hours) × $20.00

Related exercise material: **BE24.5, BE24.6, DO IT! 24.3, E24.4, E24.6, E24.7, E24.8, and E24.11.**

# Variance Reports and Balanced Scorecards

**LEARNING OBJECTIVE 4**
Prepare variance reports and balanced scorecards.

## Reporting Variances

All variances should be reported to appropriate levels of management as soon as possible. The sooner managers are informed, the sooner they can evaluate problems and take corrective action.

- The form, content, and frequency of variance reports vary considerably among companies.
- One approach is to prepare a weekly report for each department that has primary responsibility for cost control.
- Under this approach, materials price variances are reported to the purchasing department, and all other variances are reported to the production department that did the work.

The report for Xonic shown in **Illustration 24.26**, with the materials for the Xonic Tonic order listed first, illustrates this approach.

**ILLUSTRATION 24.26**

**Materials price variance report**

| Xonic | | | | | |
|---|---|---|---|---|---|
| Variance Report—Purchasing Department | | | | | |
| For Week Ended June 8, 2022 | | | | | |
| Type of Materials | Quantity Purchased | Actual Price | Standard Price | Price Variance | Explanation |
| X100 | 4,200 lbs. | $3.10 | $3.00 | $420 U | Rush order |
| X142 | 1,200 units | 2.75 | 2.80 | 60 F | Quantity discount |
| A85 | 600 doz. | 5.20 | 5.10 | 60 U | Regular supplier on strike |
| **Total price variance** | | | | **$420 U** | |

The explanation column is completed after consultation with the purchasing department manager.

Variance reports facilitate the principle of "management by exception" explained in Chapter 23. For example, the vice president of purchasing can use the report shown above to evaluate the effectiveness of the purchasing department manager. Or, the vice president of production can use production department variance reports to determine how well each production manager is controlling costs.

- In using variance reports, top management normally looks for **significant variances**.
- These may be judged on the basis of some quantitative measure, such as more than 10% of the standard or more than $1,000.

# Income Statement Presentation of Variances

In income statements **prepared for management** under a standard cost accounting system, **cost of goods sold is stated at standard cost and the variances are disclosed separately**. Unfavorable variances increase cost of goods sold. Favorable variances decrease cost of goods sold, thus increasing gross profit. **Illustration 24.27** shows the presentation of variances in an income statement. This income statement is based on the production and sale of 1,000 units of Xonic Tonic at $70 per unit. It also assumes selling and administrative costs of $3,000. Observe that each variance is shown, as well as the total net variance. In this example, variations from standard costs reduced net income by $3,000.

Standard costs may be used in financial statements prepared for stockholders and other external users.

- The costing of inventories at standard costs is in accordance with generally accepted accounting principles when there are no significant differences between actual costs and standard costs. **Hewlett-Packard** and **Jostens, Inc.**, for example, report their inventories at standard costs.
- However, if there are significant differences between actual and standard costs, the financial statements must report inventories and cost of goods sold at actual costs.

It is also possible to show the variances in an income statement prepared in the variable costing (CVP) format. To do so, it is necessary to analyze the overhead variances into variable and fixed components. This type of analysis is explained in cost accounting texts.

**ILLUSTRATION 24.27**

**Variances in income statement for management**

### Xonic
#### Income Statement
#### For the Month Ended June 30, 2022

| | | |
|---|---|---|
| Sales revenue | | $70,000 |
| Cost of goods sold (at standard) | | 52,000 |
| Gross profit (at standard) | | 18,000 |
| **Variances** | | |
| **Materials price** | $ 420 U | |
| **Materials quantity** | 600 U | |
| **Labor price** | 420 F | |
| **Labor quantity** | 1,500 U | |
| **Overhead** | 900 U | |
| **Total variance unfavorable** | | **3,000** |
| Gross profit (actual) | | 15,000 |
| Selling and administrative expenses | | 3,000 |
| Net income | | $12,000 |

# Balanced Scorecard

Financial measures (measurement in dollars), such as variance analysis and return on investment (ROI), are useful tools for evaluating performance. However, many companies now supplement these financial measures with nonfinancial measures to better assess performance and anticipate future results. For example, airlines like **Delta** and **United** use capacity utilization as an important measure to understand and predict future performance. Companies that publish the *New York Times* and the *Chicago Tribune* newspapers use circulation figures as another measure by which to assess performance. **Penske Automotive Group**, the owner of 300 dealerships, rewards executives for meeting employee retention targets. **Illustration 24.28** lists some key nonfinancial measures used in various industries.

**ILLUSTRATION 24.28**    Nonfinancial measures used in various industries

| Industry | Measure |
|---|---|
| **Automobiles** | Capacity utilization of factories.<br>Average age of key assets.<br>Impact of strikes.<br>Brand-loyalty statistics. |
| **Computer Systems** | Market profile of customer end-products.<br>Number of new products.<br>Employee stock ownership percentages.<br>Number of scientists and technicians used in R&D. |
| **Chemicals** | Customer satisfaction data.<br>Factors affecting customer product selection.<br>Number of patents and trademarks held.<br>Customer brand awareness. |
| **Regional Banks** | Number of ATMs by state.<br>Number of products used by average customer.<br>Percentage of customer service calls handled by interactive voice response units.<br>Personnel cost per employee.<br>Credit card retention rates. |

**Source:** Financial Accounting Standards Board, *Business Reporting: Insights into Enhancing Voluntary Disclosures* (Norwalk, Conn.: FASB, 2001).

Most companies recognize that both financial and nonfinancial measures can provide useful insights into what is happening in the company.

- As a result, many companies now use a broad-based measurement approach, called the **balanced scorecard**, to evaluate performance.
- The **balanced scorecard** incorporates financial and nonfinancial measures in an integrated system that links performance measurement with a company's strategic goals.

Nearly 50% of the largest companies in the United States, including **Unilever**, **Chase**, and **Walmart**, are using the balanced scorecard approach.

The balanced scorecard evaluates company performance from a series of "perspectives." The four most commonly employed perspectives are as follows.

1. The **financial perspective** is the most traditional view of the company. It employs financial measures of performance used by most firms.

2. The **customer perspective** evaluates the company from the viewpoint of those people who buy its products or services. This view compares the company to competitors in terms of price, quality, product innovation, customer service, and other dimensions.

3. The **internal process perspective** evaluates the internal operating processes critical to success. All critical aspects of the value chain—including product development, production, delivery, and after-sale service—are evaluated to ensure that the company is operating effectively and efficiently.

4. The **learning and growth perspective** evaluates how well the company develops and retains its employees. This would include evaluation of such things as employee skills, employee satisfaction, training programs, and information dissemination.

Within each perspective, the balanced scorecard identifies objectives that contribute to attainment of strategic goals. **Illustration 24.29** shows examples of objectives within each perspective.

**ILLUSTRATION 24.29**  **Examples of objectives within the four perspectives of balanced scorecard**

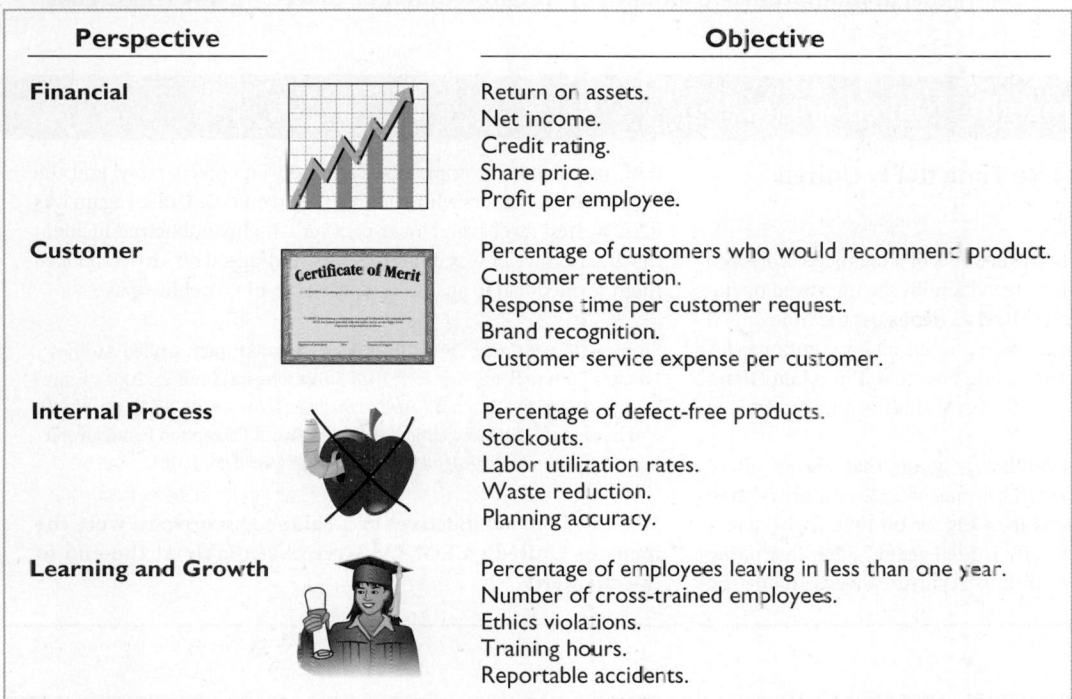

| Perspective | Objective |
|---|---|
| Financial | Return on assets.<br>Net income.<br>Credit rating.<br>Share price.<br>Profit per employee. |
| Customer | Percentage of customers who would recommend product.<br>Customer retention.<br>Response time per customer request.<br>Brand recognition.<br>Customer service expense per customer. |
| Internal Process | Percentage of defect-free products.<br>Stockouts.<br>Labor utilization rates.<br>Waste reduction.<br>Planning accuracy. |
| Learning and Growth | Percentage of employees leaving in less than one year.<br>Number of cross-trained employees.<br>Ethics violations.<br>Training hours.<br>Reportable accidents. |

The objectives are linked across perspectives in order to tie performance measurement to company goals. The financial-perspective objectives are normally set first, and then objectives are set in the other perspectives in order to accomplish the financial goals. For example, within the financial perspective, a common goal is to increase profit per dollars invested as measured by ROI.

- In order to increase ROI, a customer-perspective objective might be to increase customer satisfaction as measured by the percentage of customers who would recommend the product to a friend.

- In order to increase customer satisfaction, an internal-process-perspective objective might be to increase product quality as measured by the percentage of defect-free units.

- Finally, in order to increase the percentage of defect-free units, the learning-and-growth-perspective objective might be to reduce factory employee turnover as measured by the percentage of employees leaving in under one year.

**Illustration 24.30** illustrates this linkage across perspectives.

**ILLUSTRATION 24.30**

**Linked process across balanced scorecard perspectives**

Through this linked process, the company can better understand how to achieve its goals and what measures to use to evaluate performance.

In summary, the balanced scorecard does the following:

1. Employs both **financial and nonfinancial measures**. (For example, ROI is a financial measure; employee turnover is a nonfinancial measure.)

2. **Creates linkages** so that high-level corporate goals can be communicated all the way down to the shop floor.

3. **Provides measurable objectives for nonfinancial measures** such as product quality, rather than vague statements such as "We would like to improve quality."

4. Integrates all of the company's goals into a single performance measurement system, so that **an inappropriate amount of weight will not be placed on any single goal**.

---

**Service Company Insight**    United Airlines

PhotoDisc, Inc./
Getty Images

### It May Be Time to Fly United Again

Many of the benefits of a balanced scorecard approach are evident in the improved operations at **United Airlines**. At the time it filed for bankruptcy, United had a reputation for some of the worst service in the airline business. But when Glenn Tilton took over as United's chief executive officer, he recognized that things had to change.

He implemented an incentive program that allows all of United's 63,000 employees to earn a bonus of 2.5% or more of their wages if the company "exceeds its goals for on-time flight departures and for customer intent to fly United again." After instituting this program, the company's on-time departures were among the best, its customer complaints were reduced considerably, and the number of customers who said that they would fly United again was at its highest level ever. However, after a highly publicized incident in which a traveler was injured as he was dragged off an overbooked flight, United had to again overcome a negative public image.

**Sources:** Susan Carey, "Friendlier Skies: In Bankruptcy, United Airlines Forges a Path to Better Service," *Wall Street Journal* (June 15, 2004); Emre Serpen, "More to Maintain," *Airline Business* (November 2012), pp. 38–40; and Lewis Lazare, "How United Airlines' Brand Perception Fared Over a Year of Incidents," *Chicago Business Journal* (April 26, 2018).

**Which of the perspectives of a balanced scorecard were the focus of United's CEO? (Answer is available at the end of the chapter.)**

---

**ACTION PLAN**

- **Gross profit at standard is sales revenue less cost of goods sold at standard.**

- **Adjust standard gross profit by adding a net favorable variance or subtracting a net unfavorable variance.**

## DO IT! 4 | Reporting Variances

Polar Vortex Corporation experienced the following variances: materials price $250 F, materials quantity $1,100 F, labor price $700 U, labor quantity $300 F, and overhead $800 F. Sales revenue was $102,700, and cost of goods sold (at standard) was $61,900. Determine the actual gross profit.

### Solution

| | | |
|---|---:|---:|
| Sales revenue | | $102,700 |
| Cost of goods sold (at standard) | | 61,900 |
| Standard gross profit | | 40,800 |
| Variances | | |
| Materials price | $ 250 F | |
| Materials quantity | 1,100 F | |
| Labor price | 700 U | |
| Labor quantity | 300 F | |
| Overhead | 800 F | |
| Total variance favorable | | 1,750 |
| Gross profit (actual) | | $ 42,550 |

Related exercise material: **DO IT! 24.4, E24.10, E24.14, and E24.15.**

| Appendix 24A | # Standard Cost Accounting System |

## LEARNING OBJECTIVE *5

Identify the features of a standard cost accounting system.

A **standard cost accounting system** is a double-entry system of accounting.

- In this system, companies use standard costs in making entries, and they formally recognize variances in the accounts.
- Companies may use a standard cost system with either job order or process costing.

In this appendix. we will explain and illustrate a **standard cost, job order cost accounting system**. The system is based on two important assumptions:

1. Variances from standards are recognized at the earliest opportunity.
2. The Work in Process account is maintained exclusively on the basis of standard costs.

In practice, there are many variations among standard cost systems. The system described here should prepare you for systems you see in the "real world."

## Journal Entries

We will use the transactions of Xonic to illustrate the journal entries. Note as you study the entries that the major difference between the entries here and those for the job order cost accounting system in Chapter 15 is the **variance accounts**.

1. Purchase raw materials on account for $13,020 when the standard cost is $12,600.

| | | |
|---|---|---|
| Raw Materials Inventory | 12,600 | |
| Materials Price Variance | 420 | |
|     Accounts Payable | | 13,020 |
|       (To record purchase of materials) | | |

Xonic debits the inventory account for actual quantities at standard cost. This enables the perpetual materials records to show actual quantities. Xonic debits the price variance, which is unfavorable, to Materials Price Variance.

2. Incur direct labor costs of $31,080 when the standard labor cost is $31,500.

| | | |
|---|---|---|
| Factory Labor | 31,500 | |
|     Labor Price Variance | | 420 |
|     Factory Wages Payable | | 31,080 |
|       (To record direct labor costs) | | |

Like the raw materials inventory account, Xonic debits Factory Labor for actual hours worked at the standard hourly rate of pay. In this case, the labor variance is favorable. Thus, Xonic credits Labor Price Variance.

3. Incur actual manufacturing overhead costs of $10,900.

| | | |
|---|---|---|
| Manufacturing Overhead | 10,900 | |
|     Accounts Payable/Cash/Acc. Depreciation | | 10,900 |
|       (To record overhead incurred) | | |

The controllable overhead variance (see Appendix 24B) is not recorded at this time. It depends on standard hours applied to work in process. This amount is not known at the time overhead is incurred.

**4.** Issue raw materials for production at a cost of $12,600 when the standard cost is $12,000.

| | | |
|---|---|---|
| Work in Process Inventory | 12,000 | |
| Materials Quantity Variance | 600 | |
|     Raw Materials Inventory | | 12,600 |
|         (To record issuance of raw materials) | | |

Xonic debits Work in Process Inventory for standard materials quantities used at standard prices. It debits the variance account because the variance is unfavorable. The company credits Raw Materials Inventory for actual quantities at standard prices.

**5.** Assign factory labor to production at a cost of $31,500 when standard cost is $30,000.

| | | |
|---|---|---|
| Work in Process Inventory | 30,000 | |
| Labor Quantity Variance | 1,500 | |
|     Factory Labor | | 31,500 |
|         (To assign factory labor to jobs) | | |

Xonic debits Work in Process Inventory for standard labor hours at standard rates. It debits the unfavorable variance to Labor Quantity Variance. The credit to Factory Labor produces a zero balance in this account.

**6.** Apply manufacturing overhead to production $10,000.

| | | |
|---|---|---|
| Work in Process Inventory | 10,000 | |
|     Manufacturing Overhead | | 10,000 |
|         (To assign overhead to jobs) | | |

Xonic debits Work in Process Inventory for standard hours allowed multiplied by the standard overhead rate.

**7.** Transfer completed work to finished goods $52,000.

| | | |
|---|---|---|
| Finished Goods Inventory | 52,000 | |
|     Work in Process Inventory | | 52,000 |
|         (To record transfer of completed work to finished goods) | | |

In this example, both inventory accounts are at standard cost.

**8.** Sell the 1,000 gallons of Xonic Tonic for $70,000.

| | | |
|---|---|---|
| Accounts Receivable | 70,000 | |
| Cost of Goods Sold | 52,000 | |
|     Sales | | 70,000 |
|     Finished Goods Inventory | | 52,000 |
|         (To record sale of finished goods and the cost of goods sold) | | |

The company debits Cost of Goods Sold at standard cost. Gross profit, in turn, is the difference between sales and the standard cost of goods sold.

**9.** Recognize unfavorable total overhead variance:

| | | |
|---|---|---|
| Overhead Variance | 900 | |
|     Manufacturing Overhead | | 900 |
|         (To recognize overhead variances) | | |

Prior to this entry, a debit balance of $900 existed in Manufacturing Overhead because overhead of $10,900 was incurred but only $10,000 of overhead was applied. This entry therefore adjusts the account to a zero balance in the Manufacturing Overhead account. The information needed for this entry is often not available until the end of the accounting period.

**HELPFUL HINT**

Each debit balance in variance accounts indicates an unfavorable variance; each credit balance indicates a favorable variance.

# Ledger Accounts

**Illustration 24A.1** shows the cost accounts for Xonic after posting the entries. Note that five variance accounts, highlighted in red, are included in the ledger (see **Helpful Hint**). The six

| Raw Materials Inventory | | |
|---|---|---|
| (1) 12,600 | (4) 12,600 | |

| Materials Price Variance | |
|---|---|
| (1) 420 | |

| Work in Process Inventory | | |
|---|---|---|
| (4) 12,000 | (7) 52,000 | |
| (5) 30,000 | | |
| (6) 10,000 | | |

| Factory Labor | | |
|---|---|---|
| (2) 31,500 | (5) 31,500 | |

| Materials Quantity Variance | |
|---|---|
| (4) 600 | |

| Finished Goods Inventory | | |
|---|---|---|
| (7) 52,000 | (8) 52,000 | |

| Manufacturing Overhead | | |
|---|---|---|
| (3) 10,900 | (6) 10,000 | |
| | (9) 900 | |

| Labor Price Variance | |
|---|---|
| | (2) 420 |

| Cost of Goods Sold | |
|---|---|
| (8) 52,000 | |

| Labor Quantity Variance | |
|---|---|
| (5) 1,500 | |

| Overhead Variance | |
|---|---|
| (9) 900 | |

other accounts are the same as those illustrated for a job order cost system in Chapter 15, in which only actual costs were used.

| Appendix 24B | # Overhead Controllable and Volume Variances

## LEARNING OBJECTIVE *6

Compute overhead controllable and volume variances.

As indicated in the chapter, the total overhead variance is generally analyzed through a price variance and a quantity variance. The name usually given to the price variance is the **overhead controllable variance**; the quantity variance is referred to as the **overhead volume variance**.

## Overhead Controllable Variance

The **overhead controllable variance** shows whether overhead costs are effectively controlled.

- To compute this variance, the company compares actual overhead costs incurred with budgeted costs for the **standard hours allowed**.

- The budgeted costs are determined from a flexible manufacturing overhead budget. (The concepts related to a flexible budget were discussed in Chapter 23.)

For Xonic, the budget computation for manufacturing overhead is variable manufacturing overhead cost of $3 per hour of labor plus fixed manufacturing overhead costs of $4,400 ($52,800 ÷ 12, per Illustration 24.6). **Illustration 24B.1** shows the monthly flexible budget for Xonic.

| | A | B | C | D | E |
|---|---|---|---|---|---|
| | | | Xonic | | |
| 1 | | | | | |
| 2 | | Flexible Manufacturing Overhead Monthly Budget | | | |
| 3 | Activity Index | | | | |
| 4 | Standard direct labor hours | 1,800 | **2,000** | 2,200 | 2,400 |
| 5 | | | | | |
| 6 | Costs | | | | |
| 7 | Variable costs | | | | |
| 8 | Indirect materials | $1,800 | $ 2,000 | $ 2,200 | $ 2,400 |
| 9 | Indirect labor | 2,700 | 3,000 | 3,300 | 3,600 |
| 10 | Utilities | 900 | 1,000 | 1,100 | 1,200 |
| 11 | Total variable costs | 5,400 | 6,000 | 6,600 | 7,200 |
| 12 | | | | | |
| 13 | Fixed costs | | | | |
| 14 | Supervision | 3,000 | 3,000 | 3,000 | 3,000 |
| 15 | Depreciation | 1,400 | 1,400 | 1,400 | 1,400 |
| 16 | Total fixed costs | 4,400 | 4,400 | 4,400 | 4,400 |
| 17 | Total costs | $9,800 | $10,400 | $11,000 | $11,600 |

As shown, the budgeted costs for 2,000 standard hours are $10,400 ($6,000 variable and $4,400 fixed).

**Illustration 24B.2** shows the equation for the overhead controllable variance and the calculation for Xonic at 1,000 units of output (2,000 standard labor hours).

| Actual Overhead | − | Overhead Budgeted* | = | Overhead Controllable Variance |
|---|---|---|---|---|
| $10,900 | − | $10,400 | = | $500 U |
| ($6,500 + $4,400) | | ($6,000 + $4,400) | | |

*Based on standard hours allowed.

The overhead controllable variance for Xonic is $500 unfavorable.

- Most controllable variances are associated with variable costs, which are controllable costs.
- Fixed costs are often known at the time the budget is prepared and are therefore not as likely to deviate from the budgeted amount.

In Xonic's case, all of the overhead controllable variance is due to the difference between the actual variable overhead costs ($6,500) and the budgeted variable costs ($6,000).

Management can compare actual and budgeted overhead for each manufacturing overhead cost that contributes to the controllable variance. In addition, management can develop cost and quantity variances for each overhead cost, such as indirect materials and indirect labor.

## Overhead Volume Variance

The **overhead volume variance** is the difference between normal capacity hours and standard hours allowed times the fixed overhead rate.

- The overhead volume variance relates to whether fixed costs were under- or overapplied during the year.
- For example, the overhead volume variance answers the question of whether Xonic effectively used its factory assets.
- If Xonic produces less Xonic Tonic than normal capacity would allow, an unfavorable variance results. Conversely, if Xonic produces more Xonic Tonic than what is considered normal capacity, a favorable variance results.

**Illustration 24B.3** provides the equation for computing the overhead volume variance.

| Fixed Overhead Rate | × | ( Normal Capacity Hours | − | Standard Hours Allowed ) | = | Overhead Volume Variance |
|---|---|---|---|---|---|---|

**ILLUSTRATION 24B.3**

**Equation for overhead volume variance**

To illustrate the fixed overhead rate computation, recall that Xonic budgeted fixed overhead cost for the year of $52,800 (Illustration 24.6). At normal capacity, 26,400 standard direct labor hours are required. The fixed overhead rate is therefore $2 per hour ($52,800 ÷ 26,400 hours).

Xonic produced 1,000 units of Xonic Tonic in June. The standard hours allowed for the 1,000 gallons produced in June is 2,000 (1,000 gallons × 2 hours). For Xonic, normal capacity for June is 1,100, so standard direct labor hours for June at normal capacity is 2,200 (26,400 annual hours ÷ 12 months). The computation of the overhead volume variance in this case is as shown in **Illustration 24B.4**.

| Fixed Overhead Rate | × | ( Normal Capacity Hours | − | Standard Hours Allowed ) | = | Overhead Volume Variance |
|---|---|---|---|---|---|---|
| $2 | × | (2,200 | − | 2,000) | = | $400 U |

**ILLUSTRATION 24B.4**

**Computation of overhead volume variance for Xonic**

In Xonic's case, a $400 unfavorable volume variance results. The volume variance is unfavorable because Xonic produced only 1,000 gallons rather than the normal capacity of 1,100 gallons in the month of June. As a result, it underapplied fixed overhead for that period.

In computing the overhead variances, it is important to remember the following.

1. Standard hours allowed are used in each of the variances.
2. Budgeted costs for the controllable variance are derived from the flexible budget.
3. The controllable variance generally pertains to variable costs.
4. The volume variance pertains solely to fixed costs. Often, these volume variances arise because productive capacity exceeds what is needed to satisfy sales. This is usually beyond the control of the production manager.

# Review and Practice

## Learning Objectives Review

### 1 Describe standard costs.

Both standards and budgets are predetermined costs. The primary difference is that a standard is a unit amount, whereas a budget is a total amount. A standard may be regarded as the budgeted cost per unit of product.

Standard costs offer a number of advantages. They (a) facilitate management planning, (b) promote greater economy, (c) are useful in setting selling prices, (d) contribute to management control, (e) permit "management by exception," and (f) simplify the costing of inventories and reduce clerical costs.

The direct materials price standard should be based on the delivered cost of raw materials plus an allowance for receiving and handling. The direct materials quantity standard should establish the required quantity plus an allowance for waste and spoilage.

The direct labor price standard should be based on current wage rates and anticipated adjustments such as COLAs. It also generally includes payroll taxes and fringe benefits. Direct labor quantity standards should be based on required production time plus an allowance for rest periods, cleanup, machine setup, and machine downtime.

For manufacturing overhead, a standard predetermined overhead rate is used. It is based on an expected standard activity index such as standard direct labor hours or standard machine hours.

### 2 Determine direct materials variances.

The equations for the direct materials variances are as follows.

$$\begin{pmatrix} \text{Actual quantity} \\ \times \text{Actual price} \end{pmatrix} - \begin{pmatrix} \text{Standard quantity} \\ \times \text{Standard price} \end{pmatrix} = \begin{matrix} \text{Total} \\ \text{materials} \\ \text{variance} \end{matrix}$$

$$\begin{pmatrix} \text{Actual quantity} \\ \times \text{Actual price} \end{pmatrix} - \begin{pmatrix} \text{Actual quantity} \\ \times \text{Standard price} \end{pmatrix} = \begin{matrix} \text{Materials} \\ \text{price} \\ \text{variance} \end{matrix}$$

$$\begin{pmatrix} \text{Actual quantity} \\ \times \text{Standard price} \end{pmatrix} - \begin{pmatrix} \text{Standard quantity} \\ \times \text{Standard price} \end{pmatrix} = \begin{matrix} \text{Materials} \\ \text{quantity} \\ \text{variance} \end{matrix}$$

### 3 Determine direct labor and total manufacturing overhead variances.

The equations for the direct labor variances are as follows.

$$\begin{pmatrix} \text{Actual hours} \\ \times \text{Actual rate} \end{pmatrix} - \begin{pmatrix} \text{Standard hours} \\ \times \text{Standard rate} \end{pmatrix} = \begin{matrix} \text{Total} \\ \text{labor} \\ \text{variance} \end{matrix}$$

$$\begin{pmatrix} \text{Actual hours} \\ \times \text{Actual rate} \end{pmatrix} - \begin{pmatrix} \text{Actual hours} \\ \times \text{Standard rate} \end{pmatrix} = \begin{matrix} \text{Labor} \\ \text{price} \\ \text{variance} \end{matrix}$$

$$\begin{pmatrix} \text{Actual hours} \\ \times \text{Standard rate} \end{pmatrix} - \begin{pmatrix} \text{Standard hours} \\ \times \text{Standard rate} \end{pmatrix} = \begin{matrix} \text{Labor} \\ \text{quantity} \\ \text{variance} \end{matrix}$$

The equation for the total manufacturing overhead variance is as follows.

$$\begin{pmatrix} \text{Actual} \\ \text{overhead} \end{pmatrix} - \begin{pmatrix} \text{Overhead} \\ \text{applied at} \\ \text{standard hours} \\ \text{allowed} \end{pmatrix} = \begin{matrix} \text{Total overhead} \\ \text{variance} \end{matrix}$$

### 4 Prepare variance reports and balanced scorecards.

Variances are reported to management in variance reports. The reports facilitate management by exception by highlighting significant differences. Under a standard costing system, an income statement prepared for management will report cost of goods sold at standard cost and then disclose each variance separately.

The balanced scorecard incorporates financial and nonfinancial measures in an integrated system that links performance measurement and a company's strategic goals. It employs four perspectives: financial, customer, internal process, and learning and growth. Objectives are set within each of these perspectives that link to objectives within the other perspectives.

### *5 Identify the features of a standard cost accounting system.

In a standard cost accounting system, companies journalize and post standard costs, and they maintain separate variance accounts in the ledger.

### *6 Compute overhead controllable and volume variances.

The total overhead variance is generally analyzed through a price variance and a quantity variance. The name usually given to the price variance is the overhead controllable variance. The quantity variance is referred to as the overhead volume variance.

## Glossary Review

**Balanced scorecard**   An approach that incorporates financial and non-financial measures in an integrated system that links performance measurement and a company's strategic goals. (p. 24-20).

**Customer perspective**   A viewpoint employed in the balanced scorecard to evaluate the company from the perspective of those people who buy and use its products or services. (p. 24-20).

**Direct labor price standard**   The rate per hour that management determines should be incurred for direct labor to produce one unit of product. (p. 24-6).

**Direct labor quantity standard**   The time that management determines should be required to produce one unit of product. (p. 24-6).

**Direct materials price standard**   The cost per unit of direct materials that management determines should be incurred to produce one unit of product. (p. 24-5).

**Direct materials quantity standard**   The quantity of direct materials that management determines should be used per unit of finished goods. (p. 24-5).

**Financial perspective**   A viewpoint employed in the balanced scorecard to evaluate a company's performance using financial measures. (p. 24-20).

**Ideal standards**   Standards based on the optimum level of performance under perfect operating conditions. (p. 24-4).

**Internal process perspective**   A viewpoint employed in the balanced scorecard to evaluate the effectiveness and efficiency of a company's value chain, including product development, production, delivery, and after-sale service. (p. 24-21).

**Labor price variance**   The difference between the actual hours times the actual rate and the actual hours times the standard rate for labor. (p. 24-14).

**Labor quantity variance**   The difference between actual hours times standard rate and standard hours times the standard rate for labor. (p. 24-14).

**Learning and growth perspective**   A viewpoint employed in the balanced scorecard to evaluate how well a company develops and retains its employees. (p. 24-21).

**Materials price variance**   The difference between the actual quantity times the actual price and the actual quantity times the standard price for materials. (p. 24-11).

**Materials quantity variance**   The difference between the actual quantity times the standard price and the standard quantity times the standard price for materials. (p. 24-11).

**Normal capacity**   The average activity output that a company should experience over the long run. (p. 24-7).

**Normal standards**   Standards based on an efficient level of performance that is attainable under expected operating conditions. (p. 24-4).

*****Overhead controllable variance**   The difference between actual overhead incurred and overhead budgeted for the standard hours allowed. (p 24-25).

*****Overhead volume variance**   The difference between normal capacity hours and standard hours allowed times the fixed overhead rate. (p. 24-27).

*****Standard cost accounting system**   A double-entry system of accounting in which standard costs are used in making entries, and variances are recognized in the accounts. (p. 24-23).

**Standard costs**   Predetermined unit costs which companies use as measures of performance. (p. 24-3).

**Standard hours allowed**   The hours that should have been worked for the units produced. (p. 24-19).

**Standard predetermined overhead rate**   An overhead rate determined by dividing budgeted overhead costs by an expected standard activity index. (p. 24-7).

**Total labor variance**   The difference between actual hours times the actual rate and standard hours times the standard rate for labor. (p. 24-13).

**Total materials variance**   The difference between the actual quantity times the actual price and the standard quantity times the standard price of materials. (p. 24-10).

**Total overhead variance**   The difference between actual overhead costs and overhead costs applied to work done, based on standard hours allowed. (p. 24-16).

**Variance**   The difference between total actual costs and total standard costs. (p. 24-8).

## Practice Multiple-Choice Questions

1. **(LO 1)** Standards differ from budgets in that:
   a. budgets but not standards may be used in valuing inventories.
   b. budgets but not standards may be journalized and posted.
   c. budgets are a total amount and standards are a unit amount.
   d. only budgets contribute to management planning and control.

2. **(LO 1)** Standard costs:
   a. are imposed by governmental agencies.
   b. are predetermined unit costs which companies use as measures of performance.
   c. can be used by manufacturing companies but not by service or not-for-profit companies.
   d. All of the answer choices are correct.

3. **(LO 1)** The advantages of standard costs include all of the following **except**:
   a. management by exception may be used.
   b. management planning is facilitated.
   c. they may simplify the costing of inventories.
   d. management must use a static budget.

4. **(LO 1)** Normal standards:
   a. allow for rest periods, machine breakdowns, and setup time.
   b. represent levels of performance under perfect operating conditions.
   c. are rarely used because managers believe they lower workforce morale.
   d. are more likely than ideal standards to result in unethical practices.

**5. (LO 1)** The setting of standards is:

    **a.** a managerial accounting decision.

    **b.** a management decision.

    **c.** a worker decision.

    **d.** preferably set at the ideal level of performance.

**6. (LO 2)** Each of the following equations is correct **except**:

    **a.** Labor price variance = (Actual hours × Actual rate) − (Actual hours × Standard rate).

    **b.** Total overhead variance = Actual overhead − Overhead applied.

    **c.** Materials price variance = (Actual quantity × Actual price) − (Standard quantity × Standard price).

    **d.** Labor quantity variance = (Actual hours × Standard rate) − (Standard hours × Standard rate).

**7. (LO 2)** In producing product AA, 6,300 pounds of direct materials were used at a cost of $1.10 per pound. The standard was 6,000 pounds at $1.00 per pound. The direct materials quantity variance is:

    **a.** $330 unfavorable.

    **b.** $300 unfavorable.

    **c.** $600 unfavorable.

    **d.** $630 unfavorable.

**8. (LO 3)** In producing product ZZ, 14,800 direct labor hours were used at a rate of $8.20 per hour. The standard was 15,000 hours at $8.00 per hour. Based on these data, the direct labor:

    **a.** quantity variance is $1,600 favorable.

    **b.** quantity variance is $1,600 unfavorable.

    **c.** price variance is $3,000 favorable.

    **d.** price variance is $3,000 unfavorable.

**9. (LO 3)** Which of the following is **correct** about the total overhead variance?

    **a.** Budgeted overhead and overhead applied are the same.

    **b.** Total actual overhead is composed of variable overhead, fixed overhead, and period costs.

    **c.** Standard hours actually worked are used in computing the variance.

    **d.** Standard hours allowed for the work done is the measure used in computing the variance.

**10. (LO 3)** The equation for computing the total overhead variance is:

    **a.** actual overhead less overhead applied.

    **b.** overhead budgeted less overhead applied.

    **c.** actual overhead less overhead budgeted.

    **d.** No correct answer is given.

**11. (LO 4)** Which of the following is **incorrect** about variance reports?

    **a.** They facilitate "management by exception."

    **b.** They should only be sent to the top level of management.

    **c.** They should be prepared as soon as possible.

    **d.** They may vary in form, content, and frequency among companies.

**12. (LO 4)** In using variance reports to evaluate cost control, management normally looks into:

    **a.** all variances.

    **b.** favorable variances only.

    **c.** unfavorable variances only.

    **d.** both favorable and unfavorable variances that exceed a predetermined quantitative measure such as a percentage or dollar amount.

**13. (LO 4)** Generally accepted accounting principles allow a company to:

    **a.** report inventory at standard cost but cost of goods sold must be reported at actual cost.

    **b.** report cost of goods sold at standard cost but inventory must be reported at actual cost.

    **c.** report inventory and cost of goods sold at standard cost as long as there are no significant differences between actual and standard cost.

    **d.** report inventory and cost of goods sold only at actual costs; standard costing is never permitted.

**14. (LO 4)** Which of the following would **not** be an objective used in the customer perspective of the balanced scorecard approach?

    **a.** Percentage of customers who would recommend product to a friend.

    **b.** Customer retention.

    **c.** Brand recognition.

    **d.** Earnings per share.

***15. (LO 5)** Which of the following is **incorrect** about a standard cost accounting system?

    **a.** It is applicable to job order costing.

    **b.** It is applicable to process costing.

    **c.** It reports only favorable variances.

    **d.** It keeps separate accounts for each variance.

***16. (LO 6)** The equation to compute the overhead volume variance is:

    **a.** Fixed overhead rate × (Standard hours − Actual hours).

    **b.** Fixed overhead rate × (Normal capacity hours − Actual hours).

    **c.** Fixed overhead rate × (Normal capacity hours − Standard hours allowed).

    **d.** (Variable overhead rate + Fixed overhead rate) × (Normal capacity hours − Standard hours allowed).

## Solutions

**1. c.** Budgets are expressed in total amounts, and standards are expressed in unit amounts. The other choices are incorrect because (a) standards, not budgets, may be used in valuing inventories; (b) standards, not budgets, may be journalized and posted; and (d) both budgets and standards contribute to management planning and control.

**2. b.** Standard costs are predetermined units costs which companies use as measures of performance. The other choices are incorrect because (a) only those that are called regulations are imposed by governmental agencies, (c) standard costs can be used by all types of companies, and (d) choices (a) and (c) are incorrect.

**3. d.** Standard costs are separate from a static budget. The other choices are all advantages of using standard costs.

**4. a.** Normal standards allow for rest periods, machine breakdowns, and setup time. The other choices are incorrect because they describe ideal standards, not normal standards.

**5. b.** Standards are set by management. The other choices are incorrect because setting standards requires input from (a) managerial accountants and (c) sometimes workers, but the final decision is made by management. Choice (d) is incorrect because setting standards at the ideal level of performance is uncommon because of the perceived negative effect on worker morale.

**6. c.** Materials price variance = (Actual quantity × Actual price) − (Actual quantity (not Standard quantity) × Standard price). The other choices are correct equations.

**7. b.** The direct materials quantity variance is (6,300 × $1.00) − (6,000 × $1.00) = $300. This variance is unfavorable because more material was used than prescribed by the standard. The other choices are therefore incorrect.

**8. a.** The direct labor quantity variance is (14,800 × $8) − (15,000 × $8) = $1,600. This variance is favorable because fewer labor hours

were used than prescribed by the standard. The other choices are therefore incorrect.

**9. d.** Standard hours allowed for work done is the measure used in computing the variance. The other choices are incorrect because (a) budgeted overhead is used to calculate the predetermined overhead rate while overhead applied is equal to standard hours allowed times the predetermined overhead rate, (b) overhead is a product cost and does not include period costs, and (c) standard hours allowed, not hours actually worked, are used in computing the overhead variance.

**10. a.** Total overhead variance equals actual overhead less overhead applied. The other choices are therefore incorrect.

**11. b.** Variance reports should be sent to the level of management responsible for the area in which the variance occurred so it can be remedied as quickly as possible. The other choices are correct statements.

**12. d.** In using variance reports to evaluate cost control, management normally looks into both favorable and unfavorable variances that exceed a predetermined quantitative measure such as percentage or dollar amount. The other choices are therefore incorrect.

**13. c.** GAAP allows a company to report both inventory and cost of goods sold at standard cost as long as there are no significant differences between actual and standard cost. The other choices are therefore incorrect.

**14. d.** Earnings per share is not an objective used in the customer perspective of the balanced scorecard approach. The other choices are all true statements.

**\*15. c.** A standard cost accounting system reports both favorable and unfavorable variances. The other choices are all correct statements.

**\*16. c.** The equation to compute the overhead volume variance is Fixed overhead rate × (Normal capacity hours − Standard hours allowed). The other choices are therefore incorrect.

---

# Practice Brief Exercises

---

**1. (LO 1)** Castellen Company accumulates the following data concerning raw materials in making one quart of finished product. (1) Price—purchase price $3.00; terms 2/10, n/30; freight-in $0.25; and receiving and handling $0.10. (2) Quantity—required materials 2.7 pounds, allowance for waste and spoilage 0.3 pounds. Compute the following.

*Set direct materials standard.*

   **a.** Standard direct materials price per quart.

   **b.** Standard direct materials quantity per quart.

   **c.** Total standard materials cost per quart

### Solution

**1. a.** Standard direct materials price per quart = ($3.00 − $0.06 + $0.25 + $0.10) = $3.29

   **b.** Standard direct materials quantity per quart = (2.7 + .3) = 3 pounds

   **c.** Standard materials cost per quart = ($3.29 × 3) = $9.87

**2. (LO 2)** Spandrell Company's standard materials cost per unit of output is $12 (3 pounds × $4). During July, the company purchases and uses 5,800 pounds of materials costing $22,910 in making 2,000 units of finished product. Compute the total, price, and quantity materials variances.

*Compute direct materials variances.*

### Solution

2. Total materials variance = [(5,800 × $3.95\*) − (6,000\*\* × $4.00)] = $1,090 F

   Materials price variance = [(5,800 × $3.95) − (5,800 × $4.00)] = $290 F

   Materials quantity variance [(5,800 × $4.00) − (6,000 × $4.00)] = $800 F

   \*$22,910 ÷ 5,800; \*\*2,000 × 3

*Compute direct labor variances.*

3. **(LO 3)** Timemore Company's standard labor cost per unit of output is $34 (2 hours × $17 per hour). During August, the company incurs 1,960 hours of direct labor at an hourly cost of $17.20 per hour in making 1,000 units of finished product. Compute the total, price, and quantity labor variances.

### Solution

3. Total labor variance = [(1,960 × $17.20) − (2,000 × $17.00)] = $288 F

   Labor price variance = [(1,960 × $17.20) − (1,960 × $17.00)] = $392 U

   Labor quantity variance = [(1,960 × $17.00) − (2,000 × $17.00)] = $680 F

## Practice Exercises

*Compute materials and labor variances.*

1. **(LO 2, 3)** Hector Inc., which produces a single product, has prepared the following standard cost sheet for one unit of the product.

|  |  |
|---|---|
| Direct materials (6 pounds at $2.50 per pound) | $15.00 |
| Direct labor (3.1 hours at $12.00 per hour) | $37.20 |

During the month of April, the company manufactures 250 units and incurs the following actual costs.

|  |  |
|---|---|
| Direct materials purchased and used (1,600 pounds) | $4,192 |
| Direct labor (760 hours) | $8,740 |

### Instructions

Compute the total, price, and quantity variances for materials and labor.

### Solution

1. Total materials variance:

| (AQ × AP) | − | (SQ × SP) | = | TMV |
|---|---|---|---|---|
| (1,600 × $2.62\*) | | (1,500\*\* × $2.50) | | |
| $4,192 | − | $3,750 | = | $442 U |

\*$4,192 ÷ 1,600; \*\*250 × 6

Materials price variance:

| (AQ × AP) | − | (AQ × SP) | = | MPV |
|---|---|---|---|---|
| (1,600 × $2.62) | | (1,600 × $2.50) | | |
| $4,192 | − | $4,000 | = | $192 U |

Materials quantity variance:

| (AQ × SP) | − | (SQ × SP) | = | MQV |
|---|---|---|---|---|
| (1,600 × $2.50) | | (1,500 × $2.50) | | |
| $4,000 | − | $3,750 | = | $250 U |

Total labor variance:

| (AH × AR) | − | (SH × SR) | = | TLV |
|---|---|---|---|---|
| (760 × $11.50\*) | | (775\*\* × $12.00) | | |
| $8,740 | − | $9,300 | = | $560 F |

\*$8,740 ÷ 760; \*\*250 × 3.1

Labor price variance:

| | (AH × AR) | − | (AH × SR) | = | LPV |
|---|---|---|---|---|---|
| | (760 × $11.50) | | (760 × $12.00) | | |
| | $8,740 | − | $9,120 | = | $380 F |

Labor quantity variance:

| | (AH × SR) | − | (SH × SR) | = | LQV |
|---|---|---|---|---|---|
| | (760 × $12.00) | | (775 × $12.00) | | |
| | $9,120 | − | $9,300 | = | $180 F |

**2. (LO 3)** Manufacturing overhead data for the production of Product H by Yamato Company are as follows.   *Compute overhead variances.*

| | |
|---|---|
| Overhead incurred for 35,000 actual direct labor hours worked | $140,000 |
| Overhead rate (variable $3; fixed $1) at normal capacity of 36,000 direct labor hours | $4 |
| Standard hours allowed for work done | 34,000 |

### Instructions

Compute the total overhead variance.

### Solution

2. Total overhead variance:

| Actual Overhead | − | Overhead Applied | = | Overhead Variance |
|---|---|---|---|---|
| $140,000 | − | $136,000 | = | $4,000 U |
| | | (34,000 × $4) | | |

## Practice Problem

**(LO 2, 3)** Manlow Company makes a cologne called Allure. The standard cost for one bottle of Allure is as follows.   *Compute variances.*

| Manufacturing Cost Components | Quantity | × | Price | = | Cost |
|---|---|---|---|---|---|
| Direct materials | 6 oz. | × | $ 0.90 | = | $ 5.40 |
| Direct labor | 0.5 hrs. | × | $12.00 | = | 6.00 |
| Manufacturing overhead | 0.5 hrs. | × | $ 4.80 | = | 2.40 |
| | | | | | $13.80 |

During the month, the following transactions occurred in manufacturing 10,000 bottles of Allure.

1. 58,000 ounces of materials were purchased at $1.00 per ounce.
2. All the materials purchased were used to produce the 10,000 bottles of Allure.
3. 4,900 direct labor hours were worked at a total labor cost of $56,350.
4. Variable manufacturing overhead incurred was $15,000 and fixed overhead incurred was $10,400.

The manufacturing overhead rate of $4.80 is based on a normal capacity of 5,200 direct labor hours. The total budget at this capacity is $10,400 fixed and $14,560 variable.

### Instructions

a. Compute the total variance and the variances for direct materials and direct labor components.

b. Compute the total variance for manufacturing overhead.

**Solution**

**a.**

**Total Variance**

Actual costs incurred

| | |
|---|---:|
| Direct materials | $ 58,000 |
| Direct labor | 56,350 |
| Manufacturing overhead | 25,400 |
| | 139,750 |
| Standard cost (10,000 × $13.80) | 138,000 |
| Total variance | $ 1,750 U |

**Direct Materials Variances**

| | | | | | |
|---|---|---|---|---|---|
| Total | = | $58,000 (58,000 × $1.00) | − $54,000 (60,000* × $0.90) | = | $4,000 U |
| Price | = | $58,000 (58,000 × $1.00) | − $52,200 (58,000 × $0.90) | = | $5,800 U |
| Quantity | = | $52,200 (58,000 × $0.90) | − $54,000 (60,000 × $0.90) | = | $1,800 F |

*10,000 × 6

**Direct Labor Variances**

| | | | | | |
|---|---|---|---|---|---|
| Total | = | $56,350 (4,900 × $11.50*) | − $60,000 (5,000** × $12.00) | = | $3,650 F |
| Price | = | $56,350 (4,900 × $11.50) | − $58,800 (4,900 × $12.00) | = | $2,450 F |
| Quantity | = | $58,800 (4,900 × $12.00) | − $60,000 (5,000 × $12.00) | = | $1,200 F |

*56,350 ÷ 4,900; **10,000 × 0.5

**b.**

**Overhead Variance**

| | | | | | |
|---|---|---|---|---|---|
| Total | = | $25,400 ($15,000 + $10,400) | − $24,000 (5,000 × $4.80) | = | $1,400 U |

---

Brief Exercises, DO IT! Exercises, Exercises, Problems, Data Analytics Activities, and many additional resources are available for practice in WileyPLUS.

---

*Note:* All asterisked Questions, Exercises, and Problems relate to material in the appendices to the chapter.

---

## Questions

**1. a.** "Standard costs are the expected total cost of completing a job." Is this correct? Explain why or why not.

**b.** "A standard imposed by a governmental agency is known as a regulation." Is this correct? Explain why or why not.

**2. a.** Explain the similarities and differences between standards and budgets.

**b.** Contrast the accounting for standards and budgets.

**3.** Standard costs facilitate management planning. What are the other advantages of standard costs?

**4.** Contrast the roles of the management accountant and management in setting standard costs.

**5.** Distinguish between an ideal standard and a normal standard.

**6.** What factors should be considered in setting (a) the direct materials price standard and (b) the direct materials quantity standard?

**7.** "The objective in setting the direct labor quantity standard is to determine the aggregate time required to make one unit of product."

Is this correct? Explain why or why not. What allowances should be made in setting this standard?

**8.** How is the predetermined overhead rate determined when standard costs are used?

**9.** What is the difference between a favorable cost variance and an unfavorable cost variance?

**10.** In each of the following equations, supply the words that should be inserted for each number in parentheses.

**a.** (Actual quantity × (1)) − (Standard quantity × (2)) = Total materials variance

**b.** ((3) × Actual price) − (Actual quantity × (4)) = Materials price variance

**c.** (Actual quantity × (5)) − ((6) × Standard price) = Materials quantity variance

**11.** In the direct labor variance matrix, there are three factors: (1) Actual hours × Actual rate, (2) Actual hours × Standard rate, and

(3) Standard hours × Standard rate. Using the numbers, indicate the equations for each of the direct labor variances.

12. Mikan Company's standard predetermined overhead rate is $9 per direct labor hour. For the month of June, 26,000 actual hours were worked, and 27,000 standard hours were allowed. How much overhead was applied?

13. How often should variances be reported to management? What principle may be used with variance reports?

14. What circumstances may cause the purchasing department to be responsible for both an unfavorable materials price variance and an unfavorable materials quantity variance?

15. What are the four perspectives used in the balanced scorecard? Discuss the nature of each, and how the perspectives are linked.

16. Kerry James says that the balanced scorecard was created to replace financial measures as the primary mechanism for performance evaluation. He says that it uses only nonfinancial measures. Is this true?

17. What are some examples of nonfinancial measures used by companies to evaluate performance?

18. (a) How are variances reported in income statements prepared for management? (b) Can standard costs be used in preparing financial statements for stockholders? Explain.

*19. (a) Explain the basic features of a standard cost accounting system. (b) What type of balance will exist in the variance account when (1) the materials price variance is unfavorable and (2) the labor quantity variance is favorable?

*20. If the $9 per hour overhead rate in Question 12 includes $5 variable, and actual overhead costs were $248,000, what is the overhead controllable variance for June? The normal capacity hours were 28,000. Is the variance favorable or unfavorable?

*21. What is the purpose of computing the overhead volume variance? What is the basic equation for this variance?

*22. Alma Ortiz does not understand why the overhead volume variance indicates that fixed overhead costs are either underapplied or overapplied. Clarify this matter for Alma.

*23. John Hsu is attempting to outline the important points about overhead variances on a class examination. List four points that John should include in his outline.

# Brief Exercises

**BE24.1 (LO 1), AP** Lopez Company uses both standards and budgets. For the year, estimated production of Product X is 500,000 units. Total estimated cost for materials and labor are $1,400,000 and $1,700,000, respectively. Compute the estimates for (a) a standard cost and (b) a budgeted cost.

*Distinguish between a standard and a budget.*

**BE24.2 (LO 1), AP** Tang Company accumulates the following data concerning raw materials in making its finished product. (1) Price per pound of raw materials is net purchase price $2.30, freight-in $0.20, and receiving and handling $0.10. (2) Quantity per gallon of finished product is required materials 3.6 pounds and allowance for waste and spoilage 0.4 pounds. Compute the following.

*Set direct materials standard.*

  a. Standard direct materials price per pound of raw materials.
  b. Standard direct materials quantity per gallon.
  c. Total standard materials cost per gallon.

**BE24.3 (LO 1), AP** Labor data for making one gallon of finished product in Bing Company are as follows. (1) Price—hourly wage rate $14.00, payroll taxes $0.80, and fringe benefits $1.20. (2) Quantity—actual production time 1.1 hours, rest periods and cleanup 0.25 hours, and setup and downtime 0.15 hours. Compute the following.

*Set direct labor standard.*

  a. Standard direct labor rate per hour.
  b. Standard direct labor hours per gallon.
  c. Standard labor cost per gallon.

**BE24.4 (LO 2), AP** Simba Company's standard materials cost per unit of output is $10 (2 pounds × $5). During July, the company purchases and uses 3,200 pounds of materials costing $16,192 in making 1,500 units of finished product. Compute the total, price, and quantity materials variances.

*Compute direct materials variances.*

**BE24.5 (LO 3), AP** Mordica Company's standard labor cost per unit of output is $22 (2 hours × $11 per hour). During August, the company incurs 2,150 hours of direct labor at an hourly cost of $10.80 per hour in making 1,000 units of finished product. Compute the total, price, and quantity labor variances.

*Compute direct labor variances.*

**BE24.6 (LO 3), AP** In October, Pine Company reports 21,000 actual direct labor hours, and it incurs $118,000 of manufacturing overhead costs. Standard hours allowed for the work done is 20,600 hours. The predetermined overhead rate is $6 per direct labor hour. Compute the total overhead variance.

*Compute total overhead variance.*

*Match balanced scorecard perspectives.*

**BE24.7 (LO 4), AP** The four perspectives in the balanced scorecard are (1) financial, (2) customer, (3) internal process, and (4) learning and growth. Match each of the following objectives with the perspective it is most likely associated with: (a) factory capacity utilization, (b) employee work days missed due to injury, (c) return on assets, and (d) brand recognition.

*Journalize materials variances.*

**\*BE24.8 (LO 5), AP** Journalize the following transactions for Combs Company.

   **a.** Purchased 6,000 units of raw materials on account for $11,500. The standard cost was $12,000.

   **b.** Issued 5,600 units of raw materials for production. The standard units were 5,800.

*Journalize labor variances.*

**\*BE24.9 (LO 5), AP** Journalize the following transactions for Shelton, Inc.

   **a.** Incurred direct labor costs of $24,000 for 3,000 hours. The standard labor cost was $24,900.

   **b.** Assigned 3,000 direct labor hours costing $24,000 to production. Standard hours were 3,150.

*Compute the overhead controllable variance.*

**\*BE24.10 (LO 6), AP** Some overhead data for Pine Company are given in BE24.6. In addition, the flexible manufacturing overhead budget shows that budgeted costs are $4 variable per direct labor hour and $50,000 fixed. Compute the overhead controllable variance.

*Compute overhead volume variance.*

**\*BE24.11 (LO 6), AP** Using the data in BE24.6 and BE24.10, compute the overhead volume variance. Normal capacity was 25,000 direct labor hours.

## DO IT! Exercises

*Compute standard cost.*

**DO IT! 24.1 (LO 1), AP** Larkin Company accumulated the following standard cost data concerning product I-Tal.

   Direct materials per unit: 2 pounds at $5 per pound
   Direct labor per unit: 0.2 hours at $16 per hour
   Manufacturing overhead: Allocated based on direct labor hours at a predetermined rate of $20 per
      direct labor hour
   Compute the standard cost of one unit of product I-Tal.

*Compute materials variance.*

**DO IT! 24.2 (LO 2), AP** The standard cost of product 777 includes 2 units of direct materials at $6.00 per unit. During August, the company bought 29,000 units of materials at $6.30 and used those materials to produce 16,000 units. Compute the total, price, and quantity variances for materials.

*Compute labor and manufacturing overhead variances.*

**DO IT! 24.3 (LO 3), AP** The standard cost of product 5252 includes 1.9 hours of direct labor at $14.00 per hour. The predetermined overhead rate is $22.00 per direct labor hour. During July, the company incurred 4,000 hours of direct labor at an average rate of $14.30 per hour and $81,300 of manufacturing overhead costs. It produced 2,000 units.

   **a.** Compute the total, price, and quantity variances for labor.

   **b.** Compute the total overhead variance.

*Prepare variance report.*

**DO IT! 24.4 (LO 4), AP** Tropic Zone Corporation experienced the following variances: materials price $350 U, materials quantity $1,700 F, labor price $800 F, labor quantity $500 F, and total overhead $1,200 U. Sales revenue was $92,100, and cost of goods sold (at standard) was $51,600. Determine the actual gross profit.

## Exercises

*Compute budget and standard.*

**E24.1 (LO 1), AP** `Writing` Parsons Company is planning to produce 2,000 units of product in 2022. Each unit requires 3 pounds of materials at $5 per pound and a half-hour of labor at $16 per hour. The overhead rate is 70% of direct labor.

## Instructions

**a.** Compute the budgeted amounts for 2022 for direct materials to be used, direct labor, and applied overhead.

**b.** Compute the standard cost of one unit of product.

**c.** What are the potential advantages to a corporation of using standard costs?

**E24.2 (LO 1), AP** Hank Itzek manufactures and sells homemade wine, and he wants to develop a standard cost per gallon. The following are required for production of a 50-gallon batch.

*Compute standard materials costs.*

3,000 ounces of grape concentrate at $0.06 per ounce
54 pounds of granulated sugar at $0.30 per pound
60 lemons at $0.60 each
50 yeast tablets at $0.25 each
50 nutrient tablets at $0.20 each
2,600 ounces of water at $0.005 per ounce

Hank estimates that 4% of the grape concentrate is wasted, 10% of the sugar is lost, and 25% of the lemons cannot be used.

## Instructions

Compute the standard cost of the ingredients for one gallon of wine. (Carry computations to two decimal places.)

**E24.3 (LO 1), AP** Stefani Company has gathered the following information about its product.

*Compute standard cost per unit.*

*Direct materials.* Each unit of product contains 4.5 pounds of materials. The average waste and spoilage per unit produced under normal conditions is 0.5 pounds. Materials cost $5 per pound, but Stefani always takes the 2% cash discount all of its suppliers offer. Freight costs average $0.25 per pound.

*Direct labor.* Each unit requires 2 hours of labor. Setup, cleanup, and downtime average 0.4 hours per unit. The average hourly pay rate of Stefani's employees is $12. Payroll taxes and fringe benefits are an additional $3 per hour.

*Manufacturing overhead.* Overhead is applied at a rate of $7 per direct labor hour.

## Instructions

Compute Stefani's total standard cost per unit.

**E24.4 (LO 1, 3), AP** Service  Monte Services, Inc. is trying to establish the standard labor cost of a typical brake repair. The following data have been collected from time and motion studies conducted over the past month.

*Compute labor cost and labor quantity variance.*

| | |
|---|---|
| Actual time spent on the brake repair | 1.0 hour |
| Hourly wage rate | $12 |
| Payroll taxes | 10% of wage rate |
| Setup and downtime | 20% of actual labor time |
| Cleanup and rest periods | 30% of actual labor time |
| Fringe benefits | 25% of wage rate |

## Instructions

**a.** Determine the standard direct labor hours per brake repair.

**b.** Determine the standard direct labor hourly rate.

**c.** Determine the standard direct labor cost per brake repair.

**d.** If a brake repair took 1.6 hours at the standard hourly rate, what was the direct labor quantity variance?

**E24.5 (LO 2), AP** The standard cost of Product B manufactured by Pharrell Company includes three units of direct materials at $5.00 per unit. During June, 29,000 units of direct materials are purchased at a cost of $4.70 per unit, and 29,000 units of direct materials are used to produce 9,400 units of Product B.

*Compute materials price and quantity variances.*

## Instructions

**a.** Compute the total materials variance and the price and quantity variances.

**b.** Repeat (a), assuming the purchase price is $5.15 and the quantity purchased and used is 28,000 units.

**E24.6 (LO 3), AP** Lewis Company's standard labor cost of producing one unit of Product DD is 4 hours at the rate of $12.00 per hour. During August, 40,600 hours of labor are incurred at a cost of $12.15 per hour to produce 10,000 units of Product DD.

*Compute labor price and quantity variances.*

**Instructions**

**a.** Compute the total labor variance.

**b.** Compute the labor price and quantity variances.

**c.** Repeat (b), assuming the standard is 4.1 hours of direct labor at $12.25 per hour.

*Compute materials and labor variances.*

**E24.7 (LO 2, 3), AP** Levine Inc., which produces a single product, has prepared the following standard cost sheet for one unit of the product.

| | |
|---|---|
| Direct materials (8 pounds at $2.50 per pound) | $20 |
| Direct labor (3 hours at $12.00 per hour) | $36 |

During the month of April, the company manufactures 230 units and incurs the following actual costs.

| | |
|---|---|
| Direct materials purchased and used (1,900 pounds) | $5,035 |
| Direct labor (700 hours) | $8,120 |

**Instructions**

Compute the total, price, and quantity variances for materials and labor.

*Compute the materials and labor variances and list reasons for unfavorable variances.*

**E24.8 (LO 2, 3), AN** **Writing** The following direct materials and direct labor data pertain to the operations of Laurel Company for the month of August.

| Costs | | Quantities | |
|---|---|---|---|
| Actual labor rate | $13 per hour | Actual hours incurred and used | 4,150 hours |
| Actual materials price | $128 per ton | Actual quantity of materials purchased and used | 1,220 tons |
| Standard labor rate | $12.50 per hour | Standard hours used | 4,300 hours |
| Standard materials price | $130 per ton | Standard quantity of materials used | 1,200 tons |

**Instructions**

**a.** Compute the total, price, and quantity variances for materials and labor.

**b.** Provide two possible explanations for each of the unfavorable variances calculated above, and suggest where responsibility for the unfavorable result might be placed.

*Determine amounts from variance report.*

**E24.9 (LO 2, 3), AN** You have been given the following information about the production of Usher Co., and are asked to provide the factory manager with information for a meeting with the vice president of operations.

| | Standard Cost Card |
|---|---|
| Direct materials (5 pounds at $4 per pound) | $20.00 |
| Direct labor (0.8 hours at $10) | 8.00 |
| Variable overhead (0.8 hours at $3 per hour) | 2.40 |
| Fixed overhead (0.8 hours at $7 per hour) | 5.60 |
| | $36.00 |

The following is a variance report for the most recent period of operations.

| | | Variances | |
|---|---|---|---|
| Costs | Total Standard Cost | Price | Quantity |
| Direct materials | $410,000 | $2,095 F | $ 9,000 U |
| Direct labor | 164,000 | 3,906 U | 22,000 U |

**Instructions**

**a.** How many units were produced during the period?

**b.** How many pounds of raw materials were purchased and used during the period?

**c.** What was the actual cost per pound of raw materials?

**d.** How many actual direct labor hours were worked during the period?

**e.** What was the actual rate paid per direct labor hour?

(CGA adapted)

**E24.10 (LO 3, 4), AP** During March 2022, Toby Tool & Die Company worked on four jobs. A review of direct labor costs reveals the following summary data.

*Prepare a variance report for direct labor.*

| Job Number | Actual | | Standard | | Total |
| --- | --- | --- | --- | --- | --- |
| | **Hours** | **Costs** | **Hours** | **Costs** | **Variance** |
| A257 | 221 | $4,420 | 225 | $4,500 | $  80 F |
| A258 | 450 | 9,450 | 430 | 8,600 | 850 U |
| A259 | 300 | 6,180 | 300 | 6,000 | 180 U |
| A260 | 116 | 2,088 | 110 | 2,200 | 112 F |
| Total variance | | | | | $838 U |

Analysis reveals that Job A257 was a repeat job. Job A258 was a rush order that required overtime work at premium rates of pay. Job A259 required a more experienced replacement worker on one shift. Work on Job A260 was done for one day by a new trainee when a regular worker was absent.

**Instructions**

Prepare a report for the factory supervisor on direct labor cost variances for March. The report should have columns for (1) Job No., (2) Actual Hours, (3) Standard Hours, (4) Quantity Variance, (5) Actual Rate, (6) Standard Rate, (7) Price Variance, and (8) Explanation.

**E24.11 (LO 3), AP** Manufacturing overhead data for the production of Product H by Shakira Company, assuming the company uses a standard cost system, are as follows.

*Compute overhead variance.*

| | |
| --- | --- |
| Overhead incurred for 52,000 actual direct labor hours worked | $263,000 |
| Overhead rate (variable $3; fixed $2) at normal capacity of 54,000 direct labor hours | $5 |
| Standard hours allowed for work done | 52,000 |

**Instructions**

Compute the total overhead variance.

**E24.12 (LO 3), AP** Byrd Company produces one product, a putter called GO-Putter. Byrd uses a standard cost system and determines that it should take one hour of direct labor to produce one GO-Putter. The normal production capacity for this putter is 100,000 units per year. The total budgeted overhead at normal capacity is $850,000 comprised of $250,000 of variable costs and $600,000 of fixed costs. Byrd applies overhead on the basis of direct labor hours.

*Compute overhead variances.*

During the current year, Byrd produced 95,000 putters, worked 94,000 direct labor hours, and incurred variable overhead costs of $256,000 and fixed overhead costs of $600,000.

**Instructions**

a. Compute the predetermined variable overhead rate and the predetermined fixed overhead rate.

b. Compute the applied overhead for Byrd for the year.

c. Compute the total overhead variance.

**E24.13 (LO 2, 3), AP** **Writing** Ceelo Company purchased (at a cost of $10,200) and used 2,400 pounds of materials during May. Ceelo's standard cost of materials per unit produced is based on 2 pounds per unit at a cost $5 per pound. Production in May was 1,050 units.

*Compute variances for materials.*

**Instructions**

a. Compute the total, price, and quantity variances for materials.

b. Assume Ceelo also had an unfavorable labor quantity variance. What is a possible scenario that would provide one cause for the variances computed in (a) and the unfavorable labor quantity variance?

**E24.14 (LO 2, 4), AP** **Service** Picard Landscaping plants grass seed as the basic landscaping for business campuses. During a recent month, the company worked on three projects (Remington, Chang, and Wyco). The company is interested in controlling the materials costs, namely the grass seed, for these plantings projects.

*Prepare a variance report.*

In order to provide management with useful cost control information, the company uses standard costs and prepares monthly variance reports. Analysis reveals that the purchasing agent mistakenly purchased poor-quality seed for the Remington project. The Chang project, however, received higher-than-standard-quality seed that was on sale. The Wyco project received standard-quality seed. However, the price had increased and a new employee was used to spread the seed.

Shown below are quantity and cost data for each project.

| Project | Actual Quantity | Actual Costs | Standard Quantity | Standard Costs | Total Variance |
|---|---|---|---|---|---|
| Remington | 500 lbs. | $1,200 | 460 lbs. | $1,150 | $ 50 U |
| Chang | 400 | 920 | 410 | 1,025 | 105 F |
| Wyco | 550 | 1,430 | 480 | 1,200 | 230 U |
| Total variance | | | | | $175 U |

**Instructions**

a. Prepare a variance report for the purchasing department with the following columns: (1) Project, (2) Actual Pounds Purchased, (3) Actual Price per Pound, (4) Standard Price per Pound, (5) Price Variance, and (6) Explanation.

b. Prepare a variance report for the production department with the following columns: (1) Project, (2) Actual Pounds, (3) Standard Pounds, (4) Standard Price per Pound, (5) Quantity Variance, and (6) Explanation.

*Complete variance report.*

**E24.15 (LO 4), AN** Urban Corporation prepared the following variance report.

**Urban Corporation**
**Variance Report—Purchasing Department**
**For the Week Ended January 9, 2022**

| Type of Materials | Quantity Purchased | Actual Price | Standard Price | Price Variance | Explanation |
|---|---|---|---|---|---|
| Rogue11 | ? lbs. | $5.20 | $5.00 | $5,500 ? | Price increase |
| Storm17 | 7,000 oz. | ? | 3.30 | 1,050 U | Rush order |
| Beast29 | 22,000 units | 0.40 | ? | 660 F | Bought larger quantity |

**Instructions**

Fill in the appropriate amounts or letters for the question marks in the report.

*Prepare income statement for management.*

**E24.16 (LO 4), AP** Fisk Company uses a standard cost accounting system. During January, the company reported the following manufacturing variances.

| | | | |
|---|---|---|---|
| Materials price variance | $1,200 U | Labor quantity variance | $750 U |
| Materials quantity variance | 800 F | Overhead variance | 800 U |
| Labor price variance | 550 U | | |

In addition, 8,000 units of product were sold at $8 per unit. Each unit sold had a standard cost of $5. Selling and administrative expenses were $8,000 for the month.

**Instructions**

Prepare an income statement for management for the month ended January 31, 2022.

*Identify performance evaluation terminology.*

**E24.17 (LO 1, 4), C** The following is a list of terms related to performance evaluation.

1. Balanced scorecard
2. Variance
3. Learning and growth perspective
4. Nonfinancial measures
5. Customer perspective
6. Internal process perspective
7. Ideal standards
8. Normal standards

**Instructions**

Match each of the following descriptions with one of the terms above.

a. The difference between total actual costs and total standard costs.

b. An efficient level of performance that is attainable under expected operating conditions.

c. An approach that incorporates financial and nonfinancial measures in an integrated system that links performance measurement and a company's strategic goals.

d. A viewpoint employed in the balanced scorecard to evaluate how well a company develops and retains its employees.

e. An evaluation tool that is not based on dollars.

f. A viewpoint employed in the balanced scorecard to evaluate the company from the perspective of those people who buy its products or services.

g. An optimum level of performance under perfect operating conditions.

h. A viewpoint employed in the balanced scorecard to evaluate the efficiency and effectiveness of the company's value chain.

**E24.18 (LO 4), C** Indicate which of the four perspectives in the balanced scorecard is most likely associated with the objectives that follow.

1. Percentage of repeat customers.

2. Number of suggestions for improvement from employees.

3. Contribution margin.

4. Brand recognition.

5. Number of cross-trained employees.

6. Amount of setup time.

*Identity balanced scorecard perspectives.*

**E24.19 (LO 4), C** Indicate which of the four perspectives in the balanced scorecard is most likely associated with the objectives that follow.

1. Ethics violations.

2. Credit rating.

3. Customer retention.

4. Stockouts.

5. Reportable accidents.

6. Brand recognition.

*Identify balanced scorecard perspectives.*

**\*E24.20 (LO 5), AP** Vista Company installed a standard cost system on January 1. Selected transactions for the month of January are as follows.

1. Purchased 18,000 units of raw materials on account at a cost of $4.50 per unit. Standard cost was $4.40 per unit.

2. Issued 18,000 units of raw materials for jobs that required 17,500 standard units of raw materials.

3. Incurred 15,300 actual hours of direct labor at an actual rate of $5.00 per hour. The standard rate is $5.50 per hour. (Credit Factory Wages Payable.)

4. Performed 15,300 hours of direct labor on jobs when standard hours were 15,400.

5. Applied overhead to jobs at the rate of 100% of direct labor cost for standard hours allowed.

*Journalize entries in a standard cost accounting system.*

**Instructions**

Journalize the January transactions.

**\*E24.21 (LO 2, 3, 5), AN** Lopez Company uses a standard cost accounting system. Some of the ledger accounts have been destroyed in a fire. The controller asks your help in reconstructing some missing entries and balances.

*Answer questions concerning missing entries and balances.*

**Instructions**

Answer the following questions.

a. Materials Price Variance shows a $2,000 unfavorable balance. Accounts Payable shows $138,000 of raw materials purchases. What was the amount debited to Raw Materials Inventory for raw materials purchased?

b. Materials Quantity Variance shows a $3,000 favorable balance. Raw Materials Inventory shows a zero balance. What was the amount debited to Work in Process Inventory for direct materials used?

c. Labor Price Variance shows a $1,500 favorable balance. Factory Labor shows a debit of $145,000 for wages incurred. What was the amount credited to Factory Wages Payable?

d. Factory Labor shows a credit of $145,000 for direct labor used. Labor Quantity Variance shows a $900 favorable balance. What was the amount debited to Work in Process for direct labor used?

e. Overhead applied to Work in Process totaled $165,000. If the total overhead variance was $1,200 favorable, what was the amount of overhead costs debited to Manufacturing Overhead?

**\*E24.22 (LO 5), AP** Data for Levine Inc. are given in E24.7.

*Journalize entries for materials and labor variances.*

**Instructions**

Journalize the entries to record the materials and labor variances.

*Compute manufacturing overhead variances and interpret findings.*

**\*E24.23 (LO 6), AN** Writing The information shown below was taken from the annual manufacturing overhead cost budget of Connick Company.

| | |
|---|---|
| Variable manufacturing overhead costs | $34,650 |
| Fixed manufacturing overhead costs | $19,800 |
| Normal production level in labor hours | 16,500 |
| Normal production level in units | 4,125 |
| Standard labor hours per unit | 4 |

During the year, 4,050 units were produced, 16,100 hours were worked, and the actual manufacturing overhead was $55,500. Actual fixed manufacturing overhead costs equaled budgeted fixed manufacturing overhead costs. Overhead is applied on the basis of direct labor hours.

**Instructions**

a. Compute the total, fixed, and variable predetermined manufacturing overhead rates.

b. Compute the total, controllable, and volume overhead variances.

c. Briefly interpret the overhead controllable and volume variances computed in (b).

*Compute overhead variances.*

**\*E24.24 (LO 6), AN** Service The loan department of Calgary Bank uses standard costs to determine the overhead cost of processing loan applications. During the current month, a fire occurred, and the accounting records for the department were mostly destroyed. The following data were salvaged from the ashes.

| | |
|---|---|
| Standard variable overhead rate per hour | $9 |
| Standard hours per application | 2 |
| Standard hours allowed | 2,000 |
| Standard fixed overhead rate per hour | $6 |
| Actual fixed overhead cost | $12,600 |
| Variable overhead budget based on standard hours allowed | $18,000 |
| Fixed overhead budget | $12,600 |
| Overhead controllable variance | $1,200 U |

**Instructions**

a. Determine the following.

1. Total actual overhead cost.

2. Actual variable overhead cost.

3. Variable overhead costs applied.

4. Fixed overhead costs applied.

5. Overhead volume variance.

b. Determine how many loans were processed.

*Compute variances.*

**\*E24.25 (LO 6), AP** Seacrest Company's overhead rate was based on estimates of $240,000 for overhead costs and 24,000 direct labor hours. Seacrest's standards allow 2 hours of direct labor per unit produced. Production in May was 900 units, and actual overhead incurred in May was $19,500. The overhead budgeted for 1,800 standard direct labor hours is $18,600 ($6,000 fixed and $12,600 variable).

**Instructions**

a. Compute the total, controllable, and volume variances for overhead.

b. What are possible causes of the variances computed in part (a)?

# Problems

*Compute variances.*

**P24.1 (LO 2, 3), AP** Rogen Corporation manufactures a single product. The standard cost per unit of product is shown below.

| | |
|---|---|
| Direct materials—1 pound plastic at $7.00 per pound | $ 7.00 |
| Direct labor—1.6 hours at $12.00 per hour | 19.20 |
| Variable manufacturing overhead | 12.00 |
| Fixed manufacturing overhead | 4.00 |
| Total standard cost per unit | $42.20 |

The predetermined manufacturing overhead rate is $10 per direct labor hour ($16.00 ÷ 1.6). It was computed from a master manufacturing overhead budget based on normal production of 8,000 direct labor hours (5,000 units) for the month. The master budget showed total variable costs of $60,000 ($7.50 per hour) and total fixed overhead costs of $20,000 ($2.50 per hour). Actual costs for October in producing 4,800 units were as follows.

| | |
|---|---:|
| Direct materials (5,100 pounds) | $ 36,720 |
| Direct labor (7,400 hours) | 92,500 |
| Variable overhead | 59,700 |
| Fixed overhead | 21,000 |
| Total manufacturing costs | $209,920 |

The purchasing department buys the quantities of raw materials that are expected to be used in production each month. Raw materials inventories, therefore, can be ignored.

**Instructions**

a. Compute all of the materials and labor variances.

*a. MPV $1,020 U*

b. Compute the total overhead variance.

**P24.2 (LO 2, 3, 4), AP** Ayala Corporation accumulates the following data relative to jobs started and finished during the month of June 2022.

*Compute variances, and prepare income statement.*

| Costs and Production Data | Actual | Standard |
|---|---:|---:|
| Raw materials unit cost | $2.25 | $2.10 |
| Raw materials units | 10,600 | 10,000 |
| Direct labor payroll | $120,960 | $120,000 |
| Direct labor hours | 14,400 | 15,000 |
| Manufacturing overhead incurred | $189,500 | |
| Manufacturing overhead applied | | $193,500 |
| Machine hours expected to be used at normal capacity | | 42,500 |
| Budgeted fixed overhead for June | | $55,250 |
| Variable overhead rate per machine hour | | $3.00 |
| Fixed overhead rate per machine hour | | $1.30 |

Overhead is applied on the basis of standard machine hours. Three hours of machine time are required for each direct labor hour. The jobs were sold for $400,000. Selling and administrative expenses were $40,000. Assume that the amount of raw materials purchased equaled the amount used.

**Instructions**

a. Compute all of the variances for (1) direct materials and (2) direct labor.

*a. LQV $4,800 F*

b. Compute the total overhead variance.

c. Prepare an income statement for management. (Ignore income taxes.)

**P24.3 (LO 2, 3, 4), AN** **Writing** Rudd Clothiers is a small company that manufactures tall-men's suits. The company has used a standard cost accounting system. In May 2022, 11,250 suits were produced. The following standard and actual cost data applied to the month of May, when normal capacity was 14,000 direct labor hours. All materials purchased were used.

*Compute and identify significant variances.*

| Cost Component | Standard (per unit) | Actual |
|---|---|---|
| Direct materials | 8 yards at $4.40 per yard | $375,575 for 90,500 yards ($4.15 per yard) |
| Direct labor | 1.2 hours at $13.40 per hour | $200,925 for 14,250 hours ($14.10 per hour) |
| Overhead | 1.2 hours at $6.10 per hour (fixed $3.50; variable $2.60) | $49,000 fixed overhead $37,000 variable overhead |

Overhead is applied on the basis of direct labor hours. At normal capacity, budgeted fixed overhead costs were $49,000, and budgeted variable overhead was $36,400.

**Instructions**

a. Compute the total, price, and quantity variances for (1) materials and (2) labor.

*a. MPV $22,625 F*

b. Compute the total overhead variance.

c. Which of the materials and labor variances should be investigated if management considers a variance of more than 4% from standard to be significant?

*Answer questions about variances.*

**P24.4 (LO 2, 3), AN** Kansas Company uses a standard cost accounting system. In 2022, the company produced 28,000 units. Each unit took several pounds of direct materials and 1.6 standard hours of direct labor at a standard hourly rate of $12.00. Normal capacity was 50,000 direct labor hours. During the year, 117,000 pounds of raw materials were purchased at $0.92 per pound. All materials purchased were used during the year.

**Instructions**

a. If the materials price variance was $3,510 favorable, what was the standard materials price per pound?

*b. 4.0 pounds*

b. If the materials quantity variance was $4,750 unfavorable, what was the standard materials quantity per unit?

c. What were the standard hours allowed for the units produced?

d. If the labor quantity variance was $7,200 unfavorable, what were the actual direct labor hours worked?

e. If the labor price variance was $9,080 favorable, what was the actual rate per hour?

*f. $7.20 per DLH*

f. If total budgeted manufacturing overhead was $360,000 at normal capacity, what was the predetermined overhead rate?

g. What was the standard cost per unit of product?

h. How much overhead was applied to production during the year?

i. Using one or more answers above, what were the total costs assigned to work in process?

*Compute variances, prepare an income statement, and explain unfavorable variances.*

**P24.5 (LO 2, 3, 4), AP** [Service] [Writing] Hart Labs, Inc. provides mad cow disease testing for both state and federal governmental agricultural agencies. Because the company's customers are governmental agencies, prices are strictly regulated. Therefore, Hart Labs must constantly monitor and control its testing costs. Shown below are the standard costs for a typical test.

| | |
|---|---:|
| Direct materials (2 test tubes @ $1.46 per tube) | $ 2.92 |
| Direct labor (1 hour @ $24 per hour) | 24.00 |
| Variable overhead (1 hour @ $6 per hour) | 6.00 |
| Fixed overhead (1 hour @ $10 per hour) | 10.00 |
| Total standard cost per test | $42.92 |

The lab does not maintain an inventory of test tubes. As a result, the tubes purchased each month are used that month. Actual activity for the month of November 2022, when 1,475 tests were conducted, resulted in the following.

| | |
|---|---:|
| Direct materials (3,050 test tubes) | $ 4,270 |
| Direct labor (1,550 hours) | 35,650 |
| Variable overhead | 7,400 |
| Fixed overhead | 15,000 |

Monthly budgeted fixed overhead is $14,000. Revenues for the month were $75,000, and selling and administrative expenses were $5,000.

**Instructions**

*a. LQV $1,800 U*

a. Compute the price and quantity variances for direct materials and direct labor.

b. Compute the total overhead variance.

c. Prepare an income statement for management.

d. Provide possible explanations for each unfavorable variance.

*Journalize and post standard cost entries, and prepare income statement.*

**\*P24.6 (LO 2, 3, 4, 5), AP** Jorgensen Corporation uses standard costs with its job order cost accounting system. In January, an order (Job No. 12) for 1,900 units of Product B was received. The standard cost of one unit of Product B is as follows.

| | | |
|---|---|---:|
| Direct materials | 3 pounds at $1.00 per pound | $ 3.00 |
| Direct labor | 1 hour at $8.00 per hour | 8.00 |
| Overhead | 2 hours (variable $4.00 per machine hour; | |
| | fixed $2.25 per machine hour) | 12.50 |
| Standard cost per unit | | $23.50 |

Normal capacity for the month was 4,200 machine hours. During January, the following transactions applicable to Job No. 12 occurred.

1. Purchased 6,200 pounds of raw materials on account at $1.05 per pound.
2. Requisitioned 6,200 pounds of raw materials for Job No. 12.
3. Incurred 2,000 hours of direct labor at a rate of $7.80 per hour.
4. Worked 2,000 hours of direct labor on Job No. 12.
5. Incurred manufacturing overhead on account $25,000.
6. Applied overhead to Job No. 12 on basis of standard machine hours allowed.
7. Completed Job No. 12.
8. Billed customer for Job No. 12 at a selling price of $65,000.

**Instructions**

a. Journalize the transactions.

b. Post to the job order cost accounts.

c. Prepare the entry to recognize the total overhead variance.

d. Prepare the January 2022 income statement for management. Assume selling and administrative     d. NI $15,890
   expenses were $2,000.

*P24.7 **(LO 6), AP** Using the information in P24.1, compute the overhead controllable variance and the       *Compute overhead controllable*
overhead volume variance.        *and volume variances.*

*P24.8 **(LO 6), AP** Using the information in P24.2, compute the overhead controllable variance and the       *Compute overhead controllable*
overhead volume variance.        *and volume variances.*

*P24.9 **(LO 6), AP** Using the information in P24.3, compute the overhead controllable variance and the       *Compute overhead controllable*
overhead volume variance.        *and volume variances.*

*P24.10 **(LO 6), AP** Using the information in P24.5, compute the overhead controllable variance and the       *Compute overhead controllable*
overhead volume variance.        *and volume variances.*

# Continuing Cases

## Current Designs

 Excel

CD24  The executive team at **Current Designs** has gathered to evaluate the company's operations for the last month. One of the topics on the agenda is the special order from Huegel Hollow, which was presented in CD15. Recall that Current Designs had a special order to produce a batch of 20 kayaks for a client, and you were asked to determine the cost of the order and the cost per kayak.

Mike Cichanowski asked the others if the special order caused any particular problems in the production process. Dave Thill, the production manager, made the following comments: "Since we wanted to complete this order quickly and make a good first impression on this new customer, we had some of our most experienced type I workers run the rotomold oven and do the trimming. They were very efficient and were able to complete that part of the manufacturing process even more quickly than the regular crew. However, the finishing on these kayaks required a different technique than what we usually use, so our type II workers took a little longer than usual for that part of the process."

Deb Welch, who is in charge of the purchasing function, said, "We had to pay a little more for the polyethylene powder for this order because the customer wanted a color that we don't usually stock. We also ordered a little extra since we wanted to make sure that we had enough to allow us to calibrate the equipment. The calibration was a little tricky, and we used all of the powder that we had purchased. Since the number of kayaks in the order was fairly small, we were able to use some rope and other parts that were left over from last year's production in the finishing kits. We've seen a price increase for these components in the last year, so using the parts that we already had in inventory cut our costs for the finishing kits."

**Instructions**

**a.** Based on the comments above, predict whether each of the following variances will be favorable or unfavorable. If you don't have enough information to make a prediction, use "NEI" to indicate "Not Enough Information."

1. Quantity variance for polyethylene powder.
2. Price variance for polyethylene powder.
3. Quantity variance for finishing kits.
4. Price variance for finishing kits.
5. Quantity variance for type I workers.
6. Price variance for type I workers.
7. Quantity variance for type II workers.
8. Price variance for type II workers.

**b.** Diane Buswell examined some of the accounting records and reported that Current Designs purchased 1,200 pounds of pellets for this order at a total cost of $2,040. Twenty (20) finishing kits were assembled at a total cost of $3,240. The payroll records showed that the type I employees worked 38 hours on this project at a total cost of $570. The type II finishing employees worked 65 hours at a total cost of $796.25. A total of 20 kayaks were produced for this order.

The standards that had been developed for this model of kayak were used in CD15 and are reproduced here. For each kayak:

54 pounds of polyethylene powder at $1.50 per pound

1 finishing kit (rope, seat, hardware, etc.) at $170

2 hours of type I labor from people who run the oven and trim the plastic at a standard wage rate of $15 per hour

3 hours of type II labor from people who attach the hatches and seat and other hardware at a standard wage rate of $12 per hour.

Calculate the eight variances that are listed in part (a) of this problem.

## Waterways Corporation

(This is a continuation of the Waterways case from Chapters 14–23.)

**WC24** Waterways Corporation uses very stringent standard costs in evaluating its manufacturing efficiency. These standards are not "ideal" at this point, but management is working toward that as a goal. This case asks you to calculate and evaluate the company's variances.

*Go to WileyPLUS for complete case details and instructions.*

# Data Analytics in Action

### Data Analytics at HydroHappy

**DA24** HydroHappy's management want to see a visual comparison of its materials variances to better illustrate trends over time. For this case, you will use materials price and quantity variance data to create and analyze stacked area charts.

*Go to WileyPLUS for complete case details and instructions.*

# Expand Your Critical Thinking

### Decision-Making Across the Organization

**CT24.1** **Service** Milton Professionals, a management consulting firm, specializes in strategic planning for financial institutions. James Hahn and Sara Norton, partners in the firm, are assembling a new strategic planning model for use by clients. The model is designed for use on most personal computers and replaces a rather lengthy manual model currently marketed by the firm. To market the new model, James and Sara will need to provide clients with an estimate of the number of labor hours and computer time needed to operate the model. The model is currently being test-marketed at five small financial institutions. These financial institutions are listed below, along with the number of combined computer/labor hours used by each institution to run the model one time.

| Financial Institutions | Computer/Labor Hours Required |
|---|---|
| Midland National | 25 |
| First State | 45 |
| Financial Federal | 40 |
| Pacific America | 30 |
| Lakeview National | 30 |
| Total | 170 |
| Average | 34 |

Any company that purchases the new model will need to purchase user manuals for the system. User manuals will be sold to clients in cases of 20, at a cost of $320 per case. One manual must be used each time the model is run because each manual includes a nonreusable computer-accessed password for operating the system. Also required are specialized computer forms that are sold only by Milton. The specialized forms are sold in packages of 250, at a cost of $60 per package. One application of the model requires the use of 50 forms. This amount includes two forms that are generally wasted in each application due to printer alignment errors. The overall cost of the strategic planning model to clients is $12,000. Most clients will use the model four times annually.

Milton must provide its clients with estimates of ongoing costs incurred in operating the new planning model, and would like to do so in the form of standard costs.

### Instructions

With the class divided into groups, answer the following.

  **a.** What factors should be considered in setting a standard for computer/labor hours?

  **b.** What alternatives for setting a standard for computer/labor hours might be used?

  **c.** What standard for computer/labor hours would you select? Justify your answer.

  **d.** Determine the standard materials cost associated with the user manuals and computer forms for each application of the strategic planning model.

## Managerial Analysis

*CT24.2 Ana Carillo and Associates is a medium-sized company located near a large metropolitan area in the Midwest. The company manufactures cabinets of mahogany, oak, and other fine woods for use in expensive homes, restaurants, and hotels. Although some of the work is custom, many of the cabinets are a standard size.

One non-custom model is called Luxury Base Frame. Normal production is 1,000 units. Each unit has a direct labor hour standard of 5 hours. Overhead is applied to production based on standard direct labor hours. During the most recent month, only 900 units were produced; 4,500 direct labor hours were allowed for standard production, but only 4,000 hours were used. Standard and actual overhead costs were as follows.

| | Standard (1,000 units) | Actual (900 units) |
|---|---|---|
| Indirect materials | $ 12,000 | $ 12,300 |
| Indirect labor | 43,000 | 51,000 |
| (Fixed) Manufacturing supervisors salaries | 22,500 | 22,000 |
| (Fixed) Manufacturing office employees salaries | 13,000 | 12,500 |
| (Fixed) Engineering costs | 27,000 | 25,000 |
| Computer costs | 10,000 | 10,000 |
| Electricity | 2,500 | 2,500 |
| (Fixed) Manufacturing building depreciation | 8,000 | 8,000 |
| (Fixed) Machinery depreciation | 3,000 | 3,000 |
| (Fixed) Trucks and forklift depreciation | 1,500 | 1,500 |
| Small tools | 700 | 1,400 |
| (Fixed) Insurance | 500 | 500 |
| (Fixed) Property taxes | 300 | 300 |
| Total | $144,000 | $150,000 |

### Instructions

  **a.** Determine the overhead application rate.

  **b.** Determine how much overhead was applied to production.

   **c.** Calculate the total overhead variance, controllable variance, and volume variance.

   **d.** Decide which overhead variances should be investigated.

   **e.** Discuss causes of the overhead variances. What can management do to improve its performance next month?

## Real-World Focus

**CT24.3** **Glassmaster Company** is organized as two divisions and one subsidiary. One division focuses on the manufacture of filaments such as fishing line and sewing thread; the other division manufactures antennas and specialty fiberglass products. Its subsidiary manufactures flexible steel wire controls and molded control panels.

   The annual report of Glassmaster provides the following information.

---

### Glassmaster Company
#### Management Discussion

Gross profit margins for the year improved to 20.9% of sales compared to last year's 18.5%. All operations reported improved margins due in large part to improved operating efficiencies as a result of cost reduction measures implemented during the second and third quarters of the fiscal year and increased manufacturing throughout due to higher unit volume sales. Contributing to the improved margins was a favorable materials price variance due to competitive pricing by suppliers as a result of soft demand for petrochemical-based products. This favorable variance is temporary and will begin to reverse itself as stronger worldwide demand for commodity products improves in tandem with the economy. Partially offsetting these positive effects on profit margins were competitive pressures on sales prices of certain product lines. The company responded with pricing strategies designed to maintain and/or increase market share.

---

### Instructions

   **a.** Is it apparent from the information whether Glassmaster utilizes standard costs?

   **b.** Do you think the price variance experienced should lead to changes in standard costs for the next fiscal year?

**CT24.4** **Service** The **Balanced Scorecard Institute** is a great resource for information about implementing the balanced scorecard. One item of interest provided at its website is an example of a balanced scorecard for a regional airline.

### Instructions

Go to the Balanced Scorecard Institute website, do a search on "Examples and Success Stories," scroll down to select the Regional Airline example under Commercial Organizations, and then answer the following questions.

   **a.** What are the objectives identified for the airline for each perspective?

   **b.** What measures are used for the objectives in the customer perspective?

   **c.** What initiatives are planned to achieve the objective in the learning perspective?

## Communication Activity

**CT24.5** The setting of standards is critical to the effective use of standards in evaluating performance.

### Instructions

Explain the following in a memo to your instructor.

   **a.** The comparative advantages and disadvantages of ideal versus normal standards.

   **b.** The factors that should be included in setting the price and quantity standards for direct materials, direct labor, and manufacturing overhead.

## Ethics Case

**CT24.6** At Symond Company, production workers in the Painting Department are paid on the basis of productivity. The labor time standard for a unit of production is established through periodic time studies conducted by Douglas Management Consultants. In a time study, the actual time required to complete a specific task by a worker is observed. Allowances are then made for preparation time, rest periods, and cleanup time. Bill Carson is one of several veterans in the Painting Department.

Bill is informed by Douglas that he will be used in the time study for the painting of a new product. The findings will be the basis for establishing the labor time standard for the next 6 months. During the test, Bill deliberately slows his normal work pace in an effort to obtain a labor time standard that will be easy to meet. Because it is a new product, the Douglas representative who conducted the test is unaware that Bill did not give the test his best effort.

**Instructions**

a. Who was benefited and who was harmed by Bill's actions?

b. Was Bill ethical in the way he performed the time study test?

c. What measure(s) might the company take to obtain valid data for setting the labor time standard?

## All About You

**CT24.7** From the time you first entered school many years ago, instructors have been measuring and evaluating you by imposing standards. In addition, many of you will pursue professions that administer professional examinations to attain recognized certification. A federal commission presented proposals suggesting all public colleges and universities should require standardized tests to measure their students' learning.

**Instructions**

Answer the following questions.

a. What are possible advantages of standard testing?

b. What are possible disadvantages of standard testing?

c. Would you be in favor of standardized tests?

## Considering Your Costs and Benefits

**CT24.8** **Writing** Do you think that standard costs are used only in making products like wheel bearings and hamburgers? Think again. Standards influence virtually every aspect of our lives. For example, the next time you call to schedule an appointment with your doctor, ask the receptionist how many minutes the appointment is scheduled for. Doctors are under increasing pressure to see more patients each day, which means the time spent with each patient is shorter. As insurance companies and employers push for reduced medical costs, every facet of medicine has been standardized and analyzed. Doctors, nurses, and other medical staff are evaluated in every part of their operations to ensure maximum efficiency. While keeping medical treatment affordable seems like a worthy goal, what are the potential implications for the quality of health care? Does a focus on the bottom line result in a reduction in the quality of health care?

A simmering debate has centered on a very basic question: To what extent should accountants, through financial measures, influence the type of medical care that you receive? Suppose that your local medical facility is in danger of closing because it has been losing money. Should the facility put in place incentives that provide bonuses to doctors if they meet certain standard-cost targets for the cost of treating specific ailments?

**YES:** If the facility is in danger of closing, then someone should take steps to change the medical practices to reduce costs. A closed medical facility is of no use to me, my family, or the community.

**NO:** I don't want an accountant deciding the right medical treatment for me. My family and I deserve the best medical care.

**Instructions**

Write a response indicating your position regarding this situation. Provide support for your view.

### Answers to Insight and Accounting Across the Organization Questions

**How Do Standards Help a Business?** **Q:** How will the creation of such standards help a business or organization? **A:** Standards facilitate management planning, make employees more cost-conscious, are useful in setting prices, contribute to management control, and simplify inventory costing for financial reporting.

**Speedy Data to the Rescue!** **Q:** How do 5G and other technology reduce specific variances from standard costs? **A:** Many forms of new technology provide large amounts of factory floor data to employees almost instantaneously. This enables constant monitoring of production conditions and product quality. Labor variances as well as employee injuries can be reduced because of sensors that provide information about unsafe conditions or worker fatigue. Labor and materials variances are reduced by sensors that monitor various aspects of equipment functions and indicate whether machine output is meeting product specifications.

**What's Brewing at Starbucks?** **Q:** What implications does Starbucks' commitment to corporate social responsibility have for the standard cost of a cup of coffee? **A:** Starbucks' *Global Social Impact Report* explicitly describes its goals related to corporate social responsibility. By including measurable objectives, it signals that it is committed to meeting these goals. As a consequence of setting measurable objectives, when the company determines the standard costs of its products, it needs to factor in the costs of these programs. For example, if renewable energy costs more per kilowatt hour, then the company must include this added cost in its determination of its products' costs.

**It May Be Time to Fly United Again** **Q:** Which of the perspectives of a balanced scorecard were the focus of United's CEO? **A:** Improving on-time flight departures is an objective within the internal process perspective. Customer intent to fly United again is an objective within the customer perspective.

# Planning for Capital Investments

## Chapter Preview

Companies like **Holland America Line** (as discussed in the following Feature Story) must constantly determine how to invest their resources. Other examples: **Dell** announced plans to spend $1 billion on data centers for cloud computing. **ExxonMobil** announced that two wells off the Brazilian coast, which it had spent hundreds of millions of dollars to drill, would produce no oil. **Renault** and **Nissan** spent over $5 billion during a nearly 20-year period to develop electric cars, such as the Leaf.

The process of making such capital expenditure decisions is referred to as **capital budgeting**. Capital budgeting involves choosing among various capital projects to find those that will maximize a company's return on its financial investment. The purpose of this chapter is to discuss the various techniques used to make effective capital budgeting decisions.

# Feature Story

## Floating Hotels

Do you own a boat? Maybe you think it's a nice boat, but how many swimming pools, movie theaters, shopping malls, or restaurants does it have on board? If you are in the cruise-line business, like **Holland America Line**, you need all of these amenities and more just to stay afloat. Holland America Line is considered by many to be the leader of the premium luxury-liner segment.

**Carnival Corporation**, which owns Holland America Line and other cruise lines, is one of the largest vacation companies in the world. During one recent three-year period, Carnival spent more than $3 billion per year on capital expenditures. That's a big number, but keep in mind that Carnival estimates that at any given time there are 270,000 people (200,000 customers and 70,000 crew) on its 100 ships somewhere in the world.

The cruise industry is a tricky business. When times are good, customers are looking for ways to splurge. But when times get tough, people are more inclined to take a trip in a minivan than a luxury yacht. So, if you are a cruise-line executive, it's important to time your investments properly. For example, during one stretch of solid global economic growth, many cruise lines decided to add capacity. The industry built 14 new ships at a total price of $4.7 billion. (That's an average price of about $330 million.) But, it takes up to three years to build one of these giant vessels. Unfortunately, by the time the ships were completed, the economy was in a nosedive.

To maintain passenger numbers during the recession, cruise prices had to be cut by up to 40%. While the lower prices attracted lots of customers, that wasn't enough to offset an overall decline in revenue of 10%. The industry had added capacity at exactly the wrong time.

 Watch the *Holland America Line* video in WileyPLUS to learn more about real-world capital budgeting.

# Chapter Outline

| LEARNING OBJECTIVES | REVIEW | PRACTICE |
|---|---|---|
| **LO 1** Describe capital budgeting inputs and apply the cash payback technique. | • Cash flow information<br>• Cash payback | **DO IT! 1** Cash Payback Period |
| **LO 2** Use the net present value method. | • Equal annual cash flows<br>• Unequal annual cash flows<br>• Choosing a discount rate<br>• Simplifying assumptions<br>• Comprehensive example | **DO IT! 2** Net Present Value |
| **LO 3** Identify capital budgeting challenges and refinements. | • Intangible benefits<br>• Profitability index for mutually exclusive projects<br>• Risk analysis<br>• Post-audit of investment projects | **DO IT! 3** Profitability Index |
| **LO 4** Use the internal rate of return method. | • Comparing discounted cash flow methods | **DO IT! 4** Internal Rate of Return |
| **LO 5** Use the annual rate of return method. | • Based on accrual-accounting data | **DO IT! 5** Annual Rate of Return |

**Go to the Review and Practice section at the end of the chapter for a targeted summary and practice applications with solutions.**

**Visit WileyPLUS for additional tutorials and practice opportunities.**

# Capital Budgeting and Cash Payback

## LEARNING OBJECTIVE 1
Describe capital budgeting inputs and apply the cash payback technique.

Many companies follow a carefully prescribed process for capital expenditure decisions, known as **capital budgeting. Illustration 25.1** shows this general process.

**ILLUSTRATION 25.1**　Corporate capital budget authorization process

   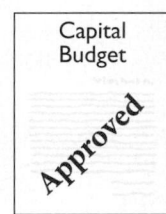

1. Project proposals are requested from departments, factories, and authorized personnel.

2. Proposals are screened by a capital budget committee.

3. Company officers determine which projects are worthy of funding.

4. Board of directors approves capital budget.

The involvement of top management and the board of directors in the process demonstrates the importance of capital budgeting decisions.

- These decisions often have a significant impact on a company's future profitability.
- Poor capital budgeting decisions can cost a lot of money and have even led to the bankruptcy of some companies.

## Cash Flow Information

In this chapter, we look at several methods that help companies make effective capital budgeting decisions. Most of these methods employ **cash flow numbers**, rather than accrual accounting revenues and expenses.

- Remember from your financial accounting course that accrual accounting records **revenues** and **expenses**, rather than cash inflows and cash outflows. In fact, revenues and expenses measured during a period often differ significantly from their cash flow counterparts.
- Accrual accounting has advantages over cash accounting in many contexts.
- **For purposes of capital budgeting, though, estimated cash inflows and outflows are the preferred inputs**.
- Ultimately, the value of all financial investments is determined by the value of cash flows received and paid.

Sometimes cash flow information is not available. In this case, companies can make adjustments to accrual accounting numbers to estimate cash flow. Often, they estimate net annual cash flow by adding back depreciation expense to net income.

- Depreciation expense is added back because it is an expense that does not require an outflow of cash.
- By adding depreciation expense back to net income, companies approximate net annual cash flow.

Suppose, for example, that Reno Company's net income of $13,000 includes a charge for depreciation expense of $26,000. Its estimated net annual cash flow would be $39,000 ($13,000 + $26,000).

**Illustration 25.2** lists some typical cash outflows and inflows related to equipment purchase and replacement.

**ILLUSTRATION 25.2**

**Typical cash flows relating to capital budgeting decisions**

**Cash Outflows**

Initial investment
Repairs and maintenance
Increased operating costs
Overhaul of equipment

**Cash Inflows**

Proceeds from sale of old equipment
Increased cash received from customers
Reduced cash outflows related to operating costs
Salvage value of equipment

These cash flows are the inputs that are considered relevant in capital budgeting decisions.

The capital budgeting decision, under any technique, depends in part on a variety of considerations:

- **The availability of funds:** Does the company have unlimited funds, or will it have to ration capital investments?

- **Relationships among proposed projects:** Are proposed projects independent of each other, or does the acceptance or rejection of one depend on the acceptance or rejection of another?

- **The company's basic decision-making approach:** Does the company want to produce an accept-reject decision or a ranking of desirability among possible projects?

- **The risk associated with a particular project:** How certain are the projected returns? The certainty of estimates varies with such issues as market considerations or the length of time before returns are expected.

## Illustrative Data

To compare the results of the various capital budgeting techniques, we use a continuing example. Assume that Stewart Shipping Company is considering an investment of $130,000 in new equipment. The new equipment is expected to last 10 years. It is estimated to have a zero salvage value at the end of its useful life. The expected annual cash inflows are $200,000, and the annual cash outflows are $176,000. **Illustration 25.3** summarizes these data.

**ILLUSTRATION 25.3**

**Investment information for Stewart Shipping example**

| | |
|---|---:|
| Initial investment | $130,000 |
| Estimated useful life | 10 years |
| Estimated salvage value | –0– |
| | |
| Estimated annual cash flows | |
|     Cash inflows from customers | $200,000 |
|     Cash outflows for operating costs | 176,000 |
| Net annual cash flow | $ 24,000 |

In the following two sections, we examine two popular techniques for evaluating capital investments: the cash payback technique and the net present value method.

## Cash Payback

The **cash payback technique** identifies the time period required to recover the cost of the capital investment from the net annual cash flow produced by the investment. **Illustration 25.4** presents the equation for computing the cash payback period **assuming equal net annual cash flows.**

$$\frac{\text{Cost of Capital}}{\text{Investment}} \div \frac{\text{Net Annual Cash}}{\text{Flow}} = \frac{\text{Cash Payback}}{\text{Period}}$$

The cash payback period in the Stewart Shipping example is 5.42 years, computed as follows (see **Helpful Hint**).

$$\$130,000 \div \$24,000 = 5.42 \text{ years}$$

The evaluation of the payback period is often tied to the expected useful life of the asset. For example, assume that at Stewart Shipping a project is unacceptable if the payback period is longer than 60% of the asset's expected useful life. The 5.42-year payback period is 54.2% ($5.42 \div 10$) of the project's expected useful life. Thus, the project is acceptable.

It follows that when the payback technique is used to decide among acceptable alternative projects, **the shorter the payback period, the more attractive the investment**. This is true for two reasons:

1. The earlier the investment is recovered, the sooner the company can use the cash funds for other purposes.
2. The risk of loss from obsolescence and changed economic conditions is less in a shorter payback period.

The preceding computation of the cash payback period assumes **equal net annual cash flows** in each year of the investment's life. In many cases, this assumption is not valid. In the case of **uneven** net annual cash flows, the company determines the cash payback period **when the cumulative net cash flows from the investment equal the cost of the investment**.

To illustrate unequal cash flows, assume that Chen Company proposes an investment in new equipment that is estimated to cost $300,000. **Illustration 25.5** shows how to use the proposed investment data to calculate the cash payback period.

**Investment data:**

| Year | Investment | Net Annual Cash Flow | Cumulative Net Cash Flow |
|---|---|---|---|
| 0 | $300,000 | | |
| 1 | | $ 60,000 | $ 60,000 |
| 2 | | 90,000 | 150,000 |
| 3 | | 90,000 | 240,000 |
| 4 | | 120,000 | 360,000 |
| 5 | | 100,000 | 460,000 |

**Determining the cash payback period:**

We can first visualize the investment data as follows.

| Year | 1 | 2 | 3 | 4 | 5 |
|---|---|---|---|---|---|
| Net Annual Cash Flow | $60,000 | $90,000 | $90,000 | $120,000 | $100,000 |
| Cumulative Value | $60,000 | $150,000 | **$240,000** | **$360,000** | $460,000 |

Because the $300,000 investment falls between the cumulative values for years 3 ($240,000) and 4 ($360,000), we next need to calculate the fraction of the year needed beyond year 3, as follows.

| | |
|---|---|
| Investment cost | $300,000 |
| Year 3 cumulative value | 240,000 |
| Additional cash flow needed during year 4 | $ 60,000 |

$$\text{Fractional year} = \frac{\text{Additional cash flow needed during year 4}}{\text{Year 4 net annual cash flow}} = \frac{\$60,000}{\$120,000} = .5$$

**Total cash payback period** = 3 years + .5 years = **3.5 years**

As Illustration 25.5 shows, at the end of year 3, cumulative net cash flow of $240,000 is less than the investment cost of $300,000, but at the end of year 4 the cumulative cash inflow of $360,000 exceeds the investment cost. The cash flow needed in year 4 to equal the investment cost is $60,000 ($300,000 − $240,000). Assuming the cash inflow occurred evenly during year 4, we divide $60,000 by the net annual cash flow in year 4 ($120,000) to determine the point during the year when the cash payback occurs. Thus, we get 0.50 ($60,000 ÷ $120,000), or half of the year, and the cash payback period is 3.5 years.

The cash payback technique may be a useful initial screening tool. It may be the most critical factor in the capital budgeting decision for a company that desires a fast turnaround of its investment because of a weak cash position. It also is relatively easy to compute and understand.

However, cash payback should not be the only basis for the capital budgeting decision.

- **It ignores the expected profitability of the project**. To illustrate, assume that Projects A and B have the same payback period, but Project A's useful life is double the useful life of Project B. Project A's earning power, therefore, is twice that of Project B's.

- A further—and major—disadvantage of this technique is that **it ignores the time value of money**. We address time value of money with the approach described in the next section.

---

**ACTION PLAN**

- **Annual cash inflows − Annual cash outflows = Net annual cash flow.**

- **Cash payback period = Cost of capital investment ÷ Net annual cash flow.**

### DO IT! 1 | Cash Payback Period

Watertown Paper Corporation is considering adding another machine for the manufacture of corrugated cardboard. The machine would cost $900,000. It would have an estimated life of 6 years and no salvage value. The company estimates that annual cash inflows would increase by $400,000 and that annual cash outflows would increase by $190,000. Compute the cash payback period.

**Solution**

| | |
|---|---:|
| Estimated annual cash inflows | $400,000 |
| Estimated annual cash outflows | 190,000 |
| Net annual cash flow | $210,000 |

Cash payback period = $900,000 ÷ $210,000 = 4.3 years

Related exercise material: **BE25.1 and DO IT! 25.1.**

---

# Net Present Value Method

**LEARNING OBJECTIVE 2**

Use the net present value method.

The time value of money can have a significant impact on a capital budgeting decision. Cash flows that occur early in the life of an investment are worth more than those that occur later—because of the time value of money. Therefore, it is useful to recognize the timing of cash flows when evaluating projects.

Capital budgeting techniques that take into account both the time value of money and the estimated net cash flows from an investment are called **discounted cash flow techniques**.

- They are generally recognized as the most informative and best conceptual approaches to making capital budgeting decisions.

- The expected net cash flow used in discounting cash flows consists of the annual net cash flows plus the estimated liquidation proceeds (salvage value) when the asset is sold for salvage at the end of its useful life.

The primary discounted cash flow technique is the **net present value method**. A second method, discussed later in the chapter, is the **internal rate of return**. At this point, **we recommend that you examine Appendix G** to review the time value of money concepts upon which these methods are based. Also, the Excel tutorial provided in WileyPLUS for this chapter demonstrates the use of the NPV (net present value) and IRR (internal rate of return) functions in Excel.

The **net present value (NPV) method** involves discounting net cash flows to their present value and then comparing that present value with the capital outlay required by the investment.

- The difference between these two amounts is referred to as **net present value (NPV)**.
- Company management determines what interest rate to use in discounting the future net cash flows. This rate, often referred to as the **discount rate** or **required rate of return**, is management's minimum acceptable rate of return on investments (discussed in a later section).
- The NPV decision rule is this: **A proposal is acceptable when net present value is zero or positive**. A zero or positive NPV indicates that the rate of return on the investment equals or exceeds (respectively) the required rate of return. When net present value is negative, the project is unacceptable.

**Illustration 25.6** shows the net present value decision criteria.

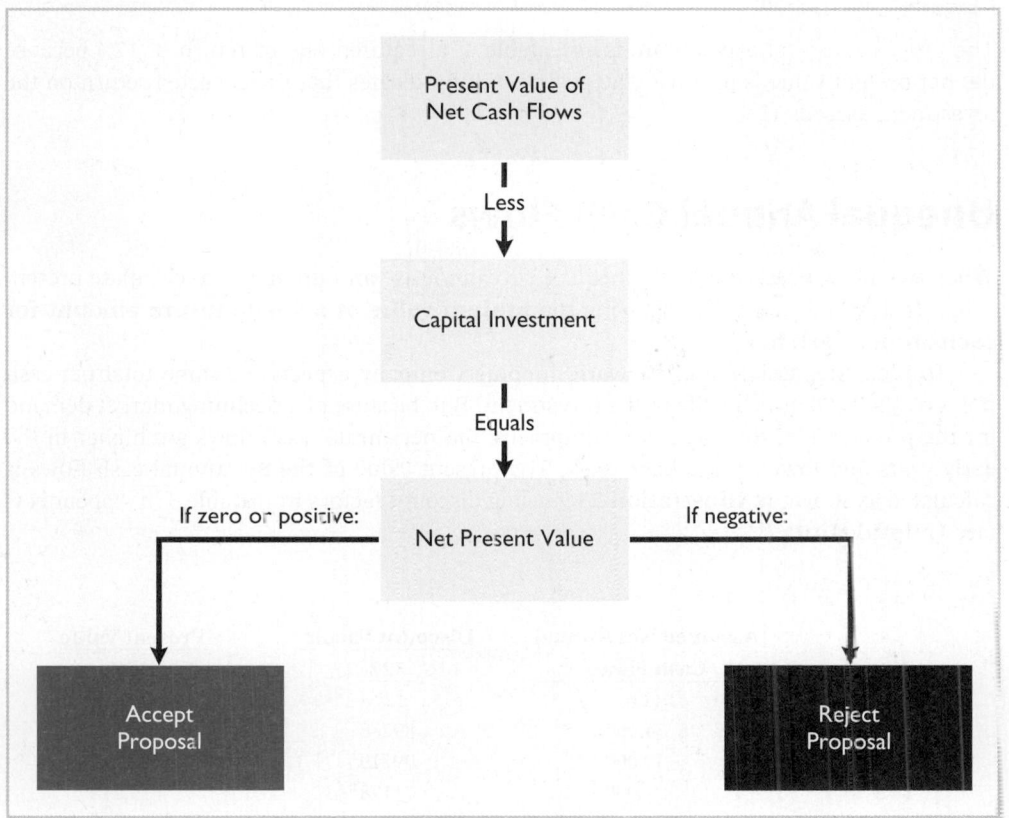

**ILLUSTRATION 25.6**

Net present value decision criteria

When making a selection among acceptable proposals, **the higher the positive net present value, the more attractive the investment**. The application of this method to two cases is described in the next two sections. In each case, we assume that the investment has no salvage value at the end of its useful life.

## Equal Annual Cash Flows

In our Stewart Shipping Company example, the company's net annual cash flows are $24,000 ($200,000 cash inflows − $176,000 cash outflows). If we assume this amount **is uniform over the asset's useful life**, we can compute the present value of the net annual cash flows by using

**HELPFUL HINT**

The ABC Co. expects equal cash flows over an asset's 5-year useful life. The discount factor it should use in determining present values if management wants a 12% return is 3.60478 (using Table 4, Appendix G).

the present value of an annuity of 1 for 10 payments (from Table 4, Appendix G). Assuming a discount rate of 12%, the present value of net cash flows is as shown in **Illustration 25.7** (rounded to the nearest dollar) (see **Helpful Hint**).

**ILLUSTRATION 25.7**

Computation of present value of equal net annual cash flows

| | Present Value at 12% |
|---|---|
| Discount factor for 10 periods | 5.65022 |
| Present value of net cash flows: | |
| $24,000 × 5.65022 | **$135,605** |

**Illustration 25.8** shows the analysis of the proposal by the net present value method.

**ILLUSTRATION 25.8**

Computation of net present value—equal net annual cash flows

| | 12% |
|---|---|
| Present value of net cash flows | $135,605 |
| Less: Capital investment | 130,000 |
| **Net present value** | **$ 5,605** |

The proposed capital expenditure is acceptable at a required rate of return of 12% because the net present value is positive. The positive NPV indicates that the expected return on the investment exceeds 12%.

## Unequal Annual Cash Flows

When net annual cash flows are unequal, we cannot use annuity tables to calculate present value. Instead, we use tables showing the **present value of a single future amount for each annual cash flow**.

To illustrate, assume that Stewart Shipping Company expects the same total net cash flows of $240,000 over the life of the investment. But, because of a declining market demand for the product over the life of the equipment, the net annual cash flows are higher in the early years and lower in the later years. The present value of the net annual cash flows is calculated as shown in **Illustration 25.9**, using discount factors from Table 3 in Appendix G (see **Helpful Hint**).

**HELPFUL HINT**

Appendix G demonstrates the use of a financial calculator to solve time value of money problems.

**ILLUSTRATION 25.9**

Computation of present value of unequal annual cash flows

| Year | Assumed Net Annual Cash Flows | Discount Factor 12% | Present Value 12% |
|---|---|---|---|
| | (1) | (2) | (1) × (2) |
| 1 | $ 34,000 | .89286 | $ 30,357 |
| 2 | 30,000 | .79719 | 23,916 |
| 3 | 27,000 | .71178 | 19,218 |
| 4 | 25,000 | .63552 | 15,888 |
| 5 | 24,000 | .56743 | 13,618 |
| 6 | 22,000 | .50663 | 11,146 |
| 7 | 21,000 | .45235 | 9,499 |
| 8 | 20,000 | .40388 | 8,078 |
| 9 | 19,000 | .36061 | 6,852 |
| 10 | 18,000 | .32197 | 5,795 |
| | **$240,000** | | **$144,367** |

Therefore, the analysis of the proposal by the net present value method is as shown in **Illustration 25.10**.

|                                      | 12%       |
|--------------------------------------|-----------|
| Present value of net cash flows      | $144,367  |
| Less: Capital investment             | 130,000   |
| **Net present value**                | **$ 14,367** |

**ILLUSTRATION 25.10**

**Computation of net present value—unequal annual cash flows**

In this example, the present value of the net cash flows is greater than the $130,000 capital investment. Thus, the project is acceptable at a 12% required rate of return.

- The difference between the present values using the 12% rate under **equal** cash flows ($135,605) and **unequal** cash flows ($144,367) is due to the pattern of the flows.

- Since more money is received sooner under this particular uneven cash flow scenario, its present value is greater.

---

### Management Insight

7506417745/
Shutterstock.com

#### Can You Hear Me—Better?

With speeds up to 100 times faster than 4G, 5G cellular technology promises great potential. In fact, many factory applications that rely on connected machines require 5G speed. But delivering 5G means that **Verizon**, **AT&T**, and **T-Mobile US** must make massive capital investments.

Investments in 5G have additional risks because companies must make choices regarding which airwave spectrum to operate in. Choosing to operate in the high-frequency range will offer superfast speeds. But, this range has significant limitations in terms of how far the signal will travel (thus requiring investing in more towers) and what it will travel through. By contrast, if a company chooses the low-band spectrum, its signal will travel long distances, but the speeds are about the same as 4G. With so much at stake, these decisions have huge implications.

A big question that nobody has answered yet is why will customers be willing to pay more for 5G than for 4G? Use of 5G will require consumers to purchase new phones—not a trivial personal investment. And if consumers do not switch quickly, telecom companies might not get the payback they need for their huge investments. In the meantime, 6G technology, which will be 10 times faster than 5G, is already being designed. This additional speed will be needed in order for autonomous cars to operate safely.

**Sources:** Sarah Krouse, "U.S. Telecom Giants Take Different Paths to 5G," *Wall Street Journal* (April 12, 2020); and River Davis, "Forget 5G for a Moment. Instead, Imagine 6G," *Wall Street Journal* (April 12, 2020).

**Why is the capital investment in 5G technology particularly risky for telecom carriers? (Answer is available at the end of the chapter.)**

---

## Choosing a Discount Rate

Now that you understand how companies apply the net present value method, it is logical to ask a related question: How is a discount rate (required rate of return) determined in real capital budgeting decisions?

- In many instances, a company uses a required rate of return equal to its **cost of capital**— that is, the rate that it must pay to obtain funds from creditors and stockholders.

- The cost of capital is a weighted average of the rates paid on borrowed funds as well as on funds provided by investors in the company's common stock and preferred stock (see **Helpful Hint**).

- If management believes a project is riskier than the company's usual line of business, the discount rate should be increased.

That is, the discount rate has two components, a cost of capital component and a risk component. Often, companies assume the risk component is equal to zero.

Using an incorrect discount rate can lead to incorrect capital budgeting decisions. Consider again the Stewart Shipping example in Illustration 25.8, where we used a discount rate of 12%. Suppose that this rate does not take into account the fact that this project is riskier than most of the company's investments. A more appropriate discount rate, given the risk, might be 15%. **Illustration 25.11** compares the net present values at the two rates. At the higher, more appropriate discount rate of 15%, the net present value is negative. The negative NPV indicates that the expected rate of return on the investment is less than the required rate of return of 15%. The company should reject the project (discount factors from Appendix G, Table 4).

**ILLUSTRATION 25.11**

**Comparison of net present values at different discount rates**

| | Present Values at Different Discount Rates | |
|---|---|---|
| | **12%** | **15%** |
| Discount factor for 10 payments | 5.65022 | 5.01877 |
| Present value of net cash flows: | | |
| $24,000 × 5.65022 | $135,605 | |
| $24,000 × 5.01877 | | $120,450 |
| Less: Capital investment | 130,000 | 130,000 |
| Positive (negative) net present value | $ 5,605 | $ (9,550) |

The discount rate is often referred to by alternative names, including the **required rate of return**, the **hurdle rate**, and the **cutoff rate**. Determination of the cost of capital varies somewhat depending on whether the entity is a for-profit or not-for-profit business. Calculation of the cost of capital is discussed more fully in advanced accounting and finance courses.

## Simplifying Assumptions

In our examples of the net present value method, we made a number of simplifying assumptions:

- **All cash flows occur at the end of each year.** In reality, cash flows will occur at uneven intervals throughout the year. However, it is far simpler to assume that all cash flows come at the end (or in some cases the beginning) of the year. In fact, this assumption is frequently made in practice.

- **All cash flows are immediately reinvested in another project that has a similar return.** In most capital budgeting situations, companies receive cash flows during each year of a project's life. In order to determine the return on the investment, some assumption must be made about how the cash flows are reinvested in the year that they are received. It is customary to assume that cash flows received are reinvested in some other project of similar return until the end of the project's life.

- **All cash flows can be predicted with certainty.** The outcomes of business investments are full of uncertainty, as the **Holland America Line** Feature Story shows. There is no way of knowing how popular a new product will be, how long a new machine will last, or what competitors' reactions might be to changes in a product. But, in order to make investment decisions, analysts must estimate future outcomes. In this chapter, we have assumed that future amounts are known with certainty.[1] In reality, little is known with certainty. More advanced capital budgeting techniques deal with uncertainty by considering the probability that various outcomes will occur.

## Comprehensive Example

Best Taste Foods is considering investing in new equipment to produce fat-free snack foods. Management believes that although demand for fat-free foods has leveled off, fat-free foods are here to stay. The estimated costs, cost of capital, and cash flows shown in **Illustration 25.12** were determined in consultation with the marketing, production, and finance departments.

**ILLUSTRATION 25.12**

**Investment information for Best Taste Foods example**

| | |
|---|---|
| Initial investment | $1,000,000 |
| Cost of equipment overhaul in 5 years | $200,000 |
| Salvage value of equipment in 10 years | $20,000 |
| Cost of capital (discount rate) | 15% |
| Estimated annual cash flows | |
| Cash inflows received from sales | $500,000 |
| Cash outflows for cost of goods sold | $200,000 |
| Maintenance costs | $30,000 |
| Other direct operating costs | $40,000 |

---

[1]One exception is a brief discussion of sensitivity analysis later in the chapter.

- Remember that we are using cash flows in our analysis, not accrual revenues and expenses.
- Thus, for example, the direct operating costs would not include depreciation expense, since depreciation expense does not use cash.

Illustration 25.13 presents the computation of the net annual cash flows of this project.

| | |
|---|---:|
| Cash inflows received from sales | $ 500,000 |
| Cash outflows for cost of goods sold | (200,000) |
| Maintenance costs | (30,000) |
| Other direct operating costs | (40,000) |
| **Net annual cash flow** | **$ 230,000** |

**ILLUSTRATION 25.13**

**Computation of net annual cash flow**

Illustration 25.14 shows computation of the net present value for this proposed investment (discount factors from Appendix G, Tables 3 and 4).

| Event | Time Period | Cash Flow | × | 15% Discount Factor | = | Present Value |
|---|---|---|---|---|---|---|
| Net annual cash flow | 1–10 | $ 230,000 | | 5.01877 | | $1,154,317 |
| Salvage value | 10 | 20,000 | | .24719 | | 4,944 |
| Less: Equipment purchase | 0 | 1,000,000 | | 1.00000 | | 1,000,000 |
| Less: Equipment overhaul | 5 | 200,000 | | .49718 | | 99,436 |
| **Net present value** | | | | | | **$ 59,825** |

**ILLUSTRATION 25.14**

**Computation of net present value for Best Taste Foods investment**

Because the net present value of the project is positive, Best Taste should accept the project.

---

# DO IT! 2 | Net Present Value

Watertown Paper Corporation is considering adding another machine for the manufacture of corrugated cardboard. The machine would cost $900,000. It would have an estimated life of 6 years and no salvage value. The company estimates that annual cash inflows would increase by $400,000 and that annual cash outflows would increase by $190,000. Management has a required rate of return of 9%. Calculate the net present value on this project and discuss whether it should be accepted.

### Solution

| | |
|---|---:|
| Estimated annual cash inflows | $400,000 |
| Estimated annual cash outflows | 190,000 |
| Net annual cash flow | $210,000 |

| | Cash Flow | × | 9% Discount Factor | = | Present Value |
|---|---|---|---|---|---|
| Present value of net annual cash flows | $210,000 | | 4.48592[a] | | $942,043 |
| Less: Capital investment | | | | | 900,000 |
| Net present value | | | | | $ 42,043 |

[a]Table 4, Appendix G, 9%, 6 years

Since the net present value is greater than zero, Watertown should accept the project.

**ACTION PLAN**

- **Recall that Estimated annual cash inflows − Estimated annual cash outflows = Net annual cash flow.**
- **Use the NPV technique to calculate the difference between net cash flows and the initial investment.**
- **Accept the project if the net present value is positive.**

Related exercise material: **BE25.2, BE25.3, DO IT! 25.2, E25.1, E25.2, and E25.3.**

# Capital Budgeting Challenges and Refinements

---

**LEARNING OBJECTIVE 3**

Identify capital budgeting challenges and refinements.

---

Now that you understand how the net present value method works, we can add some "additional wrinkles." Specifically, these are the impact of intangible benefits, a way to compare mutually exclusive projects, refinements that take risk into account, and the need to conduct post-audits of investment projects.

## Intangible Benefits

The NPV evaluation techniques employed thus far rely on tangible costs and benefits that can be relatively easily quantified. Some investment projects, especially high-tech projects, fail to make it through initial capital budget screens because only the project's tangible benefits are considered.

- **Intangible benefits** might include increased quality, improved safety, or enhanced employee loyalty.
- By ignoring intangible benefits, capital budgeting techniques might incorrectly eliminate projects that could be financially beneficial to the company.

To avoid rejecting projects that actually should be accepted, analysts suggest two possible approaches:

1. Calculate net present value ignoring intangible benefits. Then, if the NPV is negative, ask whether the project offers any intangible benefits that are worth at least the amount of the negative NPV.
2. Project conservative estimates of the value of the intangible benefits, and incorporate these values into the NPV calculation.

### Example

Assume that Berg Company is considering the purchase of a new mechanical robot to be used for soldering electrical connections. **Illustration 25.15** shows the estimates related to this proposed purchase (discount factor from Appendix G, Table 4).

**Investment information for Berg Company example**

| | | | | |
|---|---|---|---|---|
| Initial investment | $200,000 | | | |
| Annual cash inflows | $ 50,000 | | | |
| Annual cash outflows | 20,000 | | | |
| **Net annual cash flow** | **$ 30,000** | | | |
| Estimated life of equipment | 10 years | | | |
| Discount rate | 12% | | | |

| | Cash Flows | | 12% Discount Factor | | Present Value |
|---|---|---|---|---|---|
| Present value of net annual cash flows | $30,000 | × | 5.65022 | = | $ 169,507 |
| Less: Initial investment | | | | | 200,000 |
| **Net present value** | | | | | **$ (30,493)** |

Based on the negative net present value of $30,493, the proposed project is not acceptable. This calculation, however, ignores important information.

- The company's engineers believe that purchasing this machine will improve the quality of electrical connections in the company's products. As a result, future warranty costs may be reduced.

- This higher quality may translate into higher future sales.
- The new machine will be safer than the current machine.

The managers at Berg Company do not have confidence in their ability to accurately estimate these potentially higher revenues and lower costs. But Berg can incorporate this new information into the capital budgeting decision in the two ways discussed earlier.

1. Management might simply ask whether the reduced warranty costs, increased sales, and improved safety benefits have an estimated total present value to the company of at least $30,493. If yes, then the project is acceptable.

2. Analysts can estimate the annual cash flows of these benefits. In our initial calculation, we assumed each of these benefits to have a value of zero. It seems likely that their actual values are much higher than zero. Given the difficulty of estimating these benefits, however, conservative values should be assigned to them. If, after using conservative estimates, the net present value is positive, Berg should accept the project.

To illustrate, assume that Berg estimates that improved sales will increase cash inflows by $10,000 annually as a result of an increase in perceived quality. Berg also estimates that annual cost outflows would be reduced by $5,000 as a result of lower warranty claims, reduced injury claims, and fewer missed work days. Consideration of the intangible benefits results in the revised NPV calculation shown in **Illustration 25.16** (discount factor from Appendix G, Table 4).

**ILLUSTRATION 25.16**
**Revised investment information for Berg Company example, including intangible benefits**

| Initial investment | $200,000 | | |
|---|---|---|---|
| Annual cash inflows (revised) | $ 60,000 ($50,000 + $10,000) | | |
| Annual cash outflows (revised) | 15,000 ($20,000 − $5,000) | | |
| **Net annual cash flow** | **$ 45,000** | | |
| Estimated life of equipment | 10 years | | |
| Discount rate | 12% | | |

|  | Cash Flows | 12% Discount Factor | Present Value |
|---|---|---|---|
| Present value of net annual cash flows | $45,000 × | 5.65022 = | $254,260 |
| Less: Initial investment | | | 200,000 |
| **Net present value** | | | **$ 54,260** |

Using these conservative estimates of the value of the additional benefits, Berg should accept the project.

## Ethics Insight

istock.com/cgering/E+/ Getty Images

### It Need Not Cost an Arm and a Leg

Most manufacturers say that employee safety matters above everything else. But how many back up this statement with investments that improve employee safety? For example, a woodworking hobbyist, who also happens to be a patent attorney with a Ph.D. in physics, invented a mechanism that automatically shuts down a power saw when the saw blade comes in contact with human flesh. The blade stops so quickly that only minor injuries result.

Power saws injure 40,000 Americans each year, and 4,000 of those injuries are bad enough to require amputation. Therefore, you might think that power-saw companies would be lined up to incorporate this mechanism into their saws. But, in the words of one power-tool company, "Safety doesn't sell." Since existing saw manufacturers were unwilling to incorporate the device into their saws, the inventor eventually started his own company to build the devices and sell them directly to businesses that use power saws.

**Source:** Melba Newsome, "An Edgy New Idea," *Time: Inside Business* (May 2006), p. A16.

**In addition to the obvious humanitarian benefit of reducing serious injuries, how else might the manufacturer of this product convince potential customers of its worth? (Answer is available at the end of the chapter.)**

# Profitability Index for Mutually Exclusive Projects

In theory, companies should accept all projects with positive NPVs. However, companies rarely are able to adopt all positive-NPV proposals.

1. Proposals often are **mutually exclusive**.

   - This means that if the company adopts one proposal, it would be impossible or impractical to also adopt the other proposal.

   - For example, a company may be considering the purchase of a new packaging machine and is looking at various brands and models.

   - Once the company has determined which brand and model to purchase, the others will not be purchased—even though they also may have positive net present values.

2. Managers often must choose between various positive-NPV projects because of **limited resources**.

   - For example, the company might have ideas for two new lines of business, each of which has a projected positive NPV.

   - However, both of these proposals require skilled personnel, and the company determines that it will not be able to find enough skilled personnel to staff both projects.

   - Management will have to choose the project it thinks is the better option.

When choosing between alternative proposals, it is tempting simply to choose the project with the higher NPV. Consider the following example of two mutually exclusive projects. Each is assumed to have a 10-year life and a 12% discount rate (discount factors from Appendix G, Tables 3 and 4). **Illustration 25.17** shows the estimates for each project and the computation of the present value of the net cash flows.

| ILLUSTRATION 25.17 | | Project A | Project B |
|---|---|---|---|
| **Investment information for mutually exclusive projects** | Initial investment | $40,000 | $ 90,000 |
| | Net annual cash inflow | 10,000 | 19,000 |
| | Salvage value | 5,000 | 10,000 |
| | Present value of net cash flows | | |
| | ($10,000 × 5.65022) + ($5,000 × .32197) | 58,112 | |
| | ($19,000 × 5.65022) + ($10,000 × .32197) | | 110,574 |

**Illustration 25.18** computes the net present values of Project A and Project B by subtracting the initial investment from the present value of the net cash flows.

| ILLUSTRATION 25.18 | | Project A | Project B |
|---|---|---|---|
| **Net present value computation** | Present value of net cash flows | $58,112 | $110,574 |
| | Less: Initial investment | 40,000 | 90,000 |
| | Net present value | **$18,112** | **$ 20,574** |

As Project B has the higher NPV, it would seem that the company should adopt it. However, Project B also requires more than twice the original investment of Project A ($90,000 versus $40,000). In choosing between the two projects, the company should also include in its calculations the amount of the original investment.

One relatively simple method of comparing alternative projects is the **profitability index**.

- This method takes into account both the size of the original investment and the discounted cash flows.

- The profitability index is calculated by dividing the present value of net cash flows that occur after the initial investment by the amount of the initial investment, as **Illustration 25.19** shows.

| Present Value of Net Cash Flows | ÷ | Initial Investment | = | Profitability Index |
|---|---|---|---|---|

**ILLUSTRATION 25.19**
**Equation for profitability index**

- The profitability index allows comparison of the relative desirability of projects that require differing initial investments.
- Note that any project with a positive NPV will have a profitability index above 1.

The profitability index for each of the mutually exclusive projects is calculated in Illustration 25.20.

$$\text{Profitability Index} \;=\; \frac{\text{Present Value of Net Cash Flows}}{\text{Initial Investment}}$$

| Project A | Project B |
|---|---|
| $\dfrac{\$58,112}{\$40,000} = 1.45$ | $\dfrac{\$110,574}{\$90,000} = 1.23$ |

**ILLUSTRATION 25.20**
**Calculation for profitability index**

In this case, the profitability index of Project A exceeds that of Project B. Thus, Project A is more desirable. Again, if these were not mutually exclusive projects and if resources were not limited, then the company should invest in both projects since both have positive NPVs. Additional considerations related to preference decisions are discussed in more advanced courses.

# Risk Analysis

A simplifying assumption made by many financial analysts is that projected results are known with certainty. In reality, projected results are only estimates based on the forecaster's belief as to the most probable outcome.

- One approach for dealing with such uncertainty is **sensitivity analysis**.
- Sensitivity analysis uses a number of outcome estimates to get a sense of the variability among potential returns.

An example of sensitivity analysis was presented in Illustration 25.11, where we illustrated the impact on NPV of different discount rate assumptions. A higher-risk project would be evaluated using a higher discount rate.

Similarly, to take into account that more distant cash flows are often more uncertain, a higher discount rate can be used to discount more distant cash flows. Other techniques to address uncertainty are discussed in advanced courses.

---

## People, Planet, and Profit Insight

Elnur/Shutterstock.com

### Big Spenders

Investments in electricity production and transmission represent some of society's biggest capital budgeting decisions. For example, billionaire Philip Anschutz is backing a project to build a 3,000-megawatt Wyoming wind farm as well as a 730-mile transmission line that would efficiently transfer the electricity to Las Vegas, where it could then travel on existing lines to locations in California. Total cost: $9 billion. This would be the biggest wind farm in the United States except that an even bigger, 4,000-megawatt wind farm is being planned by a different group of investors. In the past, these investments were made by regulated utility companies, which were allowed to pass on their costs to customers and thus essentially guaranteed a steady revenue stream. Today, many of the biggest projects are instead being financed by private investors. These investors will be selling their electricity in energy markets driven by market demand. This provides for more potential upside on their investment but also more uncertainty regarding revenue flows.

**Source:** Russell Gold, "Investors Are Building Their Own Green-Power Lines," *Wall Street Journal* (April 6, 2017).

**How does the financing of today's big energy investments differ from big energy capital investments of the past, and what are the implications? (Answer is available at the end of the chapter.)**

# Post-Audit of Investment Projects

Well-run organizations perform post-audits of investment projects after their completion. A **post-audit** is a thorough evaluation of how well a project's actual performance matches the original projections. An example of a post-audit is seen in a situation that occurred at **Campbell Soup**. The company made the original decision to invest in the Intelligent Quisine line based on management's best estimates of future cash flows. During the development phase of the project, Campbell hired an outside consulting firm to evaluate the project's potential for success. Because actual results during the initial years were far below the estimated results and because the future also did not look promising, the project was terminated.

Performing a post-audit is important for a variety of reasons.

1. If managers know that the company will compare their estimates to actual results, they will be more likely to submit reasonable and accurate data when they make investment proposals. This reduces overly optimistic estimates by managers hoping to get pet projects approved.

2. As seen with Campbell Soup, a post-audit provides a formal mechanism by which the company can determine whether existing projects should be supported or terminated.

3. Post-audits improve future investment proposals because, by evaluating past successes and failures, managers improve their estimation techniques.

A post-audit involves the same evaluation techniques used in making the original capital budgeting decision—for example, use of the NPV method. The difference is that, in the post-audit, analysts insert actual figures, where known, and they revise estimates of future amounts based on new information. The managers responsible for the estimates used in the original proposal must explain the reasons for any significant differences between their estimates and actual results.

Post-audits are not foolproof. In the case of Campbell Soup, some observers suggested that the company was too quick to abandon the project. Industry analysts suggested that with more time and more advertising expenditures, Intelligent Quisine might have enjoyed success.

---

**ACTION PLAN**

- **Determine the present value of annual cash flows of each mutually exclusive project.**
- **Determine profitability index by dividing the present value of annual cash flows by the amount of the initial investment.**
- **Choose project with highest profitability index.**

## DO IT! 3 | Profitability Index

Taz Corporation has decided to invest in renewable energy sources to meet part of its energy needs for production. It is considering solar power versus wind power. After considering cost savings as well as incremental revenues from selling excess electricity into the power grid, it has determined the following.

|  | Solar | Wind |
|---|---|---|
| Present value of annual cash flows | $78,580 | $168,450 |
| Initial investment | $45,500 | $125,300 |

Determine the net present value and profitability index of each project. Which energy source should it choose?

**Solution**

|  | Solar | Wind |
|---|---|---|
| Present value of annual cash flows | $78,580 | $168,450 |
| Less: Initial investment | 45,500 | 125,300 |
| Net present value | $33,080 | $ 43,150 |
| Profitability index | 1.73* | 1.34** |

*$78,580 ÷ $45,500
**$168,450 ÷ $125,300

While the investment in wind power generates the higher net present value, it also requires a substantially higher initial investment. The profitability index favors solar power, which suggests that the additional net present value of wind is outweighed by the cost of the initial investment. The company should choose solar power.

Related exercise material: **BE25.5, DO IT! 25.3, and E25.4.**

# Internal Rate of Return

**LEARNING OBJECTIVE 4**

Use the internal rate of return method

The **internal rate of return method** differs from the net present value method in that it finds the **interest yield of the potential investment**.

- The **internal rate of return (IRR)** is the interest rate that causes the present value of the proposed capital expenditure to equal the present value of the expected net annual cash flows (that is, NPV equal to zero).
- Because it recognizes the time value of money, the internal rate of return method is (like the NPV method) a discounted cash flow technique.

How do we determine the internal rate of return? One way is to use a financial calculator (see Appendix G) or electronic spreadsheet (see the Excel tutorial provided in WileyPLUS) to solve for this rate. Or, we can use a trial-and-error procedure searching for a discount rate that results in an NPV equal to zero.

To illustrate, assume that Stewart Shipping Company is considering the purchase of a new front-end loader at a cost of $244,371. Net annual cash flows from this loader are estimated to be $100,000 a year for three years. To determine the internal rate of return on this front-end loader, the company finds the discount rate that results in a net present value of zero. **Illustration 25.21** shows that at a rate of return of 10%, Stewart Shipping has a positive net present value of $4,315. At a rate of return of 12%, it has a negative net present value of $4,188. At an 11% rate, the net present value is zero. Therefore, 11% is the internal rate of return for this investment (discount factors from Appendix G, Table 3).

**ILLUSTRATION 25.21** Estimation of internal rate of return

| Year | Net Annual Cash Flows | Discount Factor 10% | Present Value 10% | Discount Factor 11% | Present Value 11% | Discount Factor 12% | Present Value 12% |
|---|---|---|---|---|---|---|---|
| 1 | $100,000 | .90909 | $ 90 909 | .90090 | $ 90,090 | .89286 | $ 89,286 |
| 2 | $100,000 | .82645 | 82,645 | .81162 | 81,162 | .79719 | 79,719 |
| 3 | $100,000 | .75132 | 75,132 | .73119 | 73,119 | .71178 | 71,178 |
| | | | 248,686 | | 244,371 | | 240,183 |
| Less: Initial investment | | | 244,371 | | 244,371 | | 244,371 |
| Net present value | | | $ 4,315 | | $ –0– | | $ (4,188) |

An easier approach to solving for the internal rate of return can be used if the net annual cash flows are **equal**, as in the Stewart Shipping example. In this special case, we can find the internal rate of return using the equation provided in **Illustration 25.22**.

| Capital Investment | ÷ | Net Annual Cash Flows | = | Internal Rate of Return Factor |
|---|---|---|---|---|

**ILLUSTRATION 25.22**

Equation for internal rate of return—even cash flows

Applying this equation to the Stewart Shipping example, we find:

$$\$244{,}371 \div 100{,}000 = 2.44371$$

We then look up the factor 2.44371 in Table 4 of Appendix G in the three-payment row and find it under 11%. Row 3 is reproduced here for your convenience.

| | | | | | | | | | | |
|---|---|---|---|---|---|---|---|---|---|---|
| **Table 4 Present Value of an Annuity of 1** | | | | | | | | | | |
| **(n)** **Payments** | **4%** | **5%** | **6%** | **7%** | **8%** | **9%** | **10%** | **11%** | **12%** | **15%** |
| 3 | 2.77509 | 2.72325 | 2.67301 | 2.62432 | 2.57710 | 2.53130 | 2.48685 | **2.44371** | 2.40183 | 2.28323 |

Recognize that if the cash flows are **uneven**, then a trial-and-error approach or a financial calculator or computerized spreadsheet must be used.

Once managers know the internal rate of return, they compare it to the company's required rate of return (the discount rate). The IRR decision rule is as follows:

- **Accept the project when the internal rate of return is equal to or greater than the required rate of return.**
- **Reject the project when the internal rate of return is less than the required rate of return.**

**Illustration 25.23** shows these relationships. The internal rate of return method is widely used in practice, largely because most managers find the internal rate of return easy to interpret.

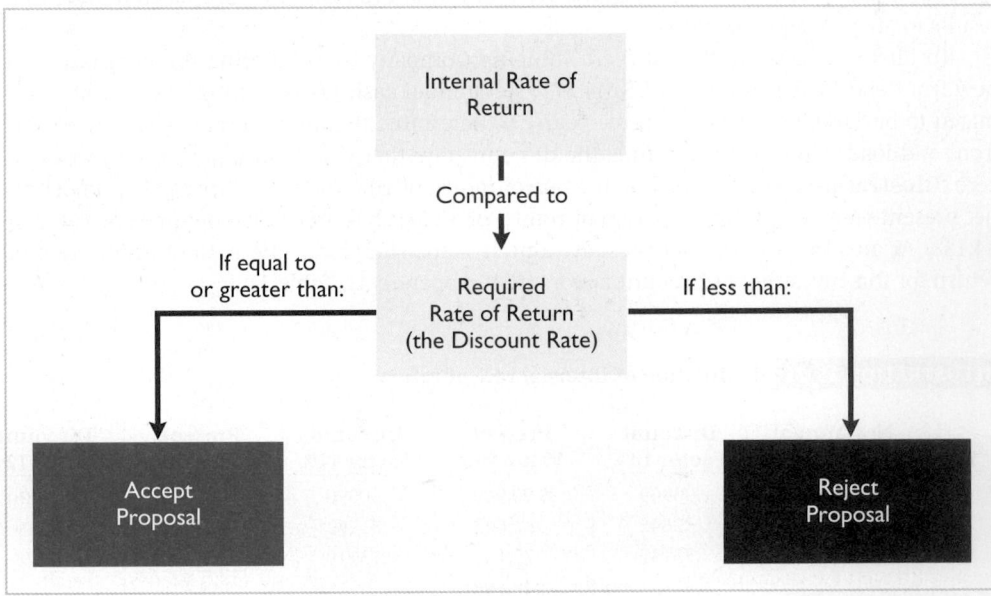

# Comparing Discounted Cash Flow Methods

**Illustration 25.24** compares the two discounted cash flow methods—net present value and internal rate of return. When properly used, either method will provide management with relevant quantitative data for making capital budgeting decisions.

| | **Net Present Value** | **Internal Rate of Return** |
|---|---|---|
| 1. Objective | Compute net present value (a dollar amount). | Compute internal rate of return (a percentage). |
| 2. Decision Rule | If net present value is zero or positive, accept the proposal. | If internal rate of return is equal to or greater than the required rate of return, accept the proposal. |
| | If net present value is negative, reject the proposal. | If internal rate of return is less than the required rate of return, reject the proposal. |

Finally, note that these capital budgeting calculations can also be performed using Excel. A big benefit of using Excel is the ability to quickly experiment with different input variables such as the number of payments, interest rates, or payment amounts. An instructional video demonstrating how to use Excel to perform capital budgeting calculations is provided in WileyPlus. The following shows a sample worksheet from that video.

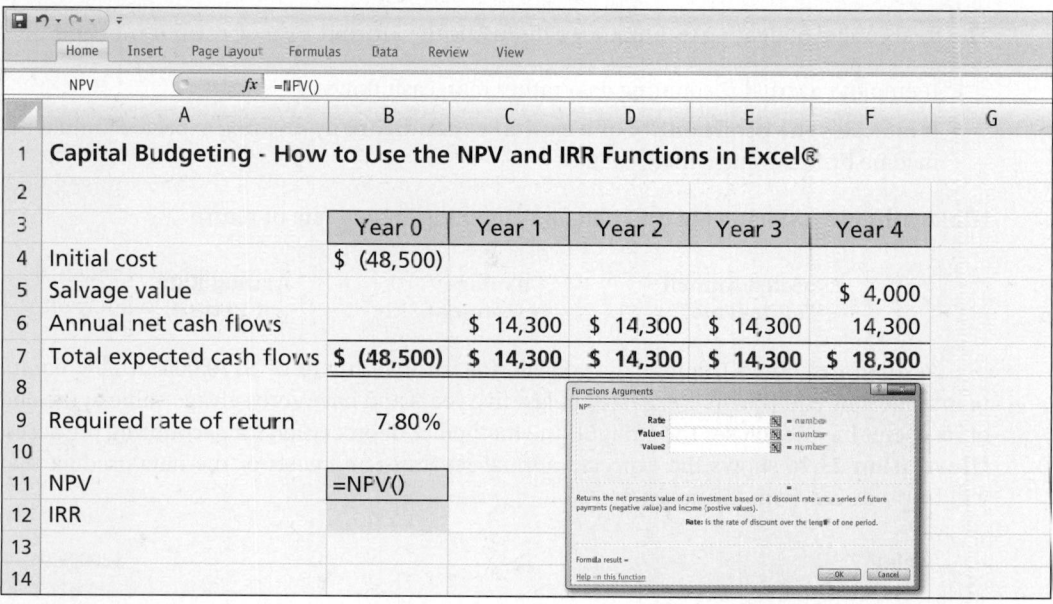

## DO IT! 4 | Internal Rate of Return

Watertown Paper Corporation is considering adding another machine for the manufacture of corrugated cardboard. The machine would cost $900,000. It would have an estimated life of 6 years and no salvage value. The company estimates that annual cash inflows would increase by $400,000 and that annual cash outflows would increase by $190,000. Management has a required rate of return of 9%. Calculate the internal rate of return on this project and discuss whether it should be accepted.

### Solution

| | |
|---|---|
| Estimated annual cash inflows | $400,000 |
| Estimated annual cash outflows | 190,000 |
| Net annual cash flow | $210,000 |

$900,000 ÷ $210,000 = 4.285714. Using Table 4 of Appendix G and the factors that correspond with the six-payment row, 4.285714 is between the factors for 10% and 11%. Since the project has an internal rate that is greater than 10% and the required rate of return is only 9%, the project should be accepted.

Related exercise material: **BE25.7, BE25.8, DO IT! 25.4, E25.5, E25.6, and E25.7.**

**ACTION PLAN**

• **Estimated annual cash inflows − Estimated annual cash outflows = Net annual cash flow.**

• **Capital investment ÷ Net annual cash flows = Internal rate of return factor.**

• **Look up the factor in the present value of an annuity table to find the internal rate of return.**

• **Accept the project if the internal rate of return is equal to or greater than the required rate of return.**

# Annual Rate of Return

---

**LEARNING OBJECTIVE 5**

Use the annual rate of return method.

---

The final capital budgeting technique we discuss is the **annual rate of return method**.

- It employs accrual accounting data rather than cash flows.
- It indicates **the profitability of a capital expenditure** by dividing expected annual net income by the average investment.

**Illustration 25.25** shows the equation for computing annual rate of return.

**ILLUSTRATION 25.25**

**Annual rate of return equation**

| Expected Annual Net Income | ÷ | Average Investment | = | Annual Rate of Return |
|---|---|---|---|---|

Assume that Reno Company is considering an investment of $130,000 in new equipment. The new equipment is expected to last five years and have zero salvage value at the end of its useful life. Reno uses the straight-line method of depreciation for accounting purposes. **Illustration 25.26** shows the expected annual revenues and costs of the new product that will be produced from the investment.

**ILLUSTRATION 25.26**

**Estimated annual net income from Reno Company's capital expenditure**

| | | |
|---|---|---|
| Sales | | $200,000 |
| Less: Costs and expenses | | |
| Manufacturing costs (exclusive of depreciation) | $132,000 | |
| Depreciation expense ($130,000 ÷ 5) | 26,000 | |
| Selling and administrative expenses | 22,000 | 180,000 |
| Income before income taxes | | 20,000 |
| Income tax expense | | 7,000 |
| Net income | | $ 13,000 |

Reno's expected annual net income is $13,000. Average investment is derived from the equation shown in **Illustration 25.27**.

**ILLUSTRATION 25.27**

**Equation for computing average investment**

$$\frac{\text{Original Investment} + \text{Value at End of Useful Life}}{2} = \text{Average Investment}$$

The value at the end of useful life is equal to the asset's salvage value, if any. For Reno, average investment is $65,000 [($130,000 + $0) ÷ 2]. The expected annual rate of return for Reno's investment in new equipment is therefore 20%, computed as follows.

$$\$13,000 \div \$65,000 = 20\%$$

Management then compares the annual rate of return with its **required rate of return** for investments of similar risk. The required rate of return is generally based on the company's cost of capital. The decision rule is:

- **A project is acceptable if its rate of return is greater than management's required rate of return**.
- **It is unacceptable when the reverse is true**.
- When companies use the rate of return technique in deciding among several acceptable projects, **the higher the rate of return for a given risk, the more attractive the investment**.

The principal advantages of this method are the simplicity of its calculation and management's familiarity with the accounting terms used in the computation. Two limitations of the annual rate of return method are:

1. It does not consider the time value of money. For example, no consideration is given to whether cash inflows will occur early or late in the life of the investment. As explained in Appendix G, recognition of the time value of money can make a significant difference between the future value and the discounted present value of an investment.

2. This method relies on accrual accounting numbers rather than expected cash flows. This is potentially problematic because valuation theories employed in finance are based on cash flows. Also, some people feel that accrual accounting numbers are more susceptible to manipulation by management (see **Helpful Hint**).

> **HELPFUL HINT**
>
> A capital budgeting decision based on only one technique may be misleading. It is often wise to analyze an investment from a number of different perspectives.

---

## Data Analytics Insight    Electronic Arts

Chris Willson/Alamy Stock Photo

### Increasing the Chances of Gaming Wins

Today's video games are infinitely more sophisticated than the games produced 25 years ago, and the costs required to develop them have skyrocketed. In 1994, **Electronic Arts** spent an unheard of $5 million developing a new game. These days, game development requires a two-year commitment by hundreds of employees and costs around $500 million. And if the game fails to attract buyers, then all of that money is gone.

How does Electronic Arts increase the likelihood of success? Big data. Because today's games are nearly all played online, the company collects data about which features of a game that players engage with the most. The company does not have to ask survey questions to collect this data but instead obtains the information from the usage data. However, when Electronic Arts first switched to this big-data approach, it quickly found out that it had more data than it could handle. Over time, the company has learned to collect only a fraction of the available data and then use it wisely.

The company's data analysis now guides the design and development of new games as well as the subsequent marketing. This dramatically reduces the risks associated with the giant capital investments involved.

**Source:** Bernard Marr, *Big Data in Practice* (Hoboken, NJ: John Wiley and Sons, 2016), pp. 273–279.

**In what ways do the capital investments of Electronic Arts benefit from data analytics? (Answer is available at the end of the chapter.)**

---

## DO IT! 5    Annual Rate of Return

Watertown Paper Corporation is considering adding another machine for the manufacture of corrugated cardboard. The machine would cost $900,000. It would have an estimated life of 6 years and no salvage value. The company estimates that annual revenues would increase by $400,000 and that annual expenses excluding depreciation would increase by $190,000. It uses the straight-line method to compute depreciation expense. Management has a required rate of return of 9%. Compute the annual rate of return.

> **ACTION PLAN**
>
> - Expected annual net income = Annual revenues − Annual expenses (including depreciation expense).
> - Average investment = (Original investment + Value at end of useful life) ÷ 2.
> - Annual rate of return = Expected annual net income ÷ Average investment.

### Solution

| | | |
|---|---:|---:|
| Revenues | | $400,000 |
| Less: | | |
| Expenses (excluding depreciation) | $190,000 | |
| Depreciation ($900,000 ÷ 6 years) | 150,000 | 340,000 |
| Annual net income | | $ 60,000 |

Average investment = ($900,000 + $0) ÷ 2 = $450,000
Annual rate of return = $60,000 ÷ $450,000 = 13.3%

Since the annual rate of return (13.3%) is greater than Watertown's required rate of return (9%), the proposed project is acceptable.

Related exercise material: **BE25.9, DO IT! 25.5, E25.8, E25.9, E25.10, and E25.11.**

# Review and Practice

## Learning Objectives Review

### 1  Describe capital budgeting inputs and apply the cash payback technique.

Management gathers project proposals from each department; a capital budget committee screens the proposals and recommends worthy projects. Company officers decide which projects to fund, and the board of directors approves the capital budget. In capital budgeting, estimated cash inflows and outflows, rather than accrual-accounting numbers, are the preferred inputs.

The cash payback technique identifies the time period required to recover the cost of the investment. The equation when net annual cash flows are equal is: Cost of capital investment ÷ Estimated net annual cash flow = Cash payback period. The shorter the payback period, the more attractive the investment.

### 2  Use the net present value method.

The net present value method compares the present value of future cash inflows with the capital investment to determine net present value. The NPV decision rule is: Accept the project if net present value is zero or positive. Reject the project if net present value is negative.

### 3  Identify capital budgeting challenges and refinements.

Intangible benefits are difficult to quantify and thus are often ignored in capital budgeting decisions. This can result in incorrectly rejecting some projects. One method for considering intangible benefits is to calculate the NPV, ignoring intangible benefits. If the resulting NPV is below zero, evaluate whether the benefits are worth at least the amount of the negative net present value. Alternatively, intangible benefits can be incorporated into the NPV calculation, using conservative estimates of their value.

The profitability index is a tool for comparing the relative merits of alternative capital investment opportunities. It is computed as Present value of net cash flows ÷ Initial investment. The higher the index, the more desirable the project.

A post-audit is an evaluation of a capital investment's actual performance. Post-audits create an incentive for managers to make accurate estimates. Post-audits also are useful for determining whether a company should continue, expand, or terminate a project. Finally, post-audits provide feedback that is useful for improving estimation techniques.

### 4  Use the internal rate of return method.

The objective of the internal rate of return method is to find the interest yield of the potential investment, which is expressed as a percentage rate. The IRR decision rule is: Accept the project when the internal rate of return is equal to or greater than the required rate of return. Reject the project when the internal rate of return is less than the required rate of return.

### 5  Use the annual rate of return method.

The annual rate of return uses accrual accounting data to indicate the profitability of a capital investment. It is calculated as Expected annual net income ÷ Amount of the average investment. The higher the rate of return, the more attractive the investment.

## Glossary Review

**Annual rate of return method**  The determination of the profitability of a capital expenditure, computed by dividing expected annual net income by the average investment. (p. 25-20).

**Capital budgeting**  The process of making capital expenditure decisions in business. (p. 25-3).

**Cash payback technique**  A capital budgeting technique that identifies the time period required to recover the cost of a capital investment from the net annual cash flow produced by the investment. (p. 25-4).

**Cost of capital**  The weighted-average rate of return that the firm must pay to obtain funds from creditors and stockholders. (p. 25-9).

**Discounted cash flow technique**  A capital budgeting technique that considers both the estimated net cash flows from the investment and the time value of money. (p. 25-6).

**Discount rate**  The interest rate used in discounting the future net cash flows to determine present value. (p. 25-7).

**Internal rate of return (IRR)**  The interest rate that will cause the present value of the proposed capital expenditure to equal the present value of the expected net annual cash flows. (p. 25-17).

**Internal rate of return (IRR) method**  A method used in capital budgeting that results in finding the interest yield of the potential investment. (p. 25-17).

**Net present value (NPV)**  The difference that results when the original capital outlay is subtracted from the discounted net cash flows. (p. 25-7).

**Net present value (NPV) method**  A method used in capital budgeting in which net cash flows are discounted to their present value and then compared to the capital outlay required by the investment. (p. 25-7).

**Post-audit**  A thorough evaluation of how well a project's actual performance matches the original projections. (p. 25-16).

**Profitability index**  A method of comparing alternative projects that takes into account both the size of the investment and its discounted net cash flows. It is computed by dividing the present value of net cash flows by the initial investment. (p. 25-14).

**Required rate of return**  Management's minimum acceptable rate of return on investments, sometimes called the discount rate or cost of capital. (p. 25-7).

**Sensitivity analysis**  An approach that uses a number of outcome estimates to get a sense of the variability among potential returns. (p. 25-15).

# Practice Multiple-Choice Questions

1. **(LO 1)** Which of the following is **not** an example of a capital budgeting decision?

   a. Decision to build a new factory.

   b. Decision to renovate an existing facility.

   c. Decision to buy a piece of machinery.

   d. All of the answer choices are capital budgeting decisions.

2. **(LO 1)** What is the order of involvement of the following parties in the capital budgeting authorization process?

   a. Factory managers, officers, capital budget committee, board of directors.

   b. Board of directors, factory managers, officers, capital budget committee.

   c. Factory managers, capital budget committee, officers, board of directors.

   d. Officers, factory managers, capital budget committee, board of directors.

3. **(LO 1)** What is a weakness of the cash payback approach?

   a. It uses accrual-based accounting numbers.

   b. It ignores the time value of money.

   c. It ignores the expected profitability of the project.

   d. It ignores both the time value of money and the expected profitability of the project.

4. **(LO 1)** Siegel Industries is considering two capital budgeting projects. Project A requires an initial investment of $48,000. It is expected to produce net annual cash flows of $7,000. Project B requires an initial investment of $75,000 and is expected to produce net annual cash flows of $12,000. Using the cash payback technique to evaluate the two projects, Siegel should accept:

   a. Project A because it has a shorter cash payback period.

   b. Project B because it has a shorter cash payback period.

   c. Project A because it requires a smaller initial investment.

   d. Project B because it produces a larger net annual cash flow.

5. **(LO 2)** Which is a **true** statement regarding using a higher discount rate to calculate the net present value of a project?

   a. It will make it less likely that the project will be accepted.

   b. It will make it more likely that the project will be accepted.

   c. It is appropriate to use a higher rate if the project is perceived as being less risky than other projects being considered.

   d. It is appropriate to use a higher rate if the project will have a short useful life relative to other projects being considered.

6. **(LO 2)** A positive net present value means that the:

   a. project's rate of return is less than the cutoff rate.

   b. project's rate of return exceeds the required rate of return.

   c. project's rate of return equals the required rate of return.

   d. project is unacceptable.

7. **(LO 2)** Which of the following is **not** an alternative name for the discount rate?

   a. Hurdle rate.

   b. Required rate of return.

   c. Cutoff rate.

   d. All of the answer choices are alternative names for the discount rate.

8. **(LO 3)** If a project has intangible benefits whose value is hard to estimate, the best thing to do is:

   a. ignore these benefits, since any estimate of their value will most likely be wrong.

   b. include a conservative estimate of their value.

   c. ignore their value in your initial net present value calculation, but then estimate whether their potential value is worth at least the amount of the net present value deficiency.

   d. either include a conservative estimate of their value or ignore their value in your initial net present value calculation, but then estimate whether their potential value is worth at least the amount of the net present value deficiency.

9. **(LO 3)** An example of an intangible benefit provided by a capital budgeting project is:

   a. the salvage value of the capital investment.

   b. a positive net present value.

   c. a decrease in customer complaints regarding poor quality.

   d. an internal rate of return greater than zero.

10. **(LO 3)** The following information is available for a potential capital investment.

| | |
|---|---:|
| Initial investment | $80,000 |
| Salvage value | 10,000 |
| Net annual cash flow | 14,820 |
| Present value of net annual cash flows | 98,112 |
| Net present value | 18,112 |
| Useful life | 10 years |

The potential investment's profitability index (rounded to two decimals) is:

   a. 5.40.          c. 1.23.

   b. 1.19.          d. 1.40.

11. **(LO 3)** A post-audit of an investment project should be performed:

   a. on all significant capital expenditure projects.

   b. on all projects that management feels might be financial failures.

   c. on randomly selected projects.

   d. only on projects that enjoy tremendous success.

12. **(LO 4)** A project should be accepted if its internal rate of return exceeds:

   a. zero.

   b. the rate of return on a government bond.

   c. the company's required rate of return.

   d. the rate the company pays on borrowed funds.

13. **(LO 4)** The following information is available for a potential capital investment.

| | |
|---|---:|
| Initial investment | $60,000 |
| Net annual cash flow | 15,400 |
| Net present value | 3,143 |
| Useful life | 5 years |

The potential investment's internal rate of return is approximately:

**a.** 5%.    **c.** 4%.

**b.** 10%.   **d.** 9%.

**14. (LO 5)** Which of the following is **incorrect** about the annual rate of return technique?

**a.** The calculation is simple.

**b.** The accounting terms used are familiar to management.

**c.** The timing of the cash inflows is not considered.

**d.** The time value of money is considered.

**15. (LO 5)** The following information is available for a potential capital investment.

| | |
|---|---|
| Initial investment | $120,000 |
| Annual net income | 15,000 |
| Net annual cash flow | 27,500 |
| Salvage value | 20,000 |
| Useful life | 8 years |

The potential investment's annual rate of return is approximately:

**a.** 21%.    **c.** 30%.

**b.** 15%.    **d.** 39%.

## Solutions

**1. d.** Choices (a), (b), and (c) are all examples of capital budgeting decisions, so choice (d) is the best answer.

**2. c.** The process of authorizing capital budget expenditures starts with factory managers, moves on to the capital budgeting committee, goes next to the officers of the firm and finally is acted upon by the board of directors. The other choices are therefore incorrect.

**3. d.** Choices (b) and (c) are both correct; therefore, choice (d) is the best answer. Choice (a) is incorrect as the use of accrual-based accounting numbers is not a weakness of the cash payback approach.

**4. b.** Project B ($75,000 ÷ $12,000) has a shorter cash payback period than Project A ($48,000 ÷ $7,000). The other choices are therefore incorrect.

**5. a.** If a higher discount rate is used in calculating the net present value of a project, the resulting net present value will be lower and the project will be less likely to be accepted. The other choices are therefore incorrect.

**6. b.** A positive net present value means that the project's rate of return exceeds the required rate of return. The other choices are therefore incorrect.

**7. d.** Choices (a), (b), and (c) are all alternative names for the discount rate; therefore, choice (d) is the best answer.

**8. d.** Choices (b) and (c) are both reasonable approaches to including intangible benefits in the capital budgeting process; therefore, choice (d) is the best answer. Choice (a) is incorrect because even though these intangible benefits may be hard to quantify, they should not be ignored in the capital budgeting process.

**9. c.** A decrease in customer complaints regarding poor quality is one example of an intangible benefit provided by a capital budgeting project. The other choices are incorrect because (a) salvage value, (b) net present value, and (d) internal rate of return are all quantitative measures, i.e., tangible.

**10. c.** ($18,112 + $80,000) ÷ $80,000 = 1.23, not (a) 5.40, (b) 1.19, or (d) 1.40.

**11. a.** A post-audit should be performed on all significant capital expenditure projects, not just on (b) financial failures, (c) randomly selected projects, or (d) tremendous successes, because the feedback gained will help to improve the process in the future and also will give managers an incentive to be more realistic in preparing capital expenditure proposals.

**12. c.** A project should be accepted if its internal rate of return exceeds the company's required rate of return, not (a) zero, (b) the rate of return on a government bond, or (d) the rate the company pays on borrowed funds.

**13. d.** ($60,000 ÷ $15,400) equals 3.8961, which corresponds with approximately 9% in Table 4 of Appendix G, not (a) 5%, (b) 10%, or (c) 4%.

**14. d.** The time value of money is not considered when applying the annual rate of return method. The other choices are correct statements.

**15. a.** $15,000 ÷ [($120,000 + $20,000) ÷ 2] = 21%, not (b) 15%, (c) 30%, or (d) 39%.

## Practice Brief Exercises

*Compute the cash payback period for a capital investment.*

**1. (LO 1)** Carson Company is considering purchasing new equipment for $600,000. Annual depreciation over the 8-year useful life of the equipment is $75,000. It is expected that the equipment will produce net annual cash inflows of $100,000 over its 8-year useful life. Compute the cash payback period.

### Solution

1. Cash payback period = $600,000 ÷ $100,000 = 6 years

**2. (LO 2)** Hilred Company is considering two different, mutually exclusive capital expenditure proposals. Project A will cost $400,000, has an expected useful life of 8 years and a salvage value of zero, and is expected to increase net annual cash flows by $80,000. Project B will also cost $400,000, has an expected useful life of 8 years and a salvage value of $100,000, and is expected to increase net annual cash flows by $70,000. A discount rate of 10% is appropriate for both projects. Compute the net present value of each project. Which project should be accepted?

*Compute net present values.*

**Solution**

2.

**Project A**

| | Cash Flows | × | 10% Discount Factor | = | Present Value |
|---|---|---|---|---|---|
| Present value of net annual cash flows | $ 80,000 | × | 5.33493 | = | $426,794 |
| Present value of salvage value | 0 | × | .46651 | = | 0 |
| | | | | | 426,794 |
| Less: Capital investment | | | | | 400,000 |
| Net present value | | | | | $ 26,794 |

**Project B**

| | Cash Flows | × | 10% Discount Factor | = | Present Value |
|---|---|---|---|---|---|
| Present value of net annual cash flows | $ 70,000 | × | 5.33493 | = | $373,445 |
| Present value of salvage value | 100,000 | × | .46651 | = | 46,651 |
| | | | | | 420,096 |
| Less: Capital investment | | | | | 400,000 |
| Net present value | | | | | $ 20,096 |

Project A has a higher net present value than Project B, and it should therefore be accepted.

**3. (LO 5)** King-Roken Company is considering investing in new automated equipment. It is expected that the equipment will increase annual revenues by $200,000 and annual expenses by $120,000 (including depreciation). The equipment will cost $540,000 and have a $20,000 salvage value at the end of its 10-year useful life. Calculate the annual rate of return.

*Calculate annual rate of return.*

**Solution**

3. The annual rate of return is calculated by dividing expected annual income by the average investment. The company's expected annual income is:

$$\$200,000 - \$120,000 = \$80,000$$

Its average investment is

$$\frac{\$540,000 + \$20,000}{2} = \$280,000$$

Therefore, its annual rate of return is:

$$\$80,000 \div \$280,000 = 28.6\%$$

# Practice Exercises

**1. (LO 1, 4)** BTMS Inc. wants to purchase a new machine for $30,000. Installation costs are $1,500. The old machine was bought 5 years ago and had an expected economic life of 10 years without salvage value. This old machine now has a book value of $2,000, and BTMS Inc. expects to sell it for that amount. The

*Calculate payback period and internal rate of return, and apply decision rules.*

new machine would decrease operating costs by $8,000 each year of its economic life. The straight-line depreciation method would be used for the new machine, for a 5-year period with no salvage value.

**Instructions**

a. Determine the cash payback period.

b. Determine the approximate internal rate of return.

c. Assuming the company has a required rate of return of 10%, state your conclusion on whether the new machine should be purchased.

(CGA adapted)

**Solution**

1. a. Total net investment = $30,000 + $1,500 − $2,000 = $29,500

    Annual net cash flow = $8,000

    Payback period = $29,500 ÷ $8,000 = 3.7 years

   b. Net present value approximates zero when discount rate is 11%.

| Item | Amount | Years | PV Factor | Present Value |
|------|--------|-------|-----------|---------------|
| Net annual cash flows | $8,000 | 1–5 | 3.69590 | $29,567 |
| Less: Capital investment | | | | 29,500 |
| Net present value | | | | $    67 |

   c. Because the approximate internal rate of return of 11% exceeds the required rate of return of 10%, the investment should be accepted.

*Calculate payback, annual rate of return, and net present value*

2. **(LO 1, 2, 5)** MCA Corporation is reviewing an investment proposal. The initial cost is $105,000. Estimates of the book value of the investment at the end of each year, the net cash flows for each year, and the net income for each year are presented in the schedule below. All cash flows are assumed to take place at the end of the year. The salvage value of the investment at the end of each year is equal to its book value. There would be no salvage value at the end of the investment's life.

**Investment Proposal**

| Year | Book Value | Annual Cash Flows | Annual Net Income |
|------|-----------|-------------------|-------------------|
| 1 | $70,000 | $45,000 | $16,000 |
| 2 | 42,000 | 40,000 | 18,000 |
| 3 | 21,000 | 35,000 | 20,000 |
| 4 | 7,000 | 30,000 | 22,000 |
| 5 | 0 | 25,000 | 24,000 |

MCA Corporation uses a 15% target rate of return for new investment proposals.

**Instructions**

a. What is the cash payback period for this proposal?

b. What is the annual rate of return for the investment?

c. What is the net present value of the investment?

(CMA-Canada adapted)

**Solution**

2. a.

| | Year | Amount | Balance |
|---|------|--------|---------|
| Initial investment | 0 | $(105,000) | $(105,000) |
| Less: Cash flow | 1 | 45,000 | (60,000) |
| | 2 | 40,000 | (20,000) |
| | 3 | 35,000 | 15,000 |

   Payback period = 2 + ($20,000 ÷ $35,000) = 2.57 years

**b.** Average annual net income = ($16,000 + $18,000 + $20,000 + $22,000 + $24,000) ÷ 5 = $20,000

Average investment = ($105,000 + $0) ÷ 2 = $52,500

Annual rate of return = $20,000 ÷ $52,500 = 38.10%

**c.**

| | Year | Discount Factor, 15% | × | Amount | = | Present Value |
|---|---|---|---|---|---|---|
| Net cash flows | 1 | 0.86957 | | $45,000 | | $ 39,131 |
| | 2 | 0.75614 | | 40,000 | | 30,246 |
| | 3 | 0.65752 | | 35,000 | | 23,013 |
| | 4 | 0.57175 | | 30,000 | | 17,153 |
| | 5 | 0.49718 | | 25,000 | | 12,430 |
| Present value of cash inflows | | | | | | 121,973 |
| Less: Initial investment | | | | | | 105,000 |
| Net present value | | | | | | $ 16,973 |

# Practice Problem

**(LO 1, 2, 5)** Cornfield Company is considering a long-term capital investment project in laser equip-ment. This will require an investment of $280,000, and it will have a useful life of 5 years. Annual net income is expected to be $16,000 a year. Depreciation is computed by the straight-line method with no salvage value. The company's cost of capital is 10%, and it desires a cash payback of 60% of a project's useful life or less. (*Hint:* Assume cash flows can be computed by adding back depreciation expense.)

*Compute annual rate of return, cash payback, and net present value.*

### Instructions

(Round all computations to two decimal places unless directed otherwise.)

**a.** Compute the cash payback period for the project.

**b.** Compute the net present value for the project. (Round to nearest dollar.)

**c.** Compute the annual rate of return for the project.

**d.** Should the project be accepted? Why or why not?

### Solution

**a.** $280,000 ÷ $72,000 ($16,000 + $56,000) = 3.89 years

**b.**

| | Present Value at 10% |
|---|---|
| Discount factor for 5 payments | 3.79079 |
| Present value of net cash flows: | |
| $72,000 × 3.79079 | $272,937 |
| Less: Capital investment | 280,000 |
| Negative net present value | $ (7,063) |

**c.** $16,000 ÷ $140,000 ($280,000 ÷ 2) = 11.4%

**d.** The annual rate of return of 11.4% is reasonable. However, the cash payback period is 78% of the project's useful life, and net present value is negative. The recommendation is to reject the project.

---

Brief Exercises, DO IT! Exercises, Exercises, Problems, Data Analytics Activities, and many additional resources are available for practice in WileyPLUS.

# Questions

1. Describe the process a company may use in screening and approving the capital expenditure budget.

2. What are the advantages and disadvantages of the cash payback technique?

3. Tom Wells claims the equation for the cash payback technique is the same as the equation for the annual rate of return technique. Is Tom correct? What is the equation for the cash payback technique?

4. Two types of present value tables may be used with the discounted cash flow techniques. Identify the tables and the circumstance(s) when each table should be used.

5. What is the decision rule under the net present value method?

6. Discuss the factors that determine the appropriate discount rate to use when calculating the net present value.

7. What simplifying assumptions were made in the chapter regarding the calculation of net present value?

8. What are some examples of potential intangible benefits of investment proposals? Why do these intangible benefits complicate the capital budgeting evaluation process? What might happen if intangible benefits are ignored in a capital budgeting decision?

9. What steps can be taken to incorporate intangible benefits into the capital budget evaluation process?

10. What advantages does the profitability index provide over direct comparison of net present value when comparing two projects?

11. What is a post-audit? What are the potential benefits of a post-audit?

12. Identify the steps required in using the internal rate of return method when the net annual cash flows are equal.

13. El Cajon Company uses the internal rate of return method. What is the decision rule for this method?

14. What are the strengths of the annual rate of return approach? What are its weaknesses?

15. Your classmate, Mike Dawson, is confused about the factors that are included in the annual rate of return technique. What is the equation for this technique?

16. Sveta Pace is trying to understand the term "cost of capital." Define the term and indicate its relevance to the decision rule under the internal rate of return technique.

# Brief Exercises

*Compute the cash payback period for a capital investment.*

**BE25.1 (LO 1), AP** Rihanna Company is considering purchasing new equipment for $450,000. It is expected that the equipment will produce net annual cash flows of $60,000 over its 10-year useful life. Annual depreciation will be $45,000. Compute the cash payback period.

*Compute net present value of an investment.*

**BE25.2 (LO 2), AN** Hsung Company accumulates the following data concerning a proposed capital investment: cash cost $215,000, net annual cash flows $40,000, and present value factor of cash inflows for 10 years 5.65 (rounded). Determine the net present value, and indicate whether the investment should be made.

*Compute net present value of an investment.*

**BE25.3 (LO 2), AP** Thunder Corporation, an amusement park, is considering a capital investment in a new exhibit. The exhibit would cost $136,000 and have an estimated useful life of 5 years. It can be sold for $60,000 at the end of that time. (Amusement parks need to rotate exhibits to keep people interested.) It is expected to increase net annual cash flows by $25,000. The company's borrowing rate is 8%. Its cost of capital is 10%. Calculate the net present value of this project to the company.

*Compute net present value of an investment and consider intangible benefits.*

**BE25.4 (LO 2, 3), AN** Caine Bottling Corporation is considering the purchase of a new bottling machine. The machine would cost $200,000 and has an estimated useful life of 8 years with zero salvage value. Management estimates that the new bottling machine will provide net annual cash flows of $34,000. Management also believes that the new bottling machine will save the company money because it is expected to be more reliable than other machines, and thus will reduce downtime. How much would the reduction in downtime have to be worth in order for the project to be acceptable? Assume a discount rate of 9%. (*Hint:* Calculate the net present value.)

*Compute net present value and profitability index.*

**BE25.5 (LO 2, 3), AN** McKnight Company is considering two different, mutually exclusive capital expenditure proposals. Project A will cost $400,000, has an expected useful life of 10 years and a salvage value of zero, and is expected to increase net annual cash flows by $70,000. Project B will cost $310,000, has an expected useful life of 10 years and a salvage value of zero, and is expected to increase net annual cash flows by $55,000. A discount rate of 9% is appropriate for both projects. Compute the net present value and profitability index of each project. Which project should be accepted?

**BE25.6 (LO 3), AN** Quillen Company is performing a post-audit of a project completed one year ago. The initial estimates were that the project would cost $250,000, would have a useful life of 9 years and zero salvage value, and would result in net annual cash flows of $46,000 per year. Now that the investment has been in operation for 1 year, revised figures indicate that it actually cost $260,000, will have a total useful life of 11 years (including the year just completed), and will produce net annual cash flows of $39,000 per year. Evaluate the success of the project. Assume a discount rate of 10%.

*Perform a post-audit.*

**BE25.7 (LO 4), AP** Kanye Company is evaluating the purchase of a rebuilt spot-welding machine to be used in the manufacture of a new product. The machine will cost $176,000, has an estimated useful life of 7 years and a salvage value of zero, and will increase net annual cash flows by $35,000. What is its approximate internal rate of return?

*Calculate internal rate of return.*

**BE25.8 (LO 4), AN** Viera Corporation is considering investing in a new facility. The estimated cost of the facility is $2,045,000. It will be used for 12 years, then sold for $716,000. The facility will generate annual cash inflows of $400,000 and will need new annual cash outflows of $150,000. The company has a required rate of return of 7%. Calculate the internal rate of return on this project, and discuss whether the project should be accepted.

*Calculate internal rate of return.*

**BE25.9 (LO 5), AP** Swift Oil Company is considering investing in a new oil well. It is expected that the oil well will increase annual revenues by $130,000 and will increase annual expenses by $70,000 including depreciation. The oil well will cost $490,000 and will have a $10,000 salvage value at the end of its 10-year useful life. Calculate the annual rate of return.

*Compute annual rate of return.*

# DO IT! Exercises

**DO IT! 25.1 (LO 1), AP** Wayne Company is considering a long-term investment project called ZIP. ZIP will require an investment of $140,000. It will have a useful life of 4 years and no salvage value. Annual cash inflows would increase by $80,000, and annual cash outflows would increase by $40,000. Compute the cash payback period.

*Compute the cash payback period for an investment.*

**DO IT! 25.2 (LO 2), AN** Wayne Company is considering a long-term investment project called ZIP. ZIP will require an investment of $120,000. It will have a useful life of 4 years and no salvage value. Annual cash inflows would increase by $80,000 and annual cash outflows would increase by $40,000. The company's required rate of return is 12%. Calculate the net present value on this project and discuss whether it should be accepted.

*Calculate net present value of an investment.*

**DO IT! 25.3 (LO 3), AP** Ranger Corporation has decided to invest in renewable energy sources to meet part of its energy needs for production. It is considering solar power versus wind power. After considering cost savings as well as incremental revenues from selling excess electricity into the power grid, it has determined the following.

*Compute profitability index.*

|  | **Solar** | **Wind** |
|---|---|---|
| Present value of annual cash flows | $52,580 | $128,450 |
| Capital investment | $39,500 | $105,300 |

Determine the net present value and profitability index of each project. Which energy source should it choose?

**DO IT! 25.4 (LO 4), AN** Wayne Company is considering a long-term investment project called ZIP. ZIP will require an investment of $120,000. It will have a useful life of 4 years and no salvage value. Annual cash inflows would increase by $80,000, and annual cash outflows would increase by $40,000. The company's required rate of return is 12%. Calculate the internal rate of return on this project and discuss whether it should be accepted.

*Calculate internal rate of return.*

**DO IT! 25.5 (LO 5), AP** Wayne Company is considering a long-term investment project called ZIP. ZIP will require an investment of $120,000. It will have a useful life of 4 years and no salvage value. Annual revenues would increase by $80,000, and annual expenses (excluding depreciation) would increase by $41,000. Wayne uses the straight-line method to compute depreciation expense. The company's required rate of return is 12%. Compute the annual rate of return.

*Calculate annual rate of return.*

# Exercises

*Compute cash payback and net present value.*

**E25.1 (LO 1, 2), AN** Linkin Corporation is considering purchasing a new delivery truck. The truck has many advantages over the company's current truck (not the least of which is that it runs). The new truck would cost $56,000. Because of the increased capacity, reduced maintenance costs, and increased fuel economy, the new truck is expected to generate cost savings of $8,000. At the end of 8 years, the company will sell the truck for an estimated $27,000. Traditionally the company has used a rule of thumb that a proposal should not be accepted unless it has a payback period that is less than 50% of the asset's estimated useful life. Larry Newton, a new manager, has suggested that the company should not rely solely on the payback approach, but should also employ the net present value method when evaluating new projects. The company's cost of capital is 8%.

## Instructions

**a.** Compute the cash payback period and net present value of the proposed investment.

**b.** Does the project meet the company's cash payback criteria? Does it meet the net present value criteria for acceptance? Discuss your results.

*Compute cash payback period and net present value.*

**E25.2 (LO 1, 2), AN** Doug's Custom Construction Company is considering three new projects, each requiring an equipment investment of $22,000. Each project will last for 3 years and produce the following net annual cash flows.

| Year | AA | BB | CC |
|------|------|------|------|
| 1 | $ 7,000 | $10,000 | $13,000 |
| 2 | 9,000 | 10,000 | 12,000 |
| 3 | 12,000 | 10,000 | 11,000 |
| Total | $28,000 | $30,000 | $36,000 |

The equipment's salvage value is zero, and Doug uses straight-line depreciation. Doug will not accept any project with a cash payback period over 2 years. Doug's required rate of return is 12%.

## Instructions

**a.** Compute each project's payback period, indicating the most desirable project and the least desirable project using this method. (Round to two decimals and assume in your computations that cash flows occur evenly throughout the year.)

**b.** Compute the net present value of each project. Does your evaluation change? (Round to nearest dollar.)

*Calculate net present value and apply decision rule.*

**E25.3 (LO 2), AN** Hillsong Inc. manufactures snowsuits. Hillsong is considering purchasing a new sewing machine at a cost of $2.45 million. Its existing machine was purchased 5 years ago at a price of $1.8 million; 6 months ago, Hillsong spent $55,000 to keep it operational. The existing sewing machine can be sold today for $250,000. The new sewing machine would require a one-time, $85,000 training cost. Operating costs would decrease by the following amounts for years 1 to 7:

| Year | 1 | $390,000 |
|------|---|----------|
| | 2 | 400,000 |
| | 3 | 411,000 |
| | 4 | 426,000 |
| | 5 | 434,000 |
| | 6 | 435,000 |
| | 7 | 436,000 |

The new sewing machine would be depreciated according to the declining-balance method at a rate of 20%. The salvage value is expected to be $400,000. This new equipment would require maintenance costs of $100,000 at the end of the fifth year. The cost of capital is 9%.

## Instructions

Use the net present value method to determine whether Hillsong should purchase the new machine to replace the existing machine, and state the reason for your conclusion.

(CGA adapted)

*Compute cash payback period and annual rate of return.*

*Compute net present value and profitability index.*

**E25.4 (LO 2, 3), AN** BAK Corp. is considering purchasing one of two new diagnostic machines. Either machine would make it possible for the company to bid on jobs that it currently isn't equipped to do. Estimates regarding each machine are provided here.

|  | Machine A | Machine B |
|---|---|---|
| Original cost | $75,500 | $180,000 |
| Estimated life | 8 years | 8 years |
| Salvage value | –0– | –0– |
| Estimated annual cash inflows | $20,000 | $40,000 |
| Estimated annual cash outflows | $5,000 | $10,000 |

### Instructions

Calculate the net present value and profitability index of each machine. Assume a 9% discount rate. Which machine should be purchased?

**E25.5 (LO 4), AN** Bruno Corporation is involved in the business of injection molding of plastics. It is considering the purchase of a new computer-aided design and manufacturing machine for $430,000. The company believes that with this new machine it will improve productivity and increase quality, resulting in an increase in net annual cash flows of $101,000 for the next 6 years. Management requires a 10% rate of return on all new investments.

*Determine internal rate of return.*

### Instructions

Calculate the internal rate of return on this new machine. Should the investment be accepted?

**E25.6 (LO 1, 4), AN** BSU Inc. wants to purchase a new machine for $29,300, excluding $1,500 of installation costs. The old machine was purchased 5 years ago and had an expected economic life of 10 years with no salvage value. The old machine has a book value of $2,000, and BSU Inc. expects to sell it for that amount. The new machine will decrease operating costs by $7,000 each year of its economic life. The straight-line depreciation method will be used for the new machine for a 6-year period with no salvage value.

*Calculate cash payback period and internal rate of return, and apply decision rules.*

### Instructions

a. Determine the cash payback period.

b. Determine the approximate internal rate of return.

c. Assuming the company has a required rate of return of 10%, state your conclusion on whether the new machine should be purchased.

(CGA adapted)

**E25.7 (LO 4), AN** Iggy Company is considering three capital expenditure projects. Relevant data for the projects are as follows.

*Determine internal rate of return.*

| Project | Investment | Annual Net Income | Life of Project |
|---|---|---|---|
| 22A | $240,000 | $15,500 | 6 years |
| 23A | 270,000 | 20,600 | 9 years |
| 24A | 280,000 | 15,700 | 7 years |

Annual net income is constant over the life of the project. Each project is expected to have zero salvage value at the end of the project. Iggy Company uses the straight-line method of depreciation.

### Instructions

a. Determine the internal rate of return for each project. Round the internal rate of return factor to three decimals.

b. If Iggy Company's required rate of return is 10%, which projects are acceptable?

**E25.8 (LO 5), AP** Service Pierre's Hair Salon is considering opening a new location in French Lick, California. The cost of building a new salon is $300,000. A new salon will normally generate annual revenues of $70,000, with annual expenses (including depreciation) of $41,500. At the end of 15 years, the salon will have a salvage value of $80,000.

*Calculate annual rate of return.*

### Instructions

Calculate the annual rate of return on the project.

**E25.9 (LO 1, 5), AP** Service Legend Service Center just purchased an automobile hoist for $32,400. The hoist has an 8-year life and an estimated salvage value of $3,000. Installation costs and freight charges were $3,300 and $700, respectively. Legend uses straight-line depreciation.

The new hoist will be used to replace mufflers and tires on automobiles. Legend estimates that the new hoist will enable its mechanics to replace 5 extra mufflers per week. Each muffler sells for $72 installed. The cost of a muffler is $36, and the labor cost to install a muffler is $16.

**Instructions**

a. Compute the cash payback period for the new hoist.

b. Compute the annual rate of return for the new hoist. (Round to one decimal.)

*Compute annual rate of return, cash payback period, and net present value.*

**E25.10 (LO 1, 2, 5), AP** Vilas Company is considering a capital investment of $190,000 in additional productive facilities. The new machinery is expected to have a useful life of 5 years with no salvage value. Depreciation is by the straight-line method. During the life of the investment, annual net income and net annual cash flows are expected to be $12,000 and $50,000, respectively. Vilas has a 12% cost of capital rate, which is the required rate of return on the investment.

**Instructions**

(Round to two decimals.)

a. Compute (1) the cash payback period and (2) the annual rate of return on the proposed capital expenditure.

b. Using the discounted cash flow technique, compute the net present value.

*Calculate payback, annual rate of return, and net present value.*

**E25.11 (LO 1, 2, 5), AP** Drake Corporation is reviewing an investment proposal. The initial cost is $105,000. Estimates of the book value of the investment at the end of each year, the net cash flows for each year, and the net income for each year are presented in the following schedule. All cash flows are assumed to take place at the end of the year. The salvage value of the investment at the end of each year is assumed to equal its book value. There would be no salvage value at the end of the investment's life.

| | | Investment Proposal | |
| | | | |
| Year | Book Value | Annual Cash Flows | Annual Net Income |
| --- | --- | --- | --- |
| 1 | $70,000 | $45,000 | $10,000 |
| 2 | 42,000 | 40,000 | 12,000 |
| 3 | 21,000 | 35,000 | 14,000 |
| 4 | 7,000 | 30,000 | 16,000 |
| 5 | 0 | 25,000 | 18,000 |

Drake Corporation uses an 11% target rate of return for new investment proposals.

**Instructions**

a. What is the cash payback period for this proposal?

b. What is the annual rate of return for the investment?

c. What is the net present value of the investment?

(CMA-Canada adapted)

# Problems

*Compute annual rate of return, cash payback, and net present value.*

**P25.1 (LO 1, 2, 5), AN** U3 Company is considering three long-term capital investment proposals. Each investment has a useful life of 5 years. Relevant data on each project are as follows.

| | Project Bono | Project Edge | Project Clayton |
| --- | --- | --- | --- |
| Capital investment | $160,000 | $175,000 | $200,000 |
| Annual net income: | | | |
| Year 1 | 14,000 | 18,000 | 27,000 |
| 2 | 14,000 | 17,000 | 23,000 |
| 3 | 14,000 | 16,000 | 21,000 |
| 4 | 14,000 | 12,000 | 13,000 |
| 5 | 14,000 | 9,000 | 12,000 |
| Total | $ 70,000 | $ 72,000 | $ 96,000 |

Depreciation is computed by the straight-line method with no salvage value. The company's cost of capital is 15%. (Assume that cash flows occur evenly throughout the year.)

**Instructions**

a. Compute the cash payback period for each project. (Round to two decimals.)

b. E $(7,312); C $2,163    b. Compute the net present value for each project. (Round to nearest dollar.)

c. Compute the annual rate of return for each project. (Round to two decimals.) (*Hint:* Use average annual net income in your computation.)

d. Rank the projects on each of the foregoing bases. Which project do you recommend?

**P25.2 (LO 1, 2, 5), AN** `Service` `Writing` Lon Timur is an accounting major at a midwestern state university located approximately 60 miles from a major city. Many of the students attending the university are from the metropolitan area and visit their homes regularly on the weekends. Lon, an entrepreneur at heart, realizes that few good commuting alternatives are available for students doing weekend travel. He believes that a weekend commuting service could be organized and run profitably from several suburban and downtown shopping mall locations. Lon has gathered the following investment information.

*Compute annual rate of return, cash payback, and net present value.*

1. Five used vans would cost a total of $75,000 to purchase and would have a 3-year useful life with negligible salvage value. Lon plans to use straight-line depreciation.

2. Ten drivers would have to be employed at a total payroll expense of $48,000.

3. Other annual out-of-pocket expenses associated with running the commuter service would include gasoline $16,000, maintenance $3,300, repairs $4,000, insurance $4,200, and advertising $2,500.

4. Lon has visited several financial institutions to discuss funding. The best interest rate he has been able to negotiate is 15%. Use this rate for cost of capital.

5. Lon expects each van to make 10 round trips weekly and carry an average of 6 students each trip. The service is expected to operate 30 weeks each year, and each student will be charged $12.00 for a round-trip ticket.

**Instructions**

a. Determine the annual (1) net income and (2) net annual cash flows for the commuter service.

b. Compute (1) the cash payback period and (2) the annual rate of return. (Round to two decimals.)

c. Compute the net present value of the commuter service. (Round to the nearest dollar.)

d. What should Lon conclude from these computations?

a. (1) $5,000

b. (1) 2.5 years

**P25.3 (LO 2, 3, 4), AN** `Service` Brooks Clinic is considering investing in new heart-monitoring equipment. It has two options. Option A would have an initial lower cost but would require a significant expenditure for rebuilding after 4 years. Option B would require no rebuilding expenditure, but its maintenance costs would be higher. Since the Option B machine is of initial higher quality, it is expected to have a salvage value at the end of its useful life. The following estimates were made of the cash flows. The company's cost of capital is 8%.

*Compute net present value, profitability index, and internal rate of return.*

|  | Option A | Option B |
|---|---|---|
| Initial cost | $160,000 | $227,000 |
| Annual cash inflows | $71,000 | $80,000 |
| Annual cash outflows | $30,000 | $31,000 |
| Cost to rebuild (end of year 4) | $50,000 | $0 |
| Salvage value | $0 | $8,000 |
| Estimated useful life | 7 years | 7 years |

**Instructions**

a. Compute the (1) net present value, (2) profitability index, and (3) internal rate of return for each option. (*Hint:* To solve for internal rate of return, experiment with alternative discount rates to arrive at a net present value of zero.)

b. Which option should be accepted?

a. (1) NPV A $16,709

  (3) IRR B 12%

**P25.4 (LO 2, 3), E** `Service` Jane's Auto Care is considering the purchase of a new tow truck. The garage doesn't currently have a tow truck, and the $60,000 price tag for a new truck would represent a major expenditure. Jane Austen, owner of the garage, has compiled the following estimates in trying to determine whether the tow truck should be purchased.

*Compute net present value considering intangible benefits.*

| | |
|---|---|
| Initial cost | $60,000 |
| Estimated useful life | 8 years |
| Net annual cash flows from towing | $8,000 |
| Overhaul costs (end of year 4) | $6,000 |
| Salvage value | $12,000 |

Jane's good friend, Rick Ryan, stopped by. He is trying to convince Jane that the tow truck will have other benefits that Jane hasn't even considered. First, he says, cars that need towing need to be fixed. Thus, when Jane tows them to her facility, her repair revenues will increase. Second, he notes that the tow truck could have a plow mounted on it, thus saving Jane the cost of plowing her parking lot. (Rick will give her a used plow blade for free if Jane will plow Rick's driveway.) Third, he notes that the truck will generate goodwill; people who are rescued by Jane's tow truck will feel grateful and might be more inclined to use her service station in the future or buy gas there. Fourth, the tow truck will have "Jane's Auto Care" on its doors, hood, and back tailgate—a form of free advertising wherever the tow truck goes. Rick estimates that, at a minimum, these benefits would be worth the following.

| | |
|---|---|
| Additional annual net cash flows from repair work | $3,000 |
| Annual savings from plowing | 750 |
| Additional annual net cash flows from customer "goodwill" | 1,000 |
| Additional annual net cash flows resulting from free advertising | 750 |

The company's cost of capital is 9%.

**Instructions**

a. NPV $(13,950)

**a.** Calculate the net present value, ignoring the additional benefits described by Rick. Should the tow truck be purchased?

b. NPV $16,491

**b.** Calculate the net present value, incorporating the additional benefits suggested by Rick. Should the tow truck be purchased?

**c.** Suppose Rick has been overly optimistic in his assessment of the value of the additional benefits. At a minimum, how much would the additional benefits have to be worth in order for the project to be accepted?

*Compute net present value and internal rate of return with sensitivity analysis.*

**P25.5 (LO 2, 3, 4), E** **Service** Coolplay Corp. is thinking about opening a soccer camp in southern California. To start the camp, Coolplay would need to purchase land and build four soccer fields and a sleeping and dining facility to house 150 soccer players. Each year, the camp would be run for 8 sessions of 1 week each. The company would hire college soccer players as coaches. The camp attendees would be male and female soccer players ages 12–18. Property values in southern California have enjoyed a steady increase in value. It is expected that after using the facility for 20 years, Coolplay can sell the property for more than it was originally purchased for. The following amounts have been estimated.

| | |
|---|---|
| Cost of land | $300,000 |
| Cost to build soccer fields, dorm, and dining facility | $600,000 |
| Annual cash inflows assuming 150 players and 8 weeks | $920,000 |
| Annual cash outflows | $840,000 |
| Estimated useful life | 20 years |
| Salvage value | $1,500,000 |
| Discount rate | 8% |

**Instructions**

a. NPV $207,277

**a.** Calculate the net present value of the project.

**b.** To gauge the sensitivity of the project to these estimates, assume that if only 125 players attend each week, annual cash inflows will be $805,000 and annual cash outflows will be $750,000. What is the net present value using these alternative estimates? Discuss your findings.

**c.** Assuming the original facts, what is the net present value if the project is actually riskier than first assumed and a 10% discount rate is more appropriate?

d. IRR 12%

**d.** Assume that during the first 5 years, the annual net cash flows each year were only $40,000. At the end of the fifth year, the company is running low on cash, so management decides to sell the property for $1,332,000. What was the actual internal rate of return on the project? Explain how this return was possible given that the camp did not appear to be successful.

# Continuing Cases

## Current Designs

**CD25** A company that manufactures recreational pedal boats has approached Mike Cichanowski to ask if he would be interested in using **Current Designs'** rotomold expertise and equipment to produce some of the pedal boat components. Mike is intrigued by the idea and thinks it would be an interesting way of complementing the present product line.

One of Mike's hesitations about the proposal is that the pedal boats are a different shape than the kayaks that Current Designs produces. As a result, the company would need to buy an additional roto-mold oven in order to produce the pedal boat components. This project clearly involves risks, and Mike wants to make sure that the returns justify the risks. In this case, since this is a new venture, Mike thinks that a 15% discount rate is appropriate to use to evaluate the project.

As an intern at Current Designs, Mike has asked you to prepare an initial evaluation of this proposal. To aid in your analysis, he has provided the following information and assumptions.

1. The new rotomold oven will have a cost of $256,000, a salvage value of $0, and an 8-year useful life. Straight-line depreciation will be used.

2. The projected revenues, costs, and results for each of the 8 years of this project are as follows.

| | | |
|---|---:|---:|
| Sales | | $220,000 |
| Less: | | |
|    Manufacturing costs | $140,000 | |
|    Depreciation | 32,000 | |
|    Shipping and administrative costs | 22,000 | 194,000 |
| Income before income taxes | | 26,000 |
| Income tax expense | | 10,800 |
| Net income | | $ 15,200 |

### Instructions

a. Compute the annual rate of return. (Round to two decimal places.)

b. Compute the payback period. (Round to two decimal places.)

c. Compute the net present value using a discount rate of 9%. (Round to nearest dollar.) Should the proposal be accepted using this discount rate?

d. Compute the net present value using a discount rate of 15%. (Round to nearest dollar.) Should the proposal be accepted using this discount rate?

## Waterways Corporation

(*Note:* This is a continuation of the Waterways case from Chapters 14–24.)

**WC25** Waterways Corporation puts much emphasis on cash flow when it plans for capital investments. The company chose its discount rate of 8% based on the rate of return it must pay its owners and creditors. Using that rate. Waterways then uses different methods to determine the best decisions for making capital outlays. Waterways is considering buying five new backhoes to replace the backhoes it now has. This case asks you to evaluate that decision, using various capital budgeting techniques.

*Go to WileyPLUS for complete case details and instructions.*

## Comprehensive Cases

**CC25.1** For this case, revisit the Greetings Inc. company presented in earlier chapters. The company is now searching for new opportunities for growth. This case will provide you with the opportunity to evaluate a proposal based on initial estimates as well as conduct sensitivity analysis. It also requires evaluation of the underlying assumptions used in the analysis.

**CC25.2** Armstrong Helmet Company needs to determine the cost for a given product. For this case, you will have the opportunity to explore cost-volume-profit relationships and prepare a set of budgets.

*Go to WileyPLUS for details and instructions for both cases.*

## Data Analytics in Action

### Using Data Visualization for Capital Budgeting Decisions

**DA25.1** Data visualization can be used to help analyze investment decisions.

**Example:** Recall the *People, Planet, and Profit Insight* box "Big Spenders" presented in the chapter. However, not all upgrades to clean energy need to be quite so large. For example, consider the following chart, which shows an investment in solar panels for a factory in Australia. The chart shows that the company will recover its solar-panel investment during 2025, during the investment's sixth year of its expected 16-year life. With an estimate of $0.12 per kilowatt hour, the annual savings will be around $6,500.

For this case, you will create line charts to analyze the present value of the solar-panel investment at different rates of return. You will also consider what other sensitivity analyses might be used with the data provided.

*Go to WileyPLUS for complete case details and instructions.*

### Data Analytics at HydroHappy

**DA25.2** HydroHappy's management believes the net present value (NPV) method provides the best information to make capital budgeting decisions. NPV analysis indicates that purchasing new forklifts will result in a higher return than retaining and overhauling the old forklifts. For this case, you will create and analyze clustered column and bar charts that will help management easily visualize which new forklift model will provide the best option for the company.

*Go to WileyPLUS for complete case details and instructions.*

## Expand Your Critical Thinking

### Decision-Making Across the Organization

**CT25.1** Luang Company is considering the purchase of a new machine. Its invoice price is $122,000, freight charges are estimated to be $3,000, and installation costs are expected to be $5,000. Salvage value of the new machine is expected to be zero after a useful life of 4 years. Existing equipment could be retained and used for an additional 4 years if the new machine is not purchased. At that time, the salvage value of the equipment would be zero. If the new machine is purchased now, the existing machine would be scrapped. Luang's accountant, Lisa Hsung, has accumulated the following data regarding annual sales and expenses with and without the new machine.

1. Without the new machine, Luang can sell 10,000 units of product annually at a per unit selling price of $100. If the new unit is purchased, the number of units produced and sold would increase by 25%, and the selling price would remain the same.

2. The new machine is faster than the old machine, and it is more efficient in its usage of materials. With the old machine, the gross profit rate will be 28.5% of sales, whereas the rate will be 30% of sales with the new machine. (*Note*: These gross profit rates do not include depreciation on the machines. For purposes of determining net income, treat depreciation expense as a separate line item.)

3. Annual selling expenses are $160,000 with the current equipment. Because the new equipment would produce a greater number of units to be sold, annual selling expenses are expected to increase by 10% if it is purchased.

4. Annual administrative expenses are expected to be $100,000 with the old machine, and $112,000 with the new machine.

5. The current book value of the existing machine is $40,000. Luang uses straight-line depreciation.

6. Luang's management has a required rate of return of 15% on its investment and a cash payback period of no more than 3 years.

### Instructions

With the class divided into groups, answer the following. (Ignore income tax effects.)

a. Calculate the annual rate of return for the new machine. (Round to two decimals.)

b. Compute the cash payback period for the new machine. (Round to two decimals.)

c. Compute the net present value of the new machine. (Round to the nearest dollar.)

d. On the basis of the foregoing data, would you recommend that Luang buy the machine? Why or why not?

## Managerial Analysis

**CT25.2** Hawke Skateboards is considering building a new factory. Bob Skerritt, the company's marketing manager, is an enthusiastic supporter of the new factory. Lucy Liu, the company's chief financial officer, is not so sure that the factory is a good idea. Currently, the company purchases its skateboards from foreign manufacturers. The following figures were estimated regarding the construction of a new factory.

| | | | |
|---|---|---|---|
| Cost of factory | $4,000,000 | Estimated useful life | 15 years |
| Annual cash inflows | 4,000,000 | Salvage value | $2,000,000 |
| Annual cash outflows | 3,540,000 | Discount rate | 11% |

Bob Skerritt believes that these figures understate the true potential value of the factory. He suggests that by manufacturing its own skateboards the company will benefit from a "buy American" patriotism that he believes is common among skateboarders. He also notes that the firm has had numerous quality problems with the skateboards manufactured by its suppliers. He suggests that the inconsistent quality has resulted in lost sales, increased warranty claims, and some costly lawsuits. Overall, he believes sales will be $200,000 higher than projected above, and that the savings from lower warranty costs and legal costs will be $60,000 per year. He also believes that the project is not as risky as assumed above, and that a 9% discount rate is more reasonable.

### Instructions

Complete the following.

a. Compute the net present value of the project based on the original projections.

b. Compute the net present value incorporating Bob's estimates of the value of the intangible benefits but still using the 11% discount rate.

c. Compute the net present value using the original estimates, but employing the 9% discount rate that Bob suggests is more appropriate.

d. Comment on your findings.

## Real-World Focus

**CT25.3 Tecumseh Products Company** has its headquarters in Ann Arbor, Michigan. It describes itself as "a global multinational corporation producing mechanical and electrical components essential to industries creating end-products for health, comfort, and convenience." The following was excerpted from the management discussion and analysis section of a recent annual report.

---

### Tecumseh Products Company
#### Management Discussion and Analysis

The company has invested approximately $50 million in a scroll compressor manufacturing facility in Tecumseh, Michigan. After experiencing setbacks in developing a commercially acceptable scroll compressor, the Company is currently testing a new generation of scroll product. The Company is unable to predict when, or if, it will offer a scroll compressor for commercial sale, but it does anticipate that reaching volume production will require a significant additional investment. Given such additional investment and current market conditions, management is currently reviewing its options with respect to scroll product improvement, cost reductions, joint ventures and alternative new products.

---

### Instructions

Discuss issues the company should consider and techniques the company should employ to determine whether to continue pursuing this project.

**CT25.4 Campbell Soup Company** is an international provider of soup products. Management is very interested in continuing to grow the company in its core business, while "spinning off" those businesses that are not part of its core operation.

### Instructions

Go to the home page of Campbell Soup Company and access its current annual report. Review the financial statements and management's discussion and analysis, and answer the following questions.

**a.** What was the total amount of capital expenditures in the current year, and how does this amount compare with the previous year? In your response, note what year you are using.

**b.** What interest rate did the company pay on new borrowings in the current year?

**c.** Assume that this year's capital expenditures are expected to increase cash flows by $60 million. What is the expected internal rate of return (IRR) for these capital expenditures? (Assume a 10-year period for the cash flows.)

## Communication Activity

**CT25.5** Refer to E25.9 to address the following.

### Instructions

Prepare a memo to Maria Fierro, your supervisor. Show your calculations from E25.9 (a) and (b). In one or two paragraphs, discuss important nonfinancial considerations. Make any assumptions you believe to be necessary. Make a recommendation based on your analysis.

## Ethics Case

**CT25.6** NuComp Company operates in a state where corporate taxes and workers' compensation insurance rates have recently doubled. NuComp's president has just assigned you the task of preparing an economic analysis and making a recommendation relative to moving the entire operation to Missouri. The president is slightly in favor of such a move because Missouri is his boyhood home and he also owns a fishing lodge there.

You have just completed building your dream house, moved in, and sodded the lawn. Your children are all doing well in school and sports and, along with your spouse, want no part of a move to Missouri. If the company does move, so will you because the town is a one-industry community and you and your spouse will have to move to have employment. Moving when everyone else does will cause you to take a big loss on the sale of your house. The same hardships will be suffered by your coworkers, and the town will be devastated.

In compiling the costs of moving versus not moving, you have latitude in the assumptions you make, the estimates you compute, and the discount rates and time periods you project. You are in a position to influence the decision singlehandedly.

**Instructions**

   **a.** Who are the stakeholders in this situation?

   **b.** What are the ethical issues in this situation?

   **c.** What would you do in this situation?

## All About You

**CT25.7** Numerous articles have been written that identify early warning signs that you might be getting into trouble with your personal debt load. You can find many good articles on this topic on the Web.

**Instructions**

Find an article that identifies early warning signs of personal debt trouble. Write a summary of the article and bring your summary and the article to class to share.

## Considering Your Costs and Benefits

**CT25.8** The March 31, 2011, edition of the *Wall Street Journal* includes an article by Russell Gold entitled "Solar Gains Traction—Thanks to Subsidies."

**Instructions**

Read the article and then answer the following questions.

   **a.** What was the total cost of the solar panels installed? What was the "out-of-pocket" cost to the couple?

   **b.** Using the total annual electricity bill of $5,000 mentioned in the story, what is the cash payback of the project using the total cost? What is the cash payback based on the "out-of-pocket" cost?

   **c.** Solar panel manufacturers estimate that solar panels can last up to 40 years with only minor maintenance costs. Assuming no maintenance costs, a 6% rate of interest, a more conservative 20-year life, and zero salvage value, what is the net present value of the project based on the total cost? What is the net present value of the project based on the "out-of-pocket" cost?

   **d.** What was the wholesale price of panels per watt at the time the article was written? At what price per watt does the article say that subsidies will no longer be needed? Does this price appear to be achievable?

## Answers to Insight and Accounting Across the Organization Questions

**Can You Hear Me—Better?  Q:** Why is the capital investment in 5G technology particularly risky for telecom carriers? **A:** The investment in 5G technology by telecom carriers is risky for a few reasons. First, it is a huge investment in new technology. Large investments are inherently uncertain, but 5G is particularly risky because companies must choose which airwave spectrum to operate in. Choosing the highest frequency, which provides the fastest data transmission, will also require significant additional investments in new towers. Choosing the lower frequency will require less investment but will not provide much improvement in service, making it less desirable to consumers. A big risk factor is that it is unclear that consumers will be willing to pay the extra money that the carriers need to make their investments pay off.

**It Need Not Cost an Arm and a Leg  Q:** In addition to the obvious humanitarian benefit of reducing serious injuries, how else might the manufacturer of this product convince potential customers of its worth? **A:** Serious injuries cost employers huge sums, which can sometimes force small companies out of business. In addition to the obvious humanitarian benefit, the manufacturer can demonstrate that this device is a sound financial investment in terms of reduced healthcare and workers' compensation costs, and fewer hours missed due to injury. Also, employers that do not have the device may ultimately be found negligent with regard to worker safety.

**Big Spenders  Q:** How does the financing of today's big energy investments differ from big energy capital investments of the past, and what are the implications? **A:** In the past, regulated utility companies made big investments in power plants and transmission lines. In exchange for being regulated, utilities companies are allowed to pass on their costs to consumers, plus an agreed-upon return on their investments. Many of today's big energy investments are being made by private investors. They sell their energy in open markets at whatever the market price is, based on supply and demand. This provides for a higher possible upside on their investment returns but also increases the uncertainty of the investments.

**Increasing the Chances of Gaming Wins  Q:** In what ways do the capital investments of Electronic Arts benefit from data analytics?  **A:** Electronic Arts spends up to $500 million on the development of a new video game. If this game is not popular, the money is wasted. To reduce this risk, the company collects large amounts of data that are generated by online-game players. This informs the company of which features of a game are the most popular with players. Electronic Arts then uses this information to develop and market its new games.

# Specimen Financial Statements: Apple Inc.

Once each year, a corporation communicates to its stockholders and other interested parties by issuing a complete set of audited financial statements. The **annual report**, as this communication is called, summarizes the financial results of the company's operations for the year and its plans for the future. Many annual reports are attractive, multicolored, glossy public relations pieces, containing pictures of corporate officers and directors as well as photos and descriptions of new products and new buildings. Yet the basic function of every annual report is to report financial information, almost all of which is a product of the corporation's accounting system.

The content and organization of corporate annual reports have become fairly standardized. Excluding the public relations part of the report (pictures, products, etc.), the following are the traditional financial portions of the annual report:

- Financial Highlights
- Letter to the Stockholders
- Management's Discussion and Analysis
- Financial Statements
- Notes to the Financial Statements

- Management's Responsibility for Financial Reporting
- Management's Report on Internal Control over Financial Reporting
- Report of Independent Registered Public Accounting Firm
- Selected Financial Data

The official SEC filing of the annual report is called a **Form 10-K**, which often omits the public relations pieces found in most standard annual reports. On the following pages, we present **Apple Inc.**'s financial statements taken from the company's 2018 Form 10-K. The complete Form 10-K, including notes to the financial statements, is available at the company's website.

**Apple Inc.**
**Consolidated Statements of Operations**
**(in millions, except number of shares which are reflected in thousands and per share amounts)**

|  | Years ended | | |
|---|---|---|---|
|  | September 29, 2018 | September 30, 2017 | September 24, 2016 |
| Net sales | $ 265,595 | $ 229,234 | $ 215,639 |
| Cost of sales | 163,756 | 141,048 | 131,376 |
| Gross margin | 101,839 | 88,186 | 84,263 |
|  |  |  |  |
| Operating expenses: |  |  |  |
| Research and development | 14,236 | 11,581 | 10,045 |
| Selling, general and administrative | 16,705 | 15,261 | 14,194 |
| Total operating expenses | 30,941 | 26,842 | 24,239 |
|  |  |  |  |
| Operating income | 70,898 | 61,344 | 60,024 |
| Other income/(expense), net | 2,005 | 2,745 | 1,348 |
| Income before provision for income taxes | 72,903 | 64,089 | 61,372 |
| Provision for income taxes | 13,372 | 15,738 | 15,685 |
| Net income | $ 59,531 | $ 48,351 | $ 45,687 |
|  |  |  |  |
| Earnings per share: |  |  |  |
| Basic | $ 12.01 | $ 9.27 | $ 8.35 |
| Diluted | $ 11.91 | $ 9.21 | $ 8.31 |
|  |  |  |  |
| Shares used in computing earnings per share: |  |  |  |
| Basic | 4,955,377 | 5,217,242 | 5,470,820 |
| Diluted | 5,000,109 | 5,251,692 | 5,500,281 |

See accompanying Notes to Consolidated Financial Statements.

**Apple Inc.**
**Consolidated Statements of Comprehensive Income**
**(in millions)**

| | Years ended | | |
| --- | --- | --- | --- |
| | September 29, 2018 | September 30, 2017 | September 24, 2016 |
| Net income | $59,531 | $48,351 | $45,687 |
| Other comprehensive income/(loss): | | | |
| Change in foreign currency translation, net of tax effects of $(1), $(77) and $8, respectively | (525) | 224 | 75 |
| Change in unrealized gains/losses on derivative instruments: | | | |
| Change in fair value of derivatives, net of tax benefit/(expense) of $(149), $(478) and $(7), respectively | 523 | 1,315 | 7 |
| Adjustment for net (gains)/losses realized and included in net income, net of tax expense/(benefit) of $(104), $475 and $131, respectively | 382 | (1,477) | (741) |
| Total change in unrealized gains/losses on derivative instruments, net of tax | 905 | (162) | (734) |
| Change in unrealized gains/losses on marketable securities: | | | |
| Change in fair value of marketable securities, net of tax benefit/ (expense) of $1,156, $425 and $(863), respectively | (3,407) | (782) | 1,582 |
| Adjustment for net (gains)/losses realized and included in net income, net of tax expense/(benefit) of $21, $35 and $(31), respectively | 1 | (64) | 56 |
| Total change in unrealized gains/losses on marketable securities, net of tax | (3,406) | (846) | 1,638 |
| Total other comprehensive income/(loss) | (3,026) | (784) | 979 |
| Total comprehensive income | $56,505 | $47,567 | $46,666 |

See accompanying Notes to Consolidated Financial Statements.

**Apple Inc.**
**Consolidated Balance Sheets**
**(in millions, except number of shares which are reflected in thousands and par value)**

| | September 29, 2018 | September 30, 2017 |
|---|---|---|
| **ASSETS:** | | |
| Current assets: | | |
| Cash and cash equivalents | $ 25,913 | $ 20,289 |
| Marketable securities | 40,388 | 53,892 |
| Accounts receivable, net | 23,186 | 17,874 |
| Inventories | 3,956 | 4,855 |
| Vendor non-trade receivables | 25,809 | 17,799 |
| Other current assets | 12,087 | 13,936 |
| Total current assets | 131,339 | 128,645 |
| | | |
| Non-current assets: | | |
| Marketable securities | 170,799 | 194,714 |
| Property, plant and equipment, net | 41,304 | 33,783 |
| Other non-current assets | 22,283 | 18,177 |
| Total non-current assets | 234,386 | 246,674 |
| Total assets | $365,725 | $375,319 |
| **LIABILITIES AND SHAREHOLDERS' EQUITY:** | | |
| Current liabilities: | | |
| Accounts payable | $ 55,888 | $ 44,242 |
| Other current liabilities | 32,687 | 30,551 |
| Deferred revenue | 7,543 | 7,548 |
| Commercial paper | 11,964 | 11,977 |
| Term debt | 8,784 | 6,496 |
| Total current liabilities | 116,866 | 100,814 |
| | | |
| Non-current liabilities: | | |
| Deferred revenue | 2,797 | 2,836 |
| Term debt | 93,735 | 97,207 |
| Other non-current liabilities | 45,180 | 40,415 |
| Total non-current liabilities | 141,712 | 140,458 |
| Total liabilities | 258,578 | 241,272 |
| | | |
| Commitments and contingencies | | |
| | | |
| Shareholders' equity: | | |
| Common stock and additional paid-in capital, $0.00001 par value: 12,600,000 shares authorized; 4,754,986 and 5,126,201 shares issued and outstanding, respectively | 40,201 | 35,867 |
| Retained earnings | 70,400 | 98,330 |
| Accumulated other comprehensive income/(loss) | (3,454) | (150) |
| Total shareholders' equity | 107,147 | 134,047 |
| Total liabilities and shareholders' equity | $365,725 | $375,319 |

See accompanying Notes to Consolidated Financial Statements.

**Apple Inc.**
**Consolidated Statements of Shareholders' Equity**
**(in millions, except number of shares which are reflected in thousands and per share amounts)**

| | Common Stock and Additional Paid-In Capital | | Retained Earnings | Accumulated Other Comprehensive Income/(Loss) | Total Shareholders' Equity |
|---|---|---|---|---|---|
| | Shares | Amount | | | |
| Balances as of September 26, 2015 | 5,578,753 | $27,416 | $92,284 | $ (345) | $119,355 |
| Net income | — | — | 45,687 | — | 45,687 |
| Other comprehensive income/(loss) | — | — | — | 979 | 979 |
| Dividends and dividend equivalents declared at $2.18 per share or RSU | — | — | (12,188) | — | (12,188) |
| Repurchase of common stock | (279,609) | — | (29,000) | — | (29,000) |
| Share-based compensation | — | 4,262 | — | — | 4,262 |
| Common stock issued, net of shares withheld for employee taxes | 37,022 | (806) | (419) | — | (1,225) |
| Tax benefit from equity awards, including transfer pricing adjustments | — | 379 | — | — | 379 |
| Balances as of September 24, 2016 | 5,336,166 | 31,251 | 96,364 | 634 | 128,249 |
| Net income | — | — | 48,351 | — | 48,351 |
| Other comprehensive income/(loss) | — | — | — | (784) | (784) |
| Dividends and dividend equivalents declared at $2.40 per share or RSU | — | — | (12,803) | — | (12,803) |
| Repurchase of common stock | (246,496) | — | (33,001) | — | (33,001) |
| Share-based compensation | — | 4,909 | — | — | 4,909 |
| Common stock issued, net of shares withheld for employee taxes | 36,531 | (913) | (581) | — | (1,494) |
| Tax benefit from equity awards, including transfer pricing adjustments | — | 620 | — | — | 620 |
| Balances as of September 30, 2017 | 5,126,201 | 35,867 | 98,330 | (150) | 134,047 |
| Cumulative effect of change in accounting principle | — | — | 278 | (278) | — |
| Net income | — | — | 59,531 | — | 59,531 |
| Other comprehensive income/(loss) | — | — | — | (3,026) | (3,026) |
| Dividends and dividend equivalents declared at $2.72 per share or RSU | — | — | (13,735) | — | (13,735) |
| Repurchase of common stock | (405,549) | — | (73,056) | — | (73,056) |
| Share-based compensation | — | 5,443 | — | — | 5,443 |
| Common stock issued, net of shares withheld for employee taxes | 34,334 | (1,109) | (948) | — | (2,057) |
| Balances as of September 29, 2018 | 4,754,986 | $40,201 | $70,400 | $(3,454) | $107,147 |

See accompanying Notes to Consolidated Financial Statements.

**Apple Inc.**
**Consolidated Statements of Cash Flows**
**(in millions)**

| | Years ended | | |
|---|---|---|---|
| | September 29, 2018 | September 30, 2017 | September 24, 2016 |
| Cash and cash equivalents, beginning of the year | $20,289 | $20,484 | $21,120 |
| Operating activities: | | | |
| Net income | 59,531 | 48,351 | 45,687 |
| Adjustments to reconcile net income to cash generated by operating activities: | | | |
| Depreciation and amortization | 10,903 | 10,157 | 10,505 |
| Share-based compensation expense | 5,340 | 4,840 | 4,210 |
| Deferred income tax expense/(benefit) | (32,590) | 5,966 | 4,938 |
| Other | (444) | (166) | 486 |
| Changes in operating assets and liabilities: | | | |
| Accounts receivable, net | (5,322) | (2,093) | 527 |
| Inventories | 828 | (2,723) | 217 |
| Vendor non-trade receivables | (8,010) | (4,254) | (51) |
| Other current and non-current assets | (423) | (5,318) | 1,055 |
| Accounts payable | 9,175 | 8,966 | 2,117 |
| Deferred revenue | (44) | (626) | (1,554) |
| Other current and non-current liabilities | 38,490 | 1,125 | (1,906) |
| Cash generated by operating activities | 77,434 | 64,225 | 66,231 |
| Investing activities: | | | |
| Purchases of marketable securities | (71,356) | (159,486) | (142,428) |
| Proceeds from maturities of marketable securities | 55,881 | 31,775 | 21,258 |
| Proceeds from sales of marketable securities | 47,838 | 94,564 | 90,536 |
| Payments for acquisition of property, plant and equipment | (13,313) | (12,451) | (12,734) |
| Payments made in connection with business acquisitions, net | (721) | (329) | (297) |
| Purchases of non-marketable securities | (1,871) | (521) | (1,388) |
| Proceeds from non-marketable securities | 353 | 126 | — |
| Other | (745) | (124) | (924) |
| Cash generated by/(used in) investing activities | 16,066 | (46,446) | (45,977) |
| Financing activities: | | | |
| Proceeds from issuance of common stock | 669 | 555 | 495 |
| Payments for taxes related to net share settlement of equity awards | (2,527) | (1,874) | (1,570) |
| Payments for dividends and dividend equivalents | (13,712) | (12,769) | (12,150) |
| Repurchases of common stock | (72,738) | (32,900) | (29,722) |
| Proceeds from issuance of term debt, net | 6,969 | 28,662 | 24,954 |
| Repayments of term debt | (6,500) | (3,500) | (2,500) |
| Change in commercial paper, net | (37) | 3,852 | (397) |
| Cash used in financing activities | (87,876) | (17,974) | (20,890) |
| Increase/(Decrease) in cash and cash equivalents | 5,624 | (195) | (636) |
| Cash and cash equivalents, end of the year | $25,913 | $20,289 | $20,484 |
| Supplemental cash flow disclosure: | | | |
| Cash paid for income taxes, net | $10,417 | $11,591 | $10,444 |
| Cash paid for interest | $ 3,022 | $ 2,092 | $ 1,316 |

See accompanying Notes to Consolidated Financial Statements.

# Appendix B

# Specimen Financial Statements: PepsiCo, Inc.

**PepsiCo, Inc.** is a world leader in convenient snacks, foods, and beverages. The following are PepsiCo's financial statements as presented in its 2018 annual report. The complete annual report, including notes to the financial statements, is available at the company's website.

**Consolidated Statement of Income**
**PepsiCo, Inc. and Subsidiaries**
**Fiscal years ended December 29, 2018, December 30, 2017 and December 31, 2016**
**(in millions except per share amounts)**

|  | 2018 | 2017 | 2016 |
|---|---|---|---|
| **Net Revenue** | $64,661 | $63,525 | $62,799 |
| Cost of sales | 29,381 | 28,796 | 28,222 |
| Gross profit | 35,280 | 34,729 | 34,577 |
| Selling, general and administrative expenses | 25,170 | 24,453 | 24,773 |
| **Operating Profit** | 10,110 | 10,276 | 9,804 |
| Other pension and retiree medical benefits income/(expense) | 298 | 233 | (19) |
| Interest expense | (1,525) | (1,151) | (1,342) |
| Interest income and other | 306 | 244 | 110 |
| Income before income taxes | 9,189 | 9,602 | 8,553 |
| (Benefit from)/provision for income taxes (See Note 5) | (3,370) | 4,694 | 2,174 |
| Net income | 12,559 | 4,908 | 6,379 |
| Less: Net income attributable to noncontrolling interests | 44 | 51 | 50 |
| **Net Income Attributable to PepsiCo** | $12,515 | S 4,857 | $ 6,329 |
| **Net Income Attributable to PepsiCo per Common Share** | | | |
| Basic | $ 8.84 | $ 3.40 | $ 4.39 |
| Diluted | $ 8.78 | $ 3.38 | $ 4.36 |
| Weighted-average common shares outstanding | | | |
| Basic | 1,415 | 1,425 | 1,439 |
| Diluted | 1,425 | 1,438 | 1,452 |

See accompanying notes to the consolidated financial statements.

**Consolidated Statement of Comprehensive Income**
**PepsiCo, Inc. and Subsidiaries**
**Fiscal years ended December 29, 2018, December 30, 2017 and December 31, 2016**
**(in millions)**

|  | 2018 | 2017 | 2016 |
|---|---|---|---|
| Net income | $12,559 | $4,908 | $6,379 |
| Other comprehensive income/(loss), net of taxes: |  |  |  |
| Net currency translation adjustment | (1,641) | 1,109 | (302) |
| Net change on cash flow hedges | 40 | (36) | 46 |
| Net pension and retiree medical adjustments | (467) | (159) | (316) |
| Net change on available-for-sale securities | 6 | (68) | (24) |
| Other | — | 16 | — |
|  | (2,062) | 862 | (596) |
| Comprehensive income | 10,497 | 5,770 | 5,783 |
| Comprehensive income attributable to noncontrolling interests | (44) | (51) | (54) |
| **Comprehensive Income Attributable to PepsiCo** | $10,453 | $5,719 | $5,729 |

See accompanying notes to the consolidated financial statements.

**Consolidated Statement of Cash Flows**
**PepsiCo, Inc. and Subsidiaries**
**Fiscal years ended December 29, 2018, December 30, 2017 and December 31, 2016**
**(in millions)**

|  | 2018 | 2017 | 2016 |
|---|---|---|---|
| **Operating Activities** |  |  |  |
| Net income | $12,559 | $ 4,908 | $ 6,379 |
| Depreciation and amortization | 2,399 | 2,369 | 2,368 |
| Share-based compensation expense | 256 | 292 | 284 |
| Restructuring and impairment charges | 308 | 295 | 160 |
| Cash payments for restructuring charges | (255) | (113) | (125) |
| Charge related to the transaction with Tingyi | — | — | 373 |
| Pension and retiree medical plan expenses | 221 | 221 | 501 |
| Pension and retiree medical plan contributions | (1,708) | (220) | (695) |
| Deferred income taxes and other tax charges and credits | (531) | 619 | 452 |
| Other net tax benefits related to international reorganizations | (4,347) | — | — |
| Net tax (benefit)/expense related to the TCJ Act | (28) | 2,451 | — |
| Change in assets and liabilities: |  |  |  |
| Accounts and notes receivable | (253) | (202) | (349) |
| Inventories | (174) | (168) | (75) |
| Prepaid expenses and other current assets | 9 | 20 | 10 |
| Accounts payable and other current liabilities | 882 | 201 | 981 |
| Income taxes payable | 333 | (338) | 329 |
| Other, net | (256) | (305) | 70 |
| **Net Cash Provided by Operating Activities** | 9,415 | 10,030 | 10,663 |

(*continues*)

|  | 2018 | 2017 | 2016 |
|---|---|---|---|
| **Investing Activities** | | | |
| Capital spending | $ (3,282) | $(2,969) | $(3,040) |
| Sales of property, plant and equipment | 134 | 180 | 99 |
| Acquisition of SodaStream, net of cash and cash equivalents acquired | (1,197) | — | — |
| Other acquisitions and investments in noncontrolled affiliates | (299) | (61) | (212) |
| Divestitures | 505 | 267 | 85 |
| Short-term investments, by original maturity: | | | |
| More than three months - purchases | (5,637) | (18,385) | (12,504) |
| More than three months - maturities | 12,824 | 15,744 | 8,399 |
| More than three months - sales | 1,498 | 790 | — |
| Three months or less, net | 16 | 2 | 16 |
| Other investing, net | 2 | 29 | 7 |
| **Net Cash Provided by/(Used for) Investing Activities** | 4,564 | (4,403) | (7,150) |
| | | | |
| **Financing Activities** | | | |
| Proceeds from issuances of long-term debt | — | 7,509 | 7,818 |
| Payments of long-term debt | (4,007) | (4,406) | (3,105) |
| Cash tender and exchange offers/debt redemptions | (1,589) | — | (2,504) |
| Short-term borrowings, by original maturity: | | | |
| More than three months - proceeds | 3 | 91 | 59 |
| More than three months - payments | (17) | (128) | (27) |
| Three months or less, net | (1,352) | (1,016) | 1,505 |
| Cash dividends paid | (4,930) | (4,472) | (4,227) |
| Share repurchases - common | (2,000) | (2,000) | (3,000) |
| Share repurchases - preferred | (2) | (5) | (7) |
| Proceeds from exercises of stock options | 281 | 462 | 465 |
| Withholding tax payments on RSUs, PSUs and PEPunits converted | (103) | (145) | (130) |
| Other financing | (53) | (76) | (58) |
| **Net Cash Used for Financing Activities** | (13,769) | (4,186) | (3,211) |
| Effect of exchange rate changes on cash and cash equivalents and restricted cash | (98) | 47 | (252) |
| **Net Increase in Cash and Cash Equivalents and Restricted Cash** | 112 | 1,488 | 50 |
| **Cash and Cash Equivalents and Restricted Cash, Beginning of Year** | 10,657 | 9,169 | 9,119 |
| **Cash and Cash Equivalents and Restricted Cash, End of Year** | $10,769 | $10,657 | S 9,169 |

See accompanying notes to the consolidated financial statements.

## Consolidated Balance Sheet
### PepsiCo, Inc. and Subsidiaries
### December 29, 2018 and December 30, 2017
### (in millions except per share amounts)

| | 2018 | 2017 |
|---|---|---|
| **ASSETS** | | |
| **Current Assets** | | |
| Cash and cash equivalents | $ 8,721 | $10,610 |
| Short-term investments | 272 | 8,900 |
| Restricted cash | 1,997 | — |
| Accounts and notes receivable, net | 7,142 | 7,024 |
| Inventories | 3,128 | 2,947 |
| Prepaid expenses and other current assets | 633 | 1,546 |
| **Total Current Assets** | 21,893 | 31,027 |
| **Property, Plant and Equipment, net** | 17,589 | 17,240 |
| **Amortizable Intangible Assets, net** | 1,644 | 1,268 |
| Goodwill | 14,808 | 14,744 |
| Other indefinite-lived intangible assets | 14,181 | 12,570 |
| **Indefinite-Lived Intangible Assets** | 28,989 | 27,314 |
| **Investments in Noncontrolled Affiliates** | 2,409 | 2,042 |
| **Deferred Income Taxes** | 4,364 | — |
| **Other Assets** | 760 | 913 |
| **Total Assets** | $77,648 | $79,804 |
| | | |
| **LIABILITIES AND EQUITY** | | |
| **Current Liabilities** | | |
| Short-term debt obligations | $ 4,026 | $ 5,485 |
| Accounts payable and other current liabilities | 18,112 | 15,017 |
| **Total Current Liabilities** | 22,138 | 20,502 |
| **Long-Term Debt Obligations** | 28,295 | 33,796 |
| **Deferred Income Taxes** | 3,499 | 3,242 |
| **Other Liabilities** | 9,114 | 11,283 |
| **Total Liabilities** | 63,046 | 68,823 |
| Commitments and contingencies | | |
| **Preferred Stock, no par value** | — | 41 |
| **Repurchased Preferred Stock** | — | (197) |
| **PepsiCo Common Shareholders' Equity** | | |
| Common stock, par value 1⅔¢ per share (authorized 3,600 shares; issued, net of repurchased common stock at par value: 1,409 and 1,420 shares, respectively) | 23 | 24 |
| Capital in excess of par value | 3,953 | 3,996 |
| Retained earnings | 59,947 | 52,839 |
| Accumulated other comprehensive loss | (15,119) | (13,057) |
| Repurchased common stock, in excess of par value (458 and 446 shares, respectively) | (34,286) | (32,757) |
| **Total PepsiCo Common Shareholders' Equity** | 14,518 | 11,045 |
| Noncontrolling interests | 84 | 92 |
| **Total Equity** | 14,602 | 10,981 |
| **Total Liabilities and Equity** | $77,648 | $79,804 |

See accompanying notes to the consolidated financial statements.

**Consolidated Statement of Equity**
**PepsiCo, Inc. and Subsidiaries**
**Fiscal years ended December 29, 2018, December 30, 2017 and December 31, 2016**
**(in millions)**

| | 2018 Shares | 2018 Amount | 2017 Shares | 2017 Amount | 2016 Shares | 2016 Amount |
|---|---|---|---|---|---|---|
| **Preferred Stock** | | | | | | |
| Balance, beginning of year | 0.8 | $ 41 | 0.8 | $ 41 | 0.8 | $ 41 |
| Conversion to common stock | (0.1) | (6) | — | — | — | — |
| Retirement of preferred stock | (0.7) | (35) | — | — | — | — |
| Balance, end of year | — | — | 0.8 | 41 | 0.8 | 41 |
| **Repurchased Preferred Stock** | | | | | | |
| Balance, beginning of year | (0.7) | (197) | (0.7) | (192) | (0.7) | (186) |
| Redemptions | — | (2) | — | (5) | — | (6) |
| Retirement of preferred stock | 0.7 | 199 | — | — | — | — |
| Balance, end of year | — | — | (0.7) | (197) | (0.7) | (192) |
| **Common Stock** | | | | | | |
| Balance, beginning of year | 1,420 | 24 | 1,428 | 24 | 1,448 | 24 |
| Share issued in connection with preferred stock conversion to common stock | 1 | — | — | — | — | — |
| Change in repurchased common stock | (12) | (1) | (8) | — | (20) | — |
| Balance, end of year | 1,409 | 23 | 1,420 | 24 | 1,428 | 24 |
| **Capital in Excess of Par Value** | | | | | | |
| Balance, beginning of year | | 3,996 | | 4,091 | | 4,076 |
| Share-based compensation expense | | 250 | | 290 | | 289 |
| Equity issued in connection with preferred stock conversion to common stock | | 6 | | — | | — |
| Stock option exercises, RSUs, PSUs and PEPunits converted[a] | | (193) | | (236) | | (138) |
| Withholding tax on RSUs, PSUs and PEPunits converted | | (103) | | (145) | | (130) |
| Other | | (3) | | (4) | | (6) |
| Balance, end of year | | 3,953 | | 3,996 | | 4,091 |
| **Retained Earnings** | | | | | | |
| Balance, beginning of year | | 52,839 | | 52,518 | | 50,472 |
| Cumulative effect of accounting changes | | (145) | | — | | — |
| Net income attributable to PepsiCo | | 12,515 | | 4,857 | | 6,329 |
| Cash dividends declared - common[b] | | (5,098) | | (4,536) | | (4,282) |
| Cash dividends declared - preferred | | — | | — | | (1) |
| Retirement of preferred stock | | (164) | | — | | — |
| Balance, end of year | | 59,947 | | 52,839 | | 52,518 |
| **Accumulated Other Comprehensive Loss** | | | | | | |
| Balance, beginning of year | | (13,057) | | (13,919) | | (13,319) |
| Other comprehensive (loss)/income attributable to PepsiCo | | (2,062) | | 862 | | (600) |
| Balance, end of year | | (15,119) | | (13,057) | | (13,919) |

*(continues)*

|  | 2018 | | 2017 | | 2016 | |
| --- | --- | --- | --- | --- | --- | --- |
|  | **Shares** | **Amount** | Shares | Amount | Shares | Amount |
| **Repurchased Common Stock** | | | | | | |
| Balance, beginning of year | **(446)** | **$(32,757)** | (438) | $(31,468) | (418) | $(29,185) |
| Share repurchases | **(18)** | **(2,000)** | (18) | (2,000) | (29) | (3,000) |
| Stock option exercises, RSUs, PSUs and PEPunits converted | **6** | **469** | 10 | 708 | 9 | 712 |
| Other | **—** | **2** | — | 3 | — | 5 |
| Balance, end of year | **(458)** | **(34,286)** | (446) | (32,757) | (438) | (31,468) |
| **Total PepsiCo Common Shareholders' Equity** | | **14,518** | | 11,045 | | 11,246 |
| **Noncontrolling Interests** | | | | | | |
| Balance, beginning of year | | **92** | | 104 | | 107 |
| Net income attributable to noncontrolling interests | | **44** | | 51 | | 50 |
| Distributions to noncontrolling interests | | **(49)** | | (62) | | (55) |
| Currency translation adjustment: | | **—** | | — | | 4 |
| Other, net | | **(3)** | | (1) | | (2) |
| Balance, end of year | | **84** | | 92 | | 104 |
| **Total Equity** | | **$ 14,602** | | $ 10,981 | | $ 11,199 |

(a) Includes total tax benefits of $110 million in 2016.
(b) Cash dividends declared per common share were $3.5875, $3.1675 and $2.96 for 2018, 2017 and 2016, respectively.

See accompanying notes to the consolidated financial statements.

# Specimen Financial Statements:
# The Coca-Cola Company

**The Coca-Cola Company** is a global leader in the beverage industry. It offers hundreds of brands, including soft drinks, fruit juices, sports drinks, and other beverages, in more than 200 countries. The following are Coca-Cola's financial statements as presented in its 2018 annual report. The complete annual report, including notes to the financial statements, is available at the company's website.

**The Coca-Cola Company and Subsidiaries**
**Consolidated Statements of Income**

| Year Ended December 31,<br>(in millions except per share data) | 2018 | 2017 | 2016 |
|---|---|---|---|
| **NET OPERATING REVENUES** | **$31,856** | $35,410 | $41,863 |
| Cost of goods sold | **11,770** | 13,255 | 16,465 |
| **GROSS PROFIT** | **20,086** | 22,155 | 25,398 |
| Selling, general and administrative expenses | **10,307** | 12,654 | 15,370 |
| Other operating charges | **1,079** | 1,902 | 1,371 |
| **OPERATING INCOME** | **8,700** | 7,599 | 8,657 |
| Interest income | **682** | 677 | 642 |
| Interest expense | **919** | 841 | 733 |
| Equity income (loss)—net | **1,008** | 1,071 | 835 |
| Other income (loss)—net | **(1,121)** | (1,764) | (1,265) |
| **INCOME FROM CONTINUING OPERATIONS BEFORE INCOME TAXES** | **8,350** | 6,742 | 8,136 |
| Income taxes from continuing operations | **1,623** | 5,560 | 1,586 |
| **NET INCOME FROM CONTINUING OPERATIONS** | **6,727** | 1,182 | 6,550 |
| Income (loss) from discontinued operations (net of income taxes of $126, $47 and $0, respectively) | **(251)** | 101 | — |
| **CONSOLIDATED NET INCOME** | **6,476** | 1,283 | 6,550 |
| Less: Net income attributable to noncontrolling interests | **42** | 35 | 23 |
| **NET INCOME ATTRIBUTABLE TO SHAREOWNERS OF THE COCA-COLA COMPANY** | **$ 6,434** | $ 1,248 | $ 6,527 |
| Basic net income per share from continuing operations[1] | **$  1.58** | $  0.28 | $  1.51 |
| Basic net income (loss) per share from discontinued operations[2] | **(0.07)** | 0.02 | — |
| **BASIC NET INCOME PER SHARE** | **$  1.51** | $  0.29[3] | $  1.51 |
| Diluted net income per share from continuing operations[1] | **$  1.57** | $  0.27 | $  1.49 |
| Diluted net income (loss) per share from discontinued operations[2] | **(0.07)** | 0.02 | — |
| **DILUTED NET INCOME PER SHARE** | **$  1.50** | $  0.29 | $  1.49 |
| **AVERAGE SHARES OUTSTANDING—BASIC** | **4,259** | 4,272 | 4,317 |
| Effect of dilutive securities | **40** | 52 | 50 |
| **AVERAGE SHARES OUTSTANDING—DILUTED** | **4,299** | 4,324 | 4,367 |

[1]Calculated based on net income from continuing operations less net income from continuing operations attributable to noncontrolling interests.

[2]Calculated based on net income (loss) from discontinued operations less net income from discontinued operations attributable to noncontrolling interests.

[3]Per share amounts do not add due to rounding.

Refer to Notes to Consolidated Financial Statements.

**The Coca-Cola Company and Subsidiaries**
**Consolidated Statements of Cash Flows**

| Year Ended December 31, | 2018 | 2017 | 2016 |
|---|---|---|---|
| (In millions) | | | |
| **OPERATING ACTIVITIES** | | | |
| Consolidated net income | $ 6,476 | $ 1,283 | $ 6,550 |
| (Income) loss from discontinued operations | 251 | (101) | — |
| Net income from continuing operations | 6,727 | 1,182 | 6,550 |
| Depreciation and amortization | 1,086 | 1,260 | 1,787 |
| Stock-based compensation expense | 225 | 219 | 258 |
| Deferred income taxes | (450) | (1,256) | (856) |
| Equity (income) loss—net of dividends | (457) | (628) | (449) |
| Foreign currency adjustments | (38) | 281 | 158 |
| Significant (gains) losses on sales of assets—net | 189 | 1,459 | 1,146 |
| Other operating charges | 558 | 1,218 | 647 |
| Other items | 682 | (269) | (224) |
| Net change in operating assets and liabilities | (1,202) | 3,464 | (225) |
| Net cash provided by operating activities | 7,320 | 6,930 | 8,792 |
| **INVESTING ACTIVITIES** | | | |
| Purchases of investments | (7,789) | (17,296) | (16,626) |
| Proceeds from disposals of investments | 14,977 | 16,694 | 17,842 |
| Acquisitions of businesses, equity method investments and nonmarketable securities | (1,040) | (3,809) | (838) |
| Proceeds from disposals of businesses, equity method investments and nonmarketable securities | 1,362 | 3,821 | 1,035 |
| Purchases of property, plant and equipment | (1,347) | (1,675) | (2,262) |
| Proceeds from disposals of property, plant and equipment | 245 | 104 | 150 |
| Other investing activities | (60) | (93) | (305) |
| Net cash provided by (used in) investing activities | 6,348 | (2,254) | (1,004) |
| **FINANCING ACTIVITIES** | | | |
| Issuances of debt | 27,339 | 29,857 | 27,281 |
| Payments of debt | (30,568) | (28,768) | (25,615) |
| Issuances of stock | 1,476 | 1,595 | 1,434 |
| Purchases of stock for treasury | (1,912) | (3,682) | (3,681) |
| Dividends | (6,644) | (6,320) | (6,043) |
| Other financing activities | (243) | (91) | 79 |
| Net cash provided by (used in) financing activities | (10,552) | (7,409) | (6,545) |
| **CASH FLOWS FROM DISCONTINUED OPERATIONS** | | | |
| Net cash provided by (used in) operating activities from discontinued operations | 307 | 111 | — |
| Net cash provided by (used in) investing activities from discontinued operations | (421) | (58) | — |
| Net cash provided by (used in) financing activities from discontinued operations | 205 | (38) | — |
| Net cash provided by (used in) discontinued operations | 91 | 15 | — |
| **EFFECT OF EXCHANGE RATE CHANGES ON CASH, CASH EQUIVALENTS, RESTRICTED CASH AND RESTRICTED CASH EQUIVALENTS** | (262) | 241 | (5) |
| **CASH, CASH EQUIVALENTS, RESTRICTED CASH AND RESTRICTED CASH EQUIVALENTS** | | | |
| Net increase (decrease) in cash, cash equivalents, restricted cash and restricted cash equivalents during the year | 2,945 | (2,477) | 1,238 |
| Cash, cash equivalents, restricted cash and restricted cash equivalents at beginning of year | 6,373 | 8,850 | 7,612 |
| Cash, cash equivalents, restricted cash and restricted cash equivalents at end of year | 9,318 | 6,373 | 8,850 |
| Less: Restricted cash and restricted cash equivalents at end of year | 392 | 367 | 295 |
| Cash and cash equivalents at end of year | $ 8,926 | $ 6,006 | $ 8,555 |

Refer to Notes to Consolidated Financial Statements.

**The Coca-Cola Company and Subsidiaries**

**Consolidated Statements of Shareowners' Equity**

| Year Ended December 31, | 2018 | 2017 | 2016 |
|---|---|---|---|
| (in millions except per share data) | | | |
| **EQUITY ATTRIBUTABLE TO SHAREOWNERS OF THE COCA-COLA COMPANY** | | | |
| **NUMBER OF COMMON SHARES OUTSTANDING** | | | |
| Balance at beginning of year | 4,259 | 4,288 | 4,324 |
| Treasury stock issued to employees related to stock compensation plans | 48 | 53 | 50 |
| Purchases of stock for treasury | (39) | (82) | (86) |
| Balance at end of year | 4,268 | 4,259 | 4,288 |
| **COMMON STOCK** | $ 1,760 | $ 1,760 | $ 1,760 |
| **CAPITAL SURPLUS** | | | |
| Balance at beginning of year | 15,864 | 14,993 | 14,016 |
| Stock issued to employees related to stock compensation plans | 467 | 655 | 589 |
| Tax benefit (charge) from stock compensation plans | — | — | 130 |
| Stock-based compensation expense | 225 | 219 | 258 |
| Other activities | (36) | (3) | — |
| Balance at end of year | 16,520 | 15,864 | 14,993 |
| **REINVESTED EARNINGS** | | | |
| Balance at beginning of year | 60,430 | 65,502 | 65,018 |
| Adoption of accounting standards[1] | 3,014 | — | — |
| Net income attributable to shareowners of The Coca-Cola Company | 6,434 | 1,248 | 6,527 |
| Dividends (per share—$1.56, $1.48 and $1.40 in 2018, 2017 and 2016, respectively) | (6,644) | (6,320) | (6,043) |
| Balance at end of year | 63,234 | 60,430 | 65,502 |
| **ACCUMULATED OTHER COMPREHENSIVE INCOME (LOSS)** | | | |
| Balance at beginning of year | (10,305) | (11,205) | (10,174) |
| Adoption of accounting standards[1] | (409) | — | — |
| Net other comprehensive income (loss) | (2,100) | 900 | (1,031) |
| Balance at end of year | (12,814) | (10,305) | (11,205) |
| **TREASURY STOCK** | | | |
| Balance at beginning of year | (50,677) | (47,988) | (45,066) |
| Treasury stock issued to employees related to stock compensation plans | 704 | 909 | 811 |
| Purchases of stock for treasury | (1,746) | (3,598) | (3,733) |
| Balance at end of year | (51,719) | (50,677) | (47,988) |
| **TOTAL EQUITY ATTRIBUTABLE TO SHAREOWNERS OF THE COCA-COLA COMPANY** | $16,981 | $17,072 | $23,062 |
| **EQUITY ATTRIBUTABLE TO NONCONTROLLING INTERESTS** | | | |
| Balance at beginning of year | $ 1,905 | $   158 | $   210 |
| Net income attributable to noncontrolling interests | 42 | 35 | 23 |
| Net foreign currency translation adjustments | 53 | 38 | (13) |
| Dividends paid to noncontrolling interests | (31) | (15) | (25) |
| Contributions by noncontrolling interests | — | — | 1 |
| Business combinations | 101 | 1,805 | — |
| Deconsolidation of certain entities | — | (157) | (34) |
| Other activities | 7 | 41 | (4) |
| **TOTAL EQUITY ATTRIBUTABLE TO NONCONTROLLING INTERESTS** | $ 2,077 | $ 1,905 | $   158 |

[1]Refer to Note 1, Note 3, Note 4 and Note 15.

Refer to Notes to Consolidated Financial Statements.

# Specimen Financial Statements:
# Amazon.com, Inc.

**Amazon.com, Inc.** is the world's largest online retailer. It also produces consumer electronics —notably the Kindle e-book reader and the Kindle Fire Tablet computer—and is a major provider of cloud computing services. The following are Amazon's financial statements as presented in the company's 2018 annual report. The complete annual report, including notes to the financial statements, is available at the company's website.

**Amazon.com, Inc.**
**Consolidated Statements of Cash Flows**
**(in millions)**

| | Year Ended December 31, | | |
| --- | --- | --- | --- |
| | 2016 | 2017 | 2018 |
| CASH, CASH EQUIVALENTS, AND RESTRICTED CASH, BEGINNING OF PERIOD | $16,175 | $19,934 | $21,856 |
| OPERATING ACTIVITIES: | | | |
| Net income | 2,371 | 3,033 | 10,073 |
| Adjustments to reconcile net income to net cash from operating activities: | | | |
| Depreciation of property and equipment and other amortization, including capitalized content costs | 8,116 | 11,478 | 15,341 |
| Stock-based compensation | 2,975 | 4,215 | 5,418 |
| Other operating expense, net | 160 | 202 | 274 |
| Other expense (income), net | (20) | (292) | 219 |
| Deferred income taxes | (246) | (29) | 441 |
| Changes in operating assets and liabilities: | | | |
| Inventories | (1,426) | (3,583) | (1,314) |
| Accounts receivable, net and other | (3,436) | (4,780) | (4,615) |
| Accounts payable | 5,030 | 7,100 | 3,263 |
| Accrued expenses and other | 1,724 | 283 | 472 |
| Unearned revenue | 1,955 | 738 | 1,151 |
| Net cash provided by (used in) operating activities | 17,203 | 18,365 | 30,723 |
| INVESTING ACTIVITIES: | | | |
| Purchases of property and equipment | (7,804) | (11,955) | (13,427) |
| Proceeds from property and equipment incentives | 1,067 | 1,897 | 2,104 |
| Acquisitions, net of cash acquired, and other | (116) | (13,972) | (2,186) |
| Sales and maturities of marketable securities | 4,577 | 9,677 | 8,240 |
| Purchases of marketable securities | (7,240) | (12,731) | (7,100) |
| Net cash provided by (used in) investing activities | (9,516) | (27,084) | (12,369) |
| FINANCING ACTIVITIES: | | | |
| Proceeds from long-term debt and other | 618 | 16,228 | 768 |
| Repayments of long-term debt and other | (327) | (1,301) | (668) |
| Principal repayments of capital lease obligations | (3,860) | (4,799) | (7,449) |
| Principal repayments of finance lease obligations | (147) | (200) | (337) |
| Net cash provided by (used in) financing activities | (3,716) | 9,928 | (7,686) |
| Foreign currency effect on cash, cash equivalents, and restricted cash | (212) | 713 | (351) |
| Net increase (decrease) in cash, cash equivalents, and restricted cash | 3,759 | 1,922 | 10,317 |
| CASH, CASH EQUIVALENTS, AND RESTRICTED CASH, END OF PERIOD | $19,934 | $21,856 | $32,173 |
| SUPPLEMENTAL CASH FLOW INFORMATION: | | | |
| Cash paid for interest on long-term debt | $ 290 | $ 328 | $ 854 |
| Cash paid for interest on capital and finance lease obligations | 206 | 319 | 575 |
| Cash paid for income taxes, net of refunds | 412 | 957 | 1,184 |
| Property and equipment acquired under capital leases | 5,704 | 9,637 | 10,615 |
| Property and equipment acquired under build-to-suit leases | 1,209 | 3,541 | 3,641 |

See accompanying notes to consolidated financial statements.

**Amazon.com, Inc.**
**Consolidated Statements of Operations**
**(in millions, except per share data)**

| | Year Ended December 31, | | |
| --- | --- | --- | --- |
| | **2016** | **2017** | **2018** |
| Net product sales | $94,665 | $118,573 | $141,915 |
| Net service sales | 41,322 | 59,293 | 90,972 |
| Total net sales | 135,987 | 177,866 | 232,887 |
| Operating expenses: | | | |
| Cost of sales | 88,265 | 111,934 | 139,156 |
| Fulfillment | 17,619 | 25,249 | 34,027 |
| Marketing | 7,233 | 10,069 | 13,814 |
| Technology and content | 16,085 | 22,620 | 28,837 |
| General and administrative | 2,432 | 3,674 | 4,336 |
| Other operating expense, net | 167 | 214 | 296 |
| Total operating expenses | 131,801 | 173,760 | 220,466 |
| Operating income | 4,186 | 4,106 | 12,421 |
| Interest income | 100 | 202 | 440 |
| Interest expense | (484) | (848) | (1,417) |
| Other income (expense), net | 90 | 346 | (183) |
| Total non-operating income (expense) | (294) | (300) | (1,160) |
| Income before income taxes | 3,892 | 3,806 | 11,261 |
| Provision for income taxes | (1,425) | (769) | (1,197) |
| Equity-method investment activity, net of tax | (96) | (4) | 9 |
| Net income | $ 2,371 | $ 3,033 | $ 10,073 |
| Basic earnings per share | $ 5.01 | $ 6.32 | $ 20.68 |
| Diluted earnings per share | $ 4.90 | $ 6.15 | $ 20.14 |
| Weighted-average shares used in computation of earnings per share: | | | |
| Basic | 474 | 480 | 487 |
| Diluted | 484 | 493 | 500 |

See accompanying notes to consolidated financial statements.

**Amazon.com, Inc.**
**Consolidated Statements of Comprehensive Income**
**(in millions)**

| | Year Ended December 31, | | |
| --- | --- | --- | --- |
| | **2016** | **2017** | **2018** |
| Net income | $2,371 | $3,033 | $10,073 |
| Other comprehensive income (loss): | | | |
| Foreign currency translation adjustments, net of tax of $(49), $5, and $6 | (279) | 533 | (538) |
| Net change in unrealized gains (losses) on available-for-sale debt securities: | | | |
| Unrealized gains (losses), net of tax of $(12), $5, and $0 | 9 | (39) | (17) |
| Reclassification adjustment for losses (gains) included in "Other income (expense), net," net of tax of $0, $0, and $0 | 8 | 7 | 8 |
| Net unrealized gains (losses) on available-for-sale debt securities | 17 | (32) | (9) |
| Total other comprehensive income (loss) | (262) | 501 | (547) |
| Comprehensive income | $2,109 | $3,534 | $ 9,526 |

See accompanying notes to consolidated financial statements.

**Amazon.com, Inc.**
**Consolidated Balance Sheets**
**(in millions, except per share data)**

| | December 31, | |
| --- | --- | --- |
| | **2017** | **2018** |
| **ASSETS** | | |
| Current assets: | | |
| Cash and cash equivalents | $ 20,522 | $ 31,750 |
| Marketable securities | 10,464 | 9,500 |
| Inventories | 16,047 | 17,174 |
| Accounts receivable, net and other | 13,164 | 16,677 |
| Total current assets | 60,197 | 75,101 |
| Property and equipment, net | 48,866 | 61,797 |
| Goodwill | 13,350 | 14,548 |
| Other assets | 8,897 | 11,202 |
| Total assets | $131,310 | $162,648 |
| **LIABILITIES AND STOCKHOLDERS' EQUITY** | | |
| Current liabilities: | | |
| Accounts payable | $ 34,616 | $ 38,192 |
| Accrued expenses and other | 18,170 | 23,663 |
| Unearned revenue | 5,097 | 6,536 |
| Total current liabilities | 57,883 | 68,391 |
| Long-term debt | 24,743 | 23,495 |
| Other long-term liabilities | 20,975 | 27,213 |
| Commitments and contingencies (Note 7) | | |
| Stockholders' equity: | | |
| Preferred stock, $0.01 par value: | | |
| Authorized shares—500 | | |
| Issued and outstanding shares—none | — | — |
| Common stock, $0.01 par value: | | |
| Authorized shares—5,000 | | |
| Issued shares—507 and 514 | | |
| Outstanding shares—484 and 491 | 5 | 5 |
| Treasury stock, at cost | (1,837) | (1,837) |
| Additional paid-in capital | 21,389 | 26,791 |
| Accumulated other comprehensive loss | (484) | (1,035) |
| Retained earnings | 8,636 | 19,625 |
| Total stockholders' equity | 27,709 | 43,549 |
| Total liabilities and stockholders' equity | $131,310 | $162,648 |

See accompanying notes to consolidated financial statements.

**Amazon.com, Inc.**
**Consolidated Statements of Stockholders' Equity**
**(in millions)**

| | Common Stock | | | | | | |
| | Shares | Amount | Treasury Stock | Additional Paid-In Capital | Accumulated Other Comprehensive Income (Loss) | Retained Earnings | Total Stockholders' Equity |
|---|---|---|---|---|---|---|---|
| Balance as of January 1, 2016 | 471 | $5 | $(1,837) | $13,394 | $ (723) | $ 2,545 | $13,384 |
| Net income | — | — | — | — | — | 2,371 | 2,371 |
| Other comprehensive income (loss) | — | — | — | — | (262) | — | (262) |
| Exercise of common stock options | 6 | — | — | 1 | — | — | 1 |
| Excess tax benefits from stock-based compensation | — | — | — | 829 | — | — | 829 |
| Stock-based compensation and issuance of employee benefit plan stock | — | — | — | 2,962 | — | — | 2,962 |
| Balance as of December 31, 2016 | 477 | 5 | (1,837) | 17,186 | (985) | 4,916 | 19,285 |
| Cumulative effect of a change in accounting principle related to stock-based compensation | — | — | — | — | — | 687 | 687 |
| Net income | — | — | — | — | — | 3,033 | 3,033 |
| Other comprehensive income (loss) | — | — | — | — | 501 | — | 501 |
| Exercise of common stock options | 7 | — | — | 1 | — | — | 1 |
| Stock-based compensation and issuance of employee benefit plan stock | — | — | — | 4,202 | — | — | 4,202 |
| Balance as of December 31, 2017 | 484 | 5 | (1,837) | 21,389 | (484) | 8,636 | 27,709 |
| Cumulative effect of changes in accounting principles related to revenue recognition, income taxes, and financial instruments | — | — | — | — | (4) | 916 | 912 |
| Net income | — | — | — | — | — | 10,073 | 10,073 |
| Other comprehensive income (loss) | — | — | — | — | (547) | — | (547) |
| Exercise of common stock options | 7 | — | — | — | — | — | — |
| Stock-based compensation and issuance of employee benefit plan stock | — | — | — | 5,402 | — | — | 5,402 |
| Balance as of December 31, 2018 | 491 | $5 | $(1,837) | $26,791 | $(1,035) | $19,625 | $43,549 |

See accompanying notes to consolidated financial statements.

# Specimen Financial Statements: Walmart Inc.

The following are **Walmart Inc.**'s financial statements as presented in the company's 2019 annual report. The complete annual report, including notes to the financial statements, is available at the company's website.

**Walmart Inc.**
**Consolidated Statements of Income**

| | Fiscal Years Ended January 31, | | |
| --- | --- | --- | --- |
| *(Amounts in millions, except per share data)* | **2019** | **2018** | **2017** |
| **Revenues:** | | | |
| Net sales | $510,329 | $495,761 | $481,317 |
| Membership and other income | 4,076 | 4,582 | 4,556 |
| Total revenues | 514,405 | 500,343 | 485,873 |
| **Costs and expenses:** | | | |
| Cost of sales | 385,301 | 373,396 | 361,256 |
| Operating, selling, general and administrative expenses | 107,147 | 106,510 | 101,853 |
| **Operating income** | 21,957 | 20,437 | 22,764 |
| **Interest:** | | | |
| Debt | 1,975 | 1,978 | 2,044 |
| Capital lease and financing obligations | 371 | 352 | 323 |
| Interest income | (217) | (152) | (100) |
| Interest, net | 2,129 | 2,178 | 2,267 |
| Loss on extinguishment of debt | — | 3,136 | — |
| Other (gains) and losses | 8,368 | — | — |
| **Income before income taxes** | 11,460 | 15,123 | 20,497 |
| Provision for income taxes | 4,281 | 4,600 | 6,204 |
| **Consolidated net income** | 7,179 | 10,523 | 14,293 |
| **Consolidated net income attributable to noncontrolling interest** | (509) | (661) | (650) |
| **Consolidated net income attributable to Walmart** | $ 6,670 | $ 9,862 | $ 13,643 |
| | | | |
| **Net income per common share:** | | | |
| **Basic net income per common share attributable to Walmart** | $ 2.28 | $ 3.29 | $ 4.40 |
| **Diluted net income per common share attributable to Walmart** | 2.26 | 3.28 | 4.38 |
| | | | |
| **Weighted-average common shares outstanding:** | | | |
| Basic | 2,929 | 2,995 | 3,101 |
| Diluted | 2,945 | 3,010 | 3,112 |
| | | | |
| **Dividends declared per common share** | $ 2.08 | $ 2.04 | $ 2.00 |

*See accompanying notes.*

**Walmart Inc.**
**Consolidated Statements of Comprehensive Income**

| | Fiscal Years Ended January 31, | | |
|---|---|---|---|
| (Amounts in millions) | 2019 | 2018 | 2017 |
| Consolidated net income | $7,179 | $10,523 | $14,293 |
| Consolidated net income attributable to noncontrolling interest | (509) | (661) | (650) |
| **Consolidated net income attributable to Walmart** | 6,670 | 9,862 | 13,643 |
| | | | |
| Other comprehensive income (loss), net of income taxes | | | |
| Currency translation and other | (226) | 2,540 | (3,027) |
| Net investment hedges | 272 | (405) | 413 |
| Cash flow hedges | (290) | 437 | 21 |
| Minimum pension liability | 131 | 147 | (397) |
| Unrealized gain on available-for-sale securities | — | 1,501 | 145 |
| Other comprehensive income (loss), net of income taxes | (113) | 4,220 | (2,845) |
| Other comprehensive (income) loss attributable to noncontrolling interest | 188 | (169) | 210 |
| **Other comprehensive income (loss) attributable to Walmart** | 75 | 4,051 | (2,635) |
| | | | |
| Comprehensive income, net of income taxes | 7,066 | 14,743 | 11,448 |
| Comprehensive (income) loss attributable to noncontrolling interest | (321) | (830) | (440) |
| **Comprehensive income attributable to Walmart** | $6,745 | $13,913 | $11,008 |

*See accompanying notes.*

**Walmart Inc.**
**Consolidated Balance Sheets**

| | As of January 31, | |
|---|---|---|
| (Amounts in millions) | 2019 | 2018 |
| **ASSETS** | | |
| **Current assets:** | | |
| Cash and cash equivalents | $ 7,722 | $ 6,756 |
| Receivables, net | 6,283 | 5,614 |
| Inventories | 44,269 | 43,783 |
| Prepaid expenses and other | 3,623 | 3,511 |
| Total current assets | 61,897 | 59,664 |
| **Property and equipment:** | | |
| Property and equipment | 185,810 | 185,154 |
| Less accumulated depreciation | (81,493) | (77,479) |
| Property and equipment, net | 104,317 | 107,675 |
| **Property under capital lease and financing obligations:** | | |
| Property under capital lease and financing obligations | 12,760 | 12,703 |
| Less accumulated amortization | (5,682) | (5,560) |
| Property under capital lease and financing obligations, net | 7,078 | 7,143 |
| | | |
| Goodwill | 31,181 | 18,242 |
| Other long-term assets | 14,822 | 11,798 |
| **Total assets** | $219,295 | $204,522 |

*(continues)*

| (Amounts in millions) | As of January 31, | |
| --- | --- | --- |
| | **2019** | **2018** |
| **LIABILITIES AND EQUITY** | | |
| **Current liabilities:** | | |
| Short-term borrowings | $  5,225 | $  5,257 |
| Accounts payable | 47,060 | 46,092 |
| Accrued liabilities | 22,159 | 22,122 |
| Accrued income taxes | 428 | 645 |
| Long-term debt due within one year | 1,876 | 3,738 |
| Capital lease and financing obligations due within one year | 729 | 667 |
| Total current liabilities | 77,477 | 78,521 |
| | | |
| Long-term debt | 43,520 | 30,045 |
| Long-term capital lease and financing obligations | 6,683 | 6,780 |
| Deferred income taxes and other | 11,981 | 8,354 |
| | | |
| Commitments and contingencies | | |
| | | |
| **Equity:** | | |
| Common stock | 288 | 295 |
| Capital in excess of par value | 2,965 | 2,648 |
| Retained earnings | 80,785 | 85,107 |
| Accumulated other comprehensive loss | (11,542) | (10,181) |
| Total Walmart shareholders' equity | 72,496 | 77,869 |
| Noncontrolling interest | 7,138 | 2,953 |
| Total equity | 79,634 | 80,822 |
| **Total liabilities and equity** | $219,295 | $204,522 |

*See accompanying notes.*

**Walmart Inc.**
**Consolidated Statements of Shareholders' Equity**

| (Amounts in millions) | Common Stock Shares | Common Stock Amount | Capital in Excess of Par Value | Retained Earnings | Accumulated Other Comprehensive Income (Loss) | Total Walmart Shareholders' Equity | Noncontrolling Interest | Total Equity |
|---|---|---|---|---|---|---|---|---|
| **Balances as of February 1, 2016** | 3,162 | $317 | $1,805 | $90,021 | $(11,597) | $80,546 | $3,065 | $83,611 |
| Consolidated net income | — | — | — | 13,643 | — | 13,643 | 650 | 14,293 |
| Other comprehensive income (loss), net of income taxes | — | — | — | — | (2,635) | (2,635) | (210) | (2,845) |
| Cash dividends declared ($2.00 per share) | — | — | — | (6,216) | — | (6,216) | — | (6,216) |
| Purchase of Company stock | (120) | (12) | (174) | (8,090) | — | (8.276) | — | (8,276) |
| Cash dividend declared to noncontrolling interest | — | — | — | — | — | — | (519) | (519) |
| Other | 6 | — | 740 | (4) | — | 736 | (249) | 487 |
| **Balances as of January 31, 2017** | 3,048 | 305 | 2,371 | 89,354 | (14,232) | 77,798 | 2,737 | 80,535 |
| Consolidated net income | — | — | — | 9,862 | — | 9,862 | 661 | 10,523 |
| Other comprehensive income (loss), net of income taxes | — | — | — | — | 4,051 | 4,051 | 169 | 4,220 |
| Cash dividends declared ($2.04 per share) | — | — | — | (6,124) | — | (6,124) | — | (6,124) |
| Purchase of Company stock | (103) | (10) | (219) | (7,975) | — | (8,204) | — | (8,204) |
| Cash dividend declared to noncontrolling interest | — | — | — | — | — | — | (687) | (687) |
| Other | 7 | — | 496 | (10) | — | 486 | 73 | 559 |

(continues)

| (Amounts in millions) | Common Stock | | Capital in Excess of Par Value | Retained Earnings | Accumulated Other Comprehensive Income (Loss) | Total Walmart Shareholders' Equity | Noncontrolling Interest | Total Equity |
|---|---|---|---|---|---|---|---|---|
| | Shares | Amount | | | | | | |
| **Balances as of January 31, 2018** | 2,952 | $295 | $2,648 | $85,107 | $(10,181) | $77,869 | $2,953 | $80,822 |
| Adoption of new accounting standards on February 1, 2018, net of income taxes | — | — | 2,361 | (1,436) | 925 | (1) | 924 | |
| Consolidated net income | — | — | — | 6,670 | — | 6,670 | 509 | 7,179 |
| Other comprehensive income (loss), net of income taxes | — | — | — | — | 75 | 75 | (188) | (113) |
| Cash dividends declared ($2.08 per share) | — | — | — | (6,102) | — | (6,102) | — | (6,102) |
| Purchase of Company stock | (80) | (8) | (245) | (7,234) | — | (7,487) | — | (7,487) |
| Cash dividend declared to noncontrolling interest | — | — | — | — | — | — | (488) | (488) |
| Noncontrolling interest of acquired entity | — | — | — | — | — | — | 4,345 | 4,345 |
| Other | 6 | 1 | 562 | (17) | — | 546 | 8 | 554 |
| **Balances as of January 31, 2019** | 2,878 | $288 | $2,965 | $80,785 | $(11,542) | $72,496 | $7,138 | $79,634 |

*See accompanying notes.*

**Walmart Inc.**
**Consolidated Statements of Cash Flows**

| (Amounts in millions) | Fiscal Years Ended January 31, | | |
|---|---|---|---|
| | 2019 | 2018 | 2017 |
| **Cash flows from operating activities:** | | | |
| Consolidated net income | $ 7,179 | $10,523 | $14,293 |
| Adjustments to reconcile consolidated net income to net cash provided by operating activities: | | | |
| Depreciation and amortization | 10,678 | 10,529 | 10,080 |
| Unrealized (gains) and losses | 3,516 | — | — |
| (Gains) and losses for disposal of business operations | 4,850 | — | — |
| Deferred income taxes | (499) | (304) | 761 |
| Loss on extinguishment of debt | — | 3,136 | — |
| Other operating activities | 1,734 | 1,210 | 206 |
| Changes in certain assets and liabilities, net of effects of acquisitions: | | | |
| Receivables, net | (368) | (1,074) | (402) |
| Inventories | (1,311) | (140) | 1,021 |
| Accounts payable | 1,831 | 4,086 | 3,942 |
| Accrued liabilities | 183 | 928 | 1,280 |
| Accrued income taxes | (40) | (557) | 492 |
| Net cash provided by operating activities | 27,753 | 28,337 | 31,673 |
| | | | |
| **Cash flows from investing activities:** | | | |
| Payments for property and equipment | (10,344) | (10,051) | (10,619) |
| Proceeds from the disposal of property and equipment | 519 | 378 | 456 |
| Proceeds from the disposal of certain operations | 876 | 1,046 | 662 |
| Purchase of available for sale securities | — | — | (1,901) |
| Payments for business acquisitions, net of cash acquired | (14,656) | (375) | (2,463) |
| Other investing activities | (431) | (77) | (31) |
| Net cash used in investing activities | (24,036) | (9,079) | (13,896) |
| | | | |
| **Cash flows from financing activities:** | | | |
| Net change in short-term borrowings | (53) | 4,148 | (1,673) |
| Proceeds from issuance of long-term debt | 15,872 | 7,476 | 137 |
| Repayments of long-term debt | (3,784) | (13,061) | (2,055) |
| Premiums paid to extinguish debt | — | (3,059) | — |
| Dividends paid | (6,102) | (6,124) | (6,216) |
| Purchase of Company stock | (7,410) | (8,296) | (8,298) |
| Dividends paid to noncontrolling interest | (431) | (690) | (479) |
| Purchase of noncontrolling interest | — | (8) | (90) |
| Other financing activities | (629) | (261) | (398) |
| Net cash used in financing activities | (2,537) | (19,875) | (19,072) |
| | | | |
| Effect of exchange rates on cash, cash equivalents and restricted cash | (438) | 487 | (452) |
| | | | |
| Net increase (decrease) in cash, cash equivalents and restricted cash | 742 | (130) | (1,747) |
| Cash, cash equivalents and restricted cash at beginning of year | 7,014 | 7,144 | 8,891 |
| Cash, cash equivalents and restricted cash at end of period | $ 7,756 | $ 7,104 | $ 7,144 |
| | | | |
| **Supplemental disclosure of cash flow information:** | | | |
| Income taxes paid | 3,982 | 6,179 | 4,507 |
| Interest paid | 2,348 | 2,450 | 2,351 |

*See accompanying notes.*

# Specimen Financial Statements: Louis Vuitton

**Louis Vuitton** is a French company and is one of the leading fashion houses in the world. Louis Vuitton has been named the world's most valuable luxury brand. Note that its financial statements are IFRS-based and are presented in euros (€). The complete consolidated financial statements, including notes to the financial statement, are available at the company's website.

|  | | Consolidated Income Statement | | |
|---|---|---|---|---|
| (EUR millions, except for earnings per share) | Notes | 2018 | 2017[1][2] | 2016[1] |
| **Revenue** | 23 | **46,826** | **42,636** | **37,600** |
| Cost of sales | | (15,625) | (14,783) | (13,039) |
| **Gross margin** | | **31,201** | **27,853** | **24,561** |
| Marketing and selling expenses | | (17,755) | (16,395) | (14,607) |
| General and administrative expenses | | (3,466) | (3,162) | (2,931) |
| Income/(loss) from joint ventures and associates | 7 | 23 | (3) | 3 |
| **Profit from recurring operations** | 23–24 | **10,003** | **8,293** | **7,026** |
| Other operating income and expenses | 25 | (126) | (180) | (122) |
| **Operating profit** | | **9,877** | **8,113** | **6,904** |
| Cost of net financial debt | | (117) | (137) | (133) |
| Other financial income and expenses | | (271) | 78 | (185) |
| **Net financial income/(expense)** | 26 | **(388)** | **(59)** | **(318)** |
| Income taxes | 27 | (2,499) | (2,214) | (2,133) |
| **Net profit before minority interests** | | **6,990** | **5,840** | **4,453** |
| Minority interests | 17 | (636) | (475) | (387) |
| **Net profit, Group share** | | **6,354** | **5,365** | **4,066** |
| **Basic Group share of net earnings per share** (EUR) | 28 | **12.64** | **10.68** | **8.08** |
| Number of shares on which the calculation is based | | 502,825,461 | 502,412,694 | 502,911,125 |
| **Diluted Group share of net earnings per share** (EUR) | 28 | **12.61** | **10.64** | **8.06** |
| Number of shares on which the calculation is based | | 503,918,140 | 504,010,291 | 504,640,459 |

(1) The financial statements as of December 31, 2017 and December 31, 2016 have been restated to reflect the retrospective application with effect from January 1, 2016 of IFRS 9 Financial Instruments. See Note 1.2.

(2) The financial statements as of December 31, 2017 have been restated to reflect the definitive allocation of the purchase price of Christian Dior Couture. See Note 2.

## Consolidated Statement of Comprehensive Gains and Losses

| (EUR millions) | Notes | 2018 | 2017[1][2] | 2016[1] |
|---|---|---|---|---|
| **Net profit before minority interests** | | **6,990** | **5,840** | **4,453** |
| Translation adjustments | | 274 | (958) | 78 |
| Amounts transferred to income statement | | (1) | 18 | - |
| Tax impact | | 15 | (49) | (9) |
| | 15,4,17 | **288** | **(989)** | **69** |
| Change in value of hedges of future foreign currency cash flows | | 3 | 372 | 47 |
| Amounts transferred to income statement | | (279) | (104) | (26) |
| Tax impact | | 79 | (77) | (1) |
| | | **(197)** | **191** | **20** |
| Change in value of the cost of hedging instruments | | (271) | (91) | (273) |
| Amounts transferred to income statement | | 148 | 210 | 180 |
| Tax impact | | 31 | (35) | 24 |
| | | **(92)** | **84** | **(69)** |
| **Gains and losses recognized in equity, transferable to income statement** | | **(1)** | **(714)** | **20** |
| Change in value of vineyard land | 6 | 8 | (35) | 30 |
| Amounts transferred to consolidated reserves | | - | - | - |
| Tax impact | | (2) | 82 | 108 |
| | | **6** | **47** | **138** |
| Employee benefit commitments: change in value resulting from actuarial gains and losses | | 28 | 57 | (88) |
| Tax impact | | (5) | (24) | 17 |
| | | **23** | **33** | **(71)** |
| **Gains and losses recognized in equity, not transferable to income statement** | | **29** | **80** | **67** |
| **Comprehensive income** | | **7,018** | **5,206** | **4,540** |
| Minority interests | | (681) | (341) | (433) |
| **Comprehensive income, Group share** | | **6,337** | **4,865** | **4,107** |

(1) The financial statements as of December 31, 2017 and December 31, 2016 have been restated to reflect the retrospective application with effect from January 1, 2016 of IFRS 9 Financial Instruments. See Note 1.2.

(2) The financial statements as of December 31, 2017 have been restated to reflect the definitive allocation of the purchase price of Christian Dior Couture. See Note 2.

**Consolidated Balance Sheet**

| ASSETS *(EUR millions)* | Notes | 2018 | 2017[1][2] | 2016[1] |
|---|---|---|---|---|
| Brands and other intangible assets | 3 | 17,254 | 16,957 | 13,335 |
| Goodwill | 4 | 13,727 | 13,837 | 10,401 |
| Property, plant and equipment | 6 | 15,112 | 13,862 | 12,139 |
| Investments in joint ventures and associates | 7 | 638 | 639 | 770 |
| Non-current available for sale financial assets | 8 | 1,100 | 789 | 744 |
| Other non-current assets | 9 | 986 | 869 | 777 |
| Deferred tax | | 1,932 | 1,741 | 2,053 |
| **Non-current assets** | | **50,749** | **48,694** | **40,219** |
| Inventories and work in progress | 10 | 12,485 | 10,888 | 10,546 |
| Trade accounts receivable | 11 | 3,222 | 2,736 | 2,685 |
| Income taxes | | 366 | 780 | 280 |
| Other current assets | 12 | 2,868 | 2,919 | 2,342 |
| Cash and cash equivalents | 14 | 4,610 | 3,738 | 3,544 |
| **Current assets** | | **23,551** | **21,061** | **19,397** |
| **Total assets** | | **74,300** | **69,755** | **59,616** |

| LIABILITIES AND EQUITY *(EUR millions)* | Notes | 2018 | 2017[1][2] | 2016[1] |
|---|---|---|---|---|
| Share capital | 15.1 | 152 | 152 | 152 |
| Share premium account | 15.1 | 2,298 | 2,614 | 2,601 |
| Treasury shares and LVMH share-settled derivatives | 15.2 | (421) | (530) | (520) |
| Cumulative translation adjustment | 15.4 | 573 | 354 | 1,165 |
| Revaluation reserves | | 875 | 1,111 | 799 |
| Other reserves | | 22,462 | 19,903 | 18,125 |
| Net profit, Group share | | 6,354 | 5,365 | 4,066 |
| Equity, Group share | | 32,293 | 28,969 | 26,388 |
| Minority interests | 17 | 1,664 | 1,408 | 1,510 |
| **Equity** | | **33,957** | **30,377** | **27,898** |
| Long-term borrowings | 18 | 6,005 | 7,046 | 3,932 |
| Non-current provisions | 19 | 2,430 | 2,484 | 2,342 |
| Deferred tax | | 5,036 | 4,989 | 4,137 |
| Other non-current liabilities | 20 | 10,039 | 9,870 | 8,497 |
| **Non-current liabilities** | | **23,510** | **24,389** | **18,908** |
| Short-term borrowings | 18 | 5,027 | 4,530 | 3,447 |
| Trade accounts payable | 21.1 | 5,314 | 4,539 | 4,184 |
| Income taxes | | 538 | 763 | 428 |
| Current provisions | 19 | 369 | 404 | 352 |
| Other current liabilities | 21.2 | 5,585 | 4,753 | 4,399 |
| **Current liabilities** | | **16,833** | **14,989** | **12,810** |
| **Total liabilities and equity** | | **74,300** | **69,755** | **59,616** |

(1) The financial statements as of December 31, 2017 and December 31, 2016 have been restated to reflect the retrospective application with effect from January 1, 2016 of IFRS 9 Financial Instruments. See Note 1.2.

(2) The financial statements as of December 31, 2017 have been restated to reflect the definitive allocation of the purchase price of Christian Dior Couture. See Note 2.

## Consolidated Statement of Changes in Equity

| (EUR millions) | Number of shares | Share capital | Share premium account | Treasury shares and LVMH-share settled derivatives | Cumulative translation adjustment | Available for sale financial assets | Hedges of future foreign currency cash flows and cost of hedging instruments | Vineyard land | Employee benefit commitments | Net profit and other reserves | Group share | Minority interests | Total |
|---|---|---|---|---|---|---|---|---|---|---|---|---|---|
| | | | | | | Revaluation reserves | | | | | Total equity | | |
| Notes | | 15.1 | | 15.2 | 15.4 | | | | | | | 17 | |
| As of December 31, 2015 | 507,139,110 | 152 | 2,579 | (241) | 1,137 | 103 | (10) | 965 | (107) | 19,762 | 24,340 | 1,460 | 25,800 |
| Impact of changes in accounting standards[1] | - | - | - | - | - | (103) | (61) | - | - | 160 | (4) | - | (4) |
| As of January 1, 2016, after restatement | 507,139,110 | 152 | 2,579 | (241) | 1,137 | - | (71) | 965 | (107) | 19,922 | 24,336 | 1,460 | 25,796 |
| Gains and losses recognized in equity | | | | | 28 | | (44) | 113 | (56) | - | 41 | 46 | 87 |
| Net profit | | | | | | | | | | 4,066 | 4,066 | 387 | 4,453 |
| Comprehensive income | - | - | - | - | 28 | - | (44) | 113 | (56) | 4,066 | 4,107 | 433 | 4,540 |
| Stock option plan and similar expenses | | | | | | | | | | 39 | 39 | 2 | 41 |
| (Acquisition)/disposal of treasury shares and LVMH share-settled derivatives | | | | (321) | | | | | | (21) | (342) | - | (342) |
| Exercise of LVMH share subscription options | 907,929 | | 64 | | | | | | | | 64 | | 64 |
| Retirement of LVMH shares | (920,951) | | (42) | 42 | | | | | | | - | | - |
| Capital increase in subsidiaries | | | | | | | | | | | - | 41 | 41 |
| Interim and final dividends paid | | | | | | | | | | (1,811) | (1,811) | (272) | (2,083) |
| Changes in control of consolidated entities | | | | | | | | | | (5) | (5) | 22 | 17 |
| Acquisition and disposal of minority interests' shares | | | | | | | | | | (58) | (58) | (34) | (92) |
| Purchase commitments for minority interests' shares | | | | | | | | | | 58 | 58 | (142) | (84) |
| As of December 31, 2016 | 507,126,088 | 152 | 2,601 | (520) | 1,165 | - | (115) | 1,078 | (163) | 22,190 | 26,388 | 1,510 | 27,898 |
| Gains and losses recognized in equity | | | | | (811) | | 245 | 36 | 30 | - | (500) | (134) | (634) |
| Net profit | | | | | | | | | | 5,365 | 5,365 | 475 | 5,840 |
| Comprehensive income | - | - | - | (811) | - | 245 | 36 | 30 | 5,365 | 4,865 | 341 | 5,206 | |
| Stock option plan and similar expenses | | | | | | | | | | 55 | 55 | 7 | 62 |
| (Acquisition)/disposal of treasury shares and LVMH share-settled derivatives | | | | (50) | | | | | | (11) | (61) | - | (61) |
| Exercise of LVMH share subscription options | 708.485 | | 53 | | | | | | | | 53 | | 53 |
| Retirement of LVMH shares | (791,977) | | (40) | 40 | | | | | | | - | | - |
| Capital increase in subsidiaries | | | | | | | | | | | - | 44 | 44 |
| Interim and final dividends paid | | | | | | | | | | (2,110) | (2,110) | (261) | (2,371) |
| Changes in control of consolidated entities | | | | | | | | | | (6) | (6) | 114 | 108 |
| Acquisition and disposal of minority interests shares | | | | | | | | | | (86) | (86) | (56) | (142) |
| Purchase commitments for minority interests' shares | | | | | | | | | | (129) | (129) | (291) | (420) |
| As of December 31, 2017 | 507,042,596 | 152 | 2,614 | (530) | 354 | - | 130 | 1,114 | (133) | 25,268 | 28,969 | 1,408 | 30,377 |
| Gains and losses recognized in equity | | | | | 219 | - | (259) | 3 | 20 | - | (17) | 45 | 28 |
| Net profit | | | | | | | | | | 6,354 | 6,354 | 636 | 6,990 |
| Comprehensive income | - | - | - | 219 | - | (259) | 3 | 20 | 6,354 | 6,337 | 681 | 7,018 | |
| Stock option plan and similar expenses | | | | | | | | | | 78 | 78 | 4 | 82 |
| (Acquisition)/disposal of treasury shares and LVMH share-settled derivatives | | | | (256) | | | | | | (26) | (282) | - | (282) |
| Exercise of LVMH share subscription options | 762,851 | | 49 | | | | | | | - | 49 | - | 49 |
| Retirement of LVMH shares | (2,775,952) | | (365) | 365 | | | | | | - | - | | - |
| Capital increase in subsidiaries | | | | | | | | | | | - | 50 | 50 |
| Interim and final dividends paid | | | | | | | | | | (2,715) | (2,715) | (345) | (3,060) |
| Changes in control of consolidated entities | | | | | | | | | | (9) | (9) | 41 | 32 |
| Acquisition and disposal of minority interests shares | | | | | | | | | | (22) | (22) | (19) | (41) |
| Purchase commitments for minority interests' shares | | | | | | | | | | (112) | (112) | (156) | (268) |
| As of December 31, 2018 | 505,029,495 | 152 | 2,298 | (421) | 573 | - | (129) | 1,117 | (113) | 28,816 | 32,293 | 1,664 | 33,957 |

(1) The financial statements as of December 31, 2017 and December 31, 2016 have been restated to reflect the retrospective application with effect from January 1, 2016 of IFRS 9 Financial Instruments. See Note 1.2.

**Consolidated Cash Flow Statement**

| (EUR millions) | Notes | 2018 | 2017[1][2] | 2016[1] |
|---|---|---|---|---|
| **I. OPERATING ACTIVITIES AND OPERATING INVESTMENTS** | | | | |
| Operating profit | | 9,877 | 8,113 | 6,904 |
| Income/(loss) and dividends from joint ventures and associates | 7 | 5 | 25 | 18 |
| Net increase in depreciation, amortization and provisions | | 2,302 | 2,376 | 2,143 |
| Other computed expenses | | (141) | (43) | (177) |
| Other adjustments | | (78) | (66) | (155) |
| **Cash from operations before changes in working capital** | | **11,965** | **10,405** | **8,733** |
| Cost of net financial debt: interest paid | | (113) | (129) | (122) |
| Tax paid | | (2,275) | (2,790) | (1,923) |
| **Net cash from operating activities before changes in working capital** | | **9,577** | **7,486** | **6,688** |
| Change in working capital | 14.2 | (1,087) | (514) | (512) |
| **Net cash from operating activities** | | **8,490** | **6,972** | **6,176** |
| Operating investments | 14.3 | (3,038) | (2,276) | (2,265) |
| **Net cash from operating activities and operating investments (free cash flow)** | | **5,452** | **4,696** | **3,911** |
| **II. FINANCIAL INVESTMENTS** | | | | |
| Purchase of non-current available for sale financial assets[a] | 8 | (445) | (125) | (28) |
| Proceeds from sale of non-current available for sale financial assets | 8 | 45 | 87 | 91 |
| Dividends received | | 18 | 13 | 55 |
| Tax paid related to non-current available for sale financial assets and consolidated investments | | (2) | - | (461) |
| Impact of purchase and sale of consolidated investments | 2 | (17) | (6,306) | 310 |
| **Net cash from (used in) financial investments** | | **(401)** | **(6,331)** | **(33)** |
| **III. TRANSACTIONS RELATING TO EQUITY** | | | | |
| Capital increases of LVMH SE | 15.1 | 49 | 53 | 64 |
| Capital increases of subsidiaries subscribed by minority interests | 17 | 41 | 44 | 41 |
| Acquisition and disposals of treasury shares and LVMH share-settled derivatives | 15.2 | (295) | (67) | (352) |
| Interim and final dividends paid by LVMH SE | 15.3 | (2,715) | (2,110) | (1,859) |
| Tax paid related to interim and final dividends paid | | (36) | 388 | (145) |
| Interim and final dividends paid to minority interests in consolidated subsidiaries | 17 | (339) | (260) | (267) |
| Purchase and proceeds from sale of minority interests | 2 | (236) | (153) | (95) |
| **Net cash from (used in) transactions relating to equity** | | **(3,531)** | **(2,105)** | **(2,613)** |
| **Change in cash before financing activities** | | **1,520** | **(3,740)** | **1,265** |
| **IV. FINANCING ACTIVITIES** | | | | |
| Proceeds from borrowings | 18.1 | 1,529 | 5,931 | 913 |
| Repayment of borrowings | 18.1 | (2,174) | (1,760) | (2,181) |
| Purchase and proceeds from sale of current available for sale financial assets[a] | 13 | (147) | 92 | (104) |
| **Net cash from (used in) financing activities** | 14.2 | **(792)** | **4,263** | **(1,372)** |
| **V. EFFECT OF EXCHANGE RATE CHANGES** | | **67** | **(242)** | **54** |
| **NET INCREASE (DECREASE) IN CASH AND CASH EQUIVALENTS (I+II+III+IV+V)** | | **795** | **281** | **(53)** |
| **CASH AND CASH EQUIVALENTS AT BEGINNING OF PERIOD** | 14.1 | **3,618** | **3,337** | **3,390** |
| **CASH AND CASH EQUIVALENTS AT END OF PERIOD** | 14.1 | **4,413** | **3,618** | **3,337** |
| **TOTAL TAX PAID** | | **(2,314)** | **(2,402)** | **(2,529)** |

(a) The cash impact of non-current available for sale financial assets used to hedge net financial debt (see Note 18) is presented under "IV Financing activities" as "Purchase and proceeds from sale of current available for sale financial assets".

(1) The financial statements as of December 31, 2017 and December 31, 2016 have been restated to reflect the retrospective application with effect from January 1, 2016 of IFRS 9 Financial Instruments. See Note 1.2.

(2) The financial statements as of December 31, 2017 have been restated to reflect the definitive allocation of the purchase price of Christian Dior Couture. See Note 2.1.

# Time Value of Money

## Appendix Preview

Would you rather receive $1,000 today or a year from now? You should prefer to receive the $1,000 today because you can invest the $1,000 and then earn interest on it. As a result, you will have more than $1,000 a year from now. What this example illustrates is the concept of the **time value of money**. Everyone prefers to receive money today rather than in the future because of the interest factor.

## Appendix Outline

### LEARNING OBJECTIVES

| | |
|---|---|
| **1.** Compute interest and future values. | • Nature of interest<br>• Future value of a single amount<br>• Future value of an annuity |
| **2.** Compute present values. | • Present value variables<br>• Present value of a single amount<br>• Present value of an annuity<br>• Time periods and discounting<br>• Present value of a long-term note or bond |
| **3.** Compute the present value in capital budgeting situations. | • Using alternative discount rates |
| **4.** Use a financial calculator to solve time value of money problems. | • Present value of a single sum<br>• Present value of an annuity<br>• Future value of a single sum<br>• Future value of an annuity<br>• Internal rate of return<br>• Useful financial calculator applications |

# Interest and Future Values

> **LEARNING OBJECTIVE 1**
> Compute interest and future values.

## Nature of Interest

**Interest** is payment for the use of another person's money. It is the difference between the amount borrowed or invested (called the **principal**) and the amount repaid or collected. The amount of interest to be paid or collected is usually stated as a rate over a specific period of time. The rate of interest is generally stated as an annual rate.

The amount of interest involved in any financing transaction is based on three elements:

1. **Principal ($p$):** The original amount borrowed or invested.
2. **Interest Rate ($i$):** An annual percentage of the principal.
3. **Time ($n$):** The number of periods over which the principal is borrowed or invested.

### Simple Interest

**Simple interest** is computed on the principal amount only. It is the return on the principal for one period (we use an annual interest rate unless stated otherwise). Simple interest is usually expressed as shown in **Illustration G.1**.

**ILLUSTRATION G.1**

**Interest computation**

| Interest | = | Principal $p$ | × | Rate $i$ | × | Time $n$ |
|---|---|---|---|---|---|---|

For example, if you borrowed $5,000 for 2 years at a simple interest rate of 12% annually, you would pay $1,200 in total interest, computed as follows.

$$\text{Interest} = p \times i \times n$$
$$= \$5,000 \times .12 \times 2$$
$$= \$1,200$$

### Compound Interest

**Compound interest** is computed on principal **and** on any interest earned that has not been paid or withdrawn. It is the return on (or growth of) the principal for two or more time periods. Compounding computes interest not only on the principal but also on the interest earned to date on that principal, assuming the interest is left on deposit.

To illustrate the difference between simple and compound interest, assume that you deposit $1,000 in Bank Two, where it will earn simple interest of 9% per year, and you deposit another $1,000 in Citizens Bank, where it will earn compound interest of 9% per year compounded annually. Also assume that in both cases you will not withdraw any cash until three years from the date of deposit. **Illustration G.2** shows the computation of interest to be received and the accumulated year-end balances.

**ILLUSTRATION G.2**   Simple versus compound interest

| Bank Two | | | | Citizens Bank | | |
|---|---|---|---|---|---|---|
| Simple Interest Calculation | Simple Interest | Accumulated Year-End Balance | | Compound Interest Calculation | Compound Interest | Accumulated Year-End Balance |
| Year 1 $1,000.00 × 9% | $ 90.00 | $1,090.00 | | Year 1 $1,000.00 × 9% | $ 90.00 | $1,090.00 |
| Year 2 $1,000.00 × 9% | 90.00 | $1,180.00 | | Year 2 $1,090.00 × 9% | 98.10 | $1,188.10 |
| Year 3 $1,000.00 × 9% | 90.00 | $1,270.00 | | Year 3 $1,188.10 × 9% | 106.93 | $1,295.03 |
| | $ 270.00 | | $25.03 Difference | | $ 295.03 | |

Note in Illustration G.2 that simple interest uses the initial principal of $1,000 to compute the interest in all three years. Compound interest uses the accumulated balance (principal plus interest to date) at each year-end to compute interest in the succeeding year—which explains why your compound interest account is larger.

Obviously, if you had a choice between investing your money at simple interest or at compound interest, you would choose compound interest, all other things—especially risk—being equal. In the example, compounding provides $25.03 of additional interest income. For practical purposes, compounding assumes that unpaid interest earned becomes a part of the principal, and the accumulated balance at the end of each year becomes the new principal on which interest is earned during the next year.

Most business situations use compound interest. Simple interest is generally applicable only to short-term situations of one year or less.

# Future Value of a Single Amount

The **future value of a single amount** is the value at a future date of a given amount invested, assuming compound interest. For example, in Illustration G.2, $1,295.03 is the future value of the $1,000 investment earning 9% for three years. The $1,295.03 is determined more easily by using the formula shown in **Illustration G.3**.

$$FV = p \times (1 + i)^n$$

**ILLUSTRATION G.3**
**Formula for future value**

where:

$FV$ = future value of a single amount
$p$ = principal (or present value; the value today)
$i$ = interest rate for one period
$n$ = number of periods

The $1,295.03 is computed as follows.

$$
\begin{aligned}
FV &= p \times (1 + i)^n \\
&= \$1,000 \times (1 + .09)^3 \\
&= \$1,000 \times 1.29503 \\
&= \$1,295.03
\end{aligned}
$$

The 1.29503 is computed by multiplying $(1.09 \times 1.09 \times 1.09)$. The amounts in this example can be depicted in the time diagram shown in **Illustration G.4**.

**ILLUSTRATION G.4** Time diagram

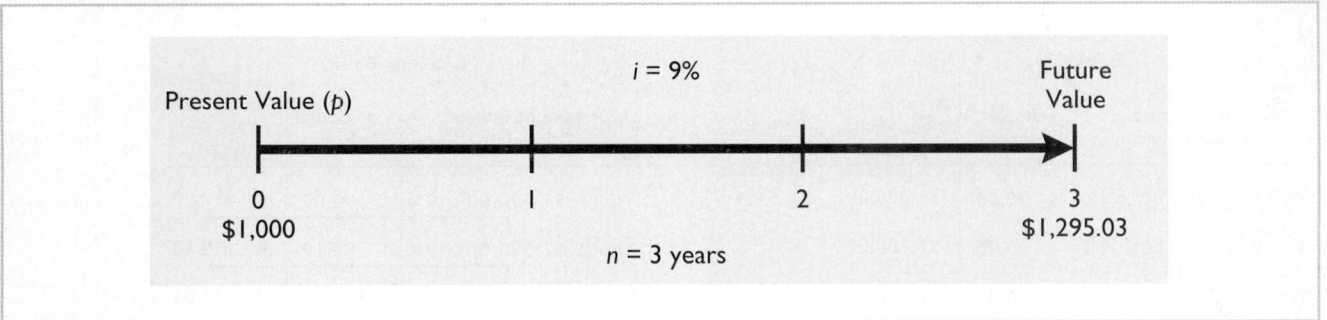

Another method used to compute the future value of a single amount involves a compound interest table. This table shows the future value of 1 for *n* periods. **Table 1** is such a table.

**TABLE 1** Future Value of 1

| (*n*) Periods | 4% | 5% | 6% | 7% | 8% | 9% | 10% | 11% | 12% | 15% |
|---|---|---|---|---|---|---|---|---|---|---|
| 0 | 1.00000 | 1.00000 | 1.00000 | 1.00000 | 1.00000 | 1.00000 | 1.00000 | 1.00000 | 1.00000 | 1.00000 |
| 1 | 1.04000 | 1.05000 | 1.06000 | 1.07000 | 1.08000 | 1.09000 | 1.10000 | 1.11000 | 1.12000 | 1.15000 |
| 2 | 1.08160 | 1.10250 | 1.12360 | 1.14490 | 1.16640 | 1.18810 | 1.21000 | 1.23210 | 1.25440 | 1.32250 |
| 3 | 1.12486 | 1.15763 | 1.19102 | 1.22504 | 1.25971 | 1.29503 | 1.33100 | 1.36763 | 1.40493 | 1.52088 |
| 4 | 1.16986 | 1.21551 | 1.26248 | 1.31080 | 1.36049 | 1.41158 | 1.46410 | 1.51807 | 1.57352 | 1.74901 |
| 5 | 1.21665 | 1.27628 | 1.33823 | 1.40255 | 1.46933 | 1.53862 | 1.61051 | 1.68506 | 1.76234 | 2.01136 |
| 6 | 1.26532 | 1.34010 | 1.41852 | 1.50073 | 1.58687 | 1.67710 | 1.77156 | 1.87041 | 1.97382 | 2.31306 |
| 7 | 1.31593 | 1.40710 | 1.50363 | 1.60578 | 1.71382 | 1.82804 | 1.94872 | 2.07616 | 2.21068 | 2.66002 |
| 8 | 1.36857 | 1.47746 | 1.59385 | 1.71819 | 1.85093 | 1.99256 | 2.14359 | 2.30454 | 2.47596 | 3.05902 |
| 9 | 1.42331 | 1.55133 | 1.68948 | 1.83846 | 1.99900 | 2.17189 | 2.35795 | 2.55803 | 2.77308 | 3.51788 |
| 10 | 1.48024 | 1.62889 | 1.79085 | 1.96715 | 2.15892 | 2.36736 | 2.59374 | 2.83942 | 3.10585 | 4.04556 |
| 11 | 1.53945 | 1.71034 | 1.89830 | 2.10485 | 2.33164 | 2.58043 | 2.85312 | 3.15176 | 3.47855 | 4.65239 |
| 12 | 1.60103 | 1.79586 | 2.01220 | 2.25219 | 2.51817 | 2.81267 | 3.13843 | 3.49845 | 3.89598 | 5.35025 |
| 13 | 1.66507 | 1.88565 | 2.13293 | 2.40985 | 2.71962 | 3.06581 | 3.45227 | 3.88328 | 4.36349 | 6.15279 |
| 14 | 1.73168 | 1.97993 | 2.26090 | 2.57853 | 2.93719 | 3.34173 | 3.79750 | 4.31044 | 4.88711 | 7.07571 |
| 15 | 1.80094 | 2.07893 | 2.39656 | 2.75903 | 3.17217 | 3.64248 | 4.17725 | 4.78459 | 5.47357 | 8.13706 |
| 16 | 1.87298 | 2.18287 | 2.54035 | 2.95216 | 3.42594 | 3.97031 | 4.59497 | 5.31089 | 6.13039 | 9.35762 |
| 17 | 1.94790 | 2.29202 | 2.69277 | 3.15882 | 3.70002 | 4.32763 | 5.05447 | 5.89509 | 6.86604 | 10.76126 |
| 18 | 2.02582 | 2.40662 | 2.85434 | 3.37993 | 3.99602 | 4.71712 | 5.55992 | 6.54355 | 7.68997 | 12.37545 |
| 19 | 2.10685 | 2.52695 | 3.02560 | 3.61653 | 4.31570 | 5.14166 | 6.11591 | 7.26334 | 8.61276 | 14.23177 |
| 20 | 2.19112 | 2.65330 | 3.20714 | 3.86968 | 4.66096 | 5.60441 | 6.72750 | 8.06231 | 9.64629 | 16.36654 |

In Table 1, *n* is the number of compounding periods, the percentages are the periodic interest rates, and the 5-digit decimal numbers in the respective columns are the future value of 1 factors. To use Table 1, you multiply the principal amount by the future value factor for the specified number of periods and interest rate. For example, the future value factor for two periods at 9% is 1.18810. Multiplying this factor by $1,000 equals $1,188.10—which is the accumulated balance at the end of year 2 in the Citizens Bank example in Illustration G.2. The $1,295.03 accumulated balance at the end of the third year is calculated from Table 1 by multiplying the future value factor for three periods (1.29503) by the $1,000.

The demonstration problem in **Illustration G.5** shows how to use Table 1.

**ILLUSTRATION G.5** Demonstration problem—Using Table 1 for *FV* of 1

> John and Mary Rich invested $20,000 in a savings account paying 6% interest at the time their son, Mike, was born. The money is to be used by Mike for his college education. On his 18th birthday, Mike withdraws the money from his savings account. How much did Mike withdraw from his account?

> **Answer:** The future value factor from Table 1 is 2.85434 (18 periods at 6%). The future value of $20,000 earning 6% per year for 18 years is **$57,086.80** ($20,000 × 2.85434).

# Future Value of an Annuity

The preceding discussion involved the accumulation of only a single principal sum. Individuals and businesses frequently encounter situations in which a **series** of equal dollar amounts are to be paid or received at evenly spaced time intervals (periodically), such as loans or lease (rental) contracts. A series of payments or receipts of equal dollar amounts is referred to as an **annuity**.

The **future value of an annuity** is the sum of all the payments (receipts) plus the accumulated compound interest on them. In computing the future value of an annuity, it is necessary to know (1) the interest rate, (2) the number of payments (receipts), and (3) the amount of the periodic payments (receipts).

To illustrate the computation of the future value of an annuity, assume that you invest $2,000 at the end of each year for three years at 5% interest compounded annually. This situation is depicted in the time diagram in **Illustration G.6**.

**ILLUSTRATION G.6** Time diagram for a three-year annuity

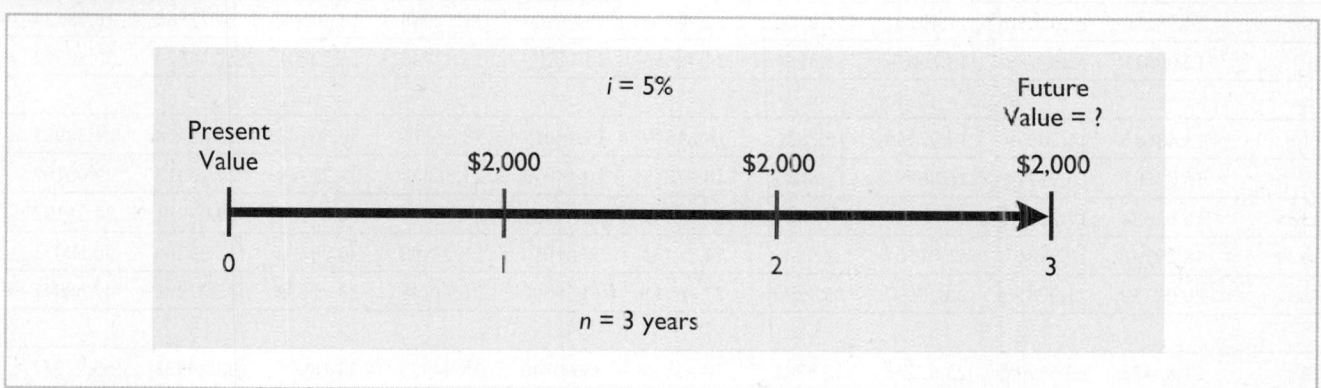

The $2,000 invested at the end of year 1 will earn interest for two years (years 2 and 3), and the $2,000 invested at the end of year 2 will earn interest for one year (year 3). However, the last $2,000 investment (made at the end of year 3) will not earn any interest. Using the future value factors from Table 1, the future value of these periodic payments is computed as shown in **Illustration G.7**.

**Future value of periodic payment computation**

| Invested at End of Year | Number of Compounding Periods | Amount Invested | × | Future Value of 1 Factor at 5% | = | Future Value |
|---|---|---|---|---|---|---|
| 1 | 2 | $2,000 | | 1.10250 | | $2,205 |
| 2 | 1 | 2,000 | | 1.05000 | | 2,100 |
| 3 | 0 | 2,000 | | 1.00000 | | 2,000 |
| | | | | **3.15250** | | **$6,305** |

The first $2,000 investment is multiplied by the future value factor for two periods (1.1025) because two years' interest will accumulate on it (in years 2 and 3). The second $2,000 investment will earn only one year's interest (in year 3) and therefore is multiplied by the future value factor for one year (1.0500). The final $2,000 investment is made at the end of the third year and will not earn any interest. Thus, $n = 0$ and the future value factor is 1.00000. Consequently, the future value of the last $2,000 invested is only $2,000 since it does not accumulate any interest.

Calculating the future value of each individual cash flow is required when the periodic payments or receipts are not equal in each period. However, when the periodic payments (receipts) are **the same in each period**, the future value can be computed by using a future value of an annuity of 1 table. **Table 2** is such a table.

**TABLE 2    Future Value of an Annuity of 1**

| (n) Payments | 4% | 5% | 6% | 7% | 8% | 9% | 10% | 11% | 12% | 15% |
|---|---|---|---|---|---|---|---|---|---|---|
| 1 | 1.00000 | 1.00000 | 1.00000 | 1.0000 | 1.00000 | 1.00000 | 1.00000 | 1.00000 | 1.00000 | 1.00000 |
| 2 | 2.04000 | 2.05000 | 2.06000 | 2.0700 | 2.08000 | 2.09000 | 2.10000 | 2.11000 | 2.12000 | 2.15000 |
| 3 | 3.12160 | 3.15250 | 3.18360 | 3.2149 | 3.24640 | 3.27810 | 3.31000 | 3.34210 | 3.37440 | 3.47250 |
| 4 | 4.24646 | 4.31013 | 4.37462 | 4.4399 | 4.50611 | 4.57313 | 4.64100 | 4.70973 | 4.77933 | 4.99338 |
| 5 | 5.41632 | 5.52563 | 5.63709 | 5.7507 | 5.86660 | 5.98471 | 6.10510 | 6.22780 | 6.35285 | 6.74238 |
| 6 | 6.63298 | 6.80191 | 6.97532 | 7.1533 | 7.33592 | 7.52334 | 7.71561 | 7.91286 | 8.11519 | 8.75374 |
| 7 | 7.89829 | 8.14201 | 8.39384 | 8.6540 | 8.92280 | 9.20044 | 9.48717 | 9.78327 | 10.08901 | 11.06680 |
| 8 | 9.21423 | 9.54911 | 9.89747 | 10.2598 | 10.63663 | 11.02847 | 11.43589 | 11.85943 | 12.29969 | 13.72682 |
| 9 | 10.58280 | 11.02656 | 11.49132 | 11.9780 | 12.48756 | 13.02104 | 13.57948 | 14.16397 | 14.77566 | 16.78584 |
| 10 | 12.00611 | 12.57789 | 13.18079 | 13.8164 | 14.48656 | 15.19293 | 15.93743 | 16.72201 | 17.54874 | 20.30372 |
| 11 | 13.48635 | 14.20679 | 14.97164 | 15.7836 | 16.64549 | 17.56029 | 18.53117 | 19.56143 | 20.65458 | 24.34928 |
| 12 | 15.02581 | 15.91713 | 16.86994 | 17.8885 | 18.97713 | 20.14072 | 21.38428 | 22.71319 | 24.13313 | 29.00167 |
| 13 | 16.62684 | 17.71298 | 18.88214 | 20.1406 | 21.49530 | 22.95339 | 24.52271 | 26.21164 | 28.02911 | 34.35192 |
| 14 | 18.29191 | 19.59863 | 21.01507 | 22.5505 | 24.21492 | 26.01919 | 27.97498 | 30.09492 | 32.39260 | 40.50471 |
| 15 | 20.02359 | 21.57856 | 23.27597 | 25.1290 | 27.15211 | 29.36092 | 31.77248 | 34.40536 | 37.27972 | 47.58041 |
| 16 | 21.82453 | 23.65749 | 25.67253 | 27.8881 | 30.32428 | 33.00340 | 35.94973 | 39.18995 | 42.75328 | 55.71747 |
| 17 | 23.69751 | 25.84037 | 28.21288 | 30.8402 | 33.75023 | 36.97351 | 40.54470 | 44.50084 | 48.88367 | 65.07509 |
| 18 | 25.64541 | 28.13238 | 30.90565 | 33.9990 | 37.45024 | 41.30134 | 45.59917 | 50.39593 | 55.74972 | 75.83636 |
| 19 | 27.67123 | 30.53900 | 33.75999 | 37.3790 | 41.44626 | 46.01846 | 51.15909 | 56.93949 | 63.43968 | 88.21181 |
| 20 | 29.77808 | 33.06595 | 36.78559 | 40.9955 | 45.76196 | 51.16012 | 57.27500 | 64.20283 | 72.05244 | 102.44358 |

Table 2 shows the future value of 1 to be received periodically for a given number of payments. It assumes that each payment is made at the **end** of each period. We can see from Table 2 that the future value of an annuity of 1 factor for three payments at 5% is 3.15250. The future value factor is the total of the three individual future value factors shown in Illustration G.7. Multiplying this amount by the annual investment of $2,000 produces a future value of $6,305.

The demonstration problem in **Illustration G.8** shows how to use Table 2.

**ILLUSTRATION G.8** Demonstration problem—Using Table 2 for *FV* of an annuity of 1

John and Char Lewis's daughter, Debra, has just started high school. They decide to start a college fund for her and will invest $2,500 in a savings account at the end of each year she is in high school (4 payments total). The account will earn 6% interest compounded annually. How much will be in the college fund at the time Debra graduates from high school?

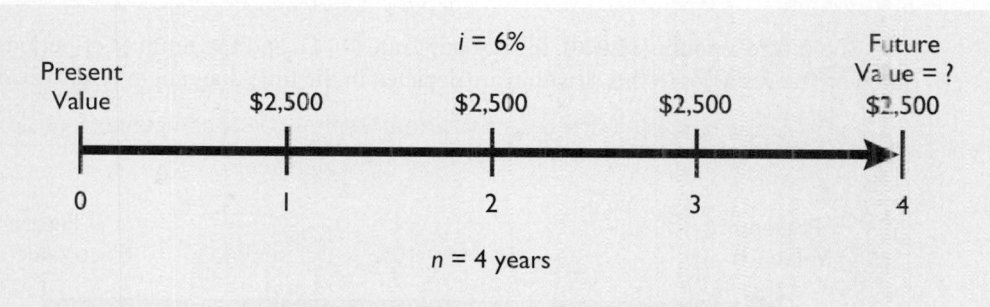

**Answer:** The future value factor from Table 2 is 4.37462 (4 payments at 6%). The future value of $2,500 invested each year for 4 years at 6% interest is **$10,936.55** ($2,500 × 4.37462).

# Present Values

**LEARNING OBJECTIVE 2**

Compute present values.

## Present Value Variables

The **present value** is the value now of a given amount to be paid or received in the future assuming compound interest. The present value, like the future value, is based on three variables: (1) the dollar amount to be received (future amount), (2) the length of time until the amount is received (number of periods), and (3) the interest rate (the discount rate). The process of determining the present value is referred to as **discounting the future amount**.

Present value computations are used in measuring many items. For example, the present value of principal and interest payments is used to determine the market price of a bond. Determining the amount to be reported for notes payable and lease liabilities also involves present value computations. In addition, capital budgeting and other investment proposals are evaluated using present value computations. Finally, all rate of return and internal rate of return computations involve present value techniques.

# Present Value of a Single Amount

To illustrate present value, assume that you want to invest a sum of money today that will provide $1,000 at the end of one year. What amount would you need to invest today to have $1,000 one year from now? If you want a 10% rate of return, the investment or present value is $909.09 ($1,000 ÷ 1.10). The formula for calculating present value is shown in **Illustration G.9**.

**ILLUSTRATION G.9**

**Formula for present value**

$$\text{Present Value } (PV) = \text{Future Value } (FV) \div (1 + i)^n$$

The computation of $1,000 discounted at 10% for one year is as follows.

$$
\begin{aligned}
PV &= FV \div (1 + i)^n \\
&= \$1{,}000 \div (1 + .10)^1 \\
&= \$1{,}000 \div 1.10 \\
&= \$909.09
\end{aligned}
$$

The future amount ($1,000), the discount rate (10%), and the number of periods (1) are known. The variables in this situation are depicted in the time diagram in **Illustration G.10**.

**ILLUSTRATION G.10**

**Finding present value if discounted for one period**

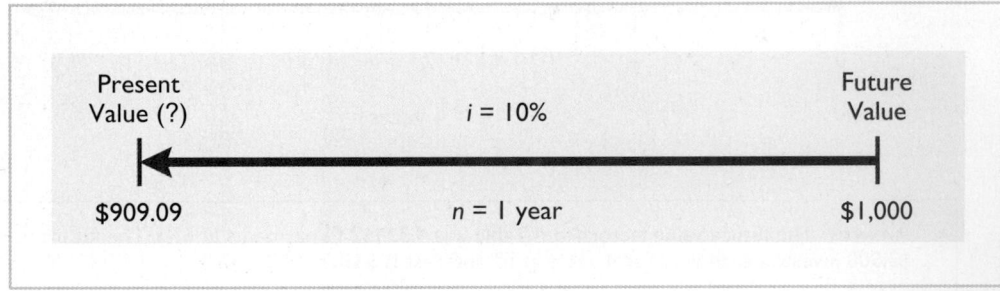

If the single amount of $1,000 is to be received **in two years** and discounted at 10%, the formula $PV = \$1{,}000 \div (1 + .10)^2$ is used, where $(1 + .10)^2$ is equal to 1.21 (1.10 × 1.10). Its present value is $826.45 ($1,000 ÷ 1.21), depicted in **Illustration G.11**.

**ILLUSTRATION G.11**

**Finding present value if discounted for two periods**

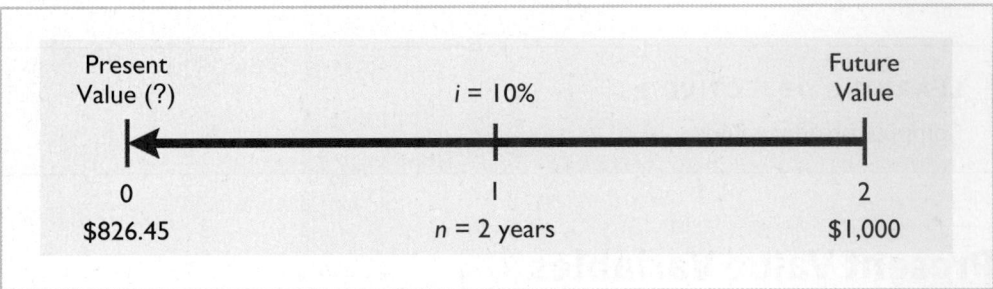

The present value of 1 may also be determined through tables that show the present value of 1 for *n* periods. In **Table 3**, *n* is the number of discounting periods involved. The percentages are the periodic interest rates or discount rates, and the 5-digit decimal numbers in the respective columns are the present value of 1 factors.

**TABLE 3**  Present Value of 1

| (*n*) Periods | 4% | 5% | 6% | 7% | 8% | 9% | 10% | 11% | 12% | 15% |
|---|---|---|---|---|---|---|---|---|---|---|
| 1 | .96154 | .95238 | .94340 | .93458 | .92593 | .91743 | .90909 | .90090 | .89286 | .86957 |
| 2 | .92456 | .90703 | .89000 | .87344 | .85734 | .84168 | .82645 | .81162 | .79719 | .75614 |
| 3 | .88900 | .86384 | .83962 | .81630 | .79383 | .77218 | .75132 | .73119 | .71178 | .65752 |
| 4 | .85480 | .82270 | .79209 | .76290 | .73503 | .70843 | .68301 | .65873 | .63552 | .57175 |
| 5 | .82193 | .78353 | .74726 | .71299 | .68058 | .64993 | .62092 | .59345 | .56743 | .49718 |
| 6 | .79031 | .74622 | .70496 | .66634 | .63017 | .59627 | .56447 | .53464 | .50663 | .43233 |
| 7 | .75992 | 71068 | .66506 | .62275 | .58349 | .54703 | .51316 | .48166 | .45235 | .37594 |
| 8 | .73069 | .67684 | .62741 | .58201 | .54027 | .50187 | .46651 | .43393 | .40388 | .32690 |
| 9 | .70259 | .64461 | .59190 | .54393 | .50025 | .46043 | .42410 | .39092 | .36061 | .28426 |
| 10 | .67556 | .61391 | .55839 | .50835 | .46319 | .42241 | .38554 | .35218 | .32197 | .24719 |
| 11 | .64958 | .58468 | .52679 | .47509 | .42888 | .38753 | .35049 | .31728 | .28748 | .21494 |
| 12 | .62460 | .55684 | .49697 | .44401 | .39711 | .35554 | .31863 | .28584 | .25668 | .18691 |
| 13 | .60057 | .53032 | .46884 | .41496 | .36770 | .32618 | .28966 | .25751 | .22917 | .16253 |
| 14 | .57748 | .50507 | .44230 | .38782 | .34046 | .29925 | .26333 | .23199 | .20462 | .14133 |
| 15 | .55526 | .48102 | .41727 | .36245 | .31524 | .27454 | .23939 | .20900 | .18270 | .12289 |
| 16 | .53391 | .45811 | .39365 | .33873 | .29189 | .25187 | .21763 | .18829 | .16312 | .10687 |
| 17 | .51337 | .43630 | .37136 | .31657 | .27027 | .23107 | .19785 | .16963 | .14564 | .09293 |
| 18 | .49363 | .41552 | .35034 | .29586 | .25025 | .21199 | .17986 | .15282 | .13004 | .08081 |
| 19 | .47464 | .39573 | .33051 | .27615 | .23171 | .19449 | .16351 | .13768 | .11611 | .07027 |
| 20 | .45639 | .37689 | .31180 | .25842 | .21455 | .17843 | .14864 | .12403 | .10367 | .06110 |

When using Table 3, the future value is multiplied by the present value factor specified at the intersection of the number of periods and the discount rate.

For example, the present value factor for one period at a discount rate of 10% is .90909, which is the value used to compute $909.09 ($1,000 × .90909) in Illustration G.10. For two periods at a discount rate of 10%, the present value factor is .82645, which is the value used to compute $826.45 ($1,000 × .82645) in Illustration G.11.

Note that a higher discount rate produces a smaller present value. For example, using a 15% discount rate, the present value of $1,000 due one year from now is $869.57 ($1,000 × .86957), versus $909.09 at 10%. Also note that the farther in the future that the future value is, the smaller the present value. For example, using the same discount rate of 10%, the present value of $1,000 due in **five years** at 10% is $620.92 ($1,000 × .62092). The present value of $1,000 due in **one year** is $909.09, a difference of $288.17.

The following two demonstration problems (**Illustrations G.12** and **G.13**) illustrate how to use Table 3.

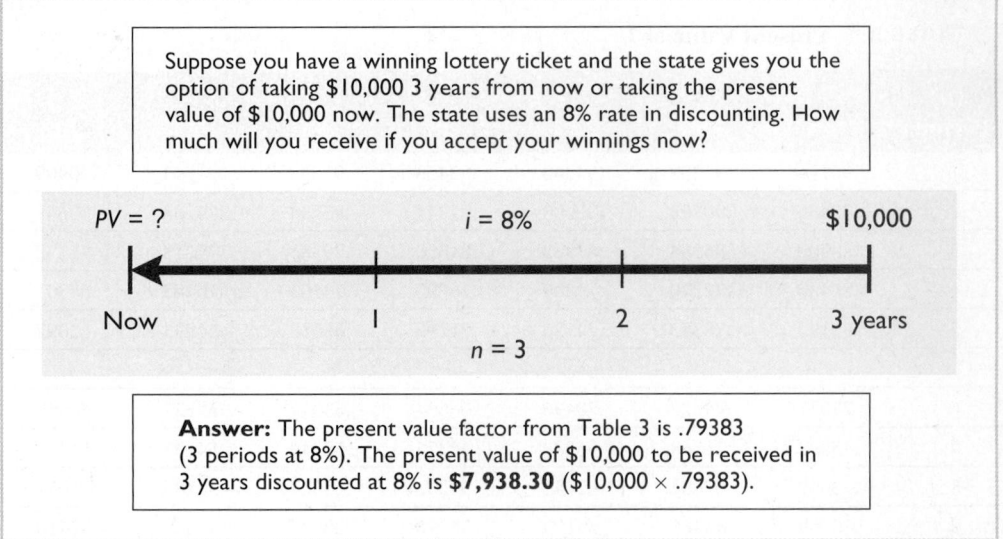

Suppose you have a winning lottery ticket and the state gives you the option of taking $10,000 3 years from now or taking the present value of $10,000 now. The state uses an 8% rate in discounting. How much will you receive if you accept your winnings now?

PV = ?          i = 8%          $10,000

Now          1          2          3 years

n = 3

**Answer:** The present value factor from Table 3 is .79383 (3 periods at 8%). The present value of $10,000 to be received in 3 years discounted at 8% is **$7,938.30** ($10,000 × .79383).

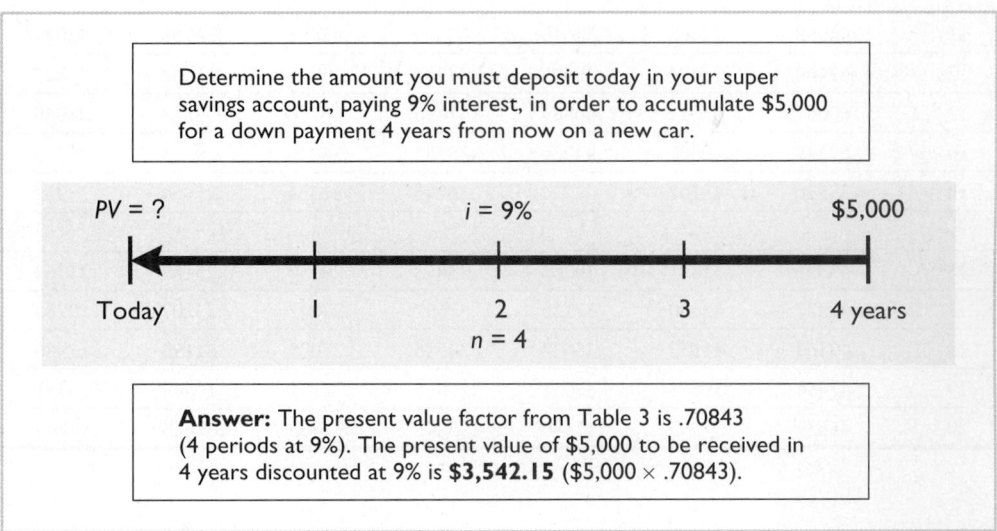

Determine the amount you must deposit today in your super savings account, paying 9% interest, in order to accumulate $5,000 for a down payment 4 years from now on a new car.

PV = ?          i = 9%          $5,000

Today          1          2          3          4 years

n = 4

**Answer:** The present value factor from Table 3 is .70843 (4 periods at 9%). The present value of $5,000 to be received in 4 years discounted at 9% is **$3,542.15** ($5,000 × .70843).

# Present Value of an Annuity

The preceding discussion involved the discounting of only a single future amount. Businesses and individuals frequently engage in transactions in which a series of equal dollar amounts are to be received or paid at evenly spaced time intervals (periodically). Examples of a series of periodic receipts or payments are loan agreements, installment sales, mortgage notes, lease (rental) contracts, and pension obligations. As discussed earlier, these periodic receipts or payments are **annuities**.

The **present value of an annuity** is the value now of a series of future receipts or payments, discounted assuming compound interest. In computing the present value of an annuity, it is necessary to know (1) the discount rate, (2) the number of payments (receipts), and (3) the amount of the periodic receipts or payments. To illustrate the computation of the present value of an annuity, assume that you will receive $1,000 cash annually for three years at a time when the discount rate is 10%. This situation is depicted in the time diagram in **Illustration G.14**. **Illustration G.15** shows the computation of its present value in this situation.

**ILLUSTRATION G.14**
Time diagram for a three-year annuity

|                        |   | **Present Value of 1** |   |                   |
| ---------------------- | - | ---------------------- | - | ----------------- |
| **Future Amount**      | × | **Factor at 10%**      | = | **Present Value** |
| $1,000 (1 year away)   |   | .90909                 |   | $  909.09         |
| 1,000 (2 years away)   |   | .82645                 |   | 826.45            |
| 1,000 (3 years away)   |   | .75132                 |   | 751.32            |
|                        |   | **2.48686**            |   | **$2,486.86**     |

**ILLUSTRATION G.15**
Present value of a series of future amounts computation

This method of calculation is required when the periodic cash flows are not uniform in each period. However, when the future receipts are the same in each period, an annuity table can be used. As illustrated in **Table 4**, an annuity table shows the present value of 1 to be received periodically for a given number of payments. It assumes that each payment is made at the end of each period.

| **TABLE 4** | **Present Value of an Annuity of 1** |

| (n) Payments | 4% | 5% | 6% | 7% | 8% | 9% | 10% | 11% | 12% | 15% |
| --- | --- | --- | --- | --- | --- | --- | --- | --- | --- | --- |
| 1 | .96154 | .95238 | .94340 | .93458 | .92593 | .91743 | .90909 | .90090 | .89286 | .86957 |
| 2 | 1.88609 | 1.85941 | 1.83339 | 1.80802 | 1.78326 | 1.75911 | 1.73554 | 1.71252 | 1.69005 | 1.62571 |
| 3 | 2.77509 | 2.72325 | 2.67301 | 2.62432 | 2.57710 | 2.53130 | 2.48685 | 2.44371 | 2.40183 | 2.28323 |
| 4 | 3.62990 | 3.54595 | 3.46511 | 3.38721 | 3.31213 | 3.23972 | 3.16986 | 3.10245 | 3.03735 | 2.85498 |
| 5 | 4.45182 | 4.32948 | 4.21236 | 4.10020 | 3.99271 | 3.88965 | 3.79079 | 3.69590 | 3.60478 | 3.35216 |
| 6 | 5.24214 | 5.07569 | 4.91732 | 4.76654 | 4.62288 | 4.48592 | 4.35526 | 4.23054 | 4.11141 | 3.78448 |
| 7 | 6.00205 | 5.78637 | 5.58238 | 5.38929 | 5.20637 | 5.03295 | 4.86842 | 4.71220 | 4.56376 | 4.16042 |
| 8 | 6.73274 | 6.46321 | 6.20979 | 5.97130 | 5.74664 | 5.53482 | 5.33493 | 5.14612 | 4.96764 | 4.48732 |
| 9 | 7.43533 | 7.10782 | 6.80169 | 6.51523 | 6.24689 | 5.99525 | 5.75902 | 5.53705 | 5.32825 | 4.77158 |
| 10 | 8.11090 | 7.72173 | 7.36009 | 7.02358 | 6.71008 | 6.41766 | 6.14457 | 5.88923 | 5.65022 | 5.01877 |
| 11 | 8.76048 | 8.30641 | 7.88687 | 7.49867 | 7.13896 | 6.80519 | 6.49506 | 6.20652 | 5.93770 | 5.23371 |
| 12 | 9.38507 | 8.86325 | 8.38384 | 7.94269 | 7.53608 | 7.16073 | 6.81369 | 6.49236 | 6.19437 | 5.42062 |
| 13 | 9.98565 | 9.39357 | 8.85268 | 8.35765 | 7.90378 | 7.48690 | 7.10336 | 6.74987 | 6.42355 | 5.58315 |
| 14 | 10.56312 | 9.89864 | 9.29498 | 8.74547 | 8.24424 | 7.78615 | 7.36669 | 6.98187 | 6.62817 | 5.72448 |
| 15 | 11.11839 | 10.37966 | 9.71225 | 9.10791 | 8.55948 | 8.06069 | 7.60608 | 7.19087 | 6.81086 | 5.84737 |
| 16 | 11.65230 | 10.83777 | 10.10590 | 9.44665 | 8.85137 | 8.31256 | 7.82371 | 7.37916 | 6.97399 | 5.95424 |
| 17 | 12.16567 | 11.27407 | 10.47726 | 9.76322 | 9.12164 | 8.54363 | 8.02155 | 7.54879 | 7.11963 | 6.04716 |
| 18 | 12.65930 | 11.58959 | 10.82760 | 10.05909 | 9.37189 | 8.75563 | 8.20141 | 7.70162 | 7.24967 | 6.12797 |
| 19 | 13.13394 | 12.08532 | 11.15812 | 10.33560 | 9.60360 | 8.95012 | 8.36492 | 7.83929 | 7.36578 | 6.19823 |
| 20 | 13.59033 | 12.46221 | 11.46992 | 10.59401 | 9.81815 | 9.12855 | 8.51356 | 7.96333 | 7.46944 | 6.25933 |

Table 4 shows that the present value of an annuity of 1 factor for three payments at 10% is 2.48685.[1] This present value factor is the total of the three individual present value factors, as shown in Illustration G.15. Applying this amount to the annual cash flow of $1,000 produces a present value of $2,486.85.

The following demonstration problem (**Illustration G.16**) illustrates how to use Table 4.

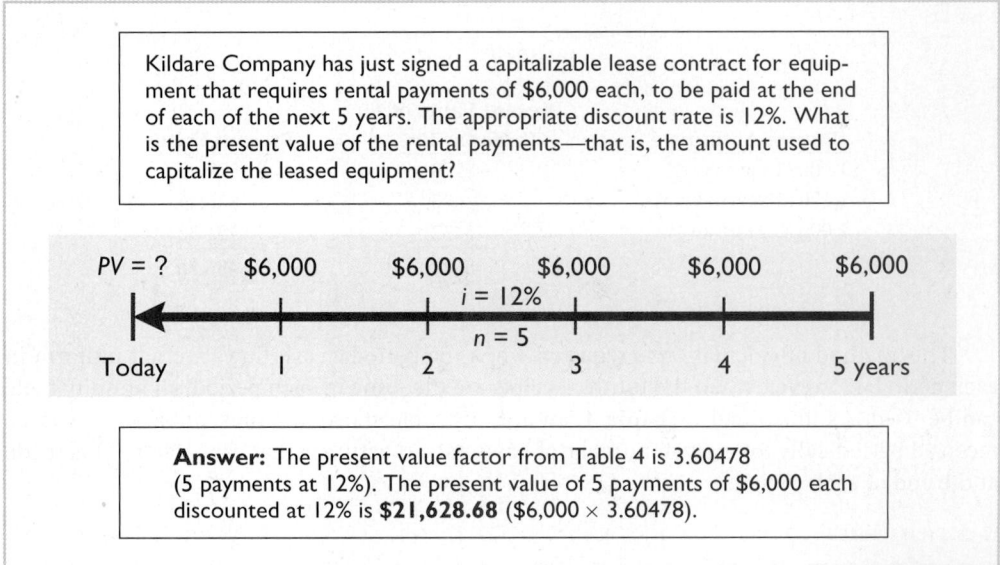

Kildare Company has just signed a capitalizable lease contract for equipment that requires rental payments of $6,000 each, to be paid at the end of each of the next 5 years. The appropriate discount rate is 12%. What is the present value of the rental payments—that is, the amount used to capitalize the leased equipment?

**Answer:** The present value factor from Table 4 is 3.60478 (5 payments at 12%). The present value of 5 payments of $6,000 each discounted at 12% is **$21,628.68** ($6,000 × 3.60478).

## Time Periods and Discounting

In the preceding calculations, the discounting was done on an annual basis using an annual interest rate. Discounting may also be done over shorter periods of time such as monthly, quarterly, or semiannually.

When the time frame is less than one year, it is necessary to convert the annual interest rate to the applicable time frame. Assume, for example, that the investor in Illustration G.14 received $500 **semiannually** for three years instead of $1,000 annually. In this case, the number of periods becomes six (3 × 2), the discount rate is 5% (10% ÷ 2), the present value factor from Table 4 is 5.07569 (6 periods at 5%), and the present value of the future cash flows is $2,537.85 (5.07569 × $500). This amount is slightly higher than the $2,486.86 computed in Illustration G.15 because interest is computed twice during the same year. That is, during the second half of the year, interest is earned on the first half-year's interest.

## Present Value of a Long-Term Note or Bond

The present value (or market price) of a long-term note or bond is a function of three variables: (1) the payment amounts, (2) the length of time until the amounts are paid, and (3) the discount rate. Our example uses a five-year bond issue.

The first variable (dollars to be paid) is made up of two elements: (1) a series of interest payments (an annuity) and (2) the principal amount (a single sum). To compute the present value of the bond, both the interest payments and the principal amount must be discounted—two different computations. The time diagrams for a bond due in five years are shown in **Illustration G.17**.

---

[1]The difference of .00001 between 2.48686 and 2.48685 is due to rounding.

ILLUSTRATION G.17 Time diagrams for the present value of a bond

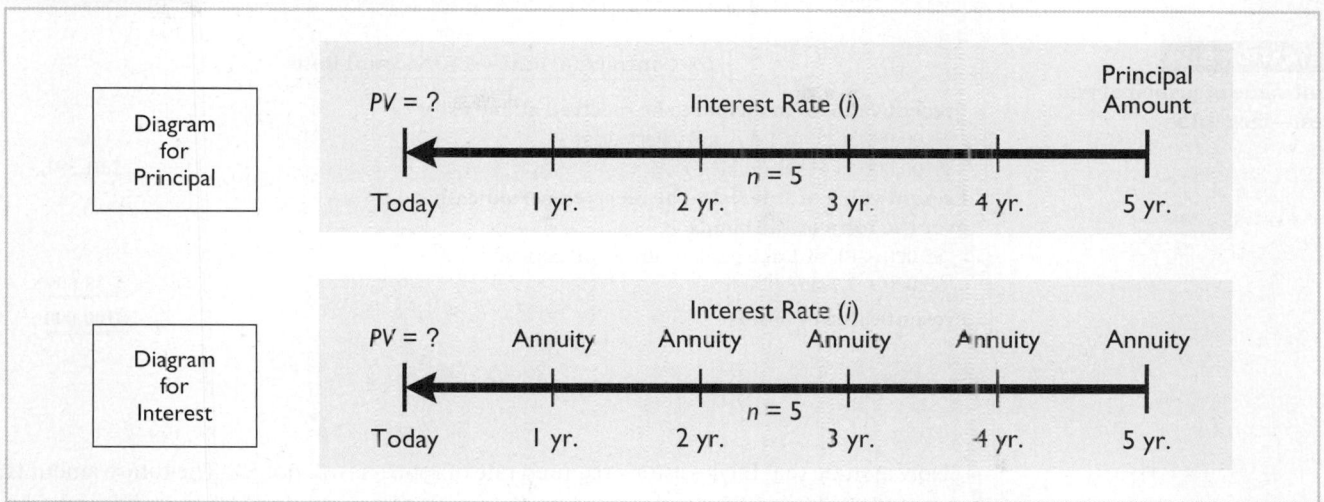

When the investor's market interest rate is equal to the bond's contractual interest rate, the present value of the bonds will equal the face value of the bonds. To illustrate, assume a bond issue of 5%, 10-year bonds with a face value of $100,000 with interest payable **annually** on January 1. If the discount rate is the same as the contractual rate, the bonds will sell at face value. In this case, the investor will receive (1) $100,000 at maturity and (2) a series of ten $5,000 interest payments ($100,000 × 5%) over the term of the bonds. The length of time is expressed in terms of interest periods—in this case, 10—and the discount rate per interest period, 5%. The time diagram in **Illustration G.18** depicts the variables involved in this discounting situation.

ILLUSTRATION G.18 Time diagram for present value of a 5%, 10-year bond paying interest annually

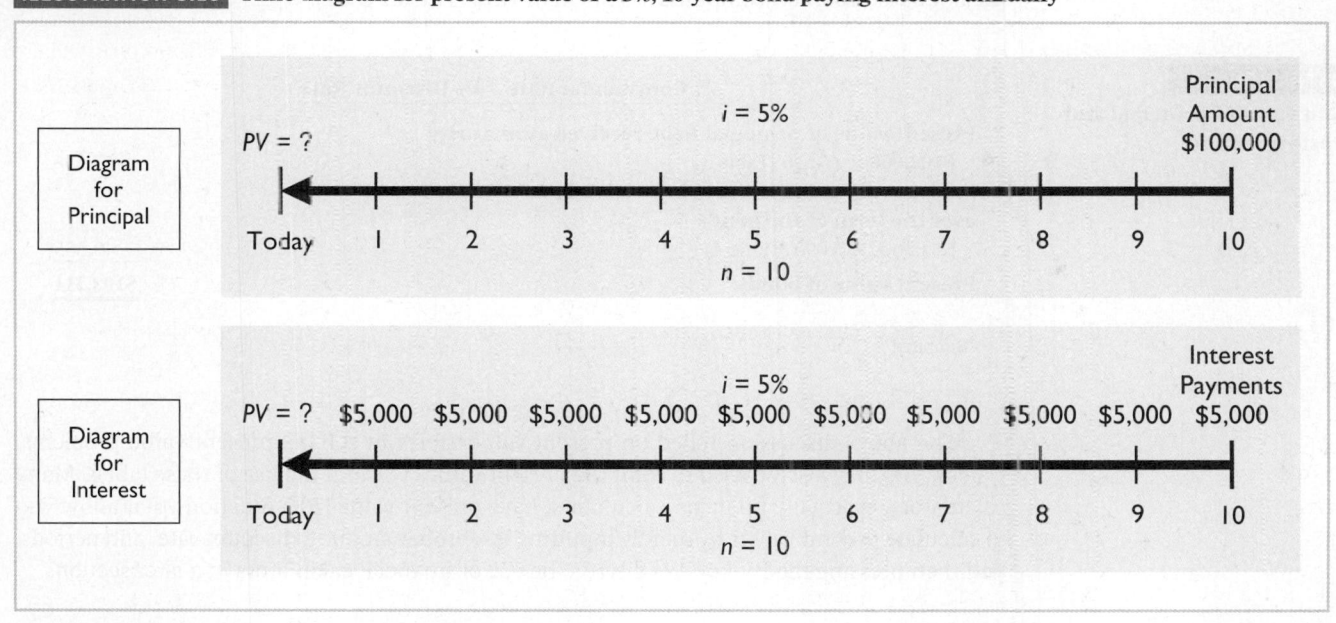

Illustration **G.19** shows the computation of the present value of these bonds.

| ILLUSTRATION G.19 |
|---|

**Present value of principal and interest—face value**

**5% Contractual Rate—5% Discount Rate**

| | |
|---|---:|
| **Present value of principal to be received at maturity** | |
| $100,000 × *PV* of 1 due in 10 periods at 5% | |
| $100,000 × .61391 (Table 3) | $ 61,391 |
| **Present value of interest to be received periodically** | |
| **over the term of the bonds** | |
| $5,000 × *PV* of 1 due periodically for 10 periods at 5% | |
| $5,000 × 7.72173 (Table 4) | 38,609* |
| **Present value of bonds** | **$100,000** |

*Rounded

Now assume that the investor's required rate of return is 6%, not 5%. The future amounts are again $100,000 and $5,000, respectively, but now a discount rate of 6% must be used. The present value of the bonds is $92,639, as computed in **Illustration G.20**.

| ILLUSTRATION G.20 |
|---|

**Present value of principal and interest—discount**

**5% Contractual Rate—6% Discount Rate**

| | |
|---|---:|
| **Present value of principal to be received at maturity** | |
| $100,000 × .55839 (Table 3) | $55,839 |
| **Present value of interest to be received periodically** | |
| **over the term of the bonds** | |
| $5,000 × 7.36009 (Table 4) | 36,800 |
| **Present value of bonds** | **$92,639** |

Conversely, if the discount rate is 4% and the contractual rate is 5%, the present value of the bonds is $108,111, computed as shown in **Illustration G.21**.

| ILLUSTRATION G.21 |
|---|

**Present value of principal and interest—premium**

**5% Contractual Rate—4% Discount Rate**

| | |
|---|---:|
| **Present value of principal to be received at maturity** | |
| $100,000 × .67556 (Table 3) | $ 67,556 |
| **Present value of interest to be received periodically** | |
| **over the term of the bonds** | |
| $5,000 × 8.11090 (Table 4) | 40,555* |
| **Present value of bonds** | **$108,111** |

*Rounded

The above discussion relied on present value tables in solving present value problems. Calculators may also be used to compute present values without the use of these tables. Many calculators, especially financial calculators, have present value (*PV*) functions that allow you to calculate present values by merely inputting the proper amount, discount rate, and periods, and then pressing the PV key. We discuss the use of financial calculators in a later section.

# Capital Budgeting Situations

### LEARNING OBJECTIVE 3
Compute the present value in capital budgeting situations.

The decision to make long-term capital investments is best evaluated using discounting techniques that recognize the time value of money. To do this, many companies calculate the present value of the cash flows involved in a capital investment.

To illustrate, Nagel-Siebert Trucking Company, a cross-country freight carrier in Montgomery, Illinois, is considering adding another truck to its fleet because of a purchasing opportunity. **Navistar Inc.**, Nagel-Siebert's primary supplier of overland rigs, is overstocked and offers to sell its biggest rig for $154,000 cash payable upon delivery. Nagel-Siebert knows that the rig will produce a net cash flow per year of $40,000 for five years (received at the end of each year), at which time it will be sold for an estimated salvage value of $35,000. Nagel-Siebert's discount rate in evaluating capital expenditures is 10%. Should Nagel-Siebert commit to the purchase of this rig?

The cash flows that must be discounted to present value by Nagel-Siebert are as follows.

Cash payable on delivery (today): $154,000.

Net cash flow from operating the rig: $40,000 for five years (at the end of each year).

Cash received from sale of rig at the end of five years: $35,000.

The time diagrams for the latter two cash flows are shown in **Illustration G.22**.

**ILLUSTRATION G.22**  **Time diagrams for Nagel-Siebert Trucking Company**

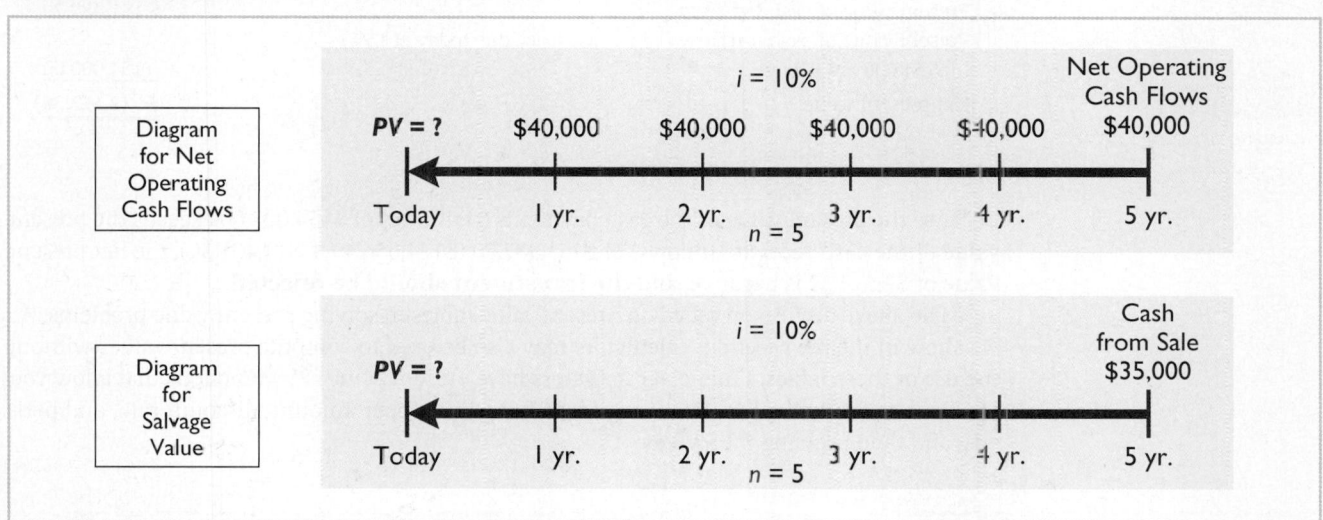

Notice from the diagrams that computing the present value of the net operating cash flows ($40,000 at the end of each year) is **discounting an annuity** (Table 4), while computing the present value of the $35,000 salvage value is **discounting a single sum** (Table 3). The computation of these present values is shown in **Illustration G.23**.

ILLUSTRATION G.23

**Present value computations at 10%**

Present Values Using a 10% Discount Rate

| | |
|---|---:|
| Present value of net operating cash flows received annually over 5 years | |
| $40,000 × PV of 1 received annually for 5 years at 10% | |
| $40,000 × 3.79079 | $ 151,631.60 |
| Present value of salvage value (cash) to be received in 5 years | |
| $35,000 × PV of 1 received in 5 years at 10% | |
| $35,000 × .62092 | 21,732.20 |
| Present value of cash **inflows** | 173,363.80 |
| Present value of cash **outflows** (purchase price due today at 10%) | |
| $154,000 × PV of 1 due today | |
| $154,000 × 1.00000 | (154,000.00) |
| Net present value | **$  19,363.80** |

Because the present value of the cash receipts (inflows) of $173,363.80 ($151,631.60 + $21,732.20) exceeds the present value of the cash payments (outflows) of $154,000.00, the net present value of $19,363.80 is positive, and **the decision to invest should be accepted**.

Now assume that Nagel-Siebert uses a discount rate of 15%, not 10%, because it wants a greater return on its investments in capital assets. The cash receipts and cash payments by Nagel-Siebert are the same. The present values of these receipts and cash payments discounted at 15% are shown in **Illustration G.24**.

**ILLUSTRATION G.24**

**Present value computations at 15%**

Present Values Using a 15% Discount Rate

| | |
|---|---:|
| Present value of net operating cash flows received annually over 5 years at 15% | |
| $40,000 × 3.35216 | $ 134,086.40 |
| Present value of salvage value (cash) to be received in 5 years at 15% | |
| $35,000 × .49718 | 17,401.30 |
| Present value of cash **inflows** | $ 151,487.70 |
| Present value of cash **outflows** (purchase price due today at 15%) | |
| $154,000 × 1.00000 | (154,000.00) |
| Net present value | **$  (2,512.30)** |

Because the present value of the cash payments (outflows) of $154,000.00 exceeds the present value of the cash receipts (inflows) of $151,487.70 ($134,086.40 + $17,401.30), the net present value of $2,512.30 is negative, and **the investment should be rejected**.

The above discussion relied on present value tables in solving present value problems. As we show in the next section, calculators may also be used to compute present values without the use of these tables. Financial calculators have present value (PV) functions that allow you to calculate present values by merely identifying the proper amount, discount rate, and periods, and then pressing the PV key.

# Using Financial Calculators

**LEARNING OBJECTIVE 4**

Use a financial calculator to solve time value of money problems.

Business professionals, once they have mastered the underlying time value of money concepts, often use a financial calculator to solve these types of problems. To use financial calculators, you enter the time value of money variables into the calculator. **Illustration G.25** shows the five most common keys used to solve time value of money problems.[2]

**ILLUSTRATION G.25**
**Financial calculator keys**

where:

| | | |
|---|---|---|
| N | = | number of periods |
| I | = | interest rate per period (some calculators use I/YR or i) |
| PV | = | present value (occurs at the beginning of the first period) |
| PMT | = | payment (all payments are equal, and none are skipped) |
| FV | = | future value (occurs at the end of the last period) |

In solving time value of money problems in this appendix, you will generally be given three of four variables and will have to solve for the remaining variable. The fifth key (the key not used) is given a value of zero to ensure that this variable is not used in the computation.

# Present Value of a Single Sum

To illustrate how to solve a present value problem using a financial calculator, assume that you want to know the present value of $84,253 to be received in five years, discounted at 11% compounded annually. **Illustration G.26** depicts this problem.

**ILLUSTRATION G.26**
**Calculator solution for present value of a single sum**

Illustration G.26 shows you the information (inputs) to enter into the calculator: N = 5, I = 11, PMT = 0, and FV = 84,253. You then press PV for the answer: −$50,000. As indicated, the PMT key was given a value of zero because a series of payments did not occur in this problem.

### Plus and Minus

The use of plus and minus signs in time value of money problems with a financial calculator can be confusing. Most financial calculators are programmed so that the positive and negative cash flows in any problem offset each other. In the present value problem above, we identified the $84,253 future value initial investment as a positive (inflow); the answer −$50,000 was shown as a negative amount, reflecting a cash outflow. If the 84,253 were entered as a negative, then the final answer would have been reported as a positive 50,000.

Hopefully, the sign convention will not cause confusion. If you understand what is required in a problem, you should be able to interpret a positive or negative amount in determining the solution to a problem.

### Compounding Periods

In the problem above, we assumed that compounding occurs once a year. Some financial calculators have a default setting, which assumes that compounding occurs 12 times a year. You

---

[2]On many calculators, these keys are actual buttons on the face of the calculator; on others, they appear on the display after the user accesses a present value menu.

must determine what default period has been programmed into your calculator and change it as necessary to arrive at the proper compounding period.

### Rounding

Most financial calculators store and calculate using 12 decimal places. As a result, because compound interest tables generally have factors only up to five decimal places, a slight difference in the final answer can result. In most time value of money problems, the final answer will not include more than two decimal places.

## Present Value of an Annuity

To illustrate how to solve a present value of an annuity problem using a financial calculator, assume that you are asked to determine the present value of rental receipts of $6,000 each to be received at the end of each of the next five years, when discounted at 12%, as pictured in **Illustration G.27**.

**Calculator solution for present value of an annuity**

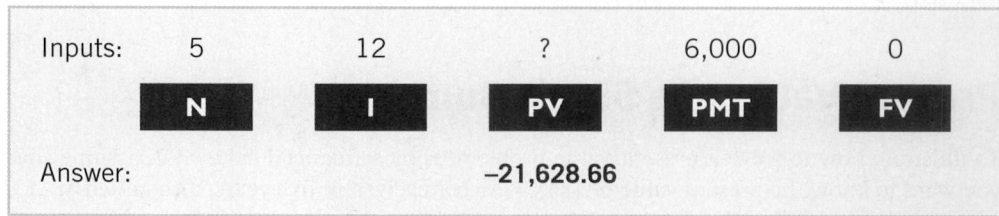

In this case, you enter N = 5, I = 12, PMT = 6,000, and FV = 0, and then press PV to arrive at the answer of −$21,628.66.

## Future Value of a Single Sum

Now let us look at an investment to illustrate how to solve a future value problem using a financial calculator. Assume that you will invest $20,000 today in a fund and you intend to leave it there for 15 years. The fund earns 7% interest. **Illustration G.28** shows how to compute the future value of the fund at the end of year 15.

**Calculator solution for future value of single sum**

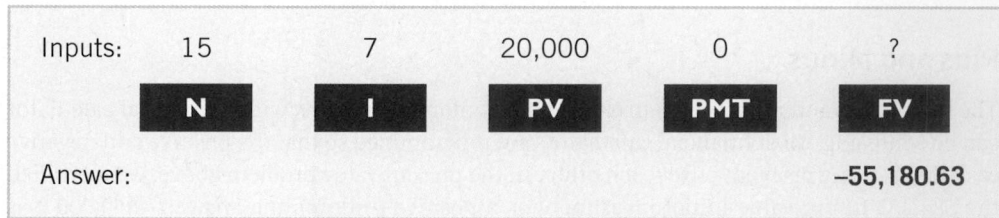

In this case, you enter N = 15, I = 7, PV = 20,000, and PMT = 0, and then press FV to calculate the future value of −$55,180.63.

## Future Value of an Annuity

You can use a financial calculator to solve a future value of an annuity problem for an annuity investment. Assume that you will invest $8,000 in a fund at the end of each of the next eight years. The fund earns 9% interest. **Illustration G.29** shows how to compute the future value of the fund at the end of the eighth year.

**ILLUSTRATION G.29**
**Calculator solution for future value of an annuity**

In this case, you enter N = 8, I = 9, PV = 0, and PMT = 8,000, and then press FV to determine the future value of −$88,227.79.

# Internal Rate of Return

You can also use these same calculator keys to compute the internal rate of return of an investment that has equal cash flows. Suppose that a purchase of a piece of equipment with a seven-year life requires an initial investment of $54,000, has positive cash flows of $7,800 per year, and has an estimated salvage value of $11,000. The computation is shown in **Illustration G.30**.

**ILLUSTRATION G.30**
**Calculator solution for internal rate of return**

In this case, you enter N = 7, PV = −54,000 (we entered as a negative, since it is an outflow), PMT = 7,800, and FV = 11,000, and then press FV to determine the answer of 4.52%. Notice that the advantage to this approach is that you arrive at a much more precise result, rather than the rough approximation provided by the present value tables. To determine the internal rate of return using your calculator for an investment with unequal cash flows, you need to employ the cash flow key (CF) and the internal rate of return key (IRR). The use of these function keys varies across calculators, so you should consult the user manual for your calculator or the manufacturer's website for specific information.

# Useful Applications of the Financial Calculator

With a financial calculator, you can solve for any interest rate or for any number of periods in a time value of money problem. Here are some examples of these applications.

## Auto Loan

Assume you are financing the purchase of a used car with a three-year loan. The loan has a 9.5% stated annual interest rate, compounded monthly. The price of the car is $6,000, and you want to determine the monthly payments, assuming that the payments start one month after the purchase. This problem is pictured in **Illustration G.31**.

**ILLUSTRATION G.31**
**Calculator solution for auto loan payments**

To solve this problem, you enter N = 36 (12 × 3), I = 9.5, PV = 6,000, and FV = 0, and then press PMT. You will find that the monthly payments will be $192.20. Note that the payment key is usually programmed for 12 payments per year. Thus, you must change the default (compounding period) if the payments are other than monthly.

## Mortgage Loan Amount

Say you are evaluating financing options for a loan on a house (a mortgage). You decide that the maximum mortgage payment you can afford is $700 per month. The annual interest rate is 8.4%. If you get a mortgage that requires you to make monthly payments over a 15-year period, what is the maximum home loan you can afford? **Illustration G.32** depicts this problem.

**ILLUSTRATION G.32**

**Calculator solution for mortgage amount**

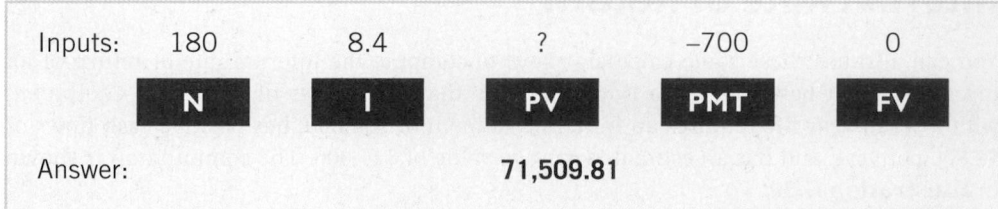

| Inputs: | 180 | 8.4 | ? | −700 | 0 |
|---|---|---|---|---|---|
| | **N** | **I** | **PV** | **PMT** | **FV** |
| Answer: | | | **71,509.81** | | |

You enter N = 180 (12 × 15 years), I = 8.4, PMT = −700, and FV = 0, and then press PV. With the payments-per-year key set at 12, you find a present value of $71,509.81—the maximum home loan you can afford, given that you want to keep your mortgage payments at $700. Note that by changing any of the variables, you can quickly conduct "what-if" analyses for different situations.

# Review

## Learning Objectives Review

### 1 Compute interest and future values.

Simple interest is computed on the principal only, while compound interest is computed on the principal and any interest earned that has not been withdrawn.

To solve for future value of a single amount, prepare a time diagram of the problem. Identify the principal amount, the number of compounding periods, and the interest rate. Using the future value of 1 table, multiply the principal amount by the future value factor specified at the intersection of the number of periods and the interest rate.

To solve for future value of an annuity, prepare a time diagram of the problem. Identify the amount of the periodic payments (receipts), the number of payments (receipts), and the interest rate. Using the future value of an annuity of 1 table, multiply the amount of the payments by the future value factor specified at the intersection of the number of periods and the interest rate.

### 2 Compute present values.

The following three variables are fundamental to solving present value problems: (1) the future amount, (2) the number of periods, and (3) the interest rate (the discount rate).

To solve for present value of a single amount, prepare a time diagram of the problem. Identify the future amount, the number of discounting periods, and the discount (interest) rate. Using the present value of a single amount table, multiply the future amount by the present value factor specified at the intersection of the number of periods and the discount rate.

To solve for present value of an annuity, prepare a time diagram of the problem. Identify the amount of future periodic receipts or payments (annuities), the number of payments (receipts), and the discount (interest) rate. Using the present value of an annuity of 1 table, multiply the amount of the annuity by the present value factor specified at the intersection of the number of payments and the interest rate.

To compute the present value of notes and bonds, determine the present value of the principal amount and the present value of the interest payments. Multiply the principal amount (a single future amount) by the present value factor (from the present value of 1 table) intersecting at the number of periods (number of interest payments) and the discount rate. To determine the present value of the series of interest payments, multiply the amount of the interest payment by the present value factor (from the present value of an annuity of 1 table) intersecting at the number of periods (number of interest payments) and the discount rate. Add the present value of the principal amount to the present value of the interest payments to arrive at the present value of the note or bond.

**3** Compute the present value in capital budgeting situations.

Compute the present values of all cash inflows and all cash outflows related to the capital budgeting proposal (an investment-type decision). If the **net** present value is positive, accept the proposal (make the investment). If the **net** present value is negative, reject the proposal (do not make the investment).

**4** Use a financial calculator to solve time value of money problems.

Financial calculators can be used to solve the same (and additional) problems as those solved with time value of money tables. Enter into the financial calculator the amounts for all of the known elements of a time value of money problem (periods, interest rate, payments, future or present value), and it solves for the unknown element. Particularly useful situations involve interest rates and compounding periods not presented in the tables.

## Glossary Review

**Annuity**   A series of equal dollar amounts to be paid or received at evenly spaced time intervals (periodically). (p. G-5).

**Compound interest**   The interest computed on the principal and any interest earned that has not been paid or withdrawn. (p. G-2).

**Discounting the future amount(s)**   The process of determining present value. (p. G-7).

**Future value of an annuity**   The sum of all the payments (receipts) plus the accumulated compound interest on them. (p. G-5).

**Future value of a single amount**   The value at a future date of a given amount invested, assuming compound interest. (p. G-3).

**Interest**   Payment for the use of another person's money. (p. G-2).

**Present value**   The value now of a given amount to be paid or received in the future, assuming compound interest. (p. G-7).

**Present value of an annuity**   The value now of a series of future receipts or payments, discounted assuming compound interest. (p. G-10).

**Principal**   The amount borrowed or invested. (p. G-2).

**Simple interest**   The interest computed on the principal only. (p. G-2).

---

## Many additional resources are available for practice in WileyPLUS.

---

## Brief Exercises

**(Use tables to solve exercises BEG.1 to BEG.23.)**

**BEG.1 (LO 1), AP**   Jozy Altidore invested $6,000 at 5% annual interest, and left the money invested without withdrawing any of the interest for 12 years. At the end of the 12 years, Jozy withdrew the accumulated amount of money. (a) What amount did Jozy withdraw, assuming the investment earns simple interest? (b) What amount did Jozy withdraw, assuming the investment earns interest compounded annually?

*Compute the future value of a single amount.*

**BEG.2 (LO 1), C**   For each of the following cases, indicate (a) what interest rate columns and (b) what number of periods you would refer to in looking up the future value factor.

*Use future value tables.*

**1.** In Table 1 (future value of 1):

|  | Annual Rate | Number of Years Invested | Compounded |
|---|---|---|---|
| Case A | 5% | 3 | Annually |
| Case B | 12% | 4 | Semiannually |

**2.** In Table 2 (future value of an annuity of 1):

|  | Annual Rate | Number of Years Invested | Compounded |
|---|---|---|---|
| Case A | 3% | 8 | Annually |
| Case B | 8% | 6 | Semiannually |

*Compute the future value of a single amount.*

**BEG.3 (LO 1), AP** Liam Company signed a lease for an office building for a period of 12 years. Under the lease agreement, a security deposit of $9,600 is made. The deposit will be returned at the expiration of the lease with interest compounded at 4% per year. What amount will Liam receive at the time the lease expires?

*Compute the future value of an annuity.*

**BEG.4 (LO 1), AP** Bates Company issued $1,000,000, 10-year bonds. It agreed to make annual deposits of $78,000 to a fund (called a sinking fund), which will be used to pay off the principal amount of the bond at the end of 10 years. The deposits are made at the end of each year into an account paying 6% annual interest. What amount will be in the sinking fund at the end of 10 years?

*Compute the future value of a single amount and of an annuity.*

**BEG.5 (LO 1), AP** Andrew and Emma Garfield invested $8,000 in a savings account paying 5% annual interest when their daughter, Angela, was born. They also deposited $1,000 on each of her birthdays until she was 18 (including her 18th birthday). How much was in the savings account on her 18th birthday (after the last deposit)?

*Compute the future value of a single amount.*

**BEG.6 (LO 1), AP** Hugh Curtin borrowed $35,000 on July 1, 2022. This amount plus accrued interest at 8% compounded annually is to be repaid on July 1, 2027. How much will Hugh have to repay on July 1, 2027?

*Use present value tables.*

**BEG.7 (LO 2), C** For each of the following cases, indicate (a) what interest rate columns and (b) what number of periods you would refer to in looking up the discount rate.

1. In Table 3 (present value of 1):

| | Annual Rate | Number of Years Involved | Discounts per Year |
|---|---|---|---|
| Case A | 12% | 7 | Annually |
| Case B | 8% | 11 | Annually |
| Case C | 10% | 8 | Semiannually |

2. In Table 4 (present value of an annuity of 1):

| | Annual Rate | Number of Years Involved | Number of Payments Involved | Frequency of Payments |
|---|---|---|---|---|
| Case A | 10% | 20 | 20 | Annually |
| Case B | 10% | 7 | 7 | Annually |
| Case C | 6% | 5 | 10 | Semiannually |

*Determine present values.*

**BEG.8 (LO 2), AP** a. What is the present value of $25,000 due 9 periods from now, discounted at 10%?

b. What is the present value of $25,000 to be received at the end of each of 6 periods, discounted at 9%?

*Compute the present value of a single amount investment.*

**BEG.9 (LO 2), AP** Messi Company is considering an investment that will return a lump sum of $900,000 6 years from now. What amount should Messi Company pay for this investment to earn an 8% return?

*Compute the present value of a single amount investment.*

**BEG.10 (LO 2), AP** Lloyd Company earns 6% on an investment that will return $450,000 8 years from now. What is the amount Lloyd should invest now to earn this rate of return?

*Compute the present value of an annuity investment.*

**BEG.11 (LO 2), AP** Robben Company is considering investing in an annuity contract that will return $40,000 annually at the end of each year for 15 years. What amount should Robben Company pay for this investment if it earns an 8% return?

*Compute the present value of an annual investment.*

**BEG.12 (LO 2), AP** Kaehler Enterprises earns 5% on an investment that pays back $80,000 at the end of each of the next 6 years. What is the amount Kaehler Enterprises invested to earn the 5% rate of return?

*Compute the present value of bonds.*

**BEG.13 (LO 2), AP** Dempsey Railroad Co. is about to issue $400,000 of 10-year bonds paying an 11% interest rate, with interest payable annually. The discount rate for such securities is 10%. How much can Dempsey expect to receive for the sale of these bonds?

*Compute the present value of bonds.*

**BEG.14 (LO 2), AP** Dempsey Railroad Co. is about to issue $400,000 of 10-year bonds paying an 11% interest rate, with interest payable annually. The discount rate for such securities is 12%. How much can Dempsey expect to receive from the sale of these bonds?

*Compute the present value of a note.*

**BEG.15 (LO 2), AP** Neymar Taco Company receives a $75,000, 6-year note bearing interest of 4% (paid annually) from a customer at a time when the discount rate is 6%. What is the present value of the note received by Neymar?

**BEG.16 (LO 2), AP** Gleason Enterprises issued 6%, 8-year, $2,500,000 par value bonds that pay interest annually on April 1. The bonds are dated April 1, 2022, and are issued on that date. The discount rate of interest for such bonds on April 1, 2022, is 8%. What cash proceeds did Gleason receive from issuance of the bonds?

*Compute the present value of bonds.*

**BEG.17 (LO 2), AP** Frazier Company issues a 10%, 5-year mortgage note on January 1, 2022, to obtain financing for new equipment. Land is used as collateral for the note. The terms provide for semiannual installment payments of $48,850. What are the cash proceeds received from the issuance of the note?

*Compute the present value of a note.*

**BEG.18 (LO 2), AP** If Colleen Mooney invests $4,765.50 now and she will receive $12,000 at the end of 12 years, what annual rate of interest will Colleen earn on her investment? (*Hint:* Use Table 3.)

*Compute the interest rate on a single amount.*

**BEG.19 (LO 2), AP** Tim Howard has been offered the opportunity of investing $36,125 now. The investment will earn 11% per year and at the end of that time will return Tim $75,000. How many years must Tim wait to receive $75,000? (*Hint:* Use Table 3.)

*Compute the number of periods of a single amount.*

**BEG.20 (LO 2), AP** Joanne Quick made an investment of $10,271.38. From this investment, she will receive $1,200 annually for the next 15 years starting one year from now. What rate of interest will Joanne's investment be earning for her? (*Hint:* Use Table 4.)

*Compute the interest rate on an annuity.*

**BEG.21 (LO 2), AP** Kevin Morales invests $7,793.83 now for a series of $1,300 annual returns beginning one year from now. Kevin will earn a return of 9% on the initial investment. How many annual payments of $1,300 will Kevin receive? (*Hint:* Use Table 4.)

*Compute the number of periods of an annuity.*

**BEG.22 (LO 3), AP** Barney Googal owns a garage and is contemplating purchasing a tire retreading machine for $12,820. After estimating costs and revenues, Barney projects a net cash inflow from the retreading machine of $2,700 annually for 7 years. Barney hopes to earn a return of 9% on such investments. What is the present value of the retreading operation? Should Barney Googal purchase the retreading machine?

*Compute the present value of a machine for purposes of making a purchase decision.*

**BEG.23 (LO 3), AP** Snyder Company is considering purchasing equipment. The equipment will produce the following cash inflows: Year 1, $25,000; Year 2, $30,000; and Year 3, $40,000. Snyder requires a minimum rate of return of 11%. What is the maximum price Snyder should pay for this equipment?

*Compute the maximum price to pay for a machine.*

**BEG.24 (LO 4), AP** Carly Simon wishes to invest $18,000 on July 1, 2022, and have it accumulate to $50,000 by July 1, 2032. Use a financial calculator to determine at what exact annual rate of interest Carly must invest the $18,000.

*Determine interest rate.*

**BEG.25 (LO 4), AP** On July 17, 2021, Keith Urban borrowed $42,000 from his grandfather to open a clothing store. Starting July 17, 2022, Keith has to make 10 equal annual payments of $6,500 each to repay the loan. Use a financial calculator to determine what interest rate Keith is paying.

*Determine interest rate.*

**BEG.26 (LO 4), AP** As the purchaser of a new house, Carrie Underwood has signed a mortgage note to pay the Nashville National Bank and Trust Co. $8,400 every 6 months for 20 years, at the end of which time she will own the house. At the date the mortgage is signed, the purchase price was $198,000 and Underwood made a down payment of $20,000. The first payment will be made 6 months after the date the mortgage is signed. Using a financial calculator, compute the exact rate of interest earned on the mortgage by the bank.

*Determine interest rate.*

**BEG.27 (LO 4), AP** Using a financial calculator, solve for the unknowns in each of the following situations.

*Various time value of money situations.*

a. On June 1, 2021, Jennifer Lawrence purchases lakefront property from her neighbor, Josh Hutcherson, and agrees to pay the purchase price in seven payments of $16,000 each, the first payment to be payable June 1, 2022. (Assume that interest compounded at an annual rate of 7.35% is implicit in the payments.) What is the purchase price of the property?

b. On January 1, 2021, Gerrard Corporation purchased 200 of the $1,000 face value, 8% coupon, 10-year bonds of Sterling Inc. The bonds mature on January 1, 2031, and pay interest annually beginning January 1, 2022. Gerrard purchased the bonds to yield 10.65%. How much did Gerrard pay for the bonds?

**BEG.28 (LO 4), AP** Using a financial calculator, provide a solution to each of the following situations.

*Various time value of money situations.*

a. Lynn Anglin owes a debt of $42,000 from the purchase of her new sport utility vehicle. The debt bears annual interest of 7.8% compounded monthly. Lynn wishes to pay the debt and interest in equal monthly payments over 8 years, beginning one month hence. What equal monthly payments will pay off the debt and interest?

**b.** On January 1, 2022, Roger Molony offers to buy Dave Feeney's used snowmobile for $8,000, payable in five equal annual installments, which are to include 7.25% interest on the unpaid balance and a portion of the principal. If the first payment is to be made on December 31, 2022, how much will each payment be?

*Determine internal rate of return.*

**BEG.29 (LO 4), AP** Renolds Corporation is considering two alternative investments in excavating equipment. Investment A requires an initial investment of $184,000, has positive cash flows of $27,500 per year, and has an estimated salvage value of $21,000. Investment B requires an initial investment of $234,000, has positive cash flows of $32,800 per year, and has an estimated salvage value of $19,000. Each piece of equipment is expected to have a 12-year useful life. Use a financial calculator to determine the internal rate of return of each project to decide which is more desirable. (Round to two decimal places, e.g., 9.74%.)

# Appendix H

# Reporting and Analyzing Investments

## Appendix Preview

Some companies believe in aggressive growth through investing in the stock of existing companies. Besides purchasing stock, companies also purchase other securities, such as bonds issued by corporations or by governments. Companies can make investments for a short or long period of time, as a passive investment, or with the intent to control another company. As you will see in this appendix, the way in which a company accounts for its investments is determined by a number of factors.

## Appendix Outline

| LEARNING OBJECTIVES | REVIEW | PRACTICE |
|---|---|---|
| 1. Explain how to account for debt investments. | • Why corporations invest<br>• Accounting for debt investments | DO IT! 1 Debt Investments |
| 2. Explain how to account for stock investments. | • Holdings of less than 20%<br>• Holdings between 20% and 50%<br>• Holdings of more than 50% | DO IT! 2 Stock Investments |
| 3. Discuss how debt and stock investments are reported in the financial statements. | • Debt securities<br>• Equity securities<br>• Balance sheet presentation<br>• Presentation of realized and unrealized gain or loss | DO IT! 3a Trading and Available-for-Sale Debt Securities<br><br>DO IT! 3b Financial Statement Presentation of Investments |

**Go to the Review and Practice Section at the end of the appendix for a review of key concepts and practice applications with solutions.**

# Accounting for Debt Investments

### LEARNING OBJECTIVE 1
Explain how to account for debt investments.

# Why Corporations Invest

Corporations purchase investments in debt or equity securities generally for one of three reasons. First, a corporation may **have excess cash** that it does not need for the immediate purchase of operating assets. For example, many companies experience seasonal fluctuations in sales. A Cape Cod marina has more sales in the spring and summer than in the fall and winter. The reverse is true for an Aspen ski shop. Thus, at the end of an operating cycle, many companies may have cash on hand that is temporarily idle until the start of another operating cycle. These companies may invest the excess funds to earn—through interest and dividends—a greater return than they would get by just holding the funds in the bank. **Illustration H.1** shows the role that such temporary investments play in the operating cycle.

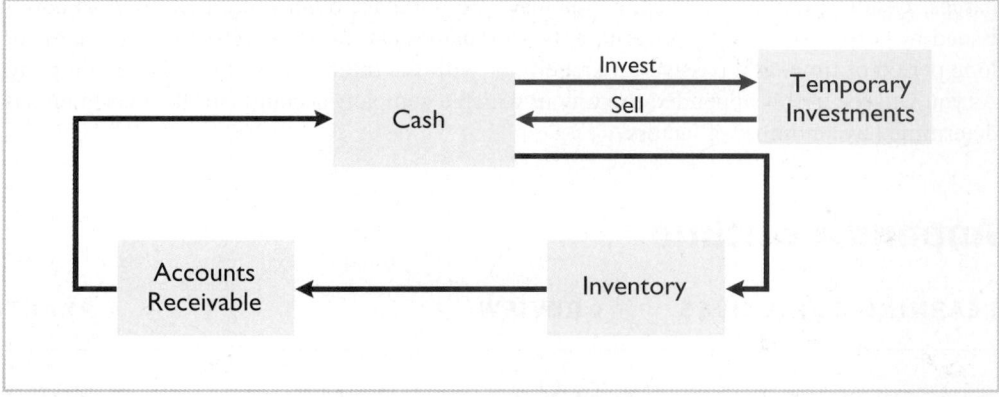

A second reason some companies such as banks purchase investments is to generate **earnings from investment income**. Although banks make most of their earnings by lending money, they also generate earnings by investing in primarily debt securities. Banks purchase investment securities because loan demand varies both seasonally and with changes in the economic climate. Thus, when loan demand is low, a bank must find other uses for its cash.

Some companies attempt to generate investment income through speculative investments. That is, they are speculating that the investment will increase in value and thus result in positive returns. Therefore, they invest mostly in the common stock of other corporations.

Third, companies also invest for **strategic reasons**. A company may purchase a noncontrolling interest in another company in a related industry in which it wishes to establish a presence. Or, a company can exercise some influence over one of its customers or suppliers by purchasing a significant, but not controlling, interest in that company. Another option is for a corporation to purchase a controlling interest in another company in order to enter a new industry without incurring the costs and risks associated with starting from scratch.

In summary, businesses invest in other companies for the reasons shown in **Illustration H.2**.

# Accounting for Debt Investments

**Debt investments** are investments in government and corporation bonds. In accounting for debt investments, companies must make entries to record (1) the acquisition, (2) the interest revenue, and (3) the sale.

## Recording Acquisition of Bonds

**At acquisition, debt investments are recorded at cost.** Cost includes all expenditures necessary to acquire these investments, such as the price paid plus brokerage fees (commissions), if any.

For example, assume that Kuhl Corporation acquires 50 Doan Inc. 8%, 10-year, $1,000 bonds on January 1, 2022, at a cost of $50,000. Kuhl records the investment as:

| | | | |
|---|---|---|---|
| Jan. 1 | Debt Investments | 50,000 | |
| | Cash | | 50,000 |
| | (To record purchase of 50 Doan Inc. bonds) | | |

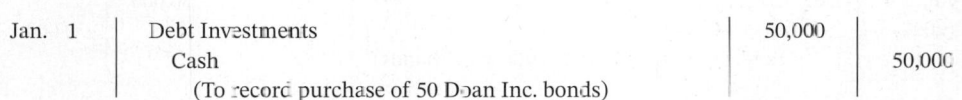

A = L + SE
+50,000
−50,000

Cash Flows
−50,000

## Recording Bond Interest

The Doan Inc. bonds pay interest of $4,000 annually on January 1 ($50,000 × 8%). If Kuhl Corporation's fiscal year ends on December 31, it accrues the interest of $4,000 earned since January 1. The adjusting entry is:

| | | | |
|---|---|---|---|
| Dec. 31 | Interest Receivable | 4,000 | |
| | Interest Revenue | | 4,000 |
| | (To accrue interest on Doan Inc. bonds) | | |

A = L + SE
+4,000
+4,000 Rev

Cash Flows
no effect

Kuhl reports Interest Receivable as a current asset in the balance sheet. It reports Interest Revenue under "Other revenues and gains" in the income statement.

Kuhl records receipt of the interest on January 1 as follows.

| | | | |
|---|---|---|---|
| Jan. 1 | Cash | 4,000 | |
| | Interest Receivable | | 4,000 |
| | (To record receipt of accrued interest) | | |

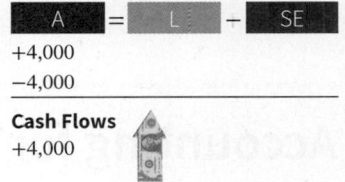

A = L + SE
+4,000
−4,000

Cash Flows
+4,000

A credit to Interest Revenue at this time would be incorrect. Why? Because the company earned and accrued the interest revenue in the preceding accounting period.

## Recording Sale of Bonds

When Kuhl Corporation sells the bond investments, it credits the investment account for the cost of the bonds. The company records as a gain or loss any difference between the net proceeds from the sale (sales price less brokerage fees) and the cost of the bonds (see **Helpful Hint**).

Assume, for example, that Kuhl receives net proceeds of $53,000 on the sale of the Doan Inc. bonds on January 1, 2023, after receiving the interest due. Since the securities cost $50,000, Kuhl has realized a gain of $3,000. It records the sale as follows.

| | | | |
|---|---|---|---|
| Jan. 1 | Cash | 53,000 | |
| | Debt Investments | | 50,000 |
| | Gain on Sale of Debt Investments | | 3,000 |
| | (To record sale of Doan Inc. bonds) | | |

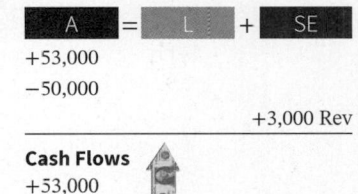

A = L + SE
+53,000
−50,000
+3,000 Rev

Cash Flows
+53,000

**HELPFUL HINT**

The accounting for short-term debt investments and long-term debt investments is similar. Any exceptions are discussed in more advanced courses.

Kuhl reports the gain on the sale of debt investments under "Other revenues and gains" in the income statement and reports losses under "Other expenses and losses."

**ACTION PLAN**
- **Record bond investments at cost.**
- **Record interest when accrued.**
- **When bonds are sold, credit the investment account for the cost of the bonds.**
- **Record any difference between the cost and the net proceeds as a gain or loss.**

## DO IT! 1 | Debt Investments

Waldo Corporation had the following transactions pertaining to debt investments.

Jan. 1, 2022 Purchased 30 $1,000 Hillary Co. 10% bonds for $30,000. Interest is payable annually on January 1.
Dec. 31, 2022 Accrued interest on Hillary Co. bonds in 2022.
Jan. 1, 2023 Received interest on Hillary Co. bonds.
Jan. 1, 2023 Sold 15 Hillary Co. bonds for $14,600.
Dec. 31, 2023 Accrued interest on Hillary Co. bonds in 2023.

Journalize the above transactions, including the accrual of interest on December 31, 2022.

### Solution

| | | | |
|---|---|---|---|
| Jan. 1 (2022) | Debt Investments | 30,000 | |
| | Cash | | 30,000 |
| | (To record purchase of 30 Hillary Co. bonds) | | |
| | | | |
| Dec. 31 (2022) | Interest Receivable | 3,000 | |
| | Interest Revenue ($30,000 × 10%) | | 3,000 |
| | (To accrue interest on Hillary Co. bonds) | | |
| | | | |
| Jan. 1 (2023) | Cash | 3,000 | |
| | Interest Receivable | | 3,000 |
| | (To record receipt of interest on Hillary Co. bonds) | | |
| | | | |
| Jan. 1 (2023) | Cash | 14,600 | |
| | Loss on Sale of Debt Investments | 400 | |
| | Debt Investments [$30,000 × (15 ÷ 30)] | | 15,000 |
| | (To record sale of 15 Hillary Co. bonds) | | |
| | | | |
| Dec. 31 (2023) | Interest Receivable | 1,500 | |
| | Interest Revenue ($15,000 × 10%) | | 1,500 |
| | (To accrue interest on Hillary Co. bonds) | | |

# Accounting for Stock Investments

**LEARNING OBJECTIVE 2**

Explain how to account for stock investments.

**Stock investments** are investments in the capital stock of corporations. When a company holds stock (and/or debt) of several different corporations, the group of securities is an **investment portfolio**.

The accounting for investments in common stock depends on the extent of the investor's influence over the operating and financial affairs of the issuing corporation (the **investee**). **Illustration H.3** shows the general guidelines.

Companies are required to use judgment instead of blindly following the guidelines.[1] We explain and illustrate the application of each guideline next.

...................................................................................................................................

[1] Among the factors that companies should consider in determining an investor's influence are whether (1) the investor has representation on the investee's board of directors, (2) the investor participates in the investee's policy-making process, (3) there are material transactions between the investor and the investee, and (4) the common stock held by other stockholders is concentrated or dispersed.

| Investor's Ownership Interest in Investee's Common Stock | Presumed Influence on Investee | Accounting Guidelines |
|---|---|---|
| Less than 20% | Insignificant | Cost method |
| Between 20% and 50% | Significant | Equity method |
| More than 50% | Controlling | Consolidated financial statements |

# Holdings of Less Than 20%

In the accounting for stock investments of less than 20%, companies use the cost method. Under the **cost method,** companies record the investment at cost and recognize revenue only when cash dividends are received.

## Recording Acquisition of Stock

At acquisition, stock investments are recorded at cost. Cost includes all expenditures necessary to acquire these investments, such as the price paid plus brokerage fees (commissions), if any.

Assume, for example, that on July 1, 2022, Sanchez Corporation acquires 1,000 shares (10% ownership) of Beal Corporation common stock at $40 per share. The entry for the purchase is:

| July 1 | Stock Investments | 40,000 | |
|---|---|---|---|
| | Cash | | 40,000 |
| | (To record purchase of 1,000 shares of Beal common stock) | | |

A = L + SE
+40,000
−40,000

Cash Flows
−40,000

## Recording Dividends

During the time the company holds the stock, it makes entries for any cash dividends received. Thus, if Sanchez Corporation receives a $2 per share dividend on December 31, the entry is:

| Dec. 31 | Cash (1,000 × $2) | 2,000 | |
|---|---|---|---|
| | Dividend Revenue | | 2,000 |
| | (To record receipt of a cash dividend) | | |

A = L + SE
+2,000
+2,000 Rev

Cash Flows
+2,000

Sanchez reports Dividend Revenue under "Other revenues and gains" in the income statement.

## Recording Sale of Stock

When a company sells a stock investment, it recognizes the difference between the net proceeds from the sale (sales price less brokerage fees) and the cost of the stock as a gain or a loss.

Assume, for instance, that Sanchez Corporation receives net proceeds of $39,500 on the sale of its Beal Corporation stock on February 10, 2023. Because the stock cost $40,000, Sanchez has incurred a loss of $500. It records the sale as:

| Feb. 10 | Cash | 39,500 | |
|---|---|---|---|
| | Loss on Sale of Stock Investments | 500 | |
| | Stock Investments | | 40,000 |
| | (To record sale of Beal common stock) | | |

A = L + SE
+39,000
−500 Exp
−40,000

Cash Flows
+39,500

Sanchez reports the loss account under "Other expenses and losses" in the income statement and shows a gain on sale under "Other revenues and gains."

# Holdings Between 20% and 50%

When an investor company owns only a small portion of the shares of stock of another company, the investor cannot exercise control over the investee. But when an investor owns between 20% and 50% of the common stock of a corporation, it is presumed that the investor has significant influence over the financial and operating activities of the investee. The investor probably has a representative on the investee's board of directors. Through that representative, the investor begins to exercise some control over the investee—and the investee company in some sense becomes part of the investor company.

For example, even prior to purchasing all of **Turner Broadcasting**, **Time Warner** owned 20% of Turner. Because it exercised significant control over major decisions made by Turner, Time Warner used an approach called the equity method. Under the **equity method, the investor records its share of the net income of the investee in the year when it is earned**. An alternative might be to delay recognizing the investor's share of net income until a cash dividend is declared. But that approach would ignore the fact that the investor and investee are, in some sense, one company, making the investor better off by the investee's net income.

Under the **equity method**, the company initially records the investment in common stock at cost. After that, it adjusts the investment account **annually** to show the investor's equity in the investee. Each year, the investor does the following. (1) It increases (debits) the investment account and increases (credits) revenue for its share of the investee's net income.[2] (2) The investor also decreases (credits) the investment account for the amount of dividends received. The investment account is reduced for dividends received because payment of a dividend decreases the net assets of the investee.

## Recording Acquisition of Stock

Assume that Milar Corporation acquires 30% of the common stock of Beck Company for $120,000 on January 1, 2022. The entry to record this transaction is:

| A | = | L | + | SE |
|---|---|---|---|---|
| +120,000 | | | | |
| −120,000 | | | | |

**Cash Flows**
−120,000

| Jan. 1 | Stock Investments | 120,000 | |
| | Cash | | 120,000 |
| | (To record purchase of Beck common stock) | | |

## Recording Revenue and Dividends

For 2022, Beck reports net income of $100,000. It declares and pays a $40,000 cash dividend. Milar must record (1) its share of Beck's income, $30,000 (30% × $100,000), and (2) the reduction in the investment account for the dividends received, $12,000 (30% × $40,000). The entries are:

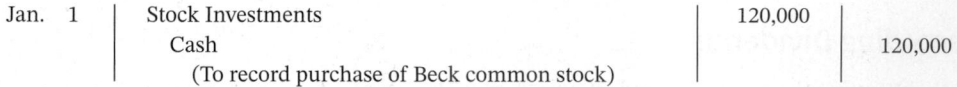

(1)

| A | = | L | + | SE |
|---|---|---|---|---|
| +30,000 | | | | |
| | | | | +30,000 Rev |

**Cash Flows**
no effect

| Dec. 31 | Stock Investments | 30,000 | |
| | Revenue from Stock Investments | | 30,000 |
| | (To record 30% equity in Beck's 2022 net income) | | |

(2)

| A | = | L | + | SE |
|---|---|---|---|---|
| +12,000 | | | | |
| −12,000 | | | | |

**Cash Flows**
+12,000

| Dec. 31 | Cash | 12,000 | |
| | Stock Investments | | 12,000 |
| | (To record dividends received) | | |

[2]Conversely, the investor increases (debits) a loss account and decreases (credits) the investment account for its share of the investee's net loss.

After Milar posts the transactions for the year, the investment and revenue accounts are as shown in **Illustration H.4**.

| Stock Investments | | | | | Revenue from Stock Investments | | |
|---|---|---|---|---|---|---|---|
| Jan. 1 | | 120,000 | Dec. 31 | **12,000** | | Dec. 31 | **30,000** |
| Dec. 31 | | **30,000** | | | | | |
| Dec. 31 | Bal. | 138,000 | | | | | |

**ILLUSTRATION H.4**

**Investment and revenue accounts after posting**

During the year, the investment account increased by $18,000. This $18,000 is explained as follows: (1) Milar records a $30,000 increase in revenue from its stock investment in Beck, and (2) Milar records a $12,000 decrease due to dividends received from its stock investment in Beck.

Note that the difference between reported revenue under the cost method and reported revenue under the equity method can be significant. For example, Milar would report only $12,000 of dividend revenue (30% × $40,000) if it used the cost method.

## Holdings of More Than 50%

A company that owns more than 50% of the common stock of another entity is known as the **parent company**. The entity whose stock is owned by the parent company is called the **subsidiary (affiliated) company**. Because of its stock ownership, the parent company has a **controlling interest** in the subsidiary company.

When a company owns more than 50% of the common stock of another company it usually prepares **consolidated financial statements**. Consolidated financial statements present the assets and liabilities of the parent and subsidiary companies. They also present the total revenues and expenses of the parent and subsidiary companies. Companies prepare consolidated statements **in addition to** the financial statements for the individual parent and subsidiary companies.

As noted earlier, prior to acquiring all of **Turner Broadcasting, Time Warner** accounted for its investment in Turner using the equity method. Time Warner's net investment in Turner was reported in a single line item—Other investments. After the merger, Time Warner instead consolidated Turner's results with its own. Under this approach, Time Warner included the individual assets and liabilities of Turner with its own assets. That is, Turner's plant and equipment were added to Time Warner's plant and equipment, its receivables were added to Time Warner's receivables, and so on. A similar sort of consolidation went on when **AOL** merged with Time Warner (see **Helpful Hint**).

**Consolidated statements are useful to the stockholders, board of directors, and management of the parent company.** Consolidated statements indicate to creditors, prospective investors, and regulatory agencies the magnitude and scope of operations of the companies under common control. For example, regulators and the courts undoubtedly used the consolidated statements of **AT&T** to determine whether a breakup of the company was in the public interest. **Illustration H.5** lists three companies that prepare consolidated statements and some of the companies they have owned.

**HELPFUL HINT**

If the parent (A) has three wholly owned subsidiaries (B, C, and D), there are four separate legal entities but only one economic entity from the viewpoint of the shareholders of the parent company.

| PepsiCo | Avis Budget Group | The Walt Disney Company |
|---|---|---|
| Frito-Lay | Avis Car Rental | Capital Cities/ABC, Inc. |
| Tropicana | Budget Car Rental | Disneyland, Disney World |
| Quaker Oats | Payless Car Rental | Anaheim Ducks |
| Pepsi-Cola | Apex Car Rentals | Anaheim Angels |
| Gatorade | Zipcar | ESPN |

**ILLUSTRATION H.5**

**Examples of consolidated companies and their subsidiaries**

**ACTION PLAN**

- Presume that the investor has relatively little influence over the investee when an investor owns less than 20% of the common stock of another corporation. In this case, net income earned by the investee is not considered a proper basis for recognizing income from the investment by the investor.

- Presume significant influence for investments of 20%–50%. Therefore, record the investor's share of the net income of the investee.

## DO IT! 2 | Stock Investments

The following are two independent situations.

1. Rho Jean Inc. acquired 5% of the 400,000 shares of common stock of Stillwater Corp. at a total cost of $6 per share on May 18, 2022. On August 30, Stillwater declared and paid a $75,000 dividend. On December 31, Stillwater reported net income of $244,000 for the year.

2. Debbie, Inc. obtained significant influence over North Sails by buying 40% of North Sails' 60,000 outstanding shares of common stock at a cost of $12 per share on January 1, 2022. On April 15, North Sails declared and paid a cash dividend of $45,000. On December 31, North Sails reported net income of $120,000 for the year.

Prepare all necessary journal entries for 2022 for (1) Rho Jean Inc. and (2) Debbie, Inc.

### Solution

| | | | | |
|---|---|---|---:|---:|
| **1.** | May 18 | Stock Investments (400,000 × 5% × $6) | 120,000 | |
| | | Cash | | 120,000 |
| | | (To record purchase of 20,000 shares of Stillwater Co. stock) | | |
| | Aug. 30 | Cash | 3,750 | |
| | | Dividend Revenue ($75,000 × 5%) | | 3,750 |
| | | (To record receipt of cash dividend) | | |
| **2.** | Jan. 1 | Stock Investments (60,000 × 40% × $12) | 288,000 | |
| | | Cash | | 288,000 |
| | | (To record purchase of 24,000 shares of North Sails' stock) | | |
| | Apr. 15 | Cash | 18,000 | |
| | | Stock Investments ($45,000 × 40%) | | 18,000 |
| | | (To record receipt of cash dividend) | | |
| | Dec. 31 | Stock Investments ($120,000 × 40%) | 48,000 | |
| | | Revenue from Stock Investments | | 48,000 |
| | | (To record 40% equity in North Sails' net income) | | |

# Reporting Investments in Financial Statements

**LEARNING OBJECTIVE 3**

Discuss how debt and stock investments are reported in the financial statements.

The value of debt and stock investments may fluctuate greatly during the time they are held. For example, in a 12-month period, the stock of **Time Warner** hit a high of $58\frac{1}{2}$ and a low of 9. In light of such price fluctuations, how should companies value investments at the balance sheet date? Valuation could be at cost, at fair value, or at the lower-of-cost-or-market value.

Many people argue that fair value offers the best approach because it represents the expected cash realizable value of securities. **Fair value** is the amount for which a security could be sold in a normal market. Others counter that unless a security is going to be sold soon, the fair value is not relevant because the price of the security will likely change again.

# Debt Securities

For purposes of valuation and reporting at a financial statement date, debt investments are classified into three categories:

1. **Trading securities** are bought and held primarily for sale in the near term to generate income on short-term price differences.
2. **Available-for-sale securities** are held with the intent of selling them sometime in the future.
3. **Held-to-maturity securities** are debt securities that the investor has the intent and ability to hold to maturity.[3]

**Illustration H.6** shows the valuation guidelines for these debt securities.

**ILLUSTRATION H.6**  **Valuation guidelines for debt securities**

| Trading | Available-for-Sale | Held-to-Maturity |
|---|---|---|
| "We'll sell within 10 days." | "We'll hold the bonds for a while to see how they perform." | "We intend to hold until maturity." |
| At fair value with changes reported in net income | At fair value with changes reported in the stockholders' equity section | At amortized cost |

## Trading Securities

Trading securities are held with the intention of selling them in a short period of time (generally less than three months and sometimes less than a full day). **Trading** means frequent buying and selling. As indicated in Illustration H.6, companies adjust trading securities to fair value at the end of each period (an approach referred to as **mark-to-market** accounting). They report changes from cost **as part of net income**. The changes are reported as **unrealized gains or losses** because the securities have not been sold. The unrealized gain or loss is the difference between the **total cost** of trading securities and their **total fair value**. Companies classify trading securities as a current asset.

As an example, **Illustration H.7** shows the costs and fair values for investments classified as trading securities for Pace Corporation on December 31, 2022. Pace has an unrealized gain of $7,000 because total fair value ($147,000) is $7,000 greater than total cost ($140,000)

**ILLUSTRATION H.7**

**Valuation of trading securities**

**Trading Securities, December 31, 2022**

| Investments | Cost | Fair Value | Unrealized Gain (Loss) |
|---|---|---|---|
| Yorkville Company bonds | $ 50,000 | $ 48,000 | $(2,000) |
| Kodak Company bonds | 90,000 | 99,000 | 9,000 |
| Total | $140,000 | $147,000 | **$ 7,000** |

**HELPFUL HINT**

Companies report an unrealized gain or loss in the income statement because of the likelihood that the securities will be sold at fair value since they are a short-term investment.

The fact that trading securities are a short-term investment increases the likelihood that Pace will sell them at fair value for a gain. Pace records fair value and the unrealized gain through an adjusting entry at the time it prepares financial statements (see **Helpful Hint**).

---

[3]This category is provided for completeness. The accounting and valuation issues related to held-to-maturity securities are discussed in more advanced accounting courses.

In this entry, the company uses a valuation allowance account, Fair Value Adjustment—Trading, to record the difference between the total cost and the total fair value of the securities. The adjusting entry for Pace is:

+7,000

+7,000 Rev

**Cash Flows**
no effect

| Dec. 31 | Fair Value Adjustment—Trading | 7,000 | |
| | Unrealized Gain or Loss—Income | | 7,000 |
| | (To record unrealized gain on trading securities) | | |

The use of the Fair Value Adjustment—Trading account enables the company to maintain a record of the investment cost. Actual cost is needed to determine the gain or loss realized when the securities are sold. The company adds the debit balance (or subtracts a credit balance) of the Fair Value Adjustment—Trading account to the cost of the investments to arrive at a fair value for the trading securities.

**The fair value of the securities is the amount companies report on the balance sheet.** They report the unrealized gain on the income statement under "Other revenues and gains." The term **income** in the account title indicates that the gain affects net income.

If the total cost of the trading securities is greater than total fair value, an unrealized loss has occurred. In such a case, the adjusting entry is a debit to Unrealized Gain or Loss—Income and a credit to Fair Value Adjustment—Trading. Companies report the unrealized loss under "Other expenses and losses" in the income statement.

The Fair Value Adjustment—Trading account is carried forward into future accounting periods. No entries are made to this account during the period. At the end of each reporting period, a company adjusts the balance in the account to the difference between cost and fair value at that time. It closes the Unrealized Gain or Loss—Income account at the end of the reporting period.

## Available-for-Sale Securities

As indicated earlier, available-for-sale securities are held with the intent of selling them sometime in the future. If the intent is to sell the securities within the next year or operating cycle, a company classifies the securities as current assets in the balance sheet. Otherwise, it classifies them as long-term assets in the investments section of the balance sheet.

Companies also report available-for-sale securities at fair value. The procedure for determining fair value and unrealized gain or loss for these securities is the same as that for trading securities. To illustrate, assume that Shelton Corporation has two securities that are classified as available-for-sale. **Illustration H.8** provides information on the cost, fair value, and amount of the unrealized gain or loss on December 31, 2022. There is an unrealized loss of $9,537 because total cost ($293,537) is $9,537 more than total fair value ($284,000).

**ILLUSTRATION H.8**

Valuation of available-for-sale securities

**Available-for-Sale Securities, December 31, 2022**

| Investments | Cost | Fair Value | Unrealized Gain (Loss) |
|---|---|---|---|
| Campbell Soup Co. bonds | $ 93,537 | $103,600 | $10,063 |
| Hershey Foods bonds | 200,000 | 180,400 | (19,600) |
| Total | $293,537 | $284,000 | $(9,537) |

Both the adjusting entry and the reporting of the unrealized loss from Shelton's available-for-sale securities differ from those illustrated for trading securities. The differences result because these securities are not going to be sold in the near term. Thus, prior to actual sale it is much more likely that changes in fair value may reverse the unrealized loss. Therefore, Shelton does not report an unrealized loss in the income statement. Instead, the company reports it as an item of other comprehensive income in the statement of comprehensive income. In the adjusting entry, Shelton identifies the fair value adjustment account with available-for-sale securities, and identifies the unrealized gain or loss account with stockholders' equity (see **Helpful Hint**). The adjusting entry for Shelton to record the unrealized loss of $9,537 is as follows.

**HELPFUL HINT**

**The entry is the same regardless of whether the securities are considered short-term or long-term.**

| Dec. 31 | Unrealized Gain or Loss—Equity | 9,537 | |
| | Fair Value Adjustment—Available-for-Sale | | 9,537 |
| | (To record unrealized loss on available-for-sale | | |
| | securities) | | |

A = ___ + SE
−9,537 Eq
−9,537

**Cash Flows**
no effect

If total fair value exceeds total cost, Shelton would record the adjusting entry as an increase (debit) to Fair Value Adjustment—Available-for-Sale and a credit to Unrealized Gain or Loss—Equity.

Shelton's unrealized loss of $9,537 would appear in the statement of comprehensive income as shown in **Illustration H.9.**

### Shelton Corporation
#### Statement of Comprehensive Income
#### For the Year Ended December 31, 2022

| | |
|---|---|
| Net income | $118,000 |
| Other comprehensive income | |
| Unrealized loss on available-for-sale securities | (9,537) |
| Comprehensive income | $108,463 |

**ILLUSTRATION H.9**

**Statement of comprehensive income**

**ETHICS NOTE**

Recently, the SEC accused investment bank **Morgan Stanley** of overstating the value of certain bond investments by $75 million. The SEC stated that, in applying fair value accounting, Morgan Stanley used its own more optimistic assumptions rather than relying on external pricing sources.

For available-for-sale securities, the company carries forward the Unrealized Gain or Loss—Equity account to future periods. At each future balance sheet date, the account is adjusted with the Fair Value Adjustment—Available-for-Sale account to show the difference between cost and fair value at that time (see **Ethics Note**).

---

## DO IT! 3a | Trading and Available-for-Sale Debt Securities

Some of Powderhorn Corporation's investment debt securities are classified as trading securities and some are classified as available-for-sale. The cost and fair value of each category at December 31, 2022, are as follows.

| | Cost | Fair Value | Unrealized Gain (Loss) |
|---|---|---|---|
| Trading securities | $93,600 | $94,900 | $1,300 |
| Available-for-sale securities | $48,800 | $51,400 | $2,600 |

At December 31, 2021, the Fair Value Adjustment—Trading account had a debit balance of $9,200, and the Fair Value Adjustment—Available-for-Sale account had a credit balance of $5,750. Prepare the required journal entries for each group of securities for December 31, 2022.

**ACTION PLAN**

- Mark trading securities to fair value and report the adjustment in current-period income.

- Mark available-for-sale securities to fair value and report the adjustment as a separate component of stockholders' equity.

### Solution

*Trading securities:*

| Unrealized Gain or Loss—Income | 7,900* | |
| Fair Value Adjustment—Trading | | 7,900 |
| (To record unrealized loss on trading securities) | | |

*$9,200 − $1,300

*Available-for-sale securities.*

| Fair Value Adjustment—Available-for-Sale | 8,350** | |
| Unrealized Gain or Loss—Equity | | 8,350 |
| (To record unrealized gain on available-for-sale | | |
| securities) | | |

**$5,750 + $2,600

# Equity Securities

The valuation and reporting of equity securities at a financial statement date depends on the levels of influence involved, as shown in **Illustration H.10**.

ILLUSTRATION H.10

**Accounting and reporting for equity securities by category**

| Category | Valuation | Unrealized Gains or Losses | Other Income Effects |
|---|---|---|---|
| Holdings less than 20% | Fair value | Recognized in net income | Dividends declared; gains and losses from sale |
| Holdings between 20% and 50% | Equity | Not recognized | Proportionate share of investee's net income |
| Holdings more than 50% | Consolidation | Not recognized | Not applicable |

When an investor has an interest of less than 20%, it is presumed that the investor has little or no influence over the investee. In such cases, if market prices are available subsequent to acquisition, the company values and reports the stock investment using the fair value method.

## Illustration of Stock Holdings Less Than 20%

At December 31, 2022, Shelton Corporation has two equity securities in which it has less than a 20% ownership interest and therefore has little or no influence over these companies. Shelton has the following cost and fair value for these two companies, as shown in **Illustration H.11**.

**ILLUSTRATION H.11**

**Computation of fair value adjustment—equity security portfolio (2022)**

| Investments | Cost | Fair Value | Unrealized Gain (Loss) |
|---|---|---|---|
| Twitter Co. | $259,700 | $275,000 | $15,300 |
| Campbell Soup Co. | 317,500 | 304,000 | (13,500) |
| Totals | $577,200 | $579,000 | $ 1,800 |

For Shelton's equity securities portfolio, the gross unrealized gain is $15,300 and the gross unrealized loss is $13,500, resulting in a net unrealized gain of $1,800. That is, the fair value of the equity securities portfolio is above cost by $1,800.

Shelton records the net unrealized gains and losses related to changes in the fair value equity securities in an Unrealized Gain or Loss—Income account. In this case, Shelton prepares an adjusting entry debiting the Fair Value Adjustment—Stock account and crediting the Unrealized Gain or Loss—Income account to record the increase in fair value and to record the gain as follows.

|  | **December 31, 2022** | | |
|---|---|---|---|
| Fair Value Adjustment—Stock | | 1,800 | |
| Unrealized Gain or Loss—Income | | | 1,800 |
| (To record unrealized gain on equity securities) | | | |

Similar to trading securities, Shelton adjusts the balance in the Fair Value Adjustment—Stock account for the difference between cost and fair value. In addition, the unrealized gain related to Shelton's equity securities is reported in the "Other revenues and gains" section of the income statement.

# Balance Sheet Presentation

In the balance sheet presentation, companies must classify investments as either short-term or long-term.

## Short-Term Investments

**Short-term investments** (also called **marketable securities**) are securities held by a company that are (1) **readily marketable** and (2) **intended to be converted into cash** within the next year or operating cycle, whichever is longer (see Helpful Hint). Investments that do not meet **both criteria** are classified as **long-term investments**.

**Readily Marketable** **An investment is readily marketable when it can be sold easily whenever the need for cash arises.** Short-term paper[4] meets this criterion because a company can readily sell it to other investors. Stocks and bonds traded on organized securities markets, such as the New York Stock Exchange, are readily marketable because they can be bought and sold daily. In contrast, there may be only a limited market for the securities issued by small corporations and no market for the securities of a privately held company.

**Intent to Convert** **Intent to convert means that management intends to sell the investment within the next year or operating cycle, whichever is longer.** Generally, this criterion is satisfied when the investment is considered a resource that the company will use whenever the need for cash arises. For example, a ski resort may invest idle cash during the summer months with the intent to sell the securities to buy supplies and equipment shortly before the next winter season. This investment is considered short-term even if lack of snow cancels the next ski season and eliminates the need to convert the securities into cash as intended.

Because of their high liquidity, companies list short-term investments immediately below Cash in the current assets section of the balance sheet. Short-term investments are reported at fair value. For example, Weber Corporation would report its trading securities as shown in **Illustration H.12**.

**Weber Corporation**
**Balance Sheet (partial)**

| Current assets | |
|---|---|
| Cash | $21,000 |
| **Debt investments (at fair value)** | **60,000** |

## Long-Term Investments

Companies generally report long-term investments in a separate section of the balance sheet immediately below "Current assets," as shown in **Illustration H.13**. Long-term investments in available-for-sale securities are reported at fair value. Investments in common stock accounted for under the equity method are reported at equity.

**Weber Corporation**
**Balance Sheet (partial)**

| Investments | | |
|---|---|---|
| Debt investment (at fair value) | $100,000 | |
| **Stock investments (at fair value)** | **50,000** | |
| **Stock investments (at equity)** | **150,000** | |
| Total investments | | $300,000 |

---

[4]Short-term paper includes (1) certificates of deposits (CDs) issued by banks, (2) money market certificates issued by banks and savings and loan associations, (3) Treasury bills issued by the U.S. government, and (4) commercial paper issued by corporations with good credit ratings.

# Presentation of Realized and Unrealized Gain or Loss

Companies must present in the financial statements gains and losses on investments, whether realized or unrealized. In the income statement, companies report gains and losses, as well as interest and dividend revenue, in the nonoperating activities section under the categories listed in **Illustration H.14.**

**ILLUSTRATION H.14**

**Nonoperating items related to investments**

| **Other Revenues and Gains** | **Other Expenses and Losses** |
|---|---|
| Interest Revenue | Loss on Sale of Investments |
| Dividend Revenue | Unrealized Loss |
| Gain on Sale of Investments | |
| Unrealized Gain | |

Companies report the cumulative amount of other comprehensive income items from the current and previous years as a separate component of stockholders' equity. To illustrate, assume that Muzzillo Inc. has common stock of $3,000,000, retained earnings of $1,500,000, and an accumulated other comprehensive loss of $100,000. **Illustration H.15** shows the financial statement presentation of the accumulated other comprehensive loss.

**ILLUSTRATION H.15**

**Unrealized loss in stockholders' equity section**

| Muzzillo Inc. | |
|---|---|
| Balance Sheet (partial) | |
| Stockholders' equity | |
| Common stock | $3,000,000 |
| Retained earnings | 1,500,000 |
| Total paid-in capital and retained earnings | 4,500,000 |
| **Accumulated other comprehensive loss** | **(100,000)** |
| Total stockholders' equity | $4,400,000 |

A classified balance sheet is shown in **Illustration H.16**. This balance sheet includes the following items (highlighted in red): short-term and long-term debt investments, stock investments, and accumulated other comprehensive income.

**ILLUSTRATION H.16**

**Classified balance sheet**

| Pace Corporation | | |
|---|---|---|
| Balance Sheet | | |
| December 31, 2022 | | |
| **Assets** | | |
| Current assets | | |
| Cash | | $   21,000 |
| **Debt investments (at fair value)** | | **147,000** |
| Accounts receivable | $ 84,000 | |
| Less: Allowance for doubtful accounts | 4,000 | 80,000 |
| Inventory, at FIFO cost | | 43,000 |
| Prepaid insurance | | 23,000 |
| Total current assets | | 314,000 |
| Investments | | |
| **Debt investments (at fair value)** | 20,000 | |
| **Stock investments (at fair value)** | 30,000 | |
| **Stock investments (at equity)** | 150,000 | |
| Total investments | | 200,000 |

| | | | |
|---|---|---:|---:|
| Property, plant, and equipment | | | |
| Land | | | 200,000 |
| Buildings | $800,000 | | |
| Less: Accumulated depreciation—buildings | 200,000 | 600,000 | |
| Equipment | 180,000 | | |
| Less: Accumulated depreciation—equipment | 54,000 | 126,000 | |
| Total property, plant, and equipment | | | 926,000 |
| Intangible assets | | | |
| Goodwill | | | 270,000 |
| Total assets | | | $1,710,000 |

### Liabilities and Stockholders' Equity

| | | | |
|---|---|---:|---:|
| Current liabilities | | | |
| Accounts payable | | | $ 185,000 |
| Federal income taxes payable | | | 60,000 |
| Interest payable | | | 10,000 |
| Total current liabilities | | | 255,000 |
| Long-term liabilities | | | |
| Bonds payable, 10%, due 2027 | | $ 300,000 | |
| Less: Discount on bonds | | 10,000 | |
| Total long-term liabilities | | | 290,000 |
| Total liabilities | | | 545,000 |
| Stockholders' equity | | | |
| Paid-in capital | | | |
| Common stock, $10 par value, | | | |
| 200,000 shares authorized, 80,000 shares | | | |
| issued and outstanding | | 800,000 | |
| In excess of par—common stock | | 100,000 | |
| Total paid-in capital | | 900,000 | |
| Retained earnings (Note 1) | | 255,000 | |
| Total paid-in capital and retained earnings | | 1,155,000 | |
| **Add: Accumulated other comprehensive income** | | **10,000** | |
| Total stockholders' equity | | | 1,165,000 |
| Total liabilities and stockholders' equity | | | $1,710,000 |

**Note 1.** Retained earnings of $100,000 is restricted for plant expansion.

---

## DO IT! 3b | Financial Statement Presentation of Investments

Identify where each of the following items would be reported in the financial statements.

1. Interest earned on investments in bonds.
2. Fair value adjustment—stock.
3. Unrealized gain or loss—equity.
4. Gain on sale of investments in stock.
5. Unrealized gain—income.

Use the following possible categories:

*Balance sheet:*

| | |
|---|---|
| Current assets | Current liabilities |
| Investments | Long-term liabilities |
| Property, plant, and equipment | Stockholders' equity |
| Intangible assets | |

*Income statement:*

| | |
|---|---|
| Other revenues and gains | Other expenses and losses |

**ACTION PLAN**

- Classify investments as current assets if they will be held for less than one year.
- Report unrealized gains or losses on trading securities in income.
- Report unrealized gains or losses on available-for-sale securities in equity.
- Report realized gains and losses on investments in the income statement as "Other revenues and gains" or as "Other expenses and losses."

**Solution**

| Item | Financial Statement | Category |
|---|---|---|
| 1. Interest earned on investments in bonds. | Income statement | Other revenues and gains |
| 2. Fair value adjustment—stock | Balance sheet | Investments |
| 3. Unrealized gain or loss—equity. | Balance sheet | Stockholders' equity |
| 4. Gain on sale of investments in stock. | Income statement | Other revenues and gains |
| 5. Unrealized gain—income. | Income statement | Other revenues and gains |

# Review and Practice

## Learning Objectives Review

### 1   Explain how to account for debt investments.

Corporations invest for three common reasons: (a) they have excess cash, (b) they view investment income as a significant revenue source, and (c) they have strategic goals such as gaining control of a competitor or supplier or moving into a new line of business.

Entries for investments in debt securities are required when companies purchase bonds, receive or accrue interest, and sell bonds.

### 2   Explain how to account for stock investments.

Entries for investments in common stock are required when companies purchase stock, receive dividends, and sell stock. When ownership is less than 20%, the cost method is used—the investment is recorded at cost. When ownership is between 20% and 50%, the equity method should be used—the investor records its share of the net income of the investee in the year it is earned.

When a company owns more than 50% of the common stock of another company, consolidated financial statements are usually prepared. These statements are especially useful to the stockholders, board of directors, and management of the parent company.

### 3   Discuss how debt and stock investments are reported in the financial statements.

Investments in debt securities are classified as trading, available-for-sale, or held-to-maturity for valuation and reporting purposes. Trading securities are reported as current assets at fair value, with changes from cost reported in net income. Available-for-sale securities are also reported at fair value, with the changes from cost reported as items of other comprehensive income. Available-for-sale securities are classified as short-term or long-term depending on their expected realization.

Investments in stock when ownership is less than 20% are reported at fair values, with changes from cost reported in net income.

Short-term investments are securities held by a company that are readily marketable and intended to be converted to cash within the next year or operating cycle, whichever is longer. Investments that do not meet both criteria are classified as long-term investments.

## Glossary Review

**Available-for-sale securities**   Securities that are held with the intent of selling them sometime in the future. (p. H-9).

**Consolidated financial statements**   Financial statements that present the assets and liabilities controlled by the parent company and the total revenues and expenses of the subsidiary companies. (p. H-7).

**Controlling interest**   Ownership of more than 50% of the common stock of another entity. (p. H-7).

**Cost method**   An accounting method in which the investment in common stock is recorded at cost and revenue is recognized only when cash dividends are received. (p. H-5).

**Debt investments**   Investments in government and corporation bonds. (p. H-3).

**Equity method**   An accounting method in which the investment in common stock is initially recorded at cost, and the investment account is then adjusted annually to show the investor's equity in the investee. (p. H-6).

**Fair value**   Amount for which a security could be sold in a normal market. (p. H-8).

**Held-to-maturity securities**   Debt securities that the investor has the intent and ability to hold to maturity. (p. H-9).

**Long-term investments**   Investments that are not readily marketable or that management does not intend to convert into cash within the next year or operating cycle, whichever is longer. (p. H-13).

**Mark-to-market**   A method of accounting for certain investments that requires that they be adjusted to their fair value at the end of each period. (p. H-9).

**Parent company**   A company that owns more than 50% of the common stock of another entity. (p. H-7).

**Short-term investments (marketable securities)**   Investments that are readily marketable and intended to be converted into cash within the next year or operating cycle, whichever is longer. (p. H-13).

**Stock investments** Investments in the capital stock of corporations. (p. H-4).

**Subsidiary (affiliated) company** A company in which more than 50% of its stock is owned by another company. (p. H-7).

**Trading securities** Securities bought and held primarily for sale in the near term to generate income on short-term price differences. (p. H-9).

## Practice Multiple-Choice Questions

1. **(LO 1)** Which of the following is **not** a primary reason why corporations invest in debt and equity securities?
   a. They wish to gain control of a competitor.
   b. They have excess cash.
   c. They wish to move into a new line of business.
   d. They are required to by law.

2. **(LO 1)** Debt investments are initially recorded at:
   a. cost.
   b. cost plus accrued interest.
   c. fair value.
   d. face value.

3. **(LO 1)** Hanes Company sells debt investments costing $26,000 for $28,000. In journalizing the sale, credits are to:
   a. Debt Investments and Loss on Sale of Debt Investments.
   b. Debt Investments and Gain on Sale of Debt Investments.
   c. Stock Investments and Gain on Sale of Stock Investments.
   d. None of the answer choices is correct.

4. **(LO 2)** Pryor Company receives net proceeds of $42,000 on the sale of stock investments that cost $39,500. This transaction will result in reporting in the income statement a:
   a. loss of S2,500 under "Other expenses and losses."
   b. loss of S2,500 under "Operating expenses."
   c. gain of $2,500 under "Other revenues and gains."
   d. gain of $2,500 under "Operating revenues."

5. **(LO 2)** The equity method of accounting for long-term investments in stock should be used when the investor has significant influence over an investee and owns:
   a. between 20% and 50% of the investee's common stock.
   b. 20% or more of the investee's common stock.
   c. more than 50% of the investee's common stock.
   d. less than 20% of the investee's common stock.

6. **(LO 2)** Assume that Horicon Corp. acquired 25% of the common stock of Sheboygan Corp. on January 1, 2022, for $300,000. During 2022, Sheboygan Corp. reported net income of $160,000 and paid total dividends of $60,000. If Horicon uses the equity method to account for its investment, the balance in the investment account on December 31, 2022, will be:
   a. $300,000.
   b. $325,000.
   c. $400 000.
   d. $340,000.

7. **(LO 2)** Assume that Horicon Corp. acquired 25% of the common stock of Sheboygan Corp. on January 1, 2022, for $300,000. During 2022, Sheboygan Corp. reported net income of $160,000 and paid total dividends of $60,000. If Horicon uses the equity method to account for its investment, what entry would Horicon make to record the receipt of the dividend from Sheboygan?
   a. Debit Cash and credit Revenue from Stock Investments.
   b. Debit Cash Dividends and credit Revenue from Stock Investments.

   c. Debit Cash and credit Stock Investments.
   d. Debit Cash and credit Dividend Revenue.

8. **(LO 2)** You have a controlling interest if:
   a. you own more than 20% of a company's stock.
   b. you are the president of the company.
   c. you use the equity method.
   d. you own more than 50% of a company's stock.

9. **(LO 2)** Which of the following statements is **false**? Consolidated financial statements are useful to determine:
   a. the profitability of specific subsidiaries.
   b. the total profitability of companies under common control.
   c. the breadth of a parent company's operations.
   d. the full extent of total obligations of companies under common control.

10. **(LO 3)** At the end of the first year of operations, the total cost of the trading securities portfolio is $120,000. Total fair value is $115,000. The financial statements should show:
    a. a reduction of an asset of $5,000 and a realized loss of $5,000.
    b. a reduction of an asset of $5,000 and an unrealized loss of $5,000 in the stockholders' equity section.
    c. a reduction of an asset of $5,000 in the current assets section and an unrealized loss of $5,000 in "Other expenses and losses."
    d. a reduction of an asset of $5,000 in the current assets section and a realized loss of $5,000 in "Other expenses and losses."

11. **(LO 3)** At December 31, 2022, the fair value of available-for-sale debt securities is $41,300 and the cost is $39,800. At January 1, 2022, there was a credit balance of $900 in the Fair Value Adjustment—Available-for-Sale account. The required adjusting entry would be:
    a. Debit Fair Value Adjustment—Available-for-Sale for $1,500 and credit Unrealized Gain or Loss—Equity for $1,500.
    b. Debit Fair Value Adjustment—Available-for-Sale for $600 and credit Unrealized Gain or Loss—Equity for $600.
    c. Debit Fair Value Adjustment—Available-for-Sale for $2,400 and credit Unrealized Gain or Loss—Equity for $2,400.
    d. Debit Unrealized Gain or Loss—Equity for $2,400 and credit Fair Value Adjustment—Available-for-Sale for $2,400.

12. **(LO 3)** If a company wants to increase its reported income by manipulating its investment accounts, which should it do?
    a. Sell its "winner" trading securities and hold its "loser" trading securities.
    b. Hold its "winner" trading securities and sell its "loser" trading securities.

c. Sell its "winner" available-for-sale securities and hold its "loser" available-for-sale securities.

d. Hold its "winner" available-for-sale securities and sell its "loser" available-for-sale securities.

13. **(LO 3)** In the balance sheet, a debit balance in Unrealized Gain or Loss—Equity is reported as a(n):

a. increase to stockholders' equity.

b. decrease to stockholders' equity.

c. loss in the income statement.

d. loss in the retained earnings statement.

14. **(LO 3)** Short-term debt investments must be readily marketable and expected to be sold within:

a. 3 months from the date of purchase.

b. the next year or operating cycle, whichever is shorter.

c. the next year or operating cycle, whichever is longer.

d. the operating cycle.

## Solutions

**1. d.** Corporations are not required to by law to invest in debt and equity securities. The other choices are reasons why corporations invest in debt and equity securities.

**2. a.** When debt investments are purchased, they are recorded at cost, not (b) cost plus accrued interest, (c) fair value, or (d) face value.

**3. b.** Credits are made to Debt Investments $26,000 and Gain on Sale of Debt Investments $2,000 ($28,000 − $26,000). The other choices are therefore incorrect.

**4. c.** Because the cash received ($42,000) is greater than the cost ($39,500), this sale results in a gain, not a loss, which will be reported under "Other revenues and gains" in the income statement. The other choices are therefore incorrect.

**5. a.** The equity method is used when the investor can exercise significant influence and owns between 20% and 50% of the investee's common stock. The other choices are therefore incorrect.

**6. b.** Horicon records the acquisition of the stock investment by debiting Stock Investments $300,000 and crediting Cash $300,000. Then, Horicon records (1) its share in Sheboygan Corp.'s net income ($160,000 × .25) by debiting Stock Investments $40,000 and crediting Revenue from Stock Investments $40,000 and (2) the reduction in the investment account for the dividends received ($60,000 × .25) by debiting Cash $15,000 and crediting Stock Investments $15,000. Thus, the balance in the investment account on December 31 will be $325,000 ($300,000 + $40,000 − $15,000), not (a) $300,000, (c) $400,000, or (d) $340,000.

**7. c.** Horicon records the receipt of the dividend from Sheboygan by debiting Cash and crediting Stock Investments. The other choices are therefore incorrect.

**8. d.** You have a controlling interest if you own more than 50% of a company's stock, not (a) 20% of a company's stock, (b) are president of the company, or (c) use the equity method.

**9. a.** Consolidated financial statements are not useful in determining the profitability of specific subsidiaries (legal entities) because consolidated financial statements represent the results of the single economic entity. The other choices are true statements.

**10. c.** The difference between the fair value ($115,000) and total cost ($120,000) of trading securities at the end of the first year would result in a reduction of an asset of $5,000 through the valuation allowance account in the current assets section and an unrealized loss of $5,000 in "Other expenses and losses." The other choices are therefore incorrect.

**11. c.** In this case, there is an unrealized gain of $1,500 because total fair value of $41,300 is $1,500 greater than the total cost of $39,800. The desired balance in the market adjustment account is $1,500 debit. The required adjusting entry considers the existing credit balance of $900 and is a debit to Fair Value Adjustment—Available-for-Sale for $2,400 ($1,500 + $900) and a credit to Unrealized Gain or Loss—Equity for $2,400 ($1,500 + $900). The other choices are therefore incorrect.

**12. c.** When a company sells its winners as related to available-for-sale securities, it has a realized gain that increases net income. Selling the winners will affect the balance in Unrealized Holding Gain or Loss—Equity, but any change in this balance does not affect net income. Choices (a) and (b) are incorrect because trading securities' gains and losses related to changes in valuation are reported in net income. Thus, when a company sells a trading security, it should have no effect on net income because the value change was recognized in net income previously. Choice (d) is incorrect because selling the losing available-for-sale securities will decrease net income.

**13. b.** A debit balance in Unrealized Gain or Loss—Equity is reported on the balance sheet as a separate component of stockholders' equity, decreasing stockholders' equity. The other choices are therefore incorrect.

**14. c.** Short-term investments are current assets that are expected to be consumed, sold, or converted to cash within one year or the operating cycle, whichever is longer. The other choices are therefore incorrect.

## Practice Brief Exercises

*Journalize entries for debt investments.*

**1. (LO 1)** Liriano Corporation purchased debt investments for 85,000 on January 1, 2022. On July 1, 2022, Liriano received cash interest of $6,800. Journalize the purchase and the receipt of interest. Assume that no interest has been accrued.

## Solution

| | | | | |
|---|---|---|---|---|
| 1. | Jan. 1 | Debt Investments | 85,000 | |
| | | Cash | | 85,000 |
| | July 1 | Cash | 6,800 | |
| | | Interest Revenue | | 6,800 |

**2. (LO 2)** On June 1, Willyjuan Company buys 2,000 shares of Minaya common stock for $57,000 cash. On October 15 Willyjuan sells the stock investments for $54,000 in cash. Journalize the purchase and sale of the common

*Journalize entries for stock investments.*

## Solution

| | | | | |
|---|---|---|---|---|
| 2. | June 1 | Stock Investments | 57,000 | |
| | | Cash | | 57,000 |
| | Oct. 15 | Cash | 54,000 | |
| | | Loss on Sale of Stock Investments | 3,000 | |
| | | Stock Investments | | 57,000 |

**3. (LO 3)** The cost of the trading securities of Dylan Company at December 31, 2022, is $46,000. At December 31, 2022, the fair value of the securities is $50,000. (a) Prepare the adjusting entry to record the securities at fair value. (b) Show the financial statement presentation at December 31, 2022.

*Prepare adjusting entry and indicate statement presentation using fair value.*

## Solution

| | | | | |
|---|---|---|---|---|
| 3. a. | Dec. 31 | Fair Value Adjustment—Trading | 4,000 | |
| | | Unrealized Gain or Loss—Income | | 4,000 |
| | | ($50,000 – $46,000) | | |

**b.**

**Balance Sheet**

Current assets

Short-term investments, at fair value      $50,000

**Income Statement**

Other revenues and gains

Unrealized gain—income      $4,000

---

# Practice Exercises

---

**1. (LO 1)** Potter Company purchased 50 Quinn Company 6%, 10-year, $1,000 bonds on January 1, 2022, for $50,000. The bonds pay interest annually. On January 1, 2023, after receipt of interest, Potter Company sold 30 of the bonds for $28,100.

*Journalize debt investment transactions, accrue interest, and record sale.*

## Instructions

Prepare the journal entries to record the transactions described above.

**Solution**

**1.**

| | 2022 | | | |
|---|---|---|---|---|
| | Jan. 1 | Debt Investments | 50,000 | |
| | | Cash | | 50,000 |
| | Dec. 31 | Interest Receivable | 3,000 | |
| | | Interest Revenue ($50,000 × 6%) | | 3,000 |
| | 2023 | | | |
| | Jan. 1 | Cash | 3,000 | |
| | | Interest Receivable | | 3,000 |
| | Jan. 1 | Cash | 28,100 | |
| | | Loss on Sale of Debt Investments | 1,900 | |
| | | Debt Investments [(30 ÷ 50) × $50,000] | | 30,000 |

*Journalize transactions for investments in stocks.*

**2. (LO 2)** Lucy Inc. had the following transactions in 2022 pertaining to investments in common stock.

Jan. 1 Purchased 4,000 shares of Morgan Corporation common stock (5% interest) for $180,000 cash.
July 1 Received a cash dividend of $3 per share.
Dec. 1 Sold 600 shares of Morgan Corporation common stock for $32,000 cash.
Dec. 31 Received a cash dividend of $3 per share.

**Instructions**

Journalize the transactions.

**Solution**

**2.**

| | Jan. 1 | Stock Investments | 180,000 | |
|---|---|---|---|---|
| | | Cash | | 180,000 |
| | July 1 | Cash (4,000 × $3) | 12,000 | |
| | | Dividend Revenue | | 12,000 |
| | Dec. 1 | Cash | 32,000 | |
| | | Stock Investments [$180,000 × (600 ÷ 4,000)] | | 27,000 |
| | | Gain on Sale of Stock Investments | | 5,000 |
| | Dec. 31 | Cash [(4,000 − 600) × $3] | 10,200 | |
| | | Dividend Revenue | | 10,200 |

*Prepare adjusting entries for fair value, and indicate statement presentation for two classes of securities.*

**3. (LO 3)** Remy Company started business on January 1, 2022, and has the following data at December 31, 2022.

| Debt Securities | Cost | Fair Value |
|---|---|---|
| Trading | $120,000 | $132,000 |
| Available-for-sale | 100,000 | 86,000 |

The available-for-sale securities are held as a long-term investment.

**Instructions**

a. Prepare the adjusting entries to report each class of securities at fair value.

b. Indicate the statement presentation of each class of securities and the related unrealized gain (loss) accounts.

**Solution**

3.

| | | | | |
|---|---|---|---|---|
| **a.** Dec. | 31 | Fair Value Adjustment—Trading | | |
| | | ($132,000 − $120,000) | 12,000 | |
| | |     Unrealized Gain or Loss—Income | | 12,000 |
| Dec. | 31 | Unrealized Gain or Loss—Equity | | |
| | | ($100,000 − $86,000) | 14,000 | |
| | |     Fair Value Adjustment—Available-for-Sale | | 14,000 |

**b.**

**Balance Sheet**

| | |
|---|---|
| Current assets | |
|   Short-term investments, at fair value | $132,000 |
| Investments | |
|   Debt investment, at fair value | 86,000 |
| Stockholders' equity | |
|   Less: Accumulated other comprehensive income | $14,000 |

**Income Statement**

| | |
|---|---|
| Other revenues and gains | |
|   Unrealized gain—income | $12,000 |

## Practice Problem

**(LO 2, 3)** In its first year of operations, DeMarco Company had the following selected transactions in stock investments (holdings less than 20%).

*Journalize transactions and prepare adjusting entry to record fair value.*

| | |
|---|---|
| June 1 | Purchased for cash 600 shares of Sanburg common stock at $24 per share. |
| July 1 | Purchased for cash 800 shares of Cey Corporation common stock at $33 per share. |
| Sept. 1 | Received a $1 per share cash dividend from Cey Corporation. |
| Nov. 1 | Sold 200 shares of Sanburg common stock for cash at $27 per share. |
| Dec. 15 | Received a $0.50 per share cash dividend on Sanburg common stock. |

At December 31, the fair values per share were Sanburg $25 and Cey $30.

### Instructions

**a.** Journalize the transactions.

**b.** Prepare the adjusting entry at December 31 to report the securities at fair value.

### Solution

| | | | | |
|---|---|---|---|---|
| **a.** June | 1 | Stock Investments | 14,400 | |
| | |   Cash (600 × $24) | | 14,400 |
| | |   (To record purchase of 600 shares of Sanburg common stock) | | |
| July | 1 | Stock Investments | 26,400 | |
| | |   Cash (800 × $33) | | 26,400 |
| | |   (To record purchase of 800 shares of Cey common stock) | | |
| Sept. | 1 | Cash (800 × $1.00) | 800 | |
| | |   Dividend Revenue | | 800 |
| | |   (To record receipt of $1 per share cash dividend from Cey Corporation) | | |

| | | | | |
|---|---|---|---|---|
| Nov. 1 | Cash (200 × $27) | | 5,400 | |
| |     Stock Investments (200 × $24) | | | 4,800 |
| |     Gain on Sale of Stock Investments | | | 600 |
| |       (To record sale of 200 shares of Sanburg | | | |
| |       common stock) | | | |
| Dec. 15 | Cash [(600 – 200) × $0.50] | | 200 | |
| |     Dividend Revenue | | | 200 |
| |       (To record receipt of $0.50 per share | | | |
| |       dividend from Sanburg) | | | |
| **b.** Dec. 31 | Unrealized Gain or Loss—Income | | 2,000 | |
| |     Fair Value Adjustment—Stock | | | 2,000 |
| |       (To record unrealized loss on trading | | | |
| |       securities) | | | |

| Investment | Cost | Fair Value | Unrealized Gain (Loss) |
|---|---|---|---|
| Sanburg common stock | $ 9,600[a] | $10,000[b] | $ 400 |
| Cey common stock | 26,400[c] | 24,000[d] | (2,400) |
| Totals | $36,000 | $34,000 | $(2,000) |

[a]400 × $24; [b]400 × $25; [c]800 × $33; [d]800 × $30

---

**Many additional resources are available for practice in WileyPLUS.**

---

## Questions

**1.** What are the reasons that companies invest in securities?

**2. a.** What is the cost of an investment in bonds?

  **b.** When is interest on bonds recorded?

**3.** Geena Jaymes is confused about losses and gains on the sale of debt investments. Explain these issues to Geena:

  **a.** How the gain or loss is computed.

  **b.** The statement presentation of gains and losses.

**4.** Heliy Company sells bonds that cost $40,000 for $45,000, including $1,000 of accrued interest. In recording the sale, Heliy books a $5,000 gain. Is this correct? Explain.

**5.** What is the cost of an investment in stock?

**6.** To acquire Gaines Corporation stock, Palmer Co. pays $61,500 in cash. What entry should be made for this investment, assuming the stock is readily marketable?

**7. a.** When should a long-term investment in common stock be accounted for by the equity method?

  **b.** When is revenue recognized under the equity method?

**8.** Stetson Corporation uses the equity method to account for its ownership of 30% of the common stock of Pike Packing. During 2022, Pike reported a net income of $80,000 and declares and pays cash dividends of $10,000. What recognition should Stetson Corporation give to these events?

**9.** What constitutes "significant influence" when an investor's financial interest is less than 50%?

**10.** Distinguish between the cost and equity methods of accounting for investments in stocks.

**11.** What are consolidated financial statements?

**12.** What are the valuation guidelines for trading and available-for-sale debt investments at a balance sheet date?

**13.** Pat Ernst is the controller of J-Products, Inc. At December 31, the end of its first year of operations, the company's investments in trading debt securities cost $74,000 and have a fair value of $70,000. Indicate how Pat would report these data in the financial statements prepared on December 31.

**14.** Pat Ernst is the controller of J-Products, Inc. At December 31, the end of its first year of operations, the company's investments in trading debt securities cost $74,000 and have a fair value of $70,000. How would Pat report the data if the investments were long-term and the debt securities were classified as available-for-sale?

**15.** Boise Company's investments in equity securities at December 31 show total cost of $202,000 and total fair value of $210,000. Boise has less than a 20% ownership interest in the equity securities. Prepare the adjusting entry.

**16.** Where is Accumulated Other Comprehensive Loss reported on the balance sheet?

**17.** Bargain Wholesale Supply owns stock in Cyrus Corporation, which it intends to hold indefinitely because of some negative tax consequences if sold. Should the investment in Cyrus be classified as a short-term investment? Why?

# Brief Exercises

**BEH.1 (LO 1), AP** Craig Corporation purchased debt investments for $40,800 on January 1, 2022. On July 1, 2022, Craig received cash interest of $1,660. Journalize the purchase and the receipt of interest. Assume no interest has been accrued.

*Journalize entries for debt investments.*

**BEH.2 (LO 2), AP** On August 1, Snow Company buys 1,000 shares of BCN common stock for $35,600 cash. On December 1, the stock investments are sold for $38,000 in cash. Journalize the purchase and sale of the common stock.

*Journalize entries for stock investments.*

**BEH.3 (LO 2), AP** Tote Company owns 25% of Toppe Company. For the current year, Toppe reports net income of $150,000 and declares and pays a $60,000 cash dividend. Record Tote's equity in Toppe's net income and the receipt of dividends from Toppe.

*Journalize transactions under the equity method.*

**BEH.4 (LO 3), AP** Cost and fair value data for the trading debt securities of Lecler Company at December 31, 2022, are $62,000 and $59,600, respectively. Prepare the adjusting entry to record the securities at fair value.

*Prepare adjusting entry using fair value.*

**BEH.5 (LO 3), AP** Cost and fair value data for the trading debt securities of Lecler Company at December 31, 2022, are $62,000 and $59,600, respectively. Show the financial statement presentation of the trading securities and related accounts.

*Indicate statement presentation using fair value.*

**BEH.6 (LO 3), AP** In its first year of operations, Machin Corporation purchased available-for-sale debt securities costing $72,000 as a long-term investment. At December 31, 2022, the fair value of the securities is $69,000. Prepare the adjusting entry to record the securities at fair value.

*Prepare adjusting entry using fair value.*

**BEH.7 (LO 3), AP** In its first year of operations, Machin Corporation purchased available-for-sale debt securities costing $72,000 as a long-term investment. At December 31, 2022, the fair value of the securities is $69,000. Show the financial statement presentation of the securities and related accounts. Assume the securities are noncurrent.

*Indicate statement presentation using fair value.*

**BEH.8 (LO 3), AP** Perth Corporation has these long-term investments: common stock of Vejas Co. (10% ownership), cost $108,000, fair value $112,000; common stock of Penn Inc. (30% ownership), cost $210,000, equity $230,000; and debt investment, cost $90,000, fair value, $150,000. Prepare the investments section of the balance sheet.

*Prepare investments section of balance sheet.*

# DO IT! Exercises

**DO IT! H.1 (LO 1), AP** Kurtyka Corporation had the following transactions relating to debt investments:

*Make entries for bond investment.*

Jan.  1, 2022   Purchased 50, $1,000, 10% Spiller Company bonds for $50,000. Interest is payable annually on January 1.

Dec. 31, 2022   Accrued interest on Spiller Company bonds.

Jan.  1, 2023   Received interest from Spiller Company bonds.

Jan.  1, 2023   Sold 30 Spiller Company bonds for $29,000.

Journalize the above transactions, including the adjusting entry for the accrual of interest on December 31, 2022.

**DO IT! H.2 (LO 2), AP** The following are two independent situations:

*Make journal entries for stock investments.*

1. Edelman Inc. acquired 10% of the 500,000 shares of common stock of Schuberger Corporation at a total cost of $11 per share on June 17, 2022. On September 3, Schuberger declared and paid a $160,000 dividend. On December 31, Schuberger reported net income of $550,000 for the year.

2. Wen Corporation obtained significant influence over Hunsaker Company by buying 30% of Hunsaker's 100,000 outstanding shares of common stock at a cost of $18 per share on January 1, 2022. On May 15, Hunsaker declared and paid a cash dividend of $150,000. On December 31, Hunsaker reported net income of $270,000 for the year.

Prepare all necessary journal entries for 2022 for (a) Edelman and (b) Wen.

*Make journal entries for trading and available-for-sale securities.*

**DO IT! H.3a (LO 3), AP** Some of Tollakson Corporation's investments in debt securities are classified as trading securities and some are classified as available-for-sale. The cost and fair value of each category at December 31, 2022, are as follows.

|  | Cost | Fair Value | Unrealized Gain (Loss) |
|---|---|---|---|
| Trading securities | $96,300 | $84,900 | $(11,400) |
| Available-for-sale securities | $59,000 | $63,200 | $ 4,200 |

At December 31, 2021, the Fair Value Adjustment—Trading account had a debit balance of $3,200, and the Fair Value Adjustment—Available-for-Sale account had a credit balance of $5,750. Prepare the required journal entries for each group of securities for December 31, 2022.

*Indicate financial statement presentation of investments.*

**DO IT! H.3b (LO 3), K** Identify where each of the following items would be reported in the financial statements.

1. Loss on sale of investments in stock.

2. Unrealized gain or loss—equity.

3. Fair value adjustment—trading.

4. Interest earned on investments in bonds.

5. Unrealized loss on trading securities.

Use the following possible categories:

*Balance sheet:*

| | |
|---|---|
| Current assets | Current liabilities |
| Investments | Long-term liabilities |
| Property, plant, and equipment | Stockholders' equity |
| Intangible assets | |

*Income statement:*

| | |
|---|---|
| Other revenues and gains | Other expenses and losses |

# Exercises

*Journalize debt investment transactions, and accrue interest.*

**EH.1 (LO 1), AP** Chopin Corporation had these transactions pertaining to debt investments:

Jan.  1  Purchased 90 Martine Co. 10% bonds (each with a face value of $1,000) for $90,000 cash. Interest is payable annually on December 31.

Dec. 31  Received annual interest on Martine Co. bonds.

31  Sold 30 Martine Co. bonds for $32,000.

**Instructions**

Journalize the transactions.

*Journalize stock investment transactions, and explain income statement presentation.*

**EH.2 (LO 2, 3), AP** Soylent Company had these transactions pertaining to stock investments:

Feb.  1  Purchased 1,200 shares of BJ common stock (2% of outstanding shares) for $8,400.

July  1  Received cash dividends of $2 per share on BJ common stock.

Sept.  1  Sold 500 shares of BJ common stock for $5,400.

Dec.  1  Received cash dividends of $1 per share on BJ common stock.

**Instructions**

a. Journalize the transactions.

b. Explain how dividend revenue and the gain (loss) on sale should be reported in the income statement.

**EH.3 (LO 2), AP** Cooper Inc. had these transactions pertaining to investments in common stock:

*Journalize transactions for investments in stock.*

Jan. 1 Purchased 1,200 shares of Gate Corporation common stock (5% of outstanding shares) for $59,200 cash.

July 1 Received a cash dividend of $7 per share.

Dec. 1 Sold 900 shares of Gate Corporation common stock for $47,200 cash.

31 Received a cash dividend of $7 per share.

**Instructions**

Journalize the transactions.

**EH.4 (LO 2), AP** On January 1, Lyon Corporation purchased a 25% equity investment in Shane Corporation for $150,000. At December 31, Shane declared and paid a $80,000 cash dividend and reported net income of $380,000.

*Journalize and post transactions under the equity method.*

**Instructions**

a. Journalize the transactions.

b. Determine the amount to be reported as an investment in Shane stock at December 31.

**EH.5 (LO 2), AP** These are two independent situations:

*Journalize entries under cost and equity methods.*

1. Sosey Cosmetics acquired 12% of the 300,000 shares of common stock of Elite Fashion at a total cost of $14 per share on March 18, 2022. On June 30, Elite declared and paid a $75,000 dividend. On December 31, Elite reported net income of $244,000 for the year. At December 31, the market price of Elite Fashion was $16 per share.

2. Williams Inc. obtained significant influence over Kasey Corporation by buying 25% of Kasey's 30,000 outstanding shares of common stock at a total cost of $11 per share on January 1, 2022. On June 15, Kasey declared and paid a cash dividend of $35,000. On December 31, Kasey reported a net income of $120,000 for the year.

**Instructions**

Prepare all the necessary journal entries for 2022 for (a) Sosey Cosmetics and (b) Williams Inc.

**EH.6 (LO 3), AP** At December 31, 2022, the trading debt securities for Gwynn, Inc. are as follows.

*Prepare adjusting entry to record fair value, and indicate statement presentation.*

| Security | Cost | Fair Value |
|---|---|---|
| A | $18,100 | $16,000 |
| B | 12,500 | 14,800 |
| C | 23,000 | 18,000 |
| Total | $53,600 | $48,800 |

**Instructions**

a. Prepare the adjusting entry at December 31, 2022, to report the securities at fair value.

b. Show the balance sheet and income statement presentation at December 31, 2022, after adjustment to fair value.

**EH.7 (LO 3), AP** Writing At December 31, 2022, available-for-sale debt securities for Gwynn, Inc. are as follows. The securities are considered to be a long-term investment.

*Prepare adjusting entry to record fair value, and indicate statement presentation.*

| Security | Cost | Fair Value |
|---|---|---|
| A | $18,100 | $16,000 |
| B | 12,500 | 14,800 |
| C | 23,000 | 18,000 |
| Total | $53,600 | $48,800 |

**Instructions**

a. Prepare the adjusting entry at December 31, 2022, to report the securities at fair value.

b. Show the statement presentation at December 31, 2022, after adjustment to fair value.

c. Pam Jenks, a member of the board of directors, does not understand the reporting of the unrealized gains or losses on trading debt securities and available-for-sale debt securities. Write a letter to Ms. Jenks explaining the reporting and the purposes it serves.

*Prepare adjusting entries for fair value, and indicate statement presentation for two classes of securities.*

**EH.8 (LO 3), AP** Weston Company has these data at December 31, 2022, the end of its first year of operations.

| Debt Securities | Cost | Fair Value |
|---|---|---|
| Trading | $110,000 | $122,000 |
| Available-for-sale | 100,000 | 96,000 |

The available-for-sale securities are held as a long-term investment.

**Instructions**

a. Prepare the adjusting entries to report each class of securities at fair value.

b. Indicate the statement presentation of each class of securities and the related unrealized gain (loss) accounts.

# Problems

*Journalize debt investment transactions.*

**PH.1 (LO 1), AP** Penn Farms is a grower of hybrid seed corn for Bend Genetics Corporation. It has had two exceptionally good years and has elected to invest its excess funds in bonds. The following selected transactions relate to bonds acquired as an investment by Penn Farms, whose fiscal year ends on December 31.

**2022**

Jan.  1   Purchased at par $600,000 of Dover Corporation 10-year, 7% bonds dated January 1, 2022, directly from the issuing corporation. The bonds pay interest annually on January 1.

Dec. 31   Accrual of interest at year-end on the Dover bonds.

Assume that all intervening transactions and adjustments have been properly recorded and the number of bonds owned has not changed from December 31, 2022, to December 31, 2024.

**2025**

Jan.  1   Received the annual interest on the Dover bonds.

      1   Sold $300,000 of Dover bonds at 110.

Dec. 31   Accrual of interest at year-end on the Dover bonds.

**Instructions**

Journalize the listed transactions for the years 2022 and 2025.

*Journalize investment transactions, prepare adjusting entry, and show financial statement presentation.*

**PH.2 (LO 1, 2, 3), AP** In January 2022, the management of Northern Company concludes that it has sufficient cash to purchase some short-term investments in debt and stock securities. During the year, the following transactions occurred.

Jan.  1   Purchased 70 $1,000, 8% TRC bonds for $70,000. Interest is payable annually on December 31.

Feb.  1   Purchased 1,200 shares of LAF common stock for $51,600.

Mar.  1   Purchased 500 shares of NCL common stock for $18,500.

July  1   Received a cash dividend of $0.80 per share on the LAF common stock.

Aug.  1   Sold 200 shares of LAF common stock at $42 per share.

Sept. 1   Received $2 per share cash dividend on the NCL common stock.

Dec. 31   Received the annual interest on the TRC bonds.

      31   Sold the TRC bonds for $75,700.

At December 31, the fair values of the LAF and NCL common stocks were $39 and $30 per share, respectively. These stock investments by Northern Company provide less than a 20% ownership interest.

## Instructions

**a.** Journalize the transactions and post to the accounts Debt Investments and Stock Investments. (Use the T-account form.)

**b.** Prepare the adjusting entry at December 31, 2022, to report the investments at fair value.

**c.** Show the balance sheet presentation of investment securities at December 31, 2022.

**d.** Identify the income statement accounts and give the statement classification of each account.

**PH.3 (LO 2, 3), AP** On December 31, 2021, the end of its first year of operations, Botani Associates owned the following securities that are held as long-term investments.

*Journalize transactions, prepare adjusting entry for stock investments, and show balance sheet presentation.*

| Common Stock | Shares | Cost |
|---|---|---|
| C Co. | 1,000 | $48,000 |
| D Co. | 5,000 | 35,000 |
| E Co. | 1,200 | 24,000 |

On this date, the total fair value of the securities was equal to its cost. The securities are not held for influence or control over the investees. In 2022, the following transactions occurred.

| | | |
|---|---|---|
| July | 1 | Received $2.00 per share semiannual cash dividend on D Co. common stock. |
| Aug. | 1 | Received $0.50 per share cash dividend on C Co. common stock. |
| Sept. | 1 | Sold 1,000 shares of D Co. common stock for cash at $9 per share. |
| Oct. | 1 | Sold 300 shares of C Co. common stock for cash at $53 per share. |
| Nov. | 1 | Received $1 per share cash dividend on E Co. common stock. |
| Dec. | 15 | Received $0.50 per share cash dividend on C Co. common stock. |
| | 31 | Received $2.20 per share semiannual cash dividend on D Co. common stock. |

At December 31, the fair values per share of the common stocks were C Co. $47, D Co. $7, and E Co. $24. These investments should be classified as long-term.

## Instructions

**a.** Journalize the 2022 transactions and post to the account Stock Investments. (Use the T-account form.)

**b.** Prepare the adjusting entry at December 31, 2022, to show the securities at fair value. Botani has less than a 20% ownership interest in all these common stocks (C Co., D Co., and E Co.).

**c.** Show the balance sheet presentation of the investments at 2022. These investments should be classified as long-term.

**PH.4 (LO 2), AP** Writing Wellman Company acquired 30% of the outstanding common stock of Grinwold Inc. on January 1, 2022, by paying $1,800,000 for 60,000 shares. Grinwold declared and paid a $0.50 per share cash dividend on June 30 and again on December 31, 2022. Grinwold reported net income of $800,000 for the year.

*Prepare entries under cost and equity methods, and prepare memorandum.*

## Instructions

**a.** Prepare the journal entries for Wellman Company for 2022, assuming Wellman cannot exercise significant influence over Grinwold. (Use the cost method.)

**b.** Prepare the journal entries for Wellman Company for 2022, assuming Wellman can exercise significant influence over Grinwold. (Use the equity method.)

**c.** The board of directors of Wellman Company is confused about the differences between the cost and equity methods. Prepare a memorandum for the board that explains each method and shows in tabular form the account balances under each method at December 31, 2022.

**PH.5 (LO 2, 3), AP** Here is Kalvin Company's portfolio of long-term stock investments at December 31, 2021, the end of its first year of operations.

*Journalize stock transactions, and show balance sheet presentation.*

| | Cost |
|---|---|
| 1,400 shares of Batone Inc. common stock | $73,500 |
| 1,200 shares of Mendez Corporation common stock | 84,000 |
| 800 shares of P. Tillman Corporation preferred stock | 33,600 |

On December 31, the total cost of the portfolio equaled the total fair value. Kalvin had the following transactions related to the securities during 2022.

Jan. 20    Sold 1,400 shares of Batone Inc. common stock at $55 per share.

    28    Purchased 400 shares of $10 par value common stock of P. Wahl Corporation at $78 per share.

    30    Received a cash dividend of $1.25 per share on Mendez Corporation common stock.

Feb.  8    Received cash dividends of $0.40 per share on P. Tillman Corporation preferred stock.

    18    Sold all 800 shares of P. Tillman preferred stock at $35 per share.

July  30    Received a cash dividend of $1.10 per share on Mendez Corporation common stock.

Sept.  6    Purchased an additional 600 shares of the $10 par value common stock of P. Wahl Corporation at $82 per share.

Dec.   1    Received a cash dividend of $1.50 per share on P. Wahl Corporation common stock.

At December 31, 2022, the fair values of the securities were:

| | |
|---|---|
| Mendez Corporation common stock | $65 per share |
| P. Wahl Corporation common stock | $77 per share |

Kalvin uses separate account titles for each investment, such as Investment in Mendez Corporation Common Stock.

**Instructions**

a. Prepare journal entries to record the transactions.

b. Prepare the adjusting entry at December 31, 2022, to report the portfolio at fair value.

c. Show the balance sheet presentation at December 31, 2022.

*Prepare a balance sheet.*

**PH.6 (LO 3), AP** The following data, presented in alphabetical order, are taken from the records of Manfreid Corporation.

| | |
|---|---|
| Accounts payable | $ 150,000 |
| Accounts receivable | 90,000 |
| Accumulated depreciation—buildings | 180,000 |
| Accumulated depreciation—equipment | 52,000 |
| Allowance for doubtful accounts | 6,000 |
| Bonds payable (10%, due 2033) | 350,000 |
| Buildings | 900,000 |
| Cash | 63,000 |
| Common stock ($5 par value; 500,000 shares authorized, 240,000 shares issued) | 1,200,000 |
| Debt investments (at fair value) | 400,000 |
| Discount on bonds payable | 20,000 |
| Dividends payable | 50,000 |
| Equipment | 275,000 |
| Goodwill | 190,000 |
| Income taxes payable | 70,000 |
| Inventory | 170,000 |
| Land | 410,000 |
| Notes payable (due 2023) | 70,000 |
| Paid-in capital in excess of par value | 464,000 |
| Prepaid insurance | 16,000 |
| Retained earnings | 310,000 |
| Stock investments (Horton Inc. stock, 30% ownership, at equity) | 240,000 |
| Stock investments (short-term, at fair value) | 128,000 |

**Instructions**

Prepare a balance sheet at December 31, 2022.

# Company Index

# Subject Index

direct materials, 24-5, 24-29
Price takers, 21-3
Price variances, 24-10
  labor price variance (LPV), 24-14, 24-15,
    24-29
  materials price variance (MPV), 24-11, 24-12,
    24-29
Prices
  bond, 10-9, 10-10–10-11
  cash equivalent, 9-3, 9-29
  market, 10-10–10-11, 11-34
  for new stock issues, 11-9
  total price variance, 24-18
Pricing, 21-1–21-48
  absorption-cost, 21-21–21-23, 21-27
  big data, 21-20
  cost considerations, 21-3
  cost-plus, 21-5–21-7, 21-27
  environmental factors, 21-3
  factors that affect, 21-3
  full-cost, 21-21, 21-27
  objectives, 21-3
  optimal, 21-20
  strategic, 21-9
  target costs and, 21-4
  target selling prices, 21-6, 21-27
  time-and-material, 21-10–21-13, 21-27
  transfer prices, 21-13–21-21, 21-27
  variable-cost, 21-8–21-9, 21-21,
    21-23–21-24, 21-27
Principal, G-2, G-14, G-21
Private accounting, 1-25, 1-28
Privately held corporations, 11-3, 11-35
Pro forma income, 13-7–13-8, 13-31
Process cost systems, 15-3
  applications, 16-3–16-4
  definition, 15-25, 16-26
  vs. job order cost systems, 16-4–16-6, 16-25
  overview, 16-3–16-5
Process costing, 16-1–16-46
  assigning manufacturing costs,
    16-7–16-9
  cost flows, 16-4, 16-6–16-7
  equivalent units, 16-9–16-12
  physical unit cost flow, 16-14, 16-20–16-21
  for service companies, 16-4
  transfer to cost of goods sold, 16-9
  transfer to finished goods, 16-8
  transfer to next department, 16-8
Process further, 20-11–20-14
Processing, just-in-time (JIT),
  17-23–17-25, 17-27
Product(s)
  allocation of activity cost pools to,
    17-10
  assigning overhead costs to, 17-10
  cost drivers per, 17-10
  joint, 20-12, 20-20
  reputational dimension, 4-22
  unprofitable, 20-16–20-18
Product costs, 14-9, 14-23, 20-8
  unit, 17-11
Product-level activities, 17-15, 17-16, 17-27
Production
  equivalent units of, 16-10
  make-or-buy decisions, 20-8–20-10
  requirements for, 22-10, 22-11
  sell-or-process further decisions, 20-11–20-14
Production budget, 22-10, 22-27

Production cost report, 16-13–16-18, 16-26
  FIFO method, 16-23–16-24
  preparation, 16-17, 16-23–16-24, 16-25
Production costs
  actual, 24-9
  unit, 16-15–16-16, 16-22, 16-26
Profit(s)
  accumulated, 11-59
  gross, 5-18–5-19, 5-20, 5-32
  merchandising, 5-19
  paper or phantom, 6-15
  retained, 11-59
  service company insights, 14-11
Profit and loss statement, 1-21
Profit centers, 23-21, 23-22–23-23, 23-31
Profit margin, 13-26, 13-31
Profitability
  cost-volume-profit (CVP) analysis,
    18-11–18-15, 19-1–19-55
  gross profit rate, 13-27, 13-31
  operating leverage and, 19-17–19-18
  people, planet, and profit insights,
    14-20, 16-12, 18-5, 19-18, 24-17, 25-15
  target costs and, 21-4
  unprofitable segments or products,
    20-16–20-19
Profitability index, 25-14–25-15, 25-22
Profitability ratios, 13-16, 13-17, 13-20, 13-
  24–13-29, 13-31
Promissory notes, 8-14, 8-15, 8-23
Property, plant, and equipment (PP&E),
  4-20–4-21, 9-3. see also Plant assets
  balance sheet section, 4-21
  in classified balance sheet, 4-19
  definition, 4-27
  GAAP vs. IFRS accounting for,
    9-49–9-50
  in notes to financial statements, 9-15
  statement presentation, 9-24–9-25
Proprietorships, 1-9, 1-28
  owner's equity accounts, 11-11
  sole, 7-3
Proving the ledgers, J-5–J-6, J-7,
  J-10, J-14
Public accounting, 1-25, 1-26, 1-28
Public Company Accounting Oversight Board
  (PCAOB), 7-3, 7-47
Public education, 10-7
Publicly held corporations, 11-3, 11-35
Pull approach, 17-24
Purchase allowances, 5-9, 5-33
Purchase discounts, 5-9–5-10, 5-27, 5-33
Purchase invoices, 5-7, 5-33
Purchase returns, 5-9, 5-33
Purchases
  on account, 1-16
  for cash, 1-16
  computation, 12-22
  on credit, 1-16, 1-17, 2-17
  of equipment, 1-16
  fraud in purchasing, 7-6
  of merchandise, 5-26–5-27
  merchandise purchases budget, 22-23, 22-24,
    22-27
  for merchandising companies, 5-17
  of office equipment, 2-15
  recording, 5-6–5-10, 5-26–5-27
  segregation of activities, 7-6
  share repurchase, 11-18

summary of transactions, 5-10
  of supplies, 1-16, 2-17
  treasury stock, 11-15–11-16
Purchases journal, J-4, J-10–J-12, J-17
Push approach, 17-23

**Q**
Qualitative factors, 20-5, 20-9
Quality control, total, 17-25
Quality of earnings, 13-7–13-8, 13-31
Quantity variances, 24-10

**R**
Rate of return
  annual, 25-20–25-21, 25-22
  internal, 25-17–25-19, 25-22, G-19
  minimum, 23-29
  required, 25-10, 25-20, 25-22
Rates of interest. see Interest rates
Ratio(s), 13-15, 13-31
Ratio analysis, 13-15–13-30, 13-31
Rationalization, 7-3
Raw materials, 6-3, 6-27, 14-8
  accumulating costs of, 15-6
  assigning costs of, 15-8–15-10
  stockpiling, 22-12
Raw materials inventory, 14-12, 15-5, 22-22
Readily marketable investments, H-13
Real accounts, 4-9, 4-27
Real estate, 1-10
Realized gain or loss, H-14–H-15
Receipts
  cash receipts controls, 7-12–7-14
  counter, 7-13
  mail, 7-14
  over-the-counter, 7-13–7-14
  petty cash, 7-17
  typical classifications, 12-4
Receivables, 8-3, 8-23
  accounting for, 8-1–8-42. see also Accounts
    receivable
  average collection period, 8-21
  in balance sheets, 8-19
  from employees, 8-3
  GAAP vs. IFRS requirements, 8-41
  interest, 8-17
  management, 8-21
  notes, 8-3, 8-14–8-18, 8-23
  in notes to financial statements, 8-20
  other, 8-3, 8-23
  as percentage of assets, 8-3
  percentage-of-receivables basis, 8-9,
    8-23
  presentation, 8-19–8-20
  trade, 8-3, 8-23
  types of, 8-3
Reconciling bank accounts, 7-19,
  7-22–7-27
Reconciling items, 12-29–12-30
Record date, 11-20, 11-35
Recording acquisition of bonds, H-3
Recording acquisition of stock, H-5, H-6
Recording bond interest, H-3
Recording dividends, H-5
Recording employer payroll taxes, I-9
Recording estimated uncollectibles, 8-7
Recording losses, 2-12
Recording payroll, I-1–I-7
Recording revenue and dividends, H-6–H-7

# RAPID REVIEW
## Chapter Content

### BASIC ACCOUNTING EQUATION (Chapter 2)

| | | | | | | | | |
|---|---|---|---|---|---|---|---|---|
| **Basic Equation** | **Assets** | = | **Liabilities** | + | | **Stockholders' Equity** | | |

| | Assets | = | Liabilities | + | Common Stock | + | Retained Earnings | + | Revenues | − | Expenses | − | Dividends |
|---|---|---|---|---|---|---|---|---|---|---|---|---|---|
| **Expanded Basic Equation** | | | | | | | | | | | | | |
| **Debit / Credit Rules** | Dr. + / Cr. − | | Dr. − / Cr. + | | Dr. − / Cr. + | | Dr. − / Cr. + | | Dr. − / Cr. + | | Dr. + / Cr. − | | Dr. + / Cr. − |

### ADJUSTING ENTRIES (Chapter 3)

| Type | | Adjusting Entry | |
|---|---|---|---|
| Deferrals | 1. Prepaid expenses | Dr. Expenses | Cr. Assets |
| | 2. Unearned revenues | Dr. Liabilities | Cr. Revenues |
| Accruals | 1. Accrued revenues | Dr. Assets | Cr. Revenues |
| | 2. Accrued expenses | Dr. Expenses | Cr. Liabilities |

**Note:** Each adjusting entry will affect one or more income statement accounts and one or more balance sheet accounts.

### INTEREST (Chapter 3)

Interest Computation

Interest = Face value of note × Annual interest rate × Time in terms of one year

### ACCOUNTING CONCEPTS (Appendix 3B)

| Fundamental Qualities | Enhancing Qualities | Assumptions | Principles | Constraint |
|---|---|---|---|---|
| Relevance | Comparability | Monetary unit | Historical cost | Cost |
| Faithful representation | Verifiability | Economic entity | Fair value | |
| | Timeliness | Periodicity | Revenue recognition | |
| | Understandability | Going concern | Expense recognition | |
| | | | Full disclosure | |

Two other important accounting concepts are materiality and consistency.

### CLOSING ENTRIES (Chapter 4)

Purpose

1. Update the Retained Earnings account in the ledger by transferring net income (loss) and dividends to retained earnings.
2. Prepare the temporary accounts (revenue, expense, dividends) for the next period's postings by reducing their balances to zero.

### ACCOUNTING CYCLE (Chapter 4)

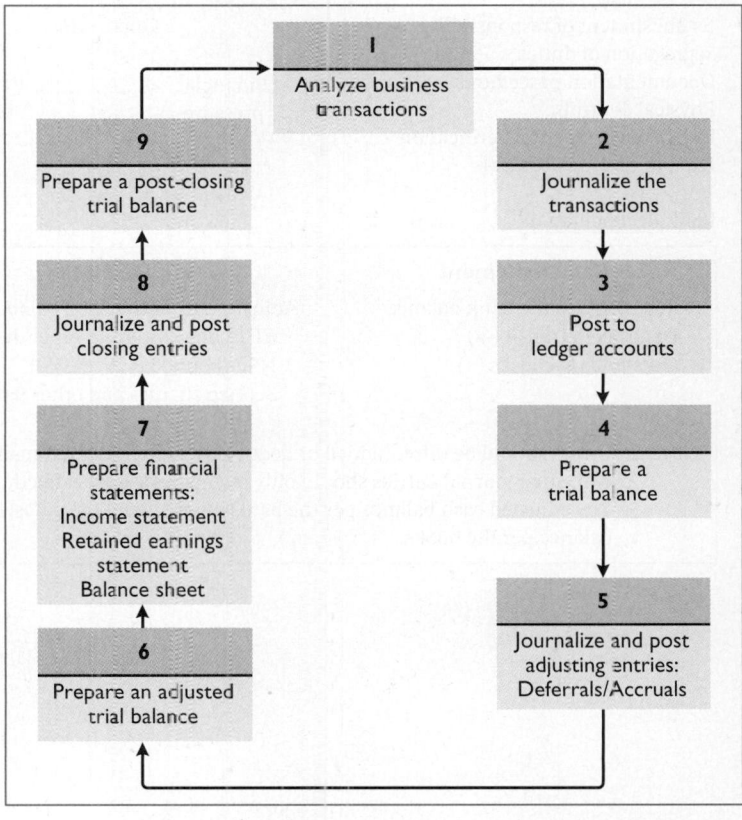

1. Analyze business transactions
2. Journalize the transactions
3. Post to ledger accounts
4. Prepare a trial balance
5. Journalize and post adjusting entries: Deferrals/Accruals
6. Prepare an adjusted trial balance
7. Prepare financial statements: Income statement, Retained earnings statement, Balance sheet
8. Journalize and post closing entries
9. Prepare a post-closing trial balance

# Chapter Content

**INVENTORY** (Chapters 5 and 6)

Ownership

| Freight Terms | Ownership of Goods on Public Carrier Resides with: |
|---|---|
| FOB shipping point | Buyer |
| FOB destination | Seller |

Perpetual vs. Periodic Journal Entries

| Event | Perpetual | Periodic |
|---|---|---|
| Purchase of goods | Inventory<br>    Cash (A/P) | Purchases<br>    Cash (A/P) |
| Freight (shipping point) | Inventory<br>    Cash | Freight-In<br>    Cash |
| Return of purchased goods | Cash (or A/P)<br>    Inventory | Cash (or A/P)<br>    Purchase Returns and Allowances |
| Sale of goods | Cash (or A/R)<br>    Sales Revenue<br>Cost of Goods Sold<br>    Inventory | Cash (or A/R)<br>    Sales Revenue<br>No entry |
| Return of sold goods | Sales Returns and Allowances<br>    Accounts Receivable<br>Inventory<br>    Cost of Goods Sold | Sales Returns and Allowances<br>    Accounts Receivable<br>No entry |
| End of period | No entry | Closing or adjusting entry required |

**FRAUD, INTERNAL CONTROL, AND CASH** (Chapter 7)

Principles of Internal Control

Establishment of responsibility
Segregation of duties
Documentation procedures
Physical controls
Independent internal verification
Human resource controls

The Fraud Triangle

Bank Reconciliation

| Per Bank Statement | Per Books |
|---|---|
| Adjustments to the bank balance<br>    Deposits in transit (+)<br>    Outstanding checks (−) | Adjustments to the book balance<br>    EFT collections and other deposits (+)<br>    NSF (bounced) checks (−)<br>    Service charges and other payments (−) |

**Note:** 1. Errors should be offset (added or deducted) on the side that made the error.
2. Adjusting journal entries should only be made for items affecting books.
3. The adjusted cash balance per the bank should equal the adjusted cash balance per the books.

# RAPID REVIEW
## Chapter Content

**RECEIVABLES** (Chapter 8)

Two Methods to Account for Uncollectible Accounts

| | |
|---|---|
| **Direct write-off method** | Record bad debt expense when the company determines a particular account to be uncollectible. |
| **Allowance method** | At the end of each period, estimate the amount of uncollectible receivables. Debit Bad Debt Expense and credit Allowance for Doubtful Accounts in an amount that results in a balance in the allowance account equal to the estimate of uncollectibles. As specific accounts become uncollectible, debit Allowance for Doubtful Accounts and credit Accounts Receivable. |

**PLANT ASSETS** (Chapter 9)

Computation of Annual Depreciation Expense

| | |
|---|---|
| **Straight-line** | $\dfrac{\text{Cost} - \text{Salvage value}}{\text{Useful life (in years)}}$ |
| **Declining-balance** | Book value at beginning of year × Declining balance rate*<br>*Declining-balance rate = 1 ÷ Useful life (in years) |
| **Units-of-activity** | $\dfrac{\text{Cost} - \text{Salvage value}}{\text{Useful life (in units)}}$ × Units of activity during year |

**Note:** If depreciation is calculated for partial periods, the straight-line and declining-balance methods must be adjusted for the relevant proportion of the year. Multiply the annual depreciation expense by the number of months expired in the year divided by 12 months.

**ISSUANCE OF BONDS** (Chapter 10)

| | |
|---|---|
| **Premium** | Market interest rate < Contractual interest rate |
| **Face Value** | Market interest rate = Contractual interest rate |
| **Discount** | Market interest rate > Contractual interest rate |

Computation of Annual Bond Interest Expense

Interest expense = Interest paid (payable) + Amortization of discount
 (OR − Amortization of premium)

**Bond Amortization** (Appendices 10A and 10B)

| | | |
|---|---|---|
| **Straight-line amortization** | $\dfrac{\text{Bond discount (premium)}}{\text{Number of interest periods}}$ | |
| **Effective-interest amortization (preferred method)** | Bond interest expense | Bond interest paid |
| | Carrying value of bonds at beginning of period × Effective-interest rate | Face amount of bonds × Contractual interest rate |

**STOCKHOLDERS' EQUITY** (Chapter 11)

No-Par Value vs. Par Value Stock Journal Entries

| No-Par Value | Par Value |
|---|---|
| Cash<br>  Common Stock | Cash<br>  Common Stock (par value)<br>  Paid-in Capital in Excess of Par |

Comparison of Dividend Effects

| | Cash | Common Stock | Retained Earnings |
|---|---|---|---|
| Cash dividend | ↓ | No effect | ↓ |
| Stock dividend | No effect | ↑ | ↓ |
| Stock split | No effect | No effect | No effect |

# Chapter Content

## STATEMENT OF CASH FLOWS (Chapter 12)

Cash flows from operating activities (**indirect method**)

| | | |
|---|---|---:|
| Net income | | |
| Add: | Amortization and depreciation | $ X |
| | Losses on disposals of assets | X |
| | Decreases in current assets | X |
| | Increases in current liabilities | X |
| Deduct: | Increases in current assets | (X) |
| | Decreases in current liabilities | (X) |
| | Gains on disposals of assets | (X) |
| Net cash provided (used) by operating activities | | $ X |

Cash flows from operating activities (**direct method**)

| | |
|---|---:|
| Cash receipts | |
| (Examples: from sales of goods and services | |
| to customers, from receipts of interest and dividends) | $ X |
| Cash payments | |
| (Examples: to suppliers, for operating expenses, | |
| for interest, for taxes) | (X) |
| Net cash provided (used) by operating activities | $ X |

## FINANCIAL STATEMENT ANALYSIS (Chapter 13)

| Discontinued operations | Income statement (presented separately after Income from continuing operations). |
|---|---|
| Changes in accounting principle | In most instances, use the new method in current period and restate previous years' results using new method. For changes in depreciation and amortization methods, use the new method in the current period, but do not restate previous periods. |

### Income Statement and Comprehensive Income

| | |
|---|---:|
| Sales | $ XX |
| Cost of goods sold | XX |
| Gross profit | XX |
| Operating expenses | XX |
| Income from operations | XX |
| Other revenues (expenses) and gains (losses) | XX |
| Income before income taxes | XX |
| Income tax expense | XX |
| Income before discontinued operations | XX |
| **Discontinued operations (net of tax)** | **XX** |
| **Net income** | **XX** |
| **Other comprehensive income items (net of tax)** | **XX** |
| **Comprehensive income** | **$ XX** |

## MANAGERIAL ACCOUNTING (Chapter 14)

### Characteristics of Managerial Accounting

| **Primary users** | Internal users |
|---|---|
| **Reports** | Internal reports issued as needed |
| **Purpose** | Special purpose for a particular user |
| **Content** | Pertains to subunits, may be detailed, use of relevant data |
| **Verification** | No independent audits |

### Types of Manufacturing Costs

| **Direct materials** | Raw materials directly associated with finished product |
|---|---|
| **Direct labor** | Work of employees directly associated with turning raw materials into finished product |
| **Manufacturing overhead** | Costs indirectly associated with manufacture of finished product |

## JOB ORDER AND PROCESS COSTING (Chapters 15 and 16)

### Types of Accounting Systems

| **Job order** | Costs are assigned to each unit or each batch of goods |
|---|---|
| **Process cost** | Costs are applied to similar products that are mass-produced in a continuous fashion |

### Job Order and Process Cost Flow

# RAPID REVIEW
## Chapter Content

### ACTIVITY-BASED COSTING (Chapter 17)

1. **Identify and classify the activities** involved in the manufacture of specific products and **allocate overhead to cost pools.**

$\downarrow$

2. **Identify the cost driver** that has a strong correlation to the costs accumulated in each cost pool and estimate total annual cost driver usage.

$\downarrow$

3. **Compute the activity-based overhead rate** for each cost pool.

$\downarrow$

4. **Assign overhead costs to products** using the overhead rates determined for each cost pool.

### COST-VOLUME-PROFIT (Chapters 18 and 19)

#### Types of Costs

| | |
|---|---|
| **Variable costs** | Vary in total directly and proportionately with changes in activity level |
| **Fixed costs** | Remain the same in total regardless of change in activity level |
| **Mixed costs** | Contain both a fixed and a variable element |

#### CVP Income Statement Format

| | Total | Per Unit | Percent of Sales |
|---|---|---|---|
| Sales | $xx | $xx | xxx% |
| Variable costs | xx | xx | xx |
| Contribution margin | xx | $xx | xx% |
| Fixed costs | xx | | |
| Net income | $xx | | |

| | |
|---|---|
| **Unit contribution margin** | = Unit selling price − Unit variable costs |

| | |
|---|---|
| **Break-even point in units** | = Fixed costs ÷ Unit contribution margin* |

| | |
|---|---|
| **Break-even point in dollars** | = Fixed costs ÷ Contribution margin ratio* |

| | |
|---|---|
| **Required sales in units for target net income** | = (Fixed costs + Target net income) ÷ Unit contribution margin |

| | |
|---|---|
| **Degree of operating leverage** | = Contribution margin ÷ Net income |

*For multiple products use weighted-average.

### INCREMENTAL ANALYSIS (Chapter 20)

1. Identify the relevant costs associated with each alternative. **Relevant costs** are those costs and revenues that differ across alternatives. Choose the alternative that maximizes net income.
2. **Opportunity costs** are those potential benefits that are given up when one alternative is chosen instead of another one. Opportunity costs are relevant costs.
3. **Sunk costs** have already been incurred and will not be changed or avoided by any future decision. Sunk costs are not relevant costs.

### PRICING (Chapter 21)

#### External Pricing

| | |
|---|---|
| **Markup percentage** | = Desired ROI per unit ÷ Total unit cost |

| | |
|---|---|
| **Target selling price** | = Total unit cost + (Total unit cost × Markup percentage) |

#### Transfer Pricing

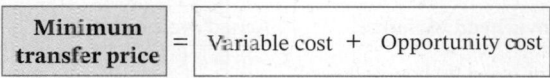

| | |
|---|---|
| **Minimum transfer price** | = Variable cost + Opportunity cost |

### BUDGETS (Chapter 22)

#### Components of the Master Budget

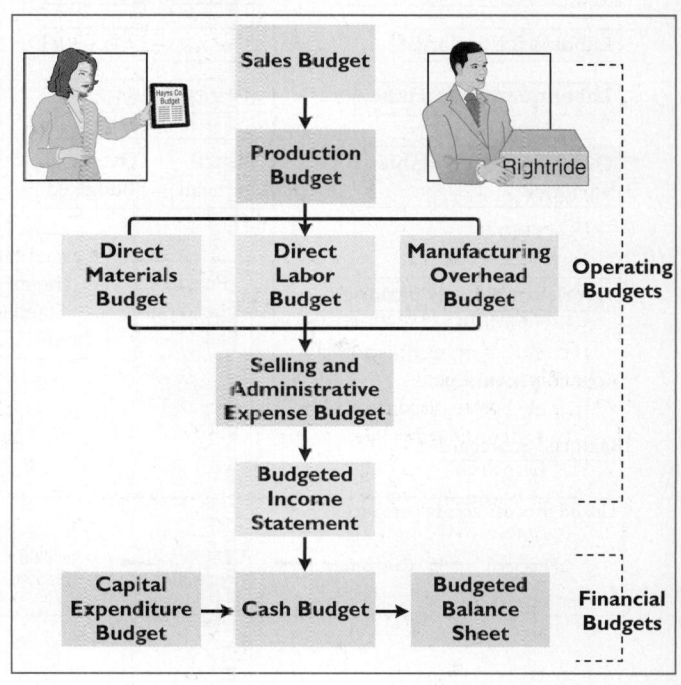

# Chapter Content

## RESPONSIBILITY ACCOUNTING (Chapter 23)

### Types of Responsibility Centers

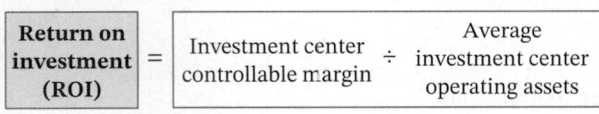

| Cost | Profit | Investment |
|---|---|---|
| Expenses only | Expenses and Revenues | Expenses and Revenues and ROI |

### Return on Investment

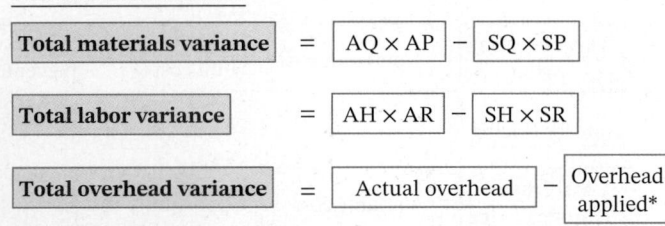

$$\text{Return on investment (ROI)} = \text{Investment center controllable margin} \div \text{Average investment center operating assets}$$

## STANDARD COSTS (Chapter 24)

### Standard Cost Variances

$$\text{Total materials variance} = (AQ \times AP) - (SQ \times SP)$$

$$\text{Total labor variance} = (AH \times AR) - (SH \times SR)$$

$$\text{Total overhead variance} = \text{Actual overhead} - \text{Overhead applied*}$$

*Based on standard hours allowed.

$$\text{Materials price variance} = (AQ \times AP) - (AQ \times SP)$$

$$\text{Materials quantity variance} = (AQ \times SP) - (SQ \times SP)$$

$$\text{Labor price variance} = (AH \times AR) - (AH \times SR)$$

$$\text{Labor quantity variance} = (AH \times SR) - (SH \times SR)$$

$$\text{** Overhead controllable variance} = \text{Actual overhead} - \text{Overhead budgeted}$$

$$\text{** Overhead volume variance} = \text{Fixed overhead rate} \times (\text{Normal capacity hours} - \text{Standard hours allowed})$$

**Appendix coverage.

### Balanced Scorecard

Linked process across perspectives:

Financial → Customer → Internal Process → Learning and Growth

## CAPITAL BUDGETING (Chapter 25)

### Annual Rate of Return

$$\text{Annual rate of return} = \text{Expected annual net income} \div \text{Average investment}$$

### Cash Payback

$$\text{Cash payback period} = \text{Cost of capital investment} \div \text{Annual cash inflow}$$

### Discounted Cash Flow Approaches

| Net Present Value | Internal Rate of Return |
|---|---|
| Compute net present value (a dollar amount). If net present value is zero or positive, accept the proposal. If net present value is negative, reject the proposal. | Compute internal rate of return (a percentage). If internal rate of return is equal to or greater than the minimum required rate of return, accept the proposal. If internal rate of return is less than the minimum rate, reject the proposal. |

# RAPID REVIEW
# Chapter Content

## INVESTMENTS (Appendix H)

Comparison of Long-Term Bond Investment and Liability Journal Entries

| Event | Investor | Investee |
|---|---|---|
| Purchase/issue of bonds | Debt Investments<br>    Cash | Cash<br>    Bonds Payable |
| Interest receipt/payment | Cash<br>    Interest Revenue | Interest Expense<br>    Cash |

Comparison of Cost and Equity Methods of Accounting for Long-Term Stock Investments

| Event | Cost | Equity |
|---|---|---|
| Acquisition | Stock Investments<br>    Cash | Stock Investments<br>    Cash |
| Investee reports earnings | No entry | Stock Investments<br>    Investment Revenue |
| Investee pays dividends | Cash<br>    Dividend Revenue | Cash<br>    Stock Investments |

Debt Investments

| | |
|---|---|
| **Trading** | Report at fair value with changes reported in net income. |
| **Available-for-sale** | Report at fair value with changes reported in other comprehensive income. |

Stock Investments

| Category | Valuation | Unrealized Gains or Losses | Other Income Effects |
|---|---|---|---|
| Holdings less than 20% | Fair value | Recognized in net income | Dividends declared; gains and losses from sale. |
| Holdings between 20% and 50% | Equity | Not recognized | Proportionate share of investee's net income. |
| Holdings more than 50% | Consolidation | Not recognized | Not applicable. |

# Financial Statements

| Order of Preparation | Date |
|---|---|
| 1. Income statement | For the period ended |
| 2. Retained earnings statement | For the period ended |
| 3. Balance sheet | As of the end of the period |
| 4. Statement of cash flows | For the period ended |

Income Statement (perpetual inventory system)

| **Name of Company**<br>**Income Statement**<br>**For the Period Ended** | | |
|---|---|---|
| Sales | | |
|   Sales revenue | $ X | |
|   Less: Sales returns and allowances | X | |
|     Sales discounts | X | |
|   Net sales | | $ X |
| Cost of goods sold | | X |
| Gross profit | | X |
| Operating expenses | | |
|   (Examples: store salaries, advertising, delivery, | | |
|   rent, depreciation, utilities, insurance) | | X |
| Income from operations | | X |
| Other revenues and gains | | |
|   (Examples: interest, gains) | X | |
| Other expenses and losses | | |
|   (Examples: interest, losses) | X | X |
| Income before income taxes | | X |
| Income tax expense | | X |
| Net income | | $ X |

| **Name of Company**<br>**Statement of Comprehensive Income**<br>**For the Period Ended** | |
|---|---|
| Net income | $XX |
| Other comprehensive income | XX |
| Comprehensive income | $XX |

Retained Earnings Statement

| **Name of Company**<br>**Retained Earnings Statement**<br>**For the Period Ended** | |
|---|---|
| Retained earnings, beginning of period | $ X |
| Add: Net income (or deduct net loss) | X |
| | X |
| Deduct: Dividends | X |
| Retained earnings, end of period | $ X |

Income Statement (periodic inventory system)

| **Name of Company**<br>**Income Statement**<br>**For the Period Ended** | | | |
|---|---|---|---|
| Sales | | | |
|   Sales revenue | | $ X | |
|   Less: Sales returns and allowances | | X | |
|     Sales discounts | | X | |
|   Net sales | | | $ X |
| Cost of goods sold | | | |
|   Beginning inventory | | X | |
|   Purchases | $ X | | |
|   Less: Purchase returns and allowances | X | | |
|   Net purchases | X | | |
|   Add: Freight-in | X | | |
|   Cost of goods purchased | | X | |
|   Cost of goods available for sale | | X | |
|   Less: Ending inventory | | X | |
|     Cost of goods sold | | | X |
| Gross profit | | | X |
| Operating expenses | | | |
|   (Examples: store salaries, advertising, delivery, | | | |
|   rent, depreciation, utilities, insurance) | | | X |
| Income from operations | | | X |
| Other revenues and gains | | | |
|   (Examples: interest, gains) | | X | |
| Other expenses and losses | | | |
|   (Examples: interest, losses) | | X | X |
| Income before income taxes | | | X |
| Income tax expense | | | X |
| Net income | | | $ X |

**Note:** Net income (loss) presented on the retained earnings statement must equal the net income (loss) presented on the income statement.

# Financial Statements

Balance Sheet

| Name of Company<br>Balance Sheet<br>As of the End of the Period | | | |
|---|---|---|---|
| **Assets** | | | |
| Current assets | | | |
| (Examples: cash, short-term investments, accounts receivable, inventory, prepaids) | | | $ X |
| Long-term investments | | | |
| (Examples: investments in bonds, investments in stocks) | | | X |
| Property, plant, and equipment | | | |
| Land | | $ X | |
| Buildings and equipment | $ X | | |
| Less: Accumulated depreciation | X | X | X |
| Intangible Assets | | | X |
| Total assets | | | $ X |
| | | | |
| **Liabilities and Stockholders' Equity** | | | |
| Liabilities | | | |
| Current liabilities | | | |
| (Examples: notes payable, accounts payable, accruals, unearned revenues, current portion of notes payable) | | | $ X |
| Long-term liabilities | | | |
| (Examples: notes payable, bonds payable) | | | X |
| Total liabilities | | | X |
| Stockholders' equity | | | |
| Common stock | | | X |
| Retained earnings | | | X |
| Total liabilities and stockholders' equity | | | $ X |

**Note:** Total assets on the balance sheet must equal total liabilities plus stockholders' equity; and, ending retained earnings on the balance sheet must equal ending retained earnings on the retained earnings statement.

Statement of Cash Flows

| Name of Company<br>Statement of Cash Flows<br>For the Period Ended | |
|---|---|
| Cash flows from operating activities | |
| Note: May be prepared using the direct or indirect method | |
| Net cash provided (used) by operating activities | $ X |
| Cash flows from investing activities | |
| (Examples: purchase/sale of long-term assets) | |
| Net cash provided (used) by investing activities | X |
| Cash flows from financing activities | |
| (Examples: issue/repayment of long-term liabilities, issue of stock, payment of dividends) | |
| Net cash provided (used) by financing activities | X |
| Net increase (decrease) in cash | X |
| Cash, beginning of the period | X |
| Cash, end of the period | $ X |

**Note:** Cash, end of the period, on the statement of cash flows must equal cash presented on the balance sheet.

# RAPID REVIEW
# Using the Information in the Financial Statements

| Ratio | Formula | Purpose or Use |
|---|---|---|
| **Liquidity Ratios** | | |
| 1. Current ratio | $\dfrac{\text{Current assets}}{\text{Current liabilities}}$ | Measures short-term debt-paying ability. |
| 2. Acid-test (quick) ratio | $\dfrac{\text{Cash + Short-term investments +}}{\text{Accounts receivable (net)}} \Big/ \text{Current liabilities}$ | Measures immediate short-term liquidity. |
| 3. Accounts receivable turnover | $\dfrac{\text{Net credit sales}}{\text{Average net accounts receivable}}$ | Measures liquidity of receivables. |
| 4. Inventory turnover | $\dfrac{\text{Cost of goods sold}}{\text{Average inventory}}$ | Measures liquidity of inventory. |
| **Profitability Ratios** | | |
| 5. Profit margin | $\dfrac{\text{Net income}}{\text{Net sales}}$ | Measures net income generated by each dollar of sales. |
| 6. Asset turnover | $\dfrac{\text{Net sales}}{\text{Average total assets}}$ | Measures how efficiently assets are used to generate sales. |
| 7. Return on assets | $\dfrac{\text{Net income}}{\text{Average total assets}}$ | Measures overall profitability of assets. |
| 8. Return on common stockholders' equity | $\dfrac{\text{Net income - Preferred dividends}}{\text{Average common stockholders' equity}}$ | Measures profitability of stockholders' investment. |
| 9. Earnings per share (EPS) | $\dfrac{\text{Net income - Preferred dividends}}{\text{Weighted-average common shares outstanding}}$ | Measures net income earned on each share of common stock. |
| 10. Price-earnings (P-E) ratio | $\dfrac{\text{Market price per share of stock}}{\text{Earnings per share}}$ | Measures the ratio of the market price per share to earnings per share. |
| 11. Payout ratio | $\dfrac{\text{Cash dividends paid on common stock}}{\text{Net income}}$ | Measures percentage of earnings distributed in the form of cash dividends. |
| **Solvency Ratios** | | |
| 12. Debt to assets ratio | $\dfrac{\text{Total liabilities}}{\text{Total assets}}$ | Measures percentage of total assets provided by creditors. |
| 13. Times interest earned | $\dfrac{\text{Net income + Interest expense + Income tax expense}}{\text{Interest expense}}$ | Measures ability to meet interest payments as they come due. |
| 14. Free cash flow | Net cash provided by operating activities – Capital expenditures – Cash dividends | Measures the amount of cash generated during the current year that is available for the payment of additional dividends or for expansion. |

www.wiley.com

WILEY